The Merriam-Webster Crossword Puzzle Dictionary

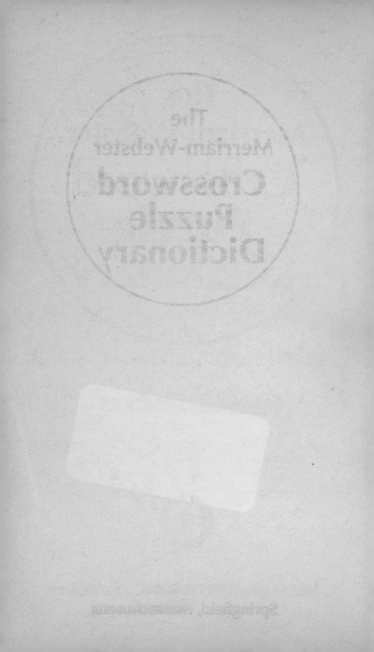

The Merriam-Webster Crossword Puzzle Dictionary

A Merriam-Webster®

MERRIAM-WEBSTER, INC., ***Publishers***
Springfield, Massachusetts

A GENUINE MERRIAM-WEBSTER

The name *Webster* alone is no guarantee of excellence. It is used by a number of publishers and may serve mainly to mislead an unwary buyer.

A Merriam-Webster® is the registered trademark you should look for when you consider the purchase of dictionaries or other fine reference books. It carries the reputation of a company that has been publishing since 1831 and is your assurance of quality and authority.

ISBN 0-87779-905-9

MADE IN THE UNITED STATES OF AMERICA

23456AG/B949392

Preface

The Merriam-Webster Crossword Puzzle Dictionary has been edited to meet the specific needs of crossword puzzle solvers. The extensive resources and editorial care that have placed Merriam-Webster® general dictionaries among the most respected and sought-after reference books in this country have been utilized in preparing this specialized dictionary.

Based on actual crossword puzzle clues, entries have been selected from Webster's Third New International Dictionary and its venerable predecessor, Webster's New International Dictionary, Second Edition, as well as from Webster's Collegiate Thesaurus, Webster's New Geographical Dictionary, Webster's New Biographical Dictionary, Webster's Ninth New Collegiate Dictionary, and Encyclopaedia Britannica, making this book one of the most comprehensive of its kind. Because of the wide range of information contained in this book, it can also be used as a source of much general reference material.

The Merriam-Webster Crossword Puzzle Dictionary is adapted from Webster's Official Crossword Puzzle Dictionary and, as such, relies on work done by the writers and editors of that book, especially by its project editor, James G. Lowe. The adaptation was carried out by Robert D. Copeland and John M. Morse with the assistance of Michael G. Belanger, Daniel J. Hopkins, and Stephen J. Perrault. Data-entry work was done by Karen L. Levister. Proofreading was done by Francine A. Roberts with additional proofreading assistance provided by Jennifer N. Cislo, Jennifer S. Goss, Peter D. Haraty, and Maria S. Sansalone.

Introduction

Main Entries

The organization of The Merriam-Webster Crossword Puzzle Dictionary is structured in accordance with the way in which crossword puzzles are constructed and solved. The main entries and their subcategories correspond to the numbered clues given in the puzzle, and the answer words that follow the main entries are possibilities for filling in the blanks provided.

Main entries appear in boldface type and are entered in alphabetical order letter by letter. Those beginning with *Mc-* are alphabetized as if spelled *Mac-;* thus **McTeague author** appears before **mad.** We have endeavored to make the range of entries as comprehensive as possible in a book of this size so as to enable the user to meet the challenges of even the most difficult puzzles.

These entries include names of persons (as biblical, famous, legendary, literary, and mythological), places (as countries, islands, mountains, rivers, states, and seas), and miscellaneous things (as chemical elements, coins, drinks, games, and wines). Also included are titles of famous books, operas, and works of art. The bulk of the main entries, however, consists of words that have synonyms or closely related words.

Entries may be a single word, a group of words, or a blank with a word or group of words (as **Damocles' ______** or **______ d'Azur**). Parts of speech are not indicated since they are not usually provided in puzzle clues.

Subcategories

When the main entry is a large category (as at **animal, composer,** and **river**), the list of answer words is broken down into alphabetically arranged subcategories for easy access. Each subcategory is introduced by an appropriate boldface italic word or words. If you want to find, for example, the name of a French composer, first look for the entry **composer** and then under it the subcategory **French.**

Subcategories may indicate various kinds of relationships to the main entry, for example, personal (father, mother, etc.), political (capital, kingdom, etc.), literary (author, character, etc.), or artistic (painter, sculptor, etc.). They may indicate a nationality, a language or dialect, or a particular example or type. Also included as subcategories are prefixes, suffixes, combining forms, and chemical symbols related to the main entry.

Answer Words

When more than one answer is possible to a clue represented by a main entry, the answer words are grouped together according to the number of letters they contain. The specific number appears in boldface before each numerical grouping, and within each grouping answer words are alphabetized. Even when only a single answer word is given, the boldface number of its letters precedes it. Answer words usually range from two to thirteen letters since longer answers are rarely asked for. However, some answers (as titles and nicknames) may consist of more than one word and may exceed thirteen letters. Some answers are not actual words; these include abbreviations, prefixes, suffixes, combining forms, and chemical symbols, which are commonly called for in crossword puzzles.

In a single list of answer words you may find grouped together words that seem unrelated to one another. This results when the answer words are of various parts of speech or are synonymous with only one meaning of a main entry that has more than one meaning. Thus, answer words, although related to the main entry, may not be synonymous with each other.

Guide Words

In order to facilitate finding a particular entry, the first main entry on each left-hand page is printed at the top of that page in larger boldface type. Likewise, the last main entry on each right-hand page is printed at the top of that page. These two guide words indicate the alphabetical range of main entries on the two pages.

Cross-References

Occasionally a reduced boldface cross-reference to another main entry is given instead of answer words. For example, at **anywise** you are directed to see **anyhow** for answer words because these two main entries are synonymous, and at **Arthur** you are referred to **King Arthur** for the answer words. These cross-references save space and allow a greater number of main entries than would otherwise be possible.

The
Merriam-Webster
Crossword
Puzzle
Dictionary

A

Aaron ***brother:*** 5 Moses ***father:*** 5 Amram ***sister:*** 6 Miriam ***son:*** 5 Abiku, Nadab 7 Eleazer, Ithamar

aback 5 short 6 sudden 7 unaware 8 suddenly, unawares 10 unawaredly 12 unexpectedly

abacus ***Chinese:*** 7 swanpan 8 shwanpan

abaft 3 aft 4 back 5 after 6 astern, back of, behind

abalienate 4 cede, deed 5 alien 6 assign, convey, remise 8 make over, sign over, transfer

abalone 5 ormer

abandon 3 fun 4 cede, drop, ease, junk, play, quit 5 chuck, leave, scrap, sport, waive, yield 6 desert, disuse, give up, laxity, maroon, reject, resign, turn up 7 cast off, discard, forsake, freedom, laxness, liberty, license, unguard 8 hand over, renounce, wildness 9 looseness, repudiate, surrender, throw over 10 exuberance, relinquish, unruliness, wantonness 11 naturalness, spontaneity, unrestraint 12 heedlessness, incontinence, unconstraint 13 impulsiveness

abandoned 4 lewd, lorn 6 wanton 7 corrupt, debased, riotous, uncouth 8 depraved, derelict, deserted, desolate, forsaken, solitary 9 debauched, dissolute, lecherous, perverted, reprobate 10 degenerate, lascivious, licentious, profligate 12 incorrigible, unprincipled

abase 4 fawn, sink 5 cower, lower, toady 6 bemean, cringe, debase, demean, demote, grovel, humble, reduce 7 degrade, truckle 8 cast down, diminish 9 downgrade, humiliate

abash 4 faze 5 abase 6 demean, humble, rattle 7 confuse 8 confound 9 discomfit, embarrass, humiliate 10 disconcert

abashment 6 unease 9 confusion 10 uneasiness 12 discomfiture, discomposure 13 disconcertion, embarrassment

abate 3 ebb 4 fall, lull, wane 5 annul, close, let up, quash, taper 6 lessen, negate, recede, reduce, relent, weaken 7 abolish, die away, die down, dwindle, ease off, nullify, slacken, subside, vitiate 8 abrogate, decrease, diminish, moderate, taper off 9 drain away, eradicate 10 annihilate, invalidate 11 exterminate

abatement 6 rebate 8 discount 9 deduction, reduction 11 subtraction

abbot ***female:*** 6 abbess

abbreviate 3 cut 7 abridge, curtail, cut back, shorten

abbreviation 7 acronym 10 abridgment, shortening

abdicate 5 demit, leave 6 reject, resign 7 abandon 8 renounce, withdraw 9 surrender, throw away 10 relinquish

abdomen 3 gut, pot 5 belly, tummy 6 middle, paunch, venter 7 midriff, stomach 8 potbelly 9 bay window 10 midsection 11 breadbasket ***combining form:*** 6 ventri, ventro ***depression:*** 5 navel

abduct 5 seize 6 kidnap, snatch 10 spirit away

abecedarian 4 tyro 7 amateur, dabbler 9 smatterer 10 dilettante

Abel ***brother:*** 4 Cain, Seth ***father:*** 4 Adam ***mother:*** 3 Eve ***slayer:*** 4 Cain

Abelard ***son:*** 9 Astrolabe ***wife:*** 7 Heloise

abele 6 poplar

aberrant 3 odd 6 errant, erring 7 deviant, devious, strange, unusual 8 abnormal, atypical, peculiar 9 anomalous, deviative, different, disparate, divergent, eccentric, untypical 11 exceptional, heteroclite

aberration 4 slip 6 lunacy, oddity, rarity 7 madness, mistake, turning 8 insanity 9 curiosity, departure, deviation, diversion, unbalance 10 alienation, deflection, divergence, insaneness 11 abnormality, derangement, distraction, psychopathy

abet 3 aid, egg 4 goad, help, prod, spur, urge 6 assist, exhort, foment, incite, stir up 8 advocate 9 encourage, instigate 11 countenance

abettor 9 accessory 10 accomplice 11 confederate, conspirator 13 coconspirator

abeyance 5 break, pause 7 latency, respite 8 dormancy, interval 10 quiescence, quiescency, suspension 11 cold storage 12 intermission, interruption

abeyant 6 latent 7 dormant, lurking 8 deferred 9 postponed, quiescent, repressed 10 suppressed 11 intermitted

abhor 4 hate 5 scorn 6 detest, loathe 7 contemn, despise, disdain 8 execrate 9 abominate

abhorrence 4 hate 6 dismay, hatred, horror 8 aversion, distaste, loathing 9 repulsion, revulsion 10 repellency, repugnance 11 abomination, detestation
abhorrent 6 horrid, odious 7 hatable, hateful 8 hateable 9 invidious, obnoxious, repellent, repugnant, revulsive 10 abominable, detestable 11 uncongenial 12 antipathetic 13 unsympathetic
Abi *father:* 9 Zechariah *husband:* 4 Ahaz *mother:* 8 Hezekiah
abide 4 bear, last, live, stay, take, wait 5 brook, cling, dwell, exist, stand, stick, tarry 6 accede, accept, adhere, cleave, endure, linger, remain, reside, suffer 7 consent, hang out, perdure, persist, receive, stomach, subsist, swallow 8 continue, tolerate 11 stick around
abiding 4 firm, sure 6 steady 7 durable, lasting 8 enduring 9 steadfast 10 perdurable, persistent 11 unfaltering, unqualified 12 never-failing, wholehearted 13 unquestioning
Abiel *grandson:* 4 Saul 5 Abner *son:* 3 Ner 4 Kish
abigail 4 maid
Abigail's husband 5 David, Nabal
ability 5 knack, might, skill 6 talent 7 address, aptness, command, faculty, know-how, mastery, prowess 8 adequacy, aptitude, capacity, deftness, facility 9 dexterity, expertise, expertism, handiness, ingenuity 10 adroitness, capability, cleverness, competence, efficiency, expertness, mastership 11 proficiency 13 qualification, qualifiedness
Abital's husband 5 David
abject 9 underfoot 11 downtrodden
abjure 4 cede 5 unsay 6 desert, disown, recall, recant 7 abandon, disavow, forsake, retract 8 forswear, palinode, renounce, take back, withdraw 9 repudiate, surrender 10 relinquish
ablaze 5 afire, aglow, fiery 6 aflame, alight 7 burning, flaming, flaring, ignited 8 aflicker 11 conflagrant
able 4 good, keen 5 alert, sharp, smart 6 au fait, brainy, clever, expert, proper, wicked 7 capable, go-ahead, skilled 8 skillful 9 brilliant, competent, effective, effectual, efficient, qualified 10 proficient 11 intelligent 12 enterprising
abnegation 6 denial 10 self-denial 12 renouncement, renunciation
Abner *cousin:* 4 Saul *father:* 3 Ner *slayer:* 4 Joab
abnormal 3 odd 5 undue, weird 6 off-key 7 deviant, offtype, unusual 8 aberrant, atypical 9 anomalous, deviative, divergent, irregular, paratypic, unnatural, unregular, untypical 11 heteroclite, uncustomary 13 heteromorphic, preternatural *combining form:* 3 mal 4 anom, poly 5 anomo, pseud 6 pseudo *prefix:* 3 dys, par 4 para
abnormality 5 lusus
abode 4 home 5 house 8 domicile, dwelling 9 residence, residency 10 commorancy, habitation
abolish 4 undo 5 abate, annul, quash 6 cancel, negate, repeal, revoke, vacate 7 blot out, nullify, rescind, vitiate, wipe out 8 abrogate, disallow, disannul 9 eradicate, extirpate 10 annihilate, circumduct, extinguish, invalidate 11 exterminate
abolitionist 4 Mott, Weld 5 Lundy, Smith, Stowe 6 Birney, Lowell, Parker, Tappan 8 Douglass, Garrison, Phillips, Whittier
abominable 6 cursed, horrid, odious 7 hateful 8 accursed, hateable 9 abhorrent, loathsome, offensive, repugnant, revolting 10 detestable
abominable snowman 4 yeti
abominate 4 damn, hate 5 abhor, curse 6 detest, loathe 8 execrate 9 objurgate
abomination 4 hate, pest 5 bogey, scorn, trial 6 hatred, horror, plague 7 bugaboo, bugbear, disdain, dislike, incubus 8 anathema, aversion, contempt, disfavor, distaste, loathing 9 annoyance, bête noire, disrelish, repulsion, revulsion 10 abhorrence, black beast, repugnance, repugnancy 11 detestation
aboriginal 6 native, savage 7 endemic 8 barbaric, primeval 9 barbarian, barbarous, primitive 10 indigenous, primordial 13 autochthonous
aborigine 3 abo 6 native
abortive 4 vain 6 futile, unripe 7 useless 8 bootless, immature, unformed 9 fruitless 10 unavailing 11 ineffective, ineffectual, unavailable 12 unproductive
abound 4 flow, teem 5 crawl, swarm
abound in *suffix:* 5 ulent
abounding 4 full, rife 5 alive 6 jammed, packed 7 replete, stuffed, teeming 8 swarming, thronged 11 overflowing
abounding in *suffix:* 3 ose, ous 4 ious
about 2 on, re 4 as to, back, in re, most, much, near, nigh, over, upon, with 5 again, anent, circa, round 6 all but, almost, anyhow, around, nearby, nearly 7 anywise, apropos, through 8 at random, backward, casually, randomly, to and fro 9 aimlessly, as regards, haphazard, in reverse 10 carelessly, concerning, near-at-hand, respecting, throughout 11 any which way, haphazardly, practically 12 circuitously 13 approximately, helter-skelter
about-face 4 turn 7 reverse 8 reversal 9 reversion, volte-face 11 reversement
above 3 o'er 4 over, past 5 aloft, supra 6 beyond 8 overhead *combining form:*

6 supero *prefix:* 3 sur 4 over 5 hyper, super, supra
above all 7 chiefly
aboveboard 4 open 7 artless 8 straight 9 ingenuous 10 forthright, scrupulous 12 plain dealing
abracadabra 4 cant 5 argot 6 jargon 7 mummery 9 gibberish 10 hocus-pocus, mumbo jumbo 13 mystification
abrade 3 bug, irk, rub 4 burn, fret, gall, rasp, wear 5 annoy, chafe, erode, grate, graze 6 bother, flurry, ruffle, scrape 7 corrade, corrode, eat away, perturb, provoke 8 exercise 9 excoriate
Abraham *birthplace:* 2 Ur *brother:* 5 Haran, Nahor *concubine:* 5 Hagar *father:* 5 Terah *grandfather:* 5 Nahor *grandson:* 4 Esau *nephew:* 3 Lot *son:* 5 Isaac, Medan, Shuah 6 Midian, Zimran 7 Ishmael *well:* 9 Beer-Sheba *wife:* 5 Sarah 7 Keturah
Abraham's bosom 4 Zion 5 bliss 6 Canaan, heaven 7 elysium, nirvana 8 empyrean, paradise 10 Civitas Dei 12 New Jerusalem
abreast 2 up 6 au fait, versed 7 versant 8 familiar, informed, up-to-date 9 au courant 10 acquainted, conversant 12 contemporary
abridge 3 cut 5 limit, slash 6 lessen, minify, narrow, reduce 7 curtail, cut back, shorten 8 condense, diminish, minimize, restrict, retrench 10 abbreviate
abridgment 3 sum 5 brief 6 aperçu, digest, précis, sketch 7 capsule, epitome, outline, summary 8 abstract, boildown, breviary, breviate, syllabus, synopsis 9 summation, summing-up 10 compendium, conspectus 12 condensation
abroad 6 afield 7 oversea 8 overseas
abrogate 4 ruin, undo, void 5 abate, annul, quash, wreck 6 cancel, negate, vacate 7 abolish, blot out, nullify, vitiate 8 dissolve 9 discharge 10 annihilate, extinguish, invalidate, obliterate
abrupt 4 curt 5 bluff, blunt, brief, brisk, crisp, gruff, hasty, quick, ready, sharp, sheer, short, steep 6 casual, crusty, snippy, speedy, sudden 7 arduous, brusque, hurried, rushing 8 headlong, informal 9 impetuous 11 precipitant, precipitate, precipitous, short-spoken, subitaneous 13 unceremonious
abruptly 5 short 6 sudden 7 asudden 8 suddenly 9 forthwith
abruptness 10 brusquerie
Absalom *commander:* 5 Amasa *father:* 5 David *mother:* 7 Maachah *sister:* 5 Tamar *slayer:* 4 Joab
abscess 4 boil, sore 5 botch, ulcer 6 lesion, pimple, trauma 7 pustule 8 furuncle 9 carbuncle
abscond 2 go 3 fly 4 flee, quit 5 break, leave, scape 6 decamp, escape 8 withdraw
absence 4 lack, need, void, want 6 dearth, defect, vacuum 7 default, drought, failure 9 privation 10 deficiency 13 insufficiency
absent 4 away, gone, lost 7 bemused, faraway, lacking, missing, omitted, wanting 8 distrait, heedless 9 forgetful 10 abstracted
absentminded 4 lost 7 bemused, faraway 8 distrait, heedless, unseeing 10 abstracted, unnoticing 11 inattentive, inconscient, preoccupied, unobserving 12 unperceiving
absent without leave 4 AWOL
absolute 4 hard, pure, real, true 5 ideal, sheer, utter 6 actual, simple 7 eternal, factual, genuine, perfect, unmixed 8 complete, despotic, flawless, infinite, outright, positive, ultimate, unflawed 9 arbitrary, autarchic, boundless, downright, fleckless, imperious, masterful, out-and-out, sovereign, tyrannous, unalloyed, undiluted, unlimited 10 autocratic, autonomous, consummate, impeccable, monocratic, tyrannical 11 categorical, dictatorial, domineering, independent, note-perfect, unmitigated, unqualified 12 indefectible, totalitarian, transcendent 13 authoritarian
absolutely 6 easily 9 doubtless 10 definitely, positively 11 doubtlessly 13 unequivocally
absolution 6 pardon 7 amnesty 11 condonation
absolutism 9 Caesarism 12 dictatorship
absolve 4 free 5 clear, spare 6 acquit, excuse, exempt, let off, shrive 7 release, relieve 8 dispense 9 discharge, exculpate, exonerate, vindicate 10 disculpate
absorb 5 imbue 6 embody, engage, imbibe, infuse, sponge 7 consume, engross, immerse, inhaust, involve 8 permeate 9 preoccupy 10 assimilate, impregnate, monopolize 11 incorporate
absorbed 4 deep, rapt 6 intent 7 engaged, wrapped 8 immersed, involved 9 engrossed, wrapped up 11 preoccupied
absorbent cotton 7 pledget
absorbing 9 consuming 10 engrossing 12 monopolizing
abstain 4 curb, deny, keep 5 forgo, spurn 6 eschew, refuse, reject 7 decline, forbear, refrain 8 abnegate, hold back, teetotal, withhold 9 constrain
abstemious 5 sober 7 ascetic, austere, sparing 9 abstinent, continent, temperate 11 self-denying
abstentious see **abstemious**

abstinence 8 sobriety 10 continence, temperance 12 renunciation
abstinent see abstemious
abstract 4 lift 5 annex, brief, filch, ideal, pinch, steal, swipe, unfix 6 detach, divide, pilfer 7 epitome, neutral, purloin, utopian 8 academic, boildown, breviary, breviate, detached, notional, separate, synopsis, uncouple 9 colorless, disengage, visionary 10 abridgment, conceptual, conspectus, disconnect, dissociate, impersonal, inconcrete 11 appropriate, impractical, speculative, theoretical, unpassioned 12 condensation, disassociate, hypothetical, transcendent 13 disinterested
abstracted 4 lost, rapt 6 absent, intent 7 bemused, faraway 8 distrait, heedless 9 engrossed, oblivious, unmindful, unminding 11 inattentive, inconscient, preoccupied 12 absentminded
abstruse 4 deep 5 heavy, ideal 6 knotty, occult, orphic, secret 7 complex 8 esoteric, hermetic, profound 9 intricate, recondite 10 acroamatic 11 complicated 12 hypothetical
absurd 5 balmy, comic, crazy, droll, funny, loony, potty, silly, wacky 6 insane 7 asinine, fatuous, foolish 8 farcical 10 irrational 11 harebrained 12 preposterous, unreasonable
absurdity 5 folly 7 inanity 8 insanity, nonsense 9 craziness, dottiness, silliness 11 foolishness, witlessness 13 senselessness
abundance 4 ease 6 enough, galore, plenty 7 lashins 8 adequacy, lashings, thriving 10 lavishness, prosperity 11 prodigality, sufficiency *Scottish:* 5 routh, rowth
abundant 4 lush, rife 5 ample, thick 6 common, lavish, plenty 7 copious, crammed, crowded, liberal, profuse, replete 8 generous, prolific 9 bounteous, bountiful, luxuriant, planteous, plentiful
abuse 3 mar, mud 4 harm, hurt 5 decry, spoil, wrong 6 damage, debase, impair, injure, mess up, misuse, rating, revile 7 calumny, corrupt, cursing, exploit, obloquy, oppress, outrage, pervert, profane, railing 8 belittle, berating, derogate, discount, ill-treat, maltreat, minimize, misapply, mistreat, reviling, swearing 9 contumely, desecrate, disparage, dispraise, invective, manhandle, misemploy, mishandle, persecute, profanity 10 defamation, depreciate, impose upon, malignment, scurrility 12 billingsgate, vilification, vituperation
abusive 5 dirty 6 odious 7 scurril 8 scurrile 9 aspersing, insulting, invective, maligning, offending, offensive, outraging, truculent, vilifying 10 affronting, scurrilous, vituperous 11 opprobrious 12 contumelious, vituperative, vituperatory
abut 4 join, line 5 flank, march, touch, verge 6 adjoin, border 8 neighbor 11 communicate
abutting 4 next 7 joining 8 adjacent, touching 9 adjoining, bordering, impinging 10 approximal, connecting, contiguous, juxtaposed 12 conterminous
abysm 4 gulf 5 chasm
abysmal 4 deep 8 infinite, profound 9 plumbless, soundless 10 bottomless, fathomless 11 illimitable, plummetless 12 unfathomable
abyss 3 pit 4 gulf, hell 5 chasm, depth, hades, Sheol 6 Tophet 7 Gehenna, inferno 8 deepness 9 perdition 10 profundity, underworld 11 netherworld 12 profoundness
academic 5 booky 6 closet 7 bookish, utopian 8 gownsman, pedantic 10 scholastic 11 book-learned, impractical, quodlibetic, speculative, theoretical
academic year part 4 term 7 quarter 8 semester 9 trimester
accede 3 let, yes 5 agree, allow 6 assent, concur, permit 7 consent 9 acquiesce, cooperate, subscribe
accelerate 5 hurry, impel, speed 6 hasten, step up 7 quicken, swiften
acceleration 7 speedup
accent 4 beat, tone 5 meter, pulse, throb 6 rhythm, stress 7 cadence 8 emphasis 9 pulsation 10 inflection, intonation *Irish:* 6 brogue *Scottish:* 4 burr *Southern:* 5 drawl
accent mark 5 acute, grave
accentuation see accent
accept 3 bow, buy, see 4 bear, take 5 adopt, agree, catch, favor, go for, grasp, yield 6 admire, endure, esteem, follow, pocket, take in 7 agree to, approve, believe, compass, receive, respect, swallow 8 assent to, bear with, hold with, tolerate, tough out 9 agree with, apprehend, approbate 10 capitulate, comprehend, understand 11 countenance, subscribe to
acceptable 4 good 6 decent 7 average 8 adequate, all right, bearable, ordinary 9 endurable, tolerable 10 sufficient 11 commonplace, supportable 12 satisfactory 13 unexceptional, unimpeachable
acceptably 4 well 5 amply, right 8 properly, suitably 9 fittingly 10 adequately, becomingly 13 appropriately
acceptant 8 suasible, swayable 9 receptive 10 responsive 11 persuadable, persuasible 13 influenceable
acceptation 5 sense 6 import 7 meaning, message, purport 10 intendment 12 signifi-

cance, significancy 13 signification, understanding
accepted 5 sound, usual 6 proper 7 chronic, correct, routine 8 habitual, orthodox, received 9 customary 10 accustomed, recognized, sanctioned 11 established 12 conventional
access 3 fit, way 4 adit, door, gust, pang, turn 5 burst, entry, onset, route, sally, spell, throe 6 attack, entreé, stitch, taking, twinge 7 flare-up, ingress, passage, seizure 8 entrance, eruption, outburst 9 admission, explosion 10 admittance
accessible 4 open 6 public, usable 9 operative 10 employable 11 practicable 12 approachable, unrestricted
accession 4 rise 5 raise 8 addition, increase 9 accretion, increment 12 augmentation
accessory 7 abettor, adjunct, fitting 8 addition, adjuvant, appendix 9 accretion, ancillary, appendage, auxiliary, increment, secondary, tributary 10 accomplice, coincident, collateral, concurrent, incidental, subsidiary 11 appurtenant, concomitant, confederate, conspirator, subordinate, subservient 12 adventitious, appurtenance, contributory 13 accompaniment, coconspirator
accident 3 hap 4 fate, luck 5 fluke 6 chance, hazard, kismet, mishap 7 destiny, fortune 8 calamity, casualty, fortuity 9 mischance 10 misfortune 12 misadventure
accidental 3 odd 5 fluky 6 casual, chance, random 7 unmeant 9 chromatic, dependent, unplanned, unwitting 10 coincident, contingent, fortuitous, undesigned, unintended, unpurposed 11 conditional, inadvertent 13 unintentional
accidentally 5 haply
acclaim 4 hail 5 cheer, éclat, exalt, glory, honor, roose 6 homage, kudize, praise 7 applaud, commend, glorify, magnify, ovation, root for 8 applause, plaudits 9 recommend, reverence 10 compliment
acclamation 8 applause, plaudits
acclimate 6 harden, season 7 toughen 9 climatize
acclimatize see acclimate
accolade 4 bays 5 award, badge, honor, kudos 7 laurels 10 decoration 11 distinction
accommodate 3 fit 4 hold, suit, tune, vary 5 adapt, alter, defer, favor, house, humor, lodge, put up, yield 6 adjust, attune, bestow, billet, change, encase, harbor, modify, oblige, square, submit, tailor 7 cater to, conform, contain, enclose, indulge, quarter 8 domicile 9 entertain, harmonize, integrate, reconcile 10 coordinate, proportion 11 convenience, domiciliate 12 reconciliate
accommodations 4 keep, room 7 housing, lodging, shelter 8 lodgment 12 room and board
accompaniment 4 mate 6 fellow 7 comrade, consort, partner 8 addition 9 accessory, associate, attendant, colleague, companion, corollary 10 assistance, complement, enrichment, equivalent, supplement 11 concomitant, enhancement 12 augmentation
accompany 4 join, lead 5 bring, guide, pilot, steer 6 attend, convoy, escort 7 combine, conduct, consort, esquire 8 chaperon 9 associate 11 consort with
accompanying 8 incident 9 ancillary, attendant, attending, satellite 10 coincident, collateral 11 concomitant
accomplice 5 aider 6 flunky, helper, stooge 7 abettor 9 accessory, assistant 11 confederate, conspirator 13 coconspirator
accomplish 3 win 4 gain 5 reach, score 6 attain, fulfil, rack up 7 achieve, fulfill, realize, succeed
accomplished 4 ripe 5 adept 6 expert 8 finished, masterly 9 all-around, many-sided, perfected, versatile, virtuosic 10 consummate, proficient
accomplishment 3 act, art 4 deed 5 craft, doing, skill, thing 6 action, finish 8 fruition 9 adeptness, expertise 10 attainment, expertness 11 achievement, acquirement, acquisition, proficiency
accord 4 deal, fuse, give, jibe, tune 5 agree, award, blend, chime, fit in, grant, merge, tally, union 6 chorus, concur, confer, square 7 concede, concert, conform, empathy, harmony 8 affinity, coalesce, coincide, dovetail, sympathy 9 agreement, harmonize, vouchsafe 10 attraction, consonance, correspond, solidarity 11 concordance 13 understanding
accordant 9 congruous 10 harmonious
accordingly 2 so 4 ergo, then, thus 5 hence 9 therefore, thereupon 12 consequently
accost 3 dog 4 dare, face, hail 5 annoy, front, greet, hound, worry 6 bother, call to, halloo, pester, salute 7 address, affront, apply to, bespeak, outface, outrage 8 approach, confront 9 challenge 10 buttonhole 11 memorialize
accouchement 7 lying in 8 childbed 11 confinement
account 3 tab, use 4 bill, deem, note, rate, view 5 avail, favor, score, story, value, worth 6 assess, esteem, reason, reckon, regard, report, repute 7 dignity, explain, expound, fitness, history, invoice, justify, recital, respect, service, utility, version 8 appraise, consider, estimate, evaluate

9 advantage, chronicle, elucidate, narrative, rationale, reckoning, relevance, statement, valuation 10 admiration, estimation, reputation, usefulness 11 consequence, distinction, explain away, explanation, rationalize 13 applicability, consideration, justification
accountable 6 liable 8 amenable 10 answerable 11 responsible
account book 6 ledger
accounting ***branch of:*** 11 bookkeeping
accouter 3 arm, rig 4 deck, gear 5 adorn, dress, equip, fix up, ready 6 attire, fit out, outfit 7 appoint, furnish, prepare, turn out 8 decorate 9 embellish
accouterment 4 gear 6 outfit, tackle 7 bravery, regalia 8 matériel, tackling 9 apparatus, equipment, machinery, trappings 11 furnishings, habiliments 12 appointments 13 paraphernalia
accredit 2 OK 3 lay 4 okay 5 refer 6 assign, attest, charge, enable, impute 7 approve, ascribe, certify, commend, empower, endorse, license 8 sanction, vouch for 9 attribute, authorize, recommend 10 commission
accretion 4 rise 5 raise 7 adjunct 8 addition, increase 9 accession, appendage, increment 10 attachment 11 enlargement 12 augmentation
accumulate 4 heap, hive, mass, pile 5 amass, hoard, lay by, lay in, lay up, stock, uplay 6 garner, gather, roll up 7 backlog, collect, lay down, store up 8 assemble, treasure 9 stockpile
accumulation 4 bank, heap, mass, pile 5 hoard, stock, store, trove 7 buildup, cumulus, reserve 9 amassment 10 collection 11 aggregation 13 agglomeration
accumulative 5 chain 8 additive, additory 9 summative 11 aggregative 12 augmentative
accuracy 9 exactness, precision 10 definition, exactitude 11 correctness, preciseness 12 definiteness
accurate 4 nice 5 exact, right 6 proper 7 certain, correct, precise 8 reliable, rigorous 9 authentic 10 dependable
accursed 6 odious 7 hateful 8 damnable 9 abhorrent, execrable, offensive, repugnant, revolting 10 abominable, detestable
accusation 6 charge 8 delation 10 allegation, indictment ***false:*** 7 calumny
accuse 3 tax 5 blame 6 charge, delate, indict 7 arraign, censure, impeach 8 denounce 9 criminate, criticize, inculpate, reprobate 11 incriminate
accustom 3 use 4 wont 5 adapt, inure 6 adjust, harden, season 9 habituate 11 acclimatize, familiarize
accustomed 5 usual 7 chronic, routine 8 accepted, everyday, habitual, standard 9 confirmed 10 habituated, regulation 11 commonplace 12 conventional
ace 3 bit, jot 4 atom, hair, iota, mite 5 crumb, minim, speck 7 whisker 8 molecule, particle 11 hairbreadth
ace and face card 7 natural 9 blackjack
acedia 5 sloth
acerb 3 dry 4 acid, sour, tart 7 acetose, caustic 9 acidulous, corrosive, sarcastic 12 archilochian
acerbate 7 envenom 8 embitter
acerbic see **acerb**
acerbity 7 acidity, sarcasm 8 acrimony, asperity, dourness, mordancy, sourness, tartness 9 harshness, roughness, surliness 10 bitterness, causticity 11 crabbedness, saturninity
Achates' companion 6 Aeneas
ache 3 yen 4 hurt, long, lust, pain, pang, pine, pity, rack, sigh 5 crave, throe, yearn 6 hanker, hunger, injury, misery, stitch, suffer, thirst, twinge 7 feel for 8 yearning 10 sorrow over 11 commiserate 13 compassionate ***Scottish:*** 5 stoun 6 stound
acheronian 5 black, bleak, drear 6 dismal, gloomy 7 joyless 8 desolate, funereal 9 cheerless
achieve 2 do 3 get, win 4 gain 5 reach, score 6 attain, finish, obtain, rack up, secure 7 acquire, execute, perform, realize 8 complete, conclude 9 actualize 10 accomplish
achievement 4 deed, feat 6 finish 7 exploit 10 attainment 11 acquirement, acquisition, tour de force
Achilles ***adviser:*** 6 Nestor ***companion:*** 9 Patroclus ***father:*** 6 Peleus ***horse:*** 7 Xanthus ***lover:*** 7 Briseis ***mother:*** 6 Thetis ***slayer:*** 5 Paris ***victim:*** 6 Hector ***vulnerable part:*** 4 heel
Achilles' heel 8 soft spot
aching 4 sore 7 algetic, hurtful, hurting, painful 10 afflictive
Achsah ***father:*** 5 Caleb ***husband:*** 7 Othniel
achy 4 sore
acicular 5 acute, peaky, piked, sharp 6 peaked 7 pointed
acid 3 dry 4 sour, tart 5 acerb 7 acerbic, acetose ***bleaching:*** 6 oxalic ***combining form:*** 3 oxy 4 acet 5 aceto ***fatty:*** 6 capric 7 caproic, stearic 8 caprylic ***found in apples:*** 5 malic ***found in cranberries:*** 7 benzoic ***found in grapes:*** 8 tartaric ***found in lemons:*** 6 citric ***found in rhubarb:*** 6 oxalic ***found in sour milk:*** 6 lactic ***indicator:*** 6 litmus ***kind:*** 5 amino, boric, iodic, malic 6 acetic, bromic, formic, nitric, oxalic, tannic 7 chloric, nitrous, silicic 8 carbolic, carbonic, chlorous, muriatic, sulfuric 9 aqua

regia 12 hydrochloric *neutralizer:* 4 base 6 alkali *tanning:* 6 tannic 8 catechin *vinegar:* 6 acetic
acid radical *combining form:* 3 oyl
acidulous 3 dry 4 sour, tart 5 acerb, sharp 6 biting 7 acerbic, acetose, cutting, piquant, pungent
Acis *lover:* 7 Galatea *slayer:* 10 Polyphemus
acknowledge 3 own 4 avow, deem, tell, view 5 admit, agree, allow, grant, let on, own up 6 accept, fess up, reveal 7 concede, confess, declare, divulge 8 announce, consider, disclose, proclaim 9 recognize
acknowledgment 6 credit 11 recognition
acme 4 apex, peak 6 apogee, climax, summit, tiptop, vertex, zenith 8 capstone, meridian, pinnacle 11 culmination
acorn *combining form:* 5 balan 6 balano *sprouter:* 3 oak
acoustic 5 aural 6 audile 8 auditory
acquaint 4 clew, clue, post, tell, warn 6 advise, fill in, inform, notify, orient, wise up 7 apprise, present 8 accustom 9 habituate, introduce
acquaintance 4 mate 5 amigo, crony 6 friend 7 comrade 8 familiar, intimacy, intimate 9 associate, companion, confidant 10 experience 11 familiarity
acquainted 6 au fait, versed 7 abreast, versant 8 familiar, informed 9 au courant 10 conversant
acquiesce 3 bow, yes 5 agree 6 accede, assent, concur 7 consent 9 reconcile, subscribe
acquiescence 9 deference 10 compliance, conformity 11 resignation 12 complaisance
acquiescent 7 passive 8 resigned, yielding 10 submissive 11 unresistant, unresisting 12 nonresistant, nonresisting
acquire 3 add, get, win 4 earn, form, gain, land, make 5 amass, annex, reach 6 garner, obtain, pick up, secure 7 bring in, collect, develop, procure 8 cumulate 9 knock down 10 accumulate
acquirement 6 finish 7 advance 8 addition 9 accretion, erudition 10 attainment 11 achievement, acquisition, advancement
acquisition see **acquirement**
acquisitive 5 itchy 6 grabby, greedy 8 covetous, desirous, grasping 10 prehensile
acquit 3 act 4 bear, free 5 carry, clear 6 behave, deport 7 absolve, comport, conduct, release 8 liberate 9 discharge, exculpate, exonerate, vindicate 10 disculpate
acres 4 land 5 manor 6 estate 7 demesne
acrid 4 sour 5 harsh, sharp 6 biting, bitter 7 austere, caustic, cutting 9 amaroidal 10 astringent
acrimonious 3 mad 5 angry, cross, irate, testy, wroth 6 cranky, ireful, wrathy, wrothy 8 wrathful, wrothful 9 indignant, irascible, splenetic 11 belligerent, contentious, quarrelsome
acrimony 5 spite 6 animus, malice, rancor 7 ill will 8 acerbity, asperity, mordancy 9 animosity, antipathy, malignity 10 bitterness 11 malevolence
Acrisius *daughter:* 5 Danae *slayer:* 7 Perseus
across 4 over 6 beyond 7 athwart 12 transversely *prefix:* 2 di 3 dia 4 over 5 trans
act 2 do 3 run 4 bear, deed, fake, feat, play, sham, work 5 bluff, doing, feign, put on, serve 6 acquit, affect, assume, behave, demean, deport 7 comport, conduct, exploit, operate, perform, portray, pretend 8 function, simulate 9 discourse, officiate, personate 10 masquerade 11 counterfeit, impersonate *suffix:* 2 cy, th 3 ade, ate, ice, ion, ism
acting 6 pro tem 7 interim 9 ad interim, temporary 10 pro tempore
actinium *symbol:* 2 Ac
action 4 case, deed, fray, suit, work 5 cause, doing 6 affray, battle, combat 7 lawsuit, process, service 8 behavior, conflict, function 9 discharge, execution, operation, procedure 10 engagement, proceeding 11 performance *combining form:* 3 cin, kin 4 cino, kine, kino 5 cinet, kinet 6 cineto, kineto, praxia, praxis *suffix:* 2 al, cy 3 ade, ing, sis 4 ance, ence, esis, ment, osis 5 ation 7 isation, ization *unwise:* 8 impolicy
action painting 7 tachism
activate 4 stir, wake 5 rally, rouse, waken 6 arouse, awaken 8 energize, vitalize
activation *combining form:* 7 kinesis
active 4 busy, live, spry, yare 5 agile, alert, alive, brisk, zippy 6 brisky, lively, nimble 7 driving, dynamic, running, working 8 animated, spirited, vigorous 9 assiduous, energetic, operative, sprightly, vivacious 11 functioning, industrious 12 enterprising
activity 8 exercise, exertion 10 exercising
actor 4 mime 5 mimic, party 6 mummer, player, sharer 7 trouper 8 partaker, thespian 9 performer 11 participant 12 impersonator, participator *name:* 3 Cox (Wally), Dix (Richard), Fox (Michael J.), Lom (Herbert), Mix (Tom), Ray (Aldo) 4 Alda (Alan, Robert), Bean (Orson), Blue (Ben), Bond (Ward), Cobb (Lee J.), Coco (James), Culp (Robert), Dean (James), Duff (Howard), Egan (Richard), Falk (Peter), Ford (Glenn, Harri-

son), Foxx (Redd), Geer (Will), Grey (Joel), Hale (Alan), Hill (Arthur), Hope (Bob), Hurt (William), Ives (Burl), Jory (Victor), Kaye (Danny), Kean (Edmund), Keel (Howard), Ladd (Alan), Lahr (Bert), Lord (Jack), Lunt (Alfred), Marx (Chico, Groucho, Harpo), Muni (Paul), Ngor (Haing S.), Peck (Gregory), Raft (George), Ryan (Robert), Shaw (Robert), Todd (Richard), Tone (Franchot), Torn (Rip), Webb (Clifton, Jack), Wynn (Ed, Keenan), York (Michael) **5** Adler (Luther), Allen (Woody), Arkin (Alan), Asner (Ed), Autry (Gene), Ayres (Lew), Barry (Gene), Bates (Alan), Beery (Noah, Wallace), Berle (Milton), Boone (Richard), Brady (Scott), Brand (Neville), Burns (George), Caine (Michael), Candy (John), Clark (Dane), Conte (Richard), Cooke (Alistair), Corey (Wendell), Cosby (Bill), Davis (Sammy Jr.), Delon (Alain), Donat (Robert), Evans (Maurice), Ewell (Tom), Finch (Peter), Flynn (Errol), Fonda (Henry, Peter), Gabin (Jean), Gable (Clark), Gould (Elliot), Grant (Cary), Gwenn (Edmund), Hardy (Oliver), Hayes (Gabby), Irons (Jeremy), Jaffe (Sam), Jones (Dean), Kazan (Elia), Keach (Stacy), Keith (Brian), Kelly (Gene), Kiley (Richard), Kline (Kevin), Lamas (Fernando, Lorenzo), Lanza (Mario), Lewis (Jerry), Lloyd (Harold), Lorre (Peter), Lukas (Paul), Lynde (Paul), March (Frederic), McCoy (Tim), Mills (John), Mineo (Sal), Moore (Victor), Nimoy (Leonard), Niven (David), Nolan (Lloyd), Nolte (Nick), Oakie (Jack), Oland (Warner), O'Neal (Patrick, Ryan), Payne (John), Pesci (Joe), Power (Tyrone), Price (Vincent), Quale (Anthony), Quinn (Anthony), Rains (Claude), Scott (George C., Randolph), Segal (George), Sheen (Charlie, Martin), Stack (Robert), Stamp (Terence), Tracy (Spencer), Tufts (Sonny), Wayne (John), Wilde (Cornel), Wills (Chill), Young (Gig, Robert) **6** Abbott (Bud), Albert (Eddie), Ameche (Don), Arness (James), Backus (Jim), Balsam (Martin), Barker (Lex), Baxter (Warner), Beatty (Warren), Begley (Ed), Bogart (Humphrey), Bolger (Ray), Bosley (Tom), Brando (Marlon), Brooks (Mel), Burton (Richard), Caesar (Sid), Cagney (James), Callan (Michael), Cantor (Eddie), Carney (Art), Chaney (Lon), Coburn (Charles, James), Colman (Ronald), Conway (Tim, Tom), Coogan (Jackie), Cooper (Gary), Cotten (Joseph), Crabbe (Buster), Cronyn (Hume), Crosby (Bing), Cruise (Tom), Culkin (Macaulay), Curtis (Tony), Dailey (Dan), Danson (Ted), Danton (Ray), Darren (James), De Niro (Robert), De Vito (Danny), Dullea (Keir), Duryea (Dan), Duvall (Robert), Ferrer (Jose, Mel), Fields (W.C.), Finney (Albert), Garner (James), Gibson (Hoot), Gorcey (Leo), Greene (Lorne, Richard), Harris (Richard), Harvey (Laurence), Hayden (Sterling), Heflin (Van), Heston (Charlton), Hingle (Pat), Holden (Bill), Howard (Trevor), Hudson (Rock), Hunter (Jeffrey, Tab), Huston (John, Walter), Jacobi (Lou), Jagger (Dean), Keaton (Buster, Michael), Knotts (Don), Kruger (Otto), Landau (Martin), Landon (Michael), Laurel (Stan), Lemmon (Jack), Lugosi (Bela), MacRae (Gordon), Malden (Karl), Martin (Dean), Marvin (Lee), Massey (Raymond), Mature (Victor), McCrea (Joel), Meeker (Ralph), Menjou (Adolphe), Morley (Robert), Morris (Wayne), Morrow (Vic), Mostel (Zero), Murphy (Audie, Eddie), Murray (Bill, Don), Nelson (Ozzie), Newley (Anthony), Newman (Paul), O'Brian (Hugh), O'Brien (Edmund, Pat), O'Toole (Peter), Pacino (Al), Parker (Fess), Poston (Tom), Powell (Dick), Reeves (Steve), Reiner (Carl, Rob), Rennie (Michael), Ritter (John, Tex), Rogers (Roy, Wayne, Will), Romero (Cesar), Rooney (Mickey), Schell (Maximilian), Sharif (Omar), Slezak (Walter), Swayze (Patrick), Talbot (Lyle), Taylor (Robert, Rod), Thomas (Danny, Richard), Toomey (Regis), Tucker (Forrest), Turpin (Ben), Vaughn (Robert), Voight (Jon), Wagner (Robert), Walker (Robert), Warden (Jack), Weaver (Dennis, Fritz), Welles (Orson), Werner (Oskar), Wilder (Gene) **7** Abraham (F. Murray), Andrews (Dana), Astaire (Fred), Aykroyd (Dan), Bellamy (Ralph), Bogarde (Dirk), Bridges (Beau, Jeff, Lloyd), Bronson (Charles), Brynner (Yul), Bushman (Francis X.), Buttons (Red), Calhern (Louis), Calhoun (Rory), Cameron (Rod), Carlson (Richard), Carroll (Leo G.), Chaplin (Charlie), Connery (Sean), Connors (Chuck, Mike), Conried (Hans), Costner (Kevin), da Silva (Howard), DeLuise (Dom), Donahue (Troy), Donlevy (Brian), Douglas (Kirk, Melvyn, Michael, Paul), Dreyfus (Richard), Edwards (Vince), Feldman (Marty), Freeman (Morgan), Garrick (David), Gazzara (Ben), Gielgud (John), Gleason (Jackie), Gossett (Louis), Granger (Farley, Stewart), Guiness (Alec), Hackman (Gene), Henreid (Paul), Hoffman (Dustin), Homeier (Skip), Homolka (Oscar), Hopkins (Anthony), Ireland (John), Janssen (David), Johnson (Don, Van), Jourdan (Louis), Jurgens (Curt), Karloff (Boris), Kennedy (Arthur, George), Klugman (Jack), Lawford (Peter), Leonard (Sheldon), MacLane (Barton), Maharis (George), Matthau (Walter), McCarey (Leo), McGavin (Darren), McQueen (Steve), Merrill (Gary), Milland (Ray), Mitchum (Robert), Montand (Yves), Navarro (Ramon), Newhart (Bob), O'Connor (Carroll, Donald), Olivier (Laurence), Palance (Jack), Paulsen (Pat), Peppard (George), Perkins (Anthony), Persoff (Nehemiah), Pickens (Slim), Pidgeon (Walter), Poitier (Sidney),

Preston (Robert), Randall (Tony), Redford (Robert), Robards (Jason), Robeson (Paul), Salvini (Tommaso), Sanders (George), Savalas (Telly), Scourby (Alexander), Selleck (Tom), Sellers (Peter), Silvers (Phil), Sinatra (Frank), Skelton (Red), Skinner (Otis), Steiger (Rod), Stewart (James), Tamblyn (Russ), Ustinov (Peter), Vallone (Raf), Van Dyke (Dick), Wallach (Eli), Widmark (Richard), Wilding (Michael), Winters (Jonathan), Woolley (Monty) 8 Basehart (Richard), Bickford (Charles), Blackmer (Sidney), Borgnine (Ernest), Buchanan (Edgar), Buchholz (Horst), Carrillo (Leo), Chandler (Jeff), Costello (Lou), Cummings (Robert), Day-Lewis (Daniel), Eastwood (Clint), Forsythe (John), Gardiner (Reginald), Garfield (John), Harrison (Noel, Rex), Hemmings (David), Holbrook (Hal), Holloway (Stanley), Jannings (Emil), Kilbride (Percy), Kingsley (Ben), Langella (Frank), Laughton (Charles), Lockhart (Gene), Marshall (E.G., Herbert), McDowell (Malcolm), McLaglen (Victor), Meredith (Burgess), Mitchell (Thomas), O'Connell (Arthur), O'Herlihy (Dan), Rathbone (Basil), Redgrave (Michael), Reynolds (Burt), Ritchard (Cyril), Robinson (Edward G.), Sarrazin (Michael), Scofield (Paul), Stallone (Sylvester), Sullivan (Barry), Von Sydow (Max), Whitmore (James) 9 Amsterdam (Morey), Barrymore (John, Lionel), Carnovsky (Morris), Carradine (David, John, Robert), Courtenay (Tom), Depardieu (Gerard), Fairbanks (Douglas), Franciosa (Anthony), Hardwicke (Cedric), Hyde-White (Wilfrid), Lancaster (Burt), MacMurray (Fred), Montalban (Ricardo), Pleasance (Donald), Robertson (Cliff, Dale), Zimbalist (Efrem) 10 Fitzgerald (Barry), Montgomery (Robert), Richardson (Ralph), Sutherland (Donald, Kiefer), Washington (Denzel) 11 Greenstreet (Sydney), Mastroianni (Marcello) 13 Kristofferson (Kris)

actor's ***quest:*** 4 part, role ***signal:*** 3 cue

actress 3 Bow (Clara), Day (Doris), Dee (Sandra), Dru (Joanne), Gam (Rita), Loy (Myrna), May (Elaine) 4 Bara (Theda), Barr (Roseanne), Cass (Peggy), Cher, Coca (Imogene), Dahl (Arlene), Duke (Patty), Eden (Barbara), Foch (Nina), Gish (Lillian), Hawn (Goldie), Holm (Celeste), Hunt (Linda, Marsha), Hyer (Martha), Kahn (Madeline), Kerr (Deborah), Lake (Veronica), Lisi (Virna), Main (Marjorie), Mayo (Virginia), Neal (Patricia), Raye (Martha), Rigg (Diana), Ross (Katharine), Rush (Barbara), Ryan (Peggy), Weld (Tuesday), West (Mae), Wood (Natalie, Peggy), Wray (Fay), York (Susannah) 5 Adams (Maude), Arden (Eve), Astor (Mary), Bates (Kathy), Bloom (Clair), Booth (Shirley), Britt (May), Bruce (Virginia), Buzzi (Ruth), Caron (Leslie), Close (Glenn), Crain (Jeanne), Davis (Bette, Geena, Judy), Dunne (Irene), Eggar (Samantha), Fonda (Jane), Gabor (Eva, Zsa Zsa), Garbo (Greta), Grant (Lee), Hagen (Uta), Hasso (Signe), Hayes (Helen), Henie (Sonja), Howes (Sally Ann), Jones (Jennifer, Shirley), Kelly (Patsy), Lange (Jessica), Leigh (Janet, Vivien), Lenya (Lotte), Loren (Sophia), Mason (Pamela), Miles (Sarah), Miles (Vera), Moore (Mary Tyler, Terry), North (Sheree), Novak (Kim), O'Hara (Maureen), Olson (Nancy), O'Neal (Tatum), Picon (Molly), Pitts (Zasu), Roman (Ruth), Saint (Eva Marie), Scott (Lizbeth, Martha), Smith (Alexis, Maggie), Storm (Gale), Tandy (Jessica), Welch (Raquel), Wiest (Dianne), Wyatt (Jane), Young (Loretta) 6 Angeli (Pier), Bacall (Lauren), Barrie (Wendy), Baxter (Anne), Bergen (Candice, Polly), Blaine (Vivian), Cannon (Dyan), Davies (Marion), Del Rio (Dolores), Dennis (Sandy), Diller (Phyllis), Duncan (Sandy), Fabray (Nanette), Farrow (Mia), Foster (Jodie), Garner (Peggy Ann), Garson (Greer), Gaynor (Mitzi), Gordon (Ruth), Grable (Betty), Grimes (Tammy), Harlow (Jean), Harper (Valerie), Harris (Julie), Hunter (Kim), Hussey (Ruth), Huston (Anjelica), Hutton (Betty), Keaton (Diane), Keeler (Ruby), Lamarr (Hedy), Lamour (Dorothy), Lasser (Louise), Laurie (Piper), Louise (Tina), Lupino (Ida), MacRae (Sheila), Malone (Dorothy), Martin (Mary), Matlin (Marlee), McGraw (Ali), Merkel (Una), Monroe (Marilyn), Moreau (Jeanne), Moreno (Rita), Oberon (Merle), O'Brien (Margaret), Palmer (Lili), Parker (Suzy), Powers (Stephanie), Prowse (Juliet), Remick (Lee), Ritter (Thelma), Rogers (Ginger), Sidney (Sylvia), Spacek (Sissy), Streep (Meryl), Taylor (Elizabeth), Temple (Shirley), Thomas (Marlo), Tiffin (Pamela), Tomlin (Lily), Turner (Kathleen, Lana), Walker (Nancy), Wilson (Marie), Wright (Teresa), Wynter (Dana) 7 Allyson (June), Andress (Ursula), Andrews (Julie), Bergman (Ingrid), Burnett (Carol), Darnell (Linda), DeCarlo (Yvonne), Dukakis (Olympia), Dunaway (Faye), Dunnock (Mildred), Fleming (Rhonda), Fricker (Brenda), Gardner (Ava), Garland (Judy), Goddard (Paulette), Grayson (Kathryn), Hayward (Susan), Hepburn (Audrey, Katharine), Jackson (Glenda), Langtry (Lillie), Learned (Michael), Lombard (Carole), Magnani (Anna), Mangano (Silvana), McGuire (Dorothy), McKenna (Siobhan), Mimieux (Yvette), Miranda (Carmen), Natwick (Mildred), Perrine (Valerie), Podesta (Rosanna), Roberts (Julia), Russell (Jane, Rosalind), Shearer (Norma), Simmons (Jean), Stevens (Stella), Swanson (Gloria), Thaxter (Phyllis), Tierney (Gene), Ullmann (Liv), Winfrey (Oprah), Winters (Shelley), Withers (Jane) 8 Anderson

(Judith), Ashcroft (Peggy), Bancroft (Anne), Bankhead (Tallulah), Basinger (Kim), Blondell (Joan), Byington (Spring), Caldwell (Zoe), Channing (Carol), Christie (Julie), Crawford (Joan), Dewhurst (Colleen), Dietrich (Marlene), Dressler (Marie), Fletcher (Louise), Fontaine (Joan), Fontanne (Lynn), Goldberg (Whoopi), Griffith (Melanie), Hayworth (Rita), Lansbury (Angela), Lawrence (Gertrude), Leachman (Cloris), Leighton (Margaret), Lindfors (Viveca), Lockhart (June), Lovelace (Linda), MacLaine (Shirley), Mercouri (Melina), Minnelli (Liza), Pfeiffer (Michelle), Pickford (Mary), Prentiss (Paula), Redgrave (Lynn, Vanessa), Rowlands (Gena), Signoret (Simone), Stanwyck (Barbara), Sullavan (Margaret), Talmadge (Norma), Thompson (Sada), Williams (Esther), Woodward (Joanne) **9** Barrymore (Ethel), Bernhardt (Sarah), Christian (Linda), Dickinson (Angie), Kellerman (Sally), Mansfield (Jayne), Moorehead (Agnes), O'Sullivan (Maureen), Pleshette (Suzanne), Plowright (Joan), Schneider (Romy), Singleton (Penny), Stapleton (Jean, Maureen), Strasberg (Susan), Streisand (Barbra), Struthers (Sally), Thorndike (Sybil), Vera-Ellen **10** Lanchester (Elsa), Montgomery (Elizabeth), Rutherford (Margaret), Tushingham (Rita) **11** de Havilland (Olivia), McCambridge (Mercedes), Riefenstahl (Leni) **12** Lollabrigida (Gina)

actual **4** hard, real, true **6** extant **7** genuine **8** absolute, bona fide, concrete, existent, material, physical, positive, tangible, unfabled **9** authentic, objective, veridical **10** legitimate, phenomenal, undeniable **12** indisputable

actuality **4** fact **5** being **7** reality **9** existence, substance **10** embodiment **11** incarnation, materiality

actually **4** very **5** truly **6** really **7** de facto **9** genuinely, veritably

actuate **4** move, stir **5** drive, impel, rouse **6** arouse, propel, set off **7** provoke, trigger **8** mobilize, vitalize **9** circulate, galvanize

act up **9** misbehave

acumen **3** wit **8** astucity, keenness **9** acuteness, sharpness **10** astuteness, shrewdness **11** discernment, penetration, percipience **12** perspicacity

acute **4** dire, high, keen **5** peaky, piked, sharp **6** argute, peaked, piping, shrill, treble, urgent **7** crucial, cutting, exigent, pointed **8** acicular, critical, incisive, piercing, shooting, stabbing **9** aciculate, acuminate, acuminous, cuspidate, desperate, knifelike, observant, sensitive, trenchant **10** perceptive **11** climacteric, penetrating, penetrative, quick-witted, sharp-witted ***combining form:*** **3** oxy

adage **3** saw **4** word **6** byword, saying, truism **7** proverb **8** aphorism, apothegm

Adah ***husband:*** **4** Esau **6** Lamech ***son:*** **5** Jabal, Jubal **7** Eliphaz

Adam ***grandson:*** **4** Enos **5** Enoch ***rib:*** **3** Eve ***son:*** **4** Abel, Cain, Seth ***teacher:*** **6** Raisel ***wife:*** **3** Eve **6** Lilith

adamant **5** rigid **8** immobile, obdurate **9** immovable, unbending, unswaying **10** inexorable, inflexible, relentless, unbendable, unyielding **12** unsubmitting

adapt **3** fit **4** suit **5** refit **6** adjust, square, tailor **7** conform **9** acclimate, reconcile **11** acclimatize, accommodate

adaptable **6** mobile, pliant, supple **7** ductile, plastic, pliable **8** moldable **9** all-around, malleable, many-sided, versatile

add **3** sum, tot **4** cast, foot, tote **5** affix, annex, tally, total **6** append, attach, figure, reckon, tack on, take on **7** augment, compute, enlarge, subjoin, summate **8** compound, increase, totalize **9** calculate

added **3** new **4** else, more **5** fresh, other **7** another, farther, further **10** additional

addendum **5** rider **7** allonge **8** addition **10** supplement

ad design **4** logo

addict **3** fan **4** bias, buff **5** hound, lover **6** adjust, junkie, votary, zealot **7** devotee, fanatic, habitué, hophead **9** habituate **10** aficionado, enthusiast, predispose

addition **4** plus, rise **5** extra, raise, rider **7** accrual, adjunct **8** addendum, appanage, increase **9** accession, accessory, accretion, extension, increment **10** accruement, supplement **12** appurtenance, augmentation ***number:*** **6** addend **7** summand

additional **3** new **4** else, more **5** extra, fresh, other **7** another, farther, further **9** accessory **12** supplemental **13** supplementary

additionally **3** too, yea, yet **4** also, more, then **5** again **6** as well, withal **7** addedly, besides, further **8** likewise, moreover **11** furthermore

additive **5** chain **8** extender **9** summative **10** cumulative **12** accumulative

addle **5** mix up **6** ball up, fuddle **7** confuse, fluster, nonplus, perplex **8** befuddle, bewilder, confound, distract, throw off **9** dumbfound

address **3** aim, air, set, sue, woo **4** hail, mien, port, send, ship, tact, talk **5** apply, court, greet, level, point, poise, remit, route, skill, speak **6** accost, attend, call to, devote, direct, pursue, relate, salute, speech **7** bearing, bespeak, consign, forward, incline, know-how, lecture, prowess, tutoyer **8** appeal to, approach, converse, deftness, demeanor, dispatch, petition, presence, talk with, transmit **9** dexterity, diplomacy, expertise 10 adroitness, allocution, buckle down, competence, deportment, efficiency 11 comportment, memorialize, proficiency, savoir faire, superscribe, tactfulness 12 apostrophize

adduce 3 lay 4 cite 5 offer 6 allege, submit, tender 7 advance, present, proffer, propose, suggest 8 document 9 exemplify 10 illustrate

add up to 4 mean 5 spell 6 denote, import, intend 7 connote, express, signify

adept 4 deft, whiz 5 crack 6 adroit, expert, master, wizard 7 skilled 8 masterly, skillful, virtuoso 9 dexterous, masterful 10 proficient 11 crackerjack 12 professional

adequacy 5 might 6 enough 7 ability 8 capacity 10 capability, competence, sufficient 13 qualification

adequate 6 common, decent, enough 8 all right 9 competent, sufficing 10 acceptable, sufficient 11 comfortable 12 satisfactory 13 unexceptional, unimpeachable

adequately 4 well 5 amply, right 6 enough 8 properly, suitably 9 fittingly 10 becomingly 13 appropriately

adhere 5 cling, stick 6 adsorb, cleave, cohere

adherence 4 bond 5 cling 7 loyalty 8 adhesion, clinging, cohesion, fidelity, stickage, sticking 9 constancy 10 attachment, concretion 11 cementation 12 faithfulness 13 agglutination

adherent 6 cohort 7 sectary 8 disciple, follower, henchman, partisan, sectator, stalwart 9 satellite, supporter *suffix:* 3 ite

adhering 8 osculant

adhesion see adherence

adhesive 5 gluey, gooey, gummy, tacky 6 clingy, cloggy, sticky 7 stickum 8 mucilage

adieu 2 by 5 congé 6 bye-bye, so long 7 cheerio, good-bye, parting 8 farewell, toodle-oo 11 leave taking

ad interim 6 acting, pro tem, supply 9 temporary 10 pro tempore

adipose 3 fat 5 fatty

adiposity 7 fatness, obesity 10 corpulence, fleshiness

adit 3 way 4 door 5 entry 6 access, entrée 7 ingress 8 entrance 9 admission 10 admittance

adjacent 5 handy 6 nearby 7 close-by 8 abutting, touching 9 adjoining, bordering 10 approximal, contiguous, convenient, juxtaposed, near-at-hand 11 close-at-hand, neighboring 12 conterminous

adjoin 4 abut, line, meet 5 march, touch, verge 6 border, butt on 8 neighbor 11 communicate

adjoining see abutting

adjourn 4 rise, stay 5 close, defer, delay 6 hold up, put off, recess, shelve 7 break up, disband, hold off, suspend 8 dissolve, hold over, postpone, prorogue 9 prorogate, terminate

adjudge 6 umpire 7 referee 9 arbitrate 10 adjudicate

adjudicate see adjudge

adjunct 5 affix 8 addition, appanage, appendix 9 accessory, accretion, appendage 10 attachment 12 appurtenance

adjust 3 fit, fix, rig 4 suit, tune 5 adapt, order, right 6 accord, attune, orient, square, tailor, tune up 7 arrange, conform, correct, rectify 8 modulate, regulate 9 habituate, harmonize, reconcile 11 accommodate

adjuvant 9 accessory, ancillary, auxiliary 10 collateral, subsidiary 11 appurtenant, subservient 12 contributory

ad-lib 9 improvise 11 extemporize, improvisate

Admetus *father:* 6 Pheres *wife:* 8 Alcestis

administer 3 run 4 deal, give 5 issue 6 direct, govern, manage, render, strike 7 conduct, deal out, deliver, dole out, execute, give out, inflict, mete out 8 carry out, dispense, share out 9 apportion, supervise 10 distribute, portion out

administrate 6 govern, render 7 execute 8 carry out

administration *system of:* 11 bureaucracy

administrator 4 exec 7 manager, officer 8 official 9 executive

admirable 6 august, worthy 8 laudable 9 deserving, estimable, meritable, praisable 11 commendable, meritorious, thankworthy 12 praiseworthy

admiral *American:* 4 Byrd, Sims 5 Dewey, Stark 6 Halsey, Nimitz 7 Zumwalt 8 Farragut, Rickover, Spruance *Confederate:* 6 Semmes *Dutch:* 5 Tromp *English:* 6 Nelson, Rodney, Vernon 7 Hawkins 8 Beaufort, Jellicoe, Villiers 11 Mountbatten *French:* 10 Villeneuve *German:* 4 Spee 6 Donitz, Raeder 7 Tirpitz *Japanese:* 4 Togo 5 Yonai 8 Yamamoto *Spanish:* 8 Menendez

admiration 5 amaze, favor 6 esteem, regard, wonder 7 account, respect 9 amazement, marveling 10 estimation, wonderment 12 appreciation

admire 5 adore, prize, value 6 esteem, regard, relish, revere 7 adulate, cherish, lionize, respect, worship 8 consider, treasure, venerate 9 delight in, reverence 10 appreciate

admirer 3 fan 6 votary 7 amateur, devotee, fancier

admission 3 way 4 adit, door 5 entry

6 access, entrée 7 ingress 8 entrance 10 admittance
admit 3 own 4 avow, take 5 agree, allow, enter, grant, let on, lodge, own up 6 fess up, harbor, permit, suffer, take in 7 concede, confess, receive, shelter 9 entertain, introduce, recognize 11 acknowledge
admittance see **admission**
admix 5 merge 6 mingle 8 comingle, immingle 9 commingle 11 intermingle
admixture 4 dash 5 alloy, shade, smack, spice, taint, tinge 7 amalgam 8 compound 9 composite 10 adulterant, denaturant 12 amalgamation
admonish 4 warn 5 chide 6 lesson, monish, rebuke 7 caution, reprove, tick off 8 call down, reproach 9 reprimand
admonishing 7 warning 8 monitory 10 cautionary, cautioning, monitorial
admonition 3 rap, wig 6 caveat, rebuke 7 caution, chiding, reproof, warning 9 reprimand 11 forewarning
ado 4 fuss, stir 5 tizzy, whirl 6 bustle, flurry, furore, pother, uproar 7 turmoil 9 confusion
adolescence 5 youth 6 spring 7 puberty 9 greenness, youthhood 10 juvenility, pubescence, springtide, springtime 12 youthfulness
adolescent 4 teen 6 teener 8 preadult, teenager
Adonijah ***brother:*** 5 Amnon 7 Absalom, Chileab ***father:*** 5 David ***mother:*** 7 Haggith ***slayer:*** 7 Benaiah
Adonis ***lover:*** 5 Venus 9 Aphrodite ***mother:*** 5 Myrrh 6 Myrrha ***slayer:*** 4 boar
adopt 4 take 6 affect, assume, take on, take up 7 embrace, espouse
adoption 8 espousal 9 embracing 11 embracement
adorable 4 lush 7 darling, lovable 8 heavenly, lovesome, luscious 9 ambrosial, delicious 10 delectable, delightful 11 scrumptious
adoration 4 love 7 passion, worship 8 devotion, idolatry 9 affection 11 idolization
adore 4 love 6 admire, dote on, esteem, revere 7 idolize, worship 8 dote upon, enshrine, venerate 9 affection, delight in, reverence
adorn 4 deck, trim 5 prank, primp, prink 6 bedeck, doll up, enrich, pretty, richen 7 bedizen, dress up, enhance, furbish, garnish, smarten 8 beautify, decorate, ornament, prettify, spruce up, titivate 9 embellish
adornment 5 decor 6 finery 7 garnish 8 ornament 9 caparison 10 decoration 11 centerpiece 13 embellishment
ad rem 7 apropos, germane 8 apposite, material, pointful, relevant 9 pertinent 10 applicable 11 applicative, applicatory
adroit 3 sly 4 deft 5 canny, handy, smart 6 astute, clever, nimble, shrewd 7 cunning 8 dextrous, skillful 9 dexterous, ingenious, workmanly 11 intelligent, quick-witted, workmanlike 13 perspicacious
adroitness 3 art 5 craft, skill 7 address, cunning, know-how, prowess, sleight 8 deftness 9 dexterity, expertise, readiness
adulation 7 acclaim, blarney 8 applause, flattery, soft soap 12 blandishment
adult 4 aged, ripe 5 grown 6 mature 7 grown-up, matured, ripened 9 full-blown, full-grown 11 full-fledged
adulterant 5 alloy 9 admixture 10 denaturant
adulterate 4 thin 5 taint 6 debase, defile, dilute, doctor, dope up, weight 7 pollute 8 denature, impurify 10 tamper with
adumbrate 3 dim, fog 4 bode, call, hint, mist, murk 5 augur, cloud, draft 6 darken, shadow, sketch 7 becloud, bespeak, betoken, obscure, outline, portend, predict, presage, suggest 8 block out, chalk out, forebode, forecast, foretell, indicate, prophesy, rough out, skeleton 9 obfuscate, prefigure 10 foreshadow, vaticinate 11 prefigurate, skeletonize 12 characterize
adumbration 4 hint, sign 5 shade, umbra 6 shadow 7 umbrage 8 penumbra 10 intimation, suggestion
advance 3 aid 4 cite, help, lend, loan, move 5 get on, march, raise, serve 6 adduce, allege, assist, course, foster, mature, prefer, uplift 7 develop, elevate, forward, further, headway, ongoing, present, proceed, promote, upgrade 8 anabasis, approach, encroach, get along, heighten, increase, overture, progress 9 encourage, evolution 11 development, furtherance, improvement, progression 12 breakthrough
advanced 7 forward, liberal, radical 8 tolerant 10 precocious 11 broad-minded, progressive
advancement 5 march 7 headway 8 progress 9 promotion 10 preference
advantage 3 use 4 boon, edge, good, lead, odds, sake 5 asset, avail, bulge, serve 6 better, profit 7 account, benefit, fitness, godsend, mastery, service, welfare 8 blessing, handicap, interest, leverage 9 allowance, head start, relevance, upper hand, well-being 10 ascendancy, domination, leadership, prosperity, usefulness 11 benediction, superiority 12 running start
advantageous 4 good 6 paying, toward, useful 7 benefic, gainful, helpful 8 favoring, remedial, salutary 9 conducive, desirable, expedient, favorable, lucrative 10 beneficial,

profitable, propitious, well-paying, worthwhile 11 moneymaking 12 remunerative
advent 6 coming 7 arrival, hearing 8 approach
adventitious 6 casual 10 accidental, contingent, fortuitous, incidental 12 supervenient
adventure 4 feat, gest, risk 5 quest, wager 6 chance 7 emprise, exploit 8 escapade 10 enterprise
adventuresome see **adventurous**
adventurous 4 bold, rash 5 brash 6 daring 7 doughty 8 intrepid, reckless 9 audacious, daredevil, foolhardy, impetuous, imprudent 11 temerarious
adversary 3 con 4 anti 5 match 7 opposer 8 opponent 9 oppugnant 10 antagonist
adverse 4 anti 7 counter, harmful, hurtful, opposed 8 contrary, negative, opposing 9 injurious, oppugnant 11 deleterious, detrimental, obstructive, unfavorable 12 antagonistic, antipathetic 13 counteractive
adversity 4 dole 6 misery, mishap 7 tragedy 8 distress 9 mischance, suffering 10 misfortune 11 contretemps
advert 4 note 5 refer 6 allude, notice, remark 7 bring up, observe 8 point out
advertent 6 arrect 7 heedful 9 attentive, intentive, observant, regardful
advertise 4 plug, puff, push 5 boost 6 blazon, report 7 build up, declare, promote, publish 8 announce, ballyhoo, proclaim 9 broadcast, publicize 10 annunciate, bruit about, promulgate
advertisement 2 ad 4 bill, plug, sign 5 blurb, flyer 6 notice, poster 7 affiche 9 billboard, broadcast, promotion, publicity 10 commercial, propaganda 11 declaration, publication 12 announcement, proclamation, promulgation 13 pronouncement
advertising 7 buildup, puffery 9 publicity
advice 4 news, word 7 caution, counsel, tidings, warning 8 guidance, teaching 10 admonition 11 information, instruction 12 intelligence
advisable 4 wise 6 seemly 7 politic, prudent 8 sensible, suitable, tactical 9 expedient
advise 4 clew, clue, post, tell, warn 6 confab, confer, fill in, huddle, inform, notify, parley, powwow, wise up 7 apprise, caution, consult, counsel 8 acquaint, forewarn 9 recommend 11 confabulate
advised 7 studied 8 designed, intended, prepense, studious 10 considered, deliberate, thought-out 11 intentional 12 premeditated
advocacy 7 defense
advocate 4 back 5 favor 6 preach, uphold 7 promote, support 8 backstop, champion, exponent, side with 9 encourage, expounder, proponent, supporter 11 countenance ***combining form:*** 4 crat ***suffix:*** 5 arian
Aeacus ***father:*** 4 Zeus ***mother:*** 6 Aegina ***son:*** 6 Peleus 7 Telamon
Aedon ***brother:*** 7 Amphion ***sister-in-law:*** 5 Niobe ***son (victim:*** 6 Itylus
Aeetes ***daughter:*** 5 Medea ***father:*** 6 Helios
Aegaeon see **Briareus**
Aegeon's wife 7 Aemilia
Aegeus'son 7 Theseus
aegis 4 ward 5 armor, guard 6 shield 7 backing, defense 8 armament, auspices, security 9 patronage, safeguard 10 protection 11 sponsorship
Aegisthus ***father:*** 8 Thyestes ***lover:*** 12 Clytemnestra ***mother:*** 7 Pelopia ***slayer:*** 7 Orestes ***victim:*** 6 Atreus 9 Agamemnon
Aegyptus ***brother:*** 6 Danaus ***father:*** 5 Belus ***mother:*** 8 Anchinoe ***son:*** 7 Lynceus
Aeneas ***companion:*** 7 Achates ***father:*** 8 Anchises ***mother:*** 5 Venus 9 Aphrodite ***son:*** 5 Iulus 8 Ascanius ***wife:*** 6 Creusa 7 Lavinia
Aeneid ***author:*** 6 Vergil, Virgil ***first words:*** 16 arma virumque cano ***hero:*** 5 Aneas
Aeolus ***brother:*** 5 Dorus 6 Xuthus ***daughter:*** 6 Canace 7 Alcyone 8 Halcyone ***father:*** 6 Hellen 8 Poseidon ***mother:*** 9 Melanippe ***son:*** 7 Athamas 9 Salmoneus
aeon 3 age 7 dog's age 8 blue moon, coon's age, eternity
aerate 3 air 6 aerify 9 oxygenate, ventilate
aerial 4 airy 5 lofty 6 towery, vapory 7 soaring, spiring, topless 8 ethereal, towering, vaporous 9 pneumatic 10 impalpable 11 atmospheric
aerie, aery, eyrie 4 nest 5 brood 9 penthouse
aeronaut 4 Fogg 5 pilot 7 aviator 8 Zeppelin 10 balloonist
Aerope ***husband:*** 6 Atreus ***lover:*** 8 Thyestes ***son:*** 8 Menelaus 9 Agamemnon
aery 6 aerial 8 ethereal 9 visionary
Aesculapius ***daughter:*** 6 Hygeia 7 Panacea ***father:*** 6 Apollo ***mother:*** 7 Coronis ***slayer:*** 4 Zeus 7 Jupiter ***son:*** 7 Machaon 9 Podalirus ***teacher:*** 6 Chiron ***wife:*** 6 Epione
Aeson ***brother:*** 6 Pelias ***son:*** 5 Jason
aesthete 10 dilettante 11 cognoscente, connoisseur
Aether's father 6 Erebus
affable 6 genial, gentle, polite 7 amiable,

cordial 8 gracious, sociable 9 congenial, courteous

affair 4 love 5 amour, thing 6 matter 7 concern, liaison, palaver, romance 8 business, intrigue 10 proceeding

affect 3 act, get 4 fake, move, sham, sway 5 bluff, carry, feign, haunt, put on, touch 6 assume, resort, strike 7 actuate, impress, inspire, pretend 8 frequent, simulate 9 influence 11 counterfeit

affectation 4 airs, lugs, pose 9 mannerism, prettyism

affected 5 put-on 6 chichi, la-di-da, too-too 7 assumed, feigned, genteel, mincing, stilted 8 involved, mannered, overnice, précieux, precious, spurious 9 concerned, conscious 10 artificial, implicated, interested 11 alembicated, overrefined, pretentious 13 self-conscious

affected with/by *combining form:* 6 pathic *suffix:* 2 ic 4 ical

affecting 6 moving 8 poignant, touching 9 troubling 10 disturbing, impressive 11 distressful, distressing

affection 4 bias, love, mark 5 savor, trait 6 doting, malady, virtue, warmth 7 ailment, concern, disease, emotion, feature, feeling, leaning, passion, quality, worship 8 devotion, disorder, fondness, interest, penchant, property, sickness, sympathy, syndrome 9 attention, attribute, character, complaint, condition, infirmity, sentiment 10 attachment, propensity, tenderness 12 predilection

affectionate 4 dear, fond, warm 6 doting, loving, tender 7 devoted 8 lovesome 11 sympathetic

affective 6 moving 7 emotive 9 emotional

affectivity 7 emotion, feeling, passion 9 sentiment

affianced 7 engaged 8 intended, plighted, promised 9 betrothed 10 contracted

affiche 4 bill 6 poster 7 placard 8 handbill

affidavit certificate 5 jurat

affiliated 4 akin 6 agnate, allied 7 cognate, connate, kindred, related 8 incident 10 connatural 11 consanguine

affiliation 5 tie-up 6 hookup 7 cahoots 8 alliance 10 connection 11 association, combination, conjunction, partnership 12 conjointment

affinity 6 simile 7 analogy 8 likeness, sympathy 9 alikeness, semblance 10 attraction, comparison, similarity, similitude 11 resemblance *combining form:* 5 phily, trope 6 philia 7 tropism

affirm 3 say, yes 4 aver, avow 5 state, vouch 6 assert, attest, avouch, depose 7 certify, declare, profess, protest, witness 9 guarantee

affirmative 2 ay 3 aye, yes 8 positive

affix 3 add 5 annex, rivet 6 append, attach, fasten 7 subjoin

afflict 3 try, vex 4 rack 5 annoy, harry, press, smite, worry, wound, wring 6 bother, harass, harrow, martyr, pester, plague, strike 7 agonize, crucify, torment, torture 9 martyrize 10 excruciate

afflicted 6 dolent, rueful, woeful 7 doleful, ruthful 8 dolorous, stricken, wretched 9 miserable, sorrowful

affliction 3 rue, woe 4 care, dole 5 cross, grief, trial 6 mishap, ordeal, regret, sorrow 7 anguish, illness 8 disorder, sickness, unhealth 9 heartache, infirmity, mischance 10 heartbreak 11 tribulation *suffix:* 4 itis

afflictive 4 dire, sore 6 aching, bitter, woeful 7 algetic, galling, hurtful, hurting, painful 8 grievous 10 calamitous, deplorable, lamentable 11 distasteful, distressing, regrettable, unfortunate, unpalatable 13 heartbreaking

affluent 4 rich 7 moneyed, opulent, wealthy

affray 3 row 5 brawl, clash, fight, melee 6 fracas 7 ruction, scuffle 8 skirmish 9 scrimmage 10 donnybrook

affright 3 awe 5 alarm, scare, spook 7 startle, terrify 9 terrorize

affront 4 face, meet, slap 6 insult, offend, slight 7 despite, offense, outrage 8 dishonor 9 aspersion, contumely, criticize, encounter, indignity 10 defamation

aficionado 3 fan 4 buff 5 hound, lover 6 addict, votary 7 devotee, habitué

afield 4 away 5 amiss, badly, wrong 6 astray

afire see **aflame**

aflame 5 afire, aglow, fiery 6 ablaze, alight 7 blazing, burning, flaming, flaring, ignited 8 aflicker 11 conflagrant

afraid 3 shy 4 wary 5 chary, jumpy, loath, scary, timid 6 aghast, averse, scared, trepid 7 afeared, anxious, ascared, fearful, uneager 8 cautious, hesitant, skittish, timorous 9 reluctant, terrified, unwilling 10 frightened 11 disinclined 12 apprehensive

afresh 3 new 4 anew, over 5 again, newly 6 de novo, lately, of late 8 once more, recently

Africa *country:* 4 Chad, Mali, Togo 5 Benin, Congo, Egypt, Gabon, Ghana, Kenya, Libya, Niger, Sudan, Zaire 6 Angola, Gambia, Guinea, Malawi, Rwanda, Uganda, Zambia 7 Algeria, Burundi, Lesotho, Liberia, Morocco, Namibia, Nigeria, Senegal, Somalia, Tunisia 8 Botswana, Cameroon, Djibouti, Ethiopia, Tanzania, Zimbabwe 9 Cape Verde, Mauritius, Swaziland 10 Ivory Coast, Madagascar, Mauritania, Mozambique, Seychelles 11 Burkina Faso,

Sierra Leone, South Africa 12 Guinea Bissau 13 Comoro Islands *ethnic group:* 3 Ibo 4 Akan, Arab, Boer, Copt, Fula, Issa, Moor, Zulu 5 Bantu, Fulah, Galla, Hausa, Kongo, Mande, Negro, Pygmy, Swazi, Wolof 6 Beduin, Berber, Fulani, Hamite, Herero, Kaffir, Kikuyu, Nubian, Somali, Tuareg, Ubangi, Yoruba 7 Ashanti, Bedouin, Bushman, Malinke, Swahili 8 Egyptian, Mandingo 9 Hottentot *language:* 3 Ibo 4 Urdu 5 Bantu, Galla, Hausa 6 Arabic, Berber, Somali, Yoruba 7 Amharic, Bambara, Swahili 8 Malagasy 9 Afrikaans

aft 6 astern

after 3 for 4 back, hind, next, past, rear 5 below, later, since 6 behind, beyond, hinder, retral 7 by and by, ensuing 8 hindmost, latterly 9 following, posterior 10 subsequent 12 postliminary, subsequently

after all 3 yet 5 still 6 though 7 howbeit, however 11 nonetheless 12 nevertheless

aftereffect 5 issue 6 result, upshot 7 outcome 8 causatum 11 consequence, eventuality

afterlife 6 beyond 8 eternity 9 hereafter

aftermath see **aftereffect**

afterward 4 next, to-be 5 later 6 behind, future, offing 7 by-and-by 8 latterly 9 hereafter 12 subsequently

afterword 8 epilogue

Agag *kingdom:* 6 Amalek *slayer:* 6 Samuel

again 4 also, anew, back, over 5 about 6 afresh, around, de novo 7 besides, further 8 once more 12 additionally *combining form:* 2 an 3 ana 4 pali *prefix:* 2 re

again and again 3 oft 4 much 5 often 8 ofttimes 10 frequently, oftentimes, repeatedly

against 4 agin 6 contra, facing, toward, versus 7 apropos, despite, vis-à-vis 8 fronting, touching 9 in spite of 10 concerning, respecting *prefix:* 2 ob 3 ant 4 anti 6 contra 7 counter

Agamemnon *avenger:* 7 Orestes *brother:* 8 Menelaus *daughter:* 7 Electra 9 Iphigenia *father:* 6 Atreus *slayer:* 9 Aegisthus *son:* 7 Orestes *wife:* 12 Clytemnestra

agape 6 aghast 7 shocked 8 dismayed 10 confounded 11 dumbfounded, overwhelmed 13 thunderstruck

agate 3 mib, taw 6 marble 7 shooter

Agave *father:* 6 Cadmus *husband:* 6 Echion *mother:* 8 Harmonia *sister:* 3 Ino 6 Semele 7 Autonoe *son:* 8 Pentheus

age 3 eon, era 4 aeon, grow, ripe, time 5 epoch, ripen 6 grow up, mature, mellow, period 7 develop 8 blue moon, caducity, eternity, maturate

aged 3 old 4 ripe 5 hoary, olden 6 mellow, senior 7 ancient, antique, elderly, matured, ripened 8 Noachian, timeworn 9 senescent, venerable 11 patriarchal 12 antediluvian

ageless 7 eternal 8 dateless, timeless 10 intemporal

agency 4 mean 5 cause, organ 6 medium 7 channel, vehicle 8 ministry 10 instrument

agenda 6 docket 7 program 8 calendar, schedule 9 timetable *entry:* 4 item

Agenor *brother:* 5 Belus *daughter:* 6 Europa *father:* 7 Antenor, Neptune 8 Poseidon *mother:* 5 Libya *son:* 6 Cadmus

agent 3 fed, spy 4 doer, mean, tool 5 actor, organ, proxy, spook 6 deputy, factor, medium 7 channel, proctor, steward, vehicle 8 assignee, attorney, executor, institor, minister, ministry 9 activator, go-between, middleman 10 instrument, procurator *combining form:* 4 stat *suffix:* 3 ant

age-old 7 ancient, antique 8 timeworn 9 venerable 12 antediluvian

agglomerate 4 heap, mass, pile 9 aggregate 11 aggregation

agglomeration 5 hoard, trove 9 aggregate, amassment 10 collection, cumulation 11 aggregation

aggrandize 5 boost, exalt, honor 6 beef up, expand, extend 7 augment, build up, dignify, enlarge, ennoble, glorify, magnify, sublime 8 heighten, increase, multiply 11 distinguish

aggravate 4 gall 5 annoy, grate, mount, peeve, pique, rouse, upset 6 burn up, deepen, nettle, worsen 7 bedevil, disturb, enhance, magnify, perturb, provoke 8 heighten, irritate 9 intensify 10 exasperate

aggravation 6 bother, pother 9 annoyance

aggregate 3 all, sum 4 body, bulk, floc 5 add up, gross, total, whole 6 amount, budget, number 7 quantum 8 entirety, quantity, totality 11 agglomerate 12 conglomerate 13 agglomeration *suffix:* 3 ery

aggregation 4 ruck 5 crowd, group, hoard, trove 6 muster 7 company 8 assembly 9 amassment, congeries, gathering 10 assemblage, collection, cumulation 11 agglomerate 12 accumulation

aggression 4 raid 5 fight, onset 6 attack 7 assault, offense 8 invasion 9 incursion, offensive, onslaught, pugnacity 10 assailment 12 belligerence 13 combativeness

aggressive 5 pushy 6 fierce 7 scrappy, vicious 8 militant 9 assertive, combative,

imperious **11** belligerent, contentious, domineering, hard-hitting
aggressiveness **11** bellicosity **12** belligerence, belligerency
aggrieve **4** hurt, pain **5** annoy, harry, worry, wrong **6** harass, injure, plague **7** afflict, oppress, torment **8** distress **9** constrain, persecute
aghast **4** agog, awed **5** agape **6** afraid, amazed, scared **7** anxious, fearful, shocked **8** appalled, dismayed, startled **9** horrified, terrified **10** astonished, confounded, frightened **11** awestricken, dumbfounded, overwhelmed **12** horror-struck **13** flabbergasted, thunderstruck
agile **4** deft, spry, yare **5** brisk, catty, lithe, zippy **6** active, adroit, limber, lively, nimble, supple, volant **7** lissome **8** dextrous **9** dexterous, sprightly
agitate **4** rile, rock **5** argue, drive, impel, peeve, shake, upset **6** bother, debate, flurry, joggle, ruffle **7** discuss, dispute, disturb, fluster, perturb, provoke, tempest, unhinge **8** convulse, irritate **9** thrash out **10** discompose, exasperate
agitation **4** flap, stew **6** bustle, dither, lather, pother, tumult **7** tempest, turmoil **9** commotion, confusion **10** turbulence
agitator **7** inciter **8** fomenter **10** instigator
Aglaia see Graces
Aglauros, Agraulos *father:* **7** Cecrops *sister:* **5** Herse **9** Pandrosos
aglow **5** afire **6** ablaze, aflame, alight, lucent **7** radiant, shining **8** aflicker, gleaming, luminous
agnate **4** akin, like **5** alike **6** allied **7** cognate, connate, kindred, related, similar **9** analogous **10** affiliated **11** consanguine **13** corresponding
agnostic **7** infidel, skeptic **11** disbeliever
ago **2** by **4** gone, past, syne, yore **5** since
agog **4** avid **5** eager **6** ardent, roused **7** excited, popeyed **9** impatient
agonize **4** fret, gall, rack **5** chafe **6** harrow, squirm, suffer, writhe **7** afflict, torment, torture, trouble **8** distress **10** excruciate
agonizing **7** intense, racking, tearing **9** harrowing, torturing, torturous **10** tormenting **12** excruciating
agony **4** pain **5** dolor **6** misery **7** passion **8** distress **9** suffering
agrarian **5** rural **6** rustic **8** agrestal, pastoral **10** campestral **12** agricultural
Agraulos see Aglauros
agree **3** yes **4** jibe, suit **5** admit, check, equal, fit in, match, tally **6** accede, accord, assent, concur, square **7** comport, concede, concert, concord, conform, consent **8** check out, coincide, dovetail **9** acquiesce, harmonize, recognize, subscribe **10** correspond **11** acknowledge
agreeable **4** nice **7** affable, welcome **8** amenable, pleasant, pleasing **9** congenial, congruous, consonant, favorable **10** compatible, consistent, gratifying **11** pleasurable, pleasureful, sympathetic
agreed **2** OK **3** aye, yea, yep, yes **4** okay **8** all right, okeydoke
agreement **4** bond, deal, pact **6** accord, treaty, unison **7** bargain, compact, concord, entente, harmony **8** contract, covenant **9** concordat **10** consonance **11** concordance
agree with **3** fit **4** suit **5** befit **6** become **10** go together
agricultural **8** agrarian *combining form:* **4** agro
agriculture **7** farming, tillage **8** agronomy **9** husbandry
Agrippina's son **4** Nero
aground **7** beached **8** stranded
Ahab *daughter:* **8** Athaliah *father:* **4** Omri *wife:* **7** Jezebel
Ahasuerus *kingdom:* **6** Persia *wife:* **6** Esther, Vashti
Ahaz *kingdom:* **5** Judah *son:* **8** Hezekiah *wife:* **3** Abi
Ahaziah *father:* **4** Ahab **5** Joram **7** Jehoram *kingdom:* **5** Judah **6** Israel *mother:* **7** Jezebel **8** Athaliah *sister:* **9** Jehosheba **11** Jehosobeath
ahead **4** alee, ante, fore **5** forth **6** before, onward **7** forward, onwards **8** forwards, previous **9** in advance **10** beforehand **11** precedently **12** antecedently
Ahinoam *father:* **7** Ahimaaz *husband:* **4** Saul **5** David *son:* **5** Amnon
aid **4** abet, hand, help, lift **6** assist, helper, relief, succor **7** ancilla, backing, comfort, help out, succour, support **8** benefact, succorer **9** assistant, attendant, coadjutor **10** assistance, benefactor, coadjutant, lieutenant, ministrant, mitigation **11** alleviation, assuagement
Aida *composer:* **5** Verdi *father:* **8** Amonasro *lover:* **7** Radames *rival:* **7** Amneris
aide **6** deputy, second **7** orderly **9** assistant, coadjutor **10** coadjutant, lieutenant
ail **4** cark **5** upset, worry **7** afflict, trouble **8** distress
ailing **3** ill, low **4** mean, weak **6** donsie, droopy, offish, poorly, sickly, unwell **8** off-color **9** enfeebled **10** indisposed **11** debilitated
ailment **3** ill **6** malady, unrest **7** disease, ferment, turmoil **8** disorder, disquiet, sickness, syndrome **9** affection, complaint, condition, infirmity **10** inquietude **11** disquietude, restiveness **12** restlessness
aim **3** try **4** cast, goal, head, mark, mean, plan, want, wish **5** angle, essay, focus, level, point, slant, train **6** aspire, design,

desire, direct, intend, strive, target, zero in 7 address, attempt, propose, purpose 8 ambition, endeavor 9 objective 11 contemplate

aimless 6 random 9 desultory, haphazard, hit-or-miss, irregular, unplanned 10 designless 11 purposeless

air 3 sky 4 aura, feel, mien, mood, port, song, tune, vent 5 state, style 6 aerate, aerify, manner, melody, reveal, strain 7 bearing, declare, divulge, express, feeling, melisma, publish, quality 8 demeanor, presence, proclaim 9 broadcast, character, semblance, ventilate 10 atmosphere, deportment 11 comportment ***combining form:*** 3 aer, atm 4 aeri, aero, atmo 5 pneum 6 pneumo 7 pneumat 8 pneumato

aircraft 5 blimp, drone, plane 6 glider 7 airship, balloon, chopper 8 aerodyne, aerostat, airplane, jetliner, zeppelin 9 dirigible 10 helicopter ***carrier:*** 7 flattop 8 birdfarm ***designer:*** 6 Fokker, Martin 7 Junkers, Tupolev 8 Northrop, Sikorsky, Yakovlev 13 Messerschmitt

airless 5 close, stivy 6 stuffy, sultry 8 stifling 10 breathless 11 suffocating

airman 5 flier, pilot 6 fly-boy 7 aviator

air movement 5 draft 7 updraft 9 downdraft

air navigation system 5 loran, navar, radar

airplane 3 jet, SST 4 STOL, VTOL 5 avion, VSTOL 6 bomber 7 fighter 8 autogiro, autogyro 9 transport ***A-bomb-dropper:*** 8 Enola Gay ***battle:*** 8 dogfight ***body:*** 8 fuselage ***commercial:*** 5 liner ***engine:*** 3 jet 6 fanjet 7 propjet 8 turbofan, turbojet 9 turboprop ***engine casing:*** 7 nacelle ***engineless:*** 6 glider ***instrument:*** 5 radar, radio 7 compass 9 altimeter, gyroscope 10 tachometer 11 transponder ***maneuver:*** 4 buzz, dive, loop, roll 8 nosedive 9 chandelle 10 barrel roll ***movement:*** 3 yaw 4 bank, spin 5 pitch 8 tailspin ***part:*** 3 fin 4 flap, nose, prop, tail, wing 5 cabin, wheel 6 engine, rudder 7 aileron 8 airscrew, elevator 9 empennage, propeller 10 stabilator, stabilizer ***pilotless:*** 5 drone ***shelter:*** 6 hangar ***target:*** 6 drogue ***vapor:*** 8 contrail

airport 5 drome, field 7 helipad 8 airdrome, airfield, heliport 9 aerodrome ***building:*** 8 terminal ***flag:*** 8 windsock ***name:***

Amsterdam: 8 Schiphol ***Atlanta:*** 10 Hartsfield ***Boston:*** 5 Logan ***Chicago:*** 5 O'Hare ***Copenhagen:*** 7 Kastrup ***Dublin:*** 7 Shannon ***London:*** 7 Gatwick 8 Heathrow ***New York:*** 3 JFK 7 Kennedy 9 La Guardia ***Paris:*** 4 Orly 8 DeGaulle 9 Le Bourget ***Rome:*** 7 Da Vinci ***Washington:*** 6 Dulles

part: 5 apron, tower 6 runway 7 taxiway

airs 4 lugs, pose, show 6 vanity 9 loftiness, mannerism, prettyism, vainglory 11 affectation, ostentation

airship 8 zeppelin 9 dirigible

airtight 8 hermetic

airwaves nuisance 6 static

airy 4 rare, thin 5 blowy, gusty, light, lofty, windy 6 aerial, bouncy, breezy, dainty, towery, vapory 7 buoyant, gaseous, soaring, spiring, tenuous 8 animated, delicate, ethereal, rarefied, spirited, supernal, towering, vaporous, volatile 9 expansive, frivolous, pneumatic, resilient, windswept 10 diaphanous 11 atmospheric, skyscraping 12 effervescent, high-spirited

Ajax's father 6 Oileus 7 Telamon

akin 4 like 5 alike 6 agnate, allied 7 cognate, connate, kindred, related, similar, uniform 8 parallel 9 analogous, consonant 10 affiliated, comparable, connatural 11 consanguine 13 corresponding

Alabama 7 capital 10 Montgomery ***college, university:*** 5 Miles 6 Auburn, Mobile 8 Tuskegee 9 Talladega 10 Huntingdon ***largest city:*** 10 Birmingham ***nickname:*** 11 Cotton State 12 Heart of Dixie ***state flower:*** 8 camellia

alacrity 8 celerity, dispatch 9 briskness, eagerness, quickness, readiness 10 enthusiasm, expedition, promptness 11 promptitude

alamo 6 poplar 10 cottonwood

a la mode 4 chic, tony 6 modish, tonish, trendy 7 dashing, stylish 9 exclusive 11 fashionable

alarm 3 SOS 4 fear 5 alert, dread, larum, panic, scare, siren, spook, upset 6 dismay, fright, horror, terror, tocsin 7 startle, terrify, warning 8 affright, frighten 9 terrorize 11 forewarning, trepidation 13 consternation

alarmable 4 edgy 8 agitable, skittery, skittish, volatile 9 excitable, startlish 11 combustible

Alaska ***capital:*** 6 Juneau ***largest city:*** 9 Anchorage ***state flower:*** 11 forget-me-not

Albania ***capital:*** 6 Tirane ***monetary unit:*** 3 lek

albatross 5 goony 6 gooney, goonie

albeit 5 while 6 much as, though 7 whereas 8 although

Alberta ***capital:*** 8 Edmonton ***university:*** 7 Calgary 10 Lethbridge

Albion 7 England

album 3 ana 6 record 7 garland, omnibus 8 register 9 anthology 10 miscellany 11 florilegium

Alcestis ***father:*** 6 Pelias ***husband:*** 7 Admetus ***rescuer:*** 8 Heracles, Hercules
alchemist 10 Paracelsus
Alcina ***sister:*** 7 Morgana 10 Logistilla ***victim:*** 6 Rogero 8 Astolpho, Ruggiero
Alcinous ***daughter:*** 8 Nausicaa ***wife:*** 5 Arete
Alcmaeon ***father:*** 10 Amphiaraus ***mother:*** 8 Eriphyle ***wife:*** 10 Callirrhoe
Alcmene ***husband:*** 10 Amphitryon ***son:*** 8 Heracles, Hercules
alcohol 4 grog 5 booze, drink, hooch, juice 6 liquor, tipple 7 spirits 9 aqua vitae, firewater ***name:*** 4 amyl 5 butyl, cetyl, ethyl 6 glycol, methyl, sterol 7 butanol, ethanol, mannite, menthol 8 glycerin, glycerol, inositol, mannitol, methanol 9 isopropyl 11 cholesterol ***used in perfumes:*** 5 nerol 7 borneol, linalol 8 farnesol, geraniol, linalool
alcoholic 4 hard 8 bibulous 9 spiritous 10 spirituous 11 dipsomaniac 12 intoxicating
alcoholic drink see under **beverage**
alcoholized 5 drunk
alcove 6 gazebo, pagoda 9 belvedere ***Japanese:*** 8 tokonoma
Alcyone ***father:*** 5 Atlas 6 Aeolus ***husband:*** 4 Ceyx ***mother:*** 7 Pleione ***sisters:*** 8 Pleiades
ale 3 nog 4 nogg
Alea 6 Athena
alehouse 3 pub 4 café 6 bistro 7 cabaret 8 beer hall 9 bierstube, brasserie, honky-tonk, nightclub 10 beer garden 11 rathskellar
Alemanus ***father:*** 7 Histion ***grandfather:*** 6 Japhet
alert 3 SOS 4 keen, warn 5 alarm, quick, ready, sharp, smart 6 brainy, bright, clever, frisky, lively, tocsin 7 heedful, knowing, mindful, wakeful 8 animated, open-eyed, spirited, vigilant, watchful 9 attentive, brilliant, mercurial, sprightly, vivacious, wide-awake 11 intelligent, quick-witted, ready-witted ***Scottish:*** 4 gleg 8 wakerife
Alexander ***birthplace:*** 5 Pella ***conquest:*** 4 Tyre 5 Egypt, Issus 6 Arbela, Greece, Persia 7 Parthia 8 Granicus ***father:*** 6 Philip ***general:*** 9 Antipater ***horse:*** 10 Bucephalus ***kingdom:*** 9 Macedonia ***mother:*** 8 Olympias ***teacher:*** 9 Aristotle ***wife:*** 6 Roxana
alfalfa 6 lucern 7 lucerne
alfresco 7 open-air, outdoor, outside 9 out-of-door 10 hypaethral
alga 6 desmid, diatom 7 seaweed ***blue-green:*** 6 nostoc ***brown:*** 4 kelp 5 fucus 8 rockweed ***combining form:*** 7 phyceae ***green:*** 8 conferva 9 chlorella ***red:*** 4 nori 7 amanori
algebra term 4 root 6 factor 8 binomial, equation, monomial, variable 9 quadratic 10 polynomial
Algeria ***capital:*** 7 Algiers ***ethnic group:*** 4 Arab 6 Berber ***monetary unit:*** 5 dinar ***port:*** 4 Oran
algetic 4 sore 6 aching 7 hurtful, hurting, painful 10 afflictive
Ali ***son:*** 5 Hasan 6 Husayn ***wife:*** 6 Fatima
alias 3 AKA 6 anonym 7 pen name 9 pseudonym 10 nom de plume 11 nom de guerre
alibi 4 plea 6 excuse 7 pretext
alien 6 exotic 7 foreign, inconnu, strange 8 estrange, outcomer, outsider, stranger, transfer 9 auslander, extrinsic, foreigner, outlander 10 extraneous, outlandish
alienate 4 part, wean 6 assign, convey, remise 8 disunify, disunite, estrange, sign over, transfer 9 disaffect 10 relinquish
alienation 6 lunacy 7 madness 8 insanity 9 unbalance 10 aberration, insaneness 11 derangement, distraction, psychopathy 12 disaffection, estrangement
alight 4 land 5 afire, aglow, fiery, perch, roost 6 ablaze, aflame, bright, settle 7 blazing, burning, deplane, detrain, flaming, flaring, glowing, ignited, set down, sit down 8 aflicker, dismount 9 effulgent, refulgent, touch down 11 conflagrant
align 4 line, true 5 range 6 adjust, line up 8 regulate 9 allineate
alike 4 akin, same 7 similar, uniform 8 parallel 9 analogous, consonant 10 comparable 13 corresponding ***combining form:*** 2 is 3 hom, iso 4 homo
alikeness 6 simile 7 analogy 8 affinity 9 semblance 10 comparison, similarity, similitude 11 resemblance
aliment 3 pap 4 food 7 pabulum 9 nutriment 10 sustenance 11 nourishment
alimentary 9 nutritive 11 nutritional
alimentary canal 7 enteron
alimentation 4 keep 5 bread 6 living 7 support 10 livelihood, sustenance 11 maintenance, subsistence
alimony see **alimentation**
alive 4 rife 5 awake, aware, fresh, quick, vital 6 active, extant, living, zoetic 7 animate, dynamic, knowing, replete, running, teeming, working 8 animated, existent, existing, sensible, sentient, swarming, thronged 9 abounding, au courant, cognizant, conscious, operative, wide-awake 11 functioning, overflowing
alkali metal 6 cesium, sodium 7 lithium 8 francium, rubidium 9 potassium
alkaline substance 3 lye, reh 4 lime, soda, usar 5 borax 6 potash 7 ammonia, antacid 8 pearl ash, saltwort 11 caustic soda

alkali's opposite 4 acid
alkalize 6 basify
alkaloid 4 base ***hallucinogenic:*** 7 harmine 9 harmaline ***medicinal:*** 5 ergot 6 heroin 7 cocaine, codeine, emetine, eserine, harmine, quinine 8 atropine, caffeine, ecgonine, lobeline, morphine 9 ephedrine, harmaline, quinidine, reserpine 11 scopolamine ***narcotic:*** 6 heroin 7 cocaine, codeine 8 morphine ***poisonous:*** 6 conine 7 tropine 8 atropine, nicotine, solanine, thebaine 9 aconitine 11 scopolamine
all 3 sum 4 each 5 every, gross, quite, total, whole 6 apiece, entire, in toto, purely, wholly 7 exactly, totally, utterly 8 complete, entirety, everyone, outright, totality 9 aggregate, everybody 10 altogether, everything ***combining form:*** 3 omn, pam, pan 4 omni, pano, pant 5 panta, panto
all-around 7 general, overall 8 complete, sweeping, synoptic 9 adaptable, many-sided, panoramic, versatile 10 consummate 11 wide-ranging 13 comprehensive
allay 4 balm, calm, ease, lull 5 quiet, still 6 settle, soothe, subdue 7 assuage, compose, lighten, mollify, quieten, relieve 8 mitigate 9 alleviate 11 tranquilize
all but 4 most, much, nigh 5 about 6 almost, nearly 8 as good as, as much as, well-nigh 11 essentially, practically 13 approximately
allegation 8 pleading 9 assertion
allege 3 lay 4 cite 5 offer, state 6 adduce, assert 7 advance, declare, present, profess
alleged 7 dubious, would-be 8 doubtful, so-called, specious, supposed 9 pretended, professed, purported, soi-disant 10 ostensible, self-styled
allegiance 5 ardor, piety 6 fealty, homage 7 loyalty 8 devotion, fidelity 12 faithfulness
allegiant 4 true 5 liege, loyal 6 ardent 7 staunch 8 constant, faithful, resolute 9 steadfast
allegory 4 myth 5 fable 7 parable 8 apologue 9 symbolism 10 figuration 12 typification
allergy 5 atopy 8 aversion, dyspathy 9 antipathy, rejection, repulsion
alleviate 4 cure, ease 5 allay 6 remedy 7 assuage, lighten, mollify, relieve 8 mitigate
alleviation 4 ease 6 relief 8 easement 10 mitigation
all-fired 5 utter 6 blamed, dashed, deuced 7 blasted, blessed, doggone, goldarn 8 infernal
alliance 5 tie-up, union 6 hookup, league 7 cahoots 9 anschluss, coalition 10 connection, federation 11 affiliation, association, combination, confederacy, conjunction, partnership, unification 12 conjointment 13 confederation
allied 4 akin 6 agnate, linked, united 7 cognate, connate, kindred, related 8 incident 10 affiliated, connatural 11 consanguine
all in 5 spent 6 bleary, effete, used up 7 drained, far-gone, worn-out 8 depleted 9 exhausted, washed-out
all in all 5 quite 6 in toto, purely, wholly 7 en masse, totally, utterly 9 generally 10 altogether, by and large, on the whole
allineate 4 line 5 align, range 6 line up
allness 8 entirety, totality
allocate 4 give 5 allot, allow 6 assign 7 earmark, mete out 9 admeasure, apportion, designate
allocution 4 talk 6 speech 7 address, lecture
allot 4 give 5 grant 6 accord, assign 7 deal out, dole out, mete out 8 allocate, dispense 9 admeasure, apportion 10 distribute
allotment 3 cut 4 bite, meed, part 5 quota, share, slice 6 ration 7 measure, partage, portion, quantum 9 allowance
all-out 5 total 9 full-blown, full-scale, unlimited 12 totalitarian
all over 10 everyplace, everywhere, far and near, far and wide, high and low, throughout
allow 3 let, lot, own 4 give 5 admit, allot, brook, grant, leave, let on, stand 6 assign, endure, fess up, permit, suffer 7 concede, confess, mete out 8 allocate, tolerate 9 admeasure, apportion 11 acknowledge
allowance 3 aid, cut, lot 4 bite, edge, help, meed, odds, part, tret 5 grant, leave, quota, share, slice 6 corody, permit, ration 7 consent, corrody, measure, partage, portion, quantum, subsidy, vantage 8 handicap, pittance, sanction 9 advantage, allotment, head start 10 assistance, concession, permission, sufferance 13 accommodation, apportionment, authorization
alloy 5 blend 6 fusion 7 amalgam, mixture 8 compound 9 admixture, composite 10 adulterant, denaturant 11 interfusion 12 amalgamation, intermixture ***brass-like:*** 6 latten, lattin ***copper-sulfur:*** 6 niello ***copper-tin:*** 6 bronze ***copper-zinc:*** 5 brass 6 tambac, tombac, tombak 8 arsedine ***gold-like:*** 6 oreide, ormolu, oroide ***gold-silver:*** 8 electrum ***iron-carbon:*** 5 steel ***iron-nickel:*** 5 invar 7 elinvar ***mercury:*** 7 amalgam ***pewter-like:*** 5 bidri ***tin-lead:*** 5 calin, terne 6 pewter, solder ***tin-zinc:*** 6 oreide, oroide ***used in jewelry:*** 6 oreide, oroide, tombac
all-powerful 8 almighty 10 omnipotent
all right 2 OK 3 aye, yea, yep, yes

4 good, jake, okay 6 agreed, decent 8 adequate, okeydoke 9 tolerable 10 acceptable 12 satisfactory

all round 7 overall 10 everyplace, everywhere, far and near, far and wide, high and low, throughout

all there 4 sane 5 lucid, right 6 normal 12 compos mentis

All the Way Home author 4 Agee

allude 4 hint 5 imply, refer 6 advert 7 bring up, suggest 8 intimate

allure 4 bait, draw, take, tole, toll, wile 5 charm, decoy, tempt 6 appeal, entice, entrap, lead on, seduce 7 attract, bewitch, enchant, glamour 8 charisma, inveigle, witchery 9 captivate, fascinate, magnetism, magnetize 10 witchcraft 11 fascination

allurement 4 bait, call, draw, pull, trap 5 decoy, snare 6 appeal, come-on 9 seduction 10 attraction, enticement, seducement, temptation 12 drawing power, inveiglement

alluring 5 siren 8 charming 9 appealing, beguiling, glamorous, seductive 10 appetizing, attractive, bewitching, enchanting 11 captivating, fascinating

ally 4 join 5 unite 6 friend, helper 7 comrade, partner 8 federate 9 affiliate, associate, bedfellow, colleague, supporter 10 accomplice 11 confederate 12 collaborator

almighty 3 God 7 Creator 10 omnipotent 11 all-powerful

almost 4 nigh 5 about 6 all but, nearly 8 as good as, as much as, well-nigh 9 nearabout, virtually 11 essentially, practically 13 approximately *Scottish:* 6 feckly

alms 7 charity 8 donation, offering 11 benefaction, beneficence 12 contribution

Aloeus *father:* 7 Neptune 8 Poseidon *mother:* 6 Canace *son:* 4 Otus 9 Ephialtes *wife:* 9 Iphimedia

aloft 4 high, over 5 above 6 upward 7 skyward 8 overhead *combining form:* 4 hyps 5 hypsi, hypso

Aloha State 6 Hawaii

alone 4 only, sole, solo 5 apart, solus 6 lonely, singly, solely, unique 7 isolate, removed 8 detached, entirely, isolated, lonesome, peerless, singular, solitary 9 matchless, unequaled, unmatched, unrivaled 10 unexampled, unexcelled 11 exclusively, unsurpassed 12 unparalleled, unrepeatable 13 unaccompanied

aloneness 8 solitude 9 isolation

along 3 too, yet 4 also 5 forth 6 as well, onward 7 besides, forward 8 likewise, moreover 11 furthermore 12 additionally

alongside 2 by 6 beside, next to 7 fornent *prefix:* 3 par 4 para

along with *combining form:* 3 sym, syn

aloof 4 cold, cool 5 proud 6 casual, chilly, frigid, offish, remote 7 distant, haughty 8 arrogant, detached, reserved, reticent, solitary 9 unbending, uncurious, withdrawn 10 disdainful, restrained, unsociable 11 constrained, indifferent, standoffish, unconcerned 12 uninterested

alp 4 peak 5 mount 8 mountain

alpaca's habitat 4 Peru 5 Andes 7 Bolivia

alpha 4 dawn 5 start 6 outset 7 dawning, genesis, opening 8 outstart 9 beginning 12 commencement

alphabet 4 ABC's 7 grammar, letters 8 elements 9 rudiments 10 principles 12 fundamentals *Arabic:* 2 ba, fa, ha, ra, ta, ya, za 3 ayn, dad, dal, gaf, jim, kaf, kha, lam, mim, nun, sad, sin, tha, waw, zay 4 alif, dhal, shin 5 ghayn *Greek:* 2 mu, nu, pi, xi 3 chi, eta, phi, psi, rho, tau 4 beta, iota, zeta 5 alpha, delta, gamma, kappa, omega, sigma, theta 6 lambda 7 epsilon, omicron, upsilon *Hebrew:* 2 he, pe 3 mem, nun, sin, taf, tav, taw, tet, vav, waw, yod, yud 4 alef, ayin, beth, caph, heth, kaph, koph, qoph, resh, shin, teth 5 aleph, cheth, gimel, lamed, sadhe, tsade, zayin 6 daleth, samekh *Old Irish:* 4 ogam 5 ogham *runic:* 7 futhark, futhorc, futhork

Alphenor's mother 5 Niobe

Alpheus *beloved:* 8 Arethusa *father:* 7 Oceanus *form:* 5 river *mother:* 6 Tethys

Alpine *animal:* 4 ibex 7 chamois *climber:* 10 alpestrian *dance:* 5 gavot 7 gavotte *dress:* 6 dirndl *goat:* 4 ibex *herdsman:* 4 senn *house:* 6 chalet *lake:* 4 Como, Iseo 5 Garda 6 Geneva, Luzern 8 Maggiore 9 Constance, Neuchatel *pass:* 3 col 5 Cenis 7 Brenner, Simplon 9 St. Bernard *peak:* 5 Blanc, Eiger 7 Bernina 8 Jungfrau 10 Matterhorn *plant:* 9 edelweiss *primrose:* 8 auricula *resort:* 5 Davos 7 Bolzano, Zermatt 8 Chamonix, Grenoble 9 Innsbruck 10 Interlaken 11 Sankt Moritz *river:* 5 Rhine, Rhone *snowfield:* 4 firn, neve *staff:* 10 alpenstock *state:* 5 Tirol, Tyrol 7 Bavaria *tunnel:* 5 Blanc, Cenis 7 Arlberg, Simplon 10 St. Gotthard *wind:* 4 bise, bora 5 foehn

already 4 even, once 6 before 7 earlier 8 formerly 9 erstwhile 10 heretofore, previously

also 3 too, yet 4 more 5 again, along, still 6 as well, withal 7 besides, further 8 likewise, moreover 9 similarly 10 in addition 11 furthermore 12 additionally

also-ran 5 loser

altar *boy:* 6 server 7 acolyte *cloth:* 4 pall 5 palla 7 frontal *hanging:* 6 dorsal, dossal, dossel *platform:* 8 predella *screen:* 7 reredos *shelf:* 6 gradin 7 gradine, retable *site:* 4 apse, bema *table:* 5 mensa *vessel:* 5 cruet, paten 7 chalice 8 ciborium 10 monstrance

alter 4 geld, turn, vary 5 adapt 6 adjust, change, jigger, modify, mutate, neuter, temper 8 moderate, modulate 9 refashion

alteration 4 turn 5 shift 6 change 8 mutation 9 variation 10 adaptation, adjustment, changeover, conversion, transition 12 modification 13 metamorphosis

altercate 4 spat, tiff 5 argue, scrap 6 bicker 7 brabble, dispute, quarrel, wrangle 8 squabble 9 caterwaul

altercation 3 row 4 tiff 6 combat, fracas 7 contest, dispute, quarrel, wrangle 8 argument, squabble 9 bickering 10 falling-out 11 controversy, embroilment

alternate 3 sub 5 proxy 6 fill-in, rotate 7 stand-in 8 periodic 9 change off, fluctuate, oscillate, recurrent, recurring, replacing, surrogate 10 equivalent, isochronal, periodical, substitute 11 isochronous, locum tenens, pinch hitter, replacement 12 intermittent

alternately 6 in lieu, rather 7 instead

alternative 5 proxy 6 choice, option 8 druthers, election 9 selection, surrogate 10 preference, substitute 11 contingency, possibility

Althaea *father:* 8 Thestius *husband:* 6 Oeneus *son:* 8 Meleager *victim:* 8 Meleager

although 4 when 5 while 6 albeit, much as 7 howbeit, whereas

altitude 6 height 9 elevation

altitudinous 4 high, tall

altogether 4 well 5 quite 6 in toto, wholly 7 en masse, exactly, totally, utterly 8 all in all, entirely 9 generally, perfectly 10 by and large, completely, on the whole, thoroughly

altruistic 6 humane 7 liberal 8 generous 9 unselfish 10 benevolent, bighearted, charitable, open-handed 11 magnanimous, noble-minded 12 eleemosynary, humanitarian 13 philanthropic

alum 4 grad 6 emetic 7 styptic 8 graduate 10 astringent

aluminum *symbol:* 2 Al

always 4 ever 7 forever 8 evermore 9 eternally 10 constantly, invariably 11 forevermore, in perpetuum, perpetually 12 continuously

amalgam see **amalgamation**

amalgamate 3 mix 4 fuse, meld 5 admix, merge, unify, unite 6 mingle 8 compound, intermix 9 interfuse 11 consolidate, intermingle

amalgamation 5 alloy, blend 6 fusion, merger 7 compost, mixture 8 compound 9 admixture, composite 10 commixture 13 consolidation

Amalthea *form:* 4 goat *horn:* 10 cornucopia *nursling:* 4 Zeus

Amasa *father:* 6 Hadlai, Jether *mother:* 7 Abigail

amass 4 bulk, hive 5 hoard, lay up, uplay 6 garner, gather, roll up 7 store up 8 cumulate 9 stockpile 10 accumulate

amassment 5 hoard, trove 9 colluvies 10 collection, cumulation 11 aggregation 12 accumulation 13 agglomeration

Amata's husband 7 Latinus

amateur 4 tyro 6 novice, tinker, votary 7 admirer, dabbler, devotee 8 beginner, neophyte, putterer 9 greenhorn, smatterer 10 apprentice, enthusiast, uninitiate 11 abecedarian

amateurish 3 raw 5 crude, green 6 clumsy, flawed 7 jackleg 8 dabbling 9 deficient, unskilled, untutored 10 dilettante, unfinished 12 dilettantist

amative 6 erotic 7 amorous 11 aphrodisiac

amaze 6 wonder 7 astound 8 astonish, surprise 9 dumbfound, marveling 10 admiration, wonderment 11 flabbergast 12 confoundment

amazement 6 wonder 8 surprise 9 marveling 10 admiration, wonderment 12 confoundment

amazing 7 strange 8 wondrous 9 marvelous, wonderful 10 astounding, miraculous, prodigious, stupendous, surprising 11 astonishing

amazon 5 harpy, scold, shrew, vixen 6 ogress, virago 8 fishwife 9 termagant, Xanthippe

ambassador 5 agent, envoy 6 legate 8 diplomat, emissary 9 messenger *papal:* 6 nuncio

ambience 6 medium, milieu 7 climate 10 atmosphere 11 environment, mise-en-scène 12 surroundings

ambiguity 7 evasion 9 equivoque, obscurity, vagueness 11 amphibology, uncertainty 12 equivocality, equivocation 13 double meaning

ambiguous 5 fishy, vague 6 opaque, unsure 7 dubious, obscure, suspect, unclear 8 doubtful 9 equivocal, tenebrous, uncertain, unsettled 10 inexplicit 11 problematic 12 questionable

ambit 5 limit, orbit, range, reach, scope, sweep 6 extent, radius 7 circuit, compass, purview 9 extension, perimeter, periphery 13 circumference

ambition 3 aim 4 goal, hope, mark, wish 5 dream, drive 6 desire, spirit, target 7 avidity, purpose 9 eagerness, intention,

objective **10** aspiration, enterprise, get-up-and-go, initiative
ambitious **4** avid, bold, keen **5** eager **8** aspiring **9** energetic, grandiose, visionary **10** aggressive **11** hard-working **12** enterprising
ambivalent see **equivocal**
amble **4** mope **5** dally, drift, mosey **6** bummel, dawdle, linger, stroll **7** saunter
ambrosial **4** lush **5** balmy, spicy, sweet, yummy **6** aromal, savory **7** darling **8** adorable, aromatic, fragrant, heavenly, luscious, perfumed, redolent **9** delicious **10** delectable, delightful **11** scrumptious
ambulant **6** roving **7** nomadic, vagrant, walking **8** vagabond **9** itinerant **11** peripatetic
ambulate **4** hoof, pace, step, walk **5** tread, troop **6** foot it **7** traipse
ambulatory see **ambulant**
ambuscade **6** ambush **10** ambushment
ambush **4** trap **5** snare **6** assail, attack, entrap, lay for, waylay **7** assault, ensnare, scupper **8** surprise **9** ambuscade
ameliorate **4** help, mend **5** amend **6** better, perk up **7** improve, relieve **8** mitigate **10** convalesce, recuperate
amenable **4** tame **6** docile, liable, pliant **7** plastic, pliable, subdued, willing **8** biddable, obedient **9** adaptable, malleable, receptive, tractable **10** answerable, responsive **11** accountable, responsible
amend **4** help **5** right **6** better, repair **7** correct, improve, rectify **9** meliorate **10** ameliorate
amends **7** redress **8** reprisal **9** indemnity, quittance **10** recompense, reparation **11** restitution **12** compensation
amenities **5** mores **6** manner **8** decorums **9** etiquette **10** civilities **11** proprieties
amenity **5** charm, frill, luxus **6** luxury **7** comfort **8** civility, courtesy, facility **9** attention, gallantry, geniality, pleasance **10** affability, amiability, betterment, cordiality, enrichment, politeness **11** convenience, enhancement, improvement, sociability **12** agreeability, extravagance, graciousness, gratefulness, pleasantness **13** agreeableness, courteousness, enjoyableness
ament **4** fool, zany **5** idiot, moron **6** catkin, cretin **7** half-wit, natural **8** imbecile **9** simpleton
amerce **4** fine **5** mulct **6** punish **8** penalize
amercement **4** fine **5** mulct **7** forfeit, penalty
American ***with Japanese-born parents:*** **5** nisei
American League ***Baltimore:*** **7** Orioles ***Boston:*** **6** Red Sox ***California:*** **6** Angels ***Chicago:*** **8** White Sox ***Cleveland:*** **7** Indians ***Detroit:*** **6** Tigers ***Kansas City:*** **6** Royals ***Milwaukee:*** **7** Brewers ***Minnesota:*** **5** Twins ***New York:*** **7** Yankees ***Oakland:*** **9** Athletics ***Seattle:*** **8** Mariners ***Texas:*** **7** Rangers ***Toronto:*** **8** Blue Jays
America, the Beautiful ***music:*** **4** Ward ***words:*** **5** Bates
americium ***symbol:*** **2** Am
Amfortas ***father:*** **7** Titurel ***opera:*** **8** Parsifal
amiability **7** amenity **9** geniality, pleasance **10** cordiality **12** gratefulness, pleasantness **13** agreeableness, enjoyableness
amiable **4** kind, mild, warm **6** benign, genial, gentle, kindly **7** affable, cordial, lenient **8** gracious, mannerly, obliging **9** courteous **10** responsive **11** complaisant, good-humored, good-natured, warm-hearted **12** good-tempered
amicable **7** pacific **8** empathic, friendly, peaceful **9** congenial, peaceable **10** harmonious, like-minded, neighborly **11** sympathetic **13** understanding
amical **8** friendly **9** congenial **10** harmonious
amid **5** among, midst **6** during **10** throughout
amigo **4** mate **6** friend **8** familiar, intimate **9** confidant **12** acquaintance
amino acid **4** dopa **6** leucin, lysine, serine, toluid, valine **7** cystein, cystine, glycine, leucine, proline, toluide **8** cysteine, dopamine, histidin, thyroxin, toluidin, tyrosine
Amis novel **8** Lucky Jim
amiss **3** bad **4** awry, poor **5** badly, wrong **6** afield, astray, faulty, flawed, guilty, rotten, sinful, unholy **7** wrongly **8** blamable, blameful, culpable, faultily **9** defective, imperfect **10** censurable **11** blameworthy, incorrectly, unfavorably **12** inaccurately **13** demeritorious, reprehensible
amity **6** comity **7** concord, harmony **8** goodwill **10** friendship, kindliness **11** benevolence **12** friendliness
Ammonite god **6** Molech
amnesty **6** pardon **10** absolution
Amnon ***father:*** **5** David ***half sister:*** **5** Tamar ***mother:*** **7** Ahinoam
Amon ***father:*** **8** Manasseh ***son:*** **6** Josiah
Amonasro's daughter **4** Aida
among **3** mid **4** amid **5** midst **7** between ***prefix:*** **5** inter
amorist **5** lover, Romeo **7** Don Juan, gallant **8** Casanova, lothario, paramour
amorous **6** erotic **7** amative, amatory, lustful **8** enamored **10** infatuated **11** aphrodisiac
amorousness **4** love **5** amour **7** passion
amorphous **8** formless, inchoate, unformed, unshaped **9** shapeless
amount **4** body, bulk, core, dose **5** add up,

equal, price, reach, run to, sense, total, touch 6 budget, burden, dosage, embody, matter, number, thrust, upshot 7 include, purport, quantum, run into, subsume 8 approach, comprise, quantity 9 aggregate, substance 12 correspond to ***owed:*** 4 debt ***Scottish:*** 4 haet 7 bittock ***small:*** 3 bit, jot 4 atom, drop, iota, mite, whit 5 minim, spark, speck, trace 7 modicum, smidgen 8 molecule, particle 9 scintilla

amour 4 love 5 lover 6 affair 7 liaison, passion, romance 8 intimacy, intrigue 10 love affair 12 entanglement, relationship

amour propre 5 pride 6 vanity 7 conceit 8 self-love, vainness 9 vainglory 10 narcissism, self-esteem, self-regard 11 self-conceit, self-respect 13 conceitedness

amphetamines 5 speed 6 dexies, hearts, uppers 7 bennies, Dexoxyn 8 greenies, pep pills, Preludin 9 Dexedrine 10 Benzedrine, Methedrine

amphibian ***burrowing:*** 9 caecilian ***extinct:*** 7 eryopid ***family:*** 7 Hylidae, Ranidae 9 Bufonidae, Proteidae, Sirenidae ***genus:*** 4 Bufo, Hyla, Rana 5 Acris, Siren 7 Aneides, Eurycea 8 Ascaphus, Ensatina, Manculus, Necturus, Triturus 9 Ambystoma, Plethodon ***legless:*** 9 caecilian ***order:*** 5 Anura 7 Caudata 9 Salientia ***tailed:*** 3 eft, olm 4 newt 7 caudate, proteus, uredele 10 salamander ***tailless:*** 4 frog, hyla, toad 8 bullfrog, tree toad 10 batrachian, salientian ***wormlike:*** 9 caecilian ***young:*** 7 tadpole 8 polliwog

Amphion ***brother:*** 6 Zethus ***conquest:*** 6 Thebes ***father:*** 4 Zeus ***mother:*** 7 Antiope ***sister:*** 5 Aedon ***wife:*** 5 Niobe

Amphitrite ***father:*** 6 Nereus ***husband:*** 7 Neptune 8 Poseidon ***mother:*** 5 Doris ***son:*** 6 Triton

Amphitryon's wife 7 Alcmene

ample 5 great, large, roomy 6 lavish, plenty 7 copious, liberal, profuse 8 abundant, generous, handsome, prodigal, spacious 9 bounteous, bountiful, capacious, plenteous, plentiful 10 commodious

amplify 5 swell 6 dilate, expand 7 develop, distend, enlarge, inflate 8 increase 9 elaborate

amplitude 4 size 5 scope, space 6 spread 7 bigness, breadth, expanse, stretch 8 distance, fullness, wideness 9 expansion, greatness, largeness, magnitude, roominess 11 sizableness 12 sizeableness, spaciousness 13 capaciousness

Amram ***father:*** 4 Bani 6 Dishon, Kohath ***wife:*** 8 Jochebed

amulet 4 juju, luck, zemi 5 charm 6 fetish, grigri, mascot 7 periapt 8 greegree, grisgris, talisman 10 lucky piece, phylactery, rabbit-foot

Amulius' brother 7 Numitor

amuse 4 wile 5 charm 6 divert 7 animate, beguile, delight, enchant, enliven 8 distract, recreate 9 entertain, fascinate

amusement 9 diversion 10 recreation 11 dissipation, distraction 13 entertainment

amusement park 7 funfair

amusement show 8 carnival

amusing 5 droll, funny 7 comical, risible 8 humorous 9 laughable, ludicrous

Amycus ***father:*** 7 Neptune 8 Poseidon ***friend:*** 8 Heracles, Hercules ***mother:*** 5 Melia

Amymone ***father:*** 6 Danaus ***son:*** 8 Nauplius

ana 5 varia 9 anecdotes 10 collection, miscellany 11 memorabilia

anabasis 5 march 7 advance, headway, ongoing 8 progress 11 advancement, proficiency

anadem 5 crown 6 wreath 7 chaplet, coronal, coronet, garland

anagogic 6 mystic, occult 8 mystical, telestic 10 symbolical 11 allegorical

analects 4 posy 5 album 7 garland, omnibus 9 anthology 10 miscellany 11 florilegium

analgesic 7 anodyne 10 anesthetic, painkiller

analogous 4 akin, like 5 alike 7 kindred, similar, uniform 8 parallel 9 consonant 10 comparable

analogue 5 match 7 cognate 8 congener, parallel 9 correlate 11 counterpart, countertype 13 correspondent

analogy 6 simile 8 affinity, likeness, metaphor 9 alikeness, semblance 10 comparison, similarity, similitude 11 resemblance

analysis 4 scan, view 5 audit 6 review, survey 7 breakup, checkup 8 exegesis, scrutiny 9 breakdown 10 dissection, inspection, resolution 11 examination 13 perlustration

analytic 4 keen 5 acute, sharp 6 subtle 7 logical 8 piercing 11 penetrating 13 ratiocinative

analyze 7 dissect, examine, inspect, resolve 8 classify 9 anatomize, break down, decompose 10 decompound, scrutinize 11 investigate

analyze grammatically 5 parse

Ananias 4 liar 6 fibber 7 fibster 8 perjurer 9 falsifier 11 storyteller 12 prevaricator ***coconspirator:*** 8 Sapphira ***father:*** 9 Nedebaeus ***wife:*** 8 Sapphira

anarch see **anarchist**

anarchism 4 riot 7 misrule 8 disorder 9 distemper

anarchist 5 rebel 8 frondeur, mutineer, revolter 9 insurgent 10 malcontent
anarchy 4 riot 5 chaos 7 misrule 8 disorder 9 distemper, mobocracy 10 ochlocracy 11 lawlessness
anathema 5 curse 6 pariah 7 bugbear, censure, malison, outcast, reproof 9 bete noire 10 black beast 11 abomination, commination, detestation, imprecation, malediction 12 condemnation, denunciation
anathematize 4 damn 5 curse 8 execrate 9 objurgate
anatomical depression 5 fossa, fovea
anatomical tube 3 vas 4 duct 5 canal
anatomist 5 Wolff 6 Harvey 8 Vesalius
anatomize 7 analyze, dissect, resolve 9 break down, decompose 10 decompound
Anaxarete's lover 5 Iphis
Anaxo ***brother:*** 10 Amphitryon ***daughter:*** 7 Alcmene ***father:*** 7 Alcaeus ***husband:*** 9 Electryon
ancestor 8 forebear, foregoer 9 ascendant, precursor, prototype 10 antecedent, antecessor, forefather, forerunner, progenitor 11 predecessor 12 primogenitor
ancestral sequence 8 pedigree 9 bloodline, genealogy
ancestry 4 race 5 blood, breed, stock 6 family, origin, source 7 descent, kindred, lineage 8 pedigree 10 derivation, extraction
Anchises' son 6 Aeneas
anchor 3 fix 4 moor 5 catch 6 fasten, secure 7 grapnel, killick, killock ***line:*** 7 catfall ***part:*** 4 ring 5 crown, fluke, shank
anchorage 4 port 5 chuck, haven, roads 6 harbor, riding 7 mooring 9 harborage, roadstead
anchors ____ 6 aweigh
ancient 3 old 4 aged 5 elder, hoary, olden 6 age-old, doting, primal, senior 7 antique, elderly, oldster 8 Noachian, oldtimer, primeval, timeworn 9 doddering, venerable 10 primordial 12 antediluvian ***combining form:*** 4 pale 5 palae, paleo 6 archae, archeo, palaeo 7 archaeo
ancient capital 4 Susa 5 Balkh, Calah, Isker, Kalhu, Ninus, Sibir 6 Bactra, Nimrud 7 Nineveh, Shushan 10 Persepolis
ancient city ***Asia Minor:*** 4 Nice, Teos 5 Tyana 6 Edessa, Nicaea 7 Antioch 13 Halicarnassus ***Babylonia:*** 4 Sura 5 Accad, Agade, Akkad, Eridu, Larsa 7 Ellasar ***Bengal:*** 4 Gaur 9 Lakhnauti ***Canaan:*** 5 Gezer ***Cyprus:*** 7 Salamis ***Egypt:*** 2 On 6 Thebes 7 Memphis 10 Heliopolis ***Etruria:*** 4 Veii ***Euphrates River:*** 7 Babylon ***Greece:*** 5 Crisa 6 Athens, Sparta 7 Calydon 10 Lacedaemon ***Ionia:*** 4 Myus, Teos 5 Chios, Samos 6 Priene 7 Ephesus, Lebedos, Miletus, Phocaea 8 Colophon, Erythrae 10 Clazomenae ***Italy:*** 5 Locri 7 Pompeii 11 Herculaneum ***Latium:*** 5 Gabii 9 Alba Longa ***Mayan:*** 4 Coba 5 Tikal ***Nile River:*** 5 Meroe ***North Africa:*** 5 Utica 8 Carthage ***Palestine:*** 4 Gaza 5 Ekron, Endor, Sodom 6 Beroea, Bethel, Gilead, Hebron 7 Jericho, Samaria 8 Ashkelon 9 Capernaum, Jerusalem ***Peloponnesus:*** 5 Tegea 6 Sparta 7 Corinth ***Sumeria:*** 2 Ur 4 Kish, Uruk 5 Erech, Larsa 6 Lagash ***Turkey:*** 5 Assos, Assus 9 Byzantium ***Yucatan:*** 5 Uxmal
ancient country ***Adriatic coast:*** 7 Illyria ***Africa:*** 10 Mauretania ***Arabian Peninsula:*** 5 Sheba ***Asia:*** 4 Aram 5 Media, Minni, Syria 7 Armenia, Ash Sham, Bactria ***Asia Minor:*** 5 Lydia, Mysia 6 Aeolis, Pontus 7 Cilicia, Phrygia 8 Bithynia ***Balkan:*** 7 Macedon 9 Macedonia ***Black Sea:*** 7 Colchis ***Dead Sea:*** 4 Edom ***Euphrates River:*** 9 Babylonia ***Europe:*** 4 Gaul 5 Dacia 6 Gallia ***gold-rich:*** 5 Ophir ***Italy:*** 6 Latium 7 Etruria ***Nile valley:*** 4 Cush ***Peloponnesus:*** 4 Elis 7 Arcadia ***Syria:*** 9 Phoenicia
ancient empire 6 Median 7 Hittite, Persian 8 Assyrian, Athenian, Chaldean, Egyptian, Seleucid 9 Ptolemaic 10 Babylonian
ancient kingdom ***Anglo-Saxon:*** 6 Wessex ***Asia:*** 4 Ghor, Ghur ***Celtic:*** 7 Cumbria ***China:*** 3 Shu ***Euphrates valley:*** 4 Hira 7 Al-Hirah ***Greece:*** 8 Pergamon, Pergamum ***North Of Assyria:*** 3 Van 6 Ararat, Urartu ***Palestine:*** 5 Judah 6 Israel ***Persian Gulf:*** 4 Elam ***Portugal:*** 7 Algarve ***Spain:*** 4 Leon 6 Aragon 7 Castile, Galicia, Granada, Navarre ***Syria:*** 4 Moab ***Welsh:*** 5 Powys ***West Sahara:*** 4 Gana 5 Ghana
ancient monument 6 sphinx 7 obelisk, pyramid
ancient royal forest 4 Dean 8 Sherwood
ancient town ***Africa:*** 4 Zama ***Armenia:*** 4 Dwin, Tvin ***Asia Minor:*** 4 Soli 5 Derbe, Issus, Soloi ***Attica:*** 6 Icaria ***Black Sea:*** 5 Olbia 9 Apollonia ***Greece:*** 4 Abae, Opus 8 Marathon ***Italy:*** 4 Elea, Luna 5 Cumae, Velia ***Latium:*** 5 Ardea, Cures ***Macedonia:*** 5 Pydna, Stobi 9 Apollonia ***Peloponnesus:*** 5 Asine ***Persia:*** 6 Hormuz 8 Harmozia ***Sicily:*** 5 Hybla ***Spain:*** 5 Munda ***Tatar:*** 5 Isker, Sibir ***Wendish:*** 5 Julin
ancilla 3 aid 4 help 6 helper 7 striker 9 assistant, attendant
ancillary 8 adjuvant, incident 9 accessory, attendant, attending, auxiliary, satellite 10 coincident, collateral, subsidiary 11 appurtenant, concomitant, subservient 12 accompanying, contributory
andiron 7 firedog

androgynous 8 bisexual 13 hermaphrodite
android 5 robot 9 automaton
Andromache ***husband:*** 6 Hector 7 Helenus, Pyrrhus 11 Neoptolemus ***son:*** 8 Astyanax, Molossus
Andromeda ***father:*** 7 Cepheus ***husband:*** 7 Perseus ***mother:*** 10 Cassiopeia ***rescuer:*** 7 Perseus
___ and warp 4 woof
anecdote 4 tale, yarn 5 story 7 episode, recital 8 relation 9 narration, narrative
anemic 4 pale 6 pallid, watery 8 waterish 9 bloodless
anent 2 re 4 in re 5 about, as for 7 apropos 8 touching 9 as regards 10 concerning 13 with respect to
anesthetic 4 dull, hard 5 rocky 7 anodyne 9 analgesic, bloodless, insensate 10 impassible, insensible, pain-killer 11 insensitive ***combining form:*** 5 caine ***medical:*** 5 ether 6 spinal 7 eucaine 8 morphine, procaine 9 halothane, novocaine 10 benzocaine, chloroform, tetracaine 11 scopolamine
anesthetized 4 dead, numb 6 asleep, numbed 8 benumbed, deadened 9 senseless, unfeeling 10 insensible 11 insensitive
anew 4 over 5 again 6 afresh, de novo, lately, of late 8 once more, recently ***combining form:*** 2 an 3 ana 4 pali ***prefix:*** 2 re
angel 6 backer, cherub, patron, surety 7 sponsor 8 backer-up 9 celestial, guarantor ***biblical:*** 5 Uriel 7 Gabriel, Michael, Raphael ***fallen:*** 7 Lucifer ***hierarchy:*** 6 powers 7 thrones, virtues 8 cherubim, seraphim 9 dominions ***of death:*** 6 Azrael
angelic 4 holy 5 godly 7 saintly 8 cherubic
Angelica ***father:*** 9 Galaphron ***husband:*** 6 Medoro ***lover:*** 7 Orlando
anger 3 ire, irk, vex 4 bile, boil, burn, fume, fury, huff, rage, rant, rave, rile 5 annoy, pique, storm, wrath 6 blow up, choler, dander, enrage, madden, nettle, offend, seethe 7 affront, bristle, dudgeon, flare up, incense, outrage, provoke, steam up, umbrage 8 boil over, irritate 9 aggravate, annoyance, infuriate 10 exasperate 11 indignation, infuriation 12 exasperation
angered easily 4 rily 5 riley 9 irascible
angle 3 aim, bow 4 axil, bend, bias, fish, hand, hint, skew, turn 5 facet, phase, slant 6 aspect, crotch 7 flexure, outlook, turning 8 flection 9 direction, viewpoint 10 standpoint ***combining form:*** 3 gon 4 goni 5 gonio 6 anguli, angulo
Anglo-Saxon ***army:*** 4 fyrd ***assembly:*** 4 moot 5 gemot 6 gemote ***coin:*** 3 ora 5 sceat 6 mancus ***council:*** 9 heptarchy ***county:*** 5 shire ***court:*** 4 moot 5 gemot 6 gemote ***crown tax:*** 4 geld ***epic:*** 7 Beowulf ***free servant:*** 5 thane, thegn ***god:*** 3 Ing ***goddess of fate:*** 4 Wyrd ***historian:*** 4 Bede ***king:*** 3 Ine, Ini 4 Edwy 5 Edgar, Edred 6 Alfred, Edmund, Edward, Egbert 8 Ethelred ***kingdom:*** 4 Kent 5 Essex 6 Mercia, Sussex, Wessex 10 East Anglia 11 Northumbria ***king's council:*** 5 witan ***letter:*** 3 edh, eth, wen, wyn 4 wynn 5 thorn ***nobleman:*** 4 earl ***poet:*** 4 scop ***prince:*** 8 atheling ***sheriff:*** 5 reeve 6 gerefa ***slave:*** 4 esne ***tenant:*** 6 geneat ***village:*** 3 ham ***warrior:*** 5 thane, thegn
angry 3 mad 4 rily, sore, waxy 5 irate, riley, upset, vexed, wroth 6 heated, ireful, put out, shirty, wrathy, wrothy 7 enraged, furious, uptight 8 choleric, incensed, maddened, worked up, wrathful, wrothful 9 indignant, perturbed, wrought up 10 aggravated, infuriated 11 acrimonious, exasperated
anguish 3 rue, woe 4 ache, care, dole, pain, pang 5 grief, throe, worry 6 regret, sorrow 7 anxiety, torment, torture 9 heartache 10 affliction, heartbreak
angular 4 bony, lank, lean 5 crude, gaunt, lanky, rough, spare 6 skinny 7 scraggy, scrawny 8 rawboned, unworked 9 roughhewn, undressed 10 unfinished, unpolished 11 unfashioned
anima 4 soul 6 pneuma, psyche, spirit 9 élan vital 10 vital force
animadversion 4 slam, slur 7 censure, obloquy 9 aspersion, criticism, stricture 10 accusation, imputation, reflection 11 insinuation 12 reprehension
animadvert 5 state, utter 6 remark 7 comment, declare, observe 10 commentate
animal 5 beast, brute, feral 6 brutal, carnal, ferine 7 beastly, bestial, brutish, critter, fleshly, sensual, swinish, wilding 8 creature, wildling ***antlered:*** 3 elk 4 axis, deer 5 moose 7 caribou 8 reindeer ***aquatic:*** 3 eel 4 fish, frog, seal 5 otter, whale 6 dugong, sea cow, walrus 7 dolphin, manatee, octopus 8 bryozoan, porpoise 9 alligator, crocodile ***arboreal:*** 2 ai 4 bird, unau 5 chimp, coati, koala, lemur, sloth 6 gibbon, monkey 7 opossum, tarsier 8 kinkajou, marmoset, squirrel 9 orangutan ***burrowing:*** 4 mole 5 brock, ratel 6 badger, gopher, marmot, rabbit 7 echidna 9 armadillo, groundhog, woodchuck ***castrated:*** 2 ox 5 capon, spado, steer 6 barrow, wether 7 gelding ***combining form:*** 2 zo 3 zoa (plural), zoo 4 zoon 6 theria (plural) 7 therium ***draft:*** 2 ox 3 yak 4 mule, oxen (plural) 5 horse 6 donkey 8 elephant ***exhibit:*** 3 zoo ***extinct:*** 3 moa 4 dodo, urus 6 quagga 7 mam-

moth **8** dinosaur, eohippus, mastodon **9** solitaire, trilobite ***female:*** **3** cow, dam, doe, ewe, hen, pen, roe, sow **4** mare, puss **5** bitch, goose, jenny, nanny, vixen **6** jennet **7** lioness ***four-footed:*** **9** quadruped ***four-limbed:*** **8** tetrapod ***free-swimming:*** **6** nekton ***hibernating:*** **4** bear, frog, toad **5** skunk, snake **7** polecat **8** chipmunk **9** groundhog, woodchuck ***horned:*** **2** ox **3** ram, yak **4** bull, goat, ibex, kudu **5** addax, ariel, badak, bison, eland, rhino **6** cattle, koodoo **7** buffalo, gazelle, giraffe, unicorn **8** antelope ***humped:*** **2** ox **3** elk, yak **4** zebu **5** bison, camel, moose ***imaginary:*** **5** snark ***insect-eating:*** **4** mole, newt **5** gecko, shrew **6** numbat **7** echidna **8** aardvark, anteater, hedgehog, pangolin, tamandua **10** salamander ***lover:*** **8** zoophile ***male:*** **3** cob, ram, tom **4** boar, buck, bull, cock, stag, stud **5** billy, steer **6** gander **7** gobbler, rooster **8** bachelor, stallion ***many-celled:*** **8** metazoan ***many-footed:*** **9** centipede, millipede ***marsupial:*** **4** tait **5** koala **6** cuscus, numbat, wombat **7** dasyure, opossum, wallaby **8** kangaroo **9** bandicoot, phalanger ***meat-eating:*** **9** carnivore ***mythical:*** **4** yale **5** hodag, Hydra, kylin **6** bunyip, dragon, kraken, sphinx **7** centaur, griffin, mermaid, Pegasus, unicorn **8** basilisk, Cerberus, Minotaur ***one-celled:*** **9** protozoan ***Peruvian:*** **5** llama **6** alpaca, vicuna ***plant-eating:*** **9** herbivore ***skin disease:*** **5** mange ***snouted:*** **5** coati, tapir **8** mongoose; (see also **animal**, *insect-eating*) ***spotted:*** **4** axis, paca **6** calico, jaguar, ocelot **7** cheetah, leopard, piebald **8** skewbald **9** dalmatian ***striped:*** **4** kudo **5** tiger, zebra **6** koodoo, quagga ***suffix:*** **4** acea (plural) **5** acean ***trail:*** **3** pug **4** foil, slot **5** spoor ***tusked:*** **6** walrus **7** warthog **8** elephant ***two-footed:*** **5** biped ***web-footed:*** **4** duck, frog, toad **5** goose, otter **6** beaver **8** duckbill, platypus ***young:*** **3** cub, kid, kit, pup **4** calf, colt, fawn, foal, joey, lamb **5** bunny, chick, kitty, poult, shoat, stirk, whelp **6** cygnet, farrow, heifer, kitten, piglet **7** bullock, gosling, lambkin **8** suckling, yeanling, yearling **9** fledgling

animal behavior ***study of:*** **8** ethology

animal fat **4** suet **6** tallow

animalism **7** lechery **9** carnality **10** sensualism, sensuality, unchastity **11** fleshliness, lustfulness **13** lecherousness

animalize **4** warp **6** debase **7** corrupt, deprave, pervert, vitiate **9** brutalize **10** bestialize, demoralize

animal life **5** fauna

animals ***suffix:*** **3** ata, ida, ini **4** idae, idea

animate **4** fire **5** cheer, drive, exalt, impel, liven, nerve, steel **6** inform, vivify **7** actuate, chirk up, enliven, hearten, inspire, quicken, refresh **8** activate, embolden, inspirit, motivate, vitalize **9** encourage, enhearten **10** invigorate, vivificate

animated **3** gay **4** cant, keen **5** alert, alive, canty, vital **6** lively, living, zoetic **7** zestful **8** spirited **9** exuberant, sprightly, vitalized, vivacious **12** high-spirited

animation **3** vim **4** brio, dash, élan, life, zing **5** oomph, verve **6** esprit, spirit

animosity **6** enmity, rancor **9** antipathy, hostility **10** antagonism

animus **4** plan, soul **6** design, enmity, intent, pneuma, psyche, rancor, spirit **7** meaning, purpose **9** antipathy, élan vital, hostility, intention **10** antagonism, intendment, vital force

Anius ***daughter:*** **4** Oeno **5** Elais **6** Spermo ***father:*** **6** Apollo ***mother:*** **5** Rhoeo

ankle **6** tarsus ***combining form:*** **4** tars **5** tarso

annals **7** history **9** chronicle

Anna's sister **4** Dido

annex **3** add, arm, cop, ell, nim, win **4** gain, hook, join, land, take, wing **5** affix, seize, steal, unite **6** append, attach, fasten, obtain, pick up, secure, take on **7** acquire, preempt, procure, purloin, subjoin **8** accroach, addition, arrogate, superadd **9** extension, sequester **10** commandeer, confiscate **11** appropriate, expropriate

Annie Oakley **4** pass

annihilate **4** raze, ruin, undo **5** abate, annul, crush, quash, quell, wrack, wreck **6** murder, negate, quench, squash, uproot **7** abolish, blot out, destroy, expunge, nullify, put down, root out, vitiate, wipe out **8** abrogate, decimate, demolish, massacre, suppress **9** eradicate, extirpate, slaughter **10** extinguish, invalidate, obliterate **11** exterminate

annihilative **7** ruinous **8** wrackful, wreckful **10** shattering **11** destructive

anniversary ***hundredth:*** **9** centenary **10** centennial ***tenth:*** **9** decennial ***thousandth:*** **10** millennial **11** millenniary

annotate **5** gloss **7** comment, explain **9** elucidate **10** commentate

announce **5** augur, sound **6** attest, blazon, herald **7** bespeak, betoken, declare, forerun, presage, present, publish, testify, witness **8** foreshow, foretell, indicate, proclaim **9** advertise, broadcast, harbinger **10** bruit about, promulgate **11** preindicate

announcement **9** broadcast **11** declaration, publication **12** proclamation, promulgation **13** advertisement

annoy **3** bug, irk, vex **4** bait, fret, gall, gnaw, miff **5** chafe, chivy, harry, peeve, tease, upset, worry **6** abrade, badger, bother, harass, heckle, hector, pester, plague, ruffle **7** agitate, bedevil, disturb, hagride, perturb, provoke **8** distress, exercise, irritate **9** beleaguer ***Scottish:*** **4** fash

annoyance **3** ire **4** pest **5** anger, trial **6** bother, irking, pester, plague, pother, vexing **7** teasing **8** distress, irritant, nuisance, vexation **9** besetment, bothering, pestering, provoking **10** affliction, botherment, harassment **11** aggravation, botheration, indignation, provocation **12** exasperation

annoying **5** pesky

annual **5** plant **6** flower, yearly **7** almanac **8** yearbook

annul **4** undo, void **5** abate, erase, quash **6** cancel, delete, efface, negate, revoke, vacate **7** abolish, blot out, expunge, nullify, redress, rescind, vitiate, wipe out **8** abrogate, dissolve **9** cancel out, discharge, frustrate **10** annihilate, counteract, extinguish, invalidate, neutralize, obliterate **11** countermand

annunciate **5** sound, state **7** declare, publish **8** proclaim **9** advertise, broadcast **10** bruit about, promulgate

anodyne **6** opiate **8** narcotic, nepenthe, sedative **9** analgesic, calmative, soporific **10** anesthetic, depressant, pain-killer **12** tranquilizer

anointing **7** unction

anomalous **6** off-key **7** deviant, foreign, strange **8** aberrant, abnormal, atypical, peculiar **9** deviative, divergent, irregular, unnatural, untypical **11** heteroclite **13** preternatural

anon **4** soon, then, when **5** again **7** by and by, shortly **8** directly **9** presently

anonym **5** alias **11** nom de guerre

anonymous **7** unknown, unnamed **8** nameless **9** incognito **10** innominate **11** unspecified **12** undesignated, unidentified, unrecognized

another **3** new **4** else, more **5** added, fresh **7** farther, further **10** additional

anschluss **5** union **6** league **8** alliance **9** coalition **10** federation **11** confederacy **13** confederation

anserine **5** silly **6** stupid **9** gooselike

answer **4** fill, meet **5** rebut, reply **6** come in, refute, rejoin, result, retort, return **7** fulfill, respond, satisfy **8** antiphon, rebuttal, response, solution **9** rejoinder **10** refutation **11** recriminate **13** countercharge

answerable **5** bound **6** liable **7** obliged **8** amenable **9** compelled, duty-bound, obligated **11** accountable, constrained, responsible

ant **5** emmet **9** carpenter ***combining form:*** **6** myrmec **7** myrmeco ***relating to:*** **6** formic ***worker:*** **6** ergate

Antaean **4** huge **5** giant **6** heroic **7** titanic **8** colossal, gigantic **9** cyclopean, Herculean **10** gargantuan

Antaeus ***father:*** **7** Neptune **8** Poseidon ***mother:*** **2** Ge **4** Gaea ***slayer:*** **8** Heracles, Hercules

antagonism **3** con **6** animus, enmity, rancor **7** discord **8** friction, opposure **9** animosity, antipathy, hostility **10** antithesis, opposition, oppugnancy, resistance **11** contrariety **12** disagreement

antagonist **3** con **4** anti **5** match **7** opposer **8** opponent **9** adversary, oppugnant

antagonistic **4** anti **6** averse, bitter **7** adverse, hostile, opposed **8** clashing, contrary, inimical, opposing **9** oppugnant, rancorous, vitriolic **10** antonymous, discordant **11** conflicting, contrariant, inconsonant **12** antipathetic, incompatible ***combining form:*** **7** enantio

ante **3** bet, pot **5** stake, wager

anteater see **animal**, ***insect-eating***

antecede **7** forerun, precede, predate **8** foredate

antecedence **8** priority **12** previousness

antecedent **4** fore **5** cause, prior **6** former, reason **8** ancestor, anterior, forebear, foregoer, occasion, previous **9** condition, foregoing, precedent, preceding, precursor, prototype **10** forerunner **11** determinant, predecessor

antedate see **antecede**

antediluvian **3** old **4** aged, fogy **5** hoary **6** age-old, fogram, fossil, square **7** ancient, antique **8** mossback, Noachian, timeworn **10** fuddy-duddy **12** old-fashioned **13** stick-in-the-mud

antelope **3** gnu, kob **4** guib, koba, kudu, oryx, poku, puku, suni, tora **5** addax, beira, beisa, bongo, eland, goral, nagor, nyala, oribi, saiga, serow, tiang **6** dik-dik, duiker, grimme, impala, lechwe, lelwel, nilgai **7** blesbok, bubalis, chamois, defassa, dibatag, gazelle, gemsbok, gerenuk, grysbok, sassaby **8** agacella, bontebok, bushbuck, reedbuck, sing-sing, steinbok **9** duikerbok, kleeneboc, sitatunga, springbok, waterbuck **10** hartebeest **12** klipspringer ***extinct:*** **7** blaubok **9** blaauwbok ***family:*** **7** Bovidae ***female:*** **3** doe ***four-horned:*** **6** chouka **7** chikara **10** chousingha ***male:*** **4** buck ***mythical:*** **4** yale ***young:*** **3** kid

antenna **4** yagi **6** aerial, dipole **8** monopole

Antenor ***father:*** **8** Aesyetes ***son:*** **6** Agenor ***wife:*** **6** Theano

anterior **4** past **5** prior **6** former **8** previous **9** foregoing, precedent, preceding **10** antecedent

Anteros ***brother:*** **4** Eros ***father:*** **4** Ares,

Mars ***mother:*** 5 Venus 9 Aphrodite ***opposite:*** 4 Eros
anthology 3 ana 4 posy 5 album 7 garland, omnibus 8 analects, delectus, treasury 10 collection, miscellany 11 compilation, florilegium
anthropoid 3 ape 6 monkey 7 gorilla, manlike, primate 8 hominoid, humanoid 10 chimpanzee
anthropologist 4 Boas, Mead 5 Black, Keith, Sapir, Tylor 6 Dubois, Frazer, Hooton, Leakey, Linton, Morgan 7 Kroeber, Wissler 8 Benedict, Washburn 10 Malinowski 11 Weidenreich, Westermarck
anti 3 con 7 adverse, opposed, opposer 8 opponent, opposing 9 adversary, oppugnant 10 antagonist 12 antagonistic, antipathetic
antiaircraft fire 4 flak
antibiotic 7 colicin 8 viomycin 9 polymyxin 10 bacitracin, novobiocin, penicillin 11 bacteriocin, tyrothricin 12 streptomycin, tetracycline
antic 4 dido, lark 5 caper, comic, prank, trick 6 frisky, frolic, lively, pranky, shines 7 bizarre, comical, foolish, playful, roguish 8 farcical, gamesome, prankful, prankish, spirited 9 fantastic, grotesque, laughable, ludicrous, sprightly 10 frolicsome, rollicking, shenanigan, tomfoolery 11 mischievous, monkeyshine
anticipate 3 see 5 await 6 divine, expect 7 foresee, preknow, presage, prevent, previse 8 forecast, forefeel, foreknow, foretell, outguess 9 apprehend, forestall, foretaste, prevision, visualize
anticipation 10 expectancy 11 expectation
anticipatory 7 atiptoe 9 expectant, expecting
Anticlea ***father:*** 9 Autolycus ***husband:*** 7 Laertes ***son:*** 7 Ulysses 8 Odysseus
antidote 4 cure 6 remedy 7 negator 9 nullifier 10 corrective 11 counterstep, neutralizer 12 counteragent 13 counteractant, counteractive
Antigone ***brother:*** 9 Polynices ***father:*** 7 Oedipus ***mother:*** 7 Jocasta ***sister:*** 6 Ismene ***uncle:*** 5 Creon
Antilochus ***father:*** 6 Nestor ***friend:*** 8 Achilles ***slayer:*** 6 Memnon
antimony 7 stibium ***combining form:*** 4 stib 5 stibi, stibo 6 stibio ***symbol:*** 2 Sb
Antiope ***father:*** 6 Asopus ***husband:*** 5 Lycus 7 Theseus ***queen of:*** 7 Amazons ***son:*** 6 Zethus 7 Amphion 10 Hippolytus
antipasto 4 whet 7 zakuska 9 appetizer 11 hors d'oeuvre
antipathetic 7 adverse, opposed 8 aversive, clashing, contrary, opposing, opposite, ungenial 9 abhorrent, antipodal, loathsome, obnoxious, oppugnant, repellent, repugnant, repulsive 10 antonymous, discordant, disgusting 11 conflicting, contrariant, distasteful, uncongenial 12 antagonistic 13 contradictory, unsympathetic
antipathy 6 animus, enmity, rancor 7 allergy, dislike 8 aversion, distaste, dyspathy 9 animosity, hostility 10 abhorrence, antagonism, repellency
antiphon 5 reply 6 answer, retort, return 7 respond 8 response 9 rejoinder
antipodal 5 polar 7 counter, reverse 8 contrary, converse, opposite 9 diametric 11 diametrical 12 antithetical 13 contradictory
antipode 6 contra 7 counter, reverse 8 contrary, converse, opposite 10 antithesis 11 counterpole 13 contradictory
antiquate 7 outdate, outmode 8 obsolete 9 obsolesce 12 superannuate
antiquated 5 dated, fusty, moldy, passé 7 antique, archaic 8 obsolete, old-timey, outmoded 10 oldfangled 12 old-fashioned
antique 3 old 4 aged 5 dated, hoary, passé 6 age-old 7 ancient, archaic 8 Noachian, old-timey, outdated, outmoded, time-worn 9 ancestral, out-of-date, venerable 10 antiquated, oldfangled 12 antediluvian, old-fashioned
antiquity ***combining form:*** 6 archae, archeo 7 archaeo
antiseptic 6 iodine 7 alcohol 8 peroxide 9 boric acid, carvacrol, germicide, merbromin 10 gramicidin 12 carbolic acid, disinfectant ***pioneer:*** 6 Lister
antisocial 7 ascetic, austere 8 eremitic, reserved, solitary 9 reclusive, withdrawn 11 introverted, standoffish 12 misanthropic
antithesis 3 con 6 contra 7 counter, reverse 8 antipode, antipole, contrary, converse, opposite, opposure 10 antagonism, opposition 11 contrariety, counterpole 13 contradictory
antithetical 5 polar 7 counter, reverse 8 contrary, converse, opposite 9 antipodal, diametric 10 antipodean 11 diametrical 13 contradictory
antlike 9 myrmecoid
Antony, Mark ***defeat:*** 6 Actium ***friend:*** 6 Caesar ***lover:*** 9 Cleopatra ***wife:*** 7 Octavia
Anubis' father 6 Osiris
anus ***combining form:*** 3 ano 5 proct 6 procta, procti, procto
anvil ***combining form:*** 5 incud 6 incudo
anxiety 4 care 5 doubt, dread, panic, worry 6 unease 7 concern 8 disquiet, distress, mistrust, suspense 9 suffering 10 solicitude, uneasiness 11 concernment, disquietude, uncertainty
anxious 4 agog, avid, keen 5 eager, scary,

upset 6 afraid, aghast, ardent, scared, uneasy 7 alarmed, fearful, jittery, worried 8 agitated, appetent, troubled 9 impatient, perturbed, terrified 10 breathless, disquieted, frightened 12 apprehensive
any 4 some
anyhow 6 random 8 at random, randomly 9 haphazard 11 any which way, haphazardly 13 helter-skelter
anytime 4 ever 5 at all
anyway 4 ever, once 5 at all
anywise see **anyhow**
A1 4 tops 5 prime 6 Grade A 8 five-star, superior 9 excellent, first rate, front-rank, number one, top-drawer 10 blue-ribbon, first-class
apace 4 fast 7 flat-out, hastily, quickly, rapidly, swiftly 8 speedily 9 posthaste 12 lickety-split 13 expeditiously
Apache chief 7 Cochise 8 Geronimo
apart 5 alone, aside 6 singly 7 asunder, isolate, removed, sky-high 8 detached, isolated, one by one 9 severally 10 separately 12 individually 13 independently, unaccompanied ***combining form:*** 4 dich 5 chori, dicho ***prefix:*** 3 dis
apart from 3 bar, but 4 save 6 except, saving 7 barring, besides 9 outside of 11 exclusive of
apartheid 10 separation, separatism 11 segregation 12 separateness
apartment 4 flat, room 5 rooms, suite 6 rental, walk-up 7 chamber, flatlet 8 lodgings, tenement
apathetic 3 dry 4 dull, limp 5 inert, stoic 6 stolid, torpid 7 callous, languid, unmoved 8 sluggish 9 impassive, untouched 10 anesthetic, insensible, phlegmatic, spiritless 11 indifferent, insensitive 12 matter-of-fact
apathy 6 acedia, phlegm, torpor 8 coldness, lethargy, obduracy, stoicism 9 disregard, inertness, lassitude, passivity, stolidity, torpidity, unconcern 10 detachment, dispassion 11 callousness, disinterest, impassivity, insouciance 12 heedlessness, indifference, listlessness 13 insensibility, insensitivity, unmindfulness
ape 4 copy, mime, mock 5 magot, mimic 6 baboon, gibbon, monkey, parody, pongid, simian 7 copycat, gorilla, imitate, take off 8 travesty 9 burlesque, orangutan 10 caricature, chimpanzee, orangoutan ***combining form:*** 6 pithec 7 pitheco 8 pithecus
aperçu 6 digest, précis, sketch, survey 7 pandect, sylloge 8 syllabus 10 compendium
aperitif 4 whet 5 drink 8 cocktail 9 appetizer
aperitive 5 sapid, tasty 6 savory 8 saporous, tasteful 9 palatable, toothsome 10 appetizing, flavorsome 13 mouthwatering
aperture 3 gap 4 gash, hole, slit, vent 5 break, chasm, cleft, slash 6 breach, outlet 7 opening, orifice, pinhole 8 puncture 10 interstice 11 perforation 13 discontinuity
apery 7 mimicry
apex 3 cap, tip, top 4 acme, cusp, noon, peak, roof 5 crest, crown, limit, point 6 apogee, climax, comble, culmen, summit, vertex, zenith 8 capsheaf, capstone, meridian, noontide, pinnacle, ultimate 9 crescendo, fastigium, sublimity 11 culmination, ne plus ultra 12 quintescence ***combining form:*** 3 ace 4 apic 5 apici, apico
Aphareus' son 4 Idas 7 Lynceus
aphorism 4 rule 5 axiom, gnome, maxim, moral 6 dictum, truism 7 brocard 8 apothegm
aphrodisia 4 itch, lust 6 desire 7 passion 9 eroticism, prurience, pruriency 11 lustfulness 13 concupiscence, lickerishness
aphrodisiac 6 erotic 7 amative, amatory, amorous
Aphrodite 5 Venus ***consort:*** 4 Ares 6 Vulcan 10 Hephaestus ***father:*** 4 Zeus 7 Jupiter ***goddess of:*** 4 love ***mother:*** 5 Dione ***son:*** 4 Eros 5 Cupid 6 Aeneas 7 Priapus
apiarist 6 beeman 9 beekeeper, beemaster
apical 3 top 7 highest, topmost 8 loftiest 9 uppermost
apiculture 10 beekeeping
apiece 3 all 4 each 5 aside 6 singly 8 one by one, per caput 9 per capita 12 individually, respectively
apish 7 slavish 9 emulative, imitative
aplomb 4 ease 5 poise 8 coolness, easiness 9 assurance, composure, sangfroid, self-trust 10 confidence, equanimity 11 nonchalance, savoir faire 13 self-assurance
apocalypse 6 oracle, vision 8 prophecy 10 revelation
apocalyptic 4 dire 5 vatic 6 mantic 7 baleful, baneful, direful, fateful, fatidic, ominous, unlucky 8 Delphian, oracular 9 ill-boding, prophetic, sibylline, vaticinal 11 prophetical, threatening 12 inauspicious
apocopate 5 elide
apocryphal 5 false, wrong 6 untrue 7 dubious 8 doubtful, spurious 9 incorrect, ungenuine 11 unauthentic
apogee 4 acme, apex, peak 6 climax, summit, zenith 8 capstone, meridian, pinnacle 11 culmination
Apollo 6 Helios 7 Phoebus ***beloved:*** 6 Cyrene, Daphne 8 Calliope ***birthplace:***

5 Delos *father:* 4 Zeus 7 Jupiter *mother:* 4 Leto 6 Latona *oracle:* 6 Delphi *sister:* 5 Diana 7 Artemis *son:* 3 Ion 7 Orpheus *temple:* 6 Delphi

Apollyon 5 devil, fiend, Satan 6 diablo 7 Lucifer, Old Nick, serpent 9 Beelzebub 10 Old Scratch 13 Old Gooseberry

apologetic 5 sorry 7 defense 8 contrite, penitent 9 regretful, repentant 10 remorseful 11 attritional, penitential 12 compunctious 13 justification

apologia 7 defense 11 elucidation, explanation 13 clarification, justification

apologue 4 myth 5 fable 7 parable 8 allegory

apology 6 excuse 7 defense, redress, regrets, support 8 espousal, mea culpa 9 admission 10 advocating, advocation, concession, confession 11 championing 13 justification

aporetic 6 show-me 9 quizzical, skeptical 11 incredulous, questioning, unbelieving 12 disbelieving

apostasy 7 perfidy 9 defection, desertion, falseness, recreancy

apostate 8 defector, recreant, renegade, runagate, turncoat 9 turnabout 13 tergiversator

apostatize 4 turn 6 defect, desert 8 renounce 9 repudiate 10 tergiverse 12 tergiversate

a posteriori 9 inducible, inductive

apostle 4 John, Jude, Paul 5 James, Judas, Peter, Silas, Simon 6 Andrew, Philip, Thomas 7 Matthew 8 Barnabas, disciple, follower, Matthias, preacher 9 missioner 10 colporteur, evangelist, missionary 11 Bartholomew 12 propagandist *of Germany:* 8 Boniface *of Ireland:* 7 Patrick *of the English:* 9 Augustine *of the French:* 5 Denis *of the Gauls:* 8 Irenaeus *of the Gentiles:* 4 Paul *of the Goths:* 7 Ulfilas *to the Indians:* 9 John Eliot

apothecary 7 chemist 8 druggist 10 pharmacist

apothegm 4 rule 5 axiom, gnome, maxim, moral 6 dictum, truism 7 brocard 8 aphorism

apotheosis 6 height 7 epitome 8 last word, ultimate 9 elevation 10 exaltation 11 deification, ennoblement, idolization, lionization 12 enshrinement, quintessence 13 dignification, glorification

appall 3 awe 4 faze 5 daunt, shake 6 dismay 7 horrify, overawe 11 consternate

appalling 5 awful 7 fearful 8 daunting, dreadful, horrible, horrific, shocking, terrible, terrific 9 dismaying, frightful 10 formidable, horrifying

appanage 5 right 9 privilege 10 birthright, perquisite 11 prerogative

apparatus 4 gear, tool 6 outfit, tackle 7 utensil 8 materiel, tackling 9 equipment, implement, machinery 10 instrument 11 habiliments 13 accouterments, paraphernalia *combining form:* 4 stat

apparel 4 clad, duds, garb, togs 5 array, dress 6 attire, clothe 7 clothes, garment, raiment 8 clothing, enclothe 10 attirement 11 habiliments

apparent 5 clear, plain 6 patent 7 evident, obvious, seeming 8 distinct, illusive, illusory, manifest, palpable, semblant 9 prominent 10 Barmecidal, noticeable, observable, ostensible 11 discernible, perceivable, unambiguous, unequivocal

apparently *combining form:* 5 quasi

apparition 5 bogey, ghost, shade, spook, umbra 6 shadow, spirit, wraith 7 eidolon, phantom, specter 8 illusion, phantasm, revenant, spectrum 13 hallucination

appeal 3 beg 4 call, lure, plea, pray, pull, suit 5 brace, charm, crave, plead 6 allure, excite, invoke, orison, prayer, sue for 7 attract, beseech, entreat, glamour, implore 8 charisma, entreaty, interest, intrigue, petition 9 fascinate, importune, magnetism, seduction 10 allurement, attraction, supplicate 11 application, fascination, imploration 12 drawing power, solicitation, supplication

appealing 5 siren 8 alluring, charming 9 seductive 10 attracting, attractive, bewitching, enchanting 11 captivating, fascinating

appear 4 look, loom, rise, seem, show 5 arise, issue, sound 6 arrive, emerge 7 emanate 11 materialize

appearance 3 air 4 face, look, mien, pose, show 5 front, guise 6 aspect, facade, facies, manner 7 bearing, seeming, showing 8 demeanor 9 semblance 10 simulacrum 11 countenance *combining form:* 5 phane, phany

appease 4 calm 6 pacify, soothe 7 assuage, content, gratify, mollify, placate, relieve, satisfy, sweeten 10 conciliate, propitiate

appellation 4 name 5 nomen, style, title 7 moniker 8 cognomen 11 designation 12 denomination

append 3 add 5 annex 6 take on 7 subjoin 8 superadd

appendage 3 arm, fin, leg, tab, tag 4 barb, flap, horn, limb, seta, tail, wing 5 extra 6 cercus 7 adjunct, antenna, elytron, stipule 8 pedipalp, pendicle, tentacle 9 accessory, auxiliary 10 collateral, incidental, supplement 12 appurtenance, nonessential

appendix 5 rider 7 adjunct, codicil

8 addendum 9 accessory 10 supplement 12 appurtenance
apperception 5 grasp 11 recognition 12 apprehension, assimilation 13 comprehension, understanding
appertain 5 apply 6 bear on, belong, relate 8 bear upon
appetence 5 taste 7 stomach
appetent 4 agog, avid, keen 5 eager 6 ardent 7 anxious, athirst, craving, lusting, thirsty 8 desirous, yearning 9 impatient 10 breathless
appetite 4 bent, bias, itch, lust, urge 5 taste 6 desire, hunger, liking 7 craving, leaning, passion, stomach 8 cupidity, fondness, gluttony, penchant, soft spot, voracity, weakness 10 proclivity, propensity 11 inclination *combining form:* 6 orexia *insatiable:* 7 bulimia
appetizer 4 whet 6 canapé, savory, tidbit 7 zakuska 8 delicacy 9 antipasto 11 hors d'oeuvre
appetizing 5 sapid, tasty 6 savory 8 saporous 9 aperitive, palatable, relishing, toothsome 10 flavorsome 13 mouthwatering
applaud 4 clap, hail, laud, root 5 bravo, cheer, extol 6 kudize, praise, rise to 7 acclaim, commend 9 recommend 10 compliment
applause 4 hand 6 bravos, cheers 7 acclaim, ovation, rooting 8 cheering, clapping, plaudits 11 acclamation
apple 4 crab, pome 6 pippin, russet 7 Baldwin, costard, Duchess, Stayman, Wealthy, Winesap 8 Cortland, greening, Jonathan, McIntosh, pearmain 9 Delicious 10 Rome Beauty 11 Granny Smith, Gravenstein, Northern Spy, Transparent *combining form:* 4 pomi *genus:* 5 Malus *juice:* 5 cider *relating to:* 5 malic
applejack 5 cider 6 brandy
apple knocker 4 hick, jake 5 yokel 6 rustic 7 bucolic, bumpkin, hayseed, hoosier, redneck 10 provincial
apple-polish 4 fawn 5 cower, toady 6 cringe, grovel, kowtow 7 honey up, truckle 8 bootlick 9 brownnose
apple-polisher 5 toady 8 bootlick, clawback, groveler, lickspit 9 brownnose, sycophant 10 bootlicker, brownnoser, footlicker 11 lickspittle
applesauce 5 fudge, hooey 6 bunkum 7 baloney, rubbish, twaddle 8 malarkey, nonsense 9 poppycock 12 blatherskite
appliance 3 use 4 play 6 usance 9 operation 10 employment 11 application *kitchen:* 4 oven 5 mixer, range, stove 7 blender, toaster 9 can opener 10 dishwasher 12 refrigerator
applicability 3 use 5 avail 7 account, fitness, utility 9 advantage, relevance 10 usefulness
applicable 3 apt, fit 4 just, meet 5 ad rem 6 seemly 7 apropos, correct, fitting, germane 8 apposite, material, pointful, relevant, suitable 9 befitting, pertinent 10 felicitous 11 applicative, applicatory, appropriate
applicant 6 seeker 7 hopeful 8 aspirant 9 candidate
application 3 use 4 heed, plea, suit 5 study 6 appeal, debate, orison, prayer, usance 8 entreaty, exercise, exertion, petition 9 appliance, attention, operation 10 employment, exercising 11 imploration, imprecation 12 deliberation, supplication 13 concentration, consideration
applicatory 5 ad rem 7 apropos, germane 8 apposite, material, pointful, relevant 9 pertinent
applied *combining form:* 6 techno
apply 3 use 4 bend, give, turn, urge 5 press 6 accost, appeal, bear on, bestow, devote, direct, employ, handle, relate, resort, take on 7 address, beseech, entreat, implore, pertain, utilize 8 approach, bear upon, exercise, petition, set about 9 appertain, importune, undertake 10 buckle down
appoint 3 arm, rig, tap 4 gear, name 5 equip 6 assign, finger, fit out, outfit 7 dress up, furbish, furnish, turn out 8 accouter, accredit, delegate, nominate 9 authorize, designate, embellish 10 commission
appointment 3 job 4 date, post, spot 5 berth, place, tryst 6 billet, office 8 position 9 situation 10 connection, engagement, rendezvous 11 assignation
apportion 3 lot 4 give 5 allot, allow, divvy, quota, serve, share, split 6 assign, bestow, divide, parcel, ration 7 deal out, dish out, dole out, measure, mete out, prorate 8 allocate, dispense, separate, share out 9 admeasure, partition 10 administer, distribute
apportionment 4 meed, part 5 quota, share 6 ration 7 measure, quantum 9 allotment, allowance
apposite 5 ad rem 6 timely 7 apropos, germane 8 material, pointful, relevant 9 pertinent 10 applicable 11 applicative, applicatory
appositeness 5 order 9 propriety 10 expediency 11 suitability
appraisal 5 stock 8 estimate, judgment 9 valuation 10 assessment, estimation, evaluation
appraise 4 rate 5 assay, audit, judge, set at, value 6 assess, survey 7 adjudge, examine, inspect, valuate 8 estimate, evaluate 10 scrutinize
appreciable 5 clear, plain 7 evident, obvi-

ous 8 apparent, concrete, manifest, material, palpable, sensible, tangible 10 detectable, observable 11 discernible, perceptible, substantial

appreciate 4 know, like, love 5 enjoy, grasp, prize, savor, value 6 admire, esteem, fathom, regard, relish 7 apprize, cherish, cognize, respect 8 treasure 9 apprehend, delight in 10 comprehend, understand

appreciation 7 tribute 9 gratitude 11 recognition, testimonial 12 gratefulness

apprehend 3 dig, nab, see 4 bust, fear, know, take, twig 5 catch, grasp, pinch, run in, seize, sense 6 absorb, accept, arrest, detain, digest, divine, fathom, pick up, take in, wise up 7 catch on, cognize, compass, foresee, make out, preknow, previse, realize 8 conceive 9 penetrate, recognize, visualize 10 anticipate, appreciate, understand

apprehensible 5 lucid 8 knowable, luminous 10 fathomable

apprehension 4 care, fear, idea 5 alarm, angst, dread, pinch, worry 6 arrest, notion, pickup, unease 7 anxiety, capture, concern, thought 8 disquiet 9 agitation, detention, misgiving 10 conception, foreboding, perception, solicitude, uneasiness 11 disquietude, premonition

apprehensive 5 alive, awake, aware 6 afraid 7 anxious, fearful, knowing 8 sensible, sentient 9 cognizant, conscious

apprentice 4 colt, tyro 6 novice, rookie 7 learner, trainee 8 beginner, freshman, neophyte, newcomer 9 novitiate 10 tenderfoot

apprenticed 5 bound 8 articled 10 indentured

apprise 4 clue, post, tell, warn 6 advise, fill in, inform, notify, reveal, wise up 8 acquaint, announce 11 communicate

apprize 5 value 6 esteem 7 cherish 8 treasure 10 appreciate

approach 4 near, nigh 5 reach, rival, touch, verge 6 accost, advise, amount, border, trench 7 address, advance, apply to, attempt, bespeak, consult 8 endeavor, overture 11 approximate

approaching 6 coming 7 nearing 8 oncoming, upcoming 11 forthcoming

approbate 5 favor 6 accept 7 approve 11 countenance

approbation 2 OK 4 okay 5 favor 6 esteem 8 approval, blessing, goodwill, sanction 10 admiration 11 benediction

approbatory 9 favorable

appropinquity 9 immediacy, proximity 10 contiguity

appropriate 3 apt, cop, due, fit 4 grab, just, lift, meet, take, true 5 annex, claim, exact, filch, grasp, pinch, right, seize, steal, swipe, usurp 6 assume, pilfer, proper, snatch, snitch, timely, useful, worthy 7 condign, desired, fitting, germane, merited, preempt, purloin 8 accroach, apposite, arrogate, deserved, eligible, entitled, relevant, rightful, suitable 9 befitting, opportune, pertinent, requisite, sequester 10 acceptable, admissible, applicable, commandeer, confiscate, convenient, felicitous, seasonable

appropriately 4 well 5 amply, right 8 properly, suitably 9 fittingly 10 acceptably, adequately, becomingly

appropriateness 3 use 5 order 7 account, aptness, fitness, service, utility 8 meetness 9 advantage, propriety, relevance, rightness 10 expediency, usefulness

appropriation 5 grant 7 stipend, subsidy 9 allotment, allowance 10 subvention

approval 2 OK 4 okay 5 favor 8 applause, blessing, sanction, suffrage 10 acceptance, compliment 11 approbation, benediction, endorsement 12 commendation

approve 2 OK 4 okay 5 clear, favor, go for 6 accept, back up, praise, ratify, uphold 7 applaud, certify, commend, condone, confirm, endorse, initial, stand by, support, sustain 8 accredit, hold with, sanction 9 approbate 10 compliment 11 countenance

approximal 8 abutting, adjacent, touching 9 adjoining, bordering 10 contiguous, juxtaposed 12 conterminous

approximate 4 near, nigh, rude 5 judge, place, rough 6 reckon 8 approach, estimate, relative 11 comparative

approximately 4 most, nigh 5 about 6 all but, almost, nearly 8 well-nigh 9 nearabout 11 practically

appurtenance 7 adjunct 8 appendix 9 accessory, appendage, equipment, furniture 11 furnishings

appurtenant 8 adjuvant 9 accessory, ancillary, auxiliary 10 collateral, subsidiary 11 subservient 12 contributory

a priori 8 dogmatic, reasoned 9 deducible, deductive, derivable

apriorism 5 posit 6 thesis 7 premise 9 postulate 10 assumption 11 postulation, presumption, supposition

apron 5 stage 8 pinafore

apropos 2 re 4 as to, in re, meet 5 about, ad rem, anent, as for 6 proper 7 germane 8 apposite, material, pointful, relevant, touching 9 as regards, pertinent, regarding 10 applicable, as respects, concerning, respecting 11 applicative, applicatory, in respect to 13 with respect to

Apsu *daughter:* 6 Lahamu *son:* 5 Lahmu *wife:* 6 Tiamat

apt 3 fit 4 just, meet 5 alert, given, prone,

quick, ready **6** bright, liable, likely, prompt, proper **7** apropos, fitting **8** apposite, disposed, inclined, relevant, suitable **9** befitting, pertinent **10** felicitous **11** appropriate
aptitude **4** bent, gift **5** flair, knack **6** genius, talent **7** ability, fitness **8** capacity, tendency **10** propensity **11** disposition
aptness **4** bent, gift **5** flair, knack, order **6** genius, talent **7** faculty, fitness **8** meetness **9** propriety, rightness **10** expediency **11** suitability
aquake **5** shaky **7** aquiver, shaking **9** quivering, shivering, trembling, tremorous, tremulant, tremulous
aqua vitae **4** grog **5** booze, drink, hooch **6** liquor, tipple **7** alcohol, spirits **9** firewater
aqueduct **5** canal **6** course **7** channel, conduit **11** watercourse
Aquila star **6** Altair
aquiver see **aquake**
Arab country **4** Iraq, Oman **5** Egypt, Libya, Qatar, Sudan, Syria, Yemen **6** Jordan, Kuwait **7** Algeria, Bahrain, Lebanon, Morocco, Tunisia **11** Saudi Arabia
arable **7** fertile **8** fruitful, tillable **10** cultivable, productive
Arachne ***father:*** **5** Idmon ***form:*** **6** spider ***mother:*** **6** Cyrene ***rival:*** **6** Athena **7** Minerva
arachnid **4** mite, tick **6** acarus, spider **8** scorpion **9** phalangid, tarantula **10** harvestman
Aran ***brother:*** **2** Uz ***father:*** **6** Dishan
arbiter **5** judge **6** umpire **7** referee **9** moderator
arbitrary **4** rash **7** erratic, wayward **8** absolute, arrogant, despotic, freakish, heedless, oracular, whimsied **9** autarchic, impetuous, tyrannous, vagarious, whimsical **10** autocratic, capricious, monocratic, tyrannical **11** dictatorial, magisterial, precipitate **12** unreasonable **13** authoritarian
arbitrate **5** judge **6** umpire **7** adjudge, mediate, referee **9** intervene **10** adjudicate **12** intermediate
arbitrator **5** judge **6** umpire **7** referee **8** mediator **9** moderator
arbor **5** bower **6** casino, gazebo **7** pergola **9** belvedere **11** summerhouse
arc **3** bow, lob **4** arch, bend **5** curve, round **7** rainbow **9** curvation, curvature
arcadia **4** Eden, Zion **6** heaven, utopia **8** paradise **9** Cockaigne, fairyland, Shangri-la **10** lubberland, wonderland **12** promised land
arcane **6** mystic, secret **8** numinous **10** cabalistic, mysterious, unknowable **11** inscrutable **12** impenetrable **13** unaccountable
Arcas ***father:*** **4** Zeus **7** Jupiter ***mother:*** **8** Callisto
arch **3** bow, coy **4** bend, hump, pert **5** chief, cocky, curve, first, fresh, roach, round, saucy, vault **6** bantam, camber, cheeky, cocket, impish **7** leading, playful, premier, roguish **8** champion, flippant, foremost, malapert **9** curvation, curvature, principal **10** coquettish **11** mischievous ***inner curve:*** **8** intrados ***kind:*** **4** flat, ogee **5** ogive, round, Tudor **6** lancet **7** rampart, trefoil **9** horseshoe, primitive, segmental **10** shouldered **11** equilateral ***outer curve:*** **8** extrados ***part:*** **8** keystone, springer, voussoir ***pointed:*** **4** ogee **5** ogive
archaeological site ***Africa:*** **8** Zimbabwe ***Crete:*** **7** Knossos ***Egypt:*** **6** Naqada **9** Al-Bahnasa **11** Oxyrhynchus ***England:*** **10** Stonehenge ***Greece:*** **7** Mycenae, Olympia ***Iraq:*** **2** Ur **4** Isin, Nuzi **5** Issin **7** Babylon, Nineveh ***Israel:*** **7** Jericho ***Italy:*** **7** Pompeii ***Turkey:*** **4** Troy **9** Hissarlik
archaeologist **5** Evans **6** Carter **7** Thomsen, Woolley, Worsaae **8** Breasted, Goodyear, Piranesi **10** Schliemann **11** Winckelmann
archaic **3** old **5** dated, passé **6** bygone **7** antique **8** outdated **9** out-of-date, primitive, unevolved **10** antiquated **11** undeveloped **12** old-fashioned ***combining form:*** **4** pale **5** palae, paleo **6** palaeo
arched **4** bent **5** bowed, round **6** curved **7** arrondi, rounded **8** arciform **11** curvilinear ***combining form:*** **3** tox **4** toxi, toxo
archer **4** Tell **5** Cupid **6** bowman **9** Robin Hood **11** Sagittarius
archery ***combining form:*** **3** tox **4** toxi, toxo
archetypal **5** ideal, model **7** classic, typical **9** classical, exemplary **12** paradigmatic, prototypical
archetype **5** ideal, model **6** mirror **7** example, pattern **8** exemplar, original, paradigm, standard **9** beau ideal, prototype **10** protoplast
archfiend **5** demon, devil, Satan **8** succubus
Archimedes' cry **6** eureka
archipelago ***Asian:*** **5** Malay ***Canada:*** **6** Arctic ***Japan:*** **4** Goto **9** Gotoretto ***Norway:*** **11** Spitsbergen ***off Scotland:*** **7** Orcades, Orkneys **13** Orkney Islands ***off South America:*** **14** Tierra del Fuego
architect **4** sire **5** maker **6** author, father **7** creator, founder **8** designer, inventor **9** generator, patriarch **10** originator ***American:*** **3** Pei **5** McKim, Stone, Weese, White **6** Breuer, Rogers, Soleri, Upjohn, Walter, Warren, Wright **7** Johnson, Latrobe, Renwick, Sturgis **8** Bulfinch, Saarinen, Sullivan, Thornton, Yamasaki **10** Richardson ***Brazilian:*** **8** Niemeyer ***English:*** **4** Shaw, Wood, Wren **5** Jones, Scott, Wyatt **6** Street, Voy-

sey 8 Vanbrugh ***Finnish:*** 5 Aalto ***French:*** 6 Perret 11 Le Corbusier ***German:*** 8 Schinkel ***German-American:*** 7 Gropius ***Italian:*** 6 Romano 7 da Vinci, Orcagna, Peruzzi, Raphael, Vignola 8 Palladio, Sangallo, Terragni 9 Sansovino 12 Michelangelo ***Japanese:*** 5 Tange ***Roman:*** 9 Vitruvius

architecture 6 design, makeup 9 formation 11 composition 12 constitution, construction ***ornament:*** 4 boss, fret 5 gutta 6 finial, pampre, patera, volute 7 cabling, console, crocket, diglyph 8 encarpus, triglyph, vignette 9 arabesque, guilloche, modillion ***style:*** 5 Doric, Greek, Ionic, Tudor 6 Gothic, Norman, Rococo 7 Baroque 8 Colonial, Georgian 9 Byzantine, Victorian 10 Corinthian, Romanesque 11 Renaissance 13 Mediterranean

archive 6 record 7 library 8 document, monument 9 athenaeum

arch-shaped 8 arciform

arctic 3 icy 4 cold, cool 5 chill, gelid, nippy 6 chilly, frosty, hiemal 7 glacial, numbing 8 freezing, hibernal 11 hyperborean ***animal:*** 3 auk, fox 4 bear, hare, seal, vole 5 sable, whale 6 ermine, marten 7 caribou, lemming 8 reindeer 9 ptarmigan ***base:*** 4 Etah (Greenland) ***bird:*** 3 auk ***cetacean:*** 7 narwhal ***current:*** 8 Labrador ***dog:*** 5 husky 7 Samoyed 8 malamute, malemute ***explorer:*** 4 Byrd, Cook 5 Bylot, Davis, Peary 6 Baffin, Bennet, Bering, Henson, Hudson, Nansen, Nobile 7 Barents, Wilkins, Wrangel 8 Amundsen 9 Ellsworth, Mackenzie, Macmillan 10 Stefansson ***forest:*** 5 taiga ***jacket:*** 5 parka 6 anorak ***people:*** 4 Lapp 5 Aleut, Yakut 6 Eskimo, Koryak, Tungus, Zyrian 7 Chukchi, Samoyed 9 Kamchadal ***sea:*** 4 Kara 6 Laptev 7 Barents, Chukchi 8 Beaufort 9 Greenland ***transport:*** 7 dogsled ***treeless plains:*** 6 tundra

ardent 3 hot 4 agog, avid, keen, true 5 eager, fiery, loyal 6 fervid, heated, intent, red-hot, strong, torrid 7 anxious, athirst, blazing, burning, earnest, fervent, flaming, intense, staunch 8 appetent, constant, desirous, faithful, powerful, resolute, sizzling, vehement, white-hot 9 allegiant, impatient, impetuous, impulsive, scorching, steadfast 10 breathless, hot-blooded, passionate 11 impassioned 12 enthusiastic

ardor 4 fire, zeal, zest, zing 5 gusto, piety, verve 6 fealty, fervor, spirit, warmth 7 avidity, loyalty, passion 8 devotion, fidelity 9 calenture, eagerness 10 allegiance, enthusiasm 12 faithfulness

arduous 4 hard 5 rough, sheer, steep, tight 6 abrupt, trying, uphill 7 labored, operose, tricksy 8 sideling, toilsome 9 difficult, laborious, strenuous 11 precipitate, precipitous

area 4 belt, zone 5 field, place, range, realm, scene, space, tract 6 domain, locale, region, sector, sphere 7 expanse 8 district, locality, province, vicinage, vicinity 9 bailiwick, territory 12 neighborhood ***combining form:*** 3 gea 4 gaea ***dark, shaded:*** 5 umbra ***unit:*** 4 acre 7 hectare

arena 5 scene 7 stadium, theater 8 coliseum 10 hippodrome 12 amphitheater

Ares 4 Mars ***consort:*** 5 Venus 9 Aphrodite ***father:*** 4 Zeus 7 Jupiter ***mother:*** 4 Enyo, Hera, Juno ***son:*** 5 Remus 7 Romulus

arête 5 crest, merit 6 virtue 7 quality 10 excellence, excellency, perfection

Arethusa's pursuer 7 Alpheus

argent 6 silver 7 silvern, silvery

Argentina ***capital:*** 11 Buenos Aires ***monetary unit:*** 4 peso

Arges 7 Cyclops ***brother:*** 7 Brontes 8 Steropes ***father:*** 6 Uranus ***mother:*** 4 Gaea

argon ***symbol:*** 2 Ar

Argonauts' leader 5 Jason

argot 4 cant 5 lingo, slang 6 jargon, patois, patter 7 dialect 10 vernacular

arguable 4 moot 7 dubious 8 doubtful 9 debatable, uncertain 10 disputable 11 problematic 12 questionable

argue 4 moot 5 claim, clash 6 assert, attest, bicker, debate, differ, hassle, object 7 agitate, bespeak, canvass, contend, discept, discuss, dispute, dissent, justify, protest, quarrel, quibble, stickle, testify, witness, wrangle 8 announce, conflict, disagree, indicate, maintain, polemize, squabble 9 thrash out 10 polemicize 11 expostulate, remonstrate

argument 3 row 4 fuss 5 theme, topic 6 debate, dustup, hassle, motive, reason, rumpus 7 dispute, polemic, sorites, subject, wrangle 8 rebuttal 10 contention, dissension, squabbling 11 controversy, disputation, embroilment 12 disagreement

argumentation 6 debate 7 dispute, mooting, oratory 8 forensic, rhetoric 9 dialectic 11 controversy, disputation

argumentative 9 litigious, polemical 11 contentious 12 disputatious 13 controversial

Argus ***father:*** 4 Zeus 7 Jupiter ***mother:*** 5 Niobe ***slayer:*** 6 Hermes 7 Mercury

argute 4 high 5 cagey, heady, savvy, sharp 6 piping, shrewd, shrill, treble 8 piercing 9 sagacious 13 perspicacious

aria 3 lay 4 hymn, lied, song 5 ditty 7 descant

Ariadne ***father:*** 5 Minos ***husband:*** 7 Theseus ***mother:*** 8 Pasiphae

arid 3 dry 4 drab, dull, sere 5 dusty, tepid 6 barren, boring, dreary 7 bone-dry, insipid, sterile, tedious, thirsty 8 bromidic, droughty, weariful 9 dryasdust, infertile, unwatered, waterless, wearisome 10 unfruitful 12 moistureless 13 uninteresting

Ariel's master 8 Prospero

Aries 3 ram

aright 4 well 5 fitly 6 justly, nicely 8 decently, properly 9 correctly, fittingly 10 decorously

arise 4 lift, soar 5 begin, get up, issue, mount, start 6 ascend, aspire, spring, uprear 7 emanate, proceed 8 commence 9 originate

Aristaeus ***father:*** 6 Apollo ***mother:*** 6 Cyrene ***son:*** 7 Actaeon ***wife:*** 7 Autonoe

aristarch 5 momus 6 carper, critic, Zoilus 7 caviler, knocker 10 criticizer 11 faultfinder

aristocracy 5 elite 6 bon ton, gentry, jet set 7 who's who 8 nobility, noblesse, smart set 9 beau monde, blue blood, gentility, haut monde 10 patricians, patriciate, upper class, upper crust 13 carriage trade

aristocrat 9 blue blood, gentleman, patrician ***ancient Greek:*** 8 eupatrid ***Russian:*** 5 boyar 6 boyard

Aristophanes play 6 Plutus 8 The Birds, The Frogs 9 The Clouds

arithmetic 4 math 8 figuring 9 ciphering, reckoning 11 calculation, computation, mathematics

Arizona ***capital:*** 7 Phoenix ***college:*** 11 Grand Canyon ***motto:*** 11 God Enriches ***nickname:*** 16 Grand Canyon State ***state bird:*** 10 cactus wren ***state flower:*** 13 saguaro cactus

Arkansas ***capital:*** 10 Little Rock ***motto:*** 13 The People Rule ***state bird:*** 11 mockingbird ***state flower:*** 12 apple blossom

arm 3 bay, ell, gun, rig 4 cove, gear, gulf, wing 5 annex, bayou, equip, firth, force, inlet, power 6 fit out, harbor, muscle, outfit, slough, weapon 7 appoint, furnish, turn out 8 accouter, strength 9 extension ***bone:*** 4 ulna 6 radius 7 humerus ***combining form:*** 6 brachi 7 brachio ***muscle:*** 6 biceps 7 triceps

armada 4 navy 5 fleet

armadillo ***genus:*** 7 Dasypus ***giant:*** 4 tatu 5 tatou ***nine-banded:*** 4 peba, peva ***relative:*** 5 sloth 8 anteater ***seven-banded:*** 6 mulita ***six-banded:*** 5 poyou 6 peludo ***small:*** 5 pichi 10 pichiciago 11 quirquincho ***three-banded:*** 4 apar 5 apara ***twelve-banded:*** 7 tatouay

armament 4 ward 5 aegis, armor, guard 6 shield 7 defense 8 security 9 safeguard 10 protection

armamentarium 4 fund 5 stock, store 6 supply 9 inventory

armchair 8 fauteuil

armed ***combining form:*** 5 hoplo

armed attendant 9 bodyguard

armed forces 4 army, navy 6 troops 8 air force, military 10 servicemen

armistice 5 truce 9 cease-fire

armor 4 mail, ward 5 aegis, cover, guard 6 shield 7 buckler, defense, shelter 8 armament, security 9 safeguard 10 protection ***arm:*** 8 brassart ***armpit:*** 8 pallette ***buttocks:*** 5 culet ***coat:*** 7 hauberk 10 brigandine ***combining form:*** 5 hoplo ***elbow:*** 6 couter 9 cubitiere ***face:*** 5 visor 6 beaver ***flexible:*** 4 mail ***foot:*** 7 sabaton, soleret 8 sabbaton, solleret ***forearm:*** 8 vambrace ***hand:*** 8 gauntlet ***head:*** 6 helmet ***horse:*** 4 bard 5 barde 6 crinet 7 peytral, peytrel, poitrel 8 chamfron, chanfron, criniere ***knee:*** 11 genouillere ***leg:*** 4 jamb 5 jambe 6 greave 7 jambeau ***mail:*** 4 coif 7 hauberk 8 chausses ***neck:*** 6 camail ***shoulder:*** 7 ailette 8 pauldron, pouldron 9 epauliere ***skirt:*** 6 tonlet ***suit:*** 7 panoply ***thigh:*** 4 tace 5 cuish, tasse 6 tasset, tuille 8 flancard 9 flanchard ***throat:*** 6 gorget

armory 4 dump 5 depot 7 arsenal 8 magazine

armpit 6 axilla 8 underarm ***Scottish:*** 5 oxter

arms 7 ensigns, warfare 8 weaponry

army 4 host, rout 5 crowd, flock, horde 6 legion, scores 7 militia 9 multitude ***combat arm:*** 5 armor 8 infantry 9 artillery ***commission:*** 6 brevet ***Fort:*** 3 Dix, Lee, Ord 4 Hood, Knox, Polk, Sill 5 Bliss, Bragg, Lewis, Meade, Riley 6 Carson, Eustis, Gordon, Monroe, Rucker 7 Belvoir, Benning, Jackson, Shafter 8 Campbell, Holabird, Huachuca, Monmouth 9 McClellan, McPherson 10 Sam Houston 11 Leavenworth ***law enforcer:*** 2 MP ***mascot:*** 4 mule ***meal:*** 4 chow, mess ***mine layer:*** 6 sapper ***NCO:*** 8 corporal, sergeant ***officer:*** 5 major 7 captain, colonel, general, warrant 10 lieutenant ***post:*** 4 base, camp, fort ***postal abbreviation:*** 3 APO ***relating to:*** 7 martial 8 military ***school:*** 3 OCS, OTS 7 academy 9 West Point ***store:*** 2 PX 10 commissary 12 post exchange ***unit:*** 5 corps, squad, troop 7 brigade, cavalry, company, platoon 8 division, regiment ***vehicle:*** 4 jeep, tank 9 half-track

Arnold's coconspirator 5 André

aroma 4 balm, odor 5 scent, smell, spice 7 bouquet, incense, perfume 9 fragrance, redolence

aromatic 5 balmy, spicy, sweet 6 savory 7 perfumy 8 fragrant, perfumed, redolent 9 ambrosial

around 4 back, near, nigh, over 5 about, again, circa 6 anyhow, extant, nearby, random 7 anywise, through 8 at random, existent, existing, randomly 9 haphazard 10 throughout 11 any which way, haphazardly 13 helter-skelter *prefix:* 4 ambi, amph, peri 5 amphi 6 circum

around-the-clock 8 constant 9 continual, incessant, perpetual 10 continuous 11 unremitting 13 uninterrupted

arouse 4 fire, stir, wake, whet 5 alert, pique, rally, waken 6 awaken, bestir, excite, incite, kindle, work up 7 inflame 9 challenge

arraign 3 tax, try 6 accuse, charge, indict 7 impeach 9 criminate, inculpate 11 incriminate

arrange 4 plan, sort 5 array, chart, order, unify 6 assort, codify, design, devise, lay out, map out, scheme, set out 7 dispose, marshal 8 organize, sequence, tabulate 9 blueprint, harmonize, integrate, methodize 10 categorize, symphonize, synthesize 11 choreograph, orchestrate, systematize

arrangement 5 order, setup 6 layout, lineup, series 8 ordering, sequence 9 structure 11 disposition 12 distribution *combining form:* 4 taxy 5 taxis 6 tactic *of five objects:* 8 quincunx *suffix:* 4 osis

arrant 4 rank 5 gross, total, utter 6 brassy, brazen 7 blatant, flat-out 8 absolute, complete, impudent, infernal, overbold 9 barefaced, downright, out-and-out, shameless, unabashed 10 unblushing

arras 7 drapery 8 tapestry

array 3 lot 4 clad, garb, pomp, show 5 batch, bunch, clump, dress, group, order 6 attire, bundle, clothe, parade 7 apparel, arrange, cluster, display, dispose, garment, marshal, panoply, raiment 8 enclothe, organize, spectrum 11 systematize

arrears 3 due 4 debt 9 liability 12 indebtedness

arrect 6 raised 7 heedful, stand-up, upright 9 advertent, attentive, intentive, observant, regardful 10 straight-up, upstanding

arrest 3 nab 4 bust, halt, jail, stay, stem, stop 5 catch, check, pinch, run in, stall 6 collar, detain, lock up, pickup, pull in, retard, stop up 7 capture, contain, seizure 8 imprison, obstruct, restrain 9 apprehend, detention, interrupt 11 incarcerate 12 apprehension

arresting 6 marked, signal 7 salient 9 affective, appealing, prominent 10 attractive, enchanting, impressive, noticeable, remarkable 11 conspicuous, outstanding

arride 6 divert, please 7 beguile, delight, gladden, gratify 8 pleasure 9 delectate, entertain

arrival 6 advent, coming 7 success 8 entrance, incoming 9 emergence 10 appearance

arrive 4 come, show 5 get in, reach 6 show up, thrive, turn up 7 prosper, succeed 8 flourish

arriviste 7 parvenu, upstart 8 roturier 12 nouveau riche

arrogance 5 pride 6 hubris, hybris, morgue 7 disdain, hauteur 9 loftiness, superbity 11 haughtiness

arrogant 5 cocky, proud, puffy, wiggy 6 lordly, snooty, snotty, stuffy 7 bloated, haughty, pompous 8 cavalier, fastuous, insolent, superior 10 disdainful, peremptory, pontifical 11 domineering, highfalutin, magisterial, overbearing 12 supercilious 13 high-and-mighty, self-important *Scottish:* 7 paughty

arrogate 4 grab, take 5 annex, seize, usurp 6 assume 7 preempt 8 accroach, take over 9 sequester 10 commandeer, confiscate 11 appropriate, expropriate

arrondi 4 bent 5 arced, bowed, round 6 arched, curved 7 rounded 8 arciform 11 curvilinear

arrow *combining form:* 3 tox 4 toxi, toxo 7 hastato *poison:* 4 upas 5 urare, urari 6 antiar, curara, curare, curari, oorali 7 woorali, woorari 8 antiarin

arrow-like 6 beloid 7 hastate 8 sagittal 9 sagittate

arrowroot 3 pia 5 araru, tuber 6 ararao 7 coontie, maranta

arroyo 3 gap 4 draw 5 brook, chasm, cleft, clove, creek, gorge, gulch, gully 6 clough, coulee, ravine, stream 7 channel

arsenal 4 dump 5 depot, store 6 armory 8 magazine 10 depository, repository, storehouse

arsenic *symbol:* 2 As

arsonist 5 firer, torch 7 firebug 10 incendiary

art 5 craft, skill, trade 6 métier 7 cunning, finesse, know-how, slyness 8 artifice, foxiness, vocation, wiliness 9 cageyness, canniness, dexterity, expertise 10 adroitness, craftiness, handicraft, profession *combining form:* 4 typy 6 techno *faddish:* 6 kitsch *style:* 2 op 3 pop 6 rococo 7 baroque, Bauhaus, Islamic, optical, surreal 8 abstract, cubistic, romantic 9 arabesque, Byzantine, Christian, classical, dadaistic, realistic 11 Renaissance 12 naturalistic, surrealistic *suffix:* 3 ery 4 ship

Artegal's wife 11 Britomartis

Artemis 5 Diana *birthplace:* 5 Delos *brother:* 6 Apollo *father:* 4 Zeus 7 Jupiter *mother:* 4 Leto 6 Latona *priestess:* 9 Iphigenia

artery 3 way 4 path, road 5 aorta, track

6 avenue, street, vessel 7 carotid, highway 8 coronary 9 boulevard 12 thoroughfare

artful 3 sly 4 foxy, oily, wily 5 suave 6 adroit, astute, crafty, smooth, tricky 7 cunning 8 guileful 9 dexterous, insidious 10 diplomatic

arthropod 3 bee, fly 4 crab, moth 6 beetle, insect, shrimp 7 lobster 8 arachnid, barnacle, chilopod, diplopod, myriapod, myriopod 9 butterfly, centipede, cockroach, millipede 10 crustacean *body segment:* 6 somite, telson 8 metamere *class:* 7 Insecta 8 Symphyla 9 Arachnida, Chilopoda, Crustacea, Diplopoda, Pauropoda *limb segment:* 6 podite 8 podomere

Arthur see King Arthur

article 2 an 3 the 4 item 5 essay, paper, point, theme, thing 6 object 7 element 10 particular 11 composition, stipulation

articled 5 bound 10 indentured

articulate 3 say 4 join, oral 5 order, utter, vocal 6 fluent, prolix, relate, sonant, spoken, voiced 7 connect, phonate 8 eloquent 9 enunciate, garrulous, harmonize, integrate, pronounce, talkative 10 coordinate 11 concatenate 12 smooth-spoken

artifice 4 play, ploy, ruse, wile 5 craft, feint, guile, trick 6 deceit, device, gambit 7 cunning, knavery, slyness 8 foxiness, trickery, wiliness 9 adeptness, cageyness, canniness, chicanery, ingenuity, rascality, stratagem 10 adroitness, cleverness, craftiness 11 skulduggery

artificial 4 fake, mock, sham 5 dummy, false, put-on 6 ersatz, forced, unreal 7 assumed, feigned, labored, man-made, pretend 8 affected, spurious 9 contrived, imitation, insincere, simulated, synthetic, unnatural 10 fabricated, factitious, fictitious, substitute

artillery 6 rocket 8 cannonry, howitzer, ordnance, weaponry

artillery plant 11 burning bush

artisan 7 builder, workman 9 carpenter, craftsman

artist 3 ace 4 whiz 5 adept 6 expert, master, wizard, wonder 8 virtuoso 10 first-rater, past master, topnotcher *garb:* 5 smock *knife:* 7 spatula *medium:* 3 oil 5 chalk, paint 6 pastel 7 tempera 8 charcoal 10 watercolor *pigment board:* 7 palette *stand:* 5 easel *workshop:* 6 studio 7 atelier (see also painter)

artless 4 free 5 naive 6 simple 7 natural 8 trusting, unartful 9 childlike, ingenuous, unstudied 10 aboveboard, forthright, unaffected, unschooled 12 unartificial, unsuspicious

arty 8 imposing 9 overblown 11 pretentious 12 high-sounding

as 3 for 5 being, since, while 7 because 11 considering

Asa *father:* 6 Abijam 7 Elkanah *grandfather:* 8 Rehoboam *grandmother:* 6 Maacah

___ as a pin 4 neat

as a rule 7 usually 8 commonly 9 generally 10 frequently, ordinarily

Ascanius 5 Iulus *father:* 6 Aeneas

ascend 4 lift, rise, soar 5 arise, climb, crest, mount, scale 6 aspire, uprear 7 upclimb 8 escalade, escalate, surmount

ascendancy 8 dominion 9 dominance, masterdom, supremacy 10 domination, prepotency 11 preeminence, sovereignty 13 preponderance

ascendant 6 master 7 regnant 8 ancestor, dominant, forebear 9 paramount, precursor, prevalent, sovereign 10 forefather, forerunner, progenitor 11 overbearing, predecessor, predominant, predominate 12 preponderant, primogenitor

ascension 4 rise 6 rising

ascent 4 rise 5 climb 6 rising 7 raising 9 elevation, uplifting

ascertain 5 learn 7 catch on, find out, unearth 8 discover 9 determine

ascetic 3 nun 4 monk 5 stern, stoic 6 hermit, severe 7 austere, eremite, recluse 8 anchoret 9 abstinent, anchorite, mortified 10 abstemious, astringent, forbearing, restrained 11 disciplined, self-abasing, self-denying *ancient Hebrew:* 6 Essene *Buddhist:* 5 bonze 7 bhikshu *early Christian:* 7 stylite *Hindu:* 4 Yogi 5 fakir, Yogin

Asclepius see Aesculapius

ascribe 3 lay 4 cite 5 refer 6 assign, charge, credit, impute 8 accredit 9 attribute

Asenath *husband:* 6 Joseph *son:* 7 Ephraim 8 Manasseh

aseptic 8 retiring 9 shrinking, unaffable, withdrawn 10 restrained 11 unexpansive

asexual 6 agamic 7 agamous *combining form:* 4 agam 5 agamo

as for 2 re 4 in re 7 apropos 8 touching 9 regarding 10 concerning, respecting

as good as 4 nigh 5 about 6 all but, almost, nearly 8 well-nigh 9 just about, nearabout 11 essentially, practically 13 approximately

ash 4 soot 7 cinders, residue 8 clinkers

ashake 6 aquake 7 aquiver, ashiver, quaking 9 quivering, shivering, trembling, tremulous

ashamed 6 abased, abject 7 abashed, hangdog, humbled 8 contrite, penitent 9 chagrined, mortified, repentant 10 humiliated 11 discomfited, embarrassed

ashen 4 gray, pale 5 faded, livid, lurid, waxen 6 doughy, pallid 7 ghostly, macabre 8 blanched, bleached 9 cinereous, colorless 10 corpselike

Asher *daughter:* 5 Serah *father:* 5 Jacob *mother:* 6 Zilpah *son:* 4 Isui 6 Beriah, Ishuah, Jimnah

Ashhur *father:* 6 Hezron *mother:* 5 Abiah

ashiver see **ashake**

Asia *country:* 4 Iran, Iraq, Laos, Oman 5 China, India, Japan, Nepal, Qatar, Syria, Yemen 6 Bhutan, Cyprus, Israel, Jordan, Kuwait, Taiwan 7 Bahrain, Lebanon, Myanmar, Vietnam 8 Cambodia, Malaysia, Maldives, Mongolia, Pakistan, Sri Lanka, Thailand 9 Indonesia, Kampuchea, Singapore 10 Bangladesh, North Korea, South Korea 11 Afghanistan, Philippines, Saudi Arabia *ethnic group:* 3 Han, Jew, Lao, Tai 4 Arab, Kurd, Moor, Shan, Thai, Turk 5 Karen, Khmer, Malay, Tajik, Tamil, Uzbek 6 Burman, Indian, Korean, Lepcha, Manchu, Mongol, Sindhi 7 Baluchi, Bengali, Chinese, Iranian, Persian, Punjabi, Tibetan 8 Armenian, Assyrian, Japanese, Javanese, Nepalese 9 Dravidian, Indo-Aryan, Pakistani, Sinhalese 10 Circassian, Montagnard, Singhalese, Vietnamese 13 Khalkha Mongol *language:* 3 Lao 4 Urdu 5 Hindi, Malay, Tamil, Uzbek 6 Arabic, Hebrew, Korean, Nepali 7 Bengali, Burmese, Khalkha, Kurdish, Persian, Tibetan, Turkish, Yiddish 8 Armenian, Japanese, Javanese, Mandarin 9 Cambodian 10 Vietnamese 15 Bahasa Indonesia

aside 4 awry 5 apart, askew 6 askant, aslant, aslope 7 askance, slantly 8 excursus, sideways 9 excursion, obliquely, slantways, slantwise 10 digression, discursion, divagation, slantingly 11 parenthesis

aside from 3 bar 4 save 6 bating, except 7 barring, besides 9 excluding, outside of 11 exclusive of

as if *combining form:* 5 quasi

asinine 5 silly 6 absurd, simple 7 fatuous, foolish, puerile, witless 8 mindless 9 brainless 10 irrational, weak-headed

ask 3 beg, bid 4 quiz, seek 5 crave, exact, query 6 appeal, demand, desire, invite 7 beseech, call for, canvass, consult, enquire, entreat, examine, implore, inquire, request, require, solicit 8 question 9 catechize, importune 11 interrogate *Scottish:* 5 speer, speir

askance 4 awry 5 askew 8 cockeyed 9 cock-a-hoop, crookedly, cynically 10 critically, doubtfully, doubtingly 11 skeptically 12 suspiciously 13 distrustfully, mistrustfully

asker 6 beggar, prayer, suitor 9 suppliant 10 petitioner, supplicant 11 supplicator

askew 4 awry 6 askant 7 askance 8 cockeyed 9 cock-a-hoop, crookedly

aslant 5 aside 6 aslope 8 sideways, sidewise 9 obliquely 11 slaunchways *combining form:* 5 plagi 6 plagio

asleep 4 dead, idle, numb 5 inert 6 dozing, numbed 7 defunct, dormant, napping 8 benumbed, deadened, inactive 9 exanimate, senseless, unfeeling 10 insensible, unanimated 11 unconscious 12 anesthetized

as long as 3 for 5 cause, since 6 seeing 7 because, whereas 11 considering

as much as 6 all but, almost 8 well-nigh 11 essentially, practically

asomatous 8 bodiless 10 discarnate, immaterial, unphysical 11 disembodied, incorporeal 13 insubstantial

aspect 4 look, mien, side 5 angle, facet, phase 7 bearing, seeming 10 appearance

asperity 5 rigor 8 acerbity, acrimony, grimness, hardness, hardship, mordancy, tartness 9 harshness, roughness 10 bitterness, difficulty, inclemency, inequality, unevenness 11 vicissitude 12 irregularity, irritability

asperous 5 harsh, rough 6 craggy, jagged, rugged, uneven 7 scraggy, unlevel 8 scabrous, unsmooth

asperse 4 slur 5 libel 6 defame, insult, malign 7 baptize, immerse, slander, traduce 8 christen, sprinkle 9 denigrate 10 calumniate, scandalize

aspersion 4 muck, slam, slur 5 abuse 7 calumny, obloquy, slander 9 invective, stricture 10 detraction, reflection 12 vituperation 13 animadversion

asphalt 7 bitumen 8 blacktop

asphyxiate 5 choke 6 stifle 7 quackle, smother 9 suffocate

aspirant 6 seeker 7 hopeful 9 applicant, candidate

aspiration 3 aim 4 goal 6 desire 8 ambition 9 objective 10 pretension 13 ambitiousness

aspire 3 aim, try 4 long, pant, rise, soar 5 arise, mount 6 ascend, hunger, thirst, uprear

aspiring 7 emulous, wanting, wishful 8 vaulting, yearning 9 ambitious

as regards 2 re 4 in re 7 apropos 8 touching 10 concerning, respecting

ass 4 donk, fool, jerk, moke 5 burro, idiot 6 donkey 8 imbecile 10 nincompoop *female:* 5 jenny *male:* 4 jack *wild Asian:* 5 kiang 6 onager 8 chigetai

assail 4 beat 5 beset, pound, storm 6 attack, buffet, fall on, oppugn, pummel, strike 7 aggress, assault 8 fall upon

assailment 5 onset 6 attack 7 assault, offense 9 offensive, onslaught 10 aggression

Assam silkworm 4 eria

assassin 3 gun 5 bravo 6 gunman, hit man 7 torpedo 8 murderer 9 cutthroat 10 gunslinger, hatchet man, triggerman ***of Caesar:*** 6 Brutus 7 Cassius ***of Garfield:*** 7 Guiteau ***of J.F. Kennedy:*** 6 Oswald ***of Lincoln:*** 5 Booth ***of Marat:*** 6 Corday ***of R.F. Kennedy:*** 6 Sirhan
assassinate 4 cool, do in, kill 6 finish, murder, rub out 7 bump off, execute, put away 8 knock off 9 liquidate
assault 3 mug, war 4 raid 5 beset, fight, onset, set-to, storm 6 assail, attack, fall on, onfall, strike 7 aggress, mugging, offense 8 fall upon, invasion 9 offensive, onslaught 10 aggression, assailment
assay 3 try 4 rate, seek 5 offer, value 6 assess, strive, survey 7 attempt, valuate, venture 8 appraise, endeavor, estimate, evaluate, struggle 9 undertake
assemblage 4 ruck 5 crowd, group 6 muster 7 company, turnout 9 gathering 10 collection 11 aggregation 12 congregation
assemble 4 call, form, make, mass, mold 5 amass, build, clump, group, shape 6 gather, muster, summon 7 cluster, collect, convene, convoke, fashion, marshal, produce, round up 8 congress, contrive 9 aggregate, forgather 10 accumulate, congregate 11 manufacture, put together
assembly 4 band, bevy, crew, ruck 5 bunch, covey, crowd, group, party, rally 6 muster, troupe 7 cluster, company, meeting 8 conclave 9 congeries, gathering 10 collection 11 association 12 congregation ***American Indian:*** 6 powwow ***ancient Greek:*** 8 ecclesia ***ancient Roman:*** 7 comitia ***anglo-Saxon:*** 4 moot 5 gemot 6 gemote 8 folkmoot, folkmote ***ecclesiastical:*** 5 synod 10 consistory ***Hawaiian:*** 3 hui ***Irish:*** 4 feis ***legislative:*** 4 diet 6 senate 8 congress 10 parliament ***medieval English:*** 7 husting ***place:*** 4 hall, room 5 agora 10 auditorium ***Russian:*** 4 duma ***witches':*** 6 sabbat 7 sabbath
assent 3 yes 5 agree 6 accede 7 consent 9 acquiesce, subscribe
assert 4 aver, avow 5 argue, claim, state, utter, voice 6 adduce, affirm, avouch, defend, depose, submit 7 advance, contend, declare, express, justify, profess, protest, publish, warrant 8 announce, constate, maintain, proclaim 9 broadcast, predicate, vindicate 10 promulgate 11 disseminate
assertive 4 sure 5 pushy 7 assured, certain, pushing 8 cocksure, emphatic, forceful, positive, sanguine 9 confident, insistent 10 aggressive, resounding 11 affirmative, self-assured 13 self-confident
assertory 5 pushy 7 pushing 8 militant 10 aggressive
assess 4 deem, levy, rate 5 assay, exact, judge, put on, set at, value, weigh 6 impose, reckon, survey 7 account, valuate 8 appraise, consider, estimate, evaluate
assessment 3 tax 4 duty, levy 5 stock 6 impost, tariff 8 estimate, judgment 9 appraisal, valuation 10 estimation, evaluation 12 appraisement
asset 6 credit 8 resource 9 advantage 11 distinction
assets 5 means, money 6 wealth 7 capital 8 bankroll, property 9 resources, valuables
assiduous 4 busy 7 moiling, operose, zealous 8 diligent, sedulous, tireless 9 laborious 11 hard-working, industrious 13 indefatigable
assiduously 4 hard 9 earnestly, intensely 10 thoroughly 11 intensively 12 exhaustively 13 painstakingly, unremittingly
assign 3 fix, set 4 cede, deed, give 5 allot, allow, refer 6 charge, convey, credit, define, impute, remise, settle 7 appoint, ascribe, lay down, mete out, station 8 accredit, allocate, make over, relegate, sign over, transfer 9 admeasure, apportion, attribute, establish, prescribe 10 pigeonhole
assignation 4 date 5 tryst 9 allotment 10 engagement, rendezvous 11 appointment, get-together
assignee 5 agent, proxy 6 deputy, factor 8 attorney
assignment 3 job 4 duty, task 5 chare, chore, stint 6 devoir 10 obligation
assimilate 5 adopt, liken, match 6 absorb, equate, imbibe, insorb 7 compare, inhaust, paragon 8 parallel 11 incorporate
assimilation 9 awareness 11 mindfulness, recognition 12 apperception 13 consciousness
assist 3 aid 4 abet, help, lift 5 do for, stead 6 relief, succor 7 comfort, help out, secours, support 8 benefact 9 cooperate
assistance 3 aid 4 help, lift 6 relief, succor 7 backing, comfort, secours, subsidy, support 9 upholding 10 subvention, supporting
assistant 3 aid 4 aide, help 5 aider 6 flunky, helper, lackey, minion, second, stooge 7 acolyte, ancilla, orderly, striker 8 adjutant, henchman 9 attendant, auxiliary, coadjutor 10 aide-de-camp, coadjutant, lieutenant 12 right-hand man
assistive 6 aidant, aiding 7 helpful 11 serviceable
assize 3 law 4 rule 5 canon, edict 6 decree 7 precept, statute 8 standard 9 ordinance, prescript 10 regulation

associate 3 pal 4 ally, chum, join, link, mate, yoke 5 buddy, crony, match, merge, unite 6 cohort, comate, couple, fellow, friend, hobnob, relate 7 bracket, combine, compeer, comrade, conjoin, connect, consort, partner 8 confrere, familiar, federate, intimate 9 affiliate, bedfellow, colleague, companion, copartner 10 accomplice, amalgamate, compatriot, complement, consociate 11 concomitant, confederate, correlative, counterpart, running mate 12 acquaintance 13 accompaniment, brother-in-arms, comrade-in-arms
associated *combining form:* 3 sym, syn
associated with *suffix:* 2 ic 4 ical
association 4 axis, bloc, club, hint 5 guild, order, tie-up, union 6 hookup, league 7 cahoots, circuit, concert, society 8 alliance, congress, overtone, relation, sodality, teamwork 9 coalition, undertone 10 conference, connection, federation, fellowship, fraternity, suggestion 11 affiliation, brotherhood, combination, conjunction, connotation, cooperation, implication, partnership 12 conjointment, organization, relationship, togetherness 13 collaboration
assort 5 class, group, order 7 arrange 8 classify, stratify 9 methodize 10 categorize, pigeonhole 11 systematize
assorted 5 mixed 6 fitted, motley, suited, varied 7 adapted, matched 8 chowchow 11 conformable, promiscuous 12 conglomerate, multifarious 13 heterogeneous, miscellaneous
assortment 4 olio 6 jumble, medley 7 mélange, variety 8 mishmash, pastiche 9 potpourri 10 hodgepodge, miscellany 11 gallimaufry
assuage 4 calm, ease 5 allay 6 pacify, soothe 7 appease, lighten, mollify, placate, relieve 8 mitigate 9 alleviate 10 conciliate, propitiate
as such 5 per se 13 intrinsically
assumably 6 likely 8 probably 9 doubtless
assume 3 act, don 4 fake, sham, take 5 bluff, feign, get on, posit, put on, seize, usurp 6 affect, draw on, expect, reckon, slip on, strike, take on 7 believe, imagine, preempt, premise, presume, pretend, suppose, suspect 8 accroach, arrogate, shoulder, simulate 9 postulate 10 commandeer, presuppose, understand 11 appropriate, counterfeit
assumed 5 put on 7 feigned 8 affected, delusory, putative, spurious 9 deceptive 10 artificial, factitious
assumption 5 posit 6 thesis 7 premise, surmise 9 apriorism, postulate 10 conjecture 11 supposition
assurance 5 nerve, troth 6 aplomb, parole, pledge, safety, surety 8 audacity, safeness, security, sureness, temerity 9 brashness, certainty, certitude, cockiness, composure, guarantee, hardiness, sangfroid, self-trust 10 brazenness, confidence, conviction, equanimity 11 presumption
assure 5 cinch 6 ensure, insure, secure 7 promise, satisfy 8 convince, persuade
assured 4 cool 6 secure 7 certain, decided 8 clear-cut, composed, definite, sanguine 9 collected, confident, unruffled 10 pronounced, undoubtful 11 unflappable 13 imperturbable, self-confident
assuredness 6 surety 9 certainty, certitude 10 confidence, conviction
Assyria *capital:* 5 Calah 7 Nineveh *city:* 4 Hara, Opis 5 Ashur, Assur, Kalhu 6 Asshur *god:* 3 Sin 4 Asur, Nabu 5 Ashur, Assur, Nusku 6 Asshur, Tammuz 7 Ninurta *goddess:* 6 Ishtar *king:* 3 Pul 6 Sargon 11 Sennacherib, Shalmaneser 12 Ashurbanipal, Assurbanipal *language:* 7 Aramaic *measure:* 4 cane, foot 5 gasab, makuk 6 artaba, gariba 7 mansion *queen:* 9 Semiramis *river:* 6 Tigris *writing:* 9 cuneiform
astatine *symbol:* 2 At
astern 3 aft 4 rear 5 abaft
Asterope *father:* 5 Atlas *mother:* 7 Pleione *sisters:* 8 Pleiades
as to 2 re 4 in re 7 apropos 8 touching 9 regarding 10 concerning, respecting
astonish 5 alarm, amaze 7 astound 8 affright, dumfound, surprise 9 dumbfound 11 flabbergast
astonishing 7 amazing 8 wondrous 9 marvelous, wonderful 10 astounding, miraculous, prodigious, stupendous, surprising 11 spectacular 12 breathtaking
astound 5 amaze 8 astonish, dumfound, surprise 9 dumbfound 11 flabbergast
astounding see **astonishing**
Astraea *father:* 4 Zeus 7 Jupiter *mother:* 6 Themis
astral 6 dreamy, starry 7 exalted, highest, stellar 8 sidereal 9 daydreamy, stellular, top-drawer, unworldly, visionary 10 top-ranking 11 daydreaming 12 otherworldly
astray 4 awry 5 amiss, badly, wrong 6 afield
astricted 5 bound 7 costive 10 obstipated 11 constipated
astringent 4 keen 5 acrid, harsh, sharp, stern, tonic 6 biting, bitter, severe, strict 7 ascetic, austere, caustic, cutting, styptic 8 incisive, roborant 11 contracting 12 constrictive
astrologer 11 Nostradamus
astrological aspect 5 trine 7 sextile 8 quartile 10 opposition 11 conjunction
astronaut 4 Ride (Sally) 5 Glenn (John),

Young (John) 6 Aldrin (Edwin), Lovell (James), Worden (Alfred) 7 Collins (Michael), Gagarin (Yuri), Schirra (Walter), Shepard (Alan), Yegorov (Boris) 8 Stafford (Thomas) 9 Armstrong (Neil), McAuliffe (Christa) 10 Tereshkova (Valentina)

astronomer ***American:*** 3 See 6 Lowell 7 Langley, Newcomb 8 Tombaugh 9 Pickering 11 Schlesinger ***Austrian:*** 13 Schwarzschild ***Dutch:*** 6 Sitter 7 Huygens ***English:*** 4 Ryle, Wren 6 Halley, Lovell 7 Lockyer, Parsons 8 Herschel ***French:*** 6 Picard 7 Laplace, Messier ***German:*** 4 Wolf 5 Vogel 6 Kepler, Muller, Struve ***Greek:*** 12 Eratosthenes ***Italian:*** 7 Galilei 12 Schiaparelli ***Persian:*** 11 Omar Khayyam ***Polish:*** 10 Copernicus ***Swedish:*** 7 Celcius ***Swiss:*** 6 Zwicky

astute 3 sly 4 deep, foxy, keen, wily 5 cagey, heady, savvy, sharp 6 argute, artful, crafty, shrewd, tricky 7 cunning, knowing 8 guileful 9 astucious, insidious, sagacious 13 perspicacious

astuteness 3 wit 6 acumen 8 keenness 10 shrewdness 11 discernment, penetration, percipience 12 perspicacity

Astyanax ***father:*** 6 Hector ***mother:*** 10 Andromache

asunder 5 apart

as usual 8 wontedly 10 habitually 11 customarily 12 consistently

asweat 5 puggy 8 perspiry 10 perspiring

as well 3 too, yet 4 also, even, just, more 7 besides, exactly 8 likewise, moreover 9 expressly, precisely 11 furthermore 12 additionally

as well as 6 beside, beyond 7 besides 12 over and above

as yet 5 so far 7 earlier, thus far 8 hitherto

asylum 4 home, port 5 cover, haven 6 covert, harbor, refuge 7 retreat, shelter 8 bughouse, loony bin, madhouse, nuthouse, security 9 harborage, sanctuary 10 booby hatch, crazy house, sanatorium 11 institution

asymmetric 6 uneven 7 unequal 8 lopsided 9 irregular 10 off-balance, unbalanced 12 overbalanced

Atalanta ***husband:*** 8 Melanion ***suitor:*** 10 Hippomenes

at all 4 ever, once 6 anyway, soever 7 anytime, anywise ***Scottish:*** 3 ava

ataraxy 8 calmness, coolness 9 composure, sangfroid 10 equanimity

atavism 9 reversion, throwback

ataxia 5 chaos, snarl 6 huddle, muddle 7 clutter 8 disarray, disorder 9 confusion

at close hand 4 near, nigh 6 nearby

atelier 6 studio 7 bottega 8 workshop

Athamas ***daughter:*** 5 Helle ***father:*** 6 Aeolus ***son:*** 7 Phrixos, Phrixus 8 Learchus ***wife:*** 3 Ino 7 Nephele

Athena, Athene 7 Minerva ***attribute:*** 3 owl 5 Aegis 7 serpent ***father:*** 4 Zeus ***names:*** 4 Alea, Nike 5 Areia 6 Ergane, Hippia, Hygeia, Itonia, Pallas, Polias 8 Apaturia 9 Parthenos, Promachos 10 Chalinitis ***shield:*** 4 Egis 5 Aegis ***statue:*** 9 Palladium ***temple:*** 9 Parthenon

athenaeum 7 library 8 archives

Athens ***citadel:*** 9 Acropolis ***founder:*** 7 Cecrops ***last king:*** 6 Codrus ***marketplace:*** 5 agora ***rival:*** 6 Sparta ***senate:*** 5 boule ***temple:*** 9 Parthenon

athirst 3 dry 4 avid, keen 5 eager 6 ardent 7 anxious, dried-up 8 appetent 9 impatient 10 dehydrated, desiccated

athlete 4 jock 6 player 7 acrobat, gymnast, tumbler

athlete's foot 8 ringworm

athletic 6 active, brawny, sinewy 8 muscular, vigorous 9 energetic, strenuous ***contest:*** 4 agon, game 5 match ***field:*** 4 oval, ring, rink 5 arena, court 7 diamond, stadium 8 gridiron ***prize:*** 3 cup 5 medal 6 trophy

athletics 5 games 6 sports 8 exercise 10 gymnastics, recreation 12 calisthenics

athwart 4 over 5 cross 6 across, beyond 9 crossways, crosswise 12 transversely

atiptoe 9 expectant, expecting 10 anticipant 12 anticipative, anticipatory

Atlas ***brother:*** 10 Prometheus ***daughter:*** 5 Hyads 6 Hyades 8 Pleiades 10 Atlantides ***father:*** 7 Iapetus ***mother:*** 7 Clymene ***race:*** 5 Titan ***wife:*** 7 Pleione

at last 7 finally

Atli ***slayer:*** 6 Gudrun ***wife:*** 6 Gudrun

atmosphere 3 air 4 aura, mood 6 aether, medium, milieu 7 ambient, climate, feeling, quality 8 ambiance, ambience 9 semblance 11 environment, mise-en-scène 12 surroundings ***stratum:*** 9 exosphere 10 ionosphere, mesosphere 11 chemosphere, ozonosphere, troposphere 12 stratosphere, thermosphere ***sun's:*** 12 chromosphere

atmospheric 4 airy 6 aerial 9 pneumatic

atoll 6 island ***equatorial area:*** 11 Baker Island ***Indian Ocean:*** 4 Male ***Kiribati:*** 4 Beru 7 Abaiang, Abemama, Apamama ***Marshall Islands:*** 4 Ebon, Mili, Ujae 6 Bikini 8 Eniwetok 9 Kwajalein ***Northern Cook Islands:*** 8 Manahiki ***North of Samoa:*** 7 Fakaofo ***Pacific:*** 5 Makin 8 Johnston 10 Butaritari, Palmerston ***Tokelau:*** 5 Atafu 10 Duke of York ***Tuamotu:*** 10 Anaa Island 11 Chain Island ***Tuvalu:*** 8 Funafuti

atom 3 bit, jot 4 iota, mite 5 minim, touch, trace 6 tittle 7 modicum, smidgen 8 particle ***charged:*** 3 ion 5 anion ***group:*** 7 radical

atomic particle 3 ion 4 beta, muon, pion 5 alpha, boson, meson 6 baryon, hadron, lepton, proton 7 fermion, hyperon, neutron, nucleon 8 electron, mesotron, neutrino, positron, thermion ***hypothetical:*** 5 quark 6 parton
atomize 4 ruin 5 smash, wreck 6 rub out 7 destroy, shatter 8 demolish, destruct, dynamite, nebulize 9 devastate, pulverize
at once 3 now 4 away 8 directly, first off, together 9 forthwith, instantly, right away 11 immediately, straightway 12 concurrently, straightaway
atone 3 pay 6 repent 7 expiate, satisfy 10 compensate, recompense
atoner 8 penitent
Atossa ***father:*** 5 Cyrus ***husband:*** 6 Darius 7 Smerdes 8 Cambyses ***son:*** 6 Xerxes
atramentous 3 jet 4 ebon, inky 5 black, ebony, raven, sable 10 pitch-black
at random 5 about 6 anyhow 7 anywise 9 haphazard 11 any which way, haphazardly 13 helter-skelter
Atreus ***brother:*** 8 Thyestes ***father:*** 6 Pelops ***mother:*** 10 Hippodamia ***slayer:*** 9 Aegisthus ***son:*** 8 Menelaus 9 Agamemnon 11 Pleisthenes ***victim:*** 11 Pleisthenes ***wife:*** 6 Aerope
atrocious 4 foul, vile 6 horrid, odious, savage 7 heinous, noisome, obscene 8 shocking 9 desperate, execrable, loathsome, monstrous, offensive, repulsive, sickening 10 abominable, despicable, disgusting, outrageous, scandalous 12 contemptible
atrocity 8 enormity, savagery 9 brutality 11 heinousness 13 monstrousness
atrophy 7 decline 8 downfall 9 decadence, downgrade 10 degeneracy, devolution 11 declination 12 degeneration 13 deterioration ***combining form:*** 4 necr 5 necro
attach 3 add, fix, tie 4 bind 5 affix, annex, rivet 6 adhere, append, fasten
attached 7 sessile
attachment 4 love 6 fealty 7 loyalty 8 adhesion, devotion, fidelity, fondness 9 adherence, affection, constancy 10 allegiance 12 faithfulness
attack 3 fit 4 raid, rush 5 beset, blitz, drive, fight, foray, onset, sally, siege, spasm, spell, storm, throe 6 access, ambush, assail, banzai, battle, charge, fall on, harass, have at, invade, irrupt, onfall, savage, sortie, strike, tackle, turn on 7 aggress, assault, besiege, bombard, offense, seizure 8 fall upon, outbreak, paroxysm 9 beleaguer, incursion, offensive, onslaught, pugnacity 10 aggression, assailment 11 bellicosity 12 belligerence 13 combativeness ***combining form:*** 5 lepsy 6 lepsia, lepsis
attacker ***combining form:*** 6 mastix
attain 3 get, win 4 gain 5 reach, score 6 rack up 7 achieve, realize 10 accomplish
attainment 11 achievement, acquirement, acquisition, realization
attempt 3 try 4 seek, stab 5 assay, essay, offer, trial 6 strive 7 venture 8 endeavor, striving, struggle 9 undertake 11 undertaking
attend 3 aid 4 hear, heed, help, mind 5 watch 6 assist, convoy, escort, listen 7 care for, conduct, hearken, oversee 8 chaperon 9 accompany, companion, supervise 11 consort with
attendant 3 aid 4 help 6 helper, lackey 7 ancilla, doorman, orderly, servant, striker 8 incident 9 ancillary, assistant, satellite 10 bridesmaid, coincident, collateral 11 chamberlain, concomitant 12 accompanying ***ancient Roman:*** 6 lictor ***in court:*** 7 bailiff 8 tipstaff
attendants 5 suite, train 7 cortege, retinue 9 entourage
attention 4 heed, mark, note 5 study 6 notice, regard, remark 7 amenity 8 courtesy, sedulity 9 assiduity, awareness, diligence, gallantry 10 absorption, cognizance, observance 11 application, engrossment, mindfulness, observation, sensibility 12 deliberation, sedulousness 13 concentration, consciousness, consideration
attention getter 4 ahem 5 gavel
attentive 5 alert, aware 6 arrect, intent 7 heedful, mindful 8 open-eyed 9 advertent, observant, open-eared, regardful 10 interested, thoughtful 11 considerate 13 concentrating
attenuate 3 sap 4 rare, slim, thin 5 blunt, reedy 6 lessen, rarefy, shrink, slight, stalky, subtle, twiggy, weaken 7 cripple, deflate, disable, slender, squinny, subtile, tenuous, unbrace 8 enfeeble, rarefied, wiredraw 9 dissipate, undermine 10 debilitate
attest 5 argue, swear, vouch 6 affirm, verify 7 bespeak, betoken, certify, point to, testify, witness 8 announce, indicate 10 asseverate
attestation 5 proof 7 witness 8 evidence 9 testament, testimony 11 testimonial 12 confirmation
attic 4 loft 6 garret 8 cockloft
at times 9 sometimes 10 now and then 11 ever and anon, now and again 12 here and there
attire 4 clad, duds, garb, togs 5 array, dress 6 clothe, outfit 7 apparel, clothes, garment, raiment 8 accouter, clothing, enclothe 11 habiliments
attirement see **clothes**
attitude 4 pose 5 stand 6 stance 7 pos-

ture **8** carriage, demeanor, position, posture **11** point of view
attitudinize **4** pose **7** pass for, pass off, posture **10** masquerade
attorney **5** agent, proxy **6** deputy, factor, lawyer **7** counsel **8** assignee **9** barrister, counselor, solicitor **10** counsellor
attract **4** draw, lure, wile **5** charm, court, tempt **6** allure, appeal, draw in, entice, invite, seduce **7** beguile, bewitch, enchant, solicit **8** interest, intrigue, inveigle **9** captivate, fascinate, magnetize
attraction **4** bait, call, draw, lure, pull **5** charm, mecca **6** appeal, liking **8** affinity, cynosure, sympathy **9** seduction **10** allurement **12** drawing power
attractive **4** cute, fair, sexy **5** bonny, dishy, siren **6** comely, lovely, luring, pretty **7** Circean, likable **8** alluring, charming, engaging, enticing, fetching, handsome, inviting, magnetic, mesmeric, tempting **9** appealing, beauteous, beautiful, beckoning, glamorous, seductive **10** bewitching, enchanting **11** captivating, fascinating, good-looking, tantalizing **13** prepossessing
attractiveness **5** charm **6** appeal, beauty, glamor
attribute **4** mark **5** refer, trait **6** assign, charge, credit, emblem, impute, symbol, virtue **7** ascribe, earmark, feature, quality **8** accredit, property **9** character
attrition **3** rue **4** ruth, wear **7** penance, remorse **8** abrasion, friction **9** penitence, penitency **10** repentance **12** contriteness
attritional **5** sorry **8** contrite, penitent **9** regretful, repentant **10** apologetic, remorseful **11** penitential
attune **7** balance, conform **9** harmonize, integrate, reconcile **10** coordinate, proportion **11** accommodate
atypical **3** odd **5** queer **7** deviant, strange **8** aberrant, abnormal, peculiar **9** anomalous, deviative, different, irregular, unnatural **11** exceptional, heteroclite **13** preternatural
auberge **3** inn **5** hotel, lodge **6** hostel, tavern **7** hospice **8** hostelry **9** roadhouse **11** caravansary, public house
Auber opera **10** Fra Diavolo
au courant **5** awake, aware **6** au fait, versed **7** abreast, knowing, versant, witting **8** familiar, informed, sentient, up-to-date **9** cognizant, conscious **10** acquainted, conversant **12** contemporary **13** up-to-the-minute
auction *Scottish:* **4** roup
audacious **4** bold, rash **5** brash, brave, saucy **6** brazen, daring **7** valiant **8** fearless, impudent, insolent, intrepid, reckless, unafraid, uncurbed, valorous **9** daredevil, dauntless, foolhardy, shameless, undaunted, venturous **10** courageous, ungoverned, unhampered **11** adventurous, impertinent, temerarious, uninhibited, untrammeled, venturesome **12** contumelious, unrestrained **13** adventuresome
audacity **4** gall **5** brass, nerve **6** mettle, spirit **7** courage **8** temerity **9** assurance, brashness, cockiness, hardihood, hardiness, impudence **10** brazenness
audible **5** aural **9** auricular
audibly **5** aloud
audience **6** public **7** hearing **8** audition **9** clientage, clientele, following **10** spectators
audile **5** aural **8** acoustic
audit **4** scan **5** check, probe **6** review, survey **7** checkup **8** analysis, scrutiny **10** inspection **11** examination **13** investigation, perlustration
audition **7** hearing **8** audience
auditory **5** aural **8** acoustic
au fait **4** able **5** right **6** decent, proper, versed **7** abreast, capable, correct, versant **8** becoming, decorous, familiar, informed **9** au courant, befitting, competent, qualified **10** acquainted, conforming, conversant
au fond **8** at bottom **9** basically, in essence **11** essentially **13** fundamentally
Augean stable **3** sty **4** sink **5** Sodom **7** cesspit **8** cesspool
auger *combining form:* **6** trypan **7** trypano
Auge's son **8** Telephus
aught **4** zero **5** zilch **6** cipher **7** nothing **8** goose egg
augment **3** wax **4** hike, rise **5** boost, build, exalt, mount, raise **6** beef up, expand, extend **7** enlarge, magnify, upsurge **8** compound, heighten, increase, manifold, multiply **10** aggrandize
augmentation **4** rise **5** annex, extra, raise **7** adjunct **8** addition, increase **9** accession, accretion, increment **10** complement, enrichment **11** enhancement **13** accompaniment
augur **4** bode, omen **7** betoken, portend, predict, presage, promise, prophet, suggest **8** forebode, forecast, foreshow, foretell, indicate, prophesy, soothsay **9** adumbrate, foretoken, predictor, prefigure **10** forecaster, foreshadow, foreteller, prophesier, vaticinate **11** Nostradamus **13** prognosticate
augury **4** omen **6** boding **7** portent, presage **8** bodement **9** foretoken **10** prognostic
august **5** grand, noble **6** lordly **7** stately **8** baronial, imposing, majestic, princely, splendid **9** grandiose **11** magnificent
___ au lait **4** café

au naturel 3 raw 4 nude 5 naked 6 unclad 8 buff-bare, stripped 9 unclothed, undressed 10 stark-naked
aura 3 air 4 feel, glow, halo, mood 5 aroma 6 nimbus 7 aureole, feeling 8 mystique, radiance 9 emanation, semblance 10 atmosphere
aural 6 audile 7 audible 8 acoustic, auditory 9 auricular
aureate 7 flowery 8 sonorous 9 bombastic, overblown 10 euphuistic, rhetorical 11 declamatory 13 grandiloquent
auricular 5 aural 7 audible
Auriga star 7 Capella
aurora 4 dawn, morn 7 dawning, morning, sunrise 8 cockcrow, daybreak
Aurora 3 Eos ***goddess of:*** 4 dawn ***husband:*** 8 Tithonus ***son:*** 6 Memnon
auslander 5 alien 7 inconnu 8 outcomer, outsider, stranger 9 foreigner
auspex 5 augur 7 prophet 8 foreseer 10 forecaster, foreteller, prophesier, soothsayer 11 Nostradamus
auspices 5 aegis 7 backing 9 patronage 11 sponsorship
auspicious 6 benign, bright, dexter, timely 7 hopeful, timeous 9 favorable, fortunate, opportune, well-timed 10 prosperous, seasonable
Austen novel 4 Emma 10 Persuasion 17 Pride and Prejudice
Auster see **Notus**
austere 4 bare, dour, grim, hard 5 acrid, bleak, grave, harsh, sharp, stern 6 bitter, severe, simple, somber 7 ascetic, serious 9 stringent, unadorned 10 astringent
Australia ***capital:*** 8 Canberra ***largest city:*** 6 Sydney ***monetary unit:*** 6 dollar
Austria ***capital:*** 6 Vienna ***dynasty:*** 8 Habsburg, Hapsburg ***monetary unit:*** 9 schilling
autarchic 4 free 8 absolute, despotic, dogmatic, separate 9 arbitrary, imperious, sovereign, tyrannous 10 autocratic, autonomous, monocratic, tyrannical 11 independent, self-reliant
authentic 4 real, true 5 pukka, right, solid, sound, valid 6 trusty 7 certain, factual, genuine 8 accurate, bona fide, credible, faithful, reliable 9 simon-pure, undoubted, veritable 10 convincing, dependable, sure-enough 11 indubitable, trustworthy 12 questionless
authenticate 6 verify 7 bear out, confirm, justify, voucher 8 validate 11 corroborate 12 substantiate
author 4 sire 5 maker 6 father, penman, proser, scribe, writer 7 creator, founder 8 inventor, novelist, prosaist 9 architect, generator, patriarch 10 originator ***American:*** 3 Bly, Nin, Poe 4 Agee, Buck, Dana, Grey, King, Mann, Rand, Roth, Uris, West 5 Aiken, Alger, Barth, Crane, Harte, Oates 5 O'Hara, Paine, Steel, Stein, Stone, Stowe, Turow, Twain, Tyler, Welty, White, Wolfe, Wylie 6 Alcott, Bellow, Cabell, Cather, Clancy, Cooper, Ferber, Harris, Hersey, Holmes, Hudson, Hughes, Irving, Jewett, Kidder, London, Mailer, Miller, Morley, Norris, Parker, Porter, Potter, Runyon, Singer, Styron, Updike, Warren, Wilder, Wilson, Wister, Wright 7 Baldwin, Beattie, Clemens, Cozzens, Farrell, Gardner, Garland, Glasgow, Heyward, Howells, Jarrell, Johnson, Kerouac, Lardner, Malamud, Masters, Mumford, Nabokov, Rexroth, Richter, Roberts, Saroyan, Sheehan, Thoreau, Thurber, Wharton 8 Anderson, Caldwell, Faulkner, Marquand, Melville, Michener, Mitchell, Remarque, Rinehart, Salinger, Sandburg, Sinclair, Spillane, Stockton, Vonnegut 9 Burroughs, Dos Passos, Hawthorne, Hemingway, Isherwood, McCullers, Steinbeck, Wodehouse, Woollcott 10 Fitzgerald, Tarkington ***Australian:*** 4 West 5 White 10 Richardson ***Austrian:*** 5 Kafka 7 Suttner 10 Schnitzler ***Canadian:*** 3 Roy 5 Kirby 6 Atwood, Davies 7 Leacock, Raddall, Richler, Service 8 Woodcock 9 de la Roche, MacLennan ***Chinese:*** 5 Han Yu ***Czech:*** 5 Capek ***Danish:*** 4 Rode, Wied 6 Jensen 7 Holberg ***Dutch:*** 6 Vondel ***English:*** 4 Amis, Ford, Lyly, Saki, Snow, Ward, West 5 Defoe, Doyle, Eliot, Hardy, James, Lewis, Lowry, Milne, Powys, Reade, Spark, Swift, Waugh, Wells, White, Woolf, Young 6 Archer, Austen, Belloc, Brontë, Bunyan, Butler, Conrad, Graves, Greene, Hilton, Huxley, Lytton, Malory, Orwell, Powell, Sayers, Sterne, Storey, Walton 7 Ballard, Burgess, Dickens, Durrell, Fleming, Follett, Forster, Golding, Kipling, Maugham, Sassoon, Shelley, Sitwell, Southey, Surtees, Tolkien, Walpole, Wyndham 8 Christie, Forester, Koestler, Lawrence, Macaulay, Meredith, Sillitoe, Smollett, Strachey, Trollope, Zangwill 9 De Quincey, Du Maurier, Goldsmith, Mansfield, Masefield, Priestley, Radcliffe, Thackeray 10 Chesterton, Galsworthy, Richardson 12 Quiller-Couch ***Finnish:*** 7 Waltari 9 Sillanpaa ***French:*** 4 Gide, Hugo, Kock, Sade, Sand, Zola 5 Camus, Dumas, Sagan, Stael, Verne, Vigny 6 Balzac, Daudet, France, Proust, Sartre 7 Cocteau, Gautier, Malraux, Mauriac, Maurois, Merimée, Rolland, Romains, Simenon 8 Beauvoir, Flaubert, Marivaux, Rabelais, Stendhal, Voltaire 9 Giraudoux 10 Maupassant, Saint-Simon 12 Robbe-Grillet ***German:*** 4 Böll 5 Grass, Hesse, Storm, Tieck, Zweig 6 Toller 7 Fontane, Richter, Wieland 8 Hoffmann, Schlegel 9 Hauptmann, Sudermann 10 Wassermann ***Greek:***

6 Lucian 11 Kazantzakis ***Hungarian:*** 5 Jokai ***Icelandic:*** 7 Laxness ***Irish:*** 5 Joyce 6 Stoker 7 Beckett, O'Connor, Russell 8 O'Faolain, Stephens 9 O'Flaherty ***Italian:*** 5 Verga 6 Silone 7 Manzoni, Moravia 8 Boccacio 9 Vittorini 10 Pirandello, Straparola ***Japanese:*** 7 Mishima 8 Kawabata, Murasaki 9 Yokomitsu, Yoshikawa ***Lebanese:*** 6 Gibran ***Norwegian:*** 3 Lie 6 Hamsun, Undset 8 Björnson, Kielland ***Norwegian-American:*** 7 Rolvaag ***Polish:*** 7 Reymont 8 Zeromski 11 Sienkiewicz ***Portuguese:*** 6 Pessoa ***Roman:*** 5 Pliny, Varro ***Russian:*** 5 Gorki 7 Andreev, Tolstoy 8 Turgenev, Zamyatin 9 Lermontov, Sholokhov 10 Dostoevsky 11 Dostoyevsky, Yevtushenko 12 Solzhenitsyn ***Scottish:*** 4 Lang 5 Scott 6 Barrie, Buchan 8 Urquhart 9 Stevenson ***Spanish:*** 6 Baroja 7 Alarcon 9 Cervantes ***Swedish:*** 7 Johnson, Rydberg 8 Lagerlof 10 Lagerkvist, Strindberg ***Swiss:*** 4 Wyss 6 Frisch 9 Spitteler ***Welsh:*** 4 Owen 5 Evans, Wynne ***Yiddish:*** 4 Asch

authoritarian 6 strict 8 dogmatic 9 dictative, stringent 10 oppressive, totalistic 11 dictatorial, doctrinaire, magisterial 12 totalitarian

authoritative 4 sure, true 5 sound 8 accepted, attested, dogmatic, official, orthodox 9 canonical, dictative, ex officio, trustable 10 dependable, ex cathedra, sanctioned 11 cathedratic, dictatorial, doctrinaire, irrefutable, magisterial, trustworthy 12 indisputable

authority 4 rule, sway 6 credit, expert, master, weight 7 command, control, mastery 8 prestige, virtuoso 9 influence 10 domination, governance, government, past master 12 jurisdiction

authorization 5 leave 6 permit 7 consent, go-ahead, mandate 8 sanction 9 allowance, clearance 10 green light, permission, sufferance

authorize 3 let 4 vest 5 allow 6 enable, invest, permit 7 approve, empower, endorse, entitle, license, qualify, warrant 8 accredit, sanction 10 commission 11 countenance

auto see **automobile**

autobiographer 9 memoirist

autobiography 4 life, vita 5 diary 6 memoir 7 journal 11 confessions

autochthonous 6 native 7 endemic 10 aboriginal, indigenous

autocracy 7 tyranny 9 despotism 12 dictatorship

autocratic 7 haughty 8 absolute, arrogant, despotic 9 arbitrary, tyrannous 10 tyrannical

autodidactic 10 self-taught 12 self-educated

autograph 3 ink 4 sign 9 signature, subscribe 11 John Hancock

autoist 6 driver 8 motorist, operator

Autolycus ***daughter:*** 8 Anticlea ***father:*** 6 Hermes 7 Mercury

automate 8 robotize

automatic 8 habitual 9 impulsive, reflexive 10 mechanical, self-acting, unprompted 11 instinctive, involuntary, perfunctory, spontaneous, unmeditated ***combining form:*** 4 self

automaton 5 golem, robot 7 android, machine

automobile 3 bus, car 5 buggy, coupe, racer, sedan 6 jalopy, tourer 7 flivver, hardtop, machine 8 dragster, motorcar, roadster, runabout ***British:*** 2 MG 6 Anglia, Austin, Jaguar 7 Bentley, Daimler, Hillman, Sunbeam, Triumph 8 Vauxhall 10 Rolls-Royce 11 Austin-Healy ***French:*** 5 Simca 7 Citroen, Peugeot, Renault ***German:*** 3 BMW 7 Porsche 10 Volkswagen 12 Mercedes-Benz ***Italian:*** 4 Fiat 6 Lancia 7 Ferrari 8 Maserati 9 Alfa-Romeo ***Japanese:*** 5 Honda, Mazda 6 Datsun, Subaru, Toyota ***Swedish:*** 4 Saab 5 Volvo

automotive pioneer 4 Benz, Ford, King, Olds 5 Evans, Roper 6 Cugnot, Duryea, Lenoir, Winton 7 Daimler, Stanley 8 Morrison

Autonoe ***father:*** 6 Cadmus ***husband:*** 9 Aristaeus ***mother:*** 8 Harmonia ***sister:*** 5 Agave ***son:*** 7 Actaeon

autonomous 4 free 8 separate 9 autarchic, sovereign 11 independent 12 self-governed, uncontrolled

autopsy 8 necropsy 10 postmortem

auto racer 8 Foyt (A. J.) 4 Hill (Graham) 5 Clark (Jim), Petty (Richard), Unser (Al, Bobby) 6 Fangio (Juan) 7 Brabham (Jack), Stewart (Jackie) 8 Andretti (Mario)

autumn casualty 3 DST (Daylight Saving Time) 6 leaves

auxiliary 4 aide 6 helper 7 reserve 8 adjutant, adjuvant 9 accessory, ancillary, assistant, coadjutor 10 additional, collateral, subsidiary 11 appurtenant, subservient 12 contributory 13 complementary, supplementary ***verb:*** 2 am, do, is 3 are, can, did, had, has, may, was 4 been, does, have, must, were, will 5 could, might, ought, shall, would 6 should

avail 3 use 5 serve 6 profit 7 account, benefit, fitness, service 9 advantage, relevance 10 usefulness 13 applicability

available 8 gettable 9 securable 10 attainable, obtainable, procurable 11 purchasable

avalanche 5 flood, slide 8 mudslide, rockfall 9 landslide, rockslide, snowslide
avarice 5 greed 7 avidity 8 cupidity, rapacity 10 greediness 12 covetousness, graspingness
avenge 5 repay, right 7 pay back, redress, requite 9 retaliate, retribute, vindicate
avengement 7 revenge 8 reprisal, requital, revanche 9 vengeance 11 counterblow, retaliation, retribution
avenue 3 way 4 path, road 5 track 6 artery, street 7 highway 9 boulevard 12 thoroughfare
aver 4 avow 5 state 6 affirm, assert, avouch, depose 7 declare, profess, protest 8 constate, maintain 9 predicate
average 3 par 4 fair, mean, norm, so-so 6 common, median, medium 8 mediocre, middling, moderate, ordinary 11 indifferent 12 intermediate
averagely 4 so-so 6 enough, fairly, rather 8 passably 9 tolerably 10 moderately
avernal 7 hellish, stygian 8 infernal, plutonic 9 cimmerian, plutonian
averse 5 balky, loath 6 afraid 7 uneager 8 backward, hesitant 9 reluctant, resistant, unwilling 10 indisposed 11 disinclined
aversion 4 fear, hate 5 dread 6 hatred, horror 7 allergy, disgust, dislike 8 disfavor, distaste, dyspathy, loathing 9 antipathy, disliking, disrelish, repulsion, revulsion 10 abhorrence, antagonism, repugnance 11 abomination, detestation, displeasure 13 indisposition
aversive 8 ungenial 9 repellent, repugnant 11 uncongenial 12 antipathetic 13 unsympathetic
avert 4 foil, turn, veer, ward 5 check, deter 6 thwart 7 deflect, forfend, obviate, prevent, rule out 8 preclude, stave off 9 forestall, frustrate
avian 8 ornithic
aviary 4 cage 6 volary 8 dovecote, ornithon 9 birdhouse, columbary, dovehouse
aviator 3 ace 5 flier, pilot 6 airman, flyboy, Wright 7 birdman, Earhart 9 Lindbergh 10 Richthofen 12 Rickenbacker
avid 4 agog, keen 5 eager 6 ardent, greedy 7 anxious, athirst, craving, thirsty, wanting 8 appetent, covetous, desirous 9 impatient 10 breathless
avidity 5 greed 7 avarice 8 cupidity, rapacity
avoid 4 bilk, duck, shun, snub 5 avert, elude, evade, shirk 6 bypass, divert, escape, eschew 7 obviate, prevent 8 preclude
avoidance 6 escape 7 come-off, elusion, evasion 8 escaping, escapism, eschewal, shunning 9 runaround *combining form:* 4 phob 5 phobo
avouch 3 own 4 aver, avow 5 admit 6 affirm, assert, depose 7 confess, confirm, declare, profess, protest 8 constate 9 predicate 11 acknowledge, corroborate
avow 3 own 4 aver 5 admit, allow, grant, let on, own up 6 affirm, assert, avouch, depose, fess up 7 concede, confess, declare, profess, protest 8 constate, maintain 9 predicate 11 acknowledge
await 4 hope 6 expect 7 count on
awake 4 stir 5 alive, aware, rouse 6 roused 7 aroused 8 sensible, sentient 9 au courant, cognizant, conscious, stirred up
awaken 4 stir, whet 5 alert, rally, rouse 6 arouse, bestir, kindle
awanting 4 sans 5 minus 7 lacking, without
award 4 give, kudo 5 badge, endow, grant, honor, kudos, medal, prize 6 accord, bestow, confer 7 concede, laurels, tribute 8 accolade 9 vouchsafe 10 blue ribbon, decoration 11 distinction *motion picture:* 5 Oscar *mystery novel:* 5 Edgar *record:* 6 Grammy *television:* 4 Emmy *theater:* 4 Tony
aware 5 alert, alive, awake 7 heedful, knowing, mindful, witting 8 informed, sensible, sentient 9 au courant, cognizant, conscious 10 conversant 12 apprehensive
awash 4 full 6 jammed, loaded, packed 7 brimful, crammed, crowded, stuffed 8 brimming 9 chock-full
away 3 far, fro, now, off 4 afar, gone, over 5 apart, aside, forth, hence 7 lacking, missing, omitted, wanting 8 directly, first off, right off 9 forthwith, instantly, therefrom 11 immediately
away from *prefix:* 2 ap 3 aph, apo
awe 4 fear 5 alarm, scare 6 fright, wonder 7 startle, terrify 8 affright, frighten 9 reverence, terrorize 10 veneration, wonderment
aweigh 5 atrip
aweless 4 bold 5 brave 7 valiant 8 fearless, intrepid, unafraid, valorous 9 dauntless, undaunted 10 courageous
awesome 4 eery 5 eerie 6 august, dreary, solemn 7 sublime 8 dreadful, imposing, terrific
awful 7 fearful 8 dreadful, horrible, horrific, shocking, terrible, terrific 9 appalling, frightful 10 formidable
awfully 4 much, very 6 hugely 7 greatly 8 whacking, whopping 9 extremely
awhile *Scottish:* 4 awee
awkward 5 gawky, inept, splay 6 clumsy, gauche, wooden 7 gawkish, halting, lumpish, unhandy, unhappy 8 bumbling, bun-

gling, ungainly **9** graceless, ham-handed, ill-chosen, lumbering, maladroit **10** blundering, bunglesome, unskillful **11** heavy-handed, splathering, unfortunate **12** discommoding, embarrassing, incommodious, inconvenient, infelicitous **13** discommodious

awning ***ancient Roman:*** **8** velarium

awry **5** amiss, askew, badly, wrong **6** afield, askant, astray **7** askance **8** cock-eyed **9** cock-a-hoop, crookedly **11** unfavorably ***Scottish:*** **5** aglee, agley

ax, axe **3** adz, can **4** adze, fire, sack **5** hache **6** bounce **7** boot out, chopper, cleaver, dismiss, hatchet, kick out **8** tomahawk **9** discharge, terminate ***blade:*** **3** bit ***double-headed:*** **6** twibil **7** twibill ***handle:*** **5** helve ***ice:*** **6** piolet

axiom **3** law **4** rule **5** gnome, maxim, moral **6** dictum, truism **7** brocard, theorem **8** aphorism, apothegm **9** principle **10** principium **11** fundamental

aye **2** OK **3** yea, yep, yes **4** okay **8** all right

Azariah ***brother:*** **7** Ahimaaz ***father:*** **4** Obod **5** Zadok **6** Nathan **7** Ahimaaz, Hilkiah, Jeroham, Johanan **8** Hoshaiah, Maaseiah **11** Jehoshaphat ***son:*** **7** Seraiah

Aztec ***capital:*** **12** Tenochtitlan ***conqueror:*** **6** Cortes, Cortez ***emperor:*** **9** Montezuma ***god:*** **4** Xipe **6** Eecatl, Meztli, Tlaloc **9** Xipetotec **11** Xiuhtecutli **12** Quetzalcoatl ***hero:*** **4** Nata ***language:*** **7** Nahuatl ***temple:*** **8** teocalli

B

baa **5** bleat

Babbitt **4** boob **8** boeotian **10** middlebrow, philistine ***author:*** **5** Lewis

babblative **5** gabby, talky **6** chatty **9** garrulous, talkative **10** loquacious **11** loose-lipped **12** loose-tongued, multiloquent

babble **3** gab, jaw, yak, yap **4** blab, chat **5** clack, prate, run on **6** burble, drivel, gibber, jabber, patter, piffle, rattle, yammer **7** blabber, blather, chatter, maunder, palaver, prattle, twaddle **8** nonsense **9** gibberish **11** jabberwocky

babbler ***Scottish:*** **7** blellum

babe **6** infant **7** neonate, newborn **8** bantling

babel **3** din **6** clamor, hubbub, jangle, racket, tumult, uproar **10** hullabaloo, tintamarre **11** pandemonium

baboon **6** chacma **8** mandrill **9** hamadryas

babushka **8** bandanna, kerchief

baby **3** tot **5** sissy, spoil **6** cocker, coddle, cosset, dote on, infant, pamper **7** bambino, cater to, indulge, neonate, newborn, papoose, toddler **8** bantling, dote upon, nursling, suckling, weakling, weanling **11** mollycoddle ***ailment:*** **5** colic, croup ***baptismal robe:*** **7** chrisom ***bed:*** **4** crib **6** cradle **8** bassinet ***bedroom:*** **7** nursery ***breechcloth:*** **6** diaper ***cap:*** **6** biggin, bonnet ***carriage:*** **4** pram **5** buggy **8** stroller **12** perambulator ***doctor:*** **12** pediatrician ***food:*** **3** pap **4** milk **6** pablum ***garment:*** **7** rompers ***Italian:*** **7** bambino ***napkin:*** **3** bib ***nurse:*** **4** nana ***outfit:*** **7** layette ***powder:*** **4** talc ***shoe:*** **6** bootee ***Spanish:*** **4** bebé, nene ***unborn:*** **5** fetus

baby grand **5** piano

babyhood **7** infancy

babyish **7** puerile **8** childish, immature **9** infantile, infantine

Babylonian **6** lavish **9** luxurious ***abode of the dead:*** **5** Aralu ***capital:*** **7** Babylon ***chaos:*** **4** Apsu ***city:*** **2** Ur **5** Accad, Akkad **6** Cunaxa, Cuthah ***crown prince:*** **10** Belshazzar ***division:*** **5** Accad, Akkad, Sumer ***earth mother:*** **6** Ishtar ***first ruler:*** **6** Nimrod ***god:*** **2** Ea, Zu **3** Anu, Bel, Hea, Sin **4** Adad, Addu, Apsu, Enzu, Irra, Nabu, Nebo **5** Alala, Alalu, Dagan, Enlil, Kingu, Lahmu, Mummu, Ninib, Siris **6** Anshar, Marduk, Namtar, Nannar, Nergal, Ramman, Tammuz **7** Shamash **8** Ningirsu ***goddess:*** **4** Gula, Nina **5** Aruru, Belit **6** Allatu, Belili, Beltis, Ishtar, Kishar, Lahamu, Ningal, Tiamat **7** Baalath, Damkina ***hero:*** **5** Adapa, Etana **9** Gilgamesh ***king:*** **6** Sargon **9** Hammurabi ***priest:*** **2** en ***priestess:*** **5** entum ***river:*** **6** Tigris **9** Euphrates ***ruler of the dead:*** **6** Nergal ***storm god:*** **4** Adad, Adda, Addu ***sun god:*** **3** Bel **7** Shamash ***tower:*** **5** Babel **8** ziggurat ***waters:*** **4** Apsu **6** Tiamat ***winged dragon:*** **6** Tiamat

baccalaureate **6** degree **8** bachelor

bacchanal 4 orgy 5 party 7 debauch 10 saturnalia 11 bacchanalia
bacchanalian 7 drunken, reveler 9 orgiastic
bacchanal's cry 4 evoe 5 evohe
Bacchus 8 Dionysus ***attendant:*** 6 maenad ***father:*** 4 Zeus 7 Jupiter ***lover:*** 5 Venus 9 Aphrodite ***mother:*** 6 Semele ***son:*** 7 Priapus ***staff:*** 7 thyrsus
Bach ***birthplace:*** 8 Eisenach ***composition:*** 5 fugue, motet, suite 6 sonata 7 cantata, chorale, partita, prelude, toccata 8 concerto, fantasia, oratorio, sinfonia ***deathplace:*** 7 Leipzig ***musical style:*** 7 baroque ***religion:*** 8 Lutheran
back 3 aid 4 abet, fund, help, hind, rear 5 about, again, dorsa (plural), round, spine, stake 6 around, assist, dorsum, hinder, rachis, recede, remote, retral, uphold 7 endorse, finance, promote, retract, retreat, reverse, sponsor, support 8 advocate, bankroll, champion, frontier, hindmost, rearward, side with 9 in reverse, posterior, retrocede, vertebrae (plural) 10 outlandish, retrograde, round about ***ailment:*** 7 lumbago 10 rheumatism ***combining form:*** 2 an 3 ana, not 4 dors, noto 5 dorsi, dorso, notus 6 opisth 7 opistho ***of a book:*** 5 spine ***of an arthropod:*** 6 tergum ***of an insect:*** 5 notum ***of the neck:*** 4 nape 6 scruff ***prefix:*** 2 re 4 post 5 retro ***relating to:*** 6 dorsal
back answer 6 retort 7 riposte 8 comeback, repartee
backbiter 9 slanderer
backbiting 5 abuse 7 calumny, obloquy, scandal, slander 8 libelous 9 invective, maligning, traducing, vilifying 10 calumnious, defamation, defamatory, detracting, detraction, detractive, scandalous, slanderous 12 belittlement, depreciation, vituperation 13 disparagement
backbone 4 grit, guts 5 moxie, nerve, spine, spunk 6 pillar, rachis 8 mainstay 9 fortitude, vertebrae (plural) 12 spinal column
backcountry 4 bush 6 sticks 7 boonies 8 frontier 9 boondocks 10 hinterland
backcourtman 5 guard
back down 4 balk 5 demur, welsh 6 beg off, cry off, recall, recant, renege, resile 7 disavow, retract, stickle 8 withdraw 9 weasel out
backer 5 angel 6 patron, surety 7 sponsor 8 promoter 9 guarantor 10 bankroller, meal ticket
backfire 6 fizzle 8 kick back, miscarry 9 boomerang 11 fall through
background 7 scenery
backhanded 7 devious 8 indirect 9 sarcastic
backing 4 help 5 aegis 7 support 8 auspices 9 patronage 10 assistance 11 sponsorship
backland see **backcountry**
backlash 5 slack 6 recoil 8 reaction
backlog 5 hoard, stock, store 7 nest egg, reserve 9 inventory, reservoir, stockpile
back of 5 abaft 6 behind
back off see **back down**
backpack 8 knapsack, packsack, rucksack 9 haversack
backpedal see **back down**
backset 5 check 7 reverse 8 reversal
backside 4 rear, rump, seat 5 fanny, hiney 6 behind, bottom, heinie 8 buttocks, derriere 9 posterior
backslide 5 lapse 6 return, revert 7 regress, relapse 9 retrovert 10 recidivate
backstabbing 7 calumny, scandal, slander 10 defamation, detraction 12 belittlement, depreciation 13 disparagement
backstairs 6 secret, sordid 7 furtive 10 scandalous
backstop 6 uphold 7 support 8 advocate, champion, side with
back talk 3 lip 4 guff, sass 5 mouth, sauce 9 impudence, insolence
backtrack 7 retrace, retreat, reverse
backward 3 shy 4 dull, slow 5 about, again, loath, round, timid 6 around, averse, demure, modest, retral, stupid 7 bashful, moronic, uneager 8 hesitant, ignorant, inverted, retarded, retiring, retrorse, reversed 9 benighted, diffident, dim-witted, in reverse, reluctant, unwilling 10 behindhand, half-witted, indisposed, retrograde, round about, slow-witted, uncultured 11 disinclined, thickheaded, undeveloped 12 feebleminded, self-effacing, simpleminded, uncultivated 13 unprogressive
backwoods see **backcountry**
backwoodsman 4 hick, jake 5 yokel 6 rustic 7 bumpkin, hillman 9 hillbilly 10 provincial
bacon ***side:*** 6 flitch, gammon ***slice:*** 6 rasher
Bacon work 12 Novum Organum
bacteria 5 cocci 7 bacilli, vibrios 8 spirilla ***culture medium:*** 4 agar ***destroyer:*** 10 antibiotic
bacterial disease 7 anthrax, leprosy, tetanus 8 syphilis 9 gonorrhea, pneumonia 10 diphtheria
bacteriologist ***American:*** 6 Enders 7 Noguchi, Theiler ***British:*** 7 Fleming ***French:*** 5 Widal 7 Nicolle, Pasteur ***German:*** 4 Cohn, Koch 5 Klebs 7 Behring, Loffler 10 Wassermann ***Japanese:*** 8 Kitazato ***Russian:*** 11 Metchnikoff ***Swiss:*** 6 Yersin
bad 3 ill, low 4 down, evil, foul, null, poor, sour, void 5 amiss, lousy, rough, rowdy,

tough, wrong 6 arrant, nocent, putrid, rancid, rotten, sinful, unruly, wicked 7 decayed, froward, harmful, hateful, hurtful, immoral, invalid, naughty, nocuous, noisome, noxious, peccant, spoiled, tainted, unhappy, unsound, vicious 8 damaging, dejected, downcast, inferior, perverse, wretched 9 abhorrent, defective, deficient, depressed, execrable, injurious, loathsome, miserable, obnoxious, offensive, putrefied, reprobate, repulsive, sickening, woebegone 10 decomposed, disgusting, disorderly, dispirited, ill-behaved, indecorous, iniquitous, unpleasant 11 deleterious, detrimental, displeasing, distasteful, distressing, downhearted, intolerable, misbehaving, mischievous, unfavorable 12 disagreeable, disconsolate, insufferable, unacceptable 13 objectionable *combining form:* 3 cac, mal 4 caco *comparative:* 5 worse *prefix:* 3 dys, mis *superlative:* 5 worst

Badebec *husband:* 9 Gargantua *son:* 10 Pantagruel

Baden, for one 3 spa

badge 3 pin 5 award, honor, kudos 6 button, emblem 7 laurels 8 accolade, insignia 10 decoration 11 distinction

badger 4 bait, ride 5 brock, chivy, hound 6 heckle, hector 8 balisaur, bullyrag *group of:* 4 cete

Badger State 9 Wisconsin

badinage 6 banter 7 joshing, kidding 8 backchat, repartee, snip-snap 9 cross talk 10 persiflage

badland 4 wild 5 waste 6 barren, desert 8 wildness 10 wilderness

badly 4 awry, illy 5 amiss, wrong 6 afield, astray 7 harshly, roughly 8 severely 9 painfully 10 rigorously 11 unfavorably *combining form:* 3 mal

badman 4 hood, thug 6 bandit, outlaw 7 bandido, hoodlum, villain 8 criminal, hooligan 9 desperado

bad mark 3 gig 7 demerit

bad-tempered 6 cranky, crusty, touchy 8 choleric 9 dyspeptic 10 ill-humored, ill-natured, tempersome 12 cantankerous

Baedeker 5 guide 6 manual 8 handbook 9 guidebook, vade mecum 10 compendium 11 enchiridion

baffle 4 balk, bilk, foil, ruin 5 addle, mix up, stump 6 muddle, puzzle, thwart 7 confuse, flummox, mystify, nonplus 8 befuddle, confound 9 dumbfound, frustrate 10 circumvent, disappoint

bafflement 9 confusion 10 perplexity

bag 3 cop, nab, net 4 grip, hook, land, nail, poke, sack 5 biddy, catch, crone, pouch, purse, seize, steal 6 beldam, collar, secure 7 capture, satchel 8 backpack, knapsack, reticule, suitcase 9 apprehend

bagatelle 6 trifle

baggage 4 gear 5 hussy, tramp, trull, wench 6 wanton 7 effects, luggage, trollop 8 slattern, strumpet

Baghdad *founder:* 6 Mansur *river:* 6 Tigris

bagnio 7 brothel 8 bordello, cathouse 10 bawdy house, whorehouse

Bagnold 4 Enid

bagpipe *part:* 5 drone 7 bourdon, chanter *sound:* 5 skirl

Bahamas' capital 6 Nassau

bail 3 dip 4 bond, lade 5 ladle, scoop 6 surety 8 guaranty, security, warranty 9 guarantee

bailiwick 5 field, realm 6 domain, sphere 7 demesne, terrain 8 district, dominion, province 9 champaign, territory 12 jurisdiction

bait 3 nag 4 lure, ride, toll, trap 5 chivy, decoy, harry, hound, leger, snare, tempt 6 allure, badger, come-on, entice, entrap, harass, heckle, hector, lead on, ledger, molest, pester, seduce 7 torment 8 bullyrag, inveigle 9 persecute 10 allurement, enticement, seducement, temptation 12 inveiglement

bake 4 burn, cook, fire, kiln 5 broil, roast 6 saggar, sagger, scorch 7 scallop, scollop, swelter

baked clay 7 ceramic

baker's dozen 8 thirteen

bakers' yeast 6 leaven

baking 3 hot 5 fiery 6 red-hot, torrid 7 burning 8 broiling, scalding, sizzling, white-hot 9 scorching *chamber:* 4 kiln, oven

baksheesh 3 tip 4 alms 5 favor 6 reward 8 gratuity

Balaam *beast:* 3 ass 6 donkey *father:* 4 Beor

balance 4 rest 5 level, poise 6 adjust, attune, make up, offset, redeem, set off, stasis 7 harmony, remains, remanet, remnant, residue 8 atone for, coolness, leavings, outweigh, residual, residuum, symmetry 9 composure, congruity, equipoise, harmonize, remainder, stability 10 compensate, equanimity, proportion, steadiness 11 consistency, countervail, equilibrium, self-control 12 counterpoise *combining form:* 5 stato

bald 4 bare, nude 5 naked, plain 6 shaven, smooth 8 glabrous, hairless 9 unadorned 11 undecorated, ungarnished 12 unornamented 13 unembellished

baldachin 4 silk 6 canopy, fabric

Balder, Baldur *father:* 4 Odin *mother:* 5 Frigg 6 Frigga *slayer:* 4 Hoth, Loke, Loki 5 Hoder, Hothr *son:* 7 Forsete, Forseti *wife:* 5 Nanna

balderdash 3 rot 4 bosh 5 bilge 6 blague, bushwa 7 eyewash, rubbish 8 claptrap, malarkey, nonsense
baldness 8 alopecia
baldpate 7 widgeon 8 skinhead
balefire 6 beacon
baleful 4 dire, evil 6 malign 7 direful, fateful, malefic, ominous 8 sinister 9 ill-boding, ill-omened 10 maleficent, pernicious 11 apocalyptic, threatening 12 unpropitious
balk 3 gag, jib, shy 4 beam, dash, foil, ruin 5 demur 6 baffle, boggle, refuse, thwart, timber 7 scruple, stickle, stumble 8 hang back 9 frustrate 10 circumvent, disappoint
balky 5 loath 6 averse, ornery 7 froward, restive, wayward 8 contrary, hesitant, perverse 9 reluctant 11 wrongheaded 12 cross-grained
ball 3 orb, wad 5 dance, globe, round 6 sphere 7 rondure 8 conglobe, ensphere 10 conglobate ***batted high:*** 3 fly ***batted straight:*** 5 liner ***combining form:*** 5 globo, spher 6 sphaer, sphero 7 sphaera, sphaero ***of thread or yarn:*** 4 clew ***ornamental:*** 6 pom-pom, pompon ***tiny:*** 7 globule
ballad 3 lay 4 lied, poem, song 7 calypso ***rhyme:*** 4 ABCB ***singer:*** 8 minstrel 10 troubadour
ballast 5 poise 6 steady 9 stabilify, stabilize 11 stabilitate
ballerina 6 dancer 7 danseur 8 coryphee, danseuse 9 figurante 11 dancing girl
ballet ***costume:*** 4 tutu 6 tights 7 leotard ***dancer:*** 7 danseur 8 coryphee, danseuse, figurant 9 ballerina, figurante ***for two:*** 9 pas de deux ***handrail:*** 5 barre ***jump:*** 4 jeté 8 ballonné 9 entrechat ***knee bend:*** 4 plié ***position:*** 6 pointe 8 attitude 9 arabesque ***step:*** 3 pas 8 glissade ***turn:*** 6 chaîné 9 pirouette
ball game see at game
balloon sail 9 spinnaker
ball-shaped 7 globoid, globose 8 globular, spheroid 9 globulous, spherical
ball up 4 clew 5 addle 6 fuddle 7 confuse, fluster 8 befuddle, bewilder, distract, throw off
ballyhoo 4 tout 6 herald, hoopla 7 trumpet 9 publicity
balm 4 lull 5 allay, aroma, cream, quiet, salve, scent, spice, still 6 cerate, chrism, settle, soothe 7 bouquet, compose, incense, perfume, unction, unguent 8 ointment 9 fragrance, redolence 11 tranquilize
balmacaan 8 overcoat
balm of Gilead 6 poplar 9 balsam fir 12 balsam poplar
balmy 4 mild, soft 5 bland, faint, spicy, sweet 6 aromal, easing, gentle, insane, savory, smooth 7 foolish, lenient, perfumy 8 aromatic, fragrant, perfumed, pleasant, pleasing, redolent, soothing 9 agreeable, ambrosial
baloney 3 rot 4 bosh, bull, bunk 5 hokum 7 hogwash, rubbish 8 nonsense
balsam poplar 9 tacamahac 10 hackmatack 12 balm of Gilead
Balthazar's gift 5 myrrh
Baltic ***native:*** 4 Lett 7 Latvian 8 Estonian 10 Lithuanian ***state:*** 6 Latvia 7 Estonia 9 Lithuania
balustrade 4 rail 7 railing 8 banister
Balzac character 6 Goriot 7 Grandet 9 Birotteau
bamboozle 4 bilk, dupe, fool, gull, hoax 5 trick 6 befool 7 chicane, swindle 8 flimflam, hoodwink 11 hornswoggle
ban 4 tabu 5 taboo 6 enjoin, forbid, outlaw 8 prohibit 9 interdict 11 forbiddance, prohibition 12 interdiction, proscription
Ban ***ally:*** 6 Arthur ***son:*** 8 Lancelot
banal 4 flat 5 bland, corny, trite, vapid 6 watery 7 insipid, sapless 8 waterish 9 hackneyed 10 namby-pamby, pedestrian, wishy-washy 11 commonplace
banality 6 cliché, truism 7 bromide 8 prosaism 9 platitude 10 prosaicism, shibboleth 11 commonplace
banana oil 5 hokum
banausic 4 blah, dull, poky 6 dreary, earthy, stodgy 7 humdrum, mundane, sensual, worldly 8 temporal 10 monotonous, pedestrian 13 materialistic
band 4 belt, club, crew, gang, gird, tape 5 bunch, corps, covey, group, party, strap, strip, troop, unite 6 concur, fillet, girdle, league, outfit, ribbon, streak, team up, troupe 7 cluster, combine, company, conjoin 8 begirdle, cincture, coadjute, engirdle, symphony 9 cooperate, orchestra 10 encincture 12 philharmonic ***combining form:*** 3 zon 4 taen, zono 5 taeni 6 taenio ***Mexican:*** 8 mariachi ***neck:*** 6 torque ***of flowers:*** 7 wreathe ***small:*** 5 combo
bandage 4 bind 5 dress 6 swathe 7 swaddle
bandanna 8 babushka, kerchief
bandeau 5 strip 6 fillet, ribbon, stripe 9 brassiere
banderilla 4 dart
banderole 4 flag, jack 6 banner, burgee, ensign, pennon 7 pennant 8 streamer
bandicoot 3 rat
bandit 6 badman, outlaw, raider, sacker 7 bandido, brigand, cateran, forager, ravager 8 marauder, pillager 9 cutthroat, desperado, holdup man, plunderer 10 freebooter, highwayman 11 bushwhacker ***of India:*** 6 dacoit
bandleader 7 maestro 8 choragus 9 conductor
bandolier 4 belt

bandwagon 3 fad 4 chic, mode, rage 5 craze, style, vogue 7 fashion
bandy 4 flip, toss 6 banter 8 exchange 11 interchange
bane 4 ruin 5 venom, virus 6 poison 7 bugaboo, bugbear, undoing 8 downfall 9 contagion, destroyer, ruination 11 destruction
baneful 4 dire 6 deadly 7 fateful, noxious, ominous 9 ill-boding, ill-omened, injurious, pestilent, unhealthy 10 pernicious 11 apocalyptic, pestiferous, threatening 12 pestilential, unpropitious
bang 3 bat, hit, pep, pop, rap 4 bash, beat, belt, blow, boom, clap, kick, push, shot, slam, sock, wham, whop 5 blast, burst, crash, noise, punch, sharp, smack, smash, sound, vigor, whack 6 thrill, wallop 7 surpass 8 smack-dab, squarely, vitality 9 explosion
Bangladesh *capital:* 5 Dacca, Dhaka *monetary unit:* 4 taka
bang-up 5 dandy 7 capital 8 five-star, top-notch, whiz-bang 9 excellent, first-rate 10 first-class 11 first-string
banish 4 oust 5 debar, eject, evict, exile, expel 6 deport, put out, run out 7 cast out, dismiss, exclude, expulse, shut out, turn out 8 displace, drive out, relegate 9 discharge, ostracize, rusticate 10 expatriate 13 excommunicate
banishment 5 exile 9 expulsion, ostracism 10 relegation 11 deportation 12 displacement
Bani's son 3 Uel 5 Amram, Rehum
banister 4 rail 7 railing 10 balustrade
bank 4 heap, hill, mass, pile, save 5 beach, coast, levee, mound, shore, stack, stash 6 invest, margin, rely on, rivage, strand 7 build on, count on, deposit, lay away, pyramid, trust in, trust to 8 depend on, lay aside, reckon on, rely upon, salt away, set aside, sock away 10 depend upon, streamside 11 calculate on 12 squirrel away
bank deal 4 loan
bankroll 4 back 5 stake 7 finance 9 grubstake 10 capitalize
bankrupt 4 bare, bust, do in, ruin 5 break, drain, strip, use up, wreck 6 divest, fold up, pauper 7 deplete, deprive, exhaust 9 pauperize 10 impoverish
bankruptcy 4 ruin 7 failure 9 depletion, sterility 10 barrenness, exhaustion
banned 7 illegal, illicit, tabooed 8 enjoined, verboten 9 forbidden 10 prohibited, proscribed
banner 4 flag, jack 6 bang-up, ensign, pennon 7 pendant, pennant 8 champion, five-star, gonfalon, gonfanon, standard, streamer, top-notch 9 banderole, excellent, first-rate, front-rank 10 blue-ribbon, first-class 11 first-string *Roman:* 7 labarum 8 vexillum
bannerol 4 flag, jack 6 ensign, pennon 7 pendant, pennant 8 streamer
banquet 4 feed 5 feast 6 dinner, junket, regale, repast, spread
banquette 4 seat 5 bench, shelf 8 platform
bantam 4 arch, fowl, grig, pert 5 saucy, small 6 little, petite 8 malapert, smallish
banter 3 fun, kid, rag, rib 4 fool, jest, jive, joke, josh, razz 5 chaff, jolly, tease 7 teasing 8 backchat, badinage, chitchat, exchange, repartee, snip-snap 9 small talk 10 persiflage 11 give-and-take
bantling 4 babe, baby 6 infant 7 neonate, newborn
baptize 3 dub 4 call, name 5 title 6 purify 7 asperse, cleanse, immerse 8 christen, sprinkle 9 designate 10 denominate
bar 3 ban, dam, pub, rod, tap 4 bate, café, curb, dive, halt, save, slab, snag, stop 5 block, brake, court, fence, ingot, limit, stick, strip 6 billet, bistro, except, hinder, impede, lounge, saloon, tavern 7 barrier, buvette, cabaret, cantina, confine, delimit, exclude, gin mill, rule out, rummery, rumshop, suspend, taproom 8 alehouse, blockade, count out, drinkery, drunkery, grogshop, lawcourt, obstacle, obstruct, pothouse, prelimit, restrict, traverse, tribunal 9 aside from, barricade, eliminate, excluding, honky-tonk, nightclub, outside of, roadblock, roadhouse 11 exclusive of, obstruction, rathskeller 12 circumscribe, watering hole *iron:* 6 rabble
barb 4 dart 5 shaft *combining form:* 3 onc 4 onch, onci, onco 5 oncho
Barbados *capital:* 10 Bridgetown *monetary unit:* 6 dollar
barbarian 3 Hun 4 Goth, rude, wild 5 brute 6 savage, Vandal 8 Visigoth 9 foreigner, Ostrogoth
barbarism 6 misuse 8 malaprop, slangism, solecism 9 neologism, vulgarism 10 corruption 11 impropriety, malapropism 13 vernacularism, vernacularity
barbarity 7 cruelty 8 atrocity 10 inhumanity
barbarous 4 fell, grim, rude, wild 5 cruel 6 brutal, fierce, Gothic, savage, unholy, vulgar, wicked 7 Hunnish, inhuman, lowbrow, uncivil, ungodly, wolfish 8 backward, fiendish, inhumane, sadistic 9 benighted, ferocious, graceless, heartless, primitive, tasteless, truculent 10 outlandish, outrageous, philistine, unmerciful 11 unchristian, uncivilized 12 uncultivated
Barbary ape 5 magot

Barbary state 5 Tunis 7 Algiers, Morocco, Tripoli
barbate 7 bearded 9 whiskered 11 bewhiskered
barber 6 shaver 7 clipper, cropper, friseur 8 coiffeur 9 coiffeuse 10 haircutter 11 hairdresser, hair stylist
Barber of Seville *author:* 12 Beaumarchais *character:* 6 Figaro, Rosina, Rosine 7 Bartolo, Basilio 8 Almaviva, Bartholo *composer:* 7 Rossini 9 Paisiello
barber's itch 8 ringworm
bard 4 muse, poet, scop 5 skald 8 jongleur, minstrel 10 Parnassian, troubadour
bardlet 6 rhymer 8 poetling, verseman 9 poetaster, poeticule, rhymester, versifier 10 versesmith 11 versemonger 12 versificator
Bard of Avon 11 Shakespeare
bare 4 bald, mere, nude, open, show, very, void 5 clear, empty, naked, stark, strip 6 barren, denude, divest, expose, peeled, reveal, unclad, unveil, vacant 7 baldish, denuded, deprive, disrobe, emptied, exhibit, exposed, uncover, unrobed, vacuous 8 bankrupt, denudate, disclose, stripped 9 dismantle, unattired, unclothed, uncovered, undressed *combining form:* 4 gymn, nudi, psil 5 gymno, psilo
barefaced 5 blunt 6 arrant, brassy, brazen 7 blatant 8 impudent, overbold 9 shameless, unabashed 10 unblushing 11 temerarious
barefoot 6 unshod 8 shoeless 9 discalced 10 unsandaled 11 discalceate
bareheaded 7 hatless
barely 4 just 6 hardly, scarce 8 scarcely
bargain 3 buy 4 bond, deal, pact, swap 5 steal, trade, truck 6 barter, dicker, haggle, higgle, palter 7 chaffer, compact, traffic 8 closeout, contract, covenant, exchange, giveaway, huckster 9 agreement, negotiate 10 compromise, convention, loss leader, pennyworth 11 transaction
barge 4 scow 5 clump, stump 6 lumber 7 galumph, stumble
baritone *American:* 5 Gorin 6 Milnes, Warren 7 MacNeil, Merrill, Reardon, Tibbett 8 Guarrera, Warfield *English:* 6 Bailey *German:* 4 Prey *Italian:* 5 Gobbi 8 Raimondi
barium *symbol:* 2 Ba
bark 3 arf, yap, yip 4 snap, woof, yelp 5 snarl *combining form:* 6 phello 7 cortico *Scottish:* 4 yaff
barkeeper see bartender
barkentine 4 ship
bark remover 4 spud 7 spudder
Barlow epic 9 Columbiad
barman see bartender
Barmecidal 8 apparent, illusive, illusory, semblant 10 ostensible
barn 6 stable 10 storehouse *area of:* 4 loft 7 hayloft
barnacle 5 leech 7 sponger 8 hanger-on, parasite 10 freeloader 11 bloodsucker 12 lounge lizard
barnstorm 4 tour 5 pilot 6 travel
Barnum *elephant:* 5 Jumbo *midget:* 8 Tom Thumb *partner:* 6 Bailey
barnyard 4 foul 5 dirty, nasty 6 coarse, filthy, smutty, vulgar 7 obscene, raunchy 8 indecent
baron 4 czar, king 5 mogul 6 tycoon 7 magnate
baronial 5 grand, noble, royal 6 august, lordly 7 stately 8 imposing, majestic 9 grandiose 11 magnificent
baroque 4 gilt, rich 6 florid, ornate, rococo 8 luscious 10 flamboyant, ornamented
Baroque *architect:* 7 Bernini 8 Boromini *composer:* 4 Bach 6 Handel 9 Scarlatti 10 Monteverdi *painter:* 6 Rubens 7 El Greco, Poussin 8 Carracci 9 Velazquez 10 Caravaggio *sculptor:* 7 Bernini, Coustou 8 Coysevox, Girardon
bar pin 9 brochette
barrack 6 billet, casern 7 caserne 8 quarters
barracuda 4 fish, spet 5 barry, senet 6 becuna, becune, picuda, sennet 10 guaguanche, guaguancho
barrage 4 hail 5 burst, salvo, storm, surge 6 shower, stream, volley 8 drumfire 9 broadside, cannonade, fusillade 11 bombardment
barrel 3 keg, run, tun 4 butt, cask, much, peck, pipe, rush, whiz 5 fleet, hurry, speed 6 hasten 7 rundlet 8 hogshead 9 great deal *maker:* 6 cooper *part:* 4 hoop 5 stave *stopper:* 4 bung *support:* 6 gantry
barrelhouse 3 zip 4 dive, rush, whiz 5 hurry, joint 6 hasten, hustle 7 hangout 9 honky-tonk
barren 3 dry 4 arid 5 bleak, stark, waste 6 desert, effete, fallow 7 badland, parched, sterile 8 desertic, heirless, impotent, infecund, wild land 9 childless, infertile, unbearing, unfertile, wasteland 10 unfruitful, untillable, wilderness 12 hardscrabble, unproductive
barricade 3 bar 4 stop, wall 5 block, fence 7 barrier, railing 8 blockade 9 blank wall, roadblock *of trees:* 6 abatis
Barrie character 4 John 5 Peter, Tommy, Wendy 7 Michael 8 Crichton 9 Tiger Lily 10 Tinker Bell 11 Captain Hook
barrier see barricade
barring 3 but 4 save 6 bating, except,

saving 9 aside from, excluding, outside of 11 exclusive of
barrister 6 lawyer 7 counsel 8 attorney
barroom 3 pub 6 lounge, saloon, tavern 7 taproom 8 dramshop, drinkery, groggery, grogshop
bar sinister 4 blot, blur, onus, slur, spot 5 brand, odium, stain 6 stigma 8 black eye
bartender 7 tapster 8 boniface 10 mixologist 12 saloonkeeper
barter 4 swap 5 trade, truck 7 bargain, traffic 8 exchange *Scottish:* 6 niffer
Bartered Bride composer 7 Smetana
Baruch *father:* 6 Nenan, Zabbai *occupation:* 6 scribe
basal 5 basic 6 bottom, lowest 7 primary, radical 8 simplest 10 bottommost, elementary, nethermost, pedimental, rudimental, underlying 11 fundamental, rudimentary 12 foundational
base 3 bad, bed, fix, low 4 evil, foot, mean, poor, prop, root, seat, ugly, vile 5 build, cheap, dirty, found, lousy, lowly, nadir, plant, set up, sorry, stand, tatty 6 bottom, common, filthy, ground, humble, paltry, scurvy, shoddy, sleazy, sordid, trashy, wicked 7 bedrock, caitiff, footing, ignoble, lowborn, low-down, servile, squalid, support 8 beggarly, buttress, cowardly, pedestal, plebeian, recreant, unwashed, unworthy, wretched 9 construct, dastardly, degrading, establish, framework, loathsome, low-minded, predicate 10 abominable, despicable, foundation, groundwork, substratum, unennobled 11 disgraceful, humiliating, ignominious 12 contemptible, meanspirited, substructure, underpinning
baseball *abbreviation:* 2 AB, AL, BA, BB, BI, CF, DH, DP, ER, FA, HR, IP, LF, LP, NL, RF, SB, SO, SS, WP 3 ERA, HSP, LOB, MVP, PCT, RBI *founder:* 9 Doubleday *glove:* 4 mitt *official:* 3 ump 6 umpire *pitch:* 4 drop, heat 5 curve, smoke 6 change, heater, sinker, slider, slurve 7 spitter 8 change-up, fadeaway, fastball, fork ball, knuckler, palm ball, spitball 9 brushback, screwball 12 change of pace, knuckle curve *player:* 6 batter 7 baseman, catcher, fielder, pitcher 9 infielder, shortstop 10 outfielder 11 left fielder 12 right fielder 13 center fielder *practice fly ball:* 5 fungo *term:* 3 bag, bat, box, fan, fly, out, run, tag, tap, tip 4 balk, ball, base, bean, bunt, cage, deck, foul, hook, line, mitt, pill, pole, save, walk 5 alley, apple, bench, bloop, clout, count, drive, error, flare, glove, homer, liner, mound, pop-up, slide, swing 6 assist, clutch, double, dugout, groove, ground, inning, inside, pop fly, pop-out, powder, putout, rubber, runner, single, strike, triple, windup 7 battery, blooper, bullpen, cleanup, diamond, floater, fly ball, home run, infield, manager, outside, pickoff, rhubarb, sidearm, squeeze, stretch 8 baseline, beanball, delivery, foul ball, grounder, keystone, outfield, pinch-hit, rosin bag, southpaw 9 full count, home plate, hot corner, line drive, sacrifice, strikeout, two-bagger 10 double play, frozen rope, ground ball, scratch hit, strike zone 11 knuckleball, pinch hitter, squeeze play, three-bagger 12 Texas leaguer
baseballer 3 Ott (Mel) 4 Cobb (Ty), Dean (Dizzy), Ford (Whitey), Foxx (Jimmy), Mays (Willie), Rose (Pete), Ruth (Babe), Ryan (Nolan) 5 Aaron (Henry), Banks (Ernie), Bench (Johnny), Berra (Yogi), Boggs (Wade), Brock (Lou), Carew (Rod), Clark (Will), Grove (Lefty), Gwynn (Tony), Kiner (Ralph), Maris (Roger), Spahn (Warren), Young (Cy), Yount (Robin) 6 Feller (Bob), Foster (George), Gehrig (Lou), Gibson (Bob), Gooden (Dwight), Herzog (Whitey), Hunter (Catfish), Koufax (Sandy), Mantle (Mickey), Morgan (Joe), Musial (Stan), Palmer (Jim), Seaver (Tom), Wagner (Honus) 4 Canseco (José) 7 Carlton (Steve), Clemens (Roger), Hornsby (Roger), Hubbell (Carl), Jackson (Reggie), Johnson (Walter), Puckett (Kirby), Schmidt (Mike), Speaker (Tris) 8 Anderson (Sparky), Clemente (Roberto), DiMaggio (Joe), Robinson (Jackie), Williams (Ted) 9 Alexander (Grover), Henderson (Rickey), Hershiser (Orel), Killebrew (Harmon), Mattingly (Don) 10 Campanella (Roy), Strawberry (Darryl), Valenzuela (Fernando) 11 Yastrzemski (Carl)
baseball team see American League; National League
baseboard 7 molding 8 skirting
baseborn 3 low 4 mean 5 lowly 6 humble 7 bastard, ignoble, natural 8 plebeian, spurious, unwashed 11 misbegotten 12 illegitimate
baseless 4 idle, vain 5 empty, false, wrong 9 pointless, senseless, unfounded, untenable 10 gratuitous, groundless, ungrounded 11 uncalled-for, unnecessary, unsupported, unsustained, unwarranted 12 indefensible 13 unjustifiable
basement 6 bottom, ground 10 foundation, groundwork, substratum 12 substructure
base on balls 4 pass, walk
bash 3 bat 4 belt, blow, slam, whop 5 crack, smack, smash, whack 6 wallop 7 blowout, shindig
Bashan *last king:* 2 Og *people:* 7 Rephaim
Bashemath *father:* 7 Ishmael *husband:* 4 Esau *sister:* 8 Nebaioth
bashful 3 coy, shy 5 mousy, timid

6 demure, modest 7 abashed 8 retiring, timorous 9 diffident, recoiling, shrinking, unassured 11 embarrassed, unassertive
basic 4 main 5 basal, chief 6 bottom 7 capital, element, primary, radical 8 rudiment 9 elemental, essential, primitive, principal 10 elementary, substratal, underlying 11 fundamental 12 foundational 13 part and parcel
basically 6 au fond 9 in essence 11 essentially 13 fundamentally
basic point 4 crux, gist 7 essence
basin 3 cwm, dip, sag 4 sink 6 cirque, hollow 7 sinkage 8 sinkhole, washbowl 9 concavity 10 depression ***liturgical:*** 5 stoup 7 piscina
basis 4 root, seat 5 axiom, heart, right 6 bottom, ground, reason 7 bedrock, essence, footing, grounds, premise, theorem, warrant 9 postulate, principle 10 assumption, foundation, groundwork, substratum 11 fundamental, presumption 12 substructure, underpinning 13 justification
bask 3 sun 4 roll 5 revel 6 wallow, welter 7 indulge, rollick 9 luxuriate
basket 5 frail 6 dosser, gabion 7 pannier
basketball ***inventor:*** 8 Naismith ***official:*** 6 umpire 7 referee ***player:*** 5 cager, guard 6 center 7 forward 8 hoopster, swingman ***team:*** 4 five 7 quintet ***term:*** 3 gun, jam, key 4 cage, dunk, pass 5 board, lay-up, press, shoot, tip-in 6 freeze, tap-off, tip-off, travel 7 dribble, keyhole, rebound, throw-in, time-out 8 alley-oop, jump ball, slam dunk 9 backboard, backcourt, field goal, free throw 11 ball control
basketballer 3 Bol (Manute) 4 Bird (Larry), Reed (Willis), West (Jerry) 5 Barry (Rick), Cousy (Bob), Ewing (Patrick), Mikan (George) 6 Baylor (Elgin), Cowens (Dave), Erving (Julius), Jordan (Michael), McAdoo (Bob), McHale (Kevin), Pippin (Scottie), Walton (Bill), Worthy (James) 7 Barkley (Charles), Frazier (Walt), Johnson (Magic), Russell (Bill), Wilkins (Dominique) 8 Auerbach (Red), Havlicek (John), Olajuwon (Akeem) 9 Robertson (Oscar) 11 Abdul-Jabbar (Kareem), Chamberlain (Wilt)
Basmath's father 7 Solomon
Basque ***cap:*** 5 beret ***game:*** 6 pelota 7 jai alai ***mountains:*** 8 Pyrenees ***province:*** 5 Alava 7 Vizcaya 9 Guipuzcoa
bass 6 singer 7 crappie, jewfish, sunfish 8 cabrilla ***American:*** 5 Hines, Ramey, Tozzi 6 Morris 7 Plishka, Robeson 8 Flagello ***Bulgarian:*** 8 Ghiaurov ***Italian:*** 5 Siepi ***Russian:*** 9 Chaliapin ***Swiss:*** 6 Corena
bassinet 4 pram 9 baby buggy 12 baby carriage, perambulator
bastard 5 cross 6 by-blow, hybrid 7 mongrel 8 baseborn, spurious, whoreson 10 fatherless, unfathered 11 chance child, misbegotten 12 filius populi, illegitimate, natural child 13 filius nullius ***combining form:*** 4 noth 5 notho
bastardize 4 warp 6 debase 7 corrupt, debauch, deprave, pervert, vitiate 9 brutalize 10 bestialize, demoralize
bastardly 4 mean 12 contemptible
baste 3 wig 4 beat, drub, lash, mill, pelt, rail, whip 5 paste, scold 6 batter, berate, larrup, pummel, stitch, thrash, wallop 7 bawl out, belabor, chew out, clobber, tell off 8 bless out 10 tongue-lash
bastille 4 jail 6 prison
bastinado 3 bat 4 bash, beat, blow 5 crack, pound, smack, smash, stick, whack 6 cudgel, thwack, wallop 8 bludgeon
bastion 7 bulwark, parapet, rampart 10 breastwork
bat 3 bag, bop, bum, gad, hag, jag 4 belt, biff, blow, bust, club, mace, roam, rove, slam, sock, tear, trot, whop, wink 5 baton, biddy, binge, blink, booze, crack, crone, drunk, mooch, smack, spree, witch 6 beldam, bender, cudgel, ramble, rantan, thwack, wander 7 meander, nictate, traipse, twinkle 8 bludgeon 9 chiropter, flying fox, gallivant, nictitate, reremouse, truncheon 10 knobkerrie, shillelagh ***combining form:*** 8 nycteris ***European:*** 7 noctule 8 serotine 9 pipistrel 11 pipistrelle ***Malaysian:*** 6 kalong
batch 3 lot, set 5 array, bunch, clump, group 6 bundle, clutch, parcel 7 cluster
bate 4 omit 6 deduct, except 7 exclude 8 moderate, restrain
bath 3 spa, tub 4 wash 5 hydro, wells 6 shower 7 springs 13 watering place ***combining form:*** 5 balne 6 balneo ***relating to:*** 7 balneal
bathe 3 lap, lip, sop, tub 4 bask, lave, soak, soap, wash 5 douse, flush, souse 6 shower
bathetic 5 mushy, soppy, stale, tired, trite 6 cliché 8 clicheéd 7 maudlin, mawkish 9 hackneyed 11 commonplace, sentimental, stereotyped, tear-jerking 13 stereotypical
bathing suit 6 bikini, trunks 7 maillot
bathroom 2 WC 6 toilet 8 lavatory
Bathsheba ***father:*** 5 Eliam ***husband:*** 5 David, Uriah ***son:*** 7 Solomon
bathtub gin 5 hooch 7 bootleg 9 moonshine 11 mountain dew
bating 3 bar, but 4 save 6 except, saving 7 barring 9 aside from, excluding, outside of 11 exclusive of
baton 4 club, mace, wand 5 billy

6 cudgel 7 war club 8 bludgeon 9 billy club, truncheon 10 nightstick
batrachian 4 frog, toad 9 amphibian 10 salientian
batter 4 beat, drub, lame, maim, maul 5 baste, pound, wreck 6 bruise, buffet, bung up, mangle, pummel, thrash, wallop 7 belabor, clobber, contuse, cripple, disable, lambast, shatter 8 lacerate, lambaste, mutilate 9 disfigure
battery 3 lot 4 body 5 array, batch, bunch, clump, group 6 bundle 7 cluster
battery terminal 5 anode 7 cathode
battle 3 tug, war 5 brush, clash, fight 6 action, assail, attack, combat, oppugn, sortie 7 assault, bombard, contend, contest 8 conflict, skirmish 9 encounter, onslaught, scrimmage 10 engagement 11 hostilities *combining form:* 5 machy
battle-ax 6 twibil 7 twibill
Battle Born State 6 Nevada
battle cry 5 motto 9 catchword *Japanese:* 6 banzai
battlement 7 parapet
battlesome 6 brawly 7 scrappy 8 brawling 9 brawlsome 11 quarrelsome
batty 4 nuts 5 crazy, wacky 6 crazed, insane, maniac, screwy 7 cracked 8 deranged 9 bedlamite
bauble 5 curio 6 gewgaw, trifle 7 bibelot, novelty, trinket, whatnot 8 gimcrack 9 objet d'art 10 knickknack
Baucis' husband 8 Philemon
bavardage 6 by-talk 8 chitchat, trifling 9 small talk
Bavaria 6 Bayern *capital:* 6 Munich *city:* 8 Augsburg, Bayreuth, Wurzburg 9 Nuremburg *king:* 6 Ludwig *patron saint:* 6 Rupert
bawd 4 drab, moll 5 poule, whore 6 harlot, hooker 8 meretrix 10 prostitute 11 nightwalker 12 streetwalker
bawdy house 4 stew 6 bagnio 7 brothel 8 bordello, cathouse, joyhouse 10 whorehouse 11 parlor house 13 sporting house
bawl 3 cry, sob 4 howl, roar, rout, wail, weep, yell, yowl 5 shout 6 bellow, boohoo, clamor, holler, scream, shriek, squall, yammer 7 blubber, bluster, screech
bawl out 3 wig 4 lash 5 scold 6 berate 7 chew out, condemn, tell off, upbraid 8 bless out, denounce 10 tongue-lash
bay 3 arm 4 cove, gulf, howl, wail 5 award, badge, bayou, bight, creek, firth, honor, inlet, kudos, quest 6 harbor, slough 7 laurels, ululate 8 accolade 10 decoration 11 distinction *Aegean Sea:* 5 Anzac *Africa:* 6 Walvis *Alaska:* 7 Glacier *Angola:* 5 Bengo, Tiger 6 Tigres *Antarctica:* 3 Ice 8 Amundsen *Arabian Sea:* 4 Qamr 5 Kamar *Argentina:* 6 Blanca *Australia:* 5 Anson, Shark 6 Botany, Sharks 9 Discovery *Baltic:* 4 Hano, Kiel 6 Danzig, Kieler 9 Pomerania 10 Pomeranian, Pommersche *Barents Sea:* 4 Kola 7 Pechora *Beaufort Sea:* 7 Prudhoe 9 Mackenzie *Bismarck Sea:* 5 Kimbe *Brazil:* 9 Guanabara *Bristol Channel:* 10 Carmarthen *California:* 5 Morro 8 Monterey, San Diego 12 San Francisco *Canada:* 5 Fundy *Cape Breton Island:* 4 Mira *Capetown:* 5 Table *Caribbean Sea:* 5 Limon 8 Chetumal *Central America:* 7 Fonseca *China:* 4 Mirs *Crete:* 4 Suda 5 Canea *Cuba:* 4 Broa, Mora, Nipe 10 Guantanamo *Dominican Republic:* 4 Ocoa *East River:* 8 Flushing *Ecuador:* 5 Manta *Egypt:* 6 Abukir 7 Aboukir *Eire:* 4 Clew 7 Brandon *English Channel:* 3 Tor 4 Lyme 5 Seine *Estonia:* 5 Parnu 6 Pyarnu *Europe:* 6 Biscay 11 Aquitanicus *Florida:* 8 Biscayne *Greenland:* 5 Disko 6 Baffin 8 Melville *Gulf of Alaska:* 3 Icy 5 Woman 12 Resurrection *Gulf of Boothia:* 5 Pelly *Gulf of California:* 5 Adair *Gulf of Guinea:* 5 Benin, Bonny 6 Biafra *Gulf of Mexico:* 5 Tampa 6 Mobile 7 Aransas 8 Campeche, Sarasota 9 Matagorda, Pensacola 10 San Antonio, Terrebonne 11 Atchafalaya, Ponce de Leon 12 Apalachicola 13 Corpus Christi *Gulf of St. Lawrence:* 5 Bonne, Gaspé *Hawaii:* 5 Koloa, Lawai *Hong Kong:* 4 Deep *Honshu:* 3 Ise 5 Mutsu, Osaka, Owari, Tokyo 6 Atsuta, Sagami *Hudson River:* 7 New York *Iceland:* 4 Faxa, Huna 8 Faxafloi *Indian Ocean:* 6 Bengal 15 Great Australian *Indonesia:* 4 Bima, Kayo 5 Saleh 8 Humboldt *Irish Sea:* 4 Luce 7 Dundalk *Jamaica:* 4 Long *Japan:* 4 Tosa *Java:* 4 Lada 5 Peper *Java Sea:* 7 Batavia 8 Djakarta *Kara Sea:* 6 Enisei 7 Yenisei *Lake Erie:* 8 Sandusky *Lake Huron:* 7 Saginaw, Thunder *Lake Michigan:* 5 Green 13 Grand Traverse *Lake Ontario:* 11 Irondequoit *Lake Superior:* 5 Huron 8 Keweenaw 9 Whitefish *landlocked:* 5 Lamon *Long Island Sound:* 6 Oyster *Madagascar:* 8 Antongil *Maine:* 5 Casco 7 Machias 9 Penobscot *Marquesas Islands:* 5 Anaho *Maryland-Virginia:* 10 Chesapeake 12 Chincoteague *Massachusetts:* 6 Boston 7 Cape Cod 8 Buzzards, Plymouth *Mediterranean:* 9 Famagusta *Mozambique:* 5 Memba, Pemba *Nantucket Sound:* 5 Lewis *New Brunswick:* 13 Passamaquoddy *Newfoundland:* 4 Hare 5 White 7 Fortune *New Guinea:* 3 Oro 5 Berau, Hansa, Milne *New Jersey:* 5 Great 6 Newark 7 Raritan 8 Barnegat *New York:* 7 Jamaica *New Zealand:* 5 Hawke 6 Tasman 11 Hauraki Gulf *North*

Carolina: 6 Onslow *North Sea:* 4 Jade 9 Jadebusen *Northwest Territories:* 5 Wager 7 Repulse 8 Franklin 9 Frobisher *Nova Scotia:* 8 Cobequid *Oregon:* 4 Coos *Philippines:* 5 Baler, Pilar, Sogod 6 Butuan *Puerto Rico:* 5 Sucia *Quebec:* 6 Ungava *Red Sea:* 4 Foul *Rhode Island:* 12 Narragansett *Russia:* 4 Amur 5 Aniva, Chaun 6 Ussuri 7 Amurski *Scotland:* 5 Enard *Sea of Japan:* 13 Peter the Great *Solomon Islands:* 4 Deep *South Africa:* 5 Algoa, False *South Carolina:* 4 Bull, Long *South China Sea:* 4 Bias, Datu, Taya 5 Dasol, Subic, Subig 6 Brunei, Paluan 7 Camranh *Spain:* 5 Cadiz 9 Gibraltar *Spitsbergen:* 5 Cross, Kings *Sri Lanka:* 4 Palk *Strait of Gibraltar:* 7 Tangier *Sumatra:* 5 Bajur 10 Koninginne *Sydney:* 6 Botany *Tasmania:* 5 Storm *Texas:* 7 Trinity *Tyrrhenian Sea:* 6 Naples 7 Paestum *Wales:* 9 Carnarvon 10 Caernarvon *Washington:* 5 Dabob 6 Skagit *Western Sahara:* 8 Rio de Oro *West Indies:* 5 Coral *White Sea:* 5 Onega *Yellow Sea:* 5 Korea

baygall 3 bog, fen 4 mire, moss, quag, sump 5 marsh, swamp 6 morass 9 swampland

bayou 3 arm, bay 4 cove, gulf 5 bight, creek, firth, inlet 6 harbor, slough *Louisiana:* 5 Macon 9 Lafourche 10 Terrebonne *Mississippi:* 9 Chickasaw

Bay State 13 Massachusetts

bay window 3 pod, pot 6 paunch 8 potbelly 11 corporation

bazoo 3 boo 4 bird, hiss, hoot, pooh, razz 7 catcall 8 pooh-pooh 9 raspberry 10 Bronx cheer

bazooka's target 4 tank

be 4 go on, hold, live, move 5 abide, exist, stand 6 endure, obtain, remain 7 breathe, persist, prevail, subsist 8 continue

beach 4 bank 5 coast, shore, wreck 6 pile up, strand 8 cast away, lakeside 9 lakeshore, shipwreck 10 oceanfront *Hawaii:* 7 Waikiki *Massachusetts:* 9 Nantasket *New York:* 10 Fire Island

___ Beach 5 Dover

beached 7 aground 8 grounded, stranded

beachhead 8 foothold

beachwear see bathing suit

beacon 5 flare 6 pharos 7 bonfire 8 balefire 9 watchfire 10 lighthouse

beak 3 neb, nib 4 bill, cape, naze, nose, peck, pick 5 point, snoot, snout 6 beezer, pecker 7 sneezer 8 foreland, headland 9 proboscis, schnozzle 10 promontory *combining form:* 5 rostr 6 rhamph, rostri, rostro 7 rhampho 8 rhynchus

beaklike part 7 rostrum

be-all and end-all 3 sum 4 pith, root, soul, tote 5 stuff, total, whole 6 bottom, marrow 7 essence 8 entirety, sum total, totality 9 aggregate, substance 10 rock bottom 12 quintessence

beam 3 can, ray 4 balk, burn, grin, rear, seat 5 fanny, gleam, shaft, shine, shoot, smile 6 behind, bottom, lintel, rafter, timber 7 radiate 8 backside, buttocks, crosstie, derriere 9 posterior

beaming 6 bright, lucent 7 fulgent, lambent, radiant 8 luminous 9 brilliant, effulgent, refulgent 12 incandescent

bean 3 dry, wax 4 bush, coco, conk, dome, head, lima, mung, navy, pole, poll, snap 5 baked, brain, broad, horse, jelly, pinto 6 belfry, coffee, frijol, kidney, noddle, noggin, noodle, string 7 frijole, jumping 9 headpiece 10 stringless *of India:* 3 urd

beano 5 bingo

Bean Town 6 Boston

beany 5 fiery 6 spunky 7 gingery, peppery 8 spirited 10 mettlesome 11 highhearted 12 high-spirited

bear 2 go 3 act, bow, jag, jam, lug, try 4 born, buck, form, go on, have, head, hump, lump, make, pack, push, quit, show, take, tote 5 abide, allow, apply, beget, birth, breed, bring, brook, bruin, carry, crowd, crush, defer, ferry, fruit, press, refer, shape, squab, stand, stick, touch, yield 6 accept, acquit, affect, attend, behave, convey, convoy, create, demean, deport, digest, endure, escort, invent, permit, pocket, relate, seller, set out, squash, squish, squush, submit, suffer 7 afflict, comport, concern, condone, conduct, deliver, display, exhibit, fashion, involve, pertain, possess, produce, squeeze, stomach, support, sustain, swallow, take off, torment, torture, turn out 8 chaperon, engender, fructify, generate, light out, multiply, parallel, shoulder, stick out, sweat out, tolerate, tough out 9 accompany, acquiesce, appertain, companion, fabricate, procreate, propagate, reproduce, strike out, transport 10 bring forth, correspond 11 consort with, countenance *Alaskan:* 5 polar 6 kodiak *Australian:* 5 koala *combining form:* 4 arct 5 arcto *family:* 7 Ursidae *genus:* 5 Ursus *kind:* 3 sun 5 black, brown, honey, koala, polar, sloth 6 kodiak 7 grizzly 10 spectacled *relating to:* 6 ursine *young:* 3 cub

bearable 7 livable 9 allowable, endurable, tolerable 10 acceptable, admissible, sufferable 11 supportable, sustainable 12 satisfactory

beard 4 barb, dare, defy, face, fuzz 5 brave, front 6 beaver, goatee 7 galways, outdare, outface, stubble, Vandyke, venture 8 imperial, whiskers 9 burnsides, challenge 11 muttonchops 12 side-whiskers *combining form:* 5 pogon 6 pogono *on* *grain:* 3 awn *pointed:* 6 goatee 7 Vandyke

bearded 5 hairy 7 barbate, goateed, stubbed, stubbly 8 unshaven 9 whiskered 11 bewhiskered

bear down 5 crush 6 defeat, reduce, subdue 7 conquer 8 vanquish 9 overpower, subjugate

bearer 5 envoy 6 coolie, porter, redcap, skycap 7 bellboy, bellhop, bellman, carrier, courier, drogher 8 cargador, emissary 9 messenger 11 internuncio *combining form:* 3 fer 4 pher, phor 5 phora, phore 6 phorae (plural), phorum

bearing 3 air, set 4 brow, look, mien, port, pose 5 birth, front, poise, stand 6 aspect, stance 7 address, conduct, display, posture 8 attitude, behavior, birthing, carriage, delivery, demeanor, presence 10 childbirth, deportment 11 comportment, parturition *combining form:* 6 ferous, gerous, parous 7 igerous, phorous

bearish 5 waspy 6 cranky, ornery 7 dubious, waspish 8 cankered, vinegary 9 crotchety, declining 10 vinegarish 11 pessimistic 12 cantankerous

bearlike 6 ursine, ursoid 8 ursiform

bear out 6 verify 7 confirm, justify 8 validate 11 corroborate 12 authenticate, substantiate

bear up 4 prop 5 brace, carry 6 uphold 7 bolster, shore up, support, sustain 8 buttress

beast 5 brute 6 animal 7 beastie, critter, varmint 8 behemoth, creature 9 quadruped *combining form:* 4 ther 5 thero 6 theria (plural), therio 7 therium

beastly 5 brute, feral 6 animal, brutal, ferine 7 bestial, brutish, swinish

beat 2 do 3 get, gyp, lam, tan, top, wag, win 4 balk, best, bilk, cane, comb, dash, drub, drum, dump, flog, foil, grub, lace, lash, lick, maul, pelt, rake, ruin, trim, wale, wave, welt, whip, whop 5 baste, baton, cheat, cozen, curry, excel, lay on, meter, outdo, paste, pound, pulse, rhyme, scoop, scour, smear, stick, stump, swing, throb, tromp, whisk 6 baffle, batter, better, buffet, chouse, cudgel, diddle, exceed, forage, hammer, larrup, muss up, pummel, rhythm, search, switch, thrash, thwart, waggle, wallop, woggle 7 belabor, buffalo, cadence, cadency, clobber, conquer, defraud, lambast, measure, nonplus, prevail, pulsate, ransack, rough up, rummage, shellac, smother, surpass, triumph, trounce 8 bludgeon, finecomb, flimflam, lambaste, malleate, outshine, outstrip, overcome, rhythmus 9 bastinado, exclusive, frustrate, fustigate, overreach, palpitate, transcend 10 circumvent, disappoint, pistol-whip

beat down 5 crush 6 defeat, reduce, subdue 7 conquer 8 vanquish 9 overpower, subjugate

beating 4 rout 5 lumps 6 defeat, hiding 7 debacle, licking 8 drubbing 9 overthrow, pulsating, thrashing 10 defeasance 11 shellacking 12 vanquishment

beatitude 5 bliss 7 ecstasy, rapture 9 happiness, transport 11 blessedness 12 blissfulness

Beatles 4 John, Paul 5 Ringo 6 George

beau 5 flame, lover, swain 6 steady 7 beloved 8 truelove, young man 9 boyfriend, inamorato 10 sweetheart

Beau Brummel 3 fop 5 dandy 7 coxcomb 8 macaroni 9 exquisite 11 petit-maître 12 lounge lizard

beau ideal 5 model 6 mirror 7 example, pattern 8 ensample, exemplar, paradigm, standard 9 archetype

Beaumarchais' hero 6 Figaro

beauteous 4 fair 5 bonny 6 comely, lovely, pretty 8 handsome 10 attractive 11 good-looking

beautiful 4 fair 5 bonny 6 choice, comely, lovely, pretty, proper, superb 7 elegant, sublime 8 glorious, gorgeous, handsome, pleasing, splendid, stunning 9 exquisite 10 attractive, eye-filling, personable 11 good-looking, resplendent, well-favored 12 eye-appealing *combining form:* 4 cali, calo 5 calli, callo

beautiful people 6 jet set 8 smart set

beautify 4 deck, trim 5 adorn, grace, prank 6 bedeck 7 dress up, garnish 8 decorate, ornament, prettify 9 embellish, glamorize

beauty 5 belle, dream, peach, toast 6 eyeful, looker, lovely 7 charmer, dazzler, stunner 8 knockout 9 eye-opener 10 goodlooker *combining form:* 4 cali, calo 5 calli, callo

beaver 5 beard 6 rodent 8 whiskers *family:* 10 Castoridae *genus:* 6 Castor *home:* 5 lodge *young:* 3 kit, pup

Beaver State 6 Oregon

becalm 4 lull 5 allay, quiet, still 6 settle, soothe 7 compose, quieten 11 tranquilize

because 2 as 3 for, now 5 being, since 6 seeing 7 whereas 8 as long as 10 inasmuch as 11 considering

because of 4 over 5 due to 7 owing to, through

Becher's father 7 Ephraim 8 Benjamin

Beckett work 4 Play, Watt 6 Molloy, Murphy 7 Endgame 9 Happy Days 14 Krapp's Last Tape 15 Waiting for Godot

becloud 3 dim, fog 4 blur 5 bedim, befog, muddy 6 darken, puzzle 7 confuse, eclipse, obscure, perplex 8 befuddle 9 obfuscate

become 2 go 3 fit, get, run, wax 4 come, grow, rise, soar, suit, turn 5 arise, befit, mount 6 go with 7 enhance, flatter 9 agree with 10 go together *suffix:* 3 ize
becoming 4 nice 5 right 6 decent, proper, seemly 7 correct, fitting 8 decorous, suitable, tasteful 9 befitting 10 attractive, conforming, flattering 11 appropriate, comme il faut *suffix:* 6 escent 7 escence
bed 3 cot 4 base, bunk, flop, rest, seat, twin 5 basis 6 bottom, cradle, double, ground, Murphy, pallet, pile in, retire, roll in, tuck in, turn in 7 bedrock, trundle 8 rollaway 10 foundation, substratum *combining form:* 4 clin 5 clino *of India:* 7 charpai, charpoy
Bedad's son 5 Hadad
bedamn 4 cuss 5 curse, swear 8 execrate 9 imprecate
bedaub 3 dab 5 smarm, smear 6 smudge 7 besmear, plaster
bedaze 4 stun 6 bemuse, benumb 7 petrify, stupefy 8 paralyze
bedazzle 4 daze 5 blind
bedbug 5 cimex 6 chinch 7 cimices (plural)
bedcover 5 quilt 6 afghan, spread 8 coverlet, coverlid 11 counterpane
bedeck 4 trim 5 adorn, prank 6 bedaub 7 bedizen, dress up, garnish 8 beautify, decorate, ornament 9 embellish
Bedeiah's father 4 Bani
bedevil 5 annoy, harry, tease, worry 6 harass, pester, plague 7 hagride, wherret 9 tantalize
bedevilment 7 trouble 8 disorder, vexation 9 confusion
bedfellow 4 ally 9 associate
bedim 3 fog 5 befog, cloud, gloom 6 darken 7 becloud, eclipse, obscure 9 obfuscate
bedlamite 3 mad, nut 4 loon, nuts 5 batty, crazy, loony 6 dement, insane, madman, maniac 7 cracked, lunatic, madling 8 demented, deranged 9 non compos
bedog 3 tag 4 tail 5 trail 6 shadow
bedouin 4 Arab 5 nomad
bedraggled 5 faded, seedy 6 shabby, tagrag 7 rundown 8 decrepit, tattered 10 down-at-heel, threadbare 11 dilapidated
bedridden 4 weak 6 feeble, infirm, laid up, sickly 7 bedfast 8 confined 13 incapacitated
bedrock 4 base, root 5 basis 6 ground 7 footing 10 foundation, groundwork, substratum 12 substructure, underpinning
bedroom 7 boudoir
bedspread 8 coverlet, coverlid 11 counterpane
bed-wetting 8 enuresis
bee *combining form:* 3 api *family:* 6 Apidae 8 Bombidae *food:* 6 nectar *genus:* 4 Apis 5 Osmia 6 Bombus 8 Ceratina 9 Megachile *glue:* 8 propolis *group:* 5 swarm 6 colony *house:* 6 apiary *kind:* 5 drone, mason, queen 6 cuckoo, mining, sewing, worker 8 honeybee, quilting, spelling 9 bumblebee, carpenter 10 leafcutter *nest:* 4 hive, skep *product:* 3 wax 5 honey *relating to:* 5 apian 8 apiarian *study of:* 8 apiology *wax cells:* 9 honeycomb
beechnuts 4 mast
beef 3 arm 4 crab, fuss, miff, thew, tiff, yaup, yawp 5 bitch, bleat, boost, brawl, brawn, force, gripe, might, power, sinew, steam, vigor 6 energy, expand, extend, muscle, squawk, yammer 7 augment, blow off, dispute, enlarge, magnify, quarrel, rhubarb 8 heighten, increase, multiply, squabble, strength 9 bellyache, bickering, strong arm 10 aggrandize, falling-out 11 altercation *cut:* 3 rib 4 loin, rump, side 5 chuck, flank, plate, round, shank 7 brisket, sirloin 10 tenderloin *grade:* 4 good 5 prime 6 choice 7 utility 8 standard 10 commercial *order:* 4 rare 6 medium 8 well-done
beefeater 6 warder, yeoman
beefheaded 4 dull 5 dense 6 stupid 10 numskulled
beefy 5 burly, hefty, husky
Beehive State 4 Utah
beekeeper 8 apiarian, apiarist 12 apiculturist
beekeeping 10 apiculture
Beeliada's father 5 David
beeline 3 nip, zip 4 whiz 5 hurry, speed 6 bullet, hustle, rocket 7 hotfoot 8 highball
Beelzebub 5 devil, fiend, Satan 6 diablo 7 Lucifer, Old Nick, serpent 8 Apollyon 10 Old Scratch 13 Old Gooseberry
beer 3 ale 4 bock, brew 5 draft, lager, stout, weiss 6 porter 7 pilsner 8 pilsener *cup:* 3 mug 4 toby 5 stein 6 flagon, seidel 7 tankard 8 schooner 9 blackjack *drinking place:* 3 inn, pub 6 saloon, tavern *ingredient:* 4 hops, malt 5 yeast 6 barley *maker:* 6 brewer *mythical inventor:* 9 Gambrinus *plant:* 7 brewery *Russian:* 5 kvass *Scottish:* 10 barley-bree, barley-broo *slang:* 4 suds *Tibetan:* 5 chang
beer hall 5 stube 8 alehouse, mughouse
Beeri *daughter:* 6 Judith *son:* 5 Hosea
beet 5 chard 6 mangel, wurzel 7 mangold *family:* 9 goosefoot
Beethoven, Ludwig van *birthplace:* 4 Bonn *opera:* 7 Fidelio *overture:* 6 Egmont 7 Leonore 10 Coriolanus, Prometheus *sonata:* 8 Kreutzer, Pastoral 9 Moonlight 10 Pathetique *symphony:* 6 Choral, Eroica 8 Pastoral

beetle 3 jut 4 hang, poke, pout 5 bulge, pouch 7 project 8 bend over, lean over, overhang, protrude, stand out, stick out ***click:*** 6 cucuyo, elater 7 firefly 8 cucubano, skipjack ***dung:*** 6 scarab 9 tumblebug ***front wing:*** 6 elytra (plural) 7 elytron ***fruit-eating:*** 8 curculio ***insect-eating:*** 7 ladybug 8 ladybird ***kind:*** 3 dor 4 bean, dorr, dung, fire, June, stag 5 click, flour, grain, tiger, water 6 carpet, chafer, dor bug, ground, May bug, meloid, museum 7 blister, cadelle, carabid, firefly, goldbug, goliath, Juno bug, vedalia 8 ambrosia, figeater, Japanese, lampyrid, passalid, pinch bug 9 bombadier, longicorn, potato bug 10 cockchafer, rhinoceros ***order:*** 10 Coleoptera ***ornamental:*** 6 scarab ***sacred:*** 6 scarab ***snouted:*** 6 weevil 7 billbug 8 curculio 9 wood borer ***young:*** 4 grub 5 larva 8 wireworm

beetlehead 4 dolt, dope 5 dunce 8 dumbbell

beetleheaded 4 dull 5 dense 6 stupid 10 numskulled

beet soup 6 borsch, borsht 7 borscht

befall 2 go 3 hap 5 break, occur 6 betide, chance, happen 7 come off, develop, fall out

befit 4 suit 6 become, go with 9 agree with 10 go together

befitting 3 apt 4 just, meet, nice 5 happy, right 6 decent, proper, seemly 7 correct 8 becoming, decorous, suitable 10 conforming, felicitous 11 appropriate, comme il faut ***suffix:*** 2 ly

befog 3 dim 4 blur 5 bedim, cloud, muddy 6 darken, puzzle 7 becloud, confuse, eclipse, obscure, perplex, stumble 8 bewilder, confound 9 obfuscate, overcloud 13 metagrobolize

befool 4 dupe, gull, hoax 5 trick 7 chicane 8 hoodwink 9 bamboozle, victimize 11 hornswoggle

before 2 to 3 ere 4 ante, once, then, till, up to 5 ahead, until 6 facing, sooner, up till 7 ahead of, already, earlier, forward, prior to 8 formerly, previous 9 erstwhile, in advance, preceding 10 heretofore, previously 11 confronting, in advance of, precedently 12 antecedently ***combining form:*** 4 fore 6 proter 7 protero ***prefix:*** 2 ob 3 pre, pro 4 ante

befoul 4 slur 5 dirty, smear 6 defame, malign 7 blacken, pollute, slander, spatter, traduce 9 bespatter, denigrate 11 contaminate

befuddle 4 daze 5 addle, mix up 6 ball up 7 confuse, fluster 8 bewilder, distract, throw off 9 bumfuzzle

befuddlement 3 fog 4 daze, haze, maze 5 mix-up 9 confusion 10 muddlement 11 muddledness

beg 3 ask, nag, sue 4 pray 5 brace, cadge, crave, plead, press, worry 6 appeal, call on, demand, invoke, obtest 7 beseech, besiege, conjure, entreat, implore, request, solicit 8 petition 9 importune 10 supplicate

begem 5 beset, jewel 7 bejewel, enjewel

beget 4 bear, sire 5 breed 6 father 7 produce 8 generate, multiply 9 procreate, propagate, reproduce 11 progenerate

begetting ***combining form:*** 4 gony

beggar 4 hobo 5 asker, tramp 6 bummer, cadger, pauper, prayer, sponge, suitor 7 moocher, sponger 8 deadbeat 9 schnorrer, suppliant 10 down-and-out, freeloader, panhandler, petitioner, supplicant 11 bindle stiff, supplicator

beggared 4 flat, poor 5 broke, needy 8 dirt poor, indigent 9 destitute 11 fortuneless, impecunious 12 impoverished

beggarly 4 mean 5 cheap, sorry 6 cheesy, measly, paltry, scurvy, shabby, trashy 7 pitiful 8 pitiable, wretched 10 despicable, despisable 12 contemptible

Beggar's Opera ***music:*** 7 Pepusch ***painting:*** 7 Hogarth ***text:*** 3 Gay

beggarweed 6 dodder, spurry 9 knotgrass

beggary 4 need, want 6 penury 7 bumming, cadging, poverty 8 mooching 9 indigence, mendicity, neediness, pauperism 10 mendicancy 11 destitution, panhandling

begin 4 open 5 arise, dig in, enter, found, set to, start 6 attack, broach, get off, launch, spring, tackle, take up, tee off 7 break in, jump off, kick off, lead off, prepare, usher in 8 commence, embark on, initiate 9 establish, institute, introduce, originate 10 embark upon, inaugurate

beginner 4 colt, tiro, tyro 6 novice, rookie 8 freshman, neophyte, newcomer 9 novitiate 10 apprentice, tenderfoot

beginning 4 dawn, rise, root 5 alpha, basal, birth, onset, start 6 anlage, origin, outset, primal, setout, source, spring, sprout 7 dawning, genesis, infancy, initial, nascent, opening 8 creation, exordium, outstart, prologue, rudiment, simplest 9 dayspring, elemental, emergence, inception, inceptive, incipient 10 appearance, elementary, incipiency, initiative, initiatory, opening gun, rudimental 11 origination, rudimentary 12 commencement, introductory ***combining form:*** 3 acr, akr 4 acro, akro, arch ***suffix:*** 6 escent

begird 3 hem 4 band, belt, ring 5 beset, round 6 circle, girdle 8 cincture, encircle, engirdle, surround 9 encompass 10 encincture

begirdle 4 band, belt 6 engird 8 cincture 10 encincture
begone 4 kite 5 scram 6 decamp, get out 7 buzz off, skiddoo, take off, vamoose 8 clear out, hightail 9 skedaddle
begrime 4 foul, soil 5 dirty 6 besoil, smirch, smooch, smudge, smutch 7 tarnish
begrudge 4 envy
beguile 4 lure, play, wile 5 bluff, fleet, while 6 betray, delude, entice, humbug, illude, jockey, juggle, seduce, take in 7 deceive, exploit, finesse, mislead 8 maneuver 10 manipulate 11 double-cross
beguiling 5 false 8 deluding, delusive, delusory 9 deceiving, deceptive 10 fallacious, misleading
Behan's autobiography 10 Borstal Boy
behave 2 do 3 act 4 bear, go on, move, quit, take, work 5 carry, react 6 acquit, demean, deport, direct, manage 7 comport, conduct, control, disport, operate, perform 8 function
behavior 6 manner 7 bearing, conduct 8 demeanor 10 deportment 11 comportment
behead 4 neck 9 decollate 10 decapitate, guillotine
beheaded noblewoman 4 Grey (Lady Jane) 6 Boleyn (Anne) 9 Catherine 10 Antoinette (Marie)
behemoth 5 giant, whale 7 mammoth, monster 9 leviathan
behemothic 4 huge 7 mammoth, titanic 8 colossal, gigantic 9 Herculean, monstrous 10 gargantuan, mastodonic 11 elephantine
behest 4 word 5 order 6 charge, demand 7 bidding, command, dictate, mandate, request 9 prompting 10 injunction 12 solicitation
behind 3 can 4 next, rump 5 abaft, after, below, fanny, hiney, infra, later, since 6 back of, bottom, heinie 7 by and by 8 backside, buttocks, derriere, latterly 9 afterward, following, posterior 10 afterwhile 12 subsequently, subsequent to ***combining form:*** 7 postero ***prefix:*** 3 met 4 meta, post 5 retro
behindhand 3 lax 4 late 5 lated, slack, tardy 6 in debt, remiss 7 belated, overdue 8 backward, careless, derelict 9 in arrears, negligent 10 delinquent, neglectful, regardless, unpunctual 11 undeveloped 12 disregardful 13 unprogressive
behold 3 see 4 espy, mark, note, view 6 descry, notice 7 discern, observe 11 distinguish ***French:*** 5 voilà ***Latin:*** 4 ecce
beholden 7 obliged 8 indebted 9 obligated
beholder 6 viewer 7 watcher, witness 8 by-sitter, looker-on, observer, onlooker 9 bystander, spectator 10 eyewitness
being 2 as 3 for, man 4 body, esse, soul 5 human, since, stuff, thing, wight 6 entity, matter, mortal, nature, object, person, seeing 7 because, essence, texture, whereas 8 as long as, creature, essentia, existent, material 9 actuality, character, existence, personage, something, substance 10 inasmuch as, individual 11 considering, personality 12 essentiality 13 individuality ***suffix:*** 2 ic 3 ant, ent 4 ical
bejewel 3 gem 5 begem, beset 7 diamond, encrust, spangle 9 bespangle
Bel ***father:*** 2 Ea ***wife:*** 5 Belit 6 Beltis
bel ___ 5 canto 6 esprit
Bel ___ 5 Paese
Bela ***father:*** 4 Beor 8 Benjamin ***son:*** 3 Ard
belabor 4 beat, drub 5 baste, pound 6 batter, buffet, pummel, thrash, wallop 7 lambast 8 lambaste
Belait 6 Europe
belated 5 dated, passé, tardy 7 antique, archaic, overdue 8 outdated, outmoded 9 out-of-date 10 antiquated, behindhand, oldfangled, unpunctual 12 old-fashioned
belch 4 burp, spew 5 eject, erupt, expel 6 irrupt 8 disgorge, eructate
beleaguer 4 gnaw 5 annoy, beset, harry, siege, storm, tease, worry 6 harass, invest, pester, plague 7 bedevil, besiege, hagride 8 blockade
belfry 7 clocher 8 carillon 9 bell tower, campanile ***dweller:*** 3 bat
Belgium ***capital:*** 8 Brussels ***commercial center:*** 4 Gent 5 Ghent ***horse breed:*** 9 Brabançon ***language:*** 6 French 7 Flemish ***monetary unit:*** 5 franc ***people:*** 7 Fleming, Flemish, Walloon ***province:*** 5 Liège, Namur 7 Antwerp, Brabant, Hainaut, Limburg 8 Flanders 10 Luxembourg ***violinist:*** 5 Ysaye
belie 4 hide, warp 5 color, twist 6 garble 7 conceal, distort, falsify, pervert 8 disguise, disprove, miscolor, misstate, negative 10 contradict, contravene, controvert 12 misrepresent
belief 3 ism 4 idea, mind, view 5 credo, creed, dogma, faith, tenet, trust 6 assent, credit 7 concept, feeling, opinion, precept 8 credence, doctrine, religion, sureness 9 assurance, certainty, certitude, principle, sentiment 10 conviction, persuasion
believable 5 solid 6 likely 7 tenable 8 credible, possible, probable, rational 9 colorable, plausible 10 convincing, creditable, impressive, meaningful, persuasive, presumable, reasonable, satisfying, supposable 11 conceivable, substantial
believe 3 buy 4 deem, feel, hold, take

5 admit, sense, think, trust 6 accept, assume, credit, expect, gather, reckon, repute 7 imagine, suppose, suspect, swallow 8 accredit, consider 10 understand

belittle 5 decry 8 derogate, diminish, discount, minimize, write off 9 criticize, discredit, disparage, dispraise, underrate 10 depreciate, undervalue 11 detract from 13 underestimate

belittlement 4 tale 7 calumny, scandal, slander 10 backbiting, defamation, detraction 12 backstabbing, depreciation 13 disparagement

bell 4 bong, peal, ring, toll 5 chime, knell

bell-bottoms 5 pants 8 trousers

bell cow 4 dean, lead 5 doyen, guide, pilot 6 leader

Bellerophon ***father:*** 7 Glaucus 8 Poseidon ***grandfather:*** 8 Sisyphus ***horse:*** 7 Pegasus ***victim:*** 7 Chimera

belles lettres 10 literature

belletrist 4 poet 6 author, writer

bellflower 9 campanula

____ belli 5 casus

bellicose 7 scrappy, warlike 8 factious, fighting, militant 9 assertive, combative, truculent 10 aggressive, pugnacious, rebellious 11 belligerent, contentious, quarrelsome 12 gladiatorial

belligerence 5 fight 6 attack 9 pugnacity 10 aggression, truculence 13 combativeness

belligerent 3 hot 6 ardent, fierce 7 hostile, scrappy, warlike, warring 8 battling, fighting, invading, militant, ructious 9 attacking, bellicose, combative, truculent 10 aggressive, pugnacious 11 contentious, hot-tempered, quarrelsome 12 antagonistic, gladiatorial

Bellini ***opera:*** 5 Norma 8 Il Pirata 9 I Puritani 12 La Sonnambula ***sleepwalker:*** 5 Amina

bell metal 6 bronze

bellow 3 bay, cry, low, moo 4 bark, bawl, roar, rout, wail, yelp 6 clamor 7 bluster

Bellow character 6 Herzog 7 Sammler 9 Henderson 10 Augie March

bell ringer 3 hit, wow 4 bang 5 smash 6 toller 7 success 12 carillonneur

bell ringing 11 campanology

bell-shaped 11 campanulate

bell sound 4 ding, dong, peal, ring, ting, toll 5 clang, knell 6 tinkle

bell tower 6 belfry 7 clocher 8 carillon 9 campanile

____ bellum 4 ante, post

bellwether 4 dean, lead 5 doyen, guide, pilot 6 leader

belly 3 gut 5 tummy 6 paunch, venter 7 abdomen, stomach ***combining form:*** 5 gastr 6 gaster, gastro, ventri, ventro 7 gastero, gastria ***Scottish:*** 4 wame

bellyache 4 beef, crab, fuss, yaup, yawp 5 bitch, bleat, colic, gripe 6 gripes, squawk, yammer 7 blow off 12 collywobbles

bellyacher 4 crab 5 crank 6 griper, grouch, kicker 7 grouser 8 grumbler 10 complainer, malcontent 11 faultfinder

belly button 5 navel

belong 2 go 3 fit, set 4 suit, vest 5 agree, befit, chime, match, tally 6 accord, become, inhere 7 indwell, pertain 9 appertain, harmonize 10 correspond

belonging ***suffix:*** 2 an, ar 3 ary, ean, ian, ine

belongings 5 goods 6 estate, things 7 effects 8 chattels, movables 10 possession

beloved 3 pet 4 baby, beau, dear, love 5 flame, honey, lover, sweet 6 steady 7 darling, sweetie 8 blue-eyed, favorite, ladylove, loveling, precious, truelove 9 boyfriend, inamorata, inamorato, sweetling 10 fair-haired, girl friend, heartthrob, sweetheart

below 4 next 5 after, infra, since, under 6 behind, nether 7 beneath 9 following 10 underneath 12 subsequent to ***combining form:*** 6 intero ***prefix:*** 3 sub 5 infra

belt 3 bat, bop 4 area, band, bash, biff, blow, gird, loop, ring, sash, slam, slug, sock, whop, zone 5 blast, smack, smash, strap, strip, tie up, tract 6 begird, cestus, circle, engird, girdle, region, wallop 7 baldric, caestus, clobber, stretch 8 begirdle, ceinture, cincture, encircle, engirdle 9 bandoleer, bandolier, territory, waistband 10 cummerbund, encincture ***celestial:*** 6 zodiac ***combining form:*** 3 zon 4 zono

belt highway 8 ring road

Belus ***brother:*** 6 Agenor ***daughter:*** 4 Dido ***father:*** 7 Neptune 8 Poseidon ***mother:*** 5 Libya ***son:*** 6 Danaus 7 Cepheus, Phineus 8 Aegyptus

belvedere 6 alcove, gazebo, pagoda 11 garden house, summerhouse

bemean 4 sink 5 abase, lower 6 debase, humble 7 degrade 8 cast down 9 humiliate

bemedaled 9 decorated 10 beribboned

bemired 4 miry, oozy 5 muddy 6 claggy, clarty

bemoan 3 rue 4 weep 6 bewail, grieve, lament, regret 7 deplore 8 complain

bemuse 4 daze, stun 5 addle 6 bedaze, benumb, puzzle 7 fluster, perplex, petrify, stupefy 8 paralyze

bemused 4 lost 6 absent 7 faraway 8 distrait 10 abstracted 11 inconscient, preoccupied 12 absentminded

bench 6 settee ***church:*** 3 pew ***outdoor:*** 6 exedra ***upholstered:*** 9 banquette

benchmark 5 gauge 7 measure 8 standard 9 criterion, yardstick 10 touchstone
bend 2 go 3 arc, bow, jut, nod, yaw 4 arch, bias, cave, curl, flex, give, hang, hook, lean, tack, turn 5 angle, apply, break, crook, curve, round, shift, stoop, throw, yield 6 beetle, buckle, devote, direct, double, fold up, inflex 7 address, crumple, dispose, flexure, incline, turning 8 collapse, flection, lean over, overhang 9 curvation, curvature, deviation 10 buckle down, deflection, predispose
bendable 6 pliant, supple 7 elastic, pliable 8 flexible
bender see binge
bending *combining form:* 7 sphingo
___ bene 4 nota
beneath 5 below, under *prefix:* 3 hyp, sub 4 hypo 5 infra
___ Benedict 4 eggs
benediction 2 OK 4 boon, good, okay 5 favor, grace 6 thanks 7 benefit, benison, godsend 8 approval, blessing 9 advantage 11 approbation 12 thanksgiving
benefact 3 aid 4 abet, help 5 do for, stead 6 assist 7 help out
benefaction 4 alms 7 charity 8 donation, offering 11 beneficence 12 contribution
beneficence see benefaction
beneficial 4 good 5 brave 6 toward, useful 7 helpful 8 favoring, salutary 9 favorable, wholesome 10 propitious 12 advantageous
beneficiary 4 heir 5 donee 6 vassal 7 legatee 9 feudatory *suffix:* 2 ee
beneficiate 5 treat 6 reduce 7 prepare, process
benefit 3 aid 4 boon, gain, good, help, sake 5 avail, build, favor, serve 6 assist, behalf, behoof, better, profit, succor 7 account, advance, further, godsend, improve, promote, relieve, welfare, work for 8 blessing, interest 9 advantage, well-being 10 ameliorate, prosperity 11 benediction 12 contribute to
benevolence 4 boon, gift 5 amity, favor 6 comity 7 largess, present 8 goodwill 10 compliment, friendship, kindliness 12 friendliness
benevolent 3 big 4 good, kind 5 lofty 6 do-good, humane, kindly 7 liberal 8 generous 10 altruistic, beneficent, bighearted, charitable, chivalrous, openhanded 11 considerate, freehearted, magnanimous 12 eleemosynary, greathearted, humanitarian, largehearted 13 compassionate, philanthropic, tenderhearted
benighted 8 backward, ignorant, untaught 9 untutored 10 illiterate, uneducated, uninformed, unlettered, unschooled 11 empty-headed, know-nothing 12 uninstructed 13 unenlightened, unprogressive
benign 4 kind, mild 6 bright, dexter, gentle, humane, kindly 7 clement 8 gracious, merciful 9 favorable, fortunate 10 auspicious, benevolent, charitable, forbearing, propitious 11 good-hearted
Benin *capital:* 9 Porto Novo *largest city:* 7 Cotonou *monetary unit:* 5 franc
benison 8 blessing 11 benediction
Benjamin *brother:* 6 Joseph *father:* 5 Jacob *mother:* 6 Rachel
bent 3 set 4 bias, gift, head, nose, turn 5 arced, bowed, flair, knack, round 6 arched, curved, genius, intent, talent 7 arrondi, decided, faculty, leaning, rounded, settled, uncinal 8 arciform, decisive, inflexed, penchant, resolute, resolved, tendency, uncinate 9 inclining 10 determined, proclivity, propensity 11 curvilinear, disposition, inclination 12 predilection *combining form:* 4 cyrt 5 ancyl, ankyl, curvi, cyrto 6 anchyl, ancylo, ankylo, campto 7 anchylo
benumb 4 daze, dull, mull, stun 5 blunt 6 bedaze, bemuse, deaden 7 petrify, stupefy 8 paralyze 11 desensitize
benumbed 6 asleep 9 senseless, unfeeling 10 insensible 11 insensitive 12 anesthetized
benzene *combining form:* 4 phen 5 pheno
Beor's son 4 Bela 6 Balaam
bequeath 4 will 5 leave 6 devise, hand on, legate, pass on 8 hand down, transmit
bequest 6 devise, legacy 11 inheritance
berate 3 jaw 4 rail, rate 5 scold 6 revile 7 bawl out, chew out, upbraid 10 tongue-lash, vituperate
berceuse 7 lullaby 10 cradlesong
bereave 3 rob 4 lose, oust 6 divest 7 deprive 10 disinherit, dispossess
bereaved 6 bereft 9 sorrowing 10 distressed
Berechiah's son 9 Zechariah
Bergen's dummy 5 Snerd 8 McCarthy
Beriah's father 5 Asher 6 Shimei, Shimhi 7 Ephraim
berkelium *symbol:* 2 Bk
Bermuda grass 4 doob
Bernice *brother:* 7 Agrippa *father:* 5 Herod *husband:* 6 Polemo *lover:* 5 Titus 9 Vespasian
berry 4 wort 5 bacca, fruit, grape, whort 6 banana, tomato 7 bramble, currant, madrona, madrone, madrono, whortle 8 allspice *combining form:* 4 cocc 5 cocci, cocco *Latin:* 6 acinus *medicinal:* 5 cubeb
berry-bearing 7 baccate 11 bacciferous
berrylike 7 baccate, coccoid
berth 3 job 4 dock, pier, post, quay, slip, spot 5 jetty, levee, place, wharf 6 billet,

office 8 position 9 situation 10 connection 11 appointment
Bertha's son 7 Orlando
beryllium *symbol:* 2 Be
beseech see **beg**
beset 3 gem, hem 4 gird, ring 5 begem, jewel, storm 6 assail, attack, circle, fall on, girdle, infest, invest, strike 7 aggress, assault, bejewel, besiege, compass, enjewel, environ, overrun 8 blockade, encircle, fall upon, surround 9 beleaguer, encompass, overswarm 10 overspread
besetment 4 pest 6 bother, pester, plague 8 irritant, nuisance 9 annoyance 10 botherment 11 botheration 12 exasperation
besetting 8 dominant, haunting 9 obsessive, principal 10 persistent
beside 2 by 3 bar, but 4 near, nigh, save 5 round 6 beyond, except, nearby, next to 7 barring 8 as well as, opposite 9 alongside, aside from, excluding, outside of 11 exclusive of 12 over and above *prefix:* 2 ep 3 eph, epi, par 4 para
besides 3 bar, but, new, too, yet 4 also, else, more, save, then 5 added, again, along, other 6 as well, beyond, except 7 barring, farther, further 8 as well as, likewise, moreover 9 aside from, excluding, otherwise, outside of 10 additional, in addition 11 exclusive of, furthermore 12 additionally, over and above
besiege 4 trap 5 beset, hem in 6 assail, attack, invest 7 assault 8 blockade, encircle, surround 9 beleaguer, encompass
besmear 3 dab, tar 4 daub, soil 5 smarm, stain, sully, taint 6 bedaub, defile, smudge 7 plaster, tarnish 8 besmirch, discolor
besmirch see **besmear**
besoil 4 foul 5 dirty, grime 6 smirch, smooch, smudge, smutch 7 begrime, tarnish
besom material 5 twigs
besotted 5 dotty, drunk 8 enamored 9 infatuate 10 infatuated
bespatter 4 slur, spot 5 smear 6 befoul, bespot, defame, malign 7 asperse, blacken, slander, traduce 9 denigrate
bespeak 3 ask 4 book, hire 6 accost, attest, desire 7 address, apply to, betoken, request, reserve, solicit, testify, witness 8 announce, approach, indicate 9 preengage
bespeckle 3 dot 6 pepper 7 freckle, stipple 8 sprinkle
best 3 gem, pip, top 4 beat, down, most, pick 5 cream, elite, excel, model, outdo, pride, prime, prize, worst 6 better, choice, defeat, exceed, flower, master 7 conquer, greater, largest, paragon, pattern, prevail, surpass, triumph 8 exemplar, nonesuch, outshine, outstrip, overcome, primrose 9 nonpareil, transcend 10 bettermost *combining form:* 6 aristo
bestial 5 brute, feral 6 animal, brutal, ferine 7 beastly, brutish, swinish
bestialize 4 warp 6 debase 7 corrupt, debauch, deprave, pervert, vitiate 9 brutalize 10 bastardize, demoralize
bestir 4 wake, whet 5 rally, rouse, waken 6 arouse, awaken, kindle 9 challenge
bestow 3 use 4 bunk, give, pack 5 apply, board, grant, house, lodge, put up, store 6 billet, confer, devote, donate, employ, handle, harbor, lavish 7 exploit, hand out, present, quarter, utilize 8 domicile, exercise, give away 9 entertain, warehouse *Scottish:* 7 propine
bestower 5 donor, giver 7 donator 9 conferrer, presenter
bestrew 3 sow 5 straw 7 disject, scatter 9 broadcast 11 disseminate
bestride 4 back 5 mount 8 straddle, striddle
bet 3 lay, pot, set 4 ante, game, play, risk 5 banco, put on, stake, wager 6 gamble, parlay *racing:* 6 exacta 8 perfecta, quinella, quiniela *taker:* 6 bookie
Betelgeuse 4 star *constellation:* 5 Orion
betel palm 5 areca
bête noire 4 hate 7 bugbear 8 anathema 10 black beast 11 abomination, detestation
bethink 4 cite, mind 6 recall, remind, retain, revive 8 remember 9 recollect, reminisce 10 retrospect
Bethuel *daughter:* 7 Rebekah *father:* 5 Nahor *mother:* 6 Milcah *son:* 5 Laban *uncle:* 7 Abraham
betide 2 go 3 hap 5 break, occur 6 befall, chance, happen 7 come off, develop, fall out
betimes 4 soon 5 early 6 timely 8 oversoon 10 seasonably 11 prematurely
betoken 4 bode, omen 5 argue, augur 6 attest 7 bespeak, portend, presage, promise, testify, witness 8 announce, forebode, foreshow, indicate 9 foretoken 10 foreshadow
betray 4 sell, show, tell, trap 5 bluff, cross, snare, spill, split 6 delude, desert, entrap, evince, humbug, illude, inform, juggle, reveal, take in, turn in, unveil 7 beguile, betoken, blab out, deceive, divulge, ensnare, mislead, sell out, uncover 8 disclose, discover, evidence, give away, indicate, manifest, renegade 10 apostatize 11 collaborate, demonstrate, double-cross
betrayal 7 treason
betrayer 3 rat 4 fink, nark 6 snitch 7 stoolie, tattler, traitor 8 informer,

squealer, turncoat **10** talebearer, tattletale **11** stool pigeon
betroth **6** pledge **8** affiance
betrothal **8** espousal **10** engagement
betrothed **6** fiancé **7** engaged, fiancée, pledged **8** intended, plighted, promised, wife-to-be **9** affianced, bride-to-be **10** contracted **11** husband-to-be
better **3** top, win **4** beat, best, good, help, more, most **5** amend, elder, excel, outdo **6** choice, exceed, senior **7** greater, improve, largest, success, surpass, triumph, victory **8** brass hat, higher-up, outshine, outstrip, superior, whip hand **9** advantage, desirable, exceeding, excellent, meliorate, transcend, upper hand **10** ameliorate, preferable, surpassing **11** exceptional, superiority
bettor **7** wagerer
between **5** among, twixt **6** atwixt **7** betwixt ***prefix:*** **5** inter, intra
betweentimes **11** at intervals
bevel **4** bias **6** biased **7** slanted **8** diagonal, slanting
beverage **3** ade, nog, pop, tea **4** mate, milk, soda **5** cider, cocoa, drink, juice, shake **6** coffee, eggnog, frappe, malted, nectar **7** potable **8** lemonade, libation, potation **9** drinkable, milk shake ***alcoholic:*** **3** ale, gin, rum **4** beer, grog, mead, wine **5** cider, julep, negus, punch, stout, toddy, vodka **6** bishop, brandy, caudle, cooler, liquor, rickey, shandy, sherry, whisky **7** liqueur, martini, sangria, tequila, whiskey **8** cocktail, highball, sillabub, sillibub, syllabub, vermouth ***Australasian:*** **4** kava ***British:*** **5** perry, stout **6** stingo ***carbonated:*** **4** cola, soda **6** rickey **8** root beer **9** ginger ale ***central Asian:*** **5** kumys **6** koumis, koumys, kumiss, kumyss **7** koumiss, koumyss ***Dutch:*** **7** schnaps **8** schnapps ***from camel's milk:*** **5** kumys **6** koumis, koumys, kumiss, kumyss **7** koumiss, koumyss ***from cow's milk:*** **5** kefir ***Greek:*** **4** ouzo **7** oenomel, oinomel, retsina, retzina ***Irish:*** **5** usque **6** poteen **7** potheen, potteen **8** usquabae, usquebae **10** usquebaugh ***medicinal:*** **6** elixir ***Mexican:*** **6** pulque **7** tequila ***of the gods:*** **6** nectar ***Oriental:*** **4** sake, saki **6** arrack, samshu ***Russian:*** **5** kefir, kvass, quass, vodka ***Scottish:*** **4** yill **6** scotch ***South American:*** **4** maté **5** yerba ***Swedish:*** **5** glogg ***Turkish:*** **4** raki ***West Indies:*** **3** rum **5** tafia
bevy **4** band, crew **5** bunch, covey, group, party **7** cluster **8** assembly
bewail **4** moan, weep **6** bemoan, grieve **7** deplore
beware **4** heed, mind **5** watch **6** attend, notice **7** look out **8** watch out
bewhiskered **7** barbate, bearded
bewilder **3** fog **4** stun **5** addle, befog, mix up **6** baffle, ball up, fuddle, muddle, puzzle **7** confuse, fluster, perplex, stumble **8** befuddle, confound, distract **9** bumfuzzle **13** metagrobolize
bewitch **3** hex **4** draw, snow, take, wile **5** charm, spell, trick **6** allure, dazzle, voodoo **7** attract, bedevil, enchant, possess **8** demonize, ensorcel, overlook **9** beglamour, captivate, ensorcell, fascinate, magnetize, sorcerize
bewitching **8** alluring, charming, magnetic, mesmeric **9** seductive **10** attractive
bewitchment **5** magic **7** sorcery **8** witchery, wizardry **9** conjuring, magicking **10** necromancy, witchcraft **11** incantation
beyond **3** new, yon **4** else, more, over, past **5** above, added, after, other **6** across, beside, yonder **7** athwart, besides, farther, further, outside, without **8** as well as **9** afterlife, hereafter, otherwise **10** additional, afterworld, otherworld **12** over and above, transversely ***combining form:*** **6** preter **7** praeter ***prefix:*** **3** met, par **4** meta, over, para **5** extra, hyper, super, trans, ultra
bias **4** bend, bent, skew **5** angle, bevel, slant **7** beveled, dispose, incline, leaning, slanted **8** diagonal, penchant, slanting **9** inclining, influence, prejudice, viewpoint **10** partiality, predispose, prepossess, proclivity, standpoint **11** disposition, inclination **12** one-sidedness, predilection
biased **6** swayed, warped **7** bigoted, colored, partial, slanted **8** disposed, inclined, one-sided, partisan, slanting **9** jaundiced, unneutral **10** influenced, interested, prejudiced **11** opinionated, predisposed, tendentious **12** prepossessed **13** unindifferent
bibelot **5** curio **6** bauble, gewgaw, trifle **7** novelty, trinket, whatnot **8** gimcrack **9** objet d'art **10** knickknack
Bible ***abbreviation:*** **2** Ex, Is, Jn, Lk, Mk, Mt, Ps **3** Col, Cor, Dan, Eph, Gal, Gen, Hab, Heb, Hos, Jas, Jer, Jon, Lam, Lev, Mal, Mic, Neh, Num, Pet, Rev, Rom, Sam, Tim, Tit **4** Deut, Ezek, Josh, Judg, Obad, Phil, Prov, Zech, Zeph **5** Chron, Thess **6** Eccles, Philem ***Apocrypha book:*** **5** Tobit **6** Baruch, Esdras, Esther, Judith **7** Susanna **8** Manasseh, Manasses **9** Maccabees ***New Testament book:*** **4** Acts, John, Jude, Luke, Mark **5** James, Peter, Titus **6** Romans **7** Hebrews, Matthew, Timothy **8** Philemon **9** Ephesians, Galatians **10** Colossians, Revelation **11** Corinthians, Philippians **13** Thessalonians ***Old Testament book:*** **3** Job **4** Amos, Ezra, Joel, Ruth **5** Hosea, Jonah, Kings, Micah, Nahum **6** Daniel, Esther, Exodus, Haggai, Isaiah, Joshua, Judges, Psalms, Samuel **7** Ezekiel, Genesis, Malachi, Numbers, Obadiah **8** Habakkuk, Jeremiah, Nehemiah,

Proverbs **9** Leviticus, Zechariah, Zephaniah **10** Chronicles **11** Deuteronomy **12** Ecclesiastes, Lamentations **13** Song of Solomon ***part:*** **4** book **5** verse **7** chapter **9** testament ***translator:*** **4** Knox **5** Eliot **6** Jerome, Luther **7** Erasmus, Tyndale, Zwingli **8** Wycliffe **9** Coverdale ***version:*** **4** Geez **5** Douay, Itala **6** Coptic, Gothic, Syriac, Targum **7** Vulgate **8** Peshitta **9** Jerusalem, King James, Masoretic, Serampore **10** New English, Septuagint

Biblical ***animal:*** **4** reem **5** daman **8** behemoth ***ascetic order:*** **6** Essene ***battle:*** **7** Jericho ***battle site:*** **10** Armageddon ***charioteer:*** **4** Jehu ***city, town:*** **2** Ai, Ur **3** Ain, Dan, Lod, Luz, Nob **4** Bela, Cana, Gath, Gaza, Nain, Nebo, Tyre, Zoar **5** Bezer, Calno, Derbe, Ekron, Endor, Gerar, Golan, Haifa, Haran, Joppa, Lydda, Ramah, Sidon, Sodom, Tekoa, Zorah **6** Ashdod, Asshur, Beroea, Bethel, Calneh, Dothan, Emmaus, Gadara, Gibeah, Gibeon, Gilgal, Hebron, Kadesh, Lystra, Mizpah, Ophrah, Rimmon, Shiloh, Shunem, Siloan, Smyrna, Tarsus **7** Antioch, Askelon, Baalbec, Bethany, Corinth, Ephesus, Ephraim, Iconium, Jericho, Jezreel, Magdala, Nineveh, Samaria, Shechem **8** Caesarea, Chorazin, Damascus, Gomorrah, Michmash, Nazareth, Philippi, Tiberias **9** Beersheba, Beth-horon, Bethlehem, Bethsaida, Capernaum, Jerusalem ***coin:*** (see at **Hebrew**) ***coney:*** **5** daman ***desert:*** **5** Sinai ***garden:*** **4** Eden **8** Paradise ***giant:*** **4** Anak, Emim **7** Goliath ***giant slayer:*** **5** David ***hill:*** **4** Zion ***hunter:*** **6** Nimrod ***judge:*** **3** Eli **4** Ehud, Elon, Jair, Tola **5** Abdon, Ibzan **6** Gideon, Samson, Samuel **7** Deborah, Othniel, Shamgar **8** Jephthah ***king:*** **2** Og **3** Asa **4** Agag, Ahab, Ahaz, Amon, Bera, Elah, Jehu, Omri, Reba, Saul **5** David, Herod, Hiram, Joash, Joram, Nadab, Pekah, Rezin, Zimri **6** Abijam, Baasha, Birsha, Hoshea, Japhia, Josiah, Jotham, Uzziah **7** Ahaziah, Amaziah, Azariah, Jehoash, Jehoram, Menahem, Shallum, Solomon **8** Hezekiah, Jehoahaz, Jeroboam, Manasseh, Rehoboam, Zedekiah **9** Jehoiakim, Zechariah **10** Jehoiachin **11** Jehoshaphat ***land:*** **3** Nod, Pul **4** Aram, Elam, Moab, Seba, Seir **5** Judah, Judea, Perea **6** Bashan, Canaan, Goshen, Israel **7** Chaldea, Galilee, Samaria **9** Palestine ***land of plenty:*** **6** Goshen ***measure:*** (see at **Hebrew**) ***mountain:*** **3** Hor **4** Ebal, Nebo, Peor, Seir **5** Horeb, Sinai, Tabor **6** Abarim, Ararat, Carmel, Gilboa, Gilead, Hermon, Moriah, Olivet, Pisgah **7** Gerizim, Lebanon ***name:*** **2** Er, Ir, Ur **3** Abi, Asa, Bel, Dan, Eli, Eri, Eve, Gad, Ham, Hen, Hod, Hul, Hur, Ira, Iri, Iru, Job, Lot, Ner, Nun, Ram, Reu, Toi, Uel, Uri, Zur **4** Abel, Adah, Adam, Agag, Ahab, Ahaz, Amon, Aran, Bela, Beor, Boaz, Buzi, Cain, Cush, Dodo, Ebal, Ebed, Eber, Eder, Ehud, Elah, Elam, Elon, Enan, Enos, Eram, Esau, Ezer, Gaal, Gadi, Gera, Guni, Hazo, Heli, Hori, Ibri, Iddo, Igal, Irad, Iram, Ishi, Izri, Jada, Jael, Jair, Jehu, Joab, Joah, Joel, John, Kish, Kore, Lael, Leah, Levi, Lois, Maon, Mark, Mary, Mica, Moab, Moza, Naam, Nebo, Neri, Noah, Obal, Obed, Oded, Ohad, Ohel, Omar, Omri, Onam, Onan, Oreb, Oren, Ozem, Ozni, Paul, Puah, Reba, Rosh, Ruth, Salu, Saph, Sara, Saul, Seth, Shem, Shua, Sodi, Suah, Susi, Tema, Tola, Ucal, Ulam, Uzai, Uzal, Uzzi, Zeeb, Zeri, Ziza, Zuar **5** Aaron, Abiel, Abner, Amasa, Amnon, Amram, Asher, Bedad, Bedan, Beeri, Caleb, Carmi, Chuza, Cozbi, David, Debir, Deuel, Dinah, Eliab, Eliam, Elias, Eliel, Eliud, Emmor, Enoch, Ephah, Ephai, Ephod, Esrom, Ethan, Ezbon, Gaham, Galal, Gazez, Gomer, Hadad, Hagar, Haggi, Haman, Hamul, Hanan, Hanun, Haran, Harum, Heber, Helah, Heleb, Helek, Helon, Hemam, Heman, Herod, Hirah, Hobab, Horam, Hosea, Ibhar, Imlah, Imnah, Isaac, Iscah, Ishui, Ithra, Ittai, Izhar, Jaasu, Jabal, Jacob, Jahdo, Jakeh, Jalam, Jalon, James, Jamin, Janna, Jared, Jarib, Jeiel, Jerah, Jered, Jesse, Jeush, Jezer, Joash, Jobab, Jogli, Jonah, Jonas, Joram, Jubal, Judah, Judas, Korah, Laban, Lahad, Lahmi, Laish, Libni, Lotan, Mahli, Mahol, Mamre, Maoch, Massa, Merab, Mered, Mesha, Micah, Moses, Mushi, Nabal, Nadab, Nahor, Naomi, Nehum, Nogah, Nohah, Ocram, Onias, Ophir, Orpah, Othni, Palal, Pallu, Palti, Pekah, Peleg, Pelet, Perez, Peter, Puvah, Rahab, Raham, Raphu, Regem, Rekem, Reuel, Rezon, Rizia, Rufus, Sacar, Sallu, Sarah, Segub, Seled, Serah, Sered, Serug, Shama, Shaul, Sheal, Sheba, Shema, Shiza, Shobi, Shuah, Shual, Shuni, Simon, Tahan, Tamar, Tarah, Tebah, Terah, Tibni, Tilon, Timna, Tubal, Uriah, Uriel, Uthai, Uzzah, Zabad, Zabdi, Zabud, Zadok, Zaham, Zebah, Zephi, Zepho, Zerah, Zibia, Zimri, Zohar **6** Abital, Achsah, Ashhur, Balaam, Baruch, Becher, Beriah, Bilhah, Binnui, Canaan, Cheran, Chesed, Daniel, Dathan, Dishan, Dishon, Elasah, Eliada, Elijah, Elisha, Elpaal, Eshban, Eshcol, Esther, Eunice, Gesham, Gideon, Gilead, Ginath, Hanani, Hannah, Hanoch, Hareph, Hebron, Hemdam, Hepher, Hezion, Hezron, Hodesh, Hoglah, Hophni, Hoshea, Hotham, Hothir, Huldah, Hupham, Hushim, Isaiah, Ishbak, Ishpah, Ishpan, Ishuah, Israel, Ithiel, Ithran, Izliah, Izziah, Jaalam, Jabesh, Jachin, Jahath, Japhia, Jashub, Jehiel, Jehush, Jemuel, Jesher, Jeshua, Jether, Jethro, Jeziel, Jezoar, Joahaz, Joakim, Joanna, Joelah,

Joiada, Joktan, Joseph, Joshah, Joshua, Josiah, Jotham, Judith, Kareah, Kemuel, Keziah, Kohath, Laadah, Lamech, Maacah, Maadai, Machir, Mahali, Mahlah, Mahlon, Malcam, Manoah, Martha, Matred, Mattan, Melech, Merari, Midian, Milcah, Miriam, Mirmah, Misham, Naamah, Naaman, Naarah, Nahash, Nahath, Nathan, Nemuel, Nepheg, Neriah, Nimrod, Ochran, Ophrah, Pagiel, Paruah, Pasach, Paseah, Peleth, Penuel, Peresh, Philip, Pilate, Pispah, Pithon, Prisca, Putiel, Raamah, Rachel, Raddai, Ramiah, Ramoth, Raphah, Reaiah, Rechab, Reuben, Rimmon, Rinnah, Rizpah, Rohgah, Salmon, Salome, Samson, Samuel, Shaaph, Shamir, Sharai, Sheber, Shelah, Shemer, Shephi, Shepho, Shilem, Shilhi, Shimea, Shimei, Shimri, Shiphi, Shobab, Shobal, Shoham, Shomer, Shuham, Simeon, Tahash, Tahath, Talmai, Thomas, Tikvah, Tirzah, Tobias, Urijah, Uzziah, Uzziel, Vaniah, Vashni, Vashti, Vophsi, Zaavan, Zabbai, Zaccur, Zalaph, Zebiah, Zephon, Zeresh, Zereth, Zeruah, Zetham, Zibiah, Zichri, Zillah, Zilpah, Zimmah, Zimran, Zippor, Zoheth, Zophah, Zuriel *patriarch:* (see at Hebrew) *people:* 6 Kenite, Levite 7 Amorite, Edomite, Elamite, Moabite 9 Israelite *plains:* 4 Maab 5 Mamre 7 Jericho *plotter:* 5 Haman *poem:* 5 psalm *pool:* 5 Gihon 6 Shelah, Siloam 8 Bethesda *priest:* 3 Eli 4 Levi 5 Aaron, Annas 8 Caiaphas *Promised Land:* 6 Canaan *pronoun:* 2 ye 3 thy 4 thee, thou 5 thine *prophet:* (see prophet entry) *Psalmist:* 5 David *punishment:* 7 stoning *queen:* 5 Sheba 6 Esther, Vashti 7 Candace, Jezebel 8 Athaliah *reproach:* 4 raca *river:* 3 Zab 4 Nile 5 Abana, Arnon 6 Abanah, Jabbok, Jordan, Kishon *sacred object:* 4 urim 7 thummin *scribe:* 6 Baruch *sea:* 3 Red 4 Dead 7 Galilee *sea monster:* 9 Leviathan *spice:* 5 aloes, myrrh 6 cassia, onycha, stacte 7 calamus 8 cinnamon, galbanum 12 frankincense *spy:* 5 Caleb *temptress:* 3 Eve 7 Delilah *thief:* 8 Barabbas *tree:* 5 cedar *valley:* 4 Baca, Elah 6 Hinnon, Kidron, Shaveh, Siddim *verb ending:* 3 eth *weed:* 4 tare *well:* 3 Ain 4 Esek 6 Jacob's *witch's home:* 5 Endor

bibliography 4 list 7 catalog, history

bibliopole 7 bookman 10 bookdealer, bookseller

bicker 3 row, war 4 spat, tiff 5 argue, clack, fight, scrap 6 argufy, battle, hassle, rattle, ruttle 7 brabble, clatter, clitter, contend, dispute, fall out, quarrel, quibble, shatter, wrangle 8 squabble 9 altercate, caterwaul

bickering 3 row 4 spat 5 run-in 6 hassle 7 dispute, quarrel, wrangle 8 squabble 11 altercation, embroilment

bicycle 4 bike 9 high-riser 11 high-wheeler *brake:* 7 caliper, coaster *for two:* 6 tandem *rider:* 6 cycler 7 cyclist *ten-speed:* 10 derailleur

bid 3 ask 4 tell, warn 5 order 6 charge, direct, enjoin, invite, summon 7 command, request 8 instruct

biddable 6 docile 7 amiable, docious 8 amenable, obedient, obliging 9 tractable 11 good-natured

bidding 4 call, word 5 order 6 behest, charge 7 command, dictate, mandate 9 summoning 10 injunction

biddy 3 bag, bat, hag 4 drab, girl, maid, trot 5 crone, witch 6 beldam

bide 4 live, stay, wait 5 dwell, tarry 6 linger, remain, reside 7 hang out 8 continue 11 stick around

bier 10 catafalque

biff 3 bop, hit 4 belt, blow, ding, nail, sock, whop 5 catch, clout, devel, pound, slosh, smack, whack 6 strike, thwack, wallop

bifold see binary

bifurcate 4 fork 5 split 6 branch, divide 8 separate 11 dichotomize, dichotomous

bifurcation 4 fork 6 branch 8 division 9 dichotomy 10 separation

big 3 fat 4 arty, bull, full, gone, lion, much, very 5 ample, awash, awful, great, heavy, hefty, husky, large, lofty, major, roomy, sated 6 biggie, bigwig, bumper, clumsy, gravid, hugely, packed, parous 7 awfully, brimful, copious, crammed, crowded, glutted, greatly, hulking, notable, replete, sizable, stuffed, swollen, weighty 8 enceinte, generous, imposing, inflated, material, oversize, pregnant, spacious 9 capacious, chock-full, distended, expectant, expecting, extensive, extremely, important, momentous, overblown, satisfied 10 benevolent, chivalrous, commodious, large-scale, meaningful, voluminous 11 considerate, heavyweight, magnanimous, overflowing, pretentious, significant, substantial 12 considerable, greathearted, high-sounding 13 comprehensive, consequential

Big Bertha's birthplace 5 Essen

Big Dipper *constellation:* 9 Ursa Major *star:* 5 Alcor, Dubhe, Merak, Mizar

bigfoot 4 Omah 9 Sasquatch

biggety 4 bold, wise 5 fresh, nervy, sassy 6 cheeky 7 forward 8 impudent 10 procacious 11 smart-alecky

bighearted 7 liberal 10 openhanded

big house 3 can, jug, pen 4 jail 5 clink 6 lockup, prison 7 slammer 8 hoosegow 11 reformatory 12 penitentiary

bight 3 arm, bay 4 cove, gulf 5 bayou, creek, firth, inlet 6 harbor, slough

bigmouthed 4 loud 10 boisterous

bigness 4 size 9 amplitude, greatness, largeness, magnitude 11 sizableness
bigot 6 maniac, racist, zealot 7 fanatic
bigoted 6 biased, narrow 9 hidebound, illiberal, lily-white 10 brassbound, intolerant, prejudiced, unenlarged 11 small-minded 12 conservative, narrow-minded
big shot 3 VIP 5 celeb, nabob 6 bigwig, fat cat 7 notable 8 big wheel 9 big cheese, celebrity, dignitary 13 high-muck-a-muck
bijouterie 6 jewels 7 jewelry 8 trinkets
bile *combining form:* 4 bili, chol 5 chole, cholo
bilge 4 bunk 5 hooey, trash 6 bushwa 7 hogwash, malarky, rubbish 8 nonsense 10 balderdash
Bilhah's son 3 Dan 8 Naphtali
Bilhan's father 7 Jediael
bilk 3 gyp, shy 4 balk, beat, dash, duck, foil, kite, ruin, shun 5 avoid, cheat, cozen, dodge, elude, evade, shake 6 baffle, chouse, diddle, double, escape, eschew, thwart 7 defraud 8 flimflam 9 frustrate, overreach 10 circumvent, disappoint
bill 3 neb, nib, tab 4 beak, bone, buck, cape, fish, head, naze, oner, peak, skin 5 check, point, score, visor 6 damage, dollar, pecker, poster 7 account, affiche, charges, invoice, ironman, placard, smacker 8 foreland, frogskin, handbill, headland 9 reckoning, smackeroo, statement 10 promontory *five-dollar:* 3 fin *of a bird:* 3 neb, nib 4 beak *one-dollar:* 4 buck *ten-dollar:* 7 sawbuck
billet 3 bar, bed, hut, job, rod 4 post, slab, spot 5 berth, board, house, ingot, lodge, place, put up, stick, strip 6 bestow, canton, harbor, office 7 quarter 8 domicile, position 9 entertain, situation 10 connection 11 appointment
billet-doux 8 mash note 10 love letter
billfold 6 wallet
billiards term 3 cue 4 foot, head, pool, rack, spot 5 break, carom, chalk, masse 6 bridge, cannon, corner, inning, miscue, pocket, string 7 bricole, cue ball, cushion, scratch 8 balkline, cue stick, rotation 9 eight ball 10 object ball
billingsgate 5 abuse 7 obloquy 9 contumely, invective 10 scurrility 12 vituperation
billion *British:* 8 milliard *combining form:* 4 giga
billionth *combining form:* 4 nano
bill of fare 4 menu 7 program 11 carte du jour
bill of lading 7 receipt
billy club 5 baton 6 cudgel 8 bludgeon 9 truncheon 10 knobkerrie, nightstick
bin 3 box 4 crib, vina 5 frame, pungi, stall 6 hamper, trough 9 container 10 receptacle *for coal:* 6 bunker *for fish:* 5 kench
binary 4 dual 5 duple 6 bifold, double, duplex 7 twofold 9 dualistic
bind 3 tie 4 frap, gird, tape 5 chain, dress, tie up 6 cement, enserf, fetter, ligate 7 bandage, confine, enchain, spancel 8 astringe, enfetter, ligature 9 constrict *bird's wings:* 6 pinion *to secrecy:* 4 tile, tyle *with twigs:* 5 withe
binding *combining form:* 5 desis
binge 3 bat, bum, bun, jag 4 bust, orgy, soak, tear, time, toot 5 blast, booze, drunk, fling, souse, spree 6 bender, ran-tan 7 blowoff, blowout, carouse, debauch, rampage, splurge, wassail 8 carousal, rowdydow 9 bacchanal, brannigan 11 bacchanalia, compotation
bingo 5 beano
Binnui *father:* 7 Henadad *son:* 7 Noadiah
biographer 9 memoirist *American:* 5 Weems 6 Parton 7 Freeman 8 Bradford, Sandburg *English:* 6 Aubrey, Morley, Walton 7 Boswell 8 Strachey *French:* 7 Maurois *German:* 6 Ludwig *Greek:* 8 Plutarch *Italian:* 6 Vasari *Roman:* 9 Suetonius
biography 3 bio 4 life, obit 5 diary, story 6 memoir 7 history, journal, letters, profile 8 obituary 11 confessions
biological category 5 class, genus, order 6 family, phylum 7 species, variety 10 subspecies
bionomics 7 ecology
birchbark 5 canoe
bird *African:* 4 coly, fink, taha, tock 5 paauw 6 barbet, bulbul, jabiru, quelea, whidah 7 courser, finfoot, marabou, ostrich, touraco 8 hornbill, oxpecker, parakeet, umbrette 9 beefeater, broadbill, francolin, napecrest, trochilus 10 hammerhead, tambourine *antarctic:* 4 skua 7 penguin 10 sheathbill *aquatic:* 3 auk, cob, ern, mew 4 cobb, coot, duck, erne, gony, gull, loon, skua, swan, teal, tern 5 booby, cahow, goose, grebe, murre, rotch, solan 6 fulmar, gannet, hagdon, petrel, puffin, rotche, scoter, wigeon 7 anhinga, dovekey, dovekie, finfoot, mallard, moorhen, pelican, penguin, skimmer, widgeon 8 alcatras, baldpate, dabchick, murrelet 9 albatross, cormorant, gallinule, guillemot, kittiwake 10 shearwater, sheathbill *arctic:* 3 auk 4 knot, skua, xema 5 murre, rotch 6 fulmar, jaeger, rotche 7 dovekey, dovekie 9 guillemot *Asian:* 4 kora, myna, ruff, smew 5 mynah, pewit, pitta 6 chukar, drongo, dunlin, hoopoe 7 courser, hill tit, lapwing, peacock, sirgang 8 accentor, dotterel, hornbill, parakeet, tragopan, wheatear 9 brambling, francolin *Australian:* 3 emu 4 kahu, koel, koil, lory 5 arara, galah, pitta 6 drongo, leipoa 7 boobook, bustard, figbird, waybung 8 bellbird, bush-

lark, cockatoo, lorikeet, lyrebird, manucode, megapode, morepork, parakeet 9 cassowary, coachwhip, frogmouth, pardalote ***blackbird:*** 3 ani, daw, pie 4 crow, merl, rook 5 amsel, merle, ousel, ouzel, raven 6 chough, magpie, thrush 7 grackle, jackdaw, redwing ***carrion-eating:*** 4 aura 5 urubu 6 condor 7 buzzard, vulture ***Central American:*** 4 guan, ibis 5 booby, macaw 6 barbet, jabiru, toucan 7 bittern, cotinga, jacamar, quetzal, tinamou 8 curassow, troupial ***chimney-nesting:*** 5 swift ***class:*** 4 Aves ***colony:*** 5 roost 7 rookery ***combining form:*** 5 ornis 6 ornith 7 ornitho 8 ornithes (plural) ***corvine:*** (see crow family below) ***crocodile:*** 9 trochilus ***crow family:*** 3 daw, jay, kae 4 rook 5 raven 6 chough, corbie, magpie 7 jackdaw ***diving:*** 3 auk 4 smew 5 grebe, murre 6 dipper, petrel 8 murrelet 9 guillemot, merganser ***European:*** 3 mag, mew, nun 4 clee, darr, gled, mall, merl, pope, rook, ruff, shag, smew, wren 5 amsel, crake, egret, finch, glede, merle, ousel, ouzel, pewit, pipit, terek, whaup 6 cuckoo, dunlin, hoopoe, linnet, martin, merlin, missel, redleg, roller, thrush 7 bustard, jackdaw, kestrel, lapwing, martlet, ortolan, redwing, ruddock, sparrow, wagtail, wryneck 8 accentor, blackcap, brantail, dabchick, dotterel, garganey, nightjar, nuthatch, peesweep, redstart, reedling, starling, throstle, wheatear, whimbrel, whinchat, woodcock 9 brambling, chaffinch, crossbill, fieldfare, stonechat 10 chiffchaff, goatsucker, kingfisher 11 lammergeier ***extinct:*** 3 moa 4 dodo, mamo 8 Diatryma 9 aepyornis, solitaire ***fabulous:*** 3 roc 5 hansa 6 simurg 7 phoenix, simurgh ***flightless:*** 3 emu, moa 4 dodo, kagu, kiwi, rhea, weka 6 kakapo, ratite, takahe 7 apteryx, ostrich, penguin, roatelo 8 Diatryma, notornis 9 cassowary ***fruit-eating:*** 4 coly 6 parrot, toucan ***game:*** 4 duck, guan, rail, sora, teal 5 brant, goose, quail, snipe 6 chukar, grouse, turkey 7 bustard, mallard, pintail, widgeon 8 baldpate, bobwhite, moorfowl, pheasant, shoveler, tragopan, wildfowl, woodcock 9 merganser, partridge, ptarmigan ***ground-dwelling:*** 5 colin, quail 6 grouse, peahen, turkey 7 chicken, peacock, peafowl 8 bobwhite, moorfowl, pheasant 9 partridge, ptarmigan ***Hawaiian:*** 2 io 3 ava, ioa, iwa 4 koae, mamo, moho, omao ***Indian:*** 4 baya, kala, koel, koil 5 sarus, shama 6 argala, bulbul, homrai, luggar 7 peacock 8 adjutant, amadavat, tragopan ***Jamaican:*** 7 vervain ***large:*** 3 emu, moa 4 guan 5 eagle 6 curlew, jabiru, willet 7 bustard, megapod, ostrich, pelican, seriema 8 curassow, megapode, shoebill ***largest:*** 7 ostrich ***Madagascar:*** 6 drongo 7 anhinga, kirombo, roatelo ***marsh:*** 4 coot, rail, sora 5 crane, snipe, stilt 8 reedling 9 gallinule ***Mexican:*** 6 jacana ***mythical:*** 3 roc 7 phoenix 9 fenghuang, feng-hwang ***New Zealand:*** 3 ihi, kea, poe, tui 4 huia, kaka, kaki, kiwi, koko, ruru, titi, weka 6 kakapo 7 apteryx 8 morepork, notornis ***nocturnal:*** 3 owl 5 cahow, owlet 7 bullbat, dorhawk 8 guacharo, nightjar 9 nighthawk 10 goatsucker ***North American:*** 3 ani, tit 4 coot, pape, sora, stib, wamp, wren 5 booby, colin, crane, egret, junco, murre, robin, swift, veery, vireo 6 chebec, darter, dunlin, fulmar, grouse, hagdon, phoebe, towhee, turkey, verdin, willet 7 anhinga, blue jay, catbird, flicker, grackle, tanager 8 bobolink, bobwhite, cardinal, killdeer, nuthatch, thrasher, titmouse, wheatear 9 chickadee, crossbill, nighthawk, partridge, snakebird 10 bufflehead 12 whippoorwill ***of Arabian Nights:*** 3 roc ***of brilliant plumage:*** 4 lory, toco, tody 5 macaw, pitta 6 oriole, parrot, toucan, trogon 7 jacamar, kirombo, minivet 8 lorikeet, parakeet, pheasant, tragopan ***of omen:*** 7 waybird ***of peace:*** 4 dove ***of prey:*** 3 owl 4 gled, hawk, kite 5 buteo, eagle, glead, glede, harpy 6 condor, elenet, falcon, osprey, raptor 7 buzzard, goshawk, harrier, kestrel, vulture 8 caracara 9 accipiter 11 lammergeier ***relating to:*** 5 avian, avine 8 ornithic ***shore:*** 3 auk 4 gull, ruff, tern 5 reeve, snipe, stilt 6 avocet, avoset, curlew, dunlin, plover, puffin, willet 7 lapwing, skimmer 8 dotterel, killdeer, redshank, whimbrel, woodcock 9 phalarope, sandpiper, turnstone ***small:*** 3 tit 4 tody, wren 5 finch, pewee, pipit, serin, sylph, vireo 6 canary, sappho, tomtit, verdin 7 manakin, sparrow 8 titmouse 9 chickadee ***songbird:*** 3 jay, tit 4 chat, crow, lark, wren 5 finch, mavie, mavis, pipit, robin, shama, veery, vireo 6 bulbul, canary, dipper, linnet, oriole, shrike, thrush 7 catbird, creeper, hill tit, kinglet, redwing, skylark, sparrow, swallow, tanager, titlark, wagtail, warbler, waxwing 8 accentor, amadavat, bobolink, brantail, cardinal, nuthatch, philomel, redstart, starling, thrasher, whinchat, woodlark 9 chickadee, stonechat 10 chiffchaff, flycatcher 11 nightingale ***South American:*** 3 ara, hia 4 anna, guan, jacu, loro, mitu, rhea, soco, toco, yeni 5 chaja, egret, macaw, potoo, sylph 6 chunga, cracid, jabiru, motmot, sappho, toucan 7 cariama, cotinga, hoatzin, jacamar, limpkin, manakin, seriema, tinamou 8 boatbill, caracara, curassow, guacharo, hoactzin, screamer, tapacolo, tapaculo, terutero, troupial 9 campanero, trumpeter ***talking:*** 4 myna 5 mynah 6 parrot ***tropical:*** 3 ani

6 barbet, drongo, motmot, quezal, toucan, trogon 7 cacique, hoatzin, jacamar, manakin, quetzal, sawbill, waxbill 8 guacharo, hoactzin, troupial ***turkey-like:*** 8 curassow ***unfledged:*** 4 eyas 5 chick 6 gorlin 8 nestling ***wading:*** 4 ibis, rail 5 crane, egret, heron, stork 6 godwit, jabiru, jacana 7 bittern, courlan, limpkin, tattler 8 boatbill, flamingo, shoebill, umbrette 9 spoonbill 10 hammerhead ***web-footed:*** 3 auk 4 duck, loon, swan 5 goose, murre 6 avocet, avoset, darter, fulmar, gannet, petrel, puffin 7 anhinga, pelican, penguin 8 shoveler 9 albatross, cormorant, guillemot, merganser, razorbill, snakebird 10 shearwater ***West Indian:*** 3 ani 4 tody

birdbrain 5 dummy, dunce, idiot, moron 7 dullard 8 dullhead, dumbbell 9 ignoramus, simpleton 10 rattlehead 11 featherhead

birdcage ***large:*** 6 aviary, volary, volery

birdlife 5 ornis 8 avifauna

bird pepper 8 capsicum

birds' eggs ***study of:*** 6 oology

bird's head ***top:*** 5 pilea (plural) 6 pileum

birr 3 pep 4 tuck 5 moxie, vigor 6 energy 7 potency 9 hardihood

birth 4 dawn, flow, rise, slip, stem 5 arise, issue, onset, start 6 outset, spring 7 bearing, emanate, genesis, opening, proceed 8 geniture, nascence, nascency, nativity, outstart 9 beginning, originate 10 derive from 12 commencement ***combining form:*** 4 toky

birth-control leader 6 Sanger

birth flower ***April:*** 5 daisy ***August:*** 9 gladiolus ***December:*** 10 poinsettia ***February:*** 8 primrose ***January:*** 9 carnation ***July:*** 8 sweet pea ***June:*** 4 rose ***March:*** 6 violet ***May:*** 15 lily of the valley ***November:*** 13 chrysanthemum ***October:*** 6 dahlia ***September:*** 5 aster

birthmark 4 mole 5 nevus, point, trait 7 feature 9 character

birthright 6 legacy 8 appanage, heritage 9 heritance, patrimony, privilege 10 perquisite 11 inheritance, prerogative

birthroot 8 trillium

birthstone ***April:*** 7 diamond 8 sapphire ***August:*** 7 peridot 8 sardonyx ***December:*** 6 zircon 9 turquoise ***February:*** 8 amethyst ***January:*** 6 garnet ***July:*** 4 ruby ***June:*** 5 agate, pearl 11 alexandrite ***March:*** 6 jasper 10 aquamarine, bloodstone ***May:*** 7 emerald ***November:*** 5 topaz ***October:*** 4 opal 10 tourmaline ***September:*** 8 sapphire 10 chrysolite

biscuit 3 bun 4 roll, rusk, snap 6 bisque, cookie 7 cracker 8 cracknel, hardtack ***Scottish:*** 4 bake

bishop ***district:*** 7 diocese ***headdress:*** 5 miter, mitre ***seat of office:*** 3 see ***skullcap:*** 9 zucchetto ***staff:*** 7 crosier, crozier ***throne:*** 8 cathedra

bishopric 3 see 7 diocese

bismuth ***symbol:*** 2 Bi

bison ***European:*** 6 wisent 7 aurochs ***family:*** 7 Bovidae ***North American:*** 7 buffalo

bistered 4 dark 5 brown, dusky, swart 6 brunet, swarth 7 swarthy 11 dark-skinned

bistro 4 café 6 nitery 7 cabaret, hot spot 8 nightery 9 nightclub, night spot 11 discotheque 13 watering place

bit 3 end, jot 4 atom, bite, curb, drop, iota, mite, time, whet 5 check, minim, scrap, space, speck, spell, while 6 bridle, hold in, morsel 7 inhibit, smidgen, stretch 8 fragment, hold back, hold down, molecule, mouthful, particle, restrain, withhold 9 constrain

bit by bit 9 gradually, piecemeal

bitch goddess 7 success

bite 3 cut, eat, lot 4 burn, chaw, chew, gnaw, part, tapa 5 bever, chack, champ, chomp, erode, mug-up, munch, piece, quota, scour, share, slice, smart, snack, stang, sting, tooth 6 crunch, morsel, nibble 7 corrode, eat away, partage, portion, scrunch 8 mouthful 9 allotment, allowance, masticate

Bithiah's husband 5 Mered

biting 5 crisp, nippy 7 cutting, ingoing, mordant 8 clear-cut, incisive 9 sarcastic, trenchant 11 penetrating

bitter 3 bad 4 acid, hard, tart 5 acerb, acrid, harsh, sharp 6 brutal, picric, rugged, severe, woeful 7 austere, divided, galling, hostile, painful 8 grievous, rigorous, virulent 9 alienated, amaroidal, rancorous, vexatious, vitriolic 10 afflictive, disturbing, unpleasant 11 distasteful, distressing, intemperate, unpalatable 12 antagonistic, disagreeable ***combining form:*** 4 picr 5 picro

bitterness 8 acrimony, asperity

bitterroot 7 dogbane

bitumen 3 tar 5 pitch 7 asphalt, naphtha 8 blacktop

bivalve 4 clam, spat 6 cockle, mussel, oyster, pholas 7 geoduck, goeduck, mollusk, pandora, piddock, scallop 10 brachiopod

bivouac 4 camp 6 encamp, laager, maroon 10 encampment

bizarre 3 odd 5 antic, queer, weird 7 curious, oddball, strange, unusual 8 peculiar, singular 9 fantastic, grotesque 10 outlandish

Bizet opera 6 Carmen

blab 3 gab, yak 4 chat, talk, tell 5 rumor 6 babble, betray, gabble, gossip, jabber,

reveal, tattle **7** chatter, divulge, palaver **8** disclose, give away
blabber **3** gab **4** chat **5** clack, drool, prate **6** babble, drivel, gabber, gabble, jabber, magpie, prater **7** blather, chatter, palaver, prattle, twaddle **8** jabberer, prattler **9** chatterer **10** chatterbox
blabbermouth **6** gabber, magpie, prater **7** windbag **8** jabberer, prattler **9** bandar-log **10** chatterbox
black **3** jet **4** ebon, foul, inky, noir, onyx **5** bleak, dirty, ebony, nasty, raven, sable, slate, soily, utter **6** bruise, dismal, dreary, filthy, gloomy, grubby, impure, pitchy, somber **7** contuse, piceous, squalid, unclean **8** absolute, charcoal, complete, funereal, outright **9** downright, out-and-out, pitch-dark **10** depressing, depressive, oppressive **11** atramentous, dispiriting ***combining form:*** **3** mel **4** atro, mela, melo **5** melam, melan **6** melano
blackball **4** veto **7** boycott, exclude **9** ostracize
black bass **7** sunfish **10** priestfish
black beast **4** hate **7** bugbear **8** anathema **9** bête noire **11** abomination, detestation
blackbird see at bird
black cohosh **7** bugbane
black crappie **7** sunfish **10** calico bass
black death **6** plague
black diamond **4** coal **8** hematite **9** carbonado
blacken **4** slur, soot **5** libel, smear **6** defame, malign, vilify **7** asperse, slander, traduce **10** calumniate
black eye **4** blot, onus, slur **5** mouse, odium, stain **6** shiner, stigma **11** bar sinister
blackfish **5** whale **6** bowfin, salmon, tautog **7** galjoen **8** luderick
Black Forest ***city:*** **10** Baden-Baden ***peak:*** **8** Feldberg ***river:*** **5** Rhine **6** Danube
black gold **3** oil **9** maldonite, petroleum
blackguard **4** heel **5** knave, rogue **6** rascal **7** lowlife, villain **9** miscreant, scoundrel
blackhead **4** clam **5** sebum **6** comedo, mussel **9** scaup duck
blackheart **9** sandpiper **12** whortleberry
blackjack **3** oak **6** coerce **7** tankard **9** scaup duck **10** sphalerite
black lead **8** graphite
black letter **6** Gothic **10** Old English
black magic **10** witchcraft
blackmail **6** extort **8** chantage **9** extortion
Black Muslim founder **5** Farad
black out **5** annul, erase, faint, swoon **6** cancel, delete, efface **7** expunge **10** obliterate
blackpoll **7** warbler
Black Prince **6** Edward
Blackshirt **7** fascist
blacksmith **4** fish **6** forger, plover **7** farrier, striker **10** horseshoer
blacktail **6** dassie **11** salmon trout
blackthorn **4** cane, plum **7** pear haw **8** cocktail
black vomit **11** hematemesis, yellow fever
blackwash **5** libel **6** malign, vilify **7** asperse, slander, traduce **9** denigrate **10** calumniate, scandalize, villainize
black widow **6** spider
bladder **3** sac **4** cyst **5** pouch **6** vesica **7** blister, vacuole **7** vesicae (plural), vesicle **8** vesicula **9** vesiculae (plural) ***combining form:*** **3** asc **4** asci, asco, cyst, phys **5** cysto, physo
blah **4** bosh, dull **5** hooey **6** bunkum, dreary, humbug, stodgy **7** humdrum **8** banausic, nonsense, pishposh, plodding **10** balderdash, monotonous, pedestrian
blamable see **blameworthy**
blame **3** rap **4** onus **5** fault, guilt, knock **6** accuse **7** censure, condemn **8** denounce, reproach **9** criticize, reprehend, reprobate **10** accusation, denunciate, imputation **12** condemnation, denunciation, reprehension ***Scottish:*** **4** wite, wyte **6** dirdum
blameless **4** good, pure **5** clean **8** innocent, unguilty **9** crimeless, exemplary, faultless, guiltless, lily-white, righteous **10** inculpable
blameworthy **5** amiss **6** guilty, sinful, unholy **8** culpable, faultful **10** censurable, delinquent, illaudable, punishable **13** reprehensible, uncommendable
blanch **4** pale **5** quail, start, white, wince **6** bleach, flinch, recoil, shrink, whiten **7** decolor, squinch
blanched **3** wan **4** ashy, pale **5** ashen, livid, waxen **6** doughy, pallid **9** colorless
Blancheflor's beloved **6** Flores, Floris
bland **4** flat, mild, soft **5** balmy, banal, suave, vapid **6** gentle, smooth, urbane, watery **7** insipid, lenient, sapless **8** waterish **10** namby-pamby, wishy-washy
blandish **3** con **4** coax **6** cajole **7** blarney, flatter, wheedle **8** soft-soap **9** sweet-talk
blandishment **3** oil **7** blarney, incense **8** flattery, soft soap **9** adulation
blank **4** skip **5** chasm, empty, utter **6** vacant **7** deadpan **8** absolute, omission **9** downright, out-and-out, oversight **11** preterition **12** inexpressive, unexpressive
blanket **3** cap **5** cover, crown **6** afghan, stroud **7** overlay **8** overcast **10** overspread ***Spanish:*** **6** sarape, serape
blankness **7** vacancy, vacuity **9** emptiness **11** vacuousness
blare **5** shout **6** scream, shriek
blaring **4** loud **7** roaring **8** piercing

10 stentorian 11 full-mouthed, stentorious 12 earsplitting
blarney 3 con, oil 4 coax 6 cajole 7 incense, wheedle 8 blandish, flattery, soft soap 9 adulation, sweet-talk 12 blandishment
blasé 5 jaded 7 knowing, worldly 8 mondaine 9 apathetic 11 indifferent, worldly-wise 12 disenchanted, disentranced, sophisticate 13 disillusioned, sophisticated
blaspheme 5 abuse, curse, swear 6 revile 7 profane
blasphemous 7 profane 12 sacrilegious
blasphemy 5 abuse 7 cursing, cussing, shaming 8 swearing 9 befouling, profanity, sacrilege, violation 10 execration 11 desecration, imprecation, profanation
blast 4 bang, beat, belt, boom, clap, dash, drub, ruin, slam, slug, toot, wham, whip 5 burst, crack, crash, smash, wreck 6 blight, wallop 7 destroy, lambast 8 lambaste 9 overwhelm
blat 6 cry out 7 exclaim 8 blurt out 9 ejaculate
blatant 4 loud 5 gaudy, overt 6 arrant, brassy, brazen, flashy, garish, patent, tawdry 7 glaring 8 impudent, overbold, strident 9 barefaced, clamorous, shameless, unabashed 10 boisterous, unblushing, vociferant, vociferous 11 loudmouthed 12 obstreperous
blather 4 bosh 5 drool, hokum, prate 6 babble, bunkum, drivel, gabble 7 blabber, prattle, twaddle 8 nonsense 10 balderdash, double-talk, flapdoodle
blaze 4 glow 5 blare, flame, flare, glare, shine 7 declare 8 announce, proclaim 10 incandesce 11 scintillate *Scottish:* 3 low 4 lowe
blazes 4 hell 5 abyss, hades, Sheol 6 Tophet 7 Gehenna, inferno 9 perdition
blazing 5 afire, fiery 6 aflame, alight, ardent, fervid, red-hot 7 burning, fervent, flaming, flaring, ignited 9 perfervid 10 passionate 11 conflagrant, impassioned
blazing star 8 tritonia 9 colicroot
blazon 5 sound 7 declare, publish 8 announce, proclaim 9 advertise, broadcast 10 annunciate, bruit about, promulgate
bleach 5 white 6 blanch, blench, whiten 7 decolor 8 peroxide
bleak 4 dour, grim, hard 5 harsh 6 dismal, dreary, gloomy, severe, somber 7 austere 8 funereal 9 stringent 10 depressing, oppressive 13 disheartening
blear 3 dim 4 blur, dull 5 faint, vague 7 obscure, shadowy, unclear 10 ill-defined, indistinct
bleary 3 dim 5 all in, faint, spent, vague 6 effete, used up 7 drained, far-gone, obscure, shadowy, unclear, worn-out 8 depleted 9 exhausted, washed-out 10 ill-defined, indistinct
bleat 3 baa 4 crab, fuss, yawp 5 gripe 6 squawk, yammer 7 blow off
bleed 4 ooze, seep, weep 5 exude, mulct, stick, sweat 6 fleece, strain 8 transude
bleeding heart 8 dicentra 11 sympathizer
blemish 3 mar 4 flaw, harm, hurt, scar, vice, wart 5 fault, spoil 6 blotch, damage, defect, impair, injure 7 blister, tarnish, vitiate 8 pockmark 13 disfigurement
blench 5 quail, start, white, wince 6 bleach, flinch, recoil, shrink, whiten 7 decolor, squinch
blend 3 mix 4 fuse, meld 5 alloy, immix, unify, unite 6 commix, fusion 7 amalgam, arrange, combine, mixture 8 coalesce, compound, conflate, immingle, intermix 9 commingle, composite, harmonize, integrate, interfuse 10 amalgamate, commixture, symphonize, synthesize 11 interfusion, orchestrate 12 amalgamation, intermixture
bless 4 laud 5 extol 6 hallow, praise 7 glorify 8 eulogize, sanctify 9 celebrate 10 consecrate, panegyrize
blessed 4 holy 6 sacred 7 saintly 8 hallowed 9 unprofane 10 sanctified 11 consecrated
blessedness 5 bliss 9 beatitude, happiness 12 blissfulness
blessing 2 OK 4 boon, good, okay 5 favor, grace 6 thanks 7 benefit, benison, godsend 8 approval 9 advantage 11 approbation, benediction 12 thanksgiving
blight 3 nip 4 dash, ruin 5 blast 7 disease
blimp 5 fatso, fatty 7 airship 8 zeppelin 9 dirigible
blind 4 daze, dull 5 decoy, drunk, front, shill 6 capper, dazzle 7 eyeless, muddled, shutter 8 bedazzle, unseeing 9 pixilated, shillaber, sightless 10 inebriated, lackluster, lusterless, visionless 11 intoxicated *combining form:* 5 typhl 6 typhlo
blind alley 6 pocket 7 dead end, impasse 8 cul-de-sac
blind god 4 Hoth 5 Cupid, Hoder, Hodur, Hothr
blindworm 6 lizard
blink 3 bat 4 wink 5 flash 7 flicker, nictate, twinkle 9 nictitate
blink at 4 omit 6 forget, ignore, slight 7 connive, neglect 8 discount, overlook 9 disregard
blip 3 box 4 cuff, slap 5 smack, spank 6 buffet, censor, screen 9 expurgate 10 bowdlerize
bliss 4 Zion 6 Canaan, heaven 7 elysium, nirvana 8 empyrean, paradise 9 beatitude, happiness 11 blessedness

blissful 5 happy 6 elated 8 beatific, ecstatic, euphoric 9 contented
blissfulness 7 ecstasy 8 euphoria 9 beatitude, happiness 10 exaltation 11 blessedness
blister 4 bleb, flay 5 blain, bulla, slash 6 canker, scathe, scorch 7 lambast, scarify, scourge, vesicle 8 lambaste, vesicate 9 castigate, excoriate ***combining form:*** 7 vesicul 8 vesiculo
blithe 3 gay 4 boon 5 jolly, merry, sunny 6 cheery, chirpy, jocund, jovial 7 gleeful 8 cheerful, chirrupy, mirthful, sunbeamy 9 lightsome 12 lighthearted
blithering 4 rank 5 gross, utter 7 blasted 8 absolute, outright, positive 9 downright, out-and-out
blithesome see blithe
blitz 4 raid 7 bombard 10 mass attack 11 bombardment
bloated 5 puffy 6 stuffy 7 pompous 8 arrogant 10 pontifical 11 magisterial 13 self-important
bloc 4 ring 5 party 7 combine, faction 9 coalition 11 combination
block 3 bar, dam, ell 4 clog, fill, plug, stop, wall, wing 5 annex, brake, choke, close 6 cut off, hinder, impede 7 barrier, congest, occlude, stopper 8 obstruct 9 barricade, extension, intercept
blockade 3 bar 4 stop, wall 5 beset, siege 6 invest 7 barrier, besiege 9 barricade, beleaguer, blank wall, roadblock
blockbuster 4 bomb
blockhead 4 dolt, dope 5 dunce, idiot, ninny 8 clodpate, dumbbell, numskull 9 simpleton 10 thickskull
blockheaded 4 dumb 5 dense, thick 6 stupid 7 doltish 10 numskulled
block out 5 close, draft 6 screen, shroud, sketch 7 outline, shut off 8 obstruct, skeleton 9 adumbrate 12 characterize
block up 4 clog, plug, stop
bloke 3 guy, man 4 chap, gent 6 fellow 9 gentleman
blond 4 fair 5 light, straw 6 flaxen, golden 7 towhead 8 platinum 9 towheaded
blood 4 gore 6 murder, origin 7 descent, lineage 8 ancestry 10 extraction ***cancer of:*** 8 leukemia ***cell:*** 3 red 4 poly 5 white 8 hemocyte, monocyte, platelet 9 corpuscle, leukocyte 10 lymphocyte 11 erythrocyte, granulocyte ***clot:*** 8 thrombus ***clotted:*** 4 gore ***coloring matter:*** 10 hemoglobin ***combining form:*** 3 hem 4 emia, haem, hema, hemi, hemo 5 aemia, haema, haemo, hemat, hemia 6 haemat, haemia, hemato, sangui 7 haemato 8 sanguini, sanguino ***disease:*** 6 anemia 8 leukemia 10 hemophilia ***factor:*** 2 RH ***feud:*** 8 vendetta ***fluid part:*** 5 serum 6 plasma ***of the gods:*** 5 ichor ***particle in:*** 7 embolus ***poisoning:*** 6 pyemia 7 toxemia 8 copremia, sapremia 10 septicemia ***pressure:*** 8 systolic 9 diastolic ***relating to:*** 5 hemal, hemic 7 hematal ***serum:*** 6 plasma ***study of:*** 10 hematology ***sugar:*** 7 glucose
bloodbath 7 carnage 8 butchery, massacre 9 slaughter
bloodless 4 dull, hard, pale 6 anemic, pallid, watery 8 waterish 9 insensate 10 anesthetic, insensible 11 insensitive
bloodletting 10 phlebotomy 11 venesection
bloodlike 8 hematoid
bloodline 6 family, strain
bloodroot 7 puccoon 8 turmeric 10 tetterwort 11 Indian paint
bloodshed ***place of:*** 8 aceldama
bloodstained 4 gory 7 imbrued 8 sanguine 10 sanguinary 11 ensanguined, sanguineous
bloodstone 10 chalcedony
bloodsucker 4 tick 5 lamia, leech 6 lizard, sponge 7 sponger, vampire 8 barnacle, hanger on, parasite 10 freeloader 12 lounge lizard
bloodthirsty 8 sanguine 9 homicidal, murdering, murderous 10 sanguinary 11 sanguineous
blood vessel 4 vein 5 aorta 6 artery 7 jugular 9 capillary ***combining form:*** 3 vas 4 angi, vasi, vaso 5 angio ***rupture:*** 6 rhexis
bloodwort 6 yarrow 8 centaury 10 herb robert 11 salad burnet
bloody 4 gory, grim 7 imbrued 8 sanguine 9 cutthroat, homicidal, murdering, murderous 10 sanguinary 11 ensanguined, sanguineous 12 slaughterous
bloom 4 blow, glow, posy 5 blush 6 flower 7 blossom, burgeon 10 effloresce
blooper 4 slip, trip 5 boner, break, error, fluff, gaffe, lapse 6 boo-boo, bungle 7 blunder, faux pas, mistake 8 solecism 9 indecorum 11 impropriety
blossom 3 bud 4 blow, glow, open, posy 5 bloom, blush, flush 6 flower, unfold 7 burgeon 10 effloresce
blot 4 blur, onus, slur, smut, spot 5 brand, odium, stain 6 stigma 7 bestain, blemish 8 black eye, discolor 11 bar sinister
blotch 6 macula, macule, mottle 7 splodge, splotch ***combining form:*** 5 macul 6 maculi, maculo
blot out 5 abate, annul, erase 6 cancel, delete, efface 7 abolish, expunge 9 eradicate, extirpate 10 annihilate, extinguish, obliterate 11 exterminate
blouse 5 middy, shirt, smock, tunic 6 basque, guimpe

bloviate 4 rant, rave 5 mouth, orate 7 declaim, soapbox 8 harangue, perorate
blow 3 bop, fan, hit, jar 4 bang, bash, belt, biff, brag, bump, cuff, gasp, gust, huff, jolt, pant, puff, slam, slug, swat, whop, wind 5 bloom, boast, break, crack, pound, prate, punch, shock, slosh, smack, smash, vaunt, waste, whack 6 flower, impact, ruffle, thwack, wallop, winnow 7 blossom, burgeon, consume, fritter, respite 8 breather, knockout, outbloom, squander 9 bastinado, collision, dissipate, gasconade, throw away 10 concussion, effloresce, frivol away, percussion, trifle away 11 rodomontade
blow-by-blow 6 minute 8 detailed, itemized, thorough 9 clocklike 10 particular
blowhard see boaster
blow in 4 come 6 arrive, show up, turn up
blowout 4 bash 6 shindy 7 shindig
blowsy 5 dowdy 6 frowsy, sordid 8 slattern 10 slatternly 13 draggletailed
blow up 4 boil, burn, fume, rage 5 anger, burst, go off 6 seethe 7 bristle, explode 8 boil over, detonate, disprove, dynamite 9 discredit
blowy 4 airy 5 gusty, windy 6 breezy
blubber 3 cry, sob 4 pipe, wail, weep 6 boohoo
bludgeon 3 bat 4 club 5 baton, billy, bully 6 cudgel, hector 7 bluster, war club 8 browbeat, bulldoze, bullyrag 9 bastinado, billy club, strong-arm, truncheon 10 intimidate, nightstick *British:* 4 cosh
blue 3 low, sea 4 down, racy 5 ocean, salty, shady, spicy 6 purple, risqué, wicked 7 profane 8 dejected, downcast, off-color 9 depressed, woebegone 10 dispirited, suggestive 11 downhearted 12 disconsolate *combining form:* 3 ind 4 cyan, indi, indo 5 cyano *dark:* 5 perse 6 indigo *grayish:* 5 merle, slate 7 celeste *greenish:* 4 aqua, bice, cyan, teal 5 beryl 6 cobalt 7 azurite 8 calamine 9 turquoise *moderate:* 5 copen *reddish:* 5 smalt 6 marine, purple, violet 7 cyanine, gentian, lobelia 8 mazarine *sky:* 5 azure 8 cerulean
___ Blue 3 Ben
blue blood 5 elite 6 aristo, gentry 7 aristoi 9 gentility, gentleman, patrician 10 aristocrat, upper class 11 aristocracy
bluebonnet 4 Scot 6 parrot 10 cornflower
Blue Boy painter 12 Gainsborough
bluecoat 3 cop 5 bobby 6 copper 8 Dogberry 9 constable, policeman
blue-eyed 8 favorite, precious 10 fair-haired
Bluegrass State 8 Kentucky
Blue Grotto site 5 Capri
bluejacket 6 sailor
blue jeans 6 denims
blue moon 3 age, eon 4 aeon 7 dog's age 8 coon's age, eternity 12 donkey's years
bluenose 4 prig 5 prude 7 puritan 8 comstock 9 Mrs. Grundy, nice Nelly 10 goody-goody
bluenosed 4 prig, prim 6 prissy, stuffy 7 prudish 8 priggish 9 Victorian 10 tight-laced 11 puritanical, straitlaced
blue-pencil 4 edit 6 delete, revise
bluepoint 6 oyster
blueprint 4 cast, plan 5 chart 6 design, devise, scheme, sketch 7 arrange, outline, project 8 game plan, strategy
blue-ribbon 3 top 5 prime 6 Grade A 7 capital 8 five-star, top-notch 9 excellent, first-rate, top-drawer 10 first-class 11 first-string
blues 5 dumps, gloom 7 dismals, sadness 9 dejection 10 depression, melancholy 11 unhappiness 12 mournfulness
bluff 3 act 4 curt, fake, fool, sham 5 blunt, feign, frank, gruff, rough, sharp, trick 6 abrupt, affect, assume, betray, candid, crusty, delude, direct, humbug, illude, snippy 7 beguile, brusque, deceive, mislead, pretend 8 snippety 9 outspoken 10 forthright, no-nonsense 11 counterfeit, double cross, plainspoken, short-spoken
blunder 4 bull, goof, mess, slip, trip 5 boner, botch, error, fluff, gaffe, gum up, lapse 6 bobble, bollix, bumble, bungle, goof up 7 blooper, louse up, mistake, stumble 8 flounder
blunderbuss 3 gun 7 bungler, firearm
blunt 4 bald, curt, dull, mull, numb 5 bluff, brief, gruff, short 6 abrupt, benumb, crusty, deaden, obtund, obtuse, snippy, snubby, weaken 7 brusque, cripple, disable, disedge, stupefy 8 enfeeble, hebetate, snippety 9 attenuate, undermine 10 debilitate 11 desensitize 12 unstrengthen
blur 3 dim, fog 4 blot, dull, mist, onus, slur, spot 5 befog, blear, brand, cloud, muddy, odium, smear, stain, taint 6 smudge, stigma 7 becloud, besmear, confuse, tarnish 8 besmirch, black eye, discolor 11 bar sinister *in printing:* 6 mackle
blurb 2 ad 4 plug, puff 6 notice 7 puffing, write-up 12 commendation
blurt 4 blat, bolt 6 cry out 7 exclaim 9 ejaculate
blush 4 glow, rose 5 bloom, color, flush, rouge 6 mantle, pinken, redden 7 blossom, crimson, roseate
bluster 4 bawl, huff, rage, roar, rout 5 blast, bully, storm 6 bellow, clamor, hector 7 dragoon 8 bludgeon, browbeat, bulldoze, bullyrag 10 intimidate
blustery 4 wild 5 rough 6 raging, stormy

7 furious 8 stormful 9 turbulent 11 tempestuous
boa 5 scarf, snake
board 4 slab 5 get on, house, lodge, put up, table 6 bestow, billet, embark, harbor 7 emplane, entrain, quarter ***artist's:*** 7 palette
board game see at game
boarding house 7 pension 8 pensione
boardwalk 9 promenade
boast 4 blow, brag, crow, puff 5 exalt, mouth, prate, preen, vaunt 7 bluster, show off, swagger 9 gasconade 11 rodomontade
boaster 6 blower, gascon 7 bragger, vaunter 8 blowhard, braggart, puckfist, rodomont 11 braggadocio, rodomontade
boastful 6 braggy 8 arrogant, braggart, vaunting 9 big-headed, conceited 11 pretentious, rodomontade 12 braggadocian, vainglorious 13 swelled-headed ***Scottish:*** 6 vaunty
boat 3 ark 4 ship 6 vessel 7 steamer ***above-water:*** 9 hydrofoil ***Arab:*** 4 dhow ***bottom projection:*** 4 keel ***British:*** 5 coble 6 wherry 7 coracle ***Canadian:*** 6 bateau ***canoe-like:*** 7 pirogue ***captain:*** 7 skipper ***cargo:*** 3 hoy 4 scow 5 barge 6 wherry 7 drogher, gabbard, gabbart, lighter 8 canaller ***Chinese:*** 4 junk 6 sampan ***dock, basin:*** 6 marina ***Dutch:*** 6 dogger, hooker, schuit, schuyt 8 bilander ***Egyptian:*** 6 sandal 8 dahabeah ***Eskimo:*** 5 kayak, umiak 6 oomiak 7 bidarka 8 bidarkee ***fishing:*** 4 dory 5 coble, smack 6 dogger, lugger 7 caravel, coracle, tartana, trawler ***flat-bottomed:*** 4 dory, keel, punt, scow 5 barge, coble 6 bateau, bugeye 7 lighter, pontoon ***French:*** 7 caravel ***front end of:*** 3 bow 4 fore, prow ***hide-covered:*** 7 coracle ***Indian:*** 4 doni 5 dhoni 7 masoola ***Indonesian:*** 4 prao, prau, proa 5 prahu ***Irish:*** 7 currach, curragh ***Italian:*** 7 gondola ***landing:*** 3 LST ***Levantine:*** 4 saic 6 caique ***mail:*** 6 packet ***Mediterranean:*** 6 settee ***motor:*** 7 cruiser, inboard 8 outboard, runabout ***narrow:*** 4 punt 5 canoe, scull, shell 7 gondola 8 canaller ***Nile river:*** 6 sandal 8 dahabeah ***on a ship:*** 3 gig 5 jolly 6 launch 7 pinnace ***Philippine:*** 5 banca, casco ***pole-propelled:*** 4 punt 7 gondola ***Polynesian:*** 4 pahi ***race:*** 7 regatta ***racing:*** 3 gig 5 scull, shell, yacht 6 torpid ***rear end of:*** 3 aft 5 stern ***river:*** 4 scow 5 barge, canoe, ferry 6 packet, sampan, wherry ***round:*** 4 gufa 5 goofa, guffa 6 goofah ***rowing:*** 4 dory 5 coble, scull, shell, skiff 6 caique, dinghy, randan ***sailing:*** 4 yawl 5 ketch, skiff, sloop, smack, yacht 6 cutter, lateen, lugger, settee 7 pinnace 8 lateener, schooner ***Scandinavian:*** 4 pram 5 praam ***Scottish:*** 5 coble 7 currach, curragh, gabbard, gabbart ***scouting:*** 7 vedette, vidette ***small:*** 3 cog 4 dory 5 coble, skiff 6 bugeye, cockle, dinghy 7 coracle, shallop ***song:*** 9 barcarole 10 barcarolle ***three-hulled:*** 8 trimaran ***three-oared:*** 6 randan ***towing:*** 3 tug ***twin-hulled:*** 9 catamaran ***two-masted:*** 4 yawl 5 ketch 8 schooner
boatman 5 poler 6 Charon 7 oarsman, paddler 8 deckhand 9 gondolier
boat-shaped 8 scaphoid 9 cymbiform, navicular ***combining form:*** 5 scaph 6 scapho ***ornament:*** 3 nef
boatswain 4 bos'n 5 bosun 6 jaeger 10 tropic bird
Boaz's wife 4 Ruth
bob 3 jig, nod, rap, tap 4 buff, crop, dock 5 bunch, float, gigue 6 weight 7 cluster, nosegay
bobbery 3 row 4 fray 5 brawl, fight, melee 6 affray, fracas, hubbub 7 ruction 10 donnybrook 11 disturbance
bobbin 4 pirn 5 quill, spool 7 spindle
bobble 4 mess 5 botch, gum up 6 bollix, bungle, goof up 7 louse up
bobby 6 copper, peeler 7 officer 9 constable, policeman
bobwhite 5 quail 9 partridge
Boccaccio ***beloved:*** 9 Fiammetta ***tales:*** 9 Decameron
bode 4 omen 5 augur 7 betoken, portend, presage, promise 8 foreshow 9 foretoken 10 foreshadow
bodement 4 omen 6 augury 7 portent, presage 9 foretoken 10 prognostic
bodiless 9 asomatous, unfleshly 10 discarnate, immaterial, unphysical 11 disembodied, incorporeal 13 insubstantial
bodily 6 carnal 7 fleshly, sensual, somatic 8 corporal, physical 9 corporeal
body 4 bulk, core, mass, mort, pith, soma 5 array, batch, bunch, clump, group, stiff, stock, torso 6 amount, budget, bundle, burden, corpse, corpus, object, parcel, staple, upshot, volume 7 cadaver, carcass, cluster, corpora (plural), purport, quantum, remains 8 physique, quantity 9 aggregate, substance ***combining form:*** 4 dema, soma, some, somi (plural) 5 somat, somia, somus 6 somata (plural), somato ***suffix:*** 2 cy
body cavity 5 cecum, sinus 6 coelom 7 abdomen 8 hemocoel
body check 5 block
bodyguard 9 attendant, protector
body of water 3 bay, sea 4 gulf, lake, pond, pool 5 bight, brook, creek, fiord, firth, fjord, inlet, ocean, river 6 lagoon 7 channel, estuary 9 reservoir
body passage 4 duct, iter, vein 5 canal 6 artery, meatus, vessel 7 trachea
body politic 5 state 6 nation

boeotian 4 boob 7 Babbitt 10 middle-brow, philistine
bog 3 fen 4 mire, quag 5 marsh, swamp 6 morass 8 quagmire 9 swampland *combining form:* 4 helo
Bogart film 6 Sahara 7 Dead End, Sabrina 8 Key Largo 10 Casablanca, High Sierra 11 The Big Sleep
bog down 5 delay 6 detain, hang up, retard, slow up 7 set back, slacken 10 decelerate
bogey 5 ghost, shade, spook 6 spirit, wraith 7 phantom, specter 8 revenant 10 apparition
boggle 3 gag, jib, shy 4 balk, mess 5 botch, demur, gum up, stick 6 bollix, bungle, cobble, goof up, strain 7 louse up, nonplus, scruple, stagger, stickle, stumble 9 dumbfound
bogus 4 fake, sham 5 false, phony, snide 6 forged, pseudo 8 spurious 9 brummagem, imitation, pinchbeck 11 counterfeit
Boheme, La *character:* 4 Mimi 7 Rodolfo *composer:* 7 Puccini *setting:* 5 Paris
Bohemian 7 beatnik, dropout 8 maverick 9 eccentric 10 iconoclast 13 nonconformist
bohunk 3 oaf 4 gawk, lout, lump 5 klutz 6 lubber, lummox 7 palooka
boil 4 bolt, burn, dash, fume, race, rage, rush, stew 5 anger, churn, fling, poach, shoot 6 blow up, bubble, charge, coddle, pimple, seethe, simmer 7 abscess, bristle, ferment, flare up, pustule, smolder 8 furuncle 9 carbuncle
boil down 8 simplify 10 streamline
boiled *combining form:* 5 cocto
boiler suit 8 coverall
boiling 3 hot 5 fiery 6 baking, red-hot 7 burning 8 scalding, sizzling 9 scorching 10 blistering
boil over 4 burn, fume, rage 5 anger 6 blow up, seethe 7 bristle, flare up
boisterous 5 noisy, rowdy 6 unruly 7 blatant, raucous, riotous 8 rowdyish, strident 9 clamorous, termagant, turbulent 10 disorderly, rollicking, rowdydowdy, tumultuous, vociferant, vociferous 11 loudmouthed, openmouthed 12 obstreperous, rambunctious
Boito opera 11 Mefistofele
bold 4 pert, wise 5 bluff, brave, fresh, nervy, sassy, saucy 6 brazen, cheeky 7 doughty, forward, valiant 8 fearless, impudent, insolent, intrepid, unafraid 9 audacious, dauntless, undaunted 10 courageous, procacious 11 impertinent, smart-alecky 12 contumelious
boldhearted 5 brave 7 doughty, valiant 8 fearless, intrepid, unafraid 9 audacious, dauntless, undaunted 10 courageous
boldness 4 gall 5 nerve 7 chutzpa 8 audacity, chutzpah, temerity 9 hardihood, impudence, insolence, insolency 10 brazenness, disrespect 12 impertinence
Bolero composer 5 Ravel
Bolivia *capital:* 5 La Paz, Sucre *monetary unit:* 4 peso
bollix 4 flub, mess 5 botch, gum up 6 bobble, bungle, fumble, goof up 7 louse up
Bolshevik 3 Red 6 commie 7 comrade 9 communist
bolshevism 9 communism
bolster 4 prop 5 brace, carry 6 bear up, buoy up, upbear, uphold 7 shore up, support, sustain 8 backstop, buttress 9 reinforce, underprop 10 strengthen
bolt 3 fly, run 4 cram, dash, flee, gulp, jump, lash, race, rush, tear 5 chase, rivet, scoot, shoot, skirr, slosh, start 6 charge, cry out, englut, gobble, guzzle, spring 7 exclaim, kingpin, make off, scamper, startle 8 blurt out 9 ejaculate, skedaddle 11 ingurgitate 13 thunderstroke
bomb 3 dud 4 bust, flop 5 blitz, lemon, loser, shell 7 failure 9 cannonade
bombard 4 pelt 5 blitz, shell 6 strike 7 assault 9 cannonade
bombardment 4 hail 5 burst, salvo 6 shower, volley 7 barrage 8 drumfire 9 broadside, cannonade, fusillade
bombardon 4 bass 7 helicon 8 bass tuba
bombast 4 rant 7 fustian 8 rhapsody, rhetoric, tumidity 9 turgidity 11 highfalutin, rodomontade
bombastic 7 aureate, flowery, swollen 8 sonorous 9 overblown 10 euphuistic, rhetorical 11 declamatory 12 magniloquent 13 grandiloquent
bombed 5 drunk 11 intoxicated
bombinate 3 hum 4 buzz 5 drone, strum, thrum 6 bumble
bombshell 8 surprise
bomb shelter 4 abri
bona fide 4 real, true 7 genuine 9 authentic, undoubted, veritable 10 sure-enough 11 indubitable
bona fides 9 good faith, sincerity 11 sincereness
bonanza 4 mine 8 eldorado, Golconda, gold mine, treasury 13 treasure trove
bonbon 5 candy 7 fondant 8 confetti (plural), confetto
bond 3 tie 4 bail, knot, link, pact, yoke 5 nexus 6 surety 7 bargain, compact 8 adhesion, clinging, cohesion, contract, covenant, guaranty, ligament, ligature, security, stickage, sticking, vinculum, warranty 9 adherence, agreement, coherence, guarantee 10 connection, connective, convention 11 transaction *combining form:* 4 desm 5 desmo

bondage 4 yoke 6 thrall 7 helotry, peonage, serfage, serfdom, slavery 9 servility, servitude, thralldom, villenage 11 enslavement, subjugation
bondsman 5 slave 7 chattel 9 mancipium
bone ***ankle:*** 5 talus 6 tarsus ***arm:*** 4 ulna 6 radius 7 humerus ***back:*** 5 spine 8 vertebra 9 vertebrae (plural) ***breast:*** 7 sternum ***calf:*** 6 fibula ***cavity:*** 5 fossa ***change into:*** 6 ossify ***cheek:*** 5 malar 6 zygoma ***chest:*** 3 rib ***collar:*** 8 clavicle ***combining form:*** 3 ost 4 osse, ossi, oste 5 osseo, osteo 6 osteon, osteus ***face:*** 5 malar, nasal 7 frontal 8 temporal ***finger:*** 7 phalanx 8 phalange ***foot:*** 6 tarsus 9 calcaneum, calcaneus 10 astragalus, metatarsus ***hand:*** 10 metacarpus ***head:*** 5 skull, vomer 7 cranium 8 parietal, sphenoid 9 occipital ***heel:*** 9 calcaneum, calcaneus ***hip:*** 5 ilium, pubis 6 pelvis 7 ischium ***jaw:*** 7 maxilla 8 mandible ***kneecap:*** 7 patella ***Latin:*** 2 os 5 ossa (plural) ***leg:*** 5 femur, tibia 6 fibula 7 patella ***lower back:*** 6 coccyx, sacrum ***middle ear:*** 5 anvil, incus 6 hammer, stapes 7 malleus, stirrup ***relating to:*** 6 osteal ***shin:*** 5 tibia ***shoulder blade:*** 7 scapula ***small:*** 7 ossicle ***thigh:*** 5 femur ***toe:*** 7 phalanx 8 phalange ***U-shaped:*** 5 hyoid ***wrist:*** 6 carpus
bonehead 5 dunce 8 clodpate, numskull 10 thick-skull
bone-like 7 osseous, osteoid
boner see **blooper**
bone up 4 cram 5 study 6 review
bong 4 bell, peal, ring, toll 5 chime, knell
boniface 8 publican, taverner 9 barkeeper, innholder, innkeeper, saloonist 12 saloonkeeper
bonkers 5 crazy 6 insane
bonny 4 fair 6 comely, lovely, pretty 9 beauteous, beautiful 10 attractive 11 good-looking
bon vivant 7 epicure, gourmet 8 gourmand 10 gastronome 11 gastronomer 12 gastronomist, man-about-town
bon voyage 8 farewell, good trip
bony 4 lank, lean 5 gaunt, lanky, spare 6 skinny 7 angular, scraggy, scrawny 8 rawboned
boo 4 hiss, hoot, razz 5 bazoo 7 catcall 8 cannabis 9 marijuana, raspberry
boob 3 oaf 4 dolt, goof, goon 5 chump, dunce 7 Babbitt, fathead 8 boeotian, dolthead, lunkhead 10 middlebrow, philistine
boo-boo see **blooper**
booby hatch 6 asylum 8 loony bin, madhouse, nuthouse 9 funny farm
booby trap 7 pitfall, springe 8 deadfall, trapfall
boodle 4 bilk, loot, mint 5 booty, cheat, cozen, prize, spoil 6 bundle, chisel, chouse, diddle, packet 7 defraud, fortune, plunder 8 flimflam 10 plunderage
boohoo 3 cry, sob 4 blub, wail, weep 7 blubber
book 4 list, tome 5 album, codex, novel, tract 6 enroll, folder, manual, scroll, volume 7 catalog, edition, leaflet, reserve, writing 8 brochure, hardback, inscribe, pamphlet, schedule, softback, treatise 9 monograph, preengage 10 compendium 11 publication ***combining form:*** 6 biblio ***of psalms:*** 7 psalter ***of public records:*** 5 liber
bookdealer 10 bibliopole 11 bouquiniste
bookie see **bookmaker**
bookish 7 learned 8 academic, literary, pedantic 9 scholarly
bookkeeping term 4 loss 5 asset, audit, check, debit, entry 6 budget, credit, income, ledger, profit 7 account, balance, expense, invoice, voucher 8 discount, interest 9 liability 12 depreciation
bookmaker 6 binder, bookie, editor 7 printer 9 publisher
book of account 6 ledger, record 7 journal 8 register
bookplate 5 label 8 ex libris
bookstall 5 kiosk 9 newsstand
boom 4 bang, clap, slam, wham 5 blast, burst, crack, crash, smash 7 thunder 10 prosperity
boomerang 8 backfire, backlash, kick back 10 bounce back
booming 6 robust 7 roaring, thrifty 8 thriving 10 prospering, prosperous 11 flourishing
boon 4 gift, good 5 favor, jolly, merry 6 blithe, jocund, jovial 7 benefit, festive, gleeful, godsend, largess, present 8 blessing, mirthful 9 advantage 10 blithesome 11 benediction, benevolence
boondocks 6 sticks 8 backland, backwash, frontier 9 backwater, backwoods 10 hinterland 11 backcountry
boor 3 oaf 4 lout 5 chuff, churl, clown, yahoo, yokel 6 lummox, mucker, rustic 7 buffoon, bumpkin, grobian, peasant 10 clodhopper
boorish 4 rude 6 coarse, rugged, vulgar 7 ill-bred, loutish, lowbred, lumpish, uncivil 8 churlish, cloddish, clownish, impolite, lubberly, swainish 9 graceless, tasteless, unrefined 10 robustious, uncultured, ungracious, unpolished 11 clodhopping, ill-mannered, uncivilized
boost 2 up 3 wax 4 hike, jump, plug, push, rise 5 put up, raise 6 beef up, expand, extend, jack up 7 augment, enlarge, magnify, promote, upgrade 8 heighten, increase, multiply 9 advertise 10 aggrandize 12 breakthrough

boot 2 ax 4 bang, fire, kick, sack, tyro 5 chase, chuck, eject, evict 6 bounce, novice, rookie, thrill 7 dismiss, extrude, kick out 8 beginner, freshman, neophyte, throw out 9 discharge, terminate 10 apprentice, tenderfoot ***kind:*** 5 kamik, wader 6 arctic, chukka, crakow, gaiter, galosh, golosh, mucluc, mukluk 7 bottine, cothurn, gambado, jodhpur, shoepac 8 balmoral, cothurni (plural), muckluck, overshoe, shoepack 9 cothurnus 10 Wellington ***Scottish:*** 8 gamashes (plural)

Boötes star 8 Arcturus

booth 5 kiosk, stall, stand

boot hill 8 cemetery 9 graveyard 12 burial ground

bootleg 3 run 5 hooch 7 smuggle 9 moonshine 10 bathtub gin, contraband 11 mountain dew

bootless 4 vain 6 futile 7 useless 8 abortive 9 fruitless 10 profitless, unavailing 11 ineffective, ineffectual 12 unproductive, unprofitable

bootlick 4 fawn 5 cower, toady 6 cringe, grovel, kowtow 7 truckle 9 brownnose 11 apple-polish

bootlicker 4 toad 5 toady 7 spaniel 8 lickspit 9 sycophant, toadeater 11 lickspittle

booty 4 loot, swag 5 prize, spoil 6 boodle 7 plunder 10 plunderage

booze 3 jag 4 grog, swig 5 binge, drink, hooch, sauce, souse, swill 6 bender, guzzle, imbibe, liquor, tipple 7 carouse, spirits, swizzle 8 liquor up 9 aqua vitae, brannigan, firewater

boozehound 4 lush, wino 5 drunk 6 sponge 7 guzzler 8 drunkard 9 inebriate

boozer see boozehound

bop 3 bat 4 bash, belt, biff, blow, sock, whop 5 pound, smack

borax 6 tincal

Bordeaux wine ***district:*** 5 Medoc 6 Graves ***grape:*** 6 Malbec, Merlot 8 Cabernet ***name:*** 5 Arsac, Ludon, Macau 6 Moulis 7 Labarde, Margaux, Pomerol 8 Cantenac, Pauillac 9 St. Julien, St. Emilion, St. Estephe, St. Laurent ***red:*** 6 claret

bordello see brothel

border 3 hem, lip, rim 4 abut, brim, edge, join, line 5 bound, brink, flank, frame, march, marge, skirt, touch, verge 6 adjoin, butt on, define, fringe, limbus, margin, trench 7 outline, selvage 8 approach, befringe, boundary, frontier, neighbor, sideline, surround 9 marchland, perimeter, periphery 11 butt against, communicate ***embroidered:*** 6 orfray 7 orphrey ***inlaid:*** 8 purfling ***raised:*** 7 coaming

bordereau 4 note 10 memorandum

bordering 8 abutting, adjacent, touching 9 adjoining 10 approximal, contiguous, juxtaposed 12 conterminous

borderland 5 march 8 frontier 9 marchland

borderline 7 unclear 8 doubtful 9 ambiguous, dubitable, equivocal, uncertain, undecided, unsettled 11 problematic

border line 8 boundary 11 demarcation

border state 8 Delaware, Kentucky, Maryland, Missouri, Virginia

bore 4 gape, gawk, gaze, pall, peer, ream, tire 5 auger, drill, ennui, glare, gloat, prick, punch, stare, weary 6 goggle, wimble 7 fatigue 8 puncture 9 perforate

boreal 3 icy 4 cold, cool 5 chill, gelid 6 arctic, chilly, frosty 7 glacial 8 freezing

Boreas ***beloved:*** 8 Orithyia ***brother:*** 5 Notus 8 Hesperus, Zephyrus ***father:*** 8 Astraeus ***mother:*** 3 Eos ***son:*** 5 Zetes 6 Calais

boredom 4 yawn 5 ennui 6 tedium 7 fatigue 8 doldrums 9 weariness

borer ***combining form:*** 6 trypan 7 trypano

Borgia 6 Alonso, Cesare 7 Rodrigo 8 Lucrezia

boring 4 dull 6 dreary, stodgy, tiring 7 humdrum, irksome, tedious 8 drudging, tiresome 10 monotonous

born 3 née 6 inbred 7 built-in 8 inherent 9 intrinsic 10 congenital, deep-seated, ingenerate ***combining form:*** 3 gen 4 gene 6 genous 7 genetic

borne by the wind 5 eolic 6 aeolic, eolian 7 aeolian

Borodin opera 10 Prince Igor

borough 4 burg, town 5 burgh 7 village 8 township ***Scottish:*** 5 brugh

bosh see bunkum

bosom 4 soul 5 heart 6 breast

bosomy 5 busty, buxom 6 chesty

boss 4 head 5 chief 6 honcho, leader, master, survey 7 headman, oversee 8 chaperon, hierarch, overlook, superior 9 chieftain, dominator, supervise 11 quarterback, superintend ***African:*** 5 bwana

bossy 8 imperial 9 imperious, masterful 10 high-handed, imperative, peremptory 11 domineering, magisterial, overbearing

botanist ***American:*** 4 Gray (Asa) 5 Sears (Paul B.) 6 Bailey (Liberty), Bessey (Charles), Carver (George W.) 7 Bartram (John), Burbank (Luther) 9 Fairchild (David) ***Austrian:*** 6 Mendel (Gregor) ***British:*** 6 Sloane (Sir Hans) ***Danish:*** 7 Warming (Johannes) ***Dutch:*** 2 De Vries (Hugo) ***German:*** 4 Cohn (Ferdinand), Mohl (Hugo Von) 5 Sachs (Julius von) ***Irish:*** 6 Harvey (William) ***Scottish:*** 5 Brown (Robert) ***Swedish:*** 8 Linnaeus (Carolus) ***Swiss:*** 6 Nageli (Karl) 8 Candolle (Augustin)

botany branch 8 algology, bryology, mycology 9 phycology 10 palynology 11 hydroponics, pteridology 12 bacteriology
botch 3 dub 4 blow, flub, mess, muck, muff, mull, muss 5 fluff, gum up, mix-up, spoil 6 bobble, boggle, bollix, bumble, bungle, cobble, foozle, fumble, goof up, mess up, mucker, muddle 7 blunder, louse up 8 bugger up, shambles 9 mishandle, mismanage 10 misconduct
botchy 5 messy 6 sloppy, untidy 8 careless, slapdash, slipshod, slovenly 10 unthorough
both *combining form:* 3 bis *prefix:* 4 ambi, amph 5 amphi
bother 3 bug, irk, vex 4 fret, pest 5 annoy, chafe, upset 6 abrade, flurry, harass, pester, plague, ruffle 7 agitate, disturb, fluster, perturb, provoke, unhinge 8 disquiet, irritant, nuisance 9 annoyance, besetment 10 discompose 11 aggravation 12 exasperation 13 inconvenience
botheration 4 pest 6 pester, plague 8 irritant, nuisance 9 annoyance, besetment 11 aggravation 12 exasperation
Botswana *capital:* 8 Gaborone *monetary unit:* 4 pula
bottle 4 vial 5 ampul, cruet, cruse, flask, phial 6 ampule, carafe, fiasco, flacon, magnum, vessel 8 decanter, jeroboam 9 container *baby's:* 6 nurser
bottle gourd 8 calabash
bottleneck 7 impasse 8 obstruct, paralyze, slowdown, throttle
bottom 3 bed 4 base, foot, seat, sole 5 basal, basic, fanny, found, hiney, nadir 6 behind, breech, heinie, lowest 7 bedrock, essence, footing, primary, rear end 8 backside, buttocks, derriere 9 establish, lowermost, posterior, predicate, underbody, undermost, underside 10 foundation, nethermost, underlying, underneath 11 fundamental 12 foundational, quintessence, substructure, undersurface
bottom dog 4 prey 6 victim 8 casualty
bottomless 4 deep 7 abysmal 8 baseless 9 plumbless, soundless, unfounded 10 fathomless, gratuitous, groundless, ungrounded 11 plummetless, uncalled-for, unwarranted 12 unfathomable
bottommost 6 lowest 9 lowermost, undermost 10 nethermost
bough 4 limb 6 branch
boulevard 3 way 4 path, road 5 track 6 artery, avenue, street 7 highway 12 thoroughfare
boulevardier 7 flaneur, trifler 9 bon vivant 12 man-about-town
bounce 2 ax 3 hop 4 fire, jump, leap, sack 5 bound, vault 6 hurdle, spring 7 boot out, dismiss, kick out, saltate 9 discharge, terminate
bounce back 7 rebound, recover 8 backfire, backlash 9 boomerang
bounce off 5 carom
bouncer 4 goon 7 chucker 8 houseman 9 muscleman, strong arm
bouncy 4 airy 7 buoyant, elastic 8 volatile 9 expansive, resilient 12 effervescent
bound 3 end, hem, hop, rim 4 edge, jump, leap, term 5 limit, skirt, vault, verge 6 border, bounce, define, demark, finite, fringe, hurdle, margin, spring 7 delimit, limited, mark out, measure, saltate 8 articled, confines, surround 9 demarcate, determine 10 delimitate, indentured, limitation 11 apprenticed
boundary 5 ambit 6 limits 7 compass 8 confines, environs, purlieus 9 precincts
bounder 3 cad, cur 6 rotter
boundless 7 endless 8 infinite 9 limitless, unlimited 10 indefinite, unmeasured 11 measureless 12 immeasurable
bounteous 4 free 5 ample 6 plenty 7 copious, liberal 8 abundant, generous, handsome 9 plenteous, plentiful, unsparing 10 freehanded, munificent, openhanded
bountiful see bounteous
Bounty captain 5 Bligh
bouquet 4 balm, kudo, posy 5 aroma, scent, spice 7 corsage, garland, incense, nosegay, orchids, perfume 9 fragrance, redolence 10 compliment 11 arrangement, boutonniere
bourgeois 10 philistine 11 middle-class 12 capitalistic
bourgeoisie 11 middle class
bout 4 tour, turn 5 shift, siege, spell, stint, trick
bovine 2 ox 3 cow, yak 4 anoa, bull, calf, gaur, neat, zebu 5 bison, gayal, steer, stirk 6 catalo, cattle, wisent 7 aurochs, banteng, buffalo, bullock, cattalo 8 longhorn *genus:* 3 Bos *sound:* 3 low, moo
bow 3 arc 4 arch, bend, lout, turn 5 angle, crook, curve, defer, round, yield 6 congee, curtsy, salaam, submit 7 flexure, succumb, turning 8 flection 9 curvation, curvature 10 capitulate 11 buckle under 12 knuckle under
bowdlerize 4 blip 6 censor, screen 9 expurgate
bowed 4 bent 5 arced, bandy, round 6 arched, curved 7 arrondi, rounded 8 arciform 9 bowlegged 11 bandy-legged, curvilinear *combining form:* 3 tox 4 toxi, toxo
bowel 3 gut 4 draw 6 paunch 10 eviscerate, exenterate
bower 5 arbor 7 pergola
bowery 7 skid row 8 skid road
bowfin 7 mudfish

bowl 5 arena, basin, jorum, mazer, stade 6 tureen, vessel 7 stadium 8 coliseum ***ornamental:*** 5 tazza
bowlegged 5 bandy
bowler 3 hat 5 derby 6 kegler 7 kegeler
Bowl game 3 Sun (El Paso) 4 Rose (Pasadena) 5 Aloha (Honolulu), Gator (Jacksonville), Peach (Atlanta), Pecan (Abilene), Sugar (New Orleans), Super 6 Cotton (Dallas), Fiesta (Tempe), Orange (Miami), Senior (Mobile) 7 Holiday (San Diego), Liberty (Memphis) 10 Bluebonnet (Houston), California (Fresno) 12 Independence (Shreveport) 7 Florida Citrus (Orlando)
bowling 7 kegling 8 kegeling ***British:*** 8 skittles ***Italian:*** 5 bocce, bocci 6 boccia, boccie ***term:*** 3 pin 4 hook, lane, spot 5 curve, frame, spare, split 6 gutter, strike, string, turkey 7 duckpin 9 candlepin
bowl over 3 wow 4 stun 5 floor 6 dismay 8 surprise 9 overwhelm 10 disconcert
box 3 bin 4 case, cell, chop, cuff, kist, loge, slap, sock 5 booth, chest, clout, crate, fight, punch, smack, spank, stall, trunk 6 buffet, carton, casket, coffin, hopper, packet, square 7 confine, enclose, package 8 canister 9 container, enclosure, rectangle 10 pigeonhole, receptacle 11 compartment ***ancient:*** 4 arca ***for a document:*** 7 hanaper ***for ammunition:*** 7 caisson ***for an official seal:*** 7 skippet
boxer 7 fighter, palooka, puncher, slugger 8 pugilist 9 flyweight 11 heavyweight, lightweight 12 bantamweight, middleweight, welterweight 13 featherweight ***champ:*** 3 Ali (Muhammad) 5 Louis (Joe), Moore (Archie), Tyson (Mike) 6 Hearns (Thomas), Holmes (Larry), Spinks (Leon, Michael), Tunney (Gene), Walker (Mickey) 7 Charles (Ezzard), Corbett (James), Dempsey (Jack), Foreman (George), Frazier (Joe), Johnson (Jack), Leonard (Sugar Ray), Sharkey (Jack), Walcott (Joe) 8 Marciano (Rocky), Robinson (Sugar Ray), Sullivan (John L.) 9 Armstrong (Henry), Holyfield (Evander), Patterson (Floyd), Schmeling (Max)
boxing 8 pugilism 10 fisticuffs 13 prizefighting ***term:*** 2 KO 3 jab, TKO 4 bell, blow, bout, duck, foul, hook, ring, rope, spar 5 break, count, feint, glove, judge, match, parry, punch, round, swing, towel 6 bucket, canvas, corner, sponge 7 low blow, referee 8 heavy bag, knockout, pugilism, speed bag, uppercut 9 knockdown 11 punching bag
boy 3 lad, son 5 gamin, sonny 6 laddie, nipper, shaver 7 gossoon 9 shaveling, stripling, youngster ***combining form:*** 3 ped 4 paed, paid, pedo 5 paedo, paido ***country:*** 5 swain ***errand:*** 5 gofer 8 lobbygow ***French:*** 6 garçon ***Latin:*** 4 puer ***mischievous:*** 6 urchin ***small:*** 3 tad ***Spanish:*** 4 niño
boyfriend 4 beau 5 beaux (plural), flame, lover, swain 6 fiancé, steady 7 beloved 8 paramour, truelove 9 inamorato 10 heartthrob, sweetheart
Boy Scout ***founder:*** 11 Baden-Powell ***gathering:*** 8 jamboree ***motto:*** 10 be prepared ***rank:*** 9 Life Scout, Star Scout 10 Eagle Scout, Tenderfoot ***unit:*** 5 troop 6 patrol
Boys Town ***founder:*** 8 Flanagan ***state:*** 8 Nebraska
B.P.O.E. member 3 Elk
Brabantio's daughter 9 Desdemona
brabble 3 gab, row 4 chat, spat, tiff 5 clack, scrap 6 bicker, cackle, hassle, jabber 7 chatter, dispute, fall out, palaver, prattle, quarrel, wrangle 8 squabble 9 bickering, brannigan, caterwaul 10 falling-out 11 altercation 12 tittle-tattle
brace 3 beg, duo 4 dyad, gird, pair, pray, prop, stay 5 plead, ready, shore, steel 6 appeal, bear up, column, couple, splent, splint, upbear, uphold 7 beseech, bolster, doublet, entreat, fortify, implore, prepare, refresh, shore up, support, sustain, twosome 8 buttress 9 importune 10 strengthen, supplicate 11 underpinner 12 underpinning 13 underpropping
bracelet 6 bangle 8 wristlet
bracing 5 tonic 9 animating 10 quickening, vitalizing 11 stimulating, stimulative 12 exhilarating, exhilarative, invigorating
bracket 3 wed 4 join, link 5 unite 6 couple, relate 7 collate, combine, compare, conjoin, connect 8 contrast 9 associate
bract 4 leaf 5 glume, palea, palet 6 paleae (plural), spathe 8 phyllary
brad 4 nail
Bradamant ***brother:*** 7 Rinaldo ***husband:*** 6 Rogero 8 Ruggiero
Bradbury's forte 5 sci-fi
brag 4 blow, crow, puff 5 boast, mouth, prate, vaunt 9 gasconade 11 rodomontade
braggadocian 8 boastful, braggart, vaunting 11 rodomontade
braggadocio 7 boaster 8 boasting, braggart, bragging 9 cockiness 10 cockalorum
braggart 6 blower 7 boaster, vaunter, windbag 8 blowhard, boastful, fanfaron, puckfist, rodomont, vaunting 11 braggadocio, rodomontade 12 braggadocian
Brahmin 7 egghead 8 highbrow 10 double-dome 12 intellectual
braid 4 plat 5 plait, queue 7 galloon, pigtail 8 soutache 10 intertwine, interweave ***gold or silver:*** 5 orris ***hemp:*** 5 tagal
brain 3 wit 4 bean, conk, head, mind 7 concuss 9 intellect 10 gray matter 12 intelligence ***bone:*** 5 skull 7 cranium

clot: 10 thrombosis *combining form:* 6 cerebr, enceph 7 cerebri, cerebro 8 cerebell 9 cerebelli, cerebello, encephalo, encephaly 10 encephalia, encephalus *gland:* 6 pineal 9 pituitary *layer:* 4 obex 6 cortex *lobe:* 6 limbic, vermis 7 frontal 8 parietal, temporal 9 occipital *membrane:* 3 pia 4 dura, tela 6 meninx 8 pia mater 9 arachnoid, dura mater *part:* 4 aula, lobe 7 medulla 8 cerebrum, thalamus 9 sensorium, ventricle 10 cerebellum, hemisphere 12 diencephalon *relating to:* 8 cerebral 10 encephalic *ridge:* 4 gyri (plural) 5 gyrus *vertebrate:* 10 encephalon *wave record:* 3 EEG *white matter:* 4 alba

brainchild 7 coinage 9 invention 11 contrivance

brainless 6 simple 7 asinine, foolish, unwitty, witless 8 mindless 9 nitwitted, senseless 10 weak-minded

brainless one 5 ament

brainpower 3 wit 5 sense 9 mentality, mother wit 12 intelligence

brainsick 4 daft 5 batty, crazy 6 crazed, insane 7 cracked, lunatic 8 demented, deranged 9 bedlamite

brainstorm 4 idea 11 inspiration

brainteaser 6 puzzle

brainwashing 10 persuasion

brainwork 7 thought 10 cogitation, reflection 11 cerebration, speculation 12 deliberation

brainy 5 alert, sharp, smart 6 bright, clever 7 knowing 9 brilliant 11 intelligent, quick-witted, ready-witted

brake 3 bar, dam 4 slow, stop 5 block 6 hinder, impede 8 obstruct 10 overslaugh

branch 4 gill, limb, rami (plural) 5 bough, brook, creek, ramus 6 ramify, runnel, stream 7 rivulet *relating to:* 5 ramal 7 ramular

branched 6 ramate, ramose, ramous 8 ramulose, ramulous *combining form:* 7 cladous

brand 4 blot, blur, logo, mark, onus, slur, spot 5 odium, stain 6 stigma 8 black eye, logotype 9 trademark 11 bar sinister

brandish 4 show 5 flash 6 expose, flaunt, parade 7 display, disport, exhibit, show off, trot out

brand-new 4 mint 5 clean, fresh 6 unused 8 pristine 9 untouched 12 spick-and-span

brandy 4 marc 5 pisco, rakia 6 cognac, grappa, kirsch, rakija 7 quetsch 8 armagnac, calvados, slivovic 9 applejack, framboise, mirabelle, slivovitz 11 aquardiente

brannigan 3 row 4 bust 5 binge, fight, spree 6 bender, hassle, ruckus 7 brabble, carouse, dispute, quarrel, wassail, wrangle 10 falling out 11 altercation

brash 4 bold 5 hasty 6 brazen, madcap, uppish, uppity 7 forward, pushful, pushing 8 reckless, tactless 9 ebullient, exuberant, hot-headed, impetuous, impolitic, maladroit, presuming, unpolitic, untactful, vivacious 10 ill-advised, incautious 11 overweening, thoughtless 12 effervescent, high-spirited, presumptuous, undiplomatic 13 inconsiderate, self-asserting, self-assertive

brashness 4 gall 5 brass, cheek, crust, nerve 8 audacity, temerity 9 assurance, hardihood, hardiness 10 confidence, effrontery 11 presumption

brass 4 gall 5 cheek, crust, nerve 9 brashness 10 confidence, effrontery 11 presumption *combining form:* 5 chalc, chalk 6 chalco, chalko

brassbound 5 brash, rigid 6 narrow, uppish, uppity 7 adamant, bigoted, forward, pushful 8 obdurate 9 illiberal, presuming, unbending 10 inexorable, inflexible, intolerant, relentless, unyielding 11 overweening, small-minded 12 narrow-minded, presumptuous, single-minded 13 self-asserting, self-assertive

brass hat 5 elder 6 better, senior 8 higher-up, superior

brass tacks 7 details

brass worker 7 brasier, brazier

brassy see **brazen**

brave 4 bold, dare, defy, face, game, good 5 gutsy, hardy, manly, noble, stout, vivid 6 daring, gritty, heroic, manful, plucky, spunky, useful 7 aweless, benefic, defiant, doughty, gallant, helpful, outdare, outface, valiant, venture 8 colorful, fearless, intrepid, resolute, spirited, stalwart, unafraid, valorous 9 audacious, challenge, dauntless, favorable, soldierly, steadfast, undaunted, unfearful, unfearing 10 beneficial, courageous, propitious, unblenched 11 boldhearted, lionhearted, unblenching, undauntable, unflinching, venturesome 12 advantageous, greathearted, stouthearted, unfrightened

Brave New World author 6 Huxley

bravery 4 grit 5 pluck 6 daring, spirit 7 courage, heroism 8 audacity, boldness 9 fortitude, gallantry 11 intrepidity 12 intrepidness *false:* 7 bravado

brawl 3 row 4 feud, fray, maul, riot, spat, tiff 5 broil, fight, melee, scrap, set-to 6 affray, bicker, dustup, fracas, hassle, mellay, rumble, tussle 7 bobbery, brabble, dispute, quarrel, ruction, scuffle, wrangle 8 dogfight, eruption, rowdydow, slugfest, squabble, struggle, upheaval 9 bickering, caterwaul, commotion, fistfight, imbroglio, scrimmage 10 donnybrook, fisticuffs, free-for-all 11 altercation, disturbance

brawn 4 beef, thew 5 might 6 muscle

brawny 5 beefy, lusty, tough 6 sinewy 8 athletic, muscular, vigorous
bray 4 buck 5 crush 6 powder 9 comminute, pulverize, triturate 12 contriturate
brazen 4 bold, loud 5 gaudy, saucy 6 arrant, brassy, flashy, garish, tawdry, tinsel 7 aeneous, blatant, chintzy, glaring 8 impudent, insolent, overbold 9 audacious, barefaced, shameless, unabashed 10 procacious, unblushing 11 impertinent 12 contumelious, meretricious
Brazil ***explorer:*** 6 Cabral ***largest city:*** 8 Sao Paulo ***monetary unit:*** 8 cruzeiro
breach 3 gap 4 hole, open, rent, rift 5 break, split 6 hiatus, lacuna, offend, schism 7 discord, disrupt, fissure, infract, interim, opening, rupture, violate 8 disunity, division, fracture, infringe, interval, trespass 9 severance, violation 10 alienation, contravene, infraction, separation, transgress 12 estrangement, infringement, interruption 13 contravention, discontinuity, transgression
bread 3 bun 4 feed, food, grub 5 money 6 cocket, living, simnel, viands 7 biscuit, edibles, nurture, support 8 victuals 9 provender 10 livelihood, provisions, sustenance 11 comestibles, maintenance, subsistence ***blessed:*** 7 eulogia 9 antidoron ***boiled:*** 4 cush 6 panada ***browned:*** 5 toast 6 sippet 7 crouton 8 zwieback ***combining form:*** 4 arto ***communion:*** 4 azym, host 5 azyme, wafer 9 eucharist ***consecrated:*** 9 eucharist ***cube:*** 7 crouton ***from heaven:*** 5 manna ***hard and crisp:*** 4 rusk 8 zwieback ***ingredient:*** 4 meal 5 flour, yeast 6 leaven ***Jewish:*** 5 matzo 6 hallah, matzoh 7 challah ***maker:*** 5 baker ***relating to:*** 6 panary ***roll:*** 5 bagel ***Scottish:*** 7 bannock ***small piece:*** 6 sippet ***soup:*** 6 panada ***spread:*** 3 jam 4 oleo 5 jelly 6 butter ***unleavened:*** 4 azym 5 azyme, matzo 6 matzoh ***with fruit and nuts:*** 7 stollen
bread and butter 4 keep 6 living 7 support 10 livelihood, sustenance 11 maintenance, subsistence 12 alimentation
breadbasket 7 stomach
breadth 5 range, reach, scope, space, sweep 6 spread 7 compass, expanse, stretch 8 distance, fullness, wideness 9 amplitude, expansion
break 3 gap 4 bust, cave, fail, flee, fold, hole, leak, plow, rent, rift, ruin 5 boner, burst, crack, crash, gaffe, rebut, scape, solve, spell, split, yield 6 befall, betide, breach, chance, convey, decode, demote, escape, fold up, get out, happen, hiatus, lacuna, offend, plow up, reduce, refute, schism, sunder 7 abscond, blooper, come off, come out, confute, crumble, crumple, declass, degrade, demerit, fall out, faux pas, fissure, infract, interim, opening, respite, rupture, shatter, time-out, violate 8 bankrupt, breather, collapse, confound, decipher, disprove, dissolve, fracture, fragment, interval 9 downgrade, interlude, pauperize 10 contravene, controvert, impoverish, transgress 11 communicate, impropriety, interregnum, opportunity, parenthesis 12 intermission, interruption 13 discontinuity
breakable 5 frail 7 fragile 8 delicate, shattery 9 frangible 11 fracturable, shatterable
breakaway 4 prop 10 escarpment, scrummager
breakdown 5 crash, smash, wreck 7 crack-up, debacle, smashup 8 analysis, collapse 10 dissection, resolution
break down 3 rot 4 wilt 5 decay, spoil, taint 6 cave in, digest, molder 7 analyze, crumble, dissect, give out, putrefy, resolve, succumb 9 anatomize, decompose 10 decompound 12 disintegrate
breaker ***combining form:*** 5 clast 7 clastic
breakfront 7 cabinet 8 bookcase
break in 5 train 8 initiate 9 interrupt
breaking up ***combining form:*** 7 schises (plural), schisis ***suffix:*** 4 lyse, lyze
breakneck 4 fast 5 fleet, hasty, quick, rapid, swift 6 speedy 10 expeditive, harefooted 11 expeditious
break out 5 erupt 6 escape 7 explode 10 burst forth
breakthrough 4 hike, rise 5 boost 7 advance, upgrade 8 increase
break through 5 burst 6 breach 7 rupture
breakup 8 analysis 10 dissection
break up 4 part 6 divide, sunder 7 disband, disjoin, disrupt, rupture 8 disjoint, disperse, dissever, dissolve, disunite, separate
breast 5 bosom, chest, heart ***animal:*** 7 brisket ***combining form:*** 3 maz 4 mast, mazo 5 masto, stern, steth 6 mastia (plural), sterno, stetho
breastbone 7 sternum
breast-feed 5 nurse 6 suckle 7 nourish
breast-shaped 9 mammiform
breastwork 7 bastion, bulwark, parapet, rampart
breath 4 blow, dash, hint 5 break, spell, trace, whiff 6 streak 7 respite, soupçon 9 suspicion 10 suggestion ***combining form:*** 4 pnea 5 pneum, pnoea 6 pneumo 7 pneumat 8 pneumato
breathe 2 be 4 live, rest, sigh 5 exist 6 exhale, expire, inhale 7 confide, inspire, respire, subsist, whisper
breather 5 break, spell 7 respite
breathing ***labored:*** 7 dyspnea

8 dyspnoea *normal:* 6 eupnea 7 eupnoea *rapid:* 8 polypnea 9 polypnoea

breathing apparatus 10 respirator *underwater:* 5 scuba

breathing orifice 8 blowhole, spiracle

breathless 4 agog, avid, keen 5 close, eager, stivy 6 ardent, stuffy, sultry 7 airless, anxious, athirst, thirsty 8 appetent, stifling 9 impatient 11 suffocating

breathtaking 8 exciting 9 thrilling 11 astonishing

Brecht play 4 Baal 7 Galileo 13 Mother Courage

breech 4 rear, rump 5 fanny 6 behind, bottom 8 backside, buttocks, derriere 9 fundament, posterior

breechclout 9 loincloth

breed 3 ilk 4 bear, grow, kind, sire, type 5 beget, cause, class, hatch, raise 6 father, induce, nature 7 produce, species, variety 8 engender, generate, multiply, muster up 9 character, cultivate, procreate, propagate, reproduce 11 progenerate

breeding 5 grace 6 polish 7 culture 9 gentility 10 refinement 11 cultivation

breeding ground 6 hotbed 8 hothouse 10 forcing bed 12 forcing house

breeze 3 zip 4 snap 5 cinch, waltz 6 zephyr 8 duck soup, kid stuff, pushover 10 child's play

breezy 4 airy 5 blowy, gusty, windy 6 casual, dégagé 7 relaxed, unfussy 8 informal 9 easygoing 11 low-pressure 13 unconstrained

breviary 5 brief 7 epitome 8 abstract, boildown, synopsis 10 conspectus 11 abridgement 12 condensation

breviloquent 4 curt 5 bluff, blunt, brief, gruff, rough, short, terse 6 abrupt, crusty 7 brusque, concise, laconic, summary 8 succinct 11 compendious 13 short and sweet

brevity 8 laconism 9 briefness, shortness, terseness 11 conciseness 12 succinctness

brew 4 loom 6 foment, gather, impend 9 forthcome, potpourri 10 miscellany

Briareus 7 Aegaeon *father:* 6 Uranus *mother:* 2 Ge 4 Gaea

bribe 3 buy, fix, sop 6 buy off, square, suborn 7 corrupt 10 tamper with

bric-a-brac 6 curios

brick 5 block *handler:* 6 hacker *layer:* 5 mason *laying:* 7 masonry *material:* 4 clay, marl *oven:* 4 kiln *pile:* 4 hack *row:* 6 course *sun-dried:* 3 bat 5 adobe *trough for carrying:* 3 hod *wooden:* 3 nog

bridal 7 spousal, wedding 8 marriage, nuptials 9 espousals

bridal wreath 6 spirea

bridge 4 span *kind:* 4 arch, draw, rope 5 swing, truss 7 bascule, covered, natural, pontoon, trestle, viaduct 10 cantilever, suspension *term:* 3 bid 4 book, east, pass, ruff, slam, suit, void, west 5 bonus, dummy, north, raise, south, trick, trump 6 double, renege, rubber 7 auction, finesse, no-trump, overbid 8 contract, jump call, redouble 9 grand slam, overtrick, singleton 10 little slam, undertrick, vulnerable

bridge-like game 5 whist 6 hearts

bridle 3 bit 4 curb, rein 5 check 6 hold in, manage 7 control, inhibit, repress 8 hold back, hold down, restrain, suppress, withhold 9 constrain

brief 4 curt 5 bluff, blunt, gruff, short, terse 6 abrupt, crusty, snippy 7 brusque, concise, epitome, laconic, passing 8 abstract, boildown, breviary, breviate, fleeting, snippety, succinct, synopsis 9 momentary, transient 10 conspectus 11 abridgement, compendiary, compendious 12 breviloquent, condensation 13 short and sweet *combining form:* 5 brevi

brig 4 jail 6 cooler, lockup, prison 7 slammer 8 stockade 9 guardroom

brigand 6 bandit, bummer, looter 7 cateran, forager 8 marauder, pillager 9 plunderer 10 depredator, freebooter

brigandage 7 pillage 11 depredation

bright 4 glad, keen 5 alert, brave, clear, light, lucid, nitid, sharp, shiny, smart, vivid 6 benign, brainy, cheery, clever, colory, dexter, lively, lucent 7 animate, beaming, blazing, flaming, fulgent, glowing, knowing, lambent, lighted, radiant 8 animated, cheerful, colorful, gleaming, luminous, lustrous, spirited, sunshiny 9 brilliant, effulgent, favorable, fortunate, refulgent, sparkling, sprightly, vivacious 10 auspicious, glistening, glittering, precocious, propitious, shimmering 11 illuminated, intelligent, quick-witted, ready-witted 12 incandescent 13 scintillating *combining form:* 6 lampro

brighten 5 cheer, shine 6 polish 7 burnish, enliven, furbish, gladden 8 illumine 10 illuminate

brightness 5 éclat 6 luster, reflet 8 radiance, radiancy, splendor 9 luminance 10 brilliance, luminosity *measure of:* 3 lux 4 phot 5 lumen 6 candle 7 candela 10 footcandle

brilliance see brightness

brilliant 4 sage, wise 5 sharp, smart 6 brainy, bright, clever, lucent 7 beaming, fulgent, knowing, lambent, radiant 8 luminous 9 effulgent, refulgent 11 intelligent, quick-witted, ready-witted 12 incandescent 13 knowledgeable

brilliantine 6 pomade

brim 3 hem 4 edge 5 brink, skirt, verge,

visor 6 border, fringe, margin 9 perimeter, periphery
brimful see brimming
brimming 3 big 4 full 5 awash 6 filled, jammed, loaded, packed 7 crammed, crowded, replete, stuffed, teeming, welling 8 swelling 9 chock-full
brimstone 6 sulfur ***combining form:*** 3 thi 4 thio
brine 3 sea 4 deep, main 5 ocean
bring 4 lead, sell 5 fetch 7 convert 8 persuade
bring about 4 make 5 cause 6 draw on, effect, secure 7 produce
bring around 6 induce, prompt 7 win over 8 convince, persuade, talk into 9 argue into 11 prevail upon
bring back 6 recall, return, revive 7 restore 8 retrieve, revivify
bring down 4 drop, fell 5 floor, level 6 ground, tumble 9 prostrate
bring forth 4 bear 7 deliver
bring forward 6 adduce 7 present, produce 9 introduce
bring in 3 get, pay, win 4 earn, gain, make, sell 5 fetch, yield 6 return 7 acquire
bringing ***suffix:*** 3 fic
bring off 6 effect 8 carry out 10 effectuate 12 carry through
bring out 3 say 4 tell 5 educe, state, utter 7 chime in, declare, deliver
bring together 4 join 5 batch, blend, merge, unify, unite 7 collect, compact, compile 9 integrate 10 synthesize 11 consolidate
bring up 4 halt, moot, rear, stop 5 breed, raise, refer, train 6 advert, allude, broach, draw up, foster, haul up, pull up 7 educate, mention, nourish, nurture 8 point out 9 cultivate, introduce 10 provide for
brink 3 hem 4 brim, edge 5 point, skirt, verge 6 border, fringe, margin 9 perimeter, periphery, threshold
briny 5 salty
brio 3 vim 4 dash, élan, zing 5 oomph, verve 6 esprit, spirit 9 animation
briolette 7 diamond
Briseis' lover 8 Achilles
brisk 4 spry, yare 5 agile, quick, zippy 6 active, adroit, lively, nimble, volant 9 sprightly
bristle 4 boil, burn, fume, rage, seta 5 anger, setae (plural) 6 blow up, chaeta, seethe 7 chaetae (plural), flare up 8 boil over ***combining form:*** 4 seti 5 chaet 6 chaeta, chaeto 7 chaetae (plural), chaetes, chaetus ***Scottish:*** 5 birse
British ***air force:*** 3 RAF ***airplane:*** 8 Spitfire ***bailiff:*** 5 reeve ***bar:*** 3 pub 5 local ***bard:*** 4 scop ***barge:*** 6 wherry ***bed:*** 4 doss ***beer:*** 6 swipes ***boat, ancient:*** 7 coracle ***boat, fishing:*** 5 coble 6 hooker ***boy:*** 6 nipper ***cathedral city:*** 3 Ely 4 York 5 Truro 6 Durham, Exeter 7 Lincoln 8 Coventry, Hereford, St. David's 9 Salisbury, Worcester 10 Canterbury, Gloucester ***Channel Island:*** 4 Sark 6 Jersey 8 Alderney, Guernsey ***china:*** 5 Spode ***coal carrier:*** 4 corf ***coin, current:*** 5 pence (plural), penny 9 halfpenny ***coin, old:*** 3 bob, ora 5 ackey, angel, crown, groat, noble 6 bawbee, florin, George, guinea, seskin, sovran, tanner, teston 7 angelot, carolus 8 farthing, shilling 9 dandiprat, halfcrown, sovereign 10 threepence ***colony, former:*** 4 Aden, Cape 5 Adana, Kenya, Malta, Natal 6 Ceylon, Cyprus, Gambia 7 Jamaica, Sarawak 9 Gold Coast, Singapore, Transvaal 10 Basutoland, New Zealand 11 Orange River, Sierra Leone 12 Bechuanaland ***conservative party:*** 4 Tory ***country gentleman:*** 6 squire ***county:*** 4 Kent, York 5 Derby, Devon, Essex, Hants, Salop 6 Dorset, Durham, Oxford, Surrey, Sussex 7 Bedford, Rutland, Suffolk, Warwick 8 Cheshire, Cornwall, Hereford, Hertford, Somerset, Stafford 9 Berkshire, Hampshire, Lancaster, Leicester, Wiltshire, Worcester 10 Cumberland, Gloucester, Shropshire 11 Westmorland ***court, local:*** 8 hustings ***court, medieval:*** 4 eyre ***cow barn:*** 4 byre ***dance, ancient:*** 6 morris ***dandy:*** 4 toff ***elevator:*** 4 lift ***farm, small:*** 5 croft ***field:*** 5 croft ***flashlight:*** 5 torch ***football:*** 5 rugby ***forest:*** 5 Arden, weald 8 Sherwood ***freeman:*** 5 ceorl, churl, thane ***game:*** 5 darts, rugby 6 soccer 7 cricket ***gasoline:*** 6 petrol ***gun:*** 4 Bren, Sten ***hat:*** 6 bowler ***hat, military:*** 5 busby ***headmaster:*** 4 beak ***horse:*** 5 screw 6 garron ***horse dealer:*** 5 coper ***hunt:*** 5 chevy, chivy ***hut:*** 6 Nissen ***idler:*** 4 spiv ***innkeeper:*** 8 publican ***jail:*** 4 gaol ***king, legendary:*** 3 Lud 4 Beli, Bran 6 Arthur 7 Artegal, Belinus, Elidure 8 Brannius ***laborer:*** 5 navvy, prole ***landowner:*** 6 squire ***language, ancient:*** 6 Celtic, Cymric 9 Brythonic ***lawyer:*** 9 barrister, solicitor ***legislature:*** 10 parliament ***letter, old:*** 3 wen 5 thorn ***liberal party:*** 4 Whig ***magistrate:*** 4 beak ***malt liquor:*** 6 porter ***measure:*** 3 ell, pin 4 boll, comb, coom, cran, goad, hand, hide, last, pool, rood, trug, yoke 5 bodge, coomb, digit, float, floor, hutch, jugum, stack, truss 6 bovate, cranne, firkin, oxgang, pottle, runlet, strike, sulung, tierce 7 rundlet, tertian, virgate 8 carucate, chaldron, puncheon 9 kilderkin, shaftment, shathmont 10 barleycorn ***molasses:*** 7 treacle ***news agency:*** 7 Reuters ***nobleman:*** 4 duke, earl, lord, peer 5 baron 6 prince 8 marquess, viscount ***nurse:*** 6 sister ***order:***

6 Garter ***ore carrier:*** 4 corf ***peasant:*** 5 churl ***peddler:*** 7 chapman ***people, early:*** 4 Celt, Jute, Pict 5 Angle, Iceni, Saxon ***poet:*** 4 scop ***policeman:*** 5 bobby 6 copper, peeler ***political party:*** 4 Tory, Whig 6 Labour ***pope:*** 8 Adrian IV ***pottery:*** 5 Spode ***prince:*** 6 Andrew 7 Charles ***princess:*** 4 Anne 8 Margaret ***printer:*** 6 Caxton ***prison:*** 7 Newgate 8 Dartmoor 13 Tower of London ***queen, ancient:*** 8 Boadicea ***racetrack:*** 5 Ascot 10 Epsom Downs ***resort:*** 4 Bath 7 Margate 8 Brighton 9 Blackpool ***rifle:*** 7 Enfield ***royal house:*** 4 York 5 Tudor 6 Stuart 7 Hanover, Windsor 9 Lancaster 11 Plantagenet ***royal residence:*** 7 Windsor ***school:*** 4 Eton 5 Rugby 6 Harrow ***school, military:*** 9 Sandhurst ***seaman:*** 6 rating ***serf:*** 4 esne 6 thrall ***solitaire:*** 8 patience ***spa:*** 4 Bath 5 Epsom 6 Buxton 7 Matlock 8 Brighton 10 Cheltenham ***stables:*** 4 mews ***stool pigeon:*** 4 nark ***streetcar:*** 4 tram ***tavern:*** 3 pub ***tax:*** 3 VAT 4 geld 6 excise ***thicket:*** 7 spinney ***tinworks:*** 8 stannary ***tobacco packet:*** 5 screw ***tourist:*** 7 tripper ***truck:*** 5 lorry ***tutor:*** 3 don ***valley:*** 4 dene ***wage earner:*** 5 prole ***weight:*** 4 keel 5 stone ***woman in the navy:*** 4 Wren ***wrench:*** 7 spanner

British Columbia ***capital:*** 8 Victoria ***largest city:*** 9 Vancouver

Britomartis 7 Artemis 8 Dictynna

brittle 5 crisp, short 7 crackly, crumbly, crunchy, friable

broach 3 pin 4 clip, moot 7 bring up, mention 9 introduce, ventilate 10 speak about

broad 4 wide 6 risqué, scopic 7 liberal, radical 8 advanced, extended, off-color, scopious, tolerant 9 expansive, extensive 10 suggestive 11 broad-minded, progressive ***combining form:*** 4 eury, lati, plat 5 platy

broadcast 3 sow 5 straw, strew 6 blazon 7 bestrew, declare, disject, publish, scatter 8 announce, proclaim, televise, transmit 9 advertise 10 annunciate, bruit about, promulgate 11 blaze abroad, declaration, disseminate, publication 12 announcement, proclamation, promulgation 13 advertisement, pronouncement

broaden 4 open 5 widen 6 expand 9 breadthen, spread out

broadloom 6 carpet

broad-minded 4 wide 7 liberal, radical 8 advanced, tolerant 11 progressive

broadside 4 hail 5 burst, salvo, storm 6 shower, volley 7 barrage 9 cannonade, fusillade 11 bombardment

broadtail 5 sheep 6 parrot 7 karakul, rosella 8 lambskin

Brobdingnagian 4 huge 5 giant 7 Antaean, mammoth, titanic 8 colossal, gigantic 9 cyclopean, monstrous 10 gargantuan

brocaded 6 broché

brocard 4 rule 5 axiom, gnome, maxim, moral 6 dictum, truism 8 aphorism, apothegm

brochette 4 spit 6 skewer

broil 4 bake, burn, cook, fray 5 brawl, fight, grill, roast 6 affray, fracas, scorch 7 bobbery, ruction, swelter 10 donnybrook, free-for-all

broiling 3 hot 5 fiery 6 baking, red-hot, torrid 7 burning 8 scalding, sizzling 9 scorching 10 sweltering

broke 4 flat, poor 5 needy, stony 8 beggared, dirt poor, indigent, strapped 9 destitute

broken-down 5 dingy, seedy, tacky 6 shabby, tagrag 8 decrepit, tattered 10 threadbare 11 dilapidated

brokenhearted 7 crushed 8 dejected 9 depressed

broker 8 mediator 9 go-between, middleman 10 interagent, interceder 11 intercessor 12 entrepreneur, intermediary, intermediate 13 intermediator

bromide 6 cliché, truism 8 banality, prosaism 9 platitude 10 prosaicism, shibboleth 11 commonplace, rubber stamp

bromidic 3 dry 4 arid, dull 5 dusty 7 insipid, tedious 8 wearifui 9 dryasdust, wearisome 13 uninteresting

bromine ***symbol:*** 2 Br

bronco 5 horse 6 cayuse 7 mustang ***Australian:*** 6 brumby

Brontë ***character:*** 9 Catherine, Rochester 10 Heathcliff ***novel:*** 8 Jane Eyre 16 Wuthering Heights ***sisters:*** 4 Anne 5 Emily 9 Charlotte

Bronx cheer 3 boo 4 hiss, razz 5 bazoo 7 catcall 9 raspberry

brooch 3 pin 4 clip

brood 3 set, sit 4 mope, seed 5 cover 6 scions 7 despond, progeny 8 children 9 offspring 11 descendants, progeniture

brook 4 bear, gill, race, rill, take 5 abide, creek, stand 6 arroyo, endure, rillet, runnel, stream, suffer 7 rivulet, stomach, swallow 8 tolerate ***Scottish:*** 6 burnie

broom 5 besom, brush, shrub, sweep, whisk 7 heather ***combining form:*** 5 scopi

broth 5 stock 6 brewis 8 bouillon, consomme ***Scottish:*** 4 bree, broo

brothel 6 bagnio 7 lupanar 8 bordello, cathouse, seraglio 9 call house 10 bawdy house, fancy house 11 parlor house 13 sporting house

brother 3 bub, kin 4 monk 5 friar 7 comrade ***French:*** 5 frère ***Italian:*** 3 fra 5 frate

8 fratello *Latin:* 6 frater *relating to:* 9 fraternal *Spanish:* 7 hermano
brotherhood 4 club 5 guild, order, union 6 league 7 society 8 sodality 10 fellowship, fraternity 11 association
brotherly 4 kind 10 cherishing 12 affectionate
Brothers Karamazov 4 Ivan 6 Alexei, Dmitri 10 Smerdyakov
brouhaha 3 din 4 coil, fuss 5 babel 6 clamor, furore, hubbub, hurrah, jangle, racket, ruckus, rumpus, shindy, tumult, uproar 8 foofaraw 9 commotion 10 hullabaloo 11 pandemonium
brow 5 frons, front 8 forehead
browbeat 3 cow 5 bully 6 harass, hector 7 bluster, dragoon 8 bludgeon, bulldoze, bullyrag 10 intimidate
brown 4 dark, sear 5 dusky, toast 6 gloomy, scorch, tanned 7 swarthy *dark:* 5 sepia, umber 9 chocolate *grayish:* 3 dun 6 bister, bistre *light:* 3 tan 4 ecru, fawn 5 beige, hazel, khaki, tawny *moderate:* 4 teak 6 sahara, sienna *reddish:* 3 bay 4 roan 5 henna 6 auburn, russet, sorrel, titian 8 chestnut *yellowish:* 6 bronze 12 butterscotch
Brown Bomber 5 Louis (Joe)
brown coal 7 lignite
brownie 3 elf, fay 5 fairy, nisse, pixie 6 sprite
Browning poem 8 Prospice 11 Pippa Passes 12 Rabbi Ben Ezra 13 Fra Lippo Lippi, My Last Duchess
brown recluse 6 spider
brownshirt 4 Nazi 12 storm trooper
browse 4 scan, shop 6 go over, peruse 7 dip into, run over 8 glance at, look over 10 glance over, run through 11 flip through, leaf through, riff through, skim through 12 thumb through 13 riffle through
bruise 4 mash, pulp 5 black, crush 6 batter, squash 7 becrush, contuse 8 abrasion, black eye 9 contusion
bruit about 6 blazon 7 declare, publish 8 announce, proclaim 9 advertise, broadcast 10 annunciate, promulgate 11 blaze abroad
bruja 3 hag, hex 5 lamia, witch 9 sorceress 10 witchwoman 11 enchantress
brume 4 film, haze, mist 5 smaze
brummagem 4 fake, sham 5 bogus, false, phony, snide 6 pseudo, tinsel 8 spurious 9 pinchbeck 11 counterfeit
brunet 4 dark 5 dusky, swart 6 swarth 7 swarthy 8 bistered
Brunhild's husband 6 Gunnar 7 Gunther
brush 4 clip, fray, kiss, skim 5 clash, graze, melee, run-in, set-to, shave, sweep 6 affray, glance, mellay, scrape 7 contact 8 skirmish 9 encounter, scrimmage, sideswipe 10 velitation *combining form:* 5 scopi
brusque 4 curt 5 bluff, blunt, brief, gruff, short 6 abrupt, crusty, snippy 8 snippety
brutal 4 hard 5 feral, harsh 6 animal, bitter, ferine, rugged, severe 7 beastly, bestial, swinish 8 rigorous 9 inclement 11 intemperate
brutalize 4 warp 6 debase 7 corrupt, debauch, deprave, pervert, vitiate 10 bastardize, bestialize, demoralize
brute 5 beast, feral 6 animal, ferine 7 beastly, bestial, swinish 8 creature
brutish 3 low 4 base, mean, vile 5 crude, feral 6 animal, coarse, ferine, scurvy 7 beastly, bestial, swinish 11 animalistic
bryophyte 4 moss 9 liverwort
Brythonic see Cymric
bubble 3 lap 4 boil, stir, wash 5 churn, dream, slosh, swash 6 burble, gurgle, seethe, simmer 7 chimera, fantasy, ferment, smolder 8 illusion 9 pipe dream
bubbly 8 effusive 9 champagne, exuberant, sparkling
buccaneer 5 rover 6 pirate, sea dog 7 corsair, sea wolf 8 picaroon, sea rover 9 sea robber 10 freebooter
buck 3 fop, guy, lug, man 4 bear, bill, bray, chap, dude, duel, gent, pack, tote 5 carry, crush, dandy, forry, fight, horse, pitch, repel, throw 6 combat, convey, dollar, fellow, oppose, powder, resist, unseat 7 contest, coxcomb, dispute, sawbuck, trestle, unhorse 8 sawhorse, traverse 9 comminute, exquisite, gentleman, pulverize, transport, triturate, withstand, workhorse 11 Beau Brummel 12 contriturate
bucket 3 fly, run 4 pail, rush, whiz 5 hurry, speed 6 barrel, hasten, hustle 7 grapple 9 clamshell
Buckeye State 4 Ohio
buckle down 5 apply, set to 6 devote, direct, fall to, jump in, wade in 7 address, pitch in 8 jump into, wade into
buckle under 3 bow 4 cave, give 5 defer, yield 6 submit 7 knuckle, succumb 10 capitulate
Buck novel 12 The Good Earth
buckram 5 stiff 6 wooden 7 stilted 9 cardboard 11 muscle-bound
buck up 5 cheer 6 solace 7 comfort, console, upraise
bucolic 4 hick, jake 5 rural, yokel 6 rustic 7 bumpkin, country, hayseed, hillman, hoosier, outland 8 agrestic, pastoral 9 chawbacon 10 campestral, out-country, provincial 11 countrified
bud 4 germ, seed 5 chick, child, spark 6 embryo 8 juvenile, young one 9 youngling, youngster *combining form:* 5 blast 6 blasto

Buddha 7 Gautama 10 Siddhartha ***Chinese:*** 2 Fo ***dialogues:*** 5 sutra ***disciple:*** 6 Ananda ***Japanese:*** 5 Amida, Amita ***mother:*** 4 Maya ***son:*** 6 Rahula ***teachings:*** 6 dharma ***wife:*** 9 Yasodhara

Buddhism 5 Daijo, Foism, Kegon 7 Lamaism 8 Hinayana, Mahayana

Buddhist ***bronze image:*** 8 Daibutsu ***chant:*** 6 mantra ***column:*** 3 lat ***dialogues:*** 5 sutra ***doctrine:*** 7 trikaya ***enlightenment:*** 6 satori ***evil spirit:*** 4 Mara ***fate:*** 5 karma ***fertility spirit:*** 6 yaksha, yakshi ***gateway:*** 5 toran 6 torana ***god:*** 4 deva ***hatred:*** 4 dosa ***hell:*** 6 Naraka ***language:*** 4 Pali ***mendicant:*** 7 bhikshu ***monastery:*** 4 tera ***monk:*** 2 bo 4 lama 5 arhat, bonze, yahan 7 bhikshu, poongee 8 poonghee, poonghie, talapoin ***monument, mound:*** 5 stupa ***novice:*** 5 goyin ***paradise:*** 4 Jodo ***religious community:*** 6 sangha ***sacred city:*** 5 Lhasa ***saint:*** 5 arhat ***school:*** 5 ritsu ***scripture:*** 9 Tripitika ***sect:*** 3 Zen 6 tendai ***shrine:*** 4 tope 5 stupa 6 dagaba, dagoba 7 chorten ***spell:*** 6 mantra ***spiritual leader:*** 4 guru 9 Dalai Lama ***state of happiness:*** 7 nirvana ***temple:*** 6 pagoda, vihara ***throne:*** 5 asana ***title:*** 7 mahatma ***tree of enlightenment:*** 2 bo 5 bodhi, pipal ***tutelary spirit:*** 6 yaksha, yakshi ***will to live:*** 5 tanha

buddy 3 pal 4 chum 5 crony 6 comate, friend 7 comrade 9 associate, companion 11 running mate

buddy-buddy 4 cozy 5 pally 6 chummy 8 intimate

budgerigar 6 parrot 8 lovebird, parakeet 9 parrakeet

budget 4 body, bulk 5 total 6 amount 7 quantum 8 quantity 9 aggregate

budtime 6 spring 10 springtide

Buenos ____ 5 Aires

buff 3 fan, rub 5 glaze, gloss, shine 6 addict, glance, polish, votary 7 burnish, devotee, furbish, habitué 10 aficionado

buffalo 4 anoa, balk, beat, bilk, dash, foil, ruin 5 bison, stump 6 baffle 7 carabao, nonplus 9 frustrate 10 circumvent, disappoint ***Philippines:*** 7 tamarao, tamarau, timarou

buffalo grass 5 grama 6 gramma

buffet 3 box 4 beat, blip, chop, cuff, drub, poke, slap, sock 5 clout, pound, punch, smack, spank 6 batter, pummel, thrash, wallop 7 belabor, lambast 8 lambaste

buffoon 4 zany 5 clown 9 harlequin 11 merry-andrew

bug 3 irk, nut, vex 4 fret, gall 5 annoy 6 bother, insect, zealot 7 fanatic, provoke, wiretap 10 enthusiast

bugaboo see bugbear

bugbear 4 bogy, fear, ogre 5 bogey 6 goblin 7 problem, specter, spectre 8 anathema, bogeyman 9 bête noire, boogeyman, hobgoblin 10 black beast 11 abomination, detestation

bugle ***blare:*** 7 tantara ***call:*** 4 mess, taps 6 sennet, tattoo 7 retreat 8 assembly, reveille

Bugs ____ 4 Baer 5 Bunny

build 3 wax 4 form, make, mold, rise 5 boost, erect, forge, frame, mount, put up, raise, run up, shape 6 expand, uprear 7 augment, enlarge, fashion, habitus, magnify, produce, throw up, upsurge 8 assemble, compound, heighten, increase, multiply, physique 9 construct, fabricate 10 aggrandize 11 manufacture 12 constitution

builder 10 contractor

builder's knot 10 clove hitch

building 3 hut 6 fabric 7 edifice 9 structure ***addition:*** 3 ell 4 wing 5 annex ***compartment:*** 3 bay 4 room 6 office ***connector:*** 9 breezeway ***farm:*** 4 barn, crib, shed, silo ***for apartments:*** 8 tenement ***for arms:*** 7 arsenal ***for fodder:*** 4 silo ***for gambling:*** 6 casino ***for grain:*** 4 silo 7 granary 8 elevator ***for horses:*** 6 stable ***for manufacture:*** 4 shop 5 plant 7 factory ***for music:*** 4 hall 10 auditorium, opera house ***for sports:*** 3 gym 4 bowl 5 arena 7 stadium 8 coliseum 9 gymnasium 10 hippodrome ***material:*** 4 iron, wood 5 adobe, brick, glass, steel, stone 6 cement 8 concrete ***medieval:*** 6 castle ***projection:*** 3 bay, ell 4 wing 5 annex 6 dormer 7 cornice ***round:*** 7 rotunda

build up 4 puff 5 erect 9 advertise, construct, establish, publicize 10 press-agent

built-in 6 inborn, inbred, innate 8 inherent 9 essential, ingrained 10 congenital, deep-seated, indwelling

bulb 3 bud 4 leek, lily, sego 5 onion, tulip 6 garlic, squill 8 daffodil, hyacinth 9 amaryllis, narcissus ***segment:*** 5 clove

bulb-like bud 4 corm 5 tuber 7 rhizome

Bulgaria ***capital:*** 5 Sofia ***monetary unit:*** 3 lev

bulge 3 jut 4 bump, edge, lump, poke, pout 5 pouch, swell 6 beetle, dilate, expand 7 distend, project 8 handicap, overhang, protrude, stand out, stick out, swelling 9 advantage, allowance, head start, outthrust 10 projection, protrusion 11 protuberate 12 protuberance

bulk 4 body, core, loom, mass 5 total 6 amount, budget, corpus, object, staple, volume 7 bigness, quantum 8 quantity, stand out 9 aggregate, greatness, largeness, magnitude, substance ***combining form:*** 4 onco 5 oncho

bull 3 big, fat 4 slip, toro, trip 5 boner, buyer, error, fluff, husky, lapse, large 6 bun-

gle 7 blooper, blunder, mistake 8 oversize *combining form:* 4 taur 5 tauri, tauro
bulldoze 3 cow 4 push 5 bully, press, shove 6 hector, hustle, jostle 7 bluster, dragoon 8 bludgeon, browbeat, bullyrag, shoulder 10 intimidate
bullet 3 fly, zip 4 whiz 5 hurry 6 barrel, dumdum, tracer *size:* 7 caliber, calibre
bull fiddle 10 contrabass, double bass
bullfighter 6 torero 7 matador, picador 8 toreador 9 cuadrilla 11 cuadrillero 12 banderillero *famous:* 6 Arruza 8 Belmonte, Joselito, Manolete 10 El Cordobes
bullfighting *arena:* 5 plaza *cheer:* 3 olé *hero:* 6 torero 7 matador 8 toreador *lancer:* 7 picador *red cloth:* 6 muleta *Spanish:* 7 corrida *team:* 9 cuadrilla
bullheaded 6 mulish 8 perverse 9 obstinate, pigheaded 10 headstrong, refractory, self-willed 11 intractable, stiff-necked 12 pertinacious
bullwork 4 moil, toil 5 grind, labor, sweat 6 drudge 7 travail 8 drudgery
bully 3 cow 4 fine, punk 5 meany 6 hector, meanie, menace, pander 7 bluster, dragoon, harrier, torment 8 ballyrag, bludgeon, browbeat, bulldoze, bullyrag, harasser, threaten 9 bulldozer, excellent, first-rate, front-rank, tormenter 10 browbeater, intimidate, macquereau, persecutor 11 antagonizer, intimidator
bullyrag see **bulldoze**
bulwark 4 fend 5 cover, guard 6 defend, screen, secure, shield 7 bastion, parapet, protect, rampart 8 fortress 9 safeguard 10 breastwork, stronghold
bum 3 beg, jag, vag 4 bust, hobo, idle, laze, lazy, loaf, loll, slug 5 binge, cadge, drunk, idler, mooch, tramp 6 bender, dawdle, loafer, loiter, lounge, slouch 7 carouse, drifter, floater, goof off, vagrant, wassail 8 derelict, dolittle, faineant, slugabed, sluggard, vagabond 9 brannigan, do-nothing, goldbrick, lazybones, panhandle 10 street arab
bumbershoot 8 umbrella
bumble 3 hum 4 buzz, muff 5 botch, drone, lurch, strum, thrum 6 bobble, bollix, bungle, fumble, mucker 7 blunder, stumble 9 bombinate
bumbling 5 inept 6 gauche, wooden 7 awkward, halting, unhandy, unhappy 9 ham-handed, maladroit 11 heavy-handed
bummer 6 bandit, beggar, cadger, looter 7 brigand, cateran, forager, moocher 8 marauder, pillager 9 plunderer 10 depredator, freebooter, panhandler
bump 3 hit, jar 4 bang, bust, jolt, knot, knur, lump, slam 5 break, bunch, carom, clash, crash, gnarl, knock, shock 6 demote, impact, jostle, reduce, strike, wallop 7 collide, declass, degrade, demerit, disrate, mudhole, pothole 8 disgrade, pumpknot, swelling 9 chuckhole, collision, downgrade 10 concussion, percussion 12 protuberance
bumpkin 4 hick, jake, rube 6 joskin, rustic 7 bucolic, hayseed, hoosier 9 chawbacon 10 clodhopper, provincial
bump off 4 do in, kill 6 finish, murder 7 execute, put away 9 liquidate 11 assassinate
Bumppo, Natty *alias:* 7 Hawkeye 10 Deerslayer, Pathfinder *creator:* 6 Cooper
bumptious 8 arrogant 9 conceited, obtrusive
bumpy 5 jerky, nubby, ridgy, rough 6 bouncy, jouncy 7 jolting
bunch 3 lot, set 4 band, bevy, body, bump, crew, knot, lump, push 5 batch, clump, covey, crowd, group, party 6 bundle, circle, clutch, parcel 7 cluster 8 assembly
bunco steerer 3 gyp 6 con man 7 diddler, sharper 8 swindler 9 defrauder, trickster 12 double-dealer 13 confidence man
bundle 3 lot, pot, set, wad 4 bale, body, mint, pile 5 array, batch, bunch, clump, group, sheaf 6 bindle, boodle, fardel, packet, parcel 7 cluster, fortune *of grain:* 5 sheaf, shock, stook *of hay:* 4 bale, wase *of sticks:* 5 fagot 6 faggot 7 fascine *small:* 8 fascicle
bungle 4 bull, flub, muff, slip, trip 5 boner, botch, error, fluff, gum up, lapse 6 bollix, foozle, goof up 7 blooper, blunder, louse up, mistake
bungler 5 klutz 8 shlemiel 9 blunderer, schlemiel 10 stumblebum 11 blunderbuss
bunglesome 6 clumsy 7 awkward
bunk 3 hut 5 board, hokum, house, lodge, put up 6 bestow, billet, harbor, humbug 7 baloney, quarter 8 domicile, nonsense 9 poppycock
bunkum 4 jazz 5 hokum 7 baloney 8 flimflam, nonsense 9 poppycock 10 balderdash
Bunyanesque 4 huge 7 mammoth, titanic 8 colossal, gigantic 9 Herculean, monstrous 10 behemothic, gargantuan, prodigious
buoy 4 prop 6 uphold 7 bolster, support, sustain 9 underprop
buoyancy 10 ebullience, exuberance, exuberancy 13 effervescence
buoyant 4 airy 6 bouncy 7 elastic 8 volatile 9 expansive, resilient 12 effervescent
burble 3 yak 4 chat, wash 5 clack, run on, slosh, swash 6 babble, bubble, gabble, gurgle, rattle, yammer 7 chatter, prattle
burden 3 tax 4 clog, duty, gist, haul, lade, load, onus, task 5 cargo, weigh 6 amount, charge, cumber, lading, lumber, saddle,

upshot, weight 7 afflict, freight, oppress, payload, purport 8 encumber, handicap, overload 9 millstone, substance 10 deadweight

burdensome 5 tough 6 taxing 7 exigent, onerous, weighty 8 exacting, grievous 9 demanding 10 oppressive

bureau 5 chest 7 dresser 10 chiffonier

bureaucrat 8 mandarin, official 11 functionary 12 civil servant

burg 6 hamlet, Podunk 7 cowtown, mudhole, village 8 hick town, tank town 11 whistle-stop 12 one-horse town 13 jerkwater town

burgee 4 flag, jack 6 banner, ensign, pennon 7 pendant, pennant 8 standard, streamer

burgeon 4 blow 5 bloom, build, mount, run up 6 expand, flower, sprout 7 augment, blossom, enlarge 8 heighten, increase, multiply, outbloom, snowball 10 effloresce

burghal 4 city 5 urban 9 municipal

burgher 3 cit 5 towny 6 towner 7 citizen, townman 8 townsman

burglar 4 yegg 5 thief 6 robber 7 yeggman *loot:* 4 swag

burglarize 3 rob 6 burgle 7 ransack 10 housebreak

burgomaster 5 mayor 10 magistrate

Burgundy wine *grape:* 5 Gamay, Pinot *red:* 8 Mercurey 10 Beaujolais *white:* 5 Rully 6 Chagny 7 Chablis 10 Montrachet 13 Pouilly-Fuissé

burial 4 tomb 5 grave 7 funeral 8 exequies 9 interment, obsequies, sepulcher, sepulture 10 entombment, inhumation *box:* 6 casket, coffin *ceremony:* 7 funeral *coffin stand:* 4 bier *mound:* 3 low 6 barrow 7 tumulus *tomb:* 9 mausoleum, sepulcher, sepulchre

burial ground 8 boot hill, cemetery 8 God's acre 9 graveyard 10 necropolis 11 polyandrium 12 memorial park, potter's field *early Christian:* 8 catacomb

burlap 5 gunny 6 fabric 7 bagging, sacking 10 wrappering *fiber:* 4 hemp, jute

burlesque 3 ape 4 mock, sham 5 farce, mimic 6 parody 7 imitate, mockery, takeoff 8 travesty 10 caricature

burly 5 beefy, hefty, husky

Burma 7 Myanmar *capital:* 7 Rangoon

burn 4 bake, beam, bite, boil, char, cook, fire, fume, kiln, melt, rage, sere 5 anger, blaze, broil, chark, creek, flame, flare, gleam, light, parch, roast, scald, shine, singe, smart, smoke, sting, toast 6 blow up, ignite, kindle, scorch, seethe, stream 7 bristle, combust, consume, cremate, flare up, inflame, radiate, smolder, sputter, swelter 8 boil over, smoulder 9 carbonize, cauterize 10 incinerate *Scottish:* 7 scowder 8 scouther

burnable 9 flammable, ignitable 11 combustible, inflammable

burned-out 7 worn-out 8 fatigued 9 destroyed, exhausted 10 broken-down 11 debilitated

burning 3 hot 4 dire 5 afire, aglow, fiery 6 ablaze, aflame, alight, ardent, fervid, heated, hectic, red-hot, torrid, urgent 7 blazing, clamant, exigent, fervent, fevered, flaming, flaring, glowing, ignited, instant, lighted 8 broiling, feverish, pressing, sizzling, white-hot 9 clamorous, scorching 10 imperative, passionate 11 conflagrant, impassioned, importunate 12 incandescent *combining form:* 4 igni *malicious:* 5 arson *relating to:* 5 pyric

burnish 3 rub 4 buff 5 glaze, gloss, shine 6 glance, polish 7 furbish

burnished 5 shiny 6 glossy, sheeny 7 shining 8 gleaming, lustrous, polished 10 glistening

burnsides 5 beard 8 whiskers 10 sideboards 11 dundrearies, muttonchops 12 side-whiskers

burp 5 belch, eruct 8 eructate

burro 3 ass 4 donk 6 donkey 7 jackass

Burroughs' hero 6 Tarzan

burrow 3 den 4 hole, lair, snug 5 couch, hovel, lodge 6 cuddle, nestle, nuzzle 7 snuggle

burst 4 bang, boom, clap, gust, rive, slam, wham 5 blast, crack, crash, erupt, flare, go off, lunge, sally, salvo, smash, storm 6 access, blow up, plunge, shiver, shower, volley 7 barrage, explode, flare-up, rupture, shatter 8 break out, detonate, drumfire, eruption, fragment, mushroom, outbreak, splinter, splitter 9 broadside, cannonade, explosion, fusillade 11 bombardment

bursting 8 erumpent *combining form:* 7 rrhexis, rrhexes (plural)

bury 4 hide, tomb 5 cache, cover, inter, plant, stash 6 coffin, entomb, inhume, screen 7 conceal, lay away, put away, secrete 8 ensconce 9 sepulcher, sepulture

bush 4 rose 5 lilac, shrub, wahoo 6 azalea, cassis, privet 7 currant, weigela 8 backland, backwash, barberry, frontier, hazelnut 9 backwater, backwoods, forsythia, manzanita, up-country 10 gooseberry, hinterland 11 pussy willow 12 rhododendron *combining form:* 5 thamn 6 thamno

bush-league 5 minor 8 mediocre 10 inadequate, second-rate

bushranger 8 woodsman 12 frontiersman

bushwa 4 bosh 5 hooey 6 bunkum 7 baloney, eyewash 8 malarkey, nonsense 9 poppycock 10 balderdash, flapdoodle

bushwhacker 6 bandit, outlaw, raider, sniper 8 woodsman 9 guerrilla

bushy 5 bosky
business 3 job 4 duty, firm, line, role, work 5 trade 6 affair, custom, matter, office, outfit, racket 7 calling, company, concern, lookout, palaver, pursuit, traffic 8 commerce, function, industry, province 9 patronage 10 employment, enterprise, occupation 13 establishment ***expense:*** 8 overhead ***syndicate:*** 6 cartel
businesslike 7 serious 9 efficient, practical 10 purposeful, systematic
businessman 6 dealer, trader, tycoon 7 magnate 8 merchant 9 tradesman 10 trafficker 12 merchandiser
buss 4 kiss, peck 5 smack 6 smooch 8 osculate
bust 3 dud, jag, nab 4 bomb, bump, fail, flop, fold, raid, ruin 5 binge, break, crash, lemon, loser, spree 6 arrest, bender, demote, fold up, pauper, reduce 7 carouse, declass, degrade, demerit, disrate, failure 8 bankrupt, disgrade 9 downgrade, pauperize 10 impoverish
bustard ***African:*** 7 korhaan 8 knorhaan ***genus:*** 4 Otis ***relating to:*** 7 otidine
bustle 3 ado, fly, run 4 flit, fuss, rush, stir, to-do 5 hurry, whirl, whisk 6 clamor, flurry, furore, hassle, hasten, hubbub, hustle, pother, tumult, uproar 7 turmoil 9 commotion, whirlpool, whirlwind 10 hurly-burly
bustling 4 busy 5 brisk, fussy 6 active, lively 7 hopping, humming, popping 9 energetic
busty 5 buxom 6 bosomy, chesty 11 full-bosomed
busy 5 fussy 6 engage, lively, occupy 7 engaged, engross, hopping, humming, immerse, popping, working 8 bustling, employed, hustling, occupied 9 assiduous, intrusive, obtrusive, officious 10 meddlesome 11 impertinent
busybody 5 prier, pryer, snook, snoop 6 butt-in, gossip, rubber 7 meddler, Paul Pry 8 informer, kibitzer, quidnunc 9 pragmatic 10 newsmonger, pragmatist, rubberneck 11 nosey Parker, rumormonger 12 gossipmonger, intermeddler
but 3 bar, yet 4 just, only, save 5 alone 6 bating, except, merely, saving, simply, solely, unless 7 barring, besides, however 8 entirely 9 aside from, excluding, outside of 11 exclusively
butcher 4 slay 9 slaughter
butcher-bird 6 shrike
butcherly 6 bloody, clumsy, savage 10 unskillful
butchery 7 carnage 8 massacre 9 bloodbath, bloodshed, slaughter
Butler, Samuel ***novel:*** 7 Erewhon 16 The Way of All Flesh ***poem:*** 8 Hudibras
butt 3 keg, tun 4 abut, cask, dupe, fool, gull, jest, join, joke, line, mark, mock, pipe 5 chump, touch, verge 6 adjoin, barrel, border, jestee, pigeon, sucker, target, victim 7 fall guy, gudgeon, mockery 8 derision, hogshead, neighbor 9 cigarette, pilgarlic 11 communicate, sitting duck 13 laughingstock
butter ***artificial:*** 4 oleo 9 margarine 13 oleomargarine ***Indian:*** 3 ghi 4 ghee ***piece:*** 3 pat ***semifluid:*** 3 ghi 4 ghee ***tree:*** 4 shea ***tub:*** 6 firkin
butterball 5 blimp, fatty 8 dumpling
butterfish 5 coney 6 gunnel
butterfly 5 diana, satyr, zebra 6 copper, morpho 7 admiral, buckeye, kallima, monarch, satyrid, skipper, sulphur, troilus, vanessa, viceroy 8 crescent, grayling, milkweed, victoria 9 aphrodite, metalmark, nymphalid, wood nymph 10 fritillary, hairstreak, parnassius 11 checkerspot, swallowtail ***bush:*** 8 buddleia ***fish:*** 6 blenny, chiton 7 gurnard ***larva:*** 11 caterpillar ***lily:*** 8 mariposa ***order:*** 11 Lepidoptera ***plant:*** 8 oncidium ***pupa:*** 9 chrysalis ***scientist:*** 13 lepidopterist
butterlike 8 butyrous 11 butyraceous
butt-in 7 meddler 8 busybody, kibitzer, quidnunc
butt in 6 horn in, meddle 7 intrude, obtrude 8 busybody, chisel in 9 interfere, interlope 10 intertrude, monkey with, tamper with 11 intermeddle
buttinsky see butt-in
buttocks 4 prat, rear, rump, seat, tail 5 fanny, hiney, nates, podex 6 behind, bottom, breech, heinie 7 hind end, hunkers, keester, keister, rear end, tail end 8 backside, derriere, haunches 9 fundament, posterior ***combining form:*** 3 pyg 4 pyga, pygo 5 pygia 6 procta
button ***Japanese:*** 7 netsuke
buttonball 8 sycamore
button-down 6 square 8 orthodox, straight 12 conventional
buttonwood 8 sycamore 13 white mangrove
buttress 4 prop, stay 5 brace, shore 6 bear up, column, upbear, uphold 7 bolster, shore up, support, sustain 11 underpinner 12 underpinning 13 underpropping
buxom 5 busty 6 bosomy, chesty 7 shapely, stacked 10 curvaceous 11 full bosomed, full-figured
buy 3 get 5 bribe 6 obtain, ransom, redeem 7 acquire, bargain, believe 8 close-out, purchase 10 pennyworth, tamper with ***Scottish:*** 4 coff
buy back 6 redeem
buyer 6 emptor, vendee 8 customer 9 purchaser
buy off 3 fix, sop 5 bribe 10 tamper with

Buzi's son 7 Ezekiel
buzz 3 hum 4 fizz, hiss, whir, whiz 5 drone, rumor, strum, thrum, whirr, whish 6 bumble, fizzle, gossip, report, rumble, sizzle, wheeze, whoosh 7 whisper 8 sibilate 9 bombinate 11 scuttlebutt
by 3 per, via 4 as to, near, nigh, over, with 5 adieu, round 6 beside, nearby, next to, so long 7 good-bye, through 8 farewell 9 alongside 11 according to
by and by 4 anon, next, soon 5 after, infra, later 7 shortly 8 directly, latterly 9 afterward, presently 10 afterwhile 12 subsequently
by and large 7 en masse 8 all in all 9 generally 10 altogether, on the whole
by dint of see by means of
bye-bye 5 adieu 6 so long 7 cheerio 8 farewell, toodle-oo
bygone 3 old 4 dead, late, lost, once, past 5 dated, olden 6 former, whilom 7 antique, archaic, belated, defunct, extinct, old-time, onetime, quondam 8 departed, sometime, vanished 9 erstwhile, out-of-date 10 antiquated, oldfangled 12 old-fashioned
by means of 3 per, via 4 with 7 through
byname 7 moniker 8 nickname 9 sobriquet 10 hypocorism
bypass 5 burke, skirt 6 detour 8 sidestep 10 circumvent
byplace 4 nook 5 niche 6 cranny
by-product 7 spin-off 8 offshoot 9 outgrowth 10 derivative, descendant
Byron work 4 Cain, Lara 5 Beppo 6 Werner 7 Don Juan, Manfred 9 The Giaour 10 The Corsair 12 Childe Harold
bystander 6 viewer 7 watcher, witness 8 beholder, looker-on, observer, onlooker 9 spectator 10 eyewitness
by stealth 7 sub rosa 8 covertly, secretly 9 furtively, privately 13 clandestinely
by virtue of see by means of
by way of see by means of
byword 3 saw 5 adage 6 phrase, saying, slogan 7 proverb 8 nickname 9 sobriquet 10 hypocorism, shibboleth 11 catchphrase
Byzantine 6 daedal, knotty 7 complex, gordian 8 involved 9 elaborate, intricate 11 complicated 12 labyrinthine 13 sophisticated ***emperor:*** 3 Leo 4 Zeno 5 Basil 6 Bardas, Justin, Phocas 7 Michael, Romanus 9 Heraclius, Justinian 10 Nicephorus, Theodosius ***empress:*** 3 Zoe 5 Irene 8 Theodora

C

cab 4 hack, taxi
cabal 3 mob 4 camp, clan, plot, ring 5 covin 6 circle, clique, scheme 7 coterie, ingroup 8 intrigue, practice 9 camarilla 10 conspiracy 11 machination
cabaletta 4 aria, song
cabalistic 6 arcane, mystic 8 numinous 9 mysterial, unguessed 10 mysterious, unknowable 11 inscrutable 12 impenetrable 13 unaccountable
caballero 6 knight 8 cavalier, horseman 9 chevalier
cabaret 4 café 6 nitery 7 hot spot 8 nightery 9 nightclub, night spot 10 supper club 11 discotheque 12 watering hole
cabbage 3 nab, nip 4 hook, lift 5 kraut, money, pinch, steal 6 collar 7 purloin 10 greenbacks, sauerkraut 11 appropriate ***disease of:*** 6 mildew, mosaic 7 root rot, yellows 8 blackleg, club root ***family:*** 4 cole, kail, kale, rape 5 colza, savoy 6 turnip 7 collard, mustard 8 broccoli, coleseed, colewort, kohlrabi, rutabaga 11 cauliflower
cabbagehead see dunce
cabdriver 4 hack 5 cabby 6 cabbie
cabin 3 cot, hut 4 camp 5 lodge, shack 6 cabana, shanty 7 cottage 9 stateroom
cabin cruiser 4 boat 9 motorboat
cabinet 7 armoire, commode 8 cupboard
cabinetmaker ***American:*** 5 Phyfe 6 Belter, Wright 7 Goddard 8 McIntire, Townsend ***English:*** 4 Adam, Hope, Kent 5 Smith 8 Sheraton 11 Hepplewhite ***French:*** 6 Boulle 8 Caffieri, Cressent ***German:*** 10 Weisweiler
cable 4 rope, wire 6 stitch
cabriolet 8 carriage
cache 4 bury, hide 5 cover, plant, stash, store 7 conceal, secrete 8 ensconce
cachet 4 rank 5 state 6 status 7 dignity, stature 8 position, prestige, standing 11 consequence

cachinnate 5 laugh
cackle 3 gab, jaw 4 blab, chat 5 clack, run on 6 babble, burble, gabble, gaggle 7 blabber, blatter, chatter, prattle
cacoëthes 5 mania
cacophonic 9 dissonant, immusical, unmusical 10 discordant, inharmonic 11 disharmonic 12 inharmonious, unharmonious 13 disharmonious
cacophonous see **cacophonic**
cacophony 10 dissonance
cactus 5 dildo, nopal 6 cereus, cholla, mescal, peyote 7 airampo, bisnaga, biznaga, opuntia, saguaro, sahuaro 8 chichipe 11 prickly pear ***fruit:*** 6 cochal
cad 3 cur 4 heel, lout 5 creep, louse 6 rotter 7 bounder 9 yellow dog
cadaver 4 body, mort 5 stiff 6 corpse 7 carcass, remains
cadaverous 5 gaunt 6 wasted 7 ghastly, ghostly, shadowy 8 skeletal, spectral 9 deathlike, emaciated, ghostlike 10 corpselike
cadence 4 beat 5 meter, pulse, rhyme, swing, throb 6 rhythm 7 measure 8 rhythmus 9 pulsation
cadency see **cadence**
cadet 4 pimp 5 bully, plebe 6 pander 8 fancy man 10 macquereau
cadge 3 beg, bum 5 mooch 6 sponge 9 panhandle
cadmium ***symbol:*** 2 Cd
Cadmus ***daughter:*** 3 Ino 5 Agave 6 Semele 7 Autonoe ***father:*** 6 Agenor ***sister:*** 6 Europa ***victim:*** 6 dragon ***wife:*** 8 Harmonia
caducity 3 age 6 old age 7 dotardy 10 dotingness, senescence 11 elderliness, senectitude
Caesar ***assassin:*** 6 Brutus 7 Cassius ***battle:*** 4 Zela 9 Pharsalus ***conquest:*** 4 Gaul ***eulogist:*** 6 Antony ***message:*** 12 veni, vidi, vici ***river:*** 7 Rubicon ***utterance:*** 9 et tu Brute ***wife:*** 7 Pompeia 8 Cornelia 9 Calpurnia
Caesarism 10 absolutism 12 dictatorship
café 5 diner 6 nitery 7 beanery, cabaret, hot spot 8 cookshop, nightery 9 lunchroom, nightclub, night spot 10 coffee shop, supper club 11 discotheque, eating house 12 luncheonette, watering hole 13 watering place
café ___ 6 au lait, filtre
cage 3 hem, mew, pen 4 coop, jail 6 immure, shut in 7 close in, enclose, envelop 8 imprison 11 incarcerate
cagey 3 sly 5 heady 6 argute, astute, shrewd 9 astucious, sagacious 13 perspicacious
cageyness 3 art 5 craft 7 cunning, slyness 8 artifice, foxiness, wiliness 9 canniness 10 artfulness, craftiness
cahoots 5 tie-up 6 hookup 8 alliance 10 connection 11 affiliation, association, combination, conjunction, partnership 12 togetherness
caiman 6 jacare 9 crocodile
Cain ***brother:*** 4 Abel, Seth ***father:*** 4 Adam ***land:*** 3 Nod ***mother:*** 3 Eve ***nephew:*** 4 Enos ***son:*** 5 Enoch ***victim:*** 4 Abel
Caine Mutiny author 4 Wouk
cajole 3 con 4 coax 7 beguile, blarney, wheedle 8 blandish, soft-soap 9 sweet-talk
cake 3 dry, set 4 coat, rime 5 cover, crust 6 harden 7 congeal, encrust, incrust 8 indurate, solidify 10 incrustate ***almond:*** 8 macaroon ***chocolate:*** 7 brownie ***coffee:*** 5 babka 6 kuchen ***cornmeal:*** 4 pone 8 tortilla ***crisp, thin:*** 5 wafer ***flat:*** 5 cooky 6 cookie ***oatmeal:*** 4 farl 5 farle, scone 7 bannock ***of food:*** 5 patty 6 pattie ***ring-shaped:*** 5 donut 6 jumbal, jumble 8 doughnut ***rum-soaked:*** 4 baba ***Scottish:*** 4 farl 5 farle, scone ***shell-shaped:*** 9 madeleine ***toasted:*** 7 crumpet ***topping:*** 5 icing 8 frosting, streusel ***twisted:*** 7 cruller ***unleavened:*** 8 tortilla ***wheat:*** 4 puri ***without flour:*** 5 torte ***without shortening:*** 6 sponge
Cakes and Ale author 7 Maugham
cakewalk 4 romp, rout 5 dance, strut 6 prance 7 runaway
calaboose 4 jail 5 clink, pokey 6 cooler, lockup, prison 8 hoosegow
Calais ***brother:*** 5 Zetes ***father:*** 6 Boreas ***mother:*** 8 Orithyia
calamitous 4 dire 5 fatal 6 woeful 7 fateful, ruinous 8 grievous 10 afflictive, deplorable, disastrous, lamentable 11 cataclysmic, distressing, regrettable, unfortunate 12 catastrophic 13 heartbreaking
calamity 4 ruin, woes 5 wreck 7 tragedy 8 disaster 9 cataclysm 10 affliction 11 catastrophe, tribulation 12 misadventure
Calamity ___ 4 Jane
calamity howler 9 Cassandra, pessimist, worrywart
calcar 4 oven
calcium ***symbol:*** 2 Ca
calculate 5 count, value 6 assess, cipher, figure, reckon 7 compute 8 appraise, estimate, evaluate 9 ascertain, determine
calculated 7 planned
calculating 3 sly 4 wary, wily 5 chary 6 artful, crafty 7 careful, cunning, guarded 8 cautious, discreet, gingerly, guileful 11 circumspect, considerate
calculating device 6 abacus ***ancient Peruvian:*** 5 quipo, quipu
calculation 8 figuring 9 ciphering, reckon-

ing **10** arithmetic, estimation **11** computation
calculus ***combining form:*** **4** lith **5** litho
Caleb ***daughter:*** **6** Achsah ***father:*** **6** Hezron **9** Jephunneh ***son:*** **3** Hur, Iru
Caledonia **8** Scotland
calembour **3** pun **11** paronomasia
calendar **4** card, sked **6** agenda, docket **7** program **8** schedule **9** programma, timetable ***abbreviation:*** **3** Apr, Aug, Dec, Feb, Fri, Jan, Mar, Mon, Nov, Oct, Sat, Sep, Sun, Tue, Wed **4** Sept **5** Thurs ***ecclesiastical:*** **4** ordo **8** menology
calenture **4** fire, zeal **5** ardor **6** fervor, hurrah **7** passion **10** enthusiasm
calf ***hide:*** **3** kip ***leather:*** **3** elk ***meat:*** **4** veal ***stray:*** **4** dogy **5** dogie ***unbranded:*** **8** maverick
Caliban **5** slave ***master:*** **8** Prospero ***witch-mother:*** **7** Sycorax
caliber **5** class, grade, merit, value, worth **6** virtue **7** quality, stature
calibrate **7** measure **9** systemize **11** standardize
California ***capital:*** **10** Sacramento ***college, university:*** **3** USC **4** UCLA **5** Biola **8** Stanford **10** Pepperdine **12** San Francisco ***colonizer:*** **6** Sutter ***fault zone:*** **10** San Andreas ***largest city:*** **10** Los Angeles ***motto:*** **6** Eureka ***nickname:*** **11** Golden State ***state flower:*** **11** golden poppy
californium ***symbol:*** **2** Cf
caliginous **3** dim **4** dark, dusk **5** dusky, murky **6** gloomy **7** obscure **9** lightless, tenebrous **13** unilluminated
Caligula's mother **9** Agrippina
caliology topic **4** nest
caliph's name **3** Ali **7** Abu Bakr
Calista's seducer **8** Lothario
calisthenics **9** exercises
call **3** bid, cry, dub **4** bawl, draw, hail, hoot, howl, lure, name, note, page, pull, roar, song, term, yell, yowl **5** augur, cause, claim, exact, greet, hallo, hollo, phone, pop in, shout, title, visit **6** accost, appeal, bellow, come by, drop by, drop in, holler, invite, look in, look up, reckon, salute, stop by, stop in, summon **7** address, baptize, convene, convoke, entitle, portend, predict, presage, round up, solicit, summons **8** assemble, christen, estimate, forecast, foretell, occasion, prophesy **9** adumbrate, challenge, designate, necessity, postulate, seduction, telephone **10** allurement, attraction, denominate, vaticinate, visitation, vociferate **11** approximate, requisition **12** drawing power **13** prognosticate
calla **4** lily
call down **5** chide **6** lesson, monish, rebuke **7** reprove, tick off **8** admonish, reproach **9** reprimand
called **6** yclept **7** ycleped
caller **5** guest **7** visitor **8** visitant
call for **3** ask **5** crave **6** demand **7** require **11** necessitate
call forth **5** evoke **6** elicit **7** conjure
calligrapher **6** penman **7** copyist **9** engrosser
calligraphist see calligrapher
calligraphy **4** hand **6** ductus, script **10** penmanship **11** handwriting
call in **6** summon **7** convene
calling **3** art, job **4** work **5** craft, trade **6** métier **7** mission, pursuit **8** business, lifework, vocation **10** employment, handicraft, occupation, profession
Calliope **4** Muse ***father:*** **4** Zeus **7** Jupiter ***mother:*** **9** Mnemosyne ***son:*** **7** Orpheus
Callisto ***lover:*** **4** Zeus **7** Jupiter ***son:*** **5** Arcas
call off **5** scrub **6** cancel
Call of the Wild ***author:*** **6** London ***dog:*** **4** Buck
call on **5** visit **7** require
callosity **8** hardness **9** thickness
callous **5** stony **8** obdurate **9** heartless, indurated, unfeeling **11** coldhearted, hardhearted, unemotional **12** case-hardened, stonyhearted **13** unsympathetic
callow **3** raw **5** fresh, green, young **6** infant, unripe **7** untried **8** immature, juvenile, unversed, youthful **9** unfledged **10** unseasoned **11** unpracticed **13** inexperienced, unexperienced
call's partner **4** beck
call up **5** draft, evoke **6** summon **8** mobilize
calm **4** cool, easy, hush, lull **5** allay, peace, quiet, relax, salve, still **6** hushed, pacify, placid, poised, sedate, serene, settle, smooth, soothe, stable, steady, stilly **7** appease, assuage, compose, halcyon, mollify, pacific, placate, resting, staunch **8** composed, inactive, peaceful, reposing, tranquil **9** collected, easygoing, impassive, possessed, quiescent, unruffled **10** nonchalant, phlegmatic, untroubled **11** tranquilize, unflappable **12** even-tempered, self-composed **13** imperturbable, self-possessed
calmant **8** quietive, sedative
calmative see calmant
calmness **6** phlegm **7** ataraxy **8** coolness **9** composure, sangfroid **10** equanimity
calumniate **5** libel **6** defame, malign, vilify **7** asperse, slander, traduce **9** denigrate **10** scandalize, villainize
calumnious **8** libelous **9** maligning, traducing, vilifying **10** backbiting, defamatory, detracting, detractive, scandalous, slanderous
calumny **7** scandal, slander **10** backbiting,

defamation, detraction, reflection **12** back-stabbing, belittlement, depreciation **13** disparagement
Calvados **6** brandy
calvary **5** cross, trial **6** ordeal **10** affliction, visitation **11** tribulation
Calypso ***beloved:*** **7** Ulysses **8** Odysseus ***island:*** **6** Ogygia
calyx part **5** sepal
camaraderie **5** cheer **7** jollity **10** affability **11** sociability **12** conviviality, friendliness
camarilla **3** mob **4** camp, clan, ring **5** cabal **6** circle, clique **7** coterie, ingroup
Cambodia **9** Kampuchea ***capital:*** **0** Pnom penh ***monetary unit:*** **4** riel
camel ***driver:*** **6** sarwan ***one-humped:*** **9** dromedary ***two-humped:*** **8** Bactrian
camel hair fabric **3** aba
camelopard **7** giraffe
Camelot **6** palace ***lord:*** **6** Arthur
Camembert **6** cheese
cameraman **6** photog **7** lensman **8** photoist **12** photographer
Cameroon ***capital:*** **7** Yaounde ***largest city:*** **6** Douala ***monetary unit:*** **5** franc
Camilla ***father:*** **7** Metabus ***slayer:*** **5** Aruns
Camille's creator **5** Dumas
camouflage **4** mask **5** cloak **8** disguise **9** dissemble **11** dissimulate
camp **3** cot, hut, mob **4** clan, ring, tent **5** cabal, cabin, lodge, shack **6** circle, clique, shanty **7** bivouac, caboose, coterie, cottage, ingroup **9** camarilla
campaigner **9** candidate
campanile **6** belfry **8** carillon **9** bell tower
campestral **5** rural **6** rustic **7** bucolic, country, outland **8** agrestic, pastoral **10** out-country, provincial **11** countrified
campus see college
Camus work **5** Rebel **6** Plague **8** Caligula, Stranger
can **4** fire **7** dismiss **9** container, discharge **10** receptacle ***combining form:*** **5** scyph **6** scyphi, scypho
Canaan **4** Zion **5** bliss **6** heaven **7** elysium, nirvana **8** empyrean, paradise ***father:*** **3** Ham ***grandfather:*** **4** Noah
Canaanite god **3** Mot **4** Baal **6** Molech, Moloch
Canace ***brother:*** **8** Macareus ***father:*** **6** Aeolus
Canada ***capital:*** **6** Ottawa ***college, university:*** **6** McGill **8** McMaster **9** Concordia ***largest city:*** **8** Montreal ***monetary unit:*** **6** dollar ***province:*** **6** Quebec **7** Alberta, Ontario **8** Manitoba **10** Nova Scotia **12** New Brunswick, Newfoundland, Saskatchewan ***provincial park:*** **5** Gaspé **7** Rondeau **9** Garibaldi
Canadian insurgent **4** Riel
canaille **3** mob **6** masses, rabble **8** riffraff, unwashed **11** proletariat
canal **4** duct **6** course **7** channel, conduit **8** aqueduct **11** watercourse ***Africa:*** **4** Suez **8** Ismailia ***Belgium:*** **6** Albert ***Canada:*** **7** Welland ***Central America:*** **6** Panama ***China:*** **5** Grand **7** Da Yunhe ***combining form:*** **4** meat **5** meato ***Florida:*** **10** Saint Lucie ***Germany:*** **4** Kiel ***Greece:*** **7** Corinth ***Massachusetts:*** **7** Cape Cod ***Michigan:*** **3** Soo ***Netherlands:*** **8** Noord Zee, North Sea **13** Amsterdam Ship ***New York:*** **4** Erie **6** Oswego **9** Champlain ***Ontario:*** **6** Rideau ***Thailand:*** **6** khlong ***Venice:*** **5** Grand
canapé spread **4** paté
canard **3** fib, lie **4** tale **5** spoof **7** falsity, untruth **8** untruism **9** falsehood **13** prevarication
canary **4** fink **6** snitch **7** stoolie **8** informer, squealer
Canary Islands **5** Ferro, Lobos, Palma **6** Gomera, Hierro **7** Inferno **8** Graciosa, Tenerife **9** Alegranza, Lanzarote
canary yellow **6** meline
cancel **3** end **4** drop, x out **5** annul, erase, scrub **6** delete, efface, negate, revoke **7** blot out, call off, expunge, redress, rescind, sublate, wipe out **8** black out **9** frustrate, terminate **10** counteract, invalidate, neutralize, obliterate **12** countercheck
cancer **5** tumor **9** carcinoma ***combining form:*** **6** carcin **7** carcino ***treatment:*** **5** X rays **7** surgery **9** radiation **12** chemotherapy
cancer-causing **12** carcinogenic ***substance:*** **10** carcinogen
cancer-like **8** cancroid
candescent **7** glowing **8** dazzling
Candia **5** Crete
candid **4** fair, just, open **5** frank, plain **6** honest **8** unbiased **9** equitable, impartial, objective, uncolored **10** aboveboard, forthright, scrupulous, unreserved **11** openhearted, unconcealed, undisguised **12** undissembled, unprejudiced **13** dispassionate, undissembling
candidate **6** seeker **7** hopeful, nominee, stumper **8** aspirant **9** applicant, dark horse **10** campaigner
Candide ***author:*** **8** Voltaire ***lover:*** **9** Cunegonde ***tutor:*** **8** Pangloss ***valet:*** **7** Cacambo
candle **6** bougie **8** bayberry ***holder:*** **6** lampad, sconce **7** menorah, pricket **9** girandole **10** candelabra **11** candelabrum ***material:*** **3** wax **4** wick **6** tallow **7** stearin **8** paraffin ***religious:*** **6** votive **7** paschal ***slender:*** **5** taper
candlefish **8** eulachon ***relative:*** **5** smelt
candlepins **7** bowling

candy 5 honey 7 sweeten 9 sugarcoat, sugar over *kind:* 4 rock 5 fudge, gundy, lolly, sweet, taffy, toffy 6 bonbon, comfit, dragée, jujube, nougat, toffee 7 brittle, caramel, fondant, gumdrop, penuche, praline 8 licorice, lollipop, lollypop, marzipan, sourball, taiglach, teiglach 9 chocolate, jelly bean, nonpareil, sweetmeat 10 confection 12 butterscotch *medicated:* 7 lozenge 9 cough drop
Canea's land 5 Crete
canine 3 dog 4 tyke 5 hound, pooch
Canis Major star 6 Sirius
Canis Minor star 7 Procyon
canker 5 stain 6 debase 7 corrupt, debauch, deprave, pervert, vitiate 9 animalize 10 bestialize, demoralize
cankered 5 waspy 6 cranky, ornery 7 bearish, waspish 8 vinegary 9 crotchety 10 vinegarish 12 cantankerous, cross-grained
canker sore 5 ulcer 6 lesion 10 ulceration
cannabis 3 pot 4 hemp 5 bhang, ganja, grass 7 hashish 9 marijuana
canned 6 pocket, potted 7 capsule 9 condensed 10 epitomized
Cannery Row author 9 Steinbeck
cannibalic 4 grim 5 cruel 6 fierce, savage 7 inhuman, wolfish 8 inhumane 9 barbarous, ferocious, truculent
canniness 3 art 5 craft 7 caution, cunning, slyness 8 artifice, foxiness, prudence, wiliness 9 cageyness, foresight 10 artfulness, craftiness, discretion, precaution, providence 11 forethought 12 discreetness
cannon 6 pom-pom 8 howitzer, ordnance 9 artillery *part:* 5 chase 6 breech 8 cascabel, trunnion *slang:* 6 pistol 10 pickpocket
cannonade 4 bomb, hail 5 blitz, burst, salvo, shell 6 shower, volley 7 barrage, bombard 8 drumfire 9 broadside, fusillade 11 bombardment
cannonball 4 dive 5 speed 7 missile
cannoneer 6 gunner
cannon fodder 8 infantry, soldiers
canny 3 sly 4 wise 5 chary, quick, sharp, slick, smart 6 adroit, clever, frugal, saving 7 cunning, knowing, sparing, thrifty 9 dexterous, ingenious, provident, stewardly 10 economical, unwasteful 11 quick-witted, sharp-witted 12 nimble-witted
canoe 6 dugout 7 pirogue, piroque *ancient:* 7 coracle *Central American:* 6 pitpan *Eskimo:* 5 kayak, umiak 6 oomiak 7 bidarka *Guianan:* 6 corial *Latin American:* 5 bungo *Malabar Coast:* 6 ballam *Maori:* 4 waka *Philippine:* 5 banca 6 baroto *Polynesian:* 4 pahi
canon 3 law 4 rule 5 dogma, edict, tenet 6 assize, decree 7 precept, statute 8 decretum, doctrine 9 ordinance 10 regulation
canonical 5 sound 8 accepted, orthodox, received 10 sanctioned 13 authoritative
canonical hour 4 none, sext 5 lauds, prime, terce 6 matins, tierce 7 vespers 8 compline
canonicals 9 vestments
can opener 9 church key
canopy 3 sky 5 cover 6 awning 7 marquee, shelter 8 covering 9 baldachin 10 baldachino 11 baldacchino *canvas:* 4 tilt
cant 3 tip 4 heel, lean, list, tilt 5 argot, idiom, lingo, slang, slant, slope 6 jargon, patois, patter, speech 7 dialect, diction, incline, lexicon, palaver, recline 8 language 9 hypocrisy 10 dictionary, pharisaism, sanctimony, Tartuffery, Tartuffism, vernacular, vocabulary 11 phraseology, terminology 12 pecksniffery
cantaloupe 5 melon 9 muskmelon
cantankerous 4 dour, sour 5 cross, huffy, waspy 6 cranky, crusty, morose, ornery 7 bearish, crabbed, prickly, waspish 8 cankered, liverish, petulant, snappish, vinegary 9 crotchety, dyspeptic, irascible, irritable 10 ill-natured, vinegarish 12 cross-grained
canter 3 bum, vag 4 gait, hobo 5 tramp 7 drifter, vagrant 8 derelict, vagabond 10 street arab 11 bindle stiff
Canterbury *archbishop:* 3 Odo 6 Anselm, Becket, Parker 7 Cranmer, Dunstan 9 Augustine
Canterbury Tales *author:* 7 Chaucer *inn:* 6 Tabard
canticle 3 ode 4 hymn, song 10 Benedicite, Benedictus, Magnificat 12 Nunc Dimittis
canticles 11 Song of Songs 13 Song of Solomon
cantilever 6 bridge 7 support
cantillate 4 sing 5 chant 6 recite
cantina 3 bar, pub 6 saloon, tavern 7 barroom, gin mill, rum hole 8 drinkery, groggery, pothouse
canton 6 billet 7 quarter 8 district, division
cantor 5 hazan 6 chazan, hazzan 7 chazzan 9 precentor
canvas 4 duck, sail, tarp, tent 6 awning 8 painting 9 tarpaulin
canvasback 4 duck
canvass 3 con, vet 4 case, drum, moot 5 argue, study 6 debate, drum up, survey 7 agitate, check up, discept, discuss, dispute, examine, inspect, solicit 9 check over, thrash out 10 scrutinize
canyon 5 cajon, chasm, gorge, gulch 6 ravine, valley 10 depression *Colorado*

River: 5 Grand *mouth:* 4 abra *Snake river:* 5 Hells

cap 3 cob, top 4 best, pass 5 beret, cover, crest, crown, trump 6 barret, beanie, climax, exceed, top off 7 blanket, overlay, surpass 8 outshine, outstrip, overcast, round off, surmount 9 culminate, finish off, transcend 10 overspread *academic:* 11 mortarboard *brimless:* 3 tam 5 beret, calot 7 calotte *clergyman's:* 5 miter, mitre 7 biretta 9 zucchetto *combining form:* 8 calyptri, calyptro *cone-shaped:* 3 taj *hoodlike:* 4 coif *hunter's:* 7 montero *jester's:* 7 coxcomb 9 cockscomb *Jewish:* 8 yarmulke *knitted:* 5 toque, tuque *military:* 4 kepi *mushroom:* 6 pileus *Muslim:* 3 taj *part:* 4 bill, brim, flap, peak 5 visor 7 earflap *Roman:* 6 pileus *Scottish:* 3 tam 5 mutch 6 bonnet 8 balmoral 9 glengarry 11 tam-o'-shanter *sheepskin:* 6 calpac, kalpak 7 calpack *Turkish:* 6 calpac, kalpak 7 calpack

capability 3 art 5 craft, might, skill 7 ability, cunning, potency 8 adequacy, capacity, efficacy 10 competence, efficiency 13 effectiveness, qualification, qualifiedness

capable 4 able, good 6 au fait, proper, wicked 9 competent, qualified *suffix:* 3 ile 4 able, ible

capacious 4 wide 5 ample, roomy 7 copious 8 abundant, spacious 10 commodious

capacitance *unit of:* 5 farad

capacity 4 bent, gift, rank 5 knack, might, place, state 6 status, talent 7 ability, caliber, faculty, footing, station, stature 8 adequacy, position, standing 9 character, situation 10 capability, competence 13 qualification, qualifiedness *unit of:* 4 gill, peck, pint 5 liter, minim, quart 6 bushel, gallon 8 fluidram 10 fluidounce, milliliter

Capaneus *slayer:* 4 Zeus *wife:* 6 Evadne

caparison 8 clothing 9 adornment

cape 4 beak, bill, head, naze, ness 5 point 8 foreland, headland, pelerine 10 promontory *clergyman's:* 7 mozetta 8 mozzetta *papal:* 5 fanon, orale

Cape *Africa:* 4 Juby, Yubi 5 Blanc 6 Blanco 7 Agulhas *Alaska:* 3 Icy 4 Nome 5 Ocean 11 Krusenstern *Algeria:* 3 Fer *Antarctica:* 3 Ann 4 Dart 5 Adare *Arctic:* 5 North 8 Nordkaap *Asia:* 5 Aniva *Australia:* 5 Byron, Otway, Sandy, Smoky 6 Arnhem 9 Van Diemen *Baffin Island:* 4 Dyer *Black Sea:* 5 Yasun *Borneo:* 4 Datu 6 Datoek *Brazil:* 4 Frio, Raso 5 Norte *California:* 9 Mendocino *Canada:* 5 North *Caribbean:* 8 Honduras *Colombia:* 5 Aguja *Costa Rica:* 5 Velas *Crete:* 5 Plaka *Croatia:* 5 Ploca 6 Planka *Cuba:* 4 Cruz 5 Maisi *Denmark:* 4 Skaw 6 Skagen *Desolación island:* 5 Pilar 6 Pillar *Djibouti:* 3 Bir *Egypt:* 5 Banas *England:* 8 Bolerium, Lands End *Florida:* 5 Sable 7 Kennedy 9 Canaveral *Greece:* 4 Busa 5 Gallo, Malea, Papas, Vouxa 6 Araxos, Maleas 7 Akritas *Guadalcanal:* 4 West *Guinea:* 5 Verga *Gulf of California:* 5 Lobos *Gulf of Guinea:* 5 Lopez *Gulf of Mexico:* 4 Rojo *Hawaii:* 5 Ka Lae, South 10 South Point 11 Diamond Head *Hispaniola:* 5 Beata *Honshu:* 3 Iro, Oma 5 Inubo, Kyoga, Nyudo *Iceland:* 4 Horn 5 North *Indonesia:* 4 Vals 5 False *Japan:* 4 Esan, Nomo, Sata, Soya 5 Erimo, Kamui *Liberia:* 5 Mount *Libya:* 3 Tin 4 Milh *Long Island Sound:* 10 Throgs Neck *Malay Peninsula:* 5 Bulat 7 Romania *Malaysia:* 4 Piai 5 Sirik *Massachusetts:* 3 Ann, Cod *Mediterranean:* 5 Ajdir *Mexico:* 4 Buey *Morocco:* 3 Sim 4 Guir, Rhir *Namibia:* 4 Fria 5 Cross *Newfoundland:* 4 Pine 5 Bauld *New Jersey:* 3 May *New Zealand:* 4 East 5 Brett, North, South, Table *North Carolina:* 4 Fear 7 Lookout 8 Hatteras *Northwest Territories:* 8 Bathurst *Nova Scotia:* 5 Canso 6 Breton *Oman:* 3 Nus 4 Hadd *Ontario:* 4 Hurd, Rich *Pakistan:* 5 Monze, Muari *Portugal:* 4 Roca *Puerto Rico:* 4 Rojo *Quebec:* 5 Gaspé *Red Sea:* 5 Kasar *Sicily:* 4 Boeo, Faro 7 Lilibeo, Passero, Pelorus *Solomon Islands:* 5 Zelee *Somalia:* 4 Asir 5 Assir, Hafun *South Africa:* 4 Seal 8 Good Hope *South America:* 4 Horn *Spain:* 3 Nao 4 Gata 5 Creus, Penas 9 Trafalgar *Syria:* 5 Basit *Taiwan:* 5 O-luan 7 Garam Bi *Tasmania:* 5 Table *Tierra del Fuego:* 5 Penas *Tunisia:* 5 Blanc *Turkey:* 3 Boz 4 Baba, Ince, Kara, Krio 6 Lectum 8 Bozburun 9 Inceburun, Karaburun *Vancouver Island:* 5 Scott *Virginia:* 5 Henry *Washington:* 5 Alava

Čapek *coinage:* 5 robot *play:* 3 R.U.R.

caper 4 dido, lark, romp 5 antic, frisk, prank, shine, trick 6 cavort, frolic, gambol 7 roguery, rollick 8 escapade, mischief 9 capriccio, devilment 10 impishness, shenanigan, tomfoolery 11 monkeyshine, waggishness

Capetown's famous son 5 Smuts

capillary 4 tube 6 vessel 8 hairlike 11 blood vessel

capital 3 top 4 cock, fine, main, rank 5 basic, chief, dandy, gross, major, prime, vital 6 assets, famous, wealth 7 glaring 8 cardinal, dominant, five-star, flagrant, topnotch 9 egregious, essential, excellent, first-rate, number one, principal, resources 10 first-class, preeminent, underlying 11 fundamental, outstanding, predominant *Admiralty Islands:* 8 Lorengau *Afghanistan:* 5 Kabul *Alberta:* 8 Edmonton *Angola:* 6 Luanda *Antigua:* 7 St. Johns

Armenia: 6 Erevan, Erivan 7 Yerevan ***Assam:*** 6 Dispur ***Azerbaijan:*** 4 Baku ***Belize:*** 8 Belmopan ***Belarus:*** 5 Minsk ***Bhutan:*** 6 Thimbu ***Bophuthatswana:*** 8 Mmabatho ***Botswana:*** 8 Gaborone ***Dominica:*** 6 Roseau ***Equatorial Guinea:*** 6 Malabo ***Estonia:*** 7 Tallinn ***Ethiopia:*** 10 Addis Ababa ***Faeroe Islands:*** 9 Thorshavn ***Falkland Islands:*** 7 Stanley ***French Guiana:*** 7 Cayenne ***Galapagos Islands:*** 12 San Cristobal ***Georgia, Republic of:*** 7 Tbilisi ***Ghana:*** 5 Accra ***Greenland:*** 7 Godthab ***Guam:*** 5 Agana ***Guinea:*** 7 Conakry ***Kazakhstan:*** 7 Alma Ata ***Kirghizia:*** 7 Bishkek ***Kiribata:*** 6 Tarawa ***Latvia:*** 4 Riga ***Lithuania:*** 7 Vilnius ***Malaysia:*** 11 Kuala Lumpur ***Manitoba:*** 8 Winnipeg ***Mauritania:*** 10 Nouakchott ***Moldova:*** 8 Kishinev ***Mongolia:*** 9 Ulan Bator ***Montserrat:*** 8 Plymouth ***Mozambique:*** 6 Maputo ***Myanmar:*** 6 Yangon ***Namibia:*** 8 Windhoek ***Newfoundland:*** 10 Saint Johns ***Northern Ireland:*** 7 Belfast ***Northern Territory:*** 6 Darwin ***North-West Frontier Province:*** 8 Peshawar ***Northwest Territories:*** 11 Yellowknife ***Nova Scotia:*** 7 Halifax ***Orange Free State:*** 12 Bloemfontein ***Papua New Guinea:*** 11 Port Moresby ***Prince Edward Island:*** 13 Charlottetown ***Puerto Rico:*** 7 San Juan ***Queensland:*** 8 Brisbane ***Réunion:*** 10 Saint Denis ***Saint Helena:*** 9 Jamestown ***Saint Lucia:*** 8 Castries ***Saskatchewan:*** 6 Regina ***Scotland:*** 9 Edinburgh ***Seychelles:*** 8 Victoria ***Shetland:*** 7 Lerwick ***Sicily:*** 7 Palermo ***Sierra Leone:*** 8 Freetown ***Sikkim:*** 7 Gangtok ***Sind:*** 7 Karachi ***Slovenia:*** 9 Ljubljana ***Solomon Islands:*** 7 Honiara ***South Australia:*** 8 Adelaide ***South-West Africa:*** 8 Windhoek ***Suriname:*** 10 Paramaribo ***Swaziland:*** 7 Mbabane ***Tadzhikistan:*** 8 Dushanbe ***Tahiti:*** 7 Papeete ***Tasmania:*** 6 Hobart ***Tibet:*** 5 Lhasa ***Tirol:*** 9 Innsbruck ***Tonga:*** 9 Nukualofa ***Transkei:*** 6 Umtata ***Turkmenistan:*** 9 Ashkhabad ***Ukraine:*** 4 Kiev ***Uruguay:*** 10 Montevideo ***Uttar Pradesh:*** 7 Lucknow ***Uzbekistan:*** 8 Tashkent ***Venda:*** 11 Thohoyandou ***Victoria:*** 9 Melbourne ***Vietnam:*** 5 Hanoi ***Wales:*** 7 Cardiff ***Western Australia:*** 5 Perth ***Yukon:*** 10 Whitehorse (see also names of individual countries and states)

capitalist 8 investor 9 bourgeois, financier, plutocrat

capitalistic 9 bourgeois

capitalize 3 aid 4 back, fund, help 5 stake 6 assist 7 finance, promote, sponsor, support 8 bankroll 9 grubstake, subsidize

capital sin see **deadly sin**

Capitol Hill sound 3 aye, nay

capitulate 3 bow 4 cave 5 defer, yield 6 submit 7 knuckle, succumb 11 buckle under 12 knuckle under

capitulation 8 dedition 9 surrender 10 submission

capper 5 blind, decoy, shill, stick 9 shillaber

capriccio 5 caper, fancy, prank 6 whimsy

caprice 3 bee 4 mood, vein, whim 5 crank, fancy, freak, habit, humor, trait, trick 6 foible, maggot, megrim, notion, temper, vagary, whimsy 7 boutade, conceit 8 crotchet 9 mannerism 11 peculiarity 12 whigmaleerie 13 inconsistency

capricious 4 iffy 5 moody 6 chancy, fickle 7 erratic, wayward 8 freakish, ticklish, unstable, variable, volatile, whimsied 9 arbitrary, fluctuant, humorsome, mercurial, uncertain, vagarious, whimsical 10 changeable, inconstant, lubricious 12 effervescent, incalculable 13 temperamental, unpredictable

capsheaf see **capstone**

capsize 4 keel 5 upset 8 collapse, overturn

capstone 4 acme, apex, peak 6 apogee, climax, summit 8 capsheaf, meridian, pinnacle 11 culmination

capsule 6 canned, pocket, potted 9 condensed 10 epitomized ***combining form:*** 4 thec 5 theci, theco

capsulize 7 enclose 8 condense

captain 7 skipper 11 four-striper ***fictional:*** 4 Ahab, Nemo 5 Bligh, Queeg ***pirate:*** 4 Kidd

Captains Courageous author 7 Kipling

caption 6 legend 7 cutline 8 overline 9 underline

captious 5 testy 6 critic, snappy 7 carping, finicky, peevish 8 caviling, contrary, critical, exacting, perverse, petulant, snappish 9 cavillous, demanding, irritable 10 censorious 12 faultfinding, overcritical 13 hypercritical

captivate 4 draw, grip, hold, take, wile 5 charm 6 allure, please 7 attract, bewitch, delight, enchant, gratify 8 enthrall 9 fascinate, magnetize, mesmerize, spellbind

captivating 8 magnetic 9 appealing, glamorous, seductive

captive 7 hostage 8 prisoner

captivity 11 confinement 12 imprisonment

capture 3 bag, get, nab 4 nail, take 5 catch, cotch 6 collar, secure 7 prehend

Capuan 4 lush 5 plush 6 deluxe 7 opulent 8 luscious, palatial 9 luxuriant, luxurious, sumptuous 11 upholstered

car 4 auto, heap 5 buggy, coach, coupe, crate, motor, sedan, wreck 6 hotrod, jalopy, junker 7 clunker, flivver, hardtop, machine, phaeton 8 dragster, motorcar, roadster,

runabout 9 limousine 10 automobile, touring car 11 convertible 12 station wagon (see also **automobile**)
caramel-like 5 chewy
caravansary 3 inn 5 hotel, lodge 6 hostel, tavern 7 auberge, hospice 8 hostelry 9 roadhouse 11 public house
carbohydrate 5 sugar 6 starch 7 glucose, lactose, sucrose 8 fructose, glycogen 9 cellulose, galactose ***suffix:*** 3 ose
carbon 4 coal, coke, soot 8 graphite, plumbago 9 lampblack ***combining form:*** 7 anthrac 8 anthraco
carbonate 6 aerate
carbon compound ***suffix:*** 2 an 3 ane, ene, yne 5 ylene
carbon copy 5 ditto 7 replica 9 duplicate, facsimile 11 replication 12 reproduction 13 reduplication
carbonize 4 burn, char
carboxyl ***suffix:*** 3 oic 4 onic
carbuncle 4 boil 6 pimple 7 abscess, pustule ***combining form:*** 7 anthrac 8 anthraco
carcass 4 body, mort 5 stiff 6 corpse, deader 7 cadaver, remains
carcinoid 5 tumor
carcinoma 5 tumor 6 cancer
card 3 wag 4 menu, sked, zany 5 joker, trump 6 agenda, docket 7 program 8 calendar, comedian, humorist, schedule 9 programma, timetable 11 carte du jour ***fortune-telling:*** 5 tarot ***spot:*** 3 pip
cardboard 5 stiff 6 unreal, wooden 7 bristol, buckram, stilted 10 unlifelike 11 muscle-bound, stereotyped, unrealistic
card-carrying 7 genuine 11 full-fledged
card game see at **game**
cardiac stimulant 7 ouabain 9 digitalis
cardialgia 9 heartburn
cardinal 5 vital 6 ruling 7 central, pivotal 9 essential 10 overriding, overruling 11 fundamental 12 constitutive
cardinal point 4 east, west 5 north, south
cardinal suffix 2 ty 4 teen
Cardinal Virtue 7 justice 8 prudence 9 fortitude 10 temperance
care 3 rue, woe 4 dole, fear, heed, mind, reck, tend, ward 5 alarm, grief, nurse, pains, serve, trial, trust, watch, worry 6 attend, charge, dismay, effort, mother, regard, regret, sorrow, strain, stress, unease, wait on 7 anguish, anxiety, concern, conduct, custody, keeping, running, tension, trouble 8 disquiet, exertion, handling, interest, suspense, tendance 9 agitation, alertness, attention, curiosity, heartache, misgiving, oversight, vigilance 10 affliction, enthusiasm, foreboding, heartbreak, intendance, management, minister to, solicitude, uneasiness 11 concernment, disquietude, disturbance, heedfulness, safekeeping, supervision 12 apprehension, guardianship, perturbation, watchfulness 13 consciousness, consideration, consternation
careen 4 sway 5 lurch, swing, weave 6 wobble 7 stagger
career 4 race, rush, tear 5 chase, speed 6 course 7 calling 8 vocation
care for 4 like, mind, tend 5 nurse 6 foster
carefree 4 wild 6 breezy 8 feckless, reckless 9 lightsome 10 free-minded, incautious, insouciant 12 happy-go-lucky, lighthearted 13 irresponsible
careful 4 safe, wary 5 chary, exact, fussy 6 intent 7 duteous, dutiful, finical, finicky, guarded, heedful, precise, prudent, studied 8 accurate, cautious, critical, discreet, gingerly, punctual 9 attentive, observant, provident, religious 10 deliberate, meticulous, particular, scrupulous 11 calculating, circumspect, considerate, foresighted, painstaking, punctilious 12 conscionable 13 conscientious
carefully 8 gingerly
careless 3 lax 4 rash, wild 5 messy, slack, unfit 6 botchy, remiss, sloppy, unneat, untidy 7 raunchy, unkempt 8 derelict, feckless, heedless, reckless, slapdash, slipshod, slovenly, uncaring 9 forgetful, incapable, negligent, oblivious, unheeding, unmindful, unrecking 10 behindhand, delinquent, disheveled, inadequate, incautious, neglectful, regardless, unthinking, unthorough 11 inadvertent, inattentive, thoughtless, unconcerned, unqualified 12 disregardful, irreflective, unfastidious, uninterested, unreflective 13 irresponsible
caress 3 pat, pet, toy 4 love, neck 5 dally, flirt 6 cocker, coddle, coquet, cosset, cuddle, dandle, fondle, nuzzle, pamper, stroke, trifle 7 indulge
caressive 7 calming 8 soothing
caretaker 9 custodian
careworn 5 drawn, jaded 6 fagged 7 haggard, pinched 8 troubled, tuckered 9 exhausted 10 distressed
cargo 4 haul, load 6 burden, lading 7 freight, payload
caricature 4 fake, mock, sham 5 farce, phony 6 parody 7 cartoon, lampoon, mockery, takeoff 8 travesty 9 burlesque, clinquant, imitation 10 pasquinade 13 laughingstock
carillon 6 belfry 9 bell tower, campanile
caritas 5 grace, mercy 6 lenity 7 charity 8 clemency
cark 3 ail 4 fret, fuss, stew 5 upset, worry 6 pother 7 trouble 8 distress
Carmen ***author:*** 7 Mérimée ***composer:***

5 Bizet *lover:* 7 Don José *toreador:* 9 Escamillo
Carmi *father:* 6 Reuben *son:* 5 Achan
carnage 8 butchery, massacre 9 bloodbath, bloodshed, slaughter
carnal 4 lewd 5 gross 6 animal, bodily, coarse, earthy, vulgar, wanton 7 earthly, fleshly, lustful, mundane, obscene, sensual, somatic, worldly 8 corporal, material, physical, sensuous 9 corporeal 10 lascivious
carnation 4 pink 5 color 6 flower
carnival *attraction:* 4 ride 6 midway 8 sideshow 10 concession *character:* 5 shill 6 barker, hawker 7 grifter, spieler *New Orleans:* 9 Mardi Gras *performer:* 4 geek
carol 4 song 6 ballad *Christmas:* 4 noel
carom 3 dap 4 skim, skip 5 graze 6 glance 8 ricochet
carotid's relative 5 aorta
carousal 3 bat, jag 4 tear 5 binge, booze, drunk, spree 6 bender 7 blowoff 9 brannigan *Scottish:* 6 splore
carouse 4 hell, riot 5 revel 6 frolic 7 roister, wassail *Scottish:* 4 birl 5 birle
carp 3 nag 4 fuss 5 cavil 6 peck at 7 henpeck
carpe ___ 4 diem
carpenter 3 ant, bee 6 joiner, wright 7 artisan, builder, workman 9 craftsman
carpentry 7 joinery
carper 5 momus 6 critic, Zoilus 7 caviler, knocker 9 aristarch 10 criticizer 11 faultfinder, smellfungus
carpet 3 mat, rug 5 tapis 6 velvet, Wilton 8 Brussels, moquette, Venetian 9 Axminster, broadloom *Afghan:* 5 Herat 6 Herati *Indian:* 4 Agra *Persian:* 4 kali 6 Kerman, Keshan, Kirman, Sarouk *Turkish:* 5 Koula, Ladik 8 Ghiordes
carpet beetle 10 buffalo bug
carpet knight 8 hedonist, sybarite
carping 6 critic, jawing 7 blaming, railing 8 blameful, captious, caviling, critical 9 cavillous, damnatory 10 censorious, upbraiding 11 criticizing, objurgatory, reproachful, reprobating, reprobatory 12 condemnatory, faultfinding, overcritical, reprehending 13 hypercritical
carrageen 7 seaweed 9 Irish moss
carrefour 5 plaza 6 square 10 crossroads
carriage 3 rig 4 pose 6 stance 7 posture, transit, voiture 8 attitude, carrying, posture 9 transport 10 conveyance 12 transporting *American:* 5 buggy 8 dearborn, rockaway 9 buckboard *attendant:* 6 flunky 7 flunkey, footman *baby:* 4 pram 5 buggy 8 stroller 12 perambulator *driver:* 4 hack 5 cabby 8 coachman *folding top:* 6 calash *four-wheeled:* 4 sado, trap 5 buggy, coupe 6 berlin, calash, fiacre, landau, surrey 7 britska, cariole, dos-a-dos, hackney, phaeton 8 barouche, britzska, brougham, carriole, carryall, clarence, dearborn, rockaway, sociable, stanhope, tarantas, victoria 9 buckboard *Indian:* 6 gharri, gharry *Javanese:* 4 sado *man-drawn:* 6 riksha 7 rikisha, rikshaw 10 jinrikisha *Philippine:* 6 calesa 7 calesin 9 carromata *Russian:* 6 drosky, troika 7 droshky 8 tarantas 9 tarantass *stately:* 7 caroche *three-horse:* 6 troika *two-wheeled:* 3 gig 4 shay, trap 5 buggy, sulky 6 calesa, chaise, dennet, hansom, herdic, whisky 7 caleche, calesin, dogcart, tilbury, whiskey 8 curricle 9 cabriolet, carromata *with attendants:* 8 equipage
carriage trade 5 elite 6 flower, gentry 7 quality 9 blue blood, gentility 10 upper class, upper crust 11 aristocracy
carrick bend 4 knot
carrier 5 envoy 6 bearer, porter, vector 7 airline, courier, drogher, vehicle 8 emissary 9 messenger 11 internuncio *combining form:* 4 pher, phor 5 phora, phore 6 phorae (plural), phorum
Carroll character 5 Alice 6 Hatter 8 Dormouse 9 March Hare 10 Mock Turtle 11 White Rabbit 12 Humpty Dumpty
carrot 4 meed, plum 5 prize 6 reward 7 guerdon, premium 8 dividend
carry 3 act, get, jag, lug 4 bear, buck, have, hump, keep, move, pack, pipe, prop, quit, send, sway, take, tote, waft 5 brace, bring, ferry, fetch, shift, stock, touch 6 acquit, affect, bear up, behave, convey, demean, deport, funnel, remove, siphon, strike, upbear, uphold 7 bolster, channel, comport, conduct, disport, impress, inspire, possess, shore up, support, sustain, traject 8 buttress, transfer, transmit 9 influence, transport
carrying *combining form:* 7 phorous
carrying case 7 holdall
carry off 4 down, kill, slay 6 cut off, finish, lay low, spirit 7 destroy, put away, take off 8 dispatch
carry on 3 run 4 go on, keep, rant, rave 5 act up, cut up, horse 6 direct, hang on, manage, ordain 7 conduct, operate, persist 9 horseplay, persevere
carry out 6 effect, govern, render 7 execute, fulfill 8 bring off, complete, finalize, transact 9 discharge, prosecute 10 administer, effectuate 12 administrate
carry over 8 postpone, transfer
carrytale 5 clack, tabby 6 gossip 8 gossiper, quidnunc 10 newsmonger 12 gossipmonger 13 scandalmonger
carry through 4 last 5 abide 6 effect, endure 7 perdure, persist 8 bring off, continue 10 effectuate

cart 4 dray, haul 5 carry 6 barrow, convey 7 tumbrel, tumbril 8 carriage 9 transport ***Indian:*** 5 tonga ***racing:*** 5 sulky
___ carte 3 a la
___ Carte 5 D'Oyly
carte blanche 3 say 5 power, right, say-so 7 license 8 free hand 9 authority 10 blank check 11 prerogative
carte d'entrée 6 ticket
carte du jour 4 menu
cartel 4 bloc, dare, defy, pool 5 chain, group, stump, trust 7 combine 8 defiance 9 challenge, syndicate 10 consortium
Carthaginian ***goddess of the moon:*** 5 Tanit 6 Tanith ***queen:*** 4 Dido 6 Elissa
cartilage 6 tissue 7 gristle ***combining form:*** 6 chondr 7 chondri, chondro
cartogram 3 map
cartographer ***English:*** 5 Smith ***Flemish:*** 6 Kremer 8 Mercator, Ortelius ***German:*** 13 Waldseemuller ***Greek:*** 7 Ptolemy
cartography 9 mapmaking
cartoonist 4 Capp (Al), Nast (Thomas), Szep 5 Davis (Jim), Gould (Chester), Kelly (Walt), Young (Chic) 6 Disney (Walt), Larson (Gary), Schulz (Charles) 7 Mauldin (Bill), Trudeau (Garry) 8 Goldberg (Rube), Groening (Matt)
cartouche 5 brown, frame 6 shield
cartridge 4 case, tube 5 shell 8 cylinder
cartwheel 4 coin 6 tumble 10 handspring
carve 3 cut 5 sculp, sever, slice, split 6 chisel, cleave, sculpt, sunder 7 dissect 8 dissever 9 sculpture
Casanova 4 wolf 5 Romeo 6 chaser, masher 7 amorist, Don Juan, gallant 8 lothario, paramour 9 ladies' man, philander, womanizer 10 lady-killer 11 philanderer
cascade 5 chute, falls, sault, spout 8 cataract 9 waterfall
case 3 con, pod, vet 4 etui, hull, husk, skin, suit, view 5 cause, event, order, shape, shell, shuck, spook, state, study 6 action, estate, oddity, repair, sample 7 canvass, check up, episode, examine, example, inspect, lawsuit, oddball 8 incident, instance, original, sampling, specimen 9 character, check over, condition, eccentric, situation 10 occurrence, scrutinize 11 eventuality 12 circumstance, illustration ***combining form:*** 4 thec 5 theca, theci, theco 6 thecae (plural), thecia (plural) 7 thecium ***grammatical:*** 6 dative 8 ablative, genitive, vocative 9 objective 10 accusative, nominative, possessive
casebearer 5 larva 11 caterpillar
case-hardened 7 callous 10 insensible
case history 6 sample 7 example 8 instance, sampling, specimen 12 illustration
casement 6 window
Casey at the Bat poet 6 Thayer
cash 4 coin, jack 5 bread, dough, money 6 mazuma, wampum 7 scratch, shekels 11 legal tender
cashier 2 ax 3 bar, can 4 cast, fire, oust, sack, shed 5 eject, expel, scrap 6 bounce, reject, shelve, slough 7 boot out, discard, dismiss, exclude, kick out 8 abdicate, jettison, pass over, throw out 9 discharge, eliminate, terminate, throw away
cash in 3 die 4 conk, drop 5 croak 6 pop off 7 kick off, succumb 8 check out, pass away
casino attendant 8 croupier
cask 3 keg, tun 4 butt, pipe 6 barrel 8 hogshead
casket 3 box 5 chest 6 coffin
Cassandra 7 seeress 9 doomsayer, pessimist, worrywart 10 prophetess 11 crepehanger ***brother:*** 7 Helenus ***father:*** 5 Priam ***lover:*** 9 Agamemnon ***mother:*** 6 Hecuba ***slayer:*** 12 Clytemnestra
casserole 4 dish
Cassiopeia ***daughter:*** 9 Andromeda ***husband:*** 7 Cepheus ***kingdom:*** 8 Ethiopia
Cassio's mistress 6 Bianca
cassock 7 soutane
cast 3 add, aim, hue, lay, sum, tot, way 4 dash, drop, face, fire, foot, form, hint, hurl, junk, kind, look, mold, plan, shed, sort, tint, tone, toss, tote, turn, type 5 chart, class, color, fling, heave, leave, level, pitch, point, scrap, shade, shape, sling, smack, throw, tinge, total, touch, trace, train, weird, yield 6 design, devise, direct, figure, launch, nature, reject, slough, stripe, visage, zero in 7 address, arrange, cashier, discard, dope out, incline, moulage, project, scatter, soupçon, summate, variety 8 abdicate, disperse, forecast, jettison, prophecy, totalize 9 blueprint, broadcast, character, prevision, prognosis, suspicion, throw away 10 distribute, expression, intimation, prediction, suggestion 11 countenance, description, foretelling 12 conformation 13 configuration
cast about 4 hunt, seek 5 quest 9 ferret out, search for, search out
cast a spell 3 hex
cast away 4 blow 5 beach, waste, wreck 6 pile up, strand 7 consume, fritter 8 squander 9 dissipate, shipwreck
castaway 5 leper 6 pariah 7 Ishmael, outcast 8 derelict 10 Ishmaelite 11 offscouring, untouchable
cast down 3 bad, low 4 down, sink 5 abase, lower 6 bemean, debase, demean, humble 7 degrade 8 dejected, downcast 9 depressed, humiliate, woebegone 10 dispirited 11 crestfallen 12 disconsolate

castigate 3 wig 4 beat, drub, flay, rail, rate 5 baste, slash 6 berate, pummel, punish, scathe, scorch, thrash 7 belabor, blister, chasten, correct, lambast, scarify, scourge, upbraid 8 chastise, lambaste, lash into, penalize 9 excoriate 10 discipline, tongue-lash
castigation 3 rod 8 punition 10 correction, discipline, punishment 12 chastisement
cast iron 7 spiegel
castle 5 manor, villa 7 chateau, mansion ***adjunct:*** 4 moat ***gate:*** 10 portcullis ***ledge:*** 7 rampart ***structure:*** 6 turret ***tower:*** 4 keep 6 donjon ***wall:*** 6 bailey 10 battlement
castle-builder 7 dreamer, utopian 8 idealist 9 ideologue, visionary
cast off 5 fling, let go, loose, untie 6 slough, unmoor 7 unhitch 8 unfasten
Castor ***brother:*** 6 Pollux 10 Polydeuces ***constellation:*** 6 Gemini ***father:*** 4 Zeus 9 Tyndareus ***mother:*** 4 Leda ***sister:*** 5 Helen ***slayer:*** 4 Idas
castor oil 9 cathartic, lubricant
cast out 4 oust 5 exile, expel 6 banish, deport 7 expulse 8 displace 9 ostracize, transport 10 expatriate
cast overboard 8 jettison
castrate 3 fix 4 geld 5 alter, unman, unsex 6 neuter 7 unnerve 8 enervate, mutilate, unstring 9 sterilize 10 emasculate 11 desexualize
castrato singer 9 Farinelli
casual 5 aloof, fluky, light, minor, petty 6 breezy, chance, degage, little, remote 7 offhand, relaxed, trivial, unfussy 8 detached, informal 9 easygoing, extempore, impromptu, impulsive, incurious, small-beer, uncurious, unplanned, withdrawn 10 accidental, contingent, fortuitous, improvised, incidental, shoestring 11 indifferent, low-pressure, spontaneous, unconcerned, unimportant 12 uninterested 13 disinterested, insignificant, unconstrained
casualty 4 prey 5 death, fatal 6 mishap, victim 8 accident, fatality, underdog 9 bottom dog, mischance 12 misadventure
casuistry 7 fallacy, sophism 8 delusion 9 deception, sophistry 12 equivocation, speciousness, spuriousness 13 deceptiveness
casus ___ 5 belli
cat 4 eyra, lion, lynx, puma, puss 5 felid, kitty, ounce, pussy 6 bobcat, cougar, feline, kaffir 7 caracal 12 mountain lion ***catlike animal:*** 5 civet, genet, zibet 6 zibeth 7 linsang ***combining form:*** 5 aelur, ailur 6 aeluro, ailuro ***disease:*** 9 distemper ***domestic:*** 3 Rex 4 Manx 5 tabby 6 calico 7 Burmese, Persian, Siamese 8 longhair 9 Himalayan, shorthair 10 Abyssinian ***extinct:*** 10 saber-tooth ***fastest:*** 7 cheetah ***female:*** 5 queen 7 lioness, tigress 9 grimalkin ***genus:*** 5 Felis ***grinning:*** 8 Cheshire ***group:*** 7 clowder ***male:*** 3 tom ***relating to:*** 6 feline ***ring-tailed:*** 6 serval ***Scottish:*** 8 baudrons ***sound:*** 3 mew 4 hiss, meow, purr, roar 5 miaou, miaow, miaul 9 caterwaul ***spotted:*** 4 pard 6 jaguar, margay, ocelot, serval 7 cheetah, leopard, panther ***striped:*** 5 tiger ***tailless:*** 4 Manx ***young:*** 6 kitten
cataclysm 4 pour, woes 5 flood, spate 6 deluge 7 niagara, torrent, tragedy 8 calamity, cataract, disaster, flooding, overflow 10 inundation 11 catastrophe 12 misadventure
cataclysmic 5 fatal 7 fateful, ruinous 10 calamitous, disastrous 12 catastrophic
catacomb 5 crypt, vault 10 undercroft
catafalque 4 bier
catalog 4 book, list, roll 5 admit, count, enter, tally 6 enroll, number, roster 7 itemize, program 8 inscribe, register, roll call, schedule, syllabus 9 enumerate, introduce, inventory 10 prospectus ***of books:*** 11 bibliotheca ***of goods:*** 9 inventory ***of saints:*** 9 hagiology
catalyst 4 goad, spur 7 impetus, impulse 8 stimulus 9 incentive, stimulant 10 incitation, incitement, motivation
catamaran 4 boat, raft
catamount 4 lynx 6 cougar
cataract 5 chute, falls, flood, sault, spate, spout 6 deluge 7 cascade, niagara, torrent 8 flooding, overflow 9 cataclysm, waterfall 10 inundation
catastrophe 3 woe 7 tragedy 8 calamity, disaster 9 cataclysm 12 misadventure
catastrophic 5 fatal 7 fateful, ruinous 10 calamitous, disastrous 11 cataclysmic
Catawba 4 wine 5 river
catcall 3 boo 4 bird, hiss, hoot, pooh, razz 5 bazoo 8 pooh-pooh 9 raspberry 10 Bronx cheer
catch 3 bag, con, fix, get, hit, nab, net, see, wed 4 ding, dupe, espy, find, fool, grab, grip, gull, hoax, hook, moor, nail, snag, sock, spot, take, trap 5 abash, benet, block, clasp, clout, grasp, hit on, marry, reach, seize, smite, snare, stick, stump, trick, whack 6 accept, anchor, arrest, baffle, clutch, collar, cut off, descry, detect, entrap, fasten, flurry, follow, put out, rattle, secure, snatch, strike, take in, tangle, turn up 7 capture, chicane, confuse, disturb, ensnare, espouse, fluster, grapple, hit upon, nonplus, perplex, prehend 8 confound, contract, entangle, flimflam, hoodwink, meet with, overhaul, overtake 9 apprehend, bamboozle, embarrass, encounter, intercept

10 comprehend, understand 12 come down with
catchall term 3 etc.
Catcher in the Rye ***author:*** 8 Salinger ***character:*** 9 Caulfield (Holden)
catcher's glove 4 mitt
catching 6 taking 10 contagious, infectious 12 communicable
catch on 3 see 4 hear 5 learn 6 tumble 7 find out, unearth 8 discover 9 ascertain, determine
catchphrase see catchword
Catch-22 author 6 Heller
catch up 4 hold 8 enthrall 9 fascinate, mesmerize, spellbind
catchword 5 maxim, motto 6 byword, phrase, slogan 9 battle cry, watchword 10 shibboleth
catchy 6 fitful, spotty, tricky 8 sporadic 9 appealing, desultory, irregular, spasmodic
catechist 7 teacher
catechize 3 ask 4 quiz 5 query 7 examine, inquire 8 question 11 interrogate
catechumen 7 convert, student
categorical 4 sure 6 direct 7 certain, decided, express 8 absolute, clean-cut, clear-cut, definite, explicit, positive, specific, ultimate 9 downright 10 definitive, forthright 11 unambiguous, unequivocal
categorize 3 peg 4 sort 5 class, group 6 assort 7 put down 8 classify, identify, nail down 10 pigeonhole
category 4 tier 5 class, genre, grade, group 6 league 8 grouping 10 pigeonhole
catenation 6 series 10 connection
catercorner 9 slantways, slantwise 10 cornerwise, diagonally 12 slantingways
caterpillar 5 larva 7 cutworm, webworm 8 armyworm, silkworm 10 casebearer ***combining form:*** 5 campa, eruci
cater to 4 baby 5 humor, spoil 6 cocker, coddle, cosset, cotton, pamper 7 gratify, indulge 11 mollycoddle
caterwaul 3 row 4 howl, meow, spat, tiff 5 miaou, miaow, miaul, scrap 6 bicker 7 brabble, fall out, quarrel, wrangle 8 squabble
catharsis 9 cleansing, purgation 10 lustration 11 expurgation 12 purification
cathartic 9 castor oil, purgative
Cathay 5 China
cathedral 5 duomo 6 church ***passage:*** 5 slype
catholic 6 cosmic, global 7 general, generic 8 eclectic 9 extensive, inclusive, planetary, universal, worldwide 10 ecumenical, large-scale 12 cosmopolitan 13 comprehensive
catholicity 10 liberality 12 universality
catholicon 6 elixir 7 cure-all, nostrum, panacea
catkin 5 ament
catlike 5 catty 6 feline 7 furtive 8 stealthy
catnap 6 siesta, snooze 10 forty winks
Cat on a Hot ___ 7 Tin Roof
cat's-paw 4 pawn, tool 6 puppet, stooge
cattail 4 rush
cattle 4 kine, neat, oxen 5 bovid 6 bovine ***breed:*** 5 Angus, Devon, Kerry 6 Durham, Jersey, Sussex 7 Brahman, Hariana, Red Poll, Sahiwal 8 Ayrshire, Charbray, Galloway, Guernsey, Hereford, Highland, Holstein, Limousin, Longhorn 9 Charolais, Red Polled, Shorthorn, Simmental 10 Brown Swiss, Charollais 11 Dutch Belted ***call:*** 4 sook 6 sookie ***castrated:*** 5 steer ***catching rope:*** 5 lasso 6 lariat ***combining form:*** 4 bovi ***cry:*** 3 low, moo ***dehorn:*** 4 poll ***disease:*** 4 loco 5 bloat 6 garget, nagana 7 anthrax, locoism, measles, murrain 8 blackleg, lumpy jaw, mastitis, staggers 10 rinderpest, Texas fever 11 brucellosis ***extinct breed:*** 9 Teeswater ***family:*** 7 Bovidae ***feed:*** 6 fodder 7 farrago ***female:*** 3 cow ***foot:*** 4 hoof ***genus:*** 3 Bos ***goddess:*** 6 Bubona ***grazing land:*** 5 range 7 pasture ***group:*** 4 herd 5 drove ***herdsman:*** 6 cowboy, drover, gaucho 7 vaquero 8 wrangler 10 cowpuncher ***hornless:*** 5 muley 6 mulley ***hybrid:*** 7 cattalo ***identification:*** 5 brand ***Indian:*** 4 dhan ***jowl:*** 6 dewlap ***male:*** 4 bull ***pen:*** 6 corral ***round up:*** 7 wrangle ***stable:*** 4 barn, byre ***steal:*** 6 rustle ***unbranded:*** 8 maverick ***wild flight:*** 8 stampede ***young:*** 4 calf ***young, motherless:*** 5 dogie
catty 4 evil, spry, yare 5 agile, brisk, zippy 6 active, bitchy, feline, lively, nimble, volant, wicked 7 catlike, furtive, hateful, vicious 8 spiteful, stealthy 9 malicious, rancorous, sprightly 10 despiteful, malevolent
Caucasian ***capital:*** 4 Baku 7 Tbilisi, Yerevan ***republic:*** 7 Armenia, Georgia 10 Azerbaijan
Caucasus ***peak:*** 6 Elbrus ***people:*** 5 Osset
caucho 3 ule 4 hule 6 rubber
caudal ***appendage:*** 4 tail ***combining form:*** 2 ur 3 uro
cause 4 call, case, goad, make, root, suit 5 breed, evoke, get up, hatch 6 action, author, draw on, effect, elicit, induce, motive, origin, reason, secure, source, spring, work up 7 creator, impulse, lawsuit, produce, provoke 8 engender, generate, muster up, occasion 9 generator, incentive, necessity 10 antecedent, bring about, inducement, obligation, originator, prime mover 11 determinant 13 consideration ***combining form:*** 4 etio 5 aetio, aitio
cause ___ 7 célèbre
caused by ***suffix:*** 2 ic 4 ical

causerie 3 rap 4 chat, chin, talk, yarn 5 prose
causing *combining form:* 7 facient, factive *suffix:* 3 fic 4 able, ible
caustic 4 keen, tart 5 acerb, acrid, acute, crisp, harsh, rough, salty, sharp, terse 6 biting, bitter, ironic, severe 7 acerbic, cutting, mordant, pungent, satiric 8 incisive, scathing, stinging, succinct 9 corrosive, sarcastic, stringent, trenchant 10 mordacious 12 archilochian *solution:* 3 lye
cauterize 4 burn, sear
caution 4 warn 6 caveat 7 warning 8 forewarn, monition, prudence 9 canniness, chariness, foresight 10 admonition, discretion, precaution, providence 11 commonition, forethought, forewarning 12 discreetness
cautionary 4 wary 6 surety 8 cautious, monitive, monitory, security 10 admonitory
cautious 4 cozy, safe, wary 5 alert, cagey, canny, chary 6 shrewd 7 careful, guarded, politic, prudent 8 discreet, gingerly, scheming, vigilant, watchful 9 judicious, provident 11 calculating, circumspect, considerate, foresighted 13 prethoughtful
cavalcade 6 parade, series 8 sequence 10 procession
cavalier 5 lofty, proud 6 knight 7 haughty 8 arrogant, horseman, insolent, superior 9 caballero 10 disdainful 11 overbearing 12 supercilious 13 high-and-mighty
cavalryman 6 lancer 7 dragoon, trooper *Algerian:* 5 spahi 6 spahee *horse:* 5 waler *Prussian:* 4 ulan 5 uhlan *Russian:* 7 cossack *Turkish:* 5 spahi 6 spahee *weapon:* 5 lance, saber 7 carbine
cave 3 bow, den 4 bend, drop, give, grot, lair 5 antre, break, defer, yield 6 fold up, grotto, hollow, submit 7 crumple, knuckle, succumb 8 collapse 9 break down 10 capitulate, subterrane 11 buckle under 12 knuckle under, subterranean *combining form:* 6 speleo *dweller:* 3 bat 4 bear, lion 6 hermit 9 Cro-Magnon 10 troglodite 11 Neanderthal *explorer:* 9 spelunker *formation:* 10 stalactite, stalagmite *France:* 7 Lascaux 10 Rouffignac 13 Gouffre Berger *Iceland:* 7 Singing *Indiana:* 9 Wyandotte *Iraq:* 8 Shanidar *Kentucky:* 7 Mammoth *New Zealand:* 7 Waitomo *rock:* 8 dolomite 9 limestone *South Africa:* 5 Cango *Spain:* 8 Altamira *study of:* 10 speleology
caveat 6 notice 7 caution, warning 8 monition 10 admonition 11 commonition, forewarning
caveat ___ 6 emptor
cave-dwelling *combining form:* 6 troglo
cavern 6 grotto 10 subterrane 12 subterranean *Capri:* 10 Blue Grotto *combining form:* 4 antr 5 antro *Montana:* 13 Lewis and Clark *New Mexico:* 8 Carlsbad *Tennessee:* 10 Cumberland *Virginia:* 5 Luray
cavernous 4 vast 6 gaping, hollow 7 chasmal, yawning 10 commodious, sepulchral 11 reverberant
caviar 3 roe 4 eggs 6 relish *source:* 6 beluga 7 sterlet 8 sturgeon
cavil 4 carp, momi (plural) 7 chicane, quibble
caviler 5 momus 6 carper, critic, Zoilus 7 knocker 9 aristarch 10 criticizer 11 faultfinder, smellfungus
caviling 4 mean 5 fussy, petty, small 6 critic, pickly 7 carping, finicky 8 captious, contrary, critical, exacting, niggling 9 demanding 10 censorious, nitpicking 12 faultfinding, overcritical 13 hairsplitting, hypercritical
cavity 3 pit 4 bore, hole, void 6 boring, hollow 7 vacuity *body:* 5 antra (plural), sinus 6 antrum 8 follicle, hemocoel *combining form:* 3 cel 4 antr, caec, ceci, ceco, cele, celo, coel 5 antro, caeci, caeco, coele, coelo *in a glacier:* 6 moulin
cavort 4 romp 5 caper, cut up, frisk 6 frolic, gambol 7 carry on, rollick 9 horseplay 10 roughhouse 11 horse around
caw 4 yaup, yawp 6 squall, squark, squawk
cay 3 key 4 isle, reef
cayenne 6 pepper *genus:* 8 Capsicum
cayman see **caiman**
Cayuga chief 5 Logan
cease 3 erd 4 halt, quit, stop 5 close 6 desist, ending, finish, period 8 conclude, give over, intermit, knock off, leave off, surcease 9 cessation, terminate 10 conclusion, desistance 11 discontinue, termination
cease-fire 5 truce 9 armistice
ceaseless 7 endless, eternal 8 constant, immortal, unending 9 continual, perpetual, unceasing 10 continuous 11 amaranthine, everlasting, never-ending, unremitting 12 interminable 13 uninterrupted
Cecrops' daughter 5 Herse 8 Aglauros 9 Pandrosos
cecum *combining form:* 5 typhl 6 typhlo
cede 4 deed 5 alien, grant, leave, waive, yield 6 accord, assign, convey, give up, remise, resign 7 abandon, concede 8 alienate, hand over, make over, sign over, transfer 9 surrender, vouchsafe 10 abalienate, relinquish
ceiling *elaborate:* 7 plafond
ceinture 4 belt, sash 6 girdle 8 cincture 9 waistband
Celaeno *father:* 5 Atlas *mother:* 7 Pleione *sisters:* 8 Pleiades
celebrate 4 fete, hymn, keep, laud 5 bless, cry up, extol 6 praise 7 glorify,

maffick, magnify, observe 8 eulogize 9 solemnize 10 panegyrize 11 commemorate
celebrated 5 famed, great, noted 6 famous 7 eminent, notable 8 renowned 9 prominent 11 illustrious 13 distinguished
celebration 4 fete, gala 6 fiesta 7 jubilee 8 festival, jamboree
célèbre 5 cause
celebrity 3 VIP 4 fame, hero, lion, name, star 5 éclat 6 renown, repute, worthy 7 big name, mahatma, notable 8 cynosure, immortal, luminary, somebody 9 notoriety, personage, superstar 10 notability, reputation
celerity 4 gait, pace 5 haste, hurry, speed 6 hustle, rustle 8 alacrity, dispatch, legerity, rapidity, velocity 9 briskness, quickness, swiftness 10 expedition, speediness
celery ***genus:*** 5 Apium ***green:*** 6 pascal ***relative:*** 6 carrot 7 parsley, parsnip ***white:*** 8 blanched ***wild:*** 8 smallage
celestial 7 blessed, elysian 8 beatific, empyreal, empyrean, ethereal, heavenly, Olympian, supernal 9 unearthly 12 otherworldly, transmundane
celestial body 3 sun 4 moon, star 5 comet 6 meteor, nebula, planet 8 asteroid 9 satellite ***hypothetical:*** 9 black hole
Celestial Empire 5 China
cell 4 room, zoid 5 cubby, zooid 7 cubicle 11 compartment ***blood:*** 8 hemocyte ***combining form:*** 3 cyt 4 cyte, cyto, phag 5 blast, gamet, phage 6 gameto, gonidi 7 gonidio ***disease:*** 6 cancer ***division:*** 7 meiosis, mitosis ***fertilized egg:*** 6 zygote ***material:*** 3 DNA, RNA 7 protein 9 chromatin, cytoplasm 10 protoplasm ***nerve:*** 6 neuron ***part:*** 4 gene 7 nucleus, vacuole 8 ribosome 10 chromosome ***reproductive:*** 3 egg 4 germ, ovum 5 sperm 6 gamete 8 gonidium
cellist ***American:*** 4 Rose 6 Lesser, Parnas 7 Nelsova, Parisot, Starker 8 Schuster ***English:*** 5 du Pré ***Russian:*** 11 Piatigorsky 12 Rostropovich ***Spanish:*** 6 Casals
cellophane 4 wrap 7 wrapper 8 wrapping 9 packaging
celluloid 4 film 7 plastic
cement 4 bind, join 5 unify, unite 6 mortar 8 concrete ***combining form:*** 4 lith ***ingredient:*** 4 lime 6 silica 7 alumina 8 magnesia, pozzolan 9 iron oxide, pozzolana
cemetery 8 boneyard, boot hill, catacomb 8 God's acre 9 graveyard 10 churchyard, necropolis 11 polyandrium 12 burial ground, memorial park, potter's field ***underground:*** 8 catacomb
cense 7 thurify
censer 8 thurible ***carrier:*** 8 thurifer
censor 4 blip, edit 5 purge 6 cut out, delete, excise, narrow, purify, screen 7 clean up, exscind 8 restrain, restrict 9 expurgate, red-pencil 10 blue-pencil, bowdlerize
censorious 6 critic 7 carping, chiding 8 captious, caviling, critical 9 cavillous, culpatory 10 accusatory, condemning, denouncing 11 reproachful 12 condemnatory, denunciatory, faultfinding, overcritical, reprehending 13 hypercritical
censurable 5 amiss, wrong 6 guilty, sinful, unholy 8 blamable, blameful, culpable, doubtful, improper, wrongful 9 incorrect 11 blameworthy 12 inadmissible, questionable, unacceptable 13 demeritorious, discreditable, objectionable, reprehensible
censure 3 rap 4 skin 5 blame, knock, scorn, scout 6 oppose, rebuke, reject, strafe 7 condemn, contemn, disdain, reprove 8 denounce, disallow, reproach 9 criticize, reprehend, reprimand, reprobate 10 denunciate, disapprove, stigmatize
centaur 6 Chiron, Nessus
Centaurus star 4 Beta 5 Alpha
Centennial State 8 Colorado
center 3 hub, mid 4 core, mean, pith, root, seat 5 focus, heart, midst, quick 6 dynamo, inside, medial, median, middle 7 central, essence, halfway, midmost 8 interior, midpoint, omphalos, polestar 9 activator, energizer, stimulant 10 focal point, middlemost 11 equidistant 12 intermediary, intermediate
centerboard 4 keel
centerfold 7 foldout 8 gatefold
centipede 9 arthropod ***class:*** 9 Chilopoda
central 3 key, mid 4 main, mean 5 basic, chief, focal 6 master, medial, median, middle, ruling, signal 7 leading, pivotal, primary, radical, salient 8 cardinal, dominant, foremost 9 essential, important, paramount 10 overriding, overruling 11 controlling, fundamental, outstanding, predominant, significant 12 all-absorbing, intermediary, intermediate, preponderant
Central African Republic ***capital:*** 6 Bangui ***monetary unit:*** 5 franc
Central America ***country:*** 6 Panama 8 Honduras 9 Costa Rica, Guatemala, Nicaragua 10 El Salvador ***ethnic group:*** 6 Indian 7 Mestizo, Spanish ***language:*** 7 Nahuatl, Spanish
centripetal 8 unifying 10 compacting 11 integrative 12 centralizing 13 concentrating, consolidating
centurion 7 officer, soldier 9 commander
century plant ***genus:*** 5 Agave
cephalalgia 8 headache
cephalopod 5 squid 7 mollusk, octopus 10 cuttlefish

Cepheus *daughter:* 9 Andromeda *kingdom:* 8 Ethiopia *wife:* 10 Cassiopeia
cerate 4 balm 5 cream, salve 6 chrism 7 unction, unguent 8 ointment
cerberus 6 custos, keeper, warden 8 claviger, guardian, watchdog 9 custodian
Cerberus *father:* 6 Typhon *form:* 3 dog *mother:* 7 Echidna
cereal 4 meal, mush 5 gruel 6 farina 7 oatmeal 8 cornmeal, porridge *grass:* 3 rye 4 corn, oats, ragi, rice 5 emmer, maize, spelt, wheat 6 barley, millet 7 sorghum 9 buckwheat *North African:* 8 couscous *Russian:* 5 kasha
cerebral 6 mental 7 psychic 8 highbrow 9 psychical 10 highbrowed 12 intellective, intellectual 13 psychological *combining form:* 5 psych 6 psycho
cerebrate 5 think 6 reason 7 reflect 8 cogitate 9 speculate 10 deliberate
cerebration 7 thought 9 brainwork 10 cogitation, reflection 11 speculation 12 deliberation
ceremonial 3 set 5 fixed, lofty, rigid, stiff 6 august, formal, ritual, solemn 7 courtly, starchy, stately, studied 8 mannered, stylized 10 liturgical 11 ritualistic
ceremonious 6 formal, moving, proper, seemly, solemn 7 stately 8 decorous, imposing, majestic, striking 9 grandiose 10 impressive 12 conventional
ceremony 4 form, rite 6 ritual 7 liturgy, service 9 formality 10 observance *Jewish:* 8 habdalah, havdalah 10 bar mitzvah, bas mitzvah 11 bath mitzvah *university:* 8 encaenia
Ceres 7 Demeter *daughter:* 10 Persephone, Proserpina, Proserpine *father:* 6 Cronus, Saturn *mother:* 3 Ops 4 Rhea
cerium *symbol:* 2 Ce
certain 3 one, set 4 firm, many, some, sure, true 5 fated, fixed 6 divers, stated, sundry 7 assured, ensured, insured, settled, several, various 8 accurate, cocksure, credible, definite, numerous, positive, provable, reliable, sanguine, surefire, unerring 9 authentic, certified, confident, doubtless, necessary, plausible, unfailing, warranted 10 dependable, guaranteed, inarguable, ineludible, inevasible, inevitable, infallible, returnless, stipulated, undeniable, unevadable, verifiable 11 confirmable, indubitable, ineluctable, inescapable, irrevocable, trustworthy, unalterable, unavoidable, undoubtable, unescapable 12 demonstrable, indefeasible, indisputable, well-grounded 13 establishable, incontestable, predestinated, predetermined, uncontestable
certainty 6 surety 8 firmness, sureness 9 assurance, certitude, dogmatism 10 confidence, conviction, positivism, steadiness 11 assuredness, staunchness 12 absoluteness, definiteness, positiveness
certificate 3 IOU 4 bond, note 6 coupon, notice, ticket 7 diploma, license, receipt, voucher 8 contract, document 9 testimony 10 credential
certifier 6 notary
certify 2 OK 4 aver, avow, okay 5 vouch 6 assert, attest, avouch 7 approve, endorse, license, profess, warrant, witness 8 accredit, guaranty, notarize, sanction 9 authorize, guarantee 10 commission
Cervantes' hero 10 Don Quixote
cesium *symbol:* 2 Cs
cessation 3 end 4 stop 5 cease, close 6 ending, finish, period 10 conclusion, desistance 11 termination
cesspool 3 den, sty 4 sink 5 Sodom 11 pandemonium 12 Augean stable
Cetus star 4 Mira
cgs unit 3 erg 4 dyne, gram, phot 5 gauss, poise, stilb 6 second, stokes 7 lambert, maxwell, oersted 10 centimeter
Chablis 4 wine 8 Burgundy
Chad *capital:* 8 N'Djamena *monetary unit:* 5 franc
chafe 3 irk, rub, vex 4 flay, fret, gall, hurt, peel, skin, wear 5 annoy, erode, graze 6 abrade, bother, damage, impair, injure, ruffle, scrape 7 corrode, inflame, provoke, scratch 8 exercise, irritate 9 excoriate
chaff 3 fun, kid, rag, rib 4 jest, joke, josh, razz 5 jolly 6 banter
chaffer 3 beg 4 coax 5 plead 6 dicker, haggle, higgle, palter 7 bargain 8 huckster
chafing 7 fretful 9 impatient, unpatient
chagrined 5 upset 6 shamed 7 ashamed, crushed 9 mortified, perturbed 11 discomposed 12 disconcerted
chain 3 row 4 bond, gyve, iron 5 group, train, trust 6 cartel, catena, fetter, hobble, series, string, tether 7 combine, manacle, shackle 8 additive, additory, handcuff, sequence 9 summative, syndicate 10 cumulative, succession 11 alternation, concatenate, consecution, progression, stereotyped 12 accumulative, conglomerate 13 concatenation, stereotypical *adjunct:* 8 sprocket *collar:* 6 torque *combining form:* 6 strept 7 strepto *gang:* 6 coffle *ornamental:* 10 chatelaine *ship's:* 3 tye *sound:* 5 clank
chain ___ 3 saw 4 gang, mail 5 smoke, store 6 letter 8 reaction
Chained Lady 9 Andromeda
chainlike 8 catenate
chain-shaped 10 catenulate
chair 4 seat 5 stool 6 rocker 7 preside *back:* 5 splat *bishop's:* 8 cathedra *portable:* 5 sedan *reclining:* 12 chaise longue, chaise lounge *royal:* 6 throne *type:* 4 club,

easy 6 morris 7 rocking 8 captain's, cogswell 9 reclining 10 ladder-back
chalcedony 4 onyx, sard 5 agate 6 jasper, quartz 9 carnelian 10 bloodstone 11 chrysoprase
chalice 3 ama, cup 5 amula, grail
chalk *combining form:* 4 calc 5 calci, calco 8 calcareo
chalk out 5 draft 6 sketch 7 outline 8 block out, rough out, skeleton 9 adumbrate 11 skeletonize 12 characterize
chalk up 3 get, win 4 gain, have 5 annex 6 obtain, pick up, secure 7 acquire, procure
challenge 3 try 4 call, dare, defi, defy, face, stir, wake, whet 5 beard, brave, claim, demur, doubt, exact, front, rally, rouse, stump, waken 6 arouse, awaken, banter, bestir, cartel, demand, kindle, strive 7 calling, dispute, outdare, protest, require, solicit, venture 8 claiming, defiance, demurral, demurrer, exacting, mistrust, question, struggle 9 demanding, objection, postulate 10 difficulty, insistence 11 importuning, requisition 12 remonstrance 13 remonstration
challenger 5 rival 8 opponent 9 adversary, contender 10 competitor, contestant
chamber 4 cell, room 5 haven, house 6 harbor, shield 7 cubicle, shelter 9 apartment *combining form:* 6 thalam 7 thalamo *in Egyptian tomb:* 6 serdab *underground:* 8 hypogeum
chambered 10 cancellate, cancellous
chamberlain 6 priest 7 officer, servant 9 attendant, treasurer
chameleon 6 lizard
chameleonic 6 fickle 10 changeable, inconstant
chamois 4 gems 5 gemse 6 shammy 7 leather 8 antelope, ruminant *habitat:* 4 Alps *Old Testament:* 6 aoudad
chamois-like animal 4 ibex 5 goral 6 gooral 7 klipbok 12 klipspringer
champ 3 gum, nip 4 bite, chew, mash, peck, pick 5 chomp, crush, mouth, munch 6 crunch, mumble, nibble 7 chumble, scrunch 8 macerate, ruminate 9 masticate
champagne 4 wine 5 color 6 bubbly *bucket:* 4 icer *center:* 5 Reims
Champagne *capital:* 6 Troyes
champaign 5 field 6 domain, sphere 7 demesne, terrain 8 dominion, province 9 bailiwick, territory
champignon 6 fungus 8 mushroom
champion 4 arch, back, boss, head 5 chief, dandy, first, prime 6 uphold 7 capital, contend, leading, premier, support, titlist 8 advocate, backstop, exponent, fight for, foremost, side with, splendid, superior, top-notch, whiz-bang 9 excellent, expounder, principal, proponent, supporter 10 blue-ribbon 11 illustrious, outstanding, titleholder 13 distinguished *medieval:* 7 paladin
championing *prefix:* 3 pro
championship 5 crown, title 7 defense, pennant 8 advocacy
chance 2 go 3 hap, hit, lot, odd 4 bump, fate, luck, meet, risk, shot, show, time 5 break, fluke, fluky, light, occur, wager 6 befall, betide, casual, gamble, happen, hazard 7 come off, fall out, fortune, offhand, opening, outlook, stumble, venture 8 accident, careless, fortuity, heedless, occasion, prospect 9 advantage, adventure, transpire 10 accidental, fortuitous, incidental, likelihood 11 opportunity, possibility, probability *even:* 6 toss-up
chancellor 5 judge 6 priest 7 adviser, officer 8 minister 9 secretary *German:* 6 Brandt, Erhard, Hitler 7 Schmidt 8 Adenauer, Bismarck
chancy 4 iffy 5 dicey, fluky, hairy, risky 6 touchy, tricky 7 erratic, unsound 8 perilous, ticklish 9 dangerous, fluctuant, hazardous, uncertain, whimsical 10 capricious, jeopardous, precarious 11 speculative, treacherous 12 incalculable 13 unpredictable
change 3 fix 4 geld, swap, turn, vary 5 alter, shift, sport, trade, unsex 6 avatar, invert, modify, mutate, neuter, reform, revamp, revert, revise, switch 7 commute, convert, inverse, novelty, replace, reverse 8 castrate, exchange, mutation, mutilate, revision, transfer 9 deviation, diversify, permutate, refashion, sterilize, transform, transmute, transpose, variation, variegate 10 aberration, alteration, conversion, divergence, innovation, substitute, transplace 11 desexualize, interchange, permutation, transfigure, vicissitude 12 metamorphose, modification, transmogrify 13 metamorphosis, transmutation *sudden:* 8 peripety 10 peripeteia
changeable 5 fluid 6 fickle, labile, mobile, pliant, shifty 7 movable, mutable, plastic, protean, unfixed 8 moveable, restless, slippery, ticklish, unstable, unsteady, variable, volatile, weathery 9 adaptable, mercurial, uncertain, unsettled 10 capricious, inconstant, lubricious 13 kaleidoscopic, temperamental
change decor 4 redo
changeless 5 fixed 6 steady 7 regular, uniform 8 constant, resolute 9 steadfast 10 invariable
change off 9 alternate
change of heart 8 reversal
change of life 9 menopause 11 climacteric
change of pace 5 pitch, shift

changeover 5 shift 10 alteration, conversion
channel 3 way 4 duct, mean, pass, pipe 5 agent, canal, carry, organ 6 agency, convey, course, funnel, groove, medium, siphon, strait 7 conduct, conduit, passage, vehicle 8 aqueduct, ministry, pipeline, transmit 10 instrument 11 watercourse ***Africa-Madagascar:*** 10 Mozambique ***Atlantic-Nantucket Sound:*** 8 Muskeget ***Atlantic-North Sea:*** 7 English ***California:*** 12 Santa Barbara ***Caribbean-Gulf of Mexico:*** 6 Yucatń ***combining form:*** 3 vas 4 vasi, vaso 5 solen 6 soleno ***Ellesmere-Greenland:*** 7 Robeson 10 Smith Sound ***Ganges:*** 5 Hugli 7 Hooghly ***Hawaii:*** 5 Kaiwi, Kauai ***Japan:*** 5 Bungo ***Long Island:*** 13 Rockaway Inlet ***Mediterranean:*** 5 Malta ***Northwest Territories:*** 9 M'Clintock ***Pakistan:*** 4 Nara ***Scotland:*** 5 Minch ***Tierra del Fuego:*** 6 Beagle ***Tigris-Euphrates:*** 11 Shatt-al-Arab ***Virginia:*** 12 Hampton Roads ***West Indies:*** 9 Old Bahama 10 Saint Lucia
channel bass 4 drum 7 redfish
"Chanson ___" 6 Triste
chanson de 5 geste
chant 4 sing, tune 8 vocalize 10 cantillate ***Gregorian:*** 9 plainsong 12 cantus firmus ***Jewish:*** 6 Hallel
chanteuse 6 singer 10 cantatrice
chanticleer 4 cock 7 rooster
chaos 4 void 5 snarl 6 ataxia, huddle, muddle 7 anarchy, clutter, misrule 8 disarray, disorder 9 confusion, mobocracy 10 ochlocracy, unruliness 11 lawlessness
Chaos ***daughter:*** 3 Nox, Nyx 4 Gaea ***son:*** 6 Erebus
chap 3 guy, man 4 gent 6 fellow 9 gentleman ***British:*** 5 bloke
chaparral 7 thicket
chaparral bird 10 roadrunner
chaperon 4 boss 5 guide 6 attend, convoy, escort, survey 7 conduct, oversee 9 accompany, companion, supervise 11 consort with, quarterback, superintend
chapfallen see **crestfallen**
chaplain 5 padre 8 sky pilot
chaplet 5 crown 6 anadem, rosary, wreath 7 coronal, coronet, garland
char 4 burn 9 carbonize
character 3 ilk, rep, VIP 4 case, fame, kind, mark, mind, name, quiz, rank, role, sign, sort, soul, type 5 chief, humor, nabob, place, point, savor, state, trait 6 bigwig, cipher, device, kidney, letter, makeup, mettle, nature, oddity, report, repute, spirit, status, stripe, symbol, temper, virtue, zombie 7 big shot, courage, feature, footing, notable, oddball, persona, quality, station, variety 8 big-timer, capacity, eminence, identity, monogram, original, position, property, standing, uniquity 9 affection, attribute, birthmark, dignitary, eccentric, intellect, reference, situation 10 complexion, notability, reputation, resolution, uniqueness 11 credentials, description, disposition, distinction, personality, temperament, testimonial 13 individualism, individuality ***chief:*** 4 hero 11 protagonist ***defect:*** 8 hamartia ***suffix:*** 3 ery
character assassination 7 calumny, scandal, slander 10 backbiting, defamation, detraction 12 backstabbing, belittlement, depreciation 13 disparagement
characteristic 4 mark, odor, sign, tang 5 badge, point, savor, smack, token, trait 6 flavor, normal, proper, virtue 7 feature, natural, quality, regular, special, typical 8 especial, peculiar, property, specific 9 affection, attribute, birthmark, character, diacritic 10 diagnostic, individual, particular 11 differentia, distinctive, singularity 13 idiosyncratic
characteristic of ***suffix:*** 2 ic, ly 3 ish, ist 4 ical 5 istic 7 istical
characterize 4 mark 5 draft 6 define, sketch 7 outline, qualify 8 block out, chalk out, describe, identify, rough out, skeleton 9 adumbrate, signalize 11 distinguish, individuate, peculiarize, personalize, singularize, skeletonize 13 differentiate, individualize
characterized by ***suffix:*** 2 al, ic 3 ful, ial, ous 4 ical
characterless 4 weak 5 sissy 6 futile 7 unmanly 8 childish, impotent 9 infantile, powerless, sissified 10 namby-pamby, panty-waist, wishy-washy
charade 7 pageant 8 disguise, pretense 10 pretension 11 make-believe
chare 3 job 4 duty, task 5 chore, stint 6 devoir 10 assignment
charge 3 ask, bid, fee, lay, tab, tax 4 bill, boil, bolt, care, clog, cost, dash, duty, fill, heap, lade, lash, load, must, need, onus, pack, pile, race, rate, rush, task, tear, tell, toll, warn, word 5 chase, choke, fling, order, ought, place, price, refer, right, shoot, trust, weigh 6 accuse, adjure, assign, behest, burden, credit, cumber, devoir, direct, enjoin, impugn, impute, indict, saddle, tariff, weight 7 arraign, ascribe, bidding, command, conduct, dictate, entrust, expense, impeach, mandate, pervade, request, running, solicit 8 accredit, business, encumber, handling, instruct, permeate, price tag, reproach, saturate 9 attribute, committal, criminate, inculpate, millstone, oversight, penetrate, percolate, reprehend, transfuse 10 commitment, deadweight, impregnate, injunction, intendance, management, obligation 11 impenetrate, incriminate, supervision

chargeable 6 liable 11 responsible
chargeless 4 free 6 gratis 8 costless 10 gratuitous 13 complimentary
charger 5 horse, mount, steed 7 courser 8 war-horse
chariness 7 caution 8 prudence
chariot 5 essed 6 esseda, essede *four-horse:* 8 quadriga *two-horse:* 4 biga
charioteer 5 drive, pilot 6 Auriga, driver
charisma 5 charm 6 allure, appeal, duende, glamor 7 glamour 8 witchery 9 magnetism 10 witchcraft 11 fascination
charitable 4 easy, good 6 benign, humane, kindly 7 clement, helpful, lenient 8 merciful, obliging, tolerant 9 indulgent 10 altruistic, benevolent, forbearing, thoughtful 11 considerate, kindhearted, sympathetic 12 eleemosynary, humanitarian 13 accommodating, philanthropic
charity 4 alms, love 5 amity, grace, mercy 6 lenity 7 caritas 8 altruism, clemency, donation, goodwill, offering 9 affection 10 attachment, humaneness, kindliness 11 benefaction, beneficence, benevolence 12 contribution, friendliness
charivari 5 babel 6 medley 8 serenade, shivaree 10 hodgepodge 11 celebration
charlatan 4 sham 5 bluff, quack 8 impostor 9 quacksalver 10 mountebank 11 four-flusher, quacksalver 12 saltimbanque
Charlemagne *brother:* 8 Carloman *father:* 5 Pepin *knight:* 4 Ivon, Oton 5 Gerin, Ivory 6 Anseis, Gerard, Gerier, Oliver, Roland, Samson 7 Olivier, paladin 8 douzeper, Engelier 9 Berengier *nephew:* 6 Roland 7 Orlando *sword:* 7 Joyeuse *traitor:* 4 Gano 7 Ganelon
Charles's Wain 9 Big Dipper
charleston 5 dance
Charley's Aunt author 6 Thomas
Charlie Brown creator 6 Schulz
Charlie McCarthy 5 dummy 6 stooge *friend:* 5 Snerd *voice:* 6 Bergen
charm 3 hex 4 draw, juju, luck, lure, rune, take, wile, zemi 5 spell, witch 6 allure, amulet, appeal, enamor, fetish, glamor, mascot, voodoo 7 attract, bewitch, enchant 8 enthrall, talisman, witchery 9 captivate, ensorcell, fascinate, magnetism, magnetize 10 allurement, attraction, phylactery, witchcraft 11 conjuration, fascination, incantation 12 gratefulness 13 agreeableness
charmed 8 enamored 9 bewitched, enchanted, entranced 10 captivated, fascinated
charmer 4 mage 5 magus 6 magian, wizard 7 warlock 8 conjurer, magician, sorcerer 9 enchanter 11 necromancer
charming 5 siren 7 drawing, winsome 8 adorable, alluring, magnetic 9 glamorous, seductive 10 attracting, attractive, enchanting 11 captivating
Charon 7 boatman 8 ferryman *father:* 6 Erebus *mother:* 3 Nox *river:* 4 Styx
Charpentier opera 6 Louise
charpoy 3 bed, cot
chart 3 map 4 cast, plan, plat, plot 5 graph, table 6 design, devise, scheme 7 arrange, dope out, project 9 blueprint 10 tabulation
charter 3 let 4 deed, hire, rent 5 lease 10 conveyance
Chartreuse 7 liqueur
chary 4 safe, wary 5 canny, loath 6 frugal, saving 7 careful, guarded, sparing, thrifty 8 cautious, discreet, gingerly, hesitant 9 inhibited, provident, reluctant, stewardly 10 economical, restrained, unwasteful 11 calculating, circumspect, considerate, constrained, disinclined
Charybdis 9 whirlpool *rock associated with:* 6 Scylla
chase 3 out, run 4 boil, bolt, dash, game, hunt, lash, prey, race, rush, tear 5 chivy, chuck, eject, evict, fling, shoot, speed, trail 6 career, charge, course, follow, pursue, quarry, venery 7 boot out, dismiss, extrude, hunting, kick out, pursuit 8 throw out
chase away 4 shoo
chaser 4 wolf 6 masher 7 Don Juan 8 Casanova 9 ladies' man, philander, womanizer 10 lady-killer 11 philanderer
chasm 3 gap 4 gulf, skip 5 abysm, abyss, blank, cleft, clove, gorge, gulch, split 6 arroyo, clough, ravine, schism 8 cleavage, omission, overlook 9 oversight 11 preterition 13 pretermission
chasmal 7 yawning 9 cavernous
chassepot 5 rifle
chaste 4 pure 5 clean, moral 6 decent, modest, proper, seemly, vestal, virgin 7 ethical 8 becoming, decorous, maidenly, spotless, virginal, virtuous 9 abstinent, continent, righteous, stainless, undefiled, unsullied 10 immaculate 11 unblemished
chasten 3 try 5 abase 6 humble, punish 7 afflict, correct 8 chastise 9 castigate, humiliate 10 discipline
chastise 4 beat 5 baste 6 pummel, punish, thrash 7 belabor, chasten, correct 9 castigate 10 discipline
chastisement 3 rod 8 punition 10 correction, discipline, punishment 11 castigation
chat 3 gab, jaw, rap, yak, yap 4 blab, chin, gush, talk, yarn 5 clack, prate, prose, run on, visit 6 babble, burble, cackle, confab, dither, gabble, gossip, jabber, parley, patter, rattle, yak-yak, yammer, yatter 7 chatter, clatter, palaver, prattle, smatter, twaddle, twitter 8 causerie, chin-chin, colloque, collo-

quy, converse, dialogue, lallygag **9** tête-à-tête, yakety-yak **11** confabulate **12** bibble-babble, conversation, tittle-tattle **13** confabulation
chateau **5** manor, villa **6** castle **7** mansion
chateaubriand **5** steak **10** tenderloin
Chateaubriand novel **4** René **5** Atala **10** Les Natchez
chatelain **6** warden **8** governor **9** castellan
chatelaine **4** hook, wife **5** clasp **8** mistress
chattel **5** slave **7** bondman **8** bondsman **9** bondslave, mancipium
chatter **3** gab, jaw, yak **4** blab, bull, chat **5** clack, prate **6** babble, burble, cackle, gabble, gibber, gossip, jabber, natter, patter, yak-yak, yammer, yatter **7** blabber, blather, blatter, blither, brabble, palaver, prattle **8** chin-chin, chitchat **9** small talk, yakety-yak **12** bibble-babble, gibble-gabble, talkee-talkee, tittle tattle
chatterbox **5** tabby **6** chewet, gabber, gossip, magpie, prater **7** blabber **8** busybody, jabberer, prattler, quidnunc **9** bandar-log, blabmouth, chatterer **10** newsmonger, tattletale **12** blabbermouth **13** scandalmonger
chatty **5** gabby, talky, wordy **9** garrulous, talkative **10** babblative, loquacious **11** loose-lipped **12** loose-tongued, multiloquent **13** multiloquious
chauffeur **5** drive **6** driver **9** transport
chauvinism **8** jingoism **10** partiality, patriotism **11** nationalism
cheap **3** bad, low **4** base, fake, mean, poor, sham, vile **5** petty, phony, sorry, tatty, wrong **6** cheesy, common, flashy, garish, measly, paltry, rotten, scurvy, shabby, shoddy, sleazy, tawdry, trashy, undear **7** chintzy, cut-rate, low-cost, pitiful, popular, reduced **8** beggarly, inferior, pitiable, rubbishy, terrible, trifling, trumpery, uncostly **9** brummagem, low-priced, rubbishly, valueless, worthless **10** despicable, despisable, reasonable, rubbishing **11** inexpensive **12** contemptible, meretricious
cheapen **5** decry, lower **7** devalue **8** mark down, write off **9** devaluate, downgrade, write down **10** depreciate, undervalue
cheap-jack **6** hawker, monger, vendor **7** higgler, packman, peddler **8** huckster, inferior, outcrier **9** worthless
cheapskate **4** skin **5** chuff, miser, stiff **7** niggard **8** muckworm, tightwad **9** skinflint **11** cheeseparer
cheat **3** con, gyp **4** beat, bilk, burn, dupe, fool, gull, hoax, ream, sell, take **5** bunco, cozen, crook, fraud, fudge, hocus, put-on, screw, short, slick **6** befool, boodle, chisel, chouse, con man, deceit, delude, diddle, extort, fleece, humbug, sucker **7** beguile, chicane, deceive, defraud, diddler, hoaxing, mislead, sharper, swindle **8** cozening, flimflam, swindler, trickery **9** chicanery, deception, defrauder, fourberie, imposture, overreach, trickster **10** dishonesty, hanky-panky **11** double-cross, highbinding **12** double-dealer **13** bamboozlement, confidence man, double-dealing ***on a check:*** **4** kite
check **2** go **3** bit, tab, try **4** balk, bill, curb, foil, halt, jibe, rein, stay, stem, stop, test, tick **5** agree, cease, prove, score, stall, tally **6** accord, arrest, baffle, bridle, damage, desist, hold in, square, thwart **7** backset, conform, examine, inhibit, obviate, prevent, repress, reverse, setback **8** dovetail, hold back, hold down, preclude, restrain, reversal, suppress, withhold **9** constrain, frustrate, interrupt **10** circumvent, correspond **11** discontinue
checklist **7** catalog **9** catalogue, inventory
checkmate **6** arrest, corner, defeat, thwart **7** counter
check over **3** con, vet **4** view **5** study **6** survey **7** canvass, check up, examine, inspect **10** scrutinize
checkup **7** medical **8** physical **10** inspection **11** examination
cheek **4** face, gall **5** brass, crust, nerve **9** brashness **10** confidence, effrontery **11** presumption ***combining form:*** **3** mel **4** melo **5** bucco
cheekbone **5** malar
cheeky **4** bold, pert, wise **5** fresh, nervy, sassy, smart **7** forward **8** impudent **11** smart-alecky
cheep **4** chip, peep **5** chirp, tweet **7** chipper, chirrup, chitter, tweedle, twitter
cheer **3** rah **4** root **5** bravo, huzza, nerve, steel **6** buck up, hoorah, hooray, hurrah, hurray, huzzah, solace **7** animate, applaud, comfort, console, hearten, upraise **8** embolden, inspirit **9** encourage, enhearten **10** strengthen ***corrida:*** **3** olé
cheerful **3** gay **4** airy, glad, rosy **5** chirk, corky, jolly, merry, riant, sunny **6** blithe, bright, chirpy, jaunty, jocund, lively **7** beamish, buoyant, radiant **8** animated, carefree, chirrupy, debonair, sunbeamy **9** lightsome, vivacious **12** lighthearted ***Scottish:*** **5** cadgy
cheerio **2** by **5** adieu **6** bye-bye, so long **7** good-bye **8** farewell, toodle-oo
cheerless **4** drab **5** bleak **6** dismal, dreary, gloomy, somber **8** funereal **9** dejecting **10** depressing, oppressive, tenebrific **11** dispiriting
cheese **3** pot **4** blue, jack **5** brick, cream, store **6** farmer **7** cottage, process **9** pineapple, smearcase ***American:*** **8** Longhorn

11 Liederkranz 12 Monterey Jack ***Belgian:*** 9 Limburger ***brown:*** 6 mysost 7 gjetost ***Canadian:*** 3 Oka ***combining form:*** 3 tyr 4 case, tyro 5 caseo ***curdling agent:*** 6 rennet, rennin ***Danish:*** 4 Tybo 5 Esrom 6 Samsoe 7 Havarti ***dish:*** 6 fondue 7 rarebit, soufflé ***Dutch:*** 4 Edam 5 Gouda 6 Leyden ***English:*** 7 cheddar, Stilton 8 Cheshire 10 Lancashire ***French:*** 4 Brie 7 fromage, Livarot 9 Camembert, reblochon, Roquefort 10 Neufchâtel 11 Pont l'Évêque, Port du Salut ***German:*** 4 kase 6 Tilsit 7 Munster 8 Muenster, Tilsiter ***Greek:*** 4 feta 7 kasseri ***green:*** 7 sapsago ***Italian:*** 6 Romano 7 fontina, ricotta 8 Bel Paese, Parmesan, pecorino 9 provolone 10 Gorgonzola, mozzarella 12 caciocavallo ***lover:*** 9 turophile ***main ingredient:*** 6 casein ***Norwegian:*** 6 mysost 7 gjetost, primost 9 gammelost, Jarlsberg, taffelost 10 Noekkelost ***Oriental:*** 4 tofu ***protein:*** 6 casein ***Scottish:*** 6 Dunlop, Orkney 7 kebbock, kebbuck ***Swedish:*** 8 graddost ***Swiss:*** 6 Saanen 7 Gruyère, sapsago 8 Vacherin 10 Emmentaler 11 Emmenthaler ***uncured:*** 7 cottage ***Welsh:*** 10 Caerphilly ***whey:*** 5 ziger 6 zieger

cheesecloth 5 gauze

cheeselike 6 caseic 7 caseous

cheeseparer 4 skin 5 chuff, miser, stiff 7 niggard 8 muckworm, tightwad 9 skinflint 10 cheapskate

cheeseparing 4 mean 5 cheap, close, tight 6 shabby, stingy 7 miserly 8 grudging 9 illiberal, niggardly, penurious 11 closefisted, tightfisted 12 parsimonious 13 penny-pinching

cheesy 4 mean, poor 5 cheap, tatty 6 common, shoddy, sleazy, trashy 7 caseous 8 rubbishy

chef d'oeuvre 7 classic 9 showpiece 10 magnum opus, masterwork 11 masterpiece, tour de force

Chekhov, Anton ***play:*** 6 Ivanov 7 Sea Gull 10 Uncle Vanya 12 Three Sisters 13 Cherry Orchard

chelonian 6 turtle 8 tortoise

chemical ***agent:*** 8 catalyst ***combining form:*** 2 is, ol, ox, yl 3 aci, hex, iod, iso, mer, ole, oxa, oxo, oyl, pyr, thi, tri, ure 4 acet, amid, amin, hept, hexa, hydr, iodo, orth, poly, pyro, quin, tetr, thio 5 aceto, amido, amino, hepta, hydro, ortho, quino, tetra, xanth 6 ammino, xantho ***combining power:*** 7 valence ***compound:*** 4 acid, base, diol, enol, imid, oxim, salt, tepa, urea 5 amide, amine, diene, ester, imide, imine, indol, orcin, oxime, purin, pyran, salol, tolan, triol 6 alkali, benzin, benzol, diamin, emodin, guanin, halide, hydrid, indole, inulin, ionone, isatin, isolog, isomer, ketone, lactam, maltol, metepa, natron, nitril, pterin, purine, pyrone, pyrrol, quinol, retene, silane, skatol, tannin, tetryl, thiram, thymol, tolane, triene, trimer, uracil, ureide, yttria, zeatin 7 barilla, benzene, benzole, cumarin, diamide, diamine, diazine, diazole, diester, flavone, guanine, heptose, hydride, indamin, indican, indoxyl, isatine, levulin, metamer, monomer, naphtol, nitrile, orcinol, oxazine, phytane, picolin, polyene, polymer, pyrrole, quinoid, quinone, salicin, skatole, steroid, taurine, terpene, thiazin, thiazol, thymine, tolidin, triazin, urethan, uridine, vitamer, xylidin 8 cephalin, cyanamid, disulfid, elaterin, fluorene, furfural, guaiacol, hematein, hexamine, indamine, isologue, kephalin, lichenin, limonene, melamine, naloxone, naphthol, palmitin, phenazin, phosphid, phthalin, picoline, piperine, pristane, quinolin, resorcin, salicine, santonin, siloxane, sodamide, sorbitol, spermine, squalene, stilbene, strontia, tautomer, thiazine, thiazole, thiophen, thiotepa, thiourea, tolidine, triazine, triazole, triptane, tyramine, urethane, vanillin, warfarin, xanthene, xanthine, xanthone, xylidine, ytterbia, zaratite, zirconia ***element:*** (see at element) ***prefix:*** 2 di 3 dia, met 4 meta ***quantity:*** 4 mole ***radical:*** 4 acyl, amyl, cyan 5 allyl, butyl, ethyl, tolyl 6 acetyl, formyl, methyl, oxalic, phenyl, propyl, toluyl 7 benzoyl ***reaction:*** 5 redox ***salt:*** 5 niter, nitre, urate, ziram 6 haloid, humate, malate, oleate, phytin 7 ferrate, formate, gallate, maleate, pectate, persalt, picrate, tannate, toluate, zincate 8 fumarate, pyruvate, racemate, selenate, silicate, stearate, tartrate, thionate, titanate, valerate, vanadate, xanthate ***suffix:*** 2 id, il, in, ol, on 3 ane, ase, ate, ein, ene, ide, ile, ine, ite, ium, oic, oin, one, ose, ous, yne 4 eine, idin, itol, oate, olic, onic 5 idine, onium, oside, ylene ***warfare agent:*** 7 tear gas 8 vesicant 10 mustard gas

chemist 7 analyst 8 druggist 10 apothecary, pharmacist ***American:*** 4 Urey 6 Remsen, Sumner 7 Onsager, Pauling, Seaborg 8 Hoffmann, Langmuir, Mulliken, Richards, Woodward ***Austrian:*** 4 Kuhn 5 Pregl ***British:*** 6 Ramsay 8 Smithson ***Dutch:*** 8 van't Hoff ***English:*** 4 Abel, Davy 5 Soddy 6 Dalton 7 Faraday 9 Priestley, Wollaston 10 Williamson ***French:*** 5 Curie 7 Moissan, Pasteur 8 Sabatier 9 Lavoisier ***German:*** 5 Haber 6 Bunsen, Liebig, Nernst, Wittig, Wohler 7 Fischer, Hofmann, Ostwald, Wallach, Wieland, Windaus, Ziegler 9 Zsigmondy 10 Erlenmeyer, Staudinger 11 Willstatter ***Italian:*** 5 Natta 8 Avogadro ***Russian:*** 7 Semenov 8 Zelinsky 9 Mendeleev ***Scottish:*** 4 Todd ***Swedish:*** 8 Svedberg ***Swiss:*** 6 Karrer, Werner (see also under **Nobel Prize Winner**)

chemist's vessel 4 vial 5 ampul, flask, phial 6 aludel, ampule, beaker, mortar, retort 7 ampoule, matrass 8 bolt head, crucible, cylinder, test tube
chemoreceptor 8 taste bud
cheongsam 5 dress
Cheops 5 Khufu 7 pyramid
Cheran's father 6 Dishon
cherish 4 keep, save 5 guard, nurse, prize, value 6 admire, defend, esteem, foster, harbor, nursle, relish, revere, shield 7 apprize, nourish, nurture, shelter 8 conserve, preserve, treasure, venerate 9 cultivate, delight in, entertain, reverence, safeguard 10 appreciate
Cherokee ***chief:*** 4 Ross ***historian:*** 7 Sequoya
cherry ***dark:*** 4 Bing ***family:*** 4 rose 8 Rosaceae ***genus:*** 6 Prunus ***hybrid:*** 4 Duke ***sour:*** 7 morello 8 amarelle ***sweet:*** 4 Bing, gean 7 mazzard, oxheart 9 Bigarreau ***wild:*** 7 marasca, mazzard 10 maraschino
cherry bomb 11 firecracker
Cherry Orchard author 7 Chekhov
cherrystone 4 clam 6 quahog
chersonese 9 peninsula
Chesed ***father:*** 5 Nahor ***wife:*** 6 Milcah
chess ***champion:*** 3 Tal 4 Euwe 6 Karpov, Lasker 7 Fischer, Smysolv, Spassky 8 Alekhine, Kasparov, Steinitz 9 Botvinnik, Petrosian 10 Capablanca ***draw game:*** 9 stalemate ***goal:*** 4 mate 9 checkmate ***move:*** 6 castle, gambit 10 fianchetto ***opening:*** 6 gambit ***piece:*** 4 king, pawn, rook 5 queen 6 bishop, knight ***risk:*** 6 gambit ***term:*** 3 net, pin 4 biff, draw, file, fork, mate, rank 5 check 6 attack, castle, gambit, skewer 7 capture, develop, end game 9 checkmate, en passant 10 fianchetto, middle game 11 combination
chest 4 kist 6 breast, bureau, coffer, lowboy, thorax, wangan, wangun 7 dresser, highboy, wanigan 8 treasury, wannigan 9 exchequer 10 chiffonier ***combining form:*** 5 stern 6 sterno, stetho, thorac 7 thoraci, thoraco
chesterfield 4 sofa 8 overcoat 9 davenport
chestnut 4 tree 5 color, horse 6 cliché, marron 10 brownstone, chinquapin ***extract:*** 6 tannin ***Polynesian:*** 4 rata ***water:*** 4 ling
cheval glass 6 mirror
chevalier 5 noble 6 knight 8 horseman 9 caballero, gentleman
chevron 6 stripe
chew 3 eat, gum 4 bite, chaw, gnaw 5 champ, chomp, chump, crump, munch 6 crunch, devour, mumble, nibble 7 chumble, consume, scrunch 8 ruminate 9 masticate
chewing gum 6 chicle
chew out 3 jaw, wig 5 scold 6 revile 7 bawl out, tell off 10 tongue-lash, vituperate
Chiang ____ 7 Kai-shek
chic 3 cry, fad 4 mode, rage 5 craze, smart, style, swank, swish, vogue 6 furore, modish, trendy, with-it 7 dashing, fashion, stylish 9 exclusive 10 dernier cri 11 fashionable
chicane 4 dupe, fool, gull, hoax, ploy, ruse, wile 5 cavil, feint, fraud, trick 6 befool, gambit 7 quibble 8 artifice, flimflam, hoodwink, maneuver, trickery 9 bamboozle, deception, stratagem, victimize 10 dishonesty, hanky-panky 11 furtiveness, highbinding 13 double-dealing
chicanery 4 plot 5 fraud 8 intrigue, trickery 11 machination
chichi 5 showy, swank 6 dressy, la-di-da 7 splashy 8 affected, overnice, peacocky, précieux, precious 10 flamboyant, peacockish 11 alembicated, overrefined, pretentious 12 orchidaceous, ostentatious
chick 3 kid 5 child 6 moppet, nipper 8 juvenile, young one 9 youngling, youngster
chickadee 8 titmouse ***family:*** 7 Paridae
Chickasaw chief 5 mingo
chicken 4 fowl, funk 5 sissy 6 coward, craven, funker 7 dastard, gutless, quitter, unmanly 8 cowardly, poltroon 9 spunkless 11 lily-livered, poltroonish, yellowbelly 12 poor-spirited 13 pusillanimous ***breed:*** 4 Java 6 Ancona, Brahma, Cochin, Lamona, Redcap, Sussex 7 Buckeye, Cornish, Dorking, Holland, Leghorn, Minorca 8 Delaware, Dominick, Langshan 9 Buttercup, Dominique, Orpington, Wyandotte 10 Australorp 11 Jersey Giant, Rock Cornish ***castrated:*** 5 capon ***cooking:*** 5 fryer 7 broiler, roaster ***disease:*** 5 gapes 8 pullorum 11 coccidiosis ***female:*** 3 hen 6 pullet ***genus:*** 6 Gallus ***male:*** 4 cock 7 rooster 8 cockerel ***pen:*** 4 coop ***small:*** 6 bantam ***sound:*** 6 cackle
chicken feed 7 peanuts 8 pittance
chicken pox 9 varicella
chickpea 8 garbanzo
chickweed 4 pink 7 potherb
chicle 3 gum 10 chewing gum
chicory 7 witloof
chide 4 rate 5 scold, sneap 6 berate, lesson, monish, rebuke 7 reprove, tick off, upbraid 8 admonish, call down, reproach 9 reprimand
chiding 3 rap, wig 6 rebuke 7 reproof 8 reproach 9 reprimand 10 admonition 12 admonishment

chief 4 arch, boss, cock, duce, head, jefe, lion, main, star 5 first, major, prime 6 bigwig, führer, honcho, leader, master, potent, primal, ruling, sachem 7 capital, headman, leading, notable, premier, primary, stellar, telling, weighty 8 bigtimer, big wheel, champion, dictator, dominant, eminence, foremost, hierarch, luminary 9 dignitary, dominator, effective, important, momentous, number one, principal, prominent 10 notability, preeminent 11 controlling, outstanding, predominant, significant 13 consequential *combining form:* 4 prot 5 proto *commander:* 4 CINC *prefix:* 4 arch 5 archi *Spanish:* 4 jefe
Chief Justice 3 Jay 4 Taft 5 Chase, Stone, Taney, Waite, White 6 Burger, Fuller, Holmes, Hughes, Vinson, Warren 8 Marshall 9 Ellsworth
chiefly 6 mainly, mostly 7 largely, overall 9 generally, primarily 11 principally 13 predominantly
chiffchaff 4 bird 7 warbler
chiffonier 5 chest 6 bureau 7 dresser
chigger 4 mite 6 chigoe, red bug
chignon 3 bun 4 knot
chilblain 4 sore 8 swelling 12 inflammation
child 3 kid 5 minor, youth 6 cherub, moppet, nipper, teener 7 dickens 8 innocent, juvenile, runabout, teenager, young one 9 sweetling, youngling, youngster 10 adolescent 11 teenybopper *combining form:* 3 ped 4 paed, paid, pedo 5 paedo, paido, tecno *gifted:* 7 prodigy *homeless:* 4 waif *parentless:* 6 orphan *Scottish:* 5 bairn *spoiled:* 4 brat *young:* 3 tot 4 baby, tike, tyke 6 infant, kiddie 8 bantling, weanling
childish 4 slow 5 naive, silly 6 simple 7 asinine, babyish, fatuous, foolish, kiddish, moronic, puerile 8 arrested, backward, immature, retarded 9 infantile, infantine *Scottish:* 7 bairnly 8 bairnish
childless 6 barren 7 sterile
childlike 6 docile, filial 7 natural 8 innocent, trustful, trusting 9 ingenuous
child's play 4 snap 5 cinch, setup 6 breeze, picnic 8 duck soup, kid stuff, pushover
Chile *capital:* 8 Santiago *chief export:* 6 copper *conqueror:* 8 Valdivia *monetary unit:* 4 peso
Chileab *father:* 5 David *mother:* 7 Abigail
chili con ____ 5 carne
Chilion *father:* 9 Elimelech *mother:* 5 Naomi
chill 3 icy 4 ague, cold, cool 5 gelid, nippy 6 arctic, chilly, deject, formal, frigid, frosty 7 distant, glacial 8 dispirit, freezing, reserved, solitary 9 disparage, withdrawn 10 abstracted, demoralize, discourage, dishearten 11 emotionless, indifferent, standoffish, unemotional 12 uninterested 13 disinterested
chiller 7 shocker 8 thriller
chilly 3 raw 4 cold 5 algid 7 coldish
chilopod 9 centipede
chime 4 bell, bong, peal, ring, toll, tune 5 knell 6 accord 7 concord, harmony 9 agreement 10 consonance 11 concordance
chime in 3 say 4 tell 5 state, utter 6 chip in 7 break in, declare, deliver 8 bring out, throw out 9 interrupt
chimera 5 dream 6 bubble 7 fantasy, rainbow 8 illusion, phantasy 9 pipe dream
Chimera *father:* 6 Typhon *mother:* 7 Echidna *slayer:* 11 Bellerophon
chimerical 6 absurd, unreal 7 fictive, utopian 8 delusive, delusory, fabulous, fanciful, illusory, mythical 9 ambitious, deceptive, fantastic, fictional, imaginary 10 fictitious 11 pretentious 12 preposterous, suppositious
chiming 7 musical 8 blending, harmonic 9 consonant, symphonic 10 harmonious 11 symphonious
chimney 3 lum 4 flue, tube 5 stack 10 smokestack *corner:* 8 fireside 9 inglenook *output:* 3 gas 4 fume, soot 5 smoke
chimpanzee 3 ape 6 monkey 7 primate 10 anthropoid *kin:* 7 gorilla
chin 3 rap 4 chat, talk, yarn 5 prose, visit 6 mentum 8 causerie, colloque, converse *combining form:* 5 genio, mento
china 6 dishes 7 ceramic 8 crockery 9 porcelain 11 earthenware *maker:* 3 Bow 5 Hizen, Imari, Spode 6 Doccia, Sèvres 7 Bristol, Chelsea, Dresden, Limoges, Meissen 8 Caughley, Haviland, Wedgwood
China *capital:* 6 Peking 7 Beijing *largest city:* 8 Shanghai *monetary unit:* 4 yuan *old name:* 6 Cathay *province:* 5 Anhui, Gansu, Hebei, Henan, Hubei, Hunan, Jilin 6 Fujian, Shanxi, Yunnan 7 Guizhou, Jiangsu, Jiangxi, Qinghai, Shaanxi, Sichuan 8 Liaoning, Shandong, Szechwan, Zhejiang 9 Guangdong 12 Heilongjiang *region:* 5 Tibet 6 Xizang 10 Nei Monggol 12 Ningxia Huizu 13 Inner Mongolia, Xinjiang Uygur
china clay 6 kaolin
chinchilla 3 fur 6 rodent
chine 5 crest, ridge 7 hogback
Chinese *administrative unit:* 2 fu 5 hsien *archway:* 6 pai-lou *aromatic root:* 7 ginseng *artichoke:* 6 crosne 7 chorogi, crosnes 8 knotroot *assembly:* 3 hui *bamboo:* 7 whangee *boat:* 4 junk 6 sampan *boat-dweller:* 3 Tan 5 Tanka *bow:* 6 kowtow *Buddha:* 2 Fo *Buddhism:* 5 Foism

cabbage: 6 pechay 7 pakchoi *card game:* 6 fan tan *cauterizing agent:* 4 moxa *civet:* 5 rasse *combining form:* 4 Sino 5 Chino 6 Sinico *conveyance:* 7 pedicab, ricksha 10 jinrikisha *date:* 6 jujube *deer:* 8 elaphure *dialect:* 2 Wu 4 Amoy 5 Hakka 6 Swatow 7 Foochow 8 Mandarin 9 Cantonese, Pekingese *dictator:* 10 Mao Tse-tung *distance unit:* 2 li *dog:* 4 chow, Peke 9 Pekingese *dulcimer:* 7 yang-kin 8 yang ch'in *dynasty:* 2 Wu 3 Ch'i, Han, Sui, Wei, Yin 4 Ch'en, Ch'in, Chou, Hsia (first), Ming, Sung, T'ang, Tsin, Yuan 5 Ch'ing, Liang, Shang 6 Manchu, Mongol, Shu Han *fabric:* 5 pekin 6 pongee, tussah 7 tsatlee 8 shantung *feminine principle:* 3 yin *festival:* 8 Ch'in Ming *feudal state:* 3 Wei *figurine:* 5 magot *food:* 6 subgum, won ton 7 foo yong *fruit:* 6 lichee, litchi, loquat 7 kumquat 8 mandarin *gambling game:* 6 fan tan *gazelle:* 6 dzeren, dzeron *god:* 4 joss, Shen 7 Shang-ti, Tien Chu *gong:* 6 tam-tam *grass:* 3 bon *gruel:* 6 congee *herb:* 5 ramee, ramie 7 ginseng *idol:* 4 joss *jute:* 7 chingma *laborer:* 6 coolie *legendary emperor:* 7 Huang Ti *liquid measure:* 5 cheng, sheng *liquor:* 6 samshu *magnolia:* 5 yulan *mandarin's residence:* 5 yamen *masculine principle:* 4 yang *military leader:* 7 warlord *money, silver:* 5 sycee *moon guitar:* 6 yue-kin 8 yueh-ch'in *musical instrument:* 3 kin 4 ch'in, pipa 5 cheng, hsiao 6 yue-kin 8 yang ch'in, yueh ch'in *nurse:* 4 amah *official:* 4 kuan 8 mandarin *official seal:* 4 chop *oil:* 4 tung *omelet:* 7 foo yong *ox:* 4 zebu *pagoda:* 2 ta 3 taa *peony:* 6 moutan *permit:* 4 chop *porcelain:* 4 chin, Ming 7 celadon, Nankeen 8 mandarin *pottery:* 4 Kuan, Ming 5 Chien 7 boccaro, tz'u-chou *prefecture:* 2 fu *puzzle:* 7 tangram *race:* 9 Mongoloid *religion:* 5 Foism 6 Taoism 8 Buddhism 12 Confucianism *rice song:* 6 yang ko *sauce:* 3 soy *secret society:* 4 tong *sheep:* 3 sha 5 urial 6 oorial *silkworm:* 6 tussah 7 tussore 9 ailanthus *string money:* 4 tiao *tea:* 5 bohea, congo, hyson 6 congou, oolong 8 souchong *temple:* 2 ta 3 taa 6 pagoda *tree:* 4 tung 6 gingko, ginkgo, loquat, wampee 7 kumquat 8 mandarin *unicorn:* 3 lin *vine:* 5 kudzu 7 yangtao *weight:* 3 fan, fen, tan 4 mace, tael 5 catty, liang, picol, picul

chink 4 rift, rima, rime 5 cleft, clink, crack, split 6 jingle, tingle, tinkle 7 fissure 8 rimation

chinquapin 3 nut 8 chestnut

chintzy 4 loud 5 cheap, gaudy 6 brazen, flashy, garish, tawdry, tinsel 7 blatant, glaring 12 meretricious

chip in 6 kick in 7 break in, chime in, pitch in 9 interrupt, subscribe 10 contribute 11 come through

chipmunk 6 hackee, rodent *family:* 8 squirrel 9 Sciuridae

chipper 3 gay 4 keen, neat, peep, snug, tidy, trig, trim 5 alert, cheep, chirm, chirp, tweet 6 bright, lively 7 animate, chirrup, chitter, orderly, tweedle, twitter 8 animated, spirited 9 shipshape, sprightly, vivacious 11 uncluttered, well-groomed 12 spick-and-span

chirk 3 gay 5 cheer 6 blithe, bright, cheery, chirpy, lively 7 animate, chipper, hearten 8 animated, cheerful, chirrupy, embolden, inspirit, sunbeamy 9 encourage, enhearten, lightsome, sprightly, vivacious 10 strengthen

chirography 4 fist, hand 6 ductus, script 10 penmanship 11 calligraphy, handwriting

chiromancy 9 palmistry

Chiron 7 centaur *father:* 6 Cronus *mother:* 7 Philyra *pupil:* 5 Jason 8 Achilles, Heracles, Hercules 9 Asclepius 11 Aesculapius

chiropody 8 podiatry

chiropractic *founder:* 6 Palmer

chiropter 3 bat

chirp 4 chip, peep 5 cheep, chirm, tweet 7 chipper, chirrup, clutter, tweedle, twitter

chirpy 5 chirk, sunny 6 blithe, cheery 8 cheerful, chirrupy, sunbeamy 9 lightsome

chirrup 4 chip, peep 5 cheep, chirm, chirp, tweet 7 chipper, chitter, tweedle, twitter

chisel 3 gyp 4 beat, bilk 5 carve, cheat, cozen, cut in, sculp 6 butt in, diddle, horn in, sculpt 7 defraud, intrude, obtrude 9 sculpture 10 intertrude

chiselly 3 bad 4 sour 6 rotten 7 unhappy 10 unpleasant 11 displeasing 12 disagreeable

chit 3 kid 4 memo, note 5 chick, child 6 moppet 8 juvenile, notandum, notation, young one 9 youngster 10 memorandum

chitchat 5 clack 6 babble, by-talk, cackle, gabble 7 chatter, prattle 8 trifling 9 bavardage, small talk 12 talkee-talkee, tittle-tattle

chitter 4 chip, peep 5 cheep, chirp, tweet 7 chipper, chirrup, tweedle, twitter

chivalric see chivalrous

chivalrous 3 big 5 lofty, manly, noble 8 generous, knightly 10 benevolent 11 considerate, magnanimous 12 greathearted

chivy, chivvy 3 try 4 bait, ride 5 chase, hound, trail 6 badger, follow, heckle, hector, pursue 7 afflict, torment 8 bullyrag

Chloe 11 shepherdess *beloved:* 7 Daphnis

chlordane 11 insecticide

chloride 4 salt 5 ester 7 muriate

chlorine *symbol:* 2 Cl

Chloris ***father:*** 7 Amphion ***husband:*** 6 Neleus 8 Zephyrus ***mother:*** 5 Niobe ***son:*** 6 Nestor
chloroform 7 anodyne, solvent 10 anesthetic
choate 4 full 5 whole 6 entire 7 perfect 8 complete, integral
chockablock 4 full 6 jammed, packed 7 brimful, crammed, crowded, jam-full, stuffed 8 bung-full 9 jam-packed
chocolate 3 bar 5 candy, cocoa, color, drink 8 beverage
Chocolate Soldier composer 6 Straus
chocolate tree 5 cacao
choice 3 fat, top 4 best, pick, rare 5 cream, elite, pride, prime, prize 6 chosen, culled, dainty, flower, option, picked, rating, select 7 elegant, finding, supreme, verdict 8 decision, delicate, druthers, election, judgment, peerless, selected, superior, volition 9 appraisal, exquisite 8 recherché 9 selection 10 evaluation, preeminent, preference, surpassing 11 alternative, superlative, unsurpassed 12 incomparable, transcendent 13 determination ***even:*** 6 toss-up
choicy 4 nice 5 fussy, picky 6 choosy 7 finical, finicky 9 finicking 10 fastidious, particular 11 persnickety
choir 6 chorus ***area:*** 4 loft 7 chancel, gallery ***assistant:*** 9 succentor ***leader:*** 6 cantor 8 choragus 9 precentor ***member:*** 9 chorister ***section:*** 4 alto, bass 5 tenor 7 soprano ***vestment:*** 4 gown, robe 5 cotta 8 surplice
choke 4 clog, fill, heap, hush, load, pack, pile, plug, stop 5 block, close, quiet, shush, still 6 charge, shut up, stifle 7 congest, occlude, quieten, silence, smother, stopper 8 obstruct, strangle, throttle 9 suffocate 10 asphyxiate
choking 8 quashing, stifling 9 quenching, squashing 10 repression, smothering, squelching, strangling 11 suppression
choleric 3 mad 4 waxy 5 angry, fiery, irate, ratty, testy, wroth 6 cranky, heated, ireful, spunky, tetchy, touchy, wrathy 7 carping 8 captious, wrathful 9 indignant, irascible, temperish 11 acrimonious, hot-tempered 12 fault-finding 13 quick-tempered
cholla 6 cactus
chomp 4 bite, chew 5 champ, chump, munch 6 crunch 7 scrunch 8 ruminate 9 masticate
choose 3 opt 4 cull, like, love, mark, pick, take, want, will, wish 5 adopt, elect, favor 6 desire, optate, opt for, please, prefer, select 7 embrace, espouse, pick out 8 handpick 9 single out
choosy 4 nice 5 fussy 7 finical, finicky 8 delicate 9 finicking 10 fastidious, particular, pernickety 11 persnickety
chop 3 box, cut, hew 4 cuff, dice, fell, hack, hash, poke, slap 5 clout, cut up, mince, smack, spank 6 buffet, hackle 8 fragment
chop-chop 4 fast 7 flat-out, hastily, quickly, rapidly 8 full tilt, promptly, speedily 9 posthaste 12 lickety-split
chophouse 10 restaurant
Chopin ***birthplace:*** 6 Poland ***instrument:*** 5 piano ***lover:*** 4 Sand (George)
chord 4 line 5 triad 6 tetrad 9 harmonize ***sequence:*** 7 cadence
chore 3 job 4 duty, task 5 stint, trial 6 devoir, effort 8 taskwork 10 assignment 11 tribulation
choreograph 6 direct 7 arrange, compose
choreographer ***American:*** 4 Feld, Lang 5 Ailey, Fosse, Shawn, Tharp 6 Fokine, Graham, Taylor, Tetley 7 de Mille, Massine, Robbins, Tamiris, Weidman 8 Humphrey 10 Balanchine, Cunningham ***English:*** 5 Tudor 6 Ashton, Weaver 9 MacMillan ***French:*** 6 Béjart, Perrot, Petipa 7 Noverre ***German:*** 5 Jooss ***Mexican:*** 5 Limon ***Russian:*** 8 Nijinska
chorography 3 map 9 mapmaking
chortle 5 laugh, tehee 6 giggle, guffaw, hee-haw, titter 7 chuckle, snicker, sniggle
chorus 4 tune 6 accord 7 concert, concord, harmony 10 consonance
chorus girl 7 chorine
chosen 4 pick 5 elect 6 picked, select 8 selected 9 exclusive
Chou ___ 5 En-Lai
chouse 3 gyp, jig 4 beat, bilk, play, ploy, ruse 5 cheat, cozen, feint, trick 6 diddle, gambit 7 defraud, gimmick, whizzer 8 artifice, flimflam
chow 4 feed, food, grub, meal 6 repast, viands 7 edibles, nurture 8 victuals 9 provender, refection 10 provisions 11 comestibles
chowchow 4 brew, hash, stew 5 mixed 6 jumble, medley, motley, relish, varied 7 mélange 8 assorted, mishmash, preserve 9 potpourri 10 hodgepodge, miscellany 11 promiscuous 12 conglomerate, multifarious 13 heterogeneous, miscellaneous
chowderhead 4 dope 5 dunce, noddy 6 noodle 7 schnook 9 lame-brain
chowhound 7 glutton 8 gourmand
chrism 3 oil 4 balm 5 cream, salve 6 cerate 7 unction, unguent 8 ointment
christen 3 dub 4 call, name, term 5 style, title 7 asperse, baptize, entitle, immerse 8 sprinkle 9 designate 10 denominate
christening 7 baptism

Christian 5 right 6 decent, proper, seemly 8 becoming, decorous 9 befitting, civilized ***denomination:*** 6 Mormon, Quaker 7 Baptist 8 Anglican, Catholic, Lutheran 9 Calvinist, Methodist 12 Episcopalian ***Eastern rite:*** 5 Uniat 6 Uniate ***Egyptian:*** 4 Copt ***love feast:*** 5 agape ***martyr, first:*** 7 Stephen ***symbol:*** 3 IHS 4 rood 5 cross 7 ichthus, ichthys
Christian Science founder 4 Eddy (Mary Baker)
___ Christie 6 Agatha
Christina's World painter 5 Wyeth
Christmas 4 Noel, Xmas, yule 8 Nativity, yuletide ***symbol:*** 7 Yule log
Christmas Carol, A ***author:*** 7 Dickens ***character:*** 7 Scrooge, Tiny Tim 8 Cratchit
Christogram 6 Chi-Rho
Christopher Robin creator 5 Milne
chromatic 8 colorful 10 accidental
chromium ***symbol:*** 2 Cr
chromosome component 3 DNA 4 gene 8 telomere 10 centromere, chromomere
chronic 5 usual 6 wonted 7 routine 8 accepted, habitual 9 confirmed, customary 10 accustomed, habituated
chronicle 4 list 5 story 6 annals, record, relate, report 7 account, history, recital, version 8 describe 9 narration, narrative, recountal
chronograph 5 watch 9 timepiece
chronometer 5 clock, watch 9 timepiece
chrysalis 4 pupa 8 covering
Chryseis ***captor:*** 9 Agamemnon ***father:*** 7 Chryses
Chrysippus ***father:*** 6 Pelops ***slayer:*** 6 Atreus 8 Thyestes
chthonian 6 Hadean 8 infernal, plutonic 9 plutonian, Tartarean 10 sulphurous
chubby 5 plump, podgy, pudgy, round, tubby 6 plumpy, rotund 8 plumpish, roly-poly 10 roundabout
chuck 4 cast, junk, quit, shed 5 chase, ditch, eject, evict, scrap 6 desert, reject, slough 7 abandon, boot out, discard, dismiss, extrude, forsake, kick out 8 jettison, renounce, throw out 9 throw away, throw over
chucker 7 bouncer 8 houseman
chuckle 5 laugh, tehee 6 giggle, guffaw, hee-haw, titter 7 chortle, snicker, sniggle
chucklehead 4 dope 5 dunce, noddy 6 noodle 7 schnook 9 lame-brain
chuff 4 boor, glum, ugly 5 churl, clown, hunks, miser, nabal, stiff, sulky, surly 6 gloomy, morose, mucker, sullen 7 crabbed, grobian, niggard, scrooge 8 muckworm 9 skinflint 10 clodhopper 12 moneygrubber
chum 3 pal 5 buddy, crony, cully 6 comate, friend 7 comrade 9 associate, companion 11 running mate
chumble 4 chew 5 champ, chomp, munch 6 crunch 7 scrunch 8 ruminate 9 masticate
chummy 4 cozy 5 close, pally, thick 8 familiar, intimate 10 buddy-buddy, palsy-walsy 12 confidential
chump 3 oaf, sap 4 boob, butt, chaw, chew, dolt, dupe, fool, goof, goon, gull, mark 5 booby, dunce, munch 6 crunch, pigeon, sucker 7 fall guy, fathead, gudgeon, scrunch 8 dolthead, lunkhead, ruminate 9 masticate
chunk 3 gob, wad 4 clod, hunk, lump 5 clump, hunch 6 nugget
chunky 5 dumpy, squat 6 chubby, rotund, stocky, stubby, stumpy 8 heavyset, thickset 11 thick-bodied
church 4 cult, fane, kirk, sect 5 creed, faith 6 temple 7 minster 8 basilica, religion 9 cathedral, communion, spiritual 10 connection, house of God, persuasion, tabernacle 12 denomination 13 house of prayer ***adjunct:*** 6 belfry 7 steeple 9 bell tower ***basin:*** 4 font 5 stoup ***bench:*** 3 pew ***bishop's:*** 9 cathedral ***Buddhist:*** 2 ta 3 taa 6 pagoda ***calendar:*** 4 ordo ***caretaker:*** 6 sexton ***chapel:*** 7 oratory ***combining form:*** 7 ecclesi 8 ecclesio ***council:*** 5 synod ***court:*** 4 Rota 10 consistory ***creed:*** 6 Nicene 8 Apostles' ***district:*** 6 parish 7 diocese ***father:*** 5 Basil 6 Jerome, Justin, Origen 7 Clement 8 Ignatius 9 Augustine 10 Chrysostom, Tertullian, theologian ***fund-raiser:*** 6 bazaar ***governing body:*** 5 curia 7 classis 10 consistory ***head:*** 4 pope 7 pontiff ***land:*** 5 grebe ***law:*** 5 canon ***member:*** 11 communicant ***Muslim:*** 6 mosque ***of a monastery:*** 7 minster ***officer:*** 5 elder, vicar 6 beadle, deacon, sexton, verger, warden 9 presbyter, sacristan ***part:*** 4 apse, bema, loft, nave 5 aisle, altar, choir 6 vestry 7 chancel, gallery, narthex, steeple 8 sacristy, transept 9 baptistry, sanctuary 10 baptistery, clerestory ***porch:*** 6 parvis 7 galilee ***pulpit:*** 4 ambo ***reader:*** 6 lector ***recess:*** 4 apse ***revenue:*** 5 tithe ***room:*** 6 vestry 8 sacristy ***Scottish:*** 4 kirk ***seat for clergy:*** 7 sedilia ***service:*** 4 mass 6 matins 7 vespers 8 evensong 9 communion ***small:*** 6 chapel ***tribunal:*** 4 Rota ***vault:*** 5 crypt
Churchill, Winston ***daughter:*** 4 Mary 5 Diana, Sarah ***father:*** 8 Randolph ***mother:*** 6 Jennie ***Order:*** 6 Garter ***phrase:*** 11 Iron Curtain ***son:*** 8 Randolph ***trademark:*** 5 cigar ***wife:*** 10 Clementine
church key 9 can opener
churchman 6 cleric, divine, parson, priest

8 clerical, minister, preacher, reverend 9 clergyman 12 ecclesiastic
churl 4 boor, clod 5 chuff, clown 6 mucker 7 grobian 10 clodhopper
churlish 4 curt, dour 5 blunt, crude, gruff, naive, surly 6 coarse, crusty 7 boorish, brusque, loutish, lowbred 8 cloddish, clownish 10 uncultured, unpolished, unschooled 11 clodhopping, uncivilized 12 discourteous
churn 4 boil, stir 6 bubble, seethe, simmer 7 ferment, smolder ***Scottish:*** 4 kirn
chute 5 falls, sault, spout 7 cascade 8 cataract 9 waterfall
Chuza's wife 6 Joanna
cicatrix 4 scar 13 scarification
Cicero ***forte:*** 7 oratory ***target:*** 8 Catiline 10 Mark Antony
Cid 4 epic, hero, play, poem 5 opera ***composer:*** 8 Massenet ***meaning:*** 4 lord ***name:*** 4 Diaz (Rodrigo, Ruy) 5 Bivar ***playwright:*** 9 Corneille ***sword:*** 6 Colada, Tizona ***wife:*** 6 Jimena, Ximena
cigar 4 toby 5 breva, stogy 6 concha, corona, Havana, Manila, stogie 7 bouquet, cheroot, culebra, Londres, regalia, trabuco 8 panatela, perfecto, pickwick, puritano 9 belvedere ***case:*** 7 humidor ***color:*** 5 claro 6 maduro 8 colorado
cigarette 3 cig, fag 4 butt 5 smoke 6 gasper 10 coffin nail
cigarfish 4 scad
cilium 4 hair, lash 7 eyelash 8 barbicel ***combining form:*** 7 blephar 8 blepharo
cimmerian 7 avernal, hellish, stygian 8 infernal, plutonic 9 plutonian 11 pandemoniac
cinch 4 snap 5 setup 6 assure, breeze, ensure, insure, picnic, secure 8 duck soup, kid stuff, pushover 10 child's play
cinchona bark extract 7 quinine
cincture 4 band, belt, gird, sash 6 begird, engird, girdle 8 begirdle, engirdle 9 waistband
cinders 3 ash 5 ashes 8 clinkers
cinema 4 film, show 5 flick, movie 7 picture 9 photoplay 11 picture show 13 motion picture, moving picture
cinereous 4 gray 5 ashen
cinnabar 3 ore 7 mineral 9 vermilion ***color:*** 3 red
cinnamon bark 6 cassia
cinnamon stone 6 garnet 8 essonite
cipher 3 zip 4 zero 5 aught, digit, ought, zilch 6 figure, naught, nobody, nought, number, reckon 7 chiffer, compute, integer, nothing, nullity, numeral, whiffet 8 estimate, goose egg, monogram, whipster 9 calculate, nonentity 11 whole number
ciphering 10 arithmetic 11 calculation, computation
circa 4 near, nigh 5 about 6 around, nearby 7 close on
circadian 5 daily 7 diurnal 9 quotidian
Circe 5 siren 9 sorceress ***brother:*** 6 Aeetes ***father:*** 3 Sol 6 Helios ***home:*** 5 Aeaea ***lover:*** 7 Ulysses 8 Odysseus ***niece:*** 5 Medea ***son:*** 5 Comus 9 Telegonus
Circean 6 luring 8 enticing, fetching, tempting
circinate 6 coiled
circle 3 hem, lot, mob, set 4 camp, clan, gird, gyre, halo, loop, push, ring, roll, turn 5 bunch, cabal, crowd, cycle, group, orbit, range, round, scope, wheel, whorl 6 begird, clique, corona, extent, girdle, gyrate, length, radius, rotary, rotate 7 compass, coterie, cronies, environ, friends, ingroup, revolve, rondure 8 comrades, encircle, surround 9 camarilla, dimension, encompass, extension, extensity, intimates 10 associates, circumduct, companions 12 acquaintance ***bisector:*** 8 diameter ***colored:*** 6 areola, areole ***combining form:*** 3 gyr 4 cycl, gyro 5 cyclo ***graph:*** 8 pie chart ***luminous:*** 4 aura, halo 6 corona, nimbus 7 aureola, aureole ***part:*** 3 arc 6 sector 8 quadrant ***small:*** 4 disk 7 annulet 8 roundlet
circlet 4 band, ring 8 bracelet, headband ***for head or helmet:*** 7 coronal, coronel
circuit 3 way 4 gyre, loop, tour, trip, turn 5 ambit, round, route, wheel, whirl 6 course, league 7 compass, journey, travels 8 gyration, rotation 9 perimeter, periphery, round trip 10 conference, revolution, roundabout 11 association, circulation 13 circumference
circuitous 7 oblique 8 circular, indirect 10 collateral, roundabout
circuit rider 9 clergyman
circular 4 bill 5 flier, flyer, gyral, round 7 annular, cycloid, discoid 8 handbill 10 circuitous ***file:*** 11 wastebasket ***motion:*** 4 eddy, gyre, spin 5 whirl 8 gyration, rotation 10 revolution ***plate:*** 4 disc, dish, disk
circularize 4 poll 9 publicize
circulate 4 flow 5 strew 6 rotate, set off, spread 7 actuate, diffuse, radiate, revolve 8 disperse, exchange, mobilize 9 propagate 10 distribute 11 disseminate, interchange
circulation 4 gyre, turn 5 round, wheel, whirl 7 circuit 8 gyration, rotation 10 revolution
circulator 6 gossip 8 gossiper, quidnunc 9 carrytale 10 newsmonger 11 rumormonger 12 gossipmonger
circumambulate 4 roam, rove 5 drift, mooch, range, stray 6 ramble, wander 7 meander 8 straggle
circumciser 5 mohel

circumcision ***Jewish:*** 5 Berit, Brith 10 Brith Milah
circumference 3 rim 5 ambit 6 border, bounds, limits, margin 7 circuit, compass 8 boundary, confines 9 perimeter, periphery
circumflex 9 diacritic
circumfuse 7 envelop 8 surround
circumjacent 11 surrounding
circumlocution 8 pleonasm, verbiage 9 tautology, verbality 10 periphrase, redundancy, roundabout 11 periphrasis 13 circumambages
circumnavigate 5 skirt 6 bypass, detour 10 circumvert
circumnavigator 4 Cook 5 Drake 8 Magellan, van Noort 9 Cavendish
circumscribe 3 bar 5 limit 6 fetter, hamper 7 confine, delimit, trammel 8 prelimit, restrict 10 delimitate
circumscribed 5 bound, fixed 6 finite, narrow, strait 7 bounded, cramped, precise 8 definite 11 determinate
circumscription 5 cramp, stint 9 restraint, stricture 10 constraint, limitation 11 confinement, restriction 12 ball and chain 13 constrainment
circumspect 4 safe, wary 5 chary 7 careful, guarded 8 cautious, discreet, gingerly 10 meticulous, scrupulous 11 calculating, considerate, punctilious
circumstance 4 fate, item 5 event, moira, thing 6 detail, factor, kismet 7 destiny, element, episode, portion 8 incident, occasion 9 component, happening 10 occurrence, particular 11 constituent
circumstantial 4 full, nice 5 close, exact 6 minute, strict 7 precise, replete 8 accurate, complete, detailed, itemized, thorough 9 clocklike 10 blow-by-blow, particular
circumvent 4 balk, beat, bilk, dash, dupe, foil, ruin 5 avoid, burke, elude, evade, skirt, trick 6 baffle, befool, bypass, detour, escape, thwart 8 hoodwink, outflank, sidestep 9 frustrate 10 disappoint
circumvolution 4 gyre, turn 5 round, wheel, whirl 7 circuit 8 gyration, rotation 10 revolution 11 circulation
circus 4 ring 5 arena 6 big top, cirque 9 spectacle 12 amphitheater ***animal:*** 4 bear, flea, lion, seal 5 horse, tiger 8 elephant ***attraction:*** 5 freak 8 sideshow ***owner:*** 6 Bailey, Barnum 8 Ringling ***performer:*** 5 clown, tamer 7 acrobat, athlete, juggler, tumbler 9 aerialist, fire eater ***worker:*** 7 rouster 10 roustabout
citadel 4 fort 7 redoubt 8 fastness, fortress 10 stronghold ***of Carthage:*** 5 Bursa, Byrsa ***Russian:*** 7 kremlin
citation 5 award 6 eulogy, reward 7 guerdon, tribute 8 encomium 9 panegyric 10 salutation
cite 4 name, tell 5 count, offer, quote 6 adduce, allege, number, recall, remind, retain, revive 7 advance, bethink, mention, present, specify 8 instance, remember 9 enumerate, recollect, reminisce 10 retrospect
citizen 5 towny 6 towner 7 burgess, burgher, subject, townman 8 national, townsman
Citizen Kane director 6 Welles
citron 4 tree 5 melon 6 yellow
citrus ***family:*** 3 rue 8 Rutaceae ***fruit:*** 4 lime 5 lemon 6 citron, orange 7 kumquat, tangelo 8 bergamot, mandarin, shaddock 9 tangerine 10 grapefruit
city 4 burg 5 urban 7 burghal 9 municipal ***Alamo:*** 10 San Antonio ***combining form:*** 5 polis ***Eternal:*** 4 Rome ***French:*** 5 ville ***heavenly:*** 4 Sion, Zion ***Latin:*** 4 urbs ***Motor:*** 7 Detroit ***of Bells:*** 10 Strasbourg ***of Bridges:*** 6 Bruges ***of Brotherly Love:*** 12 Philadelphia ***of David:*** 9 Jerusalem ***official:*** 5 mayor 7 manager 8 alderman 10 councilman ***of God:*** 6 heaven 8 paradise ***of Gold:*** 8 Eldorado ***of Kings:*** 4 Lima ***of Lights:*** 5 Paris ***of Lilies:*** 8 Florence ***of Masts:*** 6 London ***of Rams:*** 6 Canton ***of Refuge:*** 6 Medina ***of Saints:*** 8 Montreal ***of Seven Hills:*** 4 Rome ***of the dead:*** 10 Necropolis ***of Victory:*** 5 Cairo ***planner:*** 8 urbanist ***section:*** 4 slum, ward 5 block, plaza 6 barrio, ghetto, square, uptown 8 business, downtown, red-light 11 residential ***slicker:*** 4 dude ***windy:*** 7 Chicago
city-state ***Greek:*** 5 polis 6 poleis (plural)
city, town, village (see also capital) ***Afghanistan:*** 5 Balkh, Farah, Herat, Kushk ***Alabama:*** 3 Opp 4 Arab, Boaz, Elba 5 Eutaw, Selma 6 Dothan, Mobile 7 Decatur, Floraia 8 Prichard 10 Birmingham, Huntsville, Tuscaloosa ***Alaska:*** 5 Kenai, Sitka 6 Bethel, Kodiak, Valdez 9 Anchorage, Fairbanks, Ketchikan ***Albania:*** 4 Fier 5 Berat, Korce, Kukes, Vlore ***Alberta:*** 4 Olds 5 Hanna, Leduc, Taber 7 Calgary 10 Lethbridge ***Algeria:*** 4 Oran 5 Batna, Blida, Medea, Saida, Setif 6 Annaba, Bechar ***Argentina:*** 4 Azul, Goya 5 Junin, Lanus, Lujan, Merlo, Salta, Tigre 6 Parana 7 Cordoba, La Plata, Mendoza, Rosario, San Juan, Santa Fe 11 Bahia Blanca ***Arizona:*** 3 Ajo 4 Eloy, Mesa, Yuma 5 Globe, Tempe 6 Tucson 7 Sun City, Winslow 8 Glendale, Prescott 9 Flagstaff 10 Casa Grande, Scottsdale ***Arkansas:*** 4 Mena 5 Beebe, Cabot, Earle, Ozark, Wynne 9 Fort Smith, Pine Bluff, Texarkana ***Australia:*** 3 Ayr 5 Dalby, Dubbo, Unley 8 Randwick 9 Bankstown, Blacktown, Newcastle 10 Kalgoorlie, Parramatta, Sutherland, Wollongong 12 Alice Springs ***Austria:*** 4 Enns,

Graz, Linz, Wels 5 Lienz, Steyr, Traun 8 Salzburg 9 Innsbruck 10 Klagenfurt ***Azerbaijan:*** 9 Kirovabad ***Bangladesh:*** 5 Bogra, Pabna 6 Khulna 10 Chittagong ***Belarus:*** 5 Brest, Gomel, Mozyr, Pinsk 6 Grodno 7 Mogilev, Vitebsk ***Belgium:*** 3 Ath, Hal, Huy, Mol 4 Amay, Dour, Geel, Genk, Gent, Hoei, Luik, Mons, Vise 5 Aalst, Arlon, Diest, Dison, Eupen, Evere, Ghent, Gilly, Halle, Hamme, Hornu, Ieper, Jette, Jumet, Leuze, Liege, Menen, Namen, Namur, Ronse, Theux, Thuin, Uccle, Ukkel, Wavre, Ypres 6 Bruges 7 Antwerp ***Bolivia:*** 5 Oruro, Uyuni 9 Santa Cruz 10 Cochabamba ***Bosnia and Herzegovina:*** 5 Bihac, Brcko, Jajce, Tuzla 8 Sarajevo ***Botswana:*** 4 Maun 5 Kanye ***Brazil:*** 4 Codo, Para 5 Bahia, Bauru, Belem, Ceara, Natal 6 Campos, Canoas, Caxias, Ilheus, Maceio, Manaus, Olinda, Recife, Santos 7 Aracaju, Caruaru, Goiania, Jundiai, Marilia, Niteroi, Pelotas, Sao Luis, Uberaba, Vitoria 8 Campinas, Colatina, Curitiba, Londrina, Salvador, Santarem, Sao Paulo, Sorocaba, Teresina 9 Caratinga, Fortaleza, Guarulhos, Rio Grande 10 Guarapuava, Joao Pessoa, Juiz de Fora, Nova Iguacu, Pernambuco, Petropolis, Piracicaba, Santa Maria, Santo Andre, Uberlandia 11 Campo Grande, Caxias do Sul, Ponta Grossa, Porto Alegre 12 Montes Claros, Rio de Janeiro, Teofilo Otoni, Volta Redonda 13 Belo Horizonte, Campina Grande, Duque de Caxias, Florianopolis, Mogi das Cruzes, Riberiao Preto ***British Columbia:*** 5 Comox 9 Vancouver ***Bulgaria:*** 3 Lom 4 Ruse 5 Varna, Vidin 6 Burgas 7 Plovdiv 11 Stara Zagora ***Burkina Faso:*** 13 Bobo Dioulasso ***California:*** 4 Brea, Galt, Lodi, Ojai 5 Arvin, Azusa, Ceres, Chico, Chino, Dixon, Hemet, Indio, Norco, Ripon, Ukiah, Wasco, Yreka 6 Downey, Encino, Fresno, Oxnard, Pomona, Sonoma 7 Anaheim, Burbank, Compton, Fremont, Hayward, Modesto, Oakland, San Jose, Seaside, Soledad, Van Nuys 8 Berkeley, Glendale, Palo Alto, Pasadena, San Diego, Santa Ana, Stockton, Torrance, Yuba City 9 El Segundo, Hollywood, Long Beach, Menlo Park, Riverside, Sausalito 10 Carmichael, Chowchilla, Chula Vista, Culver City, Los Angeles, Pismo Beach, San Leandro, Santa Clara 11 Bakersfield, Laguna Beach, Pebble Beach, Redwood City, San Clemente, Santa Monica 12 Beverly Hills, Mission Viejo, Redondo Beach, San Francisco, Santa Barbara 13 San Bernardino, San Luis Obispo ***Cameroon:*** 4 Buea, Edea 5 Kribi, Lomie 6 Douala ***Canada:*** 5 Banff, Edson, Hanna, Leduc, Rouyn 6 Regina 7 Calgary, Halifax, Toronto, Windsor 8 Hamilton, Montreal, Moose Jaw, Victoria, Winnipeg 9 Saint John, Saskatoon, Vancouver 10 Lethbridge, Saint Johns, Sherbrooke, Thunder Bay, Whitehorse 11 Fredericton, Yellowknife 12 Peterborough 13 Charlottetown, Trois Rivieres ***Central African Republic:*** 5 Bouar ***Chad:*** 4 Sarh ***Chile:*** 4 Lebu, Lota, Tome 5 Ancud, Angol, Arica, Maipu, Penco, Rengo, Talca 10 Concepcion, Talcahuano, Valparaiso 11 Antofagasta ***China:*** 4 Amoy, Jian, Luan, Yaan 5 Hefei, Jilin, Jinan, Lhasa, Qinan, Ssuan, Wuhan, Yibin, Yumen 6 Andong, Anqing, Anshan, Anshun, Anyang, Beihai, Canton, Datong, Foshan, Fushun, Guilin, Haikou, Handan, Harbin, Hoihao, Jilong, Luzhou, Mukden, Ningbo, Pengbu, Suzhou, Urumqi, Xiamen, Xuzhou, Yanggu, Yichun, Yining, Zhangi, Zhaoan 7 Baoding, Changan, Chengdu, Dandong, Guiyang, Huainan, Jiamusi, Jiaxing, Kaifeng, Kunming, Luoshan, Luoyang, Nanking, Nanning, Shantou, Taiyuan, Wanxian, Weifang, Yizhang 8 Changchi, Changsha, Dangshan, Hangzhou, Hanzhong, Hengyang, Huangshi, Jiangmen, Jiujiang, Kueiyang, Liaoyang, Nanchang, Shanghai, Shangrao, Shaoyang, Tianshui, Zhenjing 9 Changchun, Chenjiang, Chongqing, Chungking, Huangshih, Zhenjiang 10 Jingdezhen, Laojunmiao 11 Qinhuangdao, Zhangjiakou ***Colombia:*** 4 Buga, Cali 5 Bello, Mocoa, Neiva, Ocana, Pasto, Tulua, Tunja 6 Cucuta, Ibague 7 Cienaga, Palmira, Pereira 8 Medellin, Monteria 9 Cartagena, Manizales 10 Santa Marta 11 Bucaramanga 12 Barranquilla ***Colorado:*** 5 Craig 6 Arvada, Salida 7 Alamosa, Durango, Greeley, La Junta 8 Brighton, Gunnison, Lakewood, Longmont, Loveland, Montrose, Thornton 9 Englewood, Estes Park, Leadville, Littleton, Rocky Ford 10 Broomfield, Castle Rock, Fort Lupton, Fort Morgan, Monte Vista, Northglenn, Walsenburg, Wheat Ridge 11 Fort Collins 13 Grand Junction ***Connecticut:*** 5 Byram 6 Bethel, Bolton, Darien, Easton, Granby, Groton, Haddam, Hamden, Moosup, Somers, Weston 7 Ansonia, Bethany, Danbury, Enfield, Ledyard, Meriden, Milford, Newtown, Niantic, Norwalk, Norwich, Old Lyme, Pomfret, Seymour, Tolland, Windham, Winsted, Wolcott 8 Branford, Cromwell, East Lyme, Guilford, New Haven, Simsbury, Stamford, Suffield, Westport 9 Danielson, Deep River, East Haven, Ellington, Greenwich, Harwinton, Killingly, Montville, New Canaan, Newington, New London, Pawcatuck, Rocky Hill, Southbury, Thomaston, Waterbury, Waterford, West Haven 10 Bridgeport, Brookfield, East Granby, East Haddam, Farmington, Gales Ferry, Kensington, Litchfield, New Britain, New Milford, North Haven, Plainville, Ridgefield, Stonington, Terryville, Torrington 11 Beacon Falls, East Norwalk, East Windsor, Forestville, Glastonbury, Marlborough, Middlefield, Old Saybrook, Southington, Wallingford, Willimantic 12 Collinsville, East Hartford, New Fairfield, South Norwalk, South Windsor, West Hartford, Wethersfield, Windsor Locks 13 North Branford, Thompsonville ***Croatia:*** 4 Pula 5 Sisak, Zadar 6 Rijeka, Zagreb 9 Dubrovnik ***Cuba:*** 5 Banes, Bauta 7 Holguin 8 Camaguey, Marianao, Matanzas 10 Cienfuegos ***Cyprus:*** 7 Kyrenia, Larnaca 8 Limassol 9 Famagusta ***Czechoslovakia:*** 4 Brno, Cheb 5 Decin, Nitra, Opava, Pisek, Plzen, Tabor 6 Kosice 7 Ostrava 10 Bratislava ***Delaware:*** 5 Lewes 7 Seaford 10 Harrington, Wilmington ***Denmark:*** 5 Arhus, Skive, Vejle 6 Alborg, Odense, Viborg 13 Frederiksberg ***Dominican Republic:*** 4 Azua, Bani, Moca 5 Cotui, Nagua, Neiba ***Ecuador:*** 4 Loja 5 Canar, Daule, Manta, Pinas 9 Guayaquil ***Egypt:*** 4 Giza, Idfu, Isna, Qena 5 Asyut, Benha, Disuq, Girga, Luxor, Minuf, Tahta, Tanta 6 Helwan 7 El Arish, Zagazig 8 Damanhur, Damietta, El Faiyum, Ismailia, Port Said ***Eire:*** 4 Athy, Birr, Cobh, Naas, Tuam 5 Ennis, Sligo 6 Carlow, Galway, Tralee 7 Dundalk, Kildare, Wexford, Wicklow 8 Kilkenny, Monaghan 9 Castlebar, Killarney, Tipperary, Waterford 10 Balbriggan ***England:*** 4 Bath, Eton, Hove, Ryde, York 5 Bacup, Brent, Brigg, Colne, Corby, Cowes, Egham, Eling, Esher, Eston, Goole, Leeds, Leigh, Lewes, Luton, Oadby, Poole, Ryton, Wigan 6 Bexley, Bolton, Dudley, Merton, Oldham, Torbay, Warley, Welwyn 7 Bristol, Bromley, Croydon, Hackney, Ipswich, Malvern, Norwich, Salford, Seaford, Walsall 8 Abingdon, Basildon, Brighton, Coventry, Hastings, Hatfield, Havering, Hertford, Lewisham, Plymouth, Wallsend 9 Aylesbury, Blackpool, Islington, Leicester, Liverpool, Sheffield 10 Birkenhead, Canterbury, Colchester, Manchester, Nottingham, Portsmouth, Sunderland 11 Bournemouth, Northampton, Southampton 12 Peterborough, Stoke-on-Trent, West Bromwich 13 Melton Mowbray, Middlesbrough, Southend-on-Sea, Wolverhampton ***Estonia:*** 5 Parnu, Tartu ***Ethiopia:*** 5 Aksum, Harar 6 Asmara 8 Dire Dawa ***Finland:*** 4 Kemi, Oulu, Pori 5 Espoo, Hango, Kotka, Lahti, Rauma, Turku, Vaasa 7 Tampere ***Florida:*** 4 Leto, Mims, Ojus, Tice 5 Dania, Davie, Largo, Miami, Ocala, Ocoee, Oneco, Tampa 6 DeLand 7 Hialeah, Key West, Orlando 8 Gulfport, Key Largo, Lakeland, Sarasota 9 Boca Raton, Bradenton, Fort Myers, Hollywood, Kissimmee, Palm Beach, Pensacola, Vero Beach 10 Clearwater, Cocoa Beach, Fort Pierce, Miami Beach, Titusville 11 Coral Gables, Gainesville, Key Biscayne, St. Augustine, Winter Haven 12 Apalachicola, Daytona Beach, Ft. Lauderdale, Jacksonville, Pompano Beach, St. Petersburg 13 Chattahoochee ***France:*** 3 Dax, Pau 4 Agde, Agen, Albi, Ales, Auch, Caen, Gien, Laon, Lyon, Metz, Orly, Reze, Sens, Sete, Vire 5 Arles, Arras, Auray, Auton, Avion, Berck, Blois, Bondy, Brest, Creil, Digne, Dijon, Douai, Dreux, Flers, Gagny, Laval, LePuy, Lille, Lunel, Meaux, Melun, Muret, Nimes, Niort, Noyon, Reims, Revin, Rodez, Rouen, Royan, Tours, Tulle, Vichy, Vitre 6 Amiens, Angers, Calais, Cannes, Evreux, LeMans, Nantes, Nevers, Rennes, Thiers, Toulon 7 Ajaccio, Avignon, Bethune, Bourges, LeHavre, Limoges, Lorient, Lourdes, Orleans, Roubaix 8 Bordeaux, Gentilly, Grenoble, Toulouse 9 Cherbourg, Le Creusot, Marseille, Montreuil 10 Draguignan, Strasbourg, Versailles 11 Montpellier 12 Saint Etienne 13 Aix en Provence ***Georgia:*** 4 Adel, Alma, Arco 5 Jesup, Macon, McRae 7 Calhoun 8 Americus, Marietta, Savannah, Valdosta 9 Brunswick ***Georgia, Republic of:*** 6 Batumi 7 Kutaisi, Sukhumi, Tbilisi ***Germany:*** 3 Aue, Hof, Ulm 4 Gera, Goch, Hamm, Jena, Kehl, Kiel, Koln, Marl, Suhl 5 Aalen, Ahlen, Borna, Bruhl, Calbe, Celle, Duren, Emden, Essen, Forst, Fulda, Furth, Gotha, Greiz, Hagen, Halle, Hanau, Herne, Hurth, Kleve, Lemgo, Lobau, Mainz, Neuss, Peine, Pirna, Riesa, Stade, Thale, Trier, Wesel, Zeitz 6 Aachen, Bremen, Coburg, Dachau, Dessau, Erfurt, Kassel, Lubeck, Munich, Rheydt 7 Cologne, Dresden, Koblenz, Krefeld, Leipzig, Munchen, Munster, Potsdam, Rostock, Zwickau 8 Augsburg, Bayreuth, Chemnitz, Cuxhaven, Dortmund, Duisburg, Hannover, Mannheim, Nurnburg, Wurzburg 9 Bielefeld, Brunswick, Darmstadt, Karlsruhe, Magdeburg, Nuremburg, Oldenburg, Osnabruck, Remscheid, Stuttgart, Wiesbaden, Wuppertal 10 Baden Baden, Dusseldorf, Heidelberg, Oberhausen, Regensburg, Salzgitter 11 Brandenburg, Bremerhaven, Saarbrucken 12 Braunschweig 13 Gelsenkirchen ***Ghana:*** 2 Wa 4 Axim, Keta, Tema 5 Lawra, Yendi 6 Kumasi ***Greece:*** 3 Kos 4 Arta 5 Argos, Lamia, Nemea, Volos 6 Sparta 7 Corinth 12 Thessaloniki ***Guatemala:*** 5 Coban ***Guinea:*** 4 Labe ***Hawaii:*** 4 Aiea, Hilo, Laie 5 Kapaa, Lihue, Maili 6 Kailua 7 Kaneohe, Wailuku ***Honduras:*** 5 Danli ***Hong Kong:*** 7 Kowloon ***Hungary:*** 3 Ozd 4 Eger, Gyor, Pecs 5 Abony, Bekes 6 Szeged 7 Miskolc 8 Debrecen

Idaho: 4 Buhl 5 Nampa 6 Driggs, Dubois, Weiser 7 Gooding, Orofino, Payette, Rexburg 8 Caldwell 9 Blackfoot, Pocatello, Sandpoint, Twin Falls 11 Coeur d' Alene, Grangeville, Saint Maries, Soda Springs 12 Bonners Ferry, Mountain Home, Saint Anthony 13 American Falls ***Illinois:*** 4 Dupo, Pana 5 Aledo, Alsip, Alton, Carmi, Elgin, Galva, Lacon, Niles, Olney, Pekin, Plano, Posen 6 Albion, DeKalb, Galena, Hardin, Joliet, Macomb, Moline, Paxton, Peoria, Skokie, Toulon, Urbana 7 Chicago, Decatur, Glencoe, Oak Lawn, Oquawka, Tuscola, Watseka, Wheaton 8 Carthage, Evanston, Golconda, Hennepin, Kankakee, La Grange, Monmouth, Rockford, Vandalia, Waukegan 9 Belvidere, Effingham, Galesburg, Park Ridge, Rushville, Yorkville 10 Belleville, Carbondale, Carrollton, Des Plaines, Metropolis, Northbrook, Rock Island 11 Carlinville, Jerseyville, Lindenhurst, McLeansboro, Murphysboro, Shawneetown, Taylorville 12 Edwardsville, Highland Park, Mount Carroll 13 Lawrenceville, Mount Sterling, Pinckneyville ***India:*** 3 Mau 4 Agra, Ahwa, Bhuj, Durg, Gaya, Kota, Mhow, Puri, Rewa, Tonk, Ziro 5 Adoni, Ajmer, Akola, Alwar, Arcot, Arrah, Banda, Barsi, Bidar, Bihar, Churu, Damoh, Delhi, Dewas, Eluru, Gonda, Jalna, Jammu, Karur, Miraj, Morvi, Nasik, Patan, Patna, Poona, Sagar, Satna, Sikar, Simla, Surat, Thana 6 Baroda, Bhopal, Bombay, Guntur, Howrah, Jaipur, Jhansi, Kanpur, Meerut, Mysore, Nagpur, Raipur, Rajkot, Ranchi, Ujjain 7 Aligarh, Asansol, Belgaum, Bikaner, Burdwan, Cuttack, Gauhati, Gwalior, Jodhpur, Kurnool, Lucknow, Madurai, Mathura, Nellore, Patiala, Vellore 8 Alleppey, Amravati, Amritsar, Bareilly, Bhatpara, Calcutta, Dehra Dun, Jabalpur, Jamnagar, Kakinada, Kolhapur, Ludhiana, Malegaon, Sholapur, Srinagar, Varanasi 9 Ahmadabad, Allahabad, Bangalore, Bhagalpur, Bhavnagar, Darbhanga, Gorakhpur, Hyderabad, Jullundur, Kamarhati, Mangalore, Moradabad, Nagercoil, Thanjavur, Tuticorin 10 Ahmadnagar, Chandigarh, Coimbatore, Jamshedpur, Saharanpur, Trivandrum, Ulhashagar, Vijayawada 11 Garden Reach, Muzaffarpur, Rajahmundry 12 Hubli Dharwar, Secunderabad, Shahjahanpur 13 Machilipatnam ***Indiana:*** 5 Berne, Paoli, Vevay 6 Delphi, Kokomo, Marion, Muncie, Tipton 7 Bedford, Corydon, Elkhart, La Porte, Winamac 8 Bluffton, Kentland 9 Boonville, Cannelton, Fort Wayne, New Albany, Rushville, South Bend, Vincennes 10 Brookville, Brownstown, Crown Point, Evansville, Logansport, Scottsburg, Terre Haute, Valparaiso 11 Greencastle, Noblesville, Shelbyville 12 Connersville, Lawrenceburg, Martinsville ***Indonesia:*** 4 Pati 5 Bogor, Garut, Kudus, Medan, Tegal, Turen 6 Batang, Kediri, Madiun, Malang, Manado, Padang 7 Bandung 8 Semarang, Surabaja, Tjirebon 9 Palembang, Pontianak, Surakarta 10 Pekalongan 11 Tasikmalaja 12 Bandjarmasin ***Iowa:*** 4 Adel, Tama 5 Albia, Clive, Onawa, Pella 6 Algona, Cresco, Eldora, Harlan, Keokuk, Le Mars, Red Oak, Sibley, Waukon 7 Allison, Anamosa, Carroll, Clinton, Corydon, Creston, Decorah, Denison, Dubuque, Elkader, Marengo, Osceola, Ottumwa, Wapello, Waverly 8 Camanche, Chariton, Clarinda, Ida Grove, Mount Ayr, Primghar 9 Davenport, Fort Dodge, Indianola, Keosauqua, Maquoketa, Muscatine, Oskaloosa, Storm Lake, West Union, Winterset 10 Emmetsburg, New Hampton, Rock Rapids, Spirit Lake 11 Cedar Rapids, Estherville, Fort Madison 12 Grundy Center 13 Council Bluffs, Guthrie Center ***Iran:*** 3 Qum 4 Amul, Arak, Khoi, Sari, Yazd, Yezd 5 Ahwaz, Babol, Rasht 6 Abadan, Meshed, Shiraz, Tabriz 7 Esfahan, Hamadan, Isfahan, Mashhad ***Iraq:*** 3 Ana, Kut 5 Amara, Basra, Erbil, Hilla, Mosul, Rutba 6 Kirkuk 7 An Najaf ***Ireland:*** (see *Eire*, above) ***Israel:*** 5 Afula, Haifa, Holon 8 Nazareth, Ramat Gan 9 Beersheba ***Italy:*** 4 Acri, Alba, Asti, Bari, Enna, Este, Fano, Gela, Iesi, Lodi, Lugo, Pisa 5 Adria, Agira, Anzio, Aosta, Arola, Cantu, Capua, Carpi, Crema, Cuneo, Eboli, Fermo, Fondi, Forli, Gaeta, Imola, Ivrea, Lecce, Lecco, Lucca, Massa, Melfi, Menfi, Monza, Padua, Parma, Prato, Turin 6 Assisi, Foggia, Modena, Naples, Rimini, Venice, Verona 7 Bergamo, Bolzano, Brescia, Catania, Leghorn, Palermo, Pescara, Salerno, Taranto, Trieste 8 Cagliari, La Spezia, Piacenza ***Ivory Coast:*** 6 Bouake ***Jamaica:*** 6 May Pen 10 Montego Bay ***Japan:*** 3 Ina, Ise, Ito, Ota, Tsu, Ube, Uji, Yao 4 Ageo, Anan, Gifu, Hagi, Himi, Hofu, Iida, Joyo, Kaga, Kobe, Kofu, Kure, Miki, Mito, Naha, Nara, Noda, Oita, Otsu, Saga, Saku, Soka, Tosu, Ueda, Yono 5 Akita, Atami, Beppu, Chiba, Chofu, Daito, Fukui, Hanno, Hyuga, Imari, Itami, Iwaki, Iwata, Izumi, Izumo, Kiryu, Kochi, Kyoto, Minoo, Odate, Ogaki, Okawa, Okaya, Omiya, Omuta, Osaka, Otaru, Oyama, Sabae, Saiki, Sanjo, Suita, Tenri, Urawa, Yaizu, Zushi 6 Akashi, Aomori, Himeji, Kadoma, Kurume, Matsue, Mitaka, Nagano, Nagoya, Numazu, Sasebo, Suzuka, Toyama, Yonago 7 Fukuoka, Hitachi, Ibaraki, Imabari, Iwakuni, Kawagoe, Kodaira, Kushiro, Machida, Matsudo, Morioka, Muroran, Niigata, Niihama, Nobeoka, Obihiro, Odawara, Okayama, Okazaki, Sapporo, Shimizu, Takaoka, Tottori **8** Ashikaga, Fujisawa, Fukuyama, Hachioji, Hakodate, Hirakata, Hirosaki, Ichihara, Ichikawa, Kakogawa, Kamakura, Kanazawa, Kawasaki, Koriyama, Kumagaya, Kumamoto, Maebashi, Miyazaki, Nagasaki, Neyagawa, Onomichi, Shizuoka, Takasaki, Toyonaka, Wakayama, Yamagata, Yokohama, Yokosuka **9** Amagasaki, Asahikawa, Chigasaki, Fukushima, Funabashi, Hachinohe, Hamamatsu, Hiratsuka, Hiroshima, Kagoshima, Kawaguchi, Kishiwada, Koshigaya, Kurashiki, Matsubara, Matsumoto, Matsusaka, Matsuyama, Moriguchi, Musashino, Tachikawa, Takamatsu, Takatsuki, Tokushima, Tomakomai, Toyohashi, Yamaguchi, Yokkaichi **10** Ichinomiya, Ishinomaki, Kitakyushu, Miyakonojo, Takarazuka, Utsunomiya, Yatsushiro **11** Nishinomiya, Shimonoseki **12** Higashiosaka **13** Aizuwakamatsu ***Jordan:*** **5** Irbid **6** Nablus ***Kansas:*** **4** Gove, Iola **5** Colby, Hoxie, Lakin, Leoti, Paola, Pratt **6** Atwood, Beloit, Girard, Holton, Larned, Olathe, Salina **7** Abilene, Dighton, Emporia, Garnett, Hugoton, Jetmore, Kinsley, Mankato, Oberlin, Osborne, Wichita **8** Cimarron, Goodland, La Crosse, Sublette, Wakeeney **9** Coldwater, Fort Scott, Great Bend, Oskaloosa **10** Clay Center, Hutchinson **11** Leavenworth, Smith Center, Yates Center **12** Council Grove, Overland Park **13** Medicine Lodge, Sharon Springs ***Kazakhstan:*** **6** Guryev, Uralsk **8** Balkhash, Chimkent, Dzhambul, Kyzl Orda, Pavlodar **9** Karaganda **10** Aktyubinsk **11** Tselinograd **13** Petropavlovsk, Semipalatinsk ***Kentucky:*** **4** Inez **5** Cadiz, Hyden, McKee **6** Elkton, Harlan **7** Ashland, Campton, Greenup, Hickman, Hindman, Owenton, Paducah, Stanton **8** Bardwell, Carlisle, Fort Knox, La Grange, Mayfield **9** Bardstown, Covington, Cynthiana, Eddyville, Lexington, Maysville, Owensboro, Pikeville, Pineville, Smithland, Southgate, Vanceburg, Wickliffe **10** Booneville, Frenchburg, Hawesville, Louisville, Whitesburg **11** Beattyville, Brooksville, Burkesville, Hardinsburg, Harrodsburg, Hodgenville, Leitchfield, Morganfield, Mount Olivet, Owingsville, Paintsville, Scottsville, West Liberty **12** Barbourville, Bowling Green, Catlettsburg, Flemingsburg, Hopkinsville, Madisonville, Munfordville, Prestonsburg, Russellville, Salyersville, Taylorsville **13** Elizabethtown, Mount Sterling, Nicholasville, Tompkinsville ***Kenya:*** **4** Embu **5** Nyeri **6** Kisumu, Nakuru **7** Mombasa ***Kirghizia:*** **3** Osh **5** Naryn ***Laos:*** **5** Pakse **11** Savannakhet **12** Luang Prabang ***Latvia:*** **9** Ventspils **10** Daugavpils ***Lebanon:*** **5** Sidon, Zahle ***Libya:*** **4** Homs **5** Derna, Zawia **6** Tobruk **8** Benghazi ***Lithuania:*** **6** Kaunas **8** Klaipeda ***Louisiana:*** **4** Jena **5** Amite, Arabi, Houma, Mamou, Norco, Rayne **6** Colfax, Edgard, Gretna, Minden, Ruston **7** Arcadia, Bastrop, Marrero, Oberlin **8** Bogalusa, De Ridder, Metairie, New Roads, Oak Grove, Westwego **9** Abbeville, Chalmette, Coushatta, Hahnville, Leesville, New Iberia, Opelousas, Port Allen, Thibodaux, Winnfield, Winnsboro **10** Marksville, New Orleans, Plaquemine, Shreveport **11** Farmerville, Franklinton, Lake Charles, Ponchatoula, Ville Platte **12** Natchitoches **13** Napoleonville ***Macedonia:*** **4** Stip **5** Debar, Ohrid **6** Skopje ***Madagascar:*** **8** Tamatave **9** Antsirane, Mahajanga **11** Antsiranana **12** Fianarantsoa ***Maine:*** **4** Milo, Saco **5** Eliot, Orono **6** Auburn, Bangor, Gorham **7** Berwick, Houlton, Kittery, Machias, Rumford **8** Lewiston, Portland, Rockland **9** Bar Harbor, Biddeford, Brunswick, Ellsworth, Kennebunk, Skowhegan, Wiscasset **10** South Paris **11** Millinocket, Presque Isle **13** South Portland ***Malawi:*** **5** Zomba **8** Blantyre ***Malaysia:*** **4** Ipoh **5** Gemas, Klang **6** Kelang, Penang, Pinang **11** Johore Bahru ***Mali:*** **5** Kayes, Mopti, Segou **7** Sikasso ***Maryland:*** **5** Bowie **6** Denton, Elkton, Towson **8** Bethesda, Landover, Snow Hill **9** Baltimore, Rockville **10** Beltsville, Hagerstown **11** Chestertown, College Park, Leonardtown **12** Havre de Grace, Silver Spring **13** Upper Marlboro ***Massachusetts:*** **4** Ayer **5** Acton, Athol, Lenox, Salem **6** Agawam, Boston, Dedham, Hadley, Ludlow, Malden, Monson, Natick, Saugus, Woburn **7** Danvers, Duxbury, Holyoke, Hyannis, Medford, Methuen, Needham, Raynham, Seekonk, Swansea, Taunton, Walpole, Waltham, Wareham **8** Brockton, Chicopee, Falmouth, Plymouth, Rockport, Scituate, Somerset, Uxbridge, Yarmouth **9** Attleboro, Braintree, Brookline, Deerfield, Edgartown, Fall River, Fitchburg, Haverhill, Lexington, Southwick, Tewksbury, Westfield, Wilbraham, Worcester **10** Barnstable, Framingham, Gloucester, Greenfield, Leominster, Longmeadow, New Bedford, North Adams, Swampscott, Winchendon **11** Belchertown, Easthampton, Northampton, South Hadley, Springfield **12** Mattapoisett, Provincetown, Turners Falls, West Yarmouth, Williamstown ***Mauritania:*** **4** Atar **5** Kaedi **6** Dakhla ***Mexico:*** **4** Leon **5** Ameca, Choix, Tepic **6** Celaya, Colima, Merida, Oaxaca, Puebla, Toluca **7** Durango, Guasave, Morelia, Reynosa, Tampico, Tijuana, Tlalpan, Torreon, Uruapan **8** Chetumal, Coyoacan, Culiacan, Ensenada, Mazatlan, Saltillo, Tuxtepec **9** Fresnillo, Ixtacalco, Monterrey, Queretaro, Salamanca, Tapachula 10 Cuernavaca, Hermosillo, Ixtapalapa, Xochimilco 11 Guadalajara, Nueva Laredo 12 Azcapotzalco 13 Ciudad Obregon, Coatzacoalcos, San Luis Potosi, Veracruz Llave ***Michigan:*** 3 Mio 4 Alma, Caro, Holt, Novi 5 Ionia, L'Anse, Niles 6 Adrian, Alpena, Bad Axe, Lapeer, Otsego, Paw Paw 7 Allegan, Corunna, Detroit, Gladwin, Livonia, Midland, Saginaw 8 Ann Arbor, Bessemer, Dearborn, Escabana, Grayling, Hastings, Houghton, Kalkaska, Manistee, Munising, Muskegon, Newberry, Petoskey, Sandusky 9 Big Rapids, Cheboygan, Coldwater, Hillsdale, Kalamazoo, Ludington, Menominee, Ontonagon, Port Huron, Roscommon, Ypsilanti 10 Cassopolis, Charlevoix, Eagle River, Grand Haven, Manistique, West Branch, White Cloud 11 Battle Creek, East Lansing, Grand Rapids, Harrisville, Saint Ignace 12 Crystal Falls, Highland Park, Iron Mountain, Mount Clemens 13 Mount Pleasant ***Minnesota:*** 3 Ely 4 Mora 5 Anoka, Edina, Osseo 6 Aitkin, Bagley, Benson, Chaska, Duluth, Milaca, New Ulm, Wadena, Waseca, Windom, Winona 7 Bemidji, Glencoe, Hallock, Hibbing, Luverne, Mankato, Red Wing, Clayton, Wabacha, Wheaton 8 Baudette, Brainerd, Elk River, Le Center, Mahnomen, Moorhead, Owatonna, Shakopee 9 Albert Lea, Blue Earth, Caledonia, Crookston, Elbow Lake, Fairbault, Pipestone, Saint Paul, Silver Bay 10 Ortonville, Park Rapids, Saint Cloud, Saint James, Saint Peter, Stillwater, Two Harbors 11 Bloomington, Fergus Falls, Grand Marais, Little Falls, Long Prairie, Mantorville, Minneapolis, Worthington 12 Breckenridge, Detroit Lakes, Granite Falls, Red Lake Falls, Redwood Falls ***Mississippi:*** 4 Iuka 5 Amory 6 Biloxi, Leland, McComb, Purvis, Sardis, Sumner, Tunica, Tupelo, Vaiden, Winona 7 Belzoni, Brandon, Fayette, Okolona, Quitman, Wiggins 8 Ackerman, Gulfport, Hernando, Lucedale, Meridian, Paulding, Pontotoc, Rosedale, Walthall 9 Greenwood, Indianola, Meadville, New Albany, Pittsboro, Senatobia, Vicksburg, Woodville 10 Batesville, Bay Springs, Booneville, Brookhaven, Clarksdale, Ellisville, Hazlehurst, New Auguste, Pascagoula, Port Gibson, Starkville, Waynesboro 11 Coffeeville, Hattiesburg, Leakesville, Mayersville, Poplarville, Rolling Fork, Water Valley 12 Holly Springs 13 Bay Saint Louis ***Missouri:*** 3 Ava 4 Linn 5 Eldon, Hayti, Ladue, Rolla 6 Galena, Kahoka, Neosho, Potosi 7 Hermann, Ironton, Kennett, Linneus, Osceola, Palmyra, Sedalia 8 Doniphan, Gallatin, Hannibal 9 Boonville, Camdenton, Cassville, Hartville, Hillsboro, Maryville, Maysville, New Madrid, Pineville, Tuscumbia, Warrenton 10 Kirksville, Marble Hill, Marshfield, Perryville, Saint Louis, Steelville, Unionville, West Plains 11 Keytesville, Poplar Bluff, Saint Joseph, Warrensburg 12 Saint Charles 13 Harrisonville ***Mongolia:*** 5 Kobdo 6 Darhan 10 Choybalsan ***Montana:*** 5 Havre, Libby 6 Hardin, Hysham, Polson, Scobey, Wibaux 7 Bozeman, Broadus, Choteau, Cut Bank, Ekalaka, Ryegate, Winnett 8 Billings, Glendive, Missoula, Red Lodge 9 Big Timber, Deer Lodge, Harlowton, Kalispell, Wolf Point 10 Fort Benton, Great Falls, Plentywood 13 Thompson Falls ***Montenegro:*** 8 Titograd ***Morocco:*** 4 Safi, Taza 5 Nador, Oujda 6 Agadir, Meknes 7 Kenitra 9 Marrakesh 10 Casablanca ***Mozambique:*** 5 Beira 7 Nampula 9 Quelimane, Quilimane ***Myanmar:*** 3 Pyu 4 Paan 5 Akyab, Bhamo, Chauk, Katha, Magwe, Minbu, Mogok, Tavoy 7 Bassein 8 Mandalay ***Namibia:*** 5 Outjo 6 Tsumeb 12 Keetmanshoop ***Nebraska:*** 3 Ord 5 Cozad, Omaha, Ponca, Tryon, Wahoo 6 Elwood, Gering, McCook, Minden, Mullen, Neligh, Pender, Sidney, Wilber 7 Burwell, Chadron, Fremont, Kearney, Kimball, Osceola, Tekamah 8 Beatrice, Chappell, Fairbury, Hastings, Holdrege, Ogallala, Red Cloud, Schuyler, Tecumseh, Thedford 9 Ainsworth, Benkelman, Broken Bow, Fullerton, Papillion 10 Clay Center, Hartington, Springview, Stockville 11 Grand Island, Hayes Center, North Platte, Plattsmouth ***Netherlands:*** 3 Ede, Epe, Oss 4 Echt, Tiel, Uden 5 Aalst, Assen, Delft, Emmen, Soest, Vaals, Venlo, Vught, Weert, Weesp, Zeist 6 Arnhem 7 Haarlem, Tilburg, Utrecht 8 Enschede, Nijmegen 9 Apeldoorn, Eindhoven, Groningen, Rotterdam, Zandvoort ***Nevada:*** 3 Ely 4 Elko, Reno 6 Fallon, Minden, Pioche 7 Tonopah 8 Las Vegas, Lovelock 9 Goldfield, Yerington 10 Winnemucca ***New Brunswick:*** 5 Minto 9 Dalhousie 10 Edmundston, Richibucto 12 Hopewell Cape, Perth Andover, Saint Andrews ***Newfoundland:*** 5 Burin 6 Wabana ***New Hampshire:*** 5 Derry, Keene 6 Exeter, Gorham, Nashua 7 Hanover, Laconia, Ossipee 8 Hinsdale, Seabrook 9 Littleton, Merrimack 10 Portsmouth, Woodsville ***New Jersey:*** 4 Atco, Lodi 6 Camden, Newark, Nutley, Rahway 7 Bayonne, Clifton, Hoboken, Hohokus, Paramus, Passaic, Raritan, Teaneck 8 Freehold, Metuchen, Paterson, Vauxhall, Woodbury 9 Belvidere, Bridgeton, Glassboro, Lakehurst, Maplewood, Menlo Park, Montclair, Riverside, Toms River 10 Asbury Park, Bloomfield, Cherry Hill, East Orange, Flemington, Hackensack, Mount Holly, Perth Amboy, Piscataway, Plainfield, Somerville,

West Orange 11 Mays Landing, South Orange 13 Palisades Park ***New Mexico:*** 4 Mora, Taos 5 Belen, Hobbs, Raton 6 Clovis, Deming, Grants 7 Roswell, Socorro 8 Estancia, Los Lunas, Mosquero, Portales 9 Carrizozo, Las Cruces, Lordsburg, Los Alamos, Lovington, Santa Rosa, Tucumcari 10 Alamogordo, Bernalillo, Fort Sumner 11 Albuquerque ***New York:*** 4 Elma, Ovid 5 Depew, Ilion, Islip, Le Roy, Nyack, Olean, Owego, Utica 6 Attica, Cohoes, Delmar, Elmira, Ithaca, Oneida 7 Batavia, Corning, Geneseo, Katonah, Mineola, Penn Yan, Suffern, Yonkers 8 Bay Shore, Cortland, Herkimer, Hyde Park, Lockport, Mayville, Ossining, Syracuse, Valhalla 9 Greenport, Hempstead, Patchogue, Riverhead, Rochester, Scarsdale, Schoharie 10 Binghamton, Glens Falls, Haverstraw, Huntington, Lackawanna, Lake George, Lake Placid, Mamaroneck, Massapequa, Mount Kisco, Renssalaer, Wampsville, Watervliet 11 Ballston Spa, Canajoharie, Canandaigua, Cheektowaga, Cooperstown, Farmingdale, Hudson Falls, Irondequoit, Plattsburgh, Port Chester, Saint George, Schenectady, Southampton, Watkins Glen, White Plains 12 Lake Pleasant, Little Valley, Poughkeepsie 13 Mechanicville, Port Jefferson ***New Zealand:*** 4 Hutt, Tawa 5 Levin, Taupo, Waihi 7 Dunedin 8 Auckland 12 Christchurch ***Nicaragua:*** 4 Leon 5 Boaco, Rivas ***Nigeria:*** 3 Aba, Ado, Ede, Ife, Iwo, Jos, Owo, Oyo 4 Kano, Ondo 5 Akure, Enugu, Gusau, Okene, Zaria 6 Ibadan, Ilesha, Ilorin, Kaduna, Mushin, Sokoto 7 Onitsha, Oshogbo 8 Abeokuta 9 Maiduguri, Ogbomosho 12 Port Harcourt ***North Carolina:*** 4 Dunn 5 Ayden, Elkin, Erwin, Oteen, Sylva 6 Burgaw, Dobson, Durham, Lenoir, Manteo, Marion, Shelby, Sparta, Winton 7 Bayboro, Brevard, Edenton, Kinston, New Bern, Newland, Raeford, Roxboro, Sanford, Tarboro 8 Asheboro, Beaufort, Gastonia, Snow Hill 9 Albemarle, Asheville, Charlotte, Currituck, High Point, Louisburg, Lumberton, Morganton, Pittsboro, Southport, Wadesboro, Warrenton, Wentworth 10 Burnsville, Chapel Hill, Gatesville, Greensboro, Hayseville, Laurinburg, Lillington, Lincolnton, Mocksville, Reidsville, Rockingham, Smithfield, Whiteville, Wilkesboro 11 Bakersville, Kenansville, Statesville, Swanquarter, Waynesville, Williamston, Yadkinville, Yanceyville 12 Fayetteville, Hillsborough, Murfreesboro, Robbinsville, Taylorsville, Winston Salem 13 Rutherfordton ***North Dakota:*** 4 Mott 5 Cando, Fargo, Minot, Rolla 6 Amidon, Ashley, Bowman, Formon, Lakota, Linton, Medora, Mohall 7 La Moure, Langdon 8 Bowbells, McClusky, Wahpeton, Washburn 9 Bottineau, Dickinson, Ellendale, Fessenden, Fort Yates, Hettinger, Williston 10 Carrington, Devils Lake, Grand Forks 11 Minnewaukan, New Rockford ***Northern Ireland:*** 5 Derry, Larne, Newry, Omagh 6 Antrim, Armagh 8 Limavady 9 Ballymena, Banbridge, Coleraine, Craigavon, Dungannon, Newcastle 10 Ballymoney 11 Ballycastle, Downpatrick, Enniskillen, Londonderry, Magherafelt 13 Carrickfergus ***North Korea:*** 5 Haeju, Nampo 6 Wonsan 7 Hamhung, Kaesong, Sinuiju 8 Ch'ongjin, Kimchaek 9 P'yongyang ***Norway:*** 4 Bodo 5 Hamar, Skien 6 Tromso 9 Stavanger, Trondheim ***Nova Scotia:*** 5 Digby 6 Pictou 7 Arichat, Baddeck 8 Port Hood 9 Kentville, Lunenburg, Shelburne, Westville 10 Antigonish 11 Guysborough ***Ohio:*** 4 Kent 5 Akron, Berea, Bryan, Cadiz, Carey, Eaton, Heath, Logan, Niles, Parma, Piqua, Solon, Xenia 6 Canton, Celina, Dayton, Elyria, Euclid, Kenton, Lorain, Marion, Medina, Sidney, Tiffin, Toledo 7 Ashland, Batavia, Bucyrus, Chardon, Findlay, Ironton, Oakwood, Pomeroy, Ravenna, Van Wert, Wauseon, Waverly, Wooster 8 Caldwell, Conneaut, Marietta, Paulding, Sandusky 9 Ashtabula, Cleveland, Coshocton, Mansfield, West Union 10 Cincinnati, Gallipolis, Wapakoneta, Woodsfield, Zanesville 11 Chillicothe, Circleville, Millersburg, Mount Gilead, Painesville, Port Clinton 12 New Lexington, Steubenville 13 Bellefontaine, Cuyahoga Falls, Upper Sandusky ***Oklahoma:*** 3 Ada 4 Alva, Enid 5 Altus, Atoka, Sayre, Tulsa 6 Arnett, Durant, El Reno, Guymon, Hollis, Idabel, Lawton, Madill, Mangum, Nowata, Okemah, Poteau, Taloga, Vinita, Wewoka 7 Antlers, Ardmore, Cordell, Eufaula, Newkirk, Purcell, Sapulpa, Stigler, Watonga, Waurika 8 Anadarko, Coalgate, Okmulgee, Pawhuska, Sallisaw, Stilwell 9 Chickasha, Claremore, Frederick, McAlester, Tahlequah, Wilburton 10 New Cordell, Stillwater, Tishomingo 11 Holdenville, Pauls Valley 12 Bartlesville ***Oman:*** 3 Sur 6 Matrah 7 Salalah ***Ontario:*** 4 Ajax, Wawa, York 6 Barrie, Guelph, Kenora, Minden, Picton, Sarnia, Simcoe 7 Cobourg, Gore Bay, Napanee, Sudbury, Windsor 8 Brampton, Cochrane, Goderich, North Bay, Pembroke, Prescott 9 Brantford, Kitchener, L'Original, Newmarket, Owen Sound, Walkerton 10 Belleville, Brockville, Haileybury, Parry Sound, Thunder Bay 11 Bracebridge, Fort Frances, Mississauga, Orangeville 12 Peterborough, St. Catharines ***Oregon:*** 4 Moro 5 Canby, Nyssa 6 Condon, Eugene 7 Heppner 8 Coquille, La Grande, Lakeview, Portland, Roseburg

9 Clackamas, Corvallis, Gold Beach, Hood River, Pendleton, The Dalles, Tillamook 10 Grants Pass, Prineville 11 McMinnville 12 Klamath Falls ***Pakistan:*** 5 Bannu, Bhera, Kasur, Kohat 6 Gujrat, Lahore, Mardan, Multan, Quetta, Sukkur 7 Karachi, Sialkot 8 Lyallpur, Peshawar, Sargodha 9 Hyderabad 10 Bahawalpur, Gujranwala, Rawalpindi ***Paraguay:*** 3 Ita 4 Yuty 5 Belen, Luque, Pilar ***Pennsylvania:*** 4 York 5 Avoca, Darby, Muncy, Paoli 6 Easton 7 Altoona, Bedford, Clarion, Hanover, Hershey, Laporte, Latrobe, Reading, Ridgway, Sunbury 8 Carlisle, Edinboro, Hazleton, Montrose, Scranton, Somerset, Tionesta 9 Allentown, Ebensburg, Honesdale, Jim Thorpe, Lancaster, Lewisburg, Lock Haven, Meadville, New Castle, Smethport, Wellsboro 10 Bellefonte, Bloomsburg, Brookville, Carbondale, Clearfield, Gettysburg, Greensburg, Huntingdon, Kittanning, McKeesport, Middleburg, Pittsburgh, Pottsville, Waynesburg 11 Coudersport, Stroudsburg, Tunkhannock, Valley Forge, West Chester, Wilkes Barre 12 Chambersburg, Conshohocken, Philadelphia, State College, Williamsport 13 Hollidaysburg, Kennett Square, New Bloomfield ***Peru:*** 3 Ica, Ilo 5 Ancon, Cuzco, Jauja, Junin, Lamas, Pisco, Piura, Tacna 6 Callao 8 Arequipa, Chiclayo, Trujillo ***Philippines:*** 3 Iba 4 Bago, Bais, Boac, Bogo, Cebu, Daet, Jolo, Lipa, Mati 5 Basco, Bulan, Cadiz, Danao, Davao, Digos, Gapan, Gubat, Iriga, Laoag, Ormoc, Silay, Tagum, Vigan 6 Butuan, Iloilo 7 Angeles, Bacolod, Basilan 8 Batangas, Calbayog 9 Zamboanga 13 General Santos ***Poland:*** 4 Lodz, Nysa, Pila, Zary 5 Brzeg, Bytom, Bytow, Chelm, Gubin, Ilawa, Jaslo, Konin, Kutno, Lomza, Luban, Lubin, Mlawa, Olawa, Opole, Plock, Radom, Rumia, Sanok, Sopot, Tczew, Torun, Tychy, Ursus, Zagan 6 Gdansk, Gdynia, Kielce, Lublin, Poznan, Zabrze 7 Chorzow, Gliwice, Wroclaw 8 Katowice, Szczecin 9 Bialystok, Bydgoszcz, Sosnowiec, Walbrzych 10 Ruda Slaska 11 Czestochowa 12 Bielsko Biala ***Portugal:*** 4 Faro 5 Braga, Evora 6 Oporto ***Prince Edward Island:*** 10 Summerside ***Puerto Rico:*** 5 Ponce 7 Bayamon ***Quebec:*** 4 Alma 5 Amqui, Anjou, Granb, Laval, Levis, Magog, Percé, Rouyn 6 Ham Sud, Matane, Val d'Or 7 Bedford, Lachute 8 Cap Santé, Joliette, LacBrome, Maniwaki, Montreal, Rimouski, Roberval, Sept Iles, Waterloo 9 Becancour, Cookshire, Iberville, Inverness, La Malbaie, La Prairie, Longueuil, Montmagny, Saint Jean, Tadoussac, Vaudreuil, Vercheres 10 Ayers Cliff, Baie Comeau, Chicoutimi, Huntingdon, Marieville, St. Henedine, St. Julienne, Ville Marie, Yamachiche 11 Beauharnois, Lac Megantic, L'Assomption, Louiseville, Mont Laurier, Napierville, New Carlisle, Sainte Croix, Saint Pascal 12 Loretteville, Saint Liboire, Saint Raphael 13 Baie Saint Paul, Berthierville, Chateau Richer, Coteau Landing, Drummondville, Papineauville, Riviere du Loup, Sainte Martine, Thetford Mines, Trois Rivieres ***Rhode Island:*** 7 Newport, Rumford, Warwick 8 Apponaug, Coventry, Cranston, Tiverton, Westerly 9 Hopkinton, Pawtucket 10 Woonsocket 11 West Warwick 12 Narragansett, West Kingston 13 East Greenwich ***Romania:*** 3 Dej 4 Aiud, Arad, Cluj, Deva, Husi, Iasi 5 Anina, Bacau, Buzau, Carei, Lugoj, Sibiu, Turda 6 Braila, Brasov, Galati, Oradea 7 Craiova 8 Ploiesti 9 Constanta, Timisoara ***Russia:*** 3 Kem, Ufa 4 Inta, Luga, Okha, Omsk, Orel, Orsk, Perm, Tula, Tura, Zima 5 Aldan, Artem, Chita, Ishim, Kansk, Lysva, Onega, Penza, Pskov, Rzhev, Salsk, Serov, Sochi, Sokol, Tomsk, Tulun, Volsk, Yurga 6 Bratsk, Kaluga, Kovrov, Kurgan, Rostov, Ryazan, Samara, Syzran, Tambov, Tyumen, Vyborg, Yelets 7 Angarsk, Armavir, Barnaul, Bryansk, Irkutsk, Ivanovo, Izhevsk, Kalinin, Kolomna, Lipetsk, Magadan, Nalchik, Norilsk, Rybinsk, Saransk, Saratov, Shakhty, Ulan Ude, Vologda, Yakutsk, Zhdanov 8 Belgorod, Kemerovo, Kostroma, Murmansk, Nakhodka 7 Novorod 8 Orenburg, Smolensk, Taganrog, Vladimir, Voronezh 9 Archangel, Astrakhan, Berezniki, Kiselevsk, Krasnodar, Rubtsovsk, Serpukhov, Stavropol, Syktyvkar, Ulyanovsk, Volgograd, Yaroslavl 10 Cheboksary, Dzerzhinsk, Khabarovsk, Yoshkar Ola 11 Chelyabinsk, Cheremkhovo, Cherepovets, Krasnoyarsk, Makhachkala, Novosibirsk, Prokopyevsk, Sterlitamak, Verkhoyansk, Vladikavkaz, Vladivostok 12 Magnitogorsk, Novokuznetsk, Novomoskovsk, Severodvinsk 13 Yekaterinburg ***Saskatchewan:*** 8 Moose Jaw 10 Assiniboia ***Saudi Arabia:*** 4 Jauf, Taif 5 Jidda 6 Medina ***Scotland:*** 3 Ayr 4 Alva, Caol, Dyce, Oban 5 Alloa, Annan, Beith, Cowie, Cupar, Dalry, Ellon, Kelso, Kelty, Largs, Leven, Nairn, Patna, Troon 6 Dundee 7 Glasgow 8 Aberdeen 9 Inverness ***Senegal:*** 5 Thies 6 Kaolak 7 Kaolack ***Serbia:*** 3 Bor, Nis, Pec 4 Ruma 5 Becej, Cacak, Pirot, Sabac, Senta, Vrbas, Vrsac 7 Novi Sad 8 Subotica ***Slovenia:*** 4 Bled 5 Celje, Koper, Kranj 9 Ljubljana ***Somalia:*** 3 Eil 5 Afgoi, Alula, Brava, Burao, Obbia 7 Berbera, Kismayu ***South Africa:*** 5 Brits, Ceres, De Aar, Nigel, Paarl 6 Benoni, Durban 7 Springs 8 Boksburg, Mafeking 9 Germiston, Kimberley, Uitenhage 10 East London

11 Krugersdorp, Vereeniging 12 Johannesburg 13 Port Elizabeth ***South Carolina:*** 5 Aiken, Cayce, Saxon 6 Saluda, Sumter 7 Bamberg, Gaffney, Laurens, Manning, Pickens 8 Barnwell, Beaufort, Newberry, Rock Hill, Walhalla 9 Abbeville, Allendale, Edgefield, Greenwood, Kingstree, McCormick, Ridgeland, Winnsboro 10 Charleston, Darlington, Greenville, Orangeburg, Walterboro 11 Bishopville, Myrtle Beach, Spartanburg 12 Moncks Corner 13 Bennettsville, Saint Matthews ***South Dakota:*** 5 Burke, Hayti, Leola, Murdo, Onida, Selby 6 Armour, De Smet, Dupree, Kadoka, Olivet 7 Milbank, Sturgis, Tyndall, Yankton 8 Deadwood, Elk Point, Faulkton, Highmore, Kennebec, Redfield 9 Brookings, Clear Lake, Flandreau, Lake Andes 10 Fort Pierre, Gannvalley, Plankinton, Sioux Falls, Timber Lake 12 Belle Fourche ***South Korea:*** 3 Iri 4 Yosu 5 Cheju, Masan, Mokpo, Pusan, Suwon, Taegu, Ulson, Wonju 6 Chinju, Chonju, Inchon, Kunsan, Taejon 7 Kwangju ***Spain:*** 4 Adra, Baza, Elda, Jaca, Jaen, Leon, Loja, Lugo, Olot, Reus, Vich, Vigo 5 Albox, Alcoy, Alora, Baena, Cadiz, Ceuta, Cieza, Ecija, Eibar, Elche, Gijon, Ibiza, Jodar, Lorca, Mahon, Oliva, Osuna, Palma, Ronda, Soria, Ubeda 6 Bilboa, Burgos, Cuenca, Malaga, Murcia, Oviedo 7 Almaden, Almeria, Cordoba, Durango, Granada, Seville, Tarrasa, Vitoria 8 Alicante, La Coruna, Pamplona, Sabadell, Valencia 9 Barcelona, Salamanca, Santander, Saragossa 10 Hospitalet, Valladolid 12 San Sebastion ***Sri Lanka:*** 5 Galle, Kandy 6 Jaffna 10 Batticaloa ***Sudan:*** 4 Juba 5 Kodok, Kosti 8 Omdurman ***Sweden:*** 4 Lund, Umea 5 Boden, Boras, Falun, Gavle, Lulea, Malmo, Nacka, Pitea, Solno, Vaxjo, Visby, Ystad 7 Uppsala 8 Goteborg 9 Jonkoping ***Switzerland:*** 3 Zug 4 Biel, Chur, Thun 5 Aarau, Arbon, Baden, Basel, Koniz 6 Lugano, Zurich 7 Lucerne 8 Lausanne ***Syria:*** 4 Hama, Homs 5 Idlib 6 Aleppo 7 Latakia ***Tanzania:*** 5 Lindi, Mbeya, Tanga 6 Dodoma 8 Zanzibar ***Tennessee:*** 5 Alcoa, Erwin, Rives 6 Celina, Dunlap, Loudon, Ripley, Selmer 7 Memphis, Waverly 8 Gallatin, Oak Ridge, Rutledge, Tazewell, Wartburg 9 Dandridge, Dyersburg, Hohenwald, Jacksboro, Jonesboro, Knoxville, Lewisburg, Maryville, Pikeville 10 Cookeville, Crossville, Gainesboro, Hartsville, Smithville, Sneedville, Somerville, Waynesboro 11 Blountville, Chattanooga, Clarksville, Greeneville, McMinnville, Rogersville, Sevierville, Shelbyville, Tiptonville 12 Decaturville, Elizabethton, Lawrenceburg, Madisonville, Maynardville, Murfreesboro ***Texas:*** 4 Azle, Roby, Vega, Waco 5 Alvin, Anson, Baird, Bowie, Bryan, Clute, Cuero, Emory, Ennis, Freer, Hondo, Marfa, Mexia, Olney, Ozona, Pampa, Pecos, Pharr, Plano, Sealy, Tulia, Vidor, Wylie 6 Belton, Boerne, Bonham, Burnet, Conroe, Dallas, Del Rio, Denton, El Paso, Gilmer, Goliad, Jayton, Lamesa, Laredo, Linden, Lufkin, Menard, Morton, Odessa, Quanah, Sarita, Seguin, Sinton, Tahoka, Tilden, Uvalde 7 Abilene, Anahuac, Bandera, Bastrop, Big Lake, Brenham, Cotulla, Crowell, Dalhart, Denison, Dimmitt, Farwell, Houston, Kaufman, Kountze, Lubbock, Mentone, Mertzon, Midland, Refugio, San Saba, Stanton, Van Horn, Wharton 8 Amarillo, Angleton, Beaumont, Beeville, Cleburne, Eastland, Eldorado, Floydada, Giddings, Glen Rose, Gonzales, Granbury, Groveton, Hemphill, La Grange, Lampasas, Lipscomb, Longview, McKinney, Monahans, Montague, Muleshoe, Pearsall, Perryton, Rockwall, Spearman, Stinnett 9 Arlington, Aspermont, Ballinger, Bellville, Big Spring, Brownwood, Childress, Clarendon, Corsicana, Crosbyton, Eagle Pass, Fort Davis, Fort Worth, Galveston, Groesbeck, Henrietta, Hillsboro, Jacksboro, Kerrville, Levelland, Paint Rock, Palo Pinto, Plainview, San Angelo, Sanderson, San Marcos, Silverton, Woodville 10 Brownfield, Coldspring, Falfurrias, Gatesville, George West, Jourdanton, Kingsville, Port Arthur, Port Lavaca, San Antonio, Sweetwater, Waxahachie 11 Brownsville, Floresville, Goldthwaite, Littlefield, Nacogdoches, Rocksprings, Weatherford 12 Breckenridge, Daingerfield, Fort Stockton, Hebbronville, New Braunfels, Raymondville, San Augustine, Sierra Blanca, Stephenville, Throckmorton, Wichita Falls 13 Brackettville, Corpus Christi, Hallettsville ***Thailand:*** 3 Nan, Tak 5 Phrae, Roi Et, Surin 8 Songkhla ***Tunisia:*** 4 Beja, Sfax 5 Gabes, Gafsa 7 Bizerte ***Turkey:*** 5 Adana, Bursa, Izmir, Konya, Sivas 6 Erzurm, Samsun 7 Kayseri, Malatya 8 Istanbul 9 Eskisehir, Gaziantep 10 Diyarbakir ***Turkmenistan:*** 8 Nebit Dag ***Uganda:*** 5 Jinja, Mbale 7 Entebbe ***Ukraine:*** 4 Lvov, Sumy 5 Lutsk, Rovno 6 Odessa 7 Donetsk, Kharkov, Kherson, Poltava 8 Vinnitsa, Zhitomir 9 Chernigov, Krivoy Rog, Nikolayev 10 Chernovtsy, Kirovograd, Kremenchug, Sevastopol, Simferopol, Zaporozhye ***United Arab Emirates:*** 5 Ajman, Dubai 7 Sharjah 8 Fujairah 12 Ras al Khaimah ***Uruguay:*** 4 Melo 5 Minas, Pando, Rocha, Salto ***Utah:*** 3 Loa 4 Lehi, Moab, Orem 5 Konab, Manti, Nephi, Ogden, Provo 6 Tooele 7 Parowan 8 Duchesne 9 Coalville, Panguitch 10 Castle Dale 11 Saint George ***Uzbekistan:*** 5 Nukus 6 Kokand

7 Bukhara, Fergana 8 Andizhan, Chirchik, Namangan 9 Samarkand ***Venezuela:*** 4 Coro 5 Anaco, Cagua 6 Merida 7 Cabimas, Maracay 8 Valencia 9 Maracaibo 12 Barquisimeto, San Cristobal ***Vermont:*** 5 Barre 7 Chelsea, Newfane, Rutland 8 Winooski 9 Guildhall, North Hero 10 Bennington, Burlington, Middlebury 11 Brattleboro, Saint Albans, St. Johnsbury 12 Bellows Falls ***Vietnam:*** 3 Hue 4 Vinh 5 Da Lat, Hoi An, My Tho 6 Da Nang 7 Nam Dinh, Qui Nhon 8 Haiphong, Nha Trang ***Virginia:*** 4 Tabb 5 Luray, Surry 6 Grundy, Saluda 7 Accomac, Boydton, Mathews, New Kent, Norfolk 8 Abingdon, Culpeper, Leesburg, Manassas, Montross, Nottoway, Poquoson, Powhatan, Rustburg, Tazewell 9 Arlington, Clintwood, Courtland, Dinwiddie, Eastville, Farmville, Fincastle, Goochland, Lunenburg, Lynchburg 10 Appomattox, Berryville, Front Royal, Hillsville, Jonesville, King George, Lovingston, Pearisburg, Portsmouth, Rocky Mount, Wytheville 11 Heathsville, King William, Newport News, Warm Springs 12 Prince George, Spotsylvania, Tappahannock 13 Stanardsville ***Wales:*** 4 Rhyl 5 Neath, Risca, Tenby, Tywyn 7 Cardiff, Cwmbran, Denbigh, Swansea 8 Aberdare, Bridgend 10 Llangollen ***Washington:*** 4 Omak 5 Brier, Camas, Kelso, Lacey, Pasco, Selah 6 Asotin, Colfax, Tacoma, Yakima 7 Ephrata, Everett, Pomeroy, Prosser, Seattle, Spokane 8 Bellevue, Chehalis, Colville, Okanogan 9 Cathlamet, Montesano, Ritzville, Snohomish, Wenatchee 10 Bellingham, Coupeville, Ellensburg, Goldendale, Walla Walla, Waterville 11 Port Angeles, Port Orchard 12 Friday Harbor, Port Townsend ***West Virginia:*** 5 Nitro, Welch 6 Elkins, Hamlin, Hinton, Keyser, Ripley 7 Beckley, Parsons, Weirton 8 Kingwood, Philippi, Wheeling 9 Glenville, Marlinton, Pineville, Wellsburg 10 Buckhannon, Clarksburg, Huntington, Moorefield, Morgantown, Petersburg, Saint Marys, Williamson 11 Grantsville, Harrisville, Martinsburg, Moundsville, Parkersburg 12 Middlebourne, Summersville 13 New Cumberland, Point Pleasant ***Wisconsin:*** 4 Kiel 5 Ripon, Tomah 6 Antigo, Barron, Durand, Hurley, Oconto, Racine, Wausau 7 Baraboo, Chilton, Crandon, Elkhorn, Hayward, Kenosha, Keshena, Mauston, Merrill, Oshkosh, Shawano, Viraqua, Waupaca, Wautoma 8 Appleton, Green Bay, Kewaunee, La Crosse, Montello, Phillips, Washburn, Waukesha, West Bend 9 Eau Claire, Ellsworth, Fond du Lac, Green Lake, Ladysmith, Manitowoc, Marinette, Menomonie, Milwaukee, Sheboygan, Shell Lake, Wauwatosa, West Allis, Whitehall 10 Balsam Lake, Darlington, Dodgeville, Eagle River, Grantsburg, Janesville 11 Neillsville, Sturgeon Bay 12 Stevens Point, Whitefish Bay 13 Chippewa Falls ***Wyoming:*** 4 Lusk 6 Casper, Lander 7 Laramie, Rawlins, Worland 8 Gillette, Kemmerer, Pinedale, Sheridan, Sundance 9 Wheatland 10 Green River 11 Rock Springs, Thermopolis ***Yemen:*** 5 Taizz 7 Hodeida, Mukalla ***Zaire:*** 4 Boma 6 Bukavu, Likasi 7 Kananga 9 Kisangani, Mbuji Mayi 10 Lubumbashi ***Zambia:*** 5 Kabwe, Kitwe, Mansa, Mbala, Mongu, Ndola ***Zimbabwe:*** 5 Gwelo 6 Umtali 8 Bulawayo

civet 3 cat ***African:*** 7 nandine ***Asian:*** 5 zibet 6 zibeth ***Chinese:*** 5 rasse ***East Indian:*** 6 musang 9 tangalung ***Indian:*** 6 bondar ***Madagascar:*** 5 fossa 8 fanaloka ***Malaysian:*** 8 mampalon ***relative:*** 5 genet

civic 6 public 8 national

civil 5 bland, suave 6 polite, public, urbane 7 affable, cordial, courtly, genteel, politic, refined 8 gracious, mannerly, national, obliging, well-bred 9 courteous 10 cultivated, diplomatic 12 well-mannered 13 accommodating

civility 6 comity 7 amenity, decorum 9 etiquette, propriety 10 politeness

civilization 7 culture

civilized 5 bland, suave 6 decent, polite, proper, smooth, urbane 7 refined 8 decorous 9 befitting, Christian 10 conforming 11 comme il faut 13 sophisticated

civil rights ***leader:*** 4 King ***organization:*** 4 ACLU, CORE 5 NAACP

Civil War ***admiral:*** 8 Buchanan, Farragut ***battle:*** 6 Shiloh 7 Bull Run 8 Antietam, Manassas 9 Mobile Bay, Nashville, Vicksburg 10 Cold Harbor, Gettysburg 11 Chattanooga, Chickamauga ***general:*** 3 Lee 4 Hood, Pope 5 Bragg, Buell, Ewell, Grant, Meade, Sykes 6 Hooker 7 Forrest, Jackson, Sherman 8 Burnside, Johnston, Sheridan 9 McClellan, Rosecrans, Schofield 10 Beauregard ***ship:*** 7 Monitor 9 Merrimack

civil wrong 4 tort

Civitas Dei 4 Zion 5 bliss 6 Canaan, heaven 7 elysium, nirvana 8 empyrean, paradise 12 New Jerusalem 13 Abraham's bosom

clabber 5 curds

clack 3 gab, jaw, yak 4 blab, chat 5 prate, sieve, tabby 6 babble, bicker, gabble, gossip, jabber, rattle 7 blabber, chatter, clatter, clitter, palaver, prattle, shatter 8 quidnunc, telltale 9 carrytale, yakety-yak 10 talebearer 11 rumormonger 13 scandalmonger

clad 4 face, garb, side, skin 5 array, dress

6 attire, clothe 7 apparel, garment, raiment, sheathe 8 enclothe

claim 4 call, dibs 5 argue, exact, right, share, stake, title 6 adduce, allege, assert, defend, demand 7 advance, contend, justify, purport, require, solicit, warrant 8 interest, maintain, pretense 9 assertion, challenge, postulate, privilege, vindicate 10 birthright, pretension 11 affirmation, declaration, prerogative, requisition 12 protestation

clairvoyance 3 ESP

clairvoyant 4 seer

clam 5 razor 6 gweduc, quahog 7 bivalve, coquina, geoduck, goeduck, gweduck, mollusk, quahaug, steamer 11 cherrystone *genus:* 3 Mya

clamant 4 dire 6 crying, urgent 7 burning, exigent, instant 8 pressing 9 clamorous 10 imperative 11 importunate

clamber 5 climb, crawl, scale 8 scrabble, scramble, struggle

clamor 3 din 4 bawl, roar, rout, to-do 5 babel, claim, whirl 6 bellow, bustle, debate, demand, hassle, hubbub, jangle, outcry, racket, tumult, uproar, upturn 7 agitate, bluster, dispute, ferment, turmoil 8 upheaval 9 commotion 10 convulsion, hullabaloo, hurly-burly, tintamarre 11 pandemonium

clamorous 4 dire 5 vocal 6 crying, urgent 7 begging, blatant, burning, clamant, exigent, instant, voluble 8 adjuring, eloquent, pressing, strident 9 imploring 10 articulate, boisterous, imperative, multivocal, vociferant, vociferous 11 importunate, loudmouthed, openmouthed 12 obstreperous

clamp 4 grip, hold, vise 5 clasp, grasp, gripe 6 clench, clinch, clutch, tenure 7 grapple

clamshell 6 bucket 7 grapple

clan 3 mob 4 camp, folk, race, ring 5 cabal, house, stock, tribe 6 circle, clique, family 7 coterie, ingroup, kindred, lineage 9 camarilla *emblem:* 5 totem

clandestine 3 sly 4 foxy 6 artful, covert, secret 7 furtive, illicit 8 hush-hush, stealthy 10 undercover 12 hugger-mugger, illegitimate 13 surreptitious, under-the-table

clang 3 din 4 ding, peal 5 noise 6 jangle

clangorous 5 noisy 7 rackety 8 clattery, noiseful, sonorous 10 uproarious

clap 4 bang, boom, slam, wham 5 blast, burst, crack, crash, smash 7 applaud

claptrap 4 bull 5 hokum 6 bunkum, drivel, humbug 7 baloney, twaddle 8 malarkey, nonsense 10 flapdoodle

Clare Boothe ___ 4 Luce

claret 3 red 4 wine 8 Bordeaux

clarify 5 clean, clear 6 define, purify, settle 7 analyze, cleanse, clear up, explain 8 depurate, simplify 9 break down, delineate, elucidate, formulate 10 illuminate, illustrate 13 straighten out

clarion 4 fair, fine 5 clear, sunny 8 pleasant, rainless, sunshiny 9 cloudless, unclouded 10 undarkened

clarity 4 care 6 nicety 8 accuracy, lucidity 9 clearness, fussiness, limpidity, plainness, precision, propriety 10 exactitude 11 perspicuity 12 articulation, correctitude

clash 3 jar, row, try 4 bump, fray, fret, gall, jolt, riot 5 brawl, broil, brush, crash, grate, melee, scrap, set to, shock, smash 6 action, affray, battle, fracas, impact, jangle, mellay, rumpus, wallop 7 collide, discord 8 conflict, mismatch, skirmish 9 collision, disaccord, encounter, scrimmage 10 concussion, engagement 11 embroilment 12 disharmonize

clasp 3 hug 4 clip, coil, grip, hold, take 5 clamp, grasp, gripe, press, tache 6 clench, clinch, clutch, enfold, tenure 7 embrace, grapple, squeeze 10 chatelaine

class 3 ilk 4 head, hold, kind, mark, part, rank, rate, sort, tier, type 5 allot, brand, caste, color, gauge, genre, genus, grade, grain, group, judge, order, score, stamp, style 6 assess, assign, assort, branch, divide, kidney, league, nature, reckon, regard, stripe 7 account, bracket, caliber, feather, quality, section, species, variety 8 appraise, category, consider, division, evaluate, grouping, separate 10 categorize, pigeonhole 11 description 12 denomination *Hindu:* 5 caste, varna *middle:* 11 bourgeoisie *school:* 6 junior, senior 8 freshman 9 sophomore *scientific:* 5 genus 6 genera (plural) *suffix:* 2 cy *working:* 11 proletariat

classic 3 top 4 fine 5 ideal, model, prime 6 famous 7 capital, typical, vintage 8 champion, superior, top-notch 9 classical, excellent, exemplary 10 magnum opus, masterwork, prototypal 11 chef d'oeuvre, masterpiece, tour de force 12 paradigmatic, prototypical

classification 4 sort, type 5 genre, genus, grade, order 6 family, genera (plural), phylum, rating 7 species 8 category, division, grouping, taxonomy, typology 11 arrangement

classified 6 secret 9 top secret 12 confidential

classify 4 rank, rate, sort 5 grade, group 6 assort 8 evaluate 10 categorize, pigeonhole

classy 2 in 4 tony 5 sharp, swank, swish 6 modish, tonish 7 dashing, stylish 11 fashionable

clatter 3 gab, jaw 4 chat, to-do 5 clack, run on 6 babble, bicker, clamor, dither, hassle, hubbub, pother, rattle, tumult, uproar

7 chatter, clitter, shatter, turmoil 9 commotion 10 hurly-burly *Scottish:* 7 brattle
clattery 5 noisy 7 rackety 8 noiseful, sonorous 10 clangorous, uproarious
Claudia's husband 6 Pilate
Claudio's beloved 4 Hero
Claudius *nephew:* 6 Hamlet *slayer:* 6 Hamlet 9 Agrippina *successor:* 4 Nero
claviger 6 custos, keeper, warden 8 cerberus, guardian, watchdog 9 custodian
claw 3 dig 4 nail, tear 5 chela, grasp, grope, seize, talon, uncus 6 clutch, scrape, ungual, unguis, ungula 7 scratch *combining form:* 4 chel 5 cheli, onych, ungui 6 onycho 8 onychium
clay 3 cob, pug 4 galt, leck, loam, lute, marl 5 argil, brick, earth, gault, loess, ocher, ochre, rabat 6 clunch 8 camstone *baked:* 4 bole, tile 5 adobe, brick *box:* 6 saggar, sagger *brick:* 3 bat *building:* 5 adobe *ceramic:* 10 terra-cotta *combining form:* 3 pel 4 pelo 6 argill 7 argilli, argillo 10 argillaceo *constituent:* 6 silica 7 dickite, nacrite 8 feldspar, silicate 9 kaolinite *friable:* 4 bole *in glass:* 4 tear *made of:* 7 fictile *mold:* 3 dod *porcelain:* 6 kaolin 7 kaoline *red:* 4 bole 8 laterite, sinopite *rock:* 5 shale *slab:* 3 bat *sticky:* 8 gumbotil *tobacco pipe:* 6 dudeen *watery mixture:* 4 slip *white:* 6 kaolin 7 kaoline
clay pigeon 6 target
clean 3 gut 4 dust, fair, pure, swab, tidy, trim, wash, wipe 5 dress, fresh, groom, order, purge, renew, scour, scrub, sweep 6 bright, chaste, decent, modest, neaten, police, purify, spruce, vacuum 7 clarify, freshen, furbish, shining, sinless 8 brighten, depurate, innocent, renovate, spotless, unguilty, unsoiled 9 blameless, crimeless, faultless, guiltless, sparkling, stainless, taintless, undefiled, unsullied, untainted, wholesome 10 immaculate, inculpable 11 recondition, sportsmanly, unblemished 12 spick-and-span, straighten up 13 sportsmanlike *ship's bottom:* 5 bream
clean-cut 7 express 8 definite, explicit, specific 10 definitive 11 categorical, unambiguous
cleaner see **cleanser**
cleanhanded 8 innocent
clean-limbed 4 trim 7 shapely 8 shapeful 10 statuesque, well-turned
cleanse 5 purge, rinse 6 purify, refine 7 clarify, deterge 8 depurate, lustrate, sanitize 9 disinfect, expurgate, sterilize
cleanser 3 lye 4 soap 6 bleach 9 detergent
cleansing 9 catharsis, purgation 10 lustration 11 expurgation 12 purification
Cleante *father:* 8 Harpagon *lover:* 9 Angelique
clear 3 get, net, pay, rid, win 4 bare, earn, fade, fair, fine, gain, leap, lose, make, over, pure, quit, sink, void, well 5 à fond, close, empty, exact, fully, glean, lucid, milky, overt, pay up, plain, quite, repay, solve, stark, sunny, untie, vault 6 acquit, better, gather, hurdle, limpid, lucent, obtain, patent, pay off, pick up, public, secure, settle, simple, square, vacant, vacate, vanish 7 absolve, acquire, clarify, clarion, cleanse, clean up, crystal, defined, evanish, evident, explain, improve, obvious, precise, rule out, satisfy, untwine, utterly, vacuous 8 apparent, definite, distinct, entirely, evanesce, explicit, knowable, luculent, luminous, manifest, overleap, palpable, pellucid, pleasant, rainless, scot-free, sensible, shake off, sunshiny, surmount, tangible, throw-off, unburden, unhidden, univocal, untangle 9 cloudless, disappear, discharge, eliminate, elucidate, evaporate, exculpate, exonerate, extricate, graspable, liquidate, meliorate, negotiate, perfectly, published, stabilize, tralucent, unblurred, unclouded, vindicate 10 accumulate, altogether, ameliorate, completely, disculpate, disentwine, illuminate, illustrate, opalescent, openhanded, see-through, translucid, undarkened, unentangle, unobscured, unscramble 11 appreciable, conspicuous, disencumber, disentangle, open-and-shut, perceptible, perspicuous, translucent, transparent, unambiguous, unequivocal, unperplexed 12 recognizable, transpicuous, unmistakable 13 apprehensible, uncomplicated
clearance 7 go-ahead 10 green light 13 authorization
clear away 6 remove 7 take out 9 discumber 10 disembroil 12 disembarrass
clear-cut 4 nice 5 crisp, exact, lucid, plain 6 biting, lucent 7 assured, crystal, cutting, decided, express, ingoing, precise 8 definite, distinct, explicit, incisive, luminous, manifest, pellucid, specific 9 trenchant, unblurred, undoubted 10 definitive, pronounced, undisputed 11 categorical, indubitable, penetrating, translucent, transparent, unambiguous 12 transpicuous, unquestioned
clear-eyed 10 discerning
clearheaded 10 perceptive
clear out 4 kite 5 scram 6 begone, decamp, get out 7 skiddoo, take off, vamoose 8 hightail 9 skedaddle
clear-sightedness 3 wit 6 acumen 8 astucity, keenness 10 astuteness, shrewdness 11 discernment, penetration, percipience
clear up 5 solve 6 cipher, unfold 7 clarify, dope out, explain, resolve, unravel 8 deci-

pher, dissolve 9 elucidate, figure out, puzzle out 10 illuminate, illustrate

clearwing 4 moth

cleat 4 bitt 5 cavel, chock, kevel 6 batten 7 bollard, coxcomb, dolphin

cleavage 5 chasm, cleft, split 6 schism

cleave 3 cut, hew, rip 4 chop, join, link, rend, rive, tear 5 carve, cling, sever, slice, split, stick, unite 6 adhere, cohere, divide, sunder 7 combine, conjoin, dissect, divorce 8 dissever, separate 9 associate

cleft 3 gap 4 rift, rima, rime, slit 5 chasm, chink, clove, crack, gorge, gulch, split 6 arroyo, clough, ravine, schism 7 crevice, fissure 8 cleavage, rimation *combining form:* 5 fissi, schiz 6 schizo 7 schisto

clemency 5 grace, mercy 6 lenity 7 caritas, charity 8 fairness, justness, lenience, leniency, mildness 9 endurance, tolerance 10 gentleness, indulgence, sufferance, toleration 11 forbearance 12 mercifulness 13 equitableness

clement 4 easy, kind, mild 6 benign, humane, kindly, tender 7 lenient 8 merciful, tolerant 9 benignant, indulgent 10 benevolent, charitable, forbearing 11 sympathetic 13 compassionate

clench 4 grip, grit, hold 5 clamp, clasp, grasp, gripe 6 clinch, clutch, tenure 7 grapple

Cleopatra *attendant:* 4 Iras 8 Charmian *brother:* 7 Ptolemy *husband:* 7 Ptolemy *killer:* 3 asp *lover:* 6 Antony, Caesar *river:* 4 Nile

Cleopatra's Needle 7 obelisk

clepsydra 9 timepiece 10 water clock

clerestory 7 gallery

clergyman 5 clerk, padre, vicar 6 bishop, cleric, curate, divine, father, parson, pastor, priest, rector 7 dominie, pontiff, prelate 8 chaplain, clerical, minister, ordinary, preacher, pulpiter, reverend, shepherd, sky pilot 9 churchman, predicant, pulpiteer 10 ecclesiast, evangelist, missionary, sermonizer 11 pulpitarian 12 ecclesiastic *American:* 4 Hale, King 5 Eliot, Stone, Weems 6 Dwight, Holmes, Hooker, Mather, Merton, Parker, Powell, Taylor 7 Beecher, Harvard, Russell 10 Muhlenberg *English:* 4 Ward 5 Donne, Paley, Smith 6 Cotton, Fuller, Taylor 7 Cranmer, Parsons 8 Kingsley *French:* 8 Teilhard 10 Schweitzer *home:* 5 manse 6 priory 7 rectory 8 vicarage 9 monastery, parsonage *traveling:* 12 circuit rider

cleric see clergyman

clerisy 8 literati 10 illuminati 13 intellectuals

clerk 3 nun 4 monk 5 steno 6 cleric, scribe 7 scholar 8 minister 9 clergyman, secretary 11 salesperson 12 stenographer

clerkish 4 nice 5 fussy, picky 6 choosy 7 finical, finicky 9 finicking, squeamish 10 fastidious, particular

clever 3 apt, sly 4 able, deft, good, racy, slim 5 adept, alert, canny, funny, handy, quick, ready, salty, sharp, slick, smart, witty 6 adroit, brainy, bright, crafty, expert, nimble, pretty, prompt, tricky, wicked 7 amusing, capable, cunning, knowing, piquant, risible, skilled 8 dazzling, fanciful, humorous, masterly, pleasing, skillful 9 all-around, brilliant, competent, deceitful, dexterous, facetious, ingenious, laughable, many-sided, qualified, sparkling, sprightly, versatile, whimsical, workmanly 10 neat-handed, proficient 11 coruscating, intelligent, quick-witted, ready-witted, workmanlike 12 entertaining 13 scintillating

cliché 5 stale, trite 6 truism 7 bromide 8 banality, bathetic, prosaism, timeworn 9 hackneyed, platitude 10 prosaicism 11 commonplace, stereotyped 13 stereotypical

click 2 go 4 tick 6 go over, pan out 7 come off, succeed 8 prove out

click beetle 6 elater 8 elaterid

client 6 patron 8 customer

cliff 4 crag 5 bluff, cleve, scarp 7 clogwyn 8 headland, palisade 9 precipice *Scottish:* 5 heuch, heugh

climacteric 4 dire 5 acute 7 crucial 8 critical 9 desperate, menopause 12 change of life

climate 6 medium, milieu 7 ambient 8 ambience 10 atmosphere 11 environment, mise-en-scène 12 surroundings *combining form:* 6 meteor 7 meteoro

climatize 6 harden, season 7 toughen 9 acclimate

climax 3 cap, end 4 acme, apex, peak 5 crown 6 apogee, finish, summit, top off 8 capsheaf, capstone, conclude, meridian, pinnacle, round off 9 culminate, finish off, terminate 11 culmination *in drama:* 10 catastasis

climb 4 shin, upgo 5 mount, scale, speel 6 ascend 7 clamber 8 escalade, escalate

climbing 8 scandent

climbing iron 7 crampon

clinch 3 hug 4 grip, hold 5 clamp, clasp, grasp, gripe, press 6 clutch, enfold, tenure 7 embrace, grapple, squeeze

cling 4 bond 5 stick 6 adhere, cleave, cohere 8 adhesion, cohesion, stickage, sticking 9 adherence, coherence

clingfish 6 remora

clingstone 5 peach

clink 3 can, jug 4 jail, stir 5 pokey 6 cooler, jingle, lockup, tingle, tinkle 7 chinkle, slammer 8 hoosegow 9 calaboose

clinkers 3 ash 5 ashes 7 cinders

clinquant 6 tinsel 10 glittering
Clio see **Muse**
clip 3 cut, mow, pin 4 crop, pare, skin, soak, trim 5 lower, prune, shave, shear, skive, slash, stick 6 broach, brooch, fleece, reduce 7 cut back, cut down 8 mark down 10 overcharge
clique 3 mob, set 4 camp, clan, ring 5 cabal 6 circle 7 coterie, faction, in-group 9 camarilla
cloak 4 cape, face, mask, robe, show, veil, wrap 5 cover, guise 6 facade, joseph, mantle, poncho, screen, shroud, veneer 7 blanket, curtain, dress up, manteau 8 disguise 9 dissemble, semblance 10 camouflage 11 dissimulate ***ancient Greek:*** 7 chlamys ***ancient Roman:*** 5 palla, sagum 6 abolla 7 paenula, pallium ***Arab:*** 3 aba ***combining form:*** 6 pallio ***fur:*** 7 pelisse ***hooded:*** 5 capot 6 capote 7 burnous 8 burnoose, cardinal ***Indian:*** 5 choga ***Jewish:*** 6 kittel ***liturgical:*** 4 cope ***monk's:*** 8 analabos ***Moroccan:*** 5 jelab 7 jellaba 8 djellaba ***over armor:*** 6 tabard 7 surcoat ***Spanish:*** 4 capa 5 manta ***Turkish:*** 6 dolman ***waterproof:*** 6 poncho
clobber 4 belt, slam, slug 5 blast, brain, clout, smash 6 wallop
clochard 3 vag 4 hobo 5 tramp 6 canter 7 drifter, floater, vagrant 8 roadster, vagabond 11 bindle stiff
clock 4 time 9 timepiece 11 chronometer ***ship-shaped:*** 3 nef ***water:*** 9 clepsydra
clocklike 4 full 6 minute 7 precise, regular 8 detailed, itemized, thorough 10 blow-by-blow, particular
clockmaker 10 horologist
clockwise 6 deasil 8 positive 11 right-handed
clod 3 gob, wad 4 boob, dolt, dope, hunk, lump 5 chump, chunk, clump, dummy, dunce, hunch 6 dimwit, nugget 8 dumbbell 9 blockhead, lamebrain
cloddish 7 boorish, ill-bred, loutish 8 churlish, clownish 9 unrefined 10 uncultured, unpolished 11 uncivilized
clodhopper 4 boor, hick, lout, shoe 5 chuff, churl, clown, yokel 6 mucker, rustic 7 bumpkin, grobian, hayseed, hoosier, redneck 9 chawbacon
clog 3 gum, tax, tie 4 curb, fill, lade, load, plug, stop 5 block, choke, close, leash, weigh 6 burden, charge, cumber, fetter, hamper, hobble, hog-tie, lumber, saddle 7 congest, occlude, shackle, stopper, trammel 8 encumber, obstruct 9 cumbrance, entrammel, hindrance, impedance 10 impediment 11 encumbrance
cloister 7 seclude 9 sequester
Cloister and the Hearth author 5 Reade
cloistered 7 recluse, secluse 8 hermetic, secluded 9 seclusive 11 sequestered
cloistered one 3 nun 4 monk
Clorinda ***beloved:*** 7 Tancred ***father:*** 6 Senapo ***guardian:*** 6 Arsete ***slayer:*** 7 Tancred
close 3 end 4 bang, clap, clog, face, fill, firm, halt, hard, meet, near, next, nigh, plug, quit, seal, shut, slam, stop, taut 5 abate, block, cease, choke, debar, dense, front, handy, humid, muggy, solid, stivy, taper, tense, thick, tight 6 almost, chummy, desist, ending, finale, finish, lessen, narrow, nearby, nearly, period, reduce, screen, shroud, silent, sticky, stingy, stuffy, sultry, windup, wrap up 7 airless, compact, congest, crowded, dwindle, exclude, miserly, nearest, occlude, shut off, shut out, stopper 8 abutting, adjacent, block out, complete, conclude, decrease, diminish, familiar, finalize, intimate, nearmost, obstruct, obturate, reserved, reticent, stifling, taciturn, taper off, ultimate, write off 9 adjoining, cessation, compacted, condensed, determine, drain away, encounter, immediate, nearabout, niggardly, penurious, proximate, terminate 10 breathless, compressed, conclusion, consummate, contiguous, contracted, convenient, desistance, near-at-hand 11 constricted, impermeable, neighboring, substantial, suffocating, termination, tight-lipped 12 cheeseparing, confidential, consolidated, impenetrable, parsimonious, tight-mouthed 13 pennypinching ***combining form:*** 4 pync, sten 5 plesi, pynco, steno 6 plesio
closed ***combining form:*** 5 clist 6 cleist, clisto, occlus 7 cleisto, occluso
closed-minded 4 deaf 8 unpliant 9 obstinate, pigheaded, unpliable 10 bullheaded, hardheaded, self-willed, unyielding 11 intractable
closefisted 6 stingy 7 miserly 8 clinging, grasping 9 clutching, niggardly, tenacious 13 penny-pinching
close in 3 hem, mew 4 cage, coop 5 fence, hedge 6 corral, immure 7 enclose, envelop
close-knit 8 intimate
close-lipped 6 silent 8 reserved, reticent, taciturn 12 tight-mouthed
closely 4 hard 7 sharply 8 intently, minutely 9 carefully, heedfully, mindfully 11 searchingly 12 meticulously, scrupulously, thoughtfully 13 punctiliously
close match 6 tossup
closemouthed see **close-lipped**
closeness 8 intimacy
close off 6 cut off, enisle, island 7 isolate 8 insulate, separate 9 segregate, sequester

closet 6 hushed, inside, office 7 private 8 academic 11 speculative, theoretical 12 confidential
closing 3 end, lag 4 last, stop 5 final 6 ending, finish, latest, latter, period 8 eventual, hindmost, terminal, ultimate 9 cessation 10 concluding, desistance 11 termination
closure 3 cap, lid 8 fastener 9 cessation *combining form:* 6 clisis 7 cleisis
clot 3 gel, set 4 body, jell 5 array, batch, bunch, clump, group, jelly 6 bundle, gelate 7 battery, cluster, congeal, jellify 8 coagulum, thrombus 9 coagulate 10 gelatinize *combining form:* 6 thromb 7 thrombo
cloth see fabric
clothe 3 tog 4 clad, deck, do up, garb, robe 5 array, cloak, drape, dress, endue, equip, tog up 6 attire, bedeck, invest, mantle, outfit, rig out, swathe, tog out 7 apparel, bedrape, costume, dress up, garment, raiment, vesture 8 accouter, enclothe
clothes 3 rig 4 duds, garb, rags, togs 5 array, dress, getup 6 attire, outfit, things 7 apparel, costume, raiment, rigging, toggery, vesture 8 clothing 9 vestments 10 attirement 11 habiliments *basket:* 6 hamper *civilian:* 5 mufti *relating to:* 8 vestiary
clothes moth genus 5 Tinea
clothespress 3 kas 7 armoire 8 wardrobe
clothes tree 8 costumer
cloud 3 dim, fog, tar 4 army, blur, host, rout 5 addle, befog, crowd, flock, gloom, muddy, smear, sully, taint 6 legion, muddle, puzzle, scores, shadow, smudge 7 becloud, besmear, confuse, obscure, perplex, tarnish 8 befuddle, besmirch, discolor, distract, overcast 9 adumbrate, multitude *combining form:* 4 cirr 5 cirrh, cirri, cirro, nepho, nimbo 6 cirrhi, cirrho, nephel 7 nephelo *type:* 6 cirrus, nimbus 7 cumulus, stratus 11 altocumulus, altostratus 12 cirrocumulus, cirrostratus, cumulonimbus, nimbostratus 13 stratocumulus
cloudburst 6 deluge, shower 8 downpour, rainfall
clouded 4 open 5 shady 7 dubious, unclear 8 doubtful 9 ambiguous, equivocal, uncertain, unsettled 11 problematic
cloudless 4 fair, fine 5 clear, sunny 7 clarion 8 pleasant, rainless, sunshiny 10 undarkened
cloud-like mass 6 nebula
cloudy 4 dull, hazy 5 foggy, heavy, misty, mucky, murky, mushy, vague 6 vapory 7 louring 8 lowering, nubilous, overcast, vaporous
clough 3 gap 5 chasm, cleft, clove, gorge, gulch 6 arroyo, ravine
clout 2 in 3 box, hit 4 biff, chop, cuff, ding, drag, nail, poke, pull, slam, slap, slog, slug, sock 5 paste, punch, smack, smite, whack 6 buffet, strike 9 influence
clove 3 gap 5 chasm, cleft, gorge, gulch 6 arroyo, clough, ravine
clove hitch 4 knot
cloven-footed 8 fissiped
clover 5 lotus 6 alsike, ladino, lucern 7 alfalfa, berseem, lucerne, melilot, trefoil 8 four-leaf, shamrock 9 lespedeza *family:* 3 pea *genus:* 9 Trifolium
clown 3 wag 4 boor, fool, hick, jake, mime, rube, zany 5 chuff, churl, cutup, joker 6 jester, mucker, mummer, rustic 7 bucolic, buffoon, bumpkin, farceur, grobian, hayseed, hoosier 8 comedian, jokester 9 harlequin 10 mountebank 11 merry-andrew *French:* 7 pierrot *operatic:* 5 buffo *Spanish:* 8 gracioso
clownish 3 row 4 rude, zany 6 clumsy, gauche 7 awkward, boorish, ill-bred, loutish, lumpish, uncouth 8 churlish, cloddish 9 unrefined 10 uncultured, unpolished 11 uncivilized
cloy 4 fill, glut, jade, pall, sate 5 gorge 6 stodge 7 satiate, surfeit
club 3 bat 4 mace 5 baton, billy, guild, order, union 6 bistro, cudgel, league 7 society 8 bludgeon, sodality, sorority 9 truncheon 10 fellowship, fraternity, knobkerrie, nightstick 11 association, brotherhood *Australian:* 5 waddy *college:* 8 sorority 10 fraternity *combining form:* 5 clavi 6 rhopal 7 rhopalo *Irish:* 8 shillala 10 shillelagh *women's:* 7 sorosis
clubfoot 7 talipes
cluck 4 fowl, simp 5 dunce 6 dimwit, nitwit 7 lackwit, pinhead, wantwit 9 dumb bunny 13 featherweight
clue 3 cue 4 hint, post, tell, warn, wind 6 advise, fill in, inform, notify, notion, wise up 7 apprise, inkling 8 acquaint, telltale 10 indication, intimation, suggestion
clump 3 gob, lot, set, wad 4 body, clod, hunk, lump 5 array, barge, batch, bunch, chunk, group, hunch, stump 6 bundle, jumble, lumber, nugget, parcel 7 cluster, clutter, galumph, stumble 10 hodgepodge
clump of grass 4 tuft 6 tuffet
clumsy 5 bulky, gawky, inept, splay 6 gauche, klutzy, wooden 7 awkward, hulking, lumpish, uncouth, unhandy, unhappy 8 bumbling, ungainly, unwieldy 9 graceless, ham-handed, inelegant, lumbering, maladroit 10 bunglesome 11 heavy-handed
clumsy one 3 oaf 4 lout 5 klutz 6 lummox 7 bungler
clunk 4 thud 5 clonk, thump
clunker 4 heap 5 crate, wreck 6 jalopy, junker

cluster 3 lot, set 4 band, bevy, body, crew 5 array, batch, bunch, clump, covey, group, party 6 bundle, clutch, gather, parcel 7 collect, package, round up 8 assemble, assembly, cumulate 9 aggregate, associate 10 accumulate ***combining form:*** 3 cym, kym 4 cymo, kymo

cluster bean 4 guar

clutch 3 nab, set 4 body, grab, grip, hold, keep, take 5 array, batch, bunch, catch, clamp, clasp, clump, grasp, gripe, group, seize 6 bundle, clench, clinch, harbor, parcel, snatch, tenure 7 cherish, cluster, grapple ***Scottish:*** 5 cleek 7 claucht, claught

clutter 4 hash, mash, mess, muss, ruck 5 chaos, snarl 6 ataxia, huddle, jumble, jungle, litter, medley, muddle, tumble 7 mélange, rummage, shuffle 8 disarray, disorder, mishmash, scramble 9 confusion, macedoine 10 hodgepodge 12 huggermugger

Clydesdale 5 horse

Clymene ***father:*** 7 Oceanus ***husband:*** 7 Iapetus ***mother:*** 6 Tethys ***son:*** 5 Atlas 10 Epimetheus, Prometheus

Clytemnestra ***brother:*** 6 Castor, Pollux 10 Polydeuces ***daughter:*** 7 Electra 9 Iphigenia ***father:*** 9 Tyndareus ***husband:*** 9 Agamemnon ***lover:*** 9 Aegisthus ***mother:*** 4 Leda ***slayer:*** 7 Orestes ***son:*** 7 Orestes ***victim:*** 9 Agamemnon, Cassandra

Clytie ***beloved:*** 6 Apollo ***form:*** 9 sunflower 10 heliotrope

coach 5 stage, train, tutor 8 carriage 10 instructor

coadjutant 3 aid 4 aide 9 assistant 10 aide-decamp, lieutenant

coadjute 4 band 5 unite 6 concur, league 7 combine, conjoin 9 cooperate

coadjutor see **coadjutant**

coadunation 5 union 6 merger 7 melding, merging 8 mergence 9 coalition 11 combination, unification 13 consolidation

coagulate 3 dry, gel, set 4 clot, jell 5 jelly 6 curdle, freeze, gelate, harden 7 compact, congeal, jellify, thicken 8 coalesce, concrete, condense, solidify 9 dehydrate 10 gelatinize, inspissate 11 concentrate, consolidate

coal ***combining form:*** 7 anthrac, carboni 8 anthraco ***distillate:*** 3 tar ***dust:*** 4 coom, smut, soot 5 coomb, slack ***element:*** 6 carbon ***fused leavings:*** 4 slag 7 clinker ***glowing:*** 5 ember, gleed ***hard:*** 10 anthracite ***lump:*** 3 cob ***miner:*** 7 collier ***region:*** 4 Saar ***residue:*** 4 coke ***shaly:*** 9 tasmanite ***soft:*** 6 cannel 10 bituminous

coalesce 3 mix, wed 4 fuse, join, link 5 blend, cling, merge, stick, unite 6 adhere, cleave, mingle, relate 7 bracket, combine, conjoin, connect 9 associate

coalition 4 bloc, ring 5 party, union 6 league, merger 7 combine, faction, melding, merging 8 alliance, mergence 9 anschluss 10 federation 11 coadunation, combination, confederacy, unification 13 confederation, consolidation

coarse 3 low, raw 4 foul, rude 5 caked, cakey, crass, crude, dirty, gross, lumpy, nasty, rough, rowdy, tacky 6 common, filthy, grainy, incult, smutty, vulgar 7 boorish, obscene, raffish, raunchy, uncouth 8 granular, indecent, inexpert, prentice 9 inelegant, roughneck, unrefined, vulgarian 10 uncultured 11 particulate 12 scatological, uncultivated ***food:*** 6 fodder

coast 4 bank 5 beach, drift, shore, slide 6 strand 8 littoral ***of Antarctica:*** 4 Knox ***of west Africa:*** 5 Ivory ***swampy:*** 7 maremma

coastal 8 littoral

coaster 4 sled

coat 5 layer, plate, tunic 6 blazer, duster, jacket, patina, raglan, reefer, ulster, veneer 7 cutaway, paletot 8 covering, mackinaw, tegument 9 newmarket, redingote 10 integument ***animal:*** 3 fur 4 hide, pelt, wool 6 pelage ***arctic:*** 5 parka ***fur-lined:*** 7 pelisse ***glossy:*** 5 glacé ***kind:*** 3 car, pea, top 5 frock 6 trench ***Levantine:*** 6 caftan ***medieval:*** 8 gambeson ***of arms:*** 5 crest 6 blazon, emblem, shield, tabard 7 surcoat 8 blazonry 9 escucheon 10 escutcheon ***of egg white:*** 5 glair 6 glaire ***of gold:*** 4 gild, gilt ***of mail:*** 6 byrnie 7 hauberk ***Scottish:*** 4 jupe ***seaman's:*** 5 grego ***soldier's:*** 5 frock, tunic 6 capote ***waterproof:*** 7 slicker 10 mackintosh

coating 4 film 5 layer 6 finish, patina, veneer 7 lacquer 8 covering

coax 3 con, get 4 lure, urge 5 press, tease, tempt 6 cajole, entice, fleech, induce, pester, plague 7 blarney, prevail, wheedle 8 blandish, butter up, inveigle, persuade, soft-soap 9 importune, sweet talk ***Scottish:*** 7 cuittle

cob 3 cap 4 ding, swan 5 excel, horse, outdo 6 exceed 7 surpass 8 outmatch, outshine, outstrip

cobalt ***symbol:*** 2 Co

cobble 4 make, mend, mess 5 botch, patch, snafu, stone 6 bollix, bungle, foul up, goof up, mucker, repair 7 confuse, louse up, screw up, snarl up

cobbler 3 pie 4 fish 5 drink 7 catfish, pompano 9 shoemaker 10 threadfish

cobbler's form 4 last

cobelligerent 4 ally

cobweb 3 net 4 mesh, toil, trap 8 gossamer 12 entanglement

coccyx 8 tailbone

cochineal 3 dye 6 insect

cochleate 6 spiral 11 shell-shaped

cock 3 tap 4 bank, boss, gate, head, heap, hill, lord, mass, pile, rick 5 chief, drift, mound, stack, swank, swell, valve 6 faucet, honcho, leader, master, spigot 7 headman, hydrant, pyramid, rooster, swagger 8 hierarch, mountain 9 chieftain, dominator, number one, principal 10 preeminent 11 chanticleer, pontificate
cock-a-doodle-doo 4 blow, brag, crow, puff 5 boast, mouth, prate, vaunt 9 gasconade 11 rodomontade
cock-a-hoop 4 awry 5 askew 6 askant 7 askance 8 exultant, exulting, jubilant 9 crookedly, triumphal 10 triumphant
Cockaigne 4 Zion 6 heaven, utopia 7 arcadia 8 paradise 9 fairyland, Shangri-la 10 lubberland, wonderland 12 promised land
cockalorum 8 leapfrog 11 braggadocio
cockamamy 10 incredible, ridiculous
cock-and-bull story 3 fib, lie 6 canard 7 falsity, untruth 9 falsehood 13 prevarication
cockatoo bush 9 blueberry
cockcrow 4 dawn, morn 5 light, sunup 6 aurora 7 dawning, morning, sunrise 8 daybreak, daylight
cocker 4 baby 5 humor, spoil 6 coddle, cosset, pamper 7 cater to, indulge 11 mollycoddle
cockeyed 4 awry 5 askew, boozy, drunk 6 askant 7 askance, muddled 9 crookedly, disguised, pixilated, plastered 10 inebriated 11 intoxicated
cockle 4 fret 6 dimple, riffle, ripple
cockleshell 4 boat
cockscomb see **coxcomb**
cocksure 7 certain 8 positive 9 confident
cocktail 5 Bronx, drink, zombi 6 zombie 7 martini, Sazerac, sidecar 8 aperitif, daiquiri, pink lady, salty dog, sangrita, sombrero 9 aperitive, appetizer, Manhattan 10 Bloody Mary, Margharita ***fruit:*** 9 macedoine ***gasoline:*** 7 Molotov
cocktail lounge 3 bar, pub 6 saloon, tavern 7 barroom, gin mill, taproom 8 groggery, pothouse
Cocktail Party author 5 Eliot
coconspirator 7 abettor 9 accessory 10 accomplice 11 confederate
coconut meat 5 copra
coddle 4 baby 5 humor, spoil 6 cosset, cotton, pamper 7 cater to, indulge 11 mollycoddle
code 6 cipher 7 encrypt 8 encipher ***kind:*** 3 zip 4 area 5 Morse, penal ***message in:*** 10 cryptogram
code word see **communications code word**
codicil 5 rider 8 addendum, appendix 10 supplement
codswallop 8 nonsense
coefficient 8 coacting, coactive, conjoint, synergic 10 synergetic 11 cooperative
coelenterate 5 coral 7 hydroid 9 jellyfish 10 sea anemone
coerce 3 cow 4 make, push, urge 5 beset, bully, force 6 compel, menace, oblige 8 browbeat, bulldoze, threaten 9 blackjack, constrain, terrorize 10 intimidate
coercion 5 force 6 duress, menace, threat 8 menacing 10 compulsion, constraint 11 threatening
coeval see **contemporary**
coexistent see **contemporary**
coffee ***alkaloid:*** 7 caffein 8 caffeine ***bean:*** 3 nib ***cake:*** 6 kuchen ***cup:*** 9 demitasse ***cup holder:*** 4 zarf ***French:*** 4 café ***grinder:*** 4 mill ***kind:*** 4 drip, java 5 mocha 7 arabica, instant 8 espresso ***maker:*** 6 biggin 10 percolator ***pot:*** 3 urn
coffee shop 4 café 5 diner 8 snack bar 9 hash house, lunchroom 11 eating house, greasy spoon 12 luncheonette
coffer 5 chest 8 treasury, war chest 9 exchequer
coffin 3 box 4 kist 6 casket ***carrier:*** 6 hearse 10 pallbearer ***nail:*** 9 cigarette ***stand:*** 4 bier 10 catafalque
cogency 5 force, point, punch 7 bearing, concern 8 validity 9 relevance, validness 10 connection, pertinence 13 effectiveness
cogent 5 solid, sound, valid 6 potent 7 telling, weighty 8 forceful, forcible, powerful, puissant 9 justified 10 compelling, convincing, meaningful, persuasive, satisfying 11 influential, significant, well-founded 12 constraining, satisfactory, well-grounded 13 consequential
cogitate 4 plot 5 think 6 devise, reason 7 collude, connive, imagine, reflect 8 conceive, conspire, contrive, envisage, envision, intrigue 9 cerebrate, machinate, scheme out, speculate 10 deliberate
cogitation 7 thought 9 brainwork 10 reflection 11 cerebration, speculation 12 deliberation
cogitative 7 pensive 8 thinking 9 pondering 10 meditative, reflecting, reflective, ruminative, thoughtful 11 speculative 13 contemplative
cognate 4 akin 6 agnate, allied, common 7 connate, general, generic, kindred, related 8 incident 9 universal 10 affiliated, connatural 11 consanguine
cognition 9 knowledge 10 perception ***combining form:*** 5 gnosy 6 gnosia, gnosis
cognizance 4 heed, mark, note 6 notice, regard, remark 9 attention 10 observance 11 observation
cognizant 5 alive, awake, aware 7 know-

ing, witting 8 sensible, sentient 9 au courant, conscious 12 apprehensive

cognize 4 know 5 grasp 6 fathom 9 apprehend 10 appreciate, comprehend, understand

cognomen 4 name 5 style, title 7 epithet, moniker 11 appellation, appellative, designation 12 compellation, denomination

cognoscente 5 judge 6 critic, expert 8 aesthete 9 authority 10 dilettante, proficient, specialist 11 connoisseur

cognoscible 8 knowable

cohere 2 go 4 fuse, join 5 agree, blend, check, cling, fit in, merge, stick, unite 6 accord, cleave 7 combine, comport, conform, connect 8 check out, coalesce, dovetail 9 associate 10 correspond

coherence 4 bond 5 cling, union, unity 8 adhesion, clinging, cohesion, stickage, sticking 9 congruity, integrity 10 conformity, solidarity 11 consistency

coherent 7 unified 9 connected 10 consistent

cohesion see **coherence**

cohort 4 mate 6 fellow 7 partner, sectary 8 adherent, confrere, disciple, follower, henchman, partisan, sectator 9 associate, copartner, satellite, supporter 10 consociate

coif 3 cap 4 hood 6 hairdo 8 skullcap

coiffure 6 hairdo 9 headdress *aid:* 3 net, rat 5 snood

coil 4 curl, fuss, loop, ring, turn, wind 5 helix, twine, twist 6 furore, rotate, ruckus, rumpus, shindy, spiral, tumult, uproar 7 entwine, revolve, shindig, turmoil, wreathe 8 brouhaha, foofaraw 9 commotion, corkscrew *combining form:* 4 spir 5 spiri, spiro

coiled 7 tortile 9 circinate

coin 4 mint *Afghanistan:* 3 pul *Albania:* 3 lek *Algeria:* 5 dinar 7 centime *ancient Greek:* 4 obol *ancient Muslim:* 5 dinar *ancient Roman:* 6 follis 8 denarius *Argentina:* 4 peso 7 centavo *Australia:* 4 cent 6 dollar *Austria:* 8 groschen 9 schilling *Bahamas:* 4 cent 6 dollar *Bahrain:* 4 fils 5 dinar *Barbados:* 4 cent 6 dollar *Belgium:* 5 franc 7 centime *Benin:* 5 franc *Bhutan:* 7 chetrum 8 ngultrum *Bolivia:* 7 centavo *Botswana:* 4 pula 5 thebe *Brazil:* 7 centavo 8 cruzeiro *Bulgaria:* 3 lev 8 stotinka *Burundi:* 5 franc *Cameroon:* 5 franc *Canada:* 4 cent 6 dollar *Cape Verde Islands:* 6 escudo *Chile:* 4 peso 7 centavo *China:* 3 fen 4 jiao, yuan 5 chiao *Columbia:* 4 peso 7 centavo *Costa Rica:* 5 colon *Cuba:* 4 peso 7 centavo *Cyprus:* 4 cent 5 pound *Czechoslovakia:* 5 haler 6 koruna *defective:* 4 fido *Denmark:* 3 ore 5 krone *Dominican Republic:* 4 peso 7 centavo *Ecuador:* 5 sucre 7 centavo *edge:* 7 milling *Egypt:* 7 piastre 8 millieme *Ethiopia:* 4 cent *European gold:* 5 ducat *Fiji:* 4 cent 6 dollar *Finland:* 5 penni 6 markka *former:* 3 lek, mil, pie 4 anna, besa, cash, doit, duit, kran, para, pice 5 crown, fanam, litas, mohur, paisa, rupia, shahi, toman 6 centas, heller, kopeck, macuta, pagoda, tangka 7 santims, sapeque 8 farthing, maravedi, sixpence, skilling 9 half penny, rigsdaler 10 Indian head, reichsmark, threepence 13 reichspfennig *France:* 5 franc 7 centime *Gambia:* 5 butut 6 dalasi *Germany:* 4 mark 7 pfennig *Ghana:* 4 cedi 6 pesewa *Great Britain:* 6 guinea 8 new penny 9 sovereign *Greece:* 6 lepton 7 drachma *Guatemala:* 7 centavo, quetzal *Guinea-Bissau:* 4 peso *Guyana:* 4 cent 6 dollar *Haiti:* 6 gourde 7 centime *Honduras:* 7 centavo, lempira *Hungary:* 6 forint *Iceland:* 5 eyrir, krona *India:* 5 paisa, rupee *Indonesia:* 3 sen 6 rupiah *Iran:* 4 rial *Iraq:* 4 fils 5 dinar *Ireland:* 5 penny 8 farthing *Israel:* 5 agora 6 shekel *Italy:* 4 lira *Jamaica:* 4 cent 6 dollar *Japan:* 3 rin, sen, yen *Jordan:* 3 fil 5 dinar *Kenya:* 8 shilling *Korea, North:* 3 won 4 chon *Korea, South:* 3 won *Kuwait:* 4 fils *large:* 9 cartwheel *Lebanon:* 5 livre 7 piaster, piastre *Lesotho:* 4 loti *Liberia:* 4 cent 6 dollar *Libya:* 6 dirham *Luxembourg:* 5 franc *Madagascar:* 5 franc *Malawi:* 6 kwacha 7 tambala *Malta:* 4 cent 5 pound *Mauritania:* 7 ouguiya *Mauritius:* 4 cent 5 rupee *Mexico:* 4 peso 7 centavo *Monaco:* 5 franc *Morocco:* 6 dirham *Mozambique:* 7 metical *Nepal:* 5 paisa, rupee *Netherlands:* 4 cent 6 florin, gulden *New Zealand:* 4 cent 6 dollar *Nicaragua:* 7 centavo, cordoba *Nigeria:* 4 kobo *Norway:* 3 ore 5 krone *old Hungarian:* 5 pengo *old Italian:* 5 scudo *old Swedish:* 8 skilling *Oman:* 4 rial *Pakistan:* 4 pice 5 paisa *Panama:* 6 balboa 9 centesimo *Papua-New Guinea:* 4 kina, toea *Paraguay:* 7 centimo, guarani *Peru:* 4 inti 7 centimo *Philippines:* 4 piso 7 sentimo *Poland:* 5 grosz, zloty *Portugal:* 6 escudo 7 centavo *Qatar:* 6 dirhem *Roman:* 6 aureus, bezant 7 solidus *Romania:* 3 leu *Russia:* 5 kopek 6 rouble *Rwanda:* 5 franc *San Marino:* 4 lira *Saudi Arabia:* 6 halala *Seychelles:* 4 cent 5 rupee *side of a:* 7 obverse *Sierra Leone:* 4 cent *Singapore:* 4 cent 6 dollar *South Africa:* 4 cent, rand 10 krugerrand *Spain:* 6 peseta 7 centimo *Sri Lanka:* 4 cent 5 rupee *stamping metal:* 8 planchet *Suriname:* 4 cent 6 gulden *Swaziland:* 4 cent 9 lilangeni *Sweden:* 3 ore 5 krona *Switzerland:*

5 franc 6 rappen ***Syria:*** 5 pound ***Tanzania:*** 8 shilingi ***Thailand:*** 3 att 4 baht ***thick:*** 7 piefort 8 piedfort ***Tonga:*** 6 pa'anga, seniti ***Trinidad and Tobago:*** 4 cent 6 dollar ***Tunisia:*** 5 dinar ***Turkey:*** 4 lira 5 kurus ***Uganda:*** 8 shilling ***United Arab Emirates:*** 6 dirham ***United States:*** 4 dime 5 penny 6 dollar, nickel 7 quarter 10 half dollar ***Uruguay:*** 4 peso 9 centesimo ***Vatican City:*** 4 lira ***Venezuela:*** 7 bolivar ***Western Samoa:*** 4 sene, tala ***Zambia:*** 5 ngwee 6 kwacha ***Zimbabwe:*** 4 cent 6 dollar

coinage 9 invention, neologism 10 brainchild 11 contrivance

coincide 4 jibe 5 agree, equal, match, tally 6 accord, concur 7 concert, concord 9 harmonize 10 correspond

coincident 9 ancillary, attendant, attending, satellite 10 collateral 11 concomitant 12 accompanying

coincidentally 6 at once 8 together 12 concurrently

coin-shaped 8 nummular

colander's cousin 5 sieve 6 sifter 8 strainer

cold 3 icy, raw 4 cool, dead, iced 5 algid, bleak, brisk, chill, crisp, drear, frore, gelid, nippy, polar 6 arctic, biting, chilly, dismal, frigid, frosty, frozen, gloomy, somber, wintry 7 bracing, cutting, defunct, extinct, glacial, joyless, nipping, shivery 8 chilling, comatose, deceased, departed, freezing, heatless, lifeless 9 cheerless, chillsome, exanimate, inanimate, inhibited, senseless 10 impersonal, insensible, oppressive, undersexed 11 dispiriting, emotionless, inconscious, indifferent, passionless, unconscious, unemotional 12 matter-of-fact, unresponsive 13 unimpassioned, unsympathetic ***combining form:*** 3 cry, kry 4 cryo, kryo 5 frigo 7 psychro ***common:*** 6 coryza ***symptom:*** 5 cough, fever 6 sneeze 7 catarrh

cold ___ 3 war 4 cash, cuts, feet, fish, pack, room, sore, wave 5 cream, frame, front, patch, steel, sweat, water 6 turkey 7 storage 8 shoulder

cold-blooded 7 callous 8 hardened, obdurate 9 heartless, unfeeling 10 hardboiled, impersonal 11 emotionless, hardhearted 12 matter-of-fact, stonyhearted 13 unimpassioned

cold box 4 icer

cold feet 4 fear 5 alarm, dread, panic 6 dismay, fright, horror, terror 11 trepidation 13 consternation

coldhearted see **cold-blooded**

cold-shoulder 3 cut 4 snob, snub 9 ostracize

cold storage 7 latency 8 abeyance, abeyancy, doldrums, dormancy 10 quiescence, quiescency, suspension 12 intermission, interruption

cole 4 rape 7 cabbage 8 broccoli, kohlrabi 11 cauliflower

Coleridge poem 9 Kubla Khan 10 Christabel

Colette character 4 Gigi 5 Cheri 8 Claudine

colewort 4 kale 7 cabbage

colic 5 gripe 9 bellyache 11 stomachache 12 collywobbles

coliseum 4 bowl 5 stade 7 stadium

collapse 2 go 4 bend, cave, drop, fail, flag, give, tire, wilt 5 break, crash, droop, smash, weary, wreck, yield 6 cave in, fold up, peg out, weaken 7 breakup, crack-up, crumple, debacle, deflate, exhaust, failure, founder, give out, play out, ruining, shatter, smashup, succumb, undoing 8 flake out, languish 9 break-down, cataclysm, ruination 10 disruption 11 catastrophe, destruction 12 disintegrate

collar 3 bag, cop, get, nab, nip 4 hook, lift, nail, take 5 catch, steal 6 corner, secure 7 capture, prehend 8 bottle up 11 appropriate ***armor:*** 6 gorget ***boy's:*** 4 Eton ***chain:*** 4 torc 6 torque ***horse:*** 7 bargham ***jeweled:*** 6 carcan 8 carcanet ***lace-edged:*** 6 rabato, rebato ***medieval:*** 10 chevesaile ***metal:*** 4 torc 6 torque ***Philippine:*** 7 panuelo ***pleated:*** 4 ruff ***wooden:*** 4 cang 6 cangue

collarbone 8 clavicle

collate 7 arrange, bracket, compare 8 contrast 9 integrate

collateral 3 sub 5 under 6 allied 7 cognate, kindred, oblique, related, subject 8 adjuvant, circular, incident, indirect 9 accessory, ancillary, attendant, attending, auxiliary, dependent, satellite, secondary, tributary 10 circuitous, coincident, reciprocal, roundabout, subsidiary 11 adminicular, appurtenant, concomitant, subordinate, subservient 12 accompanying, confirmative, confirmatory, contributory, verificatory 13 complementary, corresponding, corroborative, corroboratory

colleague 3 pal 4 aide, chum 5 buddy, crony 6 fellow, helper 7 compeer, partner 8 confrere, co-worker 9 assistant, associate, companion, copartner 10 compatriot, consociate, workfellow

collect 4 draw, make, rank, rein 5 array, group, infer, judge, order, raise 6 deduce, deduct, derive, gather, muster 7 cluster, compile, compose, control, dispose, make out, marshal, round up 8 assemble, conclude, congress, restrain 10 congregate, rendezvous, simmer down

collected 4 calm, cool, easy, smug, sure

5 quiet, still 6 placid, poised, serene 7 assured 8 composed, peaceful, sanguine, tranquil 9 confident, easygoing, possessed, unruffled 10 complacent, nonchalant 11 unflappable 13 imperturbable, self-possessed, self-satisfied

collection 3 ana, kit, lot 4 band, bevy, clan, crew, olio, ruck 5 bunch, clump, crowd, group, hoard, party, trove 6 medley, muster, outfit 7 cluster, company, variety 8 assembly, caboodle 9 aggregate, amassment, colluvies, congeries, gathering 10 assemblage, assortment, cumulation, miscellany 11 aggregation 12 accumulation, congregation 13 agglomeration, armamentarium ***miscellaneous:*** 4 hash, olio 6 jumble, medley 7 mélange, mixture 8 mishmash, pastiche 9 bric-a-brac, potpourri 10 hodgepodge, salmagundi 11 olla podrida ***of anecdotes:*** 3 ana ***of animals:*** 3 zoo 9 menagerie ***of artistic works:*** 6 museum 7 gallery ***of clothes:*** 8 wardrobe ***of dried plants:*** 9 herbarium ***of facts:*** 4 data ***of literary pieces:*** 5 sylva 8 analecta, analects 9 anthology ***of proper names:*** 11 onomasticon ***of reports:*** 4 file 7 dossier ***of trinkets:*** 10 bijouterie ***suffix:*** 3 ery

collective ***association, Russian:*** 5 artel ***farm, Israeli:*** 7 kibbutz ***farm, Russian:*** 7 kolkhoz

collector ***of bird's eggs:*** 8 oologist ***of books:*** 11 bibliophile ***of coins:*** 11 numismatist ***of fares:*** 9 conductor ***of phonograph records:*** 10 discophile ***of stamps:*** 11 philatelist

colleen 4 girl, lass ***country:*** 4 Eire, Erin 7 Ireland

college ***building:*** 3 gym, lab 4 dorm, hall ***campus area:*** 4 quad 10 quadrangle ***class meeting:*** 3 lab 7 lecture, seminar 8 tutorial, workshop ***degree:*** 2 AA, AB, BA, BD, BS, CE, DD, MA, MD, MM, MS 3 BLS, DST, LLB, LLD, MBA, MEd, MFA, MLS, PhD 5 LittD ***graduate:*** 6 alumna, alumni (plural) 7 alumnae (plural), alumnus ***official:*** 4 dean 5 prexy 6 bursar, regent 7 proctor, provost, trustee 8 chairman, chaplain, director 9 counselor, librarian, president, registrar ***oldest in U.S.:*** 7 Harvard ***oldest women's in U.S.:*** 12 Mount Holyoke ***permit for absence:*** 5 exeat ***relating to:*** 8 academic 10 collegiate ***social group:*** 4 frat 8 sorority 10 fraternity ***song:*** 9 alma mater ***student class:*** 4 soph 5 frosh 6 junior, senior 8 freshman 9 sophomore ***teacher:*** 3 don 4 prof 5 tutor 8 academic 9 professor 10 instructor ***term:*** 7 quarter, session 8 semester 9 trimester ***VIP:*** 4 BMOC ***woman:*** 4 coed

college athletic team ***Air Force:*** 7 Falcons ***Alabama:*** 11 Crimson Tide ***Arizona:*** 8 Wildcats ***Arizona State:*** 9 Sun Devils ***Arkansas:*** 10 Razorbacks ***Arkansas State:*** 7 Indians ***Army:*** 6 Cadets ***Auburn:*** 6 Tigers ***Baylor:*** 5 Bears ***Boston College:*** 6 Eagles ***Boston University:*** 8 Terriers ***Brigham Young:*** 7 Cougars ***Brown:*** 6 Bruins ***California:*** 11 Golden Bears ***Central Michigan:*** 9 Chippewas ***Cincinnati:*** 8 Bearcats ***Citadel:*** 8 Bulldogs ***Clemson:*** 6 Tigers ***Colgate:*** 10 Red Raiders ***Colorado:*** 9 Buffaloes ***Colorado State:*** 4 Rams ***Columbia:*** 5 Lions ***Connecticut:*** 7 Huskies ***Cornell:*** 6 Big Red ***Dartmouth:*** 8 Big Green ***Davidson:*** 8 Wildcats ***Delaware State:*** 7 Hornets ***Drake:*** 8 Bulldogs ***Duke:*** 10 Blue Devils ***Eastern Kentucky:*** 8 Colonels ***Eastern Michigan:*** 6 Hurons ***Florida:*** 6 Gators ***Florida State:*** 9 Seminoles ***Fresno State:*** 8 Bulldogs ***Furman:*** 8 Palidans ***Georgia:*** 8 Bulldogs ***Georgia Tech:*** 13 Yellow Jackets ***Harvard:*** 7 Crimson ***Hawaii:*** 15 Rainbow Warriors ***Holy Cross:*** 9 Crusaders ***Houston:*** 7 Cougars ***Howard:*** 6 Bisons ***Idaho:*** 7 Vandals ***Idaho State:*** 7 Bengals ***Illinois:*** 6 Illini ***Illinois State:*** 8 Redbirds ***Indiana:*** 8 Hoosiers ***Indiana State:*** 9 Sycamores ***Iowa:*** 8 Hawkeyes ***Iowa State:*** 8 Cyclones ***Kansas:*** 8 Jayhawks ***Kansas State:*** 8 Wildcats ***Kent State:*** 13 Golden Flashes ***Kentucky:*** 8 Wildcats ***Lehigh:*** 9 Engineers ***Louisiana State:*** 6 Tigers ***Louisiana Tech:*** 8 Bulldogs ***Maine:*** 10 Black Bears ***Maryland:*** 5 Terps 9 Terrapins ***Massachusetts:*** 9 Minutemen ***Miami (Florida):*** 10 Hurricanes ***Miami (Ohio):*** 8 Redskins ***Michigan:*** 10 Wolverines ***Michigan State:*** 8 Spartans ***Minnesota:*** 7 Gophers ***Mississippi:*** 6 Rebels ***Mississippi State:*** 8 Bulldogs ***Missouri:*** 6 Tigers ***Montana:*** 9 Grizzlies ***Montana State:*** 7 Bobcats ***Navy:*** 10 Midshipmen ***Nebraska:*** 11 Cornhuskers ***Nevada:*** 6 Rebels 8 Wolfpack ***New Hampshire:*** 8 Wildcats ***New Mexico:*** 5 Lobos ***New Mexico State:*** 6 Aggies ***North Carolina:*** 8 Tar Heels ***North Carolina State:*** 8 Wolfpack ***Northeastern:*** 7 Huskies ***Northwestern:*** 8 Wildcats ***Notre Dame:*** 13 Fighting Irish ***Ohio State:*** 8 Buckeyes ***Ohio University:*** 7 Bobcats ***Oklahoma:*** 7 Sooners ***Oklahoma State:*** 7 Cowboys ***Oregon:*** 5 Ducks ***Oregon State:*** 7 Beavers ***Pennsylvania:*** 7 Quakers ***Pennsylvania State:*** 12 Nittany Lions ***Pittsburgh:*** 8 Panthers ***Princeton:*** 6 Tigers ***Purdue:*** 12 Boilermakers ***Rhode Island:*** 4 Rams ***Rice:*** 4 Owls ***Rutgers:*** 14 Scarlet Knights ***San Diego State:*** 6 Aztecs ***San Jose State:*** 8 Spartans ***South Carolina:*** 9 Gamecocks ***South Carolina State:*** 8 Bulldogs ***Southern California:*** 7 Trojans ***Southern Illinois:*** 7 Salukis ***Southern Methodist:*** 8 Mustangs ***Stanford:*** 9 Cardinals ***Syracuse:*** 9 Orangemen ***Temple:*** 4 Owls ***Tennessee:*** 10 Volunteers ***Tennessee State:*** 6 Tigers ***Tennessee Tech:*** 12 Golden Eagles ***Texas:*** 9 Longhorns ***Texas A&M:*** 6 Aggies ***Texas Christian:*** 11 Horned Frogs ***Texas Southern:*** 6 Tigers ***Texas Tech:*** 10 Red Raiders ***Toledo:*** 7 Rockets ***Tulane:*** 9 Green Wave ***UCLA:*** 6 Bruins ***UNLV:*** 12 Runnin' Rebels ***Utah:*** 4 Utes ***Utah State:*** 6 Aggies ***Vanderbilt:*** 10 Commodores ***Villanova:*** 8 Wildcats ***Virginia:*** 9 Cavaliers ***VMI:*** 7 Keydets ***VPI:*** 8 Gobblers ***Wake Forest:*** 12 Demon Deacons ***Washington:*** 7 Huskies ***Washington State:*** 7 Cougars ***West Virginia:*** 12 Mountaineers ***William & Mary:*** 7 Indians ***Wisconsin:*** 7 Badgers ***Wyoming:*** 7 Cowboys ***Yale:*** 4 Elis 8 Bulldogs

collide 3 hit, ram 4 bump 5 carom, clash, crash, smash 6 strike 7 impinge 8 conflict

collision 4 bump, jolt 5 clash, crash, shock, smash, wreck 6 impact, pileup 7 crack-up, smashup 10 concussion, percussion 11 destruction 12 demolishment

collocate 3 set 5 place 7 arrange 8 position

collogue 5 treat 6 advise, confab, confer, huddle, parley, powwow 7 consult 11 confabulate

colloid 3 gel, sol 4 agar 8 hydrogel, hydrosol

colloque 4 chat, chin, talk, yarn 5 visit 8 converse

colloquial 6 patois, vulgar 7 vulgate 8 familiar, informal 10 vernacular

colloquium 7 palaver, seminar 10 conference, rap session

colloquy 4 chat, talk 6 parley 7 palaver, seminar 8 converse, dialogue 10 conference, rap session 12 conversation 13 confabulation

collude 4 plot 6 devise 7 connive 8 cogitate, conspire, contrive, intrigue 9 machinate, scheme out

collusion 10 complicity, connivance

colluvies 4 hash 5 hoard, trove 6 jumble, medley 7 mélange 8 mishmash, pastiche 9 amassment, potpourri 10 assortment, collection, cumulation, hodgepodge, miscellany 11 aggregation 12 accumulation 13 agglomeration

collywobbles 5 colic, gripe 9 bellyache 11 stomachache

Colombia ***capital:*** 6 Bogota ***highest peak:*** 9 Cristobal ***monetary unit:*** 4 peso

Colonel Blimp 10 fuddy-duddy 12 stuffed shirt

colonnade 4 stoa

color 3 dye, hue 4 cast, flag, glow, jack, pink, rose, show, tint, tone 5 belie, blush, flush, paint, rouge, shade, stain, tinct, tinge, twist 6 banner, ensign, mantle, pennon, pinken, redden, stance 7 crimson, distort, falsify, pennant, pigment 8 attitude, disguise, dyestuff, gonfalon, misstate, overdraw, position, standard, streamer, tincture 9 embellish, embroider, oriflamme, overpaint, overstate, semblance 10 exaggerate 12 chromaticity, misrepresent ***band:*** 5 facia, vitta 6 fascia ***combining form:*** 5 chrom 6 chromo 7 chromat 8 chromato 9 chromasia ***primary:*** 3 red 4 blue 6 yellow ***relating to:*** 9 chromatic ***secondary:*** 5 green 6 orange, purple ***soft:*** 6 pastel

Colorado ***academy, college:*** 5 Regis 10 U.S. Air Force ***capital:*** 6 Denver ***nickname:*** 15 Centennial State ***park:*** 5 Estes ***state bird:*** 11 lark bunting ***state flower:*** 9 columbine

colorant 3 dye 5 stain 7 pigment 8 dyestuff, tincture

coloration ***combining form:*** 6 chroia, chromy 7 chromia

colored 6 biased, warped 7 bigoted, partial 8 one-sided, partisan 9 jaundiced 10 prejudiced 11 tendentious 12 prepossessed ***combining form:*** 6 chroic, chrome 7 chromat, chroous 8 chromato

colorful 3 gay 5 gaudy, showy, vivid 6 bright, flashy, florid, garish 7 splashy

coloring 4 face, mask, show 5 front, guise, put-on 6 facade 8 disguise 9 hyperbole, semblance 12 embroidering, exaggeration 13 embellishment, overstatement

coloring matter ***combining form:*** 5 phyll

colorist 6 tinter

colorless 3 wan 4 ashy, drab, dull, flat, pale 5 ashen, livid, lurid, prosy, waxen, white 6 albino, doughy, pallid 7 insipid, neutral, prosaic 8 abstract, blanched, detached, lifeless, tintless 10 achromatic, impersonal, lackluster, lusterless, poker-faced 11 unpassioned 13 disinterested, dispassionate, unimaginative ***combining form:*** 4 leuc, leuk 5 leuco, leuko

colossal 4 huge, vast 7 mammoth, titanic 8 gigantic 9 cyclopean, monstrous 10 behemothic, gargantuan 11 elephantine

Colossus of 6 Rhodes

colporteur 7 apostle 9 missioner 10 evangelist, missionary 12 propagandist

colt 4 tyro 6 novice, rookie 8 beginner, freshman, neophyte, newcomer 9 fledgling, novitiate

coltish 6 elvish, frisky, impish 7 larkish, playful, puckish, waggish 10 frolicsome 11 mischievous

columbary 8 dovecote, pigeonry 9 dovehouse 11 culverhouse, pigeon house

Columbine ***beloved:*** 9 Harlequin ***father:*** 9 Pantaloon
columbium ***symbol:*** 2 Cb
Columbus ***birthplace:*** 5 Genoa ***patron:*** 8 Isabella 9 Ferdinand ***ship:*** 4 Nina 5 Pinta 10 Santa Maria ***son:*** 5 Diego ***starting point:*** 5 Palos
column 3 row 4 pier, prop 5 brace, shore 6 pillar 7 support 8 buttress, pilaster 11 underpinner 12 underpinning 13 underpropping ***base:*** 4 ordo 5 socle 6 plinth 9 stylobate ***bulge:*** 7 entasis ***female figure:*** 8 caryatid ***male figure:*** 5 atlas 7 telamon 8 atlantes (plural) ***style:*** 5 Doric, Ionic 10 Corinthian ***top:*** 7 capital 8 chapiter
coma 5 faint, sleep, swoon 6 stupor, torpor 7 languor, slumber, syncope 8 blackout, dullness, hebetude, lethargy 9 lassitude, torpidity
comate 3 pal 4 chum 5 buddy, crony 7 comrade 9 associate, companion 11 running mate
comatose 5 dopey, heavy 6 stupid, torpid 8 sluggish 9 lethargic, senseless 10 insensible, slumberous 11 inconscious, unconscious 12 hebetudinous
comb 4 grub, rake, sift, sort 5 probe, scour 6 forage, search, winnow 7 ransack, rummage 8 finecomb, separate 11 investigate ***combining form:*** 4 loph 5 lopho 6 pectin 7 pectini
combat 3 war 4 buck, duel 5 fight, repel 6 action, battle, oppose, resist, strife 7 contend, contest, dispute, service 8 traverse 9 withstand
combating ***prefix:*** 4 anti
combative 7 warlike 8 militant, vigorous 9 agonistic, bellicose, truculent 10 pugnacious 11 belligerent, contentious, quarrelsome 12 gladiatorial
combativeness 5 fight 6 attack 9 pugnacity 10 aggression 11 bellicosity 12 belligerence
combe 4 dale, glen, vale 6 valley
combination 4 bloc, pool, ring 5 party, tie-up, union 6 hookup, merger 7 cahoots, faction, melding, merging 8 alliance, mergence 9 aggregate, coalition 10 connection 11 affiliation, association, coadunation, conjunction, partnership, unification 13 consolidation ***combining form:*** 4 hapt 5 hapto
combine 3 add, mix, wed 4 band, bloc, fuse, join, link, pool, ring 5 blend, chain, group, merge, party, trust, unify, union, unite 6 cartel, concur, embody, league, mingle, relate 7 bracket, conjoin, connect, faction 8 coadjute, coalesce 9 associate, coalition, commingle, cooperate, integrate, syndicate 10 amalgamate 11 consolidate, incorporate 12 conglomerate ***Japanese:*** 8 zaibatsu
combined action 7 synergy 8 synergia
combust 4 burn 10 incinerate
combustible 4 edgy, fuel 8 agitable, burnable, skittery, skittish, volatile 9 alarmable, excitable, flammable, ignitable, startlish 11 inflammable ***material:*** 3 gas, oil 4 coal, peat, wood 6 tinder
come 4 flow, grow, near, show, stem 5 add up, arise, get in, issue, occur, reach, run to, sum to, total 6 amount, arrive, befall, betide, happen, number, show up, spring, turn up 7 advance, develop, emanate, proceed 8 approach, hail from 9 aggregate, originate, transpire 10 derive from ***a cropper:*** 4 fail, fall ***across:*** 4 find, meet 8 discover 9 encounter ***apart:*** 12 disintegrate ***at:*** 6 attack, attain ***away:*** 5 leave 6 depart ***before:*** 7 precede ***between:*** 9 interfere, interpose ***clean:*** 7 confess ***down from:*** 6 alight ***forth:*** 5 issue 6 appear, emerge ***forward:*** 9 volunteer ***from:*** 6 derive, result ***into:*** 5 enter 7 acquire ***near:*** 5 verge 8 approach ***round:*** 5 rally 7 get well, recover ***to pass:*** 5 occur 6 happen ***up:*** 5 arise ***upon:*** 4 find, meet 6 affect, attack 7 afflict 8 discover 9 encounter
comeback 6 retort 7 riposte 8 repartee
come by 3 see 4 call, gain 5 pop in, run in, visit 6 attain, drop in, look in, look up, step in 7 acquire, inherit
comedian 3 wag, wit 4 card, zany 5 comic, droll, joker 6 jester 8 funnyman, humorist, jokester, quipster
comedo 9 blackhead
comedown 4 fall, ruin 5 crash 7 descent, setback 8 collapse
come down with 3 get 5 catch 8 contract
comedy 5 humor 8 drollery 9 drollness, funniness, wittiness 10 comicality 12 humorousness
come in 5 enter, reply 6 answer, rejoin, retort, return 7 ingress, respond 9 penetrate
comely 4 fair, nice 5 bonny, sonsy 6 lovely, pretty, proper, seemly, sonsie 7 correct 8 becoming, decorous, handsome 9 beauteous, beautiful, befitting, civilized 10 attractive 11 good-looking
come off 3 hap 5 break, click, occur 6 befall, betide, go over, happen, pan out 7 develop, succeed 8 prove out
come-off 6 escape 7 elusion, evasion 8 escaping, eschewal, shunning 9 avoidance, runaround
come-on 4 bait, lure, trap 5 cheat, decoy, rogue, snare 6 con man, gypper 8 swindler 9 trickster 10 allurement, enticement, seducement, temptation 11 flimflammer

12 bunco steerer, double-dealer, inveiglement 13 confidence man
come out 4 leak 5 break, debut 6 emerge 9 transpire
come out with 3 say 4 tell 5 state, utter 7 declare, deliver
comestible 6 edible 7 eatable 8 esculent
comestibles 4 feed, food, grub 6 viands 7 edibles 8 victuals 9 provender 10 provisions
come through 6 chip in, kick in 7 pitch in, ride out, survive 9 subscribe 10 contribute
come together 4 meet 7 synapse 8 converge
comeuppance 3 due 5 lumps, merit 6 rights 7 deserts 9 deserving
comfort 3 aid 4 help, lift 5 cheer 6 assist, buck up, relief, solace, succor 7 amenity, condole, console, relieve, secours, support, upraise 8 facility, reassure 10 assistance, sympathize 11 commiserate, convenience
comfortable 4 cozy, easy, homy, snug, soft 5 comfy, cushy, homey 6 loungy 7 content, easeful, pleased, restful, welcome, well-off 8 adequate, homelike, pleasant, pleasing, well-to-do 9 agreeable, competent, satisfied, sufficing, well-fixed 10 gratifying, prosperous, sufficient, well-heeled 11 substantial 12 satisfactory
comforter 4 pouf, puff 5 quilt 9 eiderdown
comfortless 5 harsh 7 uncomfy 12 inconsolable 13 discomforting
comfy 4 cozy, easy, homy, snug, soft 5 cushy, homey 7 easeful 8 homelike 11 comfortable
comic 3 wag, wit 5 antic, droll, funny, joker 6 jester 7 risible 8 comedian, farcical, funnyman, gelastic, humorist, jokester, quipster 9 laughable, ludicrous 10 ridiculing, ridiculous *strip:* 7 funnies
comical 4 zany 5 droll, funny, silly 6 absurd, impish 7 foolish, risible, roguish, waggish 8 farcical, gelastic, sportive 9 laughable, ludicrous 10 ridiculous
coming 4 next 6 advent 7 arrival, ensuing, nearing 9 following 11 approaching *forth:* 7 issuant
comity 5 amity 7 concord, harmony 8 goodwill 10 friendship, kindliness 11 benevolence, camaraderie, comradeship 12 friendliness
comma 4 lull 5 pause 8 interval 9 pausation
command 3 bid, law 4 rule, sway, tell, warn, word 5 canon, might, order, power, skill 6 adjure, behest, charge, compel, direct, enjoin, manage 7 ability, bidding, captain, conduct, control, dictate, know-how, mandate, mastery, precept, statute 9 authority, constrain, direction, directive, expertise, expertism, ordinance 10 domination, expertness, injunction, mastership 11 instruction 12 jurisdiction *to go:* 4 mush 6 avaunt, begone, giddap *to stop:* 4 whoa 5 avast
commandeer 4 take 5 annex, seize, usurp 6 assume 7 preempt 8 accroach, arrogate 9 sequester 10 confiscate 11 appropriate, expropriate
commander 4 boss, head 6 honcho, leader, master 7 captain, general, headman, officer 8 decurion, hierarch 9 dominator
commandment 3 law 4 rule 5 edict, order 6 decree 7 mitsvah, mitzvah, precept, statute
Commedia dell' ___ 4 Arte
comme il faut 4 nice 5 right 6 decent, proper, seemly 7 correct 8 becoming, decorous 9 befitting 10 conforming
commemorate 4 keep 7 observe 8 monument 9 celebrate, solemnize 11 memorialize 13 monumentalize
commemorative 8 memorial
commence 4 open 5 arise, begin, enter, start 6 launch, take up 7 kick off, lead off 8 embark on 9 originate 10 embark upon, inaugurate
commencement 4 dawn 5 alpha, birth, onset, start 6 outset 7 dawning, genesis, opening 8 outstart 9 beginning
commend 4 hail, laud 5 extol 6 commit, kudize, praise, tender 7 acclaim, applaud, approve, confide, consign, entrust, proffer 8 hand over, relegate, turn over 10 compliment
commendable 6 worthy 8 laudable 9 admirable, deserving, estimable, meritable, praisable 11 meritorious, thankworthy 12 praiseworthy
commensurable see commensurate
commensurate 4 even 5 equal 11 symmetrical 12 proportional
comment 4 note 6 notice, remark, review 7 observe 8 critique, reviewal 9 criticism 10 animadvert 11 observation 12 obiter dictum
commerce 5 trade, truck 7 contact, traffic 8 business, congress, dealings, exchange, industry 9 communion 11 interchange, intercourse 13 communication
commercial 2 ad 8 business 10 mercantile 13 advertisement
commie 3 Red 9 Bolshevik, communist
commination 5 curse 7 malison 8 anathema 11 imprecation, malediction
commingle 3 mix 5 immix, merge, unify 8 compound, intermix 9 integrate 10 amalgamate
comminute 4 bray, buck 5 crush 6 powder 9 pulverize, triturate 12 contriturate

commiserable 4 poor 6 rueful 7 piteous, pitiful 8 pathetic, pitiable
commiserate 4 ache, pity 7 feel for 10 sympathize 13 compassionate
commiseration 3 rue 4 pity, ruth 8 sympathy 10 compassion
commission 3 bid 4 name 5 board, order 6 charge, depute, enable, enjoin 7 appoint, command, council, empower, license 8 accredit, delegate, deputize, instruct, nominate 9 authorize, designate
commit 2 do 5 allot 6 assign, invest, ordain 7 commend, confide, consign, entrust, execute, perform, pull off, trustee 8 hand over, relegate, turn over 10 perpetuate
commitment 4 duty, must, need 5 ought 6 charge, devoir 10 obligation
committal see commitment
commixture 6 fusion 7 compost 9 composite 11 interfusion
commodious 4 wide 5 ample, roomy 8 spacious 9 capacious
commodities 5 goods, items, wares 6 things 8 articles 9 vendibles 11 merchandise
common 4 flat, park, poor 5 cheap, joint, plaza, prosy, stale, tatty, trite, typic, usual 6 decent, garden, impure, mutual, normal, paltry, shared, shoddy, sleazy, square, trashy 7 defiled, general, generic, natural, prosaic, regular, routine, typical 8 adequate, all right, communal, conjoint, conjunct, déclassé, everyday, familiar, frequent, inferior, low-grade, ordinary 9 customary, pleasance, prevalent, tolerable, universal 10 desecrated, second-rate, sufficient, uneventful, unexciting 11 intermutual, second-class 12 matter-of-fact, satisfactory, second-drawer, unnoteworthy 13 unexceptional, unimpeachable, uninteresting *combining form:* 3 cen 4 caen, ceno, coen 5 caeno, coeno
commonalty 3 mob 5 plebs 6 masses, people, plebes, public, rabble 7 commune 8 populace 9 hoi polloi, multitude, plebeians 11 proletariat, rank and file, third estate
commoners see commonalty
commonition 6 caveat 7 caution, warning 11 forewarning
commonplace 5 lowly, tired, trite, usual 6 cliché, normal, truism 7 bromide, clichéd, general, inanity, mundane, natural, prosaic, regular, typical, workday 8 banality, bromidic, chestnut, everyday, ordinary, prosaism, shopworn, timeworn, well-worn, workaday 9 platitude, prevalent, triteness 10 prosaicism, shibboleth, stereotype, threadbare, uneventful 11 stereotyped 12 unnoteworthy 13 stereotypical, unexceptional
common sense 6 wisdom 8 gumption, judgment
Common Sense author 5 Paine
commorancy 4 home 5 abode, house 8 domicile, dwelling 9 residence, residency 10 habitation
commotion 3 din, row 4 coil, flap, fuss, moil, riot, stew, stir, to-do 5 hurly, storm, upset, whirl 6 bustle, clamor, dither, flurry, fracas, furore, hassle, hoopla, hubbub, hurrah, lather, outcry, pother, racket, ruckus, rumpus, shindy, tow-row, tumult, uproar, upturn 7 clatter, ferment, fluster, ruction, shindig, turmoil, whoopla 8 brouhaha, disquiet, foofaraw, rowdydow, upheaval, uprising 9 agitation, confusion 10 convulsion, hullabaloo, hurly-burly, turbulence 11 pandemonium 12 perturbation
commove 5 elate 6 excite 7 inspire 9 stimulate 10 exhilarate
communal 5 joint 6 common, mutual, public, shared 8 conjoint, conjunct 11 intermutual
commune 6 confer 8 commerce, converse, district 10 collective 12 conversation *Israeli:* 7 kibbutz *Russian:* 3 mir 7 kolkhoz
communicable 8 catching 9 expansive, garrulous, talkative 10 contagious, infectious
communicate 4 abut, join, tell 5 touch, verge 6 adjoin, border, butt on, convey, impart, pass on, reveal, signal 7 contact, divulge 8 disclose, neighbor, transmit
communication 4 talk, word 7 contact, message, missive, talking 8 commerce, converse, exchange 9 directive 10 conversing, discussing, discussion 11 interchange, intercourse 12 conversation *means:* 2 TV 4 drum, note 5 media, phone, radio 6 letter, medium, pigeon, speech 9 telegraph, telephone 10 television *system:* 8 language
communications code word 4 Alfa, Echo, Golf, Kilo, Lima, Mike, Papa, Xray, Zulu 5 Bravo, Delta, Hotel, India, Oscar, Romeo, Tango 6 Quebec, Sierra, Victor, Yankee 7 Charlie, Foxtrot, Juliett, Uniform, Whiskey 8 November
communicative 7 voluble 9 expansive, garrulous, talkative 10 loquacious
communion 4 cult, sect 5 creed, faith, truck 6 church 7 contact, traffic 8 commerce, converse, dealings, religion 10 connection, persuasion 11 intercourse 12 denomination *cloth:* 8 corporal *cup:* 3 ama 7 chalice *plate:* 5 paten
communism 8 Leninism 10 bolshevism
Communist 3 red 5 pinko 6 commie 7 comrade, Marxist 8 Leninist 9 Bolshevik, Stalinist 10 Trotskyist

Communist leader ***Chinese:*** **10** Mao Tse-tung ***Russian:*** **5** Lenin **6** Stalin **7** Trotsky **10** Khrushchev

community **4** city, town **6** people, public **7** enclave, society **12** neighborhood ***ecological:*** **10** biocenosis

commute **5** alter **6** change, travel **7** convert **8** exchange, transfer **9** transform, translate, transmute, transpose **10** compensate, substitute **11** interchange, transfigure **12** metamorphose, transmogrify

compact **4** bond, firm, hard **5** close, dense, pithy, thick, tight, unify **6** packed **7** bargain, bunched, crowded **8** compress, condense, contract, covenant **9** agreement, integrate **10** convention **11** concentrate, consolidate, transaction **12** epigrammatic ***combining form:*** **4** pycn **5** pycno

companion **3** pal **4** chum, fere, mate, twin **5** buddy, crony, match **6** attend, cohort, comate, double, escort, fellow **7** comrade, conduct, consort, partner **8** chaperon, helpmate, helpmeet **9** accompany, associate, colleague, duplicate **10** coordinate, reciprocal **11** concomitant, consort with, running mate **13** accompaniment

companionable **6** social **7** amiable **8** sociable **9** convivial **11** good-natured

companionship **7** company, society **10** fellowship

company **3** mob **4** band, club, crew, firm, gang, pack, ruck, team **5** corps, group, house, party, troop **6** attend, clique, convoy, guests, muster, outfit, troupe **7** concern, conduct, coterie, society, visitor **8** assembly, business, chaperon, visitors **9** companion, gathering **10** assemblage, collection, enterprise, fellowship **11** aggregation, association, camaraderie, comradeship **12** congregation, consociation **13** companionship, establishment

comparable **4** akin, like **5** alike **6** agnate **7** similar, uniform **8** parallel **9** consonant **13** corresponding, undifferenced

comparative **4** near **8** relative **11** approximate ***suffix:*** **2** er

compare **5** liken, match **6** equate **7** bracket, collate, paragon **8** contrast, parallel **9** correlate **10** assimilate

comparison **6** simile **7** analogy **8** affinity, likeness **9** alikeness, semblance **10** similarity, similitude **11** resemblance

compass **3** get, hem, see, win **4** gain, gird, ring **5** ambit, annex, catch, field, grasp, orbit, range, reach, round, scope, sweep **6** bounds, circle, domain, extent, girdle, limits, obtain, radius, secure, sphere, take in **7** acquire, circuit, environ, procure, purview **8** boundary, confines, encircle, environs, purlieus, surround **9** apprehend, enclosure, extension, perimeter, periphery, precincts **10** comprehend, understand **13** circumference ***kind:*** **4** gyro **5** solar **8** lensatic, magnetic ***stand:*** **8** binnacle

compassion **3** rue **4** pity, ruth **5** mercy **7** charity, empathy **8** clemency, humanity, sympathy **10** humaneness **11** benevolence **13** commiseration, fellow feeling

compassionate **4** pity, warm **6** humane, tender **7** clement, feel for **10** responsive **11** commiserate, kindhearted, softhearted, sympathetic, warmhearted

compassionless **5** stony **7** callous **8** obdurate **9** heartless, unfeeling **11** cold-blooded, hardhearted, ironhearted **12** stony-hearted

compass point **2** NE, NW, SE, SW **3** ENE, ESE, NNE, NNW, SSE, SSW, WNW, WSW **4** east, west **5** north, rhumb, south ***Scottish:*** **4** airt

compatible **6** proper **8** suitable **9** agreeable, congenial, congruous, consonant **10** consistent **11** sympathetic

compatriot **7** compeer **8** confrere **9** associate, colleague

compeer see **compatriot**

compel **4** hale, make, urge **5** drive, force **6** coerce, impose, oblige **7** concuss, enforce **9** constrain ***Scottish:*** **3** gar

compellation **4** name **5** nomen, style, title **7** moniker **8** cognomen **11** appellative, designation **12** denomination

compendious **4** curt **5** brief, short **7** compact, concise, laconic, summary **8** succinct **12** breviloquent **13** short and sweet

compendium **5** brief, guide **6** aperçu, digest, manual, précis, sketch, survey **7** pandect, sylloge **8** Baedeker, handbook, overview, syllabus **9** guidebook, vade mecum **10** abridgment, conspectus **11** enchiridion

compensate **3** pay **5** repay **6** make up, offset, redeem, set off **7** balance, guerdon, requite **8** atone for, outweigh **9** indemnify, reimburse **10** counteract, neutralize, recompense, remunerate **11** countervail **12** counterpoise

compensation **6** amends, reward, salary **7** payment, redress **8** reprisal, requital, solatium **9** indemnity, quittance **10** recompense, reparation **11** restitution

compete **3** vie **5** fight, match, rival **6** battle, strive **7** contend, contest, dispute, emulate, tourney **8** rivalize, struggle

competence **5** might **6** enough **7** ability **8** adequacy, capacity **10** capability **11** sufficiency **13** qualification, qualifiedness

competent **4** able **5** adept **6** au fait, decent, enough, proper **7** capable, skilled **8** adequate, masterly **9** qualified, sufficing

10 sufficient 11 comfortable 12 satisfactory

competition 4 game, meet 5 match, rival 6 strife 7 contest, rivalry, warfare 8 concours, conflict, corrival, striving, struggle, tug-of-war 9 emulation, rencontre

competitor 5 rival 8 corrival, opponent 9 adversary 10 antagonist, contestant

compile 4 edit 6 gather, muster, select 7 collect 8 assemble

complacence see **complacency**

complacency 5 pride 6 egoism 7 conceit, egotism 9 vainglory 10 narcissism 11 amour propre, consequence 13 conceitedness

complacent 4 smug 7 assured 8 egoistic, priggish 9 conceited, confident, egotistic 11 self-assured, self-pleased 13 self-confident, self-contented, self-possessed, self-satisfied

complain 3 nag 4 crab, fuss, kick, wail 5 gripe, grump, whine 6 grouch, grouse, murmur, pester, repine, yammer 7 grizzle, grumble, protest 9 bellyache

complainer 4 crab 5 crank 6 griper, grouch, kicker 7 grouser 8 grumbler, sourpuss 10 malcontent 11 faultfinder

complaint 3 ill 5 gripe 6 malady 7 ailment, disease, protest 8 disorder, sickness, syndrome 9 affection, condition, infirmity

complaisant 4 easy, mild 7 amiable, lenient 8 generous, obliging 9 agreeable, indulgent 11 good-humored, good-natured 12 good-tempered

complement 4 crew 7 pendant 9 correlate 10 enrichment, supplement 11 counterpart, enhancement 12 augmentation 13 accompaniment

complementary *prefix:* 7 counter

complete 3 end 4 done, full, halt 5 close, ended, gross, total, uncut, utter, whole 6 choate, entire, finish, wind up, wrap up 7 achieve, fulfill, perfect, perform, plenary, through 8 absolute, conclude, finished, integral, outright, realized, thorough, totalize, ultimate, undocked, whole-hog 9 concluded, determine, discharge, downright, full-dress, implement, out-and-out, terminate 10 accomplish, consummate, exhaustive, terminated, unabridged 11 uncondensed, unmitigated 13 thoroughgoing, unabbreviated *combining form:* 3 hol, tel 4 holo, tele, telo 5 teleo

completed 4 done, over 5 ended 7 through 8 finished 9 concluded 10 terminated

completion 3 end 6 finish *combining form:* 6 teleut 7 teleuto

complex 5 vague 6 daedal, knotty, system, varied 7 gordian, mixed-up, network, obscure 8 baffling, compound, confused, involved, puzzling 9 Byzantine, composite, confusing, elaborate, intricate 10 mysterious, mystifying, perplexing 11 bewildering, complicated, confounding 12 labyrinthine 13 heterogeneous, sophisticated

complexion 3 hue 4 tint 5 color, humor, tinge 6 makeup, nature, temper 8 tincture 9 character 11 disposition, personality, temperament 13 individualism, individuality

complexionless 4 ashy, pale 5 ashen, livid, lurid, waxen 6 doughy, pallid 8 blanched 9 colorless

compliance 8 docility 9 obedience 10 conformity 11 amenability, resignation 12 acquiescence, tractability

complicate 5 mix up, ravel, snarl, upset 6 jumble, muddle, tangle 7 perplex 8 disorder, entangle 10 disarrange

complicated 4 hard 5 fancy 6 daedal, knotty 7 complex, gordian 8 abstruse, involved 9 Byzantine, elaborate, intricate, recondite 12 labyrinthine 13 sophisticated

complicity 9 collusion 10 connivance 11 involvement

compliment 4 hail, kudo, laud 6 kudize, praise 7 acclaim, applaud, bouquet, commend, orchids, tribute 8 accolade, encomium 9 laudation, recommend 12 commendation

complimentary 4 free 6 gratis 8 costless 10 chargeless, gratuitous

comply 4 keep, mind, obey 6 follow, submit 7 conform, observe 9 acquiesce

component 4 part 6 factor 7 element 10 ingredient 11 constituent

comport 3 act 4 bear, go on, quit 5 agree, carry, check, fit in, tally 6 accord, acquit, behave, demean, square 7 conduct 8 dovetail 9 harmonize 10 correspond

comportment 3 air, set 4 mien 5 tenue 7 address, bearing, conduct 8 behavior, demeanor, presence

compose 4 balm, calm, cool, form, lull, make, rein 5 allay, quiet, relax, still, verse, write 6 becalm, create, devise, indite, invent, make up, settle, solace, soothe 7 collect, comfort, console, contain, control, dream up, repress, versify 8 comprise, melodize, mitigate, moderate, modulate, restrain, suppress, tune down 9 originate, re-collect 10 constitute, simmer down 11 tranquilize *type:* 3 set

composed 4 calm, cool, easy 5 quiet, staid, still 6 placid, poised, sedate, serene 8 tranquil 9 collected, easygoing, possessed, repressed, unruffled 10 nonchalant, suppressed 11 unflappable 13 imperturbable, self-possessed

composer 4 bard, poet 5 odist 6 author, lyrist, penman, scorer, writer 7 elegist, hymnist 8 compiler, essayist, lyricist, melodist, monodist, novelist 9 balladist, dramatist, harmonist, scenarist, songsmith, tunesmith, wordsmith 10 compositor, typesetter ***American:*** 3 Kay 4 Cage, Cash, Hill, Ives, Kern, Work 5 Arlen, Bland, Bloch, Cohan, Dylan, Friml, Glass, Gould, Grofé, Handy, Mason, Moore, Sousa, Still 6 Barber, Berlin, Cowell, Emmett, Foster, Hanson, Harris, Joplin, McKuen, Morton, Oliver, Parker, Piston, Porter, Seeger, Taylor, Varese 7 Babbitt, Brubeck, Copland, Gilbert, Gilmore, Goldman, Guthrie, Herbert, Loesser, Maxwell, Menotti, Rodgers, Romberg, Schuman, Thomson, Tiomkin 8 Billings, Burleigh, Damrosch, Gershwin, Kreisler, Sessions, Sondheim, Spalding, Williams 9 Bacharach, Bernstein, Ellington, Ledbetter, MacDowell 10 Blitzstein, Gottschalk ***Argentinian:*** 9 Ginastera ***Australian:*** 8 Grainger ***Austrian:*** 4 Berg, Wolf 5 Haydn 6 Czerny, Mahler, Mozart, Straus, Sulzer, Webern 7 Strauss 8 Bruckner, Schubert 9 Schönberg ***Belgian:*** 5 Ysaye ***Brazilian:*** 10 Villa-Lobos ***Czech:*** 3 Suk 6 Dvořák 7 Janáček, Kubelik, Smetana ***Danish:*** 7 Nielsen ***Dutch:*** 9 Sweelinck ***English:*** 4 Arne, Byrd 5 Elgar 6 Delius, Morley, Tallis, Walton, Wesley 7 Britten, Dowland, Gibbons, Purcell, Weelkes 8 Sullivan 11 Lloyd Webber ***Finnish:*** 8 Palmgren, Sibelius ***Flemish:*** 5 Dufay, Lasso 6 Lassus 8 Willaert ***French:*** 4 Indy, Lalo 5 Auber, Bizet, Dukas, Fauré, Ibert, Jarre, Lully, Ravel, Satie, Widor 6 Boulez, Campra, Franck, Gounod, Rameau, Thomas 7 Berlioz, Debussy, Delibes, Milhaud, Poulenc 8 Chabrier, Couperin, Honegger, Massenet, Messiaen 9 Offenbach ***German:*** 4 Bach, Orff 5 Bruch, Gluck, Reger, Spohr, Weber, Weill 6 Brahms, Handel, Schutz, Vogler, Wagner 7 Hassler, Richter, Silcher, Strauss 8 Schumann, Telemann 9 Beethoven, Buxtehude, Hindemith, Meyerbeer 10 Praetorius 11 Humperdinck, Mendelssohn, Stockhausen ***Hungarian:*** 5 Lehar, Liszt 6 Bartok, Kodaly, Ligeti 8 Dohnanyi ***Italian:*** 4 Peri 5 Boito, Verdi, Vinci 6 Busoni, Viotti, Vitali 7 Bellini, Corelli, Martini, Puccini, Rossini, Tartini, Vivaldi 8 Clementi, Gabrieli, Mascagni, Paganini, Respighi 9 Cherubini, Donizetti, Pergolesi, Scarlatti, Tommasini 10 Boccherini, Monteverdi, Palestrina, Ponchielli, Zingarelli 11 Frescobaldi, Leoncavallo 12 Dallapiccola ***Mexican:*** 6 Chavez ***Norwegian:*** 5 Grieg ***Polish:*** 6 Chopin 10 Paderewski, Penderecki, Wieniawski ***Romanian:*** 7 Xenakis ***Russian:*** 6 Glinka 7 Borodin 8 Glazunov, Scriabin 9 Prokofiev 10 Mussorgsky, Rubinstein, Stravinsky, Tcherepnin 11 Tchaikovsky 12 Rachmaninoff, Shostakovich ***Spanish:*** 5 Falla, Vives 6 Garcia 7 Albéniz 8 Granados, Victoria

composite 3 mix 6 hybrid 7 amalgam, complex, compost, mixture, montage 8 compound 9 immixture 10 commixture 11 combination 12 amalgamation, intermixture

composition 5 essay, paper, theme 6 design, makeup 7 article, morceau, writing 8 fantasia 9 formation 10 compromise 12 architecture, constitution, construction ***choral:*** 5 motet ***for eight:*** 5 octet ***for five:*** 7 quintet ***for four:*** 7 quartet ***for nine:*** 5 nonet ***for one:*** 4 solo 5 scena ***for seven:*** 6 septet ***for six:*** 6 sextet ***for three:*** 4 trio ***for two:*** 4 duet 6 duetto ***instrumental:*** 3 jig 4 reel 5 étude, fugue, gigue, march, rondo, suite 6 sonata 7 caprice, partita, prelude, scherzo 8 allemand, concerto, fantasia, overture, rhapsody, saraband, sinfonia, symphony, tone poem 9 capriccio, sarabande 10 intermezzo ***vocal:*** 4 aria, lied, mass, song 5 canon, carol, chant, motet, opera, round 6 arioso, ballad, chorus 7 cantata, chanson, chantey, chorale, lullaby, requiem 8 berceuse, madrigal, oratorio 9 barcarole, plainsong, spiritual 12 cantus firmus

compos mentis 4 sane 5 lucid 6 normal

composure 6 phlegm 7 ataraxy 8 calmness, coolness 9 sangfroid 10 equanimity

compound 3 mix 4 join, link 5 admix, alloy, blend, boost, immix, unite 6 commix, couple, expand, extend, fusion, make up, mingle 7 amalgam, augment, bracket, complex, compost, connect, enlarge, magnify, mixture 8 coagment, coalesce, comingle, heighten, increase, intermix, multiply 9 admixture, associate, coadunate, commingle, composite 10 aggrandize, commixture 11 intermingle 12 amalgamation ***aromatic:*** 7 depside ***chemical:*** (see at **chemical**) ***combining form:*** 5 genin ***medicinal:*** 7 quassin 8 magnesia ***protein:*** 7 peptone ***sulfur:*** 5 thiol 6 sulfid 7 sulfide, sulfone 8 sulfonal, sulfuryl, sulphide, sulphone ***volatile:*** 8 cymogene

comprehend 3 dig, get, see 4 know 5 catch, grasp 6 accept, embody, fathom, take in 7 cognize, compass, contain, embrace, include, involve, subsume 8 perceive 9 encompass 10 appreciate, understand

comprehendible 5 lucid 8 knowable, luminous 9 graspable 10 fathomable 12 intelligible 13 apprehensible

comprehensible see **comprehendible**

comprehensive 4 full, wide 5 broad 6 global 7 general, overall 8 sweeping 9 all-around, inclusive 12 encyclopedic

comprehensiveness 5 scope 7 breadth 8 fullness, wideness 9 amplitude

compress 3 jam 4 bear, cram, push 5 crowd, crush, press, stupe 6 shrink, squash, squish 7 bandage, compact, pledget, squeeze 8 condense, contract, laminate 9 constrict 11 concentrate

comprise 4 form, make 6 make up 7 compose, contain, include 10 constitute

compromise 4 mean, pact, risk 5 peril 6 hazard, menace 7 bargain, compact, imperil, jeopard 8 contract, endanger, jeopardy 9 agreement, middle way 10 golden mean, jeopardize 11 composition 12 middle ground

compulsion 4 itch, need, urge 5 drive, force 6 duress 8 coercion, exigency, violence 9 necessity 10 constraint

compulsory 8 required 9 imperious, mandatory 10 imperative, obligatory

compunction 3 rue 4 ruth 5 demur, qualm 6 squeam 7 penance, remorse, scruple 9 attrition, hesitancy, penitence, penitency 10 conscience, contrition, hesitation, repentance 12 contriteness

compunctious 5 sorry 8 contrite, penitent 9 regretful, repentant 10 apologetic, remorseful 11 attritional, penitential

computation 8 figuring 9 ciphering, reckoning 10 arithmetic, estimation 11 calculation

compute 5 total 6 cipher, figure, reckon 8 estimate 9 calculate

computer 6 abacus 7 machine 10 calculator 13 adding machine ***data:*** 7 readout 8 printout, software ***infomation:*** 4 data ***instruction:*** 5 macro ***inventor:*** 7 Babbage ***language:*** 5 ALGOL, BASIC, COBOL 7 FORTRAN ***operator:*** 9 programer 10 programmer ***type:*** 6 analog 7 digital

comrade 3 pal 4 ally, chum, mate 5 buddy, crony 6 comate, fellow, frater 7 brother, consort 8 tovarich, tovarish 9 associate, communist, companion

comstock 4 prig 5 prude 6 Grundy 7 puritan 8 bluenose 9 Mrs. Grundy, nice Nelly 10 goody-goody

con 4 anti, bilk, coax, dupe, fool, hoax, scam, view 5 learn, study, trick 6 befool, cajole, gammon, inmate, survey 7 blarney, canvass, chicane, convict, deceive, examine, inspect, opposer, swindle, wheedle 8 blandish, flimflam, hoodwink, jailbird, memorize, opponent, opposure, prisoner, soft soap 9 adversary, bamboozle, check over, oppugnant, sweet-talk 10 antagonism, antagonist, antithesis, opposition, scrutinize 11 contrariety, hornswoggle

concatenate 4 join, link 5 unite 7 connect 9 integrate 10 articulate

concave 6 arched 7 vaulted 8 bowllike 9 depressed ***combining form:*** 7 coelous

concavity 3 dip, sag 4 bowl, dent, sink 5 basin 6 hollow 7 sinkage 8 sinkhole 10 depression

conceal 4 bury, hide, veil 5 cache, cloak, cover, stash 6 occult, screen 7 secrete 8 ensconce, enshroud, palliate 10 camouflage

concealed 5 privy 6 buried, covert, hidden, secret 7 guarded 8 obscured, shrouded, ulterior 11 clandestine ***combining form:*** 4 adel 5 adelo

concede 3 own 4 avow 5 admit, allow, award, grant, let on, own up 6 accord, fess up 7 confess 9 vouchsafe 11 acknowledge

conceit 4 idea, whim 5 fancy, freak, humor, image, pride 6 egoism, megrim, notion, vagary, vanity 7 boutade, caprice, concept, egotism, thought 8 crotchet, self-love, smugness, snobbery, vainness 9 self-glory, self-pride, vainglory 10 conception, impression, narcissism, perception, self-esteem 11 amour propre, complacence, complacency, consequence, self-opinion, swelled head 12 apprehension, intellection 13 outrecuidance

conceited 4 vain 6 snobby, snooty 7 pompous, stuck up 8 snobbish 12 narcissistic, vainglorious

conceitedness 6 vanity 8 self-love, vainness 9 vainglory 10 narcissism, self-esteem 11 amour propre

conceivable 6 likely, mortal 7 earthly 8 possible, probable 9 thinkable 10 imaginable, supposable

conceive 4 form, make 5 beget, fancy, grasp, think 6 accept, assume, expect, follow, gather, ponder, vision 7 believe, compass, feature, imagine, realize, suppose, suspect 8 cogitate, envisage, envision, meditate, ruminate 9 apprehend, speculate, visualize 10 comprehend, excogitate, understand

concentrate 3 fix 4 heap, mass, meet, pile 5 focus, rivet, unify 6 fasten, fixate, gather, shrink 7 collect, compact 8 assemble, compress, condense, contract, converge 9 constrict, integrate 11 consolidate

concentrated 5 fixed, lusty, whole 6 fierce, potent, robust, strong 7 furious, intense 8 vehement 9 exclusive, exquisite, undivided 10 full-bodied, unswerving 12 undistracted

concentrating 8 unifying 10 compacting 11 centripetal, integrative 12 centralizing 13 consolidating

concentration 4 heed 5 study 6 debate 9 attention 11 application 12 deliberation 13 consideration

concept 4 idea 5 image 6 notion 7 conceit, thought 10 impression, perception 12 apprehension, intellection
conception 4 idea 5 image, start 6 notion 7 conceit, thought 9 beginning 10 impression, perception 12 apprehension, intellection
conceptual 5 ideal 8 abstract, notional 9 imaginary, visionary 10 ideational 12 transcendent
concern 4 care, firm, heed 5 doubt, worry 6 affair, gadget, matter, outfit, regard, unease, wonder 7 anxiety, company, dubiety, lookout, palaver 8 business, disquiet, interest, mistrust 9 attention, curiosity, dubiosity, misgiving, occasions, suspicion 10 enterprise, inquietude, skepticism, solicitude, uneasiness 11 carefulness, disquietude, heedfulness, incertitude, uncertainty, uncertitude 12 apprehension 13 consciousness, consideration, establishment
concerned 8 affected, involved 10 implicated, interested
concerning 2 re 4 as to, in re 5 about, anent, as for 7 against, apropos 9 as regards, regarding 10 respecting
concert 4 tune 5 agree 6 accord, chorus, concur, settle 7 arrange, benefit, concord, harmony, recital 8 coincide 9 cooperate, harmonize, negotiate 10 consonance 11 performance
concert hall 5 odeon, odeum 10 auditorium
concession 5 favor 6 gambit 9 allowance, privilege 10 compromise 12 acquiescence
conch 5 shell 6 mussel 7 mollusk
concierge 6 porter, warden 7 doorman, janitor 9 custodian 10 doorkeeper
conciliate 4 calm, ease 5 quiet 6 pacify, soothe 7 appease, assuage, mollify, placate, sweeten 10 propitiate 11 tranquilize
concise 4 curt 5 brief, pithy, short, terse 7 compact, laconic, summary 8 abridged, succinct 9 condensed 10 compressed, contracted 11 compendiary, compendious 12 breviloquent 13 short and sweet
conclude 3 end 4 draw, halt, rule, stop 5 close, infer, judge 6 decide, deduce, deduct, derive, figure, finish, gather, reason, settle, wind up, wrap up 7 collect, resolve 8 complete, ultimate 9 determine, terminate
concluding 4 last 5 final 6 latest, latter 7 closing 8 eventual, hindmost, terminal, ultimate
conclusion 3 end 4 stop 5 cease, close, finis 6 ending, epilog, finale, finish, period, windup 7 closing, closure 8 decision, epilogue, illation, judgment, sequitur 9 cessation, deduction, inference 10 desistance, resolution, settlement 11 termination 13 determination, ratiocination
conclusive 4 last 5 final 6 cogent 7 telling 8 deciding, decisive 10 compelling, convincing, definitive 11 determinant, determinate, irrefutable 12 irrefragable, unanswerable
concoct 3 mix 4 brew, cook 5 frame, hatch 6 cook up, create, devise, invent, make up, vamp up 7 dream up, hatch up 8 conceive, contrive 9 formulate, originate
concomitant 4 mate 6 fellow 7 consort 8 adjuvant, incident 9 accessory, ancillary, associate, attendant, attending, companion, satellite 10 coincident, collateral 12 accompanying 13 accompaniment, supplementary
concord 4 pact, tune 5 agree, chime, unity 6 accord, chorus, concur, treaty 7 concert, harmony, rapport 8 coincide 9 agreement, harmonize 10 consonance, convention
concordance 4 tune 5 chime 6 accord 7 harmony 9 agreement 10 consonance
concordant 8 agreeing 9 congruous 10 harmonious
concourse 6 throng 7 joining, meeting 8 junction 9 gathering 10 concursion, confluence
concrete 3 set 4 join, link 5 beton, solid, unite 6 couple, harden 7 bracket, combine, congeal, connect 8 coalesce, compound, indurate, solidify 9 associate ***component:*** 4 sand 5 water 6 gravel
concubine 7 hetaera, hetaira, odalisk 8 mistress 9 odalisque
concupiscence 4 lust 6 desire 7 passion 9 eroticism, prurience, pruriency 10 aphrodisia 11 lustfulness 13 lickerishness
concupiscent 3 hot 7 goatish, lustful, satyric 8 prurient 9 lickerish 10 lascivious, libidinous, passionate
concur 4 band, jibe 5 agree, unite 6 accord, league 7 combine, concert, concord, conjoin, go along 8 coadjute, coincide 9 cooperate, harmonize
concurrent 6 coeval 10 coetaneous, coexistent, coexisting, synchronal, synchronic 11 synchronous 12 contemporary, simultaneous
concurrently 6 at once 8 together 12 coincidently
concuss 3 jar 4 rock 5 force, shake, shock 6 coerce, compel, oblige 7 agitate, shotgun 8 convulse 9 constrain
concussion 3 jar 4 bump, jolt 5 clash, clout, crash, shock, smack 6 impact 7 beating, jarring, jolting, shaking 8 pounding 9 buffeting, collision
condemn 3 rap 4 damn, doom 5 blame, decry, knock 7 censure, convict

8 denounce, sentence 9 criticize, proscribe, reprehend, reprobate 10 denunciate

condensation 3 dew 5 brief 7 epitome, summary 8 abstract, boildown, breviary, breviate, synopsis 10 abridgment, conspectus

condense 3 sum 5 sum up 6 digest, reduce, shrink 7 abridge, capsule, compact, shorten, summate 8 boil down, compress, contract 9 capsulize, constrict, epitomize, inventory, summarize, synopsize 10 abbreviate 11 concentrate, consolidate

condescend 5 deign, stoop 6 unbend

condign 3 due, fit 4 fair, just 5 right 7 merited 8 deserved, rightful, suitable 9 requisite 11 appropriate 13 rhadamanthine

condiment 3 soy 4 salt 5 caper, curry, sauce, spice 6 catsup, pepper, relish 7 chutney, ketchup, mustard, paprika, vinegar 8 dressing, turmeric 9 seasoning 10 mayonnaise

condition 2 if 3 ill 4 case, mode 5 order, shape, state, terms 6 estate, fettle, kilter, malady, repair, status 7 ailment, disease, fitness, posture, proviso, strings 8 disorder, sickness, syndrome 9 affection, complaint, essential, exception, infirmity, necessity, provision, requisite, situation 10 limitation, sine qua non 11 requirement, reservation, stipulation 12 prerequisite 13 qualification *suffix:* 2 or, th, ty 3 dom, ery, ice, ile, ion, ism 4 ance, ancy, ence, ency, ment, ness, oses (plural), osis, ship 5 ation

conditional 4 iffy 7 reliant 8 relative 9 dependent, provisory, qualified, tentative, uncertain 10 contingent, restricted 11 provisional 12 provisionary

condolence 3 rue 4 pity, ruth 8 sympathy 10 compassion 13 commiseration

condonable 7 tenable 9 excusable, tolerable 10 acceptable, defensible, vindicable 11 justifiable, warrantable

condone 5 remit 6 excuse, pardon 7 forgive 8 overlook

conduce 4 lead, tend 7 redound 10 contribute

conduct 3 act, run 4 bear, care, head, lead, quit, show 5 guide, pilot, route, steer, tenue, usher 6 acquit, attend, behave, charge, convey, convoy, demean, deport, direct, escort, funnel, handle, keep up, manage, ordain 7 arrange, carry on, channel, company, comport, control, operate, oversee, running, traject 8 behavior, chaperon, handling, shepherd, transmit 9 accompany, companion, oversight, supervise 10 administer, deportment, intendance, management 11 comportment, supervision

conductor 5 guide 6 copper, escort, leader 7 maestro 8 conveyor, director, motorman 10 bandleader 11 impressario *American:* 4 Shaw 5 Grofé, Stock, Szell 6 Levine, Maazel, Previn, Reiner, Thomas, Walter 7 Fiedler, Monteux, Ormandy 8 Damrosch, Williams 9 Bernstein, Leinsdorf, Rodzinski, Steinberg, Stokowski 11 Kostelanetz, Mitropoulos *Australian:* 7 Bonynge *Austrian:* 4 Bohm 6 Mahler 10 von Karajan *Belgian:* 5 Ysaye *British:* 5 Solti *Canadian:* 9 MacMillan *Czech:* 7 Kubelik *English:* 4 Wood 5 Boult 7 Beecham, Malcolm, Sargent 8 Goossens 10 Barbirolli *French:* 5 Munch 6 Boulez, Pretre *German:* 4 Muck 5 Spohr, Weber 9 Klemperer, Scherchen 11 Furtwangler, Mendelssohn *Hungarian:* 5 Seidl 7 Nikisch, Richter *Indian:* 5 Mehta *Italian:* 6 Abbado 9 Toscanini *Japanese:* 5 Ozawa *Mexican:* 6 Chavez *Russian:* 12 Koussevitzky *Spanish:* 6 Iturbi *stick:* 5 baton *suffix:* 3 eer *Swiss:* 8 Ansermet

conduit 4 duct, main, pipe 5 canal 6 course 7 channel 8 aqueduct, penstock, pipeline 11 watercourse

coney 4 pika 5 hyrax 6 rabbit 10 butterfish

confab 4 chat 5 treat 6 advise, confer, huddle, parley, powwow 7 consult 8 collogue

confabulate see confab

confabulation 3 rap 4 chat, talk 6 parley 8 colloquy, converse, dialogue 10 conference, discussion 12 conversation, deliberation

confection see candy

confederacy 5 union 6 league 8 alliance 9 anschluss, coalition 10 federation

confederate 3 reb 4 ally 5 rebel, unite 6 fellow 7 abettor, partner 8 conspire 9 accessory, associate, colleague 10 accomplice 11 conspirator 12 collaborator 13 coconspirator *admiral:* 6 Semmes *capital:* 8 Richmond *color:* 4 gray *general:* 3 Lee 4 Hill, Hood 5 Bragg, Ewell, Price, Smith 6 Morgan, Stuart 7 Forrest, Hampden, Jackson, Pickett 8 Johnston 9 Pemberton 10 Beauregard, Longstreet *president:* 5 Davis *soldier:* 9 butternut *spy:* 4 Boyd (Belle) *vice-president:* 8 Stephens

confederation see confederacy

confer 4 give, meet, talk 5 allot, award, grant, speak, treat 6 accord, advise, bestow, confab, huddle, parley, powwow 7 consult, discuss, present 8 collogue, colloque, converse 10 deliberate 11 confabulate

conference 3 rap 4 loop, talk 5 synod, wheel 6 league, parley, powwow 7 circuit, meeting, palaver, seminar 8 colloquy 9 symposium 10 colloquium, discussion, rap session, round robin, round table 11 association 12 deliberation 13 confabulation

confess 3 own 4 avow, sing 5 admit, allow, grant, let on, own up 6 reveal 7 concede, divulge 8 disclose 11 acknowledge

confession 5 creed 6 avowal 7 peccavi 9 admission, statement 10 disclosure

confidant 4 mate 5 amigo 6 friend 8 familiar, intimate 11 cater-cousin 12 acquaintance

confide 4 tell 6 bestow, commit 7 breathe, commend, consign, entrust, present, whisper 8 hand over, relegate, turn over

confidence 4 gall, hope 5 brass, cheek, faith, nerve, stock, trust 6 aplomb, surety 7 courage 8 reliance, sureness 9 assurance, brashness, certainty, certitude, self-trust 10 conviction, dependence, effrontery, equanimity 11 assuredness *game:* 4 scam 5 bunco, bunko, grift, sting 7 swindle

confidence man 3 gyp 7 diddler, grifter, sharper, sharpie 8 swindler 9 defrauder, trickster 11 bunco artist 12 bunco steerer

confident 4 bold, sure 5 brash, brave, cocky, perky, pushy 6 secure, uppity 7 assured, certain, pushful 8 cocksure, fearless, intrepid, positive, sanguine, trustful, unafraid 9 dauntless, presuming, undaunted 10 brassbound, courageous, undoubtful 11 overweening, self-assured, self-reliant 12 presumptuous 13 self-assertive, self-possessed

confidential 5 close, privy, thick 6 chummy, closet, hushed, inside, secret 7 private 8 familiar, intimate 9 auricular

configuration 4 cast, form 5 shape 6 figure 7 contour, outline, pattern 12 conformation

confine 3 bar, box, end, mew, pen 4 cage, coop, crib, jail, term 5 bound, cramp, limit, orbit, range, reach, scope, sweep 6 embank, encage, extent, immure, intern, radius 7 delimit, enclose, pinfold, purview 8 bastille, boundary, imprison, localize, prelimit, restrict 9 constrain, periphery 10 delimitate, limitation 11 incarcerate 12 circumscribe 13 circumference

confinement 5 cramp 7 lying-in 8 childbed 9 captivity, restraint 10 constraint 11 restriction 12 accouchement, imprisonment 13 constrainment

confines 6 bounds, limits 7 compass 8 boundary, environs, purlieus 9 precincts

confirm 3 fix, set 4 back 5 check, prove, vouch 6 attest, ratify, uphold, verify 7 bear out, certify, justify, support 8 check out, validate 11 corroborate 12 authenticate, substantiate

confirmation 5 proof 7 witness 8 evidence 9 testament, testimony 11 attestation, testimonial

confirmed 3 set 5 fixed, sworn 7 chronic, settled 8 deep-dyed, definite, habitual, ratified 9 hard-shell 10 accustomed, deep-rooted, deep-seated, entrenched, habituated, inveterate 13 bred-in-the-bone, dyed-in-the-wool

confiscate 4 take 5 annex, seize, usurp 7 escheat, preempt 8 accroach, arrogate 9 sequester 10 commandeer 11 appropriate, expropriate

confiture 3 jam 8 conserve, preserve

conflagrant 5 afire, fiery 6 ablaze, aflame, alight 7 blazing, burning, flaming, flaring, ignited

conflagration 4 fire 5 blaze 7 inferno 9 holocaust

conflict 3 jar, war 4 bout, duel, meet, rift, vary 5 clash, fight 6 battle, combat, differ, jangle, oppose, strife 7 contest, discord, dispute, dissent, meeting, rivalry, warfare 8 argument, concours, disagree, disunity, mismatch, striving, struggle, tug-of-war, variance 9 disaccord, emulation, encounter, rencontre 10 contention, difference, dissension, dissidence 11 competition, controversy 12 disharmonize

conflicting 7 warring 8 clashing, contrary 9 dissonant 10 contending, discordant, discrepant 11 contrariant, incongruent, incongruous, inconsonant 12 antagonistic, antipathetic, disconsonant, incompatible, inconsistent, inharmonious

confluence 7 meeting 8 junction 9 concourse, gathering 10 concursion

conform 3 fit 4 jibe, mind, obey, suit, tune 5 adapt, agree, fit in, yield 6 accord, adjust, attune, comply, follow, square, submit, tailor 7 observe 8 dovetail, quadrate 9 acquiesce, harmonize, integrate, reconcile 10 coordinate, correspond, proportion, tailor-make 11 accommodate 12 reconciliate

conformable 6 fitted, suited 7 adapted, matched 8 assorted, suitable

conformation 4 cast, form 5 shape 6 figure 13 configuration

conforming 4 nice, typy 5 typey 6 decent, proper, seemly 7 uniform 8 becoming, decorous 9 befitting, civilized 11 comme il faut

conformity 7 decorum, harmony 8 affinity, legalism, normalcy 9 coherence, congruity, obedience 10 compliance, submission 11 consistency, resignation 12 acquiescence

confound 3 mix 4 faze, pose, stun 5 abash, befog, evert, mix up, rebut 6 baffle, puzzle, rattle, refute 7 confuse, confute, misdeem, mistake, perplex, stumble, stupefy **8** bewilder, disprove **9** discomfit, dumbfound, embarrass **10** controvert, disconcert, disconfirm **11** misidentify **13** metagrobolize

confounded **4** rank **5** agape, gross, utter **6** aghast, blamed, cursed, cussed, damned **7** blasted, blessed, shocked **8** absolute, dismayed, infernal, outright **9** consarned, dad-burned, execrable, out-and-out **11** dumbfounded, overwhelmed, straight-out, unmitigated **13** thunderstruck

confrere see colleague

confront **4** defy, face, meet **5** brave **6** accost, breast, oppose **9** challenge, encounter

confuse **3** fog, mix **4** blur, faze, mull, pose, warp **5** abash, addle, befog, cloud, dizzy, mix up, muddy, twist, upset, wrest **6** baffle, ball up, bemuse, flurry, foul up, fuddle, garble, jumble, mess up, muddle, puzzle, rattle, wrench **7** agitate, becloud, derange, disrupt, distort, flummox, fluster, misdeem, mislead, mistake, nonplus, perplex, perturb, pervert, snarl up **8** bedazzle, befuddle, bewilder, confound, disorder, disquiet, distract, throw off, unsettle **9** discomfit, embarrass **10** disarrange, discompose, disconcert **11** disorganize, misidentify **12** misrepresent **13** metagrobolize

confused **4** lost **5** muddy, muzzy, vague **7** at a loss, mixed up **9** perplexed **10** bewildered, topsy-turvy **12** disconcerted

confusion **3** din **4** flap, loss, mess, muck, ruin, stew **5** babel, chaos, havoc, mix-up, snafu, snarl **6** ataxia, bedlam, dither, foul-up, hubbub, huddle, jumble, lather, muddle, pother, tumult, unease **7** clutter, turmoil **8** disarray, disorder, misorder, pell-mell **9** abashment, agitation, commotion, ruination **10** hullabaloo, turbulence, uneasiness **11** bedevilment, derangement, destruction, devastation, disturbance, pandemonium **12** discomfiture, discomposure, razzle-dazzle **13** disconcertion, embarrassment

confute **4** deny **5** break, evert, rebut **8** confound, disprove **10** controvert, disconfirm

congé **3** bow **5** adieu **7** good-bye, parting **8** farewell **9** dismissal **11** leave-taking

congeal **3** dry, gel, set **4** cake, clot, curd, jell **5** jelly **6** curdle, gelate, harden **7** jellify, stiffen, thicken **8** concrete, indurate, solidify **9** coagulate **10** gelatinize

congener **3** ilk **4** kind, sort, type **5** class, genus

congenial **4** good, nice **6** amical, social **7** affable, cordial, kindred, welcome **8** amicable, friendly, gracious, pleasant, pleasing, sociable **9** agreeable, congruous, consonant, favorable **10** compatible, consistent, gratifying, harmonious **11** cooperative, pleasurable, sympathetic **13** companionable

congenital **6** inborn, inbred, innate, native **7** connate, natural **8** inherent **9** essential, ingrained, inherited, intrinsic **10** connatural, deep-seated, indigenous, indwelling, unacquired

conger **3** eel **4** pike

congeries **4** ruck **5** group **6** muster **7** company **8** assembly **9** gathering **10** assemblage, collection **11** aggregation **12** congregation

congest **3** jam **4** clog, fill, plug, stop **5** block, choke, close, crowd **7** occlude **8** obstruct

conglobate **4** ball **5** round **6** sphere **8** ensphere

conglomerate **4** heap, mass, pool **5** chain, group, mixed, trust **6** cartel, motley, varied **7** combine **8** assorted, chow-chow **9** aggregate, syndicate **11** aggregation, promiscuous **12** multifarious **13** agglomeration, heterogeneous, miscellaneous

conglomeration **5** hoard, trove **9** aggregate, amassment, colluvies **10** collection, cumulation **11** agglomerate, aggregation **12** accumulation

Congo ***capital:*** **11** Brazzaville ***monetary unit:*** **5** franc

congratulate **4** laud **6** salute **10** compliment, felicitate

congregate **4** meet, teem **5** raise, swarm **6** gather, muster **7** collect, convene **8** assemble, congress **9** forgather **10** rendezvous

congregation **4** host, mass, ruck **5** crowd, group **6** muster **7** company, meeting **8** assembly, audience **9** gathering **10** assemblage, collection

congress **4** club, diet **5** guild, synod, union **6** gather, league, muster **7** collect, society **8** assemble, assembly **9** forgather **10** congregate, fellowship, fraternity, parliament, rendezvous **11** association, brotherhood, Capitol Hill, legislature

congressman **7** senator **8** delegate **10** legislator **14** representative

congruity **9** agreement, coherence **10** conformity **11** consistency

congruous **3** apt, fit **7** fitting **9** accordant, agreeable, congenial, consonant **10** compatible, concordant, consistent, harmonious **11** appropriate, sympathetic

conjectural **7** reputed **8** putative, supposed **11** suppositive, suppository **12** hypothetical, suppositious **13** suppositional

conjecture **5** fancy, guess, infer **6** assume, theory **7** presume, pretend, sup-

pose, surmise, suspect 9 inference, speculate 11 speculation, supposition
conjoin 3 wed 4 band, knit, link, yoke 5 unite 6 concur, couple, league, relate 7 combine, connect 8 coadjute 9 associate, cooperate
conjoint 6 common, mutual, public, shared 8 coacting, coactive, communal, conjunct, synergic 10 synergetic 11 coefficient, cooperative, intermutual
conjointly 8 mutually, together
conjointment 5 tie-up, union 6 hookup 7 cahoots, wedding 8 alliance 9 coalition 10 connection 11 affiliation, association, combination, conjunction, partnership
conjugal 6 wedded 7 marital, married, nuptial, spousal 8 hymeneal 9 connubial 11 matrimonial
conjugality 7 wedlock 8 marriage 9 matrimony 12 connubiality
conjugate 4 join, link, yoke 5 yoked 6 couple, joined, linked 7 bracket, combine, conjoin, connect, coupled 8 coalesce 9 associate, connected
conjunct 5 joint 6 common, mutual, public, shared 8 communal 11 intermutual
conjunction 2 as, if, or, so 3 and, but, for, nor, tho, yet 4 as if, lest, than, then, when 5 since, tie-up, union, until, while 6 either, hookup, though, unless, whenas, whilst 7 because, neither, wedding, whereas, whether 8 alliance, although, moreover 9 coalition, therefore 10 connection 11 affiliation, association, combination, partnership 12 conjointment
conjuration 4 rune 5 charm, spell, trick 11 incantation, legerdemain
conjure 3 beg 4 pray 5 brace, crave 6 appeal, invoke 7 beseech, entreat, implore 9 importune 10 supplicate
conjurer 4 mage, seer 5 magus 6 magian, shaman, wizard 7 warlock 8 magician, sorcerer 9 enchanter, trickster, voodooist 11 illusionist, necromancer
conjuring 5 magic 7 sorcery 8 witchery, wizardry 10 necromancy, witchcraft 11 bewitchment, enchantment, legerdemain, thaumaturgy
conk 3 die, hit, rap 4 swat 5 knock 7 decease 8 pass away
con man see confidence man
connate 4 akin 6 allied, inborn, native 7 kindred, natural, related 8 incident, inherent 9 elemental, essential, inherited, intrinsic 10 affiliated, congenital, deep-seated, indigenous, indwelling, unacquired 11 consanguine
connatural see connate
connect 3 tie, wed 4 bind, join, link, yoke 5 marry, unite 6 attach, bridge, couple, fasten, relate 7 combine, conjoin 9 affiliate, associate, interlock
connected with *suffix:* 3 ast 4 aria 5 arium, orial
Connecticut *academy, college, university:* 4 Yale 7 Trinity 8 Hartford, New Haven, Wesleyan 9 Fairfield 10 Bridgeport, Quinnipiac 11 Sacred Heart, Saint Joseph 12 U.S. Coast Guard *capital:* 8 Hartford *nickname:* 11 Nutmeg State 12 Blue Law State *state bird:* 13 American robin *state flower:* 14 mountain laurel
connection 3 job 4 cult, post, seam, sect, spot 5 creed, joint, nexus, tie-in, tie-up, union 6 billet, hookup 7 joining 8 alliance, coupling, junction, juncture, position, religion 9 communion, situation 10 catenation 11 affiliation, appointment, association, combination, conjunction, partnership 12 conjointment, denomination, togetherness
connective 2 or 3 and, nor 6 either 7 neither 8 syndetic 11 conjunction, conjunctive
connivance 9 collusion 10 complicity
connive 4 plot, wink 5 blink 6 devise, wink at 7 blink at, collude 8 cogitate, conspire, contrive, intrigue 9 machinate, scheme out
connoisseur 6 expert 7 epicure, gourmet 8 aesthete, gourmand, highbrow 9 bon vivant 10 dilettante 11 cognoscente
connotation 4 hint 7 meaning 8 overtone 9 undertone 10 suggestion 11 association, implication
connote 4 hint, mean 5 imply, spell 6 import, intend 7 add up to, express, signify, suggest 8 intimate 9 insinuate
connubial 6 wedded 7 marital, married, nuptial, spousal 8 conjugal, hymeneal 11 matrimonial
connubiality 7 wedlock 8 marriage 9 matrimony 11 conjugality
conquer 3 win 4 beat, best, foil, lick, tame, whip 5 crush 6 defeat, hurdle, master, outwit, reduce, subdue, thwart 7 prevail, triumph 8 bear down, beat down, overcome, override, surmount, vanquish 9 checkmate, overpower, overthrow, overwhelm, subjugate 10 overmaster
conquest 3 win 4 rout 7 routing, subdual, triumph, victory 9 overthrow
Conrad *character:* 3 Jim 4 Axel, Lena 5 Flora, Kurtz 6 Marlow 7 Almayer 8 MacWhirr, Nostromo *work:* 5 Youth 6 Chance 7 Lord Jim, Typhoon, Victory 8 Nostromo 11 Secret Agent 14 Almayer's Folly
consanguine 4 akin 6 agnate, allied 7 cognate, connate, kindred, related 8 incident 10 affiliated, connatural

conscience 5 demur, qualm, sense 6 psyche, squeam 7 scruple 11 compunction
conscienceless 6 amoral, shifty, tricky, unfair 7 devious 12 unprincipled
conscientious 4 fair, just, true 5 exact, fussy, right 6 honest 7 careful, dutiful, heedful, upright 8 punctual, studious 9 honorable 10 meticulous, scrupulous 11 painstaking, punctilious 12 conscionable
conscionable see conscientious
conscious 5 alive, awake, aware 7 knowing, mindful, witting 8 affected, mannered, sensible, sentient, vigilant, watchful 9 attentive, au courant, cognizant 10 conversant, perceptive
consciousness 4 care, heed 6 regard 7 concern 9 awareness 11 carefulness, needfulness
conscribe, conscript 5 draft 6 enlist, enroll, muster
consecrate 5 bless 6 anoint, devote, hallow 8 dedicate, sanctify
consecrated 4 holy 6 sacred 7 blessed 8 hallowed 9 unprofane 10 sanctified *oil:* 6 chrism *thing:* 6 sacrum
consecution 3 row 5 chain, order, train 6 sequel, series 8 sequence 10 procession, succession 11 progression
consecutive 4 next 5 after, later 6 serial 7 ensuing, sequent 9 enlarging, following, succedent 10 increasing, sequential, subsequent, succeeding, successive 11 progressive 12 successional 13 subsequential
consent 3 let, yes 5 agree, allow, leave, yield 6 accede, accord, assent, comply, concur, permit 7 approve 8 sanction 9 acquiesce, agreement, allowance, subscribe 10 permission, sufferance 13 authorization, understanding
consentaneous 5 solid 9 unanimous 11 consentient
consequence 3 end 4 fame, pith, rank 5 event, honor, issue, pride, state 6 cachet, effect, egoism, import, moment, renown, repute, result, sequel, status, upshot, weight 7 conceit, dignity, egotism, outcome, stature 8 position, prestige, sequence, standing 9 aftermath, magnitude, vainglory 10 importance, narcissism, reputation 11 aftereffect, amour propre, complacence, complacency, weightiness 12 significance 13 conceitedness, momentousness
consequent 5 sound 7 logical 8 rational, sensible 9 following, resulting 10 reasonable 11 intelligent
consequential 3 big 7 weighty 8 material 9 important, momentous 10 meaningful 11 significant, substantial 12 considerable
consequently 2 so 4 ergo, then, thus 5 hence 9 therefore, thereupon 11 accordingly
conservation 4 care 6 saving 7 control, keeping 8 managing 9 attention, directing, governing, preserval, salvation 10 cherishing, husbanding, management, protection 11 safekeeping 12 preservation, sustentation
conservative 4 tory, wary 5 chary, right 6 proper 7 diehard, puritan 8 cautious, discreet, moderate, old liner, orthodox, rightist, standpat 9 temperate, unextreme 10 controlled, reasonable, restrained 11 bitter-ender, circumspect, reactionary, right-winger, standpatter, unexcessive
conserve 3 can, jam 4 save 6 keep up 7 support, sustain 8 maintain, preserve 9 confiture
consider 3 eye, see 4 deem, feel, hold, mind, muse, rate, rule, scan, view 5 fancy, infer, judge, sense, study, think, weigh 6 admire, credit, esteem, gather, look at, ponder, reason, reckon, regard 7 account, believe, bethink, examine, imagine, inspect, perpend, reflect, respect 8 cogitate, conceive, conclude, gaze upon, look upon, meditate, prescind, ruminate, think out 9 speculate, think over 10 excogitate, scrutinize 11 contemplate
considerable 3 big 4 good, tidy 5 hefty, large, major 6 active, goodly, pretty 7 notable, sizable, weighty 8 material, sensible 9 effective, extensive, important, momentous 10 large-scale, meaningful 11 efficacious, respectable, significant, substantial 13 consequential
considerably 3 far 4 well 5 quite 6 rather 8 somewhat 13 significantly
considerate 3 big 4 kind, safe, wary 5 chary, lofty 6 kindly, polite, tender 7 amiable, careful, guarded 8 cautious, discreet, generous, gingerly, obliging 9 attentive 10 benevolent, chivalrous, thoughtful 11 calculating, circumspect, complaisant, magnanimous, sympathetic, warm-hearted 12 greathearted 13 compassionate
consideration 4 heed 5 cause, favor, mercy, study 6 debate, esteem, motive, reason, regard, spring 7 account, concern, respect 9 attention, awareness 10 admiration, estimation, solicitude 11 application, forbearance, heedfulness, mindfulness 12 deliberation 13 concentration
considered 7 advised, studied, willful 8 designed, prepense, studious 9 voluntary 10 deliberate, thought-out 11 intentional 12 aforethought, premeditated
consign 4 give, send, ship 5 allot, award,

remit, route, yield **6** commit, devote **7** address, commend, confide, entrust, forward **8** dispatch, hand over, relegate, transmit, turn over **9** surrender

consist **2** be, go **3** lie **4** rest **5** abide, agree, dwell, exist, fit in **6** accord, inhere, repose, reside **7** comport, conform, consort, subsist **8** dovetail **10** correspond

consistency **7** aptness, concord, fitness, harmony **8** evenness, felicity, firmness, likeness **9** agreement, coherence, congruity **10** apposition, conformity, consonance, similarity **11** suitability

consistent **4** same, true **8** constant **9** agreeable, congenial, congruous, consonant, unfailing, unvarying **10** compatible, invariable, unchanging **11** sympathetic

consistently **7** as usual, usually **8** wontedly **10** habitually **11** customarily

console **4** calm **5** cheer, table **6** buck up, solace **7** animate, cabinet, comfort, hearten, relieve, upraise **8** inspirit **11** tranquilize

consolidate **3** mix, set **4** fuse **5** blend, merge, unify, unite **7** compact **8** compress, condense, solidify **9** integrate **10** amalgamate, strengthen **11** concentrate

consolidation **5** union **6** merger **7** melding, merging **8** mergence **9** coalition **11** coadunation, combination, unification **12** amalgamation

consonance **4** tune **5** chime **6** accord, chorus **7** concert, concord, harmony **9** agreement **11** concordance

consonant **4** akin, like **5** alike, round **6** agnate, fortis, rotund **7** chiming, musical, orotund, ringing, similar, uniform, vibrant **8** blending, harmonic, parallel, plangent, resonant, sonorant, sonorous **9** accordant, agreeable, analogous, congenial, congruous **10** coincident, comparable, compatible, consistent, harmonious, resounding **11** conformable, sympathetic, symphonious **13** corresponding ***kind:*** **4** stop, surd **5** nasal, velar **6** atonic, voiced **7** lateral, palatal, spirant **8** alveolar, bilabial, unvoiced **9** fricative, voiceless

consort **4** bear, mate, wife **5** agree, group, tally **6** accord, attend, convoy, fellow, spouse, square **7** company, comport, conduct, conform, husband **8** assembly, chaperon, dovetail **9** accompany, associate, companion, harmonize **10** correspond **11** concomitant **13** accompaniment

consortium **4** club **5** guild, order, union **6** league **7** society **8** congress **10** fellowship, fraternity **11** association

conspectus **5** brief **7** epitome **8** abstract, boildown, breviary, breviate, synopsis **10** abridgment **12** condensation

conspicuous **5** clear, plain, showy **6** marked, patent, signal **7** blatant, eminent, evident, obvious, pointed, salient **8** apparent, distinct, flagrant, manifest, striking **9** arresting, arrestive, egregious, prominent **10** celebrated, noticeable, openhanded, remarkable **11** illustrious, outstanding

conspiracy **4** plan, plot **5** cabal, covin **6** scheme **8** intrigue, sedition **9** treachery **11** machination

conspirator **7** abettor **9** accessory **10** accomplice **11** confederate

conspire **4** plot **5** cabal **6** devise **7** collude, complot, connive **8** cogitate, contrive, intrigue **9** machinate, scheme out

constancy **6** fealty **7** loyalty **8** adhesion, fidelity **9** adherence, diligence **10** attachment **12** faithfulness

constant **4** even, fast, same, true **5** fixed, liege, loyal **6** ardent, dogged, stable, steady **7** abiding, chronic, endless, equable, lasting, stabile, staunch, uniform **8** clinging, enduring, faithful, unending **9** allegiant, ceaseless, confirmed, continual, immovable, immutable, obstinate, perpetual, steadfast, unceasing, unfailing, unmovable, unvarying **10** changeless, consistent, continuous, inflexible, invariable, inveterate, persistent, persisting, unchanging, unwavering **11** everlasting, inalterable, persevering, unalterable, unremitting **12** interminable, pertinacious, unchangeable, unmodifiable **13** unfluctuating

Constantine ***birthplace:*** **4** Nish ***mother:*** **6** Helena ***son:*** **7** Crispus ***victim:*** **6** Fausta **7** Crispus ***wife:*** **6** Fausta

constantly **4** ever **6** always **10** invariably **11** perpetually **12** continuously

constellation **5** group **7** pattern **10** assemblage, collection **11** arrangement ***Altar:*** **3** Ara ***Archer:*** **11** Sagittarius ***Arrow:*** **7** Sagitta ***Balance:*** **5** Libra ***Big Dipper:*** **9** Ursa Major ***Bird of Paradise:*** **4** Apus ***Bull:*** **6** Taurus ***Centaur:*** **9** Centaurus ***Chained Lady:*** **9** Andromeda ***Chameleon:*** **10** Chamaeleon ***Champion:*** **7** Perseus ***Charioteer:*** **6** Auriga ***Clock:*** **10** Horologium ***Colt:*** **8** Equuleus ***Crab:*** **6** Cancer ***Crane:*** **4** Grus ***Cross:*** **4** Crux ***Crow:*** **6** Corvus ***Crown:*** **6** Corona ***Cup:*** **6** Crater ***Dolphin:*** **9** Delphinus ***Dove:*** **7** Columba ***Dragon:*** **5** Draco ***Eagle:*** **6** Aquila ***Fishes:*** **6** Pisces ***Fly:*** **5** Musca ***Flying Fish:*** **6** Volans ***Furnace:*** **6** Fornax ***Graving Tool:*** **6** Caelum ***Greater Dog:*** **10** Canis Major ***Hare:*** **5** Lepus ***Herdsman:*** **6** Boötes ***Horned Goat:*** **11** Capricornus ***Hunter:*** **5** Orion ***Indian:*** **5** Indus ***Keel:*** **6** Carina ***Lady in the Chair:*** **10** Cassiopeia ***Larger Bear:*** **9** Ursa Major ***Larger Dog:*** **10** Canis Major ***Lesser Dog:*** **10** Canis Minor ***Lion:*** **3** Leo ***Little Dipper:*** **9** Ursa Minor ***Little Fox:*** **9** Vulpecula ***Lizard:***

7 Lacerta ***Lyre:*** 4 Lyra ***Mariner's Compass:*** 5 Pyxis ***Monarch:*** 7 Cepheus ***Net:*** 9 Reticulum ***Painter's Easel:*** 6 Pictor ***Pair of Compasses:*** 8 Circinus ***Peacock:*** 4 Pavo ***Pump:*** 6 Antlia ***Ram:*** 5 Aries ***Rescuer:*** 7 Perseus ***River Po:*** 8 Eridanus ***Sails:*** 4 Vela ***Scorpion:*** 8 Scorpius ***Serpent:*** 7 Serpens ***Serpent Holder:*** 9 Ophiuchus ***Sextant:*** 7 Sextans ***Shield:*** 6 Scutum ***Smaller Bear:*** 9 Ursa Minor ***Square:*** 5 Norma ***Stern:*** 6 Puppis ***Swan:*** 6 Cygnus ***Table:*** 5 Mensa ***Toucan:*** 6 Tucana ***Triangle:*** 10 Triangulum ***Twins:*** 6 Gemini ***Unicorn:*** 9 Monoceros ***Virgin:*** 5 Virgo ***Water Carrier:*** 8 Aquarius ***Water Monster:*** 5 Hydra ***Water Snake:*** 6 Hydrus ***Whale:*** 5 Cetus ***Winged Horse:*** 7 Pegasus ***Wolf:*** 5 Lupus

consternate 5 daunt, shake 6 appall, dismay 7 horrify

consternation 4 fear 5 alarm, dread, panic 6 dismay, fright, horror, muddle, terror 9 confusion, trepidity 10 muddlement, perplexity 11 distraction, trepidation 12 bewilderment

constipate 6 stifle 7 trammel 8 stagnate, stultify

constituent 4 part 5 piece, voter 6 factor, member 7 element, portion 8 division, fraction 9 component, principal 10 ingredient

constitute 4 form, make 5 enact, found, set up, start 6 create, embody, make up 7 compose 8 complete, comprise, organize 9 establish, institute

constitution 3 law 4 code 5 build, canon, habit 6 design, makeup, nature 7 habitus 8 physique 9 formation, ordinance, structure 11 composition 12 architecture, construction

Constitution 12 Old Ironsides

constitutional 4 turn, walk 6 inborn, inbred, innate, ramble, stroll 7 built-in, saunter 8 inherent 9 essential, ingrained, intrinsic 10 congenital, deep-seated

Constitution State 11 Connecticut

constitutive 5 vital 8 cardinal 9 essential 11 fundamental

constrain 3 ban, bar, jam, jug 4 bear, curb, deny, hurt, jail, make, pain, push 5 check, crowd, crush, force, press 6 bridle, coerce, compel, enjoin, grieve, hold in, immure, injure, intern, oblige, squash, squish 7 abstain, concuss, confine, deprive, inhibit, refrain, shotgun, squeeze 8 aggrieve, bastille, disallow, distress, hold back, hold down, imprison, restrain, restrict, withhold 11 incarcerate

constraint 4 bond 5 check, cramp, force 6 duress 8 coercion, violence 9 restraint 10 compulsion, repression 11 confinement, restriction, suppression

constrict 4 curb, stop 5 choke, limit, strap 6 hamper, narrow, pucker, shrink 7 confine, inhibit, squeeze, tighten 8 astringe, compress, condense, contract, restrain, strangle, stultify 9 constrain 10 constipate, constringe 11 concentrate 12 circumscribe

constrictor 3 boa 5 snake 6 muscle 8 anaconda 9 sphincter, strangler

construct 4 form, make, rear 5 build, erect, forge, frame, put up, raise, set up 6 devise, uprear 7 build up, fashion, produce 8 assemble 9 establish, fabricate, hammer out 11 put together

construction 6 design, expose, makeup 8 building, exegesis 9 construal, formation 10 exposition 11 composition, explanation, explication 12 architecture, constitution

constructive 7 helpful, virtual 8 implicit 9 practical

construe 7 analyze, explain, expound 8 spell out 9 explicate, interpret, translate

consuetude 3 use 4 wont 5 habit, trick, usage 6 custom, manner, praxis 8 habitude, practice

consult 3 ask 5 refer, treat 6 advise, confab, confer, huddle, parley, powwow 7 counsel, examine 8 collogue, consider 11 confabulate

consume 2 go 3 eat, use 4 down, gulp, meal, raze, ruin, take, wolf 5 crush, drink, eat up, gorge, sew up, shift, spend, swill, use up, waste, wreck 6 absorb, devour, expend, feed on, finish, guzzle, ingest 7 destroy, engross, exhaust, fritter, put away, put down, swallow 8 gobble up, squander 9 dissipate, overwhelm, partake of, polish off, throw away 10 annihilate, extinguish, frivol away, monopolize, run through, trifle away

consumer advocate 5 Nader

consuming 9 absorbing 10 engrossing 12 monopolizing

consummate 3 end 4 able, halt, ripe 5 close, utter 6 finish, gifted, superb, wind up, wrap up 7 perfect, skilled, supreme, trained 8 absolute, complete, conclude, finished, flawless, outright, peerless, positive, talented, ultimate 9 downright, faultless, out-and-out, perfected, practiced, terminate, virtuosic 10 impeccable, inimitable 11 superlative, unmitigated 12 accomplished 13 thoroughgoing, unsurpassable

consumption 2 TB 3 use 5 decay, waste 8 phthisis 11 white plague 12 tuberculosis

contact 3 get 4 abut, meet 5 reach, touch, union 6 accord 7 harmony, oneness, rapport, taction 8 commerce, nearness, relation, tangency, touching 9 closeness, communion, proximity 10 connection,

contiguity, fellowship 11 association, contingence, impingement, intercourse, propinquity 13 communication, companionship *combining form:* 4 hapt 5 hapto
contagion 3 pox 4 bane 5 taint, venom, virus 6 miasma, poison 7 disease 9 pollution 10 corruption 13 contamination
contagious 6 catchy, taking 8 catching 10 infectious 12 communicable
contain 4 have, hold, keep, take 5 admit, house, lodge 6 embody, take in 7 collect, compose, control, embrace, include, involve, receive, repress, smother, subsume 8 comprise, restrain 9 encompass 10 comprehend, simmer down 11 accommodate
container 3 bag, bin, box, can, cup, jar, keg, mug, pod, pot, tin, tub, urn, vat 4 cage, case, cask, drum, etui, ewer, pail, sack, silo, tank, vase, vial, well 5 chest, crate, cruet, flask, glass, gourd, phial, pouch 6 basket, bottle, carafe, carton, casket, coffin, cooler, goblet, hamper, hatbox, holder, inkpot, shaker 7 bandbox, capsule, chalice, inkwell, package, pitcher, thermos 8 canister, catchall, decanter, envelope, hogshead, jerrican, puncheon 10 receptacle *liturgical:* 3 pix, pyx 7 chalice 8 ciborium
containing *suffix:* 2 ic 4 ical
contaminate 4 foul, harm, soil 5 dirty, spoil, stain, taint 6 befoul, debase, defile, infect, injure, poison 7 corrupt, deprave, pervert, pollute, tarnish, vitiate 9 desecrate 10 adulterate
conte 4 tale 5 story 9 narrative
contemn 4 hate 5 abhor, scorn, scout, spurn 7 despise, disdain 8 look down
contemplate 3 aim, eye 4 mean, mull, muse, plan, scan, view 5 study, think, weigh 6 design, intend, look at, ponder 7 examine, inspect, perpend, propose, purpose, reflect 8 consider, gaze upon, look upon, meditate, think out 9 think over 10 excogitate, scrutinize
contemplation 5 study 6 musing 7 thought 8 thinking 9 brainwork, pondering 10 cogitation, meditation, reflection, rumination 11 cerebration, speculation 12 deliberation
contemplative 6 musing 7 pensive 8 thinking, weighing 9 pondering, reasoning 10 cogitative, meditative, reflecting, reflective, ruminative, thoughtful 11 speculative
contemporary 2 up 6 coeval, extant 7 abreast, current, instant, present 8 existent, existing, todayish, up-to-date 9 au courant 10 coetaneous, coexistent, coexisting, coincident, concurrent, present-day, synchronal, synchronic 11 concomitant, synchronous 12 simultaneous 13 up-to-the-minute
contempt 5 scorn, shame 6 hatred, infamy 7 despite, disdain, mockery, sarcasm 8 aversion, defiance, despisal, disfavor, disgrace, dishonor, distaste, ignominy 9 antipathy, contumacy, discredit, disesteem, disrepute 10 opprobrium, repugnance 11 despisement 12 stubbornness 13 disparagement, recalcitrance
contemptible 3 bad, low 4 base, evil, mean, poor, vile 5 cheap, sorry 6 abject, odious, scummy, scurvy, shabby, sordid 7 hateful, ignoble, pitiful 8 beggarly, infamous, inferior, pitiable, shameful 9 abhorrent 10 abominable, despicable, despisable, detestable, disgusting 11 ignominious
contemptible one *suffix:* 3 een, eer
contemptuous 7 haughty 8 arrogant, scornful 10 disdainful 12 supercilious
contend 3 say, tug, vie, war 4 cope, face, meet, tell, urge 5 argue, brawl, claim, fight, rival 6 assert, battle, charge, combat, defend, enjoin, oppose, oppugn, report, resist 7 compete, contest, justify, warrant 8 confront, cope with, maintain 9 encounter, vindicate, withstand
___ contendere 4 nolo
content 4 cozy, gist 5 happy 6 at ease 7 appease, gratify, satisfy 9 satisfied, substance 12 significance
contention 3 war 4 feud 6 hurrah, rumpus, strife, thesis 7 discord, dispute, dissent, quarrel, rivalry, wrangle 8 argument, conflict, disunity, squabble, variance 9 discord 10 difference, dissension, dissidence 11 altercation, competition, controversy 12 contestation *Scottish:* 5 sturt
contentious 5 fiery 7 carping, froward, peppery, scrappy, warlike 8 captious, caviling, contrary, militant, perverse 9 bellicose, combative, hotheaded, impetuous, litigious, polemical, truculent 10 pugnacious 11 belligerent, quarrelsome 12 disputatious, faultfinding, gladiatorial 13 argumentative, controversial
conterminous 8 abutting, adjacent, touching 9 adjoining, bordering 10 approximal, contiguous, juxtaposed
contest 3 sue, vie 4 bout, buck, duel, feud, fray, game, meet, race, tilt 5 clash, fight, match, repel, rival, trial 6 battle, combat, debate, oppose, resist, strife, strive, trying 7 compete, contend, dispute, rivalry, testing, warfare 8 argument, concours, conflict, endeavor, skirmish, striving, struggle, tug-of-war 9 emulation, encounter, rencontre, withstand 10 engagement, tournament 11 competition *combining form:* 5 machy
contiguity 9 adjacency, confinity, immediacy, proximity 11 propinquity 13 appropinquity

contiguous 4 near, next, nigh 5 close 6 nearby 7 close-by 8 abutting, adjacent, touching 9 adjoining, bordering 10 approximal, juxtaposed, near-at-hand 11 close-at-hand, neighboring 12 conterminous

continence 6 purity, virtue 8 chastity, sobriety 10 abstinence, chasteness, moderation, temperance 13 self-restraint, temperateness

continent 4 Asia, mass, pure 5 sober 6 Africa, chaste, curbed, Europe 7 America, bridled 8 mainland 9 abstinent, Australia, inhibited, temperate 10 abstemious, Antarctica, restrained 11 abstentious 12 North America, South America *lost:* 8 Atlantis

continental pool 3 EEC 12 Common Market

contingence 5 touch 7 contact

contingency 4 pass 5 break, event, pinch 6 chance, crisis, strait 8 exigency, juncture, occasion, zero hour 9 emergency 10 crossroads 11 opportunity, possibility 12 turning point

contingent 3 odd 5 fluky 6 casual, chance, likely 7 reliant 8 possible, probable, relative 9 dependent 10 accidental, fortuitous, incidental, unforeseen 11 conditional 13 unanticipated, unforeseeable

continual 6 steady 7 abiding, endless, running, staying 8 constant, enduring, minutely, timeless, unending, unwaning 9 ceaseless, incessant, perpetual, unceasing, unfailing, unvarying 10 continuous, persistent, persisting, relentless, unchanging, unflagging 11 everlasting, unremitting 12 interminable 13 unintermitted, uninterrupted

continually 4 ever 6 always 7 forever, running 8 together 10 constantly 11 incessantly, night and day 12 successively 13 consecutively

continuance 3 run 4 stay 5 delay 6 sequel 8 duration, survival 9 constancy, longevity 10 permanence 11 persistence 12 postponement, prolongation

continuation 3 run 8 duration 9 endurance, extension 11 persistence, protraction 12 prolongation

continue 4 go on, last, ride, stay 5 abide, renew, run on 6 endure, pick up, remain, reopen, resume, retain, take up 7 carry on, outlast, outlive, perdure, persist, prolong, restart, survive 8 maintain, postpone 9 carry over, persevere 10 recommence 12 carry through

continuing 3 old 7 ongoing 8 constant, enduring, lifelong 9 long-lived, perennial 10 inveterate 11 long-lasting

continuity 6 script 8 duration, scenario 9 endurance 11 persistence

continuous see continual

continuously see continually

contort 3 wry 4 bend, warp, wind 5 curve, gnarl, twist, wring 6 deform, writhe 7 distort, grimace, torture 8 misshape

contortionist 7 acrobat

contour 4 form, line 5 curve, shape 7 outline, profile 9 lineament, lineation 10 figuration, silhouette 11 delineation

contra 5 again 6 facing, toward 7 against, counter, reverse, vis-à-vis 8 antipode, antipole, converse, fronting, opposite 9 vice versa 10 antithesis, conversely, oppositely

contraband 3 hot 5 taboo 6 banned 7 bootleg, illegal, illicit, shut out, smuggle 8 excluded 9 forbidden 10 prohibited, proscribed 11 disapproved

contract 3 get 4 bond, fail, knit, pact, sink, take 5 catch, cause, incur, lease, limit, upset 6 engage, induce, lessen, obtain, reduce, shrink, treaty, weaken 7 abridge, acquire, afflict, bargain, betroth, bring on, compact, decline, derange, dwindle, wrinkle 8 affiance, compress, condense, covenant, decrease, diminish, disorder, restrict, sicken of 9 agreement, betrothal, constrict, indispose, succumb to 10 convention, sicken with 11 concentrate, transaction 12 come down with *maritime:* 8 bottomry *part:* 6 clause 7 article, proviso

contraction 3 it's, tis 4 ain't, can't, don't, flex, isn't, won't 5 aren't, cramp, didn't, spasm 7 elision 9 reduction, shrinkage 10 abridgment 12 abbreviation *heart's:* 7 systole *poetic:* 3 e'en, e'er, o'er, 'tis 4 ne'er, 'twas 5 'twere, 'twill

contradict 4 deny 5 belie, cross, rebut 6 impugn, negate 7 dispute, gainsay 8 negative, traverse 9 disaffirm 10 contravene

contradiction 6 denial 7 paradox 8 antinomy, negation 10 gainsaying

contradictory 7 counter, reverse 8 antipode, antipole, contrary, converse, negating, opposite 9 antipodal 10 antipodean, antithesis, nullifying 11 counterpole 12 antagonistic, antithetical 13 counteractive

contraption 3 rig 6 device, gadget 7 machine 11 contrivance

contrariety 3 con 8 opposure 10 antagonism, antithesis, opposition

contrariwise 5 again 9 vice versa 10 conversely, oppositely

contrary 5 balky, polar 6 averse, ornery, unruly 7 counter, froward, restive, reverse, wayward 8 antipode, antipole, clashing, converse, opposite, perverse, recusant, stubborn 9 antipodal, diametric, dissident, obstinate, vice versa 10 antipodean, antithesis, conversely, discordant, headstrong, oppositely, rebellious, refractory 11 conflicting, counterpole, dissentient, intractable, wrongheaded 12 antagonistic, antipathetic, antithetical, contumacious, cross-grained, recalcitrant 13 contradictory, insubordinate, nonconforming, nonconformist *prefix:* 3 dis 5 retro 6 contra 7 counter

contrast 7 compare 9 diversity 10 comparison, difference, divergence

contravene 4 defy, deny 5 break, cross, fight, spurn 6 abjure, breach, combat, disown, impugn, negate, offend, oppose, reject, resist 7 exclude, gainsay, infract, violate 8 disclaim, infringe, negative, traverse 9 disaffirm, repudiate 10 contradict, transgress

contravention 3 sin 4 vice 5 crime 6 breach 7 offense 8 trespass 9 violation 10 infraction 12 infringement 13 transgression

contretemps 4 slip 6 mishap 7 tragedy 9 adversity, mischance 10 misfortune

contribute 3 aid 4 give, help, tend 5 add to 6 assist, chip in, donate, kick in, submit, supply 7 augment, conduce, fortify, pitch in, recruit, redound 9 reinforce, subscribe 10 strengthen, supplement 11 come through

contribution 4 alms, gift 5 share 7 charity, present 8 donation, offering 11 benefaction, beneficence

contributory 8 adjuvant 9 accessory, ancillary, auxiliary 10 collateral, subsidiary 11 appurtenant, subservient

contrite 5 sorry 8 penitent 9 regretful, repentant 10 apologetic, remorseful 11 attritional, penitential 12 compunctious

contriteness see contrition

contrition 3 rue 4 ruth 7 penance, remorse 9 attrition, penitence, penitency 10 repentance 11 compunction

contrivance 3 art 6 device 7 coinage, machine 8 artifice 9 apparatus, invention 10 brainchild 11 contraption

contrive 3 rig 4 fake, make, move, plan, plot 5 fix up, frame 6 cook up, devise, handle, invent, make up, scheme, vamp up, wangle 7 collude, concoct, connive, develop, dream up, fashion, hatch up, project, work out 8 cogitate, conspire, intrigue 9 elaborate, fabricate, formulate, machinate, scheme out

contrived 5 hokey 6 forced 7 labored 10 artificial

control 4 curb, rein, rule, sway 5 might, power, quell 6 adjust, bridle, corner, direct, govern, handle, manage, master, subdue 7 command, compose, contain, mastery, repress, smother, strings 8 dominate, monopoly, regulate, restrain 9 authority, supervise 10 discipline, domination 12 jurisdiction

controlled 4 tame 8 discreet, moderate 9 temperate, unextreme 10 reasonable, restrained 11 unexcessive 12 conservative

controversial 7 eristic 9 litigious, polemical 11 contentious 12 disputatious 13 argumentative

controversy 3 row 4 miff, tiff 6 debate, rumpus, strife 7 dispute, quarrel, wrangle 8 argument, squabble 9 bickering 10 contention, falling-out 11 altercation, embroilment

controvert 4 deny 5 break, rebut 6 oppugn, refute 7 confute 8 confound, disprove, question 9 challenge 10 disconfirm

contumacious 6 unruly 7 froward 8 contrary, factious, insolent, mutinous, perverse 9 insurgent, seditious 10 rebellious 13 insubordinate

contumacy 7 despite 8 contempt, defiance 12 stubbornness 13 recalcitrance

contumelious 4 bold 5 saucy 6 brazen 7 abusive, scurril 8 impudent, insolent, scurrile 9 audacious, invective, truculent 10 scurrilous, vituperous 11 impertinent, opprobrious 12 vituperative, vituperatory

contumely 4 slap 5 abuse 6 insult 7 affront, despite, obloquy 9 aspersion, indignity, invective, stricture 10 scurrility 12 billingsgate, vituperation 13 animadversion

contuse 5 black 6 bruise, injure

conundrum 3 why 6 enigma, puzzle, riddle 7 mystery, problem 10 puzzlement 13 Chinese puzzle, mystification

convalesce 4 mend 7 improve, recover 10 recuperate

convene 3 sit 4 call, meet, open 6 call in, gather, muster, summon 7 convoke, summons 8 assemble 10 congregate

convenience 4 ease 6 toilet 7 amenity, benefit, comfort

convenient 3 fit 4 good, meet, near, next, nigh 5 close, handy 6 nearby, proper, useful 7 close-by 8 adjacent, suitable 9 immediate 10 accessible, near-at-hand 11 appropriate, close-at-hand

convent 5 abbey 6 friary, priory 7 nunnery 9 monastery, sanctuary

convention 3 law 4 bond, form, pact, rule 5 canon, usage 6 accord, custom, treaty 7 bargain, compact, concord, meeting, precept 8 assembly, contract, covenant, practice 9 agreement, gathering, tradition 10 convenance 11 transaction 13 understanding

conventional 5 trite, usual 6 decent, formal, normal, proper, seemly, solemn, square 7 correct, stately 8 decorous, moderate, ordinary, orthodox, priggish, reliable, straight 9 temperate 10 button-down, ceremonial, dependable, fastidious, restrained, scrupulous 11 ceremonious, commonplace, constrained, responsible, traditional 12 conservative 13 conscientious

conventionalize 5 adapt 7 conform, stylize

converge 4 join, meet 5 focus 8 approach 9 concenter 11 concentrate

conversant 5 awake, aware 6 au fait, versed 7 abreast, knowing, witting 8 familiar, informed, sensible, sentient, up-to-date 9 au courant, cognizant, conscious 10 acquainted, perceptive, percipient 12 apprehending, apprehensive 13 comprehending

conversation 4 chat, talk 6 confab, debate, parley, speech 7 comment, talking 8 causerie, colloquy, dialogue, duologue, repartee, shoptalk 9 cross talk, discourse, tête-à-tête 10 discussion 13 confabulation

conversation piece 6 oddity 9 curiosity

converse 4 chat, chin, talk, yarn 5 polar, speak, visit 6 contra, parley 7 commune, counter, reverse 8 antipode, antipole, colloque, colloquy, contrary, dialogue, opposite 9 antipodal, communion, diametric, discourse 10 antipodean, antithesis 11 counterpole 12 antithetical 13 communication, confabulation, contradictory

conversely 6 contra 8 contrary 9 vice versa 10 contrawise, oppositely 12 contrariwise

conversion 5 shift 6 change 7 novelty, rebirth, turning 8 metanoia, mutation, reversal 9 about-face 10 alteration, changeover, innovation 11 permutation, reclamation 12 modification, regeneration 13 metamorphosis, qualification, transmutation

convert 4 lead, make, move, save, sway 5 alter, bring, forge 6 change, redeem, reform 7 commute, incline 8 persuade 9 proselyte, transform, translate, transmute, transpose 11 proselytize, transfigure 12 metamorphose, transmogrify ***Christian:*** 10 catechumen

convex 5 bowed, toric 6 arched, curved 7 bulging, gibbous, rounded

convey 3 lug 4 bear, buck, cart, cede, deed, pack, pipe, send, tote 5 bring, carry, ferry 6 assign, funnel, impart, pass on, remise, siphon 7 channel, conduct, consign, project, traject 8 make over, sign over, transfer, transmit 9 put across, transport 11 communicate

conveyance 3 car 4 auto, cart, deed, sled 5 coach, coupe, sedan, stage, wagon 7 charter, trailer, transit, vehicle 8 carriage, carrying 9 transport 10 automobile 12 transporting ***public:*** 2 el 3 bus, cab 4 taxi, tram 5 plane, train 7 ricksha, trolley 8 airplane, monorail, railroad, rickshaw 9 streetcar 10 jinricksha, jinrikisha

convict 4 find 5 felon, lifer 6 inmate, trusty 7 captive 8 criminal, jailbird, prisoner, sentence 10 malefactor

conviction 4 mind, view 5 creed, faith 6 belief, surety 7 feeling, opinion 8 doctrine, sureness 9 assurance, certainty, certitude, sentiment 10 confidence, persuasion 11 assuredness

convince 3 get 4 draw 6 assure, induce, prompt 7 satisfy, win over 8 persuade, talk into 9 argue into, prevail on 11 bring around, prevail upon

convincing 5 solid, sound, valid 6 cogent, trusty 7 telling 8 credible, faithful 9 authentic 10 persuasive, satisfying 11 trustworthy 12 satisfactory

convivial 3 gay 5 jolly, merry 6 jocund, jovial, lively, social 7 festive 8 sociable 9 vivacious 13 companionable

convocation 5 synod 7 council, meeting 8 assembly 9 gathering 10 assemblage 12 congregation

convoke 3 ask, bid, sit 4 call, meet 6 gather, invite, summon 7 collect, convene, request 8 assemble 10 congregate

convoluted 5 snaky 6 coiled 7 complex, sinuous, winding 8 flexuous, tortuous 9 meandrous 10 meandering, serpentine 11 anfractuous

convoy 4 bear 5 guard, guide, train 6 attend, defend, escort, shield 7 company, conduct, protect 9 accompany, companion, safeguard 11 consort with

convulse 4 rock 5 shake 7 agitate, concuss 8 tetanize

convulsion 3 fit 5 spasm 6 attack, clamor, outcry, tumult, uproar, upturn 7 ferment, quaking, rocking, shaking 8 disaster, laughter, upheaval 9 commotion, trembling

cook 3 fix, fry 4 bake, boil, burn, chef, melt, stew 5 broil, frame, grill, poach, roast, sauté, steam 6 braise, devise, invent, make up, scorch, simmer 7 concoct, dream up, griddle, hatch up, parboil, prepare, swelter 8 barbecue, cocinero, contrive 9 formulate

cooked 4 done ***combining form:*** 5 cocto ***with tomatoes:*** 10 cacciatore

cookery 7 cuisine 8 magirics ***expert:*** 5 Bates, Beard, Child 6 Farmer 7 Crocker 9 Claiborne

cookie 4 cake, snap 7 biscuit, brownie 8 macaroon 10 gingersnap

cooking ***appliance:*** 4 oven 5 mixer, range, stove 7 blender, toaster 10 rotisserie ***implement:*** 3 cup, pan, pot, wok 4 olla 5 ladle, sieve, spoon, whisk 6 frypan, grater, masher, sifter, tureen 7 griddle, skillet, spatula 8 colander 9 eggbeater 10 rolling pin 12 measuring cup ***room:*** 6 galley 7 kitchen

cool 3 fan, ice 4 calm, cold 5 allay, aloof,

chill, frore, gelid, nippy, sober **6** arctic, chilly, frigid, frosty, offish, placid, serene, stolid **7** assured, collect, compose, control, distant, repress **8** composed, detached, freezing, reserved, restrain, solitary, suppress, tranquil **9** collected, confident, impassive, unruffled, withdrawn **10** nonchalant, phlegmatic, simmer down, unsociable **11** indifferent, standoffish, unflappable **12** happy-go-lucky **13** imperturbable, self-possessed

cooler **3** fan **4** coop, icer, jail **6** lockup, prison **11** refrigerant **12** refrigerator

cooling device **3** fan **4** icer **6** icebox **7** freezer **12** refrigerator

coolness **6** aplomb, phlegm **7** ataraxy **8** calmness **9** composure, sangfroid **10** equanimity

coop **3** hem, mew, pen **4** cage, jail **5** cramp, fence **6** corral, shut in **7** close in, confine, enclose, envelop **9** enclosure

cooperate **5** agree, unite **6** concur, league **7** combine, conjoin, connive **8** coadjute, coincide **11** collaborate

cooperation **8** teamwork

cooperative **8** coacting, coactive, conjoint, synergic **9** concerted **10** synergetic **11** coefficient **13** collaborative, uncompetitive

coordinate **4** mate, tune **5** adapt, atune, match **6** fellow **7** conform, vis-à-vis **9** companion, harmonize, integrate, reconcile **10** proportion, reciprocal **11** accommodate **12** reconciliate

cop **3** nab **4** lift, take **5** filch, pinch, steal, swipe **7** gumshoe, officer, purloin **8** bluecoat **9** patrolman, policeman **11** appropriate

copacetic **4** fine, okay **5** dandy **12** satisfactory

cope **4** arch, bend, face **5** cover, dress, get by, match, notch, vault **6** canopy, handle, make do, manage, mantel, muzzle **8** deal with **9** encounter

copestone **5** crown

copious **4** full, lush, rich **5** ample **6** lavish, plenty **7** liberal, profuse, replete **8** abundant, generous **9** abounding, bounteous, bountiful, exuberant, luxuriant, plenteous, plentiful

cop-out **6** excuse **7** pretext, retreat

copper **4** cent, coin **5** metal, penny, token **6** cuprum **9** butterfly, policeman ***combining form:*** **4** cupr **5** chalc, chalk, cupri, cupro **6** chalko ***item:*** **4** cent **5** penny **6** kettle ***sulfate:*** **7** vitriol **9** bluestone **11** blue vitriol ***symbol:*** **2** Cu

copperhead **5** snake, viper **8** squirrel

coppice **4** bosk, wood **5** copse, grove **6** bosque, forest, growth **7** thicket **9** brushwood, underwood

copse see coppice

Copt **8** Egyptian

copula **4** link **5** union **7** coupler

copy **3** ape **4** echo, fake, mock, sham **5** ditto, mimic **6** carbon, ectype, effigy, ersatz, parody, repeat **7** emulate, imitate, replica, takeoff **8** knockoff, likeness, simulate, travesty **9** burlesque, duplicate, facsimile, imitation, replicate, reproduce **10** carbon copy, impression, simulacrum, transcribe **11** counterfeit, counterpart, reduplicate, replication **12** reproduction **13** reduplication

copyist **6** scribe **9** engrosser **10** plagiarist **12** calligrapher **13** calligraphist

copyread **4** edit

coquet **3** toy **4** fool **5** dally, flirt **6** lead on, trifle **11** string along

coquette **4** vamp **5** flirt **11** hummingbird

coquettish **3** coy **4** arch **7** roguish

coral **3** red **4** pink **5** palus, polyp **6** palule **8** skeleton **9** limestone

coral reef **5** atoll ***off Australia:*** **5** Wreck ***world's largest:*** **12** Great Barrier

cord **3** tie **4** band, lace, pile, rope, whip, wire, yarn **5** cable, nerve, stack **6** strand, string, tendon, thread **7** amentum ***twisted:*** **7** torsade

cordage **4** rope **5** ropes **7** rigging ***fiber:*** **4** bast, eruc, hemp, imbe, jute, pita **5** sisal

Corday's victim **5** Marat

Cordelia ***father:*** **4** Lear ***sister:*** **5** Regan **7** Goneril

cordial **4** warm **5** drink, sonsy **6** genial, hearty, tender **7** affable, liqueur, sincere **8** friendly, gracious, sociable **9** congenial, courteous, heartfelt **10** hospitable, responsive **11** sympathetic, warmhearted **12** wholehearted

cordiality **5** ardor, favor **6** warmth **7** amenity **8** approval, sympathy **9** geniality, mutuality, pleasance **10** amiability **12** agreeability, friendliness, pleasantness **13** agreeableness, enjoyableness

cordon **4** lace **5** braid **6** circle, ribbon **7** barrier ***blue:*** **4** chef, cook **6** ribbon **10** decoration

core **3** hub, nub **4** base, body, bulk, gist, mass, meat, pith, root **5** basis, cadre, focus, heart, midst, quick **6** amount, burden, center, corpus, middle, origin, staple, thrust, upshot **7** purport **8** midpoint **9** substance **10** foundation

corf **3** tub **4** cage **5** truck **6** basket

corium **4** skin **5** cutis, layer **6** dermis

cork **4** bark, plug, seal, stop **5** float **6** bobber **7** stopper, stopple ***combining form:*** **6** phello

corker **4** lulu **5** dandy, dilly **8** jim-dandy, knockout **9** humdinger **11** crackerjack, lalapalooza

corkscrew 4 coil, curl, wind 5 twine, twist 6 spiral 7 entwine, wreathe
cormorant 4 bird, shag 7 glutton 8 Scottish *norie:* 5 scart
corn 3 zea 4 meal, salt, samp 5 grain, maize 6 clavus, hominy 9 granulate *bread:* 4 pone 7 bannock *Indian:* 3 zea 5 maize 6 mealie *kind:* 3 pop 4 dent 5 flint, flour, sweet 6 Indian *pest:* 5 borer *piece:* 3 cob, ear 5 spike 6 kernel, nubbin
Corncracker State 8 Kentucky
corner 3 box, fix, jam, nab 4 hole, nook, trap, tree 5 angle, catch, coign, niche, seize 6 collar, cranny, dogleg, pickle, plight, recess, scrape 7 capture, dilemma, impasse, trouble 8 bottle up, monopoly 10 bring to bay 11 predicament *combining form:* 4 goni 5 gonio 6 anguli, angulo *of eye:* 7 canthus
cornerstone 4 base 5 basis 7 support 10 foundation, groundwork
cornet 4 cone, horn 5 zinke 8 woodwind 9 cornopean 10 instrument
cornflower 10 bluebonnet, bluebottle
Cornhusker State 8 Nebraska
cornice 3 cap 4 band, eave 5 crown 6 geison 7 molding 8 swanneck *combining form:* 6 geisso
cornmeal 4 masa, samp 5 atole 7 hoecake *mush:* 7 polenta
cornucopia 4 cone, horn 9 abundance 12 horn of plenty
Cornwallis *adversary:* 6 Greene *surrender site:* 8 Yorktown
corny 5 banal, stale, tired, trite 6 old hat 7 clichéd 8 shopworn 9 hackneyed 10 warmed over 11 commonplace, sentimental, stereotyped
corollary 6 effect, result, sequel, upshot 8 sequence 9 resulting 10 associated, end product, equivalent 11 aftereffect, consequence, precipitate
corona 4 halo 5 cigar, crown, glory 6 circle, rosary, wreath 7 aureola, aureole, circlet, fermata, garland
coronal see coronet
coroner 7 crowner, officer 8 examiner
coronet 4 band 5 crown 6 anadem, circle, wreath 7 chaplet, circlet, garland
Coronis *form:* 4 crow *son:* 9 Asclepius 11 Aesculapius
corporal 3 NCO 5 fanon 6 bodily, carnal 7 fleshly, somatic 8 physical
corporate 6 united 7 unified 8 combined 9 aggregate
corporeal 5 hylic, somal 6 bodily, carnal 7 fleshly, somatic 8 material, physical, sensible, tangible 9 objective 10 phenomenal 11 substantial
corps 4 band 5 party, troop 6 outfit, troupe 7 company
corpse 4 body, mort 5 bones, stiff 7 cadaver, carcass, carrion, remains *combining form:* 4 necr 5 necro
corpselike 4 dead 6 deadly 7 deathly, ghastly, ghostly, shadowy 8 deadened, deathful, spectral 10 cadaverous
corpulence 7 fatness, obesity 9 adiposity 10 fleshiness
corpulent 3 fat 5 bulky, gross, heavy, obese, plump, stout 6 fleshy, portly 7 weighty 9 overblown 10 overweight
corpus 4 body, bulk, core, mass 6 oeuvre, staple 9 substance
corpuscle 4 cell 7 hematid 8 hemocyte, monocyte 9 leukocyte 10 lymphocyte 11 erythrocyte, granulocyte
corral 3 hem, mew, pen 4 cage, coop 5 fence, hedge 6 shut in 7 close in, confine, enclose 8 surround 9 enclosure
correct 3 fit, fix 4 done, edit, mend, true 5 amend, emend, exact, right 6 adjust, better, decent, proper, punish, reform, remedy, revise, seemly 7 chasten, improve, perfect, precise, rectify, redress 8 accurate, becoming, chastise, decorous, emendate, flawless, make over, regulate 9 castigate, faultless, veracious, veridical 10 conforming, discipline, impeccable, meticulous, scrupulous 11 comme il faut, punctilious, undistorted 12 conventional *combining form:* 4 orth 5 ortho
correction 3 rod 8 punition 10 discipline, punishment 11 castigation 12 chastisement
corrective 4 cure 6 remedy 8 antidote, remedial 11 counterstep 12 counteragent 13 counteractant, counteractive
correctness 5 order 7 decorum 8 accuracy 9 coherence, congruity, exactness, precision, propriety 10 definitude, exactitude, properness, seemliness 11 orderliness, preciseness 12 decorousness, definiteness
correlate 5 match 6 analog 7 pendant 8 analogue, parallel 10 complement 11 counterpart, countertype 13 correspondent
correlative 2 if, or 3 nor 4 then 6 either 7 neither, related 10 reciprocal 13 corresponding
correspond 4 jibe, suit 5 agree, equal, match, write 6 accord, concur 7 conform, consort 8 dovetail 9 harmonize 11 communicate
correspondence 4 mail 7 letters 8 homogeny, symmetry 9 agreement, congruity 10 conformity 11 consistency *mathematical:* 7 mapping 8 function
correspondent 5 match 6 analog, pen pal, writer 7 fitting 8 analogue, parallel,

suitable **9** correlate **11** counterpart, countertype
corresponding **4** akin, like **5** alike **6** agnate **7** similar **8** parallel **9** analogous, consonant **10** comparable ***prefix:*** **7** counter
correspondingly **2** so **4** also **8** likewise **9** similarly
corrida **9** bullfight ***shout:*** **3** olé
corridor **4** hall **7** couloir, hallway, passage **10** passageway
corroborate **6** verify **7** bear out, confirm, justify **8** validate **12** authenticate, substantiate
corroborative **7** helping **9** ancillary, assisting, auxiliary **10** collateral, supportive **11** adminicular **12** confirmative, confirmatory, verificatory
corroboratory see **corroborative**
corrode **3** eat **4** bite, gnaw, rust **5** erode, scour **7** eat away **8** wear away
corrosive **5** acerb **7** acerbic, caustic **9** sarcastic **12** archilochian
corrosiveness **7** sarcasm **8** acerbity **10** causticity
corrugation **4** fold, ruck **5** plica, ridge, rivel **6** crease, furrow, rimple **7** crinkle, wrinkle
corrupt **3** low, rot **4** foul, ruin, turn, warp **5** abase, decay, snide, spoil, stain, taint, venal, wreck **6** abased, befoul, debase, defile, molder, rotten, smirch **7** baneful, crooked, crumble, debauch, degrade, deprave, devious, knavish, noxious, oblique, pervert, putrefy, tarnish, vicious, vitiate **8** bribable, degraded, depraved, infamous, perverse, two-faced **9** animalize, break down, decompose, dishonest, faithless, mercenary, miscreant, nefarious, reprobate, unethical **10** bastardize, degenerate, demoralize, flagitious, inconstant, perfidious, pernicious, unfaithful, unreliable, villainous **11** deleterious, detrimental, treacherous **12** blackguardly, disintegrate, undependable, unprincipled, unscrupulous **13** double-dealing, untrustworthy
corruptible **5** venal **7** buyable **8** bribable **11** purchasable
corruption **4** vice **7** jobbery **8** slangism, solecism **9** barbarism, depravity, vulgarism **10** immorality, wickedness **11** impropriety **13** vernacularism, vernacularity
corsair **5** rover **6** pirate, sea dog **7** sea wolf **8** picaroon, sea rover **9** buccaneer, sea robber **10** freebooter
corset **6** bodice, girdle **7** support
cortex **4** bark, peel, rind **8** peridium ***combining form:*** **7** cortico
Cortland **5** apple
corundum **4** ruby **5** emery, topaz **7** emerald **8** abrasive, amethyst, sapphire
coruscate **5** flash, gleam, glint **7** glisten, glitter, sparkle **11** scintillate
Corvino's wife **5** Celia
corybantic **3** mad **4** wild **5** rabid **7** frantic, furious **8** frenetic, frenzied **9** delirious
coryphée **6** dancer, hoofer **7** danseur **8** danseuse, figurant **9** ballerina, figurante **10** ballet girl **11** dancing girl
Cosi fan tutte composer **6** Mozart
cosmetic **4** kohl **5** henna, rouge **6** ceruse, makeup, powder **7** blusher, bronzer, mascara **8** lipgloss, lipstick **9** eye shadow **10** nail polish **11** beautifying, superficial
cosmetologist **10** beautician
cosmic **6** global **8** catholic **9** planetary, universal, worldwide **10** ecumenical **12** cosmopolitan
cosmopolitan **6** cosmic, global, smooth, urbane **8** catholic, cultured, polished **9** civilized, planetary, universal, worldwide **10** cultivated, ecumenical **11** worldly-wise **12** metropolitan **13** sophisticated
cosmos **5** world **6** nature **8** creation, universe
Cossack ***army:*** **3** Don **4** Ural **5** Kuban **6** voisko ***district:*** **6** okrugi ***land:*** **7** Ukraine ***leader:*** **5** Razin **6** ataman, hetman, Mazepa **7** Bulavin **8** Pugachev ***novel:*** **10** Taras Bulba ***village:*** **8** stanitsa, stanitza
cosset **3** pet **4** baby, love **5** humor, spoil **6** caress, cocker, coddle, cuddle, dandle, fondle, pamper **7** cater to, indulge **11** mollycoddle
cost **3** tab **4** rate, toll **5** price **6** charge, outlay, tariff **7** expense **8** price tag **11** expenditure **12** disbursement ***business:*** **8** overhead
Costa Rica ***capital:*** **7** San José ***monetary unit:*** **5** colon
costermonger **6** hawker **7** peddler **9** barrow boy, barrowman
costive **4** mean **5** bound, close, tight **6** stingy **7** miserly **9** astricted, penurious **10** hardfisted, obstipated **12** cheeseparing, parsimonious
costless **4** free **6** gratis **10** chargeless, gratuitous **13** complimentary
costly **4** dear, high **5** fancy, pricy, steep, stiff **6** pricey **7** premium **8** precious, valuable **9** excessive, expensive, priceless **10** exorbitant, inordinate, invaluable **11** extravagant, inestimable
costume **3** rig **4** garb, mode **5** dress, getup, guise, style **6** outfit, setout **7** fashion, turnout
cot **3** hut **4** camp **5** cabin, lodge, shack **6** shanty **7** cottage ***hanging:*** **7** hammock ***wheeled:*** **6** gurney
coterie **3** mob **4** camp, clan, ring **5** cabal **6** circle, clique **7** ingroup **9** camarilla
cottage **3** hut **4** camp **5** cabin, lodge,

shack 6 shanty 8 bungalow ***Russian:*** 5 dacha ***Swiss:*** 6 chalet
cotton 4 take 5 agree, grasp, toady 6 accept, coddle, kowtow 7 cater to, honey up 8 bootlick, perceive 9 apprehend, harmonize 10 comprehend, fraternize, understand ***cleaner:*** 3 gin 5 willy 6 linter, willow ***cloth:*** 4 jean, pima 5 khaki 6 canvas 7 galatea, jaconet, percale, silesia ***cloth, Indian:*** 5 Surat 6 humhum 7 dhurrie ***comb:*** 4 card ***Egyptian:*** 4 maco ***fabric:*** 3 rep 4 duck, lawn, leno, mull, repp 5 chino, crash, denim, doria, drill, manta, scrim, terry, wigan 6 calico, chintz, dimity, madras, muslin, nankin, sateen, satine 7 batiste, etamine, fustian, nankeen, nanking, organdy 8 drilling, nainsook 9 grenadine 10 seersucker ***fabric, lustrous:*** 6 sateen, satine ***fabric, sheer:*** 5 voile ***fiber, short:*** 4 noil ***fuzz remover:*** 6 linter ***knot:*** 3 nep 4 slub ***measure:*** 3 lea 4 hank, pick, yard 5 count, skein ***pad:*** 7 pledget ***pod:*** 4 boll ***refuse:*** 5 flock 8 grabbots ***seed separator:*** 3 gin ***sheet:*** 3 bat 4 batt ***thread:*** 5 lisle
Cotton State 7 Alabama
cottonwood 5 alamo 6 poplar
cottony 4 soft 5 silky 6 satiny, silken 7 velvety
Coty or Descartes 4 René
couch 3 den, put 4 lair, sink, sofa, word 5 divan, droop, lodge, lower 6 burrow, daybed, phrase 7 depress, express, let down 9 davenport, formulate 12 chesterfield
cougar 3 cat 4 puma 7 panther 9 catamount
cough 6 tussis ***drop:*** 6 troche 7 lozenge
couloir 4 hall 5 gorge 7 hallway, passage 8 corridor 10 passageway
council 4 diet 5 junta 6 senate 7 cabinet, meeting 8 assembly, conclave, congress, ministry 10 conference, federation 12 consultation ***ancient Greek:*** 5 boule ***church:*** 5 synod 10 consistory ***medieval English:*** 4 moot 5 gemot 6 gemote 7 husting 8 hustings ***Muslim:*** 5 divan, diwan ***Russian:*** 4 duma 5 douma 6 soviet ***secret:*** 5 cabal, junto ***Spanish:*** 7 cabildo
counsel 4 urge, warn 5 order 6 advice, advise, charge, direct, enjoin, lawyer, prompt 7 suggest 8 admonish, advocate, attorney 9 prescribe, recommend, reprehend 10 advisement ***British:*** 9 barrister, solicitor
count 3 add, sum, tot 4 hope, look, mean 5 tally, total, weigh 6 bank on, census, expect, figure, import, matter, number, reckon, rely on 7 build on, compute, signify, trust in, trust to 8 bank upon, depend on, estimate, militate, numerate, quantify, reckon on, rely upon 9 calculate, enumerate 10 depend upon 11 calculate on
countenance 3 mug 4 back, cast, face, look, phiz 5 favor, go for 6 accept, visage 7 approve, commend, support 8 advocate, features, hold with 9 approbate, encourage 10 expression ***combining form:*** 6 prosop 7 prosopo
counter 3 pit, vie 4 anti 5 match, polar 6 oppose 7 adverse, hostile, reverse 8 antipode, antipole, contrary, converse, impeding, opposite 9 antipodal, diametric, hindering, oppugnant 10 antipodean, antithesis 11 obstructive 12 antagonistic, antithetical 13 contradictory
counteract 3 fix 5 annul 6 negate 7 correct, rectify, redress 8 negative 9 cancel out, frustrate 10 neutralize
counteractant 4 cure 6 remedy 8 antidote 10 corrective
counteragent see **counteractant**
counterbalance 6 make up, offset, redeem, set off 7 correct, rectify 8 atone for, outweigh 10 compensate
counterblow 7 revenge 8 avenging, reprisal, requital, revanche 9 vengeance 10 avengement 11 retaliation, retribution
countercheck 5 annul 6 negate 7 redress 8 negative 9 cancel out, frustrate 10 neutralize
counterfeit 3 act, ape, gyp 4 copy, fake, hoax, sham 5 bluff, bogus, dummy, false, feign, fraud, mimic, phony 6 affect, assume, deceit, pseudo 7 feigned, imitate, pretend 8 delusive, delusory, simulate, spurious 9 brummagem, deception, deceptive, imposture, pinchbeck, pretended, simulated 10 fraudulent, misleading, simulacrum ***combining form:*** 5 pseud 6 pseudo
counterpane 6 spread 8 bedcover, coverlet 9 bedspread
counterpart 4 like 5 equal, match 6 analog 7 vis-à-vis 8 analogue, parallel 9 correlate 10 complement, coordinate, equivalent 13 correspondent
counterpoise 4 trim 6 make up, offset, redeem, set off, stasis, steady 7 balance, ballast 8 atone for, outweigh 9 stabilize 10 compensate 11 equilibrium
counterpole see **opposite**
countersign 4 word 8 password 9 watchword
countertype 5 match 6 analog 8 analogue, parallel 9 correlate 13 correspondent
countervail 4 foil 6 offset, redeem, set off, thwart 7 balance, correct, rectify 8 atone for, outweigh, overcome, surmount 9 frustrate 10 compensate
countless 6 untold 10 innumerous, numberless, unnumbered 11 innumerable

12 unnumberable *combining form:* 4 myri 5 myria, myrio

Count of Monte Cristo 6 Dantes *author:* 5 Dumas

count out 3 bar 4 bate 5 debar 6 except 7 exclude, rule out, suspend 9 eliminate

countrified 5 rural 6 rustic 7 bucolic 8 agrestic, pastoral 10 campestral, provincial

country 4 home, land, soil 5 rural 6 nation, rustic 7 bucolic, outland 8 agrestic, homeland, pastoral 10 campestral, fatherland, motherland, provincial *dance:* 4 reel *home:* 5 manor, ranch, villa 8 hacienda *music:* 9 bluegrass *road:* 4 lane, path 5 byway

country jake 4 hick, rube 5 clown 6 rustic 7 bumpkin, hayseed 9 hillbilly 10 clodhopper 12 backwoodsman

coup 4 blow, plan 5 d'etat, upset 6 putsch, stroke 8 takeover 9 stratagem

couple 3 duo 4 dyad, join, link, mate, pair, span, team, yoke 5 brace, hitch, marry, unite 6 hook up 7 bracket, combine, conjoin, connect, doublet, harness, twosome 8 coalesce

coupler 4 link, ring 7 shackle *in an organ:* 7 tirasse *railroad:* 7 drawbar

couplet 4 pair 5 twins 7 distich

coupling 4 seam 5 joint, union 7 joining 8 junction, juncture 10 connection

courage 4 grit, guts 5 heart, moxie, pluck, spunk, valor 6 mettle, spirit 7 bravery, heroism 8 audacity, backbone, boldness, firmness, tenacity, valiance, valiancy 9 assurance, fortitude, gallantry 10 resolution 11 doughtiness, intrepidity, persistence 12 fearlessness 13 dauntlessness, determination

courageous 4 bold 5 brave, fiery, stout 6 manful, plucky, spunky, strong 7 doughty, valiant 8 fearless, intrepid, unafraid, valorous 9 audacious, dauntless, tenacious, undaunted 12 high-spirited

courier 5 envoy 6 bearer, legate, nuncio 7 carrier 8 emissary 9 go-between, messenger 11 internuncio

course 3 row, run, way 4 dart, dash, duct, line, path, plan, race, road, rush, tear 5 canal, chain, chase, hurry, orbit, order, range, route, scoot, scope, speed, trend 6 career, design, hasten, hustle, manner, policy, polity, scheme, scurry, sequel, series, sprint, string, system 7 advance, channel, circuit, conduit, passage, pattern, program, regimen, routine, scamper 8 aqueduct, progress, sequence 9 procedure 10 succession 11 progression *combining form:* 4 drom 5 dromo *dinner:* 5 salad 6 entrée 7 dessert 9 blue plate *of study:* 8 syllabus 10 curriculum

courser 4 bird 7 charger 8 huntsman, war-horse

court 3 bar, woo 4 quad, yard 5 charm, judge, spark 6 allure, pursue 7 address, justice, romance 8 tribunal 9 captivate, curtilage, enclosure 10 magistrate, quadrangle, sweetheart *action:* 4 suit 5 trial 6 appeal, assize 7 hearing, inquest, lawsuit 10 proceeding *calendar:* 6 docket *call to:* 7 summons 8 subpoena 11 arraignment *circuit:* 4 eyre *crier's call:* 4 oyes, oyez *decision:* 6 assize 7 finding, verdict 8 judgment *ecclesiastical:* 4 Rota 5 Curia 10 consistory *former English:* 4 leet *Indian:* 6 durbar *kind:* 4 moot 5 civil 6 county, family 7 circuit, customs, federal, supreme 8 chancery, criminal, district, juvenile, kangaroo, superior 9 appellate, municipal 11 territorial *medieval English:* 4 eyre, moot 5 gemot 6 gemote 7 husting 8 hustings *minutes:* 4 acta *of equity:* 8 chancery *officer:* 2 DA 5 clerk, crier, judge 6 puisne 7 bailiff, justice, marshal, sheriff 10 prosecutor *order:* 4 writ 5 arret, edict 6 decree 7 summons 8 mandamus, subpoena *panel:* 4 jury *relating to:* 5 aulic 8 judicial *session:* 6 assize 7 sitting 8 sederunt

courteous 5 civil 6 polite 7 genteel 8 mannerly 9 attentive 10 thoughtful 11 considerate 12 well-mannered

courter 5 wooer 6 suitor

courtesy 5 favor 6 comity 7 amenity, service 8 chivalry, civility, kindness 9 attention, gallantry, geniality 10 affability, cordiality, indulgence 11 courtliness 12 complaisance, dispensation, graciousness 13 attentiveness, consideration

court game see under game

courtly 4 prim 5 civil, lofty, preux, stiff 6 august, formal 7 gallant, starchy, stately, stilted, studied 8 gracious, imposing 9 civilized, dignified 11 ceremonious 12 conventional

courtship 4 suit 6 wooing 7 romance *former custom of:* 8 bundling

courtyard 4 quad 5 garth, patio 6 atrium 7 cortile 9 curtilage 10 quadrangle

Cousteau, Jacques *ship:* 7 Calypso *vehicle:* 11 bathysphere

cove 3 arm, bay 4 gulf 5 bayou, bight, creek, firth, inlet 6 harbor, slough

covenant 3 vow 4 bond, pact 5 agree, swear 6 concur, pledge, plight 7 bargain, compact 8 contract 9 agreement 10 convention 11 transaction

cover 3 cap, lid 4 bury, fend, hide, hood, mask, wrap 5 brood, cache, cloak, crown, guard, guise, haven, put-on, stash, track 6 asylum, bush up, canopy, defend, enfold, enwrap, facade, harbor, hiding, refuge, safety, screen, secure, shield, shroud, travel **7** blanket, bulwark, conceal, enclose, envelop, overlay, protect, retreat, secrete, shelter **8** disguise, ensconce, overcast, pass over, security, traverse **9** harborage, safeguard, sanctuary, semblance, superpose **10** false front, masquerade, overspread **11** concealment, superimpose ***combining form:*** **8** operculi ***rooflike:*** **6** awning, canopy ***the eyes:*** **9** blindfold ***the face:*** **4** mask, veil ***the mouth:*** **6** muzzle ***with asphalt:*** **4** pave ***with cloth:*** **5** drape ***with dirt:*** **6** bemire, besoil **8** besmirch ***with jewels:*** **5** begem ***with straw:*** **6** thatch

coverall **10** boiler suit

covered ***combining form:*** **5** crypt, krypt **6** crypto, krypto

covered wagon **9** Conestoga

covering ***anatomical:*** **5** theca, velum **6** tegmen **7** velamen **8** tegument **10** integument ***close-fitting:*** **6** sheath **9** sheathing ***cloth:*** **5** sheet ***combining form:*** **4** cole, derm, steg **5** coleo, derma, stego ***flap:*** **9** operculum ***for a book:*** **6** jacket ***for a cigar:*** **7** wrapper ***for a coffin:*** **4** pall ***for a corpse:*** **6** shroud **8** cerement ***for a package:*** **7** wrapper ***for concealment:*** **10** camouflage ***for food:*** **4** cosy, cozy ***for soil:*** **5** mulch ***metal:*** **4** mail **5** armor ***of a diatom:*** **6** lorica ***of a plant ovary:*** **8** pericarp ***of a seed:*** **4** aril, case **5** testa ***of fruits:*** **4** peel, rind ***of gloom:*** **4** pall ***of grain:*** **4** hull, husk **5** chaff ***shell-like:*** **8** carapace ***thin:*** **4** film **6** patina, veneer ***waterproof:*** **4** tarp **9** tarpaulin

coverlet **6** spread **8** bedcover **9** bedspread **11** counterpane

covert **5** haven, privy **6** asylum, buried, harbor, hidden, masked, refuge, secret **7** cloaked, furtive, guarded, retreat, shelter, sub-rosa **8** hush-hush, obscured, shrouded, stealthy, ulterior **9** concealed, disguised, harborage, sanctuary **10** dissembled, undercover **11** camouflaged, clandestine **12** hugger-mugger **13** surreptitious, under-the-table

covertly **7** sub rosa **8** in camera, secretly **9** by stealth, furtively, privately **10** stealthily **12** hugger-mugger **13** clandestinely

covet **4** want, wish **5** crave **6** desire **10** desiderate

covetous **4** avid, keen **5** eager, itchy **6** grabby, greedy **7** envious, hoggish, jealous, piggish, selfish, swinish **8** desirous, esurient, grasping, grudging, ravenous **9** rapacious, voracious **10** gluttonous **11** acquisitive

covey **4** band, bevy, crew **5** bunch, group, party **7** cluster **8** assembly

covin **4** plot **5** cabal **6** scheme **8** intrigue **10** conspiracy **11** machination

cow (see also **cattle**) **4** faze, kine (plural), neat **5** abash, bossy, bully, daunt **6** appall, bovine, dismay, hector, rattle **7** bluster, dragoon **8** bludgeon, browbeat, bulldoze, bullyrag **9** discomfit, embarrass, strong-arm **10** disconcert, intimidate ***cud:*** **5** rumen ***French:*** **5** vache ***hornless:*** **5** doddy, muley **6** doddie, mulley **7** pollard ***mammary gland:*** **5** udder ***pasture:*** **7** vaccary ***pen:*** **6** corral ***shed:*** **4** barn, byre **7** shippen, shippon ***Spanish:*** **4** vaca ***young:*** **4** calf **5** stirk **6** heifer

coward **4** baby **6** craven **7** caitiff, chicken, dastard, gutless, milksop, quitter, unmanly **8** poltroon, recreant, weakling **9** fraidy-cat, jellyfish, spunkless **10** scaredy-cat **11** lily-livered, poltroonish, yellowbelly **12** invertebrate, poor-spirited **13** pusillanimous

___ Coward **4** Noel

cowardly **4** vile **6** afraid, craven, yellow **7** caitiff, chicken, fearful, gutless, panicky, unmanly **8** cravenly, poltroon, recreant, timorous **9** dastardly, spunkless, worthless **11** lily-livered, milk-livered, poltroonish **12** fainthearted, poor-spirited, white-livered **13** pusillanimous

cowboy **5** waddy **6** drover, herder, waddie **7** puncher, rancher **8** buckaroo, buckeroo, herdsman, wrangler **9** cattleman **10** cowpuncher **12** broncobuster ***contest:*** **5** rodeo ***legendary:*** **9** Pecos Bill ***leggings:*** **5** chaps ***movie:*** **6** Tom Mix **8** Cisco Kid **9** Gene Autry, Roy Rogers **15** Hopalong Cassidy ***rope:*** **5** lasso, reata, riata **6** lariat ***Spanish-American:*** **6** charro, gaucho **7** llanero, vaquero

cower **4** fawn **5** quail, toady, wince **6** blench, cringe, flinch, grovel, kowtow, recoil, shrink **7** honey up, truckle **8** bootlick **9** brownnose **11** apple-polish

cowfish **6** dugong, sea cow **7** grampus, manatee **8** sirenian

cowl **3** cop **4** hood, monk **5** amice **6** almuce **7** capuche

cowpox **8** vaccinia

cowpuncher see **cowboy**

coxcomb **3** fop **4** buck, dude **5** blood, dandy **8** macaroni **9** exquisite **11** Beau Brummel **12** lounge lizard

coy **3** shy **4** arch **5** timid **6** decent, demure, proper, seemly **7** bashful, playful **8** decorous, retiring, skittish **9** diffident, kittenish, unassured **10** capricious, coquettish **11** mischievous, unassertive **12** self-effacing

Coyote State **11** South Dakota

coypu **6** rodent ***fur:*** **6** nutria

Cozbi's father **3** Zur

cozen **3** gyp **4** beat, bilk **5** cheat **6** betray, delude, diddle, humbug, illude, take in 7 beguile, deceive, defraud, mislead, sell out, swindle 8 flimflam 11 double-cross

cozy 4 easy, safe, snug, soft 5 comfy, cushy, pally 6 chummy, secure 7 easeful 8 covering, intimate 10 buddy-buddy, palsy-walsy 11 comfortable

crab 4 beef, fuss, yaup, yawp 5 bleat, gripe 6 griper, grouch, kicker, squawk, yammer 7 decapod, grouser, growler 8 arthopod, grumbler 9 bellyache, shellfish 10 bellyacher, complainer, crosspatch, crustacean 11 faultfinder ***claw:*** 5 chela 6 nipper ***combining form:*** 6 carcin 7 carcino ***constellation:*** 6 Cancer ***genus:*** 3 Uca 6 Birgus 7 Limulus, Pagurus ***hermit:*** 8 pagurian ***kind:*** 3 pea 4 blue, king, pine, rock 5 ghost, purse 6 hermit, partan, spider 7 fiddler 9 Dungeness, horseshoe ***king, horseshoe:*** 7 limulus 8 limuloid ***relating to:*** 7 cancrid ***resembling:*** 8 cancroid

crabbed 4 dour, glum 5 blunt, gruff, huffy, sulky, surly, testy 6 cranky, crusty, gloomy, morose, sullen 7 brusque 8 choleric, snappish 9 irascible, irritable, saturnine, splenetic

crabby see crabbed

crab-like 8 cancroid

crabwise 8 sidelong, sideward, sideways 9 laterally

crack 2 go 3 gag, try 4 bang, bash, belt, blow, boom, chap, clap, jape, jest, joke, quip, rent, rift, rima, rime, shot, slam, slap, slit, snap, stab, wham, whop 5 adept, blast, break, burst, chink, cleft, crash, flash, fling, jiffy, smack, smash, split, whack, whirl 6 cranny, decode, expert, master, moment 7 crevice, decrypt, fissure, instant, skilled 8 crevasse, decipher, drollery, interval, masterly, rimation, skillful, superior 9 bastinado, excellent, masterful, witticism 10 interstice, percussion, proficient 11 split second 12 cryptanalyze 13 discontinuity

crackbrain 3 nut 4 kook 5 crank 6 cuckoo 7 lunatic 8 crackpot 9 ding-a-ling, screwball

crackdown 8 quashing 10 repression 11 suppression

cracked 3 mad 4 daft, nuts 5 batty, crazy, daffy 6 crazed, cuckoo, insane, maniac, rimose, rimous, screwy 7 lunatic 8 demented

cracker 5 wafer 7 biscuit, saltine 8 Georgian 9 Floridian

crackerjack 4 lulu 5 adept, dandy, dilly, nifty 6 corker, expert, master 7 skilled 8 jim-dandy, knockout, masterly, skillful 9 humdinger, masterful 10 proficient 11 lalapalooza

crackle 4 snap 7 sparkle 9 crepitate

crackpot 3 nut 4 case, kook, loon 5 crank, loony 6 cuckoo, madman, maniac, oddity 7 dingbat, lunatic, oddball 9 character, ding-a-ling, eccentric, harebrain, screwball

crack-up 5 crash, smash, wreck 6 pileup 7 debacle, decline, smashup 8 collapse 9 breakdown 13 deterioration

cradlesong 7 lullaby 8 berceuse

craft 3 art, job 5 skill, trade 6 métier 7 calling, cunning, know-how, slyness 8 artifice, foxiness, vocation, wiliness 9 cageyness, canniness, dexterity, expertise 10 adroitness, artfulness, profession ***combining form:*** 6 techno, techny

craftiness 3 art 7 cunning, slyness 8 artifice, foxiness, wiliness 9 cageyness, canniness 10 artfulness

craftsman 5 smith 6 carver, potter, weaver, wright 7 artisan, builder, jeweler 9 carpenter

crafty 3 sly 4 foxy, keen, wily 5 acute, sharp 6 adroit, artful, astute, clever, tricky 7 cunning, fawning 8 guileful 9 deceitful, insidious ***Scottish:*** 6 sleeky 7 sleekit

cragged 5 harsh, rough 6 jagged, rugged, uneven 7 scraggy 8 asperous, scabrous, unsmooth

craggy see cragged

cram 3 jam, ram 4 bolt, fill, gulp, heap, load, pack, tamp, wolf 5 chock, crowd, crush, drive, force, press, shove, study, stuff, wedge 6 bone up, englut, gobble, guzzle, review, squash, thrust 7 jam-pack, overeat, squeeze 11 ingurgitate

crammed 4 full 5 awash 6 jammed, loaded, packed 7 brimful, crowded, stuffed 8 brimming 9 chock-full

cramp 5 stint 7 shackle 8 confined 9 restraint, stricture 10 constraint, limitation 11 confinement, restriction 12 incommodious 13 constrainment

cramped 4 tiny 5 close, small, tight 6 little, minute, narrow 8 confined 9 two-by-four 12 incommodious

cranberry 9 vaccinium ***tree:*** 7 pembina

crane 4 bird, boom 7 derrick 9 cormorant 10 demoiselle ***arm:*** 3 jib ***genus:*** 4 Grus ***Indian:*** 5 sarus ***resembling:*** 6 gruine ***ship's:*** 5 davit ***traveling:*** 5 jenny, titan 7 goliath

Crane's hero 12 Henry Fleming

cranium 5 skull

crank 3 bee, nut 4 crab, kook 5 fancy 6 cuckoo, griper, grouch, notion, vagary 7 boutade, caprice, conceit, grouser, growler, lunatic 8 crackpot, crotchet, grumbler, sourpuss 9 ding-a-ling, harebrain, screwball 10 bellyacher, crackbrain, crosspatch 11 faultfinder

cranky 4 daft 5 crazy, cross, daffy, ratty, testy, waspy 6 crazed, cuckoo, insane, ornery, tetchy, touchy **7** bearish, cracked, froward, waspish **8** cankered, choleric, contrary, vinegary **9** crotchety, irascible, temperish **10** bad-humored, ill-humored, vinegarish **11** hot-tempered **12** cantankerous, crackbrained, cross-grained, disagreeable **13** quick-tempered

cranny **4** nook **5** niche **7** byplace

crash **3** din, jar, ram **4** bang, boom, bump, bust, clap, fail, fold, jolt, slam, wham **5** blast, break, burst, crack, shock, smash, wreck **6** impact, pileup **7** collide, crack-up, debacle, smashup **8** accident, collapse **9** breakdown, collision **10** concussion, percussion

crashing **5** gross, utter **7** blasted **8** absolute, infernal, positive **9** downright **10** confounded, consummate

crass **3** raw **4** rude **5** crude, gross, rough **6** coarse, vulgar **7** loutish, uncouth **8** churlish **9** inelegant, unrefined

crate **4** heap **5** wreck **6** jalopy, junker **7** clunker

crater **3** pit **4** hole, pock **6** cavity **7** caldera **10** depression ***Hawaiian:*** **7** Kilauea

cravat **3** tie **4** band **5** scarf **7** bandage, necktie

crave **3** ask, beg **4** ache, long, lust, pine, pray, sigh, want, wish **5** brace, covet, plead **6** appeal, demand, desire, hanker, hunger, thirst **7** beseech, call for, entreat, implore, require, suspire **9** importune **10** desiderate, supplicate **11** necessitate

craven **4** funk **6** coward, funker **7** chicken, dastard, gutless, quitter, unmanly **8** cowardly, poltroon **9** spunkless **11** lily-livered, plotroonish, yellowbelly **12** poor-spirited **13** pusillanimous

craving **4** itch, lust, urge **6** desire **7** passion **8** appetite **10** appetition

crawl **4** flow, inch, teem **5** creep, slide, snail, snake, swarm **6** abound, grovel **9** pullulate

crawling **6** repent **7** reptant

craze **3** fad **4** chic, rage **5** crack, fever, furor, mania, style, vogue **6** frenzy, furore, madden **7** derange, fashion, unhinge **8** distract **9** unbalance **10** dernier cri, enthusiasm

craziness **5** folly **7** inanity **8** insanity **9** absurdity, dottiness, silliness **11** foolishness, witlessness **13** senselessness

crazy **3** fey, mad **4** daft, gaga, loco, luny, nuts, wack **5** balmy, batty, daffy, dotty, goofy, loony, nutty, silly, wacky, whack **6** absurd, cuckoo, insane, looney, madman, maniac, screwy, teched, whacky **7** bonkers, cracked, foolish, lunatic, tetched, touched, unsound **8** crackpot, demented, deranged **9** bedlamite, possessed, senseless **10** crackbrain, moonstruck, unbalanced **11** harebrained **12** preposterous ***British:*** **5** potty **6** scatty ***Scottish:*** **3** wud

crazy house **6** asylum **8** loony bin **9** funny farm **10** booby hatch

cream **3** top **4** balm, beat, best, pick, whip **5** blast, elite, pride, prime, prize, salve **6** cerate, choice, chrism **7** clobber, unction, unguent **8** lambaste, ointment

crease **4** fold, ruck **5** plica, ridge, rivel **6** furrow, rimple **7** crinkle, wrinkle **11** corrugation

create **4** make, sire **5** found, hatch, set up, spawn, start **6** father, parent **7** compose, produce **8** conceive, engender, generate **9** establish, formulate, institute, originate, procreate **10** constitute

creation **5** world **6** cosmos, kosmos, nature **8** megacosm, universe **9** macrocosm **11** macrocosmos

creative **8** original **9** demiurgic, deviceful, ingenious, inventive **10** innovative, innovatory **11** originative **12** innovational

creator **4** sire **5** maker **6** author, father **7** founder **8** inventor **9** architect, generator, patriarch **10** originator

creature **3** man **5** beast, being, brute, human, toady **6** animal, minion, mortal, person **7** critter **8** truckler **9** personage, sycophant ***fabled:*** **3** elf, imp **4** ogre, puck **5** dwarf, fairy, giant, gnome, troll **6** dragon, goblin, merman, sprite **7** brownie, gremlin, mermaid, monster, unicorn **9** hobgoblin **10** leprechaun; (see also **monster**) ***winged:*** **4** bird, fowl **8** volatile

credence **5** faith, trust **6** belief, credit **8** reliance **10** confidence

credentials **6** papers **9** character, documents, reference **11** testimonial **13** documentation

credible **5** solid, sound, valid **6** trusty **8** faithful, rational **9** authentic, colorable, plausible **10** believable, convincing, reasonable, satisfying **11** trustworthy **12** satisfactory

credit **3** lay **4** deem, feel **5** asset, faith, honor, refer, sense, think, trust **6** assign, belief, charge, impute, notice, weight **7** ascribe, believe **8** consider, credence, prestige, reliance **9** attribute, authority, influence **10** confidence **11** recognition

creditable **7** reputed **9** colorable, estimable, plausible, reputable **10** believable **11** respectable **13** well-thought-of

credo **5** creed **6** belief **8** ideology

credulous **5** naive **6** unwary **7** dupable **8** gullible, trustful, trusting **9** accepting, believing **12** unsuspecting, unsuspicious **13** unquestioning

creed **4** cult, sect **5** credo, faith **6** belief, church **8** ideology, religion **9** communion **10** connection, persuasion **12** denomination

creek 3 ria 4 gill, race, rill 5 brook 6 arroyo, rillet, runlet, runnel, stream 7 freshet, rivulet 8 brooklet 9 streamlet
creep 4 edge, inch, lurk, slip 5 crawl, glide, shirk, skulk, slide, slink, snake, sneak, steal 6 tiptoe 7 gumshoe, slither, sniggle, wriggle 9 pussyfoot
creeping 6 repent 7 reptant ***combining form:*** 6 herpet 7 herpeto
crème de la crème 4 best 5 elite 6 gentry 7 aristoi 8 optimacy 9 blue blood, haut monde 10 upper crust 11 aristocracy
Cremona family 6 Amatis
Creon ***daughter:*** 6 Creusa, Glauce, Glauke ***sister:*** 7 Jocasta ***son:*** 6 Haemon ***victim:*** 8 Antigone
crepehanger 9 Cassandra, pessimist, worrywart
crescendo 4 acme, apex, peak 5 crest 6 apogee, climax, culmen 8 capstone, meridian 11 culmination
crescent-shaped 6 lunate 7 lunated ***body or surface:*** 8 meniscus ***combining form:*** 5 selen 6 seleni, seleno
crest 3 cap, top 4 acme, apex, noon, peak, roof 5 arête, chine, crown, ridge 6 apogee, climax, summit, vertex 7 hogback 8 pinnacle, surmount 9 crescendo, fastigium 11 culmination ***combining form:*** 4 loph 5 lophi, lopho 6 lophio ***of a wave:*** 8 whitecap
crestfallen 3 low 4 blue, down 8 cast down, dejected, downcast 9 depressed 10 dispirited 11 downhearted 12 disconsolate
Crete ***ancient city:*** 7 Cnossus, Knossos 8 Phaistos ***ancient name:*** 6 Candia ***capital:*** 5 Canea ***goddess:*** 8 Dictynna 11 Britomartis ***guard:*** 5 Talos ***king:*** 5 Minos 9 Idomeneus ***maze:*** 9 labyrinth ***monster:*** 8 Minotaur ***mountain:*** 3 Ida ***princess:*** 7 Ariadne
cretin 4 fool, zany 5 ament, idiot, moron 6 zombie 7 half-wit 8 imbecile 9 simpleton
Creusa ***father:*** 5 Priam ***husband:*** 6 Aeneas ***mother:*** 6 Hecuba ***son:*** 3 Ion 8 Ascanius
crevice 4 seam, slit 5 chink, cleft, crack, grike 6 cranny 7 fissure 8 cleavage, crevasse 10 interstice
crew 4 band, bevy, gang, team 5 bunch, covey, group, party 7 cluster, retinue 8 assembly
crib 3 bed, bin, box, hut, key 4 pony, trot, weir 5 cheat, crate, hovel, stall, steal 6 cradle, crèche, manger, pilfer 7 barrier, brothel, purloin 8 bassinet, bedstead, bordello 9 enclosure 10 plagiarism, plagiarize
cricket ***period of play:*** 7 innings ***team:*** 6 eleven ***term:*** 2 on 3 leg, off, rot 4 bowl 5 pitch 6 bowler, wicket, yorker 7 batsman, striker 9 fieldsman ***turn at bat:*** 4 over
crime 3 sin 4 evil, tort 6 breach, delict, felony 7 misdeed, offense 8 delictum, iniquity 9 diablerie, violation 10 illegality, wrongdoing 11 misdemeanor 13 transgression ***instructor:*** 5 Fagin
Crimea ***capital:*** 10 Simferopol ***city:*** 5 Kerch, Yalta 10 Sevastopol ***river:*** 4 Alma ***sea:*** 4 Azov ***strait:*** 5 Kerch
criminal 4 hood, thug 5 crook, felon 6 outlaw 7 convict, illegal, illicit, lawless, mobster 8 fugitive, gangster, jailbird, offender, unlawful, wrongful 9 racketeer, wrongdoer 10 lawbreaker, malefactor, trespasser 12 illegitimate, transgressor ***habitual:*** 8 repeater 10 recidivist
criminate 3 tax 6 accuse, charge, indict 7 arraign, impeach 9 inculpate
crimp 3 bar, bit, rub 4 friz, snag 5 check, frizz, screw 6 bridle, hamper, hold in, hurdle, rimple, ruck up, rumple 7 crinkle, crumple, inhibit, scrunch, wrinkle 8 hold back, hold down, mountain, obstacle, restrain, withhold 9 constrain 10 impediment 11 Chinese wall, obstruction
crimple 5 screw 6 ruck up, rumble 7 crinkle, crumple, scrunch, wrinkle
crimson 3 red 4 glow, pink, rose 5 blush, color, flush, rouge 6 mantle, pinken, redden
cringe 4 fawn 5 cower, quail, toady, wince 6 blench, flinch, grovel, kowtow, recoil, shrink, slaver 7 truckle 8 bootlick 11 apple-polish
crinkle 4 fold, ruck 5 crimp, plica, ridge, rivel, screw 6 crease, furrow, rimple, ruck up, rumple 7 crimple, crumple, scrunch 11 corrugation
crinkly 5 crepy 6 crepey
cripple 3 sap 4 lame, maim 5 blunt, palsy 6 disarm, mayhem, weaken 7 disable, dislimb, unbrace 8 enfeeble, mutilate, paralyze 9 attenuate, dismember, prostrate, undermine 10 debilitate, immobilize 12 incapacitate, unstrengthen
cripples' patron saint 5 Giles
crisis 4 pass 5 pinch 6 strait 8 exigency, juncture, zero hour 9 emergency 10 crossroads 11 contingency 12 turning point
crisp 5 short 6 biting 7 brittle, crumbly, crunchy, cutting, friable, ingoing 8 clear-cut, incisive 9 trenchant 11 penetrating
crisscross 9 decussate, intersect
criterion 5 gauge 7 measure 8 standard 9 benchmark, yardstick 10 touchstone
critic 5 momus 6 carper, Zoilus 7 carping, caviler, knocker 8 captious, caviling, censurer, quibbler 9 aristarch, belittler, cavillous, muckraker, nitpicker 10 censorious, disparager, mudslinger 11 faultfinder, smellfungus

critical 4 dire 5 acute, fussy 7 carping, crucial, finicky, pivotal, weighty 8 captious, caviling, decisive 9 cavillous, demeaning, desperate, important, momentous 10 belittling, censorious, conclusive, particular 11 climacteric, disparaging, significant 12 faultfinding 13 consequential, determinative ***study:*** 6 examen 8 exegesis

criticism 5 blame 6 notice, rebuke, review 7 censure, comment, opinion, reproof 8 analysis, critique, diatribe, judgment, reproval, reviewal 9 appraisal 10 assessment, commentary 11 examination, observation

criticize 3 pan, rap 4 carp 5 blame, blast, cavil, cut up, fault, knock, roast, scold 6 rebuke, scathe 7 censure, condemn, reprove 8 badmouth, denounce, lambaste 9 castigate, fustigate, reprehend, reprobate 10 denunciate

criticizer 5 momus 6 carper, Zoilus 7 caviler, knocker 9 aristarch 11 faultfinder

critique see criticism

critter 5 beast, brute 6 animal 8 creature

Crius ***father:*** 6 Uranus ***mother:*** 4 Gaea ***son:*** 8 Astraeus

croak 3 die 5 scold 6 grouch, grouse, murmur, mutter 7 grumble, quarrel 8 complain

croaking 5 gruff, husky 6 hoarse

croaky see croaking

Croatia ***capital:*** 6 Zagreb ***city:*** 5 Split 6 Osijek, Rijeka

crock 3 jar, pot 4 smut, soot 7 disable 8 potsherd 11 earthenware

crocodile 7 reptile ***bird:*** 6 plover 9 trochilus ***Indian:*** 6 gavial ***relative:*** 9 alligator ***South American:*** 6 caiman, cayman, jacare ***Southeast Asian:*** 6 muggar, mugger, muggur

Croesus' kingdom 5 Lydia

Cromwell, Oliver ***regiment:*** 9 Ironsides ***son:*** 7 Richard ***victory site:*** 6 Naseby

crone 3 hag 4 drab, trot 5 biddy, witch 6 beldam

Cronus 5 Titan 6 Saturn ***daughter:*** 4 Hera 6 Hestia 7 Demeter ***father:*** 6 Uranus ***mother:*** 4 Gaea ***sister:*** 4 Rhea 6 Cybele, Tethys ***son:*** 4 Zeus 5 Hades 7 Jupiter, Neptune 8 Poseidon ***wife:*** 4 Rhea 6 Cybele

crony 3 pal 4 chum 5 buddy 6 comate 7 comrade 9 associate, companion 11 running mate

crook 3 bow 4 bend 5 curve, round, thief 6 bandit, robber

crooked 5 lying, snaky, snide, venal 6 curved, errant, shifty, zigzag 7 bending, corrupt, curving, devious, winding 8 rambling, ruthless, tortuous, twisting 9 deceitful, dishonest, underhand 10 fraudulent, meandering, serpentine, untruthful 12 unscrupulous 13 double-dealing ***combining form:*** 5 ancyl, ankyl 6 anchyl, ancylo, ankylo 7 anchylo

crookedly 4 awry 5 askew 6 askant 7 askance 8 cockeyed 9 cock-a-hoop

croon 3 hum, low 4 lull, moan, sing, wail 6 lament, murmur

crop 3 cut, hew, mow, top 4 chop, clip, pare, snip, trim 5 prune, shave, shear, skive 7 harvest, pollard 8 fruitage, truncate 10 detruncate

cropping 7 harvest, reaping 9 gathering 10 harvesting 11 ingathering

croquet 5 roque

crosier 5 staff

cross 4 deny, mule, over, rood 5 ratty, testy, trial 6 betray, cranky, hybrid, impugn, negate, ordeal, tetchy, touchy 7 athwart, calvary, carping, gainsay, mongrel, sell out 8 captious, choleric, traverse 9 decussate, disaffirm, half blood, half-breed, hybridize, intersect, irascible, temperish 10 affliction, contradict, contravene, interbreed, transverse, visitation 11 tribulation 13 quick-tempered ***a river:*** 4 ford ***bearer:*** 8 crucifer ***combining form:*** 6 stauro ***decoration:*** 4 Iron 8 Victoria ***Egyptian:*** 4 ankh ***kind:*** 3 tau 5 Greek, Latin, papal 6 Celtic, fleury, formée, moline, pommée, potent 7 avellan, botonée, Calvary, Maltese 8 crucifix, fourchée, Lorraine, quadrate 11 patriarchal 12 Saint Andrew's 13 Saint Anthony's ***section:*** 5 slice ***stroke of a letter:*** 5 serif

crossbow 8 arbalest, arbalist

crossbreed 4 mule 6 hybrid 7 bastard, mongrel 9 half blood, half-breed, hybridize 10 interbreed

crosscut 9 decussate, intersect

cross-examination 5 grill 8 grilling 11 questioning, third degree 13 interrogation

cross-eye 6 squint 9 esotropia 10 strabismus

crossing 6 thwart 8 traverse 10 transverse 11 transversal

cross out 6 cancel, delete

crosspatch 4 crab 5 crank 6 griper, grouch 7 grouser, growler 8 grumbler, sorehead, sourpuss 10 complainer

crossroads 4 pass 5 pinch 6 crisis, strait 8 exigency, juncture, zero hour 9 carrefour, emergency 11 contingency 12 intersection, turning point ***goddess:*** 6 Hecate, Hekate, Trivia

cross-shaped 8 cruciate 9 cruciform

crossways 6 across 7 athwart 10 diagonally 12 transversely

crosswise see crossways

crotchet 4 whim 5 fancy, freak, quirk

6 megrim, vagary 7 boutade, caprice, conceit 12 eccentricity

crotchety 5 waspy 6 cranky, ornery 7 bearish, waspish 8 cankered, contrary, vinegary 10 vinegarish 12 cantankerous, cross-grained

crouch 4 bend, duck 5 cower, hunch, squat, stoop 6 huddle 10 hunker down 11 scrooch down

crow 4 blow, brag, puff 5 boast, exult, mouth, prate, vaunt 9 gasconade 11 rodomontade *colony:* 7 rookery *combining form:* 5 corax *cry:* 3 caw *family:* 3 daw, jay 4 rook 5 raven 6 chough, corvid, hoodie, magpie 7 jackdaw 8 Corvidae *genus:* 6 Corvus *Hawaiian:* 5 alala *relating to:* 7 corvine

crowbar 3 pry 5 jimmy, lever 7 gablock 8 gavelock

crowd 3 jam, lot, mob, set 4 army, bear, cram, herd, host, push, rout, ruck 5 bunch, cloud, crush, drove, flock, group, horde, press, serry, shove, swarm, troop 6 circle, gaggle, huddle, legion, rabble, scores, squash, squish, squush, throng 7 cluster, company, squeeze 8 assembly 9 congeries, gathering, multitude 10 assemblage, collection 11 aggregation 12 congregation

crowded 4 full 5 awash, close, dense, thick, tight 6 jammed, loaded, packed 7 brimful, compact, crammed, stuffed 8 brimming, populous 9 chock-full

crow-like 7 corvoid

crown 3 cap, top 4 acme, apex, peak, roof 5 cover, crest, tiara 6 anadem, climax, diadem, laurel, summit, top off, vertex, wreath, zenith 7 chaplet, coronal, coronet, garland, overlay 8 meridian, overcast, pinnacle, round off, surmount 9 culminate, fastigium, finish off 10 overspread 11 culmination *combining form:* 6 corono 7 stephan 8 stephano *Egyptian:* 7 pschent

crucial 4 dire 5 acute, vital 8 critical, decisive 9 desperate, important, necessary 10 imperative 11 climacteric

crucible 4 test 5 trial 6 ordeal 10 affliction 11 tribulation

crucifix 4 rood 5 cross

crucifixion site 7 Calvary 8 Golgotha

crucify 4 kill 5 smite 6 harrow, martyr 7 afflict, agonize, mortify, torment, torture 10 excruciate

crud 3 goo 4 gook, gunk, junk, muck 5 filth, slime, trash 6 debris, sludge 7 rubbish

crude 3 raw 4 foul, poor 5 crass, dirty, gross, rough 6 coarse, filthy, gauche, impure, native, ribald, risqué, smutty, unhewn, vulgar 7 boorish, ill-bred, loutish, lowbred, obscene, raunchy, uncouth 8 backward, barnyard, cloddish, ignorant, immature, indecent, inexpert, inferior, prentice, unformed, ungraded, unsorted, unworked 9 graceless, inelegant, roughhewn, run-of-mine, unrefined, unskilled, untrained 10 amateurish, unfinished, unpolished 11 clodhopping, ineffective 12 unproficient 13 unenlightened

cruel 4 fell, grim, mean 6 brutal, fierce, savage 7 bestial, brutish, heinous, inhuman, wolfish 8 inhumane, ruthless 9 atrocious, barbarous, ferocious, heartless, monstrous, truculent, unpitying 10 relentless 12 bloodthirsty

cruise 4 sail 6 voyage

cruiser 4 boat 7 warship 9 patrol car, powerboat

crumb 3 bit, jot 4 iota 5 ounce, scrap, shred 7 smidgen 8 particle

crumble 3 rot 5 decay, spoil, taint 6 molder 7 putrefy 8 collapse 9 break down, decompose 12 disintegrate

crumbly 5 crisp, short 7 brittle, crunchy, friable

crumple 3 wad 4 bend, cave, give 5 break, crimp, screw, yield 6 fold up, rimple, ruck up 7 crinkle, scrunch, wrinkle 8 collapse

crunch 4 chew 5 champ, chomp, chump, munch 7 chumble 8 ruminate 9 masticate

Crusader *English:* 7 Richard *French:* 6 Philip, Robert 7 Godfrey, Raymond 8 Montfort *German:* 9 Frederick *Norman:* 7 Tancred 8 Bohemund *Preacher:* 7 Bernard 14 Peter the Hermit

crusading 11 evangelical 12 evangelistic

crush 3 jam 4 bear, beat, bray, buck, cram, dash, mash, pulp, push, ruin 5 crowd, drove, horde, press, quash, quell, smash, wreck 6 béguin, bruise, defeat, pestle, powder, quench, reduce, squash, squish, squush, subdue, throng 7 abolish, blot out, conquer, contuse, destroy, passion, put down, repress, scrunch, squeeze, squelch 8 bear down, beat down, demolish, suppress, vanquish 9 comminute, multitude, overpower, pulverize, puppy love, subjugate, triturate 10 annihilate, extinguish, obliterate 11 infatuation 12 contriturate

crust 4 cake, rime

crustacean 4 crab, flea, scud 5 louse, prawn 6 isopod, shrimp, slater, sow bug 7 copepod, daphnia, decapod, lobster, pill bug 8 amphipod, anomuran, barnacle, crawfish, crayfish, macruran, ostracod, sand flea 9 arthropod, beach flea, schizopod, shellfish, water flea, wood louse 10 brachyuran, stomatopod, whale louse 11 branchiopod *aggregate of:* 5 krill *appendage:* 5 exite 6 endite 7 pleopod *body segment:* 6 somite, telson 8 metamere *claw:* 5 chela 6 pincer *covering substance:*

6 chitin *larva:* 5 alima 8 nauplius *limb segment:* 6 podite 8 podomere

crusty 4 curt, foul, rank 5 bluff, blunt, brief, dirty, gross, gruff, short, testy 6 abrupt, coarse, cranky, filthy, snippy 7 brusque, crabbed, obscene, raunchy, waspish 8 choleric, snippety 9 irascible, irritable, saturnine, splenetic 10 fescennine

crux 3 nub 4 core, gist, meat, pith 6 kernel, thrust 7 purport 9 substance

cry (see also **exclamation**) 3 sob 4 bawl, blub, call, howl, moan, pule, rage, song, wail, weep, yaup, yawp, yell, yowl 5 bleat, craze, groan, hallo, hollo, motto, mourn, on-dit, rumor, shout, sniff, trend, vogue, whine, whoop 6 boohoo, furore, gossip, holler, lament, report, rumble, scream, snivel, squawk, squeak, squeal 7 blubber, fashion, hearsay, screech, ululate, whimper 9 advertise, publicize 10 vociferate 11 scuttlebutt *bacchanals':* 4 evoe *calf:* 5 bleat *cat:* 3 mew 4 meow 5 miaou *cattle:* 3 low, moo *chick:* 4 peep 5 cheep *court:* 4 oyes, oyez *crane:* 5 clang *crow:* 3 caw *dog:* 3 arf 4 bark, woof *donkey:* 4 bray 6 hee-haw *duck:* 5 quack *frog:* 5 croak *goat:* 5 bleat *goose:* 4 honk 5 clang, cronk *hen:* 6 cackle *horse:* 5 neigh 6 nicker, whinny 7 whicker *lion:* 4 roar *owl:* 4 hoot *pig:* 4 oink 5 grunt *raven:* 5 croak, cronk *sheep:* 5 bleat *songbird:* 5 chirp, tweet *turkey:* 6 gobble

cry down 5 decry 8 belittle, derogate, diminish 9 disparage 10 depreciate 11 detract from, opprobriate

crying 4 dire 6 urgent 7 burning, clamant, exigent, heinous 8 pressing, shocking 9 atrocious, clamorous, desperate, monstrous 10 imperative, outrageous, scandalous 11 importunate

cry off 5 welsh 6 renege, resile 7 back out 8 back down 9 backpedal, backwater

cry out 4 blat, bolt 7 exclaim 9 ejaculate

crypt 4 cave, cell 5 vault 7 chamber 8 catacomb 10 undercroft 11 compartment

cryptanalyze 5 break, crack 6 decode 7 decrypt 8 decipher

cryptic 4 dark 5 murky, vague 6 opaque 7 obscure, unclear 8 abstruse, Delphian 9 enigmatic, tenebrous 10 mysterious, mystifying 12 unfathomable

crystal 5 clear, lucid 6 lucent 8 clear-cut, luminous, pellucid 9 unblurred 11 translucent, transparent 12 transpicuous *combining form:* 5 blast 6 hedron

Cry, the Beloved Country
author
5 Paton

cry up 4 laud 5 bless, extol 6 praise 7 glorify, magnify 8 eulogize 9 celebrate 10 panegyrize

Cuba *capital:* 6 Havana *chief export:* 5 sugar *monetary unit:* 4 peso *premier:* 6 Castro (Fidel)

cubbyhole 5 niche 6 recess 7 cubicle

cube 3 die 4 dice (plural)

cubic meter 5 stere

Cub Scout *rank:* 4 Bear, Wolf 6 Bobcat 7 Webelos *unit:* 3 den 4 pack

Cuchulainn *father:* 3 Lug 4 Lugh *foe:* 4 Medb 5 Maeve *kingdom:* 6 Ulster *mother:* 8 Dechtire *son:* 8 Conlaoch *victim:* 8 Conlaoch *wife:* 4 Emer

cuckoo 3 nut 4 daft, kook 5 crank, crazy, daffy, nutty 6 crazed, insane 7 cracked, lunatic 8 crackpot 9 ding-a-ling, harebrain, screwball 12 crackbrained *bird:* 3 ani

cucumber 4 pepo 6 gerkin 7 gherkin

cuddle 3 pet 4 snug 6 burrow, caress, cosset, dandle, fondle, nestle, nuzzle 7 embrace, snuggle

cuddlesome 8 huggable

cudgel 3 bat 4 cane, club, mace 5 baton, billy 6 paddle 7 war club 8 bludgeon, spontoon 9 billy club, blackjack, truncheon 10 knobkerrie, nightstick

cue 4 clue, hint 6 notion 7 inkling 8 telltale 10 indication, intimation, suggestion

cuff 3 box, hit 4 blip, chop, clip, poke, slap, sock 5 clout, punch, smack, spank 6 buffet, wallop 8 haymaker

cul-de-sac 6 pocket 7 dead end, impasse 10 blind alley

cull 4 pick 5 elect, glean 6 choose, garner, gather, optate, opt for, pick up, prefer, select 7 extract 9 single out

culminate 3 cap 5 crown 6 climax, top off 8 round off 9 finish off

culmination 4 acme, apex, noon, peak 6 apogee, climax, summit 8 meridian, pinnacle 11 ne plus ultra

culpability 4 onus 5 blame, fault, guilt

culpable 5 amiss 6 guilty, sinful, unholy 8 blamable, blameful 10 censurable 11 blameworthy, impeachable 13 demeritorious, reprehensible

cult 4 sect 5 creed, faith 6 church 8 religion 9 communion 10 connection, persuasion 12 denomination *suffix:* 3 ism

cultivable 6 arable 8 tillable

cultivatable see **cultivable**

cultivate 4 farm, grow, tend, till, work 5 breed, dress, nurse, raise 6 foster, nursle, refine 7 cherish, nourish, nurture, produce 9 propagate

cultivated 6 urbane 7 genteel, refined 8 cultured, polished, well-bred 9 courteous, distingué

cultivation 6 polish 7 culture 8 breeding 10 refinement

culture 5 class 6 polish 8 breeding, elegance, learning, urbanity 9 education, erudi-

tion, gentility **10** refinement **11** cultivation, savoir faire **12** civilization **13** enlightenment
cultured **6** urbane **7** erudite, genteel, learned, refined **8** educated, literate, polished, well-bred **9** civilized, distingué **10** cultivated **11** enlightened
culture medium **4** agar
culverhouse **8** dovecote, pigeonry **9** columbary
cumber **3** tax **4** clog, lade, load, task **6** burden, charge, saddle
cumbersome **7** awkward, unhandy **8** cumbrous, unwieldy **9** ponderous
cumbrance **4** clog **6** burden **7** trouble **9** hindrance, impedance **10** impediment
cumbrous see **cumbersome**
cum ____ salis **5** grano
cumshaw **3** tip **7** largess **8** gratuity **9** lagniappe, pourboire **10** perquisite
cumulate **4** hive **5** amass, lay up, uplay **6** garner, roll up **7** store up **9** stockpile
cumulation **5** hoard, trove **9** amassment, colluvies, stockpile **10** collection **11** aggregation **13** agglomeration
cumulative **5** chain **8** additive, additory **9** summative **10** increasing **11** multiplying
cunning **3** art, sly **4** deep, foxy, keen, wary, wily **5** acute, canny, craft, guile, savvy, sharp, skill, smart **6** adroit, artful, astute, clever, crafty, deceit, tricky **7** finesse, know-how, knowing, slyness **8** artifice, deftness, facility, foxiness, guileful, subtlety, wiliness **9** adeptness, cageyness, canniness, dexterity, dexterous, duplicity, expertise, ingenious, ingenuity, insidious, masterful, sharpness, slickness **10** adroitness, artfulness, cleverness, craftiness, shiftiness, shrewdness, trickiness **12** dissemblance **13** dexterousness, dissimulation, ingeniousness
cup **3** mug **4** toby **5** grail, jorum, stein **6** beaker, seidel **7** chalice, tankard **8** schooner ***assayer's:*** **5** cupel ***combining form:*** **5** cotyl, cyath, scyph **6** cotyli, cotylo, cyatho, scyphi, scypho ***diamond cutter's:*** **3** dop ***handle:*** **3** ear, lug ***holder:*** **4** zarf ***liturgical:*** **3** ama **5** amula, calix **7** chalice ***Scottish:*** **4** tass ***small:*** **6** noggin **7** canakin, canikin **8** cannikin **9** demitasse ***sports:*** **5** Davis, Ryder **6** Curtis **7** Stanley **8** America's, Wightman ***two-handled:*** **3** tyg
cupbearer of the gods **4** Hebe **8** Ganymede
cupboard **3** kas **5** ambry, cubby, cuddy **6** buffet, closet, larder, pantry **7** armoire, cabinet **8** credence, credenza **9** sideboard
Cupid **4** Amor, Eros **6** cherub **7** amorino **8** amoretto ***beloved:*** **6** Psyche ***brother:*** **7** Anteros ***father:*** **6** Hermes **7** Mercury ***mother:*** **5** Venus **9** Aphrodite ***title:*** **3** Dan
cupidity **4** lust **5** greed **6** desire **7** avarice, avidity, craving, passion **8** rapacity, voracity **9** eagerness **10** greediness **11** infatuation **13** rapaciousness
cupola **4** dome **5** vault **6** turret **7** furnace, lantern, lookout
cup-shaped **8** scyphate
cur **3** cad, dog **4** scum, toad **5** skunk, snake **6** rotter **7** bounder, stinker **8** riffraff, stinkard **9** yellow dog
curative **5** tonic **7** healing **8** remedial, salutary, sanative, sanatory **9** medicinal, remedying, vulnerary, wholesome **10** beneficial, corrective, medicative **11** restorative, therapeutic **12** invigorating
curb **3** bit, tie **4** clog, deny **5** check, leash, tie up **6** bridle, fetter, hamper, hobble, hogtie, hold in **7** abstain, inhibit, refrain, repress, shackle **8** hold back, hold down, restrain, suppress, withhold **9** constrain, entrammel ***British:*** **4** kerb
curd see **curdle**
curdle **4** clot, sour **5** spoil **7** clabber, thicken **9** coagulate ***Scottish:*** **6** lapper, lopper
cure **3** age **4** heal **6** physic, remedy **7** restore **8** antidote, medicant, medicine **9** pharmacon **10** corrective, medicament, medication **11** counterstep **12** counteragent **13** counteractant, counteractive ***fish:*** **6** kipper
cure-all **6** elixir **7** nostrum, panacea **10** catholicon
cureless **8** hopeless **9** incurable, insanable, uncurable **10** impossible **11** immedicable, irreparable **12** irremediable **13** uncorrectable
curio **3** toy **6** bauble, gewgaw, trifle **7** bibelot, trinket, whatnot **9** bric-a-brac, objet d'art, **10** knickknack
curiosity **6** marvel, oddity, rarity, regard, wonder **7** anomaly, concern **8** interest, nonesuch
curious **3** odd **4** nosy **5** nosey, peery, queer, weird **6** prying, quaint, snoopy **7** bizarre, oddball, strange, unusual **8** peculiar, singular **9** inquiring **11** inquisitive, inquisitory, questioning **12** disquisitive **13** inquisitorial, investigative
curium ***symbol:*** **2** Cm
curl **4** coil, friz, kink, wind **5** frizz, twine, twist **6** spiral **7** entwine, frizzle, ringlet, wreathe **9** corkscrew
curling ***match:*** **8** bonspiel ***period of play:*** **3** end ***team:*** **4** four ***term:*** **3** tee **4** hack, rink **5** house, stone
curly **5** kinky **6** frizzy
currency **4** cash **5** dough, lucre, money, scrip **11** legal tender ***premium:*** **4** agio ***unit:*** (see individual country)

current 3 run 4 eddy, flow, flux, rife, rush, tide 5 drift, flood, spate, tenor, trend 6 extant, modern, stream 7 instant, popular, present, rampant, regnant, topical 8 existent, tendency, up-to-date 9 prevalent 10 present-day, prevailing, widespread 11 fashionable 12 contemporary ***air:*** 4 gale, gust, wind 5 blast, draft 6 breeze, squall, vortex, zephyr 7 cyclone, indraft, tornado, twister, typhoon, updraft 8 outdraft 9 downdraft, hurricane, whirlwind 10 slipstream ***combining form:*** 4 rheo ***ocean:*** 7 riptide 8 undertow 9 maelstrom, whirlpool ***unit:*** 6 ampere 8 abampere 10 statampere

Currier's partner 4 Ives

curry 4 drug, whip 6 thrash 9 overwhelm

curse 4 cuss, damn, oath 5 swear 6 bedamn, plague 7 damning, malison, scourge 8 anathema, cussword, execrate 9 blaspheme, blasphemy, expletive, imprecate, objurgate, profanity, sacrilege, swearword 10 execration, pestilence 11 commination, imprecation, malediction, objurgation, profanation 12 anathematize, denunciation

cursed 6 damned, odious 7 blasted, blessed, doggone, dratted 8 damnable, infernal 9 execrable 10 confounded 13 blankety-blank

cursive 4 easy 6 fluent, smooth 7 flowing, running 10 effortless

cursory 5 brief, hasty, quick, rapid, short 7 hurried, shallow, sketchy 9 depthless 10 uncritical 11 superficial

curt 5 bluff, blunt, brief, gruff, short 6 abrupt, crusty, snippy 7 brusque, concise, laconic, summary 8 snippety, succinct 11 compendiary, compendious 12 breviloquent 13 short and sweet

curtail 3 cut 5 slash 6 lessen, minify 7 abridge, cut back, shorten 8 diminish, retrench 10 abbreviate

curtain 4 drop, veil 5 drape 6 screen 7 barrier ***doorway:*** 8 portiere ***holder:*** 3 rod ***Indian:*** 6 pardah, purdah ***rod concealer:*** 7 valance ***sash:*** 7 tieback ***stage:*** 4 drop 8 backdrop

curtains 3 end 5 death 6 demise 7 decease, drapery

curtilage 4 quad, yard 5 court 9 enclosure 10 courthouse, quadrangle

curvaceous 5 buxom 7 rounded, shapely, stacked 9 Junoesque 13 well-developed

curvation 3 arc, bow 4 arch, bend 5 round

curvature (see curvation) ***of the spine:*** 8 kyphosis, lordosis 9 scoliosis

curve 3 arc, bow 4 arch, bend, coil, curl, turn, veer, wind 5 crook, round, twist 6 convex, spiral, swerve 7 concave, flexure, rondure, sinuate ***of an arch:*** 8 extrados, intrados ***pitcher's:*** 4 hook ***plane:*** 7 cissoid, cycloid, limaçon 8 parabola, sinusoid, trochoid 9 hyperbola ***S-shaped:*** 3 ess 4 ogee 7 sigmoid

curved 4 bent 5 arced, bowed, round 6 arched 7 arcuate, arrondi, bending, crooked, embowed, falcate, rounded, twisted 8 arciform, twisting 9 declinate ***combining form:*** 4 cyrt 5 ancyl, ankyl, curvi, cyrto 6 anchyl, ancylo, ankylo, campto 7 anchylo, clastic ***implement:*** 6 sickle ***molding:*** 4 ogee ***sword:*** 8 scimitar

curvilinear see curved

curvy see curvaceous; curved

Cush ***father:*** 3 Ham ***son:*** 6 Nimrod

cushion 3 mat, pad 5 squab 6 absorb, buffer, pillow 7 bolster, hassock, pillion 8 palliate ***Indian:*** 4 gadi 5 gaddi

cushy 4 cozy, easy, snug, soft 5 comfy 7 easeful 11 comfortable

cusp 3 tip 4 apex, peak 5 point

cuspid 6 canine 8 eyetooth

cuspidate 5 acute, piked, sharp 6 peaked 7 pointed 8 acicular 9 aciculate, acuminate, acuminous

cuss 3 guy, man 4 chap, damn, oath 5 curse, swear 6 bedamn, fellow 8 execrate 9 expletive, imprecate, swearword

cussword 4 oath 5 curse, swear 9 expletive, swearword

custard 4 flan 5 apple, papaw 8 sweetsop

custodian 6 keeper, warden 7 curator, steward 8 cerberus, claviger, guardian, overseer, watchdog 9 caretaker 10 supervisor

custody 4 care, ward 5 trust 6 charge 7 keeping 10 caretaking, management, protection 11 safekeeping, supervision 12 guardianship

custom 3 use 4 want 5 habit, mores (plural), trade, trick, usage 6 manner, praxis, ritual 7 folkway, precept, traffic 8 business, habitude, practice 9 patronage 10 consuetude, tailor-made 11 made-to-order ***Latin:*** 3 mos

customary 5 usual 6 common, wonted 7 chronic, general, routine 8 accepted, everyday, familiar, frequent, habitual, orthodox, standard 10 accustomed 11 traditional 12 conventional

custom-built 10 tailor-made 11 made-to-order

customer 5 buyer 6 client, patron 7 shopper 8 consumer 9 purchaser ***aggregate of:*** 9 clientele ***frequent:*** 7 habitué

customized see custom-built

custom-made see custom-built
cut 3 hew, ilk, lop, mow, saw 4 bite, chop, clip, crop, dice, dock, fell, gash, hack, kind, nick, pare, part, reap, slit, snip, snob, snub, sort, tear, thin, trim, type 5 bevel, carve, ditch, drunk, filet, knife, lathe, lower, mince, notch, piece, prune, quota, sever, share, shave, shear, skive, slash, slice, split, stamp, wound 6 cleave, dilute, divide, fillet, hackle, incise, member, moiety, open up, parcel, pierce, reduce, scythe, sickle, sunder, trench, weaken 7 abridge, curtail, dissect, operate, partage, portion, scissor, section, segment, shorten 8 amputate, dissever, division, lacerate, mark down, retrench, separate 9 allotment, allowance, ostracize 10 abbreviate 11 description, intoxicated 12 cold-shoulder ***combining form:*** 4 sect, tomy 6 tomous ***of beef:*** 3 rib 4 loin, rump 5 baron, chine, chuck, flank, plate, roast, round, shank, steak 6 cutlet, saddle 7 brisket, sirloin 8 shoulder 9 aitchbone
cut across 8 transect 9 transcend
cut-and-dried 7 routine
cutaneous 6 dermal
cutaway 4 coat, dive
cut back 4 clip, pare 5 lower, shave, slash 6 reduce 7 abridge, curtail, shorten 8 mark down, retrench 10 abbreviate
cut down 4 clip, pare 5 lower, shave, slash 6 reduce
cute 3 sly 5 sharp 6 clever, dainty, pretty, quaint, shrewd 7 cunning 8 affected 9 ingenious 10 attractive
cut in 6 horn in 7 intrude, obtrude 8 chisel in 10 intertrude
cutlass 5 sword 7 machete
cut off 2 ax 3 axe, lop 4 kill, slay 5 block, catch, scrag 6 enisle, finish, lay low 7 destroy, isolate 8 amputate, dispatch, insulate, separate 9 intercept, segregate, sequester 10 disinherit
cut out 5 usurp 6 delete, excise, exsect, resect 7 exscind 8 displace, supplant 9 eliminate, extirpate
cutpurse 5 thief 10 pickpocket
cut short 3 bob 4 clip, crop, dock, poll 5 abort, check, shear 7 curtail
cuttable 7 sectile 8 scissile
cutter 4 boat, sled 6 editor, sleigh 7 incisor 9 cutthroat
cutthroat 3 gun 5 bravo 6 gunman, hit man 7 torpedo 8 assassin 10 gunslinger, hatchet man, triggerman
cutting 5 crisp 6 biting 7 ingoing 8 clear-cut, incisive, piercing 9 trenchant 11 penetrating ***combining form:*** 5 cidal ***edge:*** 5 blade ***remark:*** 3 dig ***tool:*** 2 ax 3 adz, axe, hob, saw 4 adze 5 knife, lathe, mower, plane, razor 6 reaper, scythe, shears, sickle 7 hatchet 8 scissors, tomahawk
cutting out ***combining form:*** 6 ectomy
cuttlefish 7 mollusk 10 cephalopod ***ink:*** 5 sepia ***relative:*** 5 squid 7 octopus
cut up 3 pan, rap 4 dice, hash, romp 5 caper, clown, horse, knock, mince 6 cavort, sliver 7 carry on, censure, condemn, show off 8 denounce 9 criticize, horse-play, misbehave, reprehend, reprobate 10 roughhouse
cutup 3 wag 4 zany 5 clown, joker 7 farceur 8 jokester
Cybele 4 Rhea ***beloved:*** 5 Attis ***brother:*** 6 Cronus ***father:*** 6 Uranus ***husband:*** 6 Cronus ***mother:*** 2 Ge 4 Gaea ***son:*** 4 Zeus 7 Jupiter, Neptune 8 Poseidon
cybernetics founder 6 Wiener
cycle 4 bike, loop, ring 5 chain, round, wheel 6 circle, course, series 7 circuit 8 sequence 10 succession, two-wheeler, velocipede
cyclone 7 tornado, twister
cyclopean 4 huge 7 Antaean, mammoth, titanic 8 colossal, gigantic 9 Herculean, monstrous 10 gargantuan 11 elephantine
Cyclops 5 Arges 7 Brontes 8 Steropes 10 Polyphemus
Cycnus ***father:*** 4 Ares, Mars ***slayer:*** 8 Hercules
Cygnus ***form:*** 4 swan ***friend:*** 7 Phaeton ***star:*** 5 Deneb
cylinder 4 drum, lock, pipe, tube 5 spool 6 barrel, bobbin, platen, roller
cylindrical 5 tubal 6 terete, tubate 7 tubular 8 tubelike, tuberoid, tubiform, tubulose, tubulous
cyma recta 4 ogee
cymbals ***dancer's:*** 3 tal 7 crotala
Cymbeline ***daughter:*** 6 Imogen ***son:*** 9 Arviragus, Guiderius
Cymric 5 Welsh 6 Celtic 9 Brythonic ***bard:*** 8 Taliesin ***Elysium:*** 6 Annwfn ***god:*** 5 Lludd ***of Elysium:*** 5 Arawn ***of the dead:*** 5 Pwyll ***of the seas:*** 3 Ler 4 Llyr 5 Dylan ***of the sky:*** 7 Gwydion ***of the sun:*** 4 Lleu, Llew ***of the underworld:*** 4 Gwyn ***goddess:*** 3 Don 9 Arianrhod ***magician:*** 6 Merlin
Cymry land 5 Wales
cynical 3 wry 6 ironic 8 sardonic
Cynthia 4 Luna, moon 5 Diana 7 Artemis
cyprian 4 jade, slut 5 hussy, tramp 6 wanton 7 jezebel, trollop 8 slattern, strumpet
Cyprus ***capital:*** 7 Nicosia ***language:*** 5 Greek 7 Turkish
Cyrano 4 poet 7 duelist ***author:*** 7 Rostand ***feature:*** 4 nose

Cyrus ***conquest:*** 5 Lydia, Media 7 Babylon ***daughter:*** 6 Atossa ***empire:*** 7 Persian ***father:*** 8 Cambyses ***son:*** 8 Cambyses
Cytherea 5 Venus 9 Aphrodite
czar 4 king 5 baron, mogul 6 prince, tycoon 7 magnate ***Russian:*** 4 Ivan 5 Basil, Peter 6 Alexis, Feodor, Fyodor 7 Michael, Romanov 8 Nicholas, Romanoff, Theodore 9 Alexander 12 Boris Godunov
czar's wife 7 czarina 8 czaritza
Czechoslovakia ***capital:*** 6 Prague ***monetary unit:*** 6 koruna

D

D.A., e.g. 4 atty
dab 3 hit, pat 4 blow, chit, lump, peck, spot 5 clout, smear 6 bedaub, blotch, smudge 7 besmear, plaster, portion, splotch
dabbler 4 tyro 7 amateur 9 smatterer 10 dilettante, uninitiate 11 abecedarian
dabbling 7 jackleg, shallow 8 ungifted 9 unskilled 10 amateurish, dilettante, unfinished 11 superficial 12 dilettantish, dilettantist
dabchick 5 grebe 9 hell-diver
Dadaist 3 Arp, Ray 4 Ball 5 Grosz, Tzara 7 Duchamp, Picabia 10 Schwitters
daedal 6 knotty 7 complex, gordian 8 involved 9 Byzantine, elaborate, intricate 11 complicated 12 labyrinthine 13 sophisticated
Daedalus 9 architect, artificer ***construction:*** 9 Labyrinth ***father:*** 6 Metion ***son:*** 6 Icarus ***victim:*** 5 Talos 6 Perdix
daffy see daft
daft 3 mad 4 loco, luny, wild 5 balmy, crazy, giddy, potty, silly 6 crazed, cuckoo, insane, maniac 7 cracked, foolish, idiotic, lunatic, unsound 8 demented, deranged, imbecile 9 bedlamite 10 unbalanced
Dag ***father:*** 7 Delling ***horse:*** 9 Skinfaksi ***mother:*** 4 Nott
Dagda ***chief god of the:*** 5 Gaels, Irish ***daughter:*** 6 Brigit ***instrument:*** 4 harp ***son:*** 6 Aengus ***wife:*** 5 Boann
dagger 4 dirk 5 skean, skeen, skene 6 bodkin 8 stiletto ***handle:*** 4 hilt ***medieval:*** 6 anlace
daily 7 diurnal 9 circadian, quotidian
dainty 4 airy, nice, rare 5 fussy, goody, light, treat 6 choice, morsel, select, tidbit, titbit 7 elegant, finical, finicky 8 delicacy, delicate, ethereal, kickshaw, superior 9 exquisite, finicking, recherché 10 delightful, diaphanous, fastidious, particular, pernickety 11 persnickety
dairy 8 creamery
dais 7 rostrum, terrace 8 platform
daisy 5 oxeye ***British:*** 10 moonflower ***Scottish:*** 5 gowan
Daisy Miller author 5 James
Daksha's father 6 Brahma
dale 4 glen 6 valley
dally 3 lag, toy 4 drag, fool, idle, play, poke 5 delay, flirt, tarry, trail 6 coquet, dawdle, frolic, lead on, linger, loiter, put off, trifle, wanton 11 string along 13 procrastinate
Dalphon's father 5 Haman
dam 3 bar 4 stay, stem, stop, weir 5 block, brake, check, choke 6 hinder, impede 7 barrier, repress 8 blockade, obstacle, obstruct, suppress 10 overslaugh
damage 3 mar 4 blot, harm, hurt, loss, ruin 5 abuse, burst, cloud, spoil, wound 6 deface, impair, injure, injury, scathe 7 blemish, destroy, marring, tarnish, vitiate 8 destruct, ill-treat, maltreat, mischief, mistreat, mutilate, sabotage 9 prejudice, vandalism 10 dilapidate, impairment ***relating to:*** 5 noxal
damaging 3 bad 4 evil 6 nocent 7 harmful, hurtful, nocuous 9 injurious 11 deleterious, detrimental, mischievous
dame 4 lady 5 woman 6 beldam, gammer, matron 7 dowager, grandam 9 matriarch
Damien's island 7 Molokai
Damkina ***husband:*** 2 Ea ***son:*** 6 Marduk
damn 4 cuss, doom, drat, durn 5 curse, swear, whoop 7 condemn, doggone 8 execrate, sentence 9 abominate, imprecate, objurgate, proscribe 10 vituperate 12 anathematize
damnable 4 dang, darn 5 gross, utter 6 blamed, cursed, cussed, odious 7 blasted, dratted, hateful 8 accursed, infernal, outright 9 abhorrent, dad-burned, downright, execrable, out-and-out 11 unmitigated

damned 4 dang, darn, durn, lost, rank, very 5 gross, utter 6 blamed, cursed, cussed, dashed, doomed 7 awfully, blasted, doggone, dratted, goldarn 8 absolute, accursed, blighted, blinding, complete, infernal, outright, whopping 9 dad-blamed, downright, execrable, extremely, out-and-out, perishing, reprobate 10 confounded, dad-blasted 11 straight-out, unmitigated 13 anathematized, blankety-blank

Damocles' ___ 5 sword

Damon's friend 7 Pythias

damp 3 wet 4 dank, dewy, mist 5 humid, juicy, moist, muggy, musty, rainy, soggy 6 clammy, moisty 7 bedewed, moisten, wettish 8 humidify, humidity, moisture

dampen 4 mute 6 deaden, muffle, sponge, stifle

damsel 3 gal 4 girl, lass, maid, miss 5 missy, wench 6 lassie, maiden, moppet 8 donzella, princess 10 demoiselle

Dan ***father:*** 5 Jacob ***mother:*** 6 Bilhah ***son:*** 6 Hushim

Danaë ***father:*** 8 Acrisius ***lover:*** 4 Zeus ***son:*** 7 Perseus

Danaus ***brother:*** 8 Aegyptus ***daughters:*** 8 Danaides ***father:*** 5 Belus ***founder of:*** 5 Argos ***grandfather:*** 7 Neptune 8 Poseidon

dance 3 hop, jig, tap 4 ball, duet, flit, foot, giga, heel, hoof, juba, leap, lope, move, reel, skit, step 5 bamba, brawl, cooch, galop, gigue, hover, lindy, mambo, mixer, polka, rumba, sally, stomp, swing, tread, valse 6 adagio, ballet, bolero, boogie, Boston, cancan, chassé, chi-chi, foot it, formal, frolic, german, hoof it, redowa, rhumba, shimmy 7 beguine, coranto, courant, flicker, flitter, flutter, hoedown, onestep, shuffle 8 Alley Cat, cakewalk, chaconne, cotillon, courante, couranto, fandango, flamenco, galliard, galopade, glissade, hula-hula, rigadoon, rigandon 9 allemande, jitterbug ***art of:*** 11 terpsichore 12 choreography ***Austrian:*** 7 ländler ***ballroom:*** 5 congo, rumba, tango 6 chacha 7 fox-trot, mazurka, twostep 8 merengue 9 cotillion 10 Charleston ***Bohemian:*** 5 polka ***Brazilian:*** 5 samba 6 maxixe 9 bossa nova ***chorus:*** 5 strut ***combining form:*** 5 chore 6 choreo, chorio ***country:*** 3 hay 8 anglaise, hornpipe ***couple:*** 5 polka ***court:*** 6 pavane 8 saraband 9 allemande, sarabande ***Cuban:*** 5 conga 8 habanera ***designer:*** 13 choreographer ***East Indian:*** 5 mudra ***English:*** 6 morris ***folk:*** 4 hora, kolo 8 hornpipe 10 tarantella, tarantelle ***formal:*** 4 prom ***French:*** 5 gavot 7 bourrée, gavotte 8 lanciers 10 carmagnole ***garment:*** 4 tutu 7 leotard ***graceful:*** 6 minuet ***Haitian:*** 4 juba ***Hungarian:*** 7 Csardas, Czardas ***Indian:*** 6 nautch ***instrument:*** 8 castanet ***Irish:*** 6 fading ***Israeli:*** 5 horah ***Italian:*** 9 rigoletto ***lively:*** 4 reel, trot 6 rhumba 7 bourrée 9 shakedown ***modern:*** 3 toe ***movement:*** 4 step 6 minuet 8 glissade 9 allemande, pirouette ***1920's:*** 10 Charleston ***old-time:*** 7 hoedown 8 chaconne ***Polish:*** 5 polka 7 mazurka 8 mazourka ***Polynesian:*** 4 hula ***round:*** 5 carol, waltz 6 carole ***shoes:*** 5 pumps 8 slippers ***slipper:*** 7 toeshoe ***slow:*** 5 pavan, pavin 6 adagio, pavane ***South American:*** 7 carioca ***Spanish:*** 4 jota 6 bolero 7 zapateo 8 cachucha, saraband ***springy:*** 3 jig ***square:*** 7 lancers 9 quadrille ***stately:*** 5 pavan 8 saraband 9 sarabande ***step:*** 3 pas 4 riff, shag 6 pickup ***voluptuous:*** 5 belly ***woman's:*** 6 cancan

dancer 6 hoofer, hopper 7 chorine, clogger, danseur, prancer, stepper 8 coryphée, danseuse, figurant 9 ballerina, chorus boy, chorus man, figurante 10 ballet girl, cakewalker, chorus girl ***American:*** 4 Feld, Lang, Tune 5 Kelly 6 Duncan, Graham, Taylor 7 Astaire, Bujones, de Mille, Gregory, Martins, Massine, McBride, St. Denis, Tamiris 8 Kirkland, Villella 9 Tallchief ***ballet:*** 6 étoile 7 soliste ***Danish:*** 8 Tomasson ***English:*** 5 Somes, Tudor 7 Markova 8 Fonteyne ***female:*** 8 devadasi ***French:*** 6 Bejart, Perrot, Petipa ***German:*** 5 Jooss ***Italian:*** 5 Grisi ***Javanese:*** 7 serimpi ***Mexican:*** 5 Limon ***Russian:*** 5 Lifar 7 Nureyev, Pavlova, Ulanova 8 Danilova, Makarova, Nijinsky, Semenova, Vaganova 10 Karasavina 11 Baryshnikov ***Scottish:*** 7 Shearer ***sword:*** 7 bouffon 8 matachin ***Zuni:*** 7 shalako

dancing 6 ballet 7 saltant 11 choregraphy, terpsichore 12 choreography ***mania:*** 9 tarantism

dandle 3 pet 4 love 6 caress, cosset, cuddle, pamper

dandruff 5 scurf 6 furfur

dandy 3 fop 4 beau, buck, dude, fine, lulu, toff 5 dilly, nifty, peach, swell 6 peachy 7 coxcomb 8 popinjay, terrific 9 excellent, first-rate, humdinger, hunky-dory, marvelous 11 Beau Brummel, crackerjack 12 lounge lizard

dang 4 darn, durn 5 utter 6 cursed, cussed, damned 7 blasted, blessed, dratted, goldarn, regular 8 absolute, outright 9 downright 10 confounded, consummate 11 unmitigated

danger 4 risk 5 peril 6 hazard, menace, plight, threat 7 pitfall 8 distress, jeopardy ***signal:*** 4 bell 5 alarm, siren 6 redeye, tocsin

dangerous 4 fell 5 dicey, grave, hairy, nasty, risky 6 chancy, scathy, unsafe,

unsure, wicked **7** parlous, serious, unsound, vicious **8** grievous, insecure, menacing, perilous **9** hazardous, unhealthy **10** jeopardous, precarious **11** threatening
dangle **4** hang **5** droop, sling, swing **6** depend **7** suspend
Daniel ***American pioneer:*** **5** Boone ***father:*** **5** David ***mother:*** **7** Abigail ***statesman:*** **7** Webster
Danish ***hero:*** **5** Ogier ***king:*** **9** Christian, Frederick ***queen:*** **9** Margrethe
dank **3** wet **4** damp **5** humid, moist **6** clammy, dampen, moisty **7** dampish, wetness, wettish **8** moisture
Dante ***beloved:*** **8** Beatrice ***birthplace:*** **8** Florence ***daughter:*** **7** Antonia ***deathplace:*** **7** Ravenna ***party:*** **6** Guelph **7** Bianchi ***patron:*** **5** Scala ***teacher:*** **6** Latini ***wife:*** **5** Gemma ***work:*** **7** Inferno **8** Commedia, Convivio **9** Vita Nuova
Dantean division **5** canto
Danton's colleague **5** Marat
Danzig **6** Gdańsk
dap **4** skim, skip **5** carom, graze **6** glance **8** ricochet
Daphne ***father:*** **5** Ladon **6** Peneus ***form:*** **10** laurel tree ***pursuer:*** **6** Apollo **9** Leucippus
Daphnis' lover **5** Chloe
dapper **4** neat, trim **5** natty, sassy **6** jaunty, rakish, spiffy, spruce, sprucy **7** bandbox, doggish, foppish, stylish **8** sparkish **11** well-groomed
dapple **4** spot **5** fleck, patch
dappled **6** dotted, motley **7** flecked, mottled, spotted **8** freckled **9** multihued **10** discolored, multicolor, variegated, versicolor **11** varicolored **12** multicolored, particolored, versicolored
Dardanelles **10** Hellespont
Dardanus ***descendants:*** **7** Trojans ***father:*** **4** Zeus **7** Jupiter ***mother:*** **7** Electra
dare **4** defi, defy, face, risk **5** beard, brave, front, stump **6** brazen, cartel, hazard **7** attempt, outface, venture **8** confront, defiance **9** challenge
daredevil see **daring**
darer **4** hero **6** risker
daring **4** bold, pert, rash, wild **5** brave, nerve **6** heroic **7** courage, heroism **8** boldness, devilish, fearless, reckless, temerity **9** audacious, daredevil, foolhardy, venturous **10** courageous, jeopardous **11** adventurous, temerarious, venturesome **13** adventuresome
Darius ***father:*** **9** Hystaspes ***son:*** **6** Xerxes ***wife:*** **6** Atossa
Darjeeling **3** tea
dark **3** dim, dun, sad, wan **4** dusk, murk **5** black, blind, brown, cloud, dingy, dusky, mirky, murky, night, shady, sooty, swart, umber, unlit, vague **6** brunet, cloudy, dismal, gloomy, opaque, somber, sombre, swarth, swarty, wicked **7** aphotic, cryptic, duskish, obscure, rayless, shadowy, stygian, subfusc, sunless, swarthy, unclear **8** abstruse, bistered, Delphian, gloomful, ignorant, mystical, sinister **9** ambiguous, enigmatic, lightless, secretive, tenebrous, unlighted **10** caliginous, indistinct, mysterious, mystifying, pitch-black **11** black-a-vised **13** unilluminated ***combining form:*** **3** mel **4** mela, melo **5** melam, melan **6** melano ***poetic:*** **4** ebon
darken **3** dim, fog **4** dull, dusk, haze, murk **5** bedim, blind, cloud, gloom, lower, shade, sully, umber **6** shadow **7** becloud, benight, blacken, eclipse, embrown, obscure, opacate, tarnish **8** melanize, overcast **9** obfuscate, overcloud **10** overshadow ***Scottish:*** **5** gloam
dark-haired ***female:*** **8** brunette ***male:*** **6** brunet
darkness **4** duck, mirk, murk **5** black, gloom, night, shade, umbra **6** shadow **7** privacy, secrecy **8** midnight, twilight
dark-skinned **5** dusky, swart **6** brunet, swarth **7** swarthy **8** bistered, melanous **11** black-a-vised
darling **3** pet **4** chou, dear, duck, love, lush **5** deary, ducky, flame, honey, loved, sweet **7** beloved, pigsney, sweetie **8** adorable, favorite, heavenly, precious **9** ambrosial **10** delectable, delightful, fair-haired, honeybunch, sweetheart
darn **4** mend **5** patch, utter **6** blamed, cursed, cussed, damned, repair **7** blasted, doggone **8** infernal, outright **9** downright **10** confounded **11** straight-out **13** blankety-blank
darn it ***French:*** **3** zut
dart **3** fly, jet, run, shy **4** barb, bolt, buzz, flit, leap, sail, scud, skim **5** arrow, bound, fling, hurry, lance, scamp, scoot, shaft, shoot, skirr, spear, speed, spurt **6** glance, hasten, scurry, spring, sprint, squirt **7** javelin, missile, scamper **8** jaculate ***barbed:*** **10** banderilla
D'Artagnan's friends **5** Athos **6** Aramis **7** Porthos
Dartmouth location **7** Hanover
darts terms **3** leg **4** bust **5** split **6** dosser, double, flight, hockey, treble **8** bull's-eye **10** clock board
Darwin **7** Charles ***ship:*** **6** Beagle ***theory:*** **9** evolution
dash **3** nip, pep, run, vim, zip **4** balk, bang, beat, bilk, boil, bolt, brio, élan, foil, hint, hurl, life, pelt, race, ruin, rush, slam, tear, tick, zing **5** ardor, blast, break, chase, crush, drive, fling, oomph, scoot, shoot, smack, speed, spice, style, throw, trace, verve

6 baffle, blight, charge, energy, esprit, hurtle, hyphen, scurry, spirit, sprint, streak, thrust, thwart, trifle 7 bravura, collide, scamper, shatter, soupçon, spatter, splotch 8 confound, tincture 9 animation, bespatter, frustrate 10 circumvent, disappoint, sprinkling, suggestion

dashboard reading 4 fuel 5 speed 7 mileage

dashing 3 gay 4 bold, chic, keen 5 alert, showy, smart, swank, swish 6 bright, dapper, jaunty, lively, modish, swanky, with-it 7 animate, rousing, stylish 8 animated, spirited 9 vivacious 11 fashionable

Das Kapital author 4 Marx

dassie 9 blacktail

dastard 4 funk 6 coward, craven, funker 7 chicken, quitter 8 poltroon 11 yellowbelly

dastardly 4 base, mean

data 5 facts, input 8 material 11 information

date 3 age, era, woo 5 court, epoch, tryst 6 cutoff, escort 7 take out 8 deadline 9 accompany 10 engagement, rendezvous 11 anniversary, appointment, assignation ***abbreviation:*** 4 appt

dated 3 old 5 passé 6 démodé, old hat 7 archaic 8 obsolete, outmoded 10 antiquated 12 old-fashioned 13 unfashionable

Dathan's father 5 Eliab

datum 4 fact

daub 4 blob, blot, spot 5 fleck, paint, smear 6 dapple, smudge, splash 7 besmear, dribble, plaster, spatter, speckle, splotch 9 variegate

daughter ***Carter's:*** 3 Amy ***Cher's:*** 8 Chastity ***Cole's:*** 7 Natalie ***Elizabeth II's:*** 4 Anne ***Fonda's:*** 4 Jane ***Ford's (Gerald):*** 5 Susan ***Garland's:*** 11 Liza Minelli ***Johnson's (Lyndon):*** 4 Lucy 5 Linda ***Kennedy's (John F.):*** 8 Caroline ***Nixon's:*** 5 Julie 6 Tricia ***Sinatra's:*** 5 Nancy

Daughter of the Moon 7 Nokomis

daunt 3 cow 6 dismay, subdue 7 conquer, horrify, terrify 8 frighten 10 disconcert, discourage, dishearten, intimidate

dauntless 4 bold, game 5 brave 8 fearless, unafraid 9 unfearful, unfearing 10 courageous, invincible 11 indomitable, lionhearted

dauntlessness 4 guts 5 heart, pluck, spunk 6 mettle, spirit 7 cojones, courage 10 resolution

davenport 4 desk, sofa 12 chesterfield

David ***commander:*** 4 Joab 5 Amasa ***companion:*** 8 Jonathan ***daughter:*** 5 Tamar ***father:*** 5 Jesse ***rebuker:*** 6 Nathan ***scribe:*** 7 Seraiah ***singer:*** 5 Heman ***son:*** 5 Amnon 7 Absalom, Solomon ***wife:*** 7 Abigail, Ahinoam 9 Bathsheba

David, for one 4 camp

David Copperfield ***author:*** 7 Dickens ***character:*** 4 Dora, Heep 5 Agnes, Uriah 6 Barkis, Betsey 7 Creakle 8 Micawber 9 Murdstone, Wickfield 10 Steerforth ***nurse:*** 8 Peggotty (Clara)

dawdle 3 lag 4 drag, idle, jauk, laze, lazy, loaf, loll, poke 5 dally, delay, tarry, trail 6 linger, loiter, lounge, put off, putter, trifle 7 fritter 8 lallygag, lollygag 13 procrastinate

dawn 4 morn 5 alpha, light, onset, start, sunup 6 aurora, outset 7 genesis, morning, opening, sunrise 8 cockcrow, daybreak, daylight, outstart 9 beginning 11 cockcrowing 12 commencement

day 3 era, sun 4 time 8 lifetime ***abbreviation:*** 3 Fri, Mon, Sat, Sun, Thu, Tue, Wed 4 Thur, Tues 5 Thurs ***before:*** 3 eve ***church calendar:*** 5 feria ***French:*** 4 jour ***German:*** 3 Tag ***holy:*** 5 feast ***hot:*** 8 scorcher ***hour:*** 4 noon ***Latin:*** 4 dies ***Spanish:*** 3 dia

day blindness 11 hemeralopia

daybreak 4 dawn, morn 5 sunup 6 aurora 7 dawning, morning, sunrise 8 cockcrow 11 cockcrowing

daydream 4 muse 5 fancy 6 revery, vision 7 fantasy, reverie 8 phantasm, phantasy

days ***fourteen:*** 9 fortnight ***of yore:*** 3 eld

daystar 3 Sol, sun 7 phoebus

daze 3 fog 4 haze, stun 5 blind, dizzy 6 bemuse, benumb, dazzle, fuddle, muddle, trance 7 confuse, mystify, petrify, stupefy 8 astonish, bedazzle, befuddle, bewilder, confound, disorder, distract, paralyze 9 dumbfound, overwhelm 10 muddlement 11 muddledness 12 befuddlement

dazed 5 woozy 6 doiled, groggy, punchy 7 witless 8 dithered

___ d'Azur 4 Cote

dazzle 5 blind, shine 8 bewilder, outshine

dazzling 6 flashy, garish 7 fulgent, glowing, radiant 9 brilliant 10 candescent

deacon 4 calf 6 cleric, doctor, layman 7 officer 10 adulterate

dead 3 dim 4 cold, dull, flat, gone, late, lost, numb 5 bleak, blind, inert, muted, passé, quiet, slain, utter 6 asleep, buried, bygone, dismal, fallen, lapsed, numbed 7 defunct, disused, exactly, expired, extinct, outworn, tedious 8 benumbed, deceased, departed, inactive, lifeless, obsolete, outmoded 9 apathetic, deathlike, exanimate, inanimate, senseless, unfeeling 10 breathless, corpselike, insensible, insentient, lackluster, lusterless, monotonous, motionless, spiritless, unanimated, unexciting 11 inoperative, insensitive, unconscious 12 anesthetized, extinguished, unresponsive ***Australian:*** 4 bung ***British:*** 5 napoo 6 napooh ***combining form:*** 4 necr 5 necro

dead duck 5 goner

deaden 4 dull, kill, mull, mute, numb, stun 5 blunt 6 benumb, dampen, muffle, obtund, opiate, stifle 7 mortify, petrify, smother, stupefy 8 paralyze 10 devitalize 11 anesthetize, desensitize

dead end 4 halt 6 pocket 7 impasse 8 cul-de-sac 10 blind alley, bottleneck, standstill

deadened 4 numb 6 asleep, corpsy, numbed 7 deathly 8 benumbed, deathful 9 deathlike, senseless, unfeeling 10 corpselike, insensible 11 insensitive 12 anesthetized

deadfall 4 trap 7 springe 9 booby trap, mousetrap

deadliness 8 fatality 9 lethality, mortality

deadlock 3 tie 4 draw 6 logjam 7 dogfall, impasse 8 standoff, stoppage 9 stalemate 10 standstill

deadly 4 dire 5 fatal, toxic 6 corpsy, lethal, mortal 7 baneful, capital, killing, noxious, ruinous, slaying 8 deathful, lethally, venomous, virulent 9 deathlike, pestilent, poisonous 10 corpselike, pernicious 11 destructive, mortiferous, pestiferous 12 pestilential

deadpan 5 blank, empty 6 vacant 12 inexpressive, unexpressive

dead shot 8 marksman

Dead Souls author 5 Gogol

dead to rights 9 red-handed

deadweight 3 tax 4 duty, load, onus, task 6 burden, charge 9 millstone

deafen 3 din

deal 4 dole, give, sale 5 allot, serve, shake, share, trade, treat 6 accord, bestow, divide, impart, lot out, parcel, strike 7 bargain, deliver, dish out, dole out, inflict, mete out, portion, scatter, wrestle 8 disburse, dispense, disperse, separate, share out 9 agreement, apportion, negotiate, partition 10 administer, distribute, measure out, portion out 11 transaction 13 understanding ***great:*** 4 lots 5 loads ***out:*** 8 dispense 9 apportion 10 administer, distribute ***secretly:*** 7 trinket ***with:*** 4 play 5 serve, treat 6 handle

dealer 4 bank 5 agent 6 banker, broker, seller, trader 8 chandler, merchant, operator 9 tradesman 10 negotiator, trafficker 11 businessman, distributer, distributor 12 merchandiser ***British:*** 6 draper, jobber, mercer 7 chapman ***card:*** 6 farmer ***horse:*** 5 coper ***women's clothing:*** 7 modiste

dealings 5 truck 7 affairs, matters, traffic 8 business, commerce, concerns 11 intercourse

dealing with ***suffix:*** 2 ic 4 ical

dean 4 head 5 doyen, guide, pilot 6 leader, priest, senior 7 officer 10 bellwether

dear 3 hon, pet 4 fond, high, lamb, love 5 honey, loved, sweet 6 costly, doting, loving, scarce 7 beloved, darling, devoted, lovable, machree, querida, special, tootsie 8 especial, favorite, loveling, lovesome, precious, valuable 9 cherished, expensive, heartfelt, sweetling 10 fair-haired, heartthrob, honeybunch, sweetheart 12 affectionate ***French:*** 4 cher 5 chère ***Irish:*** 4 agra ***Scottish:*** 2 jo

dear one ***suffix:*** 3 een

dearth 4 lack, want 6 defect, famine 7 absence, default, paucity, poverty 8 scarcity 9 privation, scantness 10 deficiency, meagerness, scantiness ***combining form:*** 5 penia

death 3 end 4 bane, exit 5 decay, night, sleep 6 demise, ending, expiry 7 decease, parting, passage, passing, quietus, silence 8 biolysis, casualty, curtains, fatality, necrosis, thanatos 9 bloodshed, departure 10 defunction, expiration, extinction, grim reaper 11 dissolution, termination 12 annihilation ***after:*** 10 posthumous ***combining form:*** 6 thanat 7 thanato ***easy:*** 10 euthanasia ***music:*** 5 dirge, elegy 8 threnody ***notice:*** 4 obit 8 obituary 9 necrology ***of tissue:*** 8 gangrene ***portending:*** 6 funest ***put to:*** 3 gas 4 hang, kill, slay 5 choke, lynch 6 murder, stifle 8 strangle, throttle 9 suffocate 11 assassinate, electrocute ***rate:*** 9 mortality ***rites:*** 7 funeral

deathless 7 abiding, eternal, lasting, undying 8 immortal 10 persisting 12 imperishable

deathlike see **deathly**

deathly 5 fatal 6 grisly, lethal, mortal 7 ghastly, haggard, macabre, stygian 8 deadened, gruesome, mortally 9 pestilent 10 cadaverous, corpselike 11 mortiferous 12 pestilential

debacle 4 rout 5 crash, smash, wreck 6 defeat 7 beating, crack-up, failure, licking, smashup 8 collapse, drubbing 9 breakdown, cataclysm, overthrow, trouncing 10 defeasance 11 shellacking 12 vanquishment

debar 4 bate 6 except, forbid, refuse 7 deprive, exclude, prevent, rule out, suspend 8 count out, preclude, prohibit 9 eliminate

debark 4 land

debase 3 mar, rot 4 harm, sink, warp 5 alloy, lower, spoil, stain, stoop, taint 6 bemean, canker, damage, defile, demean, dilute, dope up, humble, impair, injure, poison, reduce, vilify, weaken, worsen 7 corrupt, degrade, deprave, devalue, pervert, pollute, traduce, vitiate 8 cast down, dishonor 9 animalize, brutalize, humiliate, undermine 10 adulterate, bastardize, bes-

tialize, degenerate, demoralize 11 contaminate
debatable 4 moot 7 dubious 8 arguable, doubtful, mootable 9 uncertain 11 problematic 12 questionable
debate 4 fray, heed, moot 5 argue, fight, plead, rebut, study 6 hassle 7 agitate, canvass, contend, contest, discept, discuss, dispute, mooting, quarrel, wrangle 8 argument, consider, forensic, question 9 altercate, attention, dialectic, thrash out 10 toss around 11 application, controversy, disputation 12 deliberation 13 argumentation, concentration, consideration ***art of:*** 9 forensics ***expert:*** 7 eristic ***place for:*** 5 forum
debauch 4 orgy, undo, warp 5 party 6 seduce 7 corrupt, deprave, pervert, vitiate 9 bacchanal, brutalize 10 bastardize, bestialize, demoralize, saturnalia 11 bacchanalia
debauched 4 lewd 6 wanton 7 vitiate 8 depraved, vitiated 9 corrupted, dissolute, lecherous, libertine, perverted 10 lascivious, libidinous, licentious
debilitate 3 sap 5 blunt 6 weaken 7 cripple, disable, unbrace 8 enfeeble 9 attenuate, extenuate, undermine 10 devitalize 12 unstrengthen
debilitated 4 weak 6 feeble, infirm, sapped 8 burnt-out, decrepit 9 burned-out
debility 7 astheny, disease, malaise 8 asthenia, weakness 9 infirmity 10 feebleness, infirmness, sickliness 11 decrepitude 13 unhealthiness ***combining form:*** 6 asthen 7 astheno
Debir ***kingdom:*** 5 Eglon ***slayer:*** 6 Joshua
debonair 6 urbane 8 carefree, charming, graceful 10 nonchalant 12 lighthearted
Deborah's husband 9 Lappidoth
debris 4 junk, slag 5 offal, trash, waste 6 litter, refuse, rubble, spilth 7 garbage, rubbish 8 detritus, riffraff ***rock:*** 5 talus 7 eluvium 8 colluvia
debt 3 due, sin 4 evil 5 wrong 6 arrear 7 arrears, default, deficit 9 arrearage, demurrage, liability 10 obligation, wickedness 11 delinquency ***acknowledgment:*** 3 IOU 4 bill 5 check
debtless 7 solvent
debunk 6 expose, show up, unmask 7 uncloak, undress 8 discover, unshroud
Debussy's La ____ 3 Mer
debut 7 come out, opening 8 entrance, premiere 9 beginning 12 introduction
decadence 7 decline 8 downfall 9 downgrade 10 declension, degeneracy, devolution 11 declination, degradation 12 degeneration, dégringolade 13 deterioration
decadent 6 effete 8 overripe 10 degenerate
decalogue verb 5 shalt
Decameron, The ***author:*** 9 Boccaccio ***heroine:*** 8 Griselda
decamp 2 go 3 fly 4 exit, flee 5 break, leave, scape, scram 6 begone, escape, get out, retire 7 abscond, run away, skiddoo, slip off, take off 8 clear out, hightail, withdraw 9 skedaddle
decanter 6 bottle, carafe
decapitate 4 head, raze, ruin, undo 5 wrack, wreck 6 behead, unmake 7 destroy, unbuild 8 decimate, demolish 9 decollate 10 guillotine
decapod 6 shrimp 7 mollusk 10 crustacean
decathlon champ 6 Jenner (Bruce), Toomey (Bill) 7 Johnson (Rafer), Mathias (Bob) 8 Campbell (Milton), Thompson (Daley)
decay 3 ebb, rot 4 fade, sour, turn, wane 5 spoil, taint, waste 6 blight, curdle, fading, molder, wither 7 corrupt, crumble, failure, ferment, moulder, putrefy 8 putresce 9 break down, decompose 11 deteriorate 12 dilapidation, disintegrate, putrefaction 13 deterioration
decayed 3 bad 6 effete, putrid, rotten 7 carious, spoiled 8 decadent, overripe 10 degenerate
decease 3 die 4 fail, pass 5 death, sleep 6 cash in, demise, depart, expire, perish 7 passing, quietus, succumb 8 pass away 9 departure 10 defunction 11 dissolution
deceit 3 gyp 4 hoax, sham 5 fraud, guile 6 humbug 7 chicane, cunning, swindle 8 artifice, flimflam, spoofery, trickery 9 chicanery, duplicity, imposture 12 dissemblance 13 dissimulation, double-dealing
deceitful 3 sly 4 foxy, wily 5 false, lying 6 artful, crafty, fickle, hollow, shifty, sneaky, tricky 7 cunning, knavish, roguish 8 delusive, delusory, guileful, unhonest 9 dishonest, insidious, insincere, underhand 10 fallacious, mendacious, misleading, untruthful 11 treacherous, underhanded
deceivable 7 dupable 8 gullible
deceive 3 con, fob, fop, fub, lie 4 bilk, dupe, flam, fool, gaff, gull, hoax, jilt, mock, wyle 5 blind, bluff, cheat, cozen, dodge, hocus, spoof, trick 6 baffle, befool, betray, delude, humbug, illude, juggle, palter, take in 7 beguile, defraud, mislead, sell out, two-time 8 flimflam, hoodwink 9 bamboozle, four-flush 11 double-cross 12 misrepresent
deceiving 5 false 8 deluding, delusive, delusory 9 beguiling 10 fallacious, misleading
decelerate 5 delay 6 retard, slow up 7 slacken 8 slow down
decency 7 decorum, dignity, fitness 9 etiquette, propriety 10 seemliness
decent 4 fair, good, just, nice, pure

5 clean, right 6 chaste, common, enough, honest, modest, proper, seemly 7 average, correct, fitting 8 adequate, all right, becoming, decorous, spotless 9 befitting, competent, stainless, sufficing, tolerable, undefiled, unsullied 10 acceptable, conforming, immaculate, sufficient 11 comfortable, comme il faut, presentable, respectable, unblemished 12 satisfactory 13 unexceptional, unimpeachable

deception 3 gyp 4 flam, gaff, gull, hoax, hype, ruse, sham, wile 5 cheat, craft, fraud, guile, magic, put-on, spoof, trick 6 dupery, humbug, mirage 7 chicane, cunning, fallacy, fantasm, knavery, sophism 8 cheating, cozening, flimflam, illusion, intrigue, phantasm, subtlety, trickery, trumpery, wiliness 9 casuistry, chicanery, duplicity, fourberie, imposture, sophistry, treachery 10 artfulness, camouflage, defrauding, dishonesty, hanky-panky, subterfuge 11 dipsy-doodle, highbinding, indirection 12 speciousness, spuriousness 13 double-dealing ***Scottish:*** 7 blaflum

deceptive 5 false 6 artful, crafty, tricky 7 seeming, trickie 8 deluding, delusory, illusory, specious, trickish 9 beguiling 10 fallacious, misleading

deceptiveness 7 fallacy, sophism 8 delusion 9 casuistry, sophistry 12 equivocation, speciousness, spuriousness

decide 3 opt 4 rule, will 5 judge 6 figure, settle 7 adjudge, resolve 8 conclude 9 determine 10 adjudicate

decided 3 set 4 firm, flat, sure 5 fixed 6 intent 7 assured, certain, obvious, settled 8 clear-cut, cocksure, definite, explicit, positive, resolute, resolved 10 determined, pronounced 11 categorical, established, unequivocal 12 unmistakable

decimate 4 raze, ruin, undo 5 wrack, wreck 6 unmake 7 destroy, unbuild, unframe, wipe out 8 demolish, massacre 9 slaughter 10 annihilate 11 exterminate

decipher 5 break, crack, solve 6 decode, reveal, unfold 7 analyze, decrypt, resolve, unravel 8 unriddle 9 figure out, puzzle out, translate 12 cryptanalyze

decision 4 fiat 6 choice, ruling 7 resolve, verdict 8 firmness, judgment, sentence, umpirage 9 selection 10 conclusion, resolution, settlement 12 resoluteness 13 determination, purposiveness ***rabbinical:*** 9 responsum

decisive 3 set 4 bent 6 intent 7 assured, crucial, settled 8 critical, resolute, resolved 9 imperious, masterful 10 determined, imperative, peremptory 11 self-assured 13 self-confident

deck 4 trim 5 adorn, array, dress, equip, floor, prank 6 attire, blazon, clothe 7 apparel, appoint, furnish, garland, garnish 8 accouter, accoutre, beautify, decorate, emblazon, ornament, platform 9 embellish ***chief:*** 4 bos'n 9 boatswain ***high:*** 4 poop ***lowest:*** 5 orlop ***out:*** 5 fix up, primp, slick, spiff, tog up 6 doll up 7 dress up, gussy up 8 spruce up ***part:*** 7 scupper

deckhand 3 gob 6 sailor 7 rouster, swabbie

declaim 4 rant, rave 5 mouth, orate, speak, utter 6 recite 7 elocute, inveigh, soapbox 8 bloviate, harangue, perorate

declamatory 7 aureate, flowery 8 sonorous 9 bombastic, high-flown 10 euphuistic, oratorical, rhetorical 12 magniloquent 13 grandiloquent

declaration 4 word 6 avowal, oracle, report 9 broadcast, statement 10 disclosure 12 announcement 13 advertisement, pronouncement

declare 3 say, vow 4 aver, avow, deny, tell, toot, vend, vent 5 sound, state, utter, voice 6 affirm, allege, assert, assure, avouch, blazon, depone, depose, herald, report, reveal 7 chime in, deliver, divulge, express, profess, protest, publish, signify, testify 8 announce, bring out, constate, disclose, indicate, proclaim, throw out 9 advertise, broadcast, predicate, pronounce 10 annunciate, bruit about, promulgate 11 blaze abroad, come out with, disseminate ***a saint:*** 8 canonize ***in cards:*** 3 bid 4 meld ***invalid:*** 5 annul

declare off 5 welsh 6 renege, resile 7 back out 8 back down 9 backpedal, backwater

declass 4 bump, bust 5 break 6 demote, reduce 7 degrade, demerit, disrate 8 disgrade 9 downgrade

déclassé 4 hack, mean, poor 6 common 8 inferior, low-grade 10 second-rate 11 second-class 12 second-drawer

declension 8 downfall 9 decadence, downgrade 10 degeneracy 12 dégringolade

declination 6 ebbing, waning 7 failure 8 downfall 9 decadence, downgrade 10 degeneracy 12 dégringolade

decline 3 dip, ebb, jib, rot, sag, set 4 balk, dive, drop, fade, fail, fall, flag, loss, sink, slip, wane 5 abate, demur, droop, lapse, lower, slide, slope, slump, spurn 6 ebbing, go down, recede, refuse, reject, renege, waning, weaken, worsen 7 abstain, atrophy, descend, descent, dismiss, drop-off, dwindle, failure, falloff, forbear, refrain, relapse, sell-off, sinkage, subside 8 comedown, decrease, downfall, downturn, languish, lowering, toboggan, turn down 9 backslide, decadence, downgrade, downslide, downswing, downtrend, reprobate, repudiate, weakening **10** degeneracy, degenerate, depression, devolution, disapprove, disimprove, falling off, retrograde **11** backsliding, deteriorate **12** degeneration, dégringolade, disintegrate **13** deterioration ***combining form:*** **4** clin **5** clino

declivitous **6** sloped, tilted, tipped **7** leaning, oblique, pitched, sloping **8** inclined **9** inclining

declivity **3** dip **4** drop, fall **5** slope **7** descent **8** gradient **11** inclination

decode see **decipher**

decollate **4** head **6** behead **10** guillotine

decolor **5** white **6** blanch, bleach, blench, whiten **7** wash out **11** achromatize

decompose **3** rot **4** turn **5** decay, spoil, taint **6** molder **7** analyze, break up, crumble, dissect, putrefy, resolve **8** dissolve **9** anatomize, break down **12** disintegrate

decomposition ***combining form:*** **4** lyses (plural) **5** lysis

decorate **4** pink, trim **5** adorn, dress, frill, prank **6** bedeck, emboss **7** cornice, dress up, festoon, furnish, garnish, miniate, appliqué **8** beautify, emblazon, ornament **9** embellish ***a border:*** **6** purfle

decorated **6** ornate **7** adorned, wrought **9** bemedaled **10** beribboned

decoration **2** PH **3** DSC, DSM **4** bays **5** award, badge, honor, kudos, medal **6** boulle, doodad, plaque **7** laurels **8** accolade, fretting, fretwork, ornament, vignette ***cutout:*** **8** appliqué ***furniture:*** **4** buhl **8** buhlwork

decorous **3** fit **4** done, good, nice, prim **5** right **6** au fait, comely, decent, proper, seemly **7** correct, elegant, fitting **8** becoming, suitable **9** befitting, civilized, de rigueur **10** conforming **11** appropriate, respectable, well-behaved

decorously **4** well **5** fitly **6** justly, nicely **7** rightly **8** properly **9** correctly, fittingly **11** befittingly

decorousness **5** order **9** propriety **11** orderliness **12** correctitude

decorticate **4** flay, hull, peel, skin **5** scale, scalp, strip **6** denude

decorum **5** order **7** decency, dignity, modesty **9** etiquette, propriety **10** properness, seemliness **11** correctness, orderliness **12** correctitude, decorousness

decoy **4** bait, lure, toll, trap **5** blind, plant, shill, snare, stick, tempt **6** allure, capper, delude, entice, entrap, lead on, pigeon, seduce **7** deceive, mislead **8** inveigle, trickery **9** deception, shillaber **10** allurement, enticement, seducement, temptation **12** inveiglement

decrease **3** cut, ebb **4** bate, clip, drop, ease, fall, loss, sink, trim, wane **5** abate, allay, close, lower, taper, waste **6** deduct, lessen, rebate, recede, reduce, shrink **7** abridge, atrophy, curtail, cut back, cut down, dwindle, letdown, lighten, peak out, shorten, slacken, subside **8** contract, diminish, downturn, moderate, peter out, retrench, rollback, subtract, taper off **9** alleviate, drain away **10** abbreviate, diminution

decree **3** act, law, set **4** fiat, rule **5** canon, edict, enact, judge, order, tenet, ukase **6** assize, behest, charge, dictum, firman, impose, ordain, ruling **7** adjudge, appoint, bidding, command, dictate, lay down, mandate, precept, statute **8** judgment, sentence **9** directive, enactment, judgement, ordinance, prescribe, prescript **10** adjudicate, injunction, plebiscite, regulation **11** declaration **12** adjudication, announcement, proclamation, promulgation **13** pronouncement ***Muslim:*** **5** irade

decrepit **3** old **4** aged, lame, weak, worn **5** frail, seedy, tacky, tired **6** creaky, feeble, flimsy, infirm, senile, shabby, sloppy, tagrag, wasted, weakly **7** cast-off, failing, fragile, haggard, run-down, unkempt, unsound **8** slipshod **10** bedraggled, broken-down, down-at-heel, threadbare **13** insubstantial, unsubstantial

decrepitude **7** disease, malaise **8** debility **9** infirmity **10** infirmness, sickliness **13** unhealthiness

decretum **3** law **4** rule **5** canon, edict **6** assize **7** precept, statute **9** ordinance **10** regulation

decry **3** boo **4** slur **5** abuse, lower **6** lessen **7** asperse, censure, condemn, degrade, detract, devalue, run down **8** belittle, denounce, derogate, diminish, discount, mark down, minimize, take away, take from, write off **9** criticize, deprecate, devaluate, disparage, dispraise, downgrade, reprehend, reprobate, underrate, write down **10** depreciate, disapprove, undervalue **11** detract from, opprobriate

decrypt see **decipher**

decumbent **4** flat **5** prone **9** prostrate, reclining

decussate **5** cross **8** crosscut **9** intersect **10** criss-cross, intercross

dedicate **3** vow **6** devote, hallow **10** consecrate

deduce **4** draw, lead **5** infer, judge, trace **6** derive, evolve, gather **7** collect, explain, extract, make out **8** cogitate, conclude

deduct **4** bate, dock, draw, take **5** abate, allow, infer, judge **6** derive, gather, remove **7** collect, make out, take off, take out **8** abstract, conclude, discount, knock off, roll back, subtract, take away

deduction **3** cut **6** rebate **7** dockage **8** decrease, discount, illation, judgment,

sequitur, write-off **9** abatement, decrement, inference **10** conclusion **13** ratiocination
deductive **7** a priori **8** dogmatic, illative, reasoned **9** derivable **11** inferential **13** ratiocinative
deed **3** act **4** cede, fact, fait, feat, pact **5** doing, quest, thing, title **6** action, assign, convey, escrow, remise **7** charter, compact, exploit **8** alienate, contract, covenant, make over, practice, sign over, transfer **9** adventure **10** abalienate, conveyance, enterprise **11** achievement, performance, tour de force ***brutal:*** **8** atrocity ***evil:*** **3** sin **11** malefaction
deem **3** say **4** feel, hold, hope, know, tell, view **5** judge, opine, sense, think **6** credit, divine, reckon, regard **7** account, adjudge, believe **8** consider, proclaim **10** conjecture
de-emphasize **8** downplay, play down **9** soft-pedal
deep **3** low, sly **4** foxy, hard, late, rapt, wily, wise **5** abyss, acute, grave, heavy, ocean **6** artful, astute, crafty, growly, intent, middle, occult, orphic, remote, secret, shrewd, tricky **7** abysmal, complex, cunning, devious, engaged, extreme, intense, obscure, serious, unmixed **8** absorbed, abstruse, esoteric, grievous, guileful, hermetic, immersed, involved, profound **9** developed, engrossed, firmament, insidious, intensive, recondite, sagacious, unalloyed, wrapped up **10** acroamatic, bottomless, mysterious, profoundly **11** complicated, preoccupied ***combining form:*** **5** bathy ***pink:*** **5** coral
deep-dyed **5** sworn **7** settled **9** confirmed, hard-shell **10** entrenched, inveterate **13** bred-in-the-bone
deepen **4** rise **5** mount, rouse **6** darken **7** enhance, magnify, thicken **8** heighten, redouble **9** aggravate, intensate, intensify **10** strengthen
deepness **4** drop **5** abyss, depth **10** profundity
deep-rooted see **deep-dyed**
deep-sea ***combining form:*** **5** bathy
deep-seated **5** sworn **6** inborn, inbred, innate **7** connate, settled **8** inherent, profound **9** confirmed, hard-shell, ingrained, intrinsic **10** congenital, entrenched, indwelling, inveterate **13** bred-in-the-bone, dyed-in-the-wool
deep water **6** plight **7** dilemma **11** predicament
deer **3** elk, roe **4** buck, musk, stag **5** brown, moose **6** wapiti **7** caribou, venison **8** bobolink **10** camel's hair ***Asian:*** **4** axis **6** chital, sambar, sambur **7** muntjac, sambhar, sambhur **8** muntijak ***British:*** **4** hart ***combining form:*** **5** cervi ***female:*** **3** doe ***female red:*** **4** hind ***male:*** **4** hart **7** roebuck ***male red:*** **4** stag **8** staggard, staggart ***meat:*** **5** jerky **7** venison ***path:*** **3** run **5** trail ***red:*** **7** brocket ***relating to:*** **6** damine **7** cervine ***track:*** **4** slot **5** spoor ***young:*** **3** kid **4** fawn
Deerslayer ***author:*** **6** Cooper ***character:*** **11** Natty Bumppo **12** Chingachgook
deface **3** mar **4** foul, harm, ruin, scar **5** spoil **6** batter, damage, deform, injure, mangle **7** blemish, distort **8** misshape, mutilate **9** disfigure, vandalize **10** disfashion, disfeature
de facto **6** really **8** actually **9** genuinely, veritably
defalcation **4** lack **7** deficit, failing, failure **8** shortage, underage **10** deficiency, inadequacy, negligence, scantiness **13** insufficience, insufficiency
defamation **4** tale **7** calumny, scandal, slander **10** backbiting **12** backstabbing, belittlement **13** disparagement
defamatory **8** libelous **9** maligning, traducing, vilifying **10** backbiting, calumnious, detracting, detractive, scandalous, slanderous
defame **4** foul **5** abase, cloud, libel, smear **6** injure, malign, vilify **7** asperse, blemish, scandal, slander, traduce **8** dishonor, vilipend **9** blackwash, denigrate **10** calumniate, scandalize, villainize
default **4** fail, lack, omit, want **6** dearth, defect **7** absence, failure, neglect **9** oversight, privation **10** negligence **11** delinquency, dereliction **12** imperfection
defeasance **4** rout **7** beating, debacle, licking **8** drubbing **9** overthrow **11** shellacking **12** discomfiture, vanquishment
defeat **4** best, down, drub, foil, lick, loss, rout, ruin, sink, stop, undo, whip **5** check, crush, outdo, skunk, swamp, waste, whomp, worst **6** outgun, reduce, subdue **7** beating, conquer, debacle, destroy, failure, licking, nose out, outplay, outvote, repress, setback, shellac, trounce **8** outfight, outtrump, overcome, overvote, vanquish, waterloo **9** downthrow, frustrate, insuccess, overpower, overthrow, subjugate, thrashing, trouncing, unsuccess **10** nonsuccess **11** shellacking **12** discomfiture, vanquishment
defecate **5** purge, stool **6** purify, refine **7** clarify **9** discharge
defect **3** bug **4** flaw, lack, vice, want **5** botch, error, fault **6** damage, dearth, desert, foible, injury, malady **7** absence, blemish, default, failing, frailty **8** drawback, renounce, weakness **9** infirmity, privation, repudiate **10** apostatize, deficiency, tergiverse **11** shortcoming **12** imperfection, tergiversate ***timber:*** **4** knot ***visual:*** **6** myopia, squint **9** amblyopia, hyperopia **10** presbyopia, strabismus **11** hemeralopia

defection 8 apostasy 9 falseness, forsaking, recreancy 10 disloyalty 11 abandonment
defective 3 bad, ill 4 poor, sick 5 amiss, flawy 6 broken, faulty, flawed 7 damaged, lacking, unsound, wanting 8 deranged, impaired 9 corrupted, deficient, imperfect, unhealthy 10 disordered, inaccurate, inadequate, incomplete, uncomplete 12 insufficient *combining form:* 4 atel 5 atelo
defector 3 rat 7 traitor 8 apostate, recreant, renegade, runagate, turncoat 9 turnabout 13 tergiversator
defend 4 back, hold, save 5 argue, claim, cover, fight, guard 6 assert, screen, secure, shield, uphold 7 bulwark, contend, justify, protect, support, warrant 8 advocate, champion, conserve, garrison, maintain, preserve 9 safeguard, vindicate 11 rationalize
defendable see **defensible**
defendant 7 accused, libelee 8 libellee
defender 8 advocate, champion, guardian 9 protector *of people's rights:* 7 tribune
defense 4 egis, fort, ward 5 aegis, alibi, armor, guard 6 answer, excuse, sconce, shield 7 apology, bulwark, rampart, shelter 8 apologia, armament, fastness, fortress, muniment, security 9 safeguard 10 apologetic, protection, stronghold 11 exculpation, explanation 13 justification *organization:* 4 NATO 5 NORAD, SEATO *outer:* 6 tenail 8 tenaille
defenseless 8 helpless 11 unprotected
defensible 7 tenable 9 excusable 10 condonable
defer 3 bow 4 cave, stay, wait 5 adapt, delay, remit, stall, waive, yield 6 accede, adjust, hold up, put off, shelve, submit 7 adjourn, conform, hold off, knuckle, lay over, put over, succumb, suspend 8 hold over, intermit, postpone, prorogue 9 acquiesce 10 capitulate 11 accommodate, buckle under 12 knuckle under 13 procrastinate
deference 5 honor 6 homage 9 obeisance 10 compliance, submission
deferential 5 silky 6 silken 7 duteous, dutiful 9 disarming, regardful 10 respectful, saccharine 11 insinuating, insinuative 12 ingratiating, ingratiatory
defiance 4 dare 5 stump 6 cartel 7 bravado, despite 8 audacity, boldness, contempt, temerity 9 challenge, contumacy, enjoinder, hardihood, impudence, insolence 10 brazenness, effrontery, insurgency, unruliness 12 contrariness, factiousness, stubbornness
deficiency 3 sin 4 lack, want 5 fault, minus 6 dearth 7 absence, blemish, demerit, failing, failure 8 scarcity, shortage, underage 9 privation 10 inadequacy, scantiness 11 defalcation, shortcoming 12 imperfection *combining form:* 5 penia *mental:* 6 idiocy 7 amentia *oxygen:* 8 asphyxia
deficient 3 shy 5 minus, scant, short 6 faulty, flawed, meager, meagre, measly, scanty, scarce 7 bobtail, failing, lacking, unsound, wanting 8 impaired 9 defective, imperfect 10 inadequate, incomplete, uncomplete *combining form:* 6 privic
deficit 4 lack 7 failure 8 shortage, underage 10 inadequacy, scantiness 11 defalcation 13 insufficience, insufficiency
defile 3 tar 4 foul, pass, rape, soil 5 dirty, shame, smear, spoil, stain, sully, taint 6 befoul, debase, ravish 7 besmear, corrupt, outrage, pollute, profane, tarnish, violate 8 besmirch, deflower, discolor, dishonor 9 deflorate, desecrate 11 contaminate
defiled 6 impure 7 unclean 8 profaned 10 desecrated
define 3 fix, hem, rim, set 4 edge, etch, term 5 bound, limit, skirt, verge 6 assign, border 7 clarify, delimit, lay down, mark off, mark out, outline 8 surround 9 delineate, demarcate, prescribe 12 characterize
definite 3 set 4 sure 5 clear, final, fixed, sharp, solid 6 narrow 7 assured, certain, decided, express, limited, precise, settled 8 clean-cut, clear-cut, distinct, explicit, limiting, positive, specific 10 conclusive, determined, forthright, pronounced, restricted 11 categorical, determinate, established, unambiguous, unequivocal 12 unmistakable 13 circumscribed
definiteness 8 accuracy 9 exactness 10 exactitude
definitive 4 last 5 final 7 express 8 absolute, clean-cut, clear-cut, explicit, settling, specific, terminal, ultimate 10 concluding, conclusive 11 categorical, determining, unambiguous
definitiveness see **definiteness**
definitude see **definiteness**
deflect 4 bend, warp 5 avert, parry, pivot, sheer, wheel, whirl 6 detour, divert, swerve 7 deviate, diverge, hold off, keep off, refract 9 volte-face
deflection 3 yaw 4 bend, tack, turn, veer 5 curve, shift 6 double, swerve 7 bending, turning, veering 8 swerving 9 departure, diversion 10 divergence *combining form:* 7 sphingo
deflorate see **deflower**
deflower 4 rape 5 force, harry, havoc, spoil 6 defile, devast, devour, ravage, ravish 7 despoil, outrage, violate 8 desolate 9 depredate, desecrate, devastate

Defoe ***character:*** 6 Crusoe, Friday, Roxana 12 Moll Flanders ***heroine:*** 4 Moll
deform 3 mar 4 flaw, maim, warp, wind 5 spoil 6 batter, damage, deface, impair, injure, mangle 7 blemish, contort, cripple, distort, torture 8 misshape, mutilate 9 disfigure 10 disarrange
deformity 4 flaw 7 blemish, harelip 8 misshape, ugliness 10 aberration, corruption, impairment 11 abnormality, impropriety 12 irregularity, malformation
___ de France 3 île
defraud 3 gyp 4 beat, bilk, hoax, take 5 cheat, cozen, mulct, rogue, trick 6 chouse, fleece 7 swindle 8 flimflam 9 bamboozle
deft 4 neat 5 adept, agile, handy, quick 6 adroit, clever, expert, nimble 8 dextrous, skillful 9 dexterous, ingenious 10 neat-handed
deftness 7 address, prowess, sleight 9 dexterity, readiness
defunct 4 cold, dead, gone, late, lost 5 inert 6 asleep, bygone 7 extinct 8 deceased, departed, finished, inactive, lifeless, vanished 9 exanimate, inanimate
defy 4 dare, face, gibe, mock 5 beard, brave, flout, front, scorn, spurn, stump 6 cartel, ignore 7 affront, outdare, outface, venture 9 challenge
dégagé 6 breezy, casual 7 relaxed, unfussy 8 informal 9 easygoing 10 unreserved 11 low-pressure 13 unconstrained
degeneracy see degeneration
degenerate 3 rot 4 sink 5 lapse 6 effete, rotten, worsen 7 corrupt, decayed, decline, descend, vicious, vitiate 8 decadent, depraved, infamous, overripe 9 backslide, miscreant, nefarious, unhealthy 10 disimprove, flagitious, villainous
degeneration 7 atrophy, decline 8 downfall, lowering 9 decadence, depravity, downgrade 10 perversion, regression 12 dégringolade, depravedness
degradation 4 fall 7 decline, descent 11 downgrading
degrade 4 bump, bust, sink 5 abase, break, decry, lower 6 bemean, damage, debase, demean, demote, depose, expose, humble, lessen, reduce 7 corrupt, declass, demerit, deprive, detract, disrate, pervert, put down 8 belittle, cast down, derogate, diminish 9 decompose, disparage, humiliate, reduction 12 depolymerize
degree 3 peg 4 heat, rank, rate, rung, step, term, tier 5 grade, honor, notch, order, pitch, point, ratio, scale, shade, stage, stair 6 extent 7 measure, station 8 standing 9 dimension, magnitude 10 proportion ***academic:*** 2 BA, BS, MA, MD, MS 3 DDS, LLB, LLD, MBA, MFA, PhD ***highest:*** 8 cum laude 13 magna cum laude, summa cum laude ***of combining power:*** 7 valence ***of height:*** 5 grade ***of importance:*** 7 caliber, calibre ***of outward slope:*** 5 splay ***seeker:*** 9 candidate ***slight:*** 4 hair ***suffix:*** 2 ty 3 ity 4 ance, ness ***utmost:*** 4 acme
dégringolade see degeneration
___ de guerre 3 nom
dehydrate 3 dry 4 sear 5 parch 9 desiccate, exsiccate
Deianira ***brother:*** 8 Meleager ***father:*** 6 Oeneus ***husband:*** 8 Heracles, Hercules ***mother:*** 7 Althaea ***victim:*** 8 Heracles, Hercules
Deidamia ***father:*** 9 Lycomedes ***husband:*** 9 Pirithous ***son:*** 11 Neoptolemus
deific 5 godly 6 divine 7 godlike
deification 10 apotheosis
deign 5 stoop 10 condescend
Deiphobus ***brother:*** 5 Paris 6 Hector ***father:*** 5 Priam ***mother:*** 6 Hecuba ***wife:*** 5 Helen
Deirdre ***beloved:*** 5 Noisi ***father:*** 5 Felim
deity 3 god 4 deva 5 numen 6 numina (plural) 7 goddess, godhead, godhood, godling, godship 8 Almighty, divinity 12 supreme being (see also at Greek; Hindu; Norse; Roman)
deject 5 chill 8 dispirit 9 disparage 10 demoralize, discourage, dishearten
dejected 3 low, sad 4 blue, down, glum, sunk 6 gloomy, somber, sombre 7 hangdog, humbled, unhappy 8 downcast, wretched 9 cheerless, depressed, woebegone 10 despondent, spiritless 11 crestfallen, downhearted 12 disconsolate
dejection 5 dumps 7 despair 10 melancholy 12 mournfulness
Delaware ***capital:*** 5 Dover ***largest city:*** 10 Wilmington ***nickname:*** 10 First State 12 Blue Hen State, Diamond State ***state flower:*** 12 peach blossom
delay 3 lag 4 drag, hold, mire, mull, poke, slow 5 check, defer, deter, embog, stall, tarry, trail 6 dawdle, detain, hang up, hinder, hold up, impede, linger, loiter, put off, retard, shelve, slow up 7 adjourn, bog down, hold off, prolong, respite, set back, slacken, suspend 8 hangfire, hesitate, hold over, intermit, obstruct, postpone, prorogue, reprieve, slow down 9 detention, hindrance, lingering 10 decelerate, dillydally, moratorium, suspension 13 procrastinate
delaying 8 dilatory, moratory
delectable 4 lush 5 sapid, tasty, yummy 6 choice, savory 7 darling 8 heavenly, luscious, pleasing 9 ambrosial, delicious, exquisite, toothsome 10 delightful 11 scrumptious
delectation 3 joy 6 relish 7 delight, joy-

ance **8** fruition, pleasure **9** diversion, enjoyment
delegate **4** name, send **5** agent, envoy, proxy **6** assign, charge, commit, depute, deputy **7** appoint, ascribe, consign, empower, entrust **8** deputize, emissary, transfer **9** authorize, catchpole, spokesman **10** commission, mouthpiece **12** representant
delete **4** omit, x out **5** annul, blank, erase, purge **6** cancel, censor, efface, remove **7** blot out, destroy, expunge, wipe out **8** black out, cross out **9** eliminate, eradicate **10** blue-pencil, obliterate
deleterious **3** bad **6** nocent **7** harmful, hurtful, nocuous, ruinous **8** damaging **11** destructive, detrimental, mischievous, prejudicial
deletion **7** erasure **8** omission **10** deficiency
deliberate **4** cool, muse, pore, slow **5** chary, meant, study, think, weigh **6** ponder, reason, regard **7** advised, careful, heedful, laggard, planned, reflect, schemed, studied, unhasty, willful, willing, witting **8** cautious, cogitate, consider, designed, dilatory, intended, measured, meditate, mull over, prepense, ruminate, studious, talk over, turn over, unforced **9** leisurely, meditated, projected, speculate, unhurried, voluntary **10** calculated, considered, purposeful, thought-out **11** circumspect, intentional **12** aforethought, premeditated, unprescribed
deliberately **9** on purpose, purposely **10** purposedly **11** purposively
deliberation **3** rap **4** heed **5** study **6** debate **7** thought **9** brainwork **10** conference, discussion
Delibes *ballet:* **6** Sylvia **8** Coppelia, La Source *opera:* **5** Lakmé
delicacy **4** cate **5** goody, treat **6** caviar, dainty, luxury, morsel, nicety, tidbit, titbit **7** caviare **8** kickshaw **10** daintiness **11** bonne bouche
delicate **4** airy, fine, lacy, mild, nice, rare, soft, weak **5** balmy, frail, fussy, light **6** aerial, choice, dainty, flimsy, gentle, pastel, petite, queasy, select, slight, subtle, tender, touchy, tricky **7** elegant, finical, finicky, fragile, lenient, politic, refined, tactful, tenuous **8** ethereal, feathery, finespun, gossamer, graceful, hairline, shattery, superior, tactical, ticklish **9** breakable, exquisite, finicking, frangible, recherché, sensitive, squeamish **10** diplomatic, fastidious, particular, precarious **11** fracturable, persnickety, shatterable **13** hair-splitting
delicatesse **4** tact **5** poise **7** address **9** diplomacy **11** savoir faire, tactfulness
delicatessen **11** charcuterie

delicious **4** lush **5** sapid, yummy **6** choice, savory **7** darling **8** adorable, heavenly **9** ambrosial, exquisite, palatable, toothsome **10** appetizing, delectable
delight **3** joy **4** glee **5** amuse, bliss, charm, enjoy, exult, glory, mirth, revel **6** arride, divert, please, regale, relish **7** enchant, gladden, gratify, happify, jollity, joyance, rapture, rejoice, triumph **8** enravish, entrance, fruition, hilarity, jubilate, pleasure, savoring **9** delectate, enjoyment, enrapture, entertain **11** contentment, delectation **12** satisfaction *in:* **4** like, love **5** adore, enjoy, savor **6** admire **7** cherish **10** appreciate
delightful **4** lush **5** yummy **6** dreamy, savory **7** darling, elysian **8** adorable, alluring, charming, heavenly, luscious, pleasant, pleasing **9** agreeable, ambrosial **10** attractive, delectable, enchanting, gratifying **11** fascinating, scrumptious
Delilah's victim **6** Samson
delimit **3** bar **5** bound **6** demark **7** confine, mark out, measure **8** restrict **9** demarcate, determine **12** circumscribe
delineate **3** map **4** etch, limn **5** chart, image, trace **6** define, depict, render, survey **7** outline, picture, portray **8** describe **9** interpret, represent
delineation **5** story **7** account, contour, drawing, outline, picture, profile **10** silhouette **11** portraiture, presentment
delinquency **5** lapse **7** default, failure, misdeed, neglect **8** omission **9** oversight **10** misconduct **11** dereliction
delinquent **3** lax **5** slack **6** remiss **8** careless **9** negligent **10** behindhand, regardless **12** disregardful, transgressor
deliquesce **3** run **4** flux, fuse, melt, thaw **5** decay **7** liquefy **8** dissolve **9** decompose, disappear **12** disintegrate
delirious **3** mad **4** wild **5** crazy, manic, rabid **6** crazed, insane, maniac, raving **7** frantic, lunatic **8** confused, demented, deranged, ecstatic, frenetic, frenzied, rambling **9** rapturous, wandering **10** bewildered, corybantic, distracted, irrational **11** overexcited, overwrought **12** unreasonable *Scottish:* **8** brainish
delirium **5** furor **6** fervor, frenzy, ravery **7** ecstasy, jimjams, rapture
delirium ____ **7** tremens
deliver **3** say **4** bail, bear, deal, feed, find, give, hand, save, take, tell, yean **5** bring, pitch, serve, speak, state, throw, utter, whelp **6** convey, redeem, rescue, strike, supply, unbind **7** chime in, consign, declare, inflict, present, provide, release **8** bring out, dispatch, dispense, hand over, liberate, transfer, transmit, turn over **9** surrender

10 administer, bring forth, emancipate 11 come out with

deliverance 6 rescue 7 opinion, release 8 decision 10 liberation 12 disburdening

delivery 5 birth 6 rescue 7 address, bearing 8 shipment 9 rendition 10 childbirth 11 parturition 12 childbearing *combining form:* 4 toky

dell 4 dale 6 dingle, hollow, valley

Delphian 4 dark 5 vatic 6 mantic 7 cryptic, fatidic 8 oracular 9 enigmatic, prophetic, sibylline, vaticinal 10 mystifying 11 apocalyptic, prophetical

delude 5 bluff, trick 6 betray, humbug, juggle, take in 7 beguile, deceive, mislead 8 impose on 11 double-cross

deluge 3 sea, sop, wet 4 gush, pour, soak 5 douse, drown, flood, souse, spate, swamp, whelm 6 drench, engulf 7 niagara, torrent 8 cataract, downpour, flooding, inundate, overcome, overflow, submerge 9 cataclysm, overwhelm 10 cloudburst, inundation

delusion 5 dream, fancy 6 mirage 7 eidolon, fallacy, fantasy, figment, phantom, sophism 8 daydream, phantasm 9 casuistry, deception, sophistry 10 apparition, misleading 11 ignis fatuus 12 equivocation, speciousness, spuriousness 13 deceptiveness, hallucination

delusive 5 false 8 fanciful, illusory, quixotic 9 beguiling, deceiving, deceptive, fantastic, imaginary, visionary 10 chimerical, fallacious, misleading

delusory see delusive

deluxe 4 lush 5 plush 6 Capuan, choice 7 elegant, opulent 8 luscious, palatial 9 exquisite, luxuriant, luxurious, recherché, sumptuous 11 upholstered

delve 3 dig, dip 4 hole, mine, void 6 cavity, fathom, hollow, pocket, quarry, vacuum 7 vacancy, vacuity *into:* 4 sift 5 probe 7 explore 8 prospect 11 investigate

delving 5 probe, quest 7 inquest, inquiry, probing 8 research 11 inquisition 13 investigation

demagnetize 6 deperm 7 degauss

demagogue 6 leader 7 inciter 8 agitator, fomenter 9 firebrand 10 instigator 12 rabble-rouser

demand 3 ask, use 4 call, need, take, want 5 claim, crave, exact, force, order 6 compel, direct, elicit, enjoin, expect, oblige 7 call for, request, require, solicit 8 occasion 9 challenge, constrain, postulate 11 requirement, requisition

demanding 5 rigid, stern, tough 6 severe, strict, taxing, trying 7 exigent, onerous, weighty 8 grievous, rigorous 9 stringent 10 burdensome, oppressive

demarcate 5 bound, limit 6 define, set off 7 delimit, mark out, measure 8 separate, set apart 9 determine, segregate 10 delimitate 11 distinguish 12 circumscribe, discriminate 13 differentiate

demarcation 10 border line, separation 11 distinction

demean 3 act 4 bear, go on, mien, quit, sink 5 abase, carry, decry, lower 6 acquit, behave, debase, deport, humble 7 comport, conduct, degrade, detract 8 behavior, belittle, cast down, derogate 9 disparage, humiliate

demeanor 3 air, set 4 mien, port 7 address, bearing, conduct 8 behavior, carriage, portance, presence 10 deportment 11 comportment

demented 3 mad 4 luny 5 crazy, nutty 6 crazed, insane, maniac 7 lunatic, unsound 8 deranged, frenzied 9 delirious 10 hysterical, unbalanced

___ de mer 3 mal

demerit 3 sin 4 bump, bust, mark 5 break, fault 6 demote, reduce 7 declass, degrade, disrate 8 disgrade 9 downgrade 10 deficiency 11 shortcoming 12 imperfection

demesne 5 field 6 domain, estate, sphere 7 terrain 8 dominion, province 9 bailiwick, champaign, territory *house:* 5 manor

Demeter see Ceres

demigod 8 superman 10 superhuman

demise 3 die 4 drop, pass 5 death, sleep 6 cash in, depart, ending, expire 7 decease, passing, quietus, silence, succumb 8 curtains, pass away 10 defunction, expiration, extinction 11 dissolution 12 annihilation

demit 4 sink 5 couch, droop, lower 6 resign 7 depress, let down 8 abdicate, renounce, withdraw

demiurgic 8 creative, original 9 deviceful, formative, ingenious, inventive 10 innovative, innovatory 11 originative 12 innovational

demobilize 6 dispel 7 break up, disband, scatter 8 disperse, separate 9 discharge, muster out

democratic 7 popular 10 self-ruling 13 self-governing

Democratic party symbol 6 donkey

démodé 5 dated, passé 7 antique, archaic, belated 8 old-timey, outdated 9 out-of-date 12 old-fashioned

demoiselle 5 crane 6 damsel 9 damselfly 10 damselfish 11 earth pillar

demolish 4 raze, ruin, undo 5 crush, level, smash, total, wrack, wreck 6 unmake 7 destroy, unbuild, unframe 8 decimate

demolition bomb 11 blockbuster

demon 3 hag, imp 4 ogre 5 devil, fiend,

genie, ghoul, Satan, witch 7 incubus, villain, warlock 9 archfiend *Arabic:* 5 afrit 6 afreet *female:* 5 lamia 7 succuba, succubi (plural) 8 succubae (plural), succubus *Samoan:* 4 aitu *small:* 8 devilkin

demoniac see demonic

demonian see demonic

demonic 7 satanic 8 devilish, diabolic, fiendish 10 serpentine, unhallowed 11 diabolonian

demonstrate 3 try 4 mark, show, test 5 prove 6 evince, expose, ostend 7 display, exhibit, make out 8 evidence, manifest, proclaim 9 determine, establish

demonstration 4 show 5 proof 7 display 9 spectacle

demonstrative 4 here, open, that, this 7 profuse 8 effusive, outgoing 9 expansive, exuberant, outspoken 10 epideictic, outpouring, unreserved 12 unrestrained 13 unconstrained

demoralize 4 warp 5 chill, unman 6 debase, deject, weaken 7 corrupt, debauch, deprave, pervert, unnerve, vitiate 8 dispirit 9 disparage, undermine 10 bastardize, debilitate, discourage, dishearten

Demosthenes *for one:* 6 orator *oration:* 9 Olynthiac, Philippic

demote 4 bump, bust 5 break, lower 6 reduce 7 declass, degrade, demerit, disrate 8 disgrade 9 downgrade

demulcent 8 soothing 9 softening

demur 3 gag, jib, shy 4 balk 5 qualm, stick, waver 6 boggle, falter, object, oppose, squeam, strain 7 protest, scruple, stickle, stumble 8 aversion, hesitate, question 9 challenge, hesitancy, objection, vacillate 10 conscience, difficulty, hesitation, indecision, reluctance 11 compunction, deprecation, disapproval, remonstrate, uncertainty 12 protestation, remonstrance 13 remonstration, unwillingness

demure 3 coy, mim, shy 4 prim 5 timid 6 modest, silent 7 bashful 8 backward, reserved, reticent, retiring 9 diffident, unassured 11 unassertive

demurral 7 protest 8 question 9 challenge, objection 10 difficulty 12 remonstrance 13 remonstration

demurrer see demurral

den 3 sty 4 base, cave, goal, home, lair, room, sink 5 couch, lodge, Sodom 6 burrow, cavern, hollow 7 cesspit, dayroom, hideout 8 cesspool, hideaway, playroom, workroom 11 pandemonium 12 Augean stable *rabbit:* 6 warren

denial 2 no 3 nay 7 refusal, refutal 8 disproof, negation, rebuttal 9 rejection 10 abnegation, gainsaying, refutation 11 declination, repudiation 12 disallowance, renouncement, renunciation 13 contradiction, controversion

denigrate 5 libel, sully 6 darken, defame, malign, vilify 7 asperse, slander, traduce 8 belittle, tear down 10 calumniate, scandalize

denims 9 blue jeans

denizen 5 liver 6 native 7 dweller, habitué, haunter, resider 8 habitant, occupant, resident 9 indweller 10 frequenter, inhabitant

Denmark *capital:* 10 Copenhagen *monetary unit:* 5 krone

denominate 3 dub 4 call, name, term 5 style, title 7 baptize, entitle 8 christen

denomination 4 cult, name, sect 5 creed, faith, nomen, style, title 6 church 8 category, cognomen, religion 9 communion 10 persuasion 11 appellative *religious:* 6 Jewish, Muslim 7 Baptist 8 Lutheran 9 Adventist, Episcopal, Mennonite, Methodist 12 Presbyterian 13 Roman Catholic

denotation 4 name, sign 7 meaning 10 signifying

denote 4 mark, name, show 5 spell 6 import, intend 7 add up to, express 8 indicate 9 designate, insinuate, represent

denouement 6 result 7 outcome

denounce 3 rap 4 skin 5 blame, blast, decry, knock 6 accuse, scathe 7 arraign, censure, condemn, redbait, upbraid 9 criticize, reprehend, reprobate 10 denunciate, vituperate 11 incriminate 12 anathematize

de novo 4 anew, over 5 again 6 afresh 8 once more 9 over again

dense 4 dull, dumb 5 close, heavy, massy, solid, thick, tight 6 obtuse, opaque, stupid 7 compact, crammed, crowded, doltish, serried 8 blockish, imporous 9 fatheaded, jam-packed 10 numskulled 11 block-headed, thickheaded 12 impenetrable *combining form:* 4 pycn, pykn 5 pachy, pycno, pykno

dent 4 bash, nick 5 dinge, notch, tooth 6 dimple

dental structures 5 brace 6 bridge 10 bridgework

denticulate 7 serrate, serried 8 saw-edged, saw-tooth, serrated 10 saw-toothed

dentin 6 enamel

denude 4 bare 5 strip 6 divest 7 deprive, disrobe 8 bankrupt, unclothe 9 dismantle

denunciate see denounce

deny 4 curb 5 cross, forgo, rebut 6 disown, eschew, forbid, impugn, negate, refuse, refute, reject, renege 7 abstain, confute, deprive, disavow, forbear, forsake, gainsay, refrain 8 abnegate, disallow, disclaim, forswear, hold back, keep back, negative, renounce, traverse, withhold 9 constrain, disaffirm 10 contradict, contravene, controvert

depart 2 go 3 die 4 exit, flee, pass, quit 5 leave, stray 6 begone, decamp, demise, desert, differ, expire, get off, perish, ramble, recede, retire, set out, skidoo, swerve, wander 7 abandon, abscond, decease, deviate, digress, diverge, excurse, forsake, get away, pull out, skiddoo, succumb 8 divagate, pass away, withdraw

departing 7 good-bye 8 farewell 11 valedictory

department 6 branch, sphere 8 division, province 11 subdivision

departure 4 exit 5 break, death, going 6 egress, exodus, flight 7 exiting, leaving, retreat, turning 8 farewell, offgoing, outgoing, quitting 9 deviation, diversion, egression 10 aberration, decampment, deflection, divergence, setting-out, withdrawal 11 leave-taking *of a ship:* 6 sortie *point:* 7 outport

depend 4 bank, hang, lean, rely, rest, turn 5 count, hinge, sling 6 bank on, dangle, hang on, rely on, turn on 7 build on, count on, hinge on, stand on 8 reckon on 11 calculate on

dependable 4 sure, true 5 loyal, solid, tried 6 secure, steady, trusty 7 certain, staunch 8 accurate, constant, faithful, reliable, surefire 9 authentic, steadfast 11 responsible, trustworthy 12 tried and true 13 authoritative *Scottish:* 6 sicker

dependence 4 hope 5 faith, stock, trust 8 reliance

dependent 3 sub 4 iffy 5 child, under 6 minion, sponge, vassal 7 limited, reliant, relying, sponger 8 clinging, relative 9 accessory, ancillary, provisory, secondary, tributary, uncertain 10 collateral, contingent, restricted 11 appurtenant, conditional, provisional, subordinate

depict 4 draw, limn 5 image, paint 6 recite, relate, render, report, sketch 7 depaint, express, impaint, narrate, outline, picture, portray, recount 8 describe, emblazon 9 delineate, interpret, represent 12 characterize

depiction 7 picture 9 portrayal 11 portraiture, presentment

deplete 3 sap 4 draw 5 bleed, drain, empty, use up 6 expend, lessen, reduce, weaken 7 consume, disable, draw off, exhaust 8 bankrupt, decrease, diminish, draw down, enfeeble 9 undermine 10 impoverish

depleted 5 all in, spent 6 bleary, effete, used up 7 far-gone, worn-out 8 bankrupt 9 washed-out

deplorable 4 dire 5 awful 6 woeful 8 dolorous, dreadful, grievous, mournful, terrible, wretched 9 sickening 10 afflictive, calamitous, disastrous, horrifying 11 distressing, unfortunate 12 heartrending 13 heartbreaking

deplore 3 rue 4 moan, weep 5 mourn 6 bemoan, bewail, grieve, lament, regret, repent, sorrow 9 deprecate 10 disapprove, sorrow over

___ de plume 3 nom

depone 5 swear 6 assert 7 testify

___-de-pont 4 tête

deport 3 act 4 bear, go on, oust, quit 5 carry, exile, expel 6 acquit, banish, behave, demean 7 conduct, expulse 8 displace, relegate 10 expatriate

deportee 2 DP 5 exile 8 expellee

deportment 3 air, set 4 mien, port 5 tenue 7 address, bearing, conduct 8 behavior, carriage, demeanor, presence

depose 4 aver, avow, oust 5 swear 6 affirm, assert, avouch, devest, divest, remove, unmake 7 declare, decrown, profess, protest, testify, uncrown 8 constate, dethrone, discrown, displace, throw out, unthrone 9 disthrone, overthrow, predicate 11 disenthrone

deposit 3 lay, set 4 bank, drop, dump, fund, lees, pawn, stow 5 chest, dregs, lodge, place, put by, store 6 entomb, settle 7 consign, grounds 8 sediment 9 settlings 11 precipitate 13 precipitation *alluvial:* 5 delta *black:* 4 soot *calcium carbonate:* 10 stalactite, stalagmite *containing gold:* 6 placer *eggs:* 5 spawn *geologic:* 7 horizon *glacial:* 4 till 5 drift, esker 7 moraine *loam:* 5 loess *mineral:* 4 lode 10 concretion *muddy:* 6 sludge *sand:* 4 bank 5 beach *sedimentary:* 4 silt *skeletal:* 5 coral *stolen goods:* 5 fence *stream:* 8 alluvium, sediment *tooth:* 6 tartar

deposition 6 burial 7 placing 8 sediment 9 testimony 10 testifying

depository 4 bank, safe 5 attic, store, vault 7 arsenal 8 magazine 10 storehouse *for bones:* 7 ossuary

depot 4 bank, base, dump 5 store 6 armory 7 arsenal, station 8 magazine, terminal, terminus 9 warehouse 10 repository, storehouse 12 station house

deprave 4 warp 6 debase, malign 7 corrupt, debauch, pervert, vitiate 9 brutalize 10 bastardize, bestialize, demoralize

depraved 3 bad 4 evil, ugly, vile 6 putrid, rotten, warped, wicked 7 bestial, corrupt, debased, immoral, twisted, vicious, vitiate 8 degraded, perverse, vitiated 9 corrupted, debauched, miscreant, nefarious, perverted, unhealthy 10 degenerate, flagitious, villainous

depravity 4 vice 8 villainy 10 corruption, immorality, wickedness

deprecate 5 frown 6 object 7 detract

8 derogate, disfavor 9 disesteem 10 disapprove, discommend 12 disapprove of

depreciate 5 abate, abuse, decry, erode, lower 6 lessen, reduce, soften 7 cheapen, devalue, dwindle 8 belittle, decrease, derogate, diminish, discount, mark down, minimize, write off 9 devaluate, disparage, dispraise, downgrade, underrate, write down 10 devalorize, undervalue 11 detract from

depreciation 7 calumny, scandal, slander 8 discount 10 backbiting 12 backstabbing, belittlement 13 disparagement

depreciative 9 slighting 10 derogatory, detracting 11 disparaging, dyslogistic, underrating 12 undervaluing

depreciatory see **depreciative**

depredate 4 sack 5 waste 6 devour, ravage 7 despoil, pillage, plunder 8 desolate, lay waste, prey upon, spoliate 9 desecrate, devastate

depredator 6 looter, raider 7 forager, spoiler 8 marauder 10 freebooter

depress 4 damp, dash, dent, fall, sink 5 chill, couch, demit, droop, lower, slump 6 dampen, deject, dismay, indent, sadden 7 decline, let down, oppress, trouble 8 contrist, dispirit, enfeeble 9 disparage, weigh down 10 discourage, dishearten

depressant 5 black, bleak 6 dismal, dreary, gloomy 9 cheerless 10 oppressive 11 dispiriting

depressed 3 bad, low, sad 4 blue, down, glum, sunk 6 broody, gloomy, glumpy, hollow, lonely, somber 7 hippish, letdown 8 dejected, downcast 9 woebegone 10 dispirited, lugubrious, melancholy, spiritless 11 downhearted, melancholic 12 disconsolate 13 disadvantaged

depressing 3 sad 4 blue 5 black, bleak, chill 6 dismal, dreary, gloomy, somber, triste 7 joyless 8 funereal, mournful 9 saddening 10 melancholy, oppressive 11 melancholic 13 disheartening

depression 3 dip, low, pit, sag 4 drop, hole, sink, vale 5 basin, blues, crash, dumps, gloom, notch, scoop, slump 6 cavity, crater, hollow, pocket, valley 7 cyclone, decline, sadness, sinkage, sinking 8 sinkhole 9 concavity 10 melancholy, stagnation 11 unhappiness 12 mournfulness ***anatomical:*** 5 fossa, fovea 6 foveae (plural) 7 foveola, foveole 8 foveolae (plural), foveolet ***between breasts:*** 8 cleavage ***geographic:*** 7 Qattara ***in ridge:*** 3 col ***in snow:*** 8 sitzmark ***small:*** 4 dent 6 dimple

depressive see **depressant**

deprivation 4 loss 11 bereavement, deprivement, divestiture 13 dispossession

deprive 3 rob 4 bare, lose, oust 5 strip 6 denude, divest 7 bereave, disrobe 8 bankrupt, denudate, disseize 9 dismantle 10 disinherit, dispossess ***of brilliancy:*** 4 dull 6 deaden ***of courage:*** 7 unnerve ***of sensation:*** 6 benumb ***of sense and judgment:*** 9 inebriate ***of virginity:*** 8 deflower

deprive of ***prefix:*** 2 de 3 dis

depth 4 drop 5 abyss 7 lowness 8 deepness 9 acuteness 10 profundity 11 penetration 12 profoundness ***combining form:*** 4 bath 5 batho, bathy ***measure:*** 6 fathom ***measuring instrument:*** 4 gage 5 gauge ***of water:*** 5 draft 7 draught

depthless 7 cursory, shallow, sketchy 10 uncritical 11 superficial

dept. of ___ 2 ed 3 agr, com, def, int 4 comm 5 labor, state, trans 7 justice

depurate 5 clean 6 purify 7 clarify, cleanse

deputize 8 delegate 10 commission

deputy 5 agent, proxy 6 factor 8 assignee, attorney, delegate 9 catchpole 12 representant ***prefix:*** 2 co

derange 5 craze, upset 6 frenzy, madden, mess up, sicken 7 disturb, perturb, rummage, unhinge 8 disarray, disorder, distract, unsettle 9 interrupt, unbalance 10 discompose 11 disorganize

deranged 3 mad 5 crazy 6 crazed, insane, maniac 7 cracked, lunatic, unsound 8 demented 9 disturbed 10 disordered, unbalanced

derangement 6 lunacy 7 madness 8 disorder, insanity 9 confusion, unbalance 10 aberration, alienation, insaneness 11 distraction, disturbance, psychopathy, unsoundness

derby 3 hat 4 race, shoe 6 cheese 7 contest 9 horse race 10 field trial

derelict 3 bum, lax, vag 4 hobo, lorn 5 dingy, faded, leper, seedy, slack, tramp 6 pariah, remiss, shabby, unused 7 drifter, floater, Ishmael, outcast, run-down, uncouth, vagrant 8 careless, castaway, deserted, desolate, forsaken, solitary, vagabond 9 abandoned, forgotten, negligent 10 behindhand, delinquent, Ishmaelite, neglectful, regardless, street arab, threadbare, unreliable 11 dilapidated, offscouring, untouchable 12 disregardful, undependable 13 irresponsible, untrustworthy

dereliction 5 fault 7 default, failure, neglect 9 deviation, oversight 11 abandonment, delinquency, shortcoming

deride 4 lout, mock, quiz, razz, twit 5 fleer, rally, scoff, scout, taunt 7 catcall 8 ridicule

de rigueur 4 nice 5 right 6 au fait, decent, proper 7 correct 8 becoming, decorous 11 comme il faut

derision 4 butt, jest, joke, mock 5 sport 6 jestee 7 mockery 9 pilgarlic 13 laughingstock

derisive sound 3 boo 4 hiss

derivable 7 a priori 8 dogmatic, reasoned 9 deducible, deductive
derivation 4 root, well 6 origin, source, whence 7 descent 8 fountain 9 etymology 10 provenance, wellspring 11 provenience
derivative 7 spin-off 8 offshoot 9 by-product, outgrowth, secondary 10 descendant
derive 3 get 4 draw, stem, take 5 adapt, educe, infer, judge 6 deduce, deduct, evolve, gather 7 acquire, collect, emanate, make out, work out 8 arrive at, conclude 9 formulate, originate 10 excogitate
derive from 4 flow, head, rise, stem 5 arise, issue 6 spring 7 emanate, proceed 9 originate
dernier cri 3 cry, fad 4 chic, mode, rage 5 craze, style, vogue 6 furore 7 fashion 8 last word
derogate 5 decry 8 belittle, diminish, minimize, write off 9 disparage, dispraise 10 depreciate 11 detract from, opprobriate
derogatory 5 snide 8 decrying, scornful, spiteful 9 degrading, demeaning, malicious, maligning, slighting, vilifying 10 belittling, calumnious, detracting, disdainful, malevolent, pejorative 11 disparaging, dyslogistic 12 contumelious, depreciative
derout 8 stampede
derrick 5 hoist
derriere 4 beam, rear, seat 5 fanny 6 behind, bottom 7 rear end 8 backside, buttocks 9 posterior
derring-do 5 nerve 7 bravado, bravery, courage
dervish 4 monk 9 mendicant ***cap:*** 3 taj ***in Arabian Nights:*** 4 Agib ***practice:*** 7 dancing, howling 8 whirling ***wandering:*** 8 calender
descant 3 air, lay 4 aria, hymn, lied, sing, song, tune 5 ditty 6 melody, remark, strain, warble 7 discuss, dissert, measure, melisma, melodia 8 diapason, dilate on 9 discourse, expatiate, sermonize 10 dilate upon, dissertate 11 observation 12 counterpoint
Descartes' axiom 13 cogito ergo sum
descend 3 rot 4 drop, fall, pass, sink 5 lower, stoop, swoop 6 alight, derive, go down, worsen 7 decline 8 come down 9 originate 10 degenerate, disimprove, retrograde, spring from 11 deteriorate 12 disintegrate ***by rope:*** 6 rappel
descendant 3 son 5 scion 7 progeny, spin-off 8 offshoot, relative 9 by-product, outgrowth 10 derivative ***suffix:*** 3 ite
descendants 4 seed 5 brood, issue 7 progeny 8 children 9 offspring, posterity 11 progeniture
descent 3 dip 4 drop, fall 5 birth, blood, slope 6 origin 7 decline, drop-off, incline, lineage, sinking 8 ancestry, comedown, gradient, pedigree, plunging, stooping 9 declivity, downgrade 10 derivation, extraction, plummeting 11 origination 12 discomfiture ***airplane:*** 8 approach ***parachute:*** 4 jump 7 bailout
describe 4 limn 5 image, label, state 6 denote, depict, recite, relate, render, report 7 explain, express, mark out, narrate, outline, picture, portray, recount, signify 8 rehearse, vignette 9 chronicle, delineate, interpret, represent 10 illustrate 11 distinguish 12 characterize ***grammatically:*** 5 parse
description 3 ilk 4 kind, sort, tale, type, yarn 5 story 6 nature 7 account, picture, recital, variety, version 8 anecdote 9 character, chronicle, narrative, portrayal, recountal 10 recounting 11 portraiture, presentment
descry 3 see 4 espy, find, mark, note, spot, view 5 catch, hit on 6 behold, detect, spy out, turn up 7 discern, hit upon, observe 8 discover, meet with, perceive 9 encounter 11 distinguish
Desdemona ***father:*** 9 Brabantio ***husband:*** 7 Othello ***slanderer:*** 4 Iago ***slayer:*** 7 Othello
desecrate 4 sack 5 waste 6 defile, devour, ravage 7 despoil, pillage, profane 8 spoliate 9 depredate, devastate
desecration 9 blasphemy, sacrilege
desensitize 4 dull, mull, numb 5 blunt 6 benumb, deaden
desert 2 go 3 fly, rat 4 flee, quit, turn, wild 5 chuck, leave, waste 6 barren, betray, decamp, defect, depart, escape, maroon, strand, Tanami 7 abandon, abscond, badland, forsake 8 Karakumy, renounce, wild land, wildness 9 repudiate, throw over, wasteland 10 apostatize, tergiverse, wilderness 12 tergiversate ***African:*** 6 Libyan, Sahara 7 Arabian 8 Kalahari ***Arizona:*** 7 Painted ***Asian:*** 4 Gobi, Thar 6 Syrian 7 Kara Kum, Qara Qum 8 Kyzyl Kum 10 Great Sandy ***basin bottom:*** 5 playa ***beast:*** 5 camel 9 dromedary ***California:*** 6 Mohave, Mojave ***clay:*** 5 adobe ***combining form:*** 4 erem 5 eremo ***dweller:*** 4 Arab 5 nomad 6 Berber, Libyan, Malian, Nubian 8 Algerian, Egyptian, Maghrebi, Maghribi, Sudanese 11 Mauritanian ***fertile area:*** 5 oases (plural), oasis ***garb:*** 3 aba ***hallucination:*** 6 mirage ***region:*** 3 erg ***Saudi Arabia:*** 7 An Nafud ***Sudan:*** 6 Nubian ***travel group:*** 7 caravan ***valley:*** 6 bolson ***wind:*** 7 sirocco
deserted 4 bare, lorn 5 empty 6 barren, vacant 7 uncouth 8 derelict, desolate, for-

saken, solitary **9** abandoned **10** unoccupied **11** uninhabited

deserter **3** rat **4** AWOL **6** bolter **7** runaway **8** apostate, fugitive, renegade, runagate, turncoat

desertion **7** perfidy **8** apostasy **9** falseness, recreancy, treachery **11** abandonment

deserts **3** due **11** comeuppance

deserve **3** get, win **4** earn, gain, rate **5** merit **6** demand

deserved **3** due **4** just **5** right **7** condign, merited **8** rightful, suitable **9** requisite **11** appropriate **13** rhadamanthine

deserving **3** due **5** lumps, merit **6** rights, worthy **8** laudable **9** admirable, estimable, meritable, praisable **11** comeuppance, commendable, meritorious, thankworthy **12** praiseworthy

desexualize **3** fix **4** geld **5** alter, unsex **6** change, neuter **8** castrate, mutilate

desiccate **3** dry **4** fade, sear **5** decay, drain, dry up, parch, wizen **6** divest, wither **7** deplete, exhaust, shrivel **9** dehydrate **10** devitalize

desiderate **4** want, wish **5** covet, crave **6** choose, desire

design **3** aim **4** cast, draw, form, mean, mind, plan, plot, will **5** chart, decal, draft, frame, model, motif **6** animus, create, device, devise, devote, figure, intend, intent, invent, lay out, makeup, map out, motive, scheme, set out, sketch **7** arrange, diagram, dope out, drawing, execute, fashion, meaning, outline, pattern, prepare, produce, project, propose, purpose, thought, tracing **8** conation, contrive, creation, game plan, intrigue, strategy, thinking, volition **9** blueprint, construct, delineate, direction, formation, intention, invention **10** decoration, figuration, intendment, reflection **11** arrangement, composition, contemplate, delineation, disposition, machination **12** architecture, constitution, construction, deliberation ***book:*** **6** fillet **8** vignette ***carpet:*** **3** gul **9** medallion ***incised:*** **8** intaglio ***Indonesian:*** **5** batik ***inlaid:*** **6** mosaic ***of squares:*** **5** check ***openwork:*** **8** filigree ***perforated:*** **7** stencil ***raised:*** **8** repoussé ***skin:*** **6** tattoo ***textile:*** **8** polka dot ***velvety:*** **8** flocking

designate **3** dub, opt, tap **4** call, make, name, pick, term **5** allot, elect, label, style, title **6** assign, choose, denote, depute, finger, induct, select, single **7** appoint, baptize, declare, dictate, earmark, entitle, mete out, reserve, signify, specify **8** allocate, christen, identify, stand for **9** apportion, stipulate **10** decide upon **11** appropriate **12** characterize

designation **4** name **5** nomen, style, title **6** naming **8** cognomen, monicker **9** allotment **10** indicating, pigeonhole **11** appellative, identifying **12** pigeonholing

designed **7** advised, decided, studied **8** prepense, resolved, studious **10** considered, deliberate, determined, thought-out **12** aforethought, premeditated

designedly **9** on purpose, purposely **10** prepensely **11** purposively **12** deliberately **13** intentionally

designless **4** spot **6** random **9** desultory, haphazard, hit-or-miss, unplanned **12** unconsidered

desirable **6** suited **7** optimal **9** excellent, expedient

desire **3** aim, ask, yen **4** envy, eros, hope, itch, like, long, lust, pant, pine, urge, want, wish **5** covet, crave, enjoy, fancy, greed, yearn **6** asking, aspire, choice, choose, hanker, hunger, pining, thirst **7** avarice, bespeak, craving, entreat, impulse, longing, passion, request, solicit **8** appetite, cupidity, petition, rapacity, striving, yearning **9** appetency, eroticism, hankering, hungering, prurience, pruriency, thirsting **10** aphrodisia, appetition, attraction, preference **11** inclination, lustfulness **13** concupiscence, lickerishness ***combining form:*** **6** orexia ***for liquids:*** **6** thirst ***restless:*** **4** itch

desired **4** true **5** right **6** proper **7** fitting **11** appropriate

desirous **5** itchy **6** grabby, greedy **7** athirst, envious, wishful **8** appetent, covetous, grasping **10** prehensile, solicitous **11** acquisitive

desist **4** halt, quit, stop **5** cease, deval, yield **6** resign **7** abandon, abstain, forbear, hold off **8** give over, knock off, leave off, surcease **10** relinquish **11** discontinue, refrain from

desistance **3** end **4** stop **5** cease, close **6** ending, finish, period **9** cessation **10** conclusion **11** termination

desk **5** booth, stand, table **7** counter, lectern, roll top **8** lapboard **9** secretary **10** escritoire, secretaire ***adjunct:*** **8** inkstand, standish ***item:*** **3** pad **7** blotter, inkwell ***library:*** **6** carrel **7** carrell ***Scottish:*** **3** pew

desman **3** fur **4** pelt **6** mammal

___ de soie, French silk **4** peau

desolate **4** bare, dark, lorn, poor, sack **5** black, bleak, drear, empty, murky, stark, waste **6** barren, devoid, devour, dismal, gloomy, ravage, ruined, somber, vacant **7** despoil, joyless, pillage, uncouth **8** bereaved, derelict, deserted, forsaken, funereal, lay waste, lifeless, solitary, spoliate **9** abandoned, cheerless, depredate, desecrate, destitute, devastate, sorrowful **10** acheronian, unoccupied **11** dilapidated,

uninhabited 12 inconsolable, unconsolable 13 disheartening
desolation 6 sorrow 7 sadness 9 wasteland 11 abandonment
despair 4 drop 5 yield 6 give up, resign 7 abandon 8 renounce 9 surrender 10 relinquish
despairing 7 cynical, forlorn 8 hopeless 9 depressed, oppressed 10 melancholy 11 atrabilious, melancholic, pessimistic, weighed down 12 misanthropic 13 brokenhearted
desperado 6 badman, bandit, outlaw 7 bandido, convict 8 criminal 10 lawbreaker
desperate 4 dire, rash 5 acute 6 balked, crying, fierce, foiled 7 baffled, crucial, forlorn, furious, heinous, intense, vicious, violent 8 critical, headlong, hopeless, reckless, shocking, terrible, thwarted, vehement 9 atrocious, exquisite, foolhardy, monstrous, outwitted 10 frustrated, outrageous, scandalous 11 climacteric, precipitate, venturesome 12 circumvented, concentrated, overpowering 13 irretrievable, overmastering, uncollectable
despicable 3 low 4 base, mean, ugly, vile 5 cheap, sorry 6 abject, scummy, scurvy, shabby, sordid 7 ignoble 8 beggarly, infamous, wretched 9 loathsome 11 disgraceful, ignominious 12 contemptible
despisable see **despicable**
despise 4 hate, shun, snub 5 abhor, avoid, scorn, scout, spurn 6 detest, eschew, ignore, loathe, reject, slight 7 contemn, disdain 8 execrate, look down, misprize, overlook, renounce 9 abominate, disregard, repudiate
despised one 6 pariah
despisement 4 hate 5 scorn 6 hatred, malice 7 disdain, ill will 8 aversion, contempt, loathing 10 abhorrence 11 detestation, malevolence
despite 3 cut 4 harm, hate, hurt, slap, snub 5 altho, scorn 6 grudge, hatred, injury, insult, malice, rebuff, slight, spleen 7 affront, against, disdain, disgust, dislike, ill will 8 although, aversion, contempt, defiance, disfavor, distaste, loathing, spurning 9 contumacy, contumely, indignity, insolence, in spite of, malignity, rejection 10 abhorrence, incivility, malignancy 11 abomination, detestation, discourtesy, indignation, in the face of, malevolence, repudiation 12 cold shoulder, regardless of, spitefulness, stubbornness 13 disparagement, maliciousness, recalcitrance
despiteful 4 evil 5 catty 6 bitchy, wicked 7 vicious 9 malicious, rancorous 10 malevolent
despoil 4 sack 5 blast, strip, waste, wreck 6 denude, devour, ravage 7 pillage, plunder 8 desolate, spoliate 9 depredate, desecrate, devastate, strip away, wrest away
despoiler 6 looter, ruiner, sacker, vandal 7 defacer, forager, wrecker 8 marauder, pillager, ruinator 9 destroyer, plunderer, spoliator 10 depredator, freebooter
Despoina 8 mistress 10 Persephone *husband:* 5 Hades *realm:* 10 underworld
despond 3 sag 4 mope 5 brood, droop 6 give up 8 languish
despondency 5 blues, dumps, gloom 6 misery, sorrow 7 despair 9 dejection 10 blue devils, depression, melancholy
despondent 3 sad 7 forlorn 8 dejected, downcast, grieving, hopeless, mourning 9 depressed, sorrowful, woebegone 10 dispirited, melancholy 11 discouraged 12 disconsolate, disheartened
despot 4 duce 5 ruler 6 tyrant 7 autarch, emperor 8 autocrat, dictator 9 oppressor, strong man
despotic 8 absolute, tyrannic 9 arbitrary, autarchic, tyrannous 10 autocratic, monocratic, tyrannical
despotism 7 tsarism, tyranny, tzarism 8 autarchy 9 autocracy 10 domination 12 dictatorship
despotize 7 dictate, oppress 8 dominate, domineer, overlord 9 tyrannize
desquamate 4 peel 5 scale 7 peel off 8 flake off, scale off 9 exfoliate
dessert 3 ice, pie 4 cake, flan, fool, tart 5 Betty, bombe, coupe, fruit, grunt, halva, melba, slump, torte 6 afters, cheese, Danish, éclair, frappe, gateau, halvah, hermit, junket, kuchen, mousse, pastry, sorbet, sundae, trifle 7 cassata, cobbler, custard, gelatin, mazarin, parfait, pudding, sabayon, sherbet, spumone, spumoni, strudel 8 Bismarck, flummery, ice cream, marquise, napoleon, pandowdy, streusel, taiglach, teiglach, turnover 9 charlotte, cream puff, petit four, shortcake 10 blancmange, brown Betty, cheesecake, frangipane, marguerite, zabaglione 11 baked Alaska, banana split, gingerbread 12 hasty pudding, zuppa inglese *chilled:* 6 mousse *custard:* 8 zabaione, zabajone *French:* 5 bombe 6 éclair, frappe, gateau, mousse 7 mazarin, parfait, sabayon 8 marquise 9 petit four 10 blancmange, frangipane *frozen:* 5 bombe 7 parfait, sherbet 8 sherbert *German:* 6 kuchen 7 strudel *Italian:* 7 cannoli, cassata, spumone, spumoni 10 zabaglione 12 zuppe inglese *Jewish:* 8 taiglach, teiglach *pastry:* 6 quiche *soft:* 3 pud 7 pudding *Turkish:* 5 halva 6 halvah

destination 3 end, use 6 object 7 purpose 10 appointing
destine 3 fix 4 fate 6 assign, decree, devise, direct, doom to, intend 7 preform 8 dedicate, set aside 9 determine, preordain 10 foreordain 12 predetermine
destiny 3 lot 4 doom, fate, goal 5 moira, weird 6 design, future, intent, kismat, kismet 7 fortune, portion 9 intention, objective 12 circumstance
destitute 4 bare, poor, void 5 empty, needy 6 bereft, devoid 7 drained 8 bankrupt, depleted, dirt poor, divested, indigent, innocent, stripped 9 deficient, exhausted, penurious 10 bankrupted, stone-broke 11 impecunious, necessitous 12 impoverished *of water:* 9 anhydrous
destitute of *prefix:* 2 an *suffix:* 4 less
destitution 4 lack, need, want 6 dearth, penury 7 absence, poverty 9 adversity, indigence, neediness 10 misfortune
destroy 3 zap 4 doom, down, kill, raze, ruin, sack, slay, undo, wipe 5 fordo, havoc, shoot, smash, total, waste, wrack, wreck 6 cut off, finish, foredo, injure, lay low, mangle, quench, ravage, rubble, rub out, unmake 7 abolish, atomize, nullify, pillage, put away, ruinate, shatter, subvert, take off, unbuild, unframe, wipe out 8 carry off, decimate, demolish, dispatch, dissolve, dynamite, fumigate, mutilate, pull down, sabotage, tear down 9 devastate, discreate, dismantle, eradicate, extirpate, pulverize 10 annihilate, counteract, decapitate, extinguish, neutralize 11 exterminate *suffix:* 4 lyse, lyze
destroyer 4 bane, ruin 6 ruiner, tin can, vandal 7 defacer, undoing, warship, wrecker 8 downfall, ruinator 9 despoiler, ruination *combining form:* 4 cide 5 clast 7 clastic, phthora
destroying *combining form:* 5 cidal 7 clastic *prefix:* 3 ant 4 anth, anti
destruction 4 bane, loss, ruin 5 havoc 7 killing, undoing 8 downfall 9 confusion 10 impairment *combining form:* 4 lyses (plural) 5 lysis 6 clasia, clasis
destructive 5 fatal 6 deadly, lethal, mortal 7 baneful, ruinous 8 wrackful, wreckful 9 injurious 10 calamitous, disastrous, shattering 11 deleterious, detrimental
desuetude 3 end 5 cease, close 6 disuse, ending 7 closing, closure, neglect 8 disusage 9 cessation 10 conclusion, suspension 11 abandonment
desultory 6 casual, catchy, fickle, fitful, random, spotty 7 aimless, erratic, vagrant 8 shifting, sporadic, wavering 9 haphazard, hit-or-miss, mercurial, spasmodic, unplanned 10 capricious, designless, digressive, disorderly, inconstant 11 purposeless 12 unconsidered, unmethodical, unsystematic
detach 4 part, wean 5 sever, unfix 6 cut off, sunder, unhang 7 disjoin, divorce 8 abstract, dismount, disunite, separate, uncouple, withdraw 9 disengage, dismantle, dismember 10 disconnect, dissociate 11 disassemble 12 disaffiliate, disassociate
detached 5 alone, aloof, apart 6 casual, remote 7 distant, isolate, neutral, removed 8 abstract, isolated, separate, unbiased 9 colorless, incurious, uncurious, withdrawn 10 impersonal, poker-faced 11 indifferent, unconcerned, unconnected, unpassioned 12 uninterested 13 disinterested, dispassionate, unaccompanied *combining form:* 2 ap 3 aph, apo
detachment 7 divorce, rupture, split up 8 disunion, division 9 partition 10 neutrality, separation 11 dissolution, divorcement 12 unworldiness *combining form:* 5 lyses (plural), lysis
detail 4 item, list, part 5 point, thing 6 assign, relate, report 7 article, element, listing, minutia, program, specify 8 elements, minutiae (plural) 9 enumerate, stipulate 10 brass tacks (plural), particular 11 specificate, specificize 12 circumstance 13 particularize
detailed 4 full 6 minute 7 copious 8 abundant, itemized, thorough 9 clocklike 10 blow-by-blow, exhausting, exhaustive, particular 13 thoroughgoing
detain 3 nab 4 bust, curb, hold, keep, mire 5 check, delay, embog, pinch, run in 6 arrest, hang up, pick up, pull in, retard, slow up 7 bog down, inhibit, keep out, reserve, set back, slacken 8 hold back, keep back, restrain, slow down, withhold 9 apprehend 10 buttonhole, decelerate *in conversation:* 10 buttonhole
detect 4 espy, find, spot 5 catch, hit on 6 descry, turn up 7 discern, hit upon, rectify 8 discover, meet with 9 ascertain, encounter 10 demodulate
detectable 8 sensible, tangible 11 perceptible
detecting device 5 radar, sonar 6 solion 7 antenna, sferics 8 spherics 13 Geiger counter
detection 4 find 6 espial, strike 9 discovery 10 laying open, unearthing *system:* 5 radar, sofar
detective 3 tec 4 dick, G-man 5 roper 6 shamus, sleuth 7 gumshoe, shoofly 8 hawkshaw, informer, Sherlock 9 inspector 12 investigator 13 police officer *fictional:* 4 Chan (Charlie), Moto (Mr.) 5 Dupin (Auguste), Lecoq, Spade (Sam), Trent (Philip) 6 Carter (Nick), Holmes (Sherlock),

Poirot (Hercule), Wimsey (Peter) **7** Charles (Nick) **11** Father Brown
detective story writer **3** Poe (Edgar Allan) **5** Doyle (Arthur Conan), James (P.D.), Queen (Ellery), Stout (Rex) **6** Parker (Robert), Sayers (Dorothy) **7** Bentley (E.C.), Biggers (Earl), Collins (Wilkie), Fleming (Ian), Gardner (Erle Stanley), Hammett (Dashiell) **8** Chandler (Raymond), Christie (Agatha), Gaboriau (Emile), Marquand (John) **10** Chesterton (G.K.)
detent **3** dog **4** pawl **5** catch, click
detention **3** nab **5** delay, pinch **6** arrest, pickup **10** arrestment, internment **12** apprehension, imprisonment
deter **5** avert, block, debar, scare **6** divert, hinder, impede **7** forfend, inhibit, obviate, prevent, rule out, shut out, ward off **8** dissuade, frighten, obstruct, preclude, restrain, stave off **9** disadvise, forestall, turn aside **10** discourage
deterge **7** cleanse, wash off
detergent **4** soap **6** alkali **8** cleanser **9** cleansing
deteriorate **3** mar, rot **4** fade, fail, flag, sink **5** decay, dwine, spoil **6** impair, lessen, weaken, worsen **7** crumble, decline, descend **8** languish **9** decompose, undermine **10** debilitate, depreciate, disimprove, retrograde
deterioration **4** ruin **5** decay **6** dry rot, ebbing, waning **7** atrophy, decline, failure, rotting **8** decaying, downfall, spoiling **9** crumbling, decadence, downgrade, lessening **10** debasement, declension, degeneracy, impairment **12** dégringolade
determinant **4** gene, mark **5** agent, cause, trait **6** factor, reason, weight **7** radical **8** occasion **9** attribute, authority, influence **10** antecedent **11** differentia
determinate **4** spot **5** fixed, place **6** cymose, finger, narrow **7** limited, precise, settled **8** constant, definite, diagnose, identify, pinpoint **9** arbitrary, ascertain, immovable, immutable, recognize **10** definitive, inflexible, invariable, restricted **11** distinguish, established, inalterable, unalterable **12** unchangeable, unmodifiable **13** circumscribed, diagnosticate
determination **6** fixing **7** purpose, resolve **8** decision, firmness **9** resolving **10** conclusion, settlement **11** decidedness **12** resoluteness **13** purposiveness
determine **3** end, fix, see, set **4** bias, fate, halt, hear, move, rule, show **5** bound, close, drive, impel, learn, limit, prove **6** decide, direct, doom to, figure, finish, induce, ordain, settle, tumble, wind up, wrap up **7** actuate, catch on, control, delimit, destine, dispose, find out, incline, make out, mark out, measure, preform, purpose, resolve, unearth **8** complete, conclude, discover, persuade, regulate, ultimate **9** ascertain, demarcate, establish, preordain, resolve on, terminate **10** delimitate, foreordain, predestine, predispose **11** demonstrate
determined **3** set **4** bent **6** intent **7** decided, earnest, serious, settled **8** decisive, hellbent, resolute, resolved **10** purposeful, unwavering **11** unfaltering **12** unhesitating
detest **4** hate **5** abhor, spurn **6** loathe, reject **7** despise, dislike **8** execrate **9** abominate, repudiate
detestable **4** foul, vile **5** sorry **6** damned, horrid, odious **7** hateful, heinous **9** abhorrent, execrable, loathsome **10** abominable, despicable **12** contemptible
detestation **4** hate **6** hatred, horror **7** bugbear, disgust, dislike **8** anathema, aversion, loathing **9** antipathy, bête noire, repulsion, revulsion **10** abhorrence, black beast, repugnance
dethrone **6** depose, divest, unmake **7** uncrown **8** discrown, displace
detonate **5** burst, go off **6** blow up **7** explode **8** mushroom
detonator **3** cap **4** fuse, fuze **9** explosive **11** blasting cap
detour **5** avoid, skirt **6** bypass **7** deflect **9** deviation, runaround **10** circumvent, roundabout
detract **4** draw **5** decry, libel **6** divert, lessen, reduce **7** slander **8** belittle, decrease, derogate, diminish, discount, minimize, write off **9** disparage, dispraise **10** depreciate
detracting **8** libelous **9** maligning, traducing, vilifying **10** calumnious, defamatory, derogatory, pejorative, scandalous, slanderous **11** disparaging, dyslogistic **12** depreciative, depreciatory
detraction **4** harm, hurt, tale **5** libel, wrong **6** damage, injury **7** calumny, scandal, slander **8** libeling **9** aspersion, injustice, maligning, traducing **10** backbiting, slandering, sycophancy **12** backstabbing, belittlement **13** disparagement
detriment **4** harm, hurt **6** damage, injury **7** marring **8** drawback, handicap, mischief, spoiling **10** disability **12** disadvantage
detrimental **3** bad, ill **4** evil **7** adverse, harmful, hurtful, nocuous **8** damaging, negative **9** injurious **11** deleterious, mischievous, unfavorable
detritus **4** tufa, tuff **5** scree, talus **6** debris
Detroit ***county:*** **5** Wayne ***founder:*** **8** Cadillac ***lake:*** **4** Erie **10** Saint Clair ***sobriquet:*** **6** Motown **9** Motor City
de trop **5** extra, spare **6** excess **7** surplus **11** superfluent, superfluous **13** supernumerary

detruncate 3 top 4 crop 7 pollard
Deucalion ***father:*** 10 Prometheus ***kingdom:*** 6 Phthia ***mother:*** 7 Clymene ***son:*** 6 Hellen ***wife:*** 6 Pyrrha
Deuel's son 8 Eliasaph
dev, deva 3 god
Devaki's son 7 Krishna
deval 4 halt, quit, stop 5 cease 6 desist 8 give over, knock off, leave off, surcease 11 discontinue
De Valera 5 Eamon
devaluate 5 decry, lower 8 mark down, write off 9 underrate, write down 10 depreciate, undervalue
devaluation 7 atrophy, decline 8 downfall 9 decadence 10 declension, degeneracy
devalue see **depreciate**
devastate 4 sack 6 devour, ravage 7 despoil, pillage 8 desolate, lay waste, overcome, spoliate 9 depredate, desecrate, overpower, overwhelm
devastation 4 loss, ruin 5 havoc 9 confusion
devel 3 hit 4 biff, ding, nail, sock 5 clout, slosh, smite, whack 6 strike
develop 2 go 3 age, get 4 form, gain, grow, ripe 5 break, occur, phase, reach, ripen 6 attain, befall, betide, chance, dilate, enroot, evolve, expand, grow up, happen, lay out, mature, mellow, obtain, open up, thrive, unfold, unfurl 7 achieve, acquire, advance, amplify, burgeon, come off, convert, enlarge, expound, fall out, prepare, promote, prosper, realize 8 flourish, maturate 9 actualize, elaborate, establish, transpire 11 come to light, materialize 13 differentiate ***rapidly:*** 7 burgeon 8 bourgeon
development 5 phase 6 growth, phasis 7 advance, ongoing 8 ontogeny, progress, upgrowth 9 evolution, expansion, flowering, phylogeny, unfolding 11 elaboration, progression ***combining form:*** 5 plasy 6 plasia, plasto ***of life:*** 10 biogenesis
Devi 7 goddess ***consort:*** 4 Siva ***father:*** 7 Himavat ***name:*** 3 Uma 4 Kali 5 Durga, Gauri 6 Chandi 7 Parvati
deviant 6 off-key 8 aberrant, abnormal, atypical 9 anomalous, divergent, irregular, unnatural, unregular, untypical 11 heteroclite 13 preternatural
deviate 3 err, yaw 4 veer 5 sheer, stray 6 depart, swerve, wander 7 digress, diverge, pervert 9 turn aside 13 sexual pervert
deviation 3 yaw 4 bend, tack, turn 5 error, fault, lapse, shift 6 breach, change, double 7 anomaly, blunder, failing, turning, veering 9 departure, diversion 10 divergence 13 transgression
device 4 play, ploy, tool, type, wile, will 5 feint, motif, motto, shift, trick 6 design, desire, dingus, emblem, figure, gadget, gambit, hickey, motive, resort, scheme, symbol 7 gimmick, machine, pattern, project, utensil 8 artifice, creation, insignia, maneuver, resource 9 apparatus, appliance, attribute, doohickey, expedient, implement, invention, makeshift, mechanism, stratagem 10 instrument, thingumbob 11 contraption, contrivance, inclination ***automatic:*** 5 servo ***baseball:*** 11 batting cage ***binding:*** 5 clamp ***combining form:*** 4 stat ***cooking:*** 7 hibachi ***electrical:*** 8 inverter ***electronic:*** 7 vocoder ***energy changing:*** 9 converter, convertor ***fastening:*** 6 zipper ***grasping:*** 4 tong ***heating:*** 8 radiator ***hoisting:*** 5 lewis 8 lewisson ***holding:*** 4 vise 5 clamp ***in an airplane:*** 7 gosport ***irrigation:*** 6 shaduf 7 shadoof ***light-generating:*** 7 lampion ***literary:*** 5 irony ***mechanical:*** 6 gadget ***oil lamp:*** 8 pickwick ***remote-control:*** 6 selsyn 7 synchro ***respiratory:*** 8 pulmotor ***restraining:*** 8 holdback ***seed-sewing:*** 11 broadcaster ***ship's:*** 7 euphroe ***speed of rotation:*** 4 tach ***stabilizing:*** 8 gyrostat ***temperature measurement:*** 7 thermal ***warning:*** 5 siren ***weighing:*** 5 scale, trone ***wiretapping:*** 3 bug
devil 4 deil, haze, limb 5 annoy, beast, brute, demon, error, fiend, knave, rogue, Satan, scamp, tease 6 Belial, Cloots, diablo, dybbuk, pester, rascal, spirit 7 caitiff, Clootie, dickens, Lucifer, Old Nick, serpent, tempter, torment, villain 8 Apollyon, Mephisto, mischief, scalawag, Succubus 9 Archfiend, Beelzebub, cacodemon, scoundrel, skeezicks 10 blackguard, Old Scratch 11 firecracker, rapscallion 13 Old Gooseberry ***combining form:*** 6 diabol 7 diabolo
devil-devil 4 rune 5 charm, spell 11 conjuration, incantation
devilfish 3 ray 7 octopus 10 cephalopod
devilish 3 bad 4 evil 6 cursed, wicked 7 demonic, extreme, satanic 8 accursed, damnable, demoniac, demonian, diabolic, fiendish 9 excessive, execrable, nefarious 10 diabolical, iniquitous, serpentine, unhallowed, villainous 11 diabolonian, excessively
devilkin 3 imp
devil-may-care 3 gay 4 fast, rash, wild 6 rakish, sporty 7 raffish 8 rakehell, reckless
devilment see **deviltry**
devilry see **deviltry**
devil's-bones 4 dice, tats 5 cubes, ivory
deviltry 7 roguery, waggery 8 mischief 9 diablerie 11 roguishness, waggishness 12 sportiveness
devious 3 sly 4 foxy 5 stray 6 artful,

astray, crafty, errant, erring, remote, roving, secret, shifty, sneaky, tricky, unfair 7 bending, crooked, cunning, curving, erratic, obscure, removed, retired, winding 8 aberrant, guileful, indirect, lonesome, sneaking, twisting 9 diverting, underhand, wandering 10 digressing, roundabout

devise 4 cast, form, plan, plot, will 5 chart, forge, frame, leave, shape 6 cook up, create, design, invent, legacy, legate, make up, scheme, vamp up 7 arrange, bequest, collude, concoct, connive, dope out, dream up, hatch up, project 8 bequeath, cogitate, colloque, conspire, contrive, discover, intrigue, property 9 blueprint, determine, formulate, machinate, scheme for, scheme out 11 inheritance

devitalize 5 dry up 6 weaken 7 deprive, destroy 9 desiccate 10 eviscerate

devoid 4 bare 5 empty 6 barren 7 lacking, wanting 8 free from, innocent 9 deficient, destitute

devoir 3 job 4 duty, must, need, task 5 chare, chore, ought, right, stint 6 charge 9 committal 10 assignment, commitment, obligation

devolution 7 atrophy, decline, passing 8 downfall, receding, transfer 9 conferral, decadence, recession 10 declension, degeneracy, regression 12 dégringolade, retrograding, transference 13 retrogression

devolve 4 pass 8 hand down, transfer

devote 3 try, use, vow 4 bend, damn, doom, give, turn 5 apply, throw 6 addict, adjust, attach, bestow, commit, direct, donate, employ, give up, hallow, strive, take to, wrap up 7 address, attempt, confide, consign, entrust, hand out, present, provide, utilize 8 dedicate, endeavor, give away, sanctify, struggle 9 confirm in, habituate 10 buckle down, consecrate

devoted 4 dear, fond, true 5 loyal 6 ardent, doting, fervid, loving 7 zealous 8 constant, faithful, lovesome 10 thoughtful 12 affectionate ***religiously:*** 6 oblate

devotee 3 fan 4 buff 5 hound, lover 6 addict, votary 7 admirer, amateur, fancier, habitué 8 follower 9 supporter 10 aficionado, enthusiast ***suffix:*** 3 ite

devotion 4 love, zeal 5 ardor, piety 6 fealty, fervor, prayer 7 loyalty, passion 8 fidelity, fondness 9 reverence 10 allegiance, attachment, enthusiasm 12 faithfulness ***combining form:*** 5 latry ***religious:*** 6 novena

devour 3 eat 4 meal, ruin, sack, take, wolf 5 eat up, enjoy, use up, waste, wreck 6 absorb, engulf, feed on, ingest, ravage, relish 7 consume, despoil, destroy, exhaust, feast on, gloat on, pillage, revel in 8 demolish, desolate, dispatch, prey upon, spoliate, squander 9 delight in, depredate, desecrate, devastate, dissipate, feast upon, gloat over, partake of, polish off, rejoice in, swallow up 10 annihilate

devouring 4 avid 6 greedy 9 voracious ***combining form:*** 6 vorous

devout 4 holy 5 godly, pious 6 ardent, fervid, hearty 7 adoring, fervent, sincere, zealous 8 reverent, revering 9 pietistic, prayerful, religious 10 venerating, worshiping

devoutness 5 piety

dew 3 wet 5 sweat, tears 8 moisture 12 perspiration

dexter 5 right, white 6 benign, bright 9 favorable, fortunate 10 auspicious, propitious

dexterity 3 art 5 craft, skill 7 address, cunning, know-how, prowess, sleight 8 deftness 9 adeptness, expertise, readiness 10 adroitness, smoothness 12 skillfulness

dexterous 3 sly 4 deft, easy, slim 5 adept, agile, canny, coony, handy 6 adroit, artful, clever, expert, facile, nimble, smooth 7 cunning, skilled 8 masterly, skillful, sleighty 9 ingenious 10 effortless, neathanded, proficient

diablerie 3 sin 4 evil, tort 5 crime, wrong 7 devilry, roguery, sorcery, waggery 8 deviltry, iniquity, mischief, satanism 9 devilment 10 black magic, wickedness, witchcraft, wrongdoing 11 roguishness, waggishness 12 sportiveness

diablo 5 devil, fiend, Satan 7 Lucifer, Old Nick, serpent 8 Apollyon 9 Beelzebub 10 Old Scratch 13 Old Gooseberry

diabolic 4 evil 6 wicked 7 demonic, satanic 8 demoniac, demonian, devilish, fiendish 10 serpentine, unhallowed 11 diabolonian

diabolism see **diablerie**

diacritic 5 breve, haček, tilde 6 macron, proper 7 cedilla 8 dieresis, peculiar 9 diaeresis 10 circumflex, individual 11 distinctive 13 idiosyncratic ***Arabic:*** 5 hamza 6 hamzah

diadem 5 crown 6 empire 8 headband 11 sovereignty

diagnose 4 spot 5 place 6 finger 8 identify, pinpoint 9 recognize 11 determinate, distinguish

diagnostic 6 proper 8 peculiar 9 diacritic 10 indicating, indicative, individual 11 distinctive 13 idiosyncratic

diagonal 4 bias 5 bevel 6 biased 7 beveled, slanted 8 inclined, slanting 9 slantways

diagonally 8 bendwise 9 slantwise 10 cornerwise 11 catercorner, catty-corner, kitty-corner, slaunchways 12 slantingways

diagram 5 chart, graph 7 isotype 9 represent
dial 3 map, mug, pan 4 face, phiz, puss, tune 6 kisser, visage 7 control 8 features 10 manipulate 11 countenance
dialect 4 cant 5 argot, idiom, koine, lingo, slang 6 jargon, patois, patter, speech, tongue 8 language, localism 10 vernacular 11 regionalism, terminology 13 provincialism *Georgia:* 6 Gullah *London:* 7 cockney
dialectic 5 logic 6 debate 7 mooting 8 forensic 11 disputation 13 argumentation
dialogue 4 chat, talk 6 parley 8 colloquy, converse 12 conversation 13 confabulation
diameter 5 chord 8 bisector 9 thickness
diametric 5 polar 7 counter, opposed, reverse 8 contrary, converse, opposite 9 antipodal 10 antipodean 12 antithetical 13 contradictory
diamond 3 gem 5 stone 6 bright 9 brilliant, sparkling *baseball:* 7 infield *element:* 6 carbon *famous:* 4 Hope, Pitt 5 Sancy 6 Orloff, Regent 8 Braganza, Cullinan, Kohinoor 9 Excelsior 10 Great Mogul *holder:* 3 dop 4 dopp *inferior:* 4 bort 5 boart, bortz *oval:* 9 briolette *playing card:* 7 lozenge *state:* 8 Delaware *surface:* 5 facet
Diana see Artemis
Diana monkey 7 roloway
diapason 3 air, lay 4 tune 5 range, scope 6 melody, strain, warble 7 compass, descant, measure, melisma, melodia 10 tuning fork
diaper 4 didy 5 didie, nappy 6 nappie
diaphanous 5 filmy, gauzy, sheer, vague 6 flimsy 7 tiffany 8 ethereal, gossamer 11 transparent 13 insubstantial
diaphragm 4 stop 9 partition *combining form:* 5 phren 6 phreni, phreno
diarist 1 Gide (André) 5 Frank (Anne), Pepys (Samuel), Scott (Walter) 6 Burney (Fanny) 7 Boswell (James) 8 Robinson (Henry) 10 chronicler, journalist
diary 6 record 7 daybook, diurnal, journal, logbook 8 register 9 chronicle
diaskeuast 6 editor
diastase 6 enzyme
diatribe 6 tirade 7 polemic 8 harangue, jeremiad 9 criticism, philippic
dibs 4 gelt 5 blunt, brass, bread, chips, claim, dough, money, syrup, title 6 dinero, do-re-mi, rights 7 cabbage 8 pretense 10 pretension 11 reservation
dice 4 cast, shed, tats 5 bones, cubes, ivory, scrap 6 reject, slough 7 cashier, checker, discard 8 jettison, throw out 9 throw away 11 devil's-bones *combining form:* 8 astragal 9 astragalo *game:* 5 craps *losing throw:* 7 missout *singular:* 3 die *throw:* 7 boxcars 9 snake eyes
dicer 7 gambler
dichotomize 4 part 5 sever 6 divide, sunder 7 break up, disjoin, dissect 8 disjoint, disunite, separate
dichotomous 9 bifurcate
dichotomy 7 forking 9 bisection, branching, splitting 11 bifurcation
Dickens *birthplace:* 10 Portsmouth *captain:* 6 Cuttle *character:* 3 Pip, Tim 4 Dora, Gamp, Nell 5 Fagin 6 Bumble, Carton, Cuttle, Darnay, Dombey, Oliver 7 Barnaby, Defarge, Manette, Scrooge, Tiny Tim 8 Micawber, Pickwick 9 Bill Sikes, Pecksniff, Uriah Heep 10 Chuzzlewit *hero:* 6 Carton (Sidney) *nationality:* 7 English *pen name:* 3 Boz *villain:* 5 Fagin *work:* 9 Hard Times 10 Bleak House 11 Oliver Twist 12 Barnaby Rudge 15 Tale of Two Cities 16 David Copperfield 17 Great Expectations
dicker 4 deal, swap 6 barter, haggle, higgle, palter 7 bargain, chaffer 8 huckster 11 negotiation
dickey 4 weak 5 gilet, shaky 6 unsure, wobbly 8 insecure, rootless, unstable, wavering 9 fluctuant 10 shirtfront 11 vacillating
dictate 3 bid, say, set 4 lead, rule, tell, word 5 guide, order, speak, utter 6 behest, charge, decree, diktat, direct, enjoin, govern, impose, manage, ordain, recite 7 bidding, command, control, lay down, mandate, read off 8 instruct 9 directive, prescribe 10 injunction 12 prescription
dictative 8 dogmatic 11 doctrinaire, magisterial 13 authoritarian
dictator 4 duce 6 despot, tyrant 7 arbiter 8 martinet 9 oppressor, strong man 10 magistrate *German:* 6 Hitler (Adolf) *Italian:* 9 Mussolini (Benito) *military:* 8 caudillo *Spanish:* 6 Franco (Francisco)
dictatorial 4 firm 5 bossy, proud, stern 7 haughty 8 absolute, arrogant, despotic, dogmatic 9 arbitrary, imperious, masterful 10 autocratic, imperative, peremptory, tyrannical 11 doctrinaire, domineering, overbearing 12 totalitarian 13 authoritarian, authoritative
dictatorship 7 tyranny 9 autocracy, Caesarism, despotism 10 absolutism
diction 6 phrase 7 wordage, wording 8 parlance, phrasing, verbiage 9 verbalism 11 phraseology *suffix:* 3 ese
dictionary 4 cant 6 jargon 7 lexicon, palaver 8 language, wordbook 10 repository, vocabulary 11 terminology 13 reference book *compiler:* 7 Johnson (Samuel), Webster (Noah) 13 lexicographer *geographical:* 9 gazetteer *of prosody:* 6 gra-

dus *of synonyms:* 8 thesauri (plural) 9 thesaurus
dictum 4 rule 5 axiom, gnome, maxim, moral 6 saying, truism 7 brocard, opinion 8 aphorism, apothegm 9 statement 13 pronouncement
didactic 3 dry 5 moral 6 teachy 7 preachy 8 advisory, sermonic 9 hortative 10 moralizing, preceptive 11 exhortative, sermonizing
diddle 3 gyp 4 beat, bilk, hoax, idle, laze, loaf, loll, take 5 cheat, cozen, drone 6 chouse, dawdle, delude, loiter, lounge 7 defraud 8 lallygag 9 overreach, waste time
diddler 3 gyp 5 cheat 6 con man 7 grifter, sharper 9 defrauder, trickster 12 double-dealer 13 confidence man
dido 3 toy 5 curio, frill 6 bauble, gewgaw, trifle 7 bibelot, trinket, whatnot 8 furbelow, gimcrack 10 knickknack
Dido 6 Elissa *brother:* 9 Pygmalion *city founded by:* 8 Carthage *father:* 5 Belus 6 Mutton *husband:* 7 Acerbas 8 Sichaeus *lover:* 6 Aeneas
Dido and Aeneas composer 7 Purcell
die 3 ebb, pip 4 bate, conk, dado, drop, fall, fate, long, mold, pass, stop, wane 5 abate, block, cease, croak, let up, swelt 6 cash in, chance, cop out, demise, depart, expire, kick in, matrix, peg out, perish, pop off, recede 7 decease, ease off, fortune, kick off, pass out, slacken, subside, succumb 8 check out, languish, moderate, pass away, snuff out 9 disappear, grow faint *from hunger:* 6 starve *loaded:* 6 fulham, fullam
___ die 4 sine 3 bis in (twice a day), ter in (thrice a day) 6 quater in (four times a day)
die-away 4 limp 7 languid 8 listless 9 enervated 10 languorous, spiritless 11 languishing 13 lackadaisical
diehard 4 tory 5 blimp, fixed, right, white 7 Bourbon, old fogy 8 mossback, old liner, pullback, rightist, royalist, standpat, true blue 9 right wing 10 praetorian 11 bitter-ender, reactionary, reactionist, right-center, right-winger, standpatter 12 conservative, intransigent 13 reactionarist, stick-in-the-mud
___ diem 5 carpe
Dies ___ 4 Irae 7 faustus
diet 4 fast, feed 8 assembly 10 parliament
Diet of ___ 5 Worms 6 Speyer, Spires 8 Augsburg
___-dieu 4 prie
Dieu ___, British motto 10 et mon droit
differ 3 jar 4 vary 5 argue, clash 6 bicker, debate, depart, divide, oppose 7 deviate, discord, dispute, dissent, diverge, quarrel 8 conflict, disagree, squabble 9 disaccord
difference 4 know 5 clash, sever 6 change, effect, strife 7 discern, discord, dissent 8 alterity, conflict, disunity, separate, variance 9 disaccord, extricate, otherness, variation 10 contention, discrepate, dissension, divergency, severalize, unlikeness 11 controversy, discrepancy, distinction, distinguish 12 disagreement, discriminate, dissemblance, modification 13 dissimilarity, dissimilitude *slight:* 5 shade 8 hairline
different 5 other 6 divers, single, sundry, unlike 7 another, distant, diverse, several, special, unalike, unequal, unusual, various 8 discrete, distinct, opposite, peculiar, separate 9 disparate, divergent, otherwise, unsimilar 10 dissimilar, individual, particular 11 distinctive *combining form:* 3 all 4 allo 5 heter 6 hetero 7 diversi
differentiate 4 know 5 sever 7 discern 8 separate 9 extricate 10 comprehend, discrepate, severalize, understand 11 distinguish 12 discriminate
difficult 4 hard 6 uphill 7 arduous, awkward, labored, obscure, operose, problem 8 perverse, puzzling, stubborn, toilsome 9 effortful, hampering, laborious, strenuous 11 problematic *combining form:* 4 mogi *prefix:* 3 dys
difficulty 3 fix, jam 4 beef, nodi (plural) 4 pass, snag 5 cavil, demur, fight, nodus, pinch, rigor 6 bother, hassle, pickle, plight, scrape, strait 7 dilemma, dispute, pitfall, problem, protest, quarrel, trouble 8 asperity, demurral, demurrer, exigency, hardness, hardship, obstacle, quandary, question, squabble 9 bickering, challenge, emergency, objection 10 falling-out, impediment 11 altercation, arduousness, controversy, obstruction, predicament, vicissitude 12 disagreement, remonstrance 13 embarrassment, inconvenience, remonstration
diffidence 7 modesty, reserve 8 distrust 11 bashfulness
diffident 3 coy, shy 5 timid 6 demure, modest 7 bashful 8 hesitant, retiring 9 blenching, flinching, reluctant, shrinking, unassured 11 distrustful, unassertive 12 self-effacing
difform 6 uneven 7 unequal 8 lopsided 10 asymmetric 13 unsymmetrical
diffuse 3 lax 4 full, long 5 loose, slack, strew, windy, wordy 6 casual, expand, extend, lavish, prolix, random, spread 7 copious, lengthy, osmolar, osmotic, perfuse, radiate, scatter, send out, verbose 8 disperse, intersow, permeate 9 broadcast, circulate, desultory, exuberant, interlard, propagate, redundant, scattered, spreading, spread out 10 distribute, long-winded, palaverous, widespread 11 disseminate, intersperse 13 intersprinkle

diffusion 7 osmoses (plural), osmosis 9 broadcast, prolixity, spreading 10 scattering

dig 3 jab, jog, ram, run 4 grub, hole, holk, howk, like, mind, mine, poke, prod, root, sift, sink, site, spud, stab 5 delve, ditch, drive, enjoy, enter, grind, nudge, probe, punch, scoop, spade, stick 6 burrow, drudge, go into, pierce, plunge, quarry, relish, rootle, shovel, thrust, trench, tunnel 7 explore, root out, unearth 8 excavate, look into, prospect 9 delve into, hollow out, penetrate 10 excavation 11 inquire into, investigate *out:* 6 exhume *up:* 7 unearth

digest 2 go 3 sum 4 bear, cook, take 5 abide, brook, stand, sum up 6 aperçu, codify, endure, précis, sketch, survey 7 pandect, stomach, summate, swallow, sylloge 8 compress, condense, nutshell, syllabus, synopsis, tolerate 9 epitomize, inventory, summarize, synopsize 10 abridgment, compendium, comprehend, periodical 11 compilation

digestion *combining form:* 6 pepsia, peptic *good:* 7 eupepsy 8 eupepsia *poor:* 9 dyspepsia

digger 4 plow 5 miner

digit 3 toe 5 thumb 6 cipher, figure, finger, number, pinkie 7 chiffer, integer, numeral 11 whole number *abbreviation:* 2 no. *combining form:* 6 dactyl, digiti 7 dactylo, dactyly 8 dactylia 9 dactylism, dactylous

dignified 4 prim 6 proper 7 stately 8 decorous

dignify 5 erect, exalt, honor 6 uprear 7 ennoble, glorify, sublime 10 aggrandize 11 distinguish

dignitary 3 VIP 4 lion 5 chief, nabob 6 leader 7 notable 8 eminence, luminary 10 notability 13 high-muck-a-muck

dignity 4 rank 5 grace, honor, merit, poise, state, worth 6 cachet, ethics, status, virtue 7 address, decency, decorum, majesty, stature 8 elegance, grandeur, morality, nobility, position, prestige, standing 9 etiquette, grandness, nobleness, propriety 10 augustness, excellence, perfection, seemliness 11 consequence, ethicalness 12 magnificence *suffix:* 3 dom 4 ship

digress 4 roam 5 drift, stray 6 depart, ramble, swerve, wander 7 deviate, diverge, excurse 8 divagate

digression 5 aside 7 episode, excurse 8 drifting, excursus, incident, rambling, straying 9 departure, deviation, wandering 10 deflection, divagation, divergence 11 parenthesis, underaction

dike 4 bank, pond, pool 5 drain, fix up, levee, slick, spiff 6 doll up, dude up 7 barrier, deck out, doll out, dress up, gussy up 8 aboideau, causeway, spruce up 11 watercourse

dilapidate 4 do in, ruin 5 decay, wreck 6 forget, ignore, slight 7 crumble, neglect 8 bankrupt, overlook 9 decompose, disregard, shipwreck 12 disintegrate

dilapidated 5 dingy, faded, seedy, tacky 6 beat-up, marred, shabby, tagrag 7 damaged, decayed, injured, run-down 8 crumbled, impaired 10 broken-down, down-at-heel, threadbare

dilapidation 5 decay, waste 6 debris

dilate 5 swell, widen 6 expand, extend, recite 7 amplify, augment, broaden, descant, discuss, dissert, distend, enlarge, narrate, prolong, recount 8 describe, expanded, increase, lengthen, protract, rehearse 9 discourse, expatiate, sermonize 10 dissertate

dilatory 3 lax 4 slow 5 slack, tardy 6 remiss 7 laggard, unhasty 9 leisurely, negligent, unhurried 10 deliberate, neglectful

dilemma 3 box, fix, jam 4 hole, spot 6 choice, corner, pickle, plight, scrape 7 problem 8 argument, quandary 10 perplexity 11 predicament 12 bewilderment 13 mystification

dilettante 4 tyro 7 amateur, dabbler, jackleg 8 aesthete, dabbling, ungifted 9 smatterer, unskilled 10 amateurish, unfinished, uninitiate 11 abecedarian, cognoscente, connoisseur

dilettantish see amateurish

diligence 8 industry 9 assiduity 11 persistence 12 perseverance

diligent 7 operose 8 sedulous 9 assiduous 10 persistent, persisting, unflagging 11 industrious, persevering

dill plant 4 anet

dilly 3 pip 4 lulu 5 dandy, nifty, peach 6 corker, dinger, doozer, pippin, ripper, rouser 8 jim-dandy, knockout 9 humdinger 10 ripsnorter 11 crackerjack, lalapalooza

dillydally see delay

dilute 3 cut 4 thin, weak 5 alter, washy 6 debase, modify, temper, watery, weaken 7 liquefy, qualify, reduced 8 deprived, diminish, impaired, moderate, waterish, weakened 9 enfeebled, water down 10 deliquesce 11 adulterated, watered-down 12 impoverished 13 sophisticated

dim 3 fog, mat 4 blur, dark, dead, dull, dusk, fade, flat, haze, hazy, pale 5 befog, blear, blind, cloud, dusky, faint, muddy, murky, muted, vague 6 bleary, darken, gloomy 7 becloud, dislimn, eclipse, low beam, obscure, shadowy, subdued, tarnish, unclear 9 lightless, obfuscate, tenebrous 10 caliginous, ill-defined, indistinct, lacklus-

ter, lusterless 12 parking light, undetermined 13 unilluminated
dime novel 4 pulp 7 chiller, shocker 8 dreadful, thriller 10 yellowback 12 bloodcurdler, killer-diller 13 penny dreadful
dimension 4 size 5 scope, trait, width 6 aspect, extent 7 measure, quality 8 life-like 9 magnitude 10 yard lumber 11 proportions
diminish 3 ebb 4 bate, wane 5 abate, abuse, close, decry, peter, taper 6 lessen, minify, reduce, temper 7 abridge, curtail, dwindle, subside 8 belittle, decrease, derogate, minimize, moderate, taper off, write off 9 attenuate, disparage, dispraise, drain away, extenuate 10 depreciate 11 detract from
diminishing 7 calando
diminutive 3 wee 4 tiny 5 small, teeny, weeny 6 minute, teensy 9 miniature 10 teeny-weeny 11 lilliputian 12 teensy-weensy
diminutive one *suffix:* 2 el, et, ey, ia (plural), le 3 cle, ium, kin, ock, ula, ule, uli (plural) 4 ella, ette, illa, ling, ulae (plural), ulum, ulus 5 ellae (plural), illae (plural)
dimmet 4 dusk 7 evening 8 eventide, gloaming, owl-light, twilight 9 nightfall
dimple 4 fret 5 mound 6 cockle, hollow, riffle, ripple 10 depression
dim-sighted 8 purblind 9 half-blind
dimwit 4 simp 5 cluck, dunce 7 pinhead 9 dumb bunny, dumb cluck 13 featherweight
dim-witted 4 dull, slow 7 moronic 8 backward, imbecile, retarded 12 feeble-minded, simpleminded
din 3 row 5 babel, chirm, clash, music, noise, sound 6 bedlam, clamor, deafen, hubbub, jangle, racket, rattle, tumult, uproar 7 clangor, clatter, resound 8 blatancy, brouhaha, racketry 9 commotion, stridency 10 hullabaloo, percussion, tintamarre 11 pandemonium 13 clamorousness
Dinah 5 Shore *brother:* 4 Levi 6 Simeon *father:* 5 Jacob *mother:* 4 Leah
dine 3 eat, sup 4 feed
diner 3 bar 4 café 6 eatery 7 counter, hashery 8 snack bar 9 hash house 10 coffee shop, quick-lunch, restaurant 11 eating house, greasy spoon 12 lunch counter, sandwich shop
dinette *ancient Roman:* 5 oecus
ding 3 hit 4 beat, best, damn, sock 5 catch, clang, clout, outdo, outgo, whack 6 better, exceed, strike 7 surpass 8 outmatch, outshine
ding-a-ling 3 nut 4 kook 5 crank 6 cuckoo 7 lunatic 8 crackpot 9 harebrain, screwball 10 crackbrain
dinge 4 dent 5 blues, dumps, gloom 6 batter 7 sadness 9 dejection 10 depression, melancholy 11 unhappiness 12 mournfulness
dinghy 5 yacht 7 rowboat 8 life raft, sailboat
dingle 4 dale, dell 6 ravine, valley 9 storm door 10 passageway
dingus 5 gizmo 6 doodad, gadget, jigger 7 do-funny, thingum 9 doohickey 10 thingumbob 11 thingumajig
dingy 4 dark, drab, dull, mean 5 dirty, dusky, faded, murky, seedy, tacky, tired 6 gloomy, grimed, shabby, smutty, soiled 7 run-down, squalid, sullied 8 smirched 9 tarnished 10 broken-down, discolored, down-at-heel, threadbare 11 dilapidated
dinky 5 minor, small 6 lesser 8 small-fry 9 secondary, small-time 11 minor league 13 insignificant
dinner 4 fete, meal 5 feast 6 entrée, junket, regale, spread 7 banquet 8 festival, luncheon 9 breakfast, collation 10 table d'hôte *coat:* 3 tux 6 tuxedo *course:* 4 meat, soup 6 entrée 7 dessert 9 appetizer *Jewish:* 5 seder 7 sedarim (plural)
"Dinner ___" 7 at Eight
dinosaur 8 theropod 10 allosaurus 11 stegosaurus, triceratops 12 brontosaurus 13 tyrannosaurus
dinosauric 4 huge 7 mammoth 8 colossal, enormous 9 cyclopean, leviathan 10 behemothic, gargantuan, mastodonic 11 elephantine
dint 5 force, might, notch, power, sinew, vigor 6 energy, hollow, virtue 7 drive in, impress, imprint, potency 8 strength 9 puissance 10 impression 11 indentation
diocese 3 see 9 bishopric *Eastern Orthodox:* 7 eparchy *subdivision:* 6 parish
diode 9 rectifier 12 electron tube *type of:* 8 kenotron
Diomedes *city founded by:* 4 Arpi *father:* 4 Ares, Mars 6 Tydeus *foe:* 6 Aeneas, Hector *slayer:* 8 Hercules *victim:* 6 Rhesus
Dione 5 Titan *cult partner:* 4 Zeus *daughter:* 5 Venus 9 Aphrodite *father:* 7 Oceanus *lover:* 4 Zeus *mother:* 6 Tethys
Dionysus see Bacchus
Dionyza's husband 5 Cleon
Dioscuri 5 twins 6 Anaces, Anakes, Castor, Gemini, Pollux *father:* 4 Zeus 9 Tyndareus *mother:* 4 Leda *sister:* 5 Helen
dip 3 sag, set 4 bail, dish, draw, drop, duck, dunk, fall, lade, sink, skew, skid, slip, slue, tilt, veer 5 basin, depth, douse, ladle, lower, pitch, reach, sauce, scoop, sheer, slope, slump, souse, spoon, stoop 6 candle, go down, hollow, plunge, swerve, thrust, tumble 7 decline, delving, descend, descent, explore, falloff, immerse, plummet,

sinkage 8 bucket up, decrease, downturn, lowering, nose-dive, sinkhole, submerge, submerse, train off 9 concavity, declivity, downslide, downswing, downtrend, immersion 10 depression, divergence, plunge into 11 inclination *kind:* 4 clam 5 onion 10 blue cheese

diphthong 2 ae, ai, ea, ei, oe, oi, ou, oy 7 digraph 8 ligature

diploma 6 letter 7 charter, writing 8 document

diplomacy 4 tact 5 poise 7 address 10 adroitness, artfulness, settlement 11 delicatesse, savoir faire, tactfulness

diplomatic 4 wily 5 bland 6 artful, astute, crafty, polite, shrewd, smooth 7 politic, tactful 8 delicate, guileful, tactical 9 courteous 12 paleographic

diplomat's office 7 embassy

diplopod 9 millipede

dipper 3 cup 4 bird, grab 5 ladle, scoop 6 bucket, holder 10 bufflehead, water ouzel

dippy 5 crazy, silly, wacky 6 absurd, insane 7 foolish 9 fantastic 11 harebrained 12 preposterous

dipsomania 10 alcoholism

dire 5 acute, awful 6 crying, dismal, urgent, woeful 7 baleful, baneful, burning, clamant, crucial, exigent, extreme, fateful, fearful, instant, ominous, painful 8 critical, dreadful, grievous, horrible, pressing, shocking, sinister, terrible, terrific 9 appalling, cheerless, clamorous, desperate, frightful, ill-boding 10 afflictive, calamitous, deplorable, depressing, imperative, lamentable, oppressing, oppressive 11 apocalyptic, climacteric, distressing, importunate, regrettable, threatening, unfortunate 12 inauspicious, unpropitious 13 heartbreaking

direct 3 aim, bid, due, fix, lay, run, see, set 4 beam, bend, cast, dead, give, head, keep, lead, mark, next, open, show, tell, turn, warn 5 allot, apply, focus, frank, guide, issue, label, level, order, pilot, plain, point, refer, right, route, steer, throw, train 6 assign, candid, charge, custos, define, devote, divert, enjoin, escort, extend, fasten, govern, handle, lineal, linear, manage, ordain, settle, zero in 7 address, carry on, command, conduct, control, genuine, incline, nonstop, operate, oversee, present, preside, primary, project, request, through 8 dispatch, dominate, instruct, man-to-man, point out, regulate, shepherd, straight, unbroken, verbatim 9 determine, effective, firsthand, immediate, literally, literatim, out-and-out, prescribe, proximate 10 administer, buckle down, channelize, contiguous, continuous, explicitly, inevitable, proceeding, straightly, unhampered, unreserved, unswerving 11 categorical, substantive, superscribe, unconcealed, undeviating, undisguised, unequivocal, word for word 12 undissembled 13 undeviatingly, uninterrupted ***a helmsman:*** 4 conn ***proceedings:*** 7 preside

direction (see also **compass point**) 3 way 4 east, line, path, role, side, west 5 angle, north, order, point, slant, south, tenor 6 charge, course, design, sphere 7 bearing, channel, command, guiding, outlook, respect 8 guidance, pointing 9 clockwise, viewpoint 10 standpoint ***blowing:*** 7 leeward 8 windward ***combining form:*** 5 phoro ***court:*** 5 order ***for Muslims praying:*** 5 kibla 6 keblah, kildah ***horizontal:*** 7 azimuth ***main line of:*** 4 axis ***musical:*** (see **musical direction**) ***of a linear arrangement:*** 5 grain ***square dance:*** 4 call ***without fixed:*** 7 astatic

directive 4 memo, word 5 edict, ukase 6 decree, notice, ruling 7 bidding, message 8 exemplar 10 assignment, injunction, memorandum 11 instruction 13 communication, pronouncement

directly 3 due 4 anon, away, dead, soon 5 right, spang 6 at once 7 by and by, shortly 8 first off, in person, squarely, straight, verbatim 9 forthwith, instanter, instantly, literally, literatim, presently, right away 10 face-to-face, straightly 11 immediately, straight off, straightway, word for word 12 contiguously 13 undeviatingly, unqualifiedly

director 4 head 5 chief 6 leader 7 manager 9 conductor 10 supervisor

directory 4 list, ordo 5 guide, index 8 treatise 11 compilation

direful see **fearful; ominous**

dirge 4 hymn, song 6 lament 7 epicede, requiem 8 threnody 9 epicedium 11 lamentation ***Gaelic:*** 8 coronach

dirigible 7 airship 8 zeppelin 9 steerable

dirk 4 stab 5 sword 6 dagger

dirt 4 land, sand, soil, spot 5 earth, filth, fraud, grime, stain 6 gossip, gravel, ground 7 chicane, dry land, squalor 9 chicanery, deception, excrement, fourberie 10 corruption, dishonesty, hanky-panky, terra firma 11 highbinding, uncleanness 13 double-dealing, sharp practice

dirt poor 4 flat 5 broke 8 beggared, indigent 9 destitute, penurious 10 stonebroke 12 impoverished

dirty 3 low, tar 4 foul, smut, soil, wild 5 bawdy, black, dungy, grime, grimy, messy, mucky, muddy, murky, nasty, rough, smear, soily, sooty, stain, sully, taint 6 basely, befoul, begrim, besoil, coarse, dreggy, filthy, grubby, impure, raging, smirch, smooch, smudge, smudgy, smutch, smutty, soiled, sordid, stormy, vulgar 7 abusive, begrime, besmear, clouded, defiled, draggly, dullish, furious, hateful, immoral, obscene, piggish, raunchy, smoochy, smutchy, squalid, sullied, tainted, tarnish, unclean **8** begrimed, besmirch, blustery, discolor, draggled, grievous, indecent, polluted, scroungy, stormful, unchaste **9** uncleanly **10** blustering, scurrilous **11** distressing, regrettable, tempestuous **12** contaminated, contemptible, scatological **13** draggletailed

Dis see Pluto

disability **8** drawback, handicap **9** detriment

disable **3** mar, sap **4** harm, hurt, maim, ruin **5** blunt, spoil, wreck **6** batter, disarm, mangle, weaken **7** cripple, deprive, invalid, unbrace **8** enfeeble, mutilate, paralyze **9** attenuate, prostrate, undermine **10** debilitate, disqualify, immobilize **12** incapacitate, unstrengthen *a racehorse:* **6** nobble

disabuse **4** free **5** amend, emend, purge **7** correct, rectify, redress, release, unblind **8** liberate, undelude **9** disillude, enlighten, undeceive **10** illuminate **11** disillusion

disaccharide **7** lactose, maltose, sucrose

disaccord **3** jar **4** vary **5** clash **6** differ, divide, jangle, strife **7** dissent **8** conflict, disunity, mismatch, variance **10** contention, difference, dissension, dissidence **12** disharmonize

disadvantage **3** bar **4** harm, loss **6** hamper **8** blocking, drawback, handicap, obstacle **9** detriment, hindrance, prejudice **10** impediment, imposition **11** obstruction

disadvantaged **7** lacking **8** deprived **9** depressed

disadvise **5** deter **6** divert **8** dissuade **10** discourage

disaffect **4** wean **5** alien, upset **7** agitate, disturb **8** alienate, diminish, disquiet, disunify, disunite, estrange **10** discompose

disaffection **9** hostility **12** estrangement

disaffirm **4** deny **5** annul, cross **6** impugn, negate **7** gainsay, reverse **8** negative, traverse **9** repudiate **10** contradict, contravene

disagree **4** vary **5** clash **6** differ, divide **7** discord, dissent

disagreeable **3** bad **4** sour **5** waspy, whiny **6** rotten, snappy, twitty, woeful **7** helluva, peevish, pettish, unhappy, waspish **8** annoying, petulant **9** offensive, querulous **10** disturbing, unpleasant **11** displeasing, distressing

disagreement **3** row **4** spat **5** clash **7** discord, dispute, quarrel **8** variance **10** contention, difference, dissension, divergence, unlikeness **11** controversy, discrepancy, incongruity

disallow **4** deny, veto **5** debar **6** disown, refuse, reject **7** disavow, exclude, shut out **8** disclaim, keep back, withhold **9** repudiate

disallowance **6** denial **7** refusal **9** rejection

____ -disant **3** soi

disappear **2** go **4** fade **5** clear, leave **6** vanish **7** evanish **8** evanesce **9** evaporate

disappoint **4** balk, beat, bilk, dash, foil, ruin **6** baffle, defeat, thwart **9** frustrate **10** circumvent

disappointment **7** failure **9** bringdown **11** frustration

disapproval **4** veto **7** censure, dislike **9** rejection *expression of:* **3** boo **4** hiss, hoot, jeer **7** catcall **9** raspberry **10** Bronx cheer

disapprove **5** blame, decry, frown, pshaw, spurn **6** object, refuse, reject **7** censure, condemn, decline, detract, dislike, dismiss **8** denounce, disfavor, turn down **9** criticize, deprecate, disesteem, disparage, dispraise, reprehend, reprobate, repudiate **10** depreciate, discommend **11** expostulate, remonstrate

disarm **5** charm **6** allure **7** attract, bewitch, cripple, enchant, unsteel, win over **8** paralyze **9** captivate, deprive of, fascinate, prostrate **10** immobilize **12** incapacitate

disarming **5** silky **6** silken **10** saccharine **11** deferential, insinuating, insinuative **12** ingratiating, ingratiatory

disarrange **4** mess **6** jumble, mess up, mislay **7** disturb, replace, rummage **8** disorder, displace, misplace, overturn, unsettle **10** discompose **11** disorganize

disarray **5** chaos, snarl **6** ataxia, huddle, jumble, mess up, muddle, unrobe **7** clutter, derange, disturb, rummage **8** disorder, unsettle **9** confusion **10** discompose **11** disorganize

disassemble **8** dismount, separate, take down, tear down **9** dismantle, dismember, take apart

disassociate **5** unfix **6** detach **8** abstract, uncouple **9** disengage **10** disconnect

disaster **3** woe **4** rock, ruin **6** fiasco, injure, mishap **7** failure, tragedy **8** accident, calamity, casualty, distress, fatality **9** adversity, cataclysm, mischance **10** misfortune **11** catastrophe **12** misadventure

disastrous **4** dire **5** fatal **7** fateful, hapless, ruinous **8** luckless **10** calamitous **11** cataclysmic, destructive, unfortunate **12** catastrophic

disavow **4** deny **6** disown, impugn, negate, recant **8** disclaim, negative **9** repudiate

disband **4** part **5** sever **6** dispel, divide,

sunder 7 break up, disjoin, dissect, divorce, scatter 8 disjoint, disperse, dissever, dissolve, disunite, separate 9 dissipate 11 dichotomize

disbelieve 5 doubt, scorn, scout 6 eschew, reject 7 suspect 8 distrust, mistrust, question 9 discredit

disbeliever 5 cynic 7 doubter, sceptic, skeptic

disbelieving 6 show-me 8 aporetic 9 quizzical, skeptical 11 incredulous, questioning

disburden 6 unlade, unload, unship, unstow 7 discard, off-load 8 get rid of, jettison 9 discharge

disburse 3 pay 4 deal, give 5 divvy, spend 6 defray, divide, expend, lay out, lot out, outlay, pay out 7 dole out, fork out 8 dispense, disperse, shell out 9 partition 10 distribute, measure out

disbursement 4 cost 6 outlay 7 expense 11 expenditure

discard 4 cast, drop, dump, junk, oust, shed, waif 5 chuck, ditch, eject, let go, scrap, sluff, spurn 6 desert, reject, slough 7 abandon, cashier, cast off, deep-six, dismiss, forsake, wash out 8 abdicate, get rid of, jettison, lay aside, shuck off, throw out 9 repudiate, throw away

discarnate 8 bodiless 9 asomatous, unfleshly 10 immaterial, unembodied, unphysical 11 disembodied, incorporeal, nonphysical 13 insubstantial

discept 4 moot 5 argue 6 debate 7 agitate, canvass, dispute 9 thrash out 10 toss around

discern 3 see 4 know, note, view 5 sever 6 behold, descry, detect, divine, notice, remark 7 foresee, observe 8 perceive, separate 9 apprehend, ascertain, extricate 10 anticipate, difference, severalize 11 distinguish 13 differentiate

discernible 8 palpable 10 detectable, observable 11 appreciable

discerning 4 sage, wise 7 gnostic, knowing 9 clear-eyed, insighted, sagacious 10 insightful, perceptive 11 wisehearted 13 knowledgeable

discernment 3 wit 6 acumen, reason 8 keenness, sagacity 9 intuition 10 astuteness, shrewdness 11 penetration, percipience 12 perspicacity 13 sagaciousness

discharge 2 ax 3 can, pay, run 4 drop, emit, fire, flow, free, oust, pour, quit, sack, vent, void 5 annul, clear, eject, empty, expel, exude, let go, loose, pay up, quash, rheum, shoot, spare, utter 6 bounce, excuse, exempt, let fly, let off, loosen, outlet, remove, settle, square, unbind, unlade, unload, unship, unstow, vacate 7 absolve, boot out, cashier, deliver, dismiss, exclude, execute, fulfill, give off, kick out, manumit, off-load, release, relieve, removal, replace, satisfy, unchain 8 abrogate, clear off, clear out, dispense, displace, dissolve, emission, get rid of, liberate, separate, set aside, supplant, throw off 9 acquittal, bleach out, disburden, disenroll, eliminate, explosion, expulsion, liquidate, muster out, pour forth, pronounce, send forth, supersede, terminate, unloading, unshackle 10 deactivate, demobilize, disembogue, emancipate, give vent to, inactivate, liberation, separation 11 acquittance, exoneration, fulfillment 13 privilege from ***combining form:*** 5 rrhea 6 rrhoea 7 rrhagia ***concentrated:*** 7 barrage ***electrical:*** 5 spark 6 leader 8 streamer 9 lightning 12 leader stroke ***from the body:*** 5 egest 7 excrete ***simultaneous:*** 5 salvo

discinct 3 lax 5 slack 6 remiss 8 careless, derelict 9 negligent 10 behindhand, delinquent, neglectful 12 disregardful

disciple 6 cohort, zealot 7 apostle, fanatic, sectary 8 adherent, follower, henchman, partisan, sectator 9 satellite, supporter 10 enthusiast

disciplinarian 6 ramrod 8 martinet

disciplinary 7 ordered 8 punitive, punitory 9 punishing 11 castigatory

discipline 3 rod 4 curb, lead, whip, will 5 check, drill, guide, spank, teach, train 6 bridle, direct, manage, method, punish, reduce, school, subdue 7 chasten, conduct, control, correct, educate, inhibit, scourge 8 approach, chastise, instruct, overcome, penalize, punition, restrain, training 9 castigate, obedience, subjugate, will-power 10 correction, experience, punishment 11 castigation, self-command, self-control, self-mastery 12 chastisement 13 self-restraint

disclaim 4 deny 5 spurn 6 abjure, disown, recant, refuse, reject 7 disavow, gainsay, retract 8 belittle, disallow, forswear, minimize, renounce, traverse 9 challenge, criticize, deprecate, disparage, repudiate 10 contradict, contravene

disclose 3 own 4 avow, open, tell 5 admit, mouth, spill 6 betray, expose, reveal, unveil 7 blab out, confess, display, divulge, unclose, uncover 8 discover, give away, unclothe 9 make known 11 acknowledge

disclosure 6 exposé 10 confession, revelation 11 divulgation

discolor 3 tar 4 blot, dull, fade, smut, soil 5 smear, stain, sully, taint, tinge 6 defile, motley, streak 7 besmear, bestain, dappled, tarnish 8 besmirch 9 multihued 10 variegated

discoloration 5 stain *combining form:* 6 chroia
discomfit 3 irk, vex 4 faze, foil, rout 5 abash, annoy, upset 6 bother, defeat, rattle, thwart 7 confuse, disturb, perturb 8 confound 9 embarrass
discomfiture 4 rout 5 upset 6 damage, defeat, injury, unease 7 beating, debacle, descent, licking 8 comedown, disquiet, drubbing, prickles 9 abashment, agitation, commotion, confusion, overthrow 10 defeasance, uneasiness 11 frustration, shellacking 12 perturbation, vanquishment 13 embarrassment, inconvenience
discomfort 6 unease 7 malaise, misease 9 annoyance 10 uneasiness 13 embarrassment
discomforting see **uncomfortable**
discommend 5 frown 6 object 7 censure 8 admonish, disfavor 9 criticize, deprecate, disesteem, reprehend 10 disapprove
discommode 3 irk, vex 5 upset 6 bother, flurry, put out 7 fluster, perturb, trouble 8 put about 9 disoblige 13 inconvenience
discompose 3 irk, vex 5 annoy, harry, upset, worry 6 bother, dismay, flurry, harass, mess up, pester, plague, untune 7 agitate, derange, disturb, fluster, perturb, rummage, unhinge 8 disagree, disarray, disorder, disquiet, unsettle 9 embarrass 10 disarrange 11 disorganize
discomposure 6 unease 9 abashment, agitation, confusion 10 uneasiness 12 perturbation 13 embarrassment
disconcert 4 faze 5 abash, upset 6 puzzle, rattle, ruffle 7 break up, confuse, nonplus, perplex 8 bewilder, confound 9 embarrass, frustrate
disconfirm 5 break, evert, rebut 6 refute 7 confute 8 confound, disprove 10 controvert
disconnect 5 sever, unfix 6 detach 8 abstract, separate, uncouple
disconnected 7 muddled 8 inchoate 10 incoherent, incohesive 11 unorganized 12 uncontinuous
disconsolate 3 bad, low, sad 4 cold, down 5 bleak, drear 6 gloomy, somber, woeful 7 doleful, joyless, unhappy 8 dejected, downcast 9 cheerless, depressed, saddening, sorrowful, woebegone 10 depressing, melancholy 11 comfortless, crestfallen, downhearted
discontent 9 dysphoria 10 inquietude, uneasiness
discontented 5 upset 6 uneasy 7 unhappy 8 restless 9 perturbed 11 ungratified, unsatisfied
discontented one see **complainer**
discontinuance see **discontinuation**
discontinuation 3 end 5 cease, close 6 ending, finish 7 closing 9 desuetude 10 conclusion, desistance
discontinue 3 end 4 halt, quit, stop 5 cease, sever 6 desist, give up 8 break off, give over, knock off, leave off, surcease 9 terminate
discontinuity 3 gap 4 hole 5 break 6 breach, lacuna 7 opening
discontinuous 7 muddled 8 inchoate, separate 10 incoherent, incohesive 11 unconnected, unorganized
discord 3 jar 4 vary 5 clash 6 differ, divide, enmity, jangle, rancor, strife 7 unpeace 8 conflict, contrast, division, mischief, mismatch, variance 9 animosity, antipathy, collision, hostility, inharmony 10 antagonism, contention, difference, opposition 11 incongruity 12 inconsonance, polarization 13 inconsistency *goddess:* 3 Ate 4 Eris
discordant 5 harsh 7 jarring 8 clashing, contrary 9 immusical, unmixable, unmusical 10 cacophonic, inharmonic 11 cacophonous, conflicting, contrariant, incongruent, incongruous, inconsonant, quarrelsome, uncongenial 12 antagonistic, antipathetic, incompatible, inconsistent, inharmonious, unharmonious
discotheque 4 café, gogo 6 nitery 7 cabaret, hot spot 8 nightery 9 nightclub, night spot 10 supper club 12 watering hole 13 watering place
discount 4 fail, omit, take 5 abuse, decry 6 deduct, forget, ignore, lessen, rebate, slight 7 neglect, take off, take out 8 belittle, derogate, diminish, draw back, knock off, minimize, overlook, overpass, subtract, take away 9 abatement, deduction, reduction, substract, underrate 10 anticipate, depreciate 11 detract from, subtraction
discountenance 4 faze 5 abash, frown 6 object, rattle 7 confuse, reprove 8 confound, reproach 9 deprecate, embarrass 10 put to shame
discourage 3 irk, try, vex 4 damp 5 check, chill, deter, droop, scare, weigh 6 bother, dampen, deject, divert, hinder, lessen 7 afflict, depress, inhibit, prevent, trouble 8 frighten, restrain 10 demoralize
discouraging 5 black, bleak 6 dreary, gloomy 9 deterring, hindering 10 depressing, depressive, oppressive
discourse 3 act 4 play, talk 5 argue, enact, essay, orate, paper, speak, voice 6 expand, memoir, remark, sermon, speech, thesis 7 amplify, article, comment, descant, develop, enlarge, explain, expound, lecture, perform, playact 8 converse, harangue, perorate, rhetoric, speaking, tractate, treatise 9 elaborate, expatiate, monograph, person-

ate, sermonize, utterance **10** commentate, expression, monography **11** impersonate, interchange **12** conversation **13** verbalization ***art of:*** **8** rhetoric ***combining form:*** **3** log **4** logo, logy **5** logia, logue ***religious:*** **6** homily, sermon

discourteous **4** rude **7** ill-bred, incivil, uncivil **8** impolite **10** ungracious, unmannerly **11** ill-mannered, impertinent

discover **3** see **4** espy, find, hear, note, spot, tell **5** learn, mouth, spill **6** betray, debunk, descry, detect, expose, reveal, show up, tumble, unmask **7** catch on, divulge, find out, observe, publish, uncloak, unclose, undress, unearth **8** give away, perceive, proclaim, unshroud **9** advertise, ascertain, determine, encounter, make known

discovery **4** find **5** trove **6** espial, strike **7** finding **8** exposure **9** detection **10** exposition, revelation, unearthing **11** recognition

discredit **4** ruin **5** doubt, odium, shame, shoot **6** blow up, expose, infamy, show up **7** asperse, destroy, explode, obloquy **8** ignominy, puncture, reproach **9** unbelieve **10** opprobrium

discreditable **5** shady **6** shabby, shoddy **8** shameful **10** inglorious **11** ignominious

discreet **4** safe, wary **5** chary, muted, plain **6** modest, simple **7** careful, guarded, prudent, tactful **8** cautious, gingerly, moderate **9** temperate, unadorned, unextreme **10** controlled, reasonable, restrained **11** calculating, circumspect, considerate, inelaborate, unelaborate, unexcessive, unobtrusive **12** conservative, unbeautified **13** unpretentious

discrepancy **8** alterity **9** otherness, variation **10** difference, divergence, divergency, unlikeness

discrepant **7** diverse, varying **8** contrary **9** different, divergent, unmixable **11** conflicting, incongruent, incongruous, inconsonant **12** incompatible, inconsistent

discrete **8** detached, separate **9** countable **13** noncontinuous

discretion **4** tact **5** sense **6** wisdom **7** caution, secrecy **8** delicacy, judgment, prudence, wariness **9** canniness, foresight, restraint **10** providence **11** forethought

discriminate **4** know, note **5** sever **6** remark **7** analyze, compare, make out **8** contrast, perceive, separate **9** extricate **10** difference, severalize **13** differentiate

discriminating **4** wise **6** select **7** careful, prudent **8** eclectic **9** judicious, selective **10** analytical

discrimination **3** wit **5** sense **6** acumen **8** astucity, judgment, keenness **10** astuteness, shrewdness **11** percipience **12** perspicacity

discriminatory **6** biased, unfair, unjust **7** partial **8** partisan **10** prejudiced **11** inequitable **12** prepossessed

disculpate **5** clear **6** acquit **7** absolve **9** exonerate, vindicate

discursion **5** aside **8** excursus **10** divagation **11** parenthesis

discursive **6** chatty, roving **7** roaming **8** rambling **9** desultory ***group discussion:*** **11** bull session

discuss **4** moot **5** argue, parle, weigh **6** caucus, debate, parley **7** agitate, canvass, descant, expound **8** consider, converse, hash over, talk over **9** elucidate, expatiate, explicate, interpret, talk about, thrash out **10** deliberate, toss around **11** investigate ***business:*** **8** talk shop ***lightly:*** **5** bandy ***thoroughly:*** **7** exhaust

discussion **3** rap **6** confab **8** argument **10** conference **11** ventilation **12** deliberation **13** confabulation

discus thrower **6** Oerter (Al) **10** discobolus **11** Rashchupkin (Viktor)

disdain **5** abhor, pride, scorn, scout **6** morgue **7** contemn, despise, despite, hauteur **8** aversion, contempt, despisal, disprize, look down **9** antipathy, arrogance, insolence, loftiness, superbity **11** despisement, haughtiness

disdainful **5** proud **6** averse, lordly **7** haughty **8** arrogant, cavalier, insolent, scorning, scouting, spurning, superior **9** despising, rejecting **10** contemning **11** overbearing, repudiating **12** antipathetic, contemptuous, supercilious **13** high and mighty, unsympathetic

disease **3** bug, ill **5** virus **6** blight, malady, scurvy **7** ailment, anthrax, cholera, derange, endemic, illness, malaise, mycosis, purpura, rickets **8** debility, epidemic, leukemia, myxedema, paludism, pandemic, pellagra, rachitis, sickness, syndrome, zoonoses (plural), zoonosis **9** affection, black lung, complaint, condition, infirmity, sclerosis **10** alteration, blackwater, bronchitis, feebleness, impairment, infirmness, rachitides (plural), sickliness **11** decrepitude, derangement **13** unhealthiness ***animal:*** **5** mange, surra **8** enzootic, epizooty ***blood:*** **8** leucemia, leukemia, leukoses (plural), leukosis ***cabbage:*** **8** clubroot ***cattle:*** **6** cowpox **7** murrain, vaccina **8** blackleg, vaccinia ***caused by bacteria:*** **11** brucellosis ***cereal grass:*** **4** smut ***children's:*** **7** rubella **10** chicken pox ***citrus tree:*** **8** tristeza ***classification:*** **8** nosology ***combining form:*** **3** nos **4** noso, path **5** patho ***communicable:*** **12** tuberculosis ***disseminator:*** **7** carrier ***eye:*** **8** glaucoma, trachoma ***fish:*** **3** ich ***foretelling of:***

9 prognosis ***hair follicle:*** 7 sycoses (plural), sycosis ***heart:*** 11 cardiopathy ***horse:*** 4 clap 5 faroy 6 nagana, spavie, spavin 7 dourine, sarcoid 8 glanders ***identification of:*** 9 diagnosis ***industrial:*** 10 byssinosis ***infectious:*** 4 mono 6 typhus 7 malaria, tetanus, typhoid ***liver:*** 9 cirrhosis, hepatitis ***livestock:*** 7 locoism ***lung:*** 8 phthisic, phthisis 9 pneumonia ***lymph glands:*** 6 struma 8 scrofula ***metabolic:*** 4 gout ***nervous system:*** 4 kuru ***of beets:*** 8 heartrot ***of mammals:*** 10 babesiasis ***parasitic:*** 3 rot ***plant:*** 4 wilt 5 edema, scurf 6 blotch 7 frogeye 8 gummosis ***poultry:*** 7 fowlpox ***respiratory:*** 6 asthma ***sheep:*** 3 gid 7 scrapie 10 bluetongue ***skin:*** 4 acne 5 favus, hives, lupus, mange, pinta, tinea 6 eczema, tetter 7 leprosy, pemphix, prurigo, scabies 8 impetigo, keratoma, miliaria, pyoderma, ringworm, vitiligo, xanthoma 9 keratomas (plural), psoriasis, xanthomas (plural) 10 keratomata (plural), xanthomata (plural) ***suffix:*** 3 ses (plural), sis 4 itis, oses (plural), osis 5 iases (plural), iasis ***swine:*** 8 bullnose ***syphilitic:*** 5 tabes ***throat:*** 5 croup ***tropical:*** 4 pian 5 sprue 6 carate, dengue 8 psiloses (plural), psilosis ***venereal:*** 8 syphilis 9 chancroid, gonorrhea ***viral:*** 3 flu 4 noma 5 mumps, polio 6 grippe, rabies, zoster 7 ecthyma, measles, rubella, rubeola, variola 8 morbilli, psorosis, smallpox 13 poliomyelitis

diseased 6 sickly 7 fevered ***combining form:*** 3 cac 4 cace, caco ***prefix:*** 3 dys

disembark 4 land 6 alight 8 go ashore

disembarrass 3 rid 5 clear, untie 7 relieve, untwine 8 unburden, untangle 9 extricate 10 unentangle

disembodied 9 asomatous, unfleshly 10 immaterial, unphysical 11 incorporeal, nonphysical 13 insubstantial

disembogue 4 emit, flow, pour, void 6 emerge 7 give off, pour out 9 discharge

disembowel 3 gut 6 paunch, remove 7 exhaust 10 eviscerate, exenterate

disembroil 7 untwine 8 untangle 9 extricate 10 unentangle, unscramble

disemploy 2 ax 3 can 4 drop, fire, sack 5 let go 6 bounce, let out 7 boot out 9 terminate

disenchanted 5 blasé 7 knowing, worldly 8 mondaine 9 world-wise 11 worldly-wise 12 sophisticate 13 sophisticated

disencumber 5 untie 7 lighten, relieve, untwine 8 free from, untangle 9 alleviate, extricate 10 unentangle, unscramble

disengage 4 free, undo 5 loose, unfix 6 detach, unbind 7 release, unloose 8 abstract, liberate, uncouple, unfasten, unloosen 9 extricate

disentangle 4 part 5 sever, untie 6 detach, sunder 7 unravel, untwine 8 separate 9 extricate 10 unscramble 13 straighten out

disenthrall 4 free 5 loose 6 loosen, unbind 7 manumit, release, unchain 8 liberate 10 emancipate

disenthrone 6 depose, unmake 7 uncrown

disentranced see **disenchanted**

disentwine 5 untie 8 untangle 9 extricate 10 unentangle, unscramble

disesteem see **disfavor**

disfavor 5 frown, odium 6 infamy, object 7 obloquy 8 aversion, bad books, disgrace, ignominy, mistrust 9 deprecate, detriment 10 opprobrium 13 indisposition

disfigure 3 mar 4 foul 5 spoil 6 deface, deform, injure, mangle 8 mutilate

disfranchise 7 deprive 8 take away

disgorge 4 barf, spew 5 belch, eject, empty, eruct, erupt, expel, vomit 6 irrupt, spit up 7 bring up, throw up, upchuck

disgrace 4 blot, spot 5 brand, odium, shame, shend, stain 6 infamy, stigma 7 attaint, ill luck, obloquy, stigmas (plural) 8 black eye, contempt, debasing, humbling, ignominy, stigmata (plural) 9 abasement 10 debasement, misfortune, opprobrium 11 degradation, humiliation

disgraceful 5 shady 6 indign, shabby, shoddy 10 inglorious, unbecoming 11 ignominious 13 unrespectable

disgruntled 4 sore 9 uncontent 10 malcontent 11 uncontented, ungratified 12 malcontented

disguise 4 face, hide, mask, sham, show 5 belie, cloak, color, feign, front, put on 6 affect, assume, facade, garble, veneer 7 charade, conceal, dress up, falsify, obscure, pageant, pretend 8 artifice, coloring, delusion, pretense, simulate 9 deception, obfuscate 10 camouflage, false front, pretension 11 counterfeit, insincerity, make-believe 12 misrepresent, speciousness

disguisement 4 face, mask 5 cloak, color, cover, front 6 facade 8 coloring 10 false front

disgust 5 repel, shock 6 nausea, offend, reluct, revolt, sicken 7 outrage, repulse 8 aversion, nauseate 10 repugnance 13 squeamishness

disgusted 4 sick 5 fed up, tired, weary

disgusting 4 foul, vile 5 nasty 7 noisome 9 loathsome, offensive, repellent, repugnant, repulsive, revolting, sickening ***behavior:*** 11 beastliness

dish 4 food, stew, tray 5 salmi 6 shelve, tureen 7 platter 8 cup of tea, get rid of, scrapple, set aside ***baked:*** 7 soufflé ***baking:*** 7 scallop 12 scallop shell ***cheese:***

7 ramekin, rarebit **8** raclette, ramequin ***Chinese:*** **6** won ton ***deep:*** **9** casserole ***Hungarian:*** **7** goulash ***Italian:*** **7** lasagna, lasagne, ravioli ***Japanese:*** **7** sashimi, tempura **8** sukiyaki ***Mexican:*** **5** tamal **6** tamale ***Middle Eastern:*** **8** moussaka ***ornamental:*** **7** epergne ***principal:*** **6** entrée ***rice:*** **7** risotto ***rice and meat:*** **5** pilaf, pilau, pilaw **6** pilaff ***Scottish:*** **6** haggis ***shallow:*** **6** saucer

Dishan's son **2** Uz **4** Aran

disharmonic see **discordant**

disharmonious see **discordant**

disharmonize **3** jar **5** clash **6** jangle **8** conflict, mismatch

disharmony **6** strife **7** discord, unpeace **8** conflict, variance **10** contention, difference, dissension, dissention

dishearten **5** chill **6** deject **7** depress **10** demoralize

disheartening **5** black, bleak **6** dreary, gloomy, somber **8** funereal **10** depressing, depressive, despondent, oppressive **11** pessimistic

dishes **4** ware ***clay:*** **7** pottery ***porcelain:*** **5** china

dishevel **5** touse, towse **6** tousel, tousle, touzle

disheveled **5** messy **6** sloppy, untidy **7** raunchy, ruffled, unkempt **8** ill-kempt, slipshod, slovenly, straggly, uncombed **12** unfastidious

dishonest **5** false, lying, snide **6** shifty, tricky **7** corrupt, crooked, devious, furtive, knavish, oblique, roguish **8** cheating, cozening, two-faced **9** deceitful, faithless, insidious, swindling **10** defrauding, fraudulent, mendacious, perfidious, untruthful **13** double-dealing, untrustworthy

dishonesty **5** fraud **7** chicane, roguery **8** trickery **9** chicanery, deception, fourberie **10** hanky-panky **11** highbinding **13** double-dealing, faithlessness

dishonor see **disgrace**

dishonorable see **disgraceful**

Dishon's father **4** Anah

dish out **4** dole, give, hand **6** supply **7** deliver, furnish, provide **8** dispense, hand over, transfer, turn over

disillusioned see **disenchanted**

disimprison **4** free **5** loose **6** unbind **7** manumit, release, unchain **8** liberate **9** unshackle **10** emancipate

disinclination **7** dislike **8** aversion **13** indisposition, unwillingness

disinclined **3** shy **5** loath **6** afraid, averse, shying **7** balking, dubious, uneager **8** backward, boggling, doubtful, hesitant, opposing, sticking **9** objecting, reluctant, resisting, stickling, unwilling, unwishful **10** indisposed, protesting **12** antipathetic **13** unsympathetic

disinfect **7** cleanse **9** sterilize

disingenuous **3** sly **4** foxy, wily **5** false **6** artful, crafty, tricky **7** cunning, devious, feigned, oblique, unfrank **8** guileful, indirect, uncandid **9** insidious, insincere

disinherit **3** rob **4** lose, oust **6** cut off **7** bereave, deprive **9** deprive of, repudiate

disintegrate **3** rot **4** sink, turn **5** break, decay, spoil, taint **6** molder, worsen **7** crumble, decline, descend, putrefy, scatter, shatter **8** separate **9** break down, decompose **10** deliquesce, retrograde ***suffix:*** **4** lyse, lyze

disintegrating ***combining form:*** **7** clastic

disintegration ***combining form:*** **5** lyses (plural), lysis

disinter **5** dig up **6** exhume, unbury **7** unearth **8** exhumate **9** uncharnel

disinterest **6** apathy **8** lethargy **9** lassitude, unconcern **11** insouciance **12** heedlessness, indifference, listlessness **13** unmindfulness

disinterested **4** fair, just **5** aloof **6** casual, remote **7** neutral **8** abstract, detached, negative, unbiased **9** apathetic, colorless, impartial, incurious, withdrawn **10** impersonal, poker-faced **11** indifferent, unconcerned, unpassioned

disjoin **4** part **5** sever **6** divide, sunder, unglue, unlink **7** break up, divorce, unstick **8** separate

disjoint **4** part **5** sever, upset **6** divide, luxate, mess up, muddle, sunder **7** break up, rummage **8** disorder, separate **9** uncombine

disjointed **7** muddled **8** inchoate **10** incoherent, incohesive **11** unconnected, unorganized **12** uncontinuous

disk **4** chip, puck **5** wafer **6** record ***metal:*** **4** slug ***ornamental:*** **6** bangle, sequin

dislike **4** hate **6** detest, hatred, resent **8** aversion, distaste **9** prejudice **10** repugnance **11** deprecation, detestation **13** indisposition ***object of:*** **8** anathema

disliking **8** aversion **13** indisposition

dislimb **4** maim **6** mayhem **7** cripple **8** mutilate

dislimn **3** dim **5** bedim, cloud, gloom **6** darken **7** becloud, obscure **8** overcast **9** adumbrate, obfuscate

dislocate **4** move, ship **5** mix up, shift **6** jumble, remove **7** rummage **8** disorder, transfer

dislodge **5** expel **6** remove **8** drive out

disloyal **5** false **6** untrue **8** recreant **9** alienated, estranged, faithless **10** perfidious, traitorous, unfaithful **11** treacherous

disloyalty **7** falsity, perfidy, treason

9 falseness, treachery 10 infidelity 13 faithlessness
dismal 5 black, bleak 6 dreary, gloomy, somber 8 funereal 10 depressing, depressive, oppressive 13 disheartening
dismantle 4 bare, lift, raze, ruin, undo 5 annul, strip, wrack, wreck 6 denude, divest, recall, repeal, revoke 7 deprive, destroy, rescind, reverse, strip of, unbuild, uncloak 8 bankrupt, decimate, demolish, denudate, dismount, take down, wear down 10 annihilate, do away with
dismay 4 faze, fear 5 abash, alarm, appal, daunt, dread, panic, scare, shake, upset 6 appall, bother, flurry, fright, horror, puzzle, rattle, subdue, terror 7 agitate, fluster, horrify, mystify, nonplus, perplex, perturb, terrify, unhinge 8 affright, bewilder, confound, frighten 9 dumbfound, embarrass 10 discompose 11 consternate, trepidation 12 perturbation 13 consternation
dismayed 5 agape, fazed 6 aghast 7 rattled, shocked 10 confounded 11 dumbfounded, overwhelmed 13 thunderstruck
dismember 4 maim, part 5 sever 6 mangle, mayhem, sunder 7 cripple 8 dismount, mutilate, separate, take down
dismiss 2 ax 3 can, out 4 cast, drop, fire, sack, shed 5 chase, chuck, eject, evict, let go, scoff, scorn, spurn 6 bounce, depose, lay off, let out, refuse, reject, remove, retire, slough, unseat 7 boot out, cashier, contemn, decline, divorce, extrude, kick out, kiss off, put away, suspend, turn off 8 furlough, pooh-pooh, ridicule, throw out, turn away, turn down 9 reprobate, repudiate, terminate
dismissal 5 congé 6 layoff, ouster 7 removal 8 brushoff
dismount 6 alight, detach, get off 7 unhorse 8 separate, take down 10 alight from
Disney 4 Walt 10 cartoonist ***character:*** 4 Huey 5 Daisy, Dewey, Dumbo, Goofy, Louie, Pluto 6 Donald, Mickey, Minnie ***classic:*** 8 Fantasia
disobedient 6 unruly 7 naughty, willful 8 contrary 10 headstrong, rebellious 12 contumacious, obstreperous, recalcitrant 13 insubordinate
disoblige 6 offend, put out 7 affront, trouble 8 put about 9 incommode 13 inconvenience
disorder 3 ill 4 riot, turn 5 chaos, mix up, snarl, upset 6 anomie, ataxia, huddle, jumble, malady, mess up, muddle, muss up, rumple, sicken, tumble, tumult 7 ailment, anarchy, clutter, confuse, derange, disease, embroil, illness, misdeed, misrule, rummage, shuffle, turmoil, unhinge 8 disjoint, sickness, syndrome, unhealth, unsettle, upheaval 9 affection, agitation, anarchism, commotion, complaint, condition, confusion, infirmity 10 affliction, convulsion, misconduct, turbulence 11 bedevilment, misdemeanor 13 indisposition ***mental:*** 8 paranoia
disordered 4 daft 5 crazy 6 crazed, insane 7 cracked, lunatic, muddled 8 demented, deranged, inchoate 9 bedlamite 10 incoherent, incohesive 11 unconnected, unorganized 12 uncontinuous
disorderly 5 rowdy 6 unruly 7 raucous 8 rowdyish 9 termagant, turbulent 10 boisterous, rowdydowdy, tumultuous 11 rumbustious
disorderly house 6 bagnio 7 brothel 8 bordello
disorganize 5 upset 6 jumble, mess up 7 derange 8 unsettle
disoriented 4 lost
disown 4 deny 8 disclaim, renounce 9 repudiate
disparage 5 abuse, chill, decry 6 deject, slight 7 downcry, run down 8 bad mouth, belittle, derogate, minimize, write off 10 demoralize, depreciate 11 detract from
disparagement 4 tale 5 scorn 7 calumny, despite, scandal, slander 8 contempt, despisal 9 aspersion, indignity, stricture 10 backbiting, defamation, detraction, diminution, reflection 11 despisement 12 backstabbing, belittlement, depreciation 13 animadversion
disparate 6 unlike 7 diverse, unalike, unequal, various 9 different, divergent, unsimilar 11 inconsonant 12 incompatible, inconsistent
disparity 8 alterity 9 otherness 10 difference, divergence, divergency, inequality, unevenness, unlikeness
dispassionate 4 calm, cool, fair, just, open 5 aloof, equal, frank 7 neutral 8 abstract, composed, detached, judicial, unbiased 9 colorless, equitable, impartial, uncolored, unruffled 10 aboveboard, impersonal, poker-faced 11 indifferent, unflappable 12 uninfluenced, unprejudiced 13 imperturbable
dispatch 4 kill, send, ship, slay 5 eat up, haste, hurry, remit, route, scrag, speed 6 cut off, devour, finish, hasten, hustle, lay low, rustle 7 address, consign, destroy, forward, killing, message, put away, quicken, take off 8 alacrity, carry off, celerity, get rid of, goodwill, riddance, shipment, transmit 9 diligence, polish off, readiness, swiftness 10 expedition, put to death, speediness 11 promptitude
dispatch boat 5 aviso 6 packet
dispel 4 oust 5 eject 7 crumble, scatter 9 clear away, drive away

dispensable 5 minor 7 trivial 8 needless, unneeded 9 redundant 10 unrequired 11 superfluous, unessential, unimportant, unnecessary 12 nonessential
dispensary 6 clinic
dispensation 5 favor 7 service 8 courtesy, kindness, ordering 9 remission 10 indulgence, management
dispense 3 ply 4 deal, give, hand 5 spare, swing, wield 6 divide, excuse, exempt, handle, let off, let out, supply 7 absolve, deal out, deliver, dish out, dole out, furnish, mete out, portion, prorate, provide, release, relieve 8 deal with, hand over, maneuver, share out, transfer, turn over 9 apportion, discharge, partition 10 administer, distribute, manipulate, measure out, portion out
disperse 3 sow 4 deal 5 spray, strew 6 divide, lot out, spread 7 break up, diffuse, disband, disject, dole out, radiate, scatter 9 circulate, partition, propagate 10 distribute, measure out
dispersion 7 colloid 9 spreading 10 scattering *combining form:* 3 lyo
dispirit 5 chill 6 deject 7 depress 10 demoralize, discourage
dispirited 3 low, sad 4 blue, flat 8 cast down, dejected, downcast, lifeless 9 depressed, woebegone 10 melancholy 11 downhearted
dispiriting 5 black, bleak 6 dreary, gloomy 8 funereal 9 cheerless 10 depressing, depressive, oppressing
displace 4 oust 5 exile, expel, shift, usurp 6 banish, cut out, deport, depose, unmake, winkle 7 expulse, uncrown 8 crowd out, dethrone, redirect, relegate, supplant 9 transport 10 expatriate, substitute
displaced person 2 DP 6 émigré 7 evacuee, refugee 8 fugitive
display 4 open, pomp, show 5 array, flash, offer, shine 6 evince, expose, flaunt, lay out, parade, reveal, setout, spread, unfold, unveil 7 exhibit, fanfare, panoply, showing, show off, trot out, uncover 8 blazonry, brandish, describe, evidence, manifest, unclothe 9 showiness, spectacle 10 exhibiting, exhibition, pretension 11 demonstrate, ostentation 13 demonstration, manifestation
displeasing 3 bad 4 sour 6 rotten, vexing 7 irksome, unhappy 8 annoying 10 bothersome, unpleasant
displeasure 4 pain 5 anger 6 sorrow 8 aversion, vexation 10 uneasiness 11 indignation, unhappiness 13 indisposition
disport 3 act, fun 4 bear, game, go on, play, show 5 amuse, carry, flash 6 acquit, behave, demean, divert, expose, flaunt, parade 7 conduct, exhibit, jollity, pastime, show off, trot out 8 brandish, recreate 9 diversion, entertain, merriment 10 recreation
disposal 5 order 7 dumping, junking 8 bestowal, chucking, jettison, ordering, riddance, sequence 9 clearance, scrapping 10 demolition, destroying, relegation 11 arrangement, demolishing, destruction 12 throwing away, transference
dispose 4 bend, bias 5 array, order 7 arrange, incline, marshal, prepare 8 organize 9 make ready, methodize 11 systematize *of:* 4 sell 5 scrap 6 finish, handle 7 destroy, discard
disposed 4 fain 5 prone, ready 6 minded 7 willing 8 inclined
disposition 4 bent, cast, mood, tone, type, vein 5 being, humor, order, stamp, tenor 6 makeup, nature, temper 7 control, dumping, junking, leaning 8 jettison, ordering, penchant, riddance, sequence, tendency 9 character, direction, inclining, scrapping 10 complexion, management, proclivity, propensity 11 arrangement, controlling, inclination, personality, temperament 12 predilection, throwing away 13 individualism, individuality *favorable:* 8 optimism *unfavorable:* 9 pessimism
dispossess 3 rob 4 lose, oust 5 eject 6 banish, divest 7 bereave, deprive
dispossession 4 loss 6 ouster 9 privation 11 deprivation, deprivement, divestiture
dispraise 5 decry 8 belittle, derogate, diminish, minimize 10 depreciate 11 detract from, opprobriate 12 depreciation
disproportion 8 imparity, mismatch 10 inequality, unevenness
disproportionate 6 uneven 7 unequal 8 lopsided 9 irregular 10 asymmetric, off-balance, unbalanced 12 overbalanced 13 unsymmetrical
disprove 5 break, evert, rebut, shoot 6 blow up, impugn, refute 7 confute, explode 8 confound, negative, overturn, puncture, traverse 9 discredit, overthrow 10 contravene, controvert
disputable 4 moot 7 dubious 8 doubtful 9 uncertain 11 problematic
disputation 6 debate 7 mooting 8 forensic 9 dialectic 11 controversy
dispute 4 buck, duel, miff, moot, tiff 5 argue, doubt, fight, rebut, repel 6 argufy, bicker, combat, debate, hassle, oppose, refute, resist, rumpus, strife 7 agitate, canvass, confute, contend, contest, discuss, quarrel, quibble, wrangle 8 argument, conflict, mistrust, question, squabble, traverse 9 bickering, challenge, thrash out, with-

stand **10** contention, controvert, falling-out, toss around **11** altercation, controversy, embroilment ***Scottish:*** **6** threap, threep

disqualified **5** unfit **8** unfitted **9** incapable **10** ineligible, unequipped **11** incompetent

disqualify **3** bar **5** debar **6** except **7** exclude, rule out, suspend **9** deprive of, eliminate, make unfit **12** incapacitate ***as judge:*** **6** recuse

disquiet **4** care **5** upset, worry **6** bother, flurry, unease, unrest, untune **7** agitate, ailment, anxiety, concern, ferment, fluster, perturb, trouble, turmoil, unhinge **10** discompose, solicitude, uneasiness **11** concernment, restiveness **12** restlessness **13** Sturm und Drang

disquietude **4** care **5** worry **6** unease, unrest **7** ailment, anxiety, concern, ferment, turmoil **9** agitation **10** uneasiness **11** concernment, restiveness **12** restlessness **13** Sturm und Drang

Disraeli, Benjamin ***novel:*** **7** Tancred

disregard **4** fail, omit **6** apathy, forget, ignore, slight **7** blink at, neglect **8** ignoring, lethargy, omission, omitting, overlook, overpass **9** blink away, lassitude, slighting, unconcern **10** forgetting, neglecting **11** insouciance, overlooking **12** heedlessness, indifference, listlessness **13** unmindfulness

disregardful **3** lax **5** slack **6** remiss **8** careless, derelict, heedless **9** negligent **10** behindhand, delinquent, neglectful, regardless

disremember **6** forget

disreputable **4** mean **5** cheap, dingy, faded, seedy, shady, sorry **6** abject, scurvy, shabby, shoddy, sordid **7** run-down **8** beggarly, decrepit, pitiable, shameful **10** bedraggled, down-at-heel, inglorious, threadbare **11** dilapidated, ignominious **12** contemptible

disrepute **5** odium, shame **6** infamy **7** obloquy **8** disgrace, ignominy **10** opprobrium

disrespect **8** boldness **9** hardihood, impudence, insolence, insolency **10** incivility **12** impertinence, insolentness

disrespectful **4** rude **7** ill-bred, incivil, uncivil **8** impolite, impudent **10** ungracious **11** ill-mannered, impertinent

disrobe **4** bare **5** strip **6** denude, divest **7** deprive, strip of, undress **8** bankrupt, denudate, unclothe

disrupt **4** hole, open **5** upset **6** breach, mess up, muddle **7** rummage, rupture **8** disorder, unsettle **10** break apart

dissatisfaction **7** dislike **8** aversion **10** uneasiness

dissatisfactory **3** bad **4** poor **5** amiss, wrong **6** rotten

dissatisfied **5** irked, vexed **7** annoyed **8** bothered **9** uncontent **10** malcontent **11** uncontented **12** discontented, malcontented

dissect **3** cut **4** part **5** carve, probe, sever, slice, split **6** cleave, divide, pierce, sunder **7** analyze, break up, resolve **8** separate **9** anatomize, break down, decompose, penetrate **10** decompound **11** dichotomize

dissection ***of animals:*** **7** zootomy

dissemblance **5** guile **6** deceit **7** cunning **8** alterity **9** duplicity, otherness **10** difference, divergence, divergency, unlikeness

dissemble **4** mask **5** cloak, feign **7** conceal, dress up **8** disguise **10** camouflage

dissembler **8** pharisee, Tartuffe **9** hypocrite, lip server

disseminate **3** sow **5** straw, strew **6** blazon, spread **7** bestrew, declare, diffuse, publish, radiate, scatter, send out **8** announce, permeate, proclaim **9** advertise, broadcast, circulate, propagate, publicize, spread out **10** annunciate, promulgate **11** blaze abroad

dissension **6** strife **7** discord, quarrel, wrangle **8** argument, conflict, variance **9** bickering **10** contention, difference, quarreling **11** altercation, controversy

dissent **3** shy **4** balk, vary **5** demur **6** boggle, differ, divide, heresy, object, schism, strife **7** stickle **8** conflict, variance **9** misbelief **10** contention, difference, heterodoxy **11** unorthodoxy **12** nonagreement **13** nonconformism, nonconformity

dissenter **7** heretic, sectary **10** schismatic, separatist **11** misbeliever, schismatist **13** nonconformist

dissertation **6** memoir, thesis **8** tractate, treatise **9** discourse, monograph, treatment **10** monography

disservice **6** injury **8** mischief

dissever **3** cut **4** part **5** carve, slice, split **6** cleave, divide, sunder **7** divorce **8** separate **11** dichotomize

dissidence **6** heresy, schism, strife **7** discord **8** conflict **9** misbelief **10** contention, heterodoxy **11** unorthodoxy **13** nonconformism, nonconformity

dissident **7** heretic, sectary **9** differing, heretical, heterodox, sectarian **10** schismatic, separatist, unorthodox **11** contentious, misbeliever, quarrelsome, schismatist **12** unharmonious **13** nonconformist

dissimilar **6** unlike **7** diverse, unalike, unequal, various **8** contrary, opposite **9** different, divergent **10** antonymous **12** antithetical **13** contradictory

dissimilarity **8** variance **9** diversity, otherness, severance **10** difference, divergence,

divergency, unlikeness **11** incongruity **12** divarication, inconsonance **13** heterogeneity, inconsistency
dissimulate see **dissemble**
dissimulation **5** guile **6** deceit, hiding **7** cunning, masking **8** cloaking, feigning, pretense, shamming **9** duplicity, hypocrisy, secreting **10** catabolism, concealing, pharisaism, pretending, sanctimony **12** camouflaging
dissimulator see **dissembler**
dissipate **4** blow **5** waste **6** vanish **7** consume, crumble, fritter, scatter **8** evanesce, fool away, squander **9** evaporate, throw away **10** frivol away, trifle away **11** blunder away
dissociate **5** unfix **6** cut off, detach **8** abstract, alienate, estrange, uncouple
dissolute **3** lax **4** fast, wild **5** light, loose, slack **6** rakish, wanton **7** lawless, raffish, wayward **9** abandoned, reprobate **10** licentious, profligate **12** unprincipled, unrestrained **13** self-abandoned
dissolution **5** death, decay, sleep **6** demise **7** decease, divorce, passing, quietus, rupture, silence, split-up **8** curtains, division **10** detachment, profligacy **11** divorcement ***combining form:*** **3** lys **4** lysi, lyso **5** lyses (plural), lysis
dissolvable **7** soluble
dissolve **3** end **4** flux, fuse, melt, ruin, thaw, undo, void **5** annul, quash, wrack, wreck **6** recess, unfold, vacate, vanish **7** adjourn, break up, clear up, destroy, disband, immerse, liquefy, resolve, shatter, unravel **8** abrogate, decimate, decipher, demolish, destruct, fade away, get rid of, liquesce, prorogue, separate **9** decompose, figure out, lose power, prorogate, puzzle out, terminate, waste away **10** annihilate, deliquesce, do away with **13** superimposing ***suffix:*** **4** lyse, lyze
dissonance **6** strife **7** discord **8** conflict **9** cacophony **10** contention, difference **11** incongruity
dissonant **4** rude **5** harsh **6** hoarse, rugged **7** grating, jarring, raucous **8** strident **9** immusical, unmixable, unmusical **10** cacophonic, inharmonic **11** cacophonous, conflicting, incongruent, incongruous **12** incompatible, inconsistent, inharmonious
dissuade **5** deter **6** dehort, divert **10** discourage, disincline
distaff **6** female
distance **3** way **4** area, size, ways **5** ambit, orbit, piece, range, reach, route, scope, space, spell, sweep **6** course, degree, extent, length, milage, outrun, radius, spread **7** breadth, compass, expanse, mileage, outpace, purview, reserve, spacing, stretch **8** alterity, coldness, interval, outspeed, outstrip **9** amplitude, expansion, extension, otherness **10** difference, divergence, divergency, remoteness, separation, unlikeness **11** distinction, perspective **12** dissemblance **13** dissimilarity, dissimilitude ***angular:*** **8** latitude **9** longitude ***between levels:*** **4** drop ***between rails:*** **4** gage ***between supports:*** **4** span ***from bottom to top:*** **6** height ***geometric:*** **8** altitude ***greatest perpendicular:*** **6** camber ***measuring instrument:*** **8** odograph, odometer **9** pedometer, telemeter **11** range finder ***minute:*** **4** hair ***perpendicular:*** **5** depth ***shortest:*** **7** beeline **12** straight line ***the wind blows:*** **5** fetch
distant **3** far, shy **4** afar, cold, cool **5** aloof, apart **6** far-off, remote **7** diverse, faraway, haughty, obscure, removed, spacial, spatial, unalike, unequal, various **8** far-flung, isolated, off-lying, outlying, reserved, retiring, secluded, solitary **9** different, divergent, separated, unsimilar, withdrawn **10** unsociable **11** out-of-the-way, sequestered, standoffish ***combining form:*** **3** tel **4** tele, telo
distaste **7** dislike **8** aversion **9** antipathy, hostility, revulsion **10** abhorrence, repugnance **13** indisposition
distasteful **4** flat **6** bitter, odious **7** galling, insipid, painful **8** grievous, unsavory **9** loathsome, obnoxious, repellent, repugnant, repulsive, savorless, tasteless **10** abominable, afflictive, detestable, flavorless **11** ill-flavored, unpalatable **12** unappetizing
distemper **4** riot **5** mix up, paint **6** choler, muddle **7** anarchy, derange, disease, misrule, rummage **8** disorder **9** anarchism, strangles **10** affliction **11** derangement **13** panleucopenia
distend **5** bloat, swell **6** dilate, expand, extend **7** amplify, augment, enlarge, inflate **8** increase, lengthen **10** stretch out
distill **4** drib, drip, drop, weep **6** infuse, purify **7** dribble, trickle **11** concentrate
distillation apparatus **5** still **7** alembic, limbeck
distinct **4** sole **5** clear, lucid, plain **6** patent, single **7** defined, diverse, evident, express, notable, obvious, special, unusual, various **8** apparent, clear-cut, definite, especial, explicit, manifest, palpable, peculiar, separate, specific **9** different, divergent **10** individual, particular, prescribed **11** categorical, perspicuous, unambiguous, unequivocal ***combining form:*** **4** idio **5** chori **7** chorist **8** choristo
distinction **4** bays, rank **5** award, badge, class, grade, honor, kudos **6** nicety, renown **7** laurels **8** accolade, alterity, eminence, prestige **9** otherness **10** difference,

divergence, divergency, prominence, prominency, unlikeness **11** differentia, preeminence **12** significance **13** dissimilarity
distinctive **6** proper, single, unique **8** peculiar, separate **9** diacritic **10** diagnostic, individual **11** outstanding **13** idiosyncratic
distingué **6** urbane **7** genteel, refined **8** cultured, polished, well-bred **10** cultivated
distinguish **3** see **4** know, mark, note, part, spot, view **5** erect, exalt, honor, place **6** descry, finger, notice, remark, set off **7** dignify, ennoble, glorify, magnify, mark off, observe, pick out, qualify, sublime **8** diagnose, identify, perceive, pinpoint, separate **9** demarcate, extricate, recognize, signalize, single out **10** aggrandize, difference **11** determinate, individuate, singularize **12** characterize **13** diagnosticate, differentiate, individualize
distinguished **5** famed, grand, great **6** famous **7** courtly, eminent, notable, stately **8** imposing, renowned **9** dignified, prominent **10** celebrated, celebrious **11** illustrious
distort **4** bend, warp, wind **5** alter, belie, color, curve, twist, wrest **6** change, deform, garble **7** falsify, pervert, torture **8** miscolor, misshape, misstate **11** misconstrue **12** misinterpret, misrepresent
distortion **8** misshape **9** deformity
distract **5** addle, craze, mix up **6** ball up, frenzy, fuddle, harass, madden **7** confuse, derange, fluster, unhinge **8** befuddle, bewilder, confound, throw off **9** unbalance
distraction **6** lunacy **7** madness **8** insanity **9** amusement, diversion, unbalance **10** insaneness, perplexity **11** derangement, psychopathy **13** entertainment
distrait **4** lost **5** upset **6** absent **7** bemused, faraway, worried **8** harassed, troubled **9** tormented **10** abstracted **11** inattentive, inconscient, preoccupied **12** absentminded
distraught **3** mad **4** daft, nuts **5** crazy, upset **6** addled, crazed, insane **7** cracked, frantic, muddled, worried **8** agitated, confused, demented, deranged, harassed, troubled **9** flustered, perturbed, tormented **10** bewildered, nonplussed
distress **3** ail, irk, try, woe **4** ache, cark, hurt, need, pain, pang, pass, rack **5** agony, annoy, cross, dolor, grief, harry, pinch, rigor, throe, trial, upset, weigh, worry **6** bother, grieve, harass, injure, misery, pester, plague, sorrow, strain, strait, stress, twinge **7** afflict, anguish, exhaust, passion, torment, torture, trouble **8** aggrieve, calamity, exigency, hardship **9** adversity, constrain, suffering **10** affliction, difficulty, heartbreak, misfortune, visitation **11** tribulation, vicissitude ***call:*** **6** Mayday ***signal:*** **3** SOS **5** alarm
distressing **4** dire **6** woeful **8** grievous, poignant **10** afflictive, calamitous, deplorable, lamentable **11** regrettable, unfortunate **13** heartbreaking
distribute **3** lot **4** deal, give, mete **5** allot, place, strew **6** assign, assort, bestow, divide, donate, lot out, parcel, ration, spread **7** deal out, deliver, diffuse, dole out, dribble, give out, mete out, portion, present, prorate, radiate, scatter **8** allocate, classify, dispense, position, separate **9** apportion, circulate, partition, propagate, spread out **10** administer, measure out ***in a tournament:*** **4** seed
distribution **5** order **7** density **8** ordering, sequence **9** allotment, placement **10** scattering **11** arrangement, probability **12** spreading out **13** apportionment
distributor **6** jobber **7** carrier **10** wholesaler
district **4** area **5** tract **6** barrio, parcel, region, sector **7** quarter, section **8** division, locality, precinct, vicinage, vicinity **11** subdivision **12** neighborhood ***ecclesiastical:*** **5** synod **6** parish **7** diocese ***Greek:*** **4** deme ***Indian:*** **6** tahsil ***judicial:*** **7** circuit ***London:*** **4** Soho ***theater:*** **6** rialto ***Turkish administrative:*** **6** sanjak
distrust **5** doubt **7** suspect **8** wariness **9** suspicion **10** disbelieve
distrustful **4** wary **7** jealous **10** suspicious
distrusting **7** cynical **9** sceptical, skeptical **10** suspicious
disturb **4** faze, move, ship **5** alarm, fease, feaze, feeze, rouse, scare, shift, unset, upset **6** bother, damage, flurry, jumble, meddle, mess up, puzzle, remove, stir up, tamper **7** agitate, break up, derange, destroy, fluster, inquiet, perplex, replace, terrify, trouble, unhinge **8** bewilder, disorder, frighten, transfer, unsettle **9** incommode, interfere **11** intermeddle **13** inconvenience, interfere with
disturbance **6** rumpus, unrest **7** bobbery, cyclone, tornado, unquiet **9** agitating, agitation, commotion, variation **10** alteration **11** derangement **12** diastrophism, interruption ***atmospheric:*** **5** storm ***emotional:*** **8** neuroses (plural), neurosis ***mental:*** **6** frenzy **7** phrensy **8** delirium ***oceanic:*** **7** tsunami
disunify see **disunite**
disunion **6** strife **7** divorce, rupture, split-up **8** conflict, division, variance **9** partition **10** contention, detachment, difference, separation **11** divorcement
disunite **4** part, wean **5** alien **6** divide, sunder **7** break up, divorce, split up **8** alien-

ate, estrange, separate 9 fall apart, uncombine 11 dichotomize
disunity 6 strife 7 discord 8 conflict, variance 10 alienation, contention, difference
ditch 3 cut, dig, pit 4 cast, foss, junk 5 chuck, fosse, scrap 6 reject, sheuch, sheugh, trench, trough 7 abandon, cashier, discard, dismiss, foxhole 8 jettison, throw out 9 throw away 10 excavation
dither 3 gab, jaw, yak 4 chat, flap, halt, stew 5 clack, jumps, quake, run on, shake, waver 6 babble, cackle, falter, quaver, shakes, shiver, tremor, tumult 7 jitters, shivers, shudder, stagger, tremble, turmoil, twitter, whiffle, willies 8 hesitate 9 agitation, commotion, confusion, vacillate, whimwhams 10 turbulence 12 shilly-shally, wiggle-waggle 13 heebie-jeebies
dithyramb 4 hymn, poem 5 chant
dithyrambic 4 wild 5 fiery 6 ardent, fervid, torrid 7 burning, fervent, flaming 9 perfervid, rhapsodic 10 boisterous, passionate 11 impassioned
ditto 4 copy 6 carbon, repeat 7 replica 9 duplicate, facsimile 10 carbon copy 11 replication 12 reproduction 13 reduplication
ditty 3 lay 4 aria, hymn, lied, song 7 descant
diurnal 5 daily 9 circadian, ephemeral, quotidian
divagate 5 stray 6 depart, ramble, wander 7 digress, diverge, excurse
divan 4 sofa 5 couch 7 council 9 davenport 11 smoking room
diva's solo 4 aria
dive 3 bar, pub 4 dash, dump, hole, jump, leap 5 joint, lunge, pitch 6 gainer, lounge, plunge, saloon, tavern 7 barroom, decline, descend, descent, hangout, taproom 8 submerge 9 belly-flop, honky-tonk, jackknife, roadhouse 10 cannonball, submerging *position:* 4 pike, tuck 8 straight
diver 4 loon *combining form:* 4 dyta 5 dytes
diverge 4 part, vary 5 stray 6 depart, differ, ramble, swerve, wander 7 deflect, deviate, digress, excurse 8 disagree, separate 9 draw apart
divergence 7 parting, turning, variety, varying 8 alterity 9 departure, deviation, differing, otherness 10 aberration, deflection, difference, digression, separation, unlikeness 11 disagreeing, discrepancy, distinction 12 disagreement, dissemblance 13 dissimilarity, dissimilitude
divergent 6 off-key, radial, unlike 7 deviant, distant, unalike, unequal, various 8 aberrant, abnormal, atypical, contrary, opposite 9 anomalous, different, differing, disparate, irregular, radiating, spreading, unnatural, unregular, unsimilar 10 dissimilar 12 antithetical 13 contradictory
divers 4 many, some 6 sundry 7 several, various *combining form:* 4 poly, vari 5 parti, party, vario
diver's disease 5 bends 12 aeroembolism
diverse 6 unlike 7 distant, several, unalike, unequal, various 8 contrary, discrete, distinct, manifold, opposite, separate 9 different, differing, disparate, multifold, multiform, multiplex, unsimilar 10 contrasted, dissimilar 11 contrasting, contrastive 12 multifarious 13 contradictory *meanings:* 8 polysemy
diversion 3 fun 4 play 5 sport 6 levity, relish 7 disport, turning 8 pleasure, sideshow 9 amusement, departure, deviation, enjoyment, frivolity 10 aberration, deflection, recreation 11 delectation, distraction 13 entertainment
diversity 7 variety 8 multeity 10 difference, unlikeness 11 distinction, variousness 12 multiformity, multiplicity 13 dissimilarity
divert 4 turn, veer 5 alter, amuse, deter 6 swerve 7 deflect, deviate, digress 8 dissuade, distract 9 disadvise, disengage, entertain, turn aside 10 discourage *water:* 5 flume
divest 3 rob 4 bare, lose, oust 5 spoil, strip 6 denude 7 bereave, deprive, disrobe, undress 8 bankrupt, denudate, take away 9 dismantle 10 disinherit, dispossess
divide 3 cut 4 chop, deal, fork, part, vary 5 allot, carve, halve, quota, sever, share 6 assign, cleave, differ, lot out, parcel, ration, sector, sunder 7 break up, comport, discord, disjoin, dissect, dissent, divorce, dole out, furcate, portion, prorate, quarter, section, segment, share in, split up 8 allocate, classify, disagree, disburse, disjoint, dispense, disperse, disunite, fraction, graduate, separate 9 apportion, branch out, disaccord, partition, watershed 10 distribute, measure out 11 dichotomize, distinguish *into four parts:* 7 quarter *into three parts:* 7 trisect *into two parts:* 5 halve 6 bisect 9 bifurcate
divided 6 cloven 7 partite 8 multifid 9 disunited, separated *combining form:* 3 fid 4 sect 5 fissi, schiz 6 fidate, schizo, tomous 7 chorist 8 choristo
dividend 4 meed, plum 5 bonus, prize 6 carrot, return, reward 7 guerdon, premium
divider 6 bunton 7 compass 9 partition
divination 6 augury 7 insight 8 prophecy *by communication with the dead:* 10 necromancy *by dreams:* 11 oneiromancy *by figures:* 8 geomancy *by lots:* 9 sortilege

by numbers: 10 numerology *by rods:* 7 dowsing 11 rhabdomancy *by stars:* 9 astrology *combining form:* 5 mancy

divine 4 holy 5 clerk, godly, infer 6 cleric, deific, parson, priest, sacred 7 foresee, godlike, preknow, previse, suppose 8 clerical, discover, forefeel, foreknow, minister, preacher, prophesy, reverend 9 apprehend, chthonian, churchman, clergyman, marvelous, prevision, religious, visualize 10 anticipate, conjecture, superhuman, theologian 12 ecclesiastic, extramundane, transmundane 13 superphysical

Divine Comedy author 5 Dante

divining ability, for short 3 ESP

divinity 3 god 5 deity 7 godhead 8 theology *female:* 5 nymph 7 goddess

division 3 cut 4 part, unit 5 class, piece 6 member, moiety, parcel, schism 7 discord, dissent, divorce, parting, portion, rupture, section, segment, split-up 8 category, conflict, district, disunion, disunity, variance 9 disaccord, partition 10 detachment, difference, disharmony, dissidence, dissonance, separation 11 dissolution, divorcement 12 disagreement 13 apportionment *Bible:* 5 verse *book:* 7 chapter *British territorial:* 5 shire *building:* 4 wing *cell:* 7 meiosis, mitosis *city:* 4 ward 7 borough 8 precinct *combining form:* 7 kineses (plural), kinesis *contest:* 4 heat 6 inning, period *corolla:* 5 petal *country:* 5 state 6 canton 8 province 10 department, prefecture *family:* 4 side 6 branch *geologic time:* 5 epoch 6 period *hospital:* 4 ward, wing *into two:* 9 bisection 11 bifurcation, bipartition *mankind:* 4 race *meal:* 6 course *music:* 3 bar 4 line 7 measure 8 movement *opera, play:* 3 act 5 scene *poem:* 5 canto, verse 6 stanza *population:* 7 segment, stratum *race:* 3 lap 4 heat *social:* 5 caste, class, tribe *Soviet territorial:* 6 oblast 8 republic *state:* 6 county, parish *term:* 8 quotient *time:* 3 day, eon 4 week, year 5 month 6 decade, minute, moment, second 7 weekend 9 fortnight *tribal:* 4 clan *word:* 8 syllable *zodiac:* 4 sign

divisive 8 factious

divorce 4 part 5 annul, sever, split 6 cancel, sunder 7 break up, disjoin, dismiss, put away, rupture, split-up, unmarry 8 disjoint, dissever, disunion, disunite, separate 9 disaffect, partition 10 detachment, separation 11 dissolution

divot 4 turf

divulge 4 tell 5 mouth, spill 6 betray, gossip, reveal, tattle 7 blab out 8 disclose, discover, give away, proclaim 13 spill the beans

"Dixie" composer 6 Emmett

___ dixit 4 ipse

dizziness 7 vertigo

dizzy 4 daze 5 addle, dazed, giddy, inane, light, mix up, silly, undue 6 addled, ball up, fuddle, muddle, swimmy 7 asinine, confuse, dazzled, extreme, fatuous, flighty, fluster, foolish, fuddled, muddled, puzzled, reeling, stupefy 8 befuddle, bewilder, confused, heedless, skittish, swimming, throw off, towering, whirling 9 befuddled, confusing, excessive, frivolous 10 bewildered, bird-witted, confounded, distracted, exorbitant, immoderate, inordinate 11 empty-headed, extravagant, harebrained, light-headed, vertiginous 12 unmeasurable

DNA *component:* 7 adenine, guanine, thymine 8 cytosine 10 nucleotide 11 deoxyribose *segment:* 7 cistron

do 3 act, end, gyp, pay, put, set 4 bear, beat, bilk, cook, fare, feel, go on, halt, play, quit, show, suit, tire, tour, wash, work 5 break, cheat, clean, close, cover, cozen, enact, exert, get by, get on, occur, serve, shift, tonic, track 6 acquit, befall, behave, betide, chance, chouse, commit, demean, deport, diddle, effect, finish, happen, manage, render, travel, wind up, work at, wrap up 7 achieve, approve, arrange, come off, comport, conduct, defraud, develop, execute, exhaust, fall out, furbish, perform, playact, suffice, undergo, wear out 8 carry out, complete, conclude, decorate, flimflam, get along, pass over, traverse 9 determine, discourse, overreach, personate, stagger on, terminate, transpire 11 impersonate 12 stagger along 13 muddle through *away with:* 5 abate 6 banish 7 abolish 8 demolish, dissolve *without:* 5 forgo 6 forego *wrong:* 3 err

doable 8 feasible, possible

docent 7 teacher 8 lecturer, teaching 10 instructor 11 instructive

docile 4 tame 5 tawie 6 pliant 7 pliable 8 amenable, biddable, obedient 9 adaptable, teachable, tractable 10 submissive

dock 4 pier, quay, rump, slip 5 berth, jetty, levee, wharf 6 hangar, lessen, marina, reduce 7 abridge 8 platform *worker:* 6 lumper 9 stevedore 12 longshoreman

docket 4 card, sked 6 agenda 7 program 8 calendar, schedule 9 timetable

doctor 2 MD 3 fix, vet 4 load, mend 5 medic, patch, treat 6 breeze, debase, dope up, medico, repair, revamp 7 dentist, medical, rebuild, scholar, surgeon 8 overhaul 9 clinician, internist, mediciner, physician 10 adulterate, specialist 11 medicine man, recondition, reconstruct *animal:* 3 vet 12 veterinarian *children's:* 12 pediatrician *famous baby care:* 5 Spock *foot:* 10 podiatrist 11 chiropodist *heart:* 12 car-

diologist *slang:* 8 sawbones *teeth:* 7 dentist *women's:* 12 gynecologist
Doctor of the Church 5 Basil 6 Jerome 7 Ambrose, Gregory 9 Augustine 10 Athanasius
doctrinaire 6 dogged, mulish 8 dogmatic, stubborn 9 dictative, obstinate, pigheaded 10 bullheaded 11 dictatorial, magisterial, stiff-necked 12 pertinacious 13 authoritarian, authoritative
doctrine 3 ism 4 doxy 5 axiom, basic, canon, dogma, doxie, tenet 7 plenism 8 teaching 9 principle 11 fundamental, instruction *combining form:* 4 logy 5 logia *legal:* 6 cypres *occult:* 6 cabala, kabala 7 cabbala, kabbala 8 cabbalah, kabbalah *philosophical:* 8 monadism, vitalism *religious:* 8 chiliasm *suffix:* 3 ism
document 5 paper 6 record 8 evidence, monument 9 testimony 11 certificate *travel:* 8 passport
Dodavah's son 7 Eliezer
dodder 8 love vine
doddering 6 doting, senile
dodge 4 duck, jouk, slip 5 avoid, elude, evade, fence, parry, shirk, skirt, slide 6 escape, scheme, weasel 7 evasion, shuffle 8 malingar, sidestep 9 avoidance, expedient, pussyfoot 10 equivocate, tergiverse 12 short circuit, tergiversate
dodger 7 haggler 8 circular, handbill 9 throwaway
Dodger 5 Davis (Tommy) 6 Garvey (Steve), Koufax (Sandy), Snider (Duke), Sutton (Don) 8 Newcombe (Don), Robinson (Jackie) 10 Campanella (Roy) *field:* 7 Ebbetts *manager:* 6 Alston (Walter)
dodo 4 boob, dolt 5 dummy, dunce, idiot, moron 6 dimwit, nitwit 8 numskull 9 simpleton
Dodo's son 7 Eleazar, Elhanan
doe 4 deer 6 almond *young:* 3 teg
doer *suffix:* 2 er, or 3 ast, eer, ier, ist 4 ater, ster
doff 5 douse, uncap, unhat 6 remove, unhelm 7 take off
dog 3 cur, pug, pup, tag 4 bird, chap, chow, fice, mutt, peke, puli, stop, tail, tyke 5 boxer, click, feist, frank, hound, lemon, pooch, puppy, spitz, trail 6 Afghan, bawtie, bowwow, briard, canine, collie, detent, poodle, rascal, saluki, shadow, wiener, wretch 7 andiron, Maltese, mastiff, mongrel, pointer, Samoyed, spaniel, terrier, whippet 8 Airedale, inferior, keeshond, papillon, Pekinese, pinscher, spurious, wirehair 9 Chihuahua, dachshund, Dalmation, Great Dane, greyhound, Pekingese, retriever, schnauzer 10 bloodhound, Pomeranian, Weimaraner 11 frankfurter, wienerwurst 12 Newfoundland, Saint Bernard 13 cocker spaniel *Alaskan:* 8 malamute, malemiut, malemute *Australian:* 5 dingo 8 warragal, warrigal *barkless:* 7 basenji *combining form:* 3 cyn 4 cyno *Eskimo:* 5 husky *family:* 7 Canidae *FDR's:* 4 Fala *fictional:* 4 Lady 5 Astro, Pluto 6 Big Red 8 McBarker *genus:* 5 Canis *Hungarian:* 6 vizsla *hunting:* 4 alan 5 alant, hound 6 alaunt, beagle, borzoi, saluki, setter 7 harrier, pointer, redbone 8 elkhound, foxhound 9 wolfhound 10 bloodhound 11 basset hound *Indian:* 5 dhole *long-bodied:* 9 dachshund *movie:* 4 Asta, Toto 5 Benji 9 Old Yeller, Rin Tin Tin *name:* 4 Fido, Spot 5 Rover 6 Bowser *of Hades:* 8 Cerberus *Orphan Annie's:* 5 Sandy *powerful:* 11 bull mastiff *Russian:* 6 borzoi 7 Samoyed *shaggy-coated:* 8 komondor *short-legged:* 5 corgi *small:* 3 pom, pug, pup 4 alco, peke 7 whiffet 8 Pekinese 9 Chihuahua, Pekingese 10 Pomeranian *space traveler:* 5 Laika *television:* 5 Tramp 6 Lassie 9 Rin Tin Tin *terrier:* 7 scottie *three-headed:* 8 Cerberus *tiny:* 9 Chihuahua *tooth:* 4 fang *tracking:* 10 bloodhound *two-headed:* 6 Orthos *Welsh:* 5 corgi *young:* 3 pup 5 puppy, whelp
dogbane 10 bitterroot
dog days 8 canicule
dogfall 3 tie 4 draw 8 deadlock, standoff 9 stalemate
dogfight 3 row 4 fray 5 brawl, broil, melee, set-to 6 fracas 7 ruction 10 donnybrook, free-for-all
dogfish 6 bowfin, burbot 8 mud puppy *genus:* 7 Squalus
dogged 5 rigid 7 adamant 8 obdurate 9 insistent, steadfast, unbending 10 brassbound, inexorable, inflexible, persistent, persisting, persistive, relentless, unshakable 11 perseverant, persevering, unremitting 12 single-minded 13 perseverative
doggone 4 damn, darn, rank 5 utter 6 damned 7 blasted, blessed, dratted 8 absolute, infernal, outright 9 dad-burned, out-and-out 10 confounded 11 unmitigated 13 blankety-blank
dogma 5 canon, credo, creed, tenet 6 belief 8 doctrine 10 conviction, persuasion
dogmatic 7 a priori 8 reasoned 9 deducible, deductive, derivable, dictative, doctrinal 11 dictatorial, doctrinaire, magisterial 13 authoritarian, authoritative
dog-paddle 4 swim
dog's age 3 eon 4 aeon, long 8 blue moon, eternity 12 donkey's years
Dog Star 6 Sirius
dogwood 5 sumac 6 cornel 8 red osier 9 boobyalla 11 native broom

do in 4 ruin, slay 5 wreck 6 finish, murder 7 execute, exhaust, frazzle, outtire, outwear, put away, wear out 8 bankrupt, knock off, knock out 9 liquidate, prostrate, shipwreck 10 dilapidate 11 assassinate

doing 3 act 6 action ***combining form:*** 6 praxes (plural), praxia, praxis ***good:*** 10 beneficent ***suffix:*** 3 ant, ent

doit 3 bit, jot 4 damn, dram, drop, hoot, iota, whit 5 whoop 6 trifle 8 particle

doldrums 4 yawn 5 blues, dumps, ennui, gloom, slump 6 apathy, tedium 7 boredom, latency 8 abeyance, abeyancy, dormancy 9 dejection 10 depression, inactivity, quiescence, quiescency, stagnation 12 indifference, listlessness

doleful 4 down 7 piteous, pitiful, ruthful 8 cast down, dejected, downcast, grieving, mournful, mourning, wretched 9 afflicted, cheerless, depressed, miserable, plaintive, sorrowful, sorrowing, woebegone 10 dispirited, lamentable, lugubrious, melancholy 11 crestfallen, downhearted 12 disconsolate

dole out 4 deal, mete 6 divide, parcel, ration 7 mete out 8 disburse, dispense, disperse, share out 9 apportion, partition 10 administer, distribute

doll 3 Ken 6 Barbie, figure, Kewpie, puppet 10 Betsy Wetsy, Raggedy Ann 11 Raggedy Andy ***grotesque:*** 8 golliwog

dollar 4 bill, buck, oner 8 simoleon

dollop 3 nip, tot 4 dram, drop, jolt, shot, slug 5 snort 7 snifter 8 toothful

Doll's House, A ***author:*** 5 Ibsen ***heroine:*** 4 Nora

dolly 4 cart 5 truck 7 stirrer

dolomite 6 marble 9 limestone 10 bitter spar

dolor 5 agony 6 misery, sorrow 7 anguish, passion 8 distress 9 suffering

dolorous 4 dire 6 rueful, woeful 7 ruthful 8 grievous, mournful, wretched 9 afflicted, miserable, plaintive, sorrowful 10 afflictive, calamitous, deplorable, lamentable, lugubrious, melancholy 11 distressing, regrettable 13 heartbreaking

dolphin 5 whale 7 bollard 8 porpoise 9 butterfly ***combining form:*** 7 delphis

dolt 3 ass, oaf 4 boob, clod, goof 5 booby, chump, dunce 7 dullard, fathead, jughead, saphead, schnook 8 dumnkopf, lunkhead, meathead, numskull 9 blockhead ***Scottish:*** 4 coof

doltish 4 dull, dumb 5 dense, thick 6 stupid 8 blockish, duncical 9 fatheaded 11 blockheaded 12 beetleheaded

domain 4 walk 5 field, realm 6 sphere 7 demesne, terrain 8 dominion, province 9 bailiwick, champaign, territory ***nether:*** 4 hell ***transcendent:*** 6 heaven ***Turkish:*** 6 beylic, beylik

dome 4 roof 7 ceiling 12 snap fastener

domed hut 5 igloo

Domesday Book money 4 oras

domestic 4 home, tame 6 family, native 7 subdued 8 internal, national 9 household, municipal 10 indigenous, submissive

domesticate 4 tame 5 adopt, train 6 master, subdue 10 housebreak, naturalize 11 familiarize

domicile 3 hut 4 home 5 abode, board, house, lodge, put up 6 bestow, billet, harbor 7 quarter 8 dwelling 9 entertain, residence, residency 10 commorancy, habitation

domiciliate 3 hut 4 bunk, tame 5 board, house, lodge, put up 6 billet, harbor, master, reside 7 quarter

dominance 9 masterdom, supremacy 10 ascendancy, prepotence, prepotency 11 preeminence, sovereignty

dominant 4 main 5 chief, first, major 6 master, ruling 7 capital, leading, regnant, stellar, supreme 8 foremost 9 ascendant, governing, number one, paramount, prevalent, principal, sovereign 10 preeminent, prevailing, surpassing 11 outweighing, overbearing 12 overweighing, preponderant, transcendent 13 overbalancing

dominate 4 rule 5 reign 6 direct, govern, handle, manage, obsess 7 control, overtop, prevail, repress 8 domineer, look down, overarch, overlook, override 9 tower over 10 tower above ***at home:*** 12 wear the pants

domination 4 sway 5 might, power 7 command, control, mastery, strings 9 authority, masterdom, supremacy 10 ascendancy, prepotence, prepotency, suzerainty 11 preeminence, sovereignty 13 preponderancy

dominator 4 boss, cock, head 5 chief, ruler 6 honcho, leader, master 7 headman 8 hierarch 9 chieftain

domineer 4 rule 5 reign 7 prevail 11 predominate 12 preponderate

domineering 5 bossy 6 lordly 8 arrogant, imperial, insolent 9 imperious, masterful 10 highhanded, imperative, peremptory, tyrannical 11 magisterial

Dominican Republic ***capital:*** 12 Santo Domingo ***island:*** 10 Hispaniola ***monetary unit:*** 4 peso ***product:*** 5 cocoa, sugar 6 coffee 7 bauxite, tobacco

dominion 3 raj 4 rule, sway 5 field, realm, regna (plural) 6 domain, empery, regnum, sphere 7 demesne, terrain 8 property, province 9 ascendant, bailiwick, champaign, masterdom, ownership, supremacy, territory 10 ascendancy, possession, prepot-

ence, prepotency **11** preeminence, proprietary, sovereignty **13** possessorship
domino **4** mask **5** amice, visor **6** vizard **9** doughface, false face ***spot:*** **3** pip
don **3** sir **4** lord, pull **5** get on, put on **6** assume, draw on, slip on, strike, take on **7** throw on **8** huddle on
Donalbain ***brother:*** **7** Malcolm ***father:*** **6** Duncan
Donar see **Thor**
donate **4** emit, give, loan **6** bestow, devote, hansel, supply **7** hand out, handsel, present **8** give away, transfer **10** contribute
donation **3** aid **4** alms, gift, help **5** grant **7** bequest, charity, handsel, subsidy **8** offering **9** endowment **10** assistance **11** beneficence **12** contribution
donator see **donor**
Don Camillo **6** priest
Don Carlos ***author:*** **8** Schiller ***composer:*** **5** Verdi ***father:*** **6** Philip
done **5** all in, ended, right, spent **6** decent, doomed, effete, gone by, proper, used up **7** correct, drained, dressed, far-gone, through, worn-out **8** becoming, complete, decorous, depleted, finished, washed-up **9** befitting, completed, concluded, exhausted, fitted out **10** conforming, terminated ***for:*** **4** gone, sunk **5** kaput **8** finished ***poetic:*** **3** o'er
donee **7** grantee **8** receiver **9** appointor, recipient
done in **5** spent **6** effete, used up **7** fargone, worn-out **8** depleted **9** exhausted, washed-out
Don Giovanni composer **6** Mozart
Donizetti ***hero:*** **7** Roberto ***opera:*** **5** Lucia **10** Anna Bolena, La Favorita **11** Don Pasquale **12** Maria Stuarda
Don Juan **4** rake, wolf **5** Romeo **6** chaser, masher **7** amorist, gallant **8** Casanova, lothario, paramour **9** ladies' man, libertine, philander, womanizer **10** lady-killer, profligate **11** philanderer ***drama:*** **13** The Stone Guest ***home:*** **7** Seville ***mother:*** **4** Inez ***poet:*** **5** Byron
donkey **3** ass **4** fool, jerk **5** burro, idiot **7** jackass **8** imbecile **10** nincompoop ***female:*** **5** jenny
donkey's years **3** age **4** aeon **7** dog's age **8** blue moon, coon's age, eternity
donkeywork **4** moil, toil **5** grind, labor **6** drudge **7** slavery **8** drudgery, plugging
Donner see **Thor**
donnybrook **4** fray **5** brawl, fight, melee, set-to **6** affray, fracas **7** bobbery, ruction **10** free-for-all
donor **5** giver **7** donator, granter, grantor **8** bestower **9** conferrer, presenter **11** contributor
do-nothing **3** bum **4** slug **5** idler **6** loafer, slouch **8** dolittle, fainéant, slugabed, sluggard **9** lazybones
Don Quixote ***author:*** **9** Cervantes ***beloved:*** **8** Dulcinea ***companion:*** **11** Sancho Panza ***giant:*** **8** windmill ***home:*** **8** La Mancha ***horse:*** **9** Rocinante, Rosinante, Rozinante ***squire:*** **11** Sancho Panza
doodad **5** gizmo **6** dingus, gadget, jigger **7** do-funny, thingum, trinket **9** doohickey, rigamajig, thingummy **10** thingumbob **11** thingumajig
doodle **3** ass, toy **4** fool, jerk, mess **5** cheat, idiot, ninny **6** donkey, fiddle, potter, puddle, putter, tinker, trifle **7** jackass **8** imbecile, scribble **10** mess around, nincompoop
doohickey see **doodad**
doom **3** lot **4** damn, fate **5** moira, weird **6** decree, kismet **7** condemn, destine, destiny, portion, preform, tragedy **8** calamity, disaster, sentence **9** cataclysm, determine, ordinance, preordain, proscribe **10** foreordain, predestine **11** catastrophe **12** circumstance, last judgment, predetermine
doomful **4** dire **7** baleful, baneful, direful, ominous, unlucky **9** ill-boding **10** portentous **11** apocalyptic **12** inauspicious, unpropitious
doomsayer **7** killjoy **9** Cassandra, pessimist **11** crepehanger
door **3** way **4** adit **5** entry **6** access, entrée, portal **7** gateway, ingress, opening **8** entrance, entryway **9** admission **10** admittance **11** entranceway ***rear:*** **7** postern
doorkeeper **6** porter **7** gateman, ostiary
doormat **7** milksop **8** sufferer, weakling **9** jellyfish **10** namby-pamby, pantywaist **11** Milquetoast, mollycoddle
doorway **5** entry **6** portal **8** entrance, entryway **11** entranceway ***column:*** **7** trumeau **8** trumeaux (plural)
dope **4** drug **5** dunce, noddy **6** doctor, heroin, nitwit, noddle, opiate **7** cocaine **8** narcotic **9** lamebrain, marijuana **10** dunderhead **11** chowderhead, chucklehead, preparation **12** spinning bath
doped **4** high **6** stoned, zonked **7** drugged **8** hopped-up, turned on **9** spaced-out **10** tripped out
dope up **4** load **6** debase, doctor, weight **10** adulterate **12** sophisticate
dopey **5** heavy **6** stupid, torpid **7** bemused, fuddled **8** comatose, sluggish **9** lethargic **10** slumberous **12** hebetudinous
dor **6** beetle
Doric Zeus **3** Zan
Doris ***brother:*** **6** Nereus ***daughters:*** **7** Nereids ***father:*** **7** Oceanus ***husband:*** **6** Nereus

dormancy 7 latency 8 abeyance, diapause, doldrums 10 quiescence, quiescency, suspension 11 cold storage 12 intermission, interruption
dormant 6 drowsy, latent 7 abeyant, lurking, relaxed 8 immobile, inactive, sluggish 9 lethargic, potential, prepatent, quiescent 10 slow-moving 13 unprogressive
dormer 6 window
dorry 4 boat
dorsal 6 aboral 7 abaxial *combining form:* 6 opisth 7 opistho
___ d'Orsay 4 Quai
dorsum 4 back
Dorus *brother:* 6 Aeolus *father:* 6 Hellen
dose 7 measure, portion 8 quantity 10 proportion
Dos Passos trilogy 3 U.S.A.
dot 4 mark, mote, stud 5 dower, dowry, point, speck 6 bestud, pepper, period, pimple 7 freckle, speckle, stipple 8 fly-speck, sprinkle 9 bespeckle 11 intersperse 12 decimal point
dotage 8 senility 11 elderliness, senectitude
dote on 4 like 5 adore, enjoy, fancy 7 idolize, worship
doting 4 dear, fond 5 silly 6 loving, senile 7 asinine, devoted, doddery, fatuous, foolish 8 imbecile, lovesome, overfond 9 doddering 12 affectionate 13 over-indulgent
dotted 6 spotty 8 cribbled, punctate, stippled *with stars:* 4 semé
dotty 5 crazy, loony, wacky 6 absurd, insane 7 foolish 8 besotted, enamored 9 eccentric, fantastic, infatuate 10 infatuated, ridiculous 12 feebleminded, preposterous
double 3 dub, shy, yaw 4 bend, bilk, copy, dual, duck, dupe, fold, mate, shun, tack, turn, twin 5 avoid, duple, elude, evade, image, match, shift 6 bifold, binary, clench, duplex, escape, eschew, paired, ringer, wraith 7 dualize, enlarge, magnify, twofold 8 increase 9 companion, deceitful, deviation, dualistic, duplicate, insincere, replicate 10 coordinate, deflection, reciprocal, simulacrum, understudy 12 ambidextrous, hypocritical 13 spitting image *combining form:* 2 di 3 bin 4 dipl, diss 5 diphy, diplo, disso *prefix:* 2 bi 3 dis
double agent 3 spy
double-barreled 4 dual 5 duple 6 bifold, binary, duplex 7 twofold 9 dualistic
double bass 10 bull fiddle
double-cross 4 sell 5 bluff 6 betray, humbug, illude, juggle, take in 7 beguile, deceive, mislead, sell out 8 betrayal 9 four-flush
doubled *combining form:* 3 bis
double dagger 6 diesis
double-dealer 3 gyp 5 cheat 6 con man 7 diddler, sharper 8 swindler 9 defrauder 10 mountebank 11 flimflammer 13 confidence man
double-dealing 5 fraud 7 chicane 8 mala fide, trickery 9 chicanery, deception, duplicity, fourberie, insincere 10 hanky-panky, left-handed 11 highbinding 12 ambidextrous, hypocritical 13 sharp practice
double-dome 7 Brahmin, egghead 8 highbrow 12 intellectual
double-edged 5 vague 7 obscure, unclear 9 ambiguous, ancipital, equivocal, tenebrous, uncertain
double entendre 9 ambiguity, equivoque 11 amphibology 12 equivocality, equivocation
double-faced 5 vague 7 obscure, unclear 8 mala fide 9 ambiguous, equivocal, insincere, tenebrous, uncertain 10 left-handed 12 ambidextrous, hypocritical
double meaning see double entendre
double-minded 7 halting 8 hesitant, wavering 10 hesitating, indecisive, irresolute, undecisive 11 vacillating 12 ambidextrous, hypocritical
doublet 3 duo 4 dyad, pair 5 brace 6 couple, jacket 7 twosome
double-talk 4 jazz 5 hokum 6 bunkum, drivel 7 twaddle 8 flimflam, newspeak, nonsense 9 gibberish 10 balderdash 12 gobbledygook
double vision 8 diplopia
doubly *prefix:* 2 bi
doubt 5 qualm 6 wonder 7 concern, dispute, dubiety, misgive, perhaps, suspect, swither 8 distrust, mistrust, question, unbelief 9 challenge, disbelief, dubiosity, suspicion 10 skepticism 11 dubiousness, incertitude, incredulity, uncertainty, uncertitude
doubtable 4 open 7 dubious, suspect 9 ambiguous, equivocal, undecided 10 borderline 11 problematic
doubter 7 skeptic, zetetic 10 headshaker, Pyrrhonian, Pyrrhonist, unbeliever
doubtful 4 hazy, iffy, moot, open 5 fishy, shady, shaky 6 chancy, queasy, uneasy, unsure 7 clouded, dubious, obscure, suspect, unclear 8 arguable, insecure, mootable, unlikely, unstable, wavering 9 ambiguous, debatable, dubitable, equivocal, uncertain, undecided, unsettled 10 borderline, contingent, disputable, hesitating, improbable, impugnable, indecisive, precarious, suspicious, touch-and-go 11 problematic, speculative 12 questionable
doubtfulness 7 concern, dubiety 8 mistrust 9 dubiosity, dubitancy, suspicion 10 skepticism 11 uncertainty, uncertitude
doubting Thomas see doubter

doubtless 4 sure 6 easily, likely 7 certain 8 probably 9 assumably 10 absolutely, definitely, positively, presumably 13 presumptively, unequivocally
doubtlessly 4 well 5 truly 6 easily, indeed, really 8 provenly 10 absolutely, definitely, positively 11 undoubtedly 13 unequivocally
douceur 4 gift 7 present 8 gratuity
dough 4 cash 5 bread, money 8 currency 11 legal tender ***cooked in honey:*** 8 taiglach, teiglach
doughboy 11 infantryman
doughty 4 able, bold 5 brave, manly 6 plucky, spunky, strong 7 valiant 8 fearless, unafraid 9 dauntless, undaunted
doughy 4 ashy, pale 5 ashen, livid, lurid, waxen 6 pallid 8 blanched 9 colorless
do up 3 fix 4 mend, wrap 5 patch 6 doctor, repair, revamp 7 rebuild 8 overhaul 11 recondition, reconstruct
dour 4 glum, grim, hard, ugly 5 bleak, harsh, rigid, sulky, surly 6 dogged, gloomy, morose, severe, strict, sullen 7 austere, crabbed 8 rigorous 9 saturnine, stringent 10 forbidding, implacable, unyielding
douse 3 bat, bop, dip, out, sop, wet 4 doff, duck, dunk, slop, soak 5 bathe, drown, lower, plash, slosh, swash, throw 6 deluge, drench, put off, put out, quench, remove, splash, splosh 7 immerse, slacken, spatter, splurge, spurtle, take off 8 downpour, splatter, submerge, submerse 9 drenching 10 extinguish
douzeper 4 Ivon, Oton 5 Gerin, Ivory, peers 6 Anseis, Gerard, Gerier, Oliver, Roland, Samson 7 Olivier, paladin 8 Engelier 9 Berengier
dove 6 culver, pigeon 8 pacifist 10 pacificist ***call:*** 3 coo ***genus:*** 7 Columba
dovecote 6 aviary 8 pigeonry 9 birdhouse, columbary 11 culver house, pigeon house
dovehouse see **dovecote**
dovelike 4 mild, pure 6 gentle 7 lovable 9 columbine
dovetail 4 jibe 5 agree, fit in, tally 6 accord, square 8 check out 9 harmonize 10 correspond 13 interlock with
dovish 7 antiwar 8 pacifist 10 pacifistic
dowager 4 dame 6 matron 9 matriarch 10 grande dame
dowdy 4 drab, slut 5 dated, passé, tacky 6 blowsy, bygone, démodé, frowsy, frumpy, old hat, sordid, stodgy 7 archaic, traipse, vintage 8 frumpish, outdated, outmoded, slattern, slovenly 9 out-of-date, unstylish 10 antiquated, slatternly 11 draggle-tail 12 old-fashioned 13 draggletailed ***woman:*** 5 frump
dowel 3 pin, rod 5 stick
dower 3 dot 5 endow, endue 6 talent 9 crown with, endowment
dowitcher 5 snipe 8 grayback 9 brownback
down 3 bad, fur, ill, low, off, out 4 best, blue, done, drop, fell, flue, fuzz, kill, lick, lint, pile, sick, slow 5 below, ended, floor, floss, fluff, fully, level, lower, outdo, scrag, slack, throw, under, worst 6 cut off, defeat, fallen, finish, hipped, hurdle, lay low, master, nether 7 conquer, descent, destroy, flatten, for real, handout, swallow, through 8 actively, at hazard, bowl over, carry off, complete, consumed, defeated, dejected, dispatch, feathers, finished, inferior, lay aside, overcome, sluggish, suppress, surmount 9 completed, concluded, depressed, earnestly, earthward, liquidate, processed, seriously, subjacent 10 completely, dispirited, groundward, terminated, vigorously 11 netherwards 12 discomfiture ***combining form:*** 4 ptil 5 ptilo ***prefix:*** 2 de 3 cat, hyp, kat 4 cata, cath, cato, hypo, kata
down-and-outer 6 beggar, pauper, wretch
down-at-heel 5 seedy, tacky 6 shabby, tagrag 7 rundown 8 tattered 10 bedraggled, broken down, threadbare 11 dilapidated
downcast 3 bad, low, sad 4 blue, dull, glum, rout, sunk 5 moody, mopey, shaft 6 defeat, droopy, gloomy, hipped, morose 7 beating, debacle, doleful, forlorn, licking 8 dejected, drubbing, listless, soul-sick, troubled 9 depressed, heartsick, heartsore, oppressed, overthrow, woebegone 10 chapfallen, defeasance, despondent, dispirited, distressed, spiritless 11 crestfallen, discouraged, low-spirited 12 disconsolate, disheartened
downcry 5 abuse 8 belittle, derogate, diminish, discount 9 disparage, dispraise 10 depreciate 11 detract from
downfall 4 bane, ruin 7 atrophy, decline, descent, undoing 9 decadence, destroyer, ruination 10 declension, degeneracy, devolution 11 declination, destruction 12 degeneration, dégringolade 13 deterioration
downgrade 4 bump, bust 5 break, decry, lower 6 demote, reduce 7 atrophy, declass, decline, demerit, devalue, disrate 8 mark down, write off 9 decadence, devaluate, write down 10 declension, degeneracy, depreciate, devalorize, devolution, undervalue 12 degeneration, dégringolade 13 deterioration
downhearted see **downcast**
down-in-the-mouth see **downcast**
down payment 7 deposit, earnest

downpour 4 rain 6 deluge 8 rainfall 9 drenching 10 cloudburst
down quilt 5 duvet
downright 4 flat, very 5 gross, plain, utter 8 absolute, complete, positive 9 out-and-out, up-and-down 10 sure-enough 11 indubitable, unmitigated 13 thoroughgoing
downslide 3 dip, sag 4 drop, slip 5 slump 7 decline, falloff
downstage area 5 apron
downstairs 5 below 8 servants
downswing see **downslide**
down-to-earth 4 hard 5 sober 9 practical, pragmatic, realistic 10 hard-boiled, hardheaded 11 unfantastic 12 matter-of-fact, unidealistic
downtown sign 6 Main St.
downtrend see **downslide**
downtrodden 6 abject, abused 9 oppressed, underfoot 10 maltreated, mistreated, persecuted
downturn see **downslide**
downward 8 debasing 9 declining 10 descending, netherward ***combining form:*** 4 bath 5 batho
downwardly, downwards see **downward**
downy 4 soft 6 fluffy 8 feathery, soothing ***combining form:*** 4 hebe ***filler:*** 5 eider
doxy 3 ism 4 tart 5 creed, wench 6 harlot 7 opinion, trollop 8 doctrine
doyen 4 dean, lead 5 guide, maven, pilot 6 artist, expert, leader, master 8 virtuoso 9 authority 10 bellwether, master-hand, past master, proficient 12 passed master
Doyle's detective 6 Holmes
doze 3 nap 5 sleep 6 catnap, drowse 7 drop off, slumber 9 drowse off
dozy see **drowsy**
DP 6 émigré 7 evacuee, refugee 8 fugitive
drab 3 hag 4 bawd, dowd, dull, flat, slut, trot 5 biddy, bleak, crone, dingy, dowdy, faded, mousy, muddy, murky, prosy, wench, whore, witch 6 beldam, dismal, dreary, harlot, mousey 7 hustler, prosaic, subfusc, traipse 8 desolate, dullness, lifeless, slattern 9 cheerless, colorless 10 lackluster, lusterless, prostitute 11 dispiriting, draggle-tail, fille de joie, nightwalker 12 streetwalker
draconian 5 harsh, rigid 6 strict 8 rigorist, rigorous 9 stringent 10 ironhanded 12 unpermissive
Dracula author 6 Stoker (Bram)
draffy 6 drossy, no-good 7 inutile, nothing 8 unworthy 9 valueless, worthless
draft 3 tap 4 dose, plan, plot, pull, pump, swig 5 check, claim, drink, frame, press, swill, taper 6 call up, demand, design, devise, drench, enroll, induct, potion, scheme, siphon, sketch 7 compose, concoct, current, draught, harness, impress, outline, portion, prepare, project 8 block out, chalk out, contrive, muster in, rough out, skeleton, traction 9 adumbrate, allowance, conscribe, conscript, fabricate, formulate, muster out 11 delineation, skeletonize 12 characterize ***avoider:*** 6 dodger ***of a law:*** 4 bill
drag 3 lug, peg, tow, tug 4 hang, haul, poke, puff, pull, swig 5 dally, delay, draft, drain, drink, float, swill, tarry, trail 6 burden, daggle, dawdle, drench, harrow, loiter, put off, schlep, search, strain 7 ransack, sagging, schlepp, skidpan, traipse 8 drooping, friction 9 lag behind, sea anchor 10 conveyance 11 inclination 13 procrastinate ***off:*** 4 cart
dragging 4 long 7 lengthy, tedious 8 drawn-out, longsome, overlong 9 prolonged 10 protracted 12 long-drawn-out
draggle 5 trail 7 shuffle, traipse 8 besmirch
draggle-tail 4 dowd, drab, slut 5 dowdy 7 traipse 8 slattern
draggletailed 5 dowdy 6 blowsy, frowsy, sordid, untidy 8 slattern, sluttish 10 slatternly
dragnet 5 trawl
dragon 5 beast, Satan 6 wivern 8 basilisk 9 water arum 10 cockatrice ***Babylonian:*** 6 Tiamat ***biblical:*** 5 Rahab ***Canaanite:*** 3 Yam 4 Yamm 5 Lotan ***Chinese:*** 4 lung ***French:*** 8 Tarasque ***genus:*** 5 Draco ***Greek:*** 5 Ladon 9 Eurythion ***horse:*** 6 Fafner, Fafnir ***slayer:*** 4 Baal, Enki, Zeus 5 Indra 6 Cadmus, Marduk, Sigurd, Yahweh 7 Beowulf, Jupiter, Ninurta, Perseus 8 St. George 9 St. Michael 10 St. Margaret ***Sumerian:*** 3 Kur ***two-legged:*** 5 wiver 6 wivern, wyvern ***Vadic:*** 3 Ahi 6 Vritra
dragoon 3 cow 5 bully 6 harass, hector 8 browbeat, bulldoze, bullyrag 9 persecute, strong-arm, terrorize 10 cavalryman, intimidate
drag race entry 6 hot rod
drain 3 tap 4 jade, pump, sink, sump, swig, tire, vent, wear 5 bleed, draft, drink, empty, leech, sewer, swill, use up, weary 6 burden, drench, gutter, siphon, trench 7 conduit, deplete, draw off, exhaust, fatigue 8 bankrupt, draw down, wear down 9 discharge 10 impoverish 11 watercourse ***transverse:*** 7 culvert
drain away 5 abate, close, taper 6 lessen, reduce 7 dwindle 8 decrease, diminish, taper off
drained 5 all-in, spent 6 bleary, effete, used up 7 far-gone, worn-out 8 depleted 9 exhausted, washed-out
drainpipe 5 spout 9 downspout

drain pit 4 sump
dram 3 bit, nip, tot 4 dash, drop, hoot, iota, jolt, mite, shot, slug, spot, swig 5 crumb, draft, drink, ounce, shred, snort, swill 6 dollop 7 modicum, smidgen, snifter, snorter 8 particle, potation, toothful
drama 4 play 6 boards 7 theater, theatre 8 the stage 10 footlights ***former English:*** 6 masque ***Japanese:*** 3 Noh ***main part:*** 8 epitasis ***musical:*** 5 opera 8 operetta ***suspenseful:*** 11 cliff-hanger
dramatic 8 striking, theatral, theatric, thespian 10 histrionic, theatrical ***conflict:*** 4 agon ***scene:*** 4 skit
dramatis personae 4 cast
dramatist 10 playwright ***American:*** 4 Hart, Inge, Rice, Uhry 5 Albee, Mamet, Odets, Payne, Simon 6 Miller, O'Neill, Thomas, Wilson (August, Lanford) 7 Hellman, Kaufman 8 Anderson, Sherwood, Williams 11 Hammerstein, Wasserstein ***Austrian:*** 10 Schnitzler ***Belgian:*** 11 Maeterlinck ***English:*** 3 Fry, Gay 4 Rowe, Tate 5 Milne, Peele, Wilde 6 Coward, Jonson, Pinero, Pinter, Steele, Storey 7 Marlowe, Marston, Osborne, Shaffer, Webster 8 Congreve, Shadwell, Stoppard, Tourneur, Vanbrugh, Zangwill 9 Middleton, Wycherley 11 Shakespeare ***French:*** 5 Camus, Genet 6 Musset, Racine, Sardou, Sartre, Scribe 7 Anouilh, Ionesco, Labiche, Moliere, Rostand 8 Marivaux 9 Corneille, Giraudoux 12 Beaumarchais ***German:*** 5 Weiss 6 Brecht, Goethe, Kleist 8 Schiller 9 Hauptmann, Zuckmayer ***Greek:*** 8 Menander 9 Aeschylus, Euripides, Sophocles 12 Aristophanes ***Hindu:*** 8 Kalidasa ***Irish:*** 4 Shaw 5 Behan, Yeats 6 O'Casey 8 Sheridan ***Italian:*** 7 Alfieri, Giacosa, Goldoni 8 Trissino ***Japanese:*** 5 Zeami ***Norwegian:*** 5 Ibsen 8 Bjornson ***Roman:*** 7 Plautus, Terence ***Russian:*** 7 Chekhov 8 Zamyatin ***Spanish:*** 4 Vega 8 Quintero 11 Garcia Lorca ***Swedish:*** 5 Sachs 10 Strindberg ***Swiss:*** 6 Frisch
dramaturge see **dramatist**
dramaturgic see **dramatic**
drape 4 roll 5 adorn, cover 6 enfold, enwrap, sprawl, swathe, wrap up 7 curtain, swaddle 8 enswathe, envelope, spraddle, swathe in 11 spread-eagle
drapery 7 curtain 8 hangings
drastic 6 severe 7 extreme, radical 8 rigorous, vigorous 9 purgative
Dravidian language 5 Gondi, Khond, Malto, Tamil 6 Brahui, Kurukh, Telugu 8 Kanarese 9 Malayalam
draw 3 gut, lug, pen, tap, tie, tow, tug, win 4 call, edge, gain, haul, limn, lure, make, move, odds, puff, pull, pump, rise, sink, take, wile 5 alter, angle, bowel, bulge, charm, draft, drain, educe, evoke, infer, judge, paint, start, steep, taper, use up 6 allure, appeal, coulee, crayon, deduce, derive, elicit, entice, extend, gather, indite, induce, infuse, inhale, paunch, pencil, prompt, pucker, seduce, siphon, sketch 7 attract, bewitch, collect, deplete, dogfall, enchant, exhaust, extract, make out, prolong, spin out, stencil, stipple, stretch, vantage, win over 8 bankrupt, conclude, contract, convince, dead heat, deadlock, elongate, handicap, lengthen, persuade, protract, standoff 9 advantage, allowance, argue into, captivate, delineate, drain away, fascinate, formulate, head start, magnetize, represent, seduction, stalemate 10 allurement, attraction, disembowel, eviscerate, exenterate, impoverish, prolongate 11 bring around ***forth:*** 5 educe 6 elicit 7 extract ***from:*** 4 milk, pump 5 bleed ***the main features of:*** 4 etch 6 sketch 7 outline ***together:*** 3 tie 4 join, lace
draw back 5 wince 6 deduct, recede, recoil, retire 7 retreat, take off, take out 8 discount, knock off, subtract, take away 9 substract
drawback 6 defect, refund 7 trouble 8 handicap 9 detriment, hindrance 10 disability 12 disadvantage 13 inconvenience
draw down 3 get, win 4 earn, gain, make 5 drain, use up 7 acquire, bring in, deplete, exhaust 8 bankrupt 10 impoverish
drawer 9 draftsman ***for money:*** 4 till
draw in 3 get 6 induce, prompt 7 win over 8 convince, persuade, talk into 9 argue into, prevail on 11 bring around, prevail upon
drawing 4 plan 6 sketch 8 alluring, charming, magnetic 9 appealing 10 attracting, attractive, bewitching, enchanting 11 captivating, fascinating ***combining form:*** 4 gram ***humorous:*** 7 cartoon
drawing power 4 call, lure, pull 6 appeal 9 seduction 10 allurement, attraction
drawing room 5 salon 6 saloon 9 reception
drawn 4 worn 7 haggard, pinched 8 careworn
drawn-out 4 long 7 lengthy 8 dragging, extended, longsome, overlong 9 prolonged 10 protracted
draw off 3 tap 4 pump 5 bleed, draft, drain 6 remove, siphon, syphon 8 withdraw
draw on 3 don 5 cause 6 assume, effect, induce, prompt, secure 7 produce, win over 8 convince, persuade, talk into 9 argue into 10 bring about 11 bring around, prevail upon
draw out 6 extend, remove 7 extract, prolong, stretch 8 elongate, lengthen, protract 10 prolongate

draw up 4 halt, make, stop 5 draft, frame 7 prepare 9 formulate
dray 4 cart 7 travois 9 stoneboat
dray horse 4 peon 5 slave 6 drudge, slavey, toiler 11 galley slave
dread 4 fear 5 alarm, panic 6 dismay, fright, horror, terror 7 anxiety 9 trepidity 11 frightening, trepidation 13 consternation ***combining form:*** 5 phobe 6 phobia, phobic 7 phobous
dreadful 5 awful 6 tragic 7 direful, extreme, fearful, shocker 8 horrible, horrific, shocking, terrible, terrific 9 appalling, dime novel, frightful, revolting, unrefined 10 formidable, unpleasant, yellowback 11 frightening
dreadfully 4 very 6 damned 8 horribly 9 extremely 10 strikingly 11 exceedingly 12 surpassingly 13 frighteningly
dreadnought 10 battleship
dream 4 ache, long, lust, moon, pine, sigh 5 crave, fancy, ideal 6 bubble, hanker, hunger, thirst, vision 7 chimera, fantasy, imagine, rainbow, reverie, suspire 8 illusion, phantasm, phantasy 9 nightmare 10 conceive of ***combining form:*** 4 onir 5 oneir, oniro 6 oneiro ***god:*** 8 Morpheus
dreamer 6 mystic 7 utopian 8 idealist, theorist 9 ideologue, visionary 10 Don Quixote, lotus-eater 11 illusionist 13 castle-builder
dreamlike 5 vague 7 shadowy, surreal 8 nebulous
dream up 5 frame, hatch 6 devise, invent 7 concoct 8 contrive 9 formulate
dreamy 4 hazy, idle 5 ideal, nifty, super, vague 6 astral, divine, groovy, peachy 8 fanciful, glorious, pleasing, romantic 9 marvelous, unworldly, visionary, whimsical 10 delightful, idealistic, indistinct 12 otherworldly
dreary 4 blah, dull, poky 5 black, bleak 6 dismal, gloomy, somber, stodgy 7 forlorn, humdrum 8 banausic, funereal, monotone 10 depressing, depressive, enervating, monotonous, oppressive, pedestrian 11 dispiriting 12 discouraging ***Scottish:*** 5 dowie
dreck 4 junk 5 offal, swill 6 litter, refuse 7 garbage, rubbish 12 outsweepings
dredge 3 dig 5 scoop 6 deepen, search 8 excavate
dregs 3 mob 4 lees, scum 5 trash 6 masses, rabble 7 deposit, grounds 8 canaille, riffraff, sediment, unwashed 9 settlings 11 precipitate, proletariat 13 precipitation
Dreiser ***character:*** 5 Clyde 6 Carrie, Sondra 7 Roberta 10 Cowperwood ***novel:*** 8 The Stoic, The Titan 9 The Genius 12 The Financier 17 An American Tragedy
drench 3 sop, wet 4 drag, dunk, lash, pour, soak, swig, teem, wash 5 douse, draft, drain, drink, drouk, drown, souse, steep, swill 6 deluge, seethe, sodden 7 immerse, overwet, pervade 8 oversoak, saturate, submerge, waterlog 10 impregnate
dress 3 gut, rig, tan 4 bind, clad, deck, doll, duds, garb, gown, sack, tend, till, togs, trim, work 5 adorn, align, array, clean, frock, getup, guise, habit, prank, smock 6 attire, bedeck, clothe, dirndl, enrobe, outfit, sacque, setout, tailor 7 apparel, bandage, bedizen, chemise, clothes, costume, garment, garnish, raiment, turnout 8 beautify, beclothe, clothing, covering, decorate, enclothe, ornament 9 cultivate, embellish, make ready 10 attirement 11 habiliments ***a wound:*** 7 bandage ***designer:*** 4 Dior 12 Saint-Laurent ***extravagantly:*** 8 overdeck ***finically:*** 5 primp ***hair:*** 6 barber ***Hawaiian:*** 6 muumuu ***leather:*** 3 taw ***line:*** 3 horn ***mode of:*** 5 habit ***of the clergy:*** 5 cloth ***oriental:*** 9 cheongsam ***South Seas:*** 6 sarong ***with the beak:*** 5 preen ***with vulgarity:*** 7 bedizen
dress down 4 lash, rail 5 scold 6 berate 7 bawl out, tell off 10 tongue-lash
dresser 5 chest 6 bureau 10 chiffonier 11 flour bolter ***gaudy:*** 9 butterfly
dressing 5 sauce 6 catsup 7 bandage, catchup, ketchup 8 stuffing ***salad:*** 6 French 7 Italian, Russian 10 blue cheese
dressing room 8 vestiary ***church:*** 6 vestry
dressmaker 6 tailor 7 modiste 9 couturier 10 seamstress
dress up 3 tog 4 clad, mask, smug, tart 5 array, cloak, prank, preen, primp, slick, spiff 6 attire, clothe, tog out 7 apparel, deck out, doll out, smarten 8 disguise, enclothe, prettify, trick off, trick out 9 dissemble 10 camouflage 11 dissimulate
dressy 4 chic 6 formal, frilly, ornate 7 elegant, stylish 9 elaborate
Dreyfus' defender 4 Zola
drib 4 drop, weep 5 trill 6 gobbet 7 distill, droplet, globule, trickle
dribble 4 blow, drip, drop, weep 5 drool, trill, waste 6 drivel, slaver 7 consume, distill, fritter, slabber, slobber, trickle 8 pittance, salivate, squander 9 throw away 10 frivol away, trifle away 11 blunder away
driblet 4 drop 6 gobbet 7 globule 8 pittance
dried acorns 6 camata 8 camatina
dried brick 5 adobe
dried coconut meat 5 copra
dried grape 6 raisin
dried grass 3 hay
dried meat 5 jerky 7 charqui 8 pemmican

dried orchid tubers 5 salep
dried plum 5 prune
drift 3 bat, gad, run 4 bank, bent, cock, flow, flux, heap, hill, mass, mope, pile, ride, roam, rush, sail, skid, skim, tide, wash 5 amble, coast, creep, dance, float, flood, mosey, mound, range, shock, shoot, slant, slide, spate, stack, stray, tenor, trend 6 bummel, linger, motion, ramble, stream, stroll, upwaft, wander 7 current, leaning, maunder, meander, meaning, purport, pyramid, saunter 8 mountain, movement, penchant, sideslip, tendency 9 deviation, gallivant, inclining, substance 10 partiality, propensity 11 disposition, inclination, progression 12 predilection ***languidly:*** 5 swoon ***of a ship:*** 6 leeway ***unstratified:*** 4 till
drifter 3 bum, vag 4 hobo 5 rover, tramp 6 roamer 7 floater, rambler, vagrant 8 derelict, vagabond, wanderer 9 meanderer 10 street arab, temporizer 12 rolling stone
driftwood 6 jetsam 7 flotsam 8 wreckage
drill 4 bore, skid 5 prick, punch, snail 6 pierce 7 wildcat 8 exercise, practice, practise, puncture, rehearse, sideslip 9 penetrate, perforate 10 discipline ***command:*** 6 at ease 8 left face 9 about face, attention, right face
drink 3 ade, nip, sea, sip, tea 4 brew, deep, drag, grog, gulp, soak, swig, tope, toss 5 booze, draft, drain, julep, ocean, quaff, slosh, slurp, sup up, swill, toast 6 absorb, drench, guzzle, imbibe, jigger, liquid, liquor, pledge, potion, sup off, tank up, tipple 7 potable, spirits, swallow, swizzle 8 aperitif, beverage, libation, liquor up 9 aqua vitae ***after-dinner:*** 6 frappe ***British:*** 5 spree ***drugged:*** 6 mickey ***honey:*** 4 mead ***hot:*** 5 toddy 6 saloop ***liquor:*** 5 booze ***mixed:*** 3 nog 5 zombi 6 zombie ***mixer:*** 7 swirler ***noisily:*** 5 slurp ***of liquor:*** 4 dram, shot 5 snort 8 highball ***of the gods:*** 6 nectar ***Scottish:*** 6 waught ***soft:*** 7 soda pop ***tall:*** 4 fizz; (see also **beverage**)
drinkable 6 liquor 7 potable 8 beverage
drinkery 3 bar, pub 4 café 6 lounge, saloon, tavern 7 barroom, taproom
drinking 8 potation ***fountain:*** 7 bubbler ***horn:*** 6 rhyton ***spree:*** 5 binge 6 bender 8 carousal
drip 4 weep 5 trill 7 distill, dribble, spatter, spurtle, trickle 8 sprinkle
dripping 3 wet 5 runny, soppy 6 soaked, sodden, soused 7 soaking 8 drenched 9 saturated 11 wringing-wet
drippy 5 mushy, rainy, sappy, sobby, soupy 6 slushy, sobful 7 drizzly, maudlin, mawkish 11 sentimental
drive 2 go 3 dig, pep, ram, run, sic, tug 4 auto, bang, dash, élan, goad, herd, moil, move, prod, push, ride, road, roll, sink, snap, spin, spur, stab, taxi, toil, tool, trip, turn, urge 5 burst, chase, defer, force, getup, grave, guide, impel, labor, lunge, motor, pilot, pitch, pound, punch, shove, stamp, steer, stick, surge, tract, vigor, wheel, whirl 6 attack, coerce, compel, convey, exhort, hammer, plunge, propel, strain, strike, strive, thrust 7 actuate, impetus, impress, joyride, operate, produce 8 ambition, mobilize, momentum, navigate, protract, shepherd, vitality 9 chauffeur, excursion, impelling, urge along 10 charioteer, enterprise, get-up-and-go, initiative ***air:*** 4 blow ***away:*** 4 shoo 5 exile, stave 6 aroint ***back:*** 5 repel 6 defend 7 repulse ***close:*** 8 tailgate ***off:*** 6 dispel ***out:*** 8 exorcise
drivel 4 blow, bosh 5 drool, Greek, hooey, prate, waste 6 babble, gabble, jabber, slaver 7 blabber, blather, consume, dribble, fritter, prattle, rubbish, slabber, slobber, twaddle 8 cast away, claptrap, nonsense, pishposh, salivate, squander 9 gibberish, throw away 10 double-talk, flapdoodle, frivol away, trifle away 11 blunder away, jabberwocky 12 blatherskite
driveling 4 flat 5 inane, vapid 6 jejune 7 insipid, sapless 9 innocuous 10 namby-pamby, wishy-washy 12 milk-and-water
driver 5 cabby 6 cabbie, cabman, hackie, jarvey, mallet, vanman 7 autoist, hackman, spanker 8 motorist, muleteer, operator 9 chauffeur, dowitcher 10 taskmaster 11 tamping iron 12 automobilist ***fast:*** 4 jehu ***of an elephant:*** 6 mahout ***Roman:*** 10 charioteer ***truck:*** 8 teamster
driver's light 8 headlamp
driving 6 active, lively 7 dynamic 9 energetic 12 enterprising
drizzle 8 sprinkle
Dr. Jekyll and Mr.___ 4 Hyde
drogher 6 bearer, porter 7 carrier
drolerie see **drollery**
6 jester 7 comical, risible 8 comedian, farcical, funnyman, gelastic, humorist, humorous, jokester, quipster 9 burlesque, laughable, ludicrous, whimsical 10 puppet show, ridiculous
drollery 3 gag, yak 4 jape, jest, joke, quip 5 crack, humor 6 comedy 7 waggery 9 funniness, wisecrack, witticism, wittiness 10 comicality 11 comicalness 12 humorousness
drollness see **drollery**
dromedary 5 camel
drone 3 hum 4 buzz, idle, laze, loaf, loll 5 idler, strum, thrum 6 bumble, dawdle, loiter, lounge 7 bagpipe, male bee 8 parasite 9 bombinate 10 pedal point 12 diddle-daddle

dronish see drony
drony 4 lazy 7 work-shy 8 fainéant, indolent, slothful 9 easygoing, slowgoing
drool 4 guff, rave 5 prate, water 6 babble, bushwa, drivel, gabble, hot air, saliva, slaver 7 blabber, blather, dribble, enthuse, prattle, slabber, slobber, twaddle 8 claptrap, nonsense, rhapsody, salivate 10 balderdash, rhapsodize
droop 3 sag 4 fall, flag, hang, loll, sink, swag, wilt 5 couch, demit, lower, slump 6 dangle, go down, slouch, weaken 7 decline, depress, let down, subside, trollop 8 languish, pine away 11 deteriorate
droopy 3 bad 4 blue, down 6 gloomy 7 doleful 8 cast down, dejected, downcast 9 depressed 10 dispirited 11 downhearted
drop 3 die, dip, nip, sag, tot 4 down, dram, drib, dump, fall, fell, fire, iota, jolt, lose, pass, plop, quit, shot, skid, slip, slot, slug, thud, weep, wilt 5 cease, crumb, depth, floor, gutta, lapse, leave, lower, ounce, pitch, plonk, plump, plunk, scrub, shred, slide, snort, speck, spend, trill 6 bounce, cancel, cave in, crouch, curtsy, demise, depart, expire, fumble, give up, gobbet, go down, goutte, ground, lay low, peg out, plunge, pop off, reduce, resign, smitch, topple, tumble, unload, vanish 7 abandon, boot out, call off, decease, decline, deposit, descend, descent, dismiss, distill, dribble, driblet, fall off, forfeit, give out, globule, lose out, pendant, plummet, relapse, smidgen, snifter, spatter, succumb, trickle 8 bowl down, bowl over, break off, collapse, comedown, deepness, defecate, downturn, fall away, keel over, molecule, nose-dive, particle, pass away, toothful 9 backslide, break down, bring down, declivity, disappear, discharge, downslide, downswing, downtrend, knock down, prostrate, reduction, sacrifice, terminate, throw down 10 depository ***of liquid:*** 5 gutta ***saline:*** 4 tear
drop in 3 see 4 call 5 visit 6 come by, look up, stop by 8 come over
droplet 4 drib 6 gobbet 7 globule
drop off 3 sag 4 fall, slip 5 slide, slump 8 fall away
dropout's loss 7 diploma
dropsical 5 puffy, tumid, windy 6 turgid 7 swollen 8 inflated 9 flatulent, overblown, tumescent
dropsied see dropsical
dropsy 5 edema 7 hydrops 8 anasarca
dross 4 scum, slag 7 schlock 8 impurity
drossy 6 draffy, no-good 7 inutile, nothing 8 unworthy 9 worthless
drought 4 lack 6 dearth 8 scarcity, shortage
droughty 3 dry 4 arid, sere 7 bone-dry, thirsty 9 unwatered, waterless 12 moistureless
drove 4 herd, push 5 crowd, crush, flock, horde, press 6 chisel, squash, throng 9 multitude
drown 3 sop, wet 4 sink, soak, stun 5 douse, flood, souse, swamp, whelm 6 dazzle, deluge, drench, engulf 7 immerse, repress 8 inundate, overcome, overflow, submerge 9 knock over, overpower, overwhelm, prostrate, suffocate, tower over 10 extinguish
drowse 3 nod 4 doze 7 doze off, drop off, slumber
drowsy 4 dozy 6 sleepy, snoozy 7 languid, nodding 8 indolent, slumbery 9 lethargic, somnolent, soporific 10 languorous, slumberous 13 lackadaisical
drub 3 tap 4 beat, flay, lick, trim, whip 5 baste, paste, pound, score, slash, smear, stamp 6 batter, berate, buffet, pummel, scorch, thrash, wallop 7 belabor, blister, censure, scourge, shellac 8 lambaste, lash into 9 castigate, excoriate, overwhelm
drubbing 4 rout 6 defeat 7 beating, debacle, licking 9 overthrow, trouncing 10 defeasance 11 shellacking 12 vanquishment
drudge 4 grub, hack, moil, peon, plod, slog, toil, work 5 grind, labor, slave 6 slavey, toiler 7 grubber, slavery 8 bullwork, hireling, plugging 9 dray horse, mercenary, workhorse 10 donkeywork 11 galley slave
drudgery 4 moil, toil, work 5 grind, labor, sweat 7 travail 8 bullwork, plugging, taskwork 10 donkeywork
drudging 6 boring, tiring 7 irksome, tedious 8 boresome, tiresome 10 monotonous
drug 4 dope, lull 5 sulfa 6 downer, opiate, physic, poison, sulpha 7 generic, stupefy, tetanic 8 biologic, medicine, narcotic, nepenthe, pemoline, relaxant, roborant, sedative, thiazide 9 medicinal 10 medicament, medication 12 pharmaceutic ***addict:*** 6 junkie ***agent:*** 4 narc ***antibiotic:*** 8 neomycin ***calming:*** 8 sedative ***combining form:*** 8 pharmaco ***experience:*** 4 trip ***seller:*** 10 pharmacist ***sleep-inducing:*** 8 hypnotic 9 soporific
drugged 4 high 5 doped 6 stoned, zonked 8 hopped-up, turned on 9 spaced-out 10 tripped out
druggist 7 chemist 10 apothecary, pharmacist
drugstore 8 pharmacy 10 apothecary
druid 4 bard 6 priest 7 prophet 8 sorcerer ***sacred object:*** 3 oak 9 mistletoe
drum 4 cask 5 taber, tabla, tabor 6 atabal, barrel, enlist, gather, summon, tabour, tom-

tom, tymbal, tympan 7 canvass, solicit, taboret, taborin, tympani 8 cylinder, taborine, tabourer, tabouret, tympanum ***Arab:*** 6 atabal ***Indian:*** 8 mridanga ***large:*** 4 bass 6 timbal ***small:*** 5 bongo, tabor 6 tabret 7 taborin, timbrel ***string:*** 5 snare

drumfire 4 hail 5 salvo, storm 6 shower, volley 7 barrage 9 broadside, cannonade, fusillade 11 bombardment

drumhead 4 skin 7 summary

drummer 4 Rich (Buddy) 5 Krupa (Gene) 7 swagman 8 weakfish

drum up 6 invent 7 canvass, solicit 9 originate ***interest:*** 8 ballyhoo

drunk 3 fou, jag, sot 4 bust, lush, soak, tear, wino 5 binge, booze, souse, spree, tight, tipsy 6 bender, blotto, boozer, stinko, tiddly, zonked 7 guzzler, pie-eyed, squiffy, stewbum, tippler 8 squiffed 9 brannigan, inebriate 10 boozehound, inebriated 11 intoxicated

drunkard 3 sot 4 lush, soak, wino 5 rummy, stiff, toper 6 bibber, boozer, rumdum, soaker, sponge 7 drammer, fuddler, guzzler, swiller, tippler, tosspot 9 alcoholic, inebriate, swillbowl 10 boozehound 11 dipsomaniac

drunken 5 boozy, tight, tipsy 6 wobbly 7 pie-eyed 8 lurching, unsteady 10 inebriated 11 intoxicated

drupaceous fruit 4 plum 5 peach 6 almond, cherry

Drusilla ***brother:*** 8 Caligula ***father:*** 5 Herod 10 Germanicus ***husband:*** 5 Felix ***mother:*** 9 Agrippina ***sister:*** 8 Berenice 9 Agrippina

dry 3 set 4 acid, arid, bare, blot, brut, cake, dull, sear, sere, sour, tart 5 acerb, baked, dusty, empty, harsh, parch, plain, rough, slack, stoic, wizen 6 barren, harden, hoarse, modest, stingy, stolid, thirst, wither 7 acerbic, acetose, athirst, congeal, grating, insipid, jarring, parched, rasping, sapless, shrivel, sterile, tedious, thirsty 8 bromidic, discreet, droughty, indurate, rainless, scariose, scarious, solidify, strident, tearless, teetotal, weariful, withered 9 acidulous, anhydrate, anhydrous, apathetic, dehydrate, desiccate, exsiccate, impassive, juiceless, sugarless, thirsting, unadorned, unwatered, waterless, wearisome 10 dehydrated, desiccated, phlegmatic, stridulous 11 inelaborate, unemotional, ungarnished 12 matter-of-fact, moistureless, unproductive 13 unembellished, unembroidered, uninteresting, unpretentious ***biscuit:*** 7 cracker 8 hardtack ***combining form:*** 3 xer 4 xero 5 scler 6 dehydr, sclero 7 dehydro ***goods:*** 4 wear 6 linens, napery 8 clothing, textiles ***out:*** 5 sober 8 soberize ***period:*** 4 sere 6 drouth 7 drought ***wine:*** 3 sec 4 brut

dryasdust 4 arid, dull 5 dusty 6 pedant 7 insipid, prosaic, tedious 8 bromidic, pedantic, weariful 9 wearisome 10 uninspired 13 uninteresting

dry measure 4 peck, pint 5 quart 6 bushel

Dryope ***form:*** 5 lotus ***husband:*** 9 Andraemon ***sister:*** 4 Iole

dry up 4 wilt 5 mummy, wizen 6 welter, wither 7 mummify, shrivel 8 pipe down 9 desiccate, disappear 10 devitalize

dual 4 twin 5 duple 6 bifold, binary, double, duplex, paired 7 twofold

dualistic 5 duple 6 bifold, binary, double, duplex 7 twofold

dualize 4 dupe 6 double 9 duplicate

dub 4 call, flub, muff, name, term, trim 5 botch, fluff, style, title 6 bobble, boggle, bollix, double, duffer, goof up, thrust 7 baptize, blunder, entitle 8 christen, nickname, rerecord 9 designate 10 denominate

dubiety see **dubiosity**

dubiosity 5 doubt 6 wonder 7 concern 8 mistrust 9 addlement, confusion, suspicion 10 muddlement, skepticism 11 incertitude, uncertainty, uncertitude

dubious 4 moot, open 5 fishy 6 unsure 7 suspect, unclear 8 arguable, doubtful, hesitant, mootable, unlikely, untrusty 9 debatable, dubitable, equivocal, skeptical, trustless, uncertain, undecided 10 disputable, fly-by-night, improbable, unreliable 11 mistrustful, problematic, questioning, unpromising 12 questionable, undependable, undetermined 13 untrustworthy

dubitable 4 open 5 fishy 7 suspect 8 doubtful 9 ambiguous, uncertain, unsettled 10 borderline

duce 6 despot, tyrant 8 dictator 9 Mussolini, oppressor

duck 3 bob, bow, dip, shy 4 bend, bilk, dive, dunk, shun 5 avoid, dodge, douse, elude, evade, fence, parry, shirk, souse, stoop 6 double, escape, eschew, plunge 7 back out, immerse 8 sidestep, submerge, submerse 10 canvasback ***Asian:*** 5 Pekin 8 mandarin ***dabbling:*** 7 gadwall, mallard ***diving:*** 4 smew 7 pochard 9 merganser 10 bufflehead ***eggs:*** 5 pidan ***Eurasian:*** 4 smew ***European:*** 8 garganey, shelduck ***genus:*** 4 Anas ***group:*** 4 sord, team 5 brace, flock, skein 6 flight ***Hawaiian:*** 5 koloa ***hunter's screen:*** 5 blind ***male:*** 5 drake ***red-wattled:*** 7 Muscovy ***relating to:*** 7 anatine ***river:*** 4 teal 6 wigeon 7 pintail, widgeon ***scaup:*** 8 bluebill ***sea:*** 5 eider, scaup 6 scoter

duckbill 8 platypus 9 monotreme 10 mallangong

duck soup 3 pie 4 snap 5 cinch, setup

6 breeze, picnic 8 kid stuff, pushover 10 child's play
duckweed 6 lemnad
ducky 4 cute, fine 7 darling 8 pleasant, splendid 9 excellent
duct 4 pipe, tube 5 canal 6 course 7 channel, conduit 11 ink fountain, watercourse ***anatomical:*** 3 vas 4 vasa (plural) ***combining form:*** 3 vas 4 vasi, vaso
ductile 6 pliant, supple 7 plastic, pliable 8 flexible, moldable 9 adaptable, compliant, malleable, tractable ***metal:*** 4 wire
ductless gland see **endocrine gland**
ductus 4 fist, hand 6 script 10 penmanship 11 calligraphy, chirography, handwriting
dud 3 bad 4 bomb, bust, fake, flop 5 lemon, loser 7 failure 11 ineffective
dude 3 fop 4 buck 5 blood, dandy 7 coxcomb 8 macaroni 9 exquisite 10 tenderfoot 11 Beau Brummel, petit-maître 12 lounge lizard
dudgeon 4 fury, huff, miff, rage 5 pique, wrath 7 offense, umbrage 10 resentment
duds 4 togs 5 dress 6 attire, things 7 apparel, clothes, raiment 8 clothing 10 attirement 11 habiliments
due 4 debt, fair, good, just, owed 5 lumps, merit, owing, right 6 direct, earned, lawful, mature, reward, rights, unpaid 7 arrears, condign, deserts, exactly, merited, payable, payment, regular 8 adequate, deserved, directly, rightful, straight, suitable 9 arrearage, deserving, equitable, liability, requisite, scheduled, unsettled 10 recompense, satisfying, straightly, sufficient 11 appropriate, comeuppance, outstanding 12 compensation, indebtedness, satisfaction 13 rhadamanthine, undeviatingly
duel 4 buck 5 fight, repel 6 combat, oppose, resist 7 contest, dispute 8 conflict, traverse 9 withstand
duenna 8 chaperon 9 chaperone, governess
duet ***dancer's:*** 9 pas de deux
due to 4 over 7 through 9 because of
duff 5 slack 7 pudding 8 coal dust, fine coal
duffer 4 dolt, dope 5 dunce, idiot 6 dimwit 8 dumbbell, numskull 9 blockhead, ignoramus
dugout 4 abri 5 banca, canoe 7 piragua, pirogue
dukedom 5 duchy
dulcet 5 sweet 7 melodic, tuneful, winning, winsome 8 engaging, euphonic, luscious, pleasant, soothing 9 melodious 10 euphonious 11 mellisonant
dulcimer ***Chinese:*** 7 yang-kin ***Hungarian:*** 8 cimbalom ***Persian:*** 6 santir 7 santour
dull 3 bad, dim, dry, dun, mat 4 arid, blah, blue, blur, dead, down, drab, dumb, fade, flat, hard, hazy, numb, pale, poky, slow 5 befog, blear, blind, blunt, cloud, dense, dingy, dusty, heavy, inert, matte, muddy, murky, muted, prosy, thick 6 benumb, blurry, boring, cloudy, deaden, dreary, gloomy, leaden, obtund, obtuse, retard, simple, somber, stodgy, stupid, tiring, weaken 7 becloud, blunted, disedge, doltish, humdrum, insipid, irksome, louring, moronic, muffled, prosaic, stupefy, subfusc, tarnish, tedious, wash out 8 backward, banausic, bromidic, cast down, deadened, dejected, deluster, discolor, downcast, duncical, enfeeble, hebetate, hopeless, imbecile, lifeless, listless, lowering, monotone, nubilous, overcast, plodding, retarded, sluggish, weariful 9 bloodless, brainless, colorless, depressed, dim-witted, dryasdust, insensate, ponderous, unfeeling, wearisome 10 anesthetic, beef-witted, devitalize, dispirited, half-witted, impassible, indistinct, insensible, lackluster, lusterless, monotonous, numskulled, pedestrian, spiritless 11 blear-witted, desensitize, downhearted, insensitive, overclouded, thickheaded, thick-witted, unsharpened 12 disheartened, feebleminded, simpleminded 13 uninteresting ***combining form:*** 5 brady
dullard 5 dummy, dunce, idiot, moron 6 stupid 8 dumbbell 9 ignoramus, simpleton
dulled ***combining form:*** 5 ambly 6 amblyo
dullness 4 coma 5 sleep 6 apathy, stupor, torpor 7 languor, slumber 8 hebetude, lethargy, monotony 9 bluntness, denseness, lassitude, stupidity, torpidity 10 drowsiness
duly 8 properly 9 regularly 12 sufficiently
Dumas character 5 Athos 6 Aramis, Dantes 7 Camille, Porthos 9 D'Artagnan
dumb 3 mum 4 dull, mute 5 dense, quiet, thick 6 deaden, silent, stupid 7 doltish, foolish 8 duncical, reticent, taciturn, wordless 9 fatheaded, voiceless 10 numskulled, speechless, tongue-tied 11 blockheaded, thick-witted, tight-lipped 12 close-mouthed, close-tongued, inarticulate, inexpressive, tight-mouthed, unarticulate, unresponsive
dumbbell see **dullard**
dumbfound 5 amaze 6 boggle 7 astound, nonplus, stagger 8 astonish, surprise 11 flabbergast
dumbfounded 5 agape 6 aghast, amazed 7 shocked 8 confused, dismayed 10 bewildered 11 overwhelmed 13 thunderstruck
dummy 4 dolt, mock, sham 5 dunce, false, idiot, moron 6 effigy, ersatz, layout, stooge, stupid, yes-man 7 dullard 8 dullhead,

dumbbell, spurious **9** ignoramus, imitation, simpleton, simulated **10** artificial, fictitious, substitute
dump **3** sty **4** cast, drop, junk **5** chuck, depot, ditch, scrap **6** armory, pigpen, pigsty, plunge **7** arsenal, discard, eyesore **8** jettison, magazine, throw out **9** throw away
dumpling **5** blimp, fatty **8** quenelle **10** butterball
dumps **5** blues, gloom **7** sadness **9** dejection **10** depression, melancholy, the dismals **11** unhappiness **12** mournfulness
dumpy **5** squat, thick **6** chunky, slummy, squdgy, stocky, stubby **8** heavyset, thickset **9** shapeless **11** thick-bodied
dun **3** dim **4** dark, dusk, gnaw **5** annoy, brown, dusky, murky, worry **6** darken, gloomy, harass, needle, pester, plague, somber **7** bedevil, hagride, obscure **9** beleaguer, caddis fly, lightless **10** caliginous **12** grayish brown
Duncan's slayer **7** Macbeth
dunce **3** mug, oaf **4** boob, clod, dodo, dolt, dope, fool, goof, jerk, lunk, mutt, poke, simp **5** booby, chump, dummy, idiot, moron, ninny, noddy, prune **6** dimwit, donkey, duffer, nitwit, noodle, stupid, turnip, zombie **7** dullard, fathead, jackass, lackwit, muggins, pinhead, wantwit **8** bonehead, clodpate, clodpoll, dolthead, dullhead, dumbbell, imbecile, ironhead, knothead, lunkhead, numskull **9** birdbrain, blockhead, ignoramus, lamebrain, simpleton, thickhead **10** beetlehead, dunderhead, dunderpate, hammerhead, muddlehead, muttonhead, nincompoop, squarehead, thickskull, woodenhead **11** cabbagehead, chowderhead, chucklehead, knucklehead, pumpkin head **12** featherbrain, scatterbrain **13** featherweight
Dunciad author **4** Pope
duncical **4** dull, dumb **5** dense **6** stupid **7** doltish **8** blockish **9** pinheaded **10** numskulled **11** blockheaded, thickheaded
dunderhead see dunce
dunderpate see dunce
dundrearies **9** burnsides, sideburns **10** sideboards **11** muttonchops **12** sidewhiskers
dune **5** twine **8** sandbank ***area:*** **3** erg
dung **4** muck **6** manure, ordure **9** excrement ***beetle:*** **3** dor **6** scarab **9** tumblebug ***combining form:*** **4** copr, scat **5** copro, scato
dungaree fabric **5** denim
dungeon **4** cell, jail **5** vault **6** donjon, prison **9** black hole, oubliette
dunghill **6** midden
dungy **4** foul **5** black, dirty, nasty, soily **6** filthy, grubby, sordid **7** squalid, unclean
dunk **3** dip, sop **4** soak **5** douse, souse **7** immerse **8** saturate, submerge, submerse
dunlin **4** stib **9** sandpiper
duo **4** dyad, pair **5** brace **6** couple **7** doublet, twosome
dupe **3** con, job, kid, sap **4** butt, dust, fool, gull, hoax, mark, tool **5** catch, cheat, chump, cozen, patsy, slave, spoof, trick **6** befool, delude, double, outwit, pigeon, puppet, sucker **7** chicane, deceive, defraud, dualize, fall guy, gudgeon, mislead **8** flimflam, hoodwink **9** bamboozle, duplicate, victimize **11** double-cross, hornswoggle
dupery **5** cheat, fraud **7** chicane **9** chicanery, deception **10** dishonesty, hanky-panky **13** double-dealing, sharp practice
duple **4** dual **6** bifold, binary, double, duplex **7** twofold **9** dualistic
duplex see duple
duplicate **4** copy, mate, same, twin **5** ditto, equal, match **6** carbon, double, fellow **7** dualize, identic, imitate, replica **9** companion, facsimile, identical, reproduce **10** carbon copy, coordinate, equivalent, reciprocal, tantamount **11** counterpart, replication **12** reproduction ***prefix:*** **7** counter
duplicitous **6** shifty, sneaky **7** devious **8** guileful, indirect, sneaking **9** underhand **11** underhanded
duplicity **5** guile **6** deceit **7** cunning, perfidy **9** treachery **10** doubleness **12** dissemblance **13** dissimulation, double-dealing, faithlessness
durability **4** wear **11** lastingness
durable **5** stout **6** strong, sturdy **7** lasting **8** enduring **9** diuturnal, perduring, permanent, tenacious
duramen **9** heartwood
durance **9** restraint **11** confinement **12** imprisonment
duration **3** run **4** span, term, time **6** period **9** endurance **10** continuity **11** continuance, lastingness, persistence
duress **5** force **8** coercion, violence **10** compulsion, constraint
Durga see Devi
during **3** mid **4** amid, over **5** midst **10** throughout ***prefix:*** **2** di **3** dia **5** intra
durra **7** sorghum **10** guinea corn **12** Indian millet
durum **5** wheat
dusk **3** dim **4** dark **5** murky **6** darken, gloomy **7** evening, obscure **8** darkness, eventide, glooming, owl-light, twilight **9** lightless, nightfall, tenebrous **10** caliginous **12** semidarkness **13** unilluminated

dusky 3 dim 4 dark 5 black, bleak, drear, murky, swart 6 brunet, dismal, gloomy, opaque, swarth 7 joyless, obscure, swarthy 8 bistered, blackish, desolate, funereal, nubilous 9 ambiguous, cheerless, equivocal, lightless, sibylline, tenebrous 10 acheronion, caliginous, depressing 11 black-a-vised, dark-skinned, double-edged, double-faced 13 unilluminated *combining form:* 4 pheo 5 phaeo

dust 3 row 4 beat, drub, dupe, fool, gull, hoax, lick, sift, whip 5 run-in, trick 6 fracas, hassle, powder, thrash 7 chicane, confuse, dispute, quarrol, shellac 8 flimflam, hoodwink, lambaste, levigate, sprinkle 9 bamboozle, bickering, confusion, overwhelm, powdering 10 besprinkle, falling-out, sprinkling 11 altercation, disturbance, hornswoggle *combining form:* 4 coni 5 conio *Scottish:* 5 stour

dustbowl victim 4 Okie

dustup 3 row 5 run-in 6 fracas, hassle 7 dispute, quarrel 8 argument 9 bickering 10 falling-out 11 altercation

dusty 3 dim, dry 4 arid, dull 5 blowy, stale 6 barren, sordid, stormy 7 clouded, insipid, powdery, tedious 8 bromidic, weariful 9 dryasdust, miserable, wearisome, worthless 12 contemptible, unproductive, unsatisfying 13 uninteresting *Scottish:* 6 stoury

Dutch 7 trouble 8 hot water 9 Afrikaans *commune:* 3 Ede *housewife:* 4 frow *scholar:* 7 Erasmus *uncle:* 3 oom

dutiful 7 duteous 9 regardful 10 respectful 11 deferential

duty 3 job, tax, use 4 goal, levy, load, mark, must, need, onus, role, task 5 chare, chore, ought, stint 6 burden, charge, devoir, impost, object, office, target, tariff, weight 7 purpose, respect, service 8 business, function, province 9 committal, millstone, objective 10 assessment, assignment, commitment, deadweight, obligation

Duvalier's land 5 Haiti

dwarf 3 wee 4 runt, tiny 5 gnome, midge, pygmy, stunt, troll 6 midget, minify, peewee, teensy 7 manikin, minikin 8 suppress, Tom Thumb 9 miniature 10 diminutive, homunculus 11 hop-o'-my-thumb, lilliputian *combining form:* 3 nan 4 nann, nano 5 nanno *In Snow White:* 3 Doc 5 Dopey, Happy 6 Grumpy, Sleepy, Sneezy 7 Bashful *Scottish:* 7 blastie

dwarf elder 8 danewort, goutweed

dwarfish 4 tiny 6 midget 7 minikin 9 itsy-bitsy, itty-bitty, miniature 10 diminutive 11 lilliputian

dwell 3 lie, won 4 bide, live 5 abide, exist 6 inhere, reside 7 consist, hang out

dweller 5 liver 7 denizen, resider 8 habitant, occupant, resident 10 inhabitant *monastic:* 4 monk 5 friar 6 oblate *suffix:* 3 ite

dwelling 4 casa, home 5 abode, house 8 domicile 9 residence, residency 10 brownstone, commorancy, habitation *American Indian:* 4 tipi 5 hogan, tepee 6 pueblo, teepee, wigwam *clergyman's:* 5 manse 7 rectory 9 parsonage *crude:* 5 shack 6 shanty *Eskimo:* 4 iglu 5 igloo *Hindu:* 6 ashram, asrama 7 ashrama *Navaho:* 5 hogan

dwindle 3 ebb 4 fail, wane 5 abate, close, taper 6 lessen, reduce, shrink, weaken 7 decline, subside 8 decrease, diminish, taper off 9 attenuate, drain away, extenuate, fall short, waste away

dyad 3 duo 4 pair 5 brace 6 couple 7 doublet, twosome

dye 5 color, stain 6 reddle, ruddle 7 pigment 8 colorant, nigrosin, pyronine, tincture *blue:* 4 woad 6 cyanin, indigo 7 cyanine, indulin 8 indigoid, induline *for hair:* 5 henna *green:* 7 gallein *plant:* 4 chay, woad 5 chaya, sumac 6 madder *purple:* 6 orchil *red:* 5 eosin 6 eosine, kermes 7 crocein, cudbear, fuchsin, kermess, magenta 8 alizarin, anchusin, croceine, fuchsine, rhodamin, safranin 9 cochineal *reddish:* 5 henna 8 purpurin *reddish brown:* 6 orcein *violet:* 7 thionin 8 thionine *yellow:* 8 orpiment *yellowish red:* 7 achiote, annatto

dyed-in-the-wool 5 sworn 7 devoted, settled 9 confirmed, hard-shell 10 deep-rooted, deep-seated, entrenched, inveterate 13 bred-in-the-bone

dyeing process 5 batik

dyeleaves 8 inkberry 9 sweetleaf

dye red 6 ruddle

dyer's grape 8 pokeweed

dyer's mulberry 6 fustic

dyestuff see dye

dyewood 6 brasil, brazil, fustet, fustic

dying 8 expiring, moribund

dynamic 4 live 5 alive, lusty, vital 6 active 7 intense, running, working 8 forceful, forcible, vigorous 9 energetic, operative, strenuous 10 functional, red-blooded 11 functioning

dynamite 4 raze, ruin 7 destroy, shatter 8 decimate, demolish, destruct, dissolve 9 dismantle, explosive 10 annihilate *Inventor:* 5 Nobel

dynamo 6 peeler 7 hustler, rustler 8 go-getter, live wire 9 generator 11 self-starter

dysentery 4 flux 6 scours 8 diarrhea

dyslogistic 9 slighting 10 derogatory, detracting, pejorative 11 disparaging 12 depreciative, depreciatory

dyspathy 7 allergy 8 aversion
dyspepsia 7 pyrosis 9 gastritis, heartburn 11 indigestion
dyspeptic 6 morose 10 ill-humored, ill-natured, tempersome 11 bad-tempered, hot-tempered, ill-tempered
dysphoria 5 gloom, mopes 7 sadness 9 dejection 10 depression, melancholy 11 unhappiness 12 mournfulness, wretchedness
dysprosium ***symbol:*** 2 Dy
Dzhugashvili 6 Stalin

E

each 3 all, per 5 every 6 apiece 8 everyone, per caput 9 per capita
eager 3 hot 4 agog, avid, keen 5 itchy, ready 6 ardent, gung ho, heated, hungry, intent, pining, raring 7 anxious, athirst, craving, longing, restive, thirsty, wishful 8 appetent, covetous, desirous, on tiptoe, restless, yearning 9 ambitious, hankering, impatient 10 breathless, solicitous 11 acquisitive 12 enthusiastic
eagerness 4 zeal, zest, zing 5 ardor, gusto 6 fervor 7 avidity 8 alacrity, ambition, fervency, keenness 9 quickness 10 enthusiasm
eagle 4 hawk 9 accipiter ***combining form:*** 4 aeto 5 aetus ***nest:*** 4 aery 5 aerie, eyrie ***North American:*** 4 bald 6 golden 10 bald-headed ***sea:*** 3 ern 4 erne 6 osprey
eagle-eyed 7 lyncean 12 sharp-sighted
eagre 4 bore, flow, wave 5 flood
ear 4 heed, mark, note 6 notice, regard, remark 7 auricle 8 auricula 9 attention 10 observance 11 observation ***bone:*** 5 anvil, incus 6 hammer, stapes 7 malleus, stirrup ***canal:*** 5 scala ***combining form:*** 2 ot 3 aur, oto 4 auri, otic ***doctor:*** 9 otologist ***inner:*** 9 labyrinth ***middle:*** 8 tympanum ***outer:*** 5 pinna ***part:*** 4 drum, lobe 5 canal 6 tragus 7 cochlea ***relating to:*** 4 otic 5 aural 9 auricular ***science:*** 7 otology
earache 7 otalgia
eardrum 8 tympanum ***combining form:*** 6 tympan 7 tympano
___ Earhart 6 Amelia
earl 4 lord, peer 5 noble 8 nobleman 10 aristocrat
earlier 3 ere, yet 4 once 5 as yet, so far 6 before, sooner 7 already, thus far 8 formerly, hitherto, previous 9 erstwhile, preceding 10 beforehand, heretofore, previously ***combining form:*** 4 fore 6 proter 7 protero
earlier than ***prefix:*** 3 pre, pro
earliest 5 first, prime 6 maiden 7 initial, pioneer, primary 8 original, primeval, pristine ***combining form:*** 2 eo
earlike projection 3 lug
Earl of Avon 4 Eden
early 3 old 5 first, prior 6 primal, timely 7 ancient, betimes 8 germinal, original, oversoon, previous, primeval, pristine, untimely 9 preceding, premature, primative 10 antecedent, antiquated, beforehand, precocious, prevenient, primordial, seasonably 11 precipitant, prematurely ***combining form:*** 4 pale 5 palae, paleo 6 palaeo, palaio
earn 3 bag, get, net, win 4 gain, make, rate, reap 5 gross, merit, score 6 attain, come by, effect, obtain, secure 7 acquire, bring in, deserve, harvest, procure, realize, receive 8 draw down 9 knock down
earnest 4 busy, pawn, warm, zeal 5 grave, sober, staid, token 6 ardent, pledge, sedate, solemn, somber, warmth 7 serious, sincere, warrant, weighty, zealous 8 diligent, interest, pressing, security, sedulous 9 assiduous, attention, heartfelt 10 enthusiasm, intentness, no-nonsense, passionate, sobersided 11 industrious, perseverant, seriousness 12 enthusiastic, wholehearted
earnestly 4 down, hard 7 for real, soberly 8 actively, dingdong, solemnly 9 intensely, seriously, zealously 10 thoroughly 11 assiduously, intensively 12 exhaustively, thoughtfully 13 painstakingly
earnestness 7 gravity, resolve 8 decision, firmness, sobriety 10 absorption, intentness 11 engrossment, persistence, seriousness 12 deliberation, perseverance 13 concentration, determination
earnings 4 gain 5 lucre 6 income, living, profit, return 8 proceeds

ear shell 7 abalone
earshot 5 sound 7 hearing
earsplitting 4 loud 6 shrill 7 blaring, roaring 8 piercing 10 stentorian 11 full-mouthed, stentorious
earth 3 mud, orb 4 clay, clod, dirt, fill, land, loom, sand, soil, turf, vale 5 glebe, globe, humus, terra, world 6 cosmos, gravel, ground, planet, sphere 7 dry land, subsoil, terrain 8 creation, universe 9 macrocosm 10 terra firma ***combining form:*** 2 ge 3 geo 6 tellur 7 telluri, telluro ***core:*** 12 centrosphere ***god:*** 3 Geb, Keb, Seb 5 Dagan ***goddess:*** 2 Ge, Ki 4 Erda, Gaea 5 Ceres, Nintu 6 Kishar 7 Demeter, Nerthus ***relating to:*** 8 telluric 9 planetary, tellurian 11 terrestrial ***satellite:*** 4 moon ***science:*** 7 geology 9 geography ***Scottish:*** 4 yird 5 yirth
earthenware 4 delf 5 delft 7 biscuit, faience, pottery 8 crockery, majolica 9 stoneware 10 terra-cotta
earthlike 7 terrene 11 terrestrial
earthly 6 carnal, likely, mortal 7 mundane, terrene, worldly 8 material, physical, possible, probable, telluric, temporal 9 corporeal, potential, sublunary, tellurian 10 imaginable 11 conceivable, terrestrial, uncelestial, unspiritual
earthquake 5 seism, shake, shock 6 tremor 7 temblor 8 trembler, tremblor ***combining form:*** 5 seism 6 seismo ***measuring device:*** 11 seismograph, seismometer ***relating to:*** 7 seismic ***science:*** 10 seismology 11 seismometry
earthwork 4 bank, wall 7 bulwark, rampart 10 embankment 13 fortification
earthworm 7 annelid 9 brandling
earthy 3 low 5 dusty, gross, muddy, sandy 6 clayey 7 mundane, sensual, terrene, worldly 8 banausic, telluric, temporal 9 practical, pragmatic, realistic, sublunary, tellurian 10 hard-boiled, hardheaded 11 terrestrial, uncelestial, unfantastic 12 matter-of-fact 13 materialistic, unsentimental
earwax 7 cerumen
ease 3 aid, lax 4 bate, calm, dull, free, help, rest 5 allay, knock, loose, poise, relax, slack, speed 6 assist, better, deaden, loosen, relief, repose 7 abandon, assuage, calming, fluency, forward, further, improve, inertia, leisure, lighten, mollify, promote, relieve, slacken 8 calmness, deftness, diminish, dispatch, facility, idleness, mitigate, moderate, security, soothing, supinity, thriving 9 abundance, alleviate, disengage, expertise, inertness, passivity, readiness, reduction, untighten, well-being 10 adroitness, ameliorate, artfulness, cleverness, efficiency, expertness, facilitate, inactivity, mitigation, moderation, prosperity, relaxation, smoothness 11 alleviation, naturalness, spontaneity, tranquility 12 skillfulness, tranquillity
easel 5 frame, stand 7 support
easement 6 relief 9 allayment 10 mitigation 11 alleviation 13 mollification
ease off 3 ebb, lax 4 fall, wane 5 abate, let up, loose, relax, slack, unlax 6 loosen, relent, unbend, unwind 7 die away, die down, slacken, subside 8 loosen up, moderate 9 untighten
easily 4 well 6 freely, indeed, simply 7 handily, lightly, readily 8 facilely, smoothly 9 assuredly, certainly, decidedly, doubtless 10 absolutely, definitely, positively 11 competently, dexterously, doubtlessly, efficiently, undoubtedly 12 effortlessly 13 unequivocally ***combining form:*** 2 eu
east 4 Asia 6 Levant, Orient ***German:*** 3 ost
Easter 5 Pasch ***relating to:*** 7 paschal ***symbol:*** 3 egg 4 lamb 5 bunny 6 rabbit
eastern 8 oriental 9 Levantine ***countries:*** 6 Orient ***name:*** 3 Ali 4 Abou ***title:*** 3 sri
East Germany ***monetary unit:*** 7 ostmark
East Indies 9 Indonesia ***animal:*** 7 tarsier ***bark:*** 5 niepa ***bird:*** 4 baya 5 argus ***boatman:*** 6 serang ***civet:*** 6 musang ***fish:*** 5 dorab ***fruit:*** 6 durian, durion ***grass:*** 4 kans 5 glaga 6 raggee ***herb:*** 3 pia 4 chay, sola 6 sesame 7 roselle ***monkey:*** 7 hanuman 8 entelles ***musical instrument:*** 4 bina, vina ***plant:*** 2 da 4 bene, jute, sola, sunn 5 benne, kenaf 6 ambary, sesame 9 patchouli ***ship:*** 7 patamar 8 pattamar ***tree:*** 3 nim 4 dhak, neem, poon, toon 5 mahua, niepa, salai, simal, siris 6 banyan, deodar, illupi, sissoo 7 champac, hollong 8 mastwood 10 hursinghar ***warrior:*** 5 singh ***wood:*** 3 eng
easy 3 lax 4 calm, cozy, fast, glib, mild, soft, well 5 clear, comfy, cushy, light, loose, naive, plain, royal, suave 6 benign, facile, fluent, kindly, placid, poised, polite, secure, serene, simple, smooth, urbane, wanton 7 amiable, clement, courtly, cursive, evident, flowing, lenient, obvious, relaxed, well-off, whorish 8 apparent, clear-cut, composed, distinct, familiar, graceful, gullible, informal, manifest, merciful, obliging, pleasant, sociable, tolerant, tranquil, trusting, unchaste, well-to-do 9 collected, credulous, forgiving, indulgent, lethargic, possessed, well-fixed 10 charitable, diplomatic, effortless, fleeceable, forbearing, prosperous, successful, uninvolved, well-heeled 11 comfortable, complaisant, good-humored, good-natured, susceptible, sympathetic, unambitious 12 good-tempered 13 compassionate, mol-

lycoddling, self-possessed, uncomplicated, untroublesome

easygoing 3 lax 4 calm, lazy 5 drony 6 breezy, casual, dégagé, folksy, placid, poised, serene 7 affable, offhand, relaxed, unfussy, work-shy 8 carefree, careless, composed, fainéant, flexible, indolent, informal, moderate, slothful, tranquil 9 apathetic, collected, off-handed 10 unaffected, unreserved 11 indifferent, low-pressure, unambitious, unconcerned, uninhibited 12 devil-may-care, happy-go-lucky, self-composed 13 self-possessed, unconstrained

easy mark 3 sap 4 butt, dupe, fool, gull 5 chump 6 pigeon, sucker 7 fall guy 9 soft touch

easy street 8 thriving 9 abundance, well-being 10 prosperity

eat 3 sup 4 bite, chow, dine, gnaw, meal, pick, take, wolf 5 erode, feast, gorge, lunch, mouth, scoff, scour, snack, use up 6 devour, feed on, gobble, ingest, nibble 7 banquet, consume, corrode, exhaust, gorge on, swallow 8 dissolve, wear away 9 breakfast, decompose, partake of, polish off 10 gormandize, nibble away

eatable 6 edible 8 esculent 10 comestible

eater 8 consumer *combining form:* 4 phag, vora, vore 5 estes, phaga, phage 6 phagus

eating *combining form:* 4 phag 5 phago, phagy 6 phagia, vorous 7 phagous

eating place 4 café, mess 5 diner, grill 7 automat, beanery, dinette, tearoom 8 cookshop, messroom, snack bar 9 cafeteria, chophouse, lunchroom 10 coffee shop, restaurant 12 luncheonette

Ebal's father 6 Shobal

ebb 4 fade, fall, tide, wane 5 abate, let up 6 recede, relent 7 decline, die away, die down, ease off, retreat, slacken, subside 8 decrease, diminish, moderate 10 retrograde

Ebed's son 4 Gaal

Eber *father:* 6 Elpaal 7 Shashak *son:* 6 Joktan

Eblis 5 Satan *son:* 3 Tir 4 Awar 5 Dasim 8 Zalambur

ebon, ebony 3 jet 4 inky 5 black, jetty, raven, sable 9 pitch-dark 10 pitch-black 11 atramentous

éboulement 9 avalanche, landslide

ebullience 6 gaiety 7 ferment 8 buoyancy, vitality 9 agitation, animation 10 enthusiasm, excitement, exuberance, exuberancy, liveliness 12 exhilaration 13 effervescence

ebullient 5 brash 7 boiling 8 agitated 9 exuberant, vivacious 12 effervescent, high-spirited

eccentric 3 odd 4 case, coot, kook, quiz 5 crank, freak, kooky, queer, wacky, weird 6 oddity, quirky, zombie 7 bizarre, caution, curious, erratic, heretic, oddball, strange 8 bohemian, crackpot, maverick, original, peculiar, singular 9 anomalous, beeheaded, character, dissenter, fantastic, grotesque, irregular, off-center, quizzical, screwball, unnatural 10 off-balance, unbalanced, uncentered 11 exceptional 12 unconformist 13 exceptionable, idiosyncratic, nonconformist

eccentricity 5 quirk 6 oddity 10 aberration 11 peculiarity, strangeness 12 idiosyncrasy

ecclesiastic 5 clerk 6 cleric, divine, parson 8 clerical, minister, preacher, reverend 9 churchman, clergyman

ecclesiastical 5 papal 6 church 8 churchly, clerical, pastoral, priestly 9 apostolic, canonical, episcopal, prelatial, spiritual, synagogal 10 churchlike, pantheonic, pontifical, rabbinical, sacerdotal, templelike 11 churchmanly, ministerial, patriarchal, synagogical, theological 12 episcopalian, evangelistic, tabernacular

ecdysiast 6 peeler, teaser 8 stripper 10 striptease 11 stripteaser

echelon 3 row 4 file, line, rank, tier 5 queue 6 string 9 formation

echidna 5 bitis, snake, viper 8 anteater

Echidna *father:* 7 Phorcys 8 Chrysaor *mother:* 4 Ceto 10 Callirrhoe *offspring:* 5 Hydra 6 dragon, Orthus, Sphinx 7 Chimera 8 Cerberus, Chimaera

echinoderm 6 urchin 8 starfish

echo 4 ring 5 oread 6 repeat, reverb, second 7 imitate, iterate, reflect, resound, revoice 8 resonate, response 9 reiterate 10 reflection, repetition 11 reverberate 12 repercussion 13 reverberation

echoic 9 imitative 12 onomatopoeic 13 onomatopoetic

Echo's beloved 9 Narcissus

éclat 4 bang, dash, fame, pomp 5 kudos 6 luster, renown, repute 7 acclaim, display 8 applause, standing 9 celebrity, notoriety 10 brilliance, brilliancy, prominence, reputation 11 distinction, ostentation

eclectic 5 broad, fussy, mixed, picky 6 choosy, select, varied 7 derived, diverse, finicky, mingled 8 assorted, catholic, elective 9 inclusive, multiform, selective 10 discerning, fastidious, particular 11 diversified 12 multifarious 13 comprehensive, heterogeneous

eclipse 3 dim 4 murk 5 bedim, cloud, cover, excel, shade 6 darken, exceed, shadow 7 becloud, decline, obscure, surpass 8 downfall 9 adumbrate, overcloud 10 overshadow

eclogue 4 idyl, poem 5 idyll 7 bucolic
ecological 8 bionomic ***community:*** 5 biome ***succession:*** 7 subsere
ecology 7 bionomy 9 bionomics
economic 8 material 10 profitable ***doctrine:*** 12 laissez-faire ***system:*** 7 fascism 9 communism, socialism 10 capitalism 11 syndicalism 12 mercantilism
economical 4 mean 5 canny, chary, close, spare 6 frugal, saving, stingy 7 careful, miserly, prudent, sparing, thrifty 8 skimping 9 niggardly, penny-wise, penurious, provident, scrimping, stewardly 10 forehanded, unwasteful 12 cheeseparing 13 penny-pinching
economist ***American:*** 6 George, Veblen, Walker, Weaver 8 Friedman 9 Galbraith, Samuelson ***Canadian:*** 7 Leacock ***Dutch:*** 9 Tinbergen ***English:*** 4 Mill 5 Pigou 6 Keynes 7 Malthus, Ricardo ***French:*** 6 Turgot, Walras 7 Quesnay ***German:*** 5 Weber ***Scottish:*** 5 Smith ***Swedish:*** 6 Myrdal ***Swiss:*** 8 Sismondi
economize 4 save 5 skimp 6 scrimp 7 husband 8 conserve
economy 6 thrift 7 parcity 8 meanness, prudence, skimping 9 frugality, husbandry, parsimony, scrimping 10 discretion, providence, stinginess 11 carefulness, miserliness, thriftiness 13 niggardliness
ecru 5 beige
ecstasy 3 joy 5 bliss 6 frenzy, heaven 7 delight, elation, madness, rapture 8 euphoria, felicity, gladness, paradise, pleasure, rhapsody 9 beatitude, happiness, transport 10 exaltation, joyfulness 11 blessedness, delectation, enchantment, inspiration 12 blissfulness, exhilaration, intoxication 13 seventh heaven
Ecuador ***capital:*** 5 Quito ***monetary unit:*** 5 sucre
ecumenical 6 cosmic, global 7 general 8 catholic 9 inclusive, planetary, universal, worldwide 10 heaven-wide 11 all-covering 12 all-including, all-pervading, cosmopolitan 13 comprehensive
ecumenical council 4 Lyon 5 Trent 6 Nicene, Vienne 7 Ephesus, Lateran, Vatican 9 Chalcedon, Constance
eczema 6 tetter 9 malanders 10 mallenders
edacious 8 ravening, ravenous 9 voracious 10 gluttonous
eddo 4 root, taro
eddy 4 purl 5 gurge, surge, swirl, twirl, whirl, whorl 6 swoosh, vortex 8 backwash 9 backwater, maelstrom, whirlpool 10 back stream 11 back current, counterflow, counterflux ***combining form:*** 4 dino
edema 5 tumor 6 dropsy 8 anasarca, swelling
Eden 6 heaven, utopia 7 arcadia, elysium 8 paradise ***river:*** 5 Gihon 6 Pishon 8 Hiddekel 9 Euphrates
edentate 5 sloth 8 anteater 9 armadillo, toothless
Ederyn's father 4 Nudd
Edessa's king 5 Abgar
edge 3 cut, end, hem, lip, rim 4 bank, bite, brim, draw, hone, side, whet 5 bound, brink, bulge, ledge, picot, point, ridge, sidle, skirt, start, sting, verge 6 border, fringe, margin, nosing 7 acidity, outline, serrate, sharpen, vantage 8 acerbity, acridity, boundary, emborder, handicap, keenness, surround, thinness 9 acuteness, advantage, allowance, extremity, head start, knife-edge, perimeter, periphery, sharpness, threshold 10 causticity, shrillness, stringency 11 astringency, penetration 12 incisiveness
edged 5 sharp 7 crenate, cutting, vallate
edge in 4 worm 5 foist 9 insinuate 10 infiltrate
edging 3 hem 4 lace 5 braid 6 border, fringe, lacing
edgy 5 nervy, tense 6 touchy, uneasy 7 excited, restive, uptight 8 agitable, restless, skittery, skittish, volatile 9 alarmable, excitable, impatient, irritable, startlish 10 high-strung
edible 7 eatable 8 esculent 9 palatable 10 comestible ***root:*** 3 yam 4 beet, taro 6 carrot, radish, turnip 7 parsnip 8 rutabaga 11 sweet potato ***seed:*** 3 nut, pea 4 bean 6 peanut
edibles 4 food, grub 6 viands 7 nurture 8 victuals 9 provender 10 provisions 11 comestibles
edict 3 law 4 bull, fiat, rule 5 canon, order, ukase 6 decree, dictum, ruling 7 command, precept, statute 8 decretum 9 directive, manifesto, ordinance, prescript 10 instrument, regulation 12 proclamation 13 pronouncement ***papal:*** 4 bull 8 decretal
Edict of ____ 5 Milan 6 Nantes
edifice 4 pile 6 church 8 building, erection 9 structure
edify 5 teach 6 better, illume, uplift 7 educate, elevate, enhance, improve 8 illumine, instruct 9 elucidate, enlighten, irradiate 10 illuminate
edit 3 cut 4 omit 5 adapt, alter, amend, emend 6 delete, redact, refine, review, revise, reword, select 7 compile, correct, rewrite 8 assemble, copyread 9 rearrange
edition 4 copy 5 issue, print 7 reissue, version 8 printing, variorum 10 impression, reprinting 12 reproduction
editor 8 redactor 10 copyreader 11 proofreader
Edomite's ancestor 4 Esau
educate 4 rear 5 brief, teach, train

6 inform, school 7 explain, nurture 8 instruct 9 enlighten 10 discipline 12 indoctrinate
education 7 culture, science, tuition 8 breeding, coaching, guidance, learning, literacy, pedagogy, teaching, training, tutelage, tutorage, tutoring 9 erudition, knowledge, schooling, tutorship 11 instruction, learnedness, scholarship 13 enlightenment
educational 11 informative, informatory, instructive 13 informational, instructional *institution:* 6 school 7 academy, college 9 institute 10 university 12 conservatory
educator 5 tutor 7 teacher 9 professor 10 instructor *American:* 4 Mann 6 Conant 8 McGuffey *Italian:* 10 Montessori *Swiss:* 10 Pestalozzi
educe 4 drag, draw, gain, milk, pull 5 evoke, wrest, wring 6 derive, elicit, evince, evolve, extort, obtain, secure 7 distill, draw out, extract, procure 10 excogitate
eel 4 worm 5 moray, siren, snake 6 conger, murena 7 hagfish, lamprey, muraena, sniggle 8 wriggler 9 muraenoid *young:* 5 elver
eelboat 5 shuyt
eelpout 6 blenny, burbot 10 muttonfish
eely 6 slippy, wiggly 7 elusive, wriggly 8 slippery, slithery 9 wriggling
eerie 5 scary, weird 6 arcane, crawly, creepy, spooky 7 bizarre, strange, uncanny 9 fantastic, grotesque, unearthly 10 mysterious 11 frightening
efface 4 dele, x out 5 annul, erase 6 cancel, delete 7 blot out, destroy, exclude, expunge, rule out, wipe out 8 black out 9 eliminate, eradicate, extirpate 10 obliterate
effect 3 end 4 make 5 cause, enact, event, fruit, issue, yield 6 create, draw on, induce, invoke, render, result, secure, sequel, upshot 7 achieve, bring on, enforce, fulfill, outcome, perform, procure, produce, realize, turn out 8 bring off, carry out, causatum, conceive, generate, sequence 9 actualize, aftermath, corollary, implement, outgrowth, pursuance 10 accomplish, bring about, conclusion, denouement, end product 11 consequence, development, eventuality, precipitate 12 carry through, ramification, repercussion
effective 4 able 5 sound, valid 6 causal, cogent, direct, potent, useful 7 capable, dynamic, telling, virtual 8 adequate, virtuous 9 competent, efficient, operative 10 compelling, convincing 11 efficacious
effectiveness 5 force, point, power, punch, verve, vigor 7 cogency, potency 8 efficacy, strength, validity 9 validness 10 capability, efficiency 11 performance
effects 5 goods 6 things 8 chattels, movables 10 belongings 11 possessions
effectual 5 sound, valid 6 potent, strong, toothy, useful 8 decisive, powerful, virtuous, workable 9 achieving, efficient 10 conclusive, fulfilling 11 efficacious, influential, practicable 13 accomplishing, authoritative, determinative
effectuate 7 execute, fulfill 8 bring off, carry out 10 accomplish 12 carry through
effeminate 5 sappy, sissy 6 chichi, female, prissy, silken 7 epicene, foppish, unmanly 8 overnice, precious, womanish 9 pansified, sissified 10 old-maidish 12 Miss-Nancyish
effervescence 7 fizzing, foaming 8 bubbling, buoyancy 10 ebullience, ebullition, exuberance, exuberancy
effervescent 3 gay 4 airy 5 brash, jolly 6 bouncy, bubbly, lively 7 boiling, buoyant, elastic, excited, gleeful 8 animated, mirthful, volatile 9 ebullient, expansive, exuberant, hilarious, resilient, sparkling, sprightly, vivacious 12 high-spirited
effete 4 done, sere, soft, weak 5 all in, spent 6 barren, bleary, done in, used up 7 decayed, drained, far-gone, immoral, sterile, worn-out 8 consumed, decadent, decaying, depleted, fatigued, impotent, infecund, overripe 9 declining, dissolute, enfeebled, exhausted, infertile, washed-out 10 degenerate, unfruitful 11 debilitated
efficacious 6 active, potent, strong 8 forceful, forcible, powerful, puissant, virtuous 9 effective, effectual, efficient, operative 10 productive 11 influential
efficacy see **effectiveness**
efficiency see **effectiveness**
efficient 4 able 5 adept 6 expert, fitted 7 capable, skilled 8 masterly, skillful, virtuous 9 competent, effective, effectual, qualified 11 efficacious 12 businesslike
effigy 5 dummy, image 7 waxwork 8 likeness, portrait
effloresce 4 blow 5 bloom 6 flower 7 blossom, burgeon 8 outbloom
effluvium 4 odor 5 smell 6 efflux 7 exhaust 9 emanation 10 exhalation
efflux 4 flow 7 outflow 8 effusion 9 emanation
effort 3 job, try 4 task, toil, work 5 chore, essay, force, labor, might, nisus, pains, power, while 6 energy, strain 7 attempt, travail, trouble 8 endeavor, exertion, struggle, taskwork 9 puissance 11 application, elbow grease
effortful 4 hard 5 rough 6 uphill 7 arduous, labored, operose 8 toilsome 9 difficult, laborious, strenuous
effortless 4 easy 5 adept, light, ready, royal 6 expert, facile, fluent, simple,

smooth 7 cursive, flowing, running, skilled 8 masterly, skillful 10 proficient 13 untroublesome
effrontery 4 face, gall 5 brass, cheek, nerve 8 audacity, boldness, temerity 9 assurance, brashness, hardihood, impudence, insolence 10 brazenness, confidence 11 presumption 12 impertinence 13 self-assurance
effulgence 4 glow 5 blaze 8 radiance, splendor 10 brightness, brilliance, luminosity
effulgent 5 vivid 6 bright, lucent 7 beaming, lambent, radiant 8 glorious, luminous, splendid 9 brilliant 11 resplendent 12 incandescent
effuse 4 flow, gush, pour, shed 7 emanate, radiate
effusive 5 gushy 6 sloppy, slushy, smarmy 7 cloying, fulsome, gushing, profuse 8 slobbery 9 expansive, exuberant 10 outpouring, slobbering, unreserved 12 unrestrained 13 demonstrative, unconstrained
eft 4 newt 6 triton 10 salamander
egest 4 void 7 excrete 9 discharge
egg 3 ova (plural), sic 4 goad, ovum, prod, seed, spur, urge 5 drive, ovule, pique, prick, rally 6 arouse, excite, exhort, prompt, stir up 7 agitate 9 instigate, stimulate ***before maturation:*** 6 oocyte ***case:*** 5 shell 6 ovisac 7 ootheca ***combining form:*** 2 oo, ov 3 ovi, ovo ***dish:*** 6 omelet 8 omelette ***fertilized:*** 6 zygote 7 oosperm, oospore ***fish:*** 3 roe 6 caviar ***French:*** 4 oeuf ***part:*** 4 yelk, yolk 5 glair, shell, white 7 albumen, latebra 10 blastodisc ***product:*** 3 zoa (plural) 4 zoon ***white:*** 5 glair 7 albumen ***yolk:*** 6 yellow 8 vitellus
egghead 7 Brahmin 8 highbrow 10 double-dome 12 intellectual
eggplant 7 brinjal 8 brinjaul 9 aubergine
egg-shaped 4 ooid, oval 5 ovate, ovoid 6 ooidal 7 oviform
eggshell 8 cascaron
Egil's brother 6 Volund
Eglah ***husband:*** 5 David ***son:*** 7 Ithream
eglantine 7 dog rose 10 sweetbrier
Eglantine ***father:*** 5 Pepin ***husband:*** 9 Valentine
Eglon ***king:*** 5 Debir ***slayer:*** 4 Ehud
ego 4 self 6 vanity 7 conceit 10 self-esteem
egocentric 7 pompous, selfish, stuck-up 9 conceited 10 self-loving 11 self-seeking, self-serving 12 megalomaniac, narcissistic, self-absorbed, self-affected, self-centered, self-involved, vainglorious 13 individualist, self-conceited, self-concerned, self-indulgent
egoism 5 pride 6 vanity 7 conceit 9 self-glory, self-pride, vainglory 11 self-opinion 13 self-assurance
egomaniacal 7 selfish 11 self-serving 12 self-absorbed, self-centered, self-exalting, self-involved, vainglorious 13 self-concerned
egotism 5 pride 6 vanity 7 conceit 8 boasting, bragging, self-love, vainness, vaunting 9 arrogance, gasconade, gasconism, self-glory, self-pride, vainglory 10 narcissism, self-esteem 11 megalomania, self-opinion, superiority 12 boastfulness 13 conceitedness
egotistic 5 cocky, proud 7 selfish, stuck-up 8 boastful, inflated, puffed up 9 conceited 11 pretentious, self-serving 12 self-absorbed, self-centered, self-involved 13 self-concerned, self-satisfied
egregious 4 rank 5 gross, stark 6 arrant 7 blatant, capital, glaring, heinous 8 flagrant, infamous, outright, shocking 9 atrocious 10 deplorable, outrageous
egress 4 door, exit 5 issue 6 escape, exodus, outlet 7 doorway, exiting, opening, passage 8 emerging, offgoing 9 departure, emergence 10 setting-out, withdrawal
egression 4 exit 6 exodus 7 exiting 8 offgoing 9 departure 10 setting-out, withdrawal
Egypt ***capital:*** 5 Cairo ***monetary unit:*** 5 pound
Egyptian 4 Arab, Copt 6 Coptic 7 African, Arabian ***burial jar:*** 7 canopic ***Christian:*** 4 Copt ***cross:*** 4 ankh ***dam:*** 4 sudd 5 Aswan ***dancing girl:*** 4 alme 7 ghawazi (plural) 8 ghawazee (plural) ***dynasty:*** 5 Saite, Xoite 6 Hyksos, Tanite, Theban 7 Persian, Thinite 8 Memphite 9 Bubastite, Ethiopian 10 Diospolite
god:
chief: 6 Amen-Ra ***crocodile-headed:*** 5 Sebek ***falcon-headed:*** 4 Ment 5 Horus, Mentu 6 Sokari 7 Sokaris ***ibis-headed:*** 5 Thoth 6 Dhouti ***jackal-headed:*** 6 Anubis ***of chaos:*** 2 Nu ***of creation:*** 4 Ptah 5 Phtha ***of day:*** 5 Horus ***of earth:*** 3 Geb, Keb, Seb ***of evil:*** 3 Set 4 Seth 5 Sebek ***of life:*** 4 Amen, Amon 5 Ammon ***of magic:*** 5 Thoth 6 Dhouti ***of Memphis:*** 4 Ptah 5 Phtha 6 Sokari 7 Sokaris ***of pleasure:*** 3 Bes ***of procreation:*** 3 Min ***of the air:*** 3 Shu ***of the heavens:*** 5 Horus ***of the morning sun:*** 5 Horus 7 Khepera ***of the primeval flood:*** 2 Nu ***of the setting sun:*** 3 Tem, Tum 4 Atmu ***of the sun:*** 2 Ra, Re 6 Amen-Ra ***of Thebes:*** 4 Amen 6 Khensu, Khonsu ***of the underworld:*** 6 Osiris ***of war:*** 4 Ment 5 Mentu ***of wisdom:*** 5 Thoth 6 Dhouti ***ram-headed:*** 4 Amen, Amon 5 Ammon,

Khnum 6 Khnemu *snake:* 4 Apep 5 Apepi
goddess:
cat-headed: 4 Bast 5 Pakht *cow-headed:* 5 Athor 6 Hathor *lioness-headed:* 4 Bast 5 Pakht 6 Sekhet *of arms:* 4 Anta *of fertility:* 4 Isis *of love and mirth:* 5 Athor 6 Hathor *of moisture:* 6 Tefnut *of motherhood:* 4 Apet, Isis *of Thebes:* 3 Mut *of the dead:* 8 Nephthys *of the heavens:* 3 Nut *of truth and justice:* 4 Maat *queen of the gods:* 4 Sati *vulture-headed:* 3 Mut 7 Nekhebt 8 Nekhebet
king: (see **king** entry)
language: 6 Arabic, Coptic *measure:* 3 apt, dra, hen, pik, rob 4 draa, roub 5 ardab, ardeb, cubit, farde, keleh, kilah, sahme 6 artaba, aurure, feddan, keddah, robbah 7 choryos, daribah, malouah, roubouh, toumnah 8 kassabah, kharouba 10 dira baladi *month:* 4 Apap, Tybi 5 Payni, Thoth 6 Choiak, Hathor, Mechir, Mesore, Paophi 7 Pachons 9 Phamenoth, Pharmuthi *native:* 4 Arab, Copt 5 Nilot *president:* 5 Sadat 6 Nasser 7 Mubarak *queen:* 9 Cleopatra, Nefertiti *sacred bird:* 4 ibis *season:* 4 Ahet, Pert 5 Shemu *skink:* 4 adda *snake symbol:* 6 uraeus *solar disk:* 4 Aten *soul:* 2 ba, ka 3 akh *sultan:* 7 Saladin *talisman:* 6 scarab *underworld:* 4 Aaru, Duat 6 Amenti *weight:* 3 kat, oka, oke 4 heml, okia, rotl 5 artal, artel, deben, kerat, okieh, uckia 6 hamlah, kantar 7 quintal *wind:* 7 chamsin, khamsin, sirocco 8 khamseen

Ehud's victim 5 Eglon

eider 4 down, duck 8 shoreyer

eidetic 5 vivid 8 lifelike

eidolon 4 icon 5 ghost, ideal, image 7 phantom, specter 8 exemplar, phantasm

eight *combining form:* 3 oct 4 octa, octo *group of:* 5 octad, octet 6 octave, ogdoad 7 octette 8 octuplet

eighth note 6 quaver

Einstein 6 genius *birthplace:* 3 Ulm

einsteinium *symbol:* 2 Es

Eire 4 Erin 5 Ierne 7 Ireland 8 Hibernia 9 Innisfail *capital:* 6 Dublin *monetary unit:* 5 pound

ejaculate 4 blat, bolt, yell 5 eject, shout 6 cry out 7 exclaim 8 blurt out 10 vociferate

ejaculation see **exclamation**

eject 3 out 4 boot, bump, fire, oust, rout, sack, shed, spew 5 belch, chase, chuck, debar, eruct, erupt, evict, expel, spout, spurn 6 banish, disbar, irrupt, run off, squirt 7 boot out, discard, dismiss, exclude, extrude, kick out, rule out, shut out, sputter 8 disgorge, displace, drive off, throw out 9 discharge, ejaculate, eliminate, repudiate 10 dispossess

eke 4 fill 7 squeeze, stretch 10 supplement

elaborate 4 busy 5 fancy 6 daedal, dressy, evolve, expand, knotty, ornate, unfold 7 amplify, clarify, comment, complex, develop, discuss, elegant, enlarge, explain, expound, gordian 8 detailed, involved, overdone 9 Byzantine, decorated, interpret, intricate 10 overworked 11 complicated, embellished, overwrought, painstaking 12 labyrinthine

Elah *father:* 4 Uzzi 5 Caleb 6 Baasha *slayer:* 5 Zimri *son:* 6 Hoshea

Elaine *father:* 6 Pelles *lover:* 8 Lancelot 9 Launcelot *son:* 7 Galahad

Elam *capital:* 4 Susa 7 Shushan *father:* 4 Shem *king:* 12 Chedorlaomer

élan 3 vim 4 brio, dash, life, zeal, zest, zing 5 ardor, gusto, oomph, verve, vigor 6 esprit, spirit 7 impetus, potency 9 animation, eagerness 10 enthusiasm

élan vital 4 soul 5 anima 6 animus, pneuma, psyche, spirit

elapse 2 go 4 flow, pass, slip 5 glide, slide 6 expire, run out 8 pass away

Elasah's father 6 Pashur 7 Shaphan

elastic 4 airy 5 lithe 6 bouncy, garter, limber, lively, pliant, rubber, supple, whippy 7 buoyant, ductile, pliable, rubbery, soaring, springy, stretch 8 animated, flexible, moldable, spirited, stretchy, volatile 9 adaptable, ebullient, expansive, malleable, resilient, sprightly, vivacious 10 mettlesome, rubberlike 11 stretchable

elate 4 buoy 5 cheer, exalt, flush, set up 6 excite, uplift 7 cheer up, commove, delight, gladden, gratify, inspire, overjoy 8 brighten, inspirit, spirit up 9 encourage

elated 4 glad 5 happy 6 jovial 7 excited, exulted 8 ecstatic, euphoric, exultant, gladsome, jubilant, turned-on 9 overjoyed 10 enraptured 11 exhilarated, intoxicated

elater 6 beetle 8 skipjack 11 click beetle

Elatha's son 4 Bres

elation 3 joy 4 glee 7 rapture 8 buoyancy, euphoria 9 happiness, transport 10 exaltation, excitement 12 exhilaration, intoxication

Elbe tributary 4 Eger, Iser

elbow 4 push 5 ancon, joint, nudge, press, shove 6 hustle, jostle 8 bulldoze *relating to:* 7 anconal

El Camino ___ 4 Real

elder 5 prior 6 senior 7 ancient, oldster 8 brass hat, higher-up, old-timer, superior 9 presbyter 10 golden-ager 13 senior citizen *French:* 4 aîné 5 aînée

elderliness 3 age 5 years 6 old age 8 caducity 10 senescence 11 senectitude

elderly 3 old 4 aged, gray 5 aging, olden 6 senile 7 ancient 9 declining
eldorado 4 mine 7 bonanza 8 Golconda, gold mine, treasury 13 treasure-house, treasure trove
eldritch 5 eerie, weird 7 uncanny
Eleanor's husband 7 Henry II
Eleazar ***brother:*** 5 Abihu, Nadab ***father:*** 4 Dodo 5 Aaron 6 Parosh 8 Abinadab, Phinehas ***son:*** 8 Phinehas
elect 3 opt 4 cull, like, mark, name, pick, rare, take, vote, will, wish 5 admit, co-opt, judge, saved 6 accept, ballot, choice, choose, chosen, decide, optate, opt for, picked, please, prefer, settle, single, vote in 7 appoint, receive, resolve 8 conclude, destined, nominate, ordained, redeemed 9 delivered, designate, determine, exclusive, single out 10 designated, handpicked, singled out
election 6 choice 7 primary 9 balloting 10 preference 11 alternative
electioneer 5 stump 8 campaign, politick
elective 6 chosen 8 optional 9 voluntary 13 discretionary, nonobligatory
Electra ***brother:*** 7 Orestes ***father:*** 5 Atlas 7 Oceanus 9 Agamemnon ***husband:*** 7 Pylades, Thaumas ***mother:*** 6 Tethys 7 Pleione 12 Clytemnestra ***sister:*** 4 Styx 9 Iphigenia ***son:*** 6 Iasion 8 Dardanus
electric ***appliance:*** 3 fan 4 iron, oven 5 clock, drier, mixer, range, stove 6 washer 7 blender, freezer, toaster 12 refrigerator ***coil:*** 5 tesla 8 solenoid ***device:*** 4 coil, fuse, plug 6 dynamo, magnet, switch 7 battery 8 resistor, rheostat, varistor 9 amplifier, capacitor, condenser, generator, rheotrope 11 transformer ***generator:*** 6 dynamo ***particle:*** 3 ion 8 thermion ***resistance:*** 6 ohmage ***unit:*** 3 amp, ohm, rel 4 volt, watt 5 farad, henry, joule 6 abvolt, ampere 7 coulomb, faraday 8 kilovolt, kilowatt
electric current 2 AC, DC ***combining form:*** 5 potam 6 potamo ***kind:*** 6 direct 11 alternating ***power:*** 7 wattage ***strength:*** 8 amperage
electricity 5 juice, spark 7 current 8 voltaism 9 galvanism, lightning 10 enthusiasm, excitement ***kind:*** 6 static 7 current
electrify 3 jar 4 send, stun 6 excite, thrill 7 enthuse, provoke, stagger, startle
electrode 6 dynode ***negative:*** 7 cathode ***positive:*** 5 anode
electron 3 ion 7 polaron 8 negatron ***stream:*** 10 cathode ray ***tube:*** 6 triode 7 tetrode 8 dynatron, klystron
Electryon ***brother:*** 6 Mestor ***daughter:*** 7 Alcmene ***father:*** 7 Perseus ***mother:*** 9 Andromeda ***wife:*** 5 Anaxo
eleemosynary 6 humane 7 liberal 8 generous 10 altruistic, beneficent, benevolent, charitable, munificent, openhanded 12 humanitarian 13 philanthropic
elegance 4 chic, pomp, tone 5 charm, grace, style, taste 6 beauty, luxury, polish 7 culture, dignity 8 chicness, lushness, poshness, richness, splendor 10 ornateness, refinement 11 cultivation 12 magnificence, tastefulness 13 sumptuousness
elegant 4 chic, fine, posh, rare 5 grand, noble, swank 6 august, choice, classy, dainty, lovely, select, swanky, urbane 7 courtly, genteel, opulent, refined, stately 8 cultured, delicate, finished, graceful, handsome, majestic, polished, superior, tasteful 9 beautiful, exquisite, luxurious, recherché, sumptuous 10 cultivated
elegy 4 poem, song 5 dirge 6 lament, monody 7 epicede 9 epicedium ***Hebrew:*** 5 kinah
Elektra composer 7 Strauss
element 4 item, part 5 basic, facet, metal, piece, point, thing 6 aspect, detail, factor, member, sector 7 article, feature, portion, section 8 division, particle, rudiment 9 component, essential, principle 10 ingredient, particular 11 constituent, fundamental 13 part and parcel ***chemical:*** 3 tin 4 gold, iron, lead, neon, zinc 5 argon, boron, radon, xenon 6 barium, carbon, cerium, cesium, cobalt, copper, curium, erbium, helium, indium, iodine, nickel, osmium, oxygen, radium, silver, sodium 7 arsenic, bismuth, bromine, cadmium, calcium, fermium, gallium, hafnium, holmium, iridium, krypton, lithium, mercury, niobium, rhenium, rhodium, silicon, sulphur, terbium, thorium, thulium, uranium, yttrium 8 actinium, aluminum, antimony, astatine, chlorine, chromium, europium, fluorine, hydrogen, illinium, lutecium, masurium, nitrogen, nobelium, platinum, polonium, rubidium, samarium, scandium, selenium, tantalum, thallium, titanium, tungsten, vanadium 9 americium, berkelium, beryllium, columbium, germanium, lanthanum, magnesium, manganese, neodymium, neptunium, palladium, plutonium, potassium, ruthenium, strontium, tellurium, virginium, ytterbium, zirconium 10 dysprosium, gadolinium, lawrencium, molybdenum 11 californium, einsteinium, mendelevium, phosphorous 12 praseodymium 13 protoactinium ***hypothetical:*** 8 coronium
elemental 4 pure 5 basal, basic, crude, prime 6 inborn, innate, primal, simple 7 connate, primary, radical 8 inherent, intimate, simplest 9 beginning, essential, ingrained, intrinsic, primitive 10 deep-

seated, primordial, substratal, underlying 14 constitutional
elementary 4 easy 5 basal, basic 6 simple 8 simplest, unsubtle 9 beginning, essential, prefatory, primitive 10 rudimental, substratal, underlying 11 fundamental, preliminary 12 introductory
elemi 5 animé, resin 9 oleoresin
elephant 5 hathi 6 muckna, tusker 9 pachyderm ***boy:*** 4 Sabu ***driver:*** 6 mahout ***enclosure:*** 5 kraal 6 keddah ***extinct:*** 7 mammoth 8 mastodon ***female:*** 3 cow ***goad:*** 5 ankus 7 ankusha ***group:*** 4 herd ***keeper:*** 6 mahout ***male:*** 4 bull ***maverick:*** 5 rogue ***nose:*** 5 trunk 9 proboscis ***seat:*** 6 howdah ***sound:*** 4 barr 6 bellow 7 trumpet ***tooth:*** 4 tusk ***tusk:*** 5 ivory ***young:*** 4 calf
elephant-headed god 6 Ganesa 7 Ganesha
elephantine 4 huge 6 clumsy 7 awkward, mammoth 8 colossal, enormous, gigantic 9 graceless, maladroit, monstrous, ponderous 10 behemothic, gargantuan, mastodonic, prodigious, ungraceful, uninspired 11 heavy-footed, heavy-handed
elevate 4 lift, rear, rise 5 boost, elate, ensky, erect, exalt, hoist, raise 6 pick up, prefer, take up, uphold, uplift, uprear 7 advance, enhance, glorify, promote, upgrade, upraise 8 heighten 10 exhilarate
elevated 4 high 5 grand, great, lofty, moral, noble 6 aerial, formal, lifted, raised, superb 7 ethical, exalted, stately, sublime, upright, uprisen 8 eloquent, majestic, towering, upheaved, uplifted, upraised, virtuous 9 dignified, grandiose, high-flown, honorable, righteous 10 high-minded, upstanding 13 grandiloquent
elevation 4 hill, rise 5 boost, mount, raise 6 ascent, height 7 advance, raising 8 altitude, highness, mountain 9 acclivity, promotion, upgrading 10 apotheosis, preference, preferment 11 advancement, ennoblement ***indication:*** 9 bench mark
elevator 4 cage, lift, silo 5 hoist 6 lifter, raiser 7 hoister ***maker:*** 4 Otis
eleven ***combining form:*** 5 undec 6 hendec 7 hendeca
elf 3 fay 4 ouph, peri, pixy 5 fairy, nisse, ouphe, pixie 6 goblin, sprite 7 brownie, gremlin 10 leprechaun
elfin 5 child 6 urchin
elfish see **elvish**
Elgin ____ 7 marbles
Eli 4 Yale ***son:*** 6 Hophni 8 Phinehas ***successor:*** 6 Ahitub
Eli ____ 7 Whitney
Eliab ***brother:*** 5 David ***daughter:*** 7 Abihail ***father:*** 5 Helon, Pallu ***son:*** 6 Abiram, Dathan
Eliada ***father:*** 5 David ***son:*** 5 Rezon
Eliakim's father 6 Josiah 7 Hilkiah
Eliam's daughter 9 Bathsheba
Eliashib's father 4 Bani 5 Zattu 8 Elioenai
Eliathah's father 5 Heman
elicit 4 draw, milk 5 bring, cause, educe, evoke, fetch 6 derive, evince, extort 7 extract, provoke 8 bring out 9 call forth
elide 4 fail, omit, pass, skip 6 forget, ignore, slight 7 neglect 8 discount, overlook, suppress 9 disregard
Eliel's father 6 Hebron, Shimhi 7 Shashak
Eliezer's father 5 Harim, Moses 6 Zichri 7 Dodovah
eligible 3 fit 6 fitted, likely, nubile, seemly, suited, worthy 7 capable 8 suitable 9 desirable, qualified, visitable 10 acceptable, preferable 12 marriageable
Elihu ____ 4 Root, Yale
Elijah 5 Elias 7 prophet 8 Tishbite ***father:*** 5 Harim 7 Jeroham
Elimelech's wife 5 Naomi
eliminate 3 bar 4 bate, oust 5 debar, eject, erase, evict, expel, purge 6 delete, except, remove 7 dismiss, exclude, expunge, obviate, rule out, shut out, suspend, take out 8 count out 9 clear away, freeze out, liquidate
Eliot novel 6 Romola 8 Adam Bede 11 Middlemarch, Silas Marner 14 Mill on the Floss
Eliphal's father 2 Ur
Eliphaz ***father:*** 4 Esau ***mother:*** 4 Adah ***son:*** 5 Teman
Eliphelet's father 5 David 6 Hashum 7 Ahasbai 8 Adonikam
eliquate 4 melt 5 smelt
Elisabeth ***husband:*** 9 Zacharias ***son:*** 4 John (the Baptist)
Elisha ***father:*** 7 Shaphat ***servant:*** 6 Gehazi
Elishah's father 5 Javan
Elishama's father 5 David 7 Ammihud
Elisheba ***brother:*** 7 Nahshon ***father:*** 9 Amminadab ***husband:*** 5 Aaron ***son:*** 5 Abihu, Nadab 7 Eleazar, Ithamar
Elishua's father 5 David
Elissa see **Dido**
elite 3 top 4 best, pick 5 cream, elect, pride, prime, prize 6 choice, flower, gentry, jet set, select 7 aristoi, quality, society 8 optimacy, smart set 9 gentility 10 upper class, upper crust 11 aristocracy
Eliud ***father:*** 5 Achim ***son:*** 7 Eleazar
elixir 4 balm, cure 6 potion 7 arcanum, cure-all, nostrum, panacea, therapy 10 catholicon 11 therapeutic
Elizaphan see **Elzaphan**

elk 4 deer, losh 5 moose 6 sambar, sambur, wapiti
Elkanah *brother:* 5 Assir 8 Abiasaph *father:* 4 Joel 5 Korah 6 Mahath 7 Jeroham *son:* 6 Samuel *wife:* 6 Hannah 8 Peninnah
ell 3 arm 4 wing 5 annex, block 8 addition 9 extension
ellipse 4 oval 5 curve
elliptical 5 brief, ovate, short 7 concise, cryptic, summary 9 condensed, enigmatic
Elmire's husband 5 Orgon
elocution 7 oratory 8 rhetoric 11 speechcraft
elongate 4 draw 6 extend, string 7 draw out, lengthy, spin out, stretch 8 extended, lengthen, protract, wiredraw 10 lengthened
elongation 9 extension 10 production 11 lengthening, protraction
Elon's father 7 Zebulun
elope 4 flee 6 escape 7 run away
eloquence 5 force, power, vigor 6 fervor, spirit 7 passion 9 facundity 10 expression 12 expressivity, forcefulness
eloquent 4 glib, high, rich 5 lofty, vocal 6 ardent, facund, fervid, fluent, moving, potent 7 fervent, graphic, telling, voluble 8 elevated, forceful, poignant, powerful, pregnant, touching 9 affecting, revealing 10 articulate, expressive, impressive, indicative, meaningful, passionate, persuasive, suggestive 11 impassioned, sententious, significant 12 smooth-spoken 13 silver-tongued
Elpaal's father 9 Shaharaim
Elpalet's father 5 David
else 2 or 3 new 4 more 5 added, fresh, other 7 another, besides, farther, further 9 otherwise 10 additional
elucidate 5 clear, prove 7 clarify, clear up, explain 8 annotate, spell out 9 enlighten, exemplify, interpret 10 illuminate, illustrate
elude 3 fly, shy 4 bilk, duck, flee, foil, shun 5 avoid, dodge, evade 6 baffle, double, escape, eschew, outwit, thwart 9 frustrate 10 circumvate
elusion 6 escape 8 escaping, eschewal, shunning 9 avoidance, runaround
elusive 6 subtle, tricky 7 evasive, phantom 8 baffling, fleeting, fugitive, slippery 10 evanescent, intangible, mysterious 12 imponderable 13 insubstantial
elusory 5 vague 7 evasive 8 nebulous 10 intangible
elvish 5 antic 6 frisky, impish 7 coltish, larkish, playful, puckish, roguish 8 prankish, spiteful 9 kittenish 11 mischievous
elysium 4 Eden, Zion 5 bliss 6 Canaan, heaven 7 nirvana 8 empyrean, paradise 10 Civitas Dei 12 New Jerusalem
elytron 4 wing 5 scale, shard
Elzaphan's father 6 Uzziel 7 Parnach
emaciated 4 bony, lean 5 gaunt 6 skinny, wasted 7 scrawny, starved, wizened 8 skeletal, underfed 10 cadaverous
emaciation 5 tabes 7 atrophy 8 marasmus 10 starvation 11 attenuation
emanate 4 emit, flow, rise, stem 5 arise, birth, exude, issue 6 spring 7 proceed 9 originate 10 derive from
emanation 4 aura, flow 6 efflux 7 outcome 9 effluence 11 consequence
emancipate 4 free 5 loose 6 loosen, unbind 7 manumit, release, unchain 8 liberate, unfetter 9 discharge, unshackle 11 enfranchise
emancipation 7 freedom, release 10 liberation 11 deliverance
emancipator 5 Moses 7 Lincoln 9 deliverer
emasculate 3 wan 4 geld, weak 5 unman 6 soften, weaken 7 unnerve 8 boneless, castrate, enervate, impotent, unstring 9 forceless, spineless 10 devitalize, inadequate 11 ineffective, ineffectual
embalm 5 mummy 7 mummify, perfume 8 preserve
embankment 4 bund, dike, quay 5 levee, mound 7 parados 9 banquette
embargo 5 edict, order 8 blockade, stoppage 10 impediment 11 prohibition
embark 4 open 5 begin, board, enter, set to, start 6 engage, enlist, get off, take up, tee off 7 jump off 8 commence
embarrass 3 vex 4 faze 5 abash, queer, upset 6 bother, flurry, hamper, impede, rattle 7 agitate, chagrin, confuse, flummox, fluster, nonplus, perturb 8 confound, distress 9 discomfit 10 discompose, disconcert
embarrassing 7 awkward 12 discommoding, incommodious, inconvenient 13 discommodious
embarrassment 5 shame 6 strain, unease 7 chagrin 8 distress, vexation 9 abashment, agitation, confusion 10 constraint, difficulty, discomfort, uneasiness 11 humiliation 12 discomfiture, discomposure, perturbation 13 disconcertion, mortification
embassy 5 envoy 8 legation 10 ambassador
embattle 7 fortify, prepare 9 crenelate 10 crenellate
embay 6 shut in 7 shelter 8 encircle, surround
embed 3 fix, set 4 root 5 infix, lodge 7 ingrain 8 entrench
embellish 3 pad 4 deck, gild, trim 5 adorn, array, color, dress, fudge, prank 6 bedeck, blazon, emboss, enrich 7 apparel, dress up, garnish, magnify

8 beautify, decorate, ornament 9 embroider 10 exaggerate
embellishment 7 garnish, melisma, mordent 8 coloring, ornament 9 fioritura, floridity, hyperbole 11 ostentation 12 embroidering, exaggeration 13 ornamentation
ember 3 ash 4 coal 6 cinder
embezzle 4 loot 5 steal 6 pilfer, thieve 8 peculate
embitter 4 sour 7 envenom 8 acerbate 9 acidulate 10 exacerbate
emblaze 5 adorn 6 kindle 9 embellish 10 illuminate
emblazon 4 deck, laud 5 adorn, extol 7 display, glorify 8 inscribe 9 celebrate
emblem 3 bar 4 mace, sign 5 badge, crest, image, token 6 device, symbol 8 insignia, monogram 9 attribute 10 coat of arms 11 adumbration *of mercy:* 8 red cross
embodiment 6 avatar 7 epitome 9 archetype 11 incarnation 13 manifestation
embody 4 fuse, have 5 blend, merge, reify, unify, unite 6 absorb, evince, mirror, take in, typify 7 combine, compose, contain, embrace, exhibit, include, involve, realize, subsume 8 manifest 9 actualize, encompass, epitomize, exemplify, incarnate, integrate, objectify, personify, personize, represent, symbolize 10 amalgamate, assimilate, comprehend, constitute, illustrate 11 consolidate, demonstrate, emblematize, exteriorize, externalize, hypostatize, incorporate, materialize, personalize 12 substantiate
embog 4 mire 5 delay 6 detain, hang up, retard, slow up 7 set back, slacken 8 slow down 10 decelerate
embolden 5 cheer, impel, nerve, steel 6 chance, hazard 7 animate, chirk up, hearten, inspire, venture 8 inspirit 9 encourage, enhearten 10 strengthen
embolus 4 clog, clot
embosom 7 enclose 8 surround
emboss 5 adorn, raise 8 ornament 9 embellish, embroider
embouchure 5 mouth 10 mouthpiece
embowel 3 gut 4 draw 6 paunch 10 eviscerate, exenterate
embrace 3 hug 4 clip, fold, grip, have, hold, lock, wrap 5 admit, adopt, bosom, clasp, cling, cover, press, twine 6 accept, cradle, cuddle, embody, enfold, enwind, fondle, nuzzle, take in, take on, take up 7 cherish, compose, contain, embosom, enclose, entwine, envelop, espouse, include, involve, receive, snuggle, squeeze, subsume, welcome 8 comprise, encircle 9 encompass 10 comprehend 11 accommodate, incorporate
embrangle 7 confuse
embrocation 8 liniment
embroider 3 pad, sew, tat 5 color, couch, fudge 6 emboss, expand, overdo, stitch 7 amplify, build up, distend, enhance, magnify, stretch, tambour 8 decorate, ornament 9 dramatize, elaborate, embellish, overstate 10 aggrandize, exaggerate 11 hyperbolize
embroidery 4 lace 6 edging 7 cutwork, orphery, pinwork 8 couching, smocking, tapestry 10 needlework
embroil 4 mire 6 tangle 7 confuse, involve 8 disorder, distract, entangle 9 implicate
embroilment 4 tiff 6 fracas 7 dispute, quarrel, wrangle 8 squabble 9 bickering 10 falling-out 11 altercation, controversy, involvement 12 entanglement
embryo 3 bud 4 germ, seed 5 fetus, spark 7 nucleus 8 blastula, gastrula *combining form:* 5 blast 6 blasto
emend 4 edit 5 alter, right 6 polish, revise 7 correct, improve, rectify, retouch
emerald 3 gem 5 beryl, green, stone
Emerald Isle 4 Eire, Erin 7 Ireland
emerge 4 flow, loom, rise, show, stem 5 arise, issue 6 appear, derive, spring 7 come out, proceed 9 originate 11 materialize
emergency 3 fix 4 hole, pass, push 5 pinch 6 climax, clutch, crisis, strait 7 squeeze 8 juncture *money:* 5 scrip
Emerson *forte:* 5 essay *friend:* 7 Thoreau
emery 5 board 6 powder 8 abrasive, corundum
Emesh *brother:* 5 Enten *father:* 5 Enlil
émeute 4 riot 6 tumult 8 outbreak, uprising
emigrant 7 pioneer, settler 8 colonist
emigré 2 DP 5 alien, exile 7 evacuee, refugee 8 expellee, fugitive 9 immigrant 10 expatriate
Emilia *husband:* 4 Iago 7 Palamon *slayer:* 4 Iago
eminence 3 VIP 4 fame, note, peak, rise 5 chief, glory, honor, kudos, power, raise 6 bigwig, credit, height, leader, renown, repute, uprise, weight 7 dignity, notable 8 altitude, big-timer, highness, luminary, prestige 9 authority, dignitary, elevation, greatness, influence, loftiness 10 famousness, importance, notability, prepotency, projection, prominency, reputation 11 distinction, superiority
eminent 3 big 4 high 5 famed, great, large, lofty, noble, noted 6 august, famous 7 big-name, big-time, exalted, notable 8 dominant, renowned, towering 9 big league, important, well-known 10 cele-

brated, celebrious 11 conspicuous, illustrious, outstanding 13 distinguished
eminently 4 very 6 highly 7 notably 9 extremely 10 remarkably, strikingly 11 exceedingly 12 surpassingly 13 exceptionally
emir 5 chief, noble, ruler, title 8 nobleman 9 chieftain
emissary see **envoy**
emission 4 flow 9 discharge, effluvium, emanation
emit 4 beam, drip, flow, glow, ooze, pour, reek, vent, void 5 expel, exude, issue, loose, utter 6 exhale, expire, let out 7 emanate, excrete, extrude, give off, give out, radiate, release, secrete 8 evacuate, throw off 9 discharge 10 disembogue
emmer 5 grain, spelt, wheat 6 speltz
emmet 3 ant 7 pismire
Emmor's son 7 Shechem
emolliate 6 soften, weaken
emollient 7 lenient 8 lenitive, sedative, soothing
emolument 3 fee, pay 4 hire, wage 6 salary 7 guerdon, stipend 11 pay envelope 12 compensation
emote 3 act 4 gush, rage, rant 5 storm 6 take on 7 carry on, overact
emotion 3 ire, joy 4 fear, glee, hate, love 5 agony, ardor, grief, shame 6 relief, sorrow 7 ardency, despair, disgust, ecstasy, feeling, passion, sadness 8 jealousy, movement, surprise 9 affection, agitation, happiness, sentiment 11 affectivity, sensibility, sensitivity 12 excitability 13 sensitiveness ***combining form:*** 4 thym 5 thymo 6 thymia
emotional 6 ardent, moving 7 feeling, fervent, soulful 8 sentient, stirring, touching 9 affecting, affective, rhapsodic, sensitive 10 hysterical, passionate, responsive, susceptive 11 rhapsodical, softhearted, susceptible, sympathetic
emotionless 3 icy 4 cold, cool 5 chill, staid 6 frigid, torpid 7 deadpan, distant, glacial 8 reserved 9 apathetic, immovable, impassive, unfeeling 10 impersonal 11 cold-blooded, indifferent 12 matter-of-fact 13 dispassionate, unimpassioned
empathy 4 pity 6 accord, warmth 7 concord, rapport 8 affinity, sympathy 9 communion 10 compassion 12 appreciation, congeniality 13 compatibility, comprehension, fellow feeling, understanding
emperor 4 czar, king, shah, tsar, tzar 5 ruler 6 caesar, kaiser, sultan 7 monarch 8 autocrat, dictator, imperial, padishah 9 sovereign ***Japanese:*** 6 mikado 8 Hirohito
emphasis 5 focus, force 6 accent, stress, weight 9 attention 10 insistence 12 accentuation
emphasize 4 mark 5 press 6 accent, assert, charge, play up, stress 7 feature 8 pinpoint 9 highlight, italicize, punctuate, spotlight, underline 10 accentuate, underscore
emphatic 6 marked 7 decided, earnest, pointed 8 accented, forceful, positive, stressed, vigorous 9 assertive, energetic, insistent, insistive 10 aggressive, emphasized, resounding, underlined 11 accentuated, assertative
empire 4 rule, sway 5 power, realm, state 6 domain 7 demesne, kingdom, tsardom, tzardom 8 dominion, province 9 territory ***ancient:*** (see **ancient empire**)
Empire State 7 New York
empirical 7 factual 9 experient 12 experiential, experimental 13 observational
emplacement 7 battery, gallery 8 position
employ 3 add, use 4 busy, hire, work 5 apply, avail, exert, put on 6 bestow, devote, engage, handle, obtain, occupy, retain, secure, take on 7 engross, exploit, procure, utilize 8 exercise, practice
employee 4 hand, help 6 worker 7 servant 8 factotum 9 underling ***bank:*** 5 clerk, guard 6 teller ***hotel:*** 4 maid 5 clerk 7 bellboy, bellhop, doorman 9 concierge
employer 4 boss, user
employment 3 job, use 4 line, play, post, task, toil, work 5 trade, usage 6 hiring, office, usance 7 calling, mission, purpose, pursuit 8 business, engaging, exercise, exertion, function, handling, position, vocation 9 appliance, operation, situation 10 engagement, exercising, occupation 11 application, disposition, recruitment, utilization 12 exploitation
emporium 4 mall, mart, shop 5 store 6 bazaar, market 11 marketplace
empower 4 vest 5 endow 6 charge, enable, invest 7 entitle, entrust, license 8 accredit, deputize, sanction 9 authorize, privilege 10 commission
empress 5 queen ***French:*** 7 Eugenie 9 Josephine ***Japanese:*** 5 Suiko ***of India:*** 8 Victoria ***Russian:*** 4 Anna 7 czarina, tsarina, tzarina 9 Catherine, Elizabeth
empressement 6 fervor, warmth 10 cordiality
emprise 4 feat, gest 7 exploit, venture 9 adventure 11 undertaking
emptiness 4 void 6 hunger, vacuum 7 inanity, vacancy, vacuity
emptor 5 buyer 6 vendee 9 purchaser
____ emptor 6 caveat
empty 3 rid 4 bare, dumb, dump, flat, idle, pour, vain, void 5 banal, blank, clear, drain, inane, petty, silly, stark, vapid 6 barren, devoid, hollow, jejune, otiose, paltry, unload,

vacant, vacate 7 deadpan, deplete, drained, exhaust, fatuous, foolish, insipid, trivial, vacated, vacuous 8 depleted, deserted, evacuate, forsaken, ignorant, innocent, nugatory, trifling, unfilled 9 abandoned, destitute, exhausted 10 unoccupied, untenanted 11 godforsaken, ineffectual 12 inexpressive, unexpressive 14 expressionless *combining form:* 3 ken 4 keno *Scottish:* 4 toom

empty-headed 4 rude 5 dizzy, giddy, silly 6 simple, vacant 7 flighty, vacuous 8 ignorant, skittish, untaught 9 benighted, brainless, frivolous 10 illiterate, uneducated, unlettered, unschooled 11 harebrained, know-nothing 12 uninstructed 13 rattlebrained

empyreal 4 airy, holy 6 aerial, divine 7 sublime 8 heavenly 9 celestial, spiritual

empyrean 3 sky 4 Zion 5 bliss, ether 6 heaven, welkin 7 elysium, heavens, nirvana 8 heavenly, paradise 9 celestial, firmament 10 civitas Dei 12 New Jerusalem

emu 4 bird, rhea 6 ratite 9 cassowary

emulate 3 ape 4 copy 5 equal, rival 6 outvie 7 compete, imitate 8 rivalize 9 challenge

emulation 6 strife 7 contest, rivalry, warfare 8 conflict, striving, tug-of-war 9 imitation 10 contention 11 competition

emulous 5 vying 6 aiming 7 athirst 8 aspiring, striving, vaulting 9 ambitious 11 competitive

emulsifier 4 soap

enable 3 fit, let 5 allow, ready 6 permit 7 empower, entitle, license, prepare, qualify 8 accredit, sanction 9 authorize, condition 10 commission

enact 2 do 4 make, pass, play 6 decree, depict, effect, ordain, ratify 7 execute, perform, portray 8 proclaim 9 authorize, discourse, establish, institute, legislate, personate, represent 10 accomplish, bring about, constitute, effectuate 11 impersonate

enactment 3 law 6 action, assize, decree 7 statute 9 ordinance

enamel 5 glaze, gloss, paint

enamored 4 fond 5 dotty 6 loving, mashed, soft on 7 charmed, devoted, smitten 8 besotted, spoony on 9 bewitched, enchanted, entranced, infatuate 10 captivated, fascinated, infatuated, spoony over

Enan's son 5 Ahira

encamp 4 tent 6 settle 7 bivouac

encampment 6 laager 7 bivouac, hutment

encase 7 enclose, envelop, sheathe

enceinte 8 pregnant 9 expectant, expecting 10 parturient

enchain 4 bind 6 fetter

enchant 3 hex 4 draw, send, take, wile 5 charm, spell, witch 6 allure, delude, please, thrill, voodoo 7 attract, bewitch, delight 9 captivate, ensorcell, fascinate, magnetize, mesmerize, spellbind

enchanter 4 mage 5 magus 6 wizard 7 charmer, warlock 8 conjurer, magician, sorcerer 9 voodooist 11 necromancer

enchanting 5 siren 7 sirenic 8 alluring, charming 9 appealing, glamorous, seductive 10 attractive, bewitching, delectable, delightful, intriguing 11 captivating, fascinating

enchantment 3 hex 5 charm, magic, spell 7 sorcery 8 gramarye, witchery, wizardry 9 conjuring, magicking 10 necromancy, witchcraft 11 incantation

enchantress 3 hag, hex 5 bruja, Circe, lamia, Medea, witch 9 sorceress 10 witchwoman

enchiridion 4 book, text 5 guide 6 manual 8 Baedeker, handbook 9 guidebook, vade mecum 10 compendium

encincture 4 band, belt, gird 6 begird, engird, girdle 8 begirdle, engirdle

encipher 4 code

encircle 3 hem 4 band, belt, gird, halo, hoop, ring 5 girth 6 begird, engird, enlace, girdle 7 compass, embrace, enclose, environ, wreathe 8 cincture, surround 9 encompass 12 circumscribe

enclose 3 box, hem, mew, pen, rim 4 cage, coop, mure, veil, wall, wrap 5 bound, fence, hedge, limit 6 circle, closet, corral, encase, enfold, enlock, enwrap, immure, invest, shroud, shut in 7 compass, confine, contain, embosom, envelop, environ, harness 8 encircle, enshroud, ensphere, imprison, insheath, restrict, surround 9 capsulize, encompass 12 circumscribe

enclosure 3 box, haw, mew, pen, sty 4 bawn, cage, cell, coop, cote, fold, quad, tank, trap, wall, weir, yard 5 booly, booth, court, crawl, fence, kench, pound, stall 6 aviary, cancha, corral, cowpen, garden, kennel, paling, prison 7 barrier, cockpit, paddock 8 cincture, cloister, sepiment, stockade 9 cofferdam, courtyard, curtilage 10 quadrangle, sheephouse *African:* 4 boma 5 kraal *elephant:* 6 keddah

encomiast 7 praiser 8 eulogist 10 panegyrist

encomiastic 9 laudative, laudatory, praiseful 11 panegyrical

encomium 4 laud 5 kudos 6 eulogy, praise 7 acclaim, tribute 8 accolade, applause, approval, citation, plaudits 9 laudation, panegyric 10 compliment, salutation 11 acclamation 12 commendation

encompass 3 hem 4 belt, gird, have, ring 5 beset, bound 6 begird, circle,

embody, engird, girdle, take in 7 contain, delimit, embrace, enclose, environ, include, involve, subsume 8 encircle, surround 10 comprehend
encore 6 recall, repeat 8 call back 10 repetition
encounter 4 espy, face, find, fray, meet, spot 5 brush, catch, clash, close, fight, front, hit on, run-in, scrap, set-to 6 battle, descry, detect, engage, take on, turn up 7 affront, collide, contest, hit upon, meeting, quarrel 8 argument, conflict, confront, meet with, skirmish 10 contention, velitation
encourage 4 abet, back, push, stir 5 boost, cheer, favor, nerve, pique, rally, serve, steel 6 assist, assure, buck up, excite, foster, incite, induce 7 advance, animate, approve, chirk up, develop, endorse, fortify, forward, further, hearten, improve, prevail, promote, provoke, quicken, support, sustain 8 advocate, embolden, energize, inspirit, reassure, sanction 9 enhearten, galvanize, instigate, patronize, reinforce, stimulate, subsidize 10 invigorate, strengthen 11 countenance
encouragement 4 lift, push 5 boost 7 backing, support
encouraging 4 rosy 6 likely 7 hopeful, roseate 9 promising 10 promiseful 11 rose-colored
encroach 5 poach 6 invade, meddle, trench 7 impinge, intrude 8 entrench, infringe, overstep, trespass 9 interfere, interpose, intervene
encumber 3 tax 4 clog, lade, load 5 beset, block, weigh 6 burden, charge, fetter, hamper, hinder, impede, retard, saddle, weight 7 freight, oppress 8 handicap, obstruct, overload 9 incommode 10 discommode, overburden 13 inconvenience
encumbrance 4 clog, load 6 burden 8 handicap, hardship, mortgage 9 albatross 10 difficulty, impediment 12 disadvantage 13 inconvenience
encyclical 6 letter 7 general 8 circular
encyclopedic 5 broad 7 general 8 complete 9 extensive, inclusive 10 discursive 12 all-embracing, all-inclusive 13 comprehensive
encyclopedist 7 Diderot
end 3 aim, bit, tip 4 coda, goal, halt, part, quit, stop, tail, term 5 bound, cease, close, death, finis, limit, piece, scrap 5 teloi (plural), telos 6 expire, finale, finish, object, period, scotch, windup, wrap up 7 abolish, closing, closure, extreme, leaving, lineman, purpose, remnant, residue 8 boundary, complete, conclude, confines, curtains, finality, fragment, particle, surcease, terminal, terminus, ultimate 9 cessation, desuetude, determine, extremity, objective, remainder, terminate 10 borderline, completion, conclusion, desistance, expiration, limitation 11 culmination, discontinue, termination 12 consummation ***combining form:*** 3 acr, akr, tel 4 acro, akro, tele, telo
endanger 4 risk 5 peril 6 chance, expose, hazard, menace 7 imperil, jeopard, venture 8 jeopardy 10 compromise, jeopardize
endeavor 3 aim, try 4 push, seek, toil, work 5 apply, assay, essay, labor, offer, trial 6 hassle, intend, strain, strive 7 address, attempt, purpose, travail 8 exertion, striving, struggle 9 determine, undertake 11 undertaking
ended 4 done, down, over, past 7 through 8 complete, finished 9 completed 10 terminated
endemic 5 local 6 native 8 home-bred 10 aboriginal, indigenous, native-born
ending 4 stop 5 close 6 finale, finish, period, windup 7 closing 9 cessation 10 conclusion, desistance 11 termination
endive 4 herb 7 witloof 8 escarole
endless 7 eternal, forever, undying 8 constant, immortal, infinite, overlong, unending 9 ceaseless, continual, limitless, perpetual, unbounded, unceasing, unlimited 10 continuous, indefinite, unmeasured 11 amaranthine, everlasting, measureless 12 immeasurable, interminable
endmost 8 farthest, furthest
endocrine gland 5 gonad, ovary 6 pineal, testis, thymus 7 adrenal, thyroid 8 pancreas 9 pituitary 11 parathyroid 12 hypothalamus
endomorphic 6 pyknic
endorse 2 OK 4 okay, sign, visa, visé 5 vouch 6 attest, ratify, second, uphold 7 approve, certify, command, stand by, support, witness 8 accredit, advocate, champion, sanction 9 recommend 12 authenticate
endorsement 2 OK 4 fiat, visa 7 support 8 approval, sanction 9 signature
endow 4 back, fund 5 award, dower, found, grant 6 accord, bestow, confer, donate, enable, enrich, supply 7 empower, enhance, finance, promote, provide, sponsor, support 8 bequeath, heighten, organize 9 crown with, subscribe, subsidize 10 contribute
endowment 4 fund, gift 5 dower, dowry, grant, power, skill 6 talent 7 ability, chantry 8 appanage, dotation
end product 5 issue 6 effect, result, sequel, upshot 7 outcome 8 sequence 9 aftermath 11 aftereffect, consequence
endue 4 vest 5 dower, equip 6 clothe, invest, outfit 7 furnish 8 accouter 9 crown with
endurance 4 wind 5 pluck 7 stamina

8 duration, patience, strength 9 tolerance 10 continuity, toleration 11 persistence 12 continuation, perseverance
endure 2 go 4 bear, bide, last, take, wear 5 abide, allow, brook, stand 6 accept, linger, pocket, suffer 7 outlast, outlive, persist, stomach, sustain, swallow, undergo 8 bear with, continue, tolerate, tough out 9 withstand 12 carry through
enduring 3 old 4 fast, firm, sure 5 solid, sound 6 stable, steady, sturdy 7 abiding, durable, eternal, lasting, staunch 8 lifelong, resolute 9 diuturnal, long-lived, perennial, permanent, steadfast 10 continuing, inveterate, perdurable 11 long-lasting, substantial, unfaltering, unqualified 12 never-failing
Endymion ***father:*** 8 Aethlius ***lover:*** 5 Diana 6 Selene
enemy 3 foe 5 rival 7 hostile, invader 8 attacker, emulator, opponent 9 adversary, assailant, combatant, contender 10 antagonist, competitor
energetic 4 spry 5 brisk, fresh, lusty, peppy, vital, zippy 6 active, breezy, lively 7 driving, dynamic, vibrant 8 animated, spirited, tireless, vigorous 9 sprightly, strenuous, vivacious 10 aggressive, red-blooded 12 enterprising 13 indefatigable
energize 3 arm, pep 4 fuel 5 liven 6 actify, enable 7 empower, fortify, sustain 8 activate, activize, vitalize 9 reinforce 10 invigorate, strengthen
energy 2 go 3 pep, vim, zip 4 beef, birr, life, tuck 5 force, might, power, sinew, steam, vigor 6 effort, muscle, spirit 7 potency 8 activity, efficacy, strength 9 hardihood, puissance, toughness 10 mightiness 11 application 12 forcefulness, powerfulness 13 effectiveness, operativeness ***excessive:*** 7 sthenia ***unit:*** 3 erg 4 dyne, volt 5 joule 7 quantum 10 horsepower
enervate 3 sap 4 jade, tire 5 unman, weary 6 soften, weaken 7 disable, exhaust, fatigue, unnerve 8 enfeeble, unstring 10 devitalize
enfant terrible 4 limb 5 devil, rogue, scamp 6 rascal 7 villain 8 mischief, scalawag 9 skeezicks 11 rapscallion
enfeeble 3 sap 5 blunt 6 soften, weaken 7 cripple, disable, exhaust, unbrace 8 enervate 9 attenuate, undermine 10 debilitate, devitalize 12 unstrengthen
enfold 3 hug 4 gird, veil, wrap 5 clasp, cover, drape, press 6 encase, enwrap, girdle, invest, shroud, swathe 7 embrace, enclose, envelop, environ, squeeze 8 encircle, enshroud, surround 9 encompass, ensheathe
enforce 5 exact 6 compel, effect, invoke, oblige 7 execute, fulfill 9 discharge, implement, prosecute 10 accomplish, administer
enfranchise 4 free 6 rescue 7 deliver, manumit, release 8 liberate 9 extricate 10 emancipate
engage 3 tie 4 bind, busy, face, grip, hire, meet, mesh, pass, soak 5 fight, imbue, put on, troth 6 absorb, arrest, attack, battle, commit, employ, enlist, occupy, pledge, strike, take on 7 assault, betroth, engross, immerse, involve, promise 8 affiance, enthrall, interact 9 captivate, encounter, fascinate, interlace, interlock, intermesh, interplay, preoccupy, undertake ***passage:*** 4 book
engaged 4 busy, deep, rapt 6 intent 7 working, wrapped 8 absorbed, employed, immersed, intended, occupied, plighted 9 affianced, betrothed, committed, engrossed, wrapped up 10 contracted 11 preoccupied ***person:*** 6 fiancé 7 fiancée
engage in 4 wage 5 enter ***suffix:*** 3 ize
engagement 4 date, word 5 troth, tryst, visit 6 action, battle, hiring, pledge, plight 7 booking, meeting, promise 8 espousal 9 betrothal, interview 10 betrothing, employment, invitation, rendezvous 11 assignation
engaging 5 siren, sweet 6 dulcet 7 winning, winsome 8 magnetic, mesmeric 9 glamorous 10 attractive, bewitching, employment, intriguing 11 fascinating 13 prepossessing
engender 4 stir 5 beget, breed, cause, hatch, rouse 6 arouse, excite, induce, work up 7 develop, produce, provoke, quicken 8 generate, muster up, occasion 9 stimulate
engine 5 motor, turbo 7 turbine 10 locomotive ***kind:*** 3 gas, jet 5 steam 6 diesel 7 turbine 8 gasoline 9 hydraulic ***jet:*** 8 turbofan, turbojet ***part:*** 3 cam, rod 4 gear, plug, pump 5 choke 6 filter, piston 8 cylinder, manifold, throttle 9 condenser, crankcase 10 carburetor 12 transmission ***siege:*** 3 ram 12 battering ram ***sound:*** 4 chug
engineer 4 plan, plot 5 set up, swing 6 devise, driver, manage, scheme, wangle 7 arrange, finagle 8 contrive, intrigue, maneuver 9 machinate, negotiate 10 manipulate, mastermind ***kind:*** 5 civil 6 mining 8 chemical, sanitary 10 electrical, mechanical 12 aeronautical ***military:*** 6 sapper
engineers' group ***abbreviation:*** 4 IEEE
England 6 Albion 7 Britain 9 Britannia 12 Great Britain ***capital:*** 6 London ***monetary unit:*** 5 pound
English 7 British ***coin:*** 5 angel, crown, groat, pence 6 florin, guinea, seskin 7 angelet 8 farthing, shilling, sixpence, two-

pence 9 fourpence, half crown, halfpenny, sovereign 10 threepence *combining form:* 5 Anglo *farm:* 5 croft *forest:* 5 Arden 8 Sherwood *letter:* 3 zed *measure:* 3 ell, pin, rod, tun 4 comb, coom, gill, hand, hide, line, peck, pint, pipe, pole, pool, span, yard, yoke 5 chain, coomb, crane, digit, hutch, jugum, perch, point, truss 6 barrel, bovate, bushel, fathom, firkin, runlet, strike, sulung 7 furlong, quarter, rundlet, virgate 8 carucate, chaldron, hogshead, puncheon, quartern, standard 9 kilderkin 10 barleycorn *military college:* 9 Sandhurst *patron saint:* 6 George *person:* 4 chap 5 bloke 6 Briton *pirate:* 4 Kidd *princess:* 4 Anne *professor:* 3 don *royal family:* 7 Windsor *saint:* 7 Dunstan 8 Cuthbert *spa:* 4 Bath *sport:* 5 rugby 7 cricket *tavern:* 3 pub *university:* 5 Leeds 6 Oxford 9 Cambridge *weight:* 3 kip, tod 4 keel 5 barge, fagot, stand, stone, tross 6 firkin, fother, fotmal, pocket 7 quintal 8 quartern

English Channel swimmer 6 Ederle (Gertrude)

englut 4 bolt, cram, gulp, slop, wolf 5 slosh 6 gobble, guzzle 11 ingurgitate

engrave 3 cut, fix 4 etch, root 5 carve, chase, embed, infix, print 6 incise, scrive 7 enchase, impress, imprint, ingrain, insculp, instill 8 entrench, inscribe

engraver 6 chaser, etcher *German:* 5 Dürer 10 Schongauer *Italian:* 8 Raimondi

engraving 7 etching, woodcut 8 drypoint, intaglio 9 xylograph *combining form:* 5 glypt 6 glypto

engross 4 bury, busy, fill, grip, hold, soak 5 apply, sew up, write 6 absorb, arrest, engage, indite, occupy, scribe, scroll, take up 7 attract, consume, immerse, involve 8 enscroll, enthrall, inscribe 9 captivate, preoccupy 10 assimilate, monopolize 11 superscribe

engrosser 7 copyist 12 calligrapher 13 calligraphist

engulf 5 drown, flood, swamp, whelm 6 deluge, devour 7 swallow 8 inundate, overflow, submerge 9 overwhelm

enhance 4 lift, rise, suit 5 adorn, exalt, mount, raise, rouse 6 become, deepen 7 augment, elevate, flatter, magnify 8 beautify, heighten, increase, redouble 9 aggravate, embellish, embroider, intensate, intensify 10 exaggerate, strengthen

enhearten 5 cheer, nerve, steel 7 animate, chirk up 8 embolden, inspirit 9 encourage

enigma 3 why 4 crux, knot 5 rebus 6 puzzle, riddle 7 mystery, problem, puzzler, sticker 8 question 9 conundrum 10 closed book, perplexity, puzzlement 12 bewilderment, question mark 13 Chinese puzzle, mystification

enigmatic 4 dark 6 mystic 7 cryptic, obscure 8 Delphian, puzzling 10 mystifying

enisle 6 cut off 7 isolate 8 close off, insulate, separate 9 segregate, sequester

enjoin 3 ban, bid 4 deny, rule, tell, warn 5 order, taboo 6 adjure, advise, charge, decree, direct, forbid, impose, outlaw 7 caution, command, counsel, dictate, inhibit 8 admonish, disallow, forewarn, instruct, prohibit 9 interdict, prescribe

enjoy 3 own 4 fill, have, hold, like, love 5 boast, eat up, fancy, savor 6 occupy, relish, retain 7 command, possess 8 maintain 10 appreciate *a break:* 8 take five

enjoyableness 7 amenity 8 pleasure 9 geniality, pleasance 10 amiability, cordiality 12 agreeability

enjoyment 4 ease, zest 5 gusto, savor 6 relish 7 delight 8 felicity, fruition, pleasure 9 diversion 10 indulgence, recreation, relaxation 11 delectation 12 satisfaction 13 gratification

Enki *consort:* 5 Nintu *son:* 6 Ninsar

enkindle 4 fire 5 light 6 ignite 7 inflame

enlarge 3 wax 4 grow, rise 5 add to, boost, build, mount, widen 6 beef up, expand, extend 7 amplify, augment, develop, greaten, magnify, stretch, upsurge 8 heighten, increase, multiply 9 elaborate, embroider 10 aggrandize, exaggerate

enlargement 4 node 5 tumor 6 growth, nodule 8 addition, increase, swelling 9 accretion, expansion, extension *combining form:* 4 auxe 5 auxae (plural) 6 megaly 7 megalia

enlarging *combining form:* 4 micr 5 micro

enlighten 5 edify, guide, teach, train 6 advise, direct, illume, inform, school, uplift 7 apprise, educate, improve 8 acquaint, illumine, instruct 9 irradiate 10 illuminate

Enlil *father:* 2 An *mother:* 2 Ki *son:* 5 Nanna 6 Nergal, Ninazu *wife:* 6 Ninlil

enlist 4 join 5 enter 6 enroll, join up, muster, sign on, sign up 8 register 9 volunteer

enlistment 5 hitch

enliven 3 pep 4 fire, warm 5 amuse, cheer, pep up, renew, rouse 6 excite, jazz up, vivify 7 animate, inspire, quicken, refresh, restore 8 enspirit, recreate 9 entertain, galvanize, stimulate 10 exhilarate, invigorate, rejuvenate, vivificate

enmesh 4 hook, trap 5 catch 6 draw in, tangle 7 ensnarl, trammel 8 drag into, entangle 9 embrangle, implicate

enmity 4 feud, gall, hate 5 spite 6 animus, hatred, malice, rancor, spleen 7 dislike, ill will **8** aversion, bad blood, loathing **9** animosity, antipathy, hostility, malignity **10** abhorrence, alienation, antagonism, bitterness, malignancy **11** detestation, malevolence **12** disaffection, estrangement, uncordiality

ennoble **5** exalt, honor, raise **6** uplift, uprear **7** dignify, glorify, magnify, sublime **10** aggrandize **11** distinguish

ennui **4** bore, pall, tire, yawn **5** blues, dumps, weary **6** apathy, tedium **7** boredom, fatigue, languor, sadness, satiety, surfeit **8** doldrums **9** dejection, tiredness, weariness **10** depression, melancholy **11** languidness **12** listlessness

Enoch ***father:*** **4** Cain ***son:*** **10** Methuselah

Enoch Arden author **8** Tennyson

enormity **7** bigness, outrage **8** atrocity, hugeness, rankness, vastness **9** depravity, flagrancy, graveness, greatness, grossness, immensity, magnitude **11** heinousness, massiveness, seriousness, weightiness **13** atrociousness, monstrousness

enormous **3** big **4** huge, vast **5** great, large **7** immense, mammoth, titanic **8** colossal, gigantic **9** monstrous **10** gargantuan, prodigious, stupendous, tremendous

Enos ***father:*** **4** Seth ***grandfather:*** **4** Adam ***grandmother:*** **3** Eve ***uncle:*** **4** Abel, Cain

enough **6** fairly, plenty **8** adequacy, adequate, decently, passably **9** abundance, ampleness, averagely, competent, sufficing, tolerably **10** abundantly, acceptably, adequately, admissibly, competence, moderately, sufficient **11** comfortable, sufficiency **12** satisfactory, sufficiently ***poetic:*** **4** enow

enounce **3** say **5** state, utter **8** proclaim

enrage **3** ire, mad **5** anger **6** madden **7** incense, inflame, steam up, umbrage **9** infuriate

enrapture **5** charm, elate **6** allure, please, ravish, trance **7** attract, enchant, gladden, gratify, rejoice **8** enravish, enthrall, entrance **9** captivate, fascinate, transport

enrich **5** adorn, endow **6** fatten, richen **9** embellish

enroll **4** book, join, list **5** enter **6** enlist, induct, insert, join up, line up, muster, record, sign on, sign up **7** catalog, recruit **8** inscribe, register **11** matriculate

ensconce **4** bury, hide **5** cache, cover, place, plant, stash **6** locate, settle **7** conceal, install, secrete, situate **9** establish

ensemble **5** decor, group, suite, whole **6** outfit **7** costume **9** aggregate

enshroud **4** hide, veil, wrap **5** cloak **6** enfold, enwrap, invest **7** conceal, curtain, enclose, envelop

ensign **4** flag, jack **5** color **6** banner, pennon **7** pennant **8** gonfalon, standard, streamer **9** oriflamme

enslave **4** yoke **5** chain **6** thrall **7** oppress, shackle, subject **8** enthrall **9** subjugate **12** disfranchise

enslavement **4** yoke **6** thrall **7** bondage, helotry, peonage, serfdom, slavery **9** servitude, thralldom, villenage

ensnare **3** bag, net **4** hook, lure, mesh, snag, trap **5** benet, catch, decoy **6** enmesh, entice, entrap, tangle **7** capture, catch up **8** entangle, inveigle

ensnarl **6** enmesh, tangle **7** perplex, trammel **8** entangle **9** embrangle **11** intertangle

ensorcell **3** hex **5** charm, spell, witch **6** voodoo **7** bewitch, enchant

ensorcellment **5** magic **7** sorcery **8** witchery, wizardry **9** conjuring **10** necromancy, witchcraft **11** bewitchment, enchantment, incantation

ensphere **4** ball **5** round **8** conglobe **10** conglobate

ensue **4** stem **5** issue **6** attend, derive, follow, result **7** emanate, proceed, succeed **9** supervene

ensuing **4** next **5** after, later **6** coming **9** following, posterior **10** subsequent **12** postliminary **13** subsequential

ensure **5** cinch **6** secure **7** certify, warrant **9** establish, guarantee

enswathe **4** roll **5** drape **6** enwrap, wrap up **7** envelop, swaddle

entail **6** assign, confer, impose **7** require **8** transmit **11** necessitate

entangle **3** bag **4** clog, mesh, mire, trap **5** benet, catch, ravel, snare, snarl, tie up, twist **6** ball up, burden, enmesh, entrap, fetter, hamper, impede, muddle **7** capture, catch up, embroil, ensnare, ensnarl, involve, perplex, trammel **10** complicate, intertwine, interweave

entanglement **3** web **4** knot, mesh, toil **6** affair, cobweb **7** contact, liaison **8** intrigue **10** enmeshment **11** association, embroilment, ensnarement, involvement

Enten ***brother:*** **5** Emesh ***father:*** **5** Enlil

entente **6** treaty **8** alliance **9** agreement, coalition

enter **4** go in, join, list, open, post **5** admit, begin, probe, put in, set to, start **6** come in, docket, enlist, enroll, go into, inject, insert, join up, muster, pierce, record, sign on, sign up, take up **7** ingress, lead off **8** come into, commence, embark on, inscribe, register **9** introduce, penetrate **10** embark upon, inaugurate

enterprise **4** deed, feat, firm, gest, push, task **5** cause, drive, house, vigor **6** action, daring, effort, energy, hustle, outfit **7** attempt, company, concern, courage, exploit, project, pursuit, venture **8** ambition, boldness, business, campaign, endeavor, industry, interest, striving, struggle 9 adventure, eagerness 10 enthusiasm, get-up-and-go, initiative 11 corporation, speculation, undertaking 12 organization, self-reliance 13 ambitiousness, establishment, inventiveness

enterprising 4 bold, busy 5 eager 6 active, daring, hungry, lively 7 craving, dashing, driving, go-ahead, itching, lusting, pushing, zealous 8 aspiring, diligent, hustling, yearning 9 ambitious, audacious, energetic, gumptious 10 aggressive 11 adventurous, hard-working, industrious, up-and-coming, venturesome

entertain 4 host 5 amuse, board, house, lodge, put up 6 bestow, billet, divert, foster, harbor, invite, please, regale 7 cherish, delight, enliven, gladden, gratify, nourish, receive, rejoice 8 domicile, recreate

entertainer 4 host, mime 5 actor, comic 6 amuser, busker, dancer, singer 7 actress, trouper 8 comedian, minstrel ***female:*** 7 actress, diseuse, hostess 10 comedienne

entertainment 4 fete, play, show, skit 5 cheer, revue, sport 6 circus, gaiety, relief 7 banquet, concert, disport, ridotto 8 pleasure 9 amusement, diversion, enjoyment 10 recreation, relaxation 11 dissipation, distraction

enthrall 4 grip, hold 5 charm 6 absorb, engage, master, subdue 7 catch up, enchant, engross, enslave 8 intrigue 9 fascinate, mesmerize, preoccupy, spellbind, subjugate

enthuse 4 rave, send 5 drool 6 thrill 8 rhapsody 9 electrify 10 rhapsodize

enthusiasm 4 élan, fire, zeal, zest, zing 5 ardor, craze, mania, verve 6 fervor, hurrah, spirit 7 ardency, earnest, passion 8 interest 9 eagerness 10 ebullience

enthusiast 3 bug, fan, nut 4 bear, buff 5 fiend, freak, lover 6 addict, maniac, votary, zealot 7 devotee, fanatic, habitué 8 partisan 9 extremist, supporter 10 aficionado

enthusiastic 4 gaga, keen 5 eager, nutty, rabid 6 ardent, gung ho, hearty, hipped, raring 7 devoted, fervent, zealous 8 hopped-up, obsessed, spirited, vascular 10 passionate

entice 4 bait, coax, lure, toll, wile 5 charm, decoy, tempt 6 allure, cajole, entrap, lead on, seduce 8 inveigle, persuade

enticement 4 bait, lure, trap 5 decoy, snare 6 come-on 10 allurement, seducement, temptation 12 inveiglement

enticer 4 bait, vamp 5 Circe, decoy, siren 7 Lorelei, seducer, taunter, tempter 9 attractor, enchanter, temptress 10 attraction, seductress 11 enchantress, femme fatale

enticing 5 siren 6 luring 7 circean, likable 8 fetching, inviting, pleasant, pleasing, tempting, witching 9 beguiling 10 attractive, bewitching, enchanting, intriguing 11 captivating, fascinating

entire 3 all 4 full 5 gross, sound, total, whole 6 choate, intact, unhurt 7 perfect, plenary, unified 8 complete, integral, outright, unbroken, unmarred 9 compacted, undamaged, uninjured 10 integrated, unimpaired 12 concatenated, consolidated ***combining form:*** 3 hol 4 holo 7 integri

entirely 3 but 4 only, well 5 alone, fully, quite 6 solely, wholly 7 utterly 9 perfectly 10 altogether, completely, thoroughly 11 exclusively ***combining form:*** 3 pam, pan 4 pano

entirety 3 all, sum 5 gross, total, unity, whole 7 allness, complex, omneity, oneness 8 sum total, totality 9 aggregate, integrity, plenitude, wholeness 10 everything 12 collectivity, completeness, universality

entitle 3 dub, let 4 call, name, term 5 allow, style 6 enable, permit 7 baptize, empower, license, qualify 8 christen, headline, nominate 9 authorize, designate 10 denominate

entity 3 ens, sum 4 body, unit 5 being, stuff, thing, whole 6 matter, object, system 8 existent, integral, material, totality 9 existence, integrate, something, substance 10 individual

entomb 4 bury 5 inter, inurn 6 inhume, shrine 8 enshrine 9 sepulcher, sepulture 11 ensepulcher

entombment 6 burial 9 interment, sepulture 10 inhumation

entourage 5 suite, train 7 retinue, toadies 9 courtiers, followers, following, hangers-on, retainers 10 associates, attendants, sycophants

entr'acte 8 interval 9 interlude 12 intermission

entrails 4 guts 5 pluck 6 bowels, tripes, vitals 7 giblets, innards, insides, inwards, viscera 8 stuffing 9 internals 10 intestines ***combining form:*** 9 splanchno

entrammel 3 tie 4 clog, curb 5 leash 6 fetter, hamper, hobble, hog-tie 7 shackle

entrance 3 way 4 adit, door, gate 5 charm, entry, foyer, mouth 6 access, coming, entrée, please, portal, ravish 7 arrival, attract, bewitch, doorway, enchant, gladden, ingoing, ingress, opening, rejoice 8 aperture, enravish, enthrall, entryway, incoming, open door 9 admission, captivate, enrapture, fascinate, hypnotize, spell-

bind, threshold, transport 10 admittance, ingression 11 penetration
entrant 7 starter 10 competitor, contestant 11 participant
entrap 3 bag, net 4 bait, lure, toll 5 benet, catch, decoy, snare, tempt 6 allure, entice, entoil, lead on, seduce, tangle 7 catch up, ensnare 8 entangle, inveigle
entreat 3 ask, beg, bid 4 coax, pray, urge 5 crave, plead, press 6 appeal, invoke, pester, plague 7 beseech, implore, wheedle 8 blandish 9 importune 10 supplicate
entreaty 4 plea, suit 6 appeal, orison, prayer 8 petition 11 application, imploration, imprecation 12 supplication
entrée 3 way 4 adit, door 6 access 7 ingress 8 entrance, main dish 9 admission 10 admittance, main course
entrench 3 fix 4 root 5 embed, found, infix, lodge 6 define, ground, invade, settle 7 confirm, implant, ingrain 8 encroach, infringe, trespass 9 establish, interfere, intervene 10 strengthen
entrenched 5 sworn 7 settled 8 deep-dyed 9 confirmed, hard-shell 10 deep-rooted, deep-seated, inveterate 13 bred-in-the-bone, dyed-in-the-wool
entrepôt 9 warehouse 10 storehouse
entrepreneur 6 backer, broker 7 manager 8 mediator, producer, promoter 9 go-between, middleman, organizer 10 contractor, impresario, interagent, interceder, undertaker 11 intercessor 12 intermediary, intermediate 13 administrator, intermediator
entresol 9 mezzanine
entrust 4 bank, give, rely 5 allot, count, leave 6 assign, charge, commit, confer, depend, impose, reckon 7 commend, confide, consign, deliver, deposit 8 allocate, delegate, hand over, relegate, turn over
entry 3 way 4 adit, door 5 debit 6 access, credit, portal 7 doorway, ingress, opening 9 admission, threshold 10 admittance, enlistment, enrollment, ingression
entwine 4 coil, curl, lace, wind 5 braid, twist 6 enmesh, spiral 7 entwist, wreathe 8 entangle 9 corkscrew, interlace 10 interplait, intertwine, interweave
enumerate 4 list, tell 5 count, tally 6 detail, number, recite, relate 7 itemize, mention, recount, specify, tick off 8 identify 9 inventory 10 specialize 13 particularize
enunciate 3 say 4 show 5 state, utter, voice 6 affirm, intone, submit 7 advance, declare, develop, enounce, express, lay down, outline, phonate 8 announce, modulate, proclaim, vocalize 9 formulate, postulate, pronounce 10 articulate
envelop 3 hem, pen 4 cage, coop, hide, mask, roll, veil, wrap 5 cloak, drape, fence, guard, hedge 6 cocoon, corral, enfold, enwrap, immure, invest, sheath, shield, shroud, shut in, swathe, wrap up 7 enclose, protect, swaddle 8 enshroud, enswathe, surround 10 circumfuse
envenom 6 poison 7 corrupt 8 acerbate, embitter 10 exacerbate
envious 6 greedy 7 jealous, longing 8 appetent, coveting, covetous, desirous, grasping, grudging, yearning 9 green-eyed, invidious, resentful 10 begrudging, umbrageous
environ 3 hem 4 gird, ring 5 beset, fence, limit, round 6 circle, suburb 7 compass, enclose, envelop 8 encircle, go around, surround 9 encompass
environment 6 medium, milieu 7 ambient, climate, context, element, habitat, setting 8 ambience, backdrop 9 situation 10 atmosphere, background, mise-en-scène 12 surroundings *combining form:* 2 ec 3 eco, oec 4 oeco, oiko *science:* 7 ecology
environmentalist 6 Carson (Rachel) 9 ecologist
environs 6 bounds, limits 7 compass, fringes, suburbs 8 boundary, confines, locality, purlieus, vicinity 9 outskirts, precincts 12 neighborhood, surroundings
envisage 4 view 5 fancy, grasp, image, think 6 behold, regard, survey, vision 7 feature, foresee, imagine, picture, realize 8 conceive, envision, look upon 9 objectify, visualize
envision 4 view 5 dream, fancy, image, think 7 feature, foresee, imagine, picture, realize 8 conceive, summon up 9 conjure up, visualize
envoy 6 bearer, consul, deputy, legate, nuncio 7 attaché, carrier, courier 8 diplomat, emissary, minister 9 messenger 10 ambassador, councillor 11 internuncio
envy 4 long, want 5 covet, crave, yearn 6 desire, grudge, hanker 8 begrudge, grudging, jealousy 10 resentment 12 covetousness 13 invidiousness
enwrap 4 roll, veil 5 clasp, drape 6 enfold, invest, shroud, swathe 7 enclose, envelop, sheathe, swaddle 8 enshroud, enswathe
enzyme 5 ficin, lyase, renin, urase 6 kinase, ligase, lipase, mutase, papain, pepsin, rennin, urease, zymase 7 amidase, amylase, cyclase, enolase, guanase, hydrase, inulase, isozyme, lactase, maltase, oxidase, pectase, pepsine, plasmin, ptyalin, rennase, sucrase, trypsin, zymogen 8 aldolase, diastase, elastase, esterase, fumarase, lyzozyme, nuclease, protease, steapsin, thrombin, zymogene 9 biogenase, cellulase, invertase 10 amygdalase *combining form:* 3 zym 4 zyme, zymo *suffix:* 2 in 3 ase
eon see aeon

Eos see **Aurora**
épée 5 sword
epergne 5 stand 11 centerpiece
Ephah *father:* 6 Jahdai *lover:* 5 Caleb
ephelis 7 freckle
ephemeral 5 brief, short 7 passing 8 episodic, fleeting, fugitive, volatile 9 fugacious, momentary, temporary, transient 10 evanescent, short-lived, transitory, unenduring 11 impermanent
Ephialtes 5 giant *brother:* 4 Otus *father:* 6 Aloeus 8 Poseidon *mother:* 9 Iphimedia *slayer:* 6 Apollo
Ephod's son 7 Hanniel
Ephraim *brother:* 8 Manasseh *father:* 6 Joseph *grandfather:* 5 Jacob *mother:* 7 Asenath
Ephratah *husband:* 5 Caleb *son:* 3 Hur
epic 4 epos, poem, saga 5 grand, Iliad 6 Aeneid, heroic 7 Beowulf, Odyssey 8 imposing 9 narrative *suffix:* 2 ad
epicene 5 sissy 6 prissy 7 unmanly 9 pansified, sissified 10 effeminate
epicure 7 glutton, gourmet, ravener 8 gourmand, sybarite 9 bon vivant, high liver 10 gastronome 11 connoisseur, gastronomer 12 gastronomist
epicurean 4 lush 7 sensual 8 luscious, sensuous 9 luxurious 10 voluptuous 12 sensualistic
epidemic 3 flu 4 rash 6 plague 8 outbreak 10 pestilence
epidermis 4 skin 7 cuticle
epigram 4 poem 6 saying
epigrammatic 5 meaty, pithy 7 compact, concise, marrowy, piquant
epigraph 5 motto 11 inscription
epilogue 6 ending, sequel 8 follow-up, postlude 9 afterword 10 conclusion, postscript
Epimetheus *brother:* 10 Prometheus *father:* 7 Iapetus *wife:* 7 Pandora
epinard 7 spinach
episode 5 event 8 incident, occasion 9 happening 10 occurrence 12 circumstance
epistaxis 9 nosebleed
epistle 4 note 6 letter 7 missive 13 communication
epitaph 3 R.I.P. 8 hic jacet 11 inscription
epithet 4 name, term 5 title 7 agnomen, moniker 8 cognomen, monicker, nickname 9 sobriquet 11 appellation
epitome 3 sum 5 brief 6 resumé 7 summary 8 abstract, boildown, breviary, breviate, last word, synopsis, ultimate 9 summation, summing-up 10 abridgment, apotheosis, conspectus 12 condensation, quintessence
epitomize 5 sum up 6 digest, embody, mirror, typify 7 outline, summate 8 boil down, condense, nutshell, tabulate 9 capsulize, exemplify, incarnate, inventory, personify, represent, summarize, symbolize, synopsize 10 illustrate 11 emblematize, incorporate
epoch 3 age, day, era 4 date, term, time 6 period 8 interval
equable 4 even, just, same 6 stable, steady 7 orderly, regular, stabile, uniform 8 constant 9 immutable, unvarying 10 equivalent, invariable, methodical, systematic, unchanging 12 unchangeable 13 unfluctuating
equal 3 tie 4 even, fair, just, like, mate, meet, peer, same, twin 5 agree, alike, match, reach, rival 6 accord, amount, equate, even-up 7 emulate, identic, similar, uniform 8 alter ego, parallel 9 duplicate, identical, impartial, measure up, objective 10 competitor, fifty-fifty, tantamount 11 counterpart, symmetrical 12 commensurate, correspond to, proportional, unprejudiced 13 commensurable, corresponding, dispassionate, proportionate *combining form:* 2 is 3 iso 4 equi, pari 5 aequi *French:* 4 égal
equality 3 par 6 equity, parity 7 balance, égalité 8 sameness 10 adequation
Equality State 7 Wyoming
equalize 4 even 5 level 6 square 7 balance
equalizer 6 pistol 8 handicap 10 tying score
equally 6 evenly 8 squarely 10 fifty-fifty 11 impartially
equanimity 5 poise 6 aplomb, phlegm 7 ataraxy, balance 8 calmness, coolness, evenness, serenity 9 assurance, composure, equipoise, placidity, sangfroid 10 confidence, detachment 11 equilibrium, tranquility 12 tranquillity 13 self-assurance
equate 4 even 5 liken, match, treat 6 regard, relate 7 compare, paragon 8 consider, equalize, parallel, similize 9 associate, represent 10 assimilate
equestrian 5 rider 8 horseman
equidistant 3 mid 6 center, medial, median, middle 7 central, halfway, midmost 10 centermost, middlemost
equilibrium 5 poise 6 stasis 7 balance 9 equipoise, steadying 10 steadiness 12 counterpoise 13 stabilization *combining form:* 5 stato
equine 4 colt, mare 5 horse, steed
equip 3 arm, rig 4 gear 5 dress, endow, rig up 6 attire, fit out, outfit, rig out, supply 7 appoint, furnish, prepare, provide, qualify, turn out 8 accouter, accoutre
equipment 3 rig 4 gear 5 traps 6 attire, outfit, tackle, things 7 baggage, fitment 8 fittings, material, materiel, tackling

9 apparatus, machinery, trappings 10 provisions 11 accessories, attachments, habiliments, impedimenta 12 accouterment, accoutrement, provisioning 13 appurtenances, paraphernalia
equitable 4 even, fair, just, same 5 level 6 stable 8 unbiased 9 identical, impartial, objective, uncolored 10 impersonal 12 unprejudiced 13 dispassionate
equity 3 law 7 justice 8 equality, justness
equivalence 3 par 6 parity 8 equality, likeness, sameness 10 adequation 11 correlation
equivalent 4 akin, like, same 5 alike, match 6 agnate 7 identic, obverse, similar 8 parallel 9 analogous, duplicate, identical 10 comparable, reciprocal, substitute, tantamount 11 convertible, correlative, counterpart 12 commensurate 13 corresponding, proportionate
equivocal 4 hazy 5 fishy, vague 7 clouded, dubious, obscure, suspect, unclear 8 doubtful 9 ambiguous, tenebrous, uncertain, undecided 10 ambivalent, borderline, indecisive, indistinct, multivocal, unexplicit 11 problematic 12 disreputable, questionable 13 indeterminate
equivocate 3 fib, lie 5 avoid, cavil, dodge, elude, evade, fence, hedge, parry, skirt 6 escape, eschew, palter, weasel 7 falsify, quibble, shuffle 8 sidestep 9 pussyfoot 10 tergiverse 11 prevaricate 12 tergiversate
equivocation 3 fib, lie 5 lying 6 deceit 7 fallacy, fibbing, hedging, sophism 8 coloring, delusion, haggling 9 ambiguity, casuistry, deception, duplicity, quibbling, sophistry 10 distortion 11 amphibology 12 speciousness, spuriousness 13 deceptiveness, dissimulation, double meaning
equivoque 3 pun 4 quip
era 3 age, day 4 date, term, time 5 epoch, stage 6 period
eradicate 4 dele, raze 5 abate, erase, purge 6 delete, uproot 7 abolish, blot out, destroy, root out, wipe out 8 demolish 9 extirpate, liquidate 10 annihilate, extinguish 11 exterminate
Eran ***father:*** 9 Shuthelah ***grandfather:*** 7 Ephraim
erase 4 dele, x out 5 annul, blank 6 cancel, cut out, delete, efface, excise, negate, remove, rub out, scrape 7 abolish, blot out, expunge, nullify, scratch, take out, wipe out 8 black out, blank out, cross off, cross out, disannul, withdraw 9 eliminate, extirpate, sponge out, strike out 10 neutralize, obliterate
Erato see **Muse**
Erbin ***father:*** 9 Custennin ***nephew:*** 6 Arthur ***son:*** 7 Geraint
erbium ***symbol:*** 2 Er
ere 6 before
Erebus ***daughter:*** 3 Day 6 Hemera ***father:*** 5 Chaos ***home:*** 5 Hades ***sister, wife:*** 3 Nox, Nyx ***son:*** 6 Aether, Charon
Erec et ___ 5 Enide
Erechteus ***daughter:*** 8 Chthonia ***father:*** 6 Vulcan 10 Hephaestus ***mother:*** 2 Ge 4 Gaea ***slayer:*** 4 Zeus 7 Jupiter
erect 4 form, lift, make, rear 5 build, exalt, forge, frame, hoist, honor, put up, raise, run up, set up, shape, upend 6 create, effect, lifted, make up, raised, uprear 7 build up, compose, dignify, elevate, ennoble, fashion, glorify, magnify, produce, stand-up, sublime, upraise, upright 8 elevated, heighten, standing, upraised, vertical 9 construct, establish, fabricate, hammer out 10 aggrandize, bring about, straight-up, upstanding 11 distinguish, manufacture 13 perpendicular
erection 4 pile 7 edifice 8 building 9 structure
eremite 6 hermit 7 ascetic, recluse
Erewhon 6 utopia ***author:*** 6 Butler
ergo 2 so 4 then, thus 5 hence 9 therefore, thereupon 11 accordingly 12 consequently
Erichthonius ***father:*** 8 Dardanus ***son:*** 4 Tros
Eridanus star 8 Achernar
Erigone ***dog:*** 5 Maera ***father:*** 7 Icarius ***festival:*** 5 Aeora
Erin see **Eire**
Erinyes 6 Alecto, Furies 7 Megaera 9 Eumenides, Tisiphone
Eriphyle ***brother:*** 8 Adrastus ***husband:*** 10 Amphiaraus ***slayer, son:*** 8 Alcmaeon
Eris ***brother:*** 4 Ares, Mars ***daughter:*** 3 Ate ***fruit:*** 5 apple ***mother:*** 3 Nox, Nyx
Eri's father 3 Gad
ermine 3 fur 5 stoat 6 weasel
erode 3 eat, rub 4 bite, gall, gnaw, rust, wear 5 chafe, decay, grate, graze, scour 6 abrade, rub off, ruffle 7 consume, corrade, corrode, crumble, eat away, rub away 8 wear away 9 scrape off 10 scrape away 11 deteriorate 12 disintegrate
Eroica composer 9 Beethoven
Eros see **Cupid**
erotic 4 lewd, sexy 5 bawdy, spicy 6 ardent, carnal, earthy, fervid 7 amative, amatory, amorous, fervent, fleshly, sensual 8 lovesome, prurient, sensuous 9 epicurean, lecherous, lickerish, salacious 10 lascivious, passionate, voluptuous 11 aphrodisiac, impassioned 12 concupiscent
err 3 sin 4 slip, trip 5 lapse, misdo, stray 6 bungle, offend, slip up, wander 7 blunder, deviate, misplay, stumble 8 trespass 10 transgress 12 miscalculate

errand 3 job 4 task 5 chore 7 mission
errand boy 4 page 5 gofer 7 bellboy, bellhop, courier
errant 5 stray 6 roving 7 devious, erratic, naughty, ranging, roaming 8 drifting, fallible, rambling, shifting, straying 9 deviating, itinerant, wandering 10 meandering, unreliable 11 misbehaving, mischievous
erratic 4 iffy, wild 5 queer, stray, wacky, weird 6 chancy 7 bizarre, curving, devious, dubious, oddball, strange, unusual, wayward, winding 8 doubtful, freakish, peculiar, shifting, singular, unstable, variable, volatile, whimsied 9 anomalous, arbitrary, eccentric, fluctuant, irregular, mercurial, uncertain, unnatural, vagarious, wandering, whimsical 10 capricious, changeable, inconstant, meandering, roundabout, undirected 12 incalculable, inconsistent 13 idiosyncratic, unpredictable
erring see errant
erroneous 3 off 4 awry 5 amiss, askew, false, wrong 6 untrue 7 unsound 8 mistaken, specious 9 defective, incorrect, misguided 10 inaccurate
error 3 sin 4 bull, flub, muff, slip, trip 5 boner, botch, fault, fluff, lapse 6 boo-boo, bungle, fumble, howler, miscue, slipup 7 blooper, blunder, fallacy, falsity, faux pas, misplay, misstep, mistake, stumble, untruth 8 delusion, illusion, misdoing, screamer 9 falsehood, falseness, indecorum, oversight 10 inaccuracy, misreading 11 impropriety, misjudgment ***printing:*** 4 typo 6 errata (plural) 7 erratum
ersatz 4 copy, fake, mock, sham 5 dummy, false 8 spurious 9 imitation, simulated, synthetic 10 artificial, factitious, simulacrum, substitute
Erse 5 Irish 6 Celtic, Gaelic 8 Scottish
Er's father 5 Judah
erstwhile 3 old 4 late, once, past 6 before, bygone, former, whilom 7 already, earlier, onetime, quondam 8 formerly, sometime 10 heretofore, previously
eruct 4 burp, emit, spew 5 belch, eject, expel 6 irrupt 8 disgorge
erudite 7 learned 8 lettered, studious, well-read 9 scholarly 10 scholastic
erudition 4 lore 7 culture, letters, science 8 learning, literacy, pedantry 9 education, knowledge 11 bookishness, cultivation, learnedness, scholarship 12 studiousness 13 scholarliness
erupt 3 jet 4 boil, emit, hurl, spew 5 belch, burst, eject, expel, go off, spout, spurt 6 cast up, irrupt 7 cast out, explode 8 break out, detonate, disgorge, throw off, touch off 9 discharge 10 burst forth 11 extravasate
eruption 4 gust, rush 5 burst, flare, sally 6 access 7 flare-up 8 outbreak, outburst 9 commotion, explosion ***skin:*** 3 zit 4 rash 6 pimple 7 serpigo 8 exanthem
Esau ***brother:*** 5 Jacob ***country:*** 4 Edom ***descendant:*** 7 Edomite ***father:*** 5 Isaac ***father-in-law:*** 4 Elon ***grandson:*** 6 Amalek ***mother:*** 7 Rebekah ***new name:*** 4 Edom ***son:*** 5 Korha, Reuel 7 Eliphaz ***wife:*** 4 Adah 10 Aholibamah
escalade 5 climb, mount, scale 6 ascend
escalate 4 grow, upgo 5 climb, mount, scale, widen 6 ascend, expand, spread 7 broaden, enlarge, upclimb 8 heighten, increase 9 intensify
escapade 4 lark 5 antic, caper, fling, prank, spree 6 frolic, vagary 7 roguery, rollick 8 mischief
escape 3 fly, lam, shy 4 bilk, duck, flee, flit, jump, miss, shun, skip, skit, slip 5 avoid, break, burke, dodge, elude, evade, shake, skirt 6 bypass, decamp, depart, eschew, flight, outlet, vanish 7 abscond, bail out, come-off, dodging, ducking, duck out, elusion, evasion, get away, make off, release, run away 8 breakout, eschewal, shunning 9 avoidance, bypassing, departure, disappear, runaround 10 circumvent, liberation 11 deliverance, elusiveness, evasiveness 12 sidestepping 13 circumvention ***narrow:*** 9 close call 10 close shave
escargot 5 snail
escarole 6 endive
escarpment 5 cliff, slope
eschar 4 scab 5 crust 6 lesion
eschew 3 shy 4 bilk, duck, shun 5 avoid, elude, evade, forgo 6 double, escape, forego 7 abstain, forbear, refrain 8 forebear 9 sacrifice
eschewal 6 escape, shying 7 come-off, elusion, evasion 8 escaping, shirking, shunning 9 avoidance, runaround
escort 3 see 4 bear, beau, date, lead, show 5 bring, guard, guide, pilot, route, steer 6 attend, convoy, direct, fellow, squire 7 company, conduct, gallant, vis-à-vis 8 cavalier, chaperon, shepherd 9 accompany, attendant, boyfriend, companion 11 consort with
escritoire 4 desk 9 secretary 10 secretaire 11 writing desk
escrow 4 bond, deed, fund 7 deposit
esculent 6 edible 7 eatable 10 comestible
escutcheon 6 shield
Eshban's father 6 Dishon
Eshcol ***ally:*** 7 Abraham ***brother:*** 4 Aner 5 Mamre
esker 2 os 3 ose 4 kame 5 mound, ridge
Eskimo 3 Ita 4 Yuit 5 Aleut 6 Innuit ***boat:*** 5 bidar, kayak, umiak 7 bidarka ***boot:*** 5 kamik 6 mukluk ***dog:*** 5 husky

8 malamute ***dwelling:*** 5 igloo 9 barrabora ***outer garment:*** 5 parka ***sledge:*** 7 komatik
esophagus 4 tube 6 gullet, throat 7 pharynx
esoteric 5 inner 6 mystic, occult, orphic, secret 7 private 8 abstruse, hermetic, profound 9 recondite 10 acroamatic 12 confidential
ESP 9 intuition 12 clairvoyance
espadrille 4 shoe 6 sandal
espalier 7 lattice, railing, trellis
esparto 4 alfa 5 grass
especial 4 main 5 chief 7 express, notable, supreme, unusual 8 dominant, singular, specific, uncommon 9 paramount 10 individual, particular, preeminent, surpassing 11 exceptional, predominant 12 preponderant
especially 7 notably 8 in specie, markedly, uniquely 9 eminently, expressly, supremely, unusually 10 peculiarly, remarkably, singularly 12 particularly, preeminently, specifically 13 distinctively, exceptionally
espial 4 find 6 notice, strike 9 detection, discovery 10 unearthing
espionage 6 spying 8 watching 9 sleuthing 11 observation 12 surveillance
espousal 3 aid 5 troth, union 6 mating 7 support 8 adoption, advocacy, approval, ceremony, marriage 9 betrothal, embracing, promotion 10 acceptance, betrothing, engagement 11 betrothment
espouse 3 wed 4 back, mate 5 adopt, catch, marry 6 accept, take on, take up, uphold 7 approve, embrace, support 8 advocate, champion, maintain
esprit 3 vim, wit 4 brio, dash, élan, life, mind, zing 5 humor, oomph, verve 6 acumen, brains, fervor, mettle, morale, spirit 7 courage, loyalty, passion 8 devotion, tenacity 9 acuteness, animation, sharpness 10 brightness, cleverness, enthusiasm, fellowship 11 camaraderie
esprit de corps see **morale**
espy 3 see 4 find, mark, note, spot, view 5 catch, hit on, sight, watch 6 behold, descry, detect, notice, remark, take in, turn up 7 discern, hit upon, make out, observe, witness 8 meet with 9 encounter, recognize 11 distinguish
___ es Salaam 3 Dar
essay 3 try 4 seek, toil, work 5 assay, labor, offer, paper, piece, study, theme, tract, trial 6 hassle, strive, thesis 7 article, attempt, travail, venture 8 endeavor, exertion, striving, struggle, treatise 9 discourse, undertake 10 discussion, exposition 11 composition, explication, undertaking 12 dissertation
essayist ***American:*** 5 Cooke 6 Brooks 7 Cousins, Emerson 8 Repplier 10 Crevecoeur ***English:*** 4 Lamb 5 Pater, Smith 6 Ruskin, Steele 7 Addison, Hazlitt ***French:*** 9 Montaigne ***Greek:*** 8 Xenophon ***Scottish:*** 7 Carlyle
esse 5 being 9 existence
essence 3 ens, nub 4 body, crux, form, gist, pith, root, soul 5 being, fiber, fibre, stuff 6 aspect, bottom, center, entity, kernel, marrow, nature, nubbin, spirit, timber 7 element, quality, texture 8 property 9 attribute, substance 10 distillate, inwardness, rock bottom, virtuality 12 distillation, significance
essential 4 main, must 5 basal, basic, chief, prime, vital 6 inborn, inbred, innate, needed, primal, wanted 7 capital, connate, element, leading, needful, primary 8 cardinal, foremost, inherent, required, rudiment 9 condition, elemental, intrinsic, necessary, necessity, primitive, principal, requisite, right hand, substance 10 congenital, deep-seated, elementary, imperative, sine qua non, substratal, underlying 11 fundamental, necessitous, requirement 12 constitutive, precondition, prerequisite 13 indispensable, part and parcel
essentially 6 almost, au fond, really 8 actually, as good as, as much as, well-nigh 9 basically, virtually 11 practically 13 fundamentally, substantially
essonite 6 garnet 13 cinnamon stone
establish 3 fix, lay, put, set 4 base, make, moor, rest, root, show, stay 5 build, enact, endow, erect, found, infix, place, prove, rivet, set up, start, stick 6 attest, bottom, create, decree, enroot, ground, impose, secure, settle, verify 7 build up, clarify, confirm, implant, instill, make out, provide, set down 8 document, entrench, organize 9 authorize, construct, determine, formulate, hammer out, inculcate, institute, legislate, originate, predicate, prescribe 10 constitute 11 corroborate, demonstrate 12 authenticate, substantiate
establishment 4 firm 5 house 6 outfit 7 company, concern, diehard 8 business, Old Guard 9 institute, workplace 10 enterprise, foundation 11 institution 12 conservative
estate 4 case, farm, form, land, rank 5 acres, caste, class, grade, level, manor, order, place, ranch, shape, state, villa 6 quinta, repair 7 station 8 category, hacienda, mesnalty, position, property, standing 9 condition 10 plantation ***feudal:*** 4 fief 7 fiefdom ***first:*** 6 clergy ***fourth:*** 5 press ***Indian:*** 5 taluk 6 taluka ***manager:*** 7 steward 8 executor, guardian ***second:*** 6 nobles 8 nobility ***third:*** 7 commons
esteem 5 favor, honor, prize, value

6 admire, credit, liking, regard, revere 7 account, apprize, cherish, idolize, respect, worship 8 approval, consider, treasure, venerate 9 valuation 10 admiration, appreciate, estimation 12 appreciation 13 consideration

ester 6 oleate 7 acetate 8 compound 9 phosphate ***suffix:*** 4 oate

Esther ***cousin:*** 8 Mordecai ***father:*** 7 Abihail ***festival:*** 5 Purim ***Hebrew name:*** 8 Hadassah ***husband:*** 9 Ahasuerus

estimable 4 good 5 noble 6 worthy 7 admired, reputed 8 esteemed, laudable, sterling 9 admirable, deserving, honorable, meritable, praisable, reputable, respected 10 creditable 11 commendable, meritorious, respectable, thankworthy 12 praiseworthy

estimate 3 put, set, sum 4 call, cast, rank, rate 5 assay, count, fancy, guess, infer, judge, place, price, prize, round, set at, stock, value 6 assess, cipher, decide, deduce, figure, rating, reckon, settle, survey 7 adjudge, compute, imagine, suppose, surmise, valuate 8 appraise, discover, evaluate, forecast, judgment, round off, sizing up 9 appraisal, ascertain, calculate, determine, enumerate, reckoning, valuation 10 adjudicate, assessment, conjecture, evaluation, projection 11 approximate, calculation, measurement 12 appraisement

estimation 4 fame 5 favor, honor, stock 6 esteem, regard 7 account, opinion, respect 8 figuring, judgment 9 appraisal, ciphering, reckoning, valuation 10 admiration, arithmetic, assessment, evaluation, impression 11 calculation, computation 12 appraisement 13 consideration

estop 3 bar 7 prevent 8 preclude, prohibit

estrange 4 part, wean 5 alien, sever, split 6 divide, sunder 7 break up, divorce 8 alienate, disunify, disunite, separate 9 disaffect

estrangement 6 schism 7 divorce 8 division 10 alienation, withdrawal 12 disaffection

estreat 4 copy 5 exact 6 record 7 extract 9 duplicate

estuary 5 firth, frith, inlet, mouth 6 estero 10 tidal river

esurient 6 greedy, hungry 9 voracious

étagère 7 cabinet, whatnot

Etats ___ 4 Unis

etch 5 grave 6 define, depict, incise 7 engrave, impress, imprint, outline, picture, portray 8 describe, inscribe, set forth 9 delineate, represent

etcher ***American:*** 7 Pennell 8 Whistler ***French:*** 5 Redon 6 Villon ***Italian:*** 8 Piranesi ***Spanish:*** 6 Ribera ***Swiss:*** 4 Zorn

Eteocles ***brother:*** 9 Polynices ***father:*** 7 Oedipus ***mother:*** 7 Jocasta ***slayer:*** 9 Polynices

eternal 7 ageless, endless, lasting, undying 8 constant, dateless, immortal, infinite, timeless, unending 9 ceaseless, continual, deathless, immutable, permanent, perpetual, unceasing 10 immemorial, intemporal, perdurable, unchanging 11 amaranthine, everlasting, illimitable, inalterable, never-ending, sempiternal, unalterable, unremitting 12 interminable

Eternal City 4 Rome

eternally 4 ever 6 always 7 forever 8 evermore 11 forevermore, in perpetuum

eternity 3 age, eon 4 aeon, long 7 dog's age 8 blue moon, coon's age, infinity 9 afterlife 10 eviternity, infinitude, perpetuity 11 endlessness, immortality 12 infiniteness, sempiternity, timelessness

etesian 4 wind 6 annual

Ethan ___ 5 Allen, Brand, Frome

Ethan's father 5 Kishi

Ethbaal's daughter 7 Jezebel

ether 3 air, gas, sky 6 heaven 8 empyrean 10 anesthetic, atmosphere

ethereal 4 aery, airy 5 filmy, light 6 aerial, vapory 7 fragile 8 delicate, empyreal, empyrean, gossamer, heavenly, vaporish, vaporous 9 celestial, vaporlike 13 unsubstantial

ethic 5 ideal, mores, value 6 belief, morals 8 criteria, morality, standard 9 standards 10 moralities, principles

ethical 5 moral, noble 7 upright 8 elevated, virtuous 9 righteous 10 moralistic, principled, upstanding 11 right-minded

Ethiopia 9 Abyssinia ***capital:*** 10 Addis Ababa ***emperor:*** 7 Menalik 8 Selassie 9 Ras Tafari 13 Haile Selassie ***language:*** 7 Amharic ***measure:*** 3 tat 4 cubi, kuba 5 derah, messe 6 cabaho, sinjer, sinzer, tanica 7 farsakh, farsang ***monetary unit:*** 4 birr ***region:*** 4 Bale, Kefa, Welo 5 Arusi, Gojam, Harer, Shewa, Tigre 6 Gonder, Sidamo, Welega 7 Eritrea 4 Gemu, Gefa 8 Ilubabor

ethnic 5 pagan 6 racial, tribal 7 gentile, heathen, infidel, profane 8 national 9 infidelic 11 unchristian 12 non-Christian

etiolate 4 pale 6 bleach, weaken 9 colorless

etiquette 4 form 5 mores 7 conduct, decency, decorum, dignity, manners 8 behavior, protocol 9 amenities, propriety 10 civilities, convention, deportment, seemliness 11 formalities, proprieties

etna 4 lamp 7 volcano

Etruscan ***city, town:*** 4 Roma, Veii 5 Caere, Vulci 6 Arezzo 7 Clusium, Felsina, Perugia 8 Volsinii 9 Florentia, Tarquinia, Vetulonia ***deity:*** 3 Tiv, Uni 4 Turm, Usil

5 Tinia 6 Menfra, Nethun, Trithn 7 Velchan 8 Voltumna *king:* 7 Porsena, Tarquin *kingdom:* 7 Etruria
etui 4 case
etymology 6 origin 7 history, origins
etymon 4 root 5 radix
eucalypt 4 yate
eucalyptus eater 5 koala
Eucharist *container:* 3 pyx *plate:* 5 paten *service:* 4 Mass 9 Communion 11 Lord's Supper *vessel:* 8 ciborium *wafer:* 4 host 8 viaticum
___ Eulenspiegel 4 Till, Tyll
eulogistic 9 approving, laudative, laudatory, praiseful 11 approbatory, encomiastic, panegyrical 12 commendatory 13 complimentary
eulogize 4 hymn, laud 5 bless, cry up, extol 6 belaud, praise 7 applaud, glorify, magnify 8 bepraise 9 celebrate 10 panegyrize
eulogy 5 eloge 6 praise 7 oration, tribute 8 citation, encomium 9 adulation, panegyric 10 salutation 13 glorification
Eumenides see **Erinyes**
Eunice's son 7 Timothy
eunuch 7 gelding 8 castrate, castrato
euphonic 5 sweet 6 dulcet 7 melodic, tuneful 9 melodious 11 mellisonant
euphony 7 harmony
euphoria 4 glee 6 frenzy 7 ecstasy, elation, madness 10 exaltation 12 exhilaration, intoxication
Euphrosyne see **Graces**
euphuistic 7 aureate, flowery, swollen, verbose 8 colorful, elevated, sonorous 9 bombastic, elaborate, overblown 10 rhetorical 11 declamatory 12 magniloquent 13 grandiloquent
eureka 3 aha
Euridice's husband 7 Orpheus
Euripides play 3 Ion 5 Helen, Medea 6 Hecuba 7 Electra, Orestes 8 Alcestis 10 Andromache, Hippolytus 11 Trojan Women
Europa *brother:* 6 Cadmus *father:* 6 Agenor 7 Phoenix *husband:* 8 Asterius *son:* 5 Minos 8 Sarpedon
Europe 9 continent *country:* 4 Eire 5 Italy, Malta, Spain 6 France, Greece, Latvia, Monaco, Norway, Poland, Sweden 7 Albania, Andorra, Armenia, Austria, Belarus, Belgium, Denmark, Estonia, Finland, Georgia, Germany, Hungary, Iceland, Ireland, Moldova, Romania, Rumania, Ukraine 8 Bulgaria, Portugal 9 Lithuania, San Marino 10 Azerbaijan, Luxembourg 11 Netherlands, Switzerland, Vatican City 13 Liechtenstein, United Kingdom *ethnic group:* 4 Finn, Lapp, Pole, Serb, Turk, Wend 5 Croat, Czech, Dutch, Greek, Gypsy, Irish, Latin, Swede, Swiss, Welsh 6 Basque, French, German, Magyar, Polish, Scotch, Slovak 7 Catalan, English, Finnish, Fleming, Italian, Slovene, Spanish, Swedish, Walloon 8 Albanian, Andorran, Armenian, Croatian, Romanian 9 Bulgarian, Hungarian, Ukrainian 10 Macedonian, Monegasque, Phoenician 12 Byelorussian, Scandinavian *language:* 4 Lapp 5 Czech, Dutch, Greek, Irish, Latin, Welsh 6 Basque, Breton, Danish, French, Gaelic, German, Polish, Slovak 7 Catalan, English, Finnish, Flemish, Italian, Maltese, Romansh, Slovene, Spanish, Swedish, Turkish 8 Albanian, Romanian, Rumanian 9 Bulgarian, Hungarian, Icelandic, Norwegian 10 Macedonian, Portuguese 13 Serbo Croatian *mountain:* 3 Alp 8 Dolomite
europium *symbol:* 2 Eu
Euryale see **Gorgon**
Eurytus *daughter:* 4 Iole *slayer:* 8 Hercules
Euterpe see **Muse**
evacuant 6 emetic 8 diuretic, emptying 9 cathartic, purgative
evacuate 4 void 5 clear, empty, expel 6 remove 7 excrete, exhaust 8 withdraw
evacuee 2 DP 6 émigré 7 refugee 8 fugitive
evade 3 fly, shy 4 bilk, duck, flee, foil, shun 5 avoid, dodge, elude, hedge, parry, shirk 6 bypass, double, escape, eschew, outwit, thwart, weasel 7 shuffle 8 sideslip, sidestep, slip away 9 pussyfoot, turn aside 10 circumvent, equivocate, tergiverse 12 tergiversate
Evadne *father:* 5 Iphis *husband:* 8 Capaneus
evaluate 4 rank, rate 5 assay, class, gauge, grade, set at, value 6 assess, ponder, survey 8 appraise, classify, estimate 9 criticize
evaluation 5 stock 6 rating 7 judging 8 decision, estimate, judgment 9 appraisal 10 assessment, estimation 12 appraisement, appreciation, interpreting
Evander *father:* 6 Hermes 7 Mercury *mother:* 8 Carmenta 9 Carmentis *son:* 6 Pallas
evanesce 4 fade 5 clear, empty 6 dispel, vanish 7 scatter 8 disperse, dissolve 9 disappear, dissipate, evaporate 12 disintegrate
evanescent 6 fading, flying 7 cursory, melting, passing 8 fleeting, fugitive, volatile 9 ephemeral, fugacious, momentary, temporary, transient, vanishing 10 dissolving, short-lived, transitory 12 disappearing
evangelical 6 ardent, fervid 7 zealous 8 militant 9 crusading 10 missionary 11 impassioned 13 proselytizing

Evangeline ***author:*** 10 Longfellow ***beloved:*** 7 Gabriel ***home:*** 6 Acadia
evangelist 4 John, Luke, Mark 5 Moody 6 Graham, Sunday, Wesley 7 apostle, Edwards, Matthew 9 McPherson, missioner 10 colporteur, missionary, revivalist
evangelistic 9 crusading, reforming 10 missionary
evangelize 6 preach 8 homilize 9 sermonize
evaporate 4 fade 5 clear 6 vanish 7 evanish 8 evanesce, vaporize 9 disappear
evasion 5 dodge 6 escape, excuse 7 come-off, dodgery, dodging, elusion 8 escaping, escapism, eschewal, haggling, shunning 9 avoidance, quibbling, runaround
evasive 3 sly 4 eely 5 dodgy, vague 6 shifty 7 elusive, elusory, sliding, unclear 8 slippery 9 ambiguous, equivocal, shuffling 10 intangible 12 equivocating
eve 4 dusk 5 night 7 sundown
Eve ***husband:*** 4 Adam ***son:*** 4 Abel, Cain, Seth
even 3 tie, yet 4 fair, flat, just, same 5 align, equal, exact, flush, grade, level, plane, quite, still, truly 6 as well, equate, honest, indeed, really, smooth, square, stable, steady, verily 7 already, balance, equable, exactly, flatten, pancake, planate, stabile, uniform 8 balanced, constant, equalize, smoothen, so much as, straight, unvaried 9 continual, equitable, expressly, identical, precisely, unvarying 10 absolutely, comparable, consistent, continuous, fifty-fifty, positively, symmetrize, unchanging 11 undeviating 12 unprejudiced 13 fair and square, proportionate, unfluctuating ***combining form:*** 5 homal 6 homalo
evening 4 dusk 6 soiree, sunset 7 sundown 8 duskness, eventide, gloaming, twilight 9 afternoon, duskiness, nightfall ***French:*** 4 soir ***Italian:*** 4 sera ***service:*** 7 vespers ***star:*** 5 Venus 6 Hesper, Vesper 8 Hesperus
evenness 7 balance 8 equality, fairness, flatness 10 equanimity, uniformity 11 consistency
event 3 act, hap 4 case, deed, fact, feat, meet 5 issue, match, treat 6 action, affair, chance, effect, result, sequel, upshot 7 contest, delight, episode, exploit, fortune, outcome, product, sequent 8 accident, causatum, fortuity, incident, landmark, milepost, occasion, offshoot 9 aftermath, happening, milestone, outgrowth, resultant 10 occurrence, phenomenon 11 achievement, aftereffect, competition, consequence, eventuality 12 circumstance, happenstance
eventful 4 busy 9 important, momentous
eventual 3 lag 4 last 5 final 6 ending, latest, latter 7 closing, endmost, ensuing 8 hindmost, terminal, ultimate 10 concluding, consequent, inevitable, succeeding
eventuality 4 case 5 issue 6 effect, result, sequel, upshot 7 outcome 9 aftermath 11 aftereffect, consequence, contingency, possibility
eventually 3 yet 7 finally, someday 8 sometime 10 ultimately 13 sooner or later
eventuate 5 occur 6 happen, result
ever 3 too 4 once, over 5 at all, super 6 always, anyway, overly, unduly 7 anytime, anywise, forever, plaguey, usually 8 mortally, overfull, overmuch 9 eternally, extremely, immensely, regularly 10 annoyingly, constantly, consumedly, grievously, invariably 11 excessively, in perpetuum, perpetually 12 consistently, continuously
evergreen 3 fir, ivy, yew 4 ilex, pine, tree 5 cedar, holly, savin 6 laurel, myrtle, spruce 7 conifer, cypress, hemlock, juniper, redwood, sequoia 8 magnolia 9 mistletoe 12 rhododendron
Evergreen State 10 Washington
everlasting 7 endless, eternal, forever, lasting 8 constant, immortal, infinite, termless, unending 9 boundless, ceaseless, continual, limitless, permanent, perpetual, unceasing 10 continuous, perdurable 11 amaranthine, never-ending, unremitting 13 uninterrupted
evermore 6 always 9 eternally 11 in perpetuum
evert 5 upset 9 overthrow
every 3 all 4 each ***combining form:*** 3 pam, pan 4 pano ***suffix:*** 2 ly
everybody 3 all 4 each 8 everyone
everyday 5 banal, lowly, plain, usual 6 common 7 mundane, prosaic, routine, workday 8 familiar, frequent, ordinary, workaday 9 customary, plain Jane, quotidian 11 commonplace 12 unremarkable
everyplace see **everywhere**
everything 3 all ***French:*** 4 tout ***German:*** 5 alles
everywhere 7 all over, overall 8 all round, wherever 9 all around 10 far and near, far and wide, high and low, throughout
evict 3 out 4 oust 5 chase, chuck, eject, expel 6 put out 7 boot out, dismiss, extrude, kick out, shut out, turn out 8 dislodge, force out, throw out 10 dispossess
evidence 4 clue, mark, show, sign 5 index, proof, prove, token, trace 6 attest, evince, expose, ostend 7 bespeak, betoken, confirm, display, exhibit, indicia, symptom, testify, witness 8 indicate, manifest, proclaim 9 testament, testimony 10 illustrate, indication 11 attestation, demon-

strate, significant, testimonial 12 confirmation

evident 5 clear, overt, plain 6 patent 7 glaring, obvious, visible 8 apparent, distinct, manifest, palpable 9 prominent 10 noticeable, pronounced 11 unambiguous

evidently 9 outwardly, seemingly 10 apparently, officially, ostensibly 11 professedly

evil 3 bad, ill, low, sin 4 base, debt, foul, hard, tort, ugly, vice, vile 5 angry, black, catty, crime, fetid, wrong 6 malice, nocent, putrid, sinful, trying, wicked 7 badness, baleful, baneful, corrupt, devilry, harmful, hateful, hideous, hurtful, immoral, malefic, misdeed, nocuous, obscene, offense, ominous, satanic, unlucky, vicious 8 damaging, damnable, iniquity, satanism, satanity, spiteful, stinking, wrathful 9 atrocious, diablerie, diabolism, difficult, evildoing, execrable, ill-boding, ill-omened, injurious, loathsome, malicious, nefarious, offensive, rancorous, repellent, reprobate, repugnant, repulsive, revolting 10 calamitous, despiteful, disastrous, flagitious, iniquitous, malevolent, misconduct, pernicious, sinfulness, unpleasant, wickedness, wrongdoing 11 deleterious, destructive, detrimental, distasteful, maleficence, mischievous, unfavorable, unfortunate 12 disagreeable, inauspicious *combining form:* 3 mal

evildoer 3 cur 5 crook, felon 6 bad lot, sinner 7 culprit, villain 8 criminal 9 miscreant

evil spirit 3 imp 5 demon, devil, fiend 6 daemon

evince 4 mark, milk, show 5 argue, cause, educe, evoke, prove 6 attest, elicit, expose, extort, ostend 7 bespeak, betoken, confirm, display, exhibit, extract, provoke, signify 8 evidence, indicate, manifest, proclaim 9 stimulate 10 bring about, illustrate 11 demonstrate

evirate 4 geld 8 castrate 10 emasculate

eviscerate 3 gut 4 draw 5 bowel 6 paunch 7 embowel 10 disembowel, exenterate

evocative 6 moving 7 causing, weighty 8 arousing, inducing, pregnant, stirring 9 effecting, producing 10 meaningful, suggestive 11 stimulating

evoke 4 milk, stir 5 educe, raise, rally, rouse, waken 6 arouse, awaken, call up, elicit, evince, excite, extort 7 extract 8 summon up 9 call forth, conjure up, stimulate 11 summon forth

evolution 6 change, growth 8 progress, upgrowth 9 flowering, unfolding 10 biogenesis 11 development, progression

evolve 4 grow 5 educe, get at, ripen 6 change, derive, mature, obtain, open up, unfold 7 advance, develop 8 progress 9 elaborate 10 excogitate

evulse 4 pull, tear, yank 7 extract

ewe 5 sheep *young:* 6 theave

ewer 3 jug 4 vase 5 basin 7 pitcher

ex 6 former 7 without

exacerbate 5 annoy 6 worsen 7 envenom, inflame, provoke 8 embitter, heighten, irritate 9 aggravate, intensify 10 exasperate

exact 4 call, even, levy, nice, same, true, very 5 claim, force, fussy, gouge, pinch, put on, right, screw, wrest, wring 6 assess, coerce, compel, demand, extort, impose, oblige, proper, square, wrench 7 careful, correct, extract, precise, require, solicit, squeeze 8 accurate, punctual, rigorous, selfsame 9 challenge, constrain, identical, postulate, shake down 10 meticulous, scrupulous 11 painstaking, punctilious, requisition 12 conscionable 13 conscientious *combining form:* 4 orth 5 ortho

exacting 5 fussy, rigid, stern, tough 6 severe, strict, taxing, trying 7 exigent, finicky, onerous, weighty 8 critical, grievous, rigorous 9 demanding, stringent 10 burdensome, oppressive, particular

exactitude 8 accuracy 9 precision 10 definitude 11 correctness, preciseness 12 definiteness

exactly 3 all 4 bang, even, just 5 quite, right, sharp, spang, stick 6 as well, in toto, square, wholly 7 totally, utterly 8 all in all, smack-dab, squarely 9 expressly, on the nose, precisely 10 absolutely, accurately, altogether, completely, positively 12 specifically

exaggerate 3 pad 5 color, fudge 6 overdo 7 amplify, magnify, overact, romance 8 overdraw, overrate 9 embellish, embroider, overstate 10 overcharge 11 hyperbolize, romanticize

exaggeration 7 romance 8 coloring 9 hyperbole 10 caricature, stretching 11 enlargement, overdrawing 12 embroidering, overcoloring 13 amplification, embellishment, overstatement

exalt 4 fire, laud, lift 5 boost, elate, erect, extol, honor, pique, raise 6 deepen, enhalo, inform, praise, uplift, uprear 7 acclaim, animate, build up, dignify, elevate, enhance, ennoble, glorify, inspire, magnify, promote, quicken, sublime, upgrade 8 heighten, inspirit, pedestal, spirit up, stellify 9 encourage, intensify, stimulate 10 aggrandize 11 apotheosize, distinguish

exaltation 3 joy 5 bliss 6 praise 7 delight, ecstasy, elation, rapture 8 euphoria, rhapsody 9 extolment, laudation, upgrading, uplifting 10 apotheosis 11 deifi-

cation, delectation **12** exhilaration, intoxication **13** dignification, glorification
exalted **4** high **5** first, grand, lofty, noble **6** astral, august, superb **7** eminent, highest, leading, sublime **8** elevated, foremost **9** number one, prominent, top-drawer **10** top-ranking **11** high-ranking, illustrious, outstanding
examination **4** oral, quiz, scan, test, view **5** assay, audit, trial **6** review, survey **7** autopsy, canvass, checkup, hearing, inquest, inquiry, sifting, testing **8** analysis, quizzing, scanning, scrutiny **9** breakdown, check-over, diagnosis, winnowing **10** dissection, inspection **11** questioning **13** catechization, investigation, perlustration ***kind:*** **4** oral **5** final **7** medical, midterm **8** physical ***of accounts:*** **5** audit ***of a corpse:*** **7** autopsy
examine **3** ask, con, try, vet **4** pump, quiz, scan, sift, test, view **5** audit, check, grill, probe, prove, query, study **6** go over, look at, peruse, survey **7** canvass, check up, inquire, inspect, observe **8** check out, look into, look over, overhaul, question **9** catechize, check over **10** scrutinize **11** contemplate, interrogate, investigate ***eggs:*** **6** candle
examiner **6** censor, critic, tester **7** auditor, coroner **9** inspector
examining tool ***combining form:*** **5** scope
example **4** case **5** ideal, model **6** mirror, sample **7** pattern, problem **8** ensample, exemplar, instance, paradigm, sampling, specimen, standard **9** archetype **11** case history **12** illustration
exanimate **4** dead **8** lifeless **10** spiritless
exasperate **3** get, irk **4** gall, huff, rile, roil **5** peeve, pique **6** nettle, work up **7** agitate **8** irritate **9** aggravate
exasperation **4** pest **6** bother, pester, plague, pother **8** irritant, nuisance, vexation **9** annoyance, besetment **10** botherment, irritation, resentment **11** aggravation, botheration, displeasure
ex cathedra **8** official **9** ex officio **13** authoritative
excavate **3** dig **4** grub **5** scoop, spade **6** dig out, shovel **7** unearth **8** gouge out, scoop out **9** hollow out, quarry out, scrape out
excavation **3** dig, pit **4** hole, mine **5** stope **6** trench
exceed **3** top **4** beat, best, dare, pass **5** break, excel, outdo **6** better, overdo **7** outstep, overrun, presume, surpass, venture **8** outreach, outshine, outstrip, outweigh, overstep **9** overreach, transcend
exceedingly **4** very **6** hugely **7** notably, parlous, vitally **9** extremely **10** remarkably, strikingly **12** surpassingly **13** exceptionally ***prefix:*** **3** pre **5** ultra
excel **3** top **4** beat, best **5** outdo, shine **6** better, exceed **7** surpass **8** outclass, outshine, outstrip **9** transcend
excellence **5** arête, class, merit, value, worth **6** virtue **7** quality **8** fineness, goodness, niceness **10** perfection, superbness **11** distinction, superiority
excellent **3** top **4** brag, fine, good **5** bully, dandy, nobby, noble, prime, royal, smart **6** bang-up, banner, famous, Grade A, proper, superb, tip-top **7** capital, classic, premium, quality, supreme **8** champion, five-star, splendid, stunning, superior, terrific, top-notch, whiz-bang **9** classical, first-rate, front-rank, high-class, high-grade, marvelous, number one, sovereign **10** blue-ribbon, first-class **11** exceptional, first-string, magnificent, sensational, superlative, unsurpassed **12** incomparable
except **3** bar, but, yet **4** bate, kick, omit, only, save **5** debar **6** bating, beside, exempt, object, reject, saving, unless **7** barring, besides, exclude, however, outside, protest, rule out, suspend **8** count out, pass over **9** apart from, aside from, eliminate, excluding, outside of **11** exclusive of, expostulate, remonstrate
exception **5** demur **7** dissent **9** exclusion, objection
exceptionable **8** unwanted **9** unwelcome **10** ill-favored **11** undesirable **12** inadmissible, unacceptable **13** objectionable
exceptional **4** rare **6** scarce, unique **7** notable, premium, special, strange, unusual **8** distinct, singular, superior, uncommon, unwonted **9** excellent, marvelous, wonderful **10** infrequent, noteworthy, phenomenal, remarkable, unordinary **11** outstanding, uncustomary, unthinkable **12** unimaginable **13** extraordinary
exceptionally **4** very **6** hugely **7** notably, parlous, vitally **9** extremely, unusually **10** especially, remarkably, strikingly **11** exceedingly, marvelously, wonderfully **12** particularly, phenomenally, stupendously, surpassingly
excerpt **4** cite, cull, pick **5** glean, quote **6** choose, select, single **7** extract, pick out
excess **3** fat **4** plus **5** extra, flood, spare **6** de trop **7** overage, surfeit, surplus **8** overflow, overkill, overmuch, overplus, plethora **9** boundless, indulgent, limitless, overboard, overdoing, overspill, overstock, profusion, redundant, unbounded **10** immoderacy, indulgence, oversupply, Saturnalia, surplusage **11** dissipation, overbalance, overmeasure, prodigality, superfluent, superfluity, superfluous, unessential

12 extravagance, immoderation, intemperance 13 overabundance, supernumerary
excessive 4 over 5 dizzy, steep, stiff, super, undue 6 too-too 7 extreme, sky-high 8 overmuch, prodigal, towering 10 dissipated, exorbitant, immoderate, inordinate, untempered 11 extravagant, intemperate, overweening 12 supernatural, unmeasurable, unrestrained 13 overindulgent *combining form:* 4 poly *prefix:* 3 sur
excessively 3 too 4 ever, over 6 overly, unduly 7 parlous 8 overfull, overmuch 9 extremely, immensely 12 inordinately *prefix:* 5 hyper
exchange 4 swap 5 bandy, trade, truck 6 barter, change, market, switch 7 bargain, commute, pay back, replace, traffic 8 displace 10 substitute 11 reciprocate *premium:* 4 agio
exchequer 5 chest 6 coffer 8 treasury, war chest
excise 3 tax 4 toll 5 elide, slash 6 cut off, cut out, delete, exsect, remove, resect 7 exscind, root out 8 amputate 9 eradicate, expurgate, extirpate, strike out
excision 3 cut 7 erasure, removal, surgery 9 resection 11 destruction, extirpation
excitable 4 edgy 6 touchy 8 agitable, skittery, skittish, unstable, volatile 9 alarmable, mercurial, startlish 10 high-strung 11 combustible 13 temperamental
excite 4 fire, move, spur, stir 5 elate, pique, prime, rouse, set up, waken 6 appeal, arouse, stir up, thrill, turn on 7 agitate, attract, commove, disturb, innerve, inspire, perturb, provoke, quicken 8 charge up, disquiet, energize, interest, intrigue, motivate, spirit up, touch off 9 fascinate, galvanize, impassion, innervate, stimulate 10 discompose, exhilarate
excited 3 hot 4 avid 5 eager 6 hectic 7 fevered, frantic 8 aflutter
excitement 3 ado 4 stir 6 furore, warmth 8 delirium, hysteria 9 commotion 11 disturbance, pandemonium
exclaim 4 blat, bolt, roar 5 snort 6 cry out 8 blurt out, burst out 9 ejaculate
exclamation 2 ah, ai, ay, ha, hi, ho, lo, oh, ow, so 3 aah, aha, bah, boo, cry, eek, feh, fie, gee, hah, hey, hic, huh, och, oho, ooh, pah, tsk, tut, ugh, wow, yeh 4 ahem, alas, damn, dang, darn, drat, egad, gosh, heck, hell, oops, ouch, phew, pish, posh, rats, whew, yell, yipe 5 alack, bravo, faugh, golly, humph, pshaw, shout 6 clamor, hurrah, indeed, phooey, shucks 7 doggone, gee whiz, hosanna, jeepers, whoopee 9 expletive 12 interjection *of disgust:* 3 bah, feh, ugh 5 yecch 6 phooey *of dismay:* 4 oh no *of pain:* 2 ow 4 ouch *of relief:* 4 phew *of sorrow:* 4 alas 5 alack *of surprise:* 2 ah, oh 3 aha, oho, wow *of triumph:* 3 hah
exclude 3 ban, bar 4 bate 5 block, debar, estop 6 banish, disbar, except, put out 7 keep out, lock out, obviate, prevent, rule out, shut out, suspend, ward off 8 close out, count out, preclude, prohibit 9 blackball, blacklist, eliminate, ostracize *prefix:* 3 dis
excluding 3 bar, but 4 less, save 6 bating, except, saving 7 barring, besides 9 outside of 11 exclusive of
exclusive 4 chic, lone, only, pick, sole, tony 5 aloof, elect, elite, scoop, smart, swank, swish, whole 6 chosen, cliquy, picked, select, single, with-it 7 barring, dashing, high-hat, stylish 8 clannish, cliquish, limiting, selected, snobbish, unshared 9 debarring, excluding, preferred, undivided 10 individual, limitative, privileged, unswerving 11 fashionable, prohibitive, restrictive, standoffish 12 aristocratic, concentrated, undistracted
exclusively 3 but 4 only 5 alone 6 solely, wholly 8 entirely 10 completely 12 particularly
excogitate 4 mind 5 educe, study, weigh 6 derive, evolve, invent, ponder 7 develop, perpend, think up 8 consider, contrive, think out 9 think over 11 contemplate
excommunicate 8 unchurch
excoriate 3 rub 4 flay, fret, gall 5 chafe, slash 6 abrade, scathe, scorch 7 blister, scarify, scourge 8 lambaste, lash into 9 castigate
excorticate 4 peel, skin 5 scale, strip
excrement 4 dirt 5 feces 6 ordure, refuse *combining form:* 4 copr, scat 5 copro, scato *of animals:* 4 dung, muck 6 manure *of sea birds:* 5 guano
excrescence 4 wart 6 pimple 7 process 9 outgrowth, processus
excruciate 3 try 4 hurt, pain, rack 5 wound, wring 6 harrow, martyr 7 afflict, agonize, crucify, inflame, torment, torture 8 convulse, irritate
excruciating 5 acute, sharp 7 extreme, racking, rending, tearing 8 piercing, shooting, stabbing 9 agonizing, consuming, harrowing, torturing, torturous 10 tormenting
exculpate 4 free 5 clear, remit 6 acquit, excuse, let off, pardon 7 absolve, amnesty, condone, explain, forgive, justify 9 exonerate, vindicate 11 rationalize
excurse 5 stray 6 depart, ramble, wander 7 digress, diverge 8 divagate
excursion 4 ride, tour, trek, trip, walk 5 aside, jaunt, paseo, sally, tramp 6 cruise, junket, outing, safari 7 circuit, journey 9 round trip 10 digression, divagation,

expedition, one-way trip, roundabout 11 parenthesis 12 pleasure trip

excusable 6 venial 7 tenable 10 condonable, defensible, forgivable, pardonable, remittable, vindicable 11 justifiable

excuse 4 plea 5 alibi, clear, remit, shift, spare 6 acquit, cop-out, exempt, let off, pardon, reason, wink at 7 absolve, apology, condone, defense, explain, forgive, justify, pretext, regrets, relieve, stopgap 8 dispense, overlook, palliate, pass over, shrug off 9 discharge, exculpate, exonerate, extenuate, gloss over, makeshift, vindicate, whitewash 10 substitute 11 explanation, rationalize 13 justification

execrable 3 bad, low 4 base, foul, vile 6 cursed, cussed, damned 7 blasted, heinous 8 accursed, damnable, horrific, infernal 9 atrocious, loathsome, monstrous, repulsive, revolting 10 confounded, despicable, detestable, horrifying, nauseating

execrate 3 ban 4 cuss, damn, hate 5 abhor, curse, swear 6 bedamn, detest, loathe, revile 7 accurse, censure, condemn, reprove 8 denounce 9 abominate, imprecate, objurgate, reprehend, reprobate 12 anathematize

execute 2 do 3 act 4 do in, hang, kill, slay 5 cause, lynch, purge 6 finish, gibbet, govern, handle, murder, render 7 achieve, bump off, conduct, fulfill, perform, put away 8 carry out, complete, dispatch, knock off, transact 9 discharge, eliminate, implement, liquidate 10 administer, bring about, put through 11 assassinate 12 administrate

execution 6 murder 7 facture, garrote, hanging 8 garrotte 9 beheading 11 performance

executioner 6 hanger 7 hangman, headman 8 headsman

executive 4 dean 6 leader 7 manager, officer 8 director, governor, higher-up, official 9 president 10 supervisor 11 businessman 12 entrepreneur 13 administrator, businesswoman

executor 4 doer 5 agent 9 performer

exegesis 6 exposé 9 construal 10 exposition 11 explanation, explication 12 construction

exemplar 4 soul 5 ideal, model 6 mirror 7 example, pattern 8 ensample, exponent, paradigm, standard 9 archetype, prototype 12 illustration

exemplary 4 good, pure 5 ideal, model 6 worthy 7 classic, typical 8 innocent, laudable, virtuous 9 admirable, blameless, classical, guiltless, righteous 10 inculpable, prototypal, unblamable 11 commendable 12 paradigmatic, praiseworthy, prototypical

exemplify 4 cite 5 quote 6 embody, mirror, typify 7 clarify, clear up 8 spell out 9 enlighten, epitomize, personify, represent, symbolize 10 illuminate, illustrate 11 demonstrate, emblematize

exempt 4 free 5 spare 6 except, excuse, let off 7 absolve, relieve 8 dispense 9 discharge *combining form:* 6 immuno

exemption 7 freedom, release 8 immunity, impunity 9 discharge, exception

exenterate 3 gut 4 draw 5 bowel 6 paunch 7 embowel 10 disembowel, eviscerate

exercise 3 irk, ply, use, vex 4 fret, gall 5 annoy, apply, chafe, drill, exert, sit-up, sport, study, throw, train, wield 6 abrade, action, bestow, bother, employ, foster, handle, lesson, pushup, put out 7 develop, exploit, improve, prepare, problem, provoke, utilize, workout 8 activity, drilling, exertion, movement, practice, rehearse 9 athletics, condition, cultivate, operation 10 employment 11 application 12 calisthenics

exert 3 ply, use 5 apply, throw, wield 6 employ, put out, strain 8 exercise

exertion 3 use 4 toil, work 5 labor, pains, trial, while 6 effort, strain 7 trouble 8 activity, exercise, striving, struggle 9 operation 10 employment, exercising 11 application, elbow grease

exfoliate 4 peel 5 scale 8 flake off 10 desquamate

exhalation 6 breath 7 halitus 9 breathing, effluvium, emanation 10 expiration

exhale 4 blow, emit 6 expire, let out 7 breathe 10 breathe out, outbreathe

exhaust 3 fag, sap 4 do in, draw, tire 5 drain, eat up, spend, use up 6 devour, dispel, expend, finish, overdo, run out, tucker, wash up, weaken 7 consume, deplete, frazzle, outtire, outwear, overply, scatter, wear out 8 bankrupt, disperse, draw down, enfeeble, knock out, overwork 9 dissipate, overdrive, overexert, prostrate 10 debilitate, impoverish, overextend, run through

exhausted 4 beat, dead, done, limp, weak 5 all in, spent, tired 6 bleary, effete, used up 7 drained, far-gone, run-down, worn-out 8 consumed, depleted, dog-tired 9 washed-out

exhaustion 7 fatigue 8 collapse 9 lassitude, tiredness, weariness 11 prostration

exhaustive 5 total 6 all-out 7 radical 8 complete, profound, sweeping, thorough, whole-hog 9 full-blown, full-dress, full-scale, intensive, out-and-out 13 comprehensive, thoroughgoing

exhibit 3 air 4 fair, look, mark, show 5 flash, sight 6 evince, expose, flaunt, ostend, parade 7 display, disport, show off, trot out 8 brandish, evidence, manifest, pro-

claim, showcase 10 exposition, illustrate 11 demonstrate
exhibition 4 fair, show 5 sight 7 display, pageant, showing 8 offering 9 spectacle 10 exposition 12 presentation 13 demonstration, manifestation
exhilarate 4 buoy, lift 5 boost, cheer, elate, exalt, pep up, set up 6 excite, thrill, uplift 7 animate, commove, delight, enliven, gladden, inspire 8 inspirit, spirit up, vitalize 9 stimulate 10 invigorate
exhilaration 6 firing, gaiety, uplift 7 ecstasy, elation 8 euphoria, gladness 9 animation, elevation 10 exaltation, excitation, excitement, quickening 11 enlivenment, inspiration, stimulation 12 invigoration, vitalization, vivification 13 galvanization
exhort 3 sic 4 goad, prod, spur, urge 5 egg on, plead, prick 6 insist, prompt, propel 8 admonish, call upon 9 stimulate
exhume 3 dig 5 dig up 6 unbury 7 unearth 8 disinter 9 disembalm, disentomb, disinhume, uncharnel
exigency 3 fix, jam 4 need, pass, want 5 pinch, rigor 6 crisis, demand, duress, pickle, scrape, strait 7 dilemma 8 coercion, hardship, juncture, pressure, zero hour 9 necessity 10 compulsion, constraint, crossroads, difficulty, insistence 11 requirement, vicissitude 12 turning point
exigent 5 acute, tough, vital 6 crying, taxing 7 burning, clamant, instant, onerous, weighty 8 exacting, grievous, menacing, pressing 9 clamorous, demanding, insistent, necessary 10 burdensome, imperative, oppressive 11 importunate, threatening
exiguous 4 poor, thin, tiny 5 scant, skimp, small, spare 6 little, meager, narrow, scanty, scrimp, skimpy, slight, sparse 7 limited, scrimpy, slender, tenuous 8 confined 10 diminutive, restricted, straitened
exile 4 oust 5 expel 6 banish, deport, emigré 7 cast out, expulse, outcast, refugee 8 diaspora, displace, drive out, evacuate, expellee, unperson 9 exclusion, expulsion, extradite, migration, nonperson, ostracism, ostracize, transport 10 banishment, dispersion, dispossess, expatriate, relegation, scattering 11 deportation, extradition 12 displacement, expatriation ***place of:*** 7 Siberia
exist 2 am, be, is 3 are, lie 4 live, move 5 dwell 6 inhere, reside 7 breathe, consist, subsist
existence 3 ens 4 esse, life 5 being, thing 6 entity 7 reality 8 perseity 9 actuality, something 13 individuality ***combining form:*** 3 ont 4 onto
existent 4 real 5 alive, being, thing 6 actual, around, entity, living 7 instant, present 8 todayish 10 present-day 12 contemporary
existentialist writer 5 Buber, Camus 6 Marcel, Sartre 7 Jaspers 9 Heidegger 11 Kierkegaard
existing 5 alive, being, ontic 6 around, extant, living ***Latin:*** 6 in esse
exit 2 go 4 door, gate, move, quit 5 going, leave 6 depart, egress, exodus, get off, outlet, portal, retire 7 doorway, get away 8 offgoing, withdraw 9 departure, egression 10 setting-out, withdrawal
exode 5 farce 8 travesty
exodus 4 exit 6 egress, flight 7 exiting 8 offgoing 9 departure, egression, migration 10 emigration, setting-out, withdrawal
Exodus author 4 Uris (Leon)
exonerate 4 free 5 clear 6 acquit, excuse 7 absolve 9 disburden, exculpate, vindicate 10 disculpate
exorbitant 5 dizzy, undue 7 extreme 8 exacting, overmuch, towering 9 excessive, overboard 10 immoderate, inordinate, outrageous 11 extravagant, unwarranted 12 preposterous, unmeasurable
exordium 5 proem 7 preface, prelude 8 foreword, overture, preamble, prologue 9 prelusion 11 preliminary 12 introduction, prolegomenon
exotic 5 alien 7 foreign, strange, unusual 8 alluring, enticing, imported, romantic 9 different, glamorous 10 introduced, mysterious, romanesque 11 fascinating
expand 3 wax 4 grow, open, rise 5 boost, built, mount, swell, widen 6 beef up, detail, dilate, fan out, spread, unfold 7 amplify, augment, bolster, develop, distend, enlarge, inflate, magnify, prolong, stretch, upsurge 8 escalate, heighten, increase, multiply, mushroom, protract 9 discourse, elaborate, expatiate, explicate, outspread 10 aggrandize, outstretch
expanse 4 area, room 5 field, ocean, orbit, range, reach, scope, space, sweep, tract 6 domain, extent, sphere, spread 7 breadth, compass, stretch 8 distance 9 amplitude, immensity, magnitude, territory
expansion 5 space 6 growth, spread 7 breadth, stretch 8 distance, increase 9 amplitude 11 enlargement
expansive 3 big 4 airy, free, wide 5 ample, broad, great, gushy, large 6 bouncy, lavish, scopic 7 buoyant, elastic, liberal 8 effusive, extended, generous, outgoing, scopious, volatile 9 resilient 10 gregarious, openhanded, unreserved 11 extroverted 12 communicable, effervescent, unrestrained 13 communicative, demonstrative, unconstrained
expatiate 6 ramble, recite, relate, wander

7 descant, discuss, dissert, recount 8 dilate on, rehearse 9 discourse, sermonize 10 dilate upon, dissertate
expatriate 4 oust 6 banish, deport, emigré 8 displace, expellee, relegate 9 transport
expect 4 feel, hope, look, take 5 await, sense, think 6 assume, divine, gather 7 believe, count on, foresee, imagine, presume, suppose 8 foreknow 9 apprehend, count upon 10 anticipate, presuppose
expectant 3 big 5 alert, eager, heavy 6 gravid, parous 7 atiptoe, hopeful 8 childing, enceinte, open-eyed, pregnant, watchful 10 parturient 11 openmouthed 12 anticipative, anticipatory
expectation 4 hope 6 design, motive 8 prospect
expectorate 4 spit
expediency 4 step 5 order, shift 6 design, resort, tactic 7 aptness, fitness, measure, stopgap 8 meetness, recourse, resource, strategy 9 makeshift, propriety, rightness, surrogate 10 substitute 11 suitability 12 appositeness, suitableness
expedient 3 fit 4 wise 5 dodge, means, shift 6 agency, medium, refuge, resort, timely, useful 7 fitting, politic, prudent, stopgap 8 feasible, possible, recourse, resource, suitable, tactical 9 advisable, judicious, makeshift, opportune, practical, well-timed 10 beneficial, convenient, instrument, profitable, seasonable, substitute 11 appropriate, practicable, utilitarian 12 advantageous
expedite 3 hie 4 send 5 hurry, issue, speed 6 hasten 7 quicken 8 dispatch 10 accelerate, facilitate
expedition 4 trek, trip 5 haste, hurry, speed 6 hustle, rustle 7 entrada, journey, travels 8 alacrity, campaign, celerity, dispatch, goodwill 9 excursion, readiness, swiftness 10 speediness 11 promptitude, punctuality
expeditious 4 fast 5 fleet, hasty, quick, rapid, ready, swift 6 prompt, speedy 9 breakneck, effective, effectual, efficient 10 harefooted 11 efficacious
expeditiousness 5 haste, hurry, speed 6 hustle, rustle 8 celerity, dispatch 9 swiftness
expel 4 oust, spew 5 belch, eject, eruct, erupt, evict, exile 6 banish, deport, disbar, irrupt 7 blow off, blow out, cast out, drum out, exhaust, expulse, kick out, read out, turn out 8 disgorge, displace 9 ejaculate, eliminate, transport 10 expatriate ***prefix:*** 3 dis
expellee 6 emigré
expend 2 go 3 pay 4 blow, give 5 spend, use up, waste 6 finish, lay out, outlay, wash up 7 consume, exhaust, fork out 8 disburse, dispense, shell out 10 distribute, run through
expenditure 4 cost 6 outlay 12 disbursement
expense 4 cost, loss, toll 5 price 6 charge, outlay 7 forfeit 8 overhead 9 decrement, sacrifice 10 forfeiture 11 deprivation 12 disbursement
expensive 4 dear, high 6 costly 9 big-ticket 10 high-priced, immoderate 12 uneconomical
experience 3 see 4 feel, have, know, live, meet, view 5 savor, skill, taste, trial 6 accept, behold, ordeal, suffer, survey, wisdom 7 know-how, receive, sustain, undergo 8 intimacy, practice 9 encounter, go through 10 background, inwardness 11 familiarity, observation, savoir faire 12 acquaintance ***anew:*** 6 relive ***combining form:*** 7 empirio 8 empirico
experienced 3 old, vet 4 wise 6 versed 7 old-line, old-time, skilled, veteran, worldly 8 broken in, seasoned, skillful 9 practical, practiced, qualified, underwent 10 proficient 12 accomplished
experiential see empirical
experiment 3 try 4 test 5 probe, study, trial, try on, weigh 6 search, try out 7 analyze, test out 8 analysis, research, trial run 10 scrutinize 11 examination, investigate 13 investigation, trial and error ***combining form:*** 7 empirio 8 empirico
experimental 4 test 5 trial 9 empirical, temporary, tentative 11 preliminary, preparatory, provisional 13 developmental
experimentation 4 test 5 trial 8 trial run 13 trial and error
expert 3 ace, pro, wiz 4 deft, whiz 5 adept, crack, doyen, maven, mavin, swell 6 adroit, artist, master, mayvin, wizard 7 artiste, skilled, trained 8 masterly, schooled, skillful, virtuoso 9 authority, dexterous, masterful 10 master-hand, past master, proficient, specialist 11 crackerjack 12 passed master, professional ***suffix:*** 5 ician
expertise 3 art 5 craft, knack, savvy, skill 7 ability, command, cunning, finesse, know-how, mastery 9 dexterity, quickness, readiness 10 adroitness, cleverness, competence, mastership 12 skillfulness 13 ingeniousness
expertness 5 knack, skill 7 ability, command, know-how, mastery 8 facility 10 mastership
expiate 3 pay 5 amend, atone, avert 6 remedy 7 correct, rectify, redress
expiation 9 atonement
expiatory 7 atoning, lustral 9 purgative

10 lustratory **11** purgatorial **12** propitiatory **13** expurgatorial

expiration **3** end **5** death **10** exhalation **11** termination

expire **2** go **3** die **4** conk, pass **5** lapse **6** demise, depart, elapse, exhale, perish, run out **7** decease **8** pass away **10** breathe out, outbreathe

explain **4** undo **5** clear, gloss, gloze, solve **6** acquit, define **7** absolve, account, analyze, clarify, clear up, condone, justify, resolve, unravel **8** annotate, construe, decipher, footnote, spell out, unriddle, untangle **9** break down, elucidate, exculpate, exonerate, interpret, vindicate **10** illuminate, illustrate, unscramble **11** disentangle, rationalize

explain away **7** account, justify **11** rationalize

explanation **3** key **6** excuse, motive, reason **7** account, example, grounds, meaning **8** exegesis **9** construal, rationale **12** unscrambling **13** enlightenment

explanatory **8** exegetic **10** discursive **12** enlightening, illuminating, illustrative, interpretive **13** demonstrative

expletive **4** cuss, oath **5** curse, swear **8** cussword **9** swearword; (see also **exclamation**)

explicate **6** unfold **7** amplify, develop, explain, expound **8** construe, spell out **9** interpret

explication **8** exegesis **9** construal **11** development, enlargement

explicative **8** exegetic **10** scholastic **12** interpretive

explicit **4** open, sure **5** clear, exact, lucid, overt, plain **7** certain, correct, obvious, precise **8** accurate, clean-cut, clear-cut, definite, distinct, specific **10** definitive **11** categorical, perspicuous, unambiguous, unequivocal

explode **3** pop **4** fire **5** blast, burst, erupt, go off, shoot **6** blow up **7** deflate **8** break out, detonate, disprove, dynamite, mushroom, puncture **9** discharge, discredit **10** burst forth

exploit **3** act, job, use **4** blow, coup, deed, feat, gest, play, skin, soak, work **5** abuse, apply, bleed, stick, stunt **6** bestow, effort, employ, fleece, handle, jockey, parlay, stroke **7** beguile, emprise, finesse, utilize, venture **8** exercise, impose on, maneuver **9** adventure, cultivate **10** enterprise, impose upon, manipulate **11** achievement, performance, tour de force

explore **3** try **4** feel, sift, test **5** probe **6** burrow, go into, quarry, search **7** dig into, examine **8** look into, prospect, question **9** delve into, inquisite **11** inquire into, investigate

explorer ***African:*** **3** Cam, Cao **4** Park **5** Grant, Laird, Speke **6** Akeley, Burton, Lander **7** Covilha, Stanley **8** Covilhao **10** Clapperton **11** Livingstone ***American:*** **4** Byrd, Hall, Kane, Pike **5** Clark, Lewis, Peary **6** Powell, Wilkes **7** Fremont ***Antarctic:*** **4** Byrd, Cook, Ross **5** Fuchs, Ronne, Scott **6** Palmer, Rymill, Wilkes **7** Weddell, Wilkins **8** Amundsen, d'Urville **9** Ellsworth **10** Kristensen, Shackleton ***Arctic:*** **3** Rae **4** Byrd, Cook **5** Davis, Peary **6** Baffin, Bering, Henson, Hudson, Nansen, Nobile **7** Barents, Bennett, Wilkins, Wrangel **8** Amundsen **9** Mackenzie, Macmillan **10** Stefansson ***Australian:*** **7** Wilkins ***Austrian:*** **9** Weyprecht ***British:*** **12** Younghusband ***Canadian:*** **9** Mackenzie **10** Stefansson ***Danish:*** **9** Rasmussen ***Dutch:*** **6** Tasman ***English:*** **4** Cook **5** Drake, Scott, Smith **6** Baffin, Burton, Hudson **7** Raleigh, Stanley **9** Vancouver **10** Shackleton ***French:*** **7** Cartier, La Salle, Nicolet **8** Cousteau **9** Champlain, La Perouse, Marquette ***French Canadian:*** **6** Joliet **7** Jolliet **9** Iberville ***German:*** **6** Peters **7** Humbolt ***Italian:*** **5** Cabot **6** Nobile ***New Zealand:*** **7** Hillary ***Norwegian:*** **6** Nansen **8** Amundsen, Sverdrup **9** Heyerdahl ***Portuguese:*** **6** Cabral **8** Magellan ***Scottish:*** **3** Rae **4** Park, Ross **7** Thomson **11** Livingstone ***Spanish:*** **6** Balboa, Cortes, de Soto, Pinzon **7** Mendoza, Pizarro **8** Bastidas, Coronado **11** Ponce de Leon

explosion **3** pop, pow **4** bang, gust **5** blast, burst, sally **6** access **7** flare-up **8** outburst **10** detonation

explosive **3** TNT **4** bomb, mine **5** nitro, troty **6** amatol, petard, powder **7** ammonal, cordite, dunnite, grenade, lyddite **8** cheddite, dynamite, fulminic, melinite **9** fulminate **10** detonative **13** nitroglycerin ***device:*** **3** cap **4** bomb, mine **5** shell **6** petard **7** grenade **8** firework ***display:*** **9** fireworks ***expert:*** **5** Maxim ***sound:*** **3** pop, pow **4** bang, boom

exponent **6** backer **7** booster **8** advocate, champion, defender, partisan, promoter, upholder **9** supporter

expose **3** air **4** bare, open, risk, show **5** flash, peril, strip **6** debunk, flaunt, hazard, parade, reveal, show up, unfold, unmask, unveil **7** display, disport, exhibit, imperil, jeopard, lay open, publish, show off, subject, trot out, uncloak, uncover, undress **8** brandish, disclose, discover, endanger, jeopardy, muckrake, unclothe, unshroud **9** advertise, broadcast

exposé **10** revelation

exposed **4** bare, open **5** naked, prone **6** liable, likely, peeled **7** denuded, evident, menaced, subject, visible **8** apparent, manifest, revealed, stripped, unhidden **9** obnoxious, sensitive, uncovered **10** threatened **11** susceptible, unconcealed

exposition **4** fair, show **7** display, exhibit **8** analysis, exegesis **9** construal, discourse, statement **10** discussion, exhibition **11** delineation

expository **8** critical, exegetic **11** explanative, explanatory **12** interpretive

expostulate **4** kick **5** argue, fight **6** combat, debate, except, object, oppose, resist **7** discuss, dispute, protest **11** remonstrate

exposure **4** risk **5** peril **6** danger **8** jeopardy, openness **9** liability **12** helplessness, susceptivity **13** vulnerability

expound **5** state, teach **7** clarify, comment, explain, express, lecture, present **8** construe, describe, spell out **9** delineate, discourse, exemplify, explicate, interpret **10** illustrate

expounder **7** teacher **8** advocate, champion **9** proponent, supporter

express **3** air, put, say, set **4** give, mean, tell, vent, word **5** couch, crush, frame, spell, state **6** broach, convey, denote, impart, import, intend, phrase, voiced **7** add up to, connote, declare, signify, special, uttered **8** announce, clean-cut, clear-cut, definite, disclose, especial, explicit, intended, proclaim, put about, specific **9** circulate, enunciate, formulate, out-and-out, pronounce, ventilate **10** definitive, individual, particular **11** categorical, communicate, intentional, unambiguous, unqualified ***gratitude:*** **5** thank ***regret:*** **9** apologize

expression **4** cast, face, form, look, mien, show, sign, vent, word **5** idiom, issue, motto, token, voice **6** clause, phrase, symbol, visage **7** gesture **8** locution, reminder **9** eloquence, facundity, statement, utterance, verbalism, vividness **10** embodiment, indication, reflection **11** countenance, graphicness, observation **13** demonstration, manifestation ***combining form:*** **4** logy **5** logia ***facial:*** **4** grin, phiz **5** frown, scowl, smile, wince **7** grimace ***of assent:*** **3** aye, nod, yea, yes **4** okay **6** placet **9** exequator ***of sorrow:*** **4** alas, tear ***trite:*** **6** cliché **7** bromide **8** banality ***witty:*** **4** quip **8** atticism

expressionless **4** dead, dull **5** blank, empty, stony **6** stolid, vacant, wooden **7** deadpan, vacuous **9** impassive **10** lackluster **11** inscrutable

expressive **4** rich **5** vivid **6** facund, lively, poetic **7** graphic **8** eloquent, emphatic, pregnant, senseful, spirited **9** pictorial, revealing **10** meaningful, revelatory **11** sententious, significant

expressly **4** even, just **6** as well, namely **8** in specie

expressway **4** road **7** freeway, highway, parkway **8** turnpike

expropriate **4** take **5** annex, seize **7** preempt **8** accroach **9** sequester **10** commandeer, confiscate, dispossess

expulse **4** oust **5** eject **6** banish, deport **7** cast out **8** displace, relegate **9** transport

expulsion **5** exile **7** ousting, removal **8** ejection **9** ostracism **10** banishment, driving out, forcing out, relegation **11** deportation **12** displacement

expunge **4** dele, drop, omit, x out **5** annul, erase **6** cancel, delete, efface **7** blot out, destroy, discard, exclude, wipe out **8** black out **9** eradicate **10** annihilate, obliterate

expurgate **4** blip **5** purge **6** censor, purify, screen **7** cleanse **10** bowdlerize

expurgation **9** catharsis, cleansing

exquisite **3** fop **4** buck, dude, nice, rare **5** acute, blood, dandy **6** choice, dainty, fierce, select, superb **7** coxcomb, elegant, extreme, furious, intense, vicious, violent **8** delicate, finished, flawless, macaroni, superior, terrible, vehement **9** desperate, errorless, faultless, recherché **10** consummate, immaculate, impeccable

exsanguine **6** anemic **9** bloodless

exsect **6** cut out, excise

exsiccate **3** dry **4** sear **5** parch

exsuccuous **3** dry **4** sere **7** sapless **8** withered

extant **5** alive, being **6** actual, around, living **7** current, present **8** todayish **9** immediate **10** present-day **12** contemporary

extemporaneous **4** snap **6** casual **7** offhand **8** informal **9** impromptu, impulsive, unstudied **10** improvised, unprepared **11** unrehearsed **12** unthought-out

extempore see **extemporaneous**

extemporize **3** act **5** ad-lib **7** dash off, toss off **8** knock off **9** improvise **11** improvisate

extend **2** go **3** eke, run **4** draw, give, grow, make, open, pose, span, vary **5** allot, award, boost, grant, offer, range, reach **6** accord, attain, beef up, bestow, confer, donate, fan out, spread, tender, unfold **7** advance, amplify, augment, draw out, enlarge, hold out, magnify, present, proceed, proffer, project, prolong, spin out, stretch **8** allocate, continue, elongate, heighten, increase, lengthen, multiply, protract **9** outspread **10** aggrandize, outstretch, prolongate

extended ***combining form:*** **3** meg **4** mego **5** megal **6** megalo

extension **3** arm, ell **4** area, size, wing **5** ambit, annex, block, orbit, range, reach, scope, sweep **6** radius, spread **7** compass, purview, stretch **8** increase **9** magnitude **10** continuing, drawing out, elongation, production, stretch-out **11** enlargement, lengthening, prolongment, protraction **12** augmentation, continuation, prolongation, spreading out

extensity **5** ambit, orbit, range, reach, scope, sweep **6** radius **7** compass, purview

extensive **3** big **4** vast, wide **5** broad, hefty, large, major **6** scopic **7** blanket, general, immense, sizable **8** scopious, spacious **9** boundless, wholesale **10** large-scale **11** far-reaching, wide-ranging **12** considerable, far-spreading

extent **4** size, tune, writ **5** ambit, field, orbit, order, range, reach, scope, sweep, width **6** amount, degree, domain, matter, radius, sphere **7** breadth, compass, measure, purview **8** province, vicinity **9** magnitude **10** dimensions, proportion

extenuate **4** thin **5** white **6** temper, veneer, whiten **7** explain, justify, qualify, varnish **8** palliate, wiredraw **9** apologize, gloss over, gloze over, sugarcoat, whitewash **10** blanch over **11** rationalize

exterior **4** over **5** ectal, outer **6** facade **7** outmost, outside, outward, surface **8** external **9** outermost

exterminate **4** kill **5** abate **6** uproot **7** abolish, blot out, root out, wipe out **8** massacre **9** finish off, slaughter **10** annihilate, extinguish

external **3** out **4** over **5** ectal, outer **7** outmost, outside, outward **9** outermost **10** peripheral **11** superficial ***combining form:*** **3** ect **4** ecto

externalize **6** embody **8** manifest **9** incarnate, objectify, personify **12** substantiate

extinct **4** cold, dead, gone, late, lost **5** passé **6** asleep, bygone, fallen **7** archaic, defunct, disused, outworn **8** deceased, departed, lifeless, obsolete, outmoded, perished, vanished **9** collapsed **10** antiquated, overthrown, superseded, unanimated **11** disappeared, nonexistent **12** old-fashioned ***combining form:*** **4** necr **5** necro

extinction **5** death **11** destruction **12** annihilation, obliteration

extinguish **3** out **5** abate, check, crush, douse, erase, quash, quell **6** put out, quench, squash, stifle, uproot **7** abolish, blot out, blow out, destroy, expunge, put down, root out, smother, wipe out **8** suppress **9** eradicate **10** annihilate, obliterate

extirpate **4** raze **5** erase **6** cut out, efface, excise, resect, uproot **7** abolish, blot out, destroy, expunge, kill off, root out, wipe out **8** demolish **10** annihilate

extol **4** hymn, laud **5** bless, cry up, exalt **6** praise **7** applaud, commend, elevate, glorify, magnify **8** eulogize **9** celebrate **10** panegyrize

extort **3** get **4** milk, skin **5** bleed, cheat, educe, evoke, exact, force, gouge, pinch, screw, wrest, wring **6** coerce, compel, demand, elicit, evince, fleece, obtain, secure, wrench **7** squeeze **9** blackmail, shake down

extortion **8** chantage, exaction **9** blackmail

extra **3** odd **4** more, over **5** added, spare **6** de trop, rarely **7** surplus **8** markedly **9** lagniappe, unusually **10** additional, especially, noticeably, uncommonly **11** superfluent, superfluous **12** considerably, particularly, supplemental **13** supernumerary, supplementary ***prefix:*** **5** hyper, super

extract **3** dig, pry **4** cull, draw, milk, pull, tear, yank **5** educe, evoke, glean, wring **6** avulse, eke out, elicit, evince, evulse, garner, gather, pick up **7** abridge, distill, excerpt, scratch, shorten, squeeze **8** condense

extraction **5** birth, blood **6** origin **7** descent, essence, lineage **8** ancestry, pedigree **9** parentage

extraneous **5** alien, outer **6** exotic **7** foreign **9** pointless, unrelated **10** accidental, immaterial, inapposite, incidental, irrelative, irrelevant **11** impertinent, unessential **12** adventitious, inapplicable **13** inappropriate

extraordinary **3** odd **4** rare **6** unique **7** amazing, notable, unusual **8** singular, terrific, uncommon, unwonted **9** wonderful **10** noteworthy, remarkable, stupendous, tremendous **11** exceptional, unthinkable

extravagance **5** frill, luxus, waste **6** luxury **7** amenity **8** squander, unthrift **9** overdoing **10** lavishness **11** prodigality, superfluity **12** wastefulness

extravagant **4** wild **5** crazy, dizzy, outré, silly, undue **6** absurd, lavish **7** bizarre, foolish, profuse **8** prodigal, towering, wasteful **9** fantastic, ludicrous **10** immoderate, inordinate, profligate, ridiculous, unbalanced **11** exaggerated, implausible, nonsensical **12** preposterous, unmeasurable, unrestrained

extreme **3** top **4** deep, last, peak, wild **5** crest, crown, dizzy, final, limit, rabid, ultra, undue **6** ardent, climax, excess, height, moving, summit, utmost **7** ceiling, drastic, fanatic, intense, maximum, outmost, radical, violent **8** farthest, furthest, pinnacle, remotest, towering, ultraist **9** desperate, excessive, outermost, uttermost **10** immoderate, inordinate, outlandish **11** culmination, furthermost, inordinancy, intolerable, unwarranted **12** consummation, revolutional, unmeasurable, unreasonable **13** revolutionary ***degree:*** **3** nth

extremely 3 too 4 ever, over, very 6 mighty 7 parlous 8 overfull, overmuch 11 exceedingly
extremist 5 rabid, ultra 7 fanatic, radical 12 revolutional 13 revolutionary
extremity 3 arm, end, leg, tip 4 acme, apex, foot, hand, tail 5 limit, verge 6 apogee, vertex, zenith 8 terminal, terminus *combining form:* 3 acr, akr 4 acro, akro
extricate 4 free 5 clear, loose, sever, untie 6 detach, rescue 7 deliver, discern, release, resolve, unravel, untwine 8 abstract, untangle 9 clear away, disburdon, discumber, disengage 10 discrepate, disembroil, disentwine, disinvolve, severalize, unentangle, unscramble 11 disburden, disencumber, disentangle, distinguish 12 disembarrass
extrinsic 5 alien, outer 6 gained 7 foreign, outside, outward 8 acquired, external 10 accidental, extraneous
extrude 3 out 4 spew 5 chase, chuck, eject, evict 7 boot out, dismiss, kick out, project 8 throw out
exuberance 4 life, zest 5 ardor 6 spirit 7 abandon, gayness 8 buoyancy 10 friskiness, liveliness 11 zestfulness 13 sprightliness
exuberant 3 gay 4 glad, lush, rank 5 brash, happy 6 ardent, fecund, lavish, lively 7 diffuse, fertile, opulent, profuse, riotous, zestful 8 fruitful, prodigal, prolific, spirited 9 ebullient, profusive, sprightly, vivacious 10 frolicsome, passionate 12 effervescent, high-spirited
exude 4 emit, ooze, seep, weep 5 bleed, sweat 6 strain 7 emanate, secrete, trickle 8 perspire 9 discharge, percolate
exult 4 brag, crow 5 boast, gloat, glory 7 delight, rejoice, show off, triumph 8 jubilate 9 celebrate
exultant 4 glad 5 happy 6 elated, joyous 7 flushed 8 jubilant 9 cock-a-hoop, overjoyed, rejoicing, triumphal 10 cock-a-whoop, delighting
exultation 3 joy 7 delight, rapture, triumph 8 gloating 9 jubilance, rejoicing 10 jubilation
exuviate 4 molt, shed, slip 5 moult 6 slough
eye 3 orb, tab 4 gape, gaze, lamp, look, loop, mind, ring, tail, view 5 grasp, optic, sight, stare, watch 6 behold, belief, goggle, look at, ocular, oculus, peeper, regard, seeing, size up, staple, vision, winker 7 blinker, feeling, opinion 8 attitude, consider, gaze upon, judgment, look upon, position, scrutiny, thinking 9 sentiment, viewpoint 10 conception, conclusion, conviction, persuasion, rubberneck, scrutinize 11 contemplate 12 surveillance *combining form:* 3 ope, opy 4 ocul, opia, opto 5 oculo 8 ophthalm 9 ophthalma, ophthalmo 10 ophthalmia, ophthalmus *defect:* 6 myopia 9 hyperopia 10 emmetropia, presbyopia 11 astigmatism *disease:* 8 cataract, glaucoma, trachoma *doctor:* 7 oculist 11 optometrist *opening:* 5 pupil *part:* 4 iris, lens, uvea 5 pupil 6 cornea, retina, sclera *relating to:* 5 optic 7 optical *socket:* 5 orbit *Spanish:* 3 ojo
eye-catching 6 marked, signal 7 pointed, salient 9 prominent 10 noticeable, remarkable 11 conspicuous
eyedropper 7 pipette
eyeful 6 beauty, looker, lovely 7 stunner 8 knockout
eyeglass 4 lens 5 lense 7 monocle
eyeglasses 5 specs 6 lenses 7 lorgnon 8 pince-nez 9 lorgnette
eyelash 6 cilium
eyelid 8 palpebra 9 palpebrae (plural) *combining form:* 7 blephar 8 blepharo
eyepiece 4 lens 6 ocular
eye-popping 8 exciting, stirring 9 thrilling 10 exhilarant 11 astonishing 12 exhilarative
eyesore 4 mess 5 sight 6 defect, fright 7 blemish, desight 11 monstrosity
eyespot 7 disease, ocellus
eyetooth 6 canine
eyewash 3 rot 5 bilge, hooey 6 bunkum 7 twaddle 8 malarkey, nonsense
eyewitness 6 viewer 7 watcher 8 beholder, by-sitter, looker-on, observer, onlooker 9 bystander, spectator
eye worm 3 loa
eyrie see aerie
Ezbon's father 3 Gad
Ezekiel's father 4 Buzi
Ezer's father 6 Jeshua 7 Ephraim

F

Fabian 4 Shaw 8 cautious 9 socialist

fable 4 myth, tale 5 story 6 legend 7 fiction, figment 8 allegory, apologue ***animal:*** 8 bestiary

fabric 3 rep, web 4 repp 5 cloth, fiber, grain 7 texture 8 building, material, shirting 9 structure ***coarse:*** 5 crash, gunny 6 burlap, linsey, ratiné 7 cheviot, hopsack 8 homespun, osnaburg ***corded:*** 3 rep 4 repp 5 piqué 6 calico, moreen, poplin 7 pinwale 8 corduroy, paduasoy 9 bengaline ***cotton:*** 4 jean, leno 5 baize, chino, drill, scrim, swiss, wigan 6 chintz, dimity, faille, madras, muslin 7 etamine, galatea, gingham, nankeen, percale, silesia, ticking 8 chambray, dungaree, nainsook, osnaburg, tarlatan ***cotton and linen:*** 4 huck 7 fustian 9 huckaback ***crepe:*** 8 marocain ***dealer:*** 6 draper, mercer ***durable:*** 4 huck, jean 5 chino, denim, drill 6 frieze, moreen 7 lasting, ticking 8 cretonne, dungaree, osnaburg ***embroidered:*** 9 baldachin, baldaquin 10 baldachino 11 baldacchino ***finishing process:*** 8 lustring 9 mercerize 10 causterize ***flag material:*** 7 bunting ***glazed:*** 6 chintz 7 cambric, holland ***knitted:*** 6 tricot 10 balbriggan ***linen:*** 7 cambric, lockram ***looped:*** 6 bouclé ***lustrous:*** 4 silk 5 moiré, satin, surah 7 silesia, taffeta 12 brilliantine ***metallic:*** 4 lamé ***net:*** 5 tulle 8 bobbinet, illusion ***openwork:*** 4 lace 8 filigree ***ornamental:*** 4 lace 5 braid 6 ribbon 7 bunting ***pebbly-surface:*** 6 armure 8 barathea ***pile-surface:*** 5 panne, plush, terry 6 velour, velvet 7 bolivia, duvetyn, velours 8 chenille, moleskin, velveret 9 velveteen ***plaid:*** 6 tartan ***printed:*** 5 batik, toile 6 calico, chintz, damask 7 allover, challis, dornick, pintado 8 cretonne, jacquard 11 toile de jouy ***raised pattern:*** 7 brocade 10 brocatelle ***satin weave:*** 5 panne ***sheer:*** 4 lawn 5 gauze, ninon, swiss, voile 6 barege, dimity, tissue 7 batiste, chiffon, cypress, organdy, organza, tiffany 8 tarlatan ***silk:*** 4 fuji 5 pekin 6 cendal, chappe, pongee, samite, sendal 7 alamode, foulard, grogram, schappe 8 paduasoy, sarcenet, sarsenet, shantung 9 bombazine ***striped:*** 3 aba 4 abba 5 abaya, pekin 7 galatea, ticking 8 algerine 10 algerienne ***synthetic:*** 5 ninon, nylon, Orlon, rayon 6 Dacron ***twill:*** 4 jean 5 chino, drill, serge 7 foulard, galatea, nankeen, silesia, ticking 8 dungaree, shalloon 9 bombazine 10 broadcloth ***unfinished:*** 6 greige ***waterproof:*** 7 oilskin ***wool:*** 5 baize, loden, tweed 6 caddis, camlet, duffel, duffle, melton, merino, wadmad, wadmel, wadmol, witney, woolen 7 caddice, delaine, whitney, woollen 8 algerine, mackinaw, prunella 9 cassimera 10 algerienne ***wool, poor quality:*** 5 mungo 6 shoddy ***wool mixture:*** 5 tammy 6 saxony, wincey, winsey 7 drugget, ratteen 8 moquette, shalloon, zibeline ***woven:*** 4 weft 7 textile

fabricate 4 form, make 5 build, frame, shape 6 devise, invent, make up 7 concoct, fashion, produce, turn out 8 assemble, contrive 9 construct 11 manufacture

fabrication 3 fib, lie 4 opus, work 6 deceit 7 fiction, figment, product, untruth 9 falsehood

fabulist ***French:*** 10 La Fontaine ***Greek:*** 4 Esop 5 Aesop ***Indian:*** 6 Bidpai, Pilpai, Pilpay ***Roman:*** 8 Phaedrus ***Russian:*** 6 Krylov

fabulous 7 amazing 8 mythical 9 legendary, wonderful 10 astounding, exorbitant, fictitious, incredible, inordinate, outrageous, prodigious, stupendous 11 astonishing, extravagant 12 mythological ***animal:*** 6 dragon 7 centaur, unicorn ***bird:*** 3 roc 6 simurg 7 simurgh ***serpent:*** 8 basilisk 10 cockatrice

facade 4 face, mask, show 5 color, front, guise, put-on 6 veneer 8 disguise, pretense

face 3 mow, mug, top 4 cast, clad, dare, defy, gall, gaze, look, mask, meet, moue, phiz, pout, show, side, skin, veil 5 await, beard, brass, brave, cheek, cloak, close, cover, fight, front, frown, glare, guise, lower, mouth, nerve, paint, scowl, stare, watch 6 accost, border, brazen, breast, engage, expect, glower, makeup, mazard, muzzle, oppose, resist, take on, visage 7 affront, contend, grimace, outdare, seeming, sheathe, showing, venture 8 confront, disguise, features, mouthing, war paint 9 brashness, challenge, encounter, semblance, withstand 10 appearance, confidence, effrontery, expression, false front, lin-

eaments, maquillage, masquerade, simulacrum **11** countenance, physiognomy
facet **4** hand, side **5** angle, bezel, front, phase **6** aspect
facetious **5** comic, droll, funny, jolly, merry, witty **6** blithe, jocose, jocund, joking, jovial **7** comical, jesting, jocular **8** humorous **9** laughable, ludicrous **12** wisecracking
face-to-face **7** vis-à-vis
facile **4** able, deft, easy, glib **5** light, quick, royal **6** adroit, expert, fluent, simple, smooth **7** cursory, shallow, voluble **9** dexterous **10** effortless, uncritical
facilitate **3** aid **4** ease, help **6** assist **8** expedite
facility **3** aid, wit **4** bent, ease, tact, turn **5** poise, skill **7** abandon, address, amenity, comfort, fitting, leaning **8** aptitude **9** advantage, dexterity, lightness, readiness **10** smoothness **11** convenience, spontaneity **13** accommodation
facing **5** front, panel **6** before, contra, toward, veneer **7** against, vis-à-vis **8** covering, opposite, paneling **11** over against *down:* **5** prone *up:* **6** supine
facsimile **4** copy **5** ditto **6** carbon **7** replica **9** duplicate, imitation **10** carbon copy **11** replication **12** reproduction
fact **5** datum, event, truth **6** detail **7** episode, reality **8** incident **9** actuality, happening **10** observable, occurrence, particular, phenomenon **11** genuineness **12** authenticity, circumstance
faction **4** bloc, camp, part, ring, sect, side, wing **5** junto, party **7** combine **8** offshoot **11** combination
factious **7** warring **8** fighting **9** alienated, estranged, insurgent, seditious **10** contending **11** belligerent, contentious, disaffected, quarrelsome **13** insubordinate
factitious **4** sham **5** false **6** forced **7** assumed, feigned, man-made, shammed **8** affected **9** pretended, simulated, synthetic **10** artificial **13** counterfeited
factor **3** aid **4** doer, gene **5** agent, cause, maker, means, proxy **6** agency, deputy, helper **7** bailiff, element, steward **8** adjutant, assignee, attorney **9** assistant, coadjutor, component, consignee, majordomo, seneschal **10** antecedent, ingredient, instrument **11** determinant
factory **4** mill, shop **5** plant, works
factual **4** hard, true **5** valid **7** certain, genuine **8** absolute, positive **9** authentic, undoubted, veritable
faculty **4** bent, bump, gift, nose, turn **5** flair, knack, power **6** genius, talent **7** aptness, leaning **8** aptitude, capacity, function, instinct, penchant, property **12** predilection
facund **4** rich **8** eloquent, pregnant **10** expressive, meaningful **11** sententious, significant
fad **3** cry **4** chic, mode, rage, whim **5** craze, fancy, style, trend, vogue **6** furore, vagary, whimsy **7** caprice, conceit, fashion **10** dernier cri
fade **3** die, dim, ebb **4** dull, flag, melt, pale, thin **5** abate, clear, muddy **6** lessen, rarefy, vanish, weaken, wither **7** decline, dwindle, evanish, tarnish **8** diminish, dissolve, evanesce, languish, moderate **9** attenuate, disappear, evaporate **10** deliquesce **11** deteriorate
Faerie Queen, The ***author:*** **7** Spenser ***character:*** **3** Ate, Una **4** Alma **5** Guyon, Talus **6** Abessa, Amavia, Amoret, Arthur, Cambel, Duessa, Palmer **7** Artegal, Corceca, Fidessa, Maleger, Sansloy **8** Calidore, Florimel, Fradubio, Gloriana, Lucifera, Orgoglio, Satyrane **9** Archimago, Britomart **11** Britomartis
Fafner, Fafnir ***brother:*** **5** Regin **6** Fasolt, Reginn ***father:*** **8** Hreidmar ***form:*** **6** dragon ***slayer:*** **6** Sigurd **9** Siegfried ***victim:*** **6** Fasolt **8** Hreidmar
fag **4** flag, tire **5** smoke, weary **6** drudge, tucker **7** exhaust, frazzle, outtire, outwear, servant, wear out **8** knock out **9** cigarette, prostrate
fag end **4** butt **7** remnant **8** last part
fail **3** ebb, end **4** bomb, bust, flag, fold, jade, lose, miss, omit, sink, slip, wane **5** break, close, crash, drain, flunk, short **6** falter, finish, forget, ignore, lessen, run out, shrink, slight, weaken, worsen **7** blink at, bust out, decline, default, deplete, dwindle, exhaust, flummox, founder, gazette, give out, neglect, wash out **8** bankrupt, decrease, diminish, discount, languish, miscarry, overlook, overpass **9** blink away, disregard, terminate **10** impoverish **11** deteriorate
failing **3** shy **4** vice **5** fault, scant, short **6** foible, scanty, scarce **7** frailty **8** weakness **9** deficient **10** deficiency, inadequate **12** imperfection, insufficient, unsufficient
failure **3** dud **4** bomb, bust, flop, hash, lack, miss **5** botch, fault, lemon, loser **6** dearth, defeat, ebbing, fiasco, fizzle, laxity, muddle, outage, waning **7** absence, debacle, decline, default, deficit, neglect, paucity, washout **8** collapse, flagging, poorness, scarcity, shortage, underage, weakness **9** insuccess, oversight, slackness, unconcern, unsuccess **10** bankruptcy, deficiency, exhaustion, inadequacy, meagerness, negligence, nonsuccess, remissness, scantiness, skimpiness **11** declination, defalcation, delinquency, dereliction, inferiority, miscarriage, shortcoming **12** debilitation, enfeeblement, imperfection, indifference **13** deterio-

ration, insufficience, insufficiency, might-have-been

fain 4 glad 5 eager, prone, ready 6 minded 7 willing 8 desirous, disposed, inclined 11 predisposed

faint 3 dim, low, wan 4 coma, mild, pale, soft, swim, thin, weak 5 balmy, bland, blear, dusty, fuzzy, small, swoon, vague 6 bleary, feeble, gentle, hushed, smooth 7 blurred, grayout, languid, lenient, muffled, obscure, pass out, shadowy, stifled, syncope, unclear, vertigo 8 black out, listless 9 dizziness, inaudible, undefined 10 ill-defined, indistinct, undistinct

fair 4 calm, even, fine, just, mean, mild, pure, sane, show, so-so 5 balmy, blond, clean, clear, equal, light, right, ruddy, sunny, tawny 6 bazaar, blonde, candid, chaste, comely, common, dainty, decent, honest, lawful, lovely, medium, placid, pretty, square 7 average, clarion, clement, exhibit 8 balanced, carnival, charming, delicate, detached, festival, handsome, mediocre, middling, moderate, ordinary, pleasant, rainless, rational, straight, sunshine, sunshiny, tranquil, unbiased 9 beauteous, beautiful, cloudless, equitable, exquisite, impartial, objective, unclouded, uncolored 10 attractive, enchanting, exhibition, exposition, impersonal, open-minded, reasonable, sunshining, undarkened 11 good-looking, indifferent, nonpartisan, sportsmanly 12 intermediate, unprejudiced 13 disinterested, dispassionate, sportsmanlike, undistinctive, unthreatening

fair-haired 3 pet 4 dear 5 blond, loved 6 blonde 7 beloved, darling 8 blue-eyed, favorite, precious

fairness 6 equity 12 impartiality

fairy 3 elf, imp 4 pixy, puck 5 dwarf, elfin, gnome, nisse, pixie 6 goblin, kobold, sprite 7 banshee, brownie, gremlin 10 leprechaun ***king:*** 6 Oberon ***palace:*** 4 shee 5 sidhe ***queen:*** 3 Mab 7 Titania ***shoemaker:*** 10 leprechaun

fairy tale ***author:*** 5 Grimm, Wilde 8 Andersen, Perrault ***character:*** 6 Gretel, Hansel 8 Rapunzel 9 Snow White 10 Cinderella, Goldilocks

faith 4 cult, hope, sect 5 creed, stock, troth, trust 6 belief, church, credit, dogmas, tenets 8 credence, reliance, religion 9 communion, doctrines 10 confidence, connection, dependence, persuasion 12 denomination ***article of:*** 5 tenet 9 credendum

faithful 4 fast, firm, just, true 5 exact, liege, loyal, pious, right, tried 6 ardent, loving, steady, strict, trusty 7 binding, devoted, staunch 8 constant, credible, reliable, resolute, trueblue 9 allegiant, authentic, steadfast, veracious, veridical 10 convincing, dependable 11 trustworthy, undistorted 12 affectionate 13 conscientious, dyed-in-the-wool

faithfulness 5 ardor, piety 6 fealty 7 loyalty 8 adhesion, devotion, fidelity 9 adherence, constancy 10 allegiance, attachment

faithless 5 false 6 fickle, untrue 7 erratic, unloyal 8 disloyal, recreant, unstable, wavering 9 changeful 10 capricious, changeable, inconstant, perfidious, traitorous 11 fluctuating, treacherous

faithlessness 7 falsity, perfidy, treason 8 betrayal 9 treachery 10 disloyalty, infidelity

fake 3 act, gyp 4 hoax, mock, sell, sham 5 bluff, bogus, false, feign, fraud, phony, put on, snide, spoof 6 affect, assume, doctor, forged, framed, humbug, pseudo 7 falsify, pretend 8 impostor, invented, simulate, spurious 9 brummagem, charlatan, concocted, fabricate, imitation, imposture, pinchbeck, pretended, pretender, simulated 10 fabricated, fictitious, fraudulent, simulation 11 counterfeit ***combining form:*** 5 pseud 6 pseudo

fakir 7 ascetic 9 mendicant

falcon 4 hawk 5 hobby, saker 6 lanner, luggar, merlin 7 kestrel 9 peregrine ***male:*** 4 jack 6 musket, tassel, tercel 7 sakeret, tiercel 8 lanneret ***mature:*** 7 haggard, passage ***young:*** 4 eyas 5 eyess 8 brancher

falcon-headed god see at **Egyptian**

falconry 7 hawking ***equipment:*** 4 bell, hood, jess, lure 5 bewet, bewit 7 creance ***procedure:*** 3 imp 4 cope, seel

fall 3 dip, ebb, sag 4 drag, drip, drop, flop, plop, sink, skid, slip, trip, wane 5 abate, beset, crash, droop, lapse, let up, lower, pitch, plonk, plunk, slide, slump, storm, trail, yield 6 assail, attack, dangle, give up, go down, lessen, plunge, relent, sprawl, strike, submit, topple, tumble 7 aggress, assault, cascade, decline, descend, descent, die away, die down, drop off, ease off, go under, plummet, relapse, slacken, stumble, subside, succumb, wipeout 8 decrease, diminish, downcome, downfall, keel over, moderate, nose-dive 9 declivity, surrender

fallacious 3 mad 6 untrue 7 invalid 8 deluding, delusive, delusory 9 beguiling, deceiving, deceptive, illogical, sophistic 10 irrational, misleading, reasonless, unreasoned 11 nonrational 12 unreasonable

fallacy 4 idol 5 error 6 idolum 7 elusion, evasion, falsity, quibble, sophism, untruth 8 delusion 9 casuistry, deception, falsehood, falseness, quibbling, sophistry 12 equivocation, misconstrual, speciousness, spuriousness 13 deceptiveness, erroneousness, misconception

fall back 6 recede, retire 7 relapse,

retract, retreat 8 withdraw 9 retrocede 10 retrograde
fall behind 3 lag
fall flat 4 fail 5 flunk 7 bust out, flummox, wash out
fall guy 3 sap 4 butt, dupe, fish, fool, goat, gull 5 chump, patsy 6 pigeon, sucker 7 gudgeon 9 scapegoat 11 whipping boy
falling-out 3 row 4 beef, feud 5 run-in 6 hassle 7 dispute, quarrel 9 bickering 11 altercation, controversy
falloff 3 dip, sag 4 drop, slip 5 slump 7 decline 8 downturn 9 downslide, downswing, downtrend
fall out 2 go 3 row 4 spat, tiff 5 break, occur, scrap 6 betide, bicker, chance, happen, result 7 brabble, come off, develop, quarrel, wrangle 8 disagree, squabble
false 4 fake, mock, sham 5 bogus, dummy, hokey, lying, phony, snide, wrong 6 ersatz, hollow, pseudo, untrue 7 crooked, devious, seeming, unloyal, unsound 8 apostate, apparent, deluding, delusive, delusory, disloyal, recreant, renegade, specious, spurious 9 beguiling, brummagem, deceitful, deceiving, deceptive, dishonest, distorted, erroneous, faithless, illogical, imitation, incorrect, pinchbeck, simulated 10 artificial, fictitious, fraudulent, inaccurate, mendacious, misleading, ostensible, perfidious, substitute, traitorous, unfaithful, untruthful 11 backsliding, counterfeit, treacherous *combining form:* 5 pseud 6 pseudo
false face 4 mask 5 visor 6 domino, vizard
false front 4 face, mask, show, veil 5 cloak, cover 6 facade 8 disguise 10 masquerade
falsehood 3 fib, lie 4 sham, tale 5 error, fraud, story 6 canard, deceit, fakery 7 fallacy, falsity, fibbery, untruth 8 feigning, pretense, untruism 9 mendacity 10 unveracity 11 fabrication 13 dissimulation, erroneousness, prevarication, truthlessness
falseness 5 error 7 fallacy, perfidy, untruth 8 apostasy 9 defection, desertion, recreancy 10 disloyalty, infidelity
false teeth 7 denture 8 dentures
falsify 3 fib, lie 4 cook, deny, fake, warp 5 alter, belie, color, fudge, twist 6 change, doctor, garble, palter 7 contort, distort, pervert 8 miscolor, misstate, traverse 10 contradict, contravene, equivocate 11 prevaricate 12 misrepresent
falsity 3 fib, lie 4 sham, tale 5 bluff, error, story 6 canard 7 perfidy, untruth 8 untruism 9 falsehood, hypocrisy 10 disloyalty, infidelity 11 fabrication, insincerity 12 uncandidness 13 erroneousness, faithlessness, prevarication
Falstaff *companion:* 3 Nym 4 Peto 6 Pistol 8 Bardolph *composer:* 5 Verdi *creator:* 11 Shakespeare *play:* 7 Henry IV *prince:* 3 Hal *tavern:* 9 Boar's Head
Falstaffian 3 fat 6 coarse, jovial 8 boastful, humorous 9 dissolute
falter 4 halt, limp 5 lurch, quail, quake, shake, waver 6 blench, dither, flinch, quaver, recoil, shrink, topple, wobble 7 shudder, stagger, stumble, tremble, whiffle 8 hesitate, tick over 9 vacillate 12 shilly-shally
fame 4 note 5 éclat, glory, honor 6 renown, report, repute 7 acclaim 8 applause, eminence 9 celebrity, character, greatness, notoriety 10 prominence, reputation 11 acclamation, distinction, preeminence, recognition
famed 5 great, noted 7 eminent, notable 8 renowned 9 prominent 10 celebrated, celebrious 11 illustrious 13 distinguished
familiar 2 up 4 boon, cozy, easy, mate, snug 5 amigo, aware, close, fresh, thick 6 au fait, chummy, common, friend, genial, versed, wonted 7 abreast, affable, cordial, forward, mindful, prosaic, versant 8 amicable, everyday, frequent, friendly, gracious, habitual, informed, intimate, sociable 9 au courant, cognizant, confidant, conscious, customary, intrusive, obtrusive, officious 10 accustomed, acquainted, conversant, neighborly 11 cater-cousin, comfortable, commonplace, impertinent
familiarity 8 intimacy 9 awareness, cognition, knowledge 10 experience, inwardness 12 acquaintance 13 comprehension, understanding
familiarize 3 use 4 wont 5 adapt, inure 6 adjust, season 8 accustom, acquaint 9 condition, habituate
family 3 kin 4 clan, folk, home, line, race 5 brood, folks, house, issue, stirp, stock, tribe 6 ménage, strain 7 dynasty, kindred, lineage, progeny 8 domestic 9 bloodline, household, offspring *branch:* 6 stirps *lineage:* 4 tree 6 stemma 8 pedigree 9 genealogy
famished 6 hungry 7 starved 8 ravenous, starving
famous 3 top 5 great, noted 7 capital, eminent, leading, notable, popular 8 five-star, renowned, superior, top-notch 9 estimable, excellent, first-rate, honorable, notorious, prominent, reputable, well-known 10 celebrated, celebrious, first-class 11 first-string, illustrious, prestigious, redoubtable, respectable 13 distinguished, well-thought-of
fan 4 blow, buff, open, wind 5 hound, lover 6 addict, expand, extend, rooter, ruffle, spread, unfold, votary, winnow 7 admirer, amateur, devotee, habitué 8 fol-

lower **9** outspread **10** aficionado, enthusiast, outstretch ***combining form:*** **5** rhipi **6** rhipid **7** rhipido **8** flabelli ***horseracing:*** **7** turfman ***India:*** **5** punka **6** punkah ***movie:*** **7** cineast

fanatic **3** bug, nut **5** bigot, fiend, freak, rabid, ultra **6** maniac, zealot **7** extreme, radical **8** ultraist **9** extremist **10** monomaniac **12** revolutional **13** revolutionary, revolutionist

fancier **6** votary **7** admirer, amateur, devotee

fanciful **5** false, wrong **6** absurd, unreal **7** bizarre, fictive, shadowy, strange **8** fabulous, illusory, imagined, mythical, notional, romantic **9** fantastic, fictional, grotesque, imaginary, legendary **10** apocryphal, chimerical, fictitious **11** unrealistic **12** preposterous

fancy **3** bee, fad **4** idea, like, mind, whim, will **5** dream, fable, freak, humor, image, think **6** liking, megrim, mirage, notion, vagary, vision, whimsy **7** approve, boutade, caprice, chimera, conceit, concept, endorse, feature, fiction, figment, imagine, realize, whimsey **8** conceive, crotchet, daydream, delusion, envisage, envision, illusion, phantasm, phantasy, pleasure, sanction, velleity **9** capriccio, elaborate, intricate, invention, nightmare, visualize **10** conception **11** complicated, envisioning, fabrication, fata morgana, imagination, inclination **12** contrariness, envisagement, perverseness **13** hallucination, irrationality

fan dancer **4** Rand

fandango **4** ball **5** dance

fanfare **4** pomp, show **5** array, shine **6** parade **7** display, panoply **8** flourish ***trumpet:*** **6** tucket

fanlike **7** plaited, plicate

fanny **4** seat **5** hiney **6** behind, bottom, heinie **7** hind end **8** backside, buttocks, derriere **9** posterior

fanon **5** cloth, orale **7** maniple **8** corporal

fan palm **7** talipot **8** palmetto

fantasize **7** imagine **8** daydream

fantastic **3** odd **4** wild **5** crazy, loony, queer, silly, wacky **6** absurd, adroit, clever, insane, mortal, unreal **7** bizarre, fictive, foolish, massive, strange **8** cracking, delusive, delusory, fanciful, illusory, romantic, singular, towering **9** deceptive, eccentric, fictional, grotesque, imaginary, ingenious, monstrous, unearthly, whimsical **10** capricious, chimerical, fictitious, incredible, irrational, misleading, monumental, prodigious, ridiculous, stupendous, tremendous **11** extravagant, implausible, nonsensical **12** preposterous, suppositious, unbelievable, unreasonable

fantasy **4** whim **5** dream, freak **6** bubble, vagary, vision, whimsy **7** caprice, chimera, rainbow, whimsey **8** daydream, illusion, phantasm **9** imagining, nightmare, pipe dream **10** bizarrerie, conceiving **11** envisioning, imagination **12** grotesquerie

Fantine's daughter **7** Cosette

far **4** deep, long, well **5** quite **6** rather, remote **7** distant, removed **8** off-lying, outlying, somewhat **12** considerably ***combining form:*** **3** tel **4** tele, telo

far and away **4** just, very **5** quite **6** by odds **9** by all odds, decidedly, doubtless **10** absolutely, by long odds, definitely, positively **11** by a long shot, undoubtedly

far and near **7** all over, overall **8** all round **9** all around **10** everyplace, everywhere, throughout

far and wide see **far and near**

faraway **4** lost **6** absent, dreamy, remote **7** bemused, distant, removed **8** distrait, heedless, off-lying, outlying **9** oblivious, unheeding, unmindful **10** abstracted, stargazing **11** inconscient, preoccupied **12** absentminded, disregardful

farce **4** mock, sham **7** mockery **8** travesty **9** burlesque **10** caricature

farceur **3** wag **4** zany **5** clown, cutup, joker **8** jokester

farcical **5** comic, droll, funny **6** absurd **7** risible **8** gelastic **9** laughable, ludicrous **10** outrageous, ridiculous **11** extravagant **12** preposterous

fare **2** do, go **3** hie, way **4** diet, food, pass, path, rate, wend **5** get by, get on, shift, track **6** manage, push on, repair, travel **7** advance, journey, proceed **8** get along, progress **12** stagger along

farewell **2** by **3** ave, bye **5** adieu, adios, aloha, congé **6** bye-bye, so long **7** good-bye, parting **9** bon voyage, departing **11** leave-taking, valedictory

farfetched **5** queer **6** forced **7** bizarre, erratic, labored, strange **8** strained **9** eccentric, fantastic, grotesque, recherché

far-flung **6** remote **7** distant, removed **8** off-lying, outlying

farinaceous **5** mealy **7** starchy ***food:*** **4** meal **5** flour, salep **6** cereal **7** pudding, tapioca

farm **4** till **5** croft, ranch **6** grange, rancho **7** hennery **8** estancia, hacienda, hatchery, steading **9** cultivate, farmstead ***building:*** **4** barn, shed, silo ***Dutch:*** **6** bowery ***Israeli collective:*** **7** kibbutz ***Russian:*** **7** kolkhoz, sovkhoz

farmer **6** grower, tiller, yeoman **7** granger, planter, rancher **8** ranchero, ranchman **13** agriculturist ***Israeli:*** **6** halutz ***Russian:*** **5** kulak ***South African:*** **4** Boer ***tenant:*** **6** cotter **7** cottier, crofter **12** sharecropper

farming **7** tillage **8** agronomy **9** geopon-

ics, husbandry **11** agriculture, cultivation, hydroponics
faro **5** monte ***bet:*** **7** sleeper ***card:*** **4** case, hock, soda
Faroes whirlwind **2** oe
far-off **6** remote **7** distant, removed **8** outlying
farrier **5** smith **10** blacksmith
farsighted **9** hyperopic, sagacious **10** presbyopic
farther **3** now **4** else, more **5** added, fresh **6** beyond, longer, yonder **10** additional
farthest **6** utmost **7** endmost, extreme, outmost **9** outermost, uttermost
fascinate **4** draw, grip, hold, sway, take, wile **5** charm, touch **6** absorb, affect, allure, appeal, engage, excite, occupy, please, strike **7** attract, bewitch, catch up, delight, enchant, engross, gladden, impress, rejoice **8** enthrall, entrance, interest, intrigue **9** captivate, enrapture, influence, magnetize, mesmerize, preoccupy, spellbind
fascination **5** charm **6** allure, appeal, glamor **7** glamour **8** charisma, witchery **9** magnetism **10** witchcraft **11** enchantment
Fascist **4** Nazi **6** Hitler **9** Mussolini
fashion **3** cry, fad, ton, way **4** chic, form, make, mode, mold, plan, plot, rage, tone, vein, wise, wont **5** build, craft, craze, drift, erect, forge, frame, habit, modus, sculp, shape, style, thing, trend, usage, vogue **6** create, custom, design, devise, furore, manner, method, sculpt, system **7** produce, turn out **8** contrive, practice, tendency **9** bandwagon, construct, fabricate, technique **10** convention, dernier cri
fashionable **4** chic **5** smart, swank, swish **6** modish, with-it **7** a la mode, current, dashing, popular, stylish **9** exclusive, prevalent **13** up-to-the-minute
fashion designer ***American:*** **9** Gernreich (Rudi) ***Anglo-French:*** **5** Worth (Charles) ***French:*** **4** Dior **8** Givenchy (Hubert) **12** Saint-Laurent (Yves) ***Italian:*** **5** Pucci (Emilio) **7** Cassini (Oleg)
fast **3** gay, lax, set **4** diet, easy, firm, hard, held, keen, lewd, soon, sure, true, wild **5** alert, apace, bawdy, brisk, fixed, fleet, hasty, liege, light, loose, loyal, quick, rapid, slack, stuck, swift, tight, wingy **6** active, ardent, firmly, lively, presto, pronto, raking, rakish, secure, snappy, speedy, sporty, stable, starve, strong, wanton, wedged **7** fixedly, flat-out, fleetly, hastily, lustful, quickly, raffish, rapidly, riotous, satyric, solidly, staunch, swiftly, tightly, whorish **8** careless, chop-chop, constant, faithful, full tilt, heedless, indecent, promptly, rakehell, resolute, speedily, unchaste **9** breakneck, immovable, lecherous, libertine, lickerish, posthaste, salacious, tenacious **10** expeditive, harefooted, lascivious, libidinous, licentious, stationary **11** expeditious, incontinent **12** devil-may-care, inextricable, lickety-split **13** expeditiously
fasten **3** bar, bed, fix, gib, peg, pin, put, set, tie **4** bind, hank, hasp, hook, join, lash, link, lock, moor, seal, turn, weld **5** affix, apply, catch, clamp, clasp, cling, embed, focus, hitch, infix, latch, lodge, reeve, rivet, screw, stake, stick, strap, train, unite, wedge **6** adhere, anchor, attach, bundle, button, cleave, cohere, devote, direct, fixate, secure, settle, staple, zipper **7** address, connect, implant, mortise **9** concenter, establish **11** concentrate
fastener **3** pin **4** frog, snap, tack **5** catch **6** button, needle, staple, toggle **10** clothespin
fastidious **4** nice **5** fussy **6** choosy, dainty **7** choosey, finical, finicky **8** critical, exacting **9** demanding, finicking, squeamish **10** particular, pernickety **11** persnickety **13** hypercritical
fastness **4** fort **5** guard **6** adytum, castle **7** citadel, defense, redoubt, retreat, sanctum, shelter **10** protection, stronghold
fat **3** big, oil, top **4** best, bull, deep, flab, lard, pick, rich, suet, wide **5** beefy, broad, bulky, burly, cream, dumpy, elite, great, gross, heavy, husky, large, lipid, obese, pride, prime, pudgy, pursy, round, squat, stout, thick, tubby **6** brawny, choice, chunky, excess, fleshy, flower, grease, portly, rotund, stocky, stubby, tallow **7** adipose, blubber, fertile, orotund, paunchy, porcine, ringing, surfeit, surplus, vibrant, wealthy, weighty **8** blubbery, heavyset, overflow, overkill, overmuch, overplus, oversize, plethora, resonant, sonorant, sonorous, thickset **9** consonant, corpulent, overblown **10** full-bodied, overweight, potbellied, productive, prosperous, resounding **11** superfluity, upholstered **13** overabundance ***combining form:*** **3** lip **4** adip, lipo, sebi, sebo **5** adipo, lipar, steat **6** liparo, steato
fatal **5** death **6** deadly, doomed, lethal, malign, mortal **7** baleful, baneful, deathly, malefic, ruinous, unlucky **8** casualty, sinister **9** pestilent **10** calamitous, disastrous, ill-starred, maleficent, pernicious **11** cataclysmic, mortiferous **12** catastrophic, pestilential
fatality **5** death **9** virulence **10** deadliness, malignancy **11** noxiousness
fata morgana **6** mirage
fate **3** end, lot **4** doom **5** issue, karma, moira, weird **6** chance, doom to, effect, ending, kismet, result, upshot **7** destine,

destiny, fortune, outcome, portion, preform 9 determine, preordain 10 foreordain, predestine 12 circumstance, predetermine 13 inevitability
fateful 5 acute 7 crucial, ominous, ruinous 8 critical, decisive 9 ill-boding, important, momentous 10 calamitous, conclusive, disastrous 11 apocalyptic, cataclysmic, significant, threatening 12 catastrophic, inauspicious, unpropitious 13 determinative
Fates see at **Greek; Norse; Roman**
fathead 3 oaf 4 boob, dolt, goof 5 booby, chump, dunce
fatheaded 5 dense, thick 6 stupid 10 numskulled
father 2 pa 3 dad, get, pop 4 dada, make, papa, père, sire 5 beget, breed, daddy, hatch, maker, motor, mover, padre, pappy, pater, poppa, spawn 6 author, create, parent, priest 7 builder, creator, founder, produce 8 engender, generate, inventor, producer, promoter 9 architect, generator, initiator, organizer, originate, patriarch, procreate, supporter 10 encourager, ingenerate, introducer, originator, prime mover 11 inaugurator, progenerate, promulgator ***combining form:*** 4 patr 5 patri, patro ***of his country:*** 6 Cicero 10 Washington ***of history:*** 9 Herodotus ***of medicine:*** 11 Hippocrates ***of modern surgery:*** 4 Paré ***of the symphony:*** 5 Haydn ***of waters:*** 11 Mississippi
Father Brown creator 10 Chesterton
fatherland 4 home, soil 7 country
fatherless 7 bastard, natural 8 baseborn, spurious 11 misbegotten 12 illegitimate
Father Time's implement 6 scythe
fathom 4 have, know 5 grasp, plumb, probe, savvy, sound 6 pierce 7 cognize 8 perceive 9 apprehend, penetrate, plumbline, recognize 10 appreciate, comprehend, understand
fathomless 7 abysmal
fatidic 8 Delphian, oracular 9 prophetic, sibylline, vaticinal 11 prophetical
fatigue 3 irk, vex 4 jade, tire, wear 5 annoy, drain, ennui, spend, weary 6 bother, tucker, weaken 7 deplete, disable, exhaust, languor, wear out 8 weakness, wear down 9 faintness, lassitude, tiredness, weariness 10 debilitate, enervation, exhaustion, feebleness 12 debilitation, listlessness
Fatima ***father:*** 8 Mohammed, Muhammad ***husband:*** 9 Bluebeard ***step-brother:*** 3 Ali
fatness 7 obesity 9 adiposity 10 corpulence
fatten 5 plump 6 batten, enrich 7 plumpen, stouten, thicken
fatty 4 oily 5 blimp, lardy, pudge, suety 6 greasy 7 adipose 8 blubbery, dumpling, potbelly, roly-poly, strapper, unctuous 10 butterball, oleaginous, overweight ***combining form:*** 3 lip 4 adip, lipo 5 adipo, lipar 6 liparo
fatuous 4 dumb, fond 5 inane, silly 6 absurd, simple, stupid 7 asinine, foolish, idiotic, moronic, unwitty, witless 8 besotted, imbecile 9 brainless, insensate 10 infatuated, weak-headed, weak-minded 11 sheepheaded
faucet 3 tap 4 bung, cock, gate 5 spile, valve 6 spigot 7 bibcock, hydrant, petcock 8 stopcock
Faulkner ***character:*** 5 Caddy, Jason 7 Candace, Quentin 8 Benjamin ***family:*** 7 Compson ***novel:*** 8 Sartoris 9 Sanctuary, The Hamlet 11 As I Lay Dying 13 Light in August
fault 3 nag, sin 4 carp, flaw, flub, lack, onus, slip, vice 5 blame, crime, error 6 defect, foible 7 blemish, blunder, demerit, failing, frailty, mistake, offense 8 weakness 9 infirmity, liability 10 deficiency 11 culpability, shortcoming 12 imperfection 13 answerability, transgression
faultfinder 4 crab 5 grump, momus 6 critic, grouch, Zoilus
faultfinding 6 critic 8 captious, critical 9 cavillous 10 censorious, particular, pernickety 12 overcritical 13 hypercritical
faultless 4 pure 5 clean, whole 6 entire, intact 7 correct, perfect 8 flawless, innocent, unguilty 9 blameless, exquisite 10 immaculate, impeccable, inculpable 13 unimpeachable
faulty 4 sick 5 amiss, wrong 6 flawed, marred 7 damaged, defaced, inexact 8 fallible, specious 9 blemished, defective, deficient, erroneous, imperfect, imprecise, incorrect, uncorrect 10 disfigured, fallacious, inaccurate, inadequate, incomplete ***prefix:*** 3 dys
Faunus ***grandfather:*** 6 Saturn ***son:*** 4 Acis 7 Latinus
Faust ***author:*** 6 Goethe 7 Marlowe ***beloved:*** 8 Gretchen ***composer:*** 6 Gounod
faux pas 4 slip 5 boner, break, error, gaffe 6 boo-boo, bungle, howler 7 blooper, blunder, misstep, mistake, stumble 8 pratfall, screamer, solecism 9 indecorum, oversight 11 impropriety, misjudgment 12 indiscretion
favor 2 OK 3 aid, for, pro 4 back, boon, gift, help, okay 5 prize, value 6 accept, esteem, oblige, pamper, regard 7 account, approve, backing, endorse, forward, indulge, largess, present, respect, service, support 8 advocate, approval, blessing, courtesy, goodwill, hold with, kindness, resemble, sanction, simulate 9 approbate,

encourage, patronage 10 admiration, appreciate, assistance, estimation, indulgence 11 accommodate, approbation, benediction, benevolence, convenience, cooperation, countenance 12 dispensation 13 consideration, encouragement

favorable 4 good, kind, nice 5 brave, happy, lucky, white 6 benign, bright, dexter, kindly, timely, toward, useful 7 benefic, helpful, timeous, welcome 8 cheering, grateful, pleasant, pleasing, salutary 9 approving, benignant, fortunate, healthful, laudatory, opportune, praiseful, promising, well-timed, wholesome 10 auspicious, beneficial, gratifying, propitious, prosperous, reassuring 11 approbative, approbatory, encouraging, pleasureful 12 advantageous, commendatory, providential, well-disposed 13 complimentary

favoring 4 good 5 brave 6 toward, useful 7 benefic, helpful 10 beneficial, propitious 12 advantageous ***prefix:*** 3 pro

favorite 3 pet 4 dear 5 loved 6 adored, prized 7 admired, beloved, darling, popular, revered 8 blue-eyed, esteemed, laudable, pleasant, precious 9 cherished, preferred, treasured, well-liked 10 fair-haired

favoritism 4 bias 8 cronyism, nepotism 9 prejudice

fawn 3 bow, woo 4 cave, coax, door 5 abase, court, cower, crawl, defer, toady, yield 6 cajole, cotton, cringe, debase, demean, grovel, invite, kowtow, slaver, submit 7 flatter, honey up, truckle, wheedle 8 blandish, bootlick 10 ingratiate 11 apple-polish

fawning 4 mean 6 abject, humble, smarmy 7 ignoble, servile, slavish 8 toadyish, toadyism 9 adulatory, compliant, flunkyish, groveling, kowtowing, parasitic, spineless, sycophant, truckling 10 flattering, obsequious, submissive 11 bootlicking, deferential, subservient, sycophantic 12 mealy-mouthed, sycophantish

fay 3 elf 5 fairy, nisse, pixie 6 sprite 7 brownie

faze 3 vex 5 abash, annoy, daunt, worry 6 appall, bother, dismay, muddle, puzzle, rattle 7 confuse, horrify, mystify, nonplus, perplex 8 confound, irritate 9 discomfit, dumbfound, embarrass 10 disconcert

FBI director 6 Hoover

fealty 5 ardor, faith, truth 7 loyalty, support 8 devotion, fidelity, trueness 10 allegiance 11 devotedness 12 faithfulness

fear 3 awe 4 funk 5 alarm, angst, dread, panic, scare, worry 6 dismay, esteem, fright, horror, phobia, terror 7 anxiety, concern, respect 8 cold feet, disquiet, timidity 9 agitation, cowardice, misgiving, reverence, trepidity 10 foreboding 11 disquietude, trepidation 12 apprehension, cowardliness, discomposure, perturbation, presentiment, timorousness ***combining form:*** 4 phob 5 phobe, phobo 6 phobia, phobic 7 phobous ***of animals:*** 9 zoophobia ***of being buried alive:*** 11 taphephobia ***of cats:*** 12 aelurophobia, ailurophobia ***of crowds:*** 11 ochlophobia ***of darkness:*** 11 nyctophobia ***of dirt:*** 10 mysophobia ***of fire:*** 10 pyrophobia ***of heights:*** 10 acrophobia ***of men:*** 11 androphobia ***of new things:*** 9 neophobia ***of open areas:*** 11 agoraphobia ***of pain:*** 10 algophobia ***of strangers:*** 10 xenophobia ***of thunder:*** 12 brontophobia ***of water:*** 11 hydrophobia ***of women:*** 10 gynophobia

fearful 4 dire, grim 5 awful, lurid, scary, timid 6 afraid, aghast, grisly, malign, scared, uneasy 7 alarmed, anxious, ghastly, jittery, macabre, nervous, panicky, sublime, worried 8 aflutter, agitated, alarming, dreadful, gruesome, horrible, horrific, shocking, sinister, terrible, terrific, timorous 9 appalling, concerned, disturbed, frightful, perturbed, terrified 10 disquieted, formidable, frightened, horrendous, solicitous, terrifying, tremendous 11 discomposed, frightening, redoubtable 12 apprehensive

fearless 4 bold, game, sure 5 brave 6 daring 7 assured 8 intrepid, sanguine, unafraid 9 audacious, confident, dauntless 10 courageous 11 lionhearted

feasible 6 doable, likely, viable 8 possible, workable 9 practical 11 practicable

feast 3 eat 4 dine, meal 6 dinner, regale, repast, spread 7 banquet 8 potlatch ***Hawaiian:*** 4 luau ***Scottish:*** 3 foy

Feast of Lights 8 Hanukkah

Feast of Lots 5 Purim

Feast of Tabernacles 7 Sukkoth

Feast of Weeks 8 Shabuoth

feat 3 act 4 deed, gest 5 geste, stunt, trick 6 action 7 emprise, exploit, venture 9 adventure 10 enterprise 11 achievement, tour de force

feather 3 ilk 4 down, kind, sort, type 5 breed, order, pinna, plume, quill 6 fledge, fletch, pinion 7 species, variety ***combining form:*** 4 pinn, pter, ptil 5 penni, penno, pinni, ptero, ptile, ptilo ***kind:*** 4 down 5 penna, remex 6 covert 7 contour, plumule, rectrix, tectrix, tertial 8 scapular, tertiary ***part:*** 3 web 4 barb, vane 5 shaft 7 barbule 8 barbicel

featherbrained 5 dizzy, giddy, silly 7 flighty 8 skittish 9 frivolous 11 empty-headed, hare-brained 13 rattlebrained

feathered 7 pennate, plumose 8 pennated

feather-like 7 pinnate, plumate 8 pinnated

feathers 7 plumage

featherweight 4 simp 5 dunce, light 6 dimwit, nitwit 7 lackwit, pinhead, unheavy, wantwit
feature 4 item, mark 5 fancy, image, point, savor, think, trait 6 aspect, detail, factor, play up, stress, virtue, vision 7 article, element, imagine, quality, realize 8 conceive, envisage, envision, property 9 affection, attribute, birthmark, character, component, emphasize, italicize, underline, visualize 10 ingredient, particular, underscore 11 constituent
febrile 5 fiery 7 fevered, pyretic 8 feverish
feces 4 dung 5 waste 7 excreta 9 excrement ***combining form:*** 4 copr, scat 5 copro, scato
feckless 4 wild 6 remiss 7 fustian, useless 8 careless, heedless, uncaring 9 shiftless, uncareful, unheeding, unrecking, worthless 10 incautious, unpurposed, unreliable, unthinking 11 inadvertent, meaningless, purposeless, thoughtless 12 irreflective, undependable, unreflective 13 irresponsible, lackadaisical, untrustworthy
fecund 4 rich 7 fertile 8 childing, fruitful, prolific, spawning 10 productive 11 proliferant
fecundity 9 eloquence, fertility 10 expression 11 prodigality, profuseness, prolificacy 12 expressivity, fruitfulness, productivity
Federalist writer 3 Jay 7 Madison 8 Hamilton
federation 5 union 6 league 8 alliance 9 coalition 11 association, confederacy
fed up 4 sick 5 bored, tired, weary 9 disgusted
fee 3 pay, tax 4 cost, dues, hire, wage 5 price 6 charge, salary 7 expense, payment, stipend, tuition 8 retainer 9 emolument 10 recompense ***minting:*** 8 brassage 10 seignorage 11 seigniorage ***wharf:*** 7 quayage
feeble 4 puny, weak 5 frail 6 ailing, flimsy, infirm, senile, sickly, weakly 7 doddery, fragile, sapless, tenuous 8 decrepit 9 doddering 13 insubstantial
feebleminded 4 dull, slow 7 moronic 8 backward, imbecile, retarded 9 dim-witted 10 half-witted, slow-witted 12 simpleminded
feebleness 7 disease, malaise 8 debility 9 infirmity 10 infirmness, sickliness 11 decrepitude
feed 3 eat 4 find, food, give, grub, hand, meal 5 feast, graze 6 devour, fatten, fodder, ingest, repast, supply, viands 7 banquet, consume, deliver, dish out, edibles, furnish, nourish, nurture, provide, sustain 8 dispense, hand over, victuals 9 partake of, provender, refection 10 provisions ***combining form:*** 4 phag 5 phago
feed the kitty 4 ante
feel 3 air, paw 4 aura, deem, hold, know, mood 5 grope, guess, savor, sense, sound, taste, think, touch 6 assume, credit, endure, finger, fumble, handle, notice, suffer 7 believe, explore, grabble, observe, palpate, presume, suppose, surmise, suspect, undergo 8 consider, perceive 9 semblance, tactility
feeler 4 palp, test 5 probe, query 6 palpus 7 antenna, inquiry 10 intimation, prospectus 12 trial balloon
feeling 3 air 4 aura, mind, mood, vein, view 5 humor, sense, touch 6 belief, morale, notion, temper 7 emotion, opinion, outlook, passion, sensate 8 attitude, passible, reaction, sentient 9 affection, emotional, semblance, sensation, sensitive, sentiment 10 atmosphere, conviction, persuasion 11 affectivity, emotionable, palpability, sensibility, sensitivity, tangibility ***combining form:*** 5 pathy 6 pathic
feign 3 act 4 fake, sham 5 bluff, put on 6 affect, assume 7 connive, pretend 8 simulate 11 counterfeit
feint 3 jig 4 fake, hoax, play, ploy, ruse, sham, wile 5 trick 6 gambit 7 whizzer 8 maneuver 9 stratagem ***fencing:*** 5 appel ***hockey:*** 4 deke
feldspar 6 albite 8 andesine, sanidine 9 anorthite, moonstone 10 microcline, orthoclase 11 labradorite, plagioclase ***clay:*** 6 kaolin
felicitate 6 salute 7 commend 10 compliment 12 congratulate
felicitous 3 apt, fit 4 just, meet 5 happy 6 proper, timely 7 apropos, fitting 8 apposite, suitable 9 well-timed 10 applicable, seasonable 11 appropriate
feline 3 cat, tom 4 lion, lynx, pard, puma, puss 5 catty, felid, pussy, tiger 6 bobcat, cougar, jaguar, margay, ocelot, tomcat 7 catlike, cheetah, furtive, leonine, leopard, lioness, panther, tigress, wildcat 8 pussycat, stealthy ***hybrid:*** 5 liger, tigon 6 tiglon
fell 3 cut, fur, hew 4 chop, down, drop, grim, hide, kill, pelt, raze, skin, ugly 5 cruel, floor, grave, level, major 6 deadly, fierce, ground, jacket, lay low, savage, tumble 7 fearful, flatten, inhuman, mow down, serious, wolfish 8 bowl down, bowl over, grievous, horrible, horrific, inhumane 9 barbarous, bring down, dangerous, ferocious, knock down, knock over, prostrate, shoot down, throw down, truculent
Fellini film 8 Amarcord, Casanova, La Strada 9 Satyricon 11 La Dolce Vita
fellow 2 he 3 boy, bub, guy, joe, lad, man 4 bozo, buck, chap, gent, mate, peer, twin

5 bloke, match 6 codger, cohort, double, hombre, person 7 consort, partner 8 confrere 9 associate, companion, copartner, duplicate, gentleman 10 consociate, coordinate, reciprocal 11 concomitant 12 contemporary ***prefix:*** 2 co

fellowship 4 club 5 guild, order, union 6 league 7 company, society 8 alliance, sodality 10 fraternity 11 association, brotherhood, camaraderie 13 companionship

felon 8 criminal, offender 10 lawbreaker, malefactor

felt hat 6 fedora

female 4 girl 5 woman 7 womanly 8 feminine, womanish ***combining form:*** 3 gyn 4 gyne, gyno, gyny 5 gynec, gyneo, thely 6 gynaec, gynaeo, gyneco, gynous 7 gynaeco ***suffix:*** 3 ess, ine 4 ette, trix

femme fatale 5 siren 7 Lorelei 9 temptress 10 seductress

fen 3 bog 4 mire, quag 5 marsh, swamp 6 morass, slough 7 baygall 8 quagmire

fence 3 bar, hem, mew, pen 4 cage, duck, mure, stop, wall, weir 5 block, dodge, hedge, parry, shirk 6 corral, immure, paling 7 barrier, enclose, railing 8 blockade, palisade, sidestep, stockade 9 barricade, roadblock 12 circumscribe

fencer 7 duelist, épéeist 8 foilsman 9 swordsman

fencing 9 swordplay ***attack:*** 5 lunge 6 thrust 7 reprise, riposte ***defense:*** 5 parry ***movement:*** 4 volt ***ploy:*** 5 appel ***position:*** 5 prime, sixte, terce 6 octave, quarte, quinte, tierce 7 seconde, septime ***term:*** 4 jury 5 forte, lunge, piste 6 flèche, foible, pointe, touché 7 sabreur, stop cut, stop-hit 11 corps-à-corps ***touch:*** 3 cut, hit 5 punto ***weapon:*** 4 épée, foil 5 blade, guard, saber, sabre 6 pommel

fend 4 ward 5 avert, avoid, cover, guard, parry, rebut, repel 6 defend, rebuff, resist, screen, secure, shield 7 bulwark, deflect, hold off, keep off, protect, repulse, ward off 8 stave off 9 safeguard

fender 5 guard 6 buffer, shield 8 mudguard

Fenrir ***chain:*** 8 Gleipnir ***father:*** 4 Loki ***form:*** 4 wolf ***mother:*** 9 Angerboda 10 Angerbotha ***slayer:*** 5 Vidar 6 Vithar ***victim:*** 4 Odin

feral 4 wild 5 brute 6 animal, brutal, ferine, fierce, savage 7 beastly, bestial, brutish, inhuman, swinish, untamed, vicious 8 barbaric 9 barbarous, ferocious

Ferber novel 5 Giant, So Big 8 Cimarron, Show Boat, The Girls 9 Ice Palace

Ferber or Millay 4 Edna

Ferdinand ***beloved:*** 7 Miranda ***father:*** 6 Alonso ***daughter:*** 6 Joanna ***wife:*** 8 Germaine, Isabella

Ferdinand, King ***conquest:*** 7 Granada

ferment 4 boil, stir 5 churn 6 bubble, clamor, foment, leaven, outcry, seethe, simmer, tumult, unrest, upturn 7 agitate, ailment, smolder, turmoil 8 disquiet, upheaval 9 commotion 10 convulsion, inquietude 11 disquietude, restiveness 12 restlessness

fermentation 7 zymosis

fern 4 tree 5 brake, holly, royal 6 Boston 7 bracken, woodsia 8 polypody 10 maidenhair, spleenwort ***combining form:*** 6 pterid, pteris 7 pterido ***leaf:*** 5 frond

ferocious 4 fell, grim 5 brute, cruel, feral 6 brutal, fierce, savage 7 bestial, inhuman, vicious, violent, wolfish 8 inhumane, ravening, ravenous 9 barbarous, rapacious, truculent 10 implacable, relentless 12 bloodthirsty

ferret out 4 hunt, seek 5 learn, probe, quest 6 elicit 7 extract 8 discover 9 ascertain, cast about, determine, search for, search out

Ferrex's brother 6 Porrex

ferrule 3 cap, tip 4 band, knob

ferry 3 lug 4 bear, buck, pack, tote 5 carry 6 convey 9 transport

ferryman of Hades 6 Charon

fertile 4 lush, rich 6 fecund 7 bearing, copious 8 abundant, childing, creative, fruitful, pregnant, prolific, spawning, yielding 9 bountiful, ingenious, inventive, luxuriant, plenteous, producing 10 productive 11 proliferant

fertilize 6 enrich 9 pollenate, pollinate 10 impregnate, inseminate

fertilizer 4 dung, marl 5 guano 6 manure 7 compost

ferule 3 rod 5 ruler, stick 6 switch

fervent 3 hot 4 keen 5 eager, fiery 6 ardent, devout, hearty 7 blazing, burning, earnest, glowing, intense, sincere 8 vehement 9 heartfelt, perfervid 10 hot-blooded, passionate 11 impassioned 12 enthusiastic, wholehearted

fervor 4 fire, zeal 5 ardor 6 hurrah, warmth 7 passion 9 calenture, sincerity, vehemence 10 devoutness, enthusiasm, heartiness 11 earnestness

fess up 3 own 4 avow 5 admit, allow, grant, let on, own up 7 concede, confess 11 acknowledge

fester 3 rot 5 ulcer 6 rankle 7 inflame, putrefy 8 ulcerate

festina ___ 5 lente

festival 4 fair, fete, gala 5 feast, gaudy 6 fiesta 8 carnival 9 festivity 11 celebration

festive 3 gay 4 gala 5 jolly, merry

6 blithe, jocund, jovial, joyous 7 gleeful 8 mirthful 10 blithesome 12 lighthearted

festivity 5 revel 6 gaiety 7 jollity, revelry, whoopee 8 reveling 9 merriment, revelment 11 celebration, merrymaking

fetch 4 sell 5 bring 7 bring in

fetching 6 luring 7 Circean 8 alluring, enticing, tempting

fete 4 fair 5 party 6 bazaar 8 festival 9 entertain 11 celebration

fetid 4 foul, rank 6 putrid, rancid, smelly 7 rankish, reeking 8 mephitic, stinking 10 malodorous

fetish 4 idol, juju, luck, zemi 5 charm, mania, thing 6 amulet, mascot 7 periapt 8 fixation, gris-gris, penchant, talisman 9 obsession 10 phylactery

fetter 3 tie 4 clog, curb 5 leash 6 hamper, hobble, hog-tie 7 manacle, shackle, trammel 8 handcuff, restrain 9 entrammel

fettle 4 trim 5 order, shape 6 kilter, repair 7 fitness 9 condition

feud 3 row 5 run-in 6 combat, fracas 7 contest, dispute, quarrel 8 argument, squabble, vendetta 9 bickering 10 falling-out 11 altercation, controversy

feudal ***estate:*** 4 feod, feud, fief ***jurisdiction:*** 3 soc 4 soke ***laborer:*** 4 serf ***lord:*** 5 liege 8 suzerain ***service:*** 5 avera ***tax:*** 7 tallage ***tenant:*** 6 vassal 7 homager, socager, sokeman, vavasor 8 vavasour ***tenure of land:*** 6 socage ***tribute:*** 6 heriot

fever 4 ague, fire 6 dengue 7 ferment, pyrexia 9 calenture ***combining form:*** 5 febri, pyret 6 pyreto ***recurrent:*** 6 sextan 7 malaria, quartan, quintan, tertian

feverish 3 hot 5 fiery 6 fervid, heated, hectic 7 burning, excited, febrile, flushed, furious, pyretic 8 febrific, frenzied, inflamed 10 passionate 11 overwrought

fever tree 7 blue gum

few 4 rare 6 scarce, seldom, smatch 7 handful, smatter, spatter 8 sporadic, uncommon 10 infrequent, occasional, scattering, smattering, spattering, sprinkling, unfrequent ***combining form:*** 4 olig 5 oligo, pauci

____-fi 2 hi 3 sci

fiat 5 edict, order 6 decree 7 command 8 sanction 11 endorsement 12 proclamation

fib 3 lie 4 tale 5 story 6 canard, palter 7 falsify, falsity, untruth 9 falsehood, mendacity 10 equivocate 11 evasiveness, prevaricate 13 prevarication

fiber 3 web 4 noil, pita 5 grain, istle 6 fabric, strand, thread 7 texture ***brain:*** 4 pons ***coarse:*** 4 adad, jute 8 piassava ***coconut husk:*** 4 coir, kyar ***combining form:*** 2 in 3 ino 4 fibr 5 fibro ***knot:*** 3 nep ***rope:*** 5 sisal 8 henequen ***silky:*** 5 kapok ***small:*** 6 fibril ***substructure:*** 7 micelle, spongin ***synthetic:*** 5 nylon, rayon, saran, vinal ***woody:*** 4 bast ***woollike:*** 7 lanital

fibrous 4 ropy, wiry 6 sinewy 7 stringy 8 muscular

fibula 5 clasp 7 leg bone

fickle 7 flighty, moonish 8 ticklish, unstable, variable, volatile 9 mercurial 10 capricious, changeable, inconstant, lubricious, unfaithful, unreliable 12 undependable 13 temperamental

fiction 4 tale, yarn 5 fable, story 6 deceit 7 fantasy, figment 9 fish story, invention, narrative 10 concoction 11 fabrication

fictional 5 false, phony 6 unreal 7 fictive 8 fanciful, illusory 9 fantastic, imaginary 10 chimerical, fictitious 12 suppositious

fictitious 4 fake, mock, sham 5 false 6 ersatz, made-up, unreal, untrue 7 assumed, created, fictive 8 cooked-up, fanciful, illusory, invented 9 concocted, fantastic, fashioned, fictional, imaginary, simulated, trumped-up 10 artificial, chimerical, fabricated 12 suppositious ***combining form:*** 5 pseud 6 pseudo

fiddle 4 fool, mess, play 6 dabble, doodle, fidget, handle, monkey, potter, puddle, putter, tinker, trifle, violin 10 mess around

fiddle-faddle 4 bosh 5 fudge, hooey 6 bunkum, piffle 8 nonsense, pishposh 10 flapdoodle

Fidelio ***composer:*** 9 Beethoven ***hero:*** 9 Florestan ***heroine:*** 7 Leonora

____ fidelis 6 semper

fidelity 5 ardor, piety 6 fealty 7 loyalty 8 adhesion, devotion 9 adherence, constancy 10 allegiance, attachment 11 reliability, staunchness 12 faithfulness 13 dependability, steadfastness

fidget 4 play 6 fiddle, jitter, trifle 7 twiddle

fidgety 5 fussy, jumpy, nervy 6 goosey, spooky 7 jittery, nervous, restive, twitchy 8 restless, twittery 9 unrestful 10 high-strung

field 4 area, walk 5 milpa 6 domain, meadow, region, sphere 7 demesne, terrain 8 dominion, precinct, province 9 bailiwick, champaign, territory 10 department ***combining form:*** 4 agro

fieldbird 6 plover

field crop 3 hay 5 grain 6 cotton

field deity 3 Pan 4 Faun 5 Fauna

field glasses 10 binoculars

field hand 4 hoer 5 sower 6 picker 7 laborer, planter

Fielding novel 6 Amelia 8 Tom Jones 13 Joseph Andrews

field marshal ***Austrian:*** 8 Radetzky ***British:*** 6 Napier, Raglan, Wavell, Wilson 7 Roberts 8 Wolseley 9 Kitchener 10 Montgomery ***French:*** 4 Foch 6 Joffre,

Pétain *German:* 6 Keitel, Paulus, Rommel, Rupert 9 Mackensen, Rundstedt, Waldersee 10 Kesselring *Japanese:* 8 Sugiyama *Prussian:* 6 Moltke *Russian:* 7 Kutuzov, Suvorov 8 Potemkin

field mouse 4 vole

Field of Blood 8 Aceldama

field officer 5 major 7 colonel

field rat 5 metad

fiend 3 bug, nut 5 bigot, demon, devil, freak, Satan 6 diablo, maniac, zealot 7 fanatic, Lucifer, Old Nick, serpent 8 Apollyon, succubus 9 Beelzebub 10 enthusiast, Old Scratch 13 Old Gooseberry

fiendish 5 cruel 6 malign, savage, wicked 7 baleful, demonic, hellish, inhuman, malefic, satanic, vicious 8 demoniac, demonian, devilish, diabolic, infernal, sinister 9 barbarous, ferocious, malicious, malignant

fierce 4 fell, grim, wild 5 cruel 6 brutal, savage 7 brutish, enraged, furious, inhuman, intense, vicious, violent, wolfish 8 inhumane, maddened, pitiless, ruthless, terrible, tigerish, vehement 9 barbarous, bellicose, desperate, ferocious, merciless, truculent 10 aggressive, cannibalic, infuriated, pugnacious 11 belligerent

fiery 3 hot 5 afire 6 ablaze, aflame, ardent, fervid, fierce, heated, red-hot, spunky, torrid 7 blaring, blazing, burning, febrile, fervent, fevered, flaming, flaring, gingery, igneous, ignited, intense, peppery 8 broiling, feverish, inflamed, scalding, sizzling, spirited, vehement, white-hot 9 hot-headed, perfervid, scorching 10 mettlesome, passionate 11 conflagrant, impassioned 12 high-spirited

fifteen *combining form:* 8 pentadec 9 pentadeca

fifth *combining form:* 5 quint 6 quinti

fig *genus:* 5 Ficus *sacred:* 5 pipal *variety:* 5 eleme, elemi 6 Smyrna

fight 3 row, tug, war 4 beef, bout, buck, duel, feud, fray, spat, tiff 5 brawl, broil, clash, joust, melee, repel, scrap, words 6 affray, attack, battle, bicker, combat, debate, fracas, hassle, oppose, oppugn, resist, strive, tussle 7 contend, contest, crusade, dispute, quarrel, scuffle, wrangle, wrestle 8 skirmish, slugfest, squabble, struggle, traverse 9 bickering, pugnacity, withstand 10 aggression, donnybrook 11 altercation 12 belligerence, disagreement 13 combativeness *combining form:* 5 machy

fighter 2 GI 4 swad 5 boxer 7 soldier, warrior 8 pugilist, scrapper 9 man-at-arms

fighter plane 3 MiG, Roc 4 Zero 5 Sabre 6 Fokker, Hawker, Mirage, Voodoo 7 Corsair, Harrier 8 Spitfire

fighting fish 5 betta

figment 5 dream, fable, fancy 6 bubble 7 chimera, fiction 8 daydream, illusion 9 invention 11 fabrication

figurant 6 dancer, hoofer 7 danseur 8 coryphée

figuration 4 line 5 shape 7 contour, outline, profile 8 allegory 9 lineament, lineation, symbolism 10 silhouette 11 delineation

figure 3 add, sum, tot 4 cast, foot, form, rule, tote 5 build, count, digit, frame, motif, shape, total 6 cipher, decide, design, device, motive, number, reckon, settle, symbol 7 chiffer, compute, integer, numeral, outline, pattern, resolve, summate 8 conclude, estimate, physique, totalize 9 calculate, character, determine, enumerate 11 whole number 12 conformation 13 configuration *geometric:* 4 cone, cube 5 rhomb 6 circle, isogon, square 7 decagon, ellipse, hexagon, nonagon, octagon, polygon, rhombus 8 pentacle, pentagon, rhomboid, tetragon, triangle 9 rectangle 10 hexahedron, octahedron 11 icosahedron 12 dodecahedron, rhombohedron 13 quadrilateral *human:* 4 nude 5 atlas 7 telamon 8 caryatid *ornamental:* 6 statue 8 gargoyle

figure of speech 5 trope 6 aporia, simile 7 imagery, litotes 8 metaphor, metonymy 10 synecdoche

figure out 4 dope 5 crack, solve 6 decode, unfold 7 clear up, resolve, unravel 8 decipher, unriddle, untangle 9 puzzle out 10 unscramble 11 disentangle

figure skating *jump:* 4 axel, loop, lutz 5 split 6 rocker 7 bracket, counter, salchow 11 spreadeagle *spin:* 3 sit 5 camel

Fiji *capital:* 4 Suva *monetary unit:* 6 dollar

filch 3 nim, nip, rob 4 lift 5 pinch, steal, swipe 6 pilfer, snitch 7 purloin

file 3 row 4 line, rank, rasp, tier 5 queue 6 string 7 dossier, echelon

fill 3 gob, jam, jug 4 brim, clog, cloy, cram, glut, heap, jade, load, meet, pack, pall, pile, plug, sate, stop 5 block, choke, close, gorge 6 answer, bumper, charge, stodge 7 congest, engorge, occlude, satiate, satisfy, stopper, surfeit *interstices:* 3 pug 4 calk 5 chink, putty

filled 4 full 5 sated 7 replete 9 saturated

fillet 4 band, orle, tape 5 snood, strip 6 ribbon, stripe 7 bandeau, banding 8 headband *anatomical:* 9 lemniscus *architectural:* 6 cimbia, listel, reglet, taenia *combining form:* 4 taen 5 taeni 6 taenio *meat:* 10 tenderloin

fill-in 3 sub 7 stand-in 9 alternate, surrogate 10 substitute 11 locum tenens, pinch hitter, replacement, succedaneum

fill in 4 clew, clue, post, tell, warn 6 advise,

inform, insert, notify, wise up 7 apprise, throw in 8 acquaint 9 insinuate, interject, interpose, introduce 11 intercalate, interpolate

film 4 cine, haze, mist, show, skin, veil 5 brume, flick, layer, movie, smaze 6 patina 7 picture 8 pellicle 9 celluloid, photoplay 10 cinematize 11 picture show 13 motion picture, moving picture

filmy 4 fine, hazy 5 gauzy, misty, sheer, wispy 6 cloudy, dainty, flimsy 7 tiffany 8 delicate, gossamer 10 diaphanous 11 transparent

filter 4 sift 5 leach, sieve 6 purify, refine, screen, strain 8 filtrate 9 percolate

filth 4 dirt, dung, gore 6 ordure 7 squalor 9 obscenity ***combining form:*** 4 copr 5 copro

filthy 4 foul, vile 5 black, dirty, dungy, gross, mucky, nasty, soily 6 coarse, grubby, impure, ribald, sloppy, smutty, sordid, vulgar 7 obscene, raunchy, squalid, unclean 8 indecent 9 loathsome, offensive, repulsive, revolting, uncleanly, verminous 12 scatological

filthy lucre 4 cash, loot, pelf 5 dough, money 8 currency 11 legal tender

fin 4 anal 5 pinna 6 caudal, dorsal, pelvic 7 acantha, flipper, ventral 8 pectoral

finagle 5 cheat, trick 6 wangle 7 deceive, snaffle, swindle 8 engineer, maneuver 9 machinate

final 3 lag 4 last 6 ending, latest, latter 7 closing 8 crowning, decisive, eventual, hindmost, terminal, ultimate 9 finishing 10 concluding, conclusive, definitive 11 terminating

finale 3 end 5 close, finis 6 climax, ending, finish, payoff, windup 7 closing 9 cessation 10 conclusion, denouement 11 culmination, termination

finalize 3 end 5 close 6 finish, wind up 8 conclude, solidify 9 terminate 10 consummate

finance 4 back, bank, fund 5 endow, stake 7 promote, revenue, sponsor, support 8 bankroll 9 grubstake, patronize, subsidize 10 capitalize, underwrite

financial 6 fiscal, pocket 8 business, economic, monetary 9 pecuniary 10 commercial ***statement:*** 12 balance sheet

financier ***American:*** 4 Hill, Ryan, Sage 5 Baker, Eaton, Field, Gould, Grace, Green 6 Girard, Mellon, Morgan, Morris, Rogers, Yerkes 7 Peabody 10 Vanderbilt ***British:*** 6 Rhodes 7 Gresham ***French:*** 6 Necker ***German:*** 7 Schacht 10 Rothschild

finch 4 pape 5 junco, serin, zebra 6 linnet, siskin, towhee 7 bunting, chewink, redpoll 8 grosbeak, longspur

find 4 espy, give, hand, note, spot 5 catch, dig up, hit on, sight, solve 6 descry, detect, espial, locate, strike, supply, turn up 7 discern, dish out, furnish, hit upon, provide, scare up 8 discover, dispense, hand over, meet with, transfer, treasure, turn over 9 detection, discovery, encounter 10 unearthing 13 treasure trove

find out 3 see 4 hear 5 learn 6 tumble 7 catch on, unearth 8 discover 9 ascertain, determine

fine 3 tax, top 4 fair, levy, nice 5 bonny, clear, dandy, mulct, sheer, sunny 6 amerce, choice, minute, sconce, subtle 7 capital, clarion, damages, elegant, forfeit, penalty, powdery, refined 8 delicate, five-star, hairline, penalize, pleasant, rainless, splendid, sunshiny, superior, top-notch 9 beautiful, cloudless, enjoyable, excellent, first-rate, unclouded 10 amercement, assessment, first-class, impalpable, pulverized, reparation, undarkened 11 first-string 13 hairsplitting

finery 5 frill 6 gewgaw, tawdry 7 apparel, bravery, clothes, gaudery, regalia 8 foofaraw, frippery, ornament, trimming, war paint 9 full dress 10 Sunday best

finesse 3 art 4 play 5 skill 6 jockey 7 beguile, cunning, exploit 8 maneuver, subtlety 9 dexterity 10 manipulate

Fingal's Cave island 6 Staffa

finger 3 paw, tap, toy 4 feel, make, name, spot 5 digit, index, pinky, place, strum, touch 6 handle, medius, pilfer, pinkie 7 appoint, palpate 8 diagnose, identify, nominate, pinpoint 9 designate, determine, recognize 11 distinguish 13 diagnosticate ***bone:*** 7 phalanx 9 phalanges (plural) ***combining form:*** 6 dactyl, digiti 7 dactylo, dactyly 8 dactylia 9 dactylism, dactylous ***cymbal:*** 8 castanet

fingernail ***combining form:*** 4 onyx 7 onychia 8 onychium ***crescent:*** 6 lunule

fingerprint 4 arch, loop 5 whorl

finicky 4 nice 5 fussy 6 choosy, dainty, prissy 7 choosey 9 squeamish 10 fastidious, particular, pernickety 11 persnickety

finish 3 die, end 4 cool, do in, down, halt, kill, slay, stop 5 cease, close, glaze, scrag, spend, use up 6 cut off, ending, expend, finale, murder, polish, wash up, windup, wrap up 7 closing, consume, destroy, execute, exhaust, put away, surface, take off 8 carry off, complete, conclude, dispatch, finalize, knock off, terminus, ultimate 9 cessation, determine, liquidate, terminate 10 attainment, conclusion, desistance, run through 11 achievement, acquirement, acquisition, assassinate, termination ***dull:*** 3 mat 4 matt 5 matte ***second:*** 5 place ***third:*** 4 show

finished 4 done, down, over, ripe 5 ended,

suave **6** closed, smooth, urbane **7** done for, refined, through **8** complete, washed-up **9** completed, concluded, perfected, virtuosic **10** consummate, terminated **12** accomplished

finish off **3** cap **5** crown **6** climax, top off **8** round off **9** culminate

finite **5** bound **7** bounded, defined, limited **9** definable **10** restricted

Finland ***capital:*** **8** Helsinki ***monetary unit:*** **6** markka

Finlandia composer **8** Sibelius

Finnish ***bath:*** **5** sauna ***combining form:*** **5** Fenno ***epic:*** **8** Kalevala ***god:*** **6** Jumala

fin's double **7** tenspot

fir **7** conifer **9** evergreen ***genus:*** **5** Abies

fire **2** ax **3** can, pep, vim, zip **4** bake, burn, cast, dash, drop, hurl, kiln, sack, stir, toss, zeal, zest, zing **5** ardor, blaze, drive, exalt, flame, flare, fling, glare, gusto, heave, ingle, light, loose, pitch, rouse, salvo, shoot, sling, spark, throw, torch, verve, vigor **6** arouse, bounce, energy, excite, fervor, hurrah, ignite, inform, kindle, launch, spirit, thrill **7** animate, boot out, burnout, dismiss, enliven, enthuse, inferno, inflame, inspire, kick out, passion, provoke **8** enkindle, heighten **9** calenture, discharge, holocaust, intensify, terminate **10** enthusiasm, heartiness, liveliness **13** conflagration ***combining form:*** **3** pyr **4** igni, pyro ***god:*** **4** Agni, Loki **6** Vulcan **10** Hephaestus

firearm see gun

firebrand **7** hothead, hotspur **8** agitator

firebug **5** torch **8** arsonist **10** incendiary, pyromaniac

firecracker **5** squib **9** explosive **10** cherry bomb, noisemaker

firedog **7** andiron

firedrake **6** dragon

firefly **7** glowfly **12** lightning bug

fire opal **7** girasol

fireplace **5** ingle ***equipment:*** **6** fender, screen **7** andiron, fireset ***part:*** **3** hob **6** hearth, mantel

fireplug **7** hydrant

fire up **5** rouse **6** excite, ignite, incite, kindle **7** enflame, enliven, inflame, inspire, provoke **8** enkindle **9** intensify

firework **4** gerb **5** gerbe **6** fizgig, petard, rocket **8** sparkler **10** tourbillon **11** pyrotechnic, tourbillion ***cluster:*** **9** girandole

firm **3** set **4** fast, hard, sure **5** exact, fixed, house, rigid, solid, sound, stiff, tight, tough **6** outfit, secure, stable, stated, steady, stolid, strong, sturdy **7** abiding, adamant, certain, company, concern, confirm, fixedly, settled, solidly, staunch, tightly, unmoved **8** business, constant, definite, enduring, faithful, resolute, specific **9** inelastic, steadfast, tenacious **10** determined, enterprise, inflexible, stipulated, unwavering, unyielding **11** established, steadfastly, substantial, unfaltering, unqualified **12** never-failing **13** establishment

firmament **3** sky **6** welkin **7** heavens **8** empyrean

firmness **7** resolve **8** decision, security, solidity, strength, tenacity **9** constancy, soundness, stability **10** resolution, stableness, steadiness **11** decidedness **12** resoluteness **13** determination, purposiveness

first **4** arch, head **5** alpha, chief, least, prime **6** maiden, primal **7** eminent, highest, initial, leading, pioneer, premier, primary, supreme **8** champion, dominant, earliest, foremost, headmost, original, smallest **9** inaugural, initially, paramount, principal, slightest, sovereign **10** aboriginal, preeminent, primordial ***combining form:*** **4** prot **5** proto

firstborn **4** heir **5** eigne **6** eldest

first-class **3** top **4** A-one, fine **5** prime **6** tip-top **7** capital **8** five-star, superior, top-notch **9** excellent, top-drawer

first fruits **7** annates

firsthand **6** direct **7** primary **9** immediate

first man in space **7** Gagarin

first-rate see **first-class**

first showing **8** premiere

First State **8** Delaware

first-string see **first-class**

firth **3** arm, bay **4** cove, gulf **5** inlet **6** harbor, slough **7** estuary

fiscal **6** pocket **8** monetary **9** financial

fish **3** net, sap **4** butt, cast, dupe, fool, gill, hint **5** angle, chump, seine, trawl, troll **6** sucker **7** fall guy, gillnet, gudgeon, sniggle ***angler:*** **7** lophiid **9** goosefish ***aquarium:*** **4** barb **5** betta, danio, guppy, limia, platy, tetra **6** mollie **7** cichlid, gourami, rasbora **8** goldfish **9** angelfish ***basket:*** **5** creel ***catfish:*** **6** madtom **8** bullhead, bullpout, hornpout, stonecat ***cod:*** **4** cusk, hake, ling **5** torsk **6** burbot, tomcod **7** pollack, pollock ***combining form:*** **6** ichthy **7** ichthyo, ichthys ***croaker:*** **4** drum **7** corbina **8** kingfish, seatrout, weakfish **10** squeteague, squiteague ***eellike:*** **5** moray **6** conger **7** hagfish, lamprey ***eggs:*** **3** roe **5** spawn ***electric:*** **4** raad **7** torpedo **9** stargazer ***extinct:*** **10** coelacanth ***flatfish:*** **3** dab **4** butt, dace, sole **5** bream, brill, fluke **6** plaice, turbot **7** halibut **8** flounder ***food:*** **3** cod, eel, ide **4** bass, carp, cero, hake, ling, scup, shad, sole, tuna **5** jurel, perch, scrod, skate, smelt, trout **6** bonito, caviar, kipper, mullet, plaice, pompon, salmon, tautog, weever, wrasse **7** alewife, catfish, cavalla, escolar, grouper, haddock, halibut, herring, pollack, pollock, pompano, pompoon, sardine, snapper, tautaug **8** brisling, crevalle, flounder, mackerel 9 barracuda ***game:*** 4 bass, pike, tuna 5 perch, trout 6 grilse, marlin, salmon, tarpon 8 pickerel 9 swordfish ***grunt:*** 5 sargo 7 pigfish, tomtate 8 porkfish 10 bluestripe ***herring:*** 4 shad, sild 5 sprat 7 alewife, sardine 8 brisling, pilchard ***kind:*** 3 ray 4 bass, cero, chub, dory, goby, jack, pike, rudd, scup, tuna 5 balao, bream, cisco, loach, perch, porgy, sargo, shark, skate, smelt, snook, tench, tunny, wahoo 6 anabas, blenny, bonito, dorado, marlin, minnow, mullet, permit, puffer, remora, sauger, splake, sucker, tarpon, tautog, warsaw, wrasse 7 anchovy, boxfish, buffalo, cabezon, capelin, cavalla, chimera, cowfish, crappie, dolphin, grunion, haddock, hogfish, jewfish, mojarra, muddler, mudfish, oarfish, opaleye, piranha, pupfish, sardine, sawfish, sculpin, snapper, sunfish, tilapia, vendace, whiting 8 albacore, blowfish, bluefish, bluegill, bonefish, burrfish, chimaera, filefish, gambusia, grayling, halfbeak, ladyfish, lookdown, lumpfish, lungfish, mackerel, menhaden, moonfish, pickerel, pipefish, rockfish, sailfish, seahorse, skipjack, stingray, sturgeon, tilefish, topsmelt, warmouth, wolffish 9 amberjack, barracuda, greenling, jacksmelt, killifish, mummichog, pilotfish, spadefish, swordfish, topminnow, trunkfish, whitebait, whitefish 10 butterfish, flying fish, lizardfish, needlefish, parrotfish, silverside, tripletail, yellowtail 11 harvestfish, muskellunge, pumpkinseed, stickleback, triggerfish 12 schoolmaster ***luminescent:*** 9 viperfish 10 midshipman 11 hatchetfish, lanternfish ***minnow:*** 4 carp, chub, dace 6 shiner ***pan:*** 5 bream, perch, trout 7 crappie, sunfish 8 bluegill, rock bass 11 pumpkinseed ***porgy:*** 4 scup 7 pinfish 8 jolthead 10 sheepshead ***relating to:*** 7 piscine 8 ichthyic ***rockfish:*** 8 bocaccio, lionfish, rosefish 11 chilipepper ***salmon:*** 3 dog 4 chum, coho 6 sebago 7 chinook, sockeye ***spear:*** 3 gig 7 harpoon, trident ***stew:*** 8 cioppino, matelote 13 bouillabaisse ***trap:*** 3 dam 4 weir 6 eelpot 9 fishgarth ***trout:*** 5 charr 7 oquassa, rainbow 9 cutthroat 11 Dolly Varden ***young:*** 3 fry 4 parr 5 larva, smolt 6 alevin, grilse

fisherman 6 angler 8 piscator

fish hawk 6 osprey

fishhook 5 drail ***adjunct:*** 5 snell ***part:*** 4 barb 5 shank

fishing area 7 piscary

fishing line 4 trot 7 boulter, setline 8 longline, trotline ***float:*** 3 bob 5 quill 6 dobber ***leader:*** 5 snell

fishing lure 3 fly 4 herl

fishing net 5 seine, trawl

fishlike mammal 3 orc 5 whale 7 dolphin 8 porpoise

fish owl 6 ketupa

fishwife 5 harpy, scold, shrew, vixen 6 amazon, ogress, virago 9 termagant, Xanthippe

fishy 4 cold, dull 7 dubious, suspect 8 doubtful 9 ambiguous, doubtable, dubitable, equivocal, uncertain 10 suspicious

fission element 7 uranium 9 plutonium

fissure 3 gap 4 gash, hole, rent, rift, rima, rime 5 break, chasm, chink, cleft, crack, split 6 breach, schism 7 crevice, opening, rupture 8 crevasse, fracture, rimation

fist 3 job 4 grip, hand 5 grasp, index 6 clench, clutch, ductus, effort, handle, script 7 attempt 10 penmanship 11 calligraphy, chirography, handwriting

fisticuffs 4 ring 6 boxing 8 pugilism 13 prizefighting

fit 2 go 3 apt, set 4 good, hale, jibe, just, meet, sane, suit, turn, well 5 adapt, agree, frame, happy, joint, ready, right, sound, spasm, spell, tally, throe 6 access, accord, adjust, attack, become, belong, decent, go with, make up, proper, seemly, square, tailor, useful 7 capable, conform, healthy, prepare, qualify, seizure, tantrum 8 apoplexy, assemble, decorous, dovetail, eligible, paroxysm, quadrate, rightful, suitable 9 agree with, befitting, congruous, consonant, harmonize, reconcile, wholesome 10 applicable, convenient, correspond, felicitous, go together, tailor-make, well-liking 11 accommodate, appropriate ***suffix:*** 4 able, ible

fitful 6 catchy, random, spotty 8 periodic, sporadic, unstable, variable 9 desultory, haphazard, hit-or-miss, irregular, recurrent, spasmodic 10 capricious, changeable, inconstant 11 interrupted

fitness 3 use 4 trim 5 order, shape 6 fettle, kilter, repair 7 account, aptness, service, utility 8 capacity, justness, meetness 9 advantage, condition, propriety, relevance, rightness, soundness 10 expediency, usefulness 11 eligibility, suitability 12 appositeness, suitableness 13 applicability

fit out 3 arm, rig 4 gear 5 equip 6 outfit 7 appoint, furnish, turn out 8 accouter, accoutre

fitting 3 apt 4 just, meet, true 5 happy 6 proper, seemly 7 adjunct, apropos, desired, germane 8 apposite, relevant, suitable 9 accessory, accordant, befitting, pertinent 10 applicable, attachment, concordant, felicitous, harmonious 11 appropriate

Fitzgerald novel 13 The Last Tycoon 14 The Great Gatsby

five ***combining form:*** 3 pen 4 pent 5 penta 6 quinqu 7 quinque ***group of:*** 6 pentad 7 quintet ***of trumps:*** 5 pedro

five-dollar bill 3 fin
fivefold 7 quinary 9 quintuple
Five Nations 8 Iroquois ***member:*** 7 Cayugas, Mohawks, Oneidas, Senecas 9 Onondagas
five-sided figure 8 pentagon
five-year period 6 luster, lustre 7 lustrum
fix 3 buy, jam, lay, put, set, sop 4 do up, geld, make, mend, moor, root, spot, work 5 alter, bribe, catch, embed, focus, lodge, patch, place, ready, rivet, solve, stick, unsex 6 adjust, anchor, attach, buy off, change, corner, doctor, fasten, make up, neuter, pickle, plight, repair, revamp, scrape, secure, settle, square, steady, tune up 7 appoint, arrange, dilemma, ingrain, instill, prepare, rebuild, resolve, specify, work out 8 castrate, entrench, mutilate, overhaul, regulate, renovate 9 concenter, establish, stabilize, sterilize 10 tamper with 11 concentrate, desexualize, predicament, recondition, reconstruct
fixation 5 craze, mania, thing 9 obsession 11 fascination, infatuation
____ fixe 4 idée
fixed 3 pat, set 4 fast, firm, sure 5 tight, whole 6 frozen, narrow, secure, stable, stated, steady 7 abiding, certain, limited, precise, settled 8 constant, definite, enduring, immobile, immotile, immotive, resolute 9 exclusive, immovable, immutable, permanent, steadfast, tenacious, undivided, unmovable 10 inflexible, invariable, restricted, stationary, stipulated, unswerving, unwavering 11 determinate, inalterable, irremovable, unalterable, unfaltering, unqualified 12 concentrated, never-failing, unchangeable, undistracted, unmodifiable 13 circumscribed ***combining form:*** 6 aplano
fix up 5 equip, primp, slick, spiff 6 devise, doll up, supply 7 deck out, doll out, dress up, furnish, gussy up 8 contrive, spruce up 9 smarten up 11 accommodate
fizzle 4 fail, hiss 6 fiasco 7 failure, sputter
fjord ***Baffin Island:*** 9 Admiralty ***Denmark:*** 3 Ise, Lim 5 Lamme ***Iceland:*** 4 Axar, Eyja 5 Horna, Skaga, Vopna ***Norway:*** 3 Tys 4 Bokn, Nord, Salt, Stor, Tana, Vest 5 Lakse, Ranon, Sogne 9 Stavanger, Trondheim ***Spitsbergen:*** 3 Ice ***Svalbard:*** 4 Stor
flabbergast 5 amaze, shock 7 astound 8 astonish, surprise 9 dumbfound, overwhelm
flabby see **flaccid**
flaccid 4 limp, soft, weak 6 feeble, flabby, flimsy, floppy, sleazy 8 weakened, yielding
flag 3 ebb, sag 4 fade, fail, jack, sign, swag, wane, wilt 5 abate, color, droop 6 banner, burgee, colors, ensign, fanion, guidon, motion, pencel, pennon, signal, weaken 7 decline, gesture, pendant, pennant 8 bannerol, gonfalon, gonfanon, languish, penoncel, standard, streamer, tricolor 9 banderole, oriflamme, pennoncel, signalize 10 Jolly Roger 11 deteriorate
flagellate 4 flog, hide, lash, whip 5 whale 6 stripe, switch, thrash 7 scourge
flagellum 4 whip 5 shoot 6 runner, stolon 7 scourge
flagitious 6 rotten, sinful, wicked 7 corrupt, vicious 8 criminal, depraved, infamous, perverse, shameful 9 miscreant, nefarious 10 degenerate, scandalous, villainous 11 disgraceful
flagon 3 cup, mug 5 stoup 7 tankard
flagpole 4 mast 5 staff
flagrant 3 bad 4 bold, rank 5 gross 6 wanton 7 capital, glaring, heinous, obvious 8 striking 9 atrocious, egregious, monstrous 10 outrageous 11 conspicuous
flagstone 5 shale, slate
flag-waver 7 patriot 10 patrioteer 12 superpatriot
flail 4 beat, flog, skin, whip 6 strike, thrash, thresh 7 scourge
flair 4 bent, bump, gift, head, turn 5 knack 6 genius, talent 7 aptness, faculty 8 aptitude
flake 3 bit 4 chip, peel, rack, snow, tray 5 fleck, scale 6 lamina 8 fragment
flake off 4 peel 5 scale 9 exfoliate 10 desquamate
flamboyant 4 rich 5 showy, swank 6 chichi, florid, ornate, rococo 7 baroque, splashy 8 luscious, peacocky 10 peacockish 11 pretentious 12 orchidaceous, ostentatious
flame 4 beau, dear, fire, glow, love 5 ardor, blare, blaze, flare, flash, glare, honey, light, lover 7 beloved, darling, sweetie 8 ladylove, loveling, truelove 9 boyfriend, inamorata, inamorato 10 girlfriend
flamen 6 priest
flamenco 5 dance, gypsy, music
flaming 5 afire, fiery, flamy 6 ablaze, aflame, alight, ardent, flambé, red-hot 7 blazing, burning, fervent, flaring, ignited 8 white-hot 10 hot-blooded, passionate 11 conflagrant, impassioned
flammable 8 burnable 9 ignitable 11 combustible
flammable liquid 3 oil 6 acetyl 7 acetone, alcohol 8 gasoline, kerosene 10 turpentine
Flanders ***capital:*** 5 Lille ***language:*** 7 Flemish
flannelflower 7 mullein
flap 3 tab 4 clap, fold, leaf, stew 6 crisis, dither, lather, pother, tongue, tumult 7 aile-

ron, flutter, turmoil **9** agitation, commotion, confusion

flapdoodle **4** bosh **5** fudge **6** bunkum **7** rubbish **8** malarkey, nonsense **9** poppycock **12** blatherskite, fiddle-faddle

flapjack **7** hotcake, pancake **11** griddle cake

flare **4** glow **5** blaze, burst, flame, flash, torch **6** signal **7** flicker **8** eruption, outbreak, outburst

flare-up **4** gust **5** burst, sally **6** access **8** eruption, outburst **9** explosion

flaring **5** afire, fiery **6** ablaze, aflame, alight **7** blazing, burning, flaming, ignited **11** conflagrant

flash **3** ray **4** beam, burn, glow, show **5** blare, blaze, blink, crack, flame, flare, glare, gleam, glint, jiffy, shake, shine, spark **6** dazzle, expose, flaunt, glance, minute, moment, parade, quiver, second **7** display, disport, exhibit, flicker, glimmer, glisten, glitter, instant, radiate, shimmer, show off, spangle, sparkle, trot out, twinkle **8** brandish **9** breathing, coruscate **10** incandesce **11** coruscation, scintillate, split second **13** scintillation

flashy **4** loud **5** gaudy, showy **6** brazen, florid, garish, ornate, tawdry, tinsel **7** blatant, chintzy, glaring **9** sparkling **10** flamboyant, glittering **12** meretricious

flask **5** frame **6** bottle, fiasco, flacon **7** ampulla, canteen, costrel

flat **3** dim, mat **4** dead, drab, dull, even, poor **5** banal, bland, blind, broke, flush, inane, level, muted, needy, plane, prone, prosy, rooms, stale, stony, suite, vapid **6** jejune, planar, rental, smooth **7** insipid, planate, prosaic, sapless **8** dirt poor, lifeless, lodgings, strapped, tenement, unsavory **9** apartment, colorless, decumbent, destitute, downright, innocuous, penurious, prostrate, reclining, recumbent, savorless, tasteless **10** flavorless, lackluster, lusterless, monotonous, namby-pamby, procumbent, stone-broke

flatfish see at **fish**

flatland **4** mesa, moor **5** plain **6** steppe, tundra **7** plateau **9** tableland

flat-out **4** fast, rank **5** apace, utter **6** damned **7** blasted, goldarn, hastily, quickly, rapidly, swiftly **8** absolute, outright, speedily **9** out-and-out, posthaste **11** straight-out, unmitigated **12** lickety-split **13** expeditiously

flatten **3** lay **4** down, even, fell, flat **5** floor, flush, level, plane **6** deject, ground, lay low, smooth **7** depress, mow down **8** smoothen **9** bring down, knock down, prostrate

flattened at the poles **6** oblate

flatter **4** coax, suit **5** toady **6** become, cajole, praise **7** blarney, enhance, gratify, wheedle **8** blandish, bootlick, inveigle

flattery **3** oil **4** laud **6** praise **7** blarney, fawning, incense **8** cajolery, soft soap, toadying **9** adulation, laudation, truckling **10** sycophancy **11** bootlicking, compliments **12** blandishment, ingratiation

flatulent **4** vain **5** empty, gassy, tumid, windy **6** hollow, turgid **8** dropsied, inflated **9** dropsical, overblown, tumescent

Flaubert ***heroine:*** **4** Emma ***novel:*** **8** Salammbo **12** Madame Bovary

flaunt **4** show, wave **5** flash, flout, vaunt **6** expose, parade **7** display, disport, exhibit, flutter, show off, trot out **8** brandish, flourish

flavor **4** tang, zest **5** sapor, savor, smack, taste, tinge **6** relish, season **8** sapidity

flavorless **4** drab, flat **5** stale **7** insipid **8** unsavory **9** tasteless **11** distasteful, unpalatable

flavorsome **5** sapid, tasty **6** savory **9** aperitive, flavorful, palatable, relishing, toothsome **10** appetizing **11** good-tasting

flaw **3** gap, rip **4** rent, tear, vice **5** crack, fault **6** breach, defect **7** blemish, fissure **12** imperfection

flawed **4** sick **5** amiss **6** faulty, marred **7** damaged, spoiled **8** impaired **9** defective, imperfect

flawless **5** ideal, model, sound, whole **6** entire, intact **7** perfect **8** absolute, unbroken, unmarred **9** errorless, exquisite, faultless, fleckless, undamaged **10** immaculate, impeccable, unimpaired **11** note-perfect, unblemished **12** indefectible

flax **5** linen ***fiber:*** **3** tow **4** harl **5** harle **6** strick ***prepare:*** **3** ret **4** card **5** dress **6** hackle, scutch ***refuse:*** **5** hards, hurds

flaxen **5** blond, straw **6** blonde, golden

flay **4** skin **5** slash **6** assail, attack, berate, scathe, scorch **7** blister, censure, scarify, scourge **8** lambaste, lash into **9** castigate, excoriate **10** tongue-lash

flea **5** pulex **6** chigoe, jigger **7** chigger ***water:*** **7** daphnid

Fleance's father **6** Banquo

fleckless **7** perfect **8** absolute, flawless, unflawed **10** impeccable **11** note-perfect

flection **3** bow **4** bend, turn **5** angle **7** flexure, turning

Fledermaus, Die **3** bat ***character:*** **5** Adele, Falke, Frank **6** Alfred **9** Rosalinde **10** Eisenstein ***composer:*** **7** Strauss

fledgling **4** boot, colt, tyro **6** novice, rookie **8** beginner, freshman, neophyte, newcomer **10** apprentice

flee **3** fly, lam, run **4** bolt, scat, shun, skip **5** break, elude, scape, scoot, scram, skirr **6** decamp, escape **7** abscond, make off, scamper, scarper **9** skedaddle

fleece **3** web **4** bilk, clip, milk, rook, skin,

soak, wool **5** bleed, cheat, cozen, mulct, shear, stick, sweat **6** extort, hustle **7** defraud, despoil, plunder, swindle **10** overcharge

fleeceable **4** easy **5** naive **8** gullible **11** susceptible

fleecy **5** hairy **6** pilose, woolly **7** hirsute, pileous **9** whiskered

fleer **4** gibe, gird, jeer, jest, mock **5** flout, laugh, scoff, sneer, taunt **6** quip at **7** scout at **8** fugitive

fleet **3** fly, run **4** fast, flit, navy, sail, spry, wile, wing **5** agile, brisk, hasty, hurry, quick, rapid, speed, sweep, swift, while **6** armada, hasten, hustle, nimble, rocket, speedy **7** beguile **8** flotilla **9** breakneck **10** evanescent, expeditive, harefooted **11** expeditious

fleeting **5** brief **7** passing **8** fugitive, volatile **9** ephemeral, fugacious, momentary, transient **10** evanescent, short-lived, transitory

Fleming, Ian ***hero:*** **9** James Bond ***novel:*** **4** Dr. No **10** Goldfinger **11** Thunderball **12** Casino Royale

fleshly **3** lay **6** animal, bodily, carnal **7** profane, secular, sensual, somatic **8** corporal, physical, sensuous, temporal **9** corporeal, epicurean, luxurious, sybaritic **10** voluptuous **3** fat **5** beefy, gross, heavy, obese, plump, stout **6** portly **7** porcine, sarcous, weighty **9** corpulent **10** overweight ***fruit:*** **4** pome **5** bacca, berry, drupe

Fletcher's partner **8** Beaumont

flex **4** bend **5** tense **7** pliancy, tension

flexible **5** withy **6** docile, floppy, limber, pliant, supple, whippy **7** elastic, pliable, springy, stretch, willowy **8** amenable, stretchy, yielding **9** resilient, tractable **10** manageable

flexuous **5** snaky **7** sinuous, winding **8** tortuous **9** meandrous **10** circuitous, convoluted, meandering, serpentine **11** anfractuous

flick **3** hit **4** blow, cine, film, show **5** movie **6** strike **7** picture **9** photoplay **11** picture show **13** motion picture, moving picture

flicker **4** flit **5** blink, dance, flash, gleam, glint, hover, waver **7** flitter, flutter, glitter, sparkle, twinkle

flickering **7** lambent **8** unsteady

flier **3** ace **5** pilot **6** airman, fly-boy **7** aviator, birdman **8** aviatrix

flight **3** lam **4** rout, slip **5** floor, story **6** escape **7** getaway **8** breakout, escaping **10** escapement

flighty **5** dizzy, giddy, silly, swift **7** foolish **8** freakish, skittish, unstable, volatile **9** frivolous, mercurial, transient **10** capricious, changeable, inconstant **11** empty-headed, harebrained **13** irresponsible, rattlebrained

flimflam **3** gyp **4** beat, bilk, dupe, fake, fool, gull, hoax, jazz, sell, sham **5** cheat, cozen, fraud, freak, hokum, trick **6** befool, chouse, deceit, diddle, drivel, hot air, humbug, pigeon, trifle **7** chicane, deceive, defraud, eyewash, swindle **8** hoodwink, nonsense **9** bamboozle, deception, imposture, moonshine, overreach **10** balderdash, double-talk **11** hornswoggle

flimflammer **3** gyp **4** skin **5** cheat **6** con man **7** diddler, sharper **8** swindler **9** defrauder **12** double-dealer

flimsy **4** limp, thin, weak **5** filmy, frail, gauzy, sheer **6** feeble, flabby, floppy, infirm, sleazy, slight, slimsy, weakly **7** flaccid, fragile, rickety, slimpsy, tiffany, unsound **8** decrepit, delicate, gossamer **10** diaphanous, improbable, incredible **11** implausible, transparent **12** unbelievable, unconvincing

flinch **5** quail, start, wince **6** blanch, blench, recede, recoil, shrink **7** retreat, squinch **8** withdraw

fling **2** go **3** pop, try **4** boil, bolt, cast, dash, emit, fire, gibe, hurl, lash, orgy, race, rush, shot, slap, stab, tear, toss **5** binge, chase, crack, dance, heave, pitch, shoot, sling, spree, throw, whack, whirl **6** charge, launch **7** discard, rampage, sarcasm, splurge **9** disregard, overthrow

flip **3** tap **4** blow, flap, glib, pert, riff **5** drink, flick **6** riffle **8** flippant **10** somersault **11** smart-alecky

flippancy **6** levity **8** archness, pertness **9** cockiness, freshness, frivolity, lightness, sauciness **10** cheekiness, impishness, volatility **11** flightiness, playfulness, roguishness

flippant **4** flip, glib, pert

flip through **4** scan **6** browse **7** dip into, run over **8** glance at **10** glance over

flirt **3** toy **4** dart, flip, flit, fool, minx, play, toss, vamp **5** dally, flick **6** coquet, lead on, trifle, wanton **8** coquette

flit **3** fly, run, zip **4** dart, pass, rush, sail, scud, whiz, wing **5** dance, fleet, flick, float, hover, hurry, scoot, speed, sweep **6** dartle, hasten **7** flicker, flutter

flitter **3** bit **5** dance, flake, hover **7** flicker, flutter, skitter

float **3** bob, fly **4** buoy, cork, dart, hang, raft, ride, sail, scud, skim, waft, wash **5** drift, drink, flood, hover, poise, shoot, skirr **8** levitate **9** negotiate

floater **3** bum, vag **4** hobo **5** tramp **6** boomer **7** drifter, vagrant **8** derelict, vagabond

floating **5** loose **6** adrift, afloat, natant **7** buoyant, movable **8** moveable, shifting

flocculent **6** woolly

flock **3** mob **4** army, bevy, herd, host, pack, rout **5** bunch, cloud, covey, crowd, drove, group **6** flight, legion, scores, volary **9** multitude **11** aggregation

flog **3** tan **4** beat, cane, hide, lash, whip **5** birch, flail, knout, tawse, whale **6** larrup, stripe, switch, thrash **7** exhaust, scourge **10** flagellate

flood **4** bore, flow, flux, pour, rush, tide **5** drift, drown, eager, eagre, spate, swamp, whelm **6** deluge, engulf, stream **7** current, freshet, niagara, torrent **8** cataract, flooding, inundate, overflow, submerge **9** cataclysm, overwhelm **10** inundation, outgushing, outpouring

floor **4** down, drop, fell **5** level, story **6** defeat, ground, lay low **7** flatten, silence **8** audience, bowl down, bowl over **9** bring down, knock down

flop **3** dud **4** bomb, bust, fail, fall, flap **5** lemon, loser **6** fizzle **7** failure

floppy **4** limp **5** loose **6** flabby, flimsy, sleazy **7** flaccid **8** flexible

flora **6** plants **10** vegetation

flora and fauna **5** biota

Florence ***bridge:*** **12** Ponte Vecchio ***cathedral:*** **5** Duomo ***family:*** **6** Medici ***gallery:*** **6** Uffizi ***museum:*** **8** Bargello ***palace:*** **5** Pitti ***river:*** **4** Arno

florid **4** rich **5** flush, gaudy, ruddy, showy **6** ornate, rococo **7** aureate, baroque, flowery, flushed, glowing **8** figurate, luscious, rubicund, sanguine, sonorous **9** bombastic, overblown **10** euphuistic, flamboyant, rhetorical **11** declamatory, full-blooded **12** magniloquent **13** grandiloquent

Florida ***capital:*** **11** Tallahassee ***college, university:*** **4** Nova **5** Barry **6** Eckerd **7** Stetson ***discoverer:*** **11** Ponce de Leon ***Key:*** **4** Long, Vaca, West **5** Largo **7** Big Pine **9** Sugarloaf ***largest city:*** **12** Jacksonville ***motto:*** **12** In God We Trust ***nickname:*** **13** Sunshine State ***state bird:*** **11** mockingbird ***state flower:*** **13** orange blossom

florilegium **3** ana **4** posy **5** album **7** garland, omnibus **8** analects **9** anthology **10** miscellany

Florimel's husband **7** Marinel

florist's milieu **10** greenhouse

floss **3** fur **4** down, flue, fuzz, lint, pile **5** fluff

flotsam **6** jetsam **8** wreckage **9** driftwood

flounce **5** fling, frill, mince, strut **6** prance, ruffle, sashay **8** flounder, struggle

flounder **5** fling, labor, lurch **6** muddle, wallow **7** blunder, stumble **8** flatfish, struggle

flour **4** atta, bolt, meal, mill **5** grind **6** pinole, powder **9** pulverize ***beetle:*** **6** weevil

flourish **3** wax **4** brag, grow, wave **5** adorn, bloom, boast, score, swing **6** arrive, flower, stroke, thrive **7** blossom, develop, fanfare, make out, prosper, succeed **8** brandish, curlicue, decorate, ornament **9** grace note

flout **4** gibe, gird, jeer, jest, mock **5** fleer, scoff, scorn, sneer, taunt **6** deride, insult, quip at **7** jeering, mockery **9** disregard

flow **3** run **4** emit, flux, gush, hang, head, pour, rill, rise, roll, rush, stem, teem, tide, void, well **5** arise, crawl, drift, flood, issue, spate, surge, swarm **6** abound, course, gurgle, onrush, ripple, series, sluice, spring, stream **7** cascade, current, emanate, give off, indraft, outflow, proceed **8** fountain, inundate, sequence **9** discharge, originate, pullulate **10** continuity, derive from, disembogue, inundation, menstruate, succession **11** continuance, progression **12** continuation, menstruation ***combining form:*** **4** rheo **5** rrhea **6** rrhoea **7** rrhagia

flower **3** top **4** best, blow, pick, posy **5** bloom, cream, elite, pride, prime, prize **6** choice, gentry **7** aristoi, blossom, burgeon, develop, fleuron, quality, society **8** optimacy, outbloom **9** gentility **10** efflorescе, upper class, upper crust **11** aristocracy **13** inflorescence ***buttonhole:*** **11** boutonniere ***cluster:*** **4** cyme **5** spike, umbel **6** corymb, floret, raceme, spadix, thyrse **7** panicle **8** spikelet **9** capitulum, dichasium, glomerule **11** monochasium, polychasium **13** inflorescence ***combining form:*** **4** anth **5** antho, anthy, flori **6** anthes, anthus **7** anthous, florous ***cup:*** **5** calyx ***garden:*** **4** iris, lily, pink, rose **5** aster, canna, daisy, pansy, peony, phlox, poppy, tulip **6** azalia, cosmos, crocus, dahlia, orchid, violet **7** jonquil, petunia **8** camellia, daffodil, gardenia, geranium, gloxinia, hyacinth, larkspur, marigold, primrose **9** carnation, gladiolus, narcissus **10** delphinium, heliotrope **13** chrysanthemum ***opening:*** **8** anthesis ***part:*** **5** bract, calyx, ovary, ovule, petal, sepal, style **6** anther, pistil, spathe, stamen, stigma **7** corolla, nectary, pedicel, petiole **8** calyptra, filament, gynecium, peduncle, perianth ***spike:*** **5** ament **6** catkin, spadix ***stalk:*** **7** pedicel **8** peduncle ***type:*** **3** ray **4** disk **6** annual, simple **9** composite, perennial ***wild:*** **4** flag **5** bluet, daisy, gilia, vetch **6** lupine **7** anemone, arbutus, cowslip, gentian, vervain **8** bluebell, hepatica, trillium **9** buttercup, columbine, dandelion, saxifrage **10** cinquefoil **11** lady slipper **12** lady's slipper

flower arranging **7** ikebana

flowering **6** growth **8** progress, upgrowth **9** evolution, unfolding **10** evolvement **11** development, florescence, progression

flowerless plant 4 fern, moss 6 fungus, lichen 9 liverwort
flower-shaped ornament 7 fleuron
flowery 5 wordy 6 florid, ornate 7 aureate, swollen, verbose 8 sonorous 9 bombastic, overblown 10 euphuistic, rhetorical 11 declamatory 12 magniloquent 13 grandiloquent
Flowery Kingdom 5 China
flowing 4 easy 5 fluid 6 afflux, fluent, smooth 7 copious, cursive, running, streamy 8 freeform 10 effortless ***back:*** 6 reflux 8 refluent ***in:*** 6 influx 8 influent ***together:*** 7 conflux 9 confluent
flow regulator 5 valve
flub 4 mess, muff 5 boner, botch, error, fluff 6 bollix, bungle, goof up 7 blunder, louse up
fluctuate 4 sway, wave 5 swing, waver 8 undulate 9 oscillate, vacillate 10 irresolute
flue 3 fur 4 down, fuzz, lint, pile 5 floss, fluff 7 channel, dragnet, feather, fishnet, passage
fluent 4 easy, free, glib 5 fluid, vocal 6 facile, liquid, smooth 7 cursive, flowing, running, voluble 8 eloquent 9 talkative 10 articulate, effortless, loquacious 12 smooth-spoken
fluff 3 fur 4 bull, down, flub, flue, fuzz, lint, mess, muff, pile, slip, trip 5 boner, botch, error, floss, lapse 6 bollix, bungle, goof up 7 blooper, blunder, louse up, mistake
fluid 4 free 5 water 6 liquid, mobile 7 mutable, protean 8 unstable, unsteady, variable, weathery 9 changeful, unsettled 10 changeable ***combining form:*** 4 sero ***excessive:*** 5 edema
fluid pressure record 8 kymogram
fluky 3 odd 6 casual, chance 8 unsteady 9 uncertain 10 accidental, capricious, contingent, fortuitous, incidental
flume 5 chute 6 sluice, stream 7 channel
flummox 4 fail 7 confuse, perplex 8 confound 9 embarrass 10 disconcert
flunky 5 toady 7 footman, servant, steward
flurry 3 ado 4 fuss, gust, stir 5 haste, upset, whirl 6 bother, bustle, furore, pother, scurry 7 agitate, confuse, disturb, fluster, perturb, turmoil, unhinge 8 disquiet 9 agitation, confusion, whirlpool, whirlwind 10 discompose, excitement, turbulence
flush 3 lay 4 even, flat, glow, pink, rich, rose 5 bloom, blush, color, level, plane, rouge, ruddy 6 florid, mantle, pinken, redden, smooth 7 blossom, crimson, flatten, flushed, glowing, moneyed, opulent, planate, wealthy 8 abundant, affluent, rubicund, sanguine, smoothen 11 full-blooded
fluster 5 addle, dizzy, shake, upset 6 ball up, bother, flurry, fuddle, muddle, puzzle, rattle, ruffle 7 agitate, confuse, disturb, mystify, nonplus, perplex, perturb, unhinge 8 befuddle, bewilder, confound, disquiet, distract 10 discompose
flute 4 fife, roll 5 pleat 6 goffer, groove 7 chamfer, channel, flutist, piccolo, shuttle 8 recorder 9 wineglass ***combining form:*** 3 aul 4 aulo ***player:*** 5 piper 7 flutist 8 flautist
flutist ***American:*** 5 Baker, Baron 7 Robison ***British:*** 6 Galway ***French:*** 6 Rampal
flutter 4 beat, flap, flit 5 dance, hover, quake, shake, throb 6 flurry, quaver, quiver, wobble 7 flicker, flitter, pulsate, tremble, vibrate 8 disorder 9 agitation, confusion, palpitate, vibration 11 fluctuation, oscillation
flux 3 run 4 flow, fuse, melt, rush, thaw, tide 5 drift, flood, spate 6 scours, stream 7 current, flowing, liquefy, outflow 8 diarrhea, dissolve, liquesce 9 dysentery 10 deliquesce
fly 3 run, zip 4 bolt, dart, dash, flee, flit, lure, rush, sail, scud, skip, soar, whiz, wing 5 break, fleet, float, glide, hover, hurry, pilot, scape, scoot, shoot, skirr, speed, sweep, whish, whisk 6 aviate, decamp, escape, flight, hasten, hustle 7 abscond, airlift, flutter, hotfoot, make off, scamper 8 highball 9 skedaddle ***combining form:*** 3 myi 4 myia, myio 5 musci ***insect:*** 4 gnat, zimb 5 fruit, midge 6 botfly, gadfly, mayfly, tsetse 7 deerfly, sandfly, tachina 8 blackfly, dipteron, horsefly, housefly, mosquito, tachinid 10 bluebottle ***larva:*** 3 bot 4 bott 6 maggot
fly-by-night 6 unsure 7 dubious 8 untrusty 9 trustless 10 unreliable 12 questionable, undependable 13 untrustworthy
flycatcher 4 tody
flying 5 aloft, brief 6 volant 7 soaring 8 airborne, volitant
Flying Dutchman ***composer:*** 6 Wagner ***heroine:*** 5 Senta
flying fish 7 gurnard
flying fox 3 bat 6 kalong 8 fruit bat
flying horse 7 Pegasus 10 hippogriff
flying island 6 Laputa
flying lemur 6 colugo
flying mammal 3 bat
flying saucer 3 UFO
fly in the ointment 5 catch
foam 4 head, scud, scum, suds 5 froth, spume, yeast 6 lather
fob 4 seal 5 chain 6 pocket, ribbon 8 ornament
fob off 5 foist 6 palm on, put off 7 palm off
focus 3 fix, hub, put 4 meet, seat 5 heart, rivet 6 center, fasten, fixate 8 converge,

polestar **9** concenter **11** concentrate, nerve center

fodder **4** feed, food **6** forage, silage **9** provender ***crop:*** **3** hay, oat, rye **4** corn **5** maize, vetch, wheat **6** barley, clover, millet **7** alfalfa, sorghum **9** broad bean ***storage structure:*** **4** silo ***store:*** **6** ensile

foe **5** enemy, rival **8** opponent **9** adversary **10** antagonist

fog **3** dim **4** blur, daze, haze, mist, murk **5** addle, bedim, brume, cloud, muddy, vapor **6** darken, muddle, puzzle **7** becloud, confuse, eclipse, mystify, obscure, perplex, pogonip **8** bewilder, distract **9** obfuscate, overcloud **10** muddlement **11** muddledness **12** befuddlement, bewilderment

foggy **4** hazy **5** misty, murky, soupy, vague **7** brumous, muddled, obscure, tenuous **8** confused, vaporous

foghorn **8** diaphone

fogy **6** square **7** diehard **8** mossback, standpat **10** back number, fuddy-duddy **12** antediluvian, conservative, mid-Victorian **13** stick-in-the-mud

fogyish **4** tory **5** right **7** die-hard, old-line **8** orthodox **9** out-of-date **10** antiquated **11** reactionary **12** conservative, old-fashioned

foible **5** fault **7** failing, frailty **8** weakness **11** shortcoming **12** imperfection

foil **4** balk, beat, bilk, curb, dash, faze **5** sword **6** baffle, defeat, rattle, thwart, tissue **7** buffalo, repulse **8** restrain **9** discomfit, embarrass, frustrate **10** circumvent, disappoint, disconcert

foist **3** fob **4** dupe, gull, hoax, wish, worm **5** cheat, trick **6** delude, edge in, fob off, impose, palm on, work in **7** beguile, deceive, defraud, inflict, mislead, palm off, pass off, swindle, work off **8** hoodwink **9** bamboozle, insinuate, overreach **10** infiltrate

fold **3** lap, pen, ply **4** bend, bust, coat, fail, leaf, ruck, tuck **5** break, crash, drape, flock, layer, plait, pleat, plica, purse, ridge, rivel **6** crease, cuttle, double, furrow, pucker, rimple **7** confine, crinkle, crumple, embrace, entwine, envelop, flexure, overlap, plicate, wrinkle **8** surround **9** plication **11** corrugation ***combining form:*** **5** ptych **6** ptycho, valvul **7** valvulo ***skin:*** **4** ruga **5** plica, rugae (plural) **6** dewlap, plicae (plural)

folder **4** file **5** cover **6** binder **8** circular

foliage **6** growth, leaves **7** leafage, verdure **9** greenness **10** vegetation

folk **4** clan, race **5** house, laity, stock, tribe **6** family, people **7** kindred, lineage **9** relatives

folklore **4** myth **6** belief, custom, legend, mythos **9** mythology, tradition **12** superstition

folksinger **4** Baez (Joan), Ives (Burl) **5** Niles (John Jacob), White (Josh) **6** Seeger (Pete) **7** Chapman (Tracy), Guthrie (Arlo, Woody) **9** Ledbetter (Huddie)

folktale **7** märchen

follow **3** ape, dog, see, spy, tag **4** copy, hunt, keep, mind, obey, seek, tail, take **5** after, catch, chase, chivy, ensue, grasp, hound, trace, track, trail **6** accept, attend, comply, convoy, pursue, search, shadow, take in **7** conform, imitate, observe, replace, succeed **8** displace, exercise, postdate, practice, supplant **9** accompany, apprehend, supersede, supervene **10** comprehend, understand

follower **3** fan **5** freak, toady **6** addict, cohort, patron, sequel, votary **7** devotee, groupie, habitué, sectary, sequent, trailer **8** adherent, advocate, disciple, faithful, hanger-on, henchman, myrmidon, parasite, partisan, sectator, tagalong **9** dependent, satellite, supporter, sycophant **10** aficionado **11** lickspittle ***of Theodore Roosevelt:*** **9** Bull Moose ***suffix:*** **3** ite

following **4** next **5** after, below, since, suite, train **6** behind, public **7** ensuing, retinue, sequent **8** audience **9** clientage, clientele, entourage **10** sequential, subsequent, succeeding, successive **12** subsequent to

follow-up **6** sequel

folly **4** whim **6** lunacy, vanity **7** fatuity, foolery, inanity, madness **8** insanity, nonsense **9** absurdity, craziness, dottiness, silliness, stupidity **10** imprudence, indulgence **11** foolishness, witlessness

foment **3** set **4** abet, brew, goad, spur **5** nurse, raise, rouse, set on **6** arouse, excite, foster, incite, stir up, whip up **7** agitate, ferment, nurture, provoke **9** cultivate, encourage, instigate

Fomorian one-eyed giant **5** Balor

fond **4** dear, warm **5** basis, silly **6** doting, loving, tender, upbeat **7** devoted, foolish **8** enamored, lonesome, romantic, sanguine **9** indulgent **10** groundwork, infatuated, optimistic, responsive **11** sentimental, sympathetic **12** affectionate

fondle **3** hug, pet **4** love **5** clasp **6** caress, cosset, dandle **7** embrace

fondness **4** love **5** taste **6** liking, relish **8** appetite, devotion, soft spot **9** affection **10** attachment, partiality, propensity **11** inclination **12** predilection

fondness for ***combining form:*** **5** phily **6** philia ***suffix:*** **4** itis

fond of ***combining form:*** **4** phil **5** phile, philo **6** philic **7** philous

food **3** pap **4** bite, chow, diet, fare, grub, meal, meat **5** bread, manna, scoff **6** fodder, viands, vivres **7** aliment, edibles, nurture, pabulum **8** delicacy, victuals **9** nutriment, provender 10 provisions, sustenance 11 comestibles, nourishment ***combining form:*** 4 sito 6 phagia ***craving for:*** 7 bulimia ***divine:*** 8 ambrosia ***element:*** 5 sugar 6 starch 7 mineral, protein, vitamin 12 carbohydrate ***from heaven:*** 5 manna ***lover:*** 7 epicure, gourmet 8 gourmand ***provision:*** 4 mess 6 ration 7 serving ***scarcity:*** 6 famine ***waste:*** 4 orts 7 garbage

foofaraw 4 coil, fuss 6 furore, hurrah, ruckus, rumpus, shindy 8 brouhaha 9 commotion

fool 3 ass, fun, kid, rag, rib, sap, toy 4 blow, butt, dolt, dope, dupe, fish, gull, hoax, jerk, jest, joke, josh, mark, poop, razz, simp, wolf, zany 5 amble, ament, chump, clown, comic, dally, dummy, dunce, flirt, goose, idiot, jolly, loser, moron, ninny, noddy, patsy, schmo, silly, trick, waste 6 banter, befool, butt in, coquet, cretin, cuckoo, dimwit, donkey, doodle, horn in, jester, lead on, loiter, madman, meddle, monkey, motley, nincom, nitwit, pigeon, schmoe, simple, stooge, stupid, sucker, trifle, victim, wanton 7 asshead, buffoon, chicane, consume, deceive, fall guy, foolish, fritter, gudgeon, half-wit, jackass, natural, pinhead, saphead, schmuck, tomfool 8 busybody, comedian, dumbbell, easy mark, flimflam, hoodwink, imbecile, lunkhead, mooncalf, numskull, pushover, softhead, squander, underwit, womanize 9 bamboozle, birdbrain, blockhead, dissipate, interfere, interlope, philander, simpleton, throw away 10 frivol away, instrument, mess around, monkey with, nincompoop, play around, tamper with, trifle away 11 featherhead, hornswoggle, merry-andrew, ninnyhammer, rattlebrain, string along 12 featherbrain, scatterbrain 13 laughingstock

foolhardy 4 rash 6 daring 8 headlong, reckless 9 audacious, daredevil, impetuous, venturous 11 adventurous, precipitate, temerarious, venturesome 13 adventuresome

foolish 3 mad 4 daft, fond, rash, zany 5 batty, crazy, dippy, dizzy, dotty, goofy, inane, jerky, loony, loopy, sappy, silly, wacky 6 absurd, insane, simple, stupid, unwise 7 asinine, doltish, fatuous, idiotic, lunatic, moronic, offbeat, unwitty, witless 8 headless, reckless 9 brainless, fantastic, half-baked, imbecilic, laughable, ludicrous, senseless, unearthly 10 half-cocked, half-witted, idleheaded, irrational, ridiculous, unorthodox, weak-headed, weak-minded 11 harebrained, nonsensical

foolishness 4 bull, bunk 5 folly 6 lunacy 7 fatuity, inanity, waggery 8 drollery, insanity, nonsense, unwisdom 9 absurdity 10 imprudence 12 indiscretion 13 senselessness

fool's gold 6 pyrite

foot 3 add, sum, tot 4 base, cast, pace, step, tote, walk 5 dance, nadir, total, tread, troop 6 bottom, figure, hoof it, prance, tootsy 7 summate, tootsie, traipse 8 ambulate, totalize ***ailment:*** 4 corn 6 bunion, callus ***animal:*** 3 pad, paw 4 hoof 7 fetlock, flipper, pastern, trotter ***bones of:*** 5 talus, tarsi (plural) 6 cuboid, tarsal, tarsus 7 phalanx 9 calcaneus, cuneiform, navicular, phalanges (plural) 10 metatarsal ***combining form:*** 3 ped, pod, pus 4 pede, pedi, pedo, poda, pode, podo 5 podia 6 podium ***doctor:*** 10 podiatrist 11 chiropodist ***metric:*** 4 iamb 5 arsis 6 dactyl, thesis 7 anapest, pyrrhic, spondee, trochee ***part:*** 3 toe 4 arch, ball, claw, nail 5 ankle, digit, talon 6 hallux, instep

football 5 rugby 6 rugger, soccer 7 pigskin ***field:*** 8 gridiron ***foul:*** 7 holding, offside 8 clipping 12 interference ***official:*** 6 umpire 7 referee 8 linesman 9 back judge, line judge 10 field judge ***play:*** 4 dive, trap 5 sneak, sweep 6 option, screen 7 audible, counter, handoff, rollout, runback 8 dropback 9 crossbuck, off-tackle 10 buttonhook ***player position:*** 3 end 4 back 5 guard 6 center, safety, tackle 7 flanker, lineman, wideout 8 fullback, halfback, slotback, split end, tailback, tight end, wingback 9 noseguard 10 cornerback, linebacker, nose tackle 11 quarterback 12 defensive end, wide receiver ***scoring:*** 6 safety 9 field goal, touchdown 10 conversion ***starting play:*** 7 kickoff ***team:*** 6 eleven ***term:*** 4 down, kick, pass, punt, rush, snap 5 blitz, block, squad 6 fumble, huddle, onside, option, safety, spiral 7 end zone, handoff, kickoff, offside, pigskin, quarter, spinner, yardage 8 clipping, crossbar, goal line, goalpost, gridiron, halftime 9 backfield, defensive, field goal, intercept, offensive, placekick, scrimmage, touchback, touchdown 11 broken field 12 interception

footballer 4 Moon (Warren), Rice (Jerry) 5 Baugh (Sammy), Berry (Raymond), Brown (Jim), Ditka (Mike), Elway (John), Jones (Bert, Deacon), Kelly (Jim), Kosar (Bernie), Shula (Don), Starr (Bart) 6 Blanda (George), Butkus (Dick), Graham (Otto), Grange (Red), Greene (Joe), Marino (Dan), Namath (Joe), Payton (Walter), Sayers (Gale), Thorpe (Jim), Tittle (Y. A.), Unitas (Johnny) 7 Dorsett (Tony), Esiason (Boomer), Gifford (Frank), Hornung (Paul), Luckman (Sid), Montana (Joe), Simpson (O. J.) 8 Bradshaw (Terry), Nagurski (Bronko), Staubach (Roger) 9 Dickerson (Eric), Jurgensen (Sonny), Tarkenton (Fran)

footed ***combining form:*** **3** ped, pod **6** podous
footfall **4** step **5** tread
footing **4** base, rank, seat, term **5** basis, place, state **6** bottom, ground, status **7** bedrock, seating, station, warrant **8** basement, capacity, position **9** character, situation **10** foundation, groundwork, substratum
footless **6** apodal
foot lever **5** pedal **7** treadle
footlike **6** pedate **8** pediform
footpad **6** robber **10** highwayman
footprint **3** pug **4** sign, step **5** spoor, trace, track, tract **7** pugmark, vestige ***fossil:*** **7** ichnite **9** ichnolite
footslog **4** plod, slop, toil **6** stodge, trudge **8** plunther
footstep **5** spoor, track, tract **7** vestige
footstone **6** ledger **8** monument **11** grave marker
footstool **7** hassock, ottoman
fop **4** buck, dude **5** blade, blood, dandy, spark, sport, swell **6** masher **7** coxcomb, gallant **8** cavalier, macaroni, popinjay **9** exquisite **10** ladies' man, lady-killer **11** Beau Brummel, petit-maitre **12** fashion plate, lounge lizard, man-about-town
for ***prefix:*** **3** pro
forage **4** beat, comb, grub, raid, rake **5** scour **6** browse, fodder, ravage, search **7** ransack, rummage **8** finecomb, scrounge **9** pasturage; (see also **fodder**)
forager **6** raider, sacker **8** marauder, ravisher
foray **4** raid **5** harry **6** attack, harass, inroad, invade, maraud, sortie **7** overrun, pillage **8** invasion **9** incursion, irruption
forbear **4** curb, keep, shun **5** avoid, cease, evade, forgo, spare **6** bridle, desist, endure, escape, eschew, forego, suffer **7** abstain, decline, inhibit, refrain **8** restrain, tolerate, withhold **9** sacrifice
forbearance **5** grace, mercy **6** lenity **7** charity **8** clemency, lenience, leniency, mildness, patience **9** restraint, tolerance **10** abstinence, toleration
forbearing **4** easy, mild **6** gentle **7** clement, lenient, patient **8** merciful, tolerant **9** indulgent **10** charitable, thoughtful **11** considerate
Forbes hero **8** Tremaine (Johnny)
forbid **3** ban, bar **4** curb, deny, halt, stop, veto **5** block, check, debar, estop, taboo **6** enjoin, hinder, impede, outlaw, refuse **7** exclude, inhibit, obviate, prevent, rule out, shut out **8** obstruct, preclude, prohibit, restrain **9** interdict, proscribe
forbidden **5** taboo **6** banned **8** verboten **10** prohibited
Forbidden City **5** Lhasa
force **2** od **3** arm, jam, vim, vis **4** beef, cram, make, move, odyl, push, rape **5** cause, drive, exact, foist, impel, karma, might, odyle, order, pains, point, power, press, punch, sinew, speed, spoil, vigor, visit, wreak, wreck, wrest **6** coerce, compel, defile, demand, duress, effort, energy, enjoin, extort, impose, inject, legion, muscle, oblige, ravish, strain, stress **7** cogency, command, concuss, headway, impetus, inflict, outrage, potency, require, sandbag, shotgun, tension, trouble, violate **8** coercion, deflower, manpower, momentum, obligate, occasion, pressure, shoehorn, strength, validity, velocity, violence **9** constrain, deflorate, exertions, intensity, puissance, strong arm, validness, vehemence **10** compulsion, constraint ***apart:*** **5** wedge ***unit:*** **4** dyne
forced **5** rigid, stiff **6** wooden **7** labored **9** contrived, fatiguing, unnatural **10** artificial, compulsory, exhausting, factitious, far-fetched, inflexible **11** involuntary
forceful **6** cogent, mighty, potent, virile **7** dynamic, telling **8** emphatic, forcible, powerful, puissant, vigorous **9** assertive, effective, energetic, insistent **10** compelling, resounding **12** constraining
forceless **4** weak **5** wimpy **6** feeble **8** impotent **10** emasculate, inadequate **11** ineffective, ineffectual, slack-spined **12** invertebrate
force out see **expel**
forcible **6** mighty, potent **7** intense, violent **8** coercive, emphatic, militant, powerful, puissant, vehement **9** assertive **10** aggressive
Ford's folly **5** Edsel
for each **3** per
forearm bone **4** ulna **6** radius
forebear **8** ancestor **9** ascendant **10** progenitor **11** antecedents **12** primogenitor
forebode **4** omen **5** augur **7** betoken, portend, predict, presage, promise **8** foretell
foreboding **4** omen **5** dread **6** augury **7** anxiety, portent, presage, warning **9** prenotion **10** prediction, prognostic **11** premonition, presagement **12** presentiment
forecast **5** augur, guess, infer, weird **6** gather **7** foresee, portend, predict, presage, surmise **8** conclude, foreshow, foretell, prophecy, soothsay **9** adumbrate, prevision, prognosis **10** conjecture, prediction, vaticinate **13** prognosticate
forecaster **4** seer **5** augur **6** auspex, oracle **7** prophet **8** haruspex **9** predictor **10** prophesier **11** Nostradamus **13** meteorologist
foreclose **3** bar **5** debar **6** cut off, hinder **7** prevent **8** preclude

forefather see forebear
forefeel 6 divine 7 preknow, previse 9 apprehend, prevision, visualize
forefinger 5 index
forefront 8 vanguard
foregoer 7 example 8 ancestor 9 precursor, prototype 10 antecedent, antecessor 11 predecessor
foregoing 4 past 5 prior 8 anterior, previous 9 precedent, preceding 10 antecedent
forehanded 7 prudent, thrifty
forehead 4 brow 5 frons, front 8 sinciput 9 sincipita (plural) ***combining form:*** 6 fronto ***ornamental spot:*** 5 tilak
foreign 5 alien 6 exotic 7 strange 9 extrinsic, obnoxious, repellent, repugnant 10 accidental, extraneous, immaterial, inapposite, irrelative, irrelevant 11 distasteful, impertinent, incongruous, inconsonant 12 adventitious, inapplicable, incompatible, inconsistent 13 inappropriate ***combining form:*** 3 xen 4 xeno
foreigner 5 alien 7 inconnu 8 outsider, stranger
foreknow 6 divine 7 previse 8 conclude 9 apprehend, prevision, visualize 10 anticipate
foreland 4 beak, bill, cape, head, naze 5 point 8 headland 10 promontory
forelock 5 bangs, quiff 8 linchpin, split pin 9 cotter pin
foreman 4 boss 5 chief 6 gaffer, ganger, honcho, leader 7 captain, headman, manager, overman, steward 8 overseer 10 supervisor
foremost 4 arch, head, main 5 chief, first, front 7 initial, leading, premier, supreme 8 champion, headmost 9 inaugural, principal 10 preeminent
forenoon 4 morn 7 morning
forensics 6 debate 7 mooting 11 disputation 13 argumentation
foreordain 4 fate 6 doom to 7 destine, preform 9 determine 10 predestine 12 predestinate, predetermine
forerun 4 pace 6 herald 7 precede, predate, presage 8 announce, antecede, antedate 9 harbinger 10 anticipate, foreshadow
forerunner 4 mark, omen, sign 5 model, token 6 augury, author, herald 7 example, pattern, pioneer, portent, presage, symptom, warning 8 ancestor, exemplar 9 announcer, harbinger, initiator, messenger, precursor, prototype 10 antecedent, antecessor, originator, prognostic 11 anticipator, predecessor 12 announcement
foresee 4 espy 6 descry, divine 7 discern, predict, preknow, presage, previse 8 perceive, prophesy 9 apprehend, prevision, visualize 10 anticipate 13 prognosticate
foreseer 5 augur 6 auspex, oracle 7 diviner, prophet 8 haruspex 9 predictor 10 prophesier, soothsayer 11 Nostradamus
foreshadow 4 bode, hint, omen 5 augur 7 betoken, portend, presage, promise 9 adumbrate, prefigure 11 prefigurate
foresight 6 vision 7 caution 8 prudence, sagacity 9 canniness 10 discretion, perception, precaution, prescience, providence 11 discernment 12 clairvoyance
forest 4 bosk, wood 5 copse, grove, weald, woods 6 timber 7 coppice, thicket, woodlot 8 wildwood, woodland 10 timberland, wilderness ***combining form:*** 3 hyl 4 hylo ***deity:*** 5 dryad 6 sylvan 8 Sylvanus ***English:*** 5 Arden 8 Sherwood ***opening:*** 5 glade ***relating to:*** 6 sylvan ***subarctic:*** 5 taiga ***tropical:*** 5 selva 6 jungle
forestall 4 ward 5 avert, deter 7 obviate, prevent, rule out 8 preclude, stave off 10 anticipate
Forester ***hero:*** 10 Hornblower (Horatio) ***novel:*** 12 African Queen
foretell 4 bode, call, warn 5 augur 6 divine, reveal 7 declare, divulge, portend, predict, presage, promise 8 announce, disclose, proclaim, prophesy, soothsay 9 adumbrate, apprehend, prefigure 10 anticipate, vaticinate 13 prognosticate
foreteller see foreseer
forethought 5 sense 7 caution 8 gumption, judgment, prudence 9 canniness, foresight 10 discretion, precaution, providence 12 deliberation, discreetness 13 premeditation
foretime 4 past, yore 9 yesterday 10 yesteryear
foretoken 4 bode, hint, mark, note, omen, sign 5 augur, badge 6 augury, boding, herald, ostent, shadow 7 inkling, portend, portent, presage, promise, symptom, warning 8 bodement, forecast 9 harbinger, precursor 10 indication, intimation
forever 3 aye 4 ever 6 always 7 endless, eternal 8 eternity, evermore 9 endlessly, eternally 11 ceaselessly, continually, everlasting, incessantly, in perpetuum, perpetually, unceasingly 13 everlastingly
forewarning 6 caveat 7 caution 8 monition 10 admonition 11 commonition
foreword 5 proem 7 preface, prelude 8 exordium, overture, preamble, prologue 9 prelusion 12 introduction, prolegomenon
for example 2 as, e.g. 6 such as
for fear that 4 lest
forfeit 4 drop, fine, lose 5 mulct 7 penalty 9 sacrifice 10 amercement
forfend 4 ward 5 avert, deter 6 secure 7 obviate, prevent, protect, rule out, ward off 8 preclude, preserve, stave off
forge 4 beat, copy, make, mold 5 build, pound, shape 6 smithy 7 advance, fashion,

imitate, produce, turn out 8 bloomery, progress 9 construct, fabricate 11 counterfeit, manufacture, put together
forget 4 fail, omit 5 fluff 6 blow up, ignore, slight, unknow 7 blink at, neglect, unlearn 8 discount, overlook 9 blink away, disregard 11 disremember 12 misrecollect
forgetful 3 lax 5 slack 6 absent, remiss 7 bemused 8 careless, heedless 9 negligent, oblivious, unwitting 10 abstracted, neglectful 11 inattentive, thoughtless 12 absentminded
forgetfulness 5 lethe 7 amnesia 8 oblivion
forgivable 6 venial 10 pardonable
forgive 5 remit 6 excuse, pardon, slight 7 absolve, condone, neglect 8 overlook
forgo 5 leave, waive 6 eschew, give up, resign 7 abandon, forbear 8 abdicate, abnegate, renounce 9 sacrifice, surrender 10 relinquish
fork 6 bisect, branch, crotch 7 utensil *prong:* 4 tine
forlorn 4 vain 5 alone 6 bereft, futile, lonely 7 cynical 8 deserted, desolate, forsaken, helpless, homeless, hopeless, lonesome, solitary, wretched 9 abandoned, depressed, desperate, destitute, fruitless, miserable, oppressed 10 bedraggled, despairing, despondent, desponding, disordered, friendless 11 defenseless, pessimistic 12 disconsolate
form 3 law, way 4 body, cast, make, mode, mold, plan, plot, rite, rule 5 build, canon, forge, found, frame, habit, image, model, shape, style, usage 6 create, custom, design, devise, figure, invent, make up, manner, method, ritual, scheme, system 7 acquire, anatomy, compose, contour, decorum, develop, economy, fashion, liturgy, outline, precept, process, produce, profile, project, turn out 8 ceremony, comprise, organism, organize, practice, skeleton 9 construct, establish, etiquette, fabricate, formality, framework, procedure, propriety, structure 10 ceremonial, constitute, convenance, convention, proceeding, regulation, silhouette 11 manufacture 13 configuration *combining form:* 3 gen 4 gene 5 morph, plasm, plast 6 morpha, morphi (plural) 6 morpho, plasma 7 morphae (plural), morphic 8 morphism 9 morphosis *suffix:* 2 fy 3 ify
formal 3 set 4 prim 5 exact, rigid, stiff 6 dressy, proper, seemly, solemn 7 distant, nominal, orderly, precise, regular, stately, titular 8 decorous, reserved, so-called 9 essential, unbending 10 ceremonial, methodical, systematic 11 ceremonious, syntactical 12 constitutive, conventional
formality 4 form, rite 6 ritual 7 liturgy, service 8 ceremony, insignia 10 ceremonial, convenance, convention, observance
format 4 plan, size 5 shape, style 6 makeup
formation 4 form, rank 6 design, makeup 9 structure 10 production 11 arrangement, composition, development 12 architecture, construction
formative material *combining form:* 5 plasm 6 plasma
former 3 old 4 late, once, past 5 maker, prior 6 bygone, shaper, whilom 7 creator, earlier, onetime, quondam 8 anterior, previous, sometime 9 erstwhile, precedent, preceding 10 antecedent *combining form:* 6 proter 7 protero
formerly 4 erst, once 6 before, whilom 7 already, earlier 9 erstwhile 10 heretofore, previously
formidable 4 hard 5 awful, tough 6 uphill 7 arduous, fearful, labored 8 alarming, dreadful, horrific, shocking, terrible, terrific, toilsome 9 appalling, difficult, effortful, frightful, laborious, strenuous
formless 3 raw 4 rude 5 crude, rough, vague 7 chaotic, obscure, unclear 8 inchoate, unshaped 9 amorphous, shapeless, undefined, unordered 10 immaterial, indefinite, indistinct 11 unorganized
Formosa 6 Taiwan *capital:* 6 Taipei
formulate 3 put 4 make, word 5 couch, draft, frame, hatch 6 cook up, devise, draw up, invent, make up, phrase, vamp up 7 concoct, dream up, express, hatch up, prepare 8 contrive
forsake 4 quit 5 avoid, chuck, leave, spurn 6 defect, depart, desert, reject, resign 7 abandon 8 abdicate, renounce 9 throw over
forsaken 4 lorn 7 uncouth 8 derelict, deserted, desolate, solitary 9 abandoned
forsaker 8 apostate
Forseti *father:* 6 Balder *palace:* 7 Glitnir
forswear 4 deny 5 unsay 6 abjure, recall, recant, reject 7 perjure, retract 8 palinode, renounce, take back, withdraw
fort 6 castle 7 bastion, bulwark, citadel, redoubt 8 fastness, fortress, martello 10 stronghold *Baltimore:* 7 McHenry *New York:* 7 Niagara, Stanwix 8 Schuyler *Ontario:* 9 Frontenac *San Antonio:* 8 The Alamo *South Carolina:* 6 Sumter *Spanish:* 7 alcazar 8 presidio
forte 3 bag 5 thing 6 medium, métier, oyster 7 ability 8 ableness, eminency, long suit, strength 10 competence, efficiency, strong suit 11 strong point
forth 2 on 3 out 4 alee 5 ahead, along 6 onward 7 forward
forthcoming 6 future 7 affable, awaited 8 approach, expected, imminent, sociable

11 anticipated, approaching 12 approachable
for the most part 9 generally 10 on the whole
for the time being 6 pro tem 10 pro tempore
forthright 4 open 5 frank, plain 6 candid, direct, single 7 frankly 10 aboveboard 11 openhearted, undisguised, unvarnished
forthwith 3 now 4 away 5 short 6 at once, sudden 7 asudden 8 abruptly, directly, suddenly 9 instanter, instantly, right away, thereupon 11 immediately, straightway 12 straightaway
fortification 4 boma, moat, wall 5 agger, redan 6 abatis, glacis, sangar, sungar 7 barrier, parapet, rampart, ravelin, redoubt 8 barbican, enceinte, palisade 9 barricade, earthwork 10 breastwork *part:* 7 salient
fortify 3 arm 4 gird, stir 5 brace, rally, ready, renew, rouse, steel 6 arouse 7 bulwark, prepare, protect, rampart, refresh, restore 8 energize, palisade 9 encourage 10 invigorate, strengthen
fortitude 4 grit, guts, pith, sand 5 nerve, pluck, spunk, valor 6 bottom, mettle, spirit 7 bravery, courage, stamina 8 backbone, boldness, strength, tenacity, valiancy 9 constancy, endurance 10 resolution 11 intrepidity 12 fearlessness, perseverance, resoluteness, valorousness 13 dauntlessness, determination
fortress see **fort**
fortuitous 3 odd 5 fluky 6 casual, chance 10 accidental, contingent, incidental
fortuity 3 hap 4 luck 6 chance 8 accident
Fortuna 5 Tyche *symbol:* 5 wheel 6 rudder
fortunate 4 good, well 5 happy, lucky, white 6 benign, bright, dexter 9 favorable 10 auspicious, propitious 12 providential
Fortunate Islands 8 Canaries
fortune 3 lot, pot, wad 4 doom, fate, luck, mint, pile 5 worth 6 boodle, bundle, chance, hazard, packet, riches, wealth 7 destiny, portion, success 8 property 9 luckiness, resources, substance
fortune-teller 4 seer 7 palmist; (see also **foreteller**)
fortune-telling see **divination**
forty winks 3 nap 6 catnap, dog nap, siesta, snooze
forward 2 on, to 3 aid 4 abet, alee, ante, back, bold, help, pert, send, ship, wise 5 ahead, along, brash, eager, fresh, nervy, ready, relay, remit, route, sassy, saucy, serve, smart, ultra 6 cheeky, foster, hasten, onward, uphold, uppish, uppity 7 address, advance, anxious, consign, extreme, further, promote, pushful, pushing, radical, support 8 advanced, champion, dispatch, impudent, previous, transmit 9 encourage, in advance, presuming 11 overweening, precedently, smart-alecky 12 antecedently, presumptuous 13 self-asserting, self-assertive *prefix:* 4 ante
For Whom the Bell Tolls *author:* 9 Hemingway *character:* 5 Maria, Pablo, Pilar 6 Jordan
foss, fosse 4 moat 5 canal, ditch 6 trench
fossa 3 pit 6 cavity 10 depression
fossil 4 fogy 5 amber 6 square 7 antique 8 calamite, conodont, mossback 10 antiquated, fuddy-duddy 12 antediluvian, mid-Victorian 13 stick-in-the-mud *combining form:* 4 lite, lith, lyte, necr 5 necro, oryct 6 orycto *fuel:* 3 oil 4 coal, peat 9 petroleum
foster 4 back, help, rear, warm 5 favor, house, lodge, nurse, serve 6 assist, harbor, nursle, oblige, uphold 7 advance, cherish, forward, further, nourish, nurture, promote, shelter, support, sustain 8 champion 9 cultivate, encourage, entertain
foul 4 base, soil, vile 5 black, block, dirty, fetid, grime, muddy, nasty, soily 6 besoil, coarse, defile, filthy, grubby, horrid, impure, odious, putrid, rotten, smirch, smooch, smudge, smutch, smutty, vulgar, wicked 7 abusive, begrime, noisome, obscene, pollute, profane, raunchy, squalid, tarnish, unclean 8 dishonor, feculent, indecent, obstruct, polluted, stinking 9 dangerous, desecrate, entangled, loathsome, obnoxious, offensive, repellent, repugnant, repulsive, revolting, uncleanly 10 detestable, disgusting, malodorous 11 contaminate 12 scatological
foul play 5 blood 6 murder 7 killing 8 homicide, violence 12 manslaughter
found 4 base, cast, rear, rest, stay 5 begin, erect, raise, set up, start 6 bottom, create 7 fashion, support, sustain 8 commence, initiate, organize 9 establish, institute, originate, predicate
foundation 3 bed 4 base, rest 5 basis 6 bottom 7 bedrock, footing, roadbed, support, warrant 9 endowment 10 substratum 11 institution 12 organization, substructure, underpinning
foundational 5 basic 6 bottom 7 primary 10 underlying 11 fundamental
founder 4 fail, sink, sire 5 wreck 6 author, damage, go down 7 creator 8 collapse, inventor, submerge, submerse 9 architect, generator, patriarch 10 originator
fountain 3 jet 4 head, root 6 origin, source, spring, whence 8 wellhead 9 inception, reservoir 10 wellspring *nymph:* 6 Egeria
four 6 tetrad 7 quartet 10 quaternion *bag-*

ger: 5 homer 7 homerun *combining form:* 4 tetr 5 quadr, tetra 6 quadri, quadru, quater, tessar 7 tessara, tessera *gills:* 4 pint *hundred:* 5 elite 10 upper crust *inches:* 4 hand *pecks:* 6 bushel *quarts:* 6 gallon

fourberie 5 fraud 7 chicane 8 trickery 9 chicanery, deception 10 dishonesty, hanky-panky

four-flush 5 bluff 6 betray, delude, humbug, juggle, take in 7 beguile, deceive 11 double cross

four-footed animal 8 tetrapod 9 quadruped

Four Horsemen 3 War 5 Death 6 Famine 10 Pestilence

four-in-hand 3 tie 7 necktie

fourpence 5 groat

four-poster 3 bed

fourscore 6 eighty

four-sided figure 6 square 7 rhombus 9 rectangle

foursquare 7 solidly 8 quadrate 9 quadratic 10 forthright 11 quadratical 12 forthrightly

fourteen pounds 5 stone

fourth 7 quarter 8 quadrant, quartern *combining form:* 5 quadr, quart 6 quadri, quadru 7 tetarto

fowl 3 hen 4 bird, cock 5 chick, poult 6 Bantam, pullet 7 chicken, rooster; (see also **chicken; poultry**)

fox 4 fool 5 trick 6 baffle, outwit 7 confuse, Reynard 8 bewilder 9 dissemble *female:* 5 vixen *kind:* 6 corsac, corsak, fennec *Scottish:* 3 tod *young:* 3 cub

foxglove 7 mullein 8 pokeweed 9 fairy bell 10 fingerroot

fox grape 9 muscadine

foxiness 3 art 5 craft 7 cunning 8 artifice 10 cleverness

foxlike 7 vulpine

foxy 3 sly 4 deep, wily 6 artful, astute, clever, crafty, shrewd, tricky 7 cunning 8 guileful 9 deceitful, dishonest, insidious

foyer 5 lobby 8 anteroom, entrance 9 vestibule

fracas 3 row 4 feud 5 brawl, broil, fight, melee, run-in, set-to 6 affray, hassle 7 dispute, quarrel, ruction 8 squabble 9 bickering 10 donnybrook 11 altercation

fraction 3 bit, cut 4 part 5 piece, scrap 6 divide, little 7 portion, section 8 fragment

fractious 4 wild 5 cross, huffy, waspy 6 unruly 7 fretful, peevish, pettish, waspish 8 contrary, indocile, petulant, snappish 9 irritable 10 refractory 11 indomitable, intractable, quarrelsome 12 recalcitrant, ungovernable, unmanageable

fracturable 7 fragile 8 delicate, shattery 9 breakable

fracture 4 rent, rift, tear 5 break, cleft, crack, split 6 breach, schism 7 rupture, violate *combining form:* 7 rrhexis

Fra Diavolo composer 5 Auber

fragile 4 fine, thin, weak 5 crisp, frail, short 6 feeble, flimsy, infirm, slight, weakly 7 brittle, crumbly, crunchy, friable, slender, tenuous, unsound 8 decrepit, delicate, shattery

fragment 3 ace, bit, end, jot 4 atom, chip, iota, part, rive 5 burst, crumb, flake, grain, minim, piece, scrap, shard, sherd, shive, shred, smash, spall 6 morsel, shiver, sliver 7 flinder, shatter 8 particle, splinter, splitter 11 splinterize

fragmentary 4 part 6 broken 7 partial 10 fractional, incomplete 12 disorganized

fragrance 4 balm, odor 5 aroma, scent, smell, spice 7 bouquet, incense, perfume 9 redolence

fragrant 5 balmy, spicy, sweet 6 aromal, savory 7 perfumy 8 aromatic, perfumed, redolent 9 ambrosial, delicious

frail 4 puny, slim, thin, weak 5 petty 6 feeble, flimsy, infirm, sickly, slight, weakly 7 fragile, slender, tenuous, unsound 8 decrepit, delicate, shattery 9 breakable, frangible 11 fracturable, shatterable

frailty 3 sin 4 vice 5 fault 6 foible 7 failing 8 weakness 9 infirmity 11 tenuousness 12 imperfection

frame 4 body, form, make, mold, plan, sash 5 build, cause, draft, easel, erect, forge, shape, state, utter 6 cook up, deckle, devise, draw up, figure, invent, make up, system, vamp up 7 arrange, chassis, concoct, dream up, fashion, hatch up, imagine, prepare, produce 8 casement, conceive, contrive, regulate 9 cartouche, construct, fabricate, formulate *part:* 4 sill, stud 5 joist, plate

framework 4 rack 7 trestle 8 cribbing, cribwork, scaffold, skeleton, studding, studwork, trussing 9 structure *of crossed strips:* 7 lattice, trellis

France *ancient name:* 4 Gaul 6 Gallia *capital:* 5 Paris *combining form:* 5 Gallo *historic province:* 4 Foix 5 Anjou, Aunis, Bearn, Berry, Maine 6 Alsace, Artois, Marche, Poitou 7 Gascony, Guyenne, Picardy 8 Auvergne, Brittany, Burgundy, Dauphine, Flanders, Limousin, Lorraine, Lyonnais, Normandy, Provence, Touraine 9 Angoumois, Champagne, Languedoc, Nivernais, Orleanais, Saintonge, Venaissin 10 Roussillon 11 Bourbonnais, Ile de France 12 Franche Comte *monetary unit:* 5 franc

Francesca's lover 5 Paolo

franchise 4 vote 6 ballot 8 suffrage 9 exemption

frangible 7 brittle, fragile 8 delicate, shattery 9 breakable

frank 3 dog 4 fair, free, just, open 5 bluff, blunt, naive, plain 6 brazen, candid, direct, honest, hot dog, simple, single, wiener 7 natural, sincere, upright 8 man-to-man, unbiased 9 barefaced, impartial, ingenuous, outspoken 10 forthright, scrupulous, single-eyed, unmannered, unreserved 11 open-hearted, plainspoken, unconcealed, undisguised, uninhibited, unvarnished, wienerwurst

Frankenstein author 7 Shelley (Mary)

frankfurter 3 dog 6 hot dog, wiener 11 wienerwurst

Frankie's lover 6 Johnny

Frankish hero 6 Roland

Franklin ***birthplace:*** 6 Boston ***invention:*** 5 stove 8 bifocals ***pen name:*** 11 Poor Richard

frankness 6 candor 8 openness

frantic 3 mad 4 wild 5 rabid 6 insane 7 extreme, furious, violent 8 deranged, feverish, frenetic, frenzied 9 delirious, desperate 10 distraught

fraternal society 4 Elks 5 Moose 6 Eagles, Masons 10 Hibernians, Odd Fellows

fraternity 4 club 5 guild, order, union 6 league 7 company 10 fellowship 11 association, brotherhood 13 brotherliness

fraud 4 fake, hoax, sell, sham 5 cheat, faker, phony, trick 6 deceit, dupery, duping, humbug 7 chicane, defraud, swindle 8 impostor, trickery 9 chicanery, deception, fourberie, imposture, pretender 10 hanky-panky 11 bamboozling, highbinding, hoodwinking 13 bamboozlement, double-dealing, sharp practice

fraudulence 6 deceit 8 quackery, trickery 9 chicanery, deception, fourberie, phoniness 10 dishonesty

fraudulent 4 fake 5 false 7 crooked 8 cheating, guileful, quackish 9 deceitful, deceiving, deceptive, dishonest 10 fallacious

fray 3 row 4 fret 5 brawl, broil, brush, clash, fight, melee 6 combat, debate, strife, tumult 7 discord, dispute, quarrel, ruction, scuffle 8 skirmish 9 commotion, scrimmage 10 contention, dissension, donnybrook

frayed 4 worn 6 ragged 7 shreddy 10 threadbare

frazzle 4 fray, wear 5 upset 6 tucker 7 exhaust, outtire, outwear, wear out 8 knock out 9 prostrate

freak 3 bug, nut 4 whim 5 fancy, fiend, lusus 6 maniac, megrim, oddity, rarity, vagary, whimsy, zealot 7 anomaly, boutade, caprice, chimera, conceit, fanatic, monster, whimsey 8 crotchet, misshape, mutation, rara avis 9 androgyne, curiosity 10 aberration, enthusiast 11 abnormality, miscreation, monstrosity 12 malformation, whimsicality

freckle 3 dot 4 spot 7 ephelis, lentigo, speckle, stipple

free 3 lax, rid 4 open 5 clear, loose, round, unmew, unpen, untie, vocal 6 acquit, detach, exempt, gratis, loosen, ransom, redeem, rescue, unbind, uncurb, unpaid, untied, vagile 7 absolve, deliver, liberal, manumit, release, unbound, unchain, unclasp, unleash, unloose 8 autarkic, bootless, detached, generous, handsome, liberate, released, separate, sui juris, unburden, unfasten, unloosen, untether 9 autarchic, bounteous, bountiful, delivered, discharge, disengage, exculpate, exonerate, extricate, liberated, outspoken, sovereign, unchained, unchecked, unshackle, unsparing 10 autonomous, chargeless, democratic, emancipate, gratuitous, heart-whole, munificent, openhanded, self-ruling, unconfined, unenslaved, unfettered, unshackled 11 affranchise, disencumber, disentangle, disenthrall, disimprison, emancipated, enfranchise, independent, untrammeled 12 enfranchised, unregimented, unrestrained, unrestricted 13 complimentary, self-directing, self-governing, unconstrained, unrecompensed, unremunerated

freebie 4 gift, pass 7 present 8 giveaway

freebooter 5 rover 6 bandit, bummer, pirate, raider, sea dog 7 brigand, cateran, corsair, forager, sea wolf 8 marauder, picaroon, pillager

freedom 4 ease 5 right, scope, sweep 7 compass, liberty, license, release 8 facility, immunity, latitude, vagility 9 exemption, privilege 10 generosity 11 magnanimity, prerogative 12 emancipation, independence

free-for-all 4 fray 5 brawl, broil, fight, melee, spree 6 affray, fracas 7 ruction 10 donnybrook

freehanded 7 liberal 8 generous 9 bounteous, bountiful, unsparing 10 munificent, openhanded

freeloader 5 leech 6 sponge 8 barnacle, hanger-on, parasite 12 lounge lizard

freeman 4 carl 5 carle, churl, thane, thegn 6 yeoman 7 burgess, burgher, citizen

Free State 8 Maryland

free ticket 4 pass 11 Annie Oakley

freezing 3 icy 4 cold 5 chill, gelid, nippy 6 arctic, chilly, frigid, frosty 7 glacial, shivery ***combining form:*** 3 cry 4 cryo, kryo

freight 4 haul, load 5 cargo 6 burden, charge, lading 7 payload 9 transport

French ***article:*** **2** la, le, un **3** les, une ***attendant:*** **9** concierge ***back:*** **3** dos ***bed:*** **3** lit **6** couche ***boy:*** **6** garçon ***brother:*** **5** frère ***cap:*** **5** beret ***cardinal:*** **7** Mazarin **9** Richelieu ***castle:*** **7** château ***cathedral city:*** **5** Paris, Reims, Rouen **6** Amiens, Nantes, Rheims **8** Chartres ***clergyman:*** **4** abbé, curé, père ***combining form:*** **5** Gallo **6** Franco ***conjunction:*** **2** et, ou **4** mais ***couturier:*** **4** Dior **5** Patou **6** Chanel **7** Balmain **8** Givenchy **9** Courrèges, St. Laurent ***daughter:*** **5** fille ***day:*** **5** jeudi, lundi, mardi **6** samedi **8** dimanche, mercredi, vendredi ***dear:*** **4** cher ***department head:*** **7** prefect ***dream:*** **4** rêve ***dynasty:*** **5** Capet **6** Valois **7** Bourbon ***egg:*** **4** oeuf ***emblem:*** **10** fleur-de-lis ***empress:*** **7** Eugénie **9** Joséphine ***exclamation:*** **3** zut **4** eheu, hein **9** sacrebleu ***farewell:*** **5** adieu **8** au revoir ***father:*** **4** père ***forest:*** **7** Argonne, Belleau ***friend:*** **3** ami **4** amie ***game:*** **3** jeu **4** jeux (plural) ***God:*** **4** dieu ***good:*** **3** bon ***hat:*** **7** chapeau ***here:*** **3** ici ***income:*** **5** rente ***king:*** **3** roi ***language:*** **9** Provençal ***month:*** **3** mai **4** août, juin, mars, mois **5** avril **7** février, janvier, juillet ***mother:*** **4** mère ***national anthem:*** **12** Marseillaise ***opera:*** **5** Faust, Lakmé, Manon, Thaïs **6** Carmen, Mignon **7** Werther ***pancake:*** **5** crêpe ***pastry:*** **6** éclair **8** napoleon ***patron saint:*** **5** Denis ***policeman:*** **4** flic **8** gendarme ***porcelain:*** **6** Sèvres **7** Limoges ***preposition:*** **2** de **3** par, sur **4** avec, dans, pour, sans, sous ***pretty:*** **4** joli **5** jolie ***prison:*** **8** Bastille ***pronoun:*** **2** il, je, te, tu, un **3** eux, ils, mes, moi, toi, une **4** elle, nous, vous ***Protestant:*** **6** Calvin **8** Huguenot ***pupil:*** **5** élève ***queen:*** **5** reine ***rabbit:*** **5** lapin ***railroad station:*** **4** gare ***resort:*** **3** Pau **4** Nice **5** Vichy **6** Cannes, Menton **7** Antibes **8** Biarritz ***resort area:*** **7** Riviera ***restaurant:*** **6** bistro ***revolutionist:*** **5** Marat **6** Danton ***Revolution party:*** **7** Gironde, Jacobin **8** Mountain ***Revolution song:*** **5** Caira ***saint:*** **4** Joan **6** Martin ***school:*** **5** école, lycée ***sea:*** **3** mer ***season:*** **3** été **5** hiver **7** automne **9** printemps ***servant:*** **5** valet ***shop:*** **8** boutique ***shrine:*** **7** Lourdes ***singer:*** **4** Piaf **8** chanteur **9** chanteuse ***sister:*** **5** soeur ***small:*** **5** petit **6** petite ***soldier:*** **5** poilu **6** soldat, Zouave **8** chasseur ***son:*** **4** fils ***star:*** **6** étoile ***state:*** **4** état ***stock exchange:*** **6** bourse ***street:*** **3** rue ***subway:*** **5** metro ***there!:*** **5** voilà ***too much:*** **4** trop ***very:*** **4** très ***waiter:*** **6** garçon ***wartime capital:*** **5** Vichy ***water:*** **3** eau ***well:*** **4** bien ***wineshop:*** **6** bistro ***wood:*** **4** bois ***yesterday:*** **4** hier

frenetic **3** mad **4** wild **5** crazy, rabid **6** hectic **7** frantic, furious, violent **8** frenzied **9** delirious

frenzied see **frenetic**

frenzy **3** mad **4** amok, fury, rage **5** amuck, craze, furor, mania **6** madden **7** derange, madness, unhinge **8** delirium, distract, insanity **9** unbalance ***of a bull elephant:*** **4** must **5** musth

frequency unit **5** hertz **7** fresnel

frequent **5** haunt, often, usual, visit **6** affect, attend, common, infest, resort **7** hang out, overrun **8** everyday, familiar, habitual **9** customary **10** hang around

frequenter **7** denizen, habitué, haunter

fresh **3** new, raw **4** anew, bold, else, more, pert, pure, rude, wise **5** added, alive, brisk, crude, green, naive, nervy, novel, other, renew, sassy, saucy, smart, sweet, vital, vivid, young **6** bright, callow, cheeky, lively, modern, recent, unused **7** another, artless, farther, forward, further, natural, uncouth, untried **8** gleaming, impudent, neoteric, original, striking, unversed, virginal, youthful **9** new-sprung, sparkling, unspoiled **10** additional, glistening, newfangled, unseasoned **11** impertinent, modernistic, smart-alecky, unpracticed **12** invigorating, new-fashioned **13** inexperienced

freshet **5** flood, spate

freshman **4** colt, tyro **5** frosh, plebe **6** novice, rookie **8** beginner, neophyte, newcomer **9** novitiate **10** apprentice, tenderfoot

fret **3** irk, nag, rub, vex **4** cark, fray, fume, fuss, gall, gnaw, mope, stew, wear **5** annoy, brood, chafe, grate, ravel, worry **6** abrade, bother, cockle, dimple, dither, harass, nettle, plague, pother, rankle, riffle, ruffle **7** agitate, corrode, disturb, provoke, roughen, torment **8** exercise, irritate **9** excoriate **10** irritation

fretful **5** angry, cross, huffy, waspy **7** carping, chafing, peevish, pettish, waspish **8** captious, caviling, contrary, critical, perverse, petulant, restless, snappish **9** fractious, impatient, irascible, irritable, querulous, unpatient **12** faultfinding

Frey ***father:*** **5** Njord **6** Njorth ***sister:*** **5** Freya ***wife:*** **4** Gerd **5** Gerda, Gerth

Freya ***brother:*** **4** Frey ***father:*** **5** Njord **6** Njorth ***husband:*** **4** Odin

friable **5** crisp, mealy, short **7** crumbly, crunchy

fribble **5** dizzy, giddy, light **7** flighty, trifler **8** trifling **9** frivolous **11** harebrained, lightheaded

friction **7** discord, rubbing **8** abrasion **9** attrition **10** disharmony, dissension, resistance **12** disagreement

friction match **5** vesta **7** lucifer **8** locofoco

Friday's rescuer 6 Crusoe
friend 3 aid, pal 4 ally, chum, mate 5 buddy, crony, matey, serve 7 comrade, partner 8 alter ego, compadre, familiar, intimate, playmate, sidekick 9 associate, colleague, companion, confidant 10 confidante 11 cater-cousin 12 acquaintance ***French:*** 3 ami 4 amie ***Scottish:*** 3 eme ***Spanish:*** 5 amiga, amigo
Friend 6 Quaker ***founder:*** 3 Fox
friendly 5 close, pally 6 amical, chummy, loving 7 affable, amiable, cordial, devoted 8 amicable, amicably, familiar, intimate, sociable 9 congenial, favorable, receptive 10 harmonious, hospitable 11 sympathetic 12 affectionate, well-disposed
Friendly Islands 5 Tonga
friends 4 kith
friendship 5 amity 6 accord, comity, fusion, league 7 concord, empathy, harmony 8 affinity, alliance, goodwill 9 coalition 10 attraction, consonance, federation, kindliness 11 benevolence
frigate bird 3 ioa, iwa 8 alcatras ***genus:*** 7 Fregata
Frigga, Frigg ***husband:*** 4 Odin ***son:*** 6 Balder
fright 3 awe 4 fear, mess 5 alarm, dread, panic, scare, shock 6 dismay, horror, terror 7 eyesore, startle, terrify 9 terrorize, trepidity 11 trepidation
frighten 3 awe, cow 4 faze 5 alarm, daunt, scare, shock, unman, upset 6 affray, appall, dismay 7 agitate, astound, horrify, perturb, startle, terrify, unnerve 8 affright, browbeat, bulldoze, disquiet 9 terrorize 10 demoralize, discompose, disconcert, intimidate
frightful 4 grim 5 awful, scary 6 horrid 7 fearful, ghastly, hideous 8 alarming, dreadful, fearsome, horrible, horrific, shocking, terrible, terrific 9 appalling 10 formidable, horrendous
frigid 3 icy 4 cold, cool, dull 5 bleak, chill 6 arctic, chilly, frosty 7 glacial, hostile, insipid 8 freezing 9 inhibited 10 undersexed 11 emotionless, indifferent, passionless, unemotional 12 unresponsive
frill 3 air 5 jabot, luxus, ruche 6 luxury, ruffle 7 amenity, flounce, ruching 8 furbelow 11 affectation, superfluity 12 extravagance
fringe 3 hem, rim 4 brim 5 bound, brink, skirt, verge 6 border, define, edging, margin 7 fimbria 8 surround, trimming 9 perimeter, periphery
frippery 6 finery 7 bravery, regalia 8 trumpery 9 full dress 10 Sunday best 11 ostentation
frisk 4 leap, romp, skip 5 caper, dance 6 cavort, curvet, frolic, gambol, search 7 disport, rollick 9 shake down
frisky 3 gay 5 antic 6 feisty, lively 7 larkish, playful, waggish 8 gamesome, prankish, sportive 9 kittenish 10 frolicsome
fritter 4 blow 5 shred, spend, waste 7 consume 8 cast away, diminish, disperse, fool away, fragment, squander 9 dissipate, throw away 10 trifle away
frivolity 3 fun 4 game, jest, play 5 sport 6 levity, toying 8 dallying, flirting, nonsense, trifling 9 flippancy, lightness 10 coquetting 11 flightiness
frivolous 3 gay 5 dizzy, giddy, light, silly 6 toyish 7 flighty, playful, shallow, trivial 8 carefree, careless, heedless 10 bird-witted, unprofound 11 empty-headed, harebrained, superficial 13 rattlebrained
frog 4 toad 5 ranid 6 anuran 9 amphibian 10 batrachian ***combining form:*** 4 rani 7 batrach 8 batracho 9 batrachus ***family:*** 7 Ranidae ***genus:*** 4 Rana ***kind:*** 4 hyla 6 peeper 8 bullfrog, tree toad ***larva:*** 7 tadpole ***relating to:*** 6 ranine
frogmouth 8 morepork
frolic 3 fun, gay 4 hell, lark, riot, romp 5 caper, dance, frisk, merry, party, prank, revel, sport, spree, trick 6 cavort, didoes, gaiety, gambol, prance, shines 7 carouse, disport, roister, rollick, wassail 9 merriment 10 shenanigan, tomfoolery
frolicsome 3 gay 5 antic 6 frisky, impish 7 coltish, playful, roguish, waggish 8 sportive 9 sprightly 10 rollicking 11 mischievous
from ***French, Portuguese, Spanish:*** 2 de ***German:*** 3 von ***Italian:*** 2 da ***Scottish:*** 4 frae
frondeur 5 rebel 6 anarch 8 mutineer, revolter 9 anarchist, dissident, insurgent 10 malcontent
front 3 bow, van 4 brow, dare, defy, face, fore, look, mask, meet, prow, show, veil 5 beard, blind, brave, close, color, put-on 6 accost, before, facade, facing 7 forward, outdare, outface, venture 8 anterior, coloring, disguise, forehead 9 challenge, encounter 10 appearance, figurehead 11 countenance ***combining form:*** 6 antero ***prefix:*** 3 pro
frontier 4 back, bush 5 march 6 border, remote, sticks 8 backland, backwash, boundary 9 backwater, backwoods, bordering, marchland, unsettled, up-country 10 borderland, hinterland, outlandish 11 backcountry, exploratory 12 conterminous
frontiersman 5 Boone, Clark 6 Carson 7 pioneer, settler 8 Crockett 10 bushranger
fronton game 7 jai alai
front-rank 5 prime 6 Grade A 8 five-star, superior, top-notch 9 excellent, first-rate,

top-drawer **10** blue-ribbon, first-class **11** first-string
frontward **8** anterior
frost **4** hoar **6** freeze ***combining form:*** **4** crym **5** crymo
frostfish **5** smelt **6** tomcod
frost heave **5** pingo
frosting **5** icing **7** topping
frosty **3** icy **4** cold, cool, rimy **5** chill, gelid, hoary, nippy **6** chilly, frigid **7** glacial, shivery **8** freezing, reserved **10** unfriendly
froth **4** barm, foam, scum, suds, vent **5** spume, yeast **6** lather, levity **9** flippancy, frivolity, lightness
froward **5** balky, cross **6** ornery **7** peevish, restive **8** contrary, perverse, petulant **10** refractory **11** disobedient
frown **4** pout, sulk **5** glare, gloom, lower, scowl **6** glower, object **7** grimace **8** disfavor **9** deprecate, disesteem **10** disapprove
frowsy **3** lax **4** mean, rank **5** dowdy, funky, fusty, musty, slack, stale **6** blowsy, remiss, shabby, smelly, sordid **7** noisome, reeking, squalid, unkempt **8** slattern, slovenly, stinking **9** negligent **10** disheveled, disordered, malodorous, neglectful, slatternly **13** draggletailed
frozen **4** hard **5** fixed, frore, gelid, rigid, stiff **6** chilly, frigid **7** chilled **8** benumbed, immobile **9** congealed, impassive, petrified **10** mechanical, unyielding **12** refrigerated
frugal **4** mean, wary **5** canny, chary, spare **6** saving, scanty, Scotch **7** careful, prudent, sparing, thrifty **8** discreet, stinting **9** scrimping, stewardly **10** conserving, economical, meticulous, preserving, unwasteful **12** cheeseparing, parsimonious **13** penny-pinching
frugality **6** thrift **7** economy **8** prudence **9** husbandry **10** providence **11** thriftiness
fruit **5** issue, young **6** result **7** progeny **9** offspring ***citrus:*** **4** lime **5** lemon **6** citron, orange, pomelo **7** kumquat, tangelo **8** bergamot, mandarin, shaddock **9** tangerine **10** calamondin, grapefruit ***combining form:*** **4** carp **5** carpo **6** carpia (plural), carpic, carpus, fructi **7** carpium, carpous ***decay:*** **4** blet ***dried:*** **5** prune **6** raisin ***drink:*** **3** ade **5** juice, punch ***fleshy:*** **7** syconia (plural) **8** syconium ***hard-shelled:*** **3** nut **4** seed **5** gourd **7** coconut ***residue:*** **4** marc **6** pomace ***seed:*** **3** pip ***study of:*** **8** pomology **9** carpology ***subtropical:*** **3** fig **4** date, lime **5** lemon, olive **6** citron, orange **7** avocado, kumquat **9** tangerine **10** grapefruit ***sugar:*** **7** glucose **8** fructose, levulose ***temperate zone:*** **4** pear, plum, sloe **5** apple, grape, melon, peach, prune **6** casaba, cherry, loquat, quince **7** apricot, azarole, currant **8** dewberry **9** blueberry, cranberry, muskmelon, nectarine, raspberry **10** blackberry, gooseberry, loganberry, strawberry **11** boysenberry, huckleberry, pomegranate ***tropical:*** **5** guava, mango **6** ajowan, banana, papaya **7** acerola **8** breadnut, rambutan, tamarind **9** cherimoya, persimmon, pineapple **10** calamondin, mangosteen ***type:*** **3** nut **4** pepo, pome **5** berry, drupe **6** achene, legume, loment, samara **7** capsule, cypsela, silicle, silique, utricle **11** hesperidium ***undeveloped:*** **6** nubbin ***woody:*** **8** xylocarp
fruit basket **8** calathos, calathus
fruitful **4** rich **6** fecund **7** fertile **8** abundant, breeding, childing, prolific, spawning **9** abounding, plenteous, plentiful **10** productive **11** proliferant, propagating, reproducing
fruition **3** joy **7** delight, joyance **8** pleasure **9** enjoyment **10** attainment, conclusion **11** achievement, delectation, fulfillment, realization
fruitless **4** vain **6** barren, foiled, futile **7** sterile, useless **8** abortive, thwarted **9** infertile **10** unavailing **11** ineffective, ineffectual, infructuous, unavailable **12** unproductive, unprofitable
frumpy **4** drab, dull **5** dowdy, tacky **6** stodgy **8** outmoded **9** out-of-date, unstylish
frustrate **3** bar **4** balk, beat, bilk, dash, foil, halt, lick, null, ruin, vain **5** annul, block, check, cross, elude **6** arrest, baffle, blight, cancel, defeat, forbid, hinder, impede, outwit, thwart **7** buffalo, conquer, inhibit, nullify, prevent, redress **8** confound, negative, obstruct, overcome, preclude, prohibit **9** cancel out, checkmate, forestall, interrupt **10** circumvent, counteract, disappoint, neutralize
fry **5** sauté **6** sizzle
frying pan **6** spider **7** griddle, skillet
fuddle **5** mix up **6** ball up, jumble, muddle, tipple **7** confuse, fluster, stupefy **8** bewilder, distract, throw off **10** intoxicate
fuddy-duddy **4** fogy **5** Blimp, fussy **6** fogram, fossil, square **7** fusspot **8** mossback, outdated **10** fuss-budget **12** antediluvian, Colonel Blimp, mid-Victorian, stuffed shirt **13** stick-in-the-mud
fudge **3** pad **4** blur, bosh, fake **5** cheat, color, dodge, hedge, hooey, welsh **6** bunkum **7** distort, hogwash, magnify, traddle **8** contrive, nonsense, overdraw **9** embellish, embroider, overpaint, overstate, poppycock **10** exaggerate, overcharge
fuel **3** gas, oil **4** coal, coke, food, peat, wood **5** stoke **6** petrol **7** support **8** charcoal, gasoline, hypergol, kerosene **9** petroleum, stimulate **13** reinforcement
fugacious **6** flying **7** passing **8** fleeting,

volatile **9** ephemeral, momentary, transient **10** evanescent, short-lived, transitory
fugitive **2** DP **5** exile **6** emigré, outlaw **7** evacuee, lamster, passing, refugee, runaway **8** deserter, fleeting, vagabond, volatile **9** ephemeral, momentary, transient **10** evanescent, perishable, short-lived, transitory
fugue master **4** Bach
Führer, der **6** Hitler
fulfill **4** fill, meet **6** answer, effect, finish **7** achieve, execute, perform, satisfy **8** complete **9** discharge, implement **10** accomplish, effectuate
fulgent **6** bright **7** beaming, radiant, shining **8** luminous **9** brilliant
full **3** big **5** awash, jaded, plumb, round, sated, total, whole **6** choate, entire, gorged, jammed, loaded, minute, packed **7** brimful, copious, crammed, crowded, glutted, orotund, perfect, replete, satiate, stuffed, teeming **8** brimming, complete, detailed, integral, itemized, satiated, thorough **9** abounding, clocklike, jam-packed, plentiful, surfeited
full-blooded **4** rich **5** flush, ruddy **6** ardent, florid **7** flushed, genuine, glowing **8** forceful, pedigree, purebred, rubicund, sanguine **9** impelling, pedigreed, pureblood **12** thoroughbred
full bloom **8** anthesis
full-blown **4** lush, ripe **5** adult, total **6** all-out, mature **7** grown-up, matured, ripened **9** unlimited **12** totalitarian
full-bodied **5** lusty, stout **6** potent, robust, strong **9** corpulent **11** substantial
full-bosomed **5** busty, buxom **6** chesty
full dress **6** finery **7** bravery, regalia **8** frippery **10** Sunday best
full-figured **6** zaftig, zoftig
full-fledged **4** ripe **5** adult, grown **6** mature **7** genuine, grown-up, matured, ripened **12** card-carrying
full-grown **4** ripe **5** adult **6** mature **7** matured, ripened
fullness **5** scope **6** plenty **7** breadth, satiety **9** abundance, amplitude, repletion **10** perfection **12** completeness
full of ***suffix:*** **3** ose, ous **4** ious
full-scale **5** total **6** all-out **8** complete **9** unlimited **12** totalitarian
full tilt **4** fast **7** flat-out, hastily, quickly, rapidly, swiftly **8** speedily **9** posthaste **12** lickety-split **13** expeditiously
fulsome **3** fat **4** full, glib, oily **5** bland, plump, slick, soapy, suave **6** lavish, sating, smarmy, smooth **7** buttery, canting, cloying, copious, profuse **8** abundant, unctious, unctuous **9** bombastic, excessive, exuberant, repulsive, satiating, sickening, wheedling **10** disgusting, flattering, nauseating, oleaginous **11** extravagant, oily-tongued, pharisaical **12** honey-mouthed, honey-tongued, hypocritical, ingratiating, magniloquent, mealy-mouthed, pecksniffian
Fulton's steamboat **8** Clermont
fumble **3** paw **4** feel, flub, mess, muff **5** botch, error, grope **6** bobble, bollix, bungle, goof up, muddle, mumble, murmur, mutter **7** blunder, louse up, misplay, swallow **8** flounder
fume **4** boil, burn, odor, rage, reek, snit, stew **5** anger, smoke, sweat, tizzy, vapor **6** blow up, seethe, swivet **7** bristle, flare up **8** boil over **10** exhalation
fun **3** gag, kid, rag, rib **4** fool, game, glee, jest, joke, josh, play, razz **5** jolly, mirth, sport **6** banter, gaiety **7** disport, jollity, teasing, whoopee **8** hilarity, mischief, ridicule **9** amusement, diversion, high jinks, horseplay, jocundity, joviality, merriment **10** blitheness, pleasantry, recreation **13** entertainment
function **2** do, go **3** act, job, run, use **4** duty, goal, mark, role, take, task, work **5** power, react, serve **6** affair, behave, object, office, target **7** concern, faculty, operate, perform, purpose, service **8** activity, behavior, business, ceremony, occasion, province **9** objective, officiate, operation ***suffix:*** **2** cy **3** ure ***trigonometric:*** **4** sine **6** cosine, secant **7** tangent **8** cosecant **9** cotangent
functional **5** handy, utile **6** useful **7** working **9** practical **11** practicable, serviceable, utilitarian **12** occupational
functioning **4** live **5** alive **6** active **7** dynamic **9** operative
fund **4** pool **5** endow, stock, store **6** supply **7** capital, finance, reserve **9** inventory, subsidize **10** accumulate
fundament **4** beam, rear, rump, seat **6** behind, bottom **8** backside, buttocks, derriere **9** posterior **10** foundation
fundamental **3** law **4** pure **5** axiom, basal, basic, prime, vital **6** bottom, factor, primal **7** needful, primary, radical, theorem **8** cardinal, dominant **9** component, essential, formative, important, necessary, paramount, primitive, principal, principle, requisite **10** elementary, primordial, principium, substratal, underlying **11** constituent, irreducible **12** constitutive, foundational
fundamentalist **4** tory **5** right **7** diehard **8** old liner, standpat **11** bitter-ender, right-winger, standpatter **12** conservative
fundamental nature **7** essence
fund-raiser **6** dinner **8** telethon
funeral **6** burial ***car:*** **6** hearse ***director:*** **9** mortician **10** undertaker ***oration:*** **6** eulogy **8** encomium **9** panegyric ***procession:*** **6** exequy **7** cortege ***service:***

7 requiem 9 obsequies *song:* 5 dirge, elegy 7 epicede 8 threnody 9 epicedium
funereal 4 back 5 bleak, grave 6 dismal, dreary, gloomy, solemn, somber 8 mournful 10 depressing, depressive, lugubrious, oppressive 13 disheartening
fungus 4 cepe, mold, rust, smut 5 ergot, morel, yeast 6 agaric, bolete, mildew 7 amanita, truffle 8 mushroom, polypore, puffball 9 earthstar, stinkhorn, toadstool 10 champignon 11 chanterelle *combining form:* 3 myc 4 myco 5 myces, mycet 6 mycete, myceto 7 mycetes *part:* 3 cap 4 gill, umbo 5 ascus, gleba, hypha, stipe, volva 7 annulus, cortina 8 basidium, conidium, mycelium
fungus disease 3 rot 4 mold, rust, scab, smut 5 ergot, tinea 6 blight, mildew, thrush 7 mycosis 8 lumpy jaw, ringworm 12 athlete's foot *suffix:* 4 oses (plural), osis
funk 4 odor, rage, reek 5 dread, panic, smell, stink 6 coward, craven, flinch, stench 7 chicken, dastard, quitter, shirker 8 poltroon 11 yellowbelly
funky 4 foul, rank 5 musty, stale 6 frowsy, smelly 7 noisome, panicky, reeking 8 stinking 10 malodorous
funnel 4 pipe 5 carry, widen 6 convey, narrow, siphon 7 conduct, traject 8 transmit
funny 3 odd 4 zany 5 antic, comic, droll, fishy, queer 6 sneaky 7 amusing, bizarre, comical, jocular, risible, strange 8 farcical, gelastic, humorous 9 facetious, fantastic, grotesque, laughable, ludicrous 10 ridiculous 11 underhanded
funnyman 3 wag, wit 5 comic, droll, joker 6 jester 8 comedian, humorist, jokester, quipster
fur 4 down, fell, flue, hide, lint, pelt, pile, skin 5 floss, fluff, stole 6 jacket, pelage, peltry *kind:* 3 fox 4 mink, seal 5 fitch, otter, sable 6 ermine, fisher, marten, nutria, tanuki 7 raccoon 10 chinchilla *lamb:* 6 galyak, mouton 7 caracul, karakul, krimmer 9 broadtail *medieval:* 4 vair 7 miniver
furbish 3 rub 4 buff 5 glaze, gloss, shine 6 glance, polish, revive 7 burnish 8 renovate
Furies 6 Alecto 7 Erinyes, Megaera 9 Eumenides, Tisiphone
furious 3 mad 4 wild 5 angry, dirty, hasty, irate, rabid, rough, upset 6 crazed, fierce, insane, maniac, raging, stormy 7 enraged, excited, extreme, fanatic, frantic, intense, violent 8 blustery, demented, feverish, frenetic, frenzied, furibund, incensed, maddened, provoked, terrible, vehement, vigorous, wrathful 9 desperate, energetic, excessive, exquisite, fanatical, impetuous, turbulent 10 bewildered, blustering, boisterous, corybantic, distracted, hysterical, infuriated, inordinate, irrational
furl 4 curl, fold, roll, wrap 5 cover 6 enfold 7 wrinkle
furnace 4 kiln, oven 5 forge, stove 6 heater 7 smelter 8 bloomery, tryworks 11 incinerator *part:* 4 port, vent 5 bocca 6 trompe, tuyere *tender:* 6 stoker
furnish 3 arm, rig 4 feed, gear, give, hand, lend 5 array, dower, endow, endue, equip, mount, yield 6 afford, clothe, fit out, outfit, supply 7 apparel, appoint, deliver, provide, turn out 8 accouter, dispense, hand over, transfer, turn over 10 contribute
furnishings 4 gear 5 decor 9 equipment, trappings
furniture 8 equipage, hardware 9 equipment 10 furnishing *style:* 4 Adam 6 Empire 8 Colonial, Sheraton 11 chinoiserie, Chippendale, Hepplewhite
furniture designer *American:* 5 Phyfe 7 Goddard, Haldane *British:* 6 Morris 7 Gibbons, Shearer 8 Sheraton 11 Chippendale, Hepplewhite *French:* 5 Marot 6 Boulle *Scottish:* 4 Adam
furor 3 ado, cry, fad 4 chic, coil, fury, mode, rage, stir, to-do 5 craze, mania, style, vogue, whirl 6 bustle, flurry, frenzy, pother, ruckus, rumpus, uproar 7 fashion, madness, shindig 8 foofaraw 9 commotion, whirlpool, whirlwind 10 dernier cri
furore 4 stir 5 craze 6 uproar 11 controversy
furrow 3 rut 4 fold, plow, ruck 5 plica, ridge, rivel, stria, sulci (plural) 6 cleave, course, crease, groove, rimple, striae (plural), sulcus, trench 7 channel, crinkle, wrinkle 11 corrugation
furrowed 6 rugose 7 sulcate 8 sulcated, wrinkled 10 corrugated
further 3 new 4 abet, also, else, help, more, then 5 added, again, fresh, serve 6 beyond 7 advance, besides, forward, promote 8 engender, generate, moreover 9 encourage, propagate 10 additional, in addition 12 additionally
furthermore 3 and, too, yea, yet 4 also 5 along 6 as well, withal 7 besides 8 likewise, moreover
furthermost 7 extreme 8 farthest, remotest
furthest 6 utmost 7 extreme, outmost 9 outermost, uttermost
furtive 3 sly 4 foxy, wary, wily 5 catty 6 artful, covert, crafty, feline, masked, secret, shifty, sneaky, stolen, tricky 7 catlike, cloaked, cunning, sub-rosa 8 cautious, guileful, hush-hush, scheming, stealthy 9 disguised, insidious 11 calculating, circumspect, clandestine 12 hugger-mugger

13 surreptitious, under-the-table *look:* 4 peek, peep

furuncle 4 boil 7 abscess

fury 3 ire, mad 4 rage 5 anger, wrath 6 frenzy 7 madness, passion 8 acerbity, acrimony, afflatus, asperity, violence 9 vehemence 11 indignation

furze 4 whin 5 gorse *genus:* 4 Ulex 7 Genista

fuse 3 mix, run 4 flux, frit, meld, melt, thaw, weld 5 blend, merge, smelt, unify, unite 6 anneal, mingle, solder 7 compact, liquefy 8 dissolve, intermix, liquesce 9 integrate 10 amalgamate, deliquesce, interblend 11 consolidate, incorporate

fusillade 4 hail 5 burst, salvo 6 shower, volley 7 barrage 8 drumfire 9 broadside 11 bombardment

fusion 5 alloy, blend, union 6 merger 7 amalgam, mixture 8 compound 9 admixture, coalition, immixture, synthesis *combining form:* 3 zyg 4 zygo

fuss 3 ado, nag, row 4 cark, coil, crab, flap, fret, kick, miff, stew, stir, to-do, wail, yaup 5 annoy, bleat, fight, gripe, haste, hurry, speed, upset, whine, whirl, worry 6 bother, bustle, carp at, flurry, hassle, hurrah, murmur, peck at, pother, putter, racket, repine, ruckus, rumpus, shindy, squawk, yammer 7 agitate, dispute, fluster, henpeck, protest, quarrel, shindig 8 complain 9 bickering, commotion, complaint, objection, whirlpool, whirlwind 11 controversy 12 perturbation

fussbudget 8 stickler 10 fuddy-duddy 12 precisionist 13 perfectionist

fussy 4 nice 5 exact, picky 6 dainty, lively, ornate 7 careful, fidgety, finical, finicky, fretful, heedful 8 bustling, hustling 9 finicking, irritable, querulous, squeamish 10 fastidious, meticulous, particular, pernickety, scrupulous 11 painstaking, persnickety, punctilious 13 conscientious

fustian 4 rant 7 bombast, pompous, useless 8 feckless, rhapsody, rhetoric 9 worthless 10 unpurposed 11 exaggerated, highfalutin, meaningless, purposeless

fusty 4 rank 5 close, dated, fetid, moldy, musty, passé, stale 6 bygone, filthy, old hat, putrid, rancid, sloppy, smelly 7 archaic, noisome, squalid, unkempt 8 outdated 10 antiquated, disheveled, malodorous 12 old-fashioned

futile 4 idle, vain 5 empty 6 hollow, otiose 7 useless 8 abortive, bootless, hopeless, nugatory 9 frivolous, fruitless, worthless 10 inadequate, unavailing 11 ineffective, ineffectual, inefficient 12 insufficient, unprevailing, unproductive, unsuccessful

future 4 to-be 5 later 6 offing 7 by-and-by 9 afterward, hereafter 10 subsequent

Futurism *founder:* 9 Marinetti *painter:* 5 Ballo, Carra 7 Russolo 8 Boccioni, Severini *sculptor:* 8 Boccioni

fuzz 3 nap 4 blur, down, flue, lint, pile 5 floss, fluff

fuzzy 3 dim 5 faint, vague 6 bleary, blurry, frizzy 7 blurred, muddled, obscure, shadowy, unclear 8 confused 9 undefined 10 ill-defined, incoherent, indefinite, indistinct 12 inconclusive

fylfot 8 swastika

G

Gaal's father 4 Ebed
gab see **gabble**
gabbard 4 scow, ship 5 barge 7 lighter
gabber 6 magpie, prater 7 blabber 8 jabberer, prattler 9 bandar-log, blabmouth, chatterer 10 chatterbox
gabble 3 gab, jaw, yak 4 chat, talk 5 clack, drool, prate 6 drivel, gibber, gossip, jabber 7 blabber, blather, chatter, palaver, prattle, twaddle 9 yakety-yak
gabby 5 talky 6 chatty 9 garrulous, talkative 10 babblative, loquacious 11 loose-lipped 12 loose-tongued
gaberdine 4 coat, suit 5 cloth, cover, smock 7 garment
gable 4 wall 8 pediment ***ornament:*** 6 finial
Gabon ***capital:*** 10 Libreville ***monetary unit:*** 5 franc
gad 3 bat 4 band, roam, rope, rove 5 mooch, range, stray 6 ramble, wander 7 maunder, traipse 9 gallivant
Gad ***brother:*** 5 Asher ***father:*** 5 Jacob ***mother:*** 6 Zilpah ***son:*** 3 Eri 5 Ezbon, Haggi
gadfly 4 pest 6 bother, critic
gadget 4 tool 5 gizmo 6 device, dingus, doodad, hickey, jigger, widget 7 concern, dofunny, gimmick, utensil 9 apparatus, appliance, doohickey, rigamajig 11 contraption, thingamajig, thingumajig
Gadi's son 7 Menahem
gadwall 4 duck
Gaea 2 Ge ***husband:*** 6 Uranus ***offspring:*** 6 Giants, Titans, Typhon, Uranus 7 Erinyes 8 Cyclopes ***parent:*** 5 Chaos
Gaelic 4 Erse 5 Irish 6 Celtic 8 Scottish ***god:*** 3 Ler 5 Dagda ***hero:*** 5 Oisin 6 Ossian 11 Finn MacCool ***king:*** 9 Conchobar, Conchobor ***language:*** 4 Manx ***poem:*** 7 aisling ***poet:*** 4 bard, fili 6 Ossian ***queen:*** 4 Medb ***soldier:*** 4 kern 6 Fenian ***spirit:*** 7 banshee ***tale:*** 4 tain
gaff 3 fix 4 hoax, hook, spar, spur 5 abuse, fraud, trick 6 clamor, fleece, outcry, uproar 7 gimmick
gaffe 5 boner, break 7 blooper, faux pas 8 solecism 9 indecorum 11 impropriety
gag 3 jib, shy 4 balk, hoax, jape, jest, joke, keck, quip, ruse, wile 5 choke, crack, demur, heave, retch, sally, stick, trick 6 boggle, muzzle, strain 9 wisecrack, witticism
gage 6 pledge 8 security; (see also **gauge**)
Gaham ***father:*** 5 Nahor ***mother:*** 6 Reumah
Gaheris ***brother:*** 6 Gareth, Gawain ***father:*** 3 Lot ***mother:*** 8 Margawse, Morgause ***uncle:*** 6 Arthur ***victim:*** 8 Margawse, Morgause
gaiety 3 joy 4 glee 5 mirth, revel 7 jollity, revelry, whoopee 8 gladness, hilarity, radiance, reveling, vivacity 9 animation, festivity, geniality, happiness, merriment, revelment 10 liveliness 11 merrymaking
gain 3 get, net, win 4 earn, have, land, make, mend, reap 5 annex, clear, lucre, reach, score 6 attain, look up, obtain, perk up, pick up, profit, rack up, return, secure 7 achieve, acquire, bring in, clean up, improve, procure, realize 8 draw down, earnings, proceeds, windfall 9 knock down 10 accomplish
gainful 4 good, rich 6 paying 8 fruitful 9 lucrative 10 productive, profitable, satisfying, well-paying, worthwhile
gainly 8 graceful, pleasing
gainsay 4 deny 5 cross, fight 6 combat, impugn, negate, oppose, resist 7 dispute, subvert 8 disprove, negative, traverse 9 disaffirm, withstand 10 contradict, contravene, controvert
Gainsborough painting 7 Blue Boy
gait 3 run 4 lope, pace, rate, step, trot, walk 5 speed, strut 6 canter, gallop
gaiter 4 boot, shoe 8 overshoe
gala 3 gay 4 fair, fete 5 merry, party 6 festal, lively 7 festive 8 festival 9 festivity 11 celebration
Galahad ***father:*** 8 Lancelot 9 Launcelot ***mother:*** 6 Elaine ***quest:*** 9 Holy Grail
Galatea ***father:*** 6 Nereus ***husband:*** 9 Pygmalion ***lover:*** 4 Acis ***mother:*** 5 Doris
galaxy 6 nebula 8 Milky Way
Galba ***predecessor:*** 4 Nero ***successor:*** 4 Otho
gale 4 blow, gust, wind 5 blast, storm 6 squall 7 tempest 8 outburst 9 hurricane
Galen's forte 8 medicine
galilee 5 porch 6 chapel 7 portico
Galilee ***town:*** 4 Cana 7 Gergesa 8 Nazareth, Tiberias 9 Bethsaida, Capernaum

Galileo's birthplace 4 Pisa
gall 3 get, irk, rub, vex 4 face, fray, fret, rile, roil, wear 5 annoy, brass, chafe, cheek, chide, erode, grate, graze, harry, nerve, scurr, worry 6 abrade, bother, burn up, harass, ruffle, scrape 7 conceit, corrade, disturb, frazzle, inflame, provoke, scratch, torment 8 exercise, irritate 9 aggravate, arrogance, brashness, excoriate 10 confidence, effrontery ***combining form:*** 4 chol 5 chole, cholo
gallant 3 fop 4 beau, bold, buck, dude, game 5 blade, blood, brave, dandy, lover, manly, preux, Romeo, suave, swain, wooer 6 heroic, manful, suitor, urbane 7 amorist, courtly, coxcomb, Don Juan, stately 8 Casanova, gracious, lothario, paramour 9 dauntless, exquisite
gallantry 5 poise, valor 6 mettle, spirit 7 amenity, bravery, courage, heroism, prowess, suavity 8 courtesy, urbanity, valiance, valiancy 9 attention 10 resolution
gallery 5 porch 6 arcade, loggia, museum, piazza 7 balcony, passage, portico, veranda 8 audience, corridor 9 colonnade, promenade ***ancient Greek:*** 4 stoa
galley 4 boat, ship, tray 5 cuddy, proof 6 bireme 7 dromond, galliot, kitchen, trireme, unireme 9 cookhouse
Gallic 6 French
gallimaufry 4 hash, olio 6 jumble, medley 7 mélange, mixture 8 pastiche 9 potpourri 10 assortment, hodgepodge, miscellany, salmagundi
gallinaceous bird 3 hen 5 quail 6 grouse, turkey 7 chicken, hoatzin 8 curassow, megapode, pheasant 9 partridge
gallivant 3 bat, gad 4 roam, rove 5 mooch, range, stray 6 ramble, travel, wander 7 meander, traipse
gallows 5 frame 6 gibbet 7 hanging, potence ***bird:*** 7 villain 8 criminal
galore 7 aplenty, profuse 8 abundant 9 plentiful
galosh 4 boot, shoe 6 arctic 8 overshoe
Galsworthy work 7 Justice 14 The Forsyte Saga
galvanize 4 coat, move 5 pique, prime 6 arouse, excite 7 innerve, provoke, quicken 8 activate, energize, motivate, vitalize 9 innervate, stimulate
gam 3 leg, pod 5 visit
Gambia ***capital:*** 6 Banjul ***monetary unit:*** 6 dalasi
gambit 3 jig 4 move, play, ploy, ruse 5 trick 6 device 7 gimmick, whizzer 8 artifice, maneuver 9 stratagem
gamble 3 bet, lay, set 4 game, play, risk 5 put on, stake, wager 6 chance, hazard 7 venture 9 speculate
gambler 5 dicer, shark, sharp 6 bettor, player 7 sharper 8 gamester 10 speculator
gambling place 4 Reno 5 Vegas 6 casino 8 Las Vegas 10 Monte Carlo 12 Atlantic City
gambol 3 hop 4 lark, leap, romp 5 bound, caper, frisk, revel 6 cavort, frolic, spring 7 roister, rollick
Gambrinus' invention 4 beer
game 3 bet, fun, lay, set 4 bold, jest, joke, lark, play, prey 5 brave, chase, put on, sport, stake, trick, wager 6 gamble, quarry, spunky 7 contest, pastime, valiant, willing 8 fearless, intrepid, resolute, unafraid, valorous 9 amusement, dauntless, diversion, undaunted 10 courageous ***ball:*** 3 tut 4 golf, polo, pool 5 fives, rogue, rugby 6 hockey, pelota, soccer, squash, tennis 7 cricket, croquet, jai alai 8 baseball, football, handball, hardball, lacrosse, racquets, rounders, softball 9 billiards 10 basketball, volleyball 11 racquetball ***Basque:*** 6 pelota 7 jai alai ***bird:*** 5 quail 6 chukar, turkey 7 bustard 8 bobwhite, pheasant 9 partridge ***board:*** 5 chess, darts, salta 7 pachisi, reversi, squails 8 checkers 9 crokinole 10 backgammon ***card:*** 3 gin, loo, nap, pam, war 4 brag, faro, fish, skat, solo 5 monte, omber, ombre, pitch, poker, rummy, stuss, whist 6 Boston, bridge, casino, écarté, euchre, fan-tan, hearts, piquet 7 auction, bezique, canasta, cassino, cooncan, muggins, old maid, primero, reversi, setback 8 baccarat, Canfield, conquian, cribbage, Michigan, napoleon, pinochle 9 blackjack, matrimony, Newmarket, solitaire, twenty-one, vingt-et-un 11 chemin de fer ***child's:*** 3 tag 5 potsy 8 leapfrog, peekaboo 9 hopscotch ***confidence:*** 4 scam 5 bunco, bunko, sting ***court:*** 5 roque 6 pelota, squash, tennis 7 jai alai 8 handball, racquets 9 badminton 10 basketball, volleyball ***electric:*** 7 pinball ***English:*** 5 kails, rugby 7 cricket, loggats, loggets 8 draughts ***Irish:*** 6 hurley 7 hurling ***of chance:*** 4 faro, keno 5 beano, bingo, boule, craps, lotto, rondo 6 fan-tan, hazard, policy, raffle 7 lottery, rondeau 8 crack-loo, roulette 9 crackaloo ***parlor:*** 5 jacks 8 charades ***racket:*** 5 bandy 6 squash, tennis 8 lacrosse, racquets 9 badminton 11 racquetball, table tennis ***roulette-like:*** 5 boule ***rule maker:*** 5 Hoyle ***string:*** 10 cat's cradle ***table:*** 4 pool 5 craps 7 mah-jong, snooker 8 dominoes, mah-jongg, roulette 9 bagatelle, billiards 11 table tennis ***word:*** 5 rebus 6 crambo, ghosts 7 anagram, hangman 8 acrostic, charades 9 crossword, logogriph
game plan 6 design, scheme 7 project 8 strategy 9 blueprint

gamete 3 egg 4 ovum 5 sperm 8 oosphere
gamin 3 imp, tad 6 monkey, urchin
gamine 6 hoyden, tomboy
gaming cubes 4 dice
gammadion 8 swastika
gammon 3 ham 4 dupe, fool 5 bacon, feign 6 delude, humbug 7 deceive, pretend
gamut 4 note 5 range, scale 6 extent, series
gamy 4 olid, rank 5 fetid, funky 6 plucky, smelly, sordid, stinky, strong 7 noisome, reeking 10 malodorous
gander 4 fool, look 5 goose 6 glance 9 simpleton
Gandhi 6 Indira 7 Mahatma
ganef 5 thief 6 rascal
Ganesa, Ganesh ***father:*** 4 Siva 5 Shiva ***head:*** 8 elephant ***mother:*** 7 Parvati
gang 3 mob, set 4 band, crew, pack, team 5 group, horde 6 clique, outfit
gangling 4 bony 5 gaunt, lanky, rangy 6 skinny 7 spindly 9 spindling
ganglion 5 tumor 7 nucleus
gangly see **gangling**
gangrene 3 rot 5 decay 7 mortify 8 necrosis
gangster 4 goon, hood, thug 5 rough, thief, tough 6 bandit, gunman 7 mafioso, mobster 8 criminal 9 cutthroat ***girl friend:*** 4 moll
gangway 4 hall 5 aisle 7 passage 8 corridor
gannet 4 bird, ibis 5 solan
ganoid fish 3 gar 6 beluga, bowfin 8 sturgeon
Ganymede ***abductor:*** 4 Zeus 7 Jupiter ***brother:*** 4 Ilus ***father:*** 4 Tros ***function:*** 9 cupbearer
gaol 4 jail 6 prison
gap 3 col 4 hole, lull, pass, slit, slot 5 break, chasm, chink, cleft, clove, crack, gorge, gulch, pause 6 arroyo, breach, clough, cranny, hiatus, lacuna, ravine 7 caesura, crevice, fissure, interim, opening, orifice, rupture 8 aperture, cleavage, division, fracture, interval 10 separation 12 intermission, interruption 13 discontinuity
gape 3 eye, yaw 4 bore, gawk, gaze, look, ogle, peer, yawn 5 glare, gloat, stare 6 goggle 10 rubberneck
gaping 4 open 7 chasmal, yawning 9 cavernous
gar 4 fish, pike 8 billfish 10 needlefish
Garand 5 rifle
garb 4 clad 5 array, dress, getup, style 6 attire, clothe, outfit 7 apparel, garment, raiment 8 enclothe
garbage 4 junk, orts, slop 5 dregs, filth, offal, trash, waste 6 debris, kelter, litter, refuse, rubble, sewage 7 rubbish 8 riffraff ***heap:*** 6 midden
garble 4 sift, warp 5 belie, color, twist 6 jumble, mangle 7 becloud, distort, falsify, obscure, pervert 8 miscolor, misstate, mutilate 9 obfuscate 12 misrepresent
garçon 3 boy 6 waiter 7 servant
garden 3 hoe 4 Eden, farm, hall, park, plot, till, yard 5 grove, tract 8 rosarium 9 cultivate 11 commonplace ***shelter:*** 5 arbor 6 arbour
Garden City 7 Chicago
gardener 7 yardman 9 topiarist
garden house 6 alcove, gazebo, pagoda 9 belvedere
Garden State 9 New Jersey
garden tool 3 hoe 4 claw, fork, rake 5 mower, spade 6 pruner, scythe, sickle, trowel, weeder 8 clippers
Gareth ***brother:*** 6 Gawain 7 Gaheris ***father:*** 3 Lot ***mother:*** 8 Margawse, Morgause ***slayer:*** 8 Lancelot 9 Launcelot ***uncle:*** 6 Arthur ***wife:*** 6 Liones
Gargamelle's son 9 Gargantua
Gargantua ***abbey:*** 7 Theleme ***author:*** 8 Rabelais ***father:*** 12 Grandgousier ***first word:*** 5 drink ***mother:*** 10 Gargamelle ***son:*** 10 Pantagruel
gargantuan see **gigantic**
Garibaldi follower 8 redshirt
garish 4 loud 5 gaudy, showy 6 brazen, flashy, tawdry, tinsel 7 blatant, chintzy, glaring 12 meretricious
garland 3 ana, lei 4 band, posy 5 album, crown 6 anadem, wreath 7 chaplet, coronal, coronet, omnibus 8 analects 9 anthology 10 miscellany 11 florilegium
garlic 4 moly, ramp 5 clove 6 ramson
garment 4 cape, clad, coat, garb, gear, gown, robe, vest 5 array, cloak, dress, frock, habit, shirt, skirt, talar, tunic 6 attire, blouse, clothe 7 apparel, chemise, raiment 8 clothing, enclothe, vestment, wearable 10 habiliment ***Afghan:*** 6 postin 7 posteen 8 poshteen ***African:*** 6 kaross 7 dashiki ***Arab:*** 3 aba 4 haik ***British:*** 4 brat 10 mackintosh ***Burmese:*** 6 tamein ***clergy's:*** 3 alb 4 cope 7 cassock, soutane 8 vestment ***close-fitting:*** 6 girdle, tights 7 leotard ***for sleeping:*** 6 pajama 7 nightie 9 nightgown ***Greek:*** 5 tunic 6 chiton, peplos, tribon 7 chlamys 8 himation ***Hindu:*** 4 sari 5 saree ***hooded:*** 7 jellaba 8 djellaba ***Japanese:*** 6 kimono ***lace:*** 10 chemisette ***Malay:*** 6 sarong ***men's:*** 3 tie 4 vest 5 pants, shirt, socks 6 jacket, slacks 7 drawers 8 trousers ***Muslim:*** 4 izar ***outer:*** 4 cape, coat, robe, wrap 5 cloak, parka, shawl, smock, stole, wamus 6 capote, jacket, kimono, poncho, sarong, ulster, wammus 7 overall, paletot, pelisse,

surtout, sweater, topcoat, zamarra **8** overcoat, pinafore, pullover, scapular **9** coveralls, gaberdine, polonaise ***patchwork:*** **5** cento **7** khirkah ***Polynesian:*** **5** pareu **8** lavelava ***rain:*** **6** poncho **7** oilskin, slicker ***Roman:*** **4** toga **5** stola, tunic ***Scottish:*** **4** jupe, kilt **7** sporran ***sleeveless:*** **3** aba **4** cape **6** mantle, tabard ***trim:*** **7** falbala ***Turkish:*** **6** dolman ***women's:*** **4** gown **5** dress, skirt **6** blouse, vestee **7** blouson, nightie, partlet **8** negligee, peignoir, pelerine

garner **4** cull, hive, reap **5** amass, glean, hoard, lay up, store, uplay **6** gather, pick up, roll up **7** extract, granary, harvest, store up **8** cumulate, ingather **9** stockpile **10** accumulate

garnet **5** jewel, stone **6** pyrope **8** essonite ***black:*** **8** melanite ***red:*** **9** almandite

garnish **4** deck, trim **5** adorn, prank **6** bedeck **7** dress up **8** beautify, decorate, ornament **9** embellish

garret **4** loft, room **5** attic, solar **6** sollar, soller **7** mansard **8** cockloft

garrison **4** fort, post **6** occupy **7** station **10** stronghold

garrote **4** kill **5** choke **7** execute **8** strangle, throttle **9** execution

garrulous see **gabby**

garter **4** band, belt **5** snake **7** elastic **9** supporter

gas **4** fuel, fume **5** steam, vapor **6** petrol **8** gasoline **9** petroleum ***atmospheric:*** **4** neon **5** argon, oxide, ozone, xenon **6** helium, oxygen **7** krypton, methane **8** hydrogen, nitrogen ***combining form:*** **3** aer **4** mano **5** pneum **6** pneumo **7** pneumat **8** pneumato ***flammable:*** **6** butane, ethane, ethyne **7** methane, propane, propene **8** ethylene ***inert:*** **4** neon **5** argon, radon, xenon **6** helium **7** krypton ***intestinal:*** **6** flatus ***mine:*** **8** firedamp **9** blackdamp, chokedamp ***oxygen:*** **5** ozone ***toxic:*** **5** sarin **6** arsine, ketene **7** mustard, stibine, yperite **8** phosphin

gash **3** cut **4** slit **5** carve, slash, slice, split, wound **6** incise, pierce

gasket **4** band, line, ring, seal **6** sealer

gasoline **4** fuel **6** petrol ***rating:*** **6** octane

gasp **4** blow, huff, pant, puff **5** heave

Gaspar ***companion:*** **8** Melchior **9** Balthazar ***gift:*** **12** frankincense

gassy **5** windy **8** inflated, vaporous

gastronome **7** epicure, gourmet **8** aesthete, gourmand **9** bon vivant

gastronomer, gastronomist see **gastronome**

gastropod **4** slug **5** cowry, murex, snail, whelk **6** cowrie, limpet, volute **7** abalone, mollusk **8** pteropod

gat **3** gun **6** pistol **7** channel, passage

gate **3** tap, way **4** cock, door, exit **5** hatch, valve **6** faucet, portal, spigot, wicket **7** hydrant, opening, petcock **8** stopcock **9** turnstile

gatefold **6** insert **7** foldout

Gates of Hercules **9** Gibraltar

gateway **4** arch, door **5** pylon, toran **6** portal, torana **8** entrance

gather **4** brew, cull, draw, heap, herd, loom, mass, meet, pick, pile, reap, take **5** amass, bunch, flock, glean, group, horde, infer, judge, pluck, raise, shirr, stack, think, troop **6** assume, deduce, deduct, derive, expect, garner, impend, muster, pick up, take in **7** believe, cluster, collect, extract, harvest, imagine, make out, round up, suppose, suspect **8** assemble, conclude, congress **9** aggregate, forthcome **10** accumulate, congregate, rendezvous, understand

gathering **4** bevy, crew, gang, mass, ruck **5** bunch, crowd, crush, flock, group, horde, party, press, swarm **6** klatch, muster **7** company, harvest, klatsch, meeting, reaping, reunion, turnout **8** assembly, cropping, junction **9** concourse, congeries **10** assemblage, collection, concursion, confluence, harvesting **11** aggregation **12** congregation ***combining form:*** **4** fest

Gath's giant **7** Goliath

gauche **5** crude, inept **6** clumsy, wooden **7** awkward, halting, unhappy **8** bumbling **9** ham-handed, maladroit

gaucho **6** cowboy **8** herdsman ***weapon:*** **4** bola **7** machete

Gaudeamus ____ **6** igitur

gaudy **4** loud **5** crude, feast, gross, showy **6** brazen, coarse, flashy, garish, tawdry, tinsel, vulgar **7** blatant, chintzy, glaring **8** festival **9** tasteless **12** meretricious, ostentatious

gauge **5** judge, meter, scale **7** measure **8** estimate, standard **9** benchmark, criterion, yardstick **10** touchstone

Gauguin's island home **6** Tahiti

Gaul **4** Celt **6** France **9** Frenchman

Gaulish **6** French ***combining form:*** **5** Gallo ***god:*** **4** Esus **7** Taranis ***goddess:*** **8** Belisama ***priest:*** **5** druid

gaunt **4** bony, lank, lean **5** lanky, spare **6** skinny, wasted **7** angular, scraggy, scrawny **8** rawboned, skeletal **9** emaciated **10** cadaverous

gauntlet **4** dare, test **5** glove **6** cestus, ordeal **9** challenge

Gautama **6** Buddha **10** Siddhartha ***mother:*** **4** Maya ***son:*** **6** Rahula ***wife:*** **9** Yasodhara

gauze **4** film, haze, leno, mist **5** cloth, crepe, lisse, tulle **6** fabric, tissue **7** bandage, chiffon **11** cheesecloth

gauzy **5** filmy, sheer **6** flimsy **7** tiffany **8** gossamer **10** diaphanous **11** transparent

gavel 6 hammer, mallet
gavial 7 reptile 9 crocodile
gavotte 5 dance
Gawain ***brother:*** 6 Gareth 7 Gaheris ***father:*** 3 Lot ***mother:*** 8 Margawse, Morgause ***slayer:*** 8 Lancelot 9 Launcelot ***uncle:*** 6 Arthur ***victim:*** 6 Uwayne 7 Lamerok 9 Pellinore
gawk 3 oaf 4 bore, gape, gaze, lout, lump, peer 5 glare, gloat, klutz, looby, stare
gawky 5 splay 6 clumsy, gauche 7 awkward, lumpish 8 ungainly 9 lumbering
gay 4 glad, keen, wild 5 alert, bonny, brash, brave, happy, jolly, merry, queer, riant, vivid 6 blithe, bright, colory, festal, frisky, jocund, jovial, lively, rakish, sporty 7 animate, festive, forward, gleeful, playful, pushful, raffish, uranian 8 animated, colorful, mirthful, rakehell, spirited, sportive 9 confident, homophile, presuming, sprightly, vivacious 10 blithesome, brassbound, frolicsome, homoerotic, homosexual
___ Gay 4 John 5 Enola
Gaza victor 7 Allenby
gaze 3 eye, see 4 bore, gape, gawk, leer, look, ogle, peer, pore, scan, view 5 glare, gloat, stare, watch 6 goggle, look at 7 observe 8 consider, look upon
gazebo 6 alcove, pagoda 8 pavilion 9 belvedere 11 garden house, summerhouse
gazelle 3 ahu, goa 4 admi, cora, dama, kudu, mohr, oryx 5 ariel, mhorr 6 dorcus 7 chikara, corinne 8 antelope
gazette 5 paper 6 record 7 courant, journal 9 newspaper
gazetteer 5 atlas, guide
Gazez's father 5 Caleb
Ge see Gaea
gear 3 arm, cam, cog, rig 5 dress, equip, goods, stuff 6 fit out, outfit, tackle, things 7 apparel, appoint, furnish, rigging, turn out 8 accouter, accoutre, cogwheel, materiel, property, tackling 9 apparatus, equipment, machinery 10 belongings 11 accessories, habiliments, possessions 13 accouterments, accoutrements, paraphernalia
Geats ***king:*** 7 Hygelac ***prince:*** 7 Beowulf
Geb ***daughter:*** 4 Isis 8 Nephthys ***father:*** 3 Shu ***mother:*** 6 Tefnut ***sister:*** 3 Nut ***son:*** 3 Set 6 Osiris ***wife:*** 3 Nut
gecko 6 lizard
Gedaliah ***father:*** 6 Ahikam 7 Pashhur 8 Jeduthun ***slayer:*** 7 Ishmael
Gehenna 3 pit 4 hell 5 abyss, hades, Sheol 6 Tophet 7 inferno 9 perdition 10 underworld 11 netherworld
geisha wear 6 kimono
gel 3 dry, set 4 clot, jell 5 jelly 6 gelate 7 congeal, jellify 9 coagulate
gelatin 4 agar 5 jelly 7 sericin
geld 3 fix 4 spay 5 alter, unsex 6 change, neuter 8 castrate, mutilate 9 sterilize 10 emasculate 11 desexualize
gelid 3 icy 4 cold, cool 5 chill, nippy 6 arctic, chilly, frosty 7 glacial 8 freezing
gem 3 jet 4 jade, onyx, opal, ruby, sard 5 agate, amber, beryl, coral, jewel, pearl, stone, topaz 6 amulet, garnet, jasper, scarab, sphene, spinel, zircon 7 bejewel, cat's-eye, citrine, diamond, emerald, enjewel, peridot 8 amethyst, diopside, fluorite, intaglio, obsidian, sapphire, sardonyx, tigereye 9 carnelian, danburite, moonstone, phenakite, scapolite, spodumene, turquoise 10 aquamarine, cordierite, tourmaline 11 alexandrite, chrysoberyl, chrysoprase, lapis lazuli, masterpiece ***blue:*** 6 zircon 8 sapphire 9 turquoise 10 aquamarine 11 lapis lazuli ***carved:*** 8 intaglio ***changeable:*** 9 chatoyant ***cut:*** 7 navette 8 baguette, cabochon, marquise 9 brilliant ***face:*** 5 facet ***green:*** 4 jade 7 emerald, peridot, smaragd 10 chrysolite 11 chrysoprase ***red:*** 4 ruby, sard 6 garnet, pyrope, spinel 9 carnelian ***support:*** 7 setting ***weight:*** 5 carat ***yellow:*** 5 amber, topaz 6 sphene 7 citrine
Gemariah ***brother:*** 6 Ahikam ***father:*** 7 Hilkiah, Shaphan
Gemini star 6 Castor, Pollux
gemmule 3 bud 8 antelope
gemsbok 4 oryx
Gem State 5 Idaho
gemütlich see genial
gendarme 7 soldier 9 policeman
gender 3 sex 4 kind, male, sort, type 5 class 6 female, neuter
genealogy 6 stemma 7 descent, history, lineage 8 pedigree 10 family tree
general 4 wide 5 broad, typic, usual 6 common, global, normal, public, vulgar 7 generic, natural, overall, regular, routine, typical 8 everyday, sweeping 9 all-around, inclusive, prevalent, universal 11 commonplace 12 run-of-the-mill 13 comprehensive ***American:*** 3 Lee 4 Pike, Wood 5 Clark, Grant, Meade, Scott, Smith, Stark, Worth 6 Custer, Kearny, Patton, Porter, Powell, Slocum, Spaatz, Taylor 7 Bradley, Fremont, Houston, Jackson, Lejeune, Ridgway, Sherman, Twining, Wallace, Wheeler 8 Burnside, Goethals, Marshall, Mitchell, Pershing, Sheridan, Stilwell 9 MacArthur, McClellan, Rosecrans, Schofield, Wilkinson 10 Eisenhower, Vandegrift, Wainwright 11 Schwarzkopf ***American Revolutionary:*** 4 Knox, Ward 5 Gates, Wayne 6 dekalb, Greene, Morgan, Putnam 8 Moultrie, Sullivan 10 Washington ***Austrian:*** 11 Wallenstein ***British:*** 4 Gage, Howe 5 Clive, Monck, Wolfe 6 Rupert 7 Amherst, Wingate 8 Burgoyne, Cromwell 10 Abercromby,

Cornwallis, Wellington ***Carthaginian:*** 8 Hamilcar, Hannibal 9 Hasdrubal ***Chinese:*** 3 Yen 4 Feng 5 Chang ***combining form:*** 3 cen, pan 4 caen, ceno, coen, pano 5 caeno, coeno ***Confederate:*** 3 Lee 4 Hill, Hood 5 Bragg, Ewell, Price, Smith 6 Morgan, Stuart 7 Forrest, Hampton, Jackson, Pickett 8 Johnston 9 Pemberton 10 Beauregard, Longstreet ***French:*** 4 Foch 6 Moreau, Petain 7 Lefebre, Weygand 8 deGaulle, Montcalm, Saint-Cyr 9 Frontenac 10 Rochambeau ***German:*** 4 Jodl 6 Kleist 10 Ludendorff ***Greek:*** 6 Nicias 9 Miltiades 10 Alcibiades 12 Themistocles ***Japanese:*** 4 Tojo 5 Koiso 6 Yasuda 8 Yamagata 9 Yamashita ***Mexican:*** 9 Santa Anna ***Prussian:*** 11 Scharnhorst ***Roman:*** 5 Sulla 6 Caesar, Fabius, Marius, Pompey, Scipio 7 Regulus, Ricimer 8 Agricola, Lucullus, Stilicho 9 Marcellus, Sertorius 10 Theodosius 11 Cincinnatus ***Russian:*** 7 Wrangel, Zhdanov 9 Yeremenko ***Spanish:*** 4 Alba, Alva 6 Franco ***Swedish:*** 7 Wrangel

general assembly 6 plenum

generalize 5 infer, widen 6 extend, induce, spread

generally 6 mainly, mostly 7 as a rule, chiefly, en masse, largely, overall, usually 8 all in all, commonly 9 primarily 10 altogether, by and large, by ordinary, frequently, on the whole, ordinarily 11 principally 13 predominantly

generate 4 bear, make, sire 5 beget, breed, cause, get up, hatch, spawn 6 create, father, induce, parent, whip up, work up 7 develop, produce, provoke 8 engender, multiply, muster up 9 originate, procreate, propagate, reproduce 10 bring about

generic 6 common 7 general 9 universal

generosity 7 charity, largess 8 largesse 10 liberality

generous 3 big 4 free, kind 5 ample, lofty, noble 6 kindly, lavish, plenty 7 copious, helpful, liberal, profuse 8 abundant, handsome 9 bounteous, bountiful, plenteous, plentiful, unselfish, unsparing 10 altruistic, benevolent, bighearted, charitable, chivalrous, freehanded, munificent, openhanded, thoughtful, ungrudging 11 considerate, kindhearted, magnanimous

genesis 4 dawn 5 alpha, birth, start 6 origin, outset, setout 7 dawning, opening 8 outstart 9 beginning 12 commencement

genetic 10 hereditary ***material:*** 3 DNA, RNA 7 cistron 9 chromatid 10 chromosome ***term:*** 8 synapsis 9 backcross

genial 4 warm 5 jolly, merry 6 benign, blithe, gentle, jocund, jovial, kindly 7 affable, amiable, cordial 8 amicable, cheerful, friendly, gracious, sociable 9 congenial 10 neighborly

genie 4 jinn 5 afrit, jinni 6 afreet, spirit, yaksha

genitor 6 father, parent 7 creator

geniture 5 birth 8 nativity

genius 4 bent, bump, gift, head, turn 5 flair, knack 6 brains, talent, wizard 7 aptness, faculty 9 ingenuity, intellect 10 creativity 12 intelligence 13 inventiveness

Genoa's liberator 5 Doria

genre 4 kind, sort, type 5 class, style 7 species 8 category

gens 4 clan 5 group 6 family, people

Genseric's subjects 7 Vandals

genteel 4 nice, prig, prim 5 civil, noble 6 la-di-da, polite, prissy, stuffy, too-too, urbane 7 elegant, mincing, prudish, refined, stilted, stylish 8 affected, cultured, graceful, knightly, ladylike, mannerly, polished, precious, priggish, well-bred 9 courteous, distingué, Victorian 10 chivalrous, cultivated, tight-laced 11 fashionable, gentlemanly, pretentious, well-behaved 12 aristocratic, well-mannered 13 straightlaced

gentile 3 goy

gentility 5 elite 6 flower, gentry 7 aristoi, quality, society 8 breeding, optimacy 10 upper class, upper crust 11 aristocracy

gentle 4 calm, easy, kind, meek, mild, soft, tame 5 balmy, bland, faint, quiet, tamed 6 benign, genial, kindly, mellow, placid, serene, smooth, tender 7 affable, amiable, lenient 8 delicate, peaceful, pleasant, pleasing, soothing, tranquil 9 agreeable 11 softhearted, sympathetic, warmhearted 13 compassionate ***creature:*** 4 lamb

gentleman 6 aristo, fellow, mister 8 cavalier 9 blue blood, chevalier, patrician 10 aristocrat ***English:*** 6 milord ***French:*** 8 monsieur ***Hindu:*** 4 babu ***Spanish:*** 3 don 5 senor

gentleman friend 4 beau 5 swain

gentry 4 rank 5 elite 6 flower 7 aristoi, quality, society 8 optimacy 9 gentility 10 upper class, upper crust 11 aristocracy

genu 4 knee 5 joint

Genubath's father 5 Hadad

genuflect 5 kneel 6 kowtow

genuine 4 hard, real, true, very 5 plain, pucka, pukka 6 actual, dinkum, honest 7 factual, natural, sincere 8 absolute, bona fide, positive, trueborn 9 authentic, undoubted, unfeigned, veritable 10 heart-whole, sure-enough, unaffected

genus 4 kind, mode, sort, type 5 class, group, order 8 category

geode 6 cavity, nodule

geographer ***American:*** 10 Huntington ***Flemish:*** 8 Mercator ***German:*** 6 Ratzel ***Greek:*** 6 Strabo 7 Ptolemy

geologic ***period:*** **5** azoic **6** Eocene **7** Miocene, Permian **8** Cambrian, Cenozoic, Devonian, Jurassic, Mesozoic, Pliocene, Silurian, Triassic **9** Oligocene, Paleocene, Paleozoic **10** Cretaceous, Ordovician **13** Mississippian, Pennsylvanian ***study:*** **4** rock **5** earth **6** fossil
geometer **6** Euclid
geometric ***coordinate:*** **8** abscissa ***curve:*** **3** arc **6** spiral **7** cissoid, ellipse, evolute **8** parabola ***solid:*** **4** cone, cube **5** prism **7** pyramid **8** spheroid, spherule ***surface:*** **5** nappe, torus **6** toroid
geometric figure **4** cone, cube **5** prism, rhomb **6** circle, oblong, sphere, square **7** ellipse, hexagon, octagon, polygon, pyramid, rhombus **8** cylinder, heptagon, pentagon, rhomboid, spheroid, triangle **9** rectangle ***combining form:*** **5** hedra (plural) **6** hedron
geophagy **4** pica
Georgia ***capital:*** **7** Atlanta ***college, university:*** **4** Tift **5** Clark, Emory, Paine ***founder:*** **10** Oglethorpe ***nickname:*** **10** Peach State
Gera ***father:*** **4** Bela ***grandfather:*** **8** Benjamin ***son:*** **4** Ehud **6** Shimei
Geraint's wife **4** Enid
Gerda's husband **4** Frey
germ **3** bud, bug **4** seed **5** spark, spore, virus **6** embryo **7** microbe, nucleus **9** bacterium ***cell:*** **3** egg **4** ovum **5** sperm
German **4** Goth **6** Teuton ***article:*** **3** das, der, des, die ***bomber:*** **5** Gotha, Stuka ***child:*** **4** kind ***coin:*** **4** mark **5** taler **6** thaler **7** pfennig ***empire:*** **5** reich ***head:*** **4** kopf ***highway:*** **8** autobahn ***leader:*** **6** führer, kaiser ***measles:*** **7** rubella ***mister:*** **4** herr ***no:*** **4** nein ***nobleman:*** **6** Junker ***pronoun:*** **2** du, er, es **3** ich, sie, wir ***rifle:*** **6** Mauser ***weight:*** **3** lot **5** pfund, stein **8** vierling ***woman:*** **4** frau **8** fräulein
germane **5** ad rem **7** apropos, related **8** apposite, material, pointful, relevant **9** pertinent **10** applicable
Germany **11** Deutschland ***capital:*** **6** Berlin ***monetary unit:*** **4** mark; (see also **East Germany; West Germany**)
germinate **3** bud **6** evolve, sprout
Gershom, Gershon ***father:*** **4** Levi ***son:*** **5** Libni **6** Shimei
Gershwin **3** Ira **6** George ***opera:*** **12** Porgy and Bess
Gertrude ***husband:*** **8** Claudius ***son:*** **6** Hamlet
Gervaise's daughter **4** Nana
Geryon ***dog:*** **6** Orthus ***father:*** **8** Chrysaor ***mother:*** **10** Callirrhoe ***slayer:*** **8** Hercules
Gesham's father **6** Jahdai
gest, geste **4** deed, feat **7** emprise, exploit, venture **9** adventure **10** enterprise
Gestapo chief **7** Himmler
gesticulate **6** motion **7** gesture
gesture **3** act, nod **4** flag, sign **5** token **6** motion, salute, signal **8** reminder **9** signalize **10** expression, indication ***graceful:*** **9** beau geste
get **3** bag, fix, win **4** beat, come, draw, earn, gain, gall, grow, have, land, move, rile, sire, sway, turn **5** annex, breed, catch, educe, evoke, learn, peeve, reach, ready, touch, upset **6** accept, affect, arrive, attain, become, bother, burn up, collar, elicit, extort, father, induce, make up, master, obtain, pick up, secure, show up, turn up **7** acquire, bring in, capture, chalk up, compass, disturb, extract, impress, nonplus, perturb, prehend, prepare, procure, realize, receive, win over **8** contract, convince, distress, draw down, irritate, memorize, persuade, sicken of, talk into **9** aggravate, argue into, influence, knock down, prevail on, procreate **10** exasperate, sicken with **11** bring around, prevail upon, progenerate **12** come down with
get away see **get out**
getaway **3** lam **4** slip **6** escape, flight **8** breakout, escaping **10** escapement
get back **6** recoup, regain **7** recover, recruit **8** retrieve **9** repossess
get by **4** fare **5** shift **6** manage
get off **2** go **4** exit, open, quit **5** begin, leave, start **6** depart, launch, retire **7** jump off, kick off, pull out **8** commence ***prefix:*** **2** de
get out **2** go **4** exit, kite, leak **5** break, issue, leave, scram, split **6** begone, decamp, depart, egress, escape **7** publish, skiddoo, take off **8** clear out, hightail **9** skedaddle
Gettysburg general **3** Lee **5** Meade
get up **4** rise **5** arise, breed, cause, hatch, mount, stand **6** induce, uprise **7** pile out, produce, roll out, turn out **8** engender, generate, muster up, occasion, upspring **12** rise and shine
getup **2** go **3** pep, rig **4** bang, push, snap, togs **5** dress, drive, guise, punch, vigor **6** outfit, setout **7** costume **8** vitality
get-up-and-go **3** pep **4** bang, push, snap **5** drive, punch, vigor **8** ambition, vitality **10** enterprise, initiative
gewgaw **3** toy **5** curio **6** bauble, trifle **7** bibelot, novelty, trinket, whatnot **8** gimcrack **9** objet d'art **10** knickknack
geyser **5** spurt **6** spring **11** Old Faithful
Ghana ***capital:*** **5** Accra ***monetary unit:*** **4** cedi
ghastly **3** wan **4** grim, pale **5** awful **6** grisly, horrid, shadow **7** hideous, macabre **8** dreadful, gruesome, horrible, nauseant, shocking, spectral, terrible **9** appalling,

deathlike, frightful, ghostlike, sickening 10 cadaverous, corpselike, disgustful, disgusting, horrifying, nauseating, terrifying 11 frightening

ghee 3 fat 6 butter

gherkin 6 pickle 8 cucumber

ghetto 4 slum

ghost 5 shade, spook 6 shadow, spirit, wraith 7 phantom, specter 8 phantasm 10 apparition 11 poltergeist

ghostlike see ghostly

ghostly 5 eerie, scary 6 spooky 7 shadowy 8 spectral 9 deathlike 10 cadaverous, corpselike

ghoul 4 ogre 5 fiend 7 monster

GI 7 fighter, soldier, warrior 9 man-at-arms 10 serviceman

giant 4 huge, Otus 5 gross, Gyges, Hymir, jumbo, titan, troll, whale 6 Cottus, Typhon 7 Aloadae (plural), Antaeus, Cyclops, mammoth, monster, titanic 8 behemoth, Briareus, colossal, colossus, gigantic, Orgoglio 9 cyclopean, Enceladus, Ephialtes, Gargantua, Herculean, leviathan, monstrous, polypheme 10 behemothic, gargantuan ***armadillo:*** 4 tatu 5 tatou ***biblical:*** 4 Anak 7 Goliath ***cactus:*** 7 saguaro ***clam:*** 8 tridacna ***grass:*** 5 otate ***killer:*** 4 Jack 5 David ***one-eyed:*** 5 Arges 7 Cyclops 10 Polyphemus ***100-armed:*** 9 Enceladus ***100-eyed:*** 5 Argus ***perch:*** 5 begti, bekti 6 cockup ***rime-cold:*** 4 Ymer, Ymir ***sea god:*** 5 Aegir

Giant author 5 Ferber (Edna)

gibber 5 prate 6 babble, drivel, gabble, jabber, yammer 7 blather, chatter, prattle

gibberish 5 Greek 6 babble, bunkum, drivel, gabble, jabber 7 blabber, blather, mummery, palaver, prattle, twaddle 8 claptrap, nonsense 10 double-talk, hocus-pocus, mumbo jumbo 11 abracadabra, jabberwocky 12 gobbledygook

gibbet 4 hang 5 noose, scrag 7 gallows, turn off 8 string up

gibbon 3 ape, lar 6 monkey 7 primate, siamang 10 anthropoid

gibbous 6 convex, humped 7 rounded, swollen 10 humpbacked

gibe 4 gird, jeer, jest, mock, quip 5 fleer, flout, gleek, scoff, sneer 6 quip at 7 scout at 8 ridicule

Gibraltar ***colony of:*** 12 Great Britain ***conqueror:*** 5 Tarik, Tariq ***country:*** 5 Spain ***opposite:*** 5 Ceuta

Giddalti ***father:*** 5 Heman ***occupation:*** 6 singer

giddy 5 dizzy, light, silly 6 swimmy, volage, yeasty 7 flighty, fribble 8 skittish, swimming 9 fribbling, frivolous 10 bird-witted, hoity-toity 11 empty-headed, harebrained, light-headed, vertiginous 13 rattlebrained

___ Gide 5 André

Gideon ***father:*** 5 Joash ***servant:*** 5 Purah ***son:*** 9 Abimelech

Gideoni's son 6 Abidan

gift 3 set, tip 4 alms, bent, boon, bump, head, turn 5 award, favor, flair, grant, knack 6 genius, legacy, reward, talent 7 aptness, cumshaw, faculty, handout, largess, present, subsidy 8 bestowal, donation, gratuity, offering 9 lagniappe 11 benefaction, benevolence 12 contribution, presentation

gig 3 jab, job 4 boat, fool, goad, prod 5 annoy, rotor, spear 6 chaise, harass 7 demerit, provoke

gigantic 3 big 4 huge, vast 5 giant, large 7 hulking, immense, mammoth 8 colossal, enormous 9 cyclopean, monstrous 10 gargantuan, prodigious, stupendous 11 elephantine

giggle 5 laugh, tehee 6 guffaw, hee-haw, teehee, titter 7 chortle, chuckle, snicker, snigger

Gilbert and Sullivan opera 8 Iolanthe, Patience 9 Ruddigore, The Mikado 11 H.M.S. Pinafore, Princess Ida, The Sorcerer, Trial by Jury 12 The Grand Duke 13 The Gondoliers

Gil Blas author 6 Lesage

gild 5 adorn, cover, tinge 7 overlay 8 brighten 9 embellish

Gilda's father 9 Rigoletto

Gilead ***father:*** 6 Machir ***grandfather:*** 8 Manasseh ***son:*** 8 Jephthah

Gilgamesh 4 epic ***companion:*** 6 Eabani, Engidu, Enkidu ***home:*** 5 Erech ***mother:*** 6 Ninsun ***victim:*** 7 Humbaba

gill 4 race 5 brook, creek 6 runnel, stream, wattle 7 rivulet ***relating to:*** 9 branchial

gilly flower 4 pink 9 clove pink

gilt 3 hog, pig, sow 4 gold 5 swine 6 gilded, golden

gimlet 4 tool 5 drink 6 pierce 7 gum tree 8 eucalypt 10 eucalyptus ***ingredient:*** 3 gin 9 lime juice

gimmick 4 ploy, ruse, wile 5 feint, gizmo, trick 6 gadget, gambit, jigger, widget 7 concern, whizzer 8 artifice, maneuver 9 stratagem

gimpy 4 lame 7 limping 8 crippled

gin 3 net 4 sloe, trap 5 catch, rummy, snare 6 liquor 7 springe 8 Hollands

Ginath's son 5 Tibni

ginger 3 fig, pep, vim 4 herb, stir 5 liven, spice, vigor 6 mettle, revive, spirit ***cookie:*** 4 snap

gingerly 4 safe, wary 5 chary 7 careful, guarded 8 cautious, discreet 11 calculating, circumspect, considerate

gingery 5 beany, fiery 6 spunky 7 pep-

pery **8** spirited **10** mettlesome **11** high-hearted **12** high-spirited
gingham **5** cloth **6** fabric
gingiva **3** gum
ginseng **4** herb, root
Gioconda, La **8** Mona Lisa ***composer:*** **10** Ponchielli ***painter:*** **7** da Vinci (Leonardo)
giraffe **3** car **5** piano **8** ruminant **10** camelopard
girandole **6** mirror **7** earring, pendant **11** candelabrum
girasol **4** opal **8** fire opal **9** artichoke
gird **3** hem **4** band, belt, gibe, jeer, jest, ring, wrap **5** beset, brace, fleer, flout, ready, round, scoff, sneer, steel **6** circle, quip at **7** bolster, forearm, fortify, prepare, scout at, shore up, wreathe **8** begirdle, buttress, cincture, encircle, engirdle, surround **9** encompass, reinforce **10** encincture, strengthen
girdle **3** hem **4** band, bark, belt, ring, sash **5** beset, round **6** begird, cestus, circle, engird **8** ceinture, cincture, encircle, surround **9** encompass, waistband **10** encincture ***combining form:*** **3** zon **4** zono **6** pleura ***of Aphrodite:*** **6** cestus **7** caestus
girl Friday **9** secretary
girth **4** band, belt, bind, size **5** brace, cinch, strap **6** girdle **7** measure **8** cincture, encircle **10** dimensions **13** circumference
gist **4** core, meat, pith **5** sense, short **6** burden, matter, thrust, upshot **7** bearing **9** substance
gitano **5** gypsy
give **3** air, lot, pay **4** bend, cave, deal, fail, feed, find, hand, pose, sell, vend, vent **5** allot, allow, apply, award, break, grant, issue, offer, spend, throw, yield **6** accord, afford, assign, befall, bestow, betide, chance, confer, devote, direct, donate, expend, extend, fold up, happen, lay out, lot out, market, outlay, relent, render, strike, supply, tender, weaken **7** address, crumple, deliver, dish out, dole out, express, fall out, fork out, furnish, hand out, hold out, inflict, mete out, present, produce, proffer, provide, slacken **8** allocate, collapse, disburse, dispense, disperse, give away, hand over, shell out, transfer, turn over **9** admeasure, apportion, ventilate **10** buckle down, contribute, distribute
give away **4** tell **5** grant, mouth, spill **6** bestow, betray, devote, donate, reveal **7** blab out, divulge, hand out, present, unclose **8** disclose, discover
give back **4** echo **6** refund, retire, return **7** replace, restore, retreat **8** withdraw **9** reinstate
give in **5** yield **6** relent **7** indulge, succumb **9** surrender
give off **4** emit, flow, pour, vent, void **5** issue **7** release **8** throw off **9** discharge
give out **4** deal, dole, drop, emit, fail, mete, vent, wilt **5** issue **6** cave in, peg out, run out **7** release, succumb **8** collapse, throw off **9** break down
giver **5** donor **7** donator **8** bestower **9** conferrer, presenter
give up **4** cede, quit, sell **5** forgo, leave, waive, yield **6** forego, resign, vacate **7** abandon, despair, despond **8** abdicate, hand over **9** surrender **10** relinquish
gizmo see **gadget**
glabrous **4** bald **6** shaven, smooth **8** hairless **9** beardless **12** smooth-shaven
glacial **3** icy **4** cold **5** chill, gelid, nippy **6** arctic, chilly, frigid, frosty **8** freezing
glacier **3** ice **6** ice cap **8** ice sheet ***Alaska:*** **4** Muir, Taku **6** Bering ***Antarctica:*** **9** Beardmore ***deposit:*** **4** kame **5** esker **6** placer **7** moraine **8** diluvium ***fissure:*** **8** crevasse ***fragment:*** **4** berg **7** iceberg ***hill:*** **7** drumlin ***Karakoram:*** **5** Biafo **7** Baltoro ***New Zealand:*** **6** Tasman ***pinnacle:*** **5** serac
glad **4** fain **5** happy, jolly, merry **6** blithe, bright, cheery, genial, jocund, jovial, joyful, joyous **7** beaming, gleeful, pleased, radiant, tickled **8** cheerful, mirthful, pleasant, rejoiced **9** delighted, gratified **11** exhilarated **12** lighthearted
gladden **5** cheer, elate **6** arride, please **7** delight, gratify, happify, rejoice **8** pleasure
glade **5** grove, marsh **8** clearing
gladiator **7** battler, fighter **9** combatant ***Roman:*** **9** retiarius
gladly **4** fain, lief
gladness **3** joy **4** glee **5** bliss, cheer, mirth **7** jollity, joyance **9** happiness **10** joyfulness
gladstone **3** bag
glamorous **5** siren **8** alluring, charming, magnetic **9** seductive **10** attractive, bewitching, enchanting **11** captivating, fascinating
glamour **5** charm, magic **6** allure, appeal **8** charisma, witchery **9** magnetism **10** witchcraft **11** fascination
glance **3** rub **4** buff, kiss, peek, peep, skim, skip **5** brush, carom, flash, glaze, gleam, glime, glint, gloss, graze, shave, shine, touch **6** bounce, careen, polish, scrape **7** burnish, contact, furbish, glimmer, glimpse, glisten, glitter, shimmer, sparkle, twinkle **8** ricochet **9** coruscate
gland **5** gonad, liver, organ **6** thymus **7** adrenal, mammary, thyroid **8** exocrine, pancreas, prostate **9** endocrine, pituitary **11** parathyroid ***secretion:*** **7** hormone ***sex:*** **5** gonad ***swelling:*** **4** bubo
glare **4** bore, gape, gawk, gaze, glow,

peer 5 blaze, flame, flash, frown, gleam, gloat, lower, scowl, stare 6 dazzle, glower, goggle 7 glisten, glitter

glaring 4 loud, rank 5 gaudy, plain, vivid 6 brazen, flashy, garish, tawdry, tinsel 7 blatant, capital, chintzy 8 flagrant 9 egregious, obtrusive 10 noticeable 11 conspicuous, outstanding

Glasgow's patron saint 5 Mingo 9 Kentigern

glass 4 lens, pane 5 image, lense, prism 6 mirror 7 reflect 9 barometer, telescope ***combining form:*** 4 hyal, vitr 5 hyalo, vitro ***container:*** 3 jar 6 beaker, bottle ***decorative:*** 7 schmelz 8 schmelze ***drinking:*** 3 mug 5 stein 6 goblet, jigger, rummer, seidel 7 snifter, tumbler 8 schooner ***gem:*** 5 paste 6 strass ***magnifying:*** 5 loupe ***milky:*** 7 opaline ***volcanic:*** 7 perlite 8 obsidian

glasses 5 specs 6 shades 7 goggles 10 spectacles

glass-like 6 vitric 8 vitreous

glassmaker 6 blower 7 glazier, Tiffany

glassmaking ***oven:*** 4 lehr ***tool:*** 5 ponty 6 pontil 8 blowpipe

Glaucus ***father:*** 5 Minos 8 Sisyphus ***mother:*** 6 Merope 8 Pasiphae ***son:*** 11 Bellerophon

glaze 3 rub 4 buff, coat 5 glint, gloss, sheen, shine 6 enamel, glance, luster, polish 7 burnish, furbish

gleam 3 ray 4 beam, glow 5 flash, glint, sheen, shine 6 glance 7 glimmer, glisten, glitter, radiate, shimmer, sparkle, twinkle 8 radiance 11 coruscation, scintillate 13 scintillation

gleaming 5 shiny 6 glossy, sheeny 7 shining 8 lustrous, polished 9 burnished 10 glistening

glean 4 cull, reap 6 garner, gather, pick up 7 extract

glede 4 kite 6 osprey

glee 3 joy 5 mirth 6 gaiety, levity 7 delight, jollity 8 hilarity, pleasure 9 enjoyment, jocundity, joviality, merriment

gleeful 3 gay 4 boon 5 jolly, merry 6 blithe, jocund, jovial 8 mirthful 10 blithesome

glen 4 dale, vale 6 dingle, valley ***deep:*** 5 gorge 6 ravine ***Scottish:*** 5 heuch, heugh

glib 4 easy 5 slick 6 facile, fluent, smooth 7 voluble 8 eloquent, flippant, vocative, well-hung 9 talkative 10 articulate

glide 3 fly 4 flow, sail, skim, slip 5 creep, float, mouse, skate, skulk, slick, slide, slink, sneak, steal 7 gumshoe, slither 8 glissade, volplane 9 pussyfoot

glimmer 4 glow 5 flash, gleam, glint 6 glance 7 glisten, glitter, shimmer, sparkle, twinkle 9 coruscate 11 coruscation 13 scintillation

glimpse 4 look, peek, peep 5 stime 6 glance

glint 5 flash, glaze, gleam, gloss, sheen, shine 6 glance, luster, polish 7 glimmer, glisten, glitter, shimmer, sparkle, twinkle 9 coruscate 11 coruscation 13 scintillation

glissade 4 skim, slip 5 glide, slick, slide 7 slither

glisten 5 flash, gleam, glint, shine 6 glance 7 glimmer, glitter, shimmer, sparkle, twinkle 9 coruscate 11 coruscation

glitter 5 flash, gleam, glint, shine 6 glance 7 glimmer, glisten, shimmer, spangle, sparkle, twinkle 9 bespangle, coruscate 11 coruscation 13 scintillation

glittering 5 gaudy, showy 7 shining 9 brilliant, clinquant, sparkling

gloaming 3 eve 4 dusk 7 evening 8 eventide, owl-light, twilight 9 nightfall

gloat 4 bore, gape, gawk, gaze, peer 5 exult, glare, stare 6 goggle

global 5 grand 6 cosmic 7 general, overall 8 all-round, catholic 9 inclusive, planetary, universal, worldwide

globe 3 orb 4 ball 5 earth, round, world 6 planet, sphere 7 rondure ***half:*** 10 hemisphere

globule 4 bead, drib, drip, drop 6 gobbet 7 driblet, droplet 8 spherule

gloom 3 dim 4 dusk, murk 5 bedim, blues, cloud, dumps, frown, lower, scowl 6 darken, glower 7 becloud, obscure, sadness 8 darkness, overcast 9 adumbrate, dejection 10 depression, melancholy, overshadow, the dismals 11 unhappiness 12 mournfulness

gloomy 3 dim, dun, sad 4 cold, dark, dour, drab, dull, glum, ugly 5 black, bleak, drear, dusky, morne, murky, muzzy, sulky, surly 6 dismal, dreary, morose, solemn, somber, sullen 7 crabbed, joyless, obscure, stygian, unhappy 8 dejected, desolate, downcast, funereal, mournful 9 cheerless, depressed, lightless, mirthless, oppressed, saturnine, tenebrous, woebegone 10 acheronian, acherontic, caliginous, depressant, depressing, depressive, despondent, lugubrious, melancholy, oppressive, tenebrific 11 dispiriting, pessimistic 12 disconsolate, discouraging

glorify 4 hymn, laud 5 bless, cry up, erect, exalt, extol, honor 6 praise, uprear 7 dignify, ennoble, magnify, sublime 8 eulogize 9 celebrate 10 aggrandize, panegyrize

glorious 5 grand, great, noble, proud 6 divine, groovy, superb 7 radiant, sublime 8 gorgeous, lustrous, majestic, splendid, stunning 9 beautiful, brilliant, effulgent, hunky-dory, marvelous, ravishing 11 magnificent, resplendent, splendorous

glory 4 fame, halo 5 exult, honor 6 praise, renown 7 acclaim, aureole, delight, triumph 8 eminence, jubilate, splendor 9 greatness 11 distinction 12 magnificence
gloss 4 buff 5 glaze, glint, sheen, shine 6 enamel, glance, luster, polish 7 burnish, furbish, varnish 8 annotate 9 sleekness, slickness
glossary 6 clavis 7 lexicon
gloss over 5 white 6 veneer, whiten 7 falsify, varnish 8 palliate 9 extenuate, sugarcoat, whitewash 12 misrepresent
glossy 5 shiny, sleek 6 sheeny, sleeky, smarmy 7 shining 8 gleaming, lustrous, polished 9 burnished 10 glistening ***fabric:*** 4 silk 5 satin ***paint:*** 6 enamel
glove 4 mitt 5 cover 6 mitten, sheath 8 gauntlet
glow 4 pink, rose 5 blare, blaze, bloom, blush, color, flame, flare, flush, glare, rouge, shine 6 mantle, pinken, redden 7 blossom, crimson, foxfire
glower 4 gaze 5 frown, gloom, scowl, stare
glowing 3 hot 5 fiery, flush, ruddy, shiny 6 ardent, fervid, florid, heated 7 blazing, burning, candent, fervent, flaming, flushed, radiant 8 dazzling, rubicund, sanguine 10 candescent, hot-blooded, passionate 11 full-blooded, impassioned 12 enthusiastic
gloze over see **gloss over**
Gluck opera 5 Orfeo 6 Armide 7 Alceste
glucose 5 sugar
glue 3 fix 4 join 5 epoxy, paste, stick 6 adhere, attach, cement 8 adhesive, mucilage
gluey 5 gooey, gummy 6 cloggy, sticky, stodgy 8 adhesive
glum 4 dour 5 moody, sulky, surly 6 gloomy, morose, silent, sullen 7 crabbed 8 taciturn 9 depressed, oppressed, saturnine
glut 4 clog, cloy, cram, fill, jade, pall, sate 5 feast, gorge, stuff 6 stodge 7 satiate, surfeit
glutinous 4 ropy 5 gluey, gummy 6 sticky 7 viscous
glutton 3 hog, pig 5 gulch 8 gourmand 9 chowhound
gluttonous 7 hoggish, piggish 8 edacious, ravening, ravenous 9 indulgent, rapacious, voracious 11 intemperate
gluttony 7 edacity 8 gulosity
G-man 3 fed
gnarl 4 bend, knot 5 snarl, twist 6 deform 7 contort, distort
gnash 4 bite 5 grind
gnat 3 fly 4 pest 6 insect
gnaw 3 eat 4 bite, chew 5 annoy, erode, harry, scour, tease, worry 6 harass, nibble, pester, plague 7 bedevil, consume, corrode, eat away, hagride 8 wear away
gnome 3 elf, saw 4 rule 5 axiom, dwarf, maxim, moral, troll 6 dictum, goblin, sprite, truism 7 brocard 8 aphorism, apothegm
gnostic 4 sage, wise 6 sophic 7 knowing 9 insighted, sagacious 10 discerning, insightful, perceptive 13 knowledgeable
go 3 act, die, fit, fly, hie, pep, run, set, try 4 bear, bout, exit, fare, flee, give, jibe, like, move, pass, quit, shot, wend, work 5 abide, agree, apply, brook, drive, enjoy, event, fit in, fling, leave, occur, range, recur, refer, siege, spell, stint, vigor, whirl 6 accord, become, belong, decamp, demise, depart, elapse, endure, energy, escape, expire, extend, get off, happen, pan out, pop off, push on, repair, resort, retire, thrive, travel 7 abscond, advance, come off, conform, crumble, decease, episode, get away, journey, potency, proceed, prosper, pull out, push off, succeed, success, succumb, take off 8 collapse, flourish, function, incident, occasion, pass away, run along, shove off, tolerate, vitality, withdraw 9 happening, hardihood 10 correspond, get-up-and-go, occurrence ***against:*** 5 fight 6 oppose ***ahead:*** 4 lead 7 precede, proceed 8 continue, progress ***along:*** 5 agree 6 concur ***around:*** 5 avoid 7 compass 10 circumvent ***at:*** 6 attack 8 approach ***away:*** 3 off 4 exit, quit, scat, shoo 5 leave, scram 6 depart, retire ***back:*** 6 recede, return, revert 7 regress, retreat ***back on:*** 6 betray, renege 7 abandon ***back over:*** 6 review 7 retrace ***before:*** 4 lead 7 precede 8 antedate ***beyond:*** 6 exceed 7 surpass ***forward:*** 7 advance, proceed 8 continue, progress ***in:*** 5 enter 7 ingress 9 penetrate ***out:*** 4 date, exit 5 leave 6 egress ***Scottish:*** 3 gae ***through:*** 3 cut 6 endure 7 undergo 9 penetrate 10 experience ***together:*** 3 fit 4 suit 5 agree, befit 6 become 9 agree with, harmonize ***with:*** 4 date, suit 5 befit 6 escort 9 accompany
goad 3 egg, sic 4 prod, spur 5 drive, egg on, impel, prick 6 exhort, prompt, propel 7 impetus, impulse 8 catalyst, stimulus 9 impulsion, incentive, stimulant
go-ahead 4 okay 9 clearance, gumptious 10 green light 11 up-and-coming 12 enterprising 13 authorization
goal 3 aim, end, use 4 duty, mark 6 object, target 7 purpose 8 ambition, function 9 objective, quaesitum
goat 3 kid, ram 5 billy, nanny, patsy 6 alpaca, angora, nubian 7 fall guy 8 cashmere 9 scapegoat ***combining form:*** 5 capri ***female:*** 3 doe 5 nanny ***flesh:*** 6 chevon ***genus:*** 5 Capra ***Himalayan:*** 4 tahr, thar

male: 4 buck 5 billy *wild:* 4 ibex 7 markhor
goat antelope 5 goral, serow 7 chamois
goatee 5 beard 7 Vandyke
goatfish 6 mullet
goatish 3 hot 4 lewd 7 caprine, hircine, lustful, satyric 8 prurient 9 lickerish 10 lascivious, libidinous, passionate 12 concupiscent
goat-man deity 3 Pan
goat nut 6 jojoba
goatsfoot 8 goutweed
goatskin 9 chevrette
gob 3 wad 4 clod, hunk, lump, mass 5 chunk, mouth 6 nugget
gobbet 4 drip, drop 7 driblet, droplet, globule
gobble 4 bolt, cram, gulp, slop, wolf 5 slosh 6 englut, guzzle 11 ingurgitate
gobbledygook see **gibberish**
go-between 5 agent, envoy 6 broker 8 attorney, emissary, mediator 9 middleman 10 arbitrator, interagent, interceder, matchmaker, negotiator 11 intercessor 12 entrepreneur, intermediary, intermediate 13 intermediator
goblet 5 glass 6 vessel
goblin 3 elf, fay 4 bhut, bogy 5 bogie, bogle, fairy, gnome, pooka 6 booger, sprite 7 brownie 8 barghest, bogeyman
gobs 4 heap, wads 5 loads, reams, scads 6 oodles 8 slathers 10 quantities
god 4 idol 5 deity 7 creator 8 Almighty, divinity, immortal *combining form:* 3 the 4 theo *false:* 4 baal *French:* 4 dieu *Latin:* 4 deus *Spanish:* 4 dios; (see specific entries (as **Greek; Roman**) for names of specific gods and goddeses)
God Bless America composer 6 Berlin
goddess 4 idol 5 deity 8 divinity, immortal *Latin:* 3 dea; (see note at **god**)
godfather 3 don 4 capo 7 sponsor
God-fearing 5 pious 6 devout 8 reverent 9 religious
godforsaken 6 dismal 7 pitiful 8 desolate, pitiable, wretched 9 miserable, neglected 11 unfortunate
Godiva's husband 7 Leofric
godless 6 wicked 7 impious, infidel 8 agnostic 9 atheistic 11 irreligious, unreligious
godlike 6 deific, divine 8 deifical, immortal
godly 4 holy 5 pious 6 deific, devout, divine 7 angelic, saintly 9 pietistic, prayerful, religious
go down 3 dip, sag, set 4 drop, fall, fold, sink 5 droop, pitch, slump 6 cave in, plunge, submit, topple, tumble 7 crumple, decline, descend, founder, go under, succumb 8 collapse, keel over, submerge, submerse 9 surrender
God's acre 8 cemetery 9 graveyard 10 churchyard, necropolis 11 polyandrium 12 burial ground, memorial park, potter's field 13 burying ground
godsend 4 boon, good 7 benefit 8 blessing 9 advantage 11 benediction
Goethe work 5 Faust 6 Egmont, Stella 7 Clavigo 10 Prometheus
goffer 5 crimp, flute, plait
go-getter 6 dynamo, peeler 7 hustler, rustler 8 live wire 11 self-starter
goggle 3 eye 4 bore, gape, gawk, gaze, look, ogle, peer 5 glare, gloat, stare
goggles 5 specs 7 glasses 8 blinkers 10 spectacles
Gogol novel 9 Dead Souls 10 Taras Bulba
Gog's land 5 Magog
goiter 6 struma 8 swelling
gola 4 cyma 7 granary 9 storeroom, warehouse
Golconda see **gold mine**
gold 4 gilt 5 aurum, metal, money 6 riches, wealth, yellow 7 bullion, element 8 treasure *bar:* 5 ingot *combining form:* 4 auri, auro 5 chrys 6 chryso *fool's:* 6 pyrite *heraldic:* 2 or *Spanish:* 3 oro *symbol:* 2 Au
goldbrick 3 bum 4 idle, laze, lazy, loaf, loll 6 dawdle, loiter, lounge 7 shirker, slacker, slinker
Gold Bug author 3 Poe
gold cloth 4 lamé
gold-covered 4 gilt
golden 4 gilt, rich 5 blond, straw 6 blonde, flaxen, gilded, liquid, mellow, yellow 7 aureate, aureous, honeyed 8 Hyblaean
golden-ager 5 elder 6 senior 7 ancient, oldster 8 old-timer 13 senior citizen
golden apple 3 bel 6 tomato 7 hog plum
golden-apples guardian 5 Ithun 6 Ithunn
golden bough 9 mistletoe
golden-crowned accentor 8 ovenbird
goldeneye 4 duck 8 lacewing 9 merrywing
Golden Fleece seeker 5 Jason 8 Argonaut
Golden Hind captain 5 Drake
Golden Horde 6 Tatars 7 Mongols
golden horse 8 palomino
Golden State 10 California
golden wolf 6 chanco
goldfinch 8 graypate 12 yellowhammer
gold mine 7 bonanza 8 El Dorado, Golconda, treasury 13 treasure-house, treasure trove
golem 4 dolt 5 robot 7 machine 9 automaton, blockhead
golf *assistant:* 5 caddy 6 caddie *award:* 8 Ryder Cup 9 Curtis Cup, Walker Cup *club:* 4 iron, wood 5 baffy, cleek, spoon,

wedge **6** driver, mashie, putter **7** brassie, niblick, pitcher **9** metal wood, sand wedge ***club part:*** **3** toe **4** face, grip, head, heel, neck, sole **5** hosel, shaft **6** socket ***course:*** **5** links ***hazard:*** **4** trap **6** bunker **8** sand trap ***mound:*** **3** tee ***score:*** **3** par **5** bogey, bogie, eagle **6** birdie **9** albatross ***stroke:*** **3** ace **4** chip, draw, fade, hook, putt **5** drive, pitch, shank, slice **6** sclaff ***target:*** **3** cup, par, pin **4** flag **5** green **7** fairway ***term:*** **3** lie **4** ball, club, fore, hole, loft **5** divot, rough, round, swing **6** course, hazard, marker, stance, stroke **8** approach, foursome, handicap **9** backswing, downswing, flagstick **10** Vardon grip

golfer **8** linksman ***man:*** **4** Ford (Doug), Kite (Tom) **5** Boros (Julius), Faldo (Nick), Floyd (Ray), Hagen (Walter), Hogan (Ben), Jones (Bobby), Irwin (Hale), Shute (Denny), Snead (Sam) **6** Casper (Billy), Miller (Johnny), Nelson (Byron), Ouimet (Francis), Palmer (Arnold), Player (Gary), Vardon (Harry), Watson (Tom) **7** Guldahl (Ralph), Sarazen (Gene), Stewart (Payne), Trevino (Lee), Woosnam (Ian) **8** Crenshaw (Ben), Nicklaus (Jack), Weiskopf (Tom), Rodriquez (Chi Chi) **10** Middlecoff (Cary) **11** Ballesteros (Seve) ***woman:*** **4** Berg (Patty), King (Betsy) **5** Lopez (Nancy), Rawls (Betsy), Stacy (Hollis), Suggs (Louise) **6** Alcott (Amy), Carner (Joanne), Daniel (Beth), Wright (Mickey) **7** Bradley (Pat), Sheehan (Patty) **8** Zaharias (Babe) **9** Whitworth (Kathy) **10** Stephenson (Jan)

Goliath **5** giant **10** Philistine ***deathplace:*** **4** Elah ***home:*** **4** Gath ***slayer:*** **5** David

Gomer ***father:*** **7** Diblaim ***husband:*** **5** Hosea

gonad **5** gland, ovary **6** testis

gondola **3** car **4** boat **5** chair

gone **4** away, dead, left, lost **6** absent, gravid, parous **7** defunct, extinct, lacking, missing, omitted, wanting **8** childing, departed, enceinte, pregnant, vanished

gonef see **ganef**

Goneril ***father:*** **4** Lear ***husband:*** **6** Albany ***sister:*** **5** Regan **8** Cordelia ***victim:*** **5** Regan

Gone with the Wind ***author:*** **8** Mitchell ***character:*** **6** Ashley **7** Melanie **11** Rhett Butler **13** Scarlett O'Hara ***plantation:*** **4** Tara

gonfalon **4** flag **6** banner, ensign **7** pendant, pennant **8** standard **9** banderole

goo **4** crud, gook, goop, guck, gunk, muck

goober **3** nut **6** peanut

good **3** apt, fit **4** able, boon, just, meet, nice, pure **5** brave, right, sound, whole **6** adroit, au fait, clever, cogent, common, decent, humane, intact, kindly, proper, seemly, toward, useful **7** benefic, benefit, capable, fitting, gainful, godsend, healthy, helpful, welcome, welfare **8** adequate, all right, blessing, decorous, flawless, hygienic, innocent, interest, pleasant, pleasing, salutary, sensible, skillful, straight, unmarred, virtuous **9** advantage, agreeable, blameless, competent, congenial, exemplary, favorable, guiltless, healthful, incorrupt, justified, lily-white, lucrative, qualified, righteous, tolerable, undamaged, untainted, well-being, wholesome, workmanly **10** acceptable, altruistic, beneficial, benevolent, charitable, gratifying, inculpable, profitable, propitious, prosperity, salubrious, sufficient, unblamable, unimpaired, worthwhile **11** appropriate, benediction, considerate, pleasurable, pleasureful, respectable, unblemished, uncorrupted, well-behaved, well-founded, workmanlike **12** advantageous, considerable, eleemosynary, humanitarian, remunerative, salutiferous, satisfactory, well-grounded **13** philanthropic ***combining form:*** **2** eu **5** agath **6** agatho ***French:*** **3** bon ***German:*** **3** gut ***Spanish:*** **5** bueno

good-bye **4** ta-ta **5** adieu, congé **6** so long **7** cheerio, parting **8** farewell, toodle-oo **9** departing **11** leave-taking, valedictory ***French:*** **5** adieu ***German:*** **8** lebe wohl ***Japanese:*** **8** sayonara ***Spanish:*** **5** adios

Good Earth author **4** Buck

good-for-nothing **6** drafty, drossy, no-good, waster **7** fustian, inutile, nothing, rounder, useless, wastrel **8** feckless, unworthy **9** valueless, worthless **10** ne'er-do-well, profligate, scapegrace, unpurposed **11** meaningless, purposeless

good-humored see **good-natured**

good-looking **4** fair **6** comely, lovely, pretty **8** handsome **9** beauteous, beautiful **10** attractive

goodly **5** ample, large **6** comely, pretty **8** handsome **9** excellent **12** considerable

good-natured **4** easy, mild **6** genial, jovial **7** amiable, lenient **8** cheerful, obliging **9** gemütlich **10** altruistic, benevolent, charitable **11** complaisant

goodness **5** honor, merit **6** purity, virtue **7** honesty, probity **8** chastity, morality **9** integrity, rectitude, rightness **11** benevolence, uprightness **13** righteousness

goods **4** gear, line **5** stock, wares **7** effects **8** chattels, movables **9** vendibles **10** belongings **11** commodities, merchandise, possessions ***smuggled:*** **10** contraband ***stolen:*** **4** loot **5** booty **6** spoils ***thrown overboard:*** **5** lagan, ligan **6** jetsam

good-tasting **5** sapid, tasty **6** savory **8** tasteful **9** palatable, relishing, toothsome **10** appetizing, flavorsome

goodwill **5** amity, favor **6** comity **7** charity, rapport **8** alacrity, altruism, dispatch, kindness, sympathy 9 readiness, tolerance 10 expedition, friendship, generosity, kindliness 11 benevolence, helpfulness, promptitude 12 friendliness

goody 5 candy, treat 6 bonbon, dainty, morsel, tidbit, titbit 8 delicacy, kickshaw

goody-goody 4 prig 5 prude 6 Grundy 7 puritan 8 bluenose, comstock 9 Mrs. Grundy, nice Nelly

gooey 5 gluey, gummy, mushy, sappy, sobby, soupy 6 cloggy, drippy, slushy, sticky, stodgy 7 maudlin 8 adhesive 11 sentimental

goof 3 err 4 boob, dolt, mess 5 booby, botch, chump, dunce, gum up 6 bobble, bollix, bungle 7 blunder, fathead, louse up 8 dolthead, lunkhead

go off 4 blow 5 burst 7 explode 8 detonate

goofy 5 crazy, silly 6 stupid 7 foolish

gook 3 rot 4 crud, goop, gunk, muck 5 bilge, gumbo, hooey, trash 6 drivel

go on 3 act 4 bear, quit 5 carry 6 acquit, behave, demean, deport, hang on 7 carry on, comport, conduct, persist 8 continue 9 persevere

goon 3 sap 4 boob, dolt, dope, thug 7 hoodlum

gooney 9 albatross

goop 4 gook, gunk, muck 5 gumbo

goose 4 bird, dolt, poke 5 solan 9 simpleton *cry:* 4 honk, yang *genus:* 5 Anser *Hawaiian:* 4 nene *male:* 6 gander *relating to:* 8 anserine *snow:* 4 chen, wavy 5 wavey *wild:* 5 brant 7 graylag, greylag 8 barnacle, bernicle *young:* 7 gosling

goose egg 4 zero 5 aught, ought, zilch 6 cipher, naught, nought 7 nothing

gooseflesh 5 bumps 7 pimples

gopher 6 marmot, rodent 8 squirrel, tortoise

Gopher State 9 Minnesota

Gordian knot cutter 9 Alexander

Gordius' son 5 Midas

gore 4 stab, tush, tusk 5 blood, slime, wound 6 pierce

gorge 3 gap 4 cloy, fill, glut, jade, pall, sate 5 chasm, cleft, clove, flume, gulch, stuff 6 arroyo, clough, devour, gobble, guzzle, ravine, stodge 7 couloir, overeat, satiate, surfeit 11 overindulge *Arizona:* 11 Grand Canyon *China:* 7 Yangtze *Colorado:* 5 Royal

gorgeous 5 grand, plush, proud 6 lavish, lovely, pretty, superb 7 opulent, sublime 8 glorious, splendid 9 beautiful, luxurious, sumptuous 10 impressive 11 magnificent, resplendent, splendorous

Gorgon 6 Medusa, Stheno 7 Euryale *father:* 7 Phorcus, Phorcys *mother:* 4 Ceto *sentinel:* 4 Enyo 5 Deino 6 Graeae, Graiae 8 Pephredo

gorilla 3 ape 6 monkey 7 primate 10 anthropoid

Gorki drama 14 The Lower Depths

gorse 5 furze 7 juniper

gory 6 bloody 7 imbrued 8 sanguine 10 sanguinary 11 ensanguined, sanguineous 12 bloodstained

gospel 5 truth 6 truism 8 doctrine, teaching

gossamer 3 web 5 filmy, gauzy, sheer 6 flimsy 7 tiffany 10 diaphanous 11 transparent

gossip 3 cry 4 blab, buzz, chat, talk 5 clack, on-dit, prate, rumor, sieve, tabby 6 babble, claver, report, rumble, tattle 7 chatter, hearsay, prattle, rumorer 8 bigmouth, busybody, informer, quidnunc, telltale 9 carrytale, grapevine 10 circulator, mumblenews, newsmonger, talebearer 11 rumormonger, scandalizer, scuttlebutt

Gotham 7 New York

Gothic 4 rude, wild 5 crude 6 brutal, coarse, Hunnic, savage 7 Hunnish 8 barbaric 9 barbarian, barbarous 11 uncivilized

Gouda 6 cheese

gouge 3 con, dig 4 tool 5 cheat, exact, pinch, screw, wrest, wring 6 extort, wrench 7 squeeze, swindle 9 shake down 10 overcharge

goulash 4 stew 6 jumble, medley 8 mishmash

go under 4 fall, sink 6 go down, submit 7 founder, succumb 8 submerge, submerse 9 surrender

Gounod work 5 Faust 8 Ave Maria

gourd 4 pepo 5 fruit, melon 6 bottle, vessel 7 pumpkin 8 calabash, cucurbit *instrument:* 6 maraca

gourmand see glutton; gourmet

gourmet 7 epicure 9 bon vivant 10 gastronome 11 gastronomer 12 gastronomist

gout 4 blob, clot 5 spurt 6 splash 7 podagra 8 swelling

govern 3 run 4 head, lead, rule, sway 5 guide, reign, steer 6 direct, handle, manage, master, render 7 command, conduct, control, execute, oversee 8 carry out, dominate, overrule, regulate, shepherd 9 supervise 10 administer

governess 4 nana 5 nanny, nurse 6 duenna, nannie 8 mistress 9 nursemaid

government 4 rule 5 power 6 polity, regime 7 conduct, control, regency, regimen, tyranny 8 guidance, monarchy, republic 9 authority, autocracy, democracy, direction, hierarchy, oligarchy 10 management 11 aristocracy 12 dictatorship, organization *autocratic:* 7 czarism 9 despotism 10 absolutism 12 dictatorship *by a few:*

9 oligarchy ***by eight:*** 8 octarchy ***by one:*** 8 monarchy ***by three:*** 8 triarchy 11 triumvirate ***by women:*** 8 gynarchy ***combining form:*** 5 archy, cracy 6 ocracy ***official:*** 6 consul, syndic 8 diplomat 10 bureaucrat ***relating to:*** 9 political ***science:*** 8 politics ***without:*** 7 anarchy

government agency 2 VA 3 CIA, FAA, FBI, FCC, FDA, FHA, GAO, GPO, HUD, ICC, NBS, NRC, TVA 4 FEPC, NASA

governor 3 bey 4 head, lord 5 chief, nabob, pilot, ruler 6 leader, rector, regent 7 captain, manager, viceroy 8 director, official 9 executive, regulator 10 commandant, controller, magistrate ***Chinese:*** 6 tuchun ***of a fort:*** 7 alcaide 9 castellan, chatelain ***Persian:*** 6 satrap ***Turkish:*** 8 hospador

gown 4 robe, toga 5 dress, frock, habit, tunic 6 banian, banyan, camise, clothe, kimono, mantua 7 cassock, chemise, garment 8 peignoir ***hospital:*** 6 johnny

goy 7 gentile

grab 3 hog, nab 4 nail, take 5 catch, clasp, grasp, seize 6 clutch, snatch, tackle 7 grapple

grabby 5 itchy 6 greedy 8 covetous, desirous, grasping 10 prehensile 11 acquisitive

grace 4 ease 5 adorn, charm, favor, mercy 6 lenity, polish, prayer, thanks, virtue 7 caritas, charity, dignify, dignity 8 blessing, clemency, easiness, elegance, goodness, kindness, leniency, petition 9 embellish 10 indulgence, invocation, suppleness 11 benediction, forbearance 12 thanksgiving

graceful 4 airy, deft, easy 6 featly, gainly, smooth, urbane 7 elegant, flowing, genteel, refined 8 debonair, polished

graceless 4 wild 5 inept 6 vulgar 7 awkward, unhappy 8 barbaric 9 barbarian, barbarous, ill-chosen, tasteless 10 outlandish 11 unfortunate 12 infelicitous

Graces 6 Aglaia (brilliance), Charis, Thalia (bloom) 8 Charites (plural) 10 Euphrosyne (joy) ***mother:*** 5 Aegle

gracious 4 easy, kind, mild 5 preux 6 benign, clubby, genial, kindly 7 affable, amiable, cordial, courtly, gallant, starchy, stately 8 mannered, obliging, outgoing, sociable 9 benignant, bonhomous, congenial, courteous

grackle 3 jaw 7 jackdaw 9 blackbird

gradation 4 step 5 range, shade 6 ablaut, change, degree, nuance, series 8 position 9 variation 10 difference, divergence

grade 3 peg 4 lean, rank, rate, rung, sort, step, tier, tilt 5 class, group, notch, order, slant, slope, stage 6 assort, degree, estate, league 7 arrange, caliber, incline, leaning, quality 8 appraise, category, classify, evaluate, grouping

Grade A 3 top 4 fine 5 prime 7 capital 8 five-star, superior, top-notch 9 excellent, first-rate, top-drawer 10 first-class

gradient 4 lean, ramp, tilt 5 slant, slope 7 incline, leaning 11 inclination ***combining form:*** 5 cline 6 clinal

gradine 4 seat, step 5 shelf 6 chisel

gradually 8 bit by bit 9 piecemeal 10 step by step

graduate ***female:*** 6 alumna 7 alumnae (plural) ***male:*** 6 alumni (plural) 7 alumnus

Graeae, Graiae 4 Enyo 5 Deino 8 Pephredo ***father:*** 7 Phorcus, Phorcys ***mother:*** 4 Ceto ***sisters:*** 7 Gorgons

graft 4 join, mend 5 crime, scion, unite 6 attach, boodle, fasten, inarch 7 implant, topwork

grail 3 cup 7 chalice, platter

grain 3 bit, jot, rye 4 corn, iota, meal, mite, oats, rice 5 crumb, fiber, maize, speck, trace, wheat 6 barley, cereal, tittle 7 granule, smidgen, sorghum, texture 8 molecule, particle ***bundle:*** 4 bale 5 sheaf ***chute:*** 6 hopper ***ear:*** 5 spica, spike ***elevator:*** 4 silo ***mixture:*** 6 fodder ***row:*** 5 swath 7 windrow

grainy 6 coarse 8 granular

grammarian ***Roman:*** 7 Donatus

grammatical case 6 dative 8 ablative, genitive, locative, vocative 9 objective 10 accusative, nominative, possessive, subjective

grampus 5 whale 8 cetacean, scorpion 9 blackfish

Granada ***building:*** 8 Alhambra ***citadel:*** 8 Alcazaba ***last Moorish king:*** 7 Boabdil

granary 3 bin 4 gola, silo 10 repository, storehouse

grand 4 epic, huge 5 gaudy, lofty, noble, royal, showy 6 august, flashy, garish, lavish, lordly, ornate, superb 7 exalted, stately, sublime 8 baronial, elevated, gorgeous, imposing, magnific, majestic, princely, splendid, towering 9 luxurious, sumptuous 10 impressive, monumental, prodigious, stupendous, tremendous 11 magnificent 12 ostentatious

Grand Canyon ***explorer:*** 6 Powell ***state:*** 7 Arizona

grande dame 6 matron 7 dowager 9 matriarch

grandee 5 pasha 6 bashaw 8 nobleman

grandeur 4 pomp 7 dignity, majesty 8 nobility, splendor, vastness 9 greatness, largeness, loftiness, nobleness, sublimity 10 augustness 11 stateliness 12 magnificence

grand inquisitor ***Spanish:*** 10 Torquemada

grandiose 4 epic, vast 5 lofty, noble, royal, showy 6 august, cosmic, lordly 7 stately, utopian 8 imposing, majestic, princely 9 ambitious, visionary 11 magnificent, pretentious 12 ostentatious
grandmother ***Russian:*** 8 babushka ***Scottish:*** 6 gudame
grange 4 farm 5 lodge 9 farmhouse
granite 4 rock 6 aplite
Granite State 12 New Hampshire
grant 3 aid, own 4 alms, avow, cede, dole, gift, give 5 admit, allow, award, let on, own up, yield 6 accord, bestow, confer, donate, fess up, permit 7 charity, concede, confess, entitle, handout, present, subsidy 8 bequeath, donation 9 vouchsafe 10 assistance, relinquish, subvention 11 acknowledge, benefaction 12 contribution 13 appropriation
granular 5 rough, sandy 6 coarse, grainy
granule 4 pill, spot 5 grain 6 pellet 8 particle
grape 3 fox, uva 4 Bual 5 Gamay, Pinot 6 Arinto, Burger, Gentil, Merlot, muscat 7 Albillo, Aligote, Barbera, Catawba, Concord, Furmint, Niagara, sultana 8 Aleatico, Cabernet, Charbono, Delaware, Friularo, Grenache, Isabella, labrusca, malvasia, muscadel, Nebbiolo, Riesling, Semillon, Sylvaner, Thompson, Traminer, vinifera, Viognier 9 Chasselas, Lambrusco, Malvoisie, muscadine, Pinot Gris, Pinot Noir, Sauvignon, Trebbiano, zinfandel 10 Grignolino, muscadelle, Pinot Blanc, Verdicchio 11 Chenin Blanc, Mavrodaphne, Petite Sirah, scuppernong ***dried:*** 6 raisin ***drink:*** 4 wine ***pulp:*** 4 rape 6 pomace ***residue:*** 4 marc
grapefruit 6 pomelo
Grapes of Wrath ***author:*** 9 Steinbeck ***family:*** 4 Joad ***people:*** 5 Okies
grapevine 4 buzz, talk 5 on-dit, rumor 6 gossip, report, rumble 7 hearsay
graph 3 map 5 chart 6 sketch 7 diagram, outline 8 nomogram
graphic 5 clear, lucid, vivid 6 cogent, visual 7 precise, telling 8 clear-cut, definite, explicit, incisive, pictoric, striking 9 pictorial, realistic 10 compelling
graphite 4 lead 6 carbon 8 plumbago
grapnel 4 hook 6 anchor
grapple 3 nab 4 grab, grip, hold, take 5 catch, clamp, clasp, grasp, gripe, seize 6 bucket, clench, clinch, clutch, snatch, tenure, tussle 7 scuffle, wrestle
grasp 3 dig, see 4 grip, have, hent, hold, know, take 5 catch, clamp, clasp, gripe 6 accept, clench, clinch, clutch, fathom, follow, take in, tenure 7 cognize, compass, grapple 8 envisage, perceive 9 apprehend 10 appreciate, comprehend, understand
graspable 5 lucid 8 knowable 10 fathomable 12 intelligible 13 apprehensible
grasping 4 avid 5 itchy 6 grabby, greedy 8 covetous, desirous 9 extorting 10 prehensile 11 acquisitive
grass 3 pot, sod, tea 4 lawn, reed, turf, weed 6 moocah, redtop 7 herbage, panicum, pasture 8 cannabis, Mary Jane 9 cocksfoot, marijuana ***African:*** 6 imphee ***annual:*** 6 darnel 8 teosinte ***Asian:*** 7 vetiver, whangee ***Australian:*** 8 spinifex ***beach:*** 6 marram ***cereal:*** 3 oat, rye 4 milo, teff 5 kafir, maize, proso, wheat 6 kaffir, millet, sorgho 7 sorghum 8 feterita, triticum ***clump:*** 4 tuft 7 tussock ***combining form:*** 6 gramin 7 gramini ***dried:*** 3 hay ***European:*** 7 Bermuda, timothy ***fiber:*** 4 flax ***fragrant:*** 10 citronella ***giant:*** 5 otate ***Mexican:*** 7 zacaton ***pasture:*** 5 Bahia, grama ***perennial:*** 5 muhly 6 fescue, quitch, zoysia 7 esparto, galleta ***prairie:*** 8 bluestem ***second growth:*** 5 rowen ***tropical:*** 5 cogon 6 bamboo
grasshopper 4 grig 6 locust 7 katydid
grassland 3 lea 5 field 6 meadow 7 pasture, prairie ***African:*** 4 veld 5 veldt ***flat:*** 7 savanna 8 savannah ***South American:*** 5 pampa
grate 3 get, jar 4 bark, fray, gall, rasp, rile, skin 5 chafe, peeve, pique, scuff 6 abrade, burn up, nettle, scrape 7 provoke, scratch 8 irritate 9 aggravate
grateful 4 good 7 obliged, pleased, welcome 8 beholden, pleasant, renewing, solacing, thankful 9 agreeable, congenial, consoling, delicious, favorable, gratified
Gratiano ***brother:*** 9 Brabantio ***friend:*** 7 Antonio 8 Bassanio ***niece:*** 9 Desdemona ***wife:*** 7 Nerissa
gratify 4 baby, feed, sate 5 favor, feast, humor 6 arride, coddle, oblige, pamper, pander, please 7 appease, cater to, content, delight, gladden, happify, indulge, satisfy
grating 3 dry 4 grid, rasp 5 grill, harsh, rough 6 grille, hoarse 7 jarring, rasping, raucous 8 gridiron, strident 10 stridulent
gratis 4 free 8 costless 10 chargeless, gratuitous 13 complimentary
gratuitous 4 free 6 gratis, wanton 7 unasked, willing 8 baseless, costless 9 unfounded, voluntary 10 bottomless, chargeless, groundless, reasonless, ungrounded 11 uncalled-for, unwarranted 12 indefensible, supererogant 13 complimentary
gratuity 3 fee, tip 4 alms, gift, perk 5 bonus 6 reward 7 cumshaw, douceur, largess 8 donation, offering 9 baksheesh, lagniappe, pourboire 10 perquisite 11 benefaction 12 contribution

grave 3 pit, sad 4 dire, etch, fell, grim, tomb, ugly 5 awful, crypt, drive, fatal, heavy, major, pound, sober, staid, stamp, vault 6 burial, deadly, hammer, incise, sedate, severe, solemn, somber 7 austere, earnest, ghastly, impress, killing, ossuary, serious, weighty 8 catacomb, dreadful, grievous, horrible, terrible 9 dangerous, mausoleum, murderous, ponderous, saturnine, sepulcher, sepulture ***marker:*** 5 stela, stele 6 ledger 8 memorial, monument 9 footstone, headstone, tombstone 11 sarcophagus ***mound:*** 6 barrow 7 tumulus ***robber:*** 5 ghoul

gravel 4 dirt, grit, sand ***ridge:*** 5 esker

graven image 4 idol

graver 5 burin 8 sculptor

graveyard 8 boot hill, cemetery 8 God's acre 10 necropolis 11 polyandrium 12 burial ground, memorial park, potter's field 13 burying ground

gravid 6 parous 8 childing, enceinte, pregnant 9 expectant, expecting 10 parturient

gravity 6 weight 7 dignity 8 sobriety 9 heaviness, solemnity 10 importance, somberness 11 seriousness

gravy 5 juice, sauce 8 dressing, windfall ***French:*** 3 jus

gray 3 ash, old 4 aged, ashy, blah, drab, dull 5 ashen, bleak, color, hoary, slate, slaty, taupe 6 dismal, gloomy, leaden 7 elderly, grizzly, neutral 8 cinerous, gunmetal, overcast 9 colorless ***brownish:*** 7 fuscous ***combining form:*** 4 poli 5 glauc, polio 6 glauco

gray dawn 4 zinc

gray duck 7 gadwall, mallard, pintail

grayfish 7 pollack

gray matter 3 wit 4 head, mind, obex 5 brain 9 intellect

graze 3 dop, rub 4 feed, gall, harm, hurt, kiss, skim, skip, wear 5 brush, carom, chafe, erode, shave, wound 6 abrade, bruise, glance, injure, ruffle 7 contuse, corrade, pasture 8 ricochet

grease 3 fat, oil 4 lard, soil 5 smear 6 smooth 7 lanolin 9 lubricant, lubricate ***combining form:*** 4 sebi, sebo

greasy 4 oily 5 fatty, slick 6 slippy 7 pinguid 8 slippery, slithery, unctuous 10 lubricious, oleaginous

greasy spoon 4 café 5 diner 7 beanery, hashery 9 hash house, lunchroom 10 coffee shop

great 3 big, fat 4 bull, huge, vast 5 famed, grand, husky, large 6 famous, heroic 7 eminent, extreme, immense, notable, supreme, titanic 8 enormous, oversize, renowned 9 excellent, fantastic, important, prominent, wonderful 10 celebrated, celebrious, surpassing 11 illustrious, magnificent, superlative 13 distinguished ***combining form:*** 3 meg 4 mega 5 megal 6 megalo

Great Bear 9 Big Dipper, Ursa Major

Great Britain see England

Great Commoner, the 4 Pitt

Great Emancipator, the 7 Lincoln

greater 4 more, over 6 better, higher, larger 8 superior 9 overlying 11 superjacent

greatest 4 best, most 6 utmost 7 largest, noblest, supreme ***amount:*** 7 maximum

Great Expectations ***author:*** 7 Dickens ***character:*** 3 Pip 5 Biddy 7 Estella, Jaggers 8 Havisham, Magwitch

greathearted 3 big 5 brave, lofty, manly 6 heroic 7 gallant 8 fearless, generous 10 benevolent, chivalrous, courageous 11 considerate, magnanimous

Great Lake 4 Erie 5 Huron 7 Ontario 8 Michigan, Superior

Great Lake State 8 Michigan

grebe 4 bird, fowl 8 dabchick, didapper

Greece ***capital:*** 6 Athens ***monetary unit:*** 7 drachma

greed 7 avarice, avidity 8 cupidity, gluttony, rapacity, voracity 12 ravenousness

greedy 5 itchy 6 grabby 7 miserly, selfish 8 covetous, desirous, esurient, grasping 10 avaricious, gluttonous 11 acquisitive

Greek 6 babble, drivel, jabber 7 Achaean 8 Hellenic, nonsense 9 gibberish ***alien resident:*** 5 metic ***assembly:*** 5 agora, boule ***coin:*** 4 obol 5 hecte 6 lepton, stater ***column:*** 5 Doric, Ionic 10 Corinthian ***contest:*** 4 agon ***counselor:*** 6 Nestor ***cup:*** 5 kylix ***dictator:*** 7 Metaxas ***dragon:*** 9 Eurythion ***drink:*** 4 ouzo ***epic:*** 5 Iliad 7 Odyssey ***Fates:*** 6 Clotho, Moirae 7 Atropos 8 Lachesis

god:

chief: 4 Zeus ***messenger:*** 6 Hermes ***of agriculture:*** 6 Cronus ***of death:*** 8 Thanatos ***of fire:*** 10 Hephaestus ***of healing:*** 9 Asclepius ***of love:*** 4 Eros ***of marriage:*** 5 Hymen ***of physicians:*** 6 Hermes ***of the sea:*** 6 Triton 7 Oceanus 8 Poseidon ***of the sun:*** 6 Helios ***of the underworld:*** 5 Pluto ***of the wind:*** 5 Eurus, Notus 6 Aeolus, Boreas 8 Zephyrus ***of war:*** 4 Ares ***of wine:*** 8 Dionysus ***of woods:*** 3 Pan

goddess:

of agriculture: 7 Demeter ***of beauty:*** 9 Aphrodite ***of dawn:*** 3 Eos ***of discord:*** 4 Eris ***of flowers:*** 7 Chloris ***of harvests:*** 4 Rhea ***of hunting:*** 7 Artemis ***of justice:*** 7 Astraea ***of love:*** 9 Aphrodite ***of marriage:*** 4 Hera ***of night:*** 3 Nyx ***of peace:*** 5 Irene ***of retribution:*** 7 Nemesis ***of the earth:*** 2 Ge 4 Gaea, Gaia ***of the***

moon: 6 Hecate, Hekate, Selena, Selene 7 Artemis, Astarte *of the seasons:* 5 Horae *of the underworld:* 6 Hecate, Hekate *of vengeance:* 7 Nemesis *of victory:* 4 Nike *of wisdom:* 6 Athena *of witchcraft:* 6 Hecate, Hekate *of womanhood:* 4 Hera *of youth:* 4 Hebe
hero: 4 Aias, Ajax 5 Jason 7 Theseus 8 Achilles, Argonaut, Heracles, Hercules, Odysseus 9 Achilleus *historian:* 8 Xenophon 9 Herodotus 10 Thucydides *lawgiver:* 5 Draco, Solon *leader:* 9 Agamemnon *letter:* 2 mu, nu, pi, xi 3 chi, eta, phi, psi, rho, tau 4 beta, iota, zeta 5 alpha, delta, gamma, kappa, omega, sigma, theta 6 lambda 7 epsilon, omicron, upsilon *magistrate:* 6 archon *marketplace:* 5 agora *measure:* 3 ona, pik 4 bema 5 cados, chous, digit, maris, pygon, xylon 6 acaena, bachel, barile, cotula, dichas, gramme, hemina, koilon, pechys, pelame, schene 7 amphora, cyathos, diaulos, hekteus, stadion, stadium, stremma 8 condylos, daktylos, dekapode, dolichos, medimnos, metretes, palaiste, plethron, spithame, stathmos 9 oxybaphon *porch:* 4 stoa *sandwich:* 4 gyro *shield:* 5 pelta *soldier:* 7 hoplite *theater:* 5 odeon, odeum *underworld:* 5 Hades *war cry:* 5 alala *warrior:* 4 Ajax 7 Ulysses 8 Achilles, Diomedes, Odysseus 9 Agamemnon, Palamedes *weight:* 3 mna, oka 4 mina 5 litra, livre 6 diobol, kantar, obolus, stater 7 chalcon, chalque, drachma 8 diobolon, talanton *wine:* 7 retsina, retzina
green 3 raw 5 alive, fresh, plaza, virid, young 6 callow, common, infant, square, unripe 7 celadon, emerald, untried, verdant 8 immature, juvenile, pistache, unversed, youthful 9 unfledged 10 unseasoned 11 unpracticed 13 inexperienced *bluish:* 8 glaucous *combining form:* 4 verd 5 chlor, verdo 6 chloro *grayish:* 5 olive *yellowish:* 7 luteous 10 chartreuse
greenbacks 4 cash, jack 5 bread, dough, money 6 wampum 7 scratch 8 currency 11 legal tender
green-eyed 7 envious, envying, jealous 9 invidious *monster:* 8 jealousy
greenfish 7 opaleye, pollack
greenfly 5 aphid
greengage 4 plum
greenhead 3 fly 5 scaup 7 mallard
greenheart 4 tree 7 bebeeru
greenhorn 4 hick, jake, rube, tyro 5 clown 6 novice, rustic 7 bumpkin, hayseed 9 hillbilly 10 clodhopper, provincial 12 backwoodsman
greenhouse 12 conservatory
Greenland *capital:* 7 Godthab 8 Godthaab *discoverer:* 10 Eric the Red *native:* 3 Ita *settlement:* 4 Etah
green light 2 OK 7 go-ahead 9 clearance 13 authorization
Green Mansions *author:* 6 Hudson *character:* 4 Rima
green monkey 6 guenon
Green Mountain State 7 Vermont
greenness 5 youth 6 spring 7 puberty, rawness 8 verdancy, viridity 9 freshness, youthhood 10 callowness, juvenility, pubescence, springtide, springtime 11 adolescence 12 inexperience, youthfulness
green osier 7 dogwood
green plover 7 lapwing
green poppy 8 foxglove
greenroom 6 lounge
greenstone 7 diabase, diorite 8 nephrite
greet 3 cry 4 hail 6 accost, call to, salute 7 address, receive, welcome
greeting 3 ave, bow 4 hail 5 aloha, hello 6 salute 7 address, welcome 9 reception 10 salutation
gregarious 6 social 8 friendly, outgoing, sociable
gremlin 3 elf, imp 5 gnome 6 sprite
grenade 4 bomb 5 shell 7 missile 9 explosive
grenadier 4 fish 7 rattail, soldier
grenadine 4 pink, yarn 5 syrup 9 carnation
Grendel's slayer 7 Beowulf
Gretchen's lover 5 Faust
Grey's forte 7 Western
grid 5 grate 7 grating, network
griddle 3 pan 5 grill
griddle cake 7 pancake 8 flapjack
gridiron 5 field, grill 7 grating, network
grief 3 rue, woe 4 care 5 dolor, tears 6 regret, sorrow 7 anguish, chagrin, emotion, sadness, trouble 8 distress, hardship 9 bemoaning, bewailing, deploring, heartache, lamenting, suffering 10 affliction, heartbreak 11 lamentation
Grieg work 8 Peer Gynt
grievance 5 cross, rigor, trial, wrong 6 burden, injury 8 hardship 9 complaint, injustice 10 affliction 11 tribulation
grieve 3 cry, rue 4 bear, hurt, keen, moan, pain, wail, weep 5 mourn 6 bemoan, bewail, endure, injure, lament, sorrow, suffer 7 deplore 8 distress 9 constrain
grievous 3 sad 4 dire, fell, sore, ugly 5 grave, major, tough 6 bitter, taxing, woeful 7 exigent, galling, onerous, painful, serious, weighty 8 exacting 9 dangerous, demanding 10 afflictive, burdensome, calamitous, deplorable, lamentable, oppressive 11 distasteful, distressing, regrettable, unfortunate, unpalatable
grill 3 vex 4 cook, grid 5 broil, grate

7 afflict, griddle, torment 8 gridiron, question 11 third degree 12 cross-examine 13 interrogation
grilse 4 fish 6 salmon
grim 3 set 4 cold, dour, fell, firm, hard 5 angry, bleak, cruel, fixed, harsh, lurid, rigid, stern 6 dogged, fierce, grisly, mortal, savage, severe 7 adamant, austere, certain, ghastly, hideous, inhuman, macabre, ominous, wolfish 8 gruesome, horrible, inhumane, obdurate, resolute, ruthless, stubborn, terrible 9 barbarous, ferocious, loathsome, merciless, offensive, repugnant, repulsive, revolting, stringent, truculent 10 determined, forbidding, foreboding, horrifying, implacable, inevitable, inexorable, inflexible, ironfisted, off-putting, relentless, terrifying, unyielding, vindictive 11 unflinching, unforgiving
grimace 3 mop, mow, mug 4 face, moue 5 mouth, smirk, sneer 6 deform 7 contort, distort
grimalkin 3 cat, hag 6 feline
grime 4 dirt, foul, soil 5 dirty, sully 6 besoil, smirch, smooch, smudge, smutch 7 tarnish
grim reaper 5 death
grin 4 beam 5 fleer, risus, smile, smirk
grind 3 rut, vex 4 chew, grub, mill, moil, pace, plod, rote, slog, toil, work 5 crush, gnash, grate, labor, slave, sweat 6 crunch, drudge, groove, kibble 7 routine, travail 8 bullwork, drudgery, plugging 9 treadmill 10 donkeywork
grinder 4 hero 5 molar, stone, tooth 8 sandwich 9 submarine
grinding 5 harsh 6 severe 7 grating, wearing *stone:* 4 mano 6 muller, pestle
grip 4 hold, take, vice 5 clamp, clasp, grasp, seize 6 clench, clinch, clutch, duress, handle, tenure, valise 7 catch up, grapple 8 coercion, enthrall, handfast, handhold 9 fascinate, mesmerize, restraint, spellbind 10 constraint
gripe 4 beef, crab, fuss, hold, kick, yaup, yawp 5 bitch, bleat, brawl, clamp, clasp, croak, grasp 6 clench, clinch, clutch, grouch, grouse, murmur, mutter, squawk, take on, tenure, yammer 7 blow off, grapple, grumble 8 complain 9 bellyache
griper see grumbler
grippe 3 flu 7 disease 9 influenza
gripper 4 clip, hand, vice 5 clamp, clasp, tongs 6 pliers
gris-gris 5 charm, spell 6 amulet 8 talisman 11 incantation
grisly 4 grim 5 eerie, lurid, weird 6 horrid 7 ghastly, hideous, macabre, uncanny 8 gruesome, horrible, terrible 10 horrifying, terrifying
grist 3 lot 5 grain, stint 6 output 8 quantity
gristle 9 cartilage
grit 4 dirt, guts, sand, soil 5 earth, moxie, nerve, spunk 6 gravel 7 courage 8 backbone 9 fortitude
gritty 4 game 5 brave, dirty, sandy 6 plucky, soiled 8 resolute
groan 4 moan, rasp 5 creak, grate
grocery 5 store 11 supermarket ***Spanish:*** 6 bodega
grog 3 rum 5 booze, drink, hooch, juice 6 liquor, tipple 7 alcohol, spirits
groggy 4 logy, weak 5 dazed, foggy, tired 6 sleepy 7 muddled 8 sluggish
groin 4 fold 6 crotch, inguen ***combining form:*** 6 inguin 7 inguino
groom 4 comb, tidy 5 brush, clean, curry, ready, shave 6 neaten, polish, refine, toilet 7 prepare, servant 8 benedict 9 attendant 11 horsekeeper ***Chinese:*** 5 mafoo ***Indian:*** 4 syce
groove 3 rut 4 nurl, pace, rote, slot 5 canal, flute, glyph, grind, stria 6 fuller, furrow, gutter, hollow 7 chamfer, channel, routine
grope 3 pry 4 feel, poke, root, test 5 probe 6 fumble, handle, search 7 examine, explore, grabble 8 scrabble
grosbeak 4 bird 5 finch 8 haw finch
gross 3 all, big, fat, raw, sum 4 foul, mass, rank, rude 5 brute, crass, crude, heavy, obese, rough, stout, total, utter, whole 6 animal, carnal, coarse, damned, entire, fleshy, portly, smutty, vulgar 7 capital, extreme, glaring, obscene, perfect, porcine, sensual, uncouth, weighty 8 absolute, barnyard, complete, entirety, flagrant, improper, material, outright, physical, sensible, sum total, tangible, totality 9 aggregate, corporeal, corpulent, downright, egregious, excessive, inelegant, loathsome, objective, offensive, out-and-out, repulsive, revolting, unrefined 10 exorbitant, immoderate
grotesque 5 antic, comic, droll, eerie, weird 6 rococo 7 baroque, bizarre, comical, extreme, uncanny 9 fantastic, ludicrous
grotto 4 cave, hole 5 crypt, vault 6 cavern *Capri:* 4 Blue
grouch 4 crab, sulk 5 crank, croak, grump, scold 6 griper, grouse, kicker, murmur, mutter 7 crabber, grouser, growler, grumble 8 grumbler, sorehead, sourpuss 10 bellyacher, complainer, crosspatch, malcontent 11 faultfinder
ground 3 bed, why 4 base, dirt, down, drop, fell, land, rest, root, seat, soil, stay, test 5 basis, cause, earth, floor, level, proof, trial 6 bottom, reason, whyfor 7 bedrock, dry land, flatten, footing, mow down, support, sustain 8 argument, basement, but-

tress, evidence 9 bring down, establish, knock down, predicate, testimony, throw down, wherefore 10 antecedent, foundation, substratum, terra firma ***combining form:*** 2 ge 3 geo, ped 4 pedo 5 chame 6 chamae

grounded 7 beached 8 stranded

groundhog 6 marmot 9 woodchuck

groundless 4 idle 5 false 8 baseless 9 unfounded 10 bottomless, gratuitous, ungrounded 11 uncalled-for, unwarranted

groundwork 3 bed 4 base, root 5 basis 6 bottom 7 bedrock, footing, support 8 basement 10 foundation, substratum 12 substruction, substructure, underpinning

group 3 lot, set 4 band, bevy, body, clot, club, crew, gang, mess, pool, push, ruck, sect, sort, team, tier 5 array, batch, bunch, chain, class, clump, covey, crowd, grade, horde, party, place, squad, suite, trust 6 adjust, assort, bundle, cartel, circle, clique, clutch, gather, huddle, league, muster, parcel, passel 7 arrange, battery, brigade, cluster, collect, combine, company, coterie, council, dispose, echelon, platoon, round up 8 assemble, assembly, category, classify, ensemble, organize 9 congeries, gathering, harmonize, syndicate 10 assemblage, categorize, collection ***of angels:*** 4 host ***of ants:*** 6 colony ***of badgers:*** 4 cete ***of bears:*** 6 sleuth ***of bees:*** 4 hive 5 grist, swarm ***of birds:*** 6 flight, volery ***of boars:*** 7 sounder ***of cats:*** 7 clowder, clutter ***of cattle:*** 5 drove ***of chicks:*** 5 brood 6 clutch ***of clams:*** 3 bed ***of cranes:*** 5 sedge, siege ***of crows:*** 6 murder ***of ducks:*** 5 brace ***of eight:*** 5 octet ***of elephants:*** 4 herd ***of elks:*** 4 gang ***of fish:*** 5 shoal 6 school ***of five:*** 5 quint 6 pentad 7 quinary, quintet ***of four:*** 6 tetrad 7 quartet ***of foxes:*** 5 leash, skulk ***of geese:*** 5 flock, skein 6 gaggle ***of gnats:*** 5 cloud, horde ***of goats:*** 4 trip 5 tribe ***of goldfinches:*** 5 charm ***of gorillas:*** 4 band ***of greyhounds:*** 5 leash ***of grouse:*** 5 covey ***of hares:*** 4 down, husk ***of hawks:*** 4 cast ***of hounds:*** 3 cry 4 mute, pack ***of kangaroos:*** 3 mob 5 troop ***of kittens:*** 6 kendle, kindle ***of larks:*** 10 exaltation ***of leopards:*** 4 leap ***of lions:*** 5 pride ***of locusts:*** 6 plague ***of monkeys:*** 5 troop ***of mules:*** 4 span ***of nightingales:*** 5 watch ***of nine:*** 5 nonet ***of oysters:*** 3 bed ***of partridges:*** 5 covey ***of peacocks:*** 6 muster ***of pheasants:*** 3 nye 4 nest, nide ***of plovers:*** 4 wing 12 congregation ***of quail:*** 4 bevy 5 covey ***of seals:*** 3 pod 5 patch ***of seven:*** 6 pleiad, septet ***of sheep:*** 5 drove, flock ***of six:*** 5 hexad 6 hexade, sextet ***of swans:*** 4 bevy ***of swine:*** 7 sounder ***of teals:*** 6 spring ***of three:*** 4 trio 5 triad 7 ternary, trinity, triplet ***of toads:*** 4 knot ***of vipers:*** 4 nest ***of whales:*** 3 gam, pod ***of wolves:*** 4 pack ***suffix:*** 2 ad, et 3 ome 4 some

grouper 4 fish 8 rockfish 10 tripletail

grouse 5 croak, gripe, quail, scold 6 gorhen, grouch, murmur, mutter 7 gorcock, greyhen, grumble 8 complain, pheasant 9 blackcock, ptarmigan 10 whitebelly 12 capercaillie ***extinct:*** 8 heath hen ***red:*** 8 moorfowl ***strut:*** 3 lak

grouser see **grumbler**

grout 4 lees 5 dregs 6 cement, mortar 7 grounds, plaster 8 concrete

grove 3 bed 4 holt, wood 5 copse, hurst 7 boscage, coppice, orchard, thicket ***suffix:*** 3 eta (plural) 4 etum

grovel 4 fawn 5 cower, toady 6 cringe, kowtow, wallow 7 honey up, truckle 8 bootlick 9 brownnose 11 apple-polish

grow 3 age, get, run, wax 4 come, rear, rise, tend, turn 5 breed, nurse, raise, ripen, swell 6 become, expand, foster, mature, mellow, sprout, thrive 7 care for, develop, enlarge, gestate, nurture, produce 8 escalate, increase, maturate, mushroom 9 cultivate, propagate

growing 8 crescive, vegetive 10 vegetative

growl 3 grr 4 roll 5 snarl 6 mutter, rumble 7 grumble 8 complain 9 complaint

growler 3 can 4 crab, floe 5 crank, grump 6 griper, grouch 7 grouser, iceberg, pitcher 8 grumbler, sorehead, sourpuss 9 container 10 bellyacher

grow old 3 age 5 ripen 6 mature

growth 4 rise 5 swell, tumor 7 merisis 8 increase, progress, swelling 9 accretion, evolution, expansion, flowering, unfolding 10 evolvement 11 development, enlargement, progression ***malignant:*** 6 cancer ***skin:*** 3 wen 4 corn, mole, wart 6 bunion, keloid

grub 3 dig 4 beat, chow, comb, feed, food, hack, plod, poke, rake, root, slog, toil 5 grind, larva, scour, slave, spade, stump 6 burrow, drudge, forage, search, shovel, slavey, viands 7 edibles, grubber, nurture, ransack, rummage 8 excavate, finecomb, hireling, victuals 9 mercenary, provender

grubby 4 foul 5 black, dirty, grimy, nasty, soily 6 filthy, impure 7 squalid, unclean

grubstake 4 back 7 finance 8 bankroll

grudge 4 deny, envy 5 spite 6 injury, malice, refuse, spleen 7 despite, ill will 9 grievance, injustice, malignity 10 malignancy 11 malevolence 12 spitefulness

gruel 5 atole 8 porridge ***Scottish:*** 6 crowdy

gruesome see **grisly**

gruff 4 curt, dour, sour 5 bluff, blunt, husky, short, surly 6 abrupt, croaky, crusty, fierce, hoarse, morose, snippy, sullen 7 bearish, boorish, brusque, crabbed 8 churlish, croaking, snippety 9 saturnine

grumble 4 beef, crab, fuss, kick, moan, roll 5 bitch, brawl, croak, gripe, groan, growl, scold, snarl, whine 6 grouch, grouse, holler, murmur, mutter, repine, rumble, squawk 8 complain 9 bellyache

grumbler 4 crab 6 grouch 7 grouser, growler 8 sorehead 10 bellyacher, complainer, crosspatch, malcontent 11 faultfinder

grump 3 pet 4 crab, pout, sulk 5 crank 6 griper, grouch, kicker 7 growler 8 grumbler, sorehead, sourpuss 10 bellyacher

grumpy 5 moody, surly 6 crabby, cranky

guacharo 7 oilbird

Guam *capital:* 5 Agana *native:* 8 Chamorro

guanaco 5 llama 6 alpaca *kin:* 5 camel

guarantee, guaranty 3 vow 4 bail, bond, oath, seal, word 5 token, vouch 6 assure, ensure, insure, pledge, surety 7 certify, earnest, promise, warrant 8 security, warranty 9 assurance 11 undertaking

guarantor 5 angel 6 backer, patron, surety 7 sponsor 8 backer-up 11 underwriter

guard 4 fend, keep, mind, tend, ward 5 aegis, armor, cover, watch 6 attend, convoy, defend, escort, jailer, keeper, patrol, picket, screen, secure, sentry, shield, warden, warder 7 bulwark, conduct, defense, lookout, protect, turnkey 8 armament, chaperon, security, sentinel, shepherd, watchdog, watchman 9 accompany, patrolman, protector 10 protection

guarded 4 safe, wary 5 chary, privy 6 buried, covert, hidden 7 careful 8 cautious, discreet, gingerly, obscured, shrouded, ulterior 9 concealed 11 calculating, circumspect, considerate

guardhouse 4 brig 6 prison

guardian 6 custos, keeper, parent, patron, warden 7 sponsor 8 cerberus, claviger, watchdog 9 custodian, protector

guardianship 4 care, ward 5 trust 7 custody, keeping, tuition 11 safekeeping

guava 4 inga, tree 5 fruit

gudgeon 3 pin 4 fish 5 pivot 6 socket

Gudrun *brother:* 6 Gunnar 7 Gunther *father:* 5 Hetel *husband:* 4 Atli 5 Etzel 6 Sigurd 9 Siegfried

guerrilla 7 fighter, patriot, soldier 8 partisan 9 irregular 11 bushwhacker *Greek:* 6 klepht

guess 4 call, shot, stab 5 fancy, infer, think 6 deduce, reason, reckon 7 predict, presume, pretend, suppose, surmise 8 estimate 9 speculate 10 conjecture

guest 6 caller, lodger, patron, roomer 7 visitor

guff 3 jaw, lip 4 sass 5 hokum, hooey, mouth, sauce, trash 6 bunkum 7 hogwash 8 back talk, claptrap, malarkey, nonsense 9 poppycock 10 balderdash

guffaw 5 laugh, tehee 6 giggle, hee-haw, titter 7 chortle, chuckle, snicker, sniggle

guidance 7 auspice, conduct, control 9 direction 10 leadership, management

guide 3 see 4 airt, clue, dean, lead, show 5 airth, doyen, pilot, route, steer, teach, usher 6 beacon, convoy, direct, escort, leader, manage, manual, vector 7 conduct, control, marshal 8 Baedeker, chaperon, contrive, director, engineer, handbook, maneuver, navigate, shepherd 9 accompany, conductor, lead pilot, vade mecum 10 bellwether, compendium 11 enchiridion

guidebook 6 manual 8 Baedeker, handbook 9 itinerary, vade mecum 10 compendium 11 enchiridion

guided missile 3 ABM 4 Hawk, ICBM, IRBM, Nike, Thor, Zuni 5 Atlas, drone, Snark, Titan 6 Bomarc, Falcon 7 Bullpup, Polaris, Terrier 8 Redstone 9 Minuteman 10 Sidewinder

Guiderius *brother:* 9 Arviragus *father:* 9 Cymbeline

Guido's scale 2 fa, la, mi, re, ut 3 Ela, sol

guild 4 club 5 order, union 6 cartel, league 7 society 8 sodality 10 fellowship, fraternity 11 association, brotherhood

guile 4 wile 5 craft, fraud 6 deceit 7 cunning 9 duplicity 12 dissemblance

guileful 3 sly 4 deep, foxy, wily 6 artful, astute, crafty, shifty, sneaky, tricky 7 cunning, devious 8 indirect, sneaking 9 insidious, underhand 11 duplicitous, underhanded

guileless 5 naive 6 honest 7 artless, natural 8 unartful 9 ingenuous, unstudied, untutored

guillemot 3 auk 5 murre

guillotine 6 behead 9 decollate 10 decapitate

guilt 3 sin 4 onus 5 blame, crime, fault, shame 7 offense, remorse 11 culpability

guiltless 4 good, pure 5 clean 8 innocent, unguilty, virtuous 9 blameless, crimeless, exemplary, faultless, righteous 10 inculpable, unblamable

guilty 5 amiss 6 nocent, sinful, unholy, wicked 7 ashamed 8 blamable, blameful, culpable, indicted 9 impeached 10 answerable, censurable 11 accountable, blameworthy, responsible 12 incriminated

guinea fowl *genus:* 6 Numida *young:* 4 keet

guinea pig 4 cavy 6 rodent *genus:* 5 Cavia

Guinevere *husband:* 6 Arthur *lover:* 8 Lancelot 9 Launcelot

guise 3 hue, rig 4 face, mask, show 5 cloak, color, cover, dress, getup 6 facade, outfit, setout 7 costume 8 coloring 9 semblance 10 appearance

guitar *part:* 3 nut, peg 4 fret, neck 5 brace 6 bridge, string 7 peghead *player:* 7 plucker 8 strummer *small:* 3 uke 7 ukulele *soprano:* 5 tiple *tool:* 4 pick 8 plectrum

guitarist *American:* 9 Parkening *Australian:* 8 Williams *British:* 5 Bream *Italian:* 7 Ghiglia *Spanish:* 5 Yepes 6 Romero 7 Segovia

guitarlike instrument 3 uke 4 lute, vina 5 banjo, sitar 6 sancho 7 bandore, pandora, samisen, ukulele

gulch 3 gap 5 chasm, cleft, clove, gorge, gully 6 arroyo, canyon, clough, ravine

gulf 3 arm, bay, pit 4 cave, cove, eddy, well 5 abysm, abyss, bayou, bight, chasm, firth, gulch, inlet, shaft 6 cavity, harbor, hollow, ravine, slough 8 crevasse *Adriatic Sea:* 6 Venice *Aegean Sea:* 7 Saronic 8 Salonika *Africa:* 6 Guinea *Arabian Sea:* 4 Oman 7 Persian *Arctic Ocean:* 2 Ob *Australia:* 9 Van Diemen 11 Carpentaria *Baltic Sea:* 4 Riga 6 Danzig 7 Bothnia, Finland *Bering Sea:* 6 Anadyr *Canada:* 13 Saint Lawrence *Caribbean Sea:* 8 Honduras 9 Venezuela *Central America:* 6 Panama 7 Fonseca *Djibouti:* 6 Tajura 8 Tadjoura *Europe:* 7 Bothnia, Gascony 8 Gascogne *Greece:* 7 Corinth, Lepanto *Indian Ocean:* 4 Aden *Ionian Sea:* 7 Taranto *Iran:* 7 Arabian *Italy:* 5 Genoa *Mediterranean Sea:* 5 Sidra, Tunis 8 Valencia 10 Khalij Surt 11 Syrtis Major *Mexico:* 10 California *New Guinea:* 5 Papua 7 McCluer *New Zealand:* 7 Hauraki *North America:* 6 Alaska, Mexico *Northwest Territories:* 7 Boothia 8 Amundsen 9 Queen Maud *Philippines:* 4 Asid 5 Davao, Leyte, Panay, Ragay *Red Sea:* 4 Suez 5 Aqaba 11 Aelaniticus *Russia:* 8 Sakhalin *Solomon Sea:* 4 Huon, Kula 5 Vella *South China Sea:* 4 Siam 6 Tonkin 8 Lingayen, Thailand *Tyrrhenion Sea:* 7 Paestum *Yellow Sea:* 2 Bo, Po 6 Chihli

Gulf State 5 Texas 7 Alabama, Florida 9 Louisiana 11 Mississippi

gull 3 mew, sap 4 bird, dupe, fish, fool, hoax 5 chump 6 befool, pigeon, sucker 7 chicane, fall guy, gudgeon, saphead 8 flimflam, hoodwink 9 bamboozle 11 hornswoggle *relating to:* 6 larine, laroid

gullet 3 maw 4 tube 6 dewlap, ravine, throat 7 channel 9 esophagus

gullible 4 easy 5 naive 9 credulous 10 fleeceable 11 susceptible

Gulliver's Travels *author:* 5 Swift *land:* 6 Laputa 8 Lilliput 11 Brobdingnag *people:* 6 Yahoos

gully 5 gorge, gulch 6 arroyo, hollow, ravine, valley 7 couloir

gulp 4 bolt, cram, glut, slop, swig, wolf 5 slosh, stuff, swill 6 devour, englut, gobble, guzzle 7 swallow 11 ingurgitate

gum 4 chew, kino 5 botch, cheat, nyssa, stick, tuart 6 bobble, bollix, bungle, chicle, gluten, goof up, mucker, tupelo 7 bilsted, exudate, gingiva, louse up 8 adhesive, mucilage 9 sapodilla 10 eucalyptus *kind:* 6 acacia, Arabic, balata, bubble 7 chewing, dextrin *resin:* 5 myrrh 7 gamboge 8 ammoniac, galbanum, scammony 9 asafetida 12 frankincense

gummy 5 gooey 6 cloggy, sticky, stodgy 7 viscous 8 adhesive

gumption 5 sense 6 wisdom 8 judgment, sagacity 9 good sense 10 astuteness, enterprise, horse sense, shrewdness 11 common sense

gums 3 ula 8 gingivae

gumshoe 3 cop, tec 4 dick, fuzz, heat, lurk, slip 5 creep, shirk, skulk, slink, sneak, snoop, steal 6 peeler, sleuth 7 officer 8 flatfoot, hawkshaw, Sherlock 9 detective, policeman, pussyfoot 12 investigator

gun 3 gat, rod 5 rifle 6 cannon, heater, mortar, musket, pistol, weapon 7 bazooka, carbine, firearm 8 howitzer, revolver 9 derringer *antiaircraft:* 6 ack-ack, Bofors *British:* 4 sten *French:* 8 arquebus *German:* 5 Luger *mount:* 6 turret *part:* 3 pin 4 bolt, bore, butt, lock 5 sight, stock 6 barrel, breech, hammer, muzzle, safety 7 chamber, trigger 8 cylinder, magazine 9 buttstock

gunfire 4 shot 5 salvo 6 ack-ack, strafe, volley 7 barrage 9 fusillade

gung ho 4 keen 7 zealous 12 enthusiastic

Guni's father 8 Naphtali

gunk 3 goo 4 crud, gook, goop, muck

gunman 5 bravo 6 hit man 7 torpedo 8 assassin 9 cutthroat

Gunnar *brother-in-law:* 6 Sigurd *father:* 5 Hetel *sister:* 6 Gudrun *wife:* 8 Brynhild

gunnel 6 blenny 10 butterfish

gunner 7 shooter 8 marksman, rifleman 9 cannoneer 12 artilleryman

Gunther *sister:* 7 Gutrune 9 Kriemhild *slayer:* 5 Hagen *uncle:* 5 Hagen *wife:* 8 Brunhild 9 Brynhilde 11 Brunnehilde

guppy 4 fish 6 minnow

gurgle 3 lap 4 wash 5 slosh, swash 6 bubble, burble

Gurkha knife 5 kukri

gurney 3 cot 9 stretcher

guru 5 guide 6 mentor 7 teacher

gush 4 flow, pour, roll, teem 5 flood, flush, issue, spout, spurt, surge 6 sluice, spring, stream 7 emanate
gusset 4 fold 5 armor, pleat 6 insert
gust 4 gale, puff, waft, wind 5 blast, burst, draft, sally, whiff 6 access, breeze, squall 7 bluster, flare-up 8 eruption, outburst
gusto 4 élan, zeal, zest 5 ardor, heart, taste 6 fervor, palate, relish, spirit 7 delight, passion 8 pleasure 9 enjoyment 10 enthusiasm 11 delectation
gut 4 draw 5 belly, bowel, clean, dress, inner 6 paunch 7 embowel, passage, stomach 8 interior, internal, intimate, visceral 9 viscerous 10 disembowel, eviscerate, exenterate
Gutenberg ***city:*** 5 Mainz ***invention:*** 11 movable type ***partner:*** 4 Fust
gutless 6 coward, craven 7 chicken, unmanly 8 cowardly 9 spunkless 11 lily-livered, poltroonish 13 pusillanimous
guts 4 grit 5 moxie, nerve, pluck, spunk 6 mettle, spirit, tripes 7 courage, innards, insides, viscera 8 backbone, entrails, stuffing 9 fortitude, internals 10 resolution
gutsy 4 bold 5 brave, manly 6 manful, plucky, spunky 7 valiant 8 intrepid 9 unfearful 10 courageous
gutter 5 ditch, gully 6 furrow, groove, trench, trough 7 channel
guttural 4 deep 5 harsh, rough, velar 7 palatal, rasping, throaty
Guyana ***capital:*** 10 Georgetown ***monetary unit:*** 6 dollar
guzzle 4 bolt, cram, gulp, slop, soak, swig, wolf 5 booze, drink, slosh, swill 6 englut, gobble, imbibe, tank up, tipple 7 swizzle
Gwendolen's husband 7 Locrine
gymnast 7 acrobat, athlete, tumbler ***American:*** 5 Rigby (Cathy) 6 Rotton (Mary Lou), Thomas (Kurt) ***Romanian:*** 8 Comaneci (Nadia) ***Russian:*** 3 Kim (Nelly) 6 Korbut (Olga)
gymnastics 5 sport 8 exercise, tumbling 9 athletics 10 acrobatics 12 calisthenics ***apparatus:*** 3 bar 4 beam, buck, ring, rope 5 horse ***feat:*** 3 kip 4 flip 5 vault 6 tumble 9 handstand, headstand 10 handspring, headspring, somersault
gyp 4 beat, bilk, fake, hoax, sell 5 cheat, cozen, fraud, phony, spoof 6 chisel, chouse, con man, diddle, humbug, rip off 7 defraud, diddler, sharper, swindle 8 swindler 9 defrauder, imposture, overreach, trickster 10 mountebank 11 flimflammer 12 double-dealer
gypsum 8 selenite 9 alabaster
gypsy 4 caló 5 caird, nomad 6 roamer, Romany 7 tzigane, zingana, zingano 8 Bohemian, wanderer ***Spanish:*** 6 gitano
gyrate 4 roll, spin, turn 5 twirl, whirl 6 circle, rotate 7 revolve 9 pirouette, whirligig
gyration 4 turn 5 round, wheel, whirl 7 circuit 8 rotation 10 revolution 11 circulation
gyre 4 ring, spin 5 twirl, whirl 6 rotate, spiral, vortex 7 revolve 10 revolution
gyro 8 sandwich 9 gyroscope
gyve 4 bond, iron 5 chain 6 fetter 7 shackle

H

H 4 high 5 aitch 7 hundred
habeus corpus 4 writ
habilimented 4 clad 7 clothed
habilitate 5 dress 6 clothe
habit 3 rut, set, use, way 4 bent, form, mode, rote, turn, wont 5 build, dress, style, trick, usage 6 clothe, custom, groove, manner, praxis 7 carcass, contour, fashion, habitus, outline, pattern, routine 8 behavior, physique, practice, tendency 9 addiction, framework 10 consuetude, convention, proclivity 11 disposition, inclination ***riding:*** 6 joseph 8 jodhpurs ***wearer:*** 3 nun 5 rider
habitant 5 liver 7 denizen, dweller, resider 8 occupant, resident 9 indweller
habitat 4 home, site 5 abode, haunt, range 6 locale 7 station 8 locality 9 territory 11 environment 12 surroundings ***combining form:*** 2 ec 3 eco, oec 4 oeco
habitation 3 pad 4 digs, flat, home, nest, nook, roof, seat 5 abode, astre, haunt, haven, house, place, roost 6 colony, hearth 7 housing, lodging 8 domicile, dwelling, fireside, lodgment, peopling, quarters, rooftree, tenement 9 apartment, homeplace, homestead, occupancy, residence, residency
habitual 6 addict, inborn, native, steady, wonted 7 chronic, regular, routine 8 accepted, addicted, constant, frequent 9 automatic, confirmed, continual, customary, ingrained 10 accustomed, inveterate, persistent 11 established, instinctive, involuntary
habituate 3 use 4 bear, wont 5 inure 6 addict, adjust, devote, endure, season, take to 7 support 8 accustom, devote to, tolerate 9 condition, confirm in 11 familiarize
habitué 3 fan 4 buff, user 5 hound, lover 6 addict, patron, votary 7 denizen, devotee, haunter 8 customer 10 frequenter
Hacaliah, Hachaliah ***son:*** 8 Nehemiah
hacienda 4 farm 5 ranch 6 estate 10 plantation
hack 3 cab, cut, hew, old, try 4 chip, chop, dull, fell, gash, grub, jade, mean, nick, poor, taxi, trim, turn 5 cabby, cough, frame, grind, horse, notch, petty, shape, slash, slave, stale, tired, trite, usual 6 cabbie, cliché, common, drudge, haggle, lackey, mangle, slavey 7 clichéd, grating, grubber, machine, outworn, plodder, potboil, servant, taxicab, trivial 8 déclassé, hireling, inferior, low grade, mediocre, ordinary, outmoded, time-worn, well-worn 9 cabdriver, mercenary, potboiler 10 second-rate, uninspired 11 commonplace
hackneyed 4 worn 5 stale, stock, tired, trite 6 cliché 7 archaic, clichéd, worn-out 8 bathetic, everyday, obsolete, outmoded, timeworn, well-worn 9 moth-eaten, out-of-date, quotidian 10 antiquated 11 commonplace
Hadad ***father:*** 5 Bedad 7 Ishmael ***victim:*** 6 Midian
Hadadezer ***father:*** 5 Rehob ***kingdom:*** 5 Zobah
hades 3 pit 4 hell 5 Sheol 6 Tophet 7 Abaddon, Avernus, Gehenna, inferno 8 Tartarus 9 barathrum, perdition 10 underworld 11 netherworld, Pandemonium ***Babylonian:*** 5 Aralu ***god:*** 3 Dis 5 Orcus, Pluto ***guard:*** 8 Cerberus ***lake:*** 7 Avernus ***river:*** 4 Styx 5 Lethe 7 Acheron, Cocytus 10 Phlegethon
hafnium ***symbol:*** 2 Hf
hag 3 hex 4 drab, trot 5 biddy, bruja, crone, harpy, lamia, shrew, vixen, witch 6 gorgon, virago 7 grandam 8 battle-ax, fishwife, harridan, slattern 9 sorceress 10 witchwoman 11 enchantress
Hagar's son 7 Ishmael
Hagen ***father:*** 8 Alberich ***nephew:*** 7 Gunther ***slayer:*** 9 Kriemhild ***victim:*** 9 Siegfried
haggard 3 wan 4 lank, lean, pale, worn 5 ashen, drawn, faded, gaunt, spare, tired 6 fagged, pallid, skinny 7 angular, pinched, scraggy, scrawny, wearied 8 careworn, fatigued, harrowed, worn-down 9 exhausted
Haggard novel 3 She
Haggi's father 3 Gad
Haggith ***husband:*** 5 David ***son:*** 8 Adonijah
haggle 4 deal, hack 5 cavil, slash, trade 6 barter, bicker, dicker, hackle, palter 7 bargain, chaffer, dispute, quibble, stickle, wrangle 8 huckster, squabble 10 horse-trade
hail 4 ahoy 5 greet, hallo, salvo, shout, storm 6 accost, call to, hallow, holler, kudize, praise, salute, shower, volley

7 acclaim, address, applaud, barrage, call out, commend **8** come from, drumfire **9** broadside, cannonade, fusillade, originate, recommend **10** salutation **11** bombardment

hair **3** ace, bit, jot **4** hint, mite, wool **5** pilus, trace **6** nicety, trifle **7** whisker **8** fraction, particle ***animal:*** **3** fur **4** mane, pelt **8** vibrissa **9** vibrissae (plural) ***braid of:*** **5** queue **7** pigtail ***clip:*** **8** barrette ***coarse:*** **7** bristle ***combining form:*** **3** pil **4** coma, pili, pilo **5** chaet, crini, thrix, trich **6** chaeta, chaeto, tricha, trichi, tricho, trichy **7** chaetae (plural), chaetes, chaetus, trichia **8** trichous ***covering of:*** **3** wig ***facial:*** **5** beard **6** goatee **8** mustache, whiskers **9** moustache, sideburns **11** muttonchops ***fine:*** **6** lanugo ***front:*** **4** bang ***head of:*** **9** chevelure ***instrument:*** **4** comb ***knot of:*** **3** bun **6** tangle ***lock of:*** **4** curl **5** tress **7** cowlick ***loose roll:*** **4** pouf **5** pouff **6** pouffe ***matted:*** **4** shag ***ornament:*** **7** topknot ***preparation:*** **6** pomade **12** brilliantine ***relating to:*** **8** hirsutal ***root:*** **6** fibril ***set:*** **4** perm ***stiff:*** **4** seta **5** setae (plural) ***style:*** **9** pompadour ***tangled:*** **7** elflock ***tuft of:*** **7** fetlock ***unruly:*** **3** mop **7** cowlick ***without:*** **4** bald

haircutter **6** barber **7** friseur

hairdo **4** perm **7** chignon **8** bouffant

hairdresser **6** barber **7** friseur **10** beautician **13** cosmetologist

hair-raising **4** eery **5** eerie **9** thrilling **10** terrifying

hairsplitter **8** quibbler

hairstyle **2** DA **4** Afro **7** beehive, crew cut, pageboy **8** bouffont, coiffure, ducktail, ponytail

hairy **5** bushy, crude, downy, furry, fuzzy, harsh, nappy, risky, rough **6** chancy, craggy, fleecy, fluffy, jagged, lanate, pilose, rugged, shaggy, tufted, uneven, wicked, woolly **7** bristly, hirsute, pileous, scraggy, unshorn, unsound, villous **8** asperous, perilous, scabrous, strigose, unsmooth **9** dangerous, hazardous, pubescent, tomentose, unhealthy, whiskered **10** jeopardous, unpleasant **11** frightening, treacherous ***combining form:*** **4** dasy, hebe

Haiti ***capital:*** **12** Port au Prince ***export:*** **6** coffee **7** bauxite ***island:*** **10** Hispaniola ***location:*** **10** West Indies ***monetary unit:*** **6** gourde ***ruler:*** **8** Duvalier

Hajji Baba creator **6** Morier

hake **5** gadid **7** codling, whiting ***relative:*** **3** cod

halcyon **4** calm **5** happy, quiet, still **6** golden, hushed, placid, serene, stilly **8** affluent **10** kingfisher, prosperous, untroubled

Halcyone ***father:*** **6** Aeolus ***husband:*** **4** Ceyx

hale **3** fit, tug **4** draw, pull, sane, well **5** husky, right, sound, stout **6** robust **7** healthy, summons **9** strapping, wholesome

Hale character **5** Nolan

haleness **6** health

half ***prefix:*** **3** sam **4** demi, hemi, semi

half-assed **7** lacking, wanting **9** defective, deficient **10** inadequate, incomplete, uncomplete

half-breed **4** mule **5** cross **6** hybrid **7** bastard, mestizo, mongrel, mulatto **8** mixblood

halfhearted **5** tepid **8** lukewarm

half-moon **7** scalare **8** demilune **9** blue perch

halfway **3** mid **6** almost, center, medial, median, middle **7** midmost, partial **8** amenably **9** partially **10** centermost, middlemost, more or less **11** equidistant

half-wit **4** dolt, fool, zany **5** ament, idiot, moron **6** cretin **7** natural **8** imbecile **9** blockhead, simpleton

half-witted **4** dull, slow **5** silly **7** foolish, moronic **8** backward, imbecile, retarded **9** senseless **12** feebleminded, simpleminded

hall **4** dorm **5** foyer, lobby, lycea (plural) **6** lyceum **7** couloir, passage **8** building, corridor **9** dormitory **10** auditorium, living room, passageway **12** entrance room ***ancient Roman:*** **5** oecus ***exhibition:*** **5** salon ***Salvation Army:*** **7** citadel

Halley's ___ **5** comet

Hallohesh's son **7** Shallum

hallow **5** bless **6** devote, revere **8** dedicate, sanctify, venerate **10** consecrate

hallucination **6** mirage, wraith **7** fantasy, phantom **8** delusion, illusion, phantasm **11** fata morgana, ignis fatuus

hallucinogen **3** LSD **9** mescaline **10** psilocybin **11** scopolamine

halo **4** aura **5** nimbi (plural) **6** gloria, nimbus **7** aureole **8** encircle, gloriole ***combining form:*** **7** stephan **8** stephano

halogen **6** iodine **7** bromine **8** astatine, chlorine, fluorine

halt **3** end **4** lame, limp, quit, stay, stop **5** cease, check, close, hitch, lapse, stall, waver **6** arrest, desist, dither, draw up, falter, finish, haul up, hobble, pull up, wind up, wrap up **7** bring up, fetch up, stagger, suspend, whiffle **8** complete, conclude, give over, hesitate, knock off, leave off, surcease, ultimate **9** determine, interrupt, terminate, vacillate **11** discontinue

ham **4** hock **5** emote, thigh **7** buttock, overact **8** overplay, strutter **13** exhibitionist

Ham ***brother:*** **4** Shem **7** Japheth ***father:*** **4** Noah ***son:*** **4** Cush, Phut **6** Canaan **7** Mizraim

Haman's father 10 Hammedatha
Hamilcar ***conquest:*** 5 Spain ***home:*** 8 Carthage ***son:*** 8 Hannibal ***surname:*** 5 Barca
hamlet 5 moray 7 grouper, village ***Irish, Scottish:*** 7 clachan
Hamlet ***author:*** 11 Shakespeare ***beloved:*** 7 Ophelia ***castle:*** 8 Elsinore ***country:*** 7 Denmark ***friend:*** 7 Horatio ***mother:*** 8 Gertrude ***slayer:*** 7 Laertes ***uncle:*** 8 Claudius ***victim:*** 7 Laertes 8 Claudius, Polonius
Hamlet, The ***author:*** 8 Faulkner ***family:*** 6 Snopes
Hammedatha's son 5 Haman
hammer 4 beat, cock, drub, form, maul, peen, pein, pelt, toil 5 drive, erect, gavel, grave, labor, pound, set up, shape, stamp, swage, thump 6 batter, mallet, pummel, sledge, thrash, wallop 7 belabor, build up, fashion, foliate, impress, malleus, planish, trippet 8 lambaste, malleate ***type:*** 3 air 4 claw 6 sledge 8 ball peen 9 pneumatic
hammerhead 3 bat 5 dunce, shark, stork 8 clodpate, numskull 9 hog sucker 10 thickskull
Hammoleketh's brother 6 Gilead
hamper 3 bar, rub, tie 4 balk, clog, curb, foil, snag 5 block, check, crimp, leash, limit, tie up 6 battle, basket, cumber, fetter, hinder, hobble, hog-tie, hurdle, impede, lumber, retard, thwart 7 disrupt, inhibit, shackle, trammel 8 encumber, handicap, obstacle, obstruct, restrain, restrict 9 discomfit, embarrass, entrammel, frustrate
hamstring 6 hinder, impair, tendon 7 cripple, disable
Hamul's father 5 Perez 6 Pharez
Hamutal ***father:*** 8 Jeremiah ***husband:*** 6 Josiah ***son:*** 8 Jehoahaz, Zedekiah
Hanameel ***cousin:*** 8 Jeremiah ***father:*** 7 Shallum
Hanani ***brother:*** 8 Nehemiah ***father:*** 5 Heman, Immer ***son:*** 4 Jehu
Hananiah ***father:*** 4 Azur 5 Azzur, Bebai, Heman 7 Shashak 10 Zerubbabel ***son:*** 8 Jeshaiah, Pelatiah, Zedekiah
Hanan's father 4 Azel 6 Zaccur 7 Maachah, Shashak 8 Igdaliah
hand 3 aid 4 buck, feed, find, fist, furl, give, help, lift, pass, side 5 angle, facet, index, manus, phase, reach, skill, touch 6 aspect, assist, ductus, inning, pledge, relief, script, succor, supply, worker 7 ability, comfort, concern, conduct, deliver, dish out, laborer, provide, secours, support, workman 8 dispense, employee, interest, transfer, turn over 9 direction, operative, signature 10 assistance, penmanship, roustabout, workingman 11 calligraphy, chirography ***clenched:*** 4 fist ***combining form:*** 4 chir 5 cheir, chiro, palmi 6 cheiro, palmat 7 palmati ***counting zero:*** 8 baccarat ***covering:*** 5 glove 6 mitten ***declarer's:*** 7 laydown ***down:*** 8 bequeath ***gestures:*** 5 mudra ***make:*** 5 craft ***on hip:*** 6 akimbo ***part:*** 4 palm 5 thumb 6 finger ***poker:*** 5 flush 8 straight 9 full house ***protector:*** 5 glove 8 gauntlet
handbag 5 purse 8 reticule
handbill 5 flier, flyer 6 dodger, poster 7 affiche, leaflet, placard 8 circular
handbook 5 guide 6 manual 8 Baedeker 9 vade mecum 10 compendium 11 enchiridion ***religious:*** 9 catechism
handcuff 7 manacle 8 restrain ***British:*** 7 darbies (plural)
hand down 6 pass on 8 bequeath, transmit
Handel ***aria:*** 5 Largo ***birthplace:*** 5 Halle (Germany) ***opera:*** 4 Nero 5 Serse 6 Almira, Xerxes 7 Rodrigo 8 Berenice 9 Agrippina ***oratorio:*** 4 Saul 6 Esther, Joshua, Samson 7 Messiah 8 Jephthah
handicap 4 edge, load, odds 5 bulge, start 6 burden 8 drawback 9 advantage, allowance, detriment, head start 10 disability 11 encumbrance 12 disadvantage
handicraft 3 art 5 trade 6 métier 7 calling 8 vocation 10 profession
handkerchief 5 hanky 6 hankie 7 bandana 8 bandanna, mouchoir
handle 3 aim, ear, lay, paw, ply, run, try, use 4 ansa, bail, feel, grip, haft, knob, knop, name, play, take, test, wave, work 5 apply, guide, level, nomen, point, serve, shake, style, swing, title, touch, treat, wield 6 bestow, byname, byword, direct, employ, finger, govern, manage 7 act upon, conduct, control, exploit, moniker, operate, palpate, trade in, utilize 8 brandish, cognomen, deal with, dispense, dominate, doorknob, exercise, flourish, maneuver, nickname
handle-shaped 6 ansate
handling 4 care 6 charge 7 conduct, running 9 oversight 10 intendance, management 11 supervision
hand out 4 give 6 bestow, devote, donate 7 present 8 give away 10 administer
hand over 4 cede, feed, find, give 5 leave, waive, yield 6 commit, give up, resign, supply 7 abandon, commend, confide, consign, deliver, entrust, provide 8 dispense, relegate, transfer 9 deliver up, surrender 10 relinquish
handrail 8 banister
handsome 3 apt 4 chic, fair, free 5 ample, noble, smart, sonsy 6 adroit, august, comely, lovely, modish, pretty, sonsie 7 dashing, liberal, sizable, stately, stylish 8 generous, majestic 9 beauteous,

beautiful, bounteous, bountiful, unsparing 10 attractive, munificent, openhanded 11 fashionable, good-looking

handspring 6 tumble *lateral:* 9 cartwheel

handwriting 6 ductus, script 8 longhand 10 manuscript, penmanship 11 calligraphy, chirography *bad:* 10 cacography *study of:* 10 graphology

handy 4 deft 5 adept, utile 6 adroit, clever, nearby, nimble, useful, wieldy 7 close-by 8 adjacent, skillful 9 adaptable, dexterous, practical 10 beneficial, convenient, functional 11 practicable

handyman 6 jumper 8 factotum

hang 3 art, fix, jut, lop, pin, sag 4 hook, idle, lean, loll, pend, rest 5 await, cling, craft, drape, droop, float, hover, knack, lynch, noose, pause, poise, scrag, skill, sling, slope, stick, swing, trail, trick 6 adhere, attach, dangle, depend, gibbet, impend, loiter, tack up, turn on 7 execute *back:* 3 lag *loosely:* 3 sag 6 dangle

hangbird 6 oriole

hangdog 5 cowed 6 guilty 7 ashamed, pitiful 8 dejected

hanger-on 5 leech 6 sponge, sucker 7 sponger 8 barnacle, follower, parasite 9 bystander, spectator, sycophant 10 freeloader 11 bloodsucker 12 lounge lizard

hanging 7 pendent, pensile 9 declivity, pendulant, pendulous, suspended

Hanging Gardens 7 Babylon

hangings 5 arras 6 drapes 7 drapery 8 curtains, tapestry

hangout 4 dive 5 haunt, joint 6 resort 7 purlieu 9 honky-tonk 10 rendezvous 11 barrelhouse 12 watering hole

hang up 4 mire 5 delay, embog 6 detain, retard 7 achieve, bog down, set back, slacken 8 slow down 10 decelerate

hank 4 coil, loop, ring

hanker 3 yen 4 ache, long, lust, pine, sigh, wish 5 covet, crave, yearn 6 desire, hunger, thirst

hanky-panky 5 fraud 7 chicane 8 trickery 9 chicanery, deception, fourberie 11 highbinding 13 double-dealing, sharp practice

Hannah *husband:* 7 Elkanah *son:* 6 Samuel

Hannibal *defeat:* 4 Zama *father:* 8 Hamilcar *home:* 8 Carthage *surname:* 5 Barca *vanquisher:* 6 Scipio *victory:* 6 Cannae

Hanniel's father 4 Ulla 5 Ephod

Hanoch's father 6 Midian, Reuben

hansa, hanse 5 guild 6 league 11 association

Hans Brinker author 5 Dodge

Hanseatic League City 6 Bremen, Lubeck, Wismar 7 Cologne, Hamburg, Rostock

Hansen's disease 7 leprosy

Hanun's father 6 Nahash

haphazard 5 about 6 anyhow, around, chance, random 7 aimless, anywise, unaimed 8 accident, at random, careless, casually, randomly, slipshod 9 aimlessly, desultory, hit-or-miss, irregular, unplanned 10 accidental, carelessly, designless 11 any which way, unorganized 12 accidentally, unconsidered, unsystematic 13 helter-skelter

hapless 4 poor 6 woeful 7 unhappy, unlucky 8 ill-fated, untoward, wretched 9 miserable 10 ill-starred 11 star-crossed, unfortunate 12 infelicitous, misfortunate

happen 2 do, go 3 hit 4 bump, come, fall, give, luck, meet, pass, rise 5 break, light, occur 6 befall, betide, chance, drop in, tumble, turn up 7 come off, develop, fall out, stumble, turn out 8 bechance 9 transpire *again:* 5 recur *together:* 6 concur

happening 5 event, thing 7 episode 8 incident, occasion 10 occurrence 12 circumstance

happiness 3 joy 4 glee 5 bliss, cheer, mirth 6 gaiety 7 content, delight, jollity 8 felicity, gladness, pleasure 9 beatitude, enjoyment 11 delectation 12 satisfaction

happy 3 apt, fit, pat 4 glad, just, meet, nice, well 5 lucky, right 6 casual, cogent, joyful, joyous, proper, timely, upbeat 7 content, correct, fitting, pleased, telling 8 friendly, pleasant, suitable 9 befitting, congenial, contented, effective, effectual, efficient, favorable, fortunate, opportune, satisfied, well-timed 10 accidental, convincing, felicitous, fortuitous, harmonious, incidental, propitious, prosperous, seasonable 11 appropriate, efficacious 12 lighthearted

happy-go-lucky 4 cool, easy 6 blithe, casual 8 carefree, careless, cheerful, debonair, feckless, heedless, reckless 9 easygoing, lightsome 10 free-minded, insouciant, nonchalant 11 unconcerned 12 devil-may-care, light-hearted 13 lackadaisical

hara-kiri 7 seppuku, suicide 8 felo-de-se 10 self-murder 12 self-violence 13 self-slaughter

Haran *brother:* 7 Abraham *daughter:* 5 Iscah 6 Milcah *father:* 5 Terah 6 Shimei *son:* 3 Lot

harangue 4 rant, rave 5 mouth, orate 6 tirade 7 declaim, lecture, oration, soapbox 8 bloviate, diatribe, jeremiad, perorate 9 philippic 11 declamation

harass 3 irk, try, vex 4 bait, gnaw, pain, raid, ride 5 annoy, chivy, devil, foray, harry, hound, tease, worry 6 badger, heckle, hector, maraud, pester, plague, ratten, strain, stress 7 bedevil, dragoon, exhaust, fatigue,

hagride, torment, trouble **8** bullyrag, distress **9** beleaguer
harasser **5** bully **6** hector **7** harrier **9** bulldozer **10** browbeater **11** intimidator
harassment **6** irking, vexing **8** vexation **9** annoyance, bothering, provoking **10** irritation **11** aggravation, disturbance, provocation **12** exasperation, perturbation
harbinger **4** omen, sign **6** herald, symbol **7** apostle, forerun, portent, presage **8** announce, foreshow, outrider **9** precursor **10** forerunner, indication **11** preindicate
harbor **3** arm, bay, hut **4** bunk, camp, cove, gulf, hide, live, port, roof, room **5** bight, board, cabin, cover, firth, guard, haven, house, inlet, lodge, nurse, put up, roost **6** asylum, bestow, billet, covert, encamp, foster, refuge, screen, shield, take in **7** chamber, cherish, conceal, contain, nurture, protect, quarter, retreat, seaport, secrete, shelter **8** domicile **9** anchorage, entertain, safeguard, sanctuary **11** accommodate ***fee:*** **7** keelage ***Greece:*** **5** Aulis ***Guam:*** **4** Apra ***Hawaii:*** **5** Pearl ***Ireland:*** **4** Cork ***Long Island Sound:*** **8** New Haven ***Massachusetts:*** **4** Lynn **9** Annisquam ***New Jersey:*** **9** Little Egg ***Solomon:*** **4** Viru ***Washington:*** **5** Grays
hard **3** bad, set **4** dark, deep, dour, dull, fast, firm, grim, iron, near, nigh **5** amiss, badly, bleak, close, crisp, cruel, fixed, harsh, heavy, horny, madly, rocky, rough, sharp, sober, solid, stark, tight, tough, vivid **6** actual, ardent, bitter, brazen, brutal, coarse, firmly, flinty, keenly, knotty, meanly, nearby, packed, rugged, severe, sorely, sticky, strict, strong, thorny, tiring, trying, unjust, uphill, wildly **7** angrily, arduous, austere, binding, briskly, callous, closely, compact, complex, cruelly, durable, factual, fixedly, genuine, glaring, harshly, hostile, intense, irksome, labored, largely, obscure, onerous, operous, petrous, precise, roughly, rowdily, serious, sharply, slavish, solidly, tightly, tiredly, toilful, violent, wearing **8** absolute, actively, bitterly, brutally, concrete, definite, dingdong, exacting, fiercely, forcibly, frugally, granitic, grievous, grinding, indurate, intently, involved, mightily, petrosal, pitiless, positive, profound, reliable, rigorous, savagely, scabrous, severely, shabbily, snappily, stormily, strident, strongly, tempered, terrible, toilsome, unfairly, urgently, wearying **9** alcoholic, arduously, austerely, awkwardly, bloodless, compacted, demanding, difficile, difficult, earnestly, effortful, fatiguing, furiously, inclement, indurated, insensate, intensely, intensive, intricate, laborious, massively, merciless, offensive, onerously, painfully, pointedly, practical, pragmatic, punishing, realistic, resentful, resistant, searching, seriously, shameless, sprightly, straining, strenuous, stringent, unfeeling, unhandily, unsparing, viciously, violently, wearisome **10** adamantine, anesthetic, animatedly, bothersome, burdensome, compressed, cumbrously, exhausting, forbidding, forcefully, formidable, frenziedly, gruelingly, impassible, insensible, oppressive, perplexing, powerfully, rigorously, spiritedly, spirituous, sure-enough, thoroughly, toilsomely, unpleasant, unwieldily, unyielding, vigorously **11** assiduously, at close hand, complicated, difficultly, distressing, down-to-earth, exuberantly, ferociously, frantically, inequitable, insensitive, intemperate, intensively, intractable, laboriously, ponderously, rancorously, resentfully, searchingly, steadfastly, strenuously, troublesome, turbulently, unfantastic, unfavorable, unpalatable, unrelenting, unremitting, vivaciously **12** backbreaking, blood-and-guts, boisterously, burdensomely, concentrated, consolidated, cumbersomely, exhaustingly, exhaustively, incorrigible, intoxicating, matter-of-fact, meticulously, might and main, relentlessly, tumultuously ***combining form:*** **5** scler, stere **6** sclero, stereo ***to please:*** **7** finicky
hard-boiled **5** crude, rough, sober, stiff, tough **6** coarse **7** callous **8** obdurate, seasoned **9** heartless, practical, pragmatic, realistic, unfeeling **11** coldhearted, down-to-earth, unemotional, unfantastic, worldly-wise **12** matter-of-fact, stonyhearted, unidealistic **13** sophisticated, unsympathetic
harden **3** dry, set **4** cake, firm **5** adapt, enure, inure, steel **6** adjust, anneal, callus, freeze, ossify, season, temper **7** calcify, callous, compact, conform, congeal, densify, lithify, petrify, stiffen, toughen **8** accustom, concrete, indurate, sclerose, solidify **9** acclimate, climatize, fossilize, habituate **10** strengthen
hardfisted **4** mean **5** close, tight, tough **6** stingy, strong **7** save-all **9** niggardly **11** tough-minded **13** penny-pinching
hardheaded **5** sober **6** mulish **7** willful **8** perverse, stubborn **9** obstinate, practical, pragmatic, realistic **10** self-willed **11** down-to-earth, intractable, unfantastic **12** matter-of-fact, pertinacious, unidealistic
hardhearted see **hard-boiled**
hardihood **3** pep **4** birr, grit, guts, sand, tuck **5** moxie, nerve, pluck, vigor **6** energy **7** potency **8** audacity, boldness, temerity **9** assurance, brashness, cockiness, fortitude, impudence, insolence, insolency **10** brazenness, disrespect, robustness
hardly ever **6** little, rarely, seldom **7** unoften **12** infrequently, unfrequently
hardness **5** rigor **8** adamancy, asperity,

obduracy, severity 9 callosity 10 difficulty, inclemency
hardscrabble 6 barren 8 marginal 9 infertile, unbearing, unfertile 12 impoverished, unproductive
hardship 4 toil 5 peril, rigor, trial 6 danger, hazard 7 travail 8 asperity, distress, drudgery 9 adversity, mischance, privation, suffering 10 affliction, difficulty, discomfort, misfortune 11 tribulation
Hard Times author 7 Dickens
hardy 4 bold 5 brave, tough 6 brazen, daring, robust, rugged, strong 8 resolute 9 audacious
Hardy *character:* 3 Sue 4 Alec, Clym, Jude, Tess 5 Angel 8 Arabella, Eustacia, Henchard *setting:* 6 Wessex
hare 3 wat 4 fool 6 rabbit 7 leporid *Belgian:* 8 leporide *combining form:* 3 lag 4 lago *female:* 3 doe *genus:* 5 Lepus *male:* 4 buck *young:* 7 leveret
harebrained 5 balmy, crazy, dizzy, giddy, loony, silly, wacky 6 absurd, insane 7 flighty, foolish 8 skittish 9 frivolous 11 empty-headed 12 preposterous
harefooted 4 fast 5 fleet, hasty, quick, rapid, swift 6 speedy 9 breakneck 10 expeditive 11 expeditious
harem 6 serail, zenana 8 seraglio *concubine:* 3 oda 4 odah 7 odalisk 9 odalisque *room:* 3 oda 4 odah
Hareph's father 5 Caleb
Harhaiah's son 6 Uzziel
hark 4 hear, heed, mind, note 6 attend, listen, notice
harlequin 4 zany 5 clown 6 mottle 7 buffoon
Harlequin *beloved:* 9 Columbine *rival:* 7 Pierrot
harm 3 mar, sap 4 hurt, ruin 5 abuse, spoil 6 damage, ill-use, impair, injure, injury, misuse, molest 7 blemish, marring, outrage, tarnish, vitiate 8 maltreat, mischief, mistreat, sabotage 9 incommode, mischance, prejudice, undermine 10 dilapidate, discommode, disservice, impairment, misfortune 11 banefulness, noxiousness
harmful 3 bad, ill 4 evil 5 risky, toxic 6 malign, nocent, unsafe 7 baleful, baneful, hurtful, malefic, nocuous, noisome, noxious 8 damaging 9 dangerous, hazardous, injurious, malignant, unhealthy 10 pernicious 11 deleterious, detrimental, mischievous, prejudicial, troublesome, unhealthful, unwholesome 12 insalubrious
harmless 4 safe 6 unhurt 8 innocent, nontoxic 9 innocuous, innoxious 11 inobnoxious, inoffensive, unoffending, unoffensive
Harmonia *daughter:* 3 Ino 5 Agave 6 Semele 7 Autonoe *father:* 4 Ares, Mars *husband:* 6 Cadmus *mother:* 5 Venus 9 Aphrodite *son:* 9 Polydorus
harmonious 4 calm 5 sweet 6 amical, dulcet, irenic 7 chiming, chordal, musical, pacific, silvery, tuneful 8 amicable, blending, canorous, coactive, empathic, friendly, peaceful, pleasing, sonorous 9 accordant, agreeable, congenial, congruous, consonant, simpatico, symphonic 10 compatible, concinnate, concordant, empathetic, polyphonic, satisfying 11 cooperative, mellifluous, mellisonant, symmetrical, sympathetic 12 contrapuntal
harmonize 2 go 3 fit 4 jibe, tune 5 adapt, agree, blend, coapt, fit in, match, tally, unify, unite 6 accord, adjust, attune, concur, relate, square 7 arrange, concert, concord, conform 8 coincide, dovetail 9 cooperate, correlate, integrate, reconcile 10 coordinate, correspond, proportion, synthesize 11 accommodate, orchestrate 12 reconciliate
harmony 4 tune 5 chime, grace, peace, unity 6 accord, chorus, melody, unison 7 balance, concert, concord, dignity, empathy, kinship, oneness, rapport 8 affinity, diapason, elegance, sonority, symmetry 9 agreement, congruity, integrity, polyphony 10 accordance, coaptation, concinnity, conformity, consonance, musicality, proportion 11 concordance, concurrence, conformance, consistency, integration, tunefulness 12 articulation, togetherness *lack of:* 7 discord *of movement:* 8 eurythmy
Harnepher's father 6 Zophah
harness 4 gear, leaf, yoke 5 armor, hitch 6 couple, tackle 7 utilize 8 clothing 9 equipment *part:* 3 bit 4 rein 5 girth, trace 6 collar 7 blinder, crupper 9 bellyband, breeching, checkrein 12 breast collar *ring:* 6 terret, territ
harp 4 lyre 9 harmonica *Irish:* 8 clarsach
harpsichord 7 cembalo 8 clavecin
harpsichordist *American:* 6 Fuller, Kipnis, Newman 7 Marlowe, Pinkham, Valenti 11 Kirkpatrick *English:* 7 Malcolm *German:* 7 Richter 9 Leonhardt *Italian:* 7 Sgrizzi *Polish:* 9 Landowska (Wanda)
harpy 5 leech, scold, shrew, vixen 6 amazon, ogress, virago 8 fishwife, swindler 9 termagant, Xanthippe
Harpy 5 Aello 7 Celaeno, Ocypete *father:* 7 Thaumas *mother:* 7 Electra *sister:* 4 Iris
harrier 3 dog 4 hawk 5 bully 6 hector, runner 8 harasser 9 bulldozer 10 browbeater 11 intimidator
harrow 3 try 4 bait, fret, rack 5 devil, tease, wring 6 badger, heckle, hector, martyr, needle, pester 7 afflict, agonize, bedevil, crucify, torment, torture 8 irritate 9 tantalize 10 excruciate

harry 3 irk 4 gnaw, raid, sack 5 annoy, foray, havoc, tease, upset, worry 6 attack, badger, harass, maraud, pester, plague, ravage, worrit 7 assault, bedevil, despoil, disturb, hagride, perturb, pillage, torment 8 desolate, irritate, spoliate, vexation 9 beleaguer, depredate
harsh 3 dry, raw 4 dour, grim, sour, tart 5 acerb, acrid, bleak, crude, cruel, gruff, loose, rough, rusty, sharp, stark, stern, tangy 6 biting, bitter, brassy, brutal, coarse, craggy, gruffy, hoarse, jagged, rugged, severe, shaggy, shrill, uneven 7 acerbic, austere, blaring, bristly, burning, grating, jarring, mordant, pungent, rasping, raucous, scraggy, squawky, squeaky, stubbly, uncomfy, unlevel 8 asperous, exacting, granular, grinding, jangling, piercing, rigorous, scabrous, scraggly, scraping, scratchy, strident, unsmooth 9 amaroidal, dissonant, inclement, stringent, unmusical 10 astringent, discordant, irritating, stridulent, stridulous
hart 4 stag 7 red deer ***mate:*** 4 hind
Hart, Moss ***autobiography:*** 6 Act One ***collaborator:*** 7 Kaufman
hartebeest 4 tora 5 bubal 6 lelwel 7 bubalis 8 antelope ***family:*** 7 Bovidae
Hartford ***college:*** 7 Trinity ***economic activity:*** 9 insurance
Harumaph's son 7 Jedaiah
Harum's son 7 Aharhel
haruspex 5 augur 7 prophet 8 foreseer 9 predictor 10 forecaster, foreteller, prophesier, soothsayer 11 Nostradamus
harvest 2 in 3 bin 4 crop, hide, reap 5 amass, cache, hoard, stash, yield 6 garner, gather 7 bearing, collect, reaping, store up, storing, vintage 8 assemble, cropping, fruitage, ingather, squirrel, stow away 9 garnering, gathering 10 accumulate ***bug:*** 4 mite 7 chigger ***fly:*** 6 cicada ***former festival:*** 6 Lammas
harvester ***grain:*** 6 header ***of grapes:*** 8 vintager
Harvey 5 pooka 6 rabbit ***author:*** 5 Chase
Hasadiah's father 10 Zerubbabel
hash 4 chop, mess, mull, muss, stew 5 botch, mince, mix-up 6 jumble, jungle, litter, medley, mess-up, muddle, review, tumble 7 clutter, mélange, mixture, rummage 8 botchery, consider, scramble, shambles 9 patchwork, talk about 10 assortment, hodgepodge, miscellany 11 gallimaufry
Hashabiah's father 6 Kemuel 8 Jeduthun
Hashabniah's son 7 Hattush
hashish 5 bhang, ganja 6 charas 8 cannabis, narcotic ***plant:*** 4 hemp
Hashubah's father 10 Zerubbabel
hasp 6 fasten 8 fastener
Hassenuah's son 8 Hodaviah
hassle 3 row, try 4 beef, miff, spar, to-do 5 argue, brawl, cavil, essay, fight, run-in, trial, whirl 6 argufy, bicker, clamor, hubbub, pother, tumult, uproar 7 attempt, dispute, quarrel, quibble, rhubarb, turmoil, wrangle 8 endeavor, squabble, striving, struggle 9 bickering, commotion 10 hurly-burly 11 altercation, controversy
hassock 4 gadi, pouf 5 gaddi 7 cushion, ottoman 9 footstool
haste 3 run 4 dash, pace, rush 5 drive, hurry, speed 6 barrel, bucket, bustle, flurry, hustle, rocket, rustle 7 beeline, hotfoot 8 celerity, dispatch, fastness, highball, rapidity, velocity 9 fleetness, quickness, swiftness 10 expedition, nimbleness, speediness 11 hurriedness, impetuosity 12 precipitance, precipitancy 13 impetuousness, impulsiveness, precipitation
hasten 3 fly, run 4 flit, rush 5 fleet, hurry, speed 6 barrel, hustle, step up, urge on 7 hotfoot, quicken, shake up, speed up, swiften 10 accelerate
hasty 4 fast, rash 5 agile, brash, brisk, eager, fleet, quick, rapid, swift 6 abrupt, brashy, madcap, nimble, speedy, sudden 7 cursory, hurried, rushing 8 headlong, reckless, slambang, slapdash 9 breakneck, hotheaded, impatient, impetuous, irritable, quickened 10 expeditive, harefooted, ill-advised, incautious, mad-brained 11 expeditious, precipitant, precipitate, precipitous, subitaneous, thoughtless
hat 5 derby, tuque 6 cloche, fedora, panama, topper 7 bicorne, chapeau, haircap, homburg, porkpie, stetson, tricorn 8 sombrero, tricorne 9 headpiece 11 chapeau bras ***ancient Greek:*** 7 petasus ***brimless:*** 7 pillbox ***close-fitting:*** 5 toque, tuque 6 toquet, turban ***cone-shaped:*** 3 fez ***felt:*** 5 derby 6 bowler, trilby ***fur:*** 5 busby ***helmetlike:*** 4 topi 5 topee ***lightweight:*** 6 panama ***maker:*** 8 milliner ***military:*** 5 shako 6 shacko ***Muslim:*** 6 turban 7 tarbush 8 tarboosh ***Near East:*** 3 fez ***sheepskin:*** 6 calpac, kalpak 7 calpack ***soft:*** 5 toque ***straw:*** 6 boater, panama, sailor 7 bangkok 8 sombrero ***sun:*** 5 terai ***tall:*** 9 stovepipe ***wide-brimmed:*** 9 sou'wester 11 southwester ***woman's:*** 4 coif 5 beret
hatch 4 door, line, make, sire 5 breed, brood, cause, cover, frame, get up, spawn 6 cook up, create, devise, father, induce, invent, make up, parent, stroke, vamp up, work up 7 concoct, dream up, produce, provoke 8 contrive, engender, generate, incubate, occasion 9 floodgate, formulate, originate, procreate 11 compartment
hatchet 8 dispatch, tomahawk

hatchet man 3 gun 6 critic, killer 7 torpedo 8 assassin 9 cutthroat 10 highbinder
hate 5 abhor, gripe, scorn, spite 6 animus, bother, detest, horror, loathe, rancor, resent 7 bugbear, contemn, despise, disdain, disgust, dislike, ill will, trouble 8 anathema, aversion, distaste, execrate, irritant, loathing, nuisance 9 animosity, antipathy, bête noire, deprecate, grievance, hostility, repulsion, revulsion 10 abhorrence, black beast, disapprove, repugnance 11 abomination, detestation
hateful 4 evil, foul, mean, vile 5 catty, nasty 6 bitchy, bitter, horrid, malign, odious, scurvy 7 vicious 8 accursed, annoying, damnable, infamous 9 abhorrent, execrable, malicious, obnoxious, repellent, repulsive, resentful 10 abominable, despicable, despiteful, detestable, ill-natured, malevolent 11 acrimonious, blasphemous, distasteful, distressing, opprobrious, uncongenial, unspeakable 12 contemptible 13 reprehensible
Hatfield vs. ___ 5 McCoy
Hathath's father 7 Othniel
hatred 5 odium, spite 6 animus, enmity, rancor 7 dislike 8 aversion, loathing 9 animosity, antipathy, hostility, repulsion, revulsion 10 abhorrence, repugnance 11 abomination, detestation, malevolence ***combining form:*** 3 mis 4 miso ***of mankind:*** 11 misanthropy ***of marriage:*** 8 misogamy ***of women:*** 8 misogyny
hats 9 millinery
Hattush's father 8 Shemaiah 10 Hashabniah
hauberk 5 armor 9 chain mail, habergeon
haughtiness 5 pride 6 morgue 7 disdain, hauteur 9 arrogance, insolence, superbity
haughty 5 aloof, lofty, proud 6 lordly, sniffy 7 distant 8 arrogant, cavalier, detached, insolent, parvenue, reserved, scornful, sniffish, superior, toplofty 9 egotistic 10 disdainful 11 indifferent, overbearing 12 contemptuous, supercilious
haul 2 go 3 lug, tow, tug 4 cart, come, drag, draw, lift, load, move, pull, take 5 boost, cargo, hoist, raise, shift 6 burden, lading, remove 7 elevate, freight, payload ***with a tackle:*** 5 bouse, bowse
haul up 4 stop 5 hoise, hoist ***with a rope:*** 5 trice
haunches 4 beam, rump, tail 7 hind end, hunkers, rear end 8 backside, buttocks 9 fundament, posterior
haunt 4 home, howf, site 5 ghost, howff, range, shade 6 affect, linger, molest, resort, shadow, spirit, wraith 7 habitat, hang out, phantom, purlieu, specter, trouble 8 frequent, locality, phantasm 10 apparition, hang around, rendezvous 12 watering hole
haunter 7 denizen, habitué 10 frequenter
hautbois 4 oboe
hauteur see **haughtiness**
haut monde 5 elite 6 gentry 7 quality, society, who's who 8 optimacy 9 blue blood 10 patriciate 11 aristocracy 13 carriage trade
have 3 buy, eat, fix, get, let, own, see, sop, use, win 4 bear, fool, gain, hire, hold, keep, know, land, lead, must, need, pass, show, take, undo, wear 5 admit, allow, annex, beget, bribe, carry, cheat, drink, enjoy, grasp, leave, smoke, trick 6 accept, buy off, convey, defeat, embody, fathom, obtain, outfox, outwit, permit, pick up, retain, square, suborn, suffer, take in 7 achieve, acquire, carry on, chalk up, cherish, cognize, compass, compose, contain, control, embrace, execute, exhibit, include, involve, outplay, perform, possess, procure, receive, subsume, support, sustain, undergo 8 comprise, dominate, engage in, exercise, manifest, outreach, outslick, outsmart 9 apprehend, bamboozle, encompass, out-jockey, overreach, partake of 10 appreciate, categorize, comprehend, experience
haven 4 port, roof 5 cover, house, roads 6 asylum, covert, harbor, refuge, riding, shield 7 chamber, retreat, shelter 9 anchorage, harborage, roadstead, sanctuary
haversack 3 bag 4 case 8 backpack
havoc 4 loss, ruin, sack 5 waste 6 ravage 7 despoil, destroy, pillage 8 calamity, desolate, lay waste, ravaging, spoliate 9 cataclysm, confusion, depredate, desecrate, devastate, pillaging, ruination, vandalism 10 despoiling 11 catastrophe, destruction, devastation
haw 4 tree, yard 5 berry, fruit, shrub
Hawaii ***author:*** 8 Michener ***capital:*** 8 Honolulu ***discoverer:*** 4 Cook ***highest point:*** 8 Mauna Kea ***island:*** 4 Maui, Oahu 5 Kauai, Lanai 6 Niihau 7 Molokai 9 Kahoolawe ***nickname:*** 10 Aloha State ***state bird:*** 4 nene ***state flower:*** 11 red hibiscus
Hawaiian ***dance:*** 4 hula ***duck:*** 5 koloa ***feast:*** 4 luau ***god:*** 2 Ku 4 Kane, Lono 5 Wakea 7 Kanaloa ***goddess:*** 4 Pele ***goose:*** 4 nene ***instrument:*** 3 uke 7 ukulele ***lava:*** 2 aa ***neckwear:*** 3 lei ***nonnative:*** 8 malihini ***resident:*** 8 kamaaina ***thrush:*** 4 omao
hawk 4 vend 5 buteo 6 monger, osprey, peddle 7 goshawk, haggard 8 caracara, huckster, roughleg 9 accipiter ***Hawaiian:*** 2 io ***young:*** 4 eyas
hawker 6 coster, monger, pedlar, pedler, vendor 7 packman, peddler 8 falconer, pitchman
hawk-eyed 7 lyncean 12 sharp-sighted
Hawkeye State 4 Iowa

Hawthorne ***birthplace:*** 5 Salem ***novel:*** 13 The Marble Faun

Haydn oratorio 10 The Seasons 11 The Creation

hay fever 10 pollenosis, pollinosis ***cause:*** 6 pollen 7 ragweed

haymaker 3 box 4 chop, cuff, poke, sock 5 clout, punch, smack 6 buffet

hayseed see hick

haywire 4 amok 5 amuck, crazy 8 confused 10 broken-down, out of order

hazard 3 bet 4 luck, risk 5 peril, wager 6 chance, danger, gamble, menace 7 fortune, imperil, venture 8 accident, endanger, jeopardy

hazardous 5 hairy, risky 6 chancy, wicked 7 unsound 8 aleatory 9 dangerous, unhealthy

haze 3 dim, fog 4 film, mist, murk, smog 5 befog, bloom, brume, cloud, dream, fog up, smoke, vapor 6 stupor, trance 7 becloud, obscure, reverie 8 overcast 9 mistiness, murkiness, overcloud, smokiness 10 bemusement, cloudiness, muddlement 11 muddledness 12 befuddlement

hazel 3 nut 6 muffin 7 filbert 8 noisette

Hazo ***father:*** 5 Nahor ***mother:*** 6 Milcah

hazy 3 dim 5 filmy, foggy, misty, murky, mushy, smoky, vague 6 cloudy, dreamy, vapory 7 bemused, blurred, clouded, nebular, obscure, tranced, unclear 8 nebulous, vaporous 9 stuporous, uncertain 10 indefinite, indistinct

head 2 go 3 aim, top, wit 4 arch, bent, bill, boss, bump, cape, cast, cock, flow, gift, john, make, mind, naze, neck, pate, poll, rise, stem, text, turn 5 arise, brain, caput, chief, crown, first, flair, front, issue, knack, level, motif, point, poise, privy, scalp, skull, start, theme, topic, train 6 climax, crisis, direct, genius, honcho, johnny, leader, master, matter, mazard, motive, noddle, noggin, noodle, scolex, sconce, set out, talent, toilet, zero in 7 address, aptness, cranium, emanate, faculty, incline, latrine, leading, premier, proceed, subject, surpass, take off 8 argument, brainpan, champion, coiffure, director, foreland, foremost, hierarch, lavatory, light out 9 capitulum, chieftain, decollate, dominator, originate, principal, strike out 10 decapitate, derive from, gray matter, guillotine, individual, promontory 11 convenience, water closet ***area:*** 5 crown 6 temple ***back part:*** 7 occiput ***bone:*** 5 skull 7 cranium 8 parietal ***combining form:*** 5 crani 6 cephal, cranio 7 cephalo 8 cephalic 9 cephalous ***covering:*** 3 cap, hat 8 kercheif ***flower:*** 6 arnica, button ***monastery:*** 4 dean 5 abbot 8 superior ***nunnery:*** 4 dame 6 abbess 8 superior ***of hair:*** 6 fleece ***relating to:*** 8 cephalic ***shaving of:*** 7 tonsure ***skin:*** 5 scalp ***tapeworm's:*** 6 scolex ***top:*** 4 pate 5 crown

headache 6 megrim 7 problem 8 migraine 11 cephalalgia

headband 7 bandeau ***ancient Greek:*** 6 taenia 7 taeniae (plural)

headdress ***bishop's:*** 5 miter, mitre ***medieval:*** 5 barbe ***military:*** 5 busby, shako 6 helmet ***nobleman's:*** 7 coronet ***prelate's:*** 9 zucchetto ***priest's:*** 7 biretta ***royal:*** 5 crown, tiara 6 diadem ***Spanish women's:*** 8 mantilla ***women's:*** 6 bonnet; (see also hat)

headland 4 beak, bill, cape, naze, ness 5 point 10 promontory

headline 6 banner 7 feature 8 screamer

headlong 4 rash 5 hasty 6 abrupt, daring, rashly, sudden 7 hurried, rushing 8 gadarene, reckless 9 daredevil, foolhardy, impetuous 10 heedlessly, recklessly 11 precipitant, precipitate, precipitous, subitaneous

headmaster 9 principal

headshaker 7 skeptic, zetetic 9 pessimist 10 Pyrrhonian, Pyrrhonist

head-shaped 7 globose 8 capitate

head start 4 draw, edge, odds 5 bulge 7 vantage 8 handicap 9 advantage, allowance

headstone 6 ledger 8 monument 11 grave marker

headstrong 6 mulish 7 willful 8 stubborn 9 obstinate 10 refractory, self-willed 11 stiff-necked

heady 4 rash 5 cagey, giddy, smart 6 argute, astute, clever, shrewd 7 violent, willful 9 astucious, impetuous, sagacious 11 exhilarated, intoxicated 12 intoxicating

heal 4 cure, mend, scab 6 cement, remedy

healer ***combining form:*** 7 iatrist

healing 8 curative, remedial, sanative, sanatory 9 vulnerary, wholesome 11 restorative ***combining form:*** 5 iatro, iatry 7 iatrics ***goddess of:*** 3 Eir

health 7 stamina 8 euphoria, haleness, tonicity, vitality 9 soundness, well-being, wholeness

healthful 4 good 6 aiding 8 curative, hygienic, remedial, salutary, sanative 9 wholesome 10 beneficial, corrective, mitigative, profitable, salubrious 11 alleviative, restorative

healthy 3 fit 4 good, hale, iron, rosy, safe, sane, spry, well 5 agile, lusty, right, ruddy, sound, tough, whole 6 robust, rugged, strong, sturdy, vegete, viable 7 chipper, massive 8 blooming, hygienic, positive, rubicund, salutary, stalwart, thriving, vigorous 9 desirable, wholesome 10 beneficial, prosperous, salubrious, well-liking 11 flourishing, uninjurious ***Scottish:*** 5 gawsy 6 gawsie

heap 3 lot 4 bank, cock, cord, dump, fill, gobs, hill, load, lump, mass, much, pack, pile, rick, scad 5 amass, bunch, choke, clump, crate, drift, group, loads, mound, shock, stack, wreck 6 barrel, charge, gather, jalopy, junker, lumber, oodles 7 clunker, collect, deposit, jillion, million 8 assemble, cumulate, mountain, slathers, thousand, trillion 9 congeries, gathering, great deal, stockpile 10 accumulate, cumulation, quantities ***combining form:*** 5 cumul 6 cumuli, cumulo ***combustible:*** 4 pyre ***of dead bodies:*** 7 carnage

hearing 4 test 5 sound, trial 6 parley, tryout 7 earshot, meeting 8 audience, audition 9 interview 10 conference, discussion ***combining form:*** 4 acou 5 acouo, audio 6 acusia 7 acousia ***distance:*** 7 earshot

hearken 6 attend, listen

hearsay 3 cry 4 buzz, talk 5 on-dit, rumor 6 gossip, report, rumble 7 account 9 grapevine 11 scuttlebutt

heart 3 hub 4 core, guts, love, mood, pith, root, seat, soul, zest 5 ardor, bosom, focus, gusto, pluck, quick, spunk, taste 6 breast, center, mettle, palate, relish, spirit 7 courage 8 feelings, polestar 9 character 10 affections, compassion, conscience, enthusiasm, focal point ***combining form:*** 5 cardi 6 cardia, cardio 7 cardium ***contraction:*** 7 systole ***dilation:*** 8 diastole ***part:*** 6 atrium, septum 9 ventricle

heartache 3 rue, woe 4 care, pang 5 grief 6 regret, sorrow 7 anguish 10 affliction, cardialgia

heartbeat 5 pulse, throb 9 pulsation ***irregular:*** 8 arythmia

heartbreak 3 rue, woe 4 bale, care 5 agony, grief 6 regret, sorrow 7 anguish, torment 10 affliction

heartbreaking 4 dire 8 grievous 10 afflictive, calamitous, deplorable, lamentable 11 regrettable, unfortunate

heartburn 7 pyrosis 10 cardialgia

hearten 4 stir 5 cheer, nerve, rally, rouse, steel 6 arouse 7 animate, chirk up, enliven 8 energize, inspirit 9 encourage

heartfelt 4 deep, true 6 honest 7 earnest, genuine, sincere 8 bona fide, profound 9 unfeigned 11 whole-souled

heartleaf 6 ginger

heartless 5 cruel 7 callous 8 obdurate 9 unfeeling 10 hard-boiled 11 unemotional 13 unsympathetic

Heart of Dixie 7 Alabama

heartrending see **heartbreaking**

heartsease 5 pansy, viola 6 violet 9 smartweed

heart-shaped 7 cordate

heartsick 4 blue, down 8 cast down, dejected, downcast 9 depressed 10 dispirited 12 disconsolate

heartthrob 4 love 5 flame, honey, sweet 7 beloved, darling, passion 10 sweetheart

heartwood 7 duramen

hearty 4 deep, warm 5 ample 6 jovial, sailor 7 profuse, sincere 8 abundant, profound, vehement 9 approving, exuberant, flavorful, unfeigned 10 full-bodied, responsive 11 whole-souled 12 enthusiastic

heat 3 hot 4 cook, move, warm 6 excite, simmer, warmth 7 caloric, convect, furnace, hotness, inflame 8 pyrolyze ***combining form:*** 3 pyr 4 pyro 5 therm 6 calori, thermo, thermy 7 thermia ***measuring device:*** 11 colorimeter, thermometer ***quantity:*** 3 BTU

heated 3 hot, mad 4 warm, waxy 5 angry, fiery, irate, wroth 6 ardent, baking, fervid, fierce, hectic, ireful, steamy, wrathy 7 boiling, burning, fevered 8 broiling, feverish, scalding, sizzling, wrathful 9 indignant, scorching 11 acrimonious

heater 5 stove 7 furnace 8 radiator

heathbird 7 gray hen 9 blackcock 11 black grouse

heathen 5 pagan 6 ethnic 7 foreign, gentile, infidel, profane, strange 8 paganish, paganist 9 infidelic 10 unfamiliar

heat-producing 9 calorific

heave 3 gag 4 blow, cast, fire, gasp, huff, hurl, keck, pant, puff, rock, roll, toss 5 fling, labor, pitch, retch, sling, throw, vomit

heaven 3 God 4 Zion 5 bliss, glory 6 Canaan, utopia 7 arcadia, ecstasy, elysium, nirvana, rapture 8 empyrean, eternity, paradise, rhapsody 9 Cockaigne, hereafter, Shangri-la 10 afterworld, Civitas Dei, lubberland, wonderland 11 immortality, kingdom come 12 New Jerusalem, promised land 13 Abraham's bosom

heavenly 4 lush 5 yummy 6 divine, sacred 7 blessed, darling 8 adorable, empyreal, empyrean, luscious 9 ambrosial, celestial, delicious 10 delectable, delightful, enchanting 11 exceedingly, scrumptious

heavenly body see **celestial body**

heavy 3 big, fat 4 deep, drab, dull, gone, hard, loud, rich 5 acute, bulky, dopey, grave, gross, hefty, inert, obese, steep, stout, tough 6 clayey, cloggy, cloudy, clumsy, coarse, drowsy, fleshy, gravid, leaden, occult, orphic, parous, portly, secret, severe, sleepy, stupid, torpid 7 arduous, awkward, doleful, intense, labored, louring, massive, porcine, serious, unhandy, villain, weighty 8 abstruse, burdened, childing, comatose, cumbrous, enceinte, esoteric, grievous, hermetic, inactive, lowering, nubilous, overcast, pregnant, profound, sluggish, toilsome, unwieldy 9 corpulent, difficult, effortful, expectant, expecting, laborious, lethargic, lumbering, ponderous, recondite, strenuous **10** acroamatic, afflictive, burdensome, cumbersome, encumbered, formidable, lumbersome, oppressive, overweight, parturient, slumberous ***combining form:*** **4** bary, hadr **5** gravi, hadro

heavy-handed **5** inept **6** gauche, wooden **7** awkward, halting, unhappy **8** bumbling **9** maladroit, ponderous **10** uninspired

heavyhearted **3** sad **5** sorry **7** unhappy **8** mournful, saddened **10** dispirited, melancholy

heavyset **5** dumpy, thick **6** chunky, squdgy, stocky, stubby, stumpy **11** thick-bodied

heavyweight **3** VIP **4** lion **5** chief **6** big boy, leader **7** notable **8** big-timer

Hebe ***father:*** **4** Zeus **7** Jupiter ***husband:*** **8** Hercules ***mother:*** **4** Hera, Juno ***successor:*** **8** Ganymede

Heber ***father:*** **6** Beriah ***grandfather:*** **5** Asher ***mother:*** **4** Jael

hebetude **4** coma **5** sleep **6** stupor, torpor **7** languor, slumber **8** dullness, lethargy **9** torpidity

hebetudinous **5** dopey, heavy **6** stupid, torpid **8** comatose, sluggish **9** lethargic

Hebrew ***bushel:*** **4** epha **5** ephah ***coin:*** **4** beka, gera, mina, mite **5** bekah, gerah, maneh **6** lepton, shekel ***festival:*** **5** Pesah, Purim, Seder **6** Pesach, Succos, Sukkos **7** Hanukah, Sukkoth **8** Chanukah, Hanukhah, Hanukkah, Lag b'Omer, Passover, Shabuoth **9** Chanukhah, Chanukkah, Tishah-b'Ab, Yom Kippur **11** Rosh Hashana **12** Simhath Torah ***God:*** **2** El **5** Eloah, Yahwe **6** Adonai, Elohim, Yahweh **7** Jehovah ***instrument:*** **4** Asor **5** nabla, nebel ***judge:*** **6** Gideon ***lawgiver:*** **5** Moses ***letter:*** (see at **alphabet**) ***measure:*** **3** cor, hin, kab, log **4** bath, omer, seah, span **5** cubit, ephah, homer **6** finger **11** handbreadth ***month:*** **2** Ab **4** Adar, Elul, Iyar **5** Nisan, Sivan, Tebet **6** Kislev, Shebat, Tammuz, Tishri **6** Veadar (in leap year) **7** Heshvan ***patriarch:*** **3** Dan, Gad **4** Cain, Levi, Seth **5** Asher, David, Isaac, Jacob, Judah **6** Joseph, Reuben, Simeon **7** Abraham, Zebulun **8** Benjamin, Issachar, Naphtali ***sacred city:*** **5** Safad, Safed **6** Hebron **8** Tiberias **9** Jerusalem; (see also **Jewish**)

Hebron's father **6** Kohath

Hecate ***father:*** **6** Perses ***mother:*** **7** Asteria

heckle **3** nag **4** bait, faze, gibe, ride **5** chivy, hound, tease, worry **6** badger, harass, hector, molest, needle, plague, rattle **7** torment **8** bullyrag

hectic **3** red **6** fervid **7** burning, fevered, flushed **8** feverish, habitual, restless **10** persistent

hector **3** cow **4** bait, ride **5** bully, chivy, hound **6** badger **7** dragoon, harrier, swagger **8** bludgeon, braggart, browbeat, bulldoze, bullyrag, harasser

Hector ***brother:*** **5** Paris **7** Helenus, Troilus **9** Deiphobus, Polydorus ***father:*** **5** Priam ***mother:*** **6** Hecuba ***sister:*** **6** Creusa **8** Polyxena **9** Cassandra ***slayer:*** **8** Achilles ***victim:*** **9** Patroclus ***wife:*** **10** Andromache

Hecuba ***daughter:*** **6** Creusa **8** Polyxena **9** Cassandra ***father:*** **5** Dymas ***husband:*** **5** Priam ***son:*** **5** Paris **6** Hector **7** Helenus, Troilus **9** Deiphobus, Polydorus ***victim:*** **11** Polymnestor

hedge **3** mew, pen **4** cage, coop, mure, trim **5** evade, fence, guard **6** corral, hinder, immure, weasel **7** enclose, protect, shuffle **8** encircle, restrict, roadside, sidestep

hedonist **4** rake **7** epicure, gourmet **8** gourmand, sybarite **9** bon vivant, debauchee, epicurean, libertine **10** voluptuary

heebie-jeebies **5** jumps **6** dither, shakes **7** jitters, shivers

heed **3** see **4** care, hark, mark, mind, note, obey **5** study, watch **6** attend, beware, debate, listen, notice, regard, remark **7** concern, hearing, hearken, observe, respect **8** audience, consider, interest **9** attention, awareness **10** cognizance, observance **11** application, carefulness, mindfulness

heedful **5** alert, exact, fussy **6** arrect **7** careful **8** punctual **9** advertent, attentive, intentive, observant, observing **10** meticulous, scrupulous, thoughtful **11** observative, painstaking, punctilious **12** conscionable **13** conscientious

heedless **8** uncaring **9** oblivious, unmindful, unrecking **10** unthinking **11** inadvertent, inattentive, unobservant **12** unreflective

heedlessness **6** apathy **8** lethargy **9** disregard, lassitude, unconcern **11** disinterest, insouciance **12** indifference

hee-haw **4** bray **5** laugh **6** giggle, guffaw, titter **7** chortle, chuckle, snicker

heel **3** run, tip **4** cant, hock, lean, list, rest, tilt **5** knave, rogue, slant, slope **6** rascal **7** balance, incline, lowlife, recline, remains, remanet, remnant, residue, villain **8** leavings, residual, residuum **9** miscreant, remainder, scoundrel **10** blackguard ***bones:*** **8** calcanea, calcanei

heft **4** lift **5** hoist, raise, weigh **6** weight **9** heaviness

hefty **3** big **5** beefy, burly, husky, large, major **6** mighty, rugged **7** massive, sizable **8** abundant, imposing, powerful

9 extensive, good-sized, plentiful, ponderous
Heidi *author:* 5 Spyri *setting:* 4 Alps
height 4 apex, rise 6 climax, summit, zenith 7 stature 8 altitude, highness, pinnacle, tallness 9 elevation, loftiness *combining form:* 3 acr, akr 4 acro, akro, hyps 5 hypsi, hypso
heighten 3 wax 4 lift, rise 5 boost, build, mount, raise, rouse 6 better, deepen, expand, extend 7 amplify, augment, elevate, enhance, enlarge, improve, magnify, sharpen, upsurge 8 compound, increase, multiply, redouble 9 aggravate, highlight, intensate, intensify 10 aggrandize
heinous 6 crying 8 shocking 9 desperate, execrable 10 abominable, outrageous
heinousness 8 atrocity, enormity
heir 3 son 5 heres 6 haeres 7 heredes (plural), heritor 8 haeredes (plural) 9 inheritor, successor *joint:* 8 parcener
Hel, Hela *father:* 4 Loki *hall:* 7 Niflhel 8 Niflheim *mother:* 9 Angerboda
Helah's husband 5 Ashur 6 Ashhur
Heleb's father 6 Baanah
Helek's father 6 Gilead
Helenus *brother:* 5 Paris 6 Hector 7 Troilus 9 Deiphobus, Polydorus *father:* 5 Priam *mother:* 6 Hecuba *sister:* 6 Creusa 8 Polyxena 9 Cassandra *wife:* 10 Andromache
helical 6 spiral
helicopter 7 chopper 10 whirlybird *armed:* 7 gunship
Helios 6 Apollo *daughter:* 5 Circe 8 Pasiphae *father:* 8 Hyperion *mother:* 5 Theia *sister:* 3 Eos 6 Aurora, Selene *son:* 8 Phaethon
heliotrope 10 bloodstone
Heli's daughter 4 Mary
helium *symbol:* 2 He
hell see hades
Hellen *father:* 9 Deucalion *mother:* 6 Pyrrha *son:* 5 Dorus 6 Aeolus, Xuthus
hellhole 8 dystopia
hellish 7 avernal, stygian 8 infernal, plutonic 9 cimmerian, plutonian 11 pandemoniac
helm 5 steer
helmet 3 cap 5 salet 6 barbut, casque, morion, salade, sallet 7 morrion 8 burgonet, headgear *medieval:* 5 armet 6 heaume, sallet 7 basinet *part:* 7 ventail 8 aventail *sun:* 4 topi 5 topee
Heloise *husband:* 7 Abelard *son:* 9 Astrolabe
Helon's son 5 Eliab
helotry 4 yoke 6 thrall 7 bondage, peonage, serfdom 9 servitude, thralldom, villenage 11 enslavement
help 3 aid, use 4 abet, ally, back, cure, hand, lift, mend 5 amend, avail, avoid, boost, do for, serve, stead 6 assist, better, fail in, profit, relief, remedy, second, succor, uphold 7 advance, ancilla, benefit, bestead, bolster, comfort, forward, further, improve, prevent, promote, relieve, secours, service, striker, support 8 befriend, benefact, champion, minister, mitigate, palliate 9 alleviate, assistant, attendant, extricate, meliorate 10 ameliorate, assistance, facilitate 11 cooperation *forward:* 7 further *hired:* 5 labor
helper 3 aid 6 deputy, server 7 ancilla, servant 8 employee 9 assistant, associate, attendant, auxiliary 10 apprentice, benefactor 11 subordinate
helpful 4 good 5 brave 6 aidant, aidful, aiding, toward, usable 7 benefic 8 favoring, salutary 9 assistive, effective, favorable, practical 10 beneficial, profitable, propitious 11 encouraging, serviceable 12 advantageous, constructive
helping 7 portion 8 friendly 9 auxiliary
helpless 4 weak 6 feeble, futile 7 forlorn 8 desolate, forsaken, impotent 9 abandoned 10 bewildered 11 unprotected
helter-skelter 6 anyhow, around, random 7 anywise, flighty, hotfoot, turmoil 8 at random, pellmell, randomly 9 haphazard, hit-or-miss 11 any which way, haphazardly, hurry-scurry, impetuously, precipitate
helve 4 haft 6 handle
Helvetian 5 Swiss
hem 3 pen, rim 4 brim, cage, edge, gird, ring, seam, shut 5 beset, bound, brink, fence, hedge, round, skirt, verge 6 begird, border, circle, corral, define, edging, fringe, girdle, immure, margin, stitch 7 close in, enclose, envelop, selvage, shorten 8 encircle, surround 9 encompass, perimeter, periphery *turned-back:* 4 cuff
Hemam's father 5 Lotan
Heman *father:* 4 Joel *grandfather:* 6 Samuel
hematite 3 ore 10 bloodstone 12 black diamond
Hemdam's father 6 Dishon
hemlock 4 herb, tree 6 conium
hemophiliac 7 bleeder
hemp 3 kef, kif 4 kaif, keef, kief 8 cannabis *fiber:* 5 oakum
hemplike 4 towy
hen *broody:* 6 sitter *coop:* 5 cavie *spayed:* 7 poulard 8 poularde *young:* 6 pullet
hence 2 so 4 away, ergo, thus 5 since 9 therefore, thereupon 11 accordingly 12 consequently
henceforth 9 from now on, hereafter
henceforward see **henceforth**
henchman 6 cohort, lackey, minion,

stooge 7 sectary 8 adherent, disciple, follower, partisan, retainer, sectator 9 attendant, supporter

Hengist *brother:* 5 Horsa *kingdom:* 4 Kent *people:* 5 Jutes

Henley poem 8 Invictus

henpeck 3 nag 4 fuss 6 carp at

henpecked 8 uxorious

Henry II *adversary:* 6 Becket *son:* 7 Richard *surname:* 5 Anjou 11 Plantagenet *wife:* 7 Eleanor

Henry IV *surname:* 9 Lancaster *victim:* 7 Richard

Henry VIII *daughter:* 9 Elizabeth *son:* 6 Edward *surname:* 5 Tudor *victim:* 4 Anne 9 Catherine 10 Thomas More *wife:* 4 Anne, Jane 9 Catherine

Hen's father 9 Zephaniah

hepatic, hepatica 9 liverwort

Hephaestus 6 Vulcan *father:* 4 Zeus 7 Jupiter *mother:* 4 Hera, Juno *wife:* 6 Charis

Hepher's father 5 Ashur 6 Ashhur, Gilead

Hephzibah *husband:* 8 Hezekiah *son:* 8 Manasseh

Hera 4 Juno *father:* 6 Cronus, Saturn *husband:* 4 Zeus 7 Jupiter *messenger:* 4 Iris *mother:* 4 Rhea

Heracles, Hercules *beloved:* 4 Iole *brother:* 8 Iphicles *charioteer:* 6 Iolaus *father:* 4 Zeus 7 Jupiter *mother:* 7 Alcmene *son:* 6 Hyllus *victim:* 5 Hydra, Ladon 6 Geryon, Megara, Orthus 10 Nemean lion *wife:* 4 Hebe 6 Megara 8 Deianira

herald 4 hail, tout 5 crier, greet 6 signal 7 courier, forerun, precede, presage, trumpet 8 announce, ballyhoo, foreshow, outrider 9 announcer, harbinger, messenger, precursor, publicize, spokesman 10 forerunner, foreshadow 11 preindicate

heraldic *animal:* 7 gardant *border:* 4 orle *cross:* 6 fitchy, fleury, formée 7 fitchée 8 fourchée *design:* 5 giron, gyron 6 manche 7 saltier, saltire, sautoir 8 sautoire, tressour, tressure *term:* 4 ente, paty, pily 6 pattée 7 passant

heraldry 6 armory 9 pageantry *term:* 4 vert 6 moline, pommée, sejant 7 nombril, purpure, sejeant, statant

herb 4 forb, leek, mint, sage, wort 5 chive 6 allium, endive, garlic, pusley, pussly 7 campion, caraway, comfrey, gerbera, puccoon, pussley, spinach, spinage, tobacco 8 angelica, brassica, cilantro, costmary, deerweed, erigeron, gerardia, gromwell, hawkweed, marjoram, plantain, polygony, purslane, tithonia 9 buckwheat, clintonia, nemophila *African:* 7 freesia, tritoma *annual:* 4 dill, flax, okra 5 blite 6 crambe 7 bugseed, clarkia, clivers, sandbur, tampala, waxweed 8 euphrasy, sandburr, tidytips 9 bush basil 10 calliopsis *aquatic:* 6 elodea 7 nelumbo 8 hornwort *aromatic:* 5 basil, clary, thyme 6 catnip 7 catmint, chervil, monarda, oregano 8 origanum, woodruff *Asian:* 7 perilla, skirret 8 chickpea *biennial:* 11 blazing star *bitter:* 9 chamomile *bulb:* 5 onion *composite:* 8 knapweed 9 centaurea 10 bitterweed 11 bur marigold *cultivated:* 7 parsley *East Indian:* 8 pachouli, turmeric 9 patchouli, patchouly *Eurasian:* 6 mullen, squill 7 mullein *European:* 5 paris 6 axseed, betony 7 parsnip, salsify 8 earthnut, fleawort, lungwort, mandrake, oxtongue, rapeseed, samphire, snowdrop, wormwood 9 birthwort 13 Christmas rose *evergreen:* 5 galax *fragrant:* 6 cicely 7 pinesap 10 basil thyme 12 balm of Gilead *garlic:* 6 ramson *genus:* 7 solanum *Japanese:* 3 udo *leafless:* 9 broomrape *marjoram:* 6 origan *medicinal:* 6 borage, eringo, eryngo, hyssop 7 allheal, sanicle 8 blueball, camomile, centaury 9 chamomile *Mexican:* 4 chia 8 tuberose *mythical:* 4 moly *ornamental:* 8 dianthus *perennial:* 4 geum, sego 5 avens, camas, orpin, tansy 6 arnica, asarum, bennet, burnet, camass, fennel, henbit, lovage, madder, orpine, pyrola, yarrow 7 bistort, boneset, bugbane, chicory, cicoree, cudweed, dittany, dogbane, genseng, ginseng, jonquil, milfoil, pinweed, primula, quamash, redroot, rhubarb, shortia, succory, witloof 8 agrimony, boltonia, calamint, chiccory, dicentra, dropwort, eggplant, eremurus, feverfew, finochio, fireweed, gaywings, harebell, hepatica, honewort, licorice, mayapple, nutgrass, nutsedge, pokeroot, pokeweed, primrose, roseroot, sainfoin, selfheal, shinleaf, soapwort, stokesia, tarragon, toadflax, valerian 9 bloodwort, finocchio, squawroot *poisonous:* 6 conium 7 aconite, hemlock, henbane 8 veratrum *prickly:* 8 acanthus *purple:* 12 checkerbloom *Rocky mountain:* 10 bitterroot *salad:* 7 lettuce *seaside:* 8 saltwort *small-flowered:* 11 baby's breath *South African:* 12 Cape marigold *South American:* 3 oca *summer-blooming:* 11 bunchflower *tall:* 4 hemp *tropical:* 6 crinum 7 begonia, episcia, petunia 8 abelmosk, capsicum, cardamom, cardamon, cardamum *twining:* 8 lovevine *weedy:* 7 ragweed *wild garlic:* 4 moly *woody:* 8 bedstraw *yellow:* 9 celandine *yellow-rayed:* 9 calendula

herbicide 6 diquat, diuron 7 dalapon, monuron 8 picloram, simazine

Herculean 4 huge, vast 5 giant 7 immense, mammoth, titanic 8 colossal, enormous, gigantic 10 superhuman

Hercules see Heracles
herd 3 mob, run 4 lead 5 drive, drove, flock 6 gather 9 associate ***sheep:*** 6 hirsel
here and there 6 passim 7 at times 9 sometimes 11 irregularly
hereditary 9 ancestral
heredity unit 4 gene
heresy 5 error 6 schism 7 dissent, fallacy, impiety 9 defection, misbelief 10 dissidence, heterodoxy, infidelity, radicalism 11 revisionism, unorthodoxy 13 nonconformism, nonconformity
heretic 7 infidel, sectary 8 apostate, defector, recreant, recusant, renegade 9 dissenter, dissident, innovator 10 iconoclast, schismatic, separatist, unbeliever 11 misbeliever, revisionist, schismatist 12 deviationist 13 nonconformist
heretical 7 infidel 8 apostate 9 differing, dissident, heterodox, miscreant, sectarian 10 dissenting, dissentive, schismatic, unorthodox 11 disagreeing, dissentient, revisionist, unbelieving 12 misbelieving 13 nonconformist
heritage 6 legacy 9 patrimony, tradition 10 birthright
Hermes 7 Mercury ***attribute:*** 7 petasos, petasus, talaria 8 caduceus ***father:*** 4 Zeus 7 Jupiter ***mother:*** 4 Maia ***winged cap:*** 7 petasos, petasus ***winged shoes:*** 7 talaria
hermetic 4 deep 5 heavy 6 occult, secret 7 recluse, secluse 8 abstruse, airtight, profound, secluded 9 alchemist, recondite, seclusive 10 cloistered 11 sequestered
Hermia ***beloved:*** 8 Lysander ***father:*** 5 Egeus
Hermione ***father:*** 8 Menelaus ***husband:*** 7 Orestes, Pyrrhus 11 Neoptolemus ***mother:*** 5 Helen
hermit 7 eremite, recluse 8 solitary 9 anchorite
hermitage 8 hideaway 9 monastery
hernia 6 breach 7 rupture 10 protrusion ***combining form:*** 4 cele ***of the bladder:*** 9 cystocele ***support:*** 5 truss ***type:*** 6 cystic, hiatal 7 femoral 9 umbilical 10 incisional
hero 6 knight 7 demigod, paladin 8 champion 11 protagonist ***American:*** 6 Bunyan (Paul) 8 Superman ***Babylonian:*** 9 Gilgamesh ***Celtic-French:*** 7 Tristam, Tristan 8 Tristram ***Crusades:*** 7 Tancred 8 Tancredi ***English:*** 6 Arthur 7 Beowulf 9 Robin Hood ***French:*** 6 Roland 11 Charlemagne ***German:*** 5 Etzel 9 Siegfried ***Greek:*** 4 Ajax 5 Jason 7 Perseus, Ulysses 8 Achilles, Heracles, Hercules, Odysseus ***Hebrew:*** 5 David 6 Samson ***Irish:*** 9 Cuchullin 10 Cuchullain ***Italian:*** 7 Orlando ***Roman:*** 7 Romulus 8 Horatius ***Scandinavian:*** 6 Sigurd ***Scottish:*** 5 Bruce (Robert) 6 Rob Roy ***Spanish:*** 3 Cid ***Spartan:*** 8 Leonidas ***Trojan:*** 6 Aeneas, Hector
Herod ***daughter:*** 6 Salome ***father:*** 7 Antipas 9 Antipater ***kingdom:*** 5 Judea 6 Judaea ***mother:*** 6 Cyprus ***son:*** 5 Herod (Antipas) 6 Joseph 7 Pheroas 9 Phasaelus
Herodias ***daughter:*** 6 Salome ***father:*** 11 Aristobulus ***husband:*** 5 Herod (Antipas)
heroic 4 bold, huge 5 brave 6 mighty 7 extreme, radical, valiant 8 colossal, enormous, fearless, gigantic, intrepid, unafraid, valorous 9 cyclopean, dauntless, Herculean, undaunted 10 courageous
heroin 4 skag 5 horse, smack 8 narcotic 11 diamorphine
heroism 5 valor 6 spirit 7 bravery, courage, prowess 8 boldness, chivalry, nobility, valiance, valiancy 9 gallantry 11 intrepidity 12 fearlessness, valorousness
Hero's love 7 Leander
herring 8 brisling ***smoked:*** 7 bloater ***young:*** 4 brit 5 britt
Herse ***father:*** 7 Cecrops ***sister:*** 8 Aglauros ***son:*** 8 Cephalus
Hersey ***novel:*** 7 The Wall 13 A Bell for Adano ***town:*** 5 Adano
Hesione ***brother:*** 5 Priam ***father:*** 8 Laomedon ***husband:*** 7 Telamon ***rescuer:*** 8 Heracles, Hercules ***son:*** 6 Teucer
hesitant 3 shy 5 chary, loath 6 afraid, averse, wobbly 7 halting, uneager 8 backward 9 faltering, tentative, uncertain, unwilling 10 indisposed, irresolute 11 disinclined, vacillating, vacillatory 12 wiggle-waggle
hesitate 4 balk, halt 5 delay, demur, pause, stall, stick, swing, waver 6 boggle, dawdle, dither, falter, mammer 7 scruple, stagger, stammer, stickle, stutter, whiffle 8 hang back 9 temporize 10 dillydally 12 shilly-shally, wiggle-waggle 13 procrastinate
Hesperia 5 Italy, Spain 9 butterfly
Hesperides 5 Aegle 8 Erytheia, Hesperis
Hesperus 5 Venus 11 evening star ***father:*** 8 Astraeus ***mother:*** 3 Eos
Hesse novel 6 Demian 11 Steppenwolf 12 Magister Ludi
Hestia 5 Vesta ***father:*** 6 Cronus, Saturn ***mother:*** 4 Rhea
heterodox 9 dissident, heretical, sectarian 10 schismatic 13 nonconformist
heterodoxy 6 heresy, schism 7 dissent 9 misbelief 10 dissidence 13 nonconformism, nonconformity
heterogeneous 5 mixed 6 motley, varied 8 assorted, chowchow 9 disparate 12 conglomerate
hew 3 cut 4 chop, fell 5 stick 6 adhere 7 conform, cut down
hex 3 hag 4 jinx 5 bruja, charm, lamia,

queer, spell, witch **6** hoodoo, voodoo, whammy **7** bewitch, enchant **9** ensorcell, sorceress **10** Indian sign, witchwoman **11** enchantment, enchantress
heyday **4** acme **5** prime **6** spring
Hezekiah ***father:*** **4** Ahaz **7** Neariah ***mother:*** **3** Abi ***son:*** **8** Manasseh ***wife:*** **9** Hephzibah
Hezion ***grandson:*** **8** Benhadad ***son:*** **8** Tabrimon **9** Tabrimmon
Hezron's father **5** Perez **6** Pharez, Reuben
hiatus **3** gap **5** break **6** breech, lacuna **7** interim **8** aperture, interval **12** interruption
Hiawatha ***author:*** **10** Longfellow ***grandmother:*** **7** Nokomis ***mother:*** **7** Wenonah ***tribe:*** **6** Ojibwa **7** Ojibway ***wife:*** **9** Minnehaha
Hibernia **4** Eire, Erin **7** Ireland
hick **4** jake, rube **5** yokel **6** rustic **7** bucolic, bumpkin, country, hayseed **8** cornball, ruralist, ruralite **10** clodhopper, provincial
hick town **4** burg **6** Podunk **7** mudhole **11** whistlestop
hidden **5** privy **6** buried, covert, secret **7** guarded, obscure **8** obscured, shrouded, ulterior **9** concealed **11** undisclosed ***combining form:*** **5** crypt, krypt **6** crypto, krypto
hide **3** fur **4** bury, coat, fell, flog, lash, life, lurk, mask, pelt, skin, veil, whip **5** cache, cloak, cover, inter, lodge, plant, shade, stash **6** entomb, harbor, jacket, lather, mantle, occult, screen, shield, shroud, stripe, thrash **7** conceal, cover up, curtain, leather, obscure, retreat, scourge, seclude, secrete, shelter, veiling **8** ensconce **10** flagellate ***combining form:*** **4** derm **5** derma **6** dermia, dermis **9** dermatous
hideaway **3** den **4** lair **6** refuge **8** secluded **9** concealed
hideous **4** ugly **5** lurid, nasty **6** grisly, horrid **7** ghastly, hateful, macabre **8** gruesome, horrible, shocking, terrible, uncomely **9** dismaying, frightful, loathsome, ludicrous, monstrous, offensive, repellent, repugnant, repulsive, revolting, unsightly **10** disgusting, horrifying, ill-favored, ill-looking, terrifying
hideout **3** den **4** lair **5** haven **6** covert, refuge **7** retreat, shelter **9** hermitage, sanctuary
hiding place **5** cache, cover **6** covert, refuge **7** retreat
hie **2** go **4** fare, pass, wend **6** hasten, push on, repair, travel **7** journey, proceed
hiemal **6** wintry
hierarch **4** boss, cock, head **5** chief **6** honcho, leader, master **7** headman **9** chieftain
hieratic **8** priestal, priestly **9** priestish **10** priestlike, sacerdotal **12** sacerdotical
high **3** big, gay **4** acme, dear, loud, olid, rank, rick, tall, thin **5** acute, doped, drunk, fetid, grand, grave, knoll, large, lofty, noble, sharp **6** aerial, argute, bright, costly, elated, florid, height, piping, putrid, raised, rancid, remote, richly, shrill, smelly, stoned, strong, treble, whiffy, zonked **7** ancient, drugged, eminent, extreme, intense, keyed up, reeking, serious, soaring, supreme, violent **8** abstruse, arrogant, cheerful, critical, edifying, elevated, eloquent, exciting, gigantic, hopped-up, long past, nidorous, piercing, powerful, stinking, towering, turned on, vehement, wrathful **9** ambitious, climactic, excellent, expensive, imperious, important, intensive, luxurious, prominent, spaced-out **10** boisterous, malodorous, pronounced, tripped out **11** anti-cyclone, extravagant, intoxicated ***combining form:*** **4** alti
high-and-mighty **5** proud **6** lordly **8** arrogant, cavalier, insolent, superior **9** imperious **10** disdainful **11** overbearing **12** supercilious
highball **3** fly, run **4** rush, whiz **5** hurry, speed **6** barrel, hustle **7** hotfoot
highbinding **5** fraud **7** chicane **8** trickery **9** chicanery, deception, fourberie **10** dishonesty, hanky-panky **11** skulduggery
highboy **5** chest **6** bureau
highbrow **7** Brahmin, egghead **8** cerebral **10** doubledome **12** intellectual
highest **3** top **5** chief **6** apical, astral, upmost **7** exalted, supreme, topmost **9** top-drawer, uppermost **10** top-ranking ***point:*** **4** acme, apex **5** crest **6** summit, zenith **8** pinnacle
highfalutin **4** rant **6** florid **7** aureate, bombast, flowery, fustian, pompous **8** rhapsody, rhetoric **9** bombastic **10** oratorical, rhetorical **11** declamatory, pretentious
high-handed **5** bossy **8** imperial **9** arbitrary, imperious, masterful **10** imperative, peremptory **11** domineering, magisterial, overbearing
high-hat **4** snub **5** potty **6** snobby, snooty **8** snobbish **12** aristocratic
high jinks **5** revel **7** fooling, revelry, wassail, whoopee, whoopla, whoop-up **9** horseplay, revelment, rowdiness, whoop-de-do **10** roughhouse, skylarking **12** roughhousing
highlight **6** stress **7** feature **9** emphasize
high-minded **5** moral, noble **8** elevated
high-muck-a-muck **3** VIP **5** nabob **6** big boy, bigwig **7** big shot, mugwump, notable
high-pitched **6** shrill **7** shrieky **8** agitated
high-principled **5** noble **6** worthy **8** sterling **9** estimable, honorable

high roller 7 gambler, spender, wastrel 8 prodigal, unthrift 10 profligate 11 scattergood, spendthrift, waste-thrift
high sign 3 nod, tip 4 wink 5 alarm 6 signal, tipoff 7 warning
high-sounding 3 big 4 arty 7 pompous 9 overblown 10 arty-crafty 11 pretentious
high-spirited 5 beany, brash, fiery, jolly, merry 6 lively, spunky 7 gingery, peppery 8 mirthful 9 ebullient, exuberant, vivacious 10 mettlesome 12 effervescent, lighthearted
high-strung 4 taut 5 jumpy, tense, tight 6 goosey, spooky 7 fidgety, jittery, nervous, uptight 8 twittery 9 excitable, unrelaxed
hightail 4 kite 5 scram 6 begone, decamp, get out 7 skiddoo, take off 8 clear out 9 skedaddle
highway 4 path, pike, road 5 track 6 artery, avenue, street 8 turnpike 9 boulevard 12 thoroughfare ***German:*** 8 autobahn ***Italian:*** 10 autostrada
Highwayman author 5 Noyes
hike 2 up 3 wax 4 jump, rise, rove, trek, walk 5 boost, march, put up, raise, tramp, tromp 6 jack up, ramble, stroll, trapes, travel, wander 7 explore, journey, traipse, upgrade 8 backpack, footslog, increase 9 walkabout 12 breakthrough
hilarious 5 funny, merry 8 humorous, mirthful
hilarity 4 glee 5 cheer, mirth 6 gaiety 8 jocosity, laughter 9 merriment 12 cheerfulness
Hilkiah ***father:*** 4 Amzi 5 Hosah ***son:*** 7 Eliakim 8 Gemariah, Jeremiah
hill 3 kop 4 bank, bump, cock, heap, knob, pile, rick 5 butte, drift, mound, ridge, shock, slope, stack 6 cuesta, height 7 hummock, incline 8 mountain 9 elevation, monadnock ***African veld:*** 5 kopje ***Charlestown:*** 6 Bunker ***craggy:*** 3 tor ***Cuba:*** 7 San Juan ***D.C.:*** 7 Capitol ***elongate:*** 7 drumlin ***high:*** 5 mount ***level-topped:*** 4 mesa 5 butte ***of stratified drift:*** 4 kame ***rounded:*** 5 swell ***sand:*** 4 dune ***small:*** 5 knoll, kopje, mound 6 koppie ***surrounded by ice:*** 7 nunatak
hillbilly 4 rube 5 yokel 6 rustic 7 bucolic, bumpkin, hayseed 10 clodhopper 12 backwoodsman
hillock 5 knoll, mound ***British:*** 4 toft
hillside 5 slope ***Scottish:*** 4 brae
Himavat's daughter 4 Devi
hind 4 back, rear 5 after 6 retral, rustic 7 bailiff 9 posterior
hind end 4 beam, rear, rump, tail 7 hunkers 8 backside, buttocks, haunches 9 fundament, posterior
hinder 3 bar, dam, let 4 back, balk, clog, curb, mire, rear 5 after, block, brake, check, deter, embog 6 arrest, baffle, burden, cumber, fetter, hamper, hog-tie, impede, lumber, retard, retral, thwart, tramel 7 inhibit, manacle, shackle, tramell, trammel 8 blockade, handicap, obstruct, restrain 9 entrammel, frustrate, hamstring, interrupt 10 overslaugh
hindmost 3 lag 4 back, last, rear 5 after, final 6 latter, retral 7 closing 8 eventual, terminal, ultimate 9 posterior 10 concluding
hindquarters 8 haunches
hindrance 4 clog 5 block 8 drawback, obstacle 10 impediment
Hindu ***age:*** 4 yuga ***ascetic:*** 4 yogi ***caste (varna):*** 5 Sudra 6 Vaisya 7 Brahman 9 Kshatriya ***class:*** 5 caste, varna ***dancing girl:*** 8 devadesi ***demon:*** 4 Rahu 6 Ravana ***essence:*** 5 atman ***force:*** 5 karma ***garment:*** 4 sari 5 saree ***god:*** 3 dev 4 deva ***goddess:*** 4 devi ***goddess of beauty:*** 7 Lakshmi ***goddess of destruction:*** 4 Kali ***god of fire:*** 4 Agni ***god of love:*** 4 Kama ***god of the heavens:*** 7 Krishna ***god of war:*** 6 Skanda 10 Karttikeya ***god of wisdom:*** 6 Ganesa, Ganesh ***hell:*** 6 Naraka ***holy man:*** 5 sadhu 6 saddhu ***leader:*** 6 Gandhi ***lowest caste:*** 5 Sudra ***lute:*** 5 sitar ***marriage:*** 9 gandharva ***nobleman:*** 4 raja 5 rajah ***precept:*** 5 sutra, sutta ***prince:*** 4 raja 5 rajah 8 maharaja 9 maharajah ***queen:*** 4 rani 5 ranee 8 maharani 9 maharanee ***sacred thread:*** 7 upavita ***salvation:*** 7 nirvana ***scripture:*** 12 Bhagavad Gita ***social group:*** 5 caste, varna ***teacher:*** 4 guru ***term of respect:*** 5 sahib ***twice-born:*** 6 Vaisya 7 Brahman 9 Kshatriya
hinge 4 pawl 5 joint, mount 12 turning point ***kind:*** 4 butt 5 piano 10 hook-and-eye
hint 3 beg, cue, key, tip 4 cast, clue, coax, dash, fish, hair, lick, seek, sign, vein 5 angle, imply, plead, point, press, shade, smack, smell, spice, taint, taste, tinge, touch, trace, twang, whiff 6 advice, aiming, breath, notion, shadow, smatch, strain, streak, tipoff, trifle 7 connote, inkling, pointer, presage, solicit, soupçon, suggest, vestige, whisper 8 indicate, innuendo, intimate, overtone, particle, pointing, telltale, tincture 9 adumbrate, direction, importune, insinuate, prefigure, prompting, scintilla, suspicion, undertone 10 assistance, foreshadow, indication, intimation, sprinkling, suggestion 11 adumbration, association, connotation, forewarning, implication, insinuation
hinterland 4 bush 6 sticks 8 backwash, frontier, interior 9 backwater, backwoods, up-country 10 background, wilderness 11 back-country
hip 4 coxa 6 haunch, huckle ***bone:*** 5 ilium,

pubis 6 pelvis 7 ischium *cattle:* 5 thurl *combining form:* 5 ischi 6 ischio *disorder:* 8 sciatica
hippie 8 bohemian, longhair
Hippocratic ___ 4 oath
Hippodamia *father:* 8 Oenomaus *husband:* 6 Pelops 9 Pirithous 10 Peirithous *son:* 6 Atreus 8 Thyestes
Hippolytus *father:* 7 Theseus *mother:* 7 Antiope 9 Hippolyte *stepmother:* 7 Phaedra
Hippomenes' wife 8 Atalanta
Hirah's friend 5 Judah
hire 3 fee, let, pay 4 book, rent, wage 5 lease, put on, wages 6 employ, engage, salary, sublet, take on 7 charter, recruit
hireling 4 grub, hack 6 drudge, slavey 7 grubber 9 mercenary
hirsute 5 hairy 6 fleecy, pilose, shaggy, woolly 7 pileous 9 whiskered
Hispania 5 Spain 6 Iberia
hiss 3 boo 4 bird, buzz, fizz, hoot, pooh, sizz, whiz 5 bazoo, swish, whish, woosh 6 fizzle, sizzle, wheeze, whoosh 7 catcall, whisper, whistle 8 pooh-pooh, sibilate 9 raspberry
historian 8 annalist 10 chronicler *American:* 4 Webb 5 Adams, Beard, Foote 6 Durant, Malone, Miller, Muzzey, Nevins, Sarton, Sparks, Turner 7 Morison, Parkman, Ridpath, Woodson 8 Channing, Commager, Prescott, Robinson 11 Schlesinger *English:* 4 Bede, Stow, Ward 5 Acton, Grote, Wells 6 Camden, Gibbon, Namier, Stubbs 7 Hakluyt, Raleigh, Toynbee, Whewell 8 Geoffrey, Macaulay 9 Holinshed, Trevelyan *French:* 5 Renan, Taine 6 Guizot, Thiers, Volney 8 Hanotaux, Michelet *German:* 5 Ranke 7 Mommsen, Neibuhr 8 Spengler *Greek:* 8 Polybius, Xenophon 9 Dionysius, Herodotus 10 Thucydides *Italian:* 5 Croce 9 Salvemini *Jewish:* 8 Josephus *Roman:* 4 Livy 7 Sallust, Tacitus 9 Suetonius *Scottish:* 7 Carlyle 9 Robertson *Swiss:* 6 Müller *Welsh:* 7 Nennius
historical period 3 age, era 5 epoch 7 ancient 8 medieval
history 4 epic, saga, tale 5 diary, story 6 annals, memoir, report 7 account, journal, recital, version 8 relation 9 chronicle, narrative
histrionic 5 actor 6 staged 8 dramatic, theatral, thespian 10 theatrical 11 dramaturgic
hit 3 bop, rap, wow 4 bang, bash, bean, biff, blow, bump, bunt, butt, conk, cuff, ding, fill, fist, lick, luck, meet, slap, slog, slug, sock, swat, swot, wipe 5 clout, knock, light, occur, pound, skelp, smash, smite, swipe, whack 6 affect, attack, buffet, chance, happen, stress, strike, stroke, thwack, tumble 7 censure, stumble 8 bludgeon 9 collision, emphasize *baseball:* 5 homer, liner 6 double, single, triple 7 home run 9 line drive *golf ball:* 5 shank
hitch 4 jerk, lift, limp, yoke 5 thumb 6 couple, hobble 7 harness 8 stoppage 10 impediment 11 obstruction 12 entanglement
hitchhike 5 thumb
hither 4 here 6 nearer 11 to this place
hitherto 3 yet 4 here, once 5 as yet, prior, so far 6 before 7 earlier, thus far 8 formerly, previous 10 heretofore, previously
Hitler *follower:* 4 Nazi *title:* 6 Führer 7 Fuehrer *wife:* 5 Braun (Eva)
hit man 3 gun 5 bravo 7 torpedo 8 assassin, gangster 9 cutthroat 10 gunslinger
hit-or-miss 6 chance, random 7 aimless, unaimed 9 desultory, haphazard, irregular, unplanned 10 designless 12 unconsidered
hive 5 amass, lay up, uplay 6 apiary, garner, roll up 7 store up 8 cumulate 9 stockpile 10 accumulate
hoar 4 rime 5 frost
hoard 4 save 5 lay by, lay up, stash, stock, store, trove 6 garner 7 backlog, nest egg, reserve 8 squirrel, treasure 9 amassment, colluvies, inventory, reservoir, stockpile 10 accumulate, collection, cumulation 11 aggregation 12 accumulation
hoarder 5 miser
hoarfrost 4 rime
hoarse 3 dry 5 gruff, harsh, husky, rough, thick 6 croaky, rasped 7 grating, jarring, rasping, raucous, throaty 8 croaking, guttural, strident 10 discordant, stridulent, stridulous *Scottish:* 5 roupy 6 roupet
hoary 3 old 4 aged 5 stale, trite 6 age-old, remote 7 ancient, antique 8 Noachian, timeworn 9 canescent, hackneyed, venerable 12 antideluvian
hoax 3 gyp 4 dupe, fake, fool, gull, sell 5 fraud, phony, put-on, spoof, trick 6 befool, delude, humbug, take in 7 chicane, mislead 8 flimflam, hoodwink 9 bamboozle, imposture, mare's nest, victimize 11 hornswoggle
hob 4 nail 6 ferret, leader
Hobab *brother-in-law:* 5 Moses *father:* 6 Reuel
Hobbit creator 7 Tolkien
hobble 3 tie 4 clog, curb, halt, limp 5 hitch, leash 6 fetter, hamper, hog-tie, impede 7 cripple, trammel 8 obstruct 9 entrammel
hobby 7 pastime 9 avocation, diversion
hobgoblin 5 bogey 7 bugaboo
hobnail 4 stud
hobo 3 bum, vag 5 tramp 7 drifter, floater,

swagman, vagrant 8 derelict, vagabond 10 street arab

hock 4 knee, pawn 6 pledge 8 mortgage 9 hamstring 11 impignorate

hockey 6 shinny 7 shinney ***arena:*** 4 rink ***cup:*** 7 Stanley ***implement:*** 4 puck 5 stick ***official:*** 7 referee 8 linesman ***player:*** 3 Orr (Bobby) 4 Fuhr (Grant), Howe (Gordie), Hull (Bobby, Brett), wing 5 Bossy (Mike), Shore (Eddie) 6 center, Clarke (Bobby), Dryden (Ken), goalie, Harvey (Doug), Mikita (Stan), Morenz (Howie), Parent (Bernie), Potvin (Denis) 7 Bourque (Ray), forward, Gretzky (Wayne), Lafleur (Guy), Lemieux (Mario), Messier (Mark), Richard (Maurice) 8 Beliveau (Jean), Esposito (Phil, Tony), pointman, Trottier (Bryan) 10 defenseman, goalkeeper ***stick:*** 5 caman (Scottish, Irish), camog (Irish) 7 cammock (Scottish) ***team:*** 4 Jets 5 Blues, Kings 6 Bruins, Devils, Flames, Flyers, Oilers, Sabres, Sharks 7 Canucks, Rangers, Whalers 8 Capitals, Penguins, Red Wings 9 Canadiens, Islanders, Nordiques 10 Black Hawks, Maple Leafs, North Stars ***term:*** 3 box 4 cage, goal, puck, rink 5 bandy, bench, check, icing, stick 6 charge, crease, shinny 7 face-off, offside 8 blue line 9 back-check, body-check 10 center line, penalty box ***variation of:*** 9 broomball

hod 4 tray 6 trough 7 scuttle 11 coal scuttle

Hodaviah's father 8 Elioenai 9 Hassenuah

Hoder, Hoth ***brother:*** 6 Balder ***slayer:*** 4 Vali ***victim:*** 6 Balder

Hodesh's husband 9 Shaharaim

hodgepodge 4 hash 6 jumble, medley 7 mélange, mixture 8 eclectic, mishmash 9 patchwork, potpourri 10 hotchpotch, miscellany 11 gallimaufry

Hod's father 6 Zophah

hoe 4 till 9 cultivate

hog 3 pig, sow 4 boar 5 roach, swine 8 boshvark ***family:*** 6 Suidae ***female:*** 3 sow 4 gilt ***genus:*** 3 Sus ***red:*** 5 duroc ***young:*** 5 shoat, shote

hogback 5 chine, crest, ridge

Hoglah's father 10 Zelophehad

Hogni's victim 6 Sigurd

hogshead 3 keg, tun 4 butt, cask, pipe 6 barrel

hog-tie 4 clog, curb 5 leash 6 fetter, hamper, hobble 7 shackle, trammel 9 entrammel

hogwash 4 slop 5 bilge, hokum, hooey, swill 8 nonsense 9 poppycock

hoi polloi 3 mob 4 scum 5 dregs, trash 6 masses, rabble 8 populace, riffraff 9 multitude 11 proletariat

hoist 4 lift, rear, rise 5 boost, raise, winch 6 pick up, take up, uphold, uplift, uprear 7 derrick, elevate, upraise 8 windlass

hoity-toity 5 dizzy, giddy, silly 7 flighty, pompous 8 skittish 9 frivolous 11 harebrained, thoughtless 13 rattlebrained

hokum 4 bosh, jazz 5 hooey 8 flimflam, malarkey, nonsense 9 poppycock 11 foolishness

hold 3 fix, own 4 bear, deem, feel, grab, grip, halt, have, keep, last, stay, stop 5 apply, carry, clamp, clasp, cling, delay, enjoy, grasp, gripe, judge, limit, pause, poise, sense, think, value 6 accept, arrest, clench, clinch, clutch, credit, detain, esteem, harbor, prison, regard, retain, steady, tenure 7 believe, catch up, comport, contain, convene, convoke, custody, fermata, grapple, keep out, possess, reserve, support, sustain 8 conceive, consider, enthrall, keep back, maintain, preserve, purchase, restrict 9 fascinate, handclasp, mesmerize, spellbind ***as precious:*** 8 treasure ***close:*** 6 cuddle ***dear:*** 7 cherish ***from proceeding:*** 4 stay ***in check:*** 7 repress ***in common:*** 5 share ***out:*** 4 last 6 endure ***together:*** 4 bond 5 clamp 6 fasten ***wrestling:*** 8 headlock, scissors

hold back 3 bit 4 curb, deny, keep 5 check 6 bridle, detain, retain 7 abstain, inhibit, keep out, refrain, reserve 8 restrain 9 constrain

hold in 3 bit 4 curb 5 check 6 bridle 7 inhibit 8 restrain 9 constrain 10 keep silent

hold off 4 stay 5 defer, delay, rebut, remit, repel 6 rebuff, shelve 7 abstain, adjourn, repulse, suspend 8 hesitate, postpone, prorogue 9 withstand

hold up 4 halt, lift, stay 5 check, defer, delay, raise, remit, waive 6 put off 7 prevail, support, suspend, sustain 8 postpone, prorogue

hole 3 box, den, fix, gap, jam, pit 4 cave, cove, flaw, open, rent, rift, spot, vent, void 5 break, fault, niche 6 breach, burrow, cavity, corner, cranny, eyelet, hiatus, lacuna, outlet, pickle, pierce, plight, scrape, vacuum 7 dilemma, disrupt, fissure, opening, orifice, rupture, vacancy, vacuity 8 aperture 9 perforate 10 excavation, interstice 11 perforation

holiday 5 leave 6 May Day 7 festive, Flag Day 8 Arbor Day, carefree, vacation 9 Halloween 10 Father's Day, Mother's Day 12 All Saints' Day, Groundhog Day 13 St. Patrick's Day, Valentine's Day ***Alaska:*** 10 Seward's Day ***British:*** 9 Boxing Day ***Canadian:*** 11 Dominion Day, Victoria Day ***Federal:*** 8 Labor Day, New Year's 9 Christmas 11 Veterans Day 12 Armistice Day, Thanksgiving ***Hawaii:*** 8 Kuhio Day

13 Kamehameha Day *Jewish:* 8 Passover *Maryland:* 12 Defender's Day *Newfoundland:* 12 Discovery Day, St. George's Day 13 Orangemen's Day *Rhode Island:* 10 Victory Day *Texas:* 13 San Jacinto Day *Utah:* 10 Pioneer Day

holiness 5 piety 8 devotion, divinity, sanctity 12 consecration, spirituality

Holland see Netherlands

holler 3 cry 4 call, yell 5 gripe, shout 6 outcry 7 grumble 8 complain 9 complaint 10 vociferate

hollow 3 dip, sag 4 idle, sink, vain, void 5 basin, empty, false, notch, womby 6 cavity, dingle, otiose, ravine, sunken 7 channel, concave, echoing, sinkage, vacuity 8 complete, nugatory, resonant, sinkhole, sounding, thorough 9 cavernous, concavity, deceitful 10 depression, resounding, sepulchral *out:* 3 dig, gut 4 mine 5 gouge 8 excavate

holly 4 tree 5 shrub *genus:* 4 Ilex

holocaust 4 fire 7 inferno 9 sacrifice 11 destruction 13 conflagration

Holofernes' slayer 6 Judith

holy 3 god 5 pious 6 adored, devout, divine, sacred 7 angelic, awesome, blessed, revered, saintly 8 hallowed, priestly 9 glorified, pietistic, prayerful, religious, sanctuary, spiritual, unprofane, venerated, worshiped 10 reverenced, sanctified 11 consecrated, frightening *bread:* 7 eulogia 9 antidoron *combining form:* 4 hagi, hier 5 hagio, hiero *communion:* 9 eucharist *oil:* 6 chrism *person:* 5 saint 6 zaddik 8 zaddikim (plural) *Spirit:* 9 Paraclete *vessel:* 7 chalice 8 ciborium

holy place 6 shrine 7 sanctum 9 sanctuary 10 sanctorium

Holy Roman Emperor 4 Karl, Otto 5 Adolf, Franz, Henry, Louis 6 Albert, Arnulf, Conrad, Joseph, Lothar, Ludwig, Philip, Rudolf, Rupert, Wenzel 7 Charles, Francis, Leopold, Lothair 8 Heinrich 9 Ferdinand, Frederick, Friedrich, Sigismund 10 Maximilian

Holy Writ 4 Book 5 Bible 9 Scripture

homage 5 honor 7 respect, tribute 9 deference, obeisance, reverence

home 4 land, site, soil 5 abode, haunt, house, local, range 6 family, native 7 country, habitat, housing 8 domestic, domicile, dwelling, internal, locality, location, national 9 household, intestine, municipal, residence, residency 10 commorancy, fatherland, focal point, habitation, motherland 12 headquarters 13 mother country *country:* 7 cottage 8 bungalow

homely 3 dry 4 ugly 5 plain 6 direct, kindly, modest, simple 8 familiar, intimate, unpretty 10 unalluring, unhandsome 11 commonplace, inelaborate, unbeauteous, unbeautiful, unelaborate, ungarnished 12 unattractive, unornamented 13 plain-featured, unpretentious

Homer epic 5 Iliad 7 Odyssey

homesickness 9 nostalgia

homespun 6 folksy 9 practical 13 unpretentious

Home, Sweet Home *music:* 6 Bishop *words:* 5 Payne

homicidal 6 bloody 8 sanguine 9 murdering, murderous 10 sanguinary 11 sanguineous 12 bloodthirsty

homicide 5 blood 6 killer, murder, slayer 7 killing 8 foul play, murderer 9 manslayer 12 manslaughter

homilize 6 preach

homily 6 sermon 7 lecture 9 discourse 10 admonition

homogeneous 4 like, same 7 similar, uniform 10 comparable, compatible, consistent, equivalent *combining form:* 2 is 3 hol, iso 4 holo

Homo sapiens 3 man 5 flesh 7 mankind 8 humanity 9 humankind, mortality

homunculus 4 runt 5 dwarf, midge, pygmy 6 midget, peewee 7 manikin 8 Tom Thumb 11 hop-o'-my-thumb, lilliputian

honcho 4 boss, cock, head 5 chief 6 leader, master 7 headman 8 hierarch 9 chieftain

Honduras *capital:* 11 Tegucigalpa *monetary unit:* 7 lempira *neighbor:* 9 Guatemala, Nicaragua 10 El Salvador *product:* 6 coffee 7 bananas

hone 4 edge, whet 7 sharpen

honest 4 open, real, true 5 frank, plain, right 6 candid, humble, simple 7 genuine, sincere, upright 8 innocent, reliable, truthful 9 objective, reputable, unfeigned, veracious 10 forthright, heart-whole, legitimate, scrupulous, unaffected 11 undesigning 12 praiseworthy, undissembled 13 conscientious, dispassionate, unimpeachable

honesty 6 virtue 7 probity 8 goodness, justness 9 integrity, rectitude, sincerity 11 uprightness 12 incorruption, truthfulness

honey *combining form:* 4 meli, mell 5 melli *drink:* 4 mead

honey badger 5 ratel

honey bear 8 kinkajou

honeybee genus 4 Apis

honeyberry 5 genip

honey bread 5 carob

honey buzzard 4 hawk, kite, pern

honeydew 5 melon

honeyed 6 golden, liquid, mellow 8 Hyblaean 9 sweetened 11 mellifluent, mellifluous

honeysuckle 8 rewa-rewa 9 columbine 11 swamp azalea 13 pinxter flower

Hong Kong's capital 8 Victoria
honky-tonk 4 dive 5 joint 7 hangout 11 barrelhouse
honor 4 bays, fete, kudo 5 adorn, asset, award, badge, erect, exalt, glory, kudos, medal, mense 6 esteem, homage, praise, regard, trophy, uprear 7 dignify, ennoble, glorify, laurels, magnify, respect, sublime, worship 8 accolade, approval, carry out, devotion 9 adoration, adulation, deference, integrity, obeisance, privilege, recognize, reverence 10 admiration, aggrandize, blue ribbon, compliment, decoration, reputation, veneration 11 distinction, distinguish, recognition 12 incorruption
honorable 4 just, true 5 right 6 august, worthy 7 ethical, upright 8 reverend, sterling 9 dignified 10 scrupulous, worshipful 11 illustrious 13 conscientious
hood 4 cowl, hide 5 cover 6 bonnet, helmet 7 bashlyk, blinder, capouch, capuche 8 covering *clergyman's:* 6 almuce
hoodlum 4 thug 7 mobster, ruffian 8 plug-ugly 9 strong arm
hoodwink 4 dupe, fool, gull, hoax 5 blind, trick 6 befool 7 chicane 8 flimflam 9 bamboozle 10 impose upon 11 hornswoggle
hooey 4 bosh, bunk 5 bilge 6 bunkum 7 baloney 8 claptrap, malarkey, nonsense
hoof 4 boot, foot, kick, pace, walk 5 eject, troop 6 unguis, ungula 7 traipse, trample, ungulae (plural) 8 ambulate, throw out *cloven:* 5 cloot
hoofer 6 dancer 7 danseur 8 coryphée, danseuse, figurant 9 ballerina, figurante
hook 3 ear, nab, nim, nip 4 flag, gore, lift 5 catch, curve, hitch, pinch, steal 6 anchor, fasten, pilfer, scythe, secure, sickle 7 cabbage, hamulus 8 crotchet *a fish:* 4 gaff, snag *combining form:* 3 onc 4 onch, onci, onco 5 oncho *for a watch:* 10 chatelaine
hooklike 7 falcate 8 unciform *part:* 5 uncus 7 hamulus
hookup 7 cahoots, circuit 8 alliance 10 connection 11 affiliation, association, combination, conjunction, partnership
hooky 7 truancy 8 truantry
hooligan see hoodlum
hoop 4 band, ring 5 clasp 6 circle 7 circlet, enclose 8 surround 10 finger ring
Hoosier State 7 Indiana
hoot 3 boo, jot 4 bird, damn, hiss, iota, jeer, whit 5 bazoo, ounce, scrap, shout, whoop 7 catcall, modicum 8 particle, pooh-pooh 9 raspberry
hop 3 run 4 ball, jump, leap, skip, tend, trip 5 bound, dance, serve, vault 6 bounce, hurdle, spring, wait on 7 rebound, saltate, skitter 8 jump over
hope 4 look 5 await, faith, stock, trust 6 aspire, desire, expect 7 count on, promise 8 reliance 9 count upon 10 confidence *loss of:* 7 despair
hopeful 4 easy, fond, rosy 5 happy, sunny 6 bright, cheery, golden, hoping, likely, secure, seeker, upbeat 7 assured, budding, content, halcyon, roseate 8 aspirant, cheerful, cheering, sanguine 9 applicant, candidate, confident, expectant, promising, satisfied 10 auspicious, optimistic, propitious 11 encouraging, rose-colored, undisturbed, up-and-coming 12 advantageous, anticipative, Pollyannaish
hopeless 4 glum, vain 6 futile, gloomy, morose 7 forlorn 8 downcast 9 desperate, incurable, insanable, insoluble, uncurable 10 despairing, despondent, desponding, impossible 11 immedicable, ineffectual, irreparable 12 incorrigible, irredeemable, irremediable 13 uncorrectable
hoper 8 optimist 9 Pollyanna
Hophni *brother:* 8 Phinehas *son:* 3 Eli
hopped-up 4 high 6 stoned, zonked 7 drugged
___ Hopper 5 Hedda
hopping 4 busy 5 fussy 6 lively
Horae 4 Dike 6 Eirene 7 Eunomia
Horam *kingdom:* 5 Gezer *slayer:* 6 Joshua
horde 4 push 5 crowd, crush, drove, press, swarm 6 squash, throng 9 multitude
Hori's son 7 Shaphat
horizon 3 ken 4 goal, zone 5 limit, range, reach 7 purview, skyline 8 prospect
horizontal 4 flat 7 general, overall
hormone 5 kinin 6 estrin 7 estriol, estrone, gastrin, insulin, relaxin 8 autacoid, estrogen, glucagon, kallidin, secretin *female:* 8 estrogen *insect:* 7 ecdyson 8 ecdysone *pituitary:* 8 oxytocin *sex:* 6 prolan
horn 4 gore, toot 5 cornu, drink, glory, power, pride 6 antler, claxon, klaxon, shofar, tootle 7 cuckold 10 cornucopia, projection *ancient Greek:* 5 rhyta (plural) 6 rhyton *animal:* 6 antler *combining form:* 4 cera 5 ceras, cerus, corne 6 corneo *signal:* 6 typhon
___ Hornblower 7 Horatio
horn in 4 fool 6 meddle 7 intrude, obtrude 8 busybody 9 interfere, interlope 10 intertrude, monkey with, tamper with
hornlike 8 ceratoid, corneous 10 keratinous
horn-shaped 7 cornute 8 cornuted
hornswoggle 4 dupe, fool, gull, hoax 6 befool, pigeon 7 chicane 8 flimflam, hoodwink 9 bamboozle
horny 4 hard 7 callous 8 keratoid
horrible 4 grim 5 awful, lurid, nasty 6 grisly 7 fearful, ghastly, hateful, hellish, hideous 8 dreadful, gruesome, shocking,

terrible 9 abhorrent, appalling, frightful, loathsome, obnoxious, offensive, repellent, repugnant, repulsive, revolting 10 disgusting, terrifying

horrid see horrible

horrific 5 awful 7 fearful 8 dreadful, shocking, terrible 9 appalling, frightful 10 formidable

horrify 5 daunt, shake, shock 6 appall, dismay

horrifying 4 grim 5 lurid 6 grisly 7 ghastly, hideous 8 gruesome, terrible

horror 4 fear, hate, pain 5 alarm, dread, panic, shock, throe 6 dismay, fright, hatred, wrench 8 aversion, distress, loathing 9 repulsion, revulsion, trepidity 10 abhorrence, repugnance 11 abomination, detestation, trepidation

Horsa's brother 7 Hengist

hors d'oeuvre 4 whet 7 zakuska 9 antipasto, appetizer

horse 3 kid 4 buck, roam 5 act up, bronc, cut up, pacer, steed 6 bayard, bronco, brumby, equine, padnag 7 broncho, carry on, cavalry, palfrey, sawbuck, trestle, trotter 8 footrope, jackstay, palomino, skewbald, stallion, traveler ***Asian:*** 6 tarpan ***Australian-bred:*** 5 waler ***battle:*** 7 charger ***breed:*** 6 Morgan 7 Arabian, Belgian, Iceland 8 Shetland 9 Percheron 10 Lippizaner 12 Thoroughbred ***collar:*** 7 brecham, brechan ***collar part:*** 4 hame ***combining form:*** 4 hipp 5 hippo 6 hippus ***covering:*** 8 trapping ***draft:*** 10 clydesdale ***extinct:*** 8 eohippus ***farm:*** 6 dobbin ***female:*** 4 mare 5 filly ***foot part:*** 7 pastern ***gait:*** 4 trot 6 canter, gallop ***gear:*** 3 bit 4 rein 6 saddle 7 harness 9 checkrein ***leg joint:*** 7 fetlock ***leg part:*** 6 gaskin 7 gambrel ***male:*** 4 colt 8 stallion ***mark:*** 5 blaze ***naturalized:*** 7 mustang ***nervous:*** 5 shier, shyer ***of the movies:*** 6 Flicka, Silver 7 Trigger 8 Champion 11 Black Beauty ***race:*** 5 derby 6 mudder 8 Affirmed, Citation 9 Preakness 11 Seattle Slew, Secretariat 13 Belmont Stakes, Kentucky Derby ***rump:*** 7 crupper ***saddle:*** 9 Appaloosa ***small:*** 6 garron, jennet ***spotted:*** 5 Pinto 7 piebald ***tan:*** 8 palomino ***thoroughbred:*** 8 hotblood ***war:*** 8 destrier ***wild:*** 7 mustang

horseman 6 cowboy, knight 7 vaquero 8 cavalier 9 caballero, chevalier 10 equestrian

horsemanship 6 manege 10 equitation

horse opera 5 oater 7 western

horseplay 5 act up, cut up 7 carry on, fooling 8 clowning 9 high jinks, rowdiness 10 buffoonery, roughhouse, skylarking 12 roughhousing

horseshoer 6 smithy 10 blacksmith

horticulturist 7 Burbank

Horus ***brother:*** 6 Anubis ***father:*** 6 Osiris ***mother:*** 4 Isis ***victim:*** 4 Seth

hose 4 tube 5 water 8 stocking

Hosea's father 5 Beeri

Hoshaiah's son 7 Azariah 8 Jezaniah

Hoshea ***father:*** 3 Nun 4 Elah 7 Azaziah ***victim:*** 5 Pekah

hospice see hostel

hospitable 6 social 7 cordial 8 friendly 9 convivial 10 gregarious 11 cooperative

hospital 6 clinic 7 lazaret 9 infirmary ***attendant:*** 7 orderly ***ship's:*** 7 sickbay

host 4 army 5 cloud, crowd, emcee, flock 6 angels, legion, myriad, scores 7 compere 8 assemble 9 innkeeper, multitude

hostage 4 pawn 5 token 6 pledge, surety 7 earnest 8 guaranty, security 9 guarantee

hostel 3 inn 5 lodge 6 tavern, travel 7 auberge 9 roadhouse 11 caravansary, public house

hostile 3 dim, ill 4 dour, sour 5 enemy 6 bitter, fierce 7 adverse, opposed, warlike 8 contrary, inimical, militant, opposite, virulent 9 bellicose, rancorous, vitriolic 10 inimicable, pugnacious, unfriendly 11 belligerent, competitive, contentious, disaffected, unfavorable 12 antagonistic, disapproving 13 argumentative

hostility 6 animus, enmity, rancor 9 antipathy 10 antagonism

hot 5 eager, fiery, fresh, nifty, super 6 ardent, baking, banned, biting, groovy, heated, hectic, raging, stolen, sultry, torrid, tropic, unsafe, urgent 7 boiling, burning, febrile, fevered, goatish, lustful, peppery, pungent, satyric, summery, sweltry, violent, zealous 8 broiling, feverish, feverous, glorious, prurient, scalding, sizzling, tropical, vehement 9 lecherous, lickerish, marvelous, scorching 10 blistering, contraband, lascivious, libidinous, passionate, sweltering 11 radioactive 12 concupiscent

hot air 4 bosh 6 bunkum 7 blather, twaddle 8 flimflam, malarkey, nonsense 9 poppycock 10 double-talk

hot-blooded 5 fiery 6 ardent 7 blazing, burning, fervent, flaming 9 excitable 10 passionate 11 impassioned 12 high-spirited

hotchpotch see hodgepodge

hot dog 5 frank 6 weenie, weiner, wiener, wienie 7 show-off 11 frankfurter, wienerwurst

hotel 3 inn, spa 5 lodge 6 boatel, tavern 7 auberge, hospice, pension 8 motor inn 9 roadhouse 11 caravansary, public house 12 lodging house, rooming house 13 boardinghouse ***chain:*** 5 Hyatt 6 Hilton 8 Marriott, Sheraton 9 Ramada Inn 10 Holiday Inn ***inferior:*** 7 fleabag

Hoth see Hoder
Hotham's father 5 Heber
hotheaded 4 rash 5 brash, fiery, hasty 6 madcap 8 reckless 9 impetuous
Hothir's father 5 Heman
hot spot 4 café 6 nitery 7 cabaret 8 nightery 9 nightclub 10 supper club 11 discotheque 12 watering hole 13 watering place
hot springs 7 thermae
hot-tempered 5 ratty, testy 6 cranky, tetchy, touchy 7 peppery 8 choleric 9 dyspeptic, irascible 10 passionate
hot water 3 box, fix, jam 4 hole 5 Dutch 6 corner, pickle 7 dilemma, trouble 8 quagmire 10 difficulty 11 predicament
___ Houdini 5 Harry
hound 3 dog, fan 4 bait, buff, ride, tyke 5 chivy, lover 6 addict, badger, bowwow, canine, heckle, hector, votary 7 devotee, dogfish, habitué 8 bullyrag 10 aficionado *Russian:* 6 borzoi
house 3 hut, ken 4 casa, clan, firm, folk, home, race, roof, shed 5 abode, board, dwell, folks, haven, hotel, lodge, put up, stock, tribe 6 bestow, biggin, billet, casino, encase, family, harbor, ménage, outfit, shield 7 château, company, concern, contain, cottage, enclose, kindred, lineage, mansion, quarter, saltbox, shelter, theater 8 audience, business, domicile, dwelling, messuage 9 caparison, entertain, residence, residency *clergyman's:* 5 manse 7 rectory 9 parsonage *country:* 5 manor 7 cottage 8 bungalow *dog:* 6 kennel *earth:* 5 adobe *Eskimo:* 5 igloo *lower:* 8 assembly *mean:* 5 hovel *of prostitution:* 4 crib 6 bagnio 7 brothel 8 bordello *religious:* 5 abbey 6 priory 7 convent, nunnery 9 monastery *room in a:* 7 chamber *rooming:* 5 lodge *Russian:* 5 dacha *small:* 5 shack *Spanish:* 4 casa *women's (Muslim):* 5 harem
housebreak 3 rob 4 tame 5 rifle 6 subdue 7 ransack 9 knock over 10 burglarize
household 4 home 5 folks 6 common, family, ménage 8 domestic, familiar *combining form:* 2 ec 3 eco, oec 4 oeco, oiko *gods (Roman):* 5 lares 7 penates
house of God see house of worship
house of prayer see house of worship
house of worship 5 abbey, stupa 6 bethel, chapel, church, pagoda, shrine, temple 7 chantry, minster, oratory 8 basilica 9 cathedral, sanctuary 10 tabernacle 11 conventicle *Aztec:* 6 teopan 8 teocalli *Jewish:* 7 synagog 9 synagogue *Muslim:* 6 masjid, mosque, musjid
housewife 5 hussy 8 hausfrau
housing 4 case 7 shelter 9 enclosure *rundown:* 4 slum
hovel 3 hut, sty 5 hutch, shack 6 burrow, pigpen, pigsty, shanty 10 tabernacle
hover 4 flit, hang 5 cower, dance, float, poise 7 flicker, flitter, flutter 9 hang about
howbeit 3 yet 4 when 5 still, while 6 much as, though, withal 7 whereas 8 after all, although 11 nonetheless, still and all 12 nevertheless
however 3 but, yet 4 only, save 5 still 6 except, though, withal 8 after all, although 9 per contra 11 nonetheless, still and all
howl 3 bay, cry, yip 4 bark, keen, riot, wail, weep, yell, yelp 5 quest 6 scream, squall, squawl, squeal 7 blubber, protest, ululate, whimper 9 caterwaul, complaint 11 oscillation 12 sidesplitter
hoyden 6 gamine, tomboy
Hreidmar's son 5 Regin 6 Fafnir, Reginn
Hrimfaxi's rider 4 Nott
H-shaped 5 zygal
hub 4 band, bell, nave, seat 5 focus, heart 6 barrel, center 8 polestar 9 master tap 10 focal point 11 nerve center
hubbub 3 din 4 stir, to-do 5 babel, whirl 6 clamor, hassle, jangle, pother, racket, rumpus, tumult, uproar 7 turmoil 8 brouhaha 9 commotion 10 hullabaloo, hurly-burly, tintamarre 11 disturbance, pandemonium
hubristic 4 vain 5 proud 7 haughty 8 arrogant, cavalier, insolent, superior 10 disdainful 11 overbearing 12 supercilious 13 high-and-mighty
Huckleberry Finn *author:* 5 Twain *character:* 3 Jim, Tom *river:* 11 Mississippi
huckster 4 hawk, vend 5 adman 6 dicker, haggle, hawker, higgle, monger, palter, peddle, vendor 7 bargain, chaffer, higgler, packman, peddler 8 outcrier
huddle 3 don 4 lump 5 bunch, chaos, crowd, get on, hunch, put on, snarl, throw, treat 6 advise, assume, ataxia, confab, confer, crouch, draw on, jumble, parley, powwow, slip on 7 clutter, consult, cover up, meeting 8 assemble, colloque, disarray, disorder 9 confusion 10 conference, discussion 11 confabulate, scrooch down
Hudson's ship 8 Half Moon
hue 4 cast, tint, tone 5 color, shade, shape, tinge 6 aspect, outcry 10 complexion
huff 4 blow, gasp, pant, rant, rile, roil, snap 5 annoy, grate, heave, peeve, pique, storm 6 nettle, put out 7 bluster, dudgeon, flounce, inflame, inflate, offense, provoke, umbrage 8 irritate 10 resentment
huffy 5 proud, waspy 6 touchy 7 fretful, haughty, peevish, pettish, waspish 8 arrogant, cavalier, insolent, petulant, snappish, superior 9 fractious, irritable, querulous 10 disdainful 11 overbearing 12 supercilious 13 high-and-mighty

hug 5 clasp, crowd, press 6 clutch, cuddle, enfold 7 cherish, embosom, embrace, squeeze 10 felicitate 12 congratulate
huge 4 vast 5 bulky, giant, grand, great, jumbo, large, lusty, massy, Titan 6 heroic, mighty, untold 7 Antaean, immense, mammoth, massive, monster, outsize, titanic, whaling 8 colossal, enormous, gigantic, oversize, pythonic, towering, whacking, whopping 9 cyclopean, extensive, gigantean, Herculean, leviathan, monstrous, planetary, unbounded, walloping 10 behemothic, dinosauric, gargantuan, mastodonic, monumental, prodigious, tremendous, unfathomed 11 Bunyanesque, elephantine, gigantesque, magnificent, mountainous
hugeness 8 enormity 9 immensity, magnitude
hugger-mugger 4 hash, hush, mash 6 covert, jumble, jungle, litter, muddle, secret, tumble 7 clutter, furtive, jumbled, rummage, secrecy, silence, sub-rosa 8 covertly, hush-hush, in camera, scramble, secretly 9 by stealth, confusion, furtively, privately 10 mumbo jumbo, secretness, stealthily, undercover 11 clandestine 13 clandestinely
Hugo, Victor *character:* 6 Javert 7 Cosette, Fantine, Valjean 9 Esmeralda, Quasimodo
Huguenot leader 5 Condé 6 Adrets, Mornay
Huguenots composer 9 Meyerbeer
Huldah's husband 7 Shallum
hulk 4 loom, ship
hull 3 pod 4 bark, case, peel, rind, skin 5 chaff, shell, shuck 6 casing 8 covering 9 cartridge 11 decorticate
hullabaloo 3 din 5 babel 6 clamor, hubbub, jangle, racket, tumult, uproar 8 ballyhoo 10 tintamarre 11 pandemonium
Hul's father 4 Aram
hum 4 buzz, moan, purr, sing, zing 5 drone 6 bumble, melody, murmur 7 vibrate
human 4 body, life, soul 5 being, party, wight 6 mortal, person 7 hominid, mankind 8 creature, hominine, hominoid 9 enigmatic, personage 10 anthropoid, ethnologic, individual 12 ethnological *being:* 6 mortal, person 7 primate *combining form:* 7 anthrop 8 anthropo *race:* 7 mankind
humane 4 good, kind, mild 6 gentle, kindly 8 merciful 10 altruistic, benevolent, charitable 11 kindhearted, soft-hearted 12 eleemosynary 13 compassionate, philanthropic
humanitarian 4 good 10 altruistic, benevolent, charitable 12 eleemosynary 13 philanthropic
humanity 3 man, men 5 flesh 6 people 7 mankind 9 mortality 10 compassion 11 benevolence, Homo sapiens
Humbaba's slayer 9 Gilgamesh
humble 3 low 4 base, mean, meek, sink 5 abase, abash, lower, lowly, quiet 6 bemean, debase, demean, modest, simple 7 chagrin, degrade, ignoble, lowborn, lowbred, mortify, subdued 8 baseborn, cast down, plebeian, resigned, unwashed 9 compliant, discomfit, embarrass, humiliate 10 submissive, unassuming, unennobled 11 acquiescent, unobtrusive 13 insignificant, unpretentious
humbug 3 gyp, rot 4 bosh, fake, hoax, sell, sham 5 bluff, faker, fraud, hokum, phony, spoof 6 betray, bunkum, cajole, delude, drivel, illude, juggle, piffle, take in 7 beguile, deceive, mislead 8 flimflam, impostor, malarkey, nonsense, quackery 9 hypocrite, imposture, pretender 10 balderdash
humdinger 5 dandy, doozy, nifty, peach 8 jim-dandy 11 crackerjack
humdrum 4 blah, dull 6 dreary, stodgy 7 prosaic 8 banausic, monotone, monotony, plodding, workaday 10 monotonous, pedestrian
humid 4 damp, dank 5 close, moist, mucky, muggy, soggy 6 clammy, sodden, sticky, stuffy, sultry 8 stifling, vaporous 10 oppressive, sweltering
humiliate 4 sink 5 abase, lower, shame 6 bemean, debase, demean, humble 7 chagrin, degrade, mortify 8 belittle, cast down, disgrace
humming 4 busy 5 brisk, fussy 6 lively 7 hopping, popping 8 bustling, hustling
hummingbird 5 sylph 6 sappho 7 vervain 9 thorntail, trochilus *genus:* 6 Sappho
humor 3 bee, wit 4 baby, mind, mood, tone, vein, whim 5 fancy, freak, spoil 6 banter, cocker, coddle, comedy, cosset, cotton, esprit, joking, levity, makeup, megrim, nature, pamper, strain, temper, vagary 7 boutade, caprice, cater to, conceit, gratify, gruntle, indulge, jesting, kidding 8 chaffing, chitchat, crotchet, drollery, jocosity, repartee 9 character, drollness, flippancy, funniness, jocundity, lightness, wittiness 10 comicality, complexion, jocularity, jocundness, pleasantry
humorist 3 Ade, wag, wit 4 card, Nash, Shaw, Ward, zany 5 Adams, Allen, clown, comic, cutup, droll, Dunne, joker, Twain, White 6 Browne, gagman, jester, kidder, Rogers, Runyon, Thorpe 7 buffoon, Burgess, Clemens, gagster, Hubbard, Marquis, punster, Thurber 8 Aleichem, banterer, Benchley, comedian, funnyman, jokester,

Perelman, quipster **9** jokesmith, prankster **11** merry-andrew ***Canadian:*** **7** Leacock
humorous **5** funny, witty **6** jocose **7** jocular, waggish, wagsome **9** facetious
humpback **5** whale **8** kyphosis
humpbacked **7** gibbous
Humperdinck opera **15** Hansel und Gretel
humus **3** mor **4** mull, soil
hunch **3** gob, wad **4** arch, clod, lump, push, rear **5** chunk, clump, crook, fudge, shove, squat **6** crouch, curl up, huddle, jostle, nugget **11** scrooch down
Hunchback of Notre Dame **9** Quasimodo ***author:*** **4** Hugo
hundred ***combining form:*** **4** hect **5** centi, hecto **6** hecato **7** hecaton
hundredth ***combining form:*** **5** centi
Hungary ***capital:*** **8** Budapest ***dog:*** **4** puli ***ethnic group:*** **6** Magyar ***monetary unit:*** **6** forint ***national hero:*** **5** Arpad ***wine:*** **5** tokay
hunger **3** yen **4** ache, long, lust, pine, sigh **5** crave, yearn **6** famine, famish, hanker, thirst **7** craving
hungry **4** avid, poor **6** barren **7** starved **8** famished, ravenous, starving, underfed
hunk **3** gob, wad **4** clod, lump **5** chunk, clump, piece **6** nugget
hunker down **5** squat
Hunnish **4** rude, wild **6** Gothic, savage **7** uncivil **9** barbarian, barbarous **11** uncivilized **12** uncultivated
hunt **3** dog, gun, run **4** hawk, kill, prey, rout, seek **5** chase, drive, hound, quest, shoot, snare, stalk, start, track **6** battue, course, dig out, ferret, pursue, rabbit, safari, shikar **7** capture, explore, rummage **9** cast about, ferret out, search for, search out ***birds:*** **4** fowl ***illegally:*** **5** poach
hunter **5** jager, yager **6** chaser, jaeger, nimrod **7** stalker **8** chasseur, predator ***biblical:*** **6** Nimrod ***cap:*** **5** terai **7** montero ***constellation:*** **5** Orion ***cry:*** **6** yoicks **7** tallyho ***horn:*** **5** bugle ***mythological:*** **5** Orion **7** Actaeon
hunting **5** chase **6** venery **7** angling, fishing, gunning, hawking **8** coursing, falconry **9** predatory **10** predacious ***bird:*** **6** falcon ***call:*** **7** recheat ***cry:*** **7** tantivy ***dog:*** **4** alan **5** alant, hound **6** alaunt, basset, beagle, borzoi, setter **7** pointer, spaniel ***expedition:*** **6** safari
huntress **5** Diana **7** Artemis **8** Atalanta
Hupham's father **8** Benjamin
Hur ***grandson:*** **8** Bezaleel ***son:*** **8** Rephaiah
hurdle **3** bar, hop, lop, rub **4** down, jump, leap, lick, over, snag **5** bound, clear, throw, vault **6** bounce, hamper, master, spring **7** barrier, conquer, saltate **8** mountain, obstacle, overcome, overleap, surmount, traverse **9** negotiate **10** impediment **11** obstruction
hurl **4** cast, fire, rush, toss **5** drive, fling, heave, pitch, sling, throw, whirl **6** launch, thrust **8** catapult ***stones:*** **8** lapidate
hurly-burly **4** to-do **5** melee, whirl **6** clamor, hassle, hubbub, pother, tumult, uproar **7** turmoil **8** confused **9** commotion, confusion
hurrah **4** coil, fire, fuss, romp, to-do, zeal ardor, cheer, scold, spree, tease **6** fervor, furore, harass, ruckus, rumpus, shindy, uproar **7** dispute, fanfare, passion **8** argument, raillery **9** calenture, commotion **10** contention, enthusiasm **11** controversy
hurricane **5** storm **7** tornado, typhoon **8** williwaw **9** whirlwind **13** tropical storm ***tropical:*** **7** typhoon
hurried **4** fast **5** hasty **6** abrupt, sudden **7** rushing **8** headlong **9** impetuous **10** tumultuous **11** precipitant, precipitate, precipitous, subitaneous
hurry **3** fly, hie, jog, peg, run, zip **4** flit, pelt, post, rock, rush, skin, trot, whiz **5** dig in, fleet, haste, scoot, scour, skelp, skirr, skite, smoke, speed, stave, whirl, whish, whisk, whizz **6** barrel, breeze, bucket, bullet, bustle, hasten, hustle, rocket, rustle, step up, tumult, whirry **7** beeline, hotfoot, quicken, scutter, scuttle, shake up, skelter, swiften **8** celerity, dispatch, expedite, highball **9** bowl along, commotion, swiftness **10** accelerate, expedition, speediness
hurt **3** mar **4** ache, harm, pain, ruin **5** abuse, check, smart, spoil, wound, wrong **6** damage, grieve, hamper, impair, injure, injury, misuse, offend, suffer, weaken **7** afflict, blemish, damaged, outrage, tarnish, vitiate, wounded **8** aggrieve, distress, mischief, mistreat **9** constrain, detriment, prejudice, resentful, suffering **10** resentment
hurtful **4** evil, sore **6** aching **7** algetic, harmful, nocuous, painful **8** damaging **9** injurious **10** afflictive **11** deleterious, detrimental, mischievous, prejudicial **12** prejudicious
hurtle **4** rush **5** crash, fling, shoot, throw **6** clater **8** catapult **9** collision
husband **3** man **4** lord, mate, save **6** manage, mister, spouse **7** consort, hoarder **8** benedict, conserve, helpmate, helpmeet **9** other half **10** bridegroom
husbandry **6** thrift **7** economy, farming **8** prudence **9** frugality **10** management, providence **11** agriculture, thriftiness **12** conservation
hush **4** calm, lull **5** burke, quell, quiet, shush, still, whist **6** shut up, silent, stifle, stilly, whisht **7** mollify, secrecy, silence

8 choke off, suppress 9 cessation, noiseless, soundless, stillness 10 secretness 12 hugger-mugger 13 hugger-muggery, secretiveness

hush-hush 6 covert, secret 7 secrecy, silence, sub rosa 10 censorship, secretness, undercover 11 clandestine, suppression 12 confidential, hugger-mugger 13 hole-and-corner, hugger-muggery, secretiveness, surreptitious, under-the-table

Hushim ***father:*** 3 Dan ***husband:*** 9 Shaharaim

husk 3 pod 4 case, peel, skin 5 bract, carob, hoose, shell, shuck, strip ***combining form:*** 4 lepo 7 siliqui

husky 3 big, fat 4 bull 5 beefy, burly, empty, great, gruff, hefty, large, stout 6 brawny, croaky, hoarse, mighty, robust, strong, sturdy 8 croaking, gigantic, muscular, oversize, powerful, rattling, stalwart 9 Herculean, strapping, well-built 10 membranous 11 Bunyanesque

hustle 3 fly, rob, run 4 earn, move, push, rush, work 5 cheat, elbow, haste, hurry, press, shove, speed 6 gather, hasten 7 hotfoot, swindle 8 bulldoze, celerity, dispatch, shoulder 9 swiftness

hustler 4 bawd, doer, drab, moll 5 whore 6 dynamo, harlot, hooker, hummer, peeler, vendor 8 call girl, go getter, live wire, new broom 9 humdinger 10 powerhouse, prostitute 11 self-starter 12 streetwalker

hustling 4 busy 5 fussy 6 lively 7 hopping, humming, popping 9 energetic

hut 3 cot 4 camp, crib, room, shed 5 cabin, dacha, house, hovel, hutch, jacal, lodge, roost, shack 6 bestow, billet, cabana, chalet, harbor, lean-to, shanty 7 cottage, edifice, quarter 8 building, domicile ***American Indian:*** 6 wikiup 7 wickiup, wickyup ***Russian:*** 4 isba, izba ***shepherd's:*** 5 sheal, shiel 8 shealing, shieling

hutch 3 bin 4 cage 5 shack 6 locker, shanty

Huxley novel 11 Crome Yellow 13 Brave New World, Eyeless in Gaza

Hyacinthus ***father:*** 7 Amyclas ***slayer:*** 6 Apollo

hybrid 4 mule 5 cross 7 bastard, incross, mixture, mongrel 8 outcross 9 composite, crossbred, half blood, half-breed, loanblend 10 crossbreed 11 combination

hybridize 5 cross 9 cross-mate 10 crossbreed, interbreed, intercross

Hydra ***father:*** 6 Typhon ***mother:*** 7 Echidna ***slayer:*** 8 Heracles, Hercules

hydrant 3 tap 4 cock, gate 5 valve 6 faucet, spigot 7 petcock 8 fireplug, stopcock

hydraulic device 3 ram 4 jack, lift, pump 5 brake, press 8 elevator

hydrocarbon 5 xylol 6 ethane, indene, xylene ***liquid:*** 6 octane 7 retinol, styrene 8 menthene ***suffix:*** 5 ylene

hydroid 5 polyp 6 medusa, obelia 9 jellyfish, millepore

hydrometer scale 4 Brix 5 Baumé

hydrophobia 5 lyssa 6 rabies

hydroponics 11 aquiculture, tank farming

Hygeia 5 Salus ***father:*** 9 Asclepius 11 Aesculapius ***goddess of:*** 6 health

hygienic 4 good 7 healthy 8 salutary, sanitary 9 healthful, wholesome 10 salubrious

Hyllus' father 8 Heracles, Hercules

hymeneal 6 wedded 7 marital, married, nuptial, spousal 8 conjugal 9 connubial 11 matrimonial

hymn 3 lay 4 aria, laud, lied, sing, song 5 bless, carol, chant, cry up, ditty, extol, paean, trill, troll 6 choral, intone, praise, warble 7 chorale, descant, glorify, gradual, magnify 8 antiphon, canticle, doxology, eulogize 9 celebrate 10 panegyrize

hyperbole 8 coloring 12 embroidering, exaggeration 13 embellishment, overstatement

hyperbolic function 4 cosh, coth, csch, sech, sinh, tanh

hypercritical 7 carping 8 captious, caviling 9 cavillous 10 censorious 12 faultfinding

Hyperion ***daughter:*** 3 Eos 6 Aurora, Selene ***father:*** 6 Uranus ***mother:*** 2 Ge 4 Gaea ***son:*** 6 Helios ***wife:*** 5 Theia

hypnotic 6 opiate, sleepy 8 mesmeric, somnific 9 somnolent, soporific 10 somnorific 11 somniferous

hypnotize 5 charm 6 trance 8 entrance 9 mesmerize, spellbind

hypocorism 6 byname, byword 8 nickname 9 sobriquet

hypocrisy 4 cant, sham 6 humbug 7 pietism 8 glibness, quackery 9 casuistry 10 pharisaism, sanctimony, Tartuffery, Tartuffism 11 charlatanry, insincerity, religiosity 12 pecksniffery, unctiousness

hypocrite 4 sham 5 actor, faker, fraud, phony, poser, quack 6 humbug, phoney, poseur 7 bluffer, pietist, Tartufe 8 deceiver, impostor, pharisee, Tartuffe 9 charlatan, lip server, pretender 10 dissembler 11 four-flusher, masquerader 12 dissimulator

hypocritical 4 glib, oily 5 bland, false 6 smooth 7 canting 8 affected, janiform, malafide, specious, unctuous 9 casuistic, insincere, pharisaic, pietistic, religiose 10 goody-goody, left-handed, moralistic 11 dissembling, double-faced 12 ambidextrous, double-minded, mealymouthed, peck-

sniffian, smooth-spoken **13** double-dealing, doublehearted, double-tongued, sanctimonious, self-righteous, smooth-tongued
hypothesis **6** theory **8** supposal **11** supposition
hypothetical **5** ideal **7** assumed, reputed **8** abstract, doubtful, putative, supposed **11** conditional, conjectural, implication, problematic, suppositive, suppository **12** suppositious, transcendent **13** suppositional
Hypsipyle's father **5** Thoas
hyrax **4** cony **5** coney
hysterical fear **5** panic

I

Iago ***general:*** **7** Othello ***victim:*** **6** Cassio, Emilia **7** Othello **9** Desdemona ***wife:*** **6** Emilia
Iapetus ***father:*** **6** Uranus ***mother:*** **2** Ge **4** Gaea ***son:*** **5** Atlas **9** Menoetius **10** Epimetheus, Prometheus ***wife:*** **7** Clymene
Iasion ***brother:*** **8** Dardanus ***father:*** **4** Zeus **7** Jupiter ***lover:*** **5** Ceres **7** Demeter ***mother:*** **7** Electra ***son:*** **6** Plutus
ibex **3** tur **4** tahr **8** wild goat ***family:*** **7** Bovidae ***genus:*** **5** Capra
Ibhar's father **5** David
ibis-headed god **5** Thoth
Ibneiah's father **7** Jeroham
Ibnijah's son **5** Reuel
Ibri's father **7** Jaaziah
Ibsen ***character:*** **3** Ase **4** Nora **5** Brand, Hedda **7** Solness **8** Peer Gynt ***country:*** **6** Norway ***play:*** **6** Ghosts **8** Peer Gynt **11** A Doll's House, Hedda Gabler, Little Eyolf, Rosmersholm, The Wild Duck
Icarius ***brother:*** **9** Tyndareus ***daughter:*** **7** Erigone **8** Penelope ***mother:*** **10** Gorgophone
Icarus'father **8** Daedalus
ice **4** rime, sish **5** chill, frost, glace **6** freeze ***area:*** **4** rink ***combining form:*** **6** glacio **8** crystall **9** crystallo ***floating:*** **4** berg, floe ***glacial:*** **5** serac ***hanging:*** **6** icicle ***on rock:*** **7** verglas ***pinnacle:*** **5** serac
ice cream **7** spumone, spumoni, tortoni ***dish:*** **4** soda **6** frappe, sundae
iced **5** glacé **6** glazed
ice field **7** glacier
ice game **6** hockey **7** curling
ice house **4** iglu **5** igloo
Iceland ***capital:*** **9** Reykjavik ***monetary unit:*** **5** krona
Icelandic ***epic:*** **4** Edda ***hero:*** **7** Grettir
Ichabod ***father:*** **8** Phinehas ***grandfather:*** **3** Eli
Ichabod Crane's beloved **8** Caterina
icing **7** topping **8** frosting
icky **4** vile **5** nasty **6** sticky **7** noisome **8** horrible **9** loathsome, offensive, repellent, revolting, sickening **10** disgusting
icon **5** image
icy **4** cold **5** chill, gelid **6** arctic, chilly, frigid, frosty **7** glacial **8** chilling, freezing **11** emotionless, indifferent, unemotional
Idaho ***capital:*** **5** Boise ***nickname:*** **8** Gem State ***state flower:*** **7** syringa
Idas ***brother:*** **7** Lynceus ***father:*** **8** Aphareus ***slayer:*** **4** Zeus ***victim:*** **6** Castor ***wife:*** **8** Marpessa
Iddo ***father:*** **9** Zechariah ***grandson:*** **9** Zechariah ***son:*** **8** Ahinadab
idea **4** view, whim **5** fancy, guess, image **6** belief, notion, theory, vagary, whimsy **7** caprice, conceit, concept, fantasy, feeling, figment, inkling, opinion, subject, surmise, thought **8** judgment, reaction **9** sentiment, suspicion **10** assumption, brainstorm, conception, conclusion, conjecture, conviction, estimation, hypothesis, impression, perception, persuasion, reflection **11** inspiration
ideal **4** goal, very **5** jewel, model **6** mirror **7** classic, example, paragon, pattern, perfect, phoenix, typical, utopian **8** abstract, ensample, exemplar, flawless, nonesuch, notional, paradigm, standard **9** archetype, classical, exemplary, imaginary, nonpareil, visionary **10** archetypal, conceptual, ideational, prototypal **11** theoretical
idealist **7** dreamer, quixote, utopian **9** ideologue, visionary **13** castle-builder
idealistic **6** starry **7** utopian **8** poetical, quixotic, romantic **9** visionary **10** starry-eyed **11** impractical, unrealistic
identical **3** one **4** like, same, self, very **5** alike, equal, exact **8** selfsame
identification ***abbreviation:*** **2** ID ***mark:*** **5** brand, label
identify **3** tag **4** find, mark, name, spot

5 brand, place 6 finger, select 7 make out, pick out 8 diagnose, pinpoint 9 determine, establish, recognize
ideology 3 ism 4 view 5 credo, creed 7 outlook 10 philosophy
idiocy 5 folly 7 amentia, fatuity 9 stupidity
idiosyncratic 3 odd 5 queer, weird 6 proper 7 curious, erratic, oddball, strange 8 peculiar, singular 9 diacritic, eccentric 10 diagnostic, individual 11 distinctive
idiot 3 ass 4 fool, jerk, simp, zany 5 ament, dummy, dunce, moron, ninny, schmo 6 cretin, donkey, jester, motley, schmoe, stupid 7 dullard, half-wit, jackass, natural, tomfool 8 dullhead, dumbbell, imbecile, numskull 9 ignoramus, simpleton 10 nincompoop
idiotic 4 daft 6 stupid 7 foolish, moronic 9 senseless
idle 3 bum 4 laze, lazy, loaf, loll, rest, vain 5 amble, dally, drone, empty, inert, mooch, mosey, quiet, relax, sit by, tarry 6 asleep, dawdle, diddle, futile, hollow, linger, loiter, lounge, otiose, potter, repose, sleepy, stroll, unused, vacant 7 aimless, passive, saunter, sit back, useless 8 inactive, indolent, nugatory, slothful
idleness 4 laze 5 sloth 6 acedia, slouch 8 flanerie, laziness 9 indolence 12 slothfulness
idler 3 bum 4 slug 5 drone 6 loafer, slouch 8 dolittle, fainéant, slugabed, sluggard 9 do-nothing, lazybones
Idmon *daughter:* 7 Arachne *father:* 6 Apollo *mother:* 6 Cyrene
idol 3 god 4 hero, icon 5 image *Chinese:* 4 joss
idolatry 7 baalism, worship 9 adoration 11 idolization
idolize 5 adore 6 admire, dote on, revere 7 worship 8 dote upon, venerate
Idylls of the King *author:* 8 Tennyson *character:* 4 Enid 6 Arthur, Elaine, Gareth, Merlin, Vivien 7 Geraint, Lynette 8 Lancelot
iffy 5 dicey 6 chancy 7 erratic 8 doubtful 9 fluctuant, uncertain, whimsical 10 capricious 12 incalculable 13 unpredictable
Igal's father 6 Nathan 8 Shemaiah
Igdaliah's son 5 Hanan
igneous rock 4 lava 5 magma 6 basalt, gabbro, pumice, scoria 7 diabase, granite 8 obsidian, porphyry
ignis fatuus 6 mirage 8 delusion, illusion, phantasm 12 will-o'-the-wisp 13 hallucination
ignitable 8 burnable 9 flammable 11 combustible, inflammable
ignite 4 fire 5 light 6 excite, kindle 7 inflame 8 enkindle
ignited 3 lit 5 afire, fiery 6 ablaze, aflame, alight 7 blazing, burning, flaming, flaring, lighted
ignoble 3 low 4 base, mean, poor, vile 5 lowly, plain 6 abject, coarse, common, homely, humble, modest, scurvy, simple, sordid, vulgar 7 lowborn, peasant, popular, servile 8 baseborn, inferior, ordinary, plebeian, shameful, unwashed, wretched 10 despicable, inglorious, unennobled 11 disgraceful 12 dishonorable
ignominious 5 shady 6 shabby, shoddy 8 shameful 10 inglorious 11 disgraceful 12 dishonorable, disreputable 13 discreditable, unrespectable
ignominy 5 odium, scorn, shame 6 infamy 7 chagrin, despite, disdain, obloquy 8 contempt, disgrace, dishonor 9 discredit, disesteem, disrepute 10 opprobrium 13 mortification
ignoramus 4 dolt, fool 5 dummy, dunce, idiot, moron 6 nitwit, stupid 7 dullard 8 dullhead, dumbbell 9 simpleton
ignorance 7 naiveté, rawness 8 darkness 9 greenness, innocence, inscience, nescience 10 callowness, illiteracy, simpleness, simplicity 11 unawareness, uncouthness, witlessness
ignorant 3 raw 4 rude 5 crude, green, gross, naive 6 callow, simple, stupid 7 lowbrow, unaware, uncouth 8 backward, nescient, untaught 9 benighted, ingenuous, oblivious, unknowing, untutored, unwitting 10 illiterate, uncultured, uneducated, unfamiliar, uninformed, unlettered, unschooled 11 empty-headed, incognizant, know-nothing 12 inconversant, unacquainted, uninstructed
ignore 3 cut 4 fail, omit, snub 5 avoid, evade 6 forget, slight 7 blink at, neglect 8 discount, overlook, overpass 9 blink away, disregard
Igraine, Ygerne *husband:* 5 Uther 7 Gorlois *son:* 6 Arthur
iguana 6 lizard 7 tuatara
ilex 5 holly 7 holm oak
Iliad 4 epic *author:* 5 Homer *character:* 4 Ajax 5 Helen, Paris, Priam 6 Aeneas, Hector 8 Achilles, Diomedes, Odysseus 9 Agamemnon, Patroclus *city:* 4 Troy
Ilion, Ilium 4 Troy
ilk 4 kind, sort, type 5 breed, class 6 family, kidney, nature, stripe 7 variety
ill 3 bad 4 down, evil, rude, sick 5 amiss 6 malady, nocent 7 ailment, disease, harmful, hostile, hurtful, ill-bred, nocuous, noxious, uncivil 8 damaging, disorder, feverish, feverous, impolite, inimical, nauseous, sickness, syndrome 9 affection, complaint, condition, infirmity, injurious
ill-adapted 5 inapt, unfit 6 unmeet

8 unfitted, unsuited 9 ill-suited 10 unsuitable 13 inappropriate

ill-advised 4 rash 5 brash, hasty 6 madcap, unwise 8 reckless 9 hotheaded, ill-judged, impolitic, imprudent 10 incautious, indiscreet, mad-brained 11 inadvisable, inexpedient, injudicious, thoughtless, unadvisable, unexpedient 13 inconsiderate

ill-boding 4 dire 7 baleful, baneful, fateful, ominous, unlucky 9 ill-omened 11 apocalyptic 12 inauspicious, unpropitious

ill-bred 4 rude 6 rugged 7 boorish, incivil, loutish, lowbred, uncivil 8 churlish, cloddish, impolite 9 unrefined 10 uncultured, ungracious, unpolished 11 disgracious, ill-mannered, impertinent, uncivilized 12 discourteous 13 disrespectful

ill-defined 3 dim 5 blear, faint, fuzzy, vague 6 bleary 7 shadowy, unclear 9 undefined 10 indistinct

illegal 3 hot 6 banned 7 illicit, lawless 8 criminal, nonlegal, outlawed, unlawful, wrongful 9 felonious, forbidden, irregular 10 actionable, contraband, prohibited, proscribed, unlicensed 11 interdicted, unwarranted 12 illegitimate, unauthorized ***act:*** 5 crime 6 felony ***scheme:*** 4 scam

illegible 5 faint 7 obscure, unclear 10 indistinct, unreadable

illegitimacy 8 bastardy 10 illegality 11 bar sinister, illicitness 12 unlawfulness

illegitimate 6 by-blow 7 bastard, bootleg, illegal, illicit, lawless, natural 8 baseborn, criminal, spurious, unlawful, wrongful

ill-fated 7 hapless, unhappy, unlucky 8 luckless, untoward 11 star-crossed, unfortunate 12 misfortunate

ill health 7 cachexy 8 cachexia

ill-humored 5 cross 6 cranky 7 peevish 8 choleric 9 dyspeptic 10 tempersome 11 bad-tempered, hot-tempered

illiberal 4 mean 5 petty, rigid, small 6 biased, little, narrow, paltry, stingy 7 bigoted, insular, partial 8 grudging, one-sided, partisan, rigorous 9 hidebound, jaundiced, parochial, stringent 10 brassbound, intolerant, prejudiced, provincial, unenlarged, ungenerous 11 opinionated, small-minded 12 narrow-minded, uncharitable

illicit 7 bootleg, illegal, lawless 8 criminal, unlawful, wrongful 12 illegitimate

illimitable 7 endless, eternal 8 infinite 9 boundless 10 perdurable 11 measureless, sempiternal 12 immeasurable, interminable

Illinois ***capital:*** 11 Springfield ***college, university:*** 5 Barat 6 De Paul 7 Wheaton 12 Northwestern ***largest city:*** 7 Chicago ***nickname:*** 11 Sucker State 12 Prairie State ***state bird:*** 8 cardinal ***state flower:*** 6 violet

illiterate 4 rude 8 ignorant, untaught 9 benighted, unlearned, untutored 10 analphabet, uncultured, uneducated, unlettered

ill-kempt 5 messy 6 sloppy, unneat, untidy 8 careless, slipshod, slovenly, uncombed 10 disheveled

ill-mannered 4 rude 7 incivil, uncivil 8 impolite 10 ungracious 11 disgracious, impertinent 12 discourteous 13 disrespectful

ill-natured 5 cross, nasty, surly 6 crabby 8 choleric 9 dyspeptic 10 tempersome 11 bad-tempered, hot-tempered

illness 6 malady 7 ailment, disease 8 cachexia, disorder, sickness, unhealth 9 infirmity 10 affliction 13 indisposition ***mental:*** 8 dementia

illogical 3 mad 5 false 6 absurd 7 invalid, unsound 8 specious 9 plausible, senseless, sophistic 10 fallacious, irrational, reasonless, unreasoned 11 meaningless, nonrational 12 unreasonable, unscientific

ill-starred 6 malign 7 baleful, bodeful, fateful, hapless, malefic, ominous, unhappy, unlucky 8 luckless, sinister, untoward 10 foreboding, portentous 11 star-crossed, unfavorable, unfortunate, unpromising 12 misfortunate, unpropitious

ill-suited 5 inapt, unfit 6 unmeet 8 unfitted 10 unsuitable 13 inappropriate

ill-tempered 4 sour 5 cross, huffy, surly 6 crabby, grumpy 7 crabbed, grouchy, peevish, waspish 8 choleric, petulant, shrewish, snappish, vixenish 9 dyspeptic, fractious, irritable, querulous

ill-timed 5 inept 8 improper, mistimed, unseemly, untimely 10 malapropos, unbecoming, unsuitable 11 inopportune, unbefitting 12 unseasonable 13 inappropriate

ill-treat 5 abuse, harry 6 harass, misuse, molest 7 outrage 8 aggrieve, maltreat, mistreat

illude 4 bilk 5 bluff, cheat, elude 6 betray, delude, humbug, juggle, take in 7 beguile, deceive, mislead 11 double-cross

illume 5 edify, light 6 uplift 7 improve, lighten 8 illumine 9 enlighten, irradiate

illuminate 4 fire 5 clear, edify, exalt, gloss, light 6 better, define, finish, ignite, kindle, mature, polish, refine, uplift 7 clarify, clear up, ennoble, explain, expound, express, improve, lighten, perfect 8 brighten, construe 9 dramatize, elucidate, enlighten, highlight, interpret, irradiate, spotlight

illuminati 7 clerisy 8 literati 13 intellectuals

illumination 8 lighting ***unit of:*** 3 lux 4 phot 5 lumen 6 candle 7 candela 10 footcandle

illumine see illuminate

illusion 5 dream 6 bubble, mirage 7 chi-

mera, fantasy, rainbow, seeming 8 delusion, phantasm, phantasy 9 invention, pipe dream, semblance 10 appearance 11 ignis fatuus 12 will-o'-the-wisp 13 hallucination
illusionist 8 conjurer, magician 9 trickster
illusive 5 false 6 unreal 7 seeming 8 apparent
illusory 6 unreal 7 fictive, seeming 8 apparent, delusive, delusory, fanciful, illusive, semblant 9 deceptive, fantastic, fictional, imaginary, visionary 10 Barmecidal, chimerical, fictitious, misleading, ostensible
illustrate 4 mark, show 5 clear 6 embody, evince, expose, mirror, ostend, reveal, typify, vivify 7 clarify, clear up, display, enliven, exhibit, explain, expound, picture 8 disclose, discover, evidence, instance, manifest, proclaim 9 elucidate, epitomize, exemplify
illustration 4 case 6 sample 7 example, problem 8 ensample, instance, sampling, specimen
illustrative 7 graphic 8 pictoric 9 pictorial 12 iconographic
illustrator *American:* 5 Flagg 7 Burgess 8 Rockwell 9 Remington *English:* 6 Potter 7 Tenniel 9 Beardsley, du Maurier *French:* 4 Doré *German:* 5 Dürer
illustrious 5 famed, great, lofty, noted 6 famous, signal 7 eminent, exalted, notable, sublime 8 glorious, renowned, splendid, striking 9 prominent 10 celebrated, celebrious 11 conspicuous, outstanding, resplendent 13 distinguished
illustriousness 6 renown 8 eminence, prestige 10 prominence, prominency 11 distinction, preeminence
ill will 5 spite, venom 6 animus, grudge, malice, rancor, spleen 7 despite 9 hostility, malignity 10 malignancy 11 malevolence 12 spitefulness 13 maliciousness
Ilus *father:* 4 Tros *grandson:* 5 Priam *mother:* 10 Callirrhoe *son:* 8 Laomedon
image 4 copy, form, icon, idea, idol, limn 5 equal, fancy, glass, match, split, think 6 depict, double, effigy, mirror, notion, recept, render, ringer, vision 7 conceit, concept, fantasm, feature, imagine, picture, portray, realize, reflect, thought 8 conceive, describe, envisage, envision, likeness, phantasm, portrait 9 delineate, interpret, represent, semblance, visualize 10 conception, equivalent, impression, perception, simulacrum *Polynesian:* 4 tiki *Semitic:* 6 teraph 8 teraphim (plural)
imaginary 5 ideal 6 unreal 7 fancied, fictive, shadowy 8 abstract, chimeric, fanciful, illusory, imagined, notional, quixotic, spectral, visional 9 fantastic, fictional, figmental, visionary 10 chimerical, fictitious, phantasmal, phantasmic 11 imaginative 12 apparitional, hypothetical, suppositious 13 hallucinatory, unsubstantial
imagination 5 fancy 7 fantasy 8 phantasy 9 invention 10 creativity 11 inspiration 13 inventiveness, visualization
imagine 4 take 5 dream, fancy, guess, image, think 6 assume, expect, gather, vision 7 believe, feature, picture, realize, suppose, suspect 8 conceive, envisage, envision 9 fabricate, visualize 10 conjecture, understand
imbecile 3 ass 4 dolt, dull, fool, jerk, slow, zany 5 ament, idiot, moron, ninny 6 cretin, donkey 7 half-wit, jackass, moronic, natural, tomfool 8 backward, retarded 9 dim witted, simpleton 10 half-witted, nincompoop, slow-witted 12 feebleminded, simpleminded
imbibe 3 sip 4 soak, swig, toss 5 booze, drink, quaff, sup up, swill 6 absorb, guzzle, insorb, sup off, tank up, tipple 7 inhaust, swallow, swizzle 8 liquor up 10 assimilate
imbricate 3 lap 4 ride 7 overlap, overlie, shingle 8 override
imbroglio 3 row 4 miff, spat 7 dispute, quarrel 8 squabble 9 bickering 10 falling-out 11 altercation, embroilment 12 disagreement
imbue 3 dye 4 soak 5 steep, tinge 6 infuse, invest, leaven 7 ingrain, suffuse 8 permeate, saturate 9 inoculate 10 impregnate
imitate 3 ape 4 copy, echo, mime, mock 5 mimic 6 parody 7 emulate, take off 8 travesty 9 burlesque, duplicate, replicate, reproduce 11 reduplicate *combining form:* 3 mim 4 mimo
imitation 4 copy, fake, mock, sham 5 dummy, false, phony 6 ersatz 7 forgery, replica 8 likeness, spurious 9 duplicate, semblance, simulated 10 artificial, simulacrum, simulation, substitute 11 counterfeit, counterpart 12 reproduction *suffix:* 3 een 4 ette
imitative 5 apish 6 echoic 7 parodic, slavish 9 emulative 12 onomatopoeic 13 onomatopoetic
Imlah's son 7 Micaiah
immaculate 4 pure 5 clean 6 chaste, decent, modest 7 cleanly, perfect 8 flawless, innocent, spotless, unsoiled 9 errorless, exquisite, faultless, stainless, taintless, undefiled, unsullied 10 impeccable 11 unblemished
immaterial 4 airy 6 aerial 7 foreign, ghostly, psychic, shadowy 8 bodiless, ethereal, heavenly, unbodied 9 asomatous, celestial, disbodied, spiritual, unearthly, unfleshly, unworldly 10 discarnate, extraneous, impalpable, inapposite, insensible, intangible, irrelative, irrelevant, subjective,

unembodied, unmaterial, unphysical **11** disembodied, impertinent, incorporeal, nonmaterial, nonphysical **12** apparitional, imponderable, inapplicable, metaphysical, supernatural **13** insubstantial, unsubstantial

immature **3** raw **5** green, vealy, young **6** callow, infant, unripe **7** babyish, puerile **8** childish, juvenile, youthful **9** infantile, infantine, premature, unfledged **10** precocious **11** undeveloped

immaturity **6** nonage

immeasurable **7** endless **8** infinite **9** boundless, limitless, unbounded, unlimited **10** indefinite, unmeasured **11** illimitable, inestimable, measureless, uncountable **12** incalculable, unmeasurable, unreckonable

immediate **4** near, next, nigh **5** close **6** direct, nearby, urgent **7** instant, primary **9** first-hand, proximate **10** near-at-hand **11** hair-trigger **12** straightaway **13** instantaneous

immediately **3** now, PDQ **4** anon, away, soon, stat **6** at once, presto, pronto **7** shortly **8** directly, hereupon **9** forthwith, instanter, instantly, right away **11** straightway

immense **4** huge, vast **5** great, large **6** mighty **7** titanic **8** colossal, enormous, gigantic **9** monstrous **10** prodigious, tremendous

immensely **3** too **4** ever, over, very **6** overly, unduly **8** overfull, overmuch **9** extremely **11** exceedingly, excessively **12** inordinately

immensity **8** enormity, hugeness, vastness **9** magnitude **12** enormousness

immerse **3** dip **4** bury, busy, duck, dunk, sink, soak **5** bathe, douse, embed, souse **6** absorb, engage, occupy, plunge **7** asperse, baptize, engross, include **8** christen, saturate, sprinkle, submerge, submerse

immigrant **6** emigré *Israeli:* **6** halutz **7** chalutz **8** halutzim (plural) **9** chalutzim (plural) *Japanese:* **5** issei

imminent **5** loury **6** coming, likely, lowery **7** brewing, louring, nearing, ominous, pending **8** alarming, lowering, menacing, minatory, possible, probable, sinister, upcoming **9** gathering, impending, proximate **10** inevasible, inevitable **11** approaching, ineluctable, inescapable, overhanging, threatening, unavoidable, unescapable

immobile **3** set **5** fixed, inert, still **6** frozen, stable, static **8** immotile, immotive, stagnant, unmoving **9** immovable, steadfast, unmovable **10** motionless, stationary **11** irremovable

immobilize **6** disarm **7** cripple, disable **8** paralyze **9** prostrate **12** incapacitate

immoderate **5** dizzy, undue **7** extreme **8** towering **9** boundless, excessive, voracious **10** exorbitant, inordinate, untempered **11** extravagant, intemperate **12** unmeasurable, unreasonable, unrestrained **13** overindulgent

immoderation **6** excess **12** intemperance

immodest **4** bold, lewd **5** brash, gross **6** brazen **8** boastful, indecent, unchaste

immolate **4** kill **7** destroy **8** abnegate **9** sacrifice, victimize

immoral **3** bad **4** evil **5** dirty, loose, wrong **6** impure, sinful, wanton, wicked **7** corrupt, unclean, vicious **8** depraved, indecent, unchaste **9** dissolute, reprobate, uncleanly **10** iniquitous, licentious

immorality **4** vice **9** depravity **10** corruption, unchastity, wickedness

immortal **6** divine **7** abiding, endless, eternal, undying **8** enduring, timeless, unending **9** ceaseless, deathless, perpetual **11** amaranthine, everlasting, never-ending, sempiternal **12** imperishable

immotile **5** fixed **8** immobile, immotive **9** immovable, steadfast, unmovable **11** irremovable

immovable **3** pat, set **4** fast, firm **5** fixed, rigid, stuck **6** rooted, stable **7** adamant **8** constant, immobile, immotile, immotive, obdurate, unmoving **9** immutable, impassive, steadfast, unmovable **10** inflexible, invariable, stationary, unyielding

immunity **7** freedom **8** impunity **9** exemption

immunizer **7** vaccine **8** antibody

immure **3** hem, jug, pen **4** cage, coop, jail, mure, wall **5** fence, hedge **6** corral, intern **7** confine, enclose **8** bastille, cloister, imprison **9** constrain **11** incarcerate

immutable **4** firm **5** fixed **7** eternal **8** constant **9** immovable, unmovable **10** inflexible, invariable, unchanging **11** inalterable, unalterable **12** unchangeable, unmodifiable

Imnah *father:* **5** Asher *son:* **4** Kore

Imogen *father:* **9** Cymbeline *husband:* **9** Posthumus

imp **3** elf **4** brat, ouph, puck **5** cutup, demon, devil, gamin, gnome, pixie, scamp, troll **6** goblin, kobold, monkey, sprite, urchin **7** gremlin **9** hobgoblin

impact **3** hit, jar, rap **4** blow, bump, jolt, rock, slam, slap **5** brunt, clash, crash, crowd, pound, punch, quake, shake, shock, smash **6** bounce, buffet, jounce, quiver, strike, stroke, tremor, wallop **7** appulse, congest, impulse, meeting, smiting, tremble **9** collision, encounter **10** concussion, percussion

impair **3** mar, sap **4** harm, hurt **5** spoil **6** damage, debase, injure, lessen, weaken

7 blemish, cripple, tarnish, vitiate 8 enfeeble 9 prejudice, undermine
impaired 6 flawed, marred 7 damaged, spoiled 9 afflicted *prefix:* 3 dys
impale 4 spit, stab 5 lance, prick, punch, spear, spike 6 pierce, skewer, skiver 8 puncture, transfix 9 perforate 11 transpierce
impart 4 give, lend, tell 5 break, grant, share, yield 6 bestow, convey, pass on 8 disclose, transmit 11 communicate *knowledge:* 5 teach 6 inform 7 educate 8 instruct
impartial 4 even, fair, just 5 equal 7 neutral 8 unbiased 9 equitable, objective, uncolored 12 unprejudiced 13 disinterested, dispassionate
impasse 3 box, fix, jam 4 hole 6 corner, pickle, plight, pocket, scrape 7 dead end, dilemma 8 cul-de-sac, deadlock 9 stalemate 10 blind alley 11 predicament
impassioned 4 deep, warm 5 fiery, gushy, mushy 6 ardent, fervid, fierce, red-hot, torrid 7 blazing, burning, fervent, flaming, furious, glowing, gushing, intense, maudlin, violent, zealous 8 eloquent, feverish, profound, romantic, vehement, white-hot 9 perfervid 10 hot-blooded, overheated, passionate 11 dithyrambic, sentimental 12 melodramatic 13 overemotional
impassive 3 dry 4 calm, cold, cool 5 stoic 6 bovine, placid, stolid, wooden 7 callous 8 composed, hardened, reserved, reticent, taciturn 9 apathetic, collected, heartless, inanimate, indurated 10 insensible, insentient, motionless, phlegmatic, spiritless 11 cold-blooded, coldhearted, emotionless, inexcitable, insensitive, passionless, unconcerned, unemotional, unexcitable, unflappable 12 inexpressive, matter-of-fact, unexpressive, unresponsive 13 dispassionate, imperturbable, unimpressible, unsusceptible
impassivity 6 apathy, phlegm 8 stoicism 9 stolidity 13 insensibility
impatient 3 hot 4 agog, avid, edgy, keen 5 eager, harsh, hasty, itchy 6 abrupt, ardent 7 anxious, athirst, chafing, fidgety, fretful, nervous, thirsty 8 appetent, headlong, restless 9 demanding, impetuous, irascible, irritable
impeach 3 tax 6 accuse, charge, indict 7 arraign, censure 9 criminate, inculpate 11 incriminate
impeccable 4 nice 5 clean, exact, right 7 correct, perfect, precise 8 absolute, accurate, flawless, unerring, unflawed 9 errorless, exquisite, faultless, fleckless 10 immaculate, infallible 12 indefectible
impecunious 4 poor 5 needy 8 dirt poor, indigent 9 destitute, penniless, penurious 11 necessitous 12 impoverished, unprosperous
impecuniousness 4 need, want 6 penury 7 poverty 8 poorness 9 indigence, neediness, privation 11 destitution
impedance 4 clog 9 cumbrance, hindrance 10 impediment 11 encumbrance
impede 3 bar, bog, dam 4 clog, faze 5 block, brake, check, debar 6 hinder, hold up, rattle 8 obstruct 9 discomfit, embarrass
impediment 3 bar, rub 4 clog, snag 5 block, hitch 6 hamper, hurdle 8 obstacle 9 cumbrance, hindrance 10 difficulty 11 encumbrance, obstruction
impel 4 good, move, spur, urge 5 drive, force 6 compel, foment, incite, propel 7 actuate, inspire 8 mobilize, motivate 9 constrain, instigate, stimulate
impend 4 brew, hang, loom 6 gather, menace 8 approach, overhang 9 forthcome
impenetrable 4 firm, hard 5 dense, solid 6 arcane, mystic 8 numinous 9 mysterial, unguessed 10 cabalistic, impassable, impervious, mysterious, unknowable 11 impermeable, imperviable, inscrutable, substantial, ungraspable 12 incognizable, unfathomable
imperative 4 need, rule 5 acute, basic, bossy, guide, harsh, order, stern 6 crying, urgent 7 bidding, burning, claimed, clamant, command, crucial, exacted, exigent, instant 8 critical, demanded, imperial, ordering, pressing, required 9 clamorous, essential, imperious, insistent, mandatory, masterful, necessary, necessity 10 commanding, compulsory, high-handed, obligatory, peremptory 11 domineering, fundamental, importunate, magisterial, necessitous, overbearing 12 compulsatory, prerequisite
imperceptible 5 faint, vague 6 slight 7 obscure, trivial 8 fugitive 9 ephemeral, invisible, momentary 10 evanescent, impalpable, indistinct, insensible, intangible, unapparent 12 imponderable, unnoticeable, unobservable 13 inappreciable, inconspicuous, indiscernible, insignificant, unappreciable, undiscernible, unperceivable
imperceptive 7 cursory, shallow 8 slapdash 11 superficial, unobservant 12 impercipient, undiscerning, unperceiving, unperceptive
imperfect 4 sick 5 amiss 6 faulty, flawed, second 9 defective 10 defeasible, inadequate, incomplete, unfinished
imperfection 3 sin 4 flaw 5 fault 6 defect, foible 7 blemish, demerit, failing, frailty 8 weakness 10 deficiency 11 shortcoming
imperial 5 bossy, regal, royal 6 kingly 7 haughty 8 majestic 9 grandiose, imperious, masterful, sovereign 10 high-handed,

imperative, peremptory 11 domineering, magisterial, overbearing

imperil 4 risk 6 hazard, menace 7 jeopard, venture 8 endanger, jeopardy, threaten 10 compromise, jeopardize

imperious 5 bossy 6 lordly, strict, urgent 7 haughty 8 absolute, arrogant, despotic, dominant, imperial, required 9 arbitrary, mandatory, masterful, stringent 10 commanding, compulsory, high-handed, imperative, obligatory, oppressive, peremptory, tyrannical 11 dictatorial, domineering, heavy-handed, magisterial, overbearing

impermanent 7 passing 8 fleeting, fugitive, unstable 9 ephemeral, fugacious, momentary, temporary, tentative, transient 10 evanescent, short-lived, transitory

impersonal 4 cold, fair 5 equal 7 neutral 8 abstract, detached, unbiased 9 colorless, equitable, impartial, objective, uncolored 10 poker-faced 11 cold-blooded, emotionless, unpassioned 12 matter-of-fact, unprejudiced 13 disinterested, dispassionate, unimpassioned

impersonator 4 mime 5 actor, mimic 6 mummer, player 7 actress, trouper 8 thespian 9 performer, playactor 13 impressionist

impertinence 4 sass 8 audacity, boldness 9 hardihood, impudence, insolence, insolency, unfitness 10 disrespect, incivility 11 irrelevance 12 insolentness

impertinent 4 bold, busy, nosy, pert, rude 5 brash, fresh, sassy, saucy 6 brazen, prying 7 foreign, ill-bred, uncivil 8 arrogant, impolite, impudent, insolent, meddling 9 audacious, intrusive, obtrusive, offensive, officious 10 extraneous, immaterial, inapposite, irrelative, irrelevant, meddlesome, procacious, ungracious 11 ill-mannered, inquisitive, interfering, uncalled-for 12 contumelious, discourteous, inapplicable, presumptuous 13 disrespectful

imperturbability 6 phlegm 7 ataraxy 8 calmness, coolness 9 composure, sangfroid 10 equanimity

imperturbable 4 calm, cool, smug 6 placid, serene 7 unmoved 8 composed, tranquil 9 collected, impassive, unruffled, untouched 10 complacent, nonchalant, phlegmatic, unaffected 11 unflappable 13 self-satisfied

impervious 5 tight 8 hardened 10 impassable 11 impermeable, imperviable 12 impenetrable, unpierceable

impetuous 3 hot 4 rash 5 eager, fiery, hasty 6 abrupt, ardent, fervid, sudden 7 furious, hurried, restive, rushing, violent 8 headlong, vehement 9 hotheaded, impulsive 10 passionate 11 impassioned, precipitant, precipitate, precipitous, spontaneous

impetus 4 good, spur 5 force 7 impulse 8 catalyst, momentum, stimulus 9 incentive, stimulant 10 incitation, incitement, motivation

impious 6 sinful, unholy, wicked 7 froward, godless, profane, ungodly, wayward 8 contrary, indevout, perverse, undevout 9 atheistic, unduteous, undutiful 10 irreverent, scandalous, unfaithful, unhallowed 11 disobedient, irreligious, wrongheaded 12 iconoclastic, sacrilegious

impish 4 arch, pert 5 elfin, fresh, giddy, saucy 6 casual, elfish, elvish 7 coltish, offhand, playful, puckish, roguish, waggish 8 flippant, pixieish, sportive 10 frolicsome 11 free and easy, mischievous

impishness 7 devilry, roguery, waggery 8 deviltry, mischief 9 devilment 11 roguishness, waggishness 12 sportiveness

implacable 4 grim 6 mortal 8 ruthless 9 merciless 10 inexorable, ironfisted, relentless, unyielding 11 unflinching, unrelenting 12 unappeasable

implant 4 root 5 embed, imbue, infix, inset 6 enroot, infuse, leaven 7 impress, ingrain, inspire, instill, pervade 8 permeate, saturate 9 inculcate, inoculate, insinuate, introduce, penetrate 10 impregnate, inseminate 11 impenetrate

implausible 4 thin, weak 5 fishy, thick 6 flimsy 7 dubious, suspect, tenuous 8 doubtful, puzzling 10 improbable, incredible 11 problematic 12 unconvincing

implement 4 tool 6 device, effect, gadget, invoke 7 enforce, execute, fulfill, perform, realize, utensil 8 complete 9 actualize, apparatus, appliance 10 accomplish, instrument, supplement 11 contraption, contrivance ***cleaning:*** 3 mop 5 broom, brush 6 vacuum 7 sweeper 10 whiskbroom ***cutting:*** 5 knife, mower, razor 6 scythe, shears, sickle 8 scissors ***digging:*** 5 spade 6 shovel ***drawing:*** 3 pen 6 eraser, pencil 7 compass 8 charcoal, template ***eating:*** 4 fork 5 knife, spoon ***engraving:*** 5 burin 6 graver ***farm:*** 4 disc, dish, plow 6 dibber, harrow, seeder, tiller 8 gangplow, reaphook ***fireplace:*** 5 tongs 7 andiron ***fishing:*** 3 rod 4 hook 7 harpoon, trident ***garden:*** 3 hoe 4 rake 6 trowel ***grooming:*** 4 comb 5 brush 8 tweezers 10 toothbrush ***kind:*** 3 die, saw 4 file 5 brace, clamp, drill, punch, tongs 6 chisel, hammer, pliers, reamer, sander, wrench 7 hacksaw, scraper 9 blowtorch 11 screwdriver ***kitchen:*** 3 pan, pot 4 mold 5 mixer 6 kettle, mortar, pestle 7 blender, skillet, spatula ***logging:*** 4 pevy 5 peavy, peevy 6 peavey 8 cant hook ***measuring:*** 4 gage, rule 5 gauge, ruler, scale 7 caliper, divider, trammel, T-square 10 micrometer, protractor *stone:* 5 burin 6 colith 7 neolith 9 paleolith

implicate 4 mire 5 imply 6 affect, tangle 7 concern, embroil, implied, include, involve 8 implicit 11 incriminate

implication 4 hint 8 overtone 9 inference, undertone 10 suggestion 11 association, connotation

implicit 4 real 5 tacit 6 unsaid 7 genuine, implied, virtual 8 absolute, complete, inferred, unspoken 9 potential, practical, unuttered 10 undeclared, understood 11 unexpressed, unqualified

implied 5 tacit 6 unsaid 8 implicit, inferred, unspoken, wordless 9 unuttered 10 undeclared, understood

imploration 4 plea, suit 6 appeal, orison, prayer 8 entreaty, petition 11 application, imprecation 12 supplication

implore 3 ask, beg 4 coax, pray 5 crave, plead 6 appeal 7 beseech, conjure, entreat 9 importune 10 supplicate

imply 4 hint 5 point 7 connote, include, suggest 8 indicate, intimate 9 insinuate

impolite 4 rude 5 crude, rough 7 ill-bred, incivil, uncivil 10 ungracious, unmannerly, unpolished 11 disgracious, ill-mannered, uncourteous 12 discourteous 13 disrespectful

impolitic 5 brash 6 unwise 8 tactless 9 ill-judged, imprudent, maladroit, unpolitic, untactful 10 ill-advised, indiscreet 11 inadvisable, inexpedient, injudicious, unadvisable, unexpedient 12 undiplomatic

import 4 mean, pith 5 count, sense, spell, value, weigh, worth 6 convey, denote, design, intend, intent, matter, moment, object, stress, weight 7 add up to, concern, connote, express, meaning, message, purport, purpose, signify 8 emphasis, indicate 9 magnitude, objective, substance 10 importance, intendment 11 acceptation, consequence, weightiness 12 significance, significancy

importance 4 mark, note, pith 5 value, worth 6 import, moment, weight 7 account, gravity 8 eminence, priority, salience, standing 9 magnitude, substance 10 notability, prominence, reputation, worthiness 11 consequence, distinction, seriousness, weightiness 12 significance

important 3 big 5 grave, great, noted, puffy, wiggy 6 famous, marked, potent, stuffy, urgent, worthy 7 big-time, bloated, crucial, eminent, fateful, notable, pompous, salient, serious, telling, unusual, weighty 8 arrogant, eventful, material, powerful, topnotch, valuable 9 effective, essential, first-rate, front-page, memorable, momentous, ponderous, prominent 10 first-class, impressive, meaningful, noteworthy, noticeable, pontifical, remarkable, worthwhile 11 conspicuous, distinctive, exceptional, magisterial, outstanding, significant, substantial 12 considerable 13 consequential, distinguished

importune 3 beg 4 pray, urge 5 annoy, crave, plead, worry 6 appeal, invoke 7 beseech, entreat, implore, solicit, trouble 10 supplicate

impose 3 fob, set, use 4 lade, levy, wish 5 abuse, exact, foist, order, put on, visit, wreak, wreck 6 assess, burden, charge, compel, create, decree, demand, enjoin, fob off, oblige, ordain, saddle 7 command, dictate, exploit, force on, inflict, intrude, lay down, obtrude, palm off, presume, put upon, require 8 encroach, generate, infringe, trespass 9 constrain, force upon

imposing 3 big 4 arty 5 grand, noble, regal, royal 6 august, moving 7 stately 8 baronial, imperial, majestic, princely 9 grandiose, overblown 10 arty-crafty, commanding, impressive 11 magnificent, pretentious 12 high-sounding

imposition 3 tax 4 duty, fine, levy 6 burden 7 penalty 9 deception

impossible 6 absurd 8 cureless, hopeless 9 incurable, insanable, uncurable 10 infeasible, unfeasible, unworkable 11 immedicable, impractical, irreparable, unthinkable 12 inexecutable, irrealizable, irremediable, unacceptable, unattainable, unobtainable, unrealizable, unreasonable

impost 3 tax 4 duty, levy 6 tariff, weight 7 tribute 10 assessment

imposter 4 fake 5 cheat, faker, fraud, mimic, phony, quack 6 humbug 7 bluffer, shammer, shyster 8 beguiler, deceiver, imitator 9 charlatan, hypocrite, misleader, pretender, trickster 10 dissembler, mountebank 11 four-flusher, pettifogger

imposture 3 gyp 4 copy, fake, flam, hoax, ploy, ruse, sell, sham, wile 5 cheat, feint, fraud, phony, put-on, spoof, trick 6 deceit, gambit, humbug 7 forgery, sleight, swindle 8 artifice, flimflam, maneuver, pretense 9 deception, falsehood, imitation, mare's nest, stratagem 10 pretension 11 counterfeit, fabrication, make-believe

impotent 4 weak 5 frail 6 barren, effete, feeble 7 sterile 8 boneless, crippled, disabled, helpless, infecund 9 enfeebled, forceless, infertile, powerless, spineless 10 emasculate, inadequate, unfruitful 11 ineffective, ineffectual, slack-spined 12 invertebrate

impoverish 4 bust, draw, ruin 5 break, drain, use up 6 beggar, fold up, pauper 7 deplete, exhaust 8 bankrupt, draw down 9 pauperize

impoverished 4 poor 5 needy 6 scanty

8 bankrupt, beggared, indigent 9 destitute, penurious 10 stone-broke 11 impecunious

impoverishment 4 need, want 6 penury 7 poverty 8 poorness 9 indigence, neediness, privation 11 destitution

impracticable 6 unwise 7 awkward, useless 8 unusable 9 imprudent 10 impossible, infeasible, unfeasible, unworkable

impractical 5 viewy 7 useless 8 quixotic, romantic, unusable 9 visionary 10 idealistic, impossible, infeasible, ivory-tower, starry-eyed, unfeasible, unworkable 11 theoretical, unrealistic

imprecation 4 oath, plea, suit 5 curse 6 appeal, orison, prayer 7 cursing, cussing, malison 8 anathema, entreaty, petition, swearing 9 blasphemy, profanity

impregnable 4 safe 6 secure 7 guarded 8 defended, shielded 9 protected 10 invincible, unbeatable 11 indomitable

impregnate 3 sop 4 soak 5 imbue, souse, steep 6 charge, drench, infuse, leaven, seethe, sodden 7 pervade 8 permeate, saturate, waterlog 9 fertilize, inoculate, penetrate, percolate, transfuse 10 inseminate

impresario 5 agent, Carte, Hurok (Sol) 7 manager 9 Diaghilev (Sergei) 10 D'Oyly Carte

impress 3 fix, get, set 4 etch, mark, move, seal, sway 5 brand, carry, drive, exert, force, grave, infix, pique, pound, print, stamp, touch 6 affect, effect, excite, hammer, strike, thrill 7 engrave, enthuse, implant, imprint, ingrain, inspire, provoke 8 inscribe 9 electrify, establish, galvanize, inculcate, influence, stimulate

impression 4 dent, dint, idea, mark, sign 5 image, print, shock, stamp, trace, track 6 hollow, impact, notion 7 conceit, concept, edition, impress, imprint, reissue, thought, vestige 8 printing, reaction

impressionable 7 plastic, sensile 8 sensible, sentient 9 sensitive 10 affectable, responsive, susceptive 11 impressible, susceptible 13 influenceable

impressionist *composer:* 5 Ravel 7 Debussy *mimic:* 6 Little (Rich) *painter:* 5 Degas, Manet, Monet 6 Renoir, Sisley 8 Pissarro; (see also **postimpressionist**)

impressive 5 grand, noble 6 august, lavish, moving, superb 7 notable 8 gorgeous, imposing, majestic, poignant, splendid, striking, touching 9 affecting, arresting, grandiose, luxurious, sumptuous

imprimatur 7 license 8 approval, sanction

imprint 4 etch, mark 5 press, stamp 7 engrave, impress 8 inscribe 10 impression

imprison 3 jug 4 cage, curb, jail 5 check, limit 6 detain, immure, intern 7 confine, enclose 8 bastille, restrain, restrict 9 constrain 11 incarcerate 12 circumscribe

impromptu 7 offhand 9 extempore, makeshift, unstudied 10 improvised 11 extemporary, unrehearsed 13 autoschediasm, improvisation

improper 5 amiss, crude, fresh, inapt, inept, outré, rough, sassy, unapt, undue, unfit, wrong 6 gauche, unmeet 7 illicit, ungodly, unhappy 8 ill-timed, indecent, informal, tactless, uncomely, unseemly, untimely, untoward 9 incorrect, unfitting 10 inaccurate, inapposite, indecorous, indelicate, malapropos, malodorous, unbecoming, undecorous, unsuitable 11 impertinent, unbefitting 12 illegitimate, inadmissible, inapplicable, infelicitous, intempestive, unseasonable 13 inappropriate, unceremonious *prefix:* 3 mis

impropriety 5 boner, break, error, gaffe 7 blooper, faux pas 8 slangism, solecism 9 barbarism, indecorum, vulgarism 10 corruption, inelegance, unmeetness 12 unseemliness, untowardness 13 incorrectness

improve 4 edit, gain, help, mend 5 amend, edify, emend, rally, rub up 6 better, enrich, illume, look up, perk up, refine, reform, remedy, revise, revive, uplift 7 advance, augment, benefit, correct, develop, enhance, enlarge, perfect, recover, rectify, upgrade 8 illumine, increase, progress 9 cultivate, enlighten, intensify, irradiate, meliorate 10 ameliorate, convalesce, illuminate, recuperate, strengthen

improvident 6 lavish 7 profuse 8 careless, heedless, prodigal, reckless, unthrift, wasteful 9 imprudent, negligent, unthrifty 10 profligate, thriftless 11 extravagant, spendthrift 12 uneconomical

improvise 5 ad-lib 6 devise, invent 7 concoct 8 contrive 11 extemporize

improvised 7 offhand 9 extempore, impromptu, unstudied 11 extemporary, unrehearsed

imprudent 4 rash 6 unwary, unwise 7 foolish 8 reckless 10 ill-advised, incautious, indiscreet 11 inadvisable, inexpedient, injudicious, unadvisable, unexpedient 12 shortsighted

impudence 4 gall 8 audacity, boldness 9 arrogance, hardihood, insolence, insolency 10 disrespect, effrontery 11 presumption 12 impertinence, insolentness

impudent 4 bold, flip, pert, wise 5 brash, fresh, lippy, nervy, sassy, saucy, smart 6 arrant, brassy, brazen, cheeky 7 blatant, forward 8 flippant, insolent, overbold 9 audacious, barefaced, shameless, unabashed 10 procacious, unblushing

11 brazenfaced, impertinent, smart-alecky 12 contumelious 13 disrespectful
impugn 4 deny 5 cross, fight 6 assail, attack, negate, oppose, resist 7 gainsay 8 negative, traverse 9 disaffirm 10 contradict, contravene
impugnable 5 fishy, shady 7 suspect 8 doubtful 9 doubtable, equivocal, uncertain 10 borderline, suspicious 11 problematic
impulse 3 ate 4 goad, lust, push, spur, urge, whim 5 drive, force 6 impact, motive, thrust, whimsy 7 impetus, passion, whimsey 8 catalyst, excitant, stimulus 9 actuation, impulsion, incentive, stimulant 10 incitation, incitement, motivation 11 instigation
impulsive 5 hasty 6 abrupt, sudden 8 headlong, will-less 9 automatic, impetuous 10 unprompted 11 instinctive, involuntary, precipitate, spontaneous, unmeditated
impure 3 raw 4 foul, lewd, vile 5 black, crude, dirty, gross, mixed, nasty, soily 6 carnal, common, filthy, grubby, native, unholy 7 bastard, defiled, immoral, lustful, obscene, scarlet, sensual, squalid, unclean 8 immodest, indecent, polluted, profaned, prurient, unchaste, ungraded, unsorted 9 run-of-mine, uncleanly, unrefined 10 desecrated, indecorous, lascivious, unhallowed 11 adulterated
impute 3 lay 4 give, hint 5 refer 6 accuse, adduce, assign, charge, credit, impart, indict 7 ascribe 8 accredit, intimate 9 attribute
inability 9 inaptness, ineptness 10 inadequacy, inaptitude, incapacity, inefficacy, ineptitude 11 inadeptness 12 incapability, incompetence, inefficiency
inaccessible 3 far 6 closed, far-off, remote 7 distant, faraway 8 abstruse, esoteric 11 out-of-the-way, ungetatable, unreachable 12 unattainable, unobtainable
in accordance with 5 as per 10 pursuant to
inaccurate 5 false, wrong 6 faulty, untrue 7 inexact, unsound 8 specious 9 defective, erroneous, incorrect
inaction 5 drift 8 idleness, lethargy 9 indolence, inertness, slackness, torpidity 10 inactivity, quiescence 12 inactiveness, slothfulness
inactive 4 dead, idle, slow 5 inert, quiet, slack, still 6 asleep, latent, sleepy, static, supine, torpid 7 abeyant, dormant, jobless, passive 8 indolent, ossified, slothful, sluggish 9 do-nothing, lethargic, lymphatic, quiescent, sedentary, unworking 10 disengaged, motionless, unemployed, unoccupied
in addition 4 also, then 5 again 7 besides, further 8 moreover 12 additionally
inadequacy 4 lack 7 deficit, failure 8 shortage, underage 9 inability 10 deficiency, incapacity, inefficacy, scantiness 11 defalcation 12 incapability, incompetence 13 insufficience, insufficiency
inadequate 3 shy 4 weak 5 scant, short 6 meager, scanty, scarce, skimpy 7 failing, lacking, scrimpy, wanting 8 boneless, impotent 9 defective, deficient, forceless, spineless 10 emasculate, incomplete, uncomplete 11 ineffective, ineffectual, slack-spined 12 insufficient
inadmissible 5 inapt, inept, unapt 8 ill-timed, improper, unseemly, unwanted 9 unwelcome 10 ill-favored, malapropos, unbecoming 11 undesirable 12 unacceptable
inadvertent 8 careless, feckless, heedless, uncaring 9 negligent, undevised, unheeding, unplanned, unrecking, unthought 10 undesigned, unintended 13 unintentional
inadvisable 4 rash 6 unwise 7 foolish 8 careless 9 foolhardy, impolitic, imprudent, pointless 10 ill-advised, incautious, indiscreet, unsensible 11 harebrained, inexpedient, undesirable, unexpedient 13 inappropriate
inalterable 5 fixed 8 constant 9 immovable, immutable, steadfast, unmovable 10 inflexible, invariable 12 unchangeable, unmodifiable
inamorata 5 flame, honey, lover, woman 6 steady 7 beloved, sweetie 8 ladylove, mistress, paramour, truelove 10 girl friend, sweetheart
inamorato 4 beau 5 flame, lover 6 steady 7 beloved 8 truelove 9 boyfriend 10 sweetheart
inane 4 flat, idle, vain 5 blank, empty, silly, vapid 6 hollow, jejune, vacant 7 asinine, fatuous, foolish, idiotic, insipid, sapless, shallow, vacuous 8 mindless, trifling 9 driveling, frivolous, innocuous, pointless, senseless
inanimate 4 cold, dead, dull, late 5 inert 6 asleep 7 defunct, extinct 8 deceased, departed, lifeless 9 exanimate, insensate, senseless, unfeeling 10 insensible, insentient
inanity 5 folly 7 vacuity 8 insanity, unwisdom, vapidity 9 absurdity, craziness, dottiness, emptiness, frivolity, silliness 10 hollowness, triviality 11 foolishness, shallowness, witlessness 13 senselessness
inappreciable 6 meager, scanty, skimpy 7 scrimpy 10 impalpable, inadequate, insensible, intangible, unapparent 12 imponderable, insufficient, unobservable
inappropriate 5 inapt, inept, undue, unfit 6 clumsy, unmeet 8 ill-timed, improper,

unfitted, unseemly, unsuited, untimely 9 ill-suited 10 ill-adapted, indecorous, malapropos, unbecoming, unsuitable 11 inconsonant, unbefitting 12 unseasonable
inapt 4 flat 5 banal, undue, unfit 6 clumsy, gauche, jejune, unmeet 7 awkward, inadept, insipid, unhandy 8 ill-timed, improper, inexpert, unfacile, unfitted, unsuited, untimely 9 ill-suited, maladroit, unfitting 10 amateurish, ill-adapted, inadequate, malapropos, unskillful, unsuitable
in arrears 6 behind 10 behindhand
inarticulate 4 dumb, mute 5 tacit 6 silent, unsaid 7 blurred, halting, implied, unvocal 8 implicit, inferred, mumbling, unspoken, wordless 9 faltering, stammered, unuttered, voiceless 10 hesitating, incoherent, indistinct, maundering, speechless, stammering, tongue-tied, undeclared 11 unexpressed
inasmuch as 2 as 3 for, now 5 since 7 because, whereas 8 as long as 11 considering
inattentive 3 lax 5 bored 6 ennuyé, remiss 8 careless, distrait, heedless 9 forgetful, negligent, unheeding, unmindful 10 abstracted, distracted, distraught, unnoticing, unthinking, unwatchful 11 inobservant, thoughtless, unobservant, unobserving
inaugural 5 first 7 initial, leading 8 foremost, headmost 9 induction 10 initiation 11 investiture 12 installation
inaugurate 4 open 5 begin, enter, set up, start 6 get off, induct, invest, launch 7 install, instate, jump off, kick off, usher in 8 commence, dedicate, initiate 9 institute, introduce, originate 10 consecrate
inauspicious 3 bad 4 dire, evil 7 adverse, baleful, baneful, fateful, ominous, unlucky 8 sinister 9 ill-boding, ill-omened 11 threatening 12 unpropitious
inborn 6 inbred, innate, native 7 connate, natural 8 inherent 9 essential, ingrained, inherited, intrinsic 10 congenital, connatural, deep-seated, hereditary, indigenous, indwelling, unacquired
inbred 6 inborn, innate 7 connate 8 inherent 9 ingrained, intrinsic 10 congenital, deep-seated, indwelling
Inca ***beverage:*** 5 chica ***capital:*** 5 Cusco, Cuzco ***conqueror:*** 7 Pizarro ***god:*** 4 Inti 9 Viracocha 10 Pachacamac ***half-breed:*** 5 Cholo ***language:*** 8 Quechuan ***priest:*** 3 umu ***record:*** 5 quipu ***ruler:*** 9 Atahualpa, Pachacuti ***sacred object:*** 5 huaca 8 apacheta ***socioeconomic unit:*** 5 ayllu
incalculable 4 iffy, vast 6 chancy, untold 7 erratic 8 enormous, infinite 9 boundless, countless, fluctuant, limitless, uncertain, whimsical 10 capricious, unmeasured, unnumbered 11 illimitable, inestimable, innumerable, measureless, uncountable 12 immeasurable, unmeasurable
in camera 7 sub rosa 8 covertly, secretly 9 by stealth, furtively, privately 10 stealthily 12 hugger-mugger 13 clandestinely
incandescent 3 hot 5 lucid 6 ardent, bright, lucent 7 beaming, fulgent, glowing, lambent, radiant 8 luminous 9 brilliant, effulgent, refulgent
incantation 4 rune 5 chant, charm, magic, spell 7 sorcery 8 witchery, wizardry 9 conjuring, magicking 10 necromancy, witchcraft 11 bewitchment, conjuration, enchantment ***Buddhist, Hindu:*** 6 mantra
incapable 5 inept, unfit 6 unable 8 inexpert, unexpert, unfitted 9 unskilled 10 ineligible, unequipped, unskillful 11 incompetent
incapacitate 6 disarm 7 cripple, disable 8 paralyze 9 disenable, prostrate 10 disqualify, immobilize
incapacity 9 inability 10 inadequacy, inefficacy 12 incapability, incompetence
incarcerate 3 jug 4 jail 6 immure, intern 7 confine, enclose 8 bastille, imprison 9 constrain
incarnadine 3 red 4 ruby 5 ruddy 6 redden, rubify, rubric, ruddle
incarnate 5 utter 6 embody 8 embodied, manifest 9 actualize, objectify, personify, personize 11 exteriorize, externalize, materialize, personalize, unspeakable 12 substantiate
incarnation 6 avatar 7 avatara 10 embodiment ***Of Christ:*** 7 kenosis
incautious 4 bold, rash, wild 5 brash, hasty 6 madcap, unwary 7 unalert 8 carefree, careless, feckless, heedless, reckless 9 hotheaded, impetuous, impolitic, imprudent, negligent, uncareful, unguarded, unmindful 10 ill-advised, indiscreet, madbrained, neglectful, regardless, unvigilant, unwatchful 11 injudicious, thoughtless 13 inconsiderate, irresponsible
incendiary 5 torch 7 exciter, firebug 8 agitator, arsonist 10 pyromaniac 12 inflammatory
incense 3 ire, mad, oil 4 balm, burn 5 anger, aroma, scent, spice 6 arouse, enrage, homage, incite, madden ***vessel:*** 6 censer 8 thurible
incentive 4 goad, spur 5 spark 6 motive 7 impetus, impulse 8 catalyst, stimulus 9 stimulant 10 incitation, incitement, inducement, motivation 11 provocation, stimulative 13 encouragement
inception 4 root, well 5 start 6 origin, source, whence 8 fountain 9 beginning 10 derivation, initiation, provenance, wellspring 11 provenience 12 commencement
inceptive 7 initial, nascent 9 beginning,

incipient 10 initiative, initiatory 12 introductory
incertitude 5 doubt 6 wonder 7 concern, dubiety 8 mistrust 9 dubiosity, suspicion 10 indecision, skepticism 11 uncertainty
incessant 6 steady 7 endless, eternal 8 constant, timeless 9 ceaseless, continual, perpetual, unceasing 10 continuous 11 everlasting, unremitting 12 interminable
inchoate 7 muddled 8 formless, unformed, unshaped 9 amorphous, expectant, incipient, potential, shapeless 10 contingent, disjointed, disordered, incoherent, incohesive, incomplete 11 imperfected, unconnected, unorganized 12 disconnected, uncontinuous 13 discontinuous
incident 4 akin 5 event 6 agnate, allied 7 cognate, connate, episode, kindred, related 8 accident, external, occasion 9 ancillary, attendant, attending, happening, satellite 10 affiliated, collateral, connatural, occurrence 11 concomitant, consanguine 12 accompanying, circumstance
incidental 3 odd 5 fluky 6 casual, chance 8 episodic 9 accessory 10 accidental, contingent, digressive, fortuitous 11 subordinate 12 nonessential
incidentally 6 obiter 8 by the bye, by the way, casually 9 in passing 12 accidentally, fortuitously
incipient 7 initial, nascent 8 inchoate 9 beginning, inceptive 10 commencing, initiative, initiatory 12 introductory
incise 3 cut 4 etch, gash, kerf, slit 5 grave, slash, slice 6 pierce 7 engrave
incisive 4 keen, tart 5 acerb, acute, crisp, sharp, terse 6 biting 7 acerbic, caustic, concise, cutting, ingoing, laconic, mordant 8 clear-cut, drilling, piercing, scathing, slashing, succinct 9 sarcastic, trenchant 11 penetrating
incite 3 egg, set 4 abet, goad, prod, spur, urge 5 raise, rouse, set on 6 arouse, compel, excite, exhort, foment, motive, set off, stir up, whip up 7 actuate, agitate, forward, further, inflame, promote, provoke, solicit, trigger 8 motivate 9 encourage, instigate, stimulate
incitement see **incentive**
inclement 3 raw 4 hard 5 harsh, rough 6 bitter, brutal, rugged, severe, stormy 8 rigorous 10 unmerciful 11 intemperate
inclination 3 bow, nod 4 bent, bias, lean, love, mind, tilt, will 5 fancy, grade, slant, slope, taste 6 ascent, desire, liking 7 descent, incline, leaning 8 affinity, appetite, fondness, gradient, penchant, pleasure, soft spot, tendency, velleity, weakness 9 affection 10 attachment, proclivity, propensity 11 disposition 12 predilection ***rate of:*** 8 gradient
incline 3 aim, lay, tip 4 bend, bias, cant, cast, hade, heel, lean, list, look, move, sway, tend, tilt, turn 5 drive, grade, impel, level, point, slant, slide, slope, train 6 affect, direct, induce, prompt, zero in 7 address, deflect, dispose, leaning 8 gradient, persuade 9 influence, prejudice ***combining form:*** 4 clin 5 clino
inclined 3 apt 4 fain, wont 5 given, prone, raked, ready 6 biased, graded, liable, likely, minded, sloped, tilted, tipped 7 dipping, leaning, oblique, pitched, sloping, tilting, willing 8 diagonal, disposed, pitching 9 declivate 11 declivitous, predisposed ***way:*** 4 ramp
include 4 have, hold 5 admit, bound, cover 6 embody, enfold, number, take in 7 confine, contain, embrace, enclose, involve, receive, subsume 8 comprise, encircle 9 encompass 10 comprehend
inclusive 6 global 7 general, overall 8 sweeping 9 all-around, enclosing 12 encompassing, encyclopedic 13 comprehensive
incognizant 7 unaware 8 ignorant 9 oblivious, unknowing, unwitting 10 unfamiliar, uninformed 12 inconversant, unacquainted, uninstructed
incoherent 5 loose 6 broken, raving 7 muddled 8 inchoate 9 illogical 10 discordant, disjointed, disordered, incohesive, maundering, tongue-tied 11 incongruous, inconsonant, nonadhesive, unconnected, unorganized 12 disconnected, inarticulate, incompatible, inconsequent, inconsistent, inharmonious, uncontinuous 13 discontinuous
incombustible 7 apyrous 12 nonflammable
income 4 gain, take 6 profit, return 7 annuity, comings, produce, revenue 8 interest, proceeds, receipts 9 emolument
incommode 3 irk, vex 5 annoy, block 6 bother, hinder, impede, molest, plague, put out 7 disturb, trouble 8 disquiet, obstruct, put about 9 disoblige 13 inconvenience
incommodious 5 cramp 7 awkward, cramped, squeezy 8 confined 12 discommoding, embarrassing, inconvenient
incommunicable 8 reserved, taciturn 9 ineffable, withdrawn 10 restrained, untellable 11 constrained, indefinable, inenarrable, unspeakable, unutterable 12 noncommittal 13 indescribable, inexpressible, undescribable, unexpressible
incomparable 7 supreme 8 peerless, towering, ultimate 9 matchless 10 preeminent, surpassing 11 unequalable, unmatchable 12 transcendent 13 unsurpassable
incompatible 7 adverse, counter 8 con-

trary, opposite 9 antipodal, dissonant, unmixable 10 antipodean, discordant, discrepant 11 conflicting, disagreeing, incongruent, incongruous, inconsonant, unadaptable 12 antagonistic, antipathetic, antithetical, disconsonant, inconsistent, inharmonious 13 contradictory, inconformable, unconformable, unsympathetic

incompetence 9 inability, unfitness 10 disability, inadequacy, incapacity, inefficacy 12 incapability 13 insufficiency

incompetent 5 inept, unfit 8 helpless, inexpert, unexpert, unfitted 9 incapable, unskilled 10 ineligible, unequipped, unskillful 11 inefficient, unqualified 12 disqualified, insufficient *legally:* 12 inadmissible

incomplete 4 part 5 bitty, short 6 broken 7 lacking, partial, scrappy, sketchy, wanting 8 immature 9 composite, defective, deficient 10 fractional, inadequate, incoherent, uncomplete, unfinished 11 fragmentary, imperfected 12 insufficient

incompliant 5 rigid, stiff 6 mulish 8 perverse, stubborn 9 impliable, obstinate, pigheaded, resistant, unbending 10 bullheaded, headstrong, inflexible, self-willed, unflexible, unyielding 11 immalleable, intractable 12 pertinacious

incomprehensible 7 cryptic, obscure, unclear 8 abstruse 9 enigmatic 10 fathomless, mysterious, mystifying, unknowable, unreadable 11 inscrutable, ungraspable 12 impenetrable, incognizable, unfathomable, unimaginable, unsearchable 13 imperceptible, inconceivable

inconceivable 4 thin, weak 6 flimsy 10 improbable, incredible, unknowable 11 implausible, incogitable, unthinkable 12 insupposable, unbelievable, unconvincing, unimaginable

in conclusion 6 lastly 7 finally

inconclusive 4 open 9 uncertain, undecided, unsettled 10 incomplete, indecisive, indefinite, unfinished 11 ineffective

incongruous 5 alien 6 absurd 7 bizarre, foreign 9 dissonant, fantastic, grotesque, unmixable 10 discordant, discrepant, extraneous 11 conflicting, inconsonant 12 disconsonant, incompatible, inconsistent, inharmonious

inconscient 4 lost 6 absent 7 bemused, faraway 8 distrait, mindless 10 abstracted 11 preoccupied 12 absentminded

inconsequential 5 petty, small 6 measly, paltry 7 trivial 8 picayune, trifling 10 irrelevant, picayunish

inconsiderable 4 puny 5 light, minor, petty, small 6 casual, little, meager, paltry, peanut, scanty, skimpy 7 scrimpy, trivial 8 picayune, trifling 9 small-beer 10 inadequate, negligible, shoestring 11 unimportant 12 inconsequent, insufficient, unconsidered 13 inappreciable, insignificant

inconsiderate 4 rash 5 brash, hasty, sharp, short 6 madcap, unkind 8 careless, heedless, reckless 9 hotheaded 10 ill-advised, incautious, ungracious 11 precipitate, thoughtless

inconsistent 6 fickle 8 ticklish, unstable 9 dissonant, mercurial, uncertain, unmixable 10 capricious, changeable, discordant, discrepant, inconstant, lubricious 11 conflicting, incongruent, incongruous, inconsonant 12 disconsonant, incompatible, inharmonious 13 contradictory, inconformable

inconsolable 7 forlorn 8 dejected, desolate 9 heartsick 11 comfortless, heartbroken 12 disconsolate

inconspicuous 5 vague 7 obscure 10 indistinct, unemphatic 11 unobtrusive 12 unnoticeable

inconstant 5 false, light 6 fickle, shifty, untrue 7 elusive, erratic, mutable, protean, vagrant, variant, wayward 8 disloyal, slippery, ticklish, unstable, unsteady, variable, volatile, wavering 9 changeful, faithless, frivolous, mercurial, uncertain, unsettled 10 capricious, changeable, irresolute, lubricious, perfidious, traitorous, unreliable 11 chameleonic, light-minded, treacherous, vacillating 12 inconsistent, shilly-shally, undependable 13 temperamental

incontestable 4 sure 7 certain 8 positive 9 undoubted 10 undeniable 11 indubitable, irrefutable, unequivocal 12 indisputable

incontinent 4 fast, lewd 7 lustful, satyric 9 lecherous, libertine, salacious 10 lascivious, libidinous, licentious 12 unrestrained

incontrovertible 4 sure 7 certain 8 positive 10 inarguable, undeniable 11 indubitable, unequivocal 12 indisputable, undisputable 13 incontestable, uncontestable

inconvenience 3 try 4 fuss, stew 5 annoy, trial 6 bother, meddle, pother, put out 7 disturb, trouble 8 handicap, put about 9 aggravate, annoyance, disoblige, incommode, interfere 10 discomfort, discommode, discompose, exasperate 11 aggravation, awkwardness, intermeddle 12 disadvantage, discomfiture, exasperation 13 embarrassment

inconvenient 7 awkward, unhandy 8 annoying 10 bothersome, unsuitable 11 detrimental, inexpedient, inopportune, pestiferous, prejudicial, troublesome 12 discommoding, embarrassing, incommodious, unreasonable 13 discommodious

incorporate 3 mix 4 fuse, join 5 blend, merge, unite 6 absorb, embody, imbibe, insorb, mingle 7 combine, inhaust 9 integrate 10 assimilate

incorporeal 4 airy 8 bodiless 9 asomatous, spiritual 10 discarnate, immaterial, unembodied, unphysical 11 disembodied, nonmaterial, nonphysical 12 metaphysical 13 unsubstantial

incorrect 5 false, wrong 6 faulty, untrue 7 unsound 8 improper, specious 9 erroneous, imprecise 10 inaccurate, unbecoming ***combining form:*** 3 cac 4 caco ***prefix:*** 3 mis

increase 2 up 3 add, rev, wax 4 gain, grow, hike, jump, plus, push, rise, soup, teem 5 boost, build, mount, put up, raise, run up, swarm, swell 6 accrue, amount, beef up, dilate, expand, extend, gather, growth, jack up, markup 7 advance, amplify, augment, burgeon, distend, enhance, enlarge, inflate, magnify, prolong, pyramid, upgrade, upsurge 8 addition, compound, elongate, escalate, flourish, heighten, lengthen, manifold, multiply, protract, snowball 9 accession, accretion, aggravate, expansion, extension, increment, intensify, pullulate, reinforce 10 accelerate, accumulate, aggrandize, appreciate, strengthen 11 enlargement 12 augmentation, breakthrough 13 amplification ***Scottish:*** 3 eke ***suddenly:*** 4 zoom

increasing 8 crescent, crescive

incredible 4 thin, weak 5 thick 6 absurd, flimsy 8 unlikely 9 cockamamy, untenable 10 cockamamie, impossible, improbable, outlandish, ridiculous 11 implausible, incogitable, unthinkable 12 insupposable, preposterous, unbelievable, unconvincing, unimaginable 13 inconceivable

incredulity 7 unfaith 8 unbelief 9 disbelief

incredulous 4 wary 6 show-me 7 dubious 8 aporetic, doubting, hesitant 9 faithless, quizzical, skeptical, uncertain 10 suspicious 11 distrustful, distrusting, mistrustful, questioning, unbelieving, unconvinced, unsatisfied 12 disbelieving

increment 4 gain, rise 5 raise 6 growth 8 addition, increase 9 accession, accretion 11 enlargement 12 augmentation

incriminate 6 accuse, charge, indict 7 arraign, impeach, involve 9 implicate, inculpate

incrustation 4 rime, scab 5 scale 6 plaque, tarter

incubus 4 onus 5 demon 6 burden 9 nightmare 10 evil spirit

inculcate 5 infix, teach 6 impart, infuse 7 educate, implant, impress, instill 8 instruct 10 inseminate 11 communicate

inculpable 4 good, pure 5 clean 8 innocent, unguilty, virtuous 9 blameless, crimeless, exemplary, faultless, guiltless, righteous

incumbent 7 binding, leaning 8 occupant 9 overlying 12 superimposed

incur 3 get 6 induce 7 acquire, bring on 8 contract 9 encounter

incurable 8 cureless, hopeless 9 insanable 10 impossible 11 immedicable, irreparable 12 irremediable 13 irretrievable, uncorrectable, unrecoverable

incursion 4 raid 5 foray 6 attack, inroad 7 assault 8 invasion 9 irruption

incus 4 bone 5 anvil

indebted 7 obliged 8 beholden 9 duty-bound, obligated 10 honor-bound

indebtedness 3 due 4 debt 7 arrears, failure 8 beholden 9 arrearage, liability 10 bankruptcy, insolvency, nonpayment, obligation 11 delinquency

indecent 4 foul, racy 5 dirty, gross, nasty 6 coarse, filthy, impure, risqué, smutty, vulgar 7 immoral, obscene, raunchy, ungodly 8 immodest, improper, off-color, unseemly, untoward 10 indecorous, indelicate, malodorous, ridiculous, scurrilous, unbecoming, undecorous 12 scatological

indecision 5 doubt 8 to-and-fro, wavering 9 hesitancy 10 hesitation 11 uncertainty, vacillation 12 irresolution, shilly-shally

indecisive 4 open 5 shaky, vague 7 dubious, halting, unclear, unfixed 8 doubtful, hesitant, wavering 9 equivocal, faltering, tentative, uncertain, undecided, unsettled 10 borderline, hesitating, indistinct, irresolute 11 problematic, vacillating

indecorous 4 rude 5 gross, loose, rough, unfit 6 coarse, vulgar 7 uncivil, ungodly 8 immodest, impolite, improper, indecent, shameful, unlawful, unseemly, untoward 9 incorrect, inelegant, irregular, offensive, tasteless, unfitting 10 indelicate, malodorous, ridiculous, unbecoming 11 ill-mannered, unbefitting, undignified 12 discourteous 13 inappropriate

indecorum 5 boner, break, gaffe 7 blooper, faux pas 8 solecism 10 inelegance, unmeetness 11 impropriety

indeed 3 nay, yea 4 even, well 5 truly 6 easily, really, verily 7 in truth 8 forsooth, honestly 9 assuredly, certainly 10 admittedly, positively, undeniably 11 doubtlessly, undoubtedly

indefatigable 6 dogged 7 patient 8 diligent, sedulous, stubborn, tireless, untiring, vigorous 9 assiduous, energetic, steadfast, strenuous, tenacious, weariless 10 determined, persistent, relentless, unflagging, unwavering, unwearying 11 painstaking, persevering, unfaltering, unflinching, unrelenting, unweariable 13 inexhaustible

indefensible 9 untenable 10 inexpiable 11 inexcusable 12 unforgivable, unpardonable 13 unjustifiable

indefinable 5 vague 9 ineffable, uncertain 10 untellable 11 inenarrable, unspeakable, unutterable 13 indescribable, indeterminate, inexpressible, undescribable, unexpressible

indefinite 4 wide 5 broad, loose, vague 7 endless, general, inexact, obscure, unclear, unfixed 8 infinite 9 ambiguous, boundless, imprecise, limitless, unbounded, uncertain, undefined, unlimited 10 indistinct, inexplicit, unmeasured, unspecific 11 measureless 12 immeasurable, inconclusive 13 indeterminate ***article:*** 2 an ***pronoun:*** 3 all, any, few 4 each, many, most, none, some 6 anyone, nobody 7 anybody, several, someone 8 everyone, somebody 9 everybody

indehiscent fruit 3 nut 4 pepo 5 akene, berry, grain, grape, melon 6 achene, loment, samara, squash 7 pumpkin 8 cucumber 9 caryopsis 10 schizocarp

indelible 4 fast 5 fixed 7 lasting 8 enduring 9 permanent 10 inerasable, unerasable 12 ineffaceable, ineradicable, inexpungible, inextirpable, uneradicable 13 undestroyable

indelicate 3 raw 4 lewd, rude 5 crude, gross, rough 6 callow, coarse, wanton 7 uncouth, ungodly 8 impolite, improper, indecent, tactless, unseemly, untoward 9 unrefined 10 indecorous, malodorous, unbecoming

indemnify 3 pay 5 repay 7 requite 9 reimburse 10 compensate, recompense, remunerate

indemnity 6 amends 7 amnesty, redress 8 reprisal, security 9 exemption, quittance 10 protection, recompense, reparation 11 restitution 12 compensation

indentation 3 bay 4 dent, nick 5 notch, print, stamp 6 recess 7 impress, imprint

indenture 4 nick 5 notch 11 indentation

indentured 5 bound 8 articled 11 apprenticed

independent 4 free 6 closed 8 autarkic, separate 9 autarchic, sovereign 10 autonomous 11 self-reliant 12 self-centered 13 self-contained, self-sufficing, self-supported, self-sustained ***combining form:*** 4 self

indescribable 9 ineffable 10 untellable 11 indefinable, inenarrable, unspeakable, unutterable 13 inexpressible, unexpressible

indestructible 7 durable, lasting, undying 8 enduring, immortal 9 deathless, immutable, indelible, permanent, perpetual 10 changeless, inviolable, quenchless 11 unalterable 12 imperishable, ineradicable, inextirpable, irrefragable, unchangeable, unperishable, unquenchable 13 incorruptible, irrefrangible, undestroyable

indeterminate 5 vague 7 inexact, unfixed 9 uncertain, unlimited 10 indefinite, indistinct

index 4 list, mark, sign 5 table, token 7 catalog, indices (plural), indicia, symptom 8 evidence 9 catalogue

India ***bread:*** 7 chapati 8 chapatti ***butter:*** 3 ghi 4 ghee ***capital:*** 8 New Delhi ***caste:*** 5 Sudra 6 Vaisya 7 Brahman 9 Kshatriya ***female dancer:*** 8 bayadere ***harem:*** 6 zenana ***lady:*** 4 bibi 5 begum 8 memsahib ***language:*** 4 Urdu 5 Hindu, Tamil 6 Telugu 7 Bengali, Kannada, Marathi, Punjabi 8 Assamese, Gujarati, Kashmiri 9 Malayalam 10 Hindustani, Rajasthani ***largest city:*** 6 Bombay ***monetary unit:*** 5 rupee ***nurse:*** 4 amah, ayah ***outcast:*** 6 pariah ***prime minister:*** 5 Nehru 6 Gandhi ***prince:*** 4 raja, rana 5 rajah 8 maharaja 9 maharajah ***princess:*** 4 rani 5 begum, ranee ***scholar:*** 6 pandit, pundit ***screen:*** 6 purdah ***seal, stamp:*** 4 chop ***soldier:*** 4 peon 5 sepoy ***teacher:*** 4 guru ***viceroy:*** 5 nabob, nawab ***weight unit:*** 3 ser 4 cash, dhan, pank, pice, powe, rati, tank, tola 5 adpao, fanam, hubba, masha, maund, pally, pouah, ratti 6 dhurra, pagoda, pollam 7 chinnam, chittak

Indian, American ***baby:*** 7 papoose ***ball game:*** 8 lacrosse ***carrier:*** 7 travois ***Central and South American:*** 2 Ge 3 Ona 4 Cuna, Inca, Maya 5 Arara, Aztec, Carib, Olmec, Yagua 6 Arawak, Aymara, Jivaro, Omagua, Toltec, Yahgan 7 Chibcha, Quechua, Zapotec 8 Tarascan 10 Araucanian 11 Tupi-Guarani ***drink:*** 6 chicha ***food:*** 4 samp 5 maize 8 pemmican ***game:*** 6 chunky 7 chunkey ***home:*** 5 hogan, lodge, tepee 6 pueblo, teepee, wigwam 7 wickiup ***leader:*** 4 Popé 6 Wovoka 7 Cochise, Osceola, Pontiac, Sequoya 8 Geronimo, Hiawatha, Powhatan, Tecumseh 9 Massasoit 10 Crazy Horse 11 Complanter, Sitting Bull ***money:*** 5 sewan 6 wampum ***North American:*** 3 Oto, Sac, Ute 4 Cree, Crow, Hopi, Hupa, Iowa, Otoe, Pima, Pomo, Sauk, Taos, Yuma 5 Aleut, Caddo, Creek, Haida, Huron, Kansa, Kiowa, Maidu, Miami, Modoc, Omaha, Osage, Sioux 6 Apache, Cayuga, Dakota, Lenape, Mandan, Micmac, Mohawk, Munsee, Navaho, Navajo, Nootka, Ojibwa, Oneida, Paiute, Pawnee, Pueblo, Quapaw, Seneca, Siwash 7 Arapaho, Arikara, Bannock, Chilkat, Chinook, Choctaw, Dakotah, Klamath, Kutenai, Mohican, Naskapi, Natchez, Ojibway, Pontiac, Shawnee, Tlingit 8 Cherokee, Cheyenne, Chippewa, Comanche, Delaware, Illinois, Iroquois, Kickapoo, Kwakiutl, Nez Percé, Onondaga, Powhatan, Seminole, Shoshoni 9 Blackfoot,

Chickasaw, Menominee, Tsimshian, Tuscarora, Wampanoag, Winnebago 10 Assiniboin, Chiricahua, Gros Ventre, Potawatomi 11 Massachuset, Narraganset *pipe:* 7 calumet *spirit:* 5 totem 7 kachina
Indiana *college, university:* 6 De Pauw, Marion, Purdue 9 Ball State, Notre Dame *nickname:* 12 Hoosier State *state bird:* 8 cardinal *state flower:* 5 peony
indicate 3 say 4 bode, hint, mark, mean, read, show 5 argue, augur, imply, point, prove 6 attest, denote, evince, import, record, reveal 7 bespeak, betoken, connote, display, exhibit, express, presage, signify, suggest, testify, witness 8 announce, disclose, evidence, intimate, manifest, register 9 designate 10 illustrate 11 demonstrate
indication 3 cue 4 clue, hint, mark, omen, sign, type, wind 5 index, proof, token, trace 6 notion, signal, symbol 7 gesture, indicia, inkling, reading, symptom 8 evidence, reminder, telltale 9 testimony 10 expression, intimation, suggestion 11 significant 13 manifestation, prefiguration
indicative 8 denotive, evincive, indicial, symbolic 9 testatory 10 denotative, evidential, exhibitive, expressive, suggestive 11 designative, symptomatic 13 demonstrative
indicia 4 fact, mark, sign 5 index, token 7 symptom 8 evidence 9 criterion
indict 6 accuse, charge 7 arraign, impeach 9 criminate, inculpate 11 incriminate
indifference 6 apathy 8 lethargy 9 aloofness, disregard, lassitude, unconcern 10 negligence 11 disinterest, insouciance 12 carelessness, heedlessness 13 unmindfulness
indifferent 3 icy 4 cold, cool, fair, mean, numb, so-so 5 aloof, blasé, chill, equal, stoic 6 casual, frigid, medium, remote 7 average, fairish, glacial, neutral, off-hand, unmoved 8 by-the-way, careless, detached, heedless, inferior, listless, mediocre, middling, moderate, passable, unbiased, uncaring 9 apathetic, equitable, impartial, impassive, incurious, negligent, objective, uncurious, unmindful, withdrawn 10 impersonal, insensible, nonchalant, regardless, unaffected, unsociable 11 unconcerned, unemotional, unobserving 12 unimpressive, uninterested, unprejudiced 13 disinterested, dispassionate
indigence 4 lack, need, want 6 penury 7 poverty 9 neediness, privation 11 destitution
indigenous 6 inborn, innate, native 7 connote, endemic, natural 8 inherent 9 inherited 10 aboriginal, congenital, connatural, unacquired 13 autochthonous
indigent 4 poor 5 needy 6 beggar, pauper 8 dirt poor 9 destitute, penniless, penurious 11 impecunious, necessitous 12 impoverished
indigestion 9 dyspepsia
indignant 3 mad 5 angry, irate, wroth 6 heated, wrathy, wrothy 7 annoyed 8 incensed, wrathful, wrothful 9 irritated, resentful
indignation 3 ire, mad 4 fury, rage 5 anger, wrath 10 resentment
indignity 3 cut 4 slap 5 wrong 6 injury, insult, slight 7 affront, despite, outrage 9 contumely, grievance, injustice 13 disparagement
indigo 4 anil, blue
indigo bird 5 finch 7 bunting
indigo plant 4 anil
Indira Gandhi's father 5 Nehru
indirect 6 errant, shifty, sneaky 7 crooked, devious, oblique, sinuous, vagrant, winding 8 circular, guileful, sneaking, tortuous, twisting 9 deceitful, dishonest, underhand, wandering 10 circuitous, collateral, meandering, roundabout, serpentine 11 duplicitous, underhanded
indiscreet 6 unwary, unwise 9 ill-judged, impolitic, imprudent, untactful 10 ill-advised, incautious 11 injudicious 13 inconsiderate
indiscretion 4 slip 5 folly 9 incaution 10 imprudence, unwariness
indiscriminate 4 spot, wide 5 broad, mixed 6 motley, random, varied 7 aimless, jumbled, mingled, shallow 8 assorted, chowchow, confused, sweeping 9 desultory, extensive, haphazard, hit-or-miss, unplanned, wholesale 10 designless, uncritical 11 promiscuous, purposeless, superficial 12 conglomerate, multifarious, unconsidered
indispensable 5 basic, vital 6 needed 7 exigent, needful 8 cardinal 9 essential, necessary, requisite 10 imperative 11 fundamental
indisposed 3 ill, low 4 mean, sick 5 loath 6 afraid, ailing, averse, offish, poorly, sickly, unwell 7 hostile, underly, uneager 8 backward, hesitant, inimical, off-color 9 reluctant, unwilling, unwishful 11 disinclined
indisposition 6 malady 7 ailment, dislike, illness, malaise 8 aversion, bad books, disfavor, disorder, distaste, sickness, unhealth 9 disliking, disrelish, infirmity 10 affliction, reluctance 11 displeasure
indisputable 4 real, sure, true 6 actual 7 certain, evident 8 positive, unfabled 9 veridical 10 undeniable 11 indubitable,

irrefutable, unequivocal **12** irrefragable **13** incontestable, uncontestable
indistinct **3** dim **4** hazy **5** faint, misty, vague **6** bleary, cloudy **7** blurred, inexact, obscure, shadowy, unclear **8** confused **9** uncertain, undefined **10** ill-defined, indefinite **12** undetermined **13** indeterminate
indistinguishable **4** same **5** equal **7** identic **9** duplicate, identical **10** equivalent, tantamount
indite **3** pen **5** write **6** scribe **7** compose, engross **8** inscribe
individual **3** one **4** body, lone, self, sole, soul, unit **5** being, human, party, stuff, thing **6** entity, matter, mortal, object, person, proper, single **7** several, special **8** creature, especial, existent, material, peculiar, personal, separate, singular, solitary, specific **9** diacritic, existence, personage, something, substance **10** diagnostic, individual, particular, respective **11** distinctive **13** idiosyncratic ***combining form:*** **4** idio
individualist **10** egocentric
individuality **4** self **5** seity, unity **6** makeup, nature, temper **7** ipseity, oneness, selfdom **8** identity, selfhood, selfness **9** character **10** complexion, difference, singleness, uniqueness, unlikeness **11** disposition, personality, singularity, temperament **12** independence, separateness, singularness
individualize **4** mark **7** qualify, specify **9** signalize **11** distinguish, singularize **12** characterize **13** particularize
Indochina country **4** Laos **5** Burma **7** Vietnam **8** Cambodia, Thailand
indoctrinate **5** teach, tutor **7** educate **8** instruct
indolence **4** laze **5** sloth **6** slouch **7** inertia, languor **8** idleness, laziness **10** inactivity **12** slothfulness, sluggishness
indolent **4** idle, lazy **5** drony **7** work-shy **8** fainéant, inactive, slothful, sluggish **9** easygoing, slowgoing
indomitable **4** wild **6** dogged, unruly **7** staunch **8** indocile, resolute, stubborn **9** fractious, steadfast **10** impassable, invincible, unbeatable **11** impregnable, insuperable, intractable **12** inexpugnable, invulnerable, pertinacious, recalcitrant, unassailable, undefeatable, ungovernable, unmanageable **13** unconquerable, undisciplined
Indonesia ***capital:*** **7** Jakarta **8** Djakarta ***monetary unit:*** **6** rupiah ***president:*** **7** Suharto
indubitable **4** flat, real, sure, true **7** assured, certain, evident, genuine **8** bona fide, positive **9** authentic, downright, undoubted, up-and-down, veritable **10** inarguable, sure-enough, undeniable **11** irrefutable **12** indisputable, irrefragable **13** incontestable, uncontestable
induce **3** get **4** abet, draw, lead, move, sway, urge **5** breed, cause, get up, hatch, impel, infer, tempt **6** arouse, draw in, draw on, effect, elicit, incite, prompt, work up **7** actuate, inspire, procure, produce, win over **8** activate, conclude, convince, engender, generate, motivate, muster up, occasion, oversway, persuade, talk into **9** argue into, encourage, influence, prevail on
inducement **4** bait, lure **6** motive **9** incentive **10** enticement **13** consideration
induct **4** lead **6** enroll, invest **7** conduct, install, instate **8** initiate **9** introduce
inductance unit **5** henry **6** henrys (plural) **7** henries (plural)
induction **8** entrance **9** accession, inaugural, inference **10** initiation **11** investiture **12** inauguration, installation, introduction
inductive **8** Baconian, epagogic **9** inducible, prefatial, prefatory, preludial, prelusive **11** a posteriori, prefatorial, preliminary, preparative, preparatory **12** introductory
indulge **3** pet **4** baby, bask, roll **5** favor, humor, revel, spoil **6** cocker, coddle, cosset, oblige, pamper, please, regale, wallow, welter **7** cater to, delight, gratify, rollick, satisfy **9** luxuriate **11** mollycoddle
indulgence **5** favor **6** liking, luxury **7** service **8** clemency, courtesy, fondness, kindness, lenience, leniency, mildness **9** benignity, tolerance **10** benignancy, benignness, gentleness, kindliness, toleration **11** forbearance **12** dispensation, mercifulness **13** gratification
indulgence seller **5** Tezel **6** Tetzel
indulgent **4** easy, kind, mild **6** benign, kindly **7** clement, lenient **8** excusing, merciful, tolerant **9** benignant, compliant, condoning, cosseting, forgiving, pampering, pardoning **10** charitable, forbearing, permissive
indurate **3** dry, set **4** cake **5** inure **6** harden **7** confirm, congeal **8** concrete, hardened, solidify, stubborn **9** unfeeling
industrialist **6** tycoon **7** magnate
industrious **4** busy, live **6** active **7** dynamic, operose, zealous **8** diligent, sedulous **9** assiduous
industry **4** work **5** labor, trade **7** traffic **8** business, commerce **9** diligence
inebriant **5** booze, drink **6** liquor **7** alcohol, spirits **9** aqua vitae **10** intoxicant
inebriate **3** sot **4** lush, soak **5** drunk, toper **6** bibber, boozer **7** tippler, tosspot **8** drunkard
inebriated **5** drunk, tight, tipsy **7** muddled **9** disguised, pixilated **11** intoxicated
inedible **7** baneful, insipid, noxious **9** poisonous, uneatable **10** inesculent

11 unwholesome 12 indigestible, unappetizing

ineffable 4 holy 5 ideal, taboo 6 divine, sacred 8 abstract, empyreal, empyrean, ethereal, heavenly 9 celestial, spiritual 10 untellable 11 indefinable, inenarrable, unspeakable, unutterable 12 transcendent 13 indescribable, inexpressible, undescribable, unexpressible

ineffaceable 9 indelible 10 inerasable, unerasable 12 ineradicable, inexpungible, inextirpable, uneradicable

ineffective 4 vain, weak 6 futile 7 useless 8 abortive, boneless, bootless, impotent, inferior 9 forceless, fruitless, incapable, spineless, worthless 10 emasculate, inadequate, unavailing 11 incompetent, ineffectual, inefficient, slack-spined, unavailable 12 invertebrate, unproductive 13 inefficacious

ineffectiveness 9 inability 10 inadequacy, incapacity, inefficacy 12 incapability, incompetence

ineffectual see ineffective

ineffectualness see ineffectiveness

inefficacious see ineffective

inefficacy see ineffectiveness

inefficient 5 inept 8 careless, inexpert, slipshod, slovenly, unexpert, unfitted 9 incapable, unskilled, untrained 10 unprepared, unskillful 11 incompetent, ineffective, ineffectual, unqualified 12 insufficient 13 inefficacious, unworkmanlike

inelaborate 5 plain 6 modest, simple 11 undecorated, ungarnished 12 unbeautified 13 unembellished, unembroidered, unpretentious

inelastic 5 rigid, stiff 9 impliable, unbending 10 inflexible, unflexible, unyielding 11 immalleable, incompliant

inelegant 3 raw 4 rude 5 crass, crude, gross, rough 6 coarse, vulgar 7 awkward, uncouth 9 graceless, unrefined

ineligible 5 unfit 8 unfitted, unworthy 9 incapable 10 unequipped 11 incompetent, unqualified 12 disqualified

ineluctable 4 sure 5 fated 6 doomed 7 certain 9 necessary 10 ineludible, inevasible, inevitable, returnless, unevadable 11 ineluctable, inescapable, unavoidable, unescapable

ineludible 7 certain 9 necessary 10 inevasible, inevitable, returnless, unevadable 11 ineluctable, unavoidable, unescapable

inept 4 dull 5 inapt, unapt, undue, unfit 6 clumsy, gauche, wooden 7 awkward, foolish, halting, inadept, unhandy, unhappy 8 bumbling, bungling, ill-timed, improper, inexpert, unexpert, unfacile, unseemly 9 graceless, ham-handed, ill-chosen, incapable, lumbering, maladroit, unskilled 10 inadequate, malapropos, unskillful, unsuitable 11 incompetent, inefficient, undexterous, unfortunate

inequality 8 asperity, imparity, rugosity 9 disparity, roughness 10 cragginess, jaggedness, ruggedness, unevenness 12 irregularity, variableness 13 disproportion

inequitable 3 bad 5 undue, wrong 6 unfair, unjust 8 wrongful 9 arbitrary, inequable, unmerited 10 high-handed, oppressive, undeserved 11 unequitable, unrighteous

inequity 5 wrong 9 injustice 10 unfairness, unjustness

inerasable 9 indelible 12 ineffaceable, ineradicable, inexpungible, inextirpable, uneradicable

inert 4 dead, idle 5 quiet, still 6 asleep, sleepy, stolid 7 neutral, passive 8 immobile, impotent, inactive, indolent, lifeless, sluggish 9 apathetic, impassive, inanimate, lethargic, powerless 10 motionless, phlegmatic

inert gas 4 neon 5 argon, radon, xenon 6 helium 7 krypton 8 nitrogen, noble gas 13 carbon dioxide *suffix:* 2 on

inescapable see inevitable

inescapably see inevitably

inesculent 8 inedible 9 uneatable

in essence 6 au fond 7 morally 9 basically, virtually 11 essentially, practically 13 fundamentally

inessential see unessential

inestimable 6 costly 8 precious, valuable 9 priceless 10 invaluable, unmeasured 11 measureless, uncountable 12 immeasurable, incalculable, unmeasurable, unreckonable

inevitable 4 sure 5 fated 7 certain, decided, settled 8 destined 9 necessary 10 ineludible, inevasible, inexorable, inflexible, returnless, unevadable 11 ineluctable, inescapable, unavoidable, unescapable 12 foreordained, ineliminable 13 unpreventable

inevitably 8 perforce 10 helplessly, willy-nilly 11 inescapably, unavoidably, whether or no

inexcusable 8 blamable 9 untenable 10 censurable, inexpiable 11 blameworthy, intolerable, unallowable 12 criticizable, indefensible, unforgivable, unpardonable 13 impermissible, reprehensible, unjustifiable

inexhaustible 8 tireless, untiring 9 unfailing, weariless 10 unflagging, unwearying 11 unweariable 13 indefatigable

in existence 6 extant

inexorable 5 rigid 6 dogged, strict 7 adamant 8 immobile, obdurate, resolute

9 immovable, unbending 10 inflexible, relentless, unyielding 11 unrelenting 12 single-minded
inexpensive 3 low 5 cheap 6 frugal, undear 7 low-cost, popular 8 uncostly 9 low-priced 10 reasonable
inexperience 7 naiveté, rawness 8 verdancy 9 freshness, greenness, ignorance 10 callowness 13 unfamiliarity
inexperienced 3 row 5 fresh, green, inept, naive, young 6 callow 7 untried 8 ignorant, immature, inexpert, prentice, unversed 9 incapable, unskilled, untrained 10 amateurish, unfamiliar, unseasoned 11 unpracticed 12 unacquainted, unconversant
inexpert see **inexperienced**
inexplicable 3 odd 7 strange, uncanny 8 peculiar 9 ambiguous, enigmatic 10 mysterious, unsolvable 11 inscrutable, undefinable 12 unfathomable 13 indescribable, inexplainable, unaccountable, unexplainable
inexpressible 8 nameless 9 ineffable 10 untellable 11 indefinable, inenarrable, unspeakable, unutterable 13 indescribable
inexpressive 4 dull 5 blank, empty 6 vacant, wooden 7 deadpan
inexpugnable 5 fixed 6 stable 10 invincible, unbeatable 11 impregnable, indomitable, unopposable 12 invulnerable, irresistible, unassailable, undefeatable 13 unconquerable
inextricable 8 involved 9 insoluble, intricate, unsoluble 10 insolvable, unsolvable
infallible 4 sure 5 exact 7 certain, correct, perfect 8 flawless, inerrant, surefire, unerring 9 faultless, inerrable, unfailing 10 impeccable 11 indubitable 12 undeceivable
infamous 4 base, evil, vile 5 sorry 6 odious, rotten, scurvy 7 corrupt, hateful, heinous, vicious 8 ill-famed, perverse, shameful 9 abhorrent, atrocious, miscreant, nefarious, notorious, unhealthy 10 abominable, degenerate, despicable, detestable, flagitious, iniquitous, scandalous, villainous 11 disgraceful, ignominious, opprobrious 12 contemptible, disreputable
infamy 5 odium, shame 7 obloquy 8 disgrace, dishonor, ignominy 9 discredit, disesteem, disrepute, notoriety 10 opprobrium 13 notoriousness
infancy 6 nonage 8 babyhood, minority 9 childhood, juniority 10 immaturity, infanthood, juvenility
infant 4 babe, baby 5 child, green, minor, young 6 callow, unripe 7 neonate, newborn, toddler 8 bantling, immature, juvenile, nursling, youthful 9 unfledged ***bed:*** 4 crib 6 cradle 8 bassinet ***food:*** 3 pap 4 milk ***room:*** 7 nursery
infantile 7 babyish, puerile 8 childish, immature
infantryman 7 dogface 8 doughboy 11 foot soldier ***Algerian:*** 6 Zouave
infatuated 3 mad 5 dotty, silly 7 foolish 8 besotted, enamored, obsessed 9 bewitched 10 captivated, enraptured
infatuation 4 rage 5 ardor, craze, crush, folly 6 beguin 7 passion 8 devotion 9 obsession 11 fascination
in favor of 3 for, pro 4 with 10 impossible, unworkable 11 impractical 12 irrealizable, unattainable, unrealizable 13 impracticable
infect 5 taint 6 defile, infest, poison 7 pollute 11 contaminate
infection 6 plague, sepses (plural), sepsis 7 disease, illness ***fungous:*** 8 mycetoma ***skin:*** 6 herpes
infectious 5 toxic 6 taking 7 miasmic, noxious 8 catching, mephitic, virulent 9 pestilent, poisonous, vitiating 10 contagious, corrupting 11 sympathetic 12 communicable, pestilential 13 contaminating
infecund 6 barren, effete 7 sterile 8 impotent 9 infertile 10 unfruitful
infelicitous 5 inapt, inept, unapt 6 gauche 7 awkward, unhappy 9 defective, graceless, ill-chosen, imperfect, inapropos 10 deplorable, malapropos 11 regrettable, unfortunate 13 inappropriate
infer 4 draw, hint, make 5 glean, guess, judge, think 6 bestow, confer, deduce, deduct, derive, gather, induce, reason, reckon 7 collect, inflict, make out, surmise 8 conclude, construe
inference 5 guess 7 surmise 8 guessing, illation, judgment, sequitur 9 deduction, reckoning 10 assumption, conclusion, conjecture, derivation 11 presumption, supposition
inferior 3 bad, low 4 base, cull, fair, hack, mean, poor, punk, puny 5 cheap, lousy, lower, minor, petty, scrub, sorry, under 6 common, deputy, feeble, heeler, impure, junior, lesser, minion, nether, no-good, paltry, puisne, satrap, shoddy, sleazy, tawdry, tinpot, vassal 7 average, subject, unequal 8 adherent, declassé, disciple, follower, hanger-on, henchman, hireling, low-grade, mediocre, middling, ordinary, retainer, unworthy, wretched 9 attendant, auxiliary, no-account, satellite, secondary, subaltern, subjacent, sycophant, underling, valueless, worthless 10 inadequate, second-rate ***prefix:*** 3 sub 4 demi 5 infra
inferior one ***suffix:*** 3 een 4 ling 5 aster
infernal 6 Hadean 7 avernal, hellish, satanic, stygian 8 chthonic, damnable, demoniac, devilish, diabolic, fiendish, plu-

tonic 9 chthonian, plutonian, Tartarean 10 diabolical, sulphurous
inferno 3 pit 4 fire, hell 5 abyss, hades, Sheol 6 blazes, Tophet 7 Gehenna 9 holocaust, perdition 11 netherworld
Inferno *division:* 5 canto *poet:* 5 Dante *verse form:* 9 terza rima
infertile 6 barren, effete 7 drained, sterile 8 depleted, impotent, infecund 9 exhausted, unbearing, unfertile 10 unfruitful 12 hardscrabble, impoverished, unproductive
infest 4 teem 5 annoy, beset, crawl, harry, haunt, swarm, worry 6 abound, harass, pester, plague 7 overrun 8 parasite 9 overswarm 10 overspread, parasitize
infidel 5 pagan 6 ethnic 7 gentile, heathen, profane, skeptic 9 infidelic 10 unbeliever
infidelity 7 falsity, perfidy, treason 9 falseness, treachery 10 disloyalty, fickleness 11 inconstancy 13 faithlessness
infiltrate 4 leak, seep, worm 5 foist 6 edge in, work in 9 insinuate
infinite 4 vast 7 endless, eternal, immense 9 boundless, countless, limitless, perpetual, unbounded, unlimited 10 indefinite, perdurable, unmeasured 11 everlasting, illimitable, measureless, sempiternal 12 immeasurable
infirm 4 lame, weak 5 anile, frail 6 ailing, feeble, flimsy, senile, weakly 7 fragile, unsound 8 decrepit 10 irresolute 11 debilitated, vacillating 13 unsubstantial
infirmity 3 ill 5 decay 6 foible, malady 7 ailment, disease, failing, frailty, illness, malaise 8 debility, disorder, sickness, syndrome, unhealth, weakness 9 affection, complaint, condition, weakening 10 affliction, feebleness, infirmness, sickliness, unwellness 11 decrepitude 12 debilitation, diseasedness, enfeeblement 13 indisposition, unhealthiness
infix 4 root 5 embed, lodge 6 insert 7 implant, impress, ingrain, instill 8 entrench 9 inculcate 10 inseminate
inflame 3 get 4 fire, gall, good, heat, rile, roil, stir 5 grate, light, rouse 6 arouse, burn up, enrage, excite, ignite, kindle, madden, put out, redden 7 incense, provoke 8 enkindle, irritate 9 aggravate, intensify 10 exasperate
inflammable 5 fiery 6 ardent 8 burnable 9 excitable, ignitable, irascible, irritable 11 combustible
inflammation 4 gout, sore 5 felon 6 quinsy 7 catarrh, coxitis, gonitis, rickets 8 adenitis, cystitis, neuritis, pleurisy, rachitis, swelling 9 arthritis, chilblain, gastritis, phlebitis 10 combustion 12 encephalitis 13 conflagration, poliomyelitis *ear:* 6 otitis *eye:* 6 iritis 7 pinkeye 9 keratitis *horse:* 6 thrush 7 fistula, quittor 8 poll evil *intestines:* 7 ileitis 9 enteritis *suffix:* 4 itis
inflammatory 8 exciting, incitive 9 seditious 10 incendiary 11 instigative, provocative, seditionary 13 revolutionary
inflate 4 fill 5 bloat, elate, swell 6 dilate, expand, tumefy 7 amplify, distend
inflated 5 showy, tumid, windy, wordy 6 elated, prolix, turgid 7 aureate, bloated, diffuse, flowery, fustian, pompous, ranting, swollen, verbose 8 bladdery, dropsied 9 bombastic, distended, dropsical, flatulent, overblown, tumescent 10 rhetorical 11 exaggerated, pretentious, rhapsodical
inflection 4 bend, tone 5 curve 6 accent, timbre 8 tonality 9 accidence 10 intonation 11 enunciation 12 articulation 13 pronunciation
inflexible 3 set 4 grim, hard, iron 5 fixed, rigid, stiff, tough 6 dogged, strict 7 adamant, settled 8 constant, granitic, hard-line, immobile, ironclad, obdurate, rigorous, stubborn 9 immovable, immutable, impliable, inelastic, obstinate, rockbound, steadfast, unbending, unmovable 10 adamantine, brassbound, changeless, implacable, inexorable, invariable, invincible, relentless, rockribbed, unbendable, unchanging, unswayable, unyielding 11 unalterable, uncompliant, unrelenting 12 single-minded, unchangeable, unmodifiable 13 dyed-in-the-wool
inflict 4 deal, give 5 visit, wreak, wreck 6 expose, impose, strike 7 force on, subject
inflow 6 influx, inpour, inrush 9 influxion
influence 4 move, pull, sway 5 alter, bribe, carry, clout, force, impel, lobby, touch 6 affect, compel, credit, induce, modify, moment, strike, weight 7 command, control, impress, inspire, mastery 8 dominion, eminence, militate, persuade, prestige 9 authority, dominance
influenceable 8 suasible, swayable 9 acceptant, acceptive, receptive 10 responsive 11 persuadable, persuasible
influential 6 potent 8 powerful 9 effective, important
influx 6 inflow, inpour, inrush 7 illapse 8 increase 9 accession, inpouring 11 debouchment 12 augmentation
inform 3 rat 4 blab, clew, clue, fire, post, talk, tell, warn 5 endow, endue, exalt, imbue, peach, teach, train 6 advise, betray, fill in, infuse, leaven, notify, preach, snitch, squeak, squeal, tattle, turn in, wise up 7 animate, apprise, arrange, caution, educate, inspire 8 acquaint, forewarn, give away, instruct, permeate 9 advertise, enlighten 10 illuminate 11 familiarize
informal 6 breezy, casual, dégagé, simple 7 natural, private, relaxed, special, unfussy

8 familiar 9 easygoing, irregular 10 colloquial, unofficial
information 4 data (plural), fact, lore, news, word 5 datum 6 advice, notice, wisdom 7 science, tidings 9 complaint, knowledge, speerings 11 instruction 12 intelligence *second hand:* 7 hearsay *suffix:* 3 ana 4 iana
information bureau *abbreviation:* 4 USIA, USIS
informative 8 edifying 9 educative 11 educational, elucidative, explanatory, informatory, instructive 12 enlightening, illuminating 13 informational, instructional
informed 2 up 3 hip 4 wise 5 aware 6 au fait, posted, versed 7 abreast, knowing, versant 8 apprised, educated, familiar 9 au courant 10 acquainted, conversant, cultivated 11 enlightened, intelligent
informer 3 rat, spy 4 fink 5 stool 6 canary, gossip, snitch 7 stoolie, tattler, tipster 8 betrayer, busybody, squawker, squealer, telltale 10 talebearer, tattletale 11 stool pigeon
infra 4 next 5 after, below, later, under 6 behind, within 7 beneath
infract 5 break 6 breach, offend 7 violate 8 infringe 10 contravene, transgress
infraction 3 sin 4 slip 5 crime, error, lapse 6 breach 7 faux pas, offense 8 trespass 9 intrusion, violation 12 encroachment, infringement 13 contravention, transgression
infrastructure 4 base, root 5 basis 6 bottom, ground 7 bedrock, footing 10 foundation, groundwork, substratum 12 substructure, underpinning
infrequent 3 few, odd 4 rare 5 scant, stray 6 meager, scanty, scarce, seldom, sparse 7 limited, unusual 8 isolated, sporadic, uncommon, unwonted 9 scattered, spasmodic 10 occasional 11 exceptional
infringe 5 break 6 breach, defeat, impose, invade, offend, refute 7 confute, infract, intrude, obtrude, presume, violate 8 encroach, entrench, trespass 10 contravene, transgress
infuriate 3 ire, mad 5 anger 6 enrage, madden 7 incense, steam up, umbrage
infuse 4 fill, fire 5 imbue, steep 6 inform, invest, leaven 7 animate, diffuse, implant, ingrain, inspire, instill, pervade, suffuse, suggest 8 intersow, permeate, saturate 9 inculcate, inoculate, insinuate, interfuse, interlard, introduce 10 impregnate 11 intersperse 12 indoctrinate 13 intersprinkle
ingenious 3 sly 4 slim 5 acute, canny, sharp, smart 6 adroit, clever, crafty 7 cunning 8 creative, original 9 demiurgic, deviceful, inventive 11 intelligent, originative, resourceful 12 innovational
ingenuous 4 open 5 naive 6 simple, unwary 7 artless, natural, unaware 8 innocent, unartful 9 childlike, guileless, unstudied 10 unaffected, unschooled 12 unartificial
Inge play 6 Picnic 7 Bus Stop
ingest 3 eat 4 meal, take 6 absorb, devour, feed on, take in 7 consume, swallow
inglorious 5 shady 6 shabby, shoddy 8 shameful 11 disgraceful, ignominious 12 dishonorable, disreputable 13 discreditable, unrespectable
ingot 3 bar, rod 4 slap 5 stick, strip 6 billet
ingrained 7 built-in, chronic 8 inherent 10 congenital, deep-rooted, deep-seated, indwelling, inveterate
ingratiating 5 silky 6 silken 8 pleasing 9 adulatory 10 flattering, saccharine 11 deferential, sycophantic
ingredient 6 factor 7 element 9 component 11 constituent
ingress 3 way 4 adit, door, go in 5 enter, entry 6 access, come in, entrée 8 entrance 9 admission, penetrate 10 admittance
ingurgitate 4 bolt, cram, gulp, slop, wolf 5 slosh, stuff, swill 6 devour, englut, gobble, guzzle 7 swallow
inhabit 4 live 5 abide, dwell 6 occupy, people, settle, tenant 8 populate
inhabitant 5 liver 6 inmate, native 7 citizen, denizen, dweller, resider 8 indigene, resident 9 aborigine 10 autochthon *foreign:* 5 alien *indigenous:* 6 native 9 aborigine *suffix:* 3 ese, ite, ote
inhale 7 breathe, consume, respire 9 breathe in
inharmonious 6 atonal 7 jarring 9 cat-and-dog, differing, dissonant, immusical, unmusical 10 cacophonic, discordant 11 conflicting, conflictive, disagreeing, quarrelsome, uncongenial 12 antagonistic
inhere 3 lie 5 dwell, exist 6 belong, reside 7 consist
inherent 4 born 5 basic 6 inborn, innate, normal 7 built-in, connate, infixed, natural, regular, typical 8 immanent, peculiar 9 elemental, essential, ingrained, intrinsic 10 congenital, deep-seated, elementary, individual, indwelling, ingenerate
inherit 7 possess, receive, succeed
inheritance 6 devise, legacy 7 bequest 8 heritage 9 patrimony 10 birthright, entailment 13 primogeniture
inherited 6 innate, native 7 connate, natural 10 congenital, connatural, indigenous
inheritor 4 heir 7 heretor, heritor, legatee *female:* 7 heiress 8 heretrix, heritrix 10 heretrices (plural), heritrices (plural)

inhibit 3 ban 4 curb, ward 5 avert, check, taboo 6 bridle, enjoin, forbid, hinder, hold in, outlaw, reduce, retard 7 prevent, repress 8 diminish, hold back, hold down, prohibit, restrain, suppress, withhold 9 constrain
inhibited 4 cold 6 frigid 9 repressed 11 passionless 12 unresponsive
inhibition 3 ban, bar 6 hangup 9 restraint 10 impediment
inhuman 4 cold, fell 5 cruel 6 brutal, fierce, malign, savage 7 beastly, bestial, brutish, wolfish 8 devilish, fiendish, nonhuman 9 barbarous, ferocious, malicious, malignant, truculent 10 cannibalic, diabolical, impersonal, implacable, mechanical
inhumane 4 fell, grim 5 cruel 6 brutal, fierce, savage 7 wolfish 9 barbarous, ferocious, truculent
inhumation 6 burial 9 interment, sepulture 10 entombment
inhume 4 bury, tomb 5 inter, plant 6 entomb 7 lay away, put away 9 sepulcher, sepulture
inimical 3 ill 7 adverse, harmful, hostile 10 unfriendly 11 unfavorable
iniquitous 3 bad 4 evil 5 wrong 6 sinful, unjust, wicked 7 immoral, vicious 9 nefarious, reprobate
iniquity 3 sin 4 evil, tort 5 crime, wrong 9 diablerie, injustice 10 wickedness, wrongdoing
initial 5 basic, early, first, prime 6 letter, maiden 7 leading, nascent, opening, pioneer, primary 8 earliest, foremost, germinal, headmost, monogram, original 9 beginning, embryonic, incipient
initiate 4 open 5 admit, begin, enter, set up, start 6 enroll, get off, induct, invest, launch, take in, take up 7 install, kick off, usher in 8 commence 9 originate 10 inaugurate
initiation 7 baptism 9 admission, beginning, induction 10 admittance 11 origination 12 commencement, introduction
initiative 4 push 6 energy 8 ambition, aptitude, gumption 9 beginning 10 enterprise, get-up-and-go
injudicious 6 unwise 9 ill-judged, impolitic, imprudent 10 ill-advised, indiscreet 11 inexpedient
injunction 4 word 5 order 6 behest, charge 7 bidding, command, dictate, mandate 9 direction 11 prohibition
injure 3 mar 4 foul, harm, hurt, maim, pain 5 spoil, wound, wrong 6 batter, blight, bruise, damage, deface, deform, foul up, grieve, impair, mangle, offend, weaken 7 afflict, blemish, contort, cripple, disable, distort, louse up, tarnish, torment, torture, vitiate 8 aggrieve, disserve, distress, maltreat, mutilate 9 bespatter, constrain, disfigure, prejudice 12 incapacitate
injurious 3 bad 4 evil 6 nocent 7 abusive, harmful, hurtful 8 damaging 9 offensive 10 defamatory 11 detrimental
injury 3 bad, ill 4 evil, harm, hurt, loss, pain, pang, ruin 5 agony, wound, wrong 6 damage, trauma 7 outrage 8 distress, mischief 9 detriment, grievance, injustice
injustice 4 harm, hurt, ruin, tort 5 crime, wrong 6 breach, damage, injury 7 outrage 8 inequity, mischief, trespass, villainy 9 grievance, violation 10 favoritism, partiality, unfairness, wrongdoing
ink 4 sign 9 autograph, signature, subscribe
inkling 3 cue 4 clue, hint, idea, wind 6 notion 8 telltale 10 intimation, suggestion
ink or rubber 5 India
inky 3 jet 4 ebon 5 black, ebony, jetty, raven, sable 9 cimmerian, pitch-dark 10 pitch-black 11 atramentous
Inland Empire 8 Illinois
inlet 3 arm, bay, cay, voe 4 cove, gulf 5 bayou, bight, creek, fiord, firth, fjord, sound 6 harbor, slough, strait 7 estuary ***Admiralties:*** 4 Kali ***Adriatic Sea:*** 5 Vlona, Vlorë ***Aegean Sea:*** 9 Saronicus 11 Saronic Gulf 12 Gulf of Aegina ***Africa:*** 0 Walvis 12 Gulf of Guinea ***Alaska:*** 4 Cook 5 Cross, Taiya 7 Glacier 8 Chilkoot ***Aleutians:*** 5 Holtz, Nazan ***Angola:*** 5 Bengo, Tiger 6 Tigres ***Antarctica:*** 3 Ice 7 McMurdo 8 Amundsen 10 Shackleton ***Arabian Sea:*** 4 Qamr 5 Kamar ***Arctic Ocean:*** 8 Gulf of Ob ***Australia:*** 4 King 6 Botany 9 Discovery 10 Broad Sound 13 Van Diemen Gulf ***Baffin Bay:*** 8 Melville ***Baffin Island:*** 9 Admiralty ***Baltic Sea:*** 4 Hano 6 Danzig 9 Pomerania 10 Gulf of Riga, Pomeranian ***Barents Sea:*** 4 Kola 7 Pechora ***Beaufort Sea:*** 7 Prudhoe 9 Mackenzie ***Bering Sea:*** 12 Gulf of Anadyr ***Bismarck Sea:*** 5 Kimbe ***Brazil:*** 9 Guanabara ***Bristol Channel:*** 10 Carmarthen ***California:*** 5 Morro 8 Monterey, San Diego 12 San Francisco ***Canada:*** 5 Fundy 9 Howe Sound ***Cape Breton Island:*** 4 Mira ***Caribbean Sea:*** 5 Limon 8 Chetumal, Honduras 9 Venezuela ***Central America:*** 7 Fonseca ***Chile:*** 5 Otway ***China-Korea:*** 8 Huang Hai, Hwang Hai 9 Yellow Sea ***Crete:*** 4 Suda 5 Canea ***Denmark:*** 3 Ise ***Djibouti:*** 6 Tajura 8 Tadjoura ***East River:*** 8 Flushing ***Ecuador:*** 5 Manta ***Eire:*** 4 Clew 7 Brandon ***English Channel:*** 3 Tor 5 Seine 8 Plymouth ***Florida:*** 8 Biscayne 10 Saint Lucie 11 Indian River ***France-Spain:*** 6 Biscay 13 Gulf of Gascony ***Georgia:*** 8 Altamaha ***Greece:*** 13 Gulf of Corinth, Gulf of Lepanto ***Green-***

land: 6 Baffin ***Gulf of Alaska:*** 3 Icy 5 Woman 12 Resurrection ***Gulf of Mexico:*** 5 Tampa 6 Mobile 7 Aransas 8 Sarasota, Suwannee 9 Matagorda, Pensacola 10 San Antonio, Terrebonne 11 Atchafalaya, Mississippi, Ponce de Leon 12 Apalachicola 13 Corpus Christi ***Gulf of St. Lawrence:*** 5 Bonne, Gaspé ***Hawaii:*** 11 Pearl Harbor ***Honshu:*** 3 Ise 5 Osaka, Owari, Tokyo 6 Atsuta ***Hudson Bay:*** 7 Repulse ***Hudson River:*** 7 New York ***Iceland:*** 4 Axar, Eyja, Huna 5 Horna, Skaga, Vopna 8 Hunafloi ***Indonesia:*** 4 Bima 5 Saleh ***Ionian Sea:*** 7 Taranto ***Irish Sea:*** 4 Luce 7 Dundalk ***Italy:*** 11 Gulf of Genoa 14 Lagoon of Venice ***Japan:*** 4 Tosa ***Java:*** 4 Lada 5 Peper ***Java Sea:*** 7 Batavia 8 Djakarta ***Kara Sea:*** 6 Enisei 7 Yenisei ***Labrador:*** 8 Hamilton ***Lake Erie:*** 8 Put-in-Bay, Sandusky ***Lake Huron:*** 7 Saginaw, Thunder ***Lake Michigan:*** 5 Green 13 Grand Traverse ***Lake Ontario:*** 11 Irondequoit ***Lake Superior:*** 5 Huron 8 Keweenaw 9 Whitefish ***Long Island:*** 8 Rockaway ***Long Island Sound:*** 6 Oyster 8 New Haven ***Madagascar:*** 8 Antongil ***Maine:*** 5 Casco 7 Machias 9 Penobscot 12 Damariscotta ***Maryland-Virginia:*** 10 Chesapeake ***Massachusetts:*** 8 Buzzards, Plymouth 9 Annisquam ***Massachusetts Bay:*** 10 Lynn Harbor ***Mediterranean Sea:*** 8 Valencia 9 Famagusta 10 Khalij Surt 11 Gulf of Sidra, Gulf of Tunis, Syrtis Major ***Mozambique:*** 5 Memba, Pemba ***Nantucket Sound:*** 5 Lewis ***New Brunswick:*** 13 Passamaquoddy ***Newfoundland:*** 4 Hare 5 White 7 Fortune ***New Guinea:*** 3 Oro 5 Berau, Hansa 11 McCluer Gulf ***New Jersey:*** 5 Great 7 Raritan 8 Barnegat 9 Little Egg ***New York:*** 7 Jamaica ***New Zealand:*** 5 Hawke 6 Tasman ***North Carolina:*** 7 Roanoke 9 Albemarle ***Northern Ireland:*** 12 Belfast Lough ***North Sea:*** 4 Lyse 9 Hardanger ***Northwest Territories:*** 5 Wager 8 Bathurst, Franklin 9 Frobisher 12 Prince Albert ***Norway:*** 3 Tys 4 Bokn, Tana 5 Lakse, Sogne ***Norwegian Sea:*** 4 Nord, Salt, Stor, Vest 5 Ranen 8 Scoresby 9 Trondheim ***Ontario:*** 4 Owen ***Oregon:*** 4 Coos ***Philippines:*** 5 Baler, Pilar, Sogod 6 Butuan 9 Davao Gulf, Leyte Gulf, Panay Gulf ***Puget Sound:*** 4 Carr, Case ***Quebec:*** 6 Ungava ***Red Sea:*** 4 Foul ***Rhode Island:*** 12 Narragansett 13 Sakonnet River ***Russia:*** 5 Chaun 8 Sakhalin, White Sea 12 Sea of Okhotsk ***Santo Cruz Islands:*** 8 Basilisk ***Sea of Japan:*** 13 Peter the Great ***Solomon Islands:*** 4 Deep 8 Huon Gulf ***South Africa:*** 5 Table ***South Carolina:*** 4 Bull ***South China Sea:*** 4 Bias, Datu, Siam, Taya 5 Dasol, Subic, Subig 6 Brunei, Paluan 7 Camranh 8 Lingayen, Thailand ***Spain:*** 5 Cadiz ***Spitsbergen:*** 3 Ice 4 Bell 5 Kings ***Strait of Gibraltar:*** 7 Tangier ***Sumatra:*** 5 Bajur 10 Koninginne ***Tasmania:*** 5 Storm ***Tyrrhenian Sea:*** 6 Naples 7 Paestum 13 Gulf of Salerno ***Wales:*** 5 Burry ***Washington:*** 5 Dabob 6 Skagit 11 Grays Harbor

inmate 7 convict 8 occupant, prisoner 10 inhabitant

inmost part 4 core, pith 5 heart 6 center, depths, kernel, marrow 7 nucleus

inn 5 fonda, hotel, house, lodge, motel 6 hostel, posada, tavern 7 auberge, hospice 8 hostelry, wayhouse 9 roadhouse 11 caravansary, public house 13 boardinghouse ***German:*** 8 gasthaus ***Turkish:*** 6 imaret

innards 4 guts 6 tripes 7 viscera 8 entrails, stuffing

innate see **inherent**

inner 3 gut 5 close, focal 6 hidden, inside, inward, middle, secret 7 central, nuclear, private 8 familiar, interior, internal, personal, visceral 9 concealed, essential ***combining form:*** 3 ent 4 ento

innervate 4 move 5 pique, rouse 7 provoke, quicken 9 galvanize

Innisfail 4 Eire, Erin 7 Ireland

innkeeper 4 host 8 boniface, hosteler, publican

innocence 6 purity 7 naiveté 8 chastity 9 ignorance, silliness 10 simplicity 11 artlessness, sinlessness, unawareness

innocent 4 free, good, pure, void 5 clean, empty, legal, licit, naive, white 6 candid, chaste, devoid, lawful, simple 7 artless, natural, unaware 8 harmless, ignorant, unguilty, virtuous 9 blameless, childlike, crimeless, destitute, exemplary, faultless, guileless, guiltless, ingenuous, innocuous, permitted, righteous, stainless, unstained, unstudied, unsullied, untainted 10 inculpable, legitimate, tenderfoot, unaffected, unblamable, unschooled 11 inobnoxious, inoffensive, unoffending, unoffensive, white-handed 12 simpleminded, unartificial, unsuspecting

innocuous 4 flat 5 banal, bland 6 jejune, pallid 7 insipid, sapless 8 harmless 9 driveling 10 namby-pamby 11 inoffensive, unoffending, unoffensive 13 insignificant

innovation 6 change 7 novelty, wrinkle 11 vicissitude

innovative 3 new 5 novel 8 creative, original 9 demiurgic, deviceful, inventive

innovator 5 maker 7 builder 8 original, producer 9 architect, developer 10 originator

innuendo 4 clue, hint, slur 8 allusion 10 intimation 11 implication, insinuation

innumerable 4 many 6 legion, myriad, untold 9 countless, uncounted 10 numberless
Ino ***brother:*** 9 Polydorus ***father:*** 6 Cadmus ***grandfather:*** 6 Agenor ***husband:*** 7 Athamas ***mother:*** 8 Harmonia ***sister:*** 5 Agave 6 Semele 7 Autonoe ***son:*** 8 Learchus, Palaemon 10 Melicertes
inobtrusive 5 quiet, tasty 7 subdued 8 tasteful 10 restrained
inoculate 5 admit, enter, imbue, steep 6 infuse, leaven 7 implant, suffuse
inoffensive 8 harmless 9 innocuous, peaceable
inopportune 8 ill-timed, mistimed, untimely
inordinate 5 dizzy, extra, undue 6 wanton 7 extreme, surplus 8 towering 9 excessive 10 disorderly, exorbitant, gratuitous, immoderate, irrational, untempered 11 extravagant, intemperate, superfluous, uncalled-for 12 unmeasurable, unreasonable, unrestrained 13 extraordinary
in passing 6 obiter 8 by the bye, by the way 12 incidentally
in perpetuum 4 ever 6 always 7 forever 8 evermore 9 eternally 11 forevermore
inquest 5 probe 6 search 7 delving, inquiry, probing 8 research 11 examination 13 investigation
inquietude 6 unrest 7 ailment, anxiety, ferment, turmoil 10 uneasiness 11 restiveness 12 restlessness 13 Sturm und Drang
inquire 3 ask 4 seek 5 query, study 6 search 7 examine 8 question 9 catechize 10 scrutinize 11 interrogate, investigate
inquiry 5 audit, check, probe, query, quest 7 delving, hearing, probing 8 question, research, scrutiny 11 catechizing, examination, questioning 13 investigation
inquisition 4 hunt 5 probe, quest 6 search 7 delving, inquiry, probing 8 grilling, research 11 examination 13 investigation
inquisitive 4 nosy 5 peery 6 prying, snoopy 7 curious 11 questioning
inquisitor ***Spanish:*** 10 Torquemada
in re 4 as to 5 about, as for 7 apropos 9 as regards, regarding 10 as respects, concerning, respecting
in respect to see **in re**
inroad 4 raid 5 foray 6 invade 7 overrun 8 invasion 9 incursion, irruption, overswarm 12 encroachment
ins and outs 5 ropes 6 quirks 7 details 8 minutiae, oddities 11 incidentals, particulars 13 peculiarities, ramifications
insane 3 mad, off 4 daft, nuts 5 crazy, daffy, dotty, loony, manic, nutsy, nutty, rocky, silly, wacky, wrong 6 absurd, crazed, cuckoo, maniac, screwy, teched 7 cracked, foolish, lunatic, strange, tetched, touched, unsound, witless 8 demented, deranged, fanciful, mindless 9 bedlamite, brainsick, eccentric, fantastic, imaginary, visionary 10 bewildered, disordered, distracted, distraught, irrational, reasonless, ridiculous, unbalanced 11 harebrained, impractical, unrealistic 12 crackbrained, preposterous, unreasonable
insane asylum 6 bedlam 8 loony bin, madhouse, nuthouse 9 funny farm 10 booby hatch, sanatorium, sanitarium
insanity 5 folly, mania 6 dotage, frenzy, lunacy 7 madness 8 delirium, delusion, dementia, hysteria, illusion 9 acromania, craziness, dottiness, silliness, unbalance 10 aberration, alienation 11 derangement, distraction, fatuousness, foolishness, psychopathy, witlessness 13 hallucination, senselessness
insatiable 6 crying, greedy, urgent 7 exigent 8 pressing, yearning 9 clamorous, demanding, voracious 10 quenchless 11 importunate 12 unappeasable, unquenchable
inscribe 4 book, etch, list 5 enter, print, write 6 enroll 7 catalog, engrave, engross, impress, imprint 8 enscroll
inscription 5 title 6 legend 7 epigram, epitaph, heading 8 epigraph 10 enrollment
inscrutable 6 arcane, mystic, secret 8 numinous 9 mysterial, unguessed 10 cabalistic, mysterious, unknowable 12 impenetrable, unfathomable
insect 3 bee, bug, fly 6 beetle ***adult:*** 5 imago ***antenna:*** 4 palp 6 feeler ***butterfly:*** (see **butterfly** entry) ***combining form:*** 5 entom 6 entomo ***covering:*** 6 chitin ***immature:*** 4 grub, pupa 5 larva, nymph 6 larvae (plural), maggot 8 wriggler 9 chrysalis 11 caterpillar ***kind:*** 3 ant 4 flea, moth, wasp 5 aphid, scale 6 bedbug, beefly, beetle, cicada, earwig, hornet, mantid, mantis, mayfly 7 ant lion, cricket, firefly, June bug, katydid, ladybug, termite 8 honeybee, horsefly, housefly, lacewing, mosquito, stinkbug 9 bumblebee, butterfly, damselfly, dragonfly 10 silverfish, springtail 11 grasshopper 12 walkingstick ***luminous:*** 7 firefly 8 glowworm ***molt:*** 7 ecdysis ***moth:*** 4 luna 6 sphinx 8 Cecropia 10 Polyphemus ***multi-legged:*** 8 diplopod 9 centipede, millepede, millipede ***part:*** 4 palp 5 cerci (plural) 6 cercus, labium, labrum, ocelli (plural), thorax 7 antenna, maxilla, ocellus 8 antennae (plural), mandible, maxillae (plural) 9 proboscis, spiracles 10 ovipositor 11 exoskeleton ***pest:*** 4 flea, lice (plural), mite 5 louse, midge, scale 7 blowfly, termite 8 horsefly, housefly, mealybug 9 cockroach, gypsy moth 10 boll

weevil, Hessian fly, silverfish ***science:*** 10 entomology ***wingless:*** 4 flea, lice (plural) 5 louse 8 firebrat 10 silverfish 11 bristletail

insecticide 3 DDT 5 mirex, naled 6 endrin, ronnel 7 lindane, phorate 8 carbaryl, dieldrin, rotenone 9 chlordane

insecure 4 weak 5 shaky 6 dickey, infirm, unsafe, unsure, wobbly 8 hesitant, rootless, unstable, wavering 9 fluctuant, unassured, uncertain 11 questioning, unconfident

inseminate 7 implant, instill 9 fertilize 10 impregnate

insensate 4 dull, hard 5 rocky, silly 6 simple 7 fatuous, foolish, witless 8 mindless 9 bloodless, brainless, nitwitted, unfeeling 10 anesthetic, unanimated 11 sheepheaded

insensibility 4 coma 6 apathy, phlegm, torpor 8 lethargy, stoicism 12 indifference

insensible 4 cold, dead, dull, hard, numb, rapt 5 blunt, rocky, stoic 6 asleep, intent, numbed, obtuse, stolid 7 brutish, callous 8 absorbed, benumbed, comatose, deadened, hardened, obdurate 9 apathetic, bloodless, engrossed, impassive, unfeeling 10 anesthetic, phlegmatic, unapparent 11 unconscious 12 anesthetized

insensitive 4 dead, dull, hard, numb 5 aloof, rocky 6 asleep, numbed 8 benumbed, deadened 9 bloodless, unfeeling 10 anesthetic, impossible 11 indifferent, unconcerned 12 anesthetized, unresponsive 13 insusceptible, unimpressible, unsusceptible

insert 5 admit, enter, infix, inlay, inlet, inset 6 fill in 7 implant, obtrude, throw in 9 interpose 11 intercalate, interpolate

in short 7 briefly, tersely 9 concisely 10 succinctly 11 laconically

inside 5 inner 6 closet, hushed, inward, within 7 private 8 interior 11 withindoors 12 confidential ***combining form:*** 3 end 4 endo

insidious 3 sly 4 deep, foxy, wily 6 artful, astute, crafty, subtle, tricky 7 cunning, gradual 8 guileful 9 deceitful 10 fraudulent 11 treacherous

insight 6 wisdom 8 sagacity, sageness, sapience 9 intuition 10 anschauung 11 discernment, penetration 13 intuitiveness, sagaciousness, understanding

insightful 4 sage, wise 6 sophic 7 gnostic, knowing 9 sagacious 10 discerning, perceptive 11 penetrating 13 knowledgeable

insignia 4 mark, sign 5 badge 6 emblem 8 brassard 10 decoration

insignificant 4 puny 5 dinky, light, minor, petty, small 6 casual, lesser, little, paltry 7 trivial 8 inferior, small-fry, trifling 9 pointless, secondary, senseless, small-beer, small-time, unmeaning 10 shoestring 11 meaningless, minor-league, unimportant

insincere 5 false, lying 6 double, shifty, tricky 7 feigned 8 mala fide, slippery 9 deceitful, deceptive, dishonest 10 left-handed, mendacious, untruthful 11 double-faced 12 hypocritical

insinuate 4 hint, worm 5 foist, imply 6 allude, edge in, fill in, impugn, impute, insert, work in 7 ascribe, connote, implant, instill, suggest, throw in 9 introduce

insipid 3 dry 4 arid, dull, flat, mild, pale, soft, tame, thin, weak 5 banal, bland, dusty, plain, vapid 6 feeble, jejune, slight, swashy, watery 7 mundane, prosaic, sapless, subdued, tedious, tenuous 8 bromidic, lifeless, ordinary, unsavory, waterish, weariful 9 driveling, dryasdust, innocuous, pointless, savorless, tasteless, wearisome 10 flavorless, monotonous, namby-pamby, spiritless, wishy-washy 11 commonplace

insistent 4 dire 6 crying, dogged, urgent 7 burning, clamant 8 emphatic, forceful, pressing 9 assertive, clamorous, obtrusive 10 imperative, resounding 11 persevering

insolence 5 nerve 6 insult 8 audacity, boldness, contempt, rudeness 9 arrogance, hardihood, impudence 10 brazenness, disrespect, effrontery 11 haughtiness, presumption 12 impertinence

insolent 4 bold, pert, rude 5 lofty, proud, saucy 6 brazen 7 defiant, haughty, uncivil 8 arrogant, cavalier, impolite, impudent, superior 9 audacious 10 disdainful, imperative, peremptory, procacious, ungracious 11 dictatorial, impertinent, magisterial, overbearing 12 contumelious, discourteous, supercilious 13 high-and-mighty

insouciance 6 apathy 8 lethargy 9 disregard, lassitude, unconcern 11 disinterest 12 heedlessness, indifference, listlessness

insouciant 8 carefree, heedless 9 lightsome 10 free-minded 11 indifferent, unconcerned 12 happy-go-lucky, lighthearted

inspect 3 con, vet 4 view 5 check, study 6 notice, review, survey 7 canvass, check up, examine, observe 8 question 9 catechize, check over 10 scrutinize

inspiration 4 muse 6 animus, genius, vision 8 afflatus 9 brainwave, influence 10 brainstorm 13 enlightenment

inspire 3 get 4 fire, move, stir, sway 5 carry, elate, endow, endue, exalt, imbue, set up, touch 6 affect, excite, foment, incite, inhale, strike 7 animate, commove, enliven, impress, quicken 8 motivate, spirit up 9 breathe in, encourage, influence, stimulate 10 exhilarate

instability 9 shakiness 10 insecurity 11 inconstancy, unfixedness 12 unsteadiness 13 changeability, unsettledness

install 4 seat, vest 5 chair 6 induct, invest, settle 8 ensconce, enthrone, initiate 9 establish
instance 4 case, cite, item, name 5 proof 6 detail, ground, reason, sample 7 example, mention, request, specify 8 exponent, sampling, specimen 9 exemplify 10 illustrate, particular, suggestion 11 case history, instigation 12 illustration
instant 4 dire, time, wink 5 crack, flash, jiffy, point, shake, trice, while 6 minute, moment, second, urgent 7 current, exigent, present, twinkle 8 existent, juncture, occasion, pressing, todayish 9 immediate, insistent, twinkling 10 imperative, present-day
instantaneous 4 fast 5 quick, rapid 9 immediate, momentary 10 transitory 11 hair-trigger
instanter 3 now 4 away 5 right 6 at once 8 directly, first off 9 forthwith, right away 11 immediately
instantly 3 now 4 away 5 right 6 at once 8 directly, first off 9 forthwith, right away 10 pressingly
instead 4 else 6 in lieu, rather 11 alternately 13 alternatively
instigate 3 set 4 abet, fire, goad, hint, move, plan, plot, prod, spur, urge 5 impel, raise, set on 6 excite, foment, incite, scheme, stir up, whip up 7 provoke, suggest 8 motivate 9 stimulate
instill 5 imbue, infix 6 impart, infuse 7 implant 9 inculcate, introduce
instinctive 6 innate, normal 7 natural, regular, typical 8 inherent, visceral, will-less 9 automatic, intuitive, unlearned 10 congenital, unprompted, unreasoned 11 involuntary, spontaneous, unmeditated
institute 3 law 4 rule 5 begin, edict, found, set up, start 6 decree, launch, ordain 7 precept, usher in 8 decretum, initiate, organize 9 establish, introduce, ordinance, originate 10 inaugurate 12 organization
institution 4 rite 5 habit 6 custom 7 fixture 9 enactment 10 foundation 13 establishment *kind:* 6 school 7 academy, college 8 hospital 10 university
instruct 3 bid 4 lead, show, tell, warn 5 coach, drill, guide, order, pilot, steer, teach, train, tutor 6 assign, charge, define, direct, enjoin, inform, school 7 apprise, command, counsel, educate 8 acquaint, engineer 9 prescribe 10 discipline
instruction 6 advice, lesson 7 precept 8 teaching, training, tutelage 9 catechism, education, schooling 10 directions *place of:* 6 school 7 academe
instructive 8 didactic 10 moralistic, moralizing 11 educational
instrument 4 deed, gear, mean, tool 5 agent, means, organ 6 agency, device, medium, tackle 7 channel, utensil, vehicle 8 ministry 9 appliance, machinery 13 paraphernalia *aircraft:* 3 aba 5 radar, radio 7 compass 8 yawmeter 9 altimeter, gyroscope 10 altazimuth, tachometer 11 transponder *calculating:* 6 abacus 8 computer 9 slide rule *combining form:* 4 labe, stat 5 meter *graphic:* 6 camera 8 otoscope 9 telescope 10 binoculars, microscope 11 fluoroscope, stethoscope, stroboscope 12 bronchoscope, oscilloscope, spectrograph, spectroscope *measuring:* 5 clock, gauge, radar, scale, sonar 7 alidade, ammeter, balance, caliper, sextant, transit 8 quadrant 9 altimeter, astrolabe, barometer, bolometer, manometer, pedometer, sonometer, voltmeter 10 anemometer, fathometer, hydrometer, hygrometer, micrometer, radiometer, radiosonde, spirometer, tachometer, theodolite 11 chronometer, lie detector, range finder, seismograph, speedometer, thermometer 12 electroscope, galvanometer, oscillograph, oscilloscope 13 Geiger counter, potentiometer *medical:* 5 curet 6 lancet, plexor, trocar 7 curette, forceps, probang, specula (plural), tenacula (plural) 9 tenaculum *radiation-producing:* 5 laser, maser; (see also implement; musical instrument; tool)
instrumental 6 useful 7 helpful 9 conducive 11 serviceable
instrumentality 5 agent, force, means, might, organ, power 6 agency, energy, medium 7 channel, vehicle 8 ministry
insubordinate 5 rebel 6 unruly 7 riotous 8 factious, mutinous 9 seditious 10 headstrong, rebellious, refractory 11 disaffected, disobedient, dissentious, intractable, uncompliant, uncomplying 12 contumacious, recalcitrant, ungovernable
insubstantial 4 airy, puny, weak 5 frail 6 feeble, flimsy 7 fragile, tenuous, unsound 8 bodiless, decrepit 9 imaginary, unfleshly 10 intangible, unembodied 11 disembodied 12 apparitional
insufferable 7 painful 10 unbearable 11 distressing, intolerable
insufficiency 4 lack 7 failure, paucity, poverty 8 scarcity, shortage, underage 9 inability 10 inadequacy, scantiness, scarceness 11 defalcation
insufficient 3 shy 5 scant, short, unfit 6 scanty, scarce 7 failing, lacking, unequal, wanting 9 defective 10 inadequate, incomplete
insular 5 local 6 narrow 7 limited 8 confined, detached, islander, isolated, regional, secluded 9 illiberal, insulated, parochial, sectarian, sectional, small-town 10 prejudiced, provincial, restricted

insulate 6 cut off, enisle, island 7 isolate 8 close off 9 segregate, sequester
insult 4 gibe, gird, jeer, mock, rump, slap, slur 5 abase, abuse, fleer, flout, scoff, scorn, shame, sneer, taunt 6 debase, deride, humble, offend, revile 7 affront, degrade, despite, disdain, obloquy, offense, outrage 8 contempt, disgrace, ignominy, ridicule 9 contumely, humiliate, insolence 10 opprobrium 12 unpleasantry, vituperation
insurance 8 guaranty, warranty 10 protection *agency:* 7 actuary 8 adjuster 11 underwriter *term:* 6 policy 7 annuity 8 coverage 9 bordereau 11 beneficiary
insure 5 cinch, guard 6 assure, shield 7 protect 9 safeguard 10 underwrite
insurgent 5 rebel 6 anarch 8 factious, frondeur, mutineer, mutinous, revolter 9 anarchist, seditious 10 rebellious 12 contumacious 13 insubordinate
insurrection 6 mutiny, revolt 8 uprising 9 rebellion
insurrectionist 5 rebel 6 anarch 8 frondeur, mutineer, revolter 10 malcontent
insusceptible 6 immune 9 impassive, unfeeling 10 insentient 12 unresponsive
intact 5 sound, whole 6 entire, maiden, unhurt, virgin 7 perfect 8 complete, flawless, unbroken, unmarred, virginal 9 undamaged, uninjured, untouched 10 unimpaired
intangible 4 airy, rare, thin 5 vague 6 aerial, slight 8 aeriform, ethereal 10 immaterial, impalpable, unapparent 11 incorporeal
integer 5 digit 6 figure, number 7 chiffer, numeral 11 whole number
integral 3 sum 4 full 5 whole 6 choate, entire, entity, system 7 inbuilt, perfect 8 complete, inherent, totality 9 component, composite 11 constituent
integrate 3 mix, sum 4 fuse, join, link, tune 5 blend, merge, unify, unite, whole 6 attune, embody, entity, system 7 arrange, combine, compact, conform, conjoin 8 coalesce, organize, totality 9 harmonize, reconcile 10 articulate, coordinate, proportion, symphonize, synthesize 11 desegregate
integrity 5 honor 7 honesty, probity 9 constancy, soundness, wholeness 10 entireness, honestness, perfection 12 absoluteness, completeness, incorruption 13 honorableness
integument 4 coat 5 testa 7 coating, cuticle 8 covering, envelope 10 investment *combining form:* 4 derm, scyt 5 derma, scyto 6 dermia, dermis 9 dermatous
intellect 3 wit 4 mind, nous 5 brain 6 genius, pundit, reason 7 egghead, thinker 9 intuition, mentality 12 intelligence 13 comprehension, understanding
intellectual 5 brain 6 brainy, mental 7 Brahmin, egghead, psychic 8 highbrow, longhair 9 reasoning 10 double-dome, highbrowed, reflective
intelligence 3 wit 4 mind, news, word 5 brain, sense 6 acumen, advice, brains, notice, reason, wisdom 7 tidings 8 judgment, learning, sagacity 9 knowledge, mentality, mother wit, speerings 10 brainpower, shrewdness
intelligent 4 keen, wise 5 acute, alert, aware, sharp, smart, sound 6 adroit, astute, brainy, bright, clever, shrewd 7 cunning, knowing, logical 8 rational, sensible 9 brilliant, ingenious, sagacious 10 reasonable 11 quick-witted, ready-witted 13 knowledgeable, perspicacious
intelligentsia 7 clerisy 8 literati, vanguard 10 avant-garde, illuminati
intelligible 5 clear, lucid, plain 8 luminous 10 conceptual 13 supersensible, suprasensuous
intemperance 6 excess 10 debauchery 11 drunkenness 12 immoderation
intemperate 4 hard 5 harsh 6 bitter, brutal, rugged, severe 7 drunken, extreme, violent 8 bibulous, rigorous 9 bibacious, crapulous, excessive, inclement 10 gluttonous, immoderate, inordinate 12 unrestrained 13 overindulgent
intend 3 aim, try 4 mean, plan, plot 5 essay, spell 6 assign, denote, design, import, scheme, strive 7 add up to, attempt, connote, destine, express, propose, purpose, signify 8 endeavor 9 designate
intended 6 fiancé 7 engaged, fiancée 8 proposed 9 affianced, betrothed
intense 3 hot 4 deep, hard, keen 5 acute, great, vivid 6 ardent, fervid, fierce, severe, strong 7 extreme, fervent, furious, serious, vicious, violent, zealous 8 enhanced, powerful, profound, stressed, terrible, vehement 9 assiduous, desperate, excessive, exquisite 10 aggravated, emphasized, heightened 11 accentuated 12 concentrated
intensify 4 rise 5 exalt, mount, rouse 6 accent, deepen, stress 7 enhance, sharpen 8 heighten, increase, redouble 9 aggravate, emphasize 10 accentuate, aggrandize 11 concentrate
intensity 5 depth 6 energy, fervor 7 passion 8 fervency, loudness
intensive 5 eager 7 zealous 10 exhaustive 12 concentrated *pronoun:* 6 itself, myself 7 herself, himself 8 yourself 9 ourselves 10 themselves, yourselves
intent 3 aim, set 4 deep, plan, rapt, will 5 eager, fixed, sense 6 animus, design, import 7 decided, earnest, engaged, meaning, minding, purport, purpose, riveted, set-

tied, wrapped 8 absorbed, conation, decisive, diligent, immersed, resolute, resolved, sedulous, volition, watching 9 engrossed, wrapped up 10 determined
intention 3 aim, end 4 goal, hope, plan, wish 6 animus, design, desire, object, scheme 7 meaning, purpose
intentional 5 meant 7 advised, studied, willful, willing, witting 8 designed, proposed, purposed, unforced 9 designful, voluntary 10 considered, deliberate 12 premeditated, unprescribed
intentionally 9 on purpose, purposely
inter 4 bury, tomb 5 plant 6 entomb, inhume 7 lay away, put away 9 sepulcher, sepulture
interact 4 join 5 merge, unite 7 combine 9 cooperate 11 collaborate
interbreed 5 cross 9 cross-mate, hybridize
intercede 6 step in 7 mediate 9 arbitrate, interpose, intervene
intercept 4 curb, grab, stop, take 5 block, catch, check, seize 6 cut off, hinder 9 forestall, interrupt
intercessor 6 broker 8 advocate, mediator 9 go-between, middleman 12 entrepreneur
interconnect 4 join 5 blend, unite 10 anastomose, inosculate
intercourse 5 truck 7 contact, dealing, traffic 8 business, commerce, converse 9 communion 10 connection 12 conversation 13 communication
intercross 9 decussate, hybridize
interdict 3 ban 4 veto 5 taboo 6 enjoin, forbid, outlaw 8 prohibit 9 proscribe
interest 4 care, good, lure, pull 5 claim, pique, share, snare, stake, tempt 6 appeal, arouse, behalf, excite, regard 7 attract, benefit, concern, passion, welfare 9 advantage, attention, curiosity, fascinate, tantalize, titillate, well-being 10 absorption, enthusiasm, excitement, prosperity
interested 4 rapt 6 caring 7 partial 8 partisan
interfere 3 bar 4 balk, foil, fool 5 block 6 baffle, butt in, hinder, horn in, impede, meddle, step in, tamper, thwart 7 intrude, mediate, trouble 8 busybody, obstruct 9 frustrate, incommode, intervene 10 discommode, monkey with, tamper with
interim 3 gap 5 break 6 acting, breach, hiatus, lacuna, pro tem, supply 8 meantime 9 temporary 10 pro tempore
interior 3 gut 5 belly, bosom, heart, inner 6 center, inland, inside, inward, within 8 visceral 9 viscerous
interject 6 fill in 7 throw in 9 introduce
interjection ***agreement:*** 6 righto 7 right on ***attention-getter:*** 3 hey 4 ahem, psst 5 heigh ***calling pigs:*** 5 sooey ***cheer:*** 3 rah 6 hooray, hurrah, hurray ***contempt:*** 3 poh 4 pooh 5 pshaw ***disappointment:*** 4 rats 6 shucks ***disapproval:*** 3 fie ***disbelief:*** 2 aw 3 huh ***disgust:*** 3 bah, pah, ugh 4 pugh, rats 5 faugh, nerts, yecch 6 phooey ***dismay:*** 2 oy 4 oh no ***dismissal:*** 3 git ***farewell:*** 4 by-by, ciao 6 bye-bye, so long ***gratitude:*** 8 gramercy ***greeting:*** 2 hi 4 ciao 5 aloha, hello ***hesitation:*** 2 er, um ***in golf:*** 4 fore ***in hunting:*** 6 yoicks ***in marching:*** 3 hup ***joy:*** 4 whee 6 hooray, hurrah, hurray, yippee 7 whoopee ***mild apology:*** 4 oops 5 woops 6 whoops ***mild oath:*** 3 gad, gor 4 darn, drat, egad, geez, gosh, heck, jeez 5 egads, golly, zooks 6 cracky, jiminy, zounds 7 begorra, begorry, gee whiz, jeepers, jimminy 8 gadzooks, gee whizz 13 gee whillikers, gee whillikins ***of warning:*** 8 gardyloo ***O.K.:*** 5 wilco ***pain:*** 2 ow 4 ouch, yipe 5 yipes ***peace:*** 6 shalom, sholom ***regret:*** 4 alas 5 alack 8 lackaday ***relief:*** 4 phew ***request:*** 7 prithee ***silence:*** 2 sh 3 shh ***sneeze:*** 5 achoo 6 atchoo 7 kerchoo ***sorrow:*** 4 alas 5 alack 8 lackaday ***stop:*** 4 whoa ***surprise:*** 2 ah, ho, lo, oh 3 aha, huh, oho, wow 4 gosh, oops, yipe 5 blimy, yipes, zowie 6 blimey ***to a horse:*** 4 whoa 6 giddap ***toast:*** 5 salud, skoal 6 cheers, prosit 7 l'chayim ***triumph:*** 3 aha, hah 6 eureka; (see also **exclamation**)
interlace 3 mix 5 braid, twine, weave 9 alternate, interlock 10 intertwine, interweave 11 intersperse
interlard 3 mix 6 mingle 7 diffuse
interlope 4 fool 6 butt in, horn in, meddle 7 intrude 8 busybody 9 interfere 10 monkey with, tamper with 11 intermeddle
interlude 4 lull, rest 5 break, idyll, pause, spell 7 episode, respite 8 breather, entr'acte, interval, meantime 9 meanwhile
intermediary 3 mid 4 mean 5 agent, organ 6 agency, broker, center, medium, middle 7 central, channel, vehicle 8 mediator, ministry 9 go-between, middleman 10 interagent
intermediate 3 mid 4 fair, mean, so-so 6 broker, center, medium, middle, step in 7 average, between, central, fairish 8 middling 9 go-between, middleman 11 intervening 12 entrepreneur ***combining form:*** 3 mes 4 medi, meso 5 medio
intermediator 6 broker 9 go-between, middleman 12 entrepreneur
interment 6 burial 9 sepulture 10 inhumation
interminable 7 endless, eternal, lasting 8 constant, infinite, unending 9 boundless, ceaseless, continual, limitless, permanent,

perpetual, unceasing, unlimited **10** continuous **11** everlasting
intermission **4** rest, stop **5** break, pause **6** recess **7** latency, respite **8** abeyance, abeyancy, doldrums, dormancy, interval **10** quiescence, quiescency, suspension **11** cold storage, parenthesis **12** interruption
intermit **4** stay **5** check, defer, delay **6** arrest, hold up, put off **7** hold off, suspend **8** hold over, postpone, prorogue **9** interrupt
intermittent **6** broken, cyclic, fitful, serial **7** checked, iterant **8** arrested, cyclical, metrical, periodic, rhythmic, seasonal, sporadic **9** alternate, iterative, recurrent, recurring, spasmodic **10** alternated, isochronal, occasional, periodical, rhythmical **11** interrupted, isochronous
intermix **6** mingle **8** comingle, immingle **9** commingle **11** intermingle
intermixture **5** blend **7** amalgam **12** amalgamation **13** miscegenation
intern **3** jug **4** jail **6** immure **7** confine, impound, trainee **8** bastille, imprison **9** constrain
internal **3** gut **4** home **5** inner **6** inward, native **7** private **8** domestic, inherent, interior, visceral **9** intrinsic, viscerous **10** subjective *prefix:* **5** intra
internal organs **4** guts **6** vitals **7** viscera **8** entrails
international organization **2** UN **3** FAO, IAM, ICJ, IFC, ILO, ITO, ITU, OAS, WHO, WMO **4** IAAF, IABA, IAEA, IARU, IATA, ICAO, IFIP, IMCO, NATO **5** ICFTU, SEATO **6** UNESCO, UNICEF
internuncio **5** envoy **6** bearer **7** carrier, courier **8** emissary **9** messenger
interpolate **3** add **5** admit, annex, enter **6** append, fill in, insert **7** throw in **8** superadd **9** introduce **11** intercalate
interpose **4** cast, push, toss **5** shove, throw **6** butt in, fill in, insert, meddle, step in, thrust **7** intrude, mediate, obtrude, throw in **8** moderate **9** arbitrate, insinuate, intercede, interfere, intervene, introduce, negotiate
interpret **4** limn **5** gloss, image **6** decode, depict, render **7** comment, explain, expound, picture, portray **8** annotate, construe, describe, spell out **9** delineate, exemplify, explicate, represent **10** commentate
interpretation **7** meaning, reading, version **8** exegesis **9** construal, rendering **11** explanation, translation
interpretive **8** exegetic **10** expository **11** explanatory, explicatory **12** expositional
interregnum **5** break **8** interval
interrogate **3** ask **4** quiz **5** grill, query **7** examine, inquire **8** question **9** catechize
interrupt **4** halt, stay, stop **5** break, check, cut in, defer, put in, stall **6** arrest, chip in **7** break in, chime in, disturb, suspend **8** postpone **9** intercept
interruption **3** gap **4** rent, rift **5** break, pause, split **6** breach, hiatus, lacuna **7** caesura, latency
intersect **4** meet **5** cross **8** crosscut, traverse **9** decussate **10** crisscross
intersection **8** crossing, junction **10** crossroads
intersperse **7** diffuse, scatter
interval **3** gap **4** lull **5** break, comma, pause, space **6** breach, hiatus, lacuna **7** caesura, interim, respite **9** pausation **11** parenthesis ***music:*** **4** rest
intervene **4** part **5** sever **6** divide, step in **7** mediate **8** separate **9** intercede, interpose
interweave **3** mix **4** fuse, join, link **5** blend **9** associate
intestinal fortitude **4** grit, guts, sand **5** nerve, pluck, spunk **6** mettle, spirit **7** courage **8** backbone **10** resolution
intestine **3** gut **4** tube **5** bowel, canal **6** inward, viscus **7** viscera (plural) ***combining form:*** **3** col **4** coli, colo **5** enter **6** entero ***part:*** **5** cecum, colon, ileum **6** rectum **7** jejunum **8** duodenum
in the same place **6** ibidem
intimacy **7** liberty **9** closeness **10** experience **11** familiarity **12** acquaintance
intimate **3** gut **4** cozy, fond, hint, next **5** amigo, close, crony, imply, inner, pally, privy, thick **6** attest, chummy, friend, impart, loving, notify, secret, sexual **7** bespeak, betoken, comrade, connote, devoted, nearest, suggest **8** announce, familiar, inherent, visceral **9** close-knit, companion, confidant, elemental, essential, ingrained, insinuate, intrinsic, viscerous **10** deep-seated, indwelling **11** cater-cousin **12** acquaintance, confidential
intimation **3** cue **4** clue, hint, wind **5** shade, tinge, trace **6** breath, shadow, strain, streak **7** inkling **8** telltale **10** suggestion
intimidate **3** awe, cow **4** bait, ride **5** abash, alarm, bully, chivy, daunt, deter, force, hound, scare **6** badger, coerce, compel, hector, oblige **7** bluster, buffalo, dragoon, overawe, terrify **8** bludgeon, browbeat, bulldoze, bullyrag, dispirit, disquiet, frighten **9** constrain, strong-arm, terrorize
intolerant **5** irate, upset **6** averse, narrow, stuffy **7** bigoted, waspish **8** dogmatic, obdurate, outraged, snappish, worked up **9** fractious, hidebound, illiberal, impatient, irritable **10** brassbound, disdainful, inflexible, prejudiced, unenlarged **11** small-minded, unindulgent **12** antipathetic, con-

temptuous, narrow-minded, unforbearing 13 unsympathetic

intonation 4 tone 5 chant 6 accent 10 recitation

in toto 3 all 4 just 5 quite, stick 6 wholly 7 exactly, utterly 10 altogether

intoxicant 5 booze, drink 6 liquor 7 alcohol, spirits 9 aqua vitae

intoxicated 3 cut, wet 4 high 5 blind, dopey, drunk, fried, loopy, soppy, stiff, tight, tipsy 6 elated, looped, rum-dum, sloppy, sodden, soshed, stewed, stoned, tanked, zonked 7 drunken, excited, maudlin, muddled, slopped, sozzled, unsober 8 cockeyed, polluted, squiffed, turned-on 9 inebrious 11 alcoholized, exhilarated

intoxication 7 elation 8 euphoria 11 drunkenness, inebriation

intractable 4 wild 6 mulish, unruly 7 willful 8 indocile, mutinous, obdurate, perverse, stubborn 9 fractious, obstinate 10 bullheaded, headstrong, refractory, self-willed, unyielding 11 unteachable 12 pertinacious, recalcitrant, ungovernable 13 undisciplined

intransigent 5 tough 7 willful 8 stubborn 9 obstinate, unpliable 10 self-willed, unyielding 12 pertinacious

intrepid 4 bold 5 brave, hardy 6 daring, heroic 7 gallant, valiant 8 fearless, resolute, unafraid, valorous 9 audacious, dauntless, undaunted 10 courageous

intricate 4 hard 5 fancy 6 daedal, knotty 7 arduous, complex, gordian 8 involved 9 Byzantine, difficult, elaborate 11 complicated 12 labyrinthine 13 sophisticated

intrigue 4 plot 5 amour, cabal, covin 6 affair, appeal, devise, excite, scheme 7 attract, beguile, collude, connive, liaison 8 cogitate, conspire, contrive, interest, practice 9 fascinate, machinate, scheme out 10 conspiracy 11 machination

intrinsic see inherent

intrinsically 5 per se 6 as such

introduce 4 lead, moot 5 admit, begin, enter, found, set up, usher 6 broach, fill in, insert, launch, unveil, work in 7 bring up, implant, install, instill, pioneer, precede, preface, present, throw in, usher in 8 acquaint, initiate, innovate, organize 9 establish, insinuate, institute, interject, interpose, originate

introduction 5 debut, proem 7 introit, preface, prelude 8 entrance, exordium, foreword, overture, preamble, prologue, protases (plural), protasis 9 prelusion 12 prolegomenon

introductory 7 initial, nascent 8 proemial 9 beginning, prefatial, prefatory, preludial, prelusive 11 prefatorial, preliminary, preparative

intrude 5 cut in 6 bother, butt in, horn in, impose, invade, meddle, muscle, pester 7 disturb, presume 8 chisel in, encroach, entrench, infringe, trespass 9 interfere, interlope, interpose

intrusive 4 busy 7 curious 9 butting in, officious 10 meddlesome 11 impertinent 13 polypragmatic

in truth 6 indeed, really, verily 8 actually

intuition 7 insight 8 instinct 10 anschauung, sixth sense 11 second sight

inundate 5 drown, flood, swamp, whelm 6 deluge, engulf 8 overflow, submerge 9 overwhelm

inundation 4 pour 5 flood, spate 6 deluge 7 niagara, torrent 8 cataract, flooding, overflow 9 cataclysm

inure 3 use 4 wont 5 steel, train 6 harden, season 7 toughen 8 accustom 9 habituate 10 discipline 11 familiarize

inutile 6 draffy, drossy, no-good 7 nothing 8 unworthy 9 valueless, worthless

invade 4 loot, raid 5 foray 6 ravage 7 assault, overrun, pillage, plunder 8 encroach, entrench, infringe, permeate, trespass 9 overswarm 11 impenetrate

invalid 3 bad, mad 4 null, void 6 infirm, sickly 9 illogical, sophistic 10 fallacious, irrational, reasonless, unreasoned 11 nonrational, null and void 12 unreasonable

invalidate 4 undo 5 abate, annul, quash 6 offset 7 abolish, nullify 8 negative 9 discredit 10 circumduct, counteract, neutralize

invaluable 6 costly 8 precious 9 priceless 11 inestimable

invariable 4 same 5 fixed 6 steady 7 uniform 8 constant 9 continual, immovable, immutable, unfailing, unmovable, unvarying 10 consistent, inflexible, unchanging 11 inalterable, unalterable 12 unchangeable, unmodifiable

invariably 4 ever 6 always 7 forever 10 constantly 11 continually, perpetually

invasion 4 raid 5 foray 6 attack, inroad 9 incursion, intrusion, irruption, offensive 12 encroachment, entrenchment

invective 5 abuse 6 tirade 7 abusive, obloquy 8 diatribe, jeremiad, scurrile 9 contumely, damnatory, philippic, truculent 10 censorious, scurrility, scurrilous, vituperous 11 opprobrious, reproachful 12 billingsgate, condemnatory, contumelious, denunciatory, vituperation, vituperative, vituperatory

inveigh 4 kick, rail 6 except, object 7 protest 9 fulminate 11 expostulate, remonstrate

inveigle 4 bait, coax, lure, toll 5 decoy, snare, tempt 6 allure, cajole, entice, entrap, lead on, seduce 8 persuade

invent 4 coin, mint 5 frame 6 cook up,

create, design, devise, make up, patent, vamp up **7** concoct, dream up, fashion, hatch up, pioneer **8** conceive, contrive, discover, engineer, envision **9** fabricate, formulate, originate

invention **7** coinage, fiction **8** creation **10** brainchild, concoction, innovation **11** contrivance, origination

inventive **7** fertile, teeming **8** creative, fruitful, original **9** demiurgic, deviceful, ingenious **10** innovative, innovatory, productive

inventor **4** sire **5** maker **6** author, father **7** creator, founder **8** engineer, original **9** architect, generator, innovator, patriarch **10** discoverer, introducer, originator ***air brake:*** **12** Westinghouse ***air conditioning:*** **7** Carrier ***automobile:*** **7** Daimler ***ballpoint pen:*** **4** Loud ***barbed wire:*** **7** Glidden ***barometer:*** **10** Torricelli ***bifocal lens:*** **8** Franklin ***camera:*** **7** Eastman ***cash register:*** **5** Ritty ***cotton gin:*** **7** Whitney ***cylinder lock:*** **4** Yale ***dirigible:*** **8** Zeppelin ***dynamite:*** **5** Nobel ***electric battery:*** **5** Volta ***electric fan:*** **7** Wheeler ***electric organ:*** **7** Hammond ***electric razor:*** **6** Schick ***electric stove:*** **7** Hadaway ***elevator:*** **4** Otis ***fountain pen:*** **8** Waterman ***friction match:*** **6** Walker ***gyrocompass:*** **6** Sperry ***helicopter:*** **8** Sikorsky ***hot-air balloon:*** **11** Montgolfier ***incandescent lamp:*** **6** Edison ***induction motor:*** **5** Tesla ***lawn mower:*** **5** Hills ***Linotype:*** **12** Mergenthaler ***logarithm:*** **6** Napier ***machine gun:*** **7** Gatling ***microphone:*** **8** Berliner ***movable type:*** **9** Gutenberg ***parachute:*** **9** Blanchard ***pendulum clock:*** **7** Huygens ***phonograph:*** **6** Edison ***photography:*** **6** Niepce, Talbot **8** Daguerre ***piano:*** **10** Cristofori ***radio:*** **7** Marconi ***reaper:*** **9** McCormick ***revolver:*** **4** Colt ***rocket engine:*** **7** Goddard ***safety pin:*** **4** Hunt ***safety razor:*** **8** Gillette ***sewing machine:*** **4** Howe ***sleeping car:*** **7** Pullman ***spinning jenny:*** **10** Hargreaves ***steamboat:*** **5** Fitch **6** Fulton, Miller, Rumsey **8** Jouffroy ***steam engine:*** **4** Watt ***steam locomotive:*** **10** Stephenson ***stethoscope:*** **7** Laennec ***submarine:*** **7** Holland ***tank:*** **7** Swinton ***telegraph:*** **5** Morse ***telephone:*** **4** Bell ***telescope:*** **10** Lippershey ***television:*** **5** Baird **6** Nipkow **8** Zworykin **10** Farnsworth ***torpedo:*** **9** Whitehead ***vulcanized rubber:*** **8** Goodyear ***writing for the blind:*** **7** Braille ***zipper:*** **6** Judson

inventory **3** sum **4** fund, list **5** hoard, stock, store, sum up, tally **6** digest, record, supply, survey **7** account, backlog, catalog, itemize, nest egg, reserve, specify, summary, summate **8** condense, nutshell, register, tabulate **9** checklist, enumerate, epitomize, reservoir, stockpile, summarize, synopsize

inverse **4** turn **6** change, revert **7** reverse **8** contrary, opposite **9** transpose **10** transplace ***prefix:*** **2** ob

inversion **4** turn **7** reverse, turning **8** reversal **9** about-face, turnabout, volte-face **11** changeabout, reversement

invert **4** flip, turn **6** change **7** reverse, uranian, uranist **8** turn over **9** transpose **10** homosexual, transplace

invertebrate **4** weak **5** sissy **7** doormat, milksop **8** boneless, impotent, weakling **9** forceless, jellyfish, spineless **10** emasculate, inadequate, namby-pamby, panty-waist **11** ineffective, ineffectual, Milquetoast, mollycoddle, slack-spined ***kind:*** **4** worm **6** insect, sponge **7** mollusk **8** arachnid **12** coelenterate

invest **4** gird, veil, wrap **5** adorn, array, beset, dress, endow, endue, imbue, steep **6** clothe, confer, enfold, enwrap, induct, infuse, leaven, ordain, shroud **7** besiege, empower, enclose, envelop, ingrain, install, instate, suffuse

investigate **3** pry **4** poke, sift **5** probe, study **6** go into, search **7** dig into, examine, explore, inquire **8** look into, muckrake, prospect, research **9** delve into **10** scrutinize **11** inquire into

investigation **5** probe, quest **6** survey **7** delving, inquest, inquiry, probing **8** research, sounding **9** surveying **11** inquisition

investigator **4** dick **6** sleuth **7** gumshoe **8** hawkshaw, sherlock **9** detective

investiture **5** siege **8** blockage **9** inaugural, induction **10** initiation **12** inauguration, installation

inveterate **3** old, set **5** fixed, sworn **6** rooted **7** abiding, chronic, settled **8** deep-dyed, enduring, habitual, hardened, lifelong **9** confirmed, hard-shell, ingrained, long-lived, perennial **10** continuing, deep-rooted, deep-seated, entrenched, persistent, persisting **11** established

Invictus author **6** Henley

invidious **6** bitter, odious **7** envious, envying, hateful, jealous **8** libelous **9** abhorrent, green-eyed, injurious, malignant, maligning, obnoxious, repellent, repugnant, revulsive, vilifying **10** abominable, calumnious, defamatory, detestable, detracting, detractive, detractory, scandalous, slanderous

invigorate **4** stir, zest **5** brace, cheer, rally, renew, rouse **7** animate, enliven, fortify, refresh, restore **8** energize, vitalize **9** reinforce, stimulate **10** exhilarate, rejuvenate, strengthen

in vino ___ **7** veritas

inviolable **4** holy, pure **6** chaste, divine, sacred **7** blessed **8** hallowed **9** undefiled

10 sacrosanct 11 consecrated 13 incorruptible
Invisible Man, The *author:* 5 Wells
Invisible Man author 7 Ellison (Ralph)
invitation 4 call, lure 7 bidding, proffer, request 8 entreaty, proposal, stimulus 9 incentive 10 attraction, suggestion 11 proposition
invite 3 ask, bid 4 call, lure 5 tempt 6 allure, call in, entice, summon 7 request, solicit
invoice 3 tab 4 bill 5 score 7 account 9 reckoning, statement
invoke 3 beg 4 pray 5 crave, plead 6 appeal, effect 7 beseech, enforce, entreat, implore 9 implement, importune 10 supplicate
involuntary 6 forced, reflex 8 will-less 9 automatic, impulsive, unwitting 10 compulsory, unintended, unprompted 11 instinctive, spontaneous, unmeditated 13 unintentional
involve 4 mire 6 embody, engage, entail, take in, tangle 7 concern, contain, embrace, embroil, include, subsume 8 comprise, entangle 9 encompass, implicate 10 complicate, comprehend
involved 6 daedal, knotty 7 complex, gordian, muddled 8 affected, confused, enmeshed 9 Byzantine, concerned, elaborate, entangled, intricate 10 implicated, interested 11 complicated 12 labyrinthine
invulnerable 10 invincible, unbeatable 11 impregnable, indomitable
inward 5 entad, inner 6 inside, mental 8 interior, internal 9 innermore, intestine, spiritual
inwards 4 guts 6 inside, tripes, within 7 innards, insides, viscera 8 entrails, interior 9 internals
Io *father:* 7 Inachus *guard:* 5 Argus *son:* 7 Epaphus
iodine source 4 kelp
Iolcus king 5 Aeson 6 Pelias
Iole *captor:* 8 Heracles, Hercules *father:* 7 Eurytus *husband:* 6 Hyllus
ion 6 ligand *kind:* 5 anion 6 cation 8 thermion *suffix:* 3 ium 5 onium
Ion *father:* 6 Apollo *mother:* 6 Creusa *stepfather:* 6 Xuthus
Ionesco play 5 Chairs (The) 10 Rhinoceros (The) 11 Bald Soprano (The)
iota 3 bit, jot, ray 4 atom, mite, whit 5 crumb, grain, ounce, speck 6 tittle 7 smidgen 8 molecule, particle
IOU 4 debt *part:* 3 owe, you
Iowa *capital:* 9 Des Moines *college, university:* 3 Coe 5 Dordt, Drake, Loras *nickname:* 12 Hawkeye State *state bird:* 9 goldfinch *state flower:* 8 wild rose
Iphicles *brother:* 8 Heracles, Hercules *mother:* 7 Alcmene *son:* 6 Iolaus
Iphigenia *brother:* 7 Orestes *father:* 9 Agamemnon *mother:* 12 Clytemnestra *sister:* 7 Electra
Iphis' daughter 6 Evadne
Iran *capital:* 6 Tehran 7 Teheran *monetary unit:* 4 rial *oil center:* 6 Abadan
Iranian 7 Persian *language:* 5 Farsi 7 Kurdish, Persian *non-Persian people:* 5 Kurds *parliament:* 6 Majlis *sect:* 4 Shia 5 Sunni *sect member:* 6 Shiite 7 Sunnite *title:* 4 shah
Iraq *capital:* 7 Baghdad *monetary unit:* 5 dinar
irascible 5 cross, huffy, irate, ratty, surly, testy 6 cranky, ireful, snappy, tetchy, touchy 7 bristly, peevish, peppery 8 choleric, petulant, snappish 9 fractious, impatient, irritable, querulous, temperish 10 passionate 11 belligerent, hot-tempered 12 cantankerous 13 quick-tempered
Ira's father 6 Ikkesh
irate 3 mad 4 waxy 5 angry, wroth 6 ireful, wrathy, wrothy 7 enraged, furious 8 choleric, incensed, provoked, wrathful
ire 3 mad 4 fury, rage 5 anger, wrath 6 enrage, madden, temper 7 incense, steam up, umbrage 9 infuriate 10 exasperate 11 indignation 12 exasperation
Ireland see Eire
Irene 3 Pax *father:* 4 Zeus 7 Jupiter *mother:* 6 Themis
irenic 4 calm 7 pacific 8 pacifist, peaceful 9 peaceable 10 nonviolent 12 conciliatory, pacificatory
Iris *father:* 7 Thaumas *mother:* 7 Electra
Irish 4 Erse 6 Celtic, Gaelic *accent:* 6 brogue *battle cry:* 3 abu 4 aboo *cattle:* 5 Kerry *clan:* 4 sept *combining form:* 7 Hiberno *coronation stone:* 7 Lia Fail *cudgel:* 9 shillalah 10 shillelagh *death spirit:* 7 banshee *dirge:* 8 ullagone *dog:* 6 setter 7 terrier *elf:* 10 leprechaun *exclamation:* 3 aru 5 arrah *festival:* 4 feis *flag color:* 5 green, white 6 orange *flower:* 8 shamrock *girl:* 4 lass 6 lassie 7 colleen *goblin:* 5 pooka *god:* 3 Ler 5 Dagda 6 Aengus *goddess:* 4 Badb, Bodb 6 Brigit 8 Morrigan *harp:* 8 clarsach *hero:* 9 Cuchulain, Cuchullin 11 Chuchulainn *heroine:* 7 Deirdre *king:* 9 Brian Boru *lake:* 5 lough *language:* 6 Gaelic *legislature:* 4 Dail *militant force:* 3 IRA *nationalist:* 7 Parnell 8 O'Connell *nationalist society:* 8 Sinn Fein *noble:* 6 flaith *patron saint:* 7 Patrick *theater:* 5 Abbey *writing system:* 4 ogam 5 ogham; (see also **Gaelic**; **Celtic**)
Irish moss 7 seaweed 9 carrageen
irk 3 try, vex 4 fret, gall, pain 5 anger,

annoy, peeve, pique, upset 6 abrade, bother, harass, nettle, ruffle, strain, stress 7 provoke, trouble 8 distress, exercise, irritate 10 exasperate

Irma ___ 7 La Douce

iron 4 hard 5 gyves, press 6 ferrum, fetter, strong 7 adamant, manacle, shackle 8 handcuff, obdurate 9 unbending 10 adamantine, brassbound, inexorable, inflexible, relentless, unyielding ***combining form:*** 5 ferri, ferro, sider 6 sidero ***German:*** 5 eisen ***relating to:*** 6 ferric 7 ferrous ***symbol:*** 2 Fe ***wrought:*** 5 mitis

ironbound 5 harsh, rough 6 craggy, jagged, rugged, uneven 7 scraggy 8 asperous, scabrous, unsmooth

Iron City 10 Pittsburgh

ironclad 5 fixed 8 constant 9 immovable, immutable 10 inflexible, invariable 11 inalterable, unalterable 12 unchangeable

ironhanded 5 rigid 6 strict 8 rigorist, rigorous 9 draconian, stringent 12 unpermissive

ironhearted 5 stony 7 callous 8 hardened, obdurate 9 heartless, unfeeling 10 hard-boiled 11 cold-blooded 13 unsympathetic

ironic 3 wry 6 biting 7 caustic, cutting, cynical, mordant, satiric 8 sardonic 9 sarcastic, trenchant

iron ore 8 goethite, hematite, limonite, siderite, taconite 9 magnetite

Iron Pants 6 Patton

irons 5 bonds, gyves 6 chains 7 fetters 8 manacles, shackles

Iroquois tribe 6 Cayuga, Mohawk, Oneida, Seneca 8 Onondaga

irradiate 5 edify 6 illume, uplift 7 improve 8 illumine 9 enlighten 10 illuminate

irrational 3 mad 5 crazy 6 absurd, insane 7 invalid 8 demented 9 illogical, senseless, sophistic 10 fallacious, reasonless, ridiculous, unreasoned 11 nonrational 12 unreasonable

irrefutable 4 sure 7 certain 8 positive 10 conclusive, inarguable 11 indubitable 12 indisputable 13 incontestable, uncontestable

irregular 3 odd 5 queer 6 fitful, off-key, patchy, random, spotty, uneven, unique 7 aimless, deviant, devious, erratic, strange, unaimed, unequal 8 aberrant, abnormal, atypical, informal, lopsided, partisan, peculiar, singular, sporadic, unstable, unsteady, variable 9 anomalous, desultory, divergent, eccentric, guerrilla, haphazard, hit-or-miss, spasmodic, unnatural, unregular, unsettled 10 asymmetric, changeable, designless, inconstant, off-balance, unbalanced, unofficial 11 exceptional, purposeless 12 overbalanced, unconsidered, unsystematic ***combining form:*** 4 anom 5 anomo 6 anomal 7 anomali, anomalo

irregularity 7 anomaly 8 asperity, disorder 9 roughness 10 inequality, unevenness

irrelevant 7 foreign 9 unrelated 10 extraneous, immaterial, inapposite, irrelative 11 impertinent, inessential, unessential, unimportant 12 inapplicable 13 insignificant

irreligious 5 pagan 6 amoral, unholy 7 godless, impious, profane, ungodly, unmoral 8 indevout, undevout 11 blasphemous 12 sacrilegious

irreparable 8 cureless, hopeless 9 incurable, insanable, uncurable 10 impossible 11 immedicable 12 irredeemable, irremediable 13 irreclaimable, irrecoverable, irretrievable, uncorrectable, unrecoverable

irreproachable 4 good, pure 8 flawless, innocent, spotless, virtuous 9 blameless, errorless, exemplary, exquisite, faultless, guiltless, righteous 10 immaculate, impeccable, inculpable, unblamable

irresolute 6 fickle, unsure, wobbly 7 halting 8 doubtful, hesitant, unstable, wavering 9 faltering, tentative, uncertain, undecided 10 changeable, inconstant 11 fluctuating, vacillating, vacillatory 12 wiggle-waggle

irresponsible 4 wild 8 carefree, careless, feckless, reckless 9 uncareful 10 incautious, unreliable 12 unanswerable, undependable 13 unaccountable, untrustworthy

irreverent 6 unholy 7 impious, profane, ungodly 10 unhallowed

irrevocable 4 firm 5 final 9 immutable 11 unalterable 12 irreversible, unchangeable, unmodifiable, unrepealable 13 nonreversible

irrigation ditch 5 flume 6 sluice 7 acequia

irritability 6 choler 9 petulance 11 fretfulness ***abnormal:*** 8 erethism

irritable 4 edgy 5 cross, huffy, raspy, techy, testy, waspy, whiny 6 cranky, ornery, snappy, tetchy, touchy, twitty 7 fretful, peevish, pettish, prickly, raspish, waspish 8 choleric, petulant, prickish, snappish 9 fractious, impatient, irascible, querulent, querulous, splenetic 12 cantankerous, disagreeable, querulential

irritant 4 pest 6 bother, pester, plague 8 nuisance 9 annoyance, besetment 10 botherment 11 botheration 12 exasperation

irritate 3 get, irk, rub, try, vex 4 fret, gall, goad, huff, rile, roil 5 anger, annoy, chafe, grate, peeve, pique, spite 6 abrade, badger, bother, burn up, harass, hector, madden, needle, nettle, offend, put out, ruffle 7 affront, inflame, provoke 8 acerbate

9 aggravate, stimulate **10** exacerbate, exasperate
irritated 5 irate, testy 7 fretful, peevish 8 choleric 9 impatient, irascible 11 hot-tempered
irritation 4 itch, rash, sore 5 uredo 9 annoyance 10 excitation
irrupt 4 spew 5 belch, eject, eruct, expel 7 intrude 8 disgorge
irruption 4 raid 5 foray 6 inroad 8 invasion 9 incursion
I.R.S. employee 4 acct 10 accountant
Iru's father 5 Caleb
Isaac ***father:*** 7 Abraham ***mother:*** 5 Sarah ***son:*** 4 Esau 5 Jacob ***wife:*** 7 Rebekah
Isabella ***brother:*** 7 Claudio ***husband:*** 9 Vincentio
Isabella I ***country:*** 5 Spain ***home:*** 7 Castile ***husband:*** 9 Ferdinand
Isaiah's father 4 Amoz
Iscah ***brother:*** 3 Lot ***father:*** 5 Haran ***sister:*** 6 Milcah
Iseult, Isolde ***beloved:*** 7 Tristan ***husband:*** 4 Mark
Ishbak ***father:*** 7 Abraham ***mother:*** 7 Keturah
Ishbosheth's father 4 Saul
Ishi ***father:*** 6 Appaim ***son:*** 6 Zoheth
Ishmael 6 pariah 7 outcast 8 castaway, derelict, outsider 11 offscouring, untouchable ***father:*** 4 Azel 7 Abraham, Pashhur 9 Jehonanan, Nethaniah ***mother:*** 5 Hagar ***son:*** 5 Massa 8 Zebadiah
Ishmaiah's father 7 Obadiah
Ishpah's father 6 Beriah
Ishpan's father 7 Shashak
Ishtar ***brother:*** 7 Shamash ***father:*** 3 Anu, Sin ***lover:*** 6 Tammuz
Ishuah's father 5 Asher
Ishui's father 4 Saul 5 Asher
Isis ***brother:*** 6 Osiris ***father:*** 3 Geb ***husband:*** 6 Osiris ***mother:*** 3 Nut ***son:*** 4 Sept 5 Horus
Islam ***adherent:*** 6 Moslem, Muslim ***founder:*** 8 Mohammed, Muhammad ***god:*** 5 Allah ***priest:*** 4 imam ***scriptures:*** 5 Koran; (see also **Muslim**)
island 3 cay, key 4 holm, isle 5 atoll, islet 6 cut off, enisle, skerry 7 crannog, isolate 8 close off, insulate, separate 9 segregate, sequester ***Admiralty group:*** 5 Manus ***Adriatic Sea:*** 3 Vis 4 Brac, Cres, Hvar 5 Ciovo, Mljet, Solta 6 Lesina, Pharus ***Aegean Sea:*** 4 Scio 5 Chios, Khios, Samos, Thira 6 Ikaria, Lemnos, Lesbos, Limnos 7 Nikaria 8 Mitilini, Mytilene, Santorin 10 Sakis-Adasi, Susam-Adasi ***Alaska:*** 4 Adak, Atka, Attu, Kuiu 8 Wrangell ***Aleutian group:*** 3 Rat 4 Adak, Akun, Attu 5 Amlia, Kiska, Umnak 6 Kanaga, Tanaga, Unimak 8 Amchitka, Unalaska ***American Samoa:*** 3 Ofu, Tau 4 Rose 6 Swains ***Andaman Sea:*** 4 Mali 5 Tavoy ***Antarctica:*** 5 Scott, Young ***Apostle group:*** 3 Oak 4 Long, Sand 5 Outer 8 Madeline, Michigan, Stockton ***Arafura Sea:*** 5 Dolak ***Arctic Archipelago:*** 6 Baffin 8 Victoria ***Arctic Ocean:*** 5 Senja ***Australian:*** 5 Cocos 8 Tasmania ***Azores:*** 4 Pico 5 Corvo, Faial ***Bahamas:*** 3 Cat, Rum 4 Long 5 Abaco, Exuma 6 Andros, Inagua 7 Acklins, Crooked 8 Watlings 9 Eleuthera, Mayaguana 11 San Salvador ***Bahrain:*** 5 Sitra 8 Muharraq ***Balearic group:*** 5 Ibiza 7 Majorca, Menorca, Minorca 8 Mallorca ***Baltic Sea:*** 4 Moon, Muhu 5 Faron, Mukhu, Rugen, Worms 6 Vormsi 7 Gotland 8 Bornholm, Gothland, Gottland ***Barents Sea:*** 4 Bear ***Bay of Biscay:*** 2 Re ***Bay of Naples:*** 5 Capri ***Bay of Panama:*** 4 Naos ***Bering Sea:*** 5 Medny 7 Nunivak 10 Big Diomede 13 Little Diomede ***Bismarck Archipelago:*** 5 Lihir 10 New Britain ***Bristol Channel:*** 5 Lundy ***Buzzards Bay:*** 9 Cuttyhunk ***Canadian:*** 5 Banks, Devon 6 Baffin 8 Bathurst, Melville, Somerset, Victoria 9 Anticosti, Ellesmere 10 Cape Breton 11 Axel Heiberg, Southampton 12 Newfoundland, Prince Edward ***Canaries:*** 6 Gomera 7 La Palma 8 Tenerife 9 Lanzarote ***Cape Verde:*** 4 Fogo, Maio, Mayo 5 Brava, Rombo ***Caribbean Sea:*** 4 Cuba 5 Aruba, Utila, Vache 6 Tobago 7 Antigua, Curacao, Jamaica 8 Barbados, Dominica, Trinidad 10 Guadeloupe, Martinique, Puerto Rico; (see also **Virgin group**) ***Carolines:*** 5 Sorol 6 Ponape 9 Ascension ***Chagos Archipelago:*** 11 Diego Garcia ***Channel group:*** 4 Herm, Sark 5 Lihou, Sercq 6 Jersey 8 Guernsey ***Chesapeake Bay:*** 4 Deal, Kent 5 Smith, Watts ***Chukchi Sea:*** 6 Herald ***Comoro group:*** 7 Mayotte ***Congo River:*** 4 Bamu ***Cook group:*** 4 Atiu 5 Mauke ***Croatia:*** 3 Krk, Pag, Rab 5 Susak, Unije ***Cyclades:*** 3 Ios, Kea, Nio 4 Ceos, Keos, Milo 5 Delos, Melos, Milos, Naxos, Paros, Siros, Syros 6 Andros, Dhilos 7 Amorgos, Cythnos, Kithnos, Kythnos, Mykonos ***Denmark:*** 3 Als, Fyn, Mon 4 Aero, Fano, Moen, Mors 5 Alsen, Funen, Moers, Samso 8 Bornholm 13 Fanum Fortunae ***D'Entrecasteaux group:*** 8 Kaluwawa 9 Fergusson ***Dodecanese group:*** 3 Coo, Cos, Kos 4 Caso, Lero, Simi, Syme 5 Kasos, Leros, Lipso, Lisso, Patmo, Telos 6 Calino, Lipsos, Nisiro, Patmos 7 Calimno, Nisiros, Nisyros 8 Kalymnos ***East River:*** 5 Ward's 7 Welfare 9 Roosevelt ***England's:*** 7 Britian 9 Britannia 12 Great Britain ***English Channel:*** 5 Wight ***Faeroes:*** 4 Vago 5 Bordo, Sando ***Fiji:*** 4 Koro

5 Mango, Vatoa ***Florida Keys:*** 4 Long, Vaca, West 5 Largo 7 Big Pine 9 Matecumbe, Sugarloaf ***Fox group:*** 5 Umnak 6 Akutan, Unimak 8 Unalaska ***French:*** 7 Corsica 12 New Caledonia ***French Polynesia:*** 4 Rapa, Reao, Ua Pu 5 Ua Pau ***Frisian group:*** 3 Rom 4 Föhr, Sylt 5 Amrum, Juist, Mando, Texel 6 Borkum 7 Ameland 8 Langeoog, Pellworm, Vlieland 9 Helgoland, Norderney ***Futunas:*** 5 Alofi ***Galápagos:*** 5 Pinta 7 Chatham, Isabela 8 Abingdon 10 Albermarle ***Georgia:*** 5 Tybee ***Germany:*** 4 Fohr 7 Fehmarn 9 Helgoland 10 Heligoland ***Greater Antilles:*** 4 Cuba 7 Jamaica 10 Hispaniola, Puerto Rico ***Greece:*** 4 Milo, Rodi 5 Creta, Crete, Hydra, Idhra, Kriti, Rodos, Tenos, Tinos 6 Euboea, Evvoia, Hydrea, Rhodes, Rhodus 9 Negropont 10 Negroponte ***Grenadines:*** 5 Union ***Gulf of Alaska:*** 6 Kodiak ***Gulf of Bothnia:*** 5 Karlö ***Gulf of Carpentaria:*** 5 Maria 6 Groote 7 Eylandt ***Gulf of Guinea:*** 7 Sao Tomé 8 Principe, Sao Thomé 11 Saint Thomas ***Gulf of Mexico:*** 3 Cat 5 Lobos ***Gulf of Panama:*** 3 Rey ***Gulf of St. Lawrence:*** 5 Brion ***Gulf of Thailand:*** 3 Kut 5 Samui ***Haiti:*** 6 Gonave ***Hawaii:*** 4 Maui, Oahu 5 Kauai, Lanai 6 Niihau 7 Molokai 9 Kahoolawe ***Hudson Bay:*** 5 Coats ***Indian Ocean:*** 4 Mahé, Nias 5 Heard, Pemba 7 La Dique, Praslin, Réunion 8 Sri Lanka, Zanzibar 9 Mauritius 10 Madagascar ***Indonesia:*** 4 Bali, Biak, Java, Maja, Muna, Nias, Rhio, Riau, Roma, Roti, Savu, Sawu 5 Batam, Boano, Buton, Djawa, Japen, Lakor, Moena, Riouw, Rotti, Rupat, Sawoe, Solor, Sumba, Wetar, Wokam 6 Butung, Flores, Jappen, Lombok, Madura, Padang, Roepat, Romang, Soemba 7 Celebes, Madoera, Sumatra, Sumbawa 8 Boetoeng, Soembawa, Sulawesi 10 Bandanaira, Banda Neira, Sandalwood ***Inner Hebrides:*** 4 Coll, Eigg, Iona, Jura, Muck, Mull, Skye 5 Canna, Gigha, Islay, Tiree, Tyree ***Ionian group:*** 5 Corfu, Paxos, Zante 6 Cerigo, Ithaca, Leukas, Levkas 10 Santa Maura ***Iran:*** 5 Shahi ***Ireland:*** 4 Aran ***Irish Sea:*** 3 Man ***Italy:*** 4 Elba 6 Sicily 8 Sardinia ***Japan:*** 3 Iki, Uku 4 Naru, Yezo 5 Awaji, Fukae, Fukue, Hondo, Shodo 6 Honshu, Kyushu 7 Shikoku 8 Hokkaido 10 Shodoshima ***Java Sea:*** 4 Laut ***Kiribati:*** 6 Tarawa ***Kuril group:*** 4 Urup 5 Ketoi, Matua 6 Iturup 7 Etorofu, Matsuwa 8 Kunashir 9 Kunashiri ***Lake Champlain:*** 5 Grand ***Lake Erie:*** 9 North Bass, South Bass 10 Middle Bass ***Lake Huron:*** 8 Drummond 10 Manitoulin ***Lake Michigan:*** 3 Hog 4 High 6 Beaver ***Lake Ontario:*** 5 Wolfe ***Lake Superior:*** 4 Sand 6 Royale 7 Manitou ***Lake Winnipeg:*** 5 Hecla ***largest:*** 9 Greenland ***Leeward group:*** 5 Nevis 7 Antigua, Barbuda, Redonda 8 Anguilla, Sombrero 10 Montserrat, Saint Kitts 13 St. Christopher ***legendary:*** 7 Cipango ***Lesser Sundas:*** 4 Alor 5 Ombai ***Leti group:*** 3 Moa 5 Lakor ***Line group:*** 5 Flint 6 Malden, Vostok 7 Fanning, Palmyra 8 Starbuck 9 Christmas ***Long Island Sound:*** 4 City, Hart 5 Goose, Harts ***Loyalty group:*** 3 Uea 4 Lifu, Maré, Uvea 5 Lifou ***Malay Archipelago:*** 5 Kisar, Larat, Timor 6 Borneo 9 New Guinea ***Malaysia:*** 6 Penang, Pinang 13 Prince of Wales ***Malta:*** 4 Gozo ***Marianas:*** 4 Maug, Rota 5 Pagan 6 Saipan ***Marquesas group:*** 4 Eiào, Ua Pu 6 Hatutu, Hiva Oa, Ua Huka 7 Tahuata 8 Fatu Hiva, Nuku Hiva ***Marshall group:*** 5 Wotho, Wotje 8 Eniwetok 9 Kwajalein ***Massachusetts:*** 9 Nantucket ***Mediterranean Sea:*** 4 Elba 5 Corfu, Crete, Malta 6 Cyprus, Euboea, Rhodes, Sicily 7 Corsica 8 Sardinia ***Midway group:*** 4 Sand 7 Eastern ***Moluccas:*** 4 Buru 5 Ambon, Ceram, Seram 6 Boeroe ***Mozambique channel:*** 10 Juan de Nova ***Myanmar:*** 5 Daung, Kadan, Lanbi ***Narragansett Bay:*** 5 Rhode 8 Prudence 9 Aquidneck, Conanicut ***Netherlands:*** 5 Texel 7 Ameland 8 Vlieland ***Netherlands Antilles:*** 7 Curaçao ***New York:*** 4 Fire, Long 9 Gardiners, Roosevelt ***New York Bay:*** 5 Ellis 6 Staten 7 Liberty 9 Governors, Manhattan ***New Zealand:*** 5 South, White 7 Chatham, Stewart 8 D'Urville ***Niagara River:*** 4 Goat ***Nile River:*** 4 Argo, Roda, Ruda 5 Rhoda 6 Rawdah 11 Elephantine ***North Channel:*** 3 Mew ***Northern Cook group:*** 7 Penrhyn 8 Manihiki 9 Tongareva ***North Pacific:*** 4 Wake ***Northwest Territories:*** 5 Banks, Bylot, Devon 8 Bathurst, Melville 9 Ellesmere 10 Cornwallis, Resolution 13 Prince of Wales ***Norwegian:*** 8 Jan Mayen ***Norwegian Sea:*** 5 Donna, Smola, Vikna ***Nova Scotia:*** 5 Sable 10 Cape Breton ***off Alaska:*** 4 Dall 5 Kayak ***off Albania:*** 5 Sazan 6 Saseno ***off Australia:*** 4 Dunk ***off Belize:*** 9 Ambergris ***off Brazil:*** 4 Apeu 5 Rocas ***off British Columbia:*** 4 King, Pitt 9 Vancouver ***off Cape Cod:*** 8 Muskeget 9 Nantucket ***off Chile:*** 5 Guafo, Mocha ***off China:*** 5 Ma-tsu 6 Hainan, Quemoy, Taiwan ***off Crete:*** 3 Dia ***off Ecuador:*** 4 Puna ***off England:*** 3 Man 5 Wight 6 Walney ***off Florida:*** 3 Dog 4 Pine 6 Amelia 7 Pelican, Sanibel 9 Anastasia ***off France:*** 2 If ***off French Guiana:*** 6 Devil's ***off Georgia:*** 10 Cumberland 11 Saint Simons ***off Germany:*** 4 Sylt ***off Greenland:*** 5 Disko ***off Guinea:*** 5 Tombo ***off Hispaniolo:*** 5 Beata ***off Honduras:*** 5 Tigre ***off Iceland:*** 7 Surt-

sey ***off India:*** 5 Sagar ***off Ireland:*** 4 Tory 5 Clare, Clear ***off Kenya:*** 4 Lamu ***off Long Island:*** 7 Fishers ***off Louisiona:*** 5 Marsh ***off Maine:*** 4 Deer, Orrs 5 Swans 8 Monhegan 11 Mount Desert ***off Malay Peninsula:*** 6 Phuket 9 Singapore ***off Maryland:*** 10 Assateague ***off Massachusetts:*** 4 Plum 7 Naushon ***off Mexico:*** 7 Cozumel ***off Mississippi:*** 4 Horn, Ship ***off Mmozambique:*** 3 Ibo ***off New Brunswick:*** 10 Campobello ***off Newfoundland:*** 4 Bell ***off Nigeria:*** 5 Lagos ***off North Carolina:*** 5 Bodie ***off Norway:*** 5 Bomlo, Froya, Hitra, Sotra, Stord, Vardo 8 Hitteren ***off Panama:*** 5 Coiba 6 Parida ***off Poland:*** 5 Wolin 6 Wollin ***off Puerto Rico:*** 4 Crab 7 Culebra, Vieques ***off Rhode Island:*** 5 Block ***off Scotland:*** 4 Bute 5 Arran ***off South Carolina:*** 5 North 6 Parris 10 Hilton Head ***off Sri Lanka:*** 5 Delft ***off Staten Island:*** 7 Hoffman ***off Sumatra:*** 2 We 3 Weh ***off Sweden:*** 5 Graso, Oland, Vaddo ***off Syria:*** 5 Arvad, Arwad, Rouad 6 Aradus ***off Tanzania:*** 5 Mafia, Pemba ***off Tasmania:*** 5 Bruni, Bruny ***off Tunisia:*** 5 Jerba 6 Djerba, Meninx ***off Venezuela:*** 5 Aruba 7 Bonaire 8 Buen Aire ***off Virginia:*** 5 Wreck ***off Wales:*** 5 Caldy 6 Caldey ***Okinawa group:*** 4 Kume ***Orkneys:*** 3 Hoy ***Outer Hebrides:*** 5 Barra, Scarp ***Palmer Archipelago:*** 6 Anvers 7 Antwerp, Brabant ***Pearl Harbor:*** 4 Ford ***Persian Gulf:*** 4 Qeys 5 Kharg, Khark ***Philippines:*** 4 Buad, Cebu, Fuga, Ilin, Poro, Sulu 5 Balut, Batan, Bohol, Coron, Daram, Leyte, Luzon, Panay, Samal, Samar, Sugbu, Talim, Ticao, Verde 6 Negros 7 Masbate, Mindoro, Palawan, Paragua 8 Limasawa, Mindanao 10 Corregidor ***Phoenix group:*** 4 Hull, Mary 6 Birnie, Canton 9 Enderbury ***Puerto Rico:*** 4 Mona ***Quebec:*** 4 Alma ***Queen Charlotte group:*** 7 Moresby ***Red Sea:*** 5 Tiran, Zugur, Zuqar ***Russia:*** 7 Wrangel ***Ryukyu group:*** 7 Okinawa ***St. Lawrence River:*** 4 Hare 5 Jesus 8 Montreal ***San Francisco Bay:*** 5 Angel ***Santa Cruz:*** 5 Anuda, Ndeni 6 Cherry ***Sea of Japan:*** 4 Sado 5 Rebun ***Sea of Marmara:*** 4 Avsa ***second largest:*** 9 New Guinea ***Senegal:*** 5 Gorée ***Seychelles:*** 4 Mahé 7 La Digue, Praslin ***Shetland archipelago:*** 4 Unst, Yell 5 Foula ***Shumagin group:*** 4 Unga ***Sierra Leone:*** 5 Tasso ***Society group:*** 5 Eimeo, Tahaa, Tahao, Taiti 6 Moorea, Tahiti 8 Otaheite ***Solomon group:*** 4 Buka, Gizo, Savo 7 Malaita 11 Guadalcanal 12 Bougainville ***South Atlantic:*** 5 Gough 6 Gough's 11 Saint Helena ***South Korea:*** 5 Cheju ***South of Tokyo:*** 3 Iwo 7 Iwo Jima, Naka Iwo ***South Orkneys:*** 10 Coronation ***South Pacific:*** 3 Hiu 4 Niue 5 Raoul 6 Savage, Sunday 7 Norfolk 8 Pitcairn ***Spitsbergen archipelago:*** 4 Edge ***Strait of Hormuz:*** 5 Qeshm, Qishm ***Sulu Archipelago:*** 4 Jolo 5 Lapac ***Svalbard:*** 4 Hope ***Sverdrup:*** 11 Axel Heiberg 12 Amund Ringnes ***Swedish:*** 3 Ven 4 Hven 5 Hveen, Orust ***Tanzania:*** 8 Zanzibar ***Texas:*** 5 Padre ***Thames River:*** 7 Sheppey ***third largest:*** 6 Borneo ***Tierra del Fuego:*** 5 Hoste ***Tonga:*** 3 Eua, Foa 4 Uiha 5 Haano ***Treasury group:*** 4 Mono ***Truk group:*** 3 Tol 4 Haru, Moen, Udot, Uman 5 Fefan ***Tuamotu Archipelago:*** 4 Anaa 5 Chain ***Turkish:*** 5 Imroz 6 Imbros ***Tuvalu:*** 7 Nanumea 9 Nukufetau ***Tyrrhenian Sea:*** 6 Ischia 11 Montecristo ***Vanuatu:*** 3 Api, Epi, Oba 4 Aoba, Gaua, Tana, Vate 5 Efate, Maewo, Tanna ***Venezuelan:*** 5 Patos 9 La Tortuga ***Virgin group, American:*** 9 Saint John 10 Saint Croix 11 Saint Thomas ***Virgin group, British:*** 5 Peter 6 Norman 7 Anegada, Tortola 11 Jost Van Dyke ***volcanic:*** 5 Tofua 7 Iwo Jima ***Wales:*** 8 Anglesea, Anglesey, Holyhead ***Weddell Sea:*** 4 Ross 6 Hearst ***Western Samoa:*** 5 Upolu 6 Savaii ***West Indies:*** 4 Mona, Saba, Salt 5 Nevis, Peter, Saona 6 Tobago, Tortue 7 Grenada, Tortuga 8 Trinidad 9 Santa Cruz 10 Concepción, Hispaniola, Montserrat Saint Croix; (see also **Bahamas; Greater Antilles; Leeward group; Virgin group; Windward group**)***West of England:*** 7 Ireland ***West Pacific:*** 5 Dyaul, Fauro, Ocean 6 Banaba, Marcus 7 Iwo Jima, Kita Iwo 9 Minami Iwo ***Windward group:*** 10 Martinique ***with former penitentiary:*** 8 Alcatraz

island group ***Alaska:*** 3 Rat 8 Aleutian, Pribilof 9 Andreanof, Catherine ***Aleutians:*** 4 Near ***American Samoa:*** 5 Manua ***Arabian Sea:*** 9 Laccadive ***Arctic Archipelago:*** 8 Sverdrup ***Arctic Ocean:*** 8 Svalbard 12 Novaya Zemlya ***Bahamas:*** 5 Berry, Exuma 6 Bimini ***Banda Sea:*** 5 Damar ***Bangladesh:*** 5 Hatia, Hatya ***Bay of Bengal:*** 7 Andaman, Nicobar ***between England and France:*** 7 Channel ***Bismarck Archipelago:*** 4 Feni 5 Tabar, Tanga ***Bismarck Sea:*** 4 Vitu ***British:*** 7 Bermuda ***Caribbean Sea:*** 4 Swan 5 Pearl 6 Cayman, Perlas, Pigeon 8 Pichones 10 Grenadines West Indies ***Carolines:*** 3 Uap, Yap 4 Truk 5 Nomoi 7 Hogoleu ***Central Pacific Ocean:*** 4 Line 5 Samoa, Union 6 Danger, Midway 7 Phoenix, Tokelau 8 Manihiki 9 Polynesia 12 Northern Cook ***Coral Sea:*** 4 Huon ***Cuba:*** 8 Camaguey ***East of Philippines:*** 10 Micronesia ***East Siberian Sea:*** 4 Bear 8 Medvezhi ***Ecuador:*** 5 Colon 9 Galápagos ***England:*** 5 Farne ***Fiji:*** 3 Lau 7 Eastern ***Formosa Strait:*** 4 Hoko 6 Peng hu **10** Pescadores ***French:*** **5** Salut **6** Safety **9** Kerguelen ***French Polynesia:*** **3** Low **6** Tubuai **7** Austral, Paumotu, Société, Society, Tuamotu **9** Marquesas, Touamotou ***Germany:*** **8** Halligen ***Greece:*** **6** Aegean, Ionian **8** Cyclades **10** Dodecanese **11** Dodecanesus ***Hudson Bay:*** **7** Belcher ***Indian Ocean:*** **7** Aldabra ***Indonesia:*** **4** Asia, Batu, Pagi, Sula **5** Babar, Batoe, Pagai, Pageh, Penju, Spice, Wakde **6** Maluku ***Ireland:*** **4** Aran ***Japan:*** **5** Osumi ***largest:*** **5** Malay **8** Malaysia ***Lesser Antilles:*** **8** Windward ***Malay Archipelago:*** **5** Sunda **6** Soenda ***Mediterranean Sea:*** **8** Baleares, Balearic ***Moluccas:*** **3** Kai, Kei, Obi **4** Leti **5** Banda, Letti **8** Tanimbar **9** Timorlaut ***New Caledonia:*** **7** Loyalty **9** Loyalties ***North of Australia:*** **9** Melanesia ***North of British Isles:*** **5** Faroe **7** Faeroes ***North off Fiji:*** **5** Hoorn **6** Futuna ***North of Madagascar:*** **7** Aldabra **8** Farquhar ***North of New Caledonia:*** **5** Belep ***North of New Guinea:*** **8** Bismarck **9** Admiralty **11** Admiralties ***Northwest Territories:*** **5** Parry ***off Alaska:*** **3** Fox ***off Alaska Peninsula:*** **8** Shumagin ***off Cape Cod:*** **9** Elizabeth ***off eastern Asia:*** **5** Kuril **6** Kurile ***off England:*** **6** Scilly ***off Florida:*** **11** Dry Tortugas ***off Guinea:*** **3** Los **4** Loos ***off Honduras:*** **5** Bahia ***off Morocco:*** **7** Madeira ***off New Guinea:*** **3** Aru **4** Aroe ***off Nicaragua:*** **4** Corn ***off northern Africa:*** **6** Canary **8** Canaries ***off northern Australia:*** **7** Dampier ***off Sicily:*** **5** Egadi **8** Aegadian ***Outer Hebrides:*** **4** Uist ***Pago Pago's:*** **13** American Samoa ***Papua New Guinea:*** **5** Green ***Persian Gulf:*** **4** Tunb ***Philippines:*** **4** Cuyo **5** Tapul **6** Lubang **7** Basilan, Bisayas, Visayan ***Portuguese:*** **6** Azores ***Quebec:*** **8** Magdalen **9** Madeleine ***Ryukyus:*** **5** Amami ***St. Lawrence River:*** **8** Thousand ***Sea of Japan:*** **3** Oki ***Sea of Marmara:*** **5** Kizil **7** Princes **11** Kizil Adalar ***South Atlantic Ocean:*** **8** Falkland, Malvinas ***South China Sea:*** **6** Hirata **7** Paracel, Spratly ***South of New Zealand:*** **8** Auckland ***South Pacific:*** **11** Austronesia ***Sulu Sea:*** **7** Cagayan **9** Cagayanes ***Tonga:*** **5** Vavau ***Tyrrhenian Sea:*** **5** Ponza ***Venezuelan:*** **4** Aves, Bird **9** Los Roques ***West Europe:*** **12** British Isles ***West Indies:*** **6** Virgin **10** Guadeloupe ***West of French Polynesia:*** **4** Cook ***West of Scotland:*** **7** Western **8** Hebrides ***West Pacific Ocean:*** **4** Duff **5** Bonin, Mapia, Palau, Pelew **7** Ladrone, Mariana, Solomon, Vanuatu **8** Marshall, Treasury **9** Ogasawara **10** Saint David

island nation ***Atlantic Ocean:*** **9** Cape Verde ***Indian Ocean:*** **8** Malagasy, Malgache, Sri Lanka **10** Madagascar, Seychelles ***Mediterranean Sea:*** **6** Cyprus ***Mozambique Channel:*** **6** Comoro **7** Comores ***off southern China:*** **6** Taiwan ***south of Greenland:*** **7** Iceland ***West Indies:*** **4** Cuba **7** Jamaica **8** Barbados **10** Saint Lucia ***West Pacific Ocean:*** **5** Nauru ***Windward group:*** **8** Dominica

island province **12** Prince Edward

island state **6** Hawaii

isle see **island**

Ismene ***brother:*** **9** Polynices ***father:*** **7** Oedipus ***mother:*** **7** Jocasta ***sister:*** **8** Antigone ***uncle:*** **5** Creon

isochronous **8** periodic **9** alternate, recurrent, recurring **10** periodical **12** intermittent

isolate **5** alone, apart **6** cut off, detach, enisle, island, remove **7** removed, seclude **8** block off, close off, detached, insulate, pinpoint, separate **9** segregate, sequester **13** unaccompanied

Isolde see **Iseult**

Israel **4** Zion **5** Jacob **6** Canaan **9** Palestine ***capital:*** **9** Jerusalem ***district:*** **5** Haifa **7** Central, Tel Aviv **8** Northern, Southern **9** Jerusalem ***legislature:*** **7** Knesset ***monetary unit:*** **6** shekel

Israelite see **Hebrew; Jewish**

Issachar ***father:*** **5** Jacob ***mother:*** **4** Leah

issue **4** emit, flow, gush, pour, rise, seed, stem, vent **5** arise, birth, brood, child, topic **6** effect, emerge, get out, put out, result, scions, sequel, source, spring **7** descent, edition, emanate, give off, give out, outcome, problem, proceed, progeny, publish, release, subject **8** bulletin, causatum, children, question, throw off **9** offspring, originate, posterity **10** derive from, distribute, end product **11** consequence, descendants, eventuality, progeniture

Istanbul ***ancient name:*** **9** Byzantium ***business section:*** **6** Galata ***country:*** **6** Turkey ***foreign quarter:*** **4** Pera **7** Beyoglu ***park:*** **8** Seraglio ***residential section:*** **7** Uskudar

isthmus ***Africa-Asia:*** **4** Suez ***Greece:*** **7** Corinth ***North America-South America:*** **6** Panama

Italian ***article:*** **2** il, la **3** gli ***automobile:*** **4** Fiat ***cathedral:*** **5** duomo ***condiment:*** **6** tamara ***dialect:*** **6** Tuscan **8** Sicilian ***dictator:*** **9** Mussolini ***family:*** **4** Este **5** Cenci, Savoy **6** Borgia, Medici, Orsini, Pepoli, Sforza **7** Colonna, Gonzaga, Spinola **8** Visconti ***fascist:*** **10** Blackshirt ***game:*** **4** mora **5** bocce, bocci, morra **6** boccie ***gentleman:*** **3** ser **6** signor **7** signore ***highway:*** **10** autostrada ***lady:*** **5** donna **7** signora **9** signorina ***magistrate:*** **7** podesta ***opera house:*** **7** La Scala ***patriot:*** **6** Cavour, Rienzi, Rienzo **7** Mazzini **9** Garibaldi ***reformer:*** **10** Savanarola ***resort:*** **4** Lido **5** Abano, Capri **7** Locarno **8** Sorrento *road:* 6 strada *sausage:* 6 salami *soup:* 10 minestrone *square:* 6 piazza *street:* 3 via 5 corso *weight:* 5 libra, oncia

Italy *capital:* 4 Rome *monetary unit:* 4 lira

itch 4 ache, long, lust, pine, sigh, stew, urge 5 crave, yearn 6 desire, hanker, hunger, seethe, thirst 7 craving, longing, passion 8 appetite, pruritus 9 eroticism, hankering, prurience, pruriency 10 aphrodisia, appetition 11 lustfulness 13 concupiscence, lickerishness *combining form:* 4 psor 5 psoro

itching 8 pruritus 10 avaricious

itchy 5 jumpy 6 grabby, greedy 7 restive 8 covetous, desirous, grasping, prurient 10 prehensile 11 acquisitive

item 3 bit, too 4 also, more, well 5 along, entry, point, scrap, thing, topic 6 detail, matter 7 account, article, besides, element, feature, product 8 clipping, likewise, moreover 9 commodity 10 particular

itemize 4 list 5 count, tally 6 number 7 catalog, specify 8 document, spell out 9 catalogue, enumerate, inventory 10 specialize 13 particularize

iterate 5 renew, resay 6 repeat 7 reprise 10 ingeminate

Ithaca king 8 Odysseus

Ithamar's father 5 Aaron

Ithiel's father 7 Jesaiah

Ithra *son:* 5 Amasa *wife:* 7 Abigail

Ithran's father 6 Dishon, Zophah

Ithream *father:* 5 David *mother:* 5 Eglah

Ithunn's husband 5 Brage, Bragi

itinerant 6 moving, roving 7 migrant, nomadic, ranging, roaming, vagrant 8 ambulant, rambling, shifting, traveler, vagabond, wanderer 9 transient, unsettled, wandering, wayfaring 10 ambulatory 11 perambulant, peripatetic

Ittai's father 5 Ribai

Ivanhoe *author:* 5 Scott *character:* 5 Isaac 6 Cedric, Rowena, Ulrica 7 Rebecca, Wilfred 9 Robin Hood

Ivory Coast 11 Cote d'Ivoire *capital:* 7 Abidjan *monetary unit:* 5 franc

ivory-tower 6 dreamy 8 escapist 11 impractical, unpractical, unrealistic 12 nonrealistic

Ixion *descendant:* 7 Centaur *father:* 8 Phlegyas

Izhar's father 6 Ashhur, Kohath

Izliah's father 6 Elpaal

Izrahiah's father 4 Uzzi

Izri's father 8 Jeduthun

Izziah's father 6 Parosh

J

jaal goat 4 ibex
Jaazaniah's father 4 Azur 5 Azzur 7 Shaphan 8 Jeremiah
jab 3 dig, hit, jog 4 poke, prod, stab 5 nudge, prick, punch 8 puncture
Jabal ***brother:*** 5 Jubal ***father:*** 6 Lamech ***mother:*** 4 Adah
jabber 3 gab, jaw, yak 4 chat 5 clack, Greek 6 babble, drivel, gabble, gibber 7 blabber, chatter, palaver, prattle 8 nonsense 9 gibberish 11 jabberwocky
jabberer 6 gabber, gossip, magpie, prater 7 blabber 8 prattler 9 bandar-log, blabmouth, chatterer 10 chatterbox 12 blabbermouth
Jabberwocky author 7 Carroll (Lewis)
Jabesh's son 7 Shallum
jabot 4 fall 5 frill 6 ruffle
jacamar 4 bird
jacare 6 caiman 9 crocodile
___ jacet 3 hic
Jachin's father 6 Simeon
jack 2 up 3 tar 4 card, flag, hike, jump, lift, salt 5 boost, color, knave, put up, raise 6 banner, ensign, pennon, sailor, seaman 7 mariner, pendant, pennant 8 bannerol, increase, standard, streamer 9 sailorman, tarpaulin
jackal god 5 Apuat 6 Anubis
jackanapes 3 ape 6 monkey 7 coxcomb
jackass 4 dolt, donk, fool, jerk 5 burro, idiot 6 donkey 8 imbecile 10 nincompoop
jackass deer 3 kob 8 antelope
jackdaw 4 bird 7 grackle 9 blackbird
jacket 3 fur 4 coat, Eton, fell, hide, pelt, skin 5 grego, parka, wamus 6 anorak, blazer, bolero, dolman, jerkin, reefer, wammus, wampus 7 cassock, doublet, peacoat, spencer 8 camisole 10 roundabout ***armored:*** 5 acton 7 hauberk 9 habergeon ***cowboy's:*** 8 chaqueta ***Scottish:*** 4 jupe ***sleeveless:*** 4 vest 6 bolero, jerkin 9 waistcoat
jackhammer 5 drill 9 rock drill
jackknife 4 dive 6 barlow ***game:*** 11 mumblety-peg
jackleg lawyer 7 shyster 11 pettifogger
jack-of-all-trades 6 tinker 8 handyman
Jack of clubs 3 pam
jack-o'-lantern 7 pumpkin
jackpot 4 pool 5 award, kitty 7 bonanza 8 windfall 9 pot of gold
jackrabbit 4 hare
Jack's companion 4 Jill
jackstay 3 bar, rod 4 rope 5 horse 7 rigging, support
Jacob ***brother:*** 4 Esau ***daughter:*** 5 Dinah ***father:*** 5 Isaac ***father-in-law:*** 5 Laban ***mother:*** 7 Rebekah ***new name:*** 6 Israel ***son:*** 3 Dan, Gad 4 Levi 5 Asher, Judah 6 Joseph, Reuben, Simeon 7 Zebulun 8 Benjamin, Issachar, Naphtali ***variant:*** 5 James ***wife:*** 4 Leah 6 Rachel
Jacob's rod 8 asphodel
jade 3 fag, gem 4 cloy, fill, glut, minx, pall, sate, slut, snip, tire, wear 5 drain, gorge, hussy, jewel, stone, tramp, weary, wench 6 stodge, wanton 7 fatigue, jezebel, satiate, surfeit, trollop 8 malapert, saucebox, slattern, strumpet, wear down
jaded 4 full, worn 5 sated, tired, weary 6 gorged 7 glutted, satiate, wearied, wornout 8 fatigued, satiated, worn down 9 surfeited
jaeger 4 bird, skua 6 hunter 8 huntsman, rifleman 9 boatswain
Jael ***husband:*** 5 Heber ***victim:*** 6 Sisera
jag 3 bum, dag, tab 4 barb, bolt, bust, soak, tear 5 binge, booze, drunk, notch, prick, souse, spell, spree 6 bender, thrill 7 portion 8 quantity
jagged 5 erose, harsh, rough, sharp 6 craggy, hackly, rugged, uneven 7 scraggy, unlevel 8 asperous, scabrous, unsmooth
___ Jagger 4 Mick
Jaggers' ward 3 Pip
Jahaziah, Jahzeiah ***father:*** 6 Tikvah
Jahaziel's father 9 Zechariah
Jahzeel, Jahziel ***father:*** 8 Naphtali
jai alai 6 pelota ***basket:*** 5 cesta ***court:*** 6 cancha 7 fronton
jail 3 can, jug, pen 4 coop, gaol, keep, poky, stir 6 cooler, immure, intern, lockup, prison 7 confine, freezer, slammer 8 bastille, hoosegow, imprison, rock pile, stockade 9 bridewell, constrain, guardroom 11 incarcerate, reformatory 12 penitentiary
jailbird 3 con 5 loser 7 convict 8 prisoner
jailer 5 guard, screw 6 keeper, warden 7 turnkey

Jair ***father:*** 5 Segub ***grandfather:*** 6 Hezron ***son:*** 7 Elhanan 8 Mordecai
Jakeh's son 4 Agur
jakes 5 privy 8 outhouse 9 backhouse
Jalam ***father:*** 4 Esau ***mother:*** 9 Oholibama
jalopy 3 car, dog 4 auto, heap 5 crate, wreck 6 junker 7 clunker 10 automobile
jalousie 5 blind 6 window 7 shutter
jam 3 fix, ram 4 bear, bind, cram, push, tamp 5 crowd, crush, jelly, press, stuff 6 plight, scrape, squash, squish, squush 7 dilemma, squeeze 8 bar-le-duc, conserve, preserve 9 confiture, marmalade 11 predicament
Jamaica ***capital:*** 8 Kingston ***monetary unit:*** 6 dollar
Jamaican ***export:*** 3 rum ***hair style:*** 10 dreadlocks ***music:*** 3 ska 6 reggae ***nationalist:*** 6 Garvey
James ***brother:*** 4 John 5 Jesus, Joses ***cousin:*** 5 Jesus ***father:*** 7 Zebedee 8 Alphaeus ***mother:*** 4 Mary 6 Salome
James novel 10 Confidence 11 Daisy Miller, The American 12 The Europeans 13 The Bostonians, The Golden Bowl, The Tragic Muse
Jamin's father 6 Simeon
Jammy and ___ 7 Kashmir
Jane Eyre ***author:*** 6 Brontë ***lover:*** 9 Rochester
jangle 3 din, jar 4 ring 5 babel, clash 6 clamor, hubbub, racket, tumult, uproar 7 discord 8 conflict, mismatch 9 disaccord 10 hullabaloo, tintamarre 11 pandemonium 12 disharmonize
jangling 5 harsh 7 grating 9 dissonant 10 discordant
janitor 6 porter 7 charman 9 caretaker, custodian 10 doorkeeper
japan 7 varnish
Japan 5 Nihon 6 Nippon ***capital:*** 5 Tokyo ***monetary unit:*** 3 yen
Japanese ***aborigine:*** 4 Ainu ***apricot:*** 3 ume ***baron:*** 6 daimio, daimyo ***battle cry:*** 6 banzai ***Buddha:*** 5 Amida, Amita ***coin:*** 2 bu 3 rin, sen, yen 4 oban 5 koban, obang 6 kobang ***court:*** 5 dairi ***dancing girl:*** 6 geisha ***dish:*** 5 kombu 7 tempura 8 sukiyaki, teriyaki ***drink:*** 4 sake, saki ***emperor:*** 6 Mikado 8 Hirohito ***festival:*** 3 Bon ***fish:*** 3 ayu, tai 4 fugu ***garment:*** 5 haori 6 kimono ***god:*** 4 kami 5 Ebisu, Hotei 7 Daikoku, Jurojin 8 Bishamon ***goddess:*** 6 Benten 9 Amaterasu ***governor:*** 6 shogun ***grill:*** 7 hibachi ***instrument:*** 4 koto 7 samisen ***martial art:*** 4 judo 6 karate 7 jujitsu, jujutsu ***measure:*** 2 bu, go, jo, mo, ri, se, to 3 boo, cho, ken, rin, sho, sun, tan 4 hiro, koku 5 shaku, tsubo ***monastery:*** 4 tera ***money:*** 3 sen, yen ***persimmon:*** 4 kaki ***plum:*** 6 loquat ***poem:*** 5 haiku, hokku, tanka 6 haikai ***pottery:*** 7 Satsuma ***radish:*** 6 daikon ***religion:*** 6 Shinto 8 Buddhism 9 Shintoism ***rice wine:*** 4 sake, saki ***robe:*** 6 kimono ***samurai clan:*** 5 Taira 8 Minamoto ***servant:*** 6 geisha ***ship:*** 4 maru ***song:*** 3 uta ***suicide:*** 7 seppuku 8 hara-kiri, hari-kari, kamikaze ***sword:*** 5 catan 6 cattan, katana ***theater:*** 2 No 6 Kabuki ***tidal wave:*** 7 tsunami ***tree:*** 4 kiri, kozo, sugi 5 akeki, kiaki 6 hinoki, keyaki ***vehicle:*** 7 ricksha 8 rickshaw ***warrior:*** 7 samurai ***weight:*** 2 mo 3 fun, kin, rin, shi 4 kwan, niyo 5 momme 8 hiyak-kin, hiyaku-me ***wrestling:*** 4 sumo ***writing:*** 4 kana 8 hiragana, katakana ***zither:*** 4 koto
Japanese-American 5 Issei, Kibei, Nisei ***second generation:*** 6 Sansei
jape 3 gag 4 fool, jeer, jest, joke, mock, quip 5 crack, taunt 7 waggery 8 drollery 9 wisecrack, witticism
Japheth ***brother:*** 3 Ham 4 Shem ***father:*** 4 Noah ***son:*** 5 Gomer, Javan, Madai, Magog, Tiras, Tubal 7 Meshech
Japhia's father 5 David
jar 4 bump, ewer, jolt, olla, vase 5 clash, crash, cruse, quake, shake, shock, smash, upset 6 impact, jangle, jounce, tinaja, tremor 7 discord, terrine, tremble, vibrate 8 conflict, gallipot, mismatch 9 collision, container, disaccord, vibration 10 concussion 12 disharmonize ***ancient:*** 6 hydria, krater 7 amphora 8 lecythus, lekythos, lekythus ***Egyptian:*** 7 canopic ***long-necked:*** 6 goglet ***Mexican:*** 6 pinata ***Philippine:*** 5 banga
jardiniere 3 pot, urn 4 vase 5 stand 7 garnish 9 flowerpot
Jared ***father:*** 10 Mahalaleel ***son:*** 5 Enoch
jargon 4 cant 5 argot, idiom, lingo, slang 6 patois, patter, pidgin 7 chatter, dialect, lexicon, palaver, twitter 8 language 9 gibberish 10 dictionary, vernacular, vocabulary 11 terminology ***lawyer's:*** 8 legalese
jarl 4 earl 5 chief, noble 8 nobleman
jarring 3 dry 5 harsh, rough 6 hoarse 7 grating, rasping, raucous 8 strident 9 dissonant 10 discordant, stridulent, stridulous
Jashub's father 4 Bani 8 Issachar
jasmine 4 vine 5 shrub 6 flower 7 perfume
Jason ***father:*** 5 Aeson ***helper:*** 5 Medea ***lover:*** 6 Creusa, Glauce, Glauke ***quest:*** 12 Golden Fleece ***ship:*** 4 Argo ***shipmate:*** 8 Argonaut ***teacher:*** 6 Chiron 7 Cheiron ***uncle:*** 6 Pelias ***wife:*** 5 Medea
jasper 6 morlop, quartz 10 chalcedony
jaundice 4 bias 7 disease, icterus 9 prejudice ***combining form:*** 5 icter 6 ictero ***Scottish:*** 7 gulsach

jaunt 4 perk, ride, trip 5 sally 6 junket, outing, ramble 7 journey, joyride 9 excursion
jaunty 4 airy 5 light, perky 7 perkish 8 debonair 9 sprightly 10 nonchalant
java 6 coffee
Java almond 7 talisay
Java cotton 5 kapok
Java jute 5 kenaf
Javanese *carriage:* 4 sado *civet:* 5 rasse *instrument:* 5 saron 6 bonang, gender 7 gamelan *measure:* 4 paal *skunk:* 6 teledu *tree:* 4 upas 7 gondang *village:* 4 desa 5 dessa
Javan squirrel 8 jelerang
Java plum 5 jaman 6 jambul 7 jambool
javelin 5 lance, shaft, spear 6 weapon 7 assagai, assegai, harpoon
Javert's prey 7 Valjean
jaw 3 gab, wig, yak 4 chat, rail, rate, talk 5 baste, clack, prate, scold 6 babble, berate, gabble 7 chatter, prattle, upbraid 9 yakety-yak 10 tongue-lash *relating to:* 7 gnathal, gnathic
jawbone 7 maxilla 8 mandible
jawbreaker 5 candy
jay 4 bird, hick, jake, rube 5 clown, dandy 6 rustic 7 bumpkin, hayseed 9 greenhorn
Jayhawker 6 Kansan, outlaw 9 guerrilla *State:* 6 Kansas
jazz 4 guff, jive 5 bebop, swing 6 boogie 7 ragtime 8 malarkey, nonsense *up:* 7 enliven 10 popularize
jealous 5 green 7 envious, envying 8 doubting 9 demanding, green-eyed, invidious 10 possessive, possessory, suspicious 11 distrustful, mistrustful
Jecoliah's Son 6 Uzziah
Jediael's father 8 Benjamin
Jedidah *husband:* 4 Amon *son:* 6 Josiah
jeer 4 gibe, gird, jest, jibe, mock 5 fleer, flout, scoff, sneer, taunt 6 deride, quip at 7 scout at 8 ridicule
Jeeves *creator:* 9 Wodehouse *employer:* 7 Wooster (Bertie) *position:* 5 valet 6 butler
Jefferson *home:* 10 Monticello *state:* 8 Virginia
Jehiel *father:* 4 Elam 8 Hachmoni 11 Jehoshaphat *son:* 7 Obadiah 10 Shechaniah
Jehizkiah's father 7 Shallum
Jehoaddan's Son 7 Amaziah
Jehoahaz *brother:* 9 Jehoiakim *father:* 4 Jehu 6 Josiah 7 Jehoram *mother:* 7 Hamutal *son:* 5 Joash 7 Jehoash
Jehohanan *father:* 5 Bebai 6 Tobiah 8 Eliashib *son:* 7 Ishmael
Jehoiada *father:* 6 Paseah 7 Benaiah *son:* 7 Benaiah *wife:* 9 Jehosheba
Jehoiakim *father:* 6 Josiah *mother:* 7 Zebidah *son:* 10 Jehoiachin
Jehoram *brother:* 7 Ahaziah *father:* 4 Ahab 11 Jehoshaphat *kingdom:* 5 Judah *slayer:* 4 Jehu *wife:* 8 Athaliah
Jehoshaphat *father:* 3 Asa 6 Ahilud, Nimshi, Paruah *father-in-law:* 4 Ahab *son:* 4 Jehu 7 Jehoram *wife:* 8 Athaliah
Jehosheba *father:* 7 Jehoram *husband:* 8 Jehoiada *sister:* 7 Ahaziah *son:* 5 Joash
Jehovah 3 God 5 Yahwe 6 Adonai, Elohim, Yahweh
Jehozabad's father 8 Obededom
Jehozadak see **Jozadak**
Jehu 6 driver *father:* 6 Hanani 11 Jehoshaphat *grandfather:* 6 Nimshi *son:* 8 Jehoahaz *victim:* 5 Joram 7 Jehoram
Jehudijah's husband 5 Mered
Jehush *father:* 4 Esau 5 Eshek 6 Bilhan, Shimei 8 Rehoboam *mother:* 10 Oholibamah
jejune 4 dull, flat 5 banal, bland, inane, trite, vapid 7 insipid, sapless, tenuous 9 innocuous 10 namby-pamby 12 milk-and-water
Jekyll's alter ego 4 Hyde
jell 3 set 4 clot 6 gelate 7 congeal, pectize, thicken 9 coagulate 10 gelatinize
jelly 3 gel, set 4 clot, pulp 5 aspic 6 gelate, pectin, spread 7 congeal, gelatin, pectize, thicken 9 coagulate 10 gelatinize
jellyfish 3 sop 4 baby 5 sissy 6 medusa 7 acaleph, doormat, medusan, milksop 8 medusoid, weakling 10 pantywaist 11 Milquetoast, mollycoddle 12 invertebrate
Jemimah's father 3 Job
Jemuel's father 6 Simeon
jennet 3 ass 5 hinny, horse 6 donkey
jeopardize 4 risk 5 peril 6 expose, hazard, menace 7 imperil 8 endanger 10 compromise
jeopardy 4 risk 5 peril 6 danger, hazard, menace 7 imperil 8 endanger, exposure 9 liability 10 compromise
Jephthah's father 6 Gilead
Jephunneh's son 5 Caleb
jeremiad 6 lament, tirade 8 diatribe, harangue 9 complaint, philippic
Jeremiah *daughter:* 7 Hamutal *father:* 8 Hilkiath 10 Habaziniah *scribe:* 6 Baruch *son:* 8 Jaazniah
Jericho's conqueror 6 Joshua
Jerimoth *daughter:* 8 Mahalath *father:* 5 David
Jerioth's husband 5 Caleb
jerk 3 ass, lug, tic 4 fool, snap, yank 5 idiot, lurch, ninny, throw, wrest, wring 6 twitch, wrench 7 flounce, jackass, tomfool 9 vellicate 10 nincompoop
jerked beef 7 charqui
jerkin 4 coat 6 jacket 9 gyrfalcon
jerky 4 meat 5 inane, wagon 7 charqui, foolish, jolting 8 saccadic

Jeroboam ***father:*** **5** Joash, Nebat ***foe:*** **6** Abijam **8** Rehoboam ***mother:*** **6** Zeruah ***son:*** **5** Nadab **9** Zechariah
Jerome's Bible **7** Vulgate
jersey **3** cow **5** shirt **6** tricot **7** sweater **8** pullover **10** undershirt
Jerusalem **4** Sion, Zion **5** Salem **8** Holy City ***hill:*** **4** Sion, Zion **6** Moriah ***market:*** **4** souk ***mosque:*** **4** Omar ***pool:*** **6** Siloam **8** Bethesda
Jerusalem artichoke **5** tuber **7** girasol **8** girasole **9** sunflower
Jerusalem thorn **5** shrub **6** retama **7** catechu **9** horsebean
Jerusha ***father:*** **5** Zadok ***husband:*** **6** Uzziah ***son:*** **6** Jotham
Jeshaiah ***father:*** **7** Athalia **8** Hananiah, Jeduthun, Rehabiah ***son:*** **6** Ithiel
Jeshua ***father:*** **7** Jozadek ***son:*** **4** Ezer
jess **5** strap
Jesse ***daughter:*** **7** Abigail, Zeruiah ***father:*** **4** Obed ***grandfather:*** **4** Boaz ***son:*** **4** Ozem **5** David, Eliab, Elihu **6** Raddai **7** Shammah **8** Abinadab, Nethanel ***youngest son:*** **5** David
Jessica ***father:*** **7** Shylock ***husband:*** **7** Lorenzo
jest **3** fun, gag, kid, rag, rib **4** butt, game, gibe, gird, jape, jeer, joke, josh, mock, play, quip, razz **5** chaff, crack, fleer, flout, scoff, sneer, sport **6** banter, quip at **7** mockery, scout at, waggery **8** derision, drollery, ridicule **9** pilgarlic, wisecrack, witticism **13** laughing stock
jester **3** wag, wit **4** fool **5** clown, comic, droll, idiot, joker **6** motley **8** comedian, funnyman, humorist, jokester, quipster
Jesuit's founder **6** Loyola **8** Ignatius
jet **4** ebon, inky **5** black, ebony, plane, raven, sable, sprit, spurt **6** engine, splurt, squirt **8** airplane, fountain **9** pitch-dark
Jether ***father:*** **4** Ezra **6** Gideon, Zophah ***son:*** **5** Amasa
Jethro ***daughter:*** **8** Zipporah ***son-in-law:*** **5** Moses
jetsam **7** flotsam **8** wreckage **9** driftwood
jettison **4** cast, dump, junk, shed **5** scrap **6** reject, slough **7** cashier, discard, dumping, junking **8** abdicate, disposal, riddance **9** scrapping, throw away **10** discarding
jetty **4** dock, ebon, inky, pier, quay, slip **5** berth, black, ebony, groin, levee, raven, sable, wharf **9** pitch-dark **10** pitch-black
Jew **6** Essene, Semite **8** Judahite **9** Israelite
jewel **3** gem **5** adorn, begem, beset, bijou, ideal, stone **7** paragon, phoenix **8** nonesuch, ornament **9** nonpareil; (see also **gem**)
jeweler **8** lapidary, lapidist ***famous:*** **7** Tiffany
jewelry **10** bijouterie ***artificial:*** **5** glass, paste **6** strass **7** costume ***piece:*** **3** pin **4** ring **6** brooch **7** earring **8** bracelet, lavalier, necklace, tieclasp **9** lavaliere ***set:*** **6** parure
Jewish ***bread:*** **5** matzo **6** matzoh, matzos **8** afikomen ***ceremony:*** **5** berit, brith **6** berith **10** bar mitzvah ***combining form:*** **5** Judeo **6** Judaeo ***doctrine:*** **6** Mishna **7** Mishnah ***liturgy:*** **6** maarib, maariv, minhah **7** minchah **9** shaharith ***New Year:*** **11** Rosh Hashana ***organization:*** **8** Hadassah **9** B'nai B'rith ***pioneer:*** **6** halutz **7** chalutz ***prayer book:*** **6** mahzor, siddur **7** machzor ***sabbath:*** **8** Saturday ***scripture:*** **6** Talmud ***synagogue:*** **4** shul **5** schul ***teacher:*** **5** rabbi **6** Hillel; (see also **Hebrew**)
jezebel **4** jade, slut **5** hussy, tramp, trull, wench **6** wanton **7** trollop **8** slattern, strumpet
Jezebel ***father:*** **7** Ethbaal ***home:*** **5** Sidon ***husband:*** **4** Ahab ***slayer:*** **4** Jehu ***victim:*** **6** Naboth
Jezer's father **8** Naphtali
Jezreel's father **5** Hosea
jib **3** gag, shy **4** balk, sail **5** demur, stick
jibe **2** go **5** agree, fit in, tally **6** accord, square **7** conform **8** dovetail **9** harmonize **10** correspond
jiffy **5** crack, flash, hurry, shake, trice **6** minute, moment, second **7** instant **9** breathing **11** split second
jig **4** hook, play, ploy, ruse, wile **5** dance, feint, trick **6** device, gambit **7** gimmick
jigger **3** cup **4** boat **5** gizmo, glass **6** dingus, doodad, gadget, widget **7** concern, dofunny, gimmick, thingum **9** doohickey, shot glass
jiggle **5** shake **9** oscillate
jigsaw **4** tool **6** puzzle
jihad **3** war **6** strife **7** crusade, holy war **8** campaign
jilt **6** reject **7** abandon, cast off, discard
jim-dandy **5** nifty **8** knockout **9** humdinger
jimmy **3** bar, pry **4** open **5** lever **7** crowbar
jingle **4** ring, song **5** chime, chink, clink, verse **6** tinkle **7** chinkle
jinn **5** afrit, genie **6** afreet, spirit, yaksha
jinx **3** hex **5** charm, curse, spell **6** hoodoo, voodoo, whammy **7** evil eye
jitters **5** jumps, panic **6** dither, nerves, shakes **7** shivers, willies **9** whim-whams **13** heebie-jeebies
jittery **5** jumpy, nervy **6** goosey, spooky **7** fidgety, nervous **9** unrestful **10** high-strung
jive **3** kid **4** jazz, talk **5** dance, music, swing **6** jargon
Joab ***brother:*** **6** Asahel **7** Abishai ***father:***

7 Seraiah, Zeruiah ***slayer:*** 7 Benaiah ***uncle:*** 5 David ***victim:*** 5 Abner, Amasa
Joah ***father:*** 5 Asaph 6 Joahaz, Zimmah 8 Obededon ***son:*** 4 Eden
Joanna's husband 5 Chuza
Joan of Arc ***birthplace:*** 7 Domremy ***epithet:*** 7 Pucelle 13 Maid of Orleans ***victory:*** 7 Orleans
Joan's husband 5 Darby
Joash ***father:*** 4 Ahab 7 Ahaziah 8 Jehoahaz ***son:*** 6 Gideon 7 Amaziah 8 Jeroboam ***victim:*** 9 Zechariah
job 4 dupe, duty, fool, gull, hoax, line, post, spot, task, work 5 berth, chare, chore, place, stint, trade 6 befool, billet, devoir, effort, office, pigeon 7 calling, chicane, posting, pursuit 8 business, flimflam, position, sinecure, taskwork, vocation 9 bamboozle, situation, victimize 10 assignment, connection, employment, engagement, occupation, profession 11 appointment
Job ***daughter:*** 6 Keziah 7 Jemimah ***father:*** 8 Issachar ***friend:*** 6 Bildad, Zophar 7 Eliphaz ***home:*** 2 Uz
Jobab's father 5 Zerah 6 Joktan 9 Shaharaim
jobber 6 trader 10 contractor, wholesaler
job-training program 4 CETA
Jocasta ***daughter:*** 6 Ismene 8 Antigone ***husband:*** 5 Laius 7 Oedipus ***son:*** 7 Oedipus 8 Eteocles 9 Polynices
Jochebed ***brother:*** 6 Kohath ***father:*** 4 Levi ***husband:*** 5 Amram
jockey 4 play 5 rider, trick 7 beguile, exploit, finesse 8 maneuver 10 manipulate ***famous:*** 5 Baeza (Braulio) 6 Arcaro (Eddie), Murphy (Isaac), Pincay (Laffit) 7 Cauthen (Steve), Cordero (Angel), Hartack (Bill), Longden (Johnny) 8 McHargue (Darrel), Turcotte (Ron) 9 Shoemaker (Willie)
jocular 3 gay 5 comic, jolly, merry, silly, witty 6 blithe, jocose, jovial 7 comical, playful 8 cheerful, humorous, sportive 9 facetious
jocularity 4 glee 5 mirth 7 jollity 8 hilarity 9 jocundity, joviality, merriment
jocund 3 gay 5 jolly, merry 6 blithe, jovial 7 festive, gleeful, playful 8 mirthful, sportive 10 blithesome 12 lighthearted
Joel ***brother:*** 6 Nathan ***father:*** 4 Nebo 5 Ladan 6 Samuel, Zichri 7 Azariah, Pedaiah, Pethuel ***son:*** 5 Heman
jog 3 dig, jab, run 4 lope, poke, prod, trot 5 nudge, punch, shake 6 remind
jogger 6 layboy, runner
joggle 5 dowel, joint, notch, shake 6 jostle
Johanan ***father:*** 6 Josiah, Kareah, Tobiah 8 Eliashib, Elioenai, Hakkatan ***son:*** 7 Azariah
john 2 WC 4 head 5 privy 6 toilet 7 latrine 8 lavatory 11 convenience, water closet
John ***father:*** 5 Accos, Simon 10 Mattathias ***son:*** 5 Peter 9 Eupolemus 10 Mattathias; (see also **John the Baptist; John the Evangelist**)
John ***Irish:*** 4 Sean
John Hancock 9 autograph, signature
Johnson's biographer 7 Boswell
John the Baptist ***father:*** 9 Zacharias ***mother:*** 9 Elisabeth
John the Evangelist ***brother:*** 5 James ***father:*** 7 Zebedee ***mother:*** 6 Salome
join 3 fay, mix, tie, wed 4 abut, ally, bind, bond, fuse, knot, line, link, mate, weld, yoke 5 affix, blend, march, marry, merge, piece, touch, unify, unite, verge 6 attach, border, butt on, couple, enlist, enroll, fasten, relate, sign up, splice 7 bracket, combine, connect 8 coagment, coalesce, compound, concrete, neighbor 9 associate, coadunate, conjugate, integrate
joint 3 ell, hip, tie 4 butt, crux, dive, knee, link, seam 5 ankle, elbow, hinge, scarf, union, wrist 6 common, mutual, public, shared, suture 7 hangout, knuckle, shiplap 8 abutment, communal, conjunct, coupling, junction, juncture, shoulder 9 honky-tonk 10 connection ***combining form:*** 5 arthr 6 arthro, condyl 7 condylo ***disease:*** 9 arthritis 10 rheumatism ***prefix:*** 2 co
join up 5 enter 6 enlist, enroll, muster, sign up
joist 4 beam, stud 6 timber 7 sleeper, support
joke 3 fun, gag, kid, pun, rag, rib, wit, yak 4 butt, dido, fool, game, jape, jest, josh, mock, play, quip, razz 5 antic, caper, crack, humor, jolly, prank, sally, sport 6 banter, jestee, parody 7 mockery, sarcasm, waggery 8 badinage, derision, drôlerie, drollery, repartee 9 burlesque, pilgarlic, wisecrack, witticism 10 caricature 11 monkeyshine 13 laughing stock ***stale:*** 8 chestnut
joker 3 wag, wit 4 card, zany 5 clown, comic, cutup, droll 6 gagman, jester 7 farceur 8 comedian, funnyman, humorist, quipster
Jokshan ***father:*** 7 Abraham ***mother:*** 7 Keturah ***son:*** 5 Dedan, Sheba
Joktan ***brother:*** 5 Peleg ***father:*** 4 Eber ***son:*** 4 Obal 5 Ophir
jollity 3 fun 4 glee, play, romp 5 cheer, mirth, revel, sport 6 frolic, gaiety, gambol 7 disport, revelry, rollick, whoopee 8 hilarity, reveling 9 festivity, jocundity, joviality, merriment, revelment 10 blitheness, jocularity 11 merrymaking
jolly 3 fun, gay, kid, rag, rib 4 glad, jest, josh, razz 5 chaff, merry 6 banter, blithe, jocund, jovial 7 festive, gleeful, jocular, play-

ful, roguish, waggish **8** mirthful, sportive **10** blithesome, frolicsome

Jolly Roger **4** flag **6** ensign ***user:*** **6** pirate

jolt **3** jar, nip, tot **4** blow, bump, dram, drop, shot, slug **5** clash, crash, knock, shake, shock, snort **6** impact, jounce **7** snifter, startle **8** toothful **9** collision

Jonadab ***cousin:*** **5** Amnon ***father:*** **6** Rechab **7** Shimeah ***uncle:*** **5** David

Jonah **4** jinx **7** prophet ***father:*** **7** Amittai ***son:*** **5** Peter, Simon ***swallower:*** **5** whale

Jonathan ***brother:*** **7** Johanan ***father:*** **4** Jada, Saul **6** Joiada, Kareah, Uzziah **7** Absolom, Shimeah **8** Abiathar **10** Mattathias ***friend:*** **5** David

Jones, John Paul ***ship:*** **15** Bonhomme Richard ***victim:*** **7** Serapis

jongleur **4** bard **6** singer **8** minstrel **10** troubadour

jonquil **8** daffodil **9** narcissus

Jonson play **6** The Fox **7** Epicene, Volpone

Joram ***brother:*** **7** Ahaziah ***father:*** **3** Toi **4** Ahab **11** Jehoshaphat ***slayer:*** **4** Jehu ***son:*** **7** Ahaziah

Jordan ***capital:*** **5** Amman ***king:*** **7** Hussein ***monetary unit:*** **5** dinar

jorum **3** cup, jug **4** bowl

Joseph ***brother:*** (see Jacob, son) ***buyer:*** **8** Potiphar ***father:*** **5** Asaph, Jacob **9** Zacharias **10** Mattathias ***mother:*** **6** Rachel ***son:*** **5** Jesus **7** Ephraim **8** Manasseh ***wife:*** **4** Mary **7** Asenath

Joseph's coat **6** coleus **7** tampala

josh **3** fun, guy, kid, rag, rib **4** jest, joke, razz **5** chaff, jolly, tease **6** banter

Joshua's father **3** Nun

Joshua tree **5** yucca

Josiah ***father:*** **4** Amon **9** Zephaniah ***mother:*** **7** Jedidah ***son:*** **8** Jehoahaz **9** Jehoiakim

joss **4** idol **5** image

Jo's sister **3** Amy, Meg **4** Beth

jostle **3** jar, jog **4** push **5** elbow, press, shove **6** hustle **8** bulldoze, shoulder

jot **3** bit **4** atom, iota, whit **5** grain, minim, speck **6** tittle **7** modicum, smidgen, smidgin **8** particle, smidgeon

jot down **4** note **5** write

Jotham ***father:*** **6** Gideon, Jahdai, Uzziah ***mother:*** **8** Jerushah

joule component **3** org

jounce **3** jar, jog **4** bump, jolt **5** shock **6** impact, wallop **9** collision **10** concussion

journal **3** log **5** diary, organ, paper **6** record, review **7** gazette **8** magazine **9** newspaper **10** periodical

journalist **3** Bly (Nellie) **4** Will (George F.) **5** Baker (Russell) **6** Bierce (Ambrose), Ephron (Nora), Kennan (George), Murrow (Edward R.), Reston (James), Runyon (Damon), Shirer (William L.), Zenger (John Peter) **7** Cousins (Norman), Greeley (Horace), Gunther (John), Mencken (H. L.), Pearson (Drew), Tarbell (Ida), Trillin (Calvin) **8** Anderson (Jack), Atkinson (Brooks), Garrison (William Lloyd), Lippmann (Walter), Pulitzer (Joseph), Steffens (Lincoln), Thompson (Dorothy), Winchell (Walter) **9** Hohenberg (John), Watterson (Henry)

journey **2** go **3** hie **4** eyre, fare, pass, tour, trek, trip, wend **5** jaunt, sally **6** cruise, junket, push on, repair, safari, travel, voyage **7** odyssey, proceed, travels **8** progress **9** excursion **10** expedition, pilgrimage ***route:*** **9** itinerary

joust **4** tilt **5** fight **6** combat **10** tournament ***arena:*** **8** tiltyard

Jove see Jupiter

jovial see jocular

jowl **3** jaw **5** cheek **6** dewlap, wattle **8** mandible

joy **4** glee **5** bliss, mirth **6** gaiety **7** delight, ecstasy, elation, rapture **8** fruition, gladness, pleasure **9** enjoyment **11** delectation

Joyce, James ***birthplace:*** **6** Dublin ***character:*** **5** Bloom (Leopold), Bloom (Molly) **7** Dedalus (Stephen) ***work:*** **6** Exiles **7** Ulysses **9** Dubliners **13** Finnegans Wake

joyful see joyous

joyous **3** gay **4** glad **5** happy, merry **7** buoyant, festive, gleeful **8** ecstatic, mirthful **9** delighted, rapturous **12** lighthearted

Jozabad's father **6** Jeshua **7** Pashhur

Jozacar ***mother:*** **8** Shimeath ***victim:*** **5** Joash

Jozadak's son **6** Jeshua

Jubal ***father:*** **6** Lamech ***mother:*** **4** Adah

jubilant **6** elated **8** exultant, exulting **9** cock-a-hoop, triumphal **10** cock-a-whoop, triumphant

jubilate **5** exult, glory **7** delight, triumph

Judah ***brother:*** (see Jacob, son) ***father:*** **5** Jacob ***king:*** **3** Asa **4** Ahaz, Amon **5** Joash **6** Abijam, Josiah, Jotham, Uzziah **7** Ahaziah, Amaziah, Jehoram **8** Hezekiah, Jehoahaz, Manasseh, Rehoboam, Zedekiah **9** Jehoiakim **10** Jehoiachin **11** Jehoshaphat ***mother:*** **4** Leah ***son:*** **2** Er **4** Onan **6** Shelah

Judas **7** traitor ***father:*** **5** Simon **7** Chalphi **10** Mattathias ***replacement:*** **8** Matthias ***suicide place:*** **8** Aceldama, Akeldama

judge **3** put, ref, try, ump **4** call, draw, make, rule, test **5** check, court, infer **6** critic, decide, deduce, derive, gather, jurist, reckon, settle, umpire **7** arbiter, collect, justice, make out, referee **8** conclude, critique, doomster, estimate, mediator, sentence **9** arbitrate, criticize, determine **10** adjudicate, arbitrator, chancellor, magistrate, negotiator, reconciler **11** approximate, conciliator 12 intermediary ***Athenian:*** 6 dicast 7 heliast ***bench:*** 4 banc ***chamber:*** 6 camera ***gown:*** 4 robe, toga ***in Hades:*** 5 Minos 6 Aeacus 12 Rhadamanthys ***mallet:*** 5 gavel ***Muslim:*** 4 cadi 5 mufti

judgment 4 doom 5 award, sense, stock, taste 6 acumen, ruling, wisdom 7 insight, opinion, verdict 8 decision, estimate, gumption, illation, sagacity, sequitur 9 appraisal, criticism, deduction, good sense, inference 10 assessment, astuteness, conclusion, discretion, estimation, evaluation, horse sense, shrewdness 11 common sense, discernment 12 appraisement, perspicacity 13 determination, ratiocination

Judgment Day 8 doomsday

judicial 8 critical 10 judgmental ***assembly:*** 5 court ***document:*** 4 writ

judicious 4 fair, sage, sane, wise 7 prudent, sapient 8 rational, sensible 9 equitable, judgmatic, objective, sagacious 10 reasonable 13 dispassionate

Judith ***father:*** 5 Beeri ***home:*** 8 Bethulia ***husband:*** 4 Esau ***victim:*** 10 Holofernes

Judy's husband 5 Punch

jug 3 jar, pen 4 coop, ewer, jail, toby 5 gotch 6 cooler, immure, intern, lockup, prison, urceus 7 confine, pitcher 8 bastille, demijohn, imprison 9 constrain 11 incarcerate

jug band instrument 5 kazoo 6 bottle 7 washtub 9 stovepipe, washboard

Juggernaut's temple 4 Puri

juggle 5 bluff 6 betray, delude, humbug, illude, take in 7 beguile, deceive, mislead, shuffle

juice 3 sap 4 fuel, must, stum 5 cider, fluid 7 essence, vinegar 8 vitality 10 succulence 11 electricity ***combining form:*** 3 opo 4 chyl 5 chyli, chylo ***fermented:*** 4 wine 5 cider ***Scottish:*** 4 broo

juicy 4 racy 7 piquant 9 succulent

juju 4 luck, zemi 5 charm 6 amulet, fetish, mascot 7 periapt 8 talisman 10 phylactery

jujube 3 ber 7 gumdrop, lozenge

julep 5 drink

Julian's epithet 8 Apostate

Juliet ***betrothed:*** 5 Paris ***father:*** 7 Capulet ***lover:*** 5 Romeo

July 14 11 Bastille Day

jumble 3 mix, pie 4 hash, mess, olio 5 mix up, shake, snafu 6 foul up, litter, medley, mess up, muddle, muss up 7 clutter, confuse, derange, disturb, rummage, shuffle, snarl up 8 disorder, mishmash, pastiche, scramble 9 patchwork, potpourri 10 assortment, disarrange, miscellany, salmagundi 11 disorganize, gallimaufry

jumbo 4 huge 5 giant 6 mighty 7 mammoth 8 colossal, enormous, gigantic 9 cyclopean 10 prodigious 11 elephantine

jump 3 hop, lop 4 bolt, hike, jink, leap, loup 5 boost, bound, lunge, put up, raise, vault 6 bounce, hurdle, jack up, pounce, spring 7 saltate, startle 8 increase

jumper 5 dress, shirt, smock 6 blouse, jacket

jumping 7 saltant

jumping frog county 9 Calaveras

jump over 8 leapfrog

jumps 6 dither, shakes 7 jitters, shivers, willies 9 whim-whams 13 heebie-jeebies

jumpy see jittery

junction 4 seam 5 joint, union 6 suture 7 joining, meeting 8 coupling 9 concourse, gathering 10 concursion, confluence, connection

juncture 4 pass, seam 5 joint, pinch, point, union 6 crisis, moment, strait 7 instant, joining 8 coupling, exigency, zero hour 9 emergency 10 connection, crossroads 11 contingency 12 turning point

june bug 6 beetle

jungle 3 web 4 hash, knot, mash, maze, mesh 5 skein, snarl 6 jumble, litter, morass, muddle, tangle 7 clutter, mizmaze, rummage 8 mishmash, scramble 9 labyrinth

Jungle, The ***author:*** 8 Sinclair (Upton) ***locale:*** 7 Chicago

Jungle Books, The ***author:*** 7 Kipling ***character:*** 6 Mowgli ***python:*** 3 Kaa

juniper 4 cade, tree 5 cedar, larch, retem, savin

junk 4 boat, cast, dope, drug 5 offal, scrap, trash, waste 6 debris, kelter, litter, refuse, reject, slough 7 cashier, discard, garbage, rubbish, wash out 8 jettison, throw out 9 narcotics, throw away

junker 4 heap 5 crate, noble, wreck 6 jalopy 10 aristocrat

junket 4 trip 5 jaunt, sally 6 outing, picnic 9 excursion 10 roundabout

junkyard 4 dump

Juno ***bird:*** 7 peacock ***epithet:*** 6 Moneta; (see also Hera)

Junoesque 5 curvy 7 rounded 9 curvesome 10 curvaceous 11 curvilinear 13 well-developed

junta 5 group 7 council 9 committee 10 government

junto 5 cabal, group 7 coterie, faction

Jupiter 4 Jove, Zeus ***angel:*** 7 Zadkiel ***cupbearer:*** 8 Ganymede ***daughter:*** 5 Venus 7 Minerva ***epithet:*** 6 Fidius, Fulgur, Stator, Tonans 7 Pluvius ***father:*** 6 Saturn ***lover:*** 2 Io 6 Europa 8 Callisto ***mother:*** 3 Ops ***satellite:*** 2 Io 6 Europa 8 Callisto, Ganymede ***son:*** 5 Arcas 6 Castor, Pollux ***temple:*** 7 Capitol ***wife:*** 4 Juno

Jurgen *author:* 6 Cabell *trade:* 10 pawnbroker
juridical 5 legal 8 juristic
jurisdiction 3 law, see 4 sway 5 might, power, range, reach, scope, venue 6 county, domain, parish, sphere 7 command, compass, control, diocese, mastery 8 dominion, province 9 authority, bailiwick, territory 10 domination *suffix:* 3 dom
jurisprudence 3 law
jury 5 panel 9 committee *decision:* 7 verdict
just 3 all, apt, due, fit 4 even, fair, good, meet, only, true 5 equal, happy, legal, quite, right, sharp 6 as well, barely, cogent, hardly, honest, in toto, merely, proper, scarce, simply, square, wholly 7 condign, exactly, fitting, merited, totally, upright, utterly 8 all in all, deserved, faithful, rightful, scarcely, squarely, suitable, unbiased 9 befitting, equitable, expressly, honorable, impartial, justified, objective, precisely, requisite, uncolored, veracious, veridical 10 accurately, altogether, completely, felicitous, legitimate, scrupulous 11 appropriate, undistorted, well-founded 12 unprejudiced, well-grounded 13 conscientious, dispassionate, rhadamanthine
justice 3 law 5 court, judge 6 equity 7 honesty 8 evenness, fairness 10 magistrate 12 impartiality
justification 6 excuse, reason 7 account, apology, defense 8 apologia 9 rationale 10 apologetic 11 explanation
justify 5 argue, claim 6 assert, defend, excuse, uphold, verify 7 account, bear out, confirm, contend, explain, support, warrant 8 maintain, validate 9 vindicate 11 corroborate, explain away, rationalize 12 authenticate, substantiate
justly 4 well 5 fitly 6 nicely 7 rightly 8 decently, properly 9 correctly, fittingly 10 decorously 11 befittingly
jut 4 hang, poke, pout 5 bulge, jetty, pouch 6 beetle 7 project 8 bend over, lean over, overhang, protrude, stand out, stick out 9 outthrust 10 projection, protrusion 12 protuberance
jute 5 gunny 6 burlap 7 sacking *Indian:* 4 desi
Juvenal's forte 6 satire
juvenile 3 kid 5 child, green, young, youth 6 callow, infant, moppet, unripe 8 immature, young one, youthful 9 unfledged, youngling, youngster 11 undeveloped
juvenility 5 youth 7 puberty 9 greenness, youthhood 10 pubescence, springtide, springtime 11 adolescence 12 youthfulness
juxtaposed 8 abutting, adjacent, touching 9 adjoining, bordering 10 approximal, contiguous 12 conterminous

K

kabob 7 shaslik 8 shashlik 9 shashlick
kaddish 6 cantor, prayer
kady 3 hat 5 derby
Kafka, Franz ***character:*** 4 Olga 5 Samsa (Gregor) 6 Joseph (K.) ***novel:*** 7 Amerika 8 The Trial 9 The Castle
kaiser 5 ruler 7 emperor, monarch 9 sovereign
kaka 6 parrot
kakariki 6 lizard 8 parakeet
kakatoe 6 parrot 8 cockatoo
kale 4 cole 7 cabbage, collard 8 borecole, colewort
kaleidoscopic 7 diverse, various 8 colorful 10 variegated
Kali ***aspect:*** 5 Durga 7 Parvati ***husband:*** 4 Siva 5 Shiva
kalium 9 potassium
Kama ***god of:*** 4 love ***mount:*** 6 parrot 7 sparrow ***wife:*** 4 Rati
kambal 5 shawl 7 blanket
kamik 4 boot
kamikaze 7 suicide 8 airplane, suicidal
kampong 6 hamlet 7 village
Kampuchea see Cambodia
kangaroo 4 euro 6 leaper 7 bettong, wallaby 8 boongary, wallaroo 9 marsupial 10 macropodid ***herd:*** 3 mob ***male:*** 6 boomer ***young:*** 4 joey
kangaroo bear 5 koala
kangaroo rat 7 potoroo
kans 5 grass 6 glagah
Kansas ***capital:*** 6 Topeka ***college:*** 5 Tabor ***fort:*** 5 Riley ***largest city:*** 7 Wichita ***nickname:*** 14 Jayhawker State, Sunflower State ***prison:*** 11 Leavenworth
kaolin 4 clay
kapelle 5 choir 9 orchestra
kaput 6 ruined 7 done for 8 defeated, finished 9 destroyed
karakul 5 sheep
karakurt 6 spider 9 black wolf
Kareah's son 7 Johanan 8 Jonathan
karma 4 aura 5 force, power 6 spirit
kaross 3 rug 7 garment
kasha 4 mush 5 grain
katabasis 7 retreat 9 troparion
Katharina ***father:*** 8 Baptista ***suitor:*** 9 Petruchio
Katrina's suitor 9 Brom Bones 12 Ichabod Crane
katydid 6 insect 11 grasshopper
katzenjammer 6 clamor, nausea 8 hangover, headache
kava 3 awa 5 shrub 6 pepper
kayak 4 boat 5 canoe
kayo 8 knockout
Kazantzakis hero 5 Zorba
kea 6 parrot
Keats poem 5 Lamia 8 Endymion, Hyperion, Isabella, To Autumn 11 Ode to Psyche
kedge 6 anchor
keel 4 boat, drop, fall, ship 5 barge, pitch, ridge, slump, upset 6 carina, go down, plunge, topple, tumble 7 capsize 8 overturn 11 centerboard
keelbird 3 ani
keen 4 agog, avid, wail, yowl 5 acute, alert, eager, honed, nutty, sharp, smart 6 ardent, bewail, clever, fervid, gung ho, lively, shrewd 7 animate, anxious, athirst, fervent, thirsty, whetted, zealous 8 animated, appetent, spirited 9 impatient, perfervid, sensitive, sprightly, unblunted, vivacious 10 breathless, perceptive, razor-sharp 11 penetrating, penetrative, quick-witted, sharp-witted 12 enthusiastic, quick-sighted, sharp-sighted
keenness 3 wit 4 edge 6 acumen 9 sharpness 10 astuteness, shrewdness 11 discernment, penetration, percipience 12 incisiveness, perspicacity
keep 3 own, pen 4 curb, fend, have, hold, jail, mind, obey, save 5 carry, check, stock 6 bridle, comply, detain, direct, follow, hold in, living, lockup, manage, ordain, prison, retain 7 abstain, alimony, carry on, conduct, conform, control, forbear, inhibit, observe, operate, possess, refrain, reserve, support 8 conserve, hold back, hold down, maintain, preserve, restrain, withhold 9 celebrate, constrain, solemnize 10 livelihood, sustenance 11 commemorate, maintenance, subsistence
keep back 3 dam 4 deny, hold, save 6 detain, refuse, retain, retard 7 reserve 8 disallow, withhold
keeper 5 guard 6 custos, pastor, warden 7 curator 8 cerberus, claviger, guardian, watchdog 9 constable, custodian
keeping 4 care, ward 5 trust 6 charge,

saving 7 custody 9 salvation 10 caretaking 12 conservation, guardianship
keep on 7 persist 8 continue 9 persevere
keep out 3 bar 4 hold 5 debar 6 detain, retain 7 reserve 8 hold back, withhold
keepsake 5 relic, token 6 trophy 7 memento 8 giftbook, memorial, reminder, souvenir 11 remembrance 12 remembrancer
keep up 7 sustain 8 continue, maintain, preserve
keeve 3 tub, vat 4 kier 5 basin
kef 4 hemp 7 languor, tobacco 10 dreaminess 12 tranquillity
keg 3 tun 4 butt, cask, pipe 6 barrel 7 barrico 8 hogshead
kegler 6 bowler
keister, keester 7 satchel 8 buttocks, suitcase
keitloa 5 rhino
keloid 4 scar
kelp 3 ash 4 agar, alga 5 varec 7 seaweed
Kemuel ***father:*** 5 Nahor ***mother:*** 6 Milcah ***son:*** 9 Hashabiah
ken 4 view 5 grasp, range, reach, scope, sight 7 horizon, purview 10 perception
kenaf 4 hemp, jute 6 ambari 8 hibiscus
kench 3 bin 9 enclosure
Kenilworth author 5 Scott
kennel 3 den 4 pack 5 drain, house, sewer 6 gutter 7 confine, shelter 9 enclosure
keno 4 game ***similar to:*** 5 beano, bingo, lotto
Kentucky ***capital:*** 9 Frankfort ***largest city:*** 10 Louisville ***nickname:*** 14 Bluegrass State ***state bird:*** 8 cardinal ***state flower:*** 9 goldenrod
Kentucky bluegrass 3 poa
Kenya ***capital:*** 7 Nairobi ***monetary unit:*** 8 shilling
kepi 3 cap
kerchief 6 hankie 8 babushka, bandanna, headrail, kaffiyeh ***Scottish:*** 5 curch
kerf 3 cut 4 slit 5 notch 6 groove
kermis 4 fair 8 carnival, festival
kernel 3 nub, nut 4 core, crux, gist, meat, pith, seed 5 grain 6 matter, nubbin, upshot 7 nucleus 9 substance ***combining form:*** 4 cary, kary 5 caryo, karyo
Kerouac novel 6 Big Sur 9 On the Road
kestrel 4 bird, hawk 6 falcon, fanner 9 windhover
ketch 4 boat 8 sailboat
ketone 5 irone 7 acetone, camphor, muscone 8 acridone, butanone, civetone
kettle 3 pot, vat 6 vessel 7 caldron, marmite, pothole 8 cauldron, flambeau
kettledrum 5 naker, party 6 timbal, tymbal ***Arabian:*** 6 atabal
Keturah's husband 7 Abraham
kevel 5 cleat, staff 6 cudgel, hammer, timber 7 bollard
key 3 cay 4 isle, reef, tone 5 islet, pitch, vital 6 clavis, cotter, island, legend, opener, samara, spline, ticket 7 central, digital 8 critical, passport, password, solution, tonality 9 important 10 open sesame ***combining form:*** 5 clavi, clavo, cleid 6 cleido ***notch:*** 4 ward
keyboard 6 manual 7 clavier 8 pedalier 10 claviature
key fruit 6 samara
key man 9 locksmith
keynote 4 tone 5 theme, tonic 7 feature
keynoter 6 orator 7 speaker
Keystone State 12 Pennsylvania
Keziah's father 3 Job
khaki 5 cloth, color 7 uniform
khamsin 4 wind
khan 5 chief, ruler 9 chieftain, sovereign
khedive 5 ruler 7 viceroy
Khomeini, e.g. 4 imam
Ki ***brother, consort:*** 2 An ***mother:*** 5 Nammu ***son:*** 5 Enlil
kiang 3 ass
kibble 4 meal 5 grain, grind
kibbutz 4 farm 7 commune 10 collective, settlement
kibe 4 chap 5 crack 9 chilblain
kibitzer 5 prier, pryer, snoop 6 butt-in 7 meddler 8 busybody, observer, quidnunc 9 spectator 10 pragmatist, rubberneck
kick 4 bang, boot, fuss, punt, wail 5 whine 6 except, murmur, object, repine, thrill, wallop 7 grumble, protest 8 complain 11 expostulate, remonstrate
kicker 4 crab 5 crank 6 griper, grouch, punter 7 growler 8 grumbler, sorehead, sourpuss 10 complainer
kick off 4 open 5 begin, start 6 launch 8 commence, embark on, initiate 10 embark upon, inaugurate
kick out 2 ax 4 drop, fire, sack 5 chase, chuck, eject, evict 6 bounce 7 boot out, cashier, dismiss, extrude 8 throw out 9 discharge
kickshaw 3 toy 5 goody, treat 6 bauble, dainty, morsel, tidbit, titbit, trifle 8 delicacy
kid 3 bud, fun, guy, rag, rib 4 dupe, fool, gull, hoax, jest, joke, josh, razz 5 child, jolly, trick, youth 6 banter, befool, moppet 8 flimflam, hoodwink, juvenile, young one 9 bamboozle, youngling, youngster
kidnap 6 abduct, waylay 8 shanghai 10 spirit away
kidney 5 gland, organ ***combining form:*** 4 reni, reno 5 nephr 6 nephro 7 nephron, nephros ***Scottish:*** 4 neer
kidney-shaped 8 reniform

kielbasa 7 sausage
kier 3 vat
kilderkin 3 keg 4 cask 6 barrel
kilim 3 mat, rug 6 carpet
kill 3 zap 4 bane, down, hang, slay, veto 5 croak, scrag, shoot 6 cut off, finish, lay low, murder, poison, stifle 7 butcher, destroy, execute, garrote, put away, take off 8 carry off, dispatch, immolate, massacre, negative, strangle 9 non-placet, sacrifice, slaughter 10 annihilate 11 assassinate, exterminate
killer 6 gunman, hit man, slayer 7 torpedo 8 assassin, homicide, murderer ***combining form:*** 4 cide 6 ctonus
killer whale 4 orca 7 grampus
killing 5 blood 6 murder 8 foul play, homicide 9 slaughter 12 manslaughter ***combining form:*** 5 cidal ***of a race:*** 8 genocide ***of bacteria:*** 11 bactericide ***of brother:*** 10 fratricide ***of father:*** 9 parricide, patricide ***of king:*** 8 regicide ***of mother:*** 9 matricide ***of self:*** 7 suicide ***of sister:*** 10 sororicide
Kilmer poem 5 Trees
kiln 4 bake, burn, fire, oast, oven 7 furnace
kilt 5 skirt 7 filabeg, filibeg 8 fillebeg ***fabric:*** 5 plaid 6 tartan
kilter 4 trim 5 order, shape 6 fettle, repair 7 fitness 9 condition
kimono 4 gown, robe ***sash:*** 3 obi
kin 3 sib 4 clan, folk, race, sept 5 stock, tribe 6 family 7 kindred, lineage, related 8 kinsfolk, relation, relative 9 cousinage
kind 3 ilk, way 4 good, mild, sort, type, warm 5 breed, class, genre, genus, order 6 benign, gender, genial, gentle, humane, kidney, nature, stripe, tender 7 affable, amiable, clement, cordial, feather, lenient, species, variety 8 merciful, obliging, tolerant 9 benignant, character 10 altruistic, benevolent, charitable, forbearing, propitious, responsive 11 complaisant, considerate, description, good-hearted, good-humored, good-natured, openhearted, sympathetic, warmhearted 12 eleemosynary, good-tempered, humanitarian 13 compassionate, philanthropic
kindle 4 fire, move, stir, wake, whet 5 light, rally, rouse, waken 6 arouse, awaken, bestir, excite, foment, ignite, incite 7 inflame, provoke 9 challenge, instigate, stimulate
kindliness 5 amity 6 comity 8 goodwill 10 friendship 11 benevolence 12 friendliness
kindly 4 well 6 benign 7 benefic 8 friendly, gracious 9 attentive, benignant, heedfully 10 generously, neighborly 11 considerate, good-hearted 12 thoughtfully 13 considerately
kindness 5 favor 7 service 8 clemency, courtesy, goodwill, sympathy 10 indulgence 11 benevolence 12 dispensation
kindred 3 sib 4 akin, clan, folk, race, sept 5 house, stock, tribe 6 agnate, allied, family 7 cognate, connate, lineage, related 8 incident 10 affiliated, connatural 11 consanguine
king 3 rex 4 czar, tsar 5 baron, mogul, ruler 6 tycoon 7 magnate, monarch 9 sovereign ***Albanian:*** 3 Zog 7 William ***Assyrian:*** 6 Sargon 11 Sennacherib, Shalmaneser ***Babylonian:*** 6 Sargon 9 Hammurabi 10 Belshazzar ***Belgian:*** 6 Albert 7 Leopold 8 Baudouin ***Bohemian:*** 9 Wenceslas 10 Wenceslaus ***Damascus:*** 8 Benhadad ***Danish:*** 4 Abel, Eric, Gorm, Hans, John, Olaf 5 Sweyn 6 Canute, Harold, Magnus 8 Nicholas, Waldemar 9 Christian, Frederick 11 Christopher ***Dutch:*** 7 William ***Egyptian:*** 3 Tut 4 Pepi, Seti 5 Khufu, Menes, Necho 6 Cheops, Ramses 7 Harmhab, Osorkon, Psamtik, Ptolemy 8 Ikhnaton, Thothmes, Thutmose 9 Amenhotep, Sesostris 11 Tutankhamen ***English:*** 4 John 5 Henry, James 6 Alfred, Canute, Edmund, Edward, Egbert, George, Harold 7 Charles, Richard, Stephen, William 8 Ethelred 9 Athelstan, Ethelbald, Ethelbert ***French:*** 3 Odo, roi 4 John 5 Henry, Louis, Pepin, Raoul 6 Philip, Robert, Rudolf 7 Charles, Francis, Lothair 9 Hugh Capet 11 Charlemagne ***German:*** 4 Karl 5 Louis 6 Lothar, Ludwig 7 Charles, Lothair ***Greek (modern):*** 4 Paul 6 George 9 Alexander 11 Constantine ***Hawaiian:*** 10 Kamehameha ***Hungarian:*** 6 Attila ***Indian:*** 4 raja 5 rajah ***Irish:*** 9 Brain Boru ***Italian:*** 7 Humbert ***Jordanian:*** 5 Talal 7 Hussein 8 Abdullah ***Judah:*** (see at **Judah**) ***Judean:*** 5 Herod ***Lydian:*** 5 Gyges 7 Croesus 8 Alyattes ***Norwegian:*** 4 Eric, Erik, Inge, Olaf 5 Sweyn 6 Haakon, Harald, Harold, Magnus, Sigurd, Sverre ***Ostrogothic:*** 9 Theodoric ***Persian:*** 5 Cyrus 6 Darius, Xerxes ***Portuguese:*** 4 John 5 Henry, Louis, Peter 6 Carlos, Edward, Manuel, Sancho 7 Alfonso 9 Ferdinand, Sebastian ***Prussian:*** 7 Wilhelm, William 9 Frederick, Friedrich ***relating to:*** 5 regal, royal ***Saudi Arabian:*** 4 Saud 6 Faisal 9 Abdul-Aziz ***Scottish:*** 4 John 5 David, Edgar, James 6 Duncan 7 Macbeth, Malcolm, William 9 Alexander, Donalbane 10 David Bruce 11 Robert Bruce ***Spanish:*** 3 rey 5 Louis 6 Philip 7 Alfonso, Amadeus, Charles 9 Ferdinand ***Spartan:*** 8 Leonidas ***Swedish:*** 4 Eric, John 5 Oscar 6 Birger, Gustav, Haakon, Magnus 7 Charles 8 Gustavus, Waldemar 9 Frederick, Sigismund, Sten Sture ***Visigothic:*** 6 Alaric
King Arthur ***birthplace:*** 8 Tintagel ***chroni-***

cler: 8 Geoffrey *court site:* 7 Camelot 8 Caerleon *deathplace:* 6 Camlan *father:* 5 Uther *father-in-law:* 9 Laodogant, Leodegran 11 Leodegrance *foster father:* 5 Ector *jester:* 7 Dagonet *knight:* 3 Kay 4 Bors 5 Balan, Balin 6 Gareth, Gawain, Modred 7 Galahad, Geraint, Lamerok, Mordred, Tristan 8 Bedivere, Lancelot, Parsifal, Percival, Tristram 9 Percivale *lance:* 3 Ron *last abode:* 6 Avalon *last name:* 9 Pendragon *magician:* 6 Merlin *mother:* 6 Ygerne 7 Igraine *nephew:* 6 Gareth, Modred 7 Mordred *queen:* 9 Guinevere *shield:* 7 Pridwin *sister:* 7 Morgain 11 Morgan le Fay *slayer:* 6 Modred 7 Mordred *son:* 6 Modred 7 Mordred *steward:* 3 Kay *sword:* 9 Excalibur *victim:* 6 Modred 7 Mordred *wife:* 9 Guinevere

king crab 7 limulus

kingdom 5 realm 6 domain, empire 7 demesne

kingfish 4 cero 7 croaker, whiting 8 mulloway

kingfisher 4 bird 6 alcedo, dacelo 7 halcyon 10 kookaburra

kingly 5 regal, royal 6 lordly, regnal 8 imperial, majestic, powerful, puissant 9 imperious, masterful, monarchal, sovereign 10 monarchial 11 monarchical

King Philip 9 Metacomet

Kingsley play 7 Dead End 10 Men in White

Kingu *consort:* 6 Tiamat *slayer:* 6 Marduk

kink 4 bend, curl, turn, whim 5 cramp, crick, quirk, snarl, twist 6 buckle, tangle 12 imperfection

kinky 3 odd 5 outré, ultra, weird 6 far-out 7 bizarre, crooked, deviant, strange, twisted 10 outlandish

kiosk 5 booth 8 pavilion 9 newsstand 11 summerhouse

kip 3 bed 4 hide, pelt, skin 5 sleep

Kipling, Rudyard *trio:* 3 rag 4 bone 10 hank of hair *work:* 3 Kim, 6 L'Envoi 8 Gunga Din, Mandalay 10 Fuzzy Wuzzy 11 Recessional 13 Soldiers Three, The Jungle Book

kirsch 6 brandy

kirtle 4 coat, gown 5 dress, tunic

Kish *father:* 3 Ner 4 Abdi 5 Abiel, Jeiel 6 Jehiel *son:* 4 Saul

kismet 3 lot 4 doom, fate 5 moira, weird 7 destiny, portion 12 circumstance

kiss 4 buss, peck, skim 5 brush, graze, shave, smack 6 glance, smooch 8 osculate

kisser 4 face 5 mouth

Kiss sculptor 5 Rodin

kit 3 bag, box, set 6 outfit 7 package 9 container 10 collection

kitchen 6 galley 7 cuisine 8 scullery *appliance:* (see at appliance) *boss:* 4 chef; (see also cooking)

kite 4 bird, hawk, sail 5 scram 6 begone, decamp, get out 7 skiddoo, take off 8 clear out, hightail 9 skedaddle

kith 7 friends, kindred 9 neighbors

kittenish 3 coy 6 elvish, frisky, impish 7 coltish, larkish, playful, roguish 8 prankish 10 frolicsome 11 mischievous

kitty 3 cat, pot 4 pool 6 feline, stakes 7 jackpot

kiwi 4 bird 5 fruit 7 apteryx

kleptomaniac 5 thief 10 shoplifter

klutz 3 oaf 4 gawk, lout, lump 5 looby 6 lubber, lummox 7 lobster, palooka 9 schlemiel

knack 3 set 4 bent, gift, hang, head, nose, turn 5 skill, swing, trick 6 genius, talent 7 ability, aptness, command, know-how, mastery 8 facility 9 dexterity, expertise, expertism 10 expertness, mastership

knapsack 3 bag 4 case, pack 8 backpack, packsack, rucksack 9 haversack

knave 4 heel, jack 5 rogue, scamp 6 rascal, varlet 7 lowlife, villain 8 coistrel 9 miscreant, scoundrel 10 blackguard

knavery 5 fraud 8 mischief, trickery, villainy 9 rascality

knavish 5 lying 6 shifty 7 roguish 8 unhonest 9 deceitful, dishonest 10 mendacious, untruthful

knee 4 genu 5 joint *armor:* 6 poleyn *bend:* 5 kneel 9 genuflect *bone:* 7 patella

kneeler 5 stool 7 cushion 8 prie-dieu

knell 4 bong, peal, ring, toll 5 chime 6 summon 7 warning

knickknack 3 toy 4 dido 5 curio, virtu 6 bauble, gadget, gewgaw, trifle 7 bibelot, novelty, trinket, whatnot 8 gimcrack, souvenir 9 bric-a-brac, objet d'art 11 rattletraps

knife 3 cut, ulu 4 bolo, shiv, stab 5 blade, bowie, corer, gouge, panga, slice, sword 6 barong, colter, coutel, cutter, dagger, kuttar, parang, sickle 7 cleaver, couteau, machete, whittle 8 yataghan *case:* 6 sheath *maker:* 6 cutler 7 grinder *surgical:* 6 catlin 7 catling, scalpel 8 bistoury

knifelike 5 acute, sharp 8 piercing, shooting, stabbing

knight 3 dub, sir 5 eques 6 ritter 8 cavalier, chessman, horseman 9 caballero, chevalier *code:* 8 chivalry *competition:* 7 listing, tilting 8 jousting 10 tournament *flag:* 6 pennon 8 gonfalon, gonfanon *legendary:* 8 douzeper *servant:* 4 page 5 valet 6 squire *title:* 3 sir *wife:* 4 lady

knighthood 8 chivalry

knightly 5 brave, noble 7 gallant 10 chivalrous

Knight of the Round Table see King Arthur

Knight of the Rueful Countenance 10 Don Quixote

knit 4 bind, heal, join, mend, purl 5 plait, unite, weave 6 cement, stitch 7 conjoin, crochet, wrinkle 8 contract 10 intertwine

knitting 9 handiwork *material:* 4 yarn *stitch:* 3 rib 4 purl 6 garter 11 stockinette *tool:* 6 needle

knob 3 bun, bur, nub 4 bump, burr, dial, hill, lump, node, peak, umbo 5 bulge, gnarl, knoll, mound 6 button, finial, handle, nubble, pommel 7 hillock 12 protuberance *combining form:* 3 tyl 4 tylo 6 condyl 7 condylo

knobkerrie 3 bat 4 club, mace 5 billy 6 cudgel 7 war club 8 bludgeon 9 billy club, truncheon

knock 3 bob, hit, rap, tap 4 blow, bump, lick, skin, swat, tunk, wipe 5 blame, clout, pound, swipe, thump 7 censure, condemn 8 denounce 9 criticize, reprehend, reprobate 10 denunciate

knock down 3 get, win 4 drop, earn, fell, gain, make 5 floor, level 6 ground, lay low 7 acquire, bring in, flatten 8 bowl over

knocker 5 momus 6 carper, critic, Zoilus 7 caviler 9 aristarch 10 criticizer 11 faultfinder

knock off 4 do in, halt, quit, stop, take 5 cease 6 deduct, desist, finish, murder 7 execute, put away, take off, take out 8 discount, draw back, give over, leave off, subtract, surcease, take away 9 liquidate, substract 11 assassinate, discontinue

knockout 2 K.O. 4 kayo 5 dandy, peach 6 beauty, eyeful, looker, lovely 7 stunner 8 jim-dandy 9 humdinger 11 crackerjack

knock over 3 rob 4 down, drop, fell, loot 5 floor, rifle, upset, whelm 6 ground, lay low, topple 7 flatten, overset, plunder, ransack, stick up, tip over 8 bowl down, overcome, overturn 9 bring down, overpower, overthrow, overwhelm, prostrate

knoll 4 hill, knob 5 mound 7 hillock

knot 3 bow, tie, web 4 bond, bump, burr, link, loop, lump, maze, mesh, node, snag, yoke 5 bunch, gnarl, hitch, nexus, skein, snarl 6 jungle, morass, tangle 7 mizmaze 8 ligament, ligature, vinculum 9 labyrinth *in fiber:* 3 nep *kind:* 4 bend, loop, slip 5 hitch, honda 6 granny, splice, square 7 bowline

knotty 4 hard 5 rough, tough 6 daedal, rugged, sticky, uphill 7 complex, gordian, twisted 8 involved, terrible 9 Byzantine, difficult, effortful, elaborate, intricate 10 formidable 11 complicated 12 labyrinthine

knout 4 flog, lash, whip

know 3 see, wot 4 feel 5 grasp, savor, sever, taste 6 fathom, intuit, suffer 7 cognize, discern, realize, sustain, undergo 8 separate 9 apprehend, extricate, recognize 10 apperceive, appreciate, comprehend, difference, discrepate, experience, severalize, understand *Scottish:* 3 ken

knowable 5 lucid 8 luminous 9 graspable 10 cognizable, fathomable 11 cognoscible 12 intelligible 13 apprehensible

know-how 3 art 5 craft, knack, skill 7 ability, command, cunning, mastery 9 dexterity, expertise, expertism 10 adroitness, expertness, mastership

knowing 3 hep, hip 4 gash, sage, wise 5 alive, awake, aware, blasé, canny, quick, sharp, slick, smart 6 brainy, bright, clever, sophic 7 gnostic, witting, worldly 8 mondaine, sensible, sentient 9 brilliant, cognizant, conscious, insighted, observant, sagacious, world-wise 10 conversant, discerning, insightful, perceptive 11 intelligent, quick-witted, ready-witted, sharp-witted, worldly-wise 12 apprehensive, disenchanted, disentranced, nimble-witted, sophisticate 13 disillusioned, sophisticated *combining form:* 7 gnostic 9 gnostical

know-it-all 6 smarty 7 wise guy 8 wiseacre, wisehead 10 smart aleck 11 smartypants, wisecracker, wisenheimer

knowledge 4 data, lore, news 5 facts 6 wisdom 7 science 8 evidence, learning 9 cognition, education, erudition 10 cognizance 11 information, scholarship 12 intelligence 13 enlightenment *combining form:* 5 gnosy, sophy 6 gnosia, gnosis *from meditation:* 5 jnana *lack of:* 9 ignorance *mystical:* 6 gnosis *suffix:* 3 ics *systematized:* 7 science *universal:* 8 pansophy 9 pantology

knowledgeable 4 sage, wise 5 sharp, smart 6 brainy, bright, clever, sophic 7 gnostic, knowing 9 brilliant, insighted, sagacious 10 discerning, insightful, perceptive 11 intelligent, quick-witted, ready-witted

know-nothing 4 dolt, dope, rude 5 dummy, dunce, idiot 6 dimwit 7 lackwit, pinhead, wantwit 8 ignorant, untaught 9 benighted, ignoramus, untutored 10 illiterate, uneducated, unlettered 11 empty-headed

knuckle 5 joint *combining form:* 6 condyl 7 condylo

knucklehead 5 dunce 8 clodpate, numskull 10 thickskull

knuckle under 3 bow 4 cave 5 defer, yield 6 submit 7 succumb 10 capitulate

knurl 4 bead, knob, knot 5 ridge

K.O. 4 kayo 8 knockout

koan 7 paradox

kobold 5 gnome 6 goblin, spirit, sprite

Kohath ***father:*** 4 Levi ***sister:*** 8 Jochebed ***son:*** 5 Izhar
Kohinoor 7 diamond
kohlrabi 6 turnip 7 cabbage
kola 3 nut 7 extract
Kolaiah's son 4 Ahab
komatik 4 sled 6 sledge
kook 3 nut 5 crank 6 cuckoo 7 lunatic 8 crackpot 9 ding-a-ling, harebrain, screwball 10 crackbrain
kopeck 4 coin ***one hundred:*** 5 ruble
Korah ***father:*** 4 Esau 7 Eliphaz ***mother:*** 10 Oholibamah
Koran ***chapter:*** 4 sura ***revealer of:*** 7 Gabriel ***scholar:*** 5 ulama, ulema
Korea see **North Korea; South Korea**
Korean ***dynasty:*** 2 Yi ***national dish:*** 6 kimchi
kosher 3 fit 4 pure 5 clean 6 proper 7 genuine 10 legitimate
Koussevitzky 5 Serge 6 Sergei 9 conductor
kowtow 4 fawn 5 cower, toady 6 cringe, grovel 7 honey up, truckle 8 bootlick 11 apple-polish
kraal 3 hut, pen 6 corral 8 manyatta 9 enclosure
krater 6 vessel ***ovoid:*** 6 kelebe
Kriemhild ***brother:*** 7 Gunther ***husband:*** 5 Etzel 6 Attila 9 Siegfried ***slayer:*** 10 Hildebrand ***victim:*** 5 Hagen
kris 6 dagger
Krishna ***avatar of:*** 6 Vishnu ***brother:*** 8 Balarama ***father:*** 8 Vasudeva ***mother:*** 6 Devaki ***uncle:*** 5 Kansa ***victim:*** 5 Kansa
Krupp works site 5 Essen
krypton ***symbol:*** 2 Kr
kudize 4 hail 6 praise 7 acclaim, applaud, commend 9 recommend 10 compliment
kudo 7 bouquet, orchids 10 compliment
kudos 4 bays 5 award, badge, glory, honor 6 praise, renown 7 laurels 8 accolade, eminence, prestige 10 decoration, prominence, prominency 11 distinction
kudu 8 antelope
kukri 5 sword
kumquat 5 fruit ***kin:*** 6 orange
kusu 5 mouse
kuttar 6 dagger
kvass 4 beer
kylin 7 unicorn
kylix 3 cup 7 chalice
kyphosis 8 humpback 9 hunchback

L

Laadah ***father:*** **6** Shelah ***grandfather:*** **5** Judah
laager **4** camp, tent **6** encamp **7** bivouac
Laban ***daughter:*** **4** Leah **6** Rachel ***father:*** **7** Bethuel ***grandfather:*** **5** Nahor ***sister:*** **7** Rebekah
label **3** tag **4** band, mark **6** marker, ticket **8** classify ***adhesive:*** **7** sticker
labium **3** lip
labor **3** tug **4** moil, task, toil, work **5** drive, grind **6** strain, strive **7** slavery, travail **8** bullwork, drudgery, endeavor, slogging, struggle **10** birth pangs, childbirth, donkeywork **12** childbearing ***group:*** **3** AFL, CIO **5** ILGWU, union ***leader:*** **5** Hoffa, Lewis, Meany **6** Chavez **7** Gompers, Reuther **8** Randolph
laboratory ***device:*** **4** etna **5** flask **6** beaker, mortar, pestle, retort **7** pipette **8** crucible, test tube **12** Bunsen burner
laborer **3** man **4** hand, peon **5** hunky, navvy **6** bohunk, toiler, worker **7** workman **8** workhand **9** operative **10** roustabout, workingman ***Mexican:*** **7** bracero ***Oriental:*** **5** cooly **6** coolie
laborious **4** hard **5** heavy **6** uphill **7** arduous, labored, onerous, operose **8** toilsome **9** difficult, effortful, strenuous **10** burdensome
La Brea **4** pits **7** tar pits ***fossil:*** **10** sabertooth
labyrinth **3** web **4** knot, maze, mesh **5** skein, snarl **6** jungle, morass, tangle **7** mizmaze ***builder:*** **8** Daedalus ***monster:*** **8** Minotaur
labyrinthine **6** daedal, knotty **7** complex, gordian **8** involved, tortuous **9** Byzantine, elaborate, intricate **11** complicated
lace **3** net, tat, tie **4** beat, cord, lash, trim **5** adorn, braid, frill, liven, plait, twine **6** defeat, fabric, fasten, ribbon, string, thrash, thread **7** entwine, tatting **8** decorate, openwork **9** embroider **10** embroidery, intertwine, shoestring **11** needlepoint ***edge:*** **5** picot ***ground:*** **6** réseau ***into:*** **5** abuse **6** attack **7** condemn ***kind:*** **6** bobbin **7** Alençon, guipure, Maltese, Mechlin **8** Argentan, Brussels, Venetian **9** Chantilly **10** colberteen, colbertine **11** needlepoint **12** Valenciennes ***make:*** **3** tat ***pattern:*** **5** toilé
Lacedaemon **6** Sparta
lacerate **3** cut, rip **4** rend, tear **5** wound **6** mangle, pierce
lachrymose **3** sad **5** teary, weepy **7** tearful, weeping **8** mournful
lack **4** need, want **6** dearth, defect **7** absence, default, deficit, failure, require **8** shortage, underage **9** privation **10** deficiency, inadequacy, scantiness
lackadaisical **4** idle, lazy, limp **7** dieaway, languid, passive **8** fainéant, indolent, listless, romantic, slothful **9** enervated, incurious **10** languorous, spiritless
lacking **3** shy **4** away, gone, sans **5** minus, short **6** absent, devoid **7** missing, omitted, wanting, without **8** awanting **9** defective, deficient **10** inadequate, incomplete, uncomplete **12** insufficient
lackluster **3** dim, mat **4** dead, drab, dull, flat **5** blind, muted, prosy, rusty **6** leaden **7** prosaic **8** lifeless **9** colorless, tarnished
Laconian **7** Spartan ***king:*** **5** Lelex, Myles
laconic **4** curt **5** brief, pithy, short, terse **7** brusque, concise **8** succinct **11** compendiary, compendious **12** breviloquent
lacquer **5** gloss **6** finish **7** shellac, varnish
lacquered metalware **4** tole
lactate **4** salt **5** ester **7** secrete
lacteal **5** milky
lacuna **3** gap **5** break **6** breach, hiatus **7** interim **8** interval **12** interruption
lad **3** boy, son, tad **5** youth **6** shaver **9** shaveling, stripling ***Scottish:*** **6** callan **7** callant
ladder **3** run **5** scale **6** series ***adjunct:*** **4** rung **6** rundle
ladderlike **6** scalar **11** scalariform
lade **3** dip, tax **4** bail, clog, load, pack, ship, stow **5** ladle, scoop, weigh **6** burden, charge, cumber, saddle, weight **8** encumber
lading **4** haul, load **5** cargo **6** burden **7** freight, payload
ladle **3** dip **4** bail, lade **5** scoop, spoon **6** dipper
Ladon **6** dragon ***father:*** **7** Phorcus, Phorcys ***mother:*** **4** Ceto ***slayer:*** **8** Heracles, Hercules
lady ***French:*** **4** dame ***Italian:*** **5** donna **7** signora ***Muslim:*** **5** begum ***Spanish:*** **4** doña **6** senora
lady ____ **4** crab, fern, luck, palm **5** chair,

tulip 6 beetle, friend, killer 7 cracker 9 bountiful
ladybird 6 beetle 7 pintail
ladybug 6 beetle ***Australian:*** 7 vedalia
Lady Chatterley's Lover ***author:*** 8 Lawrence ***character:*** 6 Connie 7 Mellors 9 Constance
Lady of the Lake, The 5 Ellen, Nimue 6 Vivien ***author:*** 5 Scott
Lady Windermere's Fan author 5 Wilde
Laertes ***father:*** 8 Acrisius, Polonius ***sister:*** 7 Ophelia ***son:*** 7 Ulysses 8 Odysseus ***wife:*** 8 Anticlea
La Fontaine's forte 5 fable
lag 4 drag, last, poke, slow, stay, tire 5 dally, delay, final, tarry, trail 6 dawdle, deport, latest, latter, loiter, put off, retard 7 closing, slacken 8 eventual, hindmost, terminal, ultimate 10 concluding
lager 4 beer
laggard 4 slow 6 loafer, remiss 7 dawdler, unhasty 8 comatose, dawdling, delaying, dilatory, lingerer, loiterer, slowpoke, sluggish 9 apathetic, impassive, lazybones, leisurely, lethargic, loitering, slow coach, straggler, unhurried 10 deliberate, phlegmatic
La Gioconda ***composer:*** 10 Ponchielli ***painter:*** 7 da Vinci
lagniappe 3 tip 4 perk 7 cumshaw, largess, palm oil 8 gratuity 9 pourboire 10 perquisite
lagomorph 4 hare, pika 6 rabbit
lagoon 4 pond, pool 5 liman, sound 7 channel
___ La Guardia 8 Fiorello
Lahmi ***brother:*** 7 Goliath ***slayer:*** 7 Elhanan
laic 6 layman
lair 3 den 4 cave 5 couch, haunt, lodge 6 burrow 7 hideout, retreat 8 hideaway
Laius ***father:*** 8 Labdacus ***slayer, son:*** 7 Oedipus ***wife:*** 7 Jocasta
lake 3 sea 4 loch, mere, pond, pool 5 lough 6 lagoon ***Adriatic:*** 6 Varano ***Alberta:*** 6 Louise ***Algeria:*** 5 Hodna ***Alps:*** 6 Annecy ***Arizona-Nevada:*** 4 Mead ***Armenia:*** 5 Sevan 6 Gokcha, Sevang 9 Lychnitis ***Aswan's:*** 6 Nasser ***Australia:*** 4 Eyre 5 Carey, Cowan, Frome, Wells 6 Barlee 7 Amadeus, Everard, Torrens 8 Gairdner ***Austria:*** 5 Atter, Traun 6 Kammer 8 Attersee 9 Kammersee ***Bolivia:*** 5 Poopo ***Botswana:*** 5 Ngami ***British Columbia:*** 4 Pitt 5 Atlin ***California:*** 4 Mono, Tule 5 Clear, Eagle, Honey ***Cambodia:*** 8 Tonle Sap ***Canada:*** 4 Dyke 8 Manitoba ***central Africa:*** 4 Kivu 5 Mweru 6 Albert ***Central America:*** 5 Guija ***central Europe:*** 5 Leman 6 Geneva, Lugano 7 Ceresio 8 Bodensee 9 Constance ***central North America:*** 5 Rainy ***Chile:*** 4 Laja 5 Ranco ***China:*** 6 Poyang 8 Dongting ***Colorado:*** 5 Grand ***combining form:*** 4 limn 5 limni, limno 6 limnia (plural) 7 limnion ***Connecticut:*** 6 Bantam 7 Gardner 8 Highland 10 Candlewood, Pocotopaug ***Denmark:*** 5 Esrum ***east Africa:*** 6 Rudolf 7 Turkana ***east Asia:*** 5 Hanka 6 Khanka 7 Xingkai 8 Hsingkai ***east central Africa:*** 8 Victoria 10 Tanganyika ***east China:*** 2 Ho 3 Tai 5 Dalai, Hulun ***Ethiopia:*** 4 Tana, Zwai 5 Abaya, Shala, Shamo, Tsana 8 Stefanie 9 Chew Bahir ***Finland:*** 5 Inari ***Florida:*** 5 Worth 10 Okeechobee ***Germany:*** 5 Ammer, Chiem 8 Ammersee, Chiemsee ***Ghana:*** 5 Volta ***Great:*** 4 Erie 5 Huron 7 Ontario 8 Michigan, Superior ***Greece:*** 5 Bolbe, Volvi ***Guatemala:*** 7 Atitlan ***Honduras:*** 5 Yojoa ***Honshu:*** 3 Omi 4 Biwa, Suwa, Yodo ***Hungary:*** 7 Balaton 10 Plattensee ***Idaho:*** 4 Waha 5 Grays 6 Priest 11 Coeur d'Alene, Pend Oreille ***India:*** 3 Dal 5 Wular 6 Chilka ***Indonesia:*** 4 Poso, Toba 5 Ranau ***Iowa:*** 5 Storm ***Iran:*** 5 Niriz, Shahi, Urmia 8 Matianus, Urumiyeh 9 Bakhtigan ***Ireland:*** 3 Gur, Ree 4 Conn, Derg, Mask 5 Allen, Arrow, Leane ***Israel:*** 12 Bahr Tabariya, Sea of Galilee ***Israel-Jordan:*** 7 Dead Sea ***Italy:*** 4 Como, Iseo, Nemi 5 Garda 6 Albano 7 Bolsena, Perugia 8 Maggiore 9 Trasimene ***Japan:*** 4 Imba 8 Imbanuma ***Kazakh:*** 7 Balqash 8 Balkhash ***largest inland:*** 10 Caspian Sea ***Louisiana:*** 4 Soda 5 Black, White 9 Catahoula 13 Pontchartrain ***Maine:*** 3 Big 6 Sebago 9 Moosehead ***Mali:*** 4 Debo ***Manitoba:*** 4 Gods 5 Cedar, Moose 8 Winnipeg ***Mexico:*** 7 Chapala ***Michigan:*** 4 Burt ***Minnesota:*** 3 Red 4 Cass, Gull, Swan 5 Leech 6 Itasca 9 Mille Lacs 10 Minnetonka, of the Woods 11 Lac qui Parle ***Minnesota-Wisconsin:*** 5 Pepin ***Mongolian:*** 3 Har 5 Har Us, Khara 8 Khara Usu ***Montana:*** 8 Medicine ***mountain:*** 4 tarn ***Myanmar:*** 4 Inle ***Nevada:*** 4 Ruby 7 Pyramid ***New Hampshire:*** 4 Echo 5 Squam 7 Sunapee 13 Winnipesaukee ***New Jersey:*** 5 Union ***New York:*** 4 Long 5 Chazy, Keuka 6 Cayuga, George, Oneida, Otsego, Owasco, Placid, Seneca 7 Crooked, Saranac 8 Onondaga, Saratoga 10 Chautauqua 11 Canandaigua, Skaneateles ***New Zealand:*** 4 Ohau 5 Hawea, Taupo 6 Pukaki, Wanaka 8 Wakatipu ***Nicaragua:*** 7 Managua ***North Africa:*** 4 Chad ***North America:*** 9 Champlain ***Northern Ireland:*** 5 Neagh ***Northwest Territories:*** 4 Gras 5 Baker, Garry, Pelly 9 Great Bear 10 Great Slave ***Norway:*** 5 Mjosa ***Nova***

Scotia: 7 Bras d'Or ***Ontario:*** 4 Rice, Seul 5 Trout ***Oregon:*** 5 Abert 6 Crater 7 Malheur, Wallowa ***Paraguay:*** 4 Ypoa ***Peru:*** 5 Junin 13 Chinchaycocha ***Philippines:*** 4 Bato, Taal 5 Lanao 6 Bombon ***Poland:*** 5 Mamry, Mauer ***Quebec:*** 5 Minto, Payne ***Russia:*** 3 Seg 5 Chany, Ilmen, Lacha, Onega 6 Ladoga 7 Rybinsk 10 Eltonskoye 11 Ladozhskoye ***saline:*** 5 chott, shott ***Saskatchewan:*** 4 Cree 5 Ronge ***Scotland:*** 3 Ard, Awe 4 Doon, Earn, Ness, Oich, Shin, Sloy 5 Leven, Lochy, Maree, Morar, Shiel 6 Lomond ***Siberia:*** 6 Baikal, Baykal ***South Africa:*** 4 Kosi ***South America:*** 5 Merin, Mirim 8 Titicaca ***South Carolina:*** 11 Wateree Pond ***South Dakota:*** 5 Andes ***southeast Africa:*** 5 Nyasa 6 Nyassa ***southern United States:*** 5 Caddo ***southwest Europe:*** 5 Ohrid 7 Okhrida ***Sudan:*** 2 No ***Sweden:*** 5 Asnen, Roxen 6 Siljan, Vetter 7 Malaren, Vattern ***Switzerland:*** 3 Zug 4 Biel, Joux 5 Zuger 6 Bieler, Bienne, Brienz, Sarnen, Sarner, Zurich 7 Lucerne, Lungern 8 Brienzer, Zuricher 9 Neuchatel, Zurichsee ***Tadzhikistan:*** 7 Karakul ***Tanzania:*** 5 Rukwa ***Tibet:*** 4 Namu 6 Nam Tso, Tengri ***Turkey:*** 2 Ak 3 Tuz, Van 4 Bafa, Nice 5 Iznik, Sugla 6 Nicaea ***Uganda:*** 5 Kyoga ***Utah:*** 6 Powell, Sevier 9 Great Salt ***volcanic:*** 8 Ilopango ***Wales:*** 4 Bala ***Washington:*** 4 Omak 5 Moses 6 Chelan 9 Wenatchee ***western China:*** 4 Ai-pi 6 Ebinur ***western United States:*** 4 Bear 5 Tahoe ***Wisconsin:*** 5 Green 9 Winnebago ***Yellowstone National Park:*** 5 Heart, Lewis 8 Shoshone ***Zaire:*** 5 Tumba ***Zambia:*** 9 Bangweolo, Bangweulu

lake duck 7 mallard

lake herring 5 cisco

Lake poet 7 Southey 9 Coleridge 10 Wordsworth

lakes ***central North America:*** 5 Great ***Connecticut:*** 4 Twin ***Egypt:*** 5 Balah ***Maine:*** 8 Rangeley ***New Hampshire:*** 11 Connecticut ***New York:*** 6 Finger ***Saskatchewan:*** 5 Quill ***Twin:*** 8 Washinee 9 Washining ***Wisconsin:*** 4 Four

Lakmé ***aria:*** 8 Bell Song ***composer:*** 7 Delibes

Lakshmi ***husband:*** 6 Vishnu ***son:*** 4 Kama

lam 3 hit 4 beat, drub, pelt, slip 5 paste, pound 6 batter, escape, flight, hammer, pummel, thrash, wallop 7 getaway 8 breakout, escaping 10 escapement

La Mancha's knight 10 Don Quixote

lamb 4 cade, dupe, yean 5 sheep 6 cosset 8 yeanling ***leg of:*** 5 gigot

lambaste 3 pan 4 beat, drub, flay, lick, pelt, slam, slap, trim, whip 5 paste, pound, roast, scold, score, slash, smear 6 assail, attack, berate, hammer, pummel, scathe, scorch, thrash, wallop 7 blister, censure, clobber, reprove, scarify, scourge, shellac, smother 8 denounce, harangue, lash into, squabash 9 castigate, criticize, excoriate 10 tongue-lash

lambent 6 bright, lucent 7 beaming, glowing, radiant 8 luminous, lustrous 9 brilliant, effulgent, refulgent 12 incandescent

lamb of God 8 Agnus Dei

Lamb's pseudonym 4 Elia

lame 3 ill 4 halt, limp, sick, weak 6 feeble, sickly 7 cripple, halting, hipshot, limping 8 crippled, disabled 13 incapacitated

lamebrain 4 dope 5 dunce, noddy, stupe 6 noodle 7 schnook 8 dumbhead 10 dunderhead

Lamech ***daughter:*** 6 Naamah ***father:*** 9 Methusael 10 Methuselah ***son:*** 4 Noah 5 Jabal, Jubal 9 Tubalcain ***wife:*** 4 Adah 6 Zillah

lament 3 cry, rue 4 keen, moan, pine, pity, sigh, wail, weep 5 dirge, elegy, mourn 6 bemoan, bewail, grieve, plaint, regret, repent, repine 7 deplore, despair, elegize 8 jeremiad 9 complaint

lamentable 3 sad 4 dire 6 rueful, woeful 7 doleful, pitiful 8 dolesome, dolorous, grievous, mournful 9 plaintive, sorrowful 10 afflictive, calamitous, deplorable, lugubrious, melancholy 11 distressing, regrettable, unfortunate 13 heartbreaking

Lamerok ***father:*** 9 Pellinore ***lover:*** 8 Margawse ***slayer:*** 6 Gawain

lamia 3 hag, hex 5 bruja, witch 9 sorceress 10 witchwoman 11 enchantress

Lamia ***country:*** 5 Libya ***form:*** 7 serpent ***lover:*** 4 Zeus

lamina 5 blade, flake, layer, plate

lamp 3 eye, orb 4 davy 5 light, torch 6 ocular, oculus, peeper, winker 7 lantern 10 candelabra 11 candelabrum ***floor:*** 8 torchère ***hanging:*** 10 chandelier

lampblack 4 soot 6 carbon

Lampetia ***father:*** 6 Apollo, Helios ***husband:*** 9 Asclepius ***mother:*** 6 Neaera ***sister:*** 9 Phaethusa

lampoon 4 mock 5 squib 6 satire 7 pasquil 8 ridicule, satirize 10 pasquinade

lamprey 3 eel

lanai 5 porch 7 terrace, veranda

lanate 5 hairy 6 woolly

lance 3 cut 4 spit 5 blade, spear, spike 6 impale, pierce, skewer, skiver, weapon 7 javelin 8 transfix 11 transpierce

Lancelot, Launcelot ***father:*** 3 Ban ***lover:*** 6 Elaine 9 Guinevere ***son:*** 7 Galahad ***victim:*** 6 Gawain

lancer ***Prussian:*** 4 Ulan 5 Uhlan

land 3 get, win 4 dirt, gain, have, home,

soil 5 acres, annex, catch, earth, light, manor, perch, roost, shore, terra, tract 6 alight, debark, estate, ground, obtain, pick up, quinta, secure, settle 7 acquire, acreage, country, procure, set down, sit down 8 plottage 9 disembark, touch down 10 terra firma 13 mother country ***alluvial:*** 5 delta ***along a river:*** 5 carse 7 bottoms ***area:*** 7 terrain, terrene ***barren:*** 5 waste 6 desert ***combining form:*** 3 geo 4 chor, gaea 5 choro ***cultivated:*** 4 farm 5 tilth 7 tillage ***for grazing:*** 3 lea, ley 5 range 6 meadow 7 pasture ***high:*** 4 hill, mesa 7 plateau 8 mountain ***level:*** 4 mesa 5 plain 7 plateau ***low:*** 4 vale 6 valley 9 intervale ***measure:*** 3 rod 4 acre 7 centare 8 centiare ***open:*** 5 field, plain ***piece:*** 3 lot 6 estate, parcel ***reclaimed:*** 6 polder ***relating to:*** 8 agrarian ***sloping:*** 6 cuesta ***strip:*** 7 isthmus ***wet:*** 3 bog, fen 4 moor 5 marsh, swamp 6 marish 7 maremma

land east of Eden 3 Nod

landing place of the Ark 6 Ararat

landmark 5 bound, cairn 9 milestone

Land of Cakes 8 Scotland

Land of Enchantment 9 New Mexico

Land of Lakes 8 Michigan

Land of Lincoln 8 Illinois

Land of Milk and Honey 6 Israel

land of Nod 5 sleep

Land of Opportunity 8 Arkansas

Land of Plenty 6 Goshen

Land of the Midnight Sun 6 Norway

Land of the Rising Sun 5 Japan

landowner 6 squire, yeoman ***Anglo-Saxon:*** 5 thane, thegn ***Dutch:*** 7 patroon ***Scottish:*** 5 laird

landscape 5 scene 7 picture, scenery 8 painting ***gardener:*** 9 topiarist

lane 3 way 4 path, road 5 aisle, alley, byway, track 6 street 7 loaning, pathway 8 footpath 10 passageway

Langobard see Lombard

lang syne 4 past, yore 8 foretime 9 yesterday 10 yesteryear

language 4 cant 5 argot, idiom, lingo, prose, slang 6 jargon, patois, speech, tongue 7 dialect, lexicon, palaver 10 dictionary, vernacular, vocabulary 11 terminology ***ambiguous:*** 6 jargon 8 newspeak 10 double-talk ***ancient:*** 5 Greek, Latin 6 Hebrew 8 Sanskrit ***artificial:*** 2 Ro 3 Ido 7 Volapük 9 Esperanto ***classical:*** 5 Greek, Latin ***combining form:*** 5 gloss, glott 6 glosso, glotto ***expert:*** 8 linguist ***informal:*** 5 lingo, slang ***meaningless:*** 9 gibberish ***mixed:*** 6 pidgin ***pretentious:*** 6 hot air 7 bombast 8 claptrap ***regional:*** 7 dialect ***relating to:*** 10 linguistic ***Romance:*** 6 French 7 Catalan, Italian, Spanish 8 Romanian, Rumanian 10 Portuguese ***secret:*** 4 cant, code 5 argot ***structure:*** 6 syntax 7 grammar ***suffix:*** 3 ese ***written:*** 5 prose

languid 4 limp, slow, weak 5 inert 6 supine, torpid 7 die-away 8 comatose, inactive, listless, slothful, sluggish 9 apathetic, enervated, impassive, lethargic 10 languorous, phlegmatic, spiritless 11 languishing 13 lackadaisical

languishing 4 limp 6 pining 7 die-away, languid, longing 8 fainéant, indolent, listless, weakened, yearning 9 enervated, enfeebled 10 languorous, spiritless 11 debilitated 13 lackadaisical

languor 3 kef, kif 4 coma 5 blues, dumps, ennui, sleep 6 stupor, tedium, torpor 7 fatigue, slumber 8 doldrums, dullness, hebetude, lethargy 9 lassitude, torpidity, weariness 10 depression, exhaustion

languorous 3 lax 4 limp, slow 5 loose, slack 7 die-away, laggard, languid, passive, relaxed 8 dilatory, fainéant, indolent, indulged, listless, pampered, slothful 9 enervated, leisurely 10 spiritless 11 languishing 13 lackadaisical

lank 4 bony, lean 5 gaunt, lanky, spare 6 gangly, skinny 7 angular, scraggy, scrawny 8 gangling, rawboned 10 attenuated, extenuated

lanyard 4 cord, line, rope

Laocoon ***city:*** 4 Troy ***killer:*** 7 serpent

Laodamia ***father:*** 7 Acastus ***husband:*** 11 Protesilaus

Laomedon ***daughter:*** 7 Hesione ***father:*** 4 Ilus ***kingdom:*** 4 Troy ***mother:*** 8 Eurydice ***slayer:*** 8 Heracles, Hercules ***son:*** 5 Priam 8 Tithonus

Laos ***capital:*** 9 Vientiane ***monetary unit:*** 3 kip

lap 3 lip, sip 4 lave, ride, wash 5 bathe, slosh, swash 6 bubble, burble, gurgle 7 overlie, shingle 8 override 9 imbricate

lapidary 6 cutter 7 jeweler 8 engraver, polisher

lapideous 5 stony

lapillus 4 lava 6 cinder

lapin 6 rabbit

Lapiths ***foes:*** 8 centaurs ***king:*** 5 Ixion

lappet 4 flap, fold, moth 5 lapel 6 infula

Lappidoth's wife 7 Deborah

Lapsang 3 tea

lapse 3 err, sin 4 bull, slip, trip, vice 5 boner, crime, error, fluff, slide 6 breach, bungle, foible, recede, return, revert 7 blooper, blunder, decline, descend, failing, frailty, mistake, offense, subside 8 trespass 9 backslide, decadence, recession, violation 10 apostatize, declension, degenerate, devolution, recidivate, regression, retrograde 11 backsliding, deteriorate 12 degeneration 13 deterioration, retrogression, transgression

Laputan 6 absurd 9 visionary
lar 3 god 6 gibbon, spirit
larboard 4 left, port
larcenist 4 prig 5 thief 6 nimmer, robber 7 burglar, filcher, stealer 8 pilferer 9 purloiner
larceny 4 lift 5 pinch, steal, theft 7 looting, robbery 8 burglary, stealage, stealing, thievery, thieving 10 purloining ***kind:*** 5 grand, petty
lard 3 fat 6 fatten, grease 10 shortening
larder 6 pantry
large 3 big, fat 4 bull, huge, vast 5 ample, bulky, grand, great, hefty, husky, jumbo, major 6 goodly 7 extreme, immense, mammoth, massive, outsize, sizable 8 colossal, enormous, gigantic, oversize 9 excessive, extensive, monstrous 10 exorbitant, immoderate, inordinate, large-scale, monumental, prodigious, stupendous, tremendous, voluminous 11 extravagant ***combining form:*** 3 meg 4 macr, mega 5 macro, megal 6 megalo
largess 3 tip 4 boon, gift, perk 5 favor 7 cumshaw, present 8 gratuity 9 lagniappe, pourboire 10 perquisite 11 benevolence
lariat 4 rope 5 lasso, noose, reata, riata ***part:*** 5 honda, hondo ***user:*** 6 cowboy, drover 10 cowpuncher
lark 4 bird, dido 5 antic, caper, prank, shine, trick 6 frolic 7 rollick 8 carousal, escapade 10 shenanigan, tomfoolery 11 monkeyshine
larrup 4 beat, drub, dust, flog, hide, lash, lick, whip 5 mop up, whale 6 lather, stripe, thrash 7 clobber, scourge, shellac 8 lambaste 9 overwhelm 10 flagellate
larva 3 bot 4 grub, worm 5 eruca 6 dobson, maggot 7 atrocha 8 cercaria, hornworm, mealworm 10 case bearer, helgramite 11 caterpillar 12 hellgrammite ***amphibian:*** 7 tadpole ***crustacean:*** 4 zoea ***flatworm:*** 5 redia ***free-swimming:*** 7 planula ***mollusk:*** 7 veliger ***moth:*** 8 leafworm ***tapeworm:*** 6 measle
larynx 8 voice box
lasagna 5 pasta 7 noodles
lascivious 3 hot 4 fast, lewd 5 gross 6 coarse, wanton 7 goatish, lustful, obscene, satyric 8 prurient 9 lecherous, libertine, lickerish, salacious 10 libidinous, licentious, passionate 11 incontinent 12 concupiscent
lash 3 jaw, wag 4 beat, bind, boil, bolt, dash, flay, flog, hide, pour, race, rush, tear, teem, wave, whip 5 baste, chase, fling, scold, shoot, slash, whale 6 charge, drench, lather, scathe, scorch, stripe, switch, thrash, waggle, woggle 7 bawl out, blister, chew out, scarify, scourge, tell off, upbraid 8 lambaste 9 castigate, excoriate 10 flagellate
lassitude 5 blues, dumps, ennui, sleep 6 apathy, stupor, tedium, torpor 7 fatigue, languor, slumber 8 doldrums, dullness, hebetude, lethargy 9 disregard, impotence, tiredness, torpidity, unconcern, weariness 10 depression, exhaustion, torpidness 11 disinterest, insouciance 12 heedlessness, indifference, listlessness
lasso see **lariat**
last 3 end, lag 5 abide, final 6 endure, latest, latter, utmost 7 closing, dernier, extreme, perdure, persist 8 continue, eventual, furthest, hindmost, rearmost, remotest, terminal, ultimate 9 outermost, umpteenth, uttermost 10 bottommost, concluding 11 terminating ***next to:*** 6 penult 11 penultimate
last extremity 9 bitter end
lasting 3 old 6 stable 7 abiding, durable, endless, eternal 8 enduring, lifelong 9 continual, diuturnal, incessant, indelible, perduring, perennial, permanent, unceasing 10 continuing, continuous, perdurable, persisting
Last of the Goths 8 Roderick
Last of the Mohicans, The 5 Uncas ***author:*** 6 Cooper ***character:*** 4 Cora 5 Alice, Magua, Uncas 11 Natty Bumppo 12 Chingachgook
Last of the Saxons 6 Harold
Last Supper, The ***painter:*** 7 da Vinci
Las Vegas district 5 Strip
latch 4 bolt 5 catch 6 fasten 8 fastener ***British:*** 5 sneck
latchet 4 lace 5 strap, thong
late 3 new, old 4 cold, dead, once, past 5 tardy 6 asleep, bygone, former, modern, recent, whilom 7 belated, defunct, extinct, onetime, overdue, quondam 8 deceased, departed, lifeless, sometime
Late George Apley, The ***author:*** 8 Marquand
latent 4 idle 5 inert 6 hidden, unripe 7 abeyant, dormant, lurking 8 immature, inactive 9 concealed, potential, prepatent, quiescent, unmatured ***combining form:*** 5 crypt, krypt 6 crypto, krypto
later 4 anon, next, soon 5 after, infra 6 behind 7 by and by, ensuing 8 latterly, tomorrow 9 afterward, posterior 10 afterwhile, subsequent 12 postliminary, subsequently 13 subsequential
lateral 4 pass, side 8 sideways
laterally 8 crabwise, sideling, sidelong, sideward, sideways, sidewise
latest 3 lag 4 last 5 final 6 latter, newest 7 closing 8 eventual, hindmost, rearmost, terminal, ultimate 10 concluding

latex 5 paint 8 emulsion *product:* 6 balata, chicle, rubber
lath 4 slat 5 stave, stick, strip 8 forepole
lather 4 flap, flog, foam, hide, lash, moil, soap, stew, suds, whip 5 froth, spume, storm, yeast 6 bustle, clamor, dither, hassle, hubbub, pother, stripe, thrash, tumult 7 scourge, turmoil, whoopla 8 rowdydow 9 agitation, commotion, confusion
Latin 5 Roman 7 Italian 8 Hispanic *after:* 4 post *always:* 6 semper *and:* 2 et *before:* 4 ante, prae *book:* 5 liber *boy:* 4 puer *bronze:* 3 aes *brother:* 6 frater *but:* 3 sed *day:* 4 dies *dog:* 5 canis *foot:* 3 pes *force:* 3 vis *friend:* 6 amicus *god:* 4 deus *goddess:* 3 dea *grammarian:* 7 Donatus *hand:* 5 manus *is:* 3 est *law:* 3 ius, jus, lex *light:* 3 lux *peace:* 3 pax *pronoun:* 2 tu 3 ego, nos, vos *road:* 3 via 4 iter *see:* 4 vide *that is:* 5 id est *thing:* 3 res *this:* 3 hic, hoc 4 haec *thus:* 3 sic *war:* 6 bellum *wife:* 4 uxor *woman:* 6 femina *year:* 5 annus
Latin-American *country:* 4 Cuba, Peru 5 Chile 6 Brazil, Guyana, Mexico, Panama 7 Bolivia, Ecuador, Uruguay 8 Colombia, Honduras, Paraguay 9 Argentina, Costa Rica, Guatemala, Nicaragua 10 El Salvador *revolutionary:* 6 Castro (Fidel) 7 Bolivar (Simon), Guevara (Ché)
Latinus *daughter:* 7 Lavinia *father:* 6 Faunus 8 Odysseus *son-in-law:* 6 Aeneas *wife:* 5 Amata
latitude 4 play, room 5 scope, space 6 leeway, margin 7 freedom 9 elbowroom
latke 7 pancake 11 griddle cake
Latona 4 Leto *daughter:* 5 Diana 7 Artemis *father:* 5 Coeus *mother:* 6 Phoebe *son:* 6 Apollo
Latter-day Saint 6 Mormon
lattice 4 grid 5 grate 7 grating, trellis
Latvia *capital:* 4 Riga
Latvian 4 Lett *coin:* 7 santims *measure:* 4 stof 5 faden, kanne, stoff, stoof, vedro 6 kulmet, sagene, versta 8 krouchka
laud 4 hymn 5 adore, bless, cry up, extol 6 admire, praise, revere 7 flatter, glorify, magnify, worship 8 eulogize, venerate 9 celebrate, reverence 10 panegyrize
laudable 6 worthy 9 admirable, deserving, estimable, meritable, praisable 11 commendable, meritorious, thankworthy 12 praiseworthy
laugh 3 yuk 4 beam, crow, grin, ha-ha, roar 5 smile, smirk, snort, tehee, whoop 6 cackle, giggle, guffaw, hee-haw, simper, titter 7 chortle, chuckle, snicker, sniggle 10 cachinnate
laughable 4 rich 5 comic, droll, funny, witty 6 jocose 7 amusing, comical, jocular, mocking, risible 8 derisive, derisory, farcical, gelastic, humorous 9 diverting, facetious, ludicrous 10 ridiculous 12 entertaining
laughing 5 riant 8 derisive
laughingstock 4 butt, fool, jest, joke, mark, mock 5 sport 6 jestee, target 7 mockery 8 derision 9 pilgarlic
launch 4 cast, fire, hurl, open, toss 5 begin, fling, heave, pitch, set up, sling, start, throw 6 get off 7 jump off, kick off, usher in 8 commence, embark on, initiate 9 institute, introduce, originate 10 inaugurate
launching 7 lift-off, takeoff 8 blast-off
launder 4 wash 5 clean 7 cleanse
Laura's lover 8 Petrarch
laurels 4 bays 5 award, badge, honor, kudos 8 accolade 10 decoration 11 distinction
laurel tree nymph 6 Daphne
lava 2 aa 4 rock, slag 5 magma 6 latite, scoria 8 andesite, trachyte *cooled:* 8 pahoehoe *fragment:* 8 lapillus *stream:* 4 flow 6 coulee
lavalava 5 cloth, skirt
lavaliere 7 pendant 8 necklace
lavatory 2 WC 3 loo 4 head, john 5 basin, privy 6 johnny, toilet 7 latrine 8 bathroom, washroom 11 convenience, water closet
lave 3 lap, lip 4 pour, wash 5 bathe
Lavinia *father:* 7 Latinus *husband:* 6 Aeneas *mother:* 5 Amata
Lavinium's founder 6 Aeneas
lavish 4 free, lush 5 grand, spend, waste 7 opulent, profuse, riotous 8 gorgeous, prodigal, splendid, squander 9 exuberant, luxuriant, luxurious, profusive, sumptuous
law 3 act, lex 4 bill, code, doom, rule 5 axiom, canon, edict, nomos, Torah 6 assize, custom, decree, equity 7 command, dictate, justice, mandate, precept, statute, theorem 8 decretum, exigency 9 enactment, institute, necessity, ordinance, prescript, principle 10 principium, regulation 11 commandment, fundamental 12 constitution, prescription *body of:* 4 code 7 pandect 12 constitution *combining form:* 4 nomy *degree:* 3 LLB, LLD *expert:* 5 judge 6 jurist 7 justice *practitioner:* 6 lawyer 7 counsel 8 attorney *relating to:* 5 jural, legal 7 canonic 8 forensic, juristic 9 judiciary *violation of:* 3 sin 4 tort 5 crime, malum 6 felony
lawbreaker 5 felon 6 sinner 8 criminal, offender, scofflaw, violator 10 malefactor
lawcourt 3 bar 8 tribunal
lawful 3 due 5 legal, licit 7 condign 8 bona fide, innocent, rightful 9 allowable 10 legitimate
lawgiver 5 Moses, solon 10 legislator

lawlessness 4 riot 5 chaos 6 strife 7 anarchy, discord 8 conflict, variance 9 mobocracy 10 ochlocracy
lawman 7 marshal, officer, sheriff 9 policeman
Law of Moses 5 Torah 10 Pentateuch
Lawrence novel 8 Kangaroo 9 Aaron's Rod 10 The Rainbow 11 Women in Love 13 Sons and Lovers
Lawrence of ___ 6 Arabia
lawrencium *symbol:* 2 Lr
lawsuit 4 case 5 cause 6 action 10 litigation
lawyer 6 jurist, legist 7 counsel, pleader 8 advocate, attorney 9 barrister, counselor, solicitor 10 mouthpiece 12 jurisconsult, jurisprudent 13 attorney-at-law *dishonest:* 7 shyster 11 pettifogger *fictional:* 10 Perry Mason *French:* 6 avocat *Indian:* 5 vakil 6 vakeel
lawyers' patron saint 4 Ives
lax 4 ease, easy, open 5 loose, slack 6 loosen, remiss 7 ease off, lenient, slacken 8 careless, derelict 9 forgetful, negligent, oblivious, unmindful, untighten 10 behindhand, delinquent, neglectful, regardless 12 disregardful
lay 3 aim, air, bet, fix, put, set 4 aria, cast, cite, even, game, hymn, lied, play, song, tune, turn 5 ditty, flush, level, offer, place, plane, point, put on, refer, stake, stick, train, wager 6 adduce, allege, assign, charge, credit, direct, expose, gamble, impute, melody, settle, smooth, spread, strain, warble, zero in 7 address, advance, ascribe, descant, flatten, incline, measure, melisma, melodia, present, profane, secular, subject, uncover 8 accredit, diapason, smoothen, temporal, unsacred 9 attribute, establish
lay aside 4 cast, save, shed 5 chuck, ditch, put by, scrap 6 reject, slough 7 discard, neglect 8 jettison, salt away 9 throw away
lay by 4 save 5 amass, hoard, store 7 deposit 8 salt away
lay down 3 set 4 cede 5 leave, waive, yield 6 assign, decree, define, give up, impose, ordain, resign 7 abandon, dictate 8 hand over 9 establish, prescribe, surrender 10 relinquish
lay eggs 5 spawn 8 oviposit
layer 3 hen, ply 4 coat, film, seam, tier 5 paver, sheet 6 folium, lamina, veneer 7 coating, provine, stratum 8 laminate, membrane, sandwich, stratify *combining form:* 5 cline, lamin, ptych 6 lamell, lamino, ptycho, strati 7 lamelli *inner:* 6 lining *of odds:* 6 bookie 9 bookmaker *of skin:* 6 dermis 9 epidermis *outer:* 4 skin 6 veneer
lay for 6 ambush, waylay 8 surprise
lay in see **lay by**
lay low 4 down, fell, hide, kill, slay 5 floor, level, scrag 6 cut off, finish, ground 7 destroy, flatten, mow down, put away, take off 8 bowl down, bowl over, dispatch 9 knock down, knock over, throw down
layman 4 laic 7 secular
lay off 4 halt, quit, stop 5 avoid, cease 7 dismiss, measure 9 disemploy 11 discontinue
lay open 4 bare, show 6 expose, reveal 7 uncover
lay out 3 pay 4 give, plan 5 spend 6 design, expend, map out, outlay, set out 7 arrange, fork out 8 disburse, shell out
lay waste 4 ruin 6 ravage 7 destroy 8 desolate 9 devastate
lazar 5 leper
Lazarus' sister 4 Mary 6 Martha
laze 3 bum 4 idle, lazy, loaf, loll 5 sloth 6 dawdle, loiter, lounge, slouch 7 goof off 8 idleness, laziness, malinger 9 goldbrick, indolence
laziness 5 sloth 6 slouch 8 idleness 9 indolence
lazy 3 bum, lax 4 idle, loaf, loll 5 drony, inert, slack 6 dawdle, loiter, lounge, remiss, supine, torpid 7 goof off, languid, passive, work-shy 8 comatose, fainéant, inactive, indolent, listless, slothful, sluggish, trifling 9 easygoing, goldbrick, lethargic, negligent, shiftless, slowgoing
Lazy Susan 4 tray 9 turntable
lea 6 fallow, meadow 7 pasture 8 unplowed 9 grassland
leach 4 suck 7 draw out 9 lixiviate, percolate 11 bloodsucker
lead 3 get, see 4 dean, head, move, show, star 5 bring, doyen, guide, metal, pilot, route, steer, usher 6 bullet, ceruse, direct, escort, induce, leader 7 captain, conduct, convert, plumbum, precede, preface, prevail 8 graphite, persuade, shepherd 9 introduce 10 bellwether *combining form:* 5 plumb 6 molybd, plumbo 7 molybdo *ore:* 6 galena 8 galenite 9 anglesite, cerrusite *oxide:* 6 sinter *sounding:* 7 plummet *symbol:* 2 Pb
lead astray 4 undo 6 delude, entice, seduce 7 corrupt, deceive, degrade, pervert
leaden 3 dun 4 drab, dull, flat, gray 5 heavy, inert 8 dragging, lifeless, sluggish 9 plumbeous
leader 4 boss, cock, dean, duce, head, lead, lion, lord 5 chief, doyen, guide, pilot 6 bigwig, herald, honcho, master, rector 7 captain, foreman, general, headman, manager, notable 8 big-timer, big wheel, chairman, director, eminence, hierarch, luminary, superior 9 chieftain, commander, conductor, dignitary, dominator, harbinger, pace-

maker, precursor, president, principal, straw boss 10 bellwether, chairwoman, forerunner, notability, pacesetter 11 chairperson ***authoritarian:*** 10 Big Brother ***combining form:*** 4 arch ***Cossack:*** 6 ataman, hetman ***German:*** 6 führer 7 fuehrer ***Japanese:*** 6 shogun ***military:*** 7 admiral, general, warlord 9 commander 12 field marshal ***Muslim:*** 4 caid 5 calif 6 caliph, mollah, mullah ***national:*** 7 premier 9 president 12 chief of state ***religious:*** 4 pope 5 rabbi 6 bishop, priest 7 prelate 8 hierarch

leading 4 arch, head, main 5 chief, first, noted 6 famous 7 initial, popular, premier 8 champion, foremost, headmost 9 inaugural, notorious, principal, prominent, well-known

lead on 3 toy 4 bait, fool, lure, toll 5 dally, decoy, flirt, tempt 6 allure, coquet, entice, entrap, seduce, trifle, wanton 8 inveigle 11 string along

leaf 4 foil, olla, page, scan 5 blade, bract, folio, frond, petal, scale, sepal 6 browse, spathe 7 dip into, run over 8 glance at 10 glance over, run through 11 flip through, riff through, skim through 12 thumb through 13 riffle through ***aperture:*** 5 stoma ***axis:*** 6 rachis ***combining form:*** 5 phyll 6 phylla (plural), phyllo 7 phyllum ***edge:*** 9 crenation ***lily:*** 3 pad ***part:*** 4 lobe, vein 5 blade, costa, stoma 7 petiole, stipule, tendril ***pine:*** 6 needle ***scale:*** 8 ramentum ***vein:*** 5 costa

leafage 7 foliage, umbrage, verdure

leaflet 5 pinna, sheet, tract 6 folder 8 circular, pamphlet

leafy 4 lush 5 green 7 foliate, foliose, folious 8 foliated, laminate

league 4 band, bond, club, loop, tier 5 class, grade, group, guild, order, union, unite, wheel 6 concur 7 circuit, combine, conjoin, society 8 alliance, category, coadjute, division, grouping, sodality 9 anschluss, coalition, cooperate 10 conference, federation, fellowship, fraternity, pigeonhole 11 association, brotherhood, confederacy 13 confederation

Leah ***daughter:*** 5 Dinah ***father:*** 5 Laban ***husband:*** 5 Jacob ***sister:*** 6 Rachel ***son:*** 4 Levi 5 Judah 6 Reuben, Simeon 7 Zebulun 8 Issachar

leak 3 out 4 drip, ooze, seep 5 bilge, break, crack 6 escape, get out 7 come out

leaky 6 porose, porous

lean 3 jut, tip 4 bend, bony, cant, hang, heel, lank, list, look, slim, tend, thin, tilt, turn, worn 5 curve, gaunt, grade, lanky, sheer, slant, slope, spare 6 beetle, divert, meager, skinny, slight, wasted 7 angular, deflect, haggard, incline, pinched, recline, scraggy, scrawny, slender, stringy, wizened 8 bend over, gradient, overhang, rawboned, spareset 10 cadaverous

Leander's beloved 4 Hero

Leandre ***beloved:*** 7 Lucinde ***father:*** 7 Geronte

Leaning Tower site 4 Pisa

lean-to 3 hut 5 shack 7 shelter

leap 3 hop, lop 4 buck, jump, loup, over, rise, soar 5 arise, bound, caper, clear, mount, vault 6 ascend, bounce, gambol, hurdle, spring 7 saltate 8 capriole, surmount ***ballet:*** 4 jeté 9 entrechat ***by a horse:*** 7 gambade, gambado 9 ballotade

leaping light 3 arc

Lear ***daughter:*** 5 Regan 7 Goneril 8 Cordelia ***servant:*** 4 Kent

learn 3 con, get, see 4 find, hear 5 study 6 master, peruse, pick up, tumble 7 catch on, find out, realize, unearth 8 discover, memorize 9 ascertain, determine

learned 4 sage, wise 6 astute 7 bookish, erudite 8 abstruse, academic, cultured, educated, esoteric, pedantic, polymath 9 recondite, scholarly 10 cultivated, scholastic

learner 5 pupil 7 scholar, student, trainee 10 apprentice

learning 4 lore 6 wisdom 7 science 8 booklore, pedantry 9 education, erudition, knowledge 11 scholarship ***man of:*** 7 egghead, scholar, teacher 9 professor 12 intellectual

lease 3 let 4 hire, rent 7 charter 8 contract

leash 3 tie 4 bind, clog, cord, curb, rope 5 strap 6 fetter, hamper, hobble, hog-tie, tether 7 shackle, trammel 9 entrammel ***hawk's:*** 4 lune

leather 3 tan 4 hide, skin, whip 6 thrash ***kind:*** 3 kid, kip, oak 4 alum, bock, buff, calf, napa, ooze, roan 5 aluta, basil, crown, grain, japan, mocha, strap, suede, whang 6 castor, comber, latigo, levant, oxhide, patent, roller, saddle, skiver 7 buffalo, canepin, carding, chamois, hemlock, morocco, ostrich, peccary, rutland, saffian 8 capeskin, cheverel, cordovan, cordwain, shagreen ***maker:*** 6 tanner 7 tannery ***piece:*** 4 rand, welt 5 strap, thong, trank ***prepare:*** 3 sam, tan, taw 4 mull 5 curry, sammy ***soft:*** 5 aluta, mocha, suede 8 cabretta

Leatherneck 6 marine

Leatherstocking Tales, The ***author:*** 6 Cooper ***title:*** 10 The Prairie 11 The Pioneers 13 The Deerslayer, The Pathfinder

leave 2 go 3 let 4 cede, drop, exit, have, quit, will 5 allot, allow, scram, waive, yield 6 assent, assign, commit, decamp, depart, desert, devise, escape, get off, give up, legate, maroon, permit, resign, retire, strand, suffer, vacate 7 abandon, confide, consent, consign, entrust, forsake, get away, holiday, pull out 8 bequeath, emigrate, hand over, sanction, vacation, withdraw 9 allowance, apportion, surrender, terminate 10 permission, relinquish, sufferance 13 authorization

leaved 7 foliate, foliose, folious 8 foliated

leaven 5 imbue, steep, yeast 6 infuse, invest, temper, vivify 7 enliven, ingrain, qualify, quicken, suffuse 8 moderate 9 inoculate

leavening agent 5 yeast 12 baking powder

leave of absence 5 exeat 8 furlough

leave off 4 halt, quit, stop 5 cease 6 desist 8 give over, knock off, surcease 11 discontinue

leave out 4 omit, skip 5 elide 7 exclude

Leaves of Grass author 7 Whitman

leavings 4 heel, junk, lees, orts, rest 5 dregs, scrap 7 balance, remains, remanet, remnant, residue, rubbish 8 discards, portions, residual, residuum 9 fragments, remainder

Lebanon ***capital:*** 6 Beirut ***monetary unit:*** 5 pound

lecher 4 rake, roué 9 debauchee, libertine

lecherous 4 fast, lewd 7 goatish, lustful, satyric 9 libertine, salacious 10 lascivious, libidinous, licentious 11 incontinent

lectern 4 desk 5 stand

lecture 4 talk 5 scold, speak 6 preach, sermon, speech 7 address, oration, prelect 8 briefing 9 discourse 10 allocution

lecturer 6 docent, orator, reader 7 speaker, teacher 9 professor 10 praelector

Leda ***daughter:*** 5 Helen 12 Clytemnestra ***father:*** 8 Thestius ***husband:*** 9 Tyndareus ***lover:*** 4 swan, Zeus ***son:*** 6 Castor, Pollux

ledge 4 berm, lode, sill 5 berme, ridge, shelf

ledger 4 book 6 record 8 monument 9 footstone, headstone, tombstone 10 gravestone 11 grave marker

lee 5 haven 6 harbor 7 shelter

leech 4 worm 6 sponge, sucker 7 sponger 8 barnacle, hanger-on, parasite 10 freeloader 11 bloodsucker 12 lounge lizard

Leeds' river 4 Aire

leer 4 look, ogle 5 empty, fleer, smirk, sneer 6 glance 7 grimace

leery 4 wary 8 doubtful 10 suspicious 11 distrustful

lees 5 draff, dregs 6 dunder, refuse 7 deposit, grounds, vinasse 8 leavings, sediment 9 settlings 11 precipitate

leeward 8 downwind

leeway 4 play, room 5 scope, space 6 margin 8 latitude 9 elbowroom

left 4 port 8 larboard

left-handed 8 southpaw

left-hand page 5 verso

leftovers see leavings

leftward 4 levo 5 aport, laevo 8 levogyre 10 levogyrate ***go:*** 3 haw

leg 3 gam, run 4 gamb, limb, walk 5 gambe, shank 6 gammon 7 support 8 cabriole 9 appendage, drumstick ***bone:*** 4 shin 5 femur, tibia 6 fibula 7 patella ***part:*** 4 calf, crus, foot, knee, shin 5 ankle, thigh 6 cnemis

legacy 4 gift 6 devise 7 bequest 8 heritage 9 heritance, patrimony 10 birthright 11 inheritance

legal 5 licit 6 lawful 7 juridic 8 innocent 9 juridical 10 legitimate ***matter:*** 3 res 4 case, suit ***order:*** 4 writ 7 summons 8 subpoena ***party:*** 6 suitor 8 litigant 9 defendant, plaintiff ***restraint:*** 8 estoppel

legal aid group 4 ACLU

legal tender 4 cash 5 money 6 dollar 8 currency

legate 4 will 5 envoy, leave 6 deputy, devise 8 bequeath, delegate, emissary, governor 10 ambassador

legatee 4 heir 9 inheritor

legend 4 lore, myth, saga 5 fable, story 6 mythos, mythus 7 caption, fiction 8 folklore 9 mythology, tradition

legendary 6 fabled, mythic 7 fabular 8 fabulous, mythical 12 mythological

legerdemain 5 magic 8 trickery 9 conjuring

legging 5 chaps 6 puttee 7 gambade, gambado 11 spatterdash 12 antigropelos

leghorn 4 fowl 5 straw 7 chicken

legible 5 clear 8 distinct, readable

legion 4 army, host, many, rout 5 cloud, crowd, flock 6 scores, sundry 7 various 8 numerous, populous 9 multitude

legislate 5 enact

legislation 3 act, law 4 bill 7 statute

legislator 3 rep 5 solon 6 deputy 7 senator 8 lawgiver, lawmaker 9 statesman 10 politician 11 congressman

legislature 4 diet 5 house, junta 6 senate 7 council 8 assembly, congress 10 parliament ***Communist:*** 6 soviet 9 politburo, presidium ***czarist Russian:*** 4 duma ***Danish:*** 9 Folketing ***Finnish:*** 9 Eduskunta ***German:*** 9 Bundesrat, Bundestag ***Iceland:*** 7 Althing ***Israel:*** 7 Knesset ***Norway:*** 8 Storting ***one-house:*** 10 unicameral ***Poland:*** 4 Sejm ***Spain:*** 6 Cortes ***Sweden:*** 7 Riksdag ***two-house:*** 9 bicameral

legitimate 4 fair, just, true 5 legal, licit, sound, usual, valid 6 cogent, lawful, normal 7 natural, regular, typical 8 innocent, rightful 9 customary 10 recognized

leg of lamb 5 gigot

legume 3 pea, pod, soy 4 bean, guar,

seed, soya 5 pulse 6 lentil 7 soybean 9 bird's-foot, vegetable
leg up 5 boost
lei 6 wreath 7 garland 8 necklace
Leibnitz's invention 8 calculus
Leif Ericson *discovery:* 7 Vinland *father:* 4 Eric
leisure 4 ease, rest, time 6 casual, repose 10 relaxation 12 requiescence
leisurely 3 lax 4 easy, slow 5 slack 7 delayed, laggard, relaxed, restful, unhasty 8 dilatory 9 slackened, unhurried
leitmotiv 5 theme 6 motive
lemma 5 bract, theme 7 premise, theorem
lemon 3 dud 4 bomb, bust, flop 5 fruit, loser 7 failure
lemur 4 maki, vari 5 indri, locis, potto 6 aye-aye, colugo, macaco 7 half-ape, tarsier 9 babacoote
lend 4 give, loan 5 allow, grant 6 oblige 7 advance, furnish 11 accommodate
length 4 term 5 orbit, range, reach, realm, scope 6 radius 7 compass, purview, stretch, yardage 8 distance, panorama
lengthen 4 draw 6 expand, extend 7 draw out, prolong, spin out, stretch 8 elongate, increase, protract 10 prolongate *Scottish:* 3 eke
lengthy 4 long 8 dragging, drawn-out, elongate, extended, longsome, overlong 9 elongated, prolonged 10 protracted
leniency 5 mercy 8 clemency 9 tolerance 10 indulgence, toleration 11 forbearance
lenient 3 lax 4 easy, kind, mild, soft 5 balmy, bland, faint 6 benign, gentle, kindly, smooth, tender 7 amiable, clement 8 excusing, humoring, merciful, obliging, spoiling, tolerant 9 benignant, condoning, forgiving, indulgent, indulging, pampering, pardoning 10 charitable, forbearing
lenity 5 grace, mercy 7 caritas, charity 8 clemency 10 humaneness, tenderness
lens 5 glass 6 lentil 8 meniscus *kind:* 5 toric 6 convex 7 bifocal, concave 8 trifocal
lentigo 5 nevus 7 freckle
lentil 4 lens, seed 6 legume
Leofric's wife 6 Godiva
Leoncavallo opera 9 Pagliacci
leonine 8 lionlike
Leonora *alias:* 7 Fidelio *husband:* 9 Florestan
leopard 3 cat 7 panther
Leo star 7 Regulus
leper 6 pariah 7 Ishmael, outcast 8 castaway, derelict 10 Ishmaelite 11 untouchable
Leper King 7 Baldwin
Leper Priest 6 Damien
lepers' hospital 9 lazaretto
lepers' island 7 Molokai
lepidopter 4 moth 6 insect 9 butterfly
Leporello's master 11 Don Giovanni
leprechaun 3 elf 5 fairy 6 sprite *trade:* 8 cobbling
Lesage hero 7 Gil Blas
Lesbos poet 6 Sappho 7 Alcaeus
lesion 3 cut 4 flaw, sore 5 ulcer, wound 6 injury 10 impairment
Lesotho *capital:* 6 Maseru *monetary unit:* 4 loti
lessen 4 clip, crop, ease, thin, wane 5 abate, close, drain, lower, taper 6 dilute, minify, reduce, shrink, weaken 7 abridge, assuage, curtail, dwindle, lighten, relieve 8 amputate, decrease, diminish, minimize, mitigate, taper off, truncate 9 attenuate
lessening 5 letup 8 decrease, slowdown 9 abatement
lesser 3 low 5 dinky, lower, minor, small, under 6 nether 8 inferior, small-fry 9 secondary, small-time, subjacent 11 minor-league 13 insignificant
lesson 4 text 5 chide, moral, study 6 monish, rebuke 7 lecture, reading, reprove, tick off 8 admonish, call down, exercise, reproach 9 reprimand 11 instruction
lessor 6 bailor 8 landlady, landlord
let 4 have, hire, rent 5 allow, grant, lease, leave 6 permit, suffer 7 approve, certify, charter, concede, endorse, licence 8 accredit, sanction 9 authorize
letdown 5 slump 7 decline 10 depression
let go 4 emit, fire, free 6 unhand 7 dismiss, release 9 discharge
lethal 5 fatal 6 deadly, mortal, poison 7 deathly 9 pestilent, poisonous
lethargic 4 dull, idle, slow 5 dopey, heavy, inert 6 stolid, stupid, supine, torpid 7 dormant, laggard, languid, passive 8 comatose, dilatory, inactive, listless, sluggish 9 apathetic, impassive 10 languorous, phlegmatic, slumberous, spiritless 12 hebetudinous 13 lackadaisical
lethargy 4 coma 5 sleep, sloth 6 apathy, phlegm, stupor, torpor 7 inertia, languor, slumber 8 dullness, hebetude, idleness, laziness 9 disregard, inanition, indolence, inertness, lassitude, torpidity, unconcern 10 inactivity, supineness, torpidness 11 disinterest, impassivity, insouciance, passiveness
lethe 8 oblivion 13 forgetfulness
let in 5 admit
Leto see Latona
let off 5 spare 6 excuse, exempt 7 absolve, relieve 8 dispense 9 discharge
let on 3 own 4 avow, tell 5 admit, allow, grant, own up, spill 6 betray, fess up, reveal, unveil 7 concede, confess, divulge, uncover 8 disclose, give away

letter 2 ar, ef, el, em, en, ex 3 bee, cee, cue, dee, ess, gee, jay, kay, pee, tee, vee, wye, zed, zee 4 line, mail, memo, note, rune 5 aitch, print, vowel 6 report, screed, symbol 7 epistle, message, missive 8 dispatch, inscribe 9 consonant ***airmail:*** 8 aerogram ***Anglo-Saxon:*** (see **Anglo-Saxon**) ***Arabic:*** (see **alphabet**) ***Greek:*** (see **alphabet**) ***Hebrew:*** (see **alphabet**) ***kind:*** 5 chain, roman 6 italic, uncial 8 Dear John ***large:*** 7 capital 9 majuscule, upper case ***small:*** 9 lower case, miniscule
lettuce 3 cos 4 Bibb, head 6 Boston 7 iceberg, romaine, Simpson 10 butterweed
let up 3 ebb 4 fall, wane 5 abate 6 relent 7 die away, die down, ease off, slacken
letup 5 break 7 respite 9 reduction
Levant, Levantine 7 eastern
levee 4 dike, dock, pier, quay, slip 5 berth, jetty, wharf 10 embankment
level 3 aim, lay, par 4 akin, cast, down, drop, even, fell, flat, like, raze, same, tier, true, turn 5 alike, equal, floor, flush, plane, point, train 6 direct, ground, smooth, zero in 7 address, aligned, flatten, incline, mow down, planate, regular, similar, uniform 8 parallel, smoothen 9 bring down
lever 3 bar, lam, pry 4 jack 5 helve, jimmy, peavy, prize 6 peavey 7 crowbar
leverage 5 power 9 influence
leveret 4 hare
Levi ***father:*** 5 Jacob ***mother:*** 4 Leah ***son:*** 6 Kohath, Merari 7 Gershon
leviathan 4 huge 5 giant, titan, whale 7 immense, mammoth, monster 8 behemoth, enormous, gigantic 9 cyclopean 10 gargantuan 11 elephantine
Leviathan author 6 Hobbes
levitate 4 lift, rise 5 float 7 suspend
levity 5 folly, humor 8 buoyancy 9 absurdity, flippancy, frivolity, lightness, silliness
levy 3 set, tax 4 duty 5 exact, lay on, place, put on, wrest, wring 6 assess, charge, impose, impost, tariff 10 assessment
lewd 4 base, fast 5 bawdy, gross 6 coarse 7 lustful, obscene, satyric, whorish 8 improper, indecent 9 lecherous, libertine, salacious 10 indelicate, lascivious, libidinous, licentious 11 incontinent
Lewis and Clark interpreter 9 Sacagawea, Sacajawea
Lewis novel 7 Babbitt 9 Dodsworth 10 Arrowsmith, Main Street 11 Elmer Gantry
lexicographer 8 compiler ***American:*** 6 Porter 7 Webster 9 Worcester ***English:*** 4 Wyld 6 Fowler, Murray, Onions 7 Craigie, Johnson ***French:*** 6 Littré 8 Larousse
lexicon 4 cant 6 jargon 7 palaver 8 language, wordbook 9 word-hoard, wordstock 10 dictionary, vocabulary 11 onomasticon, terminology
liable 3 apt 4 open, tied 5 bound, given, prone 6 likely 7 exposed, subject 8 amenable, beatable, inclined, vincible 9 obnoxious, sensitive 10 answerable, assailable, attackable, chargeable, penetrable, vulnerable 11 accountable, conquerable, responsible, susceptible
liaison 4 bond 5 amour 6 affair 7 affaire 8 intrigue 12 relationship
liar 6 fibber 7 Ananias, fibster 8 fabulist, perjurer 9 falsifier 12 prevaricator ***female:*** 8 Sapphira
libation 5 drink 6 liquid 7 potable 8 beverage, potation
libel 6 defame, malign, vilify 7 asperse, calumny, slander, traduce 8 tear down, travesty 9 burlesque, denigrate 10 calumniate, caricature, scandalize
libelous 8 debasing 9 invidious, maligning, traducing, vilifying 10 backbiting, calumnious, defamatory, derogative, detracting, detractive, detractory, malevolent, pejorative, scandalous, slanderous
liberal 4 free, open, wide 5 ample, broad 6 lavish, plenty 7 copious, lenient, profuse, radical 8 abundant, advanced, generous, handsome, prodigal, tolerant 9 bounteous, bountiful, exuberant, indulgent, plenteous, plentiful, unsparing 10 benevolent, bighearted, charitable, forbearing, freehanded, munificent, openhanded
liberate 4 free 5 loose, remit 6 detach, loosen, unbind, unhook 7 manumit, release, unchain 8 untangle 9 discharge, unshackle 10 emancipate 12 disembarrass
liberator 7 messiah ***of Argentina:*** 9 San Martin ***of Chile:*** 8 O'Higgins ***of Ecuador:*** 5 Sucre ***of Scotland:*** 5 Bruce ***of South America:*** 7 Bolivar
Liberia ***capital:*** 8 Monrovia ***monetary unit:*** 6 dollar
Liberian ***language:*** 3 Kwa ***native:*** 3 Kru, Vai 4 Gola, Toma 5 Bassa, Grebo 6 Kruman
libertine 4 fast, lewd, rake, roué 7 lustful, satyric 9 debauchee, lecherous, salacious 10 lascivious, libidinous, licentious
liberty 5 leave 7 freedom, license 8 autonomy, delivery 10 liberation 12 emancipation, independence
libidinous 3 hot 4 fast, lewd 5 gross 6 coarse 7 goatish, lustful, obscene, satyric 8 prurient 9 lecherous, libertine, lickerish, salacious 10 lascivious, licentious, passionate 11 incontinent 12 concupiscent
Libni ***father:*** 5 Mahli 7 Gershon ***grandfather:*** 4 Levi
librarian 5 Dewey

library 7 archive 9 athenaeum 11 bibliotheca, reading room ***desk:*** 6 carrel
Libya ***capital:*** 7 Tripoli ***chief export:*** 3 oil ***largest city:*** 8 Benghazi ***monetary unit:*** 5 dinar ***father:*** 7 Epaphus ***son:*** 5 Belus 6 Agenor
license 3 let 5 allow, leave 6 enable, laxity, permit, suffer 7 certify, empower, freedom, liberty 8 accredit, passport, sanction, variance 9 authorize, looseness, slackness
licentious 3 lax 4 fast, lewd 5 loose, randy 6 amoral, animal, carnal 7 corrupt, fleshly, immoral, lustful, relaxed, satyric, sensual, unmoral 8 depraved, scabrous 9 abandoned, debauched, dissolute, lecherous, libertine, oversexed, reprobate, salacious 10 lascivious, libidinous, profligate 11 incontinent 12 unprincipled
lichen 4 moss 6 archil, litmus 7 oakmoss ***genus:*** 5 Usnea
licit 5 legal 6 lawful 8 approved, innocent, licensed 10 authorized, legitimate, sanctioned
lick 3 hit, lap, rap 4 beat, cast, dash, down, drub, flog, hint, swat, whip, wipe 5 knock, smack, smear, swipe, taste, throw, tinge, touch, trace, whiff 6 hurdle, master, thrash, tongue 7 clobber, conquer, shellac, smollop 8 lambaste, overcome, surmount 9 overwhelm
lickerish see **libidinous**
lickety-split 4 fast 5 apace 7 flat out, hastily, quickly, rapidly, swiftly 8 speedily 9 posthaste 13 expeditiously
licorice 4 root 5 candy ***pill:*** 6 cachou
lid 3 cap, top 5 cover 8 covering ***moss:*** 9 operculum
lie 3 fib 4 flam, myth, rest, tale 5 dwell, exist, fable, libel, story 6 canard, delude, inhere, palter, repose, reside 7 beguile, consist, deceive, distort, falsify, falsity, forgery, lie down, mislead, perjure, perjury, recline, untruth 8 misguide, misstate, nontruth, untruism 9 falsehood, fish story, mendacity, misinform 10 dishonesty, distortion, equivocate, exaggerate, inaccuracy, inveracity, stretch out, taradiddle 11 fraudulence, misinstruct, prevaricate 12 misstatement, song and dance
Liebestraum composer 5 Liszt
lied 4 aria, hymn, song 5 ditty 7 descant
lie down 4 rest 6 repose 7 recline 10 stretch out
lief 4 fain 6 freely, gladly 9 willingly
liege 4 true 5 loyal 6 ardent, vassal 7 staunch 8 constant, faithful, resolute 9 steadfast
lien 5 claim 6 charge 8 interest, mortgage
lieu 5 place, stead
lieutenant 3 aid 4 aide, zany 7 officer 9 assistant, coadjutor 10 aide-de-camp, coadjutant
life 3 bio, man, vim 4 body, brio, dash, élan, soul, zing 5 being, blood, human, oomph, verve 6 energy, esprit, memoir, mortal, person, spirit 8 creature, vitality 9 animation, biography, existence, personage 13 autobiography ***animal:*** 5 fauna ***animal and plant:*** 5 biota ***combining form:*** 2 bi 3 bia, bio 4 bium, bius 5 biont 6 bioses (plural), biosis, biotic ***plant:*** 5 flora ***relating to:*** 5 vital 8 biologic 10 biological ***science:*** 7 biology
life jacket 7 Mae West
lifeless 4 cold, dead, drab, dull, flat, late 5 amort, inert, prosy 6 asleep, torpid 7 defunct, extinct, prosaic 8 deceased, departed 9 colorless, exanimate, inanimate 10 lackluster, lusterless
lifelike 6 verist 8 accurate, veristic 9 realistic
life of ___ 5 Riley 8 the party
Life with Father author 3 Day
lift 2 up 3 aid, nip 4 doff, hand, heft, help, hook, jack, rear, rise, soar 5 arise, exalt, filch, heave, hoist, mount, pinch, raise, shrug, steal, surge, swipe, theft, tower 6 ascend, aspire, assist, pick up, pilfer, recall, relief, repeal, revoke, rocket, snitch, succor, take up, uphold, uprear 7 comfort, elevate, larceny, magnify, purloin, rescind, reverse, secours, support, upraise 8 levitate, stealage, stealing, thievery
lift-off 6 launch 7 takeoff 9 launching
ligament 3 tie 4 band, bond, knot, link, yoke 5 nexus 8 ligature, vinculum
ligature see **ligament**
Ligeia author 3 Poe
light 3 gay, hit 4 airy, bump, dawn, deft, easy, fair, fast, fire, lamp, land, luck, meet, morn, neon, soft 5 blond, dizzy, flash, giddy, loose, minor, perch, petty, roost, royal, small, sunny, torch 6 aurora, beacon, bright, candle, casual, chance, facile, flimsy, fluffy, happen, ignite, illume, kindle, little, meager, settle, simple, slight, smooth, strobe, swimmy, tumble, wanton 7 downing, flighty, inflame, lantern, lighten, morning, set down, sit down, slender, stumble, sunrise, trivial, unheavy, whorish 8 cheerful, cockcrow, daybreak, daylight, enkindle, illumine, luminous, skittish, swimming, trifling, unchaste 9 frivolous, small-beer, touch down 10 bird-witted, chandelier, effortless, illuminate ***combining form:*** 4 luci, phos, phot 5 lumin, photo 6 lumini, lumino ***measure:*** 3 lux 4 phot 5 lumen 6 candle 7 candela ***refractor:*** 5 prism ***relating to:*** 6 photic ***ring:*** 4 halo 6 corona 7 aureola, aureole ***science:*** 6 optics 7 photics ***source:*** 3 sun 4 lamp

light-emitting ***suffix:*** **6** escent
lighten **4** dawn, ease, fade, thin **5** allay **6** bleach, dilute, illume **7** assuage, mollify, relieve **8** brighten, illumine, mitigate **9** alleviate, attenuate, extenuate **10** illuminate
light-headed **5** dizzy, giddy **6** swimmy **7** flighty **8** swimming **9** frivolous **10** bird-witted **11** vertiginous
lighthearted **3** gay **4** glad **5** happy, jolly, merry **6** blithe, jocund, jovial, joyful, joyous, lively **7** buoyant, festive, gleeful **8** carefree, cheerful, mirthful, spirited, volatile **9** expansive, resilient, sprightly, vivacious **10** blithesome, free-minded, insouciant **12** effervescent, happy-go-lucky, high-spirited
lighthouse **5** guide, phare **6** beacon, pharos **7** warning **8** guidance **9** direction
lightless **3** dim **4** dark, dusk **5** dusky, murky **6** gloomy **7** obscure **9** tenebrous **10** caliginous **11** unillumined
lightness **6** gaiety, levity **8** buoyancy, vivacity **9** flippancy, frivolity **10** elasticity, liveliness, resiliency, volatility **11** flightiness **12** cheerfulness **13** effervescence, expansiveness
lightning bug **7** firefly
lignite **4** coal **9** brown coal
likable **6** genial **8** friendly, pleasant, pleasing **10** attractive
like **2** as **3** dig **4** akin, same, such, will, wish **5** close, elect, enjoy, equal, match **6** admire, agnate, allied, choose, esteem, please, prefer, regard, relish, select **7** approve, cognate, endorse, kindred, related, respect, similar, uniform **8** parallel, selfsame, suchlike **9** analogous, consonant, identical **10** appreciate, comparable, comprehend, equivalent, resembling ***combining form:*** **3** sym, syn **4** home **5** homeo, homoe, homoi **6** homoeo, homoio ***suffix:*** **2** ar, ic, ly **3** ine, ish, oid **4** eous, ical **5** oidal
likelihood **6** chance **11** probability
likely **3** apt **4** rosy **5** given, prone **6** liable, mortal **7** earthly, hopeful, roseate **8** inclined, possible, probable, probably **9** assumably, doubtless, promising **10** presumably, promiseful
liken **5** match **6** equate **7** compare, paragon **8** parallel **10** assimilate
likeness **4** copy, twin **5** image **6** effigy, simile **7** analogy, picture, replica **8** affinity, equality, identity, sameness **9** agreement, facsimile, semblance **10** comparison, conformity, photograph, similarity, similitude, uniformity **11** equivalence, parallelism, resemblance
likewise **2** so **3** and, too **4** also, more **5** along **6** as well, withal **7** besides **8** moreover **9** similarly **11** furthermore
liking **4** lust, mind, will **5** fancy, gusto, taste **8** affinity, appetite, fondness, penchant, pleasure, soft spot, velleity, weakness **11** inclination **12** predilection ***combining form:*** **4** phil **5** phile **6** philic **7** philous
Lilith ***husband:*** **4** Adam ***successor:*** **3** Eve
lilliputian **3** wee **4** runt, tiny **5** dwarf, midge, pygmy, teeny, weeny **6** midget, minute, peewee, teensy, teenty **7** manikin **8** Tom Thumb **10** diminutive, homunculus, teeny-weeny **12** teensy-weensy
lilt **3** air **4** sing, song, tune **5** swing
lily **3** pad **4** aloe, ixia, sego **5** calla, tiger, white, yucca **6** flower **7** leopard **8** mariposa ***combining form:*** **6** crinus
Lily ___ **4** Pons
lily of France **10** fleur-de-lis
lily-livered **6** coward, craven **7** chicken, gutless, unmanly **8** cowardly **9** spunkless **11** poltroonish **12** poor-spirited **13** pusillanimous
lily-white **4** good, pure **8** innocent, virtuous **9** blameless, exemplary, guiltless, righteous **10** inculpable
lima **4** bean, seed **7** mollusk
liman **3** bay **6** lagoon **7** estuary
limb **3** arm, fin, leg **4** twig, wing **5** bough, devil, rogue, scamp, shoot, spray, sprig **6** branch, member, rascal, switch **7** villain **8** mischief, scalawag **9** appendage
limber **5** agile, lithe, loose **6** pliant, supple **7** elastic, lissome, plastic, pliable, springy **8** flexible **9** lithesome, resilient
limbo **5** dance **6** prison **8** oblivion
lime **5** color, fruit, green **6** citrus
limen **9** threshold
limerick **4** poem **5** verse **8** fishhook ***writer:*** **4** Lear
limestone **4** malm, tufa **5** chalk **6** marble, oolite, oolith **7** coquina
lime tree **4** teil **6** linden
limit **3** bar, end, fix, rim, set **4** brim, curb, edge, term **5** brink, check, pinch, quota, verge **6** assign, border, curfew, define, hinder, lessen, margin, narrow **7** appoint, extreme, mark out, measure **8** contract, deadline, restrain, restrict **9** constrict, demarcate, determine, extremity, prescribe
limitless **4** vast **8** infinite, termless **9** unbounded **10** indefinite, unmeasured **11** innumerable, undrainable **12** immeasurable, incalculable, unfathomable **13** inexhaustible
limn **4** draw **5** image **6** depict, render, sketch **7** picture, portray **8** describe **9** delineate, interpret, represent
Limoges product **9** porcelain
limp **3** lax **4** halt, lame, wilt **5** hitch, loose, slack **6** falter, flabby, floppy, hobble, muddle, sleazy, supple, toddle, totter, waddle, wobble **7** die-away, flaccid, languid, relaxed, shuffle, stagger, stumble **9** enervated **10** languorous, spiritless

limpid 4 pure 5 clear, lucid 10 see-through 11 translucent, transparent
limping 4 halt, lame 5 gimpy 8 lameness 12 claudication
Lincoln ***assassin:*** 5 Booth ***biographer:*** 7 Masters 8 Sandburg ***debater:*** 7 Douglas ***law partner:*** 7 Herndon ***mother:*** 5 Nancy ***nickname:*** 9 Honest Abe 12 Railsplitter ***photographer:*** 5 Brady ***secretary of state:*** 6 Seward ***secretary of war:*** 7 Stanton ***wife:*** 8 Mary Todd
line 3 job, pad, ray, row, way 4 abut, file, join, path, rank, road, rope, tier, work 5 align, array, goods, march, order, queue, range, route, touch, train, verge, wares 6 adjoin, border, butt on, column, course, policy, polity, series, string 7 arrange, calling, contour, echelon, marshal, passage, profile, program, pursuit 8 business, neighbor, ordinate, sequence 9 procedure, vendibles 10 employment, figuration, occupation, silhouette, succession ***curved:*** 3 arc ***mathematical:*** 6 vector ***metrical:*** 5 verse 6 verset 8 versicle
lineage 4 clan, folk, race 5 birth, blood, house, stock, tribe 6 family, origin, stirps 7 descent, kindred 8 ancestry, pedigree
lineal 6 direct 10 hereditary
lineament 7 contour, feature, outline, profile 10 figuration, silhouette
lineation see **lineament**
lined 5 ruled 7 lineate, striate, striped 8 lineated, streaked, wrinkled
linen 4 lawn 5 cloth, toile 6 byssus, damask, dowlas, fabric, forfar, napery, sheets 7 batiste, bedding, cambric, Holland, taffeta 8 cretonne, lingerie ***fiber:*** 3 tow 4 line ***source:*** 4 flax
liner 4 ship 6 insert, vessel
Linet, Lynette ***brother:*** 6 Liones ***husband:*** 6 Gareth
linger 3 lag 4 bide, drag, mope, poke, stay, wait 5 abide, amble, dally, delay, drift, mosey, tarry 6 bummel, dawdle, loiter, put off, remain, stroll 11 stick around
lingerie 6 undies 9 underwear
lingo 4 cant 5 argot, slang 6 jargon, patois, patter 7 dialect 10 vernacular
linguist 8 polyglot 11 philologist
linguistics 9 philology
liniment 3 oil 6 lotion 8 ablution, ointment
lining 6 facing, insert 8 wainscot ***combining form:*** 6 pleura
link 3 tie 4 bond, join, knot, yoke 5 nexus, unite 6 couple, relate 7 combine, conjoin, connect 8 catenate, vinculum 9 associate, conjugate
linksman 6 golfer
linnet 5 finch
lint 3 fur 4 down, flue, fuzz, pile 5 floss, fluff 7 charpie 9 ravelings
lion 3 cat, VIP 4 king, puma 5 chief 6 big boy, cougar, leader 7 notable 8 bigtimer, eminence, luminary 9 carnivore ***group:*** 5 pride ***young:*** 3 cub
lioness headed goddess 3 Mut 6 Sekhet
lionhearted 4 bold 5 brave 7 valiant 8 fearless, intrepid, unafraid, valorous 9 dauntless 10 courageous
lionlike 7 leonine
lion monkey 7 tamarin 8 leoncito, marmoset
Lion of Judah 13 Haile Selassie
lip 3 rim 4 brim, buss, edge, kiss, lave, peck, wash 5 babble, smack 6 labium, labrum, margin, smooch 8 osculate ***relating to:*** 6 labial
lipid 3 fat, wax
lipped 7 labiate 9 bilabiate
lip server 8 pharisee, Tartuffe 9 hypocrite
liquefy 3 run 4 flux, fuse, melt, thaw, thin 6 soften 8 dissolve
liqueur 4 ouzo, raki 5 crème, noyau 6 kummel 7 cordial, curaçao, ratafia, rosolio, sloe gin 8 absinthe, anisette, prunelle 10 chartreuse, pousse-café
liquid 5 drink, fluid, sauce, water 6 golden, lotion, mellow, watery 7 honeyed 8 beverage, emulsion, Hyblaean 11 mellifluent, mellifluous ***aromatic:*** 7 eugenol 8 terpinol ***container:*** 3 cup, jug, mug 4 vial 5 glass 6 bottle, goblet 7 pitcher, tumbler ***corrosive:*** 5 oleum ***flammable:*** 3 gas, oil 5 ether, furan 6 butane, toluol 7 alcohol, dioxine, ligroin, toluene 8 furfuran, gasoline, ligroine, propenol, pyridine ***measure:*** 2 cc, ml, oz, pt, qt 3 cup, gal 4 pint 5 liter, ounce, quart 6 gallon ***medicinal:*** 8 liniment, ointment ***oily:*** 5 fusel 6 octane ***resinous:*** 6 tallol ***scented:*** 7 cologne, perfume ***thick:*** 5 sirup, syrup 8 molasses ***volatile:*** 6 hexane 7 naphtha, pentane 8 isoprene, phenetol
liquidate 3 pay 4 cool, do in, quit 5 clear, pay up, purge 6 murder, remove, settle, square 7 satisfy 8 amortize, clear off
liquor 4 grog 5 booze, drink 7 alcohol, potable, spirits 8 beverage, potation 9 aqua vitae, drinkable, firewater, inebriant, moonshine 10 intoxicant ***add:*** 4 lace 5 spike ***homemade:*** 9 moonshine 10 bathtub gin ***inferior:*** 5 hooch, smoke 6 rotgut ***kind:*** 3 gin, rum, rye 5 vodka 6 brandy, geneva, scotch 7 bourbon, whiskey 8 vermouth ***malt:*** 3 ale 4 beer 5 stout ***measure:*** 4 dram ***Mexican:*** 5 sotol 6 mescal 7 tequila ***Oriental:*** 4 sake, saki 6 arrack, samshu
liquor cabinet 10 cellarette
lissome 5 agile, lithe 6 limber, supple 8 flexible

list 3 tip 4 book, cant, file, heel, lean, menu, note, post, roll, tilt 5 count, index, slant, slope 6 agenda, detail, enroll, record, roster 7 catalog, incline, itemize, recline, specify, tick off 8 glossary, inscribe, numerate, register, roll call, schedule, tabulate 9 chronicle, enumerate, inventory 10 specialize 13 particularize
listen 4 hark, hear, heed, note 6 attend, harken 8 overhear 9 eavesdrop
listeners 8 audience
listless 4 dull, limp 6 drowsy, sleepy 7 die-away, languid 9 apathetic, enervated 10 languorous 11 languishing 13 lackadaisical
listlessness 6 apathy 8 doldrums, lethargy 9 disregard, lassitude, unconcern 11 disinterest, insouciance 12 indifference
litany 4 list 5 chant 6 ektene, prayer 7 synapte 8 rogation
literal 5 exact 7 precise 8 verbatim 11 word-for-word
literally 6 direct 8 verbatim 11 word for word
literary 7 bookish, erudite, learned 8 lettered, well-read
literary style *suffix:* 3 ese
literary work 4 book, opus, play, poem 5 cento, drama, essay, novel 10 short story
literature 4 kind 5 prose 6 poetry 7 fiction 10 nonfiction
lithe 4 lean, slim, thin 5 agile, spare 6 lissom, slight, supple, svelte 7 lissome, slender 8 graceful
lithium *symbol:* 2 Li
lithographer 4 Ives 7 Currier *French:* 5 Redon
Lithuanian 4 Balt 6 Baltic *capital:* 7 Vilnius *coin:* 6 centas
litigant 4 suer 6 suitor
litigation 4 case, suit 6 action 7 lawsuit
litter 3 bed 4 hash, junk 5 offal, trash, waste, young 6 basket, debris, jumble, jungle, muddle, refuse, tumble 7 garbage, rubbish, rummage, shuffle 8 mishmash, scramble 9 offspring, stretcher
little 3 set, wee 4 mean, puny, tiny 5 borne, light, minor, petty, short, small 6 bantam, casual, minute, monkey, narrow, paltry, petite, rarely, seldom 7 bigoted, limited, niggard, selfish, trivial, unoften 8 smallish 9 hidebound, illiberal, niggardly, secondary, small-beer 10 collateral, diminutive, fortuitous, hardly ever, incidental, provincial, shoestring, subsidiary 11 unimportant
little by little 8 inchmeal 9 gradually, piecemeal
Little Corporal 8 Napoleon
Little Dipper *constellation:* 9 Ursa Minor *star:* 5 North 7 Polaris
little finger or toe 7 minimus
Little Minister *author:* 6 Barrie *character:* 5 Gavin 6 Babbie 7 Dishart
little one *suffix:* 2 el, et, ey 2 ia (plural), ie 3 cle, ium, kin, ock, ula, ule, uli (plural) 4 ella, ette, illa, ling, ulae (plural), ulum, ulus 5 ellae (plural), illae (plural)
Little Women *author:* 6 Alcott *character:* 2 Jo 3 Amy, Meg 4 Beth *surname:* 5 March
liturgy 4 form, rite 7 service 8 ceremony 9 formality 10 ceremonial, observance
livable 4 cosy, snug 5 homey 6 viable 8 bearable, homelike 9 endurable
live 2 be, is 3 are 4 fare 5 abide, dwell, exist, green, vital 6 reside 7 breathe, dynamic, hang out, running, subsist, working
livelihood 3 art, fee, job, pay 4 keep, wage 5 bread, craft, trade 6 living, salary 7 alimony, stipend, support 9 emolument 10 handicraft, profession, sustenance 11 maintenance, subsistence
liveliness 4 brio, élan 5 verve 6 spirit 8 vibrance, vibrancy, vitality, vivacity
lively 3 gay 4 busy, fast, keen, pert, spry, yare 5 agile, alert, brisk, catty, fussy, jazzy, jolly, merry, peppy, zippy 6 active, blithe, bright, brisky, chirpy, frisky, jocund, nimble 7 animate, buoyant, chipper, dashing, driving, elastic, gleeful, hopping, humming, popping, rousing 8 animated, bustling, cheerful, chirping, chirrupy, hustling, mirthful, spirited, volatile 9 cock-a-hoop, energetic, expansive, hilarious, resilient, sprightly, vivacious
liven 5 cheer 6 vivify 7 animate, quicken
liver 4 foie 5 hepar 7 denizen 8 habitant, occupant, resident 9 indweller 10 inhabitant *combining form:* 5 hepat 6 hepato *disease:* 9 cirrhosis, hepatitis *lobster's:* 8 tomalley
liverwort 8 hepatica 9 bryophyte
livestock 6 cattle 7 animals
live wire 6 dynamo, peeler 7 hustler, rustler 8 go-getter 11 self-starter
livid 3 wan 4 ashy, pale 5 ashen, dusky, lurid, murky, waxen 6 doughy, gloomy, grisly, pallid, sultry 8 blanched 9 colorless
living 4 keep, salt 5 bread, vital 6 active, around, extant, zoetic 7 alimony, animate, dynamic, support 8 animated, existent 9 operative 10 livelihood, sustenance *combining form:* 3 ont 4 onto, vivi
living being 8 creature *combining form:* 2 zo 3 ont, zoa (plural), zoo 4 onto, zoon
living room 6 parlor 7 parlour 10 lebensraum
lizard 3 dab, eft, uma 4 adda, gila, newt, seps, uran 5 agama, anole, gecko, skink, teiid, tokay, varan, waral 6 dragon, goanna, iguana, moloch, worral, worrel 7 cheecha, monitor, reptile 8 basilisk, lacertid, slow-

worm, whiptail 9 alligator, blindworm, chameleon, crocodile 10 chuckwalla, salamander *combining form:* 4 saur 5 saura, sauro 6 sauria (plural) *genus:* 3 Uta 5 Agama 6 Ameiva, Anolis 7 Lacerta
llama 6 alpaca 7 guanaco
Lloyd's business 9 insurance
lo 4 hark, look
load 3 tax 4 bale, bear, care, cram, drag, duty, fill, glut, haul, lade, onus, pack, pile, task 5 cargo, carry, choke, drain, flood, gorge, laden, swamp, weigh 6 burden, charge, convey, cumber, debase, doctor, dope up, lading, parcel, saddle, weight 7 freight, surfeit 8 encumber, pressure, shipment 9 liability, millstone, transport
loaded 4 full 7 brimful 8 brimming 9 chock-full
loaf 3 bum 4 idle, laze, lazy 6 dawdle 9 goldbrick
loafer 3 bum 4 slug 5 idler 6 slouch 8 deadbeat, dolittle, fainéant, slugabed, sluggard 9 do-nothing, lazybones
loam 4 dirt, sand, silt, soil 7 topsoil *deposit:* 5 loess
loan 4 lend 5 prest 7 advance, imprest
loan shark 6 lender, usurer 7 Shylock 11 moneylender
loath 6 afraid, averse 7 uneager 8 hesitant 9 reluctant, unwilling 10 indisposed
loathe 4 hate 5 abhor, spurn 6 detest, refuse, reject 7 decline, despise 8 execrate 9 abominate, repudiate
loathsome 4 foul, ugly, vile 5 nasty 7 hateful, hideous 8 horrible 9 invidious, obnoxious, offensive, repellent, repugnant, repulsive, revolting 10 disgusting
lob 3 hit 4 shot, step, toss, vein 5 stair, throw
lobby 4 hall 5 foyer 8 anteroom 9 vestibule
lobe 4 flap 7 lobulus
lobo 4 wolf 10 timber wolf
lobster 10 crustacean *African:* 12 Cape crawfish *claw:* 5 chela 6 pincer *female:* 3 hen *male:* 4 cock *trap:* 3 pot 5 creel
local 6 native 7 endemic, insular, topical *combining form:* 3 top 4 topo
locale 4 area, site 5 place, scene, venue 6 region 8 district, vicinage, vicinity 11 mise-en-scène 12 neighborhood
locality 4 area, belt, home, seat, site, zone 5 field, haunt, range, tract 6 domain, region, sector, sphere 7 habitat, section 8 district, province, vicinage 9 bailiwick, territory 12 neighborhood
localize 8 pinpoint
locate 3 spy 4 espy, find, site, spot 5 place, trace 6 settle 7 situate, station, uncover 8 discover, pinpoint, position 9 establish
locating device 5 lidar, radar, sonar
location 4 area, site, spot 5 locus, place, point, scene, where 7 habitat
loch 3 bay 4 lake
lock 3 fix 4 bolt, curl, hank, tuft 5 click, latch, tress 6 bundle, fasten, secure 7 ringlet 8 fastener 9 fastening
Locke's tabula ___ 4 rasa
lockjaw 7 tetanus, trismus
Locksley Hall author 8 Tennyson
lockup 3 jug, pen 4 coop, jail 6 cooler, prison
loco 3 mad 5 crazy 6 insane
locomotive 5 cheer, dolly, train 6 engine 7 movable 8 moveable 9 camelback *small:* 5 dinky 6 dinkey *type:* 5 steam 6 diesel 8 electric
Locrine *daughter:* 7 Sabrina *father:* 4 Brut 6 Brutus *lover:* 9 Estrildis *wife:* 9 Gwendolen
locum tenens 3 sub 6 fill-in 7 stand-in 9 alternate, surrogate 10 substitute 11 pinch hitter, replacement, succedaneum
locust 5 carob 6 cicada, insect 11 grasshopper
locust bird 5 stork 7 grackle
locution 4 word 6 phrase 10 expression
lode 4 lead, vein 7 deposit
lodestar 5 guide 6 leader
lodestone 6 magnet 9 magnetite
lodge 3 cot, den, fix, hut, inn 4 camp, club, hold, lair, root, take 5 admit, board, cabin, couch, embed, hotel, house, infix, motel, put up, shack 6 accept, bestow, billet, burrow, harbor, hostel, shanty, tavern 7 auberge, contain, cottage, hospice, ingrain, quarter, receive 8 domicile, entrench, hostelry 9 entertain, roadhouse 11 accommodate, caravansary, public house
lodger 5 guest 6 renter, roomer, tenant
loess 4 loam 7 deposit
loft 3 bin 5 attic, raise 6 garret
loftiness 5 pride 6 height, morgue 7 disdain, hauteur, stature 9 arrogance, superbity
lofty 3 big 4 airy, epic, high, tall 5 grand, noble, proud 6 aerial, august, raised, superb 7 exalted, haughty, soaring, spiring, stately, sublime, topless, utopian 8 arrogant, cavalier, elevated, eloquent, generous, imposing, insolent, majestic, superior, towering 9 ambitious, grandiose, magnified, visionary 10 benevolent, chivalrous, disdainful 11 aggrandized, considerate, magnanimous, overbearing, pretentious, skyscraping 12 greathearted, supercilious
log 4 book, note, wood 5 diary, stick 6 record, timber 7 journal *mover:* 7 cantdog
logarithm inventor 6 Napier
loge 3 box 5 booth, stall 9 enclosure

logger 9 lumberman 10 lumberjack, woodcutter *legendary:* 10 Paul Bunyan
loggerhead 6 shrike, turtle
loggia 6 arcade 7 balcony, gallery
logic 6 reason 9 reasoning *specious:* 7 sophism 9 sophistry
logical 4 sane 5 clear, lucid, sound, valid 6 cogent, subtle 7 telling 8 analytic, sensible 10 compelling, convincing, reasonable
logjam 7 impasse 8 blockage, deadlock, stoppage
logo 4 mark 5 brand 9 trademark
logogriph 6 puzzle 7 anagram
logroll 4 birl
logrolling contest 5 roleo
logy 4 dull, slow 5 dopey, heavy 6 drowsy, groggy, torpid 8 listless, sluggish
Lohengrin *composer:* 6 Wagner *father:* 8 Parsifal, Parzival *wife:* 4 Elsa
loincloth *African:* 5 pagne *Hindu:* 5 dhoti, dhuti 6 dhooti *Indian:* 5 lungi 6 lungyi
Loire, city on the 5 Blois, Tours 6 Nantes 7 Orléans
Lois *daughter:* 6 Eunice *grandson:* 7 Timothy
loiter 3 bum, lag 4 drag, idle, laze, lazy, loaf, poke 5 dally, delay, tarry, trail 6 dawdle, diddle, lounge, put off
Loki *father:* 8 Farbauti *mother:* 3 Nal 6 Laufey *offspring:* 3 Hel 4 Hela 6 Fenris 7 Midgard *slayer:* 8 Heimdall *victim:* 6 Balder *wife:* 5 Sigyn 9 Angurboda
loll 3 bum 4 idle, laze, lazy 5 droop, slump, tarry 6 dawdle, diddle, slouch
Lollards' leader 6 Wyclif
lombard 6 cannon
Lombard king 5 Cleph 6 Alboin, Audoin 7 Aistulf, Aripert, Authari 9 Liudprand
London *borough:* 5 Brent 6 Barnet, Bexley, Ealing, Harrow, Sutton 7 Barking, Bromley, Chelsea, Croydon, Enfield, Hackney, Lambeth 8 Haringey, Havering, Hounslow, Lewisham 9 Greenwich, Islington, Redbridge 10 Kensington 11 Westminster *cathedral:* 7 St. Paul's *clock:* 6 Big Ben *district:* 4 Soho 5 Acton 7 Chelsea, Mayfair *gallery:* 4 Tate *policeman:* 5 bobby *prison:* 7 Newgate *river:* 6 Thames *square:* 9 Leicester, Trafalgar *street:* 4 Bond 5 Fleet 6 Strand 7 Downing 9 Whitehall 10 Piccadilly *subway:* 4 tube
London novel 9 White Fang 10 Martin Eden, The Sea Wolf 11 The Iron Heel 16 The Call of the Wild
lone 4 only, sole, solo 5 alone 6 single, unique 8 deserted, forsaken, isolated, secluded, separate, singular, solitary
lonely 4 lorn 5 alone 7 forlorn 8 deserted, homesick, lonesome, solitary
loneness 8 solitude 9 isolation
loner 6 hermit 7 outcast, recluse 8 outsider, solitary
Lone Ranger, The *creator:* 7 Striker (Fran) *helper:* 5 Tonto *horse:* 6 Silver *trademark:* 4 mask 12 silver bullet
lonesome see lonely
Lone Star State 5 Texas
long 3 age, aim, yen 4 ache, aeon, itch, lust, miss, pine, sigh, want 5 crave, dream, wordy, yearn 6 aspire, hanker, hunger, prolix, thirst 7 diffuse, dog's age, lengthy, suspire, verbose 8 blue moon, coon's age, dragging, drawn-out, eternity, extended 9 diffusive, extensive 10 protracted
long dozen 8 thirteen
long-drawn-out 7 lengthy 8 dragging 10 protracted
Longfellow poem 8 Christus, Hiawatha, Hyperion, Kavanagh 10 Evangeline 11 My Lost Youth 12 A Psalm of Life
long for 4 ache, pine, want 5 covet, crave, yearn
longing 3 yen 4 wish 6 desire, thirst 7 craving 8 appetite
Long, Long Ago composer 5 Bayly
longshoreman 9 stevedore
long-suffering 7 patient 8 humility, meekness, patience 9 lowliness 11 forbearance, patientness, resignation, subduedness
long suit 5 forte 6 medium, métier, oyster 8 eminency, strength 9 specialty 10 specialism
long-winded 5 wordy 6 prolix 7 diffuse, lasting, lengthy, verbose 9 redundant 10 palaverous
loo 6 toilet
look 3 air, mug, see 4 cast, face, gape, gawk, heed, hope, lean, leer, mien, mind, note, ogle, peek, peep, peer, seem, show, spot, tend, view 5 await, front, glare, gloat, sight, slant, sound, stare, watch 6 appear, aspect, attend, beware, divine, expect, eyeful, glance, glower, goggle, notice, regard, squint, survey, visage 7 count on, display, exhibit, express, glimpse, incline, observe, seeming 8 forecast, foretell, indicate, manifest 9 count upon 10 appearance, expression, rubberneck 11 countenance, physiognomy
look after 4 tend 6 attend 7 care for
look at 3 eye, see 4 ogle, view 6 behold 7 examine
look back 6 recall, review 7 reflect 8 remember 9 reminisce
look down 5 abhor, scorn, scout 7 contemn, despise, disdain, overtop 8 dominate, outstare 9 tower over 10 tower above
looker 6 beauty, eyeful, lovely 8 knockout
looker-on 6 viewer 7 watcher, witness 8 beholder, by-sitter, observer 9 bystander, spectator 10 eyewitness

look for 4 seek 5 await
looking glass 6 mirror
look into 5 study 7 examine, inspect 11 investigate
look out 4 mind 6 beware
lookout 4 ward 5 guard, scape, vigil, vista, watch 6 affair, cupola, picket, sentry 7 concern, palaver 8 business, prospect, sentinel, watchman 9 crow's nest, firetower, occasions, vigilance 10 observance, watchtower 9 widow's walk 11 observation, observatory, perspective 12 surveillance
loom 4 brew, bulk, hulk, near, rear, show 5 tower 6 appear, come on, emerge, gather, impend, make up, weaver 8 approach, stand out, threaten 9 forthcome ***part:*** 3 lam 4 caam 5 easer 6 heddle 7 harness, shuttle, treadle, trundle
loon 3 nut 4 bird 5 grebe
loony 3 nut 5 batty, crazy, silly, wacky 6 absurd, dement, insane, madman, maniac 7 foolish, lunatic, madling 9 bedlamite, non compos 10 Tom o' Bedlam 11 harebrained 12 preposterous
loony bin 6 asylum 8 madhouse, nuthouse 9 funny farm 10 booby hatch, crazy house
loop 3 arc, eye 4 ansa, arch, bend, coil, curl, gird, knot, ring 5 beset, curve, noose, picot, wheel 6 begird, circle, girdle, league, staple, wreath 7 circlet, circuit, compass 8 encircle, surround 9 encompass 13 circumference
looped 5 drunk 11 intoxicated
loophole 3 out 6 outlet 7 opening
loose 3 lax 4 bate, ease, easy, fast, fire, free, limp, undo, vent 5 abate, clear, let up, light, relax, shoot, slack, unbar, unfix, unpin, untie 6 flabby, remiss, unbind, unbolt, undone, unglue, unhook, unlace, unlash, unlock, unsnap, wanton 7 ease off, flaccid, manumit, relaxed, release, slacken, unchain, unclasp, unhitch, unlatch, unleash, unscrew, unstick, unstrap, whorish 8 detached, liberate, mitigate, reckless, separate, unbuckle, unbutton, unchaste, unfasten 9 alleviate, desultory, discharge, disengage, negligent, take out on, unbandage, untighten 10 capricious, disjointed, emancipate, incoherent, inconstant, unattached, unconfined, unfastened 11 disenthrall, extravagant, nonadhesive, unconnected 12 disconnected, unrestrained
loose end 6 detail 8 fragment
loose-fitting 5 baggy 6 droopy
loose-lipped see **loquacious**
loosen 3 lax 4 ease, free 5 relax, slack, untie 6 unbind 7 ease off, manumit, release, slacken, unchain 8 liberate, unbuckle, unfasten 9 discharge 10 emancipate
loosen up 5 relax 6 unbend, unwind 7 ease off
loot 3 rob 4 sack, swag 5 booty, dough, lucre, money, prize, rifle, spoil 6 boodle 7 pillage, plunder, ransack, relieve, seizure, stick up 9 knock over 10 plunderage 11 filthy lucre
looter 5 thief 6 reaver, riever 8 marauder, pillager, ravisher
lop 3 cut 4 chop, clip, jump, leap, trim 5 bound, droop, slump, vault 6 bounce, hurdle, slouch, spring 7 pendent, saltate 8 truncate
lope 3 jog, run 4 gait, romp, skip, trip 6 spring, sprint 7 skitter
lopsided 6 uneven 7 crooked, difform, unequal 8 top-heavy, unsteady 9 irregular 10 asymmetric, off-balance, unbalanced 13 unsymmetrical
loquacious 5 gabby, talky, wordy 6 chatty, prolix 7 verbose 9 jabbering, talkative 10 babblative 11 loose-lipped 12 loose-tongued, multiloquent 13 overtalkative
lord 2 Mr. 3 man, sir 4 boss, cock, earl, peer 5 noble, put on, swank, swell 6 affect, master, mister 7 husband, overawe, peacock, pretend, swagger 8 governor, nobleman, overbear 9 tyrannize ***feudal:*** 5 liege 8 seignour, suzerain ***Muslim:*** 6 sayyid
Lord High Executioner 4 Koko
Lord Jim author 6 Conrad
lordly 5 grand, noble, proud 6 august, puffed, uppity 7 haughty, swollen 8 affected, arrogant, cavalier, imposing, insolent, magnific, majestic, princely, snobbish, superior 9 egotistic, grandiose 10 disdainful 11 dictatorial, magisterial, magnificent, overbearing 12 supercilious 13 authoritarian, high-and-mighty
Lord of the Flies author 7 Golding
Lord's Prayer 9 Our Father 11 Paternoster
lore 4 myth, saga, tale 5 fable 6 custom, legend, mythos, wisdom 7 folkway, science 9 knowledge, mythology, tradition 11 information 12 old wives' tale, superstition
Lorelei 5 siren 9 temptress 10 seductress 11 femme fatale ***poet:*** 5 Heine ***river:*** 5 Rhine ***victim:*** 6 sailor 7 mariner
Lorenzo's beloved 7 Jessica
lorgnette 8 eyeglass 10 opera glass
Lorna Doone ***author:*** 9 Blackmore ***hero:*** 4 Ridd (John)
___-Lorraine 6 Alsace
lose 3 rid, rob 4 drop, fail, fall, miss, oust, slip, tine, tyne 5 clear, shake, yield 6 divest, give up, mislay 7 bereave, decline, deprive, forfeit, regress, succumb 8 misplace, shake

off, throw off, unburden **9** sacrifice, surrender

lose feathers **4** molt

loser **3** dud **4** bomb, bust, flop **5** lemon **7** also-ran, convict, failure **8** jailbird

loss **4** leak, ruin **5** havoc, waste **6** damage, defeat, injury **7** failure, forfeit **8** decrease **9** confusion, mislaying, privation, ruination, sacrifice **10** divestment, forfeiture, misplacing **11** bereavement, deprivation, deprivement, destruction

lost **4** dead, gone **6** absent, astray, bygone, damned, doomed, hidden, musing, passed, ruined **7** bemused, defunct, extinct, faraway, lacking, mislaid, missing **8** absorbed, departed, distrait, vanished **9** condemned, daydreamy, graceless **10** abstracted **11** inconscient, irrevocable, preoccupied, unconscious, unconverted **12** absent-minded, incorrigible, irredeemable, irreformable, unregenerate

Lost Horizon ***author:*** **6** Hilton ***land:*** **9** Shangri-La

lot **3** cut, ilk, set **4** bite, body, doom, fate, give, heap, kind, lump, mass, much, part, peck, plat, push, sort, type, yard **5** allow, array, batch, block, breed, bunch, clump, crowd, field, group, moira, patch, quota, share, slice, tract, weird **6** assign, barrel, bundle, circle, clutch, decree, kidney, kismet, parcel, stripe **7** cluster, destiny, feather, fortune, mete out, partage, portion, species **8** allocate, clearing, frontage **9** admeasure, aggregate, allowance, apportion, character, great deal

Lot ***father:*** **5** Haran ***sister:*** **5** Iscah **6** Milcah ***son:*** **4** Moab **5** Ammon ***uncle:*** **7** Abraham

Lotan's father **4** Seir

lothario **5** Romeo **7** amorist, Don Juan, gallant **8** Casanova, paramour

Loti, Pierre **5** Viaud

lotion **3** oil **4** balm **8** ablution, liniment, ointment

lottery **6** raffle **7** drawing **11** sweepstakes

lotus-eater **7** dreamer

loud **5** gaudy, harsh, noisy, showy **6** brassy, brazen, flashy, garish, hoarse, tawdry, tinsel, vulgar **7** blaring, blatant, booming, chintzy, glaring, pealing, raucous, ringing, roaring **8** piercing, resonant, sonorous, strident **9** deafening, obnoxious, obtrusive, offensive **10** bigmouthed, resounding, stentorian, stertorous, thunderous **11** ear-piercing, full-mouthed, fulminating, stentorious **12** ear-splitting

loudmouth **7** stentor **8** blowhard, braggart

loudspeaker **6** woofer **7** tweeter

Louise composer **11** Charpentier

Louisiana ***capital:*** **10** Baton Rouge ***largest city:*** **10** New Orleans ***nickname:*** **11** Creole State **12** Pelican State ***state flower:*** **8** magnolia ***university:*** **6** Tulane **9** Grambling

lounge **3** bar, bum, lie, pub, tap **4** idle, laze, lazy, loaf, sofa **5** dally, drift, slack **6** dawdle, loiter, saloon **7** barroom, buvette, lie down, recline, taproom

lounge lizard **3** fop **4** buck, dude **5** blood, dandy, leech **6** sponge, sucker **7** coxcomb, sponger **8** barnacle, hanger-on, macaroni, parasite **9** exquisite **10** freeloader **11** Beau Brummel, bloodsucker, petit-maître

Lourdes saint **10** Bernadette

louse **3** cur, dog, rat **4** snot, toad **5** aphid, skunk, snake **6** cootie, psylla, slater, wretch **7** stinker ***egg:*** **3** nit

louse up **4** mess, ruin **5** botch **6** bobble, bollix, bungle, mucker

lout **3** oaf **4** boor, dolt, gawk, hick, lump, mock, quiz, razz, rube, twit **5** churl, klutz, looby, rally, scout, taunt, yokel **6** deride, galoot, lubber, lummox, rustic **7** bumpkin, hayseed, lobster, palooka, peasant **8** ridicule, stinkard **10** clodhopper

Louvre masterpiece **8** Mona Lisa **11** Venus de Milo

lovable **4** dear **6** genial **7** winning, winsome **8** adorable, alluring, charming, engaging, fetching, pleasing **9** appealing, endearing, ravishing, seductive **10** attractive, bewitching, enchanting, entrancing **11** captivating, enthralling

love **3** pet **4** dear, like, lust, zeal **5** adore, amour, ardor, crush, Cupid, deify, exalt, fancy, honey, piety, prize, sweet, value **6** admire, affair, caress, cosset, cuddle, dandle, desire, enamor, fealty, fervor, fondle, liking, regard, revere **7** ardency, cherish, darling, emotion, idolize, loyalty, passion, romance, worship **8** devotion, fidelity, fondness, idolatry, treasure, venerate, yearning **9** adoration, affection, delight in, sentiment, sweetling **10** allegiance, appreciate, attachment, enthusiasm, honeybunch, sweetheart **11** amorousness, infatuation ***combining form:*** **5** phily **6** philia ***French:*** **5** amour ***Italian:*** **5** amore

love apple **6** tomato

lovebird **6** budgie, parrot **10** budgerigar

love feast **5** agape

love god **4** Amor, Eros, Kama **5** Bhaga, Cupid

love goddess **5** Athor, Freya, Venus **6** Hathor, Inanna, Ishtar **7** Astarte **9** Aphrodite, Ashtoreth

love letter **8** mash note **9** valentine **10** billet-doux

lovely **4** fair, rare **5** sweet **6** beauty, dainty, eyeful, looker, pretty **7** stunner **8** alluring, charming, delicate, engaging,

graceful, handsome, knockout 9 beauteous, beautiful, exquisite 10 attractive, bewitching, delectable, delightful, enchanting, entrancing 11 captivating, good-looking
love-potion 7 philter, philtre 11 aphrodisiac
lover 3 fan, man 4 beau, buff 5 flame, hound, leman, Romeo 6 addict, master, steady, votary 7 amorist, devotee, Don Juan, gallant, habitué 8 fancy man, lothario, mistress, paramour 9 boyfriend, inamorata, inamorato 10 aficionado, girl friend *of books:* 11 bibliophile
love song 5 canso 6 serena 8 serenade
love story 7 romance
love token 4 ring 6 amoret
loving 4 dear, fond, kind 6 ardent, erotic, tender 7 amatory, amorous, bound up, cordial, devoted, fervent 8 attached, enamored, faithful 9 attentive 10 benevolent, infatuated, passionate, solicitous 11 considerate, impassioned, warmhearted 12 affectionate *combining form:* 4 phil 5 phile, philo 6 philic 7 philous
low 3 bad, cut, moo, raw 4 base, blue, deep, down, flat, mean, neap, poor, rude, vile, weak 5 brief, broke, cheap, crass, crude, dizzy, faint, gross, needy, rough, short, under 6 abject, ailing, coarse, fallen, humble, lesser, nether, offish, poorly, scurvy, sickly, sordid, undear, unwell, vulgar, woeful 7 cut-rate, ignoble, nominal, popular, reduced, scrubby, scruffy, servile, slashed, uncouth, underly 8 atypical, baseborn, beggared, cast down, dejected, dirt poor, downcast, feverish, indigent, inferior, mediocre, moderate, off-color, plebeian, uncostly, unwashed, wretched 9 declining, depressed, destitute, inelegant, miserable, penurious, subjacent, subnormal, woebegone 10 despicable, economical, indisposed, marked down, reasonable, spiritless, subaverage, unennobled 11 crestfallen, downhearted
lowbred 7 boorish, loutish 8 churlish, cloddish, lubberly 9 unrefined 10 unpolished 11 uncivilized
low-cost 5 cheap 6 undear 7 popular 10 affordable, reasonable 11 inexpensive
low-down 4 base, mean, ugly, vile 6 scurvy 7 ignoble, servile 8 wretched 10 despicable
lowdown 4 dope 5 facts 11 information
lower 3 cut 4 clip, drop, fall, pare, peer, rail, sink 5 abase, abate, couch, decry, demit, droop, frown, gloom, scowl, shave, slash, stare, under 6 bemean, debase, demean, demote, humble, lesser, menace, nether, reduce 7 cut back, cut down, deflate, degrade, demerit, depress, descend, detrude, devalue, let down 8 cast down, inferior, mark down, overcast, submerge, threaten, write off 9 devaluate, downgrade, humiliate, subjacent *combining form:* 4 bath, cato 5 batho *prefix:* 5 infra
Lower Depths author 5 Gorki, Gorky
lowest 5 least 6 bottom 7 deepest 9 undermost 10 bottommost, nethermost, rock-bottom
lowest point 5 nadir 6 trough *on earth:* 7 Dead Sea
low-grade 4 hack, mean, poor 6 common 8 declassé, inferior 10 second-rate 11 second-class 12 second-drawer
low-key 4 soft 5 sober 7 subdued 8 softened 9 toned down
lowland 4 flat, vale 6 valley 7 bottoms *Scottish:* 6 lallan 7 lalland
Lowlander 4 Scot 8 Scotsman
lowlife 4 heel, worm 5 knave, rogue 6 mucker, no-good, rascal, wretch 7 villain 8 wormling 9 miscreant, scoundrel 10 blackguard
lowly 4 base, mean, meek 6 humble, modest 7 ignoble, mundane, prosaic, servile, workday 8 baseborn, everyday, obeisant, plebeian, retiring, unwashed, workaday
low-pitched 4 bass
low-pressure 6 casual, degagé 7 relaxed, unfussy 8 informal 9 easygoing 10 unreserved 13 unconstrained
low-priced 5 cheap 6 undear 7 popular 8 uncostly 10 reasonable 11 inexpensive
low-spirited 4 blue, down 8 dejected, downcast 9 depressed, heartsore, woebegone
low tide 3 ebb 4 neap
loyal 4 firm, true 5 liege 6 ardent, trusty 7 devoted, staunch 8 constant, faithful, resolute 9 allegiant, steadfast
loyalist 4 Tory 7 patriot
loyalty 5 ardor, truth 6 fealty 8 adhesion, devotion, fidelity, trueness 9 adherence, constancy 10 allegiance, attachment 12 faithfulness
lozenge 4 pill 5 candy 6 tablet, troche 7 diamond, rhombus, tabella 8 pastille
LSD 4 acid *user:* 8 acidhead
lubricate 3 oil 6 grease 7 moisten
lubricious 4 lewd 5 slick 6 fickle, greasy, slippy, wanton 8 slippery, slithery, ticklish, unstable, variable, volatile 9 lecherous, salacious, uncertain 10 changeable, inconstant 13 temperamental
lucent 5 clear 6 bright 7 beaming, crystal, radiant, shining 8 clear-cut, luminous, pellucid 9 brilliant, unblurred 11 unambiguous
lucid 4 sane 5 clear, right 6 bright, normal 7 beaming, crystal, lambent, radiant 8 all there, clear-cut, knowable 9 brilliant, effulgent, graspable, refulgent, unblurred 10 fathomable 11 transparent, unambigu-

ous 12 compos mentis, incandescent, intelligible, transpicuous 13 apprehensible
lucidity 3 wit 4 mind 6 reason, sanity, senses 7 clarity 8 saneness 9 clearness, plainness, soundness 12 distinctness, explicitness
Lucifer 5 devil, fiend, Satan 6 diablo 7 Old Nick, serpent 8 Apollyon 9 Beelzebub 10 Old Scratch 13 Old Gooseberry
Lucinde ***beloved:*** 7 Leandre 9 Clitandre ***father:*** 7 Geronte 10 Sganarelle
luck 3 hap, hit, lot 4 bump, juju, meet, weal, zemi 5 break, charm, fluke, light 6 amulet, chance, fetish, happen, hazard, kismet, mascot, tumble 7 fortune, godsend, periapt, stumble 8 accident, fortuity, occasion, talisman, windfall 9 advantage 10 phylactery 11 opportunity 13 fortunateness ***token:*** 5 charm 6 amulet, clover, mascot 8 talisman 9 horseshoe
luckless 7 hapless, unhappy 8 ill-fated, untoward, wretched 9 miserable 10 ill-starred 11 star-crossed, unfortunate 12 misfortunate
lucky 4 well 5 happy 6 benign 9 favorable, fortunate 10 auspicious, beneficial, felicitous, profitable, propitious 12 advantageous, providential ***Scottish:*** 5 canny
lucrative 4 good 6 paying 7 gainful 10 productive, profitable, well-paying, worthwhile 11 moneymaking 12 advantageous
Lucrezia ____ 6 Borgia
ludicrous 5 antic, awful, comic, droll, funny, silly 6 absurd 7 bizarre, comical, foolish, risible 8 farcical, gelastic 9 fantastic, grotesque, laughable
Lud's town 6 London
lug 3 box, tow 4 bear, buck, drag, draw, haul, jerk, pack, pull, snap, tote, worm, yank 5 carry, ferry 6 convey, schlep, twitch 9 transport, vellicate
luggage 4 bags 7 baggage 9 suitcases
lugubrious 3 sad 4 dour, glum 5 black, bleak 6 dismal, dreary, gloomy, morose, rueful, somber, sullen, woeful 7 doleful, joyless 8 dolesome, mournful 9 cheerless, plaintive, saturnine, sorrowful 10 depressant, depressing, lamentable, melancholy, oppressing, oppressive 11 dispiriting
lukewarm 4 cool 5 tepid 8 hesitant 9 uncertain, undecided 10 indecisive, irresolute, irresolved, unresolved, wishy-washy 11 halfhearted, uncommitted
lull 3 ebb 4 balm, calm, hush, wane 5 abate, allay, comma, let up, pause, quiet, still 6 becalm, settle, soothe, temper 7 compose, die away, die down, ease off, qualify, slacken, subside 8 abeyance, interval, moderate 9 pausation 10 quiescence 11 tranquilize
lullaby 4 song 8 berceuse 10 cradlesong ***Scottish:*** 5 baloo, balow
lumber 3 tax 4 clog, lade, load, logs, plod, slog, wood 5 barge, clump, stump, weigh 6 burden, charge, saddle, timber, trudge
lumberjack see **logger**
Lumber State 5 Maine
luminance 10 brightness
luminary 3 big, sun, VIP 4 lion, name, star 5 light, nabob 6 leader 7 big name, notable 8 big-timer, eminence, somebody 9 celebrity 10 notability 12 leading light
luminous 5 clear, lucid 6 bright, lucent 7 beaming, crystal, fulgent, lambent, radiant, shining 8 clear-cut, knowable, pellucid 9 brilliant, effulgent, graspable, refulgent, unblurred 10 fathomable 11 translucent, transparent 12 incandescent
lummox 3 oaf 4 boor, gawk, lout 5 klutz, looby 7 lobster, palooka
lump 3 bit, gob, lot, oaf, wad 4 bear, blob, bulk, chip, clod, clot, gawk, heap, hunk, knot, lout, mass, much, peck, pile, welt 5 abide, batch, block, brook, bulge, bunch, chunk, crumb, hunch, klutz, looby, piece, scrap, stand, wedge 6 barrel, digest, endure, lubber, morsel, nugget 7 lobster, palooka, portion, stomach, swallow 8 swelling 12 protuberance
lumpy 3 raw 4 rude 5 crude, rough 8 clumpish, unformed 9 roughhewn, undressed
lunacy 5 folly, mania 7 fatuity, foolery, inanity, madness 8 delirium, insanity 9 absurdity, asininity, craziness, silliness, stupidity, unbalance 10 aberration, alienation, ineptitude, insaneness 11 derangement, distraction, foolishness, psychopathy, witlessness 13 senselessness
lunatic 3 mad, nut 4 kook, loon 5 crank, crazy, loony, raver, wacky 6 absurd, crazed, cuckoo, dement, insane, madman, maniac, psycho 7 cracked, foolish, madling, unsound 8 crackpot, demented, demoniac, deranged, paranoid 9 bedlamite, ding-a-ling, energumen, fantastic, harebrain, neuropath, non compos, screwball 10 crackbrain, Tom o' Bedlam
lunch 4 meal, nosh 5 snack 6 tiffin
luncheonette, lunchroom 4 café 6 eatery 7 beanery 8 snack bar 9 cafeteria 10 coffee shop 11 eating house 12 sandwich shop
lune 5 leash
lung 5 organ 8 breather ***combining form:*** 5 pneum, pulmo 6 pneumo, pulmon 7 pulmoni, pulmono ***disease:*** 9 emphysema, pneumonia 12 tuberculosis
lunge 4 dive, stab 5 burst, drive, pitch 6 thrust

lunkhead 3 oaf 4 boob, dolt, goof 5 booby, chump, dunce
lupine 6 fierce 7 wolfish 10 bluebonnet
lurch 3 bob, yaw 4 bent, jerk, reel, rock, roll, snap, swag, sway, tilt, toss, wave, yank 5 swing, waver, weave, whirl 6 bumble, careen, falter, plunge, seesaw, swerve, teeter, tilter, topple, totter, twitch, wallow, wobble 7 blunder, leaning, stagger, stumble 8 flounder, penchant, tendency
lure 3 bag 4 bait, call, draw, fake, pull, rope, toll, trap, wile 5 blind, catch, charm, decoy, tempt, train, trick 6 ambush, appeal, cajole, come-on, draw in, draw on, entice, entrap, invite, lead on, seduce, suck-in 7 attract, beguile, bewitch, capture, con game, enchant, ensnare, gimmick, wheedle 8 blandish, delusion, illusion, inveigle 9 captivate, fascinate, incentive, seduction, siren song 10 attraction, camouflage, enticement, inducement, seducement, temptation *fishing:* 3 fly 4 herl, worm 5 spoon 6 minnow 8 bucktail
lurid 3 wan 4 ashy, grim, pale 5 ashen, livid, waxen 6 doughy, malign, sultry 7 baleful, ghastly, hideous, macabre, malefic, tabloid 8 blanched, gruesome, horrible, sinister, terrible 9 colorless 10 horrifying, maleficent, terrifying 11 sensational
lurk 4 hide, slip 5 creep, skulk, slide, slink, sneak, steal 7 gumshoe 9 pussyfoot
luscious 4 rare, rich 5 sapid, tasty, yummy 6 Capuan, choice, deluxe, florid, ornate, rococo, savory 7 baroque, darling, opulent, piquant, sensual 8 adorable, heavenly, palatial, sensuous 9 ambrosial, epicurean, exquisite, palatable 10 appetizing, delectable, delightful, flamboyant, flavorsome 11 distinctive, scrumptious, upholstered
lush 3 sot 4 rich 5 drunk, yummy 6 bibber, boozer, Capuan, deluxe 7 opulent, profuse, riotous, sensual, tippler 8 adorable, drunkard, heavenly, palatial, prodigal, sensuous 9 ambrosial, delicious, epicurean, exuberant, inebriate, luxuriant, luxurious, profusive, sumptuous 10 boozehound, delectable, delightful, voluptuous
Lusitania 4 ship 5 liner 8 Portugal
lust 3 rut, yen 4 ache, heat, itch, long, pine, urge, wish 5 crave, yearn 6 desire, fervor, hanker, hunger, libido, thirst 7 craving, lechery, passion 8 appetite, coveting, cupidity, priapism, salacity, satyrism, yearning 9 carnality, eroticism, lubricity, prurience, pruriency 10 aphrodisia, appetition, excitement, satyriasis 11 nymphomania 13 concupiscence, lecherousness
luster 4 glow 5 glaze, gleam, glint, gloss, sheen, shine 6 polish 8 radiance 9 afterglow 10 brightness, brilliance, brilliancy, effulgence, luminosity, refulgence 11 candescence, iridescence, opalescence
lusterless 3 dim, mat, wan 4 dead, drab, dull, flat 5 blind, faded, muted, prosy 7 prosaic
lustful 3 hot 4 fast, lewd 5 rutty 7 burning, goatish, itching, ruttish, satyric 8 prurient 9 lecherous, libertine, lickerish, salacious 10 hot-blooded, lascivious, libidinous, licentious, passionate 11 incontinent 12 concupiscent
lustrate 5 purge 6 purify 7 cleanse
lustration 9 catharsis, cleansing
lustrous 5 nitid, shiny 6 bright, gleamy, glossy, sheeny 7 fulgent, lambent, radiant, shining 8 gleaming, glinting, polished, splendid 9 brilliant, burnished, effulgent, refulgent, sparkling 10 glimmering, glistening 11 resplendent 12 incandescent
lusty 4 hale, huge, vast 5 hardy, vital 6 mighty, potent, robust, strong 7 dynamic, healthy, immense, massive 8 enormous, vigorous, whacking, whopping 9 energetic, strenuous 10 full-bodied, prodigious, red-blooded, tremendous
lusus 5 freak 7 monster 8 abortion 11 miscreation, monstrosity
lute 4 clay, ring, seal 6 cement 7 bandora, bandore 10 chitarrone, instrument *Arabic:* 3 oud *Greco-Roman:* 7 pandura 8 pandoura *Oriental:* 3 tar *Russian:* 7 bandura *Spanish:* 8 banduria *two-necked:* 7 theorbo
lutenist 4 Mace 6 Gallot, Mouton, Radolt 7 Bakfark, Dowland, Gautier, Perrine 8 Capirola, Gaultier
Lutetia 5 Paris
luxuriant 4 lush, posh, rank, rich 5 plush 6 Capuan, fecund, lavish 7 fertile, opulent, profuse, riotous 8 fruitful, luscious, palatial, prodigal, prolific 9 exuberant, sumptuous
luxuriate 4 bask, love, riot, roll 5 eat up, enjoy, feast, revel 6 overdo, wallow, welter 7 indulge, rollick 11 overindulge
luxurious 4 lush, posh, rich 5 awful, fancy, grand, plush, showy 6 Capuan, costly, deluxe, lavish, palace, plushy 7 opulent, sensual, stately 8 imposing, majestic, palatial, splendid 9 elaborate, epicurean, expensive, grandiose 10 impressive 11 extravagant, languishing, magnificent *situation:* 7 fat city 10 bed of roses, easy street
luxury 5 frill 6 dainty 7 amenity, comfort 8 delicacy 10 redundancy 11 superfluity 12 extravagance 13 embellishment
Lycaon *daughter:* 8 Callisto *father:* 8 Pelasgus *mother:* 8 Meliboea
Lycidas author 6 Milton

Lycomedes ***daughter:*** 8 Deidamia ***victim:*** 7 Theseus
Lycus ***brother:*** 7 Nycteus ***father:*** 7 Pandion ***slayer:*** 6 Zethus 7 Amphion ***wife:*** 5 Dirce
Lydian ***king:*** 5 Gyges 7 Croesus 8 Alyattes ***queen:*** 7 Omphale
lye 7 caustic 8 lixivium
Lynceus ***brother:*** 4 Idas ***father:*** 8 Aphareus
lynch 4 hang 6 murder
Lynette see Line
lynx 3 cat 6 bobcat 7 caracal 9 catamount
Lyra star 4 Vega
lyre 4 harp 6 kissar 10 instrument
lyric 3 ode 4 odic, poem 5 melic 6 poetic 7 melodic, musical
lyric drama 5 opera
Lysander's beloved 6 Hermia

M

Maacah ***father:*** 5 Nahor 6 Talmai 7 Absalom ***husband:*** 5 David 6 Jehiel, Machir 8 Rehoboam ***son:*** 5 Hanan 6 Abijam, Achish 7 Absalom 10 Shephatiah
Maaseiah ***father:*** 6 Jotham 7 Shallum ***son:*** 7 Azariah 8 Zedekiah 9 Zephaniah
macabre 4 grim 5 lurid 6 deadly, grisly, horrid 7 deathly, ghastly, ghostly, hideous 8 gruesome, horrible, terrible 9 deathlike, ghostlike 10 horrifying, unpleasant
macaque 6 monkey, rhesus
macaroni 3 fop 4 buck, dude 5 dandy 7 coxcomb
Macbeth ***character:*** 4 Ross 5 Angus 6 Hecate, Lennox 7 Fleance ***slayer:*** 7 Macduff ***successor:*** 7 Malcolm ***title:*** 5 thane ***victim:*** 6 Banquo, Duncan
mace 3 bat, rod 4 beat, bilk, club 5 baton, billy, staff 6 cudgel, strike 8 bludgeon 9 billy club 10 knobkerrie, nightstick
Macedonia ***capital:*** 5 Pella 6 Skopje ***king:*** 6 Philip 9 Alexander ***last king:*** 7 Perseus
machete 4 bolo 5 knife 6 guitar
Machiavelli work 9 The Prince 11 The Mandrake
machinate 4 plot 6 devise, scheme, wangle 7 collude, connive, finagle 8 cogitate, conspire, contrive, engineer, intrigue, maneuver 9 scheme out
machine 3 car 4 auto 5 buggy, golem, motor, robot 6 device 7 autocar, fashion, vehicle 8 motorcar 9 automaton 10 automobile, conveyance 11 standardize ***component:*** 3 cam 4 belt, gear, seal 5 brake, chain, screw, shaft 6 clutch, spring 7 linkage 8 coupling ***excavating:*** 7 backhoe ***humanlike:*** 5 robot ***laboratory:*** 10 centrifuge
machine-gun 6 strafe
machine gun inventor 7 Gatling
machinery 4 gear, tool 5 agent, means, organ, works 6 agency, device, gadget, medium, outfit, tackle 7 channel, utensil, vehicle 8 matériel, tackling 9 apparatus, appliance, equipment, implement 10 instrument 11 contraption, contrivance
Machir's father 6 Ammiel 8 Manasseh
mackle 4 blur
macrocosm 5 world 6 cosmos, nature 8 creation, universe
McTeague author 6 Norris
mad 3 ire 4 daft, fury, rage, rash, sore, waxy, wild 5 anger, angry, crazy, irate, irked, loony, rabid, wacky, wrath, wroth 6 absurd, enrage, heated, insane, ireful 7 cracked, enraged, foolish, frantic, furious, incense, invalid, lunatic, steam up, umbrage 8 choleric, demented, deranged, frenetic, frenzied, offended, outraged, worked up, wrathful 9 affronted, delirious, fantastic, hilarious, illogical, indignant, infuriate, senseless, sophistic 10 corybantic, exasperate, fallacious, irrational, reasonless, unbalanced
Madagascar ***capital:*** 10 Tananarive 12 Antananarivo ***export:*** 5 sugar 6 cloves, coffee 7 vanilla ***monetary unit:*** 5 franc
Madame Bovary 4 Emma ***author:*** 8 Flaubert
Madame Butterfly ***character:*** 9 Cho-Cho-San, Cio-Cio-San, Pinkerton, Sharpless ***composer:*** 7 Puccini
madcap 4 rash 5 brash, hasty 8 reckless 9 hotheaded 10 ill-advised, incautious 11 thoughtless 13 inconsiderate
Mad Cavalier 6 Rupert
madden 3 ire 5 anger, craze 6 enrage,

frenzy 7 derange, incense, possess, shatter, steam up, umbrage, unhinge 8 distract 9 infuriate, unbalance

Madeira *capital:* 7 Funchal *export:* 4 wine 5 sugar 7 bananas

made-to-order 6 custom 10 customized 11 custom-built

madhouse 5 chaos 6 asylum, bedlam 8 loony bin 9 funny farm 10 booby hatch

madman 3 ass, nut 4 bawd, fool, jerk, loon 5 idiot, loony, ninny 6 dement, donkey, maniac, psycho 7 jackass, lunatic 8 imbecile 9 bedlamite, non compos 10 nincompoop, Tom o' Bedlam

madness 4 rage 6 lunacy, rabies 7 ecstasy 8 insanity 9 unbalance 10 aberration, alienation, enthusiasm 11 derangement, distraction, psychopathy

Madonna initials 3 BVM

Madras 9 Tamil Nadu *founder:* 3 Day (Francis)

Madrid museum 5 Prado

madrigal 4 glee, poem, song 8 part-song

madrigalist *Dutch:* 8 Arcadelt *English:* 4 Byrd 6 Morley, Wilbye 7 Tomkins, Weelkes *Flemish:* 8 Willaert *Italian:* 5 Festa 7 Landini 8 Marenzio 10 Monteverdi

maelstrom 4 eddy, fury 5 storm, whirl 6 vortex 7 turmoil 9 commotion, confusion, whirlpool

maestro see **conductor**

magazine 4 dump, Life, Time 5 cache, daily, depot, organ, store 6 annual, armory, digest, review, weekly 7 arsenal, gazette, journal, McCall's, monthly, Playboy, Redbook, TV Guide 8 biweekly 9 bimonthly, newspaper, quarterly, warehouse, Woman's Day 10 depository, lumber room, periodical, repository, semiweekly, storehouse 11 publication 12 Family Circle 13 Reader's Digest

maggot 4 grub, whim 5 fancy, freak, humor, larva 6 notion, vagary 7 boutade, caprice, conceit

Magi 6 Gaspar 8 Melchior 9 Balthazar *gift:* 4 gold 5 myrrh 12 frankincense

magian 6 mystic, witchy, wizard 7 charmer, warlock 8 conjurer, sorcerer, wizardly 9 enchanter, sorcerous 11 necromancer, necromantic 12 thaumaturgic

magic 5 charm, wicca 6 augury, mystic, witchy 7 alchemy, bewitch, conjury, devilry, gramary, sorcery 8 deviltry, divining, exorcism, gramarye, satanism, witchery, witching, wizardly, wizardry 9 conjuring, diablerie, diabolism, marvelous, occultism, sorcerous, sortilege, voodooism 10 mumbo jumbo, necromancy, prodigious, remarkable, stupendous, witchcraft 11 abracadabra, bewitchment, enchantment, incantation, legerdemain, necromantic, soothsaying, thaumaturgy 12 thaumaturgic, unbelievable

magical 6 mystic, witchy 8 wizardly 9 sorcerous 10 bewitching 11 necromantic 12 thaumaturgic

Magic Flute composer 6 Mozart

magician 4 seer 5 brujo, witch 6 medium, shaman, voodoo, wizard 7 augurer, charmer, diviner, Houdini, prophet, warlock 8 conjurer, exorcist, satanist, sorcerer 9 archimage, diabolist, enchanter, exorciser, invocator, trickster, voodooist 10 soothsayer 11 illusionist, medicine man, necromancer, thaumaturge

magicking 7 sorcery 8 witchery, wizardry 9 conjuring 10 necromancy, witchcraft 11 bewitchment, enchantment, thaumaturgy

Magic Mountain, The *author:* 4 Mann *character:* 7 Castorp

magisterial 5 bossy, puffy, wiggy 6 lordly, stuffy 7 bloated, pompous 8 arrogant, dogmatic, insolent 9 dictative, imperious, important, masterful 10 disdainful, high-handed, imperative, peremptory, pontifical 11 doctrinaire, domineering, overbearing 12 supercilious 13 authoritarian, authoritative, self-important

Magister Ludi author 5 Hesse

magistrate 5 court, judge 7 bencher, justice 8 official *ancient Greek:* 5 ephor 6 archon *ancient Roman:* 5 edile 6 aedile, pretor 7 duumvir, praetor, questor 8 quaestor *Italian:* 7 podesta *Scottish:* 6 bailie *Venice (former):* 4 doge

Magna Carta *king:* 4 John *place signed:* 9 Runnymede

magnanimous 3 big 5 great, lofty, noble 7 liberal 8 generous, knightly, princely 9 forgiving, unselfish 10 altruistic, benevolent, chivalrous, highminded 11 noble-minded

magnate 4 czar, king, lion, name, peer 5 baron, mogul, nabob 6 biggie, big gun, fat cat, figure, prince, tycoon 8 big-timer, nobleman 9 personage, plutocrat

magnesium *symbol:* 2 Mg

magnet 8 terrella 9 lodestone

magnetic 7 drawing 8 alluring 9 appealing, arresting, seductive 10 attracting, attractive, bewitching, enchanting 11 captivating, charismatic, fascinating 12 irresistible *substance:* 4 iron 7 ferrite

magnetism 5 charm 6 allure, appeal, glamor 7 glamour 8 charisma, witchery 10 witchcraft 11 fascination

magnetize 4 draw, lure, take, wile 5 charm 6 allure 7 attract, bewitch, enchant 9 captivate, fascinate

magnification unit 8 diameter

magnificence 8 grandeur, splendor 13 sumptuousness
magnificent 5 grand, noble, proud 6 august, lordly, superb 7 opulent, stately, sublime 8 glorious, gorgeous, imposing, majestic, princely, splendid, standout 9 brilliant, grandiose, inspiring, luxurious, sumptuous 11 extravagant, outstanding, resplendent, splendorous, superlative 13 splendiferous
magnifier 4 lens *jeweler's:* 5 loupe
magnify 3 pad 4 hymn, laud, rise 5 add to, bless, boost, color, cry up, erect, exalt, extol, fudge, honor, mount, rouse, swell 6 beef up, deepen, dilate, expand, extend, praise, uprear 7 amplify, augment, distend, enhance, enlarge, ennoble, glorify, inflate, sublime 8 eulogize, heighten, increase, maximize, multiply, overdraw, overplay, redouble 9 aggravate, celebrate, embellish, embroider, intensate, intensify, overpaint, overstate 10 aggrandize, exaggerate, overcharge, overstress, panegyrize 13 overemphasize
magnifying *combining form:* 4 micr 5 micro
magniloquent 7 aureate, flowery, swollen 8 sonorous 9 bombastic, overblown 10 euphuistic, rhetorical 11 declamatory
magnitude 4 pith, size, tune 5 order, range 6 extent, import, matter, moment, number, volume, weight 7 bigness, caliber, measure, quality 8 enormity, hugeness, loudness, quantity, vastness, vicinity 9 greatness, immensity, largeness 10 dimensions, importance, proportion 11 consequence, sizableness, weightiness
Magnolia State 11 Mississippi
magnum opus 7 classic 10 masterwork 11 chef d'oeuvre, masterpiece, tour de force
Magog's king 3 Gog
magpie 4 bird, crow 6 gabber, prater 7 blabber 8 jabberer, prattler 9 bandar-log, blabmouth, chatterer 10 chatterbox, piping crow 12 blabbermouth 13 miscellaneous
maguey 5 agave, fiber 7 cantala
magus 6 wizard 7 charmer, warlock 8 conjurer, sorcerer 9 enchanter 11 necromancer
Magyar 9 Hungarian
Mahalath *father:* 7 Ishmael 8 Jerimoth *husband:* 4 Esau 8 Rehoboam
mah-jongg piece 4 tile
Mahli, Mahali *brother:* 5 Mushi *father:* 6 Merari
Mahlon *father:* 9 Elimelech *mother:* 5 Naomi *wife:* 4 Ruth
Mahol's son 5 Darda, Heman 6 Calcol
Maia *father:* 5 Atlas *mother:* 7 Pleione *sisters:* 8 Pleiades *son:* 6 Hermes 7 Mercury
maid 3 gal 4 girl, lass, miss 5 biddy, bonne, missy, wench 6 damsel, lassie, virgin 7 servant 8 charlady, domestic, factotum 9 charwoman, hired girl 10 au pair girl, handmaiden *lady's:* 7 abigail
maiden 3 gal 4 burd, girl, lass, miss 5 first, fresh, missy, prime, wench 6 burdie, damsel, intact, lassie, unused, virgin 7 damosel, damozel, initial, pioneer, primary, untaken, untried 8 earliest, original, virginal 10 old-maidish, spinsterly 11 husbandless, spinsterish 12 undeflowered *combining form:* 7 parthen 8 partheno *Muslim:* 5 houri *Norse mythological:* 6 valkyr 8 valkyrie, walkyrie
maidenhair tree 6 gingko, ginkgo
maidenhead 5 hymen 6 purity 9 freshness, virginity
maidenhood 9 virginity
maiden lady 7 old maid 8 spinster 10 spinstress
Maid of Astolat 6 Elaine
Maid of Orleans, The 4 Joan 7 Pucelle *author:* 8 Schiller
___ mail 3 air 5 chain
maim 4 maul 5 break 6 batter, bung up, mangle, mayhem 7 cripple, disable, dislimb 8 massacre, mutilate, paralyze 9 disfigure, dismember, hamstring
main 3 big, sea 4 blue, deep, head, line, star, very 5 brine, chief, drink, great, major, ocean, sheer, vital 7 capital, high sea, leading, stellar 8 cardinal, foremost 9 essential, paramount, principal 10 preeminent, prevailing 11 controlling, fundamental, outstanding, predominant
Maine *capital:* 7 Augusta *college:* 5 Bates, Colby 7 Bowdoin *highest point:* 10 Mt. Katahdin *largest town:* 8 Portland *motto:* 6 dirigo 7 I direct *nickname:* 11 Lumber State 13 Pine Tree State
mainstay 3 key 4 prop 5 brace, staff 6 crutch, pillar, sinews 7 standby, support 8 backbone, buttress, upholder 9 supporter, sustainer
Main Street author 5 Lewis
maintain 4 aver, avow, save 5 argue, claim, guard, right 6 affirm, assert, avouch, back up, defend, insist, keep up, manage, stress, uphold 7 care for, carry on, contend, correct, declare, husband, justify, persist, profess, protect, protest, rectify, support, warrant 8 continue, preserve 9 cultivate, emphasize, vindicate 10 provide for
maintenance 4 care, keep, salt 5 bread 6 living, upkeep 7 alimony, support 10 livelihood 11 subsistence 12 alimentation *worker:* 7 janitor 9 custodian
maize 4 milo 10 Indian corn
majestic 5 grand, noble, regal, royal 6 august, kingly, lordly 7 courtly, stately

8 elevated, imperial, imposing, kinglike, magnific, princely 9 dignified, grandiose, monarchal, sovereign 10 monarchial 11 ceremonious, magnificent, monarchical

major 3 big 4 fell, main, star, ugly 5 chief, grave, hefty, large 6 better, higher, larger 7 capital, greater, serious, sizable, stellar 8 grievous, superior 9 dangerous, extensive, principal 10 large-scale, preeminent 11 outstanding, predominant 12 considerable

Major Barbara author 4 Shaw

majority 4 edge 6 margin

make 3 act, eat, fit, fix, get, lay, net, run, set, tap, win 4 bear, brew, draw, earn, form, gain, head, mold, name, reap, sire 5 begin, build, catch, cause, clear, draft, enact, equal, erect, force, forge, frame, hatch, infer, judge, reach, ready, shape, spawn, start, write 6 attain, behave, coerce, compel, create, deduce, deduct, derive, draw on, draw up, effect, extend, father, finger, gather, intend, oblige, ordain, output, parent, secure, seduce, set out 7 achieve, acquire, appoint, bring in, clean up, collect, compose, concuss, count as, destine, fashion, harvest, perform, prepare, proceed, produce, serve as, shotgun, stretch, take off 8 assemble, break for, comprise, conclude, drag down, draw down, generate, initiate, light out, nominate, traverse 9 constrain, construct, designate, establish, fabricate, formulate, knock down, originate, procreate, strike out 10 bring about, constitute 11 manufacture, put together ***amends:*** 5 atone ***a metallic sound:*** 5 chink, clang ***a mistake:*** 3 err 4 goof ***ashen:*** 6 blanch ***a statement:*** 7 expound ***a witty remark:*** 4 jest ***bare:*** 5 strip 6 denude ***believe:*** 7 pretend ***certain:*** 6 assure 8 convince ***cheerful:*** 6 solace ***coins:*** 4 mint ***different:*** 6 change ***fast:*** 3 fix 4 gird 6 secure ***hair curly:*** 5 crimp 6 buckle ***happy:*** 5 bless 6 please 7 satisfy ***holy:*** 6 hallow ***inoperative:*** 5 annul ***into a law:*** 5 enact ***known:*** 3 air 6 expose, reveal, spread 7 declare, divulge, uncover 8 announce, disclose, proclaim ***less severe:*** 6 weaken 8 mitigate 9 attenuate ***manifest:*** 7 explain ***melodious:*** 6 attune ***merry:*** 5 cheer ***numb:*** 4 daze, stun ***presentable:*** 5 groom ***quiet:*** 4 calm 5 allay, quell 6 pacify 7 appease ***ready beforehand:*** 7 prepare ***red:*** 5 flush ***rigid:*** 5 brace 7 stiffen ***sacred:*** 8 sanctify ***slick:*** 3 oil 9 lubricate ***small:*** 8 belittle ***smaller:*** 8 compress ***strong:*** 7 fortify ***suffix:*** 2 en, fy 3 ify ***suitable:*** 5 adapt ***supremely happy:*** 7 beatify ***unclean:*** 4 soil ***understandable:*** 7 clarify ***useful:*** 7 utilize ***use of:*** 6 employ ***vigorous:*** 8 energize

make-believe 7 charade, feigned, fiction, pageant 8 disguise, pretense 9 insincere, pretender 10 pretension

make off 2 go 3 fly, run 4 bolt, flee, quit, skip 5 leave, scoot, skirr 6 decamp, depart, escape, retire 7 abscond, run away, scamper 8 withdraw 9 skedaddle

make out 2 go 3 dig, see 4 draw, show 5 catch, grasp, infer, judge, prove, score 6 accept, arrive, deduce, deduct, derive, follow, gather, take in, thrive 7 collect, compass, discern, prosper, succeed 8 conclude, flourish, get along 9 apprehend, determine, establish, interpret 10 comprehend, understand 11 demonstrate

make over 4 cede, deed 5 alien 6 assign, convey, reform, remise 7 remodel 8 alienate, renovate, transfer 10 abalienate

makeshift 6 refuge, resort 7 stopgap 8 recourse, resource 9 expedient, temporary 10 expediency, substitute 11 provisional 13 rough-and-ready

make similar to ***suffix:*** 2 fy 3 ify

make up 3 fit, fix, get, mix, pay, sue, woo 4 fuse, meld, rise 5 atone, blend, court, frame, merge, ready, spark 6 decide, derise, gather, invent, mingle, offset, pursue, redeem, set off, settle 7 address, advance, arrange, balance, compile, compose, concoct, prepare, replace, reprint 8 approach, atone for, compound, comprise, contrive, intermix, outweigh 9 formulate, improvise, interfuse 10 compensate

makeup 3 lie 4 cast, face, form, mold, plan, vein 5 fiber, grain, humor, paint, setup, shape, stamp, style 6 design, nature, powder, stripe, temper 7 fiction 8 ordering, war paint 9 blackface, character, formation 10 complexion, maquillage 11 arrangement, composition, disposition, grease paint, personality, replacement, temperament 12 architecture, compensation, constitution, construction, organization ***eye:*** 4 kohl 7 mascara ***facial:*** 5 rouge 6 powder

maladroit 5 brash, inept 6 clumsy, gauche 7 awkward, halting, unhandy 8 bumbling, bungling, tactless 9 ham-handed, impolitic, lumbering, stumbling, unpolitic, unskilled, untactful 10 blundering, left-handed, ungraceful 11 floundering, heavy-handed 12 undiplomatic

malady 3 ill 7 ailment, disease, illness 8 disorder, sickness, syndrome 9 affection, complaint, condition, infirmity 10 affliction ***suffix:*** 4 itis

malaise 7 disease 8 debility 9 infirmity 10 feebleness, infirmness, sickliness 11 decrepitude 13 unhealthiness

Malaprop creator 8 Sheridan

malapropos 5 inapt, undue 8 ill-timed, improper, mistimed, unseemly, untimely 10 unsuitable 11 ill-seasoned, inopportune,

unbefitting **12** unseasonable, unseasonably **13** inappropriate, inopportunely
malaria **6** miasma **8** paludism ***transmitter:*** **8** mosquito
malarkey **4** guff **5** hooey **6** bunkum, bushwa **7** hogwash, twaddle **8** nonsense **9** poppycock **10** balderdash **12** blatherskite
Malawi ***capital:*** **8** Lilongwe ***export:*** **3** tea **7** tobacco ***largest city:*** **8** Blantyre ***monetary unit:*** **6** kwacha
Malaysia ***capital:*** **11** Kuala Lumpur ***export:*** **3** tin **6** rubber, timber **7** palm oil
Malchiel ***father:*** **6** Beriah ***grandfather:*** **5** Asher
Malchijah, Malchiah ***father:*** **5** Harim **6** Parosh, Rechab
Malchishua's father **4** Saul
malcontent **5** crank, rebel **6** anarch, griper, grouch, kicker, unruly **7** growler **8** factious, frondeur, grumbler, mutineer, mutinous, restless, revolter, sorehead **9** alienated, anarchist, estranged, insurgent, seditious **10** bellyacher, complainer, rebellious **11** disaffected, disgruntled, disobedient, faultfinder, ungratified **12** contumacious, dissatisfied, ungovernable
mal de ___ **3** mer
Maldives capital **4** Male
maldonite **9** black gold
male **3** tom **5** fella, manly **6** manful, virile **7** manlike **9** masculine, staminate ***combining form:*** **4** andr **5** andro ***dark-haired:*** **6** brunet
malediction **5** curse **7** malison **8** anathema
malefactor **5** felon, knave, rogue **6** rascal, sinner **8** criminal, evildoer, offender **9** miscreant, scoundrel, wrongdoer **10** blackguard, lawbreaker
malefic see **malicious**
malevolence **5** spite **6** grudge, malice, spleen **7** despite, ill will **9** hostility, malignity **10** abhorrence, antagonism **11** abomination, detestation **12** spitefulness **13** maliciousness
malevolent **4** evil **6** bitchy, malign, wicked **7** baleful, hateful, hurtful, vicious **8** sinister, spiteful **9** injurious, malicious, malignant **10** despiteful
malfunction **6** glitch
Mali ***capital:*** **6** Bamako ***monetary unit:*** **5** franc ***product:*** **4** fish **6** cotton **7** peanuts
malice **4** bane, bile, hate **5** spite, venom **6** animus, enmity, grudge, hatred, poison, spleen **7** despite, ill will, umbrage **8** meanness **9** animosity, antipathy **10** bitterness, resentment **11** hatefulness, malevolence **12** spitefulness **13** invidiousness
malicious **4** evil, mean **5** catty, green, nasty, petty **6** bitchy, wicked, witchy **7** baneful, hateful, heinous, jealous, spitish **8** spiteful, venomous, virulent **9** green-eyed, poisonous, poison-pen, rancorous **10** despiteful, malevolent
maliciousness see **malevolence**
malign **4** evil, slur, soil **5** decry, libel, smear, stain, sully, taint **6** befoul, defame, defile, revile, smirch, vilify, wicked **7** asperse, baleful, baneful, blacken, detract, hateful, hostile, noxious, pollute, slander, spatter, tarnish, traduce, vicious **8** backbite, besmirch, derogate, inimical, sinister, spiteful, tear down, virulent **9** bespatter, denigrate, disparage, injurious, rancorous **10** calumniate, depreciate, despiteful, maleficent, malevolent, pernicious, scandalize, villainize, vituperate **11** deleterious, detrimental, opprobriate **12** antagonistic, antipathetic
malignant **4** evil **6** wicked **7** baleful, hateful, vicious **8** devilish, fiendish, spiteful **9** injurious, rancorous **10** despiteful, diabolical, malevolent
malison **5** curse **8** anathema **11** commination, imprecation, malediction
mall **4** lane **5** alley **6** mallet **9** concourse, esplanade, promenade **10** passageway **11** median strip
malleable **6** pliant, supple **7** ductile, plastic
malleate **4** beat **5** pound **6** hammer
mallet **6** hammer, strike
Mallothi's father **5** Heman
Malluch's father **4** Bani **5** Harim
malodorous **4** foul, gamy, high, olid, rank, vile **5** fetid, fuggy, funky, fusty, musty, nasty, reeky, rough, stale **6** frowsy, putrid, rancid, rotten, smelly, stinky, strong, whiffy **7** decayed, noisome, noxious, reeking, spoiled, stenchy, tainted, ungodly **8** improper, indecent, mephitic, polluted, stinking, unseemly, untoward **9** offensive, poisonous, stenchful **10** decomposed, indelicate, nauseating, unbecoming **11** ill-smelling **12** pestilential
Malta ***capital:*** **8** Valletta ***monetary unit:*** **5** pound ***product:*** **8** textiles
Maltese Falcon, The ***author:*** **7** Hammett ***detective:*** **5** Spade (Sam)
maltreat **5** abuse **6** ill-use, misuse **7** outrage **8** disserve
mammal **3** ass **5** camel, daman, hippo, hyrax **6** alpaca, colugo, dassie **7** bearcat, primate **8** elephant **12** hippopotamus ***African:*** **5** okapi, zebra, zoril **7** zorilla, zorille, zorillo **8** aardvark, aardwolf ***aquatic:*** **5** yapok **6** desman, dugong, narwal, yapock **7** cowfish, manatee, narwhal, platypi (plural) **8** cetacean, narwhale, platypus, porpoise, sirenian **10** platypuses (plural) ***arboreal:*** **5** lemur **6** cuscus **7** opossum

8 kinkajou, lemuroid ***Australian:*** 5 coala, koala 8 kangaroo ***burrowing:*** 8 moldwarp, starnose, suricate ***carnivorous:*** 3 cat, dog, fox 4 bear, lion, mink, seal, wolf 5 genet, hyena, otter, panda, pekan, ratel, sable, tiger 6 badger, grison, marten, racoon, teledu, walrus 7 dasyure, genette, linsang, polecat, raccoon 8 carcajou, mongoose, mungoose ***catlike:*** 5 civet ***doglike:*** 6 jackal ***extinct:*** 6 quagga 8 mastodon, stegodon ***feline:*** 4 lion 5 tiger, tigon 6 tiglon 7 leopard, lioness, tigress ***flying:*** 3 bat ***gnawing:*** 3 rat 6 beaver, rodent 7 leporid 8 squirrel ***goatlike:*** 4 tahr 6 takin ***harelike:*** 5 hyrax 7 hyraces (plural), hyraxes (plural) 8 hyracoid ***hoofed:*** 2 ox 3 cow, pig 4 deer, goat, owse, oxen (plural) 5 camel, owsen (plural), sheep, tapir 6 alpaca, ovibos 7 peccary 8 ruminant, ungulate 12 hippopotamus ***horned:*** 4 goat ***insect-eating:*** 4 mole 5 shrew 6 tanrec, tenrec 8 hedgehog ***long-necked:*** 7 giraffe ***marine:*** 3 orc 4 orca 6 walrus 7 dolphin, grampus ***marsupial:*** 9 bandicoot ***nocturnal:*** 6 wombat ***raccoon-like:*** 8 cacomixl ***ruminant:*** 4 deer 5 llama, moose, sheep 6 vicuña 7 vicugna ***small:*** 4 pika 8 hedgehog, hedgepig ***South American:*** 7 guanaco ***toothless:*** 5 sloth 8 edentate, pangolin 9 armadillo ***tropical:*** 5 coati ***unweaned:*** 8 suckling ***with flippers:*** 8 pinniped ***wolflike:*** 5 hyena 6 hyaena

mammoth 4 huge 5 giant, whale 7 monster 8 colossal, enormous, gigantic 9 leviathan, monstrous 10 behemothic, gargantuan, mastodonic 11 elephantine

Mamre's brother 4 Aner 6 Eshcol

man 2 he, Mr. 3 boy, guy 4 body, buck, chap, cuss, gent, lord, soul 5 being, brace, flesh, lover, skate 6 fellow, galoot, mister, mortal, person, police, vassal 7 bruiser, fortify, husband, John Law, officer 8 bluecoat, creature, humanity, paramour 9 boyfriend, humankind, mortality, personage 10 individual 11 Homo sapiens ***brass:*** 5 Talos, Talus ***castrated:*** 6 eunuch ***combining form:*** 4 andr 5 andro, homin 6 homini ***eccentric:*** 6 codger, geezer ***French:*** 5 homme ***Italian:*** 4 uomo ***Latin:*** 3 vir 4 homo ***Spanish:*** 6 hombre ***Yiddish:*** 6 mensch ***young:*** 3 boy, lad 8 springal 9 springald, stripling

manage 2 do 3 run 4 fare, keep 5 get by, get on, guide, shift 6 afford, direct, effect, govern, handle, ordain 7 achieve, carry on, conduct, control, execute, husband, operate, steward, succeed 8 carry out, contrive, dominate, engineer, get along, work upon 9 cultivate, stagger on, supervise 10 accomplish, administer, adulterate, bring about 11 superintend 12 riding school, stagger along 13 muddle through

management 4 care 6 charge 7 conduct, running 8 handling, intrigue 9 oversight 10 conducting, intendance 11 supervising, supervision

manager 4 exec 6 gerent 7 handler, officer 8 director, official, producer 9 conductor, executive 10 impresario, supervisor 13 administrator ***museum:*** 7 curator ***suffix:*** 3 eer

Manahath's father 6 Shobal

Man and Superman author 4 Shaw

Manassas battle 7 Bull Run

Manasseh, Manasses ***brother:*** 7 Ephraim ***father:*** 6 Hashum, Joseph 8 Hezekiah 10 Pahathmoab ***grandfather:*** 5 Jacob ***grandson:*** 6 Gilead ***mother:*** 7 Asenath ***son:*** 6 Machir

man-at-arms 2 GI 7 fighter, soldier, warrior 10 serviceman 11 fighting man

mancipium 5 slave 7 bondman, chattel 8 bondsman 9 bondslave

Mandalay author 7 Kipling

mandarin 4 duck, tree 5 elder 6 orange 8 official 9 tangerine 10 bureaucrat

mandate 4 fiat, word 5 edict, order, ukase 6 behest, charge, decree 7 bidding, command, dictate 9 authority 10 imperative, injunction 13 authorization

mandatory 6 forced 7 binding, needful 8 required 9 de rigueur, essential, imperious, necessary, requisite 10 commanding, compelling, compulsory, imperative 11 involuntary 12 irremissible 13 indispensable

mandible 3 jaw

Manette's daughter 5 Lucie

maneuver 3 jig, ply 4 move, plan, play, plot, ploy, step 5 feint, swing, trick, wield 6 design, device, gambit, handle, jockey, scheme, tactic, wangle 7 beguile, exploit, finagle, finesse, gimmick, measure 8 artifice, demarche, dispense, engineer, exercise, intrigue, movement, navigate 9 machinate, procedure, stratagem 10 manipulate, proceeding, subterfuge 11 contrivance, machination 12 manipulation

maneuvering room 8 latitude

Man for All Seasons, A ***author:*** 4 Bolt ***subject:*** 4 More

manful see manly

manganese ***ore:*** 10 pyrolusite ***symbol:*** 2 Mn

manger 4 rack 6 cratch, trough

mangle 3 mar 4 hack, iron, maul 5 press 6 batter, damage, deface, deform, impair, injure, padder 7 butcher, contort, distort 9 disfigure

mangy 5 seedy 6 shabby, sleazy, tagrag 7 scruffy, squalid 8 decrepit, tattered 9 moth-eaten 10 down-at-heel

manhandle 4 maul 5 abuse 6 batter

7 rough up 8 maltreat, mistreat 10 knock about, roughhouse, slap around

Manhattan ***purchaser:*** 6 Minuit ***school:*** 9 Juilliard ***university:*** 8 Columbia

mania 4 rage 5 craze, fancy, thing 6 fetish, hangup 7 madness, passion 8 fixation, idée fixe, insanity 9 cacoëthes, fixed idea, obsession 10 compulsion, enthusiasm 11 fascination, infatuation

maniac 3 bug, mad, nut 4 loon, wild 5 bigot, crazy, fiend, freak, loony, rabid 6 crazed, dement, insane, madman, raging, zealot 7 berserk, cracked, fanatic, frantic, furious, lunatic, madling, ranting, unsound, violent 8 demented, deranged, frenetic, frenzied 9 bedlamite, delirious, non compos 10 enthusiast

manifest 4 mark, show, told, vent 5 clear, overt, plain, shown, utter, voice 6 appear, embody, evince, expose, ostend, patent 7 display, evident, evinced, exhibit, express, obvious 8 apparent, distinct, divulged, evidence, palpable, proclaim, revealed 9 disclosed, evidenced, incarnate, objectify, personify, personize, prominent 10 illustrate, indication, noticeable 11 demonstrate, exteriorize, externalize, materialize, personalize, unambiguous

manifestation 4 show 7 display 8 epiphany 10 revelation ***combining form:*** 5 phany

manifold 5 boost 6 beef up, expand 7 augment, diverse, enlarge, magnify 8 compound, increase, multiply, numerous 9 aggregate, multiform, multiplex 10 aggrandize, multiphase 11 diversiform, polymorphic 12 multifarious, multivarious

manikin 4 puny, runt 5 dwarf, midge, pygmy 6 midget, peewee 8 Tom Thumb 10 diminutive, homunculus

Manila ***founder:*** 7 Legaspi ***victor:*** 5 Dewey

manipulate 3 ply, rig, use 4 play 5 swing, wield 6 direct, doctor, handle, jockey, juggle, manage 7 beguile, conduct, control, exploit, finesse 8 dispense, engineer, maneuver 9 machinate 10 tamper with

Manitoba ***capital:*** 8 Winnipeg ***university:*** 7 Brandon 13 Saint Boniface

mankind 5 flesh, human 6 humans, people 8 humanity 9 mortality 11 homo sapiens

like 4 male 6 virile 8 hominoid, humanoid 9 masculine 10 anthropoid

manly 4 bold, male 5 brave 6 virile 7 gallant, valiant 8 fearless, intrepid, unafraid, valorous 9 dauntless, masculine, undaunted 10 courageous

man-made 9 synthetic 10 artificial, factitious ***object:*** 8 artefact, artifact

Mann character 7 Castorp 10 Felix Krull

manner 3 use, way 4 form, kind, mien, mode, sort, tone, turn, vein, wise, wont 5 habit, modus, mores, style, trick, usage 6 custom, method, system 7 bearing, fashion, p's and q's 7 quomodo 8 behavior, decorums, demeanor, habitude, practice, protocol 9 amenities, etiquette, technique 10 civilities, consuetude, deportment, elegancies 11 affectation, formalities, peculiarity, proprieties 12 affectedness, idiosyncrasy ***combining form:*** 4 wise ***suffix:*** 2 ic, ly 4 ical

mannered 6 cutesy 8 affected 9 conscious 13 self-conscious

mannerism 4 airs, lugs, pose 7 oddness 9 prettyism, queerness 10 preciosity 11 affectation, peculiarity, singularity 12 eccentricity, idiosyncrasy 13 artificiality

mannerless 4 rude 7 ill-bred, uncivil 8 impolite 11 disgracious 12 discourteous 13 disrespectful

mannerly 5 civil 6 polite 7 civilly, genteel 8 politely 9 courteous 10 respectful 12 respectfully

Manoah's son 6 Samson

Manon composer 8 Massenet

Manon Lescaut ***author:*** 7 Prevost ***composer:*** 7 Puccini

manor 4 land 5 acres, villa 6 castle, estate, quinta 7 château 12 landed estate

manservant 5 valet 6 butler

mansion 4 hall 5 house, villa 6 castle, estate 7 château

manslaughter 5 blood 6 murder 7 bump-off, killing 8 foul play, homicide

manslayer 6 killer 8 homicide, murderer

mantic 7 fatidic 8 Delphian, oracular 9 sibylline, vaticinal 11 prophetical

mantle 4 glow, pink, rose 5 blush, color, cover, flush, rouge 6 pinken, redden 7 crimson ***combining form:*** 7 chlamyd 8 chlamydo

Manto ***father:*** 8 Tiresias ***husband:*** 7 Rhacius ***son:*** 6 Mopsus

man-to-man 4 open 5 frank 6 candid 10 unreserved 11 openhearted, unconcealed, undisguised, unvarnished 12 undissembled

mantra 2 om 4 hymn 5 chant 6 prayer 11 incantation

manual 4 text 5 guide 6 primer 7 primary 8 Baedeker, handbook, hornbook, textbook 9 guidebook, vade mecum 10 compendium 11 abecedarium, enchiridion ***religious:*** 9 catechism ***worker:*** 7 laborer

manufactory 4 mill 5 plant, works

manufacture 4 form, make, mold 5 forge, frame, shape 6 create, invent 7 fashion, produce 8 creation 9 fabricate 10 production 11 put together

manumit 4 free 5 loose 6 loosen, unbind 7 release, set free, unchain 8 liberate 9 discharge, unshackle 10 emancipate
manure 4 dung 6 ordure 7 excreta 9 excrement 10 fertilizer
manuscript 4 hand ***ancient:*** 5 codex 7 codices (plural) ***red part:*** 6 rubric
Man Without a Country, The ***author:*** 4 Hale ***character:*** 5 Nolan
many 4 much 5 monie 6 divers, legion, myriad, sundry 7 copious, diverse, several, various 8 abundant, manifold, multiple, numerous, populous 9 abounding, bounteous, bountiful, countless, multitude, plentiful 10 multiplied, voluminous 12 multifarious, multiplicate, multitudinal 13 multitudinous ***combining form:*** 4 poly 5 multi, pluri
Maon's father 7 Shammai
map 4 plan, plat 5 chart, draft, graph 6 design, lay out, set out, sketch, survey 7 arrange, diagram, drawing, explore, outline, picture, tracing 9 cartogram, delineate ***collection:*** 5 atlas ***line:*** 6 isohel 7 contour, isobath, isogone, isogram, isogriv, isohyet, isotach 8 isarithm, isocheim, isochime, isogloss, isogonal, isogonic, isograph, isopleth, isotherm ***maker:*** 12 cartographer ***making:*** 11 cartography, chorography
map projection 5 Bonne, conic 6 Albers 8 gnomonic, Mercator 9 Mollweide, polyconic 10 sinusoidal 12 orthographic 13 stereographic
maquillage 4 face 5 paint 6 makeup 8 war paint
mar 4 flaw, harm, hurt, ruin, scar, warp 5 spoil, wreck 6 bruise, damage, deface, deform, impair, injure, injury 7 blemish, scratch, tarnish, vitiate 9 prejudice ***the countryside:*** 6 litter
marabou 4 silk 5 stork 12 adjutant bird
Marat ***colleague:*** 6 Danton ***slayer:*** 6 Corday
maraud 4 raid 5 foray, harry 6 harass
marauder 6 bandit, bummer, looter, pirate, raider, sacker 7 brigand, cateran, forager, ravager, spoiler, wrecker 8 pillager, ravisher 9 buccaneer, desperado, despoiler, plunderer, spoliator 10 depredator, freebooter
marble 3 mib, mig 4 immy, migg 5 aggie, rance 6 blotch, miggle, mottle, streak 7 cipolin, glassie, steelie
Marble Faun, The ***author:*** 9 Hawthorne ***character:*** 5 Hilda 6 Kenyon, Miriam 9 Donatello ***setting:*** 4 Rome
marblehearted 5 stony 7 callous 8 hardened, obdurate 9 heartless, unfeeling 10 hard-boiled 11 cold-blooded 13 unsympathetic
march 2 go 3 hem, rim 4 abut, jibe, join, line, move 5 agree, check, fit in, get on, skirt, sling, stalk, tally, touch, verge 6 accord, adjoin, border, butt on, course, extend, fringe, parade, square, stride, travel 7 advance, headway, ongoing, proceed 8 anabasis, boundary, dovetail, frontier, get along, neighbor, outlands, parallel, progress, traverse 9 periphery, provinces, territory 10 borderland, correspond 11 advancement
March ***date:*** 4 ides ***sisters:*** 2 Jo 3 Amy, Meg 4 Beth
March Hare creator 7 Carroll
March King 5 Sousa
Mardi Gras 8 carnival 10 Fat Tuesday ***city:*** 10 New Orleans
Marduk, Merodach ***city:*** 7 Babylon ***consort:*** 8 Zarpanit 9 Sarpanitu ***father:*** 2 Ea ***victim:*** 5 Kingu
mare 3 sea 5 horse 6 equine
Mareshah's son 6 Hebron
mare's nest 3 din 4 hoax, sell 5 babel, cheat, fraud, put on, spoof 6 clamor, hubbub, humbug, racket, uproar 7 swindle 8 flimflam 9 imposture 10 hullabaloo
margarine 4 oleo
margin 3 hem, rim 4 abut, brim, edge, join, line, play, room, side 5 bound, brink, frame, scope, shore, skirt, touch, verge 6 border, fringe, leeway 7 connect, minimum, outline, selvage 8 latitude, neighbor, surround, trimming 9 elbowroom, perimeter, periphery ***of shortcoming:*** 6 leeway
Marguerite's lover 5 Faust
Marianas ***discoverer:*** 8 Magellan ***island:*** 4 Rota 5 Pagan 6 Guguan, Saipan, Tinian 7 Agrihan, Aguijan
marijuana 3 boo, pot 4 hash, hemp, weed 5 grass, joint 6 moocah, reefer 7 hashish 8 cannabis
marina 4 dock 5 basin 8 boatyard 9 esplanade, promenade
marine 5 naval 6 dipsey, dipsie, gyrene 7 abyssal, aquatic, bathyal, benthic, deep-sea, fluvial, neritic, oceanic, pelagic 8 bathybic, nautical, seagoing, seamanly 9 bathysmal, seafaring, thalassic 10 fluviatile, lacustrine, oceangoing, seamanlike 12 hydrographic, navigational 13 oceanographic ***crustacean:*** 8 barnacle ***deposit:*** 5 coral ***plant:*** 4 alga, kelp 7 seaweed
mariner 3 gob, tar 4 jack, salt 6 rating, sailor, sea dog, seaman 7 jack-tar, old salt, swabbie 8 seafarer 9 sailorman, shellback, tarpaulin 10 bluejacket
marionette 6 puppet 10 bufflehead
marital 6 wedded 7 married, nuptial, spousal 8 conjugal, hymeneal 9 connubial
maritime 7 oceanic 8 nautical 9 thalassic 12 navigational
mark 3 aim, jot, map, sap, say, see, use

4 butt, cull, dupe, duty, fish, fool, goal, gull, heed, logo, look, note, pick, read, show, sign, type, view 5 bound, brand, chart, chump, elect, grade, index, label, limit, stamp, token, trait 6 assign, attend, behold, choose, denote, emblem, evince, lay off, lay out, notice, object, optate, opt for, ostend, pigeon, prefer, rating, record, regard, select, sucker, symbol, target, victim, virtue 7 bespeak, betoken, delimit, destine, discern, exhibit, fall guy, feature, gudgeon, indicia, initial, measure, observe, pick out, purpose, qualify, quality, scratch, signify, symptom 8 ambition, evidence, function, indicate, logotype, manifest, perceive, proclaim, property, register 9 affection, attention, attribute, character, demarcate, designate, determine, objective, quaesitum, signalize, single out 10 importance, indication 11 differentia, distinction, distinguish 12 characterize *a tree:* 5 blaze *by cutting:* 4 nick 5 notch 6 scribe *distinctive:* 7 indicia 8 indicium *identifying:* 6 signet *low-water:* 5 datum *musical notation:* 6 corona 7 fermata *of insertion:* 5 caret *of omission:* 8 ellipsis 10 apostrophe *over a vowel:* 5 breve 6 accent, macron *over n:* 5 tilde *punctuation:* 4 dash 5 colon, comma 6 hyphen, period 9 semicolon *skate:* 4 cusp *time:* 5 count *under a letter:* 7 cedilla *with welts:* 4 wale

Mark *cousin:* 8 Barnabas *mother:* 4 Mary

mark down 3 cut 4 clip, pare 5 decry, lower, shave, slash 6 reduce 7 cut back, devalue 8 write off 9 devaluate 10 depreciate, underprize, undervalue

marked 5 noted 6 signal 7 pointed, salient 8 striking 9 arresting, prominent 10 noticeable, remarkable 11 conspicuous, outstanding 12 considerable 13 distinguished *man:* 4 Cain

market 4 give, sell, shop, vend 5 cheap, store 6 outlet, retail, tryste 8 showroom 9 traffic in, wholesale 11 merchandise *kind:* 4 flea 5 money, stock

marketable 3 fit 4 good 5 sound 7 selling 8 vendible 9 wholesome 10 commercial

marketplace 5 agora, bazar 6 bazaar, rialto

marksman 4 shot 7 deadeye, shooter

marl 4 clay 5 earth 9 fertilize

marlin 9 spearfish

Marlowe play 8 Edward II 9 Dr. Faustus 11 Tamburlaine 13 The Jew of Malta

marmalade fruit 6 orange, quince

marmot 10 prairie dog

Marpessa *abductor:* 4 Idas *father:* 6 Evenus

Marquand character 4 Gray, Moto 5 Apley, Wayde 6 Pulham 7 Goodwin

Marquis *cat:* 9 Mehitabel *cockroach:* 5 Archy

marriage 5 match, union 6 bridal 7 nuptial, spousal, wedding, wedlock 8 espousal, monogamy, nuptials, polygamy, polygany 9 espousals, matrimony 11 conjugality 12 connubiality *combining form:* 4 gamy 6 gamous *notice:* 5 banns *outside a group:* 7 exogamy *second:* 6 bigamy, digamy *within a group:* 8 endogamy

marriageable 6 nubile

marriage broker 9 go-between 10 matchmaker *Jewish:* 8 shadchan

marriage portion 3 dot 5 dower, dowry

marrow 4 core, meat, pith, soul 5 heart, stuff 6 bottom, kernel 7 essence 9 substance 10 virtuality 12 essentiality, quintessence

marry 3 tie, wed 4 join, link, mate, wive, yoke 5 catch, hitch 6 couple, relate, splice, spouse 7 combine, conjoin, espouse, husband 9 associate, conjugate

Mars 6 planet *combining form:* 4 areo *moon:* 6 Deimos, Phobos *relating to:* 7 martian; (see also **Ares**)

Marseillaise composer 13 Rouget de Lisle

marsh 3 bog, fen 4 mire, ooze, quag 5 bayou, glade, swail, swale, swamp 6 maskeg, morass, muskeg, slough 7 baygall, wetland 8 moorland, quagmire 9 swampland *combining form:* 4 helo 6 paludi

marshal 5 array, guide, order, rally, space, usher 6 direct, escort, muster 7 arrange, dispose, officer 8 mobilize, organize, shepherd 9 methodize 10 distribute

marshland see **marsh**

marshlight 7 spunkie 11 ignis fatuus

Martha *brother:* 7 Lazarus *sister:* 4 Mary

martial 7 warlike 8 militant, military, spirited 9 bellicose, combative 10 aggressive, mettlesome, pugnacious 11 belligerent

Martial's forte 7 epigram

Martin Chuzzlewit author 7 Dickens

Martinique *capital:* 12 Fort-de-France *discoverer:* 8 Columbus

martyr 4 Paul, rack 5 Agnes, Alban, James, Peter, saint, wring 6 George, harrow, Justin 7 afflict, agonize, crucify, Cyprian, Stephen, torment, torture 8 Ignatius, Lawrence, Polycarp, sufferer 9 Joan of Arc, Sebastian 10 excruciate *Protestant:* 6 Ridley 7 Cranmer, Latimer

marvel 6 wonder 7 miracle, portent, prodigy, stunner 9 horehound, sensation 10 phenomenon 12 astonishment

marvelous 5 awing, nifty, super, swell 6 divine, dreamy, groovy, peachy 7 amazing, awesome, ripping 8 glorious, pleasant, striking, stunning, superior, terrific, wondrous **9** agreeable, enjoyable, excellent, hunky-dory, rewarding, wonderful **10** astounding, incredible, phenomenal, prodigious, satisfying, staggering, stupendous, surprising **11** astonishing, bewildering, confounding, exceptional, pleasurable, sensational, spectacular **12** awe-inspiring, supernatural, unimaginable **13** extraordinary, inconceivable

Marx, Karl ***book:*** **10** Das Kapital ***collaborator:*** **6** Engels

Marx brother **5** Chico, Harpo, Zeppo **7** Groucho

Mary ***husband:*** **6** Clopas, Joseph **8** Alphaeus ***kinswoman:*** **9** Elisabeth ***son:*** **4** Mark **5** James, Jesus, Joses

Maryland ***academy, university:*** **7** U.S. Naval **11** Towson State **12** Johns Hopkins ***capital:*** **9** Annapolis ***largest city:*** **9** Baltimore ***nickname:*** **12** Cockade State, Old Line State

mascot **4** juju, luck, zemi **5** charm **6** amulet, bat boy, fetish **7** periapt **8** talisman **10** phylactery

masculine **4** male **5** manly **6** manful, robust, virile **7** manlike **9** unwomanly ***combining form:*** **4** andr **5** andro

masculinity **8** machismo, virility **9** manliness

mash **4** mess, pulp **6** accost, bruise, jumble, jungle, litter, muddle, suitor, tumble **7** clutter, rummage **8** scramble **10** sweetheart **12** hugger-mugger

masher **4** wolf **5** flirt **6** chaser **7** Don Juan **8** Casanova **9** ladies' man, philander, womanizer **10** lady-killer **11** philanderer

mash note **10** billet-doux, love letter

mask **4** blur, face, pose, sham, show, veil **5** block, cloak, color, cover, front, guard, guise, put-on, visor **6** aspect, defend, domino, facade, fakery, flavor, screen, shield, veneer, visard, vizard **7** dress up, frisket, muffler, posture, pretext, protect, secrete, seeming, veiling **8** coloring, disguise, pretense **9** dissemble, doughface, false face, safeguard, semblance **10** appearance, camouflage, false front, simulation **11** affectation, dissembling, dissimulate **12** disguisement **13** dissimulation

masonry **9** brickwork, stonework ***in a frame:*** **7** nogging

masquerade **4** face, pose, show, veil **5** cloak, color, cover, front **6** facade, pass as **7** pass for, pass off, posture **8** disguise **10** camouflage **12** attitudinize

mass **3** lot, sum, wad **4** bank, body, bulk, clot, core, glob, heap, hill, lump, much, pack, peck, pile **5** clump, group, mound, shock, stack, total, whole **6** corpus, nugget, object, staple, volume **7** expanse, globule, pyramid, wadding **8** assemble, mountain **9** aggregate, great deal, magnitude, stockpile, substance **10** generality **11** aggregation, proletariat **12** conglomerate ***combining form:*** **4** onco **5** oncho ***confused:*** **7** clutter **9** imbroglio ***for departed:*** **7** requiem ***ice:*** **4** calf, floe ***indefinite:*** **3** gob ***jumbled:*** **8** pell-mell, scramble ***metal:*** **5** ingot ***muddy:*** **6** sludge ***of hair:*** **3** mop ***of individuals:*** **5** crowd, horde, swarm **13** agglomeration ***part:*** **6** proper **8** ordinary ***rock:*** **4** dome ***rounded:*** **4** knob ***suffix:*** **3** ium, ome ***swollen:*** **4** cere ***tight:*** **4** knot

Massachusetts ***capital:*** **6** Boston ***college, university:*** **3** MIT **5** Clark, Curry, Smith, Tufts **6** Babson, Boston **7** Amherst, Harvard **8** Brandeis, Williams **9** Hampshire, Holy Cross, Merrimack, Radcliffe, Wellesley **11** Springfield **12** Mount Holyoke, Northeastern ***highest point:*** **10** Mt. Greylock ***nickname:*** **8** Bay State **9** Old Colony ***state bird:*** **9** chickadee

massacre **4** kill **6** mangle, murder, pogrom **8** butchery, decimate, genocide, mangling, mutilate **9** bloodbath, bloodshed, slaughter **10** annihilate, blood purge, decimation **11** exterminate, internecion

massage **3** rub **5** knead **7** rubdown

Massa's father **7** Ishmael

Massenet opera **5** Le Cid, Manon, Sapho, Thais **7** Werther

massive **4** huge, vast **5** bulky, giant, grand, heavy, hefty, hulky, jumbo, large, solid **6** mighty, mortal **7** compact, hulking, immense, mammoth, notable, weighty **8** colossal, cracking, cumbrous, enormous, gigantic, towering **9** fantastic, monstrous, ponderous **10** cumbersome, monumental, prodigious, stupendous, tremendous **11** elephantine, mountainous

master **3** get **4** best, boss, cock, down, guru, head, lick, rule, tame, whiz **5** adept, bwana, chief, crack, learn, lover, marse, ruler, sahib, swami, throw, tutor **6** artist, direct, domine, expert, genius, govern, honcho, hurdle, leader, pick up, ruling, savant, subdue, victor, wizard **7** artiste, captain, conquer, headman, maestro, overman, padrone, prevail, rabboni, regnant, skilled, subduer, triumph **8** defeater, dominant, dominate, employer, fancy man, governor, hierarch, overcome, overlord, overseer, paramour, regulate, skillful, superior, surmount, virtuoso **9** ascendant, authority, boyfriend, chieftain, conqueror, dominator, paramount, prevalent, principal, sovereign **10** proficient, subjugator, vanquisher **11** controlling, crackerjack, domesticate, domesticize, domiciliate, overbearing, predominant, predominate ***combining form:*** **4** arch

masterdom **8** dominion **9** ascendant, dominance, supremacy **10** ascendancy, domination, prepotence, prepotency **11** preeminence, sovereignty

masterful 4 deft 5 adept, bossy, crack 6 adroit, expert 7 skilled, supreme 8 absolute, despotic, dogmatic, imperial, skillful, vigorous 9 arbitrary, dexterous, dictative, energetic, imperious 10 autocratic, high-handed, imperative, peremptory, preeminent, proficient, self-willed, tyrannical 11 crackerjack, dictatorial, doctrinaire, domineering, magisterial, overbearing, superlative 12 transcendent 13 authoritarian, authoritative, high-and-mighty

masterly 5 adept, crack 6 expert 7 skilled, supreme 8 skillful 10 preeminent, proficient 11 crackerjack, superlative 12 transcendent

Master of Ballantrae 6 Durrie ***author:*** 9 Stevenson

masterpiece 7 classic 9 objet d'art 10 magnum opus 11 chef d'oeuvre, tour de force

mastery 4 sway 5 knack, might, power, skill 7 ability, command, control, know-how 8 dominion 9 authority, expertise, expertism 10 ascendancy, domination, expertness 11 superiority 12 jurisdiction

masticate 4 chew, pulp 5 champ, chomp, chump, crush, munch, smash 6 bruise, crunch, squash 7 chumble, pulpify, scrunch 8 macerate, ruminate 9 break down

mastodonic see mammoth

mast support 4 bibb

mat 3 dim, rug 4 dead, dull, felt, flat, shag 5 blind, doily, muted 6 carpet 10 lackluster, lusterless

matador 6 torero 8 toreador 11 bullfighter ***adjunct:*** 6 muleta ***move:*** 4 pase 5 faena 8 veronica

Mata Hari 3 spy

match 3 con, pit, tie, vie 4 anti, bout, game, like, meet, suit, twin 5 adapt, array, equal, event, liken, rival, touch 6 amount, double, equate, fellow, oppose 7 compare, compeer, counter, opposer, paragon, play off, stack up 8 analogue, approach, opponent, parallel 9 adversary, companion, correlate, duplicate, encounter, measure up, oppugnant, partake of 10 antagonist, assimilate, complement, coordinate, engagement, equivalent, reciprocal, supplement 11 counterpart, countertype 12 correspond to 13 correspondent, harmonize with ***friction:*** 5 fusee, fuzee 7 lucifer 8 locofoco

matchless 4 only 5 alone 6 unique 9 unequaled, unrivaled 10 inimitable 11 unparagoned 12 incomparable, unparalleled

matchmaker see marriage broker

mate 3 pal, tie, wed 4 chum, pair, peer, twin 5 amigo, breed, buddy, equal, hitch, marry, parti, sosie 6 cohort, couple, double, fellow, friend, helper, splice, spouse 7 compeer, consort, partner 8 alter ego, confrere, familiar 9 associate, companion, confidant, copartner, duplicate, procreate 10 complement, crossbreed, equivalent, reciprocal 11 cater-cousin, concomitant 12 acquaintance 13 accompaniment

maté 3 tea 5 holly 8 beverage

material 3 big 4 real, true 5 ad rem, being, cloth, gross, stuff, tapis, thing, vital 6 actual, animal, bodily, carnal, entity, fabric, matter, object 7 apropos, earthly, element, fleshly, germane, sensual, weighty, worldly 8 apposite, cardinal, palpable, physical, pointful, relevant, sensible, tangible 9 apparatus, component, corporeal, equipment, essential, important, machinery, momentous, objective, pertinent, substance 10 applicable, individual, ingredient, meaningful, phenomenal 11 applicative, applicatory, appreciable, constituent, fundamental, perceptible, significant, substantial 12 considerable 13 consequential ***building:*** 5 adobe, brick 7 plywood, shingle 8 concrete ***cementing:*** 7 plaster ***combining form:*** 3 hyl 4 hylo ***combustible:*** 8 kindling ***cushioning:*** 4 foam ***glutinous:*** 7 gelatin ***hard:*** 7 carbide ***hard covering:*** 6 stucco ***indecent:*** 4 smut ***insulating:*** 7 lagging 10 fiberglass ***leftover:*** 5 waste 7 rubbish ***petrified:*** 8 gemstone

materialistic 6 carnal, earthy 7 earthly, mundane, profane, secular, sensual, worldly

materialize 4 loom, rise, show 5 issue, reify 6 appear, embody, emerge, entify, show up, spring, typify 8 manifest 9 incarnate, objectify, personify, personize, take shape 10 pragmatize 11 exteriorize, hypostatize 12 substantiate

matériel 4 gear 6 outfit, tackle 8 tackling 9 apparatus, equipment, machinery 11 habiliments 13 accouterments, accoutrements, paraphernalia

maternal 6 mother 8 motherly

maternally related 5 enate

mathematician ***American:*** 6 Peirce, Veblen, Wiener ***British:*** 6 Stokes ***Dutch:*** 7 Huygens ***English:*** 6 Newton, Taylor, Turing, Wallis 7 Pearson, Russell 9 Whitehead ***French:*** 5 Borel, Comte, Viète 6 Galois, Pascal, Picard 7 Laplace, Vernier 8 Fournier, Painlevé, Poincaré 9 Descartes ***German:*** 5 Gauss, Wolff 6 Staudt 7 Riemann 11 Weierstrass ***Greek:*** 6 Euclid 10 Archimedes, Pythagoras ***Italian:*** 8 Volterra 10 Torricelli ***Norwegian:*** 7 Stormer ***Russian:*** 11 Lobachevsky ***Scottish:*** 4 Tait

6 Napier 8 Stirling *Swiss:* 5 Sturm 7 Steiner
mathematics ***branch:*** 7 algebra 8 calculus, geometry 10 arithmetic 12 trigonometry ***proven statement in:*** 7 theorem
___ Mather 6 Cotton 7 Richard 8 Increase
Matred ***daughter:*** 9 Mehetabel ***father:*** 7 Mezahab ***son-in-law:*** 5 Hadar
matriarch 4 dame 6 mother 7 dowager 10 grande dame 13 materfamilias
matrimonial 6 bridal, wedded 7 marital, married, nuptial, spousal 8 conjugal, hymeneal 9 connubial 11 epithalamic
matrimony 7 wedlock 8 marriage 11 conjugality 12 connubiality
matrix 3 die 6 cradle, gangue, strike 10 groundmass, truth table
matron 4 dame 7 dowager 10 grande dame, parlormaid
Mattaniah ***father:*** 4 Bani, Elam, Mica 5 Asaph, Heman, Zattu 6 Josiah 10 Pahathmoab ***grandson:*** 5 Hanan ***son:*** 6 Zaccur 8 Shemaiah
Mattatha ***father:*** 6 Nathan ***grandfather:*** 5 David
Mattathias ***father:*** 5 Simon 6 Ananos 7 Absalom, Boethus 10 Theophilus ***son:*** 8 Josephus
matter 3 pus 4 body, core, gist, head, mail, mean, meat, pith, text, to-do, tune 5 being, cause, count, motif, order, point, range, sense, stuff, theme, thing, topic, value, weigh, worry 6 affair, amount, burden, entity, extent, import, motive, object, source, upshot 7 concern, signify, subject 8 argument, business, material, vicinity 9 grievance, magnitude, substance, suppurate 10 individual 11 constituent, predicament 12 circumstance ***added to book:*** 8 addendum, appendix ***coloring:*** 3 dye 6 indigo 7 pigment 8 tinction 10 indigo blue ***combining form:*** 3 hyl 4 hylo ***decayed organic:*** 4 duff ***diffused:*** 5 vapor ***in dispute:*** 5 issue ***inferior:*** 5 trash ***waste:*** 5 dross 6 sewage 7 excreta ***white:*** 4 alba ***worthless:*** 4 slag 7 garbage
matter-of-fact 3 dry 4 cold 5 prose, prosy, sober, sound, stoic 6 earthy, stolid 7 prosaic, prosing 9 apathetic, impassive, objective, practical, pragmatic, realistic 10 hard-boiled, hardheaded, impersonal, phlegmatic, unaffected 11 cold-blooded, commonplace, down-to-earth, emotionless 12 unidealistic 13 unimpassioned, unsentimental
Matthew's father 8 Alphaeus
Mattithiah's father 4 Nebo 7 Shallum 8 Jeduthun
mattress 3 pad 4 sack ***case:*** 4 tick ***fabric:*** 7 ticking ***straw:*** 6 pallet
mature 3 age, due 4 grow, ripe, wane 5 adult, grown, olden, owing, ready, ripen, round 6 flower, grow up, mellow, season, unpaid 7 advance, blossom, decline, develop, grown-up, outgrow, overdue, payable, ripened 8 progress 9 developed, full-blown, full-grown ***combining form:*** 3 tel 4 tele, telo
maudlin 5 mushy, silly 6 addled, slushy, sticky 7 fuddled, mawkish, muddled 8 bathetic, confused, romantic 9 befuddled 11 sentimental, tear-jerking
Maugham character 4 Kear, Liza 5 Carey, Rosie, Sadie 7 Mildred 8 Craddock 10 Strickland
maul 3 paw, row 4 bang, bash, club, fray, lash, mace, whip 5 abuse, brawl, broil, flail, melee, pound, set-to 6 batter, beetle, buffet, fracas, hammer, injure, molest, sledge 7 rough up, ruction 8 dogfight, maltreat 9 manhandle 10 donnybrook
maunder 3 bat, gad 5 drift, mooch, range 6 ramble 9 gallivant
Mauritania ***capital:*** 10 Nouakchott ***monetary unit:*** 7 ouguiya
Mauritius ***capital:*** 9 Port Louis ***export:*** 5 sugar ***monetary unit:*** 5 rupee
Maurois biographee 4 Hugo, Sand 5 Byron, Dumas 6 Proust 7 Shelley 8 Disraeli
mauve 6 purple, violet
maven, mavin 5 adept 6 expert, master 8 virtuoso 9 authority 10 past master, proficient 12 professional
maverick 5 stray 8 bohemian, unmarked 9 unbranded 13 nonconformist
maw 4 crop 7 stomach 9 poppy seed
mawkish 4 flat 5 banal, mushy 6 slushy, sticky 7 cloying, maudlin 8 bathetic, romantic 9 sickening 10 lovey-dovey, nauseating 11 sentimental, tear-jerking
maxilla 3 jaw 4 bone
maxim 3 law 4 rule 5 axiom, gnome, large, moral, motto 6 dictum, saying, truism 7 brocard, precept, proverb, theorem 8 aphorism, apothegm 9 platitude, prescript 11 commonplace
maximal 3 top 6 utmost 7 highest, topmost 8 greatest
maximize 7 magnify 8 overplay 10 overstress 13 overemphasize
maximum 3 top 6 utmost 7 highest, largest, supreme, topmost 8 extremum, greatest
may 5 shrub 6 spirea 8 hawthorn
maybe 7 perhaps 8 possible, possibly 9 perchance 10 indecision 11 uncertainty
Mayflower ***document:*** 7 Compact ***passengers:*** 8 pilgrims
mayhem 4 maim 7 cripple, dislimb 8 mutilate 9 dismember

mayor 11 burgomaster ***Chicago (former):*** 5 Daley (Richard) ***New York (former):*** 9 La Guardia ***Spanish:*** 7 alcayde

Mayor of Casterbridge, The ***author:*** 5 Hardy ***character:*** 8 Henchard

maze 3 web 4 knot, mesh 5 skein, snarl 6 jungle, morass, tangle 7 confuse 8 bewilder, mishmash 9 labyrinth 10 hodgepodge, miscellany 11 gordian knot

MD 3 doc 6 doctor, medico 7 medical 8 sawbones 9 mediciner, physician

meadow 3 lea, ley 9 grassland ***low-lying:*** 5 haugh

meadow beauty 9 deer grass

meadow bird 8 bobolink

meadow chicken 8 sora rail

meadow hen 4 coot, rail 7 bittern

meadowlark 4 bird 5 acorn

meadow mushroom 6 agaric

meadow sorrel 4 dock

meager 4 bare, bony, lank, lean, mere, poor, thin 5 gaunt, lanky, scant, short, skimp, spare 6 lenten, scanty, scrimp, shabby, skimpy, skinny, slight, sparse 7 angular, minimum, scraggy, scrawny, scrimpy 8 exiguous, inferior, rawboned, scrimpit 9 deficient, miserable 10 inadequate 12 insufficient

meal 3 eat 4 chow, fare, feed, grub, take 5 board, feast, lunch, salep, snack, table 6 brunch, devour, dinner, farina, feed on, ingest, picnic, repast, spread, supper 7 consume, nooning 8 victuals 9 breakfast, collation, partake of, refection ***army:*** 4 mess

mealy 6 spotty, uneven 8 farinose 9 pollinose 11 farinaceous

mean 3 aim, low, mid, par, set, way 4 base, fair, hack, hint, mode, name, norm, pile, plan, poor, sick, so-so, ugly, want, wish 5 agent, borne, cheap, count, cruel, imply, lousy, lowly, mingy, organ, pesky, purse, rough, small, spell, tatty, tight, tough, weigh 6 agency, ailing, attest, center, common, denote, design, desire, donsie, estate, humble, import, intend, little, manner, matter, medial, medium, method, middle, narrow, offish, ornery, paltry, pocket, poorly, rugged, scrimy, scummy, scurvy, shabby, shoddy, sickly, sleazy, stingy, system, trashy, unwell, wealth, wicked 7 add up to, ashamed, average, betoken, capital, central, channel, connote, express, fairish, fashion, fortune, ignoble, limited, lowborn, miserly, nest egg, niggard, pitiful, propose, purpose, savings, scrimpy, signify, suggest, underly, vehicle 8 baseborn, beggarly, count for, déclassé, indicate, inferior, intimate, kindless, low-grade, mediocre, middling, ministry, moderate, off-color, ordinary, pitiable, plebeian, rubbishy, unwashed 9 apparatus, bastardly, designate, difficult, equipment, low-minded, machinery, niggardly, penurious, troublous, vexatious 10 despicable, despisable, formidable, indisposed, instrument, second-rate, unennobled 11 closefisted, contemplate, indifferent, ineffectual, second-class, tightfisted, troublesome 12 contemptible, intermediary, intermediate, narrow-fisted, second-drawer

meander 4 roam, rove, turn, wind 5 drift, range, snake, stray, twist 6 ramble 7 traipse 8 vagabond 9 gallivant, labyrinth

meandering 5 snaky 7 sinuous, winding 8 flexuous, tortuous 10 convoluted, serpentine 11 anfractuous

meandrous see **meandering**

meaning 3 aim 4 hint, plan 5 drift, force, point, sense, tenor, value 6 animus, design, effect, import, intent, object, syntax 7 essence, message, purport, purpose 9 intention, substance 10 definition, denotation, intendment, intimation, suggestion 11 acceptation, connotation, implication, significant 12 significance, significancy 13 signification, understanding

meaningful 4 rich 6 facund 7 weighty 8 eloquent, material, pregnant 9 important, momentous 10 expressive 11 sententious, significant, substantial 12 considerable 13 consequential

meaningless 5 blank, empty 6 vacant 7 fustian 10 unpurposed 13 insignificant

meanings ***diverse:*** 8 polysemy ***study of:*** 9 semantics

means 5 funds, money 6 agency, assets 7 quomodo 8 finances 9 apparatus, equipment, resources 10 instrument 11 wherewithal

meantime 8 interval

measly 4 poor, puny 5 petty 6 paltry 7 trivial 8 blighted, inferior, niggling, picayune, piddling, trifling 10 picayunish 12 pettifogging

measure 4 beat, bill, deal, meed, move, part, size, step, test, tune 5 bound, dance, gauge, index, limit, meter, metre, quota, rhyme, scale, share, shift, swing, weigh 6 amount, bounds, degree, effort, extent, figure, govern, melody, ration, reckon, resort, rhythm, size up, strain, survey 7 cadence, cadency, caliper, compute, delimit, mark out, melodia, portion, project, quantum, stopgap 8 calliper, estimate, indicate, maneuver, proposal, regulate, resource, rhythmus, standard 9 allotment, allowance, benchmark, calculate, calibrate, criterion, demarcate, determine, expedient, magnitude, makeshift, procedure, yardstick 10 delimitate, dimensions, indication, moderation, proceeding, proportion, temperance, touchstone 11 denominator, proposition 13 apportionment ***area:*** 4 acre 7 hectare 9 square rod 10 square foot, square inch, square mile, square yard 11 square meter ***arrow weight:*** 8 shilling ***butter:*** 4 span ***capacity:*** 4 gill, peck, pint 5 liter, minim, quart 6 bushel, gallon 8 fluidram 10 cubic meter, fluidounce, milliliter ***cloth:*** 3 ell ***combining form:*** 6 metric 8 metrical ***depth:*** 5 plumb, sound ***electrical:*** 7 coulomb ***Hebrew:*** (see at Hebrew) ***horse height:*** 4 hand ***interstellar space:*** 6 parsec ***length:*** 3 rod 4 foot, inch, mile, yard 5 cubit (ancient), meter 9 kilometer 10 centimeter ***liquid:*** 4 pint 5 pipet, quart 6 gallon 7 pipette ***metrical foot:*** 8 monopody ***mixed drinks:*** 6 jigger ***of advantage:*** 4 lead ***of comparison:*** 8 standard ***out:*** 5 batch ***paper:*** 4 ream ***printer's:*** 2 em, en 4 pica 5 point ***radioactive decay:*** 8 halflife ***rotation:*** 5 angle ***silk size:*** 8 drammage ***Spanish dry:*** 5 fanga 6 fanega ***strength of solution:*** 7 titrate ***surface:*** 3 are ***thermodynamic:*** 7 entropy 8 enthalpy ***volume:*** 9 cubic foot, cubic inch, cubic yard 10 cubic meter

Measure for Measure ***character:*** 6 Angelo, Juliet 7 Claudio, Mariana 8 Isabella 9 Vincentio ***setting:*** 6 Vienna

measurement 4 area 6 degree 8 capacity, quantity 9 dimension 11 mensuration ***rain:*** 8 udometry ***weight:*** 6 metage

measure up 3 tie 4 meet 5 equal, match, rival, touch

measuring ***combining form:*** 5 metry ***device for liquid:*** 7 venturi ***rod:*** 8 dipstick ***stick:*** 8 yardwand ***tube:*** 5 buret 7 burette

meat 4 core, food, gist, pith, pork, veal 5 flesh, jerky, sense, short, steak 6 burden, matter, thrust, upshot 7 charqui, edibles, nurture 8 victuals 9 foodstuff, provender, substance 10 provisions 11 comestibles ***broiled:*** 8 barbecue, grillade ***broth:*** 8 bouillon ***cake:*** 6 burger ***cured:*** 7 biltong ***cut:*** 3 rib 4 loin, rump 5 chuck, flank, plate, round, shank 7 brisket, sirloin 8 rib roast 9 club steak, rump roast, short loin, short ribs 10 blade roast, flank steak, round steak, T-bone steak 11 arm pot roast 12 boneless neck, pinbone steak, sirloin steak 13 blade rib roast, crosscut shank ***dealer:*** 7 butcher ***deer:*** 7 venison ***dried:*** 5 jerky ***fastening pin:*** 6 skewer ***holding rod:*** 4 spit ***juices:*** 5 gravy ***minced:*** 7 rissole ***packer:*** 5 Swift 6 Armour ***raw:*** 6 gobbet ***roasting shop:*** 10 rotisserie ***rounded mass of:*** 9 croquette ***seasoned:*** 7 sausage 8 pastrami, pastromi ***sheep:*** 6 mutton ***side:*** 8 sowbelly ***skewered:*** 5 kabab, kabob, kebob ***slice:*** 6 cutlet, rasher ***small portion:*** 6 collop ***tough part:*** 7 gristle

meat-eating 11 carnivorous

meathead 3 oaf 4 gawk, lout, lump 5 klutz, looby 6 lubber 7 palooka

Mebd ***husband:*** 6 Ailill ***victim:*** 10 Cuchulainn

Mecca ***country:*** 11 Saudi Arabia ***pilgrimage:*** 4 hadj, hajj ***port:*** 5 Jidda ***shrine:*** 5 Caaba, Kaaba

mechanic 7 artisan 9 automatic, machinist 10 uninspired

mechanism 4 gear 5 ratch, slide, steer 6 cutoff, infeed, rachet 7 ratchet 8 rackwork, signaler 9 apparatus ***bookbinder's:*** 7 gripper ***card game:*** 7 holdout ***clutch:*** 8 throwout ***dam:*** 7 tripper ***fastening:*** 5 catch ***firearm:*** 7 ejector, gunlock ***guiding:*** 5 apron ***part:*** 7 trippet ***printing:*** 8 elevator ***raising:*** 4 lift ***timepiece:*** 7 setting

meddle 3 pry 4 fool, nose 5 snoop 6 butt in, dabble, horn in, invade, kibitz, monkey, putter, tamper, tinker 7 intrude, obtrude 8 busybody, trespass 9 interfere, interlope, intervene 10 mess around, monkey with, tamper with

meddlesome 4 busy 9 intrusive, obtrusive, officious 11 impertinent 13 polypragmatic

Medea ***brother:*** 8 Absyrtus ***father:*** 6 Aeëtes ***husband:*** 5 Jason 6 Aegeus ***son:*** 6 Medeus ***victim:*** 6 Creusa, Glauce, Glauke

medial 3 mid 4 fair, moan 6 center, middle 7 average, central, fairish, halfway, midmost 8 middling, moderate 10 centermost, middlemost 11 equidistant, indifferent 12 intermediary, intermediate

median see medial

mediate 6 convey, liaise, step in 9 intercede, interfere, interpose, intervene

mediator 5 judge 6 broker 7 arbiter 9 go-between, middleman 10 interagent, interceder, peacemaker 11 intercessor

medical 3 doc 6 doctor 9 physician ***instrument:*** 11 cardiograph, stethoscope

medical treatment ***combining form:*** 5 iatry 6 iatric 7 iatrics 8 iatrical

medicament 4 cure 6 physic, remedy 9 pharmacon ***inert:*** 7 placebo

medication see medicament

medicinal 4 drug 8 biologic, salutary, sanative 12 pharmaceutic ***extract:*** 10 belladonna

medicine 4 cure 5 bromo 6 physic, remedy 7 anodyne, nostrum 8 busulfan, poultice 9 pharmacon 11 antipyretic, magical rite 12 magical power ***ball:*** 4 pill ***bottle:*** 4 vial ***branch:*** 7 surgery 8 posology 9 pathology 10 bariatrics, geriatrics, gynecology, obstetrics, pediatrics ***cathartic:*** 8 evacuant 9 purgative ***combining form:*** 5 iatro 8 pharmaco ***quantity of:*** 4 dose

6 dosage ***shell:*** 7 capsule ***soothing:*** 7 nervine 8 lenitive, sedative
medicine man 6 doctor, kahuna, shaman
medieval ***guild:*** 5 Hanse ***military unit:*** 5 lance ***study:*** 5 logic 6 trivia (plural) 7 grammar, trivium 8 rhetoric
mediocre 3 bad 4 fair, hack, mean, poor, so-so 6 common 7 average, fairish 8 inferior, middling, moderate, ordinary, passable 10 bush-league 11 commonplace
meditate 4 muse, roll 6 intend, ponder 7 purpose, revolve 8 consider, mull over, ruminate, turn over 9 reflect on 10 deliberate 11 contemplate
meditator 4 yogi 5 yogin
Mediterranean 11 Mare Nostrum 12 Mare Internum ***coastal region:*** 7 Riviera ***eastern shores:*** 6 Levant ***island:*** (see at island) ***vessel:*** 5 setee 6 settee ***wind:*** 6 solano 7 mistral, sirocco
medium 3 par 4 fair, mean, so-so 5 agent, forte, organ, radio 6 agency, métier, milieu, normal, oyster, vulgar 7 ambient, average, channel, climate, fairish, neutral, popular, vehicle 8 ambience, eminency, long suit, middling, ministry, moderate, passable, standard 9 go-between, run-of-mine, tolerable 10 atmosphere, compromise, instrument, middle-rate, strong suit, television 11 clairvoyant, environment ***nutrient:*** 7 culture ***of exchange:*** 5 money ***of radio transmission:*** 3 air 7 airwave
medley 4 brew, olio 6 jumble 7 mélange 8 pastiche 9 pasticcio, patchwork, potpourri 10 assortment, hodgepodge, miscellany 11 gallimaufry
Medusa 6 Gorgon ***father:*** 7 Phorcus, Phorcys ***mother:*** 4 Ceto ***offspring:*** 7 Pegasus 8 Chrysaor ***sister:*** 6 Stheno 7 Euryale ***slayer:*** 7 Perseus
meed 3 due 4 part, plum 5 merit, prize, quota, share 6 amount, carrot, desert, ration, reward 7 guerdon, measure, portion, premium, quantum 8 dividend 9 allotment, allowance 12 recompensing, satisfaction 13 apportionment
meek 4 mild, tame, weak 5 lowly 6 gentle, humble, modest 7 lenient, patient 8 moderate, tolerant 10 forbearing, submissive, unassuming 13 long-suffering
meerschaum 4 pipe 6 gravel 9 sepiolite
meet 3 apt, fit, hit, sit, tie 4 bump, espy, face, fair, fill, find, good, join, just, luck, open, spot 5 brave, catch, clash, close, cross, equal, event, focus, front, greet, happy, hit on, light, match, right, rival, touch, unite 6 accost, answer, chance, descry, detect, engage, happen, oppose, proper, salute, settle, suffer, take on, tumble, turn up, tussle, useful 7 affront, collide, contest, convene, fitting, fulfill, grapple, hit upon, satisfy, stumble, sustain, undergo, wrestle 8 approach, assemble, come upon, concours, conflict, confront, converge, cope with, suitable 9 concenter, conformed, encounter, equitable, impinge on, measure up, rencontre 10 applicable, congregate, convenient, experience, felicitous, provide for, reconciled 11 appropriate, competition ***a bet:*** 3 see ***a need:*** 7 suffice ***athletic:*** 8 gymkhana ***by appointment:*** 10 rendezvous
meeting 4 moot, talk 5 tryst 6 parley, powwow 7 contest, session 8 assembly, conclave, concours, conflict, congress, junction 9 concourse, encounter, gathering, rencontre 10 concursion, conference, confluence 11 competition 12 intersection ***Anglo-Saxon:*** 5 gemot 6 gemote ***place:*** 5 forum ***spiritual:*** 6 séance
Mefistofele composer 5 Boito
Megaera see Erinyes
megaphone 7 address 8 bullhorn 10 mouthpiece
Megara ***father:*** 5 Creon ***husband:*** 8 Heracles, Hercules ***king:*** 5 Nisus
megillah 5 story 6 scroll 7 account
megrim 4 urge, whim 5 fancy, freak, humor, whiff 6 whimsy 7 boutade, caprice, conceit, impulse, vertigo 8 crotchet, migraine 9 dizziness
Mehetabel ***husband:*** 5 Hadar ***mother:*** 6 Matred ***son:*** 7 Delaiah
Mehitabel 3 cat ***creator:*** 7 Marquis ***friend:*** 5 Archy
Mein Kampf author 6 Hitler
meiosis 7 litotes 12 cell division
Meistersinger 4 Folz 5 Sachs
melancholic 3 sad 6 triste 7 joyless 8 mournful 9 depressed, saddening 10 depressing
melancholy 3 sad 5 blues, dumps, ennui, gloom, sorry 6 dismal, dreary, gloomy, misery, rueful, somber, tedium, triste, woeful 7 boredom, despair, dismals, doleful, joyless, moanful, pensive, sadness, sighful, unhappy, wailful 8 dejected, dolesome, dolorous, funereal, mournful, saddened, sombrous 9 dejection, plaintive, saddening, sorrowful 10 afflicting, depressing, depression, disturbing, lachrymose, lamentable, lugubrious, perturbing, reflective, thoughtful 11 desperation, disquieting, unhappiness 12 discomposing, heavyhearted, mournfulness, wretchedness 13 miserableness
mélange see medley
Melanippe's son 6 Aeolus
Melanippus ***father:*** 7 Theseus ***slayer:*** 10 Amphiaraus ***victim:*** 6 Tydeus
Melchior ***companion:*** 6 Gaspar 9 Balthazar ***gift:*** 4 gold

Melchizedek's kingdom 5 Salem
meld 3 mix 4 fuse 5 blend, merge 6 mingle 8 compound 9 interfuse 10 amalgamate, interblend 11 intermingle
Meleager ***beloved:*** 8 Atalanta ***father:*** 6 Oeneus ***mother:*** 7 Althaea ***victim:*** 4 boar
Melech's father 5 Micah
melee 3 row 4 fray, hash, riot, stew 5 brawl, broil, brush, clash, fight 6 affray, fracas, jumble, ruckus 7 ruction, scuffle 8 dogfight, mishmash, pastiche, skirmish 9 potpourri, scrimmage 10 donnybrook, free-for-all, hodgepodge, miscellany
Melicertes ***father:*** 7 Athamas ***mother:*** 3 Ino
meliorate 4 help 5 amend 6 better, soften 7 improve
Mélisande's lover 7 Pelleas
melisma 3 air, lay 4 song, tune 6 strain, warble 7 cadenza, descant, measure 8 diapason
mellifluous 5 sweet 6 dulcet, golden, liquid, smooth 7 honeyed, silvery 8 euphonic, Hyblaean, resonant 9 accordant 13 golden-tongued, silver-tongued
mellisonant 5 sweet 6 dulcet 7 tuneful 8 euphonic 10 euphonious
mellow 3 age 4 aged 5 ripen 6 genial, golden, grow up, liquid, mature 7 develop, honeyed, matured, ripened
melodic 5 sweet, tuned 6 dulcet 7 musical, songful, tuneful 8 canorous 10 euphonious
melodious 5 lyric, sweet, tuned 6 dulcet 7 musical, songful, tuneful 8 euphonic, soundful 9 cantabile
melody 3 air, lay 4 sing, song, tune 5 canto 6 lyrics, strain, warble 7 descant, measure 8 bel canto, diapason, vocalize 11 tunefulness
melon 4 pepo 5 gourd, mango 6 casaba, papaya 7 cassaba 8 honeydew 10 cantaloupe
Melpomene see **Muse**
melt 3 rin, run 4 bake, burn, cook, flux, fuse, thaw, warm 5 blend, broil, roast, sweat 6 scorch, soften, spleen 7 liquefy, liquify, swelter 8 dissolve, liquesce, perspire, unfreeze 9 disappear 10 deliquesce ***down:*** 6 render ***together:*** 4 fuse
Melville ***character:*** 3 Pip 4 Ahab, Toby 5 Bembo, Chase 6 Cereno, Jermin, Pierre 7 Fayaway, Ishmael 8 Bartleby, Queequeg, Starbuck ***novel:*** 4 Omoo 5 Mardi, Typee 6 Pierre 7 Redburn 8 Moby Dick 11 White Jacket
member 3 cut 4 part 5 penis, piece 6 clause, moiety, parcel 7 portion, section, segment 8 division ***architectural:*** 3 fan 7 cornice ***armed forces:*** 5 cadet 6 airman, Marine, sailor 7 soldier ***chivalry order:*** 6 knight ***combining form:*** 3 mer 4 crat, mere 5 ocrat ***gang:*** 7 mobster 8 henchman 10 hatchet man ***Girl Scout:*** 7 brownie, Cadette ***household:*** 8 familiar ***legislative:*** 7 senator ***mendicant order:*** 5 friar 9 Dominican ***middle class:*** 7 burgher ***monastic order:*** 4 monk 5 friar 6 hermit ***Parliament:*** 2 MP ***political party:*** 4 Tory, Whig 7 Liberal 8 Democrat, Laborite 9 Communist, Socialist 10 Republican 12 Conservative ***secret society:*** 7 DeMolay, tongman 8 Klansman, Ku Kluxer ***senior male:*** 5 doyen ***service club:*** 4 Lion 8 Kiwanian, Rotarian ***structural:*** 4 arch ***suffix:*** 2 ad, id ***triangular:*** 5 gable
membrane 6 pleura 7 pleurae (plural) ***bodily:*** 6 serosa 7 serosae (plural) ***brain:*** 3 pia ***combining form:*** 3 vel 5 chori, hymen 6 chorio, hymeno, mening, myring 7 meningi, meningo, myringo ***diffusion through:*** 7 osmosis ***dividing:*** 5 septa (plural) 6 septum ***ear:*** 8 tympanum ***enclosing:*** 8 indusium ***thin:*** 6 lamina 7 lamella, laminae (plural) 8 lamellae (plural) ***wing:*** 8 patagium
memento 5 relic, token, trace 6 shadow, trophy 7 vestige 8 keepsake, reminder, souvenir 11 remembrance 12 remembrancer
Memnon ***father:*** 8 Tithonus ***mother:*** 3 Eos 6 Aurora ***slayer:*** 8 Achilles
memoir 3 bio 4 life 6 record, report, thesis 8 anecdote, tractate, treatise 9 biography, discourse, monograph 10 monography 11 confessions, remembrance 12 disquisition, dissertation, recollection, reminiscence 13 autobiography
memoirist 7 Boswell 10 biographer
memorable 6 rubric 9 deathless, momentous, red-letter 10 impressive, noteworthy, remembered 11 significant 13 distinguished
memorandum 4 chit, note 5 diary 6 letter, minute, notice 7 epistle, message, missive, tickler 8 dispatch, notation, reminder 9 directive 12 announcement
memorial 4 note 5 relic, token, trace 6 record, trophy 7 relique 8 keepsake, monument, reminder, souvenir 10 dedicatory, enshrining 11 celebrative, remembrance 12 consecrative, remembrancer 13 commemoration, commemorative, commemoratory ***mound:*** 4 carn 5 cairn
memorial park 8 cemetery, God's acre 9 graveyard 10 necropolis 11 polyandrium 12 burial ground, potter's field 13 burying ground
memorize 3 con, get 5 learn, study 8 remember
memory 4 mind 6 recall 8 mind's eye, souvenir 9 anamnesis, awareness, reten-

tion **10** cognizance, reflection **11** remembrance **12** recollection, reminiscence **13** concentration, consciousness, retentiveness, retrospection ***assisting:*** **8** mnemonic ***combining form:*** **4** mnem **5** mnemo **6** mnesia ***loss:*** **7** amnesia

menace **4** loom, risk **5** alarm, lower, peril, scare **6** danger, hazard, threat **7** imperil, jeopard, torment **8** endanger, frighten, jeopardy, threaten **10** jeopardize

ménage **5** folks, house **6** family **8** quarters **9** household **12** housekeeping

Menahem ***father:*** **4** Gadi ***son:*** **8** Pekahiah ***victim:*** **7** Shallum

mend **3** fix, sew **4** cure, darn, do up, gain, heal, vamp **5** patch, ready, renew **6** bushel, cobble, doctor, look up, perk up, reform, remedy, repair, revamp **7** correct, improve, patch up, rebuild, rectify, redress, restore, service **8** overhaul, renovate **9** condition, refurbish **10** ameliorate, convalesce, recuperate, rejuvenate **11** recondition, reconstruct

mendacious **5** false, lying, wrong **6** shifty **7** fibbing, knavish, roguish **8** unhonest **9** deceitful, dishonest, paltering **10** untruthful **12** equivocating **13** prevaricating

mendacity **7** dodging, fibbery, hedging **8** boggling, caviling, shifting **9** falsehood, quibbling **12** equivocation, sidestepping **13** truthlessness

mendelevium ***symbol:*** **2** Md

mendicancy **7** beggary, bumming, cadging **8** mooching, sponging **11** panhandling

mendicant **5** friar **6** beggar **7** begging

Mending Wall author **5** Frost

Menelaus ***brother:*** **9** Agamemnon ***father:*** **6** Atreus ***kingdom:*** **6** Sparta ***mother:*** **6** Aerope ***wife:*** **5** Helen

menial **5** lowly **6** humble **7** servile, slavish **8** obeisant **10** obsequious **11** subservient

Men in White author **8** Kingsley

Menlo Park inventor **6** Edison

menopause **11** climacteric **12** change of life

Menotti, Gian Carlo ***character:*** **5** Amahl ***opera:*** **9** The Consul, The Medium **12** The Telephone

men's store **12** haberdashery

mental **5** inner **6** genial **7** psychic **8** thinking **9** reasoning, spiritual **10** immaterial, telepathic **11** ideological, intelligent **12** intellective, intellectual **13** psychological ***faculty:*** **6** memory

mentality **3** wit **5** sense **6** brains **7** outlook **9** mother wit **10** brainpower **12** intelligence

mention **4** cite, name, note **5** quote, refer **6** advert, allude, detail **7** refer to, specify **8** instance **9** designate, reference **10** denominate

mentor **5** coach **7** teacher

Mentor's pupil **10** Telemachus

menu **4** card, diet **5** carte **7** regimen **10** bill of fare **11** carte du jour ***item:*** **4** soup **5** salad **6** entrée **7** dessert **9** appetizer

Mephibosheth ***father:*** **4** Saul **8** Jonathan ***mother:*** **6** Rizpah

Mephistophelian **7** satanic **8** devilish, diabolic

mephitic **4** olid **5** fetid, funky, musty **6** poison, smelly **7** noisome, noxious, reeking, stenchy **8** stinking, toxicant, venomous, virulent **9** poisonous **10** malodorous

Merab ***father:*** **4** Saul ***husband:*** **6** Adriel

Meraioth ***father:*** **6** Ahitub **8** Zerahiah ***son:*** **5** Zadok

Merari ***brother:*** **6** Kohath **7** Gershon ***daughter:*** **6** Judith ***father:*** **4** Levi ***son:*** **5** Mahli, Mushi

mercenary **4** grub, hack **5** venal **6** drudge, slavey **7** corrupt, grubber, soldier **8** hireling

merchandise **4** line, sell **5** cargo, goods, stock, trade, wares **6** deal in, job lot, market, retail **7** effects, staples, traffic **9** publicize, vendibles **11** commodities

merchandiser **9** tradesman **11** businessman

merchant **5** buyer **6** dealer, jobber, seller, trader, vender, vendor **7** peddler **8** purveyor, retailer **9** tradesman **10** specialist, trafficker, wholesaler **11** businessman, storekeeper ***guild:*** **5** hansa, hanse ***Hindu:*** **6** banian, banyan ***League:*** **9** Hanseatic ***ship:*** **5** oiler **6** argosy, coaler, galiot, packet, tanker, trader **7** collier, galliot, steamer **8** Indiaman **9** freighter ***wine:*** **7** vintner

Merchant of Venice **7** Antonio ***character:*** **6** Portia **7** Jessica, Lorenzo, Nerissa, Shylock **8** Bassanio

merciful **4** easy, kind **6** benign, humane, kindly **7** clement, lenient, sparing **8** tolerant **9** condoning, forgiving, indulgent, pardoning **10** charitable, forbearing **11** softhearted **13** compassionate

merciless **4** grim **5** cruel, harsh **6** mortal, savage, wanton **9** cutthroat, ferocious, unpitying **10** gratuitous, implacable, ironfisted, unyielding **11** uncalled-for, unflinching, unrelenting **12** unappeasable

mercurial **6** adroit, clever, fickle, mobile **7** buoyant, cunning, elastic, movable **8** ticklish, unstable, variable, volatile **9** expansive, ingenious, resilient, sprightly **10** capricious, changeable, inconstant, lubricious **12** effervescent **13** temperamental

mercury 5 azoth 9 poison ivy 11 quicksilver *ore:* 8 cinnabar *symbol:* 2 Hg

Mercury 6 planet; (see also **Hermes**)

Mercutio *friend:* 5 Romeo *slayer:* 6 Tybalt

mercy 4 pity, ruth 5 grace 6 lenity 7 caritas, charity 8 clemency, goodwill, kindness, leniency 9 benignity, tolerance 10 compassion, generosity, kindliness 11 benevolence, forbearance 13 commiseration *petition for:* 5 kyrie 8 miserere

mere 3 fen 4 bare, lake, pool, pure, very 5 marsh 9 undiluted

Mered's father 5 Ezrah

merely 3 but 4 just, only 5 quite 6 simply, wholly

Meremoth's father 4 Bani 5 Uriah

meretricious 4 loud 5 gaudy 6 brazen, flashy, garish, tawdry, tinsel 7 blatant, chintzy, glaring 8 delusive, delusory 9 deceptive, insincere 10 misleading

merge 3 mix 4 fuse, join 5 blend, unify, unite 6 mingle 7 combine 8 coalesce, compound 9 commingle, interfuse 10 amalgamate, interblend 11 consolidate, intermingle

mergence see **merging**

merger 5 union 9 coalition 11 coadunation, combination, unification 12 amalgamation 13 consolidation

merging 5 union 9 coalition 11 coadunation, combination, unification 13 consolidation

meridian 4 acme, apex, peak 6 apogee, climax, comble, summit, zenith 8 pinnacle

merit 3 due 4 earn, rate 5 arete, award, lumps, repay, value, worth 6 reward, rights, virtue 7 caliber, deserts, deserve, entitle, justify, quality, requite, stature, warrant 9 deserving 10 excellence, excellency, perfection, recompense

meritable see **meritorious**

merited 3 due 4 just 5 right 7 condign 8 deserved, rightful, suitable 9 requisite 11 appropriate 13 rhadamanthine

meritorious 6 worthy 8 laudable 9 admirable, deserving, estimable, honorable, praisable 11 commendable, thankworthy 12 praiseworthy

merlin 6 falcon 10 pigeon hawk

mermaid 7 manatee 8 sirenian 11 sirenomelus

Merodach see **Marduk**

Merope *father:* 5 Atlas 8 Oenopion *husband:* 7 Polybus 8 Sisyphus 11 Cresphontes *lover:* 5 Orion *mother:* 7 Pleione *sisters:* 8 Pleiades *son:* 7 Aepytus, Glaucus

merriment 4 glee 5 mirth, revel 6 gaiety 7 jollity, revelry, whoopee 8 hilarity, reveling 9 festivity, jocundity, joviality 10 jocularity, jubilation 13 entertainment

merry 3 gay, mad 4 boon, gean, glad, high, wild 5 happy, jolly, riant, sharp 6 blithe, jocund, jovial, joyful, joyous, lively 7 festive, gleeful, intense 8 animated, cheerful, gleesome, laughing, mirthful 9 hilarious, sprightly, vivacious 10 blithesome 12 lighthearted 13 unconstrained

merry-andrew 4 zany 5 clown 7 buffoon 9 harlequin 10 mountebank

merrymaking 5 party, revel 6 gaiety 7 jollity, revelry, whoopee 8 pleasure 9 enjoyment, festivity, revelment 10 indulgence 12 conviviality

Merry Widow composer 5 Lehar

Merry Wives of Windsor, The *character:* 3 Nym 4 Ford, Page 5 Caius 6 Fenton, Pistol 7 Slender 8 Falstaff

mesa 5 bench 7 plateau 9 cartouche, tableland

mescal 5 agave 6 cactus, liquor, maguey

mesh 3 net, web 4 knot, maze, nett 5 skein, snarl 6 accord, engage, jungle, morass, tangle 7 mizmaze, netting, network 8 entangle 9 harmonize, interlock, labyrinth 10 coordinate

Mesha *father:* 9 Shaharaim *kingdom:* 4 Moab *mother:* 6 Hodesh

Meshech's father 7 Japheth

meshuggaas 4 guff 6 drivel 7 twaddle 8 claptrap, nonsense 9 poppycock 10 balderdash

Meshullam *father:* 4 Bani 5 Zadok 9 Berechiah, Besodeiah 10 Shephatiah, Zerubbabel 12 Meshillemith *son:* 5 Sallu 7 Hilkiah

Meshullemeth *husband:* 8 Manasseh *son:* 4 Amon

mesmeric 5 siren 7 drawing 8 alluring, charming 9 glamorous 10 attractive, bewitching, enchanting 11 captivating

mesmerize 4 grip, hold 7 catch up 8 enthrall, entrance 9 fascinate, hypnotize, spellbind

Mesopotamia *civilization:* 7 Assyria 9 Babylonia *river:* 6 Tigris 9 Euphrates

mess 4 hash, mull, play 5 botch, catch, gum up, mix up, snafu, wreck 6 bobble, bollix, bungle, dabble, doodle, fiddle, fright, goof up, jumble, muddle, potter, puddle, putter, tinker, trifle 7 bitch up, confuse, desight, eyesore, louse up 8 botchery, disarray, dishevel, disorder, shambles, wreckage 9 confusion 10 disarrange, hodgepodge, miscellany 11 monstrosity *up:* 5 touse 6 tousle, touzle, untidy

message 4 note, word 5 sense 6 import, letter, report 7 epistle, evangel, meaning, mission, purport 8 dispatch, telegram 9 directive, telegraph 10 communiqué,

intendment, memorandum **11** acceptation **12** significance **13** communication, signification
Messalina's husband 8 Claudius
mess around 4 fool, idle, wolf **5** flirt **6** butt in, dabble, dawdle, doodle, fiddle, horn in, meddle, potter, puddle, putter, tinker **7** intrude **8** busybody, womanize **9** associate, interfere, interlope, manhandle, philander **10** monkey with, tamper with
messenger 4 post **5** envoy **6** herald **7** apostle, courier **8** emissary **9** character, go-between **11** internuncio **12** intermediary ***God's:*** **5** angel ***of the gods:*** **6** Hermes **7** Mercury ***Turkish:*** **6** chiaus, chouse
Messiah composer 6 Handel
messy 5 dirty, grimy **6** botchy, sloppy, unneat, untidy **7** raunchy, unkempt **8** careless, ill-kempt, slapdash, slipshod, slovenly **10** disheveled, unthorough **12** unfastidious
Mestor ***father:*** **7** Perseus ***mother:*** **9** Andromeda
metal 4 gold **5** steel, sword **6** bronze ***alloy:*** (see alloy) ***casting mold:*** **5** ingot ***corrosion:*** **4** rust ***design:*** **7** chasing ***dross:*** **4** slag ***drum:*** **8** canister ***fittings:*** **5** brass ***in mass:*** **7** bullion ***layer:*** **7** plating ***lump:*** **6** nugget ***piece:*** **4** slug ***refuse:*** **6** scoria ***sheath:*** **5** armor ***substance:*** **5** alloy ***surface scum:*** **5** dross ***thin:*** **4** foil, leaf **5** plate ***type:*** **7** quadrat ***worker:*** **5** smith **10** blacksmith
metallic element 3 tin **4** gold, iron, lead, zinc **6** barium, cobalt, copper, nickel, radium, silver, sodium **7** arsenic, bismuth, lithium, mercury, uranium **8** aluminum, platinum, tungsten, vanadium **9** magnesium, manganese, potassium, strontium **10** molybdenum
metamere 6 somite **7** segment
metamorphic ***rock:*** **5** slate **6** gneiss, marble, schist **9** quartzite, soapstone
metamorphose 3 age **5** ripen **6** change, mature **7** commute, convert, develop **9** transform, translate, transmute **11** transfigure **12** transmogrify
metamorphosis 6 change **8** changing ***combining form:*** **3** ody
Metamorphosis author 5 Kafka
metanoia 7 rebirth **10** conversion
metaphor 5 trope **6** simile **7** analogy **8** allegory **10** comparison, similitude
metaphorical compound 7 kenning
metaphysical 8 bodiless, numinous, superior **9** unearthly, unfleshly **10** discarnate, immaterial, superhuman, suprahuman **12** supermundane, supernatural, supramundane, supranatural, transcendent **13** preternatural ***poet:*** **5** Donne **7** Crashaw, Herbert, Marvell
mete 4 deal, dole, give **5** allot **6** parcel **7** portion **8** allocate, dispense **9** apportion
meteor 8 fireball **12** shooting star ***exploding:*** **5** bolis **6** bolide ***shower:*** **5** Lyrid **6** Leonid, Taurid **7** Aquarid, Geminid, Orionid, Perseid **10** Quadrantid ***suffix:*** **2** id
meteorite 8 aerolite, aerolith **10** siderolite
meter 4 beat, scan **5** rhyme, swing **6** rhythm **7** cadence, cadency, measure, versify
metheglin 4 mead **8** beverage ***ingredient:*** **5** honey
method 3 way **4** form, line, mode, modi (plural), plan, wise **5** means, modus, order, style, track **6** course, design, manner, schema, scheme, system **7** fashion, formula, pattern, process, routine, technic, wrinkle **8** practice **9** procedure, technique **11** orderliness **13** modus operandi ***careful:*** **8** strategy ***of employing troops:*** **6** tactic ***of procedure:*** **2** MO **4** game
methodical 5 exact **7** careful, orderly, precise, regular **9** organized **10** scrupulous, systematic **12** systematized
Methuselah ***father:*** **5** Enoch ***grandson:*** **4** Noah ***son:*** **6** Lamech
Methushael ***father:*** **8** Mehujael ***son:*** **6** Lamech
meticulous 4 neat **5** exact, fussy, picky **6** strict **7** careful, finicky, heedful **8** punctual, thorough **10** pernickety **11** microscopic, painstaking **12** conscionable
métier 3 art **4** mode **5** craft, forte, trade **7** calling **8** business, eminency, long suit, vocation **10** handicraft, profession, strong suit
metrical foot 4 iamb **5** iambi (plural), paeon **6** cretic, dactyl, iambic, iambus **7** anapest, pyrrhic, spondee, triseme, trochee **8** bacchius, choriamb, spondaic, tribrach, trochaic
metric unit ***area:*** **7** centare, deciare, hectare ***capacity:*** **5** liter **9** decaliter, deciliter, kiloliter **10** centiliter, hectoliter, milliliter ***length:*** **5** meter **9** decameter, decimeter, kilometer **10** centimeter, hectometer, millimeter, myriameter ***mass and weight:*** **4** gram **7** quintal **8** decagram, decigram, kilogram **9** centigram, hectogram, metric ton, milligram ***volume:*** **5** stere **9** decastere, decistere
metropolis 4 city **7** capital **13** mother country
metropolitan 5 urban **6** urbane **10** archbishop
mettle 4 guts **5** heart, pluck, spunk **6** spirit, temper **7** cojones, courage **10** resolution **12** spiritedness **13** dauntlessness
mettlesome 4 edgy **5** beany, fiery **6** spunky **7** gingery, peppery **8** skittish,

spirited **9** excitable, startlish **10** high-strung **11** high-hearted **12** high-spirited
mew **3** hem, pen **4** cage, coop, gull, molt, mure **5** fence **6** corral, immure, shut in **7** enclose **8** hideaway
mewl **4** meow **5** whine **7** whimper
Mexico ***aborigine:*** **4** Maya **5** Aztec ***coin:*** **7** centavo ***conqueror:*** **6** Cortes, Cortez ***crop:*** **5** sisal ***emperor:*** **10** Maximilian ***estate:*** **8** hacienda ***ethnic group:*** **6** Indian **7** Mestizo ***export:*** **6** coffee, cotton, sulfur **9** petroleum ***food:*** **4** masa, taco **5** chili, salsa **6** tamale **7** panocha, penuche, tostada **8** frijoles, tortilla **9** enchilada, guacamole **10** quesadilla ***house:*** **5** jacal ***language:*** **7** Spanish ***liquor:*** **7** tequila ***monetary unit:*** **4** peso ***oil enterprise:*** **5** PEMEX ***revolutionist:*** **5** Villa (Pancho) **6** Zapata **8** Carranza ***stimulant:*** **6** mescal
mezzanine **5** story **7** balcony **8** entresol
mezzo-soprano ***American:*** **5** Elias, Horne, Jones **6** Bumbry **7** Verrett **8** Troyanos, von Stade ***Austrian:*** **6** Ludwig ***English:*** **5** Baker ***Italian:*** **8** Cossotto
Miami ***bowl:*** **6** Orange ***chief:*** **12** Little Turtle ***county:*** **4** Dade ***stadium:*** **9** Joe Robbie ***team:*** **8** Dolphins
mib **5** agate **6** marble
mica **4** talc **7** biotite **8** silicate **9** muscovite
Mica ***father:*** **6** Zichri **12** Mephibosheth ***grandfather:*** **8** Jonathan
Micah ***father:*** **9** Meribbaal ***son:*** **5** Abdon
Micaiah ***father:*** **5** Imlah, Uriel **8** Gemariah ***grandfather:*** **7** Absalom ***husband:*** **8** Rehoboam ***mother:*** **5** Tamar ***son:*** **6** Abijah, Achbor
Michelangelo ***painting:*** **10** Holy Family **12** Last Judgment ***statue:*** **5** David, Moses, Pietà **7** Bacchus
Michener novel **6** Hawaii **8** Caravans, Sayonara **9** The Source **10** Centennial, Chesapeake **11** The Covenant, The Drifters **16** The Fires of Spring **18** The Bridges of Toko-ri
Michigan ***capital:*** **7** Lansing ***college:*** **4** Alma ***highest point:*** **9** Mt. Curwood ***largest city:*** **7** Detroit ***nickname:*** **9** Lake State **14** Wolverine State ***state bird:*** **5** robin ***state flower:*** **12** apple blossom
microfilm sheet **5** fiche
Micronesia ***political division:*** **4** Guam **5** Nauru **6** Tuvalu **8** Kiribati
microorganism **4** germ **5** virus **6** aerobe **7** bacilli (plural), microbe **8** bacillus, bacteria (plural), pathogen, protozoa (plural) **9** bacterium, protozoan
microphone **3** bug **4** mike ***shield:*** **4** gobo
microscope **7** magnify **9** magnifier **10** instrument ***part:*** **5** stage **6** mirror **8** eyepiece **9** objective
microscopic **4** tiny **5** small **6** minute
midday **4** noon, sext **8** noontide, noontime
middle **4** core, mean **5** waist **6** center, medial, median **7** central, halfway **8** interior **10** centermost **11** equidistant, intervening **12** intermediary, intermediate ***combining form:*** **3** mes **4** medi, meso **5** medio, mesio
Middle America country **4** Cuba **5** Haiti **6** Mexico, Panama **8** Honduras **9** Costa Rica, Guatemala, Nicaragua **10** El Salvador
Middle Atlantic State **7** New York **9** New Jersey **12** Pennsylvania
middlebrow **4** boob **7** Babbitt **10** philistine
middle class **11** bourgeoisie
middle-class **9** bourgeois
middle ear ***bone:*** **5** incus **6** stapes **7** malleus ***membrane:*** **7** eardrum **8** tympanum
Middle East country **4** Iran, Iraq, Oman **5** Egypt, Qatar, Sudan, Syria, Yemen **6** Cyprus, Israel, Jordan, Kuwait, Turkey **7** Bahrain, Lebanon **11** Saudi Arabia
Middle Kingdom **5** China
middleman **6** broker **7** bailiff **8** mediator **9** go-between **10** interagent, interceder **11** intercessor **12** entrepreneur, intermediary, intermediate **13** intermediator
Middlemarch author **5** Eliot
middle-of-the-road **8** moderate **9** soft-shell
middling **4** fair, mean, poor, so-so **6** fairly, flitch, medium, rather **7** average, fairish **8** inferior, mediocre, moderate **10** moderately, second-rate **11** indifferent **12** intermediate
midge **3** fly **4** runt **5** dwarf, pygmy **6** peewee **7** manikin **8** mannikin, Tom Thumb **10** homunculus **11** lilliputian ***larva:*** **9** bloodworm
midget **3** wee **4** runt, tiny **5** dwarf, pygmy, teeny **6** peewee, punkie, teensy **7** manikin **8** dwarfish, mannikin, Tom Thumb **9** miniature **10** diminutive, homunculus **11** lhop-o'-my-thumb, illiputian
Midian ***father:*** **7** Abraham ***mother:*** **7** Keturah
mid-Victorian **4** fogy, prig **5** prude **6** fogram, fossil, square **7** puritan **8** bluenose, mossback **9** Mrs. Grundy **10** antiquated, fuddy-duddy, goody-goody **12** old-fashioned **13** stick-in-the-mud
midwife **10** accoucheur ***Scottish:*** **5** howdy **6** howdie
mien **3** air, set **4** look, port **6** aspect, manner **7** address, bearing, seeming **8** demeanor, presence **9** mannerism **10** appearance, deportment, expression **11** comportment
miff **3** fit **4** beef, spat **5** pique, run-in **7** dis-

pute, dudgeon, offense, quarrel, rhubarb, umbrage **8** squabble **10** conniption, falling-out, resentment **11** altercation
mig **6** marble
might **3** arm **4** beef, sway, thew **5** brawn, force, means, power, sinew **6** energy, muscle **7** ability, command, control, mastery, potency, strings **8** capacity, strength **9** authority, lustiness, resources, strong arm **10** capability, competence, domination **12** forcefulness, jurisdiction, powerfulness, vigorousness **13** energeticness
mighty **4** high, huge, very **5** grand, great **6** august, heroic, hugely, moving, potent, strong, wieldy **7** eminent, immense, massive, notable, violent **8** enormous, forceful, forcible, gigantic, imposing, powerful, puissant, rattling, renowned, whacking, whopping **9** efficient, extremely, strenuous **10** impressive, monumental, prodigious, tremendous **11** efficacious, exceedingly, illustrious **12** surpassingly **13** extraordinary *combining form:* **3** din **4** dein, dino **5** deino
Mignon composer **6** Thomas
mignonette **4** herb **6** reseda
migrant **5** mover, nomad **6** mobile **7** drifter **8** traveler, wanderer
migrate **4** move, roam, rove, trek **5** drift, range, shift **6** wander **8** nomadize, transfer
migration **6** moving **8** diaspora, movement *of professionals:* **10** brain drain
migratory **5** nomad **6** errant, mobile, moving, roving **7** nomadic, ranging **9** wandering
Milan *family:* **6** Sforza **8** Visconti *opera house:* **7** La Scala
Milcah *brother:* **3** Lot *father:* **5** Haran **10** Zelophehad *husband:* **5** Nahor *son:* **7** Bethuel
mild **4** calm, easy, meek, soft, tame **5** balmy, bland, faint **6** benign, choice, dainty, docile, gentle, smooth **7** amiable, clement, lenient, subdued **8** delicate, moderate, obeisant, obliging **9** benignant, exquisite, temperate **10** forbearing, submissive
mildew **4** mold **6** fungus, growth
___ mile **7** statute **8** nautical
mileage recorder **8** odometer
milepost **5** event **6** marker **8** occasion
milestone **5** event **8** landmark, occasion
milieu **6** medium **7** ambient, climate, setting **8** ambience **10** atmosphere **11** environment, mise-en-scéne **12** surroundings
militant **5** pushy **7** fighter, martial, pushful, pushing, scrappy, warlike **8** fighting **9** assertive, assertory, bellicose, combative, truculent **10** aggressive, pugnacious **11** belligerent, contentious, quarrelsome **12** gladiatorial **13** self-assertive
military **5** troop **6** forces **7** martial, warlike **9** soldierly **10** jingoistic, servicemen **11** armed forces, soldierlike **12** chauvinistic, warmongering *base:* **4** camp, fort, post **5** depot, field **6** billet **8** barracks, garrison, quarters **10** encampment *officer:* **5** major **7** captain, colonel, general **9** brigadier **10** lieutenant *prisoner:* **3** POW *school:* **3** OCS, OTS **4** ROTC, USMA **9** West Point *sector:* **10** combat zone **11** battlefront *store:* **2** BX, PX **10** commissary *storehouse:* **5** depot, étape **6** armory **7** arsenal *supplies:* **8** matériel, ordnance *unit:* **5** corps, squad, troop **7** company, platoon **8** division, regiment **9** battalion **11** battle group *vehicle:* **4** jeep, tank **9** half-track
militate **4** tell **5** count, weigh
milk **4** draw, pump, rook, suck **5** bleed, drain, educe, empty, evoke, exact, mulct, nurse, stick, sweat, wring **6** elicit, evince, extort, fleece, suckle **7** exhaust, exploit, extract *coagulated:* **4** curd *combining form:* **4** lact **5** lacti, lacto **6** galact **7** galacto *curdled:* **5** leben **7** clabber *fermented:* **5** kefir, kumys **6** kumiss, kumyss, yogurt **7** koumiss, matzoon, yoghurt *liquid part:* **4** whey *store:* **5** dairy *sugar:* **7** lactose
milk shake **6** frappe **7** frosted
milksop **4** baby **5** sissy **6** coward **7** doormat **8** weakling **9** jellyfish **10** effeminate, namby-pamby, pantywaist **11** Milquetoast, mollycoddle
milky **4** meek, mild, tame **5** white **6** chalky, gentle **7** lacteal, lactean **8** timorous
Milky Way *combining form:* **6** galact **7** galacto
mill **4** beat, slug **5** dress, fight, plant, quern, shape, works **6** finish, thrash **7** factory, machine **11** manufactory
Miller, Arthur *play:* **9** All My Sons **10** The Misfits **12** After the Fall *salesman:* **5** Loman (Willy)
mill fever **10** byssinosis
million *combining form:* **3** meg **4** mega
millionth *combining form:* **4** micr **5** micro
Mill on the Floss author **5** Eliot
millstone **3** tax **4** duty, load, onus, task **6** burden, charge, weight **9** buhrstone **10** affliction, deadweight
Milne bear **4** Pooh
Milquetoast, Caspar *creator:* **7** Webster; (see also **milksop**)
Miltiades' victory **8** Marathon
Milton work **5** Comus **7** Lycidas **8** L'Allegro **12** Areopagitica, Paradise Lost
mime **3** act **5** actor **6** act out, player **7** trouper **8** thespian **9** performer, playactor, represent **12** impersonator *famous:* **7** Marceau (Marcel)
mimic **2** do **3** act, ape **4** copy, mock, play **5** actor, enact **6** hit off, mummer, parody, parrot, player **7** copycat, imitate, per-

form, take off, trouper **8** simulate, thespian, travesty **9** burlesque, imitation, pantomime, performer, personate, playactor **11** impersonate **12** impersonator

mimicry **4** echo, mock **5** apery **6** parody **9** imitation **10** caricature

mince **3** cut **4** chop, hash **5** cut up, strut **6** finick, sashay **7** finnick **8** moderate, restrain **9** euphemize

mincing **4** nice **5** fussy **6** dainty, la-di-da, too-too **7** finical, finicky, genteel, stilted **8** affected, delicate **9** squeamish **10** fastidious, particular, pernickety **11** persnickety

mind **3** eye, ego, wit **4** care, espy, keep, look, mood, nous, obey, soul, tend, tone, vein, view, will, wish, wits **5** brain, fancy, humor, power, study, watch, weigh, worry **6** attend, behold, belief, beware, brains, comply, descry, desire, follow, govern, liking, memory, notice, ponder, psyche, reason, sanity, senses, spirit, strain, temper **7** care for, conform, discern, dislike, faculty, feeling, look out, observe, opinion, oversee, perpend, purpose **8** consider, function, lucidity, perceive, pleasure, remember, saneness, think out, villeity, watch out **9** intellect, intention, mentality, sentiment, soundness, supervise, think over **10** brainpower, conviction, discipline, excogitate, gray matter, persuasion **11** disposition, inclination, superintend, temperament **12** intelligence, recollection **13** consciousness ***combining form:*** **3** noo **5** menti, phren, psych **6** phreni, phreno, psycho

mindful **5** alert, alive, awake, aware **7** knowing **8** sensible, vigilant **9** attentive, au courant, cognizant, conscious, observant, observing, regardful **10** conversant **12** apprehensive **13** conscientious

mindless **3** mad **4** nuts **5** nutsy, silly **6** insane, maniac, simple, stupid **7** asinine, foolish, lunatic **9** nitwitted **10** unthinking **11** sheepheaded **13** unintelligent

mine **3** dig, pit, sap **4** lode, vein, well, work **5** delve, drill, scoop **6** burrow, quarry, spring **7** bonanza, extract **8** eldorado, excavate, Golconda, treasury **10** excavation, wellspring **13** treasure-house, treasure trove ***coal:*** **8** colliery ***French:*** **4** à moi **6** le mien

mine gas **9** blackdamp, chokedamp

miner **6** digger, pitman **7** collier

mineral **5** beryl, topaz, trona **6** augite, barite, garnet, iolite, pinite, rutile, sphene, spinel, sulfur, zircon **7** apatite, azurite, bornite, calcite, citrine, coesite, cyanite, jadeite, kernite, kunzite, olivine, zeolite **8** boracite, cinnabar, dolomite, epsomite, fayalite, feldspar, fluorite, hematite, lazulite, lazurite, siderite, sodalite, stibnite, triplite, wellsite **9** aragonite, celestite, cerussite, danburite, fosterite, kaolinite, lawsonite, magnetite, malachite, muscovite, phenakite, scapolite, tridymite, turquoise, wulfenite **10** chalcedony, orthoclase, pyrrhotite, tourmaline **11** alexandrite, chrysoberyl, melanterite **12** brazilianite, chalcopyrite, tincalconite **13** rhodochrosite ***combining form:*** **3** ine, ite **4** lite, lith, lyte, xene **5** oryct **6** orycto ***flaky:*** **4** mica ***greasy:*** **4** talc **10** serpentine ***hard:*** **6** spinel **7** diamond **8** corundum ***iridescent:*** **4** opal ***nonmetallic:*** **5** boron **6** gypsum, halite **8** asbestos, graphite ***shiny:*** **4** gold **6** galena, pyrite, silver ***soft:*** **4** talc **6** gypsum **8** graphite ***transparent:*** **6** quartz

mineral water **7** seltzer

Minerva see **Athena**

mingle **3** mix **4** meld **5** merge **6** commix, make up **7** combine, concoct **8** intermix **9** socialize

mingy **4** mean **5** tight **6** stingy **7** scrimpy **8** ungiving **9** niggardly, penurious **11** closefisted

miniature **3** wee **4** copy, tiny **5** model, small, teeny, weeny **6** little, minute, teensy **8** portrait **9** itty-bitty **10** diminutive, small-scale, teeny-weeny **11** lilliputian **12** illumination

minify **5** dwarf **6** lessen, shrink **7** abridge, curtail **8** diminish

minim **3** jot **4** atom, iota **5** grain, speck **6** minute, smitch **7** modicum, smidgen **8** particle ***music:*** **8** half note, half rest

minimal **5** basic **6** lowest **8** littlest, smallest **9** slightest

minimize **5** decry, dwarf **6** reduce **7** run down **8** belittle, derogate, discount **9** disparage, dispraise **10** depreciate **11** detract from

minimum **3** dab, jot **4** hair, iota, whit **5** least, speck **6** lowest, margin **7** smidgen **8** particle, pittance, smallest

minion **4** idol, toad **6** yes-man **7** darling, spaniel **8** creature, favorite, truckler **9** sycophant, toadeater, underling **10** bootlicker **11** lickspittle, subordinate

minister **4** tend **5** agent, clerk, serve **6** cleric, curate, divine, parson **8** clerical, preacher, reverend **9** churchman, clergyman **10** ambassador **12** ecclesiastic ***of state:*** **10** chancellor

minister plenipotentiary **5** envoy

ministry **4** mean **5** agent, organ **6** agency, clergy, medium **7** channel, vehicle **10** instrument

Minnehaha's husband **8** Hiawatha

Minnesota ***capital:*** **6** St. Paul ***nickname:*** **11** Gopher State **14** North Star State ***state bird:*** **10** common loon

minor **4** fair **5** dinky, light, lower, petty, small, youth **6** casual, infant, lesser, little, medium, slight **7** average, trivial **8** inferior, mediocre, piddling, small-fry, trifling 9 dependent, secondary, small-beer, small-time 10 bush-league, second-rate, shoestring 11 indifferent, unimportant 12 unnoticeable 13 insignificant

minority 6 nonage 7 infancy 10 immaturity

minor-league 5 dinky, small 6 lesser 8 small-fry 9 secondary, small-time 11 unimportant

Minos ***daughter:*** 7 Ariadne, Phaedra ***father:*** 4 Zeus 7 Jupiter ***kingdom:*** 5 Crete ***monster:*** 8 Minotaur ***mother:*** 6 Europa ***son:*** 9 Androgeos ***wife:*** 8 Pasiphaë

Minotaur ***father:*** 4 bull ***home:*** 9 labyrinth ***mother:*** 8 Pasiphaë ***slayer:*** 7 Theseus

minstrel 4 bard, wait 6 harper, singer 7 gleeman 8 jongleur 9 balladist 10 troubadour ***end man:*** 7 Mr. Bones, Mr. Tambo

mint 3 pot, wad 4 coin, pile 6 boodle, bundle, intact, packet, unused 7 fire-new, fortune, perfect, span-new 8 brand-new, lavender, original, spang-new, unmarred 9 blue curls, bugleweed, spearmint 10 peppermint 11 spanking-new 12 spick-and-span

Minuit's purchase 9 Manhattan

minus 4 less, sans 7 lacking, wanting, without 8 awanting, subtract 10 deficiency

minute 3 jot, wee 4 full, tiny 5 crack, flash, jiffy, light, petty, shake, small, teeny, weeny 6 little, moment, second, teensy, tittle 7 careful, instant, precise, trivial 8 detailed, itemized, thorough, trifling 9 breathing, clocklike, itty-bitty, small-beer 10 blow-by-blow, meticulous, particular, scrupulous, teeny-weeny 11 lilliputian, punctilious, split second, unimportant 13 infinitesimal, insignificant

minutes 6 record 7 summary

minutiae 5 ropes 6 trivia 7 details 9 small beer 10 ins and outs, triviality 11 particulars, small change 13 small potatoes

miracle 4 feat 6 marvel, wonder 7 portent, prodigy, stunner 9 sensation 10 phenomenon

miraculous 7 amazing, strange 8 superior 9 marvelous, unearthly, wonderful 10 astounding, prodigious, staggering, superhuman, suprahuman 11 astonishing, spectacular 12 supermundane, supernatural, supramundane, supranatural 13 preternatural

mirage 8 delusion, illusion, phantasm 11 fata morgana, ignis fatuus 13 hallucination

Miranda ***father:*** 8 Prospero ***lover:*** 9 Ferdinand

mire 3 bog, fen, mud 4 muck, ooze, quag, sink, soil, trap 5 cling, delay, embog, marsh, slush, stick, swamp 6 cleave, detain, enmesh, entrap, hang up, morass, retard, slow up, tangle 7 baygall, bog down, embroil, ensnare, involve, set back, slacken 8 entangle, slow down 9 implicate

Miriam's brother 5 Aaron, Moses

mirror 5 glass, ideal, image, model 6 embody, typify 7 example, pattern, reflect 8 ensample, exemplar, paradigm, speculum, standard 9 archetype, beau ideal, body forth, epitomize, exemplify, personify, pier glass, reflector, represent, symbolize 10 illustrate 11 cheval glass, emblematize 12 looking glass ***signaling:*** 5 helio 10 heliograph, heliotrope

mirth 3 fun, joy 4 glee 5 cheer 6 gaiety, levity 7 jollity 8 gladness, hilarity 9 frivolity, happiness, jocundity, joviality, merriment, rejoicing 10 jocularity, joyfulness 12 cheerfulness

mirthful 3 gay 5 jolly, merry 6 blithe, jocund, jovial 7 festive 10 blithesome 12 lighthearted

miry 4 oozy 5 boggy, muddy

misadventure 4 bull, slip, woes 5 boner, error, lapse 6 howler, mishap 7 blunder, faux pas, tragedy 8 accident, calamity, casualty, disaster 9 cataclysm 11 catastrophe

misanthropic 7 cynical 8 reserved, solitary 9 reclusive 10 antisocial 11 standoffish

misappropriate 5 steal 8 embezzle

misbegotten 7 bastard, natural 8 baseborn, deformed, spurious 10 fatherless, unfathered 12 contemptible, illegitimate

misbehaving 3 bad 7 naughty

misbehavior 8 rudeness 10 misconduct, wrongdoing

miscalculate 3 err 8 discount, miscount, misgauge, overlook 9 disregard, overprize, overvalue 10 underprize, undervalue

miscarry 4 fail, flop 5 abort

miscellaneous 3 odd 4 many 5 mixed 6 divers, motley, sundry, varied 7 diverse, jumbled, mingled 8 assorted, chowchow, unsorted 9 different, disparate, divergent, scrambled 10 commingled, unassorted 12 conglomerate 13 heterogeneous

miscellany 3 ana 4 brew, hash, olio, posy, stew 5 album, melee, salad 6 jumble, medley, motley, muddle 7 garland, mélange, mixture, omnibus 8 analects, chowchow, mixed bag, pastiche, porridge 9 anthology, colluvies, congeries, pasticcio, patchwork, potpourri 10 assortment, cumulation, hodgepodge, hotchpotch, salmagundi 11 aggregation, combination, florilegium, gallimaufry, odds and ends, olla podrida, smorgasbord

mischance 6 mishap 7 tragedy 8 accident, casualty 9 adversity 10 misfortune 11 contretemps

mischief 3 ill 4 evil, harm, hurt, limb, ruin 5 devil, prank, rogue, scamp 6 damage, injury, rascal, strife 7 devilry, discord, dissent, outrage, roguery, trouble, villain, waggery 8 conflict, deviltry, division, hardship, scalawag, variance 9 devilment, diablerie, disaccord, skeezicks 10 contention, difference, difficulty, dissension 11 rapscallion, roguishness, waggishness 12 sportiveness

mischief-maker 3 imp 4 puck 5 devil, knave, rogue, scamp 6 rascal 7 villain 8 scalawag 9 prankster, trickster 11 rapscallion

mischievous 3 bad, ill, paw, sly 4 evil, foxy 5 antic, risky 6 artful, impish, irking, tricky, vexing, wicked 7 harmful, hurtful, irksome, larkish, naughty, playful, puckish, roguish, tricksy, waggish 8 annoying, damaging, prankish, sportive 9 bothering, injurious 10 bothersome, frolicsome, ill-behaved

mischievousness 4 evil, harm, hurt 6 injury 7 devilry, roguery, teasing, waggery 8 annoying, deviltry 9 devilment, diablerie, pestering

miscolor 4 warp 5 belie, twist 6 garble 7 distort, falsify, pervert 12 misrepresent

misconduct 10 wrongdoing 11 impropriety, malfeasance, misbehavior 12 malversation

miscreant 4 heel 5 knave, rogue 6 rascal, wretch 7 corrupt, heretic, infidel, lowlife, vicious, villain 8 depraved, infamous, perverse 9 heretical, nefarious, scoundrel, unhealthy 10 blackguard, degenerate, flagitious, unbeliever, villainous

miscue 4 miss, slip, trip 5 error, fluff, lapse 6 slipup 7 blooper, blunder, mistake

misdeed 3 sin 5 crime, wrong 7 offense 13 transgression

misdoubt 4 fear 5 dread 7 suspect 8 distrust 9 apprehend, suspicion

mise-en-scène 3 set 4 site 6 locale, medium, milieu 7 ambient, climate, setting 8 ambience, stage set 10 atmosphere 11 environment 12 stage setting, surroundings

miser 3 hog, pig 4 skin 5 chuff, hunks, nabal, piker, stiff 7 glutton, niggard, scrooge 8 muckworm, tightwad 9 skinflint 10 cheapskate

miserable 6 dolent, rueful, woeful 7 doleful, forlorn, piteous, pitiful, ruthful 8 dolorous, hopeless, shameful, wretched 9 afflicted, sorrowful, worthless 10 despairing, despondent, melancholy 12 contemptible 13 discreditable

Miserables, Les *author:* 4 Hugo *character:* 6 Javert 7 Cosette, Fantine, Valjean

miserly 4 mean 5 close, tight 6 abject, greedy, sordid, stingy 7 ignoble 8 covetous, grasping, stingily 9 penurious, scrimping 10 avaricious 11 closefisted, tightfisted 12 cheeseparing, parsimonious 13 penny-pinching

misery 3 woe 5 agony, dolor, grief 6 sorrow 7 anguish, passion, sadness, squalor 8 calamity, distress 9 adversity, dejection, privation, suffering 10 affliction, depression, desolation, melancholy 11 despondency, unhappiness 12 wretchedness

misfortune 3 woe 4 harm 5 cross, trial 7 tragedy, trouble 8 accident, calamity, casualty, disaster 9 adversity, cataclysm 10 affliction, visitation 11 catastrophe, contretemps, tribulation *Scottish:* 6 dirdum

misgiving 4 fear 5 doubt, qualm 7 anxiety, presage 8 distrust 9 prenotion, suspicion 11 premonition 12 apprehension, presentiment

misguided 5 wrong 9 erroneous 10 ill-advised

Mishael *brother:* 8 Elzaphan *cousin:* 5 Aaron *father:* 6 Uzziel

Misham's father 6 Elpaal

mishandle 5 abuse 7 pervert, rough up 10 knock about, prostitute, roughhouse, slap around

mishap 7 tragedy 8 accident, casualty 9 adversity 11 contretemps

mishmash 6 jumble, jungle, litter, medley, muddle, tumble 7 clutter, mélange, mixture, rummage 8 pastiche, scramble 9 pasticcio, patchwork, potpourri 10 hodgepodge, hotchpotch

misidentify 7 confuse 8 confound

misinterpret 3 err 7 misread

mislay 4 lose

mislead 3 lie 4 dupe, fool, lure 5 bluff, cheat, tempt 6 betray, delude, entice, illude, juggle, seduce, take in 7 beguile, deceive 8 hoodwink, inveigle 11 double-cross

misleading 5 false, wrong 8 delusive, delusory, specious 9 deceitful, deceiving, deceptive 10 fallacious, inaccurate 11 casuistical, sophistical

mismatch 3 jar 5 clash 6 jangle 7 discord 8 conflict 9 disaccord 12 disharmonize

misplace 4 lose

misrepresent 3 lie 4 gild, mask, warp 5 belie, cloak, color, dress, feign, gloss, twist, wrest 6 garble, palter, weasel, wrench 7 confuse, deceive, distort, falsify, pervert, varnish 8 disguise, simulate 9 dissemble, embellish, embroider 10 camouflage, equivocate 11 counterfeit, prevaricate

misrepresentation 3 fib, lie 4 tale 5 story 6 canard 7 falsity, untruth 8 untruism 9 falsehood

miss 3 err, gal 4 fail, girl, maid, omit 5 avoid, wench 6 damsel, escape, forget, ignore, lassie, maiden, slight 7 failure, neglect 8 discount, overlook 9 disregard
Missa Solemnis composer 9 Beethoven
misshape 4 warp, wind 6 deform 7 contort, distort, torture 9 deformity 10 distortion 12 malformation
missile 4 bolt, dart 5 arrow, shell, spear 6 bullet, rocket 10 cannonball, projectile *underwater:* 7 torpedo; (see also **guided missile**)
mission 4 goal, task 5 trade 6 errand 7 calling, embassy, purpose 8 business, legation, lifework, ministry, vocation
missionary 5 agent 7 apostle 8 emissary, promoter 10 colporteur, evangelist, revivalist 12 propagandist
Mississippi *capital:* 7 Jackson *highest point:* 9 Woodall Mt. *motto:* 14 By Valor and Arms *nickname:* 10 Bayou State 13 Magnolia State *state flower:* 8 magnolia *university:* 12 Jackson State
missive 4 memo, note 6 letter 7 epistle
Miss Julie author 10 Strindberg
Miss Lonelyhearts author 4 West
Miss-Nancyish 5 sissy 6 prissy 7 epicene, unmanly 9 pansified, sissified 10 effeminate
Missouri *capital:* 13 Jefferson City *college:* 5 Avila, Drury *nickname:* 11 Show Me State 12 Bullion State *state flower:* 9 hawthorne
misstate 4 warp 5 belie, color, twist 6 garble 7 distort, falsify, pervert
misstatement 3 fib, lie 4 tale 7 falsity, untruth 8 untruism 9 falsehood 10 taradiddle 13 prevarication
misstep 4 bull, slip 5 boner, error, fluff, lapse 6 slipup 7 blooper, blunder, faux pas
mist 3 dim, fog 4 blur, film, haze, murk 5 befog, brume, cloud, smaze 7 becloud, obscure 9 overcloud
mistake 3 err 4 bull, slip, trip 5 addle, boner, error, fluff, folly, lapse 6 boo-boo, bungle, jumble, lapsus, muddle, slight, slipup, tumble 7 blooper, blunder, confuse, neglect 8 confound, omission, omitting 9 confusion, slighting 10 inaccuracy, neglecting
mister 3 man, sir 4 lord 7 husband *French:* 8 monsieur *German:* 4 herr *Italian:* 6 signor *Spanish:* 5 senor
Mister Roberts author 6 Heggen
mistreat 5 abuse 6 ill-use 7 outrage
mistress 4 amie 5 lover, woman 6 harlot 7 bedmate, hetaira 8 dulcinea, ladylove, paramour 9 concubine, courtesan, inamorata, kept woman 10 chatelaine, girl friend *of Charles II:* 4 Gwyn (Nell) 8 Villiers (Barbara) *of Edward III:* 7 Perrers (Alice) *of Henry II (England):* 8 Clifford (Rosamund) *of Henry II (France):* 9 de Poiters (Diane) *of Louis XV:* 9 Pompadour (Madame de)
mistrust 5 alarm, doubt, scare 6 appall, dismay, wonder 7 concern, dispute, dubiety, foresee, surmise, suspect 8 frighten, question 9 apprehend, challenge, dubiosity, suspicion 10 anticipate, foreboding, skepticism 11 incertitude, uncertainty, uncertitude 12 apprehension, presentiment
mistrustful 7 jealous 10 suspicious
misty 3 dim 4 hazy 5 foggy, mushy, vague 6 cloudy, vapory 7 obscure, unclear 8 confused, vaporous 10 indistinct
misunderstanding 7 quarrel 9 imbroglio 12 disagreement
misuse 5 abuse 7 outrage, pervert 8 ill-treat, maltreat 10 prostitute *of a word:* 8 malaprop
mite 3 bit, jot 4 atom, iota 5 grain, minim, ounce, speck 6 acarid, minute, tittle 7 chigger, modicum, smidgen 8 molecule, particle, smidgeon *combining form:* 4 acar 5 acari, acaro *family:* 8 oribatid
mitigate 4 ease 5 abate, allay, relax, slake 6 lessen, soften, temper 7 assuage, lighten, mollify, relieve 8 palliate 9 alleviate, meliorate
mitigation 4 ease 6 relief 8 easement 10 moderation, palliation 11 alleviation
mitosis 12 cell division, karyokinesis *stage:* 8 anaphase, prophase 9 metaphase, telophase
mix 4 fuse, join, link, lump, meld, stir 5 blend, braid, merge, unite 6 blunge, fusion, jumble, make up, mingle, tangle, work in 7 amalgam, combine, concoct, confuse, conjoin 8 coalesce, comingle, compound, confound, immingle 9 associate, commingle, interflow, interfuse 10 amalgamate, crossbreed, inosculate, interblend 11 interfusion, intermingle, misidentify 12 amalgamation
mixable 8 miscible
mixed 6 impure, motley, varied 8 chow-chow 9 irregular 11 promiscuous 12 conglomerate, multifarious 13 heterogeneous, miscellaneous
mixed bag 4 olio 5 salad 6 jumble, medley 8 pastiche 10 assortment, hodgepodge, miscellany 11 gallimaufry
mixed-blooded person 7 mestizo, mulatto 8 octoroon 9 half-breed
mixologist 6 barman 7 tapster 9 barkeeper, bartender
mixture 4 brew, hash, olio 5 alloy, blend 6 fusion, medley 7 amalgam, compost, farrago, mélange 8 compound, mishmash, solution 9 composite, potpourri 10 concoc-

tion, confection 11 interfusion 12 amalgamation
mix up 5 addle, dizzy 6 fuddle, jumble, muddle, tumble 7 confuse, derange, disrupt, fluster, misdeem, mistake 8 befuddle, bewilder, confound, disarray, disjoint, disorder, distract 9 distemper 10 disarrange, discompose 11 disorganize, misidentify
mix-up 4 hash, mess, mull, muss 5 blend, botch, melee 6 fusion, muddle, tangle 8 botchery, compound, shambles 9 composite, confusion 11 interfusion
mizmaze 3 web 4 knot, mesh 5 skein, snarl 6 jungle, morass, tangle 9 confusion, labyrinth 12 bewilderment
mks unit 3 lux, ohm 4 mole, volt, watt 5 farad, henry, hertz, joule, lumen, meter, metre, tesla, weber 6 ampere, kelvin, newton, pascal, second 7 candela, coulomb, siemens 8 kilogram
Mnemosyne 6 Memory ***daughters:*** 5 Muses ***father:*** 6 Uranus ***lover:*** 4 Zeus ***mother:*** 2 Ge 4 Gaea
Moabite ***city:*** 3 Kir ***god:*** 7 Chemosh ***king:*** 5 Eglon, Mesha
Moab's father 3 Lot
moan 4 weep 5 groan 6 bewail, grieve, lament 7 deplore 8 complain
mob 3 set 4 camp, clan, gang, herd, push, ring, riot, rout, scum 5 cabal, crowd, crush, dregs, horde, posse, press, swarm, trash 6 circle, clique, masses, rabble, throng 7 coterie, ingroup 8 canaille, riffraff, unwashed 9 camarilla 11 proletariat
mobile 5 fluid 6 liquid, moving 7 migrant, movable, protean 8 moveable, unstable, unsteady, variable, weathery 9 all-around, changeful, many-sided, mercurial, migrative, migratory, unsettled 10 capricious, changeable, inconstant 11 migratorial
mobilize 5 drive, impel, rally 6 muster, propel, set off 7 actuate, marshal 8 activate, assemble, organize 9 circulate
Moby Dick 5 whale ***author:*** 8 Melville ***character:*** 3 Pip 6 Daggoo, Parsee 7 Ishmael 8 Queequeg, Starbuck, Tashtego ***pursuer:*** 4 Ahab ***ship:*** 6 Pequod
moccasin 3 pac 6 loafer 7 slipper 8 larrigan
mock 3 ape 4 butt, copy, defy, fake, gibe, jape, jeer, jest, joke, lout, quiz, razz, sham, twit 5 bogus, dummy, false, farce, feign, mimic, phony, quasi, rally, scout, sneer, sport, taunt 6 affect, assume, betray, delude, deride, ersatz, humbug, illude, jester, juggle, parody, pseudo 7 beguile, buffoon, deceive, imitate, mislead, sell out, take off 8 derision, ridicule, simulate, so-called, spurious, travesty 9 burlesque, disregard, imitation, pilgarlic, simulated 10 artificial, caricature, fictitious, substitute 11 counterfeit, double-cross 13 laughingstock
mockery 4 butt, jest, joke, sham 5 farce, sport 6 japery, jester, parody, satire 7 takeoff 8 derision, ridicule, travesty 9 burlesque, imitation, pilgarlic 10 caricature 13 laughingstock
mocking 8 derisive, sardonic
mode 3 cry, fad, way 4 chic, rage, vein, wise 5 craze, state, style, vogue 6 custom, furore, manner, method, status, system 7 fashion, posture 9 condition, situation, technique 10 convention, dernier cri
model 4 copy, type, very 5 dummy, frame, gauge, ideal, shape 6 design, effigy, emblem, mirror, mockup, symbol 7 classic, epitome, example, fashion, imitate, manikin, paragon, pattern, perfect, replica, typical 8 ensample, exemplar, flawless, mannikin, nonesuch, paradigm, standard 9 archetype, beau ideal, blueprint, classical, criterion, exemplary, miniature, nonpareil 10 apotheosis, embodiment, prototypal, touchstone 11 commendable 12 indefectible, paradigmatic, prototypical, quintessence, reproduction ***combining form:*** 3 typ 4 typo ***preliminary:*** 8 maquette
moderate 3 ebb 4 calm, cool, even, fair, fall, mean, mild, slow, soft, so-so, wane 5 abate, bland, let up, small, sober 6 gentle, lessen, medium, paltry, reduce, relent, slight, soften, steady, subdue, temper 7 average, chasten, control, cushion, die away, die down, ease off, equable, fairish, lighten, qualify, relieve, slacken, subside, trivial 8 attemper, constant, decrease, diminish, discreet, mediocre, middling, piddling, restrain, trifling 9 alleviate, constrain, softshell, temperate, unextreme 10 abstemious, controlled, middle-road, reasonable, restrained 11 indifferent, unexcessive 12 conservative 13 unimpassioned
moderation 7 control, measure 9 restraint 10 abstinence, limitation, temperance 13 temperateness
moderator 5 judge 7 arbiter 8 chairman, examiner, governor, mediator 10 peacemaker 11 chairperson
modern 3 new 4 late 5 fresh, novel 6 latter, recent 7 current 8 neoteric, up-to-date 9 new-sprung, prevalent 10 coincident, concurrent, newfangled, present-day, prevailing 11 concomitant 12 contemporary, new-fashioned ***combining form:*** 2 ne 3 neo
modernize 5 renew 6 update 7 refresh, restore 8 renovate 9 refurbish 10 rejuvenate
modest 3 coy, dry, shy 4 meek, nice, prim, pure 5 clean, lowly, plain, timid 6 chaste, decent, demure, humble, prissy, proper,

seemly, silent, simple, stuffy 7 bashful, prudish 8 decorous, discreet, moderate, priggish, reserved, reticent, retiring, spotless 9 diffident, stainless, temperate, unassured, undefiled, unsullied 10 immaculate, reasonable, unassuming, unboastful 11 inelaborate, puritanical, straitlaced, unassertive, unblemished, unelaborate, unpresuming, withdrawing 12 self-effacing, unornamented, unpretending 13 unembellished, unembroidered, unpretentious

Modest Proposal author 5 Swift

modesty 7 decency, pudency, reserve 8 chastity, humility, pudicity, timidity 10 diffidence

modicum 3 bit, jot 4 atom, iota, whit 5 grain, minim, ounce, scrap 7 soupçon 8 particle

modify 4 turn, vary 5 alter 6 change, mutate, temper 7 qualify 8 mitigate, moderate, restrain 9 refashion

modish 4 chic 5 smart, swank 6 with-it 7 dashing 9 exclusive 11 fashionable

Modred, Mordred ***father:*** 6 Arthur ***mother:*** 8 Margawse ***slayer, victim:*** 6 Arthur

modulate 4 sing 6 intone, temper 8 restrain

modus 3 way 4 wise 5 means 6 manner, method, system 7 fashion 9 technique

modus ___ 7 vivendi 8 operandi

mogul 4 czar, king, lord 5 baron, nabob, ruler 6 prince, tycoon 7 magnate

Mohammed see **Muhammad**

Mohawk chief 5 Brant 8 Hiawatha

Mohican chief 5 Uncas

moiety 3 cut 4 half, part 5 piece 6 member, parcel 7 element, portion, section, segment 8 division 9 component

moil 3 tug 4 grub, to-do, work 5 churn, drive, grind, labor, swirl 6 bustle, clamor, drudge, hubbub, lather, strain, strive, uproar 7 chaffer, ruction, slavery, travail, trouble, wrangle 8 drudgery, plugging, rowdydow, slogging 9 commotion, confusion 10 hurly-burly, turbulence

moira 3 lot 4 doom, fate 5 weird 6 kismet 7 destiny, portion 12 circumstance

moist 3 wet 4 damp, dank, dewy 5 gooey, humid, mushy, sappy, soggy, soupy 6 drippy, slushy, steamy, sticky, watery 7 dampish, maudlin, tearful, wettish

moisten 3 wet 6 dampen 8 humidify, saturate

moisture 5 vapor 11 tearfulness 13 precipitation ***combining form:*** 4 hygr 5 hygro

moistureless 3 dry 4 arid, sere 7 bone-dry, parched, thirsty 8 droughty 9 unwatered 10 desiccated

molar 5 tooth 7 grinder ***combining form:*** 3 myl 4 mylo

molasses 7 treacle 8 theriaca 10 blackstrap

mold 3 die, hug, lot 4 cast, form, kind, make, soil, sort, type 5 adapt, build, class, erect, forge, frame, knead, shape, stamp 6 design, fungus, growth, nature 7 fashion, pattern 8 template 9 character, construct 11 description, put together ***combining form:*** 5 plasm, plast, plasy 6 plases (plural), plasia, plasis, plasma

moldable 6 pliant, supple 7 ductile, fictile, plastic, pliable 9 adaptable, malleable

molder 3 rot 4 turn 5 decay, spoil, taint, waste 7 crumble, putrefy 9 break down, decompose 11 deteriorate 12 disintegrate

molding 4 bead, cove, gula, list, reed, tore 5 angle, congé, ogive, talon, thumb 6 baston, nebulé, reglet 7 annulet, beading, cornice, reeding 8 cincture 9 baseboard ***compound:*** 4 beak, ogie 8 cymatium 9 cyma recta 10 serpentine 11 cyma reversa ***edge:*** 5 arris ***flat:*** 4 band, face 5 bevel, splay 6 fascia, fillet, listel, regula 7 chamfer ***simple curve:*** 4 roll 5 flute, ovolo, torus 6 scotia 8 astragal

moldy 5 dated, fusty, musty, passé 6 bygone, old hat, rococo 7 ancient, archaic 8 mildewed, outdated 9 crumbling, moth-eaten 10 antiquated 12 old-fashioned

mole 4 pier, quay 5 jetty, nevus 6 burrow, tunnel 9 birthmark 10 breakwater ***combining form:*** 5 talpi

molecule 3 bit, jot 4 atom, iota 5 minim, ounce, speck 7 modicum 8 fraction, fragment, particle

molest 3 vex 4 bait, raid 5 annoy, harry, tease 6 bother, harass, heckle, pester 7 disturb, torment, trouble 9 persecute

Moll Flanders author 5 Defoe

mollify 4 calm, ease 5 allay, relax 6 pacify, soften, soothe, temper 7 appease, assuage, lighten, placate, relieve, sweeten 8 mitigate 9 alleviate 10 ameliorate, conciliate, propitiate

mollusk 6 chiton ***bivalve:*** 4 clam 6 bankia, cockle, mussel, oyster, teredo 7 geoduck, scallop 8 shipworm ***cephalopod:*** 5 squid 7 octopus 8 argonaut, nautilus 10 cuttlefish ***part:*** 6 mantle, radula, siphon ***tooth shell:*** 9 dentalium ***univalve:*** 4 slug 5 conch, cowry, murex, snail, whelk 6 cowrie, limpet, triton 7 abalone 10 nudibranch, periwinkle

mollusk-like 8 limacine

Molly ___ 7 Maguire, Pitcher

mollycoddle 4 baby 5 humor, sissy, spoil 6 cocker, cosset, pamper 7 cater to, doormat, indulge, milksop, protect 8 weakling 9 jellyfish 10 goody-goody, pantywaist 11 Milquetoast 12 invertebrate

molt 4 cast, shed, slip 6 change, slough 7 discard, ecdysis 8 exuviate
molted covering 7 exuviae
molten 6 heated, melted 7 glowing
molten rock 4 lava 5 magma
molybdenum *symbol:* 2 Mo
moment 4 pith, time 5 crack, flash, jiffy, point, shake, while 6 import, minute, second, weight 7 instant 8 juncture, occasion 9 breathing, magnitude 10 importance 11 consequence, split second, weightiness 12 significance 13 consideration
momentary 5 brief, quick, short 8 fleeting, fugitive, volatile 9 ephemeral, fugacious, transient 10 evanescent, short-lived, transitory 11 impermanent
momentous 3 big 5 grave 7 epochal, fateful, serious, weighty 8 eventful, material 9 important 10 meaningful 11 significant, substantial 12 considerable 13 consequential
momentousness 4 pith 6 import, weight 9 magnitude 10 importance 11 consequence, weightiness 12 significance
momus 6 carper, critic, Zoilus 7 caviler, knocker 9 aristarch 10 criticizer 11 faultfinder, smellfungus
Monaco *casino:* 10 Monte Carlo *prince:* 6 Ranier *princess:* 5 Grace
monad 3 one 4 atom, unit 8 zoospore
Mona Lisa 10 La Gioconda *painter:* 7 da Vinci
monarch 4 czar, king, raja, tsar, tzar 5 queen, rajah, ruler 6 kaiser, prince 7 emperor 9 potentate, sovereign
monarchical 5 regal, royal 6 kingly 8 imperial, kinglike, majestic 9 sovereign
monarch's daughter 8 princess *Portuguese, Spanish:* 7 infanta
monarch's son 6 prince *French:* 7 dauphin *Portuguese, Spanish:* 7 infante
monastery 5 abbey 6 friary, priory 7 convent, nunnery *Buddhist:* 8 lamasery *Eastern Orthodox:* 5 laura *head:* 5 abbot, prior 7 hegumen
___ Mondrian 4 Piet
monetary 6 fiscal, pocket 9 financial, pecuniary 10 numismatic
monetary rate 7 millage
monetary unit see at individual countries
money 4 bill, cash, coin, gelt, loot, pelf, swag 5 bread, chips, dough, funds, lucre, moola, rhino, rocks 6 boodle, change, dinero, mammon, mazuma, moolah, riches, specie, wampum, wealth 7 cabbage, capital, coinage, lettuce, needful, scratch, stipend 8 bankroll, currency, finances, treasure 9 resources 10 greenbacks 11 filthy lucre, legal tender
moneyed 4 rich 7 opulent, wealthy 8 affluent 10 well-heeled
moneygrubber 4 skin 5 chuff, miser, nabal, stiff 7 niggard, scrooge 8 muckworm 9 skinflint 10 cheapskate
moneymaking 6 paying 7 gainful 9 lucrative 10 profitable, well-paying, worthwhile 12 advantageous, remunerative
monger 4 hawk, rend 6 dealer, hawker, peddle, spread, trader, vendor 7 higgler, packman, peddler 8 huckster, outcrier
Mongol conqueror 9 Tamerlane 10 Kublai Khan 11 Genghis Khan, Tamburlaine
mongrel 3 cur 4 mule, mutt 5 cross 6 hybrid 7 bastard 9 crossbred, half blood, half-breed 10 crossbreed
monish 5 chide 6 rebuke 7 reprove, tick off 8 call down, reproach 9 reprimand
monition 6 caveat 7 caution, warning 11 forewarning
monitor 4 test 5 check, watch 7 adviser, observe 8 reminder 9 counselor *lizard:* 7 varanid
Monitor *designer:* 8 Ericsson *opponent:* 8 Virginia 9 Merrimack
monitory 7 warning 8 advisory 10 cautionary, cautioning, counseling 11 admonishing
monk 5 friar 7 brother 8 monastic 9 anchorite *Buddhist:* 4 lama 5 bonze *Eastern Orthodox:* 7 caloyer *Hindu:* 8 sannyasi *Roman Catholic:* 9 Dominican 10 Cistercian, Franciscan *room:* 4 cell *shaven crown:* 7 tonsure *title:* 3 dom, fra 5 padre
monkey 3 imp, sap 4 dupe, fool, gull, mark 5 cebid, gamin, small 6 bantam, butt in, ceboid, horn in, little, meddle, petite, simian, sucker, tamper, urchin, victim 7 fall guy 8 busybody, easy mark, smallish 9 interfere, interlope 10 tamper with 11 intermeddle *combining form:* 6 pithec 7 pitheco *New World:* 4 saki, titi 5 sajou 6 howler, spider, uakari, woolly 7 sapajou, tamarin 8 capuchin, marmoset, squirrel 11 douroucouli *Old World:* 4 douc, mona 5 Diana, drill, patas 6 grivet, guenon, langur, rhesus, vervet 7 colobus, hanuman, macaque 8 entellus, mandrill, mangabey, talapoin, wanderoo 9 proboscis 10 Barbary ape
monkeyshine 4 dido, lark 5 antic, caper, prank, trick 6 frolic 10 shenanigan, tomfoolery
monocratic 8 absolute, despotic 9 arbitrary, autarchic, tyrannous 10 autocratic, tyrannical
monogram 6 cipher, sketch 7 outline 8 initials
monograph 5 study 6 memoir, thesis

8 tractate, treatise 9 discourse 12 disquisition, dissertation
monopolize 3 hog 5 sew up 6 absorb, corner, manage 7 consume, control, engross
monopoly 5 trust 6 cartel, corner 7 control 9 ownership, syndicate 10 consortium 11 exclusivity
monotonous 4 blah, dull, poky, same 6 dreary, stodgy 7 humdrum, uniform 8 banausic, unvaried 10 pedestrian 11 repetitious
monotony 6 tedium 7 humdrum 8 flatness, sameness 10 uniformity
monster 4 huge, ogre 5 demon, devil, fiend, freak, giant, lusus, teras, whale 6 ogress 7 mammoth, titanic 8 abortion, behemoth, colossal, enormous, giantess, gigantic 9 hellhound, leviathan 10 behemothic, gargantuan 11 elephantine, miscreation *biblical:* 5 Rehab 8 Behemoth 9 Leviathan *combining form:* 4 pagi (plural) 5 pagus, terat 6 terato *female:* 6 Gorgon, Medusa, Scylla *fire-breathing:* 6 dragon, Typhon 7 Chimera 8 Chimaera *fowl-dragon:* 10 cockatrice *French:* 8 Tarasque *horse-fish:* 11 hippocampus *hundred-armed:* 9 Enceladus *hundred-eyed:* 5 Argus *hundred-handed:* 8 Briareus *lion-eagle:* 7 griffin *serpent-headed:* 6 gorgon *study of:* 10 teratology *three-bodied:* 6 Geryon *three-headed dog:* 8 Cerberus *two-headed dog:* 6 Orthos *water:* 6 kraken, nicker *winged dragon:* 6 wivern, wyvern *woman-bird:* 5 Harpy *woman-lion:* 6 Sphinx *woman-serpent:* 7 Echidna; (see also **dragon**)
___ monster 4 Gila
monstrosity 4 mess 5 freak, lusus, sight 6 fright 7 desight, eyesore 8 abortion 11 miscreation
monstrous 3 big 4 huge, rank, vast 5 awful, large 6 crying, mighty, mortal 7 glaring, heinous, hideous, immense, mammoth, massive, titanic 8 colossal, cracking, deformed, dreadful, enormous, gigantic, horrible, infamous, shocking, towering 9 atrocious, desperate, fantastic, malformed, unnatural 10 flagitious, gargantuan, impressive, monumental, outrageous, prodigious, scandalous, stupendous, tremendous 11 elephantine, magnificent
Montagues'enemies 8 Capulets
Montaigne's forte 5 essay
Montana *capital:* 6 Helena *highest point:* 11 Granite Peak *largest town:* 8 Billings *nickname:* 13 Mountain State, Treasure State *state flower:* 10 bitterroot
Monteverdi opera 5 Orfeo 7 Arianna
Montezuma *conqueror:* 6 Cortes, Cortez *people:* 6 Aztecs *revenge:* 8 diarrhea
month *combining form:* 4 meno *current:* 7 instant *following:* 7 proximo *Hindu:* 3 Pus 4 Asin, Jeth, Magh 5 Aghan, Chait, Sawan 6 Asargh, Bhadon, Kartik, Phagun 7 Baisakh *Jewish:* 2 Ab 4 Adar, Elul, Iyar 5 Nisan, Sivan, Tebet 6 Kislev, Shebat, Tammuz, Tishri 7 Heshvan *Muslim:* 4 Rabi 5 Rajab, Safar 6 Jumada, Sha 'ban 7 Ramadan, Shawwal 8 Muharram 9 Dhu'l-Hijja, Dhu'l-Oa'dah *preceding:* 6 ultimo
Montmartre church 10 Sacré Coeur
monument 5 relic, stela, stupa 6 ledger, record 7 chaitya, example, memento, tribute 8 archives, cenotaph, document, memorial 9 footstone, headstone, tombstone 10 gravestone 11 commemorate, grave marker, memorialize, testimonial *prehistoric:* 6 dolmen, menhir 8 cromlech, megalith
monumental 4 huge, vast 6 mighty, mortal 7 immense, mammoth, massive 8 cracking, enormous, gigantic, towering 9 fantastic, monstrous 10 prodigious, stupendous, tremendous 11 inestimable, mountainous 12 overwhelming
moocah 3 pot 5 grass 8 cannabis 9 marijuana
mooch 3 bat, beg 4 roam, rove 5 amble, cadge, drift, range, slink, sneak, steal, stray 6 ramble, sponge, wander 7 meander, saunter 8 straggle
mooching 7 beggary, bumming, cadging 9 mendicity 10 mendicancy 11 panhandling
mood 3 air 4 aura, feel, mind, tone, vein, whim 5 humor 6 aspect, spirit, strain, temper, timbre 7 caprice, emotion, feeling 8 ambiance, ambience 9 character, semblance 10 atmosphere 11 disposition, personality, temperament
moody 3 sad 4 glum 5 sulky 6 fickle, gloomy, grumpy 7 pensive 8 unstable 9 humorsome, mercurial, whimsical 10 capricious, inconstant 13 temperamental
moon 4 gape 5 dream 6 dawdle 9 satellite *combining form:* 5 selen 6 seleni, seleno *dark area:* 4 mare 5 maria (plural) *god:* 3 Sin 5 Nanna 6 Meztli *goddess:* 4 Luna 5 Diana, Tanit 6 Hecate, Hekate, Selena, Selene, Tanith 7 Artemis, Astarte
Moon and Sixpence
author
7 Maugham
mooncalf 4 dolt, fool 5 idiot, ninny 6 doodle, madman 7 jackass, tomfool 8 imbecile
moonshine 4 bosh, jake 5 hokum 6 bunkum, humbug 7 bootleg, eyewash 8 homebrew, malarkey, nonsense 10 balderdash, bathtub gin, flapdoodle 11 mountain dew 12 blatherskite

Moonstone, The ***author:*** 7 Collins ***detective:*** 4 Cuff
moor 3 bog, fen 4 fell 5 berth, catch 6 anchor, Berber, fasten, Muslim, secure 8 Moroccan ***fictional:*** 7 Othello
moose 6 cervid ***female:*** 3 cow ***male:*** 4 bull ***relative:*** 3 elk 4 deer
moot 5 argue, plead 6 broach, debate 7 agitate, bring up, canvass, discept, discuss, dispute, dubious, suggest, suspect 8 arguable, disputed, doubtful 9 debatable, introduce, thrash out, uncertain, unsettled, ventilate 10 disputable, toss around 11 problematic 12 questionable 13 controversial
mooting 6 debate 8 forensic 9 dialectic 11 disputation 13 argumentation
mop 3 mug 4 swab, wipe 5 mouth 7 grimace, shellac, trounce
mope 4 ache, pout, sulk 5 ample, brood, drift, grump, mosey 6 bummel, dawdle, grieve, linger, stroll 7 despond, saunter
mopes 5 blues, dumps 7 dismals, sadness 8 dolefuls 10 depression, melancholy 11 unhappiness 12 mournfulness
mopey 3 low 4 blue, down 6 droopy 8 cast down, dejected, downcast 9 depressed 10 dispirited, spiritless
moppet 3 bud, kid, tot 4 chit, tyke 5 chick, child, youth 8 juvenile, young one 9 youngster
mop up 4 beat, drub, dust, lick, whip 6 absorb, garner 7 shellac, trounce 8 lambaste 9 overwhelm
moral 4 good, just, pure, rule 5 axiom, gnome, maxim, noble, right 6 chaste, decent, dictum, honest, proper, teachy, truism 7 brocard, ethical, preachy, upright 8 aphorism, apothegm, didactic, elevated, sermonic, virtuous 9 honorable, righteous 10 high-minded, principled, scrupulous 11 right-minded, sermonizing 13 conscientious
morale 4 mood 5 vigor 6 esprit, spirit 9 assurance 10 confidence 13 esprit de corps
moralistic 5 noble 7 ethical 8 didactic, virtuous 9 righteous 10 principled 11 right-minded
morality 5 ethic, mores 6 virtue 7 probity 8 goodness 9 rectitude, rightness 11 saintliness, uprightness 13 righteousness
moralize 6 preach 7 lecture 9 preachify, sermonize 11 pontificate
morals 5 mores 6 ethics 9 standards
morass 3 bog, fen, web 4 knot, maze, mesh, mire, quag 5 marsh, skein, snarl, swamp 6 jungle, tangle 7 mizmaze 8 quagmire
moratorium 3 ban 5 delay 8 suspense 10 suspension
morbid 4 dark, sick 5 moody 6 gloomy, grisly, morose, sickly, sullen 7 unsound 8 diseased, gruesome 9 saturnine, unhealthy 11 melancholic, unwholesome 12 pathological
mordacious see **mordant**
mordancy 7 acidity 8 acerbity, acridity, acrimony, asperity, pungency 10 causticity, trenchancy
mordant 4 keen 5 salty, sharp 6 biting 7 burning, caustic, pungent 8 incisive, scathing 9 sarcastic, trenchant
Mordecai ***cousin:*** 6 Esther ***father:*** 4 Jair ***mother:*** 6 Esther
more 3 new, too 4 also, else, plus 5 added, again, along, extra, fresh, older, other 6 as well, better, nearer, withal 7 another, besides, farther, further, greater 8 likewise, moreover 10 additional ***combining form:*** 4 pleo, plio 5 pleio
More book 6 Utopia
moreover 3 and, too, yet 4 also, then 6 as well, withal 7 besides, further 8 likewise 11 furthermore 12 additionally
mores 6 ethics, habits 7 customs, manners 8 decorums, folkways, morality 9 amenities, etiquette 10 civilities 11 proprieties
Morgana's brother 6 Arthur
morgue 5 pride 7 disdain, hauteur 8 mortuary 9 arrogance, loftiness, superbity 11 haughtiness
moribund 5 dying, going 6 fading 7 dormant 8 decaying, expiring 10 regressing 13 deteriorating
Mormon Church ***administrative unit:*** 4 ward 5 stake ***founder:*** 5 Smith ***leader:*** 5 Young ***priest:*** 5 elder
Mormon State 4 Utah
morn see **morning**
morne 4 cold 5 black, bleak 6 dismal, gloomy 8 desolate 9 cheerless 10 depressant, depressing, depressive
morning 4 dawn 5 light, sunup 6 aurora 7 dawning, sunrise 8 cockcrow, daybreak, daylight, forenoon ***moisture:*** 3 dew 8 dewdrops ***song:*** 6 aubade
Morocco ***capital:*** 5 Rabat ***largest city:*** 10 Casablanca ***monetary unit:*** 6 dirham
moron 4 fool, zany 5 ament, dummy, dunce, idiot 6 cretin, stupid 7 dullard, halfwit 8 dullhead, dumbbell, imbecile 9 ignoramus, simpleton
moronic 4 dull 6 simple, stupid 7 brutish 8 backward, imbecile, retarded 9 dim-witted 10 half-witted, slow-witted 12 feebleminded, simpleminded
morose 4 dour, glum, sick, sour, ugly 5 gruff, sulky, surly, testy 6 cranky, crusty, gloomy, morbid, sickly, sullen 7 crabbed,

unhappy **8** choleric **9** irascible, saturnine, splenetic **10** ill-humored
Morpheus ***father:*** **6** Hypnos ***god of:*** **5** sleep
Morse code ***dash:*** **3** dah ***dot:*** **3** dit
morsel **3** bit **4** bite, tapa **5** crumb, goody, mug-up, piece, scrap, snack, taste, treat **6** dainty, tidbit, titbit **8** delicacy, fragment, kickshaw, mouthful **11** bonne bouche
mortal **3** man **4** body, grim, weak **5** awful, being, fatal, frail, human, party **6** deadly, finite, lethal, person **7** deathly, earthly, extreme, fleshly, massive, tedious **8** creature, hominine, possible, probable, ruthless, temporal, towering **9** fantastic, merciless, monstrous, personage, pestilent **10** implacable, individual, ironfisted, monumental, prodigious, relentless, stupendous, tremendous, unyielding **11** conceivable, mortiferous, unflinching, unrelenting **12** overpowering, pestilential, unappeasable
mortality **5** flesh **7** mankind **8** fatality, humanity **9** humankind, lethality **10** deadliness
mortally **4** very **7** awfully, fatally, vitally **8** terribly **9** extremely, intensely **10** dreadfully, grievously **11** exceedingly
Morte d'Arthur author **6** Malory
mortgage **4** hock, pawn **6** pledge **10** obligation
mortician **8** embalmer **10** undertaker
mortiferous **5** fatal **6** deadly, lethal, mortal **7** deathly **9** pestilent **12** pestilential
mortified **5** stern **6** severe, shamed **7** ascetic, ashamed, austere **9** chagrined
mortuary **8** tumulary **10** sepulchral **11** funeral home
mosaic **5** inlay **7** chimera **8** terrazzo **9** composite, patchwork **12** tessellation ***piece:*** **6** smalto **7** tessera **8** tesserae (plural)
Moscow ***citadel:*** **7** Kremlin ***resident:*** **9** Muscovite
Moses ***brother:*** **5** Aaron ***brother-in-law:*** **5** Hobab ***deathplace:*** **4** Nebo ***father-in-law:*** **6** Jethro ***sister:*** **6** Miriam ***son:*** **7** Eliezer, Gershom ***spy:*** **5** Caleb ***successor:*** **6** Joshua ***wife:*** **8** Zipporah
mosey **4** mope **5** amble, drift **6** bummel, linger, ramble, stroll, wander **7** saunter
Moslem see **Muslim**
mosque **6** masjid ***niche:*** **6** mihrab ***prayer caller:*** **7** muezzin ***pulpit:*** **6** mimbar ***turret:*** **7** minaret
mosquito **5** culex **7** culicid **8** culicine ***genus:*** **5** Aëdes, Culex **9** Anopheles
moss **9** bryophyte ***kind:*** **8** sphagnum ***part:*** **4** seta **7** capsule, rhizoid ***study of:*** **8** bryology
mossback **4** fogy, hick **5** yokel **6** fogram, fossil, rustic, square **7** bumpkin, hayseed **9** hillbilly **10** clodhopper, fuddy-duddy, provincial **12** antediluvian, backwoodsman, mid-Victorian **13** stick-in-the-mud
most **3** too **4** best, much, nigh, very **5** about, chief, super **6** all but, better, nearly, utmost **7** greater, highest, largest, maximum **8** greatest, majority, mightily, mortally, well-nigh **9** eminently, extremely, principal **10** remarkably **11** exceedingly, practically **12** surpassingly **13** approximately
mostly **6** mainly **7** chiefly, largely, overall, usually **9** generally, primarily **11** principally **13** predominantly
mote **3** dot **4** hill **5** point, speck **6** barrow, height **7** tumulus **8** flyspeck, particle
moth **6** tineid **7** tineoid **8** bombycid ***immature:*** **5** larva **6** larvae (plural) **11** caterpillar ***kind:*** **4** luna **7** codling, tussock **8** Cecropia, silkworm **9** browntail ***order:*** **11** Lepidoptera
moth-eaten **4** worn **5** dated, dingy, faded, moldy, passé, seedy **6** bygone, old hat, patchy, rococo, shabby, tagrag **7** archaic, raggedy, run-down, unkempt **8** decrepit, outdated, outmoded, tattered **10** antiquated, down-at-heel, threadbare **11** dilapidated
mother **2** ma **3** dam, mom **4** mama, root **5** fount, mamma, mammy, mater, momma, mommy, mummy, nurse, serve **6** mammie, origin, source, wait on **7** care for, nurture, produce, rootage **9** prototype, rootstock **10** minister to, provenance, wellspring ***combining form:*** **4** matr **5** matri, matro
mother country **4** home, land, soil **8** homeland **10** fatherland
Mother Courage author **6** Brecht
Mother of Presidents **8** Virginia
Mother of the Gods **3** Ops **4** Rhea
motif **4** head, text **5** point, theme, topic **6** design, device, figure, matter **7** pattern, subject **8** argument **13** subject matter
motion **4** flag, move, sign, stir, sway **5** swing **6** signal **7** gesture **8** carriage, movement, proposal, stirring, wavering **9** agitation, signalize **10** suggestion **11** application, fluctuation, oscillation ***combining form:*** **3** cin, kin **4** cino, kine, kino, moto **5** cinet, kinet, phoro **6** cineto, kineto, praxia, praxis **7** cinesia, kinesia
motionless **5** fixed, inert, rigid, still **6** static **8** becalmed, immobile, immotile, immotive, stagnant, unmoving **9** immovable, sedentary, steadfast, unmovable **10** stationary, stock-still, stone-still
motion picture see **movie**
motivate **4** move **5** impel, pique, rouse **6** excite, incite, induce **7** innerve, inspire, provoke, quicken **9** galvanize, influence, innervate, stimulate

motivation 4 spur 5 drive 7 impetus, impulse 8 catalyst, stimulus 9 incentive, stimulant 10 incitation, incitement 11 instigation

motive 3 aim, end 4 good, head, spur, text 5 cause, point, theme, topic 6 design, device, figure, intent, matter, object, reason, spring 7 impulse, pattern, purpose, subject 8 argument, stimulus 9 incentive, intention 10 incitement, inducement

motley 4 fool 5 idiot, mixed, salad 6 jester, jumble, medley, varied 7 dappled, diverse, mottled, piebald 8 assorted, chowchow, discolor, pastiche 9 colluvies, multihued 10 assortment, hodgepodge, miscellany, multicolor, variegated, versicolor 11 gallimaufry, promiscuous, varicolored 12 conglomerate, multicolored, multifarious, parti-colored, versicolored 13 heterogeneous, miscellaneous ***combining form:*** 5 parti, party

motor 3 car 4 auto, ride, tool 5 buggy, drive, pilot, wheel 6 engine 7 autocar, machine 10 automobile

motorbike 5 moped

motorboat 7 cruiser, inboard 8 outboard, runabout 12 cabin cruiser

motorcar 4 auto 5 buggy 10 automobile

motorcycle 7 chopper 8 minibike 9 trail bike ***adjunct:*** 7 sidecar

motorist 6 driver 7 autoist 8 operator 12 automobilist

Motown 7 Detroit

mottle 4 spot 6 blotch, marble 7 splotch

motto 3 cry 5 adage, axiom, maxim 6 byword, saying, slogan, war cry 7 precept 8 aphorism 9 battle cry, catchword, watchword 10 shibboleth 11 catchphrase, rallying cry

moue 3 mow, mug 4 face, pout 5 mouth 7 grimace 8 mouthing

mound 4 bank, cock, heap, hill, hump, mass, pile 5 cairn, drift, shock, stack 6 barrow, tumuli (plural) 7 bulwark, hillock, rampart, tumulus 8 mountain 9 elevation 10 embankment ***Buddhist:*** 5 stupa ***burial, Eastern Europe:*** 6 kurgan ***burial, Peruvian:*** 5 huaca ***of detritus:*** 4 kame ***of sand:*** 4 dune ***of stones:*** 5 cairn ***Polynesian:*** 3 ahu ***Scottish:*** 5 toman

mound-like 7 tumular

mount 2 up 3 alp, wax 4 back, hill, lift, peak, pony, rise, show, soar, upgo 5 arise, build, climb, frame, horse, put on, rouse, scale, stage, steed, stuff 6 ascend, aspire, deepen, expand, uprear 7 advance, augment, enhance, enlarge, magnify, produce, support, upclimb, upsurge 8 bestride, escalade, escalate, heighten, increase, multiply, redouble 9 aggravate, intensate, intensify 10 promontory

mountain 3 alp, lot 4 bank, dome, heap, hill, hulk, lump, mass, mesa, much, peak, peck, pile, slew 5 bluff, butte, drift, mound, shock, stack 6 hurdle, sierra 8 obstacle 10 impediment 11 obstruction ***Alaska:*** 4 Bona 7 Foraker, Sanford 8 Wrangell ***Alberta:*** 6 Castle 10 Eisenhower ***Alps' highest:*** 5 Blanc ***Angola's highest:*** 4 Moco ***Antarctica:*** 4 Mohl 7 Gardner 9 Elizabeth 12 Vinson Massif ***Appalachians:*** 10 Kittatinny ***Argentina:*** 9 Aconcagua ***Australia:*** 4 Ziel 5 Bruce 6 Cradle 9 Kosciusko ***beyond the:*** 10 tramontane 11 transalpine ***biblical:*** 5 Horeb, Tabor 6 Hermon 8 Har Tavor ***Black Hills:*** 10 Harney Peak ***Bolivia:*** 6 Sorata 8 Illimani ***Borneo:*** 8 Kinabalu, Kinabulu ***California:*** 5 Guyot 7 Palomar 8 Tuolumne 10 Buena Vista, Sonora Peak, Stanislaus ***China:*** 4 Emei, Song ***Colorado:*** 9 Pikes Peak 13 Purgatory Peak ***combining form:*** 3 ore, oro 4 oreo ***Connecticut's highest:*** 8 Frissell ***Costa Rica:*** 6 Blanco 14 Chirripó Grande ***Cyprus' highest:*** 7 Olympus, Troodos ***depression:*** 3 col ***Dominican Republic:*** 6 Duarte 8 Trujillo ***Egypt:*** 4 Musa 5 Sinai ***Fiji:*** 8 Victoria 9 Tomaniivi ***foot:*** 8 piedmont ***Gabon:*** 8 Iboundji ***Georgia:*** 8 Springer 10 Oglethorpe ***Germany:*** 7 Zollern 11 Fichtelberg ***Greece:*** 3 Ida 5 Athos, Levka 7 Helicon 9 Parnassus, Psiloriti 10 Pendelikon, Pentelicus ***Greenland:*** 9 Gunnbjørn ***Himalayas:*** 10 Kula Kangri ***India:*** 5 Japvo ***Indonesia:*** 4 Lawu 5 Kwoka, Lawoe, Raung 6 Raoeng ***Israel:*** 5 Meron 6 Carmel ***Ivory Coast:*** 5 Nimba ***Japan:*** 4 Fuji 5 Iwate 7 Fujisan 8 Fujiyama 9 Iwate-yama 10 Fuji-no-Yama ***Java:*** 5 Liman ***Jordan:*** 3 Hor 5 Haran ***Malaysia:*** 5 Ophir, Tahan 6 Ledang ***Mediterranean entrance:*** 5 Calpe 15 Rock of Gibraltar ***New York:*** 4 Bear ***North America's highest:*** 8 McKinley ***Oman:*** 4 Sham ***Pakistan:*** 9 Tirich Mir ***Papua New Guinea:*** 7 Wilhelm ***Pennine Alps:*** 4 Rosa ***Philippines:*** 3 Apo, Iba 4 Labo 5 Silay ***ridge:*** 4 spur 5 arête, crest 7 sawbuck ***Romania:*** 11 Moldoveanul ***South America:*** 7 Roraima ***South Dakota:*** 10 Custer Peak ***Syria:*** 4 Druz 5 Druze, Duruz ***Tanzania:*** 11 Kilimanjaro ***Tasmania's highest:*** 4 Ossa ***Tennessee:*** 7 Jumpoff, Lookout 11 Chimney Tops 13 Clingmans Dome ***Togo:*** 4 Agou ***Vermont:*** 11 Glastenbury ***Vietnam:*** 8 Ngoo Linh ***West Africa:*** 8 Cameroon ***western hemisphere's highest:*** 9 Aconcagua ***world's highest:*** 7 Everest; (see also **peak**)

mountain chain ***Asia:*** 8 Tien Shan ***Greece:*** 4 Oeta ***Turkey:*** 6 Taurus

mountain climbing ***equipment:*** 2 ax

3 axe, nut 5 piton 7 crampon 9 carabiner ***maneuver:*** 6 rappel 10 rappelling

mountain dew see moonshine

mountain formation 7 orogeny 9 orogenesy 10 orogenesis

mountain group ***Czechoslovakia:*** 5 Tatra 9 High Tatra ***Germany:*** 4 Harz ***Idaho:*** 10 Clearwater ***New York:*** 8 Catskill 10 Adirondack ***Sinai:*** 9 Gebel Musa ***South Dakota-Wyoming:*** 10 Black Hills ***Utah:*** 5 La Sal ***Washington:*** 7 Olympic ***Zimbabwe:*** 11 Matopo Hills 12 Matoppo Hills

mountainous 4 huge, vast 6 mighty 7 immense, mammoth, massive 8 enormous, gigantic 10 monumental, prodigious

mountain pass ***Afghanistan-Pakistan:*** 6 Khyber ***Alps:*** 5 Gries ***California:*** 4 Muir 6 Sonora ***China-Myanmar:*** 5 Namni ***Colorado:*** 3 Ute 5 Mosca, Muddy, Music, Raton ***Europe:*** 8 Moravian ***Greece:*** 5 Rupel ***Hindu Kush Mts.:*** 5 Dorah, Durah ***Pakistan:*** 5 Bolan, Gomal, Gumal ***Sierra Nevada:*** 4 Mono ***Switzerland:*** 5 Furka, Gemmi 7 Grimsel 8 Lötschen ***Tunisia:*** 4 Faïd ***Ukrainian:*** 5 Uzhok ***Wyoming:*** 5 Union

mountain range ***Alaska:*** 6 Brooks 7 Chugach 8 Wrangell ***Alaska-Canada:*** 10 Saint Elias ***Algeria:*** 3 Zab ***Alps:*** 8 Bavarian ***ancient Edom:*** 4 Seir ***Antarctica:*** 9 Ellsworth ***Appalachian:*** 4 Bald, Blue 5 Green 6 Unicoi 10 Great Smoky 12 Great Smokies ***Arizona:*** 8 Maricopa 10 Chiricahua ***Australia:*** 7 Darling 10 Macpherson ***Brazil:*** 5 Organ ***California:*** 4 Inyo 6 Nevada 7 Klamath 10 San Gabriel 13 San Bernardino ***Canada:*** 10 Laurentian ***central Asia:*** 9 Hindu Kush 11 Paropamisus ***China:*** 5 Helan ***Colorado:*** 7 San Juan ***Czechoslovakia:*** 11 East Beskids, West Beskids ***England:*** 12 Pennine Chain ***Ethiopia:*** 4 Gugu ***Eurasia:*** 8 Caucasus ***Europe:*** 4 Jura 8 Pyrenees ***France:*** 6 Vosges 8 Cévennes ***Germany:*** 4 Rhön 13 Thüringer Wald ***Greece:*** 6 Othris, Othrys, Pindus 7 Olympus 8 Taygetus ***Hawaii:*** 7 Waianae ***Himalayas:*** 8 Anapurna 9 Annapurna ***Idaho:*** 5 Lemhi 7 Wasatch ***India:*** 7 Vindhya 12 Eastern Ghats, Western Ghats ***Indonesia:*** 5 Maoke ***Iran:*** 6 Elburz ***Iran-Turkmenistan:*** 8 Kopet Dag ***Ireland:*** 7 Wicklow ***Italy:*** 9 Apennines ***Kazakhstan-Russia:*** 4 Ural ***Kirghizia:*** 4 Alai ***McKinley's:*** 6 Alaska ***Massachusetts:*** 6 Hoosac ***Mexico:*** 11 Sierra Madre ***Minnesota:*** 6 Mesabi ***New Hampshire:*** 12 Presidential ***New Jersey:*** 6 Ramapo ***New Zealand:*** 12 Southern Alps ***North Carolina:*** 5 Black ***Northern Ireland:*** 6 Mourne ***Pakistan:*** 8 Sulaiman ***Papua New Guinea:*** 6 Albert 11 Owen Stanley ***Philippines:*** 11 Sierra Madre ***Rockies:*** 11 Medicine Bow ***Russia:*** 8 Barguzin, Stanovoi ***Scandinavia:*** 5 Kölen 6 Kjølen ***South Africa:*** 9 Nieuwveld 10 Kwathlamba, Quathlamba 11 Drakensberg ***South Asia:*** 5 Ladak 6 Ladakh ***Spain:*** 6 Morena, Toledo 8 Maladeta 10 Cantabrian ***United States:*** 5 Uinta 7 Cascade 8 Gallatin, Ouachita ***Venezuela:*** 6 Mérida ***Wales:*** 8 Cambrian ***Washington:*** 6 Chelan ***Wyoming:*** 5 Teton 11 Sierra Madre ***Yosemite National Park:*** 9 Cathedral

mountains ***Algeria:*** 6 Hoggar 7 Ahaggar ***Czechoslovakia:*** 5 Tatra 9 High Tatra ***England:*** 8 Cumbrian ***Idaho:*** 10 Clearwater ***New Hampshire:*** 5 White ***New York:*** 8 Catskill 10 Adirondack ***Pennsylvania:*** 6 Pocono ***study of:*** 7 orology ***Sudan:*** 4 Nuba ***Utah:*** 5 La Sal ***Washington:*** 7 Olympic ***western North America:*** 11 Coast Ranges

mountain sickness 4 veta 7 soroche

Mountain State 7 Montana 12 West Virginia

mountain system ***Asia:*** 5 Altai 8 Himalaya 9 Himalayas ***Europe:*** 4 Alps 10 Carpathian ***Iran:*** 6 Zagros ***North Africa:*** 5 Atlas ***North America:*** 5 Rocky 7 Rockies 11 Appalachian 12 Appalachians ***Scotland:*** 9 Grampians 13 Grampian Hills ***South America:*** 5 Andes

mountebank 3 gyp 5 cheat, quack 6 con man 7 diddler, sharper 8 swindler 9 charlatan, defrauder, pretender, quackster 11 flimflammer, quacksalver 12 double-dealer, saltimbanque 13 confidence man

Mount St. Helens 7 volcano

mourn 3 rue 6 bemoan, bewail, grieve, lament, sorrow 7 protest

mournful 3 sad 4 dire 5 sorry 6 dismal, rueful, somber, triste, woeful 7 doleful, joyless, unhappy 8 dolesome, dolorous, funereal, grievous, saddened 9 plaintive, saddening, sorrowful 10 afflictive, calamitous, deplorable, depressing, dispirited, lamentable, lugubrious, melancholy 11 distressing, melancholic, regrettable, unfortunate 12 heavyhearted

mournfulness 5 blues, dumps, gloom 7 sadness 9 dejection 10 depression, melancholy, the dismals 11 unhappiness

Mourning Becomes Electra ***author:*** 6 O'Neill

mourning period ***Jewish:*** 5 shiva 6 shibah, shivah

mourning symbol 7 armband

mouse 3 pry 4 hunt, nose, poke, slip 5 creep, glide, slide, snoop, steal 6 shiner

7 explore, saunter 8 black eye, busybody *combining form:* 2 my 3 myo, mys

mouth 3 eat, gab, gob, mop, mow, yap 4 blow, brag, crow, face, guff, moue, puff, rail, rant, rave, sass, talk, tell, trap 5 boast, orate, prate, sauce, speak, spill, vaunt, voice 6 betray, mumble, palate, recite, reveal, tongue 7 blab out, declaim, divulge, grimace, soapbox, speaker, unclose 8 back talk, bloviate, disclose, discover, entrance, give away, harangue, perorate 9 gasconade, impudence, pronounce, spokesman 10 embouchure, volubility 11 rodomontade, spokeswoman 12 embouchement, spokesperson *combining form:* 3 ori, oro 4 stom 5 stoma, stome, stomi, stomo, stomy 6 stomat, stomia, stomum 7 stomata, stomate, stomato, stomous 9 stomatous

mouthing 3 mow, mug 4 face 7 grimace

mouthlike opening 5 stoma 7 stomata (plural)

mouthpiece 7 speaker 9 spokesman 11 spokeswoman 12 spokesperson

mouthward 4 orad

mouth-watering 5 sapid, tasty 6 savory, toothy 8 tasteful 9 aperitive, delicious, palatable, relishing 10 appetizing 11 good-tasting

mouthy 5 talky 9 bombastic, garrulous, talkative

movable 5 loose 6 mobile, motile, moving, roving 8 unstable, unsteady 10 changeable 11 unsteadfast

movables 5 goods 7 effects 8 chattels 10 belongings

move 2 go 3 act, hum 4 bear, blow, exit, goad, go on, lead, live, spur, step, stir, sway, turn, void 5 bring, budge, carry, drive, exist, get on, impel, leave, march, pique, rouse, shift, start, touch 6 acquit, affect, behave, convey, demean, depart, deport, excite, get off, incite, induce, kindle, motion, prompt, propel 7 actuate, advance, agitate, animate, breathe, comport, conduct, convert, disturb, get away, impress, innerve, inspire, measure, migrate, proceed, propose, provoke, pull out, replace, request, suggest, take off 8 activate, dislodge, displace, evacuate, get along, maneuver, mobilize, motivate, persuade, progress, relocate, resettle, stirring, supplant, transfer, transmit, withdraw 9 dislocate, galvanize, influence, innervate, instigate, stimulate, supersede, transport 10 proceeding

movement 3 act 4 deed, stir, time 5 tempo, trend 6 action, motion, rhythm 8 activity, dynamism, liveness, maneuver, stirring, tendency *away:* 6 exodus *combining form:* 3 cin, kin 4 cino, kine, kino 5 cinet, kinet 6 cineto, kineto 7 cinesia, kinesia *music:* 4 moto *reflex:* 5 taxis *stimulated:* 7 kinesis

movie 4 cine, film, show 5 flick 6 cinema 7 picture 9 photoplay 11 picture show 13 motion picture, moving picture *combining form:* 4 cine *cowboy:* 5 oater 7 western *short:* 4 clip 8 newsreel

movie director *American:* 3 Lee 4 Ford, Wise 5 Allen, Roach, Stone, Vidor, Wyler 6 Curtiz, Huston, Welles, Wilder 7 Coppola, Fleming, Kubrick, Nichols, Pollack, Stevens, Sturges 8 Minnelli, Scorsese 9 Hitchcock, Preminger, Spielberg, Sternberg *Austrian:* 4 Lang 8 Stroheim *French:* 4 Tati 5 Malle 6 Godard, Renoir 8 Truffaut *German:* 6 Herzog 10 Fassbinder 11 Riefenstahl *Italian:* 5 Leone 7 Fellini 8 Visconti 10 Bertolucci, Rossellini *Russian:* 10 Eisenstein *Swedish:* 7 Bergman 10 Zetterling

movie producer *American:* 5 Mayer, Roach 6 Kramer, Warner, Welles, Zanuck 7 De Mille, Goldwyn, Sennett 8 Griffith, Selznick *Austrian:* 9 Reinhardt *French:* 6 Renoir

moving 5 astir 6 mobile 7 emotive, rousing 8 arousing, exciting, gripping, pathetic, poignant, rallying, stirring, touching, unstable, unsteady 9 actuating, affecting, affective, awakening, emotional, provoking, transient 10 ambulatory, impressive 11 stimulating, unsteadfast

moving picture see **movie**

moving stairs 9 escalator

mow 3 cut, mop, mug 4 bank, clip, cock, crop, down, drop, face, fell, heap, hill, kill, moue, pile, rick, rout 5 drift, floor, level, mouth, shock, smash, stack 6 ground 7 grimace 8 bowl down, bowl over, mouthing 9 bring down, knock down, throw down

moxie 2 go 3 pep 4 birr, grit, guts, tuck 5 heart, nerve, pluck, spunk, vigor 6 energy, mettle, spirit 7 cojones, courage, potency 8 backbone 9 fortitude, hardihood 10 resolution 13 dauntlessness

Mozart *birthplace:* 8 Salzburg *cataloger:* 6 Köchel *deathplace:* 6 Vienna *opera:* 8 Idomeneo 10 Magic Flute 11 Don Giovanni 12 Cosi fan Tutte

MP's prey 4 AWOL 8 deserter

Mrs. Grundy 4 prig 5 prude 7 puritan 8 bluenose, comstock 9 nice Nelly 10 goody-goody

much 3 lot, oft 4 good, heap, long, lots, lump, many, mass, most, nigh, pack, peck, pile, scad, very 5 about, often 6 all but, almost, highly, hugely, nearly, plenty 7 greatly, notably 8 abundant, lashings, ofttimes, well-nigh 9 eminently, extremely, great deal, multitude 10 frequently, oftentimes, repeatedly *combining form:* 4 poly 5 multi

Much Ado About Nothing ***character:*** 4 Hero 7 Claudio, Don John 8 Beatrice, Benedick
much as 4 when 5 while 6 albeit, though 7 howbeit, whereas 8 although
muck 3 goo 4 crap, dirt, dung, gook, goop, grub, gunk, junk, mess, mire, murk, plod, slog, slum, soil, toil 5 dirty, filth, grime, grind, gumbo, muddy, offal, slave, slime, swill, trash, waste 6 debris, drudge, litter, manure, refuse, sludge, smirch, smooch, smudge, smutch 7 garbage, rubbish
muckamuck 3 VIP 5 nabob 6 bigwig 7 big shot, notable 8 somebody 9 dignitary 10 notability
mucker 3 cad, oaf 4 boor, punk, worm 5 botch, chuff, churl, clown, gum up, rough, rowdy, tough, yahoo 6 bobble, bollix, bungle, no-good, wretch 7 bitch up, blunder, grobian, louse up, lowlife, ruffian, toughie 8 bullyboy, wormling 9 roughneck 10 clodhopper
mucky 4 foul 5 black, dirty, dungy, humid, messy, muddy, muggy, murky, nasty, soggy 6 cloudy, filthy, grubby, sordid, sticky, sultry 7 clouded, squalid, unclean
mucous 5 slimy 6 viscid
mucronate 5 acute, piked, sharp 6 peaked 7 pointed 8 acicular 9 aciculate, acuminate, acuminous, cuspidate
mucus 9 secretion
mud 4 dirt, mire, ooze, rile, roil 5 dregs, slime 6 depths, sludge ***combining form:*** 3 pel 4 pelo
muddle 3 mix 4 blow, daze, hash, limp, mess, muck, mull, muss, rile, roil 5 addle, botch, mix up, muddy, ravel, snarl, waste 6 ataxia, drivel, foul up, fuddle, fumble, huddle, jumble, jungle, litter, mess up, mumble, murmur, muss up, mutter, tangle, tumble 7 clutter, confuse, fluster, fritter, perplex, rummage, shuffle, snarl up, stumble, stupefy, swallow 8 befuddle, bewilder, botchery, cast away, confound, disarray, disorder, distract, entangle, mishmash, scramble, shambles, squander, throw off, unsettle 9 confusion, throw away 10 complicate, disarrange, discompose, frivol away, trifle away 11 blunder away, disorganize
muddled 5 drunk, tight, tipsy, vague 6 cloudy 7 mixed-up 8 inchoate 9 disguised, pixilated 10 disjointed, disordered, incoherent, incohesive, inebriated 11 intoxicated, unconnected, unorganized 12 disconnected, uncontinuous 13 discontinuous
muddlehead 4 dolt 5 dunce, idiot, moron 6 dimwit 7 fathead 8 dumbbell 9 blockhead, simpleton 11 chowderhead
muddle through 2 do 4 fare 5 get by, get on, shift 6 manage 8 get along 9 stagger on 12 stagger along
muddy 3 dim, fog 4 base, blur, drab, dull, fade, foul, miry, oozy, pale, rile, roil, soil 5 befog, black, cloud, dirty, dungy, grime, murky, riley, roily, soily 6 cloudy, gloomy, sordid, turbid 7 becloud, begrime, bemired, confuse, squalid, subfusc, tarnish, unclean, unclear 8 confused 9 uncleanly
mudfish 6 bowfin
muezzin's faith 5 Islam
muff 4 blow, flub 5 botch, error, fluff 6 bobble, bollix, bungle, fumble, goof up 7 louse up
muffle 4 dull, mute, veil 5 shush 6 dampen, deaden, lessen, shroud, soften, stifle, subdue, wrap up 7 envelop, repress, silence, smother, squelch 8 bundle up, strangle, suppress, tone down 10 overspread
muffler 4 mask, veil 5 cloak, cover, guise, scarf 6 facade, veneer 8 disguise 10 masquerade 12 disguisement
muffler mangler 3 rut 7 pothole 9 chuckhole
mug 3 cup, mop, mow 4 boob, dolt, dope, face, fool, moue, phiz, punk, puss, thug, toby 5 dunce, grail, idiot, mouth, rough, rowdy, stein, stoup, tough 6 dimwit, mucker, seidel, visage 7 assault, chalice, grimace, ruffian, tankard 8 bullyboy, dumbbell, features, mouthing, numskull, plug-ugly, schooner 9 blockhead, ignoramus, roughneck 11 countenance
mugger 4 thug 9 assailant, assaulter
muggy 4 damp 5 humid, moist, mucky, soggy 6 moisty, sticky, sultry 7 dampish, wettish
Muhammad, Mohammed ***adopted son:*** 3 Ali ***birthplace:*** 5 Mecca ***camel:*** 5 Kaswa ***daughter:*** 6 Fatima ***deathplace:*** 6 Medina ***deity:*** 5 Allah ***father:*** 8 Abdallah, Abdullah ***father-in-law:*** 7 Abu Bakr ***flight:*** 6 hegira, hejira ***follower:*** 6 Moslem, Muslim ***horse:*** 5 Buraq 7 Alborak ***religion:*** 5 Islam ***son:*** 7 Ibrahim ***son-in-law:*** 3 Ali ***successor:*** 5 calif 6 caliph 7 Abu Bakr ***tribe:*** 7 Koreish ***uncle:*** 8 Abu Talib ***wife:*** 5 Aisha 6 Ayesha 7 Khadija
mulct 4 fine, milk, rook 5 bleed, cheat, stick, sweat 6 amerce, fleece 7 deceive, defraud, forfeit, penalty, swindle 8 penalize 10 amercement
mule 5 cross 6 hybrid 7 bastard, mongrel 9 crossbred, half blood, half-breed 10 crossbreed
muleheaded see **mulish**
mulish 5 balky 6 unruly 8 perverse, stubborn 9 obstinate, pigheaded 10 bullheaded, headstrong, inflexible, refractory, self-willed, unyielding 11 stiff-necked, wrongheaded
mull 4 hash, mess, muse, muss, numb,

poke, roll, stir 5 addle, blunt, botch, dally, delay, mix-up, tarry, think 6 ball up, bemuse, benumb, dawdle, deaden, fuddle, linger, loiter, mess-up, muddle, ponder, put off 7 confuse, crumble 8 befuddle, bewilder, botchery, cogitate, consider, distract, meditate, ruminate, shambles, throw off, turn over 9 pulverize 10 deliberate, dilly-dally 11 desensitize 13 procrastinate

mulligrubs 4 sulk 5 blues, dumps, gloom, mumps, pouts 6 grumps 7 sullens 9 dejection 10 depression, melancholy

multicolored 4 pied 6 motley 7 dappled 8 discolor 10 variegated, versicolor

multifarious 4 many 5 mixed 6 legion, motley, sundry, varied 7 diverse, various 8 assorted, chowchow, manifold, numerous, populous 10 voluminous 11 diversiform, promiscuous 12 conglomerate 13 heterogeneous, miscellaneous

multiform 7 diverse 8 manifold 11 diversiform 12 multifarious, multivarious

multiformity 7 variety 8 multeity 9 diversity 11 diverseness, variousness 12 multiplicity

multihued see **multicolored**

multilateral 9 many-sided

multiloquent 5 gabby, talky 6 chatty 9 garrulous, talkative 10 babblative, loquacious 11 loose-lipped 12 loose-tongued

multiplex see **multiform**

multiplicity 3 lot 4 mass, much, peck 6 barrel 7 variety 8 multeity 9 diversity, great deal 11 diverseness, variousness

multiply 3 wax 4 bear, rise 5 beget, boost, breed, build, mount 6 beef up, expand, extend, spread 7 amplify, augment, enlarge, magnify, produce, upsurge 8 generate, heighten, increase 9 procreate, propagate, reproduce 10 aggrandize

multitude 3 mob 4 army, host, many, rout 5 cloud, crowd, crush, drove, flock, horde, press, swarm 6 legion, oodles, public, scores, squash, throng 7 numbers

multitudinal see **multitudinous**

multitudinous 4 many 6 legion, myriad, sundry 7 various 8 manifold, numerous, populous 9 countless 10 innumerous, numberless, voluminous 11 innumerable 12 multifarious

multivocal 7 blatant 8 strident 9 clamorous, equivocal 10 boisterous, vociferant, vociferous 11 loudmouthed, openmouthed 12 obstreperous

mum 4 dumb, mute 5 still 6 silent 7 silence 8 wordless 10 speechless

mumble 4 chew 5 mouth, rumor 6 muddle, murmur, mutter 7 maunder, swallow, whisper 9 undertone 11 susurration

mumbo jumbo 7 mummery 9 gibberish 10 hocus pocus 11 abracadabra

mummer 4 mime 5 actor, mimic 6 player 7 trouper 8 thespian 9 performer, playactor 12 impersonator

mummery 6 acting 9 gibberish, hypocrisy 10 hocus pocus, mumbo jumbo 11 abracadabra

mummify 4 wilt 5 dry up, wizen 6 welter, wither 7 shrivel

mumpish 4 dour, ugly 5 sulky, surly 6 morose, sullen 9 saturnine

munch 3 eat 4 bite, chew 5 champ, chomp, chump 6 crunch 7 chumble, scrunch 8 ruminate 9 masticate

mundane 5 lowly 6 cosmic, earthy 7 earthly, prosaic, sensual, terrene, workday, worldly 8 banausic, everyday, telluric, workaday 9 sublunary, tellurian 11 commonplace, terrestrial, uncelestial 13 materialistic

municipal 4 city, home 5 urban 6 native 7 burghal 8 domestic, internal, national 9 intestine

munificent 4 free 6 lavish 7 liberal 8 generous, handsome 9 bounteous, bountiful, unsparing 10 freehanded, openhanded

munitions maker 5 Krupp

murder 4 cool, do in, hang, kill, slay 5 abate, blood, lynch, scrag 6 finish, mangle, rub out 7 abolish, blot out, destroy, execute, garrote, killing, put away, root out, smother 8 foul play, homicide, knock off, strangle, uncreate 9 eradicate, liquidate, slaughter 10 annihilate, asphyxiate, decapitate, extinguish, guillotine 11 assassinate, electrocute, exterminate 12 manslaughter ***brother:*** 10 fratricide ***father:*** 9 patricide ***king:*** 8 regicide ***mother:*** 9 matricide ***parent:*** 9 parricide ***sister:*** 10 sororicide

murderer 6 killer, slayer 7 butcher 8 assassin, homicide 9 manslayer 11 slaughterer

Murder in the Cathedral ***author:*** 5 Eliot ***character:*** 5 Henry 7 Beckett

murderous 6 brutal 9 ferocious 11 devastating 12 bloodthirsty

mure 3 pen 4 cage, wall 5 fence, hedge 6 shut in, thrust 7 close in, enclose, envelop, squeeze

murk 3 dim, fog 4 foul, haze, mist, soil 5 bedim, cloud, dirty, gloom, grime, muddy 6 besoil, darken, smirch, smudge 7 becloud, begrime, obscure, tarnish 8 darkness 9 obfuscate

murky 3 dim, dun 4 dark, drab, dull, dusk, foul 5 black, dirty, dusky, foggy, misty, muddy, nasty, roily 6 cloudy, filthy, gloomy, grubby, opaque, somber, sordid, turbid 7 obscure, squalid, subfusc, unclean 8 nubilous 9 ambiguous, equivocal, sibylline, tenebrous 10 caliginous

murmur 3 cry, hum 4 buzz, fuss, kick,

purr, talk, wail 5 croak, drone, rumor, scold, whine 6 fumble, gossip, grouch, grouse, muddle, mumble, mutter, repine, report, rumble 7 grumble, hearsay, swallow, whisper 8 complain 9 grapevine, grumbling, undertone 11 scuttlebutt, susurration

muscle 4 beef, thew 5 brawn, force, might, power, sinew 6 energy 7 potency 8 strength 9 necessity, strong arm ***arm:*** 6 biceps 7 triceps ***back:*** 9 trapezius ***calf:*** 6 soleus ***chest:*** 10 pectoralis ***combining form:*** 2 ei (plural) 3 eus, mya 6 muscul, myaria (plural) 7 musculo ***jaw:*** 8 masseter ***kind:*** 6 flexor, tensor 7 dilator, evertor, levator, rotator 8 abductor, adductor, extensor ***loin:*** 5 psoas ***neck:*** 8 platysma ***shoulder:*** 7 deltoid 10 deltoideus ***study of:*** 7 myology ***thigh:*** 8 gracilis 9 sartorius

muscle-bound 5 rigid, stiff 6 wooden 7 buckram, stilted 9 cardboard

muscular 4 ropy, wiry 5 beefy, burly, husky, stout 6 brawny, mighty, robust, sinewy, strong, sturdy, supple 7 fibrous, stringy, well-set 8 athletic, forceful, powerful, stalwart, vigorous, well-knit 9 Herculean, well-built

muse 4 bard, poet 5 study, think 6 ponder, trance 7 reflect, reverie 8 cogitate, meditate, mull over, ruminate, turn over 10 deliberate, excogitate 11 contemplate

Muse ***father:*** 4 Zeus 7 Jupiter ***mother:*** 9 Mnemosyne ***of astronomy:*** 6 Urania ***of choral song:*** 11 Terpsichore ***of comedy:*** 6 Thalia ***of dancing:*** 11 Terpsichore ***of epic poetry:*** 8 Calliope ***of history:*** 4 Clio ***of love poetry:*** 5 Erato ***of lyric poetry:*** 5 Erato ***of music:*** 7 Euterpe ***of pastoral poetry:*** 6 Thalia ***of sacred poetry:*** 8 Polymnia 10 Polyhymnia ***of tragedy:*** 9 Melpomene

museum 5 salon 7 exhibit, gallery 8 atheneum 10 collection, repository 11 pinacotheka

Mushi's father 6 Merari

mushroom 4 grow 5 burst, go off 6 blow up, expand, spread 7 explode 8 detonate ***combining form:*** 3 myc 4 myco 5 mycet 6 myceto ***edible:*** 5 morel 10 champignon 11 chanterelle ***kind:*** 6 agaric, bolete 7 inky cap, russula ***part:*** 3 cap 4 gill, ring 5 stipe, volva 6 pileus 7 annulus 8 mycelium ***poisonous:*** 7 amanita 8 death cup 9 toadstool

mushy 4 hazy, soft, weak 5 foggy, misty, pappy, pulpy, vague 6 cloudy, quaggy, spongy, sticky, vapory 7 blurred, maudlin, mawkish, pulpous, squashy, squishy, squushy 8 bathetic, effusive, romantic, sluggish, squelchy, vaporous 10 lovey-dovey 11 sentimental, tear-jerking

music ***abbreviation:*** 2 ff, mf, mp, pp, sf 3 sfz ***bass staff lines:*** 5 GBDFA ***bass staff spaces:*** 4 ACEG ***characteristic phrase:*** 9 leitmotif, leitmotiv ***chord:*** 5 tonic 8 dominant 9 augmented 10 diminished ***embellishment:*** 3 run 4 turn 5 trill 7 cadenza, mordent, roulade 8 arpeggio, flourish 9 grace note ***for eight:*** 5 octet ***for five:*** 7 quintet ***for four:*** 7 quartet ***for nine:*** 5 nonet ***for one:*** 4 solo ***for seven:*** 6 septet ***for six:*** 6 sextet ***for three:*** 4 trio ***for two:*** 3 duo 4 duet ***god:*** 6 Apollo ***hall:*** 7 cabaret, theater ***instrumental form:*** 3 jig 4 jazz, reel 5 étude, fugue, gigue, march, polka, rondo, suite, swing, waltz 6 minuet, pavane, sonata 7 bourrée, gavotte, mazurka, prelude, ragtime, toccata 8 chaconne, concerto, courante, fantasia, galliard, nocturne, overture, rhapsody, ricercar, sarabande, serenade, symphony, tone poem 9 allemande, polonaise 11 rock and roll ***medley:*** 4 olio ***morning:*** 6 aubade ***Muse:*** 7 Euterpe ***night:*** 8 nocturne, serenade ***note:*** 4 half 5 breve, minim, neume, whole 6 eighth 7 quarter 9 sixteenth ***patron saint:*** 7 Cecilia ***period:*** 6 Modern, Rococo 7 Baroque 8 Medieval, Romantic 9 Classical ***reformer:*** 5 Guido ***symbol:*** 3 bar, key 4 clef, flat, note, rest, slur, turn 5 sharp, staff 7 fermata, mordent 9 alla breve 10 accidental ***treble staff lines:*** 5 EGBDF ***treble staff spaces:*** 4 FACE ***vocal form:*** 3 air 4 aria, hymn, lied, mass, song 5 canon, chant, motet, opera, round 6 anthem, ballad 7 cantata, chanson, chorale 8 cavatina, madrigal, operetta, oratorio, serenade 9 cabaletta

musical 4 show 5 revue 6 turned 7 chiming, lyrical, melodic, songful, tuneful 8 blending, harmonic 9 consonant, melodious, symphonic 10 harmonious 11 symphonious

musical composition 4 aria, hymn, opus, solo 5 étude, fugue, motet, opera, psalm, rondo, suite 6 anthem, ballad, sonata, verset 7 cantata, chanson, chorale, prelude, requiem, toccata 8 concerto, madrigal, nocturne, operetta, oratorio, postlude, serenade, sonatina, symphony 9 bagatelle, cabaletta, interlude, toccatina 10 intermezzo

musical direction ***accented:*** 7 marcato 8 sforzato 9 sforzando ***airy:*** 7 sfogato ***as written:*** 3 sta ***bold:*** 6 audace ***brisk:*** 4 vivo 6 vivace 7 allegro, animato ***connected:*** 6 legato ***detached:*** 8 spiccato, staccato ***dignified:*** 8 maestoso ***disconnected:*** 8 staccato ***dying away:*** 7 calando ***emotional:*** 12 appassionato ***emphatic:*** 7 marcato ***evenly:*** 10 egualmente ***excited:*** 7 agitato 9 spiritoso ***fast:*** 4 vite, vivo 5 tosto 6 presto, veloce, vivace 7 allegro 10 tostamente ***faster:*** 7 stretto

11 accelerando ***fluctuating tempo:*** 6 rubato ***forcefully:*** 7 furioso ***freely:*** 9 ad libitum ***gay:*** 7 giocoso ***gentle:*** 5 dolce 7 amabile, amoroso 9 affettuso ***graceful:*** 6 adagio 8 grazioso ***half:*** 5 mezzo ***heavy:*** 7 pesante ***held firmly:*** 6 tenuto ***hurried:*** 7 agitato ***joyous:*** 7 giocoso ***less:*** 4 meno ***little:*** 4 poco ***little by little:*** 9 poco a poco ***lively:*** 4 vite 6 vivace 7 allegro, animato, giocoso 9 capriccio ***loud:*** 5 forte ***louder:*** 9 crescendo ***lovingly:*** 7 amabile, amoroso ***majestic:*** 8 maestoso ***moderate:*** 7 andante 8 moderato ***moderately loud:*** 2 mf 10 mezzo forte ***moderately soft:*** 2 mp 10 mezzo piano ***muted:*** 5 sorda, sordo ***passionless:*** 6 freddo ***plaintive:*** 7 dolente 8 doloroso ***playful:*** 7 giocoso 10 scherzando ***plucked:*** 9 pizzicato ***quick:*** 4 vite, vivo 5 tosto 6 presto, veloce, vivace 7 allegro 10 tostamente ***quickening:*** 11 affrettando ***repeat:*** 2 DC 3 bis 6 da capo ***sad:*** 7 dolente 8 doloroso ***separate:*** 6 divisi ***showily:*** 10 brilliante ***silent:*** 5 tacet ***singing:*** 9 cantabile ***sliding:*** 9 glissando ***slow:*** 5 grave, largo, tardo 6 adagio 7 andante 9 larghetto ***slowing:*** 3 rit 6 ritard 10 ritardando 11 rallentando ***smooth:*** 5 dolce 6 legato 8 grazioso ***soft:*** 5 dolce, piano ***softening:*** 10 diminuendo 11 decrescendo ***solemn:*** 5 grave ***sorrowful:*** 7 dolente 8 doloroso ***spirited:*** 4 vivo 6 audace, vivace 7 animato 9 spiritoso ***stately:*** 7 pomposo 8 maestoso ***strong:*** 5 forte ***sustained:*** 6 tenuto 9 sostenuto ***sweet:*** 5 dolce ***tender:*** 7 amabile, amoroso 10 affettuoso ***together:*** 4 a due ***tranquil:*** 7 calmato ***very fast:*** 11 prestissimo ***very loud:*** 2 ff 10 fortissimo ***very soft:*** 2 pp 10 pianissimo

musical drama 5 opera 8 operetta 9 singspiel

musical group 4 band, trio 5 choir, combo 6 chorus 7 quartet 8 ensemble, glee club, symphony 9 orchestra

musical instrument ***African:*** 5 mbira, sansa, zanza 7 kalimba, marimba ***ancient:*** 4 lyre, rote 5 crwth, rotte, shawm 6 cither, syrinx, trigon 7 cithara, mandola, pandura, panpipe, serpent, sistrum, theorbo ***Arabic:*** 3 oud 6 atabal ***bagpipe:*** 7 musette, pibroch ***biblical:*** 4 asor, harp, horn, pipe 5 flute 6 cymbal, sabeca, tabret 7 timbrel, trumpet 8 psaltery ***brass:*** 4 horn, tuba 5 bugle 6 cornet 7 althorn, clarion, helicon, saxhorn, trumpet 8 trombone 10 French horn ***Chinese:*** 3 kin ***Indian:*** 4 vina 5 sarod, sitar, veena ***Japanese:*** 4 biwa, koto 7 samisen ***keyboard:*** 5 organ, piano 6 spinet 7 celesta, cembalo, clavier 8 calliope, melodeon, virginal 9 accordion 10 clavichord, concertina, pianoforte 11 harpsichord ***medieval:*** 4 lute 5 naker, rebab, rebec, shawm, tabor 6 citole 7 cow horn, gittern, mandola, panpipe 8 cornetto, doucaine, dulcimer, gemshorn, hornpipe, Jew's harp, oliphant, recorder 9 monochord, rommelpot 10 clavichord, hurdy-gurdy ***percussion:*** 4 bell, drum 5 guiro, piano 6 cymbal, maraca 7 marimba, timbrel, tympani 8 bass drum, castanet, triangle 9 snare drum, xylophone 10 kettledrum, tambourine, vibraphone ***Persian:*** 6 santir ***pipe:*** 6 syrinx 7 bagpipe, musette, panpipe 9 cornemuse ***reed:*** 4 oboe 7 bassoon 8 clarinet 9 harmonica, saxophone 11 English horn ***Renaissance:*** 4 viol 5 regal, shawm 6 curtal, lirone, spinet 7 bagpipe, bandora, cittern, rackett, sackbut, serpent, theorbo, vihuela, violone 8 crumhorn, penorcon, recorder, virginal 9 angelique, cornamuse, orpharion, pandurina 10 bassanello, chitarrone, colascione 11 harpsichord ***Russian:*** 9 balalaika ***stringed:*** 3 oud 4 asor, harp, lute, lyre, vina, viol 5 banjo, cello, piano, rebec, sitar, viola 6 fiddle, guitar, violin, zither 7 bandora, cittern, gittern, kantele, pandura, ukulele 8 autoharp, dulcimer, mandolin 10 contrabass, double bass 11 harpsichord, violoncello ***suffix:*** 3 ina, ine ***toy:*** 5 kazoo 7 ocarina ***two-necked:*** 7 theorbo ***woodwind:*** 4 oboe 5 flute 7 bassoon, piccolo 9 flageolet, saxophone 11 English horn

musical interval 5 fifth, major, minor, sixth, third 6 ditone, fourth, octave, second 7 perfect, seventh, tritone

musical syllable 2 do, fa, la, mi, re, si, ti, ut 3 Ela, sol ***Guido's:*** 2 ut 3 Ela

musician 4 bard 5 piper 6 player 7 jazzman 8 minstrel, virtuoso 9 performer

muskeg 3 bog, fen 4 mire, quag 5 marsh, swamp 6 slough 7 baygall

musket 5 fusil 6 dragon 7 dragoon 9 flintlock, matchlock 12 muzzleloader ***medieval:*** 8 culverin

muskmelon 10 cantaloupe

Muslim, Moslem ***ascetic:*** 4 Sufi 5 fakir 7 dervish ***Bible:*** 5 Koran ***body of scholars:*** 5 ulema ***caller to prayer:*** 7 muezzin ***call to prayer:*** 4 adan, azan ***cap:*** 3 taj ***creed:*** 6 Kelima 7 Kalimah ***devil:*** 5 Eblis ***festival:*** 3 Eed 6 Bairam ***garment:*** 4 izar 5 ihram 6 chador ***god:*** 5 Allah ***holy city:*** 5 Mecca 6 Medina ***holy war:*** 5 jahad, jehad, jihad ***judge:*** 4 cadi ***lawyer:*** 5 mufti ***marriage:*** 4 mota, muta ***mendicant:*** 5 fakir ***monastery:*** 5 ribat 7 khankah ***month:*** (see at month) ***month of fasting:*** 7 Ramadan ***mosque:*** 6 masjid ***mystic:*** 4 Sufi ***nonbeliever:*** 5 Kafir 6 Kaffir ***nymph:*** 5 houri ***pilgrim:*** 4 haji 5 hadji, hajji ***pilgrimage:*** 3 haj 4 hadj, hajj ***priest:*** 4 imam ***prophet:***

8 Mohammed, Muhammad ***religion:*** 5 Islam ***saint:*** 3 pir 6 santon ***saint's tomb:*** 3 pir ***shrine:*** 5 Caaba, Kaaba 6 Kaabeh ***student:*** 5 softa ***teacher:*** 4 alim 5 mulla 6 mullah ***temple:*** 6 mosque ***title:*** 3 aga 4 agha, emir, said 5 calif, emeer, sayid 6 caliph ***tradition:*** 5 sunna 6 sunnah; (see also **mosque; Muhammad**)

muss 4 mess 5 botch, mix-up, upset 6 jumble, mess-up, muddle, rumple 7 disrupt, rummage, wrinkle 8 botchery, disarray, dishevel, disorder, shambles 10 disarrange 11 disorganize

mussel 5 naiad ***genus:*** 4 Unio 7 Mytilus 8 Anodonta ***larva:*** 9 blackhead

Mussolini, Benito 7 Fascist 8 dictator ***title:*** 4 Duce (Il)

mussy 5 messy 6 sloppy, sloven, unneat, untidy 7 unkempt 8 ill-kempt, slobbery, slovenly 10 disheveled

must 4 duty, have, need, want 5 ought 6 charge, devoir, should 9 committal, condition, essential, necessity, requisite 10 commitment, obligation, sine qua non 11 requirement 12 precondition, prerequisite

muster 4 call, roll 5 breed, cause, crowd, enter, get up, group, hatch, raise, rally 6 enlist, enroll, gather, induce, invoke, join up, number, roster, sample, sign on, sign up, summon, work up 7 collect, company, convene, develop, include, marshal, produce 8 assemble, assembly, comprise, congress, engender, generate, mobilize, occasion, organize 9 congeries, forgather, gathering, inventory 10 accumulate, assemblage, collection, congregate, rendezvous 11 aggregation, examination 12 accumulation, congregation

muster out 8 separate 9 discharge 10 demobilize

musty 4 dull, rank, sour 5 dirty, fetid, funky, moldy, stale, tired, trite 6 frowsy, old hat, smelly, whiffy 7 noisome, spoiled, squalid 8 shopworn, timeworn 10 antiquated, malodorous, threadbare

Mut ***husband:*** 4 Amen, Amon ***son:*** 5 Chons 6 Chonsu, Khonsu

mutable 5 fluid 6 fickle, mobile, shifty 7 protean 8 slippery, unstable, unsteady, variable, wavering, weathery 9 changeful, mercurial, uncertain, unsettled 10 capricious, changeable, inconstant 11 fluctuating, vacillating 12 inconsistent

mutate 4 turn, vary 5 alter 6 change, modify 7 commute 9 refashion, transform, transmute, transpose 11 transfigure 12 metamorphize, metamorphose, transmogrify

mutation 4 turn 6 change 7 novelty 9 variation 10 alteration, innovation 11 vicissitude 12 modification

mute 3 mum 4 dumb 6 dampen, deaden, muffle, reduce, silent, soften, stifle 8 silencer, wordless 9 voiceless 10 speechless 12 inarticulate, unarticulate

muted 3 dim, mat 4 dead, dull, flat 5 blind 6 silent 10 lackluster, lusterless, speechless

mutedly 6 weakly 7 faintly 9 sotto voce

mutilate 3 mar 4 geld, hurt, maim 5 alter, spoil, unsex 6 change, damage, deface, injure, mangle, mayhem, neuter 7 cripple, dislimb 8 castrate 9 disfigure, dismember, sterilize 11 desexualize

mutineer 5 rebel 6 anarch 8 frondeur, revolter 9 anarchist, insurgent 10 malcontent

mutinous 6 unruly 8 factious 9 insurgent, seditious, turbulent 10 rebellious 12 contumacious 13 insubordinate

mutiny 5 rebel 6 revolt 9 insurrect, rebellion 11 rise against 12 insurrection

mutt 3 cur, dog 4 boob, dolt, dope 5 dunce, idiot 6 dimwit 7 mongrel 8 dumbbell, numskull 9 blockhead, ignoramus

Mutt and ___ 4 Jeff

mutter 5 croak, growl, rumor, scold 6 fumble, grouch, grouse, muddle, mumble, murmur 7 grumble, swallow, whisper 9 undertone 11 susurration

muttonchops 9 burnsides, sideburns 10 sideboards 11 dundrearies 12 sidewhiskers

muttonhead 3 oaf 5 dunce, idiot 8 clodpate, numskull 9 blockhead 10 thickskull

mutual 5 joint 6 common, public, shared, united 7 related 8 communal, conjoint, conjunct 9 connected 10 associated, reciprocal, respective ***prefix:*** 2 co 5 inter

muzzle 3 gag, mug 4 face, nose, phiz 5 snout 6 nuzzle, visage 8 features, restrain 11 countenance

My Antonia author 6 Cather

My Last Duchess author 8 Browning

My Lost Youth author 10 Longfellow

myrmidon 8 follower, hireling, retainer 9 attendant, underling 11 subordinate

Myron's statue 10 Discobolus

Myrrha's son 6 Adonis

mysterious 6 arcane, mystic, occult, secret 7 cryptic, obscure, strange 8 abstruse, esoteric, numinous 9 ambiguous, enigmatic, equivocal, recondite, unguessed 10 cabalistic, unknowable 11 enigmatical, inscrutable, ungraspable 12 impenetrable, incognizable, inexplicable, unexaminable, unfathomable 13 unaccountable

mystery 5 poser 6 enigma, puzzle, riddle, secret 7 arcanum, problem, stumper 9 conundrum 10 closed book, perplexity,

puzzlement 13 Chinese puzzle, mystification *story:* 8 whodunit
mystic 4 seer 5 magic, vague 6 arcane, magian, occult, secret, witchy 7 magical, obscure 8 anagogic, esoteric, numinous, quixotic, telestic, wizardly 9 enigmatic, mysterial, sorcerous, unguessed 10 cabalistic, mysterious, unknowable 11 inscrutable, necromantic 12 impenetrable, thaumaturgic 13 unaccountable
mystical 4 deep, holy 6 covert, divine, orphic, sacred, secret 7 cryptic, furtive, sub-rosa 8 anagogic, hush-hush, orphical, profound, stealthy, telestic 9 spiritual 10 miraculous, symbolical 11 clandestine 12 hugger-mugger, supernatural, supranatural 13 hole-and-corner
mysticism 8 cabalism, quietism
mystify 6 puzzle 7 confuse, perplex 8 befuddle, bewilder 9 obfuscate
mystifying 4 dark 7 cryptic 8 Delphian 9 enigmatic
myth 4 lore, saga, tale 5 fable, story 6 legend 7 fiction, figment, parable 8 allegory, apologue, creation, folklore 9 invention, tradition 11 fabrication
mythical 6 unreal 7 created, fictive 8 fabulous, fanciful, invented 9 fantastic, fictional, imaginary, legendary, visionary 10 fictitious 12 mythological
mythological see mythical
mythologist 5 Tylor 6 Frazer 5 Miller 9 Euhemerus 10 Malinowski
mythology see myth

N

Naamah *brother:* 9 Tubalcain *father:* 6 Lamech *husband:* 7 Solomon *mother:* 6 Zillah *son:* 8 Rehoboam
Naaman *disease:* 7 leprosy *father:* 4 Bela *grandfather:* 8 Benjamin *healer:* 6 Elisha
Naam's father 5 Caleb
Naarah's husband 6 Ashhur
nab 3 nip 4 hook, nail, take 5 catch, pinch, run in, seize, steal 6 arrest, clutch, collar, detain, pickup, pull in, snatch 7 capture, grapple 9 apprehend
nabal 5 chuff, hunks, miser, stiff 7 niggard, scrooge 8 muckworm, tightwad 9 skinflint 12 moneygrubber
Nabal's wife 7 Abigail
nabob 6 biggie, bigwig, fat cat 7 notable 8 big chief, eminence 9 dignitary 10 notability
Nabokov novel 3 Ada 4 Pnin 6 Lolita, The Eye 7 Despair, The Gift 8 Mashenka, Pale Fire, The Event 10 The Defense, The Exploit
nacre 13 mother-of-pearl
nada 7 nullity, vacuity 8 nihility 11 nothingness 12 nonexistence
Nadab *brother:* 4 Kish 5 Abihu *father:* 5 Aaron, Jeiel 6 Gibeon 8 Jeroboam *mother:* 6 Maacah 8 Elisheba *slayer:* 6 Baasha
nadir 4 base, foot 6 bottom *opposite:* 6 zenith
nag 3 egg, irk, vex 4 bait, carp, fuss, goad, jade, prod, ride, urge 5 annoy, chivy, harry, hound, tease, worry 6 badger, bother, carp at, harass, heckle, hector, needle, peck at, pester, plague 7 henpeck, torment 8 harangue, irritate
Nahash's daughter 7 Abigail, Zeruiah
Nahath *father:* 5 Reuel *grandfather:* 7 Elkanah
Nahor *brother:* 5 Haran 7 Abraham *concubine:* 6 Reumah *father:* 5 Serug, Terah *grandson:* 7 Abraham *son:* 5 Terah 7 Bethuel *wife:* 6 Milcah
Nahshon *brother-in-law:* 5 Aaron *father:* 9 Amminadab *grandson:* 4 Boaz *sister:* 8 Elisheba *son:* 6 Salmon
naiad 5 nymph
naif 7 ingenue
nail 3 bag, get 4 brad, stud, tack, trap 5 catch, clone, spike, sprig 6 collar, secure, tacket, unguis, ungula 7 capture, prehend, ungulae (plural) 8 sparable *combining form:* 4 helo, onyx 5 onych, ungui 6 onycho 7 onychia 8 onychium
naive 4 easy 5 fresh 6 simple 7 artless, natural 8 gullible, innocent, original, unartful 9 ingenuous, unstudied 10 fleeceable, unaffected, unschooled 11 susceptible
naked 3 raw 4 bald, bare, mere, nude, open, pure 5 clear, sheer 6 meager, peeled, scanty, simple, unclad 7 denuded, evident, exposed, obvious, unarmed 8 buff-

bare, garbless, manifest, palpable, revealed, stripped **9** au naturel, colorless, destitute, disclosed, unclothed, uncolored, uncovered, undressed **10** discovered ***combining form:*** **4** gymn, nudi **5** gymno

Naked and the Dead author **6** Mailer

namby-pamby **3** sop **4** baby, flat **5** banal, bland, inane, sissy **6** jejune **7** doormat, insipid, milksop, sapless **8** weakling **9** driveling, innocuous, jellyfish **10** pantywaist, wishy-washy **11** Milquetoast, mollycoddle **12** milk-and-water **13** characterless

name **3** dub, nom, tab, tag, tap **4** call, cite, clan, make, race, term **5** alias, label, nomen, quote, state, style, title **6** byword, family, finger, handle, report, repute, rubric, ticket **7** appoint, baptize, declare, entitle, epithet, mention, moniker, notable, publish, specify **8** announce, christen, cognomen, identify, instance, luminary, monicker, nominate, somebody **9** advertise, celebrity, character, designate, incognito, pseudonym, recognize, sobriquet, stipulate **10** denominate, hypocorism, nom de plume, notability, reputation **11** appellation, appellative, designation ***ancient Rome:*** **7** agnomen **8** prenomen ***assumed:*** **5** alias **9** sobriquet ***combining form:*** **4** onym **7** onomato ***family:*** **8** cognomen ***fictitious:*** **9** pseudonym ***giver:*** **6** eponym

namely **5** to wit **8** scilicet **9** expressly, specially, videlicet **10** especially **12** particularly, specifically ***abbreviation:*** **3** viz

nana **5** nurse **9** nursemaid **11** nurserymaid

Nana ***author:*** **4** Zola ***mother:*** **8** Gervaise

Nanna ***brother:*** **6** Nergal, Ninazu ***father:*** **5** Enlil ***husband:*** **6** Balder ***mother:*** **6** Ninlil ***son:*** **3** Utu ***wife:*** **6** Ningal

nanny see **nana**

Naomi **4** Mara ***daughter-in-law:*** **4** Ruth **5** Orpah ***husband:*** **9** Elimelech ***meaning:*** **8** pleasant ***son:*** **6** Mahlon **7** Chilion

nap **3** nod **4** doze, rest **5** break, cover, let up, pause, relax, sleep, unlax **6** drowse, siesta, snooze **7** respite **10** forty winks

nape **6** scruff

Naphish's father **7** Ishmael

Naphtali ***brother:*** **3** Dan ***father:*** **5** Jacob ***mother:*** **6** Bilhah ***son:*** **4** Guni **5** Jezer **7** Jahzeel, Jahziel, Shallum

naphtha **7** solvent **9** petroleum

napkin **5** cloth, doily, towel **9** handcloth

napoleon **4** boot **6** pastry **8** card game **9** solitaire ***bid:*** **7** blucher **10** wellington

Napoleon ***adversary:*** **6** Nelson **7** Kutuzov **10** Wellington ***birthplace:*** **7** Ajaccio (Corsica) ***brother:*** **5** Louis **6** Jerome, Joseph, Lucien ***brother-in-law:*** **5** Murat ***deathplace:*** **8** St. Helena ***defeat:*** **7** Leipzig **8** Waterloo **9** Trafalgar ***father:*** **5** Carlo ***island of exile:*** **4** Elba **8** St. Helena ***marshal:*** **3** Ney **5** Murat, Soult **6** Suchet ***nickname:*** **14** Little Corporal ***sister:*** **5** Maria **8** Carlotta, Carolina ***victory:*** **3** Ulm **4** Jena, Lodi **5** Ligny **6** Abukir, Arcole, Wagram **7** Bautzen, Dresden, Marengo **8** Borodino **10** Austerlitz ***wife:*** **9** Josephine **11** Marie Louise

narcissism **6** vanity **7** conceit **8** self-love, vainness **9** vainglory **10** self-esteem **11** amour propre, self-conceit **13** conceitedness

narcissistic **4** vain **7** stuck-up **8** conceity **9** conceited **12** vainglorious **13** self-conceited

Narcissus ***father:*** **9** Cephissus ***mother:*** **7** Liriope ***rejected admirer:*** **4** Echo

narcotic **3** hop **4** dope, drug, junk **5** opium **6** heroin, opiate **7** anodyne, cocaine, hashish **8** hasheesh, hypnotic, morphine, nepenthe, somnific **9** somnolent, soporific **10** somnorific **11** somniferous, soporifical ***peddler:*** **6** dealer, pusher

nark **3** rat **4** fink **5** peach, stool **6** canary, inform, snitch, squeak, squeal **7** tipster **8** betrayer, informer, squeaker, squealer **10** talebearer **11** stool pigeon

narrate **4** tell, yarn **5** state, story **6** detail, dilate, recite, relate, report **7** descant, recount **8** describe, rehearse **9** discourse

narrative **4** epic, myth, saga, tale, yarn **5** fable, story **6** legend, report **7** account, history, recital, version **8** anecdote **9** chronicle ***medieval French:*** **5** roman **7** romance ***prose:*** **5** novel **7** novella

narrow **3** set **4** mean **5** close, fixed, limit, small, taper, tense **6** lessen, little, meager, paltry, strait **7** bigoted, limited, precise **8** contract, decrease, definite, obdurate, straiten **9** confining, constrict, hidebound, illiberal **10** brassbound, constringe, inexorable, inflexible, intolerant, restricted

narrowly **6** barely **8** scarcely

narrow-minded **5** petty **7** bigoted, shallow **9** hidebound, illiberal **10** brassbound, intolerant, provincial, unenlarged

nasal **6** rhinal, twangy **9** nosepiece ***combining form:*** **4** rhin **5** rhino

nascency **5** birth **6** origin

nascent **7** initial **9** beginning, inceptive, incipient **10** initiative, initiatory **12** introductory

Naseby victor **7** Fairfax **8** Cromwell

nasicorn **10** rhinoceros

nasty **4** evil, foul, icky, mean, vile **5** black, cheap, dirty, gross, snide, soily **6** coarse, filthy, grubby, horrid, impure, malign, oafish, ribald, smutty, tawdry, vulgar, wicked **7** hateful, ill-bred, obscene, raunchy, spitish, squalid, unclean, vicious **8** improper, indecent, spiteful, unseemly **9** loathsome, malicious, malignant, offensive, repugnant, repulsive, uncleanly, vexatious 10 disgusting, disturbing, indecorous, indelicate, malevolent

natant 8 swimming

Nathan *father:* 4 Bani 5 Attai, David *son:* 5 Zabad

national 4 home 5 civic, civil 6 public 7 citizen, subject 8 domestic, internal 9 intestine, municipal

National Basketball Association *Atlanta:* 5 Hawks *Boston:* 7 Celtics *Charlotte:* 7 Hornets *Chicago:* 5 Bulls *Cleveland:* 9 Cavaliers *Dallas:* 9 Mavericks *Denver:* 7 Nuggets *Detroit:* 7 Pistons *Golden State:* 8 Warriors *Houston:* 7 Rockets *Indiana:* 6 Pacers *Los Angeles:* 6 Lakers 8 Clippers *Miami:* 4 Heat *Milwaukee:* 5 Bucks *Minnesota:* 12 Timberwolves *New Jersey:* 4 Nets *New York:* 6 Knicks *Orlando:* 5 Magic *Phoenix:* 4 Suns *Portland:* 12 Trail Blazers *Sacramento:* 5 Kings *San Antonio:* 5 Spurs *Seattle:* 11 SuperSonics *Utah:* 4 Jazz *Washington:* 7 Bullets

National Football League *Atlanta:* 7 Falcons *Buffalo:* 5 Bills *Chicago:* 5 Bears *Cincinnati:* 7 Bengals *Cleveland:* 6 Browns *Dallas:* 7 Cowboys *Denver:* 7 Broncos *Detroit:* 5 Lions *Green Bay:* 7 Packers *Houston:* 6 Oilers *Indianapolis:* 5 Colts *Kansas City:* 6 Chiefs *Los Angeles:* 4 Rams 7 Raiders *Miami:* 8 Dolphins *Minnesota:* 7 Vikings *New England:* 8 Patriots *New Orleans:* 6 Saints *New York:* 4 Jets 6 Giants *Philadelphia:* 6 Eagles *Phoenix:* 9 Cardinals *Pittsburgh:* 8 Steelers *San Diego:* 8 Chargers *Seattle:* 8 Seahawks *Tampa Bay:* 4 Bucs *Washington:* 8 Redskins

national historical park *Alaska:* 5 Sitka *Idaho:* 8 Nez Percé *Kentucky-Tennessee:* 13 Cumberland Gap *Maryland-West Virginia:* 12 Harpers Ferry *Massachusetts:* 9 Minute Man *New York:* 8 Saratoga

National Hockey League *Boston:* 6 Bruins *Buffalo:* 6 Sabres *Calgary:* 6 Flames *Chicago:* 10 Black Hawks *Detroit:* 8 Red Wings *Edmonton:* 6 Oilers *Hartford:* 7 Whalers *Los Angeles:* 5 Kings *Minnesota:* 10 North Stars *Montreal:* 9 Canadiens *New Jersey:* 6 Devils *New York:* 7 Rangers 9 Islanders *Philadelphia:* 6 Flyers *Pittsburgh:* 8 Penguins *Quebec:* 9 Nordiques *St. Louis:* 5 Blues *San Jose:* 6 Sharks *Toronto:* 10 Maple Leafs *Vancouver:* 7 Canucks *Washington:* 8 Capitals *Winnipeg:* 4 Jets

nationalism 10 patriotism *excessive:* 8 jingoism 10 chauvinism

National League *Atlanta:* 6 Braves *Chicago:* 4 Cubs *Cincinnati:* 4 Reds *Houston:* 6 Astros *Los Angeles:* 7 Dodgers *Montreal:* 5 Expos *New York:* 4 Mets *Philadelphia:* 8 Phillies *Pittsburgh:* 7 Pirates *St. Louis:* 9 Cardinals *San Diego:* 6 Padres *San Francisco:* 6 Giants

national military park *Alabama:* 13 Horseshoe Bend *Arkansas:* 8 Pea Ridge *Mississippi:* 9 Vicksburg *Pennsylvania:* 10 Gettysburg *South Carolina:* 13 Kings Mountain *Tennessee:* 6 Shiloh

national monument *Alabama:* 11 Russell Cave *Alaska:* 9 Aniakchak *Arizona:* 5 Tonto 6 Navajo 7 Saguaro, Wupatki 8 Tuzigoot 10 Chiricahua, Pipe Spring, Tumacacori 11 Hohokam Pima 12 Sunset Crater, Walnut Canyon *California:* 8 Cabrillo, Lava Beds 9 Muir Woods, Pinnacles 10 Joshua Tree 11 Death Valley *Colorado:* 10 Yucca House *Colorado-Utah:* 8 Dinosaur 9 Hovenweep *Florida:* 12 Fort Matanzas 13 Fort Jefferson *Georgia:* 8 Ocmulgee 11 Fort Pulaski 13 Fort Frederica *Iowa:* 12 Effigy Mounds *Louisiana:* 12 Poverty Point *Maryland:* 11 Fort McHenry *Minnesota:* 9 Pipestone 12 Grand Portage *Nebraska:* 9 Homestead 11 Scotts Bluff *New Mexico:* 5 Pecos 7 El Morro 9 Bandelier, El Malpais, Fort Union 10 Aztec Ruins, White Sands *New York:* 11 Fort Stanwix 13 Castle Clinton *South Carolina:* 10 Fort Sumter 13 Congaree Swamp *South Dakota:* 9 Jewel Cave *Utah:* 11 Cedar Breaks 13 Rainbow Bridge *Wyoming:* 11 Devils Tower, Fossil Butte

national park *Alaska:* 6 Denali, Katmai 9 Lake Clark 10 Glacier Bay 11 Kenai Fjords, Kobuk Valley *Angola:* 4 Iona, Mupa *Arizona:* 11 Grand Canyon *Arkansas:* 10 Hot Springs *Botswana:* 5 Chobe *California:* 7 Redwood, Sequoia 8 Yosemite 11 King's Canyon *Chad:* 5 Manda *Colombia:* 5 Uraba *Colorado:* 9 Mesa Verde 13 Rocky Mountain *eastern Africa:* 10 Mount Kenya *Florida:* 8 Biscayne 10 Everglades *Hawaii:* 9 Haleakala *India:* 5 Kanha *Japan:* 5 Nikko *Kentucky:* 11 Mammoth Cave *Kenya:* 4 Meru 5 Tsavo 10 Royal Tsavo *Lake Superior:* 10 Isle Royale *Maine:* 6 Acadia *Malaysia:* 8 Kinabalu *Minnesota:* 9 Voyageurs *Montana:* 7 Glacier *Nevada:* 10 Great Basin *Oregon:* 10 Crater Lake *Poland:* 5 Ojcow, Tatra *South Africa:* 6 Kruger *South Dakota:* 8 Badlands, Wind Cave *Sri Lanka:* 4 Yala *Sweden:* 5 Sarek *Tanzania:* 5 Ruaha 9 Serengeti *Texas:* 7 Big Bend *Utah:* 4 Zion 6 Arches 11 Bryce Canyon, Canyonlands, Capitol Reef *Virginia:* 10 Shenandoah *Washington:*

7 Olympic 12 Mount Rainier 13 North Cascades *Wyoming:* 10 Grand Teton *Wyoming-Idaho-Montana:* 11 Yellowstone *Zambia:* 5 Kafue *Zimbabwe:* 13 Rhodes Inyanga, Victoria Falls

native 3 raw 4 home, wild 5 crude, local 6 impure, inborn, innate, normal, simple 7 connate, endemic, indigen, natural 8 agrarian, agrestal, domestic, indigene, inherent, internal, national, ungraded, unsorted 9 inherited, intestine, municipal 10 aboriginal, congenital, connatural, indigenous, unacquired, unaffected *Acadian Louisiana:* 5 Cajun *China:* 3 Han 9 Celestial *India:* 5 sepoy *Japan:* 9 Nipponese *London:* 7 Cockney *New England:* 4 Yank 6 Yankee *New York:* 13 Knickerbocker *suffix:* 2 er 3 ese, ier, ite, ote, yer

Native Son author 6 Wright

Nativity 4 noel, Xmas, yule 5 birth 8 yuletide 9 Christmas

natty 4 jimp 5 doggy, jimpy, sassy, smart 6 dapper, spiffy, spruce, sprucy 7 bandbox, doggish 11 well-groomed

natural 4 easy, feeb, fool, open, wild, zany 5 ament, frank, idiot, moron, naive, plain, typic, usual, white 6 candid, common, cretin, folksy, inborn, innate, native, normal, rustic, simple 7 artless, bastard, connate, general, genuine, half-wit, regular, sincere, typical 8 agrarian, agrestal, baseborn, homespun, ignorant, imbecile, inherent, innocent, spurious, unartful 9 blackjack, childlike, guileless, impulsive, ingenuous, ingrained, inherited, prevalent, primitive, simpleton, unfeigned, unlabored, unstudied, untutored, unworldly 10 congenital, fatherless, indigenous, legitimate, provincial, unacquired, unaffected, unfathered, unschooled 11 commonplace, instinctive, misbegotten, spontaneous, undesigning

naturalist *American:* 4 Muir 5 Hyatt 7 Audubon, Verrill *English:* 3 Ray 5 White 6 Darwin 7 Wallace 10 Williamson *French:* 5 Fabre 7 Lamarck, Réaumur *Scottish:* 6 Wilson 10 Richardson

nature 3 ilk, way 4 kind, sort, type 5 being, humor, shape, world 6 cosmos, figure, kidney, kosmos, makeup, stripe, temper 7 anatomy, essence, texture, variety 8 creation, essentia, megacosm, universe 9 character, framework, macrocosm, normality 10 complexion 11 description, disposition, macrocosmos, personality, temperament 12 essentiality

naught 3 nil 4 zero 5 zilch 6 cipher, ruined 7 nothing 8 goose egg 11 nonexistent, nothingness 12 nonexistence

naughty 3 bad, paw 4 evil 5 rowdy 6 unruly, wicked 7 froward, wayward, willful 8 contrary, perverse 9 ruffianly 10 disorderly, headstrong, ill-behaved, indecorous, refractory 11 disobedient, intractable, misbehaving, mischievous 12 obstreperous, recalcitrant, ungovernable

nauseate 5 abhor, repel 6 loathe, reluct, revolt, sicken 7 disgust, repulse

nauseated 4 sick 6 queasy, queazy 7 carsick 9 squeamish

nauseating 4 foul, icky 5 nasty 7 noisome 9 loathsome, offensive, repugnant, repulsive, sickening

nauseous see **nauseated**

Nausicaa *father:* 8 Alcinous *mother:* 5 Arete

nautical 5 naval 6 marine 7 oceanic 8 maritime 12 navigational *instrument:* 3 aba 7 compass, pelorus, sextant

naval hero 5 Jones, Perry 8 Farragut, Lawrence

nave 3 hub

navel 6 middle 7 nombril 9 umbilicus 11 belly button *combining form:* 6 omphal 7 omphalo

navigate 4 move, sail, walk 5 pilot, steer

navigation 6 voyage 7 passage 8 piloting, seacraft, shipping

navigational system 5 loran 6 shoran 7 teleran

navigator 5 flyer, pilot 6 airman 7 copilot *Danish:* 6 Bering *Dutch:* 6 Tasman 7 Barents *English:* 4 Cook 5 Cabot, Drake 6 Hudson 7 Gilbert, Raleigh 9 Vancouver *French:* 7 Cartier 9 La Perouse *Italian:* 5 Cabot 8 Columbus, Vespucci 9 Verrazano *Norwegian:* 4 Eric 7 Ericson 8 Ericsson *Portuguese:* 4 Dias, Diaz 6 Cabral, da Gama 8 Magellan *Spanish:* 9 Fernandez

navy 5 fleet

Nazi 9 Hitlerite 10 brownshirt *admiral:* 6 Dönitz, Raeder 7 Doenitz *air force:* 9 Luftwaffe *armed forces:* 9 Wehrmacht *collaborator:* 5 Laval 8 Quisling *concentration camp:* 6 Belsen, Dachau 9 Auschwitz 10 Buchenwald, Nordhausen *field marshal:* 5 Model 6 Keitel, Paulus, Rommel 9 Rundstedt 10 Kesselring *greeting:* 4 Heil *leader:* 3 Ley 4 Hess, Röhm 5 Roehm 6 Führer, Göring, Hitler 7 Fuehrer, Goering, Himmler 8 Goebbels, Heydrich 9 Rosenberg *police:* 2 SS 7 Gestapo *propagandist:* 8 Goebbels *submarine:* 5 U-boat *surrender signer:* 4 Jodl 6 Keitel *symbol:* 6 fylfot 8 swastika *tactic:* 10 blitzkrieg *tank:* 6 panzer

NCO 3 cpl, sgt 8 corporal, sergeant

neap 4 tide

near 2 by 4 nigh 5 about, circa, close, round 6 almost, around, beside, narrow, stingy 7 close by, closely, close on 8 adjacent, approach, stingily 9 immediate, proximate, thriftily **10** intimately **11** approximate, at close hand, closefisted ***combining form:*** **5** juxta ***prefix:*** **2** ad, ep **3** eph, epi **4** peri, pros **5** plesi **6** plesio

nearby **4** nigh **5** about, aside, circa, close, handy, round **6** around, beside **7** closeby, close on, vicinal **8** adjacent **9** immediate, proximate **10** contiguous, convenient **11** neighboring

nearest **4** next **8** proximal

nearsighted **6** myopic

neat **3** net **4** deft, nice, prim, pure, snug, tidy, trig, trim **5** clean, clear, exact, kempt, plain **6** adroit, clever, dainty, dapper, spruce, sprucy **7** chipper, correct, finicky, orderly, precise, primsie, regular, unmixed **8** accurate, spotless, straight **9** ingenious, shipshape, undiluted **10** fastidious, gratifying, immaculate, methodical, systematic **11** uncluttered, well-groomed **12** spick-and span **13** unadulterated

neb **3** ear, nib, tip **4** beak, bill, nose **6** pecker

Nebaioth ***brother:*** **5** Kedar ***father:*** **7** Ishmael

Nebraska ***capital:*** **7** Lincoln ***college, university:*** **4** Dana **5** Doane **9** Creighton ***Indian:*** **4** Otoe ***largest city:*** **5** Omaha ***state flower:*** **9** goldenrod

nebula **6** galaxy

nebulous **4** hazy **6** turbid **7** clouded **10** indistinct

necessary **5** vital **6** needed **7** certain **8** cardinal, inerrant, integral, unerring **9** essential, important, inerrable, mandatory, momentous, requisite **10** compelling, compulsory, imperative, ineludible, inevasible, inevitable, obligatory, unevadable **11** fundamental, ineluctable, inescapable, significant, unavoidable, unescapable **12** constraining, prerequisite **13** indispensable

necessitate **3** ask **4** take **5** crave **6** compel, demand **7** call for, require **9** constrain, force into

necessitous see **needy**

necessity **4** call, must, need **5** cause **6** duress **7** poverty **8** coercion, exigency, occasion **9** condition, essential, requisite **10** compulsion, constraint, obligation, sine qua non **11** needfulness, requirement **12** precondition, prerequisite **13** requisiteness

neck **3** pet **4** kiss **5** beard **6** behead, cervix, collet, fondle, smooch, strait **7** embrace **8** gorgerin **9** decollate **10** decapitate, guillotine ***back of:*** **4** nape **5** nucha **6** scruff ***ornament:*** **6** gorget, torque

necklace **4** band **5** chain **6** locket **7** rivière **8** carcanet

neckpiece **3** boa **5** scarf

necktie **5** ascot **6** cravat **10** four-in-hand ***adjunct:*** **6** tiepin **8** tie clasp

necrology **4** obit **8** obituary

necromancy **5** magic **7** sorcery **8** witchery, wizardry **9** conjuring, magicking **10** witchcraft **11** bewitchment, enchantment, thaumaturgy

necropolis **8** boneyard, boot hill, cemetery, God's acre **9** graveyard **12** burial ground

necropsy **7** autopsy **10** postmortem

need **3** use **4** call, duty, have, lack, long, must, pine, want, wish **5** claim, covet, crave, drive, exact, ought, yearn **6** charge, demand, desire, devoir, hanker, hunger, penury, thirst **7** deficit, poverty, require **8** exaction, exigency, occasion, poorness, shortage **9** committal, indigence, necessity, privation, requisite **10** commitment, compulsion, deficiency, dependence, obligation **11** destitution, requirement

neediness **4** want **6** penury **7** poverty **9** indigence, privation **11** destitution

needle **3** dun **5** annoy, tease, worry **6** harass, pester, plague **7** bedevil, hagride, obelisk, pricker, syringe ***blunt:*** **6** bodkin ***case:*** **4** etui ***combining form:*** **3** acu ***hole:*** **3** eye

needlefish **3** gar

needlelike **7** styloid **8** belonoid ***part:*** **7** acicula

needlepoint lace **7** alençon

needle-shaped **7** acerose, acerous, aciform

needlework **6** sewing **7** crochet, sampler, seaming, tatting **8** knitting **10** crocheting, embroidery

needy **4** poor **6** hard up **8** dirt poor, indigent, strapped **9** destitute, penniless, penurious **11** impecunious, necessitous **12** impoverished, unprosperous

ne'er-do-well **6** bad lot, no-good, waster **7** rounder, wastrel **9** shiftless **10** profligate, scapegrace **11** incompetent

nefarious **4** rank **5** gross **6** putrid, rotten **7** corrupt, glaring, heinous **8** flagrant, infamous, perverse **9** miscreant, monstrous **10** degenerate, detestable, outrageous, villainous

negate **4** deny, undo, void **5** abate, annul, cross, quash **6** impugn **7** abolish, gainsay, nullify, redress, vitiate **8** negative, traverse **9** cancel out, disaffirm, frustrate **10** annihilate, contradict, contravene, counteract, invalidate, neutralize **12** countercheck

negative **2** no **3** nix **4** deny, kill, veto **5** annul, cross, minus **6** impugn **7** adverse, gainsay, nullify, redress, refusal **8** abrogate, disprove, traverse **9** cancel out, disaffirm, frustrate, non-placet **10** contradict, contravene, counteract, invalidate, neutralize

11 detrimental, unfavorable ***battery terminal:*** 5 anode ***ion:*** 5 anion ***Scottish:*** 3 nae ***sign:*** 5 minus

neglect 4 fail, miss, omit, pass 5 elide, scant, scorn, shirk 6 forget, ignore, pass by, reject, slight 7 blink at, default, disdain, dismiss, failure 8 brush off, discount, omission, overleap, overlook, overpass, pass over, shrug off, slur over 9 blink away, disregard, oversight, pretermit, shrug away 10 brush aside, slough over

neglectful see **negligent**

negligee 4 gown 8 camisole 9 nightgown

negligent 3 lax 5 slack 6 remiss 7 offhand 8 careless, derelict, discinct, heedless, slipshod, slovenly 9 incurious, unheedful, unstudied 10 behindhand, delinquent, regardless, unthinking 11 inadvertent, inattentive, indifferent, thoughtless, unconcerned 12 disregardful 13 inconsiderate

negligible 4 slim 5 small 6 remote, slight 7 outside, slender 8 trifling

negotiate 4 leap, over 5 agree, clear, vault 6 adjust, handle, hurdle, manage, settle 7 arrange, bargain, compose, concert, conduct 8 complete, contract, covenant, overleap, surmount, transact 10 accomplish

Nehemiah's father 5 Azbuk 9 Hachaliah

Nehushta ***father:*** 8 Elnathan ***husband:*** 9 Jehoiakim ***son:*** 10 Jehoiachin

neigh 6 nicker, whinny 7 snicker, snigger

neighbor 4 abut, join, line 5 march, touch, verge 6 adjoin, border, butt on, corner 8 border on

neighborhood 4 area, tune 5 order, range 6 extent, matter 8 district, locality, vicinage, vicinity 9 magnitude, proximity

neighborly 6 social 7 cordial 8 amicable, friendly, gracious, sociable 10 gregarious, hospitable 11 cooperative

nematode 4 worm 7 eelworm 9 roundworm

Nemean predator 4 lion

neon 3 gas ***symbol:*** 2 Ne

neonate see **newborn**

neophyte see **newcomer**

Neoptolemus 7 Pyrrhus ***father:*** 8 Achilles ***slayer:*** 7 Orestes ***victim:*** 5 Priam ***wife:*** 8 Hermione

Nepal ***capital:*** 8 Katmandu 9 Kathmandu ***forest land:*** 5 Terai ***monetary unit:*** 5 rupee

nepenthe 6 opiate 7 anodyne 8 narcotic

Nepheg ***brother:*** 5 Korah 6 Zichri ***father:*** 5 David, Izhar

Nephele ***daughter:*** 5 Helle ***husband:*** 7 Athamas ***son:*** 7 Phrixos, Phrixus

Nephthys ***brother, husband:*** 3 Set 4 Seth

Neptune 6 planet ***satellite:*** 6 Nereid, Triton; (see also **Poseidon**)

Ner ***father:*** 5 Abiel, Jeiel ***son:*** 5 Abner

Nereides 6 Thetis 7 Galatea 10 Amphitrite ***father:*** 6 Nereus ***mother:*** 5 Doris

Nereus ***daughters:*** 8 Nereides ***emblem:*** 7 trident ***father:*** 6 Pontus ***mother:*** 2 Ge 4 Gaea ***wife:*** 5 Doris

Nergal ***brother:*** 5 Nanna 6 Ninazu ***father:*** 5 Enlil ***mother:*** 6 Ninlil

Neriah ***father:*** 8 Maaseiah ***son:*** 6 Baruch 7 Seraiah

Nerissa's husband 8 Gratiano

Nero ***birthplace:*** 4 Rome ***mother:*** 9 Agrippina ***successor:*** 5 Galba ***victim:*** 5 Lucan 6 Seneca 7 Octavia, Poppaea 9 Agrippina ***wife:*** 7 Octavia, Poppaea

Nero Wolfe creator 5 Stout (Rex)

nerve 4 face, gall, grit, guts, sand, vein 5 brass, cheek, cheer, crust, heart, moxie, spunk, steel 6 daring 7 animate, chirk up, hearten, sciatic, stamina 8 audacity, backbone, boldness, embolden, inspirit, strength, temerity 9 assurance, brashness, encourage, enhearten, fortitude, hardihood, hardiness 10 confidence, effrontery, strengthen 11 presumption ***cell:*** 6 neuron ***cell group:*** 7 ganglia (plural) 8 ganglion ***combining form:*** 4 neur 5 neura, neuro ***cranial:*** 4 vagi (plural) 5 optic, vagus 8 abducens ***ending:*** 8 receptor ***lesion:*** 8 neuritis

nerve center 3 hub 4 seat 5 focus, heart 8 polestar 10 focal point

nervous 4 edgy 5 jerky, jumpy, timid 6 feisty, goosey, spooky 7 fidgety, fretful, jittery, uptight, waspish 8 aflutter, agitated, critical, forcible, skittery, skittish, snappish, spirited, twittery, unsteady, volatile 9 difficult, excitable, irritable, querulous, unrestful 10 high-strung 12 apprehensive

nervy 4 bold, edgy, pert, wise 5 brash, fresh, jerky, jumpy, sassy, smart, tense 6 cheeky, goosey, spooky, uneasy 7 fidgety, forward, jittery, restive, twitchy, uptight 8 impudent, intrepid, twittery 9 excitable, unrestful 10 high-strung 11 smart-alecky

ness 4 cape 8 headland 10 promontory

Nessus' victim 8 Heracles, Hercules

nest 3 den 4 aery, home, lair, nidi (plural) 5 aerie, eyrie, nidus 6 nidify 7 hangout, shelter 8 smuggery 11 aggregation ***eagle's:*** 4 aery 5 aerie, eyrie ***wasp's:*** 8 vespiary

nest egg 5 hoard, stock, store 7 backlog, reserve 9 inventory, reservoir, stockpile

nestle 4 snug 5 house 6 burrow, cuddle, nuzzle 7 shelter, snuggle

Nestor ***father:*** 6 Neleus ***kingdom:*** 5 Pylos

net 4 gain, gist, make, mesh, pure 5 basic, catch, clear, seine, tulle, yield 6 maline 7 clean up, essence, malines ***combining***

form: 5 dicty 6 dictyo ***conical:*** 5 trawl ***fishing:*** 5 seine ***hair:*** 5 snood

Nethanel ***brother:*** 5 David ***father:*** 5 Jesse 7 Pashhur 8 Obededom ***son:*** 8 Shemaiah

Nethaniah's father 5 Asaph 6 Jehudi 7 Ishmael

nether 3 low 5 lower, under 6 lesser 8 inferior 9 subjacent

Netherlands ***capital:*** 9 Amsterdam ***de facto capital:*** 8 The Hague ***monetary unit:*** 6 florin, gulden 7 guilder ***patron saint:*** 10 Willibrord ***piano city:*** 3 Ede

netherworld 3 pit 4 hell 5 abyss, hades, Sheol 6 blazes 7 inferno 9 perdition 11 Pandemonium

netlike 9 reticular 10 reticulate

nettle 3 get, vex 4 huff, rile, roil 5 peeve, pique, upset 6 incite, put out, stir up 7 agitate, disturb, perturb, provoke 8 irritate 10 discompose, exasperate

nettle rash 5 hives 9 urticaria

nettlesome 5 spiny 6 thorny 7 prickly 9 irritable 10 irritating

network 3 web 4 mesh 8 gridiron 9 reticulum ***anatomical:*** 4 rete 5 retia (plural)

neurotic 6 phobic 7 nervous 8 unstable 9 obsessive 10 compulsive

neuter 3 fix 4 geld 5 alter, unsex 6 change, worker 7 sexless 8 castrate, mutilate 9 sterilize 11 desexualize 12 intransitive

neutral 4 calm, cool, easy 5 aloof 6 normal 7 hueless, relaxed 8 abstract, clinical, composed, detached, middling, unbiased 9 collected, colorless, impartial 10 achromatic, impersonal, nonchalant, pokerfaced 11 indifferent, unpassioned 13 disinterested, dispassionate

neutralize 5 annul 6 defeat, negate, offset, subdue 7 balance, conquer, nullify, redress 8 abrogate, negative, overcome, override, overrule 9 cancel out, frustrate 10 compensate, counteract, invalidate 11 countervail 12 countercheck, counterpoise

Nevada ***capital:*** 10 Carson City ***largest city:*** 8 Las Vegas ***nickname:*** 11 Silver State 14 Sagebrush State ***state flower:*** 9 sagebrush

névé 4 firn, snow

never-ending 7 endless, eternal 8 immortal 9 ceaseless 11 amaranthine, everlasting

never-failing 4 firm, sure 6 steady 7 abiding 8 enduring 9 steadfast 11 unfaltering, unqualified 12 wholehearted 13 unquestioning

nevertheless 3 but, yet 5 still 6 though, withal 7 howbeit, however 8 after all 11 still and all

nevus 4 mole 9 birthmark

new 5 fresh, novel 6 afresh, lately, modern, of late, recent 7 another, revived, strange 8 neoteric, pristine 9 first-hand, recreated, refreshed, renovated 10 additional, unfamiliar 11 modernistic, regenerated 12 unaccustomed 13 reinvigorated ***combining form:*** 2 ne 3 cen, neo, nov 4 caen, ceno, novo 5 caeno ***word:*** 7 coinage, neology 9 neologism

newcomer 4 colt, tyro 6 novice, rookie 8 beginner, chechako, freshman, neophyte 9 immigrant, novitiate 10 apprentice, tenderfoot

New Deal agency 3 CCC, NRA, TVA, WPA

Newfoundland ***capital:*** 10 Saint Johns ***discoverer:*** 5 Cabot (John) ***part:*** 8 Labrador

new gas 4 neon

New Hampshire ***capital:*** 7 Concord ***college:*** 9 Dartmouth 10 Keene State 12 Saint Anselms ***highest point:*** 12 Mt. Washington ***largest city:*** 10 Manchester ***motto:*** 13 Live Free or Die ***nickname:*** 12 Granite State ***state bird:*** 11 purple finch ***state flower:*** 11 purple lilac

New Jersey ***capital:*** 7 Trenton ***college, university:*** 4 Drew 6 Upsala 7 Rutgers 9 Princeton, Seton Hall 10 Bloomfield 11 Saint Peters ***largest city:*** 6 Newark ***nickname:*** 11 Garden State ***state bird:*** 9 goldfinch ***state flower:*** 6 violet

New Mexico ***capital:*** 7 Santa Fe ***largest city:*** 11 Albuquerque ***state bird:*** 10 roadrunner ***state flower:*** 5 yucca

news 4 dope, poop, word 5 rumor 6 advice, gossip, report, tattle 7 lowdown, tidings 9 knowledge, speerings 11 information, scuttlebutt 12 announcement, intelligence ***agency:*** 2 AP 3 UPI 4 Tass 7 Reuters

newspaper 5 daily, organ 6 review 7 journal, tabloid 8 magazine 10 periodical ***publisher:*** 6 Hearst

newt 3 eft 6 triton ***green:*** 5 ebbet

New Testament see at **Bible**

New York ***academy, college, (university):*** 3 RPI 4 Iona, Pace, SUNY 5 Keuka, Kings, Nyack, Pratt, Siena, Utica 6 CW Post, Elmira, Hunter, Ithaca, Marist, Queens, Vassar 7 Adelphi, Colgate, Cornell, Fordham, Hofstra, Niagara, St. Johns, Yeshiva 8 Brooklyn, Canisius, Columbia, Hamilton, Hartwick, Skidmore, Syracuse 9 Juilliard, Manhattan, St. Francis, St. Josephs, West Point 10 Long Island 13 Sarah Lawrence, St. Bonaventure ***capital:*** 6 Albany ***motto:*** 9 Excelsior 10 Ever Upward ***nickname:*** 11 Empire State ***state flower:*** 4 rose

New York City 6 Gotham ***borough:***

5 Bronx 6 Queens 8 Brooklyn, Richmond 9 Manhattan

New Zealand *capital:* 10 Wellington *discoverer:* 6 Tasman *monetary unit:* 6 dollar *parrot:* 3 kea

next 4 then 5 after, below, infra, later, since 6 behind, coming, second 7 by and by, closest, ensuing 8 latterly 9 afterward, following, proximate 10 afterwhile, contiguous, succeeding

nexus 3 tie 4 bond, knot, link, yoke 8 ligament, ligature, vinculum 10 connection

Nez Percé chief 6 Joseph

niagara 5 flood, spate 6 deluge 7 torrent 8 cataract, flooding, overflow 9 cataclysm 10 inundation

nib 4 beak, bill 5 tooth 6 pecker 8 pen point

nibble 4 bite, gnaw, peck, pick

Nicanor's father 9 Patroclus

Nicaragua *capital:* 7 Managua *monetary unit:* 7 cordoba *neighbor:* 8 Honduras 9 Costa Rica

nice 4 fine, good, mild, neat, rare, sage, wise 5 exact, fussy, picky, right, rigid 6 benign, chaste, choosy, comely, dainty, decent, proper, queasy, seemly, strict, subtle 7 affable, careful, clement, correct, finical, finicky, fitting, precise, refined, welcome 8 accurate, becoming, clerkish, decorous, delicate, finespun, hairline, picksome, pleasant, pleasing, precieux, precious, rigorous, suitable, virtuous 9 agreeable, befitting, congenial, enjoyable, exquisite, favorable, finicking, judicious 10 attractive, conforming, delightful, discerning, fastidious, gratifying, meticulous, oldmaidish, particular, pernickety, personable, scrupulous

niche 4 nook 5 place 6 cranny, crater, nestle, recess 7 byplace, secrete

Nicholas Nickleby author 7 Dickens

nick 4 deny, hack 5 cut in, notch, score, snipe 6 charge, record 9 indenture 11 indentation

nickname 3 tag 5 label, style 6 byword, handle 7 epithet, miscall, moniker 8 cognomen 9 sobriquet 10 hypocorism

Nicomede *conquest:* 10 Cappodocia *dramatist:* 9 Corneille *half-brother:* 6 Attale *stepmother:* 7 Arsinoë

nictate 3 bat 4 wink 5 blink 7 twinkle

nictitate see nictate

nifty 4 cool, keen, neat 5 adept, dandy, dilly, handy, peach, smart, super, swell 6 clever, corker, groovy, peachy 7 stylish 8 jim-dandy, knockout, splendid, terrific

Niger *capital:* 6 Niamey *export:* 7 uranium *monetary unit:* 5 franc

Nigeria *capital:* 5 Lagos *monetary unit:* 5 naira *people:* 3 Ibo 4 Igbo *product:* 3 tin 4 coal 5 cocoa 6 rubber

niggard 5 miser

niggardly 5 close, tight 6 scanty, stingy 7 miserly 9 penurious 11 closefisted, tightfisted 12 cheeseparing, parsimonious 13 penny-pinching

niggling 5 petty 6 measly, paltry, peanut 8 picayune, piddling, trifling 10 picayunish

nigh 2 by 4 near 5 about, circa, close, round 6 all but, almost, around, beside, nearby, nearly 7 close on 8 approach 9 immediate, proximate 10 near-at-hand 11 approximate, at close hand, practically

night blindness 10 nyctalopia

nightfall 3 eve 4 dusk, even 6 sunset 7 evening, sundown 8 eventide, gloaming, owl-light, twilight

nighthawk 6 petrel 7 bullbat 10 goatsucker *Australian:* 8 morepork

nightingale 6 thrush

nightjar 5 potoo 10 goatsucker

nightly 9 nocturnal

nightmare 5 dream, fancy, worry 6 vision 7 fantasy, incubus 8 daydream, phantasm, phantasy, succubus 12 apprehension

nightshade 7 henbane 10 belladonna *weedy:* 11 bittersweet

nightstick 3 bat 4 club, mace 5 baton, billy 6 cudgel 8 bludgeon 9 billy club, truncheon

Nike *father:* 6 Pallas *mother:* 4 Styx

nil 4 zero 6 naught, nought 7 nothing 11 nonexistent

Nile 6 Al-Bahr *dam:* 6 Makwar 9 Aswan High 10 Gebel Aulia *explorer:* 5 Baker (Sir Samuel), Bruce (James), Grant (J. A.), Speke (J. H.) *queen:* 4 Cleo 9 Cleopatra *section:* 4 Abai, Abay 5 Abbai

nilgai 8 antelope, blue bull

nimble 3 yar 4 deft, spry, yare 5 agile, alert, brisk, catty, fleet, handy, light, quick, zippy 6 active, adroit, brisky, clever, limber, lively 8 vigilant, watchful 9 dexterous, lightsome, sprightly, wide-awake

nimble-witted 3 hep 4 wise 5 canny, quick, sharp, slick, smart 7 knowing

Nimrod 6 hunter *father:* 4 Cush

Ninazu *brother:* 5 Nanna 6 Nergal *father:* 5 Enlil *mother:* 6 Ninlil

nincompoop 3 ass 4 fool, jerk 5 idiot, ninny 6 donkey 7 jackass, tomfool 8 imbecile 9 simpleton

nine 12 baseball team *combining form:* 3 non 4 nona 5 ennea *goddesses:* 5 Muses *group:* 6 ennead *inches:* 4 span *instruments:* 5 nonet

nine day devotion 6 novena

Nine Worlds 3 Hel 6 Asgard 7 Alfheim,

Midgard **8** Niflheim, Vanaheim **10** Jotunnheim **12** Muspellsheim **13** Svartalfaheim

ninny see nincompoop

Ninsun's son **9** Gilgamesh

ninth ***combining form:*** **3** non **4** nona

Nintu ***consort:*** **4** Enki ***son:*** **6** Ninsar

Ninurta ***father:*** **5** Enlil ***victim:*** **3** Kur

Ninus ***father:*** **5** Belus ***wife:*** **9** Semiramis

Niobe ***brother:*** **6** Pelops ***father:*** **8** Tantalus ***husband:*** **7** Amphion ***sister-in-law:*** **5** Aedon

nip **3** bit, dig, hop, nab **4** balk, dart, dash, dram, drop, hook, jolt, jump, lift, nail, peck, shot, slug, soak, swig **5** blast, booze, check, chill, clamp, drink, hurry, pinch, sever, snort, steal, swill **6** arrest, blight, guzzle, imbibe, snatch, tank up, thwart, tipple **7** cabbage, snifter, swizzle **8** compress, cutpurse, liquor up, piquancy, toothful **9** frustrate **10** pickpocket

nipper **3** bud, kid **4** rack **5** chick, child **6** cunner, moppet **8** brakeman, juvenile, young one **9** youngling, youngster

nipping **3** icy **4** cold, cool **5** chill, sharp **6** arctic, chilly, frosty **7** caustic, glacial, shivery **8** freezing

nipple **3** pap **4** teat **8** mammilla ***combining form:*** **4** mast **5** masto **6** papill **7** papillo

nipple-shaped **9** mammiform

Nippon **5** Japan

nippy see nipping

nirvana **4** Zion **5** bliss, dream **6** Canaan, heaven **7** elysium **8** empyrean, oblivion, paradise **10** Civitas Dei **12** New Jerusalem

nisse **3** elf, fay **5** fairy, pixie **6** kobold, sprite **7** brownie

Nisus ***betrayer, daughter:*** **6** Scylla ***father:*** **7** Pandion

nitid **6** bright, glossy **8** lustrous

nitrogen **5** azote ***combining form:*** **2** az **3** azo

nitwit **4** dope, simp **5** cluck, dunce **7** pinhead **9** dumb bunny, dumb cluck, simpleton

nix **2** no **3** nay **4** kill, nope, veto **6** naught, nought **7** nothing **8** negative

Njord, Njorth ***daughter:*** **5** Freya ***son:*** **4** Frey ***wife:*** **6** Skadhi, Skathi

no **3** nae, nay, nix **6** denial ***combining form:*** **5** nulli

no-account see no-good

Noachian **3** old **4** aged **5** hoary **6** age-old **7** ancient, antique **8** timeworn **9** venerable **12** antediluvian

Noah ***father:*** **6** Lamech **10** Zelophehad ***grandson:*** **4** Aram **6** Canaan ***great grandson:*** **3** Hul ***landing place:*** **6** Ararat ***son:*** **3** Ham **4** Shem **6** Canaan **7** Japheth

Nobel Prize Winner

chemistry:

1902: **7** Fischer ***1903:*** **9** Arrhenius ***1904:*** **6** Ramsay ***1905:*** **9** von Baeyer ***1906:*** **7** Moissan ***1907:*** **7** Buchner ***1908:*** **10** Rutherford ***1909:*** **7** Ostwald ***1910:*** **7** Wallach ***1911:*** **5** Curie ***1912:*** **8** Grignard, Sabatier ***1913:*** **6** Werner ***1914:*** **8** Richards ***1915:*** **11** Willstatter ***1918:*** **5** Haber ***1920:*** **6** Nernst ***1921:*** **5** Soddy ***1922:*** **5** Aston ***1923:*** **5** Pregl ***1925:*** **9** Zsigmondy ***1926:*** **8** Svedberg ***1927:*** **7** Wieland ***1928:*** **7** Windaus ***1929:*** **6** Harden ***1930:*** **7** Fischer ***1931:*** **5** Bosch **7** Bergius ***1932:*** **8** Langmuir ***1934:*** **4** Urey ***1935:*** **11** Joliot-Curie ***1936:*** **5** Debye ***1937:*** **6** Karrer **7** Haworth ***1938:*** **4** Kuhn ***1939:*** **7** Ruzicka **9** Butenandt ***1943:*** **6** Hevesy ***1944:*** **4** Hahn ***1945:*** **8** Virtanen ***1946:*** **6** Sumner **7** Stanley **8** Northrup ***1947:*** **8** Robinson ***1948:*** **8** Tiselius ***1949:*** **7** Giauque ***1950:*** **5** Alder, Diels ***1951:*** **7** Seaborg **8** McMillan ***1952:*** **5** Synge **6** Martin ***1953:*** **10** Staudinger ***1954:*** **7** Pauling ***1955:*** **10** du Vigneaud ***1956:*** **7** Semenov **11** Hinshelwood ***1957:*** **4** Todd ***1958:*** **6** Sanger ***1959:*** **9** Heyrovsky ***1960:*** **5** Libby ***1961:*** **6** Calvin ***1962:*** **6** Perutz **7** Kendrew ***1963:*** **7** Ziegler ***1964:*** **7** Hodgkin ***1965:*** **8** Woodward ***1966:*** **8** Mulliken ***1967:*** **5** Eigen **6** Porter **7** Norrish ***1968:*** **7** Onsager ***1969:*** **6** Barton, Hassel ***1970:*** **6** Leloir ***1971:*** **8** Herzberg ***1972:*** **5** Moore, Stein **8** Anfinsen ***1973:*** **7** Fischer **9** Wilkinson ***1974:*** **5** Flory ***1975:*** **6** Prelog **9** Cornforth ***1976:*** **8** Lipscomb ***1977:*** **9** Prigogine ***1978:*** **8** Mitchell ***1979:*** **5** Brown **6** Wittig ***1980:*** **4** Berg **6** Sanger **7** Gilbert ***1981:*** **5** Fukui **8** Hoffmann ***1982:*** **4** Klug ***1983:*** **5** Taube ***1984:*** **10** Merrifield ***1985:*** **5** Karle **8** Hauptman ***1986:*** **3** Lee **7** Polanyi **10** Herschbach ***1987:*** **4** Cram, Lehn **8** Pederson ***1988:*** **5** Huber **6** Michel **11** Deisenhofer ***1989:*** **4** Cech **6** Altman ***1990:*** **5** Corey

economics:

1969: **6** Frisch **9** Tinbergen ***1970:*** **9** Samuelson ***1971:*** **7** Kuznets ***1972:*** **5** Arrow, Hicks ***1973:*** **8** Leontief ***1974:*** **5** Hayek **6** Myrdal ***1975:*** **8** Koopmans **11** Kantorovich ***1976:*** **8** Friedman ***1977:*** **5** Meade, Ohlin ***1978:*** **5** Simon ***1979:*** **5** Lewis **7** Schultz ***1980:*** **5** Klein ***1981:*** **5** Tobin ***1982:*** **7** Stigler ***1983:*** **6** Debreu ***1984:*** **5** Stone ***1985:*** **10** Modigliani ***1986:*** **8** Buchanan ***1987:*** **5** Solow ***1988:*** **6** Allais ***1989:*** **8** Haavelmo ***1990:*** **6** Miller, Sharpe **9** Markowitz

literature:

1901: **9** Prudhomme ***1902:*** **7** Mommsen ***1903:*** **8** Bjornson ***1904:*** **7** Mistral

9 Echegaray ***1905:*** 11 Sienkiewicz ***1906:*** 8 Carducci ***1907:*** 7 Kipling ***1908:*** 6 Eucken ***1909:*** 8 Lagerlof ***1910:*** 8 von Heyse ***1911:*** 11 Maeterlinck ***1912:*** 9 Hauptmann ***1913:*** 6 Tagore ***1915:*** 7 Rolland ***1916:*** 13 von Heidenstam ***1917:*** 9 Gjellerup 11 Pontoppidan ***1919:*** 9 Spitteler ***1920:*** 6 Hamsun ***1921:*** 6 France ***1922:*** 9 Benavente ***1923:*** 5 Yeats ***1924:*** 7 Reymont ***1925:*** 4 Shaw ***1926:*** 7 Deledda ***1927:*** 7 Bergson ***1928:*** 6 Undset ***1929:*** 4 Mann ***1930:*** 5 Lewis ***1931:*** 9 Karlfeldt ***1932:*** 10 Galsworthy ***1933:*** 5 Bunin ***1934:*** 10 Pirandello ***1936:*** 6 O'Neill ***1937:*** 12 Martin du Gard ***1938:*** 4 Buck ***1939:*** 9 Sillanpaa ***1944:*** 6 Jensen ***1945:*** 7 Mistral ***1946:*** 5 Hesse ***1947:*** 4 Gide ***1948:*** 5 Eliot ***1949:*** 8 Faulkner ***1950:*** 7 Russell ***1951:*** 10 Lagerkvist ***1952:*** 7 Mauriac ***1953:*** 9 Churchill ***1954:*** 9 Hemingway ***1955:*** 7 Laxness ***1956:*** 7 Jimenez ***1957:*** 5 Camus ***1958:*** 9 Pasternak ***1959:*** 9 Quasimodo ***1960:*** 5 Perse ***1961:*** 6 Andric ***1962:*** 9 Steinbeck ***1963:*** 7 Seferis ***1964:*** 6 Sartre ***1965:*** 9 Sholokhov ***1966:*** 5 Agnon, Sachs ***1967:*** 8 Asturias ***1968:*** 8 Kawabata ***1969:*** 7 Beckett ***1970:*** 12 Solzhenitsyn ***1971:*** 6 Neruda ***1972:*** 4 Böll ***1973:*** 5 White ***1974:*** 7 Johnson 9 Martinson ***1975:*** 7 Montale ***1976:*** 6 Bellow ***1977:*** 10 Aleixandre ***1978:*** 6 Singer ***1979:*** 6 Elytis ***1980:*** 6 Milosz ***1981:*** 7 Canetti ***1982:*** 13 Garcia Marquez ***1983:*** 7 Golding ***1984:*** 7 Siefert ***1985:*** 5 Simon ***1986:*** 7 Soyinka ***1987:*** 7 Brodsky ***1988:*** 7 Mahfouz ***1989:*** 4 Cela ***1990:*** 3 Paz

peace:
1901: 6 Dunant ***1902:*** 5 Gobat 8 Ducommun ***1903:*** 6 Cremer ***1905:*** 10 von Suttner ***1906:*** 9 Roosevelt ***1907:*** 6 Moneta 7 Renault ***1908:*** 5 Bajer 9 Arnoldson ***1909:*** 9 Beernaert ***1911:*** 5 Asser, Fried ***1912:*** 4 Root ***1913:*** 10 La Fontaine ***1919:*** 6 Wilson ***1920:*** 9 Bourgeois ***1921:*** 5 Lange 8 Branting ***1922:*** 6 Nansen ***1925:*** 5 Dawes 11 Chamberlain ***1926:*** 6 Briand 10 Stresemann ***1927:*** 6 Quidde 7 Buisson ***1929:*** 7 Kellogg ***1930:*** 9 Soderblom ***1931:*** 6 Addams, Butler ***1933:*** 6 Angell ***1934:*** 9 Henderson ***1935:*** 9 Ossietzky ***1936:*** 13 Saavedra Lamas ***1937:*** 5 Cecil ***1945:*** 4 Hull ***1946:*** 4 Mott 5 Balch ***1949:*** 3 Orr ***1950:*** 6 Bunche ***1951:*** 7 Jauhaux ***1952:*** 10 Schweitzer ***1953:*** 8 Marshall ***1957:*** 7 Pearson ***1958:*** 4 Pire ***1959:*** 9 Noel-Baker ***1960:*** 7 Luthuli ***1961:*** 12 Hammarskjold ***1962:*** 7 Pauling ***1964:*** 4 King ***1968:*** 6 Cassin ***1970:*** 7 Borlaug ***1971:*** 6 Brandt ***1973:*** 8 Le Duc Tho 9 Kissinger ***1974:*** 4 Sato 8 MacBride ***1975:*** 8 Sakharov ***1976:*** 8 Corrigan, Williams ***1978:*** 5 Begin, Sadat ***1979:*** 12 Mother Teresa ***1980:*** 8 Esquivel ***1982:*** 6 Myrdal 12 Garcia Robles ***1983:*** 6 Walesa ***1984:*** 4 Tutu ***1986:*** 6 Wiesel ***1987:*** 12 Arias Sanchez ***1989:*** 9 Dalai Lama ***1990:*** 9 Gorbachev

physics:
1901: 8 Roentgen ***1902:*** 6 Zeeman 7 Lorentz ***1903:*** 5 Curie 9 Becquerel ***1904:*** 6 Strutt ***1905:*** 6 Lenard ***1906:*** 7 Thomson ***1907:*** 9 Michelson ***1908:*** 8 Lippmann ***1909:*** 5 Braun 7 Marconi ***1910:*** 11 van der Waals ***1911:*** 4 Wien ***1912:*** 5 Dalen ***1914:*** 7 von Laue ***1915:*** 5 Bragg ***1917:*** 6 Barkla ***1918:*** 6 Planck ***1919:*** 5 Stark ***1920:*** 9 Guillaume ***1921:*** 8 Einstein ***1922:*** 4 Bohr ***1923:*** 8 Millikan ***1924:*** 8 Siegbahn ***1925:*** 5 Hertz 6 Franck ***1926:*** 6 Perrin ***1927:*** 6 Wilson 7 Compton ***1928:*** 10 Richardson ***1929:*** 7 Broglie ***1930:*** 5 Raman ***1932:*** 10 Heisenberg ***1933:*** 5 Dirac 11 Schrodinger ***1935:*** 8 Chadwick ***1936:*** 4 Hess 8 Anderson ***1937:*** 7 Thomson 8 Davisson ***1938:*** 5 Fermi ***1939:*** 8 Lawrence ***1943:*** 5 Stern ***1944:*** 4 Rabi ***1945:*** 5 Pauli ***1946:*** 8 Bridgman ***1947:*** 8 Appleton ***1948:*** 8 Blackett ***1949:*** 6 Yukawa ***1950:*** 6 Powell ***1951:*** 6 Walton 9 Cockcroft ***1952:*** 5 Bloch 7 Purcell ***1953:*** 7 Zernike ***1954:*** 4 Born 5 Bothe ***1955:*** 4 Lamb 5 Kusch ***1956:*** 7 Bardeen 8 Brattain, Shockley ***1957:*** 3 Lee 4 Yang ***1958:*** 4 Tamm 5 Frank 9 Cherenkov ***1959:*** 5 Segre 11 Chamberlain ***1960:*** 6 Glaser ***1961:*** 9 Mossbauer 10 Hofstadter ***1962:*** 6 Landau ***1963:*** 5 Mayer 6 Jensen, Wigner ***1964:*** 5 Basov 6 Townes 9 Prochorov ***1965:*** 7 Feynman 8 Tomonaga 9 Schwinger ***1966:*** 7 Kastler ***1967:*** 5 Bethe ***1968:*** 7 Alvarez ***1969:*** 8 Gell-Mann ***1970:*** 4 Neel 6 Alfven ***1971:*** 5 Gabor ***1972:*** 6 Cooper 7 Bardeen 10 Schrieffer ***1973:*** 5 Esaki 7 Giaever 9 Josephson ***1974:*** 4 Ryle 6 Hewish ***1975:*** 4 Bohr 9 Mottelson, Rainwater ***1976:*** 4 Ting 7 Richter ***1977:*** 4 Mott 8 Anderson, Van Vleck ***1978:*** 6 Wilson 7 Kapitsa, Penzias ***1979:*** 5 Salam 7 Glashow 8 Weinberg ***1980:*** 5 Fitch 6 Cronin ***1981:*** 8 Schaalow, Siegbahn 11 Bloembergen ***1982:*** 6 Wilson ***1983:*** 6 Fowler 13 Chandrasekhar ***1984:*** 6 Rubbia 11 van der Meere ***1985:*** 8 Klitzing ***1986:*** 5 Ruska 6 Binnig, Rohrer ***1987:*** 6 Muller 7 Bed-

norz *1988:* 8 Lederman, Schwartz 11 Steinberger *1989:* 4 Paul 6 Ramsey 7 Dehmelt *1990:* 6 Taylor 7 Kendall 8 Friedman

physiology or medicine:
1901: 10 von Behring *1902:* 4 Ross *1903:* 6 Finsen *1904:* 6 Pavlov *1905:* 4 Koch *1906:* 5 Golgi 11 Ramon y Cajal *1907:* 7 Laveran *1908:* 7 Ehrlich 11 Metchnikoff *1909:* 6 Kocher *1910:* 6 Kossel *1911:* 10 Gullstrand *1912:* 6 Carrel *1913:* 6 Richet *1914:* 6 Barany *1919:* 6 Bordet *1920:* 5 Krogh *1922:* 4 Hill 8 Meyerhof *1923:* 7 Banting, Macleod *1924:* 9 Einthoven *1926:* 7 Fibiger *1927:* 13 Wagner-Jauregg *1928:* 7 Nicolle *1929:* 7 Eijkman, Hopkins *1930:* 11 Landsteiner *1931:* 7 Warburg *1932:* 6 Adrian 11 Sherrington *1933:* 6 Morgan *1934:* 5 Minot 6 Murphy 7 Whipple *1935:* 7 Spemann *1936:* 4 Dale 5 Loewi *1937:* 12 Szent-Gyorgyi *1938:* 7 Heymans *1939:* 6 Domagk *1943:* 3 Dam 5 Doisy *1944:* 6 Gasser 8 Erlanger *1945:* 5 Chain 6 Florey 7 Fleming *1946:* 6 Muller *1947:* 4 Cori 7 Houssay *1948:* 7 Mueller *1949:* 4 Hess 5 Moniz *1950:* 5 Hench 7 Kendall 10 Reichstein *1951:* 7 Theiler *1952:* 7 Waksman *1953:* 5 Krebs 7 Lipmann *1954:* 6 Enders, Weller 7 Robbins *1955:* 8 Theorell *1956:* 8 Cournand, Richards 9 Forssmann *1957:* 5 Bovet *1958:* 5 Tatum 6 Beadle 9 Lederberg *1959:* 5 Ochoa 8 Kornberg *1960:* 6 Burnet 7 Medawar *1961:* 6 Bekesy *1962:* 5 Crick 6 Watson 7 Wilkins *1963:* 6 Eccles, Huxley 7 Hodgkin *1964:* 5 Bloch, Lynen *1965:* 5 Jacob, Monod 6 Lwolff *1966:* 4 Rous 7 Huggins *1967:* 4 Wald 6 Granit 8 Hartline *1968:* 6 Holley 7 Khorana 9 Nirenberg *1969:* 5 Luria 7 Hershey 8 Delbruck *1970:* 4 Katz 5 Euler 7 Axelrod *1971:* 10 Sutherland *1972:* 6 Porter 7 Edelman *1973:* 6 Frisch, Lorenz 9 Tinbergen *1974:* 4 Duve 6 Claude, Palade *1975:* 5 Temin 8 Dulbecco 9 Baltimore *1976:* 8 Blumberg, Gajdusek *1977:* 5 Yalow 7 Schally 9 Guillemin *1978:* 5 Arber, Smith 7 Nathans *1979:* 7 Cormack 10 Hounsfield *1980:* 5 Snell 7 Dausset 10 Benacerraf *1981:* 5 Hubel 6 Sperry, Wiesel *1982:* 4 Vane 9 Bergstrom 10 Samuelsson *1983:* 10 McClintock *1984:* 5 Jerne 7 Koehler 8 Milstein *1985:* 5 Brown 9 Goldstein *1986:* 5 Cohen 14 Levi-Montalcini *1987:* 8 Tonegawa *1988:* 5 Black, Elion 9 Hitchings *1989:* 6 Bishop, Varmus *1990:* 6 Murray, Thomas

Nobel's invention 8 dynamite

nobility 7 peerage, royalty 8 eminence, noblesse 11 aristocracy, superiority

noble 4 peer 5 grand, lofty, moral 6 august, lordly, worthy 7 eminent, ethical, stately 8 baronial, elevated, heroical, highborn, highbred, imposing, magnific, majestic, princely, sterling, virtuous, wellborn 9 estimable, excellent, grandiose, honorable, righteous 10 high-minded, impressive, moralistic, principled 11 illustrious, magnificent, outstanding, right-minded 12 aristocratic

nobleman 4 duke, peer 5 baron 6 prince 7 baronet 8 principe ***British:*** 4 earl 8 viscount ***European:*** 7 marquis 8 marquess ***French:*** 5 comte 7 vicomte ***German:*** 4 Graf 8 burgrave, margrave 9 landgrave ***Indian:*** 6 sardar, sirdar 8 maharaja ***Italian:*** 8 marchese ***Japanese (former):*** 6 daimio, daimyo ***Scandinavian:*** 4 jarl ***Spanish:*** 7 hidalgo

noblewoman 4 lady 7 baronne, duchess, peeress 8 baroness, countess, princess ***European:*** 8 marquise ***Italian:*** 8 marchesa

nobody 4 none, zero 5 no man, no one, zilch 6 cipher 7 nothing, nullity, whiffet 8 whipster 9 nonentity

nocturnal 5 night 7 nightly 10 night piece

nocuous 3 bad, ill 6 nocent 7 harmful, hurtful 8 damaging 9 injurious 11 deleterious, detrimental, mischievous

nodding 4 dozy 6 drowsy, sleepy, snoozy 8 slumbery 9 pendulous, somnolent, soporific 10 slumberous

noddle 4 bean, head, poll 6 noggin 9 headpiece

noddy 4 dope, fool, jack, tern 5 dunce, stupe 6 fulmar, noodle 7 schnook 8 dumbhead 9 lamebrain, razorbill, simpleton

node 4 knob 5 point 11 predicament 12 entanglement, protuberance

nog 3 ale, peg, pin 5 block

Nogah's father 5 David

noggin 4 bean, head, pate, poll 6 noddle, noodle

no-good 4 worm 6 bad lot, draffy, drossy, mucker, waster, wretch 7 inutile, lowlife, nothing, rounder, wastrel 8 unworthy, wormling 9 no-account, valueless, worthless 10 ne'er-do-well, profligate, scapegrace

Nohah's father 8 Benjamin

noise 3 din 4 blab, talk 5 babel, rumor, sound 6 clamor, gossip, hubbub, racket, ruckus, rumpus, tattle, uproar 7 ruction, sonance, stridor 8 resonant 11 pandemonium

noiseless 4 hush 5 quiet, still, whist 6 silent, stilly

noisemaker 4 horn 6 rattle 7 clapper

noisette 5 hazel

noisome 4 foul, rank, vile 5 dirty, fetid, funky, fusty, musty, nasty 6 filthy, horrid, putrid, rancid, sickly 7 harmful, noxious, squalid 8 nidorous, stinking 9 offensive, repulsive, revolting, sickening, unhealthy 10 disgusting, insalutary, malodorous, nauseating, unsalutary 11 destructive, distasteful, unhealthful 12 insalubrious

noisy 4 loud 7 blatant, clamant, rackety, squeaky 8 clattery, overloud, sonorous, strident 9 clamorous, turbulent 10 boisterous, clangorous, strepitous, tumultuous, uproarious, vociferous 12 obstreperous

nomad 6 roving *Arabic:* 6 beduin 7 bedouin

nomadic 6 roving 7 vagrant 8 vagabond 9 itinerant, itinerate, wandering, wayfaring 11 perambulant, peripatetic 13 perambulatory

nom de plume see **pen name**

nomen 4 name, noun 5 style, title 7 moniker 11 appellation, appellative, designation

nomenclature 4 list, name 7 catalog 9 designate 11 appellation, designation, terminology

nominal 5 rated 6 formal 7 alleged, seeming, titular 8 apparent, so-called, trifling 9 pretended, professed 10 ostensible 11 approximate 12 substantival 13 insignificant

nominate 3 tap 4 call, name 5 offer 6 tender 7 appoint, name off, present, proffer, propose, purpose

nonage 7 infancy 8 minority 10 immaturity

nonchalant 4 cool, easy, glad 5 light 6 casual, smooth 8 careless, cheerful, composed 9 collected, unruffled 10 effortless 11 unflappable 12 lighthearted 13 imperturbable

noncleric 4 laic 6 layman

nonclerical 3 lay

nonclerics 5 laity

noncommittal 7 neutral 8 reserved 10 restrained

nonconformist 5 rebel 6 hippie 7 beatnik, heretic, sectary 8 bohemian, maverick 9 dissenter, dissident, heretical, heterodox, sectarian 10 schismatic, separatist, unorthodox 11 misbeliever, schismatist

nonconformity 6 heresy, schism 7 dissent 9 misbelief 10 dissidence, heterodoxy 11 unorthodoxy 13 individualism

nonentity 4 zero 5 aught, zilch 6 cipher, nobody 7 nothing, nullity, sad sack, whiffet 8 small fry, unperson, whipster 9 obscurity, rushlight, small beer

nonesuch 5 ideal, jewel 7 paragon 9 matchless, nonpareil, unequaled, unrivaled

nonetheless 3 yet 5 still 6 though, withal 7 howbeit, however 8 after all 11 still and all

nonexistence 4 nada 7 nullity, vacuity 8 nihility 11 nothingness

nonflammable 7 apyrous 13 incombustible

nonfunctional 7 useless 8 unusable 10 unworkable 11 impractical 13 impracticable, unserviceable

non-Hawaiian 5 haole

non-Jew 3 goy 5 goyim (plural) 7 gentile

nonmilitary 8 civilian

non-Muslim 6 giaour

no-nonsense 5 grave, sober, staid 6 sedate, solemn, somber 7 earnest, serious, weighty 10 sobersided

nonpareil see **nonesuch**

nonpartisan 4 fair, just 9 equitable, impartial, objective, uncolored 11 indifferent 12 unprejudiced 13 undistinctive

nonplus 4 balk, beat, faze 5 stick, stump, throw 6 baffle, boggle, flurry, muddle, puzzle, rattle, stymie, thwart 7 buffalo, confuse, dilemma, fluster, mystify, perplex, stagger 8 confound, overcome, paralyze, quandary 9 dumbfound, frustrate

nonprofessional 3 lay 4 laic, tyro 7 amateur, dabbler 9 smatterer 10 dilettante 11 abecedarian

nonrational 3 mad 7 invalid 9 illogical, sophistic 10 fallacious, reasonless, unreasoned 12 unreasonable

nonreligious 3 lay 7 godless, profane, secular 8 temporal

nonresistant 7 passive 8 resigned, yielding 10 submissive 11 acquiescent

nonsense 3 rot 4 blah, bosh, bull, bunk, crap, gook, guff, jazz, punk, tosh 5 bilge, drool, folly, fudge, Greek, hokum, hooey, trash 6 babble, blague, bunkum, bushwa, drivel, hot air, humbug, jabber, piffle 7 baloney, blather, eyewash, flubdub, foolery, fooling, hogwash, inanity, rubbish, trifles, twaddle 8 buncombe, claptrap, falderal, falderol, flimflam, malarkey, pishposh, slipslop, tommyrot, trumpery 9 gibberish, moonshine, poppycock 10 applesauce, balderdash, double-talk, flapdoodle, meshuggaas, tomfoolery 11 jabberwocky, whangdoodle, windbaggery 12 blatherskite, fiddle-faddle, fiddlesticks, flummadiddle 13 horsefeathers *British:* 10 codswallop

nonsensical 5 inane 6 absurd 7 foolish 9 unmeaning 12 preposterous

nonsuccess 6 defeat 7 failure

nonviolent 6 irenic 7 pacific 8 pacifist, peaceful 9 peaceable 12 pacificatory

noodle 4 bean, dope, head, poll 5 chump, dunce, ninny, noddy, stupe 6 noggin 7 schnook 8 dumbhead 9 blockhead, lamebrain, simpleton 10 dunderhead

nook 4 cove, hole 5 niche 6 alcove, corner, cranny, recess 7 byplace 9 cubbyhole
Noon Wine author 6 Porter
noose 3 tie 4 bond, hang 5 lasso, scrag, snare 6 entrap, gibbet, secure 7 turn off 8 string up
Nordhoff's partner 4 Hall
norm 3 par 4 mean, type 5 maxim, model 6 median 7 average, pattern
Norma ***composer:*** 7 Bellini ***librettist:*** 6 Romani
normal 4 mean, sane 5 lucid, right, typic, usual 6 common 7 average, general, natural, regular, typical 8 all there, ordinary, standard 9 customary, prevalent 11 commonplace 12 compos mentis
Normandy's capital 5 Rouen
Norns 5 fates, Skuld, Urdur 9 Verthandi
Norris novel 4 Blix 6 The Pit 8 McTeague 10 The Octopus
Norse ***abode of the dead:*** 8 Niflheim ***alphabet:*** 5 Runic ***archer:*** 4 Egil ***bard:*** 5 scald, skald ***chieftain:*** 4 jarl, Rolf 5 Rollo ***demon:*** 4 Mara, Surt 5 Surtr ***dragon:*** 6 Fafnir 8 Nithhogg ***epic:*** 4 Edda ***explorer:*** 4 Eric 7 Ericson 8 Ericsson ***first man:*** 3 Ask 4 Askr ***first woman:*** 5 Embla ***giant:*** 4 Egil, Wade, Wate, Ymer, Ymir 5 Aegir, Egill, Hymir, Jotun, Mimir 6 Fafnir, Jotunn ***giantess:*** 4 Egia, Norn, Nott ***god:*** 2 As, Ve 3 Asa, Ass 4 Surt, Vali, Vili 5 Aesir (plural), Surtr, Vanir (plural) 6 Hoenir, Vithar 7 Vitharr ***blind:*** 4 Hoth 5 Hoder, Hodur, Hothr ***chief:*** 4 Odin 5 Othin, Wodan, Woden, Wotan ***guardian:*** 7 Heimdal 8 Heimdall 9 Heimdallr ***messenger:*** 6 Hermod 7 Hermodr ***of beauty:*** 5 Baldr 6 Balder, Baldur ***of evil:*** 4 Loke, Loki ***of fertility:*** 4 Frey 5 Freyr ***of justice:*** 7 Forsete, Forseti ***of light:*** 3 Dag ***of peace:*** 5 Baldr 6 Balder, Baldur ***of poetry:*** 5 Brage, Bragi ***of the hunt:*** 3 Ull 4 Ullr ***of the seas:*** 5 Njord 6 Njoerd, Njorth 4 Hler 5 Aegir, Gymir ***of the sky:*** 4 Odin 5 Othin ***of thunder:*** 4 Thor 5 Donar ***of war:*** 3 Tiu, Tiw, Tyr, Zio, Ziu ***wolf:*** 6 Fenrir ***goddess:*** 3 dis 4 Saga 5 disir (plural) 7 Asynjur ***of fate:*** 3 Urd 4 Norn, Urth, Wyrd 5 Skuld 9 Verthandi ***of healing:*** 3 Eir ***of love:*** 5 Freya ***of marriage:*** 5 Frigg 6 Frigga ***of night:*** 4 Natt, Nott ***of storms:*** 3 Ran ***of the earth:*** 5 Joerd, Jorth ***of the moon:*** 5 Nanna ***of the sea:*** 3 Ran ***of the sky:*** 5 Frigg 6 Frigga ***of the underworld:*** 3 Hel 4 Hela ***of youth:*** 4 Idun 5 Ithun 6 Ithunn ***gods' abode:*** 6 Asgard ***hall of heroes:*** 8 Valhalla ***king:*** 4 Atli, Olaf ***nobleman:*** 4 jarl ***patron saint:*** 4 Olaf ***poem:*** 4 rune ***poet:*** 5 scald, skald ***rainbow bridge:*** 7 Bifrost ***sea serpent:*** 4 Wade, Wate 6 kraken 7 Midgard ***smith:*** 6 Vōlund ***tale:*** 4 saga ***toast:*** 5 skoal ***watchdog:*** 4 Garm 5 Garmr ***world's destruction:*** 8 Ragnarok ***world tree:*** 8 Ygdrasil 10 Yggdrasill
north ***combining form:*** 4 arct 5 arcto
North African ***country:*** 5 Egypt, Libya 7 Algeria, Morocco, Tunisia ***fruit:*** 3 fig 4 date ***garment:*** 4 haik ***grass:*** 4 alfa 7 esparto ***jackal:*** 4 dieb ***language:*** 6 Arabic, Berber ***Muslim sect:*** 6 Sanusi 7 Senussi ***people:*** 6 Berber, Hamite 7 bedouin ***seaport:*** 4 Oran, Sfax 6 Annaba 7 Tangier 10 Casablanca
North America ***country:*** 4 Cuba 5 Haiti 6 Canada, Mexico, Panama 7 Bahamas, Grenada, Jamaica 8 Dominica, Honduras 9 Costa Rica, Guatemala, Nicaragua 10 El Salvador, Saint Lucia 12 United States ***ethnic group:*** 5 Negro 6 Indian 7 Mestizo, Spanish ***language:*** 6 Creole, French 7 English, Nahuatl, Spanish
North Carolina ***capital:*** 7 Raleigh ***college, university:*** 4 Duke, Elon 8 Davidson 10 Wake Forest ***largest city:*** 9 Charlotte ***nickname:*** 12 Tar Heel State ***state bird:*** 8 cardinal ***state flower:*** 7 dogwood
North Dakota ***capital:*** 8 Bismarck ***largest town:*** 5 Fargo ***nickname:*** 10 Sioux State
northern 4 pike 6 boreal 11 hyperborean
northern limit of the world 5 Thule
North Korea ***capital:*** 9 Pyongyang ***monetary unit:*** 3 won
North Star State 9 Minnesota
Northwest Passage author 7 Roberts
Northwest Territories ***capital:*** 11 Yellowknife ***district:*** 8 Franklin, Keewatin 9 Mackenzie
north wind see at wind
Norway ***capital:*** 4 Oslo ***inlet:*** 5 fiord, fjord ***monetary unit:*** 5 krone ***patron saint:*** 4 Olaf ***plateau region:*** 5 fjeld
Norwegian ***goblin:*** 5 nisse ***language:*** 5 Norse 6 Bokmal 7 Bokmaal, Nynorsk, Riksmal 8 Landsmal, Riksmaal 9 Landsmaal
nose 3 pry 4 beak, bent, bump, gift, head, poke 5 aroma, flair, knack, prier, pryer, scent, smell, sniff, snift, snoop, snoot, snout, snuff 6 butt-in, genius, muzzle, nuzzle, pecker, talent 7 aptness, faculty, meddler, Paul Pry, smeller, sneezer 8 busybody, kibitzer, quidnunc, smell out 9 olfaction, proboscis, schnozzle ***combining form:*** 3 nas 4 nasi, naso 5 rhina, rhine 6 rhinus, rrhine ***kind:*** 3 pug 5 Roman 8 aquiline ***lengthener:*** 3 lie ***opening:*** 7 nostril
nosebleed 6 yarrow 9 epistaxis
nose-dive 3 dip 4 drop, fall, skid 6 plunge, tumble 7 plummet
nosegay 4 posy 7 bouquet
nosey see nosy

nosh 5 snack
Nostradamus 5 augur 6 auspex 7 prophet 8 foreseer, haruspex 9 predictor 10 forecaster, foreteller, prophesier
Nostromo author 6 Conrad
nostrum 6 elixir 7 cure-all, panacea
nosy 5 peery 6 prying, snoopy 7 curious 9 intrusive 11 inquisitive, inquisitory
not *prefix:* 2 an, il, im, in, ir, un 3 ant, dis, non 4 anth, anti
notability 3 VIP 4 lion, name 5 celeb, chief 6 leader 7 big name, big shot 8 bigtimer, eminence, luminary, somebody 9 celebrity, dignitary
notable 3 big, VIP 4 czar, king, lion, name, star 5 baron, celeb, chief, famed, great, light, mogul, nabob, nawob, power 6 big boy, biggie, big gun, bigwig, famous, fat cat, figure, leader, prince, rubric 7 big name, big shot, eminent, magnate, mugwump, pooh-bah 8 big chief, big noise, bigtimer, big wheel, eminence, great gun, luminary, renowned, somebody, striking 9 big cheese, celebrity, character, dignitary, important, muckamuck, personage, prominent, red-letter 10 celebrated, celebrious, noteworthy 11 conspicuous, heavyweight, illustrious, personality 13 distinguished, high-muck-a-muck
notarize 7 certify 8 validate
notch 3 cut, gap, peg 4 gash, mark, nick, nock, rung, step 5 cleft, grade, score, stage 6 degree, indent, record 7 scratch 8 incision, undercut 9 indenture 10 depression 11 indentation
note 3 cry, jot, see 4 call, chit, heed, mark, memo, mood, odor, show, song, tone, view 5 motif, smell, sound, tenor 6 descry, letter, regard, remark 7 comment, discern, element, epistle, jotting, missive, observe 8 annotate, eminence, indicate, perceive, reminder 9 attention, knowledge 10 cognizance, commentary, memorandum, observance, reputation 11 distinction, distinguish, information, observation 12 obiter dictum
notebook 3 log 5 diary 6 cahier 7 journal
noted 6 famous 7 eminent, leading, popular 9 prominent, well-known
noteworthy 6 patent, rubric 7 evident, notable 8 manifest, nameable 9 memorable, prominent, red-letter 10 noticeable, observable, remarkable 11 conspicuous, exceptional, outstanding 12 considerable 13 extraordinary
nothing 3 nil, nix 4 zero 5 aught, nihil, ought, zilch 6 cipher, draffy, drossy, naught, nobody, no-good, nought, trifle 7 inutile, nullity, whiffet 8 goose egg, unworthy, whipster 9 bagatelle, no-account, nonentity, valueless, worthless *French:* 4 rien *German:* 6 nichts *Latin:* 5 nihil *Spanish:* 4 nada
nothingness 4 nada, void 5 death 6 vacuum 7 nullity, vacuity 8 nihility 9 emptiness 12 nonexistence
notice 2 ad 3 see 4 care, espy, heed, mark, memo 5 favor, grasp, greet, refer, sense, sight 6 advert, descry, regard, remark, review 7 comment, concern, discern, observe, respect, thought 8 civility, critique, perceive, reviewal 9 attention, criticism, directive, recognize 10 book review, cognizance, evaluation, memorandum, observance 11 acknowledge, distinguish, information, observation 12 announcement
noticeable 6 marked, patent, signal 7 evident, obvious, pointed, salient 8 manifest, striking 9 arresting, arrestive, prominent 10 noteworthy 11 conspicuous, eye-catching, outstanding, sensational, significant, spectacular
notify 4 clew, clue, post, tell, warn 6 advise, fill in, inform, reveal, signal, wise up 7 apprise, declare, divulge, publish 8 acquaint, announce, disclose, discover, proclaim 9 broadcast 10 promulgate
notion 4 clue, hint, idea, term, whim 5 fancy, freak, humor, image 6 maggot, phrase 7 boutade, caprice, conceit, concept, inkling, thought 8 crotchet, telltale 9 knowledge 10 impression, knickknack 12 apprehension 13 understanding
notional 5 ideal 6 unreal 7 fancied, shadowy 8 fanciful, imagined 9 crotchety, imaginary, visionary, whimsical 10 conceptual 11 theoretical
notorious 5 noted 6 famous 7 leading, popular 8 ill-famed, infamous 9 prominent, well-known
Nott's horse 8 Hrimfaxi
Notus 6 Auster *brother:* 5 Eurus 6 Boreas 8 Zephyrus *father:* 6 Aeolus 8 Astraeus *mother:* 3 Eos
noun 4 name 7 nominal 11 substantive *inflectional form:* 4 case *suffix:* 2 et, ia, ic 3 ent, ery, ier, ing, ion, ist 4 ence *verbal:* 6 gerund
nourish 4 rear 5 nurse, raise 6 foster, nursle, suckle 7 bring up, build up, nurture, support 8 maintain 9 cultivate 10 breastfeed, provide for, strengthen
nourishment 3 pap 4 food, keep 6 living 7 aliment, pabulum, support 8 nutrient 10 sustenance 11 maintenance
nouveau riche 7 parvenu, upstart 8 roturier 9 arriviste
Nova Scotia *capital:* 7 Halifax *original name:* 6 Acadia, Acadie
novel 3 new, odd 5 fresh 6 modern, recent, unique 7 special, strange, unusual 8 neoteric, original, peculiar, singular,

uncommon **9** different, new-sprung **10** newfangled, unfamiliar **11** modernistic **12** new-fashioned

novelty **5** curio, sport **6** bauble, change, gewgaw, trifle **7** bibelot, newness, trinket, whatnot **8** gimcrack, mutation **9** objet d'art **10** innovation, knickknack

novice **3** cub **4** boot, colt, punk, tyro **6** greeny, rookie **7** amateur, learner, recruit, student, trainee **8** beginner, freshman, inexpert, neophyte, newcomer, prentice **9** fledgling, greenhorn, novitiate, postulant **10** apprentice, tenderfoot

Novum Organum author **5** Bacon

now **2** as **3** for **4** away **5** since, today **6** at once, hereat, seeing **7** anymore, because, present, whereas **8** as long as, directly, existing, first off, up-to-date **9** forthwith, instanter, instantly, presently, right away, sometimes **10** inasmuch as **11** considering, immediately, straightway

now and again **7** at times, betimes **9** sometimes

now and then see **now and again**

Nox, Nyx ***brother:*** **6** Erebus ***daughter:*** **3** Day **4** Eris **5** Light ***father:*** **5** Chaos ***husband:*** **6** Erebus ***son:*** **6** Charon, Hypnos **8** Thanatos

noxious **5** fetid **6** deadly, putrid, sickly **7** baneful, noisome **8** stinking **9** pestilent, unhealthy **10** insalutary, unsalutary **11** distasteful, pestiferous, unhealthful, unwholesome

nozzle **5** eject, spray **9** nose about

nuance **4** dash **5** shade, tinge, touch **6** nicety **7** soupçon **8** subtlety **9** gradation, suspicion **10** refinement, suggestion

nub **4** core, crux, gist, knob, lump, meat, pith **5** point, short **6** kernel, upshot **9** substance **12** protuberance

Nubian **8** Cushitic

nucha **4** nape

nuclear agency **3** AEC, NRC

nuclear particle **6** proton **7** neutron

nucleus **3** bud **4** core, germ, head, kern, ring, seed **5** focus, spark **6** embryo ***material:*** **8** karyotin

Nudd's son **6** Edeyrn

nude **3** raw **4** bald, bare **5** naked, stark **6** peeled, unclad **7** unrobed **8** buff-bare, stripped **9** au naturel, unattired, unclothed, uncovered, undressed **10** dishabille, stark-naked **11** garmentless

nudge **3** dig, jab, jog, toe **4** near, poke, prod **5** punch **9** ease along

nugatory **4** idle, vain **5** empty **6** hollow, otiose **7** invalid **9** worthless

nugget **3** gob, wad **4** clod, hunk, lump **5** chunk, clump, hunch

nuisance **4** harm, pest **6** bother, injury, pester, plague **7** nudnick **8** irritant, pesterer **9** besetment **10** botherment **11** botheration **12** exasperation

null **3** bad, nil **4** knur, void, zero **5** annul, empty, knurl **7** destroy, expunge, invalid, useless **9** worthless **10** obliterate **11** ineffective, ineffectual, nonexistent **13** inefficacious, insignificant

nullify **4** undo **5** abate, annul, limit, quash **6** efface, negate, offset **7** abolish, confine, vitiate **8** abrogate, restrict **10** annihilate, compensate, counteract, invalidate, neutralize **11** countervail

nullity **4** nada, zero **5** zilch **6** cipher, nobody **7** nothing, vacuity, whiffet **8** whipster **9** annulment, nonentity **11** nothingness **12** nonexistence

numb **4** dead, dull, mull **5** aloof, blunt, chill, frost **6** asleep, casual, deaden, freeze, remote **8** comatose, deadened, detached **9** incurious, insensate, senseless, stupefied, uncurious, unfeeling **10** insensible, insentient **11** desensitize, indifferent, insensitive, unconcerned, unconscious **12** anesthetized, desensitized, uninterested

number **5** add up, count, digit, run to, sum to, tally, total **6** amount, cipher, come to, figure **7** chiffer, include, integer, numeral, numeric, ordinal, run into, several, sum into **8** cardinal, numerate, paginate **9** aggregate, enumerate ***added to another:*** **6** augend ***combining form:*** **7** arithmo ***large indeterminate:*** **7** zillion ***resulting from division:*** **8** quotient ***resulting from multiplication:*** **7** product ***resulting from subtraction:*** **10** difference ***science:*** **11** mathematics ***whole:*** **7** integer

number one **4** main **5** chief, major **6** Grade A **7** capital, stellar **8** dominant, five-star, foremost, superior **9** excellent, first-rate, front-rank, numero uno, top-drawer **10** blue-ribbon, first-class, preeminent **11** first-string, outstanding, predominant

numbness **6** stupor ***combining form:*** **4** narc **5** narco

numeral **5** digit **6** cipher, figure, number **7** chiffer, integer **11** whole number

numerate **4** list, tale, tell **5** count, tally **6** number **7** tick off

numerous **3** big **4** many **5** great, large **6** legion, sundry **7** several, umpteen, various **8** populous **9** plentiful **10** voluminous **12** multifarious, multitudinal **13** multitudinous

Numitor ***brother:*** **7** Amulius ***daughter:*** **9** Rea Silvia **10** Rhea Silvia ***grandson:*** **5** Remus **7** Romulus

numskull **4** dolt **5** dunce **8** bonehead, clodpate **9** blockhead, thickhead

numskulled **5** dense, thick **6** stupid **9** fat-

headed 10 beefheaded 11 blockheaded, thickheaded, thick-witted
nunnery 7 convent 10 sisterhood ***head:*** 8 superior
Nun's son 6 Joshua
nuptial 6 bridal, wedded 7 marital, married, spousal, wedding 8 conjugal, hymeneal 9 connubial, espousals 11 matrimonial
nurse 4 feed, nana, rear, suck 5 humor, nanny, serve 6 attend, foster, mother, pamper, suckle, wait on 7 advance, care for, cherish, educate, forward, further, indulge, nourish, nurture, promote 9 cultivate 10 minister to ***children's:*** 5 nanny 6 nannie ***English:*** 11 Nightingale ***Indian:*** 4 ayah ***Oriental:*** 3 ama 4 amah
nursemaid 4 nana 5 nanny 6 minder, nannie, sitter 9 governess 10 babysitter ***Indian:*** 4 ayah ***Oriental:*** 3 ama 4 amah
nursery 6 crèche 7 brooder
nurture 4 feed, food, grub, rear 5 nurse, raise, train 6 cradle, foster, nursle, school, uphold, viands 7 bolster, bring up, cherish, edibles, educate, nourish, support, sustain 8 tutelage, victuals 9 cultivate, provender 10 discipline, provisions, upbringing 11 comestibles
nut 2 en 3 bug 4 kook, loon 5 acorn, bigot, crank, fiend, freak, issue, loony, pecan, tryma 6 almond, cashew, cuckoo, dement, madman, maniac, zealot 7 fanatic, filbert, hickory, lunatic, madling, problem, trymata (plural) 8 crackpot, question 9 bedlamite, ding-a-ling, harebrain, macadamia, non compos, pistachio, screwball 10 crackbrain, enthusiast, Tom o' Bedlam ***combining form:*** 4 cary, kary 5 caryo, karyo ***European shrub:*** 7 filbert ***of a violin bow:*** 4 frog, heel
Nut ***consort:*** 3 Geb, Keb ***daughter:*** 4 Isis 8 Nephthys ***son:*** 2 Ra 6 Osiris
nuthouse 6 asylum 8 loony bin 9 funny farm 10 booby hatch
Nutmeg State 11 Connecticut
nutria 5 coypu
nutriment 3 pap 4 food, keep 5 bread 6 living 7 pabulum, support 10 livelihood, sustenance 11 maintenance, subsistence
nutritious 9 healthful, wholesome 10 nourishing
nuts 3 mad 4 daft, wild 5 batty, crazy, wacky 6 insane, screwy 7 cracked 8 demented 10 unbalanced
nutshell 3 sum 5 sum up 6 digest 7 summate 8 condense 9 epitomize, inventory, summarize, synopsize
nutty see **nuts**
nuzzle 4 push, root, snug 5 nudge 6 burrow, cuddle, nestle, snudge, thrust 7 snoozle, snuggle
Nycteus ***brother:*** 5 Lycus ***daughter:*** 7 Antiope
nymph 5 deity, larva 6 maiden ***changed into a bear:*** 8 Callisto ***changed into a laurel:*** 6 Daphne ***changed into a rock:*** 4 Echo ***mountain:*** 5 oread ***sea:*** 6 Nereid 7 Calypso ***water:*** 5 naiad ***wood:*** 5 dryad
Nym's crony 8 Falstaff
Nyx see **Nox**

O

oaf **2** ox **3** dub **4** boob, bull, clod, dolt, gawk, goof, goon, hulk, lout, lump, slob **5** beast, booby, brute, chump, clown, dunce, klutz, looby **6** bohunk, galoot, lubber, lummox, slouch **7** bruiser, fathead, gorilla, lobster, lumpkin, palooka **8** bonehead, dolthead, lunkhead, meathead **9** blockhead, blunderer, simpleton

oak **4** tree, wood **9** broadleaf ***African:*** **7** turtosa ***family:*** **8** Fagaceae ***fruit:*** **5** acorn ***genus:*** **7** Quercus ***kind:*** **3** bur, pin, red **4** bear, cork, holm, ilex, live **5** black, holly, roble, white **6** barren, cerris, encina **7** durmast, English, moss-cup, valonia **9** blackjack ***Mexican:*** **8** chaparro ***young:*** **7** oakling **8** flittern

oar **3** row **4** pole, pull **5** rower, scull **6** paddle **7** paddler ***part:*** **4** loom, palm **5** blade, shaft **6** button, collar

oarsman **3** bow **5** rower **6** stroke **7** sculler ***director:*** **3** cox **8** coxswain

oasis **3** spa **4** wadi, wady **6** refuge, relief ***ancient:*** **4** Merv ***Egypt:*** **4** Siwa **5** Gafsa **6** Dakhla **7** Farafra **8** Ammonium ***Libya:*** **5** Mizda, Sebha **6** Sabhah **7** Gadames **8** Ghudamis ***Niger:*** **5** Bilma ***Saudi Arabia:*** **5** Hofuf, Taima **7** Al-Hufuf

oat **5** grain, grass **6** cereal ***genus:*** **5** Avena ***Scottish:*** **3** ait

oater **7** western **10** horse opera

oath **3** vow **4** cuss **5** curse, swear **6** pledge **8** cussword **9** expletive, profanity, swearword **11** affirmation ***mild:*** **3** gee **4** darn, drat, gosh **5** golly

oatmeal **6** burgoo **8** porridge ***Scottish:*** **8** drammock

Obadiah ***father:*** **4** Azel **6** Jehiel **8** Izrahiah, Shemaiah ***son:*** **8** Ishmaiah

obdurate **4** firm, hard **5** harsh, rigid, rough **6** dogged, mulish, rugged **7** adamant, callous **8** stubborn **9** heartless, immovable, unbending, unfeeling **10** brassbound, hard-boiled, inexorable, inflexible, relentless, unyielding **11** coldhearted, hardhearted, stiff-necked, unemotional **12** stonyhearted **13** unsympathetic

Obed ***father:*** **4** Boaz **6** Ephlal **8** Shemaiah ***mother:*** **4** Ruth ***son:*** **5** Jesse **7** Azariah

Obededom's father **8** Jeduthun

obedient **5** loyal **6** docile **7** duteous, dutiful, slavish **8** amenable, biddable, obeisant, yielding **9** compliant, sheeplike, tractable **10** law-abiding, submissive **11** acquiescent, subservient

obeisance **3** bow **5** congé, honor, kotow **6** curtsy, fealty, homage, kowtow, salaam **7** gesture, loyalty **9** deference, reverence **10** allegiance

Oberon ***messenger:*** **4** Puck ***wife:*** **7** Titania

Oberto composer **5** Verdi

obese **3** fat **5** gross, heavy, plump, pudgy, stout **6** fleshy, portly **7** porcine **9** corpulent **10** overweight **11** upholstered

obey **3** bow **4** heed, keep, mind **5** agree, defer, yield **6** accede, assent, comply, follow, regard, submit **7** conform, fulfill, observe, satisfy **8** carry out **9** acquiesce

obfuscate **3** dim **4** murk **5** befog, cloud, gloom **6** darken, shadow **7** becloud, contuse, obscure **8** overcast **9** adumbrate

obi **4** sash

obiter dictum **4** note **6** remark **7** comment **10** commentary **11** observation

obituary **9** necrology

object **3** aim, end, jib, use **4** balk, body, bulk, duty, goal, item, kick, mark, mass, rail, rant, rave, view **5** being, demur, frown, spurn, storm, stuff, thing **6** boggle, doodad, entity, except, gadget, matter, target, volume **7** article, dissent, protest, purpose, stickle **8** complain, disfavor, function, material **9** challenge, criticize, deprecate, disesteem, objective, substance **10** disapprove, discommend, individual

objection **5** demur **7** protest **8** demurral, demurrer, question **9** challenge, exception **10** difficulty **12** remonstrance **13** remonstration

objectionable **4** vile **5** unfit **8** unwanted **9** abhorrent, invidious, loathsome, obnoxious, offensive, repellent, repugnant, repulsive, revolting, unwelcome **10** censurable, ill-favored, unpleasant, unsuitable **11** distasteful, undesirable **12** disagreeable

objective **3** aim, end, use **4** duty, fair, goal, mark **5** gross, outer **6** object, target **7** outside, outward, purpose **8** ambition, external, function, material, physical, sensible, tangible, unbiased **9** corporeal, equitable, impartial, quaesitum, uncolored

10 impersonal, phenomenal 11 substantial 12 unprejudiced 13 dispassionate
objet d'art 5 curio, vertu (plural), virtu (plural) 6 bauble, gewgaw, trifle 7 bibelot, novelty, trinket, whatnot 8 gimcrack 10 knickknack
objurgate 4 damn 5 curse, decry 7 censure, reprove 8 execrate 9 castigate 12 anathematize
oblate 4 monk 5 offer
oblation 6 corban, korban 8 offering 9 sacrifice 12 presentation
obligated 5 bound 8 beholden, indebted
obligation 3 vow 4 call, debt, duty, must, need, oath, part 5 cause, ought, place 6 burden, charge, devoir, pledge 7 promise 8 business, contract, occasion 9 arrearage, committal, liability, necessity, restraint 10 commitment, compulsion, constraint 11 requirement 12 indebtedness
obligatory 7 binding 8 required 9 imperious, mandatory 10 compulsory, imperative
oblige 3 aid 4 help, make 5 avail, favor, force 6 assist, coerce, compel, please, profit 7 benefit, concuss, gratify, shotgun 9 constrain 10 contribute 11 accommodate
obliged 5 bound 8 beholden, grateful, indebted, thankful
obliging 4 easy, kind, mild 5 civil 7 amiable, lenient 11 complaisant, good-humored, good-natured 12 good-tempered
oblique 6 sloped, tilted, tipped 7 leaning, pitched, sloping, tilting 8 circular, inclined, indirect, pitching 9 inclining
obliterate 4 raze, x out 5 erase 6 cancel, delete, efface 7 blot out, expunge, wipe out 8 black out, cross out 10 annihilate
oblivion 5 lethe, limbo 6 pardon 7 amnesty, nirvana 13 forgetfulness, obliviousness
oblivious 7 unaware 8 absorbed, ignorant 9 forgetful, unknowing, unmindful, unwitting 10 unfamiliar, uninformed 11 incognizant, unconscious
oblong 4 oval 7 ellipse 9 elongated, rectangle 11 rectangular
obloquy 4 slam, slur 5 abuse, odium, shame 6 infamy 7 calumny, censure 8 disgrace, dishonor, ignominy 9 aspersion, contumely, discredit, disesteem, disrepute, invective, stricture 10 opprobrium, reflection, scurrility 12 billingsgate, vituperation
obnoxious 4 open, vile 5 prone 6 liable, odious 7 exposed, hateful, subject 9 abhorrent, invidious, offensive, repellent, repugnant, revulsive, sickening 10 disgusting
oboe 4 reed 7 hautboy 8 hautbois, woodwind *oriental:* 6 surnai, surnay
obscene 4 foul, lewd, rank, vile 5 bawdy, crude, dirty, gross, lurid, nasty 6 coarse, crusty, earthy, filthy, impure, ribald, risqué, smutty, sultry, vulgar 7 hideous, noisome, profane, raunchy 8 barnyard, horrible, indecent, scabrous 9 offensive, repellent, repugnant, salacious, sickening 10 disgusting, fescennine, lascivious, nauseating, scurrilous 11 foulmouthed, unprintable 12 pornographic, scatological
obscure 3 dim, far, fog, odd 4 blur, dark, dusk, fuzz, haze, hide, mask, mist, murk, veil 5 bedim, befog, belie, blear, blind, cloak, close, cloud, cover, dusky, faint, gloom, lowly, minor, murky, shade, shady, vague 6 bemask, bleary, cloudy, darken, dim out, far-off, gloomy, hidden, humble, mystic, opaque, remote, screen, secret, shadow, shroud 7 becloud, clouded, conceal, cryptic, devious, dislimn, distant, eclipse, falsify, removed, retired, shadowy, unclear, unfamed, unknown, unnoted 8 abstruse, Delphian, disguise, esoteric, lonesome, mystical, nameless, nubilous, overcast, puzzling, secluded, solitary 9 adumbrate, ambiguous, difficult, enigmatic, equivocal, illegible, lightless, obfuscate, overcloud, sibylline, tenebrous, uncertain, undefined, unheard-of 10 caliginous, camouflage, fuliginous, ill-defined, indecisive, indefinite, indistinct, mysterious, overshadow, umbrageous, unemphatic, unexplicit, unrenowned 11 double-edged, double-faced, inscrutable, out-of-the-way, sequestered, unimportant 12 inaccessible, inconclusive, inexplicable, misrepresent, uncelebrated, unfathomable, unnoticeable 13 inconspicuous, unilluminated
obsequies 5 rites 7 funeral
obsequious 6 menial 7 dutiful, fawning, servile, slavish 8 obedient, obeisant, toadying 9 parasitic 10 submissive 11 deferential, subservient, sycophantic
observance 4 heed, mark, note, rite 6 notice, regard, remark, ritual 7 liturgy, service 8 ceremony 9 attention, formality 10 ceremonial, cognizance 11 observation
observant 5 alert, awake, aware 6 arrect 7 heedful, mindful 8 watchful 9 advertent, attentive, regardful 10 thoughtful
observation 4 heed, mark, note 6 notice, regard, remark 7 comment 9 attention 10 cognizance, commentary 12 obiter dictum
observatory 5 tower 7 lookout, outlook 8 overlook *famous:* 4 Lick 6 Wilson, Yerkes 7 Palomar *instrument:* 9 telescope
observe 3 see 4 espy, keep, look, mark, mind, note, obey, twig, view 5 sight, study, watch 6 behold, comply, follow, notice, remark, revere 7 comment, conform, discern 8 perceive, venerate 9 celebrate, rev-

erence, solemnize **10** animadvert, commentate **11** commemorate
obsessed **4** held **5** beset, queer **6** dogged, hipped **7** gripped, haunted, plagued **8** harassed, overcome, troubled **9** bedeviled, bewitched, dominated, hagridden, possessed **12** prepossessed
obsession **5** craze, mania, thing **6** fetish, hang-up **8** fixation **13** preoccupation
obsolete **3** old **4** dead **5** passé **6** démodé, old hat **7** worn-out **8** old-timey, outmoded, time-worn **10** superseded **12** old-fashioned
obstacle **3** bar, dam, rub **4** bump, clog, snag, wall **5** block, catch, crimp, hitch **6** hamper, hurdle **7** barrier **8** handicap, hardship, mountain, traverse **9** hindrance **10** difficulty, impediment **11** Chinese wall, encumbrance, obstruction, vicissitude
obstinate **4** deaf **5** balky, muley, stiff, tough **6** dogged, mulish, unruly **7** crabbed, staunch, willful **8** contrary, obdurate, perverse, renitent, resolute, stubborn, unpliant **9** pigheaded, resistant, steadfast, unbudging, unpliable **10** bullheaded, hardheaded, headstrong, inexorable, inflexible, muleheaded, refractory, self-willed, unyielding **11** incompliant, intractable, opinionated, stiff-necked, wrongheaded **12** closed-minded, intransigent, pertinacious, pervicacious, recalcitrant
obstreperous **4** loud **5** noisy **6** unruly **7** blatant **8** strident **9** clamorous **10** boisterous, multivocal, vociferant, vociferous **11** disobedient, loudmouthed, openmouthed
obstruct **3** bar, dam, gag **4** clog, fill, plug, stop **5** block, brake, choke, close **6** hinder, impede, screen, shroud **7** congest, occlude, shut off, shut out, stopper, trammel **8** block out **10** bottleneck, overslaugh
obstruction **3** bar, dam, rub **4** snag **5** hitch **6** hamper, hurdle **8** mountain, obstacle **9** hindrance **10** impediment
obtain **3** buy, eke, get, win **4** earn, gain, have, reap **5** annex, reach **6** pick up, secure **7** acquire, chalk up, procure **8** purchase
obtrude **5** cut in **6** butt in, horn in, impose **7** presume **8** chisel in, infringe
obtrusive **4** busy **5** pushy **7** forward **9** bumptious, officious **10** meddlesome **11** impertinent
obtuse **4** dull, mild **5** blunt, dense, thick **6** stupid
obverse **4** face, side **5** front **10** complement
obviate **4** ward **5** avert, deter **7** forfend, prevent, rule out **8** preclude, stave off **9** forestall, interfere, interpose, intervene
obvious **5** clear, overt, plain **6** patent **7** blatant, evident, glaring **8** apparent, distinct, manifest, palpable **11** conspicuous, unambiguous, unequivocal
oca **5** tuber **6** sorrel
___O'Casey, dramatist **4** Sean
occasion **3** use **4** call, need, shot, show, time **5** basis, break, breed, cause, event, hatch, right, thing, while **6** chance, demand, excuse, ground, induce, look-in, moment, reason, squeak, work up **7** episode, instant, opening, produce, provoke, warrant **8** engender, generate, incident, milepost, muster up **9** happening, milestone, necessity **10** antecedent, foundation, obligation, occurrence **11** determinant, opportunity **12** circumstance **13** justification
occasional **3** few, odd **4** rare **6** casual, random, scarce, seldom **8** sporadic, uncommon **10** incidental, infrequent, unfrequent
Occidental **7** Western **9** Westerner
occlude **4** clog, fill, plug, stop **5** block, choke, close **7** congest, stopper **8** obstruct
occult **4** bury, deep, hide **5** cache, eerie, heavy, magic, stash, weird **6** arcane, orphic, screen, secret, voodoo **7** conceal, secrete **8** abstruse, ensconce, esoteric, hermetic, mystical, profound **9** recondite, unearthly **10** acroamatic, cabalistic, mysterious **12** supernatural ***ability:*** **3** ESP ***combining form:*** **5** crypt, krypt **6** crypto, krypto
occupant **5** liver **6** inmate, tenant **7** denizen, dweller, resider **8** habitant, resident **9** indweller **10** inhabitant ***suffix:*** **3** ite
occupation **3** job **4** line, work **5** trade **6** career, métier **7** calling, pursuit **8** business **9** occupancy, residence **10** employment, habitation, settlement
occupy **3** use **4** busy, fill, hold **5** seize **6** engage, people, tenant **7** engross, immerse, inhabit **8** populate
occur **3** hap **4** pass **6** befall, betide, chance, happen, strike **7** come off, develop, fall out **9** transpire
occurrence **2** go **3** hap **4** pass **5** event, state, thing **7** episode **8** exigency, incident, juncture, occasion **9** adventure, condition, emergency, happening, situation ***extraordinary:*** **7** miracle ***unexpected:*** **8** surprise **9** bombshell
ocean **3** sea **4** blue, deep, main **5** brine, drink **6** Arctic, Indian **7** Pacific **8** Atlantic **9** Antarctic ***movement:*** **4** tide, wave
Oceania ***country:*** **4** Fiji **8** Kiribati **9** Australia **10** New Zealand **12** Western Samoa ***ethnic group:*** **6** Fijian, Indian, Papuan, Samoan **7** British **10** Melanesian, Polynesian **11** Micronesian ***language:*** **5** Hindi, Maori **6** Fijian, Papuan, Pidgin, Samoan **7** English **10** Melanesian
oceanic **6** marine **7** pelagic **8** maritime **9** thalassic
Ocean State **11** Rhode Island

Oceanus ***daughter:*** 5 Doris 7 Oceanid 8 Eurynome ***father:*** 6 Uranus ***mother:*** 2 Ge 4 Gaea ***sister:*** 6 Tethys ***son:*** 6 Peneus 7 Alpheus ***wife:*** 6 Tethys
ocellus 3 eye 7 eyespot
ocelot 3 cat 7 wildcat
octave 4 cask, note 5 eight, scale 6 eighth
Octavia ***brother:*** 8 Augustus ***grandson:*** 8 Caligula ***husband:*** 4 Nero 6 Antony
octopus 7 mollusk 9 devilfish 10 cephalopod ***arm:*** 8 tentacle ***genus:*** 7 Polypus ***kin:*** 5 squid 10 cuttlefish
ocular 3 eye, orb 4 lamp 5 optic 6 oculus, peeper, visual, winker 7 optical, seeable, visible 8 viewable, visional
odd 4 lone, only, rare 5 extra, fluky, queer, rummy, weird 6 casual, chance, single, uneven 7 curious, erratic, oddball, strange, unusual 8 peculiar, singular, unpaired 9 eccentric, unmatched 13 idiosyncratic ***combining form:*** 5 azygo
oddball 4 case, quiz 5 queer, weird 6 oddity, weirdo, zombie 7 bizarre, curious, strange 8 original, peculiar 9 character, eccentric 10 outlandish 13 idiosyncratic
oddity 4 case, quiz 5 quirk 8 original 9 character, curiosity, eccentric 12 idiosyncrasy
odd job 5 chore
odds and ends 4 olio 5 melee 6 jumble, medley, motley, scraps 7 mélange, mixture 8 oddments, sundries 9 etceteras, leftovers, potpourri 10 assortment, hodgepodge, miscellany
ode 4 hymn, poem 5 lyric, psalm, verse
Oded's son 7 Azariah
Odets play 9 Golden Boy 10 Night Music 12 Awake and Sing, Paradise Lost 14 The Country Girl 15 Waiting for Lefty
odeum 4 hall 7 theater
Odin ***brother:*** 2 Ve 4 Vili ***daughter-in-law:*** 5 Nanna ***father:*** 3 Bor ***hall:*** 8 Valhalla ***horse:*** 8 Sleipnir ***maiden:*** 8 Valkyrie ***mansion:*** 9 Gladsheim ***mother:*** 6 Bestla ***raven:*** 5 Hugin, Munin ***ring:*** 8 Draupnir ***ship:*** 7 Naglfar 11 Skidbladnir ***son:*** 3 Tyr 4 Thor, Vali 6 Balder ***spear:*** 7 Gungnir ***sword:*** 4 Gram ***throne:*** 10 Hlidskjalf 11 Hlithskjalf ***wife:*** 4 Fria, Rind 5 Frigg 6 Frigga ***wolf:*** 4 Geri 5 Freki
odious 4 foul, vile 6 horrid 7 hateful 8 hateable 9 abhorrent, invidious 10 abominable, despicable, detestable
odium 4 blot, blur, hate, onus, slur, spot 5 brand, shame, stain 6 hatred, infamy, stigma 7 obloquy 8 black eye, disgrace, dishonor, ignominy 9 discredit, disesteem, disrepute 10 opprobrium 11 bar sinister
odontalgia 9 toothache
odor 4 funk 5 aroma, scent, smell ***combining form:*** 3 osm 4 osma, osmo ***offensive:*** 5 stink 6 stench
odorous 5 heady, sweet 6 smelly, strong 7 pungent, reeking, scented 8 aromatic, fragrant, redolent, smelling
Odysseus 7 Ulysses ***dog:*** 5 Argos ***enchantress:*** 5 Circe ***father:*** 7 Laertes ***friend:*** 6 Mentor ***harasser:*** 8 Poseidon ***herb:*** 4 moly ***kingdom:*** 6 Ithaca ***mother:*** 8 Anticlea ***son:*** 9 Telegonus 10 Telemachus ***swineherd:*** 7 Eumaeus ***voyage:*** 7 odyssey ***wife:*** 8 Penelope
Odyssey author 5 Homer
Oedipus ***brother-in-law:*** 5 Creon ***daughter:*** 6 Ismene 8 Antigone ***father:*** 5 Laius ***foster father:*** 7 Polybus ***foster mother:*** 8 Periboea ***kingdom:*** 6 Thebes ***mother:*** 7 Jocasta ***son:*** 8 Eteocles 9 Polynices 10 Polyneices ***victim:*** 5 Laius ***wife:*** 7 Jocasta
Oeneus ***kingdom:*** 7 Calydon ***son:*** 8 Meleager ***wife:*** 7 Althaea
Oenomaus ***charioteer:*** 8 Myrtilus ***daughter:*** 10 Hippodamia ***kingdom:*** 4 Pisa ***slayer:*** 6 Pelops
Oenone ***husband:*** 5 Paris ***rival:*** 5 Helen
oeuvre 4 work 6 corpus, output
of ***French:*** 2 de ***German:*** 3 aus, von
offal 4 junk 5 trash, waste 6 debris, litter, refuse, spilth 7 carrion, garbage, rubbish 9 sweepings ***fish:*** 5 gurry
off-balance 6 uneven 7 unequal 8 lopsided 9 irregular 10 asymmetric 13 unsymmetrical
off-center 9 eccentric
off-color 3 low 4 blue, mean, racy 5 broad, salty, shady, spicy 6 ailing, poorly, purple, risqué, sickly, unwell, wicked 7 underly 10 indisposed, suggestive
offend 3 sin, vex 4 gall, hurt, miff 5 break, pique, shock, sting, upset, wound 6 appall, breach, excite, insult, nettle 7 affront, disturb, horrify, infract, mortify, outrage, provoke, violate 8 aggrieve, distress, infringe, irritate, trespass 9 disoblige, displease
offender 5 felon 6 sinner 8 criminal, violator 10 lawbreaker, malefactor
offense 3 fit, pet, sin 4 huff, miff, tort 5 anger, crime, onset, pique, scene, tizzy 6 attack, catfit, delict, felony, insult, onfall 7 affront, assault, dudgeon, flare-up, misdeed, tantrum, umbrage 8 delictum, outburst 9 explosion, indignity, offensive, onslaught 10 aggression, assailment, conniption, resentment 11 displeasure, indignation, misdemeanor
offensive 3 bad 4 evil, foul, grim, icky, rank, vile 5 awful, lurid, nasty, onset 6 attack, grisly, horrid, odious, onfall 7 assault, beastly, fulsome, ghastly, hideous, noisome, obscene 8 dreadful, grue-

some, horrible, shocking, terrible, unsavory 9 abhorrent, appalling, atrocious, frightful, loathsome, onslaught, repellent, repugnant, repulsive, revolting, sickening 10 abominable, aggression, assailment, detestable, disgusting, nauseating, ungrateful, unpleasant 11 uncongenial, unpalatable, unwholesome 12 disagreeable, unappetizing 13 objectionable

offer 3 bid, lay, try 4 cite, give, pose, seek, show 5 assay, essay 6 adduce, allege, extend, strive, tender 7 advance, attempt, display, exhibit, hold out, present, proffer, propose 8 endeavor, proposal, struggle

offering 4 alms, gift 6 corban, korban, victim 7 charity, present 8 donation, oblation 9 sacrifice 11 benefaction, beneficence 12 contribution

offhand 6 casual 8 informal 9 extempore, impromptu, unstudied 10 improvised 11 extemporary, unrehearsed

office 3 job 4 duty, post, role, spot 5 berth, place 6 billet 7 station 8 business, function, position, province 9 situation 10 connection 11 appointment ***head:*** 4 boss 7 manager ***machine:*** 6 copier 9 stenotype 10 calculator, typewriter ***seeker:*** 9 candidate 10 politician ***suffix:*** 2 cy 3 ate, dom, ure 4 ship ***worker:*** 5 clerk, steno 6 typist 9 secretary 10 bookkeeper 12 stenographer

officer 3 cop 4 exec 6 noncom, police 7 John Law, manager 8 official 9 executive ***abbreviation:*** 2 Lt. 3 Adm., Col., Ens., Gen., Maj. 4 Capt., Cmdr. 5 Comdr., Lieut. ***army:*** 5 major 7 captain, colonel, general 10 lieutenant ***British:*** 9 brigadier ***court:*** 7 bailiff ***king's:*** 11 chamberlain ***law-enforcement:*** 3 cop 6 deputy, police 7 marshal, sheriff 9 constable, patrolman, policeman ***naval:*** 4 mate 6 ensign 7 admiral, captain 9 commander, commodore 10 lieutenant ***noncommissioned:*** 5 sarge 8 corporal, sergeant ***petty:*** 5 bosun, chief 6 yeoman 7 teleman 9 boatswain ***prison:*** 5 guard 6 warden

official 4 exec 7 cleared, manager, officer 8 approved, endorsed 9 canonical, cathedral, certified, executive, ex officio 10 authorized, ex cathedra, sanctioned 13 administrator, authoritative ***city or town:*** 5 mayor 8 alderman 9 selectman 10 councilman ***diplomatic:*** 5 envoy 6 consul 7 attaché 10 ambassador ***governmental:*** 6 syndic ***parish:*** 6 beadle ***sports:*** 3 ref, ump 6 umpire 7 referee 8 linesman ***university:*** 4 dean 6 bursar 7 provost 9 registrar 10 chancellor

officious 4 busy 9 intrusive, obtrusive 10 meddlesome 11 impertinent 13 polypragmatic

offing 6 future 7 by-and-by 9 aftertime, afterward, hereafter 10 background

offscouring 5 filth, leper 6 pariah, refuse 7 Ishmael, outcast 8 castaway, derelict 10 Ishmaelite 11 untouchable

offset 4 stop 5 check 6 contra, make up, redeem, set off 7 balance 8 atone for, outweigh 10 compensate 11 countervail

offshoot 5 scion 6 branch 7 spin-off 9 byproduct, outgrowth 10 derivative, descendant

offspring 3 kid, son 4 seed 5 brood, hatch, issue, scion, spawn, swarm, young 7 produce, product, progeny 8 children 9 posterity 10 descendant 11 progeniture ***combining form:*** 3 gen, ped 4 geno, paed, paid, pedo 5 paedo, paido, proli

Of Human Bondage author 7 Maugham

Of Mice and Men ***author:*** 9 Steinbeck ***character:*** 6 George, Lennie

ogee 3 ess 4 arch 5 curve 7 molding

Ogier the ___ 4 Dane

ogive 4 arch

ogle 3 eye 4 gape, gaze, leer, look 5 stare 6 goggle 10 rubberneck

ogre 5 beast, bogey, demon, giant 6 booger 7 bugbear, monster 8 bogeyman 9 boogeyman ***Algonquian:*** 7 windigo

ogress 5 harpy, scold, shrew, vixen 6 amazon, virago 8 fishwife 9 termagant, Xanthippe

Ohio ***capital:*** 8 Columbus ***college, university:*** 5 Akron, Hiram, Miami 6 Dayton 7 Antioch, Denison, Oberlin 8 Defiance, Ursuline 9 Kent State ***largest city:*** 9 Cleveland ***nickname:*** 12 Buckeye State ***state bird:*** 8 cardinal

Oholibamah ***father:*** 4 Anah ***husband:*** 4 Esau

oil 3 fat, gas 4 balm, fuel, lube, oleo 5 oleum 6 anoint, grease 7 blarney, incense, lanolin 8 flattery, soft soap 9 adulation, lubricant, lubricate, petroleum ***combining form:*** 3 ole 4 eleo, olei, oleo 5 elaeo, elaio ***consecrated:*** 6 chrism ***fragrant:*** 5 attar 6 neroli ***fuel:*** 3 gas 8 gasoline, kerosene, kerosine ***relating to:*** 5 oleic ***ship:*** 6 tanker ***well:*** 6 gusher

Oil! author 8 Sinclair

oilbird 8 guacharo

oily 5 fatty, slick, soapy, suave 6 greasy, smarmy, smooth 7 fulsome 8 unctious, unctuous 10 oleaginous

ointment 4 balm, nard 5 cream, salve 6 cerate, chrism, lotion 7 unction, unguent 8 calamine, dressing, liniment 9 demulcent, emollient 11 embrocation

OK, okay 3 aye, yea, yes 5 favor 6 agreed 7 approve, certify, endorse

8 accredit, all right, approval, blessing, sanction

Oklahoma *city:* 3 Ada 4 Enid 5 Tulsa *nickname:* 11 Sooner State *state flower:* 9 mistletoe *university:* 11 Oral Roberts

okra 4 soup 5 bendy, gumbo 8 hibiscus

old 4 aged, late, once, past 5 dated, hoary, passé, solid, stale 6 bygone, démodé, former, steady, versed, whilom 7 ancient, antique, archaic, elderly, lasting, onetime, overage, quondam, skilled, staying, veteran 8 enduring, lifelong, Noachian, outmoded, seasoned, sometime, timeworn 9 erstwhile, long-lived, perennial, perpetual, practical, practiced, primitive, venerable 10 antiquated, continuing, inveterate *Scottish:* 4 auld

old age 10 feebleness, senescence 11 decrepitude, elderliness, senectitude *combining form:* 6 geront, presby 7 geronto, presbyo *relating to:* 6 senile 8 gerontal, gerontic 9 geriatric

Old Bailey 5 court

Old Colony State 13 Massachusetts

Old Curiosity Shop author 7 Dickens

Old Dominion State 8 Virginia

Old English letter see **Anglo-Saxon**, *letter*

Old Faithful 6 geyser

old-fashioned 4 aged 5 dated, dowdy, drink, fusty, moldy, mossy, passé 6 bygone, crusty, démodé, old hat, quaint, rococo, stodgy 7 ancient, antique, archaic, belated, demoded, disused, fogyish, outworn, vintage 8 cocktail, obsolete, outdated, outmoded, unmodern 9 discarded, moss-grown, moth-eaten, out-of-date, Victorian 10 antiquated, fuddy-duddy, mossbacked

old hand 3 vet 7 veteran 9 longtimer

old hat 5 dated, stale, tired, trite 6 cliché, démodé 7 antique, archaic, clichéd, oldtime, vintage 8 shopworn, timeworn, wellworn 9 hackneyed, out-of-date 10 antiquated, oldfangled, threadbare

Old Ironsides 12 Constitution *poet:* 6 Holmes

old liner 4 tory 5 right 7 diehard 8 rightist, standpat 11 bitter-ender, right-winger, standpatter 12 conservative

Old Line State 8 Maryland

old maid 7 fusspot 8 spinster

Old Line State 13 North Carolina

Old Rough and Ready 6 Taylor

Olds' car 3 Reo

Old Scratch 5 devil, fiend, Satan 7 Lucifer, Old Nick, serpent 8 Apollyon 9 Beelzebub

old-time 5 dated 6 bygone, old hat, versed 7 antique, archaic, skilled, veteran, vintage 8 seasoned 9 practical, practiced 10 antiquated 11 experienced

old-timer 3 vet 5 elder 6 senior 7 ancient, old hand, oldster, veteran 10 golden-ager

old womanish 5 anile

Old World 6 Europe

oleaginous see **oily**

oleaster 5 olive 9 olive tree

olecranon 9 funny bone

oleo 9 margarine

oleoresin 10 turpentine

oleum 3 oil

olfaction 5 sense, smell 7 osmesis 8 smelling

olid 4 rank 5 fetid, funky 6 putrid, rancid, smelly 7 stenchy 8 mephitic, stinking 10 malodorous

olio 4 brew, hash, stew 6 medley 7 mélange, mixture 8 mishmash 9 potpourri 10 assortment, hodgepodge, miscellany 11 olla podrida

olive *genus:* 4 Olea *stuffing:* 7 pimento 8 pimiento

Oliver Twist *author:* 7 Dickens *character:* 5 Bates, Fagin, Nancy, Sikes 6 Bumble 7 Dawkins 12 Artful Dodger

olia podrida see **olio**

Ollie's pal 4 Stan

Olympian 3 god 5 lofty 7 athlete, exalted 8 majestic 10 competitor

Olympics 5 games 6 sports 9 athletics *place of origin:* 6 Athens *symbol:* 5 flame, torch

Oman *capital:* 6 Masqat, Muscat *monetary unit:* 4 rial

Omar 4 poet 7 Khayyém *country:* 6 Persia *father:* 7 Eliphaz *poem:* 8 Rubáiyát

omega 3 end 6 ending, letter *kin:* 3 zee

omelet 4 eggs *kind:* 7 foo yong, Spanish, western

omen 4 bode, sign 5 augur, token 6 augury, boding 7 auspice, betoken, portend, portent, presage, promise, warning 8 bodement, forebode, foreshow 9 foretoken 10 foreshadow, prognostic

ominous 4 dire, dour, evil, grim 6 dismal, malign 7 baleful, baneful, direful, doomful, fateful, hostile, malefic, unlucky 8 lowering, menacing, sinister 9 ill-boding, ill-omened 10 forbidding, maleficent, portentous, unfriendly 11 apocalyptic, threatening 12 inauspicious, inhospitable, unpropitious

omission 3 cut, gap 4 skip, slip 5 blank, break, chasm, error, lapse 6 hiatus, lacuna 8 eclipsis, ellipsis, overlook 9 exclusion *mark:* 5 caret 8 ellipsis 10 apostrophe

omit 3 cut 4 dele, drop, fail, skip 5 elide 6 cancel, delete, except, forget, ignore, slight 7 blink at, neglect 8 discount, leave out, overlook, overpass

Omni and Cobo 6 arenas
omnibus 3 ana 4 posy 5 album 7 garland, vehicle 8 analects 9 anthology 10 miscellany 11 florilegium *horse-drawn:* 10 shillibeer
omnipotent 3 god 5 deity 6 divine 7 godlike 8 almighty 9 unlimited 11 all-powerful
omnipresent 7 allover, endless 8 infinite, unending 9 boundless, limitless, universal 10 ubiquitous 12 immeasurable
omniscient 4 wise 7 learned 10 all-knowing
omnium-gatherum see olio
Omphale *domain:* 5 Lydia *slave:* 8 Heracles, Hercules
omphalos 5 navel 9 umbilicus 10 focal point
Omri's father 4 Imri 6 Becher 7 Michael
on 4 atop, over, upon, with 5 about, above, along, forth 7 forward
onager 5 kiang 8 catapult
Onan's father 5 Judah
once 3 odd 4 ever, late, past 5 at all 6 anyway, before, bygone, former, whilom 7 already, anywise, earlier, onetime, quondam 8 formerly, sometime *Scottish:* 4 anes 5 yince
once-over 6 glance, survey 10 inspection 11 examination
one 3 wed 4 join, link, lone, only, sole, unit 5 monad, unite 6 number, relate, single, unique, united 7 connect, numeral 8 coagment, coalesce, separate, singular, solitary 9 associate, coadunate, undivided 10 individual, particular *combining form:* 3 mon 4 heno, mono *French:* 2 un 3 une *German:* 3 ein 4 eine *prefix:* 3 uni *Scottish:* 2 ae 3 ane, yae *Spanish:* 2 un 3 uno
one and a half *combining form:* 6 sesqui
one-eyed giant 7 Cyclops 10 Polyphemus
one-handed god 3 Tiu, Tyr
one-horse town 4 burg 6 Podunk 7 mudhole 11 whistle-stop
one hundred 6 centum *years:* 7 century
O'Neill, Eugene *heroine:* 4 Anna, Nina *play:* 3 Ile 4 Gold 11 The Hairy Ape 12 Ah Wilderness, Anna Christie, Emperor Jones 13 Marco Millions 15 The Iceman Cometh 16 Strange Interlude, The Great God Brown
oneiric 6 dreamy 8 anagogic
oneness 5 unity 7 allness, unicity 8 entirety, identity, sameness, totality, uniquity 9 wholeness 10 entireness, singleness, uniqueness 11 singularity 12 completeness, selfsameness, singularness 13 identicalness, individuality
onerous 4 hard 5 heavy, hefty, tough 6 taxing, trying, unruly 7 arduous, driving, exigent, weighty 8 exacting, grievous, toilsome, unwieldy 9 demanding, difficult, laborious, ponderous 10 burdensome, cumbersome, oppressive 11 heavy-headed
oneself *combining form:* 3 aut 4 auto
one-sided 6 biased, unfair, unjust, warped 7 bigoted, colored, partial 8 lopsided, partisan, weighted 9 jaundiced 10 prejudiced
onetime 4 late, once, past 6 bygone, former, whilom 7 quondam 8 formerly 9 erstwhile
on hand 4 here 7 present
Onias' son 5 Simon
onion 4 bulb 5 cibol 7 shallot 8 eschalot *bulb:* 3 set *genus:* 6 Allium *kin:* 4 leek 6 garlic *kind:* 3 red 5 green 7 Bermuda, Danvers, Spanish *roll:* 5 bialy *young:* 8 scallion
only 3 but, one, yet 4 just, lone, mere, save, sole, solo 5 alone 6 except, merely, simply, single, solely, unique 7 however 8 entirely, peerless, separate, singular, solitary 9 matchless, unequaled, unmatched
onomasticon 7 lexicon 8 wordbook
onomatopoeic 5 mimic 6 echoic 7 mimetic, mimical 9 emulative, imitative 10 simulative
onomatopoetic see onomatopoeic
onrush see onslaught
onset 4 dawn 5 birth, start 6 attack, onfall, origin, outset, setout 7 assault, dawning, offense, opening 8 outstart 9 beginning, offensive, onslaught 10 aggression, assailment 12 commencement
onslaught 5 onset 6 attack, onfall, onrush 7 assault, offense 9 offensive 10 aggression, assailment
Ontario *capital:* 7 Toronto *university:* 4 York 5 Brock, Trent 8 McMaster
on the other hand 3 but 7 however
on the whole 7 en masse 8 all in all 9 generally 10 altogether, by and large
onto 4 atop
onus 3 tax 4 blot, blur, duty, load, slur, spot, task 5 blame, brand, fault, guilt, odium, stain 6 burden, charge, stigma, weight 8 black eye 9 millstone 10 deadweight
onward 4 alee, away 5 ahead, along, forth 7 forward
onyx 3 jet 4 inky 5 black, ebony, jetty, raven, sable 9 pitch-dark 10 chalcedony, pitchblack 11 atramentous
oodles 4 gobs, heap, slew 5 loads, scads 7 jillion 10 quantities
ooid 4 oval 5 ovate, ovoid 7 oviform
oolong 3 tea
oomph 3 vim 4 brio, dash, élan, gimp, life, push 5 drive, verve, vigor 6 esprit, pizazz,

spirit 7 pizzazz 8 strength, vitality 9 animation

ooze 3 mud 4 leak, seep, weep 5 bleed, exude, marsh, slime, sweat 6 strain 7 secrete 8 transude

opah 4 fish 5 cravo

opal 3 gem 5 glass, jewel, stone 7 girasol, hyalite 8 girasole 9 cacholong

opaque 4 dark, dull 5 dense, vague 6 cloudy, stupid 7 obscure, unclear 8 nubilous

OPEC nation 4 Iran, Iraq 5 Gabon, Libya, Qatar 6 Kuwait 7 Algeria, Ecuador, Nigeria 9 Indonesia, Venezuela 11 Saudi Arabia

open 3 cut, tap 4 ajar, bare, free, gash, hole, meet, undo, wide 5 agape, begin, break, clear, cover, frank, naked, overt, plain, prone, slash, start, swell, untie 6 billow, breach, broach, candid, dilate, expand, expose, extend, fan out, gaping, get off, launch, liable, mantle, patent, peeled, pierce, public, reveal, spread, unbolt, unfold, unlock, unseal, unshut, unstop, unveil, unwrap, usable 7 convene, denuded, jump off, kick off, outdoor, outside, release, ringent, rupture, subject, unblock, unclose, uncover, unlatch, without, yawning 8 commence, disclose, doubtful, embark on, initiate, outdoors, patulous, stripped, unbarred, unbolted, unclench, unclosed, unclothe, unlocked, unsealed 9 agreeable, ambiguous, available, dehiscent, dubitable, equivocal, obnoxious, operative, outspread, perforate, reachable, securable, sensitive, uncertain, uncovered, undecided, unimpeded, unsettled 10 accessible, attainable, embark upon, employable, inaugurate, indecisive, obtainable, out-of-doors, outstretch, overspread, unfastened 11 practicable, problematic, susceptible, unconcealed, undisguised, unvarnished 12 undissembled, unobstructed, unrestricted ***poetic:*** 3 ope ***slightly:*** 4 ajar

open-air 7 outdoor, outside 8 alfresco 9 out-of-door 10 hypaethral

open-and-shut 5 clear, plain 6 patent 7 evident, obvious 8 apparent, distinct, manifest

openhanded 4 free 5 clear, plain 6 patent 7 evident, liberal, obvious 8 apparent, distinct, generous 9 bounteous, bountiful, unsparing 10 bighearted, munificent

openhearted 4 kind, warm 5 frank, plain 6 candid

opening 2 os 3 gap, ora (plural) 4 dawn, door, gate, hole, pass, pore, rift, rima, shot, show, slit, slot, time, vent 5 birth, break, chasm, chink, cleft, crack, debut, mouth, onset, start, stoma 6 breach, chance, eyelet, lacuna, look-in, outlet, outset, setout, squeak 7 crevice, dawning, fissure, orifice, pinhole, ventage 8 aperture, crevasse, débouché, occasion, outstart, overture 9 beginning 11 opportunity ***bodily:*** 4 pore 5 hilum, hilus 7 foramen, orifice, ostiole 8 fenestra ***combining form:*** 4 pora, pore, pyle 5 stoma, stome, stomi, stomy, trema 6 stomia, stomum 7 stomata (plural), stomate, tremata (plural) ***ship's:*** 5 hatch 8 hatchway, porthole

openmouthed 5 agape 6 amazed, gaping 7 blatant 8 strident 9 clamorous 10 boisterous, multivocal, vociferant, vociferous

open sesame 3 key 6 ticket 8 passport, password

opera 7 musical ***comic:*** 5 buffa 6 bouffe ***glasses:*** 9 lorgnette ***kind:*** 4 soap 5 comic, grand, horse, space ***part:*** 3 act 4 aria 5 scena ***solo:*** 4 aria ***star:*** 4 diva 10 prima donna ***text:*** 8 libretto (see also individual titles and composers)

operate 2 go 3 act, cut, ply, run, use 4 keep, play, take, work 5 drive, pilot, react, steer, wield 6 behave, direct, handle, manage, open up, ordain 7 carry on, conduct, control, perform 8 function, maneuver 10 manipulate

operation 3 use 4 play 6 action 7 surgery 8 exercise, exertion, function 9 appliance, procedure 10 employment, exercising

operative 4 hand, live, open 5 agent, alive 6 active, usable, worker 7 dynamic, laborer, running, working, workman 8 mechanic, workhand 9 Pinkerton

operator 5 agent 6 doctor, driver 7 autoist, surgeon 8 motorist 9 conductor ***suffix:*** 3 ist 4 ster

operculum 3 lid 4 flap

operose 4 busy, hard 5 tough 6 severe 7 arduous 8 diligent, sedulous, toilsome 9 assiduous, difficult, effortful, laborious

Ophelia ***beloved:*** 6 Hamlet ***brother:*** 7 Laertes ***father:*** 8 Polonius

ophidian 5 snake 9 snakelike

Ophir's father 6 Joktan

opiate 4 dope, drug 6 deaden, sleepy 7 anodyne 8 hypnotic, narcotic, nepenthe, somnific 9 soporific 10 somnorific

opine 4 deem, hold, view 5 judge, think 6 accept, regard 7 believe, suppose

opinion 3 eye 4 idea, mind, view 5 tenet, think 6 belief, notion, theory 7 feeling, thought 8 attitude, estimate, judgment, reaction 9 sentiment 10 assumption, conclusion, conjecture, conviction, estimation, impression, persuasion 11 speculation, supposition ***express an:*** 4 vote 5 judge 9 criticize

opium 4 dope, drug 8 narcotic ***derivative:*** 6 heroin 7 codeine, meconin, narcein 8 laudanum, morphine, narceine 9 narcotine, paregoric ***prepared:*** 6 chandu ***source:*** 5 poppy

opossum 9 marsupial ***kin:*** 8 kangaroo

oppidan 8 townsman

opponent 3 con, foe 4 anti 5 enemy, match, rival 7 nemesis, opposer 9 adversary, assailant, combatant, oppugnant 10 antagonist, competitor 12 counteragent

opportune 3 fit 5 happy 6 timely 7 timeous 9 favorable, well-timed 10 auspicious, felicitous, propitious, prosperous 11 appropriate

opportunity 4 hope, pass, room, shot, show, time, turn 5 break, space, spell 6 chance, look-in, prayer, relief, squeak 7 opening 8 juncture, occasion

oppose 3 pit, vie 4 buck, duel, face 5 array, beard, fight, match, repel 6 combat, differ, object, refute, repugn, resist 7 contest, counter, dispute, play off 8 confront, contrast, traverse 9 withstand 10 contradict

opposite 2 to 4 foil 5 polar 6 contra, facing, unlike 7 antonym, counter, inverse, obverse, opposed, reverse, unalike 8 antipode, antipole, contrary, contrast, converse, separate 9 antipodal, diametric, different, divergent, unrelated, unsimilar 10 antipodean, antithesis, antonymous, dissimilar 11 contrasting, counterpole, independent, unconnected 12 antagonistic, antithetical, counterpoint 13 contradictory ***combining form:*** 7 enantio ***French:*** 8 en face de ***prefix:*** 2 ob 3 dis 5 retro 6 contra 7 counter

opposition 3 con 8 defiance 9 animosity, hostility 10 antagonism, antithesis, resistance 11 contrariety

oppress 5 harry, wrong 6 burden, harass, sadden, subdue 7 afflict, conquer, depress, outrage, torment, torture, trouble 8 aggrieve, distress, overcome 9 overthrow, persecute, subjugate

oppressive 4 hard 5 black, bleak, harsh, heavy, tough 6 dismal, gloomy, severe, somber, taxing 7 exigent, onerous, weighty 8 exacting, grievous 9 demanding 10 burdensome, depressing 11 dispiriting 12 discouraging 13 disheartening

oppressive force 4 onus, yoke 6 burden, weight 10 juggernaut

oppressor 6 despot, tyrant 8 dictator 9 strong man

opprobrious 7 abusive 8 ill-famed, infamous, scurrile 9 invective, notorious, truculent 10 scurrilous, vituperous 12 contumelious, vituperative, vituperatory

opprobrium 5 abuse, odium, scorn, shame 6 infamy 7 obloquy 8 disgrace, dishonor, ignominy 9 discredit, disesteem, disrepute 10 scurrility 12 vituperation

oppugn 3 tug, war 5 fight 6 battle 7 contend

Ops 4 Rhea ***consort:*** 6 Cronus, Saturn ***daughter:*** 5 Ceres 7 Demeter

opt 4 cull, mark, pick, take 5 elect 6 choose, decide, prefer, select 9 single out

optical 6 ocular, visual 8 visional ***instrument:*** 4 lens 5 glass, scope 7 transit 9 magnifier, optometer, periscope, telescope 10 microscope

optimist 5 hoper 7 dreamer 8 idealist, micawber 9 Pollyanna 10 positivist

optimistic 4 fond, rosy 5 merry, sunny 6 bright, hoping, upbeat 7 assured, hopeful 8 cheerful, sanguine 9 confident 12 Pollyannaish

option 5 right 6 choice 8 election 9 privilege, selection 10 preference 11 alternative, prerogative

optional 4 free 8 elective 9 voluntary 11 alternative, facultative 13 discretionary

opulence 6 plenty, riches, wealth 9 affluence

opulent 4 lush, rich 5 plush, showy, swank 6 Capuan, deluxe, lavish 7 elegant, moneyed, profuse, wealthy 8 affluent, luscious, palatial, prodigal 9 exuberant, luxuriant, luxurious, profusive, sumptuous

opuntia 6 cactus

or 4 else, gold 6 golden, yellow 9 otherwise

oracle 4 sage, seer 6 medium, vision 8 prophecy 10 apocalypse, revelation ***site:*** 6 Claros, Delphi, Didyma, Dodona 9 Epidaurus

oracular 5 vatic 6 mantic 7 fatidic 8 Delphian 9 prophetic, sibylline, vaticinal

oral 4 told 5 vocal 6 sonant, spoken, verbal, voiced 7 related, uttered 8 narrated, viva voce 9 recounted, unwritten

orange 5 color, fruit 6 citrus 8 jacinthe ***brownish:*** 6 Titian ***deep:*** 11 bittersweet ***genus:*** 6 Citrus ***kin:*** 9 tangerine 10 grapefruit ***kind:*** 4 sour 5 blood, chino, navel, Osage, sweet 7 Seville 8 bergamot, mandarin, Valencia ***seed:*** 3 pip ***skin:*** 4 rind

orangutan 3 ape 4 mias 5 pongo

orate 4 rant, rave 5 mouth, speak, spiel 7 bombast, declaim, elocute, soapbox 8 blah-blah, bloviate, harangue, perorate 9 sermonize, speechify 11 rodomontade

oration 6 sermon, speech 7 address 9 discourse ***funeral:*** 6 eulogy

orator 7 demagog, speaker 9 demagogue ***American:*** 4 Clay 5 Bryan, Henry 7 Calhoun, Douglas, Webster ***British:*** 5 Burke 8 Disraeli 9 Churchill, Gladstone 8 Mirabeau ***Greek:*** 5 Corax 8 P[illegible] 11 Demosthenes ***Roman:*** 6 Cicero

oratory 6 chapel 8 rhetoric 9 elo[illegible] eloquence 11 speechcraft

orb 3 eye 4 ball, lamp 5 globe, round 6 circle, ocular, oculus, peeper, sphere, winker

orbit 4 path 5 ambit, range, reach, scope, sweep, track 6 extent, radius ***farthest point:*** 5 apsis 6 apogee 8 aphelion ***nearest point:*** 5 apsis 7 perigee 10 pericenter, perihelion

orchard 5 copse 6 garden 8 arbustum 10 plantation

orchestra 4 band 5 combo, group 7 gamelan 8 ensemble, symphony 12 philharmonic ***leader:*** 9 conductor ***section:*** 5 brass 6 string 8 woodwind 10 percussion

orchestrate 5 blend, score, unify 7 arrange 9 harmonize, integrate 10 symphonize, synthesize

orchid 6 flower ***kind:*** 5 faham, vanda 7 calypso, pogonia 8 cattleya, oncidium 9 cymbidium 11 cypripedium ***petal:*** 3 lip 8 labellum ***product:*** 5 faham, salep ***tuber:*** 5 salep

Orcus see **Hades**

ordain 4 keep 5 order 6 decree, direct, impose, manage 7 carry on, command, conduct, dictate, lay down, operate 9 prescribe

ordeal 5 cross, trial 7 calvary 8 crucible 10 affliction, visitation 11 tribulation

order 3 bid, fix, ilk, row, set 4 case, club, fiat, gear, kind, line, plan, rank, rule, sort, tell, trim, tune, type, warn, word 5 align, array, breed, chain, edict, genus, grace, grade, guild, range, right, shape, train, union 6 adjust, behest, branch, charge, codify, decree, direct, enjoin, estate, extent, fettle, kidney, kilter, league, line up, matter, method, nature, police, repair, sequel, series, settle, status, stripe, system 7 aptness, arrange, arrayal, bidding, bracket, command, decorum, dictate, dispose, feather, fitness, mandate, marshal, pattern, probity, routine, society 8 approach, organize, regiment, regulate, sequence, sodality, tidiness, vicinity 9 allotment, amendment, arrayment, closeness, condition, following, integrity, magnitude, methodize, propriety, proration, proximity, rectitude, rightness, routinize 10 adjustment, allocation, correction, expediency, fellowship, fraternity, injunction, permission, pigeonhole, procession, properness, seemliness, streamline, succession, timeliness 11 alternation, arrangement, association, brotherhood, collocation, consecution, correctness, description, disposition, hierarchize, orderliness, progression, suitability, systematize ***good:*** 6 eutaxy ***lack of:*** 5 chaos 6 ataxia 7 anarchy, clutter 9 confusion 11 pandemonium ***of business:*** 6 agenda, docket ***of preference:*** 8 priority

orderly 4 aide, neat, snug, tidy, trig, trim 5 alike, exact 6 batman, formal 7 chipper, correct, precise, regular, uniform 8 accurate, methodic, picked up 9 shipshape 10 methodical, systematic 11 uncluttered, well-groomed 12 businesslike

ordinal 4 book 6 number ***suffix:*** 2 nd, st, th 3 eth

ordinance 3 law 4 fiat, rule 5 canon, edict 6 decree 7 precept, statute 8 decretum 9 prescript 10 capitulary, regulation

ordinary 4 so-so 5 banal, plain, trite, usual 6 common, normal 7 mundane, natural, prosaic, regular, routine 8 everyday, familiar, frequent, workaday 9 customary, plain Jane, quotidian 10 uneventful 11 commonplace 12 unnoteworthy

ordnance 4 guns 6 cannon 7 weapons 8 supplies 9 artillery 10 ammunition

ordure 9 excrement ***combining form:*** 4 copr, scat 5 copro, scato

ore 4 gold, rock 5 metal 6 copper, silver 7 mineral 8 platinum ***analysis:*** 5 assay ***deposit:*** 4 lode, vein ***excavation:*** 5 stope ***iron:*** 5 ocher 8 goethite, hematite, limonite ***lead:*** 6 galena ***process:*** 8 leaching, smelting ***refuse:*** 4 slag 5 dross, matte 6 scoria ***smelted:*** 6 speiss 7 regulus

oread 5 nymph

Oreb's slayer 6 Gideon

Oregon ***capital:*** 5 Salem ***largest city:*** 8 Portland ***nickname:*** 11 Beaver State, Sunset State 12 Webfoot State

Orel's river 3 Oka

Orestes ***father:*** 9 Agamemnon ***friend:*** 7 Pylades ***mother:*** 12 Clytemnestra ***sister:*** 7 Electra 9 Iphigenia ***victim:*** 9 Aegisthus 12 Clytemnestra ***wife:*** 8 Hermione

organ 5 agent, means 6 agency, medium, review 7 channel, journal, vehicle 8 magazine, ministry 9 newspaper 10 instrument, periodical ***ancient:*** 6 syrinx 9 hydraulus ***barrel:*** 10 hurdy-gurdy ***bodily:*** 3 ear, eye 4 lung, nose 5 gland, heart, liver 6 kidney, larynx, spleen, tongue, tonsil, viscus 9 intestine ***combining form:*** 6 viscer 7 visceri, viscero ***mouth:*** 9 harmonica ***part:*** 4 pipe, reed, stop 5 pedal, valve 6 blower 7 console, tremolo 8 keyboard, pedalier 9 wind chest ***reed:*** 8 melodeon 9 harmonium ***stop:*** 4 oboe, sext 5 gamba, quint, viola 6 dolcan, dulcet 7 bassoon, celesta, melodia, subbass, tertian 8 carillon, dulciana, gemshorn ***tactile:*** 6 feeler 8 tentacle

organ cactus 7 saguaro

organism 4 unit 5 being, biont, plant 6 animal ***disease-producing:*** 4 germ 5 virus 7 microbe 8 pathogen 9 bacterium ***single-celled:*** 5 monad 6 amoeba 9 protozoan ***suffix:*** 5 acean

organist ***American:*** 3 Fox 5 Biggs

6 Newman ***Danish:*** 9 Buxtehude ***Dutch:*** 9 Sweelinck ***English:*** 6 Wesley 7 Gibbons ***French:*** 5 Widor 6 Franck 8 Messiaen 10 Schweitzer ***German:*** 4 Bach 6 Walcha 7 Richter ***Italian:*** 7 Germani 8 Gabrieli

organization 4 body, club, unit 5 group, guild, setup 6 agency 11 arrangement, association ***college:*** 4 frat 8 sorority 10 fraternity ***criminal:*** 4 gang 5 Mafia ***fraternal:*** (see **fraternal society**) ***government:*** (see **government agency**) ***lack of:*** 5 chaos ***political:*** 4 bloc 5 party 7 apparat, machine

organize 4 form 5 array, found, order, rally, set up, start 6 create, muster 7 arrange, dispose, marshal 8 mobilize 9 construct, establish, institute, integrate, methodize, systemize 10 constitute, coordinate 11 put together

orgy 3 bat 4 romp, soak, tear 5 binge, fling, party, revel, spree 6 ran-tan 7 blow-off, carouse, debauch, rampage, splurge, wassail 8 carousal 9 bacchanal 10 saturnalia 11 bacchanalia

oriel 3 bay 6 window

orient 5 adapt, pearl, sheen 6 adjust, luster 8 acquaint 11 accommodate

Orient 4 Asia, East 7 Far East

Oriental 5 Asian 7 Asiatic, Chinese, Eastern 8 Japanese ***chieftain:*** 4 khan ***coin:*** 3 sen, yen ***dish:*** 5 pilaf ***drink:*** 3 tea 4 sake, tuba 6 arrack ***inn:*** 4 khan 5 serai 11 caravansary 12 caravanserai ***litter:*** 4 kago 5 dooly 6 doolie 9 palanquin ***market:*** 3 suq 4 souk 6 bazaar ***nana:*** 4 amah ***prince:*** 4 raja ***ruler:*** 4 khan, raja, shah 5 calif, nawab, rajah 6 caliph, sultan ***storm:*** 7 monsoon ***taxi:*** 7 ricksha 8 rickshaw 10 jinrikisha ***title:*** 4 raja 5 rajah ***weight:*** 4 tael 5 catty, liang ***worker:*** 6 coolie

orifice see **opening**

oriflamme 4 flag 5 color 6 banner, pennon 7 pendant, pennant 8 bannerol, gonfalon, standard, streamer

origin 4 root, seed, well 5 birth, blood, start 6 source, whence 7 descent, genesis, lineage 8 ancestry, fountain, nascence, nascency, pedigree 9 beginning, inception, maternity, parentage, paternity 10 derivation, extraction, provenance, wellspring ***combining form:*** 4 geny ***of a word:*** 9 etymology

original 3 new 4 case, quiz 5 first, model, novel, prime 6 maiden, mother, native, oddity, unique, zombie 7 initial, oddball, pattern, pioneer, primary 8 creative, earliest, inventor 9 archetype, character, demiurgic, deviceful, eccentric, ingenious, innovator, inventive, precedent, precursor, primitive, prototype, underived 10 archetypal, forerunner, innovative, innovatory, introducer ***prefix:*** 4 arch 5 arche, archi

originate 4 coin, flow, make, open, rise, sire, stem 5 arise, begin, birth, breed, hatch, issue, set up, spawn, start 6 create, father, launch, parent, spring 7 emanate, proceed, produce, usher in 8 come from, commence, generate, hail from, initiate, stem from 9 institute, introduce, procreate 10 derive from, inaugurate, spring from

originator 4 sire 5 maker 6 author, father 7 creator, founder 8 inventor 9 architect, generator, innovator, patriarch 10 introducer

oriole 4 bird 8 troupial ***European:*** 6 loriot ***genus:*** 7 Icterus ***golden:*** 5 pirol 6 loriot ***kind:*** 6 golden 7 orchard 8 Bullock's 9 Baltimore

Orion 6 hunter 13 constellation ***beloved:*** 3 Eos ***belt:*** 7 Ellwand ***father:*** 7 Hyrieus 8 Poseidon ***slayer:*** 5 Diana 7 Artemis ***star:*** 5 Rigel 9 Bellatrix 10 Betelgeuse

orison 4 plea, suit 6 appeal, prayer 8 entreaty, petition 11 application, imploration, imprecation 12 supplication

Orithyia ***lover:*** 6 Boreas ***son:*** 5 Zetes 6 Calais

Orlando author 5 Woolf

Orlando Furioso author 7 Ariosto

Orleans heroine 9 Joan of Arc

orlop 4 deck

ornament 3 gem 4 deck, trim 5 adorn, jewel, prank 6 bedeck, enrich, finial, tassel 7 dress up, garnish, jewelry, pendant, whatnot 8 beautify, decorate, filigree 9 embellish, embroider, lavaliere 10 lavalliere ***architectural:*** 7 crocket 10 ball-flower ***Christmas tree:*** 4 bulb 5 angel 6 tinsel ***lip:*** 6 labret ***shoulder:*** 7 epaulet

ornate 4 lush, rich 5 fancy, showy 6 florid, frilly, gilded, rococo 7 aureate, baroque, labored, opulent 8 luscious, overdone 9 elaborate, luxuriant, luxurious, sumptuous 10 flamboyant, overworked

ornery 4 mean 5 balky, nasty, waspy 6 cranky 7 bearish, froward, restive, waspish, wayward 8 cankered, contrary, perverse, stubborn, vinegary 9 crotchety 10 vinegarish 11 wrongheaded 12 cantankerous, cross-grained

ornithic 5 avian

ornithologist ***American:*** 7 Audubon, Bartram ***English:*** 5 Gould ***Scottish:*** 6 Wilson

ornithon 6 aviary

orotund 4 full, loud 5 round 7 aureate, flowery, ringing, vibrant 8 plangent, resonant, sonorant, sonorous 9 bombastic, consonant 10 euphuistic, oratorical, resounding, rhetorical, stentorian 11 declamatory 12 magniloquent 13 grandiloquent

Orpah ***husband:*** 7 Chilion ***sister-in-law:*** 4 Ruth
orphan 4 lost, waif 5 alone, Annie 6 bereft 7 cast-off, ignored 8 forsaken, slighted, solitary 9 abandoned, foundling, neglected 10 parentless, unparented
Orpheus ***father:*** 6 Apollo 7 Oeagrus ***home:*** 6 Thrace ***instrument:*** 4 lyre ***mother:*** 8 Calliope ***wife:*** 8 Euridice
ort 3 bit 5 scrap 6 morsel 7 leaving, remnant 8 leftover
orthodox 4 good, tory 5 right, sound 6 proper, square 7 correct, die-hard, fogyish, oldline 8 accepted, admitted, approved, official, received, standard, straight 9 canonical, customary 10 button-down, recognized, sanctioned 11 reactionary, traditional 12 acknowledged, conservative, conventional 13 authoritative
orthography 8 spelling
ortolan 4 sora 7 bunting 8 bobolink
Orwell novel 10 Animal Farm
oryx 7 gemsbok 8 antelope
os 4 bone 5 esker, mouth 7 orifice
oscillate 4 sway, vary 5 squeg, swing, waver 7 vibrate 9 fluctuate, pendulate
osculate 3 lip 4 buss, kiss, peck 5 smack
osier 3 rod 6 willow 7 dogwood
Osiris ***brother:*** 3 Set 4 Seth ***crown:*** 4 atef ***father:*** 3 Geb, Keb, Seb ***mother:*** 3 Nut ***scribe:*** 5 Thoth ***sister:*** 4 Isis ***slayer:*** 3 Set 4 Seth ***son:*** 5 Horus 6 Anubis ***wife:*** 4 Isis
osmium ***symbol:*** 2 Os
osmosis 4 flow 9 diffusion 10 absorption 12 assimilation
osprey 4 hawk 8 fish hawk
Ossa and ___ 6 Pelion
osseous 4 bony
ossicle 4 bone 5 incus 6 stapes 7 malleus
ossify 3 set 6 harden
ossuary 3 urn 4 tomb 5 vault
ostensible 7 alleged, seeming 8 apparent, illusive, illusory, semblant, so-called, supposed 9 pretended, professed, purported
ostentation 4 show 7 display 9 showiness
ostentatious 4 loud 5 gaudy, showy, swank 6 chichi 7 splashy 8 peacocky 10 flamboyant, peacockish 11 pretentious
ostiole 4 pore 5 mouth 7 orifice 8 aperture
ostracism 5 exile 9 expulsion 10 banishment, relegation 11 deportation 12 displacement
ostracize 3 cut 4 oust, snob, snub 5 exile, expel 6 banish, deport 7 cast out, expulse 8 displace, throw out 9 blackball 10 expatriate 12 cold-shoulder
ostrich ***female:*** 3 hen ***genus:*** 8 Struthio ***male:*** 4 cock
Ostrogoth king 9 Theodoric
otalgia 7 earache
Otello composer 5 Verdi 7 Rossini
o tempora! o ___! 5 mores
Othello ***ensign:*** 4 Iago ***lieutenant:*** 6 Cassio ***victim, wife:*** 9 Desdemona
other ***combining form:*** 3 all 4 allo 5 heter 6 hetero
others 4 rest 9 remainder ***and:*** 4 et al 6 et alii
Othniel ***brother:*** 5 Caleb ***father:*** 5 Kenaz ***wife:*** 6 Achsah
Othni's father 8 Shemaiah
otic 5 aural 8 auditory 9 auricular
otiose 4 idle, lazy, vain 5 empty 6 futile, hollow 7 surplus, useless 8 nugatory 11 inexcusable, purposeless, superfluous 13 supernumerary
Otis 7 bustard
Ottawa chief 7 Pontiac
otter ***genus:*** 5 Lutra 7 Enhydra
ottoman 4 seat 5 couch 9 footstool
Ottoman 4 Turk 7 Turkish ***ruler:*** 5 Osman 8 Suleiman
Otus 5 giant ***brother:*** 9 Ephialtes ***father:*** 6 Aloeus 8 Poseidon ***mother:*** 9 Iphimedia ***slayer:*** 6 Apollo
ouch 2 ow 3 cry 5 bezel, jewel 6 brooch, buckle 7 setting 8 bracelet, necklace 11 exclamation
ounce 3 cat 4 atom, doit, dram, drop 5 crumb, grain, minim, shred 6 weight 7 leopard, measure, smidgen 8 particle
ouph 3 elf
our ***French:*** 5 notre ***German:*** 5 unser ***Italian:*** 6 nostra
Our Town author 6 Wilder
oust 3 bar, rob 4 lose 5 eject, evict, expel 6 banish, deport, remove 7 bereave, cast out, deprive, expulse, kick out 8 displace, relegate 9 ostracize, transport 10 disinherit, dispossess
out 4 away, free, leak, show 5 break, chase, chuck, douse, eject, evict, forth, loose 6 absent, quench 7 dismiss, extrude, showing 9 transpire 10 extinguish ***of control:*** 4 wild 7 chaotic ***of gas:*** 5 tired 9 exhausted ***of line:*** 4 awry, rude 5 askew, fresh ***of place:*** 13 inappropriate ***of sorts:*** 5 cross 7 grouchy, peevish 9 irritable ***of the ordinary:*** 3 odd 7 strange, unusual
outage 7 failure 8 blackout 12 interruption
out-and-out 5 gross, sheer, utter 7 perfect 8 absolute, complete, positive 10 consummate 13 thoroughgoing
outback 4 bush 10 wilderness
outboard 5 motor
outbreak 4 dawn, rash 5 burst, flare,

onset 6 plague, revolt 8 epidemic, eruption 9 beginning 12 commencement
outbreathe 6 exhale, expire
outburst 4 gale, gust, tiff 5 flare, sally, scene, storm 6 access, fantod, frenzy, tirade 7 flare-up, rapture, tantrum, torrent 8 eruption 9 explosion
outcast 4 hobo 5 exile, leper, tramp 6 pariah 7 Ishmael, vagrant 8 castaway, derelict, vagabond 9 reprobate 10 expatriate, Ishmaelite 11 offscouring, untouchable *Japanese:* 3 eta
outclass 4 best 5 excel 7 surpass
outcome 4 fate 5 event, issue 6 effect, result, sequel, upshot 8 causatum 9 aftermath 11 aftereffect, consequence
outcrop 4 rock 5 ledge 6 basset
outcry 4 yell 5 shout 6 clamor, tumult, upturn 7 ferment 8 upheaval 9 commotion
outdare 4 defy, face 5 beard, brave, front 7 venture 9 challenge
outdated see **out-of-date**
outdo 3 top 4 beat, best, down 5 excel, trump, worst 6 better, defeat, exceed 7 surpass, upstage 9 transcend
outdoor 7 open-air 8 alfresco 10 hypaethral
outer 5 ectad, ectal 6 remote 7 surface 8 exterior, external 9 extrinsic 10 extraneous 11 superficial
outermost 4 last 5 final 7 extreme 8 farthest, furthest, remotest
outfit 3 arm, kit, rig 4 band, firm, gear 5 corps, dress, equip, getup, guise, house, party, troop 6 tackle, troupe 7 appoint, company, concern, costume, furnish 8 accouter, accoutre, business, ensemble, materiel, tackling 9 apparatus, equipment, machinery 10 enterprise 11 habiliments 12 organization 13 accouterments, accoutrements, establishment, paraphernalia
outflow 4 flux 6 efflux 8 drainage, effluent
outfox see **outwit**
outgrowth 4 tuft 5 child, issue, shoot 6 branch, effect, member, result 7 process, product, spin-off 8 offshoot, swelling 9 by-product, offspring, processus 10 derivative, descendant 11 aftereffect, consequence, enlargement, excrescence, excrescency
outhouse 5 jakes, privy 7 latrine
outing 4 trip 5 jaunt, sally 6 junket, picnic 9 excursion 10 roundabout
outland 5 rural 6 rustic 7 bucolic, country 8 agrestic, pastoral 10 campestral, provincial 11 countrified
outlandish 3 odd 4 back, wild 5 alien, kinky, queer, ultra, weird 6 remote, vulgar 7 bizarre, curious, extreme, foreign, strange, uncouth, unusual 8 barbaric, frontier, peculiar, singular 9 barbarian, barbarous, graceless, monstrous, tasteless, unsettled 10 unorthodox 11 extravagant
outlaw 3 ban 5 taboo 6 badman, bandit, enjoin, forbid, gunman 7 inhibit 8 criminal, prohibit, renegade 9 desperado, interdict
outlay 4 cost, give 5 spend 6 expend 7 expense 8 disburse 11 expenditure 12 disbursement
outlet 4 exit, hole, shop, vent 5 store 6 egress, escape 7 opening, orifice, release 8 aperture, showroom
outline 3 hem, map, rim 4 edge, form, limn, plan 5 bound, chart, draft, shape, skirt, trace 6 border, figure, fringe, margin, projet, sketch 7 contour, profile 8 skeleton, surround, syllabus 9 adumbrate 10 figuration, silhouette 11 skeletonize
outlive 7 survive
outlook 4 side, view 5 angle, scape, scene, sight, slant, vista 8 prospect 9 direction, viewpoint 10 standpoint 11 observatory, perspective, point of view
outlying 3 far 6 far-off, remote 7 distant, faraway, removed 8 far-flung
outmoded see **out-of-date**
out-of-date 3 old 5 dowdy, passé, tacky 6 démodé, frumpy, stodgy 7 antique, archaic, oldtime, vintage 8 frumpish 9 unstylish 10 antiquated 12 old-fashioned
out-of-the-way 5 aside 6 remote, secret 7 devious, obscure, removed, retired 8 lonesome
outpouring 4 flow, gush 8 effusion, outburst
output 4 crop, gain, take 5 yield 6 profit 7 harvest, produce, product 10 production
outrage 4 harm, hurt, rape, ruin 5 abuse, anger, force, spoil, wrong 6 defile, ill-use, injury, insult, misuse, offend, ravish 7 affront, oppress, violate 8 aggrieve, deflower, ill-treat, maltreat, mischief, mistreat
outrageous 5 awful, gross 6 crying, horrid, unholy, wicked 7 beastly, ghastly, obscene, ungodly 8 dreadful, flagrant, horrible, shocking, terrible 9 desperate 10 abominable, impossible 11 intolerable, unchristian, uncivilized 12 unreasonable
outré 5 kinky, ultra 7 bizarre, strange
outrigger 4 prao, prau, proa 5 canoe, prahu
outright 3 all 5 gross, total, utter, whole 6 entire 7 perfect 8 absolute, complete, positive 10 consummate 11 unmitigated 13 thoroughgoing
outrun 4 beat 6 exceed 7 surpass
outset 4 dawn 5 birth, start 7 dawning, opening 9 beginning 12 commencement
outshine see **outdo**
outside 3 bar, but, off, top 4 open, over, past, save, slim 5 after, alien, small

6 beyond, except, remove, saving, slight, utmost 7 foreign, maximal, maximum, open-air, slender, topmost 8 alfresco, exterior, external 9 apart from, excluding 10 hypaethral, negligible 11 exclusive of *prefix:* 2 ec, ex 3 ect, exo 5 extra, extro

outsider 5 alien 7 inconnu 8 stranger 9 foreigner

outsmart see **outwit**

outspoken 4 free, open 5 bluff, blunt, frank, plain, round, vocal 6 candid, direct 8 explicit, strident 10 forthright, pointblank

outspread 4 open 6 expand, extend, unfold

outstanding 3 due 4 main, star 5 chief, major, noted 6 marked, mature, signal, superb, unpaid 7 capital, notable, overdue, payable, salient, stellar 8 dominant 9 arrestive, principal, prominent, unsettled 10 noticeable, preeminent, remarkable 11 conspicuous, magnificent, predominant, superlative

outstart 4 dawn 5 birth, onset 7 dawning, opening 9 beginning 12 commencement

outstrip 3 top 4 beat, best, lose, pass 5 excel 6 better, exceed 7 surpass 8 distance

outsweepings 4 junk 5 trash, waste 6 debris, litter, refuse 7 garbage, rubbish

outward 4 over 5 ectad, ectal, overt 7 visible 8 apparent, exterior, external 10 ostensible 11 superficial

outweigh 6 make up, offset, redeem, set off 7 balance 8 atone for, overbear 10 compensate 11 countervail, overbalance

outwit 3 fox 4 dupe, foil, gull, have, hoax, undo 5 trick 6 befool 8 hoodwink 9 bamboozle, frustrate, overreach

outworn see **out-of-date**

ouzel 4 bird 6 thrush 9 blackbird

oval 4 ooid 5 track 7 ellipse 8 elliptic 9 egg-shaped 11 ellipsoidal

ovation 6 homage, praise 8 applause

oven 4 kiln, lehr, oast 5 range, stove 6 calcar

over 2 by, on 3 mid, off, too 4 amid, anew, atop, away, done, leap, past, upon, with 5 about, above, again, aloft, clear, cross, due to, ended, extra, midst, round, vault 6 across, afresh, around, beyond, de novo, during, higher, hurdle, unduly 7 athwart, greater, outside, outward, owing to, through 8 exterior, external, finished, once more, superior, surmount 9 because of, extremely, immensely, negotiate 10 throughout 11 excessively, superjacent 12 inordinately, transversely *French:* 3 sur *German:* 4 über *prefix:* 2 ep 3 eph, epi, sur 5 extra, hyper, super, supra *Spanish:* 5 sobre

overabundance 6 excess 7 surfeit, surplus 8 plethora 10 surplusage 11 superfluity

overact 3 ham, mug 4 rant 5 emote, spout

overage see **overabundance**

overall 6 global, mainly, mostly 7 chiefly, general, largely 8 sweeping 9 generally, inclusive, primarily 10 high and low, far and wide 11 principally 13 comprehensive, predominantly

overalls 5 pants 8 trousers

over and above 6 beside, beyond 7 besides 8 as well as

over and over 3 oft 4 much 5 often 8 ofttimes 10 frequently, oftentimes, repeatedly

overbearing 5 bossy, proud 6 lordly, master 7 haughty, pompous, regnant 8 absolute, arrogant, cavalier, despotic, dominant, imperial, insolent, superior 9 ascendant, imperious, masterful, paramount, prevalent, sovereign 10 autocratic, disdainful, highhanded, imperative, peremptory, tyrannical 11 magisterial, predominant, predominate 12 preponderant, supercilious 13 high-and-mighty

overblown 3 big, fat 4 arty 5 gross, heavy, obese, stout, tumid, windy 6 fleshy, portly, turgid 7 aureate, flowery, porcine 8 dropsied, imposing, inflated, sonorous 9 bombastic, corpulent, dropsical, flatulent, tumescent 10 arty-crafty, euphuistic, oratorical, rhetorical 11 declamatory, exaggerated, pretentious 12 high-sounding, magniloquent 13 grandiloquent

overbold 6 arrant, brassy, brazen 7 blatant 8 impudent 9 barefaced, shameless, unabashed 10 unblushing 11 brazenfaced

overcast 3 cap, dim 4 dull, gray, hazy 5 cloud, cover, crown, dirty, heavy 6 cloudy, darken, shadow, sullen 7 becloud, blanket, louring, obscure 8 brooding, lowering, nubilous 9 adumbrate 10 oppressive

overcharge 3 gyp, pad 4 clip, skin, soak 5 gauge, stick 6 fleece 7 magnify 9 embellish

overcoat 6 capote, raglan, ulster 7 paletot, surtout 9 balmacaan, inverness 12 chesterfield

overcome 3 win 4 beat, best, down, lick 5 drown, throw, whelm 6 defeat, hurdle, master 7 conquer, outlive, prevail, triumph 8 surmount 9 prostrate *by grief:* 8 dejected, downcast 10 dispirited 12 disconsolate 13 broken-hearted

overconfident 5 brash, cocky 6 uppity 7 pushful 9 presuming 10 brassbound 12 presumptuous

overdo 7 exhaust, fatigue 10 exaggerate

overdue 4 late 5 lated, owing, tardy 6 mature, unpaid 7 belated, payable

9 unsettled 10 behindhand, unpunctual 11 outstanding
overemphasize 7 magnify 10 exaggerate
overflow 4 brim, pour, slop, teem 5 drown, flood, slosh, spate, spill, swamp, whelm 6 deluge, engulf, excess 7 cascade, niagara, surfeit, surplus, torrent 8 cataract, flooding, inundate, plethora, spillage, submerge 9 cataclysm 10 inundation, surplusage 11 superfluity
overflowing 4 rife 5 alive, awash 7 replete, teeming 8 thronged 13 superabundant
overgrown 4 lush, rank 5 braky, copsy, dense, thick 6 brushy, jungly 7 brambly 8 thickety 9 thicketed
overhang 3 jut 4 poke, pout 5 bulge, jetty, pouch 6 beetle 7 project 8 protrude
overhaul 3 fix 4 do up, mend, take 5 catch, patch 6 doctor, repair, revamp 7 rebuild 8 renovate 11 recondition, reconstruct
overhead 5 above, aloft 7 expense
overindulgence 6 excess 8 gluttony 12 immoderation, intemperance
overindulgent 9 excessive 10 immoderate, inordinate, untempered 11 intemperate 12 unrestrained
overkill 6 excess 7 surfeit, surplus 8 plethora 10 surplusage 11 superfluity
overlap 7 shingle 9 imbricate
overlay 3 cap 4 coat 5 cover, crown 6 veneer 7 blanket 8 covering
overload 4 glut 6 excess 7 surfeit
overlook 4 boss, fail, omit, skip 5 blank, chasm 6 forget, ignore, slight, survey 7 blink at, condone, neglect 8 chaperon, discount, dominate, omission 9 blink away, chaperone, disregard, supervise 10 tower above
overlord 5 chief, ruler 8 suzerain 9 chieftain
overpass 4 fail, omit 6 bridge, forget, ignore 7 blink at, neglect 8 discount 9 blink away, disregard
overplay 6 accent 7 magnify, point up, stretch 8 maximize 9 dramatize 10 accentuate, exaggerate 11 hyperbolize
overpower 4 rout 5 crush, drown, whelm 6 defeat, master, reduce, subdue 7 conquer 8 bear down, vanquish 9 prostrate, subjugate
overreach 3 gyp 4 beat, bilk, undo 5 cheat, cozen 6 chouse, diddle, outfox, outwit 7 defraud 8 flimflam, outslick, outsmart 11 outmaneuver
override 3 lap 4 veto 7 nullify, shingle 9 imbricate
overriding 7 central, pivotal, primary 8 cardinal 9 principal
overrule 4 sway, veto 5 reign 6 govern
overrun 4 beat, drub, lick, raid, trim, whip 5 beset, foray, smear, spill, swarm 6 exceed, infest, inroad, invade, thrash 7 outstep, surpass 8 lambaste
overseas 5 alien 6 abroad, exotic 7 foreign, strange 11 transmarine, ultramarine
oversee 3 run 4 boss 5 watch 6 survey 8 chaperon 9 chaperone, supervise 11 quarterback, superintend
overseer 4 boss, head 5 chief 7 foreman, manager 8 chaperon 9 chaperone 10 supervisor
overshadow 3 dim 4 haze 5 cloud, cover 6 darken 7 becloud, obscure 9 adumbrate
overshoe 4 boot 6 arctic, galosh, patten, rubber
oversight 4 care, skip 5 aegis, blank, chasm, check, error, guard 6 charge 7 conduct, control, custody, default, failure, keeping, mistake, neglect, running 8 handling, omission, tutelage 10 ciceronage, intendance, management 11 chaperonage
overslaugh 3 bar, dam 5 block, brake 6 hinder, impede 8 obstruct
oversoon 5 early 7 betimes 8 previous, untimely 9 premature 11 prematurely
overspread 3 cap 5 beset, cover, crown 6 infest 7 blanket
overstate 3 pad 5 color, fudge 7 magnify 9 embellish, embroider 10 exaggerate
overstep 6 exceed 7 surpass 8 infringe, trespass 10 transgress
overstock 6 excess 7 surplus 9 remainder 10 surplusage
overstress 7 magnify 8 maximize 10 exaggerate
overswarm 4 raid 5 beset, foray 6 infest, inroad, invade
overt 4 open 6 patent 7 obvious, outward, visible 8 apparent, manifest
overtake 4 pass
over there 3 yon 6 yonder
overthrow 4 down, fell, oust, rout, ruin 5 purge, upset 6 defeat, depose, remove, topple, tumble, unseat 7 beating, conquer, debacle, destroy, licking, unhorse 8 dethrone, downcast, drubbing 9 liquidate, trouncing 10 defeasance 11 shellacking 12 vanquishment
overtone 4 hint 8 harmonic 10 suggestion 11 association, connotation, implication
overture 3 bid 5 proem 6 tender 7 advance, preface, prelude 8 approach, exordium, foreword, preamble, prologue, proposal 9 prelusion 11 proposition 12 introduction, prolegomenon
overturn 3 tip 4 coup, down 5 upend, upset 6 keel up, topple, tumble 7 capsize,

shake-up, unhorse **9** prostrate **10** revolution
overweening **5** brash **6** uppish, uppity **7** forward, pushful **8** arrogant **10** immoderate **12** presumptuous **13** self-assertive
overweight **3** fat **5** gross, heavy, obese, stout **6** fleshy, portly **9** corpulent
overwhelm **4** beat, bury, drub, lick, ruin, sink, trim, whip **5** crush, drown, flood, floor, lower, smear, swamp, upset, wreck **6** deluge, engulf, thrash **7** destroy, disturb, shatter, shellac, smother **8** inundate, submerge **9** devastate, downgrade, dumbfound, prostrate **10** demoralize **11** subordinate
overwhelmed **5** agape **6** aghast **7** stunned **13** thunderstruck
overword **6** burden **7** refrain
Ovid work **5** Fasti **7** Tristia **8** Heroides **13** Metamorphoses
oviform **4** ooid, oval **5** ovate **6** ooidal **9** egg-shaped
ovine **5** sheep **9** sheeplike
ovoid see oviform
ovule **3** egg ***fertilized:*** **4** seed
ovum **3** egg **6** gamete **7** egg cell
owing **3** due **6** mature, unpaid **7** overdue, payable **9** unsettled
owing to **4** over **7** through **9** because of
owl ***Australian:*** **7** boobook **8** morepork ***cry:*** **4** hoot ***kind:*** **3** elf **4** barn, gray, lulu **5** eagle, gnome, madge, pygmy, snowy **6** barred, horned **7** saw-whet, screech **9** long-eared **10** short-eared **11** great horned ***resembling:*** **8** strigine ***snowy:*** **7** harfang
Owl and Pussycat author **4** Lear
own **4** avow, have, hold **5** admit, allow, enjoy, grant, let on **6** fess up, retain **7** concede, confess, possess **11** acknowledge
owner **4** lord **8** landlady, landlord **9** possessor **10** proprietor
ownership **4** hand **5** title **8** dominion, property **10** possession **11** proprietary ***perpetual:*** **8** mortmain
ox **3** yak **4** anoa, buff, gaur, musk, zebu **5** bison, gayal, steer **6** bovine, ovibos **7** banteng, bantery, brahman, buffalo ***Asian:*** **4** zebu ***combining form:*** **4** bovi ***extinct:*** **4** urus **7** aurochs ***family:*** **7** Bovidae ***relating to:*** **6** bovine ***Scottish:*** **4** nowt, owse ***wild:*** **4** anoa, gaur **7** banteng **8** saladang, seladang
oxeye **5** daisy **6** flower
oxford **4** shoe **5** cloth, sheep
oxide ***calcium:*** **4** lime **9** quicklime ***ferric:*** **4** rust ***sodium:*** **4** soda
oxidize **4** rust
oxygen **3** air, gas **5** ozone **7** element ***discoverer:*** **9** Lavoisier ***form:*** **5** ozone ***liquid:*** **3** lox
oyster **5** forte **6** medium **7** bivalve, mollusk ***bed:*** **4** park **6** claire, cultch ***combining form:*** **5** ostre **6** ostrei, ostreo ***eggs:*** **5** spawn ***genus:*** **6** Ostrea **11** Crassostrea ***Long island:*** **9** bluepoint ***product:*** **5** pearl ***shell:*** **4** test **5** shuck ***young:*** **4** spat
oysterbird **5** tirma **10** sanderling
oysterfish **6** tautog
oyster grass **4** kelp **10** sea lettuce
Oz ***creator:*** **4** Baum ***inhabitant:*** **8** Munchkin
Ozark State **8** Missouri
Ozem ***brother:*** **5** David ***father:*** **5** Jesse **9** Jerahmeel
Ozni's father **3** Gad
Ozymandias author **7** Shelley

P

pabulum **4** food **7** aliment **8** nutrient **9** nutriment **10** sustenance **11** nourishment
pace **3** rut **4** gait, hoof, rate, step, time, walk **5** grind, speed, tempo, tread, troop **6** timing **7** example, fluency, forerun, precede, proceed, routine, traipse **8** ambulate, antecede, celerity, rapidity, regulate, velocity **9** quickness, rapidness, swiftness, treadmill
pachyderm **8** elephant
pacific **4** calm, meek, mild **6** gentle, irenic, placid, serene **8** dovelike, peaceful, tranquil **9** appeasing, peaceable
Pacificator, Great **4** Clay
Pacific Ocean discoverer **6** Balboa
pacifist **4** dove **6** irenic **8** appeaser, peaceful **9** peaceable **10** nonviolent, satyagrahi **11** peacemonger
pacify **4** calm, ease, lull **5** allay, quiet, still **6** settle, soften, soothe, subdue, temper **7** appease, assuage, mollify, placate
pack **3** jam, lot, lug, mob, ram, wad **4** bear, cram, fill, heap, load, lump, mass, much, pile, stow, tamp, tote **5** carry, choke, crowd, ferry, group, store, stuff, troop **6** barrel, bestow, bundle, charge, convey, depart **7** compact **8** compress **9** container
pack animal **3** ass **4** mule **5** burro, camel, horse, llama **6** donkey **7** jackass, sumpter **13** beast of burden
packed **4** full **5** awash **7** brimful, crowded, stuffed **8** brimming **9** chock-full
packet **3** pot, wad **4** boat, mint, pile **6** boodle, bundle, parcel **7** fortune
pact **4** bond **6** treaty **7** bargain, concord **8** alliance, covenant **9** agreement
pad **3** mat, wad **5** fudge, guard, quilt, stuff **6** muffle, shield, tablet, trudge **7** bolster, cushion, magnify, stretch **8** overdraw **9** embellish, embroider, overpaint, overstate **10** exaggerate, overcharge
paddle **3** fin, oar, row **4** pull **5** spank **6** dabble, thrash **7** flipper
pagan **7** gentile, heathen, infidel, profane **8** idolator **9** infidelic **10** unbeliever ***god:*** **4** idol
page **4** book, call, leaf **5** folio, sheet **6** locate, summon **7** writing ***left-hand:*** **5** verso ***reverse:*** **5** verso ***right-hand:*** **5** recto
pageant **4** sham, show **7** charade **8** disguise, pretense **9** spectacle **10** exhibition
Pagiel's father **5** Ocran **6** Ochran
Pagliacci ***character:*** **5** Canio, Nedda, Tonio **6** Silvio ***composer:*** **11** Leoncavallo
pagoda **2** ta **3** taa **6** alcove, gazebo, temple **9** belvedere **11** garden house, summerhouse
pail **6** bucket, piggin
pain **3** ail, irk, try **4** ache, care, hurt, pang **5** agony, cramp, grief, throe, upset, wound **6** effort, grieve, harass, harrow, injure, stitch, stress, twinge **7** afflict, agonize, anguish, crucify, provoke, torment, torture, travail, trouble **8** aggrieve, convulse, distress, lacerate **9** suffering **10** affliction, discomfort, excruciate ***abdominal:*** **5** colic ***back:*** **7** lumbago ***combining form:*** **3** alg **4** agra, algo, noci **5** agrae (plural), algia, algic **6** odynia, odynic ***ear:*** **6** otalgy **7** otalgia ***intensity unit:*** **3** dol ***muscular:*** **7** myalgia
painful **3** raw **4** sore **5** acute, sharp **6** aching, bitter **7** algetic, galling, hurting, irksome, racking **8** annoying, grievous, piercing, shooting, stabbing, stinging, unsavory **9** agonizing, harrowing, torturous, upsetting, vexatious **10** afflictive, tormenting
painkiller **6** opiate **7** anodyne **8** morphine, narcotic **9** analgesic **10** anesthetic
painstaking **5** exact, fussy **7** careful, heedful **8** diligent, exacting, punctual **9** laborious **10** meticulous, scrupulous **11** punctilious
paint **4** coat, daub, face, limn **5** color, japan, stain **6** depict, fresco, makeup **7** portray **9** delineate, represent **10** maquillage
painter **6** artist ***American:*** **4** West, Wood **5** Abbey, Henri, Hicks, Homer, Johns, Kroll, Marin, Moses, Peale, Ryder, Shahn, Sloan, Weber, Wyeth **6** Benton, Catlin, Copley, Eakins, Hassam, Hopper, Leutze, Martin, Rivers, Rothko, Stella, Stuart, Tanguy, Thorpe, Warhol **7** Allston, Bellows, Cassatt, La Farge, O'Keeffe, Parrish, Pollock, Sargent, Sheeler, Tiffany, Tworkov, Wiggins **8** Melchers, Rockwell, Sullivan, Trumbull, Whistler **9** Feininger, Remington, Twachtman, Vanderlyn **10** Motherwell, Whit-

tredge 12 Lichtenstein ***Austrian:*** 9 Kokoschka ***Belgian:*** 6 Campin 8 Magritte ***Canadian:*** 4 Kane 6 Harris, Watson 7 Jackson, Thomson 9 MacDonald ***Chinese:*** 4 Wu Li 6 Ma Yüan 7 Wang Wei 8 Yen Li-pen ***Dutch:*** 4 Hals, Lely, Maas, Maes 5 Bosch, Steen 6 Potter 7 de Hooch, de Witte, Hobbema, van Gogh, Vermeer 8 Mondrian, Ruisdael, Ruysdael, Terborch 9 Rembrandt, Wouwerman 11 Terbrugghen ***English:*** 4 John, Lear 5 Bacon, Blake, Brown, Lewis, Watts 6 Inness, Romney, Turner, Wilson 7 Hogarth, Kneller, Millais, Raeburn 8 Lawrence, Reynolds, Rossetti 9 Constable, Nicholson 12 Gainsborough ***Flemish:*** 4 Goes 6 Rubens, Weyden 7 Memling, Teniers, Van Dyck, Van Eyck 8 Breughel, Brueghel ***French:*** 4 Doré, Dufy 5 Corot, David, Degas, Leger, Manet, Monet, Puvis, Redon, Vouet 6 Braque, Breton, Claude, Clouet, Gerome, Greuze, Ingres, Le Brun, Le Nain, Millet, Renoir, Seurat, Sisley, Tanguy, Vernet 7 Bonheur, Bonnard, Cézanne, Chardin, Courbet, Daumier, Duchamp, Gauguin, Matisse, Morisot, Poussin, Rouault, Utrillo, Watteau 8 Dubuffet, Pissarro, Rousseau, Vlaminck, Vuillard 9 Delacroix, Fragonard, Géricault, Laurencin 10 Meissonier 11 Le Corbusier ***German:*** 5 Dürer, Ernst, Grosz, Nolde 6 Muller 7 Cranach, Holbein, Lochner, Schwind, Zoffany 8 Kirchner, Kollwitz 9 Grünewald, Kandinsky 10 Schongauer, Wohlgemuth ***Greek:*** 6 Zeuxis 7 Apelles 10 Polygnotus ***Irish:*** 5 Yeats ***Italian:*** 4 Reni, Rosa, Tura 5 Campi, Lippi, Piero, Sarto 6 Cosimo, Giotto, Romano, Sodoma, Titian, Vasari 7 Bellini, Chirico, Cimabue, da Vinci, Fiesole, Martini, Orcagna, Peruzzi, Raphael, Tiepolo, Uccello, Zuccari 8 Del Sarto, Fabriano, Giordano, Mantegna, Masaccio, Montagna, Perugino, Pontorno, Severini, Veronese, Vivarini 9 Carpaccio, Correggio, Francesca 10 Caravaggio, Modigliani, Signorelli, Tintoretto, Verrocchio, Zuccarelli 11 Ghirlandajo 12 Michelangelo, Parmigianino ***Japanese:*** 5 Korin 6 Sesshu ***Lithuanian:*** 7 Soutine ***Mexican:*** 6 Orozco, Rivera, Tamayo 9 Siqueiros ***Norwegian:*** 5 Munch ***Russian:*** 7 Chagall, Roerich 9 Kandinsky ***Scottish:*** 6 Ramsay 7 Nasmyth, Raeburn ***Spanish:*** 4 Dali, Goya, Gris, Miró, Sert 6 Ribera, Rincon, Tapies 7 El Greco, Herrera, Murillo, Picasso, Zuloaga 8 Zurbaran 9 Velasquez, Velazquez ***Swedish:*** 4 Zorn 6 Roslin ***Swiss:*** 4 Klee, Witz

painting 3 oil 7 acrylic, picture 10 watercolor ***circular:*** 5 tondo ***combining form:*** 6 chromy ***one-color:*** 8 monotint 10 monochrome ***plaster:*** 5 secco 6 fresco ***style:*** 6 cubism, Gothic, pop art, rococo 7 baroque, Bauhaus, dadaism, fauvism, realism 8 Barbizon, futurism 9 Byzantine, geometric, mannerism 10 avant-garde, classicism, surrealism 11 romanticism 13 expressionism, impressionism ***technique:*** 3 oil 6 fresco, gouche, pastel 7 polymer, tempera 9 encaustic 10 watercolor ***tool:*** 5 brush, easel, knife, paint 6 canvas 7 palette ***wall:*** 5 mural

pair 3 duo, two 4 dyad, join, mate, span, team, yoke 5 brace, match, unite 6 couple 7 doublet, twosome 8 geminate

Pakistan ***capital:*** 9 Islamabad ***largest city:*** 7 Karachi ***monetary unit:*** 5 rupee ***province:*** 4 Sind 6 Punjab 11 Baluchistan

pal 4 chum, mate 5 buddy, crony 6 comate, friend 7 comrade, partner 9 associate, companion 11 confederate

paladin see **douzeper**

Palal's father 4 Uzai

Palamedes ***brother:*** 6 Sforza 8 Achilles ***father:*** 8 Nauplius ***slayer:*** 7 Corinda, Ulysses 8 Odysseus

palatable 5 sapid, tasty, yummy 6 savory, toothy 8 luscious, pleasing, saporous, savorous, tasteful, tempting 9 aperitive, delicious, relishing, saporific, savorsome, toothsome 10 appetizing, delightful, flavorsome

palate 4 zest 5 gusto, heart, taste 6 relish

palatial 4 lush, rich 5 large, noble, plush 6 Capuan, deluxe, ornate 7 opulent, stately 8 luscious, splendid 9 luxuriant, luxurious, sumptuous 10 impressive 11 magnificent, upholstered

palaver 3 gas, yak 4 blab, cant, chat, guff, tack 5 clack 6 affair, babble, hot air, jargon, parley 7 chatter, concern, lexicon, lookout, prattle, seminar 8 business, colloquy, dialogue 10 colloquium, conference, discussion, rap session 12 conversation

palaverous 5 windy, wordy 6 prolix 7 diffuse, verbose 9 redundant 10 long-winded

pale 3 dim, wan 4 ashy, dull, fade, gray, sick, weak 5 ashen, faint, fence, inane, livid, lurid, muddy, pasty, stake, waxen, white 6 anemic, blanch, chalky, doughy, feeble, jejune, pallid, picket, sallow, sickly, watery, whiten 7 ghastly, insipid, tarnish, waxlike 8 blanched, encircle, waterish, whitened 9 bloodless, colorless, deathlike

paleness 6 pallor

palinode 5 unsay 6 abjure, recall, recant 7 retract 8 forswear, take back, withdraw 10 retraction 11 recantation

pall 4 bore, cloy, glut, jade, sate, tire 5 cloak, drape, ennui, gorge, weary 6 canopy, clothe, mantle, stodge 7 disgust, satiate, surfeit 8 covering 11 counterpane

palladium ***symbol:*** 2 Pd

Pallas ***brother:*** **6** Aegeus ***father:*** **7** Pandion ***slayer:*** **7** Theseus ***wife:*** **4** Styx; (see also **Athena**)
palliate **4** ease, hide, mask **5** cloak, cover, glass, gloze, salve **6** excuse, lessen, soften, temper, veneer, whiten **7** conceal, condone, cover up, lighten, qualify, varnish **8** disguise, mitigate, moderate, prettify **9** alleviate, dissemble, extenuate, glass over, gloze over, sugarcoat, whitewash
pallid **3** wan **4** ashy, dull **5** ashen, waxen **6** anemic, doughy, watery **8** blanched, waterish **9** bloodless, colorless
Pallu ***father:*** **6** Reuben ***son:*** **5** Eliab
pally **4** cozy **6** chummy **8** intimate
palm **3** tip **4** hide **5** bribe, merus, prize **6** thenar **7** conceal ***beverage:*** **4** nipa **5** assai ***fiber:*** **4** bass, bast **6** gomuti **7** bassine **8** piassava ***fruit:*** **4** date **7** coconut **11** coquilla nut ***kind:*** **3** fan, wax **4** coco, date, doom, hemp, nipa, sago **5** areca, assai, betel, datil, ivory, royal, tucum **6** gomuti, grigri, grugru, raffia, rattan **7** cabbage, feather, palmyra, talipot **8** carnauba, palmetto, piassava **12** Washingtonia ***leaf:*** **4** olla **5** frond ***starch:*** **4** sago ***vine:*** **6** rattan
palmer **7** pilgrim
Palmetto State **13** South Carolina
palm lily **2** ti
palm off **5** foist **7** deceive
Palmyra's queen **7** Zenobia
palooka **3** oaf **4** gawk, lout, lump **5** klutz **6** lubber, lummox
palpable **4** sure **5** clear, plain **6** patent **7** certain, evident, obvious, seeming, tactile **8** apparent, distinct, manifest, positive, striking, tangible **9** arresting **10** noticeable **11** perceptible, unequivocal
palpate **4** feel **5** touch **6** finger, handle
palpitate **4** beat **5** pulse, throb **6** quiver **7** flutter, pulsate **12** pitter-patter
palter **3** fib, lie **5** evade, fence **6** haggle, parley **7** bargain, chaffer, falsify **10** equivocate **11** prevaricate
Palti ***father:*** **5** Laish, Raphu ***wife:*** **6** Michal
Paltiel's father **5** Azzan
paltry **3** low, set **4** base, mean, poor, puny, vile **5** borne, cheap, petty, small, tatty, trash **6** common, little, measly, narrow, shabby, shoddy, sleazy, slight, trashy **7** limited, low-down, pitiful, rubbish, trivial **8** beggarly, inferior, picayune, piddling, rubbishy, trifling **9** worthless **10** despicable, picayunish **11** ineffectual, Mickey Mouse, unimportant **13** insignificant
Pamela author **10** Richardson
pamper **3** pet **4** baby **5** humor, spoil **6** caress, cocker, coddle, cosset, cuddle, dandle, fondle, regale, tickle **7** cater to, cherish, gratify, indulge **11** mollycoddle ***Irish:*** **6** cosher
pamphlet **5** tract **6** folder **7** booklet, leaflet **8** brochure **10** broadsheet
pan **3** rap **5** basin, blame, cut up, knock **6** attack **7** censure, condemn **8** denounce, ridicule **9** criticize, reprehend
Pan **5** Inuus **6** Faunus ***father:*** **6** Hermes ***invention:*** **6** syrinx ***lower part:*** **4** goat ***mother:*** **8** Penelope ***pipe:*** **6** syrinx ***seat of worship:*** **7** Arcadia ***son:*** **7** Silenus
panacea **4** cure **6** elixir, relief, remedy **7** cure-all, nostrum **10** catholicon
Panacea's father **9** Asclepius **11** Aesculapius
pancake **8** flapjack, slapjack ***French:*** **5** crepe ***Jewish:*** **5** latke **6** blintz **7** blintze ***Russian:*** **5** blini
Pandarus **6** archer **8** procuror ***father:*** **6** Lycaon ***slayer:*** **8** Diomedes
pandect **4** code **6** aperçu, digest, précis, sketch, survey **8** syllabus **10** compendium
pandemoniac **7** avernal, hellish, riotous, stygian **8** infernal, plutonic **9** cimmerian, plutonian
pandemonium **3** din **4** hell, sink **5** babel, Sodom **6** clamor, hubbub, jangle, racket, tumult, uproar **7** cesspit **8** cesspool, disorder **9** confusion **10** hullabaloo, tintamarre
pander **4** pimp **5** bully, cadet, cater **8** fancy man, procurer **9** procuress
Pandion ***daughter:*** **6** Procne **9** Philomela ***son:*** **6** Pallas
Pandora ***creator:*** **10** Hephaestus ***husband:*** **10** Epimetheus
pandurina **4** lute
panegyric **6** eulogy, praise **7** tribute **8** citation, encomium **9** laudation **10** salutation
panegyrical **9** laudative, laudatory, praiseful **10** eulogistic **11** encomiastic
panegyrize **4** hymn, laud **5** bless, cry up, extol **6** praise **7** glorify, magnify **8** eulogize **9** celebrate
panel **4** gore, jury **5** board, label **6** hurdle
pan-fry **5** sauté
pang **4** ache, pain, stab **5** agony, prick, spasm, throe **6** stitch, twinge **7** anguish, torment
Pangloss' pupil **7** Candide
panhandler **6** beggar
panic **4** fear, wild **5** alarm, dread, scare **6** dismay, frenzy, fright, horror, terror **8** cold feet, frighten, hysteria, stampede **11** trepidation **13** consternation
panoply **4** pomp, show **5** armor, array, shine **6** parade **7** display, fanfare
panorama **4** view **5** orbit, range, reach, scene, scope, sweep, vista **6** extent, radius **7** compass, purview **9** cyclorama
pan out **5** click **6** go over **7** come off, succeed
pant **3** aim **4** blow, gasp, gulp, huff, long,

puff, wind, wish **5** chuff, heave, throb, yearn **6** aspire, desire, hunger, thirst, wheeze **7** pulsate **9** palpitate
Pantagruel **5** giant *companion:* **7** Panurge *father:* **9** Gargantua *mother:* **7** Badebec
Pantaloon's daughter **9** Columbine
Panthea's husband **9** Abradatus
pantomime **6** ballet, dancer **7** charade **12** harlequinade
pantry **6** closet, larder **7** buttery
pants **5** jeans **6** slacks **7** drawers **8** britches, knickers, trousers
pantywaist **5** sissy **7** doormat, milksop
Panurge's companion **10** Pantagruel
Paolo's lover **9** Francesca
pap **4** food, mash, pulp, slop **5** paste, trash **7** aliment, garbage, rubbish **9** nutriment **10** sustenance **11** nourishment
papal **8** pontific **9** apostolic **10** pontifical *cape:* **5** fanon, orale *court:* **5** Curia *decree:* **8** decretal *envoy:* **6** nuncio **8** ablegate *letter:* **4** bull **10** encyclical
paper **4** card **5** essay, sheet, theme **6** letter, report **7** article, nominal **8** clerical, document **9** monograph, newspaper, wallpaper **10** memorandum **11** composition, publication **12** dissertation *arrangement:* **3** pad **6** tablet *coarse:* **9** newsprint *collection:* **4** file **7** dossier *combining form:* **6** papyro *copying:* **6** carbon *currency:* **5** scrip *measure:* **4** page, ream **5** quire, sheet *roll:* **6** scroll *scrap:* **4** chad *size:* **3** cap **4** demi, demy **5** atlas, crown, folio, legal, royal, sexto, sixmo **6** octavo, quarto **7** emperor **8** elephant, foolscap, imperial **10** typewriter *stiff:* **9** cardboard, wallboard **12** Bristol board *strong:* **5** kraft **6** manila *thin:* **4** bank **6** pelure, tissue **9** onionskin *transparent:* **8** glassine *writing:* **3** rag **6** vellum **9** parchment
paper folding *Japanese:* **7** origami
paphian **6** erotic, wanton
pappy **3** dad **4** soft **5** mushy **6** father, spongy **7** pulpous, squashy, squishy, squushy **8** squelchy, yielding **9** succulent
par **4** mean, norm **5** equal **6** median **7** average **8** equality, sameness, standard
parable **4** myth, tale **5** fable, story **8** allegory
parachute **7** bailout, skydive **8** paradrop *part:* **5** riser **6** canopy **7** harness, ripcord
paraclete **6** helper **8** advocate, consoler **9** comforter **10** Holy Spirit **11** intercessor
parade **4** brag, pomp, show **5** array, boast, flash, march, shine, strut **6** expose, flaunt, reveal **7** declare, display, disport, divulge, exhibit, fanfare, listing, marshal, panoply, publish, recital, show off, trot out **8** brandish, disclose, movement, proclaim **9** advertise, cavalcade, formation, pageantry, promenade **10** exhibition, masquerade
paradigm **5** ideal, model **6** mirror **7** example, pattern **8** ensample, exemplar, standard **9** archetype, beau ideal, prototype
paradise **4** Eden, Zion **5** bliss **6** Canaan, heaven, utopia **7** arcadia, elysium, nirvana **8** empyrean **9** Cockaigne, fairyland, Shangri-la **10** Civitas Dei, lubberland, wonderland **12** New Jerusalem, promised land
Paradise Lost author **6** Milton
paragon **3** gem **4** love, pick, tops **5** champ, cream, ideal, jewel, liken, match, model, peach, trump **6** beauty, equate, lovely **7** compare, epitome, pattern, phoenix **8** champion, exemplar, last word, nonesuch, parallel, ultimate **9** archetype, beau ideal, nonpareil **10** apotheosis, assimilate
Paraguay *capital:* **8** Asuncion *monetary unit:* **7** guarani
parallel **4** akin, even, like **5** align, alike, along, equal, liken, match **6** agnate, double, equate, line up **7** compare, similar, uniform **8** analogue **9** analogous, collimate, collocate, consonant, correlate, duplicate **10** assimilate, comparable, comparison, correspond, equivalent, similarity **11** counterpart, countertype, duplication, resemblance **13** correspondent, corresponding
parallelogram **5** rhomb **6** oblong, square **7** rhombus **8** rhomboid **9** rectangle
paralysis **5** palsy **9** impotence *combining form:* **5** lyses, lysis, plegy **6** plegia
paralyze **4** daze, maim, stun **5** close, daunt **6** appall, bemuse, benumb, deaden, disarm, dismay, weaken **7** astound, cripple, destroy, disable, horrify, nonplus, petrify, prevent, stupefy, unnerve **8** demolish, enfeeble, knock out, shut down **9** prostrate **11** flabbergast **12** incapacitate
paramount **5** above, chief **6** master **7** capital, regnant, supreme **8** cardinal, crowning, dominant, headmost, superior **9** sovereign, uppermost **10** commanding, preeminent
paramour **5** lover, Romeo **6** master **7** amorist, Don Juan, gallant **8** Casanova, fancy man, lothario, mistress **9** boyfriend, inamorata, inamorato **10** girl friend
parapet **4** wall **7** bastion, bulwark, rampart **10** battlement, breastwork *part:* **6** merlon
paraphernalia **4** gear **6** outfit, tackle **8** materiel, tackling **9** apparatus, equipment, machinery, materials, trappings **11** furnishings, habiliments **13** accouterments, accoutrements, appurtenances
paraphrase **6** reword **7** restate, version **9** rendering, summarize, translate **10** transcribe **11** restatement, translation
parasite **4** laze **5** idler, leech, toady

6 infest, sponge, sucker 7 sponger 8 barnacle, deadbeat, ectozoan, entozoan, hanger-on 9 dependent, sycophant 10 freeloader, smell-feast 11 bloodsucker

parasitic 7 fawning 8 cowering, cringing, sponging, toadying, toadyish 9 groveling, kowtowing, leechlike, truckling 11 bootlicking, freeloading, sycophantic

___ paratus 6 semper

parboil 4 stew 5 sweat 6 seethe, simmer

Parcae 5 Fates ***name:*** 4 Nona 5 Morta 6 Decuma

parcel 3 box, cut, lot 4 body, clot, deal, mete, pack, part, plot, wrap 5 allot, array, batch, bunch, clump, group, piece, quota, share, tract 6 assign, bundle, clutch, divide, member, moiety, packet, ration 7 cluster, package, portion, prorate, section, segment 8 allocate, disburse, disperse, division, fragment 9 apportion 10 distribute

parch 3 dry 4 burn, sear 5 roast, toast 6 scorch 7 shrivel 9 dehydrate, desiccate, exsiccate

parchment 5 paper 6 vellum 8 document

pardon 4 free 5 remit, spare 6 accept, excuse 7 absolve, amnesty, condone, forgive, justify, release 8 liberate, reprieve, tolerate 9 acquittal, exculpate, indemnity, remission 10 absolution, indulgence 11 exculpation, exoneration, forgiveness, vindication

pardonable 6 venial 9 excusable

pare 3 cut 4 clip, crop, flay, peel, skin, trim 5 lower, prune, scalp, shave, shear, skive, slash, strip 6 reduce, remove 7 curtail, cut back, cut down, whittle 8 diminish

parent 4 make, sire 5 cause, hatch, spawn 6 author, create, father, mother, origin 7 forbear, produce 8 ancestor, begetter, forebear, generate 9 originate, procreate 10 forefather, progenitor

parenthetically 6 obiter 8 by the bye, by the way 9 in passing

parentless 6 orphan 8 orphaned

par excellence 4 fine 5 prime 6 famous 7 classic 8 champion, superior 9 classical, number one 10 first-class 12 preeminently

pariah 5 leper 7 Ishmael, outcast 8 castaway, déclassé, derelict 10 Ishmaelite 11 offscouring, untouchable ***Japanese:*** 3 eta

Paris ***beloved:*** 5 Helen ***betrothed:*** 6 Juliet ***father:*** 5 Priam ***mother:*** 6 Hecuba ***slayer:*** 11 Philoctetes ***wife:*** 6 Oenone

Paris ***ancient name:*** 7 Lutetia ***avenue:*** 13 Champs-Elysées ***basilica:*** 10 Sacré Coeur ***cathedral:*** 9 Notre Dame ***city hall:*** 12 Hôtel de Ville ***college:*** 8 Sorbonne ***garden:*** 9 Tuileries 10 Luxembourg ***island:*** 11 Île de la Cité ***museum:*** 4 Army 5 Cluny 6 Louvre ***palace:*** 6 Louvre 7 Bourbon ***patron saint:*** 9 Geneviève ***racecourse:*** 7 Auteuil ***river:*** 5 Seine ***section:*** 8 Left Bank 9 Right Bank 10 Montmartre 12 Latin Quarter ***stock exchange:*** 6 Bourse ***subway:*** 5 Metro ***tower:*** 6 Eiffel

Parisina ***author:*** 5 Byron ***husband:*** 3 Azo ***lover:*** 4 Hugo ***slayer:*** 3 Azo

parity 7 analogy 8 equality, likeness, nearness, sameness 9 closeness 10 adequation, similarity, similitude 11 equivalence

parka 6 anorak, jacket 8 pullover

park designer 4 Vaux 6 Paxton 7 Alphand, Olmsted

parlance 4 talk 5 idiom 6 phrase, speech 7 diction, wordage, wording 8 phrasing, verbiage 9 verbalism 11 phraseology

parley 3 bet, use 4 chat, talk 5 speak, treat 6 advise, confab, confer, huddle, powwow 7 consult, discuss, meeting, utilize 8 collogue, colloquy, converse, dialogue 9 discourse 10 conference, converse in, discussion, rap session 11 confabulate 12 conversation 13 confabulation

parliament see **legislature**

parlor 5 salon

parlous 4 very 5 hairy, risky 6 chancy, damned, mighty, wicked 7 greatly 8 critical 9 dangerous, extremely, hazardous 11 exceedingly, excessively

parochial 5 petty 6 narrow 7 bigoted, insular 9 sectarian, small-town 10 provincial

parody 3 ape, rib 4 mock 5 mimic, spoof 6 satire, send-up 7 imitate, takeoff 8 ridicule, spoofery, travesty 9 burlesque, imitation 10 caricature

paronomasia 3 pun 9 calembour

parous 6 gravid 8 childing, enceinte, pregnant 9 expectant, expecting

parrot 4 copy, echo 5 mimic, polly 6 repeat 7 chatter, imitate ***kind:*** 3 ara, kea 4 jako, kaka, lory 5 macaw 6 Amazon, budgie, kakapo 8 cockatoo, lorikeet, lovebird, parakeet 9 cockatiel, parrakeet 10 budgerigar

parrot fever 11 psittacosis

parrot fish 4 loro 5 lauia 6 scarid

parry 4 duck, fend, ward 5 avert, avoid, block, dodge, evade, fence, shirk 7 deflect, prevent 8 preclude, sidestep 9 forestall

Parsifal ***composer:*** 6 Wagner ***magician:*** 8 Klingsor ***quest:*** 5 grail ***son:*** 9 Lohengrin ***temptress:*** 6 Kundry

parsimonious 4 mean 5 cheap, close, tight 6 frugal, stingy 7 miserly 9 niggardly, penurious 11 closefisted, tightfisted 12 cheese-paring 13 penny-pinching

parson 5 clerk 6 cleric, divine, rector

8 clerical, minister, preacher, reverend 9 churchman, clergyman 12 ecclesiastic
parsonage 5 manse
parson bird 3 poe, tui 4 koko
part 3 bit, cut, lot 4 bite, chip, duty, meed, role, side, some, spot, unit 5 allot, chunk, organ, piece, place, quota, scrap, sever, share, slice 6 behalf, cleave, detach, detail, divide, member, moiety, office, ration, region, sector, sunder 7 break up, disjoin, dissect, element, measure, portion, quality, quantum, quarter, section, segment 8 dissever, district, disunite, division, fraction, fragment, function, separate 9 allotment, allowance, component ***combining form:*** 3 mer 4 mere, mero, mery, toma, tome, tomy 5 meric, meris, parti 6 merous
partake 5 share 6 accept 7 receive 11 participate
Parthenon ***sculptor:*** 7 Phidias ***site:*** 9 Acropolis
partial 6 biased, unfair, warped 7 colored, half-way 8 one-sided 9 jaundiced 10 fractional, incomplete, prejudiced 11 fragmentary, predilected, predisposed ***prefix:*** 4 demi, semi
partiality 4 bent, bias 7 leaning 8 penchant, tendency 9 inclining, prejudice 10 chauvinism 11 inclination 12 one-sidedness, predilection
participant 4 aide 5 actor 6 fellow, helper, sharer 7 sharing 8 confrere 9 colleague
participate 5 share 7 partake
particle 3 ace, bit, dot, jot, ray 4 atom, damn, doit, dram, drop, hoot, iota, mite, mote, snap, spot, whit 5 atomy, crumb, fleck, grain, minim, ounce, scrap, shred, speck, whoop 6 morsel, smidge, smitch, tittle 7 dribbet, granule, modicum, smidgen 8 fragment 9 scintilla ***atomic:*** 3 ion 5 anion 6 cation ***combining form:*** 5 plast ***elementary:*** 3 psi, tau 4 kaon, muon, pion 5 boson, meson 6 baryon, hadron, lambda, lepton, photon, proton 7 fermion, hyperon, neutron, nucleon, upsilon 8 electron, mesotron, neutrino, positron ***hypothetical:*** 5 gluon, quark 6 parton 8 graviton ***suffix:*** 2 id ***virus:*** 6 virion ***with negative charge:*** 8 electron ***with positive charge:*** 6 proton 8 positron
motley 7 piebald 8 skewbald 9 multi-hued 10 variegated
particular 3 one 4 full, item, lone, nice, only, sole 5 fussy, picky, point, thing 6 dainty, detail, minute, single, unique 7 careful, correct, element, finical, finicky, precise, several, special, unusual 8 accurate, detailed, distinct, especial, exacting, itemized, separate, solitary, specific, thorough 9 clocklike, finicking 10 blow-by-blow, fastidious, individual, meticulous, pernickety, respective, scrupulous, speciality 11 appropriate, persnickety, punctilious
particularize 4 list 6 detail 7 itemize, specify 8 separate 9 enumerate, inventory, stipulate 11 specificate 13 individualize
parting 4 last 5 adieu, congé, final 7 good-bye 8 farewell 10 divergence, separation 11 leave-taking, valedictory
partisan 5 blind 6 backer, biased, cohort, warped 7 colored, devoted, devotee, die-hard, fanatic, patriot, sectary 8 adherent, advocate, champion, disciple, follower, henchman, one-sided, sectator, stalwart, upholder 9 factional, guerrilla, irregular, jaundiced, satellite, sectarian, supporter ***combining form:*** 4 crat 5 ocrat
partition 4 deal, wall 6 divide, lot out, screen 7 divorce, dole out, portion, rupture, section, split-up 8 disburse, dispense, disperse, division 9 severance 10 detachment, distribute, measure out, separation
partner 4 ally, chum, mate, wife 5 buddy, crony 6 cohort, fellow 7 comrade, husband 8 confrere, sidekick 9 assistant, associate, bedfellow, colleague, companion 10 accomplice, consociate 11 confederate ***prefix:*** 2 co
partnership 4 firm 5 tie-up 6 hookup 7 cahoots, company 8 alliance 11 association, combination, conjunction 12 consociation, togetherness 13 participation
parturient 6 gravid, parous 8 childing, enceinte, pregnant 9 expecting
parturition 5 birth 7 bearing 8 delivery 10 childbirth 12 childbearing ***combining form:*** 4 toky
party 4 ball, band, bevy, bloc, body, crew, fete, orgy, ring, side 5 actor, being, bunch, cabal, corps, covey, group, human, revel, troop, union 6 fiesta, mortal, outfit, person, sharer, soiree, troupe 7 carouse, cluster, combine, company, debauch, faction, shindig 8 alliance, assembly, carousal, creature, litigant, wingding 9 bacchanal, coalition, gathering, personage 10 detachment, individual, saturnalia 11 bacchanalia, celebration, combination, participant
parvenu 7 upstart 8 roturier 9 arriviste 12 nouveau riche
Pasha or Baba 3 Ali
Pashhur ***father:*** 5 Immer 8 Malchiah ***son:*** 8 Gedaliah
Pasiphaë ***daughter:*** 7 Ariadne, Phaedra ***husband:*** 5 Minos ***son:*** 8 Minotaur
pass 2 go 3 die, end, hap, hie, jog, top 4 beat, buck, fare, give, hand, omit, pose, wend 5 cease, lapse, occur, outdo, reach, relay, spend, while 6 crisis, demise, depart, elapse, exceed, expire, forget, hand on, happen, ignore, perish, permit, push on, repair,

roll on, slight, slip by, strait, travel **7** approve, blink at, come off, decease, develop, devolve, journey, neglect, proceed, succumb **8** bequeath, exigency, fade away, fork over, hand down, juncture, outmatch, outshine, outstrip, overlook, peter out, transmit **9** blink away, disregard, emergency, terminate, transcend, transpire, while away ***Afghanistan:*** **5** Murgh ***Afghanistan-Pakistan:*** **6** Khyber ***Alaska:*** **5** White ***Alps:*** **3** col **5** Cenis, Loibl **7** Brenner, Ljubelj, Simplon **9** St. Bernard ***California:*** **5** Cajon ***China-India:*** **9** Karakoram ***into law:*** **5** enact ***Pakistan:*** **5** Kilik ***Russian:*** **12** Caspian Gates ***Tennessee:*** **10** Cumberland ***Turkey:*** **13** Cilician Gates ***Wyoming:*** **5** South

passable **4** open **9** navigable, reachable, tolerable, unblocked **10** accessible, attainable, negotiable, travelable

passably **4** so-so **6** enough, fairly, rather **9** averagely, tolerably **10** moderately

passage **3** way **4** exit, fare, hall, line, path, road, text **5** route, shift **6** access, arcade, avenue, course, egress, strait, traject, travel, tunnel, voyage **7** areaway, channel, couloir, excerpt, hallway, journey, traject, transit **8** corridor, transfer, traverse **9** enactment, quotation **10** transition, traversing **11** transmittal **12** transference, transmission **13** transmittance ***air:*** **7** windway ***arched:*** **6** arcade ***Atlantic-Pacific:*** **9** Northwest ***combining form:*** **4** meat, pora **5** meato ***money:*** **4** fare ***roofed:*** **6** arcade **9** breezeway ***to water's edge:*** **4** ghat

Passage to India author **7** Forster

pass away **2** go **3** die **4** drop **6** cash in, demise, depart, elapse, expire, perish **7** decease, succumb

pass by **4** fail, omit **6** forget, ignore **7** neglect **8** overlook **9** disregard

passé **4** dead **5** dated **6** démodé, old hat **7** belated, demoded, disused, extinct, outworn **8** obsolete, outdated, outmoded **9** out-of-date **10** antiquated, superseded **12** old-fashioned **13** superannuated

passed master **5** maven, mavin **6** artist, expert, wizard **7** artiste **8** virtuoso **9** authority

passel **4** body, clot **5** array, batch, bunch, clump, group **6** bundle **7** battery, cluster

passenger **4** fare **8** traveler, wayfarer ***hidden:*** **8** stowaway ***vessel:*** **5** liner **7** steamer

passerine bird see **bird,** *songbird*

passing **5** death, sleep **6** demise **7** cursory, decease, elusory **8** fleeting, illusive, illusory **9** ephemeral, fugacious, momentary, transient **10** evanescent, short-lived, transitory

passion **3** ire **4** fire, fury, heat, itch, love, lust, rage, urge, zeal **5** agony, amour, anger, ardor, crush, dolor **6** béguin, desire, fervor, hurrah, misery, temper **7** craving, ecstasy, emotion, feeling, panting, rapture **8** appetite, devotion, distress, lyricism, outbreak, outburst **9** affection, calenture, eagerness, eroticism, prurience, pruriency, sentiment, suffering, transport **10** aphrodisia, appetition, dedication, enthusiasm, heartthrob, sensuality **11** affectivity, amorousness, infatuation, lustfulness **12** sensuousness **13** concupiscence, lickerishness

passionate **3** hot **5** fiery, testy **6** ardent, fervid, steamy, sultry **7** amorous, blazing, burning, excited, fervent, flaming, glowing, goatish, lustful, peppery, satyric **8** headlong, prurient, vehement **9** impetuous, irascible, lickerish, quickened, steamed up **10** hot-blooded, lascivious, libidinous, stimulated **11** high-powered, hot-tempered, precipitate **12** concupiscent, high-pressure, unrestrained **13** quick-tempered

passive **4** idle **5** inert, quiet, stoic **6** asleep, docile, latent, sleepy, stolid **7** bearing, patient **8** enduring, inactive, resigned, yielding **9** apathetic, compliant, lethargic, quiescent, tractable **10** nonviolent, phlegmatic, submissive **11** acquiescent, unresistant

pass on **3** die **6** convey, depart, expire, impart **7** decease **8** transmit **11** communicate

pass out **5** faint, swoon

pass over **4** fail, omit, pass **6** forget, ignore **7** neglect **8** overlook **9** disregard

Passover **5** Pasch ***bread:*** **4** azym **5** azyme, matzo **6** matzoh ***meal:*** **5** seder

past **2** by **3** ago, old **4** gone, late, once, yore **5** above, after, prior **6** beyond, bygone, former, gone-by, whilom **7** onetime, outside, present, quondam, without **8** anterior, foretime, lang syne, previous, sometime **9** antiquity, erstwhile, foregoing, precedent, preceding, yesterday **10** antecedent, yesteryear ***combining form:*** **6** preter **7** praeter ***prefix:*** **5** retro

pasta **5** dough, paste ***kind:*** **4** ziti **7** gnocchi, lasagna, pastina, ravioli **8** alfabeto, linguine, linguini, macaroni, rigatoni, tortelli **9** canneloni, quadrucci, spaghetti **10** malfattini, tagliolini, tortellini, vermicelli **11** cappelletti, stricchetti **12** paglia e fieno

paste **4** beat, drub, glue **5** dough, pound, stick, stuff **6** attach, batter, buffet, cement, pummel, spread, thrash, wallop **7** belabor **8** adhesive, lambaste, material

Pasternak hero **7** Zhivago

pasticcio see **pastiche**

pastiche **6** medley **7** mélange **8** mishmash **9** potpourri **10** assortment, hodge-

podge, hotchpotch, miscellany 11 gallimaufry
pastime 4 game 5 hobby, sport 9 amusement, diversion 10 recreation 13 entertainment
past master see **passed master**
pastoral 5 rural 6 rustic 7 bucolic, country, idyllic, outland 8 agrarian, agrestic, innocent 10 campestral, out-country, provincial
pastor's assistant 6 curate
pastry 3 bun, pie 4 baba, cake, flan, tart 5 torte 6 cornet, Danish, éclair, gâteau, kolach, pirogi, strata, torten (plural) 7 baklava, beignet, bouchée, dariole, fritter, gâteaux (plural), kolacky, palmier, savarin, strudel, tartlet 8 napoleon, papillon, piroshki, turnover, vacherin 9 barquette, cream puff, gugelhupf, kugelhupf, madeleine, petit four, vol-au-vent 10 cheesecake 11 profiterole 12 millefeuille ***kind:*** 4 filo, puff 5 choux, flaky 6 phyllo ***shell:*** 7 timbale 8 meringue
pasty 5 gluey 6 chalky, pallid, sickly
patch 3 bit, fix 4 do up, mend 5 cover, scrap 6 doctor, emblem, repair, revamp
patchwork 4 hash, olio, stew 5 salad 6 jumble 8 mishmash 10 hodgepodge, hotchpotch, miscellany, salmagundi
patchy 6 spotty, uneven 9 irregular
pate 4 head, poll 5 brain, crown 6 noddle, noggin, noodle
patella 7 kneecap, kneepan
patent 4 open, rank 5 clear, gross, plain 7 evident, glaring, license, obvious 8 apparent, distinct, flagrant, manifest, palpable, unclosed 9 privilege, prominent
paternal 8 fatherly
path 3 way 4 fare, lane, line, road, walk 5 byway, route, track, trail 6 artery, avenue, course, street 7 highway, passage 9 boulevard 12 thoroughfare
pathetic 3 sad 4 poor 6 moving, rueful 7 piteous, pitiful 8 pitiable 9 affecting
Pathfinder ***author:*** 6 Cooper ***hero:*** 6 Bumppo (Natty)
pathogen 4 germ 5 virus 6 fungus 9 bacterium
pathological condition ***suffix:*** 2 ia
pathos 4 pity 9 poignance, poignancy
pathway 5 track, trail 6 course
patience 4 cool 9 composure, endurance, passivity, suffering, tolerance 10 equanimity, submission, sufferance, toleration 11 forbearance, longanimity, passiveness, resignation, self-control 13 long-suffering
patient 4 case, meek 6 patron 8 enduring 9 admitting, undaunted 11 susceptible 13 long-suffering ***man:*** 3 Job
patina 4 film 6 finish 7 surface 10 coloration
patio 5 court 7 terrace 9 courtyard
patois 4 cant 5 argot, lingo, slang 6 jargon 7 dialect 10 colloquial, vernacular
patriarch 4 sire 5 maker 6 author, father, gaffer 7 creator, founder 8 inventor 9 architect, generator, graybeard 10 originator ***biblical:*** 5 David, Isaac, Jacob 7 Abraham
patrician 6 aristo 9 blue blood, gentleman 10 aristocrat
patriciate 5 elite 6 flower, gentry 7 aristoi, quality 8 optimacy 9 blue blood, gentility 10 upper crust 11 aristocracy
patrimony 6 legacy 8 heritage 9 heritance 10 birthright 11 inheritance
patriot 8 loyalist, partisan 9 flag-waver, guerrilla, irregular 11 nationalist ***overzealous:*** 5 jingo 8 jingoist 10 chauvinist
Patroclus ***friend:*** 8 Achilles ***slayer:*** 6 Hector
patrol 5 scout, watch 7 protect
patrolman 3 cop 6 police 7 John Law, officer
patrol wagon 10 Black Maria
patron 5 angel 6 avowry, backer, client, surety 7 sponsor 8 backer-up, customer
patronage 5 aegis, trade 6 custom 7 backing, subsidy, traffic 8 auspices, business, cronyism 9 clientage, clientele 10 protection 11 benefaction, sponsorship 12 guardianship 13 pork-barreling
patronize 3 use 5 deign, favor 7 protect, support 8 frequent 10 condescend
patron saint ***of beggars, cripples:*** 5 Giles ***of children:*** 8 Nicholas ***of England:*** 6 George ***of fishermen:*** 5 Peter ***of France:*** 5 Denis ***of Ireland:*** 7 Patrick ***of lawyers:*** 4 Ives ***of musicians:*** 7 Cecilia ***of Norway:*** 4 Olaf ***of physicians:*** 4 Luke ***of sailors:*** 4 Elmo 8 Nicholas ***of Scotland:*** 6 Andrew ***of shoemakers:*** 7 Crispin ***of Spain:*** 5 James 8 Santiago ***of Wales:*** 5 David ***of winegrowers:*** 7 Vincent ***of workers:*** 6 Joseph
patsy 3 sap 4 dupe, fool, goat, gull, mark 5 chump 6 pigeon, sucker, victim 7 fall guy 9 scapegoat 11 whipping boy
patter 3 jaw, yak 4 cant, chat 5 argot, clack, lingo, prate, slang 6 babble, gabble, jargon, patois 7 chatter, dialect, prattle 9 yakety-yak 10 vernacular
pattern 4 plan 5 ideal, model, motif, order 6 design, device, figure, method, mirror, motive, system 7 example 8 ensample, exemplar, original, paradigm, standard, template 11 arrangement, orderliness
paucity 4 lack 6 dearth 7 fewness, poverty 8 scarcity 10 scarceness 13 insufficiency
Paulina's husband 7 Camillo 9 Antigonus

___Paulo 3 São

Paul the Apostle ***birthplace:*** 6 Tarsus ***companion:*** 5 Silas, Titus 7 Artemas, Timothy 8 Barnabas ***original name:*** 4 Saul ***place of conversion:*** 8 Damascus ***prosecutor:*** 9 Tertullus ***teacher:*** 8 Gamaliel ***tribe:*** 8 Benjamin

paunch 3 pod 4 draw 5 belly, bowel, tummy 6 venter 7 abdomen, embowel, stomach 8 potbelly 9 bay window

pauper 4 bust, ruin 5 break 6 beggar 7 almsman, have-not, lazarus 8 bankrupt, indigent 10 down-and-out, impoverish

pauperism 4 need, want 6 penury 7 beggary, poverty 9 indigence, neediness 11 destitution

pause 3 gap 4 halt, hush, lull, stop, wait 5 break, comma, lapse, letup 6 hiatus, recess 7 caesura, respite 8 interval 9 cessation, interlude 10 hesitation, suspension 12 intermission, interruption

pave 3 lay, tar 5 cover, floor 7 overlie, surface 8 blacktop

pavement 6 tarmac 7 macadam 8 concrete, flagging, sidewalk

paw 4 feel, foot, hand 5 touch 6 finger, handle 7 palpate

pawn 4 hock, tool 5 token 6 pledge, puppet, stooge 7 earnest, warrant 8 impledge

Pax see Irene

Pax 3 Dei 6 Romana 10 Brittanica

pay 3 fee 4 give, hire, quit, wage 5 clear, remit, spend, yield 6 defray, expend, lay out, outlay, pony up, render, return, salary, settle, square, tender 7 bring in, cough up, fork out, guerdon, requite, satisfy, stipend 8 clear off, disburse, pungle up, shell out 9 discharge, emolument, indemnify, liquidate, plunk down, reimburse 10 compensate, recompense, remunerate

payable 3 due 5 owing 6 mature, unpaid 7 overdue 9 unsettled 11 outstanding

payload 4 haul 5 cargo 6 burden, lading 7 freight

payment 3 fee, tax 4 duty 6 return 7 premium 12 compensation

payoff 3 fix 5 bribe 6 climax, profit, reward 8 decisive 11 retribution

PDQ 6 at once 8 directly, right off 9 forthwith, instanter, instantly, right away 11 immediately, straightway

pea 6 legume

peace 3 pax 4 calm, ease, rest 5 order, quiet 6 repose 7 concord, harmony 8 serenity 11 tranquility 12 tranquillity

peaceable 6 irenic 7 amiable, pacific 8 amicable, friendly, pacifist 10 neighborly, nonviolent 11 complaisant 12 pacificatory

peaceful 4 cool 6 irenic, placid, steady 7 equable, pacific 8 composed, constant, pacifist 9 collected, unruffled 10 nonviolent

peacemaker 8 appeaser, mediator, placater 10 arbitrator, negotiator 11 pacificator

peace officer 3 cop 6 police 7 John Law, officer 9 patrolman, policeman

peach 3 rat 4 blab 5 dandy, nifty 6 betray, inform, snitch, squeak, squeal 8 jim-dandy 9 freestone, humdinger, nectarine 10 clingstone 11 crackerjack

Peach State 7 Georgia

peachy 4 fine, nice 6 divine 8 glorious 9 excellent, hunky-dory, marvelous

peacockish 5 showy, swank 6 chichi 7 splashy 10 flamboyant 11 pretentious

peacock-like 8 pavonine

peak 3 alp, top 4 acme, apex, bill, roof 5 abate, crest, crown, mount, visor 6 apogee, lessen, rebate, recede, summit, vertex, zenith 7 dwindle 8 capsheaf, capstone, decrease, diminish, meridian, mountain, pinnacle, taper off ***Adirondack:*** 9 Whiteface ***Africa's highest:*** 4 Kibo ***Alaska-Canada:*** 12 Mt. Saint Elias ***Andes:*** 4 Ruiz 5 Torrá ***Apennines:*** 5 Amaro ***Argentina:*** 4 Azul 5 Negra, Payún ***Bavaria:*** 5 Arber ***Berkshires:*** 10 Mt. Greylock ***Black Hills:*** 10 Mt. Rushmore ***Bolivia:*** 5 Cuzco, Tahua, Ubina 6 Sajama ***Borneo:*** 4 Raja ***California:*** 6 Sonora 7 Palomar 8 Half Dome, Mt. Shasta 9 Excelsior ***California's highest:*** 9 Mt. Whitney ***Canada:*** 5 Keele ***Canaries:*** 5 Teide 8 Tenerife ***Carpathian:*** 4 Rysy ***Catskill:*** 5 Mt. Vly 8 Mt. Pisgah ***Caucasus:*** 5 Ushba 6 Elbrus ***Chile:*** 4 Mayo, Pili 5 Paine, Pular ***Colombia:*** 4 Tama 5 Neiva ***Colorado:*** 5 Pikes 9 Purgatory ***combining form:*** 3 acr, akr 4 acro, akro ***Cuba:*** 8 Turquino ***Ecuador:*** 10 Chimborazo ***England:*** 11 Scafell Pike ***Ethiopia:*** 4 Guna 5 Holla ***France:*** 5 Pilat ***French Guiana:*** 5 Amana ***Georgia:*** 16 Springer Mountain ***Glacier National Park:*** 8 Kootenai ***Greece:*** 6 Mt. Ossa 6 Pelion ***Himalayas:*** 3 Api 5 Kamet 7 Lhotse I 8 Lhotse II 10 Gasherbrum ***Honshū:*** 4 Yari 10 Yarigatake ***Idaho:*** 13 Mt. Pend Oreille ***Iran:*** 8 Damavand ***Japan:*** 4 Sobo 5 Oyama 7 Sobozan ***Java:*** 6 Slamet ***Jordan:*** 8 Mt. Gilead ***Karakoram Range:*** 10 Masherbrum ***Karokoram Range's highest:*** 7 Dapsang 12 Godwin Austen ***Maine:*** 10 Mt. Katahdin 10 Saddleback ***Montana:*** 8 Gallatin ***Nevada:*** 5 Mt. Ely ***Newfoundland:*** 9 Gros Morne ***New Hampshire:*** 11 Mt. Monadnock ***New Zealand:*** 5 Mt. Una 6 Mt. Cook 7 Aorangi 10 Mt. Aspiring ***Oahu:*** 5 Kaala ***Oregon:*** 6 Mt. Hood ***Papua New Guinea:*** 10 Mt. Victoria ***Pennine Alps:*** 10 Matterhorn, Mont Cervin ***Philippines:*** 4 High ***Pyrenees:*** 11 de Vignemale ***Scotland:*** 8 Ben Nevis ***Spain:*** 5 Yelmo 8 Mulhacén ***Switzer-***

land: 3 Dom 4 Dôle, Tödi 5 Eiger, Mönch 6 La Dôle, Rusein 7 Pilatus 8 Jungfrau ***U.S.S.R.'s highest:*** 9 Communism ***Utah:*** 5 Kings ***Venezuela:*** 7 Mt. Icutú ***Vermont:*** 8 Haystack, Stratton 10 Mt. Ascutney 11 Mt. Mansfield ***Washington:*** 9 Mt. Olympus, Mt. Rainier 13 Mt. Saint Helens ***White Mts.:*** 12 Mt. Washington ***Wyoming:*** 10 Grand Teton 11 Elk Mountain ***Yukon:*** 4 King 7 Mt. Logan

peaked 3 wan 4 pale, sick 5 acute, drawn, piked, sharp 6 sickly 7 pointed 8 acicular 9 aciculate, acuminate, acuminous, cuspidate

peal 4 bell, bong, ring, toll 5 chime, knell

peanut 4 mani, puny 5 petty, small 6 goober, measly, paltry 8 earthnut, picayune

pear 4 Bosc 5 Anjou, Hardy 6 Comice, Garber, Seckel 7 Kieffer, LeConte 8 Bartlett ***cider:*** 5 perry

Pearl Mosque site 4 Agra

Pearl of the Pacific 4 Guam

pearly 8 nacreous

pear-shaped 8 pyriform

peasant 4 boor, carl, hick, kern, peon, serf 5 churl, knave, yokel 6 rustic 7 bumpkin, hayseed, redneck, villein 9 hillbilly ***Arab:*** 6 fellah ***Latin-American:*** 9 campesino ***Russian:*** 5 mujik 6 moujik, muzhik, muzjik

peccary 7 tayassu 8 javelina

peck 3 lip, lot, nag 4 beak, buss, fuss, kiss, much 5 smack 6 carp at, smooch 7 henpeck 8 osculate 9 great deal

pecker 3 neb, nib 4 beak, bill, nose 5 snoot, snout 9 proboscis

peculate 8 embezzle

peculiar 3 odd 5 queer, weird 6 proper, unique 7 bizarre, curious, oddball, strange, unusual 8 singular 9 diacritic, eccentric 10 diagnostic, individual 11 distinctive

peculiarity 4 mark 5 savor, trait 7 feature, quality 8 property 9 affection, attribute, character

pecuniary 6 fiscal 8 monetary 9 financial

pedagogue 5 tutor 7 teacher 12 schoolmaster

Pedaiah ***brother:*** 9 Shealtiel ***father:*** 6 Parosh 7 Kolaiah ***grandson:*** 9 Jehoiakim ***son:*** 4 Joed, Joel

pedal digit 3 toe

pedantic 3 dry 4 arid, dull 5 booky 7 bookish, donnish, erudite, inkhorn, learned 8 academic, didactic 9 dryasdust, schoolish 10 scholastic 11 book-learned

peddle 4 hawk, push, sell, vend 5 shove 6 monger 8 huckster

peddler 6 hawker, monger, pusher, vendor 7 chapman, higgler, packman, roadman 8 huckster, mongerer, outcrier 9 cheap-jack, cheap-john, piepoudre 10 colporteur 12 costermonger

pedestal part 4 base, dado 6 plinth 7 surbase

pedestrian 4 blah, dull 5 banal, heavy, inane 6 dreary, jejune, stodgy 7 humdrum, prosaic 8 banausic, monotone, plodding, truistic 10 monotonous, wishy-washy 11 commonplace 13 unimaginative

pedigree 5 blood 6 origin, stemma 7 descent, lineage 8 ancestry, purebred 9 genealogy, pureblood 10 extraction, family tree

peduncle 4 stem

peek 6 glance 7 glimpse

peel 4 bark, pare, skin 5 flake, scale, strip 8 flake off 9 exfoliate 10 desquamate 11 decorticate, excorticate

peeled 4 bare, open 5 naked 7 denuded, exposed 8 stripped 9 uncovered

peep 3 pip, spy 4 chip, look, ogle, peer 5 cheep, chirp, stare, tweet 6 glance, peek in, squeak 7 chipper, chirrup, chitter, glimpse, look-see, peek out, tweedle, twitter 8 look-over, oeillade

peeping tom 5 snoop 6 peeper, voyeur 7 prowler, snooper

peer 3 eye, pry 4 bore, gape, gawk, gaze, lord 5 equal, glare, gloat, noble, snoop, stare 6 goggle, squint 9 associate ***British:*** 4 duke, earl 5 baron 7 marquis 8 viscount ***highest:*** 4 duke ***lowest:*** 5 baron

Peer Gynt ***author:*** 5 Ibsen ***beloved:*** 7 Solveig ***composer:*** 5 Grieg ***mother:*** 3 Ase

peerless 4 only 5 alone 6 unique 8 dominant 9 matchless, nonpareil, paramount, sovereign, unequaled, unmatched, unrivaled 11 unparagoned 12 unparalleled

peeve 3 get, irk 4 miff, rile, roil 5 pique 6 nettle, put out 7 disturb, provoke 8 irritate 9 aggravate 10 exasperate

peevish 5 huffy, waspy 7 carping, fretful, pettish, waspish 8 captious, caviling, critical, petulant, snappish 9 fractious, irritable

peewee 4 runt, tiny 5 dwarf, midge, pygmy 6 midget 7 manikin, minikin 8 dwarfish, Tom Thumb 9 miniature 10 diminutive, homunculus 11 lilliputian

Peewee or Della 5 Reese

peg 3 pin 4 plod, plug 5 dowel, prong, stake, throw 6 attach 8 identify

Pegasus 5 horse, steed ***rider:*** 11 Bellerophon

Pekah ***father:*** 8 Remaliah ***slayer:*** 6 Hoshea ***victim:*** 8 Pekahiah

Pekahiah ***father:*** 7 Menahem ***slayer:*** 5 Pekah

Pelatiah's father 4 Ishi 7 Benaiah 8 Hananiah

Peleg ***father:*** 4 Eber ***son:*** 3 Reu

Peleus *brother:* 7 Telamon *father:* 6 Aeacus *half brother:* 6 Phocus *son:* 8 Achilles *victim:* 8 Eurytion *wife:* 6 Thetis

pelf 5 money, rhino, stuff 7 needful

Pelias *country:* 6 Iolcus *father:* 8 Poseidon *half brother:* 5 Aeson *son:* 7 Acastus

Pelican State 9 Louisiana

Pelion and ___ 4 Ossa

Pelleas *beloved:* 9 Mélisande *brother, slayer:* 6 Golaud

Pelles *daughter:* 6 Elaine *grandson:* 7 Galahad

pellet 3 wad 4 ball, dung, shot 5 bolus 6 bullet

Pellinore *slayer:* 6 Gawain *son:* 5 Torre 6 Dornar 7 Lamerok 8 Percival 9 Agglovale

pell-mell 5 chaos, snarl 6 ataxia, huddle, muddle, rashly 7 clutter, hotfoot 8 disarray, disorder, headlong, stampede 9 confusion, hurriedly 10 carelessly, heedlessly 11 hurry-scurry, impetuously 12 indiscreetly 13 helter-skelter, incontinently

pellucid 5 clear, sheer 6 limpid, lucent 7 crystal 8 clear-cut, luminous 9 unblurred 10 see-through 11 crystalline, translucent

Pelops *father:* 8 Tantalus *son:* 6 Atreus 8 Pittheus, Thyestes *wife:* 10 Hippodamia

pelota see jai alai

pelt 3 fly, fur 4 beat, drub, fell, hide, rush, skin, whop 5 fleet, haste, hurry, pound, scoot 6 batter, hammer, jacket, pummel, thrash, wallop 7 beeline, belabor, hotfoot

pen 3 hem, mew 4 cage, coop, crib, jail, yard 5 fence, hedge 6 cooler, corral, kennel, prison, shut in, stylus 7 close in, enclose

penalize 4 fine 5 judge, mulct 6 amerce, punish 7 chasten, condemn, correct 8 chastise 9 castigate 10 discipline

penalty 4 fine, loss 5 mulct 7 forfeit 10 amercement

penance 3 rue 4 ruth 7 remorse 9 atonement, attrition, penitence, penitency 10 contrition, repentance 11 compunction

penchant 4 bent 7 leaning 8 tendency 9 inclining 10 proclivity, propensity 11 disposition, inclination 12 predilection

pendant 4 flag, jack 5 color 6 banner, ensign, pennon 7 pennant 8 bannerol, standard, streamer 9 correlate 10 complement

pendent 7 hanging, pensile 9 pendulant, pendulous, suspended, undecided, unsettled 12 undetermined

pending 6 during 9 undecided, unsettled 12 undetermined

___ Pendragon 5 Uther

pendulous 6 wobbly 7 hanging, pendent, pensile 8 wavering 9 faltering, suspended, tentative 10 hesitating 11 vacillating

Penelope *father:* 7 Icarius *father-in-law:* 7 Laertes *husband:* 7 Ulysses 8 Odysseus *mother:* 8 Periboea *son:* 10 Telemachus *suitor:* 7 Agelaus

penetrable 6 porose, porous 8 pervious 9 permeable

penetrate 3 jab 4 bore, go in, stab 5 break, drill, drive, enter, knife, prick 6 charge, come in, insert, invade, pierce 7 ingress, pervade 8 encroach, permeate, puncture, saturate, trespass 9 insinuate, introduce, percolate, perforate, transfuse 10 impregnate

penetrating 4 keen 5 acute, crisp, sharp 6 astute, biting, shrewd 7 cutting, ingoing 8 clear-cut, incisive 9 trenchant 11 quick-witted, sharp-witted 12 quick-sighted, sharp-sighted

Peneus *daughter:* 6 Daphne *father:* 7 Oceanus *mother:* 6 Tethys

Peninnah's husband 7 Elkanah

peninsula 4 neck 10 chersonese *Alaska:* 5 Kenai 6 Seward *Australia:* 6 Tasman *Barents Sea:* 5 Kanin *British colony:* 9 Gibraltar *Canada:* 8 Labrador *Cape Cod:* 9 Race Point 12 Monomoy Point *Chile:* 5 Swett *Costa Rica:* 3 Osa *Denmark:* 7 Jutland *eastern United States:* 8 Delmarva *Estonia:* 5 Sorve *Florida:* 8 Pinellas 9 Canaveral *France:* 5 Giens *Greece:* 4 Acte 10 Chalcidice 11 Peloponnese 12 Peloponnesus *Guam:* 5 Orote *Hong Kong:* 7 Kowloon *Honshū:* 3 Izu 5 Miura *Massachusetts:* 7 Cape Ann, Cape Cod *Mexico:* 7 Yucatan 14 Baja California *Michigan:* 8 Keweenaw *Middle East:* 5 Sinai *New Guinea:* 4 Huon *New Jersey:* 9 Sandy Hook *New Zealand:* 5 Banks, Mahia *Northern Territory:* 4 Gove *Northwest Territories:* 4 Hall 7 Boothia 8 Melville *Ontario:* 5 Bruce *Persian Gulf:* 9 Ras Tanura 13 Ras at Tannurah *Quebec:* 5 Gaspé *Russia:* 4 Kola 5 Taman, Yamal 6 Kolski, Taimyr 9 Kamchatka *Scotland:* 7 Cantyre, Kintyre *South Australia:* 4 Eyre 5 Yorke 6 Yorkes *southeast Asia:* 5 Malay 9 Indochina 12 Farther India *southeastern Europe:* 6 Balkan *southwestern Asia:* 6 Arabia 7 Arabian *southwestern Europe:* 7 Iberian *Texas:* 9 Matagorda *Tierra del Fuego:* 5 Mitre *Turkey:* 8 Anatolia 9 Asia Minor *Ukraine:* 5 Kerch *Wales:* 5 Gower, Lleyn *Washington:* 7 Olympic *west Africa:* 11 Sierra Leone *Wisconsin:* 4 Door

Peninsular State 7 Florida

penis 7 phallus

penitence 3 rue 4 ruth 5 grief, qualm 6 regret, sorrow 7 anguish, penance, remorse, sadness, scruple 8 distress, humbling 10 contrition, debasement, repentance 11 compunction, degradation, humiliation, self-reproof 12 contriteness, self-reproach

penitent 5 sorry 8 contrite 9 regretful, repentant 10 apologetic, remorseful

penitentiary see **prison**

penman 5 clerk 6 author, scribe, writer 12 calligrapher 13 calligraphist

penmanship 4 hand 6 ductus, script 7 writing 11 calligraphy, chirography, handwriting

pen name 9 pseudonym 10 nom de plume ***Addison (J.):*** 4 Clio ***Arouet (F.M.):*** 8 Voltaire ***Beyle (M.H.):*** 8 Stendhal ***Blair (E.):*** 12 George Orwell ***Brontë (A.):*** 9 Acton Bell ***Brontë (C.):*** 10 Currer Bell ***Brontë (E.):*** 9 Ellis Bell ***Clemens (S.):*** 9 Mark Twain ***Dickens (C.):*** 3 Boz ***Dodgson (C.L.):*** 12 Lewis Carroll ***Dupin (A.A.):*** 10 George Sand ***Evans (M.A.):*** 11 George Eliot ***Faust (F.):*** 8 Max Brand ***Franklin (B.):*** 11 Poor Richard ***Geisel (T.):*** 7 Dr. Seuss ***Glidd (F.):*** 9 Luke Short ***Lamb (C.):*** 4 Elia ***Munro (H.H.):*** 4 Saki ***Poquelin (J.B.):*** 7 Molière ***Porter (W.S.):*** 6 O. Henry ***Ramée (M.L.):*** 5 Ouida ***Russell (G.):*** 2 AE ***Thibault (J.):*** 13 Anatole France ***Viaud (L.M.J.):*** 10 Pierre Loti

pennant 4 flag, jack 5 color 6 banner, ensign, pennon 7 pendant 8 standard, streamer 9 banderole

penniless 4 poor 5 broke 8 bankrupt 11 impecunious

pennilessness see **penury**

pennon 4 flag, jack 5 color 6 banner, ensign 8 bannerol, gonfalon, gonfanon 9 banderole, oriflamme

Pennsylvania ***battlefield:*** 10 Gettysburg ***capital:*** 10 Harrisburg ***college, university:*** 5 Gratz, Thiel 6 Drexel, Lehigh, Temple 7 La Salle 8 Alliance, Bryn Mawr, Bucknell 9 Dickinson, Lafayette, St. Joseph's, Villanova 10 Pittsburgh, Swarthmore ***nickname:*** 13 Keystone State ***state bird:*** 12 ruffed grouse ***state flower:*** 14 mountain laurel

penny pincher 5 miser, piker, stiff 7 niggard 8 tightwad 9 skinflint 10 cheapskate 11 cheeseparer 12 moneygrubber

penny-pinching 5 close, tight 6 stingy 7 miserly 9 niggardly, penurious 11 closefisted, tightfisted 12 cheeseparing, parsimonious

pensile 7 hanging, pendent 9 pendulant, pendulous, suspended

pensioner 7 retiree 8 retirant

pensive 3 sad 4 blue 6 musing 7 wistful 8 absorbed, saddened, thinking 9 pondering, withdrawn 10 abstracted, cogitative, meditative, melancholy, reflecting, reflective, ruminating, ruminative, thoughtful 11 preoccupied, speculative 13 contemplative

Pentateuch 5 Torah 6 Exodus 7 Genesis, Numbers 9 Leviticus 11 Deuteronomy

Penthesilea ***queen of:*** 7 Amazons ***slayer:*** 8 Achilles

Pentheus ***grandfather:*** 6 Cadmus ***king of:*** 6 Thebes ***mother:*** 5 Agave

Penuel ***father:*** 3 Hur 7 Shashak ***grandfather:*** 5 Judah

penumbra 5 shade 6 shadow 7 umbrage

penurious 4 poor 5 close, needy, tight 6 stingy 7 miserly 8 beggared, dirt poor, indigent 9 destitute, niggardly 10 avaricious 11 closefisted, impecunious, necessitous, tightfisted 12 cheeseparing, impoverished, parsimonious 13 penny-pinching

penury 4 need, want 7 poverty 8 poorness 9 indigence, neediness, privation 11 destitution

peon 4 serf 5 slave 6 drudge, slavey, toiler 7 laborer, peasant 9 dray horse, workhorse 11 galley slave ***Anglo-Saxon:*** 4 esne

peonage 4 yoke 6 thrall 7 bondage, helotry, serfdom, slavery 9 servitude, thralldom, villenage 11 enslavement

people 3 kin, men 4 folk 5 plebs 6 occupy, plebes, public, tenant 7 inhabit, society 8 populace, populate 9 commonage, commoners, common men, community, plebeians 10 commonalty 11 inhabitants, rank and file, third estate ***combining form:*** 4 demo, ethn 5 ethno

pep 2 go 3 vim 4 dash, push 5 getup, punch, verve, vigor 6 energy, starch 7 potency 8 vitality 9 animation, hardihood 10 get-up-and-go, liveliness

pepo 5 gourd, melon 6 squash 7 pumpkin 8 cucumber

pepper 3 dot 5 chili, speck 7 cayenne, freckle, paprika, pimento, speckle, stipple 8 capsicum, pimiento, sprinkle 9 bespeckle

peppery 4 keen, racy 5 alert, cross, fiery, spicy, zesty 6 cranky, lively, snappy, spunky 7 gingery, piquant, pungent 8 choleric, poignant, spirited 9 irascible, temperish 10 mettlesome, passionate 11 highhearted, hot-tempered 12 high-spirited 13 quick-tempered

peppy 4 keen 5 alert 6 bright, lively 7 animate 8 animated, spirited 9 sprightly, vivacious

Pepys' journal 5 Diary

Pequod ***cabin boy:*** 3 Pip ***captain:*** 4 Ahab ***harpooner:*** 6 Daggoo 8 Queequeg, Tashtego ***mate:*** 8 Starbuck

per 2 by 3 via 4 with 7 by way of, through 8 by dint of 9 by means of

perambulate 4 walk 6 stroll 8 traverse 9 promenade
per capita 3 all 4 each 5 aside 6 apiece
perceive 3 see 4 espy, feel, know, mark, mind, note, take 5 grasp, seize, sense 6 behold, descry, detect, divine, notice 7 discern, observe, realize 8 identify 9 apprehend, recognize 10 comprehend, understand
perceptible 5 clear, lucid 6 signal 8 palpable, sensible, tangible 10 cognizable, detectable, noticeable, observable 11 appreciable, conspicuous, discernible, perspicuous 12 recognizable
perception 4 idea 5 image 6 acumen, notion 7 conceit, concept, insight, thought 9 cognition 10 impression
perceptive 4 keen, sage, wise 5 acute, aware, sharp 6 sophic 7 gnostic, knowing 9 insighted, sagacious, sensitive 10 discerning, insightful, prehensile, prehensive, responsive
perch 3 bar, set 4 land 5 light, roost 6 alight, settle 7 set down, sit down, station
perchance 5 maybe 7 perhaps 8 possibly
percipience 3 wit 6 acumen 8 keenness 10 astuteness, shrewdness 11 discernment, penetration 12 perspicacity
percolate 4 ooze, seep, sift 5 exude 6 charge, filter, strain 7 pervade 8 permeate, saturate, transude 9 penetrate, transfuse 10 impregnate 11 impenetrate
percussion 3 jar 4 bump, jolt 5 clash, crash, shock 6 impact 9 collision 10 concussion ***instrument:*** (see at **musical instrument**)
Perdita ***father:*** 7 Leontes ***mother:*** 8 Hermione
perdition 3 pit 4 hell 5 abyss, hades 7 Gehenna, inferno 9 barathrum, damnation 10 underworld 11 netherworld, Pandemonium
Père Goriot author 6 Balzac
peregrination 4 trek, trip 7 journey, travels 10 expedition
peremptory 5 bossy, fixed 7 certain, decided 8 absolute, decisive, imperial, positive 9 imperious, masterful, obstinate 10 high-handed, imperative 11 domineering, magisterial, overbearing
perennial 3 old 7 durable 8 enduring, lifelong 9 continual, long-lived, permanent, perpetual, unceasing 10 continuing, inveterate, perdurable 11 long-lasting
Perez ***brother:*** 5 Zerah ***father:*** 5 Judah ***mother:*** 5 Tamar
perfect 3 fit 4 full, pure, rank, very 5 exact, gross, ideal, model, right, round, sheer, sleek, slick, sound, utter, whole 6 choate, entire, expert, intact, needed, polish, proper, refine, simple, smooth 7 express, precise, unmixed 8 absolute, complete, finished, flawless, integral, masterly, outright, positive, required, suitable, unbroken, unflawed 9 downright, excellent, fleckless, masterful, requisite, unalloyed, undamaged, undiluted, uninjured 10 consummate, impeccable, unimpaired
perfection 5 arete, ideal, merit 6 virtue 7 paragon, quality 9 integrity, wholeness 10 entireness, excellence, excellency 12 completeness
perfidious 5 false, venal 6 untrue 7 unloyal 8 disloyal, recreant 9 alienated, deceitful, dishonest, estranged, faithless, mercenary 10 traitorous, unfaithful 11 treacherous
perfidiousness see **perfidy**
perfidy 6 deceit 7 falsity, sellout, treason 8 betrayal, foul play 9 falseness, treachery 10 disloyalty, infidelity 13 faithlessness
perforate 3 pit 4 bore 5 drill, drive, prick, probe, punch 6 pierce 8 puncture 9 penetrate
perform 2 do 3 act, end 4 play, take, work 5 enact, react 6 behave, effect, finish, wind up 7 achieve, execute, fulfill, operate, playact 8 bring off, complete, function 9 discourse, implement, personate 10 accomplish, perpetrate
peformance 3 act 4 deed, feat, show, work 5 stunt 6 acting, action 7 concert, exploit, matinee 8 behavior, efficacy 9 discharge, execution 10 efficiency 11 fulfillment 12 presentation
performer 4 doer, mime 5 actor, mimic 6 mummer, player, worker 7 actress, artiste, trouper 8 thespian 9 playactor 12 impersonator ***suffix:*** 3 ant, ent
perfume 4 balm 5 aroma, cense, scent, smell, spice 6 sachet 7 bouquet, incense, odorize 9 aromatize, fragrance, redolence ***source:*** 4 musk 5 attar, myrrh, orris 6 chypre 8 bergamot
perfumer 6 Chanel
perfunctory 4 cool 5 stock, usual 6 wooden 7 cursory, routine, unaware 8 careless, standard 9 automatic 10 impersonal, mechanical 11 indifferent, involuntary, superficial, unconcerned 12 uninterested
pergola 5 arbor, bower
perhaps 5 maybe 6 theory 7 suppose 8 feasibly, possibly 9 perchance 10 conjecture, imaginably 11 conceivably, speculation
periapt 4 juju, luck, zemi 5 charm 6 amulet, fetish, mascot 8 talisman 10 phylactery
Pericles ***father:*** 10 Xanthippus ***mistress:*** 7 Aspasia ***mother:*** 8 Agariste
peril 4 risk 6 danger, hazard, menace

7 jeopard 8 endanger, exposure, jeopardy, openness 9 liability 10 compromise, jeopardize, subjection 12 endangerment

perilous 5 hairy, risky, shaky 6 chancy, touchy, wicked 7 tottery, unsound 8 delicate, dreadful, ticklish, unstable, unsteady 9 dangerous, desperate, hazardous, unhealthy 10 jeopardous 11 treacherous

___ Perilous 5 Siege

perimeter 3 hem, rim 4 brim, edge 5 ambit, brink, skirt, verge 6 border, fringe, margin 7 circuit, compass 8 boundary 9 periphery 13 circumference

period 3 age, end, era 4 days, span, stop, term, time 5 close, epoch 6 ending, season 7 closing, closure 8 duration 9 cessation 10 conclusion, generation 11 termination

periodical 5 organ 6 review 7 journal 8 magazine 9 alternate, newspaper, recurrent, recurring 10 isochronal 11 isochronous 12 intermittent

Peri opera 5 Dafne 8 Euridice

peripatetic 6 roving 7 nomadic, vagrant 8 ambulant, vagabond 9 itinerant, itinerate, wandering, wayfaring 11 perambulant

periphery see **perimeter**

periphrasis see **pleonasm**

perish 3 die, end 4 pass 5 cease 6 demise, depart, expire, vanish 7 decease, decline, go under, succumb 8 collapse, pass away 9 disappear

perjure 3 lie 5 trick 6 delude 7 deceive, mislead 8 forswear 10 equivocate 11 prevaricate

perk 4 gain, mend 6 look up 7 freshen, improve, smarten 9 percolate 10 ameliorate, convalesce, perquisite, recuperate

permanent 5 fixed 6 stable 7 abiding, durable, lasting 8 constant, enduring 9 continual, diuturnal, perduring, perennial 10 invariable, perdurable 12 imperishable

permeable 6 porose, porous 8 passable, pervious 10 penetrable

permeate 4 fill, soak 5 imbue, steep 6 charge, drench, imbrue, infuse, invade 7 diffuse, ingrain, pervade, suffuse 8 saturate 9 interfuse, penetrate, percolate, transfuse 10 impregnate, infiltrate 11 impenetrate

permissible 7 allowed 8 approved, bearable, endorsed 9 allowable, permitted, tolerable, tolerated 10 acceptable, admissible, authorized, sanctioned 11 unforbidden 12 unprohibited

permission 5 leave 6 permit 7 consent, license 8 approval, sanction 9 allowance 10 acceptance, sufferance 11 approbation, endorsement 12 acquiescence 13 authorization

permit 3 let 4 have 5 admit, allow, grant, leave 6 suffer 7 consent 8 sanction, tolerate 9 allowance, authorize 10 permission, sufferance 13 authorization

permitted 5 licit

permutation 5 sport 6 change 7 novelty 10 alteration, innovation 11 vicissitude 12 modification

pernicious 3 bad 4 evil 5 fatal, swart, toxic 6 deadly, lethal, malign, mortal, wicked 7 baleful, baneful, harmful, hurtful, killing, malefic, miasmic, noxious, ruinous 8 damaging, sinister, venomous, virulent 9 malignant, miasmatic, pestilent, poisonous 10 maleficent 11 deleterious, destructive, detrimental, devastating

Pernod flavor 5 anise 8 licorice

perorate 4 rant, rave 5 mouth 7 declaim, soapbox 8 bloviate, harangue

perpend 4 mind 5 study, weigh 6 ponder 8 consider, think out 9 think over 10 excogitate 11 contemplate

perpendicular 5 plumb 7 stand-up, upright 8 straight, vertical 10 straight-up

perpetrate 2 do 4 pull 5 wreak 6 commit, effect 7 inflict, execute, perform

perpetual 7 endless, eternal 8 constant, unending 9 ceaseless, continual, incessant, perennial, unceasing 10 continuous 11 everlasting, unremitting 12 interminable

perpetuate 4 keep 6 secure 7 bolster, support, sustain 8 conserve, eternize, maintain, preserve 10 eternalize 11 immortalize

perplex 4 balk, pose 5 amaze, befog, ravel, snarl 6 baffle, bemuse, muddle, puzzle, tangle, thwart 7 astound, confuse, ensnarl, mystify, nonplus, perturb, stumble 8 astonish, bewilder, confound, entangle, surprise 10 complicate, discompose 11 intertangle

perquisite 3 tip 5 right 6 income 7 cumshaw, largess 8 appanage, gratuity 9 lagniappe, pourboire, privilege 10 birthright 11 prerogative

per se 5 alone 6 as such, solely 8 in itself

persecute 4 bait, rack, ride 5 harry, hound, worry, wrong 6 harass, heckle, molest 7 afflict, dragoon, oppress, outrage, torment, torture 8 aggrieve

Persephone 4 Kore 10 Proserpina *father:* 4 Zeus 7 Jupiter *husband:* 5 Hades, Pluto *mother:* 5 Ceres 7 Demeter

Perseus *father:* 4 Zeus 7 Jupiter *grandfather:* 8 Acrisius *mother:* 5 Danaë *victim:* 6 Medusa 8 Acrisius *wife:* 9 Andromeda

perseverance 8 tenacity 9 diligence, endurance 11 persistence 13 steadfastness

persevere see **persist**

persevering see **persistent**

Persian *fairy:* 4 peri *fire worshiper:*

5 Parsi 6 Parsee ***governor:*** 6 satrap ***mystic:*** 4 sufi ***poet:*** 4 Omar 5 Hafiz 8 Firdausi ***prophet:*** 9 Zoroaster ***robe:*** 6 caftan ***sacred books:*** 6 Avesta ***sun-god:*** 7 Mithras ***title:*** 4 shah ***writing:*** 9 cuneiform

persiflage 6 banter 8 backchat, badinage, raillery, repartee, snip-snap

persist 4 go on, last 5 abide 6 endure, hang on, linger, obtain 7 carry on, perdure, prevail 8 continue 9 persevere 12 carry through

persistence 3 run 6 course 8 duration 9 endurance 10 continuity 11 continuance 12 continuation ***combining form:*** 6 stasia, stasis

persistent 6 dogged 7 archaic 8 enduring 9 insistent, primitive, steadfast, tenacious, unevolved 10 determined, relentless, unshakable 11 perseverant, persevering, undeveloped, unremitting 13 perseverative

persnickety 4 nice 5 fussy, picky 6 choosy 7 finicky 8 clerkish 10 fastidious

person 3 guy, man, one 4 body, chap, coot, life, self, soul 5 being, human, stick 6 entity, fellow, galoot, mortal 8 creature, specimen 10 individual ***admirable:*** 6 mensch ***ambitious:*** 8 go-getter 10 up-and-comer ***betrothed:*** 6 fiancé 7 fiancée ***clumsy:*** 5 klutz 6 kludge ***combining form:*** 6 prosop 7 prosopo ***contemptible:*** 3 cad 4 heel 5 knave 6 varlet ***distinguished:*** 3 VIP 5 great ***dressy:*** 12 clotheshorse ***eighty-year-old:*** 12 octogenarian ***energetic:*** 10 ball of fire ***guilty:*** 7 culprit ***meek:*** 7 nebbish ***ninety-year-old:*** 12 nonagenarian ***non-Jewish:*** 3 goy 7 gentile ***of mixed ancestry:*** 5 métis 7 mestizo, mulatto 8 octoroon ***one-hundred-year-old:*** 11 centenarian ***rude:*** 4 boor ***rural:*** 4 hick ***sixty-year-old:*** 12 sexagenarian ***virtuous:*** 6 zaddik 7 tzaddik ***wealthy:*** 3 nob 5 nabob

personable 6 comely 7 shapely 8 charming, handsome 10 attractive 11 good-looking

personage 3 VIP 4 body, life, soul 5 being, chief, human, nabob 6 bigwig, mortal 7 big shot, notable 8 creature, eminence, somebody 9 dignitary 10 individual, notability 11 personality

personal 3 own 5 privy 7 private, special 8 peculiar 10 individual, particular ***combining form:*** 4 idio

personal effects 5 goods, stuff, traps 6 things, tricks 10 belongings 11 possessions

personality 3 ego, VIP 5 chief, humor, nabob, seity 6 makeup, nature, temper 7 big shot, ipseity, notable, selfdom 8 eminence, identity, selfhood, selfness, somebody 9 character, dignitary, personage 10 complexion, notability 11 disposition, singularity, temperament 13 individualism, individuality

personate 2 do 3 act 4 play 5 enact 6 embody, mirror, typify 7 perform, play-act 9 discourse, epitomize, exemplify, personify, represent 10 illustrate 11 emblematize

personify 6 embody, mirror, typify 8 manifest 9 body forth, epitomize, exemplify, incarnate, objectify, represent, symbolize 10 illustrate 11 emblematize, exteriorize, externalize, materialize, personalize, reincarnate 12 substantiate

perspective 5 scape, vista 7 lookout, outlook 8 prospect 9 viewpoint

perspicacious 4 keen 5 cagey, heady 6 argute, astute, shrewd 9 astucious, sagacious 10 perceptive 11 penetrating, sharp-witted 12 quick-sighted, sharp-sighted

perspicacity 3 wit 6 acumen 8 astucity, keenness 10 astuteness, shrewdness 11 discernment, penetration, percipience

perspicuity 7 clarity 8 lucidity 9 clearness, limpidity, plainness 12 explicitness

perspicuous 5 clear, lucid 6 lucent 7 crystal 8 clear-cut, luculent, luminous, pellucid 9 unblurred 11 unambiguous

perspiration 4 work 5 sweat 9 exudation ***abnormal:*** 8 hidrosis

perspire 5 sweat 7 swelter

persuadable 8 amenable, exorable, suasible, swayable 9 acceptant, acceptive, receptive

persuade 3 win 4 coax, draw, lead, move, sway 5 bring, touch 6 affect, assure, entice, induce, prompt, reason 7 convert, entreat, impress, satisfy, win over 8 convince, talk into 9 argue into, prevail on 11 bring around, prevail upon

persuasible see **persuadable**

persuasion 3 ilk, lot 4 bias, cast, cult, mind, mold, sect, sort, type, view 5 class, creed, faith, order 6 belief, church, nature 7 feeling, opinion 8 religion 9 character, communion, prejudice, sentiment 10 cajolement, connection, conviction, partiality 11 affiliation, description 12 denomination

Persuasion author 6 Austen

pert 4 arch, bold, keen, rude, wise 5 alert, fresh, nervy, sassy, saucy, smart 6 bantam, brazen, bright, cheeky, daring, lively 7 animate, forward 8 animated, impudent, spirited 9 audacious, sprightly, vivacious 11 smart-alecky 13 disrespectful

pertain 4 join, vest 5 apply 6 bear on, belong, relate 7 combine, concern, connect 8 bear upon 9 associate

pertaining to ***suffix:*** 2 al, an, ar, ic 3 ean, ese, ial, ile, ine, ist, ory 4 ical 5 ative, istic 6 itious 7 istical

pertinacious 6 dogged, mulish 7 willful 8 perverse, stubborn 9 obstinate, tenacious 10 bullheaded, headstrong, inflexible, refractory, self-willed, unshakable, unyielding
pertinent 3 apt, fit 5 ad rem 7 apropos, germane 8 apposite, material, pointful, relevant 10 applicable, pertaining 11 applicative, applicatory, appropriate
perturb 5 upset, worry 6 bother, dismay, flurry 7 agitate, disturb, fluster, trouble 8 disquiet, unsettle 10 discompose, disconcert
Peru *capital:* 4 Lima *conqueror:* 7 Pizarro *monetary unit:* 3 sol
peruse 4 read, scan 5 study 6 survey 7 examine
pervade 4 fill 5 bathe, imbue 6 charge 8 permeate, saturate 9 penetrate, percolate, transfuse 10 impregnate 11 impenetrate
perverse 5 balky 6 cranky, mulish, ornery, putrid, rotten 7 corrupt, froward, restive, vicious, wayward 8 contrary, depraved, stubborn 9 irritable, miscreant, nefarious, obstinate, unhealthy 10 degenerate, headstrong, refractory, self-willed, unyielding, villainous 11 stiff-necked, wrongheaded 12 cross-grained, pertinacious, unreasonable
pervert 4 ruin, skew, warp 5 abuse, belie, color, twist 6 debase, garble, misuse 7 corrupt, debauch, deprave, distort, falsify, outrage 8 ill-treat, maltreat, misapply, miscolor, misstate, mistreat 9 animalize, brutalize, misemploy, mishandle 10 bastardize, bestialize, demoralize, misimprove, prostitute 12 misrepresent
pervious 6 porose, porous 9 permeable 10 penetrable
pesky 4 mean, ugly 8 annoying 9 troublous, vexatious 10 bothersome 11 troublesome
pessimist 5 cynic 7 killjoy 9 Cassandra, defeatist, doomsayer, worrywart 10 fussbudget 11 crepehanger, misanthrope
pessimistic 6 gloomy 7 cynical 10 despairing
pest 4 bane 5 worry 6 bother, pester, plague, vermin 7 heckler, nudnick, trouble 8 badgerer, irritant, nuisance, vexation 9 annoyance, besetment, tormentor
pester 4 ride 5 annoy, devil, harry, tease, worry 6 badger, bother, harass, plague 7 bedevil, hagride, torment 8 irritant, nuisance 9 annoyance, beleaguer, besetment, tantalize 10 botherment 11 botheration
pesticide 7 biocide 9 fungicide, germicide, vermicide 11 bactericide, insecticide, microbicide, rodenticide
pestiferous 6 deadly 7 baneful, noxious 9 pestilent 10 pernicious 12 pestilential
pestilence 5 curse 6 plague 7 scourge
pestilential 5 fatal 6 deadly, lethal, mortal, vexing 7 baneful, deathly, noxious 9 pestilent 10 irritating, pernicious 11 mortiferous
pestle 4 mano 5 pilum 6 muller *vessel:* 6 mortar
pet 3 hug 4 dear, love, pout, sulk 5 grump, loved 6 caress, cosset, cuddle, dandle, fondle, stroke 7 beloved, cherish, darling, embrace, indulge 8 blue-eyed, favorite
petcock 3 tap 4 gate 5 valve 6 faucet, spigot 7 hydrant 8 stopcock
peter 4 fade, fail 5 abate, cease 6 lessen, rebate, recede 7 dwindle 8 decrease, diminish, taper off 9 drain away
Peter Pan *author:* 6 Barrie *character:* 4 John 5 Wendy 7 Michael 9 Tiger Lily 10 Tinker Bell *dog:* 4 Nana *pirate:* 4 Hook, Smee
Peter the Apostle *brother:* 6 Andrew *father:* 5 Jonah *original name:* 5 Simon
Peter the Great *father:* 6 Alexis *wife:* 7 Eudoxia 9 Catherine
Pethuel's son 4 Joel
petite 3 wee 5 dwarf, small 6 bantam, little, monkey 8 smallish 9 miniature 10 diminutive 11 lilliputian
petition 3 ask, beg, sue 4 plea, pray, suit 5 plead, sue to 6 appeal, orison, prayer, sue for 7 beseech, entreat, implore, request 8 entreaty 10 supplicate 11 application, imploration, imprecation 12 supplication
Petrarch's beloved 5 Laura
Petrified Forest author 8 Sherwood
petrify 4 daze, numb, stun 5 alarm 6 appall, bedaze, bemuse, benumb, dismay 7 horrify, startle, stupefy, terrify 8 frighten, paralyze
Petruchio's wife 9 Katharina, Katharine
pettifogger 6 lawyer 7 shyster 10 bush lawyer 13 jackleg lawyer
pettish see **petulant**
petty 4 base, mean, puny 5 light, minor, small 6 casual, little, measly, paltry, peanut 7 pimping, trivial, unvital 8 childish, niggling, peddling, picayune, piddling, piffling, trifling 9 frivolous, hair-drawn, small-beer 10 irrelevant, negligible, picayunish, shoestring, ungenerous 11 impertinent, Mickey Mouse, unimportant
petty officer 6 noncom, yeoman
petulant 5 cross, huffy, sulky, testy, waspy 7 fretful, grouchy, peevish, pettish, waspish 8 snappish 9 fractious, irascible, irritable, querulous
peyote 6 cactus, mescal *drug:* 9 mescaline
Phaedra *father:* 5 Minos *husband:*

7 Theseus ***mother:*** 8 Pasiphaë ***sister:*** 7 Ariadne ***stepson:*** 10 Hippolytus
Phaëthon's father 6 Helios 7 Phoebus
phantasm 5 dream, fancy, ghost, shade 6 mirage, shadow, spirit, vision 7 eidolon, fantasy, fiction, specter 8 daydream, delusion, illusion, revenant, spectrum 9 invention, nightmare 10 apparition 11 fabrication, ignis fatuus 13 hallucination
phantom 5 ghost, shade 6 shadow, spirit 7 eidolon, specter 8 phantasm, revenant, spectrum 10 apparition
Phanuel's daughter 4 Anna
pharaoh 3 Tut 4 Coti 6 Ahmose, Ramses 7 Harmhab 8 Ikhnaton, Thutmose 9 Amenhotep, Merneptah
pharisaism 4 cant 9 hypocrisy 10 sanctimony, Tartuffery, Tartuffism 12 pecksniffery
pharisee 8 Tartuffe 9 hypocrite, lip server 10 dissembler 12 dissimulator
pharmacist 8 druggist 10 apothecary ***British:*** 7 chemist
pharos 6 beacon 10 lighthouse
Pharsalus, battle of ***vanquished:*** 6 Pompey ***victor:*** 6 Caesar
phase 4 hand, look, side, view 5 angle, color, facet, state 6 aspect 7 posture 8 position 9 condition, semblance, situation, viewpoint 10 appearance, complexion
PhD exam 5 orals
pheasant 5 argus, monal 8 tragopan
Phebe's husband 7 Silvius
Phèdre author 6 Racine
phenomenal 4 rare 5 gross 6 unique 7 unusual 8 material, physical, sensible, singular, tangible, unwonted 9 corporeal, objective 10 remarkable 11 exceptional, substantial, unthinkable 13 extraordinary
phenomenon 4 fact 5 event 6 marvel, wonder 7 anomaly, miracle, paradox, portent, prodigy, reality, stunner 9 actuality, sensation 10 experience, uniqueness 11 peculiarity, singularity, unusualness
philander 4 wolf 5 chase, dally, flirt 6 chaser, masher, pursue, trifle 7 Don Juan 8 Casanova, womanize 9 ladies' man, womanizer 10 fool around, lady-killer, mess around, play around 11 philanderer
philanthropic 4 good 6 giving, humane 8 donating 10 altruistic, benevolent, bighearted, charitable, freehanded 11 civic-minded, freehearted, kindhearted, magnanimous, openhearted 12 contributing, eleemosynary, greathearted, humanitarian
philanthropist ***American:*** 6 Girard 7 Cornell 8 Carnegie 9 Rosenwald 11 Rockefeller ***English:*** 11 Wilberforce ***Swedish:*** 5 Nobel
Philemon's wife 6 Baucis
philharmonic 4 band 8 symphony 9 orchestra
Philip of Macedonia ***father:*** 7 Amyntas ***son:*** 9 Alexander
philippic 6 tirade 8 diatribe, harangue, jeremiad
Philippics author 6 Cicero
Philippines ***capital:*** 6 Manila ***discoverer:*** 8 Magellan ***hero:*** 5 Rizal ***language:*** 7 Spanish, Tagalog, Visayan 8 Filipino ***liberator:*** 9 MacArthur ***monetary unit:*** 4 peso ***president:*** 6 Marcos
Philippi victor 6 Antony 8 Octavian
Philip the Tetrarch ***father:*** 5 Herod ***mother:*** 9 Cleopatra
philistine 4 boob, boor, lout 5 clown 7 Babbitt 8 boeotian 9 barbarian, bourgeois, vulgarian 10 capitalist, middlebrow 11 materialist
Philistine ***champion:*** 7 Goliath ***city:*** 4 Gath, Gaza 5 Ekron 6 Ashdod 8 Ashkelon ***foe:*** 5 David 6 Samson ***god:*** 5 Dagon
Philoctetes ***father:*** 5 Poeas ***victim:*** 5 Paris
Philomela 11 nightingale ***father:*** 7 Pandion ***ravisher:*** 6 Tereus ***sister:*** 6 Procne
philosopher ***American:*** 5 Adler, James, Quine, Royce 6 Langer 7 Marcuse 9 Santayana ***Arab:*** 8 Avicenna ***British:*** 7 Russell 12 Wittgenstein ***Chinese:*** 6 Lao-tsu 7 Mencius, Tai Chen 9 Confucius ***Danish:*** 11 Kierkegaard ***Dutch:*** 7 Spinoza ***English:*** 4 Mill, More 5 Bacon, Locke, Moore, Occam 6 Hobbes, Ockham 7 Bentham, Russell, Spencer, Whewell 9 Whitehead ***Finnish:*** 11 Westermarck ***French:*** 5 Comte, Taine 6 Pascal, Sartre, Valery 7 Abelard 8 Maritain, Rousseau, Teilhard 9 Descartes 10 Saint-Simon, Schweitzer ***German:*** 4 Kant, Marx 5 Hegel, Wolff 6 Fichte, Herder 7 Jaspers, Leibniz 8 Leibnitz, Spengler 9 Heidegger, Nietzsche, Schelling 12 Schopenhauer 14 Albertus Magnus ***Greek:*** 4 Zeno 5 Plato, Timon 6 Thales 7 Gorgias, Proclus 8 Diogenes, Epicurus, Longinus, Socrates 9 Aristotle 10 Anaxagoras, Democritus, Empedocles, Heraclitus, Parmenides, Protagorus, Pythagorus, Xenocrates, Xenophanes 11 Anaximander 12 Theophrastus ***Indian:*** 13 Gautama Buddha ***Irish:*** 8 Berkeley ***Italian:*** 6 Ficino ***Jewish:*** 5 Buber, Philo ***Roman:*** 6 Seneca 8 Boethius, Plotinus 9 Lucretius ***Scottish:*** 4 Hume, Mill, Reid 7 Stewart ***Spanish:*** 6 Suarez 13 Ortega y Gasset ***Swedish:*** 10 Swedenborg
philosophers' stone 6 elixir
philosophical 4 calm 8 composed, rational 9 temperate
philosophy 3 tao 4 yoga 5 deism 7 dualism, inquiry, wholism 8 stoicism 10 empiricism, pragmatism 12 Cartesianism

Phineas ***beloved:*** 9 Andromeda ***tormentors:*** 7 Harpies ***wife:*** 9 Cleopatra
Phinehas ***father:*** 3 Eli 7 Eleazar ***grandfather:*** 5 Aaron
phlegm 6 apathy 7 ataraxy 8 calmness, coolness, stoicism 9 composure, sangfroid, stolidity, unconcern 10 equanimity 11 impassivity, nonchalance
phlegmatic 3 dry 4 calm, dull 5 aloof, stoic 6 stolid 8 sluggish 9 apathetic, impassive, incurious, lethargic 11 indifferent, unconcerned
Phlegyas ***daughter:*** 7 Coronis ***father:*** 4 Ares, Mars ***son:*** 5 Ixion
phobia see **fear**
Phobos 4 moon 9 satellite ***brother:*** 6 Deimos ***father:*** 4 Ares, Mars
Phocus ***father:*** 6 Aeacus 8 Ornytion ***half brother:*** 6 Peleus 7 Telamon ***mother:*** 8 Psamathe ***slayer:*** 6 Peleus 7 Telamon ***wife:*** 7 Antiope
Phoebe 5 Diana 7 Artemis ***daughter:*** 4 Leto ***father:*** 9 Leucippus ***mother:*** 2 Ge 4 Gaea
phoebus 3 sun 7 daystar
Phoebus see **Apollo**
Phoenician ***city:*** 4 Acre, Tyre 5 Sidon ***colony:*** 8 Carthage ***god:*** 4 Baal 6 Eshmun ***goddess:*** 6 Baltis 7 Astarte
Phoenix 4 bird ***brother:*** 5 Cilix ***pupil:*** 8 Achilles ***sister:*** 6 Europa
phony 4 fake, hoax, sham 5 bogus, cheat, faker, false, fraud, put-on, snide, spoof 6 humbug, pseudo 7 swindle 8 impostor, spurious 9 brummagen, charlatan, imposture, pinchbeck, pretender 11 counterfeit
photograph 3 mug, pic 4 film, snap 5 kodak, shoot 6 glossy 7 filmize, picture, tintype 8 cinemize, likeness, snapshot 9 snapshoot ***three dimensional:*** 8 hologram
photographer 8 camerist, photoist 9 cameraman 10 shutterbug 11 snapshooter ***famous:*** 4 Haas, Hine, Riis 5 Adams, Atget, Brady, Evans, Karsh, Lange, Weber, White 6 Brandt, Coburn, Newton, Porter, Siegel, Strand, Weston 7 Emerson, Jackson, Salomon, Siskind, Thomson 8 Cosindas, Kasebier, Steichen, Steinert 9 Feininger, Leibovitz, O'Sullivan, Rejlander, Rothstein, Stieglitz 10 Cunningham, Heartfield 11 Bourke-White
photographic 5 exact, vivid 7 graphic 8 accurate, detailed 9 pictorial 11 picturesque ***solution:*** 4 hypo 5 fixer, toner 7 reducer 9 developer
phrase 3 put 4 term, word 5 couch, idiom 6 byword, slogan 7 diction, express, styling, wordage, wording 8 locution, parlance, verbiage 9 catchword, formulate, verbalism, watchword 10 expression, shibboleth
Phrixus ***father:*** 7 Athamus ***mother:*** 7 Nephele ***sister:*** 5 Helle ***wife:*** 9 Chalciope
Phrontis ***brother:*** 5 Argus, Melas 9 Cytisorus ***father:*** 7 Phrixus ***mother:*** 9 Chalciope
Phrygian ***god:*** 3 Men 4 Atys 5 Attis ***goddess:*** 6 Cybele ***king:*** 5 Midas 7 Gordius
phthisis 2 TB 11 consumption, white plague 12 tuberculosis
phylactery 4 juju, luck, zemi 5 charm 6 amulet, fetish, mascot 7 periapt 8 talisman
physic 4 cure, heal 5 purge 6 remedy 7 relieve 8 medicant, medicine 9 cathartic, purgative 10 medicament, medication
physical 5 brute, gross, lusty 6 bodily, carnal 7 fleshly, natural, somatic 8 corporal, material, sensible, tangible, visceral 9 corporeal, elemental, objective 10 elementary, phenomenal 11 substantial
physician 2 MD 3 doc 5 medic 6 doctor, medico 7 medical, surgeon 9 mediciner 10 specialist 12 practitioner ***American:*** 4 Rush, Salk 5 Minot, Spock, Still 6 Jarvik, Murphy, Weller 7 Huggins, Robbins, Theiler 8 Richards 9 Sternberg ***Arab:*** 8 Avicenna ***Austrian:*** 6 Mesmer ***Canadian:*** 5 Osler ***combining form:*** 5 iatro 7 iatrist ***English:*** 4 Ross 6 Harvey, Jenner, Willis 8 Sydenham ***French:*** 5 Widal 7 Laveran 10 Schweitzer ***German:*** 7 Sylvius ***Greek:*** 5 Galen 11 Hippocrates ***Italian:*** 7 Galvani ***slang:*** 8 sawbones ***South African:*** 7 Barnard ***Swiss:*** 10 Paracelsus; (see also **Nobel Prize Winner,** *physiology or medicine;* **surgeon**)
physicist ***American:*** 4 Rabi, Ting 5 Fermi, Gibbs, Kusch, Mayer, Pauli, Pupin, Segre, Smyth, Stern 6 Teller, Townes, Wigner 7 Goddard, Purcell 8 Einstein, Gell-Mann, McMillan, Millikan, Mulliken, Shockley, Van Allen 9 Michelson, Schwinger 11 Oppenheimer ***Austrian:*** 4 Mach 7 Doppler 11 Schrodinger ***British:*** 6 Stokes 7 Tyndall 8 Thompson ***Chinese:*** 4 Yang ***Danish:*** 4 Bohr ***Dutch:*** 6 Zeeman 7 Huygens, Lorentz, Zernike 11 Van der Waals ***English:*** 4 Snow 5 Jeans, Joule 6 Dalton, Kelvin, Newton, Powell 7 Faraday, Hodgkin, Thomson 8 Rayleigh, Robinson 9 Wollaston 10 Richardson, Rutherford, Wheatstone ***French:*** 4 Neel 5 Arago, Binet 6 Ampere, Perrin 7 Coulomb, Kastler, Reaumur 8 Lippmann ***German:*** 3 Ohm 4 Laue, Wien 5 Hertz, Stark 6 Jensen, Lenard, Nernst, Planck 7 Meitner 8 Roentgen 9 Helmholtz, Kirchhoff, Mossbauer 10 Fahrenheit, Hofstadter ***Indian:*** 5 Raman ***Irish:*** 6 Walton ***Italian:*** 5 Rossi, Volta

7 Galileo, Galvani 10 Torricelli *Japanese:* 6 Yukawa 8 Tomonaga *Mexican:* 8 Vallarta *Russian:* 4 Tamm 6 Landau 9 Prokhorov *Scottish:* 4 Tait 6 Wilson 7 Maxwell *Swedish:* 7 Rydberg 8 Angstrom, Siegbahn *Swiss:* 6 Zwicky 7 Piccard; (see also **Nobel Prize Winner**, *physics*)

physiologist *English:* 8 Starling *German:* 5 Weber, Wundt 7 Schwann 9 Helmholtz *Italian:* 11 Spallanzani; (see also **Nobel Prize Winner**, *physiology or medicine*)

physique 4 body, form 5 build, frame, habit, shape 6 figure 7 anatomy, habitus 9 structure 12 constitution 13 configuration

pianist *American:* 4 Nero, Wild 5 Arrau, Davis, Janis, Tatum, Watts 6 Duchin, Joplin, Serkin, Waller 7 Cliburn, Istomin, Ohlsson, Perahia, Winston 8 Graffman, Grainger, Horowitz, Pennario 10 Johannesen, Rubinstein *Austrian:* 6 Czerny 8 Schnabel 9 Rosenthal *Bulgarian:* 11 Weissenberg *Cuban:* 5 Bolet *English:* 4 Hess 5 Katin, Ogdon 6 Curzon *Finnish:* 8 Palmgren *French:* 6 Cortot 7 Cziffra 9 Entremont 10 Saint-Saens *German:* 5 Bülow 6 Kempff 8 Schumann 9 Gieseking *Hungarian:* 5 Liszt 6 Vasary *Italian:* 6 Busoni 8 Clementi *Polish:* 6 Chopin 7 Hofmann 9 Landowska 10 Paderewski *Russian:* 6 Berman, Gilels 7 Richter 8 Pachmann 9 Ashkenazy, Prokofiev 10 Rubinstein 12 Rachmaninoff *Spanish:* 6 Iturbi 8 Granados 10 de Larrocha *Swiss:* 4 Anda

piano 5 grand 6 softly, spinet 7 quietly, upright *builder:* 5 Knabe, Stein, Zumpe 7 Baldwin 8 Steinway 9 Bechstein 10 Chickering, Cristofori, Silbermann *inventor:* 10 Cristofori *key:* 7 digital *pedal:* 6 damper 7 celeste

Piazza Tales author 8 Melville

picaroon 5 rogue, rover, thief 6 pirate, sea dog 7 brigand, corsair, sea wolf 8 sea rover 9 buccaneer, sea robber 10 freebooter

picayune see **piddling**

Piccini's rival 5 Gluck

pick 3 top 4 beak, best, cull, gaff, mark, take 5 elect, elite, pluck, pride, prime, prize 6 choice, choose, chosen, optate, opt for, prefer, select 8 plectrum, selected 9 exclusive, single out

picket 3 peg 4 pale, post, ward 5 guard, stake, watch 6 sentry, tether 7 lookout 8 palisade, sentinel, watchman

pick handle 5 helve

pickle 3 fix, jam 4 dill, spot 5 brine 6 capers, corner, plight, scrape 7 dilemma, gherkin, trouble 8 marinate 11 predicament

pickpocket 5 thief 8 cutpurse 11 purse cutter *slang:* 3 dip

pick up 3 get 4 cull, gain, land, lift, rear 5 annex, glean, hoist, learn, pinch, raise, renew, run in 6 arrest, detain, garner, gather, master, obtain, pull in, reopen, resume, uphold, uplift, uprear 7 acquire, compass, elevate, extract, procure, restart, upraise 8 continue 9 apprehend 10 recommence

pickup 5 truck 6 arrest 9 detention 10 arrestment, hitchhiker 11 arrestation, improvement 12 acceleration, apprehension

picky 4 nice 5 fussy 6 choosy, dainty 7 finical, finicky 9 finicking 10 fastidious, particular 11 persnickety

picnic 4 snap 5 cinch 6 breeze, outing *beach:* 8 clambake

picture 4 cine, copy, draw, film, idea, limn, show 5 flick, image, movie, photo, pinup, print 6 depict, render 7 drawing, portray, tableau 8 describe, painting, portrait 9 delineate, depiction, interpret, photoplay, portrayal, represent 10 simulacrum 11 delineation, description, portraiture, presentment 13 spitting image *stand:* 5 easel

picture show 4 cine, film 5 flick, movie 9 photoplay

piddling 4 puny 5 petty 6 measly, paltry 7 trivial 8 niggling, trifling 11 Mickey Mouse

pie 4 flan, tart 5 pasty 6 [illegible], pastry 7 cobbler 8 business, crustade, turnover

piece 3 cut 4 part 6 member, moiety, parcel 7 portion, section, segment 8 division, fraction, fragment

pièce de résistance 8 main dish 9 showpiece 11 centerpiece, chef d'oeuvre, masterpiece

piecemeal 7 gradual 8 bit by bit 9 gradually 10 step-by-step

pie chart 5 graph 11 circle graph

pier 4 dock, quay, slip 5 berth, jetty, levee, wharf 6 column, pillar 8 pilaster

pierce 3 cut 4 bore, gash, gore, slit, stab 5 slash, slice, spear 6 incise, riddle, skewer 8 transfix 9 penetrate, perforate 10 run through

piercing 4 high, keen, loud, thin 5 acute, sharp 6 argute, piping, shrill, treble 7 blaring, roaring 8 shooting, stabbing 9 knifelike 10 stentorian 12 earsplitting *tool:* 3 awl

piety 5 ardor 6 fealty, fervor 7 loyalty 8 devotion, fidelity, holiness, sanctity 9 godliness, reverence 10 allegiance, devoutness 12 faithfulness

piffle 4 bosh 5 hooey 6 bunkum 7 twaddle 8 malarkey, nonsense, pishposh 10 balderdash, flapdoodle 12 blatherskite

pig 3 hog 5 swine 6 farrow, porker 7 casting, glutton *breed:* 5 Duroc 8 Tamworth

9 Berkshire, Hampshire, Yorkshire ***combining form:*** 3 hyo 7 choerus ***female:*** 3 sow 4 gilt ***feral:*** 9 razorback ***litter:*** 6 farrow ***male:*** 4 boar 6 barrow ***meat:*** 3 ham 4 pork 5 bacon 7 sausage 8 chitlins 9 chitlings 12 chitterlings ***wild:*** 7 peccary, warthog 8 babirusa 9 babirussa ***young:*** 4 gilt 5 shoat 6 farrow, piglet

pigeon 3 sap 4 dupe, fool, gull, hoax, mark 5 chump, decoy 6 culver, sucker 7 fall guy, gudgeon 8 flimflam, hoodwink 9 bamboozle, victimize 11 hornswoggle ***genus:*** 7 Columba ***house:*** 4 cote, loft ***kind:*** 4 barb, rock 5 homer 6 pouter, roller 7 carrier, crowned, dragoon, fantail, jacobin, tumbler 8 carneaux ***relative:*** 4 dove ***young:*** 5 squab

pigeonhole 4 slot, sort, tier 5 class, cubby, grade, group, niche 6 assort, league 7 catalog, cubicle 8 category, classify, grouping 9 cubbyhole 10 categorize

pigeon pea 3 dal 4 dhal, herb

piggish 6 greedy 7 selfish, swinish 10 gluttonous

pigheaded 6 mulish 7 willful 8 perverse, stubborn 9 obstinate 10 headstrong, self-willed, unyielding 11 intractable, stiff-necked

pigment 3 dye 5 color, paint, stain 8 colorant, dyestuff, tincture ***black:*** 9 lampblack ***blue:*** 4 cyan 5 azure, smalt 6 indigo 7 cyanine 8 cerulean 9 verdigris 11 ultramarine ***brown:*** 5 sepia ***umber:*** 6 bister, sienna ***combining form:*** 5 chrom 6 chromo ***dark:*** 7 melanin ***green:*** 7 celadon 8 viridian 10 biliverdin ***orange:*** 7 realgar 8 carotene ***red:*** 4 lake ***minium:*** 7 carmine, crimson, pimento, scarlet, sinopia 8 lycopene 9 bilirubin, vermilion 10 vermillion ***toxic:*** 8 gossypol ***yellow:*** 5 ocher, ochre 6 flavin, lutein 7 flavine, xanthin 8 luteolin, massicot

pigpen 3 sty 4 dump, mess

pigsty see pigpen

piker 3 bum, vag 5 miser, stiff 7 drifter, floater, niggard, vagrant 8 roadster, tightwad, vagabond 9 skinflint 10 cheapskate 11 cheeseparer 12 moneygrubber, penny pincher

pilaster 4 anta, pier 6 column, pillar

Pildash ***father:*** 5 Nahor ***mother:*** 6 Milcah

pile 3 fur, lot, mow, pot, wad 4 bank, cock, down, fill, flue, fuzz, heap, hill, lint, load, lump, mass, mint, much, pack, peck, pyre, rick 5 choke, drift, floss, fluff, hoard, mound, shock, stack 6 barrel, barrow, boodle, bundle, charge, jumble, packet 7 edifice, fortune, haycock, hayrick, pyramid, tumulus, windrow 8 erection, haystack, mountain 9 aggregate, amassment, great deal, structure 10 assemblage, collection 11 aggregation, glomeration 12 accumulation

pileous 5 hairy 6 fleecy, pilose, woolly 7 hirsute 9 whiskered

pileup 5 crash, smash 7 crack-up, smashup 8 accident 9 collision

pilfer 3 rob 4 lift 5 filch, pinch, steal, swipe 6 finger, snitch, thieve 7 purloin 11 appropriate

pilferer 4 prig 5 thief 6 nimmer 7 filcher, stealer 8 larcener 9 larcenist

pilgarlic 4 butt 5 sport 6 jestee 8 baldhead 13 laughingstock

pilgrim 5 hadji, hajji 6 palmer 8 traveler, wanderer, wayfarer ***famous:*** 5 Alden 6 Carver 8 Bradford, Brewster

pilgrimage 4 hadj, hajj, trip 7 journey

Pilgrims' interpreter 7 Squanto

Pilgrim's Progress 8 allegory ***author:*** 6 Bunyan ***hero:*** 9 Christian

pill 4 ball 5 bolus 6 pellet, pilule 7 capsule

pillage 3 nab 4 lift, loot, sack 5 filch, pinch, steal, swipe, usurp, waste 6 devour, maraud, pilfer, ravage, thieve 7 despoil, plunder, purloin 8 arrogate, desolate, spoliate 9 depredate, desecrate, devastate 10 confiscate 11 appropriate

pillager 6 looter, raider, sacker 7 forager, ravager, spoiler 8 marauder, ravisher 9 plunderer 10 freebooter

pillar 4 pier, post, prop 5 pylon, shaft, stela, stele 6 column, stelae (plural) 7 obelisk 8 backbone, mainstay, pedestal, pilaster ***combining form:*** 4 cion, styl 5 ciono, style, stylo 6 stelic, stylar

Pillar of Hercules 5 Abila, Abyla, Calpe

pillow 3 pad 7 bolster, cushion

pilose see pileous

pilot 3 ace 4 auto, dean, lead, show, tool 5 doyen, drive, flier, guide, motor, route, steer, wheel 6 airman, direct, escort, flyboy, leader 7 aviator, birdman, conduct 8 aviatrix, helmsman, shepherd

pimp 6 pander 8 fancy man, procurer

pimple 3 dot, zit 4 boil, spot, stud 6 papule 7 abscess, pustule, speckle 8 furuncle, sprinkle 9 carbuncle

pin 3 fid, peg 4 clip 5 affix, dowel, stake, thole 6 broach, brooch, cotter, fasten, secure

pinch 3 nab, nip 4 lift 5 exact, filch, gouge, run in, screw, skimp, spare, steal, stint, swipe, theft, tweak, wrest, wring 7 larceny, squeeze 8 exigency, juncture, stealing, thievery, thieving, zero hour 9 apprehend, detention, emergency, shake down 10 arrestment, crossroads, purloining

pinchbeck 4 fake, sham 5 bogus, false, phony, snide 6 pseudo 8 spurious 9 brummagen 11 counterfeit

pinch hitter 3 sub 6 fill-in 7 stand-in

9 alternate, surrogate 10 substitute 11 locum tenens, replacement, succedaneum
Pindar *home:* 6 Thebes *poems:* 4 odes
pine 4 ache, fret, long, mope, sigh 5 brood, crave, dream, yearn 6 grieve, hanker, hunger, lament, repine, thirst 7 agonize
Pine Tree State 5 Maine
pinhead 4 fool, simp 5 dense, dunce 6 dimwit, nitwit, stupid 7 doltish, lackwit, wantwit
Pinkerton 6 shamus 9 detective, operative 10 private eye
pinnacle 3 top 4 acme, apex, peak 5 crest, crown 6 apogee, climax, summit, zenith 8 capsheaf, meridian 11 culmination *of a glacier:* 5 serac
pinniped 4 seal 6 walrus
Pinocchio author 7 Collodi 9 Lorenzini
pinochle *card:* 3 ace, ten 4 jack, king, nine 5 queen *term:* 4 meld 5 widow 7 auction *two-handed:* 7 goulash
pinpoint 4 spot 5 exact, place 6 finger 7 precise 8 diagnose, identify 9 recognize 11 determinate, distinguish 13 diagnosticate
pinto 4 pied 5 overo, paint 7 painted, piebald, tobiano 8 skewbald
pint-size 3 wee 4 tiny 5 teeny, weeny 6 midget, pocket, teensy 9 miniature 10 diminutive, pocket-size
pioneer 5 first, prime 6 maiden 7 initial, primary, settler 8 colonist, earliest, original *famous:* 5 Boone, Bowie, Clark, Lewis 6 Carson, Colter 7 Bridger, Chapman, Fremont, Whitman 8 Crockett
pious 4 holy 5 godly 6 devout 8 priestly 9 pietistic, prayerful, religious
pip 3 dot 4 blip, peep, root, seed, spot 5 image, speck
pipe 3 keg, tun 4 butt, cask 5 carry 6 barrel, convey, funnel, siphon 7 channel, conduct, conduit, traject 8 hogshead *ceremonial:* 7 calumet *combining form:* 3 aul 4 aulo 5 solen 6 siphon, soleno 7 siphono *part:* 4 bowl, stem
pipe down 5 dry up, quiet 6 dumb up, shut up
pipe dream 6 bubble 7 chimera, fantasy, rainbow 8 illusion, phantasy
pipeline 7 channel, conduit 8 supplier 10 connection
piquant 4 racy, tart 5 spicy, zesty 6 biting, snappy 7 peppery, pungent 8 poignant 9 sparkling 10 appetizing
pique 3 irk 4 huff, miff, move, rile, roil 5 annoy, peeve, plume, preen, pride, rouse, snuff 6 excite, irking, nettle, put out 7 dudgeon, innerve, offense, provoke, quicken, umbrage 8 irritate, motivate, vexation 9 aggravate, annoyance, galvanize, innervate, stimulate 10 exasperate, irritation, resentment
piranha 6 caribe
pirate 5 rover 6 looter, raider, robber, sea dog 7 brigand, corsair, sea wolf 8 marauder, picaroon, pillager, sea rover 9 buccaneer, plunderer, privateer, sea robber 10 freebooter *Celtic:* 5 Fomor 8 Fomorian *flag:* 10 Jolly Roger *French:* 7 Laffite, Lafitte *Scottish:* 4 Kidd
Pirithous' wife 10 Hippodamia
pirogue 5 canoe
pirouette 4 gyre, spin 5 twirl, whirl 6 gyrate 9 whirligig
piscator 6 angler 9 fisherman
pismire 3 ant
pistol 7 handgun 8 revolver 9 derringer *case:* 7 holster
pit 3 vie 4 hell, hole 5 abyss, chasm, hades, match 6 cavity, oppose 7 counter, Gehenna, inferno, play off 9 barathrum, perdition 10 underworld 11 netherworld, Pandemonium
Pit and the Pendulum author 3 Poe
pitch 3 dip, yaw 4 cant, cast, dive, drop, fall, fire, hurl, rock, roll, swag, tilt, tone, toss 5 burst, drive, fling, heave, lunge, lurch, sling, slump, spiel, throw 6 go down, launch, plunge, seesaw, tilter, topple, tumble, unseat 7 buck off, unhorse 8 keel over 12 song and dance
pitch-black see **pitch-dark**
pitch-dark 3 jet 4 ebon, inky 5 black, ebony, jetty, raven, sable 11 atramentous
pitched 6 sloped, tilted, tipped 7 leaning, oblique, sloping, tilting 8 inclined 9 inclining
pitcher 4 ewer, olla, toby 5 cruse 7 creamer *area:* 5 mound *handle:* 3 ear 4 ansa
pitch in 5 begin, set to, start 6 chip in, fall to, jump in, kick in 8 commence, jump into, start off 9 subscribe 10 buckle down, contribute 11 come through
piteous 4 poor 6 rueful, ruined 7 pitiful 8 pathetic, pitiable 12 commiserable
pitfall 4 lure, risk, trap 5 peril, snare 6 danger, hazard 7 springe 8 deadfall, trapfall 9 booby trap, mousetrap 12 entanglement
pith 3 nub 4 core, gist, meat, pulp, root, soul 5 focus, heart 6 center, import, kernel, marrow, matter, upshot, weight 7 essence, nucleus 9 magnitude, substance 10 importance 11 consequence, weightiness 12 essentiality, significance
Pithon's father 5 Micah
pithy 4 curt 5 brief, crisp, meaty, short, terse 7 compact, concise, marrowy 8 succinct 12 epigrammatic 13 short and sweet
pitiable see **pitiful**
pitiful 3 sad 4 poor 5 cheap, sorry 6 rue-

ful, scummy, scurvy, shabby, woeful 7 forlorn, piteous 8 beggarly, pathetic, pitiable, wretched 9 miserable, sorrowful 10 despicable, despisable 12 commiserable, contemptible, heartrending

pitiless 5 cruel, stony 6 brutal, savage 8 inhumane, ruthless 9 barbarous, cutthroat, heartless, merciless, unfeeling, unpitying 10 relentless, unmerciful 11 coldhearted, hardhearted, ironhearted 12 stonyhearted 13 marblehearted

pittance 3 bit 4 mite 5 scrap, trace 6 trifle 7 dribble, driblet, smidgen

pity 3 rue 4 ache, ruth 5 mercy 7 feel for 8 clemency, sympathy 10 compassion 11 commiserate 13 commiseration

pivot 4 turn, veer, whip 5 avert, sheer, swing, wheel, whirl 6 divert, swivel 7 deflect

pivotal 3 key 5 vital 6 ruling 7 central, crucial 8 cardinal 9 essential 10 overriding

pixie 3 elf, fay 5 antic, devil, fairy, nisse, rogue, scamp 6 elvish, impish, rascal, sprite 7 brownie, coltish, playful, puckish 8 prankish, scalawag, slyboots 9 skeezicks

pixieish 5 antic 6 elvish, frisky, impish 7 playful, puckish 9 kittenish, pixilated 11 mischievous

pixilated 5 drunk 6 elvish, pranky, stoned 7 larkish, muddled, playful, puckish, roguish, waggish 9 disguised 10 frolicsome, inebriated 11 intoxicated

Pizarro *city founded:* 4 Lima *conquest:* 4 Peru *victims:* 5 Incas

placard 4 bill, post 6 poster 7 affiche 8 handbill

placate 4 calm 6 pacify, soothe 7 appease, assuage, comfort, mollify, sweeten 10 conciliate, propitiate 11 tranquilize

place 3 fix, job, lay, put, set 4 area, call, lieu, loci (plural), post, rank, site, spot, zone 5 berth, judge, locus, point, posit, state, stick, tract, where 6 billet, finger, office, reckon, region, settle, status 7 deposit, footing, install, situate, station 8 capacity, diagnose, district, estimate, identify, locality, location, pinpoint, position, standing, vicinity 9 character, establish, recognize *combining form:* 3 top 4 chor, loco, topo, topy 5 choro *of ease:* 10 bed of roses *of sin:* 5 Sodom *suffix:* 3 ary, ery, ory 4 aria (plural), oria (plural) 5 arium, orium

place-name 7 toponym

placid 4 calm, easy, mild 5 quiet, still 6 hushed, irenic, poised, serene, stilly 7 halcyon 8 composed, peaceful, tranquil 9 collected, easygoing, unruffled 10 unagitated, untroubled 12 self-composed 13 imperturbable, self-possessed

plague 3 vex 4 bane, fret, gnaw, pest, rash 5 annoy, beset, curse, harry, hound, tease, worry 6 bother, harass, hassle, hector, pester 7 afflict, bedevil, disease, hagride, scourge, torment, trouble 8 epidemic, invasion, irritant, nuisance, outbreak 9 annoyance, beleaguer, besetment 10 affliction, black death, botherment, pestilence 11 botheration, infestation

plain 3 dry, lea 4 bald, bare, moor, neat, open, pure 5 campo, clear, frank, heath, llano, stark, usual, veldt 6 candid, homely, modest, pampas, patent, severe, simple, steppe, tundra 7 austere, evident, obvious, prairie, routine, savanna, Spartan, unmixed 8 apparent, discreet, distinct, everyday, homespun, manifest, ordinary, palpable, savannah, straight, uncomely, unpretty, workaday 9 inelegant, quotidian, unadorned, undiluted 10 unaffected, unalluring, unhandsome

plainclothesman 4 dick 6 sleuth 7 gumshoe 8 hawkshaw, Sherlock 9 detective 12 investigator

plain Jane 5 usual 7 routine 8 everyday, ordinary, workaday 9 quotidian 12 unremarkable

plainness 7 clarity 8 lucidity 9 clearness, limpidity

plainsong 5 chant 12 cantus firmus

plainspoken 4 open 6 candid, direct 10 forthright 11 undisguised, unvarnished

plaintive 3 sad 6 rueful, woeful 7 doleful, elegiac, piteous, pitiful 8 dolesome, dolorous, mournful 9 sorrowful 10 lamentable, lugubrious, melancholy

plait 4 fold 5 braid, weave 7 pigtail 10 intertwine

plan 3 aim, map, way 4 cast, mean, plot 5 chart, draft, frame, order 6 animus, budget, design, devise, intend, intent, lay out, map out, method, policy, projet, scheme, set out, sketch, system 7 arrange, concert, meaning, outline, pattern, program, project, propose, purpose, regimen, work out 8 conspire, contrive, engineer, organize, platform, schedule, strategy, think out 9 blueprint, calculate, figure out, formulate, intention 10 intendment

plane 3 jet, lay 4 even, flat 5 flush, level 6 smooth 7 flatten 8 aircraft, airliner, smoothen

plane surface 4 area

planet 4 Mars 5 Earth, Pluto, Venus 6 Saturn, Uranus 7 Jupiter, Mercury, Neptune *brightest:* 5 Venus *closest to sun:* 7 Mercury *farthest from sun:* 5 Pluto *largest:* 7 Jupiter *path:* 5 orbit *red:* 4 Mars *ringed:* 6 Saturn *satellite:* 4 moon *shadow:* 5 umbra *small:* 8 asteroid *smallest:* 7 Mercury

planetary 6 global 7 immense 8 colossal, enormous 9 universal, worldwide

plangent 5 round 6 rotund 7 orotund, ringing, vibrant 8 resonant, sonorant, sonorous 9 consonant 10 resounding

plank 4 slab 5 board 6 lumber, timber 7 deposit, support

plant 3 fix, pot, set, sow 4 bury, grow, hide, mill, root, seed, tomb 5 cache, cover, imbed, inter, place, put in, stash, works 6 entomb, inhume, occult, screen 7 conceal, factory, lay away, put away, secrete 8 colonize, populate 9 cultivate ***African:*** 4 aloe 6 acacia 8 stapelia ***angiosperm:*** 5 dicot 7 monocot ***aquatic:*** 4 reed 5 lotus, sedge 7 awlwort, cattail, fanwort, papyrus 8 duckweed, eelgrass, hornwort, pondweed 9 water lily 10 watercress 11 bladderwort 12 pickerelweed ***Australian:*** 6 mallee 7 banksia 8 blackboy 10 eucalyptus ***body:*** 4 stem 7 thallus ***bract:*** 5 glume 8 phyllary ***bulbous:*** 4 lily 5 camas, onion, tulip 7 jonquil 8 hyacinth 9 narcissus ***cactus:*** 5 nopal 6 cereus, mescal 7 opuntia, saguaro 11 prickly pear ***carnivorous:*** 6 sundew 10 butterwort 12 pitcher plant 13 Venus's-flytrap ***cell layer:*** 5 suber 7 phellem ***climbing:*** 3 ivy 4 vine 5 betel, liana, vetch 6 bryony, derris, smilax 7 creeper, jasmine 8 bignonia, fumitory, moonseed, scammony, wisteria 12 morning glory ***coloring agent:*** 8 carotene 11 chlorophyll, xanthophyll ***combining form:*** 4 phyt 5 chore, cocci (plural), oecia (plural), phyta (plural), phyte, phyto ***cone-bearing:*** 3 fir, yew 4 pine 5 cedar, cycad 6 gingko, ginkgo, spruce 7 conifer, cypress, redwood 10 arborvitae, gymnosperm ***desert:*** 4 aloe 5 agave 6 cactus, cholla 8 mesquite, ocotillo 9 paloverde 11 brittlebush, Welwitschia ***disease:*** 3 rot 4 gall, mold, rust, scab, smut, wilt 5 ergot 6 blight, mildew, mosaic 7 blister 8 clubroot 9 black spot 10 black heart ***epiphyte:*** 6 orchid 8 air plant 9 bromeliad 11 Spanish moss ***evergreen:*** 3 fir 4 pine 6 spruce 7 lycopod 8 boxberry, clubmoss 9 bearberry 11 wintergreen 12 partridge pea ***extinct:*** 8 calamite ***fern:*** 5 royal 6 Boston 7 bracken 8 polypody, staghorn 10 cliffbrake, maidenhair ***flowerless:*** 4 alga, fern, kelp, moss 5 algae (plural), fungi (plural) 6 fungus, lichen 7 seaweed 8 clubmoss 9 bryophyte, equisetum, horsetail, liverwort ***fluid:*** 3 gum, sap 4 milk 5 latex, resin ***garden:*** 4 iris, ixia, lily, pink, rose 5 aster, canna, daisy, oxlip, pansy, peony, phlox, stock, tulip 6 betony, cosmos, crocus, dahlia, lupine, malope, oxalis, salvia, violet, zinnia 7 anemone, begonia, bluecap, cowslip, fuchsia, gentian, jonquil, lobelia, petunia, statice, verbena 8 bluebell, cyclamen, daffodil, foxglove, gardenia, geranium, hyacinth, larkspur, marigold, primrose, sweet pea 9 amaryllis, campanula, carnation, cineraria, gladiolus, hollyhock, ligularia, narcissus, pimpernel, portulaca, saxifrage, sunflower 10 delphinium, marguerite, mignonette, nasturtium, snapdragon 11 forget-me-not 12 rhododendron, sweet william 13 bleeding heart, chrysanthemum ***gland:*** 7 nectary ***grain:*** 3 oat, rye 4 corn, rice 5 maize, wheat 6 barley, millet 9 buckwheat ***hallucinogenic:*** 4 hemp 6 mescal 8 cannabis 9 marihuana, marijuana ***herb:*** 4 balm, mint, sage 5 basil, calla, tansy, thyme 6 catnip, cicely, fennel 7 bitters, boneset, caraway, figwort, ginseng, parsley, saffron, vanilla 8 geranium, lavender, marjoram, rosemary, valerian 9 calendula, celandine, cineraria, coriander, horehound, portulaca, spearmint, spikenard 10 elecampane, pennyroyal ***largest:*** 7 sequoia ***life:*** 5 flora ***marine:*** 4 kelp 5 fucus 7 seaweed 10 sea lettuce ***marsh:*** 4 reed 5 carex, sedge 7 bogbean, bulrush, calamus, cattail 8 red maple, sphagnum 11 loosestrife ***medicinal:*** 4 aloe, sage 5 poppy, senna, tansy 6 catnip, fennel, garlic, ipecac, nettle 7 aconite, boneset, camphor, hemlock, henbane, juniper, lobelia, mustard, parsley 8 camomile, cinchona, licorice, pilewort, wormwood 9 asafetida, chamomile, dandelion, monkshood 10 peppermint 11 assafoetida ***microscopic:*** 4 mold 6 diatom 7 euglena 8 bacteria (plural) 9 bacterium ***mushroom:*** 5 morel 7 amanita 10 champignon 11 chanterelle ***oldest:*** 11 bristlecone ***onion-like:*** 4 leek 5 chive 7 shallot 8 scallion ***opening:*** 5 stoma 7 stomata (plural) ***parasitic:*** 6 dodder, fungus 9 mistletoe 10 beechdrops ***part:*** 3 bud, nut, sap 4 bark, bulb, cell, cone, corm, leaf, pome, root, seed, stem, wood 5 drupe, fruit, grain, spore, thorn, tuber, xylem 6 catkin, flower, nectar, phloem, raceme 7 rhizome 8 lenticel 9 cellulose, cotyledon 11 chlorophyll, chloroplast 13 inflorescence ***pest:*** 5 aphid, scale 6 chafer, thrips, weevil 7 cutworm 8 fruit fly, wireworm 9 gypsy moth 10 cankerworm, leafhopper, phylloxera 11 codling moth ***poisonous:*** 4 poke, upas 5 sumac 6 castor, croton, datura 7 amantia, cassava, cowbane, henbane, lobelia, tobacco 8 foxglove, larkspur, locoweed, mayapple, oleander, pokeweed 9 baneberry, monkshood 10 belladonna, jimsonweed, manchineel, nightshade ***product:*** 3 dye, tar 4 cork, drug, food, rope 5 fiber, paper, resin, rosin 6 lumber, rubber 7 alcohol, perfume, tobacco 10 turpentine ***saprophytic:***

5 fungi (plural) 6 fungus 10 Indian pipe ***shrub:*** 3 box 5 broom, furze, lilac, sumac 6 azalea, datura, hyssop, privet, spirea 7 begonia, dogwood, spiraea 8 hawthorn, magnolia, oleander, plumbago, viburnum 9 forsythia ***succulent:*** 5 agave 6 cactus 10 bitterroot ***suffix:*** 2 ad 4 ales (plural) 5 aceae (plural), ineae (plural) ***support:*** 7 trellis ***thorny:*** 4 rose 5 briar 6 cactus, nettle, teasel, teazel, teazle 7 caltrop, thistle 8 cockspur 9 cocklebur ***tissue:*** 5 xylem 6 phloem 7 cambium, medulla 8 meristem ***unit of structure:*** 6 telome ***wild flower:*** 4 ramp 5 bluet, calla, daisy 6 adonis, lupine 7 arbutus, cowslip, gentian 8 fireweed, hepatica, toadflax, trillium 9 bloodroot, buttercup, campanula, columbine, dandelion, goldenrod ***young:*** 5 scion, shoot 6 sprout 7 cutting 8 seedling

plantlike 7 phytoid

plant louse 5 aphid

plaster 3 dab 4 coat, daub, sham 5 cover, gesso, salve, smear 6 bedaub, mortar, remedy, smudge, soothe, stucco

plastic 4 soft 5 vinyl 6 pliant, supple 7 ductile, organic, pliable 8 creative, flexible, moldable 9 adaptable, formative, malleable 10 sculptural

plat 3 lot, map 4 plan 5 chart, floor, tract 6 parcel 7 surface 8 platform

plate 4 base, coat, disc, dish, disk, tile 5 layer, paten, scute, slice 6 fascia, lamina, plaque 7 lamella, overlay

plateau 4 mesa 5 table 6 upland 9 altiplano, tableland ***arid:*** 4 puna ***barren:*** 5 field 6 paramo ***dry:*** 5 karoo 6 karroo

platform 3 map 4 bank, base, dais, deck, plan 5 forum, ledge, shelf, stage 6 design, podium, pulpit, scheme 7 balcony, pattern, rostrum 9 banquette 11 declaration ***temporary:*** 7 staging 8 scaffold ***wooden:*** 9 boardwalk

platinum ***symbol:*** 2 Pt

platitude 6 cliché, truism 7 bromide 8 banality, prosaism 10 prosaicism, shibboleth

Plato ***father:*** 7 Ariston ***literary form:*** 6 dialog 8 dialogue ***school:*** 7 Academy ***work:*** 3 Ion 4 Meno 5 Crito, Lysis 6 Laches, Phaedo 7 Apology, Gorgias 8 Phaedrus, Republic 9 Charmides, Symposium

platoon 3 lot, set 4 team, unit 5 array, batch, bunch, clump, group, squad 6 parcel 7 battery, cluster 8 division 9 formation

platter 6 salver 8 trencher

platypus 8 duckbill

plaudits 5 kudos 6 praise 7 acclaim 8 applause, encomium 11 acclamation, approbation

plausible 8 credible 10 believable, creditable

play 3 act, bet, fun, use 4 game, jest, joke, ploy, romp, room, take, wile 5 dally, drama, enact, feint, flirt, scope, serve, sport, stake, treat, trick, wager 6 cavort, comedy, device, fiddle, fidget, frolic, gambit, gamble, gambol, handle, jockey, leeway, margin, trifle 7 beguile, delight, disport, exploit, finesse, gimmick, perform, roister, rollick, twiddle 8 artifice, latitude, maneuver, pleasure, recreate 9 amusement, dalliance, discourse, diversion, elbowroom, enjoyment, pantomime, personate, stratagem 10 manipulate, recreation ***kind:*** 5 farce, opera 6 comedy 7 musical, tragedy 8 one-acter, operetta 9 melodrama, pantomime ***part:*** 3 act 5 exode, scene 8 epilogue, prologue

playact 2 do 7 perform 9 discourse, personate 11 impersonate

play down 4 mute 6 soften 9 soft-pedal 11 deemphasize

player 4 mime 5 actor, mimic 6 mummer 7 actress, trouper 8 thespian 9 performer 11 participant 12 impersonator

playful 3 gay 5 antic, jolly, merry, pixie 6 blithe, elvish, frisky, impish, jocund, joking, jovial, lively, pranky, wicked 7 coltish, dashing, gleeful, jocular, larking, larkish, puckish, roguish, waggish 8 gamesome, humorous, mirthful, pixieish, playsome, prankful, prankish, sportive 9 kittenish, pixilated, sprightly, whimsical 10 frolicsome, rollicking 11 mischievous 12 lighthearted

play off 3 pit, vie 5 match 6 oppose 7 counter

play on words 3 pun

play up 6 stress 7 feature 9 emphasize, italicize, underline 10 underscore

playwright 6 author, writer 9 dramatist 10 dramatizer, dramaturge

plaza 5 green 6 common, square 9 carrefour 11 marketplace

plea 4 suit 5 alibi 6 appeal, excuse, orison, prayer 7 apology, pretext, request 8 entreaty, overture, petition 11 application, imploration, imprecation 12 supplication ***defendant's:*** 4 nolo 6 guilty 9 not guilty

plead 3 beg, sue 4 pray 5 brace, crave 6 appeal 7 beseech, entreat, implore 9 importune 10 supplicate

pleasant 4 fair, fine, glad, good, nice 5 clear, sunny, sweet, tasty 6 cheery, genial, joyful, joyous, pretty 7 amiable, clarion, likable, welcome 8 amicable, charming, cheerful, cheering, engaging, gracious, grateful, likeable, pleasing, sunshine, sunshiny, tasteful 9 agreeable, appealing, cloudless, congenial, convivial, enjoyable, favorable, unclouded 10 delightful, gratify-

ing, undarkened *and unpleasant:* 11 bittersweet
pleasantry 3 fun 4 jest, joke 6 banter 10 jocularity
please 4 like, suit, will, wish 5 agree, amuse, elate, elect, enjoy 6 arride, choose, tickle 7 content, delight, gladden, gratify, happify, indulge, satisfy 9 delectate, titillate
pleasing 4 good, nice 5 nifty 6 comely, pretty, seemly 7 welcome, winning 8 charming, grateful, suitable 9 agreeable, congenial, favorable, palatable 10 attractive, delectable, delightful, enchanting, gratifying 11 pleasurable 12 satisfactory
pleasingly plump 6 zaftig, zoftig
pleasurable see pleasing
pleasure 3 fun, joy 4 will 5 bliss, fancy, mirth 6 arride, liking, relish 7 delight, gladden, gratify, happify, joyance 8 felicity, fruition, gladness, hedonism, velleity 9 amusement, delectate, diversion, enjoyment, happiness, merriment
pleasuremonger 8 hedonist, sybarite
pleat 4 fold 5 crimp 6 crease 7 flounce
pleated 7 plicate
plebeian 3 low 4 base, mean 5 lowly 6 coarse, common, homely, humble, vulgar 7 ignoble, ill-bred, lowborn 8 baseborn, everyday, ordinary, unwashed
plebeians see populace
plectrum 4 pick
pledge 3 row 4 bail, bond, gage, hock, oath, pass, pawn, seal, word 5 drink, swear, toast, token 6 engage, plight, surety 7 earnest, hostage, promise, warrant 8 contract, covenant, guaranty, mortgage, security, warranty 9 assurance, certainty, guarantee, undertake 11 impignorate
pledget 3 wad 8 compress
Pleiades 4 Maia 6 Merope 7 Alcyone, Celaeno, Electra, Sterope, Taygeta 8 Asterope *brightest star:* 7 Alcyone
plenteous see plentiful
plentiful 4 full, rich 5 ample 6 bumper, galore, plenty 7 copious, fertile, fulsome, liberal, opulent, profuse, teeming 8 abundant, affluent, bursting, fruitful, generous, prolific, swarming, swimming 9 abounding, bounteous, bountiful, plenteous, unstinted
plenty 3 lot 4 heap, much, pack, peck, pile 5 ample 7 copious, liberal 8 abundant, generous, mountain, opulence 9 abundance, bounteous, bountiful, great deal, plenteous, plentiful 10 cornucopia
pleonasm 8 verbiage 9 tautology, verbality 10 periphrase, redundancy, roundabout 11 periphrasis 13 circumambages
plethora 4 glut 5 flood 6 deluge, excess 7 surfeit, surplus 8 fullness, overflow, overkill, overmuch, overplus 9 repletion 10 surplusage 11 superfluity 13 overabundance
plexus 4 rete 7 network
pliable see pliant
pliant 4 limp, soft 5 lithe 6 limber, supple 7 ductile, plastic, tensile, willowy 8 flexible, moldable, workable, yielding 9 adaptable, compliant, malleable, tractable 11 manipulable 13 manipulatable
plica 4 fold, ruck 5 ridge, rivel 6 crease, furrow, rimple 7 crinkle, wrinkle 11 corrugation
plight 3 box, fix, jam, vow 4 hole, spot, word 5 swear 6 corner, engage, pickle, pledge, scrape 7 betroth, dilemma, promise 8 covenant, quandary 9 betrothal 10 difficulty, engagement 11 predicament
plighted 7 engaged 8 intended 9 affianced, betrothed 10 contracted
plod 4 grub, slog, slop, toil 5 grind, slave, tramp, tromp 6 drudge, stodge, trudge 7 trample 8 footslog, plunther
plot 4 plan 5 cabal, covin, tract 6 design, devise, parcel, scheme 7 collude, compact, connive, diagram, outline 8 cogitate, conspire, contrive, engineer, intrigue, practice, scenario 9 collusion, conniving, machinate, scheme out 10 complicity, connivance, conspiracy 11 machination
plover 4 bird 5 pewit, stilt 7 lapwing 8 dotterel, killdeer *relative:* 9 sandpiper, turnstone
plow 3 dig 4 till, turn 5 break 6 furrow, trench 8 turn over 9 cultivate *part:* 4 beam, frog 5 share 8 landside 9 moldboard
ploy 4 ruse, wile 5 feint, trick 6 device, gambit 7 gimmick 8 artifice, maneuver 9 stratagem
pluck 3 tug 4 grit, guts, pick, pull 5 cheek, heart, nerve, spunk 6 daring, mettle, snatch, spirit, tweeze 7 bravery, cojones, courage 8 gameness 10 resolution
plucky 4 bold, game 5 brave 6 spunky 7 doughty 8 fearless 9 dauntless, unfearing 10 courageous 11 undauntable
plug 3 tap 4 bung, clog, cork, fill, pack, puff, push, stop, tout 5 block, blurb, boost, choke, close, spile 7 congest, occlude, promote, puffing, stopper, stopple, tampion, tompion, write-up 8 obstruct 9 advertise
plug-ugly 3 mug 4 thug 5 rowdy, tough, yahoo 6 mucker 7 ruffian 8 bullyboy 9 roughneck
plum 5 prize 6 reward 7 guerdon, premium 8 dividend *dried:* 5 prune *kind:* 4 Agen 6 Damson, Duarte 7 bullace 8 Hortulan, Salicina 9 Green Gage, myrobalan *spiny:* 10 blackthorn
plumage 8 feathers *early:* 4 down
plumb 5 delve, probe, sound 6 fathom 7 explore, plummet 8 absolute, vertical 10 straight-up 13 perpendicular

plume 5 pique, preen, pride 7 feather 8 aigrette
plummet 3 dip 4 drop, fall, sink, skid 5 crash 6 plunge, tumble 7 decline, descend 8 collapse, decrease, nose-dive 11 precipitate
plump 3 fat 5 buxom, podgy, pudgy, round, stout, tubby 6 chubby, fleshy, portly, rotund 8 roly-poly 10 roundabout
plunder 3 rob 4 loot, swag 5 booty, prize, rifle, spoil 6 boodle 7 despoil, pillage, ransack, relieve, stick up 9 knock over
plunderage 4 loot, swag 5 booty, prize, spoil 6 boodle
plunderer 6 looter, raider, sacker 7 forager, ravager 8 marauder, pillager, ravisher 9 despoiler 10 freebooter
plunge 3 dig, dip, ram, run 4 dive, drop, fall, rush, sink, skid, stab 5 burst, douse, drive, lunge, pitch, slump, stick 6 charge, go down, thrust, topple, tumble 7 immerse, plummet 8 keel over, nose-dive, submerge
plus 4 more, over 5 asset, boost, build 6 beef up, excess, expand 7 augment, enlarge, magnify, overage, surplus 8 compound, increase 9 overstock 10 oversupply
plush 4 posh 6 Capuan, deluxe 7 opulent 8 luscious, palatial 9 luxuriant, luxurious, sumptuous 11 upholstered
Pluto 3 Dis 5 Hades ***brother:*** 4 Zeus 7 Jupiter, Neptune 8 Poseidon ***father:*** 6 Cronus, Saturn ***mother:*** 3 Ops 4 Rhea ***wife:*** 10 Persephone, Proserpina
plutonic 6 Hadean 7 avernal, hellish, stygian 8 chthonic, infernal 9 chthonian, cimmerian, Tartarean 10 sulphurous 11 pandemoniac
plutonium ***symbol:*** 2 Pu
Plutus ***father:*** 6 lasion ***god of:*** 6 riches, wealth ***mother:*** 5 Ceres 7 Demeter
ply 4 bend, fold 5 exert, layer, swing, throw, wield 6 handle, put out 7 belabor 8 dispense, exercise, maneuver 9 importune 10 manipulate
pneuma 4 soul 5 anima 6 animus, psyche, spirit 9 élan vital 10 vital force
pneumatic 4 airy 6 aerial 11 atmospheric
Pocahontas ***father:*** 8 Powhatan ***husband:*** 5 Rolfe
pock 3 pit 4 hole, spot 6 pimple 7 pustule
pocket 3 bag, nab, wee 4 hook, lift, sack, tiny 5 filch, pinch, pouch, purse, steal, swipe, weeny 6 accept, cavity 7 capsule, conceal, dead end, impasse, swallow 8 abstract, bear with, cul-de-sac, dwarfish, monetary, pint-size, tolerate, tough out 9 condensed, financial, itsy-bitsy, miniature, pecuniary 10 blind alley, diminutive ***billiards:*** 4 pool
pocket money 6 change 9 petty cash 11 small change
pocket-size 4 tiny 6 midget, minute, peewee 8 dwarfish, pint-size 9 itsy-bitsy, miniature 10 diminutive
pod 3 bag, gam, sac 4 boll, case, hull, husk, skin 5 shell, shuck 6 cocoon, paunch, school 7 capsule, silique 8 potbelly, seedcase 9 bay window 11 corporation ***combining form:*** 7 siliqui ***plant:*** 3 pea 4 bean, okra 5 chili, gumbo 6 cassia, cowpea, legume, lentil, peanut, pepper 8 capsicum, mesquite, milkweed 9 lespedeza
pod-bearing tree 5 carob 6 locust 7 catalpa
podiatry 9 chiropody
Poe, Edgar Allan ***detective:*** 5 Dupin ***poem:*** 6 Lenore 7 Israfel, To Helen, Ulalume 8 Eldorado, For Annie, The Raven 10 Annabel Lee ***tale:*** 6 Ligeia, Shadow 7 Morella, Silence 10 The Gold Bug
poem 3 ode 4 epic, epos, idyl, rime, rune, song 5 ditty, elegy, epode, idyll, lyric, rhyme, verse 6 ballad, epopee, jingle, rondel, sonnet 7 rondeau 8 limerick, madrigal ***closing:*** 5 envoi, envoy ***combining form:*** 5 stich ***division:*** 4 foot, line 5 canto, epode, stich, verse 6 stanza 7 refrain 8 epilogue, prologue ***Japanese:*** 5 haiku, tanka ***of eight lines:*** 6 octave 7 triolet ***of four lines:*** 8 quatrain ***of fourteen lines:*** 6 sonnet ***of three lines:*** 7 triplet ***pastoral:*** 7 eclogue, georgic ***short:*** 5 ditty 7 epigram
poet 4 bard, muse, scop 5 odist, skald 6 lyrist 7 elegist 8 idyllist, lyricist, satirist 9 balladist, sonneteer, sonnetist 10 Parnassian ***American:*** 3 Poe 4 Nash, Read, Tabb, Tate 5 Auden, Benét, Crane, Field, Frost, Guest, Moore, Plath, Pound, Riley, Wylie 6 Barlow, Bryant, Ciardi, Dunbar, Kilmer, Lanier, Lowell, Millay, Ransom, Seeger, Strand, Taylor, Warren, Wilbur 7 Emerson, Jeffers, Lindsay, Markham, Merrill, Nemerov, Roethke, Shapiro, Stevens, Whitman 8 Cummings, Ginsberg, MacLeish, Robinson, Teasdale, Whittier, Williams 9 Dickinson, Santayana 10 Bradstreet, Longfellow 12 Wigglesworth ***Anglo-Saxon:*** 7 Caedmon, Cynwulf 8 Cynewulf ***Arab:*** 5 Jarir ***Australian:*** 8 Paterson ***Belgian:*** 11 Maeterlinck ***Canadian:*** 5 Pratt 7 Roberts ***Chinese:*** 4 Li Po, Tu Fu ***Danish:*** 5 Evald, Ewald ***English:*** 3 Gay 4 Gray, Owen, Pope, Rowe, Tate, Wyat 5 Blake, Byron, Donne, Eliot, Keats, Noyes, Wilde, Wyatt, Young 6 Arnold, Brooke, Cowper, Dryden, Graves, Milton, Savage, Sidney, Surrey, Symons, Waller, Warton, Watson, Wotton 7 Chaucer, Herrick, Hopkins, Housman, Layamon, Patmore, Quarles, Shelley, Skelton, Southey, Spender, Spenser 8 Betjeman, Browning, Langland, Lovelace, Mere-

dith, Rossetti, Suckling, Tennyson, Thompson 9 Coleridge, Swinburne 10 Wordsworth 11 Shakespeare ***Finnish:*** 8 Runeberg ***French:*** 5 Marot 6 Musset, Valery, Villon 7 Bourget, Chenier, Gautier, Rimbaud, Ronsard 8 Malherbe, Mallarmé, Verlaine 9 Lamartine 10 Baudelaire 11 Apollinaire ***German:*** 5 Heine, Rilke, Storm 6 Goethe, Uhland 7 Walther, Wolfram 8 Schiller 9 Klopstock ***Greek:*** 5 Arion, Homer 6 Erinna, Hesiod, Pindar, Sappho 7 Thespis 8 Anacreon 9 Simonides 10 Apollonius, Theocritus ***Hindu:*** 5 Naidu 6 Tagore 8 Kalidasa ***Hungarian:*** 6 Zrinyi ***Irish:*** 5 Moore, Synge, Wolfe, Yeats 8 Stephens ***Italian:*** 4 Rosa, Vida 5 Dante, Tasso 7 Ariosto, Manzoni, Montale 8 Leopardi, Petrarch 9 D'Annunzio, Marinetti, Ungaretti ***medieval:*** 8 minstrel, trouvère, trouveur 10 troubadour ***nonsense:*** 4 Lear ***Norwegian:*** 8 Bjömson, Welhaven 9 Wergeland ***Persian:*** 4 Sadi 5 Attar, Hafiz 11 Omar Khayyam ***Roman:*** 4 Ovid 6 Horace, Vergil, Virgil 7 Juvenal, Statius 8 Catullus, Tibullus 9 Lucretius ***Russian:*** 7 Pushkin, Yesenin 9 Kheraskov, Pasternak ***Scottish:*** 4 Hogg, Muir 5 Burns, Scott 6 Ramsay 7 Thomson ***Spanish:*** 7 Jimonez ***Swedish:*** 5 Sachs 6 Tegner 8 Snoilsky 9 Karlfeldt ***Swiss:*** 9 Spitteler ***Welsh:*** 6 Thomas 7 Aneurin, Watkins

poetaster 6 rhymer, verser 7 bardlet 8 bardling, verseman 9 rhymester, versifier

poetic 5 lyric 6 bardic, dreamy 8 romantic

poetic contraction see at contraction

poet laureate 3 Pye 4 Rowe, Tate 6 Austin, Cibber, Dryden, Jonson 7 Bridges, Southey 8 Betjeman, Davenant, Day-Lewis, Shadwell, Tennyson 9 Masefield, Whitehead 10 Wordsworth

Pogo creator 9 Walt Kelly

poignancy 6 pathos

poignant 4 keen, racy 5 acute, sharp, spicy, zesty 6 moving, snappy, urgent 7 cutting, peppery, piquant, pungent 8 incisive, piercing, touching 9 affecting 10 impressive

point 3 aim, awn, bit, dot, jag, nib, tip 4 apex, barb, beak, bill, cape, cast, cusp, edge, head, hint, item, mite, mote, naze, site, snag, spot, tine, turn 5 brink, force, imply, level, locus, motif, place, prong, punch, refer, speck, spike, steer, theme, topic, trace, verge 6 allude, detail, direct, matter, moment, motive, tip-off, zero in 7 address, article, cogency, element, feature, instant, station, subject, suggest 8 argument, flyspeck, foreland, headland, indicate, juncture, location, particle, position, validity 9 birthmark, character, punctuate, situation, threshold, validness 10 particular, promontory 12 significance

Point Counter Point author 6 Huxley

pointed 5 acute, peaky, piked, sharp 6 marked, peaked, signal 7 salient 8 acicular, striking 9 aciculate, acuminate, acuminous, arresting, cuspidate, mucronate, prominent

pointer 3 dog, tip 4 dial, hint 5 arrow, steer 6 tip-off 9 indicator

pointillist 6 Seurat

point of view 5 angle 7 outlook 11 perspective

point out 8 indicate

poise 4 hang, tact 5 float, grace, hover 6 aplomb, stasis, steady 7 address, balance, ballast, dignity 8 calmness, elegance, serenity 9 assurance, diplomacy, equipoise, stabilify, stabilize 10 confidence 11 delicatesse, equilibrium, savoir faire, stabilitate, tactfulness, tranquility

poised 4 calm, easy 6 placid, serene 8 composed, tranquil 9 collected, easygoing, possessed 13 self-possessed

poison 4 bane, harm, loco, warp 5 stain, taint, toxic, toxin, venom, virus 6 debase, infect, toxine, toxoid 7 botulin, cacodyl, corrupt, debauch, deprave, destroy, envenom, pervert, vitiate 8 mephitic, toxicant, venenate, venomous, virulent 9 contagion 10 corruption, demoralize 13 contamination ***arrow:*** 4 inée 5 urare, urari 6 antiar, curara, curure 7 ouabain, woorali, woorari 8 antiarin ***combining form:*** 3 tox 4 toxi, toxo 5 toxic 6 toxico

poisoning ***food:*** 8 botulism ***lead:*** 8 plumbism

poisonous 5 fatal, toxic 6 deadly, lethal, mortal 7 baneful, miasmal, miasmic, nocuous, noxious, toxical 8 mephitic, toxicant, venenous, venomous, virulent 9 miasmatic, pestilent 10 nauseating, pernicious ***alkaloid:*** 8 nicotine 10 strychnine ***element:*** 7 arsenic

poke 3 box, dig, hit, jab, jog, jut, lag, pry 4 chop, cuff, dolt, dope, drag, nose, pout, prod, push, sock, stab, stir 5 bulge, chump, clout, dally, delay, dunce, idiot, moron, mouse, nudge, punch, rouse, shove, smack, snoop, spank, tarry, trail 6 arouse, awaken, beetle, buffet, cowboy, dawdle, dimwit, loiter, pierce, put off, putter, thrust 7 project 8 busybody

poker ***bet total:*** 3 pot ***form:*** 4 stud 8 baseball ***hand:*** 4 pair 5 flush 8 straight 9 full house 10 royal flush 13 straight flush ***stake:*** 4 ante ***term:*** 3 see 4 call, draw, open 5 raise ***token:*** 4 chip

poker-faced 5 grave, sober, staid 6 sedate, solemn, somber 7 earnest, neutral, serious

poky 4 blah, dull 6 dreary, stodgy 7 humdrum 8 banausic, monotone 10 monotonous
Poland ***capital:*** 6 Warsaw ***labor leader:*** 6 Walesa (Lech) ***monetary unit:*** 5 zloty
polar 8 opposite
pole 4 punt, spar 5 shaft, stick, stilt ***Indian:*** 5 totem ***Scottish:*** 5 caber
polecat 5 fitch, skunk 7 fitchet
polestar 3 hub 4 seat 5 focus, guide, heart 6 center 10 focal point 11 nerve center
policeman 3 cop 4 fuzz, heat 5 bobby 6 copper, peeler 7 gumshoe, John Law, officer, trooper 8 bluecoat, Dogberry, flatfoot, gendarme 9 constable, patrolman 12 peace officer ***Italian:*** 11 carabiniere ***Parisian:*** 4 flic 8 gendarme ***Spanish:*** 10 carabinero ***Turkish:*** 6 kavass 7 zaptiah, zaptieh
policy 3 wit 4 line 6 course, govern, wisdom 7 program 8 sagacity 9 procedure
polio vaccine developer 4 Salk 5 Sabin
polish 3 rub, wax 4 buff 5 glaze, glint, gloss, round, sheen, shine, sleek, slick 6 glance, luster, pumice, refine, smooth 7 brush up, burnish, culture, perfect, touch up 8 breeding, brighten 10 refinement
Polish ***dumpling:*** 7 pierogi ***patriot:*** 9 Kosciusko ***pope:*** 8 John Paul ***sausage:*** 8 kielbasa ***soldier:*** 7 Pulaski
polish off 5 eat up, shift, swill 6 devour, punish 7 consume, put away 8 dispatch
polite 5 civil 7 courtly, genteel 8 mannerly 9 attentive, courteous 10 thoughtful 11 considerate 12 well-mannered
politeness 8 chivalry, civility, courtesy
politic 4 wise 7 cunning, prudent, tactful 8 delicate, tactical 9 advisable, expedient, judicious 10 diplomatic 11 worldly-wise
political ***association:*** 4 bund ***meeting:*** 6 caucus ***party:*** 3 GOP 9 Communist, Socialist 10 Democratic, Republican ***system:*** 7 fascism 9 communism, democracy, socialism
politics ***conservative:*** 8 rightism ***liberal:*** 7 leftism
poll 4 clip, crop, head, nape 5 shear 6 noddle, noggin, noodle, survey 7 canvass
pollack, pollock 6 saithe 8 bluefish, coalfish
pollard 3 top 4 crop 8 truncate 10 detruncate
pollen-producing organ 6 stamen
pollex 5 thumb
polliwog 7 tadpole
polltaker 6 Gallup
pollute 4 foul, soil 5 dirty, taint 6 befoul, defile 7 corrupt, profane 11 contaminate
pollution 4 smog 8 impurity 10 defilement

Pollux 10 Polydeuces ***brother:*** 6 Castor ***father:*** 4 Zeus ***mother:*** 4 Leda ***sister:*** 5 Helen 12 Clytemnestra
Pollyanna 8 optimist 10 daydreamer ***author:*** 6 Porter
Pollyannaish 8 cheerful, sanguine 10 optimistic
Polonius ***daughter:*** 7 Ophelia ***slayer:*** 6 Hamlet ***son:*** 7 Laertes
poltergeist 5 ghost 6 spirit
poltroon 4 funk 6 coward, craven, funker 7 dastard, gutless, quitter, unmanly 8 cowardly 9 spunkless 11 lily-livered, yellowbelly
Polydorus ***father:*** 5 Priam 6 Cadmus ***mother:*** 6 Hecuba 8 Harmonia ***slayer:*** 8 Achilles 10 Polymestor 11 Polymnestor
polygon ***eight-sided:*** 7 octagon ***five-sided:*** 8 pentagon ***four-sided:*** 8 tetragon ***nine-sided:*** 7 nonagon ***seven-sided:*** 8 heptagon ***six-sided:*** 7 hexagon ***ten-sided:*** 7 decagon ***three-sided:*** 8 triangle ***twelve-sided:*** 9 dodecagon
Polyhymnia 4 Muse ***invention:*** 4 lyre
Polynesian 5 Maori 6 Samoan, Tongan 8 Hawaiian, Tahitian 9 Marquesan
Polynices ***brother:*** 8 Eteocles ***father:*** 7 Oedipus ***mother:*** 7 Jocasta ***wife:*** 5 Argia 6 Argeia
polyp 5 zooid 7 hydroid ***freshwater:*** 5 hydra
Polyphemus 7 cyclops ***beloved:*** 7 Galatea ***father:*** 8 Poseidon ***victim:*** 4 Acis
pome 4 pear 5 apple 6 quince 8 hawthorn
pommel 4 knob 6 finial
pomp 4 form, show 5 array, shine 6 parade, ritual 7 display, fanfare, liturgy, panoply 8 ceremony, splendor 9 formality
pompano 4 fish 6 permit 8 carangid 10 butterfish
Pompeii's volcano 8 Vesuvius
pom-pom 4 ball, tuft
pompous 4 vain 5 proud, puffy, wiggy 6 stuffy 7 aureate, bloated, flowery, stilted, stuck-up 8 arrogant, sonorous 9 bombastic, important, overblown 10 egocentric, euphuistic, hoity-toity, pontifical, rhetorical 11 declamatory, highfalutin, magisterial, pretentious
pond 4 mere 5 stank 6 lagoon, salina ***combining form:*** 4 limn 5 limni, limno
ponder 4 mind, mull, muse 5 brood, study, think, weigh 6 reason 7 perpend, reflect, revolve 8 appraise, cogitate, consider, evaluate, meditate, mull over, muse over, ruminate, think out, turn over 9 speculate, think over 10 deliberate, excogitate 11 contemplate
ponderous 4 dull 5 heavy, hefty, stiff, vapid 6 dreary, stodgy, stuffy, wooden 7 buckram, humdrum, massive, onerous,

stilted, weighty 8 plodding, unwieldy 10 burdensome, cumbersome, oppressive
poniard 6 dagger
Ponocrates' pupil 9 Gargantua
Ponte Vecchio *city:* 8 Florence *river:* 4 Arno
Pontiac's tribe 6 Ottawa
pontiff 4 pope 6 bishop
pontifical 5 puffy, wiggy 6 stuffy 7 bloated, pompous 8 arrogant, dogmatic 9 episcopal, important 11 magisterial
pony 4 crib, trot 5 horse 6 cayuse *breed:* 6 Exmoor 8 Shetland
Pooh creator 5 Milne
pooh-pooh 3 boo 4 bird, hiss, hoot, razz 5 bazoo 7 catcall, dismiss, kiss off 9 raspberry
pool 3 pot, pul 4 mere 5 chain, group, kitty, trust 6 cartel, lagoon, laguna, puddle 7 combine, jackpot 9 syndicate *player:* 7 Mosconi 13 Minnesota Fats
poor 3 bad, low 4 base, flat, hack, mean, punk 5 amiss, broke, cheap, needy, scant, skimp, spare, stony, tatty, wrong 6 common, crummy, humble, meager, paltry, rotten, rueful, scanty, scrimp, shoddy, skimpy, sleazy, sparse, trashy 7 piteous, pitiful, scrawny, scrimpy, squalid, trivial 8 bankrupt, beggared, beggarly, déclassé, exiguous, indigent, inferior, low-grade, pathetic, pitiable, rubbishy, strapped 9 deficient, destitute, insolvent, moneyless, penceless, penniless, penurious, unmoneyed 10 bankrupted, down-and-out, pauperized, second-rate, stone-broke 11 fortuneless, impecunious, indifferent, necessitous, second-class, unfavorable *combining form:* 3 mal
poorly 3 low 4 mean 6 ailing, offish, sickly, unwell 8 off-color 10 indisposed 11 undesirably 13 ineffectively
pop 3 dad, dot, gun, hit, try 4 dada, dart, ding, jump, papa, shot, slap, slog, sock, soda, stab, swat 5 break, catch, crack, daddy, drink, fling, shoot, smite, whack, whirl 6 attack, effort, father, strike 7 assault, attempt, explode, instant 8 backfire *in:* 3 see 4 call 5 visit 6 come by, drop by, look up, stop by 8 come over
pop artist 5 Blake 6 Warhol 7 Hockney, Indiana 9 Oldenburg, Wesselman
pope 3 Leo 4 John, Mark, Paul, Pius 5 Caius, Conon, Donus, Felix, Gaius, Lando, Linus, Peter, Soter, Urban 6 Adrian, Agatho, Fabian, Julius, Lucius, Martin, Sixtus, Victor 7 Anterus, Clement, Damasus, Gregory, Hadrian, Hyginus, Marinus, Paschal, Pontian, Romanus, Sergius, Stephen, Zosimus 8 Agapetus, Anicetus, Benedict, Boniface, Calixtus, Eugenius, Eusebius, Formosis, Gelasius, Hilarius, Honorius, Innocent, John Paul, Liberius, Nicholas, Pelagius, Siricius, Theodore, Vigilius, Vitalian 9 Adeodatus, Alexander, Anacletus, Callistus, Celestine, Cornelius, Densdedit, Dionysius, Eutychian, Evaristus, Hormisdas, Marcellus, Miltiades, Severinus, Silverius, Silvester, Sisinnius, Sylvester, Symmachus, Valentine, Zacharias 10 Anastasius, Melchiades, Sabinianus, Simplicius, Zephyrinus 11 Christopher, Constantine, Eleutherius, Eutychianus, Marcellinus, Telesphorus
Pope poem 10 The Dunciad 12 An Essay on Man 16 The Rape of the Lock
Popeye *accessory:* 4 pipe *baby:* 8 Sweet Pea *energizer:* 7 spinach *friend:* 5 Wimpy 8 Olive Oyl *occupation:* 6 sailor *rival:* 5 Bluto
poplar 5 abele, alamo, aspen 9 tulip tree 10 cottonwood 12 balm of Gilead *North American:* 6 balsam
Poppaea's husband 4 Nero
poppycock 3 rot 4 bosh, guff 5 bilge, hokum 6 bunkum 8 malarkey, nonsense 10 balderdash 12 blatherskite, fiddle-faddle
populace 5 plebs 6 masses, people, plebes 9 commonage, commoners, common men, plebeians 10 commonalty 11 rank and file, third estate *combining form:* 3 dem 4 demo
popular 4 rife 5 cheap, noted 6 famous, public, ruling, vulgar 7 current, favored, general, leading, rampant, regnant 8 approved, favorite 9 notorious, preferred, prevalent, prominent, well-known, well-liked 10 democratic, prevailing, widespread
populate 6 occupy, people, tenant 7 inhabit
populous 7 crowded 8 numerous
Poratha's father 5 Haman
porcelain *Chinese:* 9 Lowestoft *English:* 3 Bow 5 Derby, Spode 6 Minton 7 Bristol, Chelsea 8 Caughley, Wedgwood *French:* 6 Sèvres 7 Limoges *German:* 7 Dresden, Meissen *ingredient:* 6 kaolin 8 petuntse *Italian:* 6 Doccia *Japanese:* 5 Imari
porch 5 lanai 7 galilee, passage, veranda 8 verandah
porcine see portly
porcupine 5 porky, prick 7 echidna 8 hedgehog
porgy 4 scup 6 sparid 7 margate, pinfish 8 menhaden
Porgy and Bess composer 8 Gershwin
Porgy author 7 Heyward
pork 3 ham, pig 5 bacon, swine 8 sowbelly *cut:* 3 ham 4 jowl, loin, side 7 fatback 8 forefoot, hind foot, spare rib 9 picnic ham 10 Boston butt
pork-barreling 9 patronage
pornographic 7 obscene
porous 5 leaky 6 leachy 8 pervious

9 permeable 10 cancellate, cancellous, penetrable 13 insubstantial
porridge 4 stew 5 brose, salad 6 crowdy, sowans, sowens 7 crowdie
port 3 air, set 4 goal, mien 5 cover, haven 6 asylum, covert, harbor, refuge, riding 7 address, bearing, retreat, shelter 8 demeanor, larboard, presence 9 anchorage, harborage, roadstead, sanctuary 10 deportment 11 comportment, destination
portable 5 handy 6 mobile, wieldy
portal 4 door, gate 5 entry 7 doorway 8 entrance, entryway 11 entranceway
portcullis 3 bar 4 shut 7 grating, lattice
portend 4 bode, omen 5 augur 7 betoken, predict, presage, promise, signify 8 forebode, forecast, foreshow, foretell, indicate, prophesy 9 adumbrate, foretoken 10 foreshadow, vaticinate
portent 4 omen, sign 6 augury, boding, marvel, wonder 7 miracle, presage, prodigy, stunner 8 bodement 9 foretoken, sensation
portentous 7 pompous, weighty 8 inflated 9 marvelous 10 prodigious
porter 5 carry, hamal 6 bearer, hamaul, hammal, redcap 7 carrier, drogher 9 transport 10 doorkeeper ***airport:*** 6 skycap
Portia ***husband:*** 6 Brutus 8 Bassanio ***maid:*** 7 Nerissa
portion 3 cut, lot 4 bite, doom, fate, meed, part 5 dower, endow, moira, piece, quota, share, slice, weird 6 divide, kismet, member, moiety, parcel 7 deal out, destiny, dole out, measure, mete out, partage, prorate, quantum, segment 8 dispense, division ***largest:*** 10 lion's share ***unused:*** 8 leftover
portly 3 fat 5 heavy, obese, stout 6 fleshy 7 weighty 8 imposing 9 corpulent, overblown 10 overweight
portmanteau 9 gladstone 12 traveling bag
portrait 4 bust 5 image 6 double, ringer, statue 7 picture 10 similitude, simulacrum
portray 4 limn 5 cameo, enact, image 6 depict, render 7 picture 8 describe 9 delineate, interpret, represent
portrayal 7 picture 9 depiction 11 delineation, description, presentment
Portugal 9 Lusitania ***capital:*** 6 Lisbon ***coin:*** 7 centavo ***export:*** 4 cork, wine 8 textiles ***monetary unit:*** 6 escudo ***premier:*** 7 Salazar
pose 3 ask, dog, put, sit 4 airs, fake, give, lugs, sham 5 befog, feign, offer, query, strut 6 baffle, extend, pass as, prefer, puzzle, stance, tender 7 confuse, hold out, pass for, pass off, peacock, perplex, present, pretend, profess, proffer, propone, purport, show off, stumble, suggest 8 attitude, bewilder, carriage, confound, pretense, propound, question 9 mannerism 10 grandstand, masquerade, pretension 11 affectation, proposition 12 attitudinize
Poseidon 7 Neptune ***brother:*** 4 Zeus 5 Hades, Pluto 7 Jupiter ***consort:*** 4 Tyro 6 Medusa 7 Demeter ***father:*** 6 Cronus ***mother:*** 4 Rhea ***offspring:*** 7 Pegasus ***son:*** 5 Orion 6 Neleus, Pelias 7 Antaeus 10 Polyphemus ***weapon:*** 7 trident ***wife:*** 10 Amphitrite
posh 4 chic, tony 5 smart, swank 7 à la mode 9 exclusive 11 fashionable
posit 6 assume, thesis 7 premise, presume 9 apriorism 10 assumption, presuppose 11 presumption
position 3 job 4 rank, side, site, spot, view 5 angle, berth, color, locus, place, point, situs, slant, stand, state, where 6 belief, billet, cachet, locate, office, stance, status 7 dignity, emplace, footing, stature 8 attitude, capacity, judgment, prestige, standing 9 character, viewpoint 10 standpoint ***troops:*** 6 deploy
positive 4 firm, hard, rank, sure 5 clear, gross, sound, utter 6 actual 7 assured, certain, decided, express, factual, genuine, perfect 8 absolute, cocksure, complete, definite, emphatic, explicit, forceful, forcible, outright, specific 9 clockwise, confident, doubtless, downright, energetic, practical 10 consummate, inarguable, reasonable, sure-enough, undeniable 11 categorical, indubitable, irrefutable, right-handed, unambiguous, undoubtable, unequivocal, unmitigated 12 indisputable, irrebuttable, undisputable, unmistakable
possess 3 own 4 bear, have, hold, keep 5 carry, enjoy 6 retain
possessed 4 calm, easy 6 placid, serene 8 tranquil
possession 8 property 9 ownership 11 proprietary
possessive 7 jealous
possessive pronoun see at pronoun
possibility 2 if 9 potential 11 contingency
possible 6 latent, likely, mortal, viable 7 dormant, earthly 9 expedient, potential
possibly 5 maybe 7 perhaps 9 perchance
post 3 job, set 4 clew, clue, mail, spot, tell, warn 5 berth, place 6 advise, billet, fill in, inform, notify, office, wise up 7 apprise, placard, station 8 acquaint
poster 4 bill, sign 6 banner, notice 7 affiche, placard 8 handbill 9 billboard, broadside, signboard 12 announcement 13 advertisement
posterior 4 back, hind, rear, rump, seat, tail 5 after, later 6 behind, hinder, retral 7 ensuing, rear end, tail end 8 backside,

buttocks, hindmost, rearward 10 subsequent 13 subsequential

posterity 4 seed 5 brood, issue 6 scions 7 progeny 8 children 9 offspring 11 descendants, progeniture

posthaste 4 fast 5 fleet, quick, rapid, swift 6 speedy 7 flat-out, fleetly, quickly, rapidly, swiftly 8 full tilt, speedily 9 breakneck 10 harefooted 11 expeditious 12 lickety-split

posimpressionist painter 6 Seurat 7 Cezanne, Gauguin, Van Gogh

postmortem 7 autopsy 8 necropsy

postpone 5 defer, delay 6 hold up, put off, shelve 7 hold off, lay over, suspend 8 hold over, prorogue, reprieve 9 carry over

postulate 4 aver, call 5 claim, exact 6 affirm, assert, assume, demand, thesis 7 premise, presume, require, solicit 9 apriorism, challenge 10 assumption, presuppose 11 presumption, requisition, supposition

posture 3 sit 4 mien, mode 5 state 6 manner, stance, status 7 bearing, pass for, pass off 8 attitude, carriage 9 condition, situation 10 deportment, masquerade 12 attitudinize

posy 3 ana 5 album, bloom 6 flower 7 blossom, bouquet, corsage, garland, nosegay, omnibus 8 analecta 9 anthology 10 miscellany 11 florilegium

pot 3 bet, wad 4 ante, mint, olla, pile, weed 5 grass, kitty, stake, wager 6 boodle, bundle 7 fortune 8 cannabis 9 marihuana, marijuana, sideswipe *small:* 6 pipkin

potable 4 pure 5 clean, drink, fresh 6 liquor 8 beverage 9 drinkable

potassium 6 kalium *ore:* 6 sylvin 7 sylvine, sylvite

potato 3 yam 4 spud 5 praty, tater 6 murphy *bud:* 3 eye *cooked strips of:* 11 French fries

potbelly 5 stove 6 paunch 9 bay window

potency 3 pep 4 birr, tuck 5 force, might, power, sinew, vigor 6 energy, muscle, virtue 8 strength 9 hardihood, puissance 10 capability 13 effectiveness

potent 5 lusty 6 mighty, robust, strong, virile 8 forceful, forcible, powerful

potential 6 latent, likely 7 abeyant, dormant, lurking 8 possible, probable 9 plausible, prepotent, quiescent 10 imaginable 11 conceivable, possibility

pother 3 ado 4 cark, flap, fret, fuss, stew, stir, to-do 5 furor, whirl, worry 6 bustle, clamor, flurry, furore, hassle, hubbub, tumult, uproar 7 turmoil 9 agitation, annoyance, commotion, confusion, whirlpool, whirlwind 10 hurly-burly, turbulence

potion 7 philter, philtre

Potiphar's slave 6 Joseph

Potiphera *daughter:* 7 Asenath *son-in-law:* 6 Joseph

potpourri 4 hash 6 medley 7 mélange 8 mishmash, pastiche 9 patchwork 10 assortment, hodgepodge, miscellany, salmagundi

potshot 3 cut, dig 4 gibe, jeer 5 crack 6 insult 9 aspersion, criticism, sideswipe

potter 4 mess 6 doodle, fiddle, puddle 10 mess around *English:* 8 Wedgwood

Potter, Beatrix *creation:* 11 Peter Rabbit

potter's field 8 cemetery, God's acre 9 graveyard

pouch 3 bag, jut, sac 4 sack 5 bulge, burse 6 beetle, pocket 7 project, saccule 8 overhang, protrude, sacculus, stand out *bodily:* 5 bursa

pouf 5 quilt 9 comforter

poultice 7 plaster 8 compress, dressing 9 cataplasm

poultry 4 fowl *type:* 4 duck, swan 5 goose, quail 6 grouse, pigeon, turkey 7 chicken, ostrich, peacock 8 pheasant 9 partridge

pounce 5 swoop, talon 6 emboss, powder

pound 3 bat 4 bang, bash, beat, belt, biff, blow, drub, pelt, slam, sock 5 crack, drive, grave, smack, stamp 6 batter, buffet, hammer, pummel, thrash, wallop 7 belabor, impress 8 malleate

pound and sponge 5 cakes

pour 3 run 4 beat, emit, flow, gush, lash, rain, rill, roll, rush, teem, void 5 flood, issue, skink, spate, surge, swarm 6 decant, deluge, drench, sluice, spring, stream 7 cascade, give off, niagara, proceed, torrent 8 cataract, flooding, inundate, overflow *forth:* 6 effuse

pourboire 3 tip 7 cumshaw, largess 8 gratuity 9 lagniappe 10 perquisite

pout 3 pet 4 moue, sulk 5 bulge, grump 7 project 8 overhang, protrude

poverty 4 need, want 6 penury 7 beggary, borasca 8 poorness, scarcity 9 indigence, indigency, necessity, neediness, pauperism, privation, suffering 10 mendicancy, scarceness 11 destitution 13 destituteness, insufficience, insufficiency, pennilessness *combining form:* 5 penia

poverty-stricken see penurious

POW camp *German:* 6 stalag

powder 4 bray, buck, dust, talc 5 crush 6 talcum 8 sprinkle 9 comminute, pulverize, triturate 10 besprinkle 12 contriturate *medicinal:* 7 lupulin

power 3 arm 4 dint, sway 5 force, might, right, sinew, steam, vigor 6 energy, muscle, talent, virtue, weight 7 ability, command, control, dynamis, faculty, mastery, potence, potency, voltage 8 aptitude, capacity, dominion, dynamism, function, imperium, prestige, strength 9 authority, direction, dominance, endowment, influence, masterdom, privilege, puissance, strong arm, supremacy 10 ascendancy, birthright, capability, competence, domination, management 11 prerogative, sovereignty, superiority 12 jurisdiction, potentiality 13 effectiveness *combining form:* 5 dynam 6 dynamo *in Hindu philosophy:* 4 maya *reduction:* 8 brownout *sacred:* 4 kami *unit of:* 4 watt

powerful 4 able 5 great 6 mighty, potent, strong, wieldy 7 capable, dynamic, weighty 8 almighty, dominant, forcible, puissant, vigorous 9 competent, effective, effectual, efficient, energetic, strenuous 10 convincing, invincible 11 efficacious, influential 13 authoritative

powerless 4 weak 5 inert, unfit 6 feeble, infirm, supine 7 passive 8 decrepit, impotent, inactive, nugatory 9 incapable 11 incompetent, ineffective

powwow 4 chat, talk 5 treat 6 advise, confab, confer, huddle, parley 7 consult, meeting 8 collogue 10 conference 11 confabulate

poyou 6 peludo 9 armadillo

practicable 4 open 5 handy, utile 6 useful 9 operative 10 functional

practical 5 handy, sober, utile 6 usable, useful, versed 7 old-time, skilled, veteran 8 banausic, implicit, seasoned, sensible 9 pragmatic, realistic 10 functional, hard-boiled, hardheaded 11 down-to-earth, experienced, serviceable 12 businesslike

practically 4 most, much, nigh 5 about 6 all but, almost, nearly 8 as good as, as much as, well-nigh 9 in essence

practice 3 use, way 4 form, mode, plot, wont 5 cabal, covin, drill, habit, trick, usage 6 custom, follow, manner, method, pursue, repeat, scheme, system, usance 7 execute, fulfill, iterate, perform, process, utility 8 drilling, exercise, habitude, intrigue, rehearse 9 procedure 10 conspiracy, convenance, convention, proceeding *suffix:* 2 cy 3 ery, ics, ism

practitioner *combining form:* 4 path *suffix:* 5 ician

pragmatic 9 practical, realistic 10 hard-boiled, hardheaded, unromantic 11 down-to-earth

pragmatist 7 realist

prairie antelope 9 pronghorn

prairie apple 9 breadroot

prairie berry 9 trompillo

prairie chicken 6 grouse

prairie hen 11 clapper rail

prairie potato 9 breadroot

prairie wolf 6 coyote

praise 4 hail, hymn, laud 5 bless, cry up, erect, exalt, extol, honor, psalm, roose 6 anthem, belaud, extoll, kudize, uprear 7 acclaim, adulate, applaud, commend, dignify, enhance, ennoble, flatter, glorify, hosanna, magnify, plaudit, puffery, resound, sublime 8 eulogize, heighten, proclaim, psalmody 9 celebrate, intensify, recommend 10 aggrandize, compliment, panegyrize *expression of:* 8 accolade

praiseworthy 7 palmary 8 laudable 9 admirable, deserving, estimable, meritable 11 commendable, meritorious

prance 4 step 5 strut, tread 6 curvet, foot it, hoof it, jaunce, sashay 8 cakewalk

prank 4 deck, lark, play, trim, whim 5 adorn, antic, caper, fancy, fix up, freak, spiff, sport, trick 6 bedeck, didoes, doll up, frolic, gambol, levity, shines, vagary, wheeze, whimsy 7 caprice, conceit, deck out, doll out, dress up, fooling, garnish, gussy up, rollick 8 beautify, decorate, escapade, ornament, spruce up 9 capriccio, embellish, frivolity, high jinks, horseplay, lightness, rowdiness, smarten up 10 roughhouse, shenanigan, skylarking, tomfoolery 11 monkeyshine *Scottish:* 6 shavie

prate 3 gab, jaw, yak 4 blab, blow, brag, chat, crow, puff, yack 5 boast, clack, drool, mouth, vaunt 6 babble, drivel, gabble, jabber, waffle, yabber 7 blabber, blather, chatter, palaver, twaddle, twattle 9 gasconade, yakety-yak 11 rodomontade

prater 6 magpie 9 bandar-log, blabmouth 10 chatterbox 12 blabbermouth

prattle see prate

prattler see prater

prawn 6 shrimp 8 crevette 13 Norway lobster

praxis 3 use 4 wont 5 habit, trick, usage 6 custom, manner 8 habitude 10 consuetude

Praxiteles statue 6 Hermes 8 The Satyr

pray 3 beg 5 brace, crave, daven, doven, plead 6 appeal 7 beseech, entreat, implore 8 meditate 10 supplicate

prayer 4 plea, suit 6 appeal, beggar, litany, orison, suitor 7 angelus, begging, complin, worship 8 blessing, compline, entreaty, petition, pleading 9 adoration, imploring, suppliant 10 beseeching, supplicant 11 application, imploration, imprecation, supplicator 12 supplication *beads:* 6 rosary *ending:* 4 amen *for the dead:* 7 requiem *Jewish:* 7 kaddish, kiddush 9 kaddishim (plural) *period:* 6 novena 7 triduum *shawl:* 6 tallis, tallit 7 tallith

prayer book 6 missal 8 breviary *Jewish:* 6 mahzor, siddur 7 machzor

prayerful 4 holy 5 godly, pious 6 devout

preach 7 address, lecture 8 advocate,

homilize, moralize 9 sermonize 10 evangelize
preacher 6 cleric, divine, parson 7 evangel 8 clerical, homilist, minister, reverend 9 churchman, clergyman 10 evangelist 12 ecclesiastic
preacher bird 5 vireo
preaching friar 9 Dominican
preamble 5 proem 8 exordium, foreword, overture, prologue 12 introduction, prolegomenon
precarious 4 iffy 5 risky 6 touchy, tricky 7 dubious 8 delicate, doubtful, insecure, ticklish, unstable 9 sensitive, uncertain
precaution 8 prudence 9 foresight, safeguard 10 providence 11 forethought
precede 4 lead, pace, rank 5 forgo, usher 6 forego, herald 7 forerun, outrank 8 announce, antedate 9 introduce
precedence 8 priority
precedent 4 past 5 prior 6 former 7 example 8 anterior 9 foregoing
preceding 4 past 5 prior 6 before, former 7 ahead of, prior to 8 anterior, hitherto 9 erstwhile 10 heretofore 11 in advance of *prefix:* 4 ante
precept 3 law 4 rule 5 axiom, canon, dogma, edict, tenet 6 behest, decree 7 bidding, statute 8 decretum, doctrine 9 ordinance, principle 10 injunction, regulation 11 fundamental
preceptive 8 didactic 9 mandatory
preceptor 5 tutor 7 teacher 9 principal 10 headmaster
precinct 6 domain, region, sector, sphere 7 quarter, section 8 district, dominion, province 9 bailiwick, territory
precious 3 pet 4 dear, nice, rare, rich 5 fussy, loved, picky, showy 6 artful, chichi, choice, choosy, costly, la-di-da 7 beloved, darling, finicky, genteel, studied 8 affected, blue-eyed, favorite, overnice, prizable, valuable 9 exquisite, priceless, prizeable, recherché 10 fair-haired, fastidious, invaluable, particular
precipitancy 4 rush 5 haste 9 hastiness 10 suddenness 11 hurriedness
precipitant 5 hasty 6 abrupt, sudden 7 hurried, rushing 8 headlong 9 impetuous
precipitate 4 lees 5 dregs, event, hasty, issue, sheer, steep 6 abrupt, effect, madcap, result, sequel, sudden, upshot 7 arduous, deposit, grounds, hurried, rushing 8 headlong, sediment 9 aftermath, breakneck, hotheaded, impatient, impetuous, impulsive, overhasty, settlings 10 headstrong, refractory, unexpected, unforeseen 11 aftereffect, consequence, subitaneous
precipitation 4 hail, lees, rain, rush, snow 5 dregs, haste, sleet 7 deposit, grounds 8 sediment 9 hastiness, settlings 11 hurriedness
precipitous 5 hasty, sheer, steep 6 abrupt, sudden 7 hurried, rushing 8 headlong
précis 6 aperçu, digest, sketch, survey 7 pandect, sylloge 8 syllabus 10 compendium
precise 4 nice, very 5 exact, fixed, right, rigid 6 narrow, prissy, proper, stuffy 7 correct, genteel, limited, missish, prudish 8 accurate, definite, priggish, rigorous, specific 9 clocklike, stringent 10 particular
preciseness see **precision**
precision 4 care, need 6 timing 8 accuracy 9 exactness 10 definitude, exactitude 11 carefulness, correctness
preclude 4 quit, stop, ward 5 avert, cease, deter 7 forfend, obviate, rule out 8 stave off 9 forestall 11 discontinue
precondition 4 must 9 essential, necessity, requisite 10 sine qua non 11 requirement
precursor 6 herald 8 foregoer 9 harbinger, prototype 10 antecedent, forerunner
predate 7 forerun 8 antecede
predatory 9 rapacious, raptorial, vulturine, vulturous
predecessor 7 forbear 8 ancestor, forebear, foregoer 9 prototype 10 antecedent, forerunner
predestine see **preordain**
predetermine see **preordain**
predeterminism 8 fatalism
predicament 3 box, fix, jam 4 hole, pass, soup, spot 5 Dutch, pinch, rigor, state 6 corner, pickle, plight, scrape, strait 7 dilemma, impasse, posture, trouble 8 asperity, exigency, hardness, hardship, hot water, juncture, quagmire 9 condition, deep water, emergency, situation 10 difficulty
predicate 4 aver, avow, base, rest, stay 5 found 6 affirm, assert, avouch, depose, ground 7 declare, profess, protest 9 establish
predict 5 augur, guess, infer, judge 7 forbode, foresee, portend, suppose, surmise 8 conclude, forebode, forecast, forefeel, foreshow, foretell, prophesy, soothsay 9 adumbrate 10 conjecture, vaticinate 13 prognosticate
predictor 5 augur, weird 6 auspex 7 prophet 8 foreseer, haruspex 10 forecaster, foreteller, prophesier, soothsayer 11 Nostradamus
predilection 4 bent 7 leaning 8 penchant, tendency 9 inclining 10 proclivity, propensity
predispose 4 bend, bias, sway 6 strike 7 incline

predisposed 4 fain 5 prone, ready 7 willing 8 inclined
predisposition 4 bent 7 leaning 8 penchant, tendency 9 inclining 10 proclivity, propensity
predominant 4 main 5 chief, major 6 master 7 capital, general, primary 9 number one, paramount, principal, sovereign 11 outstanding, overbearing
predominate 4 rule 5 reign 6 master 7 regnant 9 ascendant, paramount, prevalent, sovereign 11 overbearing
preeminence 6 renown 7 primacy 8 dominion 9 masterdom, supremacy 10 ascendancy, domination 11 distinction, superiority
preeminent 4 main 5 chief, major 7 capital, stellar, supreme 8 dominant, towering, ultimate 9 number one, principal 10 surpassing 11 outstanding, unequalable, unmatchable 12 incomparable, transcendent *prefix:* 4 arch
preempt 4 take 5 annex, seize, usurp 6 assume 8 accroach, arrogate 9 sequester 10 commandeer, confiscate 11 appropriate, expropriate
preen 5 plume, pride, primp
preface 4 lead 5 proem, usher 6 prolog 8 exordium, foreword, overture, preamble, prologue 9 introduce 12 introduction
prefatory 8 proemial 9 inductive, preludial 12 introductory
prefer 3 put 4 cull, mark, pick, pose, take 5 elect 6 choose, optate, opt for, select
preference 6 choice, option 8 druthers, election 9 elevation, prelation, promotion, selection, upgrading 10 partiality
prefigure 4 hint 9 adumbrate 10 foreshadow
pregnancy 6 cyesis 9 fertility, gestation, gravidity
pregnant 4 rich 5 heavy 6 facund, gravid, parous 7 weighty 8 childing, eloquent, enceinte 9 expecting, momentous 10 expressive, meaningful, parturient 11 sententious
prehend 3 bag, get 4 nail, take 5 catch 6 collar, secure 7 capture
prehensile 6 grabby, greedy 8 covetous, desirous, grasping 11 acquisitive
preindicate 6 herald 7 forerun, presage 8 announce, foreshow 9 harbinger
prejudice 3 mar 4 bend, bias, harm, hurt, skew 5 angle, slant, spoil 6 damage, impair, injure, racism, sexism 7 bigotry, blemish, dispose, incline, leaning, tarnish, vitiate 9 influence 10 partiality 12 one-sidedness, partisanship
prejudicial 3 bad 4 evil 7 harmful, nocuous 8 damaging 9 injurious 11 deleterious, detrimental, mischievous
preknow 3 see 6 divine 7 foresee 8 forefeel 9 apprehend, visualize 10 anticipate
preliminary 5 basic 7 fitting 8 proemial, readying 9 elemental, inductive 11 fundamental 12 introductory
preliterate 9 primitive
prelude 5 proem 8 exordium, foreword, overture, prologue 12 introduction, prolegomenon
premature 5 early 8 oversoon, untimely 9 overearly
premeditated 7 advised, studied 8 designed, studious 10 considered, deliberate, thought-out
premier 4 arch, head 5 chief, first 7 leading 8 champion, foremost 9 principal
premise 5 posit 6 assume, thesis 9 apriorism, postulate 10 assumption 11 postulation, supposition
premium 4 agio, meed, plum 5 prize 6 carrot, reward 7 guerdon 8 buckshee, dividend, superior 11 exceptional
premonition 9 misgiving 10 foreboding 12 apprehension
preoccupied 4 deep, lost, rapt 6 absent, intent 7 bemused, engaged, faraway, wrapped 8 distrait, immersed 9 engrossed, forgetful, wrapped up 10 abstracted 11 inconscient 12 absentminded
preordain 4 fate 6 doom to 7 destine 9 determine 10 predestine 11 foredestine
preparation 7 fitness 8 training 9 readiness 11 compounding
preparatory 9 preludial, prelusive 11 prefatorial, preliminary
prepare 3 fit, fix, get 4 busk, gird, make 5 brace, dower, draft, endow, endue, equip, frame, prime, ready, steel, train 6 draw up, make up, outfit, supply 7 confect, dispose, fortify, furnish, provide 9 formulate 10 strengthen *for publication:* 4 edit 6 redact *leather:* 5 curry
prepared 3 set 5 ready
preponderance 8 dominion 9 ascendant, masterdom, supremacy 10 ascendancy, domination
preponderant 8 dominant, superior 9 paramount, sovereign 11 overbearing
preponderate 4 rule 5 reign 8 domineer
preposition 2 at, by, in, of, on, to, up 3 but, cum, ere, for, off, out, per, via 4 amid, down, from, into, like, onto, over, save, thru, till, unto, upon, with 5 about, above, after, along, among, anent, below, circa, since, tween, twixt, under, until 6 aboard, across, amidst, around, before, behind, beside, beyond, contra, except, gainst, inside, mongst, toward, versus, within 7 against, amongst, athwart, beneath, besides, between, betwixt, despite, outside, through,

towards, without **10** throughout, underneath

prepossess **4** bias **5** imbue **6** absorb, engage, occupy **7** engross, immerse, involve **9** influence, prejudice, preoccupy

prepossessing **10** attractive

preposterous **4** wild **5** crazy, loony, silly, wacky **6** absurd, insane **7** foolish **9** fantastic **10** irrational **11** extravagant, harebrained **12** unreasonable

preposterousness **5** folly **8** insanity **9** absurdity

prerequisite **4** must **9** condition, essential, necessary, necessity **10** imperative, sine qua non **11** necessitous, requirement

prerogative **5** right **8** appanage, immunity **9** exemption, privilege **10** birthright, perquisite

presage **4** bode, omen **5** augur **6** augury, boding, herald **7** bespeak, betoken, forerun, portend, portent, predict, promise **8** announce, bodement, forebode, forecast, foreshow, foretell, indicate, prophesy, soothsay **9** adumbrate, foretoken, harbinger, misgiving, prenotion **10** foreboding, foreshadow, prognostic, vaticinate **12** apprehensive **13** prognosticate

presbyter **5** elder **6** priest

prescience **9** foresight

prescribe **3** fix, set **6** assign, choose, decide, decree, define, impose, ordain, select, settle **7** dictate, lay down, pick out **9** determine

prescript **3** law **4** rule **5** edict **6** decree **8** decretum **9** institute, ordinance **10** regulation

prescription **3** law **4** rule **5** edict **6** decree **8** decretum **9** institute, ordinance

presence **3** air **4** look, mien, port **6** aspect **7** address, bearing, seeming **8** demeanor

present **3** aim, lay, now **4** boon, cast, cite, gift, give, head, past, pose, show **5** favor, level, offer, point, today, train **6** adduce, allege, bestow, devote, direct, donate, extant, extend, modern, tender **7** address, advance, hand out, hold out, instant, largess, proffer **8** acquaint, nowadays, todayish, up-to-date **9** introduce **12** contemporary, newfashioned

presentable **3** fit **6** decent, proper **9** befitting **11** appropriate

presentiment see **premonition**

presently **3** now **4** anon, soon **5** today **7** by and by **8** nowadays

preservation **4** care, ward **5** guard **6** saving, shield **7** defense, keeping **9** safeguard **10** husbanding **11** conservancy, safekeeping

preserve **3** can, jam **4** save **6** keep up, pickle **7** sustain **8** maintain **9** confiture

preside **3** run **4** head, keep **5** chair **6** direct, handle, manage, ordain **7** carry on, conduct, control, operate, oversee

president ***United States:*** **4** Bush (George), Ford (Gerald R.), Polk (James K.), Taft (William H.) **5** Adams (John, John Quincy), Grant (Ulysses S.), Hayes (Rutherford B.), Nixon (Richard M.), Tyler (John) **6** Arthur (Chester A.), Carter (Jimmy), Hoover (Herbert), Monroe (James), Pierce (Franklin), Reagan (Ronald), Taylor (Zachary), Truman (Harry S.), Wilson (Woodrow) **7** Harding (Warren), Jackson (Andrew), Johnson (Andrew), Johnson (Lyndon), Kennedy (John F.), Lincoln (Abraham), Madison (James) **8** Buchanan (James), Coolidge (Calvin), Fillmore (Millard), Garfield (James), Harrison (Benjamin, William H.), McKinley (William), Van Buren (Martin) **9** Cleveland (Grover), Jefferson (Thomas), Roosevelt (Franklin D., Theodore) **10** Eisenhower (Dwight D.), Washington (George)

press **3** hug, jam, ram **4** bear, cram, iron, mass, move, pack, pile, push, rice, tamp **5** clasp, crowd, crush, drive, drove, elbow, force, horde, impel, shove, stuff **6** enfold, gather, goffer, hustle, jostle, propel, sadden, sinter, squash, squish, squush, throng, thrust **7** collect, embrace, gauffer, imprint, squeeze, squelch, squoosh **8** assemble, bulldoze, shoulder **9** constrain, multitude, weigh down **10** congregate

pressing **4** dire **5** acute **6** direct, urgent **7** clamant, crucial, exigent, instant **8** critical **9** clamorous, immediate, insistent **10** imperative **11** importunate

pressure **4** push, rush **5** drive, impel **6** strain, stress **7** tension **9** overpress ***combining form:*** **4** tono **5** piezo ***instrument:*** **9** barometer ***unit:*** **3** bar **5** barye

prestige **4** rank, sway **5** power, state **6** cachet, credit, renown, status, weight **7** dignity, stature **8** eminence, position, standing **9** authority, influence **10** prominence, prominency **11** consequence, distinction

prestigious **5** famed, great **7** eminent, notable **8** renowned **9** prominent **10** celebrated **13** distinguished

presto **4** fast **7** flat-out, hastily, quickly, rapidly **8** chop-chop, full tilt **9** posthaste **12** lickety-split **13** expeditiously

presumably **6** likely **9** doubtless

presume **5** guess, opine, posit, think **6** impose, reason **7** intrude, obtrude, suppose, surmise **8** infringe **9** postulate **10** conjecture

presuming see **presumptuous**

presumption **4** face, gall **5** brass, cheek, nerve, posit **6** thesis **9** apriorism, brashness, postulate **10** confidence, effrontery

presumptuous 4 smug 5 brash, lofty 6 uppish, uppity 7 forward, pushful, pushing 9 confident 10 brassbound, complacent 11 inexcusable, overweening, self-assured

presuppose 5 guess, infer, judge, posit, think 6 assume, deduce, expect, gather, reckon 7 believe, imagine, surmise, suspect 9 postulate

presupposition 5 guess, posit 6 belief, thesis 7 surmise 8 judgment 9 apriorism, inference, judgement, postulate 10 conjecture

pretend 3 act 4 fake, sham 5 bluff, feign, guess, put on, think 6 affect, assume, delude 7 beguile, deceive, mislead, profess, purport, suppose, surmise 8 simulate

pretender 4 fake 5 faker, fraud, phony 6 humbug 8 impostor

pretense 3 air 4 face, fake, mask, sham 5 claim, cloak, color, cover, fraud, guise, title 6 deceit, facade, humbug 7 charade, pageant 8 coloring, disguise 9 deception, imposture, mannerism 10 false front, masquerade 11 affectation, make-believe

pretension 5 claim, title 7 charade, pageant 8 disguise 11 make-believe 13 ambitiousness

pretentious 3 big 4 arty 5 lofty, put-on, showy, swank, tumid 6 chichi, la-di-da, tootoo, turgid 7 aureate, feigned, flowery, genteel, mincing, pompier, splashy, stilted, utopian 8 affected, imposing, inflated, peacocky 9 bombastic, grandiose, overblown, visionary 10 arty-crafty, euphuistic, flamboyant, peacockish, rhetorical 12 high-sounding, magniloquent ***speech:*** 7 bombast

preternatural 7 deviant 8 aberrant, abnormal, atypical, numinous, superior 9 anomalous, deviative, unearthly, untypical 10 miraculous, superhuman, suprahuman 11 heteroclite 12 supermundane, supramundane

pretext 4 mask 5 alibi, cloak, cover, front, guise 6 excuse 8 pretense

pretty 4 cute, fair, good, some 5 bonny, ducky 6 adroit, bonnie, clever, comely, fairly, incony, kind of, lovely, rather, seemly, sort of, wicked 7 cunning, darling, dollish 8 handsome, skillful, somewhat 9 beauteous, beautiful 10 attractive, moderately, more or less 11 good-looking

prevail 4 beat, rule 5 reign 6 affect, master 7 conquer, impress, triumph 8 dominate, domineer, overcome, override

prevailing see prevalent

prevalent 4 rife 5 usual 6 common, master, normal, ruling, wonted 7 general, natural, popular, rampant, regnant, regular, typical 8 dominant 9 ascendant, customary, paramount, sovereign 10 accustomed, widespread 11 commonplace

prevaricate 3 fib, lie 6 palter 7 falsify 12 misrepresent

prevarication 3 fib, lie 4 tale 5 lying, story 6 canard 7 falsity 9 falsehood

prevaricator 4 liar 6 fibber 7 Ananias, fibster 8 perjurer 9 falsifier 11 storyteller

prevent 3 bar, dam 4 balk, foil, ward 5 avert, block, check, debar, deter 6 arrest, baffle, forbid, hinder, impede, thwart 7 forfend, inhibit, obviate, rule out, shut out 8 obstruct, prohibit, stave off 9 forestall, frustrate, interdict, interrupt 10 anticipate ***access:*** 9 barricade

previous 4 fore, past 5 prior 6 before, former 7 earlier, forward 8 anterior, oversoon 9 foregoing, in advance, overearly 10 antecedent, beforehand

previously 4 once 6 before 7 already, earlier, priorly 8 formerly 9 erstwhile 10 heretofore

prey 4 game 5 chase 6 quarry, victim 8 casualty, underdog 9 bottom dog

Priam ***daughter:*** 6 Creusa 8 Polyxena 9 Cassandra ***father:*** 8 Laomedon ***grandfather:*** 4 Ilus ***kingdom:*** 4 Troy ***slayer:*** 7 Pyrrhus 11 Neoptolemus ***son:*** 5 Paris 6 Hector, Lycaon 7 Helenus, Troilus 9 Deiphobus, Polydorus ***wife:*** 6 Arisbe, Hecuba

Priapus ***father:*** 7 Bacchus 8 Dionysus ***mother:*** 5 Venus 9 Aphrodite

price 3 tab 4 cost, rate, toll 6 charge, tariff 7 expense

priceless 6 costly, valued 8 precious, valuable 9 cherished, treasured 10 invaluable

prick 3 cut, jab, sic 4 bore, goad, hole, prod, slit, spur, stab, urge 5 drill, egg on, enter, pique, punch, rowel, slash, sting, thorn 6 excite, exhort, prompt, propel 8 puncture 9 perforate, stimulate

prickly 5 burry, spiny 6 nettly, thorny, tingly, twitty 7 brambly, fretful, peevish, pettish, waspish 8 annoying, petulant, snappish 9 fractious, irritable 10 bothersome, nettlesome

pride 3 fat, top 4 best, brag, crow, face, pick 5 boast, cream, elite, pique, plume, preen, scorn, vaunt 6 choice, egoism, flower, morgue 7 bighead, conceit, dignity, disdain, egotism, hauteur 8 contempt, smugness, vainness 9 arrogance, cockiness, gasconade, insolence, loftiness, self-glory, self-trust, superbity, vainglory 10 felicitate, self-esteem, self-regard 11 amour propre, haughtiness, self-opinion, self-respect 12 congratulate, snobbishness 13 condescension, self-assurance

Pride and Prejudice author 6 Austen

prier 5 snoop 6 butt-in 7 meddler, Paul Pry 8 busybody, quidnunc 10 rubberneck
priest 9 clergyman 10 chancellor 11 chamberlain ***ancient Roman:*** 6 fecial, fetial, flamen 8 pontifex ***Buddhist:*** 4 lama ***Celtic:*** 5 druid ***French:*** 4 abbé, curé ***Indian:*** 6 shaman ***military:*** 5 padre 8 chaplain ***Muslim:*** 4 imam ***of Bacchus:*** 6 maenad 9 bacchante
priestly 8 hieratic 10 sacerdotal 12 sacerdotical
prig 5 prude, thief 6 Grundy, nimmer, stuffy, wowser 7 filcher, genteel, prudish, puritan, stealer 8 bluenose, comstock, larcener, pilferer 9 larcenist, Mrs. Grundy, nice Nelly, purloiner, Victorian 10 goody-goody, tight-laced 11 puritanical, straitlaced
priggish 4 smug 6 stuffy 7 genteel, prudish 9 Victorian 10 complacent, self-loving, tight-laced 11 puritanical, self-pleased, straitlaced 13 self-contented, self-esteeming, self-righteous, self-satisfied
prim 4 neat, nice, snug, tidy 5 rigid, stiff 6 formal, proper, stuffy, wooden 7 chipper, correct, genteel, missish, orderly, precise, prudish 8 decorous, straight 9 bluenosed, shipshape, Victorian 10 ceremonial, tight-laced 11 ceremonious, puritanical, strait-laced, uncluttered, well-groomed 12 conventional
prima facie 11 self-evident
primary 4 main 5 basal, basic, chief, first 6 bottom, direct 7 initial, pioneer, radical 8 earliest, original 9 firsthand, immediate, underived 10 underlying 11 fundamental 12 foundational, underivative ***combining form:*** 4 prot 5 proto ***prefix:*** 4 arch 5 archi
primate 3 ape, man 5 human 6 monkey 7 gorilla 10 anthropoid, chimpanzee, human being 11 Homo sapiens ***nocturnal:*** 7 tarsier ***small:*** 6 galago
prime 3 top 4 best, fine, morn, move, pick 5 cream, elite, first, sunup, youth 6 aurora, choice, excite, famous, spring 7 capital, initial, morning, provoke, quicken, sunrise 8 cockcrow, daybreak, earliest, motivate, original, superior 9 dayspring, excellent, first-rate, galvanize, stimulate, underived 10 first-class, juvenility, springtide 11 adolescence
primer 4 book 6 reader 8 hornbook
primeval 10 aboriginal; (see also **primordial**)
primitive 5 basic, early 7 archaic 8 original 9 barbarian, elemental, essential, underived, unevolved 10 elementary, persistent, substratal, underlying 11 fundamental, nonliterate, preliterate, uncivilized, undeveloped 12 uncultivated ***combining form:*** 4 pale 5 palae, paleo 6 archae, archeo, palaeo, palaio 7 archaeo ***prefix:*** 4 arch 5 arche, archi
primogenitor 7 forbear 8 ancestor, forebear 9 ascendant 10 forefather
primordial 5 early, first 8 earliest, original 10 elementary 11 fundamental, undeveloped
primordium 6 anlage, origin 9 beginning
primp 5 fix up, slick, spiff 6 doll up 7 deck out, doll out, dress up, gussy up
prince ***Anglo-Saxon:*** 8 atheling ***Arab:*** 4 emir 5 emeer ***Austrian:*** 8 archduke ***Ethiopian:*** 3 ras ***Indian:*** 4 raja 5 rajah ***Muslim:*** 4 amir 5 ameer ***of demons:*** 9 Beelzebub ***of Monaco:*** 6 Ranier ***of the church:*** 8 cardinal ***of Wales:*** 7 Charles
Prince and the Pauper author 5 Twain
Prince Edward Island ***capital:*** 13 Charlottetown ***discoverer:*** 7 Cartier
Prince Igor composer 7 Borodin
princely 5 grand, noble, royal 6 august, lordly 8 baronial, imposing 9 grandiose 11 magnificent
princess ***mythical:*** 3 Ino ***of Monaco:*** 5 Grace
principal 4 arch, head, main, star 5 chief, first, major 7 capital, leading, premier, primary, stellar 8 champion, dominant, foremost 10 preeminent 11 outstanding, predominant ***combining form:*** 4 prot 5 proto ***prefix:*** 4 arch 5 archi
principium 3 law 5 axiom, basis 7 element, theorem 10 foundation 11 fundamental
principle 3 law 4 form, rule 5 axiom, basis, canon, tenet, usage 6 ground 7 precept, theorem 8 polestar 10 convention, foundation 11 fundamental
principled 5 moral, noble 7 ethical 8 virtuous 9 righteous 10 moralistic
print 4 type 5 litho, stamp, write 7 engrave, impress, publish, typeset 10 impression ***style:*** 5 roman 6 italic 7 cursive
printer ***English:*** 6 Caxton ***Italian:*** 6 Bodoni 8 Manutius (Aldus)
printers' mark see **proofreaders' mark**
printer's receptacle 7 hellbox
printing 7 edition, reissue 10 impression ***measure:*** 2 em, en 4 pica 5 agate 6 cicero ***plate:*** 6 stereo 7 linecut ***process:*** 4 roto 7 gravure ***style:*** 6 gothic
prior see **previous**
priority 5 order 8 ordering 9 supremacy 10 ascendancy, precedence
prison 3 pen 4 jail, keep 6 cooler, lockup 7 bastile, dungeon, slammer 8 bastille, stockade 11 reformatory 12 penitentiary ***California:*** 10 San Quentin ***former:*** 8 Alcatraz, Sing-Sing ***New York:*** 6 Attica 12 Rik-

ers Island *Northern Ireland:* 4 Maze *resident:* 6 inmate 7 convict 8 jailbird
prissy 6 stuffy 7 epicene, finicky, genteel, missish, prudish, unmanly 9 pansified, sissified, squeamish, Victorian 10 effeminate, fastidious, tight-laced 11 puritanical, strait-laced 12 Miss-Nancyish
pristine 4 pure 8 earliest, original
privacy 7 secrecy 9 seclusion
private 6 closet, hidden, hushed, inside, secret 7 soldier 8 discreet, personal 9 concealed 10 closed-door 12 confidential
private detective see detective
privately 7 sub rosa 8 covertly, in camera, secretly 9 by stealth 10 stealthily
privation 4 lack, loss, need, want 6 dearth, defect, losing, misery, penury 7 absence, default, poverty 8 distress, poorness 9 indigence, mislaying, neediness, suffering 10 misplacing 11 deprivement, divestiture
privilege 4 boon 5 favor, right 8 appanage 9 allowance 10 birthright, concession, perquisite 11 prerogative *pope-granted:* 6 indult
privy 2 WC 4 head, john 5 jakes 6 buried, covert, hidden, johnny, toilet 7 latrine 8 lavatory, obscured, outhouse, personal, shrouded, stealthy, ulterior 9 backhouse, concealed 11 convenience, water closet
prize 3 pry, top 4 best, loot, meed, pick, plum, swag 5 award, booty, cream, elite, jimmy, lever, spoil, value 6 boodle, carrot, choice, esteem, reward, trophy 7 cherish, guerdon, jackpot, plunder, premium 8 dividend, treasure 10 appreciate, plunderage 11 outstanding
prizefighting 8 pugilism 10 fisticuffs
pro 3 for, vet, wiz 4 whiz, with 5 adept, doyen 6 expert, master 9 authority, in favor of 10 master-hand
probable 6 likely 7 seeming 8 apparent, rational 10 reasonable
probe 3 ask 4 quiz, sift 5 query, quest, scout 6 go into 7 delving, dig into, examine, explore, feel out, inquest, inquire, inquiry 8 look into, research, sound out 9 catechize, delve into 11 inquire into, inquisition, interrogate, investigate, reconnoiter 13 investigation
probity 6 virtue 7 honesty 8 goodness 9 integrity, rectitude, rightness 11 uprightness
problem 3 nut 5 issue 6 enigma, puzzle 7 bugaboo, bugbear, dilemma, example, mystery
problematic 4 moot, open 7 dubious, suspect 8 arguable, doubtful, mootable 9 ambiguous, debatable, dubitable, uncertain, unsettled 10 disputable, indecisive, precarious 12 questionable
proboscis 4 beak, nose 5 snoot, snout 7 smeller
procedure 4 line, move, step 6 course, method, policy, polity 7 measure, program 8 demarche, maneuver
proceed 2 go 3 hie 4 fare, flow, head, move, pass, rise, stem, wend 5 arise, get on, issue, march, segue 6 push on, repair, spring, travel 7 advance, emanate, journey 8 get along, progress 9 originate 10 derive from
proceedings 8 goings-on *recorded:* 4 acta
proceeds 4 gain 5 lucre 6 profit, return 8 earnings
process 3 way 4 mode, wise 5 modus 6 manner, method, system 7 fashion, recycle, routine 9 operation, outgrowth, technique *combining form:* 4 typy *suffix:* 2 al, th 3 ing, ism, sis 4 ance, ence, esis, osis 7 ization
procession 5 order 6 parade, series 8 sequence 9 cavalcade 11 consecution *combining form:* 4 cade
proclaim 4 mark, show, vent 5 bruit, utter, voice 6 blazon, evince, herald, ostend 7 clarion, declare, exhibit, publish 8 announce, evidence, manifest, promulge 9 advertise, broadcast, ventilate 10 annunciate, bruit about, illustrate, promulgate 11 blaze abroad, demonstrate
proclivity see penchant
Procne *father:* 7 Pandion *husband:* 6 Tereus *sister:* 9 Philomela *son:* 4 Itys
procrastinate 3 lag 4 drag, poke, stay 5 dally, defer, delay, tarry 6 dawdle, linger, loiter, put off 7 prolong, suspend 8 postpone
procreate 4 bear, make, sire 5 beget, breed, hatch, spawn 6 father, mother, parent 7 produce 8 engender, generate, multiply 9 originate, propagate, reproduce
Procris' husband and slayer 8 Cephalus
Procrustean ____ 3 bed
proctor 9 supervise 10 supervisor
procure 3 get 4 draw, gain, have, land 5 annex 6 draw in, draw on, induce, obtain, pick up 7 acquire, compass, win over
prod 3 dig, jab, jog, sic 4 goad, poke, spur, urge 5 egg on, nudge, pique, prick, punch 6 excite, exhort 9 stimulate
prodigal 4 lush 6 lavish, waster 7 opulent, profuse, riotous, spender, wastrel 8 unthrift 9 exuberant, luxuriant, profusive 10 high roller, profligate, squanderer 11 scattergood, spendthrift, wastethrift
prodigious 4 huge, vast 6 mighty, mortal 7 amazing, immense, mammoth, massive 8 colossal, cracking, enormous, gigantic, towering 9 fantastic, marvelous, monstrous, wonderful 10 astounding, miracu-

lous, monumental, staggering, stupendous, surprising

produce 4 bear, form, give, grow, make, show, sire 5 beget, breed, build, cause, erect, frame, get up, hatch, mount, put on, raise, spawn, stage, yield 6 create, draw on, effect, father, output, parent, secure, work up 7 deliver, fashion, outturn, turn out 8 engender, generate, multiply, muster up 9 construct, cultivate, fabricate, originate, procreate, propagate 10 bring about 11 manufacture, put together *combining form:* 3 fer, gen 4 gene 5 genic 6 genous 7 genetic

product 5 fruit, yield 6 effect, output, result 7 harvest, outcome, outturn, turnout 8 multiple, offshoot 9 handiwork, outgrowth 11 consequence *combining form:* 3 ade, ine, ite

production 5 fruit, yield 6 output 7 outturn, turnout *combining form:* 4 geny, gony 7 genesia, poiesis 8 fication

productive 4 rich 6 fecund 7 fertile 8 childing, fruitful, prolific, spawning 11 proliferant

proem see **prologue**

profane 3 lay 4 foul 5 dirty, nasty, pagan 6 coarse, ethnic, filthy, smutty, unholy, vulgar 7 earthly, gentile, heathen, impious, infidel, mundane, obscene, raunchy, secular, ungodly, worldly 8 indecent, temporal, unsacred 9 infidelic 10 irreverent, unhallowed 11 blasphemous, terrestrial 12 sacrilegious 13 irreverential

profanity 4 oath 5 curse 7 cursing, cussing 8 swearing 9 blasphemy 10 execration 11 imprecation

profess 4 aver, avow 6 affirm, assert, avouch, depose 7 declare, protest, purport 8 constate 9 predicate

profession 3 art, job 5 craft, trade 6 career, métier 7 calling 8 vocation 10 handicraft *suffix:* 4 ship

professional 3 pro 4 paid, whiz 5 adept 6 artist, expert, master 7 artiste 8 virtuoso 9 authority 10 past master, proficient

professor 3 don 7 teacher

proffer 4 give, pose 5 offer 6 extend, tender 7 hold out, present 8 proposal 10 invitation, suggestion 11 proposition

proficiency 5 march, skill 7 advance, headway, ongoing 8 anabasis, progress 9 adeptness

proficient 4 able, whiz 5 adept, crack 6 artist, expert, master 7 artiste, capable, drilled, skilled 8 finished, masterly, skillful, virtuoso 9 authority, competent, effective, effectual, efficient, exercised, masterful, practiced, qualified 10 checked-out, consummate, past master 11 crackerjack, experienced 12 accomplished, professional

profile 4 line 7 contour, outline 9 lineament, lineation 10 figuration, silhouette

profit 3 net 4 gain, take 5 avail, lucre, serve, yield 6 output, return 7 benefit, cleanup, killing, outturn, product, receipt, turnout, work for 8 cleaning, earnings, proceeds

profitable 6 paying 7 gainful 9 lucrative 10 well-paying, worthwhile 11 moneymaking 12 advantageous, remunerative

profligate 6 bad lot, no-good, waster 7 rounder, spender, wastrel 8 prodigal, unthrift, wasteful 9 abandoned, dissolute, reprobate 10 high roller, licentious, ne'er-do-well, scapegrace, squanderer 11 scattergood, spendthrift, wastethrift

profound 3 low 4 deep, hard, wise 5 heavy 6 occult, orphic, secret 7 abysmal, intense 8 abstruse, esoteric, hermetic 9 intensive

profoundness 5 abyss, depth 8 deepness 10 profundity

profundity see **profoundness**

profuse 4 lush 6 lavish 7 copious, liberal, opulent, riotous, teeming 8 abundant, generous, prodigal, swarming 9 abounding, bounteous, bountiful, excessive, exuberant, luxuriant 10 immoderate, munificent

profusive see **profuse**

progenitor 4 sire 8 ancestor, forebear 9 ascendant 10 forefather

progeny see **posterity**

prognosis 4 cast 5 weird 8 forecast, prophecy 9 prevision 10 prediction 11 foretelling

prognostic 4 omen, sign 6 augury, boding 7 portent, presage 8 bodement 9 foretoken

prognosticate see **predict**

program 4 bill, card, line, plan, sked 5 slate 6 agenda, course, docket, policy, polity 8 calendar, schedule 9 procedure, timetable 10 bill of fare *theater:* 8 playbill

progress 2 go 4 fare, grow, move 5 get on, march 6 course, growth 7 advance, headway, ongoing, passage, proceed, promote 8 anabasis, get along, upgrowth 9 evolution, flowering, unfolding 10 evolvement 11 advancement, development, proficiency *planned:* 7 telesis

progressing 5 afoot 8 under way

progression 3 row 5 chain, order, train 6 course, growth, sequel, series 7 advance 8 sequence, upgrowth 9 evolution, flowering, unfolding 10 evolvement, succession 11 alternation, consecution, development

progressive 4 wide 5 broad 7 liberal, radical 8 advanced, stepwise, tolerant

prohibit 3 ban, bar 5 taboo 6 enjoin, forbid, outlaw 7 inhibit 9 interdict

prohibited 5 taboo 6 banned 7 illegal, illicit 8 verboten 9 forbidden

project 3 jut, see 4 cast, feat, gest, plan, poke, pout 5 bulge, chart, image, pouch, thing, think 6 affair, beetle, design, devise, extend, intend, matter, scheme, vision 7 arrange, concern, diagram, dope out, emprise, exploit, feature, imagine, prolong, propose, purpose, venture 8 business, conceive, envisage, envision, game plan, lengthen, overhang, protrude, stand out, stick out, strategy 9 adventure, blueprint, delineate, visualize 10 enterprise 11 proposition, undertaking *trivial:* 10 boondoggle

projecting 7 salient

projection 3 jut 4 bump, hook, knob, spur 5 bulge, bunch, ledge, point, spine 8 eminence, forecast, salience, swelling 9 extension, outthrust 10 prominence, protrusion

projet 4 plan 5 draft

proletariat 3 mob 4 mass 6 rabble 7 workers 8 canaille, laborers

prolific 4 rich 6 fecund 7 fertile 8 breeding, childing, fruitful, spawning, swarming 9 abounding 10 generating, productive 11 propagating, reproducing 12 reproductive

prolix 5 windy, wordy 7 diffuse, irksome, tedious, verbose 8 tiresome 9 prolonged, redundant, wearisome 10 long-winded, palaverous, protracted

prolixity 9 verbalism, verbosity, windiness, wordiness 11 verboseness

prologue 5 proem 7 preface, prelude 8 exordium, foreword, overture, preamble 9 prelusion 12 introduction, prolegomenon

prolong 4 draw, last 6 endure, extend 7 draw out, persist, spin out, stretch 8 continue, elongate, lengthen, protract

prolonged 4 long 7 lengthy 8 dragging, drawn-out, longsome, overlong 10 protracted

promenade 4 deck, walk 5 dance 6 parade, stroll 7 balcony, gallery 9 boardwalk

Prometheus *brother:* 5 Atlas 9 Menoetius 10 Epimetheus *creation:* 3 man *father:* 7 Iapetus *gift to man:* 4 fire *mother:* 7 Clymene *rescuer:* 8 Heracles, Hercules

prominence 6 renown 8 eminence, prestige, salience 10 importance, projection 11 distinction *combining form:* 8 tubercul 9 tuberculo

prominent 5 famed, great, noted 6 famous, marked, signal 7 eminent, leading, notable, popular, salient 8 renowned, striking 9 arresting, arrestive, notorious, well-known 10 celebrated, celebrious, noticeable, remarkable 11 conspicuous, illustrious, outstanding 13 distinguished *person:* 3 VIP 6 bigwig 7 grandee

promiscuous 5 mixed 6 motley, random, varied 7 aimless 8 assorted, chowchow 9 desultory, haphazard, hit-or-miss, irregular, unplanned 10 designless 11 purposeless

promise 3 vow 4 bode, oath, omen, pass, pawn, word 5 agree, augur, swear, token 6 accede, assent, assure, engage, ensure, insure, pledge, plight 7 bargain, betoken, compact, consent, earnest, portend, presage, warrant 8 contract, covenant, forebode, foreshow, security 9 assurance, foretoken, guarantee, undertake

promised land 4 Zion 6 Canaan, heaven, utopia 7 arcadia 8 paradise 9 cockaigne, fairyland, shangri-la 10 lubberland, wonderland

promising 4 rosy 6 likely 7 hopeful, roseate 11 encouraging, rose-colored

promissory note 3 IOU

promontory 4 beak, bill, cape, head, naze, peak 5 point 8 foreland, headland

promote 3 aid, cry 4 help, plug, puff, push 5 boost, serve 6 foster, impart, prefer 7 advance, build up, elevate, forward, further, upgrade 8 ballyhoo 9 advertise, encourage, publicize 10 press-agent

promoter 5 agent

promotion 7 advance, buildup, puffery 9 elevation, prelation, publicity, upgrading 10 preference, preferment 11 advancement, advertising 13 advertisement

prompt 3 apt, cue, get, sic 4 draw, fast, goad, prod, spur, urge 5 alert, egg on, prick, quick, rapid, ready, swift 6 exhort, induce, propel, speedy, timely 7 win over 8 convince, persuade, punctual, talk into

promulgate 4 toot 5 sound 7 declare, publish 8 announce, proclaim 9 advertise, broadcast 10 annunciate 11 disseminate

prone 3 apt 4 fain, flat, open 5 given, level, ready 6 liable, likely, minded, supine 7 exposed, subject, willing 8 disposed, inclined, resupine 9 decumbent, obnoxious, prostrate, reclining, recumbent, sensitive 11 predisposed, susceptible

prong 3 nib 4 fang, fork, stab, tine 5 point

pronghorn 6 cabree 8 antelope

pronoun *archaic:* 2 ye 3 thy 4 thou 5 thine *demonstrative:* 4 that, this 5 these, those *indefinite:* 3 all, any, few, one 4 both, each, none, some 5 no one, other 6 anyone, either, nobody 7 another, anybody, neither, nothing, someone 8 anything, somebody 9 everybody, something 10 everything *personal:* 2 he, it, my, we 3 her, him, his, its, our, she, you 4 hers, mine, ours, them, they, your 5 their, yours 6 theirs *possessive:* 2 my 3 her, his, its, our 4 hers, mine, ours, your 5 their, yours 6 theirs *reflexive:* 6 itself, myself 7 herself, himself, oneself, ourself 8 yourself 9 ourselves 10 themselves, yourselves *relative:* 3 who 4 that, what, whom 5 which, whose, whoso 6 whomso 7 whoever 8 whatever, whomever 9 whichever, whosoever 10 whatsoever, whomsoever 11 whichsoever

pronounce 3 say 5 speak, utter 6 recite 7 declare, phonate 9 enunciate 10 articulate

pronounced 7 assured, decided 8 clear-cut, definite

pronouncement 9 statement 11 declaration, publication 12 proclamation, promulgation

pronto 4 fast 6 at once 7 quickly 8 promptly 9 posthaste 11 immediately

pronunciation 6 speech 9 utterance *distinctive:* 4 burr 5 drawl, twang 6 accent *study:* 8 orthoepy 9 phonetics

proof 4 test 6 galley 8 argument, evidence 9 testament, testimony 10 impression 11 attestation 12 confirmation

proofreaders' mark 3 cap, rom 4 dele, ital, stet 5 caret

prop 3 leg 4 stay 5 brace, carry, shore 6 bear up, buoy up, column, upbear, uphold 7 bolster, shore up, support, sustain 8 buttress 12 underpinning

propaganda 4 hype 8 agitprop 9 publicity

propagandist 7 apostle 9 missioner 10 colporteur, evangelist, missionary

propagate 4 bear, grow 5 beget, breed, raise, strew 6 spread 7 diffuse, produce, radiate 8 disperse, generate, multiply 9 circulate, cultivate, procreate, reproduce 10 distribute 11 disseminate

propel 4 goad, move, prod, push, spur, urge 5 drive, egg on, impel, power, prick, shove 6 exhort, prompt, thrust 7 actuate

propellant 4 fuel, spur 7 impetus, impulse 8 catalyst, stimulus 9 incentive, stimulant 10 incitation, motivation 11 provocative

propeller 3 fan, oar 5 screw 6 paddle

propensity see **penchant**

proper 3 apt, due, fit 4 able, good, just, meet, nice, prig, prim, true 5 exact, happy, right 6 au fait, comely, decent, prissy, stuffy, useful 7 capable, correct, desired, fitting, genteel, missish, precise, prudish 8 accurate, becoming, decorous, peculiar, priggish, rightful, rigorous, suitable 9 befitting, competent, diacritic, qualified 10 applicable, conforming, convenient, diagnostic, felicitous, individual 11 appropriate, comme il faut, distinctive, puritanical, straitlaced *combining form:* 4 orth 5 ortho

property 4 land, mark 5 trait, worth 6 estate, realty, riches, virtue, wealth 7 feature, fortune, quality 8 dominion 9 affection, attribute, character, ownership, resources, substance 10 possession, real estate *conveyor:* 7 alienor *private:* 8 peculium *recipient:* 7 alienee *seller:* 7 Realtor *transfer:* 8 alienate

prophecy 4 cast 5 weird 6 oracle, vision 8 forecast 9 prevision, prognosis 10 apocalypse, prediction, revelation 11 foretelling

prophesier 4 seer 5 augur 6 auspex 7 prophet 8 foreseer, haruspex 9 predictor 10 forecaster, foreteller 11 Nostradamus

prophesy 5 augur 7 portend, predict, presage 8 forecast, foretell, soothsay 9 adumbrate 10 vaticinate 13 prognosticate

prophet 4 seer 5 augur 6 auspex, oracle 7 seeress 8 foreseer, haruspex 9 predictor 10 forecaster, foreteller, prophesier, soothsayer 11 Nostradamus *Major:* 6 Daniel, Isaiah 7 Ezekiel 8 Jeremiah *Minor:* 4 Amos, Joel 5 Hosea, Jonah, Micah, Nahum 6 Haggai 7 Malachi, Obadiah 8 Habakkuk 9 Zechariah, Zephaniah

prophetess 4 Anna 5 Sibyl 6 Huldah, Miriam 7 Deborah, Noadiah 9 Cassandra

prophetic 5 vatic 6 mantic, mystic 7 fatidic, strange, vatical 8 Delphian, oracular 9 sibylline, vaticinal 10 mysterious, revelatory 11 apocalyptic, prophetical

propinquity 7 kinship 8 nearness 9 closeness, immediacy, proximity 10 contiguity

propitiate 5 adapt, atone 6 adjust, pacify 7 appease, assuage, conform, content, mediate, mollify, placate, satisfy, sweeten 9 intercede, reconcile 10 conciliate

propitiatory 7 lustral 9 expiative, expiatory, purgative

propitious 4 good, rosy 5 brave, white 6 benign, bright, dexter, timely, toward, useful 7 benefic, helpful, timeous 8 favoring 9 favorable, fortunate, opportune, well-timed 10 auspicious, beneficial, prosperous, seasonable 12 advantageous

proponent 6 backer 8 advocate, champion 9 expounder, supporter

proportion 4 rate, size, tune 5 ratio, scale 6 attune, degree, extent 7 balance, conform, harmony, measure, prorate 8 symmetry

proportional 5 equal 8 relative 9 dependent 10 contingent, reciprocal 11 correlative, symmetrical 12 commensurate 13 commensurable, corresponding

proposal 3 bid 4 idea, plan 6 motion, scheme 7 outline, proffer, project 10 invita-

tion, suggestion **11** proposition ***final:*** **9** ultimatum
propose **3** aim, ask, put **4** mean, plan, pose **5** offer **6** design, intend, prefer, submit, tender **7** move for, present, purpose, request, solicit, suggest **8** nominate, propound, theorize **11** contemplate
proposition **3** put **4** pose **5** lemma, offer **6** prefer, thesis **7** premise, proffer, propose, suggest, theorem **8** proposal, propound **10** invitation, suggestion
propound **3** put **4** pose **6** prefer **7** propone, propose, suggest **11** proposition
proprietor **5** owner **6** holder **9** possessor
propriety **5** order **6** manner **7** aptness, decency, decorum, dignity, fitness **8** meetness **9** etiquette, rightness **10** expediency, properness, seemliness **11** correctness, orderliness, suitability **12** appositeness, correctitude, decorousness, suitableness
propulsion **4** fuel, push **5** drive, power
prorate **5** allot, divvy, quota, share **6** divide, parcel, ration **7** portion **9** apportion
prorogate see **prorogue**
prorogue **4** rise, stay **5** defer, delay, remit **6** hold up, put off, recess, shelve **7** adjourn, hold off **8** dissolve, hold over, postpone **9** prorogate, terminate
prosaic **4** drab, dull, flat **5** lowly, prose, prosy **6** actual, boring, common **7** factual, irksome, literal, mundane, tedious, workday **8** everyday, lifeless, ordinary, workaday **9** colorless, practical **10** lackluster, lusterless, uneventful **11** commonplace
proscenium **5** stage **9** forestage **10** foreground
proscribe **3** ban **4** damn, doom **7** condemn **8** prohibit, sentence
proscription **3** ban **5** taboo **11** forbiddance, prohibition **12** interdiction
prosecute **3** sue **5** press **6** charge, indict
prosecutor **2** DA **6** lawyer **7** accuser ***public:*** **6** fiscal
proselyte **7** convert, recruit **8** neophyte
prospect **4** mine, sift **5** probe, scape, vista **6** go into **7** dig into, explore, lookout, outlook **8** look into **9** candidate
prosper **3** dow **4** boom **5** score, yield **6** arrive, thrive **7** augment, make out, produce, succeed, turn out **8** flourish, increase
prosperity **4** boom, ease **6** growth, riches, wealth **7** arrival, benefit, success, welfare **8** interest, thriving **9** abundance, advantage, affluence, expansion, inflation, well-being **10** easy street **12** flying colors
Prospero ***daughter:*** **7** Miranda ***servant:*** **5** Ariel ***slave:*** **7** Caliban
prosperous **4** easy, rich, well **5** happy, lucky, lusty, palmy **6** robust, strong, timely **7** booming, halcyon, opulent, roaring, thrifty, timeous, wealthy, well-off **8** affluent, thriving, well-to-do **9** desirable, favorable, fortunate, opportune, well-fixed, well-timed **10** auspicious, convenient, felicitous, propitious, seasonable, successful, well-heeled **11** appropriate, comfortable, flourishing, substantial
prostitute **4** bawd, doxy, drab, moll **5** abuse, madam, poule, quean, whore **6** callet, debase, harlot, hooker, misuse, pickup, tomato, wanton **7** cocotte, corrupt, cruiser, Cyprian, debauch, deprave, hustler, joy girl, Paphian, vitiate **8** call girl, meretrix, misapply, strumpet **9** cocodette, misemploy, mishandle, party girl **10** misimprove, street girl **11** fille de joie, nightwalker **12** camp follower, streetwalker ***reformed:*** **8** Magdalen
prostitution **8** harlotry, whoredom **10** social evil **13** streetwalking ***house of:*** **7** brothel **8** bordello
prostrate **4** down, drop, fell, flat, poop **5** floor, level, prone, whelm **6** disarm, ground, lay low, tucker **7** cripple, disable, exhaust, frazzle, outtire, outwear, wear out **8** knock out, overcome, paralyze **9** decumbent, knock over, overpower, overwhelm, reclining, recumbent, throw down
protagonist **4** hero, star **5** actor **6** leader **8** advocate, champion **9** spokesman
protean **5** fluid **6** mobile **7** mutable **8** unstable, unsteady, variable, weathery **9** changeful, unsettled **10** changeable
protect **4** fend, save **5** cover, guard **6** defend, harbor, screen, secure, shield **7** bulwark, shelter **8** conserve, preserve **9** safeguard
protected **4** safe **6** immune
protection **3** pad **4** ward **5** aegis, armor, bribe, graft, guard **6** safety, shield **7** defense, squeeze **8** armament, security **9** extortion, safeguard, shakedown
protector **5** armor, guard **6** patron, shield **7** tutelar **8** guardian
protégé **4** ward **5** pupil **7** student
protein **4** zein **5** actin, opsin **6** avidin, enzyme, fibrin, globin **7** albumin, elastin, fibroin, histone, keratin, legumin, sericin **8** creatine, globulin, glutelin, prolamin, protamin, proteose, vitellin ***complex:*** **6** mucoid ***derivative:*** **7** peptone ***poisonous:*** **5** abrin, ricin ***source:*** **4** eggs, fish, meat, milk **6** cheese
pro tem **6** acting, supply **7** interim **9** ad interim, temporary **10** pro tempore
protest **4** aver, avow, kick **5** demur, fight **6** affirm, assert, avouch, combat, depose, except, object, oppose, picket, resist **7** declare, profess **8** constate, demurral, demurrer **9** challenge, objection

Protestant 5 Amish 6 Mormon, Quaker, Shaker 7 Baptist, Lollard, Pilgrim, Puritan 8 Anglican, Lutheran, Moravian 9 Adventist, Mennonite, Methodist, Unitarian 12 Episcopalian, Presbyterian ***Bohemian:*** 7 Hussite ***dissenter:*** 7 sectary ***French:*** 8 Huguenot ***martyr:*** (see at martyr)
prototypal see prototypical
prototype 5 model 8 ancestor, foregoer, original 9 archetype, precursor 10 antecedent, antecessor, forerunner, protoplast 11 predecessor
prototypical 5 ideal, model 7 classic 9 classical, exemplary 10 archetypal
protozoan 4 cell 5 ameba 6 amoeba 7 arcella, ciliate, stentor 10 flagellate, paramecium
protract see prolong
protrude 3 jut 4 poke, pout 5 bulge, pouch 6 beetle 7 project 8 overhang, stand out, stick out
protrusion 3 jut, nub 4 bump, hump 5 bulge 8 eminence, swelling 9 outthrust 10 projection 12 protuberance
protuberance see protrusion
protuberate see protrude
proud 4 vain 5 huffy, lofty, noble, wiggy 6 lordly, stuffy, superb 7 bloated, haughty, pompous, stuck-up, sublime 8 arrogant, cavalier, glorious, gorgeous, insolent, misproud, orgulous, scornful, splendid, superior, toplofty 9 conceited, hubristic, imperious, important, masterful 10 disdainful, dismissive, high-handed 11 domineering, magnificent, overbearing, pretentious, resplendent, splendorous, toploftical 12 contemptuous, narcissistic, ostentatious, proudhearted, supercilious
prove 3 try 4 show, test 5 argue, check 6 attest, verify 7 bespeak, betoken, confirm, examine, make out 8 document, indicate 9 determine, establish 11 corroborate, demonstrate 12 substantiate
provenance 4 root, well 6 origin, source, whence 8 fountain 9 inception 10 derivation, wellspring 11 provenience
provender see provisions
provenience see provenance
proverb 3 saw 4 word 5 adage, axiom, maxim 6 byword, saying
provide 4 feed, give, hand 5 cater, endow, equip 6 afford, supply 7 deliver, furnish, support 8 dispense, hand over, maintain
provided 2 if 6 if only 8 equipped
providence 6 thrift 7 caution, economy 8 prudence 9 canniness, foresight, frugality, husbandry 10 discretion, precaution 11 forethought, thriftiness 12 discreetness
provident 5 canny, chary 6 frugal, saving, Scotch 7 sparing, thrifty 9 stewardly 10 economical, unwasteful
providential 4 kind, well 5 happy, lucky 6 kindly 9 benignant, fortunate
province 4 area, duty, role, walk, work 5 field 6 domain, office, sphere 7 calling, demesne, pursuit, terrain 8 business, district, dominion, function 9 bailiwick, champaign, territory 10 department ***Greek:*** 4 nome 8 nomarchy
provincial 4 hick, jake, rube 5 clown, local, rural 6 rustic 7 bigoted, bucolic, bumpkin, country, hayseed, insular, outland, peasant 8 agrestic, pastoral 9 hidebound, parochial, sectarian, small-town 10 campestral, out-country 11 countrified
provision 4 term 6 clause 7 proviso, strings 9 condition 11 reservation, stipulation
provisional 4 iffy 7 stopgap 9 dependent, makeshift, provisory, temporary, tentative 10 contingent 11 conditional 13 rough-and-ready
provisions 4 feed, food, grub 6 viands 7 edibles, nurture 8 supplies, victuals 9 provender 11 comestibles ***dealer:*** 8 chandler
proviso see provision
provocation 6 irking, vexing 8 vexation 9 annoyance, bothering, provoking 10 harassment
provocative 4 goad, push, spur 7 impetus, impulse 8 stimulus 9 incentive 10 incitation, incitement, motivation 11 challenging
provoke 3 bug, get, irk, vex 4 abet, fire, fret, gall, move, rile, roil, stir, wake, whet 5 anger, annoy, breed, cause, chafe, exalt, get up, grate, hatch, pique, prime, raise, rally, rouse, set on, upset, waken 6 abrade, arouse, awaken, bestir, bother, excite, foment, harass, incite, induce, inform, insult, kindle, madden, put out, ruffle, stir up, thrill, whip up 7 animate, build up, enthuse, incense, inflame, innerve, inspire, outrage, perturb, produce, quicken 8 engender, exercise, generate, irritate, motivate, muster up, occasion, titivate 9 aggravate, challenge, electrify, galvanize, innervate, instigate, stimulate, titillate
provost 4 head 6 keeper 7 marshal 8 director 13 administrator
prow 3 bow 4 beak, stem 5 front
prowess 5 skill, valor 7 address, heroism, sleight 8 deftness, valiance, valiancy 9 dexterity, gallantry, readiness 10 adroitness 12 valorousness 13 dexterousness
prowl 4 hunt, pace, roam 5 creep 6 wander
proximate 4 near, next, nigh, rude 5 close, rough 6 nearby 8 imminent 9 immediate, impending 10 near-at-hand
proximity 8 nearness, vicinity 9 adja-

cency, closeness, immediacy **10** contiguity **11** propinquity **12** togetherness
proxy **5** agent, power **6** deputy, factor **8** assignee, attorney **9** authority
prude **4** prig **6** Grundy **7** old fogy, old maid, Puritan **8** bluenose, comstock **9** Mrs. Grundy, nice Nelly **10** fuddy-duddy, fuss-budget, goody-goody, spoilsport, wet blanket **12** stuffed shirt
prudence **3** wit **6** acumen, thrift, wisdom **7** caution, economy, insight **8** astucity, keenness, sagacity, sageness, sapience **9** canniness, chariness, foresight, frugality, husbandry **10** astuteness, discretion, expediency, precaution, providence, shrewdness **11** calculation, forethought, penetration, percipience, thriftiness **12** discreetness, perspicacity
prudent **4** sage, sane, wary, wise **5** canny, chary **7** politic, sapient **8** cautious, sensible, tactical **9** advisable, expedient, judicious
prudish **4** prim **5** stern **6** prissy, proper, severe, strict, stuffy **7** austere, genteel **8** priggish **9** Victorian **11** puritanical, straitlaced
prune **3** cut, lop **4** clip, crop, dolt, dope, pare, plum, thin, trim **5** brash, chump, dunce, fruit, idiot, moron, shave, shear, skive
prurience **4** itch, lust **6** desire **7** passion **9** eroticism **11** lustfulness **13** concupiscence
prurient **3** hot **4** lewd **5** bawdy **6** erotic **7** goatish, lustful, satyric, sensual **9** lickerish **10** lascivious, libidinous, passionate **12** concupiscent
pruritic **5** itchy
Prussian ***aristocrat:*** **6** Junker **12** Hohenzollern ***prime minister:*** **8** Bismarck ***ruler:*** **7** Wilhelm **9** Frederick
pry **4** lift, nose, open, peek, poke, rear, turn **5** hoist, jimmy, lever, mouse, prize, raise, snoop, twist **6** divide, pick up, take up, uphold, uplift, uprear **7** crowbar, disjoin, elevate, upraise **8** busybody, separate
psalm **3** ode **4** hymn, laud, poem, song **5** cry up, extol **6** praise **7** glorify, magnify **8** eulogize **9** celebrate ***book:*** **7** psalter ***selection:*** **6** hallel ***word:*** **5** selah
psalmist **4** poet **5** Asaph, David **6** cantor
pseudo **4** fake, mock, sham **5** bogus, false, phony, snide, wrong **8** spurious **9** brummagem, pinchbeck **11** counterfeit
pseudonym **5** alias **6** ananym, anonym **7** pen name **9** incognito, stage name **10** nom de plume **11** nom de guerre; (see also pen name)
psyche **4** mind, soul **5** anima **6** animus, pneuma, spirit **9** élan vital **10** vital force ***part:*** **2** id **3** ego **8** superego
Psyche's beloved **4** Eros **5** Cupid
psychiatrist **6** shrink ***American:*** **9** Menninger ***Austrian:*** **5** Adler ***Swiss:*** **4** Jung **9** Rorschach
psychic **6** mental **7** sensile **8** cerebral, sensible, sentient **9** sensitive, spiritual **10** responsive, susceptive, telepathic **11** impressible, susceptible **12** intellective, intellectual, supersensory **13** psychological ***American:*** **5** Cayce (Edgar) ***power:*** **3** ESP
psychoanalyst **5** Freud, Fromm **6** Horney
psychological **6** mental **7** psychic **8** cerebral **9** psychical **12** intellective, intellectual
psychologist **6** shrink ***American:*** **3** May **5** James **6** Rogers, Terman, Watson, Yerkes **7** Skinner **8** Brothers **9** Thorndike ***English:*** **4** Ward **8** Spearman, Tichener ***German:*** **5** Wundt **6** Muller, Stumpf **10** Wertheimer ***Swiss:*** **4** Jung **6** Piaget
psychopathy **6** lunacy **7** madness **8** insanity **9** unbalance **10** aberration, alienation, insaneness **11** derangement, distraction
psychotic **3** mad **5** crazy **6** insane **8** schizoid
ptarmigan **6** grouse
ptomaine **6** poison
pub **3** bar, inn **6** tavern **7** barroom, rummery, taproom **8** drinkery, groggery, grogshop
puberty **5** youth **6** spring **9** greenness, youthhood **10** juvenility, pubescence, springtide, springtime **11** adolescence ***combining form:*** **4** hebe
public **4** open **5** civic, civil, joint, state, suite, urban **6** common, mutual, people, shared, vulgar **7** general, popular, society **8** audience, communal, conjoint, conjunct, national, open-door **9** clientage, clientele, community, following, hangers-on, municipal, prevalent, universal **10** accessible, government, widespread **11** intermutual
publican **8** boniface, taverner **9** barkeeper, collector, innholder, innkeeper, saloonist **12** saloonkeeper, tax collector
publication **4** book **5** paper **7** journal **8** magazine, pamphlet **9** broadcast, newspaper **10** periodical **11** declaration ***list:*** **12** bibliography
public house **3** inn **5** hotel, lodge **6** hostel, tavern **7** auberge, hospice **8** hostelry **9** road-house **11** caravansary
publicity **4** hype, plug, puff **5** blurb **6** hoopla **7** buildup, puffery, réclame, write-up **8** ballyhoo, hard sell **9** promotion **11** advertising **12** announcement
publicize **3** cry **4** hype, plug, puff, push, tout **5** boost, bruit, extol **7** advance, build up, promote, trumpet **8** announce, headline,

skywrite 9 advertise, broadcast 10 press-agent, promulgate 11 circularize 12 propagandize
publish 3 air 4 toot, vent 5 issue, print, utter 6 broach, get out, market, put out 7 declare, express, produce 8 announce, bring out, proclaim 9 advertise, broadcast, ventilate 10 annunciate, distribute, promulgate 11 blaze abroad, disseminate
publisher 6 editor 7 printer 10 journalist
Puccini, Giacomo *heroine:* 4 Mimi *operas:* 5 Edgar, Tosca 7 Le Villi 8 La Bohème, Turandot 12 Manon Lescaut, Suor Angelica
puck 3 elf, imp 4 disk 5 fairy 6 spirit, sprite 9 hobgoblin, prankster
pucker 4 fold 5 purse 6 cockle 7 wrinkle 8 contract
puckish 5 antic 6 impish, wicked 7 larkish, playful, roguish, waggish 8 prankish, sportive 11 mischievous
pudding 4 duff 6 burgoo 7 custard, dessert, tapioca *baked:* 10 brown Betty
pudgy 5 plump, round, squab, tubby 6 chubby, plumpy, rotund, squdgy, stumpy 8 plumpish, roly-poly 10 roundabout
pueblo 4 town 7 village 8 dwelling *ceremonial room:* 4 kiva
puerile 6 boyish 7 babyish 8 childish, immature
Puerto Rico *capital:* 7 San Juan *discoverer:* 8 Columbus
puff 3 cry 4 blow, brag, crow, drag, draw, gasp, huff, pant, plug, pouf, pull, push 5 blurb, boast, boost, heave, mouth, prate, quilt, vaunt 6 praise 7 build up, puffing, write-up 8 inhaling 9 advertise, comforter, gasconade, laudation, publicize
puffer 8 blowfish 9 globefish
puffery 7 buildup 9 promotion, publicity 11 advertising 12 press-agentry
puffin 4 bird 9 sea parrot 10 shearwater
puff up 5 bloat, swell 7 inflate
puffy 5 wiggy 6 stuffy 7 bloated, pompous 8 arrogant 9 important 10 pontifical 11 magisterial 13 self-important
pug 3 bun, dog 4 nose 5 boxer, track 9 footprint
pugilism 4 ring 6 boxing 10 fisticuffs 13 prizefighting
pugilist 5 boxer 7 fighter
pugnacious 5 pushy 7 defiant, pushing, scrappy, warlike 8 brawling, militant 9 bellicose, combative, truculent 10 rebellious 11 belligerent, contentious, quarrelsome
pugnacity 5 fight 6 attack 10 aggression 12 belligerence 13 combativeness
puisne 5 judge, later 6 junior 9 associate
puissance 4 sway 5 clout, force, might, power, sinew, vigor 6 energy, muscle, virtue 7 potency 8 strength 9 influence
puissant 6 mighty, potent, ruling, strong 8 forceful, forcible, powerful 10 commanding
pukka 4 real, true 5 right 7 genuine 8 bona fide 9 authentic, simon-pure
pule 3 cry 5 whine 7 whimper
Pulitzer Prize winner, fiction *1918:* 5 Poole *1919:* 10 Tarkington *1921:* 7 Wharton *1922:* 10 Tarkington *1923:* 6 Cather *1924:* 6 Wilson *1925:* 6 Ferber *1926:* 5 Lewis *1927:* 9 Bromfield *1928:* 6 Wilder *1929:* 8 Peterkin *1930:* 7 La Farge *1931:* 6 Barnes *1932:* 4 Buck *1933:* 9 Stribling *1934:* 6 Miller *1935:* 7 Johnson *1936:* 5 Davis *1937:* 8 Mitchell *1938:* 8 Marquand *1939:* 8 Rawlings *1940:* 9 Steinbeck *1942:* 7 Glasgow *1943:* 8 Sinclair *1944:* 6 Flavin *1945:* 6 Hersey *1947:* 6 Warren *1948:* 8 Michener *1949:* 7 Cozzens *1950:* 7 Guthrie *1951:* 7 Richter *1952:* 4 Wouk *1953:* 9 Hemingway *1955:* 8 Faulkner *1956:* 6 Kantor *1958:* 4 Agee *1959:* 6 Taylor *1960:* 5 Drury *1961:* 3 Lee *1962:* 7 O'Connor *1963:* 8 Faulkner *1965:* 4 Grau *1966:* 6 Porter *1967:* 7 Malamud *1968:* 6 Styron *1969:* 7 Momaday *1970:* 8 Stafford *1972:* 7 Stegner *1973:* 5 Welty *1975:* 6 Shaara *1976:* 6 Bellow *1978:* 9 McPherson *1979:* 7 Cheever *1980:* 6 Mailer *1981:* 5 Toole *1982:* 6 Updike *1983:* 6 Walker *1984:* 7 Kennedy *1985:* 5 Lurie *1986:* 8 McMurtry *1987:* 6 Taylor *1988:* 8 Morrison *1989:* 5 Tyler *1990:* 8 Hijuelos
pull 3 don, get, lug, oar, row, tow, tug, win 4 drag, draw, gain, haul, have, jerk, land, lure, puff, push, tear, yank 5 clout, drive, heave, impel, put on, shove 6 appeal, assume, commit, evulse, obtain, paddle, pick up, secure, strain, strike, take on, wrench 7 chalk up, extract, procure 9 influence, seduction 10 allurement, attraction, perpetrate, persuasion 12 drawing power
pull down 4 raze, ruin 5 wreck 7 destroy 8 decimate, demolish, destruct, tear down 9 dismantle 10 annihilate
pullet 3 hen
pulley 5 wheel 6 sheave *watch's:* 5 fusee, fuzee
pull in 3 bit, nab 4 curb 5 check, pinch, run in 6 arrest, bridle, detain, hold in, pick up 7 inhibit 8 hold back, hold down, restrain
pulling 8 traction *cable for:* 7 towline
Pullman 3 car 7 sleeper
pull out 4 exit, quit 5 leave, pluck 6 depart, get off, retire 7 retreat, take off 8 shove off, withdraw
pull through 7 recover, ride out, survive
pullulate 4 flow, teem 5 crawl, swarm 6 abound

pull up 4 halt, stop 6 draw up, haul up
pulp 4 mash, pith 5 crush 6 bruise, squash 7 bagasse, becrush
pulpit 4 ambo 7 lectern 8 ministry, platform ***Muslim:*** 6 minbar
pulsate 4 beat, drum, pump, roar 5 pound, throb, thrum 7 vibrate 9 fluctuate, oscillate, palpitate
pulse 4 beat 5 throb 6 rhythm ***combining form:*** 6 crotic 7 sphygmo ***relating to:*** 8 sphygmic
pulverize 4 beat, bray, buck, mill, mull, ruin 5 crush, flour, grate, grind, smash, wreck 6 abrade, crunch, powder, rub out 7 atomize, break up, crumble, destroy, shatter, smatter 8 decimate, demolish, destruct, dynamite, fragment, levigate, splinter, tear down 9 comminute, micronize, triturate 11 fragmentize 12 contriturate
puma 3 cat 6 cougar
pumice 5 glass, stone
pummel 4 beat, drub, pelt 5 pound 6 batter, buffet, hammer, thrash, wallop 7 belabor
pump 3 tap 4 draw 5 draft, drain 6 siphon 7 draw off, syringe
pumpernickel 3 rye 5 bread
pumpkin 4 pepo 5 fruit 6 cushaw, squash 12 jack-o'-lantern
pun 4 joke 9 calembour, equivoque 11 paronomasia
punch 3 box, dig, hit, jab, jog, pep 4 bang, bore, cuff, poke, prod, push, slap, snap, sock, stab 5 clout, drill, drive, force, getup, nudge, paste, point, prick, smack, vigor 6 buffet, starch, strike 7 cogency 8 puncture, uppercut, validity, vitality 9 perforate, validness 13 effectiveness
punch bowl 8 monteith
puncheon 4 tool 5 stamp
puncher 5 boxer 6 cowboy
Punch's wife 4 Judy
punctilious 4 nice 5 exact, fussy 6 formal 7 careful, heedful 8 punctual 9 observant 10 meticulous, scrupulous 11 painstaking
punctual 5 exact, fussy, quick, ready 6 prompt, timely 7 careful, heedful 10 meticulous
punctuate 4 mark 5 point 6 divide 8 separate
punctuation mark 4 dash 5 brace, colon, comma 6 hyphen, parens, period 7 bracket, virgule 8 diagonal, ellipsis 9 semicolon 10 apostrophe 11 parenthesis
puncture 3 jab 4 bore, hole, stab 5 drill, prick, punch, shoot 6 blow up, riddle 7 explode 8 disprove 9 discredit, perforate 11 perforation ***surgical:*** 8 centesis
pundit 4 sage 5 swami 6 critic 7 teacher
pungency 4 tang, zest 8 piquancy
pungent 3 hot 4 keen, racy, rich, salt 5 acute, salty, sharp, spicy, tangy, zesty 6 biting, bitter, snappy 7 cutting, peppery, piquant 8 exciting, incisive, poignant 9 trenchant 11 provocative, stimulating
punish 3 fix 4 fine, whip 5 mulct, shift, swill 6 amerce, avenge 7 chasten, consume, correct, put away, put down, reprove, revenge, scourge, torture 8 chastise, lambaste, penalize 9 castigate, criticize, polish off 10 discipline
punishment 3 rod 4 fine 5 mulct 7 penalty, reproof, revenge 8 punition 9 criticism 10 amercement, avengement, correction, discipline 11 castigation 12 chastisement ***Scottish:*** 6 dirdum
punitive 5 penal 8 punitory 9 punishing 11 castigating 12 correctional, disciplinary
punk 4 bosh, colt, hood, thug 5 rough, rowdy, tough, yahoo 6 bunkum, hot air, mucker, novice, rookie 7 baloney, hogwash, hoodlum, ruffian, toughie 8 beginner, bullyboy, claptrap, neophyte, newcomer, nonsense 9 fledgling, novitiate, roughneck 10 apprentice, balderdash
punt 4 boat, kick
puny 4 weak 5 frail, petty 6 feeble, infirm, measly, paltry, sickly, weakly 7 fragile, trivial, unsound 8 decrepit, niggling, picayune, piddling, trifling 10 picayunish
pupa 9 chrysalid, chrysalis
pupil 5 cadet, tutee 7 learner, scholar, student 8 disciple ***French:*** 5 élève
puppet 4 doll, dupe, pawn, tool 5 slave 6 stooge 7 cat's-paw
puppy 3 dog 5 whelp
Purcell opera 13 Dido and Aeneas
purchase 3 buy 4 take 6 obtain 7 acquire 11 acquisition
purchaser 4 user 5 buyer 6 client, emptor, patron, vendee 7 shopper 8 consumer, customer
pure 4 good, neat 5 clean, fresh, gross, plain, sheer, total, utter 6 chaste, decent, modest, simple 7 blasted, blessed, classic, genuine, perfect, plenary, sinless, unmixed 8 absolute, complete, infernal, innocent, spotless, straight, virtuous 9 authentic, blameless, exemplary, guiltless, inviolate, out-and-out, righteous, stainless, unalloyed, undefiled, undiluted, unsullied 10 confounded, immaculate, inculpable, unblamable, unblighted, unprofaned 11 unblemished, unmitigated, unqualified 13 unadulterated
purebred 8 pedigree 9 pedigreed 10 registered 11 full-blooded 12 thoroughbred
puree 4 soup 5 paste
purely 3 all 4 just 5 quite 6 in toto, wholly 7 exactly, totally, utterly 8 all in all 10 altogether

purfle 4 trim 6 border 8 decorate, ornament
purgation 9 catharsis, cleansing 10 lustration
purgative 5 jalap 7 lustral 9 cathartic, expiatory
purge 3 rid 4 oust 5 clear, debar, eject, erase, expel 6 purify, remove 7 absolve, cleanse, dismiss, exclude, expunge, shut out, wipe out 8 disabuse, lustrate, undelude 9 eliminate, expurgate, liquidate, undeceive 11 exterminate
purification 5 grace 7 rebirth 9 atonement, catharsis, cleansing, expiation, purgation, salvation 10 absolution, lustration, redemption 11 expurgation, forgiveness 12 regeneration *sacrament:* 7 baptism
purify 5 atone, clean, purge, remit 6 filter, refine 7 absolve, baptize, clarify, cleanse, expiate 8 depurate, lustrate 9 elutriate, expurgate
purist 7 diehard, Puritan 8 Atticist 9 precisian 10 classicist 11 bitter-ender 12 conservative, precisionist
puritan 4 prig 5 prude 6 Grundy 8 bluenose, comstock 9 Mrs. Grundy, nice Nelly
puritanical 4 prim 6 narrow, prissy, strict, stuffy 7 bigoted, genteel, prudish 8 priggish, rigorous 9 blue-nosed, hidebound, illiberal, victorian 10 intolerant, tight-laced 11 straitlaced 12 narrow-minded
purity 8 chastity 9 innocence
purl 4 eddy, knit 5 gurge, swirl, whirl, whorl 6 stitch, swoosh 9 whirlpool
purlieu 5 haunt 6 resort 7 hangout
purlieus 6 bounds, limits 7 compass, suburbs 8 boundary, confines, environs 9 outskirts, precincts
purloin 5 filch, pinch, steal, swipe 6 pilfer, rip off, snitch, thieve 7 cabbage 11 appropriate
purloiner 4 prig 5 thief 6 nimmer 7 filcher, stealer 8 larcener, pilferer 9 larcenist
purple 4 blue, plum, racy 5 broad, grape, lilac, mauve, regal, salty, shady, spicy 6 florid, maroon, murrey, risqué, turgid, violet, wicked 7 flowery, pompous, stilted 8 lavender, off-color 9 bombastic, high-flown, overblown 10 oratorical, rhetorical, suggestive
Purple Heart 5 award, medal
purport 4 core, gist, meat, pith 5 drift, sense, tenor 6 burden, matter, thrust, upshot 7 meaning, message 9 substance 10 intendment 11 acceptation, connotation, implication 12 significance, significancy
purported 7 alleged, reputed, rumored 8 academic, so-called, supposed 9 pretended, professed, suspected 10 ostensible, postulated 11 presupposed, speculative
purpose 3 aim, use 4 duty, goal, mark, mean, plan 5 point 6 animus, decide, design, intend, intent, object, ponder, target 7 meaning, mission, resolve 8 ambition, conclude, consider, function, meditate, proposal 9 determine, direction, intention, objective 10 aspiration, intendment
purposeless 6 random 7 aimless, fustian, unaimed, useless 8 feckless 9 desultory, haphazard, hit-or-miss, irregular, senseless, unhelpful, unplanned, worthless 10 designless, unpurposed 11 meaningless, nonsensical, purportless 12 unprofitable
purposely 9 expressly 10 designedly, explicitly, prepensely 12 deliberately 13 intentionally
purr 3 hum 6 murmur
purse 3 bag, sum 4 knit 5 money, pouch, prize 6 pucker, wallet 7 handbag 9 clutch bag 10 pocketbook, prize money *Scottish:* 7 sporran
pursual 5 chase, quest 6 search 7 pursuit
pursue 3 woo 4 hunt, seek 5 chase, chivy, court, hound, spark, stalk, track, trail 6 badger, follow 7 address, oppress, persist 8 make up to 9 persecute, persevere
pursuit 3 job 4 hunt, line, work 5 chase, quest 6 racket, search 7 calling, seeking 8 business, reaching 9 following, obtaining 10 employment, occupation
pursy see portly
purvey 6 obtain, supply 7 provide
purview 3 ken 5 ambit, orbit, range, reach, scope, sweep 6 extent, radius 7 compass
pus 6 fester *combining form:* 2 py 3 pyo
push 3 dig, jam, lot, pep, ram, set 4 bang, bear, bump, butt, goad, move, plug, prod, snap, spur 5 boost, build, bunch, crowd, crush, drive, drove, elbow, force, getup, group, horde, hunch, impel, nudge, press, punch, shove, vigor 6 beef up, circle, expand, hustle, jostle, launch, peddle, propel, squash, squish, squush, starch, throng, thrust 8 ambition, bulldoze, compound, increase, oversell, pressure, shoulder, stimulus, vitality 9 advertise, incentive 10 aggrandize, enterprise, get-up-and-go, incitation, incitement, initiative
push around 4 bait, ride 5 bully, chivy, hound 6 badger, heckle, hector 8 bullyrag
pushful 5 brash 6 uppish, uppity 7 assured, forward, pushing 8 imposing, militant 9 assertive, assertory, confident, intrusive, obtruding, obtrusive, officious, presuming 10 aggressive 11 overweening 12 presumptuous 13 self-asserting, self-assertive

Pushkin *novel:* 12 Eugene Onegin *play:* 12 Boris Godunov
push off 2 go 4 exit, quit 5 leave 6 depart, get off 7 get away, pull out 8 withdraw
push on 2 go 3 hie 4 fare, pass, wend 6 repair, travel 7 journey, proceed
pushover 3 pie 4 snap 5 cinch, setup 6 breeze, picnic 8 duck soup, kid stuff 10 child's play
pushy see pushful
pusillanimous 6 coward, craven 7 chicken, gutless, unmanly 8 cowardly, poltroon 9 spunkless 11 lily-livered, poltroonish
puss 3 cat, kid, mug 4 face 5 child 6 kisser, kitten, moppet, nipper, visage 8 juvenile
pussyfoot 4 lurk, slip 5 creep, dodge, evade, glide, hedge, skulk, slide, slink, sneak, steal 6 weasel 7 gumshoe, shuffle 8 sidestep 10 equivocate, tergiverse 12 tergiversate
pustule 4 boil, wart 5 whelk 6 pimple 7 abscess 8 furuncle 9 carbuncle
put 3 air, fix, lay, set 4 call, give, levy, pose, turn, vent, word 5 couch, exact, focus, judge, place, rivet, state, stick 6 assess, fasten, fixate, impose, phrase, prefer, reckon, render, return, settle 7 express, propose, replace, restore, suggest 8 estimate, give back, propound 9 concenter
putative 7 reputed 8 supposed 11 conjectural, suppositive, suppository 12 hypothetical
put away 4 bury, do in, kill, slay 5 inter, plant, scrag, swill 6 cut off, entomb, finish, inhume, lay low, murder, punish 7 bump off, consume, destroy, dismiss, divorce, execute, reposit, take off, unmarry 8 carry off, dispatch, knock off 9 liquidate
put back 6 demote, return 7 replace, restore 8 give back 9 reinstate
put by 4 save 5 lay in, lay up 7 lay away 8 lay aside, salt away
put down 4 bump, bust 5 break, crush, quash, quell, shift, swill 6 demote, humble, punish, quench, squash, subdue 7 consume, declass, degrade, demerit, disrate, put away 8 disgrade, suppress 9 downgrade
put in 3 sow 4 seed 5 plant 6 insert
put off 5 delay, elude, repel 7 suspend 8 dissuade, postpone 9 frustrate 10 disconcert
put on 3 act, don, kid 4 fake, hire, pose, sham, show 5 bluff, feign, get on, mount, stage 6 affect, assume, draw on, employ, engage, slip on, strike, take on 7 mislead
put-on 3 act 4 face, fake, mask, sell, sham, show 5 cheat, cloak, cover, faked, guise, phony, posed, spoof 6 deceit, facade, parody 7 assumed, feigned 8 affected, disguise, mannered, spurious 9 deception, imposture 10 artificial, false front, masquerade
put out 3 ply, vex 4 gall, rile, roil 5 annoy, douse, exert, grate, issue, throw, wield 6 burn up, quench 7 inflame, publish, trouble 8 exercise, irritate 9 aggravate, disoblige, displease, incommode 10 discommode, dissatisfy, exasperate, extinguish 13 inconvenience
putrefy 3 rot 4 turn 5 decay, spoil, taint 6 molder 7 crumble 9 break down, decompose 12 disintegrate
putrid 3 bad 4 foul, high, olid 5 fetid 6 rancid, rotten, smelly, whiffy 7 corrupt, decayed, noisome, reeking, spoiled, vicious 8 depraved, nidorous, perverse 9 nefarious 10 malodorous *combining form:* 4 sapr 5 sapro
putter 4 club, mess 6 dawdle, doodle, fiddle, golfer, puddle, tinker 10 boondoggle
putting area 5 green
put together 4 form, join, make 5 build, erect, frame, shape, unite 7 fashion, produce 9 construct, fabricate
putty 3 mud 4 clay 6 cement
put up 3 can, hut 4 bunk, hike, jump, make, rear 5 board, boost, build, erect, forge, house, lodge, raise, set up, shape 6 bestow, billet, harbor, jack up, uprear 7 elevate, quarter 8 domicile, escalate, increase 9 construct *with:* 4 bear 5 stand 6 endure 8 tolerate
puzzle 3 why 4 foil, pose 5 addle, amaze, befog, poser, rebus, upset 6 baffle, enigma, fuddle, muddle, riddle 7 anagram, confuse, disturb, mystery, mystify, nonplus, perplex, problem, stumble 8 acrostic, befuddle, bewilder, confound, distract 9 conundrum, crossword, dumbfound, frustrate 10 closed book, disconcert, puzzlement 11 brainteaser *Chinese:* 7 tangram
puzzle out 5 break, solve 6 cipher, unfold 7 clear up, dope out, unravel 8 decipher, unriddle 9 figure out
Pygmalion *father:* 5 Belus *sister:* 4 Dido *statue, beloved:* 7 Galatea *victim:* 8 Sichaeus
pygmy 4 runt, tiny 5 dwarf, midge 6 midget, peewee 7 manikin, minikin 8 dwarfish, Tom Thumb 10 diminutive, homunculus, pocket-size 11 lilliputian
Pylades *companion:* 7 Orestes *father:* 9 Strophius *wife:* 7 Electra
pylon 4 post 5 tower 7 gateway
Pynchon novel 15 Gravity's Rainbow
pyramid 4 bank, heap, hill, mass, pile,

tomb 5 drift, mound, stack 7 windrow *builder:* 5 Khufu 6 Cheops
Pyramus' beloved 6 Thisbe
pyre 4 heap, pile
pyromaniac 8 arsonist
pyrosis 9 heartburn
pyrotechnics 9 fireworks
Pyrrha's husband 9 Deucalion
Pyrrhonian 7 doubter, skeptic, zetetic 10 unbeliever
Pyrrhus *kingdom:* 6 Epirus *victory:* 7 Asculum; (see also **Neoptolemus**)
Pythias' friend 5 Damon
python 3 boa 5 snake
pyx 3 box 4 case 5 chest 6 coffer, vessel

Q

Qatar's capital 4 Doha
Q.E.D. word 4 erat, quod
q.t., on the 8 in secret, secretly
qua 2 as 4 bird 5 heron
quack 3 cry 4 honk, sham 7 shammer 9 charlatan, pretender, quackster, simulator 10 mountebank 12 saltimbanque *combining form:* 5 pseud 6 pseudo
quad see **quadrangle**
quadra 5 frame 6 border, fillet, listel, plinth
quadragenarian 8 fortyish
quadrangle 4 yard 5 court 6 figure, square 9 courtyard, curtilage, enclosure
quadrant 6 fourth 10 instrument
quadratic 6 square 10 foursquare
quadriga 7 chariot
quadrille 5 dance, ombre 8 card game
quadrillion *combining form:* 4 peta
quadrillionth *combining form:* 5 femto
quadrivium subject 5 music 8 geometry 9 astronomy 10 arithmetic
quaestor 5 judge 8 official 9 paymaster, treasurer 10 prosecutor
quaff 3 sip 4 toss 5 drink, sup up 6 imbibe, sup off 7 swallow
quagga 3 ass
quaggy 4 soft 5 boggy, mushy, pappy, pulpy 6 spongy 7 squashy, squishy, squushy 8 squelchy, yielding
quagmire 3 bog, box, fen, fix, jam 4 hole, mire 5 marsh, swamp 6 corner, morass, pickle, plight, scrape, slough 7 dilemma 9 marshland 11 predicament
quahog 4 clam 11 cherrystone
quail 4 bird 5 colin, cower, wince 6 blanch, blench, cringe, flinch, recoil, shrink 7 massena, shudder, squinch, tremble 8 bobwhite *flock of:* 4 bevy *young:* 7 cheeper 8 squealer
quaint 3 odd 5 droll, funny, queer 7 antique, archaic, curious, oddball, strange, unusual 8 peculiar, singular 9 eccentric, laughable, whimsical 10 antiquated
quake 3 jar 5 shake, shock, waver 6 dither, quaver, quiver, shiver, tremor 7 shudder, temblor, tremble, twitter, vibrate 8 trembler, tremblor 9 fluctuate
Quaker 6 Friend 9 broadbrim *city:* 12 Philadelphia *colonizer:* 4 Penn *founder:* 3 Fox *poet:* 6 Barton 8 Whittier *state:* 12 Pennsylvania
qualification 5 might 7 ability 8 adequacy, aptitude, capacity 10 capability, competence
qualified 3 fit 4 able, good 5 fixed, tried 6 au fait, proper, proved, tested 7 capable, limited, partial, quizzed, trained 8 definite, eligible, examined, modified, reserved 9 competent 10 catechized, determined, instructed, restricted 11 conditional, disciplined
qualify 4 mark 6 assign, impute, soften 7 ascribe, certify, entitle, license, prepare 8 moderate 9 attribute, authorize
quality 4 fine, mark, rank 5 arete, class, elite, grade, merit, place, prime, savor, state, trait, value, worth 6 factor, flower, gentry, Grade A, status, virtue 7 aristoi, caliber, element, feature, footing, society, station, stature 8 capacity, five-star, position, property, standing, superior 9 affection, attribute, blue blood, character, excellent, first-rate, gentility, parameter, situation 10 blue-ribbon, excellence, first-class, patriciate, perfection, superbness *essential:* 8 suchness *suffix:* 2 cy, ty 3 ice, ity 4 ance, ancy, ence, ency, hood, ness, ship
qualm 5 demur, doubt 6 squeam, unease 7 scruple 8 mistrust 9 agitation, misgiving, objection, suspicion 10 conscience, foreboding, impatience, insecurity, reluctance, uneasiness 11 compunction, nervousness,

uncertainty 12 apprehension, perturbation, presentiment, remonstrance 13 unwillingness
qualmish 5 queer 6 queasy 9 nauseated
quandary 3 fix, jam 6 pickle, plight, scrape 7 dilemma 11 predicament
quantity 4 body, bulk, dose, unit 5 total 6 amount, budget, degree 9 aggregate ***fixed:*** 8 constant ***small:*** 3 bit, jot, ray 4 atom, dram, drop, iota, mite, whit 5 grain, scrap, shred, speck 7 modicum, smidgen
Quantrill's ____ 7 raiders
quantum 3 sum 4 body, bulk, meed, part 5 quota, share, total 6 amount, budget, ration 7 measure, portion 9 aggregate, allotment, allowance 13 apportionment ***of radiant energy:*** 6 photon ***of vibrational energy:*** 6 phonon ***theory originator:*** 6 Planck
quarantine 6 cut off 7 isolate 9 interdict, isolation
quarrel 3 row, war 4 beef, bolt, bump, dust, feud, fray, fuss, miff, spat, tiff, tile, vary 5 argue, arrow, brawl, broil, clash, fight, melee, run-in, scrap, set-to, words 6 affray, battle, bicker, chisel, differ, divide, dustup, fracas, hassle, ruckus, rumpus, squall, strife, thwart 7 bobbery, brabble, cast out, collide, contend, diamond, discord, dispute, dissent, fall out, rhubarb, ruction, scuffle, wrangle 8 catfight, conflict, squabble, to-and-fro, variance 9 altercate, bickering, brannigan, caterwaul, disaccord, imbroglio, scrimmage 10 contention, difference, difficulty, dissension, donnybrook, falling-out, free-for-all 11 altercation, battle royal, controversy, embroilment 12 disagreement
quarrelsome 6 brawly 7 adverse, counter, crabbed, hostile, scrappy, warlike 8 brawling, cankered, inimical, militant, ructious 9 bellicose, brawlsome, combative, irascible, irritable, rancorous, truculent 10 battlesome, pugnacious 11 belligerent, contentious 12 disputatious 13 argumentative
quarry 3 pit 4 game, mine, prey 5 chase, delve, pluck 6 victim 7 lozenge
quart 6 fourth ***four:*** 6 gallon ***metric:*** 5 liter, litre
quarter 3 hut 4 area, bunk, part 5 board, house, lodge, put up 6 barrio, billet, canton, fourth, harbor, sector 7 barrack, section 8 district, division, domicile, locality, precinct, quadrant 9 entertain 11 domiciliate ***circle:*** 8 quadrant ***note:*** 8 crotchet ***pint:*** 4 gill ***ship's:*** 6 fo'c'sle 10 forecastle ***year, Scottish:*** 5 raith
quarterback 4 boss 6 survey 7 oversee 9 supervise 10 footballer
quartet 4 four 6 tetrad 7 quatuor 8 foursome 10 quadruplet, quaternion
quartz 4 onyx, sard 5 agate, smoky 6 jasper, rubace 7 citrine, rubasse, sardius 8 amethyst, sardonyx, sunstone 9 cairngorm, carnelian 10 chalcedony
quash 4 undo, void 5 abate, annul, crush, quell 6 negate, quench, stifle, vacate 7 abolish, nullify, put down, repress, smother, squelch, vitiate 8 abrogate, dissolve, strangle, suppress 9 discharge
quasi 6 almost 7 seeming, virtual
Quasimodo 9 hunchback ***creator:*** 4 Hugo ***occupation:*** 10 bell ringer ***residence:*** 9 Notre Dame
quat 3 sty 4 beat, boil 6 squash 7 upstart
quaver 5 quake, shake, waver 6 dither, falter, shiver, tremor 7 shudder, tremble, twitter 8 hesitate 9 vacillate
quawk 5 heron 10 night heron
quay 4 dock, pier, slip 5 berth, jetty, levee, wharf
quean 4 bawd 5 wench, whore 6 harlot 7 hustler 8 meretrix 10 prostitute
queasy 4 open 5 fishy, queer, shady 6 qualmy 7 dubious 8 doubtful, qualmish 9 ambiguous, doubtable, nauseated, squeamish
Quebec ***college, university:*** 5 Laval, Lévis 6 McGill 9 Concordia ***largest city:*** 8 Montreal ***peninsula:*** 5 Gaspé ***vehicle:*** 7 caleche
queen 4 card 6 regina 7 goddess, monarch 8 chessman 9 sovereign ***Austria-Hungary:*** 12 Maria Theresa ***Belgian:*** 6 Astrid ***Danish:*** 8 Margaret, Margrete ***Egyptian:*** 9 Cleopatra 10 Hatshepsut ***English:*** 4 Anne, Mary 8 Victoria 9 Elizabeth ***French and English:*** 7 Eleanor ***Netherlands:*** 7 Beatrix, Juliana 10 Wilhelmina ***of heaven:*** 4 Mary, moon 7 Astarte ***of Isles:*** 6 Albion ***of Ithaca:*** 8 Penelope ***of Navarre:*** 8 Margaret ***of Scots:*** 4 Mary ***of Sheba:*** 6 Balkis ***of the Adriatic:*** 6 Venice ***of the Antilles:*** 4 Cuba ***of the East:*** 7 Zenobia ***of the fairies:*** 3 Mab 7 Titania ***of the gods:*** 4 Hera, Juno, Sati ***of the Nile:*** 9 Cleopatra ***of the North:*** 9 Edinburgh ***of the underworld:*** 3 Hel 4 Hela 10 Persephone, Proserpina ***Spanish:*** 8 Isabella ***Swedish:*** 9 Christina
Queen Anne's Lace 6 carrot
Queen of Spades ***author:*** 7 Pushkin ***composer:*** 11 Tchaikovsky
Queensland ***capital:*** 8 Brisbane ***explorer:*** 4 Cook
queer 5 droll, funny, weird 6 qualmy, queasy 7 bizarre, curious, dubious, oddball, strange, unusual 8 doubtful, obsessed, peculiar, qualmish, singular 9 eccentric, laughable, squeamish 10 outlandish
quell 5 crush, quash 6 quench, squash

7 conquer, put down 8 overcome, suppress, vanquish 9 subjugate 10 extinguish
Quemoy's neighbor 4 Amoy
quench 3 end, out 4 raze, ruin, sate 5 allay, crush, douse, quash, quell, slake, wreck 6 lessen, put out, reduce, squash 7 appease, assuage, content, destroy, gratify, lighten, put down, relieve, satiate, satisfy, shatter 8 decimate, decrease, demolish, destruct, diminish, mitigate, suppress 9 alleviate, terminate 10 extinguish
quenelle 8 meatball 9 forcemeat
quern 4 mill
querulous 5 huffy, waspy 6 crying 7 fretful, peevish, pettish, wailing, waspish, weeping 8 petulant, snappish 9 bemoaning, deploring, fractious, irritable, lamenting 10 blubbering, whimpering
query 3 ask 4 quiz 7 concern, dubiety, examine, inquire, inquiry 8 mistrust, question 9 catechize, dubiosity, dubitancy, suspicion 10 skepticism 11 interrogate, questioning, uncertainty, uncertitude 13 interrogation, interrogatory
quest 3 bay 4 howl, hunt, seek, wail 5 probe 6 search 7 delving, inquiry, probing, pursual, pursuit, seeking, ululate 8 pursuing, research 9 cast about, ferret out, pursuance, search for, search out 11 inquisition
question 3 ask, nut 4 poll, quiz 5 demur, doubt, issue, query 7 debrief, dispute, examine, inquire, inquiry, problem, protest, suspect 8 demurral, demurrer, mistrust 9 catechize, challenge, objection 10 difficulty, puzzle over 11 interrogate, wonder about 12 hesitate over, remonstrance 13 interrogation, interrogatory
questionable 4 moot 5 vague 6 unsure 7 dubious, obscure 8 arguable, doubtful, mootable, unlikely, untrusty 9 debatable, equivocal, refutable, trustless, uncertain 10 disputable, fly-by-night, improbable, unreliable 11 problematic 12 undependable
questioning 5 query 6 show-me 7 curious, inquiry 8 aporetic 9 inquiring, quizzical, skeptical 11 incredulous, inquisitive, unbelieving 12 disbelieving, disquisitive 13 interrogation, interrogatory, investigative
quetzal 4 bird, coin 6 trogon
queue 3 row 4 file, line, rank, tier 5 braid
quibble 4 carp 5 argue, cavil 6 argufy, bicker, hassle 7 chicane, dispute, wrangle 8 pettifog, squabble 9 criticize
quick 3 apt 4 able, core, deft, fast, keen, pith, root, wise 5 acute, agile, apace, brisk, canny, fleet, hasty, heart, rapid, ready, sharp, slick, smart, swift 6 abrupt, adroit, center, clever, nimble, prompt, speedy, sudden 7 capable, flat-out, hastily, knowing, rapidly, swiftly 8 speedily 9 breakneck, competent, dexterous, effective, effectual, impetuous, posthaste 10 expeditive, harefooted 11 expeditious, intelligent, quick-witted, sharp-witted 12 lickety-split, nimble-witted 13 expeditiously *combining form:* 3 oxy 5 tachy
quick bread 6 muffin 7 biscuit
quicken 4 goad, move, spur, stir, wake 5 hurry, liven, pique, rouse, speed 6 arouse, awaken, excite, hasten, induce, step up, vivify 7 actuate, animate, enliven, innerve, provoke, shake up, swiften 8 activate, energize, motivate, vitalize 9 galvanize, innervate, stimulate 10 accelerate, exhilarate, invigorate, vivificate
quickness 4 gait, pace 5 speed 8 celerity, legerity, rapidity, velocity 9 rapidness, swiftness
quicksand 3 bog 4 mire, syrt 6 syrtis
quicksilver 7 mercury 9 mercurial
quick-tempered 5 cross, ratty 6 cranky 7 peppery 8 choleric 9 irascible 10 passionate
quick-witted 3 apt, hep 4 keen, wise 5 acute, alert, canny, ready, sharp, slick, smart, witty 6 brainy, bright, clever, prompt 7 knowing 8 humorous 9 brilliant, facetious 11 intelligent, penetrating, penetrative
quid 3 cut, wad 4 chew 5 pound 9 sovereign
quiddity 6 trifle 7 essence, quibble
quidnunc see **rumormonger**
quiescent 4 calm 5 quiet, still 6 hushed, latent, placid, stilly 7 abeyant, dormant, halcyon, lurking 10 untroubled
quiet 4 calm, hush, idle, lull, stop 5 abate, allay, inert, plain, shush, still, tasty, whist 6 asleep, becalm, homely, hushed, lessen, placid, settle, shut up, silent, simple, sleepy, soothe, stilly, subdue 7 compose, halcyon, hushful, passive, silence, subdued 8 choke off, decrease, inactive, tasteful 9 cessation, noiseless, soundless, stillness 10 restrained, untroubled 11 inobtrusive, termination, tranquilize, unobtrusive
quietus 5 death, sleep 6 demise 7 decease, passing, silence 8 curtains 10 inactivity
quill 3 pen 5 spine, spool 6 bobbin 7 feather 8 plectrum
quill pig 9 porcupine
quilt 4 pouf, puff 8 bedcover 9 bedspread, comforter, eiderdown 11 counterpane *design:* 8 trapunto
quink 5 brant, goose
quintessence 4 pith, soul 5 stuff 6 bottom, marrow 7 epitome 8 last word, ultimate 9 substance 12 essentiality
quintessential 4 pith, soul 5 ideal, model, stuff 6 bottom, marrow 7 classic, essence,

typical 9 classical, exemplary, substance 10 archetypal, prototypal 12 prototypical
quintillion *combining form:* 3 exa
quintillionth *combining form:* 4 atto
quintuple 8 fivefold
quintuplets *famous:* 6 Dionne
quip 3 gag 4 gibe, gird, jape, jeer, jest, joke 5 crack, fleer, flout, sally, scoff, sneer 8 drollery 9 wisecrack, witticism
quipster 3 wag, wit 5 comic, droll, joker 6 jester 8 comedian, funnyman, humorist, jokester
quirk 4 bend, quip 5 crook 6 groove, retort 7 channel 9 mannerism 11 peculiarity
quirt 4 whip
quisling 7 traitor 8 turncoat
quit 3 act, pay 4 bear, drop, exit, halt, stop 5 carry, cease, chuck, clear, leave, pay up 6 behave, demean, depart, deport, desert, desist, get off, resign, retire, secede, settle, square 7 abandon, comport, conduct, forsake, get away, satisfy, take off 8 clear off, give over, knock off, leave off, renounce, surcease, withdraw 9 discharge, liquidate, surrender, terminate, throw over 10 relinquish 11 discontinue
quite 3 all, far 4 just, well 5 fully, in all 6 in toto, purely, rather, wholly 7 all told, exactly, totally, utterly 8 all in all, cleverly, entirely, somewhat 9 perfectly 10 altogether, completely, thoroughly
quittance 6 amends 7 redress 8 reprisal 9 indemnity 10 recompense, reparation 11 restitution 12 compensation
quitter 4 funk 6 coward, craven, funker 7 chicken 8 poltroon 11 yellowbelly
quiver 4 beat 5 flash, gleam, glint, pulse, quake, shake, throb 6 dither, glance, shiver, tremor 7 glimmer, glisten, glitter, pulsate, shimmer, shudder, sparkle, tremble, twinkle, twitter 9 palpitate
quiverleaf 5 aspen
quiver tree 4 aloe
Quixote see Don Quixote
quixotic 8 fanciful, illusory, romantic 9 fantastic, visionary 10 chimerical, idealistic 11 impractical
quiz 3 ask 4 lout, mock, razz, twit 5 query, rally, scout, taunt 6 deride, oddity, zombie 7 examine, inquire, oddball 8 original, question, ridicule 9 catechize, character, eccentric 11 interrogate
quizzical 6 show-me 7 curious, probing 8 aporetic 9 searching, skeptical 11 incredulous, inquisitive, questioning, unbelieving 12 disbelieving
quizzing glass 7 monocle
quodlibet 6 debate, medley 8 fantasia, question
quoin 5 angle, facet, wedge 6 corner 7 lozenge 8 keystone, voussoir
quoit 4 ring, rope 5 cover 6 circle
quoits 4 game *peg:* 3 hob
quondam 3 old 4 late, once, past 6 bygone, former, whilom 7 onetime 8 sometime 9 erstwhile
quorum 7 council 8 majority
quota 3 cut, lot 4 bite, meed, part 5 share, slice 6 divide, parcel, ration 7 measure, partage, portion, prorate, quantum 9 allotment, allowance, apportion
quotation 3 bid 5 offer, price 7 excerpt, passage
quotation mark *French:* 9 guillemet
quote 4 cite, list, mark 5 refer 6 adduce, notice, set off 7 excerpt
quotidian 5 daily, plain, usual 7 diurnal, routine 8 everyday, ordinary, workaday 9 circadian 12 unremarkable
Quo Vadis *author:* 11 Sienkiewicz *character:* 4 Nero 5 Lygia, Peter 8 Vinicius 9 Petronius

R

Ra ***son:*** **6** Khonsu ***wife:*** **3** Mut
Raamah ***father:*** **4** Cush ***son:*** **5** Dedan, Sheba
Rabbi Ben Ezra author **8** Browning
rabbit **4** cony **5** bunny, coney, lapin ***female:*** **3** doe ***fictional:*** **5** Fiver, Hazel, Mopsy, Peter **6** Flopsy, Harvey **7** Thumper **8** Crusader, Ricochet **9** Bugs Bunny **10** Cottontail **11** Easter Bunny ***food:*** **5** salad **6** carrot **7** lettuce
rabbitlike **8** leporine
rabble **3** mob **4** many, raff, rout, scum **5** dregs, scurf, trash **6** masses, people, polloi, public, ragtag **7** doggery **8** canaille, populace, riffraff, unwashed, varletry **9** hoi polloi, other half, tag and rag **10** commonalty, roughscuff **11** bourgeoisie, proletariat, rank and file
rabble-rouser **9** demagogue
Rabelais character **9** Gargantua **10** Pantagruel
rabid **3** mad **4** keen, wild **5** crazy, ultra **6** crazed, insane **7** extreme, fanatic, frantic, furious, radical, zealous **8** demented, deranged, frenetic, frenzied, obsessed, ultraist **9** delirious, extremist **10** corybantic **12** enthusiastic
rabies **5** lyssa **11** hydrophobia
raccoon **5** panda **10** cacomistle ***relative:*** **5** coati **10** coatimundi
race **4** boil, bolt, clan, dash, drag, folk, gill, lash, rush, tear, type **5** breed, brook, chase, creek, fling, house, shoot, speed, stock, tribe **6** career, charge, course, endure, family, nation, people, runnel, stream **7** culture, kindred, lineage, Negroid, rivulet, running, variety **8** marathon **9** Caucasian, Mongoloid ***auto:*** **5** rally **6** rallye **9** grand prix ***combining form:*** **3** gen **4** geno, phyl **5** ethno, phylo
racecourse **4** oval, turf **5** track ***combining form:*** **4** drom **5** drome, dromo
racehorse ***champion:*** **5** Kelso **6** Forego **7** Man O' War **8** Affirmed, Citation **9** Riva Ridge **10** War Admiral **11** Forward Pass, Seattle Slew, Secretariat **12** Native Dancer
Rachel ***father:*** **5** Laban ***husband:*** **5** Jacob ***servant:*** **6** Bilhah ***sister:*** **4** Leah ***son:*** **6** Joseph **8** Benjamin
rachis **4** back **5** spine **8** backbone **9** vertebrae
rachitic **5** shaky **6** wobbly **7** rackety, rickety **10** rattletrap
rachitis **7** rickets
___ Rachmaninoff **6** Sergei
racing enthusiast **8** railbird
rack **3** try **4** pain **5** frame, wring **6** harrow, martyr **7** afflict, agonize, crucify, oppress, sawbuck, torment, torture **8** distress, sawhorse **9** persecute **10** excruciate
racket **3** din **5** babel **6** clamor, hubbub, jangle, tumult, uproar **8** brouhaha **10** hullabaloo **11** pandemonium
rack up **3** win **4** gain **5** reach, score **6** attain **7** achieve, realize **10** accomplish
raconteur **11** storyteller
racy **4** blue **5** broad, fiery, salty, shady, spicy, zesty **6** purple, risqué, snappy, wicked **7** gingery, peppery, piquant, pungent **8** off-color, spirited **10** suggestive
Radames' beloved **4** Aïda
radar image **4** blip
Raddai ***brother:*** **5** David ***father:*** **5** Jesse
radiance **5** glory **8** splendor
radiant **4** glad **6** bright, cheery, lucent **7** beaming, fulgent, lambent **8** cheerful, luminous **9** brilliant, effulgent, refulgent **12** incandescent
radiate **4** beam, burn **5** gleam, shine, strew **6** spread **7** diffuse, diverge **8** disperse **9** circulate, eradicate, propagate
radiation unit **3** rem, rep **8** roentgen
radiator **6** cooler, heater **11** transmitter
radical **4** acyl, root **5** basal, basic, pinko, rabid, rebel, ultra, vital **6** bottom **7** extreme, fanatic, primary **8** advanced, agitator, cardinal, inherent, nihilist, reformer, tolerant, ultraist **9** anarchist, essential, extremist, insurgent, intrinsic **10** separatist, subversive, underlying **11** broad-minded, fundamental, out-and-outer, progressive, reactionary **12** foundational, revolutional, secessionist **13** revolutionary ***combining form:*** **2** yl **3** oyl **5** ylene ***mathematical:*** **4** surd
radicle **4** root **5** radix **9** hypocotyl
radio **8** wireless ***frequency range:*** **8** waveband
radioactive debris **7** fallout
radium ***symbol:*** **2** Ra
radius **5** ambit, orbit, range, reach, scope,

sweep 6 extent 7 compass, purview 9 extension
radix 4 base, root 6 etymon, source
radon 5 niton 6 thoron 7 actinon ***symbol:*** 2 Rn
raffish 4 fast, wild 6 sporty 8 rakehell 12 devil-may-care
raffle 4 game 6 refuse 7 lottery, rubbish, serrate 8 riffraff
raft 3 lot, mat 4 slew 5 balsa, float
rafter 4 beam, bird 10 flycatcher
rag 3 fun, jaw, kid, rib 4 fool, jive, joke, josh, rail, rant, razz 5 baste, jolly, scold, tease 9 newspaper
ragamuffin 3 bum 4 hobo, waif 5 tramp 6 loafer, orphan 7 ragshag, vagrant, wastrel 8 vagabond 9 scarecrow
rage 3 cry, fad, ire, mad 4 boil, burn, chic, fume, fury, mode, rant, whim 5 anger, craze, fancy, freak, mania, style, upset, vogue, wrath 6 blow up, frenzy, furore, seethe, vagary 7 bristle, caprice, conceit, fashion, flare up 8 acerbity, acrimony, asperity, boil over, crotchet, hysteria 9 agitation 10 dernier cri 11 indignation
ragged 4 rent, torn 5 dingy, faded, seedy 6 frayed, shabby 7 patched, shreddy, worn-out 8 battered, frazzled, tattered 10 threadbare 11 dilapidated
raging 4 wild 5 dirty, rough 6 stormy 7 furious 8 blustery 9 turbulent 10 blustering 11 tempestuous
rags 5 dress 6 attire, shreds, things 7 apparel, clothes, raiment, ribbons, tatters 8 clothing 10 attirement 11 habiliments, odds and ends
ragtag see **rabble**
ragwort 7 senecio 10 butterweed
Rahab ***husband:*** 6 Salmon ***son:*** 4 Boaz
raid 3 rob 4 loot, sack 5 foray, harry, onset, rifle, waste 6 harass, inroad, invade, maraud, pirate, ravage 7 assault, despoil, overrun, plunder 8 invasion, picaroon, spoliate 9 devastate, incursion, irruption, onslaught, overswarm
raider 6 looter, pirate, sacker 7 forager, ravager, spoiler 8 marauder, picaroon, pillager, ravisher 9 plunderer 10 freebooter 11 bushwhacker
rail 3 jaw 4 rate 5 scold 6 berate, revile 7 bawl out, upbraid 8 banister 10 balustrade, tongue-lash, vituperate
rail bird 4 sora
railing 8 banister 10 balustrade ***part:*** 8 baluster
raillery 6 satire 10 lampoonery 13 satiricalness
railroad 5 frame 9 iron horse ***car:*** 5 coach, diner, stock 6 hopper 7 caboose, gondola, Pullman ***engine:*** 10 locomotive ***station:*** 5 depot ***underground:*** 6 subway ***worker:*** 6 porter 7 fireman 8 brakeman, engineer 9 conductor 10 dispatcher 11 gandy dancer
raiment 4 clad, duds, garb, togs 5 array, dress 6 attire, clothe, things 7 apparel, clothes, garment 8 clothing, enclothe 10 attirement 11 habiliments
rain 6 mizzle, shower 7 drizzle 8 downpour ***combining form:*** 4 hyet 5 hyeto, ombro, pluvi 6 pluvia, pluvio ***fine:*** 6 serein
rainbow 3 arc 4 iris 5 gamut 7 fantasy 8 illusion, phantasy 9 pipe dream ***bridge:*** 7 Bifrost ***chaser:*** 9 visionary ***combining form:*** 4 irid 5 irido ***goddess:*** 4 Iris
rainbow fish 5 guppy, trout 6 wrasse
raincoat 3 mac 4 mack 6 poncho 7 slicker 10 mackintosh
rain gauge 8 udometer
rain leader 9 downspout
rain tree 9 monkeypod
raise 2 up 4 abet, ante, grow, hike, jack, jump, lift, pump, rear 5 boost, breed, build, erect, exalt, hoist, put up 6 foment, gather, incite, jack up, muster, pick up, stir up, take up, upbear, uphold, uplift, uprear, whip up 7 bring up, collect, elevate, enhance, inflate, produce, provoke 8 addition, assemble, congress, heighten, increase 9 accession, accretion, construct, cultivate, forgather, increment, instigate, propagate, resurrect 10 congregate, rendezvous 12 augmentation ***nap:*** 5 tease ***spirits:*** 5 elate
raisin 7 sultana
raison d' ____ 4 etre
raja 4 king 5 chief, ruler 6 prince 9 dignitary
rake 3 cad 4 beat, comb, grub, roué, tool 5 angle, scour, slope 6 forage, rascal, search 7 coxcomb, playboy, ransack, rummage 8 finecomb 9 implement, libertine 10 profligate 11 inclination
rakehell 4 fast, wild 6 rascal, sporty 7 raffish 8 rascally 9 dissolute, libertine 10 licentious, profligate 12 devil-may-care
rake's look 4 ogle
Rake's Progress engraver 7 Hogarth
rakish see **rakehell**
rally 4 fire, lout, mock, quiz, race, razz, stir, twit, wake, whet 5 harry, renew, rouse, scout, taunt, tease, waken, worry 6 arouse, awaken, bestir, deride, harass, kindle, muster, perk up, pick up 7 brace up, enliven, marshal, recover, refresh, restore 8 mobilize, organize, ridicule 9 challenge, come round, tantalize 10 invigorate
rallying cry 5 motto 6 slogan
ram 5 Aries, crash, drive, sheep, stick, stuff 6 plunge, strike, thrust 7 jam-pack, warship
Rama's wife 4 Sita
ramble 3 gad 4 roam, rove, turn, walk

5 drift, range, stray 6 depart, sprawl, stroll, wander 7 digress, diverge, excurse, meander, saunter, traipse 8 divagate, straggle 9 gallivant

rambunctious 5 rowdy 6 unruly 7 raucous 8 rowdyish 9 termagant, turbulent 10 boisterous, rowdydowdy, tumultuous

ramification 6 branch 8 offshoot 9 branching, outgrowth 11 consequence

Ramona author 7 Jackson

ramose 8 branched

ramp 5 apron, climb, storm 6 easing

rampage 4 orgy 5 binge, fling, spree 6 uproar 7 splurge, turmoil

rampageous 4 wild 6 unruly 7 riotous

rampant 4 rank, rife 6 ruling 7 current, popular, regnant 9 excessive, prevalent 10 immoderate, inordinate, widespread

rampart 7 bastion, bulwark, parapet 10 breastwork

ramshackle 7 rickety 10 dissipated 11 dilapidated

ram's mate 3 ewe

ranch 8 estancia, hacienda ***worker:*** 6 cowboy, gaucho 7 cowgirl, cowhand, cowpoke 10 cowpuncher

rancid 4 high, olid 5 fetid 6 putrid, smelly, whiffy 7 noisome, reeking 8 nidorous 10 malodorous

rancor 6 animus, enmity 9 animosity, antipathy, hostility, virulence 10 antagonism, bitterness

rancorous 4 evil 6 bitter, malign, wicked 7 hateful, hostile, vicious 8 spiteful, virulent 9 malicious, malignant, vitriolic 10 despiteful, malevolent 12 antagonistic

Rand, Ayn ***novel:*** 6 Anthem 12 Fountainhead 13 Atlas Shrugged

random 4 spot 7 aimless, anywise, unaimed 8 slapdash 9 desultory, haphazard, hit-or-miss, irregular, unplanned 10 accidental, contingent, designless, fortuitous, incidental, objectless 11 any which way, haphazardly, promiscuous, purposeless

randy 4 lewd 7 lustful, satyric 9 lecherous, libertine 10 lascivious, libidinous, licentious 11 incontinent

range 3 ken, row, run 4 area, bias, home, line, roam, rove, site, sort, span, tune, vary 5 align, ambit, drift, field, gamut, haunt, orbit, order, reach, realm, scope, space, stray, sweep, width 6 assort, circle, differ, domain, extend, extent, length, line up, matter, radius, ramble, sphere, spread, wander 7 compass, dispose, earshot, expanse, eyeshot, habitat, horizon, meander, purview, stretch 8 confines, locality, panorama, province, straggle, vicinity 9 fluctuate, gallivant, magnitude, territory

range finder 9 telemeter 10 tachymeter

rangy 5 lanky 6 gangly 7 spindly 8 gangling

rank 3 row 4 file, foul, line, lush, olid, rate, sort, tier 5 class, dirty, fetid, funky, grade, gross, grown, humid, order, place, queue, state, utter 6 assort, cachet, coarse, estate, filthy, lavish, putrid, rancid, smelly, smutty, status, string, vulgar 7 arrange, capital, dignity, echelon, footing, glaring, noisome, obscene, peerage, perfect, precede, profuse, rampant, raunchy, reeking, station, stature 8 absolute, capacity, classify, complete, evaluate, flagrant, gentrice, indecent, outright, position, positive, prestige, standing, stinking 9 character, downright, egregious, exuberant, loathsome, luxuriant, overgrown, repulsive, situation 10 consummate, malodorous, noticeable 11 consequence, conspicuous, outstanding, unmitigated ***honorary:*** 8 brevetcy ***suffix:*** 2 cy

rank and file 5 plebs 6 people, plebes 8 populace 9 commonage, commoners, common men, plebeians 10 commonalty 11 third estate

rankle 3 irk, vex 5 annoy 6 bother, fester, harass, obsess, plague 7 torment 8 irritate 9 aggravate 10 exasperate

ransack 3 rob 4 beat, comb, grub, loot, rake 5 rifle, scour 6 forage, search 7 plunder, relieve, rummage, stick up 8 finecomb

Ran's husband 5 Aegir

ransom 3 buy 4 free 6 redeem, regain 7 recover, release 8 liberate, retrieve

rant 3 jaw, rag 4 huff, rage, rail, rate, rave 5 mouth, orate, scold 6 berate 7 bawl out, bluster, bombast, declaim, fustian, soapbox 8 bloviate, harangue, perorate, rhetoric 10 vituperate 11 rodomontade

ranula 4 cyst

rap 3 bob, hit, wig 4 chat, chin, lick, skin, swat, talk, tunk, wipe, yarn 5 blame, knock, prose, swipe 6 rebuke 7 censure, chiding, condemn, reproof 8 causerie, denounce, reproach 9 criticize, reprehend, reprimand, reprobate 10 admonition, conference, denunciate, discussion

rapacious 6 fierce 8 ravening, ravenous 9 predative, predatory, raptorial, vulturine, vulturish, vulturous 10 gluttonous 11 predatorial

rapacity 5 greed 6 demand 7 avarice, avidity 8 cupidity, exaction, voracity

rape 4 cole, ruin 5 spoil 6 defile, ravage, ravish 7 debauch, despoil, outrage, plunder, seizure, violate 9 violation 10 spoliation

Rape of the Lock ***author:*** 4 Pope ***heroine:*** 7 Belinda

Raphael ***birthplace:*** 6 Urbino (Italy) ***subject:*** 7 Madonna ***teacher:*** 8 Perugino

rapid 4 fast 5 agile, brisk, fleet, hasty, quick, swift 6 nimble, speedy 7 hurried

9 breakneck, quickened 10 expeditive 11 expeditious
rapidity 4 gait, pace 5 speed 8 celerity, velocity 9 quickness, swiftness
rapids 6 dalles 10 whitewater
rapine 7 pillage, plunder 10 spoliation
Rappaccini's Daughter 8 Beatrice *author:* 9 Hawthorne
rapport 5 unity 7 concord, harmony
rapscallion see **rascal**
rap session 6 confab, parley 7 palaver 8 colloquy 10 colloquium, conference, discussion
rapt 4 deep 6 intent 7 engaged 8 absorbed, immersed 9 engrossed, wrapped up 11 preoccupied
raptorial see **rapacious**
rapture 6 heaven 7 ecstasy 8 rhapsody 9 transport 13 seventh heaven
rara ___ 4 avis
rare 3 few 4 fine, thin 6 choice, dainty, scarce, seldom, select, subtle, unique 7 elegant, subtile, tenuous, unusual 8 delicate, singular, sporadic, superior, uncommon, unwonted 9 attenuate, exquisite, recherché 10 attenuated, infrequent, occasional, unfrequent, unordinary 11 exceptional 13 extraordinary
rarefied 4 thin 6 subtle 7 subtile, tenuous 9 attenuate 10 attenuated
rarefy 4 thin 9 attenuate
rarely 5 extra 6 little, seldom 7 unoften 9 extremely, unusually 10 hardly ever
raring 4 agog, avid, keen 5 eager 6 ardent 7 anxious, athirst, thirsty 9 impatient 10 breathless
rarity 6 oddity 7 fewness 8 scarcity
rascal 5 devil, knave, rogue, scamp 7 lowlife, skellum, villain 8 mischief, scalawag 9 miscreant, scoundrel, skeezicks 10 blackguard 11 rapscallion *Irish:* 8 spalpeen
rash 5 hasty, silly 6 abrupt, daring, madcap, plague, sudden, unwary, unwise 7 foolish 8 careless, epidemic, headlong, heedless, outbreak, reckless 9 audacious, daredevil, foolhardy, hotheaded, impetuous, imprudent, impulsive, unadvised, venturous 10 ill-advised, incautious, incogitant, indiscreet, mad-brained, unthinking 11 adventurous, injudicious, precipitate, precipitous, temerarious, thoughtless, venturesome 12 unconsidered 13 adventuresome, inconsiderate
rasp 4 file 5 grate 6 scrape, wheeze 7 scratch
raspberry 3 boo 4 bird, hiss, hoot, pooh, razz 5 bazoo 7 catcall 8 pooh-pooh
raspy 3 dry 5 harsh, rough 6 hoarse, snappy 7 grating, jarring, peevish, pettish, raucous 8 petulant, prickish, snappish 9 irritable
rat 3 pad 4 fink, heel, scab 5 louse 6 defect, desert, inform, rodent, snitch, squeak, squeal 7 caitiff, stoolie 8 apostate, defector, informer, recreant, renegade, renounce, runagate, squealer, turncoat 9 bandicoot, repudiate, turnabout 10 apostatize, tergiverse 11 stool pigeon ***female:*** 3 doe
rate 3 tab 4 cost, earn, rail, rank 5 assay, class, grade, merit, price, scale, scold, set at, value 6 assess, berate, charge, degree, revile, survey, tariff 7 apprize, bawl out, chew out, deserve, upbraid, valuate 8 appraise, classify, estimate, evaluate, price tag 10 proportion, tongue-lash
rather 5 quite 6 enough, fairly, in lieu, kind of, pretty, sort of 7 instead 8 passably, somewhat 9 averagely, tolerably 10 moderately, more or less 11 alternately 12 considerably 13 alternatively
ratify 5 enact 7 approve, confirm, endorse, license 8 accredit, sanction, validate
rating 4 mark, rank 5 grade 6 rebuke 8 standing
ratio 5 scale 7 percent 8 quotient 10 proportion
ratiocination 8 judgment, sequitur 9 inference, reasoning 10 conclusion
ration 4 dole, meed, part 5 allot, quota, share 6 assign, divide, parcel 7 measure, mete out, prorate, quantum 8 allocate, division 9 allotment, allowance 10 assignment 13 apportionment
rational 4 calm, cool, sane 5 lucid, sober, sound 6 normal, stable 7 logical, prudent 8 sensible 9 judicious 10 consequent, reasonable 11 circumspect, intelligent, levelheaded
rationale 6 reason 11 explanation 13 justification
rationalize 7 explain, justify 10 account for
rattle 3 gab, jaw, yak 4 chat, faze 5 abash, addle, clack, run on, upset 6 babble, gabble 7 chatter, clatter, confuse, disturb, perplex 8 bewilder, confound, distract 9 discomfit, embarrass
rattlebrained 5 dizzy, giddy, silly 7 flighty 8 skittish 9 frivolous 11 emptyheaded
rattling 4 very 6 damned, mighty 7 parlous 8 snapping, spanking, whacking, whopping 9 extremely 11 exceedingly
ratty 5 cross, testy 6 cranky, shabby, tetchy, touchy 7 peppery, unkempt 8 choleric 9 irascible, temperish
raucous 3 dry 5 gruff, harsh, rough, rowdy 6 hoarse, unruly 7 brusque, grating, jarring, squawky 8 rowdyish, strident 9 termagant, turbulent 10 boisterous, disorderly,

rowdydowdy, stridulent, stridulous, tumultuous 11 rumbustious
raunchy 4 foul 5 dirty, messy, nasty 6 coarse, filthy, sloppy, smutty, unneat, untidy, vulgar 7 obscene, unkempt 8 ill-kempt, indecent, slipshod, slovenly 10 disheveled
ravage 3 rob 4 loot, raze, ruin, sack 5 crush, harry, havoc, spoil, strip, waste, wreck 6 devast, devour, invade 7 despoil, destroy, overrun, pillage, plunder, ransack, scourge 8 deflower, demolish, desolate, encroach, spoliate, trespass 9 depredate, desecrate, devastate, overpower, overthrow, overwhelm
rave 4 rant 5 drool, mouth, orate 7 declaim, enthuse, soapbox 8 bloviate, harangue, perorate, rhapsody 10 rhapsodize
ravel 5 snarl 6 muddle, tangle 7 perplex 8 entangle 10 complicate
ravelings 4 lint
Ravel work 6 Bolero
raven 3 jet 4 bird, ebon, inky, prey 5 black, ebony, jetty, sable 7 despoil, plunder 9 pitch-dark 10 pitch-black ***combining form:*** 5 corax ***relating to:*** 7 corvine
Raven, The ***author:*** 3 Poe ***refrain:*** 9 Nevermore
ravenous 6 hungry 7 starved 8 edacious, famished, starving 9 rapacious, voracious
ravine 3 cut, gap 4 gulf, pass 5 abyss, chasm, cleft, clove, gorge, gulch, gully, notch 6 arroyo, canyon, clough, coulee, defile, gutter, nullah 7 crevice, fissure 8 barranca, barranco, crevasse ***Mt. Washington's:*** 9 Tuckerman
ravish 3 rob 4 rape 5 spoil 6 defile 7 despoil, outrage, pillage, violate 8 deflower, entrance, overcome 9 deflorate, enrapture, transport
raw 4 nude, rude 5 crass, crude, fresh, green, gross, naked, rough, young 6 callow, coarse, impure, native, unclad, unhewn, unripe, vulgar 7 uncouth, untried 8 buff-bare, stripped, uncooked, unformed, ungraded, unsorted, untaught, unversed 9 au naturel, inelegant, roughhewn, run-of-mine, unclothed, undressed, unmatured, unrefined, untutored 10 stark-naked, unfinished, unpolished, unseasoned 11 unfashioned, unpracticed 13 inexperienced
rawboned 4 bony, lank, lean 5 gaunt, lanky, spare 6 skinny 7 angular, scraggy, scrawny
ray 4 beam, beta 5 alpha, gamma, gleam, light, manta, shaft, shine, shoot, skate, trace 6 radius, streak 7 radiate, sawfish, torpedo 8 particle 9 irradiate, radiation
raze 4 ruin, undo 5 wrack, wreck 6 unmake 7 destroy, unbuild, unframe 8 decimate, demolish
razor 3 cut 5 shave
razz 3 kid, rag, rib 4 fool, jest, joke, josh, lout, mock, quiz, twit 5 jolly, rally, scout, taunt 6 banter, deride, heckle 8 ridicule; (see also **raspberry**)
re 4 as to 5 as for 7 apropos 9 as regards, regarding 10 as respects, concerning, respecting 13 with respect to
reach 2 go 3 get, ken, run, win 4 buck, come, gain, hand, make, move, pass, show, sway 5 ambit, get at, get in, orbit, range, scope, score, sweep, touch 6 affect, arrive, attain, extend, extent, rack up, radius, show up, turn up 7 achieve, compass, contact, horizon, purview, realize, stretch 8 approach 9 extension, influence 10 accomplish
react 6 behave 7 respond
___ reaction 5 chain 7 nuclear 8 chemical
reactionary 4 fogy, tory 5 blimp, right 7 diehard, fogyish, old-line, radical 8 mossback, orthodox, rightist, royalist 11 bitter-ender, right-winger, standpatter 12 conservative
reactionist see **reactionary**
reactivate 5 renew 6 revive 8 rekindle, renovate, retrieve, revivify 9 resurrect 10 revitalize 11 resuscitate
read 3 say 4 mark, scan, show 5 proof 6 peruse, record 7 dictate 8 indicate, register ***inability to:*** 8 dyslexia
readable 7 legible
reader 6 lector, primer 8 bookworm 9 anthology
readily 4 well 6 easily, freely 7 lightly 12 effortlessly
readiness 4 ease 5 skill 7 address, fluency, prowess, sleight 8 alacrity, dispatch, facility, goodwill 9 dexterity, eloquence 10 expedition, volubility 11 promptitude
reading 7 version 9 rendition
readjust 6 modify 7 reorder 8 reorient 9 rearrange, reshuffle 10 reorganize 11 reconstruct, reorientate
ready 3 apt, fit, fix, get, set 4 fain, gird, live, make, prep 5 adept, brace, prime, prone, psych, quick, steel 6 active, expert, make up, minded, primed, prompt 7 dynamic, fortify, prepare, skilled, willing 8 adjusted, disposed, imminent, inclined, masterly, prepared, skillful 9 qualified 10 proficient, strengthen 11 predisposed
real 4 true 5 being, pucka, pukka, sound, valid 6 actual, honest 7 certain, genuine, sincere 8 bona fide, existing 9 authentic, necessary, undoubted, unfeigned, veridical 10 undeniable 12 indisputable
realism 6 verism 7 verismo

realistic 4 hard, sane 5 sober, sound 6 astute, earthy, shrewd 8 lifelike, rational, sensible, veristic 9 practical, pragmatic 10 hard-boiled, hardheaded, reasonable, unromantic 11 down-to-earth, nonacademic, pragmatical, utilitarian 12 matter-of-fact 13 unsentimental
reality 4 fact 5 truth
realize 3 win 4 gain 5 fancy, image, reach, score, think 6 attain, rack up, vision 7 achieve, feature, imagine 8 conceive, envisage, envision 10 accomplish
realm 5 orbit, range, scope, sweep 6 empire, extent, radius 7 compass, purview *suffix:* 3 dom
reanimation 7 rebirth, revival 10 renascence, resurgence 11 renaissance 12 risorgimento
reap 5 glean 6 garner, gather, thresh 7 harvest 8 ingather
rear 4 back, hind, lift, ramp, rump, seat, tail 5 after, breed, build, erect, fanny, hoist, nurse, put up, raise, set up 6 behind, bottom, foster, hinder, pick up, retral, take up, uphold, uplift 7 bring up, elevate, hind end, nurture, upraise 8 backside, buttocks, hindmost 9 construct, posterior
rear end 4 rump, seat, tail 5 fanny 6 behind, bottom 8 backside, buttocks, derriere
rearmost 4 last 5 final 6 latest, latter 7 closing 8 eventual, terminal, ultimate 10 concluding
rearrange see **readjust**
rearward 4 back 9 posterior
Rea Silvia, Rhea Silvia ***father:*** 7 Numitor ***son:*** 5 Remus 7 Romulus
reason 3 why, wit 4 mind, nous 5 cause, infer, proof, think 6 ground, motive, sanity, senses, spring, whyfor 7 account, reflect 8 argument, cogitate, logicize, lucidity, occasion, persuade, saneness 9 cerebrate, inference, intellect, rationale, soundness, speculate, wherefore 10 antecedent, deliberate 11 determinant, explanation 13 consideration, justification, ratiocination, understanding
reasonable 3 low 5 cheap, sound 6 modest, undear 7 logical, low-cost, popular 8 discreet, moderate, rational, sensible, uncostly 9 low-priced, temperate, unextreme 10 affordable, consequent, controlled, restrained 11 inexpensive, intelligent
reasoning 5 logic
reasonless 3 mad 4 daft 5 crazy 6 crazed, insane 7 cracked, invalid, lunatic 8 demented, deranged 9 bedlamite, illogical, sophistic 10 fallacious, irrational 11 nonrational
rebate 5 taper 6 lessen, reduce, refund 7 dwindle 8 decrease, diminish, discount, taper off 9 abatement, deduction, drain away, reduction 11 subtraction
Rebecca ***beloved:*** 7 Ivanhoe ***father:*** 5 Isaac
Rebekah ***brother:*** 5 Laban ***father:*** 7 Bethuel ***husband:*** 5 Isaac ***nurse:*** 7 Deborah ***son:*** 4 Esau 5 Jacob
rebel 6 anarch, mutiny, revolt, rise up 7 radical 8 attacker, debunker, frondeur, mutineer, opponent, revolter, ultraist 9 adversary, anarchist, assailant, extremist, insurgent, insurrect 10 antagonist, iconoclast, malcontent 11 rise against 13 revolutionary, revolutionist
rebellion 6 mutiny, revolt 8 sedition 10 revolution 12 insurrection
rebellious 8 mutinous 9 alienated, estranged, insurgent 11 disaffected 13 insubordinate
rebirth 7 revival 8 metanoia 10 conversion, renascence, resurgence 11 reanimation, renaissance 12 resurrection, risorgimento
rebound 7 recover 8 ricochet, snap back
rebuff 5 repel 6 reject 7 fend off, hold off, keep off, repulse, ward off 8 stave off
rebuke 3 rap, wig 5 chide, scold, scorn 6 earful, lesson, monish 7 chiding, lecture, reproof, reprove, tick off 8 admonish, call down, reproach, scolding 9 reprimand, talking-to 10 admonition 12 admonishment, dressing down 13 tongue-lashing
rebut 5 break, evert, repel 6 refute 7 confute, fend off, hold off, keep off, repulse, ward off 8 confound, disprove, stave off 10 controvert, disconfirm
recalcitrant 4 wild 6 unruly 8 opposing, stubborn, untoward 9 fractious, obstinate, resisting 11 indomitable, intractable
recall 4 cite, lift, stir 5 educe, evoke, renew, rouse, unsay, waken 6 abjure, arouse, awaken, elicit, memory, remind, repeal, retain, revive, revoke 7 bethink, extract, rescind, restore, retract, reverse 8 forswear, palinode, remember, take back, withdraw 9 anamnesis, dismantle, recollect, reinstate, reminisce 10 retrospect 12 recollection, reminiscence
recant 5 unsay 6 abjure 7 retract 8 forswear, palinode, take back, withdraw
recap 4 tire 7 retread
recapitulate 5 sum up, unite 9 summarize
recapitulation 3 sum 5 sum-up 6 précis, resumé 7 epitome, summary 9 summing-up
recede 3 ebb 4 back 5 abate, close, taper 6 depart, lessen, reduce, retire 7 dwindle, regress, retract, retreat 8 decrease, diminish, fall back, withdraw 9 drain away 10 retrograde, retrogress
receipts 6 income 7 revenue

receive 4 take 5 admit 6 take in
received 5 sound 8 accepted, orthodox 9 canonical 10 sanctioned 13 authoritative
receiver 5 donee, fence 9 treasurer
recent 3 new 4 late 5 fresh, novel 6 latest, modern 8 neoteric 9 new-sprung 10 newfangled 11 modernistic 12 new-fashioned *combining form:* 2 ne 3 cen, neo 4 caen, cene, ceno 5 caeno
receptacle 5 torus 6 cupule 8 placenta 9 container 10 repository *laundry:* 6 hamper *narrow:* 6 trough
receptive 4 open 8 amenable, friendly, suasible, swayable 9 acceptant 10 accessible, open-minded, responsive 11 persuadable, persuasible, suggestible, sympathetic
recess 5 niche 6 alcove 7 adjourn 8 dissolve, prorogue 9 prorogate, terminate
Recessional author 7 Kipling
recessive 8 retiring 9 withdrawn
recherché 3 new 4 rare 5 fresh, novel 6 choice, dainty, exotic, select 7 elegant, unusual 8 delicate, original, superior, uncommon
recidivate 5 lapse 7 relapse 9 backslide
recipe 7 formula 12 prescription
reciprocal 4 mate, twin 5 match 6 double, fellow 9 companion, duplicate 10 coordinate *combining form:* 6 allelo *prefix:* 5 inter
reciprocate 5 repay 6 retort, return 7 requite 8 exchange, serve out 9 retaliate 10 compensate, recompense 11 interchange
recital 5 story 9 discourse, narration, recountal 10 recounting 11 description *combining form:* 3 log 5 logue
recite 4 tell 5 chant, count, state 6 number, relate, report 7 narrate, recount 8 describe, rehearse 9 enumerate
reckless 4 rash, wild 5 brash, hasty 6 daring, madcap 8 carefree 9 audacious, daredevil, desperate, foolhardy, hotheaded, uncareful, venturous 10 ill-advised, incautious, mad-brained 11 adventurous, temerarious, venturesome 13 adventuresome, inconsiderate, irresponsible
reckon 3 add, put, sum 4 call, cast, deem, foot, view 5 count, guess, judge, lot on, place, total 6 bank on, cipher, figure, number, regard, rely on 7 account, build on, compute, count on, lot upon, surmise, trust in, trust to 8 bank upon, consider, depend on, estimate, rely upon 9 calculate, enumerate 10 conjecture, depend upon 11 approximate, calculate on
reckoning 3 tab 4 bill 5 score 7 account, invoice 8 figuring 9 ciphering, statement 10 arithmetic, estimation 11 calculation, computation
reclaim 7 recover, restore 9 restitute 10 rejuvenate 11 recondition, reconstruct 12 rehabilitate
recline 3 lie, tip 4 cant, heel, lean, list, rest, tilt 5 slant, slope 6 lounge, repose 7 lie down 10 stretch out
reclining 4 flat 5 prone 9 decumbent, prostrate, recumbent 10 procumbent
recluse 6 hermit 7 eremite 8 cenobite, hermetic, secluded, solitary 9 anchorite, seclusive 10 cloistered 11 sequestered *female:* 7 ancress 9 anchoress
reclusive 8 eremitic, reserved, solitary 10 antisocial 11 standoffish 12 misanthropic
recognition 6 credit 9 awareness 10 cognizance *combining form:* 5 gnosy 6 gnosia, gnosis
recognize 4 know, note, spot 5 admit, agree, place 6 finger, notice, recall, remark 7 observe 8 diagnose, identify, pinpoint, remember 11 acknowledge, determinate, distinguish
recoil 3 shy 4 balk, duck 5 dodge, quail, quake, shake, start, stick, waver, wince 6 blanch, blench, falter, flinch, shrink, swerve 7 shudder, squinch, stickle, tremble 8 hesitate, reel back
recollect 4 cite, stir 5 rally, rouse, waken 6 arouse, awaken, recall, remind, retain, revive 7 bethink 8 remember 9 reminisce 10 retrospect
recollection 6 memory, recall 9 anamnesis 11 remembrance 12 reminiscence
recommence 5 renew 6 pick up, reopen, resume, take up 7 restart 8 continue
recommend 4 hail, tout 6 advise, commit, kudize, praise 7 acclaim, applaud, consign, counsel, entrust 8 advocate 10 compliment
recommendation 6 advice 8 approval 9 character, reference 11 credentials, endorsement, testimonial
recompense 3 pay 5 award, grant, repay 6 accord, amends, offset, return, reward 7 balance, redress, requite 8 reprisal 9 indemnify, indemnity, quittance, reimburse, retaliate, vouchsafe 10 compensate, remunerate, reparation 11 reciprocate, restitution
reconcile 3 fit 4 suit, tune 5 adapt 6 adjust, attune, square, tailor 7 conform 8 quadrate 9 harmonize, integrate 10 coordinate, proportion 11 accommodate
recondite 4 dark, deep, hard 5 heavy, runic 6 mystic, occult, orphic, secret 7 cryptic, learned, obscure 8 abstruse, academic, anagogic, esoteric, hermetic, mystical, pedantic, profound 9 difficult, enigmatic, scholarly, sibylline 10 cabalistic
recondition 3 fix 4 do up, mend 5 patch 6 doctor, repair, revamp 7 rebuild, reclaim,

restore 8 overhaul 9 restitute 10 rejuvenate 12 rehabilitate
reconnoiter 5 probe, scout
reconsider 5 amend 6 review, revise 7 correct, draw off, rethink, re-treat, reweigh, sleep on 9 reexamine, think over 10 reevaluate
reconstruct 3 fix 4 do up, mend 5 patch 6 doctor, repair, retool, revamp 7 rebuild, reclaim, reorder, restore 8 overhaul, readjust, reorient 9 rearrange, reshuffle, restitute 10 rejuvenate, reorganize 12 rehabilitate
record 3 say 4 date, disc, mark, read, show 6 annals 7 archive, journal 8 archives, document, register 9 chronicle *combining form:* 4 gram 5 graph *of a meeting:* 7 minutes *of past events:* 7 history *of proceedings:* 4 acta *ship's:* 3 log 7 logbook
recorder 5 flute
record player 5 phono 9 turntable 10 phonograph
recount 4 tell 5 state 6 recite, relate, report 7 narrate 8 describe, rehearse
recoup 6 regain 7 get back, recruit 8 retrieve 9 repossess
recourse 5 shift 6 refuge, resort 7 stopgap 9 expedient, makeshift 10 expediency
recover 4 heal, mend 5 rally, renew, rewin 6 offset, perk up, redeem, regain, resume, retake, revive 7 balance, get back, improve, rebound, reclaim, recruit, refresh, restore 8 reoccupy, retrieve, snap back 9 come round, reacquire, recapture, repossess, restitute 10 bounce back, compensate, convalesce, recuperate, rejuvenate 12 rehabilitate
recreant 3 rat 5 false 6 coward, untrue 7 unloyal 8 apostate, defector, disloyal, renegade, turncoat 9 faithless, turnabout 10 perfidious, traitorous, unfaithful
recreate 4 play 5 amuse, renew, sport 6 divert 7 disport, refresh, restore 9 entertain
recreation 3 fun 4 ease, play 5 mirth, sport 6 frolic, repose 7 disport, leisure, rollick 9 amusement, diversion 13 entertainment
recrudesce 5 react, recur, renew 6 return, revert, revive 7 reoccur
recruit 4 hire, mend 5 raise, renew 6 enlist, muster, novice, recoup, regain, repair, rookie 7 draftee, get back, rebuild, recover, refresh, restore 8 beginner, enlistee, freshman, neophyte, newcomer, renovate, retrieve 9 fledgling, novitiate, repossess 10 apprentice, tenderfoot
rectifier 4 tube 5 diode 8 detector
rectify 4 mend 5 amend, emend, right 6 repair 7 correct, rebuild
rectitude 6 virtue 7 honesty, probity 8 goodness, justness, morality 9 rightness 11 uprightness 13 righteousness
rector 6 pastor 9 clergyman 10 headmaster
rectory 5 manse 9 parsonage
recumbent 4 flat 5 prone 9 prostrate, reclining
recuperate 4 gain, mend 6 look up, perk up 7 improve 10 convalesce
recur 6 repair, repeat, resort, return, revert 7 iterate 8 turn back 9 reiterate 10 recrudesce
recurrent see recurring
recurring 8 periodic 9 alternate 10 isochronal, periodical 11 isochronous 12 intermittent *combining form:* 6 ennial
red 4 laky, puce, ruby 5 gules, ocher, rouge, ruddy 6 bloody, cerise, florid, wanton 7 carmine, flushed, glowing, oxblood, radical, rubious, scarlet, stammel, vermeil 8 flagrant, sanguine 9 carnation *combining form:* 4 rhod 5 pyrrh, pyrro, rhodo 6 erythr, pyrrho 7 erythro
Red 6 commie 9 Bolshevik, Communist
redact 4 edit 5 frame 6 revise 7 compose
Red and the Black author 8 Stendhal
red ape 9 orangutan
red arsenic 7 realgar
red-backed parrot 7 grassie
red-backed sandpiper 6 dunlin 10 blackheart
Red Badge of Courage *author:* 5 Crane *hero:* 7 Fleming (Henry)
red-bellied snipe 9 dowitcher
red benjamin 9 birthroot
redbird 8 cardinal 13 summer tanager
redbird cactus 7 jewbush
red blindness 10 protanopia
red blood cell 11 erythrocyte
red-blooded 5 lusty, vital 7 dynamic 8 vigorous 9 energetic, strenuous
redbreast 4 knot 5 robin
red-breasted snipe 9 dowitcher
redbuck 6 impala
Redburn author 8 Melville
red carp 8 goldfish
red chalk 4 bole 6 ruddle
red cobalt 9 erythrite
red copper ore 7 cuprite
Red Cross *founder:* 6 Barton (Clara) *Knight:* 6 George
red currant 4 goya
redden 3 rud 4 glow, pink, rose, ruby 5 blush, color, flush, rouge, ruddy 6 mantle, pinken, rubify, rubric, ruddle 7 crimson 11 incarnadine
red dog 5 dhole, flour 8 card game
redecorate 9 refurbish
redeem 3 buy 4 free 5 loose 6 make up, offset, ransom, set off, unbind 7 balance,

manumit, release, unchain 8 atone for, liberate, outweigh 10 compensate
redeemer 6 savior 7 messiah, saviour
redemption 6 ransom 7 release 9 atonement, expiation, salvation 11 deliverance
redeye 4 rudd 7 whiskey 8 rock bass, warmouth 10 copperhead
redfish 4 drum 6 salmon 11 channel bass
red grouper 5 negre
red grouse 8 moorbird, moorfowl, moor game
red hickory 6 pignut 9 mockernut
red hind 7 graysby 8 cabrilla
red-hot 2 up 5 fiery 6 ardent, fervid 7 abreast, blazing, boiling, burning, flaming, glowing 8 scalding, sizzling, up-to-date 9 au courant, scorching 10 blistering, passionate, sweltering 11 impassioned
red hot cattail 8 chenille
red Indian paint 9 bloodroot
red ink 7 deficit
red inkberry 8 pokeweed
red ironbark 5 mugga 8 eucalypt
red iron ore 8 hematite
red lauan 8 tanguile
red lead 6 minium
red lead ore 8 crocoite
red-legged crow 6 chough
red-legged plover 9 turnstone
red-letter 6 rubric 7 notable 8 nameable 9 memorable 10 noteworthy, observable
red-light district 5 levee, stews 10 tenderloin
red mite 7 chigger
red-neck 4 hick, rube 5 yokel 6 rustic 7 bumpkin, hayseed, peasant 9 hillbilly 10 provincial 12 backwoodsman
red-necked gazelle 5 addra
redo 5 renew 6 revamp 7 remodel, restyle 8 refinish, renovate 9 reproduce, restyling 10 redecorate, repetition
red ocher 4 bole
redolence 4 balm 5 aroma, scent, spice 7 bouquet, incense, perfume 9 fragrance
redolent 5 balmy, spicy, sweet 6 aromal, savory 7 perfumy 8 aromatic, fragrant, perfumed 9 ambrosial, remindful 11 reminiscent
redouble 4 rise 5 mount, rouse 6 deepen 7 enhance, magnify 8 heighten 9 intensify
redoubt 4 fort 7 citadel 8 fastness, fortress 10 stronghold
redoubtable 5 awful, famed, great 6 famous 7 eminent, fearful 8 dreadful, horrible, horrific, renowned, shocking, terrible 9 appalling, frightful, prominent 10 celebrated 11 illustrious 13 distinguished
redound 6 accrue 7 conduce 10 contribute
red pine 4 rimu 10 Douglas fir
Red Planet 4 Mars
redpoll 6 linnet
redraft 6 revamp, review, revise, rework 7 restyle, revisal, rewrite 8 rescript, revision, work over 9 recension
redrawer 6 winder
redress 5 annul, venge 6 amends, avenge, negate 7 revenge 8 negative, reprisal 9 balancing, cancel out, frustrate, indemnity, quittance, vengeance, vindicate 10 counteract, neutralize, offsetting, recompense, reparation 11 restitution, retaliation 12 compensation, countercheck
red roe 5 coral
redroot 7 alkanet, pigweed
red sable 8 kolinsky
red silk cotton 5 simal
red silver ore 9 proustite 11 pyrargyrite
red snapper 6 rasher
red sorrel 7 roselle
red squirrel 9 chickaree
red-stalk aster 6 cocash
reduce 3 cut 4 bate, clip, diet, pare, slow 5 abate, break, crush, lower, shave, slash, taper 6 debase, defeat, demote, humble, lessen, rebate, recede, subdue, weaken 7 conquer, cripple, curtail, cut back, cut down, declass, deflate, degrade, demerit, disable, disrate, dwindle 8 bear down, beat down, decrease, diminish, discount, disgrade, enfeeble, mark down, roll back, slim down, step down, taper off, unweight, vanquish 9 downgrade, drain away, humiliate, overpower, scale down, subjugate, undermine 10 depreciate, slenderize
reductio ad ____ 8 absurdum
reduction 6 rebate 7 cutback, cutdown 8 discount, markdown 9 abatement 11 downgrading ***combining form:*** 5 lyses (plural), lysis
redundancy 8 pleonasm, tumidity, verbiage 9 inflation, prolixity, tautology, turgidity 10 flatulence, periphrase, roundabout 11 periphrasis, superfluity
redundant 5 extra, spare, windy, wordy 6 prolix 7 diffuse, surplus, verbose 9 iterating 10 long-winded, palaverous 11 reiterating, repetitious, superfluous 13 supernumerary
red vitriol 9 bieberite, colcothar
redware 7 boccaro
red whelk 6 buckie
redwing 7 gadwall
redwing blackbird 6 maizer
redwood 5 rohun 7 amboyna, sequoia 8 mahogany 10 Scotch pine
reed 4 pipe 5 arrow
reedy 4 slim, thin 6 slight, stalky, twiggy 7 slender, squinny, tenuous 9 attenuate
reef 4 lode, vein 7 bioherm
reek 4 funk 5 smell, stink 6 stench

reeking 4 rank 5 fetid, funky, fusty 6 putrid, rancid, smelly 7 noisome 10 malodorous
reel 3 bob 4 spin, sway, swim, turn 5 lurch, swing, waver, weave, whirl 6 careen, falter, teeter, topple, totter, wobble 7 stagger, stumble 8 titubate
reestablish 5 renew 6 recall, revive 7 restore 9 reinstate 11 reintroduce
reevaluate 6 review 7 rethink, re-treat, reweigh 9 think over 10 reconsider
reeve 4 ruff 6 thread 8 official 10 magistrate
reexamine see reevaluate
refashion 4 turn, vary 5 alter 6 change, modify
refection 4 feed, meal 6 repast
refectory 10 dining hall
refer 4 cite, name 5 apply, quote 6 advert, advise, allude, assign, charge, credit, hand in, impute, insert, submit 7 ascribe, bring up, mention, specify 8 accredit, instance, point out 9 attribute
referee 3 ump 5 judge 6 umpire 7 adjudge, arbiter 9 arbitrate 10 adjudicate, arbitrator
reference book 5 atlas 6 manual 7 almanac 10 dictionary 12 encyclopedia
reference guide 5 index
referendum 4 poll
refine 6 polish, smooth 7 improve, perfect
refined 4 nice 6 subtle, urbane 7 genteel 8 cultured, delicate, finespun, polished, précieux, well-bred 9 distingué 10 cultivated
refinement 5 couth, grace 6 finish, polish 7 culture, dignity, suavity 8 breeding, civility, courtesy, elegance, urbanity 10 politeness 11 cultivation
reflect 4 echo 5 glass, image, study, think, weigh 6 mirror, ponder, reason 7 sparkle 8 cogitate 9 cerebrate 10 deliberate
reflecting 7 pensive 8 lustrous 10 cogitative, meditative, ruminative, thoughtful *light:* 8 relucent *suffix:* 6 escent
reflective 7 pensive 8 thinking 9 pondering 10 cogitative, meditative, ruminative, thoughtful
reflux 6 ebbing 9 condenser, returning
reform 5 amend, emend 7 correct, improve
Reformation leader 4 Knox 6 Calvin, Luther 7 Zwingli
reformatory 3 pen 4 jail 6 cooler, lockup, prison 7 borstal 8 stockade 12 penitentiary
refractory 6 mulish 8 perverse, stubborn 9 obstinate 10 bullheaded, headstrong, self-willed, unyielding 11 intractable, stiffnecked
refrain 4 curb, deny, halt, keep, stop 5 check 6 arrest, chorus 7 forbear, inhibit 8 hold back, withhold 9 interrupt
refresh 4 rest 5 amuse, renew 6 divert, update, vivify 7 animate, enliven, quicken, restore 8 recreate, renovate 9 modernize, stimulate 10 rejuvenate
refresher 5 drink, tonic 6 bracer 9 stimulant
refrigerant 3 ice 5 freon 7 ammonia, cooling 13 carbon dioxide
refrigerator 6 fridge, icebox 9 condenser
refuge 4 port 5 cover, haven, shift 6 asylum, covert, harbor, resort, shield 7 hideout, retreat, shelter, stopgap 8 hideaway, immunity, recourse, resource 9 expedient, harborage, makeshift, sanctuary
refugee 2 DP 5 exile 6 emigré 7 evacuee 8 emigrant, fugitive 10 expatriate
refulgent 6 bright 7 beaming, radiant 8 luminous 9 brilliant
refund 5 repay 6 rebate 9 reimburse, repayment
refurbish 5 renew 6 update 7 restore, retouch 8 renovate 9 modernize 10 rejuvenate
refuse 3 jib 4 deny, dump, junk, nill 5 dreck, offal, spurn, swill, trash, waste 6 debris, kelter, litter, lumber, reject, scraps, spilth 7 decline, dismiss, garbage, rubbish 8 disallow, dustheap, keep back, riffraff, turn down, withhold 9 reprobate, repudiate, sweepings 10 disapprove
refutation 8 disproof, elenchus
refute 5 break, evert, rebut 8 confound, disprove 10 controvert, disconfirm
regain 6 recoup 7 get back, recover, recruit 8 reassume, reoccupy, retrieve 9 repossess ***possession:*** 7 replevy 8 replevin
regal 6 august, kingly 7 queenly, stately, sublime 8 glorious, imposing, kinglike, majestic, princely, splendid 9 monarchal, sovereign 10 monarchial 11 magnificent, monarchical, resplendent
regale 5 feast 6 dinner, spread 7 banquet
regalia 5 cigar 6 finery 8 frippery 9 full dress
Regan ***father:*** 4 Lear ***husband:*** 8 Cornwall ***sister:*** 7 Goneril 8 Cordelia
regard 4 care, deem, heed, mark, note, rate, view 5 assay, favor, honor, value 6 admire, assess, esteem, homage, notice, reckon, remark 7 account, concern, prizing, respect, valuing 8 approval, consider, estimate, interest 9 attention, curiosity, deference 10 admiration, cherishing, cognizance, estimation, observance, solicitude 11 approbation, carefulness, heedfulness, observation 12 appreciation, satisfaction 13 consciousness, consideration ***as perfect:*** 8 idealize

regardful 6 arrect 7 duteous 9 advertent, attentive, intentive, observant, observing
regarding 4 as to, in re 5 about, anent 6 anenst 7 apropos 10 as respects 13 with respect to
regatta 4 race 6 fabric 7 liberty
regenerate 6 reform, revive 9 reproduce
regent 5 ruler 8 governor 9 professor
regicide's victim 4 king
regimen 4 rule 9 governing 10 government
region 4 area, belt, part, walk, zone 5 field, tract 6 domain, sector, sphere 7 demesne, terrain 8 province, vicinity 9 bailiwick, territory 12 neighborhood ***elevated:*** 8 highland
regional 5 local 9 localized 10 provincial
register 3 say 4 list, mark, read, roll, show 6 enroll, record 7 catalog 8 indicate
regnant 4 rife 6 master, ruling 7 current, popular 9 paramount, prevalent, sovereign 10 prevailing, widespread
regress 6 revert 9 throw back
regret 3 rue, woe 4 care 5 demur, grief, mourn, qualm 6 bemoan, bewail, grieve, lament, repent, sorrow 7 anguish, apology, deplore, scruple 9 deprecate, heartache, penitence 10 affliction, contrition, disapprove, heartbreak 11 compunction
regretful 5 sorry 8 contrite, penitent 9 repentant 10 apologetic 11 attritional, penitential
regrettable 4 dire 6 woeful 8 grievous 10 afflictive, calamitous 11 distressing, unfortunate 13 heartbreaking
regular 3 set 4 even 5 fixed, gross, typic, usual, utter 6 common, normal, steady 7 equable, general, natural, orderly, perfect, settled, typical, uniform 8 absolute, complete, constant, methodic, ordinary, outright, positive 9 clocklike, customary, downright, prevalent 10 consummate, methodical, systematic 11 commonplace, unmitigated 12 run-of-the-mill
regulate 3 fix 5 order 6 adjust, temper, tune up 7 arrange 8 organize 9 methodize 11 systematize
regulation 3 law 4 rule 5 canon, edict 6 curfew, decree 7 precept, statute 8 decretum 9 ordinance, prescript
regulator 8 governor
Rehabiah ***father:*** 7 Eliezer ***grandfather:*** 5 Moses
rehabilitate 7 reclaim, recover, restore 11 recondition
rehearse 5 drill, state 6 recite, relate, report 7 iterate, narrate, recount 8 describe, exercise, practice 10 run through
Rehoboam ***father:*** 7 Solomon ***kingdom:*** 5 Judah 6 Israel ***mother:*** 6 Naamah
reign 4 king, rule, sway 6 govern 7 prevail 8 dominate, domineer, overrule 11 predominate 12 preponderate
reimburse 3 pay 5 repay 7 balance, requite 9 indemnify 10 compensate, remunerate
rein 4 cool 7 collect, compose, control, repress, smother 8 restrain, suppress
reinforce 4 prop 5 super 6 pillar 7 augment, bolster, enlarge, fortify, sustain 8 buttress, energize, increase, multiply 10 invigorate, strengthen
reinstate 5 renew 6 recall, return, revive 7 put back, replace, restore 8 give back 11 reestablish
reintroduce 5 renew 6 recall, revive 7 restore 11 reestablish
reinvestment 8 plowback
reiterate 5 renew, resay 6 repeat 7 reprise
reject 4 cast, jilt, junk, shed 5 debar, scrap, spurn 6 rebuff, refuse, slough 7 cashier, decline, discard, dismiss, exclude, shut out 8 jettison, throw out, turn down 9 eliminate, reprobate, repudiate, throw away 10 disapprove
rejoice 3 joy 5 exult, glory 7 gladden
rejoin 5 reply 6 answer, come in, retort 7 respond
rejoinder 5 reply 6 answer, retort, return 7 respond 8 antiphon, response
rejuvenate 5 renew 7 reclaim, recover, refresh, restore 9 modernize, refurbish 11 recondition, reconstruct
Rekem's father 6 Hebron
rekindle 5 renew 6 revive 8 renovate, retrieve, revivify 9 resurrect 10 reactivate, revitalize 11 resuscitate
relate 4 join, link, tell, yoke 5 apply, unite 6 assign, bear on, couple, credit, depict, detail, impute, render, report 7 connect, divulge, express, itemize, pertain, recount 8 bear upon, describe, disclose 9 appertain, pronounce
related 4 akin 5 alike 6 agnate, allied 7 cognate, connate, germane, kindred 8 incident 9 analogous, identical, pertinent 10 connatural 11 consanguine ***by marriage:*** 7 affined
relating to ***suffix:*** 2 al, an, ar, ic 3 ean, ese, ial, ile, ine, ist, ory 4 ical 5 ative, istic 6 itious 7 istical
relation 3 kin 7 kinsman 9 kinswoman ***on father's side:*** 6 agnate ***on mother's side:*** 5 enate
relative 2 ma, pa 3 kin, mom, sib, sis, son 4 aunt, mama, nana, papa, sibb 5 madre, mamma, mammy, momma, niece, pappy, pater, poppa, uncle 6 agnate, cousin, father, mother, nephew, parent, sister 7 brother, cognate, kinsman, sibling 8 daughter, grandson 9 dependent, kins-

woman **10** contingent, grandchild **11** approximate, conditional, grandfather, grandmother, grandparent **13** granddaughter

relatives **7** kinfolk **8** kinfolks

relax **4** ease, loll, rest **5** loose, slack **6** lollop, loosen, lounge, rest up, unbend, unwind **7** ease off, slacken **8** loosen up **9** untighten

relaxation **4** ease, rest **6** repose **7** leisure **9** amusement **11** assuagement **12** requiescence

relaxed **4** mild, soft **5** loose, slack **6** breezy, casual, dégagé, gentle **7** lenient, sinuous, unfussy **8** flexuous, informal **9** easygoing **10** unreserved **11** low-pressure

release **4** emit, free, vent **5** issue, loose, unfix, yield **6** acquit, loosen, pardon, ransom, resign, unbind, uncage, uncoil **7** give off, give out, manumit, unchain, unleash **8** liberate, throw off, unfetter, untether **9** discharge, exculpate, exonerate, surrender, take out on, unshackle **10** emancipate *conditional:* **6** parole

relegate **5** exile, expel, refer **6** banish, charge, commit, credit, deport **7** commend, confide, consign, entrust, expulse **8** accredit, displace, hand over, turn over

relent **3** ebb **4** fall, wane **5** abate, let up **7** die away, die down, ease off, slacken, subside **8** moderate

relentless **4** grim **5** cruel, rigid **6** dogged, fierce, mortal, strict **7** adamant, inhuman **8** obdurate, rigorous **9** ferocious, stringent, unbending **10** implacable, inexorable, inflexible, ironfisted, unyielding **11** unflinching **12** unappeasable

relevant **3** apt, fit **5** ad rem **6** allied, proper **7** apropos, cognate, fitting, germane, weighty **8** apposite, material, pointful, suitable **9** allowable, important, pertinent **10** admissible, applicable **11** applicative, applicatory, appropriate

reliable **4** safe **5** sound, tried, valid **6** cogent, proven, secure, trusty **7** certain, telling **8** accurate, apposite, attested, inerrant, unerring, verified **9** authentic, confirmed, validated **10** dependable **11** trustworthy **12** tried and true

reliance **4** hope **5** faith, stock, trust

relic **5** token, trace **6** shadow, trophy **7** memento, vestige **8** keepsake, memorial, reminder, souvenir **11** remembrance

relict **5** widow **8** residual

relief **3** aid **4** ease, hand, help, lift **6** assist, succor **7** comfort, secours, support **8** easement **9** allayment, softening **10** assistance, lightening, mitigation **11** alleviation, appeasement, assuagement

relieve **3** aid, rob, sub **4** ease, help, loot **5** allay, quiet, rifle, spare, spell **6** excuse, exempt, fill in, lessen, let off, reduce, soften, solace, soothe, subdue, supply, temper **7** absolve, appease, assuage, benefit, comfort, console, lighten, mollify, plunder, qualify, ransack, stick up, subvene **8** decrease, diminish, dispense, mitigate, moderate, palliate, take over **9** alleviate, discharge

religion **4** cult, sect **5** creed, faith **6** belief, church

religious **3** nun **4** holy, just, monk, true **5** godly, moral, noble, pious **6** devout, priest, sister, votary **7** ethical, staunch, upright, votress **8** faithful, monastic, votaress, votarist **9** pietistic, prayerful, steadfast ***foot-washing ceremony:*** **6** maundy ***offering:*** **8** oblation ***order member:*** **5** friar **8** cenobite

relinquish **4** cast, cede, quit, shed **5** forgo, leave, waive, yield **6** desert, forego, give up, resign **7** abandon, discard, forbear, forsake, lay down, throw up **8** abdicate, abnegate, hand over, lay aside, renounce **9** sacrifice, surrender

relish **4** like, tang, zest **5** enjoy, flair, gusto, heart, sapor, savor, smack, taste **6** admire, flavor, liking, loving, palate **7** leaning **8** enjoying, penchant, pleasure, sapidity **9** delight in, diversion, enjoyment, prejudice **10** appreciate, propensity **11** delectation

relucent **7** radiant, shining **10** reflecting

reluctant **3** shy **4** wary **5** chary, loath **6** afraid, averse **7** uneager **8** backward, cautious **9** unwilling **10** indisposed *prophet:* **5** Jonah

rely on **5** trust **7** count on **8** depend on

remain **4** bide, stay, wait **5** abide, tarry **6** linger **7** survive **11** stick around

remainder **6** excess **7** balance, residue, surplus **8** leavings, leftover, residual, residuum

remains **4** body, mort **5** stiff **6** corpse, debris, fossil **7** balance, cadaver, carcass, residue **8** leavings, residual, residuum

remark **3** see **4** heed, note **5** glass **6** notice, postil, saying **7** comment, discern, mention, observe **8** exegesis, perceive, scholium **9** assertion, attention, statement, utterance **10** animadvert, annotation, cognizance, commentary, commentate, exposition **11** observation ***in a play:*** **5** aside *witty:* **7** epigram

remarkable **4** rare **6** signal, unique **7** salient, strange, unusual, weighty **8** peculiar, singular, striking, uncommon, unwonted **9** arresting, arrestive, important, momentous, prominent **10** unordinary **11** conspicuous, exceptional, outstanding, significant, uncustomary **13** extraordinary

___ **Remarque** **5** Erich (Maria)

remedial **6** curing **7** healing **8** curative,

sanative, sanatory 9 vulnerary 11 restorative
remedy 4 cure, drug, heal 6 elixir, physic 7 cure-all, nostrum, panacea 8 antidote, biologic, medicant, medicine, specific 9 medicinal, pharmacon 10 corrective, medicament, medication 11 counterstep
remember 4 cite 5 educe, evoke 6 elicit, recall, relive, retain 9 recollect 10 retrospect
remembrance 4 gift 5 favor, relic, token 6 memory, recall, trophy 7 memento, present 8 keepsake, memorial, souvenir 0 anamnesis 12 recollection
remind 3 jog 4 warn 5 alert 6 advise, prompt 8 admonish
reminder 4 hint, memo, note, sign 5 relic, token 6 notice, trophy 7 gesture, memento, warning 8 keepsake, memorial, souvenir 10 admonition, expression, indication, intimation, memorandum, suggestion
reminisce see remember
reminiscence 6 memory, recall 9 anamnesis 12 recollection
remise 4 cede, deed 5 alien 6 assign, convey 8 alienate, make over, sign over, transfer
remiss 3 lax 4 lazy 5 slack 8 careless, derelict, fainéant, indolent, slothful 9 negligent 10 behindhand, delinquent, neglectful, regardless 12 disregardful
remit 4 send, ship, stay 5 defer, delay, route 6 excuse, hold up, pardon, put off, shelve 7 address, condone, consign, forgive, forward, hold off 8 dispatch, postpone
remnant 4 heel, rest 7 balance, oddment, residue 8 leavings, residual, residuum
remodel 6 revamp 11 reconstruct
remonstrance 5 demur 7 protest 8 demurral, demurrer, question 9 challenge, objection
remonstrate 4 kick 5 fight 6 combat, except, object, oppose, resist 7 protest 9 withstand
remonstration see remonstrance
remora 4 clog, drag 11 shark sucker, sucking fish
remorse 3 rue 6 regret 7 penance 9 attrition, penitence, penitency 10 contrition, repentance 11 compunction 12 contriteness
remorseful see regretful
remorsefulness see remorse
remote 3 far, off 4 back, slim 5 aloof, small 6 casual, far-off, secret, slight 7 devious, distant, faraway, obscure, outside, retired, slender 8 detached, far-flung, frontier, lonesome, off-lying, outlying 9 incurious, uncurious, unsettled, withdrawn 10 negligible, outlandish 11 indifferent, out-of-the-way, unconcerned 12 uninterested *combining form:* 3 tel 4 dist, pale, tele 5 disto, palea, paleo 6 palaeo, palaio
remotest 6 utmost 7 extreme, outmost 9 outermost, uttermost 11 furthermost
remove 4 doff, ship, skim 5 douse, erase, purge, shift 6 efface, put off, unseat 7 blot out, cast off, disturb, expunge, extract, take off, take out 8 dislodge, displace, displant, evacuate, take away, throw off, transfer, withdraw 9 clear away, dislocate, eliminate, eradicate, extirpate, liquidate 10 obliterate 11 exterminate *from office:* 6 depose *hair:* 8 depilate *prefix:* 2 de
removed 3 far 5 alone, aloof, apart 6 far-off, secret 7 devious, distant, faraway, isolate, obscure 8 detached, far-flung, isolated, lonesome, off-lying, outlying
remunerate 3 pay 5 award, grant, repay 6 accord 7 guerdon, requite 9 indemnify, reimburse, vouchsafe 10 recompense
remunerative 6 paying 7 gainful 9 lucrative 10 profitable, well-paying, worthwhile 11 moneymaking 12 advantageous
Remus *brother:* 7 Romulus *father:* 4 Mars *mother:* 10 Rhea Silvia *slayer:* 7 Romulus
renaissance see rebirth
renal 7 nephric
rend 3 rip 4 rive, tear 5 split 6 cleave, divide
render 3 put 4 limn, turn 5 image 6 depict, govern, return 7 execute, picture, portray 8 carry out, describe 9 delineate, interpret, represent, translate, transpose 10 administer 12 administrate *suffix:* 2 en
rendering 7 version 10 paraphrase 11 restatement, translation
rendezvous 4 date 5 haunt, raise, tryst 6 gather, muster, resort 7 collect, hangout, purlieu 8 assemble, congress 9 forgather 10 congregate, engagement 11 appointment, assignation
rendition 7 reading, version 11 translation
renegade 3 rat 5 rebel 7 heretic 8 apostate, defector, deserter, forsaker, recreant, turncoat 9 abandoner, insurgent, turnabout 10 iconoclast, schismatic 13 tergiversator
renege 5 welsh 6 cry off, resile 7 back off, back out 8 back down 9 backpedal
renew 4 mend 5 fresh, resay 6 pick up, recall, reform, reopen, repair, repeat, resume, revise, revive, take up, update 7 correct, freshen, iterate, rebuild, rectify, refresh, remodel, reprise, restart, restore 8 continue, make over, rekindle, retrieve, revivify 9 modernize, refurbish, reinstate, reiterate, resurrect 10 ingeminate, reactivate, recommence, rejuvenate, revitalize 11 reestablish, reintroduce
rennet 8 abomasum

renounce 3 rat 4 quit, turn 5 chuck, demit 6 defect, desert, resign 7 abandon, forsake 8 abdicate, disclaim 9 repudiate, throw over 10 apostatize, tergiverse
renovate 5 clean 6 revive 7 cleanse, refresh, restore 8 rekindle, retrieve, revivify 9 modernize, refurbish, resurrect 10 revitalize
renown 4 fame 5 éclat, kudos 6 repute 8 eminence, prestige 9 celebrity, notoriety 10 prominence, prominency, reputation 11 distinction, preeminence
renowned 5 famed, great 6 famous, lauded, signal 7 eminent, notable, praised 8 extolled 9 acclaimed, prominent 10 celebrated, celebrious 11 illustrious, outstanding 13 distinguished
rent 3 let 4 hire, rift, torn 5 break, lease, split 6 breach, schism, sublet 7 charter, fissure, mangled, rupture 8 fracture, sublease
rental 4 flat 5 rooms, suite 8 lodgings, tenement 9 apartment
renter 6 lessee
renunciation 6 denial 8 forgoing, yielding 9 eschewing, sacrifice, surrender 10 abjurement, forbearing, self-denial 11 forswearing
reopen 5 renew 6 pick up, resume, take up 7 restart 8 continue 10 recommence
reorder 6 retool 7 permute 8 readjust 9 rearrange, reshuffle 11 reconstruct 12 reconstitute
reorganization 7 shake-up 8 overturn, turnover
reorganize 6 retool 7 rebuild, refound 8 readjust, renovate, resettle 9 rearrange, reshuffle 10 regenerate 11 reconstruct, reestablish 12 reconstitute
reorient 6 retool 8 readjust 9 rearrange, reshuffle
repair 3 fix, hie, run 4 case, do up, fare, mend, pass, trim, turn, wend 5 apply, order, patch, recur, refer, shape 6 doctor, estate, fettle, kilter, push on, resort, revamp, travel 7 fitness, journey, proceed, rebuild, service 8 overhaul 11 recondition
reparation 6 amends, reward 7 redress 8 requital 9 atonement, indemnity, quittance 10 adjustment, recompense, settlement
repartee 3 wit 5 humor, irony 6 banter, retort, satire 7 riposte, sarcasm 8 backchat, badinage, comeback, response, snipsnap 9 rejoinder 10 back answer, persiflage
repast 4 feed, meal 9 refection
repay 5 award 6 accord, offset 7 balance, requite 9 indemnify, reimburse 10 compensate, recompense, remunerate
repeal 4 lift, void 6 recall, revoke 7 rescind, reverse 9 dismantle
repeat 4 copy, echo, harp, ring 5 chime, ditto, quote, recap, recur, renew, rerun, resay 6 parrot, recite, rehash, relate, retell, return 7 imitate, iterate, recount, restate 8 hash over, rehearse 9 duplicate, reiterate 12 recapitulate
repeater 7 firearm 10 recidivist
repeating 7 iterant
repel 4 buck 5 fight, rebut 6 combat, oppose, rebuff, reluct, resist, revolt, sicken 7 contest, disgust, dispute, fend off, hold off, keep off, ward off 8 nauseate, stave off
repellent 4 foul, vile 5 nasty 7 noisome 8 aversive, kindless, ungenial 9 invidious, loathsome, obnoxious, offensive, revolting, revulsive 10 disgusting 11 uncongenial
repent 3 rue 6 regret 7 deplore
repentance 3 rue 4 ruth 7 remorse 9 penitency 10 contrition 11 compunction 12 contriteness
repentant see **regretful**
repetition 4 copy 7 recital 8 iterance 9 rehearsal
rephrase 6 reword 7 restate
repine 4 fret, fuss, kick, wail 6 murmur 8 complain 10 discontent
replace 5 renew, shift 6 change, recoup, regain, return 7 put back, recover, restore 8 give back, retrieve, supplant, take back 9 reinstate, restitute, supersede
replacement 3 sub 6 fill-in 7 stand-in 9 alternate, surrogate 10 substitute 11 locum tenens, pinch hitter, succedaneum
replenish 5 refit, renew, stock 7 restore
replete 4 full, rife 5 alive, awash 6 jammed, loaded 7 brimful, crammed, crowded, stuffed, teeming 8 brimming, swarming, thronged 9 abounding, chock-full 11 overflowing
replica 4 copy 5 ditto 6 carbon 9 duplicate, facsimile 10 carbon copy
replicate 4 copy
reply 6 answer, come in, rejoin, retort, return 7 respond 8 response 9 rejoinder
report 3 cry 4 buzz, chat, dirt, fame, name, news, talk, word 5 brief, on-dit, rumor, state, story 6 advice, canard, gossip, impart, murmur, notice, recite, relate, review, rumble, speech, tattle 7 account, chatter, comment, hearsay, history, narrate, prating, recount, scandal, tidings, version 8 advisory, bulletin, chitchat, describe, rehearse 9 character, chronicle, grapevine, narrative, small talk, statement
reporter 7 newsman 10 journalist *inexperienced:* 3 cub
repose 3 lie 4 rest 7 leisure, lie down, recline, renewal 10 relaxation, stretch out 11 refreshment, restoration 12 requiescence

repository 5 depot, store 7 arsenal 8 magazine 10 storehouse
repossess see **regain**
reprehend 3 rap 4 rate, skin 5 blame, chide, knock, scold 6 berate, rebuke 7 censure, condemn, upbraid 8 admonish, denounce 9 criticize 10 denunciate
reprehensible 5 amiss 6 guilty, sinful, unholy 8 blameful 11 blameworthy 13 demeritorious
represent 4 body, copy, limn, mean, show 5 draft, image 6 denote, depict, embody, mirror, relate, render, sketch, typify 7 display, exhibit, express, imitate, narrate, outline, picture, portray, realize, signify, suggest 8 describe 9 body forth, delineate, epitomize, exemplify, interpret, personate, personify, symbolize 10 illustrate, substitute 11 emblematize, impersonate, personalize
representation 6 symbol 7 picture 8 likeness 9 portrayal 11 portraiture
representative 4 case 5 agent, envoy, ideal, model, typal, typic 6 deputy, sample 7 classic, example, typical 8 delegate, emissary, instance, monotype, sampling, specimen 9 catchpole, classical, exemplary 10 archetypal, prototypal 11 case history 12 illustrative, prototypical
repress 4 cool 5 shush 6 muffle 7 collect, compose, control, smother, squelch 8 restrain
repression 4 curb 5 check 7 choking, control, subdual 8 crushing, quashing, quelling, stifling 9 clampdown, crackdown, quenching, restraint, squashing 10 smothering
reprieve 7 respite
reprimand 3 rap, wig 5 chide 6 lesson, monish, rebuke 7 chiding, tick off 8 admonish, call down 10 admonition 12 admonishment
reprisal 6 amends 7 redress, revenge 8 avenging, revanche 9 indemnity, quittance, vengeance 10 avengement, recompense 11 counterblow, retaliation, retribution
reprise 5 renew, resay 7 iterate 9 reiterate
reproach 3 rap, wig 5 blame, chide, taunt 6 lesson, monish, rebuke 7 censure, chiding, upbraid 8 admonish, call down 9 discredit 10 admonition 12 admonishment
reprobate 3 bad, rap 4 evil, heel, skin 5 blame, knock, spurn, wrong 6 refuse, reject, sinful, wicked 7 censure, condemn, decline, dismiss, immoral, lowlife, vicious, villain 8 denounce, roperipe, turn down 9 abandoned, criticize, dissolute, miscreant, scoundrel 10 blackguard, disapprove, iniquitous, licentious 12 unprincipled
reproduce 4 bear, copy 5 beget, breed 7 imitate 8 generate, multiply 9 duplicate, procreate, propagate 11 reduplicate
reproduction see **replica**
reproductive cell 3 egg 4 ovum 5 sperm, spore 6 gamete 7 agamete
reproof 3 rap, wig 6 rebuke 7 chiding 8 scolding 10 admonition 12 admonishment
reprove 4 warn 5 blame, chide, scold 6 lesson, monish, punish, rebuke 7 censure, chasten, correct, counsel, tick off 8 admonish, call down, lambaste 9 criticize
reptile 5 snake 6 caiman, cayman, gavial, lizard, turtle 7 tuatara 8 hatteria, tortoise 9 crocodile, sphenodon ***combining form:*** 6 herpet 7 herpeto ***extinct:*** 8 dinosaur
republic 5 state 6 nation ***Africa:*** 4 Chad, Mali, Togo 5 Benin, Congo, Egypt, Gabon, Ghana, Kenya, Niger, Sudan, Zaire 6 Angola, Gambia, Guinea, Malawi, Rwanda, Uganda, Zambia 7 Algeria, Burundi, Comoros, Liberia, Namibia, Senegal, Somalia, Tunisia 8 Botswana, Cameroon, Djibouti, Tanzania 9 Cape Verde 10 Ivory Coast, Madagascar, Mauritania, Mozambique 11 Sierra Leone 12 Guinea-Bissau ***Asia:*** 4 Iran, Iraq, Laos 5 China, India, Syria, Yemen 6 Turkey 7 Vietnam 8 Maldives, Mongolia, Pakistan, Sri Lanka 9 Indonesia, Singapore 10 Bangladesh, North Korea, South Korea 11 Philippines ***Central America:*** 4 Cuba 5 Haiti 6 Panama 7 Ecuador 8 Honduras 9 Costa Rica, Guatemala, Nicaragua ***Europe:*** 5 Italy 6 France, Greece, Poland 7 Albania, Austria, Finland, Germany, Hungary, Iceland, Ireland, Romania, Rumania 8 Bulgaria, Portugal 9 San Marino ***Pacific:*** 5 Nauru 8 Kiribati ***South America:*** 4 Peru 5 Chile 6 Brazil, Guyana 7 Bolivia, Uruguay 8 Colombia, Paraguay 9 Argentina, Venezuela
Republican Party 3 GOP ***mascot:*** 8 elephant
Republic author 5 Plato
repudiate 4 deny 5 spurn 6 defect, desert, disown, refuse, reject 7 abandon, decline, disavow, discard, dismiss, forsake 8 disallow, disclaim, renounce, turn down 10 apostatize, disapprove, tergiverse
repugnance 4 hate 6 hatred, horror 8 aversion, loathing 11 abomination, detestation
repugnant 4 foul, vile 5 alien, nasty 6 creepy, horrid 7 foreign, noisome 8 aversive, gruesome 9 abhorrent, extrinsic, invidious, loathsome, obnoxious, offensive, repulsive, revolting, revulsive 10 disgusting
repulse 5 rebut 6 rebuff, reluct, revolt,

sicken 7 disgust, fend off, hold off, keep off, ward off 8 nauseate, stave off
repulsion see **repugnance**
repulsive see **repugnant**
reputation 4 fame, name 5 éclat 6 credit, renown, weight 8 prestige 9 authority, celebrity, character, influence, notoriety
reputed 8 putative, supposed 9 estimable 10 creditable 11 conjectural, respectable, suppositive 12 hypothetical, suppositious
request 3 ask, sue 4 pray 5 apply 6 appeal, desire, invite 7 solicit 8 entreaty, petition
Requiem for a Nun author 8 Faulkner
requin 5 shark 8 cub shark, man-eater
require 3 ask 4 call, lack, need, take, want 5 claim, crave, exact 6 demand 7 call for, solicit 11 necessitate
required 6 needed 9 mandatory 10 compulsory, obligatory 12 compulsatory
requirement 4 must, need, want 6 demand 9 condition, essential, necessity 10 sine qua non
requisite 3 due 4 just, must 5 right 6 needed 7 condign, merited, needful 8 deserved, rightful, suitable 9 condition, essential, necessity 10 sine qua non 11 appropriate 12 precondition
requisition 4 call 5 claim, exact 6 demand 7 solicit 9 challenge, postulate
requital 7 revenge 8 avenging, revanche 9 vengeance 10 avengement 11 counterblow, retaliation, retribution
requite 3 pay 5 repay 6 return 7 content, revenge, satisfy 9 indemnify, reimburse 10 compensate 11 reciprocate
reredos 6 screen 7 brazier 9 partition
rescind 4 lift 6 recall, repeal, revoke 7 reverse
rescue 4 free, save 6 ransom, redeem, regain 7 deliver, manumit, recover, release 8 conserve, liberate, preserve, retrieve 9 extricate 10 emancipate 11 disentangle 12 disembarrass
research 5 probe, quest 7 delving, inquest, inquiry, probing 11 inquisition 13 investigation
resect 6 cut out, excise 9 extirpate
resemblance 6 simile 7 analogy 8 affinity, likeness, parallel 9 alikeness 10 comparison, similarity, similitude
resemble 5 favor 8 look like, simulate
resembling *combining form:* 4 form 5 iform *suffix:* 2 ar 3 ful 4 eous, itic
resentful 4 sore 6 bitter, piqued, sullen 7 envious, jealous 9 grudgeful
resentment 4 huff, miff 5 pique, spite 6 animus, malice, rancor 7 dudgeon, ill will, offense, umbrage 9 animosity, antipathy, malignity 10 antagonism, malignancy
reservation 5 terms 7 proviso, strings
reserve 4 book, fund, hold, keep 5 hoard, stock, store 6 detain, engage, retain, supply 7 backlog, bespeak, keep out, nest egg 8 contract, hold back, keep back, withhold 9 inventory, preengage, stockpile
reserved 3 shy 5 aloof, close 6 formal, modest, offish, silent 7 bashful, distant, limited 8 eremitic, modified, reticent, solitary, taciturn 9 diffident, qualified, reclusive, withdrawn 10 antisocial, unsociable 11 ceremonious, close-lipped, constrained, standoffish, tight-lipped 12 closemouthed
reservoir 5 hoard, stock, store 7 backlog, nest egg 9 inventory, stockpile
reside 3 lie 4 live 5 dwell, exist 6 endure, inhere, occupy, people, tenant 7 consist, hang out, inhabit 8 continue, domicile
residence 4 home 5 abode, house 8 domicile, dwelling 9 occupancy 10 commorancy, habitation, occupation, settlement 11 inhabitancy 12 inhabitation
resident 5 liver 7 denizen, dweller 8 habitant, occupant 9 indweller 10 inhabitant
residential area 5 exurb 6 suburb 7 exurbia 8 suburbia
resident of *suffix:* 2 er 3 ese, ier, ite, yer
residual 4 heel 7 balance, remains, remanet, remnant 8 leavings 9 remainder
residue 3 ash 4 heel 7 balance, remains, remanet, remnant 8 bone char, leavings 9 bone black, remainder 11 animal black *from honey:* 7 slumgum *metallic:* 4 slag *mineral:* 4 calx
resign 4 cede, drop, quit 5 demit, leave, waive, yield 6 give up, submit 7 abandon 8 abdicate, hand over, renounce 9 surrender, terminate 10 relinquish
resignation 7 modesty 8 meekness, patience 9 lowliness 10 compliance, conformity, humbleness 11 forbearance, longanimity, patientness 12 acquiescence
resigned 7 passive 8 yielding 10 submissive 11 acquiescent, unresistant, unresisting
resile 6 recede, recoil 7 rebound, retract, retreat
resilient 4 airy 6 bouncy, supple, whippy 7 buoyant, elastic, springy, stretch 8 flexible, stretchy, volatile 9 expansive
resin 4 balm 5 copal, damar, roset 6 dammar 7 acrylic, copaiba *aromatic:* 6 balsam, mastic 8 sandarac *fossil:* 8 retinite *fragrant:* 4 tolu 5 elemi 6 storax, styrax 7 ladanum 8 labdanum, olibanum *gum:* 4 kino 5 myrrh 7 benzoin 8 bdellium *medicinal:* 6 guaiac 8 guaiacum *of an insect:* 3 lac *synthetic:* 8 phenolic *used by bees:* 8 propolis
resist 4 balk, buck, defy, duel, foil, stem 5 check, fight, repel 6 assail, attack, baffle,

combat, hinder, impugn, oppose, thwart 7 assault, contest, counter, dispute, gainsay 8 obstruct, traverse 9 frustrate, withstand 10 contradict, contravene
resistance unit 3 ohm
resistor 8 rheostat
resolute 3 set 4 bent, fast, true 5 loyal 6 ardent, intent, steady 7 decided, settled, staunch 8 constant, decisive, faithful, stubborn 9 allegiant, obstinate, steadfast 10 determined 12 pertinacious
resolution 4 guts 5 heart, pluck, spunk 6 mettle, spirit 7 courage 8 analysis, decision, firmness 11 decidedness 13 dauntlessness, determination, purposiveness
resolve 3 fix, rid 4 rule, work 5 break, clear, purge 6 decide, dispel, figure, settle, unfold 7 analyze, clear up, dissect, unravel, work out 8 conclude, decipher, decision, disabuse, disperse, firmness, unriddle 9 anatomize, breakdown, decompose, determine, dissipate, puzzle out 11 decidedness 13 determination, purposiveness
resonant 3 fat 4 deep, full, loud, rich 5 noisy, round 6 mellow, rotund 7 beating, booming, orotund, pulsing, ringing 8 enhanced, plangent, powerful, profound, sonorous, sounding, strident 9 pulsating, thrilling, throbbing 10 clangorous, heightened, stentorian, thundering, thunderous 11 intensified 13 reverberating
resort 2 go 3 den, inn, spa, use 4 nest, turn 5 apply, haunt, haven, hotel, lodge, recur, refer, shift 6 affect, devote, direct, employ, harbor, refuge 7 address, hang out, purlieu, retreat, riviera, stopgap, utilize 8 frequent, recourse 9 expedient, makeshift 10 substitute ***beach:*** 4 lido
resound 4 echo, hymn, laud 5 bless, cry up, extol 6 praise 7 glorify, magnify 9 celebrate
resounding 5 round 6 rotund 7 orotund, reboant, vibrant 8 emphatic, forceful, plangent, sonorant, sonorous 9 assertive, consonant
resource 3 way 4 hope, mode, step 5 dodge, means, shift 6 device, lash-up, manner, method, refuge, relief, string, system 7 fashion, measure, stopgap 8 artifice, creation 9 expedient, invention, makeshift, stratagem, surrogate
resources 5 means, worth 6 assets, riches, wealth 7 capital, fortune 8 property 9 substance
respect 3 awe 4 fear 5 favor, honor 6 admire, devoir, esteem, regard, revere 7 account, worship 8 consider, venerate 9 adoration, reverence 10 admiration, estimation, veneration 13 consideration
respectable 4 done, good, nice 5 right 6 comely, decent, proper, worthy 7 correct, reputed 8 adequate, all right, becoming, decorous 9 befitting 10 conforming, sufficient 11 appropriate 12 satisfactory 13 well-thought-of
respectful 5 civil 6 polite 7 duteous 8 gracious, obeisant, reverent 9 attentive, courteous 10 venerating 11 deferential, reverential
respecting 4 as to, in re 5 about 7 apropos 9 as regards
respire 7 breathe
respite 3 ten 4 blow, ease, lull 5 break, pause, spell 6 breath, recess 7 leisure 8 breather, reprieve 12 intermission
resplendent 5 proud 6 superb 7 blazing, flaming, glowing, sublime 8 glorious, gorgeous
respond 3 act 5 react, reply 6 answer, behave, come in, rejoin, retort, return 8 antiphon
response 5 reply 6 answer, retort, return 8 antiphon 9 rejoinder ***involuntary:*** 6 reflex 7 tropism
responsibility 4 duty, onus 6 burden, charge
responsible 6 liable 10 answerable, dependable 11 accountable
responsive 4 warm 6 tender 7 sensile 8 replying, sensible, sentient, suasible, swayable 9 acceptant, answering 11 impressible, kindhearted, persuadable, persuasible, softhearted, susceptible, sympathetic
rest 3 bed, lie, nap, nod, sit 4 base, calm, doze, ease, hang, heel, loaf, loll, lull, seat, stay 5 basis, count, found, hinge, let up, lie by, pause, peace, quiet, relax, sleep, spell, unlax 6 bottom, depend, ease up, excess, ground, lay off, lounge, repose, snooze, unbend 7 balance, breathe, ease off, footing, leisure, let down, lie down, recline, remains, remanet, remnant, seating, silence, slacken, slumber, surplus 8 interval, leavings, overplus, serenity, slack off, vacation 9 deferring, establish, placidity, predicate, remainder, stillness
restate 6 reword 8 rephrase 9 translate 10 paraphrase
restatement 7 version 9 rendering 10 paraphrase 11 translation
restaurant 4 café 5 diner 6 eatery 7 beanery, tearoom, teashop 8 teahouse 9 brasserie, cafeteria 10 coffee shop 11 coffeehouse ***worker:*** 4 chef, cook 6 busboy, waiter 7 maitre d' 8 waitress 10 dishwasher, headwaiter 12 maitre d' hotel
___ Restaurant 6 Alice's
restful 6 placid 7 easeful, relaxed 8 tranquil
restitute 6 return 7 reclaim, recover,

replace 8 take back 10 rejuvenate 11 recondition, reconstruct 12 rehabilitate
restitution 6 amends 7 redress 8 reprisal 9 indemnity, quittance 10 recompense
restive 4 edgy 5 balky, nervy, tense 6 ornery, uneasy 7 fidgety, froward, uptight, wayward 8 contrary, perverse
restiveness 7 ferment, turmoil 8 disquiet 10 inquietude 11 disquietude
restless 5 itchy, jumpy 6 fitful, fretty, uneasy 7 fidgety, fretful, jittery, nervous, unquiet 8 agitated, fretsome, troubled 9 disturbed, perturbed, spasmodic, unsettled
restlessness see **restiveness**
restorative 5 tonic 6 curing 7 healing 8 remedial, roborant, sanatory 9 remedying, vulnerary, wholesome 10 astringent
restore 4 cure, heal, save, stir 5 amend, rally, renew, right, rouse 6 arouse, better, recall, recoup, redeem, reform, regain, remedy, repair, return, revise, revive, update 7 correct, get back, improve, put back, reclaim, recover, recruit, rectify, refresh, replace 8 give back, renovate, retrieve, revivify, take back 9 modernize, refurbish, reinstate 10 rejuvenate 11 recondition, reconstruct, reestablish, reintroduce 12 rehabilitate
restrain 3 bit, gag 4 cool, curb, keep, rein, stop 5 block, check, cramp, crimp, leash 6 arrest, bridle, coarct, halter, hamper, hinder, hold in, impede, muzzle, pull in, temper 7 collect, compose, control, forbear, harness, inhibit, prevent, repress, smother 8 hold back, hold down, moderate, modulate, obstruct, suppress, underact, withhold *trade:* 7 embargo
restrained 5 quiet, tasty 7 aseptic, subdued 8 discreet, moderate, retiring, tasteful 9 shrinking, temperate, unaffable, unextreme, withdrawn 10 controlled, reasonable
restraint 5 cramp 7 durance, embargo 8 pullback 11 confinement *legal:* 5 estop
restrict 3 bar, tie 4 bind 5 limit 6 shrink 7 confine, delimit 8 prelimit 10 delimitate 12 circumscribe *a will:* 6 entail
restriction 4 curb 5 brake, check, cramp, limit, stint 7 control 10 constraint 11 confinement
restyle 6 redraw, revamp, revise, rework 7 redraft, rewrite 8 work over
result 3 end 5 close, ensue, issue 6 answer, effect, finish, sequel, upshot 7 outcome, product 8 sequence, solution 9 aftermath 10 conclusion, production 11 aftereffect, consequence, eventuality, termination *incidental:* 7 spinoff *suffix:* 7 ization
resume 4 go on 5 renew 6 keep up, pick up, recoup, regain, reopen, retake, take up 7 carry on, reclaim, recover 8 continue, reoccupy, retrieve 10 recommence
resumé 5 sum-up 7 epitome, summary 9 summation, summing-up
resurgence 7 rebirth, revival 11 reanimation 12 risorgimento
resurrect 5 raise, renew 6 revive 8 rekindle, renovate, retrieve, revivify 10 reactivate, revitalize
resurrection 7 rebirth, revival 10 renascence 11 renaissance 12 reviviscence, risorgimento
resuscitate see **resurrect**
retail 4 sell 6 market 11 merchandise
retain 3 own 4 have, hold, keep 7 possess, reserve 8 continue, hold back, keep back, preserve, remember, withhold
retainer 3 fee 6 lackey, minion 7 servant 8 employee, follower 9 dependent
retaliate 5 repay 6 avenge, punish 7 requite, revenge 10 recompense 11 reciprocate
retaliation see **reprisal**
retaliatory *prefix:* 7 counter
retard 4 balk, clog, mire 5 delay, embog, stunt 6 baffle, detain, fetter, hamper, hang up, hinder, impede, lessen, reduce, slow up 7 bog down, inhibit, set back, slacken 8 decrease, restrain, slow down 10 decelerate
retarded 3 dim 4 dull, dumb, slow 6 opaque, simple, stupid 7 moronic 8 backward, imbecile 9 dim-witted 10 half-witted, slow-witted 11 exceptional
retch 3 gag 4 keck 5 heave, vomit
retention 6 memory 7 holding, keeping, storage
reticent see **reserved**
reticulate 6 meshed, netted 10 cancellate
retinue 4 band 5 suite, train 7 company, cortege 9 entourage, following
retire 2 go 3 bed 4 drop, exit, quit 5 leave, yield 6 depart, get off, recede, resign, turn in, vacate 7 abandon, dismiss, get away, pension, retreat, take off 8 fall back, give back, run along, withdraw 9 discharge, surrender, terminate 10 pension off, relinquish 12 superannuate
retired person 7 emerita 8 emeritus
retirement allowance 7 pension
retiring 3 shy 5 timid 6 demure, modest 7 aseptic, bashful, rabbity 8 backward, reserved 9 diffident, unaffable, unassured, withdrawn 10 restrained 11 unassertive
retool 7 reequip, reorder 8 readjust, reorient 9 rearrange, reshuffle 10 reorganize
retort 3 gag, mot 4 jape, jest, joke, quip, snap 5 crack, repay, reply, sally 6 answer, come in, rejoin, return 7 respond, revenge, riposte 8 antiphon, comeback, repartee, reprisal, response 9 rejoinder

retract 4 back 5 unsay 6 abjure, disown, recall, recant, recede, revoke 7 exclude, rescind, rule out, suspend, unswear 8 fall back, forswear, palinode, take back, withdraw

retral 4 back, hind, rear 5 after 6 hinder 8 backward, hindmost 9 posterior 10 retrograde

retread 4 tire 5 recap

retreat 2 go 3 den, fly 4 back, flee, port, quit 5 cover, haven, leave, quail 6 asylum, bow out, covert, decamp, depart, escape, harbor, recede, recoil, refuge, shrink, vacate 7 abandon, back out, pull out, shelter 8 back down, crawfish, evacuate, fall back, give back, hightail, withdraw 9 climb down, harborage, sanctuary *religious:* 5 asram 6 ashram

retrench 3 cut 4 omit 5 slash 6 delete, excise, lessen, reduce 7 abridge, curtail, cut back, shorten 9 economize

retribution 3 pay 6 return 7 revenge 8 avenging, reprisal, requital, revanche 9 vengeance 10 avengement, punishment, recompense 11 counterblow *goddess of:* 3 Ate 4 Fury 7 Nemesis

retrieve 5 renew 6 recall, recoup, regain, rescue, revive 7 get back, recover, recruit, salvage 8 rekindle, renovate, revivify 9 repossess, rocurrect 10 reactivate, revitalize

retrograde 4 back, sink 5 lapse 6 invert, recede, retral, revert, worsen 7 decline, descend, inverse, relapse, retreat, reverse 8 backward, decadent, fall back, inverted, rearward 9 backslide 10 degenerate, disimprove 11 deteriorate 12 disintegrate, recapitulate

retrogress see revert

retrospect 4 cite 6 recall, remind, review, revive 7 bethink 8 remember, revision 9 reminisce 10 afterlight 13 reexamination

retrospective 6 review 8 backward 10 exhibition

return 3 lob, pay 4 gain, give 5 lucre, react, recur, renew, repay, reply, yield 6 advert, answer, bestow, come in, profit, rebate, regain, rejoin, render, retort, revert, rotate 7 bring in, put back, rebound, recover, reentry, reflect, replace, reprise, requite, respond, restore, revenue, reverse, revolve 8 antiphon, comeback, earnings, feedback, give back, proceeds, response, take back, turn back 9 reinstate, rejoinder, repayment, repercuss, restitute, retaliate, reversion 10 recompense, recrudesce, recurrence 11 reciprocate 12 reappearance, reoccurrence

Return of the Native *author:* 5 Hardy *character:* 4 Clym 8 Eustacia

Reuben *brother:* 6 Joseph *father:* 5 Jacob *mother:* 4 Leah *son:* 5 Carmi 6 Hanoch, Hezron, Phallu

Reuel *father:* 4 Esau 7 Ibnijah *mother:* 8 Basemath *son:* 5 Zerah 6 Mizzah, Nahath 7 Shammah 8 Eliasaph *son-in-law:* 5 Moses

revamp 5 patch, renew 6 redraw, repair, rework 7 rebuild, redraft, restyle, rewrite 8 make over, overhaul, renovate 11 recondition, reconstruct

reveal 3 bid, rat 4 avow, bare, blab, leak, open, show, talk, tell, vent 5 admit, break, let on, mouth, peach, spill 6 betray, expose, impart, squeak, unmask, unveil 7 bespeak, blab out, breathe, confess, declare, display, divulge, exhibit, give out, publish, unbosom, unclose, uncover, whisper 8 announce, decipher, disclose, discover, give away, unclothe 9 broadcast, uncurtain 11 acknowledge, communicate

revel 4 bask, hell, orgy, riot, roll 5 feast, gloat, spree 6 frolic, gaiety, wallow, welter 7 carouse, delight, indulge, jollity, roister, rollick, royster, wassail, whoopee, whoopla, whoop-up 8 carnival, festival 9 celebrate, festivity, high jinks, luxuriate, merriment, whoop-de-do 10 skylarking 11 merrymaking

revelation 4 tora 5 torah 6 oracle 8 epiphany, prophecy 9 discovery 10 apocalypse, disclosure 13 manifestation

reveler 8 bacchant, carouser 10 merrymaker

revelry 6 gaiety 7 jollity, wassail, whoopee, whoopla, whoop-up 8 carousal 9 festivity, high jinks, merriment, whoop-de-do 10 skylarking 11 merrymaking

revenant 5 ghost, shade 6 shadow, spirit, wraith 7 phantom, specter 8 phantasm 9 recurring 10 apparition

revenge 6 defend 7 justify, redress 8 reprisal, requital 9 vindicate 11 counterblow, retaliation, retribution

revenue 2 in 4 rent 5 gains, wages, yield 6 income, profit, return, salary 7 comings 8 earnings, interest, proceeds, receipts

reverberant 6 hollow 7 reboant 8 resonant

reverberate 4 echo, ring 5 repel 7 rebound, reflect, resound

revere 4 love 5 adore, enjoy, exalt, honor, prize, value 6 admire, esteem, hallow, regard 7 cherish, magnify, respect, worship 8 treasure, venerate 10 appreciate

revered 9 venerable

reverence 3 awe 4 fear 5 adore, dread, honor, piety 6 fealty, homage 7 loyalty, worship 8 devotion, venerate 9 deference, obeisance, solemnity *gesture of:* 3 bow 8 kneeling 11 genuflexion 12 genuflection

reverend 3 sri 4 holy 5 abbot, clerk

6 clergy, cleric, divine, parson, sacred 8 clerical, minister, preacher 9 churchman, clergyman, monsignor, venerable 11 patriarchal 12 ecclesiastic
reverent 6 devout 7 dutiful 10 respectful
reverie 4 muse 5 dream, study 6 musing, trance, vision 7 fantasy, thought 8 daydream, dreaming 10 absorption, brown study, meditation 11 abstraction, daydreaming
reversal 4 turn 5 check 6 change, switch 7 backset, setback, turning 8 backfire 9 about-face, inversion, turnabout, volte-face
reverse 4 lift, turn 5 annul, check, polar, shift, verso 6 change, contra, defeat, invert, recall, repeal, revoke 7 backset, capsize, counter, rescind, set back, subvert 8 antipode, antipole, backward, contrary, converse, disaster, exchange, opposite, overrule, overturn, transfer 9 about-face, antipodal, backwards, diametric, dismantle, overthrow, transpose, turnabout, volte-face 10 antipodean, antithesis, misfortune, right-about, transplace *prefix:* 2 de, ob 3 dis, dys
reversion 4 turn 5 lapse 6 return 7 atavism, escheat, relapse 9 about-face, throwback, turnabout, volte-face 10 right-about 11 backsliding, changeabout
revert 4 turn 5 lapse, react, recur 6 change, return 7 decline, escheat, inverse, regress, relapse 8 turn back 9 backslide, throw back, transpose 10 degenerate, recrudesce, retrograde, retrogress, transplace
revetment 7 sodwork 9 barricade 10 embankment
review 4 edit, scan 5 audit, organ, recap, study 6 notice, parade, revise, survey 7 account, brushup, checkup, comment, journal, recense, redraft, rethink, re-treat, revisal, reweigh 8 analysis, critique, magazine, rescript, revision, scrutiny 9 checkover, criticism, criticize, recension, reexamine, think over 10 afterlight, inspection, periodical, reconsider, reevaluate, reflection, retrospect 11 examination 13 reexamination, retrospection, second thought
revile 4 hate, rail, rate 5 abuse, libel, scold 6 berate, defame, malign, vilify 7 asperse, bawl out, chew out, slander, traduce, upbraid 8 backbite, disgrace, execrate, reproach 9 blaspheme 10 calumniate, tongue-lash, vituperate
revise 4 edit 5 alter, amend, emend 6 change, polish, redact, redraw, reform, revamp, review, rework, update 7 correct, improve, perfect, recense, redraft, restyle, rewrite, upgrade 8 overhaul, rescript, work over 9 recension 10 blue-pencil, reorganize
revitalize see revive
revival 7 rebirth, renewal 8 wakening 10 renascence, resurgence 11 reanimation, renaissance, restoration 12 regeneration, rejuvenation, reproduction, resurrection, reviviscence, risorgimento 13 recrudescence, resuscitation
revive 4 wake 5 rally, renew, rouse 6 arouse, exhume, recall 7 bethink, enliven, freshen, quicken, refresh, respire, restore 8 activate, energize, reawaken, rekindle, remember, renovate, retrieve, revivify, vitalize 9 galvanize, reanimate, recollect, refreshen, reinstate, resurrect, stimulate 10 reactivate, recuperate, regenerate, rejuvenate, revitalize 11 reestablish, reintroduce, resuscitate 12 reinvigorate
revivify see revive
revoke 4 lift, void 5 adeem, annul, erase 6 abjure, cancel, recall, recant, remind, renege, repeal 7 abolish, expunge, nullify, rescind, retract, reverse 8 abrogate, forswear 10 invalidate 11 countermand
revolt 4 defy, riot 5 rebel, repel 6 mutiny, offend, oppose, reluct, resist, sicken, uprise, uproar 7 boycott, disgust, repulse 8 mutineer, nauseate, overturn, renounce, sedition, uprising 9 insurrect, overthrow, rebellion 11 rise against, turn against 12 insurrection
revolter 5 rebel 6 anarch 8 frondeur, mutineer 9 anarchist, insurgent 10 malcontent
revolting 4 foul, ugly, vile 5 nasty 6 horrid 7 hideous, noisome 8 shocking 9 loathsome, offensive, repellent, repugnant, repulsive 10 disgusting, nauseating
revolution 4 gyre, reel, riot, roll, spin, turn 5 cycle, round, twirl, wheel, whirl 6 change 7 circuit, shake-up 8 disorder, gyration, overturn, rotation, sedition, turnover, uprising 9 overthrow, pirouette, rebellion
revolutionary 5 rabid, rebel, ultra 7 extreme, fanatic, radical 8 mutineer, rotating, ultraist 9 extremist, insurgent 10 malcontent ***American:*** 4 Read 5 Shays ***French:*** 5 Marat 8 Mirabeau 11 Robespierre ***Irish:*** 4 Tone ***Mexican:*** 5 Villa 6 Zapata ***Russian:*** 5 Kirov 7 Trotsky 8 Kerensky 9 Kropotkin
revolutionist see revolutionary
revolutionize 5 alter 6 change, modify, recast, redraw, reform, revamp, revise 7 remodel, restyle 8 overturn 9 overthrow, refashion, transform 11 transfigure 12 metamorphose
revolve 4 birl, chaw, gyre, muse, roll, spin, turn 5 orbit, round, wheel, whirl 6 circle, gyrate, ponder, rotate 7 agitate, circuit 8 consider, gyration, meditate, mull over, rotation, ruminate, turn over

revolver 3 gat, gun, rod 6 pistol 7 firearm, handgun
revulsion 4 hate 6 hatred, horror 8 aversion, loathing 9 repulsion 10 abhorrence, repugnance 11 abomination, detestation
reward 4 meed, plum 5 bonus, booty, crown, medal, prize 6 bounty, carrot, trophy 7 guerdon, premium 8 dividend, requital 10 compensate, honorarium, recompense, remunerate 12 compensation, remuneration
reword see **restate**
rework 6 redraw, revamp, revise 7 redraft, restyle, rewrite
rewrite see **revise**
Reynard the ___ 3 Fox
Rezon's father 6 Eliada
rhadamanthine 3 due 4 just 5 right 7 condign, merited 8 deserved, rightful, suitable 9 requisite 11 appropriate
Rhadamanthus 5 judge ***brother:*** 5 Minos ***father:*** 4 Zeus 7 Jupiter ***mother:*** 6 Europa
rhapsodic 8 ecstatic, effusive 9 emotional
Rhea 3 Ops ***daughter:*** 4 Hera, Juno 5 Ceres, Vesta 6 Hestia 7 Demeter ***father:*** 6 Uranus ***husband:*** 6 Cronus, Saturn ***mother:*** 2 Ge 4 Gaea ***son:*** 4 Zeus 5 Hades, Pluto 7 Jupiter, Neptune 8 Poseidon
rheostat 6 dimmer 8 resistor
rhesus 6 monkey 7 macaque
rhetoric 4 rant 6 speech 7 bombast, fustian, oratory 8 rhapsody 9 discourse, elocution, eloquence, verbosity 11 highfalutin, rodomontade, speechcraft 13 lexiphanicism ***term:*** 6 aporia, ecbole, simile 7 epandos, litotes 8 metaphor 10 apostrophe, digression 12 alliteration, onomatopoeia
rhetorical 4 glib 5 gassy, grand, showy, tumid, vocal, windy 6 florid, fluent, mouthy, ornate, purple, turgid 7 aureate, flowery, orotund, pompous, stilted, swollen 8 eloquent, forensic, imposing, inflated, overdone, sonorous, swelling 9 bombastic, grandiose, high-flown, overblown, tumescent 10 articulate, euphuistic, figurative, flamboyant, oratorical 11 declamatory, embellished, exaggerated, highfalutin, overwrought, pretentious 12 high-sounding, magniloquent, orchidaceous, ostentatious 13 grandiloquent
rhetorician 6 orator, writer 7 speaker ***Roman:*** 11 Quintillian
Rhine River ***city:*** 4 Bonn, Köln 5 Mainz 7 Cologne 8 Mannheim 9 Weisbaden 10 Dusseldorf ***golden ring:*** 9 Rheingold, Rhinegold ***nymph:*** 7 Lorelei ***tributary:*** 3 Aar, Ill 4 Aare, Lahn, Main, Ruhr, Waal
rhinoceros 5 badak 6 borele 7 keitloa, upeygan 8 nasicorn ***feature:*** 4 horn ***relative of:*** 5 tapir
rhizome 4 root, stem 5 shoot 6 branch
Rhode Island ***capital:*** 10 Providence ***college, university:*** 5 Brown 6 Bryant 10 Providence 11 Salve Regina ***founder:*** 8 Williams (Roger) ***nickname:*** 11 Little Rhody ***state flower:*** 6 violet
Rhodesia see **Zimbabwe**
rhombus 7 diamond, lozenge 13 parallelogram
Rhone River ***lake:*** 6 Geneva ***mountain:*** 4 Jura ***town:*** 4 Lyon 5 Arles 6 Geneva ***tributary:*** 5 Isère, Saône
rhubarb 3 row 4 beef 5 plant, run-in, set-to 7 dispute, quarrel, yawweed 8 pieplant 9 bickering 11 altercation, controversy
rhyme 4 beat, poem, rune, song 5 agree, check, meter, poesy, swing, verse 6 accord, cohere, poetry, rhythm 7 cadence, cadency, comport, conform, consist, consort, measure 8 dovetail, rhythmus 10 correspond
rhymer 4 bard, poet 5 rimer 7 bardlet 8 bardling, poetling, rimester, verseman 9 poetaster, poeticule, versifier 11 versemonger
rhymester see **rhymer**
rhythm 4 beat, lilt, time 5 meter, pulse, swing, tempo 6 accent 7 cadence, cadency, measure 8 movement, sequence
rhythmic 6 poetic 7 pulsing, regular 8 cadenced, measured, metrical 9 cadential, pulsating
rialto 4 mart 6 market 8 district, exchange
riant 3 gay 4 boon 5 jolly, merry 6 blithe, bright, jocund, jovial 7 festive, gleeful, smiling 8 cheerful, laughing, mirthful
riata 4 rope 5 lasso 6 lariat
rib 3 fun, kid, rag 4 band, bone, dike, fool, jest, joke, josh, purl, razz, stay, wale 5 chaff, costa, ridge, tease 6 banter, costae (plural), lierne ***combining form:*** 4 cost 5 costi, costo, pleur 6 pleuri, pleuro ***relating to:*** 6 costal 7 costate
ribald 5 devil, rogue, scamp 6 coarse, rascal, risqué, vulgar 7 obscene 8 indecent, mischief, scalawag, slyboots 9 skeezicks 10 irreverent 11 rapscallion
ribbon 3 bow 4 band, tape 5 braid, reins, shred, strip 6 cordon, fillet, stripe, tatter 7 bandeau, banding, binding 8 fragment, tressure 9 banderole ***combining form:*** 4 taen 5 taeni 6 taenio
rice 4 boro, paga, twig 5 arroz, bigas, canin, macan 6 branch 7 risotto ***boiled with meat:*** 5 pilaf, pilau ***combining form:*** 4 oryz 5 oryzi, oryzo ***cooked with meat:*** 7 risotto 9 jambalaya ***drink:*** 4 saki 7 pangasi ***field:*** 3 cut 4 padi 5 paddy, sawah ***husk:*** 5 lemma, shood, shude ***long-stemmed:*** 4 aman ***mountain:*** 5 smilo ***short-stemmed:*** 3 aus

rich 3 fat 4 dear, easy, high, lush, oofy, warm 5 ample, flush, heavy, meaty, plump, round, sweet, vivid 6 absurd, costly, creamy, daedal, facund, fecund, florid, fruity, hearty, mellow, monied, ornate, potent, rococo, sating, superb 7 amusing, baroque, cloying, copious, fertile, filling, moneyed, opulent, orotund, pinguid, wealthy, well-off 8 abundant, affluent, childing, eloquent, fruitful, well-to-do 9 abounding, bountiful, elaborate, laughable, luxuriant, oversweet, plentiful, satiating, sumptuous, well-fixed 10 expressive, flamboyant, meaningful, productive, prosperous, well-heeled 11 comfortable *person:* 5 Midas, nabob 7 Croesus 9 plutocrat

Richardson work 6 Pamela 8 Clarissa 15 Clarissa Harlowe

Richelieu's successor 7 Mazarin

riches 4 gold, pelf, weal 5 booty, lucre, worth 6 mammon, wealth 7 fortune 8 opulence, property, treasure 9 resources *demon of:* 6 Mammon

rick 3 mow 4 bank, cock, heap, hill, pile, ruck 5 drift, shock, stack

rickety 4 weak 5 shaky 6 feeble, senile, wobbly 7 unsound 8 rachitic, unstable, unsteady 10 ramshackle, rattletrap

ricochet 3 dap 4 skim, skip 5 bound, carom, graze 6 bounce, glance, recoil 7 rebound

rid 4 free, lose, quit, shed 5 clear, empty 6 remove, uproot 7 abolish, deliver, release, relieve 8 liberate, shake off, throw off, unburden 11 disencumber

riddle 3 pan, why 4 crux, sift 5 griph, rebus 6 enigma, pierce, puzzle, screen 7 griphus, mystery, perplex, problem 8 permeate, separate 9 conundrum, penetrate, perforate 10 puzzlement

ride 2 go 3 rib 4 auto, bait, last, lift, sail, spin, tour, trip, turn 5 chivy, coast, drift, drive, float, glide, hound, motor, tease 6 badger, banter, canter, gallop, harass, heckle, hector 7 journey, oppress, overlap, overlie, shingle, survive, torment, torture 8 bullyrag, carousel, ridicule 9 carrousel, excursion, imbricate, persecute

rider 6 clause, cowboy, jockey, knight 7 codicil 8 addendum, addition, appendix, horseman, reinsman 9 amendment 10 equestrian, supplement

ridge 3 rib, top 4 bank, brow, fold, hill, keel, reef, roll, ruck, seam, spur, wave 5 arris, chine, costa, crest, knurl, ledge, plica, quill, rivel, spine 6 crease, divide, furrow, rideau, rimple, saddle, summit 7 annulet, breaker, costula, crinkle, hogback, hummock, wrinkle 8 headland, shoulder 9 razorback 11 corrugation *gravelly:* 5 esker *on the skin:* 4 welt *sharp:* 7 hogback

ridicule 3 guy, pan 4 gibe, haze, jape, jeer, lout, mock, quiz, razz, ride, twit 5 chaff, flout, mimic, rally, roast, scoff, scout, sneer, squib, taunt 6 deride, satire 7 lampoon, mockery, pillory, sarcasm 8 derision, raillery, satirize, travesty 9 burlesque 10 caricature *god of:* 5 Momus *object of:* 4 butt 13 laughingstock

ridiculous 5 antic, comic, dotty, droll, funny, rough, silly 6 absurd, insane 7 amusing, bizarre, comical, foolish, mocking, risible, ungodly 8 derisive, derisory, farcical, gelastic, improper, indecent, unseemly 9 cockamamy, fantastic, grotesque, laughable, ludicrous 10 indecorous, irrational, outrageous, unbecoming 12 preposterous

riding *academy:* 6 manège *costume:* 5 habit *pants:* 8 jodhpurs *whip:* 4 crop 5 quirt

Rienzi composer 6 Wagner

rife 4 full, rank 5 alive, ariot 6 active, filled, strong 7 current, popular, rampant, regnant, replete, teeming 8 abundant, manifest, numerous, swarming, thronged 9 abounding, plentiful, prevalent 10 prevailing, widespread 11 overflowing

riff 4 scan, skim 6 browse

riffle 4 fret, scan, skim, wave 5 rapid, shoal 6 browse, cockle, dimple, ripple 7 dip into, run over, shuffle 8 glance at 10 glance over, run through 11 flip through, leaf through, skim through 12 thumb through

riffraff 3 mob 4 junk, mass, scum 5 dregs, offal, trash, waste 6 debris, kelter, litter, rabble, refuse, tagrag 7 garbage, rubbish 8 canaille, unwashed 11 proletariat

rifle 3 arm, gun, rob 4 loot 5 piece, steal, yager 6 furrow, groove, jaeger, weapon 7 carbine, despoil, firearm, pillage, plunder, ransack, relieve 9 chassepot *accessory:* 6 ramrod *kind:* 6 Garand, Mauser 7 Enfield 8 Browning 9 Remington 10 Winchester 11 Springfield *pin:* 4 tige

rift 3 gap 4 flaw, rent, rima, rime, rive 5 break, chasm, chink, cleft, crack, split 6 breach, cleave, divide, hiatus, schism 7 blemish, fissure, opening, rupture 8 crevasse, division, fracture, interval, rimation

rig 3 arm, fit, fix 4 gear, hoax, wind 5 dress, equip, getup, guise, trick 6 fit out, outfit, setout, tackle 7 appoint, arrange, costume, derrick, furnish, turn out 8 accouter, accoutre, carriage, equipage 9 apparatus, equipment

rigadoon 5 dance

rigamarole see **rigmarole**

rigging 3 net 4 duds, gear, togs 5 dress,

lines, ropes 6 attire, chains, tackle, things 7 apparel, clothes, raiment 8 clothing

right 3 apt, due, fit, ius, jus, now 4 away, bang, dead, done, fair, good, hale, jura (plural), just, nice, real, sane, tory, true, very, well 5 amend, amply, claim, clear, droit, emend, exact, fully, happy, legal, lucid, quite, sharp, sound, spang, title, whole 6 at once, comely, common, decent, dexter, direct, equity, highly, honest, lawful, normal, patent, proper, square, strict 7 condign, correct, diehard, exactly, fitting, fogyish, freedom, genuine, healthy, liberty, license, merited, notably, old-line, parlous, precise, rectify, redress, utterly 8 accurate, adequate, all there, appanage, becoming, bona fide, decorous, deserved, directly, easement, entirely, faithful, first off, interest, old liner, orthodox, properly, rigorous, smack-dab, squarely, standpat, straight, suffrage, suitable, suitably, usufruct 9 authentic, authority, befitting, equitable, extremely, fittingly, forthwith, franchise, honorable, instanter, perfectly, precisely, privilege, propriety, requisite, simon-pure, tolerable, undoubted, veracious, veridical, veritable, wholesome 10 acceptable, acceptably, accurately, adequately, altogether, applicable, becomingly, completely, concession, felicitous, perquisite, properness, remarkably, scrupulous, straightly, sufficient, sure-enough, well-liking 11 appropriate, bitter-ender, comme il faut, correctness, exceedingly, immediately, indubitable, prerogative, reactionary, standpatter, undistorted 12 compos mentis, conservative ***combining form:*** 4 orth, rect 5 dextr, ortho, recti 6 dextro ***feudal:*** 4 soke ***legal:*** 5 droit 8 usufruct ***royal:*** 6 regale 7 regalia (plural)

right away 3 now 6 at once 8 directly, first off, straight 9 forthwith, instanter, instantly 11 immediately, straightway

righteous 4 good, holy, just, pure 5 godly, moral, noble, pious 6 devout, worthy 7 ethical, sinless, upright 8 innocent, virtuous 9 blameless, equitable, exemplary, guiltless 10 inculpable, moralistic, principled

righteousness 6 equity, virtue 7 justice, probity 8 goodness, holiness, justness, morality 9 rectitude 11 uprightness

rightful 3 apt, due, fit 4 fair, just, true 5 legal 6 honest, lawful, proper 7 condign, fitting, merited 8 deserved, suitable 9 befitting, equitable, impartial, requisite 10 applicable, legitimate 11 appropriate

right-handed 7 dextral 8 dextrous 9 clockwise, dexterous

right-hand page 5 recto

rightist 4 tory 7 diehard 8 old liner, standpat 11 bitter-ender, reactionary, right-winger, standpatter 12 conservative

right-minded 5 moral, noble 7 ethical 8 virtuous 10 moralistic, principled

Rights of Man author 5 Paine

rigid 3 set 4 firm, hard, taut 5 fixed, solid, stein, stiff, tough 6 formal, severe, strait, strict 7 adamant, austere, buckram, hardset 8 hard-line, ironclad, obdurate, rigorist, rigorous 9 draconian, immovable, impliable, inelastic, stringent, unbending 10 adamantine, inexorable, inflexible, ironhanded, motionless, relentless, unflexible, unyielding 11 immalleable

rigidity 5 frost 6 turgor 7 buckram 8 hardness, turgency 9 stiffness ***muscular:*** 8 myotonia

rigmarole 6 ramble 8 nonsense 9 procedure 10 balderdash

Rigoletto ***composer:*** 5 Verdi ***daughter:*** 5 Gilda

rigor 5 trial 7 cruelty 8 asperity, hardness, hardship, severity 9 austerity, harshness, roughness, sharpness, sternness 10 affliction, difficulty, exactitude, strictness, visitation 11 tribulation, vicissitude 13 inflexibility

rigorous 4 hard, nice 5 exact, harsh, right, rigid, rough, stern, stiff 6 bitter, brutal, proper, rugged, severe, strait, strict 7 ascetic, correct, drastic, onerous, precise 8 accurate, exacting 9 draconian, inclement, stringent 10 burdensome, inexorable, inflexible, ironhanded, oppressive

rile 3 mud, vex 4 roil 5 anger, annoy, grate, muddy, peeve, pique, upset 6 muddle, nettle, put out 7 agitate, disturb, inflame, provoke 8 irritate 9 aggravate

rim 3 hem, lip 4 bank, boss, brim, edge, ring 5 bezel, bezil, bound, brink, skirt, verge 6 border, flange, fringe, margin, shield 7 annulus, horizon, outline 8 boundary, surround 9 perimeter, periphery ***of a basket:*** 4 hoop ***of a cask:*** 5 chime, chine ***of an insect's wing:*** 6 termen ***of a spoked wheel:*** 5 felly 6 felloe ***of a volcanic crater:*** 5 somma

rima 4 rift 5 chink, cleft, crack, split 7 fissure 8 aperture

rime 3 ice 4 cake, rift 5 chink, cleft, crack, crust, frost, split 7 encrust, fissure, incrust 10 incrustate 12 incrustation

Rimmon's son 6 Baanah, Rechab

rimple 4 fold, ruck 5 crimp, plica, ridge, rivel, screw 6 crease, furrow, ruck up, rumple 7 crimple, crinkle, crumple, scrunch, wrinkle 11 corrugation

Rinaldo ***beloved:*** 8 Angelica ***cousin:*** 7 Orlando ***father:*** 5 Aymon ***horse:*** 6 Bayard ***mother:*** 3 Aya ***sister:*** 10 Bradamante ***uncle:*** 11 Charlemagne

rind 4 bark, husk, peel, skin 5 crust ***of roast pork:*** 9 crackling

ring 3 bee, eye, hem, mob, rim 4 bail, band,

bell, bloc, bong, camp, clan, cric, ding, dirl, echo, gird, gyre, hoop, loop, peal, toll 5 anlet, arena, bague, bezel, cabal, chime, clang, cycle, group, knell, knoll, party, rigol, round, sound 6 begird, boxing, circle, clique, collar, collet, dindle, famble, girdle, staple 7 annulus, clangor, combine, compass, coterie, faction, ferrule, grommet, ingroup, resound, vibrate 8 bracelet, cincture, encircle, pugilism, surround 9 camarilla, coalition, encompass 11 combination, reverberate ***around sun or moon:*** 5 broch 6 corona ***combining form:*** 3 gyr 4 cycl, gyro 5 cyclo ***curtain:*** 3 eye ***for a compass:*** 6 gimbal ***for a lampshade:*** 4 harp 7 gallery ***harness:*** 3 dee 6 button, larigo, terret, territ ***heraldic:*** 7 annulet ***in a hinge:*** 7 gudgeon ***of chain:*** 4 link 7 belcher ***of color:*** 8 stocking ***of dots around a coin:*** 8 graining ***of leaves or flowers:*** 6 wreath 7 garland ***of light:*** 4 halo 5 glory 6 corona, nimbus 7 aureole 8 halation ***of Odin:*** 8 draupnir ***of rope or metal:*** 4 hank 6 becket 7 garland, grommet, snotter, thimble ***of two hoops:*** 5 gemel 6 gemmel, gimmal ***on a key, pocket watch or scissors handle:*** 3 bow ***on an archery target:*** 4 sous 5 souse ***relating to:*** 7 annular ***rubber, for a fruit jar:*** 4 lute ***used as a valve or diaphragm:*** 5 wafer ***used for securing a bird:*** 6 vervel ***used to enclose deer:*** 7 tinchel ***wedding:*** 4 band

Ring and the Book author 8 Browning

ringed 8 annulate, circular 9 encircled 10 surrounded

ringer 4 fake, spit 5 image 6 double 7 picture 8 impostor, portrait 9 direct hit 10 simulacrum 13 spitting image

ringing 5 round 6 bright, fervid, jangle, rotund 7 clangor, orotund, vibrant 8 decisive, plangent, resonant, sonorant, sonorous 9 consonant 10 resounding

ringleader 4 boss 5 chief 6 honcho 10 instigator, mastermind

ringlet 4 curl, lock 5 tress 7 tendril

rinse 4 lave, wash 5 douse, swill 6 douche, sluice 7 cleanse ***the mouth:*** 6 gargle

riot 4 hell, howl 5 brawl, melee, revel, smash, spree 6 attack, bedlam, clamor, émeute, excess, frolic, jumble, scream, tumult, uproar 7 anarchy, carouse, debauch, dispute, misrule, quarrel, revelry, roister, wassail 8 carousal, disorder, uprising 9 anarchism, commotion, distemper, sensation 10 donnybrook 11 disturbance

riotous 4 loud, lush, wild 5 noisy 6 lavish, stormy, wanton 7 bacchic, opulent, profuse, roaring 8 bacchian, prodigal 9 exuberant, luxuriant, profusive 10 boisterous 11 saturnalian 12 unrestrained

rip 3 cut 4 rend, rent, rive, spit, tear 5 shred, slash, split 6 attack, cleave, sunder 7 sputter 8 lacerate, splutter

ripe 3 fit 4 aged, late 5 adult, grown, ready 6 mature, mellow, timely 7 grown-up, matured, overdue 8 complete, finished 9 developed, full-blown, full-grown, perfected, virtuosic, well-timed 10 consummate, seasonable 11 full-fledged

ripen 3 age 4 grow 6 better, grow up, mature, mellow, season 7 develop, enhance, improve, perfect 8 heighten, maturate 9 intensify

ripening early 4 rath 5 rathe 8 rareripe

riposte 5 reply 6 retort, return, thrust 8 comeback, repartee 10 back answer 13 counterattack

ripping 4 fine 5 grand, nifty, super, swell 6 divine, peachy 7 capital 8 glorious, splendid, terrific 9 admirable, excellent, marvelous, wonderful 10 remarkable 11 sensational

ripple 3 cut, lap 4 curl, fret, riff, wave 5 acker 6 cockle, dimple, lipper, popple, riffle, rimple 7 crinkle, wrinkle

rip-roaring 5 noisy 6 lively 8 exciting 9 hilarious 10 boisterous, uproarious

ripsnorter 5 dandy 8 jim-dandy 9 humdinger 11 crackerjack

riptide 8 undertow

Rip Van Winkle ***author:*** 6 Irving ***dog:*** 4 Wolf

rise 2 up 3 wax 4 come, flow, grow, head, hike, lift, rear, soar, stem, well 5 awake, begin, boost, build, climb, get up, issue, mount, occur, raise, rebel, rouse, scale, sit up, stand, start, surge, swell, tower 6 ascend, ascent, aspire, awaken, befall, betide, chance, deepen, emerge, expand, growth, happen, recess, revolt, spring, thrive, uprear 7 adjourn, advance, augment, bristle, develop, elevate, emanate, enhance, enlarge, fall out, magnify, pile out, proceed, prosper, roll out, stand up, succeed, surface, turn out, upgrade, upstand, upsurge 8 addition, dissolve, eminence, heighten, increase, levitate, multiply, prorogue, redouble, upspring 9 accession, accretion, aggravate, ascension, increment, intensate, intensify, originate, prorogate, terminate, transpire 10 derive from ***above:*** 8 surmount ***abruptly:*** 9 skyrocket ***again:*** 7 resurge 9 resurrect ***against:*** 5 rebel 6 mutiny, revolt 9 insurrect ***and fall:*** 4 tide 5 heave 6 welter ***and shine:*** 5 get up 7 pile out, roll out, turn out ***gradually:*** 4 loom ***swiftly:*** 4 boil, boom 6 spring ***up:*** 4 fume, rear, well 5 rebel, swell, tower 6 ascend, revolt 9 insurrect

Rise of Silas Lapham author 7 Howells

riser 4 step

risible 5 comic, droll, funny 7 comical 8 farcical, gelastic 9 laughable, ludicrous 10 ridiculous

risk 4 dare, defy, face, luck, meet 5 beard, brave, peril, stake, wager 6 chance, danger, gamble, hazard, menace 7 fortune, imperil, jeopard, venture 8 accident, confront, endanger, exposure, jeopardy, openness 9 adventure, encounter, liability 10 compromise, jeopardize

risky 4 bold 5 hairy 6 chancy, daring, touchy, wicked 7 parlous, unsound 8 delicate, perilous, ticklish 9 dangerous, hazardous, sensitive, unhealthy 10 jeopardous, precarious 11 speculative, treacherous

risqué 3 raw 4 blue, foul, lewd, racy, sexy 5 broad, crude, dirty, gross, salty, shady, spicy 6 coarse, daring, earthy, purple, ribald, vulgar, wicked 7 naughty, obscene, raunchy 8 indecent, off-color, scabrous 9 audacious, inelegant, salacious, unrefined 10 indecorous, indelicate, suggestive

rite 4 cult, form 6 fetish, honors, office 7 liturgy, mystery, service 8 ceremony, hierurgy, occasion 9 formality, ordinance, procedure, sacrament, solemnity 10 ceremonial, initiation, observance 11 celebration, sacramental ***aborigine:*** 4 bora ***American Indian:*** 8 huskanaw 11 huskanawing ***Buddhist:*** 6 pansil ***funeral:*** 6 exequy 7 obsequy 8 exequies ***Hindu:*** 4 puja 5 pooja, sradh 6 poojah, sradha 7 sraddha ***Jewish:*** 4 bris 5 berit, briss, brith 6 berith 7 tashlik 8 tashlich 12 circumcision ***Mayan:*** 3 kex ***of initiation or purification:*** 7 baptism ***of knighthood:*** 8 accolade ***of prophecy:*** 6 augury ***of recognition of merit:*** 8 accolade; (see also **sacrament**)

ritual see **rite**

ritzy 6 modish 7 elegant, haughty 8 snobbish 9 expensive, luxurious 11 fashionable 12 ostentatious

rival 3 tie, try, vie 4 even, meet, peer, side 5 equal, fight, match, touch 6 amount, strive 7 attempt, compete, contend, contest, emulate, entrant, feuding 8 approach, emulator, opponent, rivalize, struggle 9 adversary, competing, contender, measure up, partake of 10 antagonist, competitor, contending, contestant 11 comparative, competition ***prefix:*** 3 ant 4 anth, anti

rivalry 6 strife 7 contest, warfare 8 conflict, jealousy, striving, tug-of-war 9 emulation 11 competition

rive 3 hew, rip 4 chop, plow, rend, tear 5 burst, sever, smash, split 6 cleave, divide, pierce, shiver, sunder, thrust 7 shatter 8 fracture, fragment, lacerate, separate, splinter, splitter 11 splinterize

river ***Africa:*** 4 Bomu 5 Congo, Mbomu, Zaire 6 Atbara 7 Aruwimi, Atbarah, Zambesi, Zambeze, Zambezi 9 Astaboras ***Alabama:*** 5 Coosa 6 Mobile 7 Conecuh, Perdido 9 Tombigbee 10 Tallapoosa ***Alaska:*** 5 Kobuk 6 Copper, Noatak, Tanana 7 Koyukuk, Susitna 9 Kuskokwim ***Albania:*** 4 Drin 5 Drini ***Argentina:*** 5 Negro 6 Parané 7 Matanza ***arm:*** 6 branch 9 tributary ***Asia:*** 4 Amur, Oxus 5 Indus 6 Jayhun 7 Oedanes 8 Amu Darya 9 Dyardanes 11 Brahmaputra ***Australia:*** 4 Daly 5 Roper, Yarra 6 Barwon, Culgoa, Dawson, DeGrey, Murray 7 Darling, Fitzroy, Lachlan 8 Victoria 10 Yarra Yarra ***Austria:*** 4 Enns ***bank:*** 5 levee ***Belgium:*** 5 Rupel, Senne, Weser 6 Dender, Dindar, Ourthe 8 Visurgis ***Bolivia:*** 4 Beni 5 Abuná 6 Mamoré ***Borneo:*** 5 Kajan ***bottom:*** 3 bed ***Brazil:*** 3 Ica 4 Pará, Paru 5 Negro, Xingu 6 Paraná 7 Madeira, Tapajós, Tapajoz ***British Columbia:*** 6 Skeena 10 Bella Coola ***California:*** 3 Eel, Pit 4 Kern, Yuba 6 Merced 7 Feather, Salinas, Trinity 8 Tuolumne 9 Mokelumne 10 Sacramento, Stanislaus ***Cambodia:*** 8 Tonle Sap ***Canada:*** 3 Bow 4 Back 5 Moose, Peace 6 Beaver, Fraser, Nelson, Ottawa 8 Gatineau, Saguenay 9 Athabasca, Great Fish, Mackenzie, Richelieu 11 Assiniboine ***Carolinas:*** 7 Catawba ***central Africa:*** 6 Ubangi ***central Asia:*** 6 Gandak 8 Syr Darya ***central Canada:*** 5 Slave ***central Europe:*** 4 Eger, Elbe, Labe, Ohře 5 Albis 6 Danube ***central United States:*** 3 Fox 5 Grand 6 Neosho, Platte, Wabash 8 Keya Paha, Missouri, Niobrara 9 Tennessee, Verdigris 10 Republican, Saint Croix 11 Mississippi ***channel:*** 6 alveus ***Chile:*** 3 Loa 5 Itata, Maule 6 Bío-Bío 8 Valdivia ***China:*** 2 Si, Xi, Zi 3 Bei, Hun, Wei 4 Dong 5 Baihe, Huang, Hwang, Tarim 6 Yellow 7 Kashgar, Yangtze ***Colombia:*** 4 Tomo 6 Atrato 9 Magdalena ***Colorado:*** 5 Yampa 8 Gunnison ***combining form:*** 5 fluvi, potam 6 fluvio, potamo ***Connecticut:*** 6 Thames 7 Niantic, Shepaug 9 Naugatuck 10 Farmington, Housatonic, Quinnipiac 11 Willimantic ***crossing:*** 4 ford ***current:*** 4 eddy 6 rapids ***Czechoslovakia:*** 3 Vág, Váh 4 Gran, Hron, Iser, Waag 5 Garam, Nitra 6 Jisera, Moldau, Neutra, Nyitra, Vltava ***dam:*** 4 weir ***Denmark:*** 4 Stor ***dried bed:*** 4 wadi 5 waddy ***drowned:*** 7 estuary ***East Africa:*** 4 Juba 5 Tsavo 6 Songwe ***East Asia:*** 4 Yalu 5 Amnok 7 Oryokko ***eastern United States:*** 7 Potomac ***Ecuador:*** 10 Esmeraldas ***England:*** 3 Esk, Exe, Nen, Ure 4 Aire, Avon, Eden, Nene, Ouse, Tees, Tyne, Wear 5 Swale, Trent 6 Mersey, Ribble, Thames ***Ethiopia:*** 3 Omo 4 Baro, Dawa ***Europe:*** 4 Oder 5 Saale 6 Danube, Ticino

Florida: **6** Indian **9** Kissimmee **10** Saint Johns **12** Apalachicola ***France:*** **3** Ain, Lot, Var **4** Aire, Aude, Cher, Eure, Gers, Loir, Oise, Orne, Saar, Tarn, Yser **5** Adour, Aisne, Drôme, Indre, Isère, Loire, Marne, Saare, Saône, Seine, Somme, Yonne **6** Allier, Ariège, Scarpe, Vienne **7** Durance, Garonne, La Riège **8** Charente, Dordogne ***Georgia:*** **6** Etowah, Oconee **8** Altamaha, Ocmulgee **13** Chattahoochee ***Germany:*** **3** Ems **4** Eder, Elbe, Isar, Main, Rems, Ruhr **5** Hunte, Lippe, Rhine, Spree, Werra, Weser **6** Neckar ***Germany-Poland:*** **4** Oder ***Ghana:*** **5** Volta ***god:*** **7** Alpheus, Inachus **8** Achelous ***Greece:*** **3** Iri **4** Arta **5** Lerna, Lerne **7** Alpheus, Eurotas **8** Achelous **9** Arakhthos ***hazard:*** **4** snag **6** rapids **7** Lorelei ***Honduras:*** **4** Ulúa **5** Aguán **6** Patuca ***Iberian:*** **5** Douro, Duero ***Idaho:*** **5** Lemhi ***Illinois:*** **8** Mackinaw ***India:*** **4** Sind **5** Sindh, Tapti **6** Chenab, Kaveri, Kistna **7** Cauvery, Krishna **8** Acesines, Godavari ***Indian subcontinent:*** **5** Ganga **6** Ganges ***inlet:*** **5** bayou **6** slough ***Iran:*** **3** Kor **4** Mand, Mund **5** Karun **8** Safid Rud, Sefid Rud ***Ireland:*** **3** Lee **4** Deel, Erne, Suir **5** Boyne, Clare, Foyle **6** Barrow, Liffey **7** Shannon ***Italy:*** **2** Po **4** Adda, Arno, Liri, Nera **5** Adige, Arnus, Etsch, Liris, Oglio, Padus, Piave, Tiber **6** Ollius, Rapido, Tevere, Trebia **7** Athesis, Rubicon, Secchia, Tiberis, Trebbia **8** Rubicone, Volturno ***Kansas:*** **6** Pawnee ***Kazakhstan-Russia:*** **4** Ural **5** Tobol **6** Irtysh ***Kenya:*** **4** Athi, Tana ***Kubla Khan's:*** **4** Alph ***land:*** **4** holm **5** carse, flats **7** bottoms ***Latvia:*** **2** Aa **5** Gauja ***Latvia-Lithuania:*** **7** Lielupe ***Lebanon:*** **6** Litani ***Little Rock's:*** **8** Arkansas ***living in:*** **9** rheophile ***living on the bank of:*** **8** riparian ***longest:*** **4** Nile ***Louisiana:*** **11** Atchafalaya ***Maine:*** **8** Kennebec **9** Aroostook, Penobscot ***Malaysia:*** **9** Trengganu **10** Terengganu ***Maryland:*** **8** Monocacy, Patapsco, Patuxent **9** Nanticoke ***Massachusetts:*** **7** Charles, Taunton **9** Westfield **10** Housatonic ***Mexico:*** **6** Pánuco, Sonora **7** Tabasco **8** Grijalva ***Michigan:*** **4** Cass **5** Flint, Huron **7** Detroit, Saginaw **8** Manistee, Muskegon **9** Cheboygan, Kalamazoo **10** Michigamme, Shiawassee ***Mississippi:*** **5** Pearl, Yazoo **10** Pascagoula ***Moldova-Ukraine:*** **8** Dneister ***Missouri:*** **5** Osage ***Montgomery's:*** **7** Alabama ***mouth:*** **4** lade **5** delta ***Myanmar (Burma):*** **4** Pegu **8** Chindwin, Irrawady ***Nebraska:*** **4** Loup **6** Nemaha, Platte **7** Elkhorn ***Netherlands:*** **4** Waal **5** Issel, Yssel **6** Ijssel **7** Vahalis ***New England:*** **4** Saco **6** Nashua **9** Merrimack **10** Blackstone **11** Connecticut **12** Androscoggin ***New Jersey:*** **6** Rahway **7** Passaic, Raritan **8** Tuckahoe ***New York:*** **4** East **5** Tioga **6** Hudson, Mohawk, Oneida, Oswego, Seneca **7** Chemung, Niagara **8** Chenango, Cohocton **9** Conhocton ***New Zealand:*** **7** Waikato ***Nicaragua:*** **4** Coco **7** Segovia ***Nigeria:*** **5** Benin ***North Carolina:*** **3** Haw, Tar **5** Neuse **6** Chowan **8** Alamance ***northeast North America:*** **13** Saint Lawrence ***northeast United States:*** **4** Ohio **6** Hoosic **7** Genesee, Hocking **8** Delaware, Mahoning **9** Allegheny **11** Monongahela, Susquehanna ***Northern Ireland:*** **4** Bann **6** Mourne ***North Korea:*** **5** Daido **7** Taedong ***northwest North America:*** **5** Yukon ***northwest United States:*** **5** Snake **7** Klamath **11** Pend Oreille ***Norway:*** **4** Tana, Teno ***nymph:*** **4** nais **5** naiad ***obstruction:*** **4** snag ***of fire:*** **9** Phlegeton ***of forgetfulness:*** **5** Lethe ***of ice:*** **7** glacier ***of woe:*** **7** Acheron ***Ohio:*** **5** Miami **8** Cuyahoga, Sandusky **9** Muskingum **10** Tuscarawas ***Oklahoma:*** **8** Cimarron ***Oregon:*** **5** Rogue **6** Owyhee **7** Malheur **8** McKenzie **9** Clackamas, Deschutes **10** Willamette ***Panama:*** **5** Tuira **7** Chagres ***Papua New Guinea:*** **3** Fly **5** Sepik ***Pennsylvania:*** **6** Lehigh **10** Schuylkill ***Peru:*** **5** Rímac, Santa **7** Marañón **8** Apurímac, Huallaga, Urubamba ***Philippines:*** **4** Abra, Agno **5** Pasig **7** Cagayan **8** Cotabato, Mindanao, Pampanga ***Poland:*** **3** San **7** Vistula ***Portugal:*** **4** Sado **7** Mondego ***relating to:*** **7** fluvial, potamic **9** fluminose, fluminous ***Rhode Island:*** **7** Seekonk **8** Sakonnet **10** Providence ***Romania:*** **5** Arges ***Russia:*** **2** Ob, Om **3** Don, Oka, Ufa, Usa **4** Kama, Kara, Lena, Neva, Sura, Svir **5** Onega, Terek, Volga **6** Anadyr, Angara, Belaya, Kolima, Kolyma, Ussuri, Vyatka **7** Dnieper, Pechora, Yenisei, Yenisey **8** Barguzin, Kostroma, Voronezh, Vychegda ***Russia-Ukraine:*** **6** Donets ***sacred:*** **5** Ganga **6** Ganges ***São Paulo's:*** **5** Tietê ***Scotland:*** **3** Dee, Don, Esk, Tay **4** Doon, Nith, Spey, Tyne **5** Afton, Annan, Clyde, Forth, Tweed **6** Teviot **7** Deveron **8** Findhorn ***Shanghi's:*** **7** Huang-p'u, Hwang Pu ***Sicily:*** **5** Salso **6** Simeto ***siren:*** **7** Lorelei ***South Africa:*** **4** Vaal **6** Orange ***South America:*** **3** Apa **6** Amazon **8** Amazonas, Orellana, Paraguay **9** Pilcomayo ***South Carolina:*** **6** Saluda, Santee **7** Wateree **8** Congaree ***South Dakota:*** **3** Bad ***southeast Africa:*** **7** Limpopo **9** Crocodile ***southeast Asia:*** **6** Dza-chu, Mekong **8** Lan-ts'ang ***southeast United States:*** **6** Pee Dee **7** Noxubee, Washita **8** Escambia, Ouachita, Suwannee **10** Okanoxubee ***southern United States:*** **6** Sabine ***South Korea:*** **3** Kŭm ***southwest Asia:*** **6** Jordan **9** Euphrates ***southwest United States:*** **4** Gila, Zuni **5** Pecos **8** Colorado *Spain:* 4 Ebro 6 Aragon 12 Guadalquivir *Sweden:* 4 Göta 5 Kalix *Switzerland:* 3 Aar 4 Aare 5 Reuss *Syria:* 7 Orontes *Tbilisi's:* 4 Kura *Texas:* 5 Llano 6 Brazos, Nueces 7 San Saba, Trinity 9 Guadalupe *Texas-Mexico:* 8 Rio Bravo 9 Rio Grande *tidal:* 7 estuary *Tokyo's:* 6 Sumida *Turkey:* 6 Seihun, Seyhan *Ukrainian:* 3 Bug 4 Alma *underworld:* 4 Styx 5 Lethe 7 Acheron, Cocytus 10 Phlegethon *Uruguay:* 5 Negro *Utah:* 5 Uinta, Weber 6 Jordan, Sevier *valley:* 6 strath *Venezuela:* 5 Apure, Caura 6 Caroni 7 Orinoco *Vermont:* 3 Mad 5 Onion, White 8 Winooski *Virginia:* 3 Dan 5 James 7 Rapidan 9 Nansemond 10 Appomattox, Shenandoah 12 Chickahominy, Rappahannock *wailing:* 7 Cocytus *Wales:* 4 Dyfi 5 Clwyd, Dovey, Teifi *Washington:* 6 Skagit, Yakima 9 Klickitat, Snohomish, Wenatchee *West Africa:* 5 Niger 6 Gambia 7 Senegal *West Asia:* 5 Dijla 6 Tigris 8 Hiddekel *western North America:* 8 Columbia, Flathead *western United States:* 7 Laramie 11 Yellowstone *West Virginia:* 7 Kanawha *Wisconsin:* 8 Kickapoo 9 Menominee *Wyoming:* 8 Shoshone 10 Gros Ventre 11 Medicine Bow

___ Rivera, Painter 5 Diego

river duck 4 teal 6 wigeon 7 mallard, widgeon 9 greenwing

river horse 5 hippo 12 hippopotamus

riverine 7 potamic

rivet 3 fix 4 bolt, brad, stud 5 affix 6 attach, fasten 8 fastener

rivulet 3 run 4 burn, gill, race, rill 5 bache, bayou, bourn, brook, creek 6 runlet, runnel, stream 7 channel 9 streamlet

Rizpah *father:* 4 Aiah *lover:* 4 Saul *son:* 6 Armoni 12 Mephibosheth

roach 4 fish, rock, spot 6 braise

road 3 way 4 fare, lane, line, path 5 drive, going, route, track 6 artery, avenue, career, causey, course, street 7 highway, journey, passage 8 causeway, chaussée, crossway, highroad, pavement, speedway, turnpike 9 boulevard 12 thoroughfare *along a cliff:* 8 corniche *around a city:* 6 bypass 7 beltway *bend:* 7 hairpin *edge:* 4 berm 8 shoulder *French:* 6 chemin *in or to a mine:* 4 bord 5 board 8 footrill *Irish:* 6 boreen 8 beallach *machine:* 4 harl 5 paver 6 grader 9 bulldozer *narrow (in England):* 4 loke 5 drang, drong 8 driftway *of stones:* 7 telford *raised:* 5 agger *Roman:* 3 via 4 iter *Scottish:* 4 brae 8 beallach *side:* 5 biway 6 branch 8 shunpike *Spanish:* 6 camino *surface:* 3 tar 6 bricks, gravel, stones 7 macadam 8 concrete, pavement *temporary:* 7 shoofly *zigzag:* 10 switchback

roadblock 7 barrier 8 blockade 9 barricade

road book 3 map 5 atlas 9 gazetteer, itinerary

roadhouse 3 inn 5 hotel, lodge 6 hostel, tavern 7 auberge, hospice 8 hostelry 11 caravansary

roadman 6 hawker, monger, vendor 7 drummer, higgler, packman, peddler 8 huckster, mongerer, salesman 9 canvasser

roadrunner 6 cuckoo 7 paisano

road rut 7 pothole 9 chuckhole

roam 3 bat, gad, run 4 rove, walk 5 drift, prowl, range, stray 6 ramble, stroll, travel, wander 7 meander 8 gadabout, straggle, vagabond 9 gallivant

roamer 5 gipsy, gypsy, nomad, rover 6 gadder, walker 7 drifter, rambler 8 gadabout, stroller, traveler, vagabond, wanderer 9 meanderer 12 peregrinator, rolling stone

roar 3 cry, din 4 bawl, bell, boom, bray, howl, rout, yell 5 laugh, shout 6 bellow, clamor, outcry, scream, shriek 7 bluster, rebound, ululate 9 repercuss 10 vociferate 11 reverberate *low:* 5 brool *of a boor:* 5 fream *of the surf:* 3 rut 4 rote

roast 4 bake, cook, flay, melt, razz, roti 5 broil, parch, score, slash 6 scathe, scorch 7 blister, lambast, swelter, torrefy, torrify 8 lambaste, lash into, ridicule 9 castigate, excoriate

rob 3 cop, mug 4 fake, flap, lift, loot, lose, nick, oust, pelf, roll, sack, take 5 bribe, cheat, filch, harry, heist, pinch, pluck, reave, rifle, spoil, steal, touch 6 burgle, divest, hijack, hold up, hustle, pilfer, pirate, ravage, ravish, snatch, snitch, thieve 7 bereave, defraud, deprive, despoil, pillage, plunder, purloin, ransack, relieve, stick up, swindle 8 jackroll 9 knock over, strong-arm 10 burglarize

robber 4 yegg 5 crook, thief 6 bandit, catman, pirate, rifler 7 brigand, footpad, heister, ladrone, raffles, reifier 8 hightoby, hijacker, swindler 9 holdup man 10 cat burglar, highwayman, sandbagger, stickup man 12 housebreaker *grave:* 5 ghoul *Irish:* 8 woodkern *murderous (in India and Burma):* 6 dacoit *of pedestrians:* 3 pad 7 footpad *on high seas:* 6 pirate

robbery 3 job 5 heist, theft 6 holdup, piracy 7 larceny, stickup 8 banditry *Scottish:* 4 reif

robe 3 aba 4 mant, wrap 5 cloak, cover, habit 6 caftan, clothe, mantle, revest 7 becloak, costume, garment, manteau 8 clothing, covering, dalmatic, vestment *ancient Greek tragedian's:* 5 syrma *baptismal:* 7 chrisom *bishop's:* 6 chimer 7 chimere *coronation:* 8 colobium *Eastern*

Orthodox: **10** sticharion ***Indian:*** **4** jama **6** khalat, khilat ***Jewish:*** **6** kittel ***knight's:*** **6** cyclas ***Latin:*** **5** stola ***loose:*** **5** camis, camus **6** kimona ***Mexican:*** **5** manga ***monarch's:*** **7** pluvial ***of Roman emperors:*** **6** purple ***of tartan:*** **7** arisaid ***Turkish:*** **6** dolman ***woman's:*** **5** cymar, simar, symar

Robinson Crusoe author **5** Defoe

robot **5** golem **7** android, machine **8** automata (plural) **9** automaton

Rob Roy author **5** Scott

robust **4** hale, hard, iron, rude **5** hardy, lusty, sound, stout, wally **6** browny, hearty, potent, rugged, sinewy, strong **7** booming, healthy, roaring, thrifty, valiant **8** athletic, muscular, thriving, vigorous **9** strapping **10** boisterous, full-bodied, prospering, prosperous **11** flourishing **12** concentrated

robustious **6** rugged **7** boorish, ill-bred, loutish, lumpish **8** churlish, clownish, lubberly **9** unrefined **10** unpolished

rock **3** fly, zip **4** bill, crag, oner, reel, roll, rush, slip, sway, toss **5** boner, error, fluff, geode, heave, hurry, pitch, quake, shake, speed, swing **6** barrel, bullet, bungle, dollar, gangue, hustle, miscue, rocket, slipup, totter **7** agitate, blooper, blunder, boulder, breccia, concuss, hotfoot, misstep, tremble **8** astonish, convulse, undulate **9** oscillate ***basaltic:*** **5** wacke ***cavity:*** **3** vug **4** vugg, vugh ***combining form:*** **4** lite, lith, lyte, petr, saxi **5** clast, petri, petro, phyre ***decomposed:*** **6** gossan ***fissile:*** **5** shale ***foliated:*** **8** phyllite ***formation:*** **4** sial **5** nappe **6** pluton **7** rimrock, terrane **8** isocline, syncline ***fragment:*** **8** xenolith ***fragmental:*** **8** psephite ***granular:*** **6** norite ***igneous:*** **4** lava, sial, sima **6** basalt, dunite, gabbro, ophite, pumice **7** diabase, diorite, felsite, granite, greisen, picrite, sienite, syenite **8** eruptive, felstone, obsidian, porphyry, trachyte, traprock **9** tachylyte **10** travertine ***layer:*** **8** regolith **10** mantlerock ***mass:*** **5** scree **9** batholith ***metamorphic:*** **5** slate **6** gneiss, marble, schist **8** eclogite, ganister, mylonite **9** quartzite, soapstone ***molten:*** **4** lava ***protruding:*** **5** scaur ***sedimentary:*** **4** clay, coal **5** chalk, chert, coral, flint, shale **6** pelite **8** mudstone, psammite **9** limestone, sandstone, siltstone ***silicate:*** **8** hornfels ***siliceous:*** **9** buhrstone ***soft:*** **7** tripoli ***suffix:*** **3** ite ***volcanic:*** **4** tuff **5** trass **6** basalt, taxite, terras **8** pumicate, rhyolite, tephrite

rock badger **4** cony **5** coney, hyrax

rock bass **6** redeye **8** cabrilla

rock bottom **4** pith, root, soul **5** stuff **6** lowest, marrow **7** essence **8** cheapest **9** lowermost, substance, undermost **10** nethermost

rockbound **5** rigid **7** adamant **8** obdurate **9** unbending **10** inexorable, inflexible, unyielding **12** single-minded

rocker **6** cradle **7** shoofly

rocket **3** fly, zip **4** soar, whiz **5** arise, haste, hurry, mount, smoke, surge, tower, whish **6** ascend, bullet **7** missile, shoot up **8** firework, starship ***engineer:*** **8** Von Braun ***landing:*** **7** reentry **10** splashdown ***launcher:*** **7** bazooka ***launching:*** **7** liftoff **8** blastoff

rocketry ***father of:*** **7** Goddard

rockfish **5** reina, viuva **6** gopher, rasher, tambor **7** corsair, garrupa, grouper **8** bocaccio

___ Rockne **5** Knute

rock-ribbed see **rockbound**

rockweed **4** tang **5** fucus **7** seatang, seaweed

rocky **4** dull, hard, weak **5** dizzy, reefy, shaky, stony **6** stoney, tricky, wobbly **7** petrean **8** bouldery, obdurate, ticklish, unstable, unsteady **9** bloodless, difficult, insensate, rockbound, steadfast **11** insensitive

rocky hill **3** tor

rococo **4** arty **6** florid, ornate **7** baroque **8** luscious **9** fantastic **10** flamboyant

rod **3** bar, gad, guy **4** bolt, came, cane, good, pole, scob, slab, ward **5** ingot, lytta, osier, perch, power, spoke, staff, stick, strip **6** billet, broach, carbon, etalon, pistol, raddle, skewer, switch, toggle **7** baculus, crowbar, scepter, spindle **8** punition, revolver **9** authority **10** correction, discipline, oppression, punishment **11** castigation **12** chastisement ***bundle of:*** **6** fasces ***combining form:*** **5** rhabd **6** rhabdo ***glassmaking:*** **5** punty

rodent **3** rat **4** cavy, cony, degu, hard, mole, paca, pika, utia, vole **5** cavie, coney, coypu, gundi, hutia, jutia, lerot, mouse, zokor **6** agouti, agouty, beaver, biting, cururo, gerbil, gopher, jerboa, marmot, murine, nutria, rabbit **7** chincha, hamster, lemming, leveret, muskrat **8** abrocome, capibara, capybara, chipmunk, cricetid, dormouse, gerbille, leporide, pacarana, sewellel, squirrel, tuco tuco, viscacha, vizcacha, water rat **9** guinea pig, porcupine **10** chinchilla, field mouse, prairie dog, springhare **11** kangaroo rat, meadow mouse, pocket mouse **12** pocket gopher ***aquatic:*** **5** coypu **6** beaver, coypou, nutria **7** muskrat **8** musquash ***burrowing:*** **6** gerbil, gopher **7** hamster **8** gerbille, viscacha, vizcacha ***Eurasian:*** **6** suslik ***family:*** **5** murid **6** murine **7** Muridae, sciurid **9** Sciuridae **10** Cricetidae **12** Octodontidae ***furry:*** **10** chinchilla ***genus:*** **3** Mus **5** Lepus ***relating to:*** **8** rosorial ***South American:*** **4** mara

rodeo **7** contest, roundup **9** enclosure

10 exhibition 11 competition ***animal:*** 5 horse, steer 10 Brahma bull ***event:*** 10 calf roping 11 bulldogging 12 bronco riding ***performer:*** 5 clown 6 cowboy

___ Rodin 7 Auguste

rodomontade 4 blow, brag, crow, puff, rant 5 boast, mouth, prate, pride, vaunt 6 blower, braggy, vanity 7 bluster, boaster, bombast, bragger, fustian, vaunter 8 blowhard, boastful, boasting, braggart, bragging, puckfist, rhapsody, rhetoric, vaunting 9 gasconade, vainglory 11 braggadocio

Rodomonte ***beloved:*** 8 Doralice ***slayer:*** 8 Ruggiero

Rodrigo Diaz de Bivar 5 el Cid

rod-shaped 7 virgate 8 bacillar, rhabdoid 9 bacillary, virgulate

roe 2 ra 3 ova, pea 4 deer, eggs, hart, hind 5 coral, spawn 6 caviar 7 caviare

Roentgen's discovery 4 X ray

rogation 3 law 6 decree, litany, prayer 7 inquiry 8 petition, proposal 12 supplication

___ Rogers 3 Roy 4 Will

rogue 3 boy, guy, gyp, imp 4 heel, kite 5 cheat, crank, devil, gipsy, gypsy, hempy, knave, scamp 6 beggar, canter, chiaus, coquin, harlot, rascal 7 cheater, culprit, erratic, lowlife, sharper, villain 8 mischief, picaroon, scalawag, swindler 9 defrauder, miscreant, scoundrel, skeezicks, trickster 10 blackguard, delinquent, mountebank 11 rapscallion ***relating to:*** 10 picaresque

roguery 5 fraud 7 devilry, waggery 8 deviltry, mischief, trickery 9 devilment, diablerie 11 waggishness 12 sportiveness

roguish 3 coy, sly 4 arch 5 antic, lying 6 impish, pranky, shifty, wicked 7 knavish, larkish, playful 8 espiègle, prankful, prankish 11 mischievous

roil 3 mud, vex 4 foul, rile 5 annoy, dirty, grate, muddy, peeve 6 befoul, burn up, muddle, nettle 7 blunder, disturb, inflame, pollute, provoke, turmoil 8 irritate 9 aggravate 10 exasperate 11 contaminate

roily 5 muddy, riley 6 turbid

roister 4 hell, riot 5 revel, spree 6 frolic 7 carouse, wassail

Roland 7 Orlando ***beloved:*** 4 Aude ***betrayer:*** 4 Gano 7 Ganelon ***friend:*** 6 Oliver 7 Olivier ***horn:*** 7 Olivant ***sword:*** 8 Durandal, Durendul ***uncle:*** 11 Charlemagne

role 3 bit 4 duty, face, look, part, show 5 guise 6 aspect, office 7 seeming 8 business, clothing, function, province 9 character, semblance 10 appearance

roll 3 bun, gad, rob 4 bask, bolt, bunn, clew, coil, file, flow, furl, gush, gyre, list, muse, pour, roam, rock, rota, rove, toss, turn, wind, wrap 5 drape, drift, growl, heave, pitch, range, revel, stray, surge, troll 6 bundle, circle, enwrap, goggle, grovel, gyrate, muster, ponder, ramble, roster, rotate, rumble, scroll, stream, swathe, wallow, wander, welter, whelve, wintle, wrap up 7 biscuit, brioche, catalog, envelop, grumble, indulge, revolve, rissole, rollick, swaddle, trundle 8 enswathe, involute, meditate, mull over, register, ruminate, schedule, turn over ***of coins:*** 7 rouleau ***sweet:*** 8 schnecke

roll about 6 wallow, welter

roll back 5 lower 6 reduce 7 repulse

roll call 4 list 6 roster 7 catalog 8 register, schedule

rolled 8 obvolute ***backward:*** 8 revolute ***together:*** 9 convolute

roller 4 wave 5 finer, inker, winch 6 caster, fascia, rowlet 7 breaker, carrier 8 cylinder

rollick 4 bask, lark, play, roll, romp 5 caper, frisk, revel, sport 6 cavort, frolic, gambol, wallow, welter 7 indulge 8 escapade

rollicking 3 gay 4 glad, wild 5 antic, happy, merry 6 jovial, joyful, joyous, lively 7 playful 8 cheerful 9 hilarious, sprightly 10 frolicsome 12 lighthearted

rolling stock 4 cars 6 trucks 7 coaches, engines 8 cabooses, Pullmans, sleepers, trailers 11 locomotives

rolling stone 5 rover 6 roamer 7 drifter, rambler 8 wanderer 9 meanderer

roll up 4 furl 10 accumulate

roly-poly see rotund

Roman 5 brave, Latin, papal 7 Italian ***amphitheater:*** 9 Colosseum ***assembly:*** 5 forum 6 senate 7 comitia ***building:*** 5 Forum 6 Circus 8 basilica, Pantheon ***comedy writer:*** 7 Plautus, Terence ***conspirator:*** 6 Brutus 7 Cassius 8 Catiline ***date:*** 4 Ides 7 calends, kalends ***emperors:*** 4 Nero, Otho 5 Galba, Nerva, Titus, Verus 6 Julian, Trajan 7 Hadrian, Maximus, Severus 8 Augustus, Caligula, Claudius, Commodus, Domitian, Tiberius, Valerian 9 Caracalla, Vespasian 10 Diocletian, Theodosius 11 Constantine, Valentinian ***entrance hall:*** 5 atria (plural) 6 atrium ***epic:*** 6 Aeneid ***epigrammatist:*** 7 Martial ***family:*** 7 Gracchi ***Fates:*** 4 Nona 5 Morta 6 Decuma, Parcae ***founder:*** 5 Remus 7 Romulus ***fountain:*** 5 Trevi ***garment:*** 4 toga 5 palla, sagum, stola, stole, tunic ***general:*** 5 Sulla, Titus 6 Antony, Marius, Scipio 8 Agricola

god: 4 deus

blind: 6 Plutus ***chief:*** 4 Jove 7 Jupiter ***messenger:*** 7 Mercury ***of agriculture:*** 6 Saturn ***of animals:*** 6 Faunus ***of death:*** 4 Mors ***of dreams:*** 8 Morpheus ***of fire:*** 6 Vulcan ***of gates and doors:***

5 Janus ***of healing:*** 11 Aesculapius ***of heaven:*** 6 Uranus ***of households:*** 5 Lares 7 Penates ***of love:*** 4 Amor 5 Cupid ***of medicine:*** 11 Aesculapius ***of mirth:*** 5 Comus ***of regeneration:*** 7 Priapus ***of sleep:*** 6 Somnus ***of the sea:*** 6 Pontus 7 Neptune, Proteus ***of the sun:*** 3 Sol 6 Apollo ***of the underworld:*** 3 Dis 5 Orcus, Pluto 8 Dispater ***of the wind:*** 5 Eurus, Notus 6 Aeolus, Aquilo, Auster, Boreas 8 Favonius, Zephyrus ***of war:*** 4 Mars 8 Quirinus ***of wealth:*** 6 Plutus ***of wine:*** 7 Bacchus ***of woods:*** 6 Faunus ***two-faced:*** 5 Janus
goddess: 3 dea
of agriculture: 5 Ceres ***of beauty:*** 5 Venus ***of dawn:*** 6 Aurora ***of flowers:*** 5 Flora ***of handicrafts:*** 7 Minerva ***of harvests:*** 3 Ops ***of health:*** 7 Minerva ***of hope:*** 4 Spes ***of hunting:*** 5 Diana ***of justice:*** 7 Astraea ***of love:*** 5 Venus ***of marriage:*** 4 Juno ***of night:*** 3 Nox ***of peace:*** 3 Pax ***of springs:*** 7 Juturna ***of strife:*** 9 Discordia ***of the earth:*** 6 Tellus ***of the hearth:*** 5 Vesta ***of the moon:*** 4 Luna ***of the sea:*** 10 Amphitrite ***of the underworld:*** 10 Proserpina ***of victory:*** 6 Vacuna ***of war:*** 7 Bellona ***of wisdom:*** 7 Minerva ***of womanhood:*** 4 Juno
greeting: 3 ave ***helmet:*** 5 galea 6 cassis ***hero:*** 6 Caesar 11 Cincinnatus ***hill:*** 7 Caelian, Viminal 8 Aventine, Palatine, Quirinal 9 Esquiline 10 Capitoline ***historian:*** 4 Livy 5 Nepos ***king:*** 7 Romulus, Servius, Tullius 12 Ancus Martius 13 Numa Pompilius ***military formation:*** 3 ala 6 alares (plural) 7 phalanx ***miltary unit:*** 6 cohort, legion 7 maniple ***officer:*** 9 centurion ***official:*** 5 augur, edile 6 aedile, censor, consul, lictor 7 praetor, prefect, tribune 8 irenarch, quaestor ***people:*** 5 Laeti 6 populi (plural) 7 populus, Sabines 8 plebians 9 plebeians 10 patricians ***philosopher:*** 4 Cato 6 Seneca ***physician:*** 11 Aesculapius ***port:*** 5 Ostia ***procurator:*** 6 Pilate ***racecourse:*** 6 circus ***road:*** 4 iter ***slave:*** 9 Spartacus ***statesman:*** 4 Cato 5 Pliny 6 Caesar, Cicero, Seneca 7 Agrippa 8 Augustus, Maecenas ***symbol of authority:*** 6 fasces

roman à ___ 4 clef

romance 3 woo 4 gest, love, tale 5 amour, court, fable, fancy, feign, geste, novel, story 6 affair 7 fantasy, fiction 8 stardust 10 love affair

Romance language 6 French 7 Catalan, Italian, Spanish 8 Romanian, Rumanian 9 Provençal 10 Portuguese

Romania ***capital:*** 9 Bucharest ***monetary unit:*** 3 leu

romantic 4 wild 5 ideal, mushy 6 ardent, dreamy, exotic, gothic, poetic, slushy, sticky, unreal 7 maudlin, mawkish, strange 8 bathetic, fabulous, fanciful, invented, quixotic 9 fantastic, imaginary, visionary 10 idealistic, lovey-dovey 11 extravagant, sentimental

Romany 5 gipsy, gypsy

Romeo 7 amorist, Don Juan, gallant 8 Casanova, lothario, paramour ***beloved:*** 6 Juliet ***enemy:*** 6 Tybalt ***father:*** 8 Montague ***friend:*** 8 Mercutio

Rommel, Erwin ***nickname:*** 9 Desert Fox

romp 4 play, roil, rout 5 caper, frisk 6 cavort, frolic, gambol, hoyden 7 courant, gammock, rollick, runaway, skylark

Romulus ***brother:*** 5 Remus ***father:*** 4 Mars ***mother:*** 10 Rhea Silvia ***victim:*** 5 Remus

rondure 3 orb 4 ball 5 globe, round 6 circle, sphere

rood 5 cross 8 crucifix

roof 3 hip, top 4 apex, deck, dome, flat, peak 5 cover, crest, crown, haven, house 6 cupola, harbor, palate, shield, summit, vertex 7 chamber, mansard, shelter 8 covering, housetop 9 fastigium ***automobile:*** 8 fastback ***false:*** 7 cricket ***material:*** 3 tar, tin 4 tile 5 paper, slate, straw, terne 6 copper, gravel, thatch 8 shingles ***of a cavern:*** 4 dome ***of the mouth:*** 6 palate ***part:*** 3 hip 4 eave 7 cricket ***peak:*** 3 hip ***structure:*** 9 penthouse ***type:*** 5 gable 6 cupola 7 gambrel, mansard 9 butterfly 10 jerkinhead ***vaulted:*** 4 dome

roofer 5 tiler

rook 4 bird, crow, milk 5 bleed, cheat, mulct, raven, steal, stick, sweat 6 castle, fleece 7 defraud, swindle

rookery 5 roost 8 building

rookie 4 colt, tyro 6 novice 7 recruit, trainee 8 beginner, freshman, neophyte, newcomer 9 novitiate 10 apprentice, tenderfoot

room 3 den, hut 4 aula, cell, hall, play, rein, seat, sway 5 board, divan, house, lodge, place, put up, range, roost, salon, scope, space, study 6 billet, camera, harbor, leeway, margin, reside, studio 7 boudoir, cabinet, chamber, cubicle, expanse, gallery, lodging 8 domicile, latitude 9 apartment, clearance ***ancient Roman:*** 5 atria (plural), oecus 6 atrium 7 fumaria 8 aedicule ***eating:*** 4 nook 7 cenacle, kitchen 9 refectory ***food storage:*** 6 larder, pantry ***for paintings:*** 7 gallery ***for small meetings:*** 7 seminar ***in a monastery:*** 4 cell 6 lavabo 8 locutory 9 refectory 11 calefactory ***in a prison:*** 4 cell 7 dungeon ***in a tower:*** 6 belfry ***next to dining room:*** 7 servery ***on a ship:*** 5 cabin 6 galley ***public:*** 7 theater ***round:*** 7 rotunda

room and board 7 lodging 8 lodgment
roomer 5 guest 6 lodger, tenant 7 boarder
roomy 4 wide 5 ample, broad, large, spacy 7 spacial 8 spacious 9 capacious 10 commodious
Roosevelt, F.D. ***birthplace:*** 8 Hyde Park ***dog:*** 4 Fala ***message:*** 12 fireside chat ***mother:*** 4 Sara ***predecessor:*** 6 Hoover ***program:*** 7 New Deal ***successor:*** 6 Truman ***wife:*** 7 Eleanor
roost 3 hut, sit 4 land, nest, room 5 board, house, light, lodge, perch, put up 6 alight, billet, garret, harbor, settle 7 dovecot, lodging, quarter, set down, sit down 8 domicile, dovecote 9 touch down
rooster 4 cock 5 capon, gallo 8 gamecock 11 chanticleer
root 3 dig, fix 4 base, bulb, core, grub, moot, pith, soul, stem, woll 5 basis, cheer, embed, grout, heart, infix, lodge, plant, quick, radix, shout, stuff, tuber 6 bottom, center, etymon, ground, marrow, origin, rise to, settle, source 7 applaud, bedrock, essence, footing, ingrain, radical, support 8 entrench, fountain, radicate, wellhead 9 beginning, establish, inception, substance 10 derivation, foundation ***aromatic:*** 7 ginseng ***combining form:*** 4 rhiz 5 rhiza, rhizo 6 rhizae (plural), rrhiza 7 rrhizae (plural) ***edible:*** 3 oca, oka, roi, yam 4 beet, eddo 6 carrot, ginger, radish, turnip 7 parsnip 8 rutabaga, tuckahoe ***fragrant:*** 4 khus 5 orris 6 cuscus, kuskus 7 vetiver 8 khuskhus ***main:*** 7 taproot ***medicinal:*** 5 jalap 7 ginseng, zedoary ***relating to:*** 7 radical ***starch:*** 4 arum ***tropical:*** 4 taro ***word:*** 6 etymon ***yielding red dye:*** 4 chay, choy 5 chaya, choya 6 madder
rootlet 7 radicel, radicle, rhizoid
root out 4 grub, stub 6 evulse 7 abolish, blot out, destroy, wipe out 8 demolish 9 eradicate, extirpate 10 annihilate, deracinate, extinguish 11 exterminate
Roots author 5 Haley
rope 3 gad, guy, tie, toe 4 bind, cord, hemp, line, stay 5 belay, bight, brace, cable, chord, hoose, lasso, longe, riata, sheet, widdy 6 becket, binder, fasten, halter, hawser, lariat, shroud, strand, string, tether 7 aweband, binding, bobstay, halyard, lashing, marline, outhaul, painter, towline 8 backstay, buntline, downhaul, inveigle, jackstay, lifeline, prolonge ***loop:*** 7 cringle ***maker:*** 8 strander ***mooring:*** 6 hawser ***of flowers:*** 3 lei ***saving:*** 8 lifeline ***ship's:*** 4 vang 6 parral, parrel, ratlin 7 laniard, lanyard, marline, marling, ratline, swifter 8 rattling
ropedancer 7 acrobat
rope off 6 cordon
ropes 8 minutiae 10 ins and outs, procedures, techniques
ropy 4 wiry 6 sinewy 7 fibrous, stringy 8 muscular
roque 7 croquet
rorqual 5 whale 7 finback
Rosalind's beloved 7 Orlando
rosary 5 beads 7 chaplet, garland 8 beadroll
rose 4 glow, pink 5 blush, color, flush, rouge 6 mantle, pinken, redden 7 crimson 10 erysipelas ***Chinese:*** 8 Cherokee ***combining form:*** 4 rhod 5 rhodo, roseo ***cotton:*** 7 cudweed ***feature:*** 5 thorn ***kind:*** 4 moss 5 Peace, Vogue 6 Circus, damask 7 Fashion, Granada, Iceberg, New Dawn, Pascali, Tiffany 8 Rubaiyat 9 Floradora, Montezuma, polyantha, Tropicana 10 Floribunda 11 grandiflora, Mount Shasta 12 Crimson Glory, Paul's Scarlet, Red Pinocchio 13 Golden Showers 14 Queen Elizabeth ***wild:*** 8 eglatere
roseate 3 red 4 pink 6 blushy, bright, florid, likely 7 auroral, flushed, healthy, hopeful 8 aurorean, blooming, blushful, blushing, cheerful, rubicand 9 favorable, promising 10 optimistic, promiseful
rose-colored see roseate
rosemary 4 mint 8 costmary 9 rosmarine
Rosenkavalier composer 7 Strauss
rose oil 5 attar
Rose Tattoo author 8 Williams
rosette 7 cockade 8 ornament
Rosh's father 8 Benjamin
Rosinante's master 7 Quixote (Don)
Rosmersholm author 5 Ibsen
___ Rossetti 5 Dante 9 Christina 12 Dante Gabriel ***work:*** 8 Sing-Song 11 Annus Domini, Seek and Find, Sister Helen 12 Beata Beatrix 14 The House of Life
Rossini opera 6 Otello 8 Tancredi 11 William Tell
Rostand hero 6 Cyrano
roster 4 list, roll, rota 5 slate 6 muster, scroll 7 catalog 8 beadroll, register, roll call, schedule 10 muster roll
rostrum 4 beak, dais 5 snout 6 pulpit 7 lectern, tribune 8 platform 9 proboscis
rosy see roseate
rot 3 ret 4 bosh, bull, crap, sink, turn, warp 5 bilge, chaff, decay, hooey, spoil, stain, taint, trash 6 banter, debase, fester, molder, worsen 7 corrode, corrupt, crumble, debauch, decline, deprave, descend, hogwash, pervert, putrefy, rubbish, vitiate 8 nonsense 9 animalize, break down, decompose, poppycock 10 bestialize, degenerate, demoralize, disimprove, retrograde 11 deteriorate 12 disintegrate 13 decomposition

rotary 6 circle 8 gyratory, spinning
rotate 4 gyre, pass, roll, spin, turn 5 pivot, twirl, wheel 6 circle, follow, gyrate 7 precess, relieve, revolve, succeed, trundle 8 exchange, rotiform, windmill 9 alternate 10 circumduct 11 interchange ***a log:*** 4 birl
rotation 4 gyre, turn 5 round, wheel, whirl 7 circuit, turning 8 gyration 10 revolution
rote 4 list, pace 5 grind, learn 6 course, custom, groove, memory, repeat, system 7 routine 8 practice 9 automatic, treadmill 10 memorizing, repetition 12 memorization
rotten 2 up 3 bad, bum 4 foul, poor, punk, sour 5 amiss, fetid, nasty, wrong 6 crappy, putrid 7 carrion, corrupt, decayed, spoiled, tainted, touched, unhappy, unsound, vicious 8 chiselly, depraved, perverse, unstable 9 nefarious, offensive, putrified, unhealthy 10 abominable, decomposed, degenerate, flagitious, putrescent, undermined, unpleasant, villainous 11 displeasing 12 disagreeable 13 disintegrated ***combining form:*** 4 sapr 5 sapro
rotter 3 cad, cur 7 bounder, shirker, slacker 9 yellow dog 10 blackguard
rotund 3 fat 5 beefy, buxom, dumpy, obese, plump, podgy, pudgy, round, squat, stout, thick, tubby 6 chubby, chunky, plumpy, spuddy, stocky, stubby 7 paunchy, ringing, vibrant 8 heavyset, plangent, plumpish, resonant, roly-poly, sonorant, sonorous, thickset 9 consonant, spherical 10 potbellied, resounding, roundabout
rouge 3 red 4 glow, pink, rose 5 blush, color, flush 6 mantle, pinken, redden 7 crimson
rough 3 bad, dry, raw 4 curt, firm, hard, punk, rude, wild 5 bluff, blunt, brief, brute, bumpy, crass, crude, draft, gross, gruff, hairy, harsh, heavy, raspy, rowdy, short, solid, tight, tough, uncut, yahoo 6 abrupt, broken, brushy, burred, choppy, coarse, craggy, crusty, hispid, hoarse, jagged, knotty, mucker, raging, rugged, severe, sketch, stormy, trying, uneven, unhewn, vulgar 7 arduous, boorish, brusque, cragged, furious, grating, jarring, operose, outline, rasping, raucous, ruffian, scraggy, toughie, tricksy, uncivil, uncouth, ungodly, unlevel, violent 8 asperous, block out, blustery, bullyboy, chalk out, churlish, impolite, improper, indecent, scabrous, skeleton, stormful, unformed, unseemly, unsmooth 9 adumbrate, difficult, imperfect, inclement, inelegant, ironbound, laborious, manhandle, mishandle, proximate, strenuous, turbulent, undressed, unrefined 10 blustering, boisterous, formidable, indecorous, indelicate, knock about, malodorous, ridiculous, slap around, stridulent, stridulous, tumultuous, unbecoming, undecorous, unfinished, ungracious, unpolished 11 approximate, short-spoken, skeletonize, tempestuous, unfashioned 12 characterize, discourteous ***combining form:*** 6 trachy
roughhewn 4 rude 5 crude, plain, rough 8 unformed, unworked 9 undressed 10 unfinished, unpolished 11 unfashioned 12 uncultivated
roughhouse 7 fooling, rough up 9 high jinks, horseplay, manhandle, mishandle, rowdiness 10 knock about, skylarking, slap around
roughneck see **ruffian**
roughness 7 crudity 8 acrimony, asperity 10 inequality, unevenness 12 irregularity
rough out 5 draft 6 sketch 7 outline 8 block out, chalk out, skeleton 9 adumbrate 11 skeletonize 12 characterize
rough up 9 manhandle, mishandle 10 knock about, roughhouse, slap around
round 2 by 3 arc, bow, hem, orb 4 arch, back, ball, bend, bent, bold, fast, free, full, gird, gyre, most, near, nigh, over, rich, ring, tour, turn 5 about, again, ample, arced, bowed, brisk, crook, curve, cycle, globe, harsh, large, orbed, plain, plump, podgy, pudgy, sleek, slick, tubby, vocal, wheel, whirl 6 all but, almost, arched, around, begird, beside, chubby, circle, curved, girdle, mellow, nearby, nearly, plumpy, polish, refine, rotund, smooth, sphere 7 annular, arrondi, bulbous, circuit, compass, orotund, perfect, ringing, rondure, spheric, through, vibrant 8 arciform, as good as, backward, circular, complete, conglobe, encircle, ensphere, finished, globular, gyration, plangent, plumpish, resonant, roly-poly, rotation, sonorant, sonorous, surround, vigorous, well-nigh 9 consonant, curvation, curvature, encompass, in reverse, just about, orbicular, outspoken, spherical 10 conglobate, free-spoken, resounding, revolution, throughout 11 circulation, curvilinear, cylindrical ***combining form:*** 5 globo, troch, ventr 6 trocho, ventri, ventro ***prefix:*** 4 peri
roundabout 4 tour 5 jaunt, plump, tubby 6 chubby, detour, junket, outing, plumpy, rotary, rotund 7 circuit, curving, oblique, winding 8 circular, indirect, pleonasm, plumpish, roly-poly, verbiage 9 excursion, runaround, tautology, verbality 10 circuitous, collateral, meandering, periphrase 11 periphrasis
rounded 4 bent 5 arced, bowed, curvy, round 6 arched, convex, curved, mellow 7 arrondi, gibbous 8 arciform, complete, sonorous 9 curvesome, Junoesque, perfected 10 curvaceous 11 approximate, curvilinear 13 well-developed
rounder 4 rake, roué 6 bad lot, no-good,

waster 7 wastrel 10 ne'er-do-well, profligate, scapegrace

roundly 4 most, well 5 about, à fond, fully, quite 6 all but, almost, nearly, wholly 7 bluntly, sharply, smartly, utterly 8 as good as, bitterly, candidly, entirely, promptly, well-nigh 9 just about, perfectly 10 altogether, completely, scathingly

round off 3 cap 5 crown 6 climax, top off 9 culminate, finish off

round robin 6 letter, series 7 protest 8 petition, sequence 10 tournament

round trip 4 tour 7 circuit 9 excursion

round up 5 group 6 gather 7 cluster, collect 8 assemble

rouse 4 call, move, rise, stir, wake, whet 5 alarm, awake, mount, pique, rally, waken 6 awaken, bestir, deepen, excite, foment, incite, kindle, revive, vivify 7 agitate, animate, disturb, enhance, enliven, innerve, magnify, provoke, quicken 8 heighten, motivate, redouble 9 aggravate, challenge, galvanize, innervate, instigate, intensate, intensify, stimulate

rousing 3 gay 4 keen 5 alert, brisk, peppy 6 bright, lively 7 animate, dashing 8 animated, exciting, spirited, stirring 9 inspiring, sprightly 10 exhilarant, eye-popping 11 stimulating, superlative 12 exhilarating, exhilarative, intoxicating

Rousseau work 5 Emile

roust 4 move, stir 5 pique, rouse 6 excite 7 innerve, provoke, quicken 8 motivate 9 galvanize, stimulate

roustabout 4 hand 6 worker 7 laborer, workman 8 deckhand, floorman, workhand 9 operative 10 workingman

rout 3 mob 4 army, bawl, beat, drub, dust, fuss, herd, host, lick, mass, roar, romp, root, whip 5 chase, cloud, crowd, dregs, drive, eject, expel, flock, trash 6 bellow, clamor, defeat, dig out, dispel, flight, hunt up, legion, number, rabble, scores, soiree, throng, wallop 7 beating, bluster, clobber, conquer, debacle, hunt out, licking, rummage, runaway, shellac, warming 8 cakewalk, drubbing, hunt down, lambaste, riffraff, stampede, walkaway, walkover 9 clean up on, hoi polloi, multitude, other half, overthrow, reception 10 defeasance, demoralize 11 proletariat

route 3 way 4 lead, line, path, road, send, ship, show 5 guide, pilot, remit, steer, track, trail 6 course, direct, divert, escort 7 address, channel, circuit, conduct, consign, forward, highway, journey, passage 8 dispatch, shepherd, transmit 9 direction, itinerary

routine 3 act, bit, rut 4 pace, rote 5 drill, grind, habit, plain, usual 6 course, groove, wonted 7 chronic, regular 8 accepted, everyday, habitual, ordinary, standard, workaday 9 customary, plain Jane, quotidian, treadmill 10 accustomed 11 commonplace 12 unremarkable

rove 3 gad 4 move, roam 5 drift, prowl, range, stray 6 ramble, wander 7 meander, traipse 8 vagabond 9 gallivant

rover 3 gad 5 stray 6 gadder, pirate, roamer, sea dog 7 corsair, drifter, floater, rambler, sea wolf 8 gadabout, picaroon, runabout, traveler, wanderer 9 buccaneer, itinerant, meanderer, sea robber 10 freebooter 11 peripatetic 12 rolling stone

roving 6 errant, mobile 7 nomadic, roaming, vagrant 8 rambling, vagabond 9 itinerant, itinerate, wandering, wayfaring 10 discursive 11 perambulant, peripatetic

row 3 oar 4 beef, file, fray, fuss, line, list, pull, punt, rank, sail, scud, spat, tier, tiff 5 align, brawl, broil, chain, fight, melee, mouth, order, queue, run-in, scrap, scull, set-to, swath, train 6 affray, bicker, clamor, fracas, paddle, propel, sequel, series, string 7 brabble, dispute, echelon, quarrel, rhubarb, wrangle 8 argument, sequence, squabble 9 bickering, caterwaul, commotion 10 falling-out, succession 11 altercation, consecution, disturbance, progression

rowdy 4 punk, rude 5 rough, tough, yahoo 6 mucker, unruly, vulgar 7 hoodlum, raffish, raucous, ruffian, toughie 8 bullyboy, stubborn 9 roughneck, turbulent 10 boisterous, disorderly, tumultuous 11 rumbustious

Rowena ***father:*** 7 Hengist ***guardian:*** 6 Cedric ***husband:*** 7 Ivanhoe 9 Vortigern

Roxana ***husband:*** 9 Alexander ***rival:*** 7 Statira

royal 3 top 4 easy 5 grand, light, noble, prime, regal 6 august, facile, kingly, lordly, simple, smooth, superb 7 stately 8 baronial, champion, five-star, glorious, imperial, imposing, kinglike, majestic, princely, splendid, superior 9 classical, excellent, front-rank, grandiose, monarchal, number one, sovereign 10 effortless, monarchial 11 magnificent, monarchical

royalist 4 Tory 5 blimp, white 7 Bourbon, diehard 8 Cavalier 11 reactionary

rub 3 bar, irk, vex 4 buff, fret, gall, rasp, rile, snag, wear, wipe 5 annoy, chafe, crimp, erode, glaze, gloss, grate, graze, grind, peeve, scour, scrub, shine 6 abrade, bother, glance, hamper, hurdle, nettle, polish, ruffle, scrape, smooth, stroke 7 burnish, corrade, furbish, massage, provoke 8 irritate, obstacle, traverse 9 aggravate, excoriate, hindrance 10 difficulty, exasperate, impediment 11 obstruction

Rubaiyat author 11 Omar Khayyam

rubber 4 nose 5 snoop 6 butt-in, eraser

7 Paul Pry, trouble 8 busybody, quidnunc 9 whetstone 10 caoutchouc, misfortune 11 nosey Parker 12 intermeddler ***basis:*** 5 latex ***hard:*** 7 ebonite ***synthetic:*** 8 neoprene ***tree:*** 5 Hevea 7 manihot

Rubber City 5 Akron

rubberneck 3 eye 4 gape, gaze, look, ogle 5 prier, pryer, snoop, stare 6 butt-in, goggle 7 meddler, tourist, tripper 8 busybody, kibitzer, quidnunc, sight-see 9 buttinsky, sightseer 10 pragmatist 12 intermeddler

rubbish 3 pap, rot 4 bosh, crap, junk, slop 5 bilge, dreck, dross, hooey, offal, trash, waste, wrack 6 debris, kelter, litter, pablum, refuse, rubble 7 garbage, hogwash 8 nonsense, tommyrot 9 poppycock, sweepings 11 foolishness

rubbishy 4 base, mean, poor 5 cheap, tatty 6 common, paltry, shoddy, sleazy, trashy 9 worthless

rube 4 boor, hick 5 yahoo 6 rustic 7 bucolic, bumpkin, hayseed, redneck 9 hillbilly 10 clodhopper, provincial 12 backwoodsman

rubicund 3 red 5 flush, ruddy 6 florid 7 flushed, glowing 8 sanguine 11 full-blooded

rubidium *symbol:* 2 Rb

rub out 4 do in, kill, raze, ruin 5 smash, wreck 6 finish, murder 7 bump off, destroy, put away, shatter 8 decimate, demolish, destruct, knock off 9 liquidate 10 annihilate, extinguish, obliterate 11 assassinate

rubric 3 rud 4 name, ruby 5 canon, class, nomen, ruddy, style, title 6 redden, rubify, ruddle 7 concept, notable 8 category, cognomen, nameable 9 memorable, red-letter 10 noteworthy, observable 11 appellation, appellative, designation, incarnadine 12 compellation, denomination

ruck 3 mob 4 fold, heap, mass, pile 5 crimp, crowd, group, plica, ridge, rivel, screw 6 crease, furrow, jumble, muster, pucker, rimple, rumple 7 company, crimple, crinkle, crumple, scrunch, wrinkle 9 congeries, gathering, multitude 10 assemblage, collection, generality 11 aggregation, corrugation

rucksack 4 pack 8 backpack

ruckus 3 row 4 coil, fuss, to-do 5 brawl, broil, melee, scrap 6 fracas, furore, hassle, rumpus, shindy, uproar 7 dispute, quarrel, shindig, wrangle 8 squabble 9 bickering, commotion, confusion 10 falling-out 11 altercation, controversy, disturbance

ruction see ruckus

ruddle see redden

ruddy 3 red 4 rosy, ruby 5 flush, vivid 6 blowsy, florid, lively, redden, rubify, rubric 7 bronzed, flushed, glowing 8 blooming, rubicund, sanguine 11 full-blooded, incarnadine

rude 3 ill, raw 4 curt, wild 5 bluff, crass, crude, fresh, green, gross, gruff, harsh, lumpy, rough, surly 6 abrupt, bitter, callow, clumsy, coarse, crusty, Gothic, ribald, rugged, savage, simple, stormy, unhewn, vulgar 7 angular, boorish, brusque, crabbed, Hunnish, ill-bred, incivil, inexact, loutish, natural, uncivil, uncouth 8 arrogant, barbaric, churlish, clownish, ignorant, impolite, impudent, inexpert, insolent, inurbane, tactless, unformed, unlicked, unsubtle, untaught, unversed, unworked 9 barbarian, barbarous, benighted, dissonant, elemental, imperfect, imprecise, incondite, inelegant, intrusive, makeshift, primitive, proximate, rough-hewn, truculent, turbulent, undressed, unfleshed, unrefined, unwrought 10 cacophonic, discordant, illiterate, immoderate, mannerless, meddlesome, uncultured, uneducated, unfinished, ungracious, unhandsome, unlettered, unmannered, unmannerly, unpolished, unschooled 11 approximate, cacophonous, disgracious, disharmonic, empty-headed, ill-mannered, impertinent, know-nothing, rudimentary, uncalled-for, uncivilized, uncourteous, unfashioned, unmitigated, unpracticed, unprocessed 12 discourteous, inharmonious, unconversant, uncultivated, unharmonious, uninstructed 13 disrespectful

rudiment 5 basic 6 anlage 7 element, vestige 9 beginning, essential 11 fundamental

rudimentary 5 basal, basic 7 initial 8 simplest 9 beginning, elemental, vestigial 10 elementary 11 fundamental, undeveloped ***prefix:*** 3 pro

rue 3 woe 4 care, pity, ruth 5 dolor, grief, mourn 6 bewail, grieve, lament, regret, repent, sorrow 7 anguish, deplore, penance, remorse 8 sympathy 9 heartache, penitence, penitency 10 affliction, compassion, contrition, heartbreak, repentance 11 compunction 12 contriteness

rueful 3 sad 4 poor 5 sorry 6 dolent, woeful 7 doleful, piteous, pitiful, ruthful 8 contrite, dolesome, dolorous, hopeless, mournful, pathetic, penitent, pitiable, wretched 9 afflicted, depressed, miserable, oppressed, plaintive, sorrowful 10 despairing, despondent, lamentable, lugubrious, melancholy 11 weighed down

ruff 5 frill, perch 6 collar, fringe, pigeon, ruffle 9 sandpiper 11 pumpkinseed ***female:*** 5 reeve

ruffian 4 hood, punk, thug 5 bully, rough, rowdy, tough, yahoo 6 brutal, coarse, mucker 7 gorilla, hoodlum, toughie 8 bullyboy, hooligan 9 roughneck, strong arm

ruffle 3 bug, fan, irk, rub, vex 4 blow, fret, gall, wear, wind 5 annoy, chafe, erode, frill, graze, jabot, pleat, ruche 6 abrade, bother, gather, nettle, ripple, winnow 7 agitate, corrade, dispute, disturb, provoke, stiffen, trouble, wrinkle 8 dishevel, disorder, distract, drumbeat, exercise, furbelow, irritate, skirmish 10 disarrange, discompose

Rufus'father 5 Simon

rug 3 mat 4 wrap 5 cover 6 carpet, runner 7 blanket, laprobe 8 covering ***kind:*** 3 rag, rya 6 dhurry, hooked 7 braided, flokati, Persian 8 Aubusson, Oriental 10 Savonnerie

rugby ***formation:*** 5 scrum 9 scrummage ***goal:*** 7 dropped, penalty ***period:*** 4 half ***player:*** 6 center, hooker, winger 8 standoff 9 scrum half ***scoring:*** 3 try 4 goal 10 conversion ***team:*** 7 fifteen ***term:*** 4 heel 5 match 7 convert, dribble, hand off, knock on 9 fair catch ***time-out:*** 8 stoppage ***version:*** 5 union 6 league

rugged 3 dry 4 hard, rude, wild 5 burly, hardy, harsh, heavy, husky, rough, stern, tough 6 bitter, brawny, brutal, coarse, craggy, hoarse, jagged, knotty, robust, severe, strong, sturdy, uneven 7 arduous, austere, boorish, grating, ill-bred, jarring, loutish, lumpish, operose, rasping, raucous, scraggy, unlevel 8 asperous, churlish, clownish, lubberly, muscular, rigorous, scabrous, stalwart, unsmooth, vigorous 9 difficult, inclement, laborious, strenuous, unrefined, weathered 10 formidable, robustious, stridulent, stridulous, unpolished 11 intemperate

Ruggiero ***guardian:*** 7 Atlante ***sister:*** 7 Marfisa ***slayer:*** 11 Tisaphernes ***wife:*** 10 Bradamante

ruin 4 balk, bane, beat, bilk, bust, dash, do in, doom, draw, fall, foil, harm, hurt, loss, maim, raze, sack, undo 5 break, decay, drain, havoc, spoil, use up, waste, wrack, wreck 6 baffle, beggar, blight, damage, debase, deface, devour, fold up, impair, injury, mangle, pauper, ravage, reduce, thwart, unmake 7 atrophy, break up, corrupt, decline, deplete, despoil, destroy, exhaust, outrage, pillage, unbuild, undoing, unframe, vitiate, wipe out, wrecker 8 bankrupt, calamity, clean out, collapse, decimate, demolish, desolate, dishonor, downfall, draw down, mischief, mutilate, spoliate 9 confusion, crumbling, decadence, depredate, desecrate, destroyer, devastate, disfigure, disrepair, downgrade, frustrate, overthrow, pauperize 10 circumvent, declension, degeneracy, degenerate, devolution, dilapidate, disappoint, impoverish 11 destruction, devastation, dissolution 12 degeneration 13 deterioration

ruination 4 bane, loss 5 havoc 7 undoing 8 downfall 9 confusion, destroyer 11 destruction, devastation

ruinous 5 fatal 7 fateful 8 wrackful, wreckful 10 calamitous, disastrous, pernicious, shattering 11 cataclysmic, destructive 12 annihilative, catastrophic

rule 3 law 4 lead, sway 5 axiom, bylaw, canon, edict, gnome, guide, habit, infer, judge, maxim, moral, order, reign 6 assize, course, custom, decide, decree, deduce, dictum, direct, figure, gather, govern, manage, method, regime, settle, truism 7 brocard, command, control, decorum, precept, preside, prevail, regency, regimen, resolve, statute 8 aphorism, apothegm, conclude, decretum, doctrine, dominate, domineer, dominion, overrule 9 authority, determine, etiquette, influence, ordinance, principle, procedure, propriety 10 regulation 11 fundamental ***absolute:*** 8 autarchy ***by a god:*** 8 thearchy, theonomy ***combining form:*** 4 nomy 5 archy

rule out 3 bar 4 bate, ward 5 avert, debar, deter 6 except, forbid, refuse 7 exclude, forfend, obviate, prevent, scratch, suspend 8 count out, preclude, prohibit, stave off 9 eliminate, forestall

ruler 4 king, lord 5 queen 6 archon, dynast, gerent, prince, regent, satrap, sultan 7 emperor, monarch, viceroy 8 governor, hierarch, oligarch, pentarch, princess, theocrat 9 dominator, imperator, matriarch, patriarch, potentate, sovereign 12 straightedge ***absolute:*** 6 despot, tyrant 8 autocrat, dictator, omniarch, overlord ***Arab:*** 4 amir, emir 5 emeer, sheik 6 sharif, sheikh, sherif, sultan ***Asian:*** 4 khan ***Byzantine Empire:*** 6 exarch ***combining form:*** 4 arch ***Egyptian:*** 7 pharaoh ***family:*** 7 dynasty ***Iranian:*** 4 shah ***one of four:*** 8 tetrarch ***one of seven:*** 8 heptarch ***one of three:*** 7 triarch 8 triumvir ***Persian:*** 6 satrap ***Russian:*** 4 czar, tsar, tzar ***Turkish:*** 3 bey, dey

ruling 3 law 4 rife 5 chief, edict, ukase 6 decree 7 central, current, pivotal, popular, rampant, regnant, statute 8 cardinal, decision 9 directive, prevalent 10 overriding, prevailing, widespread 11 predominant

Rumania see Romania

rumble 3 cry 4 boom, buzz, clap, peal, roar, roll, talk 5 blast, burst, crack, crash, growl, ondit, rumor 6 gossip, murmur, report, uproar 7 hearsay, quarrel, resound, thunder 9 complaint, grapevine 11 disturbance, scuttlebutt

ruminant 3 cow, yak 4 deer, goat, tahr 5 bison, camel, goral, llama, okapi, serow, sheep, takin 6 alpaca, cattle, musk ox, vicuña 7 buffalo, chamois, chewing, giraffe,

guanaco 8 antelope *stomach:* 5 rumen 6 omasum 8 abomasum 9 reticulum
ruminate 4 chew, mull, muse, roll 5 champ, chomp, chump, munch, think, weigh 6 crunch, ponder 7 chumble, reflect, revolve, scrunch 8 cogitate, consider, meditate, mull over, turn over 9 masticate 10 deliberate, excogitate 11 contemplate
ruminative 7 pensive 8 thinking 9 pondering 10 cogitative, meditative, reflecting, reflective, thoughtful 11 speculative 13 contemplative
rummage 4 beat, comb, fish, grub, hash, mash, poke, rake, rout, seek 5 mix up, scour 6 dig out, forage, hunt up, jumble, jungle, litter, mess up, muddle, search, spy out, tumble 7 clutter, disrupt, disturb, examine, hunt out, ransack 8 disarray, disorder, finecomb, hunt down, mishmash, scramble 9 ferret out, patchwork, potpourri, search out 10 collection, disarrange, discompose, hotchpotch, miscellany, scrutinize 11 disorganize
rummy 3 odd 4 lush 5 drunk, queer 6 boozer, lusher 7 bizarre, curious, guzzler, oddball, strange, swiller, tippler 8 drunkard, peculiar, singular 9 eccentric, inebriate 10 boozehound
rumor 4 blab, buzz, talk, word 5 on-dit, story 6 gossip, mumble, murmur, mutter, report, rumble, tattle 7 hearsay, tidings, whisper 9 grapevine, undertone 11 scuttlebutt, susurration
rumormonger 5 tabby 6 gossip 8 gossiper, quidnunc, telltale 9 carrytale 10 talebearer
rump 4 beam, hind, rear 5 fanny 6 behind, bottom 7 rear end 8 backside, buttocks, derriere, haunches 9 posterior *combining form:* 3 pyg 4 pyga, pygo 5 pygal, pygia
rumple 4 fold, muss 5 crimp, screw 6 tousle 7 crimple, crinkle, scrunch, wrinkle
rumpus see **ruckus**
run 2 go 3 act, dig, fly, get, ram, set, use, wax 4 bolt, come, dart, dash, flee, flit, flow, flux, fuse, gill, grow, hare, herd, hunt, keep, line, make, melt, move, pour, race, rush, shin, sink, skip, stab, tear, thaw, trip, turn, vary, work 5 apply, blend, brook, chase, creek, drift, drive, fleet, haste, hurry, range, reach, recur, refer, scoot, skirr, speed, stick, swing, tenor, trend 6 become, bustle, career, course, direct, escape, extend, gallop, govern, handle, hustle, manage, ordain, plunge, repair, resort, runnel, scorch, scurry, sprint, stream, thrust 7 bearing, bootleg, carry on, conduct, current, hotfoot, liquefy, make off, operate, proceed, retreat, rivulet, scamper, scuttle, smuggle, stretch 8 dissolve, duration, function, highball, liquesce, tendency, traverse 9 direction, endurance, skedaddle 10 continuity, contraband, deliquesce 11 continuance, persistence 12 continuation, prolongation
run across 4 meet 8 discover 9 encounter
runagate 3 rat, vag 4 hobo 5 tramp 7 drifter, floater, vagrant 8 apostate, defector, fugitive, recreant, renegade, roadster, turncoat, vagabond, wanderer 9 turnabout
run along 2 go 4 exit, quit 5 leave 6 depart, get off 7 pull out, take off 8 shove off
runaround 6 detour, escape 7 come off, elusion, evasion 8 escaping, eschewal, shunning 9 avoidance 10 roundabout
run away 4 bolt, flee 5 elope 6 desert, escape 7 abscond 8 stampede
runaway 8 decisive, deserter, fugitive
run down 3 hit 4 stop 5 decry, trace 6 pursue 7 downcry 8 belittle, derogate, diminish 9 disparage, dispraise 10 depreciate 11 detract from, opprobriate
run-down 5 dingy, seedy, tacky, tired 6 shabby, tagrag 8 decrepit, tattered, untended 9 exhausted, neglected 10 broken-down, down-at-heel, uncared-for 11 dilapidated
rune 4 poem, song 5 charm, ogham, poesy, rhyme, spell, verse 6 poetry 11 conjuration, incantation
rung 4 step 5 grade, notch, spoke, stage, stair, tread 6 degree, handle 10 crosspiece
run in 3 nab 4 bust 5 pinch, visit 6 arrest, come by, detain, drop by, look up, pick up, stop by 9 apprehend
run-in 3 row 4 tiff 5 brush, fight, set-to 6 hassle 7 dispute, quarrel, rhubarb 8 skirmish 9 bickering, encounter 10 falling-out, velitation 11 altercation
run into 4 meet 6 become 9 encounter
runnel see **rivulet**
runner 3 rug 5 agent, blade, miler, racer 6 carpet, stolon 8 operator, sprinter 9 messenger
running 4 care, easy, live, race 5 alive 6 active, charge, fluent, linear, smooth 7 conduct, cursive, dynamic, flowing, working 8 handling, roadwork, together 9 operative, oversight 10 continuous, effortless, intendance, management 11 continually, functioning, night and day, supervision 12 continuously, successively 13 consecutively *combining form:* 4 drom 5 dromo 7 dromous
running mate 3 pal 4 chum 5 buddy, crony 7 comrade 9 associate, companion
run-of-the-mill 4 fair, mean 5 typic, usual 6 common, medium, normal 7 average, general, natural, regular, typical 8 mediocre, middling, moderate, ordinary, uncommon 9 prevalent 11 commonplace,

indifferent 12 intermediate 13 unexceptional
run on 3 gab, jaw, yak 4 chat, talk 5 clack 6 babble, gabble, rattle 7 chatter, prattle 8 continue
run out 4 fail, flow, oust 5 exile, expel 6 banish, deport, elapse, expire 7 cast out, give out 8 complete, displace 9 ostracize, transport
run over 5 spill 6 exceed, repeat 7 examine 8 overbrim, overfill, overflow, rehearse
runt 5 dwarf, midge, pygmy 6 midget, peewee 7 manikin 8 Tom Thumb 10 homunculus 11 hop-o'-my-thumb, lilliputian
run through 2 go 4 scan 5 spend, use up 6 browse, expend, finish, pierce 7 consume, dip into, examine, exhaust 8 glance at, rehearse, transfix 10 glance over
runty 4 puny 5 small 7 stunted 8 dwarfish 10 diminutive, undersized 12 contemptible
run up 3 wax 4 rise 5 build, erect, mount 6 expand 7 augment, enlarge 8 increase, multiply, snowball 9 construct 10 accumulate
runway 4 path 5 strip, track, trail 6 bridge 7 channel 8 airstrip, platform
rupture 4 hole, open, part, rend, rent, rift, rive 5 break, burst, sever, split 6 breach, cleave, divide, hernia, schism, sunder 7 blowout, break up, disjoin, disrupt, dissect, divorce, fissure, parting, split-up 8 disunion, disunite, division, fracture, separate 9 partition 10 detachment, separation 11 dissolution, divorcement ***combining form:*** 7 rrhexes (plural), rrhexis
R.U.R. ***author:*** 5 Čapek (Karel) ***character:*** 5 robot
rural 6 rustic, simple 7 bucolic, country, idyllic, natural, outland 8 agrestic, arcadian, pastoral, villatic 10 campestral, out-country, provincial 11 countrified
ruse 3 jig 4 hoax, ploy, wile 5 dodge, feint, fraud, trick 6 deceit, gambit 7 gimmick 8 artifice, maneuver, trickery 9 stratagem 10 subterfuge
rush 3 fly, run 4 boil, bolt, dart, dash, flit, flow, flux, lash, race, scud, tear, tide, whiz 5 break, chase, drift, fleet, fling, flood, haste, hurry, onset, sally, scoot, shoot, spate, speed, surge 6 attack, barrel, bustle, career, charge, course, hasten, hurtle, irrupt, plunge, stream 7 assault, cattail, current 8 stampede, vanquish 9 hastiness, overpower 11 hurriedness 12 precipitance, precipitancy 13 precipitation
rushing 5 hasty 6 abrupt, sudden 7 hurried 8 headlong 9 impetuous 11 precipitant, precipitate, precipitous, subitaneous
Russian ***family:*** 7 Romanov 9 Stroganov ***monk:*** 8 Rasputin ***peasant:*** 5 kulak, mujik 6 moujik, muzhik, muzjik ***ruler:*** (see czar) ***saint:*** 15 Alexander Nevski ***villa:*** 5 dacha
rustic 3 jay, yap 4 hick, jake, rube, rude 5 churl, clown, plain, rough, rural, swain, yokel 6 farmer, joskin, simple, sturdy, sylvan, woodsy 7 artless, bucolic, bumpkin, country, granger, hayseed, hillman, hoosier, outland, peasant, plowboy, plowman, redneck, uncouth 8 agrestic, mossback, pastoral 9 chawbacon, greenhorn, hillbilly 10 campestral, clodhopper, countryman, exurbanite, husbandman, out-country, provincial 11 countrified, country jake, mountaineer 12 backwoodsman
rustle 5 haste, hurry, speed, steal, swish 6 forage, hustle, swoosh 7 crinkle 8 celerity, dispatch, susurrus 9 swiftness 10 expedition, speediness
rustler 5 thief 6 dynamo, peeler 7 hustler 8 go-getter, live wire 11 self-starter
Rustum's son and victim 6 Sohrab
rusty 3 dry 4 slow 5 harsh, hoary, inept, rough 6 hoarse, rugged 7 grating, jarring, rasping, raucous, restive 8 outmoded, strident 10 discolored
rut 4 heat, pace, rote 5 grind, track 6 estrus, furrow, groove 7 channel, routine 9 treadmill
rutabaga 5 swede 6 turnip
ruth 3 rue 4 pity 5 grief, mercy 6 regret, sorrow 7 penance, remorse, sadness 8 distress, sympathy 9 attrition, penitence, penitency 10 compassion, contrition, repentance 11 compunction
Ruth ***husband:*** 4 Boaz 6 Mahlon ***mother-in-law:*** 5 Naomi ***son:*** 4 Obed
ruthenium ***symbol:*** 2 Ru
ruthful 6 dolent, rueful, tender, woeful 7 doleful, pitiful 8 dolorous, wretched 9 afflicted, miserable, sorrowful
ruthless 4 grim 5 cruel 6 mortal, savage 8 pitiless 9 ferocious, merciless, unsparing 10 implacable, ironfisted, relentless, unyielding 11 unflinching, unrelenting 12 unappeasable
ruttish 3 hot 5 rutty 7 goatish, lustful, satyric 9 lickerish, salacious 10 lascivious, libidinous 12 concupiscent
Rwanda ***capital:*** 6 Kigali ***monetary unit:*** 5 franc

S

Sabatini novel 11 Scaramouche 12 Captain Blood
sabbatical 4 rest 5 leave
saber 5 sword
sabertooth 3 cat 5 tiger
sable 3 jet 4 dark, ebon, inky 5 black, dusky, ebony, jetty, murky, raven 6 gloomy, mammal, somber 9 pitch-dark 10 pitch-black
sabot 4 clog, shoe
sabotage 5 block, wreck 6 damage, hamper, hinder, injury 7 break up, destroy, subvert 8 obstruct, wreckage, wrecking 9 frustrate, undermine 10 impairment, subversion 11 undermining 12 subversivism
Sabra *father:* 7 Ptolemy *husband, rescuer:* 8 St. George *son:* 3 Guy 5 David 9 Alexander
Sabrina *father:* 7 Locrine *mother:* 9 Estrildis
sac 4 cyst 5 pouch
Sacar *father:* 8 Obededom *son:* 5 Ahiam
saccharine 5 sweet 6 sugary, syrupy 7 candied, cloying, honeyed, sugared 9 disarming, oversweet 11 deferential, sugarcoated 12 ingratiating
sacerdotal 8 priestly 9 religious 10 priestlike 11 ministerial
sachem 4 boss 5 chief 6 leader
sachet 3 bag 6 powder 7 perfume
sack 2 ax 3 bag, bed 4 base, drop, fire, raid, ship, wine 5 expel, pouch, strip, waste 6 bounce, devour, forage, pocket, ravage 7 boot out, cashier, despoil, dismiss, kick out, pillage 8 desolate, spoliate 9 container, depredate, desecrate, devastate, terminate
sackbut 8 trombone
sacque 6 jacket
sacrament 4 rite, sign 6 symbol 7 baptism, penance 8 ceremony 9 eucharist, matrimony 10 holy orders 12 confirmation
sacrarium 6 chapel, shrine 7 oratory, piscina 8 sacristy 9 sanctuary
sacred 4 holy 5 godly 6 immune 7 angelic, blessed, guarded, saintly 8 defended, hallowed, numinous 9 cherished, inviolate, spiritual, unprofane 10 inviolable, sacrosanct, sanctified 11 consecrated, sacramental *combining form:* 4 hagi, hier, sacr 5 hagio, hiero, sacro *monkey:* 6 baboon, rhesus 7 hanuman *place:* 7 sanctum *weed:* 7 vervain
sacrifice 4 cede, drop, give, lose 5 forgo, yield 6 devote, donate, eschew, martyr, victim 7 forbear, forfeit, offer up 8 dedicate, hecatomb, immolate, oblation, offering
sacrilege 7 impiety, offense 9 blasphemy, violation 11 desecration, irreverence, profanation
sacrilegious 7 impious, profane, ungodly 10 irreverent 11 blasphemous, irreligious
sacristan 6 sexton
sacristy 6 vestry
sacrosanct 6 sacred 8 esteemed, regarded 9 inviolate, respected 10 inviolable
sad 4 blue, down 5 drear, dumpy, sorry 6 dismal, dreary, gloomy, morose, triste, woeful 7 doleful, dumpish, joyless, piteous, pitiful, unhappy 8 dejected, desolate, dolorous, downbeat, downcast, grieving, mournful, pathetic, pitiable, saddened, tristful 9 depressed, mirthless, sorrowful, woebegone 10 afflicting, depressing, dispirited, lamentable, melancholy 11 melancholic 12 heavyhearted
sadden 7 depress, oppress 9 weigh down
saddle 3 tax 4 lade, load, task 5 weigh 6 burden, charge, cumber, hamper, impede, impose, weight 7 aparejo, inflict 8 encumber, restrict *adjunct:* 7 stirrup *covering:* 7 mochila *part:* 6 cantle, pommel 8 tapadera, tapadero *strap:* 5 cinch, girth 6 latigo 7 harness
sadness 3 woe 4 funk 5 blues, dinge, downs, dumps, gloom, grief, mopes 6 misery, sorrow 7 anguish, dismals, megrims 8 doldrums, dolefuls, glumness, mourning 9 dejection, dysphoria, moodiness 10 blue devils, depression, desolation, melancholy 11 despondency, forlornness, melancholia, unhappiness 12 downcastness, hopelessness, listlessness, mournfulness 13 sorrowfulness
safari 4 hunt, trek, trip 7 caravan 10 expedition
safe 4 wary 5 chary 6 intact, secure, unhurt 7 careful, guarded, healthy 8 cautious, defended, discreet, gingerly, guarding, harmless, innocent, riskless, shielded, unharmed 9 innocuous, protected, shel-

tered, shielding, uninjured, unscathed, wholesome **10** inviolable, protecting, scatheless, sheltering **11** calculating, circumspect, considerate, impregnable, inoffensive, uninjurious **12** invulnerable, safeguarding, unassailable, unthreatened

safety **5** cover **7** defense, shelter **8** security **9** assurance **10** protection **13** inviolability

sag **3** dip **4** bend, drop, flag, flap, flop, sink, slip, swag, wilt **5** basin, droop, slide, slump **6** dangle, hollow, slouch **7** decline, drop off, falloff, sinkage, sinking **8** downturn, fall away, settling, sinkhole **9** concavity, downslide, downswing, downtrend **10** depression

saga **4** edda, epic, tale **5** story **6** legend **9** narrative

sagacious **4** sage, wise **5** cagey, heady, smart **6** argute, astute, clever, shrewd **7** gnostic, knowing, prudent, sapient **8** critical **9** astucious, far-seeing, insighted, judicious **10** discerning, insightful, perceptive **11** intelligent **13** knowledgeable, perspicacious

sagacity **5** grasp **6** wisdom **7** insight **8** prudence, sageness, sapience, wiseness **10** perception **11** discernment, penetration, sensitivity **13** comprehension, judiciousness, understanding

sagamore **5** chief **6** sachem

sage **4** mint, sane, wise **5** acute **6** expert, master, nestor, savant, sophic **7** gnostic, knowing, learned, probing, prudent, sapient, scholar, wise man **8** polymath, profound, sensible **9** insighted, judgmatic, judicious, sagacious **10** discerning, insightful, perceptive **11** penetrating, philosophic **13** knowledgeable ***Hindu:*** **5** rishi **6** pandit **7** mahatma

Sagebrush State **6** Nevada

sage cock **6** grouse

Sage of ___ ***Chelsea:*** **7** Carlyle ***Concord:*** **7** Emerson ***Emporia:*** **5** White ***Ferney:*** **8** Voltaire ***Monticello:*** **9** Jefferson ***Pylos:*** **6** Nestor

sagging **8** swayback

Sagittarius **6** archer **7** centaur **13** constellation

saguaro **6** cactus

saharan **3** dry **4** arid, sere **6** barren **8** deserted

sail **3** fly **4** boat, dart, flit, scud, skim, wing **5** fleet, float, mizen, shoot, skirr, sweep, yacht **6** cruise, mizzen **7** spencer **9** spinnaker ***triangular:*** **3** jib **5** genoa

sailboat **4** bark, yawl **5** ketch, skiff, sloop **8** skipjack

sailing vessel **4** bark, brig, saic **5** xebec **6** barque **7** frigate, galleon **8** schooner **10** barkentine, brigantine

sailor **3** tar **4** jack, salt **5** jacky **6** seaman, swabby **7** jack-tar, mariner, swabbie, yachter **8** seafarer, shipmate **9** tarpaulin, yachtsman **10** bluejacket ***British:*** **5** limey ***fictional:*** **6** Sinbad ***patron saint:*** **4** Elmo ***song:*** **6** chanty **7** chantey **9** barcarole

saint ***biography:*** **11** hagiography ***list:*** **9** hagiology; (see also **patron saint**)

Saint, the **12** Simon Templar ***creator:*** **9** Charteris (Leslie)

Saint Anthony's cross **3** tau

Saint Elmo's Fire **9** corposant

Saint Joan author **4** Shaw

Saint John's bread **5** carob

saintly **4** holy **5** godly, pious **6** devout, seraph, worthy **7** angelic, upright **8** seraphic, virtuous **9** righteous

Saint Paul's Church (London) ***designer:*** **4** Wren

Saint Peter's Basilica ***architect:*** **7** Bernini **12** Michelangelo ***sculpture:*** **5** Pietè

Saint Vitus' dance **6** chorea

sake **3** end **4** good **5** drink **7** purpose

salaam **3** bow **8** greeting

salacious **4** fast, lewd **7** lustful, satyric **9** lecherous, libertine **10** lascivious, libidinous, licentious **11** incontinent

salad **4** brew, hash, stew, toss **5** chef's **6** Caesar **7** mélange ***item:*** **3** egg **4** bean, cuke, herb **5** cress, fruit, olive, onion **6** carrot, celery, cheese, endive, pepper, potato, radish, tomato **7** anchovy, cabbage, crouton, lettuce, parsley, spinach **8** chick-pea, coleslaw, cucumber, garbanzo, mushroom, scallion **10** watercress **11** cauliflower

salamander **3** eft **4** newt **8** mudpuppy, waterdog ***Mexican:*** **7** axolotl

salient **6** marked, moving, signal **7** obvious, weighty **8** striking **9** arresting, arrestive, important, intrusive, obtrusive, pertinent, prominent **10** impressive, noticeable, pronounced, remarkable **11** conspicuous, outstanding, significant

saline **4** salt **5** briny, salty **8** brackish **10** saliferous

saliva **4** spit **5** water **6** slaver, sputum **7** spittle

salivate **5** drool **6** drivel, slaver **7** dribble, slabber, slobber

___ Salk **5** Jonas

sallow **3** wan **4** pale **6** willow, yellow

sally **3** gag **4** gust, jape, jest, joke, quip **5** burst, crack, jaunt **6** junket, outing **7** flare-up **8** drollery, eruption, outburst **9** excursion, explosion, wisecrack, witticism

salmagundi see **hodgepodge**

salmon **4** parr, pink **5** smolt **6** grilse **7** essling, geelbec, sockeye **9** brandling ***female:*** **4** raun ***male:*** **6** kipper ***smoked:*** **3** lox

Salmon ***father:*** 3 Hur 7 Nahshon ***grandfather:*** 5 Caleb ***son:*** 4 Boaz
Salmoneus ***brother:*** 7 Athamas 8 Sisyphus ***daughter:*** 4 Tyro ***father:*** 6 Aeolus ***mother:*** 7 Enarete
Salome ***composer:*** 7 Strauss ***father:*** 5 Herod ***husband:*** 6 Philip 7 Zebedee 11 Aristobulus ***mother:*** 8 Herodias ***son:*** 4 John 5 James
salon 4 hall, shop 5 suite 6 parlor 9 apartment, reception
saloon 3 bar 4 hall 6 tavern 7 barroom, cantina, gallery, taproom 8 drinkery
salt 3 tar 4 jack, keep, NaCl 5 brine, salty 6 sailor, saline, seaman 7 jack-tar, mariner 8 salinize 9 sailorman, tarpaulin 10 saliferous
salt away 4 save 5 lay by, lay in, lay up, put by 8 lay aside
saltpeter 5 niter, nitre
saltworks 6 salina 7 saltern
salty 4 blue, racy 5 briny, broad, shady, spicy 6 purple, risqué, saline, wicked 7 caustic, mordant 8 brackish, off-color, scathing 9 trenchant 10 mordacious, saliferous, suggestive
salubrious 4 good 7 bracing, healthy 8 hygienic, salutary 9 healthful, wholesome 11 stimulating 12 invigorating
Salus see **Hygeia**
Salu's son 5 Zimri
salutation 2 hi 4 hail 5 hello 7 Dear Sir 8 greeting ***Arab:*** 6 salaam ***French:*** 5 salut ***German:*** 4 heil ***Hawaiian:*** 5 aloha ***Italian:*** 4 ciao ***Latin:*** 3 ave ***Spanish:*** 4 hola
salute 4 hail, heil 5 greet 6 accost, call to 7 address 8 greeting
salvage 4 save 6 ransom, redeem, regain, rescue 7 deliver, reclaim, recover 8 retrieve
salvation 6 saving 7 keeping 9 preserval 11 conservancy, safekeeping 12 conservation, preservation, sustentation
Salvation Army founder 5 Booth
salve 3 aid 4 balm 5 cream 6 cerate, chrism, remedy 7 unction, unguent 8 ointment 9 emollient, lubricant
salver 4 tray
salvo 4 hail 5 burst, spray, storm 6 shower, volley 7 barrage, tribute 9 broadside, cannonade, discharge, fusillade 11 bombardment, testimonial 12 appreciation
samaritan 6 helper 8 welldoer 10 benefactor
same 4 idem, like, very 5 equal, exact 7 coequal, identic, similar 8 constant 9 duplicate, identical, unfailing, unvarying 10 comparable, consistent, equivalent, invariable, tantamount, unchanging
Samoa's capital 4 Apia 8 Pago Pago
samovar 3 urn
sampan 4 boat 5 skiff
sample 4 case, part, sign, unit 5 piece 7 element, example, portion, segment 8 fragment, instance, sampling, specimen 10 indication, individual 11 case history, constituent 12 illustration
Samson ***betrayer:*** 7 Delilah ***birthplace:*** 5 Zorah ***deathplace:*** 4 Gaza ***father:*** 6 Manoah ***tribe:*** 3 Dan
Samson Agonistes author 6 Milton
Samuel ***father:*** 7 Elkanah ***grandson:*** 5 Heman ***mother:*** 6 Hannah
samurai 7 soldier, warrior ***code:*** 7 bushido
sanctify 5 bless 6 hallow 10 consecrate
sanctimonious 5 false 7 canting 9 deceiving, pharisaic 11 pharisaical 12 hypocritical, pecksniffian 13 self-righteous
sanction 2 OK 4 fiat, okay 5 leave 6 permit, ratify 7 approve, certify, consent, endorse, license, support 8 accredit, approval 9 allowance, authorize 10 commission, permission, sufferance 11 approbation, endorsement 12 confirmation, ratification 13 authorization, encouragement
sanctity 8 holiness 9 godliness 11 saintliness, uprightness 13 righteousness
sanctuary 4 port 5 bamah, cover, haven, oasis 6 asylum, covert, harbor, refuge, shrine 7 retreat, sanctum, shelter 9 harborage, holy place
sanctum 6 shrine 9 holy place, sanctuary
sandal 4 zori 8 huarache, huaracho ***winged:*** 7 talaria (plural)
sandbar 4 reef, spit 7 tombolo
sand hill 4 dune
sandpiper 4 knot, ruff, stib 5 reeve, terek 6 dunlin, teeter
sandstone deposit 6 flysch
sandwich 3 BLT, sub 4 club 5 hoagy 6 hoagie 7 grinder 9 submarine ***combining form:*** 6 burger
sandy 6 beachy, gritty 7 arenose, arenous 8 sabulose, sabulous
sane 3 fit 4 good, hale, sage, well, wise 5 lucid, right, sober, sound 6 cogent, normal 7 healthy, logical, prudent, sapient 8 all there, balanced, oriented, rational, sensible 9 judgmatic, judicious, wholesome 10 compelling, convincing, reasonable, well-liking 11 levelheaded 12 compos mentis
San Francisco ***hill:*** 3 Nob 7 Russian ***tower:*** 4 Coit
sangfroid 6 phlegm 7 ataraxy 9 aloofness, composure, unconcern 10 equanimity 11 self-control 12 indifference
sanguinary 4 gory 6 bloody 7 imbrued 9 homicidal, murdering, murderous 12 bloodstained, bloodthirsty
sanguine 4 gory 5 flush, ruddy 6 bloody, florid, secure, upbeat 7 assured, flushed,

glowing, hopeful, imbrued **8** rubicund **9** confident, expectant, homicidal, murdering, murderous **10** optimistic, undoubtful **11** full-blooded, self-assured **12** bloodstained, bloodthirsty, Pollyannaish, undespairing **13** self-confident

sanitary **5** clean **8** hygienic **9** healthful

sanity **3** wit **4** mind **6** reason, senses **8** lucidity, saneness **9** soundness **12** intelligence **13** comprehension

Sanskrit **5** Indic **8** language ***dialect:*** **4** Pali ***epic:*** **8** Ramayana ***school:*** **3** tol ***Scripture:*** **4** Veda

Santa Lucia composer **5** Denza

sap **4** dupe, fool, gull, mark, ruin **5** blunt, chump, drain, wreck **6** pigeon, sucker, weaken **7** cripple, deplete, destroy, disable, exhaust, fall guy, saphead, unbrace **8** enervate, enfeeble, knock out **9** attenuate, schlemiel, undermine **10** debilitate

Saph's slayer **8** Sibbecai

sapid **5** tasty **6** savory **8** saporous **9** aperitive, palatable, relishing, toothsome **10** appetizing, flavorsome

sapience see **sagacity**

sapient see **sagacious**

sapling **4** tree **5** youth

Sapphira ***coconspirator, husband:*** **7** Ananias

Sappho ***forte:*** **6** poetry ***island:*** **6** Lesbos

sappy **5** crazy, loony, mushy, silly, soupy **6** absurd, drippy, insane, slushy, sticky **7** foolish, maudlin, mawkish **8** bathetic **11** harebrained, sentimental

Saracen **4** Arab **6** Muslim ***hero:*** **9** Rodomonte

Sarah ***husband:*** **7** Abraham ***maid:*** **5** Hagar ***son:*** **5** Isaac

sarcasm **3** wit **4** gibe, jest **5** humor, irony, scorn **6** rancor, satire **7** mockery **8** acerbity, acrimony, mordancy, raillery, repartee, ridicule, sneering **9** invective, sharpness **10** causticity, lampooning **13** corrosiveness ***writer:*** **7** ironist

sarcastic **3** dry **4** tart **5** acerb, sharp **6** biting, ironic **7** acerbic, caustic, cutting, cynical, jeering, mocking, mordant, pungent, satiric **8** incisive, sardonic, scathing, scornful, stinging **9** corrosive, trenchant

sarcophagus **4** tomb **6** coffin

sardine **4** sild **7** herring **8** pilchard

Sardinia's capital **8** Cagliari

sardonic **3** wry **6** ironic **7** caustic, cynical, jeering, mocking, satiric **8** derisive, scornful, sneering **9** corrosive, sarcastic, saturnine **10** disdainful **12** contemptuous

sarong **5** skirt **7** garment

Sarpedon ***brother:*** **5** Minos **12** Rhadamanthus ***father:*** **4** Zeus **7** Jupiter ***mother:*** **6** Europa **8** Laodamia

Sartre work **4** Kean **6** Nausea **7** The Wall **8** The Flies **10** Baudelaire, Saint Genet

sash **4** belt **6** girdle **8** ceinture, cincture **9** waistband

sashay **4** perk **5** mince, strut **6** prance **7** flounce, swagger

Saskatchewan's capital **6** Regina

sass **4** guff **5** cheek, mouth, sauce **8** back talk, saucebox **9** insolence, sassiness **12** impertinence

sassafras **3** tea **6** saloop

sassy **4** bold, pert, wise **5** doggy, fresh, lippy, natty, nervy, smart **6** brazen, cheeky, dapper, spiffy, spruce, sprucy **7** bandbox, doggish, forward **8** impudent, malapert, sparkish **9** audacious, unabashed **11** smart-alecky, well-groomed

Satan **5** beast, demon, deuce, devil, fiend, viper **6** diablo **7** Lucifer, Old Nick, serpent, villain **8** Apollyon, devil-god, renegade, succubus **9** archfiend, Beelzebub **10** Old Scratch **13** Old Gooseberry

satanic **4** evil **6** wicked **7** demonic **8** demoniac, demonian, devilish, diabolic, fiendish **9** saturnine **10** serpentine, unhallowed **11** diabolonian

satanism **9** diabolism

satchel **3** bag **4** case **5** pouch **6** valise

sate **4** cloy, fill, glut, jade, pall **5** gorge, stuff **6** stodge **7** overeat, satiate, surfeit **8** overfill **9** overstuff

satellite **4** moon **6** cohort, minion **7** sectary, sputnik **8** adherent, disciple, favorite, follower, henchman, incident, partisan, sectator **9** ancillary, attendant, attending, supporter ***of Jupiter:*** **2** Io **6** Europa **8** Callisto, Ganymede ***of Mars:*** **6** Deimos, Phobos ***of Neptune:*** **6** Nereid, Triton ***of Saturn:*** **4** Rhea **5** Dione, Janus, Mimas, Titan **6** Phoebe, Tethys **7** Iapetus **8** Hyperion **9** Enceladus ***of Uranus:*** **5** Ariel **6** Oberon **7** Miranda, Titania, Umbriel

satiate see **sate**

satire **5** irony, spoof, squib **6** banter, parody **7** mockery, pasquil, takeoff **8** chaffing, raillery, ridicule, spoofery, travesty **10** causticity, lampoonery, pasquinade, persiflage

satiric **6** ironic **7** caustic, mocking **8** chaffing, farcical, ironical, spoofing **9** bantering, parodying **10** lampooning, ridiculing

satirist ***English:*** **5** Swift **7** Marston ***French:*** **8** Rabelais, Voltaire ***Greek:*** **8** Menippus ***Roman:*** **6** Horace **7** Juvenal, Persius **9** Petronius

satirize **4** mock **5** spoof **6** parody **7** cartoon, censure, lampoon **8** ridicule

satisfaction **6** amends **8** pleasure **9** atonement **10** attainment **11** contentment, fulfillment, restitution **13** gratification

satisfactory **2** OK **4** fair, good, okay **5** solid, sound, valid **6** cogent, decent, enough 8 adequate, all right, passable 9 competent, sufficing, tolerable 10 acceptable, convincing, sufficient 11 comfortable 13 unexceptional

satisfy 3 pay 4 fill, meet, quit, sate, suit 5 clear, humor, pay up, serve 6 answer, assure, induce, pacify, please, settle, square 7 appease, content, fulfill, gladden, gratify, indulge, placate, satiate, suffice, win over 8 clear off, convince, inveigle, persuade, pleasure 9 conform to 10 comply with

satrap 5 ruler 7 viceroy 8 governor, henchman 11 subordinate

saturate 3 sop, wet 4 soak, wash 5 bathe, imbue, madid, probe, souse, steep 6 charge, douche, drench, infuse, pierce, soaked, sodden, soused 7 instill, pervade, soaking, sopping, suffuse 8 drenched, dripping, permeate, waterlog 9 inoculote, penetrate, percolate, transfuse

Saturn see Cronus

saturnalia 4 orgy 5 party 7 debauch 9 bacchanal 11 bacchanalia

saturnine 4 dark, dour, glum, ugly 5 grave, staid, sulky, surly 6 gloomy, moping, morose, silent, solemn, somber, sullen 7 crabbed, serious 8 funereal, reserved, taciturn

satyric 4 lewd 5 horny, randy 7 goatish, lustful 8 prurient 9 lecherous, libertine, lickerish, salacious 10 lascivious, libidinous, licentious, passionate 12 concupiscent

sauce 4 guff, sass 5 mouth 6 relish 7 topping 8 back talk, pertness 9 condiment, impudence ***kind:*** 3 soy 4 hard, lear, mole 5 bercy, chili, curry, dashi, gravy, melba, pesto, salsa 6 catsup, chivry, Mornay, panada, Robert, tartar, tomato 7 catchup, chutnee, chutney, ketchup, marengo, Newburg, piquant, soubise, supreme, tartare, velouté 8 béchamel, duxelles, marinara, matelote, noisette, normande, normandy, poivrade, poulette, ravigote, remolade 9 bearnaise, lyonnaise, mariniere, remoulade 10 bordelaise, Provençale 11 hollandaise, vinaigrette

saucy see sassy

Saudi Arabia ***capital:*** 6 Riyadh ***monetary unit:*** 5 riyal

Saul ***concubine:*** 6 Rizpah ***daughter:*** 5 Merab 6 Michal ***father:*** 4 Kish ***son:*** 8 Jonathan ***successor:*** 5 David ***uncle:*** 3 Ner ***wife:*** 7 Ahinoam

saunter 4 mope, roam, rove, walk 5 amble, drift, mosey, tarry 6 bummel, linger, loiter, ramble, stroll, wander 7 meander 8 ambulate

sausage 5 wurst 6 banger, kishka, kishke, salami, Vienna, wiener 7 baloney, bologna, boloney, chorizo, saveloy 8 cervelat, chaurice, drisheen, kielbasa, pemmican 9 bratwurst, frankfort, frankfurt, pepperoni, Thuringer 10 knackwurst, knockwurst, liverwurst, mortadella 11 frankforter, frankfurter

sausage-shaped 10 botuliform

savage 4 fell, grim, rude, wild 5 brute, cruel, feral, harsh, rabid, rough 6 bloody, brutal, fierce, Gothic, Hunnic, rugged 7 bestial, brutish, Hunnish, inhuman, untamed, vicious, wolfish 8 barbaric, inhumane, primeval, ravenous, unbroken 9 barbarian, barbarous, butcherly, ferocious, heartless, murderous, primitive, rapacious, truculent, unsubdued, voracious 10 implacable, relentless 11 coldhearted, uncivilized, unharnessed, unrelenting 12 bloodthirsty, uncontrolled, uncultivated, unsocialized

savanna 5 plain 9 grassland

savant 4 sage 7 scholar, wise man

save 3 bar, but, yet 4 bank, keep, only, Stow 5 cache, guard, hoard, lay by, lay in, lay up, put by, set by, skimp, spare 6 bating, defend, except, keep up, manage, rescue, saving, scrimp, shield, unless 7 barring, besides, collect, deliver, deposit, however, husband, lay away, protect, reclaim, reserve, salvage, store up, sustain, unchain 8 conserve, lay aside, maintain, preserve, salt away, squirrel 9 aside from, economize, excluding, safeguard, stash away, stockpile, unshackle 10 accumulate 11 exclusive of

saving 3 but 6 beside, except 7 barring, besides, sparing, thrifty 9 aside from, except for, excluding, preserval, provident, salvation, stewardly 10 economical, husbanding, unwasteful 11 conservancy, safekeeping 12 conservation, preservation, sustentation

savoir faire 4 tact 5 grace, poise, taste 6 aplomb 7 address, dignity, manners 8 elegance 9 blaséness, diplomacy 10 confidence, experience, refinement 11 delicatesse, tactfulness 13 self-assurance

savor 4 feel, know, mark, tong 5 sapor, scent, smack, smell, taste, tinge, trait 6 flavor, relish, virtue 7 feature, quality 8 property, sapidity 9 affection, attribute, character 10 experience

savory 5 balmy, sapid, spicy, sweet, tasty 6 aromal 7 flavory, gustful, perfumy 8 aromatic, fragrant, perfumed, pleasing, redolent, tempting 9 ambrosial, aperitive, palatable, relishing, toothsome 10 appetizing, flaversome

saw 3 hew 4 word 5 adage 6 byword, saying 7 proverb

____ saw 3 bow, jig, pit, rip 4 band, buck, buzz, fret, hack, whip 5 chain, crown,

saber **6** coping, scroll **7** compass, keyhole **8** circular, crosscut
sawbuck **5** horse **7** trestle **9** workhorse
sawhorse see **sawbuck**
saw-toothed **7** serrate, serried **8** serrated **11** denticulate
Saxon ***serf:*** **4** esne ***warrior:*** **5** thane
say **4** aver, avow, cite, give, mark, most, much, nigh, read, show, talk, tell **5** about, mouth, quote, speak, state, utter, voice **6** affirm, almost, assert, nearly, recite, record, remark, repeat **7** breathe, chime in, comment, declare, deliver, express, phonate, protest **8** announce, bring out, decision, indicate, proclaim, register, throw out **9** authority, enunciate, just about, pronounce **10** animadvert, articulate
saying **3** mot **4** word **5** adage, axiom, maxim **6** byword, dictum, truism **7** proverb
scab **5** crust **6** eschar **13** strikebreaker
scabbard **6** sheath
scabby **4** mean **5** scaly **7** blotchy **10** scurrilous
scabrous **5** downy, harsh, rough, scaly **6** craggy, jagged, knobby, knotty, rugged, scabby, scurfy, thorny, uneven **7** bristly, prickly, scraggy, unlevel **8** asperous, unsmooth
scads **3** lot **4** gobs, heap, much, slew, wads **5** loads, reams **6** oodles **7** jillion, million, umpteen, zillion **8** slathers, thousand, trillion **9** great deal, multitude **10** quantities
scaffold **5** stage **7** staging **8** platform
Scala, La ***city:*** **5** Milan ***production:*** **5** opera
scalawag see **scamp**
scald **4** bard, boil, burn, poet **6** scorch
scale **4** peel, rate, skin, upgo **5** climb, flake, gauge, mount, ratio, scute, strip **6** ascend, degree, scutum, squama **7** chip off, measure **8** escalade, escalate, flake off, spall off **9** exfoliate **10** desquamate, proportion **11** decorticate, excorticate ***auxiliary:*** **7** vernier ***earthquake:*** **7** Richter ***temperature:*** **6** Kelvin **7** Celsius **10** centigrade, Fahrenheit
scallion **4** leek **5** onion **7** shallot
scalp **4** skin **5** cheat **6** trophy
scalpel **5** knife **7** dissect
scamp **5** devil, joker, pixie, rogue **6** rascal, ribald **7** villain **8** mischief, scalawag, slyboots **9** prankster, skeezicks **11** rapscallion
scamper **3** fly, run **4** bolt, dash, flee, scud, shin, skip **5** scoot, shoot, skirr **6** scurry, sprint **7** dash off, make off, rush off, scuddle, scuttle, tear off, whip off, whiz off **8** hurry off, light out **9** hasten off, hurry away, skedaddle, speed away
scan **3** eye **4** view **5** audit **6** browse, review, survey **7** perusal, run over **8** analysis, glance at, scrutiny **9** check-over **10** glance over, inspection, run through **11** examination, flip through, leaf through, observation, riff through, skim through **12** thumb through
scandal **4** tale **7** calumny **8** reproach **9** aspersion, discredit, disrepute **10** backbiting, defamation, detraction
scandalize **4** slur **5** libel, shock, smear **6** defame, malign **7** asperse, slander **9** denigrate **10** calumniate
scandalmonger **5** tabby **6** gossip **8** gossiper, quidnunc, telltale **9** backbiter, carrytale, muckraker **10** talebearer
scandalous **7** heinous **8** libelous, shocking **9** atrocious, desperate, maligning, monstrous, traducing, vilifying **10** backbiting, calumnious, defamatory, detracting, detractive, outrageous, slanderous
Scandinavia **6** Norway, Sweden **7** Denmark, Finland, Iceland
Scandinavian see **Norse**
scant **4** poor **5** chary, close, short, skimp, spare, stint, tight **6** meager, meagre, scarce, scrimp, skimpy, sparse **7** scrimpy, wanting **8** exiguous **9** deficient **10** inadequate **12** insufficient
scantiness **4** lack **6** dearth **7** deficit, failure, paucity, poverty **8** scarcity, shortage, sparsity, underage **10** deficiency, inadequacy, scarceness, sparseness **11** defalcation **13** insufficience, insufficiency
scanty see **scant**
scapegoat **4** mark **5** patsy **6** target, victim **7** fall guy **11** whipping boy
Scapin **5** rogue, valet ***author:*** **7** Molière ***employer:*** **7** Léandre
scar **3** cut, mar **4** flaw, scab **5** score **6** damage, deface, defect, keloid **7** blemish, blister, scratch **8** cicatrix, pockmark **9** cicatrize, disfigure **13** disfigurement ***on a seed:*** **5** hilum
scarab **6** beetle
scaramouch see **scamp**
scarce **3** few, shy **4** just, rare **5** scant, short **6** barely, hardly, scanty, seldom **7** failing, wanting **8** sporadic, uncommon **9** curtailed, deficient, shortened, truncated **10** inadequate, infrequent, occasional **12** insufficient
scarceness see **scantiness**
scarcity see **scantiness**
scare **3** awe **5** alarm, panic, spook **6** freeze, fright **7** horrify, petrify, shake up, startle, terrify **8** affright, frighten, paralyze **9** terrorize
scarf **3** boa **5** ascot, fichu, nubia, plaid, shawl, stole **8** babushka, liripipe ***Latin-American:*** **6** tapalo ***long:*** **6** rebozo
Scarlet Letter, The ***author:*** **9** Haw-

thorne *character:* 5 Pearl, Roger 6 Arthur, Hester
Scarlet Pimpernel author 5 Orczy
Scarlett's home 4 Tara
scary 6 afraid, aghast, spooky 7 anxious, fearful 8 spookish 9 terrified 10 frightened
scat 4 flee, jazz 5 scoot, scram 7 singing
scathe 4 flay 5 slash 6 scorch 7 blister, scarify, scourge 8 lambaste, lash into 9 castigate, excoriate
scathing 5 salty 6 brutal 7 burning, caustic, mordant, searing 9 scorching, trenchant 10 mordacious, sulphurous
scatological 4 foul 5 dirty, nasty 6 coarse, filthy, smutty, vulgar 7 obscene, raunchy 8 indecent
scatter 3 sow 4 cast, part, shed 5 sever, straw, strew 6 dispel, divide, splash 7 bestrew, break up, disband, discard, disject, diverge, spatter 8 dispense, disperse, separate, splatter, sprinkle 9 broadcast, dissipate 10 besprinkle, distribute 11 disseminate
scatterbrained 5 dizzy, giddy, silly 7 flighty, foolish 9 frivolous
scavenge 5 clean 7 cleanse, collect, extract, salvage
scavenger 5 hyena 7 vulture
scenario 4 plot 6 script 7 outline 10 screenplay
scene 3 set 4 site, spot, view 5 arena, field, place, sight, vista 6 locale, milieu, sphere 7 compass, culture, outlook, setting, tableau 8 backdrop, hangings, locality, location, stage set 10 background 11 environment, mise-en-scène 12 stage setting
scenery 3 set 5 decor, props 7 setting 8 stage set 9 furniture 10 properties 11 furnishings, mise-en-scène 12 stage setting
scent 4 balm, nose, odor 5 aroma, smell, sniff, snuff, spice, whiff 7 bouquet, essence, incense, odorize, perfume 9 aromatize, fragrance, redolence
scepter 4 mace 5 baton, staff 11 sovereignty
schedule 4 list, roll, sked, time 5 chart, slate, table 6 agenda, docket, record, roster 7 catalog, program 8 calendar, register, roll call 9 catalogue, timetable
scheme 4 plan, plot 5 cabal, order 6 design, device, devise 7 collude, connive, project 8 cogitate, conspire, contrive, game plan, intrigue, ordering, practice, proposal, strategy 9 blueprint, expedient, machinate 10 conspiracy 11 arrangement, contrivance, machination
schism 4 rent, rift 5 break, chasm, cleft, split 6 breach, heresy 7 dissent, fissure, rupture 8 cleavage, division, fracture 10 dissidence, divergence, heterodoxy, separation 11 unorthodoxy 12 estrangement
schizoid 5 split
schlemiel 4 fool 7 bungler 10 ne'er-do-well
schlepp 3 lug 4 drag, haul, jerk
schmaltzy 5 showy 6 florid 11 sentimental
scholar 4 sage 5 pupil 6 savant 7 bookman, student, wise man 8 literati (plural), polymath 10 classicist *Hindu:* 6 pundit *Muslim:* 5 ulama, ulema
scholarly 7 erudite, learned, trained 8 educated, studious 10 scholastic 12 intellectual
scholarship 7 science 8 learning 9 education, erudition, knowledge 11 eruditeness, learnedness
scholastic 5 booky 6 versed 7 bookish, erudite, learned 8 academic, lettered, literary, pedantic 9 scholarly 10 conversant 11 book-learned, quodlibetic *life:* 8 academia
school 3 gam, pad 4 lead, show 5 guide, shoal, teach, train 6 direct, inform, manage 7 academy, advance, college, control, educate 8 instruct 9 cultivate 10 discipline *French:* 5 école, lycée *grounds:* 6 campus *Jewish:* 5 heder 7 yeshiva 8 yeshivah *judo:* 4 dojo *organization:* 3 PTA, PTO *religious:* 8 seminary *term:* 7 quarter 8 semester
schoolbook 4 text 6 primer, reader 7 speller
School for Scandal author 8 Sheridan
schooner 4 ship 5 stein, stoup 6 goblet, seidel 7 tumbler
science 4 lore 6 wisdom 8 learning 9 education, erudition, knowledge 11 information, scholarship *combining form:* 4 logy 5 logia, sophy *of agriculture:* 8 agronomy *of animals:* 7 zoology *of armorial bearings:* 8 heraldry *of criminal punishment:* 8 penology *of environment:* 7 ecology *of fermentation:* 8 zymology *of government:* 8 politics *of health:* 7 hygiene 9 hygienics *of heredity:* 8 genetics *of human behavior:* 10 psychology *of lawmaking:* 8 nomology *of measuring time:* 8 horology 10 chronology 11 chronometry *of motion:* 8 kinetics *of mountains:* 7 orology *of nutrition:* 8 sitology *of plants:* 6 botany *of projectiles:* 10 ballistics *of soils:* 8 agrology *of the earth:* 7 geology *of time:* 10 chronology 11 chronometry *of tumors:* 8 oncology *suffix:* 3 ics
scientific classification 8 taxonomy
sci-fi writer 5 Verne 6 Asimov 8 Bradbury, Heinlein, Sturgeon
scimitar 5 saber, sword

scintilla 3 jot 4 iota 5 trace 8 particle
scintillate 5 flash, gleam, glint 6 glance 7 glimmer, glisten, glitter, shimmer, sparkle, twinkle 9 coruscate
scoff 3 boo 4 gibe, jeer, jest, mock, twit 5 fleer, flout, rally, scorn, sneer, taunt 6 deride, quip at 7 contemn, despise, disdain, scout at 8 pooh-pooh, ridicule
scold 3 jaw, rag, wig 4 chew, lash, rail, rant, rate 5 baste, blame, brace, chide, croak, grill, grunt, harpy, hound, shrew, vixen 6 amazon, berate, grouch, grouse, harass, murmur, mutter, ogress, rebuke, revile, tongue, virago 7 bawl out, blister, censure, chew out, grumble, reprove, tell off, upbraid 8 admonish, denounce, execrate, fishwife, lambaste, objurate, reproach 9 criticize, dress down, excoriate, reprehend, reprimand, reprobate, termagant, Xanthippe 10 tongue-lash, vituperate
sconce 4 head, poll 5 cover 6 noggin, noodle, screen 7 shelter 11 candlestick
scoop 3 dig, dip 4 bail, beat, grub, lade, lift 5 gouge, ladle, spade 6 dig out, gather, pick up, shovel 8 excavate 9 exclusive
scoot 3 fly, run, zip 4 bolt, dash, flee, rush, shin, skip 5 fleet, hurry, scram, skirr 6 barrel, bustle, hasten, hustle, scurry, sprint 7 beeline, make off, scamper 8 highball 9 skedaddle
scope 4 area, play, room 5 ambit, orbit, range, reach, sweep 6 extent, leeway, margin, radius 7 breadth, compass, purview 8 fullness, latitude, wideness 9 amplitude, elbowroom, extension
Scopes trial lawyer 5 Bryan 6 Darrow
scorch 4 bake, burn, cook, flay, melt 5 broil, roast, slash 6 scathe, seethe, simmer 7 blister, scarify, scourge, swelter 8 lambaste, lash into 9 castigate, excoriate
score 3 cut, tab, win 4 bill, flay, gain, gash, goal, line, mark, nick, slit 5 cleft, notch, reach, slash, tally, total 6 arrive, attain, furrow, groove, grudge, rack up, record, scathe, scorch, scotch, thrive 7 account, achieve, invoice, make out, prosper, realize, ream out, scarify, scourge, scratch, succeed 8 flourish, lambaste, lash into 9 castigate, excoriate, reckoning, serration, statement 10 accomplish
scorn 4 gibe, jeer, mock, pooh 5 abhor, flout, scoff, scout, taunt 6 gibing 7 contemn, despise, despite, disdain, jeering, mockery 8 contempt, derision, despisal, flouting, look down, ridicule, scoffing, taunting 11 despisement 13 disparagement
Scorpius star 7 Antares
Scotch cocktail 6 Rob Roy
Scotland's capital 9 Edinburgh
Scott, Sir Walter ***novel:*** 6 Rob Roy 7 Ivanhoe, Waverly 8 The Abbot 9 Woodstock 10 Kenilworth 11 Redgauntlet, The Talisman ***poem:*** 7 Marmion
Scottish ***child:*** 5 bairn ***hero:*** 5 Bruce 7 Wallace ***hill:*** 4 brae ***outlaw:*** 6 Rob Roy ***patron saint:*** 6 Andrew ***plaid:*** 6 tartan ***pudding:*** 6 haggis ***spirit:*** 5 kelpy 6 kelpie
scoundrel see scamp
scour 3 eat, fan, fly 4 beat, bite, comb, find, flit, flux, gnaw, grub, rake, rout, seek 5 erode, fleet, hurry, range, rifle, scrub, smoke, speed 6 bullet, forage, rocket, search 7 beeline, corrode, eat away, look for, ransack, rummage 8 finecomb, highball, wear away 9 ferret out 13 fine-tooth comb
scourge 3 hit 4 flay, flog, hide, lash, sack, whip, whop 5 curse, flail, knout, slash, waste, whale 6 lather, plague, ravage, scathe, scorch, stripe, thrash 7 blister, despoil, pillage, scarify 8 desolate, lambaste, lash into, spoliate 9 castigate, depredate, desecrate, devastate, excoriate 10 flagellate, pestilence
Scourge of God 6 Attila
scouting group 3 BSA, GSA
scow 3 hoy 5 barge 6 garvey 7 lighter
scowl 5 frown, gloom, lower 6 glower
scrabble 6 scrawl 7 clamber, scratch 8 scramble, scribble, squiggle
scraggy 4 bony, lank, lean 5 gaunt, harsh, lanky, rough, spare 6 jagged, rugged, skinny, uneven 7 angular, dwarfed, scrawny, scrubby, spindly, stunted, unlevel 8 asperous, gangling, rawboned, scabrous, skeletal 9 spindling, undersize
scram 4 kite 6 begone, decamp, get out 7 skiddoo, take off 8 clear out, hightail 9 skedaddle
scramble 4 hash 6 jumble, jungle, litter, muddle, ramble, scurry, sprawl, tumble 7 clamber, clutter, rummage, scuttle, shuffle 8 mishmash, scrabble, straggle
scrap 3 bit, end, jot, ort, row 4 cast, chip, dump, fray, junk, shed, spat, tiff, whit 5 brawl, broil, crumb, fight, set-to, shred, speck, waste, whoop 6 affray, bicker, fracas, reject, slough, smitch, tittle 7 bobbery, brabble, cashier, cutting, discard, fall out, quarrel, scuffle, wrangle 8 fragment, jettison, leftover, particle, squabble, throw out 9 caterwaul, scrappage, throw away
scrape 3 fix, jam, rub 4 hole, rasp, spot 5 chafe, get by, grate, graze, grind, pinch, screw, scuff, shave, skimp, spare, stint 6 abrade, corner, pickle, plight, scrimp 7 dilemma, scratch, trouble 8 get along, struggle 11 predicament
scrappy 6 brawly 7 warlike 8 brawling, militant 9 bellicose, brawlsome, combative, truculent 10 battlesome, pugnacious 11 belligerent, contentious, quarrelsome
scratch 4 claw, rake, rasp 5 grate, score

6 scotch, scrape, scrawl 8 scrabble, scribble, squiggle
scrawl 6 doodle 7 scratch 8 inscribe, scrabble, scribble, squiggle
scrawny 4 bony, lank, lean 5 gaunt, lanky, spare 6 skinny 7 angular, scraggy 8 rawboned
scream 3 cry, yip 4 howl, riot, roar, wail, yell, yowl 5 blare, shout 6 bellow, screak, shriek, shrill, squeak, squeal 7 grumble, protest, screech 8 complain 9 caterwaul
screech 4 hoot 6 pierce, screak, scream, shriek, shrill, squeal
screen 4 blip, bury, fend, hide, sift, sort 5 cache, cloak, close, cover, guard, shade, sieve, stash 6 censor, choose, defend, embosk, riddle, secure, select, shadow, shield, shroud 7 bulwark, conceal, cover up, extract, pick out, protect, seclude, secrete, shut off, shut out, sort out, umbrage, wall off 8 blindage, block out, disguise, ensconce, obstruct, separate 9 expurgate, filter out, inumbrate, safeguard, winnow out 10 bowdlerize, camouflage ***Japanese:*** 5 shoji
screw 5 crimp, exact, gouge, pinch, skimp, spare, stint, wrest, wring 6 extort, rimple, ruck up, rumple, scrape, scrimp, skinch, wrench 7 crimple, crinkle, crumple, scrunch, squeeze, wrinkle 8 thumbkin 9 shake down
screwy 3 mad 4 daft, nuts 5 wacky 6 insane 7 cracked, lunatic, unsound 10 unbalanced
scribble 5 write 6 scrawl, scribe 7 jot down, scratch 8 scrabble, squiggle
scribe 5 clerk, write 6 author, writer 7 copyist 9 secretary
scrimmage 4 fray 5 brawl, broil, brush, clash, fight, melee, set-to 6 affray, fracas, mellay 7 scuffle 8 skirmish 10 donnybrook, free-for-all
scrimp 4 save 5 stint 6 save up, scrape 9 economize
script 4 hand, text 10 penmanship 11 calligraphy, chirography, handwriting
scrivener 6 notary, scribe, writer 7 copyist
scrooge 5 miser 7 niggard 8 muckworm, tightwad 9 skinflint 10 cheapskate 12 moneygrubber
scrub 3 rub 4 buff, drop, wash 5 brush, scour 6 cancel, mallee, maquis, polish 7 call off, cleanse 8 inferior 9 chaparral, secondary, subaltern, underling 11 subordinate
scruff 4 nape, neck
scruffy 5 seedy, tacky 6 shabby, tagrag 7 run-down, scrubby 8 tattered 10 down-at-heel, threadbare
scrumptious 5 yummy 8 adorable, heavenly, luscious 9 ambrosial, delicious 10 delectable, delightful
scruple 3 bit, jot 4 atom, balk, fret, iota 5 demur, grain, qualm, scrap, shred, worry 7 modicum 8 particle, question 9 faltering, hesitancy 11 compunction
scrupulous 4 just, true 5 exact, fussy, right 6 honest, strict 7 careful, heedful, upright 8 critical, punctual 9 honorable 10 fair-minded, fastidious, meticulous, upstanding 11 painstaking, punctilious 12 conscionable 13 conscientious
scrutinize 3 eye 4 comb, scan 5 audit, probe, study, watch 6 peruse, survey 7 analyze, canvass, check up, dig into, dissect, examine, eyeball, inspect 8 consider, look over, pore over 9 check over 11 contemplate, perlustrate
scrutiny 3 eye 4 scan 5 audit, watch 6 look-in, review, survey 7 look-see 8 analysis, eagle eye, lookover 9 check-over 10 inspection 11 examination 12 surveillance 13 perlustration
scuba diver 7 frogman 8 aquanaut
scuff 6 scrape 7 scratch, shamble, shuffle
scuffle 3 row 4 cuff, fray 5 brawl, broil, fight, scrap, set-to 6 affray, fracas, shovel, tussle 7 bobbery, grapple, shamble, shuffle, wrestle
scull 3 oar, row 4 boat 6 propel
sculpt 5 carve 6 chisel
sculptor ***American:*** 4 Gabo, Taft 5 Pratt, Segal, Smith, Story 6 Aitkin, Calder, French, Powers, Zorach 7 Noguchi 8 Lachaise, Lipchitz, Nadelman, Nevelson 9 Mestrovic, Remington ***Czech:*** 6 Stursa ***Danish:*** 11 Thorvaldsen, Thorwaldsen ***Dutch:*** 6 Sluter ***English:*** 5 Moore, Watts 7 Epstein, Flaxman 8 Hepworth ***French:*** 3 Arp 4 Bloc 5 Rodin 6 Dubois, Houdon 7 Maillol, Pevsner 9 Bartholdi, Roubillac ***Greek:*** 5 Myron 7 Phidias 10 Polyclitus, Praxiteles 11 Polycleitus ***Italian:*** 5 Leoni, Salvi 6 Canova, Pisano, Robbia 7 Bernini, Cellini, da Vinci, Orcagna, Quercia 8 Ghiberti, Vittoria 9 Donatello, Sansovino 10 Verrocchio 12 Michelangelo ***Rhodian:*** 9 Polydorus ***Rumanian:*** 8 Brancusi ***Russian:*** 7 Zadkine ***Swedish:*** 6 Milles ***Swiss:*** 10 Giacometti
scum 3 cur, mob 5 dregs, dross, skunk, snake, trash 6 masses, rabble, refuse 7 stinker 8 canaille, riffraff, unwashed
scummy 3 low 4 base, mean, vile 5 cheap, sorry 6 scurvy, shabby 8 beggarly, pitiable 10 despicable, despisable 12 contemptible
scurrilous 4 foul 5 dirty, gross, nasty 6 coarse, filthy, smutty, vulgar 7 abusive, obscene, raunchy 8 indecent 9 insulting, invective, offending, offensive, outraging,

truculent **10** outrageous, vituperous **11** opprobrious **12** blackguardly, contumelious, vituperative, vituperatory

scurry **3** fly, run **4** dart, dash, shin, tear **5** scoot, shoot **6** sprint **7** scamper, scuffle, scutter, scuttle, skelter

scurvy see **scummy**

scut **4** tail

scuttlebutt **4** buzz, talk **5** on-dit, rumor **6** gossip, report, rumble **7** hearsay **9** grapevine

Scylla **4** rock ***father:*** **5** Nisus ***lover:*** **5** Minos; (see also **Charybdis**)

scythe handle **5** snath **6** snathe

sea **4** blue, deep, main **5** brine, briny, drink, ocean ***Antarctica:*** **4** Ross **5** Davis **7** Weddell **8** Amundsen ***Arctic:*** **4** Kara **7** Chukchi **8** Beaufort, Karskoye **9** Chuckchee, Norwegian **11** Chukotskoye **12** East Siberian ***Asia-Europe:*** **5** Black ***Asia Minor:*** **7** Icarian ***Atlantic:*** **5** North **7** Weddell **9** Caribbean ***Australia-Indonesia:*** **7** Arafura ***Balkan Peninsula-Italy:*** **8** Adriatic ***Bay of Bengal:*** **7** Andaman ***China-Korea:*** **5** Huang, Hwang **6** Yellow ***combining form:*** **3** mer **4** mari **5** pelag **6** pelago **7** thalass **8** thalasso ***Corsica-Italy:*** **10** Tyrrhenian ***Denmark-Norway:*** **8** Skagerak **9** Skagerrak ***Denmark-Sweden:*** **8** Kattegat ***England-Ireland:*** **5** Irish ***Fiji:*** **4** Koro ***France-Italy:*** **8** Ligurian ***Greece:*** **5** Crete ***Greece-Italy:*** **6** Ionian ***Greece-Turkey:*** **6** Aegean **8** Thracian ***Honshu:*** **6** Sagami ***Indian Ocean:*** **4** Savu, Sawu **5** Timor **7** Arabian ***Indonesia:*** **4** Bali **6** Flores ***inland:*** **3** Red **4** Aral **7** Caspian ***Japan:*** **3** Iyo, Suo **6** Inland ***largest island:*** **7** Caspian ***Malay Archipelago:*** **5** Banda ***Mexico:*** **6** Cortes ***Netherlands:*** **6** Wadden ***North Atlantic:*** **8** Sargasso ***Northern Europe:*** **6** Baltic, Ostsee **8** Suevicum **10** Baltiskoye ***North Pacific:*** **6** Bering ***Novaya Zemlya-Svalbard:*** **7** Barents ***off Scotland:*** **8** Hebrides ***off Sweden:*** **5** Aland ***Pacific:*** **4** Java **5** China, Coral **6** Maluku **7** Celebes, Eastern, Molucca, Solomon **9** East China, Moluksche **10** South China ***Russia:*** **5** White **7** Okhotsk ***Russia-Ukraine:*** **4** Azov **9** Azovskoye ***South Pacific:*** **4** Ross **6** Tasman **8** Amundsen ***Turkey:*** **7** Marmara **9** Propontis ***West Pacific:*** **5** Ceram, Japan **8** Bismarck **10** Philippine

sea anemone **7** actinia

seabird see **bird,** ***aquatic***

sea channel **6** strait **7** euripus

sea cucumber **7** trepang **11** holothurian

sea dog see **sailor**

sea duck **5** eider, scaup **6** scoter **9** merganser

sea eagle **3** ern **4** erne **6** osprey

seafood dish **4** clam, crab, tuna **5** scrod **6** oyster, shrimp **7** lobster, scallop

seagoing **8** maritime, nautical

seal **5** sigil, stamp **6** cachet, signet **7** sticker ***bearded:*** **6** makluk ***eared:*** **5** otary ***female:*** **3** cow **5** matka ***herd:*** **3** pod **5** patch ***male:*** **8** seecatch ***young:*** **3** pup

sealant **4** lute **6** luting

sea lily **7** crinoid

seam **4** bond **5** joint, union **7** joining **8** coupling, junction, juncture **10** connection

seaman see **sailor**

sea monster **3** Orc ***legendary:*** **6** kraken

seamount ***flat-topped:*** **5** guyot

seamy **5** dirty, rough, seedy **6** sordid **12** disreputable

séance **7** meeting, session, sitting ***holder:*** **6** medium

seaport ***Adriatic:*** **5** Split **6** Spljet ***Aegean:*** **5** Vathy ***Alaska:*** **9** Anchorage ***Albania:*** **5** Vlona, Vlorë ***Algeria:*** **4** Bona, Oran **5** Arzew **6** Annaba **9** Arsenaria, Cherchell, Shershell ***Angola:*** **6** Lobito **7** Cabinda **8** Benguela **9** Mocamedes ***Argentina:*** **7** La Plata ***Australia:*** **4** Eden **5** Bowen **8** Brisbane, Wallaroo **10** Wollongong ***Azores:*** **5** Horta ***Balearic:*** **5** Ibiza ***Baltic:*** **5** Visby ***Belgium:*** **6** Ostend ***Benin:*** **6** Kotonu **7** Cotonou ***Black Sea:*** **6** Odessa ***Bosnia and Herzegovina:*** **4** Omis ***Brazil:*** **3** Rio **4** Para **5** Bahia, Belem, Natal **6** Recife, Santos **8** Salvador **10** Pernambuco **11** Pôrto Alegre, São Salvador **12** Rio de Janeiro ***Bulgaria:*** **5** Varna ***Cameroon:*** **5** Campo, Duala, Kampo, Kribi ***Canaries:*** **8** Arrecife ***Celebes:*** **7** Makasar **8** Macassar, Makássar ***Chile:*** **4** Lebu, Lota **5** Ancud, Arica **8** Coquimbo **10** Valparaiso ***China:*** **4** Amoy **6** Lushun, Xiamen ***Colombia:*** **6** Lorica **9** Cartagena ***Corsica:*** **5** Calvi ***Costa Rica:*** **10** Puntarenas ***Crimean:*** **10** Sevastopol ***Croatia:*** **4** Senj **5** Zadar **9** Dubrovnik ***Cuba:*** **5** Banes ***Cyprus:*** **7** Limasol **8** Limassol **9** Famagusta ***Delaware:*** **5** Lewes ***Denmark:*** **5** Arhus, Ronne, Vejle **6** Aarhus, Alborg **7** Aalborg **8** Elsinore ***Djibouti:*** **4** Obok **5** Obock **6** Tajura **8** Tadjoura ***Ecuador:*** **5** Manta **9** Guayaquil ***Egypt:*** **4** Said **8** Al Qusayr, Al Quseir, El Qoseir **10** Alexandria ***Eire:*** **6** Dingle, Tralee **10** Balbriggan ***England:*** **10** Portsmouth ***Equatorial Guinea:*** **4** Bata ***Eritrea:*** **4** Aseb ***Estonia:*** **5** Parnu **6** Pyarnu **7** Tallinn ***Ethiopia:*** **4** Zula ***Finland:*** **3** Abo **4** Kemi, Oulu, Pori, Vasa **5** Hango, Kotka, Rauma, Turku, Vaasa **8** Uleaborg **10** Bjorneborg ***Florida:*** **5** Miami, Tampa **9** Pensacola **12** Apalachicola, Jacksonville ***France:*** **4** Meze, Nice **5** Havre, Nizza **6** Calais, Cannes, Toulon **7** Dunkirk, Le Havre, Lorient **8** Bordeaux,

Boulogne 9 Cherbourg, Dunkerque, Marseille 10 Marseilles ***French Polynesia:*** 7 Papeete ***Georgia:*** 9 Brunswick ***Georgia, Republic of:*** 4 Poti ***Germany:*** 4 Kiel 5 Emden, Husum 6 Wismar 8 Cuxhaven 11 Bremerhaven 13 Wilhelmshaven ***Ghana:*** 4 Keta 6 Kwitta ***Greece:*** 4 Kimi, Kyme 5 Pylos, Syros, Volos 7 Piraeus 8 Peiraeus ***Guatemala:*** 7 San José 10 Livingston ***Gulf of Aden:*** 5 Alula ***Haiti:*** 5 Cayes 8 Aux Cayes ***Honduras:*** 8 Trujillo ***India:*** 3 Goa 4 Puri 5 Marud 6 Old Goa 9 Jagannath 10 Juggernaut ***Ionian:*** 5 Corfu ***Iran:*** 4 Jask 7 Bushehr, Bushire ***Iraq:*** 5 Basra ***Israel:*** 4 Acre, Akko, Elat, Yafa 5 Accho, Eilat, Elath, Haifa, Jaffa, Joppa 9 Ptolemais, Sycaminum ***Italy:*** 4 Bari 5 Anzio, Gaeta, Genoa, Pizzo, Trani 6 Naples, Pesaro, Venice 7 Leghorn, Rapallo, Salerno, Taranto, Trieste, Venedig 8 Sorrento 10 Senigallia ***Ivory Coast:*** 4 Tabu 5 Tabou ***Jamaica:*** 10 Montego Bay ***Japan:*** 5 Kochi, Rumoi, Ujina, Uraga 6 Sasebo 7 Fukuoka 8 Nagasaki, Yokohama ***Java:*** 5 Tegal, Tuban 8 Samarang, Semarang, Surabaja, Tjirebon ***Jordan:*** 5 Akaba, Aqaba, Elath 6 Aelana ***Latvian:*** 9 Ventspils ***Lebanon:*** 5 Saida 7 Tripoli ***Libya:*** 4 Homs 5 Khoms 6 Tobruk ***Lithuanian:*** 5 Memel 8 Klaipeda ***Madagascar:*** 8 Tamatave ***Maine:*** 7 Belfast 8 Portland ***Malaysia:*** 4 Miri, Weld 5 Pekan 6 Melaka, Pinang 7 Malacca 10 George Town ***Massachusetts:*** 9 Fall River ***Mauritius:*** 5 Louis ***Mediterranean:*** 4 Gaza, Oran, Said 5 Genoa, Haifa, Jaffa 6 Bayrut, Beirut 7 Algiers, Bizerte, Catania, Tripoli 8 Benghazi 9 Barcelona 10 Alexandria, Marseilles ***Mexico:*** 8 Acapulco, Veracruz ***Minorca:*** 5 Mahon ***Moluccas:*** 5 Ambon ***Montenegro:*** 5 Kotov ***Morocco:*** 3 Sla 4 Safi, Sale 5 Ceuta, Saffi 6 Agadir 7 Larache, Tangier 10 Casablanca ***Mozambique:*** 5 Beira, Pemba 6 Amelia, Xai Xai 11 Porto Amelia ***New Hampshire:*** 10 Portsmouth ***New Zealand:*** 8 Auckland ***Nicaragua:*** 5 Brito ***Nigeria:*** 8 Harcourt ***Niger mouth:*** 5 Bonny ***North Korea:*** 4 Yuki 5 Unggi ***Norway:*** 4 Bodo, Moss 5 Vadso 6 Tromso 9 Stavanger, Trondheim, Trondhjem 11 Fredrikstad ***Oman:*** 3 Sur 5 Sohar 6 Matrah ***Pakistan:*** 5 Pasni ***Peru:*** 3 Ilo 4 Eten 5 Paita, Pisco ***Poland:*** 6 Gdynia 7 Gdingen, Stettin 8 Szczecin ***Portugal:*** 4 Faro 5 Lagos 6 Oporto 7 Funchal 9 Lacobriga ***Puerto Rico:*** 5 Ponce ***Russia:*** 3 Kem 5 Anapa, Sochi 6 Vyborg 11 Kaliningrad, Vladivostok ***Ryukyu:*** 4 Naha, Nawa ***Sakhalin Island:*** 8 Korsakov ***Saudi Arabia:*** 4 Wejh 5 Jidda, Qatif, Yanbu, Yenbo 6 Juddah 7 Djeddah ***Scotland:*** 3 Ayr 4 Oban 5 Alloa, Largs, Leven 6 Dundee ***Sicily:*** 5 Avola 7 Messina, Palermo 8 Syracuse ***Slovenia:*** 5 Kopar, Koper, Piran ***Somalia:*** 7 Berbera, Kismayu 9 Chisimaio ***South Africa:*** 6 Durban 8 Cape Town, Kaapstad ***South Carolina:*** 10 Charleston ***South Korea:*** 5 Mason, Mokpo 6 Inch'on, Jinsen 7 Masampo 8 Chemulpo ***Spain:*** 4 Adra, Noya, Vigo 5 Cadiz, Gadir, Gijon, Marin 6 Abdera 8 Alicante 9 Cartagena, Las Palmas ***Sri Lanka:*** 10 Batticaloa ***Sumatra:*** 6 Padang ***Sweden:*** 4 Umea 5 Gavle, Lulea, Malmo, Pitea, Ystad 8 Göteborg 10 Gothenburg ***Tanzania:*** 5 Lindi, Tanga ***Thailand:*** 4 Trat 8 Bang Phra ***Tunisia:*** 4 Sfax 5 Gabes 7 Bizerte, Safaqis ***Turkey:*** 4 Rize 5 Coruh, Sinop 6 Coroch ***Ukrainian:*** 7 Kherson ***U.S. Virgin Islands:*** 8 St. Thomas ***Vanuatu:*** 4 Vila ***Vietnam:*** 6 Da Nang 7 Tourane 8 Haiphong, Nha Trang ***Virginia:*** 10 Portsmouth ***Yemen:*** 5 Mocha, Mokha 7 Hodeida; (see also **seaport capital**)

seaport capital 4 Aden, Apia, Lomé, Suva 5 Accra, Adana, Alger, Dakar, Lagos 6 Banjul, Belize, Bissão, Bissau, Boston, Dublin, Eblana, Havana, Juneau, Kuwait, Lisbon, Maputo, Masqat, Muscat, Roseau 7 Algiers, Batavia, Colombo, Icosium, Jakarta, Moresby, San Juan 8 Al-Jazā'ir, Al-Kuwait, Bathurst, Castries, Djakarta, Freetown, Hamilton, Helsinki, Honolulu, Kingston, La Habana, Monrovia, Valletta 9 Annapolis, Mogadishu, Nukualofa, Porto-Novo, Reykjavik, Singapore 10 Bridgetown, Daressalem, Libreville, Mogadiscio, Paramaribo 11 Dar es Salaam, Port of Spain 12 Port-au-Prince

sear 3 dry 5 parch 6 burn up, scorch, sizzle 7 shrivel 9 cauterize, dehydrate, desiccate, exsiccate

search 4 beat, comb, grub, hunt, peer, rake, scan, seek 5 check, delve, frisk, quest, rifle, scour, study 6 ferret, forage, pry out 7 examine, hunting, inspect, manhunt, pursual, pursuit, ransack, rummage, run down, seeking 8 finecomb, look over, pursuing, scavenge, scout out, skirmish 9 cast about, ferret out, pursuance, scrimmage, shake down 10 scrutinize 11 scout around 13 fine-tooth comb ***for gold:*** 7 fossick

sea robber 5 rover 6 pirate 7 corsair 8 picaroon 9 buccaneer 10 freebooter

sea rover see **sea robber**

seasickness 8 mal de mer 9 naupathia

season 3 fit 4 fall, salt, term, time 5 spice, steel, train 6 autumn, harden, pepper, period, school, spring, summer, winter 7 prepare, toughen 8 marinade, marinate

9 acclimate, climatize 10 case harden, discipline 11 acclimatize

seasonable 3 apt 6 timely 7 apropos, timeous 8 relevant 9 favorable, opportune, pertinent, well-timed 10 auspicious, convenient, propitious, prosperous 11 appropriate

seasoning 4 herb, sage, salt 5 spice 6 fennel, garlic, pepper 7 cayenne, mustard, paprika 9 condiment

seat 3 bed, hub, put, sit 4 base, beam, rest 5 basis, focus, heart, place, usher 6 behind, bottom, center, settee 7 footing, fulcrum 8 backside, basement, buttocks, derriere, polestar 9 establish, fundament, posterior 10 focal point, foundation, groundwork 11 nerve center ***church:*** 3 pew ***on a camel or elephant:*** 6 howdah ***upholstered:*** 9 banquette

sea urchin 7 echinus 8 echinoid

seaweed 4 agar, alga, kelp 5 dulse 6 murlin 7 henware 9 carrageen 11 badderlocks ***brown:*** 6 fucoid 8 gulfweed, rockweed, sargasso ***edible:*** 4 ulva 7 redware ***purple:*** 9 carrageen, Irish moss

Sea Wolf, The ***author:*** 6 London ***captain:*** 10 Wolf Larsen ***ship:*** 5 Ghost

Sebastian ***brother:*** 6 Alonso ***sister:*** 5 Viola

secede 4 quit 5 leave 8 withdraw

seclude 4 hide 6 closet, immure, retire, screen 7 confine, enclose, isolate, shut off 8 cloister, separate, withdraw 9 sequester

seclusion 7 privacy 8 solitude 9 aloneness, isolation 10 detachment, retirement, separation, withdrawal 11 privateness 12 separateness

second 3 aid 4 abet, back, wink 5 flash, jiffy, trice 6 assist, minute, moment 7 endorse, instant, support 9 twinkling ***combining form:*** 4 deut 5 deuto 6 deuter 7 deutero

secondary 3 sub 5 dinky, minor, scrub, small, under 6 lesser 7 derived, subject 8 borrowed, derivate, inferior, small-fry 9 accessory, dependent, resultant, small-time, subaltern, tributary, underling 10 collateral, consequent, derivative, secondhand, subsequent 11 minor-league, subordinate, subservient ***prefix:*** 3 sub

second-class 4 hack, mean, poor 6 common 8 déclassé, inferior, low-grade

secondhand 4 used, worn 7 derived 8 borrowed

second-rate see **second-class**

second-string 3 sub 10 substitute

secrecy 4 hush 7 silence, stealth 8 hush-hush 10 censorship, covertness, subterfuge 11 concealment, furtiveness

secret 4 deep 5 heavy, sneak 6 covert, hidden, occult, orphic, remote 7 devious, furtive, obscure, removed, retired, subrosa 8 abstruse, esoteric, hermetic, hush-hush, lonesome, mystical, profound, screened, stealthy, unavowed 9 concealed, recondite 10 acroamatic, classified, restricted, undeclared, undercover 11 clandestine, out-of-the-way, underhanded 12 confidential, hugger-mugger 13 surreptitious, under-the-table ***combining form:*** 5 crypt, krypt 6 crypto, krypto

secret agent 3 spy 8 emissary

secretaire 4 desk 10 escritoire

secretary 4 desk 5 clerk 6 scribe 10 amanuensis, escritoire ***king's:*** 10 chancellor

secrete 4 bury, hide 5 cache, cover, exude, plant, stash 6 screen 7 conceal, deposit 8 ensconce, withhold

secret society 3 KKK 4 Poro, tong 5 Mafia 7 camorra 10 Ku Klux Klan

sect 4 cult 5 creed, faith 6 church 8 religion 9 communion 10 connection, persuasion 12 denomination

sectarian 5 local 7 insular 8 splinter 9 dissident, heretical, heterodox, parochial, small-town 10 provincial, schismatic, unorthodox 13 nonconformist

sectary 5 bigot, rebel 6 cohort, hippie 7 beatnik, heretic, liberal, radical 8 adherent, bohemian, disciple, follower, henchman, maverick, partisan, sectator 9 dissenter, dissident, satellite, supporter, Young Turk 10 schismatic, separatist 11 misbeliever, schismatist 13 nonconformist, revolutionary

section 3 cut 4 area, belt, part, zone 5 field, piece, slice, split, tract 6 divide, member, moiety, parcel, region, sector, sphere 7 break up, portion, quarter, segment 8 district, division, locality, precinct, separate, vicinity 9 territory 11 subdivision ***combining form:*** 4 tome, tomy

sector 7 quarter, section 8 district, precinct

secular 3 lay 7 profane 8 temporal, unsacred 11 nonclerical 12 nonreligious

secure 3 bag, fix, get, set 4 bind, fast, fend, firm, gain, have, iron, land, lock, make, moor, nail, safe, sure, take 5 annex, catch, cause, chock, cinch, clamp, cover, fixed, guard, rivet, solid, sound, tight, tried 6 anchor, assure, cement, clinch, collar, defend, draw on, effect, ensure, fasten, insure, obtain, pick up, pinion, pledge, screen, shield, stable, strong, trusty 7 acquire, assured, bulwark, capture, chalk up, prehend, procure, produce, protect, settled, staunch, tie down 8 balanced, reliable, riskless, sanguine 9 confident, safeguard, tenacious 10 batten down, bring about, dependable, underwrite, undoubtful

11 established, self-assured, trustworthy 12 tried and true 13 self-confident

security 4 bail, bond, pawn, ward 5 aegis, armor, guard, token 6 pledge, safety, shield, surety 7 defense, earnest, warrant 8 armament, firmness, guaranty, safeness, strength, warranty 9 assurance, guarantee, safeguard, soundness, stability 10 protection, stableness, steadiness 13 certification

sedan 3 car 4 auto, limo 10 automobile

sedate 4 calm 5 grave, sober, staid 6 placid, proper, seemly, serene, solemn, somber 7 earnest, serious, weighty 8 composed, decorous, tranquil 9 collected, dignified, unruffled 10 no-nonsense, sobersided 13 dispassionate, imperturbable

sedative 4 balm 7 calmant 8 barbital, hyoscine, pacifier, quietive 9 calmative 10 depressant 11 barbiturate 12 sleeping pill, tranquilizer

sedentary 4 lazy 7 settled 8 inactive 10 stationary

sediment 4 lees, silt, slag 5 draff, dregs, dross 6 scoria 7 bottoms, deposit, grounds, heeltap 9 recrement, settlings 11 precipitate 13 precipitation ***layer:*** 5 varve

sedition 4 coup 6 action, mutiny, putsch, revolt, strike 7 protest, treason 8 uprising 9 coup d'etat, rebellion 10 alienation, revolution 12 disaffection, estrangement, insurrection

seditious 7 lawless, violent 8 disloyal, factious, mutinous 9 alienated, dissident, faithless, insurgent 10 perfidious, rebellious, traitorous 11 disaffected, treacherous

seduce 4 bait, coax, lure, rape, ruin, undo 5 decoy, tease, tempt, train 6 allure, betray, delude, entice, entrap, lead on, ravish 7 corrupt, debauch, deceive, degrade, enslave, mislead, pervert, violate 8 deflower, entrance, inveigle 9 overpower, overwhelm

seducer 7 Don Juan 8 lothario

seduction 4 call, draw, lure, pull, rape, ruin 6 appeal 9 siren song, violation 10 allurement, attraction, corruption, perversion, ravishment, seducement, temptation 11 deflowering

seductive 5 siren 7 drawing, vampish 8 alluring, magnetic 9 desirable 10 attracting, attractive, bewitching, enchanting 11 captivating, fascinating, provocative

seductress 5 siren 7 Lorelei 9 temptress 11 femme fatale

sedulous 4 busy 6 active 7 operose 8 diligent, hustling 9 assiduous 10 persistent 11 industrious, persevering, unremitting

see 4 call, date, espy, gape, gaze, have, hear, know, lead, look, mark, mind, note, peek, peep, peer, scan, show, take, twig, vide, view 5 catch, fancy, glare, grasp, guide, learn, pilot, pop in, probe, route, sight, stare, steer, study, think, visit, watch, weigh 6 accept, attend, behold, come by, descry, direct, divine, drop by, drop in, escort, follow, go with, look in, look up, notice, pierce, ponder, remark, step in, stop by, stop in, suffer, take in, tumble, vision 7 catch on, conduct, discern, examine, feature, find out, foresee, glimpse, imagine, inspect, look out, make out, observe, preknow, previse, realize, sustain, take out, undergo, unearth 8 appraise, come over, conceive, consider, discover, envisage, envision, forefeel, foreknow, perceive, shepherd, watch out 9 accompany, apprehend, ascertain, determine, penetrate, prevision, recognize, visualize 10 anticipate, comprehend, experience, scrutinize, understand 11 distinguish 12 discriminate

seed 3 bud, sow 4 core, germ 5 brood, image, issue, ovule, plant, put in, spark 6 embryo, kernel, notion, scions 7 conceit, concept, nucleus, progeny 8 children, rudiment 9 offspring, posterity 10 conception, impression 11 descendants, progeniture ***aromatic:*** 6 fennel ***coating:*** 5 testa 6 testae (plural) ***combining form:*** 3 gon 4 cocc, gono, spor 5 cocci, cocco, sperm, spori, sporo 6 sperma, spermi, spermo 7 spermae (plural), spermat 8 spermato ***covering:*** 4 aril ***medicinal:*** 7 ignatia ***of a bean:*** 7 haricot ***of an herb:*** 3 pea, soy 4 soya 7 soybean ***of a vine:*** 6 peanut ***palm tree:*** 6 jarina ***poisonous:*** 10 castor bean ***prickly:*** 6 bonduc ***vessel:*** 3 pod 5 fruit, pyxis 7 pyxides, pyxidia (plural), silicle, siliqua 8 pyxidium, sillique

seedcase 3 pod

seedy 5 dingy, faded, messy, tired 6 droopy, shabby, untidy, wilted 7 rundown, sagging, unkempt, wilting 8 decrepit, drooping, flagging, slovenly, tattered 9 neglected, overgrown 10 bedraggled, down-at-heel, threadbare

seek 3 dig, try 4 fish, hunt, nose, root 5 assay, delve, essay, mouse, offer, quest, sniff 6 strive 7 attempt, bird-dog 8 endeavor, smell out, struggle 9 cast about, ferret out, search for, search out, undertake

seem 4 hint, look 5 imply, sound 6 appear 7 suggest 8 intimate, resemble 9 insinuate

seeming ***combining form:*** 5 quasi

seemly 4 nice 5 right 6 decent, proper 7 correct 8 becoming, decorous, pleasing 9 befitting, congenial, congruous, consonant 10 compatible, conforming, consistent 11 comme il faut

seep 4 drip, flow, leak, ooze, weep 5 bleed, exude, sweat 6 strain 8 transude

seer 5 augur 6 auspex 7 prophet 8 foreseer, haruspex 9 predictor 10 forecaster, foreteller 11 Nostradamus

seesaw 3 yaw 4 cant, lean, list, rock, roll, swag, sway, tilt, toss 5 lurch, pitch 6 teeter, tilter 7 bascule, incline

seethe 3 sop 4 boil, burn, fret, fume, rage, soak, stew, stir, teem 5 anger, churn, erupt, souse, steam, steep, swarm 6 abound, blow up, bubble, drench, simmer, sizzle, sodden 7 bristle, ferment, flare up, parboil 8 boil over, overflow, saturate, waterlog 10 bubble over, impregnate

see-through 5 clear 6 limpid 8 pellucid 11 translucent, transparent

segment 3 cut 4 part 5 piece 6 divide, member, moiety, parcel, set off 7 isolate, portion, seclude, section 8 division, separate 10 categorize

sego 4 lily

segregate 6 choose, cut off, enisle, island, select, single 7 isolate 8 close off, insulate, separate 9 sequester 10 disconnect

segregation 9 apartheid, isolation, seclusion 10 jim crowism, separation, separatism 12 separateness 13 ghettoization

Segub's father 4 Hiel 6 Hezron

seidel 3 cup, mug 5 stein, stoup

seine 3 net 5 trawl

seismologist 7 Richter

seize 3 nab 4 grab, take 5 annex, catch, grasp, usurp 6 abduct, arrest, clutch, kidnap, occupy, secure, snap at, snatch, strike 7 afflict, capture, grapple, impound, preempt 8 accroach, arrogate, carry off, overtake, take over 9 apprehend, latch onto, sequester, spirit off 10 commandeer, confiscate, fasten onto, spirit away 11 appropriate, expropriate

seizure 3 fit 4 turn 5 spell, throe 6 access, attack, taking 9 breakdown 10 convulsion

seldom 3 few 4 rare 6 hardly, little, rarely, scarce 7 unoften 8 scarcely, sporadic, uncommon 10 hardly ever, infrequent, occasional 11 irregularly 12 infrequently, occasionally, sporadically

select 3 top 4 best, cull, fine, mark, pick, rare, take 5 elect, elite 6 choice, choose, chosen, culled, dainty, optate, opt for, picked, prefer, single 7 elegant, favored 8 blue-chip, delicate, eclectic, screened, superior 9 exclusive, exquisite, preferred, recherché, single out, weeded out 11 winnowed out

selection 5 draft 6 acumen, choice, option 7 culling, excerpt, insight, picking 8 choosing, drafting, election 10 preference 11 alternative, discernment

selective 5 fussy, picky 6 choosy 7 choosey, finicky 8 eclectic 10 particular, scrupulous

Seled's father 5 Nadab

Selene 4 Luna 6 Hecate 7 Artemis *beloved:* 8 Endymion *brother:* 6 Helios *father:* 8 Hyperion *mother:* 4 Thea

selenium *symbol:* 2 Se

self 3 ego *combining form:* 3 aut 4 auto

self-acting 9 automatic

self-assertive 4 bold, sure 6 uppish, uppity 7 forward, pushful, pushing 8 cocksure, militant 9 audacious, intrusive, obtrusive, officious, presuming 10 aggressive, meddlesome 11 impertinent, overweening 12 presumptuous

self-assurance 6 aplomb 8 coolness 9 composure, sangfroid, self-trust 10 confidence, equanimity 13 collectedness

self-assured 4 smug 6 secure 8 sanguine 9 confident 10 undoubtful

self-complacent 4 smug 8 priggish

self-composed 4 calm, easy 6 placid, poised, serene 8 tranquil 9 collected, possessed

self-confidence 6 aplomb, hutzpa 7 chutzpa, hutzpah 8 chutzpah, sureness 9 assurance, cockiness, self-trust 12 sanguineness 13 self-assurance

self-confident 5 cocky, janty 6 jaunty, securo 7 assured, cockish 8 sanguine 10 undoubtful

self-conscious 4 prim 5 stiff 6 formal, uneasy 7 anxious, flaunty, stilted 8 affected, mannered 9 ill at ease 10 artificial 12 ostentatious

self-control 4 will 7 balance, dignity, reserve 9 stability, willpower 10 constraint, discipline

self-defense 4 judo 6 aikido, karate 7 jujitsu, jujutsu

self-destruction 7 suicide 8 felo-de-se, hara-kiri

self-discipline 4 will 9 willpower

self-effacing 3 shy 5 timid 6 modest 7 bashful, rabbity 8 backward, retiring 9 diffident, unassured 11 unassertive

self-esteem 5 pride 6 vanity 7 conceit 10 narcissism 11 amour propre

self-evident 5 clear, plain 7 obvious 8 manifest 10 prima facie 12 unmistakable

self-explanatory 5 clear, plain 7 evident, obvious 8 manifest

self-governing 7 popular 10 autonomous, democratic

self-importance 5 pride 6 egoism 7 conceit, egotism 9 arrogance, pomposity, vainglory

self-important 5 puffy, wiggy 6 stuffy 7 bloated, pompous 8 arrogant 10 pontifical 11 magisterial

self-indulgent 9 sybaritic 10 hedonistic, sybaritish 11 sybaritical
self-interest 6 egoism
selfish 6 stingy 7 hoggish, hoglike 8 egoistic 9 egotistic 10 egocentric 11 egomaniacal
self-love 6 vanity 7 conceit, narcism 8 vainness 9 vainglory 10 narcissism 11 amour propre 13 conceitedness
self-possessed 4 calm, easy 5 aloof 6 placid, poised, serene 8 composed, reserved, tranquil 9 collected, easygoing
self-proclaimed 9 soi-disant 10 self-styled
Self-Reliance author 7 Emerson
self-respect 5 pride 11 amour propre
self-righteous 7 canting 9 pharisaic 11 pharisaical 12 hypocritical, pecksniffian 13 sanctimonious
self-sacrificing 6 kindly 8 generous, selfless 9 unselfish 10 charitable 13 philanthropic
self-satisfied 4 smug 8 priggish 10 complacent
self-seeking 7 selfish 8 egoistic, selfhood 9 egotistic 10 egocentric 11 egomaniacal
self-service *combining form:* 5 teria
self-serving see **self-seeking**
self-starter 6 dynamo, peeler 7 hustler, rustler 8 go-getter, live wire
self-styled 5 quasi 7 would be 8 so-called 9 self-given, soi-disant
self-taught 12 autodidactic
sell 3 net 4 draw, hawk, mart, sale, vend 5 bring, fetch, trade, yield 6 barter, betray, deal in, market, peddle, retail, return 7 auction, bring in, command, realize, traffic 8 exchange
sell out 4 dump, move 5 cross 6 betray, delude, humbug, take in, unload 7 beguile, deceive, mislead 8 close out 9 four-flush, sacrifice 11 double-cross
semblance 3 air 4 aura, face, feel, look, mask, mood, pose, show, veil 5 front, guise 6 aspect, facade, simile, veneer 7 analogy, feeling, seeming, showing 8 affinity, disguise, likeness 9 alikeness 10 appearance, atmosphere, comparison, false front, masquerade, similarity, similitude, simulacrum 11 resemblance
Semele *father:* 6 Cadmus *mother:* 8 Harmonia *sister:* 3 Ino 5 Agave 7 Autonoe *son:* 7 Bacchus 8 Dionysus
semi 4 demi, half, hemi 6 partly 7 partial
seminar 8 colloquy 10 colloquium, conference
Seminole chief 7 Osceola
Semiramis *husband:* 5 Ninus *kingdom:* 7 Babylon
Semite 3 Jew 4 Arab 6 Hebrew 7 Maobite 8 Assyrian 9 Canaanite 10 Babylonian, Phoenician
Senapo *daughter:* 8 Clorinda *kingdom:* 8 Ethiopia
senate 7 council 8 assembly 11 legislature
senator 5 solon 8 lawmaker 10 legislator
send 4 mail, post, rush, ship 5 relay, remit, route 6 assign, commit, export, launch, thrill 7 address, advance, airmail, consign, enthuse, forward, mission, traject 8 allocate, delegate, dispatch, expedite, transmit 9 electrify *back:* 6 remand *forth:* 4 emit 7 emanate
senectitude see **senescence**
Senegal *capital:* 5 Dakar *monetary unit:* 5 franc
senescence 6 old age 8 caducity 11 elderliness, senectitude
senile 3 old 4 aged, weak 5 aging 6 doting, feeble 7 ancient, doddery 8 decrepit, doddered 9 doddering, enfeebled, senescent, shattered
senility 6 dotage 7 decline 8 caducity 10 senescence
senior 5 doyen, elder 6 better 7 ancient, doyenne, oldster 8 brass hat, higher-up, old-timer, superior 10 golden-ager
Sennacherib *father:* 6 Sargon *kingdom:* 7 Assyria *slayer, son:* 8 Sharezer 11 Adrammelech
sensation 4 bomb 5 sense 6 marvel, wonder 7 feeling, miracle, portent, prodigy, stunner 8 response 9 bombshell 10 impression, perception, phenomenon 11 sensibility, sensitivity 13 consciousness, sensitiveness *combining form:* 8 esthesio 9 aesthesio
sensational 3 hot 5 boffo, juicy, livid, lurid, smash 6 coarse, divine, groovy, marked, signal, sultry, vulgar 7 colored, piquant, pointed, pungent, rousing, salient, sensory, sensual, tabloid 8 crashing, glorious, slambang, smashing, stunning 9 arresting, hunky-dory, marvelous, prominent, sensatory, sensitive, sensorial, superfine 10 impressive, noticeable, remarkable 11 conspicuous, extravagant, outstanding
sense 3 wit 4 core, deem, feel, gist, hold, know, meat, pith 5 focus, short, smell, think 7 believe, feeling, meaning, message, nucleus, purport, realize 8 consider, gumption, judgment, perceive, prudence 9 awareness, foresight, mentality, mother wit, substance 10 anticipate, brainpower, cognizance, discretion, intendment 11 acceptation, discernment, penetration, recognition 12 appreciation, intelligence, significance, significancy 13 comprehension, consciousness, signification, understanding

Sense and Sensibility author 6 Austen
senseless 4 cold, dead, numb, surd 5 silly 6 asleep, numbed, simple, wooden 7 foolish, trivial, unaware, unwitty, witless 8 benumbed, comatose, deadened, mindless 9 brainless
senselessness 5 folly 7 inanity 8 insanity 9 absurdity, craziness, dottiness, silliness, stupidity 11 foolishness, witlessness 12 illogicality
sense organ 3 ear, eye 4 nose, skin 6 tongue
sensibility 5 heart, sense 7 emotion, feeling, insight 8 keenness 9 affection, sensation 11 discernment, penetration, sensitivity
sensible 4 good, sage, sane, wise 5 alive, awake, aware, gross, smart, solid, sound 6 noting, patent, seeing 7 evident, knowing, logical, obvious, prudent, sapient, sizable, witting 8 concrete, imaginal, manifest, material, palpable, physical, rational, sentient, tangible 9 au courant, cognizant, conscious, corporeal, judgmatic, judicious, objective, observing, remarking, sensitive, weighable 10 consequent, conversant, detectable, observable, perceiving, perceptual, phenomenal, reasonable, responsive
sensitive 4 keen, open, sore 5 acute, aware, prone, sharp, tense 6 liable, seeing, touchy, tricky 7 exposed, feeling, knowing, nervous, psychic, sensile, sensory, sensual, subject 8 affected, delicate, disposed, inclined, sensible, sentient, ticklish, unstable 9 cognizant, conscious, emotional, impressed, irritable, obnoxious, sensatory, sensorial 10 high-strung, influenced, insultable, perceiving, perceptive, precarious, responsive, susceptive, umbrageous 11 emotionable, impressible, predisposed, sensational, susceptible 13 understanding
sensitive plant 6 minosa *family:* 3 pea
sensual 4 lush 6 animal, carnal, earthy 7 fleshly, mundane, sensory, worldly 8 banausic, luscious, sensuous, temporal 9 epicurean, luxurious, sensatory, sensitive, sensorial 10 voluptuous 11 irreligious, sensational, unspiritual 13 materialistic
sensuous 4 lush 6 carnal, fleshy 7 bacchic, fleshly, sensual 8 luscious 9 dionysiac, Dionysian, epicurean, luxurious, sybaritic 10 hedonistic, voluptuous 12 sensualistic 13 self-indulgent
sentence 4 damn, doom, rule 5 blame, judge 6 devote, ordain, punish 7 adjudge, condemn 8 denounce, penalize 9 proscribe 10 adjudicate
sententious 4 rich 5 crisp, pithy, terse 6 facund 7 concise, piquant 8 eloquent, pregnant 10 aphoristic, expressive, meaningful 11 significant
sentiment 3 eye 4 bias, mind, view 6 belief 7 emotion, feeling, leaning, opinion, passion, posture 8 penchant, position, tendency 9 affection, inclining, sensation 10 conception, conviction, partiality, persuasion, propensity 11 affectivity, disposition, inclination 12 emotionalism
sentimental 4 soft 5 gooey, gushy, inane, moist, mushy, sappy, sobby, soupy, sweet, vapid 6 dreamy, drippy, jejune, loving, slushy, sobful, sticky, sugary, syrupy, tender 7 gushing, insipid, maudlin, mawkish 8 bathetic, effusive, romantic, schmalzy 9 misty-eyed, nostalgic, rosewater 10 lovey-dovey, moonstruck, namby-pamby, passionate, saccharine, soft boiled, sugar-candy 11 tear-jerking 12 affectionate 13 demonstrative
sentimentalist 5 softy 6 softie
sentimentality 4 mush 7 schmalz 8 schmaltz
sentinel see **sentry**
sentry 4 ward 5 guard, watch 6 picket 7 lookout, outpost 8 sentinel, watchman
separate 3 one 4 comb, free, know, lone, only, part, sift, sole, sort 5 apart, halve, ravel, sever, split 6 cut off, detach, dispel, divide, enisle, island, single, sunder, unglue, unique, unjoin, unknit, unlink, winnow 7 break up, discern, disjoin, dislink, dispart, dissect, diverse, divorce, isolate, quarter, rupture, scatter, several, split up, unravel, various 8 alienate, autarkic, close off, detached, diffract, discrete, disjoint, disperse, dissever, dissolve, distinct, disunify, disunite, estrange, insulate, peculiar, solitary, splinter, uncouple, unmingle, unsolder 9 autarchic, different, discharge, disengage, disrelate, extricate, muster out, segregate, sequester, sovereign, uncombine 10 autonomous, demobilize, difference, discrepate, disengaged, disgregate, dissociate, particular, severalize 11 compartment, dichotomize, disassemble, discontinue, distinctive, distinguish, independent 12 disaggregate, disconnected, discriminate 13 differentiate *flax:* 7 hatchel *into filaments:* 6 sleave
separation 6 schism 7 breakup, divorce, parting, rupture, split-up 8 disunion, disunity, division, shedding 9 apartheid, dichotomy, dispersal, partition 10 detachment, diffluence, diremption, dissection, separatism, trichotomy 11 disjointure, disjunction, disrelation, dissolution, divorcement, segregation 12 dissociation 13 disconnection, sequestration
separatism 9 apartheid 11 segregation
separatist 7 heretic, sectary 9 dissenter, dissident 10 schismatic 11 misbeliever, schismatist 13 nonconformist
sepia 3 ink 4 gray 5 brown
sepulcher 4 bury, tomb 5 grave, inter,

plant 6 burial, entomb, inhume 7 lay away, put away
sequel 3 end, row 5 chain, close, issue, order, train 6 effect, ending, finish, result, series, upshot 7 closing, outcome 8 causatum, epilogue, sequence 9 aftermath, finishing 10 succession 11 aftereffect, alternation, consecution, consequence, development, eventuality, progression, termination 12 continuation
sequence 3 row 5 chain, issue, order, train 6 effect, result, sequel, series, upshot 7 outcome 8 disposal, grouping, ordering 9 aftermath, cavalcade, placement 10 procession, succession 11 aftereffect, alternation, arrangement, consecution, disposition, eventuality, progression 12 distribution
sequential 6 serial 9 succedent 10 succeeding, successive 11 consecutive 12 successional
sequester 4 hide, take 5 annex, seize 6 attach, cut off, enisle, island 7 impound, isolate, preempt, seclude, secrete 8 accroach, arrogate, cloister, close off, insulate, separate 9 segregate 10 commandeer, confiscate, dispossess 11 appropriate, expropriate
seraglio 5 harem 6 bagnio 7 brothel, lupanar 8 bordello
Serah's father 5 Asher
Seraiah *brother:* 6 Baruch 7 Othniel *father:* 5 Asiel, Kenaz 7 Hilkiah 9 Tanhumeth *grandson:* 4 Jehu 6 Jeshua *son:* 4 Joab 7 Jozadak 9 Joshibiah
seraphic 4 pure 7 angelic, sublime
sere 3 dry 4 arid 5 parch 7 bone-dry, thirsty 8 droughty 9 unwatered, waterless 12 moistureless
Sered's father 7 Zebulun
serene 4 calm, easy 5 quiet, still 6 placid, poised 7 resting 8 composed, tranquil
serf 4 esne, peon 5 churl, helot, slave 6 thrall 7 villein *freeborn:* 7 colonus
series 3 row, run, set 4 tier 5 chain, group, scale, train 6 catena, column, parade, sequel, string 8 category, sequence 9 cavalcade, gradation 10 procession, succession 11 alternation, consecution, continuance, progression 12 continuation
serious 4 fell, grim, hard, ugly 5 grave, heavy, major, sober, staid, stern, tough 6 intent, sedate, severe, solemn, somber, steady 7 arduous, austere, earnest, intense, operose, pensive, unfunny, weighty 8 grievous, menacing, resolute, sobering 9 dangerous, difficult, humorless, important, laborious, strenuous, unamusing 10 determined, formidable, meditative, no-nonsense, poker-faced, purposeful, reflective, sobersided, thoughtful, unhumorous 11 significant, steady-going, threatening 12 businesslike 13 contemplative
sermon 6 homily, preach, tirade 7 lecture 8 harangue 9 preaching 10 preachment 11 exhortation
sermonize 6 preach 7 descant, discuss, dissert 8 dilate on, homilize, moralize 9 discourse, expatiate, preachify 10 dilate upon, dissertate, evangelize
serpent 5 devil, fiend, Satan, snake 6 dipsas *combining form:* 4 ophi 5 ophio, ophis *fabled:* 8 basilisk *mythical:* 10 cockatrice *sound:* 4 hiss
serpentine 5 snaky 7 crooked, demonic, devious, satanic, sinuous, winding 8 demoniac, demonian, devilish, diabolic, fiendish, flexuous, tortuous 9 meandrous, snakelike 10 convoluted, meandering
serrated 6 scored 7 notched, serried, toothed 8 indented, saw-edged, sawtooth 10 saw-toothed 11 denticulate
Serug *father:* 3 Reu *son:* 5 Nahor
servant 4 maid 5 valet 6 butler, menial 7 famulus, footman 8 domestic, handmaid, houseboy, houseman, servitor 9 attendant 11 chamberlain, chambermaid *India:* 4 syce *kitchen:* 8 scullion
serve 3 act, fit, use 4 make, play, suit, take, work 5 avail, nurse, put in, spend, treat 6 foster, handle, mother, profit, wait on 7 advance, benefit, care for, forward, further, promote, satisfy, service, suffice, undergo, work for 8 deal with, function, minister 9 advantage, encourage, officiate 10 minister to
service 3 use 4 duty, rite 5 avail, cater, favor 6 action, combat, ritual 7 account, fitness, liturgy 8 ceremony, courtesy, fighting, kindness 9 advantage, formality, relevance 10 active duty, ceremonial, indulgence, observance, usefulness 12 dispensation 13 applicability
servile 3 low 4 base, mean, ugly, vile 6 abject, menial, scurvy, sordid 7 ignoble, passive, slavish, toadish 8 obedient, obeisant 9 groveling 10 despicable, obsequious, submissive 11 bootlicking, subservient, unresisting
servility 4 yoke 7 bondage, helotry, peonage, serfage, serfdom, slavery 9 servitude, thralldom 11 enslavement
serving 6 dollop 7 portion
sesame 3 til *grass:* 4 gama *seed:* 8 gingelly
session 6 assize 7 meeting, sitting *combining form:* 4 fest
set 3 aim, dry, fit, fix, gel, kit, lay, lot, put 4 firm, jell, park, sink 5 affix, array, batch, brood, bunch, crowd, fixed, group, place, put on, ready, rigid, scene, sited, stick 6 anchor, belong, circle, clique, gelate, go

down, harden, impose, placed, rooted, secure, stated 7 arrange, certain, cluster, congeal, decided, deposit, descend, dictate, emplace, express, faction, install, jellify, lay down, limited, located, prepare, scenery, situate, specify, station, valuate 8 appraise, ensconce, estimate, evaluate, fastened, grouping, prepared, resolute, resolved, situated, solidify, specific 9 confirmed, designate, establish, prescribe, specified, stipulate, tenacious, unbending 10 assortment, determined, entrenched, gelatinize, inflexible, positioned, prescribed, stipulated, unyielding 11 established, mise-en-scène *a gem:* 6 collet *right:* 7 redress

set apart 7 isolate, seclude 8 dedicate

set aside 4 void 5 annul 8 overrule

set back 4 mire 5 delay, embog 6 detain, hang up, retard, slow up

setback 5 check 6 defeat, rebuff 7 reverse 8 comedown, obstacle, reversal 9 hindrance 10 impediment, regression

set down 4 land 5 light, perch, roost 6 alight, record 9 establish, touch down

set fire to 4 burn 6 ignite 7 emblaze, inflame

set free 7 manumit, unloose 8 liberate, unloosen, untangle 10 emancipate

Seth *brother:* 4 Abel, Cain *father:* 4 Adam *mother:* 3 Eve *son:* 4 Enos

set off 5 start 7 actuate, balance 8 activate, atone for, outweigh 9 circulate 10 compensate 11 countervail 12 counterpoise

set out 4 head, plan 5 start, state 6 design, intend 7 arrange, present, take off 9 undertake

Set's victim 6 Osiris

setting 5 scene 7 scenery 11 mise-en-scène *for a stone:* 4 ouch

settle 3 fix, lay, pay, put 4 calm, land, lull 5 allay, clear, light, pay up, perch, place, quiet, roost, stick, still 6 alight, becalm, clinch, decide, soothe, square, wind up 7 arrange, clean up, compose, concert, install, resolve, satisfy, set down, sit down 8 clear off, colonize, conclude, ensconce 9 determine, discharge, establish, negotiate, reconcile, touch down 11 tranquilize

settlement 7 quietus, village 8 decision 9 agreement 10 conclusion, habitation, resolution 13 determination *Israeli:* 6 moshav

settler 7 pioneer 8 colonist 9 colonizer

set-to 3 row 4 fray 5 brawl, broil, brush, fight, run-in, scrap 6 affray, fracas, hassle 7 bobbery, dispute, quarrel, rhubarb, scuffle 8 skirmish 9 bickering, encounter 10 falling-out, velitation 11 altercation

set up 4 blow, open, rear 5 elate, erect, found, put up, raise, stand, start, treat 6 create, excite, launch 7 build up, commove, inspire, start up, usher in 8 generate, initiate, organize, spirit up 9 construct, establish, hammer out, institute, introduce, originate

seven *combining form:* 4 hept, sept 5 hepta, septi *group of:* 6 heptad 8 hebdomad

seventeenth century 8 seicento

sever 3 cut 4 chop, part 5 carve, slice, split 6 cleave, divide, sunder 7 break up, dissect, divorce 8 disjoint, separate

severe 3 raw 4 dear, dour, grim, hard, sore 5 acute, bleak, grave, harsh, heavy, rigid, sharp, smart, sober, stern, tough 6 bitter, brutal, crimpy, rugged, savage, stormy, strict, wintry 7 arduous, ascetic, austere, drastic, extreme, hostile, intense, onerous, painful, serious, weighty 8 blustery, exacting, rigorous, toilsome 9 difficult, effortful, inclement, laborious, mortified, strenuous, stringent 10 astringent, blistering, blustering, forbidding, inflexible, iron-willed, oppressive, unpleasant, unyielding 11 disciplined, heavy-handed, intemperate, restrictive 12 disagreeable, inhospitable

sew 4 darn, mend, seam 5 baste 6 needle, stitch, suture

sewing *aid:* 7 thimble *case:* 4 etui *kit:* 5 hussy 9 housewife

sewing-machine inventor 4 Howe (Elias)

sexless 6 neuter 7 epicene

sex manual 9 Kama-sutra

sexton 9 custodian, sacristan

sexual *combining form:* 3 gam, gon 4 gamo, gono

sexual desire 4 eros

sexy 4 blue, racy 5 broad, salty, shady, spicy 6 erotic, purple, risqué 8 off-color 10 suggestive

Sganarelle *brother:* 6 Ariste *daughter:* 7 Lucinde *ward:* 7 Leonore 8 Isabelle *wife:* 7 Martine

Shaaph *father:* 5 Caleb 6 Jahdai *mother:* 6 Maacah

shabby 4 bare, mean, poor 5 cheap, dingy, dowdy, faded, mangy, ratty, seedy, shady, sorry, tacky, tired 6 ruined, scummy, scurvy, shoddy, sleazy, sordid, tagrag 7 outworn, rickety, ruinous, run-down, scrubby, scruffy, squalid, worn-out, wrecked 8 beggarly, decaying, decrepit, desolate, dog-eared, pitiable, shameful, slipshod, tattered 9 abandoned, miserable, moth-eaten, neglected, worm-eaten 10 bedraggled, broken-down, despicable, despisable, disfigured, down-at-heel, inglorious, ramshackle, threadbare 11 dilapidated, disgraceful, ignominious 12 contemptible, deteriorated, dishonorable, disreputable

13 deteriorating, discreditable, unrespectable
shack 3 cot, hut 4 camp 5 cabin, hovel, lodge 6 shanty 7 cottage
shackle 3 tie 4 clog, curb, gyve, lash, rope 5 bilbo, bonds, chain, gyves, irons, leash, strap 6 anklet, chains, collar, fetter, hamper, hobble, hog-tie, pinion, secure 7 enchain, fetters, garrote, leg-iron, manacle, trammel 8 bracelet, handcuff 9 entrammel
shad 4 fish 7 clupeid, herring
shade 3 hue 4 cast, hint, tint, tone, veil 5 bogey, color, cover, ghost, spice, tinge, trace, umbra 6 awning, nuance, screen, shadow, spirit, streak 7 dimness, phantom, shelter, soupçon, specter, umbrage 8 darkness, penumbra, phantasm, tincture 9 blackness, gradation, intensity, inumbrate, obscurity, suspicion, variation 10 apparition, difference, saturation, suggestion 11 adumbration, distinction, obscuration
shadow 3 dim, dog, tag 4 haze, hint, tail 5 bedim, bedog, cloud, relic, shade, shady, smack, tinge, touch, trace, trail, umbra 6 breath, screen, shaded, spirit, wraith 7 becloud, eidolon, memento, obscure, phantom, predict, specter, suggest, umbrage, umbrous, vestige 8 forecast, foretell, overcast, penumbra, phantasm, revenant, shadowed, tincture 9 adumbrate, inumbrate, overcloud, prefigure, suspicion 10 apparition, intimation, suggestion, umbrageous 11 adumbration, prefigurate *combining form:* 3 sci 4 scia, scio, skia
shadowy 3 dim 4 dark 5 faint, vague 7 ghostly 8 adumbral 10 indistinct
shady 4 blue, dark, racy 5 bosky, broad, dusky, fishy, salty, spicy 6 purple, risqué, shabby, shoddy, wicked 7 clouded, shadowy, suspect, umbrous 8 doubtful, off-color, screened, shadowed, shameful 9 equivocal, sheltered, uncertain, undecided 10 impugnable, indecisive, inglorious, suggestive, suspicious, umbrageous 11 disgraceful, ignominious 12 dishonorable, disreputable 13 discreditable
shaft 3 cut, jab, ray, rod 4 axle, barb, beam, dart, pole, stem 5 arrow, lance, shoot, spear 6 thrust 7 chimney, potshot 8 short end *of a vehicle:* 5 thill
shag 3 mat, nap, rug 5 chase, fetch 7 thicket 9 cormorant
shaggy 5 bushy, rough 7 thrummy, unkempt
shake 3 jar, jog, rid 4 deal, flit, jerk, jolt, lose, rock, roil, slip, whip 5 avoid, churn, clear, crack, daunt, elude, flash, jiffy, quail, quake, shock, trill, upset, waver, worry 6 appall, bother, bounce, dismay, dither, escape, jiggle, joggle, jostle, jounce, minute, moment, outwit, quaver, quiver, rattle, ruffle, second, shimmy, shiver, stir up, tremor, wiggle 7 agitate, chatter, commove, concuss, disturb, flicker, flitter, flutter, horrify, instant, perturb, shudder, stagger, temblor, tremble, twitter, unnerve, vibrate 8 convulse, disorder, disquiet, throw off, tremblor, unburden, unsettle, unstring 9 breathing, fluctuate, oscillate, palpitate 10 discompose, earthquake 11 consternate, split second
shake down 5 frisk, gouge, pinch, screw, wrest, wring 6 extort, search, wrench 7 squeeze
Shakespeare, William *mother:* 9 Mary Arden *play:* 6 Hamlet, Henry V 7 Henry IV, Henry VI, Macbeth, Othello 8 King John, King Lear, Pericles 9 Cymbeline, Henry VIII, Richard II 10 Coriolanus, Richard III, The Tempest 11 As You Like It 12 Julius Caesar, Twelfth Night *theater:* 5 Globe *wife:* 12 Anne Hathaway
Shakespearean actor 4 Kean 5 Evans 7 Garrick, Gielgud, Olivier 8 Macready
shaky 4 weak 6 aquake, ashake, dickey, infirm, unsure, wobbly 7 aquiver, dubious, quaking, quivery, rackety, rickety, suspect, tottery, trembly, unclear, unsound 8 doubtful, insecure, rachitic, rootless, unstable, unsteady, wavering 9 fluctuant, quivering, tottering, trembling, tremorous, tremulous, uncertain, unsettled 10 indecisive, precarious, rattletrap 11 problematic, vacillating
shale 4 rock 5 slate
shallot 4 herb, tube 5 onion 8 eschalot
shallow 4 idle, vain 5 empty, petty, shoal 6 hollow, paltry 7 cursory, flighty, sketchy, surface, trivial 8 trifling 9 depthless 10 bird-witted, shallowish, uncritical 11 superficial
shallows 6 lagoon
Shallum *father:* 5 Shaul, Zadok 6 Jabesh, Josiah, Sismai, Tikvah 8 Colhozeh, Naphtali 9 Hallohesh *mother:* 6 Bilhah *nephew:* 8 Jeremiah *slayer:* 7 Menahem *son:* 6 Mibsam 7 Hilkiah 8 Maaseiah *victim:* 9 Zechariah
shalom 5 peace 8 farewell, greeting
sham 3 act, ape, lie 4 cant, copy, fake, hoax, mock, sell 5 bluff, bogus, cheat, dummy, false, farce, feign, phony, put on, snide, spoof 6 affect, assume, create, deceit, ersatz, facade, fakery, invent, pseudo 7 assumed, feigned, imitate, mislead, mockery, plaster, pretend 8 affected, flimflam, simulate, so-called, spurious, travesty 9 brummagem, burlesque, deception, hypocrisy, imitation, imposture, pinchbeck, simulated, synthetic 10 artificial, caricature, false front, fictitious, pharisaism, sanctimony, substitute, Tartuffery, Tartuffism 11 adulterated, counterfeit, make believe

12 pecksniffery ***combining form:*** 5 pseud 6 pseudo
Shamariah see Shemariah
Shama's father 6 Hotham
Shamash 6 sun-god ***father:*** 3 Sin ***sister:*** 6 Ishtar ***wife:*** 2 Ai 3 Aya
shamble see shuffle
shambles 4 mess 5 botch, mix-up 6 mess-up, muddle 8 botchery, wreckage 9 confusion
shame 5 abash, guilt, odium 6 infamy 7 chagrin, obloquy 8 disgrace, dishonor, ignominy 9 discredit, disesteem, disrepute 10 opprobrium 11 self-reproof 12 self-reproach 13 embarrassment, mortification
shameless 4 bold, lewd 6 arrant, brassy, brazen, cheeky 7 blatant 8 immodest, impudent, overbold 9 abandoned, audacious, bald-faced, barefaced, dissolute, unabashed 10 high-handed, outrageous, profligate, unblushing 11 brazenfaced, disgraceful 12 presumptuous
Shamgar's father 5 Anath
Shamir's father 5 Micah
Shammah ***brother:*** 5 David ***father:*** 4 Agee 5 Jesse, Reuel ***grandfather:*** 4 Esau 7 Ishmael ***son:*** 7 Jonadab 8 Jonathan
Shammai's father 4 Onam 5 Ezrah, Rekem
Shammua ***father:*** 5 David, Galal 6 Bilgah, Zaccur ***mother:*** 9 Bathsheba ***son:*** 4 Abda
Shamsherai's father 7 Jeroham
shanghai 6 abduct, kidnap
Shangri-la 4 Zion 6 heaven, utopia 7 arcadia 8 paradise 9 Cockaigne, fairyland 10 lubberland, wonderland 12 promised land
shank 3 leg 4 shin, stem 5 stalk, tibia
shanty 3 cot, hut 4 camp 5 cabin, hovel, lodge, shack 7 cottage
shape 3 fit 4 case, cast, form, look, make, mold, plan, trim 5 build, forge, frame, order, state, whack 6 aspect, devise, estate, fettle, figure, kilter, repair, tailor, work up 7 fashion, fitness 8 assemble 9 condition, construct, fabricate, semblance 10 appearance 12 conformation 13 configuration ***combining form:*** 5 morph 6 morpho
shapeable 4 soft 6 pliant 7 ductile
shapeless 8 formless, inchoate, unformed 9 amorphous, unshapely
shapely 4 trim 5 buxom 6 comely 7 regular, rounded 8 balanced, clean-cut 9 Junoesque 10 curvaceous, statuesque, well-turned 11 clean-limbed, full-figured, symmetrical 12 proportioned
Shaphan ***grandson:*** 8 Gedaliah ***son:*** 6 Ahikam 8 Gemariah 9 Jaazaniah
Shaphat ***father:*** 4 Hori 5 Adlai 8 Shemaiah ***son:*** 6 Elisha
Sharai's father 4 Bani
share 3 cut, lot 4 bite, meed, part 5 claim, quota, slice, stake 6 assign, divide, parcel, quotum, ration 7 deal out, dole out, give out, measure, mete out, partage, partake, portion, prorate, quantum, rake-off 8 dispense, interest, quotient 9 allotment, allowance, apportion 10 commission, experience, percentage, proportion 11 participate 13 apportionment
shared 5 joint 6 common, mutual, public 8 communal, conjoint, conjunct ***prefix:*** 2 co
Sharezer ***father, victim:*** 11 Sennacherib
shark 5 cheat 8 swindler ***kind:*** 4 blue, gata, haye, mako, sand, tope 5 nurse, tiger, whale, white 7 basking, dogfish, leopard 8 mackerel, maneater, thresher 9 porbeagle 10 great white, hammerhead ***skin:*** 8 shagreen
sharp 3 hep, sly 4 acid, cute, fast, high, keen, sour, thin, tony, trig, wise 5 acrid, acute, alert, blunt, canny, harsh, honed, peaky, piked, quick, short, slick, smart, swank, swish 6 adroit, argute, biting, bitter, brainy, bright, clever, nimble, peaked, piping, severe, shrewd, shrill, snappy, tonish, treble 7 austere, caustic, dashing, exactly, intense, knowing, odorous, pointed, prickly, stylish, whetted 8 acicular, drilling, incisive, original, piercing, shooting, stabbing, stinging, virulent 9 aciculate, acuminate, acuminous, agonizing, amaroidal, brilliant, cuspidate, ingenious, knifelike, precisely, sensitive, unblunted, unethical, vitriolic 10 accurately, astringent, paralyzing, perceptive, ungracious 11 acrimonious, double-edged, intelligent, penetrating, penetrative, quick-witted, ready-witted, resourceful, suffocating, thoughtless 12 excruciating, nimble-witted, quick-sighted 13 inconsiderate, strong-scented, unceremonious ***combining form:*** 3 oxy 5 acuto
sharp-edged 8 cultrate
sharpen 4 edge, file, hone, whet 5 dress, grind, strop 6 stroke
sharper 3 gyp 5 cheat 6 con man 7 diddler 8 swindler 9 defrauder, trickster 10 mountebank 12 double-dealer
sharpie see sharper
sharpness 4 edge 6 acumen 8 acrimony, keenness 12 incisiveness
sharpshooter 8 marksman
sharp-sighted 4 keen 5 acute 7 lyncean 8 hawk-eyed, lynx-eyed 9 eagle-eyed 11 penetrating, penetrative, quick-witted
sharp-witted 3 hep 4 keen, wise 5 acute, canny, quick, slick, smart

6 shrewd 7 knowing 10 discerning 11 intelligent
Shashai's father 4 Bani
Shashak's father 6 Elpaal
shatter 4 dash, raze, rend, rive, ruin, snap 5 break, burst, clack, crack, crash, crush, shoot, smash, split, wrack, wreck 6 bicker, crunch, rattle, shiver 7 clatter, clitter, destroy 8 decimate, demolish, destruct, fragment, splinter, splitter 9 pulverize 10 annihilate 11 fragmentize, splinterize 12 disintegrate
shatterable 5 frail 7 fragile 8 delicate, shattery 9 breakable, frangible 11 fracturable
Shaul's father 6 Simeon
shave 3 cut 4 clip, crop, kiss, pare, skim, trim 5 brush, graze, lower, prune, shear, shred, skive, slash 6 glance, reduce, scrape, sliver 7 cut back, cut down, shingle, tonsure, whittle 8 mark down
shaveling 3 boy, lad, son, tad 6 laddie 9 stripling
shaver 3 boy, lad 5 child, razor 6 barber 9 youngster
shawl 4 maud, wrap 5 cloak, manta 6 chadar, chador, sarape, serape 7 blanket, tallith
shawm's descendant 4 oboe
Shawnee chief 8 Tecumseh 9 Cornstalk
Shaw play 6 Geneva 7 Candida 9 Pygmalion, Saint Joan 11 Misalliance 12 Major Barbara
sheaf 6 bundle 7 cluster
Sheal's father 4 Bani
Shealtiel ***father:*** 4 Neri 8 Jeconiah ***son:*** 10 Zerubbabel
shear 3 cut, mow 4 barb, clip, crop, pare, snip, trim 5 prune, shave, skive 6 barber 8 manicure
Shearjashub's father 6 Isaiah
shears 8 scissors
shearwater 4 bird 6 hagdon, haglet 7 skimmer
sheath 4 case, skin 5 cover 8 scabbard ***combining form:*** 4 cole 5 coleo, theca
sheathe 4 case, clad, face, side, skin, wrap 5 cover, panel 6 encase, jacket 7 envelop 8 surround
Sheba ***father:*** 6 Bichri ***queen:*** 6 Balkis
shebang 3 hut 6 affair 8 business
Sheber ***father:*** 5 Caleb ***mother:*** 6 Maacah
Shebuel ***father:*** 5 Heman 7 Gershom ***grandfather:*** 5 Moses
Shecaniah ***father:*** 6 Jehiel 8 Jehaziel ***son:*** 7 Hattush 8 Shemaiah ***son-in-law:*** 6 Tobiah
Shechem's father 5 Hamor 6 Gilead 8 Shemidah
shed 3 hut 4 abri, cast, doff, drop, junk, molt, slip 5 scrap 6 divest, reject, slough 7 cashier, cast off, discard, ecdysis, take off 8 exuviate, jettison, throw out 9 throw away
Shedeur's son 6 Elizur
sheen 5 glaze, glint, gloss, shine 6 finish, luster, polish 9 shininess
sheeny see shiny
sheep 5 dumba, ovine ***Australian:*** 7 jumbuck ***breed:*** 5 Tunis 6 Dorper, Dorset, Merino, Navajo, No-Tail, Oxford, Panama, Romney 7 Cheviot, Colbred, Karakul, Lincoln, Ryeland, Suffolk 8 Columbia, Cotswold, Polwarth 9 Hampshire, Leicester, Montadale, Southdown 10 Corriedale, Debouillet 11 Rambouillet ***coat:*** 4 wool 6 fleece ***disease:*** 3 gid 5 braxy 6 sturdy ***female:*** 3 ewe ***male:*** 3 ram 6 wether ***meat:*** 6 mutton ***relating to:*** 5 ovine ***Scottish:*** 9 blackface ***skin:*** 4 slat ***sound:*** 5 bleat ***tender of:*** 8 shepherd ***wild:*** 3 sha 5 urial 6 aoudad, argali, bharal, nahoor, oorial 7 bighorn, mouflon 8 moufflon ***young:*** 3 teg 4 hogg, lamb
sheepish 4 meek 5 timid 7 abashed, bashful 9 diffident 11 embarrassed
sheepskin 4 roan 5 basil 6 mouton 7 diploma 9 parchment ***prepare:*** 3 taw
sheer 3 dip 4 airy, pure, skew, slue, thin, turn, veer, whip 5 avert, filmy, gauzy, pivot, steep, utter, wheel, whirl 6 abrupt, arrant, divert, flimsy, simple, swerve 7 chiffon, deflect, perfect, unmixed 8 absolute, complete, gossamer, outright 9 out-and-out, unalloyed, undiluted 10 diaphanous, see through 11 precipitate, precipitous, transparent, unmitigated
sheet 4 leaf, page, sail 5 cover, linen, paper 9 newspaper ***combining form:*** 6 pallio
sheet ____ 3 ice 4 film 5 glass, metal, music 6 anchor
Shehariah's father 7 Jeroham
Shelah ***father:*** 5 Judah 8 Arphaxad ***son:*** 4 Eber
Shelemiah ***father:*** 5 Cushi 6 Abdeel, Binnui 8 Hananiah ***son:*** 5 Jucal 6 Irijah 8 Hananiah
Sheleph's father 6 Joktan
Shelesh's father 5 Helem
shelf 4 bank, edge, reef, sill 5 ledge, shoal 6 gradin, mantel 7 gradine 8 sandbank
shell 3 pod 4 boat, bomb, case, hull, husk, rake, skin 5 blitz, conch, shuck 6 pepper 7 bombard, capsule, grenade, mollusk 9 cannonade, cartridge ***combining form:*** 5 conch 6 concho, ostrac 7 ostraca, ostraco ***defective:*** 3 dud ***explosive:*** 4 bomb ***layer:*** 5 nacre ***ornamental:*** 5 cowry 6 cowrie ***study:*** 10 conchology

shellac 4 beat, drub, lick, rout, trim, whip 5 resin, smear 6 defeat, thrash 7 smother, trounce 8 lambaste, vanquish
Shelley ***elegy:*** 7 Adonais ***poem:*** 7 Alastor 8 Queen Mab, The Cloud 10 Ozymandias, To a Skylark
shellfish 4 clam, crab 5 conch, cowry, prawn 6 cockle, limpet, mussel, oyster, triton 7 abalone, lobster, mollusk, scallop 8 barnacle 10 crustacean
shell out 3 pay 4 give 5 spend 6 expend, outlay 8 disburse
shell-shaped 6 spiral 9 cochleate
Shelomi's son 6 Ahihud
Shelomith ***father:*** 5 Dibri, Izhar 8 Rehoboam 9 Josiphiah 10 Zerubbabel ***mother:*** 6 Maacah
shelter 3 den, hut, lee 4 abri, cote, fold, hide, port, roof, shed, tent 5 arbor, benab, bower, cloak, cover, haven, house, shack, tower 6 asylum, burrow, covert, defend, harbor, refuge, shield 7 chamber, defense, foxhole, hideout, hospice, housing, lodging, pergola, pillbox, protect, retreat 8 hideaway, security 9 dwellings, harborage, hermitage, hidey-hole, sanctuary 10 quarterage, retirement ***for a car:*** 6 garage ***for aircraft:*** 6 hangar ***for cows:*** 4 barn, byre ***toward:*** 4 alee
shelve 4 dish, drop, stay, tilt 5 defer, delay, stock, waive 6 give up, hold up, put off 7 hold off 8 hold over, postpone, prorogue
Shem ***brother:*** 3 Ham 7 Japheth ***father:*** 4 Noah
Shemaiah ***father:*** 4 Joel 7 Delaiah 8 Adonikam, Nethanel, Obededom 9 Elizaphan, Shecaniah ***son:*** 5 Uriah 6 Urijah 7 Delaiah, Obadiah
Shemariah's father 4 Bani 5 Harim 8 Rehoboam
Shema's father 4 Joel 6 Hebron
Shemer's father 5 Mahli
Shemida's father 6 Gilead
Shemuel's father 4 Tola 7 Ammihud
shenanigan 4 game, lark, play, ploy, ruse, wile 5 antic, caper, prank, stunt, trick 6 device, didoes, frolic, shines 7 fast one, gimmick, whizzer 8 goings-on, maneuver 9 stratagem 10 tomfoolery 11 legerdemain, monkeyshine
Shenazzar's father 8 Jeconiah 10 Jehoiachin
Sheol see hades
Shephatiah ***father:*** 5 David 6 Maacah, Mattan 11 Jehoshaphat ***mother:*** 6 Abital
shepherd 3 see 4 lead, show, tend 5 guide, pilot, route, steer, watch 6 direct, escort, leader 7 conduct 8 guardian ***dog:*** 6 Collie ***stick:*** 4 kent 5 crook, staff
Shephi, Shepho ***father:*** 6 Shobal
Sheridan play 7 Pizarro 9 The Critic, The Rivals
sheriff 6 lawman 7 marshal, officer ***aide:*** 6 deputy
Sherlock Holmes 6 sleuth 7 gumshoe 8 hawkshaw 9 detective 12 investigator ***creator:*** 5 Doyle ***sidekick:*** 6 Watson
sherry 4 fino, wine 7 oloroso 11 amontillado
Sheshai's father 4 Anak
Sheshan's servant 5 Jarha
shibboleth 3 tag 6 byword, clich'e, phrase, slogan, truism 7 bromide 8 banality, password, prosaism 9 catchword, platitude, watchword 10 prosaicism 11 catchphrase
shield 4 fend, roof, ward 5 aegis, armor, cover, guard, haven, house 6 defend, harbor, screen, secure 7 buckler, bulwark, protect, shelter 8 defilade 9 safeguard 10 escutcheon ***band:*** 4 fess ***bullfighter's:*** 9 burladero ***combining form:*** 4 scut 5 aspid, scuti 6 aspido ***large:*** 5 pavis 6 pavise ***light:*** 5 targe ***part:*** 4 boss, umbo 7 bordure ***Roman:*** 6 scutum 7 clipeus, testudo
shield-like 7 peltate, scutate 9 scutiform
shift 3 yaw 4 bend, bout, move, stir, tack, time, tour, turn, vary 5 alter, budge, get by, got on, spell, stint, trick 6 change, make do, manage, remove, swerve 7 disturb, replace, shuffle 8 get along, relocate, transfer 9 deviation, dislocate 10 alteration, changeover, conversion, deflection, transition
shiftless 4 lazy
shifty 5 cagey, lying, shady 6 crafty, sneaky, tricky 7 cunning, devious, dodging, elusive, evasive, furtive, knavish, mutable, roguish 8 guileful, indirect, slippery, sneaking, unhonest, unstable, unsteady, variable 9 collusive, conniving, deceitful, dishonest, insidious, shuffling, uncertain, underhand 10 changeable, fraudulent, inconstant, mendacious, untruthful 11 duplicitous, treacherous, underhanded 12 equivocating 13 prevaricative, prevaricatory
Shilem's father 8 Naphtali
Shilhi ***daughter:*** 6 Azubah ***grandson:*** 11 Jehoshaphat
shill 5 blind, decoy, stick 6 capper
shilling 3 bob
shilly-shally 4 halt 5 waver 6 dither, falter, wobbly 7 halting, stagger, whiffle 8 hesitate, to-and-fro, wavering 9 faltering, hesitancy, vacillate, whiffling 10 hesitating, hesitation, indecision 11 vacillating, vacillation, vacillatory 12 irresolution
Shilshah's father 6 Zophah
Shimea ***brother:*** 5 David ***father:*** 5 David, Jesse ***son:*** 7 Jonadab 8 Jonathan
Shimeam's father 7 Mikloth

Shimei ***brother:*** 8 Conaniah, Cononiah 10 Zerubbabel ***father:*** 4 Bani, Gera, Kish 6 Hashum, Jahath 7 Gershon 8 Jeduthun ***grandfather:*** 4 Levi

Shimeon's father 5 Harim

shimmer 5 flash, gleam, glint, spark 7 glimmer, glisten, glitter, spangle, sparkle, twinkle 8 blinking, sparking 9 coruscate 11 coruscation, scintillate 13 scintillation

shimmy 5 dance, shake 7 chemise, vibrate

Shimrath's father 6 Shimei

Shimri's father 5 Hosah 8 Shemaiah 9 Elizaphan

Shimrith's son 9 Jehozabad

Shimron's father 8 Issachar

shin 3 run 4 dash 5 scoot, tibia 6 scurry, sprint 7 scamper

shindig 4 ball, bash, coil, fête, gala, to-do 5 dance, party 6 affair, furore, ruckus, rumpus, shindy, uproar 7 shebang 8 foofaraw 9 commotion

shine 3 ray, rub 4 beam, buff, burn, glow, pomp, show 5 array, flare, flash, glare, glaze, gleam, glint, gloss, sheen 6 finish, glance, luster, parade, polish 7 burnish, display, fanfare, furbish, glimmer, glisten, panoply, radiate, sparkle, twinkle 9 luminesce 10 incandesce

shiner 4 fish 8 black eye, cyprinid

Shinto gods 4 kami

shiny 6 glossy, sheeny 7 fulgent 8 gleaming, lustrous, polished 9 burnished 10 glistening

ship 4 boat, move, send 5 remit, route, shift 6 direct, export, remove 7 address, consign, disturb, forward, freight 8 dispatch, transfer, transmit ***ancient:*** 5 knorr 6 galley 7 galleon, trireme ***attendant:*** 7 steward ***beam:*** 7 carling, keelson ***berth:*** 4 dock, slip ***boat:*** 6 dinghy ***body:*** 4 hull ***cabin:*** 9 stateroom ***commercial:*** 5 liner, oiler 6 argosy, tanker, trader 9 freighter ***crew member:*** 4 hand, mate 5 bosun 6 purser, sailor ***deck:*** 4 boat, main, poop 5 orlop 6 bridge 10 forecastle ***fishing:*** 6 lugger 7 trawler ***fleet:*** 6 armada ***floor:*** 4 deck ***front:*** 3 bow 4 prow, stem 8 cutwater ***hoister:*** 4 boom 5 davit 7 capstan ***kitchen:*** 6 galley ***left side:*** 4 port 8 larboard ***merchant:*** (see commercial) ***military:*** 6 cutter, PT boat 7 carrier, cruiser 9 destroyer, submarine ***officer:*** 4 mate 5 bosun 6 purser 7 captain, steward ***of the desert:*** 5 camel ***part:*** 3 bow 4 beam, deck, helm, hold, hull, keel, mast, stem 5 bilge, hatch, stern 6 bridge, rudder 7 scupper ***partition:*** 7 bulwark 8 bulkhead ***personnel:*** 4 crew ***platform:*** 9 crow's nest, gangboard, gangplank ***post:*** 4 mast 7 bollard ***prison:*** 4 brig ***projection:*** 7 sponson ***rear:*** 5 stern ***record:*** 3 log ***right side:*** 9 starboard ***room:*** 4 brig 5 cabin 6 galley ***rope:*** 4 line 7 halyard ***sailing:*** 4 brig, dhow, prao, prau, proa, yawl 5 ketch, prahu, sloop, xebec 6 chebec, lugger 7 caravel, galleon 8 bilander, schooner ***spar:*** 6 bumkin ***steerer:*** 4 helm 6 tiller ***storage area:*** 4 hold ***submersible:*** 9 submarine 11 bathyscaphe ***to the rear of:*** 3 aft 5 abaft 6 astern ***valve:*** 7 seacock ***window:*** 4 port 8 porthole

Shiphi's father 5 Allon

Shiphtan's son 6 Kemuel

shipment 5 cargo 8 delivery

Ship of Fools author 6 Porter

ships ***group of:*** 4 navy 5 fleet, flota 6 armada 8 flotilla

shipshape 4 neat, snug, tidy, trig, trim 7 chipper, orderly 11 spic-and-span, uncluttered, well-groomed 12 spick-and-span

shire 5 horse 6 county 8 district

shirk 4 duck, lurk, shun, slip 5 creep, dodge, fence, parry, skulk, slink, sneak, steal 6 bypass, eschew 8 sidestep

shirker see **slacker**

shirt 4 sark 6 camisa, camise, jersey 7 garment 8 guernsey, pullover ***armored:*** 6 byrnie ***hair:*** 6 cilice ***kind:*** 3 tee 4 polo 5 dress, sport ***Scottish:*** 4 jupe

shirty 3 mad 4 waxy 5 angry, irate, wroth 6 heated, ireful, wrathy 8 choleric, wrathful

Shiva, Siva ***consort:*** 3 Uma 4 Devi, Kali 5 Durga, Gauri 6 Ambika, Chandi 7 Parvati 9 Haimavati ***son:*** 6 Ganesa, Skanda 7 Ganesha 10 Karttikeya

shiver 4 rive 5 burst, quake, shake, smash 6 dither, quaver, quiver, tremor 7 shatter, shudder, tremble, twitter 8 fragment, splinter, splitter 11 splinterize

Shiza's son 5 Adina

shoal 3 bar 4 bank, hook, reef, spit 7 barrier, sandbar, shallow, tombolo 8 sandbank, sand reef, seamount 9 coral reef 11 barrier reef, superficial

Shobab ***father:*** 5 Caleb, David ***mother:*** 6 Azubah 9 Bathsheba

Shobal's father 3 Hur 4 Seir

Shobi's father 6 Nahash

shock 3 jar 4 bank, bump, cock, hill, jolt, pile, rick 5 clash, crash, floor, mound, quake, shake, smash, stack 6 appall, impact, insult, offend, sicken, trauma, tremor 7 astound, disgust, horrify, outrage, pyramid, shake up, startle, temblor 8 astonish, knock out, nauseate, surprise, tremblor 9 collision, electrify, stockpile 10 concussion, earthquake, percussion, scandalize, traumatism 11 prostration 12 stupefaction

shock absorber 6 spring 7 dashpot, snubber

shocking 5 awful, lurid 6 crying, horrid

7 burning, direful, fearful, glaring, heinous 8 dreadful, horrible, horrific, shameful, terrible 9 appalling, atrocious, desperate, frightful, monstrous 10 formidable, outrageous, scandalous 11 disgraceful, unspeakable

shoddy 4 base, mean, poor 5 cheap, dingy, seedy, shady, tacky, tatty 6 common, paltry, shabby, sleazy, trashy 7 rundown, scruffy 8 rubbishy, shameful 9 makeshift, scambling 10 broken-down, down-at-heel, inglorious 11 dilapidated, disgraceful, ignominious 12 dishonorable, disreputable 13 discreditable

shoe 3 bal, pac 4 boot, clog, geta, mule, pump 5 gilly, plate, sabot, tegua, wedge 6 brogan, brogue, buskin, crakow, gaiter, galosh, gillie, loafer, oxford, patten, sandal 7 chopine, ghillie, slipper, sneaker 8 balmoral, moccasin, platform, plimsoll 9 brodequin, pampootie, spectator 10 clodhopper, espadrille ***accessory:*** 4 horn, tree 6 polish ***armored:*** 8 solleret ***athlete's:*** 7 sneaker ***form:*** 4 last, tree ***kind:*** 8 elevator, open-toed 10 high-heeled ***part:*** 3 tip, toe 4 arch, heel, lace, lift, sole, vamp 5 shank, upper 6 box toe, collar, foxing, insole, lining, throat, tongue 7 counter, outsole 8 backstay ***protective:*** 6 galosh, rubber ***Roman:*** 6 caliga, sandal ***shiner:*** 6 polish 9 bootblack ***wooden:*** 5 sabot 7 chopine

shoeless 6 unshod 8 barefoot

shoemaker 5 soler 7 cobbler, crispin ***patron saint:*** 7 Crispin ***Scottish:*** 6 souter

Shogun author 7 Clavell

Shoham's father 7 Jaaziah

Shomer ***father:*** 5 Heber ***son:*** 9 Jehozabad

shoo-in 9 sure thing

shoot 3 bud, fly, gun, ray 4 beam, bolt, dart, dash, fire, lash, race, raze, ruin, rush, sail, scud, skim, spew, tear 5 blast, chase, fling, float, loose, photo, shaft, skirr, snipe, spurt, wrack, wreck 6 branch, charge 7 destroy, explode, project, shatter 8 decimate, demolish, destruct, disprove, puncture 9 discharge, discredit 10 annihilate, photograph ***combining form:*** 5 blast, thall 6 blasto, thalli, thallo

shooting 5 acute, sharp 7 gunplay 8 piercing, stabbing 9 knifelike

shooting star 6 meteor 8 fireball

shoot up 4 soar 6 rocket 9 skyrocket

shop 4 hunt 5 store 6 market, outlet 8 boutique, emporium, showroom

shoplift 3 bag, cop 4 palm 5 pinch, steal, swipe 6 pilfer, rip off, snitch

shop owner 3 cit 8 merchant, retailer 10 proprietor

shopworn 5 stale, tired, trite 6 cliché 7 clichéd 8 overused 9 hackneyed 10 overworked 13 stereotypical

shore 4 bank, prop, stay 5 beach, brace, brink, carry, coast 6 bear up, column, rivage, strand, upbear, uphold 7 bolster, support, sustain 8 buttress, littoral, seacoast 9 coastland, coastline, riverbank, riverside, waterside 10 embankment, waterfront 11 underpinner 12 underpinning

shorebird see at **bird**

short 3 shy 4 core, curt, gist, meat, pith 5 aback, bluff, blunt, brief, crisp, dumpy, gruff, scant, sharp, skimp, spare, squat, stint, terse, thick 6 abrupt, amount, burden, chunky, crusty, low-set, meager, scanty, scarce, skimpy, snippy, sparse, stubby, sudden, thrust, upshot 7 asudden, brittle, brusque, compact, concise, crumbly, crunchy, curtate, failing, fragile, friable, lacking, laconic, needing, pointed, purport, scrimpy, slender, squatty, summary, unaware, wanting 8 abridged, abruptly, delicate, exiguous, lessened, snippety, succinct, suddenly, thickset, unawares 9 curtailed, decreased, decurtate, deficient, forthwith, irascible 10 diminished, inadequate, ungracious 11 abbreviated, compendiary, compendious 12 breviloquent, insufficient, unexpectedly, unsufficient 13 inconsiderate, unceremonious ***combining form:*** 5 brevi 6 brachy

shortage 4 lack 5 pinch 6 dearth 7 deficit, failure 8 underage 10 deficiency, inadequacy, scantiness

shortcoming 3 sin 5 fault 7 demerit 10 deficiency 12 imperfection

shortcut 6 bypass, cutoff

shorten 3 bob, cut 4 clip, dock 5 elide, slash 6 lessen, reduce, shrink 7 abridge, bobtail, curtail, cut back, excerpt 8 compress, condense, contract, decrease, diminish, minimize, retrench, truncate 10 abbreviate

shorthand 11 stenography ***method:*** 5 Gregg 6 Pitman

shorthanded 7 wanting 11 undermanned 12 understaffed

shortly 4 anon, soon 6 pronto 7 briefly, by and by, in brief, quickly, tersely 8 directly 9 concisely, presently 10 succinctly 11 laconically

shortness 7 brevity

shortsighted 6 myopic

short-spoken 4 curt 5 bluff, blunt, brief, gruff 6 abrupt, crusty, snippy 7 brusque 8 snippety

short-tempered 5 testy 6 touchy 9 irascible

Shoshoni chief 8 Washakie 9 Pocatello

shot 2 go 3 nip, pop, try 4 dram, drop, jolt, show, slug, stab, time 5 break, carom, crack, fling, snort, whack, whirl 6 chance

7 snifter 8 occasion, toothful 11 opportunity

shoulder 4 edge, push, side 5 elbow, press, shove 6 axilla, hustle, jostle 8 bulldoze *bone:* 7 scapula 8 clavicle *combining form:* 2 om 3 omo *covering:* 6 tippet 8 scapular *muscle:* 7 deltoid *relating to:* 7 humeral 8 scapular

shoulder blade 7 scapula

shout 3 cry 4 bark, bawl, bray, call, howl, roar, yell 5 blare, whoop 6 bellow, clamor, holler, scream, shriek 7 exclaim 10 vociferate

shove 3 dig, jab, jam 4 cram, poke, prod, push 5 drive, elbow, press 6 hustle, jostle, peddle, propel, thrust 8 bulldoze, shoulder

shovel 3 dig 4 grub 5 scoop, scuff, spade 6 dig out 7 scuffle, shamble, shuffle 8 excavate

shoveler 4 duck 9 broadbill

shovelhead 7 catfish

shove off 2 go 4 exit, quit 5 leave 6 depart, get off 7 pull out, take off 8 run along

show 3 air, get, say, see 4 cine, come, fair, film, lead, look, loom, mark, pomp, read 5 array, flash, flick, front, get in, guide, mount, movie, offer, pilot, prove, revue, sport, stage, steer, vaunt 6 appear, arrive, blazon, chance, direct, emerge, escort, evince, expose, flaunt, lay out, look-in, ostend, parade, record, reveal, set out, submit, turn up, unveil 7 conduct, display, disport, divulge, exhibit, fanfare, make out, panoply, picture, present, produce, proffer, project, seeming, trot out 8 brandish, disclose, evidence, flourish, indicate, manifest, occasion, proclaim, register, shepherd 9 determine, establish, photoplay, represent, semblance, spectacle 10 appearance, exhibition, exposition, illustrate, simulacrum 11 demonstrate, materialize, opportunity, performance 13 demonstration, motion picture, moving picture

Show Boat *author:* 6 Ferber *composer:* 4 Kern

showcase 7 exhibit, vitrine

shower 3 tub 4 hail, rain, wash 5 bathe, burst, party, salvo, spray, storm 7 barrage, shatter, spatter 8 downpour, rainfall 9 broadside, cannonade, fusillade 10 cloudburst 11 bombardment

showman 8 producer *famous:* 4 Cody 6 Barnum

Show Me State 8 Missouri

show off 4 brag 5 boast, flash 6 expose, flaunt, parade 7 display, disport, exhibit, swagger, trot out 8 brandish

showoff 6 hotdog 7 hotshot 13 exhibitionist

showpiece 3 gem 5 jewel, prize 11 chef d'oeuvre, masterpiece

show up 3 get 4 come 5 get in, reach 6 arrive, debunk, expose, turn up, unmask 7 uncloak, undress 8 discover, unshroud 9 discredit 10 invalidate

showy 3 gay 4 arty, loud 5 gaudy, jazzy, swank 6 chichi, flashy, garish, ornate, sporty, tawdry 7 opulent, splashy 8 gorgeous, overdone, peacocky 9 luxurious, sumptuous 10 flamboyant, peacockish 11 overwrought, pretentious, resplendent, sensational 12 meretricious, orchidaceous, ostentatious

shrapnel 8 fragment 10 projectile

shred 3 bit, dag, rag 4 iota 5 crumb, grate, ounce, scrap, shave, speck 6 sliver 7 modicum, smidgen 8 fragment, particle

shrew 5 harpy, scold, vixen, witch 6 amazon, ogress, rodent, virago 8 fishwife, she-devil, spitfire 9 termagant, Xanthippe

shrewd 3 sly 4 cagy, foxy, keen, tidy, wise 5 acute, cagey, canny, heady, sharp, slick, smart 6 argute, astute, clever, crafty, polite, smooth 7 knowing, probing, prudent 8 piercing, sensible 9 astucious, ingenious, judicious, sagacious 10 farsighted 11 foresighted, intelligent, penetrating, quick-witted 13 perspicacious

shriek 3 cry 4 yell 5 blare, shout 6 screak, scream, shrill, squawk, squeal 7 screech

shrill 4 high, keen, thin 5 acute, sharp 6 argute, piping, scream, shriek, squeal, treble 7 screech 8 piercing, strident

shrimp 4 runt 5 prawn 10 crustacean *combining form:* 5 caris

shrine 3 box 4 tomb 5 altar 6 temple 7 sanctum 9 holy place, reliquary, sanctuary 10 sanctorium *Buddhist:* 5 stupa 6 dagoba

shrink 3 shy 4 fail, funk, wane 5 cower, demur, quail, slink, start, wince 6 blanch, blench, boggle, cringe, crouch, flinch, huddle, recede, recoil, retire, weaken, wither 7 dwindle, retreat, scruple, squinch 8 compress, condense, contract, draw back, withdraw 9 constrict, fall short, shrivel up, waste away 11 concentrate

shrinking 3 shy 5 timid 7 aseptic 8 retiring 9 unaffable, withdrawn 10 restrained 11 unexpansive

shrive 4 free 5 purge 6 pardon 7 confess

shrivel 4 wilt 5 dry up, parch, wizen 6 welter, wither

Shropshire Lad author 8 Houseman

shroud 3 lop 4 hide, veil, wrap 5 cloak, close, cover, shade 6 enfold, enwrap, invest, screen 7 enclose, envelop, shut off, shut out 8 block out, cerement, obstruct 9 cerecloth

shrouded 5 privy 6 buried, covert, hidden 7 guarded 8 obscured, ulterior 9 concealed
shrub 3 lop 4 bush 5 elder, erica, hazel, plant, prune 6 cercis, muskit, privet 7 arboret, dyeweed, guayule 8 barberry, bluewood, boxthorn, inkberry, ironweed, rosebush 9 bearberry 10 bladdernut *Asian:* 4 bago 5 ramee, ramie 6 kerria 8 caragana, japonica 10 beauty bush *climbing:* 7 jasmine *combining form:* 5 thamn 6 thamno *desert:* 5 retem 6 alhagi 7 ephedra *dwarf:* 6 bonsai *East Indian:* 3 aal 4 sunn *European:* 4 cade 8 woodbind, woodbine *evergreen:* 3 box, kat, yew 4 ilex, khat, titi 5 furze, heath, holly, pyxie, savin, taxus, thuja, thuya, toyon, yapon 6 kalmia, laurel, myrtle, nandin, protea, sabine, savine, yaupon 7 boxwood, heather, jasmine, juniper, rosebay 8 lambkill, oleander, rosemary, tamarisk *flowering:* 5 lilac, ribes, tiara, wahoo 6 azalea, daphne, laurel, myrtle, spirea, wicopy 7 chamise, chamiso, fuchsia, mahonia, maybush, rhodora, spiraea, weigela 8 magnolia, mezereon, mezereum, nineback, oleander, oleaster, shadblow, shadbush, snowball, snowbell, snowbush, tomillo, viburnum, wistaria, wisteria *fragrant:* 4 mint, sage 5 thyme 8 rosemary 10 basil thyme *genus:* 4 Inga 7 Solanum 8 Euonymus *hardwood:* 6 cornel *Mexican:* 8 ocotillo *ornamental:* 6 privet 7 deutzia, jetbead, syringa, woodwax 9 bluebeard *pasture:* 8 cowberry *prickly:* 4 whin 5 briar, chico, furze, gorse 7 bramble, rhamnus 8 hawthorn, mesquite 9 buckthorn *South American:* 4 coca 7 rhatany *thicket:* 6 maquis 7 macchia 9 chaparral *tropical:* 4 kava 5 guava, henna 7 camelia, lantana 8 buddleia, camellia, gardenia 10 frangipani *West Indian:* 4 anil 7 acerola
shrug 6 jacket 7 gesture *off:* 5 evade 8 minimize
Shua *father:* 5 Heber *son-in-law:* 5 Judah
Shuah *father:* 7 Abraham *mother:* 7 Keturah
Shual's father 6 Zophah
shuck 3 pod 4 case, cast, hull, husk, junk, peel, shed, skin 5 chuck, ditch, scrap, shell, strip 6 reject, slough 7 discard 8 jettison 11 decorticate
shudder 5 quake, shake 6 dither, gyrate, quaver, quiver, shimmy, shiver, tremor 7 frisson, tremble, twitter
shuffle 4 hash, limp, mash 5 dodge, evade, hedge, scuff 6 jumble, jungle, litter, mess up, muddle, shovel, tumble, weasel 7 clutter, disrupt, disturb, rummage, shamble, stumble 8 disarray, disorder, mishmash, sidestep 9 dislocate, pussyfoot 10 disarrange, discompose, equivocate, tergiverse 11 disorganize 12 tergiversate
Shuham's father 3 Dan
shun 3 shy 4 duck, snub 5 avoid, elude, evade 6 double, escape, eschew, refuse, reject 7 decline, disdain
Shuni's father 3 Gad
shunt 4 move, turn 5 avert, shift 6 change, divert, switch 7 deflect, head off, shuttle 8 transfer 9 sidetrack
shush 4 hush 5 quiet, still 6 muffle, shut up 7 repress, silence, squelch 8 choke off, strangle, suppress
shut 4 lock, seal 5 close 6 fasten 7 confine 10 batten down *loudly:* 4 slam
Shute, Nevil *novel:* 7 Marazan 9 Pied Piper 10 On the Beach 11 So Disdained
Shuthelah's father 7 Ephraim
shut in 3 hem, pen 4 cage, coop, mure, wall 5 fence 6 immure 7 close in, confine, enclose, envelop 8 imprison
shut-in 7 invalid 12 convalescent
shut out 3 bar 5 close 6 screen, shroud 7 exclude 8 obstruct
shutter 5 blind 6 screen
shuttle 5 shunt 6 bobbin 9 alternate
shuttlecock 4 bird 6 birdie
shut up 3 gag 4 hush 5 dry up, quiet, shush, still 6 dumb up 7 dummy up, silence 8 choke off, pipe down 9 quiet down
shy 3 coy, gag, jib, pot 4 balk, bilk, duck, meek, shun, wary 5 avoid, chary, demur, elude, evade, loath, quail, scant, short, timid 6 afraid, averse, blench, boggle, demure, double, escape, eschew, modest, recoil, scanty, scarce, shrink 7 bashful, failing, fearful, lacking, nervous, potshot, rabbity, scruple, stickle, stumble, uneager, wanting 8 backward, cautious, hesitant, inturned, reserved, retiring, sheepish, skittish, timorous 9 conscious, deficient, diffident, introvert, reluctant, sideswipe, unassured, unwilling 10 backhanded, inadequate, indisposed, shamefaced, suspicious 11 circumspect, disinclined, introverted, unassertive 12 apprehensive, insufficient, introversive, self-effacing, unsufficient 13 self-conscious
Shylock 6 usurer 9 loan shark *daughter:* 7 Jessica
shyster 11 pettifogger
Siam see Thailand
Siamese coin see coin, *Thailand*
sib 3 kin 4 akin 6 sister 7 brother, kindred, related 8 relative
Sibbecai's victim 4 Saph
Sibelius composition 9 Finlandia
Siberian *antelope:* 5 saiga *dog:* 5 husky *gulf:* 2 Ob *native:* 5 Tatar, Yakut 6 Tar-

tar 9 Mongolian ***plain:*** 6 steppe ***storm:*** 5 buran ***tent:*** 4 yurt
sibilate 4 buzz, fizz, hiss, whiz 5 swish, whisk 6 fizzle, sizzle, wheeze 7 whisper
sibling 6 sister 7 brother
sibyl 4 seer 7 prophet 10 prophetess 13 fortune-teller
sic 2 so 4 abet, goad, prod, spur, thus, urge 5 egg on, favor, prick 6 exhort, prompt, propel 7 agitate 8 catalyze, inspirit 9 instigate
Sicilian ***secret organization:*** 5 Mafia ***volcano:*** 4 Etna
Sicily's capital 7 Palermo
sick 3 ill 4 down, mean, weak 5 amiss, fed up, funny, lousy, peaky, rocky, tired, weary 6 ailing, faulty, flawed, laid up, morbid, morose, peaked, rotten, unwell, wobbly 7 fevered 8 confined, diseased 9 defective, disgusted, imperfect, tottering, unhealthy 10 disordered, indisposed 11 debilitated
sicken 5 repel, upset 6 reluct, revolt 7 derange, disgust, repulse, unhinge 8 disorder, nauseate, unsettle
sickle 5 blade, mower 8 crescent
sickly 3 ill, low 4 down, mean, puny, weak 5 pecky 6 ailing, morbid, morose, offish, peaked, poorly, unwell 7 noisome, noxious, underly 8 diseased, off-color 9 unhealthy 10 indisposed, insalutary, unsalutary 11 unhealthful, unwholesome 12 insalubrious
sickness 3 ill 6 malady 7 ailment, disease, illness 8 disorder, syndrome, unhealth 9 affection, complaint, condition, infirmity 10 affliction, unwellness 12 diseasedness 13 indisposition, unhealthiness
sic transit gloria ___ 5 mundi
side 4 clad, face, hand, part, skin 5 angle, facet, flank, phase, slant, stand 6 aspect, sector, stance 7 outlook, posture, sheathe 8 attitude, position 9 direction, viewpoint 10 standpoint 11 disposition ***combining form:*** 5 later, pleur 6 lateri, latero, pleuri, pleuro ***sheltered:*** 3 lee
sideboard 5 table 6 buffet 8 credence ***for wine:*** 8 cellaret 10 cellarette
sideboards see **sideburns**
sideburns 9 burnsides 10 sideboards 11 dundrearies, muttonchops
side by side 8 together ***combining form:*** 3 par 4 para
sidekick 3 pal 7 partner 9 assistant, companion
sidereal 6 astral, starry 7 stellar
side road 5 byway 8 bystreet, shunpike
sidestep 4 duck 5 avoid, burke, dodge, evade, fence, hedge, parry, shirk, skirt 6 bypass, weasel 9 pussyfoot 10 circumvent, equivocate 12 tergiversate
sidetrack 5 shunt 6 divert, switch
sidewalk 6 paving 7 walkway 8 pavement 9 banquette
sidewhiskers see **sideburns**
side with 4 back 6 uphold 7 support 8 advocate, backstop, champion
sidle 4 ease, edge, slip 7 saunter
siege 4 bout 5 spell 6 attack 7 seizure 9 onslaught
Siegfried ***mother:*** 9 Sieglinde ***slayer:*** 5 Hagen ***sword:*** 7 Balmung ***vulnerable spot:*** 4 back 8 shoulder ***wife:*** 9 Kriemhild
Sienkiewicz novel 8 Quo Vadis
sierra 4 fish 5 range
siesta 3 nap 5 sleep 6 catnap, dog nap, snooze 10 forty winks
sieve 4 sift 5 clack, tabby 6 gossip, screen 8 colander, gossiper, quidnunc, strainer 10 talebearer
Sif's husband 4 Thor
sift 4 bolt, comb, cull, sort 5 probe, sieve 6 filter, go into, screen, winnow 7 dig into, explore 8 filtrate, look into, prospect, separate 9 delve into 11 inquire into, investigate
sigh 3 sob 4 ache, blow, gasp, howl, long, lust, moan, pant, pine, roar 5 crave, dream, groan, sough, whine 6 exhale, hanker, hunger, murmur, thirst, wheeze 7 breathe, respire, suspire, whisper, whistle
sight 3 aim, eye, spy 4 espy, look, mess, view 5 scene 6 fright, seeing, vision 7 eyesore, outlook 11 monstrosity ***combining form:*** 4 opsy 5 opsia, opsis ***relating to:*** 5 optic 6 ocular, visual 7 optical
sightseer 7 tourist 10 rubberneck
sign 3 cue, ink 4 flag, hint, mark, omen, show 5 index, proof, token, trace 6 motion, signal, symbol 7 earmark, endorse, exhibit, gesture, indicia, initial, symptom, vestige, warning 8 evidence, exponent, reminder 9 autograph, character, indicator, subscribe 10 expression, indication, suggestion 11 attestation 13 gesticulation, symbolization ***commercial:*** 4 neon ***directional:*** 5 arrow ***of the zodiac:*** (see **zodiac sign**)
signal 3 cue 4 flag 5 alarm, alert, siren 6 beckon, famous, marked, motion, tocsin, wigwag 7 eminent, gesture, salient 8 high sign, movement, peculiar, renowned, striking 9 arresting, arrestive, prominent 10 individual, noticeable, remarkable 11 conspicuous, distinctive, illustrious, outstanding ***distress:*** 3 SOS 6 Mayday
signature 3 ink 4 name, sign 9 autograph, subscribe 11 John Hancock ***flourish:*** 6 paraph
signet 4 ring, seal 5 stamp
significance 4 pith 5 merit, sense 6 credit, import, moment, virtue, weight 7 meaning, message, purport 8 prestige

9 authority, influence, magnitude 10 excellence, importance, intendment, perfection 11 acceptation, consequence, weightiness

significant 3 big 4 rich 5 sound, valid 6 cogent, facund 7 telling, weighty 8 eloquent, forceful, material, powerful 9 important, momentous 10 compelling, convincing, expressive, meaningful 11 sententious, substantial 12 considerable 13 consequential

signification 4 gist 5 sense 6 import 7 essence, meaning, message, purport 8 implying 9 substance 10 intendment 11 acceptation, implication 12 construction 13 understanding

signify 4 bear, mean, show 5 carry, count, spell, weigh 6 convey, denote, import, intend, matter 7 add up to, bespeak, connote, express, purport

sign over 4 cede, deed 5 alien 6 assign, remise 8 alienate, make over, transfer 10 abalienate

sign up 4 join 5 enter 6 enlist, enroll, join up, muster

Sigurd ***horse:*** 5 Grani ***slayer:*** 5 Hogni ***victim:*** 6 Fafnir ***wife:*** 6 Gudrun

Sigyn's husband 4 Loki

silage 6 fodder

silence 3 gag 4 calm, dumb, hush, lull, mute 5 death, quash, quell, quiet, shush, sleep, still 6 dampen, deaden, demise, muffle, muzzle, shut up, squash 7 decease, passing, quietus, secrecy, squelch 8 choke off, curtains, hush-hush, quietude, suppress 9 quietness, stillness

silent 3 mum 4 dumb, hush, mute 5 close, muted, quiet, still, tacit, whist 6 curbed, stilly 7 checked, hushful 8 reserved, reticent, taciturn, unspoken, unvoiced, wordless 9 inhibited, noiseless, secretive, soundless, unuttered, voiceless 10 incoherent, restrained, speechless, tongue-tied, unsociable 11 close-lipped, shut-mouthed, tight-lipped, unexpressed 12 close-mouthed, close-tongued, inarticulate, tight-mouthed

silhouette 4 line 6 shadow 7 contour, outline, profile 9 lineament, lineation 10 figuration 11 delineation

silicon ***symbol:*** 2 Si

silk 5 fiber, honan 7 foulard 8 sarcenet, sarsenet ***fabric:*** 4 gros 5 caffa, ninon, Pekin, satin, surah, tulle 6 cendal, mantua, pongee, samite, sendal, tussah 7 taffeta, tussore ***factory:*** 8 filature ***hat:*** 6 topper ***maker:*** 4 worm 7 thrower ***raw:*** 5 grège 6 greige ***source:*** 6 cocoon ***waste:*** 4 noil 5 floss ***wild:*** 6 tussah 7 tussore ***yarn:*** 4 tram

silkworm 3 eri 6 bombyx, tussah 7 tussore 8 bombycid

sill 5 bench, ledge, shelf 9 threshold

silliness 5 folly 7 inanity 8 insanity 9 absurdity, craziness, dottiness 11 foolishness, witlessness 12 illogicality 13 senselessness

silly 3 off 4 daft 5 crazy, daffy, dizzy, empty, funny, giddy, loony, sappy, wacky 6 absurd, insane, simple, unwise 7 asinine, fatuous, flighty, foolish, unwitty, vacuous, witless 8 ignorant 9 fantastic, nitwitted, senseless 10 bird-witted, irrational, weak-headed, weak-minded 11 empty-headed, harebrained, light-headed, sheep-headed 12 preposterous, unreasonable 13 rattle-brained, unintelligent

silt 4 scum, soil 5 dregs 7 deposit, residue 8 sediment

silver 4 coin 5 money, shiny 6 argent, dulcet 7 bullion, element 8 argentum, flatware, lustrous, sterling 9 argentine, tableware ***relating to:*** 5 lunar 8 argentic 9 argentine, argentous ***symbol:*** 2 Ag

silverfish 6 insect, tarpon

silver fox 5 caama

silversmith 6 Revere

silver-tongued 4 glib 7 voluble 8 eloquent

silvery 6 argent 7 frosted, shining 9 argentate, argentine, argentous, brilliant 10 glittering, shimmering

Silvia's beloved 9 Valentine

Simeon ***father:*** 5 Jacob ***mother:*** 4 Leah ***son:*** 4 Ohad 6 Nemuel

simian 3 ape 6 monkey 10 anthropoid

similar 4 akin, like 5 alike 6 agnate 7 uniform 8 parallel, suchlike 9 analogous, consonant 10 comparable, reciprocal 11 correlative 13 complementary, corresponding ***combining form:*** 3 hol, hom 4 holo, home, homo 5 homeo, homoe, homoi 6 homoeo, homoio

similarity 6 simile 7 analogy 8 affinity, likeness, parallel 9 alikeness, closeness, collation, semblance 10 comparison, similitude, synonymity 11 association, coincidence, correlation, resemblance

similarly 2 so 4 also 8 likewise

simile 7 analogy 8 affinity, likeness, metaphor 9 alikeness, semblance 10 comparison, similarity, similitude 11 resemblance ***word:*** 2 as 4 like

similitude 4 copy 6 double, simile 7 analogy, replica 8 affinity, likeness, metaphor 9 alikeness, semblance 10 comparison, similarity 11 resemblance

simmer 4 boil, stew, stir 5 churn 6 bubble, seethe 7 ferment, parboil, smolder

simmer down 4 cool 7 collect, compose, control, repress, smother, subside 8 restrain, suppress 9 quiet down, re-collect

Simon ***brother:*** 5 Jesus 6 Andrew

father: 5 Jonah *new name:* 5 Peter *son:* 5 Judas, Rufus 9 Alexander
Simon ___ 5 Magus 6 Legree 8 of Cyrene 9 the Zealot
Simon Maccabeus *father:* 10 Mattathias *nickname:* 6 Thassi *slayer:* 7 Ptolemy
simp 5 dunce 6 dimwit, nitwit 7 lackwit, pinhead, wantwit 13 featherweight
simper 5 smirk
simple 4 dull, dumb, dupe, easy, mere, pure, slow, soft 5 crass, dense, dopey, light, naive, plain, royal, sheer, silly, stark 6 doting, facile, modest, smooth, spoony, stupid 7 artless, asinine, fatuous, foolish, idiotic, moronic, natural, perfect, unmixed, unwitty, witless 8 absolute, backward, childish, discreet, gullible, ignorant, imbecile, mindless, retarded, trusting, unartful, untaught 9 brainless, childlike, credulous, dim-witted, ingenuous, nitwitted, senseless, unalloyed, unstudied 10 effortless, half-witted, illiterate, slow-witted, unaffected, uneducated, unschooled, weak-headed, weak-minded 11 fundamental, inelaborate, sheepheaded, undecorated, unelaborate, unmitigated, unqualified 12 feebleminded, unartificial, unbeautified, uncompounded, unornamented 13 inexperienced, unadulterated, unintelligent, unpretentious, untroublesome *combining form:* 3 api 4 aplo, hapl 5 haplo
simpleminded 4 dull, slow 6 stupid 7 moronic 8 imbecile, retarded 9 dim-witted 10 half-witted, slow-witted
simpleton 4 dolt, fool, zany 5 ament, dummy, dunce, idiot, moron 6 cretin, stupid 7 bungler, dullard, half-wit, natural 8 dullhead, dumbbell, imbecile 9 ignoramus
simplify 6 reduce 7 abridge, clarify, clean up, cut down, shorten 8 boil down 10 disinvolve, streamline, unscramble 11 disentangle 13 straighten out
simply 3 but 4 just, only 6 merely
simulacrum 4 copy, face, show, spit 5 guise, image 6 double, ersatz, ringer 7 picture, seeming, showing 8 portrait 9 imitation, semblance 10 appearance 13 spitting image
simulate 3 act, ape 4 copy, fake, pose, sham 5 bluff, favor, feign, mimic, put on 6 affect, assume 7 imitate, play-act, pretend 8 resemble 11 counterfeit
simulated 4 fake, mock, sham 5 dummy, false, phony 6 ersatz 8 spurious 9 imitation 10 artificial, fictitious, substitute
simultaneous 6 coeval 8 agreeing 10 coetaneous, coexistent, coexisting, coinciding, concurrent, concurring, synchronal, synchronic 11 synchronous 12 contemporary
simultaneously 6 at once 8 together 12 coincidently, concurrently
sin 3 err 4 debt, evil, tort 5 crime, fault, wrong 6 offend 7 demerit 8 iniquity, trespass 9 diablerie 10 deficiency, transgress, wickedness, wrongdoing 11 shortcoming 12 imperfection *deadly:* 4 envy, lust 5 anger, pride, sloth 8 gluttony 12 covetousness
Sin 7 moon-god *daughter:* 6 Ishtar *son:* 7 Shamash *wife:* 6 Ningal
since 2 as 3 for 4 next 5 after, below 6 behind, seeing 7 because, whereas 8 as long as 9 following 10 inasmuch as 11 considering 12 subsequent to *Scottish:* 4 syne
sincere 4 dear, open, real, true 5 frank, meant, plain 6 actual, candid, devout, hearty, honest 7 genuine, serious 8 bona fide, faithful, heartful, truthful 9 authentic, heartfelt, unfeigned 10 aboveboard, forthright, heart-whole, unaffected 11 undesigning, whole-souled 12 frankhearted, undissembled, wholehearted 13 unpretentious
sincerity 6 candor 8 goodwill 9 bona fides, good faith 11 earnestness
sinecure 4 snap 5 cinch
sine qua non 4 must 9 condition, essential, necessity, requisite 11 requirement 12 precondition, prerequisite
sinew 5 force, might, power 6 energy, muscle, tendon 7 potency 8 strength
sinewy 4 ropy, wiry 5 tough 6 brawny, strong, sturdy 7 fibrous, stringy 8 athletic, muscular 9 tenacious
sinful 3 bad, low 4 base, evil, vile 5 amiss, wrong 6 guilty, unholy, wicked 7 immoral, peccant, vicious 8 blamable, blameful, culpable, damnable, shameful 9 reprobate 10 censurable, iniquitous 11 blameworthy, disgraceful 13 demeritorious, reprehensible
sing 3 hum 4 hymn, lilt, lull, tune 5 carol, chant, croon, yodel 6 intone, warble 7 confess, descant, lullaby 8 serenade, vocalize 10 cantillate
singe 4 burn, char 6 scorch
singer 4 alto, bass 5 tenor 6 cantor 7 crooner, soloist, songman, soprano 8 baritone, choirboy, songster, vocalist 9 balladeer, balladier, chorister *cabaret:* 11 chansonnier *female:* 9 chanteuse, chantress 10 cantatrice *opera:* 4 diva 5 buffa, buffo *religious:* 6 cantor
singing *exercise:* 7 solfège *group:* 4 duet, trio 5 choir 6 chorus 7 quartet *voice:* 4 alto, bass 5 tenor 7 soprano 8 baritone 9 contralto 12 mezzo-soprano
single 3 hit, one 4 free, lone, only, open, sole 5 frank, plain, unwed 6 candid, maiden, screen, unique, virgin 7 base hit, special 8 celibate, distinct, especial, sepa-

rate, singular, solitary, specific, unshared 9 exclusive, unmarried 10 individual, particular, spouseless, unattached, unfettered ***combining form:*** 3 apl, mon 4 aplo, hapl, mono 5 haplo ***prefix:*** 3 uni

single-minded 4 open 5 frank, plain, rigid 6 candid 7 adamant, bigoted, die-hard 8 obdurate 9 unbending 10 brassbound, inexorable, inflexible, relentless, unyielding

single out 4 cull, mark, pick, take 5 elect 6 choose, optate, opt for, prefer, select

singular 3 odd 4 lone, only, rare, sole, solo 5 alone, queer, weird 6 unique 7 bizarre, certain, curious, oddball, strange, unusual 8 definite, discrete, peculiar, solitary, uncommon, unwonted 9 exclusive 10 individual, outlandish, particular, respective, unexampled, unordinary 11 exceptional 13 extraordinary

singularity 5 seity, unity 7 ipseity, oneness, selfdom 8 identity, selfhood, selfness 10 singleness 11 personality 13 individualism, individuality, particularity

singularize 4 mark 7 qualify 9 signalize 11 distinguish, individuate 12 characterize 13 individualize

sinister 4 dark, dire, evil 6 malign 7 baleful, doomful, fateful, malefic, ominous 8 lowering, menacing 9 ill boding, ill-omened, malicious 10 maleficent, portentous 11 apocalyptic, threatening 12 inauspicious, unpropitious

sink 3 dip, pit, ram, rot, run, sag, set, sty 4 dive, pool, stab 5 abase, basin, demit, drive, droop, lower, slump, Sodom, stoop 6 bemean, debase, demean, go down, hollow, humble, plunge, thrust, worsen 7 cesspit, decline, degrade, depress, descend, founder, go under, let down, subside, torpedo 8 cast down, cesspool, hellhole, submerge, submerse 9 concavity, humiliate 10 degenerate, depression, disimprove, retrograde 11 deteriorate, pandemonium 12 Augean stable, disintegrate

sinker 4 drop 5 pitch 6 weight

sinkhole 3 dip, sag 5 basin 6 hollow 8 cesspool 9 concavity 10 depression

sinless 4 pure 8 innocent

Sinn ____ 4 Fein

sinuous 4 wavy 5 shaky 7 twisted, winding 8 flexuous, tortuous 9 meandrous 10 convoluted, meandering, serpentine 11 anfractuous, snake-shaped

sinus 6 cavity, hollow, recess

Sioux 6 Dakota ***chief:*** 8 Red Cloud 10 Crazy Horse 11 Sitting Bull

sip 4 toss 5 drink, quaff, sup up, taste 6 imbibe, sup off 7 swallow

siphon 3 tap 4 draw, pipe, pump 5 carry, draft, drain 6 convoy, funnel 7 channel, conduct, draw off, traject 8 transmit

sir 4 lord 5 title 6 knight, mister 9 gentleman

sire 4 lord 5 beget, breed, hatch, maker, spawn 6 author, create, father, parent 7 creator, founder, produce 8 generate, inventor 9 architect, generator, originate, patriarch, procreate 10 originator 11 progenerate

siren 4 vamp 7 charmer, drawing, enticer, Lorelei 8 alluring, magnetic 9 seductive, temptress 10 attracting, attractive, bewitching, enchanting, seductress 11 captivating, fascinating, femme fatale

Siren 5 Ligea 8 Leucosia 10 Parthenope ***German:*** 7 Lorelei

siren song 4 bait, lure, trap 5 decoy, snare 6 come-on 10 allurement, enticement, seducement, temptation

sissy 4 baby 6 prissy 7 doormat, epicene, milksop, unmanly 8 weakling 9 jellyfish 10 effeminate, pantywaist 11 Milquetoast, mollycoddle

sister 3 nun 4 girl 7 sibling 8 relative

Sister Carrie author 7 Dreiser

sisterly 7 sororal

Sisyphus ***brother:*** 7 Athamas 9 Salmoneus ***father:*** 6 Aeolus ***mother:*** 7 Enarete ***son:*** 7 Glaucus

sit 4 meet, open, pose, rest, seat 5 brood, cover, perch, squat 6 settle 7 convene, install, posture 8 ensconce

Sita ***abductor:*** 6 Ravana ***husband, rescuer:*** 4 Rama

sit down 4 land 5 light, perch, roost 6 alight, settle 9 touch down

site 3 dig 4 home, spot 5 haunt, locus, place, point, range, scene, where 6 locale 7 habitat, station 8 locality, location, position

sit-in 7 protest

sitting 6 séance 7 session ***prolonged:*** 8 sederunt

Sitting Bull's tribe 5 Sioux

sitting duck 4 butt, mark 6 target

situate 3 put, set 4 site 5 place 6 locate 8 position

situation 3 job 4 mode, post, rank, site, spot 5 berth, locus, place, point, state, where 6 billet, office, status 7 bargain, footing, posture, station 8 location, position, standing 9 condition

situs 5 place

Siva see Shiva

six ***combining form:*** 3 hex, sex 4 hexa, sexi 5 sexti ***group of:*** 5 hexad 6 hexade, sestet, sextet 7 sestole, sextole 8 sestolet, sextette 9 sextuplet ***on a die:*** 4 sice ***relating to:*** 6 senary

sixfold 9 sextuplex

six-shooter 3 gun 6 pistol 8 revolver
sixth sense 3 ESP
sizable 3 big 4 good 5 hefty, large, major 8 sensible 9 extensive 10 giant-sized, large-scale 11 respectable 12 considerable
size 4 area, body, bulk, mass 5 width 6 extent, height, length, spread, volume 7 bigness, breadth, expanse, measure, stretch 9 amplitude, dimension, extension, greatness, largeness, magnitude 10 dimensions, proportion 11 measurement
sizzle 3 fry 4 buzz, fizz, hiss, sear, whiz 5 swish, whish 6 wheeze, whoosh 8 sibilate
sizzling 3 hot 5 fiery 6 baking, red-hot, torrid 7 burning 8 broiling, scalding, white-hot 9 scorching
skald 4 bard, poet
Skanda 6 war-god ***brother:*** 6 Ganesa 7 Ganesha ***father:*** 4 Siva 5 Shiva
skate 4 fish, skid 5 glide, slide 6 fellow ***blade:*** 6 runner ***kind:*** 6 figure, hockey
skating site 3 ice 4 rink
skedaddle 3 fly, run 4 bolt, flee, kite, skip 5 scoot, scram, screw, skirr, split 6 begone, cut out, decamp, get out 7 make off, scamper, skiddoo, take off, vamoose 8 clear out, hightail
skeleton 5 bones, draft, frame 6 sketch 7 diagram, outline 9 framework ***marine:*** 5 coral, shell
skeptic 5 cynic 7 doubter, scoffer, zetetic 8 agnostic 10 headshaker, Pyrrhonian, Pyrrhonist, questioner, unbeliever 11 disbeliever
skeptical 6 show-me 7 cynical 8 aporetic, doubtful, doubting 9 quizzical 10 dissenting, suspicious 11 incredulous, mistrustful, questioning, unbelieving 12 disbelieving, freethinking
skepticism 5 doubt, qualm 6 wonder 7 concern, dubiety 8 mistrust 9 dubiosity, suspicion 11 incertitude, uncertainty
skerry 4 isle, reef
sketch 4 draw, line, plot 5 draft, trace 7 aperpçu 6 depict, design, detail, lay out, map out, précis, survey 7 develop, diagram, outline, pandect, sylloge 8 block out, chalk out, rough out, skeleton, syllabus 9 adumbrate, blueprint, delineate 10 compendium 11 skeletonize 12 characterize 13 diagrammatize
sketchy 5 rough 7 cursory, shallow 8 skeletal 9 depthless 11 superficial
skew 3 dip 4 bias, skid, slip, slue, veer 5 angle, sheer, slant, slide 6 swerve 8 train off
skewer 3 rod 4 spit 5 lance, spear, spike 6 impale, skiver 8 transfix 9 brochette 11 transpierce
ski 5 glide, slide ***lift:*** 4 J-bar, T-bar 5 chair 7 gondola
skid 3 dip 4 drop, fall, skew, slue, veer 5 sheer, slide 6 plunge, tumble 7 plummet, spinout 8 nose-dive
skid row 4 slum 6 bowery
skier ***American:*** 4 Kidd 5 Mahre ***Austrian:*** 6 Proell 7 Klammer, Schranz ***expert:*** 6 kanone ***French:*** 5 Killy ***Italian:*** 6 Theoni ***Swedish:*** 8 Stenmark
skiff 4 boat 7 rowboat
skiing ***area:*** 3 run 5 slope ***cross-country:*** 7 touring ***event:*** 6 schuss, slalom 8 downhill 11 giant slalom ***horse-drawn:*** 9 skijoring ***kind:*** 6 Alpine, Nordic ***position:*** 7 vorlage ***technique:*** 6 wedeln 8 snowplow, traverse ***turn:*** 7 christy 8 christie
skill 3 art 5 craft, knack 7 ability, address, command, cunning, know-how, mastery, prowess, sleight 8 deftness 9 dexterity, expertise, expertism, readiness 10 adroitness, expertness, mastership 13 dexterousness ***combining form:*** 6 techno, techny ***suffix:*** 3 ics 4 ship
skillet 3 pan 6 frypan, spider 9 frying pan
skillful 4 deft, good 5 adept, crack 6 adroit, clever, daedal, expert, master, pretty, wicked 7 learned, skilled, versant 8 masterly 9 masterful, workmanly 10 proficient, well-versed 11 crackerjack, workmanlike
skim 3 dap, fly 4 dart, kiss, sail, scud, skip 5 brush, carom, float, graze, shave, shoot, skirr 6 glance 8 ricochet
skimpy 3 shy 4 poor 5 scant, short, spare 6 meager, scanty, scarce, scrimp, sparse 7 failing, scrimpy, wanting 8 exiguous 9 deficient 10 inadequate 12 insufficient
skim through 4 scan 6 browse 8 glance at 10 glance over
skin 3 fur, gyp, pod, rap 4 clad, clip, face, fell, hide, pare, peel, pelt, rind, side, soak 5 blame, cheat, cover, fleet, haste, hurry, knock, miser, nabal, scale, stick, stiff, strip 6 barrel, bucket, bullet, con man, fleece, hasten, hustle, sheath, slough 7 beeline, censure, condemn, diddler, grifter, niggard, scrooge, sharper, sheathe 8 denounce, highball, swindler, tightwad 9 criticize, defrauder, dermatous, excoriate, reprehend, reprobate, sheathing 10 cheapskate, denunciate, overcharge 11 cheeseparer, decorticate, excorticate, flimflammer ***animal:*** 4 coat, hide, pelt 6 hackle, peltry ***bird:*** 7 pteryla ***combining form:*** 3 cut 4 cuti, derm, scyt 5 derma, dermo, dermy, scyto 6 dermat, dermia, dermis 7 cutaneo, dermata (plural), dermato, epiderm 8 epidermo ***depression:*** 6 dimple ***disease:*** 4 acne 5 hives, mange 6 eczema 10 dermatitis

dry: 5 scurf *fold:* 5 plica *layer:* 5 derma 6 corium, dermis 7 corneum, cuticle 9 epidermis *opening:* 4 pore *protuberance:* 4 mole, wart 6 pimple *rabbit:* 5 coney *relating to:* 6 dermal 9 cuticular, epidermal *seal:* 5 sculp *spot:* 7 freckle *tumor:* 3 wen

skinflint 5 chuff, miser, nabal 7 niggard 8 muckworm, tightwad 10 cheapskate 11 cheeseparer

skink 4 soup 6 lizard

skinny 4 bony, lank, lean 5 gaunt, lanky, spare, weedy 6 twiggy 7 angular, scraggy, scrawny 8 rawboned, skeletal 9 emaciated

Skin of Our Teeth author 6 Wilder

skip 3 dap, fly, hop, run 4 bolt, flee, jump, leap, lope, skim, trip 5 blank, bound, caper, carom, chasm, frisk, graze, scoot, skirr 6 bounce, cavort, curvet, gambol, glance, spring 7 make off, scamper, skitter 8 omission, overlook, ricochet 9 oversight, skedaddle 10 hippety-hop

skipjack 3 top 4 fish 6 beetle 8 sailboat

skipper 6 leader 7 captain 9 commander

skirl 6 scream, shriek

skirmish 4 fray 5 brush, clash, melee, run-in, set-to 6 affray, ambush, attack, mellay 7 assault 9 encounter, scrimmage 10 velitation

skirr 3 fly, run 4 bolt, dart, flee, sail, scud, skim, skip 5 float, scoot, shoot 7 make off, scamper 9 skedaddle

skirt 3 hem, rim 4 brim, duck, edge, skip 5 avoid, bound, brink, burke, dodge, elude, evade, hedge, verge 6 border, bypass, define, detour, escape, fringe, ignore, margin 7 garment 8 sidestep, surround 9 perimeter, periphery 10 circumvent, equivocate *ballet:* 4 tutu *feature:* 3 hem 4 slit *long:* 4 maxi *Scottish:* 4 kilt *short:* 4 mini *style:* 5 A-line

skit 3 act 4 jibe 5 caper, taunt 6 parody, shtick, sketch 7 schtick 9 burlesque

skitter 3 hop 4 lope, skip, trip 6 spring

skittery see **skitterish**

skittish 4 edgy 5 dizzy, giddy 7 flighty, nervous, restive 8 agitable, unstable, volatile 9 alarmable, excitable, frivolous, startlish 10 capricious, unreliable

skivvies 9 underwear

skoal 5 drink, toast

skua 4 bird 6 jaeger

skulduggery 8 foul play, trickery

skulk 4 lurk, slip 5 creep, shirk, slink, sneak, steal 7 gumshoe 9 pussyfoot

skull 4 bone, head, mind 5 brain 7 cranium 8 brainpan 9 braincase *back of:* 7 occiput *bone:* 5 vomer 6 zygoma 7 ethmoid, frontal 8 parietal, sphenoid, temporal *jawless:* 9 calvarium *joint:* 6 suture *part:* 3 jaw 5 inion 6 basion

skullcap 5 calot 6 beanie, pileus 7 calotte 8 yarmulke 9 calvarium, zucchetto

skunk 3 cur, dog 4 beat, drub, lick, scum, snot, toad, whip 5 snake 6 thrash 7 polecat, shellac 8 conepate, lambaste 9 overwhelm *genus:* 8 Mephitis

sky 5 azure 6 heaven, welkin 7 heavens 8 empyrean 9 firmament *combining form:* 4 uran 5 urano *sky-blue:* 5 azure 8 cerulean 9 caerulean

sky chief 5 pilot

skylarking 5 revel 7 fooling, revelry, wassail, whoopee, whoopla, whoop-up 9 high jinks, horseplay, revelment, rowdiness, whoop-de-do 10 roughhouse 12 roughhousing

skylight 6 window

skyline 7 horizon

sky pilot 5 padre 6 cleric, divine, parson 8 chaplain, clerical, minister, preacher 9 churchman, clergyman 12 ecclesiastic

skyrocket 4 rise, soar 5 climb 7 shoot up 8 upspring

sky sighting 3 UFO

slab 3 bar, rod 4 tile 5 ingot, slice, stick, strip 6 billet

slabber 5 drool 6 drivel, slaver 7 dribble 8 salivate

slack 3 lax, off 4 down, ease, lazy, slow, soft, weak 5 inert, loose, relax 6 feeble, infirm, loosen, remiss, slow-up 7 ease off, laggard, passive, relaxed 8 careless, derelict, dilatory, fainéant, inactive, indolent, slothful, slowdown, sluggish, stagnant, unsteady 9 leisurely, lethargic, negligent, untighten

slacken 3 ebb, lax 4 ease, fall, mire, wane 5 abate, delay, embog, let up, loose, relax 6 detain, hang up, loosen, relent, retard, slow up 7 bog down, die away, die down, ease off, set back, subside 8 moderate, slow down 9 untighten 10 decelerate

slacker 5 idler 6 loafer 7 shirker, slinker 8 slugabed, sluggard 9 goldbrick

slag 4 lava 5 dross 6 cinder, debris, scoria

slake 5 allay 6 deaden, quench 7 crumble, hydrate, satisfy

slam 3 bat, dig, hit, jab, rap 4 bang, bash, beat, belt, blow, boom, clap, ding, drub, flay, mace, slug, slur, swat, wham 5 blast, burst, crack, crash, fling, knock, pound, slash, slate, smack, smash, swipe, whack 6 batter, cudgel, hammer, scathe, strike, thwack, wallop 7 clobber, obloquy, potshot, scourge 8 lambaste, lash into 9 aspersion, bastinado, castigate, stricture

slammer 3 jug, pen 4 jail 6 cooler, prison

slander 4 hurt, slur, tale 5 belie, libel, smear 6 assail, attack, damage, defame, injure, malign 7 asperse, calumny, scandal, traduce 8 muckrake, roorback, strumpet, tear down **9** black wash, denigrate **10** backbiting, calumniate, defamation, detraction, muckraking **11** mud-slinging **12** back-stabbing, belittlement, depreciation **13** disparagement

slang **4** cant **5** argot, lingo **6** jargon, patois, patter **7** dialect **10** vernacular

slant **3** aim, tip **4** bank, bend, bias, cant, heel, lean, list, side, skew, tilt, veer, warp **5** angle, aside, bevel, color, focus, grade, point, slope, splay, train, twist **6** aslope, direct, orient, swerve **7** decline, descend, deviate, distort, diverge, incline, leaning, outlook, recline **8** gradient, sideways, sidewise **9** direction, influence, obliquely, prejudice, viewpoint **10** standpoint **11** concentrate, inclination **12** predilection ***combining form:*** **4** clin **5** clino

slap **3** box, hit, pop, try **4** bash, blip, chop, cuff, drub, flay, poke, shot, slam, stab, swat, wham **5** clout, crack, fling, punch, score, slash, smack, spank, whack, whirl **6** buffet, insult, scathe, strike **7** affront, despite, scourge **8** haymaker, lambaste, lash into **9** castigate, contumely, indignity

slapdash **5** messy **6** botchy, random, sloppy, untidy **7** aimless **8** careless, slipshod, slovenly **9** desultory, haphazard, hit-or-miss, irregular **10** designless, unthorough

slaphappy **7** foolish **8** carefree, reckless **10** punch-drunk

slash **3** cut **4** clip, flay, gash, hack, pare, slit **5** lower, shave, slice **6** hackle, haggle, incise, pierce, reduce, scathe, scorch **7** abridge, blister, curtail, cut back, cut down, scarify, scourge, shorten **8** lambaste, lash into, mark down, retrench **9** castigate, excoriate **10** abbreviate

slasher **5** knife, razor, sword **9** swordsman **12** swashbuckler

slat **4** lath **5** board, stave, strip **6** louver **7** airfoil **9** sheepskin

slate **4** gray, list, rock, tile **6** record, tablet, ticket **7** shingle **8** schedule **9** designate

slaughter **4** kill, maim, slay **6** mangle, murder **7** butcher, carnage, torture, wipe out **8** butchery, decimate, hecatomb, massacre, mutilate **9** bloodbath, bloodshed **10** annihilate **11** destruction, exterminate **12** annihilation

slaughterhouse **8** abattoir

Slav **4** Pole, Serb, Sorb, Wend **5** Croat, Czech **6** Bulgar, Slovak **7** Russian, Serbian, Slovene **8** Bohemian, Croatian, Moravian **9** Bulgarian, Ruthenian, Ukrainian

slave **4** grub, help, peon, plod, serf, slog, toil **5** grind, helot **6** drudge, menial, thrall, toiler, vassal **7** bondman, chattel, servant **8** bondsman **9** dray horse, mancipium, workhorse ***feudal:*** **4** serf ***harem:*** **9** odalisque ***liberated:*** **8** freedman ***Muslim:*** **8** Mameluke ***Spartan:*** **5** helot

slave driver **6** tyrant **8** martinet, rawhider **10** taskmaster **11** Simon Legree

slaver **4** fawn, spit **5** cower, drool, toady, water **6** cringe, drivel, grovel, kowtow, saliva **7** dribble, honey up, slabber, slobber, spittle, truckle **8** bootlick, salivate

slavery **4** moil, toil, work, yoke **5** grind, labor **6** drudge, thrall **7** bondage, helotry, peonage, serfdom **8** bullwork, drudgery, plugging **9** servitude, thralldom, villenage **10** donkeywork

Slavic apostle **5** Cyril **9** Methodius

slavish **3** low **4** hard, tame **5** apish, heavy, rough **6** knotty, menial, rugged **7** operose, servile, subdued **8** obeisant, wretched **9** difficult, emulative, imitative, laborious, miserable, spineless, strenuous **10** formidable, obsequious, uninspired, unoriginal **11** subservient

slay **4** do in, down, kill **6** cut off, finish, lay low, murder **7** butcher, destroy, execute, put away **8** dispatch, knock off **9** liquidate, slaughter **11** assassinate

slayer **4** bane **6** killer **8** homicide, murderer

sleazy **3** low **4** mean, thin **5** cheap, dingy, seedy, tacky, tatty **6** cheesy, common, flabby, flimsy, floppy, paltry, shabby, shoddy, slight, trashy **7** flaccid, run-down, tenuous **9** gossamery **10** broken-down, down-at-heel **11** dilapidated **12** disreputable

sled **4** luge, pung **6** sleigh **7** coaster, travois **8** toboggan ***Russian:*** **6** troika

sled dog **5** husky **8** malamute

sledge **6** hammer, sleigh ***Eskimo:*** **7** komatik

sleek **4** oily **5** round, slick **6** glassy, glossy, polish, refine, smarmy, smooth **7** perfect **8** lustrous, polished **10** glistening

sleep **3** nap **4** coma, doze, rest **5** death, relax, sopor **6** demise, repose, siesta, snooze, torpor **7** decease, languor, passing, quietus, shut-eye, silence, slumber **8** dullness, hebetude, lethargy **9** lassitude, torpidity **10** defunction, torpidness **11** dissolution, slumberland ***bringer:*** **7** sandman ***combining form:*** **4** hypn, narc **5** hypno, narco, somni ***god:*** **6** Hypnos, Hypnus, Somnus

sleeper **4** beam **7** Pullman, support **8** dormeuse, long shot

sleeping **4** abed **7** dormant **8** comatose ***disease:*** **10** narcolepsy

sleeplessness **8** insomnia

sleepwalker **12** somnambulist

sleepy **4** dozy **5** dazed, dopey, inert, quiet **6** drowsy, opiate, snoozy, torpid **7** nodding, passive, poppied, yawning

8 comatose, hypnotic, inactive, listless, narcotic, oscitant, sleeping, sluggish, slumbery, somnific 9 heavy-eyed, lethargic, somnolent, soporific 10 nepenthean, slumbering, slumberous, somnorific 11 somniferous

sleigh 4 pung, sled 6 sledge

sleight 4 play, ploy, ruse, wile 5 skill, trick 6 device 7 address, gimmick, prowess 8 artifice, deftness, maneuver 9 dexterity, readiness, stratagem 10 adroitness 13 dexterousness

sleight of hand 5 magic, trick 9 dexterity 11 legerdemain

slender 4 lean, slim, thin, trim 5 lithe, reedy, scant, short, small 6 remote, scanty, scarce, skinny, slight, stalky, svelte, twiggy 7 outside, spindly, squinny, tenuous, wanting 8 slimmish 9 attenuate, deficient 10 inadequate, negligible 12 insufficient

sleuth 3 tec 4 dick 7 gumshoe 8 hawkshaw, Sherlock 9 detective 10 private eye 12 investigator

slice 3 cut, lot 4 bite, gash, part, slit 5 carve, quota, sever, share, slash, split 6 cleave, incise, pierce, sunder 7 dissect, partage, portion, segment 8 dissever 9 allotment, allowance

slick 4 oily, slip, wise 5 canny, fix up, glide, quick, round, sharp, sleek, slide, smart, soapy, spiff 6 doll up, glossy, greasy, polish, refine, slippy, smarmy, smooth 7 deck out, doll out, dress up, fulsome, gussy up, knowing, perfect, slither 8 glissade, slippery, slithery, spruce up, unctious, unctuous 10 lubricious, oleaginous 11 quick-witted, sharp-witted

slicker 4 dude 6 gypper 7 cheater, diddler, oilskin, sharper 8 raincoat, swindler 9 defrauder, trickster 11 flimflammer

slide 3 dip, sag 4 drop, fall, flow, lurk, move, skid, slip 5 chute, coast, crawl, creep, drift, glide, shift, shirk, skate, skulk, slick, slink, slump, sneak, spill, steal 6 stream, tumble 7 decline, drop off, fall off, slither 8 downturn, fall away, glissade 9 downswing, downtrend

slight 4 fail, omit, skip, slim, thin 5 flout, reedy, scoff, small 6 flimsy, forget, ignore, remote, sleazy, stalky, subtle, twiggy 7 blink at, contemn, despise, neglect, outside, slender, squinny, tenuous 8 delicate, discount, overlook, overpass, smallish 9 attenuate, blink away, disregard, gossamery, pint-sized 10 negligible

slim 4 thin 5 canny, lithe, reedy, small 6 adroit, clever, narrow, remote, skinny, slight, stalky, svelte, twiggy 7 cunning, lissome, outside, slender, squinny, tenuous 9 attenuate, dexterous, ingenious, lithesome 10 negligible

slim down 4 diet 6 reduce 10 slenderize

slime 3 mud 4 muck, ooze, scum, slum 6 sludge *combining form:* 3 myx 4 myxa, myxo

slimy 4 oozy, vile 7 viscous

sling 4 cast, fire, hang, hurl, sock, toss 5 fling, heave, march, pitch, stalk, throw 6 dangle, depend, launch, stride 7 suspend 8 catapult

slink 4 lurk 5 creep, shirk, skulk, slide, sneak, steal 6 weasel 7 gumshoe, sneaker 8 sneaksby 9 pussyfoot

slip 3 dip, lam, sag 4 bull, dock, drop, fall, lose, lurk, molt, pier, quay, shed, sink, skid, trip 5 berth, boner, crash, creep, erode, error, fluff, glide, jetty, lapse, levee, mouse, shake, shirk, skulk, slick, slide, slink, slump, sneak, steal, wharf 6 bungle, escape, flight, go down, slough, soften, topple 7 blooper, blunder, decline, drop off, fall off, faux pas, getaway, gumshoe, mistake, plummet, slither 8 breakout, downturn, escaping, exuviate, fall away, glissade, nose-dive, prolapse, throw off 9 downslide, downswing, downtrend, pussyfoot

slipper 4 mule, shoe 5 brake, romeo, scuff 6 juliet, sandal 8 babouche, pantofle

slippery 3 icy 4 eely, oily 5 slick 6 greasy, lubric, shifty 7 mutable 8 slithery, unstable, unsteady, variable 9 uncertain 10 changeable, inconstant, lubricious

slipshod 5 messy, tacky 6 botchy, faulty, shabby, shoddy, sloppy, tagrag, unneat, untidy 7 inexact, raunchy, scrubby, scruffy, unkempt 8 careless, fouled-up, ill-kempt, messed-up, slapdash, slovenly, tattered 9 botched-up, haphazard, imperfect, neglected, negligent, slaphappy 10 bedraggled, disheveled, down-at-heel, inaccurate

slipup 5 boner, error, fluff, lapse 6 bungle, miscue 7 blooper, blunder, mistake 9 oversight

slit 3 cut 4 gash, rent, tear 5 slash, slice 6 incise, pierce 7 opening 8 roulette

slither 4 lurk, slip 5 creep, glide, prowl, sidle, slick, slide, slink, snake, sneak, steal 8 glissade, undulate

slithery 5 slick 6 greasy, slippy 8 slippery 10 lubricious

sliver 5 carve, shave, shred, slice 6 haggle 8 splinter

slob 4 boor, clod 6 sloven

slobber 4 gush 5 drool 6 drivel, slaver 7 dribble, slabber 8 salivate

sloe 4 plum 10 blackthorn

slog 3 hit 4 ding, grub, plod, slop, sock, toil 5 catch, clout, grind, slave, smite, whack 6 drudge, stodge, strike, trudge 8 plunther

slogan 4 word 5 idiom, motto 6 byword, phrase 8 locution 9 catchword, watchword **10** expression, shibboleth **11** catchphrase

sloop **4** boat, dray **8** longboat, sailboat

slop **3** mud, pap **4** bolt, cram, food, gulp, plod, slog, toil, wolf **5** douse, plash, slosh, spill, squab, swash **6** englut, gobble, guzzle, pablum, splash, splosh, stodge, trudge **7** rubbish, spatter, splurge, spurtle **8** footslog, plunther, splatter **11** ingurgitate

slope **3** tip **4** bend, cant, heel, lean, list, rise, skew, swag, sway, tilt **5** grade, pitch, scarp, slant **6** ascent, escarp, glacis **7** descent, incline, leaning, recline, versant **8** gradient **9** acclivity, declivity, deviation, obliquity **10** deflection **11** inclination, obliqueness *combining form:* **5** cline **6** clinal

sloppy **4** poor, soft **5** drunk, gushy, messy **6** botchy, clumsy, unneat, untidy **7** awkward, gushing, muddled, unkempt **8** careless, effusive, ill-kempt, mediocre, slapdash, slipshod, slobbery, slovenly **9** disguised, pixilated **10** amateurish, disheveled, inebriated, slobbering, unthorough **11** intoxicated

slosh **3** bat, lap **4** bang, bash, belt, blow, bolt, cram, dash, gulp, gush, roar, rush, slam, slop, wash, wolf **5** churn, crack, douse, plash, pound, smack, swash, whirl **6** babble, bubble, burble, englut, gobble, gurgle, guzzle, ripple, splash, wallop **7** spatter, splurge, spurtle **8** splatter **9** bespatter **11** ingurgitate

slot **5** niche, notch, track, trail **6** groove, keyway **7** keyhole, opening, passage **10** pigeonhole

sloth **4** laze **6** acedia, apathy, idling, lazing, slouch **7** languor, loafing **8** idleness, laziness, lethargy **9** faineancy, heaviness, indolence, lassitude, torpidity **10** ergophobia **11** inattention, languidness **12** heedlessness, listlessness, slothfulness, sluggishness **13** shiftlessness *three-toed:* **2** ai *two-toed:* **4** unav

slothful **4** idle, lazy **5** drony **7** work-shy **8** fainéant, indolent **9** easygoing, slowgoing

slouch **3** bum, hat, lop, oaf, sag **4** bend, gawk, laze, lean, loaf, loll, lout, lump, slug, wilt **5** droop, idler, klutz, looby, sloth, slump, stoop **6** loafer, lounge, lubber **7** saunter, shamble, shuffle, trollop **8** dolittle, fainéant, idleness, laziness, meathead, slugabed, sluggard **9** do-nothing, indolence, lazybones **12** slothfulness, sluggishness

slough **3** arm, bay, bog, fen, mud **4** cast, cove, gulf, junk, mire, molt, shed, slip, sump **5** bayou, firth, inlet, marsh, scrap, swamp **6** harbor, morass, reject **7** cashier, discard **8** exuviate, jettison, quagmire, throw out **9** marshland, swampland, throw away

sloven **5** messy **6** sloppy, untidy **7** unkempt **8** careless, ill-kempt, slipshod, uncombed **10** disheveled

slow **3** low, off **4** down, dull, late, poky **5** brake, rusty, slack, tardy **6** leaden, retard, simple, steady, stupid **7** halting, laggard, lagging, limited, reduced, unhasty **8** backward, crawling, dawdling, delaying, dilatory, dragging, flagging, measured, plodding, retarded, sluggish, stagnant **9** dim-witted, leisurely, snaillike, unhasting, unhurried **10** deliberate, half-witted, snail-paced, straggling, unhurrying

slowpoke **5** snail **6** lagger **7** dawdler, laggard **8** lingerer, loiterer **9** slow coach, straggler

sludge **3** mud **4** mire, muck, ooze, slob **5** slime **8** sediment

slue **3** dip **4** skew, turn, veer **5** sheer **6** swerve **8** train off

sluff **7** discard

slug **3** bum, hit, nip, tot **4** belt, dram, drop, jolt, shot, slam **5** blast, idler, larva, smash, snail, snort **6** loafer, slouch, sloven, wallop **7** clobber, slacker, snifter **8** dolittle, fainéant, toothful **9** do-nothing, lazybones *genus:* **5** Limax

sluggard **3** bum **5** idler **6** loafer, slouch **7** dawdler, laggard, lie-abed, shirker **8** dolittle, fainéant, slowpoke, slugabed **9** do-nothing, goldbrick, lazybones, slow coach **10** sleepyhead

slugger **5** boxer **6** batter, hitter

sluggish **3** off **4** down, lazy, logy, slow **5** dopey, heavy, slack, stiff **6** draggy, leaden, stupid, torpid **7** costive, lumpish **8** comatose, dragging, slothful **9** apathetic, lethargic, stupified **10** slumberous **12** hebetudinous

sluice **4** flow, gush, pour, roll, soak, wash **5** douse, flush, surge **6** drench, stream

slum **4** dump **6** ghetto **7** skid row

slumber **4** coma, doze **5** sleep **6** drowse, stupor, torpor **7** lanquor **8** dullness, hebetude, lethargy **9** lassitude, torpidity

slumberous see **sleepy**

slump **3** dip, lop, sag **4** drop, fall, flag, loll, slip **5** droop, pitch, slide **6** cave in, go down, plunge, slouch, topple, tumble **7** decline, drop off, falloff, trollop **8** collapse, downturn, fall away, keel over **9** downslide, downswing, downtrend, recession **10** depression, stagnation

slur **4** blot, blur, lisp, onus, slam, spot **5** brand, odium, smear, stain **6** befoul, defame, insult, malign, slight, stigma **7** blacken, obloquy, traduce **8** black eye, tear down **9** aspersion, bespatter, denigrate, stricture **10** calumniate

slurp **4** suck **5** lap up, slosh, smack, swill **6** guzzle **8** wolf down

slush 3 mud 4 mire, muck, snow 5 grout 6 drivel
sly 4 deep, foxy, lurk, slim, wily 5 cagey, canny, creep, shady, skulk, slick, slide, slink, smart, sneak, steal 6 adroit, artful, astute, clever, covert, crafty, shifty, smooth, subtle, tricky 7 crooked, cunning, devious, furtive, gumshoe, slanter, unfrank, vulpine 8 guileful, scheming, slippery, stealthy 9 designing, dexterous, dishonest, ingenious, insidious, masterful, predatory, subdolous, underhand 11 calculating, clandestine, underhanded 12 disingenuous, unscrupulous 13 Machiavellian
slyboots see scamp
slyness 3 art 5 craft 7 cunning 8 artifice, foxiness, wiliness 9 cageyness, canniness 10 artfulness, craftiness
smack 3 bat, bop, box, lip 4 bash, belt, biff, blip, blow, buss, chop, cuff, dash, hint, kiss, lick, peck, reek, slap, sock, tang 5 clout, crack, punch, sapor, savor, smash, smell, spank, stink, taste, tinge, trace 6 buffet, flavor, relish, smooch 7 soupçon, suggest 8 osculate, resemble, sapidity, tincture 9 suspicion 10 sprinkling
small 3 off, set, wee 4 mean, puny, slim, tiny 5 borne, dinky, light, minor, petty, short 6 bantam, lesser, little, minute, monkey, narrow, paltry, petite, remote, slight 7 cramped, limited, outside, slender, trivial 8 picayune, piddling, pint-size, trifling 9 miniature, minuscule, secondary, two-by-four 10 diminutive, negligible, picayunish, undersized 11 ineffectual, minor-league, unimportant 12 inconsequent 13 insignificant ***amount:*** see particle ***combining form:*** 4 lept, micr, mini, olig, parv 5 lepto, oligo, parvi, parvo
small fry 4 kids 8 children
small-minded 4 mean 6 narrow 7 bigoted 9 hidebound, illiberal 10 brassbound, intolerant, unenlarged
smallness ***abnormal:*** 6 nanism 8 dwarfism
small one ***suffix:*** 2 el, et, ey, ia (plural), ie 3 cle, ium, kin, ock, ula, ule, uli (plural) 4 ella, ette, illa, ling, ulae (plural), ulum, ulus 5 ellae (plural), illae (plural)
smallpox 7 variola
small talk 6 babble, banter 7 chatter, prattle 8 babbling, badinage, chitchat, repartee, trifling 9 bavardage, prattling
smalt 4 blue 5 glass
smarmy 4 oily 5 sleek, slick, soapy 6 glassy, glossy, sleeky 7 fulsome 8 polished, unctious, unctuous 10 oleaginous
smart 3 hep 4 ache, bite, bold, burn, chic, hurt, pain, pert, trig, wise 5 alert, canny, fresh, nervy, prick, quick, sassy, saucy, sharp, slick, sting, swank, swish 6 brainy, bright, cheeky, clever, dapper, modish, shrewd, spruce, suffer, tingle, with-it 7 dashing, knowing, stylish 8 impudent 9 brilliant, exclusive, sprightly 11 fashionable, intelligent, quick-witted, ready-witted, sharp-witted
smart aleck 7 show-off, wise guy 8 wiseacre 9 know-it-all 11 wisecracker, wisenheimer 12 grandstander 13 exhibitionist
smart-alecky 4 wise 5 fresh, nervy, sassy 6 cheeky 8 impudent 9 bold-faced 10 procacious
smarten 5 fix up, primp, slick, spiff 6 doll up, spruce 7 deck out, doll out, dress up, gussy up 8 spruce up
smart set 3 ton 5 elite 6 bon ton 7 aristoi, society, who's who 10 blue bloods, upper crust 11 aristocracy, Four Hundred
smash 3 hit, jar, wow 4 bang, bash, belt, blow, boom, bump, clap, jolt, raze, rive, ruin, slam, slug, sock, wham, whop 5 blast, burst, clash, crack, crash, shock, whack, wreck 6 impact, pileup, shiver, wallop 7 clobber, crack-up, debacle, destroy, shatter, smashup 8 collapse, decimate, demolish, destruct, fragment, knockout, splinter, splitter, tear down 9 bastinado, breakdown, collision, sensation, succès fou 10 annihilate, bell ringer, percussion 11 splinterize
smashup 5 crash, wreck 6 pileup 7 crack-up, debacle 8 collapse 9 breakdown
smattering 3 few 7 handful 10 sprinkling
smear 3 dab, rub, tar 4 beat, coat, daub, drub, foil, lick, slur, soil, trim, whip 5 cover, smarm, stain, sully, taint 6 bedaub, befoul, defame, defile, malign, smirch, smudge, spread, thrash 7 asperse, blacken, overlay, plaster, repulse, shellac, slander, smother, tarnish 8 besmirch, discolor, lambaste 9 bespatter, denigrate, frustrate 10 calumniate, overspread
smell 4 funk, hint, nose, odor, reek 5 aroma, scent, sense, smack, sniff, snuff, stink, trace, whiff 6 detect, stench 7 soupçon 8 tincture 9 fragrance, redolence, suspicion 10 intimation, suggestion ***combining form:*** 3 osm 4 osma, osmo
smell, sense of 9 olfaction, osphresis
smelly 4 olid, rank 5 fetid, funky, reeky 6 foetid, putrid, rancid, stinky 7 noisome, reeking, stenchy 8 stinking 10 malodorous
smelt 4 flux, slag 6 reduce, refine, speise, speiss, tomcod 7 scorify 8 sparling 9 sand borer, sand lance, whitebait, sand lance
smidgen see particle
smile 4 beam, grin 6 simper
smirch see smudge
smirk 4 grin, leer 5 fleer, sneer 6 simper
smitch see particle
smite 3 bat, hit, try 4 belt, dash, ding, slog,

sock 5 catch, clout, whack 6 harrow, martyr, strike 7 afflict, agonize, clobber, crucify, torment, torture 10 excruciate
smithereens 6 pieces 9 fragments, particles
smitten 6 mashed, soft on 8 enamored, spoony on 10 spoony over
smoke 4 cure, floc, fume 8 fumigate 9 cigarette
smoking material 3 pot 4 hash 5 cigar, joint 6 reefer 7 hashish, tobacco 9 cigarette, cigarillo, marihuana, marijuana
smolder 4 boil, stir 5 burst, churn, erupt 6 bubble, seethe, simmer 7 explode, ferment 9 fulminate
smooch 3 lip 4 buss, foul, kiss, peck, soil 5 dirty, grime, smack 6 besoil, smirch, smudge, smutch 7 begrime, tarnish 8 osculate
smooth 3 lay 4 bald, easy, even, fair, flat, mild, soft 5 balmy, bland, faint, flush, level, light, plane, preen, round, royal, sleek, slick, suave 6 evenly, facile, flatly, fluent, gentle, glossy, polish, polite, refine, simple, sleeky, trowel, urbane, velure 7 courtly, cursive, flatten, flowing, jagless, lenient, perfect, planate, running 8 glabrate, glabrous, hairless, soothing, unbroken, waveless 9 agreeable, civilized, courteous, uniformly 10 effortless, rippleless, unwrinkled *combining form:* 3 lio 4 leio, liss 5 lisso
smoothen 3 lay 4 even 5 flush, level, plane 7 flatten
smooth-spoken 5 vocal 6 fluent 8 eloquent 10 articulate
smorgasbord 4 hash 6 jumble, medley 7 mélange 8 mishmash, pastiche 9 potpourri 10 hodgepodge, miscellany 11 gallimaufry
smother 4 beat, cool, cork, drub, lick, rein, trim, whip 5 choke, quash, quell, smear 6 hush up, muffle, quench, stifle, thrash 7 clobber, collect, compose, control, quackle, repress, shellac, squelch 8 lambaste, restrain, suppress 9 suffocate 10 asphyxiate
smudge 3 dab 4 daub, foul, soil 5 dirty, grime, smear, stain, sully, taint 6 bedaub, besoil, blotch, defile, smirch 7 begrime, besmear, plaster, splotch, tarnish 8 besmirch
smug 4 tidy 5 slick 6 spruce 8 priggish 10 complacent 11 self-pleased 13 self-contented, self-satisfied
smuggle 3 run 7 bootleg 10 contraband
smut 4 blot, soil 5 dirty, smear, stain, taint 6 defile 7 bestain 8 besmirch, discolor
smutty 4 foul 5 dirty, nasty 6 coarse, filthy, vulgar 7 obscene, raunchy 8 indecent 12 scatological
Smyrna 5 Izmir
snack 3 tea 4 bite, nosh, tapa 5 mug-up 6 morsel 9 collation 11 refreshment
snag 3 bar, rub 4 clog, curb, drag 5 brake, crimp 6 hamper, hold-up, hurdle 8 obstacle, traverse 10 impediment 11 obstruction
snail 8 escargot, ramshorn, slowpoke 9 band shell
snake 3 boa, cur, dog 4 scum, snot, toad 5 crawl, creep, prick, skunk, slide 6 python 7 serpent, slither 8 anaconda, ophidian, undulate ***combining form:*** 4 ophi 5 ophio, ophis ***poisonous:*** 3 asp 4 habu 5 adder, cobra, coral, krait, mamba, viper 6 elapid, taipan 7 rattler 8 cerastes, pit viper, ringhals 10 bushmaster, copperhead, fer-de-lance 11 cottonmouth 13 water moccasin ***South African:*** 5 aboma
snakebird 6 darter 7 anhinga
snake crane 7 cariama
snake-eater 7 markhor 8 mongoose 13 secretary bird
snakelike 7 anguine 8 ophidian
snakeroot 7 bugbane 10 wild ginger 11 blazing star
snakeweed 7 bistort 13 poison hemlock
snakewood 9 nux vomica 10 frangipani
snaky 7 sinuous, winding 8 flexuous, tortuous 9 meandrous 10 convoluted, meandering, serpentine 11 anfractuous
snap 3 bit, jot, lug, pep, pie 4 bang, bark, dram, drop, hoot, iota, jerk, push, yank 5 cinch, drive, getup, grain, lurch, punch, setup, vigor 6 breeze, picnic, starch, twitch 7 crackle, modicum 8 duck soup, fragment, kid stuff, particle, pushover, sinecure, vitality 9 soft touch, vellicate 10 child's play
snap back 7 rebound, recover
snape 5 taper
snappy 4 fast, racy, tony, trig 5 fleet, hasty, huffy, quick, rapid, raspy, ready, sharp, smart, spicy, swank, swift, swish, zesty 6 lively, prompt, speedy, twitty 7 dashing, peppery, piquant, pungent, raspish, stylish 8 animated, petulant, poignant, prickish 9 breakneck, fractious, irritable, vivacious 10 harefooted 11 expeditious
snare 4 bait, lure, trap 5 catch, decoy, tempt 6 come-on, enmesh, entrap, seduce, tangle 7 catch up, chicane, ensnarl, involve, springe, trammel 8 entangle 9 chicanery, deception, embrangle 10 allurement, enticement, entrapment, seducement, temptation 12 inveiglement
snarl 3 jam, web 4 bark, gnar, knot, maze, mesh, muck 5 chaos, gnarr, ravel, skein, swarm 6 ataxia, huddle, jungle, morass, muddle, tangle 7 clutter, mizmaze, perplex 8 disarray, disorder, entangle, mishmash 9 confusion, intricacy, labyrinth 10 com-

plexity, complicate **11** intertangle **12** complication, entanglement **13** intricateness
snatch **3** nab **4** grab, jerk, nail, take, yank **5** catch, cotch, nip up, seize **6** clutch, whip up, wrench **7** grapple
sneak **3** cur, sly **4** heel, lurk, slip, toad, worm **5** crawl, creep, glide, knave, louse, prowl, shirk, skulk, skunk, slide, slink, steal **6** covert, secret, tiptoe, weasel **7** furtive, gumshoe, hangdog, reptile, slither, smuggle, sub-rosa **8** hush-hush, slyboots, stealthy **9** pussyfoot, scoundrel **10** blackguard, undercover **11** clandestine
sneaky **6** shifty **7** devious **8** guileful, indirect **9** underhand **11** duplicitous, underhanded
sneer **4** gibe, gird, grin, jest, pish **5** fleer, flout, scoff, smile, smirk **6** quip at **7** detract, scout at **8** belittle **9** disparage, underrate
snicker **5** laugh, tehee **6** giggle, guffaw, hee-haw, titter **7** chortle, chuckle
snide **4** fake, sham **5** bogus, false, phony **6** pseudo **7** corrupt, crooked **8** spurious **9** brummagem, dishonest, pinchbeck **11** counterfeit
sniff **4** nose **5** scent, smell
snifter **3** nip, tot **4** dram, drop, jolt, shot, slug **5** snort **8** toothful
snippety see **snippy**
snippy **4** curt **5** bluff, blunt, brief, gruff, short **6** abrupt, crusty **7** brusque
snit **3** fit **4** flap, fume, huff, stew **5** panic, pique, sweat, tizzy **6** dither, frenzy, swivet, taking **7** seizure **10** conniption
snitch **3** cop, nip, rat **4** beak, hook, lift, tell **5** filch, peach, pinch, steal, swipe **6** inform, squeal, tattle **7** purloin, tattler, tipster **8** betrayer, informer, squealer **11** stool pigeon
snob **5** toady **6** poseur **7** high-hat, parvenu, tinhorn, upstart **8** popinjay **9** sycophant
snobbish **5** aloof, potty, ritzy **6** remote, snooty, snotty, uppish, uppity **7** haughty, high-hat, pompous **9** high-flown **10** hoity-toity **11** patronizing, pretentious **12** supercilious **13** condescending
snook **5** cobia **6** robalo **12** sergeant fish
snoop **3** pry, spy **4** mess, nose, peek, peep, peer, poke **5** mouse, prier, pryer, stare **6** butt-in, meddle **7** intrude, meddler, Paul Pry **8** busybody, quidnunc **9** detective, inspector, interfere **10** rubberneck
snooper **3** spy **7** meddler **9** detective, inspector **12** investigator
snoopy **4** nosy **5** peery **6** prying **7** curious **11** inquisitive, inquisitory **13** inquisitorial
snoot see **snout**
snooty see **snobbish**
snooze **3** nap **5** doze **6** catnap, dog nap, siesta **10** forty winks
snort **3** nip, tot **4** dram, drop, jolt, shot, slug **7** snifter **8** toothful
snot **3** cur, dog, pig, rat, sod **4** puke, scum, toad **5** knave, louse, rogue, skunk, snake **6** wretch **7** high-hat, lowlife, reptile, stinker, villain **8** stinkard **9** scoundrel, stinkaroo
snout **4** beak, nose **6** pecker **7** smeller *combining form:* **6** rhynch **7** rhyncho **8** rhynchus
snow *combining form:* **4** chio **5** chion **6** chiono *glacial:* **4** firn, névé *melted:* **5** slush *pellet:* **7** graupel *ridge:* **8** sastruga, zastruga
snow apple **8** mushroom
snowball **3** wax **4** rise **5** build, mount, run up **6** expand **7** augment, upsurge **8** increase, multiply
snowberry **6** biolly
snowbird **9** fieldfare, ivory gull
Snow-Bound author **8** Whittier
snow eater **7** chinook
snow finch **9** brambling
snow goose **4** wavy **5** wavey
snow grouse **9** ptarmigan
snowlike **7** niveous
snowstorm **8** blizzard
snub **3** cut **5** spite, swank **6** slight **7** high-hat, put down **9** ostracize **12** cold-shoulder
snuff **4** kill, nose, odor **5** aroma, pinch, scent, smell, sniff **6** rappee **8** maccaboy
snug **4** cosy, cozy, easy, neat, soft, tidy, trig, trim **5** comfy, cushy **6** burrow, cuddle, nestle, nuzzle **7** chipper, croodle, easeful, orderly **9** shipshape **11** comfortable
snuggle **5** spoon **6** burrow, cuddle, curl up, huddle, nestle, nuzzle
so **3** sae **4** also, ergo, much, then, thus, very **5** hence **6** thusly **7** awfully, parlous **8** likewise **9** extremely, similarly, therefore, thereupon **11** accordingly, exceedingly **12** consequently
soak **3** wet **4** clip, lush, skin, swig **5** douse, drink, imbue, souse, steep **6** boozer, drench, fleece, infuse, seethe **7** guzzler, immerse, insteep, overwet **8** bedrench, drunkard, permeate, saturate, submerge **9** penetrate **10** impregnate, overcharge *flax:* **3** ret
soap **4** suds **7** flatter *hard:* **7** castile *ingredient:* **3** lye
soapbox **4** rant, rave **5** mouth, orate **7** declaim **8** bloviate, harangue, perorate
soaproot **8** sand lily
soapstone **8** steatite
soapwood **8** wild pear
soapwort **7** cowherd **11** bouncing Bet
soar **2** up **3** fly **4** lift, rise **5** arise, climb, mount, shoot **6** ascend, aspire, rocket, uprear **7** shoot up **9** skyrocket

sob 3 cry 4 blub, wail, weep 6 boohoo 7 blubber

sober 4 calm, cool, hard, soft 5 grave, staid 6 low-key, placid, proper, sedate, serene, solemn 7 earnest, serious, subdued, weighty 8 composed, decorous, forgoing, low-keyed, moderate, rational, reserved, softened, tranquil 9 abstinent, collected, continent, eschewing, inhibited, practical, pragmatic, realistic, temperate, toned down 10 abnegating, abstaining, abstemious, controlled, forbearing, hard-boiled, hardheaded, no-nonsense, reasonable, refraining, restrained 11 abstentious, constrained, disciplined, down-to-earth 12 matter-of-fact, unidealistic 13 imperturbable, self-possessed, unimpassioned

sobriety 7 gravity 9 soberness 10 abstinence, continence, sedateness, temperance 11 seriousness

sobriquet 6 byname, byword 8 nickname 10 hypocorism

so-called 6 formal 7 alleged, nominal, titular 8 supposed 9 pretended, professed, purported 10 ostensible

soccer ***cup:*** 5 World ***official:*** 7 referee 8 linesman ***player:*** 6 booter, goalie, kicker, winger 7 forward, link man, striker, sweeper 8 defender, fullback, halfback 10 goalkeeper ***player of renown:*** 4 Pele ***term:*** 3 net 4 boot, chip, kick, trap 6 corner, header, tackle, volley 7 dribble, kickoff, throw-in 8 back-heel, free kick, goal kick, goal line 9 touchline 10 center spot, corner flag, corner kick 11 dropped ball, halfway line, penalty kick, penalty spot

sociable 5 close 6 genial 7 cordial 8 familiar, gracious, intimate 9 congenial, convivial 10 gregarious 11 good-natured

social 6 genial 7 amusing, cordial 8 friendly, gracious, pleasant 9 convivial 10 gregarious, hospitable 11 pleasurable 12 entertaining 13 companionable ***class:*** 5 caste

Social Contract author 8 Rousseau

socialist ***American:*** 4 Debs (Eugene) 6 Ripley (George), Thomas (Norman) ***English:*** 4 Webb (Sidney) 6 Morris (William) ***French:*** 7 Viviani (René) ***German:*** 4 Marx (Karl) 6 Engels (Friedrich) 9 Luxemburg (Rosa) 10 Liebknecht (Wilhelm)

socialize 3 mix 5 party 6 mingle 9 associate

social worker 4 Riis (Jacob), Wald (Lillian D.) 6 Addams (Jane) 7 Alinsky (Saul D.), Lathrop (Julia C.)

society 4 club 5 elite, guild, order, union 6 flower, gentry, league, masses, people, public 7 aristoi, company, quality, who's who 8 populace, sodality 9 community 10 fellowship, fraternity, patriciate, upper class, upper crust 11 aristocracy, association, brotherhood 13 companionship ***girl:*** 3 deb 9 debutante ***high:*** 9 beau monde, haut monde

Society Islands ***capital:*** 7 Papeete ***discoverer:*** 7 Queirós

sociologist ***American:*** 4 Ward 5 Balch, Whyte 6 Du Bois, Summer 7 Johnson, Riesman ***English:*** 7 Spencer ***French:*** 8 Durkheim ***German:*** 5 Weber ***Italian:*** 6 Pareto ***Swedish:*** 6 Myrdal

sock 3 bop, box, hit 4 bash, belt, blow, chop, cuff, ding, slap, slog 5 clout, punch, smack, smash, whack 6 argyle, buffet, strike, thwack 8 stocking

socks 4 hose 7 hosiery

Socrates ***birthplace:*** 6 Athens ***poison:*** 7 hemlock ***pupil:*** 5 Plato ***wife:*** 8 Xantippe

sodality 4 club 5 guild, order, union 6 league 7 society 10 fellowship, fraternity 11 association, brotherhood

sodden 3 wet 4 soak 5 soppy, souse, steep 6 drench, seethe, soaked, soused 7 soaking, sopping 8 drenched, dripping, saturate, waterlog 9 saturated 11 wringing-wet

Sodi's son 7 Gaddiel

sodium 7 natrium ***symbol:*** 2 Na

Sodom and ___ 8 Gomorrah

sofa 5 couch, divan 7 ottoman 9 banquette

Sofia native 6 Bulgar 9 Bulgarian

soft 4 cozy, easy, mild, snug 5 balmy, bland, comfy, cushy, downy, faint, mushy, pappy, pulpy, silky, silly, sleek, sober, wooly 6 doughy, flabby, fleshy, gentle, low-key, pliant, quaggy, satiny, silken, simple, smooth, spongy, spoony, tender, woolly 7 cottony, easeful, fatuous, foolish, lenient, pillowy, pliable, pulpous, squashy, squishy, subdued, velvety, witless 8 cushiony, formless, low-keyed, moderate, squelchy, wool-like, workable, yielding 9 malleable, temperate, toned down 10 weak-headed, weak-minded 11 comfortable 12 compressible

soft-cover 9 paperback

soft hail 7 graupel

softhearted 4 warm 6 tender 10 responsive 11 sympathetic 13 compassionate

soft palate 5 velum

soft-pedal 6 dampen, hush up, muffle, subdue 7 conceal, cushion, silence 8 disguise, play down, suppress, tone down, tune down 11 de-emphasize

soft-soap 3 con 4 coax 6 cajole 7 blarney, flatter, wheedle 8 blandish 9 sweet-talk

Sohrab and Rustum author 6 Arnold

soil 3 mud, tar 4 daub, dirt, foul, home, land, loam, mess, muck, murk 5 crock, dirty, earth, glebe, grime, muddy, smear, stain, sully, taint 6 bedaub, defile, ground, smirch, smooch, smudge, smutch 7 begrime, besmear, country, drabble, draggle, dry land, pedocal, pollute, regosol, tarnish 8 bedabble, besmirch, discolor, homeland, laterite, lithosol, pedalfer, planosol, rendzina, sierozem, solonets, solonetz 10 fatherland, motherland, terra firma 11 contaminate ***aggregate:*** 3 ped ***clay:*** 5 gault ***combining form:*** 2 ge 3 geo, ped 4 agro, pedo ***dark:*** 9 chernozem ***deposit:*** 5 loess 7 eluvium ***infertile:*** 6 podsol, podzol ***layer:*** 4 gley, sola (plural) 5 solum ***prairie:*** 8 brunizem ***rich:*** 6 hotbed ***soft:*** 4 mool ***tropical:*** 7 latosol

sojourn 4 stay, stop 5 abide, tarry, visit 6 linger 7 layover 8 stopover 9 tarriance

Sol 3 sun 7 daystar, phoebus ***horse:*** 4 Eous 5 Ethon 9 Erythreos; (see also Helios)

solace 5 cheer 6 buck up 7 comfort, console, upraise

solar disk 4 Aten

solarium 7 sunroom

solder 4 weld 5 braze

soldier 2 GI 4 swad 5 perdu 6 perdue 7 dogface, fighter, pandoor, pandour, pikeman, private, trooper, warrior 8 doughboy, fusileer, fusilier, partisan, rifleman 9 free lance, guerrilla, man-at-arms, mercenary 10 carabineer, serviceman 11 condottiere, fighting man, infantryman ***ancient Greece:*** 7 hoplite, peltast ***British:*** 5 Tommy 7 redcoat ***cavalry:*** 6 hussar 8 chasseur ***Celtic:*** 4 kern 5 kerne ***Confederate:*** 3 reb ***French:*** 5 poilu 6 Zouave ***German:*** 5 jerry ***Greek:*** 6 evzone 7 palikar ***India:*** 5 jawan, sowar 7 jemadar, jemidar ***irregular:*** 8 guerilla 9 guerrilla ***Prussian:*** 4 ulan 5 uhlan ***Turkish:*** 8 janizary 9 janissary

sole 3 one 4 lone, only 5 alone, unwed 6 bottom, single, unique 8 separate, singular, unshared 9 exclusive

solecism 5 boner, break, gaffe 7 blooper, faux pas 8 slangism 9 indecorum, vulgarism 11 impropriety

solemn 4 full 5 grand, grave, sober, staid 6 august, formal, sedate, somber 7 earnest, plenary, serious, stately, weighty 8 majestic 10 ceremonial, impressive, no-nonsense, sobersided 11 ceremonious, magnificent

solemnize 4 keep 5 honor 7 dignify, observe 8 venerate 9 celebrate 11 commemorate

solicit 3 ask, beg 4 call, drum, tout, turn 5 apply, claim, exact, refer 6 demand, desire, drum up, resort 7 beseech, bespeak, canvass, implore, request, require 9 challenge, postulate 11 requisition

solicitous 4 avid, keen 5 eager 6 ardent, raring 7 anxious, athirst, thirsty 8 appetent 9 impatient

solicitude 4 care, heed 5 qualm, worry 6 regard, unease 7 anxiety, concern, scruple 8 disquiet 9 attention 10 uneasiness 11 compunction, concernment 12 presentiment, watchfulness 13 consideration

solid 4 firm, hard 5 sound 6 cogent, firmly, hardly, secure, square, stable 7 telling 9 compacted, unanimous 10 convincing

solidarity 5 union, unity 6 esprit, fixity 7 oneness 8 cohesion, firmness 9 integrity 10 singleness 12 cohesiveness, togetherness 13 esprit de corps, undividedness

solidify 3 dry, set 4 cake 6 harden 7 congeal 8 compress, concrete, contract, indurate

solitary 3 one 4 lone, lorn, only 5 alone, aloof 6 hermit, lonely, offish, single, unique 7 distant, recluse, uncouth 8 derelict, deserted, desolate, eremitic, forsaken, lonesome, reserved, separate, singular 9 abandoned, reclusive, withdrawn 10 antisocial, insociable, particular, unattended, unexampled, unsociable 11 standoffish 12 misanthropic, unrepeatable 13 companionless, unaccompanied

solitude 8 loneness 9 aloneness, isolation, seclusion 10 detachment, loneliness, quarantine, retirement, withdrawal 11 confinement 12 lonesomeness, separateness

solo 4 lone 5 alone

Solomon ***brother:*** 8 Adonijah ***daughter:*** 7 Taphath 8 Basemath ***father:*** 5 David ***kingdom:*** 6 Israel ***mother:*** 9 Bathsheba ***son, successor:*** 8 Rehoboam ***victim:*** 4 Joab 8 Adonijah

Solomon Islands' capital 7 Honiara

solution 6 answer, result ***salt:*** 6 saline

solve 3 fix 4 work 5 break 6 decide, settle, unfold 7 clear up, dope out, explain, unravel, work out 8 construe, decipher, unpuzzle, unriddle 9 determine, elucidate, enlighten, figure out, interpret, puzzle out

Somalia ***capital:*** 9 Mogadishu ***monetary unit:*** 8 shilling

somatic 6 bodily, carnal 7 fleshly 8 corporal, physical 9 corporeal

somber 3 dim 4 dark, dusk 5 black, bleak, dusky, grave, murky, staid 6 dismal, dreary, gloomy, sedate, solemn 7 earnest, obscure, serious, weighty 8 funereal 9 lightless, tenebrous 10 caliginous, depressing, depressive, no-nonsense, sobersided, tenebrific 11 dispiriting

somniferous see **sleepy**

somnolent see **sleepy**

Somnus ***brother:*** 4 Mors ***god of:*** 5 sleep ***mother:*** 3 Nox

song 3 air, cry, lay 4 aria, call, glee, hymn, lied, note 5 ditty, lyric, paean, piece, poesy, rhyme, verse 6 ballad, melody, poetry 7 calypso, chanson, descant 8 alleluia, cavatina ***biblical:*** 8 canticle ***boat:*** 9 barcarole 10 barcarolle ***combining form:*** 4 melo ***French:*** 7 chanson ***funeral:*** 5 dirge ***German:*** 4 lied 6 lieder (plural) ***lamentation:*** 8 threnode, threnody ***medieval:*** 8 sirvente ***morning:*** 6 aubade ***of joy:*** 5 paean ***operatic:*** 4 aria 8 cavatina 9 cabaletta ***Portuguese:*** 4 fado ***sacred:*** 5 psalm ***sailor's:*** 6 chanty 7 chantey, shantey ***short:*** 8 canzonet ***wedding:*** 8 hymeneal

song and dance 5 pitch, spiel

songbird see at **bird**

Song of Myself author 7 Whitman

Song of Solomon 9 Canticles

songwriter 8 composer, lyricist

Sonja ___ 5 Henie

Sonnambula composer 7 Bellini

sonnet ***developer:*** 8 Petrarch ***part:*** 5 octet 6 octave, sestet

Son of the Middle Border author 7 Garland

sonorous 5 noisy, round 6 rotund 7 aureate, flowery, orotund, rackety, ringing, vibrant 8 clattery, noiseful, plangent, resonant, voiceful 9 bombastic, consonant, overblown 10 euphuistic, oratorical, resounding, rhetorical, uproarious 11 declamatory 12 magniloquent 13 grandiloquent

Sooner State 8 Oklahoma

soothe 3 pat 4 balm, calm, hush, lull 5 allay, salve, still 6 becalm, pacify, settle, subdue 7 comfort, compose, console, massage, mollify, placate 11 tranquilize

soothsay 5 augur 7 portend, predict, presage 8 forecast, foretell, prophesy 9 abumbrate 13 prognosticate

soothsayer 5 augur 6 auspex 7 prophet 8 foreseer, haruspex 9 predictor 10 forecaster, foreteller, prophesier ***ancient Roman:*** 6 auspex 8 haruspex ***blind:*** 8 Tiresias; (see also **prophet**)

sop 3 buy, fix, wet 4 have, soak 5 bribe, douse, drown, sissy, souse, steep 6 buy off, deluge, drench, seethe, sodden, square 7 doormat, douceur 8 gratuity, saturate, waterlog, weakling 10 namby-pamby, pantywaist, tamper with 11 Milquetoast, mollycoddle

Sopater's father 7 Pyrrhus

sophic 4 sage, wise 7 gnostic, knowing 9 insighted, sagacious 10 discerning, insightful, perceptive 13 knowledgeable

sophism see **sophistry**

sophisticate 6 debase 10 adulterate 11 disillusion

sophisticated 5 adult, blasé, bored, couth, jaded, salty, suave 6 daedal, knotty, mature, smooth, svelte, urbane 7 complex, cynical, gordian, knowing, worldly 8 involved, mondaine, schooled, seasoned, well-bred 9 Byzantine, elaborate, intricate, practiced, skeptical, world-wise 10 world-weary 11 experienced, worldly wise 12 cosmopolitan, disenchanted, disentranced, labyrinthine 13 disillusioned

sophistry 7 fallacy 8 delusion 9 ambiguity, casuistry, deception 12 equivocation, speciousness, spuriousness 13 deceptiveness

Sophocles play 4 Ajax 7 Electra 8 Antigone 10 Oedipus Rex

Sophonisba ***brother:*** 8 Hannibal ***father:*** 9 Hasdrubal ***husband:*** 6 Syphax

soporiferous 6 opiate 8 hypnotic, narcotic, somnific 9 somnolent 10 somnorific 12 somnifacient

soporific 4 dozy 6 drowsy, opiate, sleepy, snoozy 7 calming, nodding, numbing 8 hypnotic, narcotic, sedative, slumbery 9 deadening, somnolent 10 anesthetic, quietening, slumberous 11 somniferous 12 somnifacient 13 tranquilizing

soprano ***American:*** 4 Pons 5 Costa, Gluck, Moffo, Price, Sills 6 Arroyo, Battle, Callas, Curtin, Donath, Farrar, Garden, Norman, Peters, Piazza, Resnik 7 Farrell, Kirsten, Stevens, Traubel 8 Ponselle ***Australian:*** 5 Melba 10 Sutherland ***Austrian:*** 7 Rysanek 8 Sembrich ***Canadian:*** 7 Stratas ***French:*** 7 Crespin ***German:*** 6 Leider 7 Lehmann 11 Schwarzkopf ***Italian:*** 5 Freni, Grisi, Patti 6 Scotto 7 Tebaldi 10 Tetrazzini 11 Ricciarelli ***Mexican:*** 8 Cruz-Romo ***Norwegian:*** 8 Flagstad ***Rumanian:*** 8 Cotrubas ***Spanish:*** 7 Caballe 8 Berganza 12 de los Angeles ***Swedish:*** 4 Lind 7 Nilsson; (see also **mezzo-soprano**)

sorcerer 4 mage 5 magus 6 wizard 7 charmer, warlock 8 conjurer, conjuror, magician 9 enchanter, voodooist 11 necromancer

sorceress 3 hag, hex 5 bruja, Circe, lamia, witch 10 witchwoman

sorcery 5 magic 8 diablery, witchery, witching, wizardry 9 conjuring 10 necromancy, witchcraft 11 bewitchment, enchantment, incantation, thaumaturgy ***African:*** 3 obe, obi 4 obia 5 obeah

sordid 3 low 4 base, foul, mean, vile 5 black, dirty, dowdy, nasty, seamy 6 blowsy, filthy, frowsy, grubby, impure, scurvy, sodden 7 ignoble, low-down, servile, squalid, unclean 8 slattern, wretched 9 uncleanly 10 despicable, slatternly

sore 5 angry, vexed 6 aching, bitter 7 algetic, chancre, hurtful, hurting, painful 9 rancorous, resentful 10 afflictive

sorehead 4 crab 6 griper, grouch 7 grouser, growler 8 grumbler, sourpuss 10 complainer, malcontent
sorrel 4 dock 7 roselle
sorrow 3 rue, sob, woe 4 care, moan 5 agony, dolor, grief, groan, mourn 6 grieve, misery, regret 7 anguish, remorse, sadness 8 distress, grieving, mourning 9 dejection, heartache, suffering 10 affliction, depression, heartbreak, melancholy 11 lamentation, unhappiness 12 mournfulness, wretchedness
sorrowful 6 dolent, rueful, tragic, triste, woeful 7 doleful, ruthful 8 dolesome, dolorous, mournful, tragical, tristful, wretched 9 afflicted, miserable, plaintive 10 lamentable, lugubrious, melancholy
sorry 3 bad, sad 4 mean, poor 5 cheap 6 cheesy, paltry, scummy, scurvy, shabby, shoddy 7 scruffy, unhappy 8 beggarly, contrite, mournful, penitent, pitiable, saddened, trifling, wretched 9 miserable, regretful, repentant 10 apologetic, despicable, despisable, inadequate, melancholy, remorseful 11 attritional, disgraceful, penitential 12 compunctious, contemptible, heavyhearted
sort 3 ilk, lot, set 4 body, comb, cull, kind, pick, sift, type 5 array, batch, class, group, order, suite 6 choose, clutch, parcel, riddle, screen, select, stripe, winnow 7 battery, catalog, species, unravel, variety 8 classify, separate 9 catalogue, character 10 categorize, pigeonhole
sortie 5 sally
sortilege 7 sorcery 8 witchery 10 divination
so-so 4 fair 6 enough, fairly, medium, rather, subpar 7 average, fairish 8 mediocre, middling, moderate, passable, passably, somewhat 9 averagely, tolerably 10 moderately 11 indifferent 12 run-of-the-mill
sot 4 lush 5 drunk 6 bibber, boozer 7 guzzler, tippler 8 drunkard 9 inebriate 10 boozehound
sotto voce 3 low 5 aside 6 softly, weakly 7 faintly, mutedly, quietly 9 mufflediy, privately 11 mutteringly
souchong 3 tea
sough 4 sigh 7 suspire
soul 4 life, pith 5 anima, being, bosom, heart, human, stuff, wight 6 animus, bottom, breast, marrow, mortal, person, pneuma, psyche, spirit 7 essence 8 creature, noumenon, vitality 9 élan vital, personage, substance 10 conscience, individual, virtuality, vital force 11 personality 12 essentiality, quintessence ***combining form:*** 4 thym 5 psych, thymo 6 psycho
sound 3 fit 4 firm, hale, look, ping, sane, seem, well 5 audio, exact, music, noise, plumb, probe, right, sober, solid, valid, whole 6 appear, cogent, fathom, intact, secure, stable, unhurt 7 correct, declare, earshot, feel out, healthy, hearing, logical, perfect, precise, publish, sonance, sonancy, telling 8 accepted, accurate, announce, flawless, orthodox, proclaim, rational, received, sensible, unbroken, unmarred 9 advertise, broadcast, canonical, errorless, faultless, resonance, undamaged, uninjured, vibration, wholesome 10 annunciate, consequent, convincing, impeccable, promulgate, reasonable, sanctioned, satisfying, unimpaired 11 disseminate, intelligent, right-minded, sober-minded, unblemished, well-founded 12 satisfactory, well-grounded 13 authoritative, reverberation ***combining form:*** 3 son 4 phon, soni, sono 5 audio, audit, phone, phony 6 audito, phonia ***high-pitched:*** 4 ping, ting ***of a horn:*** 7 tantara ***of disapproval:*** 7 catcall ***pleasant:*** 7 euphony ***quality:*** 6 timbre ***repeating:*** 7 ratatat 8 rataplan ***resounding:*** 8 resonant ***ringing in ears:*** 8 tinnitus ***rustling:*** 8 froufrou ***science:*** 6 sonics 7 phonics ***throaty:*** 8 guttural
Sound ***Alaska:*** 5 Cross ***Antarctica:*** 7 McMurdo ***Australia:*** 4 King 5 Broad ***Bahamas:*** 5 Exuma ***Canada:*** 4 Howe 6 Nansen ***Connecticut-New York:*** 10 Long Island ***English Channel:*** 8 Plymouth ***Georgia:*** 8 Altamaha ***Greenland:*** 5 Smith ***Gulf of Mexico:*** 8 Suwannee 11 Mississippi ***Massachusetts:*** 8 Vineyard 9 Nantucket ***New England:*** 11 Block Island ***North Carolina:*** 4 Core 5 Bogue 7 Pamlico, Roanoke 9 Albemarle, Currituck ***Northwest Territories:*** 4 Peel 8 Melville 9 Lancaster 12 Prince Albert ***Norwegian Sea:*** 8 Scoresby ***Ontario:*** 4 Owen ***Scotland:*** 3 Hoy 4 Jura, Mull 5 Inner ***Spitsbergen:*** 4 Bell ***Washington:*** 5 Puget
Sound and the Fury, The ***author:*** 8 Faulkner ***character:*** 5 Benjy, Caddy, Jason 7 Quentin ***family:*** 7 Compson
soundness 3 wit 4 mind 6 health, reason, sanity, senses 8 lucidity, security, strength 9 stability
sound off 7 speak up 8 speak out
soup ***beet:*** 6 borsch 7 borscht ***bowl:*** 6 tureen ***clear:*** 5 broth 8 bouillon, consommé, julienne ***cold:*** 8 gazpacho 11 vichyssoise ***curry:*** 12 mulligatawny ***okra:*** 5 gumbo ***seafood:*** 7 chowder ***thick:*** 5 gumbo, puree 6 bisque, burgoo ***vegetable:*** 10 minestrone
soupçon see particle
soupy 5 mushy, sobby 6 drippy, slushy, sticky 7 maudlin, mawkish 11 sentimental, tear-jerking
sour 3 bad, dry 4 acid, keen, tart 5 acerb,

acrid, sharp, tangy **6** acidic, bitter, rotten, turned **7** acerbic, acetose, unhappy **8** acescent, vinegary **9** acidulous, fermented

source **4** dawn, rise, root, well **5** cause, fount, onset, start **6** mother, origin, parent, rising, spring, whence **7** dawning, opening, rootage **8** fountain, starting, wellhead **9** beginning, inception, paternity, rootstock **10** antecedent, authorship, birthplace, derivation, provenance, wellspring **11** determinant, origination, provenience **12** fountainhead

sourness **7** acidity **8** acerbity **10** discontent

sourpuss **4** crab **5** crank **6** griper, grouch, kicker **7** grouser, killjoy **8** sorehead **10** complainer

south ***combining form:*** **3** not **4** noto **5** austr **6** austro ***French:*** **3** sud

South Africa ***capital:*** **8** Cape Town, Pretoria **12** Bloemfontein ***colonizer:*** **9** Pretorius ***enclave:*** **7** Lesotho ***largest city:*** **12** Johannesburg ***monetary unit:*** **4** rand ***settlers:*** **5** Boers

South America ***country:*** **4** Peru **5** Chile **6** Brazil, Guyana **7** Bolivia, Ecuador, Surinam, Uruguay **8** Colombia, Paraguay, Suriname **9** Argentina, Venezuela ***ethnic group:*** **5** Negro **6** Aymara, Creole, Indian **7** Mestizo, Mulatto, Quechua, Spanish **10** Amerindian, Portuguese ***language:*** **6** Aymara **7** Guarani, Quechua, Spanish **10** Portuguese

South Carolina ***capital:*** **8** Columbia ***college, university:*** **5** Coker **6** Furman **7** Clemson ***nickname:*** **13** Palmetto State ***state flower:*** **13** yellow jasmine

South Dakota ***capital:*** **6** Pierre ***largest town:*** **10** Sioux Falls ***nickname:*** **11** Coyote State **13** Sunshine State

southerly **7** austral

South Korea ***capital:*** **5** Seoul ***monetary unit:*** **3** won

South-West Africa **7** Namibia ***capital:*** **8** Windhoek

south wind see at **wind**

souvenir **5** relic, token **6** trophy **7** memento **8** keepsake, memorial, reminder **11** remembrance **12** remembrancer

sovereign **4** fine, free **5** regal, royal **6** kingly, master, regent **7** capital, guiding, highest, padshah, regnant **8** autarkic, champion, dominant, five-star, kinglike, loftiest, majestic, padishah, separate **9** ascendant, autarchic, classical, directing, excellent, monarchal, number one, paramount, prevalent **10** autonomous, blue-ribbon, commanding, first-class, monarchial **11** independent, monarchical, overbearing, predominant, predominate **12** preponderant, self-governed

soviet **7** council **9** committee

sow **4** seed, toss **5** drill, fling, plant, put in, straw, strew **7** bestrew, disject, scatter **9** broadcast **11** disseminate ***combining form:*** **3** hyo **7** choerus

spa **5** baths, hydro, wells **6** resort, waters **7** springs **13** watering place ***Czech:*** **6** Bilina **8** Karlsbad ***English:*** **4** Bath **6** Buxton **9** Harrogate ***German:*** **3** Ems **5** Baden **6** Bad Ems **9** Kissingen

space **4** area, room **6** cavity, spread **7** breadth, expanse, stretch **8** distance, interval, universe **9** amplitude, expansion

spaced-out **4** high **5** doped **6** stoned, zonked **7** drugged **8** hopped-up, turned on

spacious **3** big **4** vast, wide **5** ample, great, large, roomy **7** immense **8** enormous, extended **9** boundless, expansive, extensive

spade **3** dig **4** grub **5** scoop **6** dig out, shovel **8** excavate

Spade, Sam **9** detective ***creator:*** **7** Hammett

Spain ***ancient name:*** **8** Hispania ***capital:*** **6** Madrid ***former leader:*** **6** Franco ***monetary unit:*** **6** peseta

spall **4** chip **5** flake **8** fragment

span **4** term, time **8** duration, interval

spangle **4** trim **5** adorn, flash, gleam **7** glimmer, glisten, glitter, shimmer, sparkle, twinkle **8** decorate, ornament **9** coruscate **11** scintillate

Spaniard **9** Castilian

Spanish ***combining form:*** **7** Hispano ***hero:*** **3** Cid **8** Palmerin ***penal settlement:*** **8** presidio ***saint:*** **7** Dominic **8** Ignatius ***title:*** **5** señor **6** señora **8** señorita ***wine:*** **4** sack

Spanish fly **9** cantharis

spank **3** box **4** blip, cuff, slap, sock **5** clout, punch, smack **6** buffet

spar **3** box **5** stall **7** dispute, wrangle **8** longeron ***ship's:*** **6** bumkin, sprite **7** boomkin, jibboom, spright, yardarm **8** bowsprit

spare **4** bony, lank, lean, poor, save **5** extra, gaunt, lanky, lay by, lay in, lay up, pinch, put by, scant, screw, short, skimp, stint **6** de trop, excess, excuse, exempt, let off, meager, scanty, scrape, scrimp, skimpy, skinny **7** absolve, angular, lay away, relieve, scraggy, scrawny, scrimpy, surplus **8** dispense, exiguous, lay aside, rawboned, salt away **9** discharge **11** superfluent, superfluous

sparing **4** wary **5** canny, chary, tight **6** frugal, saving, Scotch, stingy **7** thrifty **8** ungiving **9** provident, stewardly **10** eco-

nomical, unwasteful **11** tightfisted **12** parsimonious
spark **3** bud, woo **4** beau, germ, seed **5** court, lover, swain, wooer **6** embryo, incite, suitor **7** gallant **8** activate
sparker **5** swain, wooer **6** suitor
sparkle **5** flash, gleam, glint **6** glance **7** glimmer, glisten, glitter, shimmer, twinkle **9** coruscate **11** coruscation, scintillate **13** scintillation
sparkling **6** lively **8** animated **9** brilliant **12** effervescent
sparling **5** smelt
sparse **4** poor, rare **5** scant, skimp **6** meager, scanty, scarce, scrimp, skimpy **7** scrimpy **8** exiguous, sporadic, uncommon **9** dispersed, scattered **10** infrequent, occasional
Sparta **10** Lacedaemon ***country:*** **7** Laconia ***hero, king:*** **8** Leonidas ***opponent:*** **6** Athens
Spartacus ***author:*** **4** Fast (Howard) ***slayer:*** **7** Crassus
spasm **3** fit **4** pang **5** burst, crick, throe ***muscular:*** **6** clonus
spasmodic **6** catchy, fitful, spotty **8** sporadic, spurtive **9** desultory
spat **3** row **4** beef, miff, tiff **5** fight, scrap **6** bicker, hassle **7** brabble, dispute, fall out, quarrel, wrangle **8** squabble **9** bickering, caterwaul **10** falling-out **11** altercation
spate **4** flow, flux, pour, rain, rush, tide **5** drift, flood, river, spurt **6** deluge, series, stream **7** current, torrent **8** cataract, flooding, overflow **9** cataclysm **10** inundation
spatter **3** few **4** slop, slur, spit, spot **5** douse, plash, slosh, smear, swash **6** befoul, bespot, defame, malign, smatch, sparge, splash, splosh **7** asperse, blacken, handful, splurge, spurtle, traduce **9** denigrate **10** scattering, smattering, sprinkling
spawn **4** make, sire **5** hatch **6** create, father, parent **7** produce **8** generate **9** originate, procreate
speak **4** talk, tell **5** blurt, drawl, mouth, orate, shout, spout, utter, voice **6** assert, convey, intone, mumble, murmur, mutter, parley **7** address, declaim, declare, descant, lecture, phonate, prelect, whisper **8** converse, dilate on, intonate, perorate, splutter, vocalize **9** discourse, expatiate, verbalize ***confusedly:*** **8** splutter ***for:*** **7** testify ***hesitantly:*** **7** stammer
speaker **9** spokesman **10** mouthpiece
spear **4** bore, pike, ream, spit **5** drill, gouge, lance, spike, stick **6** impale, pierce, skewer, skiver **7** fishgig, harpoon, leister, trident **8** transfix **9** penetrate **11** transpierce
special **4** rare **6** unique **7** express **8** peculiar, uncommon **9** earmarked **10** designated, particular **11** distinctive, exceptional
specialist ***suffix:*** **5** ician
specialize **4** list **7** itemize **9** enumerate, inventory **13** particularize
species **4** kind, sort, type **5** breed, class, order
specific **3** set **6** strict **7** express, limited **8** clean-cut, clear-cut, definite, especial, explicit, reserved **10** individual, particular **11** categorical, unambiguous
specify **3** fix, set **4** cite, list, name **5** limit **6** detail, settle **7** itemize, mention, pin down, precise **8** instance **9** condition, determine, enumerate, establish, inventory, stipulate **13** particularize
specimen **4** case, sort, type **6** sample **7** example, neotype, variety **8** instance, sampling **12** illustration ***animal or plant:*** **8** holotype ***typical:*** **8** topotype
specious **4** idle, vain **5** empty, false, wrong **6** hollow, untrue **7** seeming, unsound **8** apparent, nugatory **9** beguiling, colorable, erroneous, illogical, incorrect, plausible **10** inaccurate
speciousness **7** fallacy, sophism **8** delusion **9** casuistry, deception, sophistry **12** equivocation
speck **3** bit, dot, jot **4** atom, iota, mite, mote, tick **5** crumb, grain, point **6** pepper, smitch **7** freckle, stipple **8** molecule, particle, pinpoint, sprinkle
speckle **3** dot **4** spot, stud **5** flake, fleck **6** dapple, pepper, pimple **7** stipple **8** sprinkle
spectacle **4** show **7** display, pageant **10** exhibition **13** demonstration ***combining form:*** **4** cade
spectacular **5** stagy **7** amazing **8** dramatic, striking, wondrous **9** marvelous, thrilling, wonderful **10** astounding, eye-popping, histrionic, miraculous, prodigious, staggering, stupendous, theatrical **11** astonishing, sensational
spectator **4** seer **5** gazer **6** viewer **7** watcher, witness **8** beholder, observer, onlooker **9** bystander, perceiver **10** eyewitness
Spectator, The ***author:*** **6** Steele **7** Addison
specter **5** ghost, shade, umbra **6** shadow, spirit **7** eidolon, phantom **8** phantasm, revenant **10** apparition
spectral **6** ghosty, spooky **7** ghastly, ghostly, phantom, shadowy **9** deathlike, ghostlike, unearthly **10** cadaverous, corpselike, shadowlike **11** disembodied, phantomlike
spectrum **5** bogey, ghost, shade **6** spirit **7** eidolon **8** phantasm, revenant **10** apparition

speculate 5 study, think, weigh 6 reason, review 7 reflect 8 cogitate, theorize 9 cerebrate 10 deliberate, excogitate
speculation 6 review, theory 7 perhaps, suppose, thought 8 studying, weighing 9 brainwork 10 conjecture
speculative 5 pensy 6 closet, musing 7 curious, pensive 8 academic, thinking 9 inquiring 10 reflecting, ruminating, thoughtful 11 questioning, theoretical
Spedding biographee 5 Bacon
speech 4 talk 5 idiom, voice 6 debate, parley, tongue 7 address, dialect, lecture, monolog, oration, voicing 8 harangue, language, parlance, speaking, uttering 9 discourse, monologue, utterance 10 allocution, expressing, expression, vernacular, vocalizing 11 declamation 12 articulation, vocalization 13 verbalization
speechcraft 7 oratory 8 rhetoric 9 elocution
speechless 3 mum 4 dumb, mute 6 silent 7 aphonic
speed 3 aid, fly, rev, run, zip 4 clip, ease, gait, pace, race, rush, tear, whiz 5 chase, haste, hurry, tempo, woosh 6 barrel, bucket, burn up, career, course, goad on, hasten, hustle, rustle, smooth, spur on, step up, whoosh 7 quicken, swiften 8 alacrity, celerity, dispatch, expedite, fastness, highball, legerity, rapidity, velocity 9 fleetness, quickness, rapidness, swiftness 10 accelerate, cannonball, expedition, facilitate
speedy 4 fast 5 agile, brisk, fleet, hasty, quick, rapid, ready, swift 6 nimble, prompt, raking 8 hasteful 9 breakneck 10 harefooted 11 expeditious
spell 2 go 3 bit, fix, hex 4 bout, time, tour, turn 5 charm, shift, stint, throe, trick, while 6 access, attack, period, streak, voodoo 7 bewitch, enchant, relieve, seizure, stretch 9 ensorcell 11 conjuration, incantation
spellbind 4 grip, hold 5 charm 7 catch up 8 enthrall 9 fascinate, mesmerize
spelling 11 orthography ***bad:*** 10 cacography
spell out 7 explain, expound 8 construe 9 explicate, interpret
spend 3 pay 4 blow, drop, give, pass 5 use up, waste 6 lay out, outlay 7 consume, exhaust, fork out, hand out, splurge 8 disburse, shell out, squander 9 dissipate, throw away, while away 10 contribute, run through ***wisely:*** 7 husband
spender 6 waster 7 wastrel 8 prodigal, unthrift 10 high roller, profligate, squanderer 11 scattergood, wastethrift
spendthrift see spender
spent 5 all in 6 bleary, effete, used up 7 drained, far-gone, worn-out 8 depleted 9 exhausted, washed-out
spew 4 gush 5 belch, eject, eruct, erupt, expel, flood, vomit 6 irrupt, spit up 7 bring up, throw up, upchuck 8 disgorge
sphere 3 orb 4 ball, walk 5 field, globe, realm, round 6 circle, domain 7 demesne, rondure, terrain 8 conglobe, dominion, province 9 bailiwick, champaign, territory 10 conglobate 12 jurisdiction
spherical 5 round 6 global 7 globate, globose, globous 8 globated, globular 9 orbicular ***combining form:*** 5 globo
Sphinx ***builder:*** 6 Khafre ***father:*** 6 Typhon ***head:*** 3 man, ram 4 hawk 5 woman ***mother:*** 7 Echidna ***query:*** 6 riddle ***site:*** 4 Giza 6 Thebes
spice 4 balm, cast, dash, hint, lick 5 aroma, clove, scent, smack, smell, taste, tinge, touch, trace 6 ginger, nutmeg 7 bouquet, incense, perfume 8 cinnamon 9 fragrance, redolence
Spice Islands 8 Moluccas
spick-and-span 3 new 4 mint, neat, snug, tidy, trig, trim 5 clean, fresh 6 spruce 7 chipper, orderly 8 brand-new 9 shipshape 11 uncluttered, well-groomed
spicy 4 blue, racy 5 broad, fiery, salty, shady, sweet, zesty 6 aromal, purple, risqué, savory, snappy, wicked 7 gingery, peppery, perfumy, piquant, pungent, scented, zestful 8 aromatic, fragrant, off-color, perfumed, poignant, redolent, spirited 9 ambrosial 10 suggestive 12 high spirited 13 sophisticated
spider 6 frypan 7 araneid, skillet 8 arachnid 9 frying pan 10 black widow ***combining form:*** 6 arachn 7 arachno
spider monkey 7 sapajou
spiel 4 line 5 pitch 12 song and dance
spieler 6 gypper 7 cheater, diddler, grifter, sharper, slicker 8 swindler 9 defrauder 11 flimflammer 12 double-dealer
spigot 3 tap 4 cock, gate 5 valve 6 faucet 7 hydrant, petcock 8 stopcock
spike 5 lance, piton, spear 6 impale, skewer, skiver 8 transfix 11 transpierce
spile 4 bung 5 spout 8 forepole
spill 4 drip, drop, slop, tell 5 mouth, spray, squab 6 betray, reveal, splash 7 blab out, divulge, dribble, overrun, run over, spatter 8 disclose, discover, give away, overfill, overflow, well over
Spillane detective 11 Hammer, Mike
spin 4 gyre, reel, ride, swim, turn 5 dizzy, drive, giddy, mix up, swirl, twirl, wheel, whirl 6 gyrate, muddle, rotate 7 fluster, revolve, vibrate 9 oscillate, pendulate, pirouette, whirligig ***a log:*** 4 birl ***out:*** 4 draw 6 extend 7 prolong, stretch 8 elongate, lengthen, protract 10 prolongate
spinal column 6 rachis ***curvature:*** 7 lor-

doma 8 lordosis *part:* 8 vertebra; (see also spine)
spindle 3 pin, rod 5 newel 6 rachis
spindly 5 lanky, rangy 6 gangly
spine 4 back 6 rachis 8 backbone 9 vertebrae
spineless 4 weak 8 impotent 9 weak-kneed 10 emasculate, inadequate, weak-willed 11 ineffective, ineffectual 12 invertebrate
spin-off 8 offshoot 9 by-product, outgrowth 10 derivative, descendant
___ Spinoza 6 Baruch
spinster 7 old maid 10 maiden lady
spiny 6 thorny 7 prickly 8 echinate 10 nettlesome
spiral 4 coil, curl, wind 5 helix, twine, twist 7 entwine, helical, helices (plural), wreathe 8 gyroidal, volution 9 cochleate, corkscrew *combining form:* 3 gyr 4 gyro 5 helic 6 helico
spire 4 coil, curl 5 twist, whorl 6 sprout 7 steeple 8 pinnacle 9 germinate
spirit 3 pep, vim, zip 4 brio, dash, élan, gimp, grog, guts, life, mood, snap, soul, tone, zeal, zing 5 anima, ardor, drive, force, heart, might, moxie, oomph, pluck, power, shade, spunk, umbra, verve, vigor 6 animus, daimon, energy, esprit, fervor, ginger, mettle, morale, pneuma, psyche, shadow, starch, temper, timbre, wraith 7 cojones, courage, eidolon, passion, phantom, specter, spectre 8 phantasm, revenant, strength, vitality 9 animation, briskness, character, élan vital, substance 10 apparition, enthusiasm, get-up-and-go, liveliness, resolution, vital force 13 dauntlessness *away:* 6 abduct, kidnap, snatch *combining form:* 4 thym 5 psych, thymo 6 psycho, thymia 7 pneumat 8 pneumato *evil:* 5 afrit, demon 6 afreet 7 erlking, shaitan, sheitan *female:* 5 nymph 7 banshee, banshie, nymphet *good:* 7 eudemon 8 eudaemon *Hopi:* 7 kachina, katcina *Persian:* 4 peri
spirited 3 hot 4 avid, bold, game, keen 5 alert, beany, brave, eager, fiery, nervy, peppy, sharp 6 ardent, bright, gritty, lively, plucky, spunky 7 animate, chipper, fervent, gingery, peppery, valiant, zealous 8 animated, cheerful, fearless, intrepid, resolute 9 audacious, dauntless, sprightly, vivacious 10 courageous, mettlesome, passionate 11 high-hearted 12 enthusiastic
spirits 5 booze, drink 6 liquor, tipple 9 aqua vitae, firewater *low:* 5 blues 8 doldrums 10 blue devils, melancholy
spiritual 4 high 5 lofty 6 church, mental, sacred 7 saintly 8 bodiless, cerebral, churchly, elevated, mystical, numinous, platonic 9 unfleshly 10 discarnate, high-minded, immaterial, unphysical 11 disembodied, incorporeal, nonmaterial, nonphysical 12 metaphysical, supernatural, supramundane
spiritualist 6 mystic
spit 5 lance, spear 6 impale, saliva, skewer, skiver, slaver, sputum 7 spatter, sputter 8 splutter, transfix 9 brochette 11 expectorate
spite 6 grudge, malice, rancor, spleen 7 ill will, revenge 9 vengeance 10 malignancy 11 malevolence 12 vengefulness 13 maliciousness
spiteful 4 evil 5 catty 6 malign, wicked 7 cattish, hostile, vicious 9 malicious, malignant, rancorous 10 malevolent, vindictive 12 antagonistic
Spitta biographee 4 Bach
spitting image 4 twin 6 double, ringer 7 picture 8 portrait 10 simulacrum
spittoon 8 cuspidor
splash 3 sop, wet 4 slop, soak 5 douse, drown, slosh, spray, swash, throw 6 dabble, drench, squirt 7 spatter, splurge, spurtle 8 sprinkle
splatter 4 slop 5 douse, plash, slosh, swash 6 splosh 7 splurge, spurtle
spleen see spite
splendor 4 pomp 5 adorn, glory, value, worth 6 beauty 8 grandeur 10 brilliancy, excellence 12 magnificence
splice 3 tie 4 join, mate 5 unite
splinter 4 rive 5 burst, smash, spail, spale 6 shiver 7 shatter 8 fragment
split 3 cut, rip 4 part, rend, rent, rift, rima, rime, rive, tear 5 break, carve, chasm, chink, cleft, crack, sever, slice 6 breach, cleave, cloven, divide, schism, sunder 7 break up, disjoin, dissect, divorce, fissate, fission, fissure, rupture 8 cleavage, dissever, fracture, rimation, separate 10 alienating, estranging 11 dichotomize *combining form:* 5 schiz 6 schizo 7 schisto
splotch 4 blob, blot, spot 5 fleck, stain 6 bespot, dapple, marble, motley, mottle 9 harlequin, variegate
splurge 4 orgy, slop 5 binge, douse, fling, plash, slosh, spree, swash 6 splash, splosh 7 rampage, spatter, spurtle 8 splatter 12 extravagance
spoil 3 mar, rot 4 baby, grab, harm, haul, hurt, loot, rape, ruin, sack, swag, take, turn 5 booty, decay, favor, force, humor, louse, prize, queer, snafu, taint, waste, wreck 6 boodle, cocker, coddle, cosset, damage, defile, impair, injure, molder, oblige, pamper, ravage, ravish 7 blemish, cater to, crumble, destroy, indulge, outrage, pillage, plunder, putrefy, tarnish, violate, vitiate 8 deflower, demolish, desolate, pickings, spoliate 9 break down, decompose, deflorate, depre-

date, desecrate, devastate **10** plunderage, spoliation **11** acquisition, mollycoddle

spoilsport **7** killjoy

spoke **3** bar, rod **5** chock, stake **8** baluster **11** obstruction

sponge **5** leech, mooch **7** moocher **8** parasite **10** freeloader *material:* **8** mesoglea *opening:* **6** oscula (plural), oscule **7** osculum, ostiole

sponger **5** leech **7** moocher **8** parasite **10** freeloader

spongy **4** soft **5** mushy, pappy, pulpy **6** quaggy **7** pulpous, squashy, squishy **8** squelchy, yielding

sponsor **5** angel **6** backer, patron, surety **8** advocate, backer-up, champion, Maecenas, mainstay, promoter, upholder **9** guarantor, preferrer, supporter **10** benefactor

sponsorship **5** aegis **7** backing **8** auspices **9** patronage

spontaneous **7** natural, offhand **8** unforced **9** automatic, extempore, impromptu, impulsive, unstudied **10** improvised, unprompted **11** instinctive, unmeditated **13** unconstrained

spontoon **3** bat **4** club, mace **5** baton, billy **6** cudgel **8** bludgeon **9** billy club, truncheon **10** nightstick

spoof **4** dupe, fake, fool, hoax, sell, sham **5** cheat, farce, phony, put-on, trick **6** befool, deceit, parody, send-up **7** chicane, takeoff **8** flimflam, hoodwink **9** bamboozle, deception, imposture **11** hornswoggle

spook **3** spy **5** agent, alarm, ghost, scare **6** fright **7** specter, startle, terrify **8** affright, frighten **9** terrorize **10** ghostwrite **13** undercover man

spooky **5** eerie, jumpy, nervy, weird **6** goosey **7** fidgety, jittery, nervous, ominous, uncanny **8** twittery **9** unearthly, unrestful **10** high-strung

spool **4** wind **6** bobbin, holder

spoon **3** pet, woo **4** neck **5** court, ladle, scoop **7** scraper

spoonbill **8** shoveler **9** ruddy duck **10** paddlefish

Spoon River Poet **7** Masters

spoony **5** silly **6** simple **7** fatuous, foolish, unwitty, witless **10** weak-headed, weak-minded **11** sheepheaded *over/on:* **6** mashed **7** smitten **8** enamored

spoor **4** step **5** track, tract **7** vestige **8** footstep **9** footprint

sporadic **3** few **4** rare **6** catchy, fitful, scarce, seldom, single, spotty **8** separate, uncommon **9** desultory, irregular, spasmodic **10** infrequent, occasional, unfrequent

sport **3** fun **4** game, jest, joke, mock, play **6** frolic, racing, trifle **7** mockery, show off **9** diversion, high jinks, horseplay, pilgarlic **10** recreation *indoor:* **6** boxing, hockey, squash **7** bowling **8** handball **9** wrestling **10** acrobatics, basketball, gymnastics **11** racquetball, table tennis ***Olympic:*** **4** judo **6** boxing, diving, hockey, rowing **7** archery, cycling, fencing, shot put **8** canoeing, football, high jump, long jump, marathon, shooting, swimming, yachting **9** decathlon, pole vault, water polo, wrestling **10** basketball, gymnastics, pentathlon, triple jump, volleyball **11** discus throw, hammer throw **12** javelin throw, steeplechase **13** weightlifting *water:* **6** diving, rowing **7** sailing, surfing **8** canoeing, swimming, yachting *winter:* **6** hockey, skiing **7** curling, lugeing, skating **8** biathlon, sledding **10** ski jumping **11** bobsledding, tobogganing

sporting house **6** bagnio **7** brothel **8** bordello, seraglio

sportive **5** antic **6** frisky, impish **7** larkish, playful, roguish, waggish **8** gamesome **10** frolicsome **11** mischievous

sportiveness **7** devilry, roguery, waggery **8** deviltry, mischief **9** devilment

spot **3** fix, jam, job, nip, see **4** drop, espy, find, iota, mite, onus, post, site, slug, whit **5** brand, catch, fleck, hit on, locus, place, point, speck **6** blotch, corner, dapple, descry, detect, dollop, finger, macula, mottle, office, pickle, pimple, plight, random, scrape, stigma, turn up **7** aimless, dilemma, freckle, hit upon, smidgen, spatter, speckle, splotch, station, unaimed **8** diagnose, flyspeck, identify, location, maculate, meet with, particle, pinpoint, position **9** bespatter, encounter, haphazard, hit-or-miss, irregular, recognize, situation, unplanned **10** connection, designless **11** determinate, distinguish, predicament *combining form:* **5** macul **6** maculi, maculo

spotless **4** pure **5** clean **6** chaste, decent, modest **7** cleanly **8** hygienic, sanitary, unsoiled **9** undefiled, unsullied **10** immaculate **11** unblemished

spotted eagle ray **6** obispo

spouse **4** mate, wife **5** hubby **7** consort, husband

spout **5** chute, falls, sault **6** nozzle **7** cascade **8** cataract **9** waterfall

sprain **4** pull, tear, turn **5** break, throw, twist **6** wrench **7** stretch **8** fracture **9** dislocate

sprawl **4** loll **5** drape, slump **6** extend, lounge, ramble, slouch, spread **7** stretch **8** scramble, straddle, straggle **11** spread-eagle

spray **3** fog **4** hose **7** aerosol **8** atomizer, fumigate, nebulize

spread **3** jam, lay, set, sow **4** deal, oleo, open, pâté, push **5** feast, jelly, noise, space, splay, strew, sweep **6** butter, dinner, expand, extend, fan out, pass on, peddle, regale, retail, unfold **7** banquet, breadth, diffuse, expanse, overrun, perfuse, pervade, radiate, scatter, slather, stretch, suffuse **8** bedcover, coverlet, dispense, disperse, distance, mushroom, permeate, transmit **9** amplitude, broadcast, circulate, diffusion, dissipate, expansion, extension, profusion, propagate **10** distribute, outstretch **11** communicate, counterpane, disseminate, enlargement ***on:*** **5** apply

spree **3** bat, jag **4** bust, hell, orgy, riot, tear **5** binge, fling, revel **6** bender, frolic, rantan **7** carouse, rampage, roister, splurge, wassail **8** carousal

sprig **4** brad, heir **5** dowel, scion **6** figure **7** pintail **9** ruddy duck

sprightly **3** gay **4** keen, yare **5** agile, alert, antic, brisk, perky, sharp, smart, zippy **6** active, breezy, brisky, clever, frisky, lively, nimble, volant **7** animate, coltish, playful, pungent **8** animated, spirited, sportive **9** vivacious **10** frolicsome, keen-witted, rollicking, unpedantic **11** quick-witted **13** scintillating

spring **3** hop, lop **4** bolt, come, flow, head, jump, leap, loom, lope, rise, root, skip, stem, trip, well **5** arise, begin, birth, bound, cause, fount, hatch, issue, start, vault, youth **6** appear, arrive, bounce, emerge, geyser, hurdle, motive, origin, reason, source, tittup, uncoil, updive, vernal **7** budtime, come out, emanate, impetus, proceed, puberty, rebound, saltate, skitter, startle **8** come from, commence, excitant, fountain, stimulus, wellhead **9** greenness, originate, stimulant, youthhood **10** derive from, incitement, juvenility **12** fountainhead, youthfulness ***back:*** **6** resile ***combining form:*** **4** cren **5** creno

springe **5** snare **7** pitfall **8** deadfall, trapfall **9** booby trap, mousetrap

springlike **6** vernal

springy **6** supple, whippy **7** elastic, stretch **8** flexible, stretchy **9** recoiling, resilient **10** rebounding

sprinkle **3** dot **4** dust, spot **5** shake, speck, strew **6** pepper, powder, sparge **7** asperse, drizzle, freckle, scatter, speckle, stipple **9** bespeckle

sprint **3** run **4** dash, shin **5** scoot **6** scurry **7** scamper

sprite **3** elf, fay **5** fairy, nisse, pixie **7** brownie ***water:*** **5** kelpy **6** kelpie

spritz **3** jet **5** spurt **6** squirt

sprout **3** bud **4** grow **5** scion, shoot **6** ratoon, sucker **8** offshoot **9** germinate ***combining form:*** **4** clad **5** blast, clado **6** blasto, blasty **7** blastic

spruce **4** trim **5** natty, sassy **6** dapper, spiffy **11** well-groomed ***up:*** **5** slick, spiff **6** doll up **7** deck out, gussy up

spry **4** yare **5** agile, brisk, quick, ready, sound, zippy **6** active, brisky, lively, nimble, prompt, robust, volant **7** healthy **8** vigorous **9** energetic

spud **6** potato **8** spade lug

spume **4** foam, suds **5** froth, yeast **6** lather

spunk **4** grit, guts, sand **5** heart, moxie, nerve, pluck **6** mettle, spirit **7** cojones, courage **8** backbone **9** fortitude **10** doggedness, resolution **13** dauntlessness

spunky **4** bold **5** beany, brave, fiery, gutsy **6** plucky **7** doughty, gingery, peppery **8** fearless, spirited **9** dauntless, unfearing **10** courageous, mettlesome **11** high-hearted, undauntable **12** high-spirited

spur **3** sic **4** goad, prod, stir, urge **5** egg on, favor, prick, rally, rouse, rowel **6** arouse, awaken, exhort, prompt, propel **7** impetus, impulse **8** catalyst, excitant, stimulus **9** actuation, incentive, instigate, stimulant **10** activation, incitation, incitement, motivation **11** countenance

spurious **4** fake, mock, sham **5** bogus, dummy, false, phony, put-on, snide **6** ersatz, pseudo, unreal **7** assumed, bastard, feigned, pretend **8** affected, baseborn **9** brummagem, imitation, pinchbeck, pretended, simulated, ungenuine **10** apocryphal, artificial, substitute **11** counterfeit, make-believe, misbegotten, unauthentic **12** illegitimate ***combining form:*** **4** noth **5** notho, pseud **6** pseudo

spurn **5** flout, scoff, scorn, scout, sneer **6** refuse, reject **7** conspue, contemn, decline, despise, disdain, dismiss **8** turn down **9** reprobate, repudiate **10** disapprove

spurt **3** jet **5** spout, surge **6** spritz, sprout, squirt

sputter **3** pop **4** fizz, hiss, rage, rant, rave, spit **6** gibber, jabber **7** bluster, crackle

spy **5** agent, scout, snoop, spook **6** beagle, sleuth **7** gumshoe **8** informer, saboteur **9** detective **12** investigator **13** undercover man ***name:*** **4** Boyd (Belle), Hari (Mata) **5** André (John)

Spy, The ***author:*** **6** Cooper

spying **9** espionage

squab **5** couch **6** pigeon **7** cushion

squabble see spat

squalid **3** low **4** base, foul, mean, ugly, vile **5** black, dingy, dirty, nasty, seedy, soily **6** filthy, frowzy, grubby, impure, scurvy, shabby, shoddy, sleazy, sloppy **7** ignoble, low-down, run-down, scrubby, unclean, unkempt **8** slipshod, slovenly, wretched **10** broken-down, despicable, disheveled, slatternly **11** dilapidated **12** disreputable

squall 3 caw, yap, yip 4 bark, bawl, beef, feud, howl, roar, wail, yaup, yawp, yell, yelp, yowl 5 brawl, croak, fight, shout 6 bellow, hassle, shriek, squeal 7 dispute, quarrel, screech 9 bickering 10 falling-out 11 altercation
squander 4 blow 5 waste 7 consume, fritter 8 fool away, unthrift 9 dissipate, overdoing, throw away 10 frivol away, lavishness, trifle away 11 prodigality, prodigalize 12 extravagance, extravagancy, wastefulness
squanderer see **spender**
square 3 fit, fix, pay, sop 4 bang, boxy, even, fair, fogy, have, jibe, just, quit, suit 5 adapt, agree, bribe, clear, equal, exact, fit in, green, pay up, plaza, right, sharp, spang 6 accord, adjust, buy off, common, fogram, fossil, settle, tailor 7 balance, boxlike, conform, exactly, satisfy 8 check out, clear off, coincide, dovetail, mossback, orthodox, quadrate, smack-dab, straight, unbiased 9 discharge, equitable, harmonize, impartial, liquidate, objective, precisely, quadratic, reconcile 10 accurately, button-down, correspond, fuddy-duddy 12 conventional 13 stick-in-the-mud
squash 3 jam 4 cram, mash, pepo, pulp 5 crush, gourd, press, quell 7 put down, squeeze, squelch, squidge 8 suppress 10 annihilate, extinguish ***variety:*** 5 acorn 6 cushaw, cymlin, Sibley, turban 7 cymling, dunkard, Hubbard, scallop 8 cymbling, pattypan, zucchini 9 butternut, cocozelle, crookneck 10 Marblehead
squat 5 dumpy, hunch, stoop, thick 6 chunky, crouch, hunker, stocky, stubby 8 heavyset, thickset 10 hunker down 11 thick-bodied
squawfish 4 chub 8 cyprinid
squawk 3 caw, yap, yip 4 beef, crab, fuss, yaup, yawp 5 bitch, bleat, gripe 6 yammer 7 protest 8 complain
squeak 3 rat 4 pipe, shot, show, talk, time 5 grate, peach 6 change, inform, look-in, scream, snitch 7 opening, screech 8 occasion 11 opportunity
squeal 3 rat, yip 4 howl, rasp, talk, yell, yowl 5 bitch, bleat, creak, grate, gripe, peach 6 inform, screak, scream, shriek, shrill, snitch, squawk 7 screech 8 complain
squealer 4 fink 6 canary, snitch 7 ratfink, tipster 8 betrayer, informer 10 talebearer 11 stool pigeon
squeamish 5 dizzy, fussy, queer, shaky, upset 6 dainty, qualmy, queasy 7 finical, finicky 8 nauseous 9 finicking, nauseated, unsettled 10 fastidious, particular, pernickety 11 persnickety, vertiginous
squeamishness 6 nausea
squeeze 3 hug, jam 4 bear, cram, push 5 clasp, crowd, crush, exact, gouge, juice, pinch, press, screw, wrest, wring 6 eke out, enfold, extort, squash, squish, squush, wrench 7 embrace, extract, scratch 8 compress, contract 9 shake down
squelch 5 shush 6 muffle, squash, squish, stifle 7 repress, squidge 8 strangle, suppress
squib 4 fire 6 filler 7 lampoon 8 scribble, shoot off 9 detonator
squid 7 calamar, mollusk 8 calamary 10 cephalopod ***kin:*** 7 octopus 10 cuttlefish
squiggle 4 worm 6 scrawl, writhe 7 scratch 8 scrabble, scribble
squinch 5 quail, start, wince 6 blanch, blench, recoil, shrink
squint 4 bent 5 trend 10 hagioscope, strabismus
squire 5 judge, lover 6 escort, lawyer 7 gallant 9 accompany
squirm 4 toss, worm 6 wiggle, writhe 7 agonize, wriggle
squirrel 5 hoard, stash ***African:*** 5 xerus ***red:*** 9 chickaree
squirrel-like 8 sciuroid
squirt 3 jet, pup 4 pour 5 puppy, sprat, spray, sprit, spurt, surge, twerp 6 splurt, spritz, stream 7 spatter
squish 3 jam 4 bear, push 5 crush, press 7 squeeze, squelch
squishy 4 soft 5 pulpy 6 quaggy, spongy 7 pulpous 8 squelchy
Sri Lanka ***capital:*** 7 Colombo ***export:*** 3 tea 6 rubber ***former name:*** 6 Ceylon ***monetary unit:*** 5 rupee
SRO 7 sellout
SS chief 7 Himmler
S-shaped 7 sigmoid 9 sigmoidal
stab 2 go 3 dig, pop, ram, run, try 4 dirk, poke, shot, sink, slap 5 crack, drive, fling, prick, prong, punch, spear, stick, whack, whirl 6 dagger, pierce, plunge, thrust 7 bayonet, poniard 8 puncture, stiletto
Stabat ____ 5 Mater
stabile 6 steady 9 sculpture 10 stationary
stabilize 3 fix, set 4 prop 5 poise 6 fixate, secure, settle, steady 7 balance, ballast, support, sustain
stable 3 set 4 even, fast, firm, safe, sure 5 fixed, solid, sound 6 poised, secure, steady, strong, sturdy 7 lasting, staunch, uniform 8 balanced, constant, enduring, resolute 9 diuturnal, perduring, permanent, steadfast, unvarying 10 perdurable, unchanging, unshakable
stack 4 bank, cock, heap, hill, load, mass, pile 5 drift, mound 7 pyramid
stadium 4 bowl 5 arena 6 garden 8 coliseum 9 gymnasium
staff 3 rod 4 club, prop, rung, wand

6 cudgel 7 support *bishop's:* 7 crosier, crozier *medical:* 8 caduceus
stage 4 give, open, play, rung, show, step 5 grade, level, mount, notch, phase, put on 6 degree, period 7 execute, perform, present, produce *direction:* 4 exit 5 enter 6 exeunt *scenery:* 8 backdrop *show:* 4 play 5 drama, revue 7 musical 9 burlesque 10 vaudeville *signal:* 3 cue *whisper:* 5 aside
stage set 5 scene 7 scenery, setting 11 mise-en-scène
stagger 4 halt, reel, sway 5 amaze, floor, lurch, shift, stump, swing, waver, weave, wheel 6 boggle, careen, dither, falter, puzzle, teeter, topple, totter, wobble 7 astound, nonplus, perplex, shatter, stumble, whiffle 8 astonish, bowl over, hesitate, paralyze, titubate 9 devastate, dumbfound, knock over, overpower, overwhelm, vacillate
stagnant 5 stale 6 static 8 immobile, unmoving 10 motionless, stationary
stagnate 6 stifle 7 trammel 8 stultify, vegetate
staid 4 cool, smug 5 grave, sober 6 formal, sedate, solemn, somber, stuffy 7 earnest, serious, starchy, weighty 8 composed, decorous, priggish
stain 3 dye, tar 4 blot, blur, daub, flaw, onus, slur, smut, soil, spot 5 brand, color, crock, odium, smear, sully, taint, tinge 6 bedaub, blotch, debase, defect, defile, embrue, imbrue, smirch, smudge, smutch, stigma 7 besmear, blemish, corrupt, debauch, deprave, pervert, pigment, tarnish 8 besmirch, black eye, colorant, discolor, dyestuff, tincture *combining form:* 5 macul 6 maculi, maculo
staircase *handrail:* 8 banister *outdoor:* 6 perron *post:* 5 newel 8 baluster
stake 3 bet, lay, pot, set 4 ante, back, game, play 5 claim, put on, share, wager 6 gamble 7 finance 8 bankroll, interest 10 capitalize
stale 4 rank 5 dusty, fetid, fusty, moldy, musty, tired, trite 6 cliché, smelly 7 clichéd, noisome, reeking, stenchy 8 shopworn, timeworn 9 hackneyed 10 malodorous 11 commonplace, stereotyped
stalemate 3 tie 4 draw 7 dogfall 8 deadlock, standoff
stalk 4 hunt, prey 5 chase, drive, march, sling, track 6 ambush, follow, pursue, stride, walk up 8 flush out *flower:* 8 peduncle *leaf:* 7 petiole
stall 4 halt 5 booth, brake, check, kiosk, stand 6 arrest, put off 7 hold off 11 compartment
stalwart 4 bold 5 brave, husky, stout, tough 6 brawny, sinewy, strong, sturdy 7 valiant 8 athletic, fearless, intrepid, muscular, unafraid, valorous 9 dauntless, tenacious, undaunted 10 courageous
stamen *combining form:* 4 andr 5 andro 9 stemonous *part:* 6 anther 8 filament
stamina 9 endurance, tolerance 10 toleration
stammer 6 gibber, jabber 7 sputter, stutter 8 hesitate, splutter
stamp 3 ilk, lot 4 cast, etch, kind, mint, mold, seal, sort, type 5 clomp, clump, drive, grave, infix, pound, print, tromp 6 hammer, incuse, stripe 7 impress, imprint, sticker, trample 8 hallmark, inscribe 9 character 10 impression
stampede 4 bolt, dash, rout, rush, tear 5 chase, fling, shoot 6 charge 8 pell-mell
stamps 7 postage
stance 4 pose 5 color 7 posture 8 attitude, carriage, position, positure
stanch 4 stem, stop
stanchion 4 prop 5 brace 7 support
stand 4 bear, take 5 abide, booth, brook, kiosk, treat 6 endure, suffer 7 stomach, swallow 8 attitude, position, tolerate *artist's:* 5 easel *having three legs:* 6 tripod, trivet *ornamental:* 7 étagere *stiffly:* 7 bristle
standard 3 law, par 4 flag, jack, mean, norm, rule 5 axiom, color, gauge, ideal, model 6 assize, banner, belief, ensign, median, mirror, pennon 7 average, example, measure, pattern, pennant 8 bannerol, ensample, exemplar, paradigm, streamer 9 archetype, banderole, beau ideal, benchmark, criterion, principle, yardstick 10 touchstone 11 fundamental
stand-in 3 sub 6 second 9 alternate, assistant, surrogate 10 substitute 11 locum tenens, pinch hitter, replacement, succedaneum
standing 4 rank, term 5 place 6 cachet, status 7 dignity, footing, station, stature 8 capacity, position, prestige 9 character, situation 11 consequence
standoff see stalemate
standoffish 5 aloof 7 distant 8 eremitic, reserved, solitary 9 reclusive, withdrawn 10 antisocial, insociable, unsociable 12 misanthropic
stand out 3 jut 4 bulk, loom, poke, pout 5 bulge, pouch 6 beetle 7 project 8 overhang, protrude
standpatter 4 tory 7 diehard 8 old liner, rightist 11 bitter-ender, right-winger 12 conservative
standpoint 4 side 5 angle, slant 7 outlook 9 direction
standstill 4 halt, stop 5 check, pause 6 arrest 8 deadlock 9 cessation
Stanley Kowalski's wife 6 Stella
Stan's pal 5 Ollie

stanza 7 strophe ***combining form:*** 5 stich ***of eight lines:*** 6 octave 8 octonary ***of four lines:*** 6 ballad 8 quatrain ***of six lines:*** 6 sestet, sextet 7 sextain ***of three lines:*** 6 tercet 7 triplet 8 tristich ***Persian:*** 8 rubaiyat

star 4 main, nova 5 actor, chief, major, novae (plural) 6 étoile 7 actress, capital 8 asterisk, dominant 9 principal 10 preeminent 11 outstanding, predominant ***bright:*** 4 Vega 5 Deneb, Rigel, Spica 6 Altair, Pollux, Sirius 7 Antares, Canopus, Capella, Procyon 8 Arcturus 9 Aldebaran, Archernar, Fomalhaut 10 Beta Crucis, Betelgeuse 11 Alpha Crucis 12 Beta Centauri 13 Alpha Centauri ***combining form:*** 4 astr 5 aster, astro 6 astero, sidero ***five-pointed:*** 8 pentacle ***giant:*** 10 Betelgeuse ***six-pointed:*** 8 hexagram ***suffix:*** 2 id

starch 2 go 3 pep 4 bang, push, snap 5 drive, getup, punch, vigor 6 amylum 7 stiffen 8 vitality ***combining form:*** 4 amyl 5 amylo

star-crossed 6 doomed 7 hapless, unhappy, unlucky 8 ill-fated, luckless, untoward 10 ill-starred 11 unfortunate 12 misfortunate

Stardust composer 10 Carmichael

stare 3 eye 4 bore, gape, gawk, gaze, look, ogle, peer 5 gloat 6 goggle 7 fisheye 10 rubberneck

stark 3 raw 4 bare, firm, nude, pure 5 bleak, clear, empty, naked, quite, rigid, sheer, stout, utter 6 barren, robust, strict, unclad, vacant, wholly 8 absolute, complete, desolate, stripped 9 au naturel, out-and-out 10 absolutely

starry 6 astral 7 stellar 8 sidereal 9 stellular

Star-Spangled Banner writer 3 Key

start 4 bolt, dawn, draw, edge, jump, leap, odds, open 5 alpha, arise, begin, bound, bulge, crank, enter, found, onset, quail, set up, wince 6 blanch, blench, bounce, create, embark, flinch, get off, launch, outset, recoil, setout, shrink, spring, take up, tee off 7 actuate, dawning, genesis, infancy, kickoff, opening, pioneer, proceed, squinch, trigger, vantage 8 activate, commence, drawback, embark on, handicap, initiate, organize 9 advantage, allowance, beginning, establish, institute, originate 10 inaugurate 12 commencement

startle 3 awe 4 bolt, jolt, jump 5 alarm, scare, shock, spook 8 affright, astonish, frighten, surprise

starved 6 hungry 8 famished, ravenous, underfed

stash 4 bury, hide 5 cache, hoard, plant 7 conceal, secrete 8 ensconce, squirrel

stasis 5 poise 7 balance 9 equipoise 11 equilibrium

state 3 air, put, say 4 aver, mode, rank, tell, vent 5 opine, place, utter 6 affirm, assert, cachet, define, recite, relate, report 7 declare, deliver, dignity, enounce, explain, expound, express, footing, narrate, posture, recount 8 attitude, bring out, capacity, describe, position, prestige, set forth, standing 9 character, condition, elucidate, enunciate, interpret, situation, ventilate 11 body politic ***subdivison:*** 6 county ***suffix:*** 2 cy, th 3 ate, dom, ery, ion, ism, ity 4 ance, ancy, ence, ency, hood, ment, ness, oses (plural), osis, ship 5 ation 7 isation, ization

State abbreviation ***Alabama:*** 2 AL 3 Ala. ***Alaska:*** 2 AK 4 Alas. ***Arizona:*** 2 AZ 4 Ariz. ***Arkansas:*** 2 AR 3 Ark. ***California:*** 2 CA 3 Cal. 5 Calif. ***Colorado:*** 2 CO 3 Col. 4 Colo ***Connecticut:*** 2 CT 4 Conn. ***Delaware:*** 2 DE 3 Del. ***Florida:*** 2 FL 3 Fla. ***Georgia:*** 2 GA ***Hawaii:*** 2 HI ***Idaho:*** 2 ID 3 Ida. ***Illinois:*** 2 IL 3 Ill. ***Indiana:*** 2 IN 3 Ind. ***Iowa:*** 2 IA, Io. ***Kansas:*** 2 KS 3 Kan., Kas. 4 Kans. ***Kentucky:*** 2 KY 3 Ken. ***Louisiana:*** 2 LA ***Maine:*** 2 ME ***Maryland:*** 2 MD ***Massachusetts:*** 2 MA 4 Mass. ***Michigan:*** 2 MI 4 Mich. ***Minnesota:*** 2 MN 4 Minn. ***Mississippi:*** 2 MS 4 Miss. ***Missouri:*** 2 MO ***Montana:*** 2 MT 4 Mont. ***Nebraska:*** 2 NE 3 Neb. 4 Nebr. ***Nevada:*** 2 NV 3 Nev. ***New Hampshire:*** 2 NH ***New Jersey:*** 2 NJ ***New Mexico:*** 2 NM 4 N. Mex. ***New York:*** 2 NY ***North Carolina:*** 2 NC 4 N. Car. ***North Dakota:*** 2 ND 4 N. Dak. ***Ohio:*** 2 OH ***Oklahoma:*** 2 OK 4 Okla. ***Oregon:*** 2 OR 3 Ore. 4 Oreg. ***Pennsylvania:*** 2 PA 4 Penn. 5 Penna. ***Rhode Island:*** 2 RI ***South Carolina:*** 2 SC 4 S. Car. ***South Dakota:*** 2 SD 4 S. Dak. ***Tennessee:*** 2 TN 4 Tenn. ***Texas:*** 2 TX 3 Tex. ***Utah:*** 2 UT ***Vermont:*** 2 VT 4 Verm. ***Virginia:*** 2 VA 4 Virg. ***Washington:*** 2 WA 4 Wash. ***West Virginia:*** 2 WV 3 W. Va. ***Wisconsin:*** 2 WI 3 Wis. 4 Wisc. ***Wyoming:*** 2 WY 3 Wyo.

stately 5 grand, noble, preux, regal, royal 6 august, formal, kingly, lordly, solemn 7 courtly, gallant 8 gracious, imperial, imposing, magnific, majestic, princely 9 dignified, grandiose 10 ceremonial 11 ceremonious, magnificent

statement 3 tab 4 bill, vent, word 5 score, voice 6 dictum 7 account, invoice, recital 9 narrative, reckoning, testimony, utterance 10 deposition, expression 11 description 12 vocalization 13 verbalization ***introductory:*** 7 preface 8 foreword, prologue

stateroom 5 cabin

statesman 10 politician ***American:*** 3 Hay (John Milton) 4 Clay (Henry), Hull (Cordell), Otis (James), Root (Elihu) 5 Henry (Patrick), Lodge (Henry C.) 6 Morris (Gouverneur), Sumner (Charles) 7 Hancock (John), Kellogg (Frank B.), Lansing (Robert), Sherman, Stimson (Henry L.), Webster (Daniel) 8 Franklin, Hamilton, Pinckney, Randolph (E.J.), Rutledge (John), Trumbull 10 Stettinius (E. R.) ***Australian:*** 9 Wentworth ***Austrian:*** 6 Renner 7 Kaunitz 8 Dollfuss 10 Metternich 13 Schwarzenberg ***Canadian:*** 4 King 7 Laurier 8 Thompson 9 Macdonald, Mackenzie ***Chinese:*** 3 Yen 4 Kung, Wang, Yuan 9 Sun Yat-Sen ***Dutch:*** 6 de Witt 7 Grotius, Stikker ***East German:*** 8 Ulbricht ***English:*** 3 Fox 4 Eden, More, Peel, Pitt, Vane 5 Cecil, North 6 Morley, Sidney, Temple, Wolsey 7 Halifax, Reading, Russell, Stanley, Stewart, Warwick 8 Cromwell, Disraeli, Robinson, Villiers 9 Cavendish, Churchill, Gladstone, Salisbury, Strafford, Wellesley 10 Palmerston, Rockingham, Sunderland, Walsingham, Wellington 11 Chamberlain, Shaftesbury 12 Chesterfield ***Finnish:*** 9 Stahlberg ***French:*** 5 Sully 6 Guizot, Thiers, Turgot 7 Herriot, Mazarin, Schuman, Viviani 8 Hanotaux 9 Lafayette, Millerand, Richelieu 10 Clemenceau 11 Tocqueville ***German:*** 5 Wirth 10 Stresemann ***German-Danish:*** 9 Struensee ***Greek:*** 6 Zaimes, Zaimis 8 Pericles 9 Aristides 11 Cleisthenes, Demosthenes 12 Themistocles ***Israeli:*** 5 Begin, Dayan ***Italian:*** 6 Cavour, Crispi 7 Orlando 11 Machiavelli ***Japanese:*** 5 genro, Kanoe 6 Kanoye ***Norwegian:*** 6 Nansen ***Polish:*** 7 Zaleski 9 Pilsudski 10 Paderewski ***Prussian:*** 5 Stein ***Roman:*** 4 Cato 6 Cicero, Pompey, Seneca 7 Agrippa 8 Gracchus, Maecenas 9 Symmachus ***Russian:*** 5 Witte 7 molotov 8 Potemkin 9 Vyshinsky ***Scottish:*** 4 Knox ***South American:*** 9 San Martin ***Swiss:*** 4 Ador 5 Welti

static 5 fixed, inert, rigid, stuck 6 stable, steady, sticky 7 stabile, stalled, stopped 8 constant, immobile, inactive, stagnant, unmoving 9 immovable 10 unchanging 13 unfluctuating

station 3 set 4 post, rank, site, spot 5 depot, locus, place, point, state, where 6 assign 7 appoint, footing 8 capacity, standing 9 character

stationary 5 fixed 6 static 8 immobile, stagnant, unmoving 9 immovable 10 motionless, stock-still

statue ***base:*** 6 plinth 8 pedestal ***gigantic:*** 8 Colossus ***Greek:*** 5 atlas 7 telamon 8 caryatid ***religious:*** 5 Pietà ***small:*** 8 figurine

statuesque 4 trim 7 shapely 10 well-turned 11 clean-limbed

stature see status

status 4 rank 5 merit, place, worth 6 cachet, rating, renown 7 caliber, dignity, footing, posture, quality 8 capacity, eminence, position, prestige, standing 9 character, condition, situation 10 prominence 11 consequence, distinction

statute 3 act, law 4 rule 5 canon, edict 6 assize, decree 7 precept 8 decretum 9 enactment, ordinance 10 regulation

staunch 4 fast, firm, sure, true 5 liege, loyal 6 ardent, secure, stable, strong 8 constant, faithful, resolute 9 allegiant, steadfast

stave off 4 ward 5 avert, block, deter, parry, rebut, repel 6 rebuff 7 forfend, obviate, prevent, repulse, rule out, ward off 8 preclude 9 forestall

stay 3 lag 4 base, bide, halt, live, prop, rest, stop, wait 5 abide, brace, check, dally, defer, delay, dwell, found, remit, shore, tarry, visit 6 arrest, bottom, column, ground, linger, loiter, put off, remain, shelve 7 adjourn, sojourn, support, suspend 8 buttress, hold over, intermit, postpone, prorogue, stop over 9 establish, interrupt, predicate 10 dillydally, hang around 11 stick around

steadfast 4 firm, sure, true 5 fixed, liege, loyal, rigid 6 ardent 7 abiding, adamant, patient, staunch 8 constant, enduring, faithful, immobile, immotile, immotive, obdurate, resolute, stubborn 9 allegiant, immovable, unbending, unmovable 10 inexorable, inflexible, relentless, unwavering, unyielding 11 irremovable, unfaltering, unflinching, unqualified 12 never-failing, single-minded, wholehearted 13 unquestioning

steady 3 set 4 beau, even, fast, sure 5 fixed, flame, liege, lover, loyal, poise 6 ardent, stable, static 7 abiding, ballast, beloved, certain, durable, equable, stabile, staunch, uniform 8 constant, enduring, faithful, ladylove, reliable, resolute, truelove, unshaken 9 allegiant, boyfriend, inamorata, inamorato, stabilify, stabilize, unvarying 10 changeless, girl friend, sweetheart, unchanging, unswerving, unwavering 11 unfaltering 12 unchangeable, unflickering, wholehearted 13 unfluctuating

steak 4 club, cube 5 chuck, flank, round, T-bone 6 rib eye 7 sirloin 9 Delmonico, hamburger, Salisbury 10 tenderloin 11 porterhouse 13 chateaubriand

steal 3 cop, nab, nim, nip, rob 4 glom, grab, hook, kite, lift, loot, lurk, slip, take 5 annex, creep, filch, glide, grasp, heist, mooch, mouse, pinch, poach, prowl, rifle, seize, shirk, sidle, skulk, slide, slink, sneak, swipe, theft **6** burgle, collar, fleece, hijack, pilfer, pocket, rustle, smouch, snatch, snitch, thieve, tiptoe **7** bargain, gumshoe, larceny, pillage, plunder, purloin **8** shanghai, shoplift, thievery, thieving **9** pussyfoot **10** burglarize **11** appropriate ***a vehicle:*** **6** hijack **8** highjack

stealing **7** larceny ***combining form:*** **5** klept **6** klepto

stealthy **3** sly **4** wily **5** catty, quiet, sneak **6** covert, crafty, feline, secret, shifty, silent, slinky, sneaky **7** catlike, cunning, furtive, sub-rosa **8** hush-hush, skulking, slinking, sneaking **9** noiseless **10** pantherine, pantherish, undercover **11** clandestine **12** hugger-mugger **13** surreptitious

steam **5** force, might, power, sinew **6** energy, muscle **7** potency **8** strength **9** puissance ***combining form:*** **5** atmid **6** atmido

steam bath **5** sauna

steamboat structure **5** texas

steamer **4** boat, clam, ship

steam organ **8** calliope

steamship abbreviation **2** SS

steed **5** horse **7** charger

steel **4** gird **5** brace, cheer, nerve, rally, ready **6** buck up **7** animate, chirk up, fortify, hearten, prepare **8** embolden, inspirit **9** encourage, enhearten, reinforce **10** strengthen

steep **3** sop **4** high, soak **5** dizzy, imbue, lofty, sheer **6** abrupt, drench, infuse **7** arduous, extreme, suffuse **8** elevated, saturate **9** excessive **10** exorbitant, immoderate, impregnate, inordinate **11** precipitate, precipitous

steeple **5** spire **6** flèche

steer **3** see, tip **4** lead, show **5** guide, pilot, point, route **6** direct, escort, tip-off **7** channel, conduct **8** shepherd ***a racing rowboat:*** **3** cox **8** coxswain ***a ship:*** **4** conn, helm, luff **7** boxhaul

stein **3** cup, mug **5** stoup **6** goblet, seidel **7** tankard

Steinbeck novel **10** Cannery Row, East of Eden **12** Of Mice and Men, Tortilla Flat **13** Grapes of Wrath

Steinway product **5** piano

stellar **4** main **5** chief, major **6** astral, starry **7** capital, shining **8** dominant, gleaming, luminous, lustrous, sidereal, starlike **9** principal **10** preeminent **11** outstanding, predominant

stem **4** flow, head, rise, stop **5** arise, check, issue **6** arrest, spring, stanch **7** control, emanate, proceed **8** peduncle **9** originate **10** derive from ***covering:*** **5** ocrea ***plant:*** **4** halm **5** haulm ***suffix:*** **3** ome ***underground:*** **5** tuber **7** rhizoma, rhizome

stench **4** funk, reek **5** smell, stink

stenchful see **smelly**

stentorian **4** loud **5** rough **7** blaring, orotund, roaring **8** gravelly, piercing **9** clamorous **10** loud-voiced, vociferous **11** full-mouthed, loudmouthed **12** earsplitting **13** clarion-voiced

step **3** act **4** hoof, move, pace, rung, walk **5** dance, grade, notch, spoor, stage, stair, track, tract, tread, troop **6** action, degree, prance **7** measure, traipse **8** ambulate **9** footprint, procedure **10** proceeding ***dance:*** **3** pas ***one of a series:*** **6** gradin **7** gradine

step-by-step **7** gradual **9** piecemeal

stepmotherly **8** novercal

steppe **5** plain ***Kazakhstan:*** **6** Kirgiz **10** Betpak-Dala

Steppenwolf author **5** Hesse

stereotypical **4** hack **5** stale, trite **6** cliché, common **7** clichéd **8** bathetic, shopworn, timeworn **9** hackneyed **11** commonplace

sterile **3** dry **4** arid, bare, dead, flat **5** stale, vapid **6** barren, effete, fallow, jejune **7** insipid, worn-out **8** desolate, impotent, infecund **9** fruitless, infertile **10** uncreative, unfruitful, uninspired, unoriginal, unprolific **12** unproductive

sterilize **3** fix **4** geld, spay **5** alter, unsex **6** change, neuter **8** caponize, castrate, mutilate, sanitate, sanitize **10** emasculate, poulardize

sterilized **7** aseptic

sterling **4** pure, true **5** noble **6** worthy **9** estimable, honorable

stern **4** grim **5** sober, stony **6** flinty, severe, strict **7** ascetic, austere **9** mortified **10** astringent, implacable, inexorable, inflexible **11** unrelenting

Sterope ***father:*** **5** Atlas ***mother:*** **7** Pleione ***sisters:*** **8** Pleiades

Stevenson novel **9** Kidnapped

stew **4** boil, brew, cark, flap, fret, fume, fuss, hash, olio, olla, slum, snit **5** civet, daube, salmi, sweat, tizzy, worry **6** burgoo, dither, jumble, lather, medley, paella, pother, ragout, salmis, scouse, seethe, simmer, swivet, tumult **7** goulash, mélange, parboil, puchero, turmoil **8** mishmash, mulligan, pot-au-feu **9** agitation, Brunswick, cassoulet, commotion, confusion, pasticcio, potpourri **10** capilotade, hodgepodge, hotchpotch, miscellany, turbulence **11** olla podrida, ratatouille, slumgullion

steward **6** manage **7** manager

Stheno see **Gorgon**

stick **3** bar, dig, fix, gag, get, jib, lay, nod, put, ram, rod, run, set, shy **4** balk, beat, clip, glue, milk, pole, rook, sink, skin, slab, soak, stab **5** affix, baton, bleed, blind, cling, decoy, demur, drive, ingot, mulct, paste,

place, shill, strip, stump, sweat **6** adhere, attach, billet, boggle, capper, cement, cleave, cohere, fasten, fleece, plunge, settle, strain, thrust **7** buffalo, nonplus, scruple, stumble **9** establish, shillaber **10** overcharge *combining form:* **5** rhabd **6** rhabdo
stick around **4** bide, stay, wait **5** abide, tarry **6** linger, remain
sticker **4** seal **5** stamp
stick-in-the-mud **4** fogy **6** fogram, fossil, square **8** mossback **10** fuddy-duddy
stick out **3** jut **4** bear, poke, pout, push, take **5** abide, brook, bulge, pouch, stand **6** beetle, endure, strike **7** project, protend, stomach, support **8** overhang, protrude, tolerate **9** outthrust **10** outstretch
stick up **3** rob **4** loot **5** rifle **7** plunder, ransack, relieve **9** knock over
sticky **4** hard **5** gluey, gooey, gummy, heavy, humid, muggy, mushy, rough, soggy, tacky **6** cloggy, knotty, resiny, rugged, slushy, stodgy, sultry, viscid **7** maudlin, mawkish, operose, viscous **8** adhesive, bathetic, resinous, romantic **9** difficult, laborious, strenuous **10** formidable **11** sentimental, tear-jerking
stiff **3** dry, set **4** arid, body, dull, hard, lush, mort, skin **5** drunk, miser, nabal, rigid, stark, steep, stock, tense, undue **6** boozer, corpse, mulish, wooden **7** buckram, cadaver, carcass, extreme, guzzler, muddled, niggard, scrooge, stilted, studied, swiller **8** drunkard, hardened, tightwad, towering **9** cardboard, disguised, excessive, impliable, inebriate, inelastic, obstinate, petrified, pixilated, resistant, skinflint, unbending **10** boozehound, bullheaded, cheapskate, exorbitant, hardheaded, immoderate, inebriated, inflexible, inordinate, mechanical, self-willed, unflexible, unyielding **11** extravagant, immalleable, incompliant, intoxicated, intractable **12** closed-minded, pertinacious
stiffen **6** harden, tauten **7** bolster, buckram, support, thicken **8** rigidify, solidify **9** constrict, formalize, stabilize **10** immobilize
stifle **4** mute **5** burke, choke **6** dampen, deaden, hush up, muffle **7** smother, trammel **8** stagnate, stultify, suppress **9** suffocate **10** asphyxiate
stigma **4** blot, blur, onus, slur, spot **5** brand, odium, shame, stain, taint **6** smudge, smutch **8** black eye, disgrace, dishonor, tainting **11** bar sinister **12** besmirchment
stigmatize **7** censure **8** denounce, identify **9** designate
still **3** too, yet **4** also, balm, calm, even, hush, lull, more **5** allay, along, quiet, shush, whist **6** as well, becalm, hushed, placid, serene, settle, shut up, silent, though, withal **7** besides, compose, deathly, halcyon, howbeit, however, hushful, silence **8** after all, choke off, likewise, moreover, peaceful, quietude, stagnant, tranquil **9** deathlike, noiseless, quietness, soundless **10** motionless, untroubled **11** furthermore, nonetheless, tranquilize, unperturbed **12** additionally, nevertheless
stilt **4** bird, pole **8** longlegs
stilted **4** prim **6** formal, la-di-da, too-too, wooden **7** aureate, buckram, flowery, genteel **8** affected, decorous, sonorous **9** bombastic, cardboard **10** euphuistic
stilt-like bird **6** avocet
stimulant **4** goad, spur **7** caffein, impetus, impulse **8** caffeine, catalyst, excitant **9** incentive **10** incitation, incitement, motivation
stimulate **4** move **5** pique, rouse, set up **6** arouse, excite, vivify **7** commove, enliven, innerve, inspire, provoke, quicken **8** activate, dynamize, energize, motivate, spirit up, vitalize **9** galvanize, innervate **10** exhilarate
stimulus **4** goad, push, spur **5** boost, cause **6** motive, urging **7** impetus, impulse, piquing **8** catalyst, stressor **9** incentive **10** excitement, incitation, incitement, inducement, invitation, motivation, propellant **11** instigation, provocation, provocative **13** encouragement
sting **4** bite, burn **5** smart
stinging **8** aculeate
stingy **4** mean **5** close, scant, tight **6** frugal, narrow, scrimy **7** chinchy, costive, miserly, niggard, save-all, scrimpy, sparing, thrifty **8** pinching, ungiving **9** niggardly, penny-wise, penurious **10** economical, hardfisted, hardhanded, ironfisted, pinchpenny, ungenerous **11** closefisted, tightfisted **12** cheeseparing, parsimonious **13** narrowhearted, penny-pinching
stink **4** funk, reek **5** smell **6** stench **7** malodor **8** malaroma
stinker **3** cur, dog **4** scum, snot **5** skunk, snake
stinking see **smelly**
stinky see **smelly**
stint **2** go **3** job **4** bout, duty, task, time, tour, turn **5** chare, chore, cramp, pinch, scant, screw, share, shift, short, skimp, spare, spell, trick **6** amount, devoir, scrape, scrimp, skinch **8** quantity **9** allotment, stricture **10** assignment, limitation **11** restriction
stipend **3** fee, pay **4** hire, wage **5** award **6** salary **7** payment **9** emolument **13** consideration
stipple **3** dot **5** speck **6** pepper, streak **7** freckle, speckle **8** sprinkle **9** bespeckle
stipulate **5** state **6** detail **7** provide, specify **9** designate **13** particularize

stipulation 5 limit, terms 7 proviso, strings 9 provision
stir 3 ado, can, din, jug, mix, pen, set 4 abet, boil, fuss, jail, keep, moil, move, rout, wake, whet 5 awake, churn, drive, impel, raise, rally, rouse, roust, set on, waken, whirl 6 arouse, awaken, bubble, bustle, excite, flurry, foment, furore, hubbub, incite, kindle, motion, pother, seethe, simmer, tumult, whip up 7 actuate, agitate, ferment, inspire, provoke, quicken 8 activate, energize, movement, vitalize 9 agitation, challenge, commotion, galvanize, instigate, stimulate 11 disturbance, pandemonium
stirrup 6 stapes
stithy 5 anvil
stock 4 clan, folk, fund, have, hope, keep, race 5 carry, faith, hoard, house, tribe, trust 6 family, supply 7 backlog, furnish, kindred, lineage, nest egg, reserve 8 estimate, judgment, reliance 9 appraisal, inventory, reservoir 10 assessment, confidence, dependence, estimation, evaluation
stockade 3 can, jug 4 coop, jail 6 cooler, lockup, prison 8 hoosegow 9 calaboose, guardroom
stock exchange 6 bourse
stockings 4 hose 7 hosiery
stockpile 4 bank, heap, hill, hive, mass 5 amass, drift, hoard, lay up, mound, stack, store, uplay 6 garner, roll up 7 backlog, nest egg, pyramid, reserve, store up 8 cumulate, mountain 9 inventory, reservoir 10 accumulate
stocky 3 fat 5 bunty, cobby, dumpy, lumpy, plump, pudgy, short, squab, squat, thick 6 chuffy, chumpy, chunky, low-set, squdgy, stubby, stuggy, stumpy 7 lumpish 8 heavyset, thickset 9 corpulent 11 thick-bodied
stodge 4 cloy, fill, flut, jade, pall, plod, sate, slog, slop, toil 5 gorge 6 trudge 7 filling, satiate, surfeit 8 footslog, plunther
stodgy 4 blah, dull 5 dowdy, dumpy, gluey, gooey, gummy, heavy, tacky 6 boring, claggy, clarty, cloggy, dreary, frumpy, sticky 7 humdrum, weighty 8 banausic, frumpish, outmoded, pedantic, plodding 9 hidebound, out-of-date, ponderous, unstylish 10 monotonous, pedestrian, unexciting
stoic 3 dry 5 aloof 7 patient, Spartan 8 detached, resigned 9 apathetic, impassive 10 phlegmatic 11 indifferent, indomitable, unconcerned
stoicism 4 grit, guts, sand 5 pluck 6 apathy 8 backbone 9 fortitude, stolidity 11 impassivity 13 insensibility ***founder:*** 4 Zeno
stoke 4 feed, poke, stir, tend 6 supply
Stoker, Bram ***novel:*** 7 Dracula
stolid 3 dry 4 dull, dumb, slow 5 blunt, dense, inert 6 bovine, obtuse, supine 7 passive 8 inactive, rocklike 9 apathetic, impassive 10 phlegmatic
stomach 3 gut 4 bear, craw, take 5 abide, belly, brook, stand, taste, tummy 6 digest, endure, paunch, venter 7 abdomen, swallow 8 appetite, tolerate 9 appetence ***combining form:*** 5 gastr 6 gaster, gastro, ventri, ventro 7 gastero, gastria ***enzyme:*** 6 pepsin, rennin ***muscle:*** 7 pylorus ***ruminant:*** 5 rumen 6 omasum 8 abomasum 9 reticulum ***Scottish:*** 4 kyte
stomachache 5 colic, gripe 6 misery 8 distress 12 collywobbles
stomp 5 tramp 7 trample
stone 3 gem 4 buhr, rock 5 lapis, logan, stane 6 pebble, testis 7 boulder, lapides (plural), surface 8 calculus ***base:*** 6 plinth ***block of:*** 8 monolith ***combining form:*** 4 lite, lith, lyte ***cosmic:*** 6 meteor 9 chondrite, meteorite ***for grinding grains:*** 6 metate ***fruit:*** 5 drupe ***memorial:*** 7 obelisk ***monument:*** 8 megalith ***of a fruit:*** 3 pit 6 pyrene ***precious:*** 6 ligure
___ Stone 7 Blarney, Rosetta
stonecrop 5 sedum
stoned 4 high 5 boozy, doped, drunk 6 canned, lushed, zonked 7 drugged, muddled 8 hopped-up, turned on, wiped out 9 disguised, pixilated, plastered, spaced-out 10 inebriated, tripped out 11 intoxicated
stonelike 7 lithoid
Stooge 3 Moe (Howard) 5 Curly (Howard), Larry (Fine)
stool pigeon 3 rat 4 fink, nark, pimp, sing 5 peach 6 canary, inform, snitch, squeak, squeal 7 tipster
stoop 3 dip 4 duck, sink, thaw 5 deign, favor, kneel, porch, relax 6 accord, crouch, oblige, unbend 7 concede, descend, portico 10 condescend 11 accommodate
stop 3 bar, can, dam, end, see 4 balk, call, clog, fill, halt, plug, quit, stay, stem, wall 5 block, brake, cease, check, choke, close, stall, tarry 6 arrest, cut off, desist, draw up, ending, haul up, hinder, kibosh, lay off, pull up, stanch 7 barrier, break up, bring up, closing, congest, disrupt, occlude, prevent, shut off, sojourn, suspend, turn off 8 blockade, knock off, leave off, obstruct, surcease 9 barricade, cessation, interrupt, roadblock, terminate 10 conclusion, desistance, standstill 11 discontinue, refrain from, termination ***blood:*** 6 stanch ***up:*** 4 cork, plug 7 occlude 8 obturate
stopgap 5 shift 6 refuge, resort 8 recourse, resource 9 expedient, makeshift 10 expediency, substitute 11 provisional

stopover 5 visit 7 sojourn 9 tarriance ***for troops:*** 5 étape

stoppage 6 strike ***combining form:*** 5 stasi 6 stases (plural), stasia, stasis ***work:*** 6 hartal, strike

stopper 4 clog, fill, plug 5 block, choke, close 7 congest, occlude 8 obstruct

store 3 bin 4 fund, hive, pack, shop, tank 5 amass, cache, depot, hoard, lay up, stash 6 bestow, bought, garner, market, outlet, roll up, shoppe, supply 7 arsenal, backlog, deposit, nest egg, reserve 8 cumulate, emporium, magazine, mothball, showroom, squirrel 9 inventory, reservoir, stockpile, warehouse 10 accumulate, depository, repository ***candle:*** 9 chandlery ***in a silo:*** 6 ensile 8 ensilage ***shoe:*** 7 bootery

storehouse 5 depot 7 arsenal, granary 8 magazine 10 depository, repository

storekeeper 8 merchant

storeroom 6 larder, pantry 7 buttery

storm 4 hail, to-do 5 beset, buran, burst, salvo 6 assail, attack, bustle, clamor, easter, fall on, hassle, hubbub, pother, strike, volley 7 aggress, assault, barrage, clatter, ruction, typhoon 8 drumfire, fall upon 9 broadside, cannonade, commotion, fusillade 10 hurly-burly 11 bombardment

storm trooper 10 brownshirt

stormy 4 foul, wild 5 dirty, dusty, murky, rough 6 raging 7 furious, howling, roaring 8 blustery 9 turbulent 10 blustering, rip-roaring 11 tempestuous, threatening

story 3 fib, lie 4 tale, yarn 5 conte, fable 6 canard, legend, report 7 account, falsity, fiction, märchen, untruth, version 8 allegory, anecdote, folktale 9 chronicle, fairy tale, falsehood, narration, narrative 11 description, fabrication 13 prevarication ***involved:*** 8 megillah ***moral:*** 7 parable ***short:*** 5 conte 8 anecdote

storyteller 4 liar 6 fibber 8 fabulist 9 raconteur

stoup 4 font 5 basin 6 flagon 7 tankard

stout 3 fat 4 bold, hard 5 brave, heavy, obese, tough 6 fleshy, heroic, portly, strong, sturdy 7 porcine, valiant, weighty 8 fearless, intrepid, resolute, stalwart, valorous 9 corpulent, steadfast, tenacious 10 courageous, invincible, overweight 11 indomitable, thick-bodied

Stout detective 5 Wolfe (Nero)

stouthearted 4 bold 5 brave 7 doughty, valiant 8 fearless, intrepid, unafraid 9 dauntless, undaunted 10 courageous

stove 4 kiln 5 range 8 potbelly

stow 4 pack 6 steeve 9 warehouse

stower 9 stevedore

Stowe work 4 Dred

strabismus 6 squint

straddle 6 ramble, sprawl, stride 8 bestride, scramble, sprangle 11 spread-eagle

straggle 4 roam, rove 5 drift, range, stray 6 ramble, wander 7 maunder, meander

straight 4 fair, good, neat, pure 5 plain, right 6 at once, direct, honest, linear, square 7 unmixed 8 directly, first off, orthodox 9 forthwith, instanter, right away, undiluted 10 aboveboard, button-down, forthright, unmodified 11 immediately 12 concentrated, conventional, plain dealing 13 unadulterated, undeviatingly, uninterrupted ***combining form:*** 4 orth, rect 5 ortho, recti

straightaway 3 now 6 at once 8 directly, first off 9 forthwith, instanter 11 immediately

straightedge 5 razor

straighten 5 align 6 unbend, uncurl ***up:*** 4 tidy

straightforward 5 frank 6 candid, direct, honest 7 precise 8 clearcut 9 outspoken 11 undeviating

strain 3 air, irk, lay, try, tug 4 hint, mind, moil, mood, ooze, pull, seep, toil, tone, tune, vein, work 5 drive, labor, shade, sweat, tinge, touch, trace 6 harass, melody, streak, stress, strive, warble 7 descant, measure, melisma, soupçon, tension, trouble 8 diapason, distress, pressure, transude 9 suspicion 10 suggestion

strait 4 bind, pass 5 pinch 6 crisis 7 squeeze 8 exigency, hardship, juncture 9 crossroad, emergency 10 difficulty, perplexity 11 contingency ***Adriatic Sea-Ionian Sea:*** 7 Otranto ***Africa-Madagascar:*** 10 Mozambique ***Alaska:*** 3 Icy ***Alaska-Russia:*** 6 Bering ***Albania-Greece:*** 5 Corfu ***Asia-Europe:*** 11 Dardanelles ***Atlantic-Baffin Island:*** 5 Davis ***Atlantic-Gulf of Mexico:*** 7 Florida ***Atlantic-Mediterranean:*** 9 Gibraltar ***Atlantic-Nantucket Sound:*** 8 Muskeget ***Atlantic-North Sea:*** 7 English ***Atlantic-Pacific:*** 5 Drake 8 Magellan ***Atlantic-Saint Lawrence:*** 5 Cabot ***Baffin Island-Quebec:*** 6 Hudson ***Bering Sea-Sea of Okhotsk:*** 5 Kuril 6 Kurile ***Bismarck Sea-Solomon Sea:*** 6 Vitiaz ***Canada:*** 3 Rae 5 Dease ***East China Sea:*** 5 Korea 8 Tsushima ***East China-South China:*** 6 Taiwan 7 Formosa ***England-France:*** 5 Dover ***Flores Sea-Indian Ocean:*** 4 Sape ***Flores Sea-Savu Sea:*** 4 Alor ***Indian Ocean-Java Sea:*** 5 Sunda ***India-Sri Lanka:*** 4 Palk ***Indonesia:*** 4 Alas, Alor, Bali 5 Tioro 6 Lombok 7 Dampier, Makasar 8 Makassar, Surabaja ***Inner Hebrides:*** 5 Tiree ***Iran-Oman:*** 6 Hormuz ***Italy:*** 7 Messina ***Japan:*** 4 Yura 5 Bungo, Kitan 7 Hayasui ***Japan-Sakhalin Island:*** 4 Soya ***Lake Huron:*** 10 Mississagi ***Lake Huron-Lake Michigan:*** 8 Mackinac ***Malay Archipelago:*** 5 Wetar ***Malaysia-Singapore:*** 6 Johore ***Malay-Sumatra:*** 7 Malacca ***New Jersey-Staten Island:*** 7 van Kull ***New South Wales-Tasmania:*** 4 Bass ***New Zealand:*** 4 Cook ***Northwest Territories:*** 6 Barrow 8 Franklin, Victoria 13 Prince of Wales ***Nova Scotia:*** 5 Canso ***Pacific-San Francisco Bay:*** 10 Golden Gate ***Pacific-South China Sea:*** 5 Luzon ***Philippines:*** 5 Bohol, Tanon 6 Iloilo 7 Basilan ***Russia:*** 4 Kara ***Suvu Sea-Timor Sea:*** 4 Roti ***Sea of Azov-Black Sea:*** 5 Kerch 7 Enikale ***Sea of Japan:*** 5 Tatar ***Solomon Islands:*** 12 Bougainville ***South China Sea:*** 7 Mindoro 9 Singapore ***Turkey:*** 8 Bosporus 9 Karadeniz ***Vancouver-Washington:*** 10 Juan de Fuca ***Wales:*** 5 Menai ***Washington Sound:*** 4 Haro

straitlaced 4 prig, prim 6 narrow, prissy, strict, stuffy 7 genteel, prudish 8 priggish, rigorous 9 hidebound, Victorian 10 intolerant 11 puritanical 12 narrow-minded

strand 4 bank 5 beach, coast, shore, wreck 6 pile up 8 cast away 9 shipwreck

strange 3 new, odd 5 alien, crazy, fishy, funny, kinky, kooky, nutty, outré, queer, weird 6 exotic, far-out, freaky, quaint 7 amazing, bizarre, curious, erratic, oddball, offbeat, uncanny, uncouth, unknown, unusual 8 aberrant, abnormal, atypical, peculiar, romantic, singular, wondrous 9 eccentric, fantastic, grotesque, marvelous, wonderful 10 astounding, miraculous, mysterious, off-the-wall, outlandish, stupendous, surprising, unfamiliar 11 astonishing, exceptional, spectacular 12 unaccustomed 13 idiosyncratic ***combining form:*** 3 xen 4 xeno

Strange Interlude author 6 O'Neill

stranger 4 unco 5 alien 7 inconnu, visitor 8 outcomer, outsider, wanderer 9 auslander, foreigner, immigrant, transient

strangle 5 burke, choke, shush 6 garote, muffle, quelch 7 garotte, garrote 8 suppress, throttle

strapping 6 robust

stratagem 4 play, plot, ploy, ruse, wile 5 feint, trick 6 device, gambit 8 artifice, intrigue, maneuver 10 conspiracy 11 machination

strategy 4 plan 6 design, scheme 7 project 8 game plan 9 blueprint

stratum 3 bed 5 layer

Strauss ***opera:*** 6 Salome 7 Elektra 13 Rosenkavalier ***tone poem:*** 7 Don Juan 10 Don Quixote

straw 3 sow 5 blond 6 flaxen, golden, thatch ***braided:*** 6 sennit ***bundle:*** 8 windling ***Japanese:*** 4 toyo ***mat:*** 6 tatami ***plaited:*** 7 leghorn

stray 3 err, gad 4 roam, rove 5 range 6 depart, errant, ramble, random, wander 7 deviate, devious, digress, diverge, erratic, excurse, meander, runaway, traipse 8 divagate, sporadic 9 gallivant, wandering

streak 4 hint, spot, vein 5 fleck, shade, tinge, touch, trace 6 dapple, marble, mottle, strain, strake, stripe 7 striate 8 tincture 9 suspicion, variegate 10 intimation, suggestion ***of color:*** 5 vitta

streaked 8 brindled, grizzled

stream 3 run 4 burn, flow, flux, gill, gush, pour, race, roll, rush, tide 5 bourn, brook, creek, drift, flood, spate, surge 6 bourne, branch, rindle, runlet, runnel, sluice 7 current, rivulet 8 affluent ***combining form:*** 5 fluvi 6 fluvio ***rapid:*** 7 torrent ***small:*** 4 sike, syke ***verbal:*** 10 blue streak

streamer 4 flag, jack 5 color 6 banner, ensign, pennon 7 pendant, pennant 8 banderol, bannerol, standard

streamline 8 simplify

street 3 way 4 drag, path, road 5 drive, track 6 artery, avenue, ruelle 7 highway, roadway 9 boulevard 12 thoroughfare ***border:*** 7 curbing ***material:*** 6 cobble 7 asphalt 11 cobblestone ***narrow:*** 4 wynd ***show:*** 5 raree

streetcar 4 tram 7 trolley

Streetcar Named Desire, A ***author:*** 8 Williams ***character:*** 6 Stella 7 Blanche, Stanley

Street Scene author 4 Rice

strength 5 brawn, force, might, power, sense, sinew 6 burden, energy, muscle 7 potency, purport 8 firmness, security 9 soundness, stability, substance, toughness 10 stableness, steadiness, sturdiness

strengthen 4 beef, gird 5 brace, ready, sinew, steel 6 anneal, tone up 7 animate, chirk up, ensteel, fortify, hearten, prepare, support, toughen 8 embolden, energize, fortress, inspirit 9 encourage, enhearten, reinforce, undergird 10 invigorate

strenuous 4 hard, mean 5 lusty, tough, vital 6 uphill, wicked 7 dynamic, operose, toilful 8 toilsome, vigorous 9 difficult, effortful, energetic, Herculean, laborious

Strephon 8 shepherd ***beloved:*** 5 Chloe 6 Urania

stress 3 irk, try 4 pain 5 pinch 6 accent, burden, harass, import, play up, strain, weight 7 feature, tension, trouble 8 emphasis, pressure 9 emphasize, italicize, underline 10 importance, underscore 12 accentuation ***in poetry:*** 5 ictus

stretch 3 run 4 area, draw, time 5 fudge, range, reach, scope, space, spell, sweep, tract, while 6 extend, extent, length, limber,

region, spread, supple, whippy 7 breadth, compass, draw out, elastic, expanse, magnify, prolong, purview, spin out, springy, tighten 8 distance, elongate, flexible, lengthen, protract 9 amplitude, dimension, embellish, embroider, expansion, overstate, resilient 10 exaggerate *on a frame:* 6 tenter *out:* 3 lie 4 rest 6 repose, sprawl
stretchable 7 elastic, tensile 8 tensible
stretched 4 taut
stretcher 5 dooly 6 dhooly, gurney, leader, litter 7 tail fly 8 tall tale
strew 3 sow 4 dust 5 cover 6 pepper, spread 7 diffuse, disject, radiate, scatter 8 disperse, sprinkle 9 broadcast, circulate, dissipate, propagate 10 distribute 11 disseminate
strict 4 dour, grim, just, true 5 harsh, right, rigid, tough 8 exacting, faithful, rigorous 9 draconian, unsparing, veracious, veridical 10 forbidding, hard-boiled, ironhanded, oppressive 11 undistorted 12 unpermissive
stricture 4 slam, slur 5 cramp, stint 7 obloquy 9 aspersion 10 limitation, reflection 11 restriction 12 ball and chain 13 animadversion
stride 5 march, sling, stalk 8 straddle
strident 4 loud 5 harsh 6 hoarse 7 blatant, dinsome, grating, jarring, rasping, raucous, squawky 9 clamorous 10 boisterous, stentorian, stertorous, vociferant, vociferous 11 loudmouthed 12 obstreperous
strife 4 fray 5 brawl, broil, fight 6 affray, combat, fracas 7 contest, discord, dispute, dissent, quarrel, rivalry, warfare, wrangle 8 argument, conflict, disunity, squabble, tug-of-war, variance 9 disaccord, emulation 10 contention, difference, dissension, dissidence 11 altercation, competition, controversy
strike 3 hit, pop, rap 4 bang, bash, beat, dash, deal, ding, give, kick, knap, mace, poke, rack, slam, slap, slog, slug, sock, swat, whap, whop 5 beset, carry, clout, crash, flick, knack, knock, occur, punch, smack, smite, storm, swipe, thump, whack 6 affect, assail, attack, cudgel, fall on, fillip, hammer, harrow, pummel, thrash 7 afflict, aggress, assault, deliver, impress, inflict, inspire, percuss, torment, torture 8 fall upon 9 detection, discovery, influence
striking 5 showy, vivid 6 cogent, marked, signal 7 salient, telling 8 forceful, powerful 9 arresting, arrestive, prominent 10 compelling, noticeable, remarkable 11 conspicuous, outstanding
Strindberg play 6 Easter 8 Comrades 9 Miss Julie, The Father 10 Master Olaf 12 Dance of Death, Gustavus Vasa, The Creditors
string 3 row 4 file, line, rank, tier 5 chain, order, queue, shift, train 6 refuge, resort, sequel, series 7 echelon, stopgap 8 recourse, resource, sequence 9 expedient, makeshift 10 substitude, succession *up:* 4 hang 5 noose, scrag 6 gibbet
string along 3 toy 4 fool 5 dally, flirt 6 coquet, lead on, trifle, wanton
stringent see strict
stringy 4 ropy, wiry 6 sinewy 7 fibrous 8 muscular
strip 3 bar, rod 4 band, bare, doff, flay, husk, peel, sack, skin, slab 5 ingot, scale, stick, waste 6 billet, denude, devest, divest, expose, fillet, flitch, ravage, ribbon 7 bandeau, banding, deprive, disrobe, pillage, take off, uncover, undress 8 bankrupt, denudate, desolate, spoliate, unclothe 9 depredate, desecrate, devastate, dismantle 11 decorticate, excorticate *leather:* 5 thong *of wood:* 4 lath, slat *skin:* 6 flench, flense
stripe 3 ilk 4 band, flog, hide, kind, lash, sort, type, whip 5 breed, order, whale 6 fillet, kidney, lather, ribbon, strake, streak, thrash 7 bandeau, banding, feather, scourge, species, variety 10 flagellate
stripling 3 boy, lad
stripper 6 peeler, teaser 9 ecdysiast
stripteaser see stripper
strive 3 try, tug, vie 4 cope, moil, seek, toil, work 5 assay, essay, labor, offer 6 resist, strain 7 attempt, travail 8 endeavor, struggle 9 undertake
stroke 3 hit, pet 4 hone, whet 6 caress, soothe 8 apoplexy 9 heartbeat
stroll 4 mope, muck, turn, walk 5 amble, drift, mosey, paseo 6 bummel, linger, ramble 7 saunter
stroller 4 pram 5 tramp 6 go-cart 7 vagrant
strong 4 fast, firm, hard, rich, sure 5 hardy, large, lusty, stout, tough 6 ardent, brawny, heroic, mighty, potent, robust, rugged, secure, sinewy, stable, sturdy, wieldy 7 durable, staunch, unmixed 8 enduring, forceful, muscular, powerful, stalwart, straight, vigorous 9 strapping, tenacious, undiluted 10 able-bodied, full-bodied, spirituous 12 concentrated
strong-arm 5 bully 6 bounce, hector 7 dragoon 8 bludgeon, browbeat, bulldoze, bullyrag 9 terrorize 10 intimidate
strongbox 6 coffer
stronghold 4 fort 7 citadel, redoubt 8 fastness, fortress
strong point 5 forte
strong suit 5 forte 6 medium, métier, oyster 8 eminency
strontium *symbol:* 2 Sr
strophe 6 stanza
structure 4 form, pile 5 build, frame 6 fabric, format, makeup, system 7 anat-

omy, complex, edifice, network **8** building, erection, skeleton **9** framework **10** morphology **11** arrangement, composition **12** construction ***combining form:*** **5** morph **6** morpho

struggle **3** try, vie **4** agon **5** assay, essay, offer, trial **6** hassle, strive, tussle **7** attempt, compete, grapple, scuffle **8** endeavor, flounder, striving **9** undertake **11** undertaking

strumpet **4** jade, slut **5** hussy, tramp, trull, wench **6** harlot, wanton **7** jezebel, trollop **8** slattern

strut **6** flaunt, parade, prance, sashay **7** flounce, peacock, swagger

stub **4** snag **5** fence, guard **6** strike **9** pulverize

stubborn **5** balky, rigid, stunt **6** dogged, mulish, ornery, wilful **7** adamant, bullish, wayward, willful **8** obdurate **9** obstinate, pigheaded, steadfast, unbending **10** bullheaded, headstrong, inexorable, inflexible, rebellious, refractory, relentless, unyielding **11** intractable **12** cantankerous, contumacious, single-minded

stubby **5** dumpy, puggy, squat **6** chumpy, chunky, squdgy, stocky, stuggy, stumpy **7** puggish **8** heavyset **11** thick-bodied

stuck-up **4** vain **8** conceity **9** conceited **12** narcissistic, vainglorious

stud **3** dot **4** male, nail, post, spot **5** cleat **6** button, pillar, pimple **7** speckle, upright **8** sprinkle

student **5** pupil **6** premed **7** protégé ***college:*** **13** undergraduate ***combining form:*** **3** log **5** logue ***female:*** **4** coed ***first-year:*** **8** freshman ***fourth-year:*** **6** senior ***French:*** **5** élève **8** étudiant ***military:*** **5** cadet ***Muslim:*** **5** softa ***naval officer:*** **5** middy **10** midshipman ***of a guru:*** **5** chela ***placement:*** **8** tracking ***second-year:*** **9** sophomore ***third-year:*** **6** junior ***wandering:*** **7** goliard

studio **4** shop **7** atelier, bottega **8** workroom, workshop

Studs Lonigan creator **7** Farrell

study **3** con, vet **4** heed, mind, muse, view **5** learn, weigh **6** debate, lesson, musing, ponder, survey, trance **7** analyze, canvass, check up, examine, inspect, reverie **8** consider, exercise, memorize, think out, weighing **9** attention, check over, pondering, think over **10** excogitate, meditation, rumination, scrutinize **11** abstraction, application, contemplate **12** deliberation **13** concentration, consideration, contemplation ***combining form:*** **5** sophy ***group:*** **7** seminar ***hard:*** **4** cram ***suffix:*** **3** ics

stuff **3** jam, ram **4** cram, pith, soul, tamp **5** being, crowd, gorge **6** entity, marrow, matter, object, things **7** essence, jam-pack **8** material, overcram, overfill **9** substance **10** individual, virtuality **12** essentiality, quintessence

stuffed shirt **4** prig, smug **5** Blimp, prude **7** diehard **10** fuddy-duddy **12** Colonel Blimp

stuffing **3** gut, tar **6** tripes **7** innards, insides, inwards, pudding, viscera **8** dressing, entrails **9** internals

stuffy **4** dull, prim **5** close, fuggy, heavy, humid, stivy, thick, wiggy **6** narrow, prissy, proper, shut-up, stodgy, sultry **7** airless, bloated, genteel, humdrum, pompous, prudish **8** arrogant, priggish, stagnant, stifling **9** hidebound, illiberal, important, Victorian **10** breathless, oppressive, pontifical, tight-laced **11** magisterial, puritanical, straitlaced, suffocating **12** narrow-minded **13** self-important

stultify **4** dull **5** check **6** deaden, impair, stifle, weaken **7** inhibit, nullify, repress, smother, trammel **8** enfeeble, restrain, stagnate, suppress **9** suffocate **10** constipate, discourage, invalidate

stumble **3** err, sin **4** slip, trip **5** demur, error **6** falter **7** blunder, scruple, stagger, stammer **8** hesitate

stump **3** get **4** beat, dare, defi, defy **5** barge, stick **6** cartel, lumber **7** buffalo, galumph, nonplus **8** defiance **9** challenge

stun **4** daze **5** amaze **6** bedaze, bemuse, benumb, dazzle **7** astound, nonplus, petrify, stupefy **8** bewilder, knock out, paralyze **11** flabbergast

stunt **4** curb, feat **5** check, dwarf, runty, trick **6** impair, runted **7** runtish, scrunty **8** hold back, suppress

stupefy **4** daze, dull, faze **5** addle, blunt **6** bedaze, bemuse, benumb, rattle **7** nonplus, petrify **8** hebetate, paralyze

stupendous **7** amazing, massive **8** cracking, towering, wondrous **9** fantastic, marvelous, monstrous, wonderful **10** astounding, miraculous, monumental, prodigious, staggering **11** astonishing, spectacular

stupid **4** dull, dumb, slow **5** brute, crass, dense, dopey, dummy, dunce, heavy, idiot, moron, silly, thick **6** dummel, goosey, oafish, simple, torpid **7** asinine, brutish, doltish, dullard, fatuous, foolish, idiotic, lumpish, pinhead **8** backward, blockish, comatose, dullhead, dumbbell, dummkopf, duncical, ignorant, retarded, sluggish **9** blear-eyed, fatheaded, half-assed, ignoramus, imbecilic, lethargic, lumbering, pinheaded, simpleton **10** beefheaded, beef-witted, half-witted, numskulled, slow-witted, slumberous **11** blockheaded, thickheaded, thick-witted **12** beetleheaded, hammerheaded, hebetudinous **13** chuckleheaded

stupor **4** coma **5** sleep **6** torpor **7** languor, slumber **8** dullness, hebetude, lethargy, narcosis **9** lassitude, torpidity **10** anesthesia **13** insensibility ***combining form:*** **4** narc **5** narco

sturdy **5** sound, stout, tough **6** strong **7** healthy **8** stalwart **9** tenacious **11** substantial

sturgeon **6** beluga ***roe:*** **6** caviar **7** caviare

Sturm und Drang **6** unrest **7** ailment, ferment, turmoil **8** disquiet **10** inquietude **11** disquietude, restiveness **12** restlessness

St. Vitus' ___ **5** dance

sty **3** den, pen **4** dump, sink **5** Sodom **6** pigpen **7** cesspit, piggery **8** cesspool

stygian **7** avernal, hellish **8** infernal, plutonic **9** cimmerian, plutonian **11** pandemoniac

style **3** fad, way **4** chic, mode, rage, tone, vein **5** craze, decor, thing, vogue **6** manner **7** fashion, wording **9** designate **10** dernier cri **11** appellation, appellative ***hair:*** **4** coif **8** coiffure ***suffix:*** **5** esque

stylish **2** in **3** mod, new **4** chic, posh, tony, trig **5** doggy, natty, nifty, ritzy, sassy, sharp, showy, sleek, slick, smart, swank, swell **6** chichi, classy, dapper, dressy, modern, modish, new-day, rakish, snappy, snazzy, spiffy, tonish, trendy, with-it **7** à la mode, dashing, doggish, swagger **8** spiffing, up-to-date **9** exclusive **10** newfangled **11** fashionable, modernistic, pretentious **12** new-fashioned, ostentatious

Stymphalides' slayer **8** Heracles, Hercules

styx **5** nymph, river **7** hateful ***father:*** **7** Oceanus ***ferryman:*** **6** Charon ***location:*** **5** Hades ***mother:*** **6** Tethys

Suah's father **6** Zophah

suave **5** bland, slick **6** genial, polite, smooth, urbane **7** affable, cordial, courtly, fulsome, politic, refined, tactful, worldly **8** cultured, gracious, polished, sociable, unctuous, well-bred **9** courteous, distingué **10** cultivated, diplomatic, soft-spoken **12** ingratiating **13** sophisticated

sub **5** under **6** fill-in **7** stand-in **9** alternate, dependent, secondary **10** collateral **11** locum tenens, pinch hitter, replacement

subaltern **8** inferior **9** secondary, underling

subdue **5** crush, quash, quell **6** defeat, master, quench, reduce **7** conquer, put down, squelch **8** bear down, beat down, suppress, vanquish **9** overpower, subjugate

subdued **4** soft, tame **5** quiet, sober **6** low-key, mellow **7** neutral, serious **8** low-keyed, softened, tasteful, tempered **9** moderated, toned down **10** controlled, restrained, submissive **11** inobtrusive, unobtrusive

subjacent **3** low **5** lower, under **6** lesser, nether **8** inferior

subject **3** apt **4** core, head, meat, open, text **5** motif, point, prone, theme, topic, under **6** expose, liable, likely, matter, motive **7** citizen, exposed, lay open, problem, servile, slavish, uncover **8** argument, material, notional, question **9** dependent, leitmotif, leitmotiv, obnoxious, secondary, sensitive, substance, tributary **10** collateral **11** subordinate, subservient, susceptible

subjective **6** biased **10** prejudiced

subjugate see **subdue**

sublime **4** holy **5** erect, exalt, grand, honor, ideal, lofty, noble, proud **6** august, divine, sacred, superb **7** dignify, ennoble, exalted, glorify, magnify, stately **8** elevated, glorious, gorgeous, majestic, splendid **9** spiritual **10** aggrandize **11** distinguish, magnificent, resplendent, splendorous **12** transcendent **13** splendiferous

submerge **3** dip **4** duck, dunk, sink, soak **5** douse, drown, flood, souse, swamp, whelm **6** deluge, drench, engulf, go down **7** founder, go under, immerse **8** inundate, overflow, saturate

submerse see **submerge**

submissive **4** tame **6** menial **7** obeying, servile, slavish, subdued, unerect **8** resigned, uxorious, yielding **9** complying **10** bowing down **11** acquiescent, conformable, subservient, unresistant, unresisting **12** nonresistant, nonresisting

submit **3** bow **4** cave, fall **5** bring, defer, offer, refer, yield **6** go down, hand in, send in, tender **7** deliver, go under, knuckle, present, proffer, provide, succumb, suggest **8** theorize **9** surrender **10** capitulate **11** buckle under **12** knuckle under

subordinate **5** minor, scrub, under **7** adjunct, subject **8** adjuvant, inferior, pargergal **9** accessory, auxiliary, dependent, satellite, secondary, subaltern, tributary, underling **10** collateral, subsidiary

suborn **6** incite, induce **9** instigate

sub rosa **8** covertly, in camera, secretly **9** by stealth, furtively, privately **10** stealthily **12** hugger-mugger **13** clandestinely

subscribe **3** ink, yes **4** sign **5** agree, favor **6** accede, adhere, assent **7** approve, consent, endorse **8** sanction **9** acquiesce, autograph, signature **10** contribute

subsequent **4** next **5** after, later **6** serial **7** ensuing **9** following, posterior, resultant, resulting, succedent **10** sequential, succeeding, successive **11** consecutive ***prefix:*** **4** post

subservient **4** mean **6** abject, menial **7** fawning, ignoble, servile, slavish **8** adjuvant, cowering, cringing, obeisant, resigned **9** accessory, ancillary, auxiliary, compliant, truckling **10** collateral, obsequious, submissive **11** acquiescent

subside **3** ebb **4** fall, lull, wane **5** abate, let up **7** die away, die down, ease off, slacken **8** moderate

subsidiary **5** minor **6** back-up **8** adjuvant **9** accessory, ancillary, tributary **10** collateral

subsidize **4** back, fund, help **5** endow **7** finance, promote

subsidy **4** gift **5** grant **6** reward **10** subvention **13** appropriation

subsist **2** be **4** live, move **7** breathe

subsistence **4** keep, salt **5** bread **6** living **7** alimony, support **10** sustenance **11** maintenance **12** alimentation

substance **3** nub **4** body, bulk, core, crux, gist, mass, meat, pith, soul **5** being, drift, focus, heart, point, sense, short, stuff, tenor, thing, worth **6** amount, bottom, burden, center, corpus, entity, import, kernel, marrow, matter, nubbin, object, riches, staple, thrust, upshot, wealth **7** essence, fortune, meaning, nucleus, purport **8** additive, material, property, strength, sum total **9** resources **10** individual, virtuality **12** essentiality, quintessence ***combining form:*** **3** hyl **4** hylo **5** phane, state ***transparent:*** **6** hyalin **7** hyaline

substantial **3** big **4** easy, snug, well **5** gross, solid **6** strong **7** weighty, well-off **8** material, physical, sensible, tangible, well-to-do **9** corporeal, important, momentous, objective, well-fixed **10** meaningful, phenomenal, prosperous, well-heeled **11** comfortable, significant **12** considerable

substantiate **3** try **4** test **5** prove **6** embody, verify **7** bear out, confirm, justify **8** manifest, validate **9** incarnate, objectify, personify, personize **11** corroborate, demonstrate, exteriorize, externalize, materialize, personalize **12** authenticate

substantive **4** firm, noun, real **5** solid **8** definite **9** essential

substitute **4** mock, sham, swap **5** dummy, false, locum, other, proxy, trade **6** back-up, change, deputy, double, ersatz, fill-in, refuge, resort, second, switch **7** another, replace, reserve, standby, stand-in, stopgap **8** exchange, recourse, resource, spurious, supplant **9** alternate, expedient, imitation, makeshift, simulated, surrogate **10** additional, artificial, expediency, suppletory, understudy **11** alternative, locum tenens, pinch hitter, replacement, succedaneum ***combining form:*** **5** pseud **6** pseudo ***suffix:*** **4** ette

substratum **4** base, core, meat, root, seat **5** basis, stuff **6** bottom, ground **7** bedrock, footing **10** foundation, groundwork **12** underpinning

substructure **4** base, seat **5** basis **6** bottom **10** foundation, groundwork

subsume **4** have **6** embody, take in **7** contain, embrace, include, involve **9** encompass **10** comprehend

subterfuge **5** cheat, fraud **6** dupery **7** chicane **8** trickery **9** chicanery, deception **10** dishonesty **11** highbinding **13** double-dealing

subterranean **4** cave **6** cavern, grotto **9** underfoot **10** underearth **11** underground

subtile **4** rare, thin **7** elusive, tenuous **8** rarefied

subtle **3** sly **4** deep, fine, foxy, nice, wily **6** artful, astute, crafty **7** cunning, logical, refined **8** analytic, delicate, finespun, guileful, hairline, skillful **9** dexterous, insidious **10** analytical

subtract **4** take **6** deduct **7** take off, take out **8** discount, draw back, knock off, take away

subtraction **6** rebate **8** discount **9** abatement ***word:*** **7** minuend **9** remainder

suburbs **7** fringes **8** environs, outskirt, purlieus

subversion **8** sabotage, wreckage, wrecking **10** destroying **11** demolishing, destruction, undermining

subvert **4** ruin **5** upset, wreck **6** debase **7** corrupt, deprave, destroy **8** demolish, overturn, sabotage **9** overthrow, undermine

subway ***British:*** **4** tube **11** underground ***French:*** **5** métro

succeed **2** go **4** boom **5** click, ensue, score **6** arrive, follow, go over, pan out, thrive, win out **7** catch on, come off, make out, prevail, prosper, triumph **8** flourish, get ahead, prove out **9** supervene **10** accomplish

success **3** hit **7** arrival, killing, triumph, victory **10** attainment, prosperity **11** achievement

successful **5** smash **7** notable **8** smashing, thriving **10** noteworthy, prosperous **11** flourishing

succession **3** row **5** chain, cycle, order, round, suite, train **6** course, sequel, series, string **8** sequence **11** consecution

succinct **4** curt **5** blunt, brief, short, terse **7** brusque, concise, laconic, summary **11** compendiary, compendious **12** breviloquent

succor **3** aid **4** hand, help, lift **6** assist, relief **7** comfort, secours, support **8** ministry **10** assistance, sustenance **11** maintenance, nourishment **12** ministration

succubus **5** demon, devil, fiend, Satan **9** archfiend

succulent **5** juicy, sappy

succumb **3** bow, die **4** cave, drop, fall, pass, wilt **5** defer, yield **6** cash in, cave in, demise, depart, expire, go down, peg out, perish, resign, submit 7 decease, give out, go under, knuckle 8 collapse, pass away 9 break down, surrender 10 capitulate 11 buckle under 12 knuckle under

such 4 akin, like, said, that 5 alike 7 similar 8 parallel 9 aforesaid, analogous 10 comparable, equivalent 13 corresponding

suck 3 lap, sip 4 draw 5 nurse 6 absorb, imbibe, inhale

sucker 3 gyp, sap 4 beat, bilk, dupe, fool, gull, mark 5 cheat, chump, cozen, leech 6 diddle, pigeon, sponge 7 defraud, fall guy, saphead, sponger 8 barnacle, hanger-on, parasite 9 schlemiel 10 freeloader

suckle 5 nurse 7 nourish 10 breast-feed

Sudan ***capital:*** 8 Khartoum ***monetary unit:*** 5 pound

sudden 4 fast 5 fleet, hasty, rapid, swift 6 abrupt 7 hurried, rushing 8 headlong 9 forthwith, impetuous, quickened 11 precipitant, precipitate, precipitous, subitaneous

suds 4 beer, foam, soap 5 froth, spume 6 lather

sue 3 woo 5 court, spark 6 appeal 7 address, implead 8 litigate, make up to, petition

suer 8 litigant

suet 3 fat 6 tallow ***combining form:*** 5 steat 6 steato

Suez Canal ***builder:*** 9 de Lesseps ***city:*** 8 Ismailia, Port Said

suffer 3 bow, let, see 4 bear, have, know, lump, take 5 abide, admit, allow, brook, leave, stand, yield 6 accept, endure, permit, submit 7 agonize, anguish, receive, stomach, sustain, swallow, undergo 8 tolerate 9 acquiesce 10 experience 11 countenance

sufferance 5 leave 6 permit 7 consent 8 sanction 10 permission 13 authorization

sufferer 6 victim ***combining form:*** 4 path

suffering 5 agony, dolor 6 misery 7 passion 8 distress 9 adversity 10 misfortune ***combining form:*** 5 pathy 6 pathic

suffice 2 do 5 serve 6 enough

sufficient 3 due 5 ample 6 common, decent, enough, plenty 8 adequacy, adequate, all right, pleasing 9 agreeable, competent, plenteous, plentiful, tolerable 10 acceptable, competence 11 comfortable 12 commensurate, satisfactory 13 commensurable, proportionate, unexceptional ***poetic:*** 4 enow

suffix ***adjective:*** 2 al, an, ar, er, ic, ly 3 ant, ary, ean, ent, ese, est, eth, fic, ful, ial, ian, ile, ine, ish, ist, oid, ory, ose, ous 4 able, eous, ible, ical, ious, less 5 ative, istic, oidal, ulent 6 escent, itious 7 istical ***noun:*** 2 ad, al, cy, ee, er, et, il, on, or, th, ty 3 ade, ana, ant, ard, ata, ate, dom, een, eer, ery, ese, ice, ics, ier, ile, ine, ing, ion, ism, ist, ite, ity, ium, ive, ode, oma, ome, one, ote, sis 4 ance, ancy, ence, ency, esis, ette, etum, iana, itis, ling, ment, ness, osis, ship, ster, trix, tron 5 arian, arium, aster, ation, iasis, ician, onium, orium, tress 7 escence, isation, ization ***verb:*** 2 ed, en, fy, le 3 ate, ify, ing, ise, ize 4 lyse, lyze

suffocate 5 burke, choke, stive 6 stifle 7 quackle, smother 8 strangle 10 asphyxiate

suffrage 4 vote 5 voice 6 ballot 9 franchise

suffragist 4 Howe (Julia) 5 Stone (Lucy) 7 Anthony (Susan B.), Stanton (Elizabeth) 9 Pankhurst (Emmeline)

suffuse 5 imbue, steep 6 invest, leaven 7 ingrain 9 inoculate, interject, interpose, introduce

sugar 6 aldose, fucose, xylose 7 glucose, lactose, maltose, mannose, pentose, sorbose, sucrose, sweeten 8 fructose, furanose, levulose 10 saccharose ***combining form:*** 3 lyx 4 gluc, glyc, lyxo, sucr, thre 5 gluco, glyco, sucro, threo 7 sacchar 8 sacchari, saccharo ***from palm sap:*** 7 jaggery ***Mexican:*** 7 panocha, panoche ***source:*** 4 beet, cane, corn 5 maple ***suffix:*** 3 ose 5 ulose

sugarcane refuse 7 bagasse

sugarcoat 5 candy, honey, white 6 veneer, whiten 7 sweeten, varnish 8 palliate 9 extenuate, gloss over, gloze over, whitewash 10 blanch over, edulcorate

suggest 3 put 4 hint, pose 5 imply, point 6 prefer, submit 7 connote, propose 8 indicate, intimate, propound, theorize 9 adumbrate, insinuate

suggestion 3 cue 4 clue, hint, vein, wind 5 shade, smack, tinge, trace 6 advice, strain 7 inkling, proffer 8 allusion, innuendo, overtone, proposal, reminder, telltale 9 suspicion, undertone

suggestive 4 blue, racy, sexy 5 broad, salty, shady, spicy 6 erotic, purple, risqué, wicked 8 off-color 9 evocative

suicidal pilot 8 kamikaze

suicide 8 felo-de-se, hara-kiri 10 self-murder 13 self-slaughter ***Japanese:*** 7 seppuku

suit 2 do, go 3 fit 4 case, jibe, plea 5 adapt, agree, befit, cause, check, serve, tally 6 accord, action, adjust, appeal, asking, become, go with, orison, please, prayer, square, tailor 7 conform, enhance, flatter, lawsuit, request, satisfy, suffice 8 check out, entreaty, petition, quadrate 9 agree with, reconcile 10 go together, requesting, soliciting, tailor-make 11 accommodate, application, imploration, imprecation 12 solicitation, supplication 13 harmonize with *type:* 4 zoot 6 monkey, vested 9 paternity 10 pin-striped 11 class action

suitable 3 apt, due, fit 4 good, just, meet, nice 5 happy, right 6 proper, seemly, useful 7 condign, fitting, merited 8 deserved, eligible, rightful 9 requisite 10 convenient, felicitous 11 appropriate

suitcase 3 bag 4 grip 6 valise

suite 3 lot, row, set 4 body, flat, sort 5 array, batch, chain, group, rooms, train 6 clutch, parcel, rental, sequel, series, string 7 battery, lodging, retinue 8 chambers, sequence, tenement 9 apartment, entourage, following

suitor 4 beau 5 asker, lover, spark, swain, wooer 7 gallant, sparker 8 cavalier, paramour 9 boyfriend 10 petitioner

sulfur 9 brimstone *combining form:* 3 thi 4 thio

sulk 4 mope, pout 5 brood, frown, gloom, grump, scowl 6 glower

sulky 4 cart, dour, glum 5 huffy, moody, surly, testy 6 cranky, gloomy, morose, touchy 7 crabbed 9 irritable, querulous, saturnine 12 cantankerous

sullen 4 dour, glum, mean, sour, ugly 5 black, cross, moody, pouty, surly 6 crabby, gloomy, grumpy, morose 7 crabbed, cynical, fretful, hostile, mumpish, peevish, pouting 8 frowning, lowering, petulant, scowling 9 glowering, saturnine, tenebrose, tenebrous 10 ill-humored, malevolent, sourpussed, tenebrific 11 pessimistic

Sullivan's partner 7 Gilbert

sully 3 tar 4 soil 5 shame, smear, stain, taint 6 defile 7 besmear, pollute, tarnish 8 besmirch, discolor, disgrace

Sultan of Swat 8 Babe Ruth

sultry 3 hot 5 close, humid, livid, lurid, mucky, muggy, soggy, stivy 6 baking, red-hot, sticky, stuffy, torrid 7 airless, burning, tabloid 8 broiling, sizzling, smothery, stifling 9 scorching 10 breathless, sweltering 11 sensational

sum 3 add, all, tot 4 bulk, mass, tote 5 gross, total, whole 6 amount, digest, entity, figure, resumé, system 7 epitome 8 condense, entirety, integral, nutshell, totality, totalize 9 aggregate, epitomize, integrate, inventory, synopsize *small:* 7 peanuts 8 pittance

Sumatra *country:* 9 Indonesia *highest peak:* 8 Kerintji *largest city:* 5 Medan *shrew:* 4 tana

Sumerian *city:* 2 Ur 4 Umma *dragon:* 3 Kur *god:* 2 An 3 Abu, Kur, Utu 4 Enki 5 Enlil, Lahar, Nanna, Nintu 6 Dumuzi, Nergal, Ninazu 7 Enkimdu *goddess:* 2 Ki 6 Ningal, Ninlil

summarize 5 brief, recap 6 digest, resumé 8 condense, nutshell 9 epitomize, inventory, synopsize 10 retrograde 12 recapitulate

summary 4 curt 5 brief, short, terse 6 aperçu, précis, resumé 7 compact, compend, concise, epitome, laconic, outline, roundup, rundown 8 drumhead, overview, scenario, succinct, synopses (plural), synopsis 9 compacted, inventory 11 compendiary, compendious 12 breviloquent

summerhouse 6 alcove, gazebo, pagoda 9 belvedere

summery 7 estival 8 aestival

summit 3 top 4 acme, apex, peak, roof 5 crest, crown 6 apogee, climax, vertex, zenith 8 capsheaf, capstone, meridian, pinnacle 9 fastigium 11 culmination *combining form:* 3 ace, acr, akr 4 acro, akro, apic 5 apici, apico

summon 3 bid 4 beck, call, cite 5 order 6 beckon, call in, enjoin, muster 7 command, conjure, convene, convoke, subpena 8 assemble, subpoena

sump 3 bog, fen 4 mire, quag 5 marsh, swamp 6 morass, slough 8 quagmire 9 swampland

sumptuous 4 lush, rich 5 grand, plush 6 Capuan, deluxe, lavish, superb 7 opulent 8 gorgeous, imposing, luscious, palatial, splendid 9 grandiose, luxuriant, luxurious 10 impressive 11 resplendent 12 awe-inspiring

sun 3 orb, Sol 4 bask, star 7 daystar, phoebus 8 daylight, insolate, luminary, radiance 9 radiation 13 celestial body *combining form:* 4 heli 5 helio *disk:* 4 Aten *god:* 2 Ra 3 Lug, Sol, Tem, Utu 4 Amen, Atmu, Atum, Inti, Lleu, Llew, Lugh, Utug 5 Horus, Sunna, Surya 6 Apollo, Babbar, Helios, Marduk 7 Khepera, Ninurta, Phoebus, Shamash 8 Hyperion, Merodach

Sun Also Rises, The *author:* 9 Hemingway *character:* 6 Ashley (Brett), Barnes (Jake)

sunder 3 cut, rip 4 rend, rive 5 break, carve, sever, slice, split 6 cleave, divide 7 break up, disjoin, disrupt, dissect, divorce 8 disjoint, dissever, disunite, separate 11 dichotomize

sundew 7 drosera

sundial part 6 gnomon

sundries 7 notions 8 oddments 9 etceteras 11 odds and ends

sundry 4 many, some 6 divers, legion 7 diverse, several, various 8 manifold, numerous, populous 9 different 10 voluminous 12 multifarious, multitudinal 13 miscellaneous, multitudinous

sunfish 4 opah 8 bluegill

Sunflower State 6 Kansas

sun-god see at sun
Sun King 8 Louis XIV
sunny 4 fair, fine, warm 5 clear, happy 6 blithe, bright, cheery, chirpy, golden 7 clarion 8 cheerful, chirrupy, pleasant, rainless 9 brilliant, cloudless, lightsome, unclouded 10 undarkened
sunrise 4 dawn, morn 5 light 6 aurora 7 dawning, morning 8 cockcrow, daybreak, daylight *goddess:* 3 Eos 6 Aurora
sun-room 8 solarium
sunset 3 eve 4 dusk 7 evening 8 twilight
Sunset State 6 Oregon
Sunshine State 7 Florida 11 South Dakota
sunspot portion 5 umbra 8 penumbra
sunup see sunrise
sup 3 eat 4 dine 5 drink, quaff 6 imbibe 7 swallow 8 mouthful
superannuate 6 retire 7 outdate, outmode 8 obsolete 9 antiquate, obsolesce 10 pension off
superb 4 best, fine, rich 5 grand, lofty, noble, prime, proud, super 7 elegant, exalted, optimal, optimum, opulent, rousing, stately, sublime, supreme 8 crashing, elevated, glorious, gorgeous, imposing, majestic, slambang, splendid, standout 9 excellent, marvelous, wonderful 11 magnificent, outstanding, resplendent, sensational, splendorous, superlative 13 splendiferous
supercilious 5 proud 6 lordly, sniffy, snifty, snippy, snuffy 7 haughty 8 arrogant, cavalier, insolent, sneering, sniffish, snobbish, superior 10 disdainful 11 overbearing 13 high-and-mighty
superficial 5 hasty, shoal 6 casual, slight 7 cursory, general, shallow, sketchy, surface 8 skin-deep, smattery 9 depthless 10 uncritical
superfluity 5 frill, luxus 6 excess, luxury 7 amenity, surfeit, surplus, teeming 8 overflow, overkill, overmuch, overplus, plethora, swarming 10 surplusage 11 overflowing, prodigality 12 extravagance 13 overabundance
superfluous 4 over 5 extra, spare 6 de trop, excess 7 surplus, unasked, useless 8 needless, unneeded, unwanted 9 excessive, redundant 10 gratuitous 11 dispensable, uncalled-for, unnecessary 12 nonessential
superhuman 6 divine 7 demigod, uncanny 8 numinous 9 unearthly, unnatural 10 miraculous 13 extraordinary, preternatural
superintend 4 boss 5 guide 6 direct, manage, survey 7 control, oversee 8 chaperon, overlook 10 administer 11 quarterback
superintendence 4 care 6 charge 7 conduct, running 8 handling 9 authority, direction, oversight 10 management, presidence
superior 4 fine, head, lord, over, rare 5 above, dandy, elder, lofty, major, prime, proud, upper 6 better, choice, dainty, famous, higher, select, senior 7 capital, elegant, greater, haughty, premium, primary, unusual 8 arrogant, brass hat, cavalier, delicate, dominant, five-star, higher-up, insolent, numinous 9 excellent, exquisite, first-rate, marvelous, overlying, recherché, unearthly 10 disdainful, first-class, miraculous, noteworthy, preeminant, preferable, remarkable, suprahuman 11 exceptional, first-string, heavyweight, overbearing, predominant 13 high-and-mighty, preternatural
superiority 6 better 7 victory 8 whip hand 9 advantage, dominance, seniority, supremacy, upper hand 10 ascendancy
superjacent 4 over 6 higher 7 greater 9 overlying
superlative 4 best 8 finished, peerless, standout 10 consummate 11 magnificent, outstanding 12 accomplished
superlative degree *suffix:* 3 est
Superman 9 Clark Kent *cartoonist:* 7 Shuster *girl friend:* 8 Lois Lane
supernatural 5 magic 6 divine 7 uncanny, unusual 8 heavenly, numinous 9 celestial, spiritual, unearthly 10 miraculous, paranormal, phenomenal 12 metaphysical 13 extraordinary
supernatural being 3 elf, god 5 angel, deity, demon, fairy, gnome, nymph, troll 6 seraph, spirit 7 banshee, goddess 10 leprechaun *Muslim:* 4 jinn *Persian:* 4 peri
supernumerary 5 extra, spare 6 de trop, excess 7 surplus
supersede 7 replace, succeed 8 displace, outplace, set aside, supplant
supervene 5 ensue 6 follow 7 succeed
supervise 3 run 4 boss 5 guide, steer 6 direct, govern, manage, survey 7 conduct, control, monitor, oversee, proctor, referee 8 chaperon, overlook 10 administer 11 quarterback
supervision 4 care 6 charge 7 conduct, running 8 handling 9 oversight 10 intendance, management
supervisor 7 foreman
supine 5 inert, prone, slack 6 abject 7 passive 8 inactive, indolent 11 indifferent
supper club 4 café 6 nitery 7 cabaret, hot spot 8 nightery 9 night spot
supplant 4 oust 5 eject, expel, usurp 6 bounce, cut out 7 cast out, replace 8 crowd out, displace, force out, outplace 9 overthrow, supersede
supple 4 wiry 5 agile, lithe, withy 6 limber,

nimble, pliant, whippy 7 ductile, elastic, lissome, plastic, pliable, springy, stretch, willowy 8 flexible, graceful, moldable, stretchy 9 adaptable, lithesome, malleable, resilient

supplement 3 add, eke 5 rider 6 append 7 adjunct, codicil 8 addendum, addition, appendix 9 accessory 10 complement

suppliant 5 asker 6 beggar, prayer, suitor 9 solicitor 10 petitioner

supplicant see **suppliant**

supplicate 3 beg, sue 4 pray 5 crave, plead 6 appeal, invoke 7 beseech, entreat, implore, solicit 8 petition 9 importune

supplication 4 plea, suit 6 appeal, orison, prayer 8 entreaty, petition 11 application, imploration, imprecation

supplies 8 matériel 9 materials

supply 3 fit, man 4 feed, find, fund, give, hand, help 5 cache, equip, hoard, stock, store 6 outfit, purvey, succor 7 deliver, fulfill, furnish, provide, reserve, surplus 8 dispense, hand over, transfer, turn over 9 inventory, provision, reservoir, stockpile 12 accumulation

support 3 aid 4 back, base, bear, hand, help, keep, lift, prop, root, side, stay, take 5 abide, adopt, boost, brace, bread, brook, carry, favor, shore, strut, truss 6 anchor, assist, bear up, behalf, buoy up, column, crutch, defend, endure, girder, living, pillar, relief, second, succor, suffer, upbear, uphold, verify 7 alimony, applaud, approve, backing, bolster, bracing, comfort, confirm, embrace, endorse, espouse, footing, fortify, fulcrum, nourish, nurture, pull for, secours, shore up, stiffen, sustain, toehold 8 advocate, backstop, buttress, champion, foothold, mainstay, maintain, sanction, side with, underpin 9 encourage, reinforce, underprop 10 assistance, foundation, livelihood, provide for, strengthen, sustenance 11 corroborate, maintenance, subsistence, underpinner 12 alimentation, sustentation, underpinning

supporter 4 ally 6 cohort, patron 7 booster, sectary 8 adherent, advocate, champion, disciple, exponent, follower, henchman, partisan, sectator 9 expounder, proponent, satellite ***combining form:*** 4 crat 5 ocrat ***suffix:*** 3 ite

suppose 4 deem, take 5 allow, guess, infer, judge, opine, think 6 assume, expect, gather, reckon, repute, theory 7 believe, imagine, perhaps, presume, pretend, surmise, suspect 8 conclude, consider 10 conjecture, understand 11 speculation

supposition 5 posit 6 theory, thesis 7 premise, surmise 9 apriorism, postulate 10 assumption, conjecture, estimation, hypothesis 11 postulation, presumption, speculation

suppositious 6 unreal 7 dubious, fictive, reputed 8 doubtful, fanciful, illusory, putative, spurious 9 fantastic, fictional, imaginary, pretended, simulated 10 chimerical, fictitious, fraudulent 11 conjectural 12 hypothetical, questionable

suppress 4 cool, curb, hide, kill, rein, stop 5 burke, check, choke, crush, drown, dwarf, quash, quell, shush, spike, stunt 6 arrest, censor, cut off, hush up, muffle, quench, retard, squash, stifle, subdue 7 abolish, collect, compose, conceal, control, destroy, prevent, put down, silence, smother, squelch, swallow 8 prohibit, restrain, slap down, strangle, withhold 9 overpower, overthrow 10 annihilate, extinguish

supra 5 above

supremacy 4 sway 5 power 7 control, mastery 8 dominion 9 ascendant, authority, dominance, masterdom 10 ascendancy, domination, mastership, prepotence, prepotency 11 preeminence, sovereignty, superiority 12 predominance, principality 13 preponderance, preponderancy, transcendence

supreme 4 last 5 alone, chief, final 6 master, superb, utmost 7 highest, maximum, perfect 8 absolute, crowning, foremost, peerless, towering, ultimate 9 excellent, marvelous, paramount, sovereign, unequaled, unmatched, unrivaled 10 preeminent, surpassing 11 unequalable, unmatchable, unsurpassed 12 incomparable, transcendent, unparalleled 13 unsurpassable

Supreme Being 3 God 5 Allah 7 creator, Jehovah 11 the Almighty

surcease 3 end 4 halt, quit, rest, stop 6 desist 7 refrain, suspend 8 give over, knock off, leave off, postpone 9 cessation 11 discontinue

sure 3 set 4 fast, firm, safe 5 cocky, fixed 6 indeed, secure, stable, steady, strong 7 abiding, certain, staunch 8 absolute, arrogant, cocksure, definite, enduring, inerrant, positive, reliable, surefire, unerring, unshaken 9 confident, convinced, inerrable, steadfast 10 convincing, dependable, infallible, undeniable, unshakable, unwavering 11 indubitable, trustworthy, unequivocal, unfaltering, unqualified 12 indisputable, never-failing, wholehearted 13 incontestable, uncontestable, unquestioning

sure thing 6 shoo-in, winner 9 certainty

surety 4 bail, bond 5 angel 6 backer, patron, pledge 7 sponsor 8 backer-up, guaranty, security, warranty 9 certainty, certitude, guarantee, guarantor 10 confidence, conviction

surface 3 top 4 face, pave, rise, skin

5 cover, facet 6 come up, facing, finish, patina, veneer 7 outside 8 covering, exterior 11 superficial
surfeit 4 cloy, fill, glut, jade, pall, sate 5 gorge, stall 6 excess, stodge 7 replete, satiate, satisfy, surplus 8 overfill, overflow, overkill, overmuch, overplus, plethora 10 surplusage 11 overindulge, superfluity 13 overabundance
surge 4 flow, gush, pour, rise, roll, rush, wave 5 swell 6 billow, sluice, stream 7 upswell
surgeon 8 sawbones ***American:*** 4 Mayo, Reed 6 Thorek 8 McDowell ***British:*** 6 Hunter ***English:*** 5 Paget 6 Lister ***French:*** 4 Paré ***heart:*** 7 Barnard ***South African:*** 7 Barnard ***Swiss:*** 6 Kocher
surgery 9 operation ***instrument:*** 5 clamp, curet, lance, probe 6 gorget, lancet, splint, stylet, trocar 7 forceps, scalpel
surgical removal 8 ablation ***combining form:*** 6 ectomy
surly 4 dour, glum, rude, ugly 5 cross, gruff, sulky 6 crusty, grumpy, morose, sullen 7 bearish, boorish, crabbed, haughty, waspish 8 churlish, snappish 9 fractious, irritable, saturnine 10 ungracious 11 ill-mannered 12 discourteous
surmise see **suppose**
surmount 3 cap, top 4 best, down, leap, lick, over 5 clear, crest, crown, excel, outdo, throw, vault 6 better, finish, hurdle, master, outtop 7 conquer, surpass 8 outstrip, outtower, overcome, overleap 9 negotiate, terminate, transcend
surpass 3 cap, cob, top 4 beat, best, pass, rank 5 excel, outdo, outgo, trump 6 better, exceed, outrun, outvie 7 eclipse, outpace, outrank, outstep 8 distance, outclass, outmatch, outpoint, outrange, outrival, outshine, outstrip, outweigh, overstep 9 transcend 10 outperform, overshadow 11 outdistance
surplice 5 cotta, ephod 8 vestment
surplus 5 extra, spare 6 de trop, excess 7 overage, reserve, surfeit 8 overflow, overkill, overmuch, plethora 9 overstock, remainder 10 oversupply 11 superfluent, superfluity, superfluous 13 overabundance, supernumerary
surprise 4 faze, grab, stun 5 amaze, catch, floor, grasp, seize 6 ambush, dismay, lay for, rattle, waylay, wonder 7 astound, capture, nonplus, stagger, startle, stupefy 8 astonish, bewilder, bowl over, confound, dry-gulch, overcome 9 amazement, bushwhack, discomfit, dumbfound, overpower 10 disconcert 11 flabbergast 12 astonishment
surrender 4 cede, fall 5 leave, waive, yield 6 commit, give in, give up, go down, resign, submit 7 abandon, concede, consign, go under, succumb 8 dedition, hand over, yielding 9 relenting 10 capitulate, relinquish, submission, succumbing 11 appeasement 12 capitulation ***sign:*** 9 white flag
surreptitious see **stealthy**
surrogate 3 sub 6 deputy, fill-in, refuge, resort 7 stand-in, stopgap 8 recourse, resource 9 alternate, expedient, makeshift 10 expediency, substitute 11 alternative, locum tenens, pinch hitter, replacement, succedaneum
surround 3 hem, rim 4 edge, gird, loop, ring 5 bezel, bound, limit, round, skirt, verge 6 begird, border, circle, engulf, fringe, girdle, margin 7 compass, confine, embosom, enclave, enclose, envelop, environ, outline 8 encircle 9 encompass 10 circumvent 12 circumscribe
surrounding 5 about 12 circumjacent ***prefix:*** 4 peri 6 circum
surroundings 6 medium, milieu 7 ambient, climate 8 ambience 10 atmosphere 11 environment, mise-en-scène
surveillance 3 eye, tab 4 tout 5 vigil, watch 7 lookout 8 eagle eye, scrutiny, stakeout 9 vigilance
survey 3 con, vet 4 boss, rate, scan, view 5 assay, audit, set at, study, value 6 aperçu, assess, digest, précis, review, search, sketch 7 canvass, check up, examine, inspect, oversee, pandect, preview, sylloge, valuate 8 analysis, appraise, chaperon, estimate, evaluate, overlook, scrutiny, syllabus 9 check over, supervise 10 compendium, inspection, scrutinize 11 examination, quarterback, superintend 13 perlustration
survive 4 last 6 endure, revive 7 carry on, outlast, outlive, outwear, persist, recover, ride out 8 continue, live down 11 come through, pull through
Surya 6 sun-god ***son:*** 4 Manu, Yama 5 Karna 6 Asvins 7 Sugriva ***temple site:*** 7 Konarak
susceptible 4 easy, open 5 naive, prone 6 liable 7 exposed, sensile, subject 8 disposed, gullible, inclined, sensible, sentient 9 obnoxious, receptive, sensitive 10 fleeceable, responsive, vulnerable 11 impressible, predisposed 12 nonresistant
Susi's son 5 Gaddi
suspect 4 open 5 doubt, guess, shaky, think 6 assume, expect, gather, unsure 7 believe, dubious, imagine, suppose, unclear 8 conceive, distrust, doubtful, misdoubt, mistrust 9 doubtable, uncertain 10 disbelieve, understand 11 problematic
suspend 3 bar 4 bate, hang, stay, stop 5 debar, defer, delay, hover, sling 6 dangle,

depend, except, hold up, put off, shelve 7 adjourn, exclude, hold off, rule out 8 count out, intermit, postpone, prorogue 9 eliminate 11 discontinue
suspended 7 hanging, pendant, pensile 8 dangling, swinging 9 pendulant, pendulous
suspenders 6 braces 8 galluses
suspense 5 worry 6 unease 7 anxiety, concern, mystery 11 uncertainty 12 apprehension
suspension 4 stop 5 delay 7 latency 8 abeyance, abeyancy, doldrums, dormancy, stoppage 9 remission 10 moratorium, quiescence, quiescency 11 cold storage, withholding 12 intermission, interruption
suspicion 4 cast, hint 5 doubt, shade, smell, tinge, touch, trace, whiff 6 wonder 7 concern, dubiety 8 distrust, mistrust 9 dubiosity, misgiving 10 foreboding, intimation, skepticism, suggestion 11 incertitude, uncertainty, uncertitude
suspicious 4 wary 5 chary, leery, queer, shaky 6 unsure 7 careful, dubious, jealous, suspect 8 cautious, doubtful, watchful 9 doubtable, skeptical, uncertain 10 borderline 11 distrustful, mistrustful, problematic, unbelieving 12 questionable
suspire 4 sigh
sustain 4 bear, feed, prop, save 5 abide, brace, brook, carry, stand 6 bear up, buoy up, endure, foster, hold up, keep up, succor, suffer, upbear, uphold 7 bolster, confirm, nourish, nurture, prolong, receive, shore up, stomach, support, undergo 8 buttress, continue, preserve, tolerate 9 underprop, withstand 10 experience, strengthen
sustenance 3 pap 4 food, keep, meat, salt 5 bread 6 living, viands 7 aliment, alimony, pabulum, support 9 nutriment 10 livelihood 11 maintenance, nourishment, subsistence 12 alimentation
susurration 6 mumble, murmur, mutter, rustle 7 whisper 9 undertone
suture 4 line, seam 6 stitch
swab 3 mop 5 clean
swaddle 4 roll, wrap 5 drape 6 enwrap, swathe, wrap up 7 bandage, envelop 8 enswathe
swag 3 yaw 4 flag, loot, tilt, wilt 5 booty, droop, lurch, money, pitch, prize, spoil 6 boodle, seesaw, tilter 7 plunder 10 plunderage
swagger 4 brag, cock, lord 5 boast, strut, swank, swash, swell 7 bluster, peacock 8 flourish 11 pontificate, swashbuckle
swain 4 beau 5 lover, spark, wooer 6 suitor 7 admirer, sparker 9 boyfriend
swallow 3 sip 4 bear, bolt, down, gulp, take 5 abide, brook, drink, quaff, stand 6 absorb, accept, digest, endure, imbibe, ingest 7 believe, consume, stomach 8 bear with, tolerate 11 ingurgitate
swamp 3 bog, fen 4 mire, moss, muck, quag 5 drown, flood, glade, marsh, whelm 6 deluge, engulf, morass, muskeg, slough 7 baygall, bottoms 8 inundate, overcome, overflow, quagmire, submerge 9 marshland, overwhelm ***Everglades:*** 10 Big Cypress ***Georgia:*** 10 Okefenokee ***North Carolina-Virginia:*** 6 Dismal 11 Great Dismal
Swamp Fox 6 Marion
swan ***female:*** 3 pen ***male:*** 3 cob 4 cobb ***young:*** 6 cygnet
Swanhild ***father:*** 6 Sigurd ***mother:*** 6 Gudrun
swank 4 cock, lord, tony, trig 5 sharp, showy, swell, swish 6 chichi, classy, lively, snappy, tonish, trendy, with-it 7 peacock, splashy, stylish, swagger 8 peacocky 10 flamboyant, peacockish 11 pontificate, pretentious 12 orchidaceous, ostentatious
swap 5 trade, truck 6 barter, change, switch 7 bargain, traffic 8 exchange 10 substitute
swarm 4 flow, host, teem 5 crawl, crowd, flock, group, horde 6 abound, throng 7 overrun 9 multitude, pullulate 10 congregate
swarthy 4 dark 5 dusky 8 bistered 11 black-a-vised, dark-skinned
swash 3 lap 4 dash, slop 5 douse, plash, slosh 6 bubble, burble, gurgle, splash, splosh 7 bluster, spatter, splurge, spurtle, swagger 8 splatter
swat 3 bat, box, hit, rap 4 belt, blow, cuff, lick, slog, slug, sock 5 clout, knock, smack, smash, smite, swipe, whack 6 buffet, strike, wallop 7 clobber
swathe see **swaddle**
sway 3 get 4 bend, bias, move, rock, rule 5 carry, lurch, might, power, range, reach, reign, scope, sweep, swing, touch, waver, weave 6 affect, careen, direct, govern, manage, spread, strike, totter, waddle, wobble 7 command, dispose, expanse, impress, incline, inspire, mastery, stagger, stretch, strings 8 overrule 9 amplitude, authority, dominance, influence, oscillate, pendulate, vacillate 10 domination, predispose 11 fluctuation 12 jurisdiction
swear 3 vow 4 bind, cuss, damn, oath, rail, rant 5 abuse, curse 6 adjure, affirm, assert, attest, bedamn, depone, depose, pledge, plight, revile, vilify 7 declare, promise, testify 8 covenant, cussword, execrate 9 blaspheme, expletive, imprecate 10 asseverate, vituperate
swearword 4 cuss, oath 5 curse 9 expletive, obscenity 10 scurrility

sweat 4 emit, fume, milk, moil, ooze, rook, seep, snit, stew, toil, weep, work 5 bleed, exude, grind, labor, mulct, stick, tizzy 6 fleece, strain, swivet 7 excrete, slavery, travail 8 bullwork, drudgery, perspire, transude 10 donkeywork *combining form:* 4 hidr 5 hidro
sweater 8 cardigan, pullover, slipover
sweat out 2 go 4 bear, lump, take, wait 5 abide, brook, stand 6 endure 7 stomach 8 tolerate
sweaty 3 wet 6 clammy, sticky 7 labored 8 perspiry 10 perspiring
Sweden *capital:* 9 Stockholm *monetary unit:* 5 krona
Swedish Nightingale 4 Lind (Jenny)
sweep 3 fly 4 flit, sail, wing 5 ambit, broom, clean, clear, drive, fleet, orbit, range, reach, scope, surge 6 extent, radius 7 compass, purview 9 extension
sweeping 6 all-out 7 blanket, general, overall 8 whole-hog 9 all-around, extensive, inclusive, out-and-out, wholesale 12 all-embracing 13 comprehensive, thoroughgoing
sweepings 4 dust, junk 5 trash, waste 6 debris, litter, refuse 7 garbage, rubbish
sweet 5 candy, honey, spicy 6 aromal, dulcet, lovely, savory, sugary, syrupy 7 angelic, dessert, melodic, odorous, perfumy, scented, winning, winsome 8 aromatic, engaging, euphonic, fragrant, heavenly, loveling, luscious, perfumed, pleasant, pleasing, redolent 9 agreeable, ambrosial, beautiful, delicious 10 delectable, delightful *combining form:* 4 glyc 5 glyco
Sweet ___, song 7 Adeline
sweeten 5 candy, honey, sugar 6 pacify, refine, soften, solace 7 appease, assuage, lighten, mollify, placate, relieve 9 sugarcoat, sugar over 10 conciliate, propitiate
sweet potato 3 yam
sweet-talk 3 con 4 coax 6 banter, cajole 7 blarney, wheedle 8 blandish, soft-soap
swell 4 cock, grow, keen, lord, neat, pout, puff 5 bloat, bulge, dandy, nifty, pouch, super, surge, swank 6 billow, blow up, dilate, expand, groovy, tumefy 7 amplify, augment, balloon, distend, inflate, peacock, swagger, upsurge 8 increase, overblow, terrific 9 marvelous, wonderful *British:* 3 nob 4 toff
swelled head 5 pride 6 egoism 7 conceit, egotism 9 arrogance, vainglory 10 narcissism 11 amour propre 13 conceitedness
swelling 3 sty 4 bubo, gall, node 5 edema, tumid, tumor 6 bunion, growth 7 aureate, flowery, gibbous 8 tubercle 9 bombastic, carbuncle, chilblain, tumescent 10 euphuistic, rhetorical 12 inflammation, magniloquent 13 grandiloquent
sweltering 3 hot 5 fiery 6 baking, sultry, torrid 7 burning 8 broiling, sizzling 9 scorching
swerve 3 dip, err 4 skew, slue, turn, veer 5 sheer, shift, stray, waver 6 depart, totter, wander 7 deflect, deviate, digress, diverge 8 train off
swift 4 fast 5 fleet, hasty, quick, rapid, ready 6 prompt, raking, snappy, speedy, sudden 7 flat-out, fleetly, quickly, rapidly 8 full tilt, headlong, promptly, speedily 9 breakneck 10 harefooted
___ Swift 3 Tom 8 Jonathan *character:* 8 Gulliver
swiftness 4 gait, pace 5 haste, hurry, speed 6 hustle, rustle 8 celerity, dispatch, rapidity, velocity 9 quickness, rapidness 10 expedition, speediness
swig 4 drag, pull 5 booze, draft, drink, swill 6 guzzle, imbibe, tipple 7 swizzle
swill 4 slop, swig, tope 5 booze, draft, drink, offal, rinse, slops, trash, waste 6 debris, guzzle, refuse, spilth, tank up, tipple 7 consume, garbage, hogwash, put away, put down, rubbish, swizzle 9 polish off
swim 4 reel, spin, turn 5 float, swoon, whirl 9 dizziness
swimmer 7 natator
swimming stroke 5 crawl 7 dolphin, trudgen 9 butterfly, dogpaddle
swindle 3 con, gyp 4 beat, bilk, dupe, fake, hoax, rook, scam, sell, sham, skin 5 bunco, cheat, cozen, fraud, phony, rogue 6 chouse, diddle, humbug 7 defraud 8 flimflam 9 imposture, victimize
swine see hog
swing 3 ply, wag 4 beat, hang, rock, roll, sway, turn, veer, wave, whip 5 avert, flail, knack, lurch, meter, pivot, rhyme, sheer, trick, weave, wheel, whirl, wield 6 careen, divert, handle, jiggle, rhythm, rotate, stroke, switch, waggle, wiggle, wigwag, wobble 7 cadence, cadency, deflect, measure, revolve, stagger, vibrate 8 brandish, dispense, maneuver, undulate 9 fluctuate, oscillate, pendulate 10 manipulate
swinish 5 brute, feral, gross 6 animal, brutal, coarse, ferine, greedy 7 beastly, bestial, boarish, brutish, porcine, sensual
swipe 3 cop, hit, nab, rap 4 blow, conk, hook, lick, lift, swat, wipe 5 draft, heist, knock, pinch, steal 6 pilfer, snatch, snitch, strike
swirl 4 eddy, purl, roll 5 curve, gurge, twist, whirl, whorl 6 swoosh, vortex 9 whirlpool 11 convolution
swish 2 in 4 buzz, fizz, flog, hiss, tony, whiz 5 smart, swank, whisk 6 classy, fiz-

zle, sizzle, tonish, trendy, wheeze, whoosh, with-it 7 stylish 8 sibilate 9 exclusive

Swiss Family Robinson author 4 Wyss

switch 3 rod, wag 4 beat, flog, lash, swap, wand, wave, whip 5 shift, shunt, trade, whisk 6 change, strike, waggle, woggle 7 scourge 8 exchange 9 sidetrack 10 substitute

Switzerland *capital:* 4 Bern *largest city:* 6 Zurich *monetary unit:* 5 franc

swivel 4 turn 5 swing

swivet see **snit**

swizzle see **swig**

swollen 5 bulgy, tumid 6 turgid 7 aureate, bulbous, bulging, flowery, pompous 8 enlarged, inflated, varicose 9 bombastic, distended, tumescent 10 euphuistic, rhetorical 12 magniloquent 13 grandiloquent *combining form:* 4 phys 5 physo

swoon 4 coma, daze, fade 5 drown, faint 6 torpor 7 die away, pass out, rapture, syncope 8 black out

swoosh 4 eddy, gush, purl 5 gurge, swirl, whirl, whorl

sword 4 épée, foil, kris, pata 5 estoc, saber 6 barong, bilboa, creese, rapier, toledo 7 cutlass 8 claymore, falchion, scimitar, yataghan

sword of ____ 8 Damocles

sword-shaped 8 ensiform

sworn 6 avowed 7 devoted, settled 8 affirmed 9 confirmed, hard-shell 10 deep-rooted, deep-seated, entrenched, inveterate

sybarite 7 epicure 8 hedonist 10 voluptuary

sybaritic 6 carnal 7 sensual 8 sensuous 9 epicurean, luxurious 10 apolaustic, hedonistic, voluptuous 13 self-indulgent

sycophancy 7 calumny, scandal, slander 8 toadying 10 backbiting, defamation, detraction 12 backstabbing, belittlement, depreciation 13 disparagement

sycophant 5 toady 6 flunky, lackey, minion, stooge, yes-man 7 defamer, fawning 8 bootlick, cowering, cringing, groveler, lickspit, parasite, toadying, toadyish 9 easy rider, flatterer, groveling, kowtowing, parasitic, slanderer 10 bootlicker, self-seeker 11 bootlicking, lickspittle 13 apple-polisher

sycophantic 7 fawning, servile, slavish 8 cowering, cringing, toadying, toadyish 9 groveling, kowtowing, parasitic, truckling 10 defamatory, obsequious, slanderous 11 bootlicking

Sycorax's son 7 Caliban

syllable 3 bit, jot 4 atom, iota, whit 5 crumb, ounce, shred 7 modicum 8 particle *deletion:* 7 apocope *last:* 6 ultima *lengthening of:* 7 ectasis *next to last:* 6 penult *shortening:* 7 elision, systole *stressed:* 5 arsis

syllabus 6 aperçu, digest, précis, sketch, survey 7 epitome, outline, pandect, summary 8 abstract, headnote, synopsis 10 compendium

sylvan 5 bosky, woody 6 rustic, wooded *deity:* 3 Pan 4 Faun 5 dryad, satyr 6 Faunus 7 Silenus 8 Arethusa, Silvanus, Sylvanus

symbol 4 logo, mark, note, sign, type 5 badge, motif, stamp, token 6 design, device, emblem, figure, mascot 7 pattern 9 attribute, character 10 indication *chemical:* see individual element*Egyptian:* 4 ankh *musical:* 4 clef, flat, hold, note, rest, turn 5 presa, shake, sharp, trill 7 fermata, mordent, natural 8 arpeggio 9 crescendo 10 diminuendo 11 decrescendo

symbolic 10 emblematic 11 allegorical

symbolist poet 7 Rimbaud 8 Mallarmé, Verlaine

symbolize 6 embody, mirror, typify 7 express, signify 9 body forth, epitomize, exemplify, personify, represent 10 illustrate 11 emblematize

symmetrical 5 equal 7 regular 8 balanced 12 commensurate, proportional 13 commensurable

symmetry 5 order 7 balance, harmony 8 equality, evenness 9 agreement, congruity 10 conformity, proportion, regularity 11 arrangement

sympathetic 4 kind, warm 6 benign, humane, kindly, tender 8 amenable, favoring, friendly 9 agreeable, approving, benignant, congenial, congruous, consonant, favorable, receptive 10 compatible, consistent, responsive 11 kindhearted, softhearted, warmhearted 12 appreciating, well-disposed 13 compassionate, comprehending, understanding

sympathize 4 ache, pity 7 condole, feel for 10 appreciate, comprehend, understand 11 commiserate 13 compassionate

sympathy 3 rue 4 pity, ruth 5 heart 6 accord, warmth 7 empathy, harmony 8 affinity, kindness 9 agreement 10 benignancy, benignness, compassion, condolence, kindliness, tenderness 11 sensitivity 13 commiseration

symphonic 7 chiming, musical 8 blending, harmonic 9 consonant 10 harmonious

symphony 4 band 7 concord, harmony 9 orchestra 10 consonance 11 concert band 12 philharmonic

symptom 4 mark, note, sign 5 index, token 7 indicia 8 evidence 10 indication 11 significant

symptoms 8 syndrome

synagogue 8 assembly, building 9 community 12 congregation
synchronize 5 agree 6 concur 8 coincide
synchronous 6 coeval 8 existing 10 coetaneous, coexistent, coexisting, concurrent 11 concomitant 12 contemporary, simultaneous
syncope 4 coma 5 faint, swoon 8 blackout
syndicate 4 pool 5 chain, group, trust, union 6 cartel 7 combine 11 association, partnership 12 conglomerate, organization
syndrome 3 ill 6 malady 7 ailment, disease 8 disorder, sickness 9 affection, complaint, condition, infirmity 11 concurrence
synergic 8 coacting, coactive, conjoint
synod 4 body 7 council, meeting 8 assembly 10 convention, judicatory 11 convocation
synopsis 5 brief 7 epitome, summary 8 abstract, boildown, breviary, breviate 10 abridgment, conspectus 12 condensation
synopsize 3 sum 5 sum up 6 digest 7 summate 8 condense, nutshell 9 epitomize, inventory, summarize
synthesis 5 blend, union 11 combination 13 incorporation
synthesize 5 blend, unify 7 combine 9 harmonize, integrate
synthetic 7 man-made 10 artificial, fabricated
Syria *capital:* 8 Damascus *monetary unit:* 4 lira 5 pound
Syrinx 5 nymph 7 panpipe *pursuer:* 3 Pan
syrup 4 corn 5 maple 7 sorghum 8 molasses *almond-flavored:* 6 orgeat
syrupy 5 gooey, moist, mushy, sappy, sobby, sweet 6 drippy, dulcet, slushy, sticky 7 maudlin 11 sentimental
system 3 sum, way 4 code, mode, plan, wise 5 modus, order, setup, whole 6 entity, manner, method, scheme 7 complex, fashion, network, pattern, process, regimen 9 technique 10 regularity 11 arrangement, disposition, orderliness
systematic 7 logical, ordered, orderly, regular 8 arranged, methodic 9 organized 10 analytical, methodical 12 businesslike
systematize 5 array, order 6 adjust, codify 7 arrange, catalog, dispose, marshal 8 classify, organize, regiment 9 methodize
system of weights 4 troy 11 avoirdupois

T

tab 3 eye, tag 4 bill, cost, rate 5 check, price, score, watch 6 charge, tariff 7 account, invoice 8 eagle eye, price tag, scrutiny 9 reckoning, statement 12 surveillance
tabard 4 cape, coat 5 tunic 7 pendant
tabby 3 cat 6 feline, gossip 7 rumorer 8 gossiper, quidnunc, telltale 9 carrytale 10 newsmonger, talebearer 12 gossipmonger 13 scandalmonger
tabellion 6 scribe
tabernacle 6 church, temple 10 house of God 13 house of prayer
tabes 7 atrophy, wasting
Tabitha's Greek name 6 Dorcas
table 4 fare, list 5 bench, board, chart, stand 6 buffet, record, teapoy, upland 7 counter, plateau 8 mahogany 9 sideboard ***ornament:*** 7 epergne 11 centerpiece ***spread:*** 4 oleo 6 butter ***wheeled:*** 4 cart ***writing:*** 4 desk 9 secretary 10 escritoire
table game see at **game**
tableland 4 mesa 6 upland 7 plateau ***Alabama-West Virginia:*** 10 Cumberland ***Arizona:*** 5 Kanab 6 Kaibob ***England:*** 8 Dartmoor ***India:*** 5 Malwa; (see also **plateau**)
tablet 3 bar, pad 4 cake, disk, pill, slab 5 panel, slate 6 troche 7 lozenge ***combining form:*** 4 plac 5 pinac, pinak, placo 6 pinaco ***ornamental:*** 9 cartouche ***stone:*** 5 stela, stele ***writing:*** 3 pad 7 fanfold 8 triptych
tableware 4 cups 5 bowls, forks 6 dishes, knives, plates, silver, spoons 7 glasses, saucers
tabloid 5 livid, lurid, short 9 newspaper 11 sensational
taboo 3 ban 4 don't 6 enjoin, forbid, outlaw 7 inhibit 8 prohibit, sanction 9 interdict, restraint 10 inhibition, limitation, regulation 11 forbiddance, prohibition, reservation, restriction 12 interdiction, proscription
tabor 4 drum
taboret 5 stand, stool 7 cabinet
Tabrimmon ***father:*** 6 Hezion ***son:*** 8 Benhadad
tabula ____ 4 rasa
tabulation 5 chart, tally
tache 5 clasp 6 buckle
tacit 6 silent, unsaid 7 assumed, implied 8 hinted at, implicit, inferred, unspoken, unvoiced 9 alluded to, intimated, suggested, unuttered 10 undeclared, understood 11 unexpressed 12 inarticulate
taciturn 5 close 6 silent 7 laconic 8 reserved, reticent, wordless 10 silentious 11 close-lipped, tight-lipped 12 closemouthed
Tacitus work 7 Annales 8 Germania 9 Historiae
tack 3 pin, yaw 4 bend, brad, link, nail, turn 5 shift 6 double, swerve, zigzag 7 tangent 9 deviation 10 alteration, deflection, digression
tackle 3 rig 4 gear 5 throw 6 attack, burton, outfit, take on 7 lineman, rigging 8 matériel, set about 9 apparatus, equipment, machinery, undertake 10 footballer, plunge into 11 clothesline, habiliments 13 accouterments, paraphernalia
tacky 5 cheap, crude, dingy, dowdy, faded, gaudy, messy, seedy 6 blowsy, frowsy, frumpy, shabby, sloppy, sticky, stodgy, tagrag, untidy 7 run-down, unkempt 8 frumpish, outmoded, slovenly 9 incorrect, inelegant, out-of-date, tasteless, unstylish 10 broken-down, down-at-heel, threadbare, unbecoming, unsuitable 11 dilapidated
tact 5 poise, skill 6 acumen 7 finesse, suavity 8 civility, courtesy, deftness, urbanity 9 diplomacy, gallantry 10 adroitness, perception, politeness, smoothness 11 delicatesse, savoir faire, sensitivity
tactful 4 deft 5 suave 6 adroit, urbane 7 politic, skilled 8 delicate, discreet, polished, skillful 9 sensitive 10 diplomatic, perceptive
tactical 4 wise 7 politic, prudent 8 delicate 9 advisable, expedient 10 diplomatic, short-range
tactics 4 plan 6 method, system 9 maneuvers
tactile 8 palpable, tangible 9 touchable
taction 5 touch 7 contact 9 palpation
tad 3 bit, boy, lad, son 5 child 6 laddie 9 shaveling, stripling
tadpole 8 polliwog, pollywog
taffy 5 candy 8 flattery
tag 3 dog, end 4 flap, game, tail 5 bedog, label, trail 6 cliché, follow, shadow, ticket,

truism 7 bromide 8 banality, prosaism 9 platitude 10 prosaicism, shibboleth
tagrag 5 dingy, faded, seedy, tacky 6 shabby 7 run-down 10 bedraggled, down-at-heel, threadbare 11 dilapidated
Tahan's father 7 Ephraim
Tahash's father 5 Nahor
Tahath's father 5 Bered 7 Eleadah
Tahiti ***capital:*** 7 Papeete ***painter:*** 7 Gauguin
tail 3 dog, end, eye, tag 4 butt, rear 5 bedog, cauda, hound, trail 6 follow, pursue, shadow 7 hind end, rear end 8 backside, buttocks 9 posterior ***relating to:*** 6 caudal ***short:*** 4 scut
tailed 7 caudate
tailless 7 acaudal, anurous 8 ecaudate
tailor 3 fit, sew 4 suit 5 adapt, alter, style 6 adjust, sartor, square 7 conform, shape up 8 clothier, dovetail, quadrate, seamster 9 reconcile 11 accommodate ***Hindu:*** 5 darzi 6 durzee
taint 3 hue, rot, tar 4 blur, foul, harm, hurt, smut, soil, turn 5 brand, cloud, color, decay, dirty, smear, spoil, stain, sully 6 befoul, damage, defile, molder, smudge, smutch 7 besmear, blacken, crumble, pollute, putrefy, tarnish 8 besmirch, discolor 9 break down, decompose, discredit 10 stigmatize 11 contaminate
taipan 5 snake 8 merchant
Taiwan 7 Formosa ***capital:*** 6 Taipei
taj 3 cap
Taj Mahal 9 mausoleum ***builder:*** 9 Shah Jahan ***site:*** 4 Agra
take 3 bag, buy, cut, eat, get, gyp, nab, use, win 4 bear, beat, bilk, cull, down, draw, grab, grip, haul, pick 5 abide, admit, annex, brook, catch, charm, cheat, clasp, cozen, grasp, seize, share, stand, think, treat 6 accept, allure, assume, choose, clutch, collar, deduct, devour, endure, follow, gather, income, ingest, obtain, opt for, prefer, secure, select, snatch, strike, suffer 7 attract, believe, call for, capture, consume, defraud, enchant, grapple, imagine, receive, require, stomach, suppose, swallow 8 arrogate, contract, deal with, discount, flimflam, knock off, proceeds, purchase, receipts, subtract, tolerate 9 apprehend, captivate, fascinate, partake of, single out, substract 10 commandeer, comprehend, confiscate, sicken with, understand 11 appropriate 12 come down with ***account of:*** 6 notice ***advantage of:*** 5 abuse 7 exploit ***after:*** 6 follow 8 resemble ***apart:*** 7 analyze, dissect 9 dismantle ***care:*** 6 beware ***care of:*** 3 fix 4 tend 5 nurse 6 attend ***exception:*** 6 object ***five:*** 4 rest ***from:*** 7 deprive, detract 8 subtract ***it easy:*** 5 relax ***on the:*** 7 corrupt ***part:*** 4 join 5 share 11 participate ***place:*** 5 occur 6 happen ***the cake:*** 3 win ***to:*** 4 like ***to task:*** 5 scold 7 reprove ***turns:*** 9 alternate ***unawares:*** 8 surprise
take away 5 decry, wrest 6 deduct, remove 7 deprive, detract 8 belittle, derogate, diminish, discount, draw back, knock off, minimize, subtract, withdraw, write off 9 disparage, substract 10 depreciate 11 detract from
take back 5 unsay 6 abjure, recall, recant, return 7 replace, restore, retract 8 forswear, palinode, withdraw 9 repossess, restitute
take down 5 lower 6 reduce, tackle 8 dismount 9 dismantle, dismember 11 disassemble
take in 3 see 4 fool, have 5 admit, bluff, catch, grasp, trick 6 absorb, accept, betray, delude, embody, follow, illude 7 beguile, compass, contain, deceive, embrace, include, involve, receive, subsume 8 flimflam 9 apprehend, encompass, four-flush 10 assimilate, comprehend, understand 11 double cross
take off 2 go 3 ape 4 doff, down, exit, head, kill, kite, mock, quit, slay 5 douse, leave, mimic, scram 6 begone, decamp, deduct, depart, finish, get out, lay low, parody, remove, set out 7 destroy, get away, imitate, pull out, put away, skiddoo, vamoose 8 clear out, discount, dispatch, draw back, hightail, light out, subtract, withdraw 9 burlesque, skedaddle, strike out, substract
takeoff 4 jato, rato 6 launch, parody, send-up 7 lift-off 8 blast-off, travesty 9 burlesque 10 caricature ***area:*** 3 pad 6 runway
take on 3 add, don 4 face, hire, meet, pull 5 adopt, annex 6 append, assume, employ, engage, strike 7 embrace, espouse, subjoin 9 encounter
take out 4 date, vent 5 loose 6 deduct, remove 7 release, unleash 8 discount, draw back, knock off, subtract, withdraw 9 clear away, eliminate, substract
take over 5 seize, spell, usurp 7 relieve
take up 3 use 4 lift, open, rear 5 adopt, begin, enter, hoist, raise, renew, set to, start 6 assume, resume, tackle, uphold, uplift, uprear 7 elevate, embrace, espouse, kick off, restart, upraise 8 commence, continue, initiate 10 recommence
talc 4 mica 6 powder 7 agalite 8 steatite 9 soapstone
tale 3 fib, lie, sum 4 myth, saga, tote, yarn 5 fable, story, total, whole 6 canard, legend 7 calumny, falsity, fiction, scandal, slander, untruth 8 anecdote, entirety, sum total, totality, untruism 9 aggregate, falsehood, narration, narrative 10 backbiting, defamation, detraction 12 backstabbing, belittle-

ment, depreciation **13** disparagement, prevarication ***epic:*** **4** saga ***woeful:*** **8** jeremiad
talebearer **4** fink **5** tabby **6** canary, gossip, snitch **7** rumorer, tattler, tipster **8** gossiper, informer, quidnunc, squealer **10** newsmonger **11** rumormonger, stool pigeon **13** scandalmonger
talent **4** bent, gift, nose **5** craft, flair, forte, money, skill **6** genius **7** aptness, faculty **9** endowment, expertise
Tale of Two Cities, A ***author:*** **7** Dickens ***character:*** **6** Carton (Sidney), Darnay (Charles) **7** Defarge, Manette (Alexander), Manette (Lucie)
Tales of a Traveller author **6** Irving
Tales of a Wayside Inn author **10** Longfellow
Tales of Hoffman composer **9** Offenbach
talipot **4** palm
talisman **4** juju, luck, zemi **5** charm, saffi **6** amulet, fetish, mascot, saphie **7** periapt **10** phylactery
Talisman, The ***author:*** **5** Scott
talk **3** gab, rap, yak **4** blab, buzz, chat, chin, sing, yarn **5** on-dit, prate, rumor, run on, speak, utter, voice **6** babble, dialog, gabble, gossip, parley, patter, powwow, report, speech, squeal, tattle **7** address, chatter, declaim, gabfest, hearsay, lecture, prattle **8** causerie, colloque, colloquy, converse, dialogue, harangue, perorate, vocalize **9** discourse, grapevine, hold forth, speechify, utterance, verbalize **10** allocution, discussion **11** scuttlebutt **12** conversation, deliberation **13** confabulation, verbalization ***about:*** **7** discuss ***back:*** **4** sass ***combining form:*** **3** log **4** logy **5** logia, logue ***foolish:*** **4** bunk **6** babble **7** chatter, palaver ***indistinctly:*** **6** mumble, mutter ***over:*** **7** discuss ***slowly:*** **5** drawl ***small:*** **8** chitchat ***wildly:*** **4** rant, rave
talkative **4** glib **5** gabby, vocal **6** chatty, fluent, mouthy **7** gossipy, voluble **9** garrulous **10** babblative, loquacious **11** loose-lipped **12** loose-tongued, multiloquent **13** multiloquious
tall **4** high **5** lanky, lofty, rangy **8** towering **11** skyscraping **12** altitudinous
tallow **3** fat **4** suet **6** grease ***combining form:*** **4** sebi, sebo **5** stear, steat **6** stearo, steato
tally **4** jibe **5** agree, count, fit in, match, score **6** accord, number, square **7** balance, catalog, conform, itemize **8** numerate **9** catalogue, enumerate, harmonize, inventory **10** correspond
Talmai ***daughter:*** **6** Maacah ***father:*** **4** Anak ***grandson:*** **7** Absalom
talon **4** claw
talus **5** ankle, scree, slope
tam **3** cap
Tamar ***brother:*** **7** Absalom ***father:*** **5** David **7** Absalom ***father-in-law:*** **5** Judah ***half brother:*** **5** Amnon ***husband:*** **2** Er ***seducer:*** **5** Amnon ***son:*** **5** Perez, Zerah
tamarisk **4** atle **5** athel, atlee
tambour **3** cup **4** bell, drum, wall **7** drummer
tambourine **4** dove, drum **7** timbrel
Tamburlaine the Great author **7** Marlowe
tame **4** meek, mild **6** docile, gentle, master, pliant **7** pliable, subdued, trained **8** amenable, biddable, broken in, domestic, obedient **9** tractable **10** submissive **11** domesticate, domesticize, domiciliate, housebroken **12** domesticated
Taming of the Shrew, The ***character:*** **6** Bianca **8** Baptista **9** Katharina, Petruchio
Tammany boss **5** Tweed
Tammuz' lover **6** Ishtar
tam-o'-shanter **3** cap
tamp **3** jam, mat, ram **4** cram, pack **5** pound, stuff
tampion **4** plug
tan **3** sun, taw **4** beat, ecru, flog, whip **5** beige, brown, toast **6** bronze, darken, thrash
tanager **4** bird, yeni
Tancred, Tancredi ***beloved:*** **8** Clorinda ***father:*** **3** Odo ***mother:*** **4** Emma ***victim:*** **8** Clorinda
tandem **4** pair **8** carriage
tang **3** nip **4** bite, odor, zest **5** aroma, sapor, savor, smack, taste **6** flavor, relish **8** piquancy, pungency, sapidity **9** spiciness
tangible **7** tactile **8** embodied, material, palpable, physical, sensible **9** corporeal, touchable **10** detectable, observable, phenomenal **11** appreciable, discernible, perceptible, substantial
tangle **3** mat, web **4** knot, maze, mesh, muck, trap **5** benet, catch, mix up, ravel, skein, snare, snarl **6** entrap, foul up, jungle, morass, muddle **7** catch up, embroil, ensnare, ensnarl, involve, mizmaze, perplex **9** implicate, labyrinth **10** complicate
Tanglewood Tales author **9** Hawthorne
tango **5** dance
tank **3** vat **5** basin **7** cistern, pachuca, vehicle **8** aquarium **9** container, reservoir ***American:*** **7** Sherman ***German:*** **6** panzer ***part:*** **6** turret
tankard **3** mug **5** stoup **6** flagon **9** blackjack
tanker **4** ship **5** oiler
Tannhäuser composer **6** Wagner
tantalize **4** bait, gnaw **5** annoy, harry,

taunt, tease, worry **6** harass, pester, plague **7** bedevil, hagride, torment **9** beleaguer, frustrate
Tantalus ***daughter:*** **5** Niobe ***father:*** **4** Zeus ***son:*** **6** Pelops
tantamount **4** same **5** alike, equal **8** selfsame **9** duplicate, identical **10** equivalent
tantara **5** blare **7** fanfare
tantivy **4** rush **6** gallop **8** headlong
tantrum **3** fit
Tanzania ***capital:*** **11** Dar es Salaam ***monetary unit:*** **8** shilingi
Taoism founder **6** Lao Tzu
tap **3** bar, bob, hit, pub, rap **4** cock, draw, name, pump, tunk **5** draft, drain, knock, nudge, thump, valve **6** faucet, finger, siphon, spigot, strike **7** appoint, barroom, draw off, hydrant, petcock **8** nominate, stopcock **9** designate
tape **4** band, belt, bind **5** strip **6** fillet, record, ribbon **7** bandage, measure ***kind:*** **5** inkle **6** ferret **7** masking **8** adhesive **9** measuring ***machine:*** **8** recorder
taper **4** wick **5** abate, close, spire **6** lessen, reduce **7** dwindle **8** decrease, diminish **9** drain away
tapering **5** conic, spiry **6** terete **7** conical, pointed **8** fusiform, subulate **9** acuminate
tapestry **5** arras, kilim **6** dossal **7** curtain, Gobelin, hanging ***pattern:*** **7** cartoon ***tool:*** **6** broché
tapeworm **6** taenia **8** parasite ***body:*** **8** strobila ***combining form:*** **4** taen **5** taeni **6** taenio ***head:*** **6** scolex
Taphath's father **7** Solomon
tapioca **7** cassava, pudding
Tappuah's father **6** Hebron
taproom **3** bar, pub **6** saloon, tavern
tapster **6** barman **7** barmaid **9** barkeeper, bartender **10** mixologist
tar **4** jack, pave, salt, soil **5** pitch, smear, stain, sully, taint **6** defile, sailor, seaman **7** asphalt, besmear, mariner **8** besmirch **9** sailorman
taradiddle **3** fib, lie **5** story **6** canard **7** falsity **9** falsehood **13** prevarication
tarantella **5** dance
tarantula **6** spider
Taras Bulba author **5** Gogol
tarboosh **3** fez, hat
tardy **3** lax **4** late, slow **7** belated, delayed, laggard, overdue **8** detained, dilatory **10** behindhand, delinquent, unpunctual
tare **4** seed **5** vetch **6** weight
target **3** aim **4** butt, goal, mark **6** object, victim **9** objective, quaesitum **11** sitting duck ***center:*** **8** bull's-eye ***shooter's:*** **10** clay pigeon
Tar Heel State **13** North Carolina
tariff **3** tab, tax **4** cost, duty, levy, rate **5** price **6** charge, impost **8** price tag **10** assessment
Tarkington, Booth ***character:*** **6** Penrod
tarn **4** lake, pool
tarnish **3** dim, mar, tar **4** dull, fade, foul, harm, hurt, pale, soil **5** dirty, grime, muddy, smear, spoil, sully, taint **6** besoil, damage, impair, injure, smirch, smudge, smutch **7** begrime, besmear, blemish **8** besmirch, discolor
taro **4** dalo, eddo, gabe, gabi **5** aroid, tania **6** yautia **7** dasheen, malanga ***product:*** **3** poi
tarpaulin **4** jack, salt **5** cover **6** sailor, seaman **7** mariner **9** sailorman
tarpon **4** fish **5** oxeye
tarry **3** lag **4** bide, drag, poke, stay, wait **5** abide, dally, delay, trail, visit **6** linger, loiter, put off, remain **8** stop over **11** stick around **13** procrastinate
Tarshish's father **6** Bilhan
tarsus **5** ankle
tart **3** dry, pie **4** acid, sour **5** acerb, sharp **6** pastry **7** acerbic, acetose, piquant, pungent **9** acidulous
Tartar **6** Mongol **7** Turkish **8** Mongolic **9** Mongolian
Tartuffe author **7** Molière
Tarzan ***creator:*** **9** Burroughs (Edgar Rice) ***mate:*** **4** Jane
task **3** job **4** duty, lade, load, toil, work **5** chare, chore, labor, stint, weigh **6** burden, charge, devoir, errand, lumber, saddle, weight **7** mission, project **8** encumber **10** assignment **11** undertaking
Tasmanian **4** wolf **5** devil
Tasmania's capital **6** Hobart
tassel **4** tuft **5** adorn **6** fringe **7** pendant **8** ornament
taste **3** eat, sip, try **4** dash, feel, hint, tang, zest **5** grace, gusto, heart, sapor, savor, smack, tinge, touch, whiff **6** degust, flavor, liking, palate, polish, relish, trifle **7** finesse, stomach **8** appetite, elegance, fondness, sapidity, soft spot, tincture, weakness **9** appetence **10** experience, partiality, refinement, sprinkling **11** inclination ***combining form:*** **6** geusia ***kind:*** **4** salt, sour **5** sweet **6** bitter ***lacking:*** (see **tasteless**) ***organ:*** **3** bud
tasteless **4** dull, flat, wild **5** bland, vapid **6** vulgar **7** insipid **8** barbaric, unsavory **9** barbarian, barbarous, graceless, inelegant, savorless, unrefined **10** flavorless, outlandish, unflavored, unpolished **11** ill-flavored, unpalatable **12** unappetizing **13** uninteresting
tasty **5** sapid **6** savory, toothy **9** palatable, relishing, toothsome **10** appetizing, flavorsome
Tate **7** Gallery

tatou 9 armadillo
tatter 3 rag, rip 4 tear 5 shred
tattered 5 dingy, seedy, tacky 6 frayed, ragged, shabby, tagrag 7 run-down, shreddy 8 frazzled 10 bedraggled, broken-down, threadbare 11 dilapidated
tattle 4 blab, buzz, talk 5 rumor 6 gossip, report 7 hearsay 9 grapevine 11 scuttlebutt
tattler see **talebearer**
tattletale see **talebearer**
tatty 4 base, mean, poor 5 cheap 6 common, paltry, shoddy, sleazy, trashy 8 rubbishy
taunt 4 gibe, lout, mock, razz, twit 5 scout, tease 6 deride 7 provoke 8 reproach, ridicule
taurine 6 bovine
Taurus 4 bull ***star:*** 9 Aldebaran
taut 5 close, tense, tight
tautology 8 pleonasm, verbiage 9 verbality 10 periphrase, redundancy, roundabout 11 periphrasis 13 circumambages
tavern 3 bar, inn, pub 5 hotel, lodge 6 bistro, hostel, saloon 7 auberge, barroom, hospice, taproom 8 alehouse, drinkery, hostelry 9 roadhouse 11 caravansary, public house 12 watering hole
taverner 8 boniface, publican 9 barkeeper, innholder, innkeeper, saloonist 12 saloonkeeper
taw 5 stake 6 marble
tawdry 4 loud 5 gaudy 6 brazen, flashy, garish, tinsel 7 blatant, chintzy, glaring 12 meretricious
tawny 3 tan 4 dark 5 brown 6 tanned ***combining form:*** 5 fusco, pyrrh, pyrro 6 pyrrho
tax 4 duty, lade, levy, load, onus, scot, toll 5 abuse, tithe 6 assess, burden, cumber, impost, saddle, strain, tariff, weight 7 tollage, tribute 8 encumber 10 assessment, deadweight ***agency:*** 3 IRS ***feudal:*** 7 scutage, tallage ***kind:*** 4 geld 5 sales, tithe 6 excise, income 7 chevage, prisage 8 property 9 surcharge ***on salt:*** 7 gabelle ***rate:*** 10 assessment
taxi 3 cab, car 4 hack
taxing 5 tough 6 trying 7 exigent, onerous, weighty 8 exacting, grievous 9 demanding 10 burdensome, oppressive
Taygeta ***father:*** 5 Atlas ***mother:*** 7 Pleione ***sisters:*** 8 Pleiades
tazza 3 cup 4 vase
Tchaikovsky, Peter ***ballet:*** 8 Swan Lake 10 Nutcracker ***opera:*** 12 Eugene Onegin 13 Queen of Spades
tea 5 drink, party 6 repast 8 beverage 9 marijuana, reception ***black:*** 5 bohea, oopak, pekoe 8 souchong ***cake:*** 6 cookie ***genus:*** 4 Thea ***ingredient:*** 8 caffeine ***kind:*** 4 herb, Java 5 Assam, black, bohea, green, hyson, ledum, pekoe 6 Ceylon, congou, oolong 7 cambric 8 souchong 9 sassafras ***of India:*** 10 Darjeeling
teach 5 coach, train, tutor 6 impart, school 7 educate, instill 8 instruct 9 enlighten, inculcate 12 indoctrinate
teacher 4 guru, prof 5 coach, guide, tutor 6 docent, master, mentor, pedant 7 edifier, maestro, trainer 8 educator, magister 9 pedagogue, preceptor, professor 10 instructor 12 schoolmaster ***Hindu:*** 5 swami ***Jewish:*** 5 rabbi 7 rabboni ***Muslim:*** 3 pir 5 mulla 6 mollah, mullah ***religious:*** 8 mystagog 9 catechist
Tea for Two composer 7 Youmans
team 4 club, crew, gang, join, pair, side, yoke 5 group, squad, wagon 8 carriage ***baseball:*** 4 nine ***basketball:*** 4 five 7 quintet ***football:*** 6 eleven ***kind:*** 2 JV 6 jayvee 7 varsity ***supporter:*** 3 fan
tear 3 cut, rip, run 4 bolt, dash, gash, lash, race, rend, rift, rive, rush, slit 5 chase, fling, sever, shoot, shred, slash, speed, split 6 career, charge, cleave, course, incise, sunder, tatter 8 lacerate
tear down 4 raze, ruin, slur 5 smear, wrack, wreck 6 defame, malign 7 asperse, destroy, shatter, slander 8 demolish, destruct 9 denigrate 10 annihilate, calumniate, scandalize
tearful 3 sad 5 weepy 6 crying 7 bawling, sobbing, weeping 8 mourning 9 lamenting, sniveling 10 blubbering, lachrymose
tear-jerking 5 mushy 6 slushy, sticky 7 maudlin, mawkish 8 bathetic, romantic 11 sentimental
teary see **tearful**
tease 3 kid, rip 4 gnaw, josh, twit 5 annoy, chaff, harry, taunt, worry 6 harass, pester, plague 7 bedevil 8 ridicule 9 beleaguer
Tebah ***father:*** 5 Nahor ***mother:*** 6 Reumah
teched 4 daft 5 batty, crazy 6 crazed, insane 7 cracked, lunatic 8 demented, deranged 9 bedlamite
technicality 6 detail 8 loophole
technique 3 way 4 mode, wise 5 modus 6 manner, method, system 7 fashion ***combining form:*** 4 urgy
tectonic 10 structural
ted 5 strew 6 spread 7 scatter
tedious 3 dry 4 arid, dull 5 dusty 6 boring, tiring 7 insipid, irksome 8 boresome, bromidic, drudging, weariful 9 dryasdust, wearisome 13 uninteresting
tedium 4 yawn 5 ennui 7 boredom 8 doldrums, dullness, monotony
teem 4 flow 5 crawl, swarm 6 abound 9 pullulate
teeming 4 lush, rife 5 alive 6 aswarm

7 replete 8 swarming, thronged 9 abounding 11 overflowing

teen 5 youth 8 juvenile 9 youngster 10 adolescent

tee off 4 open 5 begin, drive, enter, start 6 take up 8 commence, initiate

teeter 5 lurch 6 falter, seesaw, topple, totter, wobble 7 stagger, stumble

teeth ***false:*** 8 dentures ***grinding:*** 7 bruxism ***having:*** 7 dentate ***problem:*** 5 decay 6 caries 8 overbite ***relating to:*** 6 dental; (see also **tooth**)

teq 3 doe 4 deer 5 sheep

tegua 8 moccasin

teju 6 lizard

telamon 5 atlas ***counterpart:*** 8 caryatid

Telamon ***brother:*** 6 Peleus ***father:*** 6 Aeacus ***half-brother:*** 6 Phocus ***son:*** 4 Ajax 6 Teucer

Telegonus ***father:*** 7 Ulysses 8 Odysseus ***mother:*** 5 Circe

telegraph 4 wire 5 cable 6 signal ***code:*** 5 Morse

Telemachus ***Father:*** 7 Ulysses 8 Odysseus ***mother:*** 8 Penelope

telephone 4 buzz, call, dial, ring 5 phone 6 ring up ***inventor:*** 4 Bell

Telephus ***father:*** 8 Heracles, Hercules ***mother:*** 4 Auge

telescope 5 glass 8 compress, condense, spyglass

television 2 TV 4 tube 5 video 8 boob tube ***antenna:*** 10 rabbit ears ***award:*** 4 Emmy ***British:*** 5 telly ***frequency:*** 3 UHF, VHF ***interference:*** 4 snow ***network:*** 3 ABC, BBC, CBS, NBC, NET, PBS ***pioneer:*** 5 Baird 8 Zworykin ***program:*** 4 news, show 5 rerun 6 series, sitcom 7 western 8 game show 9 broadcast, docudrama, soap opera ***tube:*** 4 kine 9 kinescope

tell 3 bid, say 4 clew, clue, post, tale, warn 5 mouth, order, spill, state, tally, utter 6 advise, betray, charge, direct, enjoin, fill in, inform, notify, number, relate, reveal, wise up 7 blab out, command, declare, divulge, narrate 8 bring out, disclose, discover, give away, instruct, numerate

teller 5 clerk 7 cashier, counter 8 informer, narrator

telling 5 solid, sound, valid 6 cogent 10 convincing, satisfying 12 satisfactory

tell off 3 jaw 4 rail 5 scold 6 berate, revile 7 bawl out, chew out, upbraid 8 call down 10 tongue-lash, vituperate

tell on 6 snitch, tattle

telltale 3 cue 4 clue, hint, wind 5 clack, tabby 6 gossip, notion 7 inkling 8 gossiper, quidnunc 9 carrytale 10 indication, intimation, newsmonger, suggestion, talebearer 12 gossipmonger 13 scandalmonger

tellurian 6 earthy 7 earthly, mundane, terrene, worldly 9 sublunary 11 terrestrial, uncelestial

tellurium ***symbol:*** 2 Te

Tema's father 7 Ishmael

temblor 5 quake, shake, shock 6 quaker, tremor 10 earthquake

temerarious 4 rash 6 daring 8 heedless, reckless 9 audacious, daredevil, foolhardy, imprudent, venturous 10 incautious 11 adventurous, injudicious, venturesome 13 adventuresome

temerity 4 gall 5 nerve 6 daring 8 audacity, rashness 9 assurance, brashness, hardihood, hardiness 11 impetuosity 12 heedlessness, impertinence, recklessness 13 foolhardiness

temper 4 curb, mind, mood, tone, vein 5 humor 6 dilute, makeup, season, soften, spirit, strain, timbre 7 passion 8 moderate, modulate, restrain, tone down 10 complexion 11 personality 13 individualism, individuality

temperament 4 mood 5 humor 6 makeup, nature 9 character 10 complexion 11 disposition, personality

temperamental 5 moody 6 fickle 8 ticklish, unstable, variable, volatile 9 humorsome, mercurial, uncertain 10 capricious, changeable, inconstant

temperance 7 control, measure 8 sobriety 9 austerity 10 abstinence, continence, moderation 11 refrainment, self-control 12 moderateness ***advocate of:*** 6 Nation 7 Willard

temperate 4 calm, even 5 sober 6 modest, steady 8 discreet, moderate 9 abstinent, continent, regulated, unextreme 10 abstemious, controlled, reasonable, restrained 11 abstentious, unexcessive 12 conservative 13 unimpassioned

temperature 4 heat 5 fever 6 warmth 9 intensity

tempest 4 gale, rage, wind 5 storm 6 tumult, uproar 9 commotion, hurricane

Tempest, The ***character:*** 5 Ariel 7 Caliban, Miranda 8 Prospero 9 Ferdinand

tempestuous 4 wild 5 rough 6 raging, stormy 7 furious, violent 8 blustery 9 turbulent, unbridled 10 blustering, tumultuous

temple 4 fane 6 church 10 house of God, tabernacle 13 house of prayer ***ancient:*** 4 naos 5 speos 8 pantheon ***Aztec:*** 6 teopan 8 teocalli ***Buddhist:*** 2 ta 3 taa, wat ***Eastern:*** 6 pagoda ***Greek:*** 6 hieron 9 Parthenon ***sanctuary:*** 5 cella 6 adytum 10 penetralia

tempo 4 pace, rate, time 5 speed 6 rhythm ***fast:*** 6 presto 7 allegro ***moder-***

ate: 7 andante ***slow:*** 5 grave, lento 6 adagio
temporal 3 lay 6 earthy 7 mundane, profane, secular, sensual, worldly 8 banausic, unsacred 13 materialistic
temporary 6 acting, pro tem, supply 7 interim 9 ad interim, transient 10 pro tempore
tempt 3 woo 4 bait, lure, risk, vamp 5 decoy, train 6 allure, entice, entrap, invite, lead on, seduce 7 solicit 8 inveigle 9 tantalize
temptation 4 bait, lure, trap 5 decoy, snare 6 come-on 10 allurement, enticement, seducement 12 inveiglement
temptress 4 vamp 5 siren 7 Delilah, Lorelei 10 seductress 11 femme fatale
ten ***cents:*** 4 dime ***combining form:*** 3 dec, dek 4 deca, deka 5 decem ***dollars:*** 7 sawbuck ***mills:*** 4 cent ***thousand:*** 6 myriad ***years:*** 6 decade
tenacious 3 set 4 fast, firm, true 5 fixed, stout, tight, tough 6 dogged, secure, strong, sturdy, viscid 7 viscose, viscous 8 resolute, stalwart, stubborn 9 obstinate, steadfast 10 bulldogged, persisting 11 bulldoggish, persevering 12 pertinacious
tenacity 8 firmness 10 resolution 11 persistence
tenant 6 holder, lessee, occupy, people, renter 7 boarder, dweller, inhabit 8 occupant, populate 9 collibert ***feudal:*** 4 leud 6 bordar, vassal 7 socager, sokeman ***Indian:*** 7 chakdar ***Irish:*** 7 cottier
tenantable 7 livable 9 habitable, lodgeable 10 occupiable 11 inhabitable
Ten Commandments 9 Decalogue
tend 4 care, lean, look, mind, till, work 5 dress, labor, nurse, serve, watch 7 care for, conduce, incline, redound 8 minister 10 contribute
tendency 3 run 4 bent, bias 5 drift, tenor, trend 7 current, leaning 8 penchant 9 inclining 10 proclivity, propensity 11 disposition, inclination 12 predilection ***combining form:*** 5 phily 6 philia ***suffix:*** 4 itis
tendentious 6 biased 7 colored, partial 8 one-sided, partisan 10 prejudiced
tender 4 fond, give, mild, pose, soft, sore, warm 5 offer 6 extend, gentle, humane, loving, submit 7 hold out, lenient, present, proffer, propose 8 yielding 9 forgiving 10 benevolent, charitable, responsive 11 considerate, kindhearted, softhearted, sympathetic, warmhearted 12 affectionate 13 commiserative, compassionate
tenderfoot 4 colt, tyro 6 novice, rookie 8 beginner, freshman, neophyte, newcomer 9 novitiate 10 apprentice
Tender Is the Night author 10 Fitzgerald
tendon 4 band, cord 5 sinew
tendril 4 curl 6 cirrus 7 ringlet
tenebrific 5 black, bleak 6 dismal, dreary, gloomy, somber 8 funereal 10 oppressive 11 dispiriting 13 disheartening
tenebrous 3 dim 4 dark, dusk 5 dusky, murky, vague 6 gloomy 7 obscure, unclear 9 ambiguous, equivocal, lightless, sibylline, uncertain 10 caliginous, unexplicit 13 unilluminated
tenement 4 flat 5 rooms, suite 6 rental 7 lodging 8 building 9 apartment
tenet 3 ism 5 canon, dogma 8 doctrine
tenfold 6 denary
Tennessee ***capital:*** 9 Nashville ***college, university:*** 5 Bryan 10 Vanderbilt ***largest city:*** 7 Memphis ***nickname:*** 14 Volunteer State ***state flower:*** 4 iris
tennis ***award:*** 8 Davis Cup ***item:*** 3 net 4 ball 6 racket 7 racquet ***kind:*** 5 table 7 doubles, singles 8 platform ***score:*** 4 love 5 deuce ***serve:*** 3 ace ***shoe:*** 7 sneaker ***stroke:*** 3 cut, lob 4 chop, drop 5 serve, slice 6 volley 8 backhand, forehand ***term:*** 3 let, set 5 court, fault 7 service 9 advantage, backcourt
tennis champ 4 Ashe (Arthur), Borg (Bjorn), Graf (Steffi), King (Billie Jean), Noah (Yannick), Wade (Virginia) 5 Budge (Don), Court (Margaret Smith), Evert (Chris), Laver (Rod), Lendl (Ivan), Perry (Fred), Seles (Monica), Vilas (Guillermo), Wills (Helen) 6 Agassi (André), Austin (Tracy), Becker (Boris), Edberg (Stephan), Fraser (Neale), Gibson (Althea), Kramer (Jack), Tilden (Bill) 7 Connors (Jimmy), Emerson (Roy), Lacoste (Rene), McEnroe (John), Nastase (Ilie) 8 Connolly (Maureen), Gonzalez (Pancho), Newcombe (John), Rosewall (Ken), Sabatini (Gabriela), Wilander (Mats) 11 Navratilova (Martina)
Tennyson poem 4 Maud 7 Ulysses 8 Tiresias 10 Enoch Arden, In Memoriam 12 Locksley Hall
tenor 3 run 4 body, mood, tone 5 drift, voice 6 singer 7 current, meaning, purport 8 tendency 9 substance ***American:*** 5 Lanza 6 Peerce, Tucker 8 Melchior 9 McCormack, McCracken ***Canadian:*** 7 Vickers ***Czech:*** 6 Slezak ***German:*** 10 Wunderlich ***Italian:*** 5 Gigli 6 Caruso 7 Corelli 8 Bergonzi 9 del Monaco, di Stefano, Pavarotti ***Spanish:*** 7 Domingo 8 Carreras ***Swedish:*** 5 Gedda 8 Bjorling 9 Bjoerling
tenpins 7 bowling
tense 4 edgy, taut 5 nervy, tight 6 uneasy 7 anxious, jittery, restive, uptight 8 strained ***grammatical:*** 4 past 6 future 7 perfect, present 8 preterit 9 preterite 10 pluperfect 11 progressive

tension 6 nerves, strain, stress, unease 7 anxiety 8 pressure, tautness 9 agitation 10 discomfort, uneasiness 11 nervousness, uptightness
tent 4 camp 5 bivvy, cover, lodge 6 canopy, encamp, laager, maroon 7 bivouac, shelter ***Eskimo:*** 5 tupik ***kind:*** 3 pup 4 bell, pawl, yort 5 Baker, tepee 6 teepee, wigwam 7 kibitka, marquee, wickiup 8 pavilion, umbrella ***maker:*** 4 Omar ***material:*** 6 canvas ***part:*** 3 fly, guy, peg 4 pole
tentacle 3 arm 6 feeler
tentative 4 test 5 trial 6 wobbly 7 halting 8 hesitant 9 faltering, makeshift, provisory, uncertain 10 irresolute 11 conditional, provisional, vacillating, vacillatory 12 provisionary
tenth 5 tithe ***combining form:*** 4 deci
tenuous 4 rare, slim, thin, weak 5 reedy 6 feeble, flimsy, slight, stalky, subtle, twiggy 7 slender, squinny, subtile 8 ethereal, rarefied 9 attenuate 10 attenuated 11 implausible 13 insubstantial, unsubstantial
tenure 4 grip, hold, term 5 clamp, clasp, grasp, gripe 6 clench, clinch, clutch, estate 7 grapple ***feudal:*** 7 burgage
tepid 4 mild, warm 7 warmish 8 lukewarm, milk-warm 9 temperate 11 halfhearted, indifferent
tequila source 6 mescal
Terah's son 5 Abram, Haran, Nahor 7 Abraham
teras 7 monster
terbium ***symbol:*** 2 Tb
Terentia's husband 6 Cicero
Tereus ***son:*** 4 Itys ***wife:*** 6 Procne
tergiversate 3 rat 4 turn 5 dodge, evade, hedge 6 defect, desert, weasel 7 shuffle 8 renounce, sidestep 9 pussyfoot, repudiate 10 apostatize, equivocate
term 3 dub 4 call, name, span, time, word 5 bound, hitch, spell 6 detail, period, tenure 7 article, baptize, stretch 8 christen, duration 9 designate 10 denominate, limitation, particular
termagant 5 harpy, rowdy, scold, shrew, vixen 6 amazon, ogress, unruly, virago 7 raucous 8 fishwife 5 rowdy 9 turbulent, Xanthippe 10 boisterous, disorderly, rowdydowdy, tumultuous 11 rumbustious
terminable 6 finite 7 endable, limited 9 limitable
terminal 3 end, lag 4 last 5 depot, final 6 latest, latter 7 closing, station 8 eventual, hindmost, ultimate 10 concluding ***negative:*** 7 cathode ***positive:*** 5 anode
terminate 2 ax 3 end 4 drop, fire, halt, quit, rise, sack, stop 5 close, leave 6 bounce, finish, recess, resign, wind up, wrap up 7 abolish, adjourn, boot out, cashier, dismiss, kick out 8 complete, conclude, dissolve, prorogue, ultimate 9 determine, discharge, prorogate 10 extinguish 11 discontinue
terminology 4 cant 6 jargon 7 lexicon, palaver 8 language 10 dictionary, vocabulary
termite 3 ant
tern 4 trio 5 scray 8 schooner ***genus:*** 6 Sterna
ternary 6 triple 9 threefold
terpsichore see **Muse**
terrace 4 bank, dais, deck, roof, step 5 bench, porch 7 balcony, portico 8 platform
terra-cotta 4 clay 7 pottery
terra firma 4 dirt, land, soil 5 earth 6 ground 7 dry land
terrain 4 turf, walk 5 field 6 domain, sphere 7 demesne 8 dominion, province 9 bailiwick, champaign, territory 10 topography
terrapin 6 turtle
terrestrial 6 earthy 7 earthly, mundane, profane, prosaic, secular, terrene, worldly 8 telluric 9 earthlike, sublunary, tellurian 10 earthbound
terrible 3 bad 4 grim, hard 5 awful, heavy, tough 6 fierce, grisly, horrid, severe 7 arduous, fearful, furious, ghastly, hideous, intense, macabre, vicious, violent 8 dreadful, gruesome, horrible, horrific, shocking, toilsome, vehement 9 appalling, desperate, difficult, exquisite, frightful, laborious, strenuous 10 formidable, horrifying ***combining form:*** 3 din 4 dein, dino 5 deino
terrier 3 dog ***kind:*** 3 fox 4 blue, bull, Skye 5 cairn, Irish, Welsh 6 Boston 8 Airedale, Lakeland 9 Yorkshire
terrific 5 super, swell 6 superb 7 fearful 8 dreadful, glorious, horrible, horrific, shocking 9 appalling, frightful, marvelous, upsetting, wonderful 10 formidable 11 magnificent, sensational, terrorizing
terrify 3 awe 4 stun 5 alarm, scare 7 startle 8 affright, frighten 9 terrorize
terrifying 4 grim 6 grisly, horrid 7 ghastly, hideous, macabre 8 gruesome, horrible, terrible 10 horrifying
territory 4 area, belt, land, turf, walk, zone 5 field, tract 6 domain, region, sphere 7 demesne, terrain 8 dominion, province 9 bailiwick, champaign
terror 4 fear 5 alarm, dread, panic 6 dismay, fright, horror 9 trepidity 11 fearfulness, trepidation 13 consternation
terrorist 4 thug 6 bomber 7 Jacobin 8 alarmist
terrorize 3 cow 5 alarm, bully, scare 6 fright, hector 7 dragoon 8 affright, bludg-

eon, browbeat, bulldoze, bullyrag, frighten 9 strong-arm 10 intimidate
terry 4 loop 6 fabric 8 toweling
terse 4 curt, taut 5 brief, crisp, pithy, short 7 compact, concise, laconic, summary 8 succinct 11 compendiary, compendious 12 breviloquent
tertiary 5 third
tessera 3 die 4 tile 6 tablet, ticket
test 3 try 4 exam, quiz 5 assay, check, essay, final, prove, trial, try on 6 sample, trying, try out, verify 7 confirm, examine, mid-term, proving 8 sounding, trial run 10 experiment 11 demonstrate, examination 12 experimental
testa 4 coat 5 shell 8 episperm 10 integument
testament 4 will 5 proof 7 witness 8 evidence 9 scripture, testimony 11 attestation, testimonial 12 confirmation
tester 5 frame 6 canopy, prover 7 assayer
testifier 7 witness 8 deponent 9 proselyte
testify 5 argue, swear 6 attest, depone, depose 7 bespeak, betoken, point to, witness 8 announce, indicate
testimonial 5 proof, salvo, token 6 salute 7 tribute, witness 8 evidence, memorial, monument 9 character, reference, testament 10 indication 11 attestation, credentials 12 appreciation, confirmation
testimony 5 proof 7 witness 8 evidence 10 indication 11 affirmation, attestation 12 confirmation 13 documentation
testy 5 cross, ratty 6 cranky, tetchy, touchy 7 grouchy 8 choleric 9 irascible, irritable, temperish 10 ill-humored 12 cantankerous 13 quick-tempered
tetanus 7 lockjaw, trismus
tetchy see testy
tête-à-tête 4 chat, coze, talk 7 vis-à-vis 8 causerie 10 discussion 12 conversation
tether 3 tie 4 bind, rope 5 cable, chain, scope 6 fasten
Tethys ***daughters:*** 9 Oceanides ***father:*** 6 Uranus ***husband:*** 7 Oceanus ***mother:*** 2 Ge 4 Gaea 5 Terra
tetrad 4 four 7 quartet, quatuor 8 foursome 9 quartetto 10 quaternion
Teucer ***father:*** 7 Telamon 9 Scamander ***stepbrother:*** 4 Ajax
Teutonic 6 German 8 Germanic ***language:*** 5 Dutch 6 Danish, German, Gothic 7 English, Flemish, Frisian, Swedish 9 Afrikaans, Norwegian
Texas ***capital:*** 6 Austin ***college, university:*** 3 SMU 4 Rice 5 Lamar, Wiley 6 Baylor ***largest city:*** 7 Houston ***nickname:*** 13 Lone Star State ***state flower:*** 10 bluebonnet
text 4 head 5 motif, point, theme, topic 6 matter, motive 7 subject 8 argument 13 subject matter
textbook 6 manual, primer
textile 6 fabric ***dealer:*** 6 mercer ***machine:*** 8 calender ***shop:*** 7 mercery ***treat:*** 9 mercerize
texture 3 web 5 being, fiber 6 fabric, nature 7 essence
Thackeray novel 9 Pendennis 10 Vanity Fair 11 Henry Esmond
Thailand 4 Siam ***capital:*** 7 Bangkok ***language:*** 3 Lao ***monetary unit:*** 4 baht 5 tical ***temple:*** 3 wat
Thaïs 7 hetaera 9 courtesan ***author:*** 6 France (Anatole) ***composer:*** 8 Massenet
thalassic 6 marine 7 oceanic 8 maritime
Thalia see Graces; Muse
thallium ***symbol:*** 2 Tl
Thanatopsis author 6 Bryant
Thanatos 5 death ***brother:*** 6 Hypnos ***mother:*** 3 Nyx
thankful 7 obliged 8 grateful 12 appreciative
thanks 2 ta 5 grace 8 blessing 9 gratitude 11 benediction 12 appreciation, thanksgiving
Thanksgiving 5 feast 7 holiday ***first celebrant:*** 6 Indian 7 Pilgrim ***food:*** 6 turkey
thatch 4 roof 5 cover
that is 2 i.e. ***Latin:*** 5 id est
Thaumas ***daughter:*** 4 Iris 5 Aello, Harpy 7 Celaeno, Ocypete ***daughters:*** 7 Harpies ***father:*** 6 Pontus ***mother:*** 2 Ge 4 Gaea ***wife:*** 7 Electra
thaumaturgic 5 magic 6 magian, mystic, witchy 7 magical 8 wizardly 9 sorcerous 11 necromantic
thaumaturgy 5 magic 7 sorcery 8 witchery, wizardry 9 conjuring 10 necromancy, witchcraft 11 bewitchment, enchantment, incantation
thaw 3 run 4 flux, fuse, melt 7 liquefy 8 dissolve, liquesce 10 deliquesce
the 7 article ***French:*** 2 la, le 3 les ***German:*** 3 das, der, die ***Italian:*** 2 il, la ***Spanish:*** 2 el, la 3 las, los
Thea ***daughter:*** 6 Selene ***father:*** 6 Uranus ***husband:*** 8 Hyperion ***mother:*** 2 Ge 4 Gaea
theater 4 hall 5 drama, house, odeum, stage 6 boards 9 playhouse 10 footlights ***award:*** 4 Tony ***entrance:*** 5 foyer, lobby ***Greek:*** 5 odeum ***movie:*** 6 cinema ***outdoor:*** 7 drive-in ***part:*** 3 box, pit 4 loge 5 skene, stage, wings 7 balcony, parodos, parquet 10 proscenium
theatrical 5 stagy 6 staged 8 affected, dramatic, mannered, thespian 10 artificial, histrionic 11 dramaturgic, exaggerated 12 melodramatic ***agent:*** 6 Morris ***device:*** 4 prop ***group:*** 6 troupe

Theban Eagle 6 Pindar
Thebes ***founder:*** 6 Cadmus ***king:*** 5 Laius 7 Oedipus ***queen:*** 7 Jocasta
theft 4 lift 5 pinch, steal 6 piracy 7 larceny, robbery, robbing, swiping 8 burglary, filching, stealage, stealing, thievery, thieving 9 pilferage, pilfering 10 purloining ***combining form:*** 5 klept 6 klepto
The Golden 3 Ass 4 Bowl 5 Bough 6 Fleece, Legend
theme 4 head, text 5 essay, motif, paper, point, topic 6 matter, motive, thesis 7 article, subject 8 argument 11 composition 13 subject matter
Themis ***father:*** 6 Uranus ***goddess of:*** 3 law 7 justice ***husband:*** 4 Zeus 7 Jupiter ***mother:*** 2 Ge 4 Gaea
then 2 so 4 also, anon, ergo, thus, when 5 again, hence 7 besides, further 9 therefore, thereupon 10 in addition 11 accordingly 12 additionally, consequently
thence 4 away 7 thereof 9 therefrom
theologian ***American:*** 7 Edwards, Niebuhr, Tillich, Walther ***Dutch:*** 6 Jansen ***English:*** 4 Bede 5 Pusey, Watts 6 Alcuin, Wesley 8 Langston, Pelagius, Wycliffe ***French:*** 6 Calvin 7 William 8 Sabatier ***German:*** 6 Rahner 7 Eckhart 9 Niemoller 14 Albertus Magnus ***Greek:*** 9 Zygomalas ***Italian:*** 7 Aquinas, Socinus ***Scottish:*** 10 Duns Scotus ***Spanish:*** 6 Suarez 7 Vitoria 8 Servetus ***Swedish:*** 9 Soderblom ***Swiss:*** 5 Barth, Vinet
Theologica 5 Summa
theological ***school:*** 8 seminary ***virtue:*** 4 hope 5 faith 7 charity
theorbo 4 lute 8 archlute
theorem 3 law 4 rule 5 axiom 9 principle 10 principium 11 fundamental
theoretical 5 ideal 8 abstract, academic, notional, unproved 11 conjectural, speculative 12 hypothetical, transcendent 13 problematical, suppositional
theorize 6 submit 7 suggest 9 postulate
theory 7 perhaps, premise, suppose, surmise 8 supposal 10 conjecture, hypothesis 11 speculation, supposition ***astronomical:*** 7 big bang ***combining form:*** 4 logy 5 logia, ology ***suffix:*** 3 ism
therapy 9 treatment ***combining form:*** 5 pathy 6 pathic
therefore 2 so 4 ergo, then, thus 5 hence 11 accordingly 12 consequently
therefrom 6 thence
thereupon 4 then 6 at once
therm 7 calorie
thermal 3 hot 4 warm ***unit:*** 3 Btu 6 degree 7 calorie
thermometer 9 indicator ***kind:*** 7 Celsius, Reaumur 10 centigrade, Fahrenheit
Thersander's father 9 Polynices
Thersites' slayer 8 Achilles
The Saint 12 Simon Templar
the same 4 idem 5 ditto 8 likewise 9 identical
thesaurus 7 lexicon 10 dictionary ***editor:*** 5 Roget
Theseus ***father:*** 6 Aegeus ***mother:*** 6 Aethra ***slayer:*** 9 Lycomedes ***son:*** 10 Hippolytus ***victim:*** 6 Sciron 8 Minotaur 10 Procrustes ***wife:*** 7 Phaedra
thesis 5 essay, point, posit 6 belief, memoir 7 premise 8 tractate, treatise 9 apriorism, discourse, monograph, postulate 10 contention, exposition, monography 11 postulation, proposition, supposition 12 disquisition, dissertation
thespian 4 mime 5 actor, mimic 6 mummer, player 7 trouper 8 dramatic, theatral, theatric 9 performer, playactor 10 histrionic, theatrical 11 dramaturgic 12 impersonator
Thespis' forte 5 drama 7 tragedy
Thessalian hero 5 Jason 8 Achilles
the Terrible 4 Ivan
"The Thinker" sculptor 5 Rodin
Thetis 6 Nereid ***father:*** 6 Nereus ***husband:*** 6 Peleus ***mother:*** 5 Doris ***son:*** 8 Achilles
theurgist 8 magician
thew 4 beef 5 brawn, might, power, sinew 6 muscle 8 strength
thick 3 fat 4 dull, dumb, wide 5 broad, bulky, burly, close, dense, dumpy, husky, obese, squat 6 chummy, chunky, flimsy, obtuse, stocky, stupid 7 compact, crammed, crowded, doltish, massive, viscous 8 blockish, duncical, familiar, heavyset, intimate 10 numskulled ***combining form:*** 4 dasy, hadr 5 hadro, pachy
thicket 4 bosk, bush, wood 5 clump, copse, grove 6 bosket, tangle 7 boscage, coppice, spinney 9 brushwood, chaparral ***Scottish:*** 4 rone
thickness 5 layer 7 density 9 callosity
thief 3 dip, nip 4 prig 5 ganef 6 bandit, lifter, looter, nimmer, pirate, robber 7 booster, burglar, filcher, stealer 8 hijacker, larcener, pilferer 9 larcenist, purloiner 10 cat burglar, pickpocket, shoplifter 12 housebreaker
thieve 3 nip 4 hook, lift 5 filch, pinch, steal, swipe 6 pilfer, snitch 7 purloin
thievery see theft
thievish 9 larcenous
thigh 3 ham 5 flank 6 gammon ***bone:*** 5 femur ***combining form:*** 3 mer 4 mero 5 cruro, merus 6 femoro ***relating to:*** 6 crural
thimble 3 cup 5 cover
thin 3 cut 4 fine, high, lank, lean, puny, rare, slim, weak 5 acute, gaunt, lanky,

reedy, sharp, spare, wispy **6** argute, dilute, flimsy, meager, piping, rarefy, shrill, skinny, slight, sparse, stalky, treble, twiggy, watery, weaken **7** scrawny, slender, squinny, subtile, tenuous **8** piercing, rarefied, rawboned, skeletal, twiglike, wiredraw **9** attenuate, extenuate **10** attenuated **11** implausible, watered-down **12** unconvincing **13** unsubstantial ***combining form:*** **4** lept **5** lepto

thing **2** go **3** act, cry, fad **4** deed, item, mode, rage **5** being, craze, doing, event, mania, point, stuff, style, vogue **6** action, affair, detail, entity, fetish, furore, matter, object **7** article, concern, element, episode, fashion **8** business, existent, fixation, incident, material, occasion **9** existence, happening, obsession, substance **10** dernier cri, individual, occurrence, phenomenon ***additional:*** **5** bonus ***in law:*** **3** res ***insignificant:*** **6** trifle ***rare:*** **4** oner ***single:*** **4** unit ***suffix:*** **2** ia (plural) **3** ant, ory **4** oria (plural) **5** orium ***to do:*** **3** job **5** chore ***unusual:*** **5** freak **6** oddity ***worthless:*** **4** junk **5** waste

thingamajig **5** gizmo **6** dingus, doodad, gadget, jigger **7** dofunny **9** doohickey **10** thingumbob

things **4** duds, togs **5** dress, goods, stuff, traps **6** attire, tricks **7** apparel, clothes, effects, plunder, raiment **8** chattels, clothing, movables **10** attirement, belongings, habiliment, possession ***for sale:*** **11** merchandise

think **4** deem, feel, mull, muse **5** brood, fancy, guess, study, weigh **6** assume, expect, gather, ideate, ponder, reason **7** believe, imagine, perpend, presume, realize, reflect, suppose, surmise, suspect **8** cogitate, conceive, consider, envisage, envision, logicize, meditate, ruminate **9** cerebrate, speculate, visualize **10** conjecture, deliberate, excogitate, logicalize **11** contemplate, rationalize ***out:*** **4** plan ***piece:*** **7** article

third **8** tertiary ***combining form:*** **4** trit **5** trito ***power:*** **4** cube

third degree **5** grill **8** grilling **13** interrogation

third estate **5** plebs **6** people, plebes **8** populace **9** commonage, commoners, plebeians **10** commonalty **11** rank and file

Third Man, The ***author:*** **6** Greene

thirst **3** yen **4** ache, itch, long, lust, pine **5** crave, yearn **6** hanker, hunger

thirsty **3** dry **4** agog, arid, avid, keen, sere **5** eager **6** ardent **7** anxious, athirst, bone-dry, parched **8** appetent, droughty **9** impatient, unwatered, waterless **12** moistureless

this and that **8** oddments, sundries **9** etceteras **11** odds and ends

Thisbe's lover **7** Pyramus

This Side of Paradise author **10** Fitzgerald

thistle **4** weed **7** caltrop ***Russian:*** **10** tumbleweed

thistlebird **9** goldfinch

thither **3** yon **5** there **6** yonder

thole **3** peg, pin

___ Thomas, Welsh author **5** Dylan

Thomas à ___ **6** Becket, Kempis

Thomas' Greek name **7** Didymus

Thomas opera **6** Mignon

Thompson **5** Sadie **7** Dorothy, Francis

thong **4** lace, lash, rein **5** romal, strap, strip **7** amentum, babiche, latchet **8** whiplash

Thor **5** Donar ***father:*** **4** Odin ***god of:*** **7** thunder ***hammer:*** **8** Mjollnir ***mother:*** **5** Jordh, Jorth

thorax **5** chest

Thoreau, Henry David ***friend:*** **7** Emerson ***work:*** **6** Walden

thorium ***symbol:*** **2** Th

thorn **5** briar, brier, spine **7** acantha, spinule **9** annoyance **10** irritation ***combining form:*** **4** spin **5** spini, spino **6** acanth **7** acantho, spinoso **8** acanthus

thorny **5** sharp, spiny **6** tricky **7** prickly, spinate **9** difficult, vexatious **10** nettlesome **11** troublesome

thorough **4** full **6** minute **8** complete, detailed, itemized, whole-hog **9** clocklike **10** blow-by-blow, exhaustive

thoroughbred **5** horse **8** pedigree, purebred **9** pedigreed, pureblood **11** full-blooded

thoroughfare **3** way **4** drag, path, road **5** track **6** artery, avenue, street **7** highway **9** boulevard

thoroughgoing **4** rank **5** gross, utter **8** absolute, complete, outright, whole-hog **9** out-and-out **10** consummate, exhaustive **11** straight-out, unmitigated

though **3** yet **5** still, while **6** albeit **7** however, whereas **8** after all **11** nonetheless **12** nevertheless

thought **4** idea, mind **5** image **6** musing, notion **7** concept, opinion **9** brainwork, pondering **10** cogitation, conception, meditation, reflection, rumination **11** cerebration, speculation **12** deliberation, intellection **13** contemplation ***combining form:*** **3** log **4** logo

thoughtful **6** polite **7** careful, gallant, heedful, logical, mindful, pensive, serious **8** gracious, rational, studious, thinking **9** attentive, courteous, pondering, regardful **10** cogitative, meditative, reflecting, reflective, ruminative, solicitous **11** considerate **12** intellectual **13** contemplative

thoughtless **4** rash, rude **5** brash, hasty

6 madcap 7 selfish 8 careless, feckless, heedless, impolite, reckless, uncaring 9 hotheaded, unheeding, unrecking 10 ill-advised, incautious, mad-brained, ungracious, unthinking 11 inadvertent 12 discourteous, irreflective, unreflective 13 inconsiderate

thousand ***combining form:*** 4 kilo ***dollars:*** 5 grand ***years:*** 10 millennium

thousandth 10 millesimal ***combining form:*** 5 milli

thrall 4 yoke 7 bondage, helotry, peonage, serfdom, slavery 9 servitude, villenage 11 enslavement

thrash 4 beat, drub, flog, hide, lash, lick, maul, pelt, whip 5 paste, pound, smear, whale 6 batter, buffet, larrup, pummel, stripe, wallop 7 belabor, scourge, shellac 8 lambaste 10 flagellate

thrash out 4 moot 5 argue 6 debate 7 agitate, canvass, discept, discuss, dispute 10 kick around, toss around

thread 4 line, vein, yard 5 fiber, reeve, weave 6 strand, stream, string 8 filament ***ball of:*** 4 clew, clue ***combining form:*** 3 mit, nem 4 fili, mito, nema, neme, nemo 5 nemat 6 nemata (plural), nemato ***dental:*** 5 floss ***holder:*** 6 bobbin ***kind:*** 4 silk, yarn 5 floss, lisle, watap 6 cotton, lingel 8 surgical ***loose:*** 8 raveling 9 ravelling ***surgical:*** 5 seton 6 catgut, suture

threadbare 4 hack, worn 5 dingy, faded, seedy, stale, tacky, tired, trite 6 cliché, frayed, ragged, shabby, tagrag 7 clichéd, run-down, worn-out 8 bathetic, shopworn, tattered, timeworn, well-worn 10 down-at-heel 11 commonplace, dilapidated

threadlike 6 filose

threads 8 clothing

threat 6 duress, menace 7 warning

threaten 3 cow 4 warn 5 augur 6 menace 7 caution, portend, presage 8 browbeat, bulldoze, forebode, forewarn 10 intimidate

three 4 trey 5 crowd ***combining form:*** 3 ter, tri ***group of:*** (see **threesome**)

threefold 6 thrice, triple

Three Musketeers 5 Athos 6 Aramis 7 Porthos ***author:*** 5 Dumas

Threepenny Opera, The ***author:*** 6 Brecht ***music:*** 5 Weill

threescore 5 sixty

Three Sisters, The 4 Olga 5 Irina, Masha ***author:*** 7 Chekhov

Three Soldiers author 9 Dos Passos

threesome 4 trio 5 triad, trine 6 triple, triune, troika 7 trinity 11 triumvirate

three-wheeler 8 tricycle

threnody 5 dirge, elegy

thresh 4 beat, flog, whip 5 flail 6 strike

threshold 3 eve 4 edge, gate 5 brink, limen, point, verge

thrice 9 threefold ***a day:*** 3 t.i.d. 8 ter in die

thrift 7 economy 8 prudence 9 frugality, husbandry 11 economizing

thriftiness see **thrift**

thrifty 5 canny, chary 6 frugal, robust, saving 7 booming, roaring, sparing 8 thriving 9 provident, stewardly 10 conserving, economical, preserving, prospering, prosperous, unwasteful 11 flourishing

thrill 4 bang, boot, kick, send 6 excite, wallop 7 enthuse 9 electrify, galvanize 10 excitement 11 titillation

thriller 6 gothic 7 chiller, mystery, shocker 9 dime novel 13 penny dreadful

thrive 2 go 4 boom, grow 5 score 6 arrive 7 develop, make out, prosper, succeed 8 flourish

throat 3 maw 4 gula, tube 6 groove, gullet 7 channel, weasand, weazand ***combining form:*** 3 der 4 dero 6 bronch 7 broncho ***inflammation:*** 5 croup 6 angina, quinsy 10 laryngitis ***relating to:*** 8 guttural ***upper:*** 4 gula ***warmer:*** 5 scarf

throb 4 ache, beat 5 pulse 7 pulsate 9 palpitate

throe 3 fit 4 ache, pain, pang 5 spell 6 access, attack, stitch, twinge 7 seizure 10 convulsion

thrombus 4 clot

throne 4 apse, seat 5 chair, gaddi, power 8 cathedra 11 sovereignty

throng 4 host, pack, push 5 bunch, crowd, crush, drove, flock, group, horde, press 6 squash 9 multitude

throttle 5 choke 7 garrote 8 strangle 11 accelerator

through 2 by 3 per, via 4 done, over, past, with 5 about, due to, ended, round 6 around, direct 7 by way of, done for, owing to 8 by dint of, complete, finished, straight, washed-up 9 because of, by means of, completed, concluded 10 by virtue of, terminated, throughout 13 uninterrupted ***prefix:*** 2 di 3 dia, per

throughout 3 mid 4 amid, over 5 about, midst, round 6 around, during 7 all over, overall 10 everyplace, everywhere, far and near, far and wide, high and low ***combining form:*** 3 hol 4 holo

Through the Looking Glass ***author:*** 7 Carroll ***character:*** 5 Alice

throw 3 peg, put 4 cast, fire, hurl, toss 5 fling, heave, pitch, sling 6 launch, propel, unseat 7 buck off, project, unhorse ***in the towel:*** 4 quit 6 give up

throw away 4 blow, cast, junk, shed 5 scrap, waste 6 reject, slough 7 cashier, consume, discard, fritter 8 jettison, squander

throw back 6 reject, revert 7 regress 10 retrogress
throwback 7 atavism 9 reversion
throw down 4 fell 5 level 6 lay low 8 bowl over 9 knock over, overthrow, prostrate ***the gauntlet:*** 4 defy 9 challenge
throw off 3 rid 4 emit, lose, shed, slip, vent 5 addle, eject, expel, issue, mix up, shake 6 ball up 7 confuse, fluster, give out, release 8 befuddle, bewilder, distract, unburden ***the track:*** 6 derail 7 confuse, mislead
throw out 4 cast, junk, shed 5 addle, chuck, eject, evict, mix up, scrap 6 ball up, reject, slough 7 cashier, confuse, discard, dismiss, extrude, fluster 8 befuddle, bewilder, distract, jettison
throw up 4 barf 5 heave, vomit 7 upchuck 8 disgorge 10 jerry-build
thrush 4 bird 5 robin, veery 8 bluebird ***European:*** 5 mavis, ouzel 6 mistle 9 blackbird, mistletoe 11 nightingale
thrust 3 dig, jab, ram, run 4 core, gist, meat, pith, push, sink, stab 5 drive, sense, short, shove, stick 6 burden, plunge, propel, upshot 7 intrude, purport, riposte 9 substance
thug 3 mug 4 goon, hood, punk 5 bully, rough, rowdy, tough, yahoo 6 gunman, mucker 7 hoodlum, mobster, ruffian 8 gangster, hooligan, plug-ugly 9 cutthroat, roughneck, strong arm 10 hatchet man
thulium ***symbol:*** 2 Tm
thumb 5 digit, hitch 6 pollex 8 pollices (plural) 9 hitchhike
thumb through 4 scan 6 browse 7 dip into, run over 8 glance at 10 glance over
thunder 4 bang, roar 6 rumble 8 rumbling 11 fulmination ***combining form:*** 5 bront 6 bronto, ceraun 7 cerauno, kerauno
thunderbolt 9 lightning
thunderclap see thunder
thunder lizard 10 brontosaur
thunderstruck 5 agape 6 aghast 7 shocked, stunned 8 dismayed 9 staggered 10 bewildered, confounded 11 dumbfounded, overwhelmed
Thurber character 11 Walter Mitty
thurify 5 cense
thus 2 so 3 sic 4 ergo, then 5 hence 9 therefore, thereupon, thus and so 11 accordingly 12 consequently ***French:*** 5 ainsi
Thus Spoke Zarathustra ***author:*** 9 Nietzsche
thwack 3 bop 4 biff, blow, sock, whop 5 crack, pound, smack, whack
thwart 4 balk, beat, bilk, curb, dash, foil, ruin 6 arrest, baffle, scotch, stymie 8 traverse 9 checkmate, crosswise, frustrate 10 circumvent, disappoint, transverse 11 transversal
Thyestes ***brother:*** 6 Atreus ***daughter:*** 7 Pelopia ***father:*** 6 Pelops ***mother:*** 10 Hippodamia ***son:*** 9 Aegisthus
Tiamat ***husband:*** 4 Apsu ***slayer:*** 6 Marduk
tiara 5 crown 6 diadem 9 headdress
Tibetan ***animal:*** 3 yak 5 manul ***coin:*** 5 tanga ***gazelle:*** 3 goa ***monk:*** 4 lama ***people:*** 6 Bhotia, Sherpa
Tibet's capital 5 Lhasa
tibia 8 shinbone
Tibni's father 6 Ginath
tic 5 spasm 6 twitch 9 twitching
tick 6 credit, insect 8 arachnid, parasite 11 bloodsucker ***combining form:*** 4 acar 5 acari, acaro
ticker 4 bomb 5 clock, heart, watch
ticket 3 key, tag 4 vote 5 label, slate 6 ballot 8 passport, password 10 open sesame 12 carte d'entrée ***seller:*** 7 cashier, scalper
tickle 4 stir 5 amuse, tease, touch 6 arouse, excite, please, tingle 7 delight, gratify, provoke 9 stimulate, titillate
ticklish 5 risky, rocky 6 fickle, touchy, tricky 8 delicate, unstable, variable, volatile 9 mercurial, sensitive, uncertain 10 capricious, changeable, inconstant, precarious
tick off 4 list 5 chide 6 monish, rebuke 7 reprove 8 admonish, call down, numerate, reproach 9 enumerate, reprimand
tidal flood 4 bore 5 eagre
tidbit 5 goody, treat 6 dainty, morsel 8 delicacy, kickshaw 11 bonne bouche
tide 4 flow, flux, rush 5 drift, flood, spate, surge 6 stream 7 current, holiday ***lowest:*** 4 neap ***type:*** 3 ebb, low 4 high, neap 5 flood 6 spring
tidings 4 news, word 6 advice 7 message 9 speerings 11 information 12 intelligence
tidy 4 neat, snug, trig, trim 7 chipper, orderly 9 shipshape 11 uncluttered, well-groomed 12 spick-and-span
tie 3 rod, wed 4 band, bind, bond, cord, draw, gird, join, knot, lash, link, mate, moor, rope, yoke 5 ascot, cinch, equal, jabot, leash, marry, match, nexus 6 attach, cravat, fasten, fetter, hamper, hobble, secure, splice 7 connect, dogfall, shackle, trammel, truss up 8 deadlock, fastener, ligament, ligature, standoff, vinculum 9 entrammel, fastening, stalemate 10 attachment, four-in-hand
tier 3 row 4 file, line, rank 5 class, grade, group, queue, story 6 league, string 7 echelon 8 category, grouping
tiff 3 row 4 spat 5 run-in, scrap 6 bicker 7 brabble, dispute, fall out, quarrel, rhubarb,

wrangle 8 squabble 9 bickering, caterwaul 10 falling-out 11 altercation

tiffany 5 gauze 11 cheesecloth

tiger 3 cat 6 feline 9 carnivore *young:* 3 cub

tight 3 set 4 fast, firm, hard, snug, taut, trim 5 cheap, close, dense, drunk, fixed, tense, thick 6 firmly, secure, stingy 7 compact, crowded, drunken, fixedly, miserly, solidly 9 niggardly, penurious, tenacious 10 contracted, inebriated 11 closefisted, constricted, intoxicated, steadfastly 12 cheeseparing, parsimonious 13 pennypinching

tightfisted see stingy

tight-lipped 5 close 6 silent 8 reserved, reticent, taciturn 12 closemouthed, close-tongued

tightwad 4 skin 5 miser, nabal, stiff 7 niggard, scrooge 9 skinflint 10 cheapskate 11 cheeseparer

Tikvah's son 7 Shallum 8 Jahaziah

tile 3 hat 5 brick, guard, plate, slate 6 domino, tegula 7 abacula, tessera *roofing:* 7 pantile

till 2 to 3 sow 4 plow, tend, turn, up to, work 5 until 6 before, harrow 7 prior to 9 cultivate 11 in advance of

tillable 6 arable 10 cultivable 12 cultivatable

tillage 4 farm, land 5 crops 11 cultivation

tiller 4 helm 6 farmer, rudder 7 steerer

Tilon's father 6 Shimon

tilt 3 tip, yaw 4 cant, cock, heel, lean, list, swag 5 grade, lurch, pitch, slant, slope 6 seesaw 7 incline, leaning, recline 8 gradient 11 inclination

timbal 4 drum 10 kettledrum

timber 3 log 4 balk, beam, tree, wood 5 board, joist, plank, trees, weald, woods 6 forest, girder, lumber, rafter 8 woodland *decay:* 4 dote, doze *joint:* 4 coak *mine:* 5 stull *Philippine:* 5 lauan *ship's:* 3 rib 4 bibb, keel, mast, skeg 7 stemson 8 sternson *supporting:* 4 stud 6 purlin, putlog, rafter 8 puncheon *uncut:* 8 stumpage *wolf:* 4 lobo

timbre 4 mood, tone 6 spirit, temper

timbrel 4 drum 10 tambourine

time 2 go 3 age, bit, day, era 4 book, bout, date, hour, pace, plan, shot, show, span, term, tour, turn 5 break, clock, epoch, set up, shift, space, spell, stint, tempo, trick, while 6 chance, look-in, moment, period, season, squeak 7 instant, opening, program, stretch 8 duration, occasion, schedule 11 opportunity *ahead of:* 5 early *combining form:* 5 chron, semic 6 chrono 8 chronous *gone by:* 4 past 9 yesterday *long:* 3 age, eon, era 4 aeon *of day:* 4 dawn, dusk, noon 5 night 6 sunset 7 evening, morning, sunrise 8 daybreak, twilight 9 afternoon *olden:* 4 yore 10 yesteryear *period:* 3 age, day, eon, era 4 aeon, hour, week, year 5 epoch, month 6 decade, minute, moment, second 7 century, instant 9 fortnight 10 millennium *present:* 3 now *relating to:* 8 temporal *short:* 5 jiffy 6 moment, second 7 instant *suffix:* 2 ad *to come:* 6 future 8 tomorrow *waste:* 4 loaf 5 dally 6 loiter

time and again 3 oft 5 often 8 ofttimes 10 frequently, oftentimes, repeatedly 11 over and over

timeless 7 ageless, endless, eternal 8 dateless, unending 9 ceaseless, continual, perpetual, unceasing 10 intemporal 11 everlasting, unremitting 12 interminable

timely 3 fit 4 meet, soon 5 early 6 likely, prompt, proper 7 betimes, fitting, timeous 8 punctual, suitable 9 favorable, opportune, promising, well-timed 10 auspicious, propitious, prosperous, seasonable, seasonably 11 appropriate

Time Machine, The *author:* 5 Wells

Time magazine founder 4 Luce 6 Hadden

Time of Your Life, The *author:* 7 Saroyan

timepiece 5 clock, watch 7 horloge, sundial 8 horologe 9 clepsydra 11 chronograph, chronometer, chronoscope

timetable 4 card, plan, sked 6 agenda, docket 7 program 8 calendar, schedule

timeworn 3 old 4 aged, hack 5 hoary, stale, trite 6 age-old 8 Noachian 9 hackneyed, venerable 12 antediluvian

time zone, U.S. 7 central, eastern, Pacific 8 mountain

timid 3 coy, shy 4 mild, wary 5 chary, mousy, pavid 6 afraid, demure, gentle, modest, yellow 7 bashful, chicken, fearful, halting, nervous, panicky, rabbity 9 diffident, faltering, milk-toast, mouselike, shrinking, tentative, unassured, uncertain 10 irresolute 11 unassertive, vacillating, vacillatory 12 apprehensive, fainthearted

Timna *brother:* 5 Lotan *father:* 4 Seir *son:* 6 Amalek

Timon's servant 7 Flavius

timorous 5 timid 7 fearful 8 quailing, undaring 9 quivering, recoiling, shivering, shrinking, trembling 10 shuddering

Timothy's associate 4 Paul

tin 3 box, can 5 metal 7 element, stannum 9 container *combining form:* 5 stann 6 stanni, stanno *mining region:* 8 stannary *relating to:* 7 stannic 8 stannous *sheet:* 6 latten *symbol:* 2 Sn

tincture 3 dye 4 cast, hint, tint 5 color, shade, stain, tinge, touch, trace 6 streak

8 colorant, dyestuff 10 complexion, intimation, suggestion
tinder 4 punk 8 kindling
tine 5 point, prong, spike 6 branch
tinge 3 dye, hue 4 cast, hint, tint, tone 5 color, shade, tinct, touch, trace 6 strain 8 tincture 10 complexion, intimation, sprinkling, suggestion
tinker 3 fix 4 mend, mess 6 doodle, fiddle, mender, potter, puddle, putter, repair 9 repairman 10 mess around
tinkle 3 gab, gas, jaw, yak 4 chat, ting 5 chink, clack, clink, plink 6 babble, jangle, jingle, rattle, tingle 7 chatter, prattle
tinny 4 thin 5 cheap, harsh 8 metallic
Tin Pan Alley acronym 5 ASCAP
tinsel 4 loud 5 gaudy 6 brazen, flashy, garish, tawdry 7 blatant, chintzy, glaring 8 ornament 9 clinquant 12 meretricious
tint 3 dye, hue 4 cast, tone, wash 5 color, shade, tinge, touch 7 touch up 8 tincture 10 coloration, complexion 12 pigmentation
tiny 3 wee 5 bitsy, dwarf, minim, pygmy, small, teeny, weeny 6 midget, minute, peewee, pocket, teensy, teenty, weensy 7 minikin 8 dwarfish, pint-size 9 itsy-bitsy, itty-bitty, miniature, minuscule 10 diminutive, minuscular, pocket-size, teeny-weeny 11 lilliputian, microscopic 12 teensy-weensy 13 infinitesimal
tip 3 cap, cue, top 4 apex, cant, clue, cusp, heel, hint, lean, list, peak, perk, tilt 5 point, slant, slope, steer, upset 6 advice, top[illegible] 7 cumshaw, incline, largess, overset, pointer, recline 8 forecast, gratuity, overturn, turn over 9 baksheesh, knock over, logniappe, overthrow, pourboire 10 perquisite, prediction 11 information ***combining form:*** 3 acr, akr 4 acro, akro, apic 5 apici, apico
tip-off 4 hint 5 point, steer 7 pointer, warning 8 giveaway, jump ball 10 indication
Tippecanoe and ___ too 5 Tyler
tippet 4 band, barb, cape 5 scarf
tipple 3 bib, sip 4 grog, soak, swig 5 booze, drink, swill 6 guzzle, imbibe, liquor, spirit, tank up 7 swizzle 8 liquor up 9 aqua vitae, firewater
tippler 3 sot 4 lush, soak 5 drunk, toper 6 bibber, boozer 7 tosspot 8 drunkard 9 inebriate
tipstaff 7 bailiff
tipster 4 fink, nark 6 canary, snitch 7 tattler 8 betrayer, informer, squealer 10 talebearer 11 stool pigeon
tipsy 5 drunk, tight 7 drunken 8 unsteady 10 inebriated 11 intoxicated
tiptoe 5 creep, steal 7 gumshoe 9 pussyfoot
tirade 4 rant 5 abuse 6 screed 7 censure 8 berating, diatribe, harangue, jeremiad 9 invective, philippic 10 revilement 11 rodomontade 12 condemnation, denunciation, vituperation 13 tongue-lashing
tire 3 sap 4 bore, hoop, jade, pall, poop, wear 5 drain, ennui, weary, wheel 6 tucker, weaken 7 exhaust, fatigue, wear out 8 enervate, enfeeble, wear down 10 debilitate ***airless:*** 4 flat 7 blowout ***kind:*** 4 bias, snow 6 radial 7 retread 9 whitewall
tiredness 7 fatigue 8 collapse 9 lassitude, weariness 10 exhaustion 11 prostration
tireless 4 busy 6 active 8 untiring 9 wearilless 10 unflagging, unwearying 11 unweariable 12 enthusiastic 13 indefatigable, inexhaustible
Tiresias 4 seer 10 soothsayer
tiresome 4 dull, hard 6 boring, jading, tiring 7 irksome, onerous, tedious 8 boresome, drudging 9 difficult, wearisome 10 burdensome, oppressive
Tirhanah ***father:*** 5 Caleb ***mother:*** 6 Maacah ***uncle:*** 9 Jerahmeel
Tiriac of tennis 3 Ion
tiring see tiresome
Tirol, Tyrol ***capital:*** 9 Innsbruck ***country:*** 7 Austria ***mountains:*** 4 Alps
Tirzah's father 10 Zelophehad
Tisiphone see Erinyes
tissue 3 web 4 mesh 5 fiber, gauze, paper 6 fabric ***anatomical:*** 4 tela 5 fiber 6 diploe 8 ganglion 10 epithelium ***combining form:*** 4 hist 5 histi, histo, hypho 6 histio ***connective:*** 6 stroma, tendon 9 cartilage ***kind:*** 3 fat 5 nerve 6 muscle 7 nervous 8 muscular 10 connective, epithelial ***layer:*** 6 dermis 7 stratum ***plant:*** 4 bast, wood 5 xylem 6 phloem
Titan ***father:*** 6 Uranus ***female:*** 4 Rhea 6 Tethys, Themis ***male:*** 6 Cronus 7 Iapetus, Oceanus ***mother:*** 2 Ge 4 Gaea
Titan, The ***author:*** 7 Dreiser
Titania's husband 6 Oberon
titanic 4 huge 5 great 6 mighty 8 colossal, enormous, gigantic 9 cyclopean, Herculean, monstrous 10 gargantuan, tremendous
titanium ***symbol:*** 2 Ti
tithe 3 tax 5 tenth
Tithonus ***beloved by:*** 3 Eos ***father:*** 8 Laomedon
title 3 dub, due 4 call, deed, dibs, name, term 5 claim, merit, nomen 7 baptize, caption, heading 8 christen, cognomen, pretense 9 designate 10 denominate, pretension 11 appellation, appellative, designation 12 championship, compellation, denomination ***Dutch:*** 7 mynheer ***ecclesiastic:*** 8 reverend ***feminine:*** 2 Ms. 3 Mrs. 4 dame, lady, ma'am, miss 5 madam 6 milady, missus 8 mistress ***French:***

6 madame 8 monsieur 12 mademoiselle *German:* 4 Frau, Herr 8 Fraulein *holder:* 5 noble 8 champion *Indian:* 3 sri 4 raja, shri 5 sahib 7 bahadur *Islamic:* 6 sayyid 9 ayatollah *Italian:* 5 donna 6 signor 7 signora 9 signorina *monk's:* 3 fra 7 brother *of nobility:* 3 sir 4 Duke, Earl, King, Lord, sire 5 Baron, Count, Queen 6 Prince 7 Baronet, Marquis 8 Archduke, Princess, Viscount *Oriental:* 4 khan *Persian:* 5 mirza

titmouse 4 bird 6 tomtit, verdin 7 bushtit 9 chickadee

tittor 5 laugh, tehee 6 giggle, guffaw, heehaw 7 chortle, chuckle, snicker

tittle 3 bit, jot 4 atom, iota, mite 5 minim, speck 6 smitch 7 smidgen 8 particle

titular 6 formal 7 nominal 8 so-called

Tityus *father:* 4 Zeus *slayer:* 6 Apollo

Tiu see Tyr

tizzy 4 fume, snit, stew 5 sweat 6 dither, swivet

T-man 5 agent 8 revenuer

TNT 8 dynamite 9 explosive

to 2 at 3 ere, for 4 ante, till 5 until 6 before, toward, up till 7 against, ahead of, prior to 8 opposite, touching 9 preceding 11 in advance of *be sure:* 6 indeed 9 certainly *prefix:* 2 ac, ad, af, ag, al, ap, as, at *Scottish:* 3 tae *wit:* 3 viz 6 namely 8 scilicet

toad 4 agua, hyla, scum 6 anuran, peeper 7 crapaud, stinker 8 lickspit, truckler 9 amphibian, sycophant 10 batrachian, bootlicker, footlicker 11 lickspittle *combining form:* 7 batrach 8 batracho 9 batrachus *genus:* 4 Bufo

toady 4 fawn 5 cower, kotow 6 cringe, flunky, grovel, kowtow 7 honey up, truckle 8 bootlick, lickspit, truckler 9 brownnose, sycophant 10 bootlicker, footlicker 11 apple-polish, lickspittle

To Althea from ___ 6 Prison *author:* 8 Lovelace

toast 5 bread, brown, drink, skoal 6 cheers, pledge, prosit, salute 7 wassail *Jewish:* 7 lehayim 8 lechayim *kind:* 5 melba 6 French 8 zwieback

toastmaster 2 MC 5 emcee

To a Waterfowl author 6 Bryant

tobacco 4 leaf, weed *cask:* 8 hogshead *chewing:* 4 chaw, quid *Cuban:* 4 capa *ingredient:* 3 tar 8 nicotine *juice:* 6 ambeer *kind:* 4 shag 5 bogie, snuff 6 bright, burley 7 caporal, perique, Turkish 9 broadleaf, mundungus *pipe:* 4 heel 6 dottle *rolled:* 5 cigar *Turkish:* 7 latakia

Tobacco Road author 8 Caldwell

to be *Latin:* 4 esse

Tobias *father:* 5 Tobit *son:* 8 Hyrcanus

toboggan 4 sled 7 coaster

toby 3 cup, mug 5 cigar

tocsin 3 SOS 4 sign 5 alarm, alert 6 alarum, signal

today 3 now 7 present 8 nowadays 9 presently

toddle 4 walk 6 stroll 7 saunter

toddy 3 sap 5 drink

to-do 4 coil, fuss 5 whirl 6 clamor, furore, hassle, hubbub, hurrah, pother, ruckus, rumpus, shindy, tumult, uproar 7 turmoil 9 commotion 10 hurly-burly

toe 3 tip 5 digit, touch *big:* 6 hallux *combining form:* 6 dactyl, digiti 7 dactylo, dactyly 8 dactylia 9 dactylion, dactylous *little:* 7 minimus

toehold 7 footing

toffee 5 candy

toga 4 gown, robe, wrap 5 tunic

together 6 at once, joined, united 7 jointly 8 mutually 10 conjointly 11 concertedly 12 coincidently, collectively, concurrently *prefix:* 2 co 3 col, com, con, cor, sym, syn

togetherness 5 union 7 cahoots 8 alliance, cohesion 10 connection, solidarity 11 affiliation, association, combination, conjunction, partnership

Togo *capital:* 4 Lome *monetary unit:* 5 franc

tog out 5 fix up, slick, spiff 6 doll up 7 dress up, gussy up 8 spruce up 9 smarten up

togs 4 duds 5 dress 6 attire, things 7 apparel, clothes, raiment 8 clothing 10 attirement, habiliment

To Have and to Hold author 8 Johnston

To His Coy Mistress author 7 Marvell

toil 3 net, tug 4 grub, plod, slog, slop, work 5 drive, grind, labor, slave, sweat 6 drudge, stodge, strain, strive, trudge 7 travail 8 bullwork, drudgery, footslog, plunther, slogging

toiler 4 peon 5 slave 6 drudge, slavey 9 dray horse, workhorse 11 galley slave

toilet 4 head, john 5 dress, privy 6 johnny 7 latrine 8 bathroom, lavatory 11 convenience, water closet *British:* 3 loo

toilsome 4 hard 6 uphill 7 arduous, labored, operose 9 difficult, effortful, laborious, strenuous

Toi's son 5 Joram 7 Hadoram, Jehoram

Tokay 4 wine

token 4 mark, pawn, sign 5 index, relic 6 pledge, trophy 7 earnest, gesture, indicia, memento, minimal, symptom, warrant 8 evidence, keepsake, memorial, reminder, security, souvenir 9 indicator 10 expression, indication 11 remembrance 12 remembrancer

Tokyo *formerly:* 3 Edo
Tola's father 4 Puah 8 Issachar
tolerable 2 OK 4 fair 6 common, decent 7 livable 8 adequate, all right, bearable 9 endurable 10 acceptable, sufferable, sufficient 11 presentable, respectable, supportable, sustainable 12 satisfactory
tolerably 4 so-so 6 enough, fairly, pretty, rather 8 passably 9 averagely 10 moderately
tolerance 7 stamina 8 clemency, lenience, leniency, patience 9 endurance 10 indulgence, resistance, steadiness, sufferance 11 forbearance 13 steadfastness
tolerant 4 easy 5 broad 7 clement, lenient, liberal 9 condoning, forgiving, indulgent 10 charitable, forbearing, open-minded, permissive 11 broad-minded, progressive, sympathetic 13 understanding
tolerate 4 bear, take 5 abide, allow, brook, stand 6 accept, endure, permit, suffer 7 condone, stomach, swallow 8 bear with, tough out 11 countenance
Tolkien creature 3 Ent 6 Hobbit
toll 3 tax 4 bait, bell, bong, cost, lure, peal, ring 5 chime, decoy, knell, price, tempt 6 allure, charge, entice, entrap, lead on, seduce 7 expense, lockage 8 inveigle
tollbooth 11 customhouse
Tolstoy novel 11 War and Peace 12 Anna Karenina
tomato 5 fruit 9 love apple
tomb 4 bury 5 grave, inter, plant 6 burial, inhume 7 lay away, put away 8 mausolea (plural) 9 mausoleum, sepulcher, sepulture 11 ensepulcher *ancient Egyptian:* 7 mastaba 8 mastabah *circular:* 6 tholoi (plural), tholos *empty:* 8 cenotaph
tomboy 6 gamine, hoyden
Tom Brown's School Days *author:* 6 Hughes
tombstone 6 ledger 8 memorial, monument 11 grave marker *inscription:* 3 RIP 8 hic jacet
tome 4 book 6 volume
tomfool 3 ass 4 fool, jerk 5 crazy, idiot, loony, ninny, silly 6 absurd, donkey, insane 7 foolish, jackass 8 imbecile 9 fantastic 10 nincompoop 11 harebrained 12 preposterous
tomfoolery 4 dido, lark 5 antic, caper, prank, shine, trick 6 frolic 7 hogwash, rubbish, twaddle 8 claptrap, malarkey, nonsense 9 poppycock 10 balderdash, shenanigan 11 monkeyshine 12 blatherskite
Tom Jones author 8 Fielding
tommyrot 4 bash, bull, crap 5 bilge, hooey, trash 7 hogwash, rubbish 8 nonsense
Tom o'Bedlam 3 nut 4 loon 5 loony 6 dement, madman, maniac 7 lunatic, madling 9 bedlamite, non compos
tomorrow 6 future, mañana
Tom Sawyer *author:* 5 Twain *character:* 5 Becky 8 Huck Finn, Injun Joe 9 Aunt Polly 10 Muff Potter
Tom Thumb 4 runt 5 dwarf, midge, pygmy 6 midget, peewee 7 manikin 10 homunculus 11 lilliputian
ton 3 fad 4 chic, rage 5 craze, style, vogue 6 furore 7 fashion
tone 3 hue 4 cast, mode, mood, tint, vein 5 color, humor, pitch, shade, style, tinge 6 accent, manner, spirit, strain, temper, timbre 7 fashion 10 inflection *combining form:* 4 phon 5 phono
toned down 4 mute, soft 5 sober 6 low-key, mellow 7 subdued 8 low-keyed, softened
tongue 4 lick 6 glossa, lingua, speech 7 dialect 8 language 10 vernacular *click of:* 3 tch *combining form:* 4 glot 5 gloss, lingu 6 glossa, glosso, lingua, lingui, linguo 7 glossia
tongue-lash 3 wig 4 lash, rail 5 scold 6 berate 7 bawl out, chew out, tell off, upbraid
tonguelike part 7 languet
tonic 5 sharp 7 bracing 8 renewing, roborant 9 animating 10 astringent, quickening, refreshing, vitalizing 11 restorative, stimulating, stimulative 12 exhilarating, exhilarative, invigorating 13 strengthening *extract:* 4 cola 9 berberine
tonsorialist 6 barber
tony 2 in 4 chic 5 swank, swish 6 modish 7 a la mode, stylish 9 exclusive 11 fashionable
too 4 also, ever, more, over, very 5 along 6 as well, highly, overly, unduly, withal 7 awfully, besides, greatly, notably 8 likewise, moreover, overfull, overmuch 9 extremely, immensely 10 remarkably, strikingly 11 exceedingly, excessively, furthermore 12 additionally, exorbitantly, immoderately, inordinately, unmeasurably 13 exceptionally
tool 3 awl, zax 4 pawn 5 drive 6 puppet, rimmer, stooge 7 cat's-paw, hayfork, machine, rounder, utensil 8 picklock 9 implement, mechanism 10 instrument *axlike:* 3 adz *barrel making:* 5 croze 6 crozer *boring:* 5 auger, drill *carving:* 6 veiner *cleaving:* 4 froe *cobbler's:* 3 awl *cutting:* 2 ax 3 adz, axe, saw 4 adze 5 knife 6 shears 8 billhook *digging:* 4 pick 7 mattock *engraving:* 5 burin 7 scauper *farm:* 6 seeder *filing:* 4 rasp 7 riffler *garden:* 3 hoe 4 rake 5 spade 6 trowel, weeder *grasping:* 6 pincer 7 tweezer 8 tweezers *prehistoric:* 5 flint

6 eolith *pruning:* 6 shears 8 secateur *rubbing:* 9 burnisher *scooping:* 6 router *toothed:* 3 saw 7 rippler *woodworking:* 3 saw 5 bevel, plane 6 chisel, hammer
toot 3 bat, jag 4 bust, tear 5 binge, drunk, sound, spree 6 bender 7 blowoff, carouse
tooth 5 molar 7 incisor 8 bicuspid, premolar *combining form:* 4 dent, odon, odus 5 denti, dento, odont 6 odonta, odonto, odonty 7 dentate, odontes, odontia *cuspid:* 6 canine 8 dogtooth, eyetooth *cutting:* 10 carnassial *decay:* 6 caries *doctor:* 7 dentist *pointed:* 4 fang 6 canine, cuspid *small:* 9 denticle *surface:* 5 mensa
toothless 8 edentate
toothsome 5 sapid, tasty 6 savory 8 pleasant, pleasing, tasteful 9 agreeable, delicious, palatable, relishing 10 appetizing, attractive 11 good-tasting
top 3 cap, tip 4 acme, apex, beat, best, clip, crop, cusp, dock, face, fine, head, peak, pick, roof 5 cream, crest, crown, elite, excel, outdo, point, pride, prime, prize 6 apical, better, choice, climax, exceed, height, summit, utmost, vertex 7 capital, highest, maximal, maximum, outside, pollard, surface, surpass 8 five-star, loftiest, outshine, outstrip, pinnacle, superior, surmount 9 excellent, fastigium, first-rate, transcend, uppermost 10 first-class 11 culmination, first-string *combining form:* 3 acr, akr 4 acro, akro
tope 3 nip 4 soak 5 booze, drink, shark 6 guzzle, imbibe, tank up, tipple 7 swizzle 8 liquor up
toper 3 sot 4 lush, soak 5 drunk 6 bibber, boozer 7 tippler, tosspot 8 drunkard 9 inebriate
Tophet 4 hell 5 hades, Sheol 6 blazes 7 Gehenna, inferno 9 barathrum, perdition 10 underworld 11 Pandemonium
topic 4 head, text 5 issue, motif, point, theme 6 matter, motive 7 subject 8 argument 11 proposition 13 subject matter
top-notch 4 fine 5 prime 7 capital 8 five-star, superior 9 excellent, first-rate 10 first-class 11 first-string
top off 3 cap 5 crown 6 climax 8 round off 9 culminate, finish off
topography 7 terrain
topple 4 drop, fall 5 lurch, pitch, slump, upset 6 falter, go down, plunge, teeter, totter, tumble, wobble 7 overset, stagger, stumble, tip over, unhorse 8 keel over, overturn, turn over 9 knock over, overthrow
topsy-turvy 8 cockeyed, inverted, unhinged 10 disjointed, disordered, down-side-up, upside-down 11 disarranged
toque 3 cap, hat
tor 4 hill, peak 5 mound 8 pinnacle
torch 7 firebug 8 arsonist, flambeau 10 incendiary
toreador 6 torero 7 matador 11 bullfighter
torment 3 try 4 bait, hurt, pain, rack 5 smite, wring 6 harass, harrow, heckle, molest, plague 7 afflict, agonize, crucify, torture, trouble 8 distress 9 persecute 10 excruciate
torn 4 rent 7 mangled 9 lacerated
tornado 7 cyclone, twister 9 whirlwind
toro 4 bull
torpedo 3 gun 4 mine 6 gunman, hit man 8 assassin 9 cutthroat, explosive 10 gunslinger, hatchet man, projectile, triggerman
torpid 5 dopey 8 comatose, sluggish 9 lethargic 10 slumberous 12 hebetudinous
torpor 4 coma 5 sleep 6 stupor 7 languor 8 dullness, hebetude, lethargy 9 lassitude, passivity, stolidity 10 stagnation 12 listlessness
torque 5 chain, twist 6 collar
torrent 5 flood, spate 6 deluge 7 niagara 8 cataract, flooding, overflow 9 cataclysm 10 inundation, outpouring
torrid 3 hot 5 fiery 6 ardent, fervid, heated, red-hot, sultry 7 blazing, burning, flaming 8 broiling, scalding, sizzling, white-hot 9 scorching 10 hot-blooded, passionate, sweltering 11 impassioned
tort 3 sin 4 evil 5 crime, wrong 8 iniquity 9 diablerie 10 wrongdoing
tortilla 4 cake, taco
Tortilla Flat author 9 Steinbeck
tortoise 6 turtle 8 terrapin 9 chelonian *freshwater:* 4 emyd *shell:* 8 carapace
tortuous 5 snaky 7 sinuous, winding 8 flexuous, involute, involved 9 meandrous 10 convoluted, meandering, serpentine 11 anfractuous, vermiculate
torture 3 try 4 hurt, maim, rack, warp 5 smite, wring 6 deform, harrow, mangle 7 afflict, agonize, contort, crucify, distort, oppress, torment 8 misshape, mutilate 10 excruciate
tory 5 right 7 diehard, fogyish, old-line 8 loyalist, old liner, orthodox, rightist, stand-pat 11 bitter-ender, reactionary, right-winger, standpatter 12 conservative
Tosca *character:* 5 Mario 7 Scarpia *composer:* 7 Puccini
___ Toscanini 6 Arturo
tosh 5 bilge, hooey 6 bunkum 7 eyewash 8 malarkey, nonsense, pishposh
toss 4 cast, fire, flip, hurl, rock, roll 5 bandy, drink, fling, heave, pitch, quaff, sling, throw 6 imbibe, launch, seesaw, squirm, writhe 7 agonize
tosspot see tippler

tot 3 add, nip, sum 4 cast, dram, drop, foot, jolt, shot, slug 5 child, snort, total 6 figure 7 snifter, summate, toddler
totable 8 portable
total 3 add, all, sum 4 body, bulk, cast, come, foot, full, tale 5 add up, equal, gross, run to, smash, sum to, utter, whole, wreck, yield 6 all-out, amount, budget, entire, figure, number 7 crack up, destroy, full-out, overall, perfect, plenary, quantum, run into, stack up, sum into, summate 8 absolute, complete, comprise, demolish, entirety, outright, positive, quantity, result in 9 aggregate, consist of, full-blown, full-scale, inclusive, out-and-out, unlimited 10 consummate, unreserved 11 unmitigated 13 comprehensive, thoroughgoing *combining form:* 3 hol 4 holo
totalitarian 6 all-out 7 full-out 8 absolute 9 full-blown, full-scale, unlimited 11 dictatorial 13 authoritarian
totality 3 all, sum 4 tale 5 gross, whole 6 entity, system 7 allness, oneness 8 entirety, integral 9 aggregate, integrate, wholeness 10 entireness 12 completeness
totalize 3 add, sum, tot 6 figure 7 summate
tote 3 add, lug 4 bear, buck, cart, haul, pack 5 carry, ferry 6 convey, figure 7 summate 9 transport
totem 4 clan, pole 6 emblem
To the Lighthouse author 5 Woolf
totter 4 reel 5 lurch, wheel 6 falter, topple, wobble 7 stagger, stammer 8 titubate
touch 3 dab, pat, paw, rub 4 abut, dash, feel, hand, hint, join, line, meet, move, palm, stir, sway 5 brush, carry, graze, march, probe, shade, smack, thumb, tinge, verge 6 adjoin, affect, amount, arouse, border, butt on, caress, excite, finger, fondle, handle, streak, strike, stroke 7 contact, feeling, impress, inspire, palpate, quicken, taction, toy with, verge on 9 influence, palpation, stimulate, tactility *combining form:* 6 thigmo
touchable 7 tactile 8 palpable, tangible
touch down 4 land 5 light, perch, roost 6 alight, settle 9 six points
touching 2 to 4 as to, in re 5 about, anent, as for 6 moving, tender 7 against, apropos, meeting, piteous, pitiful 8 abutting, adjacent, pitiable, poignant, stirring 9 adjoining, affecting, as regards, bordering, impinging 10 approximal, as respects, concerning, contiguous, impressive, juxtaposed, responsive 11 overlapping, sympathetic, tear-jerking 12 conterminous 13 compassionate
touchstone 4 test 5 check, gauge, proof, scale, trial 7 measure 8 standard 9 barometer, benchmark, criterion, yardstick 13 demonstration
touch up 4 do up 5 fix up 6 polish 7 brush up, improve, perfect
touchy 5 cross, dicey, miffy, ratty, risky, testy 6 cranky, tetchy, tricky, unsafe 7 harmful 8 choleric, delicate, ticklish, volatile 9 hazardous, irascible, sensitive, temperish 10 precarious 11 thin-skinned 13 oversensitive, quick-tempered, temperamental, unpredictable
tough 3 bad, fit, mug 4 goon, hard, hood, punk, taut, thug 5 bully, fixed, hardy, harsh, lusty, rigid, rough, rowdy, stiff, stout, teuch, teugh, yahoo 6 accept, anneal, flinty, ghetto, mucker, mulish, narrow, robust, rugged, severe, strict, strong, sturdy, taxing, trying, unsafe, uphill, viscid 7 arduous, drastic, exigent, healthy, hoodlum, labored, onerous, ruffian, steeled, toilful, viscose, viscous, weighty 8 bullyboy, exacting, grievous, hardcase, hardened, hard-line, hooligan, obdurate, plug-ugly, rigorous, seasoned, stalwart, stubborn, toilsome, vigorous 9 arbitrary, confirmed, dangerous, demanding, difficult, effortful, hard-shell, immutable, inner city, laborious, obstinate, pigheaded, resistant, roughneck, strenuous, tenacious 10 bullheaded, burdensome, disorderly, hard-bitten, hard-boiled, hardfisted, hardhanded, hardheaded, headstrong, inflexible, oppressive, refractory, self-willed, unyielding 11 conditioned, intractable, procrustean, unalterable, unbreakable 12 pertinacious, withstanding
toughen 6 anneal, harden, season 7 develop 9 acclimate, climatize 10 strengthen 11 acclimatize
toughie 4 punk 5 heavy, rough, rowdy, yahoo 6 mucker 7 ruffian 8 bullyboy 9 roughneck
toupee 3 wig 6 peruke, wiglet 7 periwig, wiggery
tour 4 bout, time, trip, turn 5 round, shift, spell, stint, trick 6 travel, troupe 7 circuit 9 round trip 10 roundabout
tour de force 4 deed, feat 7 classic, exploit 10 magnum opus, masterwork 11 achievement, chef d'oeuvre, masterpiece
tour guide 8 cicerone
tourist 7 tripper, visitor 8 traveler 9 sightseer, traveller 10 day-tripper, rubberneck 12 excursionist
tournament 4 tilt 5 joust 7 tourney
tousle 4 mess, muss 6 rumple 8 dishevel, disorder
tout 4 laud, plug 5 vigil, watch 6 herald, praise 7 acclaim, lookout, promote, trumpet 8 ballyhoo, proclaim 9 publicize, vigilance
tow 3 lug, tug 4 drag, draw, haul, pull

toward 6 contra, facing 7 against, apropos, benefic, helpful, vis-à-vis 8 favoring, fronting 9 favorable, regarding 10 beneficial, propitious ***prefix:*** 2 ac, ad, af, ag, al, ap, as, at, il, im, in, ir 4 pros ***suffix:*** 2 ad
towel word 3 his 4 hers
tower 5 spire 7 overtop 8 dominate, look down, overlook ***Babylonian:*** 8 ziggurat ***on a mosque:*** 7 minaret ***small:*** 6 turret
towering 4 airy, high, tall 5 dizzy, lofty, undue 6 aerial 7 extreme, massive, soaring, spiring, supreme 8 ultimate 10 exorbitant, immoderate, inordinate, monumental, preeminent, prodigious, stupendous, surpassing, tremendous 11 extravagant, skyscraping 12 altitudinous, overpowering, overwhelming, transcendent
towhee 5 finch
to wit 3 viz 6 namely 8 scilicet 9 videlicet
town 4 burg 6 podunk 7 borough, village ***medieval:*** 5 bourg
town and ___ 4 gown 7 country
townsman 3 cit 6 townee 7 burgher, citizen, oppidan
town square ***Italian:*** 6 piazza
toxic 6 poison 8 mephitic, venomous, virulent 9 poisonous
toxin 5 venin, venom 6 poison
toy 3 pet 4 fool, play 5 curio, dally, flirt, sport, tease 6 bauble, caress, coquet, cosset, cuddle, dandle, frolic, gewgaw, lead on, popgun, trifle, wanton 7 bibelot, disport, dreidel, novelty, trinket, whatnot 8 gimcrack, pinwheel 9 plaything 10 fiddle with, knickknack 11 string along
trace 4 hint, mark 5 relic, shade, smell, tinge, track, trail, tread, whiff 6 nuance, shadow, strain, streak 7 memento, soupçon, vestige 9 suspicion 10 intimation
trachea 8 windpipe
track 3 dog, way 4 drag, find, mark, path, road, sign, step, tail, walk 5 chase, cover, print, spoor, trace, trail, tread 6 artery, avenue, follow, pursue, shadow, street, travel 7 footway, highway, imprint, monitor, pathway, vestige 8 footpath, footstep, hunt down, pass over, smell out, traverse 9 footprint ***combining form:*** 4 ichn 5 ichno
track-and-field event 4 dash, race 7 shot put 8 footrace, high jump, long jump 9 broad jump, decathlon, pole vault, relay race 10 heptathlon, pentathlon, triple jump 11 discus throw 12 steeplechase
tract 3 lot 4 area, belt, plat, plot, zone 6 parcel, region 7 portion, terrain 9 territory
tractable 6 docile, pliant 7 pliable, subdued 8 amenable, biddable, flexible, obedient 10 manageable
tractate 6 memoir, thesis 8 treatise 9 discourse, monograph 10 monography 12 disquisition, dissertation
trade 3 art 4 deal, sell, swap, work 5 craft, truck 6 barter, change, custom, market, métier, peddle, switch 7 bargain, calling, pursuit, traffic 8 business, commerce, exchange, industry, merchant, vocation 9 patronage 10 employment, handicraft, occupation, profession, substitute 11 merchandise ***illicit:*** 11 black market ***suffix:*** 3 ery
trademark 4 logo 5 brand 8 logotype
trade route 7 sea-lane
tradition 4 lore, myth 6 custom, legacy, legend, mythos 8 folklore, heritage 9 mythology 10 convention
traditional 3 old 4 oral 5 fixed, usual 6 common, spoken, verbal 7 popular 8 habitual, orthodox 9 ancestral, customary, unwritten 10 immemorial 11 established, word-of-mouth 12 acknowledged, conventional, tralatitious
traditionalist 6 purist 9 precisian 12 precisionist
traditionalistic 4 tory 5 right 7 die-hard, fogyish, old-line 8 orthodox 11 reactionary 12 conservative
traduce 5 libel 6 betray, defame, malign, vilify 7 asperse, slander, violate 8 disgrace 9 denigrate 10 calumniate, scandalize
Trafalgar commander 6 Nelson
traffic 4 push, swap 5 fence, trade, truck 6 barter, custom, deal in, travel 7 bargain, bootleg 8 business, commerce, dealings, exchange, industry 9 communion, patronage 11 black-market, intercourse
trafficker 6 dealer, trader
tragedy 3 lot 4 blow, woes 5 curse, shock 6 mishap 8 calamity, disaster 9 adversity, cataclysm, mischance 10 misfortune 11 catastrophe, contretemps 12 misadventure
trail 3 dog, lag, tag 4 drag, flag, halt, path, plod, poke, tail 5 bedog, chase, chivy, dally, delay, tarry, trace, track 6 dawdle, falter, follow, linger, loiter, pursue, shadow, trudge 7 draggle, footway, gumshoe, pathway, traipse 8 footpath, footwalk 10 bridle path ***emigrant:*** 6 Oregon ***Florida:*** 7 Tamiami ***Georgia-Maine:*** 11 Appalachian ***Indian:*** 5 Great
trailer truck 4 semi
train 3 aim, lay, row, run 4 bait, cast, head, line, lure, tier, toll, turn 5 chain, coach, decoy, level, order, point, scale, shape, suite, teach, tempt 6 allure, course, direct, entice, harden, lead on, school, season, seduce, sequel, series, thread, zero in 7 develop, educate, incline, retinue 8 accustom, instruct, inveigle, sequence 9 cultivate, entourage, following, gradation, habituate

10 discipline, succession 11 alternation, consecution, progression

training 7 tuition 8 teaching, tutelage 9 education, schooling 11 instruction *horses:* 6 manege

train off 3 dip 4 skew, slue, veer 5 sheer 6 swerve

traipse 3 gad 4 dowd, drab, drag, hoof, pace, roam, rove, slut, step, walk 5 dowdy, drift, mooch, range, trail, tread, troop 6 foot it, ramble, wander 7 draggle, meander 8 ambulate, slattern 9 gallivant 11 draggle-tail

trait 4 mark 5 point, savor 6 virtue 7 feature, quality 8 property 9 affection, attribute, birthmark, character 11 denominator

traitor 5 Judas 6 Arnold 8 betrayer, quisling, renegade, renegado, traditor, turncoat

traitorous 5 false 6 untrue 7 unloyal 8 apostate, disloyal, mutinous, recreant, renegade 9 alienated, estranged, faithless, seditious 10 perfidious, rebellious, unfaithful 11 disaffected, treacherous, unpatriotic

traject 4 pipe 5 carry 6 convey, funnel, siphon 7 channel, conduct 8 transmit

tram 3 car 7 trolley 9 streetcar

trammel 3 tie 4 bind, clog, curb 5 leash, limit 6 enmesh, fetter, hamper, hobble, hogtie, stifle 7 confine, enchain, ensnarl, manacle, shackle 8 entangle, handcuff, stagnate, stultify 9 embrangle, entrammel 12 circumscribe

tramontane 7 foreign 10 outlandish 11 transalpine

tramp 3 vag 4 hike, hobo, jade, plod, thud, walk 5 march, stamp, stomp 6 ramble, stodge, stroll, trudge 7 drifter, floater, saunter, traipse, vagrant 8 derelict, footslog, vagabond 9 walkabout 10 street arab

trample 5 pound, stamp, stomp, tromp 7 tread on 8 override

trance 4 muse 5 study 6 ravish 7 reverie 8 enravish, hypnosis 9 enrapture, transport 10 brown study

tranquil 4 calm, easy 5 quiet, still 6 irenic, placid, poised, serene, stable, steady 7 pacific, restful 8 composed, peaceful 9 collected, easygoing 13 self-possessed

tranquilize 4 balm, calm, hush, lull 5 quiet, still 6 becalm, sedate, settle, soothe, subdue 7 compose

tranquilizer 6 downer, opiate 8 diazepam, pacifier, sedative 10 depressant

transaction 4 bond, pact 7 bargain, compact, dealing 8 contract, covenant 9 agreement 10 convention

transcend 3 top 4 beat, best 5 excel, outdo 6 better, exceed 7 surpass 8 outshine, outstrip

transcendent 5 ideal 7 perfect, supreme 8 abstract, towering 10 consummate, preeminent, surpassing 11 theoretical, unequalable, unmatchable 12 hypothetical, incomparable 13 unsurpassable

Transcendentalist 7 Emerson, Thoreau

transcribe 4 copy 5 write 6 record 9 translate 13 transliterate

transfer 4 cede, deed, feed, find, give, hand, move, ship 5 alien, carry, shift 6 assign, change, convey, remise, remove, supply 7 convert, deliver, devolve, disturb, provide 8 alienate, dispense, hand over, make over, relocate, sign over, turn over 9 carry over, dislocate 10 abalienate

transfix 4 spit 5 lance, spear, spike 6 impale, skewer, skiver

transform 5 alter 6 change, mutate 7 commute, convert 8 denature 12 metamorphize, metamorphose

transformation 5 shift 10 alteration, changeover, conversion

transfuse 6 charge 7 pervade 8 permeate, saturate 9 penetrate, percolate 10 impregnate 11 impenetrate

transgress 3 sin 5 break 6 breach, offend 7 infract, violate 8 infringe, overstep, trespass 10 contravene

transient 7 passing 8 fleeting, flitting, fugitive, temporal, unstable, volatile 9 ephemeral, fugacious, momentary, temporary 10 evanescent, short-lived, transitory 11 impermanent 12 momentaneous 13 insubstantial

transit 5 shift 6 travel 7 passage 8 carriage, carrying 9 transport 10 alteration, conveyance 12 transporting

transition 5 shift 6 change, growth 7 passage 8 progress 9 evolution 10 alteration, conversion 11 development 13 metamorphosis

transitory see **transient**

translate 3 put 4 turn 6 change, render, reword 7 commute, convert, restate 8 rephrase 9 interpret 10 paraphrase 12 metamorphose

translation 7 version 9 rendering 10 paraphrase 11 restatement

translucent 5 clear, lucid 6 limpid 7 crystal, obvious 8 apparent, clear-cut, luminous, pellucid 9 unblurred 10 see-through *combining form:* 4 hyal 5 hyalo

transmarine 7 oversea 8 overseas

transmission 7 gearbox *combining form:* 8 phoreses (plural), phoresis

transmit 4 pipe, send, ship 5 break, carry, radio, route 6 convey, funnel, hand on, impart, pass on, siphon 7 address, channel, conduct, consign, forward, instill, traject 8 bequeath, dispatch, hand down

transmogrify see **transform**

transmute see **transform**

transoceanic message 9 cablegram

transparent 5 clear, filmy, gauzy, lucid, plain, sheer 6 flimsy, limpid, lucent 7 crystal, tiffany 8 clear-cut, gossamer, luminous, pellucid 9 tralucent, unblurred 10 diaphanous, see-through, translucid 11 crystalline, translucent ***combining form:*** 4 hyal 5 hyalo 7 diaphan 8 diaphano

transpire 3 hap, out 4 leak 5 occur 6 befall, betide, chance, happen 7 develop

transport 3 lug, wow 4 bear, buck, move, oust, pack, send, slay, tote 5 ardor, carry, exile, expel, ferry, truck 6 banish, convey, deport, excite, fervor, heaven, ravish, stir up, thrill, trance, uplift 7 agitate, cast out, delight, ecstasy, elevate, expulse, inflame, passion, provoke, quicken, rapture, transit, vehicle 8 carriage, carrying, displace, enravish, entrance, relegate, rhapsody 9 carry away, enrapture, happiness, stimulate 10 conveyance, enthusiasm, imparadise

transportation 6 moving 7 hauling, transit, vehicle 8 carriage, carrying 10 conveyance

transpose 4 turn 6 change, invert, render, revert 7 commute, convert, inverse, reverse 12 metamorphose

transubstantiate see transform

transude 4 ooze, seep, weep 5 bleed, sweat 6 strain

Transvaal ***capital:*** 8 Pretoria ***natives:*** 7 Bushmen 10 Hottentots ***resource:*** 4 gold

transversal 4 bent 6 thwart 8 crossing 9 crosswise 12 intersecting

transverse 5 cross 6 across, thwart 7 crossed, oblique 8 crossing, diagonal 9 crosswise

trap 3 net 4 bait, lure, plot, ploy, ruse, snag, tree, wile 5 benet, catch, decoy, feint, snare 6 ambush, come-on, gambit, tangle 7 catch up, ensnare 8 artifice, birdlime, entangle, intrigue, maneuver 9 ambuscade, stratagem 10 allurement, conspiracy, enticement, seducement, temptation 11 machination 12 inveiglement ***an animal:*** 8 deadfall

trappings 4 gear 5 dress 10 decoration 13 embellishment

Trappist 4 monk ***writer:*** 6 Merton (Thomas)

trash 3 mob, rot 4 bosh, crap, junk, plod, scum, slog, slop, toil 5 bilge, dregs, hokum, offal, waste, wreck 6 bunkum, debris, kelter, litter, masses, rabble, refuse, shlock, stodge, trudge 7 garbage, rubbish 8 canaille, claptrap, doggerel, dustheap, footslog, leavings, malarkey, nonsense, plunther, riffraff, unwashed 9 sweepings, vandalize 11 proletariat

trash can 7 dustbin

trashy 4 base, mean, poor 5 cheap, tatty 6 common, cruddy, paltry, shoddy, sleazy 8 rubbishy 9 third-rate

trauma 4 blow 5 shock, upset 6 stress 8 collapse 11 disturbance

travail 4 moil, task, toil, work 5 grind, labor, pains 6 drudge 7 slavery 8 bullwork, drudgery, plugging, struggle 10 birth pangs, childbirth 11 parturition 12 childbearing, contractions

travel 2 go 3 hie 4 fare, pass, roam, tour, trek, wend 5 cover, cross, jaunt, track 6 move on, push on, repair, voyage 7 explore, journey, passage, proceed, process, traffic, transit 8 pass over

travelable 8 passable 9 navigable 10 negotiable

traveling library 10 bookmobile

traverse 3 bar, rub 4 buck, deny, duel, snag, walk 5 cover, cross, fight, repel 6 combat, hamper, hurdle, impugn, negate, oppose, patrol, resist, thwart, travel 7 contest, dispute, gainsay 8 crossing, negative, obstacle, pass over 9 crosswise, disaffirm, withstand 10 contradict, contravene, crisscross, impediment 11 obstruction, perambulate

travesty 3 ape 4 mock, sham 5 farce, mimic 6 parody 7 imitate, mimicry, mockery, take off 8 ridicule 9 burlesque 10 caricature, distortion 12 exaggeration ***satanic:*** 9 Black Mass

Traviata, La ***character:*** 7 Alfredo, Germont 8 Violetta ***composer:*** 5 Verdi

trawl 3 net 4 fish 5 troll 7 setline

tray 6 salver, server 7 platter 8 teaboard ***revolving:*** 9 lazy Susan

treacherous 5 false, hairy, Punic, risky 6 chancy, tricky, untrue, wicked 7 unloyal, unsound 8 disloyal, perilous, recreant, ticklish 9 betraying, dangerous, deceptive, faithless, hazardous, unhealthy 10 jeopardous, misleading, perfidious, precarious, traitorous, unfaithful 12 falsehearted

treachery 7 perfidy, sellout, treason 9 falseness 10 disloyalty, infidelity 11 double cross 13 double dealing, faithlessness

treacle 5 syrup 6 remedy 8 molasses

tread 4 hoof, pace, step, walk 5 dance, march, stamp, stomp, trace, track, tramp, tromp, troop 6 foot it, hoof it, prance, stride 7 traipse, trample 8 ambulate

treadle 5 lever, pedal

treadmill 3 rut 4 pace, rote 5 grind 6 groove 7 routine

treason 6 deceit 7 perfidy 8 betrayal, sedition 9 duplicity, treachery 10 disloyalty, misprision 13 deceitfulness, faithlessness, seditiousness

treasure 4 find, plum, save 5 catch, guard, pearl, prize, trove, value 6 esteem, revere 7 apprize, cherish, idolize, worship 8 con-

serve, preserve, venerate **9** reverence **10** appreciate
Treasure Island ***author:*** **9** Stevenson ***narrator:*** **10** Jim Hawkins
treasurer **6** bursar, purser **11** chamberlain
Treasure State **7** Montana
treasure trove **4** find, mine **7** bonanza **8** eldorado, Golconda, gold mine
treasury **4** mine **5** chest **6** coffer, museum **7** bonanza, gallery **8** archives, eldorado, Golconda, gold mine, war chest **9** exchequer **10** depositary, depository, repository, storehouse ***state:*** **4** fisc
treat **3** use **5** goody, nurse, serve **6** advise, confab, confer, dainty, doctor, do with, handle, huddle, manage, morsel, parley, physic, powwow, regard, tidbit, titbit **7** care for, consult **8** collogue, deal with, delicacy, kickshaw, medicate, medicine **10** minister to **11** bonne bouche, confabulate ***animals:*** **3** vet ***leather:*** **3** tan, taw **6** shammy, shamoy **7** chamois, tanning
treatise **4** book **6** memoir, thesis **7** writing **8** argument, tractate **9** discourse, monograph **10** discussion, exposition, monography **12** disquisition, dissertation ***combining form:*** **3** log **4** logy **5** logia, logue ***suffix:*** **3** ics
treatment **4** care **7** therapy ***combining form:*** **6** praxes (plural), praxis
treaty **4** pact **6** accord **7** charter, compact, concord **8** contract, covenant **9** agreement, concordat **10** convention
treble **4** high, thin **5** acute, sharp **6** argute, piping, shrill **8** piercing
tree ***African:*** **4** akee, cola, shea **5** limba, sassy **6** baobab **7** avodire, bubinga **8** sasswood **9** berberine ***Asian:*** **4** dhak, upas **6** banyan, kamala ***Australian:*** **7** blue gum **8** lacewood, quandong **9** casuarina ***branch:*** **5** bough ***Brazilian:*** **3** apa **7** arariba, seringa, wallaba ***Chinese:*** **4** tung **5** yulan **6** gingko, ginkgo, litchi **7** kumquat ***citrus:*** **4** lime **5** lemon **6** orange **8** bergamot **10** calamondin ***combining form:*** **3** dry **4** dryo **5** dendr **6** dendra (plural), dendro **7** dendron ***coniferous:*** **3** fir, yew **4** pine **5** alder, cedar, larch **6** spruce **7** cypress, hemlock, juniper, redwood, sequoia ***dwarf:*** **8** arbuscle **10** chinquapin ***East Indian:*** **4** neem, poon, teak, toon **6** banyan, deodar, durian, durion **7** amboina, amboyna, cajaput, cajeput, cajuput, champac, champak, deodara **11** chaulmoogra ***elm:*** **4** wych ***Ethiopian:*** **5** cusso, kusso **6** kousso ***Eurasian:*** **5** abele, rowan **6** medlar ***European:*** **5** osier **8** bourtree, caprifig ***European oak:*** **7** murmast ***evergreen:*** **3** fir, yew **4** atle, pine, titi **5** athel, bunya, carob, cedar, piñon, taxus, thuja, thuya **6** arbute, cullay, dahoon, jarrah, loquat, mallee, pinyon, sapota **7** arbutus, camphor, conifer, inkwood, juniper, lentisk, madrona, madrone, madrono, peebeen, quillai, redwood, sequoia **8** eucalypt, loblolly, longleaf, tamarisk **9** balsam fir **12** balm of Gilead ***evergreen oak:*** **6** encina ***fig:*** **5** pipal **6** peepul ***flowering:*** **5** sumac **6** acacia, sumach **7** dogwood **8** sourwood ***hardwood:*** **3** oak **5** beech, birch, ebony, maple **6** cherry, copalm, cornel, walnut **7** bilsted, hickory, shittah **8** chestnut, mahogany **9** primavera ***Japanese:*** **4** kaki **7** zelkova ***linden:*** **8** basswood ***mulberry:*** **8** sycamine ***North African:*** **5** babul **7** babbool ***nut-bearing:*** **4** cola, kola **5** hazel, pecan, piñon **6** almond, cashew **7** buckeye, filbert, hickory **9** pistachio ***oak:*** **5** roble **8** bluejack ***oil-yielding:*** **3** ebo **4** eboe, tung **7** cajaput, cajeput, cajuput ***ornamental:*** **3** box **5** holly **6** gingko, ginkgo, mimosa, myrtle, redbud **8** laburnum, magnolia **9** poinciana **12** rhododendron ***palm:*** **4** coco, nipa **5** ratan **6** cohune, gomuti, grugru, pinang, raffia, raphia, rattan **7** babassu, coquito, talipot **8** carnauba, ladypalm ***Peruvian:*** **8** cinchona ***Philippine:*** **4** dita, pili **6** bataan, molave **7** tindalo **10** calamondin ***resinous:*** **10** candlewood ***shade:*** **3** elm, oak **5** maple **6** linden **8** sycamore **10** chinaberry ***softwood:*** **5** alamo **6** tupelo **8** black gum, corkwood; (see also **coniferous**) ***South American:*** **3** apa **4** ombu **7** wallaba **8** oiticica **9** Brazil nut ***swamp:*** **11** bald cypress ***tropical:*** **4** akee, ohia, sago, teak **5** areca, assai, balsa, cacao, ceiba, genip, lehua, mahoe, mamey, mamie **6** acajou, balata, baobab, bustic, citrus, degame, degami, fustic, kabiki, mammee, mammey, padauk, padouk, santol, souari **7** arnotto, bebeeri, genipap, logwood, majagua, mameyes, palmyra, quassia, soursop **8** allspice, barbasco, cocobola, cocobolo, jelutong, mahogany, mangrove, milkwood, palmetto, porkwood, rosewood, simaruba, soapbark, sweetsop, tamarind **9** candlenut, cherimoya, jacaranda **10** breadfruit, manchineel **11** candleberry, coconut palm ***trunk:*** **4** bole ***willow:*** **5** osier, sauch, saugh **6** poplar ***young:*** **7** sapling
trefoil **4** leaf **6** clover
trek **4** trip **7** journey, travels **10** expedition
trellis **6** screen **7** lattice
tremble **3** jar **5** quake, shake **6** dither, quaver, quiver, shiver, tremor **7** shudder, twitter, vibrate ***Scottish:*** **4** dirl
tremblor see **temblor**
tremendous **4** huge, vast **5** awful **6** mighty, mortal **7** fearful, immense, massive, titanic **8** colossal, cracking, dreadful, enormous, gigantic, horrible, shocking, terrible, terrific, towering **9** appalling, fantastic,

frightful, monstrous **10** formidable, monumental, prodigious, stupendous
tremolo **7** vibrato
tremor **3** jar **5** quake, shake, shock **6** dither, quaver, quiver, shiver **7** shudder, temblor, tremble, twitter, vibrate **8** tremblor **10** earthquake ***muscular:*** **8** dystaxia ***Scottish:*** **6** dindle
tremulous **5** aspen, quaky, shaky **6** aguish, aquake, ashake **7** aquiver, ashiver, quaking, quivery, shaking, shivery **9** quivering, shivering, trembling, tremorous, tremulant, vibrating **11** palpitating
trench **4** sink **5** ditch, drain, drill, fosse, gully, verge **6** border, furrow, trough **8** approach ***Caribbean:*** **6** Cayman ***combining form:*** **5** bothr **6** bothro
trenchant **5** acrid, crisp, salty **6** biting **7** caustic, cutting, ingoing, mordant, probing, satiric **8** clear-cut, incisive, piercing, sardonic, scathing **9** sarcastic **10** mordacious, razor-sharp **11** penetrating
trencher **4** tray **7** platter
trend **3** fad, run **4** flow, mode, rage, wind **5** craze, drift, style, swing, tenor, vogue **6** furore **7** current, fashion **8** movement, tendency **9** direction **10** dernier cri
trendy **2** in **3** hep, hip **4** tony **5** faddy **6** modish, tonish, with-it **7** a la mode, faddish, stylish **11** fashionable, ultramodern
Trent's Last Case author **7** Bentley
trepidation **4** fear **5** alarm, dread, panic **6** dismay, fright, horror, terror **13** consternation
trepidity **4** fear **5** alarm, dread, panic **6** dismay, fright, horror, terror **13** consternation
trespass **3** err, sin **5** lapse, poach **6** breach, invade, offend **7** intrude **8** encroach, entrench, infringe, invasion **9** interlope, intrusion, obtrusion, violation **10** infraction, transgress **11** intermeddle **12** encroachment, infringement **13** contravention, transgression
tress **4** curl, hair, lock **5** braid, plait
trestle **4** buck **5** horse **7** sawbuck **8** sawhorse **9** workhorse
tret **9** allowance
triad **4** trio **5** trine **6** triple, triune, troika **7** trinity **9** threesome **11** triumvirate
trial **3** try, woe **4** care, test **5** agony, cross, essay, grief, rigor, worry **6** hassle, misery, ordeal, sorrow **7** anguish, attempt, calvary, trouble **8** crucible, distress, endeavor, hardship, striving, struggle **9** adversity, suffering **10** affliction, difficulty, experiment, heartbreak, misfortune, visitation **11** tribulation **12** experimental
trial balloon **6** feeler
trial run **4** test **10** experiment
triangle type **5** right **6** obtuse **7** scalene **9** isosceles **11** equilateral
triangular **6** cuneal **7** cuneate, hastate ***combining form:*** **6** trigon **7** trigono
tribal unit **7** phratry
tribe **4** clan, folk, race **5** house, stock **6** family **7** kindred, lineage ***combining form:*** **4** phyl **5** phylo
tribulation **5** cross, trial **6** ordeal **7** calvary **8** crucible, wronging **10** affliction, oppression, visitation **11** persecution
tribunal **3** bar **5** court **8** lawcourt
tributary **3** sub **5** minor, under **7** subject **8** influent **9** dependent, satellite, secondary **10** collateral **11** subordinate
tribute **5** salvo **6** eulogy **8** citation, encomium **9** panegyric **10** salutation **11** recognition, testimonial **12** appreciation ***feudal:*** **6** heriot
trice **4** wink **5** shake **6** moment, second **7** instant **9** twinkling **11** split second
trick **3** jig **4** bout, dupe, feat, fool, gull, hang, hoax, lark, play, ploy, ruse, sham, tour, turn, wile **5** antic, blind, bluff, caper, craft, cully, curve, dodge, feint, fraud, knack, prank, shaky, shift, slick, spell, stall, stint, stunt **6** chouse, device, didoes, frolic, gambit, outwit, praxis, scheme, shines, touchy **7** boutade, chicane, dodgery, finagle, gimmick, sleight **8** artifice, escapade, flimflam, hoodwink, maneuver, outtrump, skin game, unstable **9** bamboozle, deception, defective, diversion, stratagem, victimize **10** expediency, red herring, shenanigan, tomfoolery, unreliable **11** contrivance, hornswoggle, monkeyshine **12** undependable **13** practical joke, untrustworthy ***Scottish:*** **6** shavie
trickery **5** cheat, fraud **7** chicane, knavery **8** hokypoky **9** chicanery, deception, fourberie **10** hanky-panky **11** double-cross, highbinding **13** double-dealing, sharp practice
trickle **4** drib, drip, drop, weep **5** trill **7** distill, dribble
trickster **5** cheat **6** con man **7** cheater, diddler, grifter, sharper **8** conjurer, magician, swindler **9** defrauder **11** flimflammer, illusionist **12** double-dealer
tricksy **5** rough, tight **6** trying **7** arduous **8** prankish
tricky **3** sly **4** foxy, wily **5** rocky **6** artful, astute, crafty, quirky, shifty, touchy **7** cunning **8** delicate, delusive, delusory, gimmicky, guileful, ticklish, unstable **9** deceitful, deceptive, difficult, dishonest, insidious, sensitive **10** misleading, precarious **12** undependable
trident **5** spear **7** scepter
tried **6** proved, secure, tested, trusty **7** staunch **8** approved, faithful, reliable

9 certified, steadfast 10 dependable 11 trustworthy
tried and true 6 secure, trusty 8 reliable 10 dependable 11 trustworthy
trifle 3 toy 4 fico, fool, mash, muck, play 5 curio, dally, flirt, use up, waste 6 bauble, burn up, coquet, fiddle, fidget, gewgaw, lead on, misuse, mucker, wanton 7 bibelot, consume, fribble, fritter, novelty, trinket, twiddle, whatnot 8 fool away, gimcrack, kickshaw, play with, squander 9 dissipate, objet d'art, philander, throw away 10 frivol away, knickknack, mess around, potter away 11 prodigalize, string along
trifolium 6 clover 8 shamrock
trig 4 chic, neat, prim, snug, tidy, trim 5 sharp, smart, swank 6 classy, modish, snappy 7 chipper, dashing, orderly, stylish 9 shipshape 11 fashionable, spic-and-span, uncluttered, well-groomed 12 spick-and-span
triggerman 3 gun 5 bravo 6 gunman, hit man 7 torpedo 8 assassin 9 cutthroat 10 gunslinger, hatchet man
trigonometric function see at **function**
trill 4 drib, drip, drop, weep 5 shake 7 distill, dribble, trickle
trillion *combining form:* 4 tera, treg 5 trega
trillionth *combining form:* 4 pico
trim 3 cut, fit 4 beat, clip, crop, deck, drub, lick, neat, pare, snug, tidy, trig, whip 5 adorn, order, prank, prune, shape, shave, shear, skive 6 barber, bedeck, dapper, fettle, kilter, repair, ricrac, spruce, sprucy, thrash 7 chipper, dress up, fitness, garnish, orderly, shapely, shellac 8 beautify, clean-cut, decorate, lambaste, manicure, ornament, rickrack, shapeful 9 condition, embellish, shipshape 10 statuesque, well-turned 11 clean-limbed, spic-and-span, streamlined, uncluttered, well-groomed 12 spick-and-span *a tree:* 5 prune 7 pollard
trine see triad
Trinidad and Tobago *capital:* 11 Port of Spain *monetary unit:* 6 dollar
trinity see **triad**
trinket 5 curio 6 bauble, gewgaw, tinsel, trifle 7 bibelot, novelty, whatnot 8 frippery, gimcrack, kickshaw, nicknack 9 plaything 10 knickknack
trinkets 10 bijouterie
trio *of goddesses:* 5 Fates 6 Furies, Graces; (see also **triad**)
trip 3 hop, run 4 bull, lope, skip, slip, tour, trek 5 boner, error, fluff, lapse 6 bungle, spring 7 blooper, blunder, journey, mistake, skitter, stumble, travels 10 expedition
tripes 4 guts 7 innards, insides, inwards, viscera 8 entrails, stuffing 9 internals
triple 4 trio 5 triad, trine 6 treble, triune, troika 7 trinity 9 threesome 11 triumvirate
Triple Crown winner *1919:* 9 Sir Barton *1930:* 10 Gallant Fox *1935:* 5 Omaha *1937:* 10 War Admiral *1941:* 9 Whirlaway *1943:* 10 Count Fleet *1946:* 7 Assault *1948:* 8 Citation *1973:* 11 Secretariat *1977:* 11 Seattle Slew *1978:* 8 Affirmed
tripped out 4 high 5 doped 6 stoned, zonked 7 drugged 8 hopped-up, turned on, wiped out 9 spaced-out
Triptolemus *father:* 6 Celeus *gift to man:* 5 grain *mother:* 9 Metaneira
Tristan, Tristam *beloved:* 6 Iseult, Isolde
triste 3 sad 7 joyless 8 mournful 9 saddening 10 depressing, melancholy 11 melancholic
Tristram Shandy author 6 Sterne
trite 3 set 4 dull, flat, hack 5 banal, chain, corny, musty, stale, stock, tired, vapid 6 cliché, common, jejune, old hat, used-up 7 clichéd, drained, prosaic, worn-out 8 bathetic, bromidic, mildewed, ordinary, shopworn, timeworn, well-worn 9 hackneyed 10 threadbare 11 commonplace, stereotyped 13 platitudinous, stereotypical
triton 3 eft 4 newt 10 salamander
Triton 6 merman *attribute:* 5 conch *father:* 7 Neptune 8 Poseidon *mother:* 10 Amphitrite
triturate 4 bray, buck 5 crush, grind 6 powder 9 comminute, pulverize
triumph 3 joy, win 4 beat, best, gain 5 exult, glory 6 master 7 conquer, delight, prevail, prosper, succeed, victory 8 conquest, jubilate, overcome, reveling, surmount 9 exultance, festivity, jubilance 10 ascendancy, exultation, jubilation 11 surmounting, vanquishing 12 vanquishment
triumphal see **triumphant**
triumphant 8 exultant, exulting, jubilant 9 rejoicing
triumvirate see **triad**
Triumvirate, First *member:* 6 Caesar, Pompey 7 Crassus
Triumvirate, Second *member:* 6 Antony 7 Lepidus 8 Octavius
triune see **triad**
trivet 4 rack 5 stand 6 tripod
trivia 8 minutiae 9 small beer 11 small change 13 small potatoes
trivial 4 puny 5 light, minor, petty 6 casual, little, measly, paltry, slight 7 shallow 8 captious, picayune, trifling 9 fribbling, frivolous, small-beer 10 negligible, picayunish, shoestring 11 Mickey Mouse, superficial, unimportant 13 insignificant
troche 6 tablet 7 lozenge 8 pastille
troglodyte 7 caveman 11 cave dweller
troika 8 carriage; (see also **triad**)

Troilus ***beloved:*** 8 Cressida ***father:*** 5 Priam ***mother:*** 6 Hecuba ***slayer:*** 8 Achilles
Troilus and ___ 8 Cressida, Criseyde
Trojan ***horse builder:*** 5 Epeus ***king:*** 5 Priam ***priest:*** 7 Laocoon ***soothsayer:*** 7 Helenus 9 Cassandra ***warrior:*** 5 Paris 6 Aeneas, Agenor, Hector 9 Euphorbus
Trojan Horse builder 5 Epeus 6 Epeius
troll 4 fish, lure, roll, sing 5 angle, dwarf, giant
trolley 3 car 4 cart, tram 8 carriage 9 streetcar
Trollope, Anthony ***novel:*** 11 Ayala's Angel, Phineas Finn 12 Phineas Redux 13 The Claverings
trombone 4 wind 5 brass 7 sackbut
tromp 4 beat, drub, hike, pelt, slog 5 pound, stamp, stomp, tramp 6 batter, buffet, pummel, thrash, trudge 7 belabor, trample 8 lambaste
troop 4 army, band, hoof, host, pace, step, walk 5 corps, tread 6 foot it, forces, legion, outfit 7 company, traipse 8 ambulate, assembly, military, soldiers 9 gathering, multitude 10 collection, combatants, servicemen 11 armed forces
trope 5 irony 6 simile 8 metaphor, metonymy 10 synecdoche
Trophonius ***brother:*** 8 Agamedes ***temple site:*** 6 Delphi
trophy 5 relic, token 7 memento 8 keepsake, memorial, reminder, souvenir 11 remembrance 12 remembrancer
tropical 3 hot 4 warm 6 jungly, sultry, torrid 10 equatorial
tropical cyclone see typhoon
tropical storm see typhoon
Tropic of Cancer author 6 Miller
Tros' son 4 Ilus 8 Ganymede
trot 3 jog 4 crib, gait, lope, pony 11 translation
troth 8 espousal 10 engagement
trot out 4 show 5 flash 6 expose, flaunt, parade 7 display, disport, exhibit, show off 8 brandish
Trotsky, Leon ***associate:*** 5 Lenin
troubadour 4 bard, poet 6 rhymer 8 jongleur, minstrel, musician 9 balladist, rhymester
trouble 3 ado, ail, irk, try, vex 4 care, cark, fret, fuss, pain 5 annoy, Dutch, harry, haunt, pains, rowel, trial, upset, while, worry 6 bother, bustle, effort, flurry, harass, kiaugh, pester, plague, pother, put out, strain, stress 7 afflict, agitate, disturb, intrude, perturb, torment 8 disquiet, distress, exertion, hardship, hot water, impose on, irritate, mischief, put about, vexation 9 disoblige, incommode 10 difficulty, discommode, discompose, disconcert, impose upon 11 bedevilment, elbow grease, predicament 13 inconvenience
troublemaker 6 heller 7 hellion, inciter 8 agitator, inflamer 10 instigator
troublesome 4 mean, ugly 5 pesky 6 vexing, wicked 7 painful 8 alarming, annoying 9 upsetting, vexatious 10 bothersome, disturbing 11 disquieting
troublous 4 mean, ugly 5 pesky 6 stormy, wicked 9 turbulent, vexatious
trough 3 hod 4 bowl, tank 5 basin, drain 6 manger, vessel 7 channel 9 container ***combining form:*** 5 bothr 6 bothro
trounce 4 beat, drub, rout, trim, whip 5 whomp 6 thrash, wallop 7 clobber, shellac 9 overwhelm
troupe 4 band 5 corps, party 6 outfit 7 company
trouper 4 mime 5 actor, mimic 6 mummer, player 7 artiste 8 thespian 9 performer, playactor 11 entertainer 12 impersonator
trousers 5 pants 6 slacks 8 britches ***tartan:*** 5 trews
trout ***kind:*** 3 sea 4 char, lake 5 brook, brown, river 7 rainbow 8 speckled 9 steelhead
Trovatore, Il ***character:*** 7 Azucena, Leonora, Manrico 11 Count di Luna ***composer:*** 5 Verdi
trove 5 hoard 9 amassment, colluvies 10 collection, cumulation 11 aggregation 12 accumulation 13 agglomeration
Troy 5 Ilium ***epic of:*** 5 Iliad ***excavator:*** 10 Schliemann ***founder:*** 4 Ilus ***modern site:*** 9 Hissarlik; (see also Trojan)
truant 4 idle 7 shirker 8 shirking 13 irresponsible
truce 4 lull 5 letup, pause, peace 6 accord 7 respite 9 armistice, cease-fire
truck 3 van 4 swap 5 lorry, trade 6 barter, handle, peddle, retail 7 bargain, traffic 8 commerce, dealings, exchange ***military:*** 6 camion
truckers' communicators 3 CBs
truckle 3 tag 4 fawn, tail 5 cower, toady, trail 6 cringe, follow, grovel, kowtow 7 honey up, succumb 8 bootlick 11 apple-polish
truckler 4 toad 5 toady 7 spaniel 8 lickspit 9 sycophant, toadeater 10 bootlicker, footlicker 11 lickspittle
truculent 4 fell, grim 5 cruel, harsh, rough, sharp 6 cowing, fierce, savage, severe 7 abusive, inhuman, scrappy, warlike, wolfish 8 bullying, inhumane, militant, scathing, scurrile 9 barbarous, bellicose, combative, ferocious, invective, trenchant, vitriolic 10 pugnacious, scurrilous, terrifying, vituperous 11 belligerent, browbeating, contentious, frightening, opprobrious, quarrelsome,

terrorizing 12 contumelious, gladiatorial, intimidating, vituperative, vituperatory
trudge 4 plod, slog, slop, toil, trek 6 stodge 8 footslog, plunther
true 4 just, real, very 5 liege, loyal, right, sooth, valid 6 actual, ardent, honest, kosher, strict, trusty 7 factual, genuine, precise, staunch, unfaked, upright 8 accurate, bona fide, constant, faithful, resolute, rightful, unfabled 9 allegiant, authentic, honorable, steadfast, trustable, undoubted, unfeigned, veracious, veridical, veritable 10 creditable, dependable, legitimate, sure-enough, undeniable 11 appropriate, indubitable, trustworthy, undesigning, undistorted 12 indisputable, undissembled 13 authoritative ***combining form:*** 2 eu 4 orth 5 ortho
true-blue 5 loyal 8 faithful 10 unswerving
truism 4 rule 5 axiom, gnome, maxim, moral 6 cliché, dictum, gospel, verity 7 brocard, bromide 8 aphorism, apothegm, veracity 9 platitude 10 shibboleth 11 commonplace
Truk Island 3 Tol 4 Moen, Udot, Uman 5 Fefan 6 Dublon
truly 3 yea 4 even, very, well 6 easily, indeed, really, surely, verily 7 de facto 8 actually 9 genuinely, veritably 10 absolutely, positively 11 confidently, doubtlessly, undoubtedly
Truman, Harry S ***birthplace:*** 5 Lamar (Missouri) ***predecessor:*** 3 FDR ***successor:*** 3 DDE
trump 3 cap, top 4 beat, best, pass, ruff 5 excel, outdo 6 better 7 manille, surpass 8 clincher, outstrip, spadille
trumpery 4 base, mean, poor 5 bilge, cheap, hokum 6 bunkum, bushwa, cheesy, common, paltry, shoddy, trashy 7 twaddle 8 claptrap, flimflam, malarkey, nonsense, rubbishy 10 double-talk
trumpet 4 horn, tout 6 herald 8 ballyhoo ***call:*** 6 sennet ***ram's horn:*** 6 shofar
trumpeter 4 Hirt 5 André, Davis 6 Alpert, Voisin 7 Schwarz 9 Armstrong, Gillespie
truncate 3 lop, top 4 crop 5 shear 6 cut off 7 abridge, pollard 10 abbreviate
truncheon 3 bat 4 club, mace 5 billy 6 cudgel 8 bludgeon 9 billy club 10 knobkerrie, nightstick
trundle 3 bed, tub 4 bowl, cart, haul, push, roll 5 churn, wheel 6 lumber
trunk 3 box 4 body, case, stem 5 chest, torso 7 channel, circuit, luggage ***elephant:*** 9 proboscis ***tree:*** 4 bole
truss 3 tie 4 bind, pack 5 brace 7 support 9 supporter 10 strengthen
trust 4 care, hope, pool, rely, ward 5 chain, faith, group, lot on, stock 6 assume, bank on, belief, cartel, charge, commit, credit, rely on 7 build on, combine, confide, consign, count on, custody, keeping, presume 8 bank upon, credence, depend on, reckon on, reliance, rely upon, sureness 9 assurance, certainty, certitude, syndicate 10 confidence, conviction, dependence, depend upon 11 calculate on, safekeeping 12 conglomerate, guardianship, positiveness ***Scottish:*** 6 lippen
trustworthy 4 true 5 exact, tried, valid 6 honest, secure 7 upright 8 accurate, credible, faithful, reliable 9 authentic, realistic, veracious 10 convincing, dependable, scrupulous 12 tried and true 13 authoritative
trusty 4 firm 5 sound, tried 6 secure, stable 7 convict, turnkey 8 credible, faithful, reliable 9 authentic 10 convincing, dependable 11 predictable, responsible 12 tried and true
truth 5 axiom, maxim, sooth 6 candor, gospel, verity 7 lowdown, reality, veritas 8 veracity 9 precision, rightness 11 genuineness 12 authenticity, veridicality 13 veraciousness, veritableness ***goddess:*** 4 Maat ***serum:*** 11 scopolamine
truthful 4 real 5 frank 6 candid, honest 7 factual, sincere, veridic 8 accurate 9 realistic, veracious, veridical
truthfulness 5 truth 6 verity 8 veracity 12 veridicality 13 veraciousness
try 2 go 3 aim, irk, pop, vex 4 pain, rack, seek, shot, slap, stab, test 5 annoy, assay, check, crack, essay, exert, fling, offer, prove, trial, whack, whirl, wring 6 aspire, bother, harass, harrow, hassle, martyr, strain, stress, strive 7 afflict, agonize, attempt, crucify, test out, torment, torture, trouble 8 distress, endeavor, striving, struggle 9 undertake 10 excruciate, experiment
trying 5 rough, tight, tough 6 sticky, taxing, tricky, vexing 7 arduous, exigent, irksome, onerous, tricksy, weighty 8 annoying, exacting 9 demanding, strenuous 10 bothersome, burdensome, irritating, oppressive 11 troublesome
try out 8 audition
tryst 4 date 7 meeting 10 engagement, rendezvous 11 appointment, assignation
tsetse fly 8 glossina
tsunami 9 tidal wave
tub 3 vat 4 bath, wash 5 keeve 6 shower 8 dumpling 10 butterball
tuba 7 helicon
Tubalcain ***father:*** 6 Lamech ***mother:*** 6 Zillah
Tubal's father 7 Japheth
tubby 5 plump, podgy, pudgy 6 chubby, plumpy, rotund 8 plumpish, roly-poly 10 roundabout
tube 2 TV 4 duct, hose, pipe 5 buret,

pipet 6 siphon, subway, tunnel, vessel 7 burette, conduit, cuvette, pipette, syringe 8 pipe-line ***anatomical:*** 3 vas 4 duct, vasa (plural) 7 salpinx 9 salpinges (plural) ***combining form:*** 5 solen 6 siphon, soleno, syring 7 siphoni, siphono, syringo

tuber 4 bulb, corm, stem 6 potato 7 rhizome

tuberculosis 2 TB 8 phthisis 11 consumption, white plague

tuck 2 go 3 pep 4 birr, chow, eats, feed, food, grub, meat 5 bread, moxie, scoff, vigor 6 energy, viands 7 potency 9 hardihood, provender

tucker 4 poop, wilt 5 gruel 7 exhaust, frazzle, tire out, wear out 8 knock out 9 prostrate

tuft 5 clump, mound 7 cluster ***combining form:*** 4 loph 5 lophi, lopho 6 lophio ***of feathers:*** 7 panache ***of hair:*** 4 tate ***ornamental:*** 6 pompon ***vascular:*** 6 glomus

tufted 8 floccose

tug 3 lug, tow, war 4 drag, draw, haul, moil, pull, toil, work 5 drive, fight, labor 6 battle, oppugn, strain, strive 7 contend

tug-of-war 6 strife 7 contest, rivalry, warfare 8 conflict, striving 9 emulation 11 competition

tuition 8 teaching, training, tutelage 9 education, schooling 11 instruction

tumble 3 dip, hit 4 bump, down, drop, fall, fell, hash, hear, luck, mash, meet, skid, trip 5 floor, learn, level, light, mix up, pitch, snafu, upset 6 chance, foul up, go down, happen, jumble, litter, mess up, muddle, muss up, plunge, topple 7 catch on, clutter, confuse, descend, disturb, find out, flatten, overset, plummet, rummage, shuffle, snarl up, unearth, unhorse 8 bowl down, bowl over, come down, disarray, discover, disorder, keel over, mishmash, nose-dive, overturn, scramble, unsettle 9 ascertain, bring down, determine, knock down, knock over, overthrow 10 disarrange, discompose

tumbler 5 glass 11 cartwheeler

tumbrel 4 cart 5 wagon 7 vehicle 8 dumpcart

tumescent 6 turgid 7 aureate, bloated, bulging, flowery, swollen 8 dropsied, inflated, swelling 9 bombastic, dropsical, flatulent, overblown 10 euphuistic, rhetorical 12 magniloquent 13 grandiloquent

tumid see **tumescent**

tummy 3 gut 5 belly 6 paunch, venter 7 abdomen, stomach

tumor 3 wen 4 cyst 5 myoma 6 emerod, glioma, lipoma, myxoma 7 desmoid, emeroid, myeloma, neuroma, osteoma, sarcoma 8 blastoma, hepatoma, lymphoma, neoplasm, teratoma 9 carcinoma ***benign:*** 7 fibroid, fibroma ***combining form:*** 3 oma 4 cele, myom, onco 5 myomo, omato (plural), oncho 6 gangli 7 ganglio ***hard:*** 8 scirrhus ***soft:*** 5 gumma

tumult 3 din 4 flap, stew, to-do 5 babel, noise, whirl 6 clamor, dither, hassle, hubbub, jangle, lather, outcry, pother, racket, uproar, upturn 7 ferment, turmoil 8 disorder, paroxysm, seething, upheaval 9 agitation, commotion, confusion, maelstrom 10 convulsion, hullabaloo, hurly burly, turbulence 11 disturbance, pandemonium 12 unsettlement

tumultuous 5 rowdy 6 unruly 7 raucous 8 rowdyish 9 termagant, turbulent 10 boisterous, disorderly, rowdydowdy 11 rumbustious

tumulus 4 hill 5 mound 6 barrow 7 hillock

tun 3 keg, vat 4 butt, cask, pipe 6 barrel 8 hogshead

tune 3 air, fix, lay 4 dial, sing, sync 5 carol, chant, chime, order, range, synch 6 accord, adjust, chorus, extent, matter, melody, strain, warble 7 concert, concord, conform, descant, harmony, measure, melisma, melodia 8 diapason, regulate, vicinity, vocalize 9 agreement, harmonize, integrate, magnitude, reconcile 10 consonance, coordinate, proportion 11 accommodate, composition, concordance 12 neighborhood, reconciliate

tuneful 5 sweet, tuned 6 dulcet 7 lyrical, melodic, musical, songful 8 euphonic 9 melodious 10 euphonious 11 mellisonant

tungsten 7 wolfram

tunic 5 gipon, jupon 6 caftan, kaftan, kirtle ***Greek:*** 6 chiton

tunicate 4 salp 5 salpa 6 salpid 8 ascidian, doliolid 9 sea squirt

Tunisia ***monetary unit:*** 5 dinar ***ruins:*** 8 Carthage

tunnel 4 tube 6 burrow 7 conduit 8 crawlway ***Alps:*** 7 Simplon ***France:*** 4 Rove ***Hudson river:*** 7 Holland, Lincoln ***Nevada:*** 5 Sutro ***railroad:*** 6 Hoosac 7 Cascade

tunny 4 tuna 7 bluefin

Turandot ***character:*** 3 Liu 5 Calaf ***composer:*** 7 Puccini ***suitor:*** 5 Calaf

turban 6 pugree 7 pugaree, puggree 8 bandanna, puggaree 9 headdress

turbid 4 dark 5 dense, mucky, muddy, murky, riley, roily, smoky, thick 6 cloudy, opaque 7 clouded, obscure

turbulence 3 din 4 flap, stew 5 babel, fight 6 dither, fracas, lather, pother, tumult, uproar 7 turmoil 9 agitation, commotion, confusion 10 unruliness 11 pandemonium

turbulent 4 fast, wild 5 roily, rough, rowdy 6 raging, stormy, unruly 7 boiling, furious, howling, moiling, raucous, riotous, roaring, ruffled 8 agitated, blustery, brawling, mutinous, rowdyish, stormful, swirling 9 clamorous, convulsed, stirred up, termagant **10** blustering, boisterous, disorderly, rip-roaring, roisterous, roughhouse, rowdy-dowdy, tumultuous **11** rumbustious, tempestuous, uninhibited **12** rambunctious **13** tempest-tossed

turf **3** sod **4** area **5** divot, track **6** region, sphere, swarth **7** terrain **9** racetrack, territory

turgid see **tumescent**

turkey ***disease:*** **9** blackhead ***female:*** **3** hen ***head growth:*** **5** snood **7** dewbill ***male:*** **3** tom **7** gobbler ***throat pouch:*** **6** wattle ***young:*** **5** poult

Turkey ***capital:*** **6** Ankara ***largest city:*** **8** Istanbul ***monetary unit:*** **4** lira **5** pound

turkey buzzard **4** aura

Turkey in the ____ **5** Straw

Turkish ***empire:*** **7** Ottoman ***governor:*** **4** vali ***inn:*** **6** imaret ***music:*** **9** janissary ***palace:*** **5** serai ***province:*** **7** vilayet ***soldier:*** **5** nizam **8** janizary **9** janissary ***sultan:*** **5** Ahmet, Selim **7** Bajazet, Ilderim ***sword:*** **8** yataghan ***title:*** **3** aga, bey **4** agha **5** pasha **6** vizier

turmeric **4** herb **5** spice **8** curcumin **9** bloodroot

turmoil **4** flap, moil, riot, stew, to-do **5** whirl **6** clamor, dither, hassle, hubbub, lather, pother, strife, tumult, unease, unrest, uproar **7** anxiety, ferment, garboil **8** disorder, disquiet, distress, upheaval **9** agitation, commotion, confusion **10** disruption, hurly burly, inquietude, turbulence, uneasiness **11** anxiousness, disquietude, jitteriness, nervousness, restiveness **12** restlessness **13** Sturm und Drang

turn **3** aim, yaw, zag, zig **4** bend, bias, bout, cast, eddy, grow, gyre, plow, reel, roll, sour, spin, swim, tack, tour, vary, veer, whip, wind **5** alter, angle, avert, curve, orbit, pivot, point, refer, round, sheer, shunt, spell, stint, swing, swirl, train, twirl, twist, upset, weave, whirl **6** become, change, circle, defect, desert, detour, direct, divert, gyrate, hang on, invert, modify, mutate, obvert, plow up, render, repair, resort, revert, rotate, sicken, sprain, switch, swivel, wrench, zero in, zigzag **7** circuit, convert, deflect, derange, deviate, digress, diverge, flexure, hinge on, inverse, passade, reflect, reverse, revolve **8** disorder, flection, gyration, mutation, renounce, reversal, rotation, unsettle **9** about-face, deviation, oscillate, pirouette, rechannel, refashion, repudiate, reversion, sidetrack, translate, transpose, variation, volte-face **10** alteration, apostatize, change into, circumduct, deflection, double back, revolution, right-about, tergiverse, transplace **11** changeabout, reversement **12** modification, tergiversate ***combining form:*** **4** trop **5** trope, tropy **6** tropic **7** trophic, tropism, tropous ***to stone:*** **8** lapidify

turnabout **3** rat **6** coward **7** quitter, reverse **8** apostate, defector, recreant, renegade, reversal, runagate **9** about-face, reversion, volte-face **10** backslider, right-about **11** changeabout, reversement **13** tergiversator

turn aside or away **4** skew, veer, ward **5** avert, shunt **6** divert **7** deflect, shuttle

turn back **5** react, recur, repel **6** return, revert **10** recrudesce

turncoat **3** rat, spy **7** quisler, traitor **8** apostate, betrayer, defector, deserter, quisling, recreant, renegade, runagate **9** straggler, turnabout **13** tergiversator

turn down **4** veto **5** spurn **6** refuse, reject **7** decline, dismiss **9** reprobate, repudiate **10** disapprove

turned on **4** high **5** doped **6** stoned, zonked **7** drugged **8** hopped-up **9** spaced-out **10** tripped out

turn in **3** bed **5** rat on **6** betray, retire **7** deliver, produce **8** hand over, inform on

turning point **4** crux **5** pivot **6** climax, crisis **8** landmark

turnip **5** swede **8** rutabaga ***Scottish:*** **4** neep

turnip-shaped **8** napiform

turn left **3** haw

Turn of the Screw, The ***author:*** **5** James ***character:*** **5** Flora, Miles **10** Peter Quint ***composer:*** **7** Britten

turn over **4** feed, find, give, hand, muse, plow, roll **5** break, upset **6** assign, commit, give up, plow up, ponder, supply, topple **7** commend, confide, consign, deliver, entrust, furnish, overset, provide, revolve **8** delegate, meditate, ruminate, transfer **9** overthrow **10** deliberate, relinquish

turnpike **4** road **7** highway, tollway **8** toll road

turn right **3** gee

turn up **3** get **4** come, espy, find, show, spot **5** catch, get in, hit on, pop in, reach **6** appear, arrive, descry, detect, louden, roll in, show up **7** hit upon, uncover, unearth **8** meet with **9** encounter, track down **11** materialize

Turnus ***beloved:*** **7** Lavinia ***slayer:*** **6** Aeneas

turpentine **7** galipot, solvent, thinner ***ingredient:*** **6** pinene ***tree:*** **4** pine **9** terebinth

turret **5** tower **8** bartizan

turtle **8** terrapin, tortoise **9** chelonian ***edible part:*** **7** calipee **8** calipash ***sea:*** **6** ridley **8** hawkbill ***shell:*** **8** carapace ***shell part:*** **8** plastron

Tuscany ***city:*** **4** Pisa **8** Florence ***river:*** **4** Arno ***tower:*** **4** Pisa ***wine:*** **7** chianti

tusk 4 fang 5 ivory, tooth
tussle 4 spar 5 scrap 6 hassle 7 grapple, scuffle, wrestle 8 skirmish
tutelage see tuition
tutor 5 coach, teach 6 docent, mentor 7 teacher 9 pedagogue 10 instructor
Tut's tomb discoverer 6 Carter
TV see television
twaddle 3 jaw, yak 4 bosh, chat 5 clack, drool, prate, run on 6 babble, dither, drivel, gabble, hot air 7 blabber, blather, chatter, prattle 8 claptrap, malarkey, nonsense, tommyrot, wish-wash 9 poppycock 10 balderdash
Twain biographer 5 Paine
tweak 3 jog 4 jerk, pull 5 pinch 6 snatch, twitch
Twelfth Night character 5 Maria, Viola 6 Olivia 8 Malvolio 9 Sebastian, Toby Belch
twelve *combining form:* 5 dodec 6 dodeca
twenty *combining form:* 4 icos 5 icosa, icosi
twerp 4 brat, fool, jerk 5 sprat 6 squirt 7 upstart
twibil 2 ax 3 axe 8 battle-ax 9 battle-axe
twice 3 bis 7 twofold *combining form:* 2 di 3 bis *prefix:* 2 bi 3 dis
twice a day 3 b.i.d. 8 bis in die
twice a year 8 biannual
Twice-Told Tales author 9 Hawthorne
twig 5 shoot, sprig 6 branch *bundle of:* 5 fagot 6 faggot
twiggy 4 slim, thin 5 reedy 6 slight, stalky 7 slender, squinny, tenuous 9 attenuate
twilight 3 end, eve 4 dusk 5 gloom 6 sunset 8 gloaming, glooming, owl light 9 attenuate, nightfall
Twilight of the Gods 8 Ragnarok
twill 5 cloth, serge, weave 6 fabric 9 gabardine 11 herringbone
twin 4 dual, like, mate 5 match 6 bifold, binary, double, fellow, paired 7 matched, similar, twofold 8 matching 9 companion, duplicate, identical 10 coordinate, reciprocal *combining form:* 5 didym 6 didymo
Twin Cities 6 St. Paul 11 Minneapolis
twine 4 coil, curl, wind 5 twist 6 enmesh, spiral, tangle 7 entwine, wreathe 8 entangle 9 corkscrew 10 interweave
twinge 4 ache, pain, pang 5 throe 6 stitch
twinkle 3 bat 4 wink 5 blink, flash, gleam, glint, light, shake, shine, trice 6 minute, moment, second 7 flicker, glimmer, glisten, glitter, instant, light up, nictate, shimmer, sparkle 9 coruscate, nictitate, twinkling 10 illuminate 11 coruscation, scintillate, split second 13 scintillation
twin stars 6 Castor, Pollux
twirl 4 gyre, spin 5 whirl 6 gyrate 9 pirouette, whirligig
twist 3 wry 4 coil, curl, slub, turn, warp, wind, wisp 5 belie, color, gnarl, pivot, quirk, thraw, twine, wring 6 garble, intort, spiral, sprain, squirm, torque, widdle, wrench, writhe 7 contort, distort, entwine, falsify, intwine, pervert, wreathe, wriggle 8 miscolor, misstate, squiggle 9 corkscrew 12 misrepresent *combining form:* 4 spir 5 spiri, spiro
twisted 3 wry 4 awry 5 askew 6 knurly, thrawn, warped 7 tortile
twister 7 cyclone, tornado 9 whirlwind
twit 4 jive, josh, lout, mock, quiz, razz 5 blame, chide, rally, scout, taunt, tease 6 deride 7 censure, reprove 8 reproach, ridicule 9 reprehend
twitch 3 lug, nip 4 jerk, snap, yank 5 grasp, lurch, pinch, pluck, tweak 6 clutch, snatch 9 vellicate
twitter 3 gab, jaw 4 chat, chip, peep 5 cheep, chirp, quake, run on, shake, tweet 6 babble, cackle, dither, quaver, quiver, rattle, shiver, tremor 7 chatter, chipper, chirrup, chitter, prattle, shudder, tremble, tweedle
twittery 5 jumpy, nervy 6 goosey, spooky 7 fidgety, jittery, nervous 9 flustered 10 high-strung
two 3 duo 4 duet, pair 5 twain 6 couple *combining form:* 2 dy 3 bis, duo, dyo *divide into:* 4 fork 6 bisect 9 bifurcate *prefix:* 2 bi 3 twi
twofold 4 dual, twin 5 binal, duple 6 binary, double, duplex, dyadic, paired 9 dualistic *combining form:* 2 di 4 dipl 5 diphy, diplo 6 diphyo
Two Gentlemen of Verona *character:* 5 Julia 6 Silvia, Thurio 7 Proteus 9 Valentine
two-horned 10 bicornuate
twosome 3 duo 4 dyad, pair 5 brace 6 couple 7 doublet
two-time 5 bluff 6 delude, humbug, illude, juggle, take in 7 beguile, deceive, mislead 11 double-cross
two-wheeler 4 bike 5 cycle 7 bicycle 10 velocipede
two-winged 9 dipterous
Two Years Before the Mast author 4 Dana
Tybalt *cousin:* 6 Juliet *family:* 7 Capulet *slayer:* 5 Romeo *victim:* 8 Mercutio
Tyche *goddess of:* 7 fortune
tycoon 4 czar, king 5 baron, mogul, nabob 6 prince 7 magnate
tyke 3 dog 5 child, hound 6 canine 7 mongrel
tympanum 7 eardrum 9 middle ear

Tyndareus ***kingdom:*** 6 Sparta ***wife:*** 4 Leda
type 3 cut, ilk, lot, way 4 cast, form, kind, mold, sort 5 breed, class, genre, order, print, serif, stamp 6 kidney, nature, stripe 7 feather, species, variety 8 category 9 character 10 persuasion 11 description ***bar:*** 4 slug ***combining form:*** 5 morph 6 morpho ***jumbled:*** 2 pi 3 pie ***measure:*** 2 em, en 4 pica 5 point ***set:*** 7 compose ***setter:*** 10 compositor ***size:*** 4 pica 5 agate, pearl ***stroke:*** 5 serif ***style:*** 5 roman 6 Gothic, italic 7 Fraktur 8 boldface, sanserif 9 lightface, sans serif ***tray:*** 6 galley
Typee ***author:*** 8 Melville ***character:*** 4 Toby
typewriter ***part:*** 3 key 6 platen, spacer ***type size:*** 4 pica 5 elite
Typhon 3 Set 7 monster 8 Typhoeus ***offspring:*** 6 Sphinx 7 Chimera 8 Cerberus, Chimaera ***wife:*** 7 Echidna
typhoon 9 hurricane 13 tropical storm
typical 5 ideal, model, usual 6 common, normal, old hat 7 classic, general, natural, regular 9 classical, exemplary, prevalent 11 commonplace
typical of ***suffix:*** 2 ic, ly 3 ish, ist 4 ical 5 istic 7 istical
typify 6 embody, mirror 9 body forth, epitomize, exemplify, personify, represent, symbolize 10 illustrate 11 emblematize
typo 5 error 8 misprint
typographer 7 printer 10 compositor
Tyr 3 Tiu ***brother:*** 4 Thor ***father:*** 4 Odin ***god of:*** 3 war ***mother:*** 5 Jordh, Jorth
tyrannical 5 harsh 6 brutal 8 absolute, despotic 9 arbitrary, autarchic, roughshod 10 autocratic, monocratic, oppressive
tyrannize 5 crush 7 dictate, oppress, shackle, trample 8 dominate, domineer, overlord 9 despotize, terrorize
tyrannous 6 lordly 8 absolute, despotic 9 arbitrary, autarchic, fascistic 10 autocratic, monocratic 12 totalitarian
tyranny 7 fascism 8 totality 9 autocracy, despotism, terrorism 10 absolutism, domination, oppression 12 dictatorship
tyrant 4 duce 6 despot 8 autocrat, dictator 9 oppressor, strong man 12 totalitarian
Tyrian ___ 6 purple
tyro 4 colt 6 novice, rookie 7 amateur, dabbler 8 beginner, freshman, neophyte, newcomer 9 novitiate, smatterer 10 apprentice, dilettante, tenderfoot, uninitiate 11 abecedarian
Tyrol see Tirol
Tzar see czar

U

übermensch 7 overman 8 superman
ubiquitous 7 allover 9 universal 10 everywhere 11 omnipresent
Uel's father 4 Bani
Uganda ***capital:*** 7 Kampala ***monetary unit:*** 8 shilling
ugly 3 bad, low 4 base, dour, fell, foul, glum, mean, ugly, vile 5 awful, cross, grave, major, pesky, plain, sulky, surly, toady 6 cranky, gloomy, homely, morose, sordid, sullen, wicked 7 bizarre, crabbed, hideous, ignoble, low-down, serious, servile, vicious 8 grievous, gruesome, uncomely, unlovely, wretched 9 dangerous, grotesque, repelling, repugnant, repulsive, saturnine, troublous, unsightly, vexatious 10 despicable, ill-favored, ill-looking, uninviting, unpleasing 11 ill-tempered, threatening, troublesome, unbeautiful 12 unattractive
Ugly Duckling author 8 Andersen
ugni blanc 4 wine 9 Trebbiano
ukase 5 edict, order 6 decree, ruling 7 command 9 directive 12 proclamation
Ukraine ***capital:*** 4 Kiev ***folk dance:*** 5 gopak ***soldier:*** 7 cossack
Ulalume author 3 Poe
Ulam's father 5 Eshek
ulcer 4 sore ***kind:*** 6 peptic 8 duodenal ***mouth:*** 10 canker sore
uliginous 3 wet 4 damp, oozy 5 moist, muddy 6 swampy
ulna 5 cubit 7 cubitus, forearm
Ulrica 5 sibyl, sybil, witch
Ulster hero 4 Emer, Medb 5 Cu Roi, Etain, Noisi 6 Ailill, Fergus 7 Cathbad, Conaire, Da Derga, Deirdre 8 MacDatho 9 Conchobar, Cuchullin, Finnabair 10 Cuchulainn
ulterior 4 dark 5 later, privy 6 buried, covert, future, hidden, latent 7 cryptic, further, guarded, obscure, remoter, thither 8 obscured, shrouded 9 ambiguous, concealed, enigmatic, equivocal 10 subsequent, succeeding 11 undisclosed
ultimate 3 end, lag 4 dire, last 5 basic, close, final, grand, lofty 6 finish, latest, latter, utmost, wind up, wrap up 7 closing, epitome, exalted, extreme, maximum, sublime, supreme 8 absolute, complete, conclude, earliest, empyreal, empyrean, eventual, farthest, hindmost, last word, original, terminal, towering 9 determine, elemental, terminate 10 apotheosis, concluding, consummate, preeminent, surpassing 11 categorical, fundamental, unequalable, unmatchable 12 incomparable, quintessence, transcendent 13 unsurpassable
ultimatum 5 order 6 demand, threat
ultra 5 kinky, outré, rabid 6 beyond, far-out 7 extreme, fanatic, forward, radical 9 excessive, extremist, fanatical 10 outlandish 11 extravagant
ultraconservative 4 tory 5 blimp, white 7 Bourbon, diehard 8 royalist 9 right-wing 11 reactionary, reactionist 13 reactionarist
ultraist 5 rabid 7 extreme, fanatic, radical 9 extremist
ultramarine 7 new blue, oversea 8 overseas 10 French blue 11 lapis lazuli, transmarine
ululate 3 bay 4 hoot, howl, wail, yelp 5 quest 6 bewail, lament 7 screech
Ulysses ***author:*** 5 Joyce ***character:*** 5 Bloom, Molly 6 Boylan 7 Dedalus (Stephen); (see also **Odysseus**)
umber 5 brown, shade 6 darken, shadow 8 grayling 9 hammerkop
umbilicus 4 core 5 heart, hilum, navel ***combining form:*** 6 omphal 7 omphalo
umbra 4 fish 5 ghost, shade 6 shadow 7 eidolon, phantom 8 darkness, phantasm, revenant 10 apparition
umbrage 3 ire 4 fury, huff, miff, rage 5 anger, doubt, pique, shade, trace, umbra, wrath 6 enrage, irking, madden, offend, screen, shadow 7 dudgeon, foliage, incense, leafage, offense, pretext, steam up, verdure 8 nettling, vexation 9 annoyance, infuriate, provoking, semblance, suspicion 10 irritation, resentment 11 displeasure 12 exasperation
umbrageous 5 shady 6 shaded, shadow 7 shadowy 8 shadowed 9 resentful 11 belligerent
umbrella 5 guard, shade 6 brolly, pileus, screen 7 parasol, shelter 10 protection 11 bumbershoot ***large:*** 4 gamp
umbrous 5 shady 6 shaded, shadow 7 shadowy 8 shadowed
umph see **oomph**
umpire 5 judge 7 adjudge, arbiter, ref-

eree 9 arbitrate 10 adjudicate, arbitrator *call:* 3 out 4 balk, ball, safe 6 strike
unabashed 6 arrant, brassy, brazen 7 blatant 8 impudent, overbold 9 barefaced, shameless 10 unblushing 11 brazenfaced
unabbreviated see **unabridged**
unable 8 helpless, impotent 9 incapable 11 incompetent, inefficient, unqualified 13 incapacitated
unabridged 5 uncut, whole 6 entire, intact 8 complete, undocked 11 uncondensed, whole-length 13 unabbreviated
unacceptable 4 poor 7 boorish 8 below par, unwanted 9 unwelcome 10 ill-favored, unpleasing, unsuitable 11 undesirable 12 inadmissible 13 below standard, exceptionable, objectionable
unaccompanied 4 bare, sole 5 alone, apart 6 single 7 isolate, removed 8 detached, isolated
unaccomplished 7 jackleg 8 dabbling, ungifted 9 unskilled 10 amateurish, dilettante, incomplete, unfinished 12 dilettantish, dilettantist
unaccountable 6 arcane, mystic 7 strange 8 numinous 9 mysterial, unguessed 10 cabalistic, mysterious, unknowable 11 inscrutable 12 impenetrable, inexplicable, unfathomable 13 inexplainable, irresponsible, unexplainable
unaccustomed 3 new 6 unused 7 strange 8 uncommon 10 unfamiliar
unacquainted 7 strange, unaware, unusual 8 ignorant 9 oblivious, unknowing, unwitting 10 unfamiliar, uninformed 11 incognizant 12 inconversant, uninstructed 13 inexperienced
unacquired 6 inborn, innate, native 7 connate, natural 9 inherited 10 congenital, connatural, indigenous
unadorned 3 dry 4 bald, bare 5 naked, plain, stark 6 rustic, simple 7 austere 11 undecorated, unelaborate, ungarnished 12 unbeautified, unornamented 13 unembellished, unembroidered, unpretentious
unadulterated 4 neat, pure 5 plain, sheer 6 honest, simple 7 genuine, perfect, sincere, unmixed 8 absolute, straight 9 unalloyed, undiluted 11 unmitigated, unqualified
unadvisable see **inadvisable**
unaffable 7 aseptic 8 retiring 9 shrinking, withdrawn 10 restrained 11 unexpansive
unaffected 4 easy, real 5 naive, plain 6 rustic, simple 7 artless, natural, sincere 9 ingenuous, unstudied, untouched, untutored 10 unschooled 12 unartificial, uninfluenced
unafraid 4 bold, cool, sure 5 brave 7 assured, defiant, valiant 8 composed, fearless, intrepid, valorous 9 audacious, confident, dauntless, undaunted 10 courageous 13 imperturbable
unaimed 6 random 7 aimless 9 desultory, haphazard, hit-or-miss, unplanned 10 designless 11 purposeless 12 unconsidered
unalike 7 distant, diverse, unequal, various 9 different, disparate, divergent, unsimilar 10 dissimilar
unalloyed 4 deep, pure 5 sheer, solid 6 simple, virgin 7 genuine, perfect, unmixed 8 absolute 9 undiluted 11 unmitigated, unqualified 13 unadulterated
unalluring 5 plain 6 homely 8 uncomely, unpretty 10 unhandsome 11 unbeauteous, unbeautiful 12 unattractive
unalterable see **inalterable**
unambiguous 5 clear, lucid, plain 6 patent 7 crystal, evident, express, obvious 8 apparent, clean-cut, clear-cut, definite, distinct, explicit, luminous, manifest, palpable, pellucid, specific 9 unblurred 10 definitive 11 categorical, translucent, transparent 12 transpicuous
unanimated 4 cold, dead, dull, flat 5 vapid 6 asleep 7 insipid
unanimous 5 solid 6 agreed, united 8 agreeing, univocal 10 concordant, concurrent, harmonious 11 consentient 13 consentaneous
unappeasable 4 grim 6 mortal 8 ruthless 9 insatiate, merciless, unsatiate 10 implacable, insatiable, ironfisted, quenchless, relentless, unyielding 11 unflinching, unrelenting 12 unquenchable 13 unsatisfiable
unappetizing 4 flat 7 insipid 8 unsavory 9 savorless, tasteless 10 flavorless 11 distasteful, ill-flavored, unpalatable 12 unattractive 13 uninteresting
unappreciative 9 thankless 10 ungrateful, unthankful
unapproachable 5 aloof 6 offish 7 distant, stately 8 reserved 9 unbending, withdrawn 10 insociable, unsociable 11 standoffish, ungetatable, unreachable 12 inaccessible, unattainable
unarm see **disarm**
unarmed 4 bare 5 inerm 8 unbarbed 11 defenseless *combining form:* 5 anopl 6 anoplo
unartful 5 naive 6 simple 7 artless, natural 9 ingenuous, unstudied 10 unaffected, unschooled 12 unartificial
unarticulate see **inarticulate**
unasked 5 unbid 6 wanton 8 arrogant, impudent, unbidden, unsought, unwanted 9 uninvited, unwelcome, voluntary 10 gratuitous 11 overbearing, spontaneous,

uncalled-for, unrequested 12 presumptuous, supererogant, unacceptable

unassailable 5 stout, tough 6 secure, strong, sturdy 8 stalwart 9 tenacious 10 invincible, unbeatable 11 impregnable, indomitable 12 inexpugnable, invulnerable, undefeatable 13 inconquerable, unconquerable

unassertive 3 shy 4 meek 5 timid 6 modest 7 bashful, rabbity 8 backward, retiring 9 diffident, unassured 12 self-effacing

unassuming 3 shy 4 meek 5 lowly 6 humble, modest, simple 7 natural 8 retiring

unassured 3 shy 5 timid 6 modest, unsafe, unsure 7 bashful, rabbity 8 backward, insecure, retiring 9 diffident 10 unreliable 11 unassertive, unconfident 12 self-effacing, undependable 13 untrustworthy

unattached 4 free 5 loose 6 single 9 unmarried

unattractive 4 rude, ugly 5 plain 6 homely 8 frumpish, uncomely, unpretty 9 unlikable 10 unalluring, ungracious, unhandsome, unlikeable 11 unbeauteous, unbeautiful

unauthentic 7 bastard 8 spurious 9 ungenuine 10 apocryphal

unavailing 4 vain 6 futile 7 useless 8 abortive, bootless, gainless 9 fruitless 11 ineffective, ineffectual 12 unproductive

unavoidable 7 certain 9 necessary 10 ineludible, inevasible, inevitable, returnless, unevadable 11 ineluctable, inescapable, unescapable

unavoidably 8 perforce 10 helplessly, inevitably, willy-nilly 11 inescapably, whether or no

unaware 5 aback, short 6 sudden 7 unready 8 ignorant, suddenly 9 oblivious, unknowing, unwitting 10 unfamiliar, uninformed, unprepared 11 incognizant 12 inconversant, unacquainted, unexpectedly, uninstructed

unawares 5 aback, short 8 suddenly 12 unexpectedly

unbalance 5 craze 6 frenzy, lunacy, madden 7 derange, madness, unhinge 8 distract, insanity 10 aberration, alienation, insaneness 11 derangement, distraction, instability, psychopathy

unbalanced 3 mad 4 daft 5 batty, wacky 6 crazed, insane, uneven 7 unequal, unsound 8 demented, deranged, lopsided 9 irregular 10 asymmetric 13 unsymmetrical

unbeautiful 4 ugly 5 plain 6 homely 7 hideous 8 uncomely, unpretty 9 unsightly 10 ill-favored, ill-looking, unalluring, unhandsome 12 unattractive

unbecoming 4 rude 5 inapt, inept, rough, undue 6 clumsy, gauche, indign, unmeet 7 awkward, beneath, ungodly 8 improper, indecent, uncomely, unseemly, untimely, untoward, unworthy 9 incorrect, inelegant, maladroit 10 indecorous, indelicate, malapropos, malodorous, undecorous, unsuitable 11 disgraceful, unbefitting 12 unattractive, unseasonable 13 inappropriate

unbefitting see unbecoming

unbelievable 4 thin, weak 5 thick 6 flimsy 8 fabulous 9 fantastic 10 improbable, incredible 11 implausible, incogitable, unthinkable 12 insupposable, unconvincing, unimaginable 13 inconceivable, unsubstantial

unbeliever 5 pagan 6 giaour 7 atheist, doubter, heretic, infidel, scoffer, skeptic, zetetic 8 agnostic 10 headshaker, Pyrrhonian, Pyrrhonist 11 free-thinker

unbelieving 6 show-me 8 aporetic, doubting 9 quizzical, skeptical 11 distrusting, incredulous, questioning 12 disbelieving

unbending 5 aloof, rigid, stern, stiff 6 offish 7 distant 8 obdurate, reserved, resolute 9 impliable, inelastic, withdrawn 10 brassbound, inexorable, inflexible, insociable, relentless, unflexible, unsociable, unswayable, unyielding 11 immalleable, incompliant, standoffish 12 single-minded

unbiased 4 fair, just 5 aloof, equal 8 detached, tolerant 9 equitable, impartial, objective, uncolored 12 uninterested, unprejudiced 13 dispassionate

unbidden 7 unasked 8 unsought 9 uninvited 11 unrequested

unbind 4 free, undo 5 loose, unfix, untie 6 detach, loosen, ungird 7 absolve, deliver, manumit, release, unchain, unloose 8 dissolve, liberate, unfasten, unloosen, unswathe 9 discharge, disengage, unshackle 10 emancipate

unblamable 4 good, pure 8 innocent, virtuous 9 exemplary, guiltless, righteous 10 inculpable

unblemished 4 pure 5 clean, sound, whole 6 chaste, decent, intact, modest, unhurt 7 perfect 8 flawless, spotless, unmarred 9 stainless, undamaged, undefiled, uninjured, unsullied 10 immaculate, unimpaired

unblock 3 ope 4 open, undo 6 unshut, unstop 7 unclose

unblunted 4 keen 5 honed, sharp 7 whetted 10 razor-sharp

unblurred 5 clear, lucid 7 crystal 8 clear-cut, luminous, pellucid 11 translucent, transparent, unambiguous 12 transpicuous

unbolt 4 open 5 unbar, unpin 6 loosen, unlock 8 unfasten

unbosom 4 open, tell 6 betray, reveal, unveil 7 divulge, unclose, uncover 8 disclose, discover 9 uncurtain
unbound 4 free 5 loose 10 unconfined, unfastened
unbounded 4 huge, open 7 endless 8 infinite 9 boundless, limitless, unchecked, unlimited 10 indefinite, unmeasured 11 measureless 12 immeasurable, uncontrolled, unrestrained
unbridled 4 free 5 loose 7 violent 9 dissolute, unchecked 10 licentious, ungoverned 11 uninhibited 12 uncontrolled, unrestrained
unbroken 3 one 5 solid, sound, whole 6 entire, intact, single, unhurt 7 perfect, untamed 8 straight, unmarred, unplowed 9 continual, undamaged, undivided, uninjured, unsubdued 10 continuous, unimpaired 13 uninterrupted
unburden 3 rid 4 ease, lose 5 clear, empty 6 unload 7 relieve 8 shake off, throw off 9 discharge 11 disencumber
uncalled-for 4 rude 5 silly 6 absurd, wanton 7 foolish, incivil, unasked, uncivil 8 baseless, impolite, needless, unneeded 9 intrusive, officious, unfounded, unneedful 10 bottomless, gratuitous, groundless, ungracious, ungrounded, unrequired 11 disgracious, ill-mannered, impertinent, inessential, unessential, unnecessary, unwarranted 12 discourteous, preposterous, supererogant 13 disrespectful
uncanny 4 eery 5 eerie, scary, weird 6 creepy, spooky 7 ghostly, strange 9 unearthly, unnatural 10 mysterious, superhuman 11 supernormal, supranormal 12 supernatural 13 superordinary
uncared-for 7 run-down 8 untended 9 neglected
uncareful 4 wild 8 feckless, reckless 10 incautious 13 irresponsible
uncaring 8 feckless, heedless 9 oblivious, unheeding, unrecking 10 unthinking 11 inadvertent, thoughtless 12 irreflective, unreflective
unceasing 7 endless, eternal 8 constant, unending 9 ceaseless, continual, incessant, perpetual 10 continuous 11 everlasting, unremitting 12 interminable 13 uninterrupted
unceremonious 4 curt 5 bluff, blunt, sharp, short 6 abrupt 8 familiar, informal 9 irregular 10 ungracious, unofficial 11 thoughtless 13 inconsiderate
uncertain 4 asea, dark, hazy, iffy, moot, open 5 fluky, vague 6 chancy, fickle, fitful, queasy, shifty, unsure, wobbly 7 dubious, erratic, halting, mutable, obscure, protean, suspect, unclear 8 aleatory, arguable, doubtful, flickery, hesitant, insecure, mootable, slippery, ticklish, unstable, unsteady, variable, volatile 9 ambiguous, debatable, equivocal, faltering, fluctuant, mercurial, sibylline, tenebrous, tentative, undecided, unsettled, whimsical 10 borderline, capricious, changeable, disputable, inconstant, indecisive, indefinite, irresolute, lubricious, precarious, unexplicit 11 problematic, vacillating, vacillatory 12 incalculable, questionable, undependable, unexpectable, wiggle-waggle 13 indeterminate, problematical, temperamental, unforeseeable, unpredictable, untrustworthy
uncertainty 5 doubt, maybe, query, worry 6 bother, gamble, wonder 7 anxiety, concern, dubiety, reserve, trouble 8 disfaith, disquiet, distress, distrust, mistrust, suspense 9 agitation, dubiosity, dubitancy, suspicion 10 hesitation, skepticism, uneasiness 12 doubtfulness, perturbation
unchain 4 free 5 loose 6 loosen, unbind 7 manumit, release 8 liberate 9 discharge, unshackle 10 emancipate
unchangeable 4 fast 5 fixed 7 eternal 8 constant 9 immovable, immutable, unmovable 10 inflexible, invariable 11 inalterable, unalterable 12 unmodifiable
unchanging 4 even, same 6 stable, static, steady 7 equable, eternal, forever, settled, stabile, uniform 8 constant 9 immutable, steadfast, unfailing, unvarying 10 consistent, invariable, stationary 13 unfluctuating
unchaste 4 easy, fast, lewd 5 bawdy, dirty, light, loose 6 coarse, impure, wanton 7 haggard, immoral, obscene, scarlet, unclean 9 uncleanly
unchecked 4 free 5 loose 7 rampant 9 unbounded, unbridled 11 uninhibited
uncivil 4 rude, wild 5 crass, crude, rough 6 brutal, coarse, crusty, Gothic, rugged, savage 7 Hunnish, ill-bred, incivil 8 barbaric, clownish, impolite 9 barbarian, barbarous 10 indecorous, ungracious, unsuitable 11 disgracious, ill-mannered, impertinent, uncivilized, uncourteous 12 discourteous, uncultivated 13 disrespectful
uncivilized 4 rude, wild 6 brutal, Gothic, Hunnic, rugged, savage, unholy, wicked 7 boorish, Hunnish, ill-bred, loutish, lowbred, ungodly 8 barbaric, churlish, cloddish 9 barbarian, barbarous, unrefined 10 outrageous, uncultured, unmannerly, unpolished 12 uncultivated 13 unenlightened
unclad see unclothed
uncle *Dutch:* 3 oom *Scottish:* 3 eme *Spanish:* 3 tio
unclean 4 foul, tref, vile 5 black, dirty, nasty, soily 6 common, filthy, grubby, impure 7 defiled, immoral, obscene, squalid 8 polluted, profaned, unchaste 10 desecrated 11 unwholesome

unclear 3 dim 4 hazy, open 6 bleary, blurry, opaque, unsure 7 dubious, obscure, shadowy, suspect 8 doubtful, nebulose, nebulous 9 ambiguous, equivocal, tenebrous, uncertain, undefined, unsettled 10 ill-defined, indistinct, unexplicit 11 problematic
Uncle Remus creator 6 Harris
Uncle Tom's Cabin *author:* 5 Stowe *character:* 5 Eliza, Topsy 6 Legree (Simon) 9 Little Eva
Uncle Vanya author 7 Chekhov
uncloak 6 debunk, expose, show up, unmask 7 undress 8 discover, unshroud
unclothe 5 strip 6 denude, devest, divest, expose, reveal, unveil 7 display, disrobe, uncloak, uncover, undress 8 disclose 10 dishabille
unclothed 3 raw 4 nude 5 naked 6 unclad 8 buff-bare, stripped 9 au naturel, undressed 10 stark-naked
unclouded 4 fair, fine, open 5 clear, sunny 7 clarion 8 pleasant, rainless, sunshiny 10 undarkened
uncluttered 4 neat, snug, tidy, trig, trim 7 chipper, orderly 9 shipshape 11 spic-and-span, well-groomed 12 spick-and-span
uncolored 4 fair, just 5 equal 8 unbiased 9 equitable, impartial, objective 12 unprejudiced 13 dispassionate
uncombed 5 messy 6 sloppy, unneat, untidy 7 unkempt 8 ill-kempt, slipshod, slovenly 10 disheveled 12 unfastidious
uncombine 4 free, part 5 loose, sever 6 divide, sunder 7 disjoin 8 disjoint, dissever, disunite, separate 11 dichotomize
uncomely 4 ugly 5 inapt, inept, plain, undue 6 homely 7 hideous 8 improper, indecent, unpretty, untimely 9 unsightly 10 ill-favored, ill-looking, malapropos, unalluring, unbecoming, unhandsome, unsuitable 11 unbeauteous, unbeautiful, unbefitting 12 unattractive 13 inappropriate
uncomfortable 4 sick 5 harsh 6 queasy, uneasy 7 prickly 8 easeless, scratchy 11 distressing 13 disconcerting
uncommon 3 few, odd 4 rare 5 novel 6 choice, scarce, seldom, unique 7 special, strange, unusual 8 esoteric, especial, singular, sporadic, unwonted 10 infrequent, occasional, remarkable, unfrequent, unordinary 11 exceptional, unthinkable 12 unaccustomed, unimaginable 13 extraordinary
uncommunicative 4 dumb 5 aloof, close 6 offish, silent 7 distant, private 8 reserved, reticent, taciturn 9 unbending, withdrawn 10 insociable, unsociable 11 close-lipped, standoffish, tight-lipped 12 closemouthed, close-tongued, tight-mouthed
uncompassionate 5 stony 7 callous 8 obdurate 9 heartless, unfeeling 10 hard-boiled 11 coldhearted, hardhearted, unemotional 12 stony-hearted 13 unsympathetic
uncompliant 5 rigid 8 obdurate 9 untending 10 brassbound, inexorable, inflexible, unswayable, unyielding 12 single-minded
uncomplicated 5 basic, plain 6 honest, simple 10 elementary
uncomplimentary 9 slighting 10 derogatory, detracting, pejorative 11 disparaging, dyslogistic 12 depreciative, depreciatory
uncomprehensible see incomprehensible
uncompromising 4 firm 5 rigid, stern, tough 6 strict 7 extreme 8 hard-line, obdurate 9 unbending 10 brassbound, determined, inexorable, inflexible, relentless, unyielding 11 uncompliant 12 intransigent, single-minded
unconcealed 4 bare, open 5 frank, overt, plain 6 candid 8 apparent 11 openhearted, undisguised, unvarnished 12 undissembled 13 undissembling
unconcern 4 cool 6 apathy 8 coolness, lethargy 9 disregard, lassitude 11 disinterest, insouciance, nonchalance 12 heedlessness, indifference, listlessness 13 unmindfulness
unconcerned 4 cool 5 aloof 6 casual, remote 8 composed, detached 9 apathetic, collected, incurious, lethargic, uncurious, unmindful, withdrawn 10 nonchalant 11 indifferent 12 uninterested 13 disinterested
unconditional 4 free 5 frank, utter 6 simple 8 absolute, explicit, termless 10 unreserved
unconfined 3 lax 4 free 5 loose 9 boundless, limitless, unlimited 12 unrestrained
uncongenial 8 aversive, kindless 9 repellent, repugnant, unlikable 10 discordant, unpleasing 11 displeasing, inconsonant 12 antipathetic, inharmonious, unattractive, unharmonious 13 unsympathetic
unconnected 5 gappy 7 muddled 8 detached, inchoate, rambling, separate 10 disjointed, disordered, incoherent, incohesive 11 unorganized 12 uncontinuous 13 discontinuous
unconquerable 6 secure 9 resistant 10 impassable, invincible, unbeatable 11 impregnable, indomitable, insuperable 12 inexpugnable, invulnerable, unassailable, undefeatable
unconscionable 5 undue 6 unholy, wicked 7 extreme, ungodly 8 towering 9 barbarous, excessive 10 exorbitant, immoderate, inordinate, outrageous 11 extravagant, unchristian, uncivilized, unwarranted 12 unmeasurable, unprinci-

pled, unreasonable, unscrupulous **13** unjustifiable, unwarrantable
unconscious 3 out 4 cold 5 brute 6 asleep, blotto, torpid 7 out cold, stunned, unaware 8 comatose, ignorant, mindless 10 insensible
unconsciousness 4 coma 5 faint 6 torpor, trance
unconsidered 4 puny, rash 5 brash, hasty, petty, small 6 paltry, random 7 aimless, trivial 8 picayune, reckless, trifling 9 desultory, haphazard, hit-or-miss, hotheaded, unadvised, unplanned 10 designless, ill-advised, incautious, objectless 11 promiscuous, thoughtless 12 inconsequent
unconsolable see **inconsolable**
unconstrained 4 easy, free 6 casual, dégagé, simple 7 natural, relaxed, unfussy 8 familiar, informal, outgoing 9 easygoing, expansive 10 unreserved 11 low-pressure 13 demonstrative
unconstraint 4 ease 7 abandon, freedom, naiveté 10 simplicity 11 naturalness, spontaneity 13 impulsiveness, ingenuousness
uncontrollable 4 wild 6 unruly 8 indocile 9 fractious 11 indomitable, intractable 12 recalcitrant, unmanageable 13 insuppressive, irrepressible, uncontainable, undisciplined
uncontrolled 4 free, wild 5 loose 9 irregular, unbounded, unmanaged 10 hysterical, licentious, ungoverned 11 unregulated 12 unrestrained
unconventional 3 odd 5 loose, outré, queer 6 casual 7 devious, offbeat, strange, unusual 8 Bohemian, informal 10 unorthodox 13 unceremonious
unconversant 3 raw 5 green, young 6 callow 7 untried 8 unversed 9 unfleshed 10 unseasoned 11 unpracticed 13 inexperienced
unconvincing 4 thin, weak 5 fishy, thick 6 flimsy 10 improbable, incredible 11 implausible 12 unbelievable 13 inconceivable, unsubstantial
uncooked 3 raw
uncork 6 unplug 7 release
uncorrectable 8 cureless, hopeless 9 incurable, insanable, uncurable 10 impossible 11 immedicable, irreparable 12 irremediable 13 unrecoverable
uncorrupted 4 pure 5 naive 6 virgin 8 innocent, pristine 9 unspoiled
uncouple 3 cut 5 loose, unfix 6 detach 8 abstract, unfasten 9 disengage 10 disconnect, dissociate 12 disassociate
uncourteous 4 rude 7 uncivil 8 impolite 10 ungracious 11 disgracious, ill-mannered, impertinent, uncalled-for 13 disrespectful
uncouth 3 odd, raw 4 lorn, rude 5 crass, crude, gross, queer, rough, rummy 6 coarse, quaint, vulgar 7 awkward, bizarre, boorish, curious, erratic, ill-bred, loutish, oddball, strange, uncivil 8 backwood, derelict, deserted, desolate, forsaken, impolite, solitary, ungainly 9 abandoned, eccentric, inelegant, unrefined 10 uncultured, unpolished 11 disgracious, ill-mannered, impertinent, uncalled-for 12 discourteous, uncultivated 13 disrespectful *person:* 3 oaf 4 boor, lout 5 yokel 6 bumkin, rustic 7 bumpkin
uncover 4 bare, open, tell 5 strip 6 betray, denude, detect, divest, expose, remove, reveal, unmask, unveil 7 display, divulge, lay open, subject, unbosom, unclose, undrape, unearth 8 disclose, unclothe 9 uncurtain
uncovered 4 bare, open 5 naked 6 peeled 7 denuded, exposed 8 stripped, unmasked
uncritical 6 casual 7 cursory, inexact, offhand, shallow, sketchy 8 careless, slipshod 9 depthless, imprecise 10 inaccurate 11 perfunctory, superficial
uncrown 6 depose, unmake 8 dethrone, discrown, displace 9 disthrone 11 disenthrone
unction 3 oil 4 balm 5 cream, salve 6 cerate, chrism 7 suavity 8 ointment
unctuous 3 fat 4 oily 5 fatty, slick, soapy, suave 6 greasy, smarmy 7 fulsome 10 oleaginous
uncultivated 3 raw 4 arid, rude, wild 5 crass, crude, feral, gross, rough 6 coarse, desert, fallow, Gothic, incult, native, savage, sloven 7 deserty, Hunnish, natural, uncivil 8 agrarian, agrestal, barbaric 9 barbarian, barbarous, inelegant 11 uncivilized
uncultured 3 raw 4 rude 5 crass, crude, gross, rough 6 coarse, incult, vulgar 7 artless, boorish, ill-bred, loutish, lowbred, uncouth 8 churlish, cloddish 9 unrefined 10 unpolished 11 clodhopping, uncivilized
uncurbed 9 audacious 10 ungoverned, unhampered 11 uninhibited, untrammeled 12 uncontrolled, unrestrained
uncustomary 4 rare 6 unique 7 unusual 8 singular, uncommon, unwonted 10 unordinary 11 exceptional, unthinkable 13 extraordinary
uncut 5 whole 6 entire 8 complete, undocked 10 full-length, unabridged 11 uncondensed, whole-length 13 unabbreviated
undamaged 5 sound, whole 6 intact, unhurt 8 flawless, unbroken, unmarred 9 uninjured 10 unimpaired 11 unblemished
undaring 5 timid 8 timorous
undarkened 4 fair, fine 5 clear, sunny

7 clarion 8 pleasant, rainless, sunshiny 9 cloudless, unclouded
undaunted 4 bold 5 brave 7 Spartan, valiant 8 fearless, intrepid, valorous 9 audacious, confident 10 courageous 11 unconquered
undeceive 5 purge 8 disabuse, undelude 11 disillusion
undecided 4 moot, open 6 unsure 7 dubious, pendent, pending, unclear 8 doubtful, wavering 9 equivocal, uncertain, unsettled 10 borderline, indecisive 12 undetermined
undecipherable 9 illegible 10 unreadable
undecisive see indecisive
undeclared 5 tacit 6 secret, unsaid 7 implied 8 implicit, inferred, unspoken, wordless 9 unuttered 10 understood 11 unexpressed
undecorated 5 plain 6 homely, simple 9 unadorned 11 inelaborate, ungarnished 12 unbeautified, unornamented 13 unembellished, unembroidered
undefiled 4 pure 5 clean 6 chaste, decent, intact, modest, virgin 8 innocent, spotless, virtuous 9 stainless, unsullied 10 immaculate 11 unblemished
undefined 3 dim 5 faint, vague 6 bleary 7 obscure, shadowy, unclear 10 indistinct 12 undetermined
undemonstrated 7 untried 8 unproved, untested 11 unpracticed
undemonstrative 3 icy 4 calm, cold, cool 5 aloof, chill 6 frigid 7 aseptic, distant, glacial, laconic 8 reserved, retiring 9 shrinking, unaffable, withdrawn 10 restrained, unsociable 11 emotionless, indifferent, standoffish, unemotional, unexpansive 12 uninterested
undeniable 4 real, true 6 actual 7 certain 8 positive, unfabled 9 veridical 10 inarguable 11 indubitable, unequivocal 12 indisputable, undisputable 13 incontestable, uncontestable
undependable 5 trick 6 casual, tricky, unsafe, unsure 7 dubious, erratic 8 untrusty 9 trustless, unassured 10 fly-by-night, unreliable 12 questionable 13 irresponsible, untrustworthy
under 3 low, sub 5 below, lower, neath 6 lesser, nether 7 beneath, subject 8 inferior 9 dependent, secondary, subjacent, tributary 10 collateral, underneath 11 subordinate *prefix:* 3 hyp, sub 4 hypo
underage 4 lack 7 deficit, failure 8 shortage 10 deficiency, inadequacy, scantiness 11 defalcation 13 insufficience, insufficiency
undercarriage 5 frame 6 struts 8 supports 9 framework 11 landing gear
undercover 6 covert, secret 7 furtive, sub rosa 8 hush-hush 11 clandestine 12 hugger-mugger 13 hole-and-corner, surreptitious, under-the-table *person:* 3 spy 4 mole 5 agent, spook 9 detective 10 counterspy 12 counteragent
undercroft 5 crypt, vault 7 chamber 8 catacomb
underdeveloped 7 dwarfed, stunted 8 backward 10 behindhand 13 unprogressive
underdog 4 prey 5 loser 6 victim 8 casualty 9 dark horse
underdone 4 rare
underestimate 8 disprize, minimize 9 underrate 10 undervalue
undergarment 3 bra 4 slip 5 teddy 6 bodice, briefs, cilise, corset, girdle, shorts, skivvy, undies 7 chemise, dessous, drawers, panties, step-ins 8 flimsies, knickers, lingerie, pretties, skivvies 9 brassiere, petticoat, underwear 10 foundation
undergo 3 bow, see 4 bear, have, know, pass 5 abide, carry, defer, serve, yield 6 endure, submit, suffer 7 sustain 8 tolerate 10 experience
undergoer *suffix:* 2 ee
undergraduate 4 coed 6 junior, senior 7 student 8 freshman 9 sophomore
underground 5 train 6 hidden, secret, subway 7 beneath, illegal, off-beat 8 hypogeal, hypogean 9 underfoot 10 undercover, underearth 11 disapproved 12 subterranean 13 surreptitious 14 counterculture
underhand 3 sly 4 mean, wily 5 shady 6 crafty, secret, shifty, sneaky, tricky, unfair 7 crooked, cunning, devious, furtive, hangdog, oblique, stealth 8 guileful, indirect, sinister, sneaking 9 deceitful, dishonest, insidious 10 circuitous, fraudulent 11 duplicitous
underhanded 3 sly 4 mean 5 shady 6 secret, shifty, sneaky, unfair 7 devious 8 guileful, indirect, sneaking, unfairly 9 deceitful 10 circuitous, fraudulent 11 clandestine, duplicitous, shorthanded, undermanned 12 understaffed
underived 5 prime 7 primary 8 original 9 primitive
underlease 6 sublet 8 sublease, underlet
underlet 6 sublet 8 sublease 10 underlease
underlie 4 bear 7 subtend, support
underline 4 mark 6 legend, play up, stress 7 caption, feature 9 emphasize, italicize 10 underscore
underling 5 scrub 6 menial, minion 8 inferior 9 secondary, subaltern 11 subordinate 12 poor relation
underlying 5 basal, basic, vital 6 bottom, covert 7 crucial, needful, obscure, primary, radical 8 cardinal, critical, implicit 9 elemen-

tal, essential, necessary, primitive **10** elementary, substratal **11** fundamental **12** foundational **13** indispensable
Under Milk Wood author **6** Thomas
undermine **3** sap **4** cave, foil, ruin **5** blunt, drain, erode, wreck **6** impair, thwart, weaken **7** cripple, disable, founder, subvert, unbrace **8** enfeeble, sabotage, supplant **9** attenuate, frustrate **10** debilitate, demoralize **12** unstrengthen
undermost **6** bottom, lowest **9** lowermost **10** bottommost, nethermost, rockbottom
underneath **4** sole **5** below **6** bottom, secret **9** underside **10** undercover **12** undersurface **13** surreptitious ***prefix:*** **5** intra
underpin **4** base, prop, root, seat, stay **5** brace, shore **7** justify, support **8** buttress, maintain **12** substantiate
underpinning **4** base, prop, root, seat, stay **5** basis, brace, shore **6** column, ground **7** bedrock, footing, seating, support **8** buttress **10** foundation, groundwork, substratum **12** substruction, substructure **13** underpropping
underpowered **4** slow, weak **6** anemic **8** sluggish
underprivileged **4** poor **5** needy **7** hapless, unlucky **8** deprived, ill-fated **9** depressed **10** ill-starred **11** handicapped, unfortunate **12** impoverished **13** disadvantaged
underprize **5** decry, lower **7** devalue **9** devaluate, write down **10** depreciate, devalorize, undervalue
underprop **4** stay **5** brace, shore **6** buoy up, uphold **7** bolster, support, sustain **8** buttress
underpropping **4** prop, stay **5** brace, shore **6** column **7** support **8** buttress
underrate **5** decry, lower **7** devalue **8** discount, mark down, write off **9** devaluate, write down **10** depreciate, devalorize, undervalue **13** underestimate
underscore **6** play up, stress **7** feature **9** emphasize, italicize, underline
undersexed **4** cold **6** frigid **9** inhibited **11** passionless **12** unresponsive
underside **4** sole **6** bottom **10** underneath **12** undersurface ***combining form:*** **6** infero
undersized **4** puny **5** dwarf, runty, scrub, small **6** little **7** scrubby, stunted
understand **3** con, dig, get, ken, see **4** have, know, sabe, take, twig **5** catch, fancy, grasp, guess, infer, savvy, seize, sense, think **6** accept, assume, deduce, expect, fathom, figure, follow, gather, reason, take in **7** believe, cognize, discern, imagine, presume, realize, suppose, surmise, suspect **8** conceive, conclude, consider, perceive **9** apprehend, interpret, penetrate **10** appreciate, comprehend, conjecture
understandable **3** lay **5** clear, lucid, plain **6** simple **7** popular **8** clear-cut, exoteric, knowable, luminous **9** graspable, unblurred **10** fathomable **11** unambiguous **12** intelligible **13** apprehensible
understanding **3** ken, wit **4** deal, idea **5** grasp, sense **6** accord, humane, import, kindly, notion, reason, treaty **7** compact, concept, empathy, entente, insight, knowing, meaning, message, purport **8** attitude, contract, daylight, judgment, sympathy **9** agreement, awareness, diagnosis, intellect, intuition, knowledge, tolerance **10** acceptance, intendment **11** acceptation, discernment, intelligent, penetration, sympathetic **12** apprehension, intelligence, significance, significancy **13** comprehension, signification
understatement **7** litotes
understood **5** clear, lucid, tacit **6** unsaid **7** implied **8** implicit, inferred, unspoken, wordless **9** unuttered **10** undeclared **11** unexpressed
understudy **6** double **7** stand-in **10** substitute **11** replacement
undertake **2** do, go **3** try **4** dare, pass, seek **5** assay, begin, essay, offer, start **6** accept, assume, engage, incept, pledge, strive, take on, take up **7** attempt, certify, emprise, execute, perform, promise, warrant **8** commence, contract, covenant, endeavor, struggle
undertaker **8** embalmer **9** mortician **12** entrepreneur
undertaking **3** job, try **4** task **5** essay, trial **6** cautio, charge, effort, hassle, scheme, voyage **7** attempt, calling, emprise, emprize, project, venture **8** covenant, endeavor, striving, struggle **9** adventure **10** enterprise **11** proposition
under-the-table **6** covert, secret **7** furtive, sub-rosa **8** stealthy **10** undercover **11** clandestine **13** surreptitious
undertone **4** hint **5** aside, rumor **6** mumble, murmur, mutter **7** inkling, subtone, whisper **8** overtone **10** suggestion **11** association, connotation, implication, susurration
undertow **4** eddy **6** vortex **7** current, riptide, sea puss **8** seapoose, sea purse
undervalue see **underrate**
underwater **9** submarine **10** subaquatic, subaqueous ***breathing apparatus:*** **5** scuba ***captain:*** **4** Nemo ***chamber:*** **7** caisson ***device:*** **8** paravane ***missile:*** **7** torpedo ***sound detector:*** **5** sonar
underwear see **undergarment**

underwood 5 frith 7 boscage, coppice 10 underbrush 11 undergrowth
underworld 4 hell 5 abyss, hades, Orcus, Sheol 6 Erebus, Tophet 7 Gehenna, inferno, xibalba 8 gangland 9 barathrum 11 netherworld, Pandemonium *boatman:* 6 Charon *deity:* 3 Dis 4 Bran 5 Pluto 6 Osiris 8 Dispater *goddess:* 6 Hecate 10 Persephone *organization:* 5 Mafia *relating to:* 8 chthonic *watchdog:* 8 Cerberus
underwrite 4 back, sign 6 assure, insure, pay for 7 endorse, finance, sponsor, support 9 subscribe
undesigning 4 real, true 6 honest, simple 7 artless, genuine, sincere 9 unfeigned 10 heart-whole 12 undissembled
undesirable 8 unwanted 9 unwelcome 10 ill-favored 12 inadmissible, unacceptable 13 exceptionable, objectionable
undesired 8 unsought, unwanted, unwished 9 unwelcome 10 quenchless
undestroyable see indestructible
undetermined 3 dim 5 faint, unset, vague 6 bleary 7 dubious, obscure, pendent, pending, shadowy, unclear 8 aoristic, doubtful 9 equivocal, undecided, undefined, unsettled 10 ill defined, indistinct
undeveloped 5 crude 6 latent 7 archaic 8 backward, immature, juvenile 9 primitive, unevolved 10 behindhand, persistent 13 unprogressive
undiluted 4 mere, neat, pure 5 plain, sheer 6 simple 7 perfect, unmixed 8 absolute, straight 9 unalloyed 11 unmitigated, unqualified 13 unadulterated
undiplomatic 5 brash 8 tactless 9 impolitic, maladroit, unpolitic, untactful
undisciplined 4 wild 6 unruly, wanton 8 untoward 9 fractious, untrained 11 intractable 12 recalcitrant, ungovernable, unmanageable
undisclosed 6 hidden, sealed, secret 8 ulterior 12 confidential
undisguised 4 bald, open 5 frank, overt, plain 6 candid 9 barefaced 11 openhearted, unconcealed, unvarnished 12 undissembled 13 undissembling
undissembled 4 open, real, true 5 frank, plain 6 candid, honest 7 genuine, sincere 9 unfeigned 10 heart-whole 11 openhearted, unconcealed, undesigning, undisguised, unvarnished
undistinguished 5 gross 6 common 8 mediocre, noteless 9 unnotable 12 unnoteworthy
undistorted 4 just, true 5 clear, right 6 strict 8 faithful 9 veracious, veridical
undivided 3 one 5 fixed, total, whole 6 entire, intact 8 complete, unbroken 10 continuous, unswerving 12 concentrated, undistracted
undo 3 ope 4 have, open, raze, ruin 5 abate, annul, loose, quash, unfix, untie, wrack, wreck 6 defeat, diddle, negate, outfox, outwit, seduce, unbind, unmake, unshut, unsnap, unstop 7 abolish, debauch, destroy, nullify, unblock, unbuild, unclose, unframe, unloose, unravel, vitiate 8 abrogate, decimate, demolish, outreach, outslick, outsmart, unfasten, unloosen 9 disengage, outjockey, overreach 10 annihilate, invalidate, outgeneral 11 outmaneuver
undoing 4 bane, ruin 8 downfall 9 destroyer, overthrow, ruination 11 destruction
undoubtedly 4 well 5 truly 6 easily, indeed, really, surely 7 frankly 11 doubtlessly, indubitably
undoubtful 6 secure 7 assured 8 sanguine 9 confident 11 self-assured 13 self-confident
undress see unclothe
undressed 3 raw 4 nude, rude 5 crude, naked, rough 6 unclad, unhewn 8 buffbare, stripped, unformed, unworked 9 au naturel, roughhewn, unclothed 10 starknaked, unfinished, unpolished 11 unfashioned
undue 5 dizzy, inapt, inept, unapt 7 extreme 8 ill-timed, improper, towering, untimely 9 excessive, unfitting 10 exorbitant, immoderate, inordinate, unsuitable 11 extravagant, unwarranted 12 unreasonable, unseasonable 13 inappropriate, unjustifiable, unwarrantable
undulant fever 11 brucellosis
undulate 4 roll, swag, sway, wave 5 snake, swing 6 ripple 7 slidder, slither 9 fluctuate
unduly 3 too 4 ever, over 6 overly 8 overfull, overmuch 9 extremely, immensely 11 excessively 12 inordinately
undutiful 7 impious
undying 7 ageless, endless, eternal 8 immortal, unending 9 continual, deathless, unceasing 10 continuing, persistent 12 imperishable, interminable, unquenchable
uneager 3 shy 5 loath 6 afraid, averse 8 backward, hesitant 9 reluctant, unwilling 10 indisposed 11 disinclined
unearth 3 dig, see 4 hear, show 5 delve, learn 6 exhume, expose, reveal, tumble 7 catch on, exhibit, find out, uncover 8 disclose, discover 9 ascertain, determine
unearthly 4 eery 5 balmy, crazy, eerie, loony, silly, wacky, weird 6 absurd, insane, spooky 7 awesome, foolish, uncanny, ungodly 8 numinous, superior, terrific 9 appalling, fantastic 10 miraculous, mysterious, outlandish, superhuman, suprahu-

man 12 preposterous, supermundane, supernatural, supranatural 13 preternatural
unease 4 care 5 worry 6 unrest 7 anxiety, concern, tension, trouble 8 disquiet 9 abashment, confusion 10 discomfort, discontent, solicitude 11 concernment, displeasure, disquietude, uptightness 12 apprehension, discomfiture, discomposure 13 disconcertion, embarrassment
uneasiness see **unease**
uneasy 4 edgy 5 nervy, shaky, tense 6 unsure 7 anxious, awkward, careful, fidgety, restive, suspect, unquiet, uptight, worried 8 agitated, doubtful, restless 9 ambiguous, concerned, difficult, disturbed, doubtable, perturbed, uncertain, unrestful, unsettled 10 borderline, disquieted, precarious, solicitous, unpeaceful, untranquil 13 uncomfortable
uneducated 4 rude 6 simple 8 ignorant, untaught 9 benighted, untutored 10 illiterate, unlettered, unschooled 11 empty-headed, know-nothing 12 uninstructed
unembellished 3 dry 5 plain 6 simple 7 austere, prosaic 9 unadorned 11 undecorated, unelaborate, ungarnished 12 unbeautified, unornamented 13 unembroidered, unpretentious
unembroidered see **unembellished**
unemotional 3 dry, icy 4 cold, cool 5 chill, stoic, stony 6 frigid 7 callous, glacial, stoical 8 obdurate 9 heartless, impassive, unfeeling 10 hard-boiled, phlegmatic 11 coldhearted, hardhearted, indifferent 12 stonyhearted 13 dispassionate, unsympathetic
unemployed 4 free, idle 5 fired 6 otiose, unused 7 jobless, laid off 8 inactive, workless 9 unengaged 10 unoccupied
unending 7 eternal, undying 8 constant, immortal, timeless 9 ceaseless, continual, perpetual 10 continuous 11 amaranthine, everlasting, unremitting 12 interminable 13 uninterrupted
unenlightened 7 heathen 8 backward, ignorant 9 benighted 13 unprogressive
unenthusiastic 4 cold, cool 8 lukewarm 9 apathetic, unexcited 10 spiritless 11 perfunctory 12 uninterested
unequal 5 impar 6 uneven, unfair, unjust, unlike 7 distant, diverse, unalike, various 8 inferior, lopsided, variable 9 different, disparate, divergent, irregular, unsimilar 10 asymmetric, dissimilar, off-balance 11 fluctuating 12 overbalanced 13 unsymmetrical *combining form:* 4 anis 5 aniso
unequalable 7 supreme 8 towering, ultimate 10 preeminent, surpassing 11 unmatchable 12 incomparable, transcendant 13 unsurpassable
unequaled 4 only 5 alone 6 unique 7 supreme 8 nonesuch, peerless 9 matchless, unmatched, unrivaled 10 surpassing 11 unparagoned 12 unparalleled 13 unprecedented
unequipped 5 unfit 8 unfitted 9 incapable 10 ineligible, unprepared 11 incompetent, unqualified 12 disqualified
unequivocal 5 clear, plain 6 direct, patent 7 certain, decided, evident, obvious 8 apparent, definite, distinct, explicit, manifest, palpable, positive 10 undeniable 11 categorical, indubitable 12 indisputable, undisputable 13 incontestable, uncontestable
unerasable see **inerasable**
unerring 4 dead, sure, true 5 exact 7 certain, correct, precise 8 accurate, reliable 9 unfailing 10 dependable, infallible 11 trustworthy
unescapable see **inevitable**
unessential 8 needless, unneeded 9 extrinsic, unneedful 10 unrequired 11 dispensable, uncalled-for, unimportant, unnecessary 13 insubstantial
unethical 5 venal, wrong 6 amoral 7 corrupt, immoral 9 mercenary 10 praetorian 12 unprincipled, unscrupulous
unevadable see **inevitable**
uneven 3 odd 4 wavy 5 bumpy, erose, harsh, jaggy, rough 6 craggy, jagged, patchy, rugged, spotty, unfair, unjust, unlike 7 scraggy, streaky, unequal, unlevel, varying 8 asperous, lopsided, scabrous, scraggly, scratchy, unsmooth 9 anomalous, differing, disparate, irregular 10 asymmetric, discrepant, ill-matched, off-balance, unbalanced 11 fluctuating 12 inconsistent, overbalanced 13 unsymmetrical
unevenness 4 bump, wave 7 anomaly 8 asperity, imparity 9 disparity, roughness 10 inequality 12 irregularity 13 disproportion
uneventful 6 common 7 prosaic 8 ordinary 11 commonplace 12 unnoteworthy 13 unexceptional
unexampled 4 lone, only, sole, solo 5 alone 6 unique 8 singular, solitary 12 unrepeatable
unexceptional 5 usual 6 common, decent 7 prosaic, regular 8 adequate, all right, ordinary 9 tolerable 10 acceptable, sufficient, uneventful 11 commonplace 12 satisfactory, unnoteworthy 13 unimpeachable
unexcited 4 calm 5 level, stoic 7 stoical 8 tranquil
unexciting 4 dead, dull, tame 6 boring 7 prosaic 13 uninteresting
unexpectedly 5 aback, short 6 sudden 7 unaware 8 abruptly, suddenly, unawares 10 unawaredly 12 accidentally

unexpended 6 saving 7 reserve, surplus 8 left over 9 remaining
unexperienced see inexperienced
unexpired 5 alive, valid 8 left over 9 operative, remaining
unexplicit 4 hazy 5 vague 7 obscure, unclear 8 nebulous, nubilous 9 ambiguous, equivocal, tenebrous, uncertain 10 indistinct
unexpressed 5 tacit 6 silent, unsaid 7 implied 8 implicit, inferred, unspoken, wordless 9 unuttered, voiceless 10 undeclared, understood
unfadable 4 fast 7 sunfast 9 colorfast
unfaded 5 fresh 6 bright
unfailing 4 same, sure 6 deadly 7 certain 8 constant, reliable, surefire, unerring 9 unvarying 10 consistent, infallible, invariable, unchanging, unflagging 13 inexhaustible
unfair 4 foul, hard 5 wrong 6 biased, shabby, uneven, unjust 7 devious, unequal 8 wrongful 9 dishonest, inequable, unethical 11 inequitable, underhanded, unequitable, unrighteous 12 dishonorable
unfairness 5 wrong 8 inequity 9 injustice 10 unjustness
unfaithful 5 false 6 untrue 7 infidel, traitor, unloyal 8 disloyal, recreant, turncoat 9 faithless 10 adulterous, inaccurate, perfidious, traitorous 11 treacherous 13 untrustworthy
unfaltering 4 firm, sure, true 5 brave 6 steady 7 abiding 8 enduring, unerring 9 steadfast 11 unqualified 12 never-failing, wholehearted 13 unquestioning
unfamiliar 3 new 6 exotic 7 curious, foreign, strange, unaware, unknown 8 ignorant, peculiar 9 oblivious, unknowing, unwitting 10 remarkable, uninformed 11 incognizant 12 inconversant, unaccustomed, unacquainted, uninstructed
unfamiliarity 9 ignorance, innocence, inscience, nescience 11 unawareness 13 unknowingness
unfashionable 5 dated, passé 6 démodé 8 outmoded 9 out-of-date
unfasten 4 free, open, undo 5 loose, unbar, unfix, unpin, untie 6 detach, loosen, unbind, unlace, unlock, unsnap 7 unhitch, unloose 8 unanchor, unloosen, untether 9 disengage
unfathomable 7 abysmal 8 profound 9 plumbless, soundless 10 bottomless, fathomless, mysterious, unknowable 11 inscrutable, ungraspable 12 impenetrable, incognizable
unfavorable 3 bad, ill 4 evil, foul, poor 6 averse, unfair, unkind 7 adverse, awkward, froward, hostile, unhappy 8 backward, contrary, inimical, negative, sinister, unkindly 11 detrimental *prefix:* 3 dys
unfavorably 4 awry 5 amiss, badly, wrong 6 afield, astray
unfearful 4 bold 5 brave 7 valiant 8 fearless, intrepid, valorous 9 audacious, dauntless, undaunted 10 courageous
unfeasible 10 impossible, infeasible, unworkable 11 impractical 12 irrealizable, unattainable, unrealizable 13 impracticable
unfeeling 4 cold, dead, dull, hard, numb 5 crass, cruel, harsh, stern, stony, surly, tough 6 asleep, brutal, leaden, marble, numbed, severe, stolid, unkind 7 callous 8 benumbed, churlish, deadened, exacting, hardened, obdurate, pitiless, ruthless 9 apathetic, bloodless, crotchety, heartless, inanimate, indurated, insensate, merciless, senseless, unamiable, uncordial 10 hard-boiled, insensible, insentient 11 cold-blooded, coldhearted, hardhearted, insensitive, ironhearted, unemotional 12 anesthetized, cantankerous, curmudgeonly, roughhearted, stonyhearted 13 marblehearted, unsusceptible, unsympathetic
unfeigned 4 open, real, true 6 hearty, honest 7 genuine, natural, sincere 9 heartfelt 11 undesigning 12 undissembled, wholehearted
unfertile see infertile
unfinished 3 raw 4 rude 5 crude, rough 6 unhewn 7 jackleg, sketchy 8 dabbling, unformed, ungifted, unworked 9 imperfect, roughhewn, undressed, unskilled 10 amateurish, dilettante, incomplete, unpolished 11 unfashioned 12 dilettantish, dilettantist
Unfinished Symphony composer 8 Schubert
unfit 3 bad 4 sick 5 inapt, inept, wrong 6 faulty, unmeet 7 awkward, unhandy 8 bungling, disabled, improper, inexpert, unsuited 9 ill-suited, incapable, maladroit 10 blundering, discordant, ill-adapted, ineligible, unbecoming, unequipped, unskillful, unsuitable 11 handicapped, heavyhanded, incompetent, incongruous, inefficient, maladjusted, uncongenial, unqualified 12 disqualified, incompatible, infelicitous, inharmonious, unproficient 13 inappropriate, incapacitated *Jewish law:* 4 tref 6 trefah 7 terefah
unfitting 5 inapt, inept, unapt 8 improper, unseemly 10 malapropos, unbecoming, unsuitable 13 inappropriate
unfix 4 undo 5 loose 6 detach, loosen, unbind 7 unloose 8 abstract, dissolve, uncouple, unfasten, unloosen, unsettle 9 disengage 10 disconnect, dissociate 12 disassociate
unflagging 6 steady 8 constant, tireless, untiring 9 weariless 10 unwearying

11 unweariable 13 indefatigable, inexhaustible
unflappable 4 cool, easy 7 relaxed 8 composed 9 collected, unruffled 10 nonchalant 13 imperturbable
unflawed 7 perfect 8 absolute, flawless 9 fleckless 10 impeccable 11 note-perfect 12 indefectible
unfledged 5 green, young 6 callow, infant, unripe 8 immature, juvenile, youthful 11 undeveloped, unfeathered
unflexible see inflexible
unflinching 4 firm, grim 5 level 6 mortal 7 staunch 8 resolute, ruthless 9 merciless, steadfast 10 implacable, ironfisted, relentless, unwavering, unyielding 11 unrelenting 12 unappeasable
unfluctuating 4 even 6 stable, steady 7 equable, stabile, uniform 8 constant 9 unvarying 10 unchanging
unfold 4 open, show 5 break, burst, solve 6 deploy, evince, evolve, expand, expose, extend, fan out, flower, reveal, spread, unfurl, unroll, untuck, unwrap 7 blossom, clear up, develop, display, divulge, dope out, exhibit, explain, release, resolve, unravel 8 decipher, disclose, dissolve, evidence, manifest, unriddle 9 elaborate, explicate, figure out, outspread, puzzle out 10 outstretch 11 demonstrate
unforbearing 9 impatient 10 intolerant 11 unindulgent
unforced 4 easy 7 natural, willful, willing, witting 9 voluntary 10 deliberate 11 intentional 12 unprescribed
unforeseen 6 sudden 10 accidental, unexpected
unforgivable 9 untenable 10 inexpiable 11 inexcusable 12 indefensible, unpardonable 13 unjustifiable
unformed 4 rude 5 crude, rough 6 callow, unhewn 8 formless, inchoate, unshaped, unworked 9 amorphous, roughhewn, shapeless, uncreated, undressed 10 unfinished, unpolished 11 undeveloped, unfashioned
unfortunate 3 bad, ill, sad 4 dire, poor 5 inept 6 woeful, wretch 7 awkward, hapless, malefic, unhappy, unlucky 8 grievous, ill-fated, luckless, untoward, wretched 9 graceless, ill-chosen, miserable 10 afflictive, calamitous, deplorable, ill-starred, lamentable 11 distressing, regrettable, starcrossed 12 inauspicious, infelicitous, misfortunate, unsuccessful 13 heartbreaking
unfounded 4 idle, vain 8 baseless 9 deceptive, dishonest 10 bottomless, chimerical, gratuitous, groundless, mendacious, misleading, ungrounded, untruthful 11 uncalled-for, unwarranted
unfrequented 5 empty 6 lonely 8 isolated, solitary
unfriendly 3 ill 4 cold, cool, foul 5 chill 6 bitter, chilly, fierce, frosty, remote 7 hostile 8 inimical, unsocial 10 inimicable
unfruitful 6 barren, effete, wasted 7 sterile, useless 8 impotent, infecund 9 infertile 12 unproductive, unprofitable
unfurl 4 open 6 spread, unfold, unroll, unwind 7 develop
unfurnished 4 bare 6 vacant
unfussy 6 casual, common, dégagé 7 relaxed 8 informal 9 easygoing 10 unreserved 11 low-pressure 13 unconstrained
ungainly 5 gawky, lanky, splay 6 clumsy 7 awkward, boorish, lumpish, uncouth 8 clownish, lubberly, unlicked, unwieldy 9 lumbering, maladroit 10 blundering 11 elephantine, splathering
ungarnished 3 dry 5 plain 6 modest, simple 9 unadorned 11 inelaborate, unelaborate 12 unornamented 13 unembellished, unembroidered
ungenerous 4 mean, puny 5 close, harsh, nasty, petty, small, tight 6 paltry, peanut, shabby, stingy 7 miserly 8 grudging, picayune, trifling, ungiving 9 niggardly, penurious 12 inconsequent, parsimonious 13 pennypinching
ungenuine 7 bastard 8 spurious 10 apocryphal 11 unauthentic
ungiving 4 mean 5 close, tight 6 stingy 7 miserly, save-all 9 niggardly, penurious 11 tightfisted 12 parsimonious
ungodly see unholy
ungovernable 4 wild 6 unruly 7 froward 8 untoward 9 fractious, unbridled 10 disorderly, headstrong, rebellious 11 intractable 12 recalcitrant, unmanageable 13 irrepressible, undisciplined
ungoverned 8 uncurbed 9 audacious 10 unhampered 11 uninhibited, untrammeled 12 unrestrained
ungraceful 5 lanky 6 clumsy 7 angular, awkward, halting 8 untoward 9 inelegant
ungracious 4 hard, rude 5 gruff, sharp, short 7 uncivil 8 churlish, impolite, snappish 9 offensive 10 unmannerly, unpleasant 11 disgracious, ill-mannered, impertinent, thoughtless, uncalled-for, uncourteous 12 discourteous, unattractive 13 disrespectful, inconsiderate, unceremonious
ungraded 3 raw 5 crude 6 impure, native 8 unsorted 9 run-of-mine, unrefined
ungraspable 10 unknowable 12 impenetrable, incognizable, unfathomable
ungrateful 4 foul 6 unkind 7 hideous 8 horrible 9 loathsome, offensive, repellent, repugnant, repulsive, revolting, thankless 10 disgusting, unthankful 13 unappreciated

ungratified 9 uncontent 10 discontent, malcontent 11 disgruntled, uncontented, unsatisfied 12 discontented, dissatisfied, malcontented
ungrounded 8 baseless 9 unfounded 10 bottomless, gratuitous, groundless, uninformed 11 uncalled-for, unwarranted 12 uninstructed
unguarded 6 unwary 7 unalert 8 careless 9 imprudent 10 incautious, unvigilant, unwatchful 11 defenseless, thoughtless, unprotected
unguent 4 balm 5 cream, salve 6 cerate, ceroma, chrism 7 unction 8 ointment 9 lubricant
ungulate 3 hog, pig 4 deer 5 horse, tapir 6 hoofed 8 amblypod, elephant 10 rhinoceros
unhallowed 6 impure, unholy 7 demonic, impious, profane, satanic, ungodly 8 demoniac, demonian, devilish, diabolic, fiendish 10 desecrated, irreverent, serpentine 11 diabolonian 13 irreverential
unhampered 4 free 5 loose 6 direct 8 uncurbed 9 audacious, expedited 10 ungoverned 11 expeditious, uninhibited, untrammeled 12 unrestrained
unhandsome 4 mean, rude 5 plain 6 homely 7 ill-bred, uncivil 8 impolite, uncomely, unpretty 10 unalluring, unbecoming, ungracious 11 disgracious, ill-mannered, impertinent, unbeauteous, unbeautiful 12 discourteous, unattractive 13 disrespectful
unhandy 5 inapt, inept, unapt 6 clumsy, gauche, wooden 7 awkward, halting, inadept, unhappy 8 bumbling, cumbrous, inexpert, unfacile, unwieldy 9 ham-handed, maladroit, ponderous 10 cumbersome, unskillful 11 undexterous 12 inconvenient, unproficient
unhappiness 3 woe 5 blues, dolor, dumps, gloom, grief, worry 6 misery, mishap, sorrow, unrest 7 dismals, ill-luck, sadness 9 dejection 10 depression, melancholy 12 mournfulness, wretchedness
unhappy 3 bad, sad 4 evil, sour 5 black, bleak, inept, sorry 6 clumsy, dismal, dreary, gauche, gloomy, rotten, wooden 7 awkward, halting, joyless, unhandy, unlucky 8 bumbling, chiselly, dejected, ill-fated, luckless, mournful, saddened, untoward, wretched 9 cheerless, graceless, ill-chosen, maladroit, woebegone 10 depressant, ill-starred, melancholy, oppressive, unpleasant 11 dispiriting, displeasing, heavy-handed, melancholic, star-crossed, unfortunate 12 disagreeable, heavyhearted, inauspicious, infelicitous, misfortunate
unharmed 4 safe 6 unhurt 9 unscathed 10 scatheless
unharness 6 disarm, divest, ungear 7 outspan, unhitch, unhorse, unstrap 8 untackle
unhealthiness 7 disease, illness, malaise 8 debility, disorder, sickness 9 infirmity 10 affliction, feebleness, infirmness, sickliness 11 decrepitude 12 diseasedness 13 indisposition
unhealthy 3 bad, ill 4 sick 5 hairy, risky 6 chancy, infirm, putrid, queasy, rotten, sickly, unhale, wicked 7 corrupt, noisome, noxious, unsound, vicious 8 depraved, diseased, perilous, perverse 9 dangerous, hazardous, nefarious 10 degenerate, flagitious, insalutary, jeopardous, unsalutary, villainous 11 treacherous, unwholesome 12 insalubrious
unheard-of 3 new 7 obscure, strange, unfamed, unknown, unnoted 8 nameless 10 unrenowned 12 uncelebrated 13 extraordinary, unprecedented
unheeding 4 deaf 8 careless, feckless, heedless, ignoring, uncaring 9 unrecking 10 unnoticing, unthinking, unwatchful 11 inadvertent, inattentive, inobservant, insensitive, thoughtless, unobservant, unobserving 12 disregarding, irreflective, unperceiving, unreflective
unhesitating 4 free 5 ready 8 haltless 9 immediate 10 forthright 12 wholehearted
unhinge 4 turn 5 craze, upset 6 bother, flurry, frenzy, madden, sicken, untune 7 agitate, derange, disturb, fluster, perturb 8 disorder, disquiet, distract, unsettle 9 unbalance 10 discompose
unholy 5 amiss, rough 6 guilty, impure, sinful, wicked 7 corrupt, impious, profane, raucous, ungodly 8 blamable, blameful, culpable, dreadful, fiendish, god-awful, improper, indecent, shocking, unseemly, untoward 9 atheistic, atrocious, barbarous, frightful, malicious, unearthly 10 censurable, indecorous, indelicate, irreverent, malodorous, outrageous, scandalous, unbecoming, undecorous, unhallowed 11 blameworthy, unbelieving, unchristian, uncivilized 13 demeritorious, irreverential, reprehensible
unhorse 5 pitch, throw 6 topple, tumble, unseat 7 buck off, overset 8 dislodge, dismount, overturn, unsaddle 9 overthrow
unhurried 4 easy, slow 7 laggard, unhasty 8 dilatory 9 leisurely 10 deliberate
unhurt 4 safe 5 sound, whole 6 entire, intact 7 perfect 8 unbroken, unharmed, unmarred 9 undamaged, uninjured 10 unimpaired
unicity 7 oneness 8 uniquity 10 singleness, uniqueness
unicorn ***antelope:*** 5 takin ***Chinese:*** 5 kilin, kylin 6 chi-lin ***fish:*** 7 narwhal
unidealistic 4 hard 5 sober 9 practical,

pragmatic, realistic **10** hard-boiled, hard-headed **11** down-to-earth, unfantastic **12** matter-of-fact

unification **5** union **6** hookup, merger **7** joining, linkage, melding, merging **8** alliance, coupling, mergence **9** coalition **10** connection **11** affiliation, coadunation, combination **12** interlocking **13** consolidation

uniform **4** akin, even, like, suit **5** alike, blues, dress, equal, khaki, level **6** agnate, livery, outfit, stable, steady, whites **7** equable, ordered, orderly, regular, similar, stabile **8** constant, parallel **9** analogous, consonant, unvarying **10** comparable, compatible, consistent, invariable, monotonous, unchanging **11** homogeneous **13** corresponding, unfluctuating *combining form:* **2** is **3** iso

uniformity **7** oneness **8** equality, evenness, monotony, sameness

uniformly **6** always, evenly, flatly, smooth **8** smoothly

unify **3** tie **4** bind **5** blend, merge, order, unite **6** cement **7** arrange, compact **8** coalesce, organize **9** harmonize, integrate **10** articulate, centralize, symphonize, synthesize **11** concatenate, concentrate, consolidate, orchestrate, systematize

unilluminated **3** dim **4** dark, dusk **5** dusky, murky **6** gloomy **7** obscure **9** lightless, tenebrous **10** caliginous

unimaginable **4** rare **6** unique **7** unusual **8** singular, uncommon, unwonted **10** incredible, unknowable, unordinary **11** exceptional, incogitable, unthinkable **12** insupposable, unbelievable **13** extraordinary, inconceivable

unimaginative **4** dull **7** limited, literal, prosaic **10** pedestrian

unimpaired **4** free **5** fresh, sound, whole **6** entire, intact, unhurt **7** perfect **8** unbroken, unmarred **9** undamaged, uninjured

unimpassioned **4** calm, cold **5** sober, stoic **6** placid, steady, stolid **8** moderate, tranquil **9** impassive, temperate **10** impersonal, phlegmatic **11** cold-blooded, emotionless **12** matter-of-fact

unimpeachable **6** common, decent **8** adequate, all right **9** blameless, faultless, tolerable **10** acceptable, sufficient **12** satisfactory **13** unexceptional

unimportant **5** light, minor, petty, small **6** casual, little, paltry **7** trivial **9** small-beer **10** negligible, shoestring **13** insignificant

unindifferent **6** biased **7** colored, partial **8** one-sided, partisan **9** jaundiced, unneutral **10** prejudiced **11** tendentious **12** prepossessed

uninformed **7** unaware **8** ignorant **9** oblivious, unknowing, unwitting **10** unfamiliar **11** incognizant **12** inconversant, unacquainted, uninstructed

uninhabited **4** wild **5** empty **6** desert, vacant **8** deserted, desolate

uninhibited **3** lax **4** free, open **5** loose **8** uncurbed **9** audacious **10** boisterous, ungoverned, unhampered **11** untrammeled **12** unrestrained

uninitiate **4** tyro **7** amateur, dabbler **9** smatterer **10** dilettante **11** abecedarian

uninjured **5** sound, whole **6** entire, intact, unhurt **7** perfect **8** unbroken, unmarred **9** undamaged **10** unimpaired

uninspired **4** dull **6** stodgy **7** sterile **9** ponderous **10** uncreative, unoriginal **11** elephantine, heavy-footed, heavy-handed, noncreative, uninventive **13** unoriginative

uninstructed **4** rude **7** unaware **8** ignorant, untaught **9** benighted, oblivious, unknowing, untutored, unwitting **10** illiterate, uneducated, unfamiliar, uninformed, unlettered **11** empty-headed, incognizant, know-nothing **12** inconversant, unacquainted

unintelligent **4** dumb **5** brute **6** obtuse, simple, stupid, unwise **7** asinine, fatuous, foolish, vacuous, witless **8** ignorant, mindless **9** brainless, insensate, senseless **10** irrational, weak-headed, weak-minded

unintended see unintentional

unintentional **6** chance, random **9** causeless, haphazard, undevised, unplanned, unthought, unwitting **10** accidental, undesigned, unexpected, unforeseen, unpurposed, unthinking **11** inadvertent, purposeless, unlooked-for **13** unanticipated

uninterested **5** aloof **6** casual, remote **8** detached **9** incurious, uncurious, withdrawn **11** indifferent, unconcerned

uninteresting **3** dry **4** arid, drab, dull, flat **5** dusty, stale **6** boring, jejune, prolix, stupid **7** humdrum, insipid, tedious **8** bromidic, tiresome, weariful **9** colorless, dryasdust, wearisome **10** unexciting

uninterrupted **6** direct **7** endless, eternal, through **8** constant, straight, unending **9** ceaseless, continual, incessant, perpetual, unceasing **10** continuous **11** everlasting, unremitting **12** interminable

uninvited **7** unasked **8** unbidden, unsought **11** unrequested

union **4** bloc, club, seam **5** alloy, group, guild, hansa, hanse, joint, order **6** enosis, fusion, league, merger **7** amalgam, joining, melding, merging, society **8** alliance, congress, coupling, junction, juncture, marriage, mergence, sodality, together **9** anschluss, coalition **10** connection, federation, fellowship **11** association, brotherhood, coadunation, coalescence, combination, confederacy, unification 13 confederation, consolidation ***combining form:*** 3 zyg 4 gamy, zygo 6 gamous ***labor:*** 3 AFL, CIO, UAW 5 ILGWU ***of two gametes:*** 7 zygoses (plural), zygosis

Union Of Soviet Socialist Republics see U.S.S.R.

unique 3 odd, one 4 lone, only, rare, sole, solo 5 alone, queer 6 single 7 special, strange, unusual 8 peculiar, peerless, separate, singular, solitary, uncommon, unwonted 9 matchless, unequaled, unmatched, unrivaled 10 particular, unexampled, unordinary 11 exceptional, unparagoned 12 unparalleled, unrepeatable 13 extraordinary

uniqueness 4 mark, note 6 import, moment, oddity 7 oneness, unicity 10 notability, quaintness, singleness 11 curiousness, peculiarity, singularity, strangeness, unusualness 12 memorability, significance

___-Unis 5 Etats

unit 3 one 4 item 5 digit, group, monad, whole 6 entity 7 element, measure 10 individual ***administrative:*** 6 agency, bureau 8 district ***boy scout:*** 5 troop ***educational:*** 6 course ***military:*** (see at military) ***of acceleration:*** 3 gal ***of action:*** 7 episode ***of advertising space:*** 4 line 6 column 7 milline ***of a fire department:*** 9 battalion ***of an element:*** 4 atom 8 molecule ***of angular measure:*** 6 radian 7 centrad ***of area:*** 4 acre 6 morgen 7 hectare ***of astronomical distance:*** 6 parsec 9 light-year ***of brightness:*** 5 stilb 7 lambert ***of capacity:*** 2 cc, ml 4 gill, peck, pint 5 liter, litre, minim, ounce, quart 6 bushel, firkin, gallon 8 fluidram ***of computer information:*** 3 bit ***of conductance:*** 3 mho 7 siemens ***of distance:*** 4 mile 5 meter 7 furlong ***of electricity:*** 3 amp 4 volt, watt 6 ampere 7 coulomb ***of electromotive force:*** 4 volt ***of energy:*** 3 erg 5 joule 7 quantum 8 watthour ***of explosive force:*** 7 megaton ***of fineness:*** 5 carat, karat ***of fluidity:*** 3 rhe ***of force:*** 4 dyne 6 newton 7 poundal ***of frequency:*** 5 hertz 7 fresnel ***of grain:*** 5 sheaf 6 thrave ***of heat:*** 3 BTU 5 therm 7 calorie ***of illumination:*** 3 lux 4 phot ***of inductance:*** 5 gauss, henry ***of length:*** 3 mil 4 foot, inch, yard 5 fermi, meter 6 micron ***of loudness:*** 4 phon, sone 7 decibel ***of lumber:*** 9 board foot ***of magnetic flux:*** 5 weber 7 maxwell ***of magnetic induction:*** 5 tesla ***of magnetic intensity:*** 5 gamma 7 oersted ***of magnetomotive force:*** 7 gilbert ***of pressure:*** 3 bar 4 torr 5 barye 10 atmosphere ***of radiation:*** 3 rad 8 roentgen ***of radioactivity:*** 5 curie ***of resistance:*** 3 ohm ***of solar radiation:*** 7 langley ***of sound absorption:*** 5 sabin ***of speech:*** 4 word 6 toneme 7 phoneme 8 morpheme, syllable ***of speed:*** 3 CPS, MPH, RPM 4 knot ***of temperature:*** 6 degree, kelvin ***of time:*** 3 day 4 beat, bell, hour, week 5 month 6 minute, season, second 8 svedberg ***of viscosity:*** 5 poise ***of weight:*** 3 ton 4 dram, gram, tael 5 carat, grain, ounce, pound, stein, tonne 6 drachm, kantar 7 gigaton, kiloton, millier, quintal, scruple ***ancient Roman:*** 5 libra ***Asian:*** 5 Picul, tical 6 cattie, miskal ***British:*** 3 tod ***Chinese:*** 5 liang ***Hebrew:*** 5 gerah ***Indian:*** 3 ser 4 tola ***Muslim:*** 4 rotl ***Russian:*** 4 pood ***Turkish:*** 3 oka, oke ***of work:*** 3 erg 5 ergon, joule ***social:*** 4 clan 5 tribe 6 family 7 chapter

unite 3 add, mix, sew, tie, wed 4 ally, band, bind, bond, fuse, join, knit, link, weld 5 blend, graft, marry, merge, unify 6 adhere, adjoin, attach, cement, concur, couple, gather, league, mingle, relate, solder, splice 7 combine, conjoin, connect 8 assemble, coadjute, coalesce, compound, copulate, federate 9 affiliate, aggregate, associate, commingle, cooperate 10 amalgamate, federalize 11 concentrate, confederate, incorporate 12 conglutinate

United Arab Emirates 5 Ajman, Dubai 7 Sharjah 8 Abu Dhabi, Fujairah

United Kingdom ***capital:*** 6 London ***monetary unit:*** 5 pound ***part:*** 5 Wales 7 England 8 Scotland

unities, dramatic 4 time 5 place 6 action

unity 5 union 7 concord, harmony, oneness, rapport 8 identity, sodality, soleness, uniquity 9 agreement, communion, congruity 10 singleness, solidarity, uniformity, uniqueness 11 conformance, conjunction, singularity 12 selfsameness, singularness 13 individuality

universal 3 all 5 broad, total, whole 6 common, cosmic, entire, global 7 allover, general, generic 8 catholic, ecumenic, sweeping 9 extensive, planetary, unlimited, worldwide 10 ecumenical, ubiquitous 11 omnipresent 12 all-embracing, all-inclusive, all-pervading, cosmopolitan ***combining form:*** 3 omn 4 omni

universe 3 all 5 world 6 cosmos, nature, system 8 creation, megacosm 9 macrocosm 11 macrocosmos ***combining form:*** 4 cosm 5 cosmo

unjust 4 hard 5 cruel, wrong 6 unfair, wicked 7 unequal 8 improper, wrongful 9 dishonest, inequable 10 iniquitous 11 inequitable, unequitable, unrighteous

unjustifiable 5 undue 7 invalid 9 untena-

ble **10** inexpiable **11** inexcusable, unwarranted
unkempt **5** messy **6** frowsy, frowzy, shaggy, sloppy, unneat, untidy **7** ruffled, tousled **8** draggled, ill-kempt, scraggly, slipshod, slovenly, strubbly, uncombed **10** disarrayed, disheveled **12** unfastidious
unkind **3** bad, ill **4** mean, vile **5** cruel, harsh, rough, stern **6** severe **8** ungenial **9** inclement **10** ungenerous, ungracious **11** unfavorable
unknit **4** undo **5** ravel, relax, untie **7** unravel
unknowable **6** arcane, mystic **8** mystical, numinous **9** enigmatic, mysterial, unguessed **10** cabalistic, mysterious **11** inscrutable, ungraspable **12** impenetrable, incognizable, unexaminable, unfathomable, unimaginable **13** inconceivable
unknowing **7** unaware **8** ignorant **9** oblivious, unwitting **10** unfamiliar, uninformed **11** incognizant **12** inconversant, unacquainted, uninstructed
unknown **6** nobody, secret **7** obscure, strange, unfamed, unnoted **8** nameless **9** anonymous, incognito, unheard-of **10** unfamiliar, unrenowned **12** uncelebrated *Scottish:* **6** unkent
unlawful **7** bootleg, illegal, illicit, lawless **8** criminal, improper, wrongful **9** irregular, nefarious **10** contraband, flagitious, iniquitous **11** black-market, intolerable **12** illegitimate **13** exceptionable, objectionable
unlearned **7** natural **8** ignorant, untaught **9** inerudite, unbookish, untutored **10** illiterate, uneducated, unstudious **11** instinctive, unscholarly
unleash **4** free, vent **5** loose **7** release
unless **3** but **4** save **6** except, saving **7** without **9** excepting
unlettered see **uneducated**
unlike **7** distant, diverse, unequal, various **9** different, disparate, divergent, unsimilar **10** dissimilar
unlikely **5** unfit **7** dubious **8** doubtful **10** improbable, unsuitable **11** unpromising **12** questionable, unattractive
unlikeness **8** alterity, contrast **9** otherness **10** difference, divergence, divergency **11** discrepancy, distinction **12** disagreement, dissemblance **13** dissimilarity, dissimilitude, inconsistence
unlimited **4** vast **5** total **6** all-out **7** endless, full-out **8** infinite **9** boundless, full-blown, full-scale, unbounded, undefined, universal **10** indefinite, unconfined, unmeasured **11** measureless, untrammeled **12** immeasurable, totalitarian, unrestricted **13** indeterminate
unload **4** drop, dump, land **5** empty, unbox **6** debark, remove, unlade, unpack, unship, unstow **7** deliver, lighten, off-load, relieve, uncrate **8** jettison **9** disburden, discharge, disembark, liquidate, stevedore **11** disencumber
unloose, unloosen **4** undo **5** unfix **6** unbind **7** unrivet **8** unfasten **9** disengage
unloyal see **disloyal**
unlucky **3** bad, ill **4** dire **7** baleful, baneful, direful, doomful, fateful, hapless, ominous, unhappy **8** ill-fated, tragical, untoward **9** ill-boding, ill-omened **10** calamitous, disastrous, ill-starred **11** apocalyptic, cataclysmic, star-crossed, unfortunate **12** catastrophic, misfortunate
unman **4** undo **5** abase, crush, drain, unfit **7** degrade, deplete, exhaust, unnerve **8** castrate, enervate, paralyze, unstring **9** prostrate **10** disqualify, emasculate, impoverish
unmanageable **4** wild **6** unruly **7** restive **8** indocile **9** fractious **10** disorderly **11** indomitable, intractable **12** recalcitrant, ungovernable **13** undisciplined
unmanly **5** sissy **6** coward, craven, prissy **7** chicken, epicene, gutless **8** childish, cowardly, poltroon **9** pansified, sissified, spunkless **10** effeminate **11** lily-livered **12** Miss-Nancyish, poor-spirited **13** pusillanimous
unmannered **4** open, rude **5** frank, plain **6** candid **7** boorish, ill-bred, uncivil **8** impolite, man-to-man **10** ungracious, unmannerly **11** disgracious, openhearted, undisguised, unvarnished **12** discourteous, undissembled **13** disrespectful
unmarred **5** sound, whole **6** entire, intact, unhurt **7** perfect **8** pristine, unbroken
unmarried **4** lone, sole **5** unwed **6** single **10** spouseless
unmask **6** debunk, expose, reveal, show up, unveil **7** uncloak, undress **8** disclose, discover, unshroud
unmatchable **7** supreme **8** towering, ultimate **10** preeminent, surpassing **11** unequalable **12** incomparable, transcendent **13** unsurpassable
unmatched **3** odd **4** only **5** alone **6** unique **8** peerless, unpaired **9** matchless, unequaled, unrivaled **11** unparagoned **12** unparalleled
unmerciful **5** cruel **8** pitiless, ruthless **9** merciless, unpitying **10** relentless
unmethodical **7** cursory, erratic **9** desultory
unmindful **7** unaware **8** careless, heedless **9** forgetful, negligent, oblivious, unwitting **10** neglectful **11** inattentive
unmistakable **4** flat, open **5** clear, frank, plain **6** patent **7** evident, express **8** apparent, distinct, manifest, palpable, univocal
unmitigated **4** mere, pure, rank **5** gross,

sheer, utter **6** arrant, damned, simple **7** perfect, unmixed **8** absolute, clearcut, complete, outright **9** out-and-out, unalloyed, undiluted **10** unmodified **11** straight-out, unqualified **13** thoroughgoing, unadulterated

unmixed **4** deep, mere, neat, pure **5** plain, sheer, utter **6** simple **7** perfect, sincere **8** absolute, straight **9** unalloyed, undiluted **11** unmitigated, unqualified **13** unadulterated

unmodern **3** old **5** dated, passé **7** antique, archaic, old-time, vintage **9** out-of-date **10** antiquated, oldfangled **12** old-fashioned

unmodifiable **5** fixed **8** constant, straight **9** immovable, immutable, unmovable **10** inflexible, invariable **11** inalterable, unalterable **12** unchangeable

unmovable see **immovable**

unmoved **4** calm, cool, firm **5** stony **6** serene **7** adamant **8** obdurate, stubborn, unshaken **9** apathetic, impassive

unmoving **5** inert **6** static **8** immobile, stagnant **10** stationary

unnamed **8** nameless **9** anonymous **10** innominate **12** undesignated

unnatural **6** off-key **7** deviant, uncanny **8** abnormal **9** anomalous, divergent, irregular, unregular **10** superhuman **11** supernormal, supranormal **13** superordinary

unneat **5** messy **6** sloppy, untidy **7** unkempt **8** careless, ill-kempt, slipshod, slovenly, uncombed **12** unfastidious

unnecessary **6** excess, lavish **7** profuse, surplus **8** needless, prodigal **9** redundant **10** gratuitous, unrequired **11** inessential, superfluous, uncalled-for, unessential

unneeded see **unnecessary**

unnerve **3** sap **5** unman, upset **6** weaken **7** agitate, perturb **8** bewilder, castrate, confound, distract, enervate, enfeeble, unstring **9** undermine **10** emasculate

unneutral **6** biased, warped **7** colored, partial **8** one-sided, partisan **9** jaundiced **10** prejudiced **11** tendentious **12** prepossessed

unnoted **7** obscure, unfamed, unknown **8** nameless **9** unheard-of **10** unobserved, unremarked, unrenowned **12** uncelebrated, unconsidered

unobservant **9** unheeding **10** unnoticing, unwatchful **11** inattentive **12** unperceiving

unobserving see **unobservant**

unobstructed **4** open **5** clear **8** unclosed

unobtrusive **5** quiet, tasty **7** subdued **8** tasteful **10** restrained

unoccupied **4** free, idle **5** empty **10** unemployed

unofficial **8** informal **9** irregular **13** unceremonious

unorganized **7** muddled **8** inchoate **10** disjointed, disordered, incoherent, incohesive **11** unconnected **12** disconnected, uncontinuous **13** discontinuous

unoriginal **3** dry **4** arid, dull **5** staid **6** barren, stodgy, stuffy **7** prosaic, sterile, unfired **10** uncreative, uninspired **11** noncreative, uninventive

unornamented **3** dry **5** plain **6** simple **9** unadorned **11** inelaborate, unelaborate, ungarnished **12** unbeautified **13** unembellished, unembroidered

unorthodox **9** dissident, heretical, sectarian **10** schismatic **13** nonconformist

unorthodoxy **6** heresy, schism **7** dissent **9** disbelief **10** dissidence **13** nonconformism, nonconformity

unpaid **3** due **5** owing **6** mature **7** overdue, payable **8** freewill, wageless **9** unsettled, voluntary, volunteer **10** gratuitous **11** outstanding **13** uncompensated, unrecompensed, unremunerated

unpalatable **4** flat, thin, weak **5** washy **6** bitter, watery **7** galling, insipid, painful **8** grievous, nauseous, unsavory **9** loathsome, savorless, sickening, tasteless **10** afflictive, flavorless **11** distasteful, ill-flavored **12** unappetizing

unparalleled **5** alone **6** unique **8** peerless **9** matchless, unequaled, unmatched, unrivaled

unperceiving see **unobservant**

unpermissive **5** rigid **6** strict **8** rigorist, rigorous **9** draconian, stringent **10** ironhanded

unphysical **8** bodiless **9** asomatous **10** discarnate, immaterial, unembodied **11** disembodied, incorporeal, nonmaterial

unpierceable **10** impervious **11** impregnable **12** impenetrable

unpitying **9** merciless **10** unmerciful

unplanned **6** random **7** aimless, unaimed **9** desultory, haphazard, hit-or-miss, undevised, unthought **10** designless, undesigned, unintended, unpurposed **11** inadvertent, purposeless **12** unconsidered **13** unintentional

unpleasant **3** bad **4** sour **5** seamy **6** rotten **7** unhappy **11** displeasing, distasteful **12** disagreeable ***combining form:*** **3** cac **4** caco

unpliable **6** mulish **8** perverse, stubborn **9** obstinate, pigheaded **10** bullheaded, headstrong, self-willed **12** pertinacious

unplug **3** ope **4** open **6** uncork **7** unblock **10** disconnect

unpolished **4** rude **5** crude, rough **6** unhewn **7** boorish, ill-bred, incivil, loutish, lowbred, uncivil **8** churlish, cloddish, impolite, unformed, unworked 9 roughhewn, undressed, unrefined 10 uncultured, unfinished, ungracious 11 clodhopping, disgracious, ill-mannered, uncivilized, unfashioned 12 discourteous 13 disrespectful

unpracticed 3 raw 5 fresh, green 6 callow 7 untried 8 untested, unversed 13 inexperienced

unpredictable 4 iffy 6 chancy 7 erratic 9 fluctuant, uncertain, whimsical 10 capricious

unprejudiced 4 fair, just 5 equal 8 unbiased 9 equitable, impartial, objective, uncolored 13 dispassionate

unpressed 7 wrinkly

unpretentious 5 plain 6 modest, simple 10 unaffected 11 inelaborate, unelaborate, ungarnished 12 unbeautified 13 unembellished

unpretty 5 plain 6 homely 8 uncomely 10 unalluring, unhandsome 11 unbeauteous, unbeautiful 12 unattractive

unprincipled 5 venal 7 corrupt, crooked 9 abandoned, dishonest, dissolute, mercenary, reprobate, unethical 10 licentious, praetorian, profligate 12 unscrupulous

unproductive 4 vain 6 barren, futile 7 useless 8 impotent, infecund 9 fruitless, infertile, unbearing, unfertile 10 unavailing 11 ineffectual, unavailable 12 hardscrabble

unprofitable 4 idle, vain 7 useless

unprogressive 8 backward, ignorant 9 benighted 10 behindhand 11 undeveloped 13 unenlightened

unpropitious 4 dire 7 adverse, baleful, baneful, counter, fateful, ominous, unlucky 9 ill-boding, ill-omened 11 threatening 12 antagonistic

unprosperous 3 low 4 poor 5 broke, needy 8 indigent 9 destitute, penurious 11 fortuneless, impecunious 12 impoverished

unprotected 6 unsafe 8 helpless, insecure 9 unguarded 10 undefended, unshielded 11 defenseless, unsheltered

unproved 7 untried 8 untested

unpunctual 4 late 5 lated, tardy 7 belated, overdue 10 behindhand

unqualified 4 firm, pure, rank, sure 5 clear, gross, sheer, unfit, utter 6 entire, simple, steady 7 abiding, blasted, blessed, express, perfect, unmixed 8 absolute, complete, enduring, explicit, infernal, unfitted 9 incapable, out-and-out, steadfast, unalloyed, undiluted, unlimited, unskilled 10 confounded, ineligible, unequipped, unreserved, unsuitable 11 incompetent, unfaltering, unmitigated 12 never-failing, wholehearted 13 unadulterated, unconditional

unquenchable 9 insatiate, unsatiate 10 insatiable

unquestionable 4 flat, real, true, very 7 certain, genuine 8 bona fide, positive 9 authentic, downright, undoubted, up-and-down 10 sure-enough 11 established, well-founded 12 well-grounded

unquestioning 4 firm, sure 5 fixed 6 steady 7 abiding 8 enduring, unshaken 9 steadfast 10 unshakable 12 never-failing

unravel 5 break, solve 6 unfold, unknit 7 dope out, resolve, unsnarl 8 decipher, dissolve, unriddle, untangle 9 extricate, figure out, puzzle out 11 disentangle

unreadable 9 illegible

unreal 7 fictive 8 chimeric, fanciful, illusory 9 fantastic, fictional, imaginary 10 chimerical, fictitious 12 suppositious *combining form:* 5 pseud 6 pseudo

unrealistic 8 fanciful 10 ivory-tower 11 impractical, unpractical 12 ivory-towered 13 ivory-towerish

unreasonable 3 mad 5 loose, undue 7 invalid 8 improper, overmuch, unlawful, wrongful 9 arbitrary, excessive, illogical, sophistic 10 fallacious, immoderate, inordinate, irrational, peremptory, reasonless, unrightful 11 incongruous, nonrational, unwarranted

unreasoned 3 mad 7 invalid 9 illogical, sophistic 10 fallacious, irrational, reasonless 11 nonrational

unrecompensed 6 unpaid 13 uncompensated

unrefined 3 raw 4 rude 5 crass, crude, gross, rough 6 coarse, impure, native, vulgar 7 boorish, ill-bred, loutish, lowbred, natural, uncouth 8 churlish, cloddish, ungraded, unsorted 9 inelegant, roughcast, roughhewn, run-of-mine, undressed 10 uncultured, unpolished 11 clodhopping, uncivilized, unprocessed

unreflective 8 careless, feckless, heedless, uncaring 9 unheeding 10 unthinking 11 inadvertent, thoughtless

unrehearsed 7 offhand 9 extempore, impromptu, unstudied 10 improvised 11 extemporary

unrelated 8 discrete, separate 9 disjoined

unrelenting 4 grim 6 mortal 8 ruthless 9 merciless 10 implacable, ironfisted, unyielding 11 unflinching 12 unappeasable

unreliable 5 false, slick 6 fickle, shifty, tricky, unsafe, unsure, untrue 7 dubious, inexact 8 slippery, untrusty 9 faithless, trustless, unassured 10 fly-by-night, inaccurate, inconstant, perfidious, unfaithful 11 vacillating 12 falsehearted 13 untrustworthy

unreligious 7 godless

unremarkable 5 plain, usual 7 routine 8 everyday, ordinary, workaday 9 plain Jane, quotidian

unremitting 7 endless 8 constant, unending 9 ceaseless, continual, perpetual, unceasing 12 interminable 13 uninterrupted
unremorseful 7 unsorry 10 impenitent, regretless, uncontrite
unremunerated 6 unpaid
unrenowned 7 obscure, unfamed, unknown, unnoted 8 nameless 9 unheard-of 12 uncelebrated
unrepentant 7 unsorry 10 impenitent, regretless, uncontrite 11 remorseless
unrepresentative 7 deviant 8 aberrant, abnormal, atypical 9 anomalous, untypical 11 heteroclite
unrequested 7 unasked 8 unbidden, unsought 9 uninvited
unrequired 8 needless, unneeded 9 omissible, unneedful 11 dispensable, inessential, uncalled-for, unessential, unnecessary 12 nonessential
unreserved 4 open 5 frank, plain 6 breezy, candid, casual, dégagé 7 relaxed, unfussy 8 informal, outgoing, outright 9 easygoing, expansive 11 low-pressure, openhearted, unconcealed, undisguised, unvarnished 12 undissembled 13 demonstrative, unconstrained
unresolved 8 hesitant, wavering 9 faltering, uncertain 10 hesitating, indecisive, irresolute, undecisive 11 vacillating 12 shilly-shally
unrespectable 5 shady 6 shabby, shoddy 8 shameful 10 inglorious 11 disgraceful, ignominious
unresponsive 4 cold 6 frigid 9 inhibited 10 insentient, undersexed 11 insensitive, passionless 13 insusceptible, unimpressible, unsusceptible
unresponsiveness 6 apathy, phlegm 8 stoicism 9 stolidity 11 impassivity 13 insensibility
unrest 5 chaos 6 tumult 7 ailment, anarchy, ferment, turmoil, unquiet 8 disorder, disquiet, upheaval 9 agitation, commotion, confusion 10 convulsion, inquietude, turbulence 11 disquietude, restiveness 13 Sturm und Drang
unrestrained 4 free, open 5 bluff, blunt, frank, loose 6 candid 7 brusque, rampant 8 outgoing, reinless, uncurbed 9 audacious, excessive, expansive 10 forthright, immoderate, inordinate, ungoverned, unhampered, untempered 11 intemperate, plainspoken, uninhibited, untrammeled 13 demonstrative, overindulgent
unrestraint 4 ease 7 abandon 11 naturalness, spontaneity 13 impulsiveness
unrestricted 4 free, open 6 public 10 accessible
unrighteous 6 unfair, unjust 9 inequable 11 inequitable, unequitable
unripe 5 green, young 6 callow, infant 8 immature, juvenile, youthful 9 unfledged
unrivaled 4 only 5 alone 6 unique 8 peerless 9 matchless, unmatched 11 unparagoned 12 unparalleled
unrobe see unclothe
unroll 6 extend, uncoil, unfurl, unwind 7 open out
unromantic 4 cool, hard 5 sober 9 practical, pragmatic, realistic 10 hard-boiled, hardheaded 11 down-to-earth 12 matter-of-fact 13 unsentimental
unruffled 4 calm, cool 6 serene 8 composed, tranquil 9 collected 10 nonchalant 11 unflappable 13 imperturbable
unruly 4 hard, wild 5 rowdy, tough 7 froward, naughty, raffish, raucous, wayward 8 contrary, indocile, perverse, rowdyish, untoward 9 fractious, obstinate, ruffianly, termagant, turbulent 10 boisterous, disorderly, rampageous, rebellious, rowdy-dowdy, tumultuous 11 disobedient, indomitable, intractable, rumbustious 12 contumacious, incorrigible, obstreperous, rambunctious, recalcitrant, ungovernable, unmanageable 13 insubordinate, undisciplined
unsacred 3 lay 7 profane, secular 8 temporal
unsafe 5 risky, shaky 6 chancy 7 erratic, tottery, unsound 8 insecure, perilous, unstable 9 dangerous, hazardous, unassured, uncertain 10 jeopardous, unreliable 12 undependable 13 untrustworthy
unsaid 5 tacit 7 implied 8 implicit, inferred, nonvocal, unspoken, wordless 9 unuttered 10 undeclared, understood 11 unexpressed
unsalutary 7 noisome, noxious 9 unhealthy 11 unhealthful, unwholesome 12 insalubrious
unsatisfactory 3 bad, bum 4 poor, punk 5 amiss, wrong 6 rotten
unsatisfiable 9 insatiate 10 quenchless
unsavory 4 flat 7 insipid 9 tasteless 10 flavorless 11 distasteful, ill-flavored, unpalatable 12 unappetizing
unsay 6 abjure, recall, recant 7 retract 8 forswear, palinode, take back, withdraw
unscathed 4 safe 8 unharmed
unscented 8 odorless
unschooled 5 naive 6 simple 7 artless, natural 8 ignorant, untaught 9 benighted, ingenuous, unstudied, untutored 10 illiterate, unaffected, uneducated, unlettered 11 emptyheaded, know-nothing 12 unartificial, uninstructed
unscramble 5 untie 7 untwine 8 untangle 9 extricate 10 disembroil, disentwine,

unentangle 11 disencumber, disentangle 12 disembarrass
unscrupulous 5 shady, venal 6 crafty 7 corrupt, crooked 8 improper, scheming, sinister, unseemly, wrongful 9 deceitful, dishonest, mercenary, underhand, unethical 10 praetorian 12 questionable, unprincipled
unseasonable 5 inapt, inept, unapt, undue 8 ill-timed, improper, mistimed, untimely 10 malapropos, unbecoming 11 inopportune, unfortunate 12 inauspicious, inconvenient, infelicitous 13 inappropriate
unseasoned 3 raw 5 fresh, green, young 6 callow 7 untried 8 unversed 9 unfleshed 11 unpracticed 13 inexperienced
unseat 5 pitch, throw 6 depose, remove 7 buck off, unhorse 8 dethrone
unseemliness 9 indecorum 10 inelegance 11 impropriety
unseemly 5 crude, inapt, inept, rough, rowdy, unapt 6 coarse 7 raffish, ungodly 8 ill-timed, improper, indecent, untoward 9 inelegant, ruffianly, unrefined 10 indecorous, indelicate, malapropos, malodorous, unbecoming, undecorous, unsuitable 11 unbefitting 13 inappropriate
unseen 9 invisible
unsentimental see **unromantic**
unserviceable 7 useless 11 impractical 12 unfunctional 13 nonfunctional
unsettle 4 turn 5 upset 6 bother, flurry, jumble, sicken 7 agitate, derange, disturb, fluster, perturb, rummage, trouble, unhinge 8 disarray, disorder, disquiet 9 incommode 10 disarrange, discommode, discompose 11 disorganize
unsettled 3 due 4 back, open 5 fluid 6 mature, mobile, queasy, remote, uneasy, unpaid 7 clouded, dubious, mutable, overdue, payable, pendent, pending, protean, unclear, unquiet 8 doubtful, frontier, restless, unstable, unsteady, variable, weathery 9 changeful, dubitable, uncertain, undecided, unrestful 10 changeable, indecisive, unpeaceful, untranquil 11 outstanding, problematic 12 undetermined
unsex 3 fix 4 geld 5 alter 6 change, neuter 8 castrate, mutilate 9 sterilize 11 desexualize
unshackle 4 free 5 loose 6 loosen, unbind 7 manumit, release, unchain 8 liberate 9 discharge 10 emancipate
unshakable 4 firm, sure 5 fixed 6 steady 7 abiding 9 steadfast 10 unwavering 11 unfaltering 12 never-failing 13 unquestioning
unshaped 8 formless, inchoate, unformed 9 amorphous
unshared 4 sole 6 single 9 exclusive
unship 6 unlade, unload, unstow 7 offload 9 disburden, discharge
unshod 8 barefoot, shoeless 10 unsandaled
unshroud 6 debunk, expose, show up, unmask 7 uncloak, undress 8 discover
unshut 3 ope 4 open, undo 6 unstop 7 unblock, unclose
unsightly 4 drab, dull, ugly 7 hideous 8 uncomely 9 ill-shaped, unshapely 10 ill-favored, ill-looking, lackluster, unesthetic 11 unbeautiful
unsimilar 6 unlike 7 distant, diverse, unalike, unequal, various 9 different, disparate, divergent
unskilled 5 green, inept 7 amateur, jackleg 10 amateurish 12 dilettantish, dilettantist 13 unworkmanlike
unskillful 5 inapt, inept, unapt 6 clumsy, gauche 7 awkward, inadept, unhandy, unready 8 inexpert, unexpert, unfacile, unfitted 9 butcherly, incapable 11 incompetent, inefficient, undexterous, unqualified 12 unproficient 13 unworkmanlike
unsleeping 5 alert 7 wakeful 8 open-eyed, vigilant, watchful 9 wide-awake
unsmooth 5 harsh, rough 6 craggy, jagged, ruffly, rugged, uneven 7 scraggy, unlevel 8 asperous, scabrous
unsnarl see **untangle**
unsociable 3 shy 4 cool 5 aloof, timid 6 offish, remote, shut-in 7 distant, prickly 8 brooding, reserved, solitary, standoff 9 diffident, exclusive, secretive, sensitive, unbending, withdrawn 11 indifferent, standoffish 12 inaccessible
unsoiled 5 clean 7 cleanly 8 spotless 9 taintless, unsullied 10 immaculate
unsophisticated 5 crude, green, naive 6 callow, simple 7 artless, genuine, natural, uncouth 9 ingenuous, untutored, unworldly 10 unaffected, unschooled 12 unartificial
unsorted 3 raw 5 crude, mixed 6 impure, motley, native, varied 8 ungraded 9 unrefined 11 promiscuous 12 multifarious 13 heterogeneous, miscellaneous
unsought 7 unasked 8 unbidden, unwanted, unwished 9 undesired, uninvited, unwelcome 11 unrequested
unsound 3 mad 4 daft, weak 5 batty, false, frail, hairy, risky, wrong 6 chancy, crazed, faulty, flawed, flimsy, infirm, insane, untrue, weakly, wicked 7 cracked, damaged, fragile, lunatic 8 decrepit, demented, deranged, perilous, specious 9 dangerous, erroneous, hazardous, imperfect, incorrect, unhealthy 10 inaccurate, jeopardous, unbalanced 11 treacherous 13 insubstantial, unsubstantial *mentally:* 6 insane
unsparing 4 free 6 severe 7 liberal

8 generous, handsome 9 bounteous, bountiful 10 freehanded, munificent, openhanded

unspeakable 6 odious 7 hateful 9 atrocious, loathsome, obnoxious, offensive, repellent, repugnant, repulsive, revolting 10 disgusting, outrageous 11 distasteful 13 inexpressible, unexpressible

unspoiled 6 intact, virgin 8 pristine, untapped, virginal 9 undefiled, untouched

unspoken 4 mute 5 tacit 6 hinted, silent, unsaid 7 implied 8 implicit, inferred, unstated, unvoiced, wordless 9 intimated, suggested, unuttered 10 undeclared, understood 11 unexpressed

unstable 4 weak 5 fluid, rocky, shaky 6 dickey, fickle, mobile, moving, shifty, tricky, unsure, wobbly 7 buoyant, dubious, elastic, protean, suspect 8 doubtful, freakish, insecure, rootless, slippery, ticklish, volatile, wavering, weathery 9 ambiguous, changeful, fluctuant, mercurial, resilient, uncertain, unsettled 10 borderline, capricious, inconstant, lubricious, precarious 11 vacillating 12 effervescent 13 temperamental

unsteady 5 fluid, rocky, tippy 6 jiggly, mobile, moving, shifty, wobbly 7 movable, mutable, protean, rickety, tottery 8 slippery, staggery, tittuppy, variable, weathery 9 changeful, uncertain, unsettled 10 changeable, inconstant *British:* 5 wonky

unsteel 5 unarm 6 disarm 7 win over

unstop 3 ope 4 open, undo 6 uncork, unplug, unshut 7 unblock, unclose

unstow 6 unlade, unload, unship 7 offload 9 disburden, discharge

unstrengthen 3 sap 5 blunt 6 weaken 7 cripple, disable, unbrace 8 enfeeble 9 attenuate, undermine 10 debilitate

unstudied 5 naive 6 simple 7 artless, natural, offhand 8 unversed 9 extempore, impromptu, ingenuous, unlearned, untutored 10 improvised, unaffected, unschooled 11 extemporary, spontaneous, unrehearsed 12 unartificial

unstylish 5 dowdy, tacky 6 démodé, frumpy, stodgy 8 frumpish, outmoded 9 out-of-date

unsubstantial 4 thin, weak 5 frail, shaky 6 feeble, flimsy, infirm, weakly 7 fragile, tenuous, unsound 8 bodiless, decrepit, insecure 9 spiritual 10 immaterial, improbable, incredible, unembodied, unphysical 11 implausible, incorporeal, nonmaterial, nonphysical 12 metaphysical, unbelievable, unconvincing, undependable 13 inconceivable

unsuccess 4 bomb, flop 6 defeat 7 failure, reverse, setback

unsuitable 5 inapt, inept, undue, unfit 6 unmeet 7 unhappy 8 ill-timed, improper, unfitted, untimely 9 ill-suited 10 ill-adapted, unbecoming 11 unbefitting 13 inappropriate

unsuited 5 inapt, unfit 6 unmeet 8 unfitted 10 ill-adapted, inadequate 12 inadmissible, unacceptable 13 disappointing, inappropriate, objectionable

unsullied 4 pure 5 clean 6 chaste, decent, modest 7 cleanly 8 spotless, unsoiled 9 stainless, taintless, undefiled 10 immaculate 11 unblemished

unsure 4 open, weak 5 shaky 6 dickey, wobbly 7 dubious, unclear 8 doubtful, insecure, rootless, unstable, untrusty, wavering 9 fluctuant, trustless, unassured, uncertain, undecided 10 borderline, indecisive, suspicious, unreliable 11 problematic, unconfident, vacillating 12 questionable, undependable 13 untrustworthy

unsurpassable 7 supreme 8 towering, ultimate 10 preeminent 12 transcendent

unsusceptible 9 impassive 10 insentient 11 insensitive 12 unresponsive

unsuspecting 6 unwary 9 credulous

unsuspicious see unsuspecting

unswayable 5 rigid 8 obdurate 10 inflexible, relentless, unyielding 11 uncompliant 12 single-minded

unswerving see unfaltering

unsymmetrical 6 uneven 7 unequal 8 lopsided 9 irregular 10 off-balance 12 overbalanced

unsympathetic 4 cold, cool 6 frigid 7 callous 8 aversive, kindless, lukewarm, obdurate, ungenial 9 heartless, repellent, repugnant, unfeeling, unlikable 10 dislikable, hard-boiled, unpleasant, unpleasing 11 coldhearted, displeasing, halfhearted, hardhearted, indifferent, uncongenial, unemotional 12 stonyhearted 13 disinterested

untactful 5 brash 9 impolitic, maladroit, unpolitic 12 undiplomatic

untamed 4 wild 5 feral 9 unsubdued

untangle 7 unsnarl, untwine, untwist 9 discumber, extricate 10 disembroil, disentwine, unscramble 11 disencumber 12 disembarrass

untapped 6 virgin 8 virginal 9 unspoiled, untouched

untaught 8 ignorant 9 benighted, untutored 10 illiterate, uneducated, unlettered, unschooled 11 empty-headed, know-nothing 12 uninstructed

untempered 9 excessive 10 immoderate, inordinate 12 unrestrained 13 overindulgent

untended 7 run-down 9 neglected 10 uncared-for

Unter den ___ 6 Linden

untested 7 untried 8 unproved 11 unpracticed
unthankful 9 thankless 10 ungrateful
unthinkable 4 rare 6 unique 7 unusual 8 singular, uncommon, unwonted 10 incredible, unordinary 11 exceptional 13 extraordinary
unthinking 8 careless, feckless, heedless, uncaring 9 unheeding 11 inadvertent, thoughtless 12 irreflective, unreflective
unthorough 5 messy 6 botchy, sloppy, untidy 8 careless, slapdash, slipshod, slovenly
unthought 9 undevised, unplanned 10 undesigned, unintended, unpurposed 11 inadvertent 13 unintentional
unthrift 5 waste 6 lavish, waster 7 spender, wastrel 8 prodigal, squander 9 overdoing 10 high roller, lavishness, profligate, squanderer 11 improvident, prodigality, scattergood 12 extravagance, extravagancy, wastefulness
unthrifty 6 lavish 8 prodigal, wasteful 10 thriftless 11 extravagant, improvident
untidy 5 messy 6 botchy, sloppy, unneat 7 unkempt 8 careless, ill-kempt, slapdash, slipshod, slovenly, uncombed 10 disheveled, unthorough 12 unfastidious
untie 6 loosen, unknot, unlace, unlash 8 unstring 9 extricate 10 disembroil, disentwine, unentangle, unscramble 11 disencumber, disentangle 12 disembarrass
untighten 3 lax 4 ease 5 loose, relax, slack 6 loosen 7 ease off, slacken
until 2 to 4 till, up to 5 since 6 before 7 prior to 11 in advance of
untimely 4 soon 5 early, inapt, unapt, undue 8 ill-timed, improper, mistimed, oversoon, previous 9 overearly, premature 10 malapropos, unsuitable 11 ill-seasoned, inopportune 12 intempestive, unseasonable 13 inappropriate
untiring 8 tireless 9 weariless 10 unflagging, unwearying 11 unweariable 13 indefatigable, inexhaustible
untold 4 huge, vast 6 mighty 7 immense, mammoth, titanic 8 enormous, gigantic 9 countless, monstrous, uncounted, unrelated 10 innumerous, numberless, prodigious, unnumbered 11 innumerable, uncountable 12 unnumberable
untouchable 5 leper 6 pariah 7 Ishmael, outcast 8 castaway, déclassé, derelict, outcaste, outsider 10 Ishmaelite 11 offscouring
untouched 4 pure 5 sound, whole 6 entire, intact, virgin 7 perfect 8 flawless, pristine, unmarred, untapped, virginal 9 undamaged, unspoiled 11 unblemished
untoward 4 wild 5 rough 6 unruly 7 hapless, ungodly, unhappy, unlucky 8 ill-fated, improper, indecent, indocile, luckless, unseemly 9 fractious 10 ill-starred, indecorous, indelicate, unbecoming, undecorous 11 intractable, star-crossed, unfortunate 12 misfortunate, recalcitrant, ungovernable, unmanageable 13 undisciplined
untrained see **unskilled**
untrammeled 8 uncurbed 9 audacious 10 ungoverned, unhampered 11 uninhibited 12 unrestrained
untried 3 raw 5 fresh, green 6 callow, unripe 8 immature, unproved, untested, unversed 9 half-baked 10 unseasoned 11 unpracticed 12 unconversant 13 inexperienced
untroubled 4 calm 5 quiet, still 6 hushed, placid, stilly 7 halcyon
untroublesome 4 easy 5 light, royal 6 facile, simple, smooth 10 effortless
untrue 5 false, wrong 7 inexact, unloyal, unsound 8 disloyal, forsworn, perjured, recreant, specious 9 erroneous, faithless, imprecise, incorrect, unprecise 10 inaccurate, perfidious, traitorous, unfaithful 11 treacherous ***combining form:*** 5 pseud 6 pseudo
untruism 3 fib, lie 4 tale 5 story 6 canard 7 bouncer 9 falsehood 13 prevarication
untrustworthy 6 unsafe, unsure 7 dubious 9 unassured 10 fly-by-night, unreliable 12 questionable, undependable
untruth 3 fib, lie 4 tale 5 error, story 6 canard 7 fallacy, falsity 9 falsehood, falseness 13 erroneousness, prevarication
untruthful 5 false, lying, wrong 6 shifty 7 knavish, roguish 8 delusive, delusory, unhonest 9 deceitful, deceptive, dishonest, incorrect 10 inaccurate, mendacious, misleading
untruthfulness 7 fibbery 9 falsehood, mendacity 10 unveracity
untune 5 upset 6 bother, flurry 7 agitate, disturb, fluster, perturb, unhinge 8 disquiet 10 discompose
untutored see **unschooled**
untwine see **untangle**
untwist see **untangle**
untypical see **unusual**
unusable 7 useless 11 impractical 12 unfunctional 13 nonfunctional
unused 4 idle 6 vacant
unusual 3 odd 4 rare 6 freaky, quaint, unique 7 bizarre, curious, deviant, oddball, strange 8 aberrant, abnormal, freakish, peculiar, singular, uncommon, unwonted 9 anomalous, eccentric, untypical 10 outlandish, unordinary 11 exceptional, unthinkable 12 unimaginable 13 extraordinary ***combining form:*** 4 anom 5 anomo

unusually 5 extra 6 rarely 8 uncommon 9 extremely 10 uncommonly
unutterable 5 awful 7 awesome 8 wondrous 9 marvelous, wonderful 10 incredible, prodigious 13 inexpressible, unexpressible
unuttered see **unspoken**
unvaried 5 alike 7 uniform 10 monotonous
unvarnished see **undisguised**
unvarying see **unchanging**
unveil see **uncover**
unversed 3 raw 5 fresh, green 6 callow 7 untried 9 unfleshed 10 unseasoned 11 unpracticed 12 unconversant 13 inexperienced
unvigilant 6 unwary 7 unalert 9 unguarded 10 incautious, unwatchful
unvital 5 petty 6 paltry, peanut 7 trivial 8 piddling, trifling 12 inconsequent
unvoiced see **unspoken**
unwanted see **unwelcome**
unwarranted 5 undue 8 baseless 9 unfounded 10 bottomless, gratuitous, groundless, ungrounded 11 uncalled-for 12 unreasonable 13 unjustifiable
unwary 4 rash 5 brash, hasty 7 unalert 8 reckless 9 credulous, hotheaded, unadvised, unguarded 10 ill-advised, incautious, unvigilant 11 thoughtless 12 unsuspecting, unsuspicious 13 inconsiderate
unwashed 3 low, mob 4 base, mean, scum 5 dregs, lowly, trash 6 humble, masses, rabble 7 ignoble, lowborn 8 baseborn, canaille, plebeian, riffraff 10 unennobled 11 proletariat
unwasteful 5 canny, chary 6 frugal, saving 7 sparing, thrifty 9 provident, stewardly 10 economical
unwatchful 7 unalert 9 unguarded, unheeding 10 incautious, unnoticing, unvigilant 11 inattentive, inobservant, unobservant, unobserving 12 unperceiving
unwatered 3 dry 4 arid, sere 7 bone-dry, thirsty 8 droughty 9 waterless 12 moistureless
unwavering see **unfaltering**
unwearying 6 steady 8 constant, tireless, untiring 9 unceasing, weariless 10 unflagging 12 interminable 13 indefatigable, inexhaustible
unwed see **unmarried**
unwelcome 7 unasked 8 unsought, unwanted, unwished 9 obnoxious, repellent, undesired 10 ill-favored, unpleasant, unpleasing 11 distasteful, undesirable 12 inadmissible, unacceptable 13 exceptionable, objectionable
unwell 3 ill, low 4 mean, sick 5 frail, rocky, shaky 6 ailing, feeble, infirm, offish, poorly, queasy, sickly, weakly, wobbly 7 underly 8 off-color, qualmish 9 squeamish 10 indisposed
unwholesome 4 foul 6 sickly 7 baneful, harmful, hideous, hurtful, noxious, obscene 8 horrible 9 injurious, offensive, repellent, repulsive, unhealthy 10 disgusting, insalutary, pernicious, unsalutary 11 deleterious, detrimental, unhealthful 12 insalubrious
unwieldy 5 bulky, heavy 6 clumsy 7 awkward, massive, onerous, unhandy 8 cumbrous 9 lumbering, ponderous 10 burdensome, cumbersome 11 encumbering 12 inconvenient, unmanageable
unwilling 4 loth 5 loath 6 afraid, averse 7 uneager 8 backward, hesitant 9 reluctant 10 indisposed 11 disinclined
unwind 5 relax, unlax 6 unbend, unreel, unroll 7 ease off 8 loosen up
unwise 5 inane, inept, naive 7 fatuous, foolish, unsound, witless 8 childish, immature 9 ill-judged, impolitic, imprudent, misguided, senseless 10 ill-advised, indiscreet 11 impractical, injudicious, thoughtless, undesirable, unfortunate 13 inappropriate, unintelligent
unwished see **unwelcome**
unwishful 4 loth 5 loath 6 afraid, averse 7 uneager 8 backward, hesitant 9 reluctant 10 indisposed 11 disinclined
unwitting 7 unaware 8 ignorant 9 forgetful, oblivious, unknowing, unmindful 10 unfamiliar, uninformed 11 incognizant 12 inconversant, unacquainted, uninstructed
unwitty 5 silly 6 simple 7 asinine, fatuous, foolish, witless 8 mindless 9 brainless 10 weak-headed, weak-minded
unwonted 4 rare 6 unique 7 unusual 8 singular, uncommon 10 unordinary 11 exceptional, unthinkable 12 unimaginable 13 extraordinary
unworkable 7 useless 10 impossible, infeasible, unfeasible 11 impractical 12 unfunctional 13 nonfunctional
unworked 4 rude 5 crude, rough 6 unhewn 8 unformed 9 roughhewn, undressed 10 unfinished, unpolished 11 unfashioned
unworkmanlike 5 inept 8 inexpert, unexpert 9 incapable, unskilled 10 unskillful 11 incompetent, inefficient
unworldly 5 naive 6 astral, dreamy, simple 7 artless, natural 9 daydreamy, ingenuous, unstudied, untutored, visionary 10 unaffected, unschooled 11 daydreaming 12 unartificial
unworthy 6 drossy, no-good 7 inutile, nothing 9 no-account, valueless, worthless
unwrap see **uncover**
unwrinkled 6 smooth
unwritten 4 oral 6 spoken, verbal 11 traditional, word-of-mouth

unwrought see unworked
unyielding 4 firm, grim, hard 5 fixed, rigid, stern, stiff, tough 6 mortal, mulish 8 hard-core, hard-line, obdurate, ruthless, stubborn 9 impliable, inelastic, merciless, obstinate, pigheaded 10 bullheaded, headstrong, implacable, inexorable, inflexible, ironfisted, refractory, relentless, self-willed, unflexible, unswayable 11 immalleable, incompliant, intractable, uncompliant, unflinching, unrelenting 12 pertinacious, single-minded, unappeasable
unyoke 5 untie 6 unbind, unlink 7 disjoin, outspan, unhitch
up 4 hike, jump, lift, rise, soar 5 arise, boost, mount, raise 6 ascend, aspire, au fait, red-hot, uprear, versed 7 abreast, versant 8 familiar, increase, informed 9 au courant 10 acquainted, conversant, down-to-date 12 contemporary *prefix:* 2 an 3 ana, sur
up-and-coming 4 keen 5 alert, eager, ready 7 go-ahead 9 gumptious 12 enterprising
upbear 4 prop 5 brace, carry 7 bolster, shore up, support, sustain 8 buttress
upbeat 4 fond 8 sanguine 10 optimistic 12 Pollyannaish
upbraid 4 lash, rate 5 scold 6 berate, revile 7 bawl out, chew out 8 bless out 10 tongue-lash, vituperate
upchuck 4 barf, spew 5 vomit 6 spit up 7 bring up, throw up 8 disgorge
upcoming 7 nearing 8 foreseen 11 approaching, prospective
up-country 4 bush 6 sticks 8 backland, backwash, frontier 9 backwater, backwoods, boondocks 10 hinterland
update 5 renew 7 refresh, restore 8 renovate 9 modernize, refurbish 10 rejuvenate
Updike novel 10 Rabbit, Run, The Centaur, Bech is Back 11 Rabbit Redux 12 Rabbit at Rest, Rabbit is Rich
upend 4 beat, drub, lick, trim, whip 6 wallop 7 clobber, shellac, trounce 9 overwhelm
upgrade 3 wax 4 hike, rise 5 boost 6 prefer 7 advance, elevate, promote 8 increase 12 breakthrough
upgrowth 8 progress 9 evolution, flowering, unfolding 10 evolvement 11 development, progression
upheaval 6 change, clamor, outcry, tumult, upturn 7 ferment, heaving 8 churning, disaster, stirring 9 cataclysm, commotion 10 alteration, convulsion 11 catastrophe
uphill 4 hard 6 rugged 7 arduous, labored, operose 8 toilsome 9 difficult, effortful, laborious, strenuous
uphold 3 aid 4 back, help, lift, prop, rear 5 brace, carry, hoist, raise 6 assist, bear up, buoy up, defend, pick up, take up, upbear, uplift, uprear 7 bolster, elevate, justify, shore up, support, sustain, upraise 8 advocate, backstop, buttress, champion, maintain, side with 9 underprop, vindicate
upland 5 table 7 plateau
uplift 4 rear 5 edify, hoist, raise 6 illume, pick up, take up, uphold, uprear 7 elevate, improve, upraise 8 illumine 9 enlighten, irradiate 10 illuminate
upon 4 atop *prefix:* 2 ep 3 eph, epi
upper class 5 elite 6 flower, gentry 7 quality, society, who's who 9 blue blood, gentility 11 aristocracy
upper crust see upper class
upper hand 6 better 7 victory 9 advantage 11 superiority
uppermost 3 top 6 apical 7 highest 8 loftiest
uppity 5 brash 7 forward, pushful, pushing 9 presuming 11 overweening 12 presumptuous 13 self-asserting, self-assertive
upraise 4 lift, rear 5 cheer, hoist 6 buck up, pick up, solace, take up, uphold, uplift, uprear 7 comfort, console, elevate
uprear 4 lift, rise, soar 5 arise, build, erect, exalt, hoist, honor, mount, put up, raise 6 ascend, aspire, pick up, take up, uphold, uplift 7 dignify, elevate, ennoble, glorify, magnify, sublime, upraise 9 construct 10 aggrandize 11 distinguish
upright 4 fair, good, just, pure, true 5 erect, moral, noble 6 arrect, honest, raised 7 ethical, stand-up 8 elevated, virtuous 9 blameless, equitable, exemplary, honorable, impartial, righteous 10 high-minded, principled, scrupulous, straight-up, upstanding 13 conscientious ***combining form:*** 4 orth 5 ortho
uprightness 6 virtue 7 honesty, probity 8 morality, nobility 9 integrity, rectitude 12 reputability
uprising 6 revolt 9 rebellion 10 revolution 12 insurrection
uproar 3 din 4 coil, to-do 5 babel, brawl, broil, chaos, furor, melee, whirl 6 clamor, fracas, furore, hassle, hubbub, jangle, pother, racket, ruckus, rumpus, shindy, tumult 7 shindig, turmoil 8 brouhaha, disorder, foofaraw 9 commotion, confusion 10 hullabaloo, hurly-burly, tintamarre, turbulence 11 pandemonium
uproarious 5 noisy 7 rackety 8 clattery, noiseful, sonorous 10 clangorous
uproot 4 move 5 abate, shift 6 uptear 7 abolish, blot out, destroy, replace, subvert, wipe out 8 demolish, displace, overturn, supplant, uncreate 9 eradicate, extirpate, overthrow, supersede 10 annihilate, transplant 11 exterminate
upset 3 ail 4 bend, cark, turn 5 curve, lay

up, mix up, unman, worry 6 bother, flurry, invert, jumble, muddle, sicken, suffer, topple, tumble 7 afflict, agitate, derange, disturb, fluster, invalid, perturb, reverse, rummage, tip over, trouble, unhinge, unnerve 8 bewilder, confound, disarray, disorder, disquiet, distract, distress, overturn, turn over, unsettle 9 indispose, knock over, overthrow 10 debilitate, disarrange, discompose 12 incapacitate

upshot 4 core, gist, meat, pith 5 event, issue, sense, short 6 burden, climax, effect, ending, finish, result, sequel, thrust 7 outcome, purport 9 aftermath, substance 10 completion, conclusion 11 aftereffect, consequence, culmination, eventuality, termination

upside-down 5 snafu 7 chaotic, haywire, jumbled, mixed-up 8 confused, fouled-up, inverted, reversed 10 downside-up, topsy-turvy 13 helter-skelter

upspring 4 flow, head, rise 5 arise, get up, issue 6 uprise 7 emanate, proceed, stand up 9 originate 10 derive from

upstanding see upright

upstart 3 cad 4 boor, lout, slob 5 comer, rowdy 6 mucker 7 bounder, parvenu 8 outsider, roturier 9 arriviste, roughneck, vulgarian 11 guttersnipe 12 nouveau riche 13 social climber

upsurge 3 wax 4 rise 5 build, mount 6 expand 7 augment, enlarge 8 heighten, increase, multiply

uptight 4 edgy 5 nervy, tense 6 uneasy 7 restive

uptightness 6 unease 7 tension

up till 2 to 5 until 6 before 7 prior to 11 in advance of

up to 4 till 5 until 6 before 11 in advance of

up-to-date 6 modern, modish, red-hot, timely 7 abreast, a la mode, dashing, fitting, stylish 8 advanced, suitable 9 au courant, expedient, opportune 10 convenient 12 contemporary

Urania see Muse

Uranus *mother, wife:* 2 Ge 4 Gaea *offspring:* 6 Titans 8 Cyclopes *overthrower, son:* 6 Cronus

urban 4 city, town 5 civic 6 public 7 burghal, oppidan, popular, village 9 inner city, municipal 12 metropolitan

urbane 5 bland, civil, suave 6 poised, smooth 7 affable, genteel, refined 8 balanced, cultured, gracious, obliging, polished, well-bred 9 civilized, courteous, distingué 10 cultivated 12 cosmopolitan, metropolitan

urbanize 6 citify

urchin 3 imp 4 brat 5 child, gamin, scamp, whelp 7 dickens, mudlark 8 bratling 10 ragamuffin, street arab 11 guttersnipe, hobbledehoy *combining form:* 6 echino

Urdur, Urth see Norn

urge 3 egg, sic 4 coax, goad, itch, lust, prod, push, rush, sick, spur 5 drive, egg on, hurry, impel, press, prick, set on, shove, tar on, tarre 6 cajole, compel, desire, exhort, hustle, incite, motive, needle, prompt, propel, spring 7 craving, impulse, passion, provoke, solicit, wheedle 8 appetite, blandish, pressure 9 constrain, encourage, incentive 10 appetition 12 high-pressure

urgency 8 entreaty, exigence, instancy, pressure 10 insistence 11 importunity

urgent 6 crying 7 burning, clamant, driving, instant 8 pressing 9 clamorous, demanding, impelling, insistent 10 imperative 11 importunate

Uriah, Urijah *father:* 8 Shemaiah *slayer:* 9 Jehoiakim *son:* 8 Meremoth *wife:* 9 Bathsheba

Uriel 9 archangel *father:* 6 Kohath *grandson:* 6 Abijah

Uris, Leon *novel:* 6 Exodus 9 Battle Cry 13 The Angry Hills

Uri's son 5 Geber 7 Bezalel

urn 4 vase 7 samovar *Greek:* 7 amphora

Ursa Major 9 Great Bear

Ursa Minor 10 Little Bear *star:* 7 Polaris

Ur's son 7 Eliphal

Uruguay *capital:* 10 Montevideo *monetary unit:* 4 peso

usable 4 open 9 operative 10 accessible, functional

usage 3 way 4 form, lead, wont 5 habit, trick 6 choice, custom, manner, praxis 7 guiding, process 8 ceremony, guidance, habitude, practice 9 formality, procedure 10 convenance, convention, preference, proceeding *combining form:* 4 nomo

use 3 ply, run, way 4 duty, goal, mark, need, play, take, talk, wont, work 5 apply, avail, habit, inure, serve, speak, treat, trick, value, wield, worth 6 bestow, custom, demand, employ, govern, handle, manage, manner, object, parley, praxis, profit, target 7 account, benefit, control, exploit, fitness, operate, purpose, service, utility, utilize 8 accustom, ceremony, deal with, efficacy, exercise, exertion, function, habitude, impose on, occasion, practice, regulate 9 advantage, appliance, formality, habituate, objective, operation, relevance 10 converse in, employment, exercising, impose upon, manipulate 11 application, familiarize 12 adaptability, availability 13 applicability

used 8 shopworn 10 secondhand

used up 5 all in, spent 6 bleary, effete 7 drained, far-gone, worn-out 8 depleted 9 exhausted, washed-out

useful 3 fit 4 good, meet 5 brave, handy,

utile 6 proper, toward 7 benefic, helpful 8 favoring, suitable 9 favorable, practical 10 beneficial, convenient, functional, propitious 11 appropriate, practicable, serviceable 12 advantageous

usefulness 7 account, service, utility 9 advantage, relevance 13 applicability

useless 4 vain 6 futile 7 fustian, inutile 8 abortive, unusable 10 unavailing, unpurposed, unworkable 11 impractical, ineffective, ineffectual, unavailable 12 unfunctional, unproductive 13 impracticable, nonfunctional, unserviceable

user 6 addict 7 pothead 8 utilizer *suffix:* 4 ster

use up 3 eat 4 draw 5 drain, spend 6 devour, expend, finish 7 consume, deplete, exhaust 8 bankrupt, draw down 10 impoverish, run through

usher 4 lead 7 precede, preface 9 introduce

usher in 5 set up 6 launch 8 initiate 9 institute, introduce, originate 10 inaugurate

U.S.S.R *capital:* 6 Moscow *leader:* 6 Stalin (Joseph) 7 Kosygin (Aleksei) 8 Andropov (Yuri), Brezhnev (Leonid), Podgorny (Nikolai) 9 Chernenko (Konstantin), Gorbachev (Mikhail) 10 Khrushchev (Nikita) *monetary unit:* 5 ruble *republic:* 5 Uzbek 6 Kazakh, Kirgiz, Latvia, Russia 7 Armenia, Estonia, Georgia, Tadzhik, Turkmen, Ukraine 8 Moldavia 9 Lithuania 10 Azerbaijan, Belorussia

usual 4 rife 5 plain, typic 6 common, normal, wonted 7 chronic, current, general, natural, regular, routine, typical 8 accepted, everyday, familiar, ordinary, workaday 9 customary, plain Jane, prevalent, quotidian 10 accustomed, prevailing 11 commonplace 12 unremarkable

usually 7 as a rule 8 commonly, wontedly 9 sometimes 10 by ordinary, frequently, now and then, ordinarily 11 customarily, now and again 12 consistently, once and again

usurer 7 Shylock 9 loan shark

usurp 6 assume, cutout 7 preempt 8 accroach, arrogate, displace, supplant 10 commandeer 11 appropriate

Utah *capital:* 12 Salt Lake City *college, university:* 10 Weber State 12 Brigham Young *neighbor:* 5 Idaho 6 Nevada 7 Arizona, Wyoming 8 Colorado *nickname:* 11 Mormon State 12 Beehive State *state flower:* 8 sego lily

utensil 4 fork, tool 5 knife, spoon 8 coquille, teaspoon 9 implement 10 instrument *cooking:* see at **kitchen**

uterus 4 womb

Uther Pendragon *son:* 6 Arthur *wife:* 6 Ygerne 7 Igraine

utile 5 handy 6 useful 9 practical 10 functional 11 practicable, serviceable

utilitarian 4 hard 7 practic 9 practical, pragmatic, realistic 10 unromantic 11 down-to-earth, pragmatical 12 matter-of-fact, unidealistic *philosopher:* 4 Mill 7 Bentham

utility 3 use 7 account, fitness, service 9 advantage, relevance 10 usefulness

utilize 3 use 5 apply 6 bestow, employ, handle 7 advance, exploit, forward, further, promote 8 exercise

utmost 3 top 7 extreme, maximal, maximum, outside 8 damndest, darndest, farthest, furthest, remotest 9 damnedest, darnedest

utopia 4 Zion 6 heaven 7 arcadia 8 paradise 9 Cockaigne, dreamland, fairyland, Shangri-la 10 dreamworld, lubberland, never-never, wonderland 12 promised land

Utopia author 4 More

utopian 5 ideal, lofty 6 edenic 7 dreamer 8 abstract, arcadian, idealist 9 ambitious, grandiose, ideologue, visionary 10 idealistic, impossible, millennial, unfeasible 11 pretentious 12 otherworldly 13 castle-builder, impracticable

Uttar Pradesh *capital:* 7 Lucknow *country:* 5 India

utter 3 say 4 blue, dang, darn, durn, pure, rank, talk, tell 5 black, blank, gross, sheer, speak, stark, state, total, voice 6 arrant, blamed, dashed, deuced 7 blasted, blessed, chime in, declare, deliver, doggone, flat-out, goldarn, perfect, regular 8 absolute, all-fired, blighted, blinding, bring out, complete, crashing, infernal, outright, positive, throw-out, vocalize 9 dad-blamed, dad-burned, downright, out-and-out, verbalize 10 blithering, confounded, consummate, dad-blasted, double-dyed 11 come out with, straight-out, unmitigated, unqualified 13 blankety-blank, thoroughgoing

utterance 4 talk, vent, word 5 parol, voice 6 speech 8 speaking, vocalism 9 discourse, statement 10 expression 12 articulation, vocalization 13 verbalization

utterly 3 all 4 just, well 5 à fond, fully, plumb, quite 6 in toto, purely, wholly 7 exactly, totally 8 all in all, entirely 9 perfectly 10 altogether, completely, thoroughly

uttermost 7 extreme 8 farthest, furthest, remotest

Utu 6 sun-god *father:* 5 Nanna *mother:* 6 Ningal

Uzai's son 5 Palal

Uzal's father 6 Joktan
Uzbek capital 8 Tashkent
Uzzah ***father:*** 6 Shimei 8 Abinadab ***son:*** 6 Shimea
Uzzi ***father:*** 4 Bani 5 Bukki 6 Michri ***son:*** 4 Elah 8 Zerahiah
Uzziah ***father:*** 5 Harim, Shaul 7 Amaziah ***son:*** 6 Jotham 8 Jonathan
Uzziel ***brother:*** 5 Amram, Izhar ***father:*** 6 Kohath 8 Harhaiah, Jeduthun ***grandfather:*** 4 Levi ***son:*** 6 Sithri 7 Mishael 8 Elzaphan 9 Elizaphan

V

vacancy 4 void 6 vacuum 7 vacuity 8 voidness 9 blankness, emptiness 11 vacuousness 12 desertedness
vacant 4 bare, idle, void 5 blank, clear, empty, inane, stark, unlet 6 unused 7 deadpan, untaken, vacuous, witless 8 unfilled 10 tenantless, unoccupied 11 emptyheaded, thoughtless 12 inexpressive, unexpressive
vacate 4 quit, void 5 annul, clear, empty, leave, quash 6 give up, repeal, revoke 7 abandon, rescind, retract, reverse 8 abrogate, dissolve, part from, part with 9 discharge 10 relinquish
vacation 4 rest, trip 5 break, leave 6 recess 7 holiday, respite, time off 8 furlough 12 intermission ***resort:*** 3 spa
vacationer 7 tourist, tripper
vaccination 4 shot 7 booster 9 injection 11 inoculation
vaccine 4 shot 5 serum ***inventor:*** 6 Jenner
vacillate 3 wag 4 halt, swag, sway 5 dally, waver 6 dawdle, dither, falter, seesaw, teeter, waggle, wigwag, wobble 7 stagger, swither, whiffle 8 hesitate 9 alternate 12 fiddle-faddle, shilly-shally, teeter-totter, wiggle-waggle
vacillating 4 weak 5 shaky, timid 6 dickey, fickle, unsure, wobbly 7 erratic, halting, unfixed 8 dallying, dawdling, doubtful, doubting, hesitant, insecure, rootless, shifting, stalling, unstable, unsteady, volatile, wavering 9 demurring, eccentric, faltering, fluctuant, mercurial, pendulous, tentative, uncertain, unsettled, weak-kneed, whiffling 10 changeable, hesitating, inconstant, indecisive, irresolute, undecisive, unresolved 11 fluctuating, oscillating 12 double-minded, shilly-shally, wiggle-waggle 13 dillydallying
vacillation 5 doubt 8 dallying, demurral, stalling, to-and-fro, wavering 9 hesitancy 10 hesitation, indecision 12 irresolution, shilly-shally 13 dillydallying
vacuity 4 hole, nada, void 6 cavity, hollow 7 inanity, nullity, vacancy 8 bareness, dullness, nihility, voidness 9 blankness, bleakness, emptiness, inaneness, stupidity 10 barrenness, hollowness 11 nothingness, vacuousness 12 desolateness, nonexistence
vacuous 4 bare, dull, void 5 blank, clear, empty, inane, silly, stark 6 stupid, vacant 7 foolish, shallow 11 empty-headed, superficial
vacuousness 7 vacancy, vacuity 8 voidness 9 blankness, emptiness
vacuum 4 void 5 space 9 emptiness
vacuum tube 5 diode 6 triode 7 pentode, tetrode ***casing:*** 4 bulb ***suffix:*** 4 tron
vade mecum 5 guide 6 manual 8 Baedeker, handbook 9 guidebook 10 compendium 11 enchiridion
vadimonium 4 bond 6 pledge 8 contract, security
___ **Vadis** 3 Quo
vagabond 3 bum 4 hobo, roam, rove 5 drift, gypsy, piker, range, rogue, rover, stiff, stray, tramp 6 beggar, boomer, canter, picaro, ramble, roamer, roving, wander 7 drifter, floater, gangrel, meander, migrant, nomadic, swagger, swagman, traipse, tramper, vagrant 8 bohemian, clochard, derelict, picaroon, roadster, runabout, runagate, straggle, traveler, wanderer 9 itinerant, itinerate, straggler, transient, wandering, wayfaring 10 street arab 11 perambulant, peripatetic, Weary Willie 13 parambulatory
vagarious 5 kinky 7 erratic 8 freakish, whimsied 9 arbitrary, whimsical 10 capricious 12 unreasonable
vagary 3 bee 4 kink, whim 5 dream, fancy, freak, humor, quirk 6 megrim 7 bou-

tade, caprice, conceit, fantasy 8 crotchet, day-dream

vagrancy 6 roving 7 hoboism, roaming 8 nomadism, rambling 9 itineracy, wandering 10 itinerancy

vagrant see **vagabond**

vague 3 dim 4 hazy 5 blear, faint, foggy, misty, muddy, mushy 6 bleary, blurry, cloudy, dreamy, opaque, vapory 7 bleared, obscure, shadowy, unclear, unplain 8 nebulous, vaporous 9 ambiguous, dreamlike, equivocal, tenebrous, uncertain 10 ill-defined, indefinite, indistinct, unexplicit 12 undetermined 13 indeterminate, unsubstantial

vain 4 idle, puny, void 5 empty, pensy, petty, proud 6 futile, hollow, otiose, paltry 7 foppish, haughty, stuck-up, trivial, useless 8 abortive, arrogant, boastful, bootless, conceity, dandyish, delusive, delusory, egoistic, nugatory, trifling 9 conceited, fruitless, valueless, worthless 10 egocentric, misleading, profitless, unavailing 11 coxcombical, ineffective, ineffectual, unavailable 12 narcissistic, self-exalting, unproductive, unprofitable, vainglorious 13 inefficacious, self-conceited, self-important, swollen-headed

vainglorious 7 stuck-up 8 boastful, bragging, conceity, insolent, vaunting 9 conceited 10 disdainful 12 narcissistic, supercilious 13 self-conceited

vainglory 5 pride 6 egoism 7 bombast, conceit, egotism 8 parading 9 arrogance, flaunting, self-glory, self-pride 10 exhibition 11 haughtiness, self-opinion 12 boastfulness

vainness see **vanity**

valance 5 drape 7 curtain, drapery

vale 4 dale, glen 5 combe 6 valley 8 farewell

valediction 7 good-bye 8 farewell

valedictory 7 good-bye, parting 8 farewell 9 departing

valentine 4 card 7 beloved 10 sweetheart

Valentine ***beloved:*** 6 Silvia ***sister:*** 8 Margaret ***slayer:*** 5 Faust ***twin brother:*** 5 Orson ***wife:*** 9 Clerimond

valet 3 man 4 goad 7 servant 10 manservant

Vali ***father:*** 4 Odin ***guardian of:*** 7 justice ***mother:*** 4 Rind 5 Rindr ***victim:*** 5 Hoder

valiance see **valor**

valiant see **valorous**

valid 4 just, true 5 legal, licit, solid, sound 6 cogent, lawful, potent, strong 7 telling 8 attested, decisive, verified 9 confirmed, effective, effectual 10 acceptable, conclusive, convincing, definitive, determined, persuasive, satisfying 11 established 12 corroborated, demonstrated, satisfactory 13 determinative, substantiated

validate 5 prove 6 ratify, verify 7 approve, bear out, confirm, endorse, justify, probate 8 legalize, sanction 11 corroborate, rubber-stamp 12 authenticate, substantiate

validity 5 force, point, punch 7 cogency, gravity, potency 8 efficacy 9 soundness 13 effectiveness

validness see **validity**

valise 3 bag 4 grip 7 luggage 8 gripsack, suitcase

Valjean's pursuer 6 Javert

Valkyrie 6 maiden 8 Brynhild

valley 4 dale, dell, glen, vale 5 basin, combe, gorge, gully, swale 6 canyon, dingle, hollow, ravine, rincon 10 depression ***Africa-Asia:*** 4 Rift 9 Great Rift ***Alps:*** 11 Grindelwald ***ancient Greece:*** 5 Nemea ***arid:*** 6 bolson ***California:*** 4 Napa 5 Death, Squaw 8 Imperial, Yosemite 11 San Fernando ***Dead Sea area:*** 6 Arabah ***Dominican Republic:*** 5 Cibao ***Egypt:*** 6 Kharga ***Eire:*** 5 Avoca ***England:*** 5 Doone ***Greece:*** 5 Tembi, Tempe ***India:*** 4 Kulu 5 dhoon ***Israel:*** 4 Elah ***Lebanon:*** 4 Bika ***moon:*** 5 rille ***New York:*** 6 Sleepy 12 Sleepy Hollow ***Pennsylvania:*** 7 Nittany ***Scotland:*** 7 Glen Roy ***steep:*** 6 ravine ***Switzerland:*** 5 Hasli ***Virginia:*** 10 Shenandoah ***volcanic:*** 5 atrio ***Washington:*** 11 Grand Coulee

vallum 4 wall 7 rampart

Valmiki's epic 8 Ramayana

valor 4 guts, sand 6 mettle, spirit 7 bravery, courage, heroism, prowess 8 backbone, tenacity, valiance, valiancy 9 fortitude, gallantry 10 resolution

valorous 4 bold 5 brave 7 doughty, valiant 8 fearless, intrepid 9 audacious, dauntless, undaunted 10 courageous

valuable 4 dear 6 costly, prized, worthy 7 admired 8 esteemed, precious, property 9 expensive, priceless, respected, treasured 11 appreciated

valuate 4 rate 5 assay, set at 6 assess, survey 8 appraise, estimate

valuation 4 cost 5 price, worth 6 charge, rating 7 account, opinion 8 estimate, judgment 9 appraisal 10 assessment, estimation 12 appraisement

value 4 cost, rate 5 assay, gauge, merit, price, prize, set at, worth 6 assess, charge, esteem, figure, reckon, revere, survey, virtue 7 account, apprize, caliber, care for, cherish, compute, expense, quality, stature 8 appraise, estimate, treasure, venerate 9 appraisal, reverence 10 appreciate, assessment ***Scottish:*** 4 feck

valueless 6 draffy, drossy, no-good 7 inutile, nothing 8 unworthy 9 worthless

valve 3 tap 4 cock, gate 6 faucet, poppet,

spigot 7 hydrant, petcock, shutoff 8 stopcock *cardiac:* 6 mitral 8 bicuspid
vamoose 4 kite, scat 5 scram 6 begone, decamp, get out 7 skiddoo, take off 8 clear out, hightail 9 skedaddle
vamp 3 fix 4 do up, mend 5 fix up, flirt, frame, patch, siren 6 cook up, devise, invent, make up, repair 7 brush up, charmer, concoct, dream up, enticer, furbish, hatch up, rebuild, touch up 8 contrive, coquette, overhaul 9 formulate, inveigler, refurbish, temptress 10 gold digger, seductress 11 enchantress, femme fatale, recondition, reconstruct
vampire 3 bat 7 Dracula 9 Nosferatu 11 bloodsucker
van 3 car 4 head, lead 5 truck, wagon 6 leader 7 vehicle
vandal 4 lout 6 looter, ruiner 7 defacer, hoodlum, ravager, ruffian, spoiler, wrecker 8 hooligan, pillager, ruinator 9 despoiler, destroyer, plunderer, spoliator 10 devastator, iconoclast
vandalize 3 mar 5 trash, wreck 6 deface, rip off, tear up 7 destroy
Vandal king 8 Genseric
Vandyke 5 beard
vane 3 arm 9 indicator 11 weathercock
vanguard 9 forefront
Vaniah's father 4 Bani
vanilla 7 extract
vanish 3 die 4 fade, melt 5 clear 8 dissolve, evanesce, melt away 9 disappear, evaporate 13 dematerialize
vanity 6 egoism 7 conceit 8 self-love 9 vainglory
Vanity Fair author 9 Thackeray
vanquish 4 beat 5 crush 6 defeat, humble, reduce, subdue 7 conquer, subvert, trample 8 bear down, beat down, overturn, surmount 9 overpower, subjugate
vanquisher 5 champ 6 master, victor, winner 7 subduer 8 champion, defeater 9 conqueror 10 subjugator
vanquishment 4 rout 6 defeat 7 beating, debacle, licking, mastery, subdual 8 drubbing 9 overthrow, trouncing 10 defeasance 11 shellacking, subjugation
vantage 4 draw, edge, odds 5 bulge, start 8 deadwood, handicap 9 allowance, head start
vapid 4 dull, flat, weak 5 inane 6 jejune 7 insipid, sapless 9 driveling, innocuous, milk-toast, tasteless 10 flavorless, namby-pamby, wishy-washy 13 unimaginative, uninteresting
vapor 3 fog, gas 4 haze, mist, smog 5 brume, cloud, smoke, steam 6 breath, nimbus *combining form:* 3 atm 4 atmo, mano 5 atmid 6 atmido 7 pneumat 8 pneumato *condensed:* 3 dew *frozen:* 4 rime 5 frost *noxious:* 6 miasma
vaporize 4 boil 9 evaporate
vaporous 4 airy, hazy 5 foggy, gassy, misty, mushy, vague, wispy 6 aerial, cloudy, unreal 7 gaseous 8 ethereal, illusory 13 unsubstantial
vaquero 6 cowboy 8 herdsman
varia 10 miscellany
variable 5 fluid 6 fickle, fitful, mobile, shifty 7 mutable, protean, unequal 8 slippery, ticklish, unstable, unsteady, volatile, weathery 9 changeful, irregular, mercurial, spasmodic, uncertain, unequable, unsettled, ununiform 10 capricious, changeable, inconstant 13 temperamental
variance 6 change, strife 7 discord, dissent 8 conflict, disunity, division, severing 9 deviation, disaccord, sundering, variation 10 contention, difference, dissension, dissidence, separation 11 fluctuation
variation 4 turn 5 shift 6 change 8 mutation, variance 9 disparity 10 alteration, deflection, difference, divergence 11 discrepancy 12 modification 13 dissimilarity
varicolored see variegated
varicose 7 cirsoid, dilated, swollen
varied 5 mixed 6 motley 8 assorted, chowchow 11 promiscuous 12 conglomerate, multifarious 13 heterogeneous, miscellaneous
variegated 4 pied 5 pinto 6 calico, motley, mottle 7 checked, dappled, flecked, freaked, marbled, mottled, piebald, spotted 8 discolor, skewbald, speckled, stippled, streaked 9 checkered, multihued, spattered 10 multicolor, parti-color, polychrome, versicolor 11 varicolored 12 multicolored, parti-colored, versicolored 13 polychromatic
variety 3 ilk 4 kind, rank, sort, type 5 grade 6 medley, nature, stripe 7 species 8 multeity 9 character, diversity, variation 10 assortment, miscellany 11 description, diverseness, variousness 12 multiformity, multiplicity 13 heterogeneity
various 4 many, some 6 divers, legion, sundry, unlike, varied 7 certain, distant, diverse, several, unalike, unequal, variant, varying 8 assorted, changing, discrete, distinct, numerous, peculiar, populous, separate 9 different, disparate, divergent, unsimilar 10 dissimilar, individual, omnigenous, voluminous 11 distinctive 12 multifarious, multitudinal 13 heterogeneous, miscellaneous, multitudinous
varlet 5 knave 6 rascal 9 scoundrel
varmint 6 animal, rascal 7 critter
varnish 4 coat 5 glaze, japan, white 6 veneer, whiten 7 shellac 8 palliate 9 extenuate, gloss over, gloze over, sugar-

coat, whitewash **10** blanch over ***component:*** **5** resin
vary **3** run **4** part, turn **5** alter, range **6** change, depart, differ, divide, extend, modify, mutate **7** deviate, digress, discord, dissent, diverge, qualify **8** disagree, modulate, separate **9** disaccord, refashion
vase **3** jar, urn **4** ewer **6** crater, krater, vessel **7** amphora, potiche **8** boughpot
Vashni's father **6** Samuel
Vashti's husband **6** Xerxes **9** Ahasuerus
vassal **4** esne, leud, serf **5** helot, liege, slave **6** tenant, varlet **7** bondman, feodary, homager, peasant, servant, subject **8** liegeman **9** dependent, underling **11** beneficiary, subordinate ***high-ranking:*** **7** vavasor **8** vavasour ***office:*** **5** feoff
vast **3** big **4** huge, wide **5** ample, broad, giant, large **6** cosmic **7** immense, titanic **8** colossal, enormous, far-flung, gigantic, spacious, whopping **9** capacious, expansive **10** monumental, tremendous, widespread **12** astronomical
vastness **8** enormity, hugeness **9** immensity, magnitude **12** enormousness
vat **3** tub, tun **4** back, beck, cask, kier, tank **5** keeve, kieve **6** barrel, vessel **7** cistern **8** cauldron ***cheese:*** **7** chessel
vatic **6** mantic **7** fatidic **8** Delphian, oracular **9** prophetic, sibylline **11** apocalyptic, prophetical
Vatican ***chapel:*** **7** Sistine ***church:*** **11** Saint Peter's ***ruler:*** **4** Pope ***site:*** **4** Rome
vaticinal see vatic
vaticinate **4** call **5** augur **7** portend, predict, presage **8** forecast, foretell, prophesy **9** adumbrate **13** prognosticate
vaudeville **4** song **5** revue **7** variety **9** burlesque **13** entertainment
vaudevillian **5** actor, comic **6** dancer, singer **7** acrobat **9** performer **11** entertainer
vault **3** hop, lop, pit **4** arch, cave, dome, jump, leap, over, rise, room, soar, tomb **5** bound, clear, crypt, mount **6** ascend, bounce, cavern, cellar, hurdle, spring, upleap **7** saltate **8** catacomb, overjump, overleap, surmount, upspring **9** negotiate **10** undercroft
vaulting **7** emulous **8** aspiring **9** ambitious **12** enthusiastic **13** opportunistic
vaunt **4** blow, brag, crow, puff **5** boast, mouth, prate **6** expose, flaunt, parade **7** display, exhibit, show off **8** brandish **9** gasconade **11** rodomontade
Ve ***brother:*** **4** Odin, Vili ***victim:*** **4** Ymir
veal **4** calf ***cutlet:*** **9** schnitzel ***roasted:*** **10** fricandeau ***shank:*** **8** osso buco
vector **7** carrier
Vedic ***god:*** **4** Agni, Soma, Vayu **5** Aditi, Bhaga, Dyaus, Indra, Mitra, Rudra **6** Aditya, Varuna **7** Savitar ***goddess:*** **4** Usas **5** Ushas ***hymn:*** **6** mantra ***language:*** **8** Sanskrit ***writing:*** **7** Samhita
veer **3** dip, yaw **4** skew, slue, turn, whip **5** avert, pivot, sheer, shift, twist, wheel, whirl **6** depart, divert, swerve **7** bear off, deflect, deviate, digress, diverge **8** angle off, train off **9** volte-face
vega **5** plain **6** meadow
vegetable **3** pea, soy, yam **4** bean, beet, corn, kale, leek, okra, soya, taro, wort **5** chive, cress, green, onion, plant **6** carrot, celery, cowpea, endive, garlic, lentil, peanut, pepper, potato, radish, sorrel, squash, tomato, turnip **7** cabbage, chayote, dullard, lettuce, mustard, parsley, parsnip, pumpkin, rhubarb, salsify, shallot, soybean, spinach **8** broccoli, collards, cucumber, eggplant, kohlrabi, lima bean, rutabaga, scallion **9** artichoke, asparagus, muskmelon **10** watermelon **11** cauliflower, horseradish, sweet potato ***dish:*** **5** salad ***mold:*** **5** humus ***oyster:*** **7** salsify ***pear:*** **7** chayote ***seller:*** **6** grocer **7** grocery **12** costermonger ***sponge:*** **5** luffa ***spread:*** **4** oleo **9** margarine
vegetarian **9** herbivore
vegetate **4** idle, laze **8** languish, stagnate **9** hibernate
vegetation **5** flora **6** growth, plants **7** verdure **8** greenery ***floating:*** **4** sudd **8** pleuston
vehement **3** hot **4** wild **5** rabid **6** ardent, fervid, fierce, hearty, heated, lively, potent **7** fervent, frantic, furious, intense, vicious, violent, zealous **8** emphatic, forceful, powerful, terrible **9** delirious, desperate, energetic, exquisite, perfervid **10** passionate, pronounced **11** impassioned **12** concentrated
vehicle **3** bus, car, van **4** auto, tool **5** agent, buggy, means, organ, sedan, wagon **6** agency, medium, vector **7** carrier, channel **8** ministry **9** implement, transport **10** automobile, conveyance, instrument ***baby's:*** **4** pram **8** carriage, stroller ***child's:*** **4** bike **5** trike **7** bicycle, scooter **8** tricycle ***combining form:*** **6** mobile ***farm:*** **4** wain **7** tractor ***horse-drawn:*** **4** cart, dray **5** buggy, lorry, sulky, wagon **6** hansom, landau **8** carriage ***military:*** **4** jeep, tank ***one-wheeled:*** **8** unicycle ***passenger:*** **3** bus, cab, car **4** auto, taxi **7** ricksha ***public:*** **3** bus **4** tram **5** train **6** subway **7** omnibus, trolley ***Roman:*** **7** chariot ***winter:*** **4** sled **6** sleigh **8** snowplow
veil **4** hide, mask, wrap **5** cloak, color, cover, front, guise **6** enfold, enwrap, facade, invest, mantle, screen, shroud **7** blanket, conceal, cover up, curtain,

enclose, envelop, secrete 8 calyptra, coloring, disguise, enshroud 10 camouflage, false front, overspread, spread over ***Muslim:*** 7 yashmak ***netting:*** 6 maline 7 malines
vein 3 way 4 hint, line, lode, mind, mode, mood, seam, tone, tube, vena 5 humor, shade, style, tenor, tinge, touch, trace 6 fettle, manner, nature, spirit, strain, streak, temper, vessel 7 channel, fashion 8 tincture 9 character, suspicion 10 complexion, suggestion 11 disposition, temperament ***combining form:*** 3 ven 4 veni, veno 5 phleb 6 phlebo ***deposit:*** 3 ore ***fluid:*** 5 blood ***leaf:*** 3 rib ***leg:*** 7 saphena ***neck:*** 7 jugular ***small:*** 6 venule ***varicose:*** 5 varix
velar 7 palatal
veldt 5 plain 6 meadow 9 grassland
velitation 5 bruch, run-in, set-to 8 skirmish 9 encounter
velleity 4 mind, will, wish 5 fancy 6 liking 8 pleasure, volition 11 inclination
vellicate 3 jig, lug, nip 4 jerk, snap, yank 5 lurch, pinch 6 fidget, jiggle, twitch
velocipede 4 bike 5 cycle 7 bicycle 10 two-wheeler
velocity 3 bat 4 gait, pace 5 haste, hurry, speed 7 headway, impetus 8 celerity, dispatch, momentum, rapidity 9 quickness, rapidness, swiftness 10 expedition
velum 4 veil 8 membrane
velvet 5 cloth 6 fabric, profit 8 winnings ***on:*** 4 rich, safe 7 wealthy
velvety 4 soft 5 plush, silky, sleek, slick 6 glossy, plushy, satiny, silken, smooth 7 cottony 10 velutinous
venal 4 hack, paid 6 sordid 7 buyable, corrupt, crooked, ignoble, vicious 8 bribable, hireling, infamous 9 mercenary, nefarious, unethical 10 flagitious, iniquitous, praetorian 11 corruptible, purchasable 12 unprincipled, unscrupulous
vend 4 give, hawk, sell, toot 5 sound 6 blazon, market, monger, peddle 7 declare, publish 8 announce, huckster, proclaim 9 advertise, broadcast 10 promulgate
vendee 5 buyer 6 emptor 9 purchaser
vendetta 4 feud 9 blood feud
vendible 7 salable 8 sellable 10 marketable
vendibles 5 goods, wares 11 commodities, merchandise
vendor 6 duffer, hawker, seller 7 higgler, packman, peddler, roadman 8 huckster, merchant, outcrier, salesman 9 cheap-jack, cheap-john
vendue 4 sale 7 auction
veneer 4 face, mask, show, veil 5 cover, front, gloss, white 6 facade, whiten 7 coating, varnish 8 disguise, palliate 9 extenuate, gloss over, gloze over, sugarcoat, whitewash 10 blanch over, false front
venerable 3 old 4 aged 5 hoary 6 age-old, sacred 7 ancient, antique, elderly, honored, revered, stately 8 imposing, Noachian, reverend, timeworn 9 admirable, dignified, estimable, honorable 10 reverenced, worshipful 11 patriarchal, reverential 12 antediluvian
venerate 5 adore, honor 6 revere 7 idolize, worship 9 reverence
veneration 3 awe 5 dulia, honor 6 esteem, homage 7 respect, worship 9 reverence
venery 4 game 5 chase 7 hunting
venesection 10 phlebotomy 12 bloodletting
Venetian ***boat:*** 7 gondola ***boatman:*** 9 gondolier ***canal:*** 3 rii (plural), rio ***ruler:*** 4 doge ***street:*** 5 canal
Venezuela ***capital:*** 7 Caracas ***monetary unit:*** 7 bolivar
Venezuelan ***herdsman:*** 7 llanero ***liberator:*** 7 Bolivar ***people:*** 5 Carib 6 Timote
venge 7 redress 9 vindicate
vengeance 6 return 7 revenge 8 avenging, reprisal, requital, revanche 9 repayment 10 avengement 11 counterblow, retaliation, retribution
vengeful 7 hostile 8 inimical, wreakful 9 rancorous 10 vindictive 12 antagonistic
venial 5 minor 7 trivial 8 harmless, trifling 9 allowable, excusable, tolerable 10 forgivable, pardonable, remittable 13 insignificant
Venice of the East 7 Bangkok
Venice of the North 9 Stockholm
Veni, Creator ____ 8 Spiritus
venireman 5 juror
venison 4 deer
veni, vidi, ____ 4 vici
venom 4 bane 5 virus 6 poison, rancor 7 ill will, vitriol 9 contagion, malignity, virulence
venomous 5 toxic 6 deadly, malign, poison 7 baleful, malefic 8 mephitic, toxicant, viperish, viperous, virulent 9 malignant, poisonous, viperlike 10 maleficent, malevolent
vent 3 air, put 4 emit, give, hole, slit, slot 5 issue, loose, state, utter, voice 6 assert, outlet 7 cast out, declare, exhaust, express, give off, give out, opening, orifice, release, unleash 8 aperture, throw off 9 discharge, statement, take out on, utterance 10 expression 12 articulation, vocalization 13 verbalization
venter 3 gut 5 belly 6 paunch 7 abdomen, stomach
ventilate 3 air, put 4 give, moot 5 state 6 broach, debate, go into, take up, talk of 7 bring up, discuss, express, publish 8 rap

about, talk over 9 advertise, broadcast, introduce, thresh out 10 deliberate
ventral area 7 abdomen *combining form:* 5 gastr 6 gaster, gastri, gastro 7 gastero
ventricle 7 chamber *combining form:* 4 cele, coel 5 coele
ventriloquist *companion:* 5 dummy *famous:* 6 Bergen
venture 3 bet, try 4 dare, defy, face, feat, gest, risk 5 beard, brave, crack, fling, front, peril, stake, wager 6 banter, chance, expose, gamble, hazard 7 attempt, emprise, exploit, imperil, jeopard, lay open, operate, outdare, outface, play for 8 endanger, jeopardy 9 adventure, challenge, speculate 10 enterprise, jeopardize 11 speculation, undertaking
venturesome 4 bold, rash 5 brave, stout 6 daring, sturdy 8 overbold, reckless, stalwart 9 audacious, daredevil, foolhardy 11 adventurous, temerarious
venturous see **venturesome**
venue 4 side, site 5 place 6 ground, locale
Venus 6 planet, Vesper 8 Hesperus; (see also **Aphrodite**)
Venus de ____ 4 Milo
veracious 4 just, true 5 right, valid 6 direct, strict 8 accurate, faithful, truthful 9 veridical 11 true-tongued, undeceitful, undeceptive, undistorted, unvarnished 12 truth-telling 13 truth-speaking
veracity 4 fact 5 truth 6 gospel, truism, verity 7 honesty 8 accuracy 9 actuality, exactness, frankness 11 correctness, factualness 12 truthfulness, veridicality
veranda 5 lanai, porch 6 piazza 7 balcony, gallery, portico
verb *auxiliary:* 2 am, be, do, is 3 are, can, did, had, has, may, was 4 have, must, were, will 5 could, might, shall, would 6 should *form:* 6 active, gerund 7 passive 10 infinitive, participle *kind:* 10 transitive 12 intransitive *linking:* 6 copula *mood:* 8 optative 10 imperative, indicative 11 subjunctive *suffix:* (see at **suffix**) *tense:* 4 past 6 aorist, future 7 perfect, present 9 predicate 10 pluperfect
verbal 4 oral 6 spoken 7 literal 8 verbatim 9 unwritten 11 traditional, word-for-word, word-of-mouth
verbalism 6 phrase 7 diction, styling, wordage, wording 8 parlance, phrasing, verbiage 9 prolixity, verbosity, windiness, wordiness 10 prolixness 11 phraseology, verboseness
verbalization 4 talk 6 speech 8 speaking 9 discourse, utterance
verbalize 3 air, say 4 give, talk, vent, word 5 speak, state, utter, voice 7 express 8 vocalize 9 ventilate
verbatim 5 close, exact 6 direct, strict, verbal 7 exactly, literal, precise 8 directly, faithful 9 literally, literatim, precisely 10 accurately 11 word-for-word
verbiage 6 phrase 7 diction, wordage, wording 8 parlance, phrasing, pleonasm 9 floridity, tautology, verbalism, verbality, verbosity 10 floridness, periphrase, redundancy, roundabout 11 periphrasis, phraseology
verbose 5 windy, wordy 6 prolix 7 diffuse, flowery 9 redundant 10 long-winded, palaverous, pleonastic 11 tautologous 12 magniloquent, periphrastic 13 grandiloquent
verboseness see **verbosity**
verbosity 7 bombast 8 verbiage 9 prolixity, verbalism, windiness, wordiness 10 prolixness, redundancy 11 verboseness
verboten 5 taboo 6 banned 8 outlawed 9 forbidden 10 disallowed, prohibited, unlicensed 11 disapproved 12 unauthorized, unsanctioned
verdant 3 raw 5 green 6 grassy
verdict 6 ruling 7 finding, opinion 8 decision, judgment
Verdi opera 4 Aida 6 Ernani, Oberto, Otello 7 Nabucco 8 Don Carlo, Falstaff 9 Rigoletto 10 La Traviata 11 Il Trovatore
verdure 5 green 7 foliage, leafage, umbrage 8 greenery 10 vegetation
verge 3 hem, lip, rim 4 abut, brim, edge, join, lean, line 5 bound, brink, march, point, skirt, touch 6 adjoin, border, butt on, fringe, margin, tend to, trench 7 incline, outline, selvage, touch on 8 approach, neighbor, surround 9 threshold, touch upon 10 border line, tend toward 11 butt against, communicate
Vergil *epic:* 6 Aeneid *poems:* 8 Bucolics, Georgics
veridical see **veracious**
verification 5 proof 12 confirmation
verify 3 try 4 test 5 prove 6 settle 7 bear out, confirm, justify 8 document, validate 9 establish 11 corroborate, demonstrate 12 authenticate, substantiate
verily 3 yea 4 even 5 truly 6 indeed
verisimility 5 color 12 plausibility
veritable 4 real, true, very 6 actual 7 factual, genuine 8 bona fide, undenied 9 authentic, undoubted, unrefuted 10 sure-enough 11 indubitable
verity 5 truth 6 gospel, truism 8 veracity 12 truthfulness, veridicality 13 veraciousness
vermeil 4 ruby
vermiform 8 wormlike
vermilion 3 red
vermin 4 lice, mice, rats 5 fleas 7 bedbugs

verminous 6 filthy 7 noxious 9 offensive
Vermont ***capital:*** 10 Montpelier ***college, university:*** 7 Norwich 10 Middlebury, St. Michaels ***state bird:*** 12 hermit thrush ***state flower:*** 9 red clover
vernacular 4 cant 5 argot, idiom, lingo, slang 6 jargon, patois, patter, speech, tongue, vulgar 7 dialect, vulgate 8 language 10 colloquial 12 mother tongue
vernacularism 8 slangism, solecism 9 barbarism, vulgarism 10 corruption 11 impropriety
vernal 6 spring 10 springlike
Verne, Jules ***character:*** 4 Fogg (Phileas), Nemo 12 Passepartout ***submarine:*** 8 Nautilus
versant 2 up 6 au fait 7 abreast 8 familiar, informed 9 au courant 10 acquainted
versatile 4 able 5 handy 6 adroit, facile, gifted, mobile 7 elastic, plastic, pliable, skilled 8 flexible, skillful, talented 9 adaptable, all-around, dexterous, many-sided 10 conversant 11 well-rounded
verse 3 lay, ode 4 epic, poem, rune, song 5 lyric, poesy, rhyme, stich 6 ballad, jingle, poetry, sonnet, stanza 11 familiarize ***analysis:*** 8 scansion ***four-line:*** 8 quatrain ***six-line:*** 6 sestet ***three-line:*** 6 tercet ***two-line:*** 7 couplet ***writer:*** 4 poet, (see also poem)
versed 2 up 3 old, vet 5 adept 6 au fait 7 abreast, old-time, skilled, versant, veteran 8 familiar, informed, seasoned 9 au courant, competent, practical, practiced 10 acquainted, conversant 11 experienced
verseman 4 bard, poet 6 rhymer 9 poetaster, rhymester, versifier 12 balladmonger
versicolor see **variegated**
versifier see **verseman**
version 4 tale 5 story 6 report 7 account, history, reading 9 chronicle, narrative, rendering, rendition, rewording 10 paraphrase 11 restatement, translation 12 condensation 13 clarification, restipulation
versus 3 con 6 contra 7 against, vis-à-vis 11 over against
vertebra 4 bone ***combining form:*** 7 spondyl 8 spondyli (plural), spondylo 9 spondylus ***kind:*** 6 dorsal, lumbar, sacral 8 cervical, thoracic
vertebrae 4 back 5 spine 6 rachis 8 backbone 12 spinal column
vertebrate 6 animal ***characteristic:*** 5 spine 7 cranium ***kind:*** 4 bird, fish, frog 5 shark 6 mammal 7 lamprey, reptile
vertex 3 cap, top 4 apex, peak, roof 5 crest, crown 6 apogee, summit, tip-top, zenith 9 fastigium
Verthandi see **Norn**
vertical 5 erect, plumb, sheer, steep 7 upright 9 up-and-down 10 straight-up 13 perpendicular ***combining form:*** 4 orth 5 ortho
vertiginous 5 dizzy, giddy, light 6 rotary, swimmy 8 swimming 11 light-headed
vertigo 6 megrim 9 dizziness
verve 3 pep, vim, zip 4 brio, dash, élan, fire, life, zest, zing 5 gusto, oomph 6 bounce, esprit, spirit, spring 8 buoyancy, vivacity 9 animation 10 elasticity, liveliness, resiliency
very 2 so 3 too 4 bare, mere, most, much, real, same, true 5 ideal, model, pesky, quite, super, truly 6 damned, highly, hugely, mighty, really 7 awfully, de facto, genuine, greatly, notably, parlous, precise, vitally 8 actually, bona fide, mightily, mortally, rattling, selfsame, snapping, spanking, terribly, whacking, whopping 9 authentic, eminently, extremely, genuinely, identical, tellingly, undoubted, veritable, veritably 10 dreadfully, insatiably, remarkably, strikingly, sure-enough, thoroughly 11 exceedingly, indubitable 12 surpassingly 13 exceptionally ***French:*** 4 très ***German:*** 4 sehr ***Scottish:*** 3 gey
vesicle 3 sac 4 cyst 6 cavity 7 bladder, blister
Vesper 5 Venus 8 Hesperus 11 evening star
vespers 6 prayer 7 service 8 evensong
___ **Vespucci** 7 Amerigo
vessel 3 ama, can, cup, jar, pan, pot, pyx, tub, urn 4 boat, bowl, drum, ewer, pail, ship, tank, tube, vase, vein 5 canal, craft, cruse, laver 6 artery, barrel, bottle, bucket, firkin, flagon, kettle, krater, pottle, situla 7 cresset, pitcher 8 crucible 10 receptacle ***combining form:*** 3 vas 4 ange, angi, vasi, vaso 5 angia (plural), angio 6 angium, arteri, vascul 7 arterio, vasculo ***drinking:*** 3 cup, mug 4 toby 5 cylix, flask, glass, gourd, kylix, stein, stoup 6 goblet, seidel 7 tankard, tumbler ***Indian:*** 4 lota 5 lotah ***sailing:*** (see at **ship**) ***Scottish:*** 3 cog 6 cootie, quaich, quaigh 7 yetling
vest 4 coat 6 belong, invest, jacket, weskit 7 empower, pertain 9 appertain, authorize, waistcoat
Vesta see **Hestia**
vestal 3 nun 4 pure 6 chaste, virgin 8 virginal
vestibule 4 hall 5 entry, foyer, lobby 6 portal 7 narthex, portico 8 anteroom, entryway 11 antechamber 12 entrance hall
vestige 3 rag, tag 4 path, step 5 relic, scrap, spoor, trace, track, tract, trail 6 shadow 7 memento, remains, remnant 8 footstep 9 footprint, remainder
vestment 3 alb 4 cope, garb, gown, pall, robe 5 amice, cotta, dress, fanon, orale, stole, tunic 6 rochet, sakkos 7 cassock,

garment, maniple, pallium, tunicle 8 chasuble, cincture, dalmatic, parament, surplice 9 phelonion *ancient Hebrew:* 5 ephod
vestry 4 room 6 closet 8 sacristy
vesture 5 cover 6 clothe 7 apparel, costume, envelop, garment 8 clothing
Vesuvius 7 volcano
vetch 4 tare *bitter:* 3 ers 5 ervil
veteran 4 wise 6 expert, master, versed 7 old hand, old-time, skilled, worldly 8 oldtimer, seasoned 9 longtimer, practical, practiced 10 past master 11 experienced 13 sophisticated
veto 3 nix 4 deny, kill 6 defeat, forbid, refuse, reject 7 decline 8 disallow, negative, prohibit 9 blackball, non-placet
vex 3 bug, ire, irk 4 chaw, fret, gall 5 anger, annoy, chafe, tease 6 abrade, bother, plague 7 provoke, torment 8 exercise 9 embarrass, infuriate
vexation 6 irking 9 annoyance, bothering, provoking 10 harassment, irritation 11 aggravation, bedevilment, provocation
vexatious 4 mean, ugly 5 pesky 6 wicked 9 troublous 11 troublesome
via 2 by 3 per 4 over, road, with 5 along 7 by way of, passage, through 8 by dint of 9 by means of 10 by virtue of
viable 6 doable 8 feasible, possible, workable 11 practicable
viaduct 6 bridge
vial 5 ampul, flask, glass, phial 6 ampule, beaker, bottle, vessel 7 ampoule 8 test tube
viands 4 eats, fare, feed, food, grub 7 edibles, nurture 8 victuals 9 provender 10 provisions 11 comestibles
viator 8 traveler, wayfarer
vibrant 5 alive, round, vital 6 rotund 7 orotund, ringing 8 plangent, resonant, sonorant, sonorous 9 consonant 10 resounding
vibrate 3 jar 4 rock 5 quake, shake, trill, twang 6 shiver, tremor 7 shudder, tremble
vibration 4 vibe 5 quake, shake, trill 6 quaver, quiver, tremor 7 flutter, shaking 8 fremitus 9 trembling 11 oscillation *Scottish:* 6 dindle
vicar 6 priest 8 minister 9 clergyman
Vicar of Wakefield *author:* 9 Goldsmith *character:* 8 Primrose
vice 3 ill, sin 4 evil, flaw 5 fault, wrong 6 defect, foible 7 blemish, failing, frailty 9 depravity, indecency 10 corruption, debasement, debauchery, immorality, perversion, unchastity, wickedness 11 shortcoming
vice-president 4 veep 9 executive *American:* 4 Burr, Bush, Ford, King 5 Adams, Agnew, Dawes, Gerry, Nixon, Tyler 6 Arthur, Colfax, Curtis, Dallas, Garner, Hamlin, Hobart, Morton, Quayle, Truman, Wilson 7 Barkley, Calhoun, Clinton, Johnson, Mondale, Sherman, Wallace, Wheeler 8 Coolidge, Fillmore, Humphrey, Marshall, Tompkins, Van Buren 9 Fairbanks, Hendricks, Jefferson, Roosevelt, Stevenson 11 Rockefeller 12 Breckinridge
viceroy 5 nabob, ruler 6 exarch, satrap 7 khedive 8 governor 9 butterfly
vice versa 10 contrawise, conversely 12 contrariwise
vicinage 4 area 8 district, locality, vicinity 12 neighborhood
vicinity 4 area 5 range 6 extent, matter, region 8 district, locality, nearness, vicinage 9 magnitude, proximity 12 neighborhood
vicious 4 evil, mean, wild 5 feral, wrong 6 fierce, malign, putrid, rotten, savage, sinful, wicked 7 brutish, corrupt, furious, hateful, immoral, intense, violent 8 depraved, infamous, perverse, spiteful, terrible, vehement 9 desperate, malicious, malignant, miscreant, nefarious, rancorous, reprobate 10 degenerate, despiteful, flagitious, iniquitous, malevolent, villainous 12 blood-thirsty
vicissitude 5 rigor, trial 6 change 7 novelty, variety 8 asperity, hardness, hardship, mutation, reversal 9 adversity, diversity, mischance 10 affliction, difficulty, innovation, misfortune 11 permutation, progression, tribulation, ups and downs
victim 4 butt, dupe, fool, gull, mark, prey 5 chump 6 pigeon, quarry, sucker 7 fall guy, gudgeon 8 casualty, offering, underdog 9 bottom dog, sacrifice
victimize 4 dupe, fool, gull, hoax 5 trick 6 pigeon 8 flimflam, hoodwink, immolate 9 bamboozle, sacrifice 11 hornswoggle
victor 3 top 5 champ, first 6 master, winner 7 subduer 8 champion, defeater 9 conquerer 10 subjugator, vanquisher
Victoria, Queen *family:* 7 Hanover *father:* 6 Edward *husband:* 6 Albert *son:* 6 Edward
Victorian 4 prig, prim 6 prissy, stuffy 10 old-maidish, tight-laced 11 puritanical, straitlaced 12 old-fashioned
victory 3 win 6 better 7 command, control, mastery, success, triumph 8 conquest, dominion, walkaway, walkover, whip hand 9 advantage, supremacy, upper hand 11 subjugation, superiority *costly:* 7 Pyrrhic *easy:* 8 cakewalk, walkaway *monument:* 4 arch 13 Arc de Triomphe *reward:* 6 spoils *sign:* 3 vee *symbol:* 4 flag 6 laurel, wreath
Victory author 6 Conrad
victuals 4 chow, eats, feed, food, grub 6 viands 7 edibles 9 provender 10 provisions 11 comestibles
___ Vidal 4 Gore

videlicet 3 viz 5 to wit 6 namely 8 scilicet
vie 3 pit 5 match, rival 6 oppose, outvie 7 compete, contend, contest, counter, play off 9 challenge
Viennese ***city hall:*** 7 Rathaus ***family:*** 8 Hapsburg ***palace:*** 7 Hofburg ***park:*** 6 Prater
Vientiane's land 4 Laos
Vietnam ***Capital:*** 5 Hanoi ***monetary unit:*** 4 dong
Vietnamese New Year 3 Tet
view 3 aim, con, eye, see, vet 4 deem, espy, goal, look, mark, mind, plan, scan 5 audit, scene, sight, study, vista 6 behold, belief, descry, design, look at, notice, notion, object, regard, review, survey 7 canvass, check up, discern, examine, feeling, inspect, observe, opinion, outlook, picture, scenery 8 analysis, consider, gaze upon, look upon, panorama, perceive, prospect, scrutiny 9 check over, objective, sentiment 10 conviction, inspection, persuasion, scrutinize 11 contemplate, distinguish, examination, perlustrate 13 perlustration
viewable 6 ocular, visual 7 seeable, visible
viewer 7 watcher, witness 8 beholder, bysitter, looker-on, observer, onlooker 9 bystander, spectator 10 eyewitness
viewing instrument 5 glass, scope 7 glasses 9 telescope 10 binoculars, microscope ***combining form:*** 5 scope
viewpoint 3 eye 4 side 5 angle, slant, stand 7 outlook, posture 8 attitude, position 9 direction 10 estimation, standpoint 11 perspective
vigil 4 tout 5 watch 7 lookout 12 surveillance, watch and ward
vigilance see vigil
vigilant 4 agog, avid, keen 5 acute, alert, awake, aware, eager, sharp 7 anxious, wakeful 8 open-eyed, watchful 9 attentive, sharp-eyed, wide-awake 10 unsleeping
vignette 5 scene 6 sketch 7 picture 8 ornament
vigor 3 pep, vim, zip 4 bang, beef, birr, dash, fire, push, snap, tuck, zing 5 drive, force, getup, might, moxie, oomph, power, punch, steam 6 bounce, energy, muscle, spirit, starch 7 ability, potency 8 dynamism, strength, virility, vitality 9 hardihood, lustiness, manliness, puissance, soundness 10 capability, enterprise, get-up-and-go 11 healthiness
vigorous 5 brisk, hardy, husky, lusty, proud, stout, tough, vital 6 hearty, lively, potent, robust, sinewy, strong, sturdy 7 dashing, driving, dynamic, healthy, zealous 8 athletic, bouncing, muscular, powerful, slashing, spirited 9 energetic, exuberant, masterful, strenuous 10 mettlesome, red-blooded, survigrous 11 hard-driving, hard-hitting 13 rough-and-ready
Viking see Norse
vile 3 low 4 base, evil, foul, mean, ugly 5 gross, nasty 6 coarse, horrid, sordid, vulgar 7 debased, ignoble, low-down, noisome, obscene, servile, squalid 8 depraved, wretched 9 abhorrent, corrupted, debauched, loathsome, offensive, perverted, repugnant, repulsive, revolting 10 despicable, disgusting 12 contemptible
Vili ***brother:*** 2 Ve 4 Odin ***victim:*** 4 Ymir
vilify 5 abuse, libel 6 assail, attack, berate, defame, malign, misuse 7 asperse, outrage, slander, traduce 8 denounce, mistreat, tear down 9 denigrate 10 calumniate, villainize
villa 5 manor 6 castle, estate 7 chateau, mansion
village 4 burg, town 5 bourg, thorp 6 hamlet 7 townlet ***African:*** 4 dorp, stad 5 kraal ***Indian:*** 6 bustee, pueblo ***Japanese:*** 4 mura ***Jewish:*** 6 shtetl ***Malay:*** 7 campong, kampong ***Russian:*** 3 mir
Village Blacksmith author 10 Longfellow
villain 4 heel 5 devil, heavy, knave, rogue, scamp 6 meanie, rascal, sinner 7 lowlife 8 criminal, evildoer, mischief, offender, roperipe, scalawag 9 miscreant, reprobate, scoundrel, skeezicks 10 blackguard, malefactor 11 rapscallion ***classic:*** 4 Iago
villainous 6 putrid, rotten 7 corrupt, debased, heinous, vicious 8 contrary, infamous, perverse 9 abandoned, atrocious, dissolute, miscreant, nefarious, offensive, perverted 10 degenerate, detestable, flagitious, outrageous, profligate 13 objectionable
villainy 5 crime 9 depravity
villein 7 peasant 8 villager
villenage 4 yoke 6 thrall 7 bondage, helotry, peonage, serfdom, slavery 9 servitude, thralldom 11 enslavement
vim 4 brio, dash, élan, kick, life, push, zing 5 oomph, verve 6 esprit, pepper, spirit 9 animation
vinaigrette 3 box 4 cart 5 sauce, wagon 6 bottle
vinculum 3 tie 4 bond, knot, link, yoke 5 nexus 8 ligament, ligature
vindicable 6 venial 7 tenable 9 excusable 10 condonable, defensible 11 inoffensive, justifiable, warrantable
vindicate 4 free 5 argue, claim, clear, guard, prove, venge 6 acquit, assert, avenge, defend, refute, second, shield, uphold 7 absolve, bear out, confute, contend, justify, protect, redress, revenge, support, warrant 8 advocate, disprove, main-

tain, plead for 9 exculpate, exonerate 10 disculpate 11 rationalize
vindictive 5 nasty 6 malign 8 punitive, spiteful, vengeful, wreakful 9 malicious, malignant, merciless 10 implacable, relentless, revengeful 11 unrelenting
vine 3 hop, ivy, pea 4 gogo, soma 5 betel, buaze, guaco, kudzu, liana, liane, luffa, maile 6 cowage, cowpea, loofah, maypop 7 chayote, climber, copihue, creeper, cupseed 8 catbrier, clematis 10 chile-bells 11 bittersweet ***combining form:*** 4 viti ***East Indian:*** 6 pikake
vinegar 3 vim 6 acetum 8 sourness ***combining form:*** 4 acet 5 aceto ***relating to:*** 6 acetic ***steep in:*** 6 pickle
vinegarish 4 sour 5 waspy 6 bitter, cranky, ornery 7 bearish, waspish 8 cankered 9 crotchety, irascible 12 cantankerous, cross-grained
Vinegar Joe 8 Stilwell
vinegary 4 sour 6 acetic 7 acetose, acetous
vineyard 7 grapery ***French:*** 3 cru
Vinland discoverer 7 Ericson 8 Ericsson
vintage 3 old 4 crop, wine 5 dated, passé 6 démodé 7 antique, archaic, classic, harvest 8 outdated, outmoded 9 classical 10 antiquated 12 old-fashioned
Viola ***brother:*** 9 Sebastian ***husband:*** 6 Orsino
Viola da ___ 5 gamba
violate 3 err, sin 4 rape 5 break, force, spoil 6 breach, defile, offend, ravish 7 infract, outrage 8 deflower, infringe, overpass, trespass 9 deflorate, disregard, trample on 10 contravene, transgress 11 trample upon
violation 5 break, crime, wrong 6 breach 7 offense 8 defacing, trespass 9 blasphemy, sacrilege 10 defacement, illegality, infraction 11 desecration, misdemeanor, profanation 12 encroachment, infringement 13 contravention, transgression
violence 4 fury, riot 5 clash, force 6 attack, duress, frenzy, tumult, uproar 7 assault, rampage 8 coercion, foul play, savagery, struggle 9 onslaught 10 compulsion, constraint
violent 5 acute, harsh, rough 6 fierce, mighty, potent, strong 7 cutting, extreme, furious, intense, vicious 8 forceful, forcible, piercing, powerful, terrible, vehement 9 desperate, exquisite, splitting 10 immoderate, inordinate 11 destructive 12 concentrated
violently 4 hard 5 madly 6 wildly 8 fiercely, stormily 9 furiously, ruinously 10 frenziedly 11 combatively, frantically, turbulently 12 tumultuously 13 destructively
violet 5 mauve 6 flower, purple
violin 6 fiddle 10 instrument ***kind:*** 4 bass 5 Amati, cello, Strad 7 quinton 10 double bass, Guarnerius, Stradivari 12 Stradivarius ***part:*** 3 bow, nut, peg, rib 4 neck 5 belly 6 bridge, corner, pegbox, saddle, scroll, string 8 chin rest, purfling 11 fingerboard ***precursor:*** 5 gigue, rabab, rebec 6 vielle
violinist ***American:*** 5 Elman, Fodor, Rabin, Ricci, Stern 6 Midori, Powell, Rosand 7 Heifetz, Menuhin, Szigeti 8 Kreisler, Milstein, Spalding, Zukofsky 9 Zimbalist ***Belgian:*** 5 Ysaye 8 Grumiaux ***Canadian:*** 6 Staryk ***Czech:*** 3 Suk ***French:*** 12 Francescatti ***German:*** 9 Hindemith ***Hungarian:*** 6 Tatrai 7 Joachim ***Israeli:*** 7 Perlman 8 Zukerman ***Italian:*** 6 Viotti 7 Corelli, Vivaldi 8 Paganini 9 Geminiani ***Romanian:*** 6 Enesco ***Russian:*** 8 Oistrakh
violin maker 4 Salo 5 Amati 7 Maggini 8 Guarneri 10 Stradivari
VIP 4 lion 6 biggie, bigwig, fat cat, leader 7 big shot, notable, someone 8 big wheel, luminary, somebody 9 big cheese
viper 3 asp 5 adder, snake 10 bushmaster, copperhead, fer-de-lance 11 rattlesnake
virago 5 harpy, scold, shrew, vixen 6 amazon, ogress 8 fishwife 9 termagant, Xanthippe
Virgil see **Vergil**
virgin 3 new 4 pure 5 fresh, unwed 6 intact, maiden, single, vestal 8 celibate, innocent, primeval, pristine, unmarred, untapped 9 abstinent, unmarried, unspoiled, unsullied, untouched 10 spouseless 12 undeflowered ***combining form:*** 7 parthen 8 partheno
virginal 4 pure 6 intact, maiden 8 untapped 9 unspoiled, untouched 12 undeflowered
Virgin Goddess 5 Diana 7 Artemis
Virginia ***capital:*** 8 Richmond ***college, institute, university:*** 7 Hampton 8 Richmond 11 Old Dominion 13 Randolph Macon 14 William and Mary ***nickname:*** 11 Old Dominion ***state bird:*** 8 cardinal
Virginian, The ***author:*** 6 Wister ***character:*** 7 Trampas
Virgin Islands of the U.S. 6 St. John 7 St. Croix 8 St. Thomas
virginity 6 purity 8 chastity 10 chasteness, maidenhead, maidenhood
Virgin Queen 10 Elizabeth I
Virgo star 5 Spica
viridity 5 youth 9 freshness, greenness, innocence
virile 4 male 5 manly 6 manful, potent, robust 7 driving, manlike, mannish 8 decisive, forceful 9 energetic, masculine
virose 5 fetid 6 poison 9 poisonous

virtual 5 basic 8 implicit 9 essential, practical 11 fundamental 12 constructive
virtuality 4 pith, soul 5 stuff 6 bottom, marrow 7 essence 9 substance 12 essentiality, quintessence
virtually 6 almost, nearly 7 morally 8 actually 9 basically, in essence 10 absolutely 11 essentially, practically 13 fundamentally
virtue 4 dint, mark 5 arête, merit, piety, trait, value, vigor, worth 7 caliber, feature, potency, probity, quality, stature 8 efficacy, goodness, morality, property 9 affection, attribute, character, puissance, rectitude, rightness 10 excellence, excellency, perfection 11 uprightness 13 effectiveness, effectualness, righteousness *cardinal:* 4 hope 5 faith 7 charity, justice 8 prudence 9 fortitude 10 temperance
virtuosic 4 ripe 6 expert 8 finished 9 masterful, perfected 10 consummate 12 accomplished
virtuoso 4 whiz 6 artist, expert, master, musico, wizard 7 artiste, dabster 8 musician 9 authority 10 past master 12 professional
virtuous 4 good, pure 5 moral, noble 6 worthy 7 ethical, sinless 8 innocent, spotless 9 blameless, effective, effectual, efficient, exemplary, faultless, guiltless, righteous, unsullied, untainted 10 inculpable, moralistic, principled, unblamable 11 efficacious, right-minded, untarnished
virulent 5 sharp, toxic 6 biting, bitter, malign, poison 7 cutting, hateful, hostile 8 mephitic, scathing, spiteful, stabbing, toxicant, venomous 9 malignant, poisonous, rancorous, vitriolic 10 unfriendly 12 antagonistic
virus 4 bane, germ 5 venom 6 poison 9 contagion, infection
vis 5 force, might, power
visage 3 mug 4 cast, face, look, phiz 6 kisser 8 features 10 expression 11 countenance
vis-à-vis 6 contra, facing, toward, versus 7 against 8 fronting, opposite 9 tête-à-tête 10 coordinate 11 counterpart, over against
viscera 4 guts 7 innards, insides, inwards 8 entrails, stuffing 9 internals *combining form:* 9 splanchno
visceral 3 gut 5 inner 8 interior, internal, intimate 9 intuitive 11 instinctive, instinctual
viscid see **viscous**
viscount 4 peer 7 sheriff 8 nobleman
viscous 4 ropy, sizy 5 gummy, slimy, stiff, thick, tough 6 sticky 9 glutinous, semifluid, tenacious
vise 4 grip, tool 5 clamp
Vishnu 4 Hare, Hari *avatar:* 4 Rama 5 Kurma 6 Buddha, Matsya, Vamena, Varaha 7 Krishna 9 Narasinha *consort:* 3 Sri 4 Shri 7 Lakshmi *home:* 4 Meru
visible 4 seen 6 ocular, visual 7 seeable 8 apparent, viewable
Visigoth *conquest:* 4 Rome *king:* 6 Alaric
vision 3 eye 4 muse 5 dream, fancy, image, sight, think 6 beauty, oracle, seeing 7 fantasy, feature, imagine, realize 8 conceive, daydream, envisage, eyesight, phantasm, phantasy, presence, prophecy 9 nightmare, visualize 10 apocalypse, apparition, phenomenon, revelation *combining form:* 4 opsy, opto 5 opsia, opsis 6 optico *deceptive:* 6 mirage *defect:* (see at eye) *in bright light:* 8 photopia *in dim light:* 8 scotopia *relating to:* 5 optic 6 visual 7 optical *without:* 5 blind
visionary 5 ideal, lofty, noble 6 astral, dreamy, musing 7 dreamer, exalted, radical, utopian 8 idealist 9 ambitious, daydreamy, grandiose, ideologue, unworldly 10 abstracted, idealistic 11 daydreaming, impractical, pretentious 12 otherworldly 13 castle-builder, introspective
visionless 4 dark 5 blind 7 eyeless 9 sightless 10 stone-blind
Vision of Sir Launfal, The author 6 Lowell
visit 3 gam, see 4 call, chat, chin, pain, stay, talk, yarn 5 pop in, run in, tarry, wreak, wreck 6 avenge, bother, come by, drop by, drop in, impose, look in, look up, punish, reside, step in, stop by, stop in 7 afflict, force on, inflict, sojourn, trouble 8 colloque, come over, converse, frequent, stopover 9 force upon, tarriance *often:* 8 frequent
visitation 4 call 5 cross, trial 6 ordeal 7 calvary 8 calamity, crucible, disaster 9 mischance 10 affliction 11 catastrophe, tribulation
visitor 5 guest 6 caller 7 company, invitee
vison 4 mink
visor 4 bill, mask, peak 6 domino, vizard 8 eyeshade 9 doughface, false face
vista 4 view 5 range, scape, scene, scope, sight 6 survey 7 lookout, outlook 8 panorama, prospect 11 perspective
visual 5 optic 6 ocular 7 optical, seeable, visible 8 viewable, visional 11 discernible, perceivable, perceptible
visualize 3 see 4 view 5 fancy, image, think 6 call up, divine 7 feature, foresee, imagine, picture, preknow, previse, realize 8 conceive, envisage, envision, forefeel, foreknow 9 apprehend, conjure up, objectify, prevision 10 anticipate
vital 5 alive, lusty 6 living, needed, zoetic 7 animate, dynamic, needful 8 animated, cardinal, integral, required, vigorous 9 breathing, energetic, essential, requisite, strenuous 10 red-blooded 11 fundamen-

tal 12 constitutive, prerequisite 13 indispensable
vital force 4 soul 5 anima 6 animus, pneuma, psyche, spirit 9 élan vital
vitality see vigor
vitalize 5 liven, pep up 6 actify, excite, vivify 7 animate, enliven, provoke, quicken 8 activate, activize, dynamize, energize 9 galvanize, stimulate 10 invigorate, strengthen
vitally 4 very 6 hugely 7 notably, parlous 9 extremely 10 remarkably, strikingly 11 exceedingly 12 surpassingly 13 exceptionally
vitals see viscera
vitamin 6 biotin, niacin 7 choline, folacin 8 carotene, inositol, thiamine 9 cobalamin, folic acid, pyridoxal 10 calciferol, pyridoxine, riboflavin, tocopherol 12 ascorbic acid, bioflavonoid, meso-inositol
Vito Nuova, La *author:* 5 Dante
vitellus 4 yolk
vitiate 3 mar 4 harm, hurt, soil, undo 5 abate, annul, quash, spoil, sully, taint 6 damage, debase, defile, impair, injure, negate 7 abolish, blemish, corrupt, debased, debauch, deprave, nullify, pervert, tarnish 8 abrogate, depraved 9 brutalize, corrupted, debauched, perverted, prejudice 10 annihilate, bastardize, bestialize, demoralize, invalidate
vitreous 6 glassy
vitriol 7 sulfate 9 virulence
vitriolic 6 bitter 7 hostile 8 virulent 9 rancorous 12 antagonistic
vituperate 4 lash, rail, rate 5 abuse, curse, scold 6 bark at, berate, malign, revile, yell at 7 asperse, bawl out, chew out, condemn, growl at, upbraid 8 lambaste 10 tongue-lash
vituperation 5 abuse, blame 7 censure, obloquy 8 scolding 9 contumely, invective 10 revilement, scurrility 12 billingsgate 13 tongue-lashing
vituperative 6 severe 7 abusive, railing 8 critical, scolding, scurrile 9 invective, truculent 10 censorious, scurrilous 11 opprobrious 12 contumelious
vivacious 3 gay 4 cant, keen 5 alert, brash, canty, zesty 6 breezy, lively 7 animate, playful, vibrant 8 animated, spirited, sportive 9 ebullient, exuberant, sprightly 10 frolicsome 12 effervescent, high-spirited
vivacity see verve
Vivaldi, Antonio *epithet:* 12 il prete rosso, the red priest
____ vivant 3 bon
vivarium 3 zoo
vivid 3 gay 4 keen, rich 5 acute, alive, brave, sharp 6 bright, colory, lively, living 7 graphic, intense 8 animated, colorful, dramatic, eloquent, spirited, vigorous 9 pictorial 10 expressive, meaningful, theatrical 11 dramaturgic, picturesque 12 photographic
vivify 5 liven, renew 6 excite, revive 7 animate, enliven, quicken, refresh, restore 9 galvanize
vixen 3 fox, nag 5 harpy, scold, shrew 6 amazon, ogress, virago 8 fishwife 9 termagant, Xanthippe
viz 5 to wit 6 namely 8 scilicet 9 videlicet
vizard 4 mask 5 visor 6 domino 9 doughface, false face
vocabulary 4 cant 5 words 6 jargon 7 lexicon, palaver 8 language 9 wordhoard, word-stock 10 dictionary 11 phraseology, terminology
vocal 4 oral 6 fluent, sonant, spoken, voiced 7 uttered, voicing 8 eloquent 9 expressed, intonated, outspoken 10 articulate, expressing, expressive, free-spoken
vocalic 5 vowel 6 vowely 9 vowellike
vocalist 6 singer 8 songster 9 performer 11 entertainer
vocalization 5 mouth, voice 6 speech 7 diction, voicing 8 mouthing, sounding, speaking, uttering 9 utterance 11 enunciation 12 articulation 13 verbalization
vocalize 4 sing, talk, tune 5 chant, speak, utter, voice 6 convey, impart, let out 7 express 9 enunciate, pronounce, verbalize 11 communicate
vocal organ 6 larynx *bird:* 6 syrinx
vocation 3 art, job 4 work 5 craft, trade 6 métier 7 calling, mission 8 lifework 10 handicraft, occupation, profession
vocative 4 case 6 fluent 7 voluble 9 garrulous
vociferate 3 cry 4 call, yell 5 hallo, hollo, shout 6 holler
vociferous 4 loud 5 noisy 6 shrill 7 blatant, dinsome 8 strident 9 clamorous 10 boisterous, multivocal 11 distracting, loudmouthed, openmouthed 12 obstreperous
vogue 3 cry, fad 4 chic, mode, rage 5 craze, style, trend 6 bon ton, furore 7 fashion 10 dernier cri 11 stylishness
voice 3 put, say 4 talk, tell, vent 5 say-so, sound, speak, utter 6 phrase, speech 7 present, recount 8 vocalize 9 enunciate, formulate, pronounce, statement, utterance, verbalize 10 articulate, expression *combining form:* 4 phon 5 phone, phono, phony 6 phonia *female:* 4 alto 5 mezzo 7 soprano 9 contralto *high:* 5 tenor 7 soprano 8 falsetto *in grammar:* 6 active 7 passive *Latin:* 3 vox *male:* 4 bass 5 tenor 8 baritone *quality:* 5 pitch 6 timbre *quiet:* 7 whisper *relating to:* 5 vocal 8 phonetic *without:* 4 dumb, mute

voice box 6 larynx
voiced 4 oral 5 vocal 6 sonant, spoken 10 articulate
voiceless 3 mum 4 dumb, mute 6 silent 10 speechless 12 inarticulate, unarticulate
void 3 bad, gap 4 bare, emit, flow, hole, null, pour 5 abyss, annul, clear, drain, eject, empty, quash, scant, short 6 bereft, cavity, devoid, hollow, remove, vacant, vacate, vacuum 7 denuded, deplete, give off, invalid, negated, vacuity, vacuous 8 abrogate, deprived, dissolve, evacuate, innocent, throw out 9 destitute, discharge, eliminate 10 disembogue
voiture 3 car 8 carriage
volage 5 dizzy, giddy 7 flighty 9 frivolous 10 bird-witted 11 empty-headed, harebrained 13 rattlebrained
volant 4 spry, yare 5 agile, brisk, catty, zippy 6 active, lively, nimble 9 sprightly
volary 6 aviary 8 birdcage
volatile 4 airy, edgy 6 bouncy, fickle, lively 7 buoyant, elastic, flighty, protean 8 agitable, fleeting, flippant, fugitive, skittery, skittish, ticklish, unstable, variable 9 alarmable, ephemeral, excitable, expansive, explosive, frivolous, fugacious, mercurial, momentary, resilient, startlish, transient 10 capricious, changeable, evanescent, inconstant, lubricious, short-lived, transitory 11 impermanent, light-minded 12 effervescent 13 temperamental
volatility 6 levity 9 animation, flippancy, frivolity, lightness 11 flightiness, inconstancy, instability, variability 13 changeability, mercurialness, sprightliness
volcanic ***crater:*** 4 maar ***explosion:*** 8 eruption ***glass:*** 8 obsidian ***matter:*** 3 ash 4 lava, tufa, tuff 5 magma, trass 6 scoria ***mound:*** 4 cone 7 hornito ***passage:*** 6 throat 7 conduit ***vent:*** 8 fumarole 9 solfatara
volcano 8 mountain ***Alaska:*** 11 Mount Katmai ***Andes:*** 5 Omate 12 Huaina Putina ***Antarctica:*** 11 Mount Erebus ***Azores:*** 4 Alto ***California:*** 10 Lassen Peak ***Canaries:*** 5 Teide 8 Tenerife ***Colombia:*** 5 Huila, Pasto 6 Purace 7 Galeras ***Costa Rica:*** 4 Poás 5 Barba, Irazú ***Ecuador:*** 8 Cotopaxi ***extinct:*** 5 Iriga 8 Mauna Kea 9 Mount Popa 10 Mount Kenya ***Guatemala:*** 4 Agua 5 Fuego 7 Atitlán ***Hawaii:*** 8 Mauna Loa ***Honshū:*** 4 Nasu 5 Asama, Azuma 8 Nasudake 9 Asamayama ***Iceland:*** 5 Askja, Hekla ***Indonesia:*** 7 Tambora 9 Gunung Awu 10 Peak of Bali 11 Gunung Agung ***island:*** 8 Krakatau, Krakatoa ***Italy:*** 8 Vesuvius 9 Stromboli ***Japan:*** 3 Aso 5 Unzen 6 Asosan ***Java:*** 4 Gede 5 Bromo, Gedeh, Kelud, Salak ***Madeira:*** 5 Ruivo ***Martinique:*** 10 Mount Pelee ***Mexico:*** 6 Colima 7 Orizaba 9 Paricutin 12 Popocatepetl ***New Zealand:*** 7 Ruapehu 9 Ngauruhoe ***Philippines:*** 4 Taal 10 Mount Mayon 13 Mount Pinatubo ***Saint Vincent:*** 9 Soufrière ***Sicily:*** 4 Etna 5 Aetna ***Solomons:*** 5 Balbi ***South America:*** 5 Lanin, Maipo ***Sumatra:*** 5 Dempo
___ volente 3 Deo
volition 4 will 6 choice, desire, option 8 election 9 selection 10 preference
volley 4 hail, shot 5 burst, round, salvo, storm 6 shower 7 barrage 8 drumfire
volplane 5 glide
Volpone 3 fox ***author:*** 6 Jonson ***servant:*** 5 Mosca
Volsung ***grandson:*** 6 Sigurd 9 Siegfried ***great-grandfather:*** 4 Odin ***son:*** 7 Sigmund
Voltaire ***drama:*** 5 Zaïre 6 Alzire, Brutus, Mèrope, Oedipe 7 Mahomet 8 Tancrède ***novel:*** 5 Zadig 7 Candide ***real name:*** 6 Arouet (François Marie)
volte-face 4 turn, veer, whip 5 avert, pivot, sheer, wheel, whirl 6 divert 7 deflect, reverse 8 reversal 9 about-face, face about, reversion, turnabout 10 right-about 11 changeabout, reversement
voluble 4 glib 6 fickle, fluent 8 vocative 9 talkative 13 silver-tongued
volume 4 body, book, bulk, mass, size, tome 6 amount, object 7 content 8 capacity, loudness, quantity
voluminous 4 full, many 6 legion, sundry 7 several, various 8 numerous 12 multifarious, multitudinal 13 multitudinous
Volumnia's son 10 Coriolanus
Völund 5 smith 7 Wayland ***brother:*** 4 Egil 5 Egill
voluntary 4 free 5 opted 6 chosen 7 elected, willful, willing, witting 8 elective, optional, unforced 10 autonomous, deliberate, volitional 11 independent, intentional 12 unprescribed
volunteer 5 offer 6 enlist ***hospital:*** 12 candy striper
Volunteer State 9 Tennessee
voluptuous 4 lush 6 wanton 7 sensual 8 luscious, sensuous 9 abandoned, dissolute, epicurean, excessive, indulgent, luxurious 10 dissipated 12 sensualistic
volute 6 scroll, spiral
volution 5 twist, whorl
vomit 3 gag 4 barf, spew 5 eject, expel, retch 6 spit up 7 bring up, throw up, upchuck 8 disgorge 11 regurgitate
vomiting 6 emesis
Von Flotow opera 6 Martha
Von Stroheim film 5 Greed 13 Blind Husbands, Grand Illusion
voodoo 3 hex 4 jinx, mage 5 charm, magus, obeah, spell, witch 6 whammy, wiz-

ard 7 bewitch, enchant, warlock 8 conjurer, magician, sorcerer 9 enchanter, ensorcell 10 Indian sign 11 necromancer

voodooist 4 mage 5 magus 6 wizard 7 charmer, warlock 8 conjurer, magician, sorcerer 9 enchanter 11 necromancer

Vophsi's son 5 Nahbi

voracious 4 avid 6 greedy, hungry, sating 7 gorging 8 covetous, edacious, grasping, ravening, ravenous 9 devouring, rapacious, satiating 10 gluttonous, insatiable, surfeiting 11 acquisitive

vorago 5 abyss, chasm

vortex 4 eddy, gyre 5 spout, whirl 6 spiral 9 maelstrom, whirlpool

votary 3 fan 4 buff 5 freak, hound, lover 6 addict, zealot 7 admirer, amateur, devotee, fancier, habitué 8 disciple 10 aficionado

vote 4 poll 5 elect 6 ballot, choice, choose, decide, ratify, ticket 7 opinion 8 election, suffrage 9 franchise *affirmative:* 3 aye, nod, yea, yes 6 placet *kind:* 5 proxy, straw, voice 6 secret 7 write-in 10 plebiscite, referendum *negative:* 2 no 3 nay *right to:* 8 suffrage 9 franchise

voter 7 chooser, elector *kind:* 8 absentee

vouch 5 prove 6 assure, attest, uphold, verify 7 certify, confirm, support, witness 9 guarantee 11 corroborate 12 substantiate

voucher 4 chit 5 proof 7 receipt 9 affidavit 10 credential 11 certificate

vouchsafe 4 give 5 award, deign, favor, grant, stoop 6 accord, oblige 7 concede 10 condescend 11 accommodate

vow 4 oath, swan 5 swear 6 assert, pledge, plight, prayer 7 declare, promise 8 covenant

vowel 5 vocal 6 letter *kind:* 4 long 5 glide, schwa, short 9 diphthong *omission:* 7 aphesis 11 contraction *variation:* 6 ablaut, umlaut

vowely 5 vocal 7 vocalic

voyage 4 tour, trip 6 cruise, travel 7 journey 9 excursion 10 expedition, pilgrimage

voyeur 6 peeper 10 peeping Tom

Vronski's lover 12 Anna Karenina

Vulcan see **Hephaestus**

vulgar 3 low, raw 4 base, rude, vile, wild 5 crass, crude, dirty, gross, nasty, rough 6 coarse, public, ribald, smutty, spoken 7 general, obscene, popular, profane, uncouth 8 barbaric, barnyard, improper, indecent, unseemly 9 barbarian, barbarous, graceless, idiomatic, incorrect, inelegant, loathsome, offensive, repulsive, revolting, tasteless, unrefined 10 colloquial, indecorous, indelicate, outlandish, ungraceful, unpolished, vernacular 12 scatological

vulgarism 8 slangism, solecism 9 barbarism 10 corruption 11 impropriety 13 vernacularism, vernacularity

vulgate 6 patois 10 colloquial, vernacular

Vulgate translator 6 Jerome

vulnerability 8 exposure, openness, weakness 9 liability 11 vincibility

vulnerable 4 open, weak 6 liable 7 exposed

vulnerary 6 curing 7 healing 8 curative, remedial, sanative, sanatory 9 remedying, wholesome 11 restorative

vulpine 3 sly 4 foxy, wily 6 artful, astute, crafty, tricky 7 cunning 8 guileful 9 insidious

vulture 4 hook, lift 5 filch, pinch, steal, swipe 6 condor, snitch 7 buzzard 8 aasvogel 11 lammergeier *food:* 7 carrion

vulturine 9 predative, predatory, rapacious, raptorial 10 predacious 11 predatorial

W

wacky 3 mad 4 nuts 5 crazy, loony, silly 6 absurd, crazed, insane 7 cracked, foolish, lunatic 9 demented, deranged 11 hare-brained 12 preposterous

wad 3 gob, pot 4 bomb, clod, hunk, lump, mint, pile 5 chunk, clump, hunch 6 boodle, bundle, nugget, packet 7 fortune

waddy 3 peg 4 club 5 stick 6 cowboy 7 rustler

wade 4 ford, plod *into:* 6 attack

wadi 3 bed 4 wash 5 gully 6 ravine

wafer 4 cake, disk 7 cracker

waft 4 gust, puff, wave 5 drift, float, whiff

wag 3 wit 4 beat, card, lash, wave, zany 5 clown, comic, cutup, droll, joker, shake 6 jester, kidder, madcap, switch, twitch, waggle, wiggle, wigwag, woggle 7 farceur, show-off 8 comedian, funnyman, humorist, jokester, quipster 9 oscillate, prankster 11 wisecracker

wage 3 fee, pay 4 hire, take 6 income, return, reward, salary 7 stipend 8 earnings, receipts 9 emolument 10 recompense 12 compensation, remuneration

wager 3 bet, lay, pot, set 4 ante, game, play, risk 5 put on, stake 6 chance, gamble, hazard, impone 7 venture 9 adventure

waggery 3 gag 4 jape, jest, joke, quip 5 crack 7 devilry, roguery 8 deviltry, drollery, mischief 9 devilment, wisecrack, witticism 10 impishness 11 roguishness, waggishness 12 sportiveness

waggish 4 arch, pert 5 antic, comic, droll, funny, saucy, witty 6 impish, jocose 7 comical, jocular, playful, puckish, roguish 8 humorous, prankish, sportive 9 facetious, laughable, ludicrous 10 frolicsome 11 mischievous

waggle 4 beat, lash, sway, wave 6 switch, waddle, wobble

Wagner, Richard *birthplace:* 7 Leipzig *deathplace:* 6 Venice *father-in-law:* 5 Liszt *opera:* 6 Rienzi 8 Parsifal 9 Lohengrin, Siegfried 10 Die Walküre, Tannhäuser 12 Das Rheingold *recurring theme:* 9 leitmotif, leitmotiv *wife:* 5 Minna 6 Cosima

wagon 3 car, van 4 cart, dray, wain 5 gilly 6 telega 7 fourgon, vehicle

wah 5 panda

wahoo 4 fish 5 shrub 8 basswood, mackerel 11 burning bush

waif 5 stray 7 vagrant 8 wanderer 9 foundling

wail 3 bay, cry, sob 4 bawl, blub, fuss, howl, keen, kick, weep, yowl 5 quest, whine 6 boohoo, murmur, repine, squall 7 blubber, ululate 8 complain

wailful 6 rueful, woeful 7 doleful 8 dolesome, mournful 9 plaintive, sorrowful 10 lamentable, lugubrious, melancholy

wain 5 wagon

waistband 4 belt, sash 6 girdle 8 ceinture, cincture

waistcoat 4 vest 6 jerkin

wait 4 bide, stay 5 abide, nurse, serve, tarry 6 expect, linger, mother, remain 7 care for, foresee 10 anticipate, minister to 11 stick around

waiter 6 garçon 7 servant 9 attendant

Waiting for ___ 5 Godot, Lefty

waive 4 cede, stay 5 allow, defer, delay, grant, leave, yield 6 give up, hold up, put off, resign, shelve 7 abandon, concede, hold off, suspend 8 hand over, hold over, postpone 9 surrender 10 relinquish

wake 4 stir, whet 5 arise, get up, rally, renew, rouse 6 arouse, bestir, kindle 7 freshen, roll out 9 challenge

wakeful 5 alert 8 restless, vigilant, watchful 9 sleepless

waken see wake

Walden author 7 Thoreau

wale 3 rib 4 weal, welt 5 ridge, wheal, whelk

Wales 5 Cymru *capital:* 7 Cardiff *language:* 6 Cymric *Latin name:* 7 Cambria *patron saint:* 5 David

walk 3 leg, run 4 foot, hike, hoof, pace, plod, race, reel, slog, step, turn 5 amble, field, march, mince, strut, stump, tramp, tread, troop 6 airing, domain, foot it, lumber, parade, ramble, sphere, stride, stroll, strunt, toddle, trudge 7 alameda, demesne, saunter, stretch, terrain, traipse 8 ambulate, dominion, province, traverse 9 bailiwick, champaign, promenade, territory 11 base on balls, perambulate 12 deambulation

walkaway 4 romp, rout

walking shorts 8 Bermudas

walking stick 4 cane 5 staff 6 kebbie 8 ashplant
walk out 5 leave 6 strike
walkway 4 path 7 catwalk 9 promenade *ancient Greek:* 4 stoa
wall 3 bar, hem 4 cage, coop, stop 5 block, fence, hedge 6 corral, immure 7 barrier, close in, enclose, envelop 8 blockade 9 barricade, roadblock ***hanging:*** 8 tapestry ***protective:*** 7 parapet ***top of:*** 6 coping
wallaba tree 3 apa
wallaby 8 kangaroo
wallet 8 billfold 10 pocketbook ***items:*** 5 bills
wallop 3 bat, bop, jar 4 bang, bash, beat, belt, blow, boot, bump, drub, jolt, kick, lick, pelt, slam, slug, trim, whip, whop 5 baste, blast, clash, crash, paste, pound, shock, smack, smash 6 buffet, impact, pummel, thrash, thrill, thwack 7 belabor, shellac, trounce 8 lambaste 9 collision 10 percussion
walloping 4 huge 5 giant 7 immense, mammoth, monster 8 colossal, enormous, gigantic 10 gargantuan, prodigious
wallow 4 bask, roll 5 enjoy, lurch, revel 6 welter 7 blunder, indulge, rollick, stumble 8 flounder 9 delight in, luxuriate
___ Walpole, writer 6 Horace
walrus 6 mammal ***relative:*** 4 seal ***tooth:*** 4 tusk
___ Walton, writer 5 Izaak
waltz 3 zip 6 breeze
Waltz King 7 Strauss
Wampanoag chief 9 Massasoit, Metacomet 10 King Philip
wampum 5 beads, money, sewan 6 shells
wan 4 ashy, pale, weak, worn 5 ashen, livid, waxen 6 anemic, doughy, pallid, sickly 7 haggard 8 blanched, bleached, boneless, impotent 9 bloodless, colorless, forceless, spineless, washed-out 10 cadaverous, emasculate 11 ineffective, ineffectual, slack-spined 12 invertebrate
wand 3 rod 4 pole, tube 5 baton, staff *combining form:* 5 rhabd 6 rhabdo
wander 3 bat, bum, err, gad 4 roam, roll, rove 5 amble, drift, gypsy, mooch, range, stray, tramp 6 depart, gander, ramble, stroll 7 deviate, digress, diverge, excurse, maunder, meander, saunter, traipse 8 divagate, straggle, vagabond 9 gallivant
wanderer 5 nomad, rover 6 errant, roamer 7 drifter, pilgrim, rambler, tzigane, vagrant 9 meanderer 12 rolling stone
wane 3 ebb 4 fail, fall 5 abate, let up 6 relent, shrink, weaken 7 decline, die away, die down, dwindle, ease off, slacken, subside 8 moderate 9 fall short, waste away
wangle 7 finagle 8 engineer, maneuver, outflank 9 machinate, overreach 10 outgeneral 11 outmaneuver
want 4 lack, must, need, wish 5 covet, crave, ought 6 dearth, defect, demand, desire, penury, should 7 absence, default, poverty, require 8 exigency, poorness 9 indigence, necessity, neediness, privation 10 desiderate, inadequacy, meagerness, scantiness, skimpiness 11 destitution, requirement 12 exiguousness 13 insufficiency
wanting 3 shy 4 away, gone, sans 5 minus, scant, short 6 absent, scanty, scarce 7 failing, lacking, missing, omitted, without 9 defective, deficient 10 inadequate, incomplete, uncomplete 12 insufficient, unsufficient
wanton 3 lax, toy 4 doxy, easy, fast, fool, jade, slut 5 cruel, dally, flirt, hussy, light, loose, slack, tramp, trull, wench 6 coquet, harlot, lead on, trifle 7 baggage, cyprian, jezebel, trollop, unasked, wayward, whorish 8 contrary, perverse, slattern, spiteful, strumpet, unchaste 9 malicious 10 gratuitous, malevolent, prostitute 11 string along, uncalled-for 12 supererogant
wapiti 3 elk 4 deer, stag
war 3 tug 4 feud 5 fight 6 battle, combat, oppugn, strife 7 contend, crusade 8 struggle ***German:*** 5 krieg 10 blitzkrieg ***god:*** 3 Tyr 4 Ares, Mars, Odin 5 Wodan, Woden ***goddess:*** 4 Enyo 5 Anath 6 Inanna, Ishtar 7 Bellona ***Latin:*** 6 bellum ***Muslim:*** 5 jehad, jihad ***relating to:*** 7 martial
War and Peace ***author:*** 7 Tolstoy ***composer:*** 9 Prokofiev
warble 3 air, lay 4 sing, tune 6 melody, strain 7 descant, measure, melisma, melodia 8 diapason
warbler 7 kinglet 8 songster 9 blackpoll 11 gnatcatcher ***European:*** 10 chiffchaff
war club 3 bat 4 mace 5 baton 6 cudgel 8 bludgeon 9 truncheon 10 knobkerrie
war cry 5 motto 6 slogan ***Greek:*** 5 alala
ward 4 balk, care, fend, foil, halt, stay, turn 5 aegis, armor, avert, block, check, deter, guard, parry, rebut, repel, trust, watch 6 divert, picket, rebuff, sentry, shield, stymie, thwart 7 custody, defense, deflect, fend off, forfend, hold off, keeping, keep off, lookout, obviate, prevent, repulse, rule out 8 armament, preclude, security, sentinel, stave off, watchman 9 forestall, frustrate, interrupt, safeguard 10 protection 11 safekeeping 12 guardianship
warden 6 custos, jailer, keeper, ranger 8 cerberus, claviger, guardian, watchdog 9 custodian
wardrobe 4 room 5 trunk 6 closet 12 clothespress

ware 4 shun 5 avoid, awake, aware, cloth, goods 7 fabrics, knowing, pottery 8 sensible 9 cognizant, conscious
warehouse 4 pack, stow 5 étape, guard, store 6 bestow 7 protect, shelter, storage 8 entrepôt 11 accommodate ***oriental:*** 6 godown
wares 4 line 5 goods 9 vendibles 11 commodities, merchandise
warfare 6 strife 7 contest, rivalry 8 conflict, striving 9 emulation 11 competition ***combining form:*** 5 machy
warhorse 7 charger, courser
warlike 7 hawkish, martial, warring 8 battling, fighting, militant, military, ructious 9 bellicose, combative, truculent 10 contending, pugnacious 11 belligerent, contentious, quarrelsome 12 gladiatorial
warlock 4 mage 5 magus 6 wizard 7 charmer 8 conjurer, magician, sorcerer 9 enchanter, voodooist 11 necromancer
warm 4 heat 5 tepid 6 ardent 7 affable, cordial, fervent, sincere, zealous 8 gracious 9 heartfelt 10 passionate, responsive 11 kindhearted, softhearted, sympathetic 12 enthusiastic, wholehearted 13 compassionate ***air:*** 7 thermal
warmed-over 5 stale, tired, trite 6 old hat 7 clichéd 8 shopworn, timeworn, well-worn 9 hackneyed, twice-told
warmhearted 4 kind, warm 6 benign, kindly, tender 8 outgoing 9 benignant 10 responsive 11 sympathetic 13 compassionate
warn 3 bid, tip 4 clew, clue, post, tell 5 alert, guide, order 6 advise, beacon, charge, direct, enjoin, fill in, inform, monish, notify, wise up 7 apprise, caution, command, counsel 8 acquaint, instruct
warning 3 tip 4 hint 6 advice, caveat 7 caution, counsel, sematic 8 guidance, monition, monitory 10 admonition, admonitory, cautionary, cautioning, monitorial, suggestion 11 admonishing, commonition ***legal:*** 6 caveat
War of the Worlds author 5 Wells
warp 4 bend, kink, wind 5 color, twist, wrest 6 debase, deform, garble, wrench 7 confuse, contort, corrupt, debauch, deprave, distort, pervert, torture, vitiate 8 miscolor, misshape 9 brutalize 10 bastardize, bestialize, demoralize 12 misrepresent
warrant 4 back, pawn, word 5 argue, basis, claim, state, token 6 affirm, assert, assure, defend, ensure, insure, pledge, secure 7 call for, certify, contend, earnest, justify, require, sponsor 8 guaranty, maintain, mittimus, security 9 assurance, guarantee, stipulate, vindicate 10 foundation
warranty 4 bail, bond 6 surety 8 guaranty, security 9 guarantee
warrior 2 GI 4 hero, swad 7 fighter, soldier 9 man-at-arms 10 serviceman 11 fighting man ***female:*** 6 Amazon ***Japanese:*** 7 samurai
Warsaw ***castle:*** 5 Zamek ***river:*** 7 Vistula
warship see ship, *military*
wart 6 lesion 7 verruca
wary 4 safe 5 canny, chary, leery 6 frugal, saving, scotch 7 careful, guarded, sceptic, skeptic, sparing, thrifty 8 cautious, discreet, doubting, gingerly, vigilant, watchful 9 provident, stewardly 10 suspicious, unwasteful 11 calculating, circumspect, considerate, distrustful
wash 3 lap, lip, tub 4 lave, ride, suds 5 bathe, clean, drift, float, slosh, swash 6 bubble, burble, gurgle, shower, sluice 7 launder, shampoo
washed-out 5 all in, spent 6 bleary, effete, used up 7 drained, far-gone, worn-out 8 depleted 9 exhausted
washed-up 4 done 7 done for, through 8 finished
washing 4 bath 6 lavage 8 ablution ***ceremonial:*** 6 lavabo
Washington ***capital:*** 7 Olympia ***largest city:*** 7 Seattle ***nickname:*** 12 Chinook State 14 Evergreen State ***state bird:*** 9 goldfinch ***state flower:*** 12 rhododendron
Washington, D.C. designer 7 L'Enfant
Washington's home 11 Mount Vernon
Washington Square author 5 James
wash out 4 cast, fail, flop, junk, shed 5 elute, scrap 6 reject, slough 7 cashier, discard, flummox 8 jettison 9 throw away
wasp 6 hornet, vespid
waspish 5 huffy, sharp 6 cranky, ornery 7 bearish, crabbed, fretful, peevish, pettish 8 cankered, contrary, perverse, petulant, snappish, spiteful 9 crotchety, fractious, impatient, irritable, malicious, querulous 10 vinegarish 12 cantankerous, cross-grained
waspy see waspish
wassail 3 bat 4 bust, hell, riot, soak, tear 5 binge, revel, spree 6 bender, frolic, rantan 7 carouse, revelry, roister, whoopee, whoopla, whoop-up 8 carousal 9 high jinks, revelment 10 skylarking
waste 4 blow, fail, junk, sack, wane, wild 5 offal, trash 6 barren, debris, desert, devour, drivel, kelter, litter, ravage, refuse, sewage, shrink, trifle, weaken 7 badland, consume, despoil, dwindle, fritter, garbage, pillage, rubbish, sullage 8 cast away, desolate, emaciate, fool away, misspend, riot away, spoilage, spoliate, squander, unthrift, wild land, wildness 9 depredate, desecrate, devastate, dissipate, fall short, overdoing,

sweepings, throw away **10** frivol away, lavishness, muddle away, potter away, trifle away, wilderness **11** blunder away, dribble away, prodigality, prodigalize **12** extravagance, extravagancy ***allowance:*** **4** tret ***from a mine:*** **7** mullock ***time:*** **5** dally **6** dawdle, footle, piddle

waste away **4** fail, wane **5** dwine **7** atrophy, decline

wasted **4** worn **5** gaunt **6** meager **7** wizened **8** skeletal, withered **9** emaciated, shriveled **10** cadaverous

wasteful **6** lavish **8** prodigal **10** thriftless **11** extravagant, improvident

wastefulness **8** squander, unthrift **9** overdoing **10** lavishness **11** prodigality **12** extravagance, extravagancy

wasteland **4** wild **6** barren, desert **8** wildness **10** wilderness

Waste Land author **5** Eliot

waster **5** idler **6** loafer, no-good **7** lounger, rounder, spender, wastrel **8** prodigal, unthrift **9** fritterer **10** dissipater, high roller, ne'er-do-well, profligate, scapegrace, squanderer **11** scattergood, spendthrift

wastrel **3** rip **4** rake, roué **5** idler, knave, rogue, scamp **6** lecher, loafer, no-good, rascal **7** lounger, rounder, spender **8** prodigal, scalawag, unthrift **9** fritterer, libertine, scoundrel **10** blackguard, black sheep, dissipater, high roller, ne'er-do-well, profligate, scapegrace, squanderer **11** rapscallion, scattergood, spendthrift

watch **3** eye, see, spy, tab **4** look, mind, scan, tend, tout, ward **5** guard, vigil **6** attend, follow, picket, sentry **7** care for, examine, eyeball, inspect, lookout, monitor, surveil **8** eagle eye, scrutiny, sentinel, watchman **9** timepiece, vigilance **10** scrutinize **11** chronograph, chronometer **12** surveillance ***chain:*** **3** fob ***maker:*** **10** horologist

watchdog **6** custos, keeper, warden **8** cerberus, claviger, guardian **9** custodian

watcher **6** viewer **7** guarder, lookout, witness **8** beholder, by-sitter, guardian, looker-on, observer, onlooker **9** bystander, spectator **10** eyewitness ***combining form:*** **6** scopus

watchfire **6** beacon

watchful **4** wary **5** alert, chary, quick, ready **6** prompt **7** wakeful **8** cautious, open-eyed, vigilant **9** wide-awake **10** unsleeping **11** circumspect ***Scottish:*** **5** tenty **6** tentie

watchman **4** ward **5** guard **6** picket, sentry **7** lookout **8** sentinel

watch out **4** mind **6** beware **7** look out

watchtower **7** lookout **10** lighthouse

watchword **6** slogan **10** shibboleth **11** catchphrase, countersign

water **5** fluid **6** dilute, liquid **7** moisten **8** irrigate, moisture, snowmelt ***body:*** **3** bay, sea **4** gulf, lake, pool **5** ocean **6** lagoon, strait **9** reservoir ***combining form:*** **4** aqua, aqui, aquo, hydr **5** hydat, hydro **6** hydato, limnia (plural) **7** limnion ***French:*** **3** eau ***goddess:*** **4** Nina **7** Anahita, Anaitis ***Latin:*** **4** aqua ***Spanish:*** **4** agua

water buffalo **4** arna **7** carabao ***female:*** **5** arnee

water clock **9** clepsydra

water closet **2** WC **4** head, john **5** privy **6** johnny, toilet **7** latrine **8** lavatory **11** convenience ***British:*** **3** loo

watercourse **4** duct **5** canal **6** course **7** channel, conduit **8** aqueduct, headrace, tailrace

water cow **7** manatee

water eagle **6** osprey

watered-down **4** thin, weak **5** washy **6** dilute, watery **7** diluted **8** waterish

water elephant **12** hippopotamus

waterfall **4** eddy **5** chute, falls, sault, shoot, spout, surge **6** rapids, riffle, vortex **7** cascade **8** cataract **9** whirlpool ***California:*** **8** Yosemite ***Canada:*** **5** Grand ***Canada-U.S.:*** **7** Niagara ***former Nile:*** **5** Ripon ***Kentucky:*** **5** Great **10** Cumberland ***Niagara:*** **8** American, Canadian **9** Horseshoe ***Oregon:*** **9** Multnomah ***Snake river:*** **4** Twin **8** Shoshone ***world's highest:*** **5** Angel ***Yellowstone:*** **5** Tower ***Zambezi:*** **8** Victoria

waterfinder **6** dowser

water hole ***desert:*** **5** oasis

water horse **6** kelpie **11** hippocampus

watering hole **3** bar, pub **4** café **5** haunt, oasis **6** lounge, nitery, resort, saloon, tavern **7** barroom, cabaret, hangout, hot spot, purlieu **8** drinkery, nightery **9** nightclub, nightspot **10** rendezvous, supper club **11** discotheque

water jar **4** ewer, lota, olla **5** banga, lotah **6** hydria, kalpis

waterless **3** dry **4** arid, sere **7** bone-dry, thirsty **8** droughty **9** unwatered **12** moistureless ***combining form:*** **6** anhydr **7** anhydro

waterlog **3** sap **4** soak **5** souse, steep **6** drench, sodden **7** insteep **8** saturate

water nymph **4** lily **5** naiad **6** Nereid **7** Oceanid **9** dragonfly ***female:*** **5** nixie

water oscillation **6** seiche

water pipe **5** hooka **6** hookah **8** narghile, nargileh

water plant **7** aquatic **10** hydrophyte

water rat **4** vole **6** rodent **7** muskrat

water spirit **6** undine

waterspout **6** funnel **10** cloudburst

water sprite see **water nymph**

water tank **7** cistern

waterwheel **5** noria **6** sakieh

watery 4 pale, thin, weak 5 banal, bland, vapid, washy 6 anemic, dilute, jejune, pallid, sluicy 7 diluted, insipid, sapless 9 bloodless 10 namby-pamby, wishy-washy
wattle 3 rod 4 pole 10 interweave
wattle and ___ 4 daub
wave 3 wag 4 beat, flap, lash 6 marcel, ripple, switch, waggle, woggle 7 flutter, ripplet 8 brandish, undulate ***combining form:*** 3 cym, kym 4 cymo, kymo ***large:*** 7 tsunami
waver 4 halt, trim 5 hedge, shift 6 dither, falter, palter, seesaw, teeter 7 flicker, stagger, whiffle 8 hesitate 9 vacillate 12 shilly-shally, wiggle-waggle
wavering 4 weak 5 shaky 6 dickey, unsure, wobbly 7 halting 8 insecure, rootless, to-and-fro, unstable 9 faltering, fluctuant, hesitancy, vacillant, whiffling 10 hesitating, hesitation, indecision 11 vacillating, vacillation, vacillatory 12 irresolution, shilly-shally, wiggle-waggle
Waverly author 5 Scott
wavy pattern 5 moiré
wax 3 get, run 4 come, grow, hike, rise, turn 5 boost, build, lipid, mount 6 become, expand 7 augment, enlarge, upgrade, upsurge 8 heighten, increase, multiply, paraffin, simonize ***combining form:*** 3 cer 4 cero
waxen 3 wan 4 ashy, pale 5 ashen, livid 6 doughy, pallid 8 blanched 9 colorless
waxlike 9 ceraceous
way 3 ilk 4 adit, door, kind, lane, mode, path, road, sort, type, wise, wont 5 alley, breed, class, entry, habit, modus, order, route, style, track, trick, usage 6 access, artery, avenue, course, custom, entrée, manner, method, praxis, street, system 7 fashion, ingress, species, variety 8 distance, entrance, habitude, practice 9 admission, boulevard, technique 10 admittance, consuetude 12 thoroughfare ***combining form:*** 3 ode
wayfaring 6 roving 7 nomadic, vagrant 8 vagabond 9 itinerant, itinerate, wandering 11 perambulant, peripatetic 13 perambulatory
waylay 6 ambush 8 surprise
Way of All Flesh author 6 Butler
Way of the World author 8 Congreve
way or sea ___ 5 farer
wayward 5 balky 6 fickle, ornery 7 erratic, froward, restive 8 contrary, freakish, perverse, unstable, variable, whimsied 9 arbitrary, vagarious, whimsical 10 capricious, inconstant 11 wrongheaded 12 cross-grained
we ***French:*** 4 nous ***German:*** 3 wir ***Italian:*** 3 noi ***Spanish:*** 8 nosotros
weak 3 wan 4 puny, thin 5 faint, frail, shaky, washy 6 dickey, dilute, feeble, flimsy, infirm, sickly, unsure, watery, wobbly 7 diluted, fragile, rickety, sapless, spindly, unsound 8 boneless, decrepit, impotent, insecure, rootless, thewless, unstable, wavering 9 enfeebled, fluctuant, forceless, powerless, spineless, uncertain 10 emasculate, improbable, impuissant, inadequate, incredible, irresolute, unreliable 11 debilitated, implausible, ineffective, ineffectual, slack-spined, vacillating, watered-down 12 invertebrate, unbelievable, unconvincing, undependable 13 insubstantial, unsubstantial ***combining form:*** 4 lept 5 lepto 6 asthen 7 astheno
weaken 3 cut, sap 4 fade, fail, flag, thin, wane 5 blunt, unman 6 damage, dilute, impair, infirm, injure, lessen, reduce, shrink, soften 7 cripple, decline, disable, dwindle, unbrace, unnerve 8 enervate, enfeeble, languish, minimize, paralyze 9 attenuate, fall short, undermine, waste away 10 debilitate, emasculate 11 deteriorate 12 incapacitate, unstrengthen
weak-kneed 5 timid 6 wobbly 8 wavering 9 faltering, uncertain, whiffling 10 irresolute 11 vacillating 12 double-minded, wiggle-waggle
weakling 3 sop 4 baby, butt, drip, mark 5 sissy 6 misfit, sucker 7 doormat, milksop, sad sack 8 mama's boy, pushover 9 jellyfish 10 mother's boy, namby-pamby, pantywaist, sissy-pants 11 Milquetoast, mollycoddle 12 invertebrate 13 sissy-britches
weakness 5 taste 6 foible, liking 7 frailty 8 adynamia, appetite, fondness, soft spot 12 Achilles' heel
weal 4 wale, welt 5 ridge, wheal, whelk 6 stripe 7 welfare 9 well-being
weald 5 woods 6 forest, timber 8 woodland 10 timberland
wealth 4 mean, pelf 5 goods, worth 6 assets, estate, mammon, riches 7 capital, fortune 8 golconda, holdings, nabobism, opulence, property 9 resources, substance 11 possessions ***combining form:*** 4 plut 5 pluto
Wealth of Nations author 5 Smith
wealthy 4 rich 7 moneyed, opulent 8 affluent
wean 5 alien, spean 8 alienate, disunify, disunite, estrange 9 disaffect
weapon 3 gun 4 bola, bolo, club, dart, dirk, épée, foil, mace, nuke, pike 5 arrow, knife, lance, rifle, saber, sabre, sling, spear, sword 6 dagger, magnum, musket, pistol, poleax, rapier 7 bazooka, carbine, firearm, halberd, halbert, javelin, machete, missile, poleaxe, shotgun, trident 8 battle-ax, catapult, crossbow, petronel, revolver, spon-

toon, tomahawk 9 battle-axe, blackjack, boomerang, derringer 11 blunderbuss 13 brass knuckles
weapons 7 arsenal
wear 3 rub 4 fray, gall, jade, tire 5 chafe, drain, erode, graze, grind, weary 6 abrade, ruffle, tatter 7 corrode, fatigue, frazzle
wear away 3 eat 4 bite, gnaw 5 erode, scour 6 abrade 7 corrode
wear down 4 jade, tire 5 drain, weary 6 weaken 7 exhaust, fatigue
weariness 5 ennui 7 fatigue 9 lassitude, tiredness 10 exhaustion
wearisome see tiresome
wear out 3 fag 4 poop 6 tucker 7 exhaust, frazzle, outtire 8 knock out, overstay, overtoil 9 prostrate
weary 4 bore, jade, pall, sick, tire, worn 5 drain, fed up, jaded, tired 6 tucker, weaken 7 fatigue 8 enfeeble, fatigued, footsore, footworn, overtire, overwork, wear down, worn down 9 disgusted 10 debilitate
weasand 6 gullet, throat 8 windpipe
weasel 5 dodge, evade, hedge, slink, sneak, stoat 6 ermine, ferret 7 shuffle, sneaker 8 sidestep, sneaksby 9 pussyfoot 10 equivocate, tergiverse 12 tergiversate ***Scottish:*** 8 whittret
weather 5 clime 7 climate ***combining form:*** 6 meteor 7 meteoro
weathercock 4 vane
weave 4 reed, spin, sway 5 braid, lurch, swing, twill 6 careen, damask, pleach, raddle, tissue, wattle, wobble 7 stagger, texture
Weaver of Raveloe 6 Marner (Silas)
web 3 net 4 knot, maze, mesh 5 fiber, skein, snare, snarl, toils 6 cobweb, fabric, jungle, meshes, morass, tangle 7 ensnare, mizmaze, network, texture 8 entangle 9 labyrinth 10 enmeshment, entrapment 11 embroilment, ensnarement, involvement 12 entanglement ***combining form:*** 5 hypho ***of a feather:*** 5 vexil 8 vexillum
Weber opera 6 Oberon 9 Euryanthe 13 Der Freischütz
___ Webster 4 Noah 6 Daniel
wed 3 tie 4 join, link, mate, yoke 5 catch, marry, unite 6 marrow, relate, splice 7 combine, conjoin, connect, espouse 9 associate
wedded 7 marital, married, nuptial, spousal 8 conjugal, hymeneal 9 connubial 11 matrimonial
wedding 6 bridal 7 spousal 8 espousal, marriage, nuptials
wedding anniversary ***fifteenth:*** 7 crystal ***fifth:*** 6 wooden ***fiftieth:*** 6 golden ***first:*** 5 paper ***seventy-fifth:*** 7 diamond ***tenth:*** 3 tin ***twentieth:*** 5 china ***twenty-fifth:*** 6 silver
wedge-shaped 7 cuneate, sphenic
wedlock 8 marriage 9 matrimony 11 conjugality 12 connubiality
wee 4 tiny 5 teeny 6 minute, teensy, weensy 7 teentsy 9 miniature 10 diminutive, teeny-weeny 11 lilliputian 12 teensy-weensy
weed 4 dock, tare 5 chess 6 darnel, dodder, lupine, nettle, sorrel, teasel 7 burdock, burseed, hemlock, mullein, solanum, thistle, tobacco 8 amaranth, charlock, gromwell, purslane, toadflax 9 cocklebur, dandelion, glasswort, goldenrod, horsetail, knotgrass, marijuana, poison ivy, poison oak, stickseed 10 cinquefoil ***European:*** 6 spurry 7 spurrey 8 pingrass ***killer:*** 8 paraquat 9 herbicide ***Western:*** 4 loco
week 8 hebdomad ***two weeks:*** 9 fortnight
weep 3 cry, sob 4 blub, drib, drip, drop, moan, ooze, seep, wail 5 bleed, exude, greet, sweat, trill 6 bemoan, bewail, boohoo, grieve, lament, strain 7 blubber, deplore, distill, dribble, trickle 8 transude
weepy 5 teary 7 maudlin, tearful 10 lachrymose
weevil 4 boll 7 billbug 8 curculio ***tropical:*** 7 zyzzyva
weft 3 web 4 pick, woof, yarn 6 fabric, thread
weigh 3 tax 4 lade, load, mind, rate, tare 5 count, study 6 burden, charge, cumber, lumber, ponder, saddle, weight 7 balance, perpend 8 appraise, consider, encumber, evaluate, militate, think out 9 think over 10 excogitate 11 contemplate
weigh down 5 press 6 sadden 7 depress, oppress
weight 3 tax 4 duty, lade, load, onus, pith, task 6 burden, charge, credit, cumber, debase, import, lumber, moment, saddle 7 potency 8 efficacy, encumber, prestige 9 authority, influence, magnitude, millstone 10 adulterate, importance 11 consequence 12 forcefulness, forcibleness, powerfulness, significance ***allowance:*** 4 tare, tret 7 scalage ***apothecary:*** 4 dram 5 grain, pound 7 scruple ***Asian:*** 6 cattie ***combining form:*** 3 bar 4 baro ***gem:*** 5 carat ***measure of:*** 3 ton 4 dram, gram 5 grain, ounce, pound 7 long ton, scruple 8 kilogram, short ton 9 metric ton ***system:*** 3 net 4 troy 6 metric 10 apothecary 11 avoirdupois
weightiness 4 pith 6 import, moment, weight 9 magnitude 10 importance 11 consequence 12 significance
weight lift 5 press 6 snatch 12 clean and jerk
weighty 3 big, fat 5 grave, gross, heavy, hefty, obese, sober, staid, stout, tough 6 fleshy, portly, sedate, severe, solemn, somber, taxing 7 earnest, exigent, massive,

onerous, porcine, serious 8 cumbrous, exacting, grievous, material 9 corpulent, demanding, important, momentous, ponderous 10 burdensome, cumbersome, meaningful, no-nonsense, oppressive, overweight, sobersided 11 significant, substantial 12 considerable 13 consequential

weir 3 dam 9 fishgarth

weird 3 lot, odd 4 cast, doom, eery, fate 5 awful, eerie, moira, queer 6 creepy, kismet, spooky 7 bizarre, curious, destiny, eldrich, fearful, oddball, portion, strange, uncanny, uncouth 8 dreadful, eldritch, forecast, haunting, horrific, peculiar, prophecy, singular, supernal 9 eccentric, prevision, prognosis, unearthly, unnatural 10 mysterious, outlandish, prediction 11 foretelling, inscrutable 12 awe-inspiring, circumstance, supernatural 13 preternatural

welcome 4 hail 5 greet 6 genial 7 cordial 8 pleasant, pleasing 9 agreeable, congenial, favorable 10 contenting, gratifying, satisfying 11 pleasurable, pleasureful, sympathetic

weld 5 unite 6 solder 11 consolidate

welfare 4 good 7 benefit, fortune, success 8 interest 9 advantage, happiness, well-being 10 prosperity

welkin 3 sky 7 heavens 9 firmament

well 3 far, fit 4 easy, hale, sane 5 amply, clear, fitly, fully, happy, lucky, quite, right, sound, truly 6 aright, freely, indeed, justly, kindly, likely, nicely, origin, rather, really, source, wholly 7 happily, healthy, lightly, perhaps, readily, rightly, roundly, utterly 8 decently, entirely, facilely, fountain, possibly, probably, properly, smoothly, somewhat, suitably 9 correctly, favorably, fittingly, fortunate, inception, perfectly, tolerably, wholesome 10 acceptably, adequately, altogether, becomingly, completely, decorously, generously, pleasantly, prosperous, provenance, swimmingly, thoroughly 11 approvingly, befittingly, comfortable, doubtlessly, fortunately, provenience, substantial 12 considerably, effortlessly, fountainhead, prosperously, providential, satisfyingly, successfully 13 appropriately, significantly *combining form:* 2 eu

well-being 4 ease, good 7 benefit, welfare 8 euphoria, interest, thriving 9 abundance, advantage 10 easy street, prosperity

well-bred 6 urbane 7 genteel, refined 8 cultured, polished 9 distingué 10 cultivated

well-developed 5 curvy 7 rounded 9 curvesome, Junoesque 10 curvaceous 11 curvilinear

well-disposed 8 friendly 9 receptive 11 sympathetic

Welles movie 7 Macbeth, Othello 11 Citizen Kane, Touch of Evil

well-favored 4 fair 6 comely, lovely, pretty 8 handsome 9 beauteous, beautiful 10 attractive 11 good-looking

well-fixed see well-to-do

well-founded 4 good, just 5 meaty, pithy, sound, valid 6 cogent 7 telling 8 rational, reasoned 9 justified 10 reasonable 11 fundamental, substantial

well-groomed 4 neat, snug, tidy, trig, trim 5 doggy, natty, sassy 6 dapper, spiffy, spruce, sprucy 7 chipper, doggish, orderly 8 sparkish 9 shipshape 11 spic-and-span, uncluttered 12 spick-and-span

wellhead see wellspring

well-heeled see well-to-do

Wellington *horse:* 10 Copenhagen *victory:* 7 Vitoria 8 Talavera, Waterloo 9 Salamanca

well-known 5 noted 6 famous 7 leading, popular 9 important, notorious, prominent 11 conspicuous, outstanding

well-liked 7 favored, popular 8 favorite 9 preferred

well-mannered 5 civil 6 polite 7 genteel 9 courteous

well-nigh 4 most, much, nigh 5 about 6 all but, almost, nearly 8 as good as, as much as 11 essentially, practically

well-off see well-to-do

well-paying 7 gainful 9 lucrative 10 profitable, worthwhile 11 moneymaking 12 advantageous, remunerative

well-proportioned see well-turned

wellspring 4 root 6 origin, source 8 fountain 9 inception 10 provenance 11 provenience 12 fountainhead

well-thought-of 7 reputed 9 estimable, reputable 10 creditable 11 respectable

well-timed 7 timeous 9 favorable, opportune 10 auspicious, propitious, prosperous, seasonable

well-to-do 4 easy, rich 7 wealthy 8 affluent 10 prosperous 11 comfortable, substantial

well-turned 4 trim 7 shapely 8 shapeful 10 statuesque 11 clean-limbed

well-worn 5 stale, tired, trite 9 hackneyed 10 threadbare 11 commonplace, stereotyped

welsh 6 cry off, renege, resile 7 back off, back out 8 back down 9 backpedal, backwater 10 declare off 11 crawfish out

Welsh see Cymric

welt 4 wale, weal 5 ridge, wheal, whelk

welter 4 bask, roll, wilt 5 dry up, mummy, revel, wizen 6 wallow, wither 7 indulge, mummify, rollick, shrivel 9 luxuriate

___ Welty, writer 6 Eudora
wen 4 cyst 6 growth 11 excrescence
wench 3 gal 4 girl, jade, lass, maid, miss 5 hussy, missy, tramp, trull 6 damsel, lassie, maiden, wanton 7 jezebel, servant, trollop 8 slattern, strumpet
wend 2 go 3 hie 4 fare, pass 6 push on, repair, travel 7 journey, proceed
werewolf 11 lycanthrope
Werther's beloved 5 Lotte
Wesleyan 9 Methodist
West 8 Occident
West African ***baboon:*** 5 drill 8 mandrill ***city:*** 5 Accra, Dakar, Lagos ***country:*** 4 Togo 5 Benin, Gabon, Ghana 6 Gambia, Guinea 7 Liberia, Nigeria, Senegal 8 Cameroon 10 Ivory Coast 11 Sierra Leone ***fetish:*** 4 juju ***native:*** 3 Ibo 5 Hausa 7 Ashanti
western 5 oater 9 shoot-em-up 10 horse opera
Western organization 3 OAS 4 NATO
Western Samoa ***capital:*** 4 Apia ***monetary unit:*** 4 tala
West Germany ***capital:*** 4 Bonn
West Indies ***boat:*** 7 drogher ***country:*** 4 Cuba 5 Haiti 7 Grenada, Jamaica 8 Dominica 10 Saint Lucia 13 Bahama Islands ***language:*** 6 Creole, French 7 English, Spanish
West Point ***father of:*** 6 Thayer ***freshman:*** 5 plebe ***student:*** 5 cadet
West Virginia ***capital:*** 10 Charleston ***nickname:*** 13 Mountain State ***state bird:*** 8 cardinal ***state flower:*** 12 rhododendron
west wind see at wind
wet 3 dew, sop 4 damp, dank, lave, soak, wash 5 bedew, douse, drown, drunk, madid, moist, rainy, rinse, soggy, soppy, souse, water 6 dampen, deluge, drench, drippy, soaked, sodden, soused, sweaty, vapory 7 moisten, slopped, soaking, sopping 8 drenched, dripping, humidify, irrigate, saturate 9 saturated 10 inebriated 11 intoxicated ***combining form:*** 4 hygr 5 hygro
wet blanket 7 killjoy 10 spoilsport
wether 4 goat 5 sheep
wetland 3 bog, fen 5 marsh, swamp
whack 2 go 3 bat, hit, pop, try 4 bash, blow, ding, shot, slap, slog, sock, stab, whop 5 catch, crack, fling, smack, smash, whirl 6 strike, thwack, wallop 7 stagger
whale 4 flog, hide, lash, whip 5 giant 6 stripe, thrash 7 mammoth, monster, scourge 8 behemoth 9 leviathan 10 flagellate ***arctic:*** 7 bowhead ***combining form:*** 3 cet 4 ceto ***group:*** 3 pod ***killer:*** 4 orca ***kind:*** 3 sei 4 blue 5 right, sperm 6 baleen, beluga, killer 7 narwhal, rorqual 8 cachalot ***tale:*** 8 Moby Dick ***toothed:*** 9 blackfish ***young:*** 4 calf
whalebone 6 baleen
wham 4 bang, boom, clap, slam 5 blast, burst, crack, crash, smash
whammy 3 hex 4 jinx 6 hoodoo, voodoo 10 Indian sign
wharf 4 dock, pier, quay, slip 5 berth, jetty, levee
Wharton novel 10 Ethan Frome 12 House of Mirth
whatnot 5 curio 6 bauble, gewgaw, trifle 7 bibelot, novelty, trinket 8 gimcrack 9 objet d'art 10 knickknack
wheal 4 wale, welt 5 whelk 6 strake, streak, stripe
wheat 5 durum, emmer, spelt, trigo 6 speltz 7 einkorn ***beard:*** 3 awn ***beat:*** 6 thresh ***chaff:*** 4 bran ***crushed:*** 6 bulgur ***disease:*** 4 rust, smut
wheedle 3 con 4 coax 6 cajole 7 blarney 8 blandish, soft-soap 9 sweet-talk
wheel 4 auto, gyre, loop, reel, tire, tool, tum, veer, whip 5 avert, cycle, dolly, drive, motor, pilot, pivot, round, sheer, whirl 6 circle, divert, league, totter 7 circuit, deflect, stagger 8 gyration, rotation, titubate 9 volte-face 10 charioteer, conference, revolution 11 association, circulation ***combining form:*** 5 troch 6 trocho ***part:*** 3 hub, rim 5 spoke ***rim:*** 5 felly 6 felloe ***spoke:*** 6 radius ***toothed:*** 3 cog 4 gear
wheel-like 8 rotiform
wheelman 6 driver 7 cyclist 8 helmsman
wheel-shaped 5 round 7 trochal 8 circular
wheeze 4 buzz, fizz, hiss, lark 5 antic, caper, prank, swish, trick 6 didoes, fizzle, frolic, shines, sizzle, whoosh 7 whisper 8 sibilate 10 shenanigan 11 monkeyshine
whelk 4 wale, weal, welt 5 wheal
whelm 5 drown, flood, swamp 6 deluge, engulf 8 inundate, overcome, overflow, submerge 9 knock over, overpower, overwhelm, prostrate
whelp 3 boy, cub, pup 4 girl 5 child, puppy
when 4 anon 5 again, while 6 albeit, much as, though 7 howbeit, whereas 8 although
where 4 site, spot 5 locus, place, point 7 station, whither 8 location, position 9 situation
whereas 2 as 3 for, now 4 when 5 since, while 6 albeit, much as, seeing, though 7 because, howbeit 8 although, as long as 10 inasmuch as 11 considering
wherefore 3 why 5 proof 6 ground, reason, whyfor 8 argument
wherewithal 5 means, money 9 resources
wherry 4 boat 5 barge 7 rowboat
whet 4 edge, hone, stir, wake 5 rally,

rouse, waken 6 arouse, awaken, bestir, kindle 7 sharpen, zakuska 9 antipasto, appetizer, challenge 11 hors d'oeuvre
whiff 4 dash, hint 5 shade, smack, tinge, trace 6 breath, trifle 7 soupçon 8 tincture
whiffet 4 zero 5 zilch 6 cipher, nobody 7 nothing, nullity 8 whipster 9 nonentity
whiffle 4 halt 5 waver 6 dither, falter 7 stagger 8 hesitate 9 vacillate 12 shilly-shally, wiggle-waggle
while 2 as 3 bit 4 pass, time, when 5 fleet, pains, space, spell, spend 6 albeit, effort, moment, much as, though 7 beguile, howbeit, instant, stretch, trouble, whereas 8 although, exertion, occasion
whim 3 bee 4 idea 5 dream, fancy, freak, humor 6 megrim, vagary, vision 7 boutade, caprice, conceit, fantasy, thought 8 crotchet 11 disposition, inclination
whimper 3 cry 4 mewl, pule 5 whine
whimsical 4 iffy 6 chancy 7 erratic, wayward 8 freakish, whimsied 9 arbitrary, fluctuant, uncertain, vagarious 10 capricious 12 incalculable 13 unpredictable
whimsy 4 idea 5 dream, fancy, freak, humor 6 megrim, vagary, vision 7 boutade, caprice, conceit, fantasy, thought 8 crotchet 9 capriccio 11 disposition, inclination
whine 4 fuss, kick, pule, wail 6 murmur, repine, snivel, yammer 7 whimper 8 complain
whinny 5 neigh 6 nicker 7 whicker
whiny 5 raspy, waspy 6 snappy, twitty 7 peevish, raspish, waspish 8 snappish 9 irritable, querulous
whip 3 set 4 abet, beat, cane, drub, dust, flog, hide, lash, lick, rout, trim, turn, veer 5 avert, blast, curry, mop up, pivot, quirt, raise, set on, sheer, upend, whale, wheel, whirl, whisk, whomp 6 cudgel, defeat, divert, foment, incite, lather, stir up, stripe, subdue, switch, thrash, wallop 7 curbash, deflect, kurbash, overrun, provoke, rawhide, scourge, shellac, trounce 8 bludgeon, courbash, kourbash, lambaste, overcome, vanquish 9 bastinado, instigate, overwhelm 10 flagellate 13 cat-o'-nine-tails ***braided:*** 10 blacksnake ***combining form:*** 6 mastig, mastix 7 mastigo ***riding:*** 4 crop
whippersnapper see whiffet
whipping boy 4 goat 5 patsy 7 fall guy 9 scapegoat
whippy 6 supple 7 elastic, springy, stretch 8 flexible, stretchy 9 resilient
whir 3 fly 4 buzz 5 chirr 6 chirre 7 revolve, vibrate
whirl 2 go 3 ado, pop, try 4 eddy, flit, fuss, gyre, moil, reel, shot, slap, spin, stab, stir, swim, turn, veer, whip, whiz 5 avert, crack, fleet, fling, gurge, hurry, pivot, round, sheer, speed, stave, storm, twirl, whack, wheel, whish, whisk 6 barrel, bullet, bustle, divert, flurry, furore, gyrate, hassle, hubbub, pother, swoosh, vortex 7 circuit, clatter, deflect, ruction, stagger, whoopla 8 gyration, rotation, rowdydow 9 commotion, maelstrom, pirouette 10 hurly-burly, revolution 11 circulation
whirligig 4 gyre, spin 6 beetle, gyrate 8 carousel 9 carrousel, pirouette 12 merry-go-round
whirlpool 3 ado 4 eddy, fuss, purl, stir 5 gurge, whorl 6 bustle, flurry, furore, pother, swoosh, vortex 8 vortices (plural) 9 maelstrom, whirlwind ***combining form:*** 4 dino
whirlwind 2 oe 3 ado 4 fuss, stir 6 bustle, flurry, furore, pother, whirly 7 tornado 9 dust devil, hurricane, rainspout, sand spout 10 sand column, waterspout
whish 3 fly 4 buzz, fizz, flit, hiss, whiz 5 fleet, hurry, speed, stave, whirl 6 bullet, fizzle, sizzle, wheeze 7 whisper 8 sibilate
whisk 3 fly, zip 4 beat, flit, whip, whiz 5 hurry, speed 6 barrel, bullet
whisker 3 ace 4 hair 11 hairbreadth
whiskered 5 hairy 6 fleecy, pilose, woolly 7 barbate, bearded, hirsute, pileous
whiskers 5 beard 6 beaver
whiskey 3 rye 5 hooch, usque 6 hootch, Scotch 7 bourbon 8 usquabae, usquebae ***with beer chaser:*** 11 boilermaker
whisper 4 buzz, dash, fizz, hint, hiss, whiz 5 rumor, shade, swish, tinge, touch, trace, whiff 6 breath, fizzle, mumble, murmur, mutter, rustle, sizzle, wheeze, whoosh 7 breathe, confide 8 sibilate 9 suspicion, undertone 11 susurration
whist 4 game, hush 5 quiet, still 6 silent, stilly 7 hushful 9 noiseless, soundless ***card hand:*** 10 Yarborough
whistle 4 pipe 5 flute 6 signal
whit 3 bit, jot 4 atom, damn, hoot, iota 5 shred, whoop 7 modicum 8 particle
white 5 hoary, milky 6 albino, benign, blanch, bleach, blench, bright, dexter 7 decolor 8 palliate 9 canescent, extenuate, favorable, fortunate, gloss over, gloze over, sugarcoat 10 auspicious, blanch over, decolorize, propitious ***combining form:*** 3 alb 4 albo, cali, calo, leuc, leuk 5 callo, leuco, leuko ***egg's:*** 5 glair 6 glaire 7 albumen
white cliffs of ___ 5 Dover
White Fang author 6 London
White House ***designer:*** 5 Hoban ***first occupant:*** 5 Adams
white lightning 7 bootleg 9 moonshine 10 bathtub gin 11 mountain dew
whiten 3 dim 4 dull, fade, pale 5 frost 6 blanch, bleach, blench, silver, veneer

7 decolor, grizzle, lighten, varnish 8 etiolate, palliate 9 extenuate, gloss over, gloze over, sugarcoat 10 blanch over, decolorize
white plague 2 TB 8 phthisis 11 consumption 12 tuberculosis
whitewash 6 veneer 7 varnish 8 palliate 9 extenuate, gloss over, gloze over, sugarcoat 10 blanch over
whither 5 where 7 whereto 9 whereunto 11 whereabouts
whiting 4 fish, hake
Whitsunday 9 Pentecost
whittle 3 cut 4 pare 5 carve, shape
whiz 3 fly, zip 4 buzz, fizz, flit, hiss, zoom 5 adept, hurry, speed, swish, whirl, whish, whisk 6 bullet, expert, fizzle, master, sizzle, wheeze, whoosh, wizard 7 whisper 8 sibilate, virtuoso 10 past master 12 professional
whole 3 all, fit, sum 4 full, hale, sane 5 fixed, gross, right, sound, total 6 choate, entire, entity, intact, system, unhurt, unrent 7 gestalt, perfect, plenary 8 complete, entirety, flawless, integral, outright, sum total, totality, unbroken, unmarred 9 aggregate, exclusive, integrate, undamaged, undivided, uninjured, untouched 10 unimpaired, unswerving 11 unblemished 12 concentrated, undistracted *combining form:* 3 hol, pan 4 holo, pano, toti 7 integri
wholehearted 4 sure 6 ardent, hearty, steady 7 abiding, earnest, fervent, genuine, serious, sincere 8 bona fide, enduring 9 authentic, heartfelt, steadfast, unfeigned 10 passionate, unwavering 11 impassioned, unfaltering, unqualified 13 unquestioning
whole-hog 8 complete, thorough 9 full-dress 10 exhaustive 13 thoroughgoing
wholeness 5 vigor 6 health 7 allness, oneness 8 entirety, haleness, totality 9 integrity, soundness 10 entireness, heartiness, perfection, robustness 11 healthiness 12 completeness
whole note 9 semibreve
whole number 5 digit 6 cipher, figure 7 chiffer, integer, numeral
wholesome 3 fit 4 good, hale, safe, sane, well 5 right, sound 6 curing 7 healing, healthy 8 curative, hygienic, remedial, salutary, sanative, sanatory 9 healthful, remedying, vulnerary 10 salubrious, well-liking 11 restorative
wholly 3 all 4 just, well 5 fully, quite 6 in toto, purely 7 exactly, roundly, totally, utterly 8 all in all, entirely 9 perfectly 10 altogether, completely, thoroughly *combining form:* 4 toti
whomp 4 beat, drub, whip 5 smear 6 thrash, wallop 7 shellac, trounce 8 lambaste
whoopee 3 fun 5 revel 6 gaiety 7 jollity, revelry, wassail 8 reveling 9 festivity, high jinks, merriment, revelment 10 skylarking 11 merrymaking
whoopla 4 to-do 5 revel, whirl 6 clamor, hassle, pother, tumult, uproar 7 revelry, turmoil, wassail 9 commotion, high jinks, revelment 10 hurly-burly, skylarking
whop 3 bat, bop 4 bash, beat, biff, blow, drub, sock 5 baste, pound, smack, whack 6 batter, buffet, hammer, pummel, thwack, wallop 7 belabor 8 lambaste
whopping 4 huge, much, very 6 damned, highly, hugely, mighty 7 awfully, immense 8 colossal, enormous, gigantic 10 gargantuan, prodigious 11 exceedingly
whorl 4 eddy, purl 5 gurge, swirl 6 swoosh 9 whirlpool *combining form:* 7 spondyl 8 spondylo
why 5 proof 6 enigma, ground, puzzle, reason, riddle 7 mystery 8 argument 9 conundrum, wherefore 10 puzzlement 13 Chinese puzzle, mystification
wicked 3 bad 4 blue, evil, mean, racy, ugly 5 antic, broad, hairy, pesky, risky, salty, shady, spicy, wrong 6 adroit, au fait, chancy, clever, cursed, impish, malign, pranky, purple, risqué, sinful, unholy 7 hateful, heinous, immoral, larkish, playful, roguish, ungodly, unsound, vicious 8 fiendish, off-color, perilous, prankful, prankish, spiteful 9 barbarous, dangerous, hazardous, malicious, malignant, rancorous, reprobate, troublous, unhealthy, vexatious 10 despiteful, iniquitous, jeopardous, malevolent, outrageous, suggestive 11 mischievous, treacherous, troublesome, unchristian, uncivilized
wickedness 3 sin 4 debt, evil, vice 5 wrong 9 depravity 10 corruption, immorality
wicker 3 rod 4 twig 5 osier, withe
wicket 4 arch, door, gate, hoop 6 window
wickiup 3 hut 5 lodge, tepee 7 shelter
wide 5 ample, broad, roomy 6 scopic, sweepy 7 liberal, radical 8 advanced, extended, scopious, spacious, tolerant 9 capacious, expansive, extensive 10 commodious 11 broad-minded, progressive *combining form:* 4 eury, lati
widen 4 ream 6 dilate 7 broaden 9 breadthen
wideness 5 scope 7 breadth 8 fullness 9 amplitude
widespread 4 rife 6 ruling 7 current, popular, rampant, regnant 9 prevalent 10 prevailing
widget 5 gizmo 6 gadget, jigger 7 gimmick
width 5 ambit, orbit, range, scope 6 circle,

length, radius 7 breadth, compass 8 panorama 9 extension
wield 3 ply 5 exert, swing, throw 6 handle, put out 7 conduct, control 8 dispense, exercise, maneuver 10 manipulate ***the gavel:*** 7 preside
wieldy 6 mighty, strong 8 powerful
wiener 3 dog 5 frank 6 hot dog 11 frankfurter, wienerwurst
wife 3 Mrs. 4 mate 5 bride 6 matron, missis, missus, spouse 7 consort, dowager 8 helpmate, helpmeet 9 other half ***Latin:*** 4 uxor ***of a rajah:*** 4 rani 5 ranee
wifely 7 uxorial
wig 3 jaw, rap 4 rail, rate 5 scold 6 berate, peruke, rebuke, revile, toupee 7 bawl out, chiding, reproof, upbraid 8 reproach 9 reprimand 10 admonition, tongue-lash 12 admonishment
wiggle 4 worm 6 squirm, writhe 8 squiggle ***Scottish:*** 5 hotch
wight 5 being, human 6 mortal, person 8 creature 9 personage 10 human being, individual
wigwam 3 hut 5 lodge, tepee
wild 3 mad 4 fast 5 crazy, dirty, feral, rabid, rough, waste 6 barren, brutal, desert, ferine, Gothic, raging, rakish, savage, stormy, unruly, vulgar 7 badland, frantic, furious, Hunnish, natural, raffish, uncivil, untamed, vicious 8 agrarian, agrestal, barbaric, blustery, carefree, feckless, frenetic, frenzied, rakehell, reckless, stormful, untoward 9 barbarian, barbarous, delirious, fantastic, fractious, graceless, tasteless, turbulent, uncareful, unsubdued, wasteland 10 blustering, corybantic, incautious, outlandish, wilderness 11 extravagant, intractable, tempestuous, uncivilized 12 devil-may-care, preposterous, recalcitrant, uncultivated, ungovernable, unmanageable 13 irresponsible, undisciplined ***combining form:*** 5 agrio
wild ass 5 kiang 6 onager
Wild Duck author 5 Ibsen
wildebeest 3 gnu
wilderness 5 waste 6 barren, desert 7 badland 9 backlands, wasteland 10 hinterland 11 backcountry
Wilder play 7 Our Town
wild-eyed 6 raving 7 radical 9 visionary
wild ox 4 anoa
wile 4 draw, ploy, ruse 5 charm, feint, guile, trick 6 allure, deceit, device, gambit 7 attract, beguile, bewitch, chicane, cunning, enchant, gimmick 8 artifice, maneuver, trickery 9 captivate, chicanery, fascinate, magnetize, stratagem 13 dissimulation
wiliness 3 art 5 craft 7 cunning, slyness 8 artifice, foxiness 9 cageyness, canniness 10 artfulness, craftiness
will 4 like, mind, wish 5 elect, fancy, leave 6 choose, devise, legate, liking, please 8 bequeath, pleasure, velleity, volition 9 testament 10 discipline 11 inclination, self-command, self-control, self-mastery 13 determination, self-restraint ***addition:*** 7 codicil ***maker:*** 8 testator 9 testatrix ***without:*** 9 intestate
willful 6 dogged, mulish, unruly 7 decided 8 factious, perverse, resolved, stubborn, unforced 9 obstinate, pigheaded, purposive, voluntary 10 deliberate, determined, headstrong 11 intentional, intractable, stiff-necked, wrongheaded 12 contumacious, pertinacious, unprescribed
Williams play 10 Camino Real 13 The Rose Tattoo
William Tell composer 7 Rossini
willies 5 jumps 6 creeps, dither, shakes 7 jitters, shivers 9 whim-whams 13 heebie-jeebies
willing 3 apt 4 fair, game, open 5 prone, ready 6 minded, prompt 7 forward, witting 8 disposed, inclined, unforced 9 agreeable, compliant, favorable, voluntary 10 deliberate 11 intentional, predisposed 12 unprescribed
willow 5 osier, salix 6 sallow ***flower cluster:*** 6 catkin ***kind:*** 5 crack, pussy, white 6 basket 7 weeping
willowy 4 tall 5 lithe 6 pliant 7 slender 8 graceful
wilt 3 sag 4 drop, flag, swag 5 droop, dry up, mummy, wizen 6 cave in, peg out, welter, wither 7 give out, mummify, shrivel, succumb 8 collapse 9 break down
wily 3 sly 4 deep, foxy 6 artful, astute, clever, crafty, shrewd, tricky 7 cunning, knowing 8 guileful 9 insidious, sagacious
wimble 4 bore 5 auger, brace, scoop 6 gimlet
Wimbledon's game 6 tennis
wimple 4 veil, wrap 6 ripple
win 3 get 4 beat, earn, gain, have, make, take 5 annex, reach, score, yield 6 attain, defeat, obtain, pick up, rack up, secure 7 achieve, acquire, bring in, chalk up, conquer, procure, produce, realize, triumph, victory 8 conquest, drag down, draw down, overcome 9 knock down 10 accomplish ***over:*** 6 disarm, induce 8 convince, persuade, talk into 9 prevail on
wince 5 cower, quail, start 6 blanch, blench, cringe, flinch, recoil, shrink 7 squinch
wind 3 fan, nil 4 bend, blow, clue, coil, curl, gale, gird, gust, hint, reel, warp, wrap 5 curve, spool, twine, twist, weave 6 breath, breeze, circle, deform, enlace, girdle, naught, notion, nought, ruffle, spiral, winnow, zephyr 7 contort, distort, enclose,

entwine, envelop, inkling, meander, monsoon, nothing, torture, wreathe 8 easterly, encircle, misshape, surround, westerly 9 corkscrew 10 indication, intimation, suggestion ***cold:*** 4 bise, bora 6 sansar, sarsar 7 mistral, pampero, wulliwa 8 williwaw, willywaw ***combining form:*** 4 anem 5 anemo, venti, vento ***east:*** 5 Eurus ***gentle:*** 6 breeze, zephyr 7 cat's-paw ***hot:*** 6 samiel, shamal, simoom, solano 7 sirocco ***instrument:*** 3 sax 4 horn, oboe, tuba, vane 5 flute 7 bassoon, trumpet 8 trombone 10 anemometer 11 weather vane ***into:*** 8 aweather ***measure of speed:*** 4 knot ***Mediterranean:*** 7 etesian 8 levanter ***north:*** 6 Boreas ***scale:*** 8 Beaufort ***south:*** 5 Notus 6 Auster ***southwest:*** 8 libeccio ***stormy:*** 4 gale 7 cyclone, tornado, twister 9 hurricane 11 northeaster ***warm:*** 4 föhn 5 foehn 7 chinook ***west:*** 6 zephyr 8 Zephyrus

winding 5 snaky 6 spiral 7 bending, coiling, crooked, curving, devious, sinuous 8 flexuous, indirect, tortuous, twisting 9 meandrous 10 circuitous, convoluted, meandering, roundabout, serpentine 11 anfractuous

window 3 bay, eye 4 pane 5 oriel 6 dormer 7 fenster, lucarne, luthern, opening 8 aperture, casement, jalousie ***cover:*** 5 blind 7 curtain, shutter ***French:*** 7 fenetre ***over a door:*** 7 transom 8 fanlight ***part:*** 4 came, pane, sash, sill 5 frame ***projecting:*** 3 bay 5 oriel ***relating to:*** 9 fenestral ***roof's:*** 6 dormer 8 skylight ***Scottish:*** 7 winnock ***ship's:*** 4 port 8 porthole ***ticket:*** 7 guichet

windpipe 6 throat 7 trachea ***combining form:*** 6 bronch, trache 7 bronchi, broncho, tracheo 8 bronchio

windrow 4 bank, heap, hill, mass, pile 5 drift, mound, stack 6 furrow 7 pyramid 8 mountain

wind up 3 end 4 halt 5 close 6 finish, settle, wrap up 7 clean up 8 complete, conclude 9 determine, terminate

windup 3 end 5 close 6 ending, finale, finish 10 conclusion

windy 4 airy 5 blowy, brisk, fresh, gusty, tumid, wordy 6 breezy, drafty, prolix, turgid 7 diffuse, verbose 8 blustery, dropsied, inflated 9 dropsical, flatulent, overblown, redundant 10 palaverous

wine 4 vino 5 drink, juice 8 beverage ***aromatized:*** 8 vermouth 9 hippocras, Quinquina ***beverage:*** 5 clary, mulse, negus, punch 6 bishop 8 sangaree 9 hippocras ***bottle:*** 6 fiasco, magnum 8 decanter, jeroboam ***cabinet:*** 8 cellaret ***cask:*** 3 tun, vat 4 butt, pipe 8 puncheon ***cellar:*** 6 bodega ***combining form:*** 2 en 3 eno, oen 4 oeno ***discoverer:*** 4 Noah ***disorder:*** 5 casse ***distillate:*** 6 brandy, cognac ***dry:*** 3 sec 4 brut ***film:*** 8 beeswing ***flavor:*** 4 mull ***fortified:*** 4 port 6 Malaga, sherry 7 Madeira, marsala ***fragrance:*** 7 bouquet ***golden:*** 4 Bual 7 Amoroso, Madeira, Moscato, Oloroso, Sercial 8 Bucellas, Moscatel, muscatel ***lover:*** 9 oenophile 11 oenophilist ***maker:*** 7 vintner 8 vigneron 13 viticulturist ***merchant:*** 7 vintner ***pitcher:*** 4 olpe 5 olpae (plural) 8 oenochoe ***red:*** 4 port, tent 5 Gamay, Macon, Marco, Medoc, Rioja 6 Aleyor, Barolo, Beaune, claret, Volnay 7 Almissa, Barbera, Chianti, Falerno, Inferno, Margaux 8 Aleatico, Alicante, Ambonnay, Bordeaux, Gragnano, Julienas, Nebbiolo, Sassella 9 Adlesberg, Hermitage, Lambrusco, Pinot Noir, St. Emilion, zinfandel 10 Barbaresco, Beaujolais, Roussillon, Sangiovese, Valtellina, Verdicchio 11 Affenthaler, Mavrodaphne, Petite Sirah 12 Valpolicella ***relating to:*** 5 vinic 6 vinous ***residue:*** 4 marc ***rice:*** 4 sake ***richness:*** 4 body ***sediment:*** 4 lees 5 dregs ***shop:*** 6 bistro, bodega ***sparkling:*** 4 sekt 8 cold duck, mousseux, Spumante 9 champagne, Lambrusco ***specialist:*** 9 enologist 10 oenologist ***spiced:*** 9 hippocras ***steward:*** 9 sommelier ***study of:*** 7 enology 8 oenology ***sweet:*** 4 Bual, port, tent 5 Almus, Tokay 6 Albana, canary, d'Yquem, Malaga, muscat 7 Almissa, bastard, Catawba, Madeira, malmsey, marsala, Moscato, Oloroso, Orvieto, Vouvray 8 Aleatico, Alicante, Malvasia, Moscatel, muscadel, muscatel, sauterne 9 Sauternes 11 Mavrodaphne, scuppernong ***sweeten:*** 4 mull ***unfermented:*** 4 must ***vessel:*** 3 ama 5 amula 7 chalice ***white:*** 4 hock, sock 5 Almus, Rhine, Soave 6 Alella, Barsac, Gentil, Graves, Saumur, Valmur 7 Banyuls, Catawba, Chablis, Chacoli, Conthey, Dezaley, Falerno, Moselle, Orvieto, Vouvray 8 Aiglerie, Amarante, Bordeaux, Frascati, Riesling, Semillon, Sylvaner, Traminer, Vaudesir, vermouth 9 champagne, Hermitage, Meursault, Neuchatel, Sansevero, Teneriffe, Zeltinger 10 Hochheimer, Montrachet 11 Chenin Blanc, Niersteiner, Rudesheimer, scuppernong 12 Geisenheimer 13 liebfraumilch ***year:*** 7 vintage

wing 3 ala, arm, ell, fly 4 flit, limb, sail 5 annex, block, bulge, fleet, pinna, sweep 9 expansion, extension 10 projection, protrusion 12 prolongation, protuberance ***combining form:*** 3 ali 4 pter 5 ptera, ptero 6 pterus, pteryg 7 pterous, pterygo ***relating to:*** 4 alar 5 alary 6 pteric

winged 5 alate 7 pennate ***horse:*** 7 Pegasus

wingless 7 apteral 8 apterous

winglike 4 alar 7 aliform *part:* 3 ala 4 alae (plural)
wink 3 bat 5 blink, shake, trice 6 minute, moment, second 7 instant, nictate, twinkle 9 nictitate, twinkling 11 split second
winner 6 victor 8 champion 9 conqueror
Winnie-the-Pooh *author:* 5 Milne *character:* 3 Roo 5 Kanga 6 Piglet, Tigger
winning 5 sweet 6 dulcet, profit 8 conquest, engaging
winnow 3 fan 4 blow, comb, sift, sort, wind 6 delete, remove, ruffle 8 separate
winsome 5 sweet 6 dulcet 7 lovable, winning 8 adorable, cheerful, engaging, lovesome
winter 6 season *French:* 5 hiver *Spanish:* 8 invierno
Winter's Tale character 7 Camillo, Leontes, Perdita 8 Florizel, Hermione 9 Polixenes
wintry 3 icy 4 cold 5 hoary, snowy 6 frigid, hiemal, stormy 8 hibernal, storming
wipe 3 mop 4 x out 5 abate, annul, erase, towel 6 cancel, delete, efface 7 abolish, blot out, expunge 8 black out, decimate, massacre 9 eradicate, extirpate, slaughter 10 annihilate, extinguish, obliterate 11 exterminate
wire 3 rod 4 cord, line 5 cable 6 thread 7 message 8 telegram 9 telegraph *measure:* 3 mil 5 gauge
wireless 5 radio
wiry 4 lean, ropy 6 sinewy 7 fibrous, stringy 8 muscular
Wisconsin *capital:* 7 Madison *college, university:* 5 Ripon 9 Marquette *largest city:* 9 Milwaukee *nickname:* 11 Badger State *state bird:* 5 robin *state flower:* 6 violet
wisdom 4 lore 5 sense 7 insight, science 8 gumption, judgment, sagacity, sageness, saneness, sapience 9 good sense, knowledge 10 horse sense, shrewdness 11 common sense, information 12 perspicacity 13 judiciousness, sagaciousness *combining form:* 5 sophy
wise 3 hep, hip, way 4 bold, clew, clue, flip, keen, mode, pert, post, sage, sane, tell, warn, wily 5 acute, alert, aware, brash, cagey, canny, cocky, fresh, lippy, modus, nervy, quick, sassy, saucy, sharp, slick, smart 6 advise, artful, astute, bright, cheeky, crafty, fill in, inform, manner, method, notify, shrewd, smooth, sophic, system, tricky 7 apprise, cunning, fashion, forward, gnostic, knowing, politic, prudent, sapient 8 acquaint, arrogant, discreet, flippant, impudent, insolent, sensible, slippery, tactical 9 advisable, bold-faced, expedient, insighted, intuitive, judgmatic, judicious, provident, sagacious 10 cogitative, discerning, insightful, perceptive, procacious, reflective, thoughtful 11 foresighted, impertinent, intelligent, quick-witted, sharp-witted, smart-alecky 12 nimble-witted 13 contemplative, knowledgeable, perspicacious *person:* 4 sage 6 savant 7 scholar
wiseacre see **wise guy**
wisecrack 3 gag 4 jape, jest, joke, quip 5 sally 7 waggery 9 witticism
wise guy 6 smarty 9 know-it-all 10 smart aleck 11 smarty-pants
Wise Men see **Magi**
wish 4 hope, like, long, want, will 5 covet, crave, elect, fancy, foist, yearn 6 desire, expect, impose, please 7 longing 10 desiderate
wishbone 7 furcula 8 furculum
wishful 5 eager 7 longing 8 desirous
wishy-washy 4 weak 5 banal, bland, vapid 6 jejune, watery 7 insipid, languid, sapless 8 listless, waterish 9 enervated, savorless 10 flavorless, namby-pamby, pantywaist, spiritless 13 characterless
wisp 5 strip 6 streak 7 handful 8 fragment
wispy 5 frail 8 nebulous
wisteria 4 fuji, vine
Wister novel 12 The Virginian
wistful 3 sad 7 pensive 10 meditative, melancholy
wit 3 ESP, wag 4 head, mind 5 brain, comic, droll, grasp, humor, joker, sense 6 acumen, brains, esprit, jester, reason, sanity, satire, senses, wisdom 7 balance, insight, punster, sensing 8 astucity, comedian, funnyman, humorist, jokester, keenness, lucidity, prudence, quipster, repartee, sagacity, sageness, saneness, sapience, wordplay 9 alertness, awareness, mentality, smartness, soundness 10 astuteness, brainpower, brilliance, cleverness, divination, gray matter, perception, shrewdness 11 discernment, penetration, percipience, rationality 12 apprehension, clairvoyance, intelligence, perspicacity 13 comprehension, sagaciousness, understanding
witch 3 hag, hex 4 drab, trot 5 biddy, bruja, charm, crone, lamia, spell 6 beldam, voodoo 7 enchant 8 magician, sorcerer 9 ensorcell, sorceress 11 enchantress *companion:* 3 cat *group:* 5 coven *male:* 6 wizard 7 warlock *meeting:* 6 sabbat *Scottish:* 6 cummer *vehicle:* 5 broom
witchcraft 5 charm, magic 6 allure, appeal, voodoo 7 glamour, hexerei, sorcery 8 charisma, witchery, wizardry 9 conjuring, magnetism 10 black magic, necromancy 11 enchantment, fascination, incantation, thaumaturgy
witch hazel 8 hornbeam 11 tobaccowood, winterbloom *lotion:* 9 hamamelin

witchy 5 magic 6 magian, mystic 7 magical 8 wizardly 9 sorcerous 11 necromantic 12 thaumaturgic
with 2 by, on 3 for, per, pro, via 4 over, upon 5 about 7 by way of, through 8 by dint of 9 by means of, in favor of 10 by virtue of ***French:*** 4 avec ***German:*** 3 mit ***Italian:*** 3 con ***Latin:*** 3 cum ***prefix:*** 2 co 3 col, com, con, cor, sym, syn
withal 3 too, yea, yet 4 also, more 5 still 6 as well, though 7 besides, howbeit, however 8 after all, moreover 9 per contra 11 furthermore, nonetheless 12 additionally, nevertheless
withdraw 2 go 4 exit, quit 5 leave, quail, unsay 6 abjure, depart, get off, recall, recant, recede, recoil, remove, retire, secede, shrink 7 get away, retract, retreat, take off, take out 8 fall back, forswear, give back, palinode, run along, take away, take back
withdrawal 4 exit 6 egress, exodus 7 exiting, pullout, retreat 8 offgoing 9 departure, egression 10 setting-out ***from reality:*** 6 autism
withdrawn 4 cool 5 aloof 6 casual, offish, remote 7 aseptic, distant 8 detached, reserved, retiring, solitary 9 incurious, shrinking, unaffable, uncurious 10 restrained, unsociable 11 indifferent, standoffish, unconcerned, unexpansive 12 uninterested ***from reality:*** 8 autistic
wither 3 age, dry 4 wane, wilt 5 dry up, mummy, wizen 6 shrink, welter 7 decline, mummify, shrivel
withered 4 sere 8 shrunken
withhold 3 bit 4 curb, deny, keep 5 check 6 bridle, detain, refuse, retain 7 abstain, forbear, inhibit, keep out, refrain, reserve 8 disallow, keep back, restrain 9 constrain
within 4 into 5 among 6 inside 7 indoors, inwards 8 interior ***combining form:*** 3 end, ent 4 endo, ento ***prefix:*** 2 il, im, in, ir 5 infra, inter, intra, intro
with-it 2 in 4 tony 5 swank, swish 6 modish, tonish, trendy 7 à la mode, stylish 11 fashionable
without 4 open, past, sans 5 after, minus 6 beyond 7 lacking, open air, outside, wanting 8 awanting, outdoors 10 out-of-doors ***combining form:*** 4 lipo ***Latin:*** 4 sine ***suffix:*** 4 less
with respect to 2 re 4 as to 5 as for 7 apropos 8 touching 9 as regards, regarding 10 concerning
withstand 4 bear, buck, duel 5 abide, fight, repel 6 combat, endure, oppose, resist, suffer 7 contest, dispute 8 tolerate, traverse
withy 4 twig 5 osier 6 branch, willow
witless 4 daft 5 crazy, silly 6 crazed, insane, simple, stupid 7 asinine, cracked, unwitty 8 demented, deranged, mindless 9 bedlamite, brainless, nitwitted, senseless 10 reasonless, weak-headed, weak-minded
witlessness 5 folly 7 inanity 8 insanity 9 absurdity, craziness, dottiness, silliness 11 foolishness 13 senselessness
witness 3 see 4 view 5 argue, proof, vouch 6 attest, viewer 7 bespeak, betoken, certify, testify, watcher 8 announce, beholder, by-sitter, evidence, indicate, looker-on, observer, onlooker 9 bystander, spectator, testament, testimony 11 attestation, testimonial 12 confirmation
witticism 3 gag, pun 4 jape, jest, joke, quip 5 crack 7 waggery 8 drollery 9 wisecrack
wittiness 5 humor 6 comedy 8 drollery 9 drollness, funniness
witting 4 ware 5 alive, awake, aware 7 knowing, willful, willing 8 sensible, sentient, unforced 9 cognizant, conscious, voluntary 10 deliberate 11 intentional
witty 5 funny 6 clever, jocose 7 amusing, jocular, probing, risible 8 humorous, piercing 9 diverting, facetious, sparkling 10 ridiculous 11 penetrating 12 entertaining 13 scintillating
witty saying 3 mot 4 quip 7 epigram 8 facetiae (plural)
wiz 6 artist, expert, master 8 virtuoso 9 authority 10 past master
wizard 4 mage, sage, whiz 5 magus 6 artist, expert, master 7 warlock 8 conjurer, magician, sorcerer, virtuoso 9 archimage, authority, enchanter 10 past master, proficient 11 necromancer
wizardly 5 magic 6 magian, mystic, witchy 7 magical 9 sorcerous 11 necromantic 12 thaumaturgic
Wizard of Menlo Park 6 Edison
Wizard of Oz ***author:*** 4 Baum ***character:*** 7 Dorothy 9 Scarecrow 10 Tin Woodman 12 Cowardly Lion ***dog:*** 4 Toto
wizardry 5 magic 7 sorcery 8 witchery 9 conjuring, magicking 10 necromancy, witchcraft 11 bewitchment, enchantment, incantation
wizen 3 dry 4 wilt 5 dry up, mummy 6 welter, wither 7 mummify, shrivel
wobble 4 sway 5 lurch, quake, shake, swing, waver, weave 6 careen, dither, falter, quaver, quiver, shimmy, shiver, teeter, topple, totter 7 shudder, stagger, stumble
wobbly 4 weak 5 shaky 6 dickey, unsure 7 halting, rackety, rickety, shaking 8 hesitant, insecure, rachitic, rootless, unstable, unsteady, wavering 9 faltering, fluctuant, tentative, uncertain 10 irresolute, rattletrap 11 vacillating, vacillatory 12 wiggle-waggle

Wodehouse character 6 Jeeves, Psmith 7 Wooster 8 Mulliner
Woden see Odin
woe 3 rue 4 care 5 grief 6 misery, regret, sorrow 7 anguish, sadness, trouble 9 bemoaning, bewailing, deploring, heartache 10 affliction, heartbreak 11 lamentation, unhappiness 12 wretchedness
woebegone 3 low 4 blue, down, worn 5 black, bleak 6 dismal, dreary, gloomy, shabby 8 dejected, downcast, funereal 9 depressed 10 depressing, dispirited, lugubrious, melancholy, oppressive, tenebrific 11 crestfallen, dilapidated, dispiriting, downhearted 12 disconsolate
woeful 3 sad 4 dire 5 grave, wrung 6 dismal, dolent, paltry, racked, rueful 7 crushed 8 dejected, dolesome, dolorous, downcast, grievous, harrowed, mournful, overcome, stricken, tortured, wretched 9 afflicted, depressed, heartsick, miserable, plaintive, sorrowful 10 afflictive, calamitous, deplorable, dispirited, lamentable, lugubrious, melancholy 11 distressing, downhearted, low-spirited, regrettable, unfortunate 12 disconsolate, inconsolable 13 heartbreaking, unprecedented
wold 5 plain
wolf 4 bolt, cram, grub, gulp, lobo, roué, slop 6 canine, chaser, coyote, englut, gobble, guzzle, lecher, masher 7 amorist, Don Juan, rounder 8 Casanova, lothario, womanize 9 ladies' man, libertine, philander, womanizer 10 fool around, lady-killer, mess around, play around, profligate 11 ingurgitate, philanderer ***combining form:*** 3 lyc 4 lyco ***genus:*** 5 Canis ***group:*** 4 pack ***young:*** 5 whelp
wolfish 4 fell, grim 5 cruel 6 fierce, lupine, savage 7 inhuman 8 inhumane 9 barbarous, ferocious, truculent
wolverine 8 carcajou ***European:*** 7 glutton ***genus:*** 4 Gulo
Wolverine State 8 Michigan
woman 4 dame, lady 5 madam 6 female, matron 8 mistress ***attractive:*** 5 belle 6 beauty, eyeful, looker 7 stunner 8 knockout ***Australian:*** 4 bint ***combining form:*** 3 gyn 4 gyne, gyno, gyny 5 gynec, gyneo 6 gynaec, gynaeo, gyneco, gynous 7 gynaeco ***courageous:*** 7 heroine ***dignified:*** 6 matron 7 dowager 10 grande dame ***dowdy:*** 5 frump ***Dutch:*** 4 vrow 5 vrouw ***English:*** 6 milady ***first, biblical:*** 3 Eve ***first, mythological:*** 7 Pandora ***French:*** 5 femme ***German:*** 4 frau 8 fräulein ***Hawaiian:*** 6 wahine ***Indian:*** 5 squaw ***intellectual:*** 12 bluestocking ***Italian:*** 5 donna 7 signora ***lewd:*** 5 hussy 6 harlot, wanton 7 trollop ***little:*** 3 Mrs. 4 wife ***old:*** 3 hag 4 dame 5 crone 6 beldam, carlin, gammer, granny ***pregnant:*** 7 gravida ***resembling:*** 8 gynecoid ***royal:*** 5 queen 8 princess ***sailor:*** 4 Wave ***scheming:*** 7 jezebel ***servant:*** 4 maid ***slovenly:*** 8 slattern ***soldier:*** 3 Wac ***Spanish:*** 4 doña 6 senora ***strong:*** 6 amazon, virago ***unmarried:*** 4 miss 6 maiden 8 spinster ***young:*** 4 girl, lass 6 lassie, maiden
womanize 4 wolf 9 philander 10 fool around, mess around, play around
womanizer 4 wolf 6 chaser, masher 7 Don Juan 8 Casanova 9 ladies' man, philander 10 lady-killer 11 philanderer
womb 6 uterus ***combining form:*** 4 metr, uter 5 metra, metro, utero 6 hyster, metria (plural) 7 hystero, metrium
wombat 9 marsupial
women ***hatred of:*** 8 misogyny ***organization of:*** 3 DAR, NOW 7 sorosis 8 sorority
Women in Love author 8 Lawrence
wonder 3 awe 5 amaze, doubt 6 marvel 7 concern, dublety, miracle, portent, prodigy, stunner 8 mistrust 9 amazement, dubiosity, marveling, sensation, suspicion 10 admiration, phenomenon, skepticism 11 incertitude, uncertainty, uncertitude 12 astonishment, bewilderment
wonderful 5 great, super, swell 6 divine, groovy, peachy 7 amazing, strange 8 glorious, terrific, wondrous 9 marvelous 10 astounding, miraculous, staggering, stupendous, surprising 11 astonishing, sensational
wondrous 7 amazing, strange 9 marvelous, wonderful 10 astounding, miraculous, stupendous, surprising 11 astonishing, spectacular
wont 3 apt, use, way 5 habit, inure, trick, usage 6 custom, manner 8 accustom, habitude, practice 9 habituate 10 consuetude 11 familiarize
wonted 5 usual 7 chronic, routine 8 accepted, habitual 9 customary 10 accustomed
woo 3 sue 5 court, spark 6 pursue 7 address 8 make up to 10 sweetheart
wood 5 weald 6 forest, lumber, timber 10 timberland ***combining form:*** 3 hyl, xyl 4 hylo, lign, xylo 5 ligni, ligno, xylon, xylum ***decayed:*** 4 punk ***eater:*** 7 termite ***for burning:*** 5 fagot 6 tinder 8 kindling ***golf:*** 5 spoon 6 driver 7 brassie ***hard:*** 3 elm, eng, oak 4 ebon, poon, rata, teak 5 beach, birch, ebony, maple 6 cherry, walnut 8 chestnut, mahogany, sycamore ***imperfection:*** 4 knot 5 gnarl ***kind:*** 5 xylem 6 phloem ***made of:*** 5 treen ***pattern in:*** 5 grain 6 figure ***product:*** 3 tar 5 paper 10 turpentine ***soft:*** 4 pine
wood alcohol 6 methyl 8 methanol
woodchuck 6 marmot 9 groundhog

wood coal 7 lignite
wooded 5 bosky 6 sylvan 8 sylvatic
wooden 4 dull 5 inept, stiff, treen 6 clumsy, gauche 7 buckram, halting, stilted, unhandy 8 bumbling 9 cardboard, ham-handed, maladroit 11 heavy-handed, muscle-bound
woodland 5 weald, woods 6 forest, timber
wood nymph 5 dryad
woodpecker 7 flicker, piculet, wryneck 9 sapsucker ***genus:*** 5 Picus ***kind:*** 5 downy, green, hairy 8 imperial, pileated 9 redheaded 11 ivory-billed ***relating to:*** 6 picine 8 piciform
woodsman 6 logger, ranger 7 bushman 8 forester 11 bushwhacker
wood sorrel 3 oca 6 oxalis
woodsy 6 rustic, sylvan
woodwind 4 oboe 5 flute 7 bassoon 8 clarinet 9 saxophone 10 instrument
woodworker 9 carpenter 12 cabinetmaker
woody 6 xyloid 8 ligneous; (see also wooded)
Woody Allen film 5 Alice, Zelig 7 Bananas, Sleeper 9 Annie Hall, Interiors, Manhattan, Radio Days, September 12 Love and Death
wooer 4 beau 5 spark, swain 6 suitor 7 sparker
woof 4 weft, yarn 5 weave 6 fabric, thread 7 texture
wool 3 fur 4 coat, hair 6 fleece ***coarse:*** 3 abb ***combining form:*** 3 lan 4 erio, lani, lano ***cut:*** 5 shear ***fabric:*** 4 felt 5 baize, crepe, serge, tweed 6 covert, kersey, mohair, poplin, shoddy, velour 7 duvetyn, flannel, worsted 8 cashmere, chenille 9 gabardine 10 broadcloth ***fat:*** 7 lanolin ***kind:*** 4 hogg 6 angora, hogget, virgin ***low-quality:*** 5 mungo 6 shoddy ***matted:*** 7 daglock, taglock ***musk-ox:*** 6 qiviut ***process:*** 7 carding 8 skirting ***source:*** 4 goat, lamb 5 camel, llama, sheep
woolly 5 hairy 6 fleecy, lanate, lanose, pilose 7 hirsute, lanated, pileous 9 whiskered
woozy 4 sick, weak 5 dizzy 6 blurry 8 nauseous
word 3 cry, put, say, vow 4 buzz, news, oath, talk, tell, term 5 order, rumor, state 6 advice, behest, charge, convey, gossip, pledge, plight, report, rumble, saying 7 bidding, command, dictate, express, hearsay, mandate, message, promise, tidings, vocable, warrant 8 locution 9 assurance, directive, formulate, guarantee, speerings, statement, utterance 10 commitment, expression, injunction 11 countersign, declaration, information, scuttlebutt 12 announcement, intelligence 13 communication, pronouncement ***combining form:*** 3 log 4 logo, onym 7 onomato ***connective:*** 11 conjunction ***group:*** 6 clause, phrase 8 sentence ***misused:*** 8 malaprop 11 malapropism ***naming:*** 4 noun ***new:*** 7 coinage 9 neologism ***of action:*** 4 verb ***of honor:*** 4 oath 7 promise ***origin:*** 9 etymology ***part:*** 8 syllable ***root:*** 6 etymon ***scrambled:*** 7 anagram ***shortened:*** 11 contraction 12 abbreviation ***square:*** 10 palindrome ***with opposite meaning:*** 7 antonym ***with same meaning:*** 7 synonym ***with some pronunciation:*** 7 homonym 9 homophone ***with some spelling:*** 7 homonym 9 homograph
wordbook 7 lexicon 8 libretto 9 thesaurus 10 dictionary
word for word 8 verbatim
wordiness 8 verbiage 9 prolixity, verbalism, verbosity, windiness 10 prolixness 11 verboseness
word-of-mouth 4 oral 6 spoken, verbal 9 unwritten
wordy 4 glib 5 turnid, windy 6 prolix, turgid 7 diffuse, verbose, voluble 8 inflated 9 bombastic, flatulent, garrulous, redundant, talkative 10 long-winded, loquacious, palaverous, rhetorical
work 2 go 3 act, fix, job, run, tug, use 4 duty, line, moil, opus, take, tend, till, toil 5 chore, craft, dress, drive, grind, labor, react, solve, sweat, trade 6 behave, drudge, effort, handle, métier, racket, strain, strive 7 calling, operate, perform, pursuit, resolve, slavery, travail, trouble 8 bullwork, business, drudgery, exertion, function, plugging, slogging, striving, vocation 9 cultivate 10 employment, handicraft, occupation, profession ***combining form:*** 3 erg 4 ergo ***together:*** 9 cooperate 11 collaborate ***unit:*** 3 erg 5 joule
workaday 4 dull 5 lowly, plain, usual 7 mundane, prosaic, routine 8 everyday, ordinary 9 quotidian 11 commonplace
worker 4 doer, hand 6 toiler, wallah 7 artisan, laborer 8 employee, mechanic, operator 9 craftsman, operative 10 roustabout ***combining form:*** 5 ergat 6 ergato ***fellow:*** 7 comrade, partner 9 colleague ***group:*** 4 crew, gang 5 shift, staff, union ***hard:*** 5 slave 6 beaver, drudge ***itinerant:*** 6 boomer 7 migrant ***slow:*** 7 plodder ***unskilled:*** 4 peon 7 jackleg, laborer
working 4 busy, live 5 alive 6 active 7 dynamic, engaged, running 8 employed, occupied 9 operative 11 functioning ***not:*** 5 kaput 6 broken
workless 4 idle 7 jobless 10 unemployed
workman see **worker**

work out 3 fix 5 solve, train 7 resolve 8 exercise
workout 8 exercise, practice
work over 4 redo 6 beat up, redraw, rehash, revamp, revise, rework 7 redraft, restyle, rewrite 9 manhandle
workroom 3 lab 4 shop 6 studio 7 atelier 10 laboratory
works 4 mill 5 plant 7 factory
Works and Days author 6 Hesiod
world 5 earth, globe 6 cosmos, kosmos, nature, planet 8 creation, megacosm, universe 9 macrocosm 11 macrocosmos *combining form:* 4 cosm 5 cosmo
worldly 5 blasé 6 earthy 7 earthly, knowing, mundane, sensual, terrene 8 banausic, mondaine, telluric, temporal 9 sublunary, tellurian 11 terrestrial 12 disenchanted, sophisticate 13 disillusioned, materialistic, sophisticated
World War I *battle:* 5 Marne, Somme, Ypres 6 Verdun 7 Jutland, Lemberg 10 Tannenberg *battle line:* 9 Siegfried *hero:* 4 York 8 Pershing 12 Rickenbacker *treaty:* 10 Versailles
World War II *admiral:* 6 Halsey, Nimitz *alliance:* 4 Axis 6 Allies *battle:* 5 Anzio, Bulge 6 Bataan, Midway, Tarawa, Warsaw 7 Iwo Jima, Okinawa 8 Normandy 10 Stalingrad *general:* 6 Patton, Rommel 7 Bradley 10 Eisenhower, Montgomery *hero:* 6 Murphy *journalist:* 4 Pyle *vehicle:* 4 jeep *weapon:* 5 A-bomb 6 rocket
worldwide 6 cosmic, global 8 catholic 9 planetary, universal 10 ecumenical 12 cosmopolitan *combining form:* 5 globo
worm 3 eel, loa, lug 4 grub, nema 5 borer, fluke, leech 6 edge in, maggot, mucker, no-good, squirm, wiggle, work in, wretch, writhe 7 carbora, distome, lowlife, serpent, triclad, wriggle 8 helminth, nematode, squiggle 9 insinuate, planarium, trematode 10 infiltrate *combining form:* 5 nemat, vermi 6 nemato, scolec, scolex 7 scoleco 8 helminth 9 helmintho *marine:* 3 lug 4 naid 6 nereis, palolo 7 annelid, tubifex 11 chaetognath *parasitic:* 5 fluke, leech 7 ascarid, ascaris, cestode, filaria 8 strongyl, trichina *relating to:* 7 vermian *resembling:* 11 helminthoid
worm-eaten 6 pitted 7 decayed, worn-out 10 antiquated
worn 5 drawn, erose, jaded, tired, weary 6 eroded 7 haggard, pinched, wearied 8 careworn, fatigued
worn-out 4 sere 5 all in, spent, stale, tired, trite 6 bleary, effete, used up 7 clichéd, drained, far-gone 8 depleted 9 exhausted, hackneyed, washed out 10 threadbare 11 stereotyped
worried 8 distrait, harassed, troubled 9 tormented 10 distracted, distraught, distressed
worry 3 ail, dun, nag, tew, try, vex 4 care, cark, fret, fuss, gnaw, stew, test 5 annoy, beset, harry, tease, trial, upset 6 bother, harass, needle, pester, plague, pother, unease 7 afflict, anguish, anxiety, bedevil, disturb, hagride, oppress, torment, torture, trouble 8 aggrieve, distress 9 beleaguer, tantalize 10 solicitude, uneasiness 11 concernment, disquietude *without:* 8 carefree
worrywart 7 fusspot 9 Cassandra, pessimist 11 crepehanger
worse 4 less 6 poorer 8 inferior
worsen 3 rot 4 sink 6 debase 7 decline, degrade, descend 10 degenerate, retrograde 11 deteriorate
worship 4 love 5 adore 6 dote on, revere 7 idolize, lionize, liturgy 8 dote upon, idolatry, venerate 9 adoration, affection, reverence 10 veneration 11 idolization *combining form:* 5 latry *object of:* 3 god 4 icon, idol *place of:* 5 altar 6 church, mosque, shrine, temple 9 cathedral, synagogue
worshiper 6 votary 7 devotee 8 disciple *combining form:* 5 later
worst 4 beat, best, down 5 least, outdo 6 defeat, lowest
worsted 4 yarn 5 serge 6 fabric, poplin 9 gabardine
wort 4 herb 5 plant
worth 4 mark, note 5 merit, price, value 6 moment, riches, wealth 7 account, caliber, fortune, quality, stature 8 property 9 resources, substance, valuation
worthless 4 mean 5 junky, sorry 6 draffy, drossy, no-good, trashy 7 fustian, inutile, nothing, useless 8 feckless, unworthy 9 cheapjack, incapable, valueless 11 incompetent, meaningless, purposeless, unqualified 12 contemptible
worthwhile 4 good 6 paying 7 gainful 9 lucrative 10 profitable, well-paying 11 moneymaking 12 advantageous, remunerative
worthy 4 good 5 noble 6 divine 8 laudable, pleasing, precious, sterling 9 admirable, deserving, desirable, estimable, honorable, meritable, praisable, priceless 10 invaluable, satisfying 11 commendable, meritorious
Wotan see Odin
Wouk novel 14 The Caine Mutiny
wound 3 cut 4 blow, harm, hurt 6 damage, injure, injury, lesion, trauma 8 lacerate 10 laceration *combining form:* 7 traumat 8 traumato *discharge:* 3 pus *sign:* 4 scab, scar 5 blood 7 blister
wow 3 hit 4 bang 5 smash 7 success 9 succès fou 10 bell ringer 11 exclamation
Wozzeck composer 4 Berg

wrack 4 kelp, raze, ruin, undo 5 wreck 6 unmake 7 destroy, seaweed, unbuild, unframe 8 decimate, demolish
wraith 5 ghost, shade, spook 6 shadow, spirit 7 phantom, specter 8 phantasm 10 apparition
wrangle 3 row 4 spat, tiff 5 argue, fight, scrap 6 argufy, bicker, fracas, hassle 7 brabble, dispute, fall out, quarrel, quibble 8 squabble 9 bickering, caterwaul 11 altercation
wrangler 6 cowboy 9 disputant
wrap 4 mask, roll, veil 5 cloak, drape, paper, shawl 6 enfold, invest, muffle, shroud, swathe 7 blanket, enclose, envelop, muffler, swaddle 8 bundle up, enshroud, enswathe, wax paper 10 camouflage
wrapped up 4 deep, rapt 6 intent 7 engaged 8 absorbed, immersed 9 engrossed 11 preoccupied
wrapper 4 gown 5 cover, shawl 6 jacket
wrap up see wind up
wrath 3 ire 4 fury, rage 5 anger 8 acerbity, acrimony, asperity 10 resentment 11 indignation
wrathful 3 mad 4 waxy 5 angry, irate, wroth 6 heated, ireful, wrothy
wreak 5 exact, visit, wreck 6 impose 7 force on, inflict 9 force upon
wreath 3 lei 4 bays 5 crown, torse 6 anadem, laurel 7 chaplet, coronal, coronet, garland
wreathe 4 coil, curl, wind 5 twine, twist 6 spiral 7 contort, entwine 9 corkscrew
wreck 3 dog 4 do in, heap, hulk, raze, ruin, undo 5 beach, crash, crate, smash, total, visit, wrack, wreak 6 damage, impose, jalopy, junker, pileup, ravage, strand, unmake 7 clunker, crack-up, debacle, despoil, destroy, disable, force on, inflict, plunder, smashup, subvert, unbuild, unframe 8 bankrupt, cast away, collapse, decimate, demolish, sabotage 9 breakdown, force upon, undermine, vandalize
wreckage 6 jetsam 7 flotsam 8 sabotage 9 driftwood 10 subversion 11 undermining
wrench 3 wry 4 pull, tool, turn, warp 5 exact, force, gouge, pinch, screw, twist, wrest, wring 6 coerce, compel, extort, garble, sprain 7 distort, pervert, squeeze 9 constrain, shake down 12 misrepresent *kind:* 6 monkey 7 ratchet
wrest 3 wry 4 warp 5 exact, gouge, pinch, screw, twist, wring 6 extort, garble, wrench 7 confuse, distort, extract, pervert, squeeze 9 shake down 12 misrepresent
wrestle 4 moil, toil 5 essay, exert, fight, labor 6 strain, strive, tussle 7 contend, grapple, scuffle, stretch, travail 8 endeavor, struggle
wrestling *hold:* 4 lock 6 nelson 8 headlock, scissors *kind:* 4 sumo *term:* 3 pin 4 fall 5 throw 8 takedown
wretch 3 cur, dog 4 scum, snot, toad, worm 5 devil, knave, rogue, skunk, snake 6 mucker, no-good, rascal, rotter 7 caitiff, lowlife, stinker, villain 8 scalawag, stinkard, wormling 9 scoundrel, stinkaroo 10 blackguard, ne'er-do-well 11 rapscallion
wretched 3 low 4 base, mean, vile 6 abject, dismal, dolent, paltry, rueful, scurvy, sordid, woeful 7 doleful, forlorn, ignoble, piteous, pitiful, ruthful, servile 8 dolorous, hopeless, pitiable 9 afflicted, miserable, sorrowful 10 despairing, despicable, despondent, melancholy
wretchedness 3 woe 6 misery 11 unhappiness
wriggle 4 worm 6 squirm, writhe 8 squiggle
wring 3 wry 4 rack 5 exact, gouge, pinch, screw, wrest 6 extort, harrow, martyr, wrench 7 afflict, agonize, torment, torture 10 excruciate *the neck:* 5 scrag
wringing-wet 5 soppy 6 soaked, sodden, soused 7 soaking, sopping 8 drenched, dripping 9 saturated
wrinkle 4 fold, line, ruck, ruga, seam 5 crimp, plica, ridge, rivel, screw 6 crease, furrow, method, rimple, ruck up, rumple 7 crimple, crinkle, crumple, novelty, scrunch, shrivel 9 crow's foot 10 innovation 11 corrugation
wrinkled 5 lined 6 rugate, rugose, rugous, rumply 8 rugulose
wrist 5 joint 6 carpus *bone:* 6 carpal, hamate, lunate 8 capitate, pisiform 9 navicular 10 triangular 11 multangular *combining form:* 4 carp 5 carpo
writ 5 breve, brief, order, tales 6 capias, elegit, venire 7 mandate, precipe, summons, warrant 8 document, mandamus, mittimus, praecipe, replevin, subpoena 10 certiorari, distringas, injunction 12 habeas corpus
write 3 ink, jot, pen 4 draw, note, sign 5 chalk, draft 6 author, indite, pencil, scrawl, scribe 7 compose, dot down, engross, scratch 8 inscribe, scribble 10 correspond
write down 4 note 6 record
write off 5 decry, lower 6 cancel 7 devalue, downcry, run down 8 belittle, derogate, discount, mark down, minimize 9 devaluate, disparage, downgrade, underrate 10 depreciate, undervalue 11 detract from
writer 4 poet 6 penman, scribe 7 penster

8 composer, novelist ***bad:*** 4 hack ***combining form:*** 7 grapher; (see also **author**)

writhe 4 bend, curl, toss, worm 5 twist 6 squirm, wiggle 7 agonize, contort, distort, wriggle 8 squiggle

writing 4 book, hand 5 essay, paper, print, prose, words 6 letter, script 7 epistle 8 document, longhand 9 allograph, signature 10 literature, manuscript, penmanship 11 calligraphy, composition, inscription, publication ***character:*** 6 letter 9 cuneiform 10 hieroglyph ***combining form:*** 4 gram 6 grapho, graphy 7 graphia ***for the blind:*** 7 braille ***instrument:*** 3 pen 5 chalk, quill 6 pencil, stylus ***kind:*** 5 prose, verse 6 poetry ***sacred:*** 5 Bible, Koran 6 Talmud, Tantra 9 scripture ***secret:*** 4 code ***surface:*** 5 board, paper, slate 6 scroll 9 parchment

wrong 3 bad, ill, off, sin 4 awry, debt, evil, harm, hurt, poor, tort 5 abuse, amiss, badly, crime, false, inapt, unfit 6 afield, astray, injure, injury, offend, rotten, sinful, untrue, wicked 7 immoral, oppress, outrage, vicious 8 aggrieve, ill-treat, improper, inequity, iniquity, maltreat, mistaken, mistreat 9 diablerie, erroneous, grievance, incorrect, injustice, misguided, persecute, reprobate, unfitting 10 inaccurate, iniquitous, unfairness, unjustness, unsuitable, wickedness 11 unfavorably 12 infelicitous 13 inappropriate ***prefix:*** 3 mis

wrongdoer 5 felon 6 sinner 8 criminal, offender 9 miscreant 10 malefactor

wrongdoing 3 sin 4 evil, tort 5 crime 7 misdeed, offense 8 iniquity 9 diablerie, violation 10 misconduct 11 malefaction, misbehavior

wrongful 7 illegal, illicit, lawless 8 criminal, unlawful 12 illegitimate

wrongheaded 5 balky 6 mulish, ornery 7 froward, restive, wayward 8 contrary, perverse, stubborn 9 obstinate 10 self-willed 11 stiff-necked 12 cross-grained, pertinacious

wrought 4 made 6 formed, shaped, worked 7 created 8 finished, hammered 9 fashioned, processed 10 ornamented 12 manufactured ***up:*** 7 excited, stirred

wry 4 bent 5 twist, wrest, wring 6 ironic, wrench 7 cynical, twisted 8 sardonic

wryneck 10 woodpecker

Wuthering Heights ***author:*** 6 Brontë ***character:*** 7 Hindley 9 Catherine 10 Heathcliff

Wycliffite 7 Lollard

Wyoming ***capital:*** 8 Cheyenne ***nickname:*** 13 Equality State ***state bird:*** 10 meadowlark

X

x 3 chi, ten 4 kiss, mark 5 annul, cross, erase, error, times, wrong 6 cancel, delete, efface 7 blot out, expunge, mistake, wipe out 8 abscissa, black out 9 signature 10 obliterate

Xanadu *country:* 5 China *river:* 4 Alph

xanthic 6 yellow 9 yellowish

Xanthippe 3 nag 5 harpy, scold, shrew, vixen 6 nagger, ogress, virago 8 fishwife 9 termagant *husband:* 8 Socrates

xanthous 6 yellow

xebec 4 boat, ship 6 vessel 10 pirate ship

xenium 4 gift 7 present

xenon *symbol:* 2 Xe

Xenophon work 8 Anabasis 9 Cyropedia, Hellenica

Xeres 4 wine 5 Jerez 6 sherry

xerophyte 6 cactus

xerosis 7 dryness

Xerxes *defeat:* 7 Salamis *father:* 6 Darius *kingdom:* 6 Persia *mother:* 6 Atossa *wife:* 6 Esther

Xmas 4 Noel, yule 8 Nativity, yuletide 9 Christmas

X ray *discoverer:* 8 Roentgen *science:* 9 radiology 13 roentgenology

xurel 4 scad 6 saurel

xyloid 5 woody 8 ligneous

xylophone 5 saron, vibes 7 gambang, gamelan, marimba 8 gamelang, gigelira, sticcado 10 vibraphone

xystus 4 stoa, walk 5 porch 7 portico, terrace

Y

yacht 4 boat, race, sail, ship 5 craft 6 cruise, sonder 8 keelboat
yahoo 4 lout, punk 5 brute, clown, rough, rowdy, tough 6 mucker, savage 7 bumpkin, ruffian, toughie 8 bullyboy 9 roughneck
Yahweh 3 God 6 Jahvah 7 Jehovah
yak 2 ox 3 gab, jaw 4 blab, chat 5 clack, laugh, prate 6 babble, gabble, jabber, sarlak, sarlyk, yammer 7 blabber, buffalo, chatter, palaver, prattle
yakety-yak 3 gab, jaw 4 blab, chat 5 clack, prate 6 babble, gabble, jabber 7 blabber, chatter, palaver, prattle
Yale 3 Eli 4 lock 10 university
Yalta participant 6 Stalin 9 Churchill, Roosevelt
yam 3 ube, ubi 5 tugui 6 igname, potato 7 boniata 11 sweet potato
yammer 3 cry, gab, jaw, yak 4 chat, crab, fuss, yaup, yawp, yell 5 bleat, clack, gripe, whine, yearn 6 babble, clamor, gabble, squawk 7 chatter, grumble, prattle 8 complain 9 bellyache, yakety-yak
yank 3 lug, tug 4 grab, jerk, pull, snap, tear 5 hoick, lurch 6 clutch, evulse, snatch, twitch 7 extract 9 vellicate
yap 4 bark, hick, jake, yelp 5 clown, mouth, scold 6 bowwow, rustic 7 bumpkin, chatter, hayseed 9 hillbilly 10 clodhopper, provincial 12 backwoodsman
yard 4 lawn, quad, spar 5 court, garth, patio, stick 9 curtilage, enclosure 10 playground, quadrangle ***enclosed:*** 5 garth, patio ***five and one-half:*** 3 rod ***part of:*** 4 foot, nail ***shelter:*** 6 gazebo ***sixteenth of:*** 4 nail ***two hundred and twenty:*** 7 furlong
yardstick 5 gauge 7 measure 8 standard 9 benchmark, criterion 10 touchstone
yare 4 spry 5 agile, brisk, catty, ready 6 active, brisky, lively, nimble, volant 9 sprightly
yarn 3 rap 4 chat, chin, garn, tale, talk 5 fiber, floss, grain, prose, story, visit 6 caddis, cotton, crewel, strand, thread 7 caddice, genappe, schappe 8 anecdote, causerie, colloque, converse 9 narration, narrative ***ball of:*** 4 clew, clue ***coil:*** 5 skein 6 skeane ***cotton:*** 10 candlewick ***for fastening a sail:*** 6 roband, robbin ***woolen:*** 6 crewel, worset 7 worsted 8 shetland
yate 8 eucalypt
yaw 4 bend, gape, swag, tack, tilt, turn, veer, yawn 5 lurch, pitch, shift 6 double, seesaw, swerve, tilter 7 deviate 9 deviation 10 deflection
yawn 4 gape 5 ennui 6 tedium 7 boredom 8 doldrums
yawning 5 bored 6 gaping 7 chasmal 8 oscitant 9 cavernous
yawp 3 bay, caw, cry 4 bawl, crab, fuss, gape 5 bleat, gripe 6 squall, squark, squawk, yammer 8 complain
yea 2 ay, OK 3 aye, nay, too, yes, yet 4 also, even, more, okay 5 along, truly 6 agreed, assent, as well, indeed, really, verily 7 besides 8 all right, likewise, moreover, positive 11 affirmative 12 additionally
yeanling 3 kid 4 lamb 7 newborn
year ***academic:*** 7 session ***combining form:*** 6 ennial ***division:*** 5 month 6 season 9 trimester ***kind:*** 4 leap 5 lunar, solar 6 fiscal 8 calendar, sidereal, tropical 12 astronomical ***Latin:*** 5 annus ***Scottish:*** 7 towmond, towmont
yearbook 5 annal 6 annual 7 almanac, annuary
yearling 4 colt
Yearling ***author:*** 8 Rawlings ***character:*** 4 Jody
yearly 6 annual 8 annually
yearn 3 yen 4 ache, burn, long, lust, pant, pine, sigh, wish 5 covet, crave, dream 6 desire, grieve, hanker, hunger, thirst, yammer
yearning 4 wish 5 eager 6 desire, hanker 7 craving, wistful 8 homesick, lovesick
years ***eight:*** 9 octennial ***five:*** 7 lustrum 12 quinquennial, quinquennium ***four:*** 11 quadrennial, quadrennium ***one hundred:*** 7 century 9 centenary 10 centennial ***one thousand:*** 10 millennium ***ten:*** 6 decade 9 decennary, decenniad, decennial, decennium ***three:*** 9 triennial, triennium
yeast 3 bee 4 barm, foam, suds 5 froth, spume 6 lather, leaven 7 ferment
yeasty 5 dizzy, giddy, light 6 frothy 7 flighty 8 restless 9 exuberant, fribbling, frivolous 11 light-headed
Yeats ***beloved:*** 9 Maud Gonne ***birthplace:*** 6 Dublin ***play:*** 7 Deirdre 9 Purga-

tory 12 The Herne's Egg *poem:* 9 Byzantium 11 Lapis Lazuli
yegg 5 thief 6 robber 7 burglar 8 criminal 11 safecracker
yell 3 cry, yip 4 call, howl, roar, wail, weep, yowl 5 cheer, hallo, hollo, shout, whoop 6 bellow, bemoan, bewail, clamor, holler, lament, outcry, scream, shriek, squall, squeal, yammer 7 deplore, roaring 10 vociferate
yellow 4 mean 5 amber, blake, favel, lemon, ochre 6 coward, craven, flavid, flaxen, golden, sallow 7 gutless, mustard, saffron, unmanly, xanthic 8 cowardly, xanthous 9 jaundiced, spunkless 11 lily-livered 12 dishonorable 13 pusillanimous *brownish:* 3 dun 5 aloma, amber, straw 6 manila *combining form:* 4 flav 5 chrys, flavo, luteo, xanth 6 chryso, xantho *dye:* 5 morin 6 orlean 7 annatto 9 morindone *greenish:* 5 olive 6 acacia 10 chartreuse
yellowbelly 3 rat 4 funk 6 coward, craven, funker 7 chicken, dastard, quitter 8 poltroon
yellow dog 3 cad, cur 6 rotter 7 bounder
yellowhammer 5 ammer, finch, skite 6 gladdy 7 bunting, flicker, yeldrin 8 yoldring
yellowish brown 4 gold 7 mustard 9 butternut 12 butterscotch
Yellowstone attraction 4 bear 6 geyser 11 Old Faithful
yelp 3 cry, yap, yip 4 bark 5 boast, shout 6 outcry, squeal 8 complain
Yemen *capital:* 4 San'a *monetary unit:* 4 rial 5 dinar, riyal
Yemen, People's Democratic Republic of *capital:* 4 Aden *monetary unit:* 5 dinar
yen 4 ache, long, lust, pine, sigh, urge 5 crave, yearn 6 desire, hanker, hunger, thirst 7 craving, longing
yeoman 5 churl, clerk 6 farmer 7 freeman 8 retainer 9 assistant, attendant, beefeater, landowner 10 freeholder 11 subordinate
yeomanly 5 brave, loyal 6 sturdy 8 faithful 9 laborious 11 hardworking
yes 2 OK 3 aye, yea, yeh, yep, yup 4 okay, yeah 5 agree 6 accede, agreed, assent, gladly 7 consent, exactly 8 all right 9 acquiesce, assuredly, certainly, precisely, subscribe, willingly 11 affirmation, affirmative, undoubtedly *French:* 3 oui *German:* 2 ja *Italian:* 2 si *Russian:* 2 da *Spanish:* 2 si
yes-man 5 dummy, toady 6 minion, stooge 7 spaniel 8 bootlick, groveler, truckler 9 sycophant 10 bootlicker
yesterday 4 past, yore 8 foretime *French:* 4 hier
yesteryear 4 past, yore 8 foretime
yet 3 but, too 4 also, even, more, only, save 5 along, so far, still 6 as well, except, though, withal 7 besides, earlier, finally, further, howbeit, however, someday, thus far 8 after all, hitherto, likewise, moreover, sometime, somewhen 10 eventually, ultimately 11 furthermore, nonetheless, still and all 12 additionally, nevertheless
Yevtushenko poem 7 Babi Yar
Ygerne see **Igraine**
yield 3 bow, net, pay 4 bear, bend, cave, cede, cess, crop, emit, fail, fold, give, obey, quit, vent 5 admit, agree, allow, award, break, bring, defer, eject, grant, leave, offer, repay, waive 6 accede, accord, afford, bounty, buckle, comply, fold up, give up, impart, output, profit, relent, render, resign, return, reward, soften, submit, supply, tender 7 abandon, bring in, concede, consent, crumple, deliver, furnish, harvest, hold out, indulge, knuckle, outturn, produce, product, proffer, provide, revenue, succumb, truckle, turnout 8 collapse, hand over 9 acquiesce, discharge, surrender 10 capitulate, production, recompense, relinquish 11 buckle under 12 knuckle under
yielding 4 meek, soft, waxy 5 mushy, pappy, pulpy 6 feeble, flabby, limber, pliant, quaggy, spongy, supple 7 bearing, flaccid, flexile, passive, squashy, squishy, squushy 8 flexible, resigned, squelchy 9 tractable 10 manageable, submissive 11 acquiescent, unresistant, unresisting 12 nonresistant, nonresisting *combining form:* 6 ferous
yin and ____ 4 yang
yip 4 howl, yell, yelp, yowl 6 scream, squeal
yoke 3 tie, wed 4 bail, bond, join, knot, link, pair, span, team 5 bangy, hitch, marry, nexus, unite 6 banghy, couple, inspan, tackle 7 bondage, combine, conjoin, connect, harness, helotry, oppress, peonage, serfage, serfdom, slavery 8 ligament, ligature, vinculum 9 associate, conjugate, servility, servitude, thralldom 10 oppression 11 enslavement *combining form:* 3 zyg 4 zygo *part:* 5 oxbow
yokel 3 oaf 4 boor, clod, hick, jake, rube 6 rustic 7 bucolic, bumpkin, hayseed 8 Abderite 9 chawbacon, hillbilly 10 clodhopper 12 backwoodsman
yolk 6 center, yellow 7 essence *combining form:* 6 lecith, vitell 7 lecitho, vitello *egg:* 8 vitellus
yon see **yonder**
yonder 5 there 7 farther, further, thither
yore 4 past 8 foretime 10 yesteryear
you 2 ye 3 one 4 thee, thou *French:* 2 te, tu 4 vous *German:* 2 du 3 sie
young 3 fry, new, raw 4 baby, rude, tyro, weak 5 brood, fresh, green 6 callow,

infant, junior, litter, unripe 7 untried 8 childish, immature, juvenile, unformed, unversed, youthful 9 unfledged, unfleshed 10 unfinished, unseasoned 11 unpracticed 13 inexperienced *animal:* 3 cub, fry, pup 4 calf, colt, fawn, foal, joey, lamb 5 puppy *bird:* 5 chick *hare:* 7 leveret *sheep, goat:* 6 yeelin 8 yeanling

younger 6 junior

youngling see youngster

Young Lions author 4 Shaw

youngster 3 boy, cub, kid, lad, tad, tot 4 girl, lass, tike 5 chick, child 6 moppet, shaver, urchin 8 juvenile *suffix:* 4 ling

youth 5 prime 6 spring 7 puberty 8 juvenile, teenager 9 fledgling, stripling 10 adolescent, callowness, immaturity, juvenility, pubescence, springtide, springtime 11 adolescence 12 inexperience *ancient Greek:* 7 ephebos, ephebus *goddess of:* 4 Hebe *mythological:* 6 Adonis, Apollo, Icarus 8 Ganymede *time of:* 9 salad days; (see also youngster)

youthful 5 fresh, green, young 6 boyish, callow, infant, junior, maiden, unripe, virgin 7 puerile 8 immature, juvenile, virginal 9 beardless, unfledged

yowl 3 cry, yip 4 bawl, howl, wail, yell, yelp 6 scream, squall, squeal

yucca 5 palma 9 bear grass

Yugoslavia *capital:* 8 Belgrade *monetary unit:* 5 dinar *president:* 4 Broz, Tito *republic:* 6 Serbia 7 Croatia 8 Slovenia 9 Macedonia 10 Montenegro

Yukon *capital:* 10 Whitehorse *region:* 8 Klondike *town:* 6 Dawson

yule 4 Noel, Xmas 8 Nativity, yuletide 9 Christmas 13 Christmastide

Z

Zabbai *father:* 5 Bebai *son:* 6 Baruch

Zabud's father 6 Nathan

Zaccur *father:* 4 Imri 5 Asaph 7 Jaaziah 9 Mattaniah *son:* 5 Hanan

Zacharias *father:* 9 Barachias *son:* 4 John 6 Joseph *wife:* 9 Elisabeth

Zadoke *daughter:* 7 Jerusha *father:* 5 Baana, Immer 6 Ahitub 8 Meraioth *grandson:* 6 Jotham *son:* 7 Ahimaaz, Shallum

Zaire *capital:* 8 Kinshasa *former name:* 5 Congo 12 Belgian Congo

zakuska 4 whet 9 antipasto, appetizer 11 hors d'oeuvre

Zalmunna's slayer 6 Gideon

Zambia *capital:* 6 Lusaka *monetary unit:* 6 kwacha

zampogna 7 bagpipe, panpipe

zany 3 wag 4 card, fool 5 ament, clown, comic, crazy, cutup, dotty, idiot, joker, moron, nutty 6 cretin 7 buffoon, farceur, half-wit, pranker 8 clowning, clownish, comedian, funnyman, humorist, imbecile, jokester 9 harlequin, prankster, simpleton, trickster

Zauberflöte composer 6 Mozart

zeal 4 fire, zest 5 ardor, gusto 6 desire, energy, fervor, hurrah, spirit 7 avidity, passion, urgency 8 devotion, keenness 9 calenture, eagerness, intensity, readiness, sincerity, vehemence 10 enthusiasm, fanaticism, fierceness 11 earnestness, seriousness

zealot 3 bug, nut 5 bigot, fiend, freak 6 maniac, votary 7 devotee, fanatic, sectary 8 adherent, disciple, follower, partisan 10 enthusiast

zealous 4 avid, keen, warm 5 afire, eager, fired, nutty, rabid 6 ardent, fervid, gung ho, hearty 7 devoted, earnest, fanatic, fervent 8 frenetic, obsessed, wild-eyed 9 dedicated, possessed 12 enthusiastic

Zebadiah *father:* 6 Asahel 7 Jeroham 11 Meshelemiah *uncle:* 4 Joab

Zebah's slayer 6 Gideon

Zebedee *son:* 4 John 5 James *wife:* 6 Salome

zebra 4 duaw *extinct:* 6 quagga *resembling:* 7 zebrine, zebroid

Zebulun *brother:* 4 Levi 5 Judah 6 Simeon *father:* 5 Jacob *mother:* 4 Leah *son:* 4 Elon 5 Sered 7 Jahleel

zecchino 6 sequin

Zechariah *daughter:* 3 Abi 6 Abijah *father:* 4 Elam, Iddo 5 Bebai, Hosah 7 Isshiah 8 Jehoiada, Jeroboam, Jonathan 9 Berechiah 11 Jeberechiah, Jehoshaphat, Meshelemiah *grandson:* 8 Hezekiah *slayer:* 7 Jehoram, Shallum *son:* 4 Iddo 8 Jahaziel

Zedekiah ***brother:*** 8 Jehoahaz ***father:*** 6 Josiah 8 Hananiah, Jeconiah, Maaseiah 9 Chenaanah ***mother:*** 7 Hamutal
Zeeb's slayer 6 Gideon
zenana 5 harem, harim 8 seraglio
zenith 4 acme, apex, peak 6 apogee, climax, height, summit, vertex 8 capstone, meridian, pinnacle 11 culmination ***opposite:*** 5 nadir
Zenobia ***husband:*** 9 Odenathus ***kingdom:*** 7 Palmyra
Zeno follower 5 stoic
Zephaniah ***father:*** 8 Maaseiah ***son:*** 6 Josiah
Zephi, Zepho ***father:*** 7 Eliphaz ***grandfather:*** 4 Esau
Zephon's father 3 Gad
Zephyrus 4 wind 6 breeze 8 west wind ***father:*** 6 Aeolus 8 Astraeus ***mother:*** 3 Eos 6 Aurora ***wife:*** 4 Iris
zeppelin 5 blimp 7 airship 9 dirigible
Zerah ***brother:*** 5 Perez ***father:*** 5 Judah, Reuel 6 Simeon ***grandfather:*** 4 Esau ***mother:*** 5 Tamar
Zerbino ***beloved:*** 8 Isabella ***friend:*** 7 Orlando ***sister:*** 7 Ginevra ***slayer:*** 11 Mandricardo
Zeresh's husband 5 Haman
zero 2 oh 3 aim, lay, nil, nul 4 cast, head, nowt, turn, void 5 aught, blank, empty, level, ought, point, train, zilch 6 cipher, direct, naught, nobody, nought 7 address, nothing, nullity, scratch, whiffet 8 goose egg, whipster 9 nonentity
Zeruah ***husband:*** 5 Nebat ***son:*** 8 Jeroboam
Zerubbabel ***daughter:*** 9 Shelomith ***father:*** 7 Pedaiah ***grandfather:*** 10 Jehoiachin ***son:*** 4 Ohel
Zeruiah ***brother:*** 5 David ***sister:*** 7 Abigail ***son:*** 4 Joab 6 Asahel 7 Abishai
zest 4 edge, élan, tang, zeal 5 ardor, gusto, heart, taste 6 fervor, flavor, palate, relish 7 delight, ecstasy, elation, passion 8 piquancy, pleasure 9 eagerness, enjoyment 10 enthusiasm 11 delectation 12 satisfaction
zesty 4 racy 5 spicy 6 breezy, hearty, snappy 7 peppery, piquant, pungent 8 poignant
Zetes ***brother:*** 6 Calais ***father:*** 6 Boreas ***mother:*** 8 Orithyia ***slayer:*** 8 Heracles, Hercules
zetetic 6 seeker 7 doubter, skeptic 10 headshaker, pyrrhonian, pyrrhonist, unbeliever
Zethus ***brother:*** 7 Amphion ***father:*** 4 Zeus 7 Jupiter ***mother:*** 7 Antiope
Zeus 7 Jupiter ***brother:*** 5 Hades 8 Poseidon ***daughter:*** 3 Ate 4 Hebe, Kore 5 Helen, Irene 6 Athena 7 Artemis, Astraea 9 Aphrodite 10 Persephone, Proserpina 12 Clytemnestra ***father:*** 6 Cronus ***lover:*** 2 Io 4 Leda, Leto, Maia 5 Danae, Dione, Metis 6 Aegina, Europa, Latona, Semele, Themis 7 Alcmene, Antiope, Demeter 8 Callisto, Eurynome ***messenger:*** 4 Iris ***mother:*** 4 Rhea ***nurse:*** 8 Cynosura ***oracle:*** 6 Dodona ***shield:*** 5 aegis ***sister:*** 4 Hera, Juno 6 Hestia ***son:*** 4 Ares 5 Arcas, Argus, Minos 6 Aeacus, Apollo, Hermes, Zethus 7 Amphion, Perseus 8 Dionysus, Heracles, Hercules, Sarpedon, Tantalus ***tree:*** 3 oak ***wife:*** 4 Hera, Juno 5 Metis 6 Themis
Zibiah ***husband:*** 7 Ahaziah ***son:*** 7 Jehoash
Zichri ***father:*** 5 Asaph 6 Shimei 7 Jeroham, Shashak ***son:*** 4 Joel 7 Amasiah, Eliezer 10 Elishaphat ***victim:*** 8 Maaseiah
zigzag 4 tack, turn 5 angle, crank, weave 7 chevron 8 flexuose, flexuous
zilch 4 zero 5 aught, ought 6 cipher, naught, nobody, nought 7 nothing, nullity, whiffet 8 goose egg, whipster 9 nonentity
Zillah ***husband:*** 6 Lamech ***son:*** 9 Tubalcain
Zilpah's son 3 Gad 5 Asher
zimarra 5 cloak 7 cassock, soutane
Zimbabwe ***capital:*** 6 Harare ***former name:*** 8 Rhodesia
Zimran ***father:*** 7 Abraham ***mother:*** 7 Keturah
Zimri ***father:*** 5 Zerah ***grandfather:*** 5 Judah ***victim:*** 4 Elah
zinc ***impure oxide:*** 5 tutty ***ingot:*** 7 spelter ***ore:*** 6 blende 10 sphalerite ***symbol:*** 2 Zn
zing 3 pep, vim, zip 4 brio, dash, élan, life, snap 5 ardor, force, oomph, verve, vigor 6 energy, esprit, spirit 9 animation, eagerness 10 enthusiasm
zingel 5 perch
Zion 5 bliss 6 canaan, heaven, Israel, utopia 7 arcadia, elysium, nirvana 8 empyrean, paradise 9 cockaigne, fairyland, Shangri-la 10 Civitas Dei, wonderland 12 New Jerusalem, promised land 13 Abraham's bosom
Zionist ***American:*** 5 Szold ***English:*** 8 Zangwill ***German:*** 6 Nordau ***Israeli:*** 5 Buber 8 Weizmann
zip 3 fly, pep, vim 4 dash, rush, snap, whiz, zing 5 force, hurry, speed, waltz, whisk 6 breeze, bustle, energy, hasten, hustle
zipper 8 fastener
Zipporah ***father:*** 5 Reuel 6 Jethro ***husband:*** 5 Moses ***son:*** 7 Eliezer, Gershom
Zippor's son 5 Balak
zippy 4 keen, spry, yare 5 agile, alert, brisk, catty, ready 6 active, brisky, lively, nimble, snappy 7 dynamic, intense 8 forceful 9 sprightly

zircon 6 jargon 7 jargoon *variety:* 7 jacinth 8 hyacinth, starlite
zirconium *symbol:* 2 Zr
zither *Chinese:* 3 kin *Japanese:* 4 koto
Ziza *father:* 8 Rehoboam *mother:* 6 Maacah
zodiac sign 3 Leo (the Lion) 5 Aries (the Ram), Libra (the Balance), Virgo (the Virgin) 6 Cancer (the Crab), Gemini (the Twins), Pisces (the Fishes), Taurus (the Bull) 7 Scorpio (the Scorpion) 8 Aquarius (the Water Bearer) 9 Capricorn (the Goat) 11 Sagittarius (the Archer)
zoetic 5 alive, vital 6 living 7 animate 8 animated
Zohar *father:* 6 Simeon *son:* 6 Ephron
Zoheth's father 4 Ishi
Zoilus 5 momus 6 carper, critic 7 caviler, knocker 9 aristarch, belittler 10 criticizer 11 faultfinder, smellfungus
Zola, Emile *work:* 4 Nana 6 Verité 7 J'accuse 8 Germinal 9 La Débâcle 10 L'Assommoir 13 Thérèse Raquin
zombie 5 drink, snake 6 python 8 cocktail
zone 4 area, band, belt 5 tract 6 region, sector 7 section, segment 9 territory *ecological:* 7 ecotone
zonked 4 high 5 doped, drunk, tight 6 stoned 7 drugged, drunken 8 hopped-up, turned on 9 spaced-out 10 inebriated, tripped out 11 intoxicated
zoologist *American:* 5 Hyatt 6 Kinsey, Osborn 7 Ditmars, Merriam *British:* 6 Darwin, Huxley 7 Medawar 9 Lankester *Dutch:* 10 Swammerdam *French:* 6 Cuvier *German:* 7 Haeckel, Spemann *Norwegian:* 6 Nansen *South African:* 5 Broom *Swedish:* 8 Linnaeus
zoophyte 5 coral 6 sponge 7 hydroid 8 bryozoan 9 gorgonian 10 sea anemone 12 invertebrate
Zoroastrian *demon:* 4 deva *god:* 10 Ahura Mazda *sacred writings:* 6 Avesta
zucchetto 7 calotte 8 skullcap
Zur *brother:* 4 Kish *daughter:* 5 Cozbi *father:* 5 Jeiel
Zuriel's father 7 Abihail
zweiback 5 bread, toast 7 biscuit
zygomatic bone 5 malar 9 cheekbone
zygote 6 oocyst 7 oosperm

NOTES

NOTES

NOTES

NOTES

NOTES

NOTES